THE ENCYCLOPEDIA OF FILM

James Monaco and the editors of BASELINE

James Pallot
Senior Editor

Virgin

First published in Great Britain in 1992 by
Virgin Books
an imprint of Virgin Publishing Ltd
338 Ladbroke Grove
London W10 5AH

A catalogue record for this book is available from the British Library

ISBN 1 85227 384 4 (hardback)
0 86369 593 0 (paperback)

First published in the United States in 1991 by Perigee Books,
The Putnam Publishing Group, New York

Printed and bound in Great Britain by
Butler & Tanner Ltd, Frome and London

By James Monaco and the Editors of BASELINE

Senior Editor
James Pallot

Associate Editors
Jane Klain
Tom Weiner

Staff Writers
Charles Epstein
Stuart Kauffman

Assistant Editor
John Miller-Monzon

Editorial Assistant
Robert Weisfeld

The Editors wish to acknowledge the contributions of

Judith Israel and Paul Rosovsky

and extend their special thanks to

Laura Ash, Curtis Church, Judith Garvin, Peter Hajduk, David Henry, Jo Imeson, Blair Lavey, José Rodrìguez, Annie Gerson Swanson, Lucia Tarbox, and Meta Wheattle.

Other books by James Monaco

The New Wave: Truffaut, Godard, Chabrol, Rohmer, Rivette
How To Read A Film
Celebrity
Media Culture
Alain Resnais
American Film Now: The People, The Power, The Money, The Movies
The French Revolutionary Calendar
The Connoisseur's Guide to the Movies
Who's Who in American Film Now

Introduction

All of a sudden, 30 years have passed.

When I first began writing about movies in the early 60s, there was a feverish excitement to the subject. It's hard to describe the thrill we all experienced then of constant discoveries; the anticipation of the next great work or the next direction; the visceral pleasure of arguing out a new esthetic, more important, a new politics. The revelations seemed to come faster than we could deal with them. Movies didn't just comment on our lives back then; they motivated them, and not because we were "film buffs"—cinema was in the streets.

Being a filmgoer or a "cinephile" in the 60s was more an active profession than the passive hobby it seems today. There were no courses where you had to learn the received opinions from the PhDs; you were free to make them up as you went. There were traditions and rules, but they were there to be broken, or played with, or rediscovered as great art. There were so many ways to be new or creative or rebellious: for Americans, European art cinema; for Europeans, American movies-as-art; non-narrative cinema; independent narrative cinema; not one, but several third-world cinemas; the documentary, *cinéma vérité*, even docudrama; black cinema and black comedy; naive genres and self-conscious genres and parodies of self-conscious genres; new sounds and images, new music and colors. A truly revolutionary generation of discovery and invention.

What a feast it was!

We live in a different time now. Free espresso at intermission in china demitasses has been replaced by profit-center Diet Pepsi in non-biodegradable styrofoam. As Alain Tanner put it with prescience at the beginning of this "post-something" period: "We live in a time of normalization, where exchange is permitted and nothing changes."

In the 90s, film is a mature culture—like the music and art and other popular cultures which were born in the 60s. I guess that's not so bad. What we lose in excitement, we make up in a high level of general quality. As an industry, film is better off today. The average movie, American or European, is more sharply written, better shot, more colorfully acted—perhaps even more entertaining—than the average movie of the 60s.

Filmgoers now have more control over their own experience. No longer limited to theaters and occasional broadcast TV airings, they can choose from tens of thousands of videotapes, thousands of videodiscs, hundreds of airplane flights, and scores of cable and satellite channels. Many more distribution "windows" have opened in the last ten years, and those windows can't help but bring new light and air into the film community, eventually.

The art, right now, is about to enter a period of rapid development, spreading into new areas, developing new ways of speaking. What was once a mass theatrical medium is becoming more personal and private. These new channels of communication have had a marked effect on the business of film, even if it is too soon to declare that they have changed the art. It's hard for me now to think of movies as separate from TV, videotape, videodiscs, and soon, interactive CDs. But all of these new media remain simply means of distribution. The people who make our images and sounds still do their most "significant" work for the big screen even if we more often experience it on the small screen. It will take time (and a little more technology) before the art adapts itself to more intense and private ways of seeing.

The Lumière and Méliès of this new art have already appeared: you can see good demonstrations of the power of the new medium in the CD-Roms and videodiscs published by Voyager/Criterion and Warner Interactive Media. Like Lumière and Méliès, these companies have only begun to explore the possibilities of what we might as well call "Hypermedia," but the key differences are clear: the artist now shares control of the work with the observer, who, in turn, is presented with a far richer range of possibilities from which to choose. The spectator makes the great leap from experiencing to experimenting. Film—the singular 20th-century art—synthesized all the 19th-century arts: theater, music, painting, narrative. Its 21st-century descendant admits the viewer as a full participant in that community.

This new thing sounds to me very much like a Godard film, as conceived in the spirit of Fellini. It should go without saying that the more we invent the more we remember the past. And that, after all, is the purpose of *The Encyclopedia of Film*.

Early in 1991, as this book was about to go to press, I watched an hour of Stanley Kubrick's *2001: A Space Odyssey* on TV in the company of my children, Andrew and Charles, both 12, and Margaret, 10. These kids, like most young people today, have grown up in an ocean of cinematic images and sounds. As preteens, they are more sophisticated about techniques, narrative, dialogue—the stuff of movies—than I was at twice their age. And they not only know, they do. At their age, my only means of technical expression was a Brownie Hawkeye (although thanks to my Uncle Anthony I was already familiar with the Victorian mysteries of the darkroom). They were experimenting with the integration of images and text writing children's books at the age of five. Now, they and their friends entertain themselves by writing/programming HyperCard games/stories. All that's left is to lay in the audio and video tracks. (I haven't yet told them that's doable because I can't afford the hardware—yet.)

But they'd never seen *2001* before. They were entranced. It was an epiphany, I think. "Dad, when was this made? It looks like yesterday!" Now, it's true, their attention was focused on the special effects. After (albeit short) lifetimes of *Star Wars* and Nintendo they were finally exposed to the source of it all, a film made 25 years earlier, and I think they began to understand that the past is father to the future.

I hope you'll regard *The Encyclopedia of Film* as your guide to some of the fathers and mothers in our movie past (and present) with whom you may be less familiar.

Like modern filmmakers, we are mindful of our predecessors. I still remember that day in 1965 when I first discovered Georges Sadoul's twin paperbacks, *Dictionnaire des Cinéastes* and *Dictionnaire des Films*. Leslie Halliwell's *Filmgoer's Companion* (1965) was a landmark in its time, and we are still impressed with the prodigious effort Ephraim Katz put into his *Film Encyclopedia* (1979). David Thomson's *A Biographical Dictionary of Film* (1975) remains highly readable and Richard Roud's collection, *Cinema: A Critical Dictionary* (2 volumes, 1980) contains many interesting essays by a wide variety of critics. BASELINE's own *Who's Who in American Film Now* (1987) eschewed commentary in favor of credits, listing data on over 11,000 personnel.

The Encyclopedia of Film is a BASELINE book: all the filmographical and biographical data have been distilled from BASELINE's databases which, as of publication date, listed credits for more than 750,000 filmmakers from the most acclaimed writers, producers and directors, to the least-known grips, gaffers and bit-part players. Because the credit lists in *The Encyclopedia of Film* have been produced from the databases, you can be sure that they are as complete as it is possible to make them. (Note well: we have edited some filmographies for reasons of length, especially those of non-contemporary figures.) You'll therefore find some interesting details as you read.

The 3,000 filmmakers we have selected for inclusion here represent less than one-half of one percent of the total film community, past and present. Although you'll find all the important historical filmmakers, we've concentrated on contemporaries, those artists about whom it is most difficult to find information elsewhere. These are the people who are most likely to shape developments in the future. Although we've made cuts based on historical period, we have tried to be as unbiased as possible geographically: film is a truly international art; we hope *The Encyclopedia of Film* reflects this. You may be interested to know, as well, that we had originally intended to include numerous survey articles on national cinemas and genres, institutions, companies, technical terms and the like. In our effort to provide the most information at a price you can afford, these enhancements were left on the cutting room floor. You'll see them soon, on BASELINE, or at a bookstore near you. *The Encyclopedia of Film* went to press in March 1991. Because BASELINE tracks all projects in production, data should be reliably complete through June 30, 1991.

Like the films which are its subject, *The Encyclopedia of Film* is very much a collaborative effort. More than 60 writers and editors have contributed to the work. We hope the book is both broader in scope and more precise as a result of the talents of this able and varied crew. We know they bring a multinational perspective to the book. I'm grateful to all the editors and contributors (especially Paul Rosovsky and Judith Israel, who were Managing Editor and Senior Editor of BASELINE during much of the preparation of the book); to our agent, Mitchell Rose, who helped to conceive the project; and to our editor at Putnam, Eugene Brissie, whose care and patience has been much appreciated. I also owe much thanks to Jo Imeson, Executive Vice President of BASELINE and an essential collaborator for eight years, for her sure and constant managerial hand.

I'm especially grateful to Senior Editor, James Pallot, who managed a massive project with both literate intelligence and filmic fortitude. His attention to detail as well as his wit have made *The Encyclopedia of Film* a much better book than it might otherwise have been. His sense of proportion and style inform nearly every page.

Now that you know something about the team that has brought this book to publication, we invite your participation, too. Unlike most other books, encyclopedias are living projects, changing as they grow. The first edition of any encyclopedia is at best a first draft. If you should find any lacunae, or have suggestions for future inclusions, we invite you to correspond with us at the address below.

James Monaco
New York
March 1991

Note to the Reader

This book consists of biographical/critical sketches followed, where appropriate, by a list of film credits. Although we have made every effort to ensure that filmographies are as extensive as possible, the size of the volume prohibits us from providing complete credits for every individual. In general, we have given fuller coverage to contemporary figures whose careers remain, as yet, undocumented; for others, whose achievements have been exhaustively covered elsewhere, we have provided a representative selection of films.

Credit listings consist mostly of feature-length fiction or documentary films which have enjoyed theatrical release. Short films, when included, are noted accordingly. Each title is followed by the year of its initial release, whether in the US or elsewhere. If the film earned an Academy Award or an Award nomination for the individual concerned, that information is included in abbreviated form (please check the table below).

If a person performs only one professional function—actor, cinematographer, etc.—then his filmography will consist simply of titles and dates. If, on the other hand, he wears more than one filmmaking hat, his exact involvement on each film will be indicated in parentheses after the year of release. Abbreviations are listed below.

Films are listed in overall chronological sequence; where several films share the same year of release, they have been sorted alphabetically to aid searching. Major foreign films are listed in their language of origin, separated by a slash from their English-language release title (or, where appropriate, a translation of the original title). Slashes are also used to indicate alternate titles for English-language films.

About BASELINE

BASELINE was founded in 1983 to provide online databases and other information services to the film and TV industries. The world's largest source of information about film and TV, the company now has professional clients around the world in more than thirty countries. More than 25 separate databases list information on hundreds of thousands of film and TV cast and crew members; more than 100,000 films, TV series, specials, movies and episodes; more than 5,000 films and TV shows currently in production; more than 15,000 companies active in the industry. Additional services include online news, financial figures and communications. More information about BASELINE is available by calling 1.800.CHAPLIN or writing to us at 838 Broadway, New York, NY 10003 or 8929 Wilshire, Beverly Hills, CA 90211. Many BASELINE services are also available on Mead Data Central's Nexis service.

A Note on the Type

The Encyclopedia of Film is set in Times Roman, perhaps the most durable typeface of the 20th century, whose original 1931 design was supervised by Stanley Morison for *The Times* of London. The WordPerfect files were output by AGC Sedgwick, Princeton, NJ.

Credit Abbreviations

a	actor appearance [1]
ad	assistant director
adapt	adaptation
add	additional
anim	animator
anim.d	animation director
art d	art director
assoc	associate
asst	assistant
cam.op	camera operator
chor	choreography
consult	consultant
cont	continuity
cost	costume design wardrobe
d	director co-director
dial	dialogue
ed	editor
exec	executive
fx	special visual effects
fx ph	special effects photography
fx prod	visual effects producer
m	music composer [2]
m.arr	music arranger
m.cond	music conductor
m.dir	music director
m.perf	music performer
m.prod	music producer
orch	orchestration
p	producer co-producer
pd	production designer
ph	director of photography
prod.asst	production assistant
prod.man	production manager
props	property master
sc	screenplay co-screenplay
sets	set design set decoration
song	song composer [2] song performer
sup	supervisor
tech.sup	technical supervisor
u.man	unit manager
2u	2nd unit

(1) For animated films, "a" may indicate that the actor provided a voice-over only.

(2) In some cases, "m" or "song" indicates that a composer's work was used in a film, though it was not written specifically for that film.

NB These abbreviations may be combined in different ways, e.g. "exec.p" for executive producer, "add.dial" for additional dialogue, etc. The letters "uncred," followed by any of the above, indicates the person concerned performed the function indicated but did not receive on-screen credit for the work.

Academy Award Abbreviations

Each abbreviation is preceded by "AA" (for Academy Award) or "AAN" (for Academy Award Nomination).

BA	Best Actor/Actress
BAD	Best Art Direction/Production Design/Set Decoration
BASF	Best Animated Short Film
BCD	Best Costume Design
BD	Best Directing
BDOC	Best Documentary Feature
BED	Best Film Editing
BFLF	Best Foreign Language Film
BM	Best Music Score (Adaptation or Original)
BP	Best Picture
BPH	Best Cinematography
BS	Best Song
BSA	Best Supporting Actor/Actress
BSC	Best Screenplay (Original or Adapted)
BSF	Best Live Action Short Film
BSFX	Best Special Visual Effects
BSS	Best Song Score
BST	Best Story
HON	Honorary Award
SHORT DOC	Best Documentary Short
TECH	Scientific or Technical Award

Contributors and Editors

AB Alexander Batchan, a New-York based journalist and critic, has lectured on Soviet cinema and culture and contributed articles to *Cineaste*, *Wide Angle* and *Film Comment*.

AGS Annie Gerson Swanson is editor of BASELINE's INPRO (Feature Films in Production) database and has contributed to publications including *Premiere* magazine and the *Cinebooks Motion Picture Annual*.

ATJ Andrew Jefchak teaches film at Aquinas College in Grand Rapids, MI; he is a longtime film critic for the Grand Rapids *Press* and has contributed to *Magill's Cinema Annual*.

BKG Barry Grant teaches film at Brock University in Ontario, Canada; he has edited several books, including *Planks of Reason: Essays on the Horror Film*, and is a contributor to the *New Encyclopedia of Science Fiction*.

CAN Chon A. Noriega is a doctoral candidate in Modern Thought and Literature at Stanford University, writing his dissertation on Chicano cinema; he has contributed to *Cinema Journal* and *Magill's Cinema Annual*.

CD Charles Derry is the co-ordinator of Film Studies at Wright University in Dayton, Ohio, and the author of *Dark Dreams: A Psychological History of the Modern Horror Film* and *The Suspense Thriller: Films in the Shadow of Alfred Hitchcock*.

CDM Clodualdo del Mundo, Jr., is a screenwriter and teaches in the Communication Arts Department at La Salle University, Manila.

CL Christine List is an instructor of Film and Video at Chicago State University, where she teaches a course on images of blacks and Latinos in the cinema. She has contributed to *Jump Cut* and *Afterimage*.

CRB Charles Ramirez Berg teaches Film Studies at the University of Texas at Austin and is the author of the forthcoming *The Cinema of Solitude*, a study of Mexican film from 1967 to 1983.

CSE Caron Schwartz Ellis holds an MA from the University of Colorado, where she wrote her thesis on Vietnam war films.

DC Dan Curran is a Chicago-based filmmaker and writer; he was formerly a writer and editor for the *Motion Picture Guide* and editor-in-chief of the Cinebooks guide to *Foreign Films*.

DD David Desser is a Professor of Cinema Studies and Speech Communications at the University of Illinois at Urbana-Champaign; he is the author of *The Samurai Films of Akira Kurosawa* and *The Eros Plus Massacre: An Introduction to the Japanese New Wave Cinema*.

DFD David Donnelly is currently completing his PhD at the University of Massachusetts at Amherst and will soon be joining the faculty of the School of Communication at the University of Houston.

DG Douglas Gomery lives in Washington, D.C., teaches at the University of Maryland and has written *The Hollywood Studio System* and contributed to *Seeing Through Movies*.

DGS Dan Streible is a doctoral candidate in film at the University of Texas at Austin, currently writing a history of prize-fight films; he is also an editor for the *Velvet Light Trap*.

DH David Henry is production coordinator for BASELINE.

DLY Donald Yonker is a freelance writer and researcher based in Manhattan.

DMB Diane Borden is a Professor of Film and Literature at the University of the Pacific in Stockton, CA; among her publications are critical studies of De Sica's *Bicycle Thief* and Bergman's *Wild Strawberries*.

DT Doris Toumarkine is a staff reporter for the *Hollywood Reporter* and has written on film and video for *Spy*, *Billboard* and *New York Newsday*; she is a longtime contributing editor to *Film Journal*.

DW Dennis West teaches film at the University of Idaho and is a frequent contributor to *Cineaste* magazine. He has been published on Latin American film in *Film Criticism* and *Latin American Research Review*.

ES Eric Schaefer is a doctoral candidate in film at the University of Texas at Austin and an editor for the *Velvet Light Trap*.

JAG Joseph Gomez teaches English and Multi-Disciplinary Studies at North Carolina State University and is the author of books on Ken Russell and Peter Watkins.

JCP Jim Potter is a doctoral candidate in film at Northwestern University.

JDP James Pallot holds an MA in critical theory from the University of Southampton, England, and continued his graduate studies at St. Catherine's College, Oxford. He is publications manager for BASELINE and contributing editor for film to the *Universal Almanac*.

JDK Jane Klain is editor of BASELINE's BIOS (Biographies) database. A former editor of the *International Motion Picture Almanac* and *International Television & Video Almanac*, she has been a theater and film reviewer for *Good Times* magazine since 1985.

JFK Jeffrey Klenotic is a doctoral candidate in Communications at the University of Massachusetts at Amherst, working on the history of film marketing and exhibition.

JKWL Jenny Kwok Wah Lau, a doctoral candidate at the University of Illinois, has written and lectured on Chinese and Hong Kong film and has contributed to publications including *Asian Cinema*.

JM James Monaco is the founder and president of BASELINE. He has written several books on film, including *The New Wave*, *How to Read a Film* and *American Film Now*.

JMM John Miller-Monzon is a filmmaker and assistant editor of BASELINE's PHOTOPLAY (Released Feature Films) database. He is an MFA candidate in directing and screenwriting at Columbia University.

JN James Naremore is Director of Film Studies at Indiana University and the author of *The Filmguide to Psycho*, *The Magic World of Orson Welles* and *Acting in the Cinema*.

KG Kevin Gillogly is a freelance journalist and screenwriter based in Los Angeles.

KJ Karen Jaehne is a Manhattan-based independent producer and an editor at *Cineaste* magazine.

KJH Kevin Jack Hagopian, formerly editor of the *Film Literature Index*, is a doctoral candidate in Communication Arts at the University of Wisconsin-Madison. He has published articles in *The Velvet Light Trap*, *The Quarterly Journal of Film and Video*, *Wide Angle* and *Films and Filmmakers*.

KMM Mike Mashon is a doctoral candidate in film at the University of Texas at Austin and an editor for the *Velvet Light Trap*.

LCE Linda Ehrlich teaches Japanese at the University of Tennessee/Knoxville and has contributed articles to the *East-West Film Journal*, the *Journal of Film and Video* and *Cinemaya*.

LM Laurence Miller is Professor of Psychology at Western Washington University, where he specializes in the psychology of *film noir*; he has contributed to publications including *Cinema Journal*.

LR Lenny Rubenstein is a Manhattan-based freelance writer and researcher who specializes in war, espionage and anarchic humor; he is the author of *The Great Spy Films* and co-editor of *The Cineaste Interviews*.

MCJ Mary C. Johnson holds a PhD in English and Film from Ohio State University and teaches at Florida State University in Tallahassee.

MDM Mark D. McKennon is a Boston University graduate in Broadcasting and the author of *The Dream Machine: Computers and Robots in the Movies*.

MN Markus Nornes has completed graduate studies at the University of Southern California Film School, has worked for the East-West Center's Film Program and has been published in *Film Quarterly* and the *Hawaii International Film Festival Viewer's Guide*.

PB Paul Brenner is a doctoral candidate in Cinema Studies at New York University and has contributed to publications including *Film Journal* and *Magill's Survey of Cinema*; his short stories have appeared in several magazines and his 16mm films have been shown at festivals in New York and Chicago.

PP Phil Pantone is editor and co-publisher of the Chicago-based *Flicker Film Journal* and a writer and researcher for *The Motion Picture Guide*.

PR Peter Ruppert teaches film at Florida State University and is the author of *Reader in a Strange Land; the Activity of Reading Literary Utopias*. He has contributed articles to *Cineaste* and *Cinema Journal*.

RAH Robert A. Haller is the Director of Anthology Film Archives in Manhattan and the editor of *Brakhage Scrapbook*, as well as the curator of film for the Museum of Staten Island.

RCB Richard Bartone teaches film at the William Paterson College of New Jersey.

RDH Roger Hagedorn teaches French at the University of South Dakota; he is a frequent contributor to *Wide Angle* and is film editor for *Schatzkammer*, a publication for teachers of German.

RH Rosemary Heather is a freelance film writer and researcher currently living in London.

RJB Robin Blaetz is completing a Mellon post-doctoral fellowship in the Theater and Film Studies Department of Emory University and is working on a book about the representation of Joan of Arc in popular culture.

RM Ruth McCormick teaches film at Columbia University and is a former editor of *Cineaste*. She has translated and edited a critical study of *Fassbinder* and contributed to *American Film*, *Jump Cut* and *Women in Film*.

RW Robert Weisfeld is an editorial assistant at BASELINE and an illustrator/writer/ performance artist.

SKK Stuart Kauffman is a writer/researcher for BASELINE and recently received his MA in Cinema Studies from New York University. He has made several short films and is co-editor of *Cinema-File* magazine.

TKB Kay Beck teaches film theory and economics at Georgia State University. She chairs the Georgia Film Board and has contributed to publications including the *International Journal of Women's Studies*.

TW Tom Wiener is author of *The Book of Video Lists* and a former senior editor at *American Film* magazine.

TZ Tony Zaza is co-editor of *The Family Guide to Movies on Video* and a reviewer for the *TV and Movie Guide*, published weekly by the National Catholic News Service.

VMC Virginia Clark is an editor at Simon & Schuster and has been on the staff of the American Film Institute and the Library of Congress. She is the author of *Aldous Huxley and Film*, as well as numerous articles, and editor of *What Women Wrote: Scenarios 1912-1926*.

WWD Wheeler Winston Dixon is Director, Film Studies, at the University of Nebraska, Lincoln. Among his books are *Terence Fisher: The Critical Reception* and *The "B" Directors: A Biographical Directory*.

Abbott, Bud • Actor • Born William A. Abbott, Asbury Park, NJ, October 2, 1895; died 1974. The thinner half, opposite Lou Costello, of one of the top comedy teams of the 1940s. The duo was formed when Abbott, selling tickets at a burlesque theater, was pulled in as a last-minute substitute for Costello's indisposed straight man. Their most famous routine, "Who's On First?," was originally done on film in *The Naughty Nineties* (1945). • *One Night in the Tropics* 1940; *Buck Privates* 1941; *Hold That Ghost* 1941; *In the Navy* 1941; *Keep 'Em Flying* 1941; *Pardon My Sarong* 1942; *Ride 'Em Cowboy* 1942; *Rio Rita* 1942; *Who Done It?* 1942; *Hit the Ice* 1943; *It Ain't Hay* 1943; *In Society* 1944; *Lost in a Harem* 1944; *Bud Abbott and Lou Costello in Hollywood* 1945; *Here Come the Co-eds* 1945; *The Naughty Nineties* 1945; *Little Giant* 1946; *The Time of Their Lives* 1946; *Buck Privates Come Home* 1947; *The Wistful Widow of Wagon Gap* 1947; *Abbott and Costello Meet Frankenstein* 1948; *Mexican Hayride* 1948; *The Noose Hangs High* 1948; *Abbott and Costello Meet the Killer, Boris Karloff* 1949; *Africa Screams* 1949; *Abbott and Costello in the Foreign Legion* 1950; *Abbott and Costello Meet the Invisible Man* 1951; *Comin' Round the Mountain* 1951; *Abbott and Costello Meet Captain Kidd* 1952; *Jack and the Beanstalk* 1952; *Lost in Alaska* 1952; *Abbott and Costello Go to Mars* 1953; *Abbott and Costello Meet Dr. Jekyll and Mr. Hyde* 1953; *Abbott and Costello Meet the Keystone Cops* 1954; *Abbott and Costello Meet the Mummy* 1955; *Dance With Me Henry* 1956; *Entertaining the Troops* (archival footage) 1989.

Abraham, F. Murray • Actor • Born Pittsburgh, PA, October 24, 1940. *Educ.* University of Texas; Herbert Berghof Studio, New York. Experienced stage actor, occasionally in films. Abraham's bravura performance as Salieri in *Amadeus* (1984) has surprisingly not lead to more substantial screen roles. • *The Sunshine Boys* 1975 (a); *All the President's Men* 1976 (a); *The Ritz* 1976 (a); *The Big Fix* 1978 (a); *Scarface* 1983 (a); *Amadeus* 1984 (a) **(AABA)**; *The Name of the Rose* 1986 (a); *La Rosa dei Nomi* 1987 (a); *Personal Choice* 1988 (a); *An Innocent Man* 1989 (a); *La Nuit du serail* 1989 (a); *Performance Pieces (short)* 1989 (a); *Russicum* 1989 (a); *Slipstream* 1989 (a); *La Batalla de los Tres Reyes* 1990 (a); *Bonfire of the Vanities* 1990 (uncred.a); *Cadence* 1990 (a); *Eye of the Widow* 1991 (a).

Abrahams, Jim • Director, screenwriter; also producer, actor. • Born Shorewood, WI, May 10, 1944. *Educ.* University of Wisconsin, Madison. Cofounder, with college friends Jerry and David Zucker, of the Kentucky Fried Theater in Madison, WI, in 1969. The trio subsequently moved their satirical group to Los Angeles and made their first venture into feature filmmaking with *The Kentucky Fried Movie* (1977), a series of absurd, vulgar and (mostly) funny send-ups of popular culture. Most of their subsequent work has been in a similar vein. *Airplane!* (1980), *Top Secret!* (1984) and *The Naked Gun* (1988) pay satirical homage respectively to the disaster film, the spy film and the police film. Trademark features are rugged, but notoriously stiff, second echelon actors from the 1950s (e.g. Robert Stack, Leslie Nielsen, Peter Graves) and corny but often hilarious running verbal and visual gags.

Like his creative partners, Abrahams has ventured into a solo career, making his directing debut with the slightly more restrained and traditional comedy, *Big Business* (1988), and serving as executive producer of director John Waters's *Cry-Baby* (1990). See also Zucker, David. • *The Kentucky Fried Movie* 1977 (a,sc); *Airplane!* 1980 (a,d,exec.p,sc); *Top Secret!* 1984 (d,exec.p,sc,lyrics "Spend This Night With Me"); *Ruthless People* 1986 (d); *Big Business* 1988 (d); *The Naked Gun - From the Files of Police Squad!* 1988 (exec.p,sc); *Cry-Baby* 1990 (exec.p); *Welcome Home, Roxy Carmichael* 1990 (d).

Abuladze, Tengiz • Director, screenwriter. • Born Kutaisi, Georgia, USSR, January 31, 1924. *Educ.* Chota Rustaveli Theatre Institute, Tbilisi, Georgia (directing); VGIK, Moscow. Documentary and narrative filmmaker whose *Repentance* (1984) stirred considerable controversy for its semi-allegorical critique of Stalinism. • *Lurdzha Magdany/Magdana's Donkey* 1955 (d); *Ya, Babushka, Illiko & Illarion/I, Grandmother, Illiko & Illarion* 1963 (d,sc); *Molba/Prayer* 1967 (d,sc); *Monanieba/Repentance* 1984 (d,sc).

Acin, Jovan • Director, screenwriter • Born Belgrade, Yugoslavia, May 23, 1941. *Educ.* Academie des Beaux Arts, Paris (architecture); Academy of Theatre, Film, Radio and Television Arts, Belgrade (film direction). Acin worked in Algeria and France after leaving Yugoslavia following a clash with the authorities over his controversial first feature, *The Concrete Rose* (1975). In 1986 he won international praise for the bittersweet reminiscence of post-war Yugoslavia, *Hey Babu Riba*. • *The Concrete Rose* 1975 (d); *Bal na vodi/Hey Babu Riba* 1986 (d,sc,from memories).

Ackland, Joss • Actor • Born London, February 29, 1928. *Educ.* Central School of Speech and Drama, London. Prolific stage performer with the Old Vic and the Mermaid Theater companies who made his professional debut in 1945, only entering films in the late 1960s (after an uncredited film debut in *Seven Days to Noon* 1950). Ackland's most recent memorable screen roles include Greta Scacchi's scheming husband in *White Mischief*, Don Masino Croce in Michael Cimino's *The Sicilian* (both 1987) and the villainous South African diplomat Arjen Rudd, in *Lethal Weapon 2* (1989).

A musical comedy star in the West End productions of *A Little Night Music*, *Evita*, *Peter Pan* and *Jean Seberg*, Ackland won acclaim for portraying C.S. Lewis in the British TV production, *Shadowlands* (1985). • *Seven Days to Noon* 1950 (uncred.a); *Crescendo* 1969; *The House That Dripped Blood* 1970; *Mr. Forbush and the Penguins* 1971; *Villain* 1971; *The Happiness Cage* 1972; *England Made Me* 1973; *Hitler: The Last Ten Days* 1973; *The Black Windmill* 1974; *The Little Prince* 1974; *Spys* 1974; *One of Our Dinosaurs Is Missing* 1975; *Operation Daybreak* 1975; *Royal Flash* 1975; *Silver Bears* 1977; *Watership Down* 1978; *Who Is Killing the Great Chefs of Europe?* 1978; *Saint Jack* 1979; *The Apple* 1980; *Rough Cut* 1980; *A Zed and Two Noughts* 1985; *Lady Jane* 1986; *New World* 1986; *The Sicilian* 1987; *White Mischief* 1987; *It Couldn't Happen Here* 1988; *Popielusko* 1988; *Lethal Weapon 2* 1989; *Dimenticare Palermo* 1990; *The Hunt For Red October* 1990; *Tre Colonne in Cronaca* 1990; *The Object of Beauty* 1991.

Adam, Ken • Production designer • Born Berlin, February 1921. *Educ.* London University (architecture); Bartlett School of Architecture, London. Acclaimed art director who, besides his noted collaborations with Stanley Kubrick, helped define the look of the 60s spy thriller. Immigrated to England in 1934. • *The Brass Monkey* 1948 (draftsman); *The Queen of Spades* 1948 (draftsman); *Third Time Lucky* 1948 (draftsman); *This Was a Woman* 1948 (draftsman); *Obsession* 1949 (asst.art d); *Your Witness* 1950 (asst.art d); *Captain Horatio Hornblower* 1951 (asst.art d); *The Crimson Pirate* 1952 (asst.art d); *The Intruder* 1953 (asst.art d); *The Master of Ballantrae* 1953 (assoc. art d); *Around the World in 80 Days* 1956 (art d—Europe); *Child in the House* 1956 (art d); *Helen of Troy* 1956 (asst.art d); *Spin a Dark Web* 1956 (art d); *Star of India* 1956 (asst.art d); *Curse of the*

Demon 1958 (art d); *Gideon's Day* 1958 (art d); *The Angry Hills* 1959 (art d); *Ben-Hur* 1959 (research); *Beyond This Place* 1959 (art d); *John Paul Jones* 1959 (ship designer); *The Rough and the Smooth* 1959 (pd); *Ten Seconds to Hell* 1959 (art d); *In the Nick* 1960 (pd); *Let's Get Married* 1960 (pd); *The Trials of Oscar Wilde* 1960 (pd); *The Hellions* 1961 (initial designs); *Dr. No* 1962 (pd); *Sodoma e Gomorra/Sodom and Gomorrah* 1962 (pd); *In the Cool of the Day* 1963 (pd); *Dr. Strangelove; or, How I Learned to Stop Worrying and Love the Bomb* 1964 (pd); *The Long Ships* 1964 (initial designs); *Woman of Straw* 1964 (pd); *The Ipcress File* 1965 (pd); *Thunderball* 1965 (pd); *Funeral in Berlin* 1966 (pd); *You Only Live Twice* 1967 (pd); *Chitty Chitty Bang Bang* 1968 (pd); *Goodbye, Mr. Chips* 1969 (pd); *The Owl and the Pussycat* 1970 (production design supervisor); *Sleuth* 1972 (pd); *The Last of Sheila* 1973 (pd); *Barry Lyndon* 1975 (pd) **(AABAD)**; *Madam Kitty* 1975 (pd); *The Seven Per-Cent Solution* 1976 (pd); *The Spy Who Loved Me* 1977 (pd) **(AANBAD)**; *Moonraker* 1979 (pd); *Pennies From Heaven* 1981 (assoc.p,visual consultant); *Agnes of God* 1985 (pd); *King David* 1985 (pd); *Crimes of the Heart* 1986 (pd); *The Deceivers* 1988 (pd); *Dead-Bang* 1989 (pd); *The Freshman* 1990 (pd).

Adams, Brooke • Actress • Born New York, NY, February 8, 1949. *Educ.* High School for the Performing Arts, New York; School of the American Ballet, New York. Former juvenile stage actress whose adult movie career took off with a well-received performance, opposite Richard Gere and Sam Shepard, in Terence Malick's *Days of Heaven* (1978). Although she has starred in Philip Kaufman's *Invasion of the Body Snatchers* (1978), and repeated her off-Broadway role in the film version of Kevin Wade's romantic comedy *Key Exchange* (1985), Adams's recent work has been sidetracked to mostly horror films and supernatural thrillers. • *Death Corps* 1975; *Days of Heaven* 1978; *Invasion of the Body Snatchers* 1978; *Cuba* 1979; *A Man, a Woman and a Bank* 1979; *Tell Me a Riddle* 1980; *Utilities* 1981; *The Dead Zone* 1983; *Haunted* 1983; *Almost You* 1984; *Key Exchange* 1985; *The Stuff* 1985; *Man on Fire* 1987; *The Unborn* 1991.

Adams, Maud • *aka* Maude Adams • Actress • Born Maud Wikstrom, Lulea, Sweden, February 12, 1945. Former model who has the distinction of being the only woman to have starred opposite "James Bond" more than once. • *The Christian Licorice Store* 1971; *U-Turn* 1973; *The Man With the Golden Gun* 1974; *The Diamond Mercenaries* 1975; *Rollerball* 1975; *Laura, les ombres de l'été* 1979; *Tattoo* 1981; *Target Eagle* 1982; *Octopussy* 1983; *Jane and the Lost City* 1987; *The Women's Club* 1987; *Angel III: The Final Chapter* 1988; *Deadly Intent* 1988; *Hell Hunters* 1988; *La Nuit du serail* 1989; *Pasion de Hombre* 1989; *The Kill Reflex* 1990; *Silent Night, Deadly Night 4: Initiation* 1990.

Addams, Dawn • Actress • Born Felixstowe, England, September 21, 1930; died May 7, 1985, London. *Educ.* RADA, London. Leading lady of several romantic films of the 1950s; co-stars included Charles Chaplin, Spencer Tracy and David Niven. • *Night Into Morning* 1951; *The Unknown Man* 1951; *Plymouth Adventure* 1952; *Mizar* 1953; *The Moon Is Blue* 1953; *The Robe* 1953; *Young Bess* 1953; *Khyber Patrol* 1954; *Return to Treasure Island* 1954; *Riders to the Stars* 1954; *Secrets d'Alcove* 1954; *Le Vicomte de Bragelonne* 1955; *A King in New York* 1957; *Londra Chiama Polo Nord* 1957; *The Silent Enemy* 1958; *Die Tausend Augen des Dr. Mabuse/The 1,000 Eyes of Dr. Mabuse* 1960; *Come Fly With Me* 1962; *Blues For Lovers* 1966; *The Vampire Lovers* 1970; *The Vault of Horror* 1973.

Addinsell, Richard • Composer • Born London, January 13, 1904; died November 15, 1977, London. *Educ.* Hartford College, Oxford. Scored numerous British historical and period films and won international recognition for his popular "Warsaw Concerto" from the 1940 film, *Dangerous Moonlight/Suicide Squadron*. After writing incidental music for the stage, Addinsell first went to Hollywood in the early 1930s and returned to England to become a mainstay of the British film industry from the late 30s to the mid-60s, writing the music for such period films as *Goodbye, Mr. Chips* (1939), *Gaslight* (1940), *A Christmas Carol* (1951), *The Prince and the Showgirl* (1957) and *A Tale of Two Cities* (1958) as well as the more contemporary, *The Roman Spring of Mrs. Stone* (1961) and *Life at the Top* (1965). • *Fire Over England* 1936 (m); *Goodbye, Mr. Chips* 1939 (m); *Gaslight* 1940 (m); *Dangerous Moonlight/Suicide Squadron* 1941 (m); *Under Capricorn* 1949 (m); *The Black Rose* 1950 (m); *A Christmas Carol* 1951 (m); *Encore* 1951 (m); *Tom Brown's Schooldays* 1951 (m); *Beau Brummell* 1954 (m); *The Prince and the Showgirl* 1957 (m); *A Tale of Two Cities* 1958 (m); *Macbeth* 1960 (m); *The Roman Spring of Mrs. Stone* 1961 (m); *Waltz of the Toreadors* 1962 (m); *Life at the Top* 1965 (m); *The Sea Wolves* 1980 (song).

Addison, John • Composer • Born West Chobham, Surrey, England, March 16, 1920. *Educ.* Royal Academy of Music, London (composition, oboe, clarinet and piano). Versatile, prolific talent who entered films in the late 1940s and quickly proved equally adept at scoring comedy and drama. Addison hit a creative peak a decade later with the British film renaissance, composing sprightly classical melodies as well as moody jazz scores for the "angry young man" films of the 1960s, as in his significant contribution to Tony Richardson films, including *Look Back in Anger* (1959), *The Entertainer* (1960), *A Taste of Honey* (1961), *The Loneliness of the Long Distance Runner* (1962) and the Oscar-winning *Tom Jones* (1963). • *The Man Between* 1953 (m); *The Red Beret* 1953 (m); *The Black Knight* 1954 (m); *High and Dry* 1954 (m); *Make Me an Offer* 1954 (m); *The Cockleshell Heroes* 1955 (m); *Touch and Go* 1955 (m); *Private's Progress* 1956 (m); *Three Men in a Boat* 1956 (m); *All at Sea* 1957 (m); *Lucky Jim* 1957 (m,m.cond); *Look Back in Anger* 1959 (m); *The Entertainer* 1960 (m); *A Taste of Honey* 1961 (m,m.cond); *The Loneliness of the Long Distance Runner* 1962 (m); *Tom Jones* 1963 (m,m.cond) **(AABM)**; *Guns at Batasi* 1964 (m,m.cond); *The Amorous Adventures of Moll Flanders* 1965 (m,m.cond); *The Loved One* 1965 (m); *A Fine Madness* 1966 (m,m.cond); *Torn Curtain* 1966 (m); *The Honey Pot* 1967 (m); *The Charge of the Light Brigade* 1968 (m); *Country Dance* 1970 (m); *Start the Revolution Without Me* 1970 (m); *Mr. Forbush and the Penguins* 1971 (m); *Sleuth* 1972 (m) **(AANBM)**; *Luther* 1974 (m,m.dir); *Ride a Wild Pony* 1975 (m); *Joseph Andrews* 1976 (m); *The Seven Per-Cent Solution* 1976 (m); *Swashbuckler* 1976 (m); *A Bridge Too Far* 1977 (m,m.dir); *Highpoint* 1979 (m); *Strange Invaders* 1983 (m); *Code Name: Emerald* 1985 (m); *Grace Quigley* 1985 (m); *To Die For* 1989 (m).

Adjani, Isabelle • Actress; also producer. • Born Germany, June 27, 1955. One of France's leading actresses who first earned critical praise at age 17 as a member of the Comédie Française. Adjani gained immediate stardom with her first major film role, in François Truffaut's *The Story of Adèle H.* (1975), and went on to appear in films by noted international directors including André Téchiné (*Barocco* 1976), Werner Herzog (*Nosferatu* 1979), James Ivory (*Quartet* 1981) and Carlos Saura (*Antonieta* 1981). *Camille Claudel* (1989), her first film as producer, was directed by former companion Bruno Nuytten, by whom she has a son. • *Le Petit Bougnat* 1969 (a); *Faustine et le bel été* 1971 (a); *La Gifle/The Slap* 1974 (a); *L'Histoire d'Adèle H./The Story of Adèle H.* 1975 (a) **(AANBA)**; *Barocco* 1976 (a); *Le Locataire/The Tenant* 1976 (a); *Violette et François* 1977 (a); *The Driver* 1978 (a); *Nosferatu, Phantom der Nacht/Nosferatu* 1978 (a); *Les Soeurs Brontë* 1978 (a); *Possession* 1981 (a); *Quartet* 1981 (a,song); *Tout feu, tout flamme* 1981 (a); *Antonieta* 1982 (a); *L'Eté meurtrier/One Deadly Summer* 1982 (a); *Mortelle Randonnée* 1982 (a);

Subway 1985 (a); *Ishtar* 1987 (a); *Camille Claudel* 1988 (a,p) **(AANBA)**; *Lung Ta: Les cavaliers du vent* 1990 (a).

Adler, Buddy • Producer; also executive. • Born E. Maurice Adler, New York, NY, June 22, 1909; died July 12, 1960. *Educ.* Columbia; University of Pennsylvania, Philadelphia. Production chief at 20th Century-Fox from 1956 until his death, Adler began his career writing shorts for MGM, became a producer for Columbia in 1947, and sired an Oscar-winning best picture in 1953 with *From Here to Eternity*. Although most of the films he produced were solid commercial hits such as *Love Is a Many Splendored Thing* (1955), *Anastasia* (1956) and *South Pacific* (1958), Adler was also responsible for the hard-hitting drug melodrama, *A Hatful of Rain* (1957). Married to leading lady Anita Louise (aka Anita Fremault) until his death. • *The Dark Past* 1948 (p); *Tell It to the Judge* 1949 (p); *No Sad Songs For Me* 1950 (p); *A Woman of Distinction* 1950 (p); *The Harlem Globetrotters* 1951 (p); *Saturday's Hero* 1951 (p); *Last of the Comanches* 1952 (p); *Paula* 1952 (p); *From Here to Eternity* 1953 (p) **(AABP)**; *Salome* 1953 (p); *Violent Saturday* 1954 (p); *House of Bamboo* 1955 (p); *The Left Hand of God* 1955 (p); *The Lieutenant Wore Skirts* 1955 (p); *Love Is a Many Splendored Thing* 1955 (p) **(AANBP)**; *The Revolt of Mamie Stover* 1955 (p); *Soldier of Fortune* 1955 (p); *Anastasia* 1956 (p); *The Bottom of the Bottle* 1956 (p); *Bus Stop* 1956 (p); *A Hatful of Rain* 1957 (p); *Heaven Knows, Mr. Allison* 1957 (p); *The Inn of the Sixth Happiness* 1958 (p); *South Pacific* 1958 (p).

Adler, Stella • *aka* Stella Ardler • Teacher, actress; also stage director. • Born New York, NY, 1902. One of America's foremost acting coaches, and one of few Americans to have studied the "method" with its originator, Constantin Stanislavsky; former students include Marlon Brando, Robert De Niro, Warren Beatty and Harvey Keitel. • *Love on Toast* 1937 (a); *Shadow of the Thin Man* 1941 (a); *My Girl Tisa* 1948 (a).

Adlon, Percy • Director, producer; screenwriter. • Born Munich, Germany, June 1, 1935. *Educ.* Munich University (art, theater history, German). Thoughtful, stylish director who began his career in repertory theater but soon graduated to editing and narrating literary programs for German radio. He began working in TV in 1970, and made several shorts and documentaries before being commissioned in 1978 to make a full-length television film, *The Guardian and His Poet*, about Swiss poet Robert Walser and his publisher/mentor. Well received at several major film festivals, *Guardian* paved the way for Adlon to make his first feature, *Celeste* (1981), a painstaking recreation of the last days of Marcel Proust as witnessed by his maid.

Adlon's first major international acclaim came with *Sugarbaby* (1985), an off-beat love story featuring a subway conductor and a portly female mortician. It was praised for its joyful portrayal of sexual desire on the part of an unglamorous, overweight woman (played by Marianne Sagebrecht, who was also at the center of two later Adlon films, *Bagdad Cafe* 1987 and *Rosalie Goes Shopping* 1989). Adlon's wife Eleanore has produced all but one of his films and wrote the script for *Bagdad Cafe*. • *Celeste* 1981 (d,sc); *Letze Funf Tage/The Last Five Days* 1982 (d); *Die Schaukel/The Swing* 1983 (d,sc); *Zuckerbaby/Sugarbaby* 1985 (d,p,sc,story); *Bagdad Cafe* 1987 (d,p,sc,story); *Rosalie Goes Shopping* 1989 (d,p,sc).

Adrian • *aka* Gilbert A. Adrian • Costume designer • Born Adrian Adolph Greenberg, Naugatuck, CT, March 3, 1903; died September 13, 1959. *Educ.* New York School for Applied and Fine Arts. Long-time chief MGM designer who created both glamorous and stylishly "plain" wardrobes for such leading ladies as Joan Crawford (*Our Blushing Brides* 1930, *Grand Hotel* 1932), Greta Garbo (*Anna Christie* 1930, *Queen Christina* 1933, *Anna Karenina* 1935, *Camille* 1937, *Two-Faced Woman* 1941) and Katharine Hepburn (*The Philadelphia Story* 1940, *Woman of the Year* 1942). Adrian established his own fashion company in 1942. He had started designing costumes for the Broadway-bound musicals, *Grand Hotel* and *Camelot* when he died. Married to Janet Gaynor from 1939 until his death. • *The Eagle* 1925 (cost); *Her Sister From Paris* 1925 (cost); *Fig Leaves* 1926 (cost); *Gigolo* 1926 (cost); *The Volga Boatman* 1926 (cost); *The Angel of Broadway* 1927 (cost); *The Country Doctor* 1927 (cost); *The Forbidden Woman* 1927 (cost); *Vanity* 1927 (cost); *The Wreck of the Hesperus* 1927 (cost); *The Blue Danube* 1928 (cost); *Chicago* 1928 (cost); *The Masks of the Devil* 1928 (cost); *Midnight Madness* 1928 (cost); *Skyscraper* 1928 (cost); *A Woman of Affairs* 1928 (cost); *The Bridge of San Luis Rey* 1929 (cost); *Dynamite* 1929 (cost); *The Godless Girl* 1929 (cost); *The Kiss* 1929 (cost); *The Trial of Mary Dugan* 1929 (cost); *Anna Christie* 1930 (cost); *The Divorcee* 1930 (cost); *A Lady's Morals* 1930 (cost); *Madam Satan* 1930 (cost); *Our Blushing Brides* 1930 (cost); *Grand Hotel* 1932 (cost); *Red Dust* 1932 (gowns); *Smilin' Through* 1932 (cost); *Queen Christina* 1933 (cost); *The Barretts of Wimpole Street* 1934 (cost); *The Merry Widow* 1934 (cost); *Anna Karenina* 1935 (cost); *Mark of the Vampire* 1935 (cost); *Naughty Marietta* 1935 (cost); *Broadway Melody of 1936* 1936 (cost); *The Great Ziegfeld* 1936 (cost); *Romeo and Juliet* 1936 (cost); *Rose Marie* 1936 (cost); *Camille* 1937 (cost); *Maytime* 1937 (cost); *Marie Antoinette* 1938 (cost); *The Philadelphia Story* 1940 (cost); *Two-Faced Woman* 1941 (cost); *Ziegfeld Girl* 1941 (cost); *Woman of the Year* 1942 (cost).

Agee, James • Critic; also screenwriter, novelist. • Born James Rufus Agee, Knoxville, TN, November 27, 1909; died May 16, 1955, New York, NY. Noted American author whose early death at age 45 and posthumously published works elevated him to the mythic status of romantic literary hero-victim. Agee's best known books include the compelling documentary collaboration with photographer Walker Evans, *Let Us Now Praise Famous Men* (1941) which chronicled the hard lives of Alabama sharecroppers, and the autobiographical, Pulitzer Prize-winning novel, *A Death in the Family*, posthumously published in 1957.

As a film critic, Agee made a name for himself with his intelligent, elegant prose in *Time* and *The Nation* during the 1940s. In 1948 he gave up reviewing to co-write John Huston's *The African Queen* (1951) and to script on his own the bizarre cult favorite, Charles Laughton's *The Night of the Hunter* (1955).

The two-volume *Agee on Film*—the first part (1958) containing his acclaimed film criticism, the second (1960) his screenplays—was published posthumously. *All the Way Home*, Tad Mosel's Pulitzer Prize-winning stage adaptation of *A Death in the Family*, was presented on Broadway in 1961 and later served as the basis for the film version in 1963. • *The Quiet One* 1949 (commentary,dial); *The African Queen* 1951 (sc) **(AANBSC)**; *Crin Blanc le cheval sauvage* 1952 (commentary—English-language version); *Face to Face* 1952 (a,sc); *Genghis Khan* 1952 (commentary—English-language version); *In the Street (short)* 1952 (d); *Green Magic* 1955 (sc,commentary—English-language version); *The Night of the Hunter* 1955 (sc); *All the Way Home* 1963 (from novel *A Death in the Family*).

Agostini, Philippe • Director of photography; also director. • Born Paris, August 11, 1910. Noted stylist who first gained attention with his striking black-and-white cinematography for Robert Bresson's *Les anges du péché* (1943) and *Les dames du Bois de Boulogne* (1945); Agostini also shot Jules Dassin's gritty *Rififi* in 1955. He began directing in the 1950s, turning out mostly pedestrian films of religious content. • *Itto* 1935 (cam.op); *Un Carnet de Bal* 1937 (cam.op); *Le Ruisseau* 1938 (cam.op); *Tempête sur l'Asie/Storm Over Asia* 1938 (cam.op); *Le Jour Se Lève/Daybreak* 1939 (cam.op); *Remorques/Storm Waters* 1941 (cam.op); *Les Deux Timides* 1942 (ph); *Lettres d'Amour* 1942 (ph); *Le Mari-*

age de Chiffon 1942 (ph); *Les Anges du péché* 1943 (ph); *Douce* 1943 (ph); *Les Dames du Bois de Boulogne* 1945 (ph); *Les Portes de la nuit/Gates of the Night* 1946 (ph); *Sylvie et le Fantôme* 1946 (ph); *Monseigneur* 1949 (ph); *Pattes Blanches* 1949 (ph); *Topaze* 1950 (ph); *La Nuit est mon royaume* 1951 (ph); *Le Plaisir* 1951 (ph); *Leur dernière nuit* 1953 (ph); *Ordinations (short)* 1954 (d); *Du Rififi chez les hommes/Rififi* 1955 (ph); *Si Paris nous etait conté* 1955 (ph); *La Mariée est Trop Belle* 1956 (sc); *Paris Palace Hotel* 1956 (ph); *Les Trois font la paire* 1957 (ph); *Le Naif aux quarante enfants* 1958 (d,sc); *Dialogue des Carmélites* 1960 (d,uncred.); *Tu es Pierre* 1960 (d,sc); *Recontres* 1961 (d,d,sc); *La Soupe aux poulets* 1963 (d); *La Petite fille è la recherche du Printemps* 1971 (d); *Grandeur Nature* 1974 (d).

Agutter, Jenny • Actress • Born Taunton, England, December 20, 1952. Talented, atypically beautiful teenage lead who made a smooth transition to adult roles. • *East of Sudan* 1964; *A Man Could Get Killed* 1966; *Gates to Paradise* 1967; *Star!* 1968; *I Start Counting* 1969; *The Railway Children* 1970; *Walkabout* 1971; *The Eagle Has Landed* 1976; *Logan's Run* 1976; *Dominique* 1977; *Equus* 1977; *China 9, Liberty 37* 1978; *The Riddle of the Sands* 1979; *Sweet William* 1979; *An American Werewolf in London* 1981; *Amy* 1981; *The Survivor* 1981; *Secret Places* 1985; *Dark Tower* 1989; *Child's Play 2* 1990; *Darkman* 1990; *King of the Wind* 1990.

Aherne, Brian • Actor • Born King's Norton, England, May 2, 1902; died February 10, 1986, Venice, FL. *Educ.* Malvern College, England (architecture). Charming, classically handsome leading man who gained attention in several British silents before going to Hollywood in 1933. Memorable in the supporting role of the Emperor Maximilian, in *Juarez* (1939). Aherne was married to actress Joan Fontaine from 1939 to 1945. • *Shooting Stars* 1927; *Song of Songs* 1933; *The Fountain* 1934; *What Every Woman Knows* 1934; *I Live My Life* 1935; *Sylvia Scarlett* 1935; *Beloved Enemy* 1936; *The Great Garrick* 1937; *Merrily We Live* 1938; *Captain Fury* 1939; *Juarez* 1939 **(AANBSA)**; *Hired Wife* 1940; *The Lady in Question* 1940; *My Son, My Son* 1940; *Vigil in the Night* 1940; *The Man Who Lost Himself* 1941; *Skylark* 1941; *Smilin' Through* 1941; *My Sister Eileen* 1942; *A Night to Remember* 1942; *First Comes Courage* 1943; *Forever and a Day* 1943; *What a Woman!* 1943; *The Locket* 1946; *Angel on the Amazon* 1948; *Smart Woman* 1948; *Titanic* 1953; *A Bullet Is Waiting* 1954; *Prince Valiant* 1954; *The Swan* 1956; *The Best of Everything* 1959; *Susan Slade* 1961; *Sword of Lancelot* 1963; *The Cavern* 1965; *Rosie* 1967.

Aiello, Danny • Actor • Born Danny Louis Aiello, Jr., New York, NY, June 20, 1933. Experienced Broadway performer before entering films at the age of 40 in *Bang the Drum Slowly* (1973). Aiello has since established himself as a leading New York character actor in a wide variety of roles, from the adulterous and unsympathetic husband in Woody Allen's *The Purple Rose of Cairo* (1985) to the confused and trapped pizzeria owner in Spike Lee's *Do the Right Thing* (1989). • *Bang the Drum Slowly* 1973; *The Godfather, Part II* 1974; *The Front* 1976; *Fingers* 1977; *Bloodbrothers* 1978; *Defiance* 1980; *Hide in Plain Sight* 1980; *Chu Chu and the Philly Flash* 1981; *Fort Apache, the Bronx* 1981; *Amityville II: The Possession* 1982; *Deathmask* 1983; *Old Enough* 1984; *Once Upon a Time in America* 1984; *Key Exchange* 1985; *The Protector* 1985; *The Purple Rose of Cairo* 1985; *The Stuff* 1985; *Man on Fire* 1987; *Moonstruck* 1987; *The Pick-Up Artist* 1987; *Radio Days* 1987; *The January Man* 1988; *White Hot* 1988; *Do the Right Thing* 1989 **(AANBSA)**; *Harlem Nights* 1989; *Making "Do the Right Thing"* 1989; *Russicum* 1989; *The Closer* 1990; *Jacob's Ladder* 1990; *Once Around* 1991; *Hudson Hawk* 1991; *29th Street* 1991.

Aimée, Anouk • Actress • Born Françoise Sorya Dreyfus, Paris, April 27, 1932. *Educ.* Bauer-Therond Dramatic School, Paris. Sultry, enigmatic leading lady of several classic European films of the 1950s and 60s. Formerly married to actor Albert Finney. Aimée is most widely known for her leading role in *A Man and A Woman* (1966), opposite Jean-Louis Trintignant, a romantic icon of the 1960s. • *La Maison sous la mer* 1946; *La Fleur de l'age* 1947; *Les Amants de Vérone* 1948; *The Golden Salamander* 1949; *Conquêtes du froid (short)* 1951; *Noche de Tormenta* 1951; *La Bergère et le ramoneur* 1952; *The Man Who Watched Trains Go By* 1952; *Le Rideau cramoisi* 1952; *Forever My Heart* 1954; *Contraband Spain* 1955; *Ich suche dich* 1955; *Les Mauvaises Rencontres* 1955; *Nina* 1956; *Pot Bouille* 1957; *Tous peuvent me tuer* 1957; *Montparnasse 19* 1958; *La Tête contre les murs* 1958; *La Dolce Vita* 1959; *Les Dragueurs* 1959; *The Journey* 1959; *Il Giudizio Universale* 1961; *L'Imprévu* 1961; *Lola* 1961; *Quai Notre Dame* 1961; *Le Farceur* 1962; *Sodoma e Gomorra/Sodom and Gomorrah* 1962; *Il Giorno più corto* 1963; *Les Grands chemins* 1963; *Otto e Mezzo/8 1/2* 1963; *Il Successo* 1963; *Il Terrorista* 1963; *Liola* 1964; *Le Voci bianche* 1964; *La Fuga* 1965; *Il Morbidone* 1965; *Lo Scandalo* 1965; *La Stagioni del nostro amore* 1965; *Un Homme et une femme/A Man and a Woman* 1966 **(AANBA)**; *Model Shop* 1968; *Un Soir un Train* 1968; *The Appointment* 1969; *Justine* 1969; *Si c'était à refaire* 1976; *Mon premier amour* 1978; *Salto Nel Vuoto* 1980; *La Tragedia di un Uomo Ridicolo/The Tragedy of a Ridiculous Man* 1981; *Qu-est-ce qui fait courir David?/What Makes David Run?* 1982; *Le Général de l'Armée Morte* 1983; *Success Is the Best Revenge* 1984; *Viva la Vie!* 1984; *Un Homme et une femme: Vingt ans déjà/A Man and a Woman: 20 Years Later* 1986; *Arrivederci e Grazie* 1988; *La Table tournante* 1988; *Bethune: The Making of a Hero* 1990; *Il y a des jours... et des lunes* 1990.

Aitken, Harry E. • Executive; also exhibitor. • Born Waukesha, WI, 1870; died 1956. Early film mogul who lured D.W. Griffith away from Biograph and helped fund and distribute *The Birth of a Nation* (1915). After creating the independent Majestic Pictures in 1911, Aitken formed Mutual the follwing year and in 1915 Triangle Pictures Corporation—named for directors Griffith, Chaplin and Ince. The company lasted, ironically, for three years, and Aitken left the film business in 1920.

Akerman, Chantal • Director; also actress, screenwriter. • Born Brussels, Belgium, June 1950. *Educ.* Institut Supérieur des Arts du Spectacle et Techniques de Diffusion (INSAS), Brussels; International University, Paris (theater). Considered one of the most significant independent filmmakers of the 1970s and 80s, Akerman's pronounced visual style, influenced by structuralism and minimalism, offers astute insights into women's role in modern culture.

Akerman's interest in film was sparked at the age of 15 by a viewing of Jean-Luc Godard's *Pierrot le Fou*, prompting her to enroll in the Belgian film school, INSAS. After about two years' study she quit school, eager to begin making films rather than sitting in a classroom. Akerman saved money from clerical and waitressing jobs to make several short films which received minimal recognition.

It was not until she moved to New York in 1972 that Akerman began to develop her distinctive visual style and to deal with those themes which have dominated her work thus far. In America she became acquainted with the films of the avant-garde, specifically those of Michael Snow, which influenced her perception of the relationship between film, space and time. Her first two features, *Hotel Monterey* (1972) and *Je Tu Il Elle* (1974), with their studiously static camerawork and minimal dialogue, were early indications of the visual style which came to full flowering in *Jeanne Dielman, 23 quai du Commerce, 1080 Bruxelles* (1975). This 200 minute, minimally plotted film scrutinized three days in the life of a woman (Delphine Seyrig) who adheres to a regimented schedule of cleaning, cooking and caring for her teenage son. Every day she also takes in one male caller to make ends meet. On the third day her schedule is interrupted, and she later experiences an orgasm with her male caller. Her response to these unfathomable alterations in her routine is to thrust a pair of scissors into the man's throat.

Reception for *Jeanne Dielman* was mixed. It was criticized by many as a boring and meaningless minimalist exercise; Akerman's defenders, however, were awed by her visual aesthetic and use of real time to emphasize the routine of Seyrig's world. Thanks to the film's exposure, Akerman was able to secure financial backing from the Gaumont company and from German TV for *Les Rendezvous d'Anna* (1978). Her first semi-commercial effort, it featured popular French actors Aurore Clément and Jean-Pierre Cassel in a story of a female director treking across Europe to promote her latest film. Again, static camerawork and minimal dialogue created a sense of alienation which mirrored the emptiness and insincerity of the protagonist's encounters.

After failing to raise $25 million for an adaptation of Isaac Bashevis Singer's 1969 novel *The Manor*, Akerman returned to independent production with *All Night Long* (1982), an insightful drama contrasting romantic illusions with harsh realities. Akerman's most accessible film to date is *Golden Eighties* (1986), a satire of musicals set completely within the confines of a Brussels shopping mall. Here too her concern is with idealized notions of romance; unlike her earlier works, however, the central story is complemented by several subplots and the film's pacing is a little more sprightly. Akerman's signature camera does remain static, providing a unique perspective on the structured world of the shopping mall.

In 1988 Akerman returned to New York to film *American Stories/Food, Family and Philosophy*, an exploration of her Jewish heritage through a series of stories told by immigrants. To support herself, Akerman has held a number of teaching posts; she has stated a desire to make more commercially viable films because of the financial constraints now on independent production. PP • *La Chambre (short)* 1972 (a,d,sc); *Hotel Monterey* 1972 (d,sc); *Je Tu Il Elle* 1974 (a,d,sc); *Jeanne Dielman, 23 quai du Commerce, 1080 Bruxelles* 1975 (d,sc); *Nuit et Jour/News From Home* 1977 (a,d,sc,commentary); *Les Rendez-Vous d'Anna* 1978 (d,sc,dial); *5% de Risque* 1980 (a); *Toute une nuit/All Night Long* 1982 (d,sc); *Les Années 80* 1983 (d,sc,lyrics); *On Tour With Pina Bausch* 1983 (d,sc); *L'Homme à la Valise* 1984 (a,d,sc); *Paris vu par...vingt ans Aprés* 1984 (d,sc—*J'ai Faim, J'ai Froid*); *Elle a passé tant d'heures sous les Sunlights* 1985 (a); *Golden Eighties* 1986 (d,sc,lyrics); *Letters Home* 1986 (d); *Seven Women—Seven Sins* 1987 (d,sc—"Sloth"); *Histoires d'Amérique/American Stories* 1988 (d,sc); *Les Ministères de l'art* 1988 (a); *Un jour Pina m'a demandé* 1988 (d).

Albert, Eddie • Actor • Born Edward Albert Heimberger, Rock Island, IL, April 22, 1908. *Educ.* University of Minnesota. Personable character actor from radio and the stage who entered films in 1938, reprising his stage role as the star pitcher for a military college's baseball team in *Brother Rat*. In his long and varied stage, screen and television career, Albert's roles have ranged from amiable best friend of the romantic lead, charming and not so charming con men and even outright villians. He was most memorable as the photographer in *Roman Holiday* (1953) and the reformed alcoholic in *I'll Cry Tomorrow* (1955).

In the 1960s Albert co-starred with Eva Gabor on TV's long-running "Green Acres" (1965-71) and returned to films as Cybill Shepherd's impeccably Waspish father in *The Heartbreak Kid* (1972). Married to actress Margo from 1945 until her death in 1985. Their son Edward Albert is also an actor. • *Brother Rat* 1938; *Four Wives* 1939; *On Your Toes* 1939; *An Angel From Texas* 1940; *Brother Rat and a Baby* 1940; *A Dispatch From Reuters* 1940; *My Love Came Back* 1940; *Four Mothers* 1941; *The Great Mr. Nobody* 1941; *Out of the Fog* 1941; *Thieves Fall Out* 1941; *The Wagons Roll at Night* 1941; *Eagle Squadron* 1942; *Treat 'Em Rough* 1942; *Bombardier* 1943; *Ladies' Day* 1943; *Lady Bodyguard* 1943; *Strange Voyage* 1945; *The Perfect Marriage* 1946; *Rendezvous With Annie* 1946; *Hit Parade of 1947* 1947; *Smash-Up, the Story of a Woman* 1947; *Time Out of Mind* 1947; *The Dude Goes West* 1948; *You Gotta Stay Happy* 1948; *The Fuller Brush Girl* 1950; *Meet Me After the Show* 1951; *U.S.S. Tea Kettle* 1951; *Actors and Sin* 1952; *Carrie* 1952; *Roman Holiday* 1953 **(AANBSA)**; *The Girl Rush* 1955; *I'll Cry Tomorrow* 1955; *Oklahoma!* 1955; *Attack!* 1956; *The Teahouse of the August Moon* 1956; *The Joker Is Wild* 1957; *The Sun Also Rises* 1957; *The Gun Runners* 1958; *Orders to Kill* 1958; *The Roots of Heaven* 1958; *Beloved Infidel* 1959; *The Two Little Bears* 1961; *The Young Doctors* 1961; *The Longest Day* 1962; *Madison Avenue* 1962; *Who's Got the Action?* 1962; *Miracle of the White Stallions* 1963; *Captain Newman, M.D.* 1964; *Seven Women* 1965; *The Heartbreak Kid* 1972 **(AANBSA)**; *Escape to Witch Mountain* 1974; *The Longest Yard* 1974; *McQ* 1974; *The Take* 1974; *Birch Interval* 1975; *The Devil's Rain* 1975; *Hustle* 1975; *Whiffs* 1975; *Moving Violation* 1976; *The Concorde - Airport '79* 1979; *Foolin' Around* 1979; *Yesterday* 1979; *How to Beat the High Cost of Living* 1980; *Take This Job and Shove It* 1981; *The Act* 1982; *Yes, Giorgio* 1982; *Dreamscape* 1984; *Stitches* 1985; *Head Office* 1986; *Terminal Entry* 1987; *The Big Picture* 1989; *Brenda Starr* 1989; *Deadly Illusion* 1989.

Albertson, Jack • Actor • Born Lynn, MA, 1910; died November 25, 1981. Veteran character player, and one of only three actors (along with Melvyn Douglas and Paul Scofield) to win the "triple crown" of awards (Oscar, Emmy and Tony). • *Top Banana* 1954; *Bring Your Smile Along* 1955; *Over-Exposed* 1955; *The Harder They Fall* 1956; *The Unguarded Moment* 1956; *You Can't Run Away From It* 1956; *Don't Go Near the Water* 1957; *Man of a Thousand Faces* 1957; *Monkey on My Back* 1957; *Teacher's Pet* 1958; *Never Steal Anything Small* 1959; *Days of Wine and Roses* 1962; *Lover Come Back* 1962; *Period of Adjustment* 1962; *Who's Got the Action?* 1962; *Kissin' Cousins* 1964; *Roustabout* 1964; *A Tiger Walks* 1964; *How to Murder Your Wife* 1965; *The Flim-Flam Man* 1967; *Changes* 1968; *How to Save a Marriage and Ruin Your Life* 1968; *The Subject Was Roses* 1968 **(AABSA)**; *Justine* 1969; *Rabbit, Run* 1970; *Squeeze a Flower* 1970; *The Late Liz* 1971; *Willy Wonka and the Chocolate Factory* 1971; *Pickup on 101* 1972; *The Poseidon Adventure* 1972; *Dead and Buried* 1981; *The Fox and the Hound* 1981.

Alcaine, Jose Luis • Director of photography • Born Tangier, Algeria, December 26, 1938. *Educ.* Escuela Oficial de Cinematografia, Madrid. Prolific Spanish cinematographer who has worked with directors Vicente Aranda (*El Lute* 1987) and Manuel Guttierez Aragon (*Malaventura* 1988); best known in the US for the crisp color of Pedro Almodovar's *Women on the Verge of a Nervous Breakdown* (1988). • *El Niño Es Nuestro* 1972; *Corazón Solitario* 1973; *Vera* 1973; *Yo la Vì Primero* 1974; *País S.A.* 1975; *Quién Puede Matar a un Niño?* 1975; *Ya Soy Mujér* 1975; *Retrato de Familia* 1976; *Díos Bendiga Cada rincón de Esta Casa* 1977; *El Puente* 1977; *Così come sei/Stay as You Are* 1978; *Oro Rojo* 1978; *Soldados* 1978; *Vámonos, Bárbara* 1978; *La Campanada* 1979; *Marián* 1979; *La Triple mort du troisième personnage* 1979; *La Muchacha de las Bragas de Oro* 1980; *Demonios en el Jardín/Demons in the Garden* 1982; *El Sur* 1983; *Akelarre* 1984; *El Caso Almeria* 1984; *Tasio* 1984; *La Corte de Faraón* 1985; *Los Paraises Perdídos* 1985; *La Regina del Mate* 1985; *Rustler's Rhapsody* 1985; *El Caballero del Dragón* 1986; *Hay Que Deshacer la Casa* 1986; *Mambru Se Fué a la Guerra* 1986; *La Mitad del Cielo* 1986; *Viaje a Ninguna Parte* 1986; *Barbablú Barbablú* 1987; *Jarrapellejos* 1987; *El Lute I* 1987; *El Lute II* 1988; *Malaventura* 1988; *Mujeres al Borde de un Ataque de Nervios/Women on the Verge of a Nervous Breakdown* 1988; *El Mar y el Tiempo* 1989; *El Mono Loco/The Mad

Monkey 1989; *Atame!/Tie Me Up! Tie Me Down!* 1990; *Áy, Carmela!* 1990; *Solo o en Compañía de Otros* 1991.

Alcoriza, Luis • Director; also screenwriter, actor. • Born Badajóz, Spain, 1920. Co-wrote many of Luis Buñuel's Mexican classics. Alcoriza's own films as director have had little international success. • *El Gran Calavera* 1949 (a,sc); *Los Olvidados/The Young and the Damned* 1950 (sc); *La Híja Del Engaño* 1951 (sc); *El Bruto/The Brute* 1952 (sc); *El/This Strange Passion* 1952 (sc); *La Ilusión Viaja En Tranvía/Illusion Travels By Streetcar* 1954 (sc); *El Río y la Muerte/Death and the River* 1954 (sc); *La Mort en ce jardin/Death in the Garden* 1956 (sc); *Untouched* 1956 (sc); *La Fièvre Monte à El Pao/Fever Mounts in El Pao* 1959 (sc); *El Angel Exterminadór/The Exterminating Angel* 1962 (sc); *Tlayucan* 1962 (d,sc); *La Puerta (short)* 1968 (d); *Preságio* 1974 (d,sc); *Terrór y Encajes Negros* 1986 (d,sc); *Lo Que Importa Es Vivír* 1989 (d,sc).

Alcott, John • Director of photography • Born London, c. 1931; died July 28, 1986, Cannes, France. Highly acclaimed cinematographer, especially for his four collaborations with Stanley Kubrick. • *Whistle Down the Wind* 1961 (focus puller); *2001: A Space Odyssey* 1968 (add.ph); *A Clockwork Orange* 1971 (ph); *Little Malcolm and His Struggle Against the Eunuchs* 1974 (ph); *Barry Lyndon* 1975 (ph) **(AABPH)**; *Overlord* 1975 (ph); *Disappearance* 1977 (ph); *March or Die* 1977 (ph); *Who Is Killing the Great Chefs of Europe?* 1978 (ph); *The Shining* 1980 (ph); *Terror Train* 1980 (ph); *Fort Apache, the Bronx* 1981 (ph); *The Beastmaster* 1982 (ph); *El Triúnfo de un Hombre Llamado Caballo* 1982 (ph); *Vice Squad* 1982 (ph); *Under Fire* 1983 (ph); *Greystoke: The Legend of Tarzan, Lord of the Apes* 1984 (ph); *Miracles* 1984 (ph); *Baby: The Secret of the Lost Legend* 1985 (ph); *No Way Out* 1987 (ph); *White Water Summer* 1987 (ph).

Alda, Alan • Actor; also director, screenwriter. • Born New York, NY, January 28, 1936. *Educ.* Fordham University, New York (English); Cleveland Playhouse, OH. Son of actor Robert Alda whose break came with a starring role in the Broadway hit *The Owl and the Pussycat.* Best known for his 11 years as Hawkeye Pierce on the TV series "M*A*S*H" (1972-83), for which he wrote and directed numerous episodes, Alda has also made his mark in features. As director and actor, he has defined the role of the tolerant, good-natured, intelligent, middle-class, middle-aged American male for the 1980s and 90s. • *Gone Are the Days* 1963 (a); *Paper Lion* 1968 (a); *The Extraordinary Seaman* 1969 (a); *Jenny* 1969 (a); *The Mephisto Waltz* 1970 (a); *The Moonshine War* 1970 (a); *To Kill a Clown* 1972 (a); *California Suite* 1978 (a); *Same Time, Next Year* 1978 (a); *The Seduction of Joe Tynan* 1979 (a,sc); *The Four Seasons* 1981 (a,d,sc); *Sweet Liberty* 1986 (a,d,sc); *A New Life* 1988 (a,d,sc); *Crimes and Misdemeanors* 1989 (a); *Betsy's Wedding* 1990 (a,d,sc).

Aldo, G. R. • Director of photography • Born Aldo Graziati, Scorze, Italy, January 1, 1902; died 1953, Rome. Post-war Italian cinematographer hailed for the superb black-and-white compositions of films like *La Terra Trema* (1948) and *Umberto D* (1952). Aldo was killed in a car accident during the shooting of Luchino Visconti's *Senso* (1954). • *La Symphonie Fantastique* 1942 (cam.op); *La Chartreuse de Parme* 1948 (ph); *La Terra Trema* 1948 (ph); *Les Dernières jours de Pompei* 1949 (ph); *Miracolo a Milano/Miracle in Milan* 1950 (ph); *Tre storie proibite* 1951 (ph); *Othello* 1952 (ph); *Umberto D* 1952 (ph); *Stazione Termini/Indiscretion of an American Wife* 1953 (ph); *La Provinciale* 1953 (ph); *Senso/The Wanton Còntessa* 1954 (ph).

Aldredge, Theoni V. • Costume designer • Born Theoni Vachlioti, Salonika, Greece, August 22, 1932. *Educ.* Goodman Theater School of Drama, Chicago. Stage designer who entered films in the mid-1960s and has proven effective with everything from sumptuous period pieces (*The Great Gatsby* 1974) to contemporary thrillers (*The Fury* 1978) and outlandish comedies (*Ghostbusters* 1984). Married to actor Tom Aldredge. • *The Great Gatsby* 1974 (cost) **(AABCD)**; *Harry and Walter Go to New York* 1976 (cost); *Network* 1976 (cost); *Semi-Tough* 1977 (cost,cost); *The Cheap Detective* 1978 (cost,cost); *Eyes of Laura Mars* 1978 (cost); *The Fury* 1978 (cost); *The Champ* 1979 (cost,pd); *The Rose* 1979 (cost); *Can't Stop the Music* 1980 (cost); *A Change of Seasons* 1980 (cost—Shirley MacLaine); *Circle of Two* 1980 (cost); *Loving Couples* 1980 (cost); *Rich and Famous* 1981 (cost); *Annie* 1982 (cost); *Monsignor* 1982 (cost); *Ghostbusters* 1984 (cost); *Moonstruck* 1987 (cost); *We're No Angels* 1989 (cost); *Stanley and Iris* 1990 (cost).

Aldrich, Robert • Director; also producer. • Born Cranston, RI, August 9, 1918; died December 5, 1983, Los Angeles, CA. *Educ.* University of Virginia (economics). Famed for his macho mise-en-scène and resonant reworkings of classic action genres, Robert Aldrich became a model for many younger directors in the 1960s and 70s.

Dropping out of college and the career in banking or politics expected by his prominent Republican family (John D. Rockefeller, Jr. was an uncle), Aldrich entered film as a clerk at RKO in 1941. He rose through the ranks as a second assistant director, first assistant (working with Chaplin and Renoir, among others), production manager, studio manager and writer under contract to Enterprise Studios (1946-48).

In the early 1950s, Aldrich directed episodes of several TV series before finally making his feature film debut in 1953. He produced most of the films he directed and also contributed to their screenplays. His work aggressively confronted controversial social and political issues. Taking uncompromising positions in familiar genres and revising genre conventions, Aldrich challenged both the studio system and audience expectations.

Aldrich's dominant themes are man's efforts to prevail against both impossible odds and institutional oppression. In *Apache* (1954), the only tribal leader left unconquered after the defeat of Geronimo refuses to be subjugated by the white man but is also, ultimately, alienated from his own people. Aldrich returned to the same subject 18 years later in *Ulzana's Raid* (1972), in which Apache leader Ulzana breaks the reservation's institutional constraints, vowing to recapture lost land. In depicting the brutal savagery of the white soldiers, who are oblivious to the hostility they cause, Aldrich refuses to allow his characters the traditional redemption offered by the western genre.

In *The Big Knife* (1955), the Hollywood studio system is shown as nurturing dictatorial leaders who push individuals to compromise and suicide (the film contains blatant allusions to real-life moguls Harry Cohn and Jack Warner). *Whatever Happened to Baby Jane?* (1962) and *The Legend of Lylah Clare* (1968) continued to present a Hollywood breeding jealousy and empty myths rooted in egomania.

In *Attack!* (1956), the combination of cowardice and political compromise displayed by military officers destroys the common soldiers under their command. *Attack!* was criticized for Aldrich's violent, often frantic mise-en-scène: a soldier's arm is slowly crushed under a tank, for example, in a shot that can be taken as a metaphor for the results of institutional military incompetence.

The Dirty Dozen (1967) reiterates Aldrich's contemptuous view for a military machine which dehumanizes its subjects in order to make them capable of killing. The violent "heroics" of Robert Jefferson (Jim Brown)—dropping grenades that engulf trapped German officers in flames—illustrates how vicious men become under adversity.

Cynicism and pessimism permeate Aldrich's work. In the fatalistic *Kiss Me Deadly* (1955), private detective Mike Hammer attempts to track down the "great whatsit," a suitcase-sized atomic device which has been stolen by a spy; but the spy's greedy mistress opens the case, unleashing the device's deadly power in an apocalyptic finale. The film is arguably the director's most aesthetically striking and original, a hyper-kinetic reworking of the film noir genre that has become something of a cult favorite.

The abuse of institutional power motivates a terrorist in the political thriller *Twilight's Last Gleaming* (1977). A rogue general captures a nuclear missile silo and demands that the President read on national TV a Joint Chiefs of Staff memo admitting that over 50,000 Americans and 100,000 Southeast Asians died in a war the government knew America could never win. He insists that the President restore public confidence by calling the Vietnam war a "theatrical holocaust perpetrated by the criminally negligent." In Aldrich's cynical world-view, the Joint Chiefs sacrifice the President in order to maintain the credibility of the military complex.

On a smaller scale, *Hustle* (1975) reflects Aldrich's bleak vision of institutional betrayal. Gus, a police detective, can't win justice for the parents of a girl who accidentally drowned after an orgy with a protected leader of organized crime. Gus breaks the law to effect vengeance for the girl's father, then is himself killed by a petty criminal holding up a convenience store.

All The Marbles (1981), Aldrich's last film, was largely neglected by critics and audiences. It depicts two women wrestlers who confront the greed, sexism and humiliation of the wrestling world. Aldrich explicitly equates the physical abuse suffered by the women in the ring with the social abuse they suffer struggling for success and respect in a male-dominated field. RCB • *Pardon My Past* 1945 (ad); *The Southerner* 1945 (ad); *The Story of G.I. Joe* 1945 (ad); *The Strange Love of Martha Ivers* 1946 (ad); *Body and Soul* 1947 (ad); *The Private Affairs of Bel Ami* 1947 (ad); *Arch of Triumph* 1948 (ad); *Force of Evil* 1948 (ad); *So This Is New York* 1948 (ad); *Caught* 1949 (ad); *The Red Pony* 1949 (ad); *A Kiss For Corliss* 1950 (ad); *The White Tower* 1950 (ad); *The Big Night* 1951 (a); *M* 1951 (ad); *New Mexico* 1951 (ad); *Of Men and Music* 1951 (ad); *The Prowler* 1951 (ad); *Ten Tall Men* 1951 (assoc.p); *When I Grow Up* 1951 (prod.man); *Abbott and Costello Meet Captain Kidd* 1952 (ad); *The First Time* 1952 (assoc.p); *Limelight* 1952 (ad); *Big Leaguer* 1953 (d); *Apache* 1954 (d); *Vera Cruz* 1954 (d); *World For Ransom* 1954 (d,p); *The Big Knife* 1955 (d,p); *Kiss Me Deadly* 1955 (d,p); *Attack!* 1956 (d,p); *Autumn Leaves* 1956 (d); *The Gamma People* 1956 (story); *The Angry Hills* 1959 (d); *Ten Seconds to Hell* 1959 (d,sc); *The Last Sunset* 1961 (d); *Sodoma e Gomorra/Sodom and Gomorrah* 1962 (d); *What Ever Happened to Baby Jane?* 1962 (d,p); *Four For Texas* 1963 (d,p,sc,story); *Hush...Hush, Sweet Charlotte* 1964 (d,p); *The Flight of the Phoenix* 1965 (d,p); *The Dirty Dozen* 1967 (d); *The Killing of Sister George* 1968 (d,p); *The Legend of Lylah Clare* 1968 (d,p); *Whatever Happened to Aunt Alice?* 1969 (p); *Too Late the Hero* 1970 (d,p,sc,story); *The Grissom Gang* 1971 (d,p); *Ulzana's Raid* 1972 (d); *The Emperor of the North Pole* 1973 (d); *The Longest Yard* 1974 (d); *Hustle* 1975 (d,p); *The Choirboys* 1977 (d); *Twilight's Last Gleaming* 1977 (d); *The Frisco Kid* 1979 (d); *All the Marbles* 1981 (d).

Alea, Tomás Gutiérrez • Director, screenwriter • Born Havana, Cuba, December 11, 1928. *Educ.* University of Havana (law); Centro Sperimentale di Cinematografia, Rome. Cuba's greatest director, Alea was much influenced by Italian neorealism during his studies in Rome. He returned to Cuba in 1953 and joined the radical "Nuestro Tiempo" cultural society, becoming active in the film section.

In 1955 Alea co-directed with Julio García Espinosa, another member of the society, the 16mm documentary short *El Mégano*, which was seized by Fulgencio Batista's police because of its political content. Soon after the Cuban Revolution in 1959 Alea co-founded the national revolutionary film institute ICAIC ("Instituto del Arte y Industria Cinematografica"); he has remained a pillar of the organization ever since.

Alea's diverse creative personality has led him to experiment with a broad range of styles and themes. His first feature, *Stories of the Revolution* (1960), employs a neorealist style to present three dramatic sketches depicting the armed insurrection against Batista. The finest of Alea's historical films, *The Last Supper* (1976), draws on Afro-Cuban musical motifs and the literary style of magic realism to recreate an 18th-century slave revolt.

Alea has also made three satiric comedies that explore the legacy of bourgeois society in post-revolutionary Cuba. The madcap adventure *The Twelve Chairs* (1962) satirizes greed and bureaucracy, as does the Hollywood-influenced black comedy *Death of a Bureaucrat* (1966). In *The Survivors* (1979), an aristocratic family resorts to cannibalism in its efforts to remain isolated from the Revolution.

The stresses and strains in Cuba's revolutionary society were explored in two dramatic works, *Memories of Underdevelopment* (1968) and *Up to a Certain Point* (1984). *Memories*, Alea's masterpiece, blends documentary and drama to create a sensitive portrait of a politically uncommitted intellectual in the early days of the Revolution. The director's latest feature, *Letters From the Park* (1988), explores yet another genre, the romantic period piece.

Alea has written or co-scripted all his features and, in accordance with ICAIC's collective approach to filmmaking, has served as active advisor on two of the institute's most stylistically innovative films: *El otro Francisco*, directed by Sergei Giral, and *De cierta manera*, directed by Sara Gómez. He has also authored a book of film theory, *Dialectica del espectadór* (1982). DW • *El Mégano* (short) 1955 (d); *Esta Tierra Nuestra* (short) 1959 (d,sc); *Asemblea General* (short) 1960 (d,sc); *Historias de la Revolución/Stories of the Revolution* 1960 (d,sc); *Muerte al invasor* (short) 1961 (d,sc); *Las Doce Sillas/The Twelve Chairs* 1962 (d,sc); *Cumbite* 1964 (d,sc); *La Muerte de an Burocrata/Death of a Bureaucrat* 1966 (d,sc); *Papeles son Papeles* 1966 (idea); *Memorias del Subdesarollo/Memories of Underdevelopment* 1968 (d,sc); *Una Pelea Cubana Contra los Demonios* 1971 (d,sc); *El Arte del tobaco* 1974 (d,sc); *La Última Cena/The Last Supper* 1976 (d,sc,story); *Los Sobrevivientes/The Survivors* 1979 (d,sc); *Hasta Cierto Punto/Up to a Certain Point* 1984 (d,sc); *Se Permuta* 1985 (idea); *Cartas del Parque/Letters From the Park* 1988 (d,sc).

Aleandro, Norma • Actress; also screenwriter, author. • Born Argentina, 1941. Distinguished South American stage talent (actress, playwright, director) and TV performer who gained international recogniton, including being named best actress at Cannes, for her riveting performance in the Oscar-winning *The Official Story* (1985). • *La Tregua* 1974 (a); *Tobi* 1978 (a); *La Historia Oficiál/The Official Story* 1985 (a); *Gaby—A True Story* 1987 (a) (**AANBSA**); *Cousins* 1989 (a); *Cién Veces No Debo* 1990 (a); *Vital Signs* 1990 (a).

Alekan, Henri • Director of photography • Born Paris, February 10, 1909. *Educ.* Conservatoire des Arts et Métiers, Paris; Institut d'Optique. One of France's most distinguished and versatile cinematographers. Alekan became an assistant camera operator in 1929 and graduated to director of photography as a member of the French Resistance (he had escaped from prisoner-of-war camp in 1940). While he made his mark with directors such as René Clément (*Battle of the Rails* 1946), Jean Cocteau (*Beauty and the Beast* 1945) and Marcel Carné (*La Marie du port* 1949) in the 1940s, his later color work proved equally memorable.

Alekan is best known to contemporary audiences, however, for his lyrical return to black-and-white in Wim Wenders's *Wings of Desire* (1987). • *Mollenard* 1937 (ph); *Les Petites du Quai aux Fleurs* 1944 (ph); *La Belle et la Bête/Beauty and the Beast* 1945 (ph); *La Bataille du Rail/The Battle of the Rails* 1946 (ph); *Les Maudits* 1947 (ph); *Les Amants de Vérone* 1948 (ph); *Anna Karenina* 1948 (ph); *Une si jolie petite plage/Riptide* 1949 (ph); *La Marie du Port* 1940 (ph); *Juliette ou la clef des Songes* 1951 (ph); *Paris est toujours*

Paris 1951 (ph); *Le Fruit défendu* 1952 (ph); *Imbarco a Mezzanotte* 1952 (ph); *Roman Holiday* 1953 (ph); *Le Port de Désir/The House on the Waterfront* 1954 (ph); *Les Héros sont fatigués* 1955 (ph); *Le Cas du Dr. Laurent* 1956 (ph); *Austerlitz* 1960 (ph); *Un, deux, trois, quatre!/Black Tights* 1960 (ph); *Five Miles to Midnight* 1963 (ph); *Topkapi* 1964 (ph); *Lady L* 1965 (ph); *The Poppy Is Also a Flower* 1966 (ph); *Triple Cross* 1966 (ph); *Mayerling* 1968 (ph); *L'Arbre de Noël* 1969 (ph); *Figure in a Landscape* 1970 (ph); *Soleil Rouge* 1971 (ph); *L'Ombre et la nuit* 1978 (ph); *The Territory* 1981 (ph); *La Belle Captive* 1982 (ph); *Het Dak van de Walvis* 1982 (ph); *Der Stand der Dinge/The State of Things* 1982 (ph); *La Truite/The Trout* 1982 (ph); *Une Pierre dans la bouche* 1983 (ph); *Unser Nazi* 1984 (a); *Wundkanal* 1984 (ph); *Dorenavant tout sera comme d'habitude* 1985 (a); *Esther* 1986 (ph); *Der Himmel über Berlin/Wings of Desire* 1987 (ph); *Im Exil der Ertrunkenen Tiger (short)* 1988 (ph); *Berlin Jerusalem* 1989 (ph); *J'écris dans l'espace* 1989 (ph).

Alexander, Jane • Actress • Born Jane Quigley, Boston, MA, October 28, 1939. *Educ.* Sarah Lawrence College, Bronxville; University of Edinburgh. Much-lauded stage performer whose relatively few screen appearances have yielded four Oscar nominations. Alexander made her film debut in 1970, reprising her Tony Award-winning performance as prize fighter Jack Johnson's white mistress in *The Great White Hope*.

Often cast as forthright, plain characters, Alexander is noted for the seemingly effortless simplicity and unmannered honesty of her work. Although always dependable and sympathetic, she was exceptional as the mother in the understated, but harrowing, nuclear holocaust drama *Testament* (1983) and affecting as Eleanor Roosevelt in the television films *Eleanor and Franklin* (1976) and *Eleanor and Franklin: The White House Years* (1977). • *The Great White Hope* 1970 (a) **(AANBA)**; *A Gunfight* 1971 (a); *The New Centurions* 1972 (a); *All the President's Men* 1976 (a) **(AANBSA)**; *The Betsy* 1978 (a); *Kramer vs. Kramer* 1979 (a) **(AANBSA)**; *Brubaker* 1980 (a); *Night Crossing* 1981 (a); *Testament* 1983 (a) **(AANBA)**; *City Heat* 1984 (a); *Sweet Country* 1986 (a); *Square Dance* 1987 (a,exec.p); *Building Bombs* 1989 (a).

Alexandrov, Grigori • Director; also actor, screenwriter, editor. • Born Grigori Mormonenko, Yekaterinburg, Russia, February 23, 1903; died December 1983, USSR. Began his film career as an assistant to Sergei Eisenstein, with whom he co-directed both *October* (1928) and *The General Line* (1929). Alexandrov then accompanied the master on his trip to the West, directing the experimental short *Romance sentimentale* in Paris in 1930. (Production funds were raised on the strength of Eisenstein's being a co-director, though the film is really the work of Alexandrov and cinematographer Eduard Tissé.) From France the group moved first to the US (where Eisenstein's plans to film Dreiser's *An American Tragedy* fell through) and then Central America, where Eisenstein shot the bulk of his subsequently abandoned Mexican project (the film was edited and completed by Alexandrov and released as *Que Víva Mexico* in 1979).

Back in the USSR, Alexandrov made a name for himself as a director of effervescent musical comedies, notably *The Joyous Fellows* (1933), which stand out from the social realist works produced by his contemporaries. After succeeding Eisenstein as artistic director of Mosfilm in 1944, Alexandrov turned more to the Stalinist line. He continued to gain acclaim abroad with *Meeting on the Elbe* (1949) and *Glinka* (1952), both starring his wife Lyubov (Luba) Orlova. • *Bronenosets "Potyomkin"/Battleship Potemkin* 1925 (ad); *Oktyabar/October* 1928 (d,sc); *Generalnaya Linya/The General Line/Old and New* 1929 (d,sc); *Romance sentimentale (short)* 1930 (d); *Vstrecha na Elbe/Meeting on the Elbe* 1949 (d); *Kompozitor Glinka/Glinka* 1952 (d,sc); *Que Víva Mexico* 1979 (d,ed).

Alland, William • Producer; also actor. • Born Delmar, DE, March 4, 1916. Member of Orson Welles's Mercury Theater. Alland played the inquiring reporter in *Citizen Kane* (1941) before turning to producing. • *Citizen Kane* 1941 (a); *Macbeth* 1948 (a); *The Black Castle* 1952 (p); *Flesh and Fury* 1952 (story); *The Raiders* 1952 (p); *It Came From Outer Space* 1953 (p); *The Lawless Breed* 1953 (p,story); *The Stand at Apache River* 1953 (p); *Chief Crazy Horse* 1954 (p); *The Creature From the Black Lagoon* 1954 (p); *Dawn at Socorro* 1954 (p); *Four Guns to the Border* 1954 (p); *Johnny Dark* 1954 (p); *The Creature Walks Among Us* 1955 (p); *Revenge of the Creature* 1955 (p,story); *Tarantula* 1955 (p); *This Island Earth* 1955 (p); *The Mole People* 1956 (p); *The Deadly Mantis* 1957 (p,story); *A Gun For a Coward* 1957 (p); *The Lady Takes a Flyer* 1957 (p); *The Land Unknown* 1957 (p); *As Young As We Are* 1958 (p,story); *The Colossus of New York* 1958 (p); *The Party Crashers* 1958 (p); *Raw Wind in Eden* 1958 (p); *The Space Children* 1958 (p); *Look in Any Window* 1961 (d,p); *The Lively Set* 1964 (p,story); *The Rare Breed* 1966 (p); *Vérités et Mensonges/F For Fake* 1973 (a).

Allégret, Yves • *aka* Yves Champlain • Director; also screenwriter. • Born Paris, October 13, 1907; died January 31, 1987, Paris. Leading figure of post-WWII French cinema. Allégret revived the "poetic realism" which had colored French film of the 1930s with a trilogy of grim dramas—*Dédée* (1948), *Riptide* (1949) and *The Cheat* (1950)—all written by Jacques Sigurd. *Dédée* made a star of Simone Signoret, Allégret's wife from 1944 to 1949 and the mother of his actress daughter Catherine. His brother Marc was also a director. • *Tobie est un Ange* 1941 (d); *Les Deux Timides* 1942 (d); *La Boîte aux Rêves* 1945 (d,sc); *Les Démons de l'Aube* 1946 (d); *Dédée* 1948 (d,sc); *Une si jolie petite plage/Riptide* 1949 (d); *Manéges/The Cheat* 1950 (d); *Les Miracles n'ont lieu qu'une fois* 1951 (d); *Nez de Cuir* 1951 (d,sc); *La Jeune folle* 1952 (d); *Les Sept péchés capitaux/The Seven Deadly Sins* 1952 (d); *Les Orgueilleux* 1953 (d,sc); *Mam'zelle Nitouche* 1954 (d,sc); *Oasis* 1955 (d); *La Meilleure part* 1956 (d,sc); *Méfiez-vous Fillettes* 1957 (d); *Quand la femme s'en mêle* 1957 (d); *La Fille de Hambourg/Port of Desire* 1958 (d); *L'Ambitieuse* 1959 (d); *La Chien de Pique* 1960 (d,sc); *Konga Yo* 1962 (d,sc); *Germinal* 1963 (d); *Johnny Banco* 1967 (d,sc); *L'Invasion* 1970 (d); *Orzowei* 1975 (d); *Mords pas on t'aime* 1976 (d,sc).

Allen, Dede • Editor • Born Dorothea Carothers Allen, Cleveland, OH, 1925. *Educ.* Scripps College, Claremont, CA. One of the most distinguished American editors of the post-war era. Has worked often with Arthur Penn. • *Terror From the Year 5,000* 1958 (ed); *Odds Against Tomorrow* 1959 (ed); *The Hustler* 1961 (ed); *America, America* 1963 (ed); *Bonnie and Clyde* 1967 (ed); *Rachel, Rachel* 1968 (ed); *Alice's Restaurant* 1969 (ed); *Little Big Man* 1970 (ed); *Slaughterhouse-Five* 1971 (ed); *Serpico* 1973 (ed); *Visions of Eight* 1973 (ed); *Dog Day Afternoon* 1975 (ed) **(AANBED)**; *Night Moves* 1975 (ed); *The Missouri Breaks* 1976 (ed); *Slap Shot* 1977 (ed); *The Wiz* 1978 (ed); *Reds* 1981 (ed,exec.p) **(AANBED)**; *Mike's Murder* 1982 (ed); *Harry & Son* 1984 (ed); *The Breakfast Club* 1985 (ed); *Off Beat* 1986 (ed); *The Milagro Beanfield War* 1988 (ed); *Let It Ride* 1989 (ed); *Henry & June* 1990 (ed).

Allen, Irving • Producer, director • Born Poland, November 24, 1905; died December 17, 1987, Encino, CA. *Educ.* Georgetown University. Entered film as an editor at Universal, Paramount and Republic in 1929. During the 1940s, Allen directed a number of superb shorts which often won more acclaim than his low-budget features. In 1950 he wisely shifted from the director's chair to the producer's, and soon after formed Warwick Productions with Albert R. Broccoli, making films in both US and England. Turning solo producer in 1960, Allen was responsible for the Matt Helm series, *The Silencers* (1966), *The Ambushers* (1967) and *The Wrecking Crew* (1968). • *Forty Boys and a Song* (short) 1942 (d) **(AANBSF)**; *Strange Voyage* 1945 (d); *Avalanche* 1946 (d); *Climbing the Matterhorn (short)* 1947 (d,p)

(**AABSF**); *High Conquest* 1947 (d,p); *16 Fathoms Deep* 1948 (d,p); *Chase of Death (short)* 1949 (d,p) (**AANBSF**); *The Man on the Eiffel Tower* 1949 (p); *New Mexico* 1951 (p); *Slaughter Trail* 1951 (d,p); *The Red Beret* 1953 (p); *The Black Knight* 1954 (p); *Hell Below Zero* 1954 (p); *The Cockleshell Heroes* 1955 (p); *Prize of Gold* 1955 (p); *Odongo* 1956 (exec.p); *Safari* 1956 (exec.p); *Zarak* 1956 (p); *Fire Down Below* 1957 (p); *High Flight* 1957 (p); *Interpol* 1957 (p); *The Man Inside* 1958 (p); *No Time to Die* 1958 (p); *The Bandit of Zhobe* 1959 (p); *Killers of Kilimanjaro* 1960 (p); *Genghis Khan* 1965 (p); *Murderers' Row* 1966 (p); *The Silencers* 1966 (p); *The Ambushers* 1967 (p); *The Desperados* 1968 (p); *Hammerhead* 1968 (p); *The Wrecking Crew* 1968 (p); *Cromwell* 1970 (p); *Eyewitness* 1970 (exec.p).

Allen, Irwin • Producer, director; also screenwriter. • Born New York, NY, June 12, 1916. *Educ.* CCNY; Columbia (journalism). After a career as magazine editor, Hollywood newspaper columnist and literary agent, entered films as a producer in 1951. Since winning an Oscar for the documentary, *The Sea Around Us* (1952), Allen has specialized in adventure, sci-fi and/or disaster films (*The Big Circus* 1959, *The Lost World* 1960, *Voyage to the Bottom of the Sea* 1961). Standouts include the silly but commercially successful and thoroughly engrossing *The Poseidon Adventure* (1972) and *The Towering Inferno* (1974). As a television producer he has been responsible for the popular adventure series, "Voyage to the Bottom of the Sea" (1964-67), "Lost in Space" (1965-67), "Land of the Giants" (1968-69) and "The Swiss Family Robinson" (1975). • *A Girl in Every Port* 1952 (p); *The Sea Around Us* 1952 (commentary,cont,d,p) (**AABDOC**); *Dangerous Mission* 1954 (p); *The Animal World* 1956 (d,p,sc); *The Story of Mankind* 1957 (d,p,sc); *The Big Circus* 1959 (p,sc,story); *The Lost World* 1960 (d,p,sc); *Voyage to the Bottom of the Sea* 1961 (d,p,sc,story); *Five Weeks in a Balloon* 1962 (d,p,sc); *The Poseidon Adventure* 1972 (live action d,p); *The Towering Inferno* 1974 (d,p) (**AANBP**); *The Swarm* 1978 (d,p); *Beyond the Poseidon Adventure* 1979 (d,p); *When Time Ran Out* 1980 (p).

Allen, Jay Presson • *aka* Sarah Schiff • Screenwriter; also producer, playwright. • Born Jacqueline Presson, Fort Worth, TX, March 3, 1922. Highly skilled scenarist (especially with adaptations) who in the 1960s and 70s turned out a number of superior scripts with strong, female protagonists, often winning awards for the actresses portraying them. A successful playwright (*The Prime of Miss Jean Brodie*, *40 Carats*, *Tru*), Allen created and was executive producer on the well regarded television series, "Family" (1976-80) and since 1980 has also produced or served as executive producer on several interesting features (*Prince of the City* 1981, *Deathtrap* 1982). Married since 1955 to producer Lewis M. Allen. • *Wives and Lovers* 1963 (from play *The First Wife*); *Marnie* 1964 (sc); *The Prime of Miss Jean Brodie* 1969 (sc,from play); *Cabaret* 1972 (sc) (**AANBSC**); *Travels With My Aunt* 1972 (sc); *Funny Lady* 1975 (sc); *It's My Turn* 1980 (exec.p); *Just Tell Me What You Want* 1980 (p,sc,from novel); *Prince of the City* 1981 (exec.p,sc) (**AANBSC**); *Deathtrap* 1982 (exec.p,sc); *Lord of the Flies* 1990 (sc).

Allen, Joan • Actress • Born Rochelle, IL, August 20, 1956. *Educ.* Eastern Illinois University; Western Illinois University. Founding member of Chicago's Steppenwolf Theater Company who won a Tony for her Broadway debut in Lanford Wilson's *Burn This* (1988) and went on star as the feminist exemplar of the 1980s in Wendy Wasserstein's *The Heidi Chronicles* (1989). Although her film work has been sporadic and her roles mostly mousey secondary characters, Allen was memorable as Kathleen Turner's high school friend in *Peggy Sue Got Married* (1986) and as Jeff Bridges's steadfast wife in *Tucker: The Man and His Dream* (1988). She was outstanding in the television presentation of Arthur Miller's *All My Sons* (1987). • *Compromising Positions* 1985; *Manhunter* 1986; *Peggy Sue Got Married* 1986; *Tucker: The Man and His Dream* 1988; *In Country* 1989.

Allen, Karen • Actress • Born Carrollton, IL, October 5, 1951. *Educ.* George Washington University, Washington, DC; University of Maryland; Washington Theatre Lab, Washington DC; Lee Strasberg Institute, New York. Talented, under-used actress best remembered as Harrison Ford's tough-talking "partner" in *Raiders of The Lost Ark* (1981). • *National Lampoon's Animal House* 1978; *Manhattan* 1979; *The Wanderers* 1979; *Cruising* 1980; *A Small Circle of Friends* 1980; *Raiders of the Lost Ark* 1981; *Shoot the Moon* 1981; *Split Image* 1982; *Starman* 1984; *Until September* 1984; *Terminus* 1986; *Backfire* 1987; *The Glass Menagerie* 1987; *Scrooged* 1988; *Animal Behavior* 1989; *Sweet Talker* 1991.

Allen, Lewis • Director • Born Shropshire, England, December 25, 1905; died 1986. *Educ.* Tettenhall College, Staffordshire. After a career as stage actor and director in England and later the US, apprenticed at Paramount and directed his first feature film in 1944, the chilling, subdued ghost story, *The Uninvited.* Although British, he filmed two slices of Americana (*Our Hearts Were Young and Gay* 1944, *Those Endearing Young Charms* 1945) early in his career. Later he added an exciting aura of menance to B-films: *Desert Fury* (1947), the tautly suspenseful *Suddenly* (1954) and the psychological melodrama, *Whirlpool* (1959). • *Our Hearts Were Young and Gay* 1944 (d); *The Uninvited* 1944 (d); *Those Endearing Young Charms* 1945 (d); *The Unseen* 1945 (d,p); *The Perfect Marriage* 1946 (d); *Desert Fury* 1947 (d); *The Imperfect Lady* 1947 (d); *Sealed Verdict* 1948 (d); *So Evil My Love* 1948 (d); *Chicago Deadline* 1949 (d); *Appointment With Danger* 1951 (d); *Valentino* 1951 (d); *At Sword's Point* 1952 (d); *Suddenly* 1954 (d); *A Bullet For Joey* 1955 (d); *Illegal* 1955 (d); *Another Time, Another Place* 1958 (d); *Whirlpool* 1959 (d).

Allen, Lewis M. • Producer • Born Lewis Maitland Allen, Berryville, VA, 1922. *Educ.* University of Virginia. Respected Broadway producer of quality plays, such as *The Ballad of the Sad Cafe* and *I'm Not Rappaport*, who entered films in the early 1960s with film adapatations of stage works (*The Connection* 1961, *The Balcony* 1963, *Fortune and Men's Eyes* 1971). Often off-beat, controversial or simply interestingly artistic, Allen's films rarely play it safe, but rather maintain the same high standards found in his theater productions. He produced both film versions of *Lord of the Flies* (1963 and 1990). Since 1955, married to screenwriter-producer Jay Presson Allen whose work he has often produced. • *The Connection* 1961 (p); *The Balcony* 1963 (p); *Lord of the Flies* 1963 (p); *Fahrenheit 451* 1966 (p); *The Queen* 1968 (exec.p); *Fortune and Men's Eyes* 1971 (p); *Never Cry Wolf* 1983 (p); *1918* 1985 (exec.p); *On Valentine's Day* 1986 (exec.p); *End of the Line* 1987 (p); *O.C. and Stiggs* 1987 (exec.p); *Swimming to Cambodia* 1987 (exec.p); *Miss Firecracker* 1989 (exec.p); *Lord of the Flies* 1990 (exec.p).

Allen, Nancy • Actress • Born New York, NY, June 24, 1950. *Educ.* High School for the Performing Arts, New York (dance); Quintano's School for Young Professionals. Adept at projecting a simultaneously vulnerable and hard-edged exterior, Allen began her career in TV commercials at the age of 15 and made her film debut as Jack Nicholson's aloof hippy interlocutor in *The Last Detail* (1973). She subsequently played in a series of films by husband Brian DePalma (since divorced), notably *Dressed to Kill* (1980) and *Blow Out* (1981), and, after several duds, scored a huge success as the non-metalic partner of *Robocop* (1987). • *The Last Detail* 1973; *Forced Entry* 1975; *Carrie* 1976; *I Wanna Hold Your Hand* 1978; *1941* 1979; *Home Movies* 1979; *Dressed to Kill* 1980; *Blow Out* 1981; *Strange Invaders* 1983; *The Buddy System* 1984; *Not For Publication* 1984; *The Philadelphia Experiment* 1984; *Terror in the Aisles* 1984; *Robocop* 1987; *Sweet Revenge* 1987; *Poltergeist III* 1988; *Limit Up* 1989; *Robocop 2* 1990.

Allen, Woody • Director, actor, screenwriter; also comedian, author, musician. • Born Allen Stewart Konigsberg, Brooklyn, NY, December 1, 1935. *Educ.* CCNY; NYU. Woody Allen, winner of a best director Oscar for *Annie Hall* (1977) and two Academy Awards for best screenplay, is one of a handful of American filmmakers who can wear the label "auteur." Allen has almost complete control over his work, a condition assured by the relationship he forged with Orion Pictures in the early 1980s. His films, be they dramas or comedies, are remarkably personal and are permeated with Allen's preoccupations in art, religion and love.

After a semester at New York University (where he reportedly failed a film course), Allen began a successful career in comedy by joining the "Tonight Show" as a gag writer and providing comedic material for TV stars like Ed Sullivan, Sid Caesar and Art Carney. In 1961, Allen, exploiting a rebellious and guilt-ridden urban Jewish mentality, soon began performing his own material as a standup comic and became a well-known figure on the Greenwich Village club circuit, on records and on college campuses.

In 1965, Allen made his feature film acting and writing debut with director Clive Donner's farce *What's New, Pussycat?* Shortly thereafter he debuted as filmmaker-of-sorts by re-tooling a minor Japanese spy thriller with his own storyline and with English dialogue dubbed by American actors. The amusing result was *What's Up Tiger Lily?* (1966) which, along with the James Bond spoof *Casino Royale* (1967), which he co-wrote and acted in, launched Allen on one of the most successful and unusual filmmaking careers of recent history.

In 1966 Allen's first play, *Don't Drink the Water*, was produced on Broadway. In 1969 he made two short films for a CBS TV special: *Cupid's Shaft*, a parody of Chaplin's *City Lights*, and a loose adaptation of *Pygmalion* which saw Allen—characteristically—impersonating a rabbi. Most importantly that year, Allen directed, co-wrote and starred in *Take the Money and Run*, a loosely structured, hilarious send-up of gangster movies. Allen also wore all three hats for the two visually inventive screen comedies which followed: *Bananas* (1971), a south-of-the-border satire that lambastes both politics and mass media; and *Everything You Always Wanted to Know About Sex* (*but were afraid to ask)* (1972), a series of skits loosely related to a title borrowed from a self-help book popular at the time.

In 1972, Allen adapted from his own play and acted in the *Casablanca* spoof, *Play it Again, Sam*, directed by Herbert Ross. He returned to directing with *Sleeper* (1973), a sight-gag-studded comedy in which Allen plays a kind of Jewish Rip Van Winkle who, after being frozen for 200 years, wakes up in a futuristic America ("worse than California").

Love and Death (1975) showed the first clear signals that Allen was questioning the comedy genre, his own stature as a filmmaker and his own intellectual and creative capabilities. A spoof of the Napoleonic wars featuring persistent references to history, Russian culture and innumerable classic films, it suggested Allen's higher aspirations and need for acceptance as a "serious" filmmaker and thinker.

The year 1977 saw a step toward more serious territory with the bittersweet *Annie Hall.* While still a comedy, the film embraces more sophisticated narrative devices (Allen as hero, for instance, addresses the camera). It's also a more personal film, with the director/screenwriter/star tackling themes and problems closer to his own experience. Allen's screen persona in *Annie Hall* reflected his real-life status at the time: a New York Jewish entertainer with a "shiksa" girlfriend (Diane Keaton), an outsider looking in on the exclusive worlds of both Hollywood and the gentile. For many, *Annie Hall* remains the quintessential Allen movie: personal and thoughtful at the same time that it's sharply satiric and entertaining. The film won four Oscars, two of which (best director and best original screenplay) went to Allen himself.

After an acting stint in *The Front* (1976), Allen shifted gears, moving away from the familiar send-ups, quirky satire and laughable neuroses and anxieties of his comedies. Focusing on the starchy world of the Wasp, Allen wrote and directed his first drama, *Interiors* (1978), an intimate Bergmanesque probing of angst and betrayal within an upper-class family. Here the world that had so humorously intimidated Allen in *Annie Hall* was confronted in dead earnest. Although the film brought Allen Oscar nominations for best director and screenplay, some critics felt he had betrayed his comic vision in a sophomoric quest for "artistic respectability."

Manhattan (1979), with its lush Gershwin score and ensemble of actors/friends, marked a return to comedy peppered with autobiographical and romantic elements. The handsome black-and-white Panavision film generated some controversy because Allen's love interest on celluloid was an underage Mariel Hemingway.

Stardust Memories (1980), a slightly self-indulgent, Felliniesque fantasy, starred Allen as a celebrity struggling with the burden of fame. *A Midsummer Night's Sex Comedy* (1982) was the first Allen film to feature Mia Farrow, who has since been his companion; again, it was an homage—this time, a comic one—to Ingmar Bergman.

Zelig (1983) combined Allen's continued fascination with celebrity and his growing interest in cinematic technique and trickery. The piece brilliantly sends up the documentary genre, seamlessly merging new footage with old and recreating vintage newsreels and sound recordings. *Broadway Danny Rose* (1984), a more intense collaboration with Mia Farrow, again saw Allen in his "lovable shnook" role, here a show-biz nobody. *The Purple Rose of Cairo* (1985), like *Zelig* a technical tour de force, has a Depression-era matinee idol (Jeff Daniels) stepping off the screen into the life of a repressed, exploited fan (Mia Farrow).

Apart from the music-filled, elegiac *Radio Days* (1987), a memoir of growing up in Brooklyn, and the goofy "Oedipus Wrecks" segment of the omnibus film *New York Stories* (1989), Allen returned to adult drama in the last half of the decade. *Hannah and Her Sisters* (1986), a knowing, Chekhovian look at New York family relationships, won Allen his second Oscar for best screenplay. *September* (1987), a finely acted but bloodless drama, and the intensely Bergmanesque *Another Woman* (1988), starring Gena Rowlands in a virtuosic role as a betrayed wife, marked Allen's return to a world of emotionally bereft upper-class Wasps. Arguably the most pessimistic of Allen's dramas was 1989's *Crimes and Misdemeanors*, whose grim denouement leaves mediocrity triumphant and evil unchallenged.

Alice (1990) was possibly the filmmaker's first "New Age" comedy, a marriage of the comic and serious in which a disaffected Mia Farrow resorts to spiritual means to confront Wasp angst. The film, their eleventh together, casts Farrow as a female take on the familiar flustered, neurotic, desperate, self-conscious character once played by Allen himself.

In addition to his impressive body of film work, Allen is an experienced author and accomplished musician. His *Getting Even* is a collection of comic essays previously published in *The New Yorker. Without Feathers* is a collection of short fiction. For many years, Allen has taken time out to play clarinet once a week at the New York jazz club Michael's Pub.

While the comedies are always upbeat and the dramas rich in detail, most of Allen's films are fiercely personal. They betray his yearning for physical beauty, knowledge and intellectual and professional acceptance. His obsessions with his own Judaism, the Wasp world that eludes the Jew, and the balm of psychiatry—which may or may not chase these devils—are also never far beneath the surface of his work.

With so much of the filmmaker himself up on the screen, it is not surprising that Allen has remained unusually guarded and protected in his private life.

As consistent as he is in the themes he chooses, so is he in the way he lives and works.

Allen so values his privacy that he is virtually absent from the media; he is loath to travel and always remains close to New York. He rarely appears in photographs or is seen in public and has consistently refused interviews. Nevertheless, Allen has enjoyed fruitful professional relationships with co-writer Marshall Brickman, cinematographers Gordon Willis and Carlo Di Palma, producers Jack Rollins and Charles Joffe, production designers Mel Bourne and Santo Loquasto and editors Ralph Rosenblum and Susan Morse, as well as with the actors/friends who populate his film world.

Unique among contemporary filmmakers, Allen has found a way to produce with "mainstream" money and to have distributed by the studio organizations a continuous stream of personal films, shot and edited just the way he wants them, far away from the Hollywood orbit, seldom earning large amounts at the box-office. A remarkable businessman as well as artist, he has protected himself with low budgets that allow him to reach his like-minded, intelligent, mostly urban audience on a regular basis. DT • *What's New, Pussycat?* 1965 (a,sc); *What's Up Tiger Lily?* 1966 (a,assoc.p,d,sc,voice dubbing,special material); *Casino Royale* 1967 (a,sc); *Don't Drink the Water* 1969 (from play); *Take the Money and Run* 1969 (a,d,sc); *Bananas* 1971 (a,d,sc); *Everything You Always Wanted To Know About Sex* (*but were afraid to ask)* 1972 (a,d,sc); *Play It Again, Sam* 1972 (a,sc,from play); *Sleeper* 1973 (a,d,sc,m,m.perf); *Love and Death* 1975 (a,d,sc); *The Front* 1976 (a); *Annie Hall* 1977 (a,d,sc) **(AANBA,AABSC,AABD)**; *Woody Allen: An American Comedy* 1977 (a); *Interiors* 1978 (d,sc) **(AANBSC,AANBD)**; *Manhattan* 1979 (a,d,sc) **(AANBSC)**; *Stardust Memories* 1980 (a,d,sc); *A Midsummer Night's Sex Comedy* 1982 (a,d,sc); *Zelig* 1983 (a,d,sc); *Broadway Danny Rose* 1984 (a,d,sc) **(AANBD,AANBSC)**; *The Purple Rose of Cairo* 1985 (d,sc) **(AANBSC)**; *Hannah and Her Sisters* 1986 (a,d,sc) **(AANBD,AABSC)**; *Radio Days* 1987 (a,d,sc) **(AANBSC)**; *September* 1987 (d,sc); *Another Woman* 1988 (d,sc); *Crimes and Misdemeanors* 1989 (a,d,sc) **(AANBD,AANBSC)**; *New York Stories* 1989 (a,d,sc "Oedipus Wrecks"); *Alice* 1990 (d,sc); *Scenes From a Mall* 1991 (a).

Alley, Kirstie • Actress • Born Wichita, KS, January 12, 1955. *Educ.* Kansas State University of Agriculture and Applied Science; University of Kansas. First known as the bald and beautiful Lt. Saavik in *Star Trek II: The Wrath of Khan* (1982). Alley replaced Shelly Long in a starring role on TV's popular "Cheers" in 1987 and is best known on the big screen for *Look Who's Talking* (1989). Projecting intelligence and presence, independence as well as vulnerability, Alley is quickly becoming the Mary Tyler Moore of the 1990s. Married to actor Parker Stevenson. • *Star Trek II: The Wrath of Khan* 1982; *Champions* 1983; *Blind Date* 1984; *Runaway* 1984; *Summer School* 1987; *Shoot to Kill* 1988; *Look Who's Talking* 1989; *Loverboy* 1989; *Look Who's Talking Too* 1990; *Madhouse* 1990; *Sibling Rivalry* 1990.

Allyson, June • *aka* Ella Geisman • Actress; also singer, dancer. • Born Bronx, NY, October 7, 1917. Vivacious MGM musical star of the 1940s with a softly husky voice and a wistful girl-next-door quality. After a successful career on Broadway, Allyson appeared in several shorts and then made her feature debut, recreating her peppy ingenue role in the film version of the 1941 Broadway musical, *Best Foot Forward* (1943). Usually cast as sweet and wholesome types, Allyson matured into supportive wife roles in the 50s until she switched gears to play the shrewish wife in *The Shrike* (1955). Married to Dick Powell from 1945 until his death in 1963. • *Best Foot Forward* 1943 (a); *Girl Crazy* 1943 (a); *Thousands Cheer* 1943 (a); *Meet the People* 1944 (a); *Music For Millions* 1944 (a); *Two Girls and a Sailor* 1944 (a); *Her Highness and the Bellboy* 1945 (a); *The Sailor Takes a Wife* 1945 (a); *The Secret Heart* 1946 (a); *Till the Clouds Roll By* 1946 (a); *Two Sisters From Boston* 1946 (a); *Good News* 1947 (a); *High Barbaree* 1947 (a); *The Bride Goes Wild* 1948 (a); *The Three Musketeers* 1948 (a); *Words and Music* 1948 (a); *Little Women* 1949 (a); *The Stratton Story* 1949 (a); *The Reformer and the Redhead* 1950 (a); *Right Cross* 1950 (a); *Too Young to Kiss* 1951 (a); *The Girl in White* 1952 (a); *Battle Circus* 1953 (a); *Remains to Be Seen* 1953 (a); *Executive Suite* 1954 (a); *The Glenn Miller Story* 1954 (a); *Woman's World* 1954 (a); *The McConnell Story* 1955 (a); *The Shrike* 1955 (a); *Strategic Air Command* 1955 (a); *The Opposite Sex* 1956 (a); *You Can't Run Away From It* 1956 (a); *Interlude* 1957 (a); *My Man Godfrey* 1957 (a); *Stranger in My Arms* 1959 (a); *They Only Kill Their Masters* 1972 (a); *Et la terreur commence* 1978 (a).

Almendros, Nestor • *aka* John Nestor • Director of photography; also director. • Born Barcelona, Spain, October 30, 1930. *Educ.* Havana University (philosophy, literature); CCNY (film); Centro Sperimentale di Cinematografia, Rome (cinematography). Award-winning international cinematographer who came to prominence in the 1960s and 70s with his crisp, brilliant colors for films by François Truffaut and Eric Rohmer. In the 80s, while continuing to produce superior images for the likes of Robert Benton and Martin Scorsese, Almendros also directed a couple of piercing interview-documentaries, particularly *Improper Conduct* (1983, with Orlando Jimenez-Leal), about individual expression in Castro's Cuba. He has authored an acclaimed book on cinematography, *A Man with a Camera* (1980). • *Paris Vu Par.../Six in Paris* 1965 (ph—"St. Germain-des-Prés," "Place de l'Etoile"); *La Collectionneuse* 1966 (ph); *Wild Racers* 1968 (ph); *Ma nuit chez Maud/My Night at Maud's* 1969 (ph); *More* 1969 (ph,art d); *Domicile conjugal/Bed and Board* 1970 (ph); *L'Enfant sauvage/The Wild Child* 1970 (ph); *Le Genou de Claire/Claire's Knee* 1970 (ph); *Les Deux Anglaises et le Continent/Two English Girls* 1971 (ph); *L'Amour, l'après-midi/Chloe in the Afternoon* 1972 (ph); *La Vallée* 1972 (ph); *L'Oiseau Rare* 1973 (ph); *Poil de Carotte* 1973 (ph); *Cockfighter* 1974 (ph); *Femmes Au Soleil* 1974 (ph); *General Idi Amin Dada* 1974 (ph); *La Gueule ouverte* 1974 (ph); *Mes Petites Amoureuses* 1974 (ph); *L'Histoire d'Adèle H./The Story of Adèle H.* 1975 (ph); *Maîtresse* 1975 (ph); *Cambio de Sexo* 1976 (ph); *Gentleman Tramp* 1976 (ph); *Des Journées Entières dans les Arbres* 1976 (ph); *La Marquise d'O...* 1976 (ph); *L'Homme qui aimait les femmes/The Man Who Loved Women* 1977 (ph); *Madame Rosa* 1977 (ph); *La Chambre Verte/The Green Room* 1978 (ph); *Days of Heaven* 1978 (ph) **(AABPH)**; *Goin' South* 1978 (ph); *Koko le gorille qui parle* 1978 (ph); *Perceval le gallois* 1978 (ph); *L'Amour en Fuite/Love on the Run* 1979 (ph); *Kramer vs. Kramer* 1979 (ph) **(AANBPH)**; *The Blue Lagoon* 1980 (ph) **(AANBPH)**; *Le Dernier Metro/The Last Metro* 1980 (ph); *Sophie's Choice* 1982 (ph) **(AANBPH)**; *Still of the Night* 1982 (ph); *Vivement Dimanche/Confidentially Yours* 1982 (ph); *Mauvaise Conduite/Improper Conduct* 1983 (d,sc); *Pauline à la Plage/Pauline at the Beach* 1983 (ph); *Places in the Heart* 1984 (ph); *Heartburn* 1986 (ph); *Nadine* 1987 (ph); *Imagine: John Lennon* 1988 (ph—new interview footage); *Nadie Escuchaba/Nobody Listened* 1988 (d,p,sc); *New York Stories* 1989 (ph—"Life Lessons").

Almodóvar, Pedro • *aka* Patti Diphusa • Director, screenwriter; also composer, actor. • Born Calzada de Calatrava, La Mancha, Spain, September 25, 1951. Even before his first international hit, *What Have I Done to Deserve This?* (1984), Pedro Almodóvar had become one of Spain's most popular directors, achieving cult status at a time when Spanish films accounted for less than one-fifth of a shrinking domestic market. His appearance signaled a new wave in a national cinema that had already undergone dramatic changes since Franco's death in 1975.

In 1967 Almodóvar moved to Madrid, where he worked as a clerk at the National Telephone Company between

1970 and 1980, and took an active part in the city's emerging artistic underground. He acted with the avant-garde theater group "Los Goliardos"; wrote comic strips, articles and stories for underground papers; published parodic memoirs under the pen name "Patti Diphusa" (a ficticious international porn star); and took part in the *movida madrileña* ("Madrid upsurge") in rock 'n' roll, recording and performing with his own band. In 1974 Almodóvar shot his first film in Super-8, *Dos Putas, o Historia de Amor que Termina en Boda*. This and other shorts were followed by a Super-8 feature in 1978, *Folle, Folle, Folleme, Tim*, and a 16mm feature (blown up to 35mm) in 1980, *Pepi, Luci, Bom and Other Girls Like Mom*. Since then he has written and directed seven 35mm features, as well as continuing to publish Diphusa's highly popular memoirs.

The films of Almodóvar, an openly gay director, are camp melodramas that feature a battery of homosexual, bisexual and transexual characters and are steeped in post-Franco Spanish subculture. The director speaks for a new generation that rejects Spain's political past for the pursuit of immediate pleasure. "I never speak of Franco," he says. "The stories unfold as though he had never existed because for people who are 15 or 20 years old today, all their points of reference, their traumas, the specters of their past are unrelated to the dictatorship." His postmodern style reflects the spirit of these youths, known as *pasotas*, or "those who couldn't care less."

Almodóvar's influences include classic American melodramas, Spanish black comedies of the 1950s by directors such as Fernan Gomez and Luis Garcia Berlanga, and, in his use of the non-rational, the work of Luis Buñuel. Beneath their sometimes frenzied surface, each of his films touches on a social problem; male violence is a recurrent concern, and many of his features focus sympathetically on the plight of contemporary Spanish women. Almodóvar's cinema of excess, however, is too multi-layered—and too suffused by the irrational—to adopt a conventional moral stance or to suggest solutions. CAN • *La Caída de Sódoma (short)* 1974 (d); *Dos Putas, o Historia de Amor que Termina en Boda (short)* 1974 (d); *Homenaje (short)* 1975 (d); *El Sueño (short)* 1975 (d); *El Estrella (short)* 1976 (d); *Complementos (short)* 1977 (d); *Sexo Va (short)* 1977 (d); *Folle, Folle, Fólleme, Tim* 1978 (d); *Salomé (short)* 1978 (d); *Pepi, Luci, Bom y Otras Chicas del Montón/Pepi, Luci, Bom and Other Girls Like Mom* 1980 (d,sc); *Laberinto de Pasiones/Labyrinth of Passion* 1982 (a,d,sc,pd); *Entre Tinieblas/Dark Habits* 1983 (d,sc,song); *Qué He Hecho Yo Para Merecer Esto?/What Have I Done to Deserve This?* 1984 (d,sc); *Trayler para Amantes de lo Prohibido (short)* 1985 (d); *Mátador* 1986 (d,sc); *La Ley del Deseo/Law of Desire* 1987 (d,sc,m,song); *Mujeres al Borde de un Ataque de Nervios/Women on the Verge of a Nervous Breakdown* 1988 (d,sc); *Átame!/Tie Me Up! Tie Me Down!* 1990 (d,sc).

Alonso, Maria Conchita • Actress; also singer. • Born Cuba, 1957. Began her career as a beauty-pageant winner (Miss Teenager of the World 1971, Miss Venezuela 1975) and subsequently became one of South America's best-selling recording artists. Alonso established herself as one of Hollywood's leading Hispanic actresses with her role in *Moscow on the Hudson* (1984), opposite Robin Williams. • *Moscow on the Hudson* 1984 (a,song); *A Fine Mess* 1986 (a); *Touch and Go* 1986 (a); *Extreme Prejudice* 1987 (a); *The Running Man* 1987 (a); *Colors* 1988 (a); *Vampire's Kiss* 1988 (a); *Predator 2* 1990 (a).

Alonzo, John A. • Director of photography; also director. • Born Dallas, TX, 1934. Versatile cinematographer equally at home with controlled period drama (*Chinatown* 1974), Steven Spielberg pyrotechnics (*Close Encounters of the Third Kind* 1977) and more lyrical, rural scapes (*Sounder* 1972, *Tom Horn* 1980). Alonzo made a competent, though overlooked, directorial debut with the anarchic, pre-"WKRP," radio-station comedy, *FM* (1977). • *Bloody Mama* 1970 (ph); *Vanishing Point* 1970 (ph); *Harold and Maude* 1971 (ph); *Get to Know Your Rabbit* 1972 (ph); *Lady Sings the Blues* 1972 (ph); *Pete 'n' Tillie* 1972 (ph); *Sounder* 1972 (ph); *Conrack* 1973 (ph); *Hit* 1973 (ph); *The Naked Ape* 1973 (ph); *Chinatown* 1974 (ph) **(AANBPH)**; *Farewell, My Lovely* 1975 (ph); *The Fortune* 1975 (ph); *I Will...I Will...For Now* 1975 (ph); *Once Is Not Enough* 1975 (ph); *The Bad News Bears* 1976 (ph); *Beyond Reason* 1977 (ph); *Black Sunday* 1977 (ph); *Close Encounters of the Third Kind* 1977 (add.ph); *FM* 1977 (d); *Which Way Is Up?* 1977 (ph); *Casey's Shadow* 1978 (ph); *The Cheap Detective* 1978 (ph); *Norma Rae* 1978 (ph); *Tom Horn* 1980 (ph); *Back Roads* 1981 (ph); *Zorro, The Gay Blade* 1981 (ph); *Blue Thunder* 1983 (ph); *Cross Creek* 1983 (ph); *Scarface* 1983 (ph); *Runaway* 1984 (ph); *Terror in the Aisles* 1984 (ph); *Out of Control* 1985 (ph); *50 Years of Action!* 1986 (a,ph); *Jo Jo Dancer, Your Life Is Calling* 1986 (ph); *Nothing in Common* 1986 (ph); *Overboard* 1987 (ph); *Real Men* 1987 (ph); *Physical Evidence* 1988 (ph); *Steel Magnolias* 1989 (ph); *The Guardian* 1990 (ph); *Internal Affairs* 1990 (ph); *Navy Seals* 1990 (ph).

Altman, Robert • Director; also screenwriter, producer. • Born Kansas City, MO, February 20, 1925. *Educ.* University of Missouri (engineering). Long recognized in Europe as a true "auteur," Robert Altman brings an ironic, irreverent gaze to bear on traditional American values. His style is full of quirks and surprises, all the more unusual in light of his early training in television and industrials.

Altman's apprenticeship began in 1947 in his native Kansas City with the Calvin Company, a leading producer of industrial films. *The Delinquents* (1957), his first feature, was followed by *The James Dean Story* (1957), a docudrama that mapped out his intentions of using film to explore the reality behind pop culture icons.

From 1957 to 1965 Altman worked in Hollywood on a wide variety of television programs including "Combat," "Alfred Hitchcock Presents," and "Bonanza"; his resistance to conformity, however, delayed his progression into feature filmmaking for another decade. *Countdown* (1968) and *That Cold Day in the Park* (1969) garnered some critical attention, but Altman's career took a dramatic turn with *M*A*S*H* (1970), a box-office and critical smash which won the Palme d'Or at Cannes. Success led him to form his own Lion's Gate production company—complete with state-of-the-art editing and sound recording facilities—where the creative process was once described as "controlled chaos."

Altman's ensuing films, *Brewster McCloud* (1970), *McCabe & Mrs. Miller* (1971), *The Long Goodbye* (1973) and *Thieves Like Us* (1974), added to his reputation as an artist but were all disappointments at the box-office. *Nashville* (1975) won back the audience, was nominated for several Oscars, and invariably appears on critics' "Best of the 1970s" lists for its layered narrative, breezy character treatment and witty music. The accolades stopped with *Buffalo Bill and the Indians* (1976), Altman's bicentennial film which explored the marketing of American history. His feud with producer Dino de Laurentiis over its editing led to his dismissal from *Ragtime* (1981), eventually directed by Milos Forman.

Altman debuted as a producer with *Welcome to L.A.* (1976), by his protégé Alan Rudolph, and *The Late Show* (1977), by screenwriter Robert Benton, both films echoing his fondness for quirky characters and situations. Altman's own directorial style continued to evolve and diversify with *Three Women* (1977), which won Shelley Duvall the best actress prize at Cannes, the freewheeling satire *A Wedding* (1978) and *Quintet* (1979), an obscurely poetic film set in a snowbound post-apocalyptic world. Two comedies of this period, the offbeat romance *A Perfect Couple* (1979) and *Health* (1980), a send-up of America's health food craze, ran into distribution problems and were not widely seen. His final Lion's Gate film, *Popeye* (1980), was a stillborn cartoon recreation.

In 1981 Altman sold his Lion's Gate plant and turned his attention to the theater. He staged and then filmed the drama *Come Back to the 5 & Dime Jimmy Dean, Jimmy Dean* (1982); *Secret Honor* (1984) portrayed Richard Nixon (Philip Baker Hall) delivering an "apologia pro vita sua" monologue; and *Streamers* (1983), a film of David Rabe's play about stateside barracks life in the early days of the Vietnam War, garnered some critical support and a Venice Film Festival award for its ensemble cast. Paradoxically, Altman is now again carving a niche in the small screen, having worked on several made-for-TV productions including *The Caine Mutiny Court-Martial* (1988) and *Tanner '88* (1988). KJ • *Bodyguard* 1948 (story); *The Delinquents* 1957 (d,p,sc); *The James Dean Story* 1957 (d,ed,p); *Countdown* 1968 (d); *That Cold Day in the Park* 1969 (d); *Brewster McCloud* 1970 (d); *Events* 1970 (a); *M*A*S*H* 1970 (d) **(AANBD)**; *McCabe & Mrs. Miller* 1971 (d,sc); *Images* 1972 (d,sc); *The Long Goodbye* 1973 (d); *California Split* 1974 (d,p); *Thieves Like Us* 1974 (d,sc); *Nashville* 1975 (d,p) **(AANBD)**; *Buffalo Bill and the Indians, or Sitting Bull's History Lesson* 1976 (d,p,sc); *Welcome to L.A.* 1976 (p); *The Late Show* 1977 (p); *Three Women* 1977 (d,p,sc,idea); *Remember My Name* 1978 (p); *A Wedding* 1978 (d,p,sc,story); *A Perfect Couple* 1979 (d,p,sc); *Quintet* 1979 (d,p,sc,story); *Rich Kids* 1979 (exec.p); *Health* 1980 (d,p,sc); *Popeye* 1980 (d); *Endless Love* 1981 (a); *Before the Nickelodeon: The Early Cinema Of Edwin S. Porter* 1982 (a); *Come Back to the 5 & Dime Jimmy Dean, Jimmy Dean* 1982 (d); *Streamers* 1983 (d,p); *Secret Honor* 1984 (d,p); *Fool For Love* 1985 (d); *Jatszani Kell* 1985 (assoc.p); *Aria* 1987 (d,sc "Les Boreades"); *Beyond Therapy* 1987 (d,sc); *O.C. and Stiggs* 1987 (d,p); *The Moderns* 1988 (assistance); *Hollywood Mavericks* 1990 (a); *Vincent and Theo* 1990 (d).

Alton, John • Director of photography • Born Hungary, October 5, 1901. In the Americas from 1924, Alton shot his first films in Argentina in the 1930s and began his prolific Hollywood career with *The Courageous Dr. Christian* (1940). He demonstrated a masterful command of chiaroscuro with his work for Anthony Mann (*T-Men* 1947, *Border Incident* 1949, etc.).

In the following decade Alton shot a series of films for Allan Dwan, as well as four of Vincente Minnelli's glossy MGM productions. He is the author of *Painting with Light* (1949). • *Closed Door/Puerta Cerrada* 1939; *The Courageous Dr. Christian* 1940; *Dr. Christian Meets the Women* 1940; *Remedy For Riches* 1940; *Three Faces West* 1940; *The Devil Pays Off* 1941; *Forced Landing* 1941; *Melody For Three* 1941; *Mr. District Attorney in the Carter Case* 1941; *Power Dive* 1941; *Affairs of Jimmy Valentine* 1942; *Ice-Capades Revue* 1942; *Johnny Doughboy* 1942; *Moonlight Masquerade* 1942; *Pardon My Stripes* 1942; *The Sultan's Daughter* 1943; *Atlantic City* 1944; *Enemy of Women* 1944; *The Lady and the Monster* 1944; *Lake Placid Serenade* 1944; *Storm Over Lisbon* 1944; *Girls of the Big House* 1945; *A Guy Could Change* 1945; *Love, Honor, and Goodbye* 1945; *Song of Mexico* 1945; *Affairs of Geraldine* 1946; *The Ghost Goes Wild* 1946; *The Madonna's Secret* 1946; *The Magnificent Rogue* 1946; *One Exciting Week* 1946; *Bury Me Dead* 1947; *Driftwood* 1947; *Hit Parade of 1947* 1947; *The Pretender* 1947; *T-Men* 1947; *The Trespasser* 1947; *Winter Wonderland* 1947; *Wyoming* 1947; *Canon City* 1948; *He Walked By Night* 1948; *Hollow Triumph* 1948; *Raw Deal* 1948; *The Spiritualist* 1948; *Border Incident* 1949; *The Crooked Way* 1949; *Red Stallion in the Rockies* 1949; *Reign of Terror/The Black Book* 1949; *Captain China* 1950; *Devil's Doorway* 1950; *Father of the Bride* 1950; *Grounds For Marriage* 1950; *Mystery Street* 1950; *An American in Paris* 1951; *Father's Little Dividend* 1951; *It's a Big Country* 1951; *The People Against O'Hara* 1951; *Talk About a Stranger* 1952; *Washington Story* 1952; *Battle Circus* 1953; *Count the Hours* 1953; *I, the Jury* 1953; *Take the High Ground* 1953; *Duffy of San Quentin* 1954; *Escape to Burma* 1954; *Passion* 1954; *Silver Lode* 1954; *The Steel Cage* 1954; *Witness to Murder* 1954; *The Big Combo* 1955; *Pearl of the South Pacific* 1955; *Tennessee's Partner* 1955; *The Catered Affair* 1956; *Slightly Scarlet* 1956; *Tea and Sympathy* 1956; *The Teahouse of the August Moon* 1956; *Designing Woman* 1957; *The Brothers Karamazov* 1958; *Lonelyhearts* 1958; *Elmer Gantry* 1960; *Twelve to the Moon* 1960.

Alton, Robert • Choreographer; also director, dancer. • Born Robert Alton Hart, Bennington, VT, January 28, 1903; died June 12, 1957. *Educ.* Mordkin Ballet and Dramatic School, New York. Former chorus boy and featured dancer who went on to stage the musical numbers for Cole Porter's *Anything Goes* (1934) and *Panama Hattie* (1940) and almost all of Rodgers and Hart's post-Balanchine Broadway shows including *Pal Joey* (1940). Under long-term contract to MGM from the 1940s, while continuing to choreograph occasional Broadway musicals, Alton was a versatile, though never groundbreaking, dance director who did his finest work—such as the Fred Astaire/Judy Garland routines in *Easter Parade* (1948)—for individuals rather than large groups. His two solo directing efforts are for the most part forgettable. • *You'll Never Get Rich* 1941 (chor); *Bathing Beauty* 1944 (chor); *Broadway Rhythm* 1944 (chor); *Ziegfeld Follies* 1946 (chor); *Merton of the Movies* 1947 (d); *Easter Parade* 1948 (chor); *The Pirate* 1948 (chor); *Words and Music* 1948 (chor); *Pagan Love Song* 1950 (d); *Call Me Madam* 1953 (chor); *The Country Girl* 1954 (chor); *There's No Business Like Show Business* 1954 (chor); *White Christmas* 1954 (chor); *The Girl Rush* 1955 (assoc.p,chor).

Alvarez, Santiago • Filmmaker • Born Havana, Cuba, March 18, 1919. *Educ.* University of Havana (philosophy); Columbia (psychology); Jefferson School (English). As a young man, Santiago Alvarez studied in the US and worked there at menial jobs. After his return to Cuba in the mid-1940s, he worked as a music archivist in a TV station and participated in the activities of the Cuban communist party and "Nuestro Tiempo," a political-cultural society.

With no formal training as a filmmaker, Alvarez made his first documentaries at the age of 40, in the wake of the Revolution. He was a founding member of ICAIC, the Cuban film institute established in 1959.

Though he has directed one fiction feature and headed ICAIC's Latin American Newsreel division, Alvarez's reputation is as a brilliant and innovative documentary filmmaker. His highly partisan political themes, such as anti-imperialism and support for Fidel Castro and the Revolution, are expressed in an eclectic style that draws on creative improvisation. In his famous anti-imperialist satire, *LBJ* (1968), and other documentary shorts produced in the 1960s, the filmmaker employed a "nervous montage" approach that stressed a skillful use of sound and creative editing techniques to tie together a fast-paced collage of disparate "found" materials such as cartoons, still photos, and clips from Hollywood movies.

Among the best known of Alvarez's documentary features are *79 primaveras* (1969), a poetic tribute to Ho Chi Minh; and *De America soy hijo...y a ella me debo* (1972) and *Y el cielo fué tomado por asalto* (1973), which both chronicle Castro's international tours. DW • *Un Año de Libertad* 1960 (d); *Escambray* 1961 (d); *Muerte al invasor* 1961 (d); *Forjadores de la páz* 1962 (d); *Ciclón* 1963 (d); *Now* 1965 (d); *Segunda declaración de la Habana* 1965 (d); *Solidaridád Cuba y Vietnam* 1965 (d); *Abríl de Girón* 1966 (d); *Cerro pelado* 1966 (d); *Escalada del chantaje* 1967 (d); *Golpeando en la selva* 1967 (d); *La Guerra olvidada* 1967 (d); *Hanoi martes 13* 1967 (d); *Hasta la victoria siempre* 1967 (d); *LBJ* 1968 (d); *79 primaveras* 1969 (d); *Despegue a las 18:00* 1969 (d); *Once por cero* 1970 (d); *Piedra sobre piedra* 1970 (d); *El Sueño del Pongo* 1970 (d); *Cómo, por qué y para qué se asesina un general?* 1971 (d); *La Estampida* 1971 (d); *El Pájaro del faro* 1971 (d); *De America soy hijo...y a ella me debo* 1972 (d); *El Tígre saltó y mató, pero morirá... morirá* 1973 (d); *Y el cielo fué tomado por asalto* 1973 (d); *60 minutos con el primer mundiál de boxeo amateur* 1974 (d); *Los Cuatro puentes* 1974 (d); *Abríl de Vietnam en al año del gato* 1975 (d); *El Primer Delgado* 1975 (d); *Los Dragones de Ha-Long* 1976 (d); *Luanda ya no es de San Pablo* 1976 (d); *Maputo: Meridiano novo* 1976 (d); *Morir por la patria es vivir* 1976 (d); *El Sol no se puede tapar con un dedo* 1976 (d); *El Tiempo es el viento* 1976 (d); *Mi Hermano Fidel* 1977 (d); *El Octubre de todos* 1977 (d); *Y la noche se hízo arcoiris* 1978 (d); *El Gran salto al vacio* 1979 (d); *Tengo fe en tí* 1979 (d); *La Guerra necessaria* 1980 (d); *26 es también 19* 1981 (d); *Comenzó* • a retumbar el Momotombo 1981 (d); *La Importancia universal del hueco* 1981 (d); *Tiempo libre a La Roca* 1981 (d); *A Galope sobre la historia* 1982 (d); *Nova sinfonía* 1982 (d); *Operación Abríl del Caribe* 1982 (d); *Biografía de un carnavál* 1983 (d); *Las Campañas también puedan doblar mañana* 1983 (d); *Los Refugiados de la cueva del muerto* 1983 (d,sc); *Grácias, Santiago* 1984 (d).

Alwyn, William • Composer • Born Northampton, England, November 7, 1905; died September 12, 1985, Southwold, England. *Educ.* Royal Academy of Music, London. Prolific English composer whose film work began in documentaries in 1936. Alwyn scored over 100 films including the Carol Reed classics *Odd Man Out* (1947) and *The Fallen Idol* (1948). • *The True Glory* 1945 (m); *Odd Man Out* 1947 (m); *Escape* 1948 (m); *Fallen Idol* 1948 (m); *So Evil My Love* 1948 (m); *The Winslow Boy* 1948 (m); *The Mudlark* 1950 (m); *I'll Never Forget You* 1951 (m.dir); *Lady Godiva Rides Again* 1951 (m); *The Crimson Pirate* 1952 (m); *The Promoter* 1952 (m); *Malta Story* 1953 (m); *The Man With a Million* 1953 (m); *The Master of Ballantrae* 1953 (m); *Personal Affair* 1953 (m); *Bedevilled* 1954 (m); *The Seekers* 1954 (m); *Svengali* 1954 (m); *The Ship That Died of Shame* 1955 (m); *Safari* 1956 (m); *Zarak* 1956 (m); *I Accuse!* 1957 (m); *Fortune Is a Woman* 1958 (m); *A Night to Remember* 1958 (m); *The Silent Enemy* 1958 (m); *Shake Hands With the Devil* 1959 (m); *Third Man on the Mountain* 1959 (m); *Killers of Kilimanjaro* 1960 (m); *The Naked Edge* 1961 (m); *Burn, Witch, Burn* 1962 (m); *In Search of the Castaways* 1962 (m); *Life For Ruth* 1962 (m); *The Running Man* 1963 (m).

Amato, Giuseppe • Producer; also director, screenwriter. • Born Giuseppe Vasaturo, Naples, Italy, August 24, 1899; died 1964. Former actor turned influential producer. • *Cinque a Zero* 1932 (p); *Ma l'Amor mio non Murore* 1938 (d,p,sc); *I Grandi Magazzini* 1939 (p); *Rose Scarlatte, Melodie Eterne* 1940 (p); *La Cena delle Beffe* 1941 (p); *Quattro Passi fra la Nuvole/Four Steps in the Clouds* 1942 (d,p,sc); *Campo de'Fiori* 1943 (p,sc,story); *Malia* 1945 (d,sc); *Natale al Campo* 1948 (p,sc); *Domani è troppo Tardi* 1950 (p); *Francesco Giullare di Dio/Flowers of St. Francis* 1950 (p); *Paris est toujours Paris* 1951 (p); *La Presidentessa* 1952 (p); *Umberto D* 1952 (p); *Donne Proibite* 1953 (d,p); *Retour de Don Camillo* 1953 (assoc.p); *Gli Ultimi Cinque Minuti* 1955 (d,p); *Seven Hills of Rome* 1957 (story); *Nella città l'inferno* 1958 (p); *La Dolce Vita* 1959 (p); *Un Maledetto Imbroglio* 1959 (p); *Morte di un bandito* 1961 (d).

Ameche, Don • Actor • Born Dominic Felix Amici, Kenosha, WI, May 31, 1908. *Educ.* University of Wisconsin (law); Columbia College. Hollywood leading man of the 1930s and 40s (often opposite Alice Faye) who enjoyed renewed popularity in the 1980s. • *Ladies in Love* 1936; *One in a Million* 1936; *Ramona* 1936; *Sins of Man* 1936; *Fifty Roads to Town* 1937; *Love Is News* 1937; *Love Under Fire* 1937; *You Can't Have Everything* 1937; *Alexander's Ragtime Band* 1938; *Gateway* 1938; *Happy Landing* 1938; *In Old Chicago* 1938; *Josette* 1938; *Hollywood Cavalcade* 1939; *Midnight* 1939; *The Story of Alexander Graham Bell* 1939; *Swanee River* 1939; *The Three Musketeers* 1939; *Down Argentine Way* 1940; *Four Sons* 1940; *Lillian Russell* 1940; *Confirm or Deny* 1941; *The Feminine Touch* 1941; *Kiss the Boys Goodbye* 1941; *Moon Over Miami* 1941; *That Night in Rio* 1941; *Girl Trouble* 1942; *The Magnificent Dope* 1942; *Happy Land* 1943; *Heaven Can Wait* 1943; *Something to Shout About* 1943; *Greenwich Village* 1944; *Wing and a Prayer* 1944; *Guest Wife* 1945; *It's in the Bag* 1945; *So Goes My Love* 1946; *That's My Man* 1947; *Sleep, My Love* 1948; *Slightly French* 1949; *A Fever in the Blood* 1961; *Picture Mommy Dead* 1966; *The Boatniks* 1970; *Suppose They Gave a War and Nobody Came?* 1970; *Trading Places* 1983; *Cocoon* 1985 (**AABSA**); *Harry and the Hendersons* 1987; *Cocoon: The Return* 1988; *Coming to America* 1988; *Things Change* 1988; *Oscar* 1991.

Ames, Leon • *aka* Leon Wycoff • Actor • Born Leon Waycoff, Portland, IN, January 20, 1903. Pleasant-looking, dapper character actor best known for his paternal roles, who made his screen debut as the romantic hero in *Murders in the Rue Morgue* (1932). Having served a long stage and screen apprenticeship in minor and then supporting roles, Ames co-starred as the harrassed head of the Smith household in Vincente Minnelli's *Meet Me in St. Louis* (1944) and was immediately typecast as forceful but warm and benevolent fathers. Although he gave a strong performance as the shrewd prosecuting attorney in *The Postman Always Rings Twice* (1946), he returned to his paternal role on the television series, "Life with Father" (1953-55) and "Father of the Bride" (1961-62). • *The Cannonball Express* 1932; *The Famous Ferguson Case* 1932; *Murders in the Rue Morgue* 1932; *Stowaway* 1932; *That's My Boy* 1932; *Thirteen Women* 1932; *Uptown New York* 1932; *Alimony Madness* 1933; *Forgotten* 1933; *The Man Who Dared* 1933; *The Ship of Wanted Men* 1933; *Get That Man* 1935; *Mutiny Ahead* 1935; *Reckless* 1935; *Rescue Squad* 1935; *Strangers All* 1935; *45 Fathers* 1937; *Charlie Chan on Broadway* 1937; *Dangerously Yours* 1937; *Death in the Air* 1937; *Murder in Greenwich Village* 1937; *Cipher Bureau* 1938; *Come on Leathernecks* 1938; *International Settlement* 1938; *Island in the Sky* 1938; *Mysterious Mr. Moto* 1938; *Secrets of a Nurse* 1938; *The Spy Ring* 1938; *Strange Faces* 1938; *Suez* 1938; *Walking Down Broadway* 1938; *Calling All Marines* 1939; *Code of the Streets* 1939; *Fugitive at Large* 1939; *I Was a Convict* 1939; *Legion of Lost Flyers* 1939; *Man of Conquest* 1939; *The Marshal of Mesa City* 1939; *Mr. Moto in Danger Island* 1939; *Pack Up Your Troubles* 1939; *Panama Patrol* 1939; *Risky Business* 1939; *East Side Kids* 1940; *Ellery Queen and the Murder Ring* 1941; *No Greater Sin* 1941; *Crime Doctor* 1943; *The Iron Major* 1943; *Meet Me in St. Louis* 1944; *The Thin Man Goes Home* 1944; *Thirty Seconds Over Tokyo* 1944; *Son of Lassie* 1945; *They Were Expendable* 1945; *Weekend at the Waldorf* 1945; *Yolanda and the Thief* 1945; *The Cockeyed Miracle* 1946; *The Great Morgan* 1946; *Lady in the Lake* 1946; *No Leave, No Love* 1946; *The Postman Always Rings Twice* 1946; *The Showoff* 1946; *Alias a Gentleman* 1947; *Merton of the Movies* 1947; *Song of the Thin Man* 1947; *Undercover Maisie* 1947; *A Date With Judy* 1948; *On an Island With You* 1948; *The Velvet Touch* 1948; *Ambush* 1949; *Any Number Can Play* 1949; *Battleground* 1949; *Little Women* 1949; *Scene of the Crime* 1949; *The Big Hangover* 1950; *Crisis* 1950; *Dial 1119* 1950; *The Happy Years* 1950; *The Skipper Suprised His Wife* 1950; *Watch the Birdie* 1950; *Cattle Drive* 1951; *It's a Big Country* 1951; *On Moonlight Bay* 1951; *Angel Face* 1952; *By the Light of the Silvery Moon* 1953; *Let's Do It Again* 1953; *Sabre Jet* 1953; *Peyton Place* 1957; *The Absent-Minded Professor* 1960; *From the Terrace* 1960; *Son of Flubber* 1963; *The Misadventures of Merlin Jones* 1964; *The Monkey's Uncle* 1965; *On a Clear Day You Can See Forever* 1970; *Tora! Tora! Tora!* 1970; *Toklat* 1971; *Hammersmith Is Out* 1972; *Timber Tramps* 1973; *The Meal* 1975; *Just You and Me, Kid* 1979; *Testament* 1983; *Jake Speed* 1986; *Peggy Sue Got Married* 1986.

Amfitheatrof, Daniele • Composer; also conductor. • Born St. Petersburg, Russia, October 29, 1901; died 1983. *Educ.* Royal Academy of Music, Rome. Symphony conductor who scored his first film in Italy (Max Ophuls's *La Si-*

gnora di Tutti 1934) before immigrating to the US in 1937. Amfitheatrof signed with MGM in 1939 and scored numerous films for various studios over the next three decades. Highlights include *Letter From an Unknown Woman* (1948), *The Desert Fox* (1951) and *Major Dundee* (1965). • *La Signora di Tutti* 1934 (m); *And One Was Beautiful* 1940 (m); *Keeping Company* 1940 (m); *The Man From Dakota* 1940 (m); *The Get-Away* 1941 (m); *Andy Hardy's Double Life* 1942 (m); *Calling Dr. Gillespie* 1942 (m); *Dr. Gillespie's New Assistant* 1942 (m); *Northwest Rangers* 1942 (m); *Cry Havoc* 1943 (m); *Dr. Gillespie's Criminal Case* 1943 (m); *Harrigan's Kid* 1943 (m); *High Explosive* 1943 (m); *Lassie Come Home* 1943 (m); *Lost Angel* 1943 (m); *A Stranger in Town* 1943 (m); *Days of Glory* 1944 (m); *I'll Be Seeing You* 1944 (m); *Guest Wife* 1945 (m) **(AANBM)**; *Miss Susie Slagle's* 1945 (m); *The Beginning or the End* 1946 (m); *O.S.S.* 1946 (m); *Song of the South* 1946 (m) **(AANBM)**; *Suspense* 1946 (m.dir); *Temptation* 1946 (m); *The Virginian* 1946 (m); *Ivy* 1947 (m); *The Lost Moment* 1947 (m); *The Senator Was Indiscreet* 1947 (m); *Singapore* 1947 (m); *Smash-Up, the Story of a Woman* 1947 (m); *Another Part of the Forest* 1948 (m); *Letter From an Unknown Woman* 1948 (m); *Rogue's Regiment* 1948 (m); *You Gotta Stay Happy* 1948 (m); *The Fan* 1949 (m); *House of Strangers* 1949 (m); *Backfire* 1950 (m); *The Capture* 1950 (m); *The Damned Don't Cry* 1950 (m); *Devil's Doorway* 1950 (m); *Under My Skin* 1950 (m); *Angels in the Outfield* 1951 (m); *Bird of Paradise* 1951 (m); *The Desert Fox* 1951 (m); *The Painted Hills* 1951 (m); *Storm Warning* 1951 (m); *Tomorrow Is Another Day* 1951 (m); *The Big Heat* 1953 (m); *The Naked Jungle* 1954 (m); *The Last Hunt* 1955 (m); *Trial* 1955 (m); *The Mountain* 1956 (m); *The Unholy Wife* 1957 (m); *Fraulein* 1958 (m); *From Hell to Texas* 1958 (m); *A Spanish Affair* 1958 (m,song); *Edge of Eternity* 1959 (m,m.cond); *Major Dundee* 1965 (m,song); *Friday the 13th—A New Beginning* 1985 (song).

Amidei, Sergio • *aka* Sergei Amidei • Screenwriter; also producer. • Born Trieste, October 30, 1904. A significant contributor to the Italian neorealist movement, thanks to his work on films by Vittorio De Sica (*Shoeshine* 1946), Renato Castellani (*Under the Sun of Rome* 1948) and, most notably, Roberto Rossellini. Of his seven collaborations with Rossellini, the neorealist classics *Paisan* (1946) and *Open City* (1945), and the later *General Della Rovere* (1959), stand out. • *La Notte delle Beffe* 1939 (sc); *Roma, città aperta/Open City* 1945 (sc,story) **(AANBSC)**; *Paisan* 1946 (sc) **(AANBSC)**; *Sciuscia/Shoeshine* 1946 (sc) **(AANBSC)**; *Anni Difficili* 1947 (sc); *La Macchina ammazzacattivi* 1948 (sc); *Sotte il Sole di Roma/Under the Sun of Rome* 1948 (sc); *Stromboli* 1949 (sc); *Domenica d'Agosto* 1950 (p,story); *Paris est toujours Paris* 1951 (sc,story); *Ragazze di Piazza di Spagna* 1952 (sc,story); *Villa Borghese* 1953 (idea); *Secrets d'Alcove* 1954 (sc); *Die Angst/Fear* 1955 (sc); *Il Bigamo* 1955 (sc,story); *Picasso* 1955 (p,sc); *Il Momento Piu Bello* 1957 (sc,story); *Il Generale Della Rovere/General Della Rovere* 1959 (sc) **(AANBSC)**; *Era Notte a Roma* 1960 (sc); *Viva l'Italia* 1960 (sc); *Liolà* 1964 (sc); *La Vita Agra* 1964 (sc); *La Fuga* 1965 (sc,story); *Detenuto in Attesa di Giudizio* 1971 (sc); *La Piu Bella Serata Della Mia Vita* 1972 (sc); *Un Borghese Piccolo Piccolo* 1977 (sc); *Le Temoin* 1978 (sc.adapt); *Storie di Ordinaria Follia/Tales of Ordinary Madness* 1981 (sc,story); *La Nuit de Varennes* 1982 (sc).

Anchia, Juan Ruiz • See Ruiz-Anchia, Juan.

Anderson, Eddie "Rochester" • *aka* Eddie Anderson • Actor • Born Oakland, CA, September 18, 1905; died 1977. Best remembered as a regular on "The Jack Benny Show," Anderson also had the lead in Vincente Minnelli's all-black musical *Cabin in the Sky* (1943). • *What Price Hollywood?* 1932; *The Green Pastures* 1936; *Rainbow on the River* 1936; *Three Men on a Horse* 1936; *Bill Cracks Down* 1937; *Melody For Two* 1937; *On Such a Night* 1937; *One Mile From Heaven* 1937; *Over the Goal* 1937; *White Bondage* 1937; *Exposed* 1938; *Going Places* 1938; *Gold Diggers in Paris* 1938; *Jezebel* 1938; *Kentucky* 1938; *Rebellious Daughters* 1938; *Reckless Living* 1938; *Strange Faces* 1938; *Thanks For the Memory* 1938; *You Can't Take It With You* 1938; *Honolulu* 1939; *Man About Town* 1939; *You Can't Cheat an Honest Man* 1939; *Buck Benny Rides Again* 1940; *Love Thy Neighbor* 1940; *Birth of the Blues* 1941; *Kiss the Boys Goodbye* 1941; *Topper Returns* 1941; *Tales of Manhattan* 1942; *Cabin in the Sky* 1943; *The Meanest Man in the World* 1943; *What's Buzzin' Cousin?* 1943; *Broadway Rhythm* 1944; *Brewster's Millions* 1945; *I Love a Bandleader* 1945; *The Sailor Takes a Wife* 1945; *The Showoff* 1946; *It's a Mad, Mad, Mad, Mad World* 1963.

Anderson, Gilbert M. • Actor; also director, producer. • Born Max Aronson, Little Rock, AR, March 21, 1882; died January 20, 1971. Appeared in Edwin S. Porter's ground-breaking 1903 short *The Great Train Robbery* and later co-founded Essanay, where he starred in and directed the "Bronco Billy" series. • *The Messenger Boy's Mistake* 1902 (a); *The Great Train Robbery* 1903 (a); *What Happened in the Tunnel (short)* 1903 (ph); *The Life of an American Cowboy* 1905 (a); *Raffles, the American Cracksman* 1905 (a,d); *An Awful Skate* 1907 (a,d); *The Bandit King* 1907 (a,d,p); *The Bandit Makes Good* 1907 (a,d,p); *Ben Gets a Duck and Is Ducked* 1907 (d,p); *Western Justice* 1907 (a,d); *The Best Man Wins* 1909 (a,d); *The Black Sheep* 1909 (a,d); *The Heart of a Cowboy* 1909 (a,d); *The Indian Trailer* 1909 (a,d); *Judgment* 1909 (a,d); *Mexican's Gratitude* 1909 (a,d); *The Spanish Girl* 1909 (a,d); *A Tale of the West* 1909 (a,d); *Away Out West* 1910 (a,d); *Bronco Billy's Redemption* 1910 (a,d); *The Cowboy and the Squaw* 1910 (a,d); *The Desperado* 1910 (a,d); *The Flower of The Ranch* 1910 (a,d); *The Forest Ranger* 1910 (a,d); *An Outlaw's Sacrifice* 1910 (a,d); *Pals of the Range* 1910 (a,d); *The Pony Express Rider* 1910 (a,d); *The Silent Message* 1910 (a,d); *Take Me Out to the Ball Game* 1910 (d,sc); *Under Western Skies* 1910 (a,d); *Western Chivalry* 1910 (a,d); *Across the Plains* 1911 (a,d); *The Border Ranger* 1911 (a,d); *Bronco Billy's Adventure* 1911 (a,d); *The Cowboy Coward* 1911 (a,d); *The Faithful Indian* 1911 (a,d); *The Lucky Card* 1911 (a,d); *The Outlaw and the Child* 1911 (a,d); *Alkali Bests Bronco Billy* 1912 (a,d); *Alkali Ike's Boarding House* 1912 (d); *Bronco Billy Outwitted* 1912 (a,d); *An Indian's Friendship* 1912 (a,d); *The Smuggler's Daughter* 1912 (a,d); *Alkali Ike's Misfortunes* 1913 (d); *Bronco Billy's Oath* 1913 (a,d); *The Three Gamblers* 1913 (a,d); *Bronco Billy's Indian Romance* 1914 (a,d); *The Calling of Jim Barton* 1914 (a,d); *His New Profession (short)* 1914 (a); *Andy of the Royal Mounted* 1915 (a,d); *Bronco Billy's Marriage* 1915 (a,d); *Bronco Billy's Vengeance* 1915 (a,d); *The Champion* 1915 (a); *His Regeneration (short)* 1915 (d); *Bronco Billy and the Revenue Agent* 1916 (a,d); *Shootin' Mad* 1918 (a,d); *Any Night* 1922 (prod.sup); *Ashes* 1922 (d); *The Greater Duty* 1922 (a,d).

Anderson, Dame Judith • Actress • Born Frances Margaret Anderson, Adelaide, Australia, February 10, 1898. Leading Broadway star of the 1920s and 30s, in films from 1933. Best remembered as Mrs. Danvers in Hitchcock's *Rebecca* (1940). • *Blood Money* 1933; *Forty Little Mothers* 1940; *Rebecca* 1940 **(AANBSA)**; *Free and Easy* 1941; *King's Row* 1941; *Lady Scarface* 1941; *All Through the Night* 1942; *Edge of Darkness* 1943; *Stage Door Canteen* 1943; *Laura* 1944; *And Then There Were None* 1945; *The Diary of a Chambermaid* 1946; *Specter of the Rose* 1946; *The Strange Love of Martha Ivers* 1946; *Pursued* 1947; *The Red House* 1947; *Tycoon* 1947; *The Furies* 1950; *Salome* 1953; *The Ten Commandments* 1956; *Cat on a Hot Tin Roof* 1958; *Cinderfella* 1960; *Macbeth* 1960; *Don't Bother to Knock* 1961; *A Man Called Horse* 1970; *Inn of the Damned* 1974; *Star Trek III: The Search For Spock* 1984; *Hitchcock, Il Brivido del Genio* 1985; *Impure Thoughts* 1986.

Anderson, Kevin • Actor • Born Illinois, January 13, 1960. *Educ.* Goodman Theater School of Drama, Chicago. Member of Chicago's acclaimed Steppenwolf Theater who originated the role of Phillip in the Chicago, off-Broadway and London productions of Lyle Kessler's *Orphans* and reprised the part in Alan Pakula's 1987 screen adaptation. Anderson also starred opposite Vanessa Redgrave in the 1989 Broadway revival of *Orpheus Descending*. • *Risky Business* 1983; *Pink Nights...Hot Pink* 1985; *Orphans* 1987; *A Walk on the Moon* 1987; *Miles From Home* 1988; *In Country* 1989; *Sleeping With the Enemy* 1991.

Anderson, Lindsay • Director; also critic. • Born Bangalore, India, April 17, 1923. *Educ.* Wadham College, Oxford. "If you truly love human beings, you have to be able to be angry with them," Lindsay Anderson once said. An angry idealist and cerebral iconoclast, he has implied—at least in his early work—that the first step toward redeeming a corrupt system of values lies in contemplating its destruction.

Anderson served in WWII in a British Army Rifles unit and the Intelligence Corps. After graduation from Oxford, he co-founded *Sequence*, an influential film magazine, with writer Gavin Lambert and future directors Tony Richardson and Karel Reisz. He subsequently discovered American film, most notably the works of John Ford, which influenced his early affinity for the poetic aspects of cinema.

Anderson began his film career in 1948, making documentaries for industrialist Richard Sutcliffe. He continued to work in the non-fiction field through the 1950s, directing an Oscar-winning short, *Thursday's Children* (1953), about the efforts of deaf children to learn to communicate, and *Every Day Except Christmas* (1957), a tribute to the merchants of Covent Garden. In these films and his writings, Anderson promoted the Free Cinema movement, which explored the universal significance of mundane events and the relationship of art to working class experience.

In 1957 Anderson became director of the Royal Court Theatre; his work there and at other venues embraced Shakespeare and Chekhov, as well as contemporary playwrights such as David Storey. Anderson's first feature, *This Sporting Life* (1963), was adapted by Storey from his novel about a troubled rugby star and coal miner; it is an extension of Anderson's documentarian concerns.

If... (1968) marked a fierce revisionist departure. In this icy ode to rites of passage, Anderson paints a scathing portrait of the English private school system, using it as a thinly disguised metaphor for society as a whole. The film was the first of a trilogy (*O Lucky Man!* 1973, *Britannia Hospital* 1982) featuring the character of Mick Travis (Malcolm McDowell), who cavorts and lurches through a modern England characterized by absurdity and decay. *O Lucky Man!* leads Travis into a series of encounters with the military and medical establishments, the industrial hierarchy and, finally, the media—in the shape of a director (played by Lindsay Anderson) looking for a star for the film we have just been watching. *Brittania Hospital* is a nightmarishly comic indictment of the British medical system of the 1980s, whose decay is again representative of society as a whole.

In 1981 Anderson completed a well-received documentary study, *About John Ford*. *The Whales of August* (1988) is an elegy to old age that pairs legendary actresses Lillian Gish and Bette Davis as housebound sisters on the Maine coast. It displays neither the the lyrical realism of his early career nor the abrasive satire of his later films. His most recent work, *Glory! Glory!* (1989), a made-for-cable-TV film, sent up the televangelist phenomenon in more typical, unreserved Anderson style. But the director's iconoclasm has in recent years seemed to yield to an awareness of the intractability of the problems he once railed against. MDM • *Meet the Pioneers* (short) 1948 (a,d,ed); *Idlers That Work* (short) 1949 (a,d); *Three Installations* (short) 1952 (a,d); *Wakefield Express* (short) 1952 (d); *O Dreamland* (short) 1953 (d); *Thursday's Children* (short) 1953 (d,sc); *Trunk Conveyor* (short) 1954 (a,d); *The Children Upstairs (short)* 1955 (d); *Foot and Mouth (short)* 1955 (d); *Green and Pleasant Land (short)* 1955 (d); *Henry (short)* 1955 (d); *A Hundred Thousand Children (short)* 1955 (d); *Every Day Except Christmas* (short) 1957 (d,sc); *This Sporting Life* 1963 (d); *Raz Dwa Trzy—The Singing Lesson (short)* 1967 (d); *The White Bus (short)* 1967 (d); *If...* 1968 (d,p); *Inadmissible Evidence* 1968 (a); *75 Years of Cinema Museum* 1972 (a); *O Lucky Man!* 1973 (a,d,p); *In Celebration* 1974 (d); *Nighthawks* 1978 (collaboration); *Chariots of Fire* 1981 (a); *Britannia Hospital* 1982 (d); *The Whales of August* 1987 (d).

Anderson, Maxwell • Playwright; also screenwriter. • Born Atlantic City, NJ, December 15, 1888; died 1959. *Educ.* University of North Dakota; Stanford. Noted playwright who occasionally wrote directly for the screen. Highlights of Anderson's original film work include *All Quiet on the Western Front* (1930, with Del Andrews and George Abbott) and Hitchcock's *The Wrong Man* (1956); of his numerous plays adapted for the screen by others, Michael Curtiz's *The Private Lives of Elizabeth and Essex* (1939) and John Huston's *Key Largo* (1948) stand out. • *What Price Glory?* 1926 (from play); *The Cockeyed World* 1929 (from play *Tropical Twins*); *Saturday's Children* 1929 (from play); *All Quiet on the Western Front* 1930 (sc) **(AANBSC)**; *Rain* 1932 (sc); *Washington Merry-Go-Round* 1932 (story); *Death Takes a Holiday* 1934 (sc); *We Live Again* 1934 (sc); *Maybe It's Love* 1935 (from play); *So Red the Rose* 1935 (sc); *Mary of Scotland* 1936 (from play); *Winterset* 1936 (from play); *The Private Lives of Elizabeth and Essex* 1939 (from play *Elizabeth the Queen*); *Saturday's Children* 1940 (from play); *The Eve of St. Mark* 1944 (from play); *Knickerbocker Holiday* 1944 (from play); *Joan of Arc* 1948 (sc,from play *Joan of Lorraine*); *Key Largo* 1948 (from play); *What Price Glory?* 1952 (from play); *The Bad Seed* 1956 (from play); *The Wrong Man* 1956 (sc,from story "The True Story of Christopher Emmanuel Balestrero"); *Ben-Hur* 1959 (sc); *Never Steal Anything Small* 1959 (from play *Devil's Hornpipe*); *Anne of the Thousand Days* 1969 (from play).

Anderson, Michael • Director • Born London, January 30, 1920. Intelligent, dependable director who through the 1950s and 60s made a series of war films, notably *The Dam Busters* (1955) and the spy thriller, *The Quiller Memorandum* (1966), occasionally taking a break from the battle to helm such literary adaptations as *1984* (1955), *Around the World in 80 Days* (1956) and *The Shoes of the Fisherman* (1968). Father of actor Michael Anderson, Jr. • *Private Angelo* 1949 (d); *Waterfront* 1950 (d); *Hell Is Sold Out* 1951 (d); *Dial 17 (short)* 1952 (d); *Night Was Our Friend* 1952 (d); *The House of the Arrow* 1953 (d); *Will Any Gentleman?* 1953 (d); *The Dam Busters* 1955 (d); *1984* 1955 (d); *Around the World in 80 Days* 1956 (d) **(AANBD)**; *Yangtse Incident* 1957 (d); *Chase a Crooked Shadow* 1958 (d); *Shake Hands With the Devil* 1959 (d,p); *The Wreck of the Mary Deare* 1959 (d); *All the Fine Young Cannibals* 1960 (d); *The Naked Edge* 1961 (d); *Flight From Ashiya* 1964 (d); *Wild and Wonderful* 1964 (d); *Operation Crossbow* 1965 (d); *The Quiller Memorandum* 1966 (d); *The Shoes of the Fisherman* 1968 (d); *Pope Joan* 1972 (d); *Conduct Unbecoming* 1975 (d); *Doc Savage, The Man of Bronze* 1975 (d); *Logan's Run* 1976 (d); *Dominique* 1977 (d); *Orca...Killer Whale* 1977 (d); *Bells* 1982 (d); *Murder By Phone* 1983 (d); *Second Time Lucky* 1984 (d); *Troupers* 1985 (assoc.p); *Separate Vacations* 1986 (d); *La Boutique de l'orfèvre* 1989 (d); *Millennium* 1989 (d).

Andersson, Bibi • Actress • Born Birgitta Andersson, Stockholm, Sweden, November 11, 1935. *Educ.* Royal Dramatic Theater School, Stockholm. Major star of the Swedish cinema of the 1950s and 60s. Andersson was appearing on stage at Malmö when discovered by Ingmar Bergman, who was casting for a 1951 Bris soap commercial. She went on to became a staple of the director's stock company, distinguishing herself in such films as *Wild Strawberries* (1957), *Brink* *of Life* (1958), for which she was named best actress at Cannes, and *The Devil's Eye* (1959). Her finest work may be *Persona* (1966), Bergman's masterpiece about a mute actress (Liv Ullman and her nurse (Andersson) who gradually switch minds and identities.

Andersson's big bid for stardom outside Sweden came with John Huston's *The Kremlin Letter* (1970), generally underrated by critics. She made a successful shift to character roles with *I Never Promised You a Rose Garden* (1977), a disturbing study of schizophrenia with Andersson as a compassionate psychologist. • *Sommarnattens Leende/Smiles of a Summer Night* 1955; *Sista Paret Ut* 1956; *Det Sjunde Inseglet/The Seventh Seal* 1957; *Smultronstallet/Wild Strawberries* 1957; *Ansiktet/The Magician* 1958; *Nara Livet/Brink of Life* 1958; *Djavulens Oga/The Devil's Eye* 1960; *For att Inte Tala om Alla Dessa Kvinnor/All These Women* 1964; *Duel at Diablo* 1966; *Persona* 1966; *Flickorna/The Girls* 1968; *En Passion/The Passion of Anna* 1969; *The Kremlin Letter* 1970; *Storia di una Donna* 1970; *Beroringen/The Touch* 1971; *Appelkriget* 1972; *Ingmar Bergman* 1972; *Mannen fran andra Sidan* 1972; *Afskedens Time* 1973; *La Rivale* 1974; *Scenes From a Marriage* 1974; *Aegget ar Lost* 1975; *Blondy* 1975; *Il Pleut sur Santiago* 1975; *I Never Promised You a Rose Garden* 1977; *L'Amour en Question* 1978; *An Enemy of the People* 1978; *Picassos Aventyr* 1978; *Barnfoerbjudet* 1979; *The Concorde—Airport '79* 1979; *Du ar inte klok, Madicken* 1979; *Kristoffers Hus* 1979; *Quintet* 1979; *Twee Vrouwen* 1979; *Madicken pa Junibacken* 1980; *Marmeladupproret* 1980; *Jag rodnar* 1981; *Berget pa manens baksida* 1983; *Exposed* 1983; *Med Lill-Klas i kappsacken* 1983; *Raskenstam* 1983; *Svarte Fugler* 1983; *Sista Leken* 1984; *Huomenna* 1986; *Babette's gastebud/Babette's Feast* 1987; *Los Dueños del silencio* 1987; *Svart gryning* 1987; *Fordringsagare* 1989.

Andersson, Harriet • Actress • Born Stockholm, Sweden, January 14, 1932. Sensual, stunningly beautiful member of Ingmar Bergman's troupe, in many of the director's early classics. It is Andersson's publicity still, from Bergman's *Summer with Monika* (1952), that Jean-Pierre Léaud steals in François Truffaut's *The 400 Blows* (1959). Married to director Jörn Donner. • *Medan Staden Sover/While the City Sleeps* 1950; *Franskild* 1951; *Sommaren Med Monika/Monika/Summer With Monika* 1952; *Gycklarnas Afton/Sawdust and Tinsel/The Naked Night* 1953; *En Lektion i Karlek/A Lesson in Love* 1954; *Kvinnodrom/Dreams/Journey Into Autumn* 1955; *Sommarnattens Leende/Smiles of a Summer Night* 1955; *Sista Paret Ut* 1956; *Sasom i en Spegel/Through a Glass Darkly* 1961; *Alksande Par/Loving Couples* 1964; *Att Alska/To Love* 1964; *For att Inte Tala om Alla Dessa Kvinnor/All These Women* 1964; *The Deadly Affair* 1967; *Flickorna/The Girls* 1968; *Anna* 1970; *Den Vita Vaggen* 1974; *Monismanien 1995* 1975; *Hempa's Bar* 1977; *Linus* 1979; *La Sabina* 1979; *Fanny och Alexander/Fanny and Alexander* 1982; *Raskenstam* 1983; *Sommarkvallar pa jorden* 1987; *Himmel og Helvede* 1988; *Blankt Vapen* 1990.

Andress, Ursula • Actress • Born Bern, Switzerland, March 19, 1936. Smoldering international star whose big break came with the role of Honey in the first James Bond movie, *Dr. No* (1962). • *Dr. No* 1962; *Four For Texas* 1963; *Fun in Acapulco* 1963; *Nightmare in the Sun* 1965; *Once Before I Die* 1965; *She* 1965; *What's New, Pussycat?* 1965; *The Blue Max* 1966; *Casino Royale* 1967; *Le Dolci signore* 1967; *Perfect Friday* 1970; *Soleil Rouge/Red Sun* 1971; *The Loves and Times of Scaramouche* 1975; *The Sensuous Nurse* 1976; *Doppio Delitto* 1977; *Spogliamoci cosí senza Pudor...* 1977; *Letti Selvaggi* 1978; *La Montagna del dio Cannibale* 1978; *Tigers in Lipstick* 1978; *The 5th Musketeer* 1979; *Clash of the Titans* 1981; *Liberté, Egalité, Choucroute* 1985; *Klassezamekunft* 1989.

Andrews, Dana • Actor • Born Carver Dana Andrews, Collins, MS, January 1, 1912. *Educ.* Pasadena Playhouse; Sam Houston State Teacher's College. Solid (sometimes to the point of being wooden), average-Joe leading man of the 1940s who specialized in earnest, embittered and/or disillusioned characters. Having worked as an accountant and a singer, Andrews entered films in the early 1940s as supporting player in westerns. After portraying the brooding victim of a lynch mob in *The Ox-Box Incident* (1943), his career took off and he starred in a succession of strong vehicles often as flawed heroes.

Most memorable in urban settings, Andrews successfully teamed up with director Otto Preminger and co-star Gene Tierney for *Laura* (1944) and *Where the Sidewalk Ends* (1950) and was equally superb as the re-adjusting bombadier in *The Best Years of Our Lives* (1946) and as the unflinchingly honest prosecuting attorney in Elia Kazan's *Boomerang* (1947). With his career on the wane in the 1950s, Andrews starred in prestige TV showcases and headlined a daytime soap opera, "Bright Promise" in the late 1960s. • *Kit Carson* 1940; *Lucky Cisco Kid* 1940; *Sailor's Lady* 1940; *The Westerner* 1940; *Ball of Fire* 1941; *Belle Starr* 1941; *Swamp Water* 1941; *Tobacco Road* 1941; *Berlin Correspondent* 1942; *Crash Dive* 1943; *The North Star* 1943; *The Ox-Bow Incident* 1943; *Laura* 1944; *The Purple Heart* 1944; *Up in Arms* 1944; *Wing and a Prayer* 1944; *Fallen Angel* 1945; *State Fair* 1945; *A Walk in the Sun* 1945; *The Best Years of Our Lives* 1946; *Canyon Passage* 1946; *Boomerang* 1947; *Daisy Kenyon* 1947; *Night Song* 1947; *Deep Waters* 1948; *The Iron Curtain* 1948; *No Minor Vices* 1948; *Sword in the Desert* 1949; *Edge of Doom* 1950; *My Foolish Heart* 1950; *Where the Sidewalk Ends* 1950; *The Frogmen* 1951; *I Want You* 1951; *Sealed Cargo* 1951; *Assignment—Paris* 1952; *Duel in the Jungle* 1954; *Elephant Walk* 1954; *Smoke Signal* 1954; *Strange Lady in Town* 1954; *Three Hours to Kill* 1954; *Comanche* 1955; *Beyond a Reasonable Doubt* 1956; *While The City Sleeps* 1956; *Spring Reunion* 1957; *Zero Hour!* 1957; *Curse of the Demon* 1958; *Enchanted Island* 1958; *The Fearmakers* 1958; *The Crowded Sky* 1960; *Madison Avenue* 1962; *Battle of the Bulge* 1965; *Brainstorm* 1965; *Crack in the World* 1965; *In Harm's Way* 1965; *The Loved One* 1965; *The Satan Bug* 1965; *Town Tamer* 1965; *Johnny Reno* 1966; *Il Cobra* 1967; *The Frozen Dead* 1967; *Hot Rods to Hell* 1967; *The Devil's Brigade* 1968; *Innocent Bystanders* 1972; *Airport 1975* 1975; *Take a Hard Ride* 1975; *The Last Tycoon* 1976; *Born Again* 1978; *Good Guys Wear Black* 1978; *Prince Jack* 1984.

Andrews, Edward • Actor • Born Griffin, GA, October 9, 1914; died March 8, 1985, Palisades, CA. *Educ.* University of Virginia. Stage-trained character player who made a memorable screen debut as the disingenuous power broker in *The Phenix City Story* (1955) and went on to play both innocent dupes and clever business sharks. • *The Phenix City Story* 1955; *The Harder They Fall* 1956; *Tea and Sympathy* 1956; *Tension at Table Rock* 1956; *These Wilder Years* 1956; *Three Brave Men* 1956; *The Unguarded Moment* 1956; *Hot Summer Night* 1957; *The Tattered Dress* 1957; *Trooper Hook* 1957; *The Fiend Who Walked the West* 1958; *Night of the Quarter Moon* 1958; *The Absent-Minded Professor* 1960; *Elmer Gantry* 1960; *Love in a Goldfish Bowl* 1961; *The Young Doctors* 1961; *The Young Savages* 1961; *40 Pounds of Trouble* 1962; *Advise and Consent* 1962; *Son of Flubber* 1963; *The Thrill of It All* 1963; *The Brass Bottle* 1964; *Good Neighbor Sam* 1964; *Kisses For My President* 1964; *The Man From Galveston* 1964; *Send Me No Flowers* 1964; *A Tiger Walks* 1964; *Youngblood Hawke* 1964; *Fluffy* 1965; *Birds Do It* 1966; *The Glass Bottom Boat* 1966; *The Trouble With Girls* 1969; *How to Frame a Figg* 1970; *Tora! Tora! Tora!* 1970; *$1,000,000 Duck* 1971; *Avanti!* 1972; *Charley and the Angel* 1972; *Now You See Him, Now You Don't* 1972; *Seniors* 1978; *The Final Countdown* 1980; *Gremlins* 1984; *Sixteen Candles* 1984.

Andrews, Harry • Actor • Born Harry Fleetwood Andrews, Tonbridge, Kent, England, November 10, 1911; died March 6, 1989, Salehurst, England.

Educ. Wrekin College, England. Lean, strong-jawed and frequently bearded supporting player and distinguished Shakespearan stage actor who entered films in the early 1950s. Throughout his long, prolific career, Andrews frequently played tough military types or severe, no-nonsense characters, but he brilliantly played against type as a flashy homosexual in Joe Orton's black comedy, *Entertaining Mr. Sloane* (1970). • *The Red Beret* 1953; *The Black Knight* 1954; *The Man Who Loved Redheads* 1954; *Alexander the Great* 1956; *Helen of Troy* 1956; *A Hill in Korea* 1956; *Moby Dick* 1956; *I Accuse!* 1957; *Saint Joan* 1957; *The Devil's Disciple* 1959; *Solomon and Sheba* 1959; *Circle of Deception* 1961; *Barabbas* 1962; *Lisa* 1962; *55 Days at Peking* 1963; *Nine Hours to Rama* 1963; *633 Squadron* 1964; *Nothing But the Best* 1964; *The Agony and the Ecstasy* 1965; *The Hill* 1965; *Sands of the Kalahari* 1965; *The Truth About Spring* 1965; *Modesty Blaise* 1966; *The Night of the Generals* 1966; *The Deadly Affair* 1967; *I'll Never Forget What's 'Is Name* 1967; *The Long Duel* 1967; *The Charge of the Light Brigade* 1968; *A Dandy in Aspic* 1968; *The Night They Raided Minsky's* 1968; *Play Dirty* 1968; *The Sea Gull* 1968; *Battle of Britain* 1969; *A Nice Girl Like Me* 1969; *Country Dance* 1970; *Entertaining Mr. Sloane* 1970; *Too Late the Hero* 1970; *Wuthering Heights* 1970; *I Want What I Want* 1971; *Nicholas and Alexandra* 1971; *The Nightcomers* 1971; *The Ruling Class* 1972; *L'Uomo della Mancha* 1972; *The Last Days of Man on Earth* 1973; *The Mackintosh Man* 1973; *Man at the Top* 1973; *Theatre of Blood* 1973; *The Internecine Project* 1974; *The Blue Bird* 1976; *The Passover Plot* 1976; *Sky Riders* 1976; *Crossed Swords* 1977; *Equus* 1977; *The Big Sleep* 1978; *Death on the Nile* 1978; *The Medusa Touch* 1978; *Superman* 1978; *Watership Down* 1978; *Hawk The Slayer* 1980; *Mesmerized* 1986.

Andrews, Julie • Actress; also singer. • Born Julia Elizabeth Wells, Walton-on-Thames, England, October 1, 1935. Wholesome, popular star of the 1960s and 70s who began her career touring in musical revues with her mother and stepfather and whose lilting, sweet soprano voice and prim British charm won her kudos as a Broadway musical star. Although she lost all three film roles she created on Broadway (*The Boyfriend* 1954, *My Fair Lady* 1956 and *Camelot* 1960) to non-singers in their film incarnations, Andrews nevertheless scored a triumph by winning an Oscar for her film debut, *Mary Poppins* (1964) competing against Audrey Hepburn who starred in the film of *My Fair Lady*.

A box-office star after appearing in the blockbuster musical *The Sound of Music* (1965), followed by the less successful large-scale musical vehicles, *Star!* (1968) and *Darling Lili* (1970), Andrews attempted to break away from her goody-goody stereotyping by appearing in less wholesome, non-musical fare (e.g. Hitchcock's *Torn Curtain* 1966). However, it was only through her subsequent collaborations with second husband Blake Edwards (e.g. *The Tamarind Seed* 1974, *Victor/Victoria* 1982, *That's Life!* 1986) that she proved herself a deft comedienne and a warm dramatic actress. As "Julie Edwards," she has written two highly-regarded children's books. • *The Rose of Baghdad* 1949 (a); *The Americanization of Emily* 1964 (a); *Mary Poppins* 1964 (a) **(AABA)**; *The Sound of Music* 1965 (a) **(AANBA)**; *Hawaii* 1966 (a); *Torn Curtain* 1966 (a); *Thoroughly Modern Millie* 1967 (a); *Star!* 1968 (a); *Darling Lili* 1970 (a,song); *The Tamarind Seed* 1974 (a); *10* 1979 (a); *Little Miss Marker* 1980 (a); *S.O.B.* 1981 (a); *Victor/Victoria* 1982 (a) **(AANBA)**; *The Man Who Loved Women* 1983 (a); *Duet For One* 1986 (a); *That's Life!* 1986 (a).

Angeli, Pier • Actress • Born Anna Maria Pierangeli, Cagliari, Sardinia, Italy, June 19, 1932; died September 10, 1971, Beverly Hills, CA. Petite, gentle-looking lead of the 1950s discovered while studing in Rome by French director Léonide Moguy who then co-starred her in *Tomorrow Is Too Late* (1950) opposite Vittorio de Sica. Angeli was put under contract by MGM and starred as a soulful Italian war bride in Fred Zinnemann's *Teresa* (1951), but aside from playing Rocky Graziano's wife in *Somebody Up There Likes Me* (1956) and a circus girl in *Merry Andrew* (1958), she subsequently found few other worthy projects. Her emotional entanglements and physical accidents helped put her career into a tailspin and before her death she appeared in sexploitation and horror films. Married from 1954 to 1959 to Vic Damone. Twin sister of actress Marisa Pavan. • *Domani è troppo Tardi/Tomorrow Is Too Late* 1950; *The Light Touch* 1951; *Teresa* 1951; *The Devil Makes Three* 1952; *Sombrero* 1953; *The Story of Three Loves* 1953; *Flame and the Flesh* 1954; *The Silver Chalice* 1954; *Port Afrique* 1956; *Somebody Up There Likes Me* 1956; *The Vintage* 1957; *Merry Andrew* 1958; *Sodoma e Gomorra/Sodom and Gomorrah* 1962; *Battle of the Bulge* 1965; *Rey de Africa* 1967; *Love Me, Love My Wife* 1971.

Angelopoulos, Theo • Director, screenwriter • Born Theodoros Angelopoulos, Athens, Greece, 1936. *Educ.* IDHEC, Paris. Angelopoulos trained as a lawyer before attending IDHEC, and began his film career as a critic. His early work as a director was largely historically based and includes a trilogy (*Days of '36* 1972, *The Travelling Players* 1975, *The Hunters* 1977) which chronicles the history of Greece from the mid-1930s onward. His later work, better known internationally, draws more on ancient history and myth but retains a key political dimension. *Voyage to Cythera* (1984) is a poignant, exquisitely composed drama about an ageing exile who returns to Greece—it earned a best original screenplay award at Cannes for Angelopoulos and co-writers Tonino Guerra and Theo Valtinos; *The Beekeeper* (1986) features a landmark performance from Marcello Mastroianni as a gloomy, retired teacher who picks up an enigmatic hitchiker during a road trip. Angelopoulos is a major director with a distinctive vision and a finely honed style who has been sadly neglected by American distributors and by most American critics. • *I Ekpombi* 1968 (d,sc); *Anaparastasis* 1970 (d,sc); *I Meres tou 36/Days of 36* 1972 (d,sc); *O Thiassos/The Travelling Players* 1975 (d,sc); *I Kinigi/The Hunters* 1977 (d,sc); *O Megalexandros/Alexander the Great* 1980 (d,sc); *Athens, 1982* 1982 (d,sc); *Taxidi stin Kythera/Voyage to Cythera* 1984 (d,sc,story); *Melissokomos Petheni—O Alles Mythos, Enas* 1986 (a); *O Melissokomos/The Beekeeper* 1986 (d,sc); *Topio Stin Omichli/Landscape in the Mist* 1988 (d,sc,story); *L'Heritage de la chouette* 1989 (a).

Anger, Kenneth • Filmmaker; also author, actor. • Born Santa Monica, CA, 1932. One of the major figures of the avant-garde "New American Cinema" of the 1950s and 60s, Kenneth Anger grew up in Hollywood (he acted in *A Midsummer Night's Dream* 1935) and was allegedly making films before the age of ten (e.g. *Who Has Been Rocking My Dream Boat?* 1941). After meeting famed underground filmmaker Harry Smith in 1947, Anger completed his first important work, *Fireworks* (1947), over two weekends. This personal psychodrama received a public screening and critical acclaim in 1949 at Jean Cocteau's "Festival of the Damned" in Biarritz. Its protagonist, played by Anger himself, is a guilt-ridden homosexual who dreams of being viciously beaten by a group of sailors. His punishment leads to images of sexual liberation and fertility. *Fireworks* ends with Anger asleep with another man, the dream only temporarily abating his internal anguish over his homosexuality.

Anger shot his next major work, *Eaux d'Artifice* (1953), in the gardens of the Villa d'Este in Tivoli, Italy. *Eaux d'Artifice* is a beautifully photographed, single-character exercise in symbolism. Wandering through the garden, a woman in baroque evening dress becomes frightened by hypnotic fountains and ominous gargoyles and tries to flee the labyrinth. The film begins with her emergence from a spurting fountain and ends as water engulfs her.

During Anger's childhood, his grandmother, a costume mistress in Hollywood, had told him scandalous stories about film stars and executives. This gossip shaped *Hollywood Babylon*, Anger's book of scandal and sexual decadence which was first published in France in 1958. (Anger issued a followup, *Hollywood Babylon II*, in 1984.)

Before leaving France, Anger completed 20 minutes of *The Story of O* (1958-61), footage he claims is still locked in the Cinémathèque Française because the character "O" was played by the 20-year-old daughter of the then-Minister of Finance.

Inauguration of the Pleasure Dome (1954, 1966) depicts an imaginative world of gods invoked and controlled by the untamed desires of Lord Shiva and his female self, the Scarlet Woman. It has been shown in several versions, including one with three-screen projection. Lord Shiva's mythical world is paced with ritualistic pomp, from the slow entrance of the gods and the deceitful intoxication of Pan to the orgiastic finale set among the flames of hell.

Thirteen popular songs from the period provide the framework for Anger's most influential film, *Scorpio Rising* (1962-64). Each song is juxtaposed ironically with startling visual images. The song "Blue Velvet" accompanies men ritualistically dressing up in blue jeans and leather. As we hear the lyrics to "I Will Follow Him" we see a montage of images that includes Adolf Hitler at military rallies, disciples following Jesus Christ in DeMille's silent film *The King of Kings*, Marlon Brando leading a motorcycle gang in *The Wild One* and Anger's Scorpio figure directing his followers in a motorcycle race. While these juxtapositions may seem jejeune to contemporary audiences, the "poetic" symbolism of *Scorpio Rising* was striking to the audiences of the new art houses in America in the early 60s.

Invocation of My Demon Brother (1969) presents a pastiche of images as seen through the mind's eye of a male albino: marijuana smoked through a skull pipe; soldiers in Vietnam; a burning cat; naked males wrestling in bed; and Mick Jagger performing on stage. Inserted throughout are shots of Anger as Magus, performing occult rites on stage in celebration of the Autumnal Equinox.

Anger made *Invocation* with scraps of footage originally photographed for *Lucifer Rising* (1980). His childhood fascination with fairy tales led to a lifelong dedication to the occult, specifically Aleister Crowley's religion, Thelema. In *Lucifer Rising* the forces of nature (volcanic eruptions, lightning, turbulent water, an eclipse of the moon) awaken Lucifer. Anger includes numerous symbols drawn from alchemy and imagistic references to the cosmology of Crowley. Photographed in Egypt, Germany and England at the sites of sun worship by ancient cultures, *Lucifer Rising* culminates with the spiritual rebel of the title conjuring up a luminous flying object over the pyramids and pharaohs of Egypt.

Anger equates filmmaking with "casting a spell," or invocation. *Lucifer Rising* marks his attempt to move from the solipsistic visions and images of his earlier films to the invocation of a higher spiritual and intellectual order. RCB • *Who Has Been Rocking My Dream Boat?* 1941 (a); *Fireworks* 1947 (a,d,idea,ph,p); *Eaux D'Artifice* 1953 (d,idea,p); *Le Jeune homme et la mort (short)* 1953 (d); *Inauguration of the Pleasure Dome* 1954,1966 (a,d,idea,p); *The Story of O* 1958-61 (d,sc); *Sorpio Rising* 1962-64 (d,idea,p); *Invocation of My Demon Brother* 1969 (a,d,idea,p); *Lucifer Rising* 1980 (a,d,p,sc,ph,ed,ad); *He Stands in a Desert Counting the Seconds of His Life* 1985 (a).

Anhalt, Edward • Screenwriter; also producer. • Born New York, NY, March 28, 1914. *Educ.* Columbia. After working as a journalist and documentary filmmaker for Pathé and CBS-TV, teamed with his wife Edna Anhalt (née Richards) during WWII to write pulp fiction. After the war, they graduated to writing screenplays for thrillers, beginning with *Bulldog Drummond Strikes Back* (1947). Anhalt has since proved himself a versatile, consistently effective (and reputedly speedy) scenarist, superb at contemporary urban thrillers (*Panic in the Streets* 1950), war dramas (*The Young Lions* 1958), historical epics (*Becket* 1964) and much of everything in between. • *The City* 1939 (assoc.ph); *Bulldog Drummond Strikes Back* 1947 (sc); *The Gentleman From Nowhere* 1948 (sc); *The Crime Doctor's Diary* 1949 (sc,story); *Panic in the Streets* 1950 (story) **(AABST)**; *The Member of the Wedding* 1952 (sc); *The Sniper* 1952 (sc,story) **(AANBST)**; *Not As a Stranger* 1955 (sc); *The Pride and the Passion* 1957 (sc,story); *In Love and War* 1958 (sc); *The Restless Years* 1958 (sc); *The Young Lions* 1958 (sc); *The Sins of Rachel Cade* 1961 (sc); *The Young Savages* 1961 (sc); *A Girl Named Tamiko* 1962 (sc); *Girls! Girls! Girls!* 1962 (sc); *Wives and Lovers* 1963 (sc); *Becket* 1964 (sc) **(AABSC)**; *Boeing Boeing* 1965 (sc); *The Satan Bug* 1965 (sc); *Hour of the Gun* 1967 (a,sc); *The Boston Strangler* 1968 (sc); *In Enemy Country* 1968 (sc); *The Madwoman of Chaillot* 1969 (sc); *Jeremiah Johnson* 1972 (sc); *Luther* 1974 (sc); *The Man in the Glass Booth* 1974 (sc); *Escape to Athena* 1979 (sc); *Green Ice* 1981 (sc); *The Holcroft Covenant* 1985 (sc).

Ann-Margret • Actress; also singer, dancer. • Born Ann-Margaret Olsson, Valsjobyn, Jamtland, Sweden, April 28, 1941. *Educ.* Northwestern University. Glamourous, red-headed siren who was discovered by George Burns while a cabaret performer and subsequently typecast in teenage sex-kitten roles throughout the 1960s. Ironically, it was a film in which Ann-Margret appeared nude that brought her critical respect and her first Academy Award nomination: as the distraught "older woman" opposite Jack Nicholson in *Carnal Knowledge* (1971).

Since her marriage in 1967 to her personal manager, the former actor Roger Smith, and since her life-threatening fall from a stage in 1972, she has ventured into more interesting projects and has displayed a vulnerable sensitivity and warmth under her rather hard exterior beauty, while still continuing to perform as the sexy singer-dancer in stage spectaculars. • *A Pocketful of Miracles* 1961; *State Fair* 1962; *Bye Bye Birdie* 1963; *Kitten With a Whip* 1964; *The Pleasure Seekers* 1964; *Viva Las Vegas* 1964; *Bus Riley's Back in Town* 1965; *The Cincinnati Kid* 1965; *Once a Thief* 1965; *Made in Paris* 1966; *Murderers' Row* 1966; *Stagecoach* 1966; *The Swinger* 1966; *Il Profeta* 1967; *C.C. and Company* 1970; *R.P.M.* 1970; *Carnal Knowledge* 1971 **(AANBSA)**; *Un Homme Est Mort/The Outside Man* 1973; *The Train Robbers* 1973; *Tommy* 1975 **(AANBA)**; *Folies bourgeoises/The Twist* 1976; *Joseph Andrews* 1976; *The Last Remake of Beau Geste* 1977; *The Cheap Detective* 1978; *Magic* 1978; *The Villain* 1979; *Middle Age Crazy* 1980; *I Ought to Be in Pictures* 1981; *Lookin' to Get Out* 1982; *The Return of the Soldier* 1982; *Vice Squad* 1982; *Twice in a Lifetime* 1985; *52 Pick-Up* 1986; *A Tiger's Tale* 1987; *A New Life* 1988.

Annakin, Ken • Director; also screenwriter, producer. • Born Beverley, East Yorkshire, England, August 10, 1914. Began his film career making short documentaries, and in the postwar years mounted his first features, quickly proving himself an effective craftsman of both comedy and drama. In the 1950s Annakin crafted some intrinsically British films and began working for Disney, notably *The Swiss Family Robinson* (1960). By the 1960s he was specializing in sprawling, big-budget adventures and a series of long-distance marathon comedies beginning with *Those Magnificent Men in Their Flying Machines* (1965). • *The Way Ahead* 1944 (ad); *Make Fruitful the Land* 1945 (d); *Broken Journey* 1948 (d); *Here Come the Huggetts* 1948 (d); *Miranda* 1948 (d); *Quartet* 1948 (d); *Huggetts Abroad* 1949 (d); *Landfall* 1949 (d); *Vote For Huggetts* 1949 (d); *Double Confession* 1950 (d); *Trio* 1950 (d); *Hotel Sahara* 1951 (d); *The Planter's Wife* 1952 (d); *The Story of Robin Hood* 1952 (d); *The Sword and the Rose* 1953 (d); *The Seekers* 1954 (d); *You Know What Sailors Are* 1954 (d); *Value For Money* 1955 (d); *Loser Takes All* 1956 (d); *Three Men in a Boat* 1956 (d); *Across the Bridge* 1957 (d); *Nor the Moon By Night* 1958 (d); *Mission in Morocco* 1959 (story); *Third Man on the Mountain* 1959 (d); *The Swiss Family Robinson* 1960 (d); *The Hellions* 1961 (d); *Very Important Person* 1961 (d); *Crooks Anonymous* 1962 (d); *The Fast*

Lady 1962 (d); *The Longest Day* 1962 (d); *The Informers* 1963 (d); *Battle of the Bulge* 1965 (d); *Those Magnificent Men in Their Flying Machines* 1965 (d,sc) **(AANBSC)**; *The Long Duel* 1967 (d,p); *The Biggest Bundle of Them All* 1968 (d); *Monte Carlo or Bust!* 1969 (d,p,sc); *Call of the Wild* 1972 (d); *Paper Tiger* 1975 (d); *The 5th Musketeer* 1979 (d); *Cheaper to Keep Her* 1980 (d); *The Pirate Movie* 1982 (d); *The New Adventures of Pippi Longstocking* 1988 (d,p).

Annaud, Jean-Jacques • Director, screenwriter • Born Draveil, France, October 1, 1943. *Educ.* Vaugirard School; IDHEC, Paris; Sorbonne, Paris (literature). A former award-winning director of TV commercials whose debut, *Black and White in Color* (1976)—about a group of French colonialists in West Africa circa 1914—was ignored in his own country but became a surprise hit in the US, winning an Oscar as best foreign film. A specialist in earnest, period adaptations, Annaud subsequently made *Quest For Fire* (1981), a grueling portrait of primitive man that earned him two César awards, and *The Name of the Rose* (1986), a medieval tale of monastery murder via Umberto Eco. He also scored a grand international success with *The Bear* (1988), a somewhat saccharin, but engrossing portrait of the title character's struggle against hunters, told from the point-of-view of the bear. Has worked often with screenwriter Gerard Brach. • *La Victoire en chantant/Black and White in Color* 1976 (d,sc); *Je suis timide, mais je me soigne/Too Shy to Try* 1978 (sc); *Coup de Tête/Hot Head* 1979 (d,sc,adapt); *Quest For Fire* 1981 (d); *The Name of the Rose* 1986 (a); *L'Ours/The Bear* 1988 (d).

Anouilh, Jean • Playwright; also screenwriter, director. • Born Bordeaux, France, June 23, 1910; died October 3, 1987, Lausanne, Switzerland. Leading figure of post war French theater who contributed to the scripts of several noted films (e.g. *Monsieur Vincent* 1945) and adapted several of his own plays for the screen (*Pattes Blanches* 1949, *Caroline Cherie* 1954, etc). Anouilh also directed two films; *Le Voyageur sans baggage* (1943), from his acclaimed play, and the noirish *Deux sous de violettes* (1951). Father of actress Catherine Anouilh. • *Le Voyageur sans bagage* 1943 (d); *Anna Karenina* 1948 (sc); *Pattes Blanches* 1949 (sc,from play); *Caroline Cherie* 1950 (adapt); *Monsoon* 1952 (from play); *Waltz of the Toreadors* 1962 (from play); *Becket* 1964 (from play *Becket, ou l'honneur de Dieu*).

Anspach, Susan • Actress • Born New York, NY, November 23, 1939. *Educ.* Catholic University, Washington, DC. Blonde leading lady from the stage, in relatively few films. Anspach hit a peak in the early 1970s with *Five Easy Pieces* (1970) and *Blume in Love* (1973) and was superb in Dusan Makavayev's disturbing, hilarious *Montenegro* (1981). • *Five Easy Pieces* 1970; *The Landlord* 1970; *Play It Again, Sam* 1972; *Blume in Love* 1973; *The Big Fix* 1978; *Running* 1979; *The Devil and Max Devlin* 1981; *Gas* 1981; *Montenegro* 1981; *Misunderstood* 1984; *Blue Monkey* 1987; *Into the Fire* 1987; *Blood Red* 1989; *Back to Back* 1990; *The Rutanga Tapes* 1990.

Antonelli, Laura • Actress • Born Pola, Italy (now Pula, Yugoslavia), c. 1941. Voluptuous, radiant European screen siren of the 1970s. Antonelli appeared in numerous Italian sex farces but made more distinguished outings in Claude Chabrol's *High Heels!* (1972), Luchino Visconti's swan song, *The Innocent* (1976) and Ettore Scola's *Passion of Love* (1981). • *Bali* 1970; *A Man Called Sledge* 1970; *Sans Mobile Apparent* 1971; *Docteur Popaul/High Heels!* 1972; *Malizia/Malicious* 1973; *Peccato Veniale* 1973; *Sessomatto* 1973; *Lovers and Other Relatives* 1974; *Mio Dio, come sono Caduta in Basso* 1974; *La Divina Creatura* 1975; *L'Innocente/The Innocent* 1976; *Mogliamante/Wifemistress* 1977; *Letti Selvaggi* 1978; *Tigers in Lipstick* 1978; *Il Malato Immaginario* 1979; *Passione d'amore/Passion of Love* 1981; *Sesso e volentieri* 1982; *Till Marriage Do Us Part* 1982; *Porca vacca!* 1983; *Viuulentemente Mia* 1983; *Tranches de Vie* 1984; *La Gabbia* 1985; *Grandi Magazzini* 1985; *La Venexiana* 1986; *Rimini Rimini* 1987; *Roba da Ricchi* 1987; *L'Avaro* 1990.

Antonioni, Michelangelo • Director; also screenwriter. • Born Ferrara, Italy, September 29, 1912. *Educ.* University of Bologna (economics); Centro Sperimentale di Cinematografia, Rome (direction). Antonioni began writing about film as a student at Bologna University, mercilessly criticizing the fatuous Italian comedies of the 1930s. In 1940, he studied direction at the Centro Sperimentale in Rome. Two years later, he collaborated on consecutive films as a scriptwriter, first with Roberto Rossellini and then Enrico Fulchignoni. His first directorial effort was a documentary, *Gente del Po*, begun in 1943 and completed in 1947. For two other documentaries in the late 40s he solicited music from Giovanni Fusco, whose scores enhanced Antonioni's own pessimism.

Antonioni's minimalist, yet poignant style, which critics described as "structured absence," and his disdain for vulgar commercialism, made him an important influence on post-neorealist Italian cinema. His first feature, *Story of a Love Affair* (1950), uses complex camerawork to tell the simple tale of a wealthy woman whose husband dies. The approach would typify his subsequent work.

The Vanquished (1952), a portrait of juvenile • delinquents in post-war Europe, displeased the Italians by depicting their youngsters as neo-Fascists; censors in France and England banned one portion of the film. Antonioni's episode of the anthology film *Love in the City* (1953) dealt with suicide, a preoccupation that also provided the uneasy resolution to *The Girl Friends* (1955), a study of several women and their disappointing relationships with men.

After the release of *The Outcry* (1957), a study of the inept men of the Po Valley, Antonioni's developing assurance with the medium led him to look beyond the proletarian subjects favored by neorealism. *L'Avventura* (1959) began a phase of non-narrative, psychological cinema, examining the barren eroticism of a bourgeoisie which had abandoned its traditional social and cultural values. The film attracted a political critique that equated Antonioni's work with the writings of André Gide. Critics commonly unite the thematic concerns of *L'Avventura*, *La Notte* (1961) and *L'Eclisse* (1962) as a trilogy in which mankind reaches—unsuccessfully—for love as the last refuge in the modern world.

A stranded humanist faces the intimidations of technology in *The Red Desert* (1964), in which Antonioni had an entire landscape painted red to underline his theme of despair. Heroine Monica Vitti's palpable frustration signaled the end of her four-film collaboration with Antonioni, which had made her an international star.

Blow-Up (1966) marked Antonioni's departure from Italy to "swinging London," where he dramatized the paradoxes of its nervous hip consciousness. The film's finale—a ball-less tennis match—became a reference point of 60s cinema. The success of *Blow-Up* (Antonioni won the National Society of Film Critics' best director award) brought the director to California for *Zabriskie Point* (1970), an elegaic view of the intersection of materialism and hippiedom. *The Passenger* (1975) features Jack Nicholson as an American reporter who adopts the identity of a deceased fellow guest in a North African hotel. The director's virtuoso use of Gaudi's architecture echoes the unresolved angles of the protagonist's world. Neither *Mystery of Oberwald* (1980) nor *Identification of a Woman* (1982) found distribution in the US.

In 1985, Antonioni suffered a heart attack that left him partially paralyzed. Since then, several projects have been announced, only to be stifled in the early stages of development. KJ • *I Due Foscari* 1942 (sc,ad); *Un Pilota Ritorna* 1942 (sc); *Les Visiteurs du soir/The Devil's Envoys* 1942 (ad); *Caccia tragica* 1947 (sc); *Gente del Po (short)* 1947 (d,sc); *N.U. (short)* 1948 (d,sc); *Oltre l'oblio (short)* 1948 (d,sc); *Roma-Montevi-*

deo (short) 1948 (d,sc); *L'Amorosa menzogna (short)* 1949 (d,sc); *Bomarzo (short)* 1949 (d,sc); *Ragazze in bianco (short)* 1949 (d,sc); *Superstizione (short)* 1949 (d,sc); *Cronaca di un Amore/Story of a Love Affair* 1950 (d,sc,story,uncred.ed); *La Funivia del Faloria (short)* 1950 (d,sc); *Sette canne e un vestito (short)* 1950 (d,sc); *La Villa dei mostri (short)* 1950 (d,sc); *Lo Sceicco Bianco/The White Sheik* 1952 (story); *I Vinti/the Vanquished* 1952 (d,sc,story); *Amore in Città/Love in the City* 1953 (d,sc,from story—"Tentato Suicidio/When Love Fails"); *La Signora Senza Camelie/Camille Without Camellias* 1953 (d,sc,story,uncred.ed); *Le Amiche/The Girl Friends* 1955 (d,sc); *Uomini in più* 1955 (p); *Il Grido/The Outcry* 1957 (d,sc,story); *Questo nostro mondo* 1958 (tech.ad); *La Tempesta* 1958 (uncred.2u d); *L'Avventura* 1959 (d,sc,story); *La Notte* 1961 (d,sc,story); *L'Eclisse/The Eclipse* 1962 (d,sc,story); *Deserto Rosso/The Red Desert* 1964 (d,sc,story); *I Tre Volti/The Three Faces of a Woman* 1965 (d); *Blow-Up* 1966 (d,sc) **(AANBD)**; *Zabriskie Point* 1970 (d,sc,story,uncred.ed); *The Passenger* 1975 (d,sc,ed); *Il Mistero di Oberwald/The Mystery of Oberwald* 1980 (d,sc,electronic editor); *Chambre 666* 1982 (a); *Identificazione di una donna/Identification of a Woman* 1982 (d,sc,story,ed).

Apted, Michael • Director; also producer. • Born Aylesbury, Buckinghamshire, England, February 10, 1941. *Educ.* Downing College, Cambridge (law, history). Began his career with England's Granada Television as a researcher and then director, notably of the long-running soap, "Coronation Street." Apted's first feature was *The Triple Echo* (1973), an off-beat wartime romance in which Oliver Reed falls for an AWOL soldier disguised as a woman. He followed it with *Stardust* (1974), chronicling the rise and fall of a Beatles-like pop group.

The critical success of *Agatha* (1979) and *Coal Miner's Daughter* (1980) earned Apted access to bigger stars and bigger budgets; he directed Sigourney Weaver in *Gorillas in the Mist* (1988), based on the African experiences of Dian Fossey. Apted has also continued to make smaller films such as the adolescent comedy gem *Kipperbang* (1982) and the documentaries *28 Up* (1985) and *Bring on the Night* (1985). • *7 Up (short)* 1963 (assistant to Paul Almond); *The Triple Echo* 1973 (d); *Stardust* 1974 (d); *The Squeeze* 1977 (d); *Agatha* 1979 (d); *Stronger Than The Sun* 1979 (d); *Coal Miner's Daughter* 1980 (d); *Continental Divide* 1981 (d); *Kipperbang* 1982 (d); *Gorky Park* 1983 (d); *Firstborn* 1984 (d); *The River Rat* 1984 (exec.p); *28 Up* 1985 (d,p); *Bring on the Night* 1985 (d); *Spies Like Us* 1985 (a); *Critical Condition* 1987 (d); *Gorillas in the Mist* 1988 (d); *The Long Way Home* 1989 (d); *Class Action* 1990 (d).

Arbuckle, "Fatty" • *aka* Roscoe Arbuckle, William B. Goodrich • Actor, director; also screenwriter, producer. • Born Roscoe Conkling Arbuckle, Smith Center, KS, March 24, 1887; died June 29, 1933, New York, NY. Corpulent, baby-faced, former "Keystone Cop" who later became internationally popular as a comedian in two-reelers of his own. Falstaffian in size, if not subtlety, Arbuckle wrote, produced and directed a host of short slapstick films, several of which featured a young Buster Keaton.

At the height of his fame in 1921, when he was reportedly earning $1,000 a day, Arbuckle was charged with the death of a young actress-model named Virginia Rappe after an orgiastic drinking party. He had allegedly been making sexual advances to her when she suffered a ruptured bladder, dying several days later.

Arbuckle was tried three times (the first two resulting in hung juries) and finally acquitted of manslaughter in 1923 due to lack of evidence. However, the mud from the scandal stuck; his career was virtually over and his films banned. As a response to this and other film-star scandals, Hollywood set up the Hays Office to censor itself and protect its image. Over the next decade Arbuckle directed a Marion Davies feature and Eddie Cantor's first films under the pseudonym William B. Goodrich. • *The Sanitarium* 1910 (a); *A Bandit* 1913 (a); *Fatty's Day Off* 1913 (a); *Fatty's Flirtation* 1913 (a); *The Gangsters* 1913 (a); *The Gypsy Queen* 1913 (a); *Help! Help! Hydrophobia!* 1913 (a); *Love and Courage* 1913 (a); *Mabel's New Hero* 1913 (a); *Mother's Boy* 1913 (a); *The Noise From the Deep* 1913 (a); *Passions He Had Three* 1913 (a); *A Quiet Little Wedding* 1913 (a); *The Alarm* 1914 (d,a); *A Brand New Hero* 1914 (d,a); *Fatty Again, Leading Lizzie Astray* 1914 (d,a); *Fatty and the Heiress* 1914 (d,a); *Fatty's Debut* 1914 (d,a); *Fatty's Gift* 1914 (d,a); *Fatty's Jonah Day* 1914 (d,a); *Fatty's Magic Pants* 1914 (d,a); *Fatty's Wine Party* 1914 (d,a); *A Film Johnnie* 1914 (a); *His Favorite Pastime* 1914 (a); *In the Clutches of the Gang* 1914 (a); *The Knockout* 1914 (a); *The Masquerader* 1914 (a); *The Rounders* 1914 (a); *A Rural Demon* 1914 (a); *The Sea Nymphs* 1914 (a); *The Sky Pirate* 1914 (d,a); *A Suspended Ordeal* 1914 (a); *Tango Tangles* 1914 (a); *Fatty and the Broadway Stars* 1915 (d,a); *Fatty and Minnie He-Haw* 1915 (d,a); *Fatty's Faithful Fido* 1915 (d,a); *Fatty's New Role* 1915 (d,a); *Fickle Fatty's Fall* 1915 (d,a); *The Little Teacher* 1915 (a); *Mabel and Fatty's Married Life* 1915 (a); *Mabel and Fatty's Wash Day* 1915 (a); *That Little Band of Gold* 1915 (d,a); *The Village Scandal* 1915 (d,a); *When Love Took Wings* 1915 (d,a); *Bright Lights/The Lure of Broadway* 1916 (d,a); *A Cream Puff Romance/A Reckless Romeo* 1916 (d,a); *Fatty and Mabel Adrift* 1916 (d,a); *He Did and He Didn't/Love and Lobsters* 1916 *His Alibi* 1916 (d,a); *His Wife's Mistake* 1916 (d,a); *The Other Man* 1916 (d,a); *The Waiter's Ball* 1916 (d,a); *The Butcher Boy* 1917 (d,a); *A Country Hero* 1917 (d,a); *Fatty at Coney Island* 1917 (d,a); *His Wedding Night* 1917 (d,a); *His Wedding Night* 1917 (d,a); *Oh Doctor!* 1917 (d,a); *The Rough House* 1917 (d,a); *The Bell Boy* 1918 (d,a); *The Cook* 1918 (d,a); *Good Night Nurse* 1918 (d,a); *Moonshine* 1918 (d,a); *Out West* 1918 (d,a); *Back Stage* 1919 (d,a); *A Desert Hero* 1919 (d,a); *The Hayseed* 1919 (d,a); *Love* 1919 (d,a); *The Garage* 1920 (d,a); *Party* 1920 (a); *Brewster's Millions* 1921 (a); *Gasoline Gus* 1921 (a). Films directed under pseudonym "William Goodrich" (shorts unless noted): *The Moonshiners* 1916; *The Fighting Dude* 1925; *The Movies* 1925; *The Tourist* 1925; *Cleaning Up* 1926; *Fool's Luck* 1926; *His Private Life* 1926; *My Stars* 1926; *The Red Mill* (feature) 1927; *Special Delivery* (feature) 1927; *Up a Tree* 1930; *Won By a Neck* 1930; *The Back Page* 1931; *Beach Pajamas* 1931; *Honeymoon Trio* 1931; *The Lure of Hollywood* 1931; *Marriage Rows* 1931; *Smart Work* 1931; *The Tamale Vendor* 1931; *Anybody's Goat* 1932; *Bridge Wives* 1932; *Gigolettes* 1932; *Hollywood Luck* 1932; *Keep Laughing* 1932; *It's a Cinch* 1932; *Moonlight and Cactus* 1932; *Niagara Falls* 1932.

Arcand, Denys • Director, screenwriter • Born Deschambault, Quebec, Canada, June 25, 1941. *Educ.* University of Montreal (history). Montreal-based Denys Arcand is one of Canada's most successful screenwriter-directors. Arcand was raised in a strict Catholic home (his mother had wanted to be a Carmelite nun) and spent nine years in Jesuit school. He produced his first film, the short *Seul ou avec d'Autres* (1962), while at university.

After graduation, Arcand went to work for the National Film Board of Canada where, between 1964 and 1965, he made a trilogy of short historical documentaries about the early explorers and settlers of North America. In 1970 he directed *On est au coton*, a feature-lenghth documentary about abuses in the textile industry that was officially banned, allegedly because of its "biased" point of view. Another politically-oriented documentary followed, *Québec: Duplessisz et Après...* (1972).

In 1972 Arcand directed his first fiction feature, *Une Maudite Galette*, an ironic thriller involving theft and murder. *Rejeanne Padovani* (1973), set against the construction of Montreal's Ville-Marie superhighway, also dealt with murder and greed. For *Gina* (1975), the director drew upon his experiences filming *On est au coton* to fashion a tale of violence and revenge about a stripper and a film crew working on a documentary about the textile industry.

Following some work for TV and the production of a controversial documentary for the National Film Board about Quebec's 1980 referendum for secession from Canada, Arcand returned to features with *Le Crime d'ovide plouffe* (1984) and his breakthrough film, *The Decline of the American Empire* (1986).

Marked by Arcand's typically cynical humor, *Decline* focuses on a group of Québeçois artists and intellectuals—four men and four women—coming to grips with the problems of sexuality, success, fidelity, intimacy and aging in contemporary society. Mirroring the baby-boomer angst of John Sayles's *Return of the Secaucus Seven* and Lawrence Kasdan's *The Big Chill*, *Decline* became Canada's biggest worldwide screen success. A hit on the festival circuit and with critics and filmgoers in the States, the film won nine Génies (the Canadian Oscar), the "Fipresci" prize at Cannes and an Oscar nomination for best foreign language film. (Paramount even announced the development of a US remake.)

Jesus of Montreal (1988) is a tragicomic account of a group of struggling Montreal actors who support themselves by giving revisionist nighttime performances of a passion play. The film was allegedly inspired by an actor who auditioned for *Decline*; he told Arcand that he was portraying Jesus in an old French play being performed for tourists visiting the city's famed Mont Royal peak. The director became fascinated with the lives of these Montreal artists who made a living as biblical figures by night and in beer commercials and porno films by day.

A dazzling mix of passion play drama, Catholic ideology and contemporary satire, *Jesus of Montreal* takes an unblinking look at the plight of the struggling actor. It is a highly personal work, influenced by Arcand's rigorous Catholic education and disillusionment with the church, and reflecting his view that "the Catholic hierarchy is completely opposed to Christ's purest teachings." DT • *Seul ou avec d'Autres* (short) 1962 (d); *On est au coton* 1970 (d); *Une Maudite Galette* 1972 (d); *Québec: Duplessisz et Après...* 1972 (d,sc); *Rejeanne Padovani* 1973 (d,sc,ed); *Gina* 1975 (d,sc); *Le Crime d'ovide plouffe* 1984 (d,sc); *Le Déclin de l'empire Américain/The Decline of the American Empire* 1986 (d,sc); *Un Zoo la nuit/Night Zoo* 1987 (a); *Jésus de Montréal/Jesus of Montreal* 1989 (a,d,sc).

Archer, Anne • American actress • Born August 25, 1947. *Educ.* Claremont College, CA (theater arts). Dark-haired, attractive performer with sultry, smiling eyes who rejuvenated her career with a best supporting actress Oscar nomination as the sexy and sympathetic wife any man would be a fool to stray from in *Fatal Attraction* (1987). Daughter of actress Marjorie Lord and actor John Archer. • *The Honkers* 1971; *Cancel My Reservation* 1972; *The All-American Boy* 1973; *Trackdown* 1975; *Lifeguard* 1976; *Good Guys Wear Black* 1978; *Paradise Alley* 1978; *Hero at Large* 1980; *Raise the Titanic* 1980; *Green Ice* 1981; *Too Scared to Scream* 1982; *Waltz Across Texas* 1983; *The Naked Face* 1985; *The Check Is in the Mail* 1986; *Fatal Attraction* 1987 **(AANBSA)**; *Love at Large* 1990; *Narrow Margin* 1990; *Eminent Domain* 1991.

Ardant, Fanny • Actress • Born Monte Carlo, 1949. Statuesque leading lady in European films of the 1980s, and companion to Francois Truffaut in the director's last years. • *Les Chiens* 1978; *La Femme d'à côté/The Woman Next Door* 1981; *Les Uns et les autres/Bolero* 1981; *Vivement Dimanche!/Confidentially Yours* 1982; *Benvenuta* 1983; *La Vie est un roman/Life Is a Bed of Roses* 1983; *L'Amour à mort* 1984; *Un Amour de Swann/Swann, in Love* 1984; *Desiderio* 1984; *Les Enragés* 1984; *L'Été Prochain* 1984; *Conseil de Famille/Family Business* 1986; *Mélo* 1986; *Le Paltoquet* 1986; *La Famiglia/The Family* 1987; *Paura e Amore/Fear and Love* 1988; *Pleure pas my love* 1988; *Australia* 1989.

Arden, Eve • Actress • Born Eunice Quedens, Mill Valley, CA, April 30, 1912; died November 12, 1990, Beverly Hills, CA. Best known for her delivery of snappy, sarcastic dialogue in films such as 1945's *Mildred Pierce*, which earned her an Oscar nomination as best supporting actress. Arden had honed her sardonic powers on the stage and, after being typecast in more than 20 films in three years, attempted to break the stereotype by returning to Broadway in the musical *Very Warm For May* (1939) and the revue *Two For the Show* (1940); she also created the warm, yet tart-tongued single teacher, Miss Brooks, first on radio (from 1948), then on the successful TV series "Our Miss Brooks" (1952-56), and then on film (1956). Her acid delivery was again put to good use when she played the principal in the 1978 film, *Grease*. • *The Song of Love* 1929; *Oh, Doctor!* 1937; *Stage Door* 1937; *Cocoanut Grove* 1938; *Having Wonderful Time* 1938; *Letter of Introduction* 1938; *At the Circus* 1939; *Big Town Czar* 1939; *Eternally Yours* 1939; *The Forgotten Woman* 1939; *Women in the Wind* 1939; *A Child Is Born* 1940; *Comrade X* 1940; *No, No, Nanette* 1940; *She Couldn't Say No* 1940; *Slightly Honorable* 1940; *Bedtime Story* 1941; *The Last of the Duanes* 1941; *Manpower* 1941; *Obliging Young Lady* 1941; *San Antonio Rose* 1941; *She Knew All the Answers* 1941; *That Uncertain Feeling* 1941; *Whistling in the Dark* 1941; *Ziegfeld Girl* 1941; *Hit Parade of 1943* 1943; *Let's Face It* 1943; *Cover Girl* 1944; *The Doughgirls* 1944; *Earl Carroll Vanities* 1945; *Mildred Pierce* 1945 **(AANBSA)**; *Pan-Americana* 1945; *Patrick the Great* 1945; *The Kid From Brooklyn* 1946; *My Reputation* 1946; *Night and Day* 1946; *The Arnelo Affair* 1947; *The Song of Scheherazade* 1947; *The Unfaithful* 1947; *The Voice of the Turtle* 1947; *One Touch of Venus* 1948; *The Lady Takes a Sailor* 1949; *My Dream Is Yours* 1949; *Paid in Full* 1949; *Whiplash* 1949; *Curtain Call At Cactus Creek* 1950; *Tea For Two* 1950; *Three Husbands* 1950; *Goodbye, My Fancy* 1951; *We're Not Married* 1952; *The Lady Wants Mink* 1953; *Our Miss Brooks* 1956; *Anatomy of a Murder* 1959; *The Dark at the Top of the Stairs* 1960; *Sergeant Deadhead* 1965; *The Strongest Man in the World* 1975; *Grease* 1978; *Pandemonium* 1981; *Under the Rainbow* 1981; *Grease 2* 1982.

Ardolino, Emile • Director • Born Queens, NY. *Educ.* Queens College (English, speech, theater). Experienced TV director, mostly of theater and dance specials. Ardolino had directed Mikhail Baryshnikov, as well as Meryl Streep and William Hurt for Joseph Papp productions, before scoring a huge hit with *Dirty Dancing* (1987). • *He Makes Me Feel Like Dancin'* 1983 (d,p) **(AABDOC)**; *Dirty Dancing* 1987 (d); *Chances Are* 1989 (d); *Three Men and a Little Lady* 1990 (d).

Argento, Dario • Director; also screenwriter, producer, composer. • Born Rome, 1943. Contemporary purveyor of stylish horror films who began writing and directing at the age of 24. Son of Salvatore Argento, who has produced a number of his films. • *Oggi a Me...Domani a Te!* 1968 (sc); *C'era una Volta il West/Once Upon a Time in the West* 1969 (story); *Un Esercito di 5 Uomini* 1969 (sc); *Metti, una Sera a Cena* 1969 (sc); *L'Uccello dalle Piume di Cristallo* 1969 (d,sc); *Cat O' Nine Tails* 1971 (d,sc,story); *Quattro Mosche di Velluto Grigio* 1971 (d,sc); *Profondo Rosso/Deep Red* 1975 (d,sc); *Suspiria* 1976 (d,m,sc); *Dawn of the Dead* 1978 (sc consult,m,sound mixer—post-prod); *Inferno* 1980 (d,sc,story); *Sotto gli occhi dell'Assassino* 1982 (d,sc,story); *Creepers* 1985 (d,p,sc); *Demoni/Demons* 1985 (p,sc); *Demoni 2—L'Incubo Ritorna/Demons 2—The Nightmare Is Back* 1986 (p,sc); *Opera* 1987 (d,sc); *La Chiesa* 1988 (p,sc,story); *Two Evil Eyes* 1990 (d,p,sc—*The Black Cat*).

Arkin, Alan • Actor; also director. • Born New York, NY, March 26, 1934. *Educ.* Los Angeles City College; Los Angeles State College; Bennington College (drama). Highly versatile performer from the stage who has turned in a bevy of superlative comic performances since making his feature debut as a stranded Soviet submariner afloat in the USA in *The Russians Are Coming, the Russians Are Com-*

ing (1966). Arkin proved his dramatic skills as the sensitive, deaf-mute protagonist of *The Heart Is a Lonely Hunter* (1968), and has since been in top form as Sigmund Freud in *The Seven Per-cent Solution* (1976), opposite Peter Falk in *The In-Laws* (1979), and as the title character of the darkly humorous *Simon* (1980).

Arkin made his feature directorial debut with a competent adaptation of Jules Feiffer's stage hit, *Little Murders* (1971), which he also directed on Broadway, but has curiously helmed only one other film. • *The Last Mohican (short)* 1966 (a); *The Russians Are Coming, the Russians Are Coming* 1966 (a) **(AANBA)**; *Wait Until Dark* 1967 (a); *Woman Times Seven* 1967 (a); *The Heart Is a Lonely Hunter* 1968 (a) **(AANBA)**; *Inspector Clouseau* 1968 (a); *T.G.I.F. (short)* 1968 (d); *The Monitors* 1969 (a); *Popi* 1969 (a); *Catch-22* 1970 (a); *Little Murders* 1971 (a,d); *Last of the Red Hot Lovers* 1972 (a); *Freebie and the Bean* 1974 (a); *Rafferty and the Gold Dust Twins* 1974 (a); *Hearts of the West* 1975 (a); *The Seven Per-Cent Solution* 1976 (a); *Fire Sale* 1977 (a,d); *Improper Channels* 1979 (a); *The In-Laws* 1979 (a,exec.p); *The Magician of Lublin* 1979 (a); *Simon* 1980 (a); *Chu Chu and the Philly Flash* 1981 (a); *Full Moon High* 1981 (a); *Deadhead Miles* 1982 (a); *The Last Unicorn* 1982 (a); *The Return of Captain Invincible* 1982 (a); *Bad Medicine* 1985 (a); *Big Trouble* 1985 (a); *Joshua Then and Now* 1985 (a); *Coupe De Ville* 1990 (a); *Edward Scissorhands* 1990 (a); *Havana* 1990 (a); *The Rocketeer* 1991 (a).

Arkoff, Samuel Z. • Producer • Born Fort Dodge, IA, June 12, 1918. *Educ.* University of Iowa; University of Colorado; Loyola University, Chicago, IL (law). Co-founder (with James H. Nicholson) of American International Pictures, serving as producer or executive on over 200 of the low-budget exploitation films—monster movies, motorcycle films and beach-party pictures geared to the teenage audience—that made the studio famous. Arkoff also gave fresh talent such as Francis Ford Coppola (*Dementia 13* 1963), Martin Scorsese (*Boxcar Bertha* 1972) and Woody Allen (*What's Up, Tiger Lily?* 1966) the opportunity to direct some of their early feature films. • *The She-Creature* 1956 (p); *Reform School Girl* 1957 (p); *Attack of the Puppet People* 1958 (exec.p); *The Bonnie Parker Story* 1958 (exec.p); *Hell Squad* 1958 (exec.p); *High School Hellcats* 1958 (exec.p); *Hot Rod Gang* 1958 (exec.p); *How to Make a Monster* 1958 (exec.p); *Machine Gun Kelly* 1958 (exec.p); *Night of the Blood Beast* 1958 (exec.p); *The Spider* 1958 (exec.p); *Submarine Seahawk* 1958 (exec.p); *Suicide Battalion* 1958 (exec.p); *Tank Battalion* 1958 (p); *Teenage Caveman* 1958 (exec.p); *Terror From the Year 5,000* 1958 (exec.p); *War of the Colossal Beast* 1958 (exec.p); *A Bucket of Blood* 1959 (exec.p); *Diary of a High School Bride* 1959 (exec.p); *The Ghost of Dragstrip Hollow* 1959 (exec.p); *The Headless Ghost* 1959 (exec.p); *Horrors of the Black Museum* 1959 (exec.p); *Road Racers* 1959 (exec.p); *Tank Commandos* 1959 (exec.p); *La Maschera del demonio* 1960 (exec.p—American version); *Beach Party* 1963 (exec.p); *I Tre volti della paura* 1963 (exec.p); *Bikini Beach* 1964 (p); *The Comedy of Terrors* 1964 (p); *Pajama Party* 1964 (p); *Beach Blanket Bingo* 1965 (p); *Dr. Goldfoot and the Bikini Machine* 1965 (p); *How to Stuff a Wild Bikini* 1965 (p); *Sergeant Deadhead* 1965 (p); *The Big T.N.T. Show* 1966 (exec.p); *Fireball 500* 1966 (p); *The Ghost in the Invisible Bikini* 1966 (p); *Wild in the Streets* 1968 (p); *Angel, Angel Down We Go* 1969 (p); *Das Ausschweifende Leben des Marquis De Sade* 1969 (p); *Angel Unchained* 1970 (exec.p); *Bloody Mama* 1970 (exec.p); *The Dunwich Horror* 1970 (exec.p); *Up in the Cellar* 1970 (p); *Wuthering Heights* 1970 (p); *The Abominable Doctor Phibes* 1971 (exec.p); *Bunny O'Hare* 1971 (exec.p); *Who Slew Auntie Roo?* 1971 (p); *Dillinger* 1973 (exec.p); *Madhouse* 1974 (exec.p); *Cooley High* 1975 (exec.p); *Dragonfly* 1975 (exec.p); *The Food Of The Gods* 1975 (exec.p); *Hennessy* 1975 (exec.p); *Return to Macon County* 1975 (exec.p); *Futureworld* 1976 (exec.p); *The Great Scout & Cathouse Thursday* 1976 (exec.p); *A Matter of Time* 1976 (exec.p); *Empire of the Ants* 1977 (exec.p); *The Island of Dr. Moreau* 1977 (exec.p); *The People That Time Forgot* 1977 (exec.p); *The Town That Dreaded Sundown* 1977 (exec.p); *The Norseman* 1978 (exec.p); *Our Winning Season* 1978 (exec.p); *The Amityville Horror* 1979 (exec.p); *Chomps* 1979 (exec.p); *Dressed to Kill* 1980 (exec.p); *How to Beat the High Cost of Living* 1980 (exec.p); *The Final Terror* 1981 (exec.p); *Up the Creek* 1983 (exec.p).

Arkush, Allan • Director • Born New York, NY, April 30, 1948. *Educ.* Franklin and Marshall College, Lancaster, PA; NYU (film). A graduate of Roger Corman's school for future Hollywood directors, Arkush's films are generally better than their titles suggest. He has directed often for TV, including episodes of "Moonlighting" and "St. Elsewhere." • *Hollywood Boulevard* 1976 (d,ed); *Grand Theft Auto* 1977 (2u d); *Deathsport* 1978 (assoc.ed,d); *Rock 'n' Roll High School* 1979 (d,story); *Heartbeeps* 1981 (d); *Get Crazy* 1983 (d); *Caddyshack II* 1988 (d).

Arlen, Harold • *aka* Harold Arluck • Composer; also songwriter. • Born Hyman Arluck, Buffalo, NY, February 15, 1905; died April 23, 1986, New York, NY. Wrote a number of popular Hollywood songs, including "Stormy Weather," "Accentuate the Positive" and "That Old Black Magic." Nominated nine times for the best song Oscar, Arlen won once, for "Over the Rainbow" (1939). • *Let's Fall in Love* 1934 (song); *Gold Diggers of 1937* 1936 (song); *The Singing Kid* 1936 (song); *Stage Struck* 1936 (song); *Strike Me Pink* 1936 (song); *At the Circus* 1939 (m,song); *The Wizard of Oz* 1939 (song) **(AABS)**; *Blues in the Night* 1941 (m) **(AANBS)**; *Cairo* 1942 (song); *Star Spangled Rhythm* 1942 (song) **(AANBS)**; *Cabin in the Sky* 1943 (m) **(AANBS)**; *The Sky's the Limit* 1943 (song) **(AANBS)**; *Here Come the Waves* 1944 (song) **(AANBS)**; *Up in Arms* 1944 (m) **(AANBS)**; *Casbah* 1948 (m) **(AANBS)**; *Dark City* 1950 (song); *The Petty Girl* 1950 (song); *Macao* 1952 (lyrics "One for My Baby"); *The Farmer Takes a Wife* 1953 (song); *The Country Girl* 1954 (song); *A Star Is Born* 1954 (song) **(AANBS)**; *Gay Purr-ee* 1962 (song).

Arletty • Actress • Born Léonie Bathiat, Courbevoie, France, May 15, 1898. Sophisticated star of the 1930s and 40s, particularly memorable for her roles in four classics of "poetic realism": *Hôtel du Nord* (1938), *Daybreak* (1939), *The Devil's Envoys* (1942) and *Children of Paradise* (1945). Arletty was jailed as a collaborator for a short time after WWII because of an affair with a German officer. • *Un Chien qui rapporte* 1931; *Das Schöne Abenteuer* 1932; *Wälzerkrieg* 1933; *Pension Mimosas* 1934; *La Garconne* 1936; *Faisons un rêve* 1937; *Les Perles de la Couronne* 1937; *Hôtel du Nord* 1938; *Circonstances attenuantes* 1939; *Fric-Frac* 1939; *Le Jour Se Lève/Daybreak* 1939; *Madame Sans-Gène* 1941; *Les Visiteurs du soir/The Devil's Envoy* 1942; *Les Enfants du Paradis/Children of Paradise* 1945; *Portrait d'un Assassin* 1949; *L'Amour Madame* 1951; *Le Grand Jeu* 1953; *L'Air de Paris* 1954; *Huis clos/No Exit* 1954; *Un Drôle de Dimanche* 1958; *Maxime* 1958; *The Longest Day* 1962; *Les Volets Clos* 1972; *Carné: l'Homme à la Camera* 1980.

Arliss, George • Actor • Born George Augustus Andrews, London, April 10, 1868; died 1946. August London and New York stage performer who entered films in 1921 and specialized in playing the great historical figures—such as *Disraeli* (1921 and 1929), *Alexander Hamilton* (1931) and *Voltaire* (1933)—that had made him famous in the theater. Arliss occasionally appeared with his wife, Florence Montgomery Arliss; their son Leslie was a screenwriter and director. • *The Devil* 1921 (a); *Disraeli* 1921 (a); *The Man Who Played God* 1922 (a); *The Ruling Passion* 1922 (a); *The Green Goddess* 1923 (a); *$20 a Week* 1924 (a); *Disraeli* 1929 (a) **(AABA)**; *The Green Goddess* 1930 (a) **(AANBA)**; *Old English* 1930 (a); *Alexander Hamilton* 1931 (a,story); *The Millionaire* 1931 (a); *The*

Man Who Played God 1932 (a); *A Successful Calamity* 1932 (a); *The Adopted Father* 1933 (a); *The King's Vacation* 1933 (a); *Voltaire* 1933 (a); *The House of Rothschild* 1934 (a); *The Last Gentleman* 1934 (a); *Cardinal Richelieu* 1935 (a); *Doctor Syn* 1937 (a).

Armendariz, Pedro • Actor • Born Churubusco, Mexico, May 9, 1912; died 1963. *Educ.* California Polytechnic Institute. Virile leading man of the 1940s and 50s. One of Mexico's top stars, Armendariz appeared in a number of Emilio Fernandez films, notably *Maria Candelaria* (1943), as well as numerous Hollywood and European productions. Memorable in several John Ford films (*The Fugitive* 1947, *Three Godfathers* 1949, etc.) and as the title character of Luis Bunuel's *El Bruto* (1952). His son, Pedro Armendariz, Jr., is also an actor. • *Maria Candelaria* 1943; *Alma de Bronze* 1944; *The Fugitive* 1947; *Fort Apache* 1948; *Maclovia* 1948; *Three Godfathers* 1949; *Tulsa* 1949; *We Were Strangers* 1949; *The Torch* 1950; *El Bruto* 1952; *Border River* 1954; *The Littlest Outlaw* 1955; *The Conqueror* 1956; *Diane* 1956; *The Big Boodle* 1957; *The Little Savage* 1959; *The Wonderful Country* 1959; *Francis of Assisi* 1961; *Captain Sinbad* 1963; *From Russia With Love* 1963.

Armstrong, Gillian • Director; also screenwriter, producer. • Born Melbourne, Australia, December 18, 1950. *Educ.* Swinburne College of Advanced Education (film and TV); Australian Film and Television School, Sydney. While studying at Swinburne College, Armstrong took part in various aspects of film production, ranging from designing costumes to acting as "tea girl" to director Fred Schepisi on his segment of the anthology film, *Libido* (1973). In 1971 Armstrong wrote, produced, and directed her first film, an 8-minute short, *Roof Needs Mowing*.

Following work as an editor in 1972, Armstrong won a scholarship the next year to the Australian Film and Television School as part of the school's "interim training scheme for directors." There she completed three short films, including *Gretel* (1973), a 27-minute work based on a Hal Porter story. *Gretel* was an official entry in the 1974 Grenoble International Festival of Short Films.

After leaving film school, Armstrong made what was to be the first in a trilogy of works, made over a period of 13 years, exploring the coming of age of three young Australian women: *Smokes and Lollies* (1975) was followed five years later by *Fourteen's Good, Eighteen's Better*, which received an Atom Award for best educational short film; the trilogy was completed with *Bingo, Bridesmaids and Braces* (1988).

In 1976 Armstrong's *The Singer and the Dancer* was awarded the Australian Film Institute Award for best short film and the Greater Union Award for best fiction film. *The Singer and the Dancer* draws parallels between the lives of an unsatisfied older woman and a young woman clearly destined for the same unfortunate path; it marked the beginning of a long working relationship with both cinematographer Russell Boyd and editor Nick Beauman.

Armstrong's concern with free-thinking, independent women was central to her critically acclaimed debut feature, *My Brilliant Career* (1978). The winner of seven AFI Awards, including best direction and best film, and the British Critics' Award for best first feature, *My Brilliant Career* tells the story of a young woman determined to pursue her intellectual and literary ambitions in turn-of-the-century Australia.

Following the release of Armstrong's second feature, the new-wave musical *Starstruck* (1982), the director was invited to Los Angeles by the Ladd Company to discuss potential future collaborations. The meetings led to the production of Armstrong's first American film, MGM/UA's *Mrs. Soffel* (1984), the true-life story of the wife of a Pittsburgh prison warder (Diane Keaton) who falls in love with a convicted murderer (Mel Gibson).

A strong female character was again at the center of the director's fourth feature, *High Tide* (1987), about a chance encounter between a rootless mother and her daughter, whom she had abandoned many years before. The film also marked the reunion of Armstrong and actress Judy Davis, the star of *My Brilliant Career*, and featured the director in a cameo role as a cabaret backup singer. *High Tide* received the best film award from the Houston Film Festival and the Grand Prix from the Festival International de Créteil.

Maintaining her concern for native issues by focusing her cinematic eye on local artisans, Armstrong has consistently displayed her wide-ranging interests and abilities in several documentaries made for the Craft Council of Australia. AGS • *Roof Needs Mowing (short)* 1971 (d,e,sc); *Gretel (short)* 1973 (d,sc); *One Hundred a Day (short)* (d,sc) 1973; *Satdee Night (short)* 1973 (d); *Smokes and Lollies (short)* 1975 (a,d); *The Singer and the Dancer (short)* 1976 (d,p,sc); *My Brilliant Career* 1978 (d); *A Busy Kind of Bloke (short)* 1980 (a,d,sc); *Fourteen's Good, Eighteen's Better (short)* 1980 (d,p,sc); *Touch Wood (short)* 1980 (d,sc); *Starstruck* 1982 (d,m); *Having a Go (short)* 1983 (d); *Not Just a Pretty Face (short)* 1983 (d,sc); *Mrs. Soffel* 1984 (d); *High Tide* 1987 (d); *Bingo, Bridesmaids and Braces (short)* 1988 (d,p); *Fires Within* 1991 (d).

Arnheim, Rudolf • Theoretician; also psychologist, educator. • Born Berlin, July 15, 1904. Educ. University of Berlin. Perceptive early film theorist, some of whose ideas now seem antique, but whose collection of essays written in the 1930s, *Film As Art* (1957), continues to sell. In the US from 1940 (and a citizen since 1946), Arnheim has been a professor at Sarah Lawrence College and the University of California, Berkeley, and is the author of several other books on art, notably *Art and Visual Perception: A Psychology of the Creative Eye* (1954) and *Toward a Psychology of Art* (1966).

Arnold, Edward • Actor • Born Günther Edward Arnold Schneider, New York, NY, February 18, 1890; died April 26, 1956, Encino, CA. Prolific, popular character player who began his career on the stage and, between 1915 and 1919, starred in numerous westerns for Essanay Studio. The portly, distinguished-looking actor returned to films in the sound era, first in crime melodramas, then as a priest in *The White Sister* and a sheik in *The Barbarian* (both 1933) before finding his special niche portraying all kinds of tycoons: as an alcoholic millionaire (*Sadie McKee* 1934), a lumber tycoon (*Come and Get It* 1936) and a sinister munitions king (*Idiot's Delight* 1939).

With his cool stare and facile, jovial laugh, Arnold also excelled at playing public officials and corrupt politicians (*Mr. Smith Goes to Washington* 1939) as well as biographical personages (Louis XIII in *Cardinal Richelieu* 1935; Diamond Jim Brady in *Diamond Jim* 1935 and again in *Lillian Russell* 1940; and Daniel Webster in *All That Money Can Buy* 1941), even rising to the rank of President of the United States on the radio series, "Mr. President." • *The Cost* 1920; *Afraid to Talk* 1932; *Okay America* 1932; *Rasputin and the Empress* 1932; *The Barbarian* 1933; *Her Bodyguard* 1933; *I'm No Angel* 1933; *Jennie Gerhardt* 1933; *Roman Scandals* 1933; *Secret of the Blue Room* 1933; *Whistling in the Dark* 1933; *The White Sister* 1933; *Biography of a Bachelor Girl* 1934; *Hide-Out* 1934; *Madame Spy* 1934; *Million Dollar Ransom* 1934; *The President Vanishes* 1934; *Sadie McKee* 1934; *Thirty Day Princess* 1934; *Unknown Blonde* 1934; *Wednesday's Child* 1934; *Cardinal Richelieu* 1935; *Crime and Punishment* 1935; *Diamond Jim* 1935; *The Glass Key* 1935; *Remember Last Night?* 1935; *Come and Get It* 1936; *Meet Nero Wolfe* 1936; *Sutter's Gold* 1936; *Blossoms on Broadway* 1937; *Easy Living* 1937; *John Meade's Woman* 1937; *The Toast of New York* 1937; *The Crowd Roars* 1938; *You Can't Take It With You* 1938; *Idiot's Delight* 1939; *Let Freedom Ring* 1939; *Man About Town* 1939; *Mr. Smith Goes to Washington* 1939; *The Earl of Chicago* 1940; *Johnny Apollo* 1940; *Lillian Russell* 1940; *Slightly Honorable* 1940; *All That Money Can Buy* 1941; *Design For Scandal* 1941; *The Devil and Daniel Webster/All That Money Can Buy* 1941;

Johnny Eager 1941; *The Lady From Cheyenne* 1941; *Meet John Doe* 1941; *Nothing But the Truth* 1941; *The Penalty* 1941; *Unholy Partners* 1941; *Eyes in the Night* 1942; *The War Against Mrs. Hadley* 1942; *The Youngest Profession* 1943; *Janie* 1944; *Kismet* 1944; *Main Street After Dark* 1944; *Mrs. Parkington* 1944; *Standing Room Only* 1944; *The Hidden Eye* 1945; *Weekend at the Waldorf* 1945; *Janie Gets Married* 1946; *Mighty McGurk* 1946; *My Brother Talks to Horses* 1946; *No Leave, No Love* 1946; *Three Wise Fools* 1946; *Ziegfeld Follies* 1946; *Dear Ruth* 1947; *The Hucksters* 1947; *Big City* 1948; *Big Jack* 1948; *Command Decision* 1948; *Three Daring Daughters* 1948; *Wallflower* 1948; *John Loves Mary* 1949; *Take Me Out to the Ball Game* 1949; *Annie Get Your Gun* 1950; *Dear Wife* 1950; *The Skipper Suprised His Wife* 1950; *The Yellow Cab Man* 1950; *Dear Brat* 1951; *Belles on Their Toes* 1952; *City That Never Sleeps* 1953; *Man of Conflict* 1953; *Living It Up* 1954; *The Ambassador's Daughter* 1956; *The Houston Story* 1956; *Miami Expose* 1956; *Entertaining the Troops* 1989 (archival footage).

Arnold, Jack • Director; also producer, actor. • Born New Haven, CT, October 14, 1916. *Educ.* Ohio State University; AADA, New York. Former stage and film actor who, after filming numerous documentaries for the US State Department, the Army and private industry, began making low-budget features in the early 1950s, concocting some of that era's classic science fiction-horror films, notably *It Came From Outer Space* (1953), *The Creature From the Black Lagoon* (1954) and *The Incredible Shrinking Man* (1957). In the following decades, Arnold made fewer and less impressive features (with the exception of the clever satire, *The Mouse That Roared* 1959), and turned his attention increasingly to TV. • *The Masked Angel* 1928 (a); *Enlighten Thy Daughter* 1933 (a); *Danger Patrol* 1937 (a); *Blind Alibi* 1938 (a); *Crime Ring* 1938 (a); *Mr. Doodle Kicks Off* 1938 (a); *Tarnished Angel* 1938 (a); *This Marriage Business* 1938 (a); *The Day the Bookies Wept* 1939 (a); *Fixer Dugan* 1939 (a); *Sued For Libel* 1939 (a); *Danger on Wheels* 1940 (a); *Enemy Agent* 1940 (a); *Framed* 1940 (a); *Millionaires in Prison* 1940 (a); *Lucky Devils* 1941 (a); *Mexican Spitfire's Baby* 1941 (a); *Tillie the Toiler* 1941 (a); *Juke Box Jenny* 1942 (a); *Junior G-Men of the Air* 1942 (a); *You're Telling Me* 1942 (a); *With These Hands* 1950 (d,p) **(AANBDOC)**; *Girls in the Night* 1953 (d); *The Glass Web* 1953 (d); *It Came From Outer Space* 1953 (d); *The Creature From the Black Lagoon* 1954 (d); *The Man From Bitter Ridge* 1955 (d); *Red Sundown* 1955 (d); *Revenge of the Creature* 1955 (d); *Tarantula* 1955 (d,story); *Outside the Law* 1956 (d); *The Incredible Shrinking Man* 1957 (d); *The Lady Takes a Flyer* 1957 (d); *Man in the Shadow* 1957 (d); *The Monolith Monsters* 1957 (story); *The Tattered Dress* 1957 (d); *High School Confidential* 1958 (d); *Monster on the Campus* 1958 (d); *The Space Children* 1958 (d); *The Mouse That Roared* 1959 (d); *No Name on the Bullet* 1959 (d,p); *Bachelor in Paradise* 1961 (d); *A Global Affair* 1964 (d); *The Lively Set* 1964 (d); *Hello Down There* 1969 (d); *Black Eye* 1974 (d); *Boss Nigger* 1975 (d,p); *The Games Girls Play* 1975 (d); *The Swiss Conspiracy* 1975 (d); *Into the Night* 1985 (a).

Arquette, Rosanna • Actress • Born New York, NY, August 10, 1959. Petite, quirky lead with a winsome sensuality who, after playing adolescent girls on numerous TV shows in the late 1970s, came into her own as the star of several off-beat, independent movies of the 1980s. Granddaughter of TV humorist Cliff Arquette ("Charley Weaver") and daughter of actor Lewis Arquette, she has excelled at playing slightly spacey women torn between the desire for adventure and a concern for social convention. • *More American Graffiti* 1979; *G.O.R.P.* 1980; *S.O.B.* 1981; *Baby, It's You* 1983; *Off the Wall* 1983; *After Hours* 1985; *The Aviator* 1985; *Desperately Seeking Susan* 1985; *Silverado* 1985; *8 Million Ways to Die* 1986; *Nobody's Fool* 1986; *Amazon Women on the Moon* 1987; *Le Grand bleu/The Big Blue* 1988; *Black Rainbow* 1989; *New York Stories* 1989; *Wendy Cracked a Walnut* 1990; *Flight of the Intruder* 1991.

Artaud, Antonin • Poet, theorist; also screeenwriter, actor. • Born Marseille, France, September 4, 1896; died 1948, Ivry-sur-Seine, France. Avant-garde theorist whose book *The Theater and Its Double* (1938) expresses his ideas on the "theater of cruelty." Artaud also wrote on the cinema as well as scripting and acting in several films. He turned in a memorable cameo as Marat in Abel Gance's *Napoléon* (1927). • *L'Argent* 1927 (a); *Napoléon* 1927 (a); *La Passion de Jeanne d'Arc/The Passion of Joan of Arc* 1927 (a); *Liliom* 1934 (a); *Königsmark* 1935 (a); *Le Manque* 1977 (narrative text); *Le Rouge de Chine* 1978 (dial).

Arthur, Jean • Actress • Born Gladys Georgianna Greene, New York, NY, October 17, 1908. After a brief time on the New York stage, made her feature film debut in John Ford's *Cameo Kirby* (1923) and appeared as an ingenue in numerous low-budget silent westerns and comedy shorts. Arthur's smooth transition to sound was aided by her sexy, husky, almost croaking, voice and she won immense popularity in John Ford's *The Whole Town's Talking* (1935).

A deft commedienne and tom-boyish, prickly romantic heroine, she hit her peak playing a string of down-to-earth, independent, often working-woman types, and co-starring in three celebrated Frank Capra films: *Mr. Deeds Goes to Town* (1936), *You Can't Take It With You* (1938) and *Mr. Smith Goes to Washington* (1939). With her increased prestige, Arthur chose her later roles wisely, her last decade of work including Billy Wilder's superior romantic-comedy *A Foreign Affair* (1948) and the George Stevens classics: *Talk of the Town* (1942), *The More the Merrier* (1943) and *Shane* (1953), her final film. • *Cameo Kirby* 1923; *Biff Bang Buddy* 1924; *Bringin' Home the Bacon* 1924; *Fast and Fearless* 1924; *Thundering Romance* 1924; *Under Fire* 1924; *Drug Store Cowboy* 1925; *The Fighting Smile* 1925; *Hurricane Horseman* 1925; *A Man of Nerve* 1925; *Seven Chances* 1925; *Tearin' Loose* 1925; *The Block Signal* 1926; *Born to Battle* 1926; *The College Boob* 1926; *The Cowboy Cop* 1926; *Double Daring* 1926; *The Fighting Cheat* 1926; *Lightning Bill* 1926; *Thundering Through* 1926; *Twisted Triggers* 1926; *The Broken Gate* 1927; *Flying Luck* 1927; *Horse Shoes* 1927; *Husband Hunters* 1927; *The Masked Menace* 1927; *The Poor Nut* 1927; *Brotherly Love* 1928; *Sins of the Fathers* 1928; *Wallflowers* 1928; *Warming Up* 1928; *The Canary Murder Case* 1929; *The Greene Murder Case* 1929; *Half Way to Heaven* 1929; *The Mysterious Dr. Fu Manchu* 1929; *The Saturday Night Kid* 1929; *Stairs of Sand* 1929; *Danger Lights* 1930; *Paramount on Parade* 1930; *The Return of Dr. Fu Manchu* 1930; *The Silver Horde* 1930; *Street of Chance* 1930; *Young Eagles* 1930; *Ex-Bad Boy* 1931; *The Gang Buster* 1931; *The Lawyer's Secret* 1931; *The Virtuous Husband* 1931; *The Past of Mary Holmes* 1933; *The Defense Rests* 1934; *Most Precious Thing in Life* 1934; *Whirlpool* 1934; *Diamond Jim* 1935; *If You Could Only Cook* 1935; *Party Wire* 1935; *Public Hero Number One* 1935; *The Public Menace* 1935; *The Whole Town's Talking* 1935; *Adventure in Manhattan* 1936; *The Ex-Mrs. Bradford* 1936; *More Than a Secretary* 1936; *Mr. Deeds Goes to Town* 1936; *Easy Living* 1937; *History Is Made at Night* 1937; *The Plainsman* 1937; *You Can't Take It With You* 1938; *Mr. Smith Goes to Washington* 1939; *Only Angels Have Wings* 1939; *Arizona* 1940; *Too Many Husbands* 1940; *The Devil and Miss Jones* 1941; *Talk of the Town* 1942; *A Lady Takes a Chance* 1943; *The More the Merrier* 1943 **(AANBA)**; *The Impatient Years* 1944; *A Foreign Affair* 1948; *Shane* 1953; *George Stevens: A Filmmaker's Journey* 1985 (archival footage).

Arzner, Dorothy • Director; also screenwriter, editor. • Born San Francisco, CA, January 3, 1900; died 1979. A jack of all trades, Arzner grew up in Hollywood working in a restaurant owned by her father, and later worked as a WWI ambulance driver, newspaper copy editor, stenographer, script clerk and assistant film editor. Her work for director Fred Niblo on *Blood and Sand* (1922) convinced James Cruze to let her edit *The Covered Wagon* (1923). Arzner went on to edit *Ruggles of Red Gap* (1923), *Merton of the Movies* (1924) and *Old Ironsides* (1926) for Cruze, also functioning as his co-scenarist on the latter film.

Paramount finally gave Arzner a chance to direct with 1927's *Fashions For Women*. She proved herself a competent "assignment" director, and by 1929 had turned out five films, including one of the quintessential "flapper" pictures, *The Wild Party* (1929), starring Clara Bow. Her most interesting work, however, came in the early 1930s, particularly in *Christopher Strong* (1933) and *Merrily We Go to Hell* (1932).

Christopher Strong features Katharine Hepburn as an aviatrix, modelled on Amelia Earhart, who falls in love with a married man, Christopher Strong (Colin Clive). When she becomes pregnant by Strong, Hepburn's flier purposely crashes her plane to earth during a test flight, killing both herself and her unborn child. The film's bleak subtext—the independent woman must die because she has flouted moral convention—is complemented by stunning visuals echoing both Lubitsch's *Trouble in Paradise* and Lang's *Dr. Mabuse Der Spieler*.

Craig's Wife (1936) offered Rosalind Russell a meaty role as a shrew who drives away husband and friends with her incessant need to control the people and things around her; in contrast to the Broadway play on which the film is based, *Craig's Wife* treats the heroine sympathetically, raising her to almost tragic status.

Dance, Girl, Dance (1940) features Lucille Ball in one of her best straight performances, as a vain stripper who accepts the grimy environment in which she works with no illusions. Although visually unremarkable, its critique of the inherent sexism of the world of burlesque was far ahead of its time.

Arzner's little known last film, *First Comes Courage* (1943), was directed for Columbia and starred Merle Oberon. Oberon plays a Norwegian double agent who pretends to be in love with occupying Nazi commandant Carl Esmond in order to pry secrets from him. (She is really in love with fellow freedom fighter Brian Aherne.) The film contains a number of remarkable set pieces, including the memorable Nazi wedding of Esmond and Oberon, which takes place in a converted chapel with a regiment of SS officers in attendance; *Mein Kampf* is substituted for the Bible, and vows are exchanged in the name of Hitler rather than God. At the end of the film Oberon decides against returning to the safety of England with Aherne, choosing instead to remain in Norway and continue the struggle against fascism. Significantly, the love sequences with Aherne are the weakest elements of the narrative; Arzner portrays Oberon as a courageous woman who lives by her wits and neither welcomes nor depends on the aid of a man.

During WWII Arzner directed instructional films for the WACS. She later drifted into commercial work, making TV ads and industrial films, and taught at UCLA. She died in 1979. Although she left behind an uneven body of work, her films are notable for their targeting of issues which have come to concern contemporary women directors such as Lizzie Borden, Joyce Chopra and Agnès Varda. WWD • *The Covered Wagon* 1923 (ed); *Ruggles of Red Gap* 1923 (ed); *The Breed of the Border* 1924 (sc); *Inez From Hollywood* 1924 (ed); *Merton of the Movies* 1924 (ed); *The No-Gun Man* 1924 (sc,story); *Red Kimono* 1925 (sc); *When Husbands Flirt* 1925 (sc); *Old Ironsides* 1926 (ed,sc); *Fashions For Women* 1927 (d); *Get Your Man* 1927 (d); *Ten Modern Commandments* 1927 (d); *Manhattan Cocktail* 1928 (d); *The Wild Party* 1929 (d); *Anybody's Woman* 1930 (d); *Paramount on Parade* 1930 (d); *Sarah and Son* 1930 (d); *Honor Among Lovers* 1931 (d); *Working Girls* 1931 (d); *Merrily We Go to Hell* 1932 (d); *Christopher Strong* 1933 (d); *Nana* 1934 (d); *Craig's Wife* 1936 (d); *The Bride Wore Red* 1937 (d); *Dance, Girl, Dance* 1940 (d); *First Comes Courage* 1943 (d).

Ashby, Hal • Director; also editor. • Born Ogden, UT, c. 1929; died December 27, 1988, Malibu, CA. Ashby began his film career, thanks to the California State Department of Unemployment, as a mimeograph-machine operator at Universal Studios in 1957. He rose to become a full-fledged editor within a decade and was given his first chance to direct in 1970, when Norman Jewison was unable to carry out his assignment on *The Landlord*. Ashby went on to earn commercial and critical success, and gained a reputation as a gentle, amiable director who paid meticulous attention to casting. • *The Cincinnati Kid* 1965 (ed); *The Loved One* 1965 (ed); *The Russians Are Coming, the Russians Are Coming* 1966 (ed) **(AANBED)**; *In the Heat of the Night* 1967 (ed) **(AABED)**; *Gaily, Gaily* 1969 (assoc.p); *The Landlord* 1970 (d); *Harold and Maude* 1971 (d); *The Last Detail* 1973 (d); *Shampoo* 1975 (d); *Bound For Glory* 1976 (d); *Coming Home* 1977 (d) **(AANBD)**; *Being There* 1979 (d); *Second-Hand Hearts* 1980 (d); *Let's Spend the Night Together* 1982 (d); *Lookin' to Get Out* 1982 (a,d); *The Slugger's Wife* 1985 (d); *8 Million Ways to Die* 1986 (d).

Ashcroft, Dame Peggy • Actress • Born Peggy Ashcroft, Croydon, England, December 22, 1907. Distinguished English stage actress, occasionally in films. • *The 39 Steps* 1935; *Rhodes of Africa* 1935; *The Nun's Story* 1959; *Secret Ceremony* 1968; *Three Into Two Won't Go* 1969; *Sunday Bloody Sunday* 1971; *The Pedestrian* 1974; *Hullabaloo Over Georgie and Bonnie's Pictures* 1979; *Caught on a Train* 1980; *A Passage to India* **(AABSA)** 1984; *When the Wind Blows* 1986; *Madame Sousatzka* 1988; *She's Been Away* 1989.

Ashley, Elizabeth • *aka* Elizabeth Cole • Actress • Born Ocala, FL, August 30, 1939. *Educ.* Los Angeles State University; Neighborhood Playhouse, New York. Gifted, spirited Broadway lead of the early 1960s (*Take Her She's Mine*, *Barefoot in the Park*) who, after only a few films, usually as vixens or hard-edged women, took a five-year hiatus from the screen. Since returning in 1971, Ashley has played mostly supporting or character parts. Divorced from actors James Farentino and George Peppard. • *The Carpetbaggers* 1964; *Ship of Fools* 1965; *The Third Day* 1965; *Hawaii* 1966; *The Marriage of a Young Stockbroker* 1971; *Paperback Hero* 1973; *Golden Needles* 1974; *Rancho Deluxe* 1974; *92 in the Shade* 1975; *The Great Scout & Cathouse Thursday* 1976; *Coma* 1978; *Windows* 1980; *Paternity* 1981; *Split Image* 1982; *Dragnet* 1987; *Dangerous Curves* 1988; *Vampire's Kiss* 1988.

Asp, Anna • Production designer • Born Sweden, 1946. *Educ.* Academy of Fine Arts, Stockholm; Dramatic Institute, Stockholm (art direction). Scandinavian art director who designed the later films of Ingmar Bergman, earning an Oscar for *Fanny and Alexander* (1982). Asp's other notable work includes Andrei Tarkovsky's final film (shot in Sweden), *The Sacrifice* (1986), and Bille August's *Pelle the Conqueror* (1987). • *Giliap* 1973 (art d); *Ansikte mot ansikte/Face to Face* 1976 (art d); *Paradistorg* 1977 (art d); *Hostsonaten/Autumn Sonata* 1978 (sets); *Min Alskade* 1979 (pd); *Barnens o* 1980 (art d); *Fanny och Alexander/Fanny and Alexander* 1982 (pd,art d) **(AABAD)**; *Avskedet* 1983 (art d); *After the Rehearsal* 1984 (art d); *Ake och hans Varld* 1984 (pd); *Offret-Sacrificatio/The Sacrifice* 1986 (art d); *Pelle Erobreren/Pelle the Conqueror* 1987 (pd); *Katinka* 1988 (art d).

Asquith, Anthony • *aka* "Puffin" • Director; also screenwriter. • Born London, November 9, 1902; died February 21, 1968. *Educ.* Winchester and Balliol College, Oxford. With H.G. Wells, G.B. Shaw and others, founded London's Film Society in 1925 and, after a filmmaking apprenticeship in Hollywood, returned to England as a director in 1928. Along with Alfred Hitchcock, Asquith was a major force in the British cinema during the 1930s and 40s. Beginning with his directing debut, *Shooting Stars* (co-directed with A.V. Bramble, 1927) which utilized experimental visual effects and *A Cottage on Dartmoor* (1930), a portrait of British life, Asquith became recognized for his tasteful, restrained and civilized quasi-documentary portraits of British life and manners.

With his film version of Shaw's *Pygmalion* (co-directed with Leslie Howard, 1938), Asquith also began turning out expertly crafted theatrical adaptations, the finest of which is the delicious *The Importance of Being Earnest* (1952). In 1938 he began a profitable collaboration with playwright-screenwriter Terrence Rattigan and created emotional studies of people under stress including, perhaps their finest joint work, *The Way to the Stars* (1945) as well as *The Winslow Boy* (1948) and *The Browning Version* (1950). They continued to work together through Asquith's last film, *The Yellow Rolls-Royce* (1964). Son of liberal prime minister Lord Herbert Asquith. • *Shooting Stars* 1927 (d,sc,story,ed); *Boadicea* 1928 (ad); *Underground* 1928 (d,sc); *The Runaway Princess* 1929 (d,sc); *A Cottage on Dartmoor* 1930 (a,d,sc); *Tell England* 1931 (d,sc); *Dance Pretty Lady* 1932 (d,sc,adapt); *Marry Me* 1932 (sc); *Letting in the Sunshine* 1933 (sc); *The Lucky Number* 1933 (d); *The Unfinished Symphony* 1934 (adapt,d); *Brown on Resolution* 1935 (d); *Moscow Nights* 1935 (d,sc); *Pygmalion* 1938 (d); *Blind Dogs (short)* 1939 (d,sc); *French Without Tears* 1939 (d); *Channel Incident (short)* 1940 (d,p); *Freedom Radio* 1940 (d); *Quiet Wedding* 1940 (d); *Cottage to Let* 1941 (d); *Rush Hour (short)* 1941 (d,sc); *Uncensored* 1942 (d); *The Demi-Paradise* 1943 (d); *We Dive at Dawn* 1943 (d); *Welcome to Britain* 1943 (d); *Fanny By Gaslight* 1944 (d); *Two Fathers (short)* 1944 (d,sc); *The Way to the Stars* 1945 (d); *While the Sun Shines* 1947 (d); *The Winslow Boy* 1948 (d); *The Browning Version* 1950 (d); *The Woman in Question* 1950 (d); *The Importance of Being Earnest* 1952 (d,sc); *The Final Test* 1953 (d); *The Net* 1953 (d); *Carrington V.C.* 1954 (d); *The Young Lovers* 1954 (d); *On Such a Night (short)* 1955 (d); *The Doctor's Dilemma* 1958 (d,p); *George Bernard Shaw* 1958 (a,uncred.); *Orders to Kill* 1958 (d); *Libel* 1959 (d); *The Millionairess* 1960 (d); *Guns of Darkness* 1962 (d); *Two Living, One Dead* 1962 (d); *An Evening With the Royal Ballet* 1963 (d); *The V.I.P.s* 1963 (d); *The Yellow Rolls-Royce* 1964 (d).

Assante, Armand • Actor • Born New York, NY, October 4, 1949. *Educ.* AADA, New York. Versatile lead and supporting player, more than capable in comedy and superior in macho dramas such as *I, the Jury* (1981) and Sidney Lumet's *Q&A* (1990). • *Paradise Alley* 1978; *Prophecy* 1979; *Little Darlings* 1980; *Love & Money* 1980; *Private Benjamin* 1980; *I, the Jury* 1981; *Unfaithfully Yours* 1983; *Belizaire the Cajun* 1985; *The Penitent* 1988; *Animal Behavior* 1989; *Eternity* 1990; *Q&A* 1990; *The Marrying Man* 1991.

Astaire, Fred • Actor, dancer; also singer, choreographer. • Born Frederick Austerlitz, Omaha, NB, May 10, 1899; died June 22, 1987, Los Angeles, CA. *Educ.* Alvienne School of Dance. Together with his partner Ginger Rogers, Astaire helped re-define musical comedy in the 1930s. A dancer of unmatched grace and sophistication, he was also a capable dramatic player and a singer of some charm.

Astaire started touring the vaudeville circuit at age seven and began a successful Broadway dancing career, partnered by his sister Adele, in 1917. He made his first (small) film appearance opposite Joan Crawford in *Dancing Lady* (1933), despite the famous verdict on his Hollywood screen test: "Can't act. Slightly bald. Can dance a little." His partnership with Rogers began shortly afterwards and lasted through ten films; among her successors were Lucille Bremer, Rita Hayworth, Eleanor Powell and Cyd Charisse. • *Dancing Lady* 1933 (a); *Flying Down to Rio* 1933 (a); *The Gay Divorcee* 1934 (a); *Roberta* 1935 (a,chor); *Top Hat* 1935 (a); *Follow the Fleet* 1936 (a); *Swing Time* 1936 (a); *A Damsel in Distress* 1937 (a); *Shall We Dance* 1937 (a); *Carefree* 1938 (a); *The Story of Vernon and Irene Castle* 1939 (a); *Broadway Melody of 1940* 1940 (a); *Second Chorus* 1940 (a); *You'll Never Get Rich* 1941 (a); *Holiday Inn* 1942 (a); *You Were Never Lovelier* 1942 (a); *The Sky's the Limit* 1943 (a,chor); *Yolanda and the Thief* 1945 (a); *Blue Skies* 1946 (a); *Ziegfeld Follies* 1946 (a); *Easter Parade* 1948 (a); *The Barkleys of Broadway* 1949 (a); *Let's Dance* 1950 (a); *Three Little Words* 1950 (a); *Royal Wedding* 1951 (a); *The Belle of New York* 1952 (a); *The Band Wagon* 1953 (a); *Daddy Long Legs* 1955 (a,chor); *Funny Face* 1957 (a,chor); *Silk Stockings* 1957 (a); *On the Beach* 1959 (a); *The Pleasure of His Company* 1961 (a); *The Notorious Landlady* 1962 (a); *Finian's Rainbow* 1968 (a); *A Run on Gold* 1969 (a); *That's Entertainment!* 1974 (a); *The Towering Inferno* 1974 (a) (**AANBSA**); *The Amazing Dobermans* 1976 (a); *That's Entertainment Part 2* 1976 (a); *Un Taxi mauve* 1977 (a); *Imposters* 1979 (song); *Ghost Story* 1981 (a); *Pennies From Heaven* 1981 (song); *Can She Bake a Cherry Pie?* 1983 (song); *George Stevens: A Filmmaker's Journey* 1985 (a); *Going Hollywood: The War Years* 1988 (a); *Hotel Terminus: Klaus Barbie, His Life and Times* 1988 (song); *Loverboy* 1989 (song).

Astor, Mary • Actress • Born Lucille Vasconsellos Langhanke, Quincy, IL, May 3, 1906; died September 25, 1987, Woodland Hills, CA. Durable leading lady of the 1920s, 30s and 40s, best remembered as the homicidal, but seemingly sympathetic, Brigid O'Shaughnessy in *The Maltese Falcon* (1941). Astor was at the center of a scandal in 1936, when her suit for custody of her daughter Marylyn led to the disclosure of a personal diary, allegedly documenting her liaisons with a number of prominent Hollywood figures. • *John Smith* 1922; *The Man Who Played God* 1922; *The Rapids* 1922; *The Bright Shawl* 1923; *Hollywood* 1923; *The Marriage Maker* 1923; *Puritan Passions* 1923; *Second Fiddle* 1923; *Success* 1923; *Woman-Proof* 1923; *Beau Brummell* 1924; *The Fighting American* 1924; *The Fighting Coward* 1924; *Inez From Hollywood* 1924; *Oh, Doctor!* 1924; *The Price of a Party* 1924; *Unguarded Women* 1924; *Don Q, Son of Zorro* 1925; *Enticement* 1925; *The Pace That Thrills* 1925; *Playing With Souls* 1925; *The Scarlet Saint* 1925; *Don Juan* 1926; *Forever After* 1926; *High Steppers* 1926; *The Wise Guy* 1926; *No Place to Go* 1927; *Rose of the Golden West* 1927; *The Rough Riders* 1927; *The Sea Tiger* 1927; *The Sunset Derby* 1927; *Two Arabian Knights* 1927; *Dressed to Kill* 1928; *Dry Martini* 1928; *Heart to Heart* 1928; *Romance of the Underworld* 1928; *Sailor's Wives* 1928; *Three-Ring Marriage* 1928; *New Year's Eve* 1929; *Woman From Hell* 1929; *Holiday* 1930; *Ladies Love Brutes* 1930; *The Lash* 1930; *The Runaway Bride* 1930; *Behind Office Doors* 1931; *Other Men's Women* 1931; *The Royal Bed* 1931; *The Sin Ship* 1931; *Smart Woman* 1931; *White Shoulders* 1931; *The Lost Squadron* 1932; *Men of Chance* 1932; *Red Dust* 1932; *A Successful Calamity* 1932; *Those We Love* 1932; *Convention City* 1933; *Jennie Gerhardt* 1933; *The Kennel Murder Case* 1933; *The Little Giant* 1933; *The World Changes* 1933; *The Case of the Howling Dog* 1934; *Easy to Love* 1934; *The Man With Two Faces* 1934; *Return of the Terror* 1934; *Upperworld* 1934; *Dinky* 1935; *I Am a Thief* 1935; *Man of Iron* 1935; *Page Miss Glory* 1935; *Red Hot Tires* 1935; *Straight From the Heart* 1935; *And So They Were Married* 1936; *Dodsworth* 1936; *Lady From Nowhere* 1936; *The Murder of Dr. Harrigan* 1936; *Trapped By Television* 1936; *Hurricane* 1937; *The Prisoner of Zenda* 1937; *Listen, Darling* 1938; *No Time to Marry* 1938; *Paradise For Three* 1938; *There's Always a Woman* 1938; *Woman Against Woman* 1938; *Midnight* 1939; *Brigham Young, Frontiersman* 1940; *Turnabout* 1940; *The Great Lie* 1941 (**AABSA**); *The Maltese Falcon* 1941; *Across the Pacific* 1942; *The Palm Beach Story* 1942; *Thousands Cheer* 1943; *Young Ideas* 1943; *Blonde Fever* 1944; *Meet Me in St. Louis* 1944; *Claudia and David* 1946; *Cass Timberlane* 1947; *Cynthia* 1947; *Desert Fury* 1947; *Fiesta* 1947; *Act of Violence* 1948; *Any Number Can Play* 1949; *Little Women* 1949; *A Kiss Before Dying* 1956; *The Power and the Prize* 1956; *The Devil's Hairpin* 1957; *This Happy Feeling* 1958; *Stranger in My Arms* 1959; *Return* *to Peyton Place* 1961; *Hush... Hush, Sweet Charlotte* 1964; *Youngblood Hawke* 1964.

Astruc, Alexandre • Director; also novelist, critic, screenwriter. • Born Paris, July 13, 1923. *Educ.* Sorbonne, Paris (literature, law). Theorist turned filmmaker who championed the notion of the *caméra-stylo/camera-pen*, arguing that film should "write" in its own language as opposed to that of the theater or literature. Astruc's films as a director, beginning with *Les Mauvaises Rencontres* in 1955, emphasize style over substance, often to their detriment. 1958's *Une Vie*, however, is a fine adaptation from the novel by Maupassant, beautifully photographed by Claude Renoir. • *Le Rideau cramoisi (short)* 1952 (d,sc); *Les Mauvaises Rencontres* 1955 (d); *Une Vie* 1958 (d,sc); *La Proie pour l'ombre* 1960 (d); *L'Education sentimentale* 1962 (d); *La Longue marche* 1966 (d); *Flammes sur l'Adriatique* 1968 (d); *La Jeune Fille assassinée* 1974 (a); *Sartre par lui-même* 1979 (d).

Attenborough, Sir Richard • Director, actor; also producer. • Born Cambridge, England, August 29, 1923. *Educ.* RADA, London. Short, and eventually stout, character player who made a smooth transition to the director's chair in the late 1960s. With his vulnerable baby face, Attenborough entered film while still a RADA student as the faint-hearted seaman in *In Which We Serve* (1942) and, although often typecast as weak or blustery youths, he displayed his versatility as the menacing psychotic hood in the superb *Young Scarface/Brighton Rock* (1947), as the laboror sent to coventry in the social drama *The Angry Silence* (1959) and most notably as the pathetic, accommodating kidnapper in *Seance on a Wet Afternoon* (1964).

Frustrated by the British film industry, Attenborough teamed with actor-writer Bryan Forbes in 1959 to form Beaver Films, which produced a slew of small, ambitious and often socially-conscious features often directed by Forbes. Since his boisterous directing debut, *Oh! What a Lovely War* (1969), Attenborough has helmed several other films, most of which tackle social and political issues, some as large-scale epics with star-studded casts. In 1982, he realized a long-held dream to film the life of *Gandhi* but has fared less well with his subsequent overblown "prestige" projects. • *In Which We Serve* 1942 (a); *Schweik's New Adventures* 1943 (a); *Hundred Pound Window* 1944 (a); *Journey Together* 1945 (a); *A Matter of Life and Death* 1946 (a); *School For Secrets* 1946 (a); *Young Scarface/Brighton Rock* 1947 (a); *Dancing With Crime* 1947 (a); *The Man Within* 1947 (a); *The Guinea Pig* 1948 (a); *London Belongs to Me* 1948 (a); *Boys in Brown* 1949 (a); *The Lost People* 1949 (a); *Morning Departure* 1950 (a); *Hell Is Sold Out* 1951 (a); *The Magic Box* 1951 (a); *Father's Doing Fine* 1952 (a); *The Gift Horse* 1953 (a); *Eight O'Clock Walk* 1954 (a); *The Ship That Died of Shame* 1955 (a); *The Baby and the Battleship* 1956 (a); *Brothers in Law* 1956 (a); *Private's Progress* 1956 (a); *The Scamp* 1957 (a); *Danger Within* 1958 (a); *Dunkirk* 1958 (a); *The Man Upstairs* 1958 (a); *Sea of Sand* 1958 (a); *The Angry Silence* 1959 (a,p); *I'm All Right Jack* 1959 (a); *Jet Storm* 1959 (a); *S.O.S. Pacific* 1959 (a); *The League of Gentlemen* 1960 (a); *Only Two Can Play* 1961 (a); *Whistle Down the Wind* 1961 (p); *All Night Long* 1962 (a); *The Dock Brief* 1962 (a); *The L-Shaped Room* 1962 (p); *The Great Escape* 1963 (a); *Guns at Batasi* 1964 (a); *Seance on a Wet Afternoon* 1964 (a,p); *The Third Secret* 1964 (a); *The Flight of the Phoenix* 1965 (a); *The Sand Pebbles* 1966 (a); *Doctor Dolittle* 1967 (a); *The Bliss of Mrs. Blossom* 1968 (a); *Only When I Larf* 1968 (a); *Oh! What a Lovely War* 1969 (d,p); *10 Rillington Place* 1970 (a); *David Copperfield* 1970 (a); *The Last Grenade* 1970 (a); *Loot* 1970 (a); *The Magic Christian* 1970 (a); *A Severed Head* 1970 (a); *Young Winston* 1972 (d,p); *And Then There Were None* 1975 (a); *Brannigan* 1975 (a); *Conduct Unbecoming* 1975 (a); *Rosebud* 1975 (a); *A Bridge Too Far* 1977 (d); *Shatranj ke Khilari/The Chess Players* 1977 (a); *Magic* 1978 (d); *The Human Factor* 1979 (a); *Gandhi* 1982 (d,p) **(AABD)**; *A Chorus Line* 1985 (d); *Mother Teresa* 1985 (a,consultant); *Cry Freedom* 1987 (d,p).

Atwill, Lionel • Actor • Born Lionel Alfred William Atwill, Croydon, England, March 1, 1885; died 1946. British stage actor who came to America in 1916 and starred as a romantic lead on Broadway. Although Atwill made his screen debut in 1916, he is best known as the suavely menacing villian (most often a sinister mad doctor) of countless Hollywood horror films of the 1930s and 40s, most notably *Doctor X* (1932), *The Mystery of the Wax Museum* (1933), *The Hound of the Baskervilles* (1939). • *Eve's Daughter* 1918 (a); *For Sale* 1918 (a); *The Highest Bidder* 1921 (a); *Indiscretion* 1921 (a); *Doctor X* 1932 (a); *The Silent Witness* 1932 (a); *Murders in the Zoo* 1933 (a); *The Mystery of the Wax Museum* 1933 (a); *The Secret of Madame Blanche* 1933 (a); *Secret of the Blue Room* 1933 (a); *The Solitaire Man* 1933 (a); *Song of Songs* 1933 (a); *The Sphinx* 1933 (a); *The Vampire Bat* 1933 (a); *The Age of Innocence* 1934 (a); *Beggars in Ermine* 1934 (a); *The Firebird* 1934 (a); *The Man Who Reclaimed His Head* 1934 (a); *Nana* 1934 (a); *One More River* 1934 (a); *Stamboul Quest* 1934 (a); *Captain Blood* 1935 (a); *The Devil Is a Woman* 1935 (a); *Mark of the Vampire* 1935 (a); *The Murder Man* 1935 (a); *The Rendezvous* 1935 (a); *Absolute Quiet* 1936 (a); *Lady of Secrets* 1936 (a); *Till We Meet Again* 1936 (a); *The Great Garrick* 1937 (a); *The Lancer Spy* 1937 (a); *The Last Train From Madrid* 1937 (a); *The Road Back* 1937 (a); *The Wrong Road* 1937 (a); *The Great Waltz* 1938 (a); *Three Comrades* 1938 (a); *Balalaika* 1939 (a); *The Gorilla* 1939 (a); *The Hound of the Baskervilles* 1939 (a); *The Mad Empress* 1939 (a); *Mr. Moto Takes a Vacation* 1939 (a); *The Secret of Dr. Kildare* 1939 (a); *Son of Frankenstein* 1939 (a); *The Sun Never Sets* 1939 (a); *The Three Musketeers* 1939 (a); *Boom Town* 1940 (a); *Charlie Chan in Panama* 1940 (a); *Charlie Chan's Murder Cruise* 1940 (a); *Girl in 313* 1940 (a); *The Great Profile* 1940 (a); *Johnny Apollo* 1940 (a); *Man-Made Monster* 1941 (a); *Cairo* 1942 (a); *The Ghost of Frankenstein* 1942 (a); *Junior G-Men of the Air* 1942 (a); *The Mad Doctor of Market Street* 1942 (a); *Night Monster* 1942 (a); *Pardon My Sarong* 1942 (a); *Sherlock Holmes and the Secret Weapon* 1942 (a); *The Strange Case of Dr. Rx* 1942 (a); *To Be or Not to Be* 1942 (a); *Frankenstein Meets the Wolf Man* 1943 (a); *Captain America* 1944 (a); *Crime, Inc.* 1944 (a); *House of Frankenstein* 1944 (a); *Lady in the Death House* 1944 (a); *Raiders of Ghost City* 1944 (a); *The Secrets of Scotland Yard* 1944 (a); *Fog Island* 1945 (a); *House of Dracula* 1945 (a); *Genius at Work* 1946 (a); *Lost City of the Jungle* 1946 (a).

Audiard, Michel • Screenwriter; also director, novelist. • Born Paris, May 15, 1920; died July 27, 1985, Dourdan, France. Turned out over 130 films for most of the top French directors during a 35-year career which began in 1949. A fine dialogue writer, especially for actor Jean Gabin, Audiard was also a capable director. • *Les Trois Mousquetaires/The Three Musketeers* 1953 (sc); *Maigret Tend un Piège* 1957 (adapt,dial); *Les Misérables* 1957 (sc,adapt); *Retour de Manivelle* 1957 (dial); *Le Rouge est mis* 1957 (sc); *Les Grandes Familles* 1958 (sc); *Mélodie en sous-sol* 1962 (sc,dial); *La Métamorphose des cloportes* 1965 (dial); *Johnny Banco* 1967 (sc); *Elle boit pas, elle fume pas, elle drague pas...mais elle cause!* 1970 (d,sc); *Le Cri du Cormoran le Soir Au-Dessus des Jonques* 1971 (d,sc); *Le Drapeau Noir Flotte Sur La Marmite* 1971 (d,sc); *Elle cause plus...elle flingue* 1972 (d,sc); *Bon Baisers à Lundi* 1974 (d,sc); *Comment Réussir Quand On Est Con Et Pleurnichard* 1974 (d,sc); *Vive la France* 1974 (d,sc); *L'Incorrigible* 1975 (sc); *Le Corps de Mon Ennemi* 1976 (sc); *L'Animal* 1977 (sc,dial); *Le Grand Escogriffe* 1977 (sc); *Mort d'un pourri* 1977 (sc,dial); *Tendre Poulet/Dear Inspector* 1977 (sc); *Le Cavaleur* 1978 (sc,dial); *Les Egouts du Paradis* 1978 (dial); *Flic ou voyou* 1979 (sc,dial); *On a volé la cuisse de Jupiter/Jupiter's Thigh* 1979 (sc); *L'Entourloupe* 1980 (sc); *Est-ce bien raisonnable?* 1980 (dial); *Pile ou Face*

1980 (sc); *Garde à Vue* 1981 (dial); *Mortelle Randonnée* 1982 (sc); *Les Morfalous* 1983 (sc); *Canicule* 1984 (sc); *La Cage aux folles III: "Elles" se marient* 1985 (sc,dial); *On Ne Meurt Que 2 Fois* 1985 (sc).

Audran, Stéphane • Actress • Born Collette Suzanne Dacheville, Versailles, France, 1939. Delicately beautiful international star who came to prominence starring in films directed by her second husband, Claude Chabrol. (Audran had been previously—and briefly—married to Jean-Louis Trintingant.) Combining cool sophistication with smoldering sensuality, Audran gave impeccable performances in Chabrol's *Le boucher* (1969) and *La Rupture* (1970) and seemed equally at home in the surrealist environs of Luis Buñuel's *The Discreet Charm of the Bourgeoisie* (1972).

Audran continued to work prolifically through the 1980s, receiving renewed critical praise as the title character of Gabriel Axel's Oscar-winner *Babette's Feast* (1987). • *Les Cousins* 1959; *Les Bonnes Femmes* 1960; *Les Godelureaux* 1960; *Landru/Bluebeard* 1962; *L'Oeil du Malin/The Third Lover* 1962; *Le Tigre Aime la Chair Fraiche* 1964; *Marie-Chantal Contre le Docteur Kha* 1965; *Paris Vu Par.../Six in Paris* 1965; *La Ligne de Démarcation* 1966; *Le Scandale/The Champagne Murders* 1966; *Les Biches* 1967; *La Femme Infidèle* 1968; *Le Boucher* 1969; *La Dame dans l'auto avec des lunettes et un fusil* 1970; *La Rupture* 1970; *Aussi Loin Que L'Amour* 1971; *Juste avant la nuit/Just Before Nightfall* 1971; *Sans Mobile Apparent* 1971; *Le Charme Discret de la Bourgeoisie/The Discreet Charm of the Bourgeoisie* 1972; *Un Meurtre est un Meurtre* 1972; *Les Noces Rouges/Blood Wedding* 1973; *Comment Reussir Quand On Est Con Et Pleurnichard* 1974; *Le Cri Du Coeur* 1974; *Vincent, François, Paul...et les Autres* 1974; *And Then There Were None* 1975; *The Black Bird* 1975; *Les Liens de sang* 1977; *Mort d'un pourri* 1977; *Silver Bears* 1977; *Des Teufels Advokat* 1977; *Violette Nozière* 1977; *Eagle's Wing* 1978; *Le Gagnant* 1979; *Le Soleil en face* 1979; *The Big Red One* 1980; *Le Coeur à l'Envers* 1980; *Coup de Torchon/Clean Slate* 1981; *Le Choc* 1982; *Mortelle Randonnée* 1982; *Paradis pour tous* 1982; *La Scarlatine* 1983; *Le Sang des Autres/The Blood of Others* 1984; *Les Voleurs de la nuit* 1984; *La Cage aux folles III: "Elles" se marient* 1985; *La Gitane* 1985; *La Nuit Magique* 1985; *Poulet au Vinaigre/Cop au vin* 1985; *Suivez mon regard* 1985; *Babette's gastebud/Babette's Feast* 1987; *Corps z'a corps* 1987; *Les Predateurs de la nuit* 1987; *Les Saisons du plaisir* 1987; *Manika* 1988; *Sons* 1989; *Jours tranquilles à Clichy/Quiet Days in Clichy* 1990; *La Messe en si mineur* 1990.

August, Bille • Director, screenwriter; also director of photography. • Born Denmark, 1948. *Educ.* Christer Stroholm's Photography School, Stockholm, Sweden (commercial photography); Danish Film Institute. Former cinematographer who gained international attention as a director with *Twist and Shout* (1985), an endearing piece of nostalgia about two teens in the early 1960s. As in *Pelle the Conqueror* (1987), August has displayed a talent for sensitively portraying the everyday problems of ordinary people. He was chosen by Ingmar Bergman to direct *Good Intentions*, scripted by Bergman, about the early relationship between his parents. • *Hemat i Natten* 1977 (ph); *Honning Maane* 1978 (d,sc,story); *Man kan inte Valdtas* 1978 (ph); *Karleken* 1980 (ph); *Tomas-et Barn, du Ikke Kan Naa* 1980 (ph); *The Grass Is Singing* 1981 (ph); *Zappa* 1983 (d,sc); *Twist and Shout* 1985 (d,sc); *Pelle Erobreren/Pelle the Conqueror* 1987 (d,sc).

Aumont, Jean-Pierre • Actor • Born Jean-Pierre Salomons, Paris, January 5, 1909. *Educ.* Paris Conservatoire. Handsome, romantic Continental lead for over five decades. Aumont began his career on the French stage, scoring a triumph in Cocteau's *La Machine Infernale* (1934). He entered film in France in the early 1930s and, after fighting with the Free French Army and earning both the legion of honor and the croix de guerre, made his Hollywood debut in *Assignment in Brittany* (1943). Aumont has alternated between stage and film and US and international productions. His most representative roles came as the suave, philandering magician, Marco the Magnificent, in *Lili* (1953) and as an aging matinee idol in Truffaut's valentine to filmmaking, *Day For Night* (1973). Married to actresses Blanche Montel, Maria Montez and—twice—Marisa Pavan, he is also the brother of director François Villiers and father of actress Tina Aumont. • *Le Voleur* 1934; *L'Equipage* 1935; *Cargaison Blanche* 1937; *Hôtel du Nord* 1938; *Assignment in Brittany* 1943; *The Cross of Lorraine* 1943; *Heartbeat* 1946; *The Song of Scheherazade* 1947; *Siren of Atlantis* 1948; *Lili* 1953; *Charge of the Lancers* 1954; *Hilda Crane* 1956; *The Seventh Sin* 1957; *John Paul Jones* 1959; *The Enemy General* 1960; *The Devil at 4 O'Clock* 1961; *Les Sept péchés capitaux/The Seven Deadly Sins* 1962; *Five Miles to Midnight* 1963; *Carnival of Crime* 1964; *El Coleccionista de Cadaveres* 1968; *Castle Keep* 1969; *L'Homme Au Cerveau Greffe* 1972; *La Nuit Américaine/Day For Night* 1973; *Porgi l'Altra Guancia* 1974; *Catherine et Cie/Catherine and Co.* 1975; *The Happy Hooker* 1975; *Mahogany* 1975; *Des Journées Entières dans les Arbres* 1976; *Et la terreur commence* 1978; *Two Solitudes* 1978; *Something Short of Paradise* 1979; *Nana* 1982; *La Java des ombres* 1983; *Le Sang des Autres/The Blood of Others* 1984; *On a Volé Charlie Spencer!* 1986; *Sweet Country* 1986; *Johnny Monroe* 1987; *A notre regrettable époux* 1988.

Aurenche, Jean • Screenwriter • Born Pierrelatte, France, September 11, 1904. Entered films in the early 1930s, wrote his first feature in 1936 and began a fruitful, lasting collaboration with co-writer Pierre Bost on *Douce* (1943). The team wrote numerous scripts for directors Claude Autant-Lara (*The Devil in the Flesh* 1947, *The Red Inn* 1951), Réné Clément (*The Walls of Malapaga* 1949, *Forbidden Games* 1952, *Gervaise* 1955) and Jean Delannoy (*La Symphonie pastoral* 1946, *God Needs Men* 1950).

Though the work of Bost and Aurenche came to typify the "quality" films so despised by the New Wave directors, their earlier screenplays had often been iconoclastic, dealing with sordid subject matter and espousing progressive politics. After a series of generally undistinguished films in the 1960s, the team re-established its critical reputation with two fine, intricate dramas for Bertrand Tavernier, *The Watchmaker* (1973) and *The Judge and the Assassin* (1976). • *Douce* 1943 (sc); *La Symphonie Pastorale* 1946 (sc,adapt); *Le Diable au corps/Devil in the Flesh* 1947 (adapt); *La Mura di Malapaga/The Walls of Malapaga* 1949 (sc.adapt); *Dieu a besoin des hommes/God Needs Men* 1950 (sc); *L'Auberge Rouge/The Red Inn* 1951 (sc,adapt); *Jeux interdits/Forbidden Games* 1952 (sc); *Les Sept péchés capitaux/The Seven Deadly Sins* 1952 (sc—"Lust"); *Les Orgueilleux* 1953 (sc,dial); *Le Blé en Herbe* 1954 (sc); *Rouge et Noir* 1954 (sc); *Gervaise* 1955 (sc); *La Traversée de Paris* 1956 (sc); *En cas de malheur* 1958 (sc); *L'Horloger de St. Paul/The Watchmaker of St. Paul* 1973 (sc); *Que la fête commence...* 1974 (sc); *Le Juge et l'assassin/The Judge and the Assassin* 1976 (sc); *Coup de Torchon* 1981 (sc); *L'Etoile du nord* 1982 (sc); *Un Amour de Swann/Swann in Love* 1984 (a); *De guerre lasse* 1987 (sc); *Fucking Fernand* 1987 (sc); *Le Palanquin des larmes* 1988 (sc).

Auric, Georges • Composer • Born Lodève, France, February 15, 1899; died July 23, 1983, Paris. *Educ.* Paris Conservatoire. A respected composer before sound came to the movies, Auric's first film score was for Jean Cocteau's seminal *The Blood of a Poet* (1930). He subsequently composed over 100 film scores for numerous directors including Henri-Georges Clouzot, John Huston and Max Ophuls. • *Entr'acte* 1924 (a); *Le Sang d'un poéte/The Blood of a Poet* 1930 (m); *A Nous la Liberté* 1931 (m); *Lac aux Dames* 1934 (m); *Captain Blood* 1935 (m); *Les Mystères de Paris* 1935 (m); *Sous les yeux de l'Occident* 1936 (m); *L'Alibi* 1937 (m); *La Danseuse rouge* 1937 (m); *Un Déjeuner de soleil* 1937 (m); *Gribouille* 1937 (m); *Le Messa-*

ger 1937 (m); *Orage* 1937 (m); *Tamara la complaisante* 1937 (m); *L'Affaire Lafarge* 1938 (m); *Entrée des Artistes* 1938 (m); *Huilor (short)* 1938 (m); *La Mode revée (short)* 1938 (m); *Les Oranges de Jaffa (short)* 1938 (m); *La Rue sans joie* 1938 (m); *Son oncle de Normandie* 1938 (m); *Macao, l'enfer du jeu* 1940 (m); *Les Petits riens* 1941 (m); *L'Assassin a peur la nuit* 1942 (m); *La Belle aventure* 1942 (m); *Monsieur la Souris* 1942 (m); *Opera-Musette* 1942 (m); *L'Eternel Retour/The Eternal Return* 1943 (m); *Le Bossu* 1944 (m); *La Belle et la Bête/Beauty and the Beast* 1945 (m); *Caesar and Cleopatra* 1945 (m); *Dead of Night* 1945 (m); *François Villon* 1945 (m); *La Part de l'ombre* 1945 (m); *La Septième Porte* 1946 (m); *La Symphonie Pastorale* 1946 (m); *Torrents* 1946 (m); *Hue and Cry* 1947 (m); *Les Jeux sont faits* 1947 (m); *La Rose et le roseda (short)* 1947 (m); *Ruy Blas* 1947 (m); *L'Aigle a Deux Têtes/Eagle With Two Heads* 1948 (m); *Another Shore* 1948 (m); *Aux yeux du souvenir* 1948 (m); *Corridor of Mirrors* 1948 (m); *It Always Rains on Sunday* 1948 (m); *Les Noces de Sable* 1948 (m); *Les Parents Terribles* 1948 (m); *The Queen of Spades* 1948 (m); *Silent Dust* 1948 (m); *Ce siècle a cinquante ans* 1949 (m); *Maya* 1949 (m); *Passport to Pimlico* 1949 (m); *The Spider and the Fly* 1949 (m); *Les Amants de Bras-Mort* 1950 (m); *Cage of Gold* 1950 (m); *Caroline Cherie* 1950 (m); *Fes (short)* 1950 (m); *Orphée/Orpheus* 1950 (m); *The Galloping Major* 1951 (m); *Kermesse au soleil (short)* 1951 (m); *Nez de Cuir* 1951 (m); *La Fete A Henriette* 1952 (m); *The Lavender Hill Mob* 1952 (m); *Moulin Rouge* 1952 (m); *The Open Window (short)* 1952 (m); *La P... respectueuse* 1952 (m); *La Chair et le Diable* 1953 (m); *L'Esclave* 1953 (m); *Roman Holiday* 1953 (m); *Le Salaire de la Peur/The Wages of Fear* 1953 (m); *The Titfield Thunderbolt* 1953 (m); *Cheri Bibi* 1954 (m); *The Divided Heart* 1954 (m); *Father Brown* 1954 (m); *The Good Die Young* 1954 (m); *Nagana* 1954 (m); *Abdullah the Great* 1955 (m); *The Bespoke Overcoat (short)* 1955 (m); *La Chaleur du foyer (short)* 1955 (m); *La Femme et le fauve (short)* 1955 (m); *Gervaise* 1955 (m); *Les Hussards* 1955 (m); *Lola Montès* 1955 (m); *Rififi* 1955 (m); *Walk Into Paradise* 1955 (m); *Les Aventures de Till l'Espiegel* 1956 (m); *Le Mystère Picasso/The Mystery of Picasso* 1956 (m); *Les Sorcières de Salem* 1956 (m); *Bonjour Tristesse* 1957 (m); *Celui Qui Doit Mourir* 1957 (m); *Les Espions* 1957 (m); *Heaven Knows, Mr. Allison* 1957 (m); *Notre-Dame de Paris/The Hunchback of Notre Dame* 1957 (m,song); *The Story of Esther Costello* 1957 (m); *Les Bijoutiers du Clair de Lune* 1958 (m); *Christine* 1958 (m); *Dangerous Exile* 1958 (m); *Next to No Time* 1958 (m); *The Journey* 1959 (m); *S.O.S. Pacific* 1959 (m); *Sergent X...* 1959 (m); *Le Testament d'Orphée/The Testament of Orpheus* 1959 (m); *La Princesse de Cleves* 1960 (m); *Bridge to the Sun* 1961 (m); *Les Croulants se portent bien* 1961 (m); *Aimez-vous Brahms?/Goodbye Again* 1961 (m.dir); *The Innocents* 1961 (m); *Rendez-vous de minuit* 1961 (m); *Das Brennende Gericht* 1962 (m); *Carillons sans joie* 1962 (m); *Smash en direct (short)* 1962 (m); *The Mind Benders* 1963 (m); *La Communale* 1965 (m); *La Sentinelle endormie* 1965 (m); *Thomas l'Imposteur* 1965 (m); *La Grande vadrouille* 1966 (m); *The Poppy Is Also a Flower* 1966 (m); *Ce pays dont les frontieres no sont que fleurs (short)* 1968 (m); *Therese and Isabelle* 1968 (m); *L'Arbre de Noel* 1969 (m).

Autant-Lara, Claude • Director • Born Luzarches, France, August 5, 1903. *Educ.* Ecole des Beaux Arts, Paris. Left-leaning figure who directed the French versions of several Hollywood films in the early 1930s. Autant-Lara established himself in the 1940s with a string of impressive films including *Lettres d'amour* (1942) and the first screen adaptation of Raymond Radiguet's *Devil in the Flesh* (1947). Though his later works appear dated alongside those of the New Wave, Autant-Lara's career began with a series of avant-garde shorts, including *Construire un feu* (1926), the first film to achieve a "widescreen" effect through the use of an anamorphic lens. • *Construire un feu (short)* 1926 (d); *Local Boy Makes Good* 1931 (d, French version); *Parlor, Bedroom and Bath* 1931 (d, French version); *Le Gendarme est sans pitié (short)* 1932 (d); *The Passionate Plumber* 1932 (d, French version); *Ciboulette* 1933 (d); *My Partner Mr. Davis* 1936 (d); *Le Ruisseau* 1938 (d); *Fric-Frac* 1939 (d); *Lettres d'Amour* 1942 (d); *Le Mariage de Chiffon* 1942 (d); *Douce* 1943 (d); *Sylvie et le Fantôme* 1946 (d); *Le Diable au corps/Devil in the Flesh* 1947 (d); *Occupe-toi d'Amélie* 1949 (d); *L'Auberge Rouge/The Red Inn* 1951 (adapt,d); *Les Sept péchés capitaux/The Seven Deadly Sins* 1952 (d); *Le Bon Dieu sans Confession* 1953 (d); *Le Blé en Herbe* 1954 (d,sc); *Rouge et Noir* 1954 (d); *Marguérite de la Nuit* 1956 (d); *La Traversée de Paris* 1956 (d); *En cas de malheur* 1958 (d); *Le Joueur* 1958 (d); *La Jument verte* 1959 (d); *Le Bois des Amants* 1960 (d); *Les Regates de San Francisco* 1960 (d); *Le Comte de Monte Cristo/The Count of Monte Cristo* 1961 (d); *Vive Henri IV... Vive l'Amour!* 1961 (d); *Tu ne tueras point* 1962 (d); *Le Magot de Josefa* 1963 (d); *Le Meurtrier* 1963 (d); *Le Journal d'une Femme en Blanc* 1965 (d); *Nouveau Journal d'une Femme en Blanc* 1966 (d); *Le Plus vieux métier du monde/The Oldest Profession* 1967 (d); *Le Franciscain de Bourges* 1968 (d); *Les Patates* 1969 (d); *Gloria* 1977 (d,sc,adapt).

Auteuil, Daniel • Actor • Born Algeria, January 24, 1950. Offbeat looking lead and supporting player, best known in the US as Yves Montand's buffoonish and pathetic sidekick, Ugolin, in *Jean de Florette* (1985) and *Manon of the Spring* (1986). For the French version of the hit comedy *Look Who's Talking* (1989), Auteuil provided the voice of infant Mikey (performed by Bruce Willis in the original). • *Monsieur Papa* 1977; *La Nuit de Saint-Germain des Près* 1977; *L'Amour violé/Rape of Love* 1978; *Les Héros n'ont pas froid aux oreilles* 1978; *A nous deux* 1979; *Bête mais discipline* 1979; *Les Sous-Doués* 1980; *Les Hommes préfèrent les grosses* 1981; *Pour 100 Briques, T'as plus rien maintenant* 1982; *Que les gros salaires lèvent le doigt!!!* 1982; *L'Indic* 1983; *L'Amour en Douce* 1984; *L'Arbalete* 1984; *Les Fauves* 1984; *Palace* 1984; *Petit Con* 1984; *Jean de Florette* 1986; *Manon des sources/Manon of the Spring* 1986; *Le Paltoquet* 1986; *Quelques jours avec moi* 1988; *Look Who's Talking* 1989; *Romuald et Juliette/Mama, There's a Man in Your Bed* 1989; *Lacenaire* 1990.

Autry, Gene • Actor; also singer, songwriter, producer. • Born Tioga, TX, September 29, 1907. Durable and popular singing cowboy, usually accompanied by his trusty horse, Champion. • *The Phantom Empire* 1925 (a); *In Old Santa Fe* 1934 (a); *Melody Trail* 1935 (a); *The Sagebrush Troubadour* 1935 (a); *The Singing Vagabond* 1935 (a); *Tumbling Tumbleweeds* 1935 (a); *The Big Show* 1936 (a); *Comin' Round the Mountain* 1936 (a); *Guns and Guitars* 1936 (a); *Oh, Susanna!* 1936 (a); *Red River Valley* 1936 (a); *Ride, Ranger, Ride* 1936 (a); *The Singing Cowboy* 1936 (a); *Boots and Saddles* 1937 (a); *Git Along Little Dogies* 1937 (a); *Manhattan Merry-Go-Round* 1937 (a); *The Old Corral* 1937 (a); *Public Cowboy No. 1* 1937 (a); *Rootin' Tootin' Rhythm* 1937 (a); *Round-Up Time in Texas* 1937 (a); *Springtime in the Rockies* 1937 (a); *Yodelin' Kid From Pine Ridge* 1937 (a); *Gold Mine in the Sky* 1938 (a); *Man From Music Mountain* 1938 (a); *The Old Barn Dance* 1938 (a); *Prairie Moon* 1938 (a); *Rhythm of the Saddle* 1938 (a); *Western Jamboree* 1938 (a); *Blue Montana Skies* 1939 (a); *Colorado Sunset* 1939 (a); *Home on the Prairie* 1939 (a); *In Old Monterey* 1939 (a); *Mexicali Rose* 1939 (a); *Mountain Rhythm* 1939 (a); *Rovin' Tumbleweeds* 1939 (a); *South of the Border* 1939 (a); *Carolina Moon* 1940 (a); *Gaucho Serenade* 1940 (a); *Melody Ranch* 1940 (a); *Rancho Grande* 1940 (a); *Ride, Tenderfoot, Ride* 1940 (a); *Shooting High* 1940 (a); *Back in the Saddle* 1941 (a); *Down Mexico Way* 1941 (a); *Ridin' on a Rainbow* 1941 (a,song) **(AANBS)**; *Sierra Sue* 1941 (a); *The Singing Hill* 1941 (a); *Sunset in Wyoming* 1941 (a); *Under Fiesta Stars* 1941 (a); *Bells of Capistrano* 1942 (a); *Call of the Canyon* 1942 (a); *Cowboy*

Serenade 1942 (a); *Heart of the Rio Grande* 1942 (a); *Home in Wyomin'* 1942 (a); *Stardust on the Sage* 1942 (a); *Sioux City Sue* 1946 (a); *The Last Round-Up* 1947 (a); *Robin Hood of Texas* 1947 (a); *Saddle Pals* 1947 (a); *Trail to San Antone* 1947 (a); *Twilight on the Rio Grande* 1947 (a); *The Big Sombrero* 1948 (a); *The Strawberry Roan* 1948 (a); *The Cowboy and the Indians* 1949 (a); *Loaded Pistols* 1949 (a); *Riders in the Sky* 1949 (a); *Riders of the Whistling Pines* 1949 (a); *Rim of the Canyon* 1949 (a); *Beyond the Purple Hills* 1950 (a); *Blazing Sun* 1950 (a); *Cow Town* 1950 (a); *Gene Autry and the Mounties* 1950 (a); *Indian Territory* 1950 (a); *Mule Train* 1950 (a); *Sons of New Mexico* 1950 (a); *Hills of Utah* 1951 (a); *Silver Canyon* 1951 (a); *Texans Never Cry* 1951 (a); *Valley of Fire* 1951 (a); *Whirlwind* 1951 (a); *Apache Country* 1952 (a); *Barbed Wire* 1952 (a); *Blue Canadian Rockies* 1952 (a); *Night Stage to Galveston* 1952 (a); *The Old West* 1952 (a); *Wagon Team* 1952 (a); *Goldtown Ghost Riders* 1953 (a); *Last of the Pony Riders* 1953 (a); *On Top of Old Smoky* 1953 (a); *Pack Train* 1953 (a); *Saginaw Trail* 1953 (a); *Winning of the West* 1953 (a); *It's Showtime* 1976 (a); *Semi-Tough* 1977 (song); *Some Kind of Hero* 1982 (song); *Great Balls of Fire* 1989 (song).

Avakian, Aram • Director, editor • Born New York, NY, April 23, 1926; died January 17, 1987, New York, NY. *Educ.* Yale; Sorbonne, Paris. Edited *Girl of the Night* (1960), noted as an early example of an American film using freeze-frame and jump-cut techniques. As a director, Avakian helmed several first rate adaptations, notably *The End of the Road* (1970) from John Barth's novel. • *Satchmo the Great* 1957 (assoc.ed); *Girl of the Night* 1960 (ed); *Lad: A Dog* 1962 (d); *Lilith* 1964 (ed); *Andy* 1965 (ed); *Mickey One* 1965 (ed); *You're a Big Boy Now* 1967 (ed); *The End of the Road* 1970 (d,sc); *Cops and Robbers* 1973 (d); *11 Harrowhouse* 1974 (d); *The Next Man* 1976 (ed); *Honeysuckle Rose* 1980 (ed).

Avalon, Frankie • Singer; also actor. • Born Francis Thomas Avallone, Philadelphia, PA, September 18, 1939. Pop-rock singer of the late 1950s who turned to films. Best remembered for light "beach" movies, usually with Annette Funicello. • *Jamboree* 1957 (a); *The Alamo* 1960 (a); *Guns of the Timberland* 1960 (a); *Saiyu-ki* 1960 (a); *Sail a Crooked Ship* 1961 (a); *Voyage to the Bottom of the Sea* 1961 (a); *Panic in Year Zero* 1962 (a); *Beach Party* 1963 (a); *Drums of Africa* 1963 (a); *Operation Bikini* 1963 (a); *El Valle de las espadas* 1963 (a); *Bikini Beach* 1964 (a); *Muscle Beach Party* 1964 (a); *Beach Blanket Bingo* 1965 (a); *Dr. Goldfoot and the Bikini Machine* 1965 (a); *I'll Take Sweden* 1965 (a); *Sergeant Deadhead* 1965 (a); *Ski Party* 1965 (a); *Fireball 500* 1966 (a); *Skidoo* 1968 (a); *The Take* 1974 (a); *Grease* 1978 (a,song); *Yotz im'kavua* 1979 (songs); *Shifshuf Naim* 1981 (song); *Back to the Beach* 1987 (a,co-exec.p,song); *Good Morning, Vietnam* 1987 (song); *Born on the Fourth of July* 1989 (song); *She's Out of Control* 1989 (song); *Troop Beverly Hills* 1989 (a); *Betsy's Wedding* 1990 (song).

Avery, Tex • Director, animator • Born Fred B. Avery, Dallas, TX, 1907; died 1980. Influential figure who directed some of Hollywood's finest animated films of the 1940s and 50s, creating such memorable characters as Chilly-Willy the penguin and Droopy the dog. Avery's cartoons—often scripted by Heck Allen—offered a slightly more absurd and anarchic alternative to the work of his contemporaries Chuck Jones and Friz Freleng. • *Happy-Go-Nutty* 1944; *Screwball Squirrel* 1944; *The Shooting of Dan McGoo* 1945; *The Cat That Hated People* 1948; *Little Rural Riding Hood* 1949; *Symphony in Slang* 1951; *T.V. of Tomorrow* 1953; *The Three Little Pups* 1953; *Uncensored Cartoons* 1981; *Porky Pig in Hollywood* 1986.

Avildsen, John G. • Director; also screenwriter, editor, director of photography. • Born Chicago, IL, 1936. *Educ.* NYU (English). Competent Hollywood craftsman who worked as a production manager, assistant director and cinematographer before graduating to director in the late 1960s. Avildsen's early output included the sly, often overlooked sex comedy, *Guess What We Learned in School Today?* (1970), *Joe* (1970)—which brought him and star Peter Boyle to widespread attention—and *Rocky* (1976), which earned the best director and best picture Oscars. His later work includes the commercially successful "Karate Kid" pictures as well as the 1989 schoolroom drama, *Lean on Me*, noted for a fine central performance by Morgan Freeman. • *Greenwich Village Story* 1963 (a); *Black Like Me* 1964 (asst to Carl Lerner); *Mickey One* 1965 (asst.prod.man); *Okay Bill* 1968 (d,sc,ph,ed); *Out of It* 1969 (ph); *Cry Uncle* 1970 (d,ph); *Guess What We Learned in School Today?* 1970 (d,ph); *Joe* 1970 (d,ph); *The Stoolie* 1972 (d,ph); *Save the Tiger* 1973 (d); *Foreplay* 1974 (d); *W. W. and the Dixie Dancekings* 1974 (d); *Rocky* 1976 (d) **(AABD)**; *Slow Dancing in the Big City* 1978 (d,ed,cam.op,p); *The Formula* 1980 (d,ed); *Neighbors* 1981 (d,ed); *Traveling Hopefully (short)* 1982 (d,sc) **(AANSHORT DOC)**; *A Night in Heaven* 1983 (d,ed); *The Karate Kid* 1984 (d,ed); *The Karate Kid Part II* 1986 (d,ed); *Happy New Year* 1987 (d); *For Keeps* 1988 (d,ed); *The Karate Kid Part III* 1989 (d,ed); *Lean on Me* 1989 (d,ed,exec.p); *Rocky V* 1990 (d,ed).

Avnet, Jon • Producer • Born Brooklyn, NY, November 17, 1947. *Educ.* University of Pennsylvania; Wharton School of Business; Sarah Lawrence College, Bronxville, NY; AFI, Los Angeles (directing). First made his name as a producer, in partnership with Steve Tisch, of issue-oriented TV movies such as *The Burning Bed* (1984). Avnet's big-screen projects have included 1983's commercial hit, *Risky Business*. In 1986 he formed the Avnet/Kerner Company with Jordan Kerner. • *Checkered Flag or Crash* 1977 (assoc.p); *Coast to Coast* 1980 (p); *Deal of the Century* 1983 (exec.p); *Risky Business* 1983 (p); *Less Than Zero* 1987 (p); *Funny About Love* 1990 (p); *Men Don't Leave* 1990 (2u d,p).

Axel, Gabriel • Director, sreenwriter • Born Paris. *Educ.* Royal Theater Drama School, Denmark. Works in theater, film and TV, and divides his time between France and Denmark. Axel scored his first international success with the Oscar-winning, gastronomical comedy-drama *Babette's Feast* (1987). • *Guld Og Gronne Skove* 1959 (d); *Tre piger i Paris* 1963 (d); *Den Rode Kappe* 1967 (d,sc); *Det Kaere Legetoj* 1968 (d,p,sc); *Med Kaerlig Hilsen* 1971 (d,sc); *Familien Gyldenkaal* 1975 (d); *Alt paa et Braet* 1976 (d,sc); *Babette's gastebud/Babette's Feast* 1987 (d,sc.adapt); *Christian* 1989 (d,sc).

Axelrod, George • Screenwriter; also director, producer. • Born New York, NY, June 9, 1922. Consistently effective scenarist whose often witty and always acute examinations of American social mores produced several superior films of the 1950s and 60s. Outstanding credits include *The Seven Year Itch* (1955), adapted from his stage hit, Blake Edwards's *Breakfast at Tiffany's* (1961) and John Frankenheimer's *The Manchurian Candidate* (1962). Axelrod's directorial efforts (*Lord Love a Duck* 1966, *The Secret Life of an American Wife* 1968), though equally superb, have unfortunately been overlooked. After a decade hiatus he returned to film work in 1979. • *Phfft* 1954 (sc,story); *The Seven Year Itch* 1955 (sc,from play); *Bus Stop* 1956 (sc); *Will Success Spoil Rock Hunter?* 1957 (from play); *Breakfast at Tiffany's* 1961 (sc) **(AANBSC)**; *The Manchurian Candidate* 1962 (p,sc); *Paris When It Sizzles* 1963 (p,sc); *Goodbye, Charlie* 1964 (from play); *How to Murder Your Wife* 1965 (p,sc); *Lord Love a Duck* 1966 (d,p,sc,story); *The Secret Life of an American Wife* 1968 (d,p,sc); *The Lady Vanishes* 1979 (sc); *The Holcroft Covenant* 1985 (sc); *The Fourth Protocol* 1987 (sc.adapt).

Aykroyd, Dan • Actor, comedian; also screenwriter, producer. • Born Daniel Edward Aykroyd, Ottawa, Ontario, Canada, July 1, 1952. *Educ.* Carleton College, Ottowa (criminology). Popular comic star who began his career with the

Toronto company of the Second City comedy troupe. Aykroyd first came to prominence on the "Saturday Night Live" TV show, and after a decade of humerous romps, earned an Oscar nomination for his first dramatic role, as the dutiful son in *Driving Miss Daisy* (1989). Married to actress Donna Dixon. • *Love at First Sight* 1977 (a); *1941* 1979 (a); *Mr. Mike's Mondo Video* 1979 (a); *The Blues Brothers* 1980 (a,sc); *Neighbors* 1981 (a); *Doctor Detroit* 1982 (a); *It Came From Hollywood* 1982 (a); *Nothing Lasts Forever* 1982 (a); *Trading Places* 1983 (a); *Twilight Zone - the Movie* 1983 (a); *Ghostbusters* 1984 (a,sc); *Indiana Jones and the Temple of Doom* 1984 (a); *Into the Night* 1985 (a); *Spies Like Us* 1985 (a,sc,story); *One More Saturday Night* 1986 (exec.p); *Dragnet* 1987 (a,sc,songs); *Caddyshack II* 1988 (a); *The Couch Trip* 1988 (a); *The Great Outdoors* 1988 (a); *My Stepmother Is an Alien* 1988 (a); *Driving Miss Daisy* 1989 (a) **(AANBSA)**; *Ghostbusters II* 1989 (a,sc,from characters); *Loose Cannons* 1989 (a,song); *Masters of Menace* 1991 (a); *Nothing But Trouble* 1991 (a,d,sc).

Ayres, Lew • *aka* Lewis Ayer • Actor; also filmmaker. • Born Minneapolis, MN, December 28, 1908. *Educ.* University of Arizona (medicine). Star of the pacifist classic *All Quiet on the Western Front* (1930) whose career faded during WWII after he declared himself a conscientious objector. Ayres later produced the religious documentaries *Altars of the East* (1955) and *Altars of the World* (1976). Married to actresses Lola Lane from 1931 to 1933 and Ginger Rogers from 1934 to 1941. • *The Kiss* 1929 (a); *All Quiet on the Western Front* 1930 (a); *Common Clay* 1930 (a); *The Doorway to Hell* 1930 (a); *East Is West* 1930 (a); *Heaven on Earth* 1931 (a); *The Iron Man* 1931 (a); *Many a Slip* 1931 (a); *Spirit of Notre Dame* 1931 (a); *Up For Murder* 1931 (a); *The Cohens and Kellys in Hollywood* 1932 (a); *The Impatient Maiden* 1932 (a); *Night World* 1932 (a); *Okay America* 1932 (a); *Don't Bet on Love* 1933 (a); *My Weakness* 1933 (a); *State Fair* 1933 (a); *Cross Country Cruise* 1934 (a); *Let's Be Ritzy* 1934 (a); *Servant's Entrance* 1934 (a); *She Learned About Sailors* 1934 (a); *The Lottery Lover* 1935 (a); *Silk Hat Kid* 1935 (a); *Spring Tonic* 1935 (a); *Hearts in Bondage* 1936 (d); *Lady Be Careful* 1936 (a); *The Leathernecks Have Landed* 1936 (a); *Murder With Pictures* 1936 (a); *Panic on the Air* 1936 (a); *Shakedown* 1936 (a); *The Crime Nobody Saw* 1937 (a); *Hold Em' Navy* 1937 (a); *The Last Train From Madrid* 1937 (a); *Holiday* 1938 (a); *King of the Newsboys* 1938 (a); *Rich Man, Poor Girl* 1938 (a); *Scandal Street* 1938 (a); *Spring Madness* 1938 (a); *Young Dr. Kildare* 1938 (a); *Broadway Serenade* 1939 (a); *Calling Dr. Kildare* 1939 (a); *Ice Follies* 1939 (a); *Remember?* 1939 (a); *The Secret of Dr. Kildare* 1939 (a); *These Glamour Girls* 1939 (a); *Dr. Kildare Goes Home* 1940 (a); *Dr. Kildare's Crisis* 1940 (a); *Dr. Kildare's Strange Case* 1940 (a); *The Golden Fleecing* 1940 (a); *Dr. Kildare's Victory* 1941 (a); *Dr. Kildare's Wedding Day* 1941 (a); *Maisie Was a Lady* 1941 (a); *The People vs. Dr. Kildare* 1941 (a); *Fingers at the Window* 1942 (a); *The Dark Mirror* 1946 (a); *The Unfaithful* 1947 (a); *Johnny Belinda* 1948 (a) **(AANBA)**; *The Capture* 1950 (a); *New Mexico* 1951 (a); *No Escape* 1953 (a); *Altars of the East* 1955 (p); *Advise and Consent* 1962 (a); *The Carpetbaggers* 1964 (a); *The Biscuit Eater* 1972 (a); *The Man* 1972 (a); *Battle For the Planet of the Apes* 1973 (a); *Altars of the World* 1976 (d,ed,ph,narration,p); *End of the World* 1977 (a); *Battlestar Galactica* 1978 (a); *Damien - Omen II* 1978 (a).

Azéma, Sabine • Actress • Born Paris. *Educ.* Paris Conservatoire. Began her acting career under the aegis of Jean Anouilh and has won two Césars (the French Oscar), for Bertrand Tavernier's *A Sunday in the Country* (1984) and Alain Resnais's *Mélo* (1986). Azéma also appeared in Resnais's *Life Is a Bed of Roses* (1983) and *Love Unto Death* (1984). • *Le Chasseur de Chez Maxim's* 1977; *La Dentellière/The Lacemaker* 1977; *La Vie est un roman/Life Is a Bed of Roses* 1983; *L'Amour à mort/Love Unto Death* 1984; *Un Dimanche à la Campagne/A Sunday in the Country* 1984; *Mélo* 1986; *La Puritaine* 1986; *Zone Rouge* 1986; *Cinq jours en juin* 1989; *Vanille Fraise* 1989; *La Vie et rien d'autre/Life and Nothing But* 1989; *Trois Années* 1990.

Aznavour, Charles • *aka* Charles Aznavurian • Singer; also actor, composer. • Born Shahnour Varenagh Aznavourian, Paris, May 22, 1924. Short, tough, popular singer of the 1950s who effortlessly turned to films, most formidably as Charlie Koller in François Truffaut's New Wave classic *Shoot the Piano Player* (1960). • *Le Testament d'Orphée/The Testament of Orpheus* 1959 (a); *Tirez Sur le Pianiste/Shoot the Piano Player* 1960 (a); *Scaramouche* 1963 (song); *La Métamorphose des cloportes* 1965 (a); *Candy* 1968 (a); *Un Beau Monstre* 1970 (a); *The Games* 1970 (a); *Le Temps des Loups* 1970 (a); *Les Intrus* 1971 (a,sc); *La Part des Lions* 1971 (a); *The Blockhouse* 1973 (a); *Golden Ophelia* 1974 (song); *And Then There Were None/Ten Little Indians* 1975 (a); *Hustle* 1975 (songs); *Betty Blokk-Buster Follies* 1976 (song); *Folies bourgeoises/The Twist* 1976 (a); *Sky Riders* 1976 (a); *Die Blechtrommel/The Tin Drum* 1979 (a); *Ciao, Les Mecs* 1979 (a); *Collections Privées* 1979 (a); *The Golden Lady* 1979 (songs); *Edith et Marcel* 1982 (lyrics); *Les Fantômes du Chapelier* 1982 (a); *Qu-est-ce-qui fait courir David?/What Makes David Run?* 1982 (a,lyrics); *Too Scared to Scream* 1982 (song); *Der Zauberberg* 1982 (a); *Le Bal* 1983 (songs); *Viva la Vie!* 1984 (a); *Mauvais sang/Bad Blood* 1986 (song); *Yiddish Connection* 1986 (a,sc,story); *Mangeclous* 1988 (a); *Migrations* 1988 (a); *Il Maestro* 1989 (a).

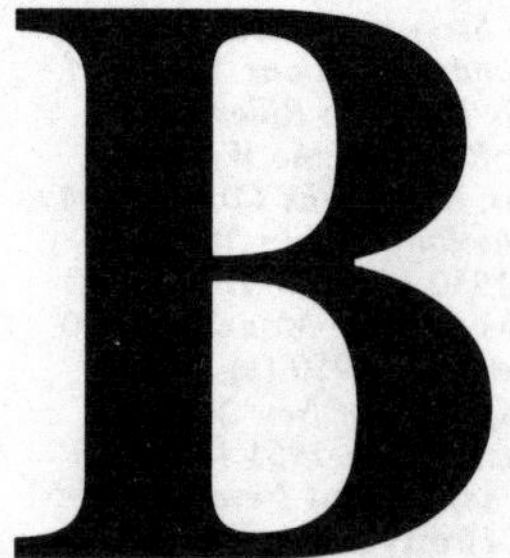

B, Beth • American filmmaker • *Educ.* Art Institute of Chicago; School of Visual Arts, New York. Together with husband Scott, among the best-known New York underground filmmakers of the late 1970s and early 80s. As a team the B's turned out numerous 8mm films, two of which were feature-length, and the highly stylized 16mm feature, *Vortex* (1982), an art-house success starring punk performer Lydia Lunch. The couple have since separated to pursue individual careers. • *The Offenders* 1980 (d,sc); *Vortex* 1982 (d,sc,ed); *Salvation! Have You Said Your Prayers Today?* 1987 (d,p,sc,post-prod,sup,m,sup, sound,song); *Belladonna (short)* 1989 (d). *(short)* 1989 (d).

B, Scott • Filmmaker • Born Scott Billingsly, US. *Educ.* University of Wisconsin, Madison; St. Cloud State College, MN. See B, Beth. • *The Offenders* 1980 (d,sc); *Vortex* 1982 (a,d,sc,ed).

Babenco, Hector • Director; also producer, screenwriter. • Born Hector Eduardo Babenco, Buenos Aires, Argentina, February 7, 1946. Hector Babenco became Brazil's leading post-*cinema nôvo* director in the 1970s and an acclaimed Hollywood director in the 80s. All his films deal with social issues, and are best seen as personal and subjective accounts of "marginalized" people—the homeless, prostitutes, political prisoners, homosexuals.

Born to poor Russian and Polish Jewish immigrant parents, Babenco was 18 when he left Argentina on a "divine mission," inspired by Beat and existential writers, to "know the world." For seven years he traveled throughout Africa, Europe and the Americas, working at odd jobs. In Spain and Italy he pursued his interest in film, working as an extra in spaghetti westerns.

In 1971 Babenco emigrated to Brazil to make films. Having grown up watching Hollywood and European films with subtitles, he was impressed by the new, indigenous Brazilian cinema. The year he arrived, however, Brazil's rightist military regime instituted strict censorship, forcing most *cinema nôvo* directors into exile. Babenco, who had never formally studied cinema, spent the next four years filming documentaries, shorts and commercials while he worked on his first feature, *King of the Night* (1975).

His next film, *Lúcio Flávio* (1978), made at the height of political repression in Brazil, depicted the life and death of a real-life thief/folk hero who had threatened to expose the police death squads. Although Babenco used dream sequences and attached a disclaimer to the film in order to appease the censors, he was the target of death threats and his house in São Paulo was machine-gunned. In addition, the prisoner who had killed the real Lúcio Flávio for the police was himself murdered on the eve of the film's opening. Despite these intimidations, *Lúcio Flávio* became Brazil's fourth-highest grossing feature, reviving the fortunes of the Brazilian film industry and picking up both the New York and the Los Angeles film critics' Award for best foreign film. Babenco became disillisioned, however, when he realized that the film had brought no concrete political changes.

Babenco's first international success was *Pixote* (1981), about the plight of Brazil's three million abandoned children. The director originally intended to film a documentary, and had completed 200 hours of interviews with children in reformatories. When he was refused further access, however, he turned to the streets and hired slum children to portray themselves. The result, although scripted, displays a documentary-like attention to detail and perspective. Rather than having the children read lines, Babenco built scenes around improvisation workshops that allowed them to contribute their own experiences to the picture.

Babenco's next two projects were English-language films. With *Kiss of the Spider Woman* (1985), he had difficulty finding American investors and was forced to defer salaries for himself and the lead actors. Its success (star William Hurt won an Oscar for his performance) ensured major Hollywood studio support for *Ironweed* (1987). Ironically, Babenco's experience in the US convinced him that Brazilian political censorship offered greater artistic freedom than Hollywood's economic censorship and studio bureaucracy. CAN • *King of the Night* 1975 (d); *Lúcio Flávio* 1978 (d); *Pixote* 1981 (d,sc); *Kiss of the Spider Woman* 1985 (d) **(AANBD)**; *Besame Mucho* 1987 (p); *Ironweed* 1987 (d).

Bacall, Lauren • Actress • Born Betty Joan Perske, New York, NY, September 16, 1924. *Educ.* AADA, New York. Tough-talking, husky-voiced leading lady who broke into films at the age of 19 opposite Humphrey Bogart in *To Have and Have Not* (1944). She subsequently married Bogart, 25 years her senior, creating a formidable team on and off screen. Like Garbo and Dietrich before her, Bacall's androgynous beauty made possible a wide variety of roles, from the wealthy, enigmatic Vivian in *The Big Sleep* (1946), to the distraught wife in the melodramatic *Written on the Wind* (1956), to her award-winning Broadway performance in *Applause* (1970).

In 1974, after an eight year hiatus, Bacall returned to the screen in *Murder on the Orient Express*, making a smooth transition to playing older women. Her autobiography, *Lauren Bacall, By Myself*, was published in 1979. Married to second husband, Jason Robards, Jr. from 1961 to 1969. • *To Have and Have Not* 1944; *Confidential Agent* 1945; *The Big Sleep* 1946; *Two Guys From Milwaukee* 1946; *Dark Passage* 1947; *Key Largo* 1948; *Bright Leaf* 1950; *Young Man With a Horn* 1950; *How to Marry a Millionaire* 1953; *Woman's World* 1954; *Blood Alley* 1955; *The Cobweb* 1955; *Written on the Wind* 1956; *Designing Woman* 1957; *The Gift of Love* 1958; *North West Frontier* 1959; *Sex and the Single Girl* 1964; *Shock Treatment* 1964; *Harper* 1966; *Murder on the Orient Express* 1974; *The Shootist* 1976; *Health* 1980; *The Fan* 1981; *Appointment With Death* 1988; *John Huston* 1988; *Mr. North* 1988; *Tree of Hands* 1989; *Misery* 1990.

Bacharach, Burt • Composer; also songwriter. • Born Kansas City, MO, May 12, 1929. *Educ.* McGill University, Montreal; Tanglewood; Mannes School of Music; Music Academy of the West. Toured Army bases during the Korean War as a uniformed concert pianist and served stints as an accompanist with several performers before coming to attention as the conductor-arranger for Marlene Dietrich during her international concert tour. Although his songs and scores had adorned several fine films beginning in 1957 (collaborating with lyricist Hal David on such memorable tunes as "Alfie" and "What the World Needs Now"), Bacharach gained acclaim for his work on *Butch Cassidy and the Sundance Kid* (1969), which included the infectious "Raindrops Keep Falling on My Head" and as the composer of catchy, syncopated pop songs for Dionne Warwick and Jack Jones during the 1960s and 70s. Bacharach established himself as a popular solo performer and continued his prolific career into the 80s, making distinguished contributions to such films as *Arthur* (1981) while his pop standards ("Wives and Lovers," "Baby, It's You," "The Look of Love," "Close to You," etc.) continue to be used in countless films. • *Lizzie* 1956 (song); *The Sad Sack* 1957 (song); *The Blob* 1958 (song); *Country Music Holiday* 1958 (song); *What's New, Pussycat?* 1965 (m,song) **(AANBS)**; *After the Fox* 1966 (m); *Alfie* 1966 (song) **(AANBS)**; *Promise Her Anything* 1966 (song); *Casino Royale* 1967 (m) **(AANBS)**; *The April Fools* 1969 (song); *Bob & Carol & Ted & Alice* 1969 (song); *Butch Cassidy and the Sundance Kid* 1969 (m,m.dir,m) **(AABM,AABS)**; *Something Big* 1971 (m); *Lost Horizon* 1973 (m,m.cond); *Arthur* 1981 (m,song) **(AABS)**; *Night Shift* 1982 (m,song); *Best Defense* 1984 (m,song); *Arthur 2 on the Rocks* 1988 (m,songs).

Bachelet, Jean • Director of photography • Born Azans, France, October 8, 1894. Former newsreel photographer who moved on to features with Jean Renoir's first film *La Fille de l'eau* (1924). Subsequently shot many of the director's classics. • *La Fille de l'eau* 1924; *Nana* 1926; *Charleston (short)* 1927; *La Petite marchande d'allumettes* 1928; *Tire-au-Flanc* 1928; *L'Arlésienne* 1930; *La Petite Lise* 1930; *Crainquebille* 1934; *Madame Bovary* 1934; *Sans Famille* 1934; *Les Bas-Fonds/The Lower Depths* 1936; *Le Crime de Monsieur Lange* 1936; *La Règle du jeu/The Rules of the Game* 1939; *Nous les Gosses* 1941; *Tire-au-Flanc* 1950; *Les Mains Sales* 1951; *La Rue des Bouches peintes* 1955.

Bacon, Kevin • Actor • Born Philadelphia, PA, July 8, 1958. *Educ.* Manning Street Actor's Theatre, Philadelphia. Talented performer from the New York stage who came to attention as the confused rich kid with a drinking problem in *Diner* (1982), and established himself in *Footloose* (1984), his first featured role. Alternating between the stage and screen, Bacon has proved equally adept at comedy and drama; he was memorable as the overwrought yuppie dad in the contemporary comedy, *She's Having a Baby* (1988), and as the young filmmaker in the underrated satire, *The Big Picture* (1989). Married to actress Kyra Sedgwick. • *National Lampoon's Animal House* 1978; *Starting Over* 1979; *Friday the 13th* 1980; *Hero at Large* 1980; *Forty Deuce* 1981; *Only When I Laugh* 1981; *Diner* 1982; *Enormous Changes at the Last Minute* 1983; *Footloose* 1984; *Quicksilver* 1986; *End of the Line* 1987; *Planes, Trains and Automobiles* 1987; *White Water Summer* 1987; *Criminal Law* 1988; *She's Having a Baby* 1988; *The Big Picture* 1989; *Flatliners* 1990; *Tremors* 1990; *He Said, She Said* 1991; *Queens Logic* 1991.

Baddeley, Hermione • Actress; also comedienne. • Born Hermione Clinton-Baddeley, Broseley, England, November 13, 1906; died August 19, 1986, Los Angeles, CA. *Educ.* Margaret Morris School of Dance and Drama. Celebrated star of the English and American stage, in films since 1928, and best know to younger audiences as the sodden, cynical and very funny Mrs. Naugatuck on the TV series "Maude".

• *Dear Mr. Prohack* 1949; *Passport to Pimlico* 1949; *A Christmas Carol* 1951; *Tom Brown's Schooldays* 1951; *The Pickwick Papers* 1952; *Women Without Men* 1956; *Room at the Top* 1958 **(AANBSA)**; *Jet Storm* 1959; *Midnight Lace* 1960; *Mary Poppins* 1964; *The Unsinkable Molly Brown* 1964; *Do Not Disturb* 1965; *Harlow* 1965; *Marriage on the Rocks* 1965; *The Adventures of Bullwhip Griffin* 1967; *Happiest Millionaire* 1967; *The Aristocats* 1970; *The Black Windmill* 1974; *Chomps* 1979; *There Goes the Bride* 1979; *The Secret of Nimh* 1982.

Badger, Clarence G. • Director • Born San Francisco, CA, June 8, 1880; died 1964. *Educ.* Boston Polytechnic Institute. Began his career in 1915 writing scripts for Allen Curtis and soon graduated to directing two-reel romantic comedies, starring Gloria Swanson and Bobby Vernon, for Mack Sennett. In 1918, Badger moved to Goldwyn and directed his first features, including several Will Rogers vehicles. He worked for various producers from the early 1920s, averaging three to four pictures a year and specializing in light romantic comedy. Badger's best known work is *It* (1927), adapted from the novel by Elinor Glyn and starring Clara Bow. • *Teddy at the Throttle* 1916 (d); *Day Dreams* 1918 (d); *The Floor Below* 1918 (d); *Friend Husband* 1918 (d); *The Kingdom of Youth* 1918 (d); *A Perfect Lady* 1918 (d); *The Venus Model* 1918 (d); *Almost a Husband* 1919 (d); *Daughter of Mine* 1919 (d); *Jubilo* 1919 (d); *Leave It to Susan* 1919 (d); *Sis Hopkins* 1919 (d); *Strictly Confidential* 1919 (d); *Through the Wrong Door* 1919 (d); *Cupid, the Cowpuncher* 1920 (d); *Honest Hutch* 1920 (d); *Jes' Call Me Jim* 1920 (d); *The Strange Boarder* 1920 (d); *Water, Water, Everywhere* 1920 (d); *Boys Will Be Boys* 1921 (d); *Doubling For Romeo* 1921 (d); *Guile of Women* 1921 (d); *A Poor Relation* 1921 (d); *An Unwilling Hero* 1921 (d); *The Dangerous Little Demon* 1922 (d); *Don't Get Personal* 1922 (d); *Quincy Adams Sawyer* 1922 (d); *The Man Alone* 1923 (sc,story); *Potash and Perlmutter* 1923 (d); *Red Lights* 1923 (d); *Your Friend and Mine* 1923 (d); *One Night in Rome* 1924 (d); *Painted People* 1924 (d); *The Shooting of Dan McGrew* 1924 (d); *Eve's Secret* 1925 (d); *The Golden Princess* 1925 (d); *New Lives For Old* 1925 (d); *Paths to Paradise* 1925 (d); *The Campus Flirt* 1926 (d); *Hands Up!* 1926 (d); *Miss Brewster's Millions* 1926 (d); *Rainmaker* 1926 (d); *It* 1927 (d); *Kiss in a Taxi* 1927 (d); *Man Power* 1927 (d); *Senorita* 1927 (d); *She's a Sheik* 1927 (d); *Swim, Girl, Swim* 1927 (d,p); *The Fifty-Fifty Girl* 1928 (d); *Hot News* 1928 (d); *Red Hair* 1928 (d); *Three Week-Ends* 1928 (d); *Paris* 1929 (d); *The Bad Man* 1930 (d); *Murder Will Out* 1930 (d); *No, No, Nanette* 1930 (d); *Sweethearts and Wives* 1930 (d); *The Hot Heiress* 1931 (d); *Party Husbands* 1931 (d); *Woman Hungry* 1931 (d); *When Strangers Marry* 1933 (d); *Rangle River* 1939 (d,p).

Badham, John • Director; also producer. • Born Luton, England, August 25, 1939. *Educ.* Yale; Yale School of Drama. After much TV work, Badham made his solo feature debut with *The Bingo Long Traveling All-Stars and Motor Kings* (1976), a film well ahead of its time, and achieved his major breakthrough with *Saturday Night Fever* (1977), one of the signature films of its decade.

A smooth director with an unobtrusive style, Badham has dealt with such topical social issues as euthanasia (*Whose Life Is It Anyway?* 1981) and nuclear strategy (*WarGames* 1983), though his more recent films have become increasingly escapist. His witty *Short Circuit* (1986) became a children's classic of the 1980s. • *Sunshine Part II* 1975 (d); *The Bingo Long Traveling All-Stars and Motor Kings* 1976 (d); *Saturday Night Fever* 1977 (d); *Dracula* 1979 (d); *Whose Life Is It Anyway?* 1981 (d); *Blue Thunder* 1983 (d); *WarGames* 1983 (d); *American Flyers* 1985 (d); *Short Circuit* 1986 (d); *Stakeout* 1987 (d,exec.p); *Disorganized Crime* 1989 (exec.p); *Bird on a Wire* 1990 (d); *The Hard Way* 1991 (d).

Baggot, King • Director, actor • Born St. Louis, MO, 1880; died July 11, 1948, Hollywood, CA. Rugged, handsome star of action and adventure movies who was among the first performers to be billed by name. Baggot later turned to directing, most impressively with *Tumbleweeds* (1925), starring cowboy star William S. Hart. He helmed his last film in 1928 and two years later resumed his acting career as a character player. • *Ivanhoe* 1913 (a); *An Oriental Romance* 1915 (a); *The Eagle's Eye* 1918 (a); *The Man Who Stayed at Home* 1919 (a); *The Cheater* 1920 (a); *The Hawk's Trail* 1920 (a); *The Butterfly Girl* 1921 (a); *Cheated Love* 1921 (d); *The Girl in the Taxi* 1921 (a); *Luring Lips* 1921 (d); *Moonlight Follies* 1921 (d); *Nobody's Fool* 1921 (d); *A Dangerous Game* 1922 (d); *Human Hearts* 1922 (d); *The Kentucky Derby* 1922 (d); *Kissed* 1922 (d); *The Lavender Bath Lady* 1922 (d); *Crossed Wires* 1923 (d,story); *The Darling of New York* 1923 (d,story); *Gossip* 1923 (d); *The Love Letter* 1923 (d); *The Thrill Chaser* 1923 (a); *The Town Scandal* 1923 (d); *The Gaiety Girl* 1924 (d); *The Tornado* 1924 (d); *The Whispered Name* 1924 (d); *The Home Maker* 1925 (d); *Raffles, the Amateur Cracksman* 1925 (d); *Tumbleweeds* 1925 (d); *Lovey Mary* 1926 (d); *Down the Stretch* 1927 (d); *The Notorious Lady* 1927 (d); *Perch of the Devil* 1927 (d); *The House of Scandal* 1928 (d); *Romance of a Rogue* 1928 (d); *The Czar of Broadway* 1930 (a); *Once a Gentleman* 1930 (a); *Scareheads* 1931 (a); *Sweepstakes* 1931 (a); *Afraid to Talk* 1932 (a); *Police Court* 1932 (a); *Father Brown, Detective* 1934 (a); *Chinatown Squad* 1935 (a); *It Happened in New York* 1935 (a); *Mississippi* 1935 (a); *Come Live With Me* 1941 (a).

Bailey, John • Director of photography • Born Moberly, MO, August 10, 1942. *Educ.* University of Santa Clara, CA; Loyola University, Chicago; USC Film School, Los Angeles; University of Vienna. Superior color cinematographer who has enjoyed multi-film associations with directors Lawrence Kasdan and Paul Schrader. With production designer Eiko Ishioka and composer Philip Glass, Bailey shared a prize at Cannes for best artistic contribution for his stunning work on Schrader's *Mishima: A Life in Four Chapters* (1985). • *Premonition* 1972 (ph); *End of August* 1974 (ph); *Legacy* 1975 (ph); *The Mafu Cage* 1978 (visual consultant); *Boulevard Nights* 1979 (ph); *The Riddle of the Sands* 1979 (sc); *Winter Kills* 1979 (add.ph,cam.op); *American Gigolo* 1980 (ph); *Ordinary People* 1980 (ph); *Continental Divide* 1981 (ph); *Honky Tonk Freeway* 1981 (ph); *Cat People* 1982 (ph); *That Championship Season* 1982 (ph); *The Big Chill* 1983 (ph); *Without a Trace* 1983 (ph); *The Pope of Greenwich Village* 1984 (ph); *Racing With the Moon* 1984 (ph); *Mishima: A Life in Four Chapters* 1985 (ph); *Silverado* 1985 (ph); *Brighton Beach Memoirs* 1986 (ph); *Crossroads* 1986 (ph); *Light of Day* 1987 (ph); *Swimming to Cambodia* 1987 (ph); *Tough Guys Don't Dance* 1987 (visual consultant); *The Accidental Tourist* 1988 (ph); *Vibes* 1988 (ph); *Hollywood Mavericks* 1990 (cam.op); *My Blue Heaven* 1990 (ph).

Bainter, Fay • Actress • Born Los Angeles, CA, December 7, 1892; died 1968. Broadway actress who made her screen debut in 1934 and, four years later, earned simultaneous Academy Award nominations for best supporting actress (*Jezebel*) and best actress (*White Banners* both 1938). Often in matriarchial roles, Banter was also acclaimed for *The Children's Hour* (1961), her last film Mother of actor Richard Venable. • *This Side of Heaven* 1934; *Make Way For Tomorrow* 1937; *Quality Street* 1937; *The Soldier and the Lady* 1937; *The Arkansas Traveler* 1938; *Jezebel* 1938 **(AABSA)**; *Mother Carey's Chickens* 1938; *The Shining Hour* 1938; *White Banners* 1938 **(AANBA)**; *Daughters Courageous* 1939; *The Lady and the Mob* 1939; *Our Neighbors, the Carters* 1939; *Yes, My Darling Daughter* 1939; *A Bill of Divorcement* 1940; *Maryland* 1940; *Our Town* 1940; *Young Tom Edison* 1940; *Babes on Broadway* 1941; *Journey For Margaret* 1942; *Mrs. Wiggs of the Cabbage Patch* 1942; *The War Against Mrs. Hadley* 1942; *Woman of the Year* 1942; *Cry Havoc* 1943; *The Heavenly Body* 1943; *The Human Comedy* 1943; *Presenting Lily Mars* 1943; *Salute to the Marines* 1943; *Dark Waters* 1944; *Three Is a Family* 1944; *State Fair* 1945; *The*

Kid From Brooklyn 1946; *The Virginian* 1946; *Deep Valley* 1947; *The Secret Life of Walter Mitty* 1947; *Give My Regards to Broadway* 1948; *June Bride* 1948; *Close to My Heart* 1951; *The President's Lady* 1953; *The Children's Hour* 1961 **(AANBSA)**.

Baker, Carroll • Actress • Born Johnstown, PA, May 28, 1931. *Educ.* St. Petersburg Junior College; Actors Studio. Talented former dancer, first cast in provocative roles such as *Baby Doll* (1956). After playing the title character in *Harlow* (1965), and starring in a string of European sexploitation movies, the possibility of transcending her earlier reputation as a screen sex kitten seemed to disappear.

In the 1980s Baker began appearing in more promising material (*Star '80* 1983, *Native Son* 1986), turning in a fine performance as Annie Phelan in *Ironweed* (1987). Married from 1955 to 1969 to Jack Garfein who directed her in *Something Wild* (1961). Mother of actress Blanche Baker. • *Easy to Love* 1953; *Baby Doll* 1956 **(AANBA)**; *Giant* 1956; *The Big Country* 1958; *But Not For Me* 1959; *The Miracle* 1959; *Bridge to the Sun* 1961; *Something Wild* 1961; *How the West Was Won* 1962; *The Carpetbaggers* 1964; *Cheyenne Autumn* 1964; *The Greatest Story Ever Told* 1965; *Harlow* 1965; *Mister Moses* 1965; *Sylvia* 1965; *Jack of Diamonds* 1967; *Orgasmo* 1968; *Captain Apache* 1971; *The Devil Has Seven Faces* 1974; *Andy Warhol's Bad* 1976; *La Moglie di mio padre* 1976; *The World Is Full of Married Men* 1979; *Watcher in the Woods* 1980; *Red Monarch* 1983; *Star 80* 1983; *The Secret Diary of Sigmund Freud* 1984; *Native Son* 1986; *Ironweed* 1987; *Kindergarten Cop* 1990.

Baker, Joe Don • Actor • Born Groesback, TX, February 12, 1936. *Educ.* North Texas State College, Denton; Actors Studio. Rugged, burly character actor with a deceptively benign Southern twang. Baker first came to attention as Steve McQueen's wheeler-dealer brother in Sam Peckinpah's *Junior Bonner* (1972), and is equally memorable as the avenging sheriff, Buford Pusser, in *Walking Tall* (1973). • *Guns of the Magnificent Seven* 1969; *Adam at 6 A.M.* 1970; *Welcome Home, Soldier Boys* 1971; *Wild Rovers* 1971; *Junior Bonner* 1972; *Charley Varrick* 1973; *The Outfit* 1973; *Walking Tall* 1973; *Golden Needles* 1974; *Framed* 1975; *Mitchell* 1975; *Crash* 1976; *Checkered Flag or Crash* 1977; *The Pack* 1977; *Speedtrap* 1977; *Wishbone Cutter* 1978; *Joysticks* 1982; *Wacko* 1983; *The Natural* 1984; *Final Justice* 1985; *Fletch* 1985; *Getting Even* 1986; *The Killing Time* 1987; *Leonard, Part 6* 1987; *The Living Daylights* 1987; *Criminal Law* 1988; *The Children* 1990.

Baker, Josephine • Singer; also entertainer. • Born St. Louis, MO, June 3, 1906; died 1975. Child performer of the Harlem stage who graduated to Broadway and then conquered Europe with her effervescent—and mildly salacious—music hall act. At the peak of her success and popularity (she was for a time the highest-paid entertainer on the continent), Baker appeared in a series of films, including a silent short (*La folie du jour* 1927, her debut), two silent features and several sound films. Of the latter the stand-out is *Zouzou* (1934), in which she starred opposite Jean Gabin and which was superbly directed by Marc Allégret.

The year 1989 saw a resurgence of interest in the expatriate star, largely fueled by the publication of two biographies: *Jazz Cleopatra* by Phyllis Rose and *Josephine Baker* by Patrick O'Connor. • *La folie du jour* 1927; *Zouzou* 1934; *Princess Tam Tam* 1935.

Baker, Kathy • Actress • Born Kathy Whitton Baker, Midland, TX, June 8, 1950. *Educ.* California Institute of the Arts (acting); University of California, Berkeley (French); Cordon Bleu, France. Fetching, versatile actress who began her career at age ten, dropped out of the acting program at college, and went to France for several years to study the fine art of *haute cuisine*. After returning to the US, Baker won an Obie award as May in Sam Shepard's *Fool for Love* (1983) and garnered acclaim for her big screen dramatic performances opposite Michael Keaton (*Clean and Sober* 1988) and Robert DeNiro (*Jacknife* 1989). • *The Right Stuff* 1983; *A Killing Affair* 1986; *My Sister's Keeper* 1986; *Street Smart* 1987 (AANBSA); *Clean and Sober* 1988; *Permanent Record* 1988; *Dad* 1989; *Jacknife* 1989; *Edward Scissorhands* 1990; *Mister Frost* 1990.

Baker, Rick • *aka* Richard Baker • Special effects makeup artist; also actor. • Born Richard A. Baker, Binghamton, NY, December 8, 1950. The man behind the men and women of numerous faces and often the man in the mask himself. Baker worked his way up from chief lab assistant for makeup artist Dick Smith to be a puppet designer and made his debut as a special effects makeup artist in 1972. He has conjured everything from werewolves (*An American Werewolf in London* 1981) to a remarkably convincing reproduction of old age (*The Autobiography of Miss Jane Pittman* 1974). Baker often makes film appearances camouflaged by his own makeup, most often as gorillas (*The Thing With Two Heads* 1972, the title role in *King Kong* 1976, *The Kentucky Fried Movie* 1977 and *The Incredible Shrinking Woman* 1981). He also designed the special effects makeup for, and appeared in, Michael Jackson's "Thriller" video. • *The Thing With Two Heads* 1972 (a); *King Kong* 1976 (tech.ad); *The Zebra Force* 1976 (makeup); *The Incredible Melting Man* 1977 (makeup); *The Kentucky Fried Movie* 1977 (a); *Star Wars* 1977 (makeup 2u); *It's Alive 2* 1978 (makeup); *The Double McGuffin* 1979 (story); *The Howling* 1980 (makeup consultant); *Madhouse* 1980 (a); *Tanya's Island* 1980 (beast design); *An American Werewolf in London* 1981 (makeup) **(AAMAKE-UP)**; *The Funhouse* 1981 (makeup); *The Incredible Shrinking Woman* 1981 (a,design "Sidney"); *Making Michael Jackson's Thriller* 1983 (makeup); *Videodrome* 1983 (makeup); *Greystoke: The Legend of Tarzan, Lord of the Apes* 1984 (cost.design,makeup) **(AANMAKE-UP)**; *Starman* 1984 (Starman transformation); *Cocoon* 1985 (consultant); *Into the Night* 1985 (a); *My Science Project* 1985 (Tyrannosaurus Rex sequence consultant); *Teen Wolf* 1985 (a); *Max mon amour* 1986 (chimpanzee consultant); *Ratboy* 1986 (Ratboy design); *Harry and the Hendersons* 1987 (monster designer—"Harry") **(AAMAKE-UP)**; *It's Alive III: Island of the Alive* 1987 (baby design); *Coming to America* 1988 (makeup) **(AANMAKE-UP)**; *Gorillas in the Mist* 1988 (assoc.p,makeup); *Moonwalker* 1988 (makeup); *Missing Link* 1989 (makeup); *Gremlins 2: The New Batch* 1990 (p,fx sup).

Baker, Roy Ward • *aka* Roy Baker • Director; also producer. • Born London, 1916. *Educ.* City of London School. Veteran British director who crafted several fine films in the 1950s, notably the superior tale of the Titanic, *A Night to Remember* (1958). A superior stylist who uses imaginative editing to heighten suspense, Baker hit a critical peak in the 1960s with such varied fare as the offbeat western *The Singer Not the Song* (1960) and the sci-fi favorite, *Quatermass and the Pit/Five Million Years to Earth* (1967). He turned to TV in the mid-1960s, directing episodes of "Danger Man," "The Saint" and "The Avengers." • *The October Man* 1947; *Highly Dangerous* 1950; *I'll Never Forget You* 1951; *Don't Bother to Knock* 1952; *Night Without Sleep* 1952; *Inferno* 1953; *Passage Home* 1955; *A Night to Remember* 1958; *The One That Got Away* 1958; *The Singer Not the Song* 1960; *Two Left Feet* 1963; *The Anniversary* 1967; *The Scars of Dracula* 1970; *The Vampire Lovers* 1970; *Dr Jekyll & Sister Hyde* 1971; *Dr. Jekyll and Sister Hyde* 1971; *Asylum* 1972; *And Now the Screaming Starts* 1973; *The Vault of Horror* 1973; *Dracula and the 7 Golden Vampires* 1975; *The Monster Club* 1981.

Baker, Sir Stanley • Actor; also producer. • Born Ferndale, Rhondda Valley, Wales, February 8, 1927; died June 28, 1976. Commanding Welsh leading man who began his career as a teen in 1943 and throughout the 1950s bristled through a series of British actioners and crime thrillers of uneven merit, playing tough villains and criminals. *The Cruel*

Sea (1953) established Baker as a screen presence and won him a long-term Rank contract. In the late 50s and early 60s he broke out of his typecasting in several exceptional films by both Cy Endfield and Joseph Losey (*Blind Date* 1959, *Accident* 1967) and co-produced several of his own films. He was knighted in 1976, just before his death. • *Undercover* 1943 (a); *All Over the Town* 1949 (a); *Captain Horatio Hornblower* 1951 (a); *The Cruel Sea* 1953 (a); *Knights of the Round Table* 1953 (a); *The Red Beret* 1953 (a); *The Beautiful Stranger* 1954 (a); *The Good Die Young* 1954 (a); *Hell Below Zero* 1954 (a); *Richard III* 1955 (a); *Alexander the Great* 1956 (a); *Child in the House* 1956 (a); *Helen of Troy* 1956 (a); *A Hill in Korea* 1956 (a); *Hell Divers* 1957 (a); *Campbell's Kingdom* 1958 (a); *Sea Fury* 1958 (a); *The Angry Hills* 1959 (a); *Blind Date* 1959 (a); *Jet Storm* 1959 (a); *Yesterday's Enemy* 1959 (a); *The Criminal* 1960 (a); *The Guns of Navarone* 1961 (a); *Eva* 1962 (a); *A Prize of Arms* 1962 (a); *Sodoma e Gomorra/Sodom and Gomorrah* 1962 (a); *A la Française* 1963 (a); *Zulu* 1963 (a,p); *Sands of the Kalahari* 1965 (a,p); *Accident* 1967 (a); *Robbery* 1967 (a,p); *The Italian Job* 1969 (a); *Where's Jack?* 1969 (a,p); *The Games* 1970 (a); *The Last Grenade* 1970 (a); *Perfect Friday* 1970 (a); *Popsy Pop* 1970 (a); *Una Lucertola con la Pelle di Donna* 1971 (a); *Innocent Bystanders* 1972 (a); *Orzowei* 1975 (a); *Zorro* 1975 (a); *Petita Jimenez* 1976 (a).

Bakshi, Ralph • Animation director, screenwriter; also producer. • Born Haifa, Palestine, October 26, 1938. From the sexually explicit *Fritz the Cat* (1972) to the racially controversial *Coonskin* (1975) and the historically conscious music-history saga, *American Pop* (1981), Bakshi's animated features are anything but escapist fantasies. Adult fare, his films are all the more effective because they tackle issues not usually associated with cartoons.

With *Heavy Traffic* (1973), Bakshi intercut animation with live action sequences and with his fantasy films, *Wizards* (1977) and *Lord of the Rings* (1978), he pioneered in the use of rotoscoping, the tracing of live-action figures to create a new realism in animation. Bakshi has also encountered controversy and plaudits for his Saturday morning cartoon series, "Mighty Mouse: The New Adventures" (1987-89). • *Fritz the Cat* 1972 (adapt,d); *Heavy Traffic* 1973 (d,sc); *Coonskin* 1975 (d,sc,stills); *Wizards* 1977 (d,p,sc); *The Lord of the Rings* 1978 (d); *American Pop* 1981 (d,p); *Hey, Good Lookin'* 1982 (d,p,sc); *Cannonball Run II* 1983 (animation sequences); *Fire and Ice* 1983 (d,from characters,p).

Balaban, Bob • Actor; also director. • Born Robert Balaban, Chicago, IL, August 16, 1945. *Educ.* Colgate University, Hamilton, NY; NYU (film). Diminutive supporting player who began working with Chicago's Second City troupe while still in high school. Although he has played a range of roles, Balaban is at his best as unsympathetic bureaucratic types. He has directed for the stage (e.g. *Girls, Girls, Girls* at the New York Shakespeare Festival in 1980) and TV ("Tales From the Darkside" 1983, etc.) and made his feature directorial debut with the stylish, overlooked black comedy, *Parents* (1989). Cousin of director Burt Balaban and nephew of the late studio head Barney Balaban. • *Me, Natalie* 1969 (a); *Midnight Cowboy* 1969 (a); *Catch-22* 1970 (a); *Making It* 1970 (a); *Report to the Commissioner* 1975 (a); *Close Encounters of the Third Kind* 1977 (a); *Girlfriends* 1978 (a); *First Love* 1979 (a); *Altered States* 1980 (a); *Absence of Malice* 1981 (a); *Prince of the City* 1981 (a); *Whose Life Is It Anyway?* 1981 (a); *2010* 1984 (a); *In Our Hands* 1984 (a); *End of the Line* 1987 (a); *Funny* 1988 (a); *Dead-Bang* 1989 (a); *Parents* 1989 (d); *Alice* 1990 (a).

Balasko, Josiane • Actress; also director, screenwriter. • Born Paris, 1950. Writer and performer with the Parisian theater group "Splendid" who initiated her popular screen career in 1976. Balasko directed her first feature, *All Mixed Up*, in 1985 and is best known to international audiences as the emotionally satisfying, but physically unattractive, mistress of Gérard Depardieu in Bertrand Blier's *Too Beautiful For You* (1989). • *Une Fille Unique* 1976 (a); *Le Locataire/The Tenant* 1976 (a); *Dites-lui que je l'aime* 1977 (a); *Nous irons tous au paradis* 1977 (a); *Pauline et l'Ordinateur* 1977 (a,dial); *Les Bronzes* 1978 (a); *Les Héros n'ont pas froid aux oreilles* 1978 (a); *Les Petits calins* 1978 (a); *Les Bronzes font du Ski* 1979 (a); *Retour en force* 1980 (sc); *Les Hommes préfèrent les grosses* 1981 (a,sc); *Hôtel des Amériques* 1982 (a); *Le Père Noël est une Ordur* 1982 (a,sc); *Papy Fait de la Résistance* 1983 (a); *Signes Extérieurs de Richesse* 1983 (a); *Petit Con* 1984 (a); *La Smala* 1984 (a); *Tranches de Vie* 1984 (a); *Le Vengeance du serpent à plumes* 1984 (a); *Sac de Noeuds/All Mixed Up* 1985 (a,d,sc); *Les Frères Pétard* 1986 (a); *Nuit d'ivresse* 1986 (a,sc,from play); *Les Keufs* 1987 (a,d,exec.p,sc.adapt,dial); *Sans peur et sans reproche* 1988 (a); *Trop belle pour toi/Too Beautiful For You* 1989 (a); *Doctor Apfelgluck* 1991 (a).

Balázs, Béla • Theoretician, screenwriter; also poet, director. • Born Herbert Bauer, Szeged, Hungary, August 4, 1884; died 1949. Wrote and directed several films but is best known for his theoretical tomes, *The Visible Man* (1924) and *Theory of the Film* (1945). Balász championed the new medium, stressing its purely visual capacity and its ability to reveal human emotions through subtle physical gestures. • *Das Mädchen Mit den Fünf Nullen* 1927 (sc); *Die Dreigroschenoper/The Threepenny Opera* 1931 (sc.adapt); *Almodo Ifjusag* 1974 (from novel); *Modre Z Nebe* 1983 (from book).

Balcon, Sir Michael • Producer; also distributor. • Born Michael Balcon, Birmingham, England, May 19, 1896; died 1977. Influential production executive who gave Alfred Hitchcock his first solo directing job (*The Pleasure Garden* 1925) and later founded Gainsborough Pictures, which produced many of Hitchcock's early classics as well as Robert Flaherty's *Man of Aran* (1933). He also headed Gaumont-British, MGM-British and Ealing Studios. Father of former actress Jill Balcon, whose son is actor Daniel Day-Lewis. • *The White Shadow* 1923 (p); *Woman to Woman* 1923 (p); *The Passionate Adventure* 1924 (p); *The Pleasure Garden* 1925 (p); *The Lodger* 1926 (p); *The Mountain Eagle* 1926 (p); *Downhill* 1927 (p); *Easy Virtue* 1927 (p); *The Ghost Train* 1927 (p,p); *Aunt Sally* 1933 (p); *Falling For You* 1933 (p); *It's a Boy* 1933 (p); *Sleeping Car* 1933 (p); *Soldiers of the King* 1933 (p); *The Camels Are Coming* 1934 (p); *Jew Süss* 1934 (p); *The Man Who Knew Too Much* 1934 (p); *Man of Aran* 1934 (p); *The 39 Steps* 1935 (p); *Things Are Looking Up* 1935 (p); *Everybody Dance* 1936 (p); *Good Morning, Boys* 1936 (p); *Jack of All Trades* 1936 (p); *The Man Who Lived Again* 1936 (p); *Sabotage* 1936 (p); *Secret Agent* 1936 (p); *Windbag the Sailor* 1936 (p); *A Yank at Oxford* 1938 (p); *Convoy* 1940 (p); *Next of Kin* 1942 (p); *Undercover* 1943 (p); *Champagne Charlie* 1944 (p); *Dead of Night* 1945 (p); *Half-Way House* 1945 (p); *The Overlanders* 1946 (p); *Hue and Cry* 1947 (p); *Nicholas Nickleby* 1947 (p); *It Always Rains on Sunday* 1948 (p); *Saraband For Dead Lovers* 1948 (p); *Scott of the Antarctic* 1948 (p); *Kind Hearts and Coronets* 1949 (p); *Passport to Pimlico* 1949 (p); *Whisky Galore* 1949 (p); *The Blue Lamp* 1950 (p); *The Man in the White Suit* 1951 (p); *The Lavender Hill Mob* 1952 (p); *The Cruel Sea* 1953 (p); *The Square Ring* 1953 (exec.p); *The Divided Heart* 1954 (p); *Lease of Life* 1954 (p); *The Feminine Touch* 1955 (p); *The Ladykillers* 1955 (p); *All at Sea* 1957 (p); *Dunkirk* 1958 (p); *The Scapegoat* 1959 (p); *Sammy Going South* 1963 (exec.p); *Tom Jones* 1963 (exec.p).

Baldwin, Alec • Actor • Born Amityville, NY, April 3, 1958. *Educ.* George Washington University, Washington, DC (political science); NYU (drama); Lee Strasberg Institute, New York. Versatile, handsome lead who first came to attention in the TV series "Knots Landing." A conscientious screen performer, Baldwin has proved equally adept at comedy (*Married to the Mob* 1988) and drama (*The Hunt For Red October* 1990); he also turned in bravura performances on Broadway as a slick corporate raider in Caryl Churchill's antic satire, *Serious Money*, and off-Broadway as a befuddled newlywed in Craig Lucas's comic fairy tale, *Prelude To A Kiss*. Brother of actor William Baldwin. • *Forever, Lulu* 1986; *Beetlejuice* 1988; *Married to the Mob* 1988; *She's Having a Baby* 1988; *Talk Radio* 1988; *Working Girl* 1988; *Great Balls of Fire* 1989; *Alice* 1990; *The Hunt For Red October* 1990; *Miami Blues* 1990; *The Marrying Man* 1991.

Ball, Lucille • Actress • Born Lucille Desiree Ball, Celeron, NY, August 6, 1911; died April 26, 1989, Los Angeles, CA. *Educ.* John Murray Anderson-Robert Milton Drama School, New York. Carrot-topped, husky-voiced and rubber-faced clown; one of America's most beloved TV comediennes and one of Hollywood's most astute businesswomen. After failing to crash into show business on the New York stage in the late 1920s, Ball began her Hollywood career in 1933 in walk-on and bit parts and then as a glamorous Goldwyn showgirl in Eddie Cantor musicals.

Finally winning some notice as a tough, aspiring actress in *Stage Door* (1937), in the 40s Ball proved adept at playing jaded sophisticates in the college musicals *Too Many Girls* (1940) and *Best Foot Forward* (1943) and excelled as a hard-hearted nightclub star in the Damon Runyon melodrama-fable, *The Big Street* (1942). Signing with MGM, she starred in film versions of hit Broadway musicals, often opposite Bob Hope or Red Skelton, but never achieved true stardom and turned her attention to radio in the late 40s.

After the success of her CBS radio show, "My Favorite Husband" (1947-51), in which she played a wacky housewife, the network asked her to develop a TV comedy series. She and Cuban bandleader/husband Desi Arnaz (married 1940-1960) responded by creating "I Love Lucy," an instant success which quickly became the number one series on TV and ran from 1951 to 1957. Innovative for being filmed (in front of a live audience) when all other comedies were broadcast live, the shows were also a goldmine since Ball and Arnaz wisely owned all the rights to the films after the initial broadcast and racked up profits from syndication rights for reruns (unheard of in the early 1950s). The show was reincarnated as a series of specials, "Lucy-Desi Comedy Hour" (1957-60).

Her success was equally great when she went solo (taking her stock company of TV regulars with her) on "The Lucy Show" (1962-68) and "Here's Lucy" (1968-74). Ball earned four Emmy Awards and a further nine nominations, and was awarded the Kennedy Center Honors in 1986. Her second husband was comedian-manager Gary Morton. Mother of Lucie Arnaz and Desi Arnaz, Jr. • *Carnival* 1935; *I Dream Too Much* 1935; *Bunker Bean* 1936; *Chatterbox* 1936; *The Farmer in the Dell* 1936; *Follow the Fleet* 1936; *That Girl From Paris* 1936; *Don't Tell the Wife* 1937; *Stage Door* 1937; *The Affairs of Annabel* 1938; *Annabel Takes a Tour* 1938; *Go Chase Yourself* 1938; *Having Wonderful Time* 1938; *Joy of Living* 1938; *Next Time I Marry* 1938; *Room Service* 1938; *Beauty For the Asking* 1939; *Five Came Back* 1939; *Panama Lady* 1939; *That's Right, You're Wrong* 1939; *Twelve Crowded Hours* 1939; *Dance, Girl, Dance* 1940; *The Marines Fly High* 1940; *Too Many Girls* 1940; *You Can't Fool Your Wife* 1940; *A Girl, a Guy and a Gob* 1941; *Look Who's Laughing* 1941; *The Big Street* 1942; *Seven Days Leave* 1942; *Valley of the Sun* 1942; *Best Foot Forward* 1943; *Du Barry Was a Lady* 1943; *Thousands Cheer* 1943; *Meet the People* 1944; *Without Love* 1945; *Easy to Wed* 1946; *Lover Come Back* 1946; *Two Smart People* 1946; *Ziegfeld Follies* 1946; *Her Husband's Affairs* 1947; *Lured* 1947; *Easy Living* 1949; *Miss Grant Takes Richmond* 1949; *Sorrowful Jones* 1949; *Fancy Pants* 1950; *The Fuller Brush Girl* 1950; *The Magic Carpet* 1951; *The Long, Long Trailer* 1954; *Forever, Darling* 1956; *The Facts of Life* 1960; *Critic's Choice* 1963; *A Guide For the Married Man* 1967; *Yours, Mine and Ours* 1968; *Mame* 1974; *Entertaining the Troops* 1989.

Ballard, Carroll • Director • Born Los Angeles, CA, October 14, 1937. *Educ.* UCLA (film). Aside from the lush, stirring *The Black Stallion* (1979) and the intriguing nature tale, *Never Cry Wolf* (1983), Ballard's output has been disappointingly sparse. • *Harvest* 1967 (p); *Star Wars* 1977 (cam.op); *The Black Stallion* 1979 (d); *Never Cry Wolf* 1983 (d); *Nutcracker: The Motion Picture* 1986 (d).

Ballard, Lucien • Director of photography • Born Miami, OK, May 6, 1908; died October 1, 1988, Rancho Mirage, CA. *Educ.* University of Oklahoma; University of Pennsylvania, Philadelphia. Highly distinguished and versatile cinematographer of several black-and-white classics who began his career as an editor and assistant cameraman with Paramount. After working as secondary photographer of both *Morocco* (1930) and *The Devil Is a Woman* (1935), Ballard was moved to the front ranks for the third of his four collaborations with Josef von Sternberg, *Crime and Punishment* (1935). He then worked on numerous second-echelon Columbia films during the late 1930s and early 40s. Ballard came into his own as an acclaimed black-and-white cinematographer with Stanley Kubrick's *The Killing* (1956) and as a specialist in lush, outdoor color for the action and Western films of Henry Hathaway, Sam Peckinpah and Budd Boetticher with whom he worked multiple times. He also shot several films starring Merle Oberon, to whom he was married from 1945 to 1949. • *Morocco* 1930 (add.ph); *Crime and Punishment* 1935 (ph); *The Devil Is a Woman* 1935 (add.ph); *Times Square Lady* 1935 (p); *Craig's Wife* 1936 (ph); *The King Steps Out* 1936 (ph); *Devil's Playground* 1937 (ph); *Girls Can Play* 1937 (ph); *I Promise to Pay* 1937 (ph); *Racketeers in Exile* 1937 (ph); *The Shadow* 1937 (ph); *Venus Makes Trouble* 1937 (ph); *Flight to Fame* 1938 (ph); *Highway Patrol* 1938 (ph); *The Lone Wolf in Paris* 1938 (ph); *Penitentiary* 1938 (ph); *Blind Alley* 1939 (ph); *Coast Guard* 1939 (ph); *Let Us Live* 1939 (ph); *The Villain Still Pursued Her* 1940 (ph); *Wild Geese Calling* 1941 (ph); *Orchestra Wives* 1942 (ph); *The Undying Monster* 1942 (ph); *Whispering Ghosts* 1942 (ph); *Bomber's Moon* 1943 (ph); *Holy Matrimony* 1943 (ph); *Tonight We Raid Calais* 1943 (ph); *The Lodger* 1944 (ph); *Sweet and Low Down* 1944 (ph); *This Love of Ours* 1945 (ph); *Temptation* 1946 (ph); *Night Song* 1947 (ph); *Berlin Express* 1948 (ph); *Fixed Bayonets* 1951 (ph); *The House on Telegraph Hill* 1951 (ph); *Let's Make It Legal* 1951 (ph); *Diplomatic Courier* 1952 (ph); *Don't Bother to Knock* 1952 (ph); *Night Without Sleep* 1952 (ph); *O. Henry's Full House* 1952 (ph); *Return of the Texan* 1952 (ph); *The Desert Rats* 1953 (ph); *The Glory Brigade* 1953 (ph); *Inferno* 1953 (ph); *New Faces* 1954 (ph); *Prince Valiant* 1954 (ph); *The Raid* 1954 (ph); *The Killer Is Loose* 1955 (ph); *The Magnificent Matador* 1955 (ph); *Seven Cities of Gold* 1955 (ph); *White Feather* 1955 (ph); *The Killing* 1956 (ph); *A Kiss Before Dying* 1956 (ph); *The Proud Ones* 1956 (ph); *Band of Angels* 1957 (ph); *I Married a Woman* 1957 (ph); *The Unholy Wife* 1957 (ph); *Anna Lucasta* 1958 (ph); *Buchanan Rides Alone* 1958 (ph); *City of Fear* 1958 (ph); *Murder By Contract* 1958 (ph); *Al Capone* 1959 (ph); *The Bramble Bush* 1960 (ph); *Desire in the Dust* 1960 (ph); *Pay or Die* 1960 (ph); *The Rise and Fall of Legs Diamond* 1960 (ph); *Marines, Let's Go* 1961 (ph); *The Parent Trap* 1961 (ph); *Susan Slade* 1961 (ph); *Ride the High Country* 1962 (ph); *The Caretakers* 1963 (ph) **(AANBPH)**; *Take Her, She's Mine* 1963 (ph); *Wall of Noise* 1963 (ph); *Wives and Lovers* 1963 (ph); *The New Interns* 1964 (ph); *Roustabout* 1964 (ph); *Boeing Boeing* 1965 (ph); *Dear Brigitte* 1965 (ph); *The Sons of Katie Elder* 1965 (ph); *An Eye For an Eye* 1966 (ph); *Nevada Smith* 1966 (ph); *Hour of the Gun* 1967 (ph); *How Sweet It Is* 1968 (ph); *The Party* 1968 (ph); *Will Penny* 1968 (ph); *True Grit* 1969 (ph); *The Wild Bunch* 1969 (ph); *The Ballad of Cable Hogue* 1970 (ph); *Elvis That's the Way It Is* 1970 (ph); *The Hawaiians* 1970 (ph); *Arruza* 1971 (ph); *A Time For Dying* 1971 (ph); *What's The Matter With Helen?* 1971 (ph); *The Get-*

away 1972 (ph); *Junior Bonner* 1972 (ph); *Lady Ice* 1973 (ph); *Thomasine & Bushrod* 1974 (ph); *Three the Hard Way* 1974 (ph); *Breakheart Pass* 1975 (ph); *Breakout* 1975 (ph); *Drum* 1976 (ph); *From Noon Till Three* 1976 (ph); *Mikey and Nicky* 1976 (end sequence ph); *St. Ives* 1976 (ph); *Rabbit Test* 1978 (ph).

Ballhaus, Michael • Director of photography • Born Berlin, August 5, 1935. Distinguished cinematographer who developed an interest in film after a relative, director Max Ophuls, allowed him to watch the filming of *Lola Montès* (1955). In 1970 Ballhaus shot the first of some 15 films for R.W. Fassbinder, before moving to the US in 1982. He has since worked with John Sayles, Volker Schlöndorff, Mike Nichols and—most notably—Martin Scorsese. • *Whity* 1970 (ph); *Sand* 1971 (ph); *Warnung Vor Einer Heiligen Nutte/Beware of a Holy Whore* 1971 (ph); *Die Bitteren Tränen der Petra von Kant/The Bitter Tears of Petra on Kant* 1972 (ph); *Tschetan, der Indianerjunge* 1973 (ph); *Martha* 1974 (ph); *Faustrecht der Freiheit/Fox and His Friends* 1975 (ph); *Mother Kusters Goes to Heaven* 1975 (ph); *Sommergäste* 1975 (ph); *Adolf & Marlene* 1976 (ph); *Also es war so...* 1976 (ph); *Chinesisches Roulette/Chinese Roulette* 1976 (ph); *Ich will doch nur, dass Ihr mich liebt/I Only Want You To Love Me* 1976 (ph); *Satansbraten/Satan's Brew* 1976 (ph); *Frauen in New York* 1977 (ph); *Bolwieser/The Stationmaster's Wife* 1978 (ph); *Despair* 1978 (ph); *Deutschland im Herbst/Germany in Autumn* 1978 (ph,cam.op); *Die Ehe der Maria Braun/The Marriage of Maria Braun* 1978 (a,ph); *Die Erste Polka* 1978 (ph); *Der Kleine Godard* 1978 (a); *Deutscher Frühling* 1979 (ph); *Kaleidoskop: Valeska Gert, Nur zum Spass-nur zum Spiel* 1979 (ph); *Der Aufstand/The Uprising* 1980 (ph); *Gross und Klein* 1980 (ph); *Malou* 1980 (ph); *Looping* 1981 (ph); *Dear Mr. Wonderful* 1982 (ph); *Heller Wahn* 1982 (ph); *Der Zauberberg* 1982 (ph); *Baby, It's You* 1983 (ph); *Edith's Tagebuch* 1983 (ph); *Aus der Familie der Panzereschen (short)* 1984 (ph); *Das Autogram* 1984 (ph); *Heartbreakers* 1984 (ph); *Old Enough* 1984 (ph); *Reckless* 1984 (ph); *After Hours* 1985 (ph); *Private Conversations* 1985 (a); *The Color of Money* 1986 (ph); *Under the Cherry Moon* 1986 (ph); *Broadcast News* 1987 (ph) **(AANBPH)**; *The Glass Menagerie* 1987 (ph); *Dirty Rotten Scoundrels* 1988 (ph); *The House on Carroll Street* 1988 (ph); *The Last Temptation of Christ* 1988 (ph); *Working Girl* 1988 (ph); *The Fabulous Baker Boys* 1989 (ph) **(AANBPH)**; *GoodFellas* 1990 (ph); *Postcards From the Edge* 1990 (ph); *Guilty By Suspicion* 1991 (ph); *What About Bob?* 1991 (ph).

Balsam, Martin • Actor • Born Bronx, NY, November 4, 1919. *Educ.* Dramatic Workshop of the New School for Social Research, New York; Actors Studio. Celebrated character player who entered films with *On the Waterfront* (1954), after considerable stage and TV experience. Particularly memorable in *Twelve Angry Men* (1957), as the doomed private dick Arbogast in *Psycho* (1960), and as the studio chief in *The Carpetbaggers* (1964). Since the mid-1970s Balsam has appeared mostly in TV. • *On the Waterfront* 1954; *Time Limit!* 1957; *Twelve Angry Men* 1957; *Marjorie Morningstar* 1958; *Al Capone* 1959; *Middle of the Night* 1959; *Psycho* 1960; *Ada* 1961; *Breakfast at Tiffany's* 1961; *Cape Fear* 1962; *Citta Prigioniera* 1962; *Who's Been Sleeping in My Bed?* 1963; *The Carpetbaggers* 1964; *Seven Days in May* 1964; *The Bedford Incident* 1965; *Harlow* 1965; *A Thousand Clowns* 1965 **(AABSA)**; *After the Fox* 1966; *Hombre* 1967; *The Good Guys and the Bad Guys* 1969; *Me, Natalie* 1969; *Trilogy* 1969; *Catch-22* 1970; *Little Big Man* 1970; *Tora! Tora! Tora!* 1970; *The Anderson Tapes* 1971; *Confessione di un Commissario di Polizia al Procuratore Della Repubblica* 1971; *The Man* 1972; *Il Consigliori* 1973; *The Stone Killer* 1973; *Summer Wishes, Winter Dreams* 1973; *Corruzione al Palazzo di Giustizia* 1974; *Murder on the Orient Express* 1974; *The Taking of Pelham 1, 2, 3* 1974; *Mitchell* 1975; *All the President's Men* 1976; *Two-Minute Warning* 1976; *The Sentinel* 1977; *Silver Bears* 1977; *Cuba* 1979; *The House on Garibaldi Street* 1979; *There Goes the Bride* 1979; *The Salamander* 1981; *Innocent Prey* 1983; *The Goodbye People* 1984; *Death Wish 3* 1985; *St. Elmo's Fire* 1985; *The Delta Force* 1986; *Whatever It Takes* 1986; *Private Investigations* 1987; *Two Evil Eyes* 1990.

Bancroft, Anne • *aka* Anne Marno • Actress • Born Anna Maria Louisa Italiano, Bronx, NY, September 17, 1931. *Educ.* AADA, New York; Actors Studio; AFI Woman's Directing Workshop. Intelligent, multi-award-winning performer who after considerable TV work went to Hollywood as a 20th Century-Fox starlet. Bancroft appeared in B features before returning to New York and making a name for herself as a serious Broadway actress in *Two For the Seesaw* (1958) and *The Miracle Worker* (1960). When she returned to Hollywood for the film version of the latter in 1962, Bancroft was in demand as a mature dramatic star of emotional depth as well as a deft comedienne, and she appeared in a string of popular and critical successes lasting through the 1980s. Standout Bancroft films include *The Graduate* (1967)—as the wealthy seductress Mrs. Robinson—*The Turning Point* (1977) and *Agnes of God* (1985). She made her directing and screenwriting debut with the 1979 comedy, *Fatso*. Married since 1964 to Mel Brooks with whom she co-starred in *Silent Movie* (1976) and *To Be or Not to Be* (1983). • *Don't Bother to Knock* 1952 (a); *The Kid From Left Field* 1953 (a); *Tonight We Sing* 1953 (a); *Treasure of the Golden Condor* 1953 (a); *Demetrius and the Gladiators* 1954 (a); *Gorilla at Large* 1954 (a); *The Raid* 1954 (a); *The Last Frontier* 1955 (a); *A Life in the Balance* 1955 (a); *The Naked Street* 1955 (a); *New York Confidential* 1955 (a); *Nightfall* 1956 (a); *Walk the Proud Land* 1956 (a); *The Girl in Black Stockings* 1957 (a); *The Restless Breed* 1957 (a); *The Miracle Worker* 1962 (a) **(AABA)**; *The Pumpkin Eater* 1964 (a) **(AANBA)**; *Seven Women* 1965 (a); *The Slender Thread* 1965 (a); *The Graduate* 1967 (a) **(AANBA)**; *Young Winston* 1972 (a); *The Prisoner of Second Avenue* 1974 (a); *The Hindenburg* 1975 (a); *Silent Movie* 1976 (a); *Lipstick* 1976 (a); *The Turning Point* 1977 (a,chor "Anna Karenina") **(AANBA)**; *Fatso* 1979 (a,d,sc); *The Elephant Man* 1980 (a); *To Be or Not to Be* 1983 (a,song); *Garbo Talks* 1984 (a); *Agnes of God* 1985 (a) **(AANBA)**; *'night, Mother* 1986 (a); *84 Charing Cross Road* 1986 (a); *Torch Song Trilogy* 1988 (a); *Bert Rigby, You're a Fool* 1989 (a).

Bancroft, George • Actor • Born Philadelphia, PA, September 30, 1882; died October 2, 1956, Santa Monica, CA. *Educ.* US Naval Academy, Annapolis, MD. Burly supporting player and unlikely romantic lead who entered film in the early 1920s and distinguished himself in several works by director Josef von Sternberg, notably the seminal gangster film *Underworld* (1927) and the brilliantly photographed *The Docks of New York* (1928). • *The Journey's End* 1921; *The Prodigal Judge* 1922; *Driven* 1923; *The Deadwood Coach* 1924; *Teeth* 1924; *Code of the West* 1925; *The Pony Express* 1925; *The Rainbow Trail* 1925; *The Splendid Road* 1925; *The Enchanted Hill* 1926; *Old Ironsides* 1926; *The Runaway* 1926; *Sea Horses* 1926; *The Rough Riders* 1927; *Tell It to Sweeney* 1927; *Too Many Crooks* 1927; *Underworld* 1927; *White Gold* 1927; *The Docks of New York* 1928; *The Dragnet* 1928; *The Showdown* 1928; *The Mighty* 1929; *Thunderbolt* 1929 **(AANBA)**; *The Wolf of Wall Street* 1929; *Derelict* 1930; *Ladies Love Brutes* 1930; *Paramount on Parade* 1930; *Rich Man's Folly* 1931; *Scandal Sheet* 1931; *Lady and Gent* 1932; *The World and the Flesh* 1932; *Blood Money* 1933; *Elmer and Elsie* 1934; *Hell-Ship Morgan* 1936; *Mr. Deeds Goes to Town* 1936; *Wedding Present* 1936; *A Doctor's Diary* 1937; *John Meade's Woman* 1937; *Racketeers in Exile* 1937; *Angels With Dirty Faces* 1938; *Submarine Patrol* 1938; *Each Dawn I Die* 1939; *Espionage Agent* 1939; *Rulers of the Sea* 1939; *Stagecoach* 1939; *Green Hell* 1940; *Little Men* 1940; *North West Mounted Police* 1940; *When the Daltons Rode* 1940; *Young Tom Edison* 1940; *The Bugle Sounds* 1941; *Texas* 1941; *Syncopation* 1942; *Whistling in Dixie* 1942.

Banderas, Antonio • Actor • Born Malaga, Spain, 1960. *Educ.* School of Dramatic Art, Malaga. Handsome leading man who first attracted international attention in the films of Pedro Almodóvar. Banderas has also appeared in more conventional dramas, including Carlos Saura's *The Stilts* (1984), Felix Rotaeta's gruesome and riveting *The Pleasure of Killing* (1987) and *Baton Rouge* (1988), directed by former Almodóvar assistant Rafaél Moleón. • *Laberinto de Pasiones/Labyrinth of Passion* 1982; *Pestañas Postizas* 1982; *El Señor Galindez* 1983; *El Caso Almería* 1984; *Los Zancos/The Stilts* 1984; *Casa Cerrado* 1985; *La Corte de Faraón* 1985; *Requiem por un Campesino Español* 1985; *27 Horas* 1986; *Matador* 1986; *Así Como Habían Sido* 1987; *La Ley del Deseo/The Law of Desire* 1987; *El Placér de Matar/The Pleasure of Killing* 1987; *Baton Rouge* 1988; *Mujeres al Borde de un Ataque de Nérvios/Women on the Verge of a Nervous Breakdown* 1988; *Si Te Dicen Que Caí* 1989; *Átame!/Tie Me Up! Tie Me Down!* 1990; *Contra el Viento* 1990.

Bankhead, Tallulah • Actress • Born Huntsville, AL, January 31, 1903; died December 12, 1968, New York, NY. Beauty queen turned stage star, who was far more famous for her tempestous personality than for her on-screen performances. Bankhead is best remembered for her deep, raspy, sultry voice, her theatrical habit of calling everyone "Daaahling," her spicy repartee and her flamboyant, hard-drinking, uninhibited lifestyle.

Bankhead was known as a compelling and colorful stage actress (*The Little Foxes* 1939, *The Skin of Our Teeth* 1943, *Private Lives* 1947) in both England and the US and excelled at playing sophisticated bitches. Her most memorable screen role, however, was as the indifferent journalist in Hitchcock's *Lifeboat* (1944), for which the New York Drama Critics named her best actress. In 1952 she penned *Tallulah, My Autobiography*. • *Thirty a Week* 1918; *When Men Betray* 1918; *His House in Order* 1928; *The Cheat* 1931; *My Sin* 1931; *Tarnished Lady* 1931; *The Devil and the Deep* 1932; *Faithless* 1932; *Make Me a Star* 1932; *Thunder Below* 1932; *Stage Door Canteen* 1943; *Lifeboat* 1944; *A Royal Scandal* 1945; *Main Street to Broadway* 1953; *Die! Die! My Darling!* 1965; *The Daydreamer* 1966.

Banks, Leslie • Actor • Born West Derby, England, June 9, 1890; died 1952. *Educ.* Oxford. Noted British stage performer who made an immediate impact in his first screen role, as the demented hunter in *The Most Dangerous Game* (1932); Banks also starred in Hitchcock's 1934 version of *The Man Who Knew Too Much*. • *The Most Dangerous Game* 1932; *I Am Suzanne* 1933; *Strange Evidence* 1933; *The Man Who Knew Too Much* 1934; *Sanders of the River* 1935; *Fire Over England* 1936; *Farewell Again* 1937; *Wings of the Morning* 1937; *Jamaica Inn* 1939; *Henry V* 1944; *Madeleine* 1950; *Your Witness* 1950.

Banky, Vilma • Actress • Born Vilma Lonchit, Nagyrodog, Hungary, January 9, 1898. European silent screen star brought to Hollywood by Sam Goldwyn in 1925 and publicized as "The Hungarian Rhapsody." Married to matinee idol Rod LaRoque from 1927 until his death in 1969. • *Im letzten Augenblick* 1920; *Das Auge des Toten* 1921; *Galathea* 1921; *Schattenkinder des Glücks* 1922; *Hotel Potemkin* 1924; *Das Schöne Abenteuer* 1924; *Das Verbotene Land* 1924; *Der Zirkuskönig* 1924; *Das Bildnis* 1925; *The Dark Angel* 1925; *The Eagle* 1925; *Soll man heiraten?* 1925; *The Son of the Sheik* 1926; *The Winning of Barbara Worth* 1926; *Magic Flame* 1927; *The Night of Love* 1927; *The Awakening* 1928; *Two Lovers* 1928; *This Is Heaven* 1929; *A Lady to Love* 1930; *Die Sehnsucht jeder Frau* 1930; *Der Rebell* 1932.

Bannen, Ian • Actor • Born Airdrie, Scotland, June 29, 1928. *Educ.* Ratcliffe College, Leicestershire. Supporting player and occasional lead of British and American films since 1956. Bannen has lately specialized in abrasive and even psychotic characterizations; he was memorable in *The Flight of the Phoenix* (1965) and more recently as the eccentric, cantankerous grandfather in John Boorman's war memoir, *Hope and Glory* (1987). • *Private's Progress* 1956; *Behind the Mask* 1958; *Macbeth* 1960; *Psyche '59* 1964; *The Flight of the Phoenix* 1965 **(AANBSA)**; *The Hill* 1965; *Mister Moses* 1965; *Penelope* 1966; *Lock Up Your Daughters!* 1969; *Too Late the Hero* 1970; *Fright* 1971; *La Spina Dorsale del Diavola* 1971; *The Mackintosh Man* 1973; *The Offence* 1973; *Identikit* 1974; *Il Viaggio* 1974; *Bite the Bullet* 1975; *Sweeney* 1976; *Watcher in the Woods* 1980; *Eye of the Needle* 1981; *Night Crossing* 1981; *Gandhi* 1982; *Gorky Park* 1983; *The Prodigal* 1983; *Defence of the Realm* 1985; *Lamb* 1985; *The Courier* 1987; *Hope and Glory* 1987; *George's Island* 1989; *Streghe* 1989; *The Big Man* 1990; *Ghost Dad* 1990.

Bara, Theda • Actress • Born Theodosia Goodman, Cincinnati, OH, 1890; died 1955. Voluptuous silent star whose fabricated exotic (and erotic) persona was an early product of the movie industry's publicity machine. • *Carmen* 1915 (a); *The Clemenceau Case* 1915 (a); *Destruction* 1915 (a); *The Devil's Daughter* 1915 (a); *A Fool There Was* 1915 (a); *The Galley Slave* 1915 (a); *Kreutzer Sonata* 1915 (a); *Lady Audley's Secret* 1915 (a); *Sin* 1915 (a); *The Two Orphans* 1915 (a); *East Lynne* 1916 (a); *The Eternal Sapho* 1916 (a); *Gold and the Woman* 1916 (a); *Her Double Life* 1916 (a); *Romeo and Juliet* 1916 (a); *The Serpent* 1916 (a); *Under Two Flags* 1916 (a); *The Vixen* 1916 (a); *Camille* 1917 (a); *Cleopatra* 1917 (a); *The Darling of Paris* 1917 (a); *Heart and Soul* 1917 (a); *Her Greatest Love* 1917 (a); *The Rose of Blood* 1917 (a); *The Tiger Woman* 1917 (a); *Madame Du Barry* 1918 (a); *Salome* 1918 (a); *The She-Devil* 1918 (a); *The Soul of Buddha* 1918 (a,story); *Under the Yoke* 1918 (a); *When a Woman Sins* 1918 (a); *La Belle Russe* 1919 (a); *Kathleen Mavourneen* 1919 (a); *The Light* 1919 (a); *The Lure of Ambition* 1919 (a); *The Siren's Song* 1919 (a); *When Men Desire* 1919 (a); *A Woman There Was* 1919 (a); *The Unchastened Woman* 1925 (a).

Barber, Frances • Actress • Born Wolverhampton, England, May 13, 1958. *Educ.* Bangor University, Gwynedd, Wales (English, drama); Cardiff University, South Glamorgan, Wales (theater). Barber has performed on stage and TV and in films by Peter Greenaway (*A Zed and Two Noughts* 1985) and Nicholas Roeg (*Castaway* 1986). Probably best known to US audiences as Rosie in Stephen Frears's *Sammy and Rosie Get Laid* (1987). • *The Missionary* 1981; *Acceptable Levels* 1983; *Those Glory Glory Days* 1983; *A Zed and Two Noughts* 1985; *Castaway* 1986; *Prick Up Your Ears* 1987; *Sammy and Rosie Get Laid* 1987; *We Think the World of You* 1988; *Chambre à part* 1989; *Duck (short)* 1989.

Barbera, Joseph • *aka* Joe Barbera • Animator; also producer. • Born Joseph R. Barbera, New York, NY, 1911. *Educ.* NYU; American Institute of Banking. Former magazine cartoonist who joined MGM in 1937 after an application to the Disney studios was unsuccessful. With fellow MGM employee William Hanna, Barbera earned a place in animation history by creating the ever-popular "Tom and Jerry" characters in 1940, producing more than 100 of the cat-and-mouse shorts over the next two decades.

Hanna and Barbera were appointed heads of the MGM cartoon department in 1955 and, when the department was cut two years later, left in order to set up Hanna-Barbera productions. The company was a huge success, turning out limited-animation series such as "The Flintstones" and "Yogi Bear" directly for TV.

The team re-entered the feature film market in 1990 with the release of the full-length animated film, *Jetsons: The Movie*. • *Yankee Doodle Mouse* 1943 (anim,p); *Mouse Trouble* 1944 (anim,p); *Quiet Please* 1945 (anim,p); *The Cat Concerto* 1946 (anim,p); *Kitty Foiled* 1947 (anim,p); *The Little Orphan* 1948 (anim,p); *Professor Tom* 1948 (anim,p); *Two Mouseketeers* 1951 (anim,p); *Johann Mouse* 1952 (anim,p); *Good Will to Men* 1955 (anim,p) **(AANBASF)**; *Mouse For Sale* 1955 (anim,p); *Invitation to the*

Dance 1956 (anim); *One Droopy Knight* 1957 (anim,p) **(AANBASF)**; *Life With Loopy* 1960 (anim,p); *Just a Wolf at Heart* 1962 (anim,p); *Hey There, It's Yogi Bear* 1964 (d,p,sc); *A Man Called Flintstone* 1966 (d,p); *Project X* 1968 (p); *Charlotte's Web* 1972 (p); *Mother, Jugs & Speed* 1976 (exec.p); *Chomps* 1979 (p,sc,story); *Attack of the Phantoms* 1980 (exec.p); *Heidi's Song* 1982 (p); *Escape From Grumble Gulch* 1983 (d); *Gobots: Battle of the Rock Lords* 1986 (exec.p); *Jetsons: The Movie* 1990 (d,p).

Bardem, Juan Antonio • Director, screenwriter • Born Juan Antonio Bardem-Muñoz, Madrid, Spain, July 2, 1922. *Educ.* Instituto de Investigaciones y Experiencias Cinematográficas, Madrid. Internationally acclaimed figure who in the 1950s, with former classmate Luis-García Berlanga, developed a filmmaking style known as "estética franquista." The object of the movement was to avoid political censorship by couching criticisms of Franco's regime in satirical terms. Bardem, nevertheless, was jailed after making the neorealist-influenced *Death of a Cyclist* (1955), a film which, along with *Calle Mayor* (1956), won him international acclaim. Bardem was also responsible—through his production company Uninci—for Luis Buñuel's return to Spain for the making of *Viridiana* (1961). • *Muerte de un Ciclista/Death of a Cyclist* 1955 (adapt,dial,d); *Calle Mayor* 1956 (d,sc); *Pantaloons* 1956 (sc); *La Venganza* 1958 (d); *Sonatas* 1959 (d); *A las Cinco de la Tarde* 1960 (d); *Los Inocentes* 1962 (d); *Nunca Pasa Nada* 1963 (d); *Los Pianos Mecánicos* 1965 (d); *El Último Día de la Guerra* 1969 (d,sc); *Varietes* 1971 (d,sc); *Behind the Shutters* 1973 (d); *La Corrupción de Chris Miller* 1973 (d); *L'Ile Mystérieuse* 1973 (d,sc); *Foul Play* 1976 (d); *El Poder del Deseo* 1976 (d); *El Perro* 1977 (a); *El Puente* 1977 (d); *Siete Días de Enero* 1979 (d,sc); *Adíos, Pequeña* 1986 (a); *Lorca, la Muerte de un Poeta* 1987 (d,sc).

Bardot, Brigitte • Actress; also singer. • Born Camille Javal, Paris, September 28, 1934. International sex symbol of the 1950s and 60s. A model turned actress, Bardot appeared in several films before achieving instant stardom in Roger Vadim's *And God Created Woman* (1956). Though most of her performances have been as scantily-clad objects in routine movies, she has also appeared in more intelligent films, such as Jean-Luc Godard's self-referential *Contempt* (1963), in which she plays a character named Camille Javal (her real name).

Bardot retired from the screen in 1974 and has since devoted her time to animal rights causes, leading an increasingly reclusive lifestyle. Her first two husbands were director Roger Vadim (1952-57) and actor Jacques Charrier (1959-63), and her son Nicholas Charrier is an actor. • *Les Dents longues* 1952 (a); *Manina, La Fille Sans Voile* 1952 (a); *Le Trou Normand* 1952 (a); *Act of Love* 1953 (a); *Le Portrait de son Père* 1953 (a); *Si Versailles m'était conté/Royal Affairs in Versailles* 1954 (a); *Tradita* 1954 (a); *Doctor at Sea* 1955 (a); *Le Fils de Caroline Cherie* 1955 (a); *Frou-Frou* 1955 (a); *Futures Vedettes* 1955 (a); *Cette Sacrée Gamine* 1956 (a); *En effeuillant la Marguérite* 1956 (a); *Et Dieu...Créa la Femme/And God Created Woman* 1956 (a); *Les Grandes Maneuvres* 1956 (a); *Helen of Troy* 1956 (a); *La Lumière d'en Face* 1956 (a); *La Mariée est Trop Belle* 1956 (a); *Mio Figlio Nerone* 1956 (a); *Une Parisienne* 1957 (a); *Les Bijoutiers du Clair de Lune/The Night Heaven Fell* 1958 (a); *En cas de malheur* 1958 (a); *Babette s'en va-t-en Guerre/Babette Goes to War* 1959 (a); *La Femme et le Pantin* 1959 (a); *Le Testament d'Orphée/The Testament of Orpheus* 1959 (a); *Voulez-vous danser avec moi?/Come, Dance With Me!* 1959 (a); *La Vérité/The Truth* 1960 (a); *La Bride sur le Cou* 1961 (a); *Vie Privée/A Very Private Affair* 1961 (a); *Le Repos du Guerrier* 1962 (a); *Le Mépris/Contempt* 1963 (a); *Une Ravissante Idiote/A Ravishing Idiot* 1964 (a); *Témoignage sur Bardot-Godard ou Le parti des choses (short)* 1964 (a); *Dear Brigitte* 1965 (a); *Víva María* 1965 (a); *Masculin-Feminin* 1966 (a); *Histoires Extraordinaires/Spirits of the Dead* 1968 (a); *Shalako* 1968 (a); *Les Femmes* 1969 (a); *Les Novices* 1970 (a); *L'Ours et la poupée* 1970 (a); *Boulevard du Rhum* 1971 (a); *Les Pétroleuses* 1971 (a); *Film Portrait* 1972 (collaboration); *Don Juan 1973 ou si Don Juan était une femme* 1973 (a); *L'Histoire très bonne et très joyeuse de Colinot Trousse chemise* 1973 (a).

Barish, Keith • Producer • Born Los Angeles, CA. Began his film career as executive producer of the Franco Zeffirelli melodrama *Endless Love* (1981); subsequent projects of note include Alan Pakula's *Sophie's Choice* (1982) and Hector Babenco's adaptation of William Kennedy's *Ironweed* (1987). • *Endless Love* 1981 (exec.p); *Sophie's Choice* 1982 (p); *Misunderstood* 1984 (exec.p); *9 1/2 Weeks* 1986 (exec.p); *Big Trouble in Little China* 1986 (exec.p); *Ironweed* 1987 (p); *Light of Day* 1987 (p); *The Monster Squad* 1987 (exec.p); *The Running Man* 1987 (exec.p); *The Serpent and the Rainbow* 1988 (exec.p); *Her Alibi* 1989 (p); *Fire Birds* 1990 (exec.p).

Barkin, Ellen • Actress • Born Bronx, NY, c. 1954. *Educ.* High School for the Performing Arts, New York; Hunter College, New York (history, drama); Actors Studio. Established herself as a strong supporting actress in the early 1980s and soon graduated to a succession of interesting, off-beat leading roles. Although she has proved herself a disciplined, versatile talent, Barkin is nevertheless usually cast in films which emphasize her "steamy" sex appeal; she is best known for her performances as a starchy assistant D.A. opposite Dennis Quaid in *The Big Easy* (1986) and as a suspected serial killer opposite Al Pacino in *Sea of Love* (1989). Married to actor Gabriel Byrne, opposite whom she starred in *Siesta* (1987). • *Diner* 1982; *Tender Mercies* 1982; *Daniel* 1983; *Eddie and the Cruisers* 1983; *Enormous Changes at the Last Minute* 1983; *The Adventures of Buckaroo Banzai: Across the 8th Dimension* 1984; *Harry & Son* 1984; *Terminal Choice* 1985; *The Big Easy* 1986; *Desert Bloom* 1986; *Down By Law* 1986; *Made in Heaven* 1987; *Siesta* 1987; *Johnny Handsome* 1989; *Sea of Love* 1989; *Switch* 1991.

Barnes, George • American director of photography • Born 1893; died 1953. Shot his first feature in 1918 and went on to work with such illustrious directors as King Vidor, Henry King, Frank Capra, Alfred Hitchcock and Cecil B. DeMille. Barnes also served as a mentor to Gregg Toland, who went on to become one of Hollywood's finest cinematographers. Married to Joan Blondell from 1932 to 1936. • *The Haunted Bedroom* 1919; *The False Road* 1920; *Hairpins* 1920; *Her Husband's Friend* 1920; *The Bronze Bell* 1921; *The Heart Line* 1921; *Opened Shutters* 1921; *Conquering the Woman* 1922; *Dusk to Dawn* 1922; *Peg o' My Heart* 1922; *The Real Adventure* 1922; *Woman, Wake Up!* 1922; *Alice Adams* 1923; *Desire* 1923; *The Love Piker* 1923; *Janice Meredith* 1924; *Yolanda* 1924; *The Dark Angel* 1925; *The Eagle* 1925; *The Teaser* 1925; *Zander the Great* 1925; *Mademoiselle Modiste* 1926; *The Son of the Sheik* 1926; *The Winning of Barbara Worth* 1926; *The Devil Dancer* 1927 **(AANBPH)**; *Magic Flame* 1927 **(AANBPH)**; *The Night of Love* 1927; *Venus of Venice* 1927; *The Awakening* 1928; *Our Dancing Daughters* 1928 **(AANBPH)**; *Sadie Thompson* 1928 **(AANBPH)**; *Two Lovers* 1928; *Bulldog Drummond* 1929; *Condemned* 1929; *The Rescue* 1929; *This Is Heaven* 1929; *The Trespasser* 1929; *A Lady's Morals* 1930; *One Heavenly Night* 1930; *Raffles* 1930; *What a Widow!* 1930; *The Devil to Pay* 1931; *Five and Ten* 1931; *Street Scene* 1931; *The Unholy Garden* 1931; *Blondie of the Follies* 1932; *The Greeks Had a Word For Them* 1932; *Polly of the Circus* 1932; *Sherlock Holmes* 1932; *Society Girl* 1932; *The Wet Parade* 1932; *Broadway Bad* 1933; *Footlight Parade* 1933; *Goodbye Again* 1933; *Havana Widows* 1933; *Peg o' My Heart* 1933; *Dames* 1934; *Flirtation Walk* 1934; *Gambling Lady* 1934; *He Was Her Man* 1934; *The Kansas City Princess* 1934; *Massacre* 1934; *Smarty* 1934; *Broadway Gondolier* 1935; *Gold Diggers of 1935* 1935; *I Live For Love* 1935; *In Caliente* 1935; *The Irish in Us*

1935; *Stars Over Broadway* 1935; *Traveling Saleslady* 1935; *Black Legion* 1936; *Cain and Mabel* 1936; *Love Begins at Twenty* 1936; *The Singing Kid* 1936; *The Barrier* 1937; *Ever Since Eve* 1937; *Hollywood Hotel* 1937; *Marked Woman* 1937; *Varsity Show* 1937; *The Beloved Brat* 1938; *Gold Diggers in Paris* 1938; *Love, Honor, and Behave* 1938; *Devil's Island* 1939; *Jesse James* 1939; *Our Neighbors, the Carters* 1939; *Stanley and Livingstone* 1939; *Free, Blonde, and 21* 1940; *Girl From Avenue A* 1940; *Hudson's Bay* 1940; *Maryland* 1940; *Rebecca* 1940 **(AABPH)**; *The Return of Frank James* 1940; *Ladies in Retirement* 1941; *Meet John Doe* 1941; *Remember the Day* 1941; *That Uncertain Feeling* 1941; *Unholy Partners* 1941; *Broadway* 1942; *Nightmare* 1942; *Once Upon a Honeymoon* 1942; *Rings on Her Fingers* 1942; *Mr. Lucky* 1943; *Frenchman's Creek* 1944; *Jane Eyre* 1944; *None But the Lonely Heart* 1944; *The Bells of St. Mary's* 1945; *The Spanish Main* 1945 **(AANBPH)**; *Spellbound* 1945 **(AANBPH)**; *From This Day Forward* 1946; *Sister Kenny* 1946; *Mourning Becomes Electra* 1947; *Sinbad the Sailor* 1947; *The Boy With Green Hair* 1948; *The Emperor Waltz* 1948; *Force of Evil* 1948; *Good Sam* 1948; *No Minor Vices* 1948; *The File on Thelma Jordan* 1949; *Samson and Delilah* 1949 **(AANBPH)**; *Let's Dance* 1950; *Mr. Music* 1950; *Riding High* 1950; *Here Comes the Groom* 1951; *The Greatest Show on Earth* 1952; *Just For You* 1952; *Road to Bali* 1952; *Somebody Loves Me* 1952; *Something to Live For* 1952; *Little Boy Lost* 1953; *The War of the Worlds* 1953.

Barouh, Pierre • Musician, actor; also director, producer • Born France. As musician and record producer, Pierre Barouh had an important influence on French popular music of the 60s and 70s, playing a major role in introducing the Brazilian samba to Europe. An actor in Claude Lelouch's landmark *A Man and a Woman* (1966, he played the husband with the guitar and cigar), Barouh also made important contributions to the score. (Francis Lai was credited.) In 1970, he produced and directed *Ça Va, Ça Vient*, a leisurely and infectious portrait of a group of Parisian workers and their families which became a cult favorite. He has continued to combine music and film in a remarkable funky, friendly mix the Brazilians call "Saravah." JM • *Le Gendarme de Saint-Tropez/The Gendarme of St Tropez* 1964 (a); *Un Homme et une femme/A Man and a Woman* 1966 (a,song); *Vivre pour vivre/Live For Life* 1967 (song); *Treize Jours en France/Challenge in the Snow* 1968 (songs); *Ca Va, Ca Vient/It Comes, It Goes* 1970 (d,sc); *Si c'était à refaire/Second Chance* 1976 (song); *Ben et Benedict/Ben and Benedict* 1977 (song); *Le Divorcement* 1979 (d,m,sc); *Il y a des jours...et des lunes/There Were Days and Moons* 1990 (a,m).

Barr, Jean-Marc • French actor • Born 1960. *Educ.* UCLA; Sorbonne, Paris; Paris Conservatoire; Guildhall School of Music and Drama, London (acting). Handsome, classically trained actor who made his film debut as Absolom in Bruce Beresford's 1985 biblical bomb, *King David*. Barr earned his first leading role as champion diver Jacques Mayol in Luc Besson's *The Big Blue* (1988), a huge hit in France which failed to find an international audience. • *The Frog Prince* 1985; *King David* 1985; *Hope and Glory* 1987; *Le Grand bleu/The Big Blue* 1988; *Le Brasier* 1991.

Barrault, Marie-Christine • Actress • Born Paris, March 21, 1944. *Educ.* Paris Conservatoire. Luminous, versatile performer in several films by Eric Rohmer and memorable as one of the lovers in *Cousin, Cousine* (1975). She is the niece of actor Jean-Loius Barrault. • *Ma nuit chez Maud/My Night at Maud's* 1969; *Les Intrus* 1971; *Cousin, Cousine* 1975 **(AANBA)**; *John Glueckstadt* 1975; *Du Coté des Tennis* 1976; *L'Etat sauvage/The Savage State* 1977; *The Medusa Touch* 1978; *Perceval le gallois* 1978; *Même les mômes ont du vague à l'Ame* 1979; *Een Vrouw Tussen Hond en Wolf* 1979; *Ma Chérie* 1980; *Stardust Memories* 1980; *Josephs Tochter* 1983; *Eine Liebe in Deutschland/A Love in Germany* 1983; *Les Mots pour le dire* 1983; *Table For Five* 1983; *Un Amour de Swann/Swann in Love* 1984; *Jean-Louis Barrault—A Man of the Theater* 1984; *Louise...l'Insoumise* 1984; *La Meilleur de la Vie* 1984; *Pianoforte* 1984; *Le Pouvoir du Mal* 1985; *Le Soulier de Satin* 1985; *Vaudeville* 1985; *Le Jupon rouge* 1987; *Adieu, je t'aime* 1988; *Daniya, Jardin del Harem* 1988; *No Blame* 1988; *L'Oeuvre au noir/The Abyss* 1988; *Prisonnières* 1988; *Sanguinés* 1988; *Une Été d'orage* 1989; *Dames Galantes* 1990.

Barreto, Bruno • Brazilian director, screenwriter • Born 1955. Scored an international hit with *Doña Flor and Her Two Husbands* (1977), a comedy of sexual manners starring Sonia Braga, but has otherwise turned out unexceptional entertainment. Barreto made his English-language directorial debut with the political thriller *A Show of Force* (1990), starring Amy Irving with whom he has a child. • *A Estrela sobe* 1974 (d,sc); *Doña Flor e Seus Dois Maridos/Doña Flor and Her Two Husbands* 1977 (d,sc); *Amada Amante* 1979 (d); *Kiss Me Goodbye* 1982 (from sc—*Doña Flor and Her Two Husbands*); *Gabriela* 1983 (d,sc); *Alem Da Paixao* 1985 (d,sc); *Where the River Runs Black* 1986 (line p.—Rio de Janeiro); *Romance de Empregada* 1988 (d); *A Show of Force* 1990 (d).

Barry, John • Composer; also musician. • Born J.B. Prendergast, York, England, 1933. Former rock 'n' roll performer and producer best known for his many "James Bond" scores. Most of Barry's film work reflects his earlier leanings but he is equally at home with less contemporary settings, as evidenced by the award-winning *The Lion in Winter* (1968). Divorced from actress-singer Jane Birkin. • *The L-Shaped Room* 1962 (m); *From Russia With Love* 1963 (m); *Zulu* 1963 (m); *Goldfinger* 1964 (m); *Seance on a Wet Afternoon* 1964 (m,m.cond); *The Ipcress File* 1965 (m); *King Rat* 1965 (m,m.cond); *The Knack...and How to Get It* 1965 (m,m.cond); *Mister Moses* 1965 (m,m.cond); *Thunderball* 1965 (m); *Born Free* 1966 (m,song) **(AABM,AABS)**; *The Chase* 1966 (m,m.cond); *The Quiller Memorandum* 1966 (m,m.cond,song); *The Whisperers* 1967 (m); *You Only Live Twice* 1967 (m); *Boom!* 1968 (m); *Deadfall* 1968 (a,m,m.cond,m.arr,song); *The Lion in Winter* 1968 (m,m.dir) **(AABM)**; *Petulia* 1968 (m); *The Appointment* 1969 (song); *Midnight Cowboy* 1969 (m,m.sup); *On Her Majesty's Secret Service* 1969 (m); *Monte Walsh* 1970 (m); *Murphy's War* 1970 (m); *Diamonds Are Forever* 1971 (m); *The Last Valley* 1971 (m); *Mary, Queen of Scots* 1971 (m) **(AANBM)**; *They Might Be Giants* 1971 (m); *Walkabout* 1971 (m); *Alice's Adventures in Wonderland* 1972 (m); *Follow Me!* 1972 (m); *A Doll's House* 1973 (m); *The Dove* 1974 (m); *The Man With the Golden Gun* 1974 (m); *The Tamarind Seed* 1974 (m,song); *The Day of the Locust* 1975 (m); *King Kong* 1976 (m); *Robin and Marian* 1976 (m); *The Deep* 1977 (m); *The White Buffalo* 1977 (m,m.dir); *The Betsy* 1978 (m); *The Black Hole* 1979 (m,m.dir); *Game of Death* 1979 (m,m.dir,song); *Hanover Street* 1979 (m); *Moonraker* 1979 (m,song); *Night Games* 1979 (m); *Saint Jack* 1979 (song); *Starcrash* 1979 (m,m.dir); *Touched By Love* 1979 (m); *When You Comin' Back, Red Ryder?* 1979 (song); *Inside Moves* 1980 (m); *Raise the Titanic* 1980 (m); *Somewhere in Time* 1980 (m,m.cond); *Body Heat* 1981 (m,m.dir); *The Legend of the Lone Ranger* 1981 (m,song); *Frances* 1982 (m,m.dir); *Hammett* 1982 (m,m.dir); *Mike's Murder* 1982 (m); *The Golden Seal* 1983 (m,song); *High Road to China* 1983 (m); *Murder By Phone* 1983 (m); *Octopussy* 1983 (m,m.dir,song); *The Cotton Club* 1984 (m); *Until September* 1984 (m); *Jagged Edge* 1985 (m,m.dir); *Morons From Outer Space* 1985 (song); *Out of Africa* 1985 (m) **(AABM)**; *A View to a Kill* 1985 (m,m.cond,song); *The Golden Child* 1986 (m); *Howard the Duck* 1986 (m,m.cond); *A Killing Affair* 1986 (m); *My Sister's Keeper* 1986 (m); *Peggy Sue Got Married* 1986 (m,m.cond); *Hearts of Fire* 1987 (m); *The Living Daylights*

1987 (m,m,song); *Masquerade* 1988 (m,m.cond); *Dances With Wolves* 1990 (m).

Barrymore, Drew • Actress • Born Los Angeles, CA, February 22, 1975. Appeared in TV commercials before reaching the age of one and gained international exposure as Gertie, the cute little sister in *E.T.* (1982). Daughter of John Barrymore, Jr. • *Altered States* 1980; *E.T., the Extra-Terrestrial* 1982; *Firestarter* 1984; *Irreconcilable Differences* 1984; *Stephen King's Cat's Eye* 1985; *Far From Home* 1989; *See You in the Morning* 1989.

Barrymore, Ethel • Actress • Born Ethel May Blythe, Philadelphia, PA, August 15, 1879; died 1959. A Broadway lead from 1900 who, while her brothers John and Lionel were becoming film stars, established herself as "the first lady of the American stage." Barrymore's screen performances were sporadic, but included an outstanding role in *Rasputin and the Empress* (1932), which co-starred both her brothers. She began making more film appearances in character roles in the 1940s, winning a best supporting actress Oscar for *None But the Lonely Heart* (1944) opposite Cary Grant. • *The Final Judgment* 1915; *The Awakening of Helena Richie* 1916; *The Kiss of Hate* 1916; *An American Widow* 1917; *The Call of Her People* 1917; *The Eternal Mother* 1917; *The Greatest Power* 1917; *Life's Whirlpool* 1917; *The Lifted Veil* 1917; *The White Raven* 1917; *Our Mrs. McChesney* 1918; *The Divorcee* 1919; *Rasputin and the Empress* 1932; *Public Hero Number One* 1935; *None But the Lonely Heart* 1944 **(AABSA)**; *The Spiral Staircase* 1946 **(AANBSA)**; *The Farmer's Daughter* 1947; *Moss Rose* 1947; *Night Song* 1947; *The Paradine Case* 1947 **(AANBSA)**; *Moonrise* 1948; *Portrait of Jennie* 1948; *The Great Sinner* 1949; *Pinky* 1949 **(AANBSA)**; *The Red Danube* 1949; *That Midnight Kiss* 1949; *It's a Big Country* 1951; *Kind Lady* 1951; *The Secret of Convict Lake* 1951; *Deadline U.S.A.* 1952; *Just For You* 1952; *Main Street to Broadway* 1953; *The Story of Three Loves* 1953; *Young at Heart* 1955; *Johnny Trouble* 1957.

Barrymore, John • Actor; also author. • Born John Blythe, Philadelphia, PA, February 15, 1882; died 1942. The youngest of the Barrymores and, of the three, the most brilliant and the most beautiful.

Barrymore worked as a cartoonist on a New York newspaper and spent some time in Paris before making his stage debut in 1903. Tall, stately and seductive, with an unforgettable voice and a truly grand theatrical manner, he became a leading matinee idol; known as the "Great Profile," he was a fine Shakesperean actor as well as an accomplished light comedian.

His film performances, beginning with *An American Citizen* (1913), were more varied than those of his siblings. He carried several silent films, both romantic (*Don Juan* 1926) and otherwise (*Dr. Jekyll and Mr. Hyde* 1920). Much of his work is timeless and impressive, some of it overcooked ham. By 1933, when he played a parody of himself in *Dinner at Eight*, his addiction to drink had begun to take its toll; a faltering memory required cue cards to be held up on set. But his genius flared brilliantly elsewhere: *Grand Hotel, A Bill of Divorcement* (both 1932), *Topaze, Counsellor-at-Law* (both 1933), *Twentieth Century* (1934).

Barrymore died penniless in 1942. He was married four times, and his spouses included the volatile Michael Strange, a writer/poetess who matched him for temperament and eccentricity; and two actresses, Delores Costello and Diane Barry. Daughter Diana (1921-60) and son John, Jr. (b. 1932) had unimpressive careers as actors and shared some of their father's destructive tendencies—Diana's autobiography, *Too Much, Too Soon* (1957), was made into a 1958 film with Errol Flynn portraying Barrymore. • *An American Citizen* 1913; *The Man From Mexico* 1914; *Are You a Mason?* 1915; *Raffles, the Amateur Cracksman* 1917; *On the Quiet* 1918; *Here Comes the Bride* 1919; *The Test of Honor* 1919; *Dr. Jekyll and Mr. Hyde* 1920; *The Lotus Eater* 1921; *Sherlock Holmes* 1922; *Beau Brummell* 1924; *Don Juan* 1926; *The Sea Beast* 1926; *The Beloved Rogue* 1927; *When a Man Loves* 1927; *Tempest* 1928; *Eternal Love* 1929; *General Crack* 1929; *The Show of Shows* 1929; *The Man From Blankley's* 1930; *Moby Dick* 1930; *The Mad Genius* 1931; *Svengali* 1931; *Arsene Lupin* 1932; *A Bill of Divorcement* 1932; *Grand Hotel* 1932; *Rasputin and the Empress* 1932; *State's Attorney* 1932; *Counsellor at Law* 1933; *Dinner at Eight* 1933; *Night Flight* 1933; *Reunion in Vienna* 1933; *Topaze* 1933; *Long Lost Father* 1934; *Twentieth Century* 1934; *Romeo and Juliet* 1936; *Bulldog Drummond Comes Back* 1937; *Bulldog Drummond's Revenge* 1937; *Maytime* 1937; *Night Club Scandal* 1937; *True Confession* 1937; *Bulldog Drummond's Peril* 1938; *Hold That Coed* 1938; *Marie Antoinette* 1938; *Romance in the Dark* 1938; *Spawn of the North* 1938; *The Great Man Votes* 1939; *Midnight* 1939; *The Great Profile* 1940; *The Invisible Woman* 1941; *Playmates* 1941; *World Premiere* 1941.

Barrymore, Lionel • Actor; also director. • Born Lionel Blythe, Philadelphia, PA, April 28, 1878; died November 15, 1954. *Educ.* Art Students League, New York. Eldest of the famed Barrymore siblings. Unlike his brother John and sister Ethel, Lionel did little acting for the theater. He made his stage debut as an infant as part of his parents' (Herbert Blythe/Maurice Barrymore and Georgia Drew) act and was a leading player by age 22. His first film roles were in D.W. Griffith shorts, beginning with *The Battle* (1911), and he worked primarily with MGM from 1926; he continued to act despite being confined to a wheelchair for the last 15 years of his life due to crippling arthritis and a serious leg injury. Barrymore gave one of his finest performances as a dying aristocrat in *Dinner at Eight* (1933) and is also fondly remembered for *Camille* (1933), *You Can't Take It With You* (1938) and *It's a Wonderful Life* (1946), among others.

Barrymore was a writer of both fiction and non-fiction, an accomplished painter and a capable film director, earning an Oscar as an alcoholic lawyer in *A Free Soul* (1931), based on the memoirs of reporter Adela Rogers St. John. • *The Informer* 1912; *Judith of Bethulia* 1913; *The Seats of the Mighty* 1914; *The Curious Conduct of Judge Legarde* 1915; *The Flaming Sword* 1915; *A Modern Magdalen* 1915; *The Romance of Elaine* 1915; *Wildfire* 1915; *A Yellow Streak* 1915; *The Brand of Cowardice* 1916; *Dorian's Divorce* 1916; *The Quitter* 1916; *The Upheaval* 1916; *The End of the Tour* 1917; *His Father's Son* 1917; *Life's Whirlpool* 1917 (d,sc); *The Millionaire's Double* 1917; *The Copperhead* 1920; *The Devil's Garden* 1920; *The Master Mind* 1920; *The Great Adventure* 1921; *Jim the Penman* 1921; *Boomerang Bill* 1922; *The Face in the Fog* 1922; *The Enemies of Women* 1923; *The Eternal City* 1923; *Unseeing Eyes* 1923; *America* 1924; *I Am the Man* 1924; *Meddling Women* 1924; *Children of the Whirlwind* 1925; *Fifty-Fifty* 1925; *The Girl Who Wouldn't Work* 1925; *The Iron Man* 1925; *A Man of Iron* 1925; *The Splendid Road* 1925; *The Wrongdoers* 1925; *The Barrier* 1926; *The Bells* 1926; *Brooding Eyes* 1926; *The Lucky Lady* 1926; *Paris at Midnight* 1926; *The Temptress* 1926; *Body and Soul* 1927; *The Show* 1927; *The Thirteenth Hour* 1927; *Women Love Diamonds* 1927; *Drums of Love* 1928; *The Lion and the Mouse* 1928; *River Woman* 1928; *Road House* 1928; *Sadie Thompson* 1928; *West of Zanzibar* 1928; *Alias Jimmy Valentine* 1929; *His Glorious Night* 1929 (d,m); *The Hollywood Revue of 1929* 1929; *Madame X* 1929 (d) **(AANBD)**; *The Mysterious Island* 1929; *The Unholy Night* 1929 (d); *Free and Easy* 1930; *The Rogue Song* 1930 (d,p); *A Free Soul* 1931 **(AABA)**; *Guilty Hands* 1931; *Ten Cents a Dance* 1931 (d); *The Yellow Ticket* 1931; *Arsene Lupin* 1932; *Broken Lullaby* 1932; *Grand Hotel* 1932; *Mata Hari* 1932; *Rasputin and the Empress* 1932; *The Washington Masquerade* 1932; *Christopher Bean* 1933; *Dinner at Eight* 1933; *Looking Forward* 1933; *Night Flight* 1933; *One Man's Journey* 1933; *Should Ladies Behave?* 1933; *The Stranger's Return* 1933; *Sweepings* 1933; *Carolina* 1934; *The Girl From Missouri* 1934; *This Side* *of Heaven* 1934; *Treasure Island* 1934; *Ah, Wilderness!* 1935; *David Copperfield* 1935; *The Little Colonel* 1935; *Mark of the Vampire* 1935; *The Return of Peter Grimm* 1935; *The Devil-Doll* 1936; *The Gorgeous Hussy* 1936; *The Road to Glory* 1936; *The Voice of Bugle Ann* 1936; *Camille* 1937; *Captains Courageous* 1937; *A Family Affair* 1937; *Navy, Blue and Gold* 1937; *Saratoga* 1937; *Test Pilot* 1938; *A Yank at Oxford* 1938; *You Can't Take It With You* 1938; *Young Dr. Kildare* 1938; *Calling Dr. Kildare* 1939; *Let Freedom Ring* 1939; *On Borrowed Time* 1939; *The Secret of Dr. Kildare* 1939; *Dr. Kildare Goes Home* 1940; *Dr. Kildare's Crisis* 1940; *Dr. Kildare's Strange Case* 1940; *The Bad Man* 1941; *Dr. Kildare's Victory* 1941; *Dr. Kildare's Wedding Day* 1941; *Lady Be Good* 1941; *The Penalty* 1941; *The People vs. Dr. Kildare* 1941; *Calling Dr. Gillespie* 1942; *Dr. Gillespie's New Assistant* 1942; *Tennessee Johnson* 1942; *Dr. Gillespie's Criminal Case* 1943; *A Guy Named Joe* 1943; *Between Two Women* 1944; *Since You Went Away* 1944; *Three Men in White* 1944; *The Valley of Decision* 1945; *It's a Wonderful Life* 1946; *The Secret Heart* 1946; *Three Wise Fools* 1946; *Dark Delusion* 1947; *Duel in the Sun* 1947; *Key Largo* 1948; *Down to the Sea in Ships* 1949; *Malaya* 1949; *Right Cross* 1950; *Bannerline* 1951; *Lone Star* 1952; *Main Street to Broadway* 1953.

Bartel, Paul • Actor, director; also producer, screenwriter. • Born Brooklyn, NY, August 6, 1938. *Educ.* UCLA (theater arts); Centro Sperimentale di Cinematografia, Rome (directing). Paul Bartel is a visual satirist who has directed a range of bawdy, violent, sophisticated and nearly always controversial films. His work is distinguished primarily by its subject matter rather than by its style.

Bartel's interest in film began at the age of nine. He went to the movies often, frequently at a film club which showed 16mm prints of silent and classic works. By the age of eleven, animation had captured his imagination. Influenced by Disney's *Pinocchio* and *Fantasia*, Bartel decided that he wanted to direct animated films. At 13, he spent a summer working at New York's UPA animation studio.

While a student at UCLA, Bartel produced several animated shorts and documentaries. Upon graduation, he received a Fullbright scholarship to study film direction in Rome. One of the short theatrical films he produced while in Italy, *Progetti*, was presented at the 1962 Venice Film Festival.

For a few years, Bartel directed military films and documentaries. While working as an assistant production manager at a New York firm, he wrote, shot and directed a few scenes which eventually grew into a theatrical short titled *The Secret Cinema*. This and a follow-up short, *Naughty Nurse*, were seen by Roger Corman's brother, Gene, who hired Bartel to direct a low-budget horror feature called *Private Parts* (1972). Poorly marketed, the film was largely ignored.

Roger Corman then hired Bartel as a second unit director on *Big Bad Mama* (1974). That film's success led to Bartel's next directing job, *Death Race 2000* (1975), a spoof of the *Cannonball Run* road-race pictures that proved a box-office winner.

Bartel was unsuccessful in trying to persuade Corman to finance his project, *Eating Raoul* (1982), so the director shot a ten-minute teaser to seduce potential investors. The story, which satirized greed, decadence and superficial middle-class values, culminating in off-camera cannibalism, interested no-one. Finally, Bartel's parents agreed to finance the film. Unable to find a distributor for the finished picture, Bartel entered it in Filmex, the Los Angeles Film Festival; *Eating Raoul* enjoyed a sensational response, prompting 20th Century-Fox to pick it up for distribution and going on to become a cult classic.

Of his subsequent films, *Lust in the Dust* (1984) is the most important. A black comedy intended to satirize the western, the film is marred by an inconsistent tone which depletes its comic energy. His most recent release, *Scenes From the Class Struggle in Beverly Hills* (1989), is a modern, sexually explicit Restoration comedy that highlights the cultural disparity between rich and poor in Beverly Hills. The film's effectiveness as a bedroom farce is undermined by constant intercutting, which disturbs the spatial continuity on which the genre depends.

Although Bartel's works often shock, his courageous choices push back convention, challenging mainstream cinema's dependence upon formula. Should *Bland Ambition*, his planned sequel to *Eating Raoul*, be produced, it will be anything but a typical follow-up; nothing about Bartel is predictable. MCJ • *Progetti (short)* 1962 (d); *The Secret Cinema (short)* 1967 (d); *Hi, Mom!* 1970 (a); *Private Parts* 1972 (d); *Big Bad Mama* 1974 (2u d); *Death Race 2000* 1975 (d); *Cannonball* 1976 (a,d,sc); *Eat My Dust* 1976 (a); *Hollywood Boulevard* 1976 (a); *Grand Theft Auto* 1977 (a); *Mr. Billion* 1977 (a); *Piranha* 1978 (a); *Roger Corman: Hollywood's Wild Angel* 1978 (a); *Rock 'n' Roll High School* 1979 (a); *Eating Raoul* 1982 (a,d,sc); *Heart Like a Wheel* 1982 (a); *Trick or Treats* 1982 (a); *White Dog* 1982 (a); *Get Crazy* 1983 (a); *Lust in the Dust* 1984 (d); *Not For Publication* 1984 (a,d,sc,song); *Into the Night* 1985 (a); *Sesame Street Presents: Follow That Bird* 1985 (a); *Chopping Mall* 1986 (a); *Killer Party* 1986 (a); *The Longshot* 1986 (d); *Amazon Women on the Moon* 1987 (a); *Munchies* 1987 (a); *Mortuary Academy* 1988 (a); *Shakedown* 1988 (a); *Out of the Dark* 1989 (a,exec.p); *Pucker Up and Bark Like a Dog* 1989 (a); *Scenes From the Class Struggle in Beverly Hills* 1989 (a,d,sc,story); *Gremlins 2: The New Batch* 1990 (a); *The Pope Must Die* 1991 (a).

Barthelmess, Richard • Actor • Born New York, NY, May 9, 1895; died 1963, Long Island, NY. *Educ.* Trinity College, Hartford CT. "The most beautiful face of any man who ever went before the camera," said Lillian Gish of her co-star in two D.W. Griffith films, *Broken Blossoms* (1919) and *Way Down East* (1920). Barthelmess remained a popular leading man through the 1920s and played supporting roles in sound films before retiring in 1942. • *Snow White* 1916; *War Brides* 1916; *Bab's Burglar* 1917; *Bab's Diary* 1917; *The Eternal Sin* 1917; *For Valour* 1917; *The Moral Code* 1917; *Nearly Married* 1917; *The Seven Swans* 1917; *The Soul of Magdalen* 1917; *The Valentine Girl* 1917; *Hit-the-Trail Holliday* 1918; *The Hope Chest* 1918; *Rich Man, Poor Man* 1918; *Sunshine Nan* 1918; *Boots* 1919; *Broken Blossoms* 1919; *The Girl Who Stayed at Home* 1919; *I'll Get Him Yet* 1919; *Peppy Polly* 1919; *Scarlet Days* 1919; *Three Men and a Girl* 1919; *The Idol Dancer* 1920; *The Love Flower* 1920; *Way Down East* 1920; *Experience* 1921; *Tol'able David* 1921; *The Bond Boy* 1922; *Just a Song at Twilight* 1922; *The Seventh Day* 1922; *Sonny* 1922; *The Bright Shawl* 1923; *The Fighting Blade* 1923; *Fury* 1923; *Twenty-One* 1923; *Classmates* 1924; *The Enchanted Cottage* 1924; *The Beautiful City* 1925; *New Toys* 1925; *Shore Leave* 1925; *Soul-Fire* 1925; *The Amateur Gentleman* 1926; *Just Suppose* 1926; *Ranson's Folly* 1926; *The White Black Sheep* 1926; *The Drop Kick* 1927; *The Patent Leather Kid* 1927 **(AANBA)**; *The Little Shepherd of Kingdom Come* 1928; *The Noose* 1928 **(AANBA)**; *Out of the Ruins* 1928; *Scarlet Seas* 1928; *Wheel of Chance* 1928; *Drag* 1929; *The Show of Shows* 1929; *Weary River* 1929; *Young Nowheres* 1929; *The Dawn Patrol* 1930; *The Lash* 1930; *Son of the Gods* 1930; *The Finger Points* 1931; *The Last Flight* 1931; *The Cabin in the Cotton* 1932; *Central Airport* 1933; *Heroes For Sale* 1933; *Massacre* 1934; *Midnight Alibi* 1934; *A Modern Hero* 1934; *Four Hours to Kill* 1935; *Only Angels Have Wings* 1939; *The Man Who Talked Too Much* 1940; *The Mayor of 44th Street* 1942; *The Spoilers* 1942.

Bartholomew, Freddie • Actor • Born Frederick Llewellyn, London, March 28, 1924. Popular child star of the 1930s, adept at very young aristocrats and period roles. Later went into advertising. • *Fascination* 1930; *Lily Christine* 1932; *Anna Karenina* 1935; *David Copperfield* 1935; *Professional Sol-*

dier 1935; *The Devil Is a Sissy* 1936; *Little Lord Fauntleroy* 1936; *Lloyd's of London* 1936; *Captains Courageous* 1937; *Kidnapped* 1938; *Listen, Darling* 1938; *Lord Jeff* 1938; *Spirit of Culver* 1939; *Two Bright Boys* 1939; *The Swiss Family Robinson* 1940; *Tom Brown's School Days* 1940; *Naval Academy* 1941; *Cadets on Parade* 1942; *Junior Army* 1942; *A Yank at Eton* 1942; *The Town Went Wild* 1944; *Sarge Goes to College* 1947; *Sepia Cinderella* 1947; *St. Benny the Dip* 1951.

Bartkowiak, Andrzej • Director of photography • Born Lódz, Poland, c. 1950. *Educ.* Lódz Film School. Noted for the gritty, urban compositions of his collaborations with Sidney Lumet, but equally at home with glossier fare such as *Terms of Endearment* (1983). • *Deadly Hero* 1976; *Prince of the City* 1981; *Deathtrap* 1982; *The Verdict* 1982; *Daniel* 1983; *Terms of Endearment* 1983; *Garbo Talks* 1984; *Prizzi's Honor* 1985; *The Morning After* 1986; *Power* 1986; *Nuts* 1987; *Twins* 1988; *Family Business* 1989; *Q&A* 1990; *Off and Running* 1991.

Barty, Billy • Actor • Born Pennsylvania, c. 1910. *Educ.* Los Angeles City College; Los Angeles State. Perhaps the most recognized dwarf actor of the last 50 years. • *Alice in Wonderland* 1933; *Out All Night* 1933; *A Midsummer Night's Dream* 1935; *The Undead* 1957; *Harum Scarum* 1965; *Pufnstuf* 1970; *The Day of the Locust* 1975; *The Amazing Dobermans* 1976; *W.C. Fields and Me* 1976; *The Happy Hooker Goes to Washington* 1977; *Foul Play* 1978; *The Lord of the Rings* 1978; *Firepower* 1979; *Skatetown, USA* 1979; *Being Different* 1981; *Hardly Working* 1981; *Under the Rainbow* 1981; *Night Patrol* 1984; *Legend* 1985; *Tough Guys* 1986; *Body Slam* 1987; *Masters of the Universe* 1987; *Off the Mark* 1987; *Rumpelstiltskin* 1987; *Snow White* 1987; *Willow* 1988; *Lobster Man From Mars* 1989; *UHF* 1989; *The Rescuers Down Under* 1990; *Life Stinks* 1991.

Baryshnikov, Mikhail • Dancer, actor; also choreographer. • Born Riga, Latvia, USSR, January 27, 1948. *Educ.* School of the Theater Opera Ballet; Vaganova School, Leningrad. One of the world's greatest dancers, Baryshnikov defected to the West in 1974 and has subsequently divided his time among film, theater and dance, collaborating with some of the leading artists of the day. He is a capable screen actor, but his greatest contributions to such films as *The Turning Point* (1977) and *White Nights* (1985) are his dancing and choreography.

Baryshnikov has been a principal dancer with the American Ballet Theater (1974-78) and the New York City Ballet (1978-79) and served as the ABT's artistic director through the 1980s. Father of a child by actress Jessica Lange. • *The Turning Point* 1977 (a,chor—"Aurora's Wedding," "Le Corsaire") (**AANBSA**); *When I Think of Russia* 1980 (a); *That's Dancing!* 1985 (a); *White Nights* 1985 (a,add.chor); *Dancers* 1987 (a,chor—"Giselle"); *The Cabinet of Dr. Ramirez* 1991 (a); *Company Business* 1991 (a).

Basehart, Richard • Actor • Born Zanesville, OH, August 31, 1914; died September 17, 1984, Los Angeles, CA. Entered film by way of Broadway in 1947, making his mark in the gritty *He Walked by Night* (1948) and proving his versatility in several international productions, notably Federico Fellini's poignant masterpiece *La Strada* (1954). Basehart married actress Valentina Cortese in 1951. • *Cry Wolf* 1947; *Repeat Performance* 1947; *He Walked By Night* 1948; *Reign of Terror* 1949; *Roseanna McCoy* 1949; *Tension* 1949; *Outside the Wall* 1950; *Fixed Bayonets* 1951; *Fourteen Hours* 1951; *The House on Telegraph Hill* 1951; *Decision Before Dawn* 1952; *La Mano dello Straniero* 1953; *Titanic* 1953; *Avanzi di Galera* 1954; *The Good Die Young* 1954; *La Strada* 1954; *Il Bidone* 1955; *Canyon Crossroads* 1955; *La Vena d'Oro* 1955; *Finger of Guilt* 1956; *Moby Dick* 1956; *Arrivederci Dimas* 1957; *Time Limit!* 1957; *The Brothers Karamazov* 1958; *Jons und Erdme* 1959; *Five Branded Women* 1960; *For the Love of Mike* 1960; *Portrait in Black* 1960; *Visa to Canton* 1960; *Hitler* 1962; *The Savage Guns* 1962; *Kings of the Sun* 1963; *Four Days in November* 1964; *The Satan Bug* 1965; *Chato's Land* 1972; *Rage* 1972; *And Millions Will Die* 1973; *The Terror of Dr. Chancey* 1975; *The Island of Dr. Moreau* 1977; *Shenanigans* 1977; *Being There* 1979; *Bix* 1981.

Basevi, James • Production designer • Born Plymouth, England, 1890. In Hollywood from 1925 as an art director, Basevi spent over a decade (1926-38) as a special effects artist before returning to design. He was head of the art department at 20th Century-Fox from the early 1940s and worked with John Ford, William Wellman and Henry King, among others. • *The Big Parade* 1925; *The Circle* 1925; *Confessions of a Queen* 1925; *Fine Clothes* 1925 (color consultant); *The Tower of Lies* 1925; *Dance Madness* 1926; *The Temptress* 1926; *Wuthering Heights* 1939 (**AANBAD**); *The Long Voyage Home* 1940; *The Westerner* 1940 (**AANBAD**); *Tobacco Road* 1941; *The Gang's All Here* 1943 (**AANBAD**); *Heaven Can Wait* 1943; *The Ox-Bow Incident* 1943; *The Song of Bernadette* 1943 (**AABAD**); *Jane Eyre* 1944; *The Lodger* 1944; *The Purple Heart* 1944; *The Sullivans* 1944; *Wilson* 1944; *The Keys of the Kingdom* 1945 (**AANBAD**); *Claudia and David* 1946; *The Dark Corner* 1946; *My Darling Clementine* 1946; *The Brasher Doubloon* 1947; *Captain From Castile* 1947; *Duel in the Sun* 1947; *The Late George Apley* 1947; *Fort Apache* 1948; *She Wore a Yellow Ribbon* 1949; *Three Godfathers* 1949; *Wagonmaster* 1950; *Across the Wide Missouri* 1951; *The People Against O'Hara* 1951; *Battle Circus* 1953; *Island in the Sky* 1953; *East of Eden* 1955.

Basinger, Kim • Actress • Born Athens, GA, December 8, 1953. *Educ.* Neighborhood Playhouse, New York. Pouty blonde lead of the 1980s who has primarily been used for ornamental purposes (*9 1/2 Weeks* 1986, *Batman* 1989); Robert Altman tried to stretch her dramatic talents a little further in *Fool For Love* (1985). A former superstar model, Basinger's career took off after appearing as "Bond girl" Domino Petachi in *Never Say Never Again* (1983). • *Hard Country* 1981; *Mother Lode* 1982; *The Man Who Loved Women* 1983; *Never Say Never Again* 1983; *The Natural* 1984; *Fool For Love* 1985; *9 1/2 Weeks* 1986; *No Mercy* 1986; *Blind Date* 1987; *Nadine* 1987; *My Stepmother Is an Alien* 1988; *Batman* 1989; *The Marrying Man* 1991.

Bass, Saul • Title designer; also director, animator. • Born New York, NY, May 8, 1920. *Educ.* Art Students League, New York; Brooklyn College, NY. Bass revolutionized the design of film title sequences, beginning with Otto Preminger's *Carmen Jones* (1954). He pioneered the use of animation techniques to achieve a range of psychological and emotional effects unobtainable with conventional straight type. His collaborations with Preminger and Alfred Hitchcock were outstanding, particularly *Vertigo* (1958), *Psycho* (1960) and *Bunny Lake Is Missing* (1965). • *Bonjour Tristesse* 1957 (title design); *Cowboy* 1958 (title design); *Vertigo* 1958 (title design); *Anatomy of a Murder* 1959 (title design); *North By Northwest* 1959 (title design); *Exodus* 1960 (title design); *Psycho* 1960 (title design); *Spartacus* 1960 (title design); *West Side Story* 1961 (title design); *Advise and Consent* 1962 (title design); *Walk on the Wild Side* 1962 (title design); *It's a Mad, Mad, Mad, Mad World* 1963 (main title design); *Bunny Lake Is Missing* 1965 (title design); *Phase IV* 1974 (d); *The Human Factor* 1979 (title design); *Broadcast News* 1987 (title design); *Big* 1988 (title design); *The War of the Roses* 1989 (title design); *GoodFellas* 1990 (titles).

Bates, Alan • Actor • Born Alan Arthur Bates, Allestree, Derbyshire, England, February 17, 1934 . Powerful British actor who came to prominence in the 1960s along with other angry young leading men, Albert Finney and Tom Courtenay. Bates gained acclaim for his first major screen role, in *The Entertainer* (1960), and soon emerged as one of the English-language cinema's most arresting talents. He has worked with the major British and American directors of his time including John Schlesinger (*A Kind of Loving* 1962, *Far From the Madding Crowd* 1967), Lindsey Anderson (*In Celebration* 1974, *Brittania Hospital* 1982), Ken Russell (*Women in Love* 1969) and Joseph Losey (*The Go-Between* 1971). In the 1980s he portrayed several elder homosexual characters (*Nijinsky* 1980, *We Think the World of You* 1988 and the Schlesinger-directed TV film *An Englishman Abroad* 1983). • *It's Never Too Late* 1956; *The Entertainer* 1960; *Whistle Down the Wind* 1961; *A Kind of Loving* 1962; *The Caretaker* 1963; *The Running Man* 1963; *Nothing But the Best* 1964; *Zorba the Greek* 1964; *Georgy Girl* 1966; *Le Roi de Coeur* 1966; *Far From the Madding Crowd* 1967; *Rece Do Gory* 1967; *The Fixer* 1968 **(AANBA)**; *Women in Love* 1969; *A Day in the Death of Joe Egg* 1970; *Three Sisters* 1970; *The Go-Between* 1971; *Impossible Object* 1973; *Butley* 1974; *In Celebration* 1974; *Royal Flash* 1975; *The Shout* 1978; *An Unmarried Woman* 1978; *The Rose* 1979; *Nijinsky* 1980; *Quartet* 1981; *Britannia Hospital* 1982; *The Return of the Soldier* 1982; *An Englishman Abroad* 1983; *The Wicked Lady* 1983; *Dr. Fischer of Geneva* 1984; *Duet For One* 1986; *A Prayer For the Dying* 1987; *We Think the World of You* 1988; *Force Majeure* 1989; *102 Boulevard Haussmann* 1990; *Docteur M.* 1990; *Hamlet* 1990; *Mister Frost* 1990.

Baxter, Anne • Actress • Born Michigan City, IN, May 7, 1923; died December 12, 1985, New York, NY. *Educ.* Theodora Irvine's School of the Theater. Debuted on Broadway at the age of 13 and began her film career in 1940. A lasting, polished performer, Baxter was able to play the sweet and wholesome good girl (e.g. Orson Welles's *The Magnificent Ambersons* 1942) as well as the suspect bad girl (e.g. Fritz Lang's *The Blue Gardenia* 1953), and is best remembered as Bette Davis's scheming protege in *All About Eve* (1950). Her grandfather was architect Frank Lloyd Wright. • *The Great Profile* 1940; *Twenty Mule Team* 1940; *Charley's Aunt* 1941; *Swamp Water* 1941; *The Magnificent Ambersons* 1942; *The Pied Piper* 1942; *Crash Dive* 1943; *Five Graves to Cairo* 1943; *The North Star* 1943; *Guest in the House* 1944; *The Sullivans* 1944; *Sunday Dinner For a Soldier* 1944; *A Royal Scandal* 1945; *Angel on My Shoulder* 1946; *The Razor's Edge* 1946 **(AABSA)**; *Smoky* 1946; *Blaze of Noon* 1947; *Mother Wore Tights* 1947; *Homecoming* 1948; *The Luck of the Irish* 1948; *The Walls of Jericho* 1948; *Yellow Sky* 1948; *You're My Everything* 1949; *All About Eve* 1950 **(AANBA)**; *A Ticket to Tomahawk* 1950; *Follow the Sun* 1951; *My Wife's Best Friend* 1952; *O. Henry's Full House* 1952; *The Outcasts of Poker Flat* 1952; *The Blue Gardenia* 1953; *I Confess* 1953; *Bedevilled* 1954; *Carnival Story* 1954; *The Come On* 1955; *One Desire* 1955; *The Spoilers* 1955; *The Ten Commandments* 1956; *Three Violent People* 1956; *Chase a Crooked Shadow* 1958; *Cimarron* 1960; *Summer of the Seventeenth Doll* 1960; *Walk on the Wild Side* 1962; *The Family Jewels* 1965; *Frauen, die Durch die Holle Gehen* 1966; *The Busy Body* 1967; *Fools' Parade* 1971; *The Late Liz* 1971; *Jane Austen in Manhattan* 1980; *The Architecture of Frank Lloyd Wright* 1983; *Hitchcock, Il Brivido del Genio* 1985.

Baxter, Warner • Actor • Born Columbus, OH, March 29, 1891; died 1951. Entered movies in 1918 and emerged as a star in his first sound film, *In Old Arizona* (1929), playing the Cisco Kid. A capable lead through the 1930s, Baxter suffered a sharp career decline following a nervous breakdown in the early 40s. His final films were mostly low-budget affairs. He was married to silent screen performer Winifred Bryson. • *All Woman* 1918; *Cheated Hearts* 1921; *First Love* 1921; *The Love Charm* 1921; *Sheltered Daughters* 1921; *The Girl in His Room* 1922; *A Girl's Desire* 1922; *Her Own Money* 1922; *If I Were Queen* 1922; *The Ninety and Nine* 1922; *Blow Your Own Horn* 1923; *In Search of a Thrill* 1923; *St. Elmo* 1923; *Alimony* 1924; *Christine of the Hungry Heart* 1924; *The Female* 1924; *The Garden of Weeds* 1924; *His Forgotten Wife* 1924; *Those Who Dance* 1924; *The Air Mail* 1925; *The Awful Truth* 1925; *The Best People* 1925; *The Golden Bed* 1925; *Rugged Water* 1925; *A Son of His Father* 1925; *Welcome Home* 1925; *Aloma of the South Seas* 1926; *The Great Gatsby* 1926; *Mannequin* 1926; *Mismates* 1926; *Miss Brewster's Millions* 1926; *The Runaway* 1926; *The Coward* 1927; *Drums of the Desert* 1927; *Singed* 1927; *The Telephone Girl* 1927; *Craig's Wife* 1928; *Danger Street* 1928; *Ramona* 1928; *Three Sinners* 1928; *The Tragedy of Youth* 1928; *West of Zanzibar* 1928; *A Woman's Way* 1928; *Behind That Curtain* 1929; *Happy Days* 1929; *In Old Arizona* 1929 **(AABA)**; *Linda* 1929; *Romance of the Rio Grande* 1929; *Thru Different Eyes* 1929; *The Arizona Kid* 1930; *Renegades* 1930; *Such Men Are Dangerous* 1930; *The Cisco Kid* 1931; *Daddy Long Legs* 1931; *Doctors' Wives* 1931; *The Squaw Man* 1931; *Surrender* 1931; *Their Mad Moment* 1931; *Amateur Daddy* 1932; *Man About Town* 1932; *Six Hours to Live* 1932; *42nd Street* 1933; *As Husbands Go* 1933; *Dangerously Yours* 1933; *I Loved You Wednesday* 1933; *Paddy, the Next Best Thing* 1933; *Penthouse* 1933; *Broadway Bill* 1934; *Grand Canary* 1934; *Hell in the Heavens* 1934; *Stand Up and Cheer* 1934; *Such Women Are Dangerous* 1934; *King of Burlesque* 1935; *One More Spring* 1935; *Under the Pampas Moon* 1935; *The Prisoner of Shark Island* 1936; *The Road to Glory* 1936; *The Robin Hood of El Dorado* 1936; *To Mary—With Love* 1936; *White Hunter* 1936; *Slave Ship* 1937; *Vogues of 1938* 1937; *Wife, Doctor, and Nurse* 1937; *I'll Give a Million* 1938; *Kidnapped* 1938; *Barricade* 1939; *The Return of the Cisco Kid* 1939; *Wife, Husband, and Friend* 1939; *Earthbound* 1940; *Adam Had Four Sons* 1941; *Crime Doctor* 1943; *The Crime Doctor's Strangest Case* 1943; *Lady in the Dark* 1944; *Shadows in the Night* 1944; *The Crime Doctor's Courage* 1945; *The Crime Doctor's Warning* 1945; *Crime Doctor's Manhunt* 1946; *Just Before Dawn* 1946; *The Crime Doctor's Gamble* 1947; *The Millerson Case* 1947; *The Gentleman From Nowhere* 1948; *The Crime Doctor's Diary* 1949; *The Devil's Henchman* 1949; *Prison Warden* 1949; *State Penitentiary* 1950.

Baye, Nathalie • Actress • Born Mainneville, France, July 6, 1948. *Educ.* Paris Conservatoire. Former dancer who began her film career playing François Truffaut's assistant in *Day for Night* (1973). By the end of the decade, after two more Truffaut films and finely controlled performances in Bertrand Tavernier's *A Week's Vacation* (1980) and Claude Goretta's *A Girl from Lorraine* (1980), Baye had emerged as one of her country's leading actresses. Among her internationally known films are Bob Swaim's slick thriller *La Balance* (1982) and *The Return of Martin Guerre* (1982), opposite Gerard Depardieu. • *La Nuit Américaine/Day For Night* 1973; *La Gueule ouverte* 1974; *Un jour la fête* 1975; *L'Homme qui aimait les femmes* 1977; *Monsieur Papa* 1977; *La Chambre Verte* 1978; *Mon premier amour* 1978; *La Mémoire courte* 1979; *Je vais craquer!* 1980; *La Provinciale/A Girl From Lorraine* 1980; *Sauve qui peut la vie* 1980; *Une Semaine de vacances/A Week's Vacation* 1980; *Beau Père* 1981; *L'Ombre Rouge* 1981; *La Balance* 1982; *J'ai Epousé Une Ombre* 1982; *Le Retour de Martin Guerre/The Return of Martin Guerre* 1982; *Notre Histoire* 1984; *Rive Droite, Rive Gauche* 1984; *Beethoven's Nephew* 1985; *Detective* 1985; *Lune de Miel* 1985; *De guerre lasse* 1987; *En toute innocence* 1988; *La Baule les pins* 1990; *Giocodi Massacro* 1990; *The Man Inside* 1990; *Un Week-end sur deux* 1990.

Bazin, André • Critic, theorist • Born Angers, France, April 8, 1918; died 1958. Key post war film theorist whose influential two-volume collection of essays *What Is Cinema?* (1967) explores the relationship between film and reality, championing such masters of the long take and mise-en-scène as Jean Renoir and Orson Welles.

A mentor to the young, delinquent François Truffaut, Bazin co-founded in 1951 *Les Cahiers du Cinéma*, the still-prominent film journal that became the primary forum for the writings of the New Wave critics. His other works include the posthumously published *Jean Renoir* (1973) and *Orson Welles: A Critical View* (1978).

Beals, Jennifer • Actress • Born Chicago, IL, December 19, 1963. Appealing, intelligent performer who caused a stir in her debut, *Flashdance* (1983), but has since appeared in little of note. • *Flashdance* 1983; *The Bride* 1985; *La Partita* 1988; *Split Decisions* 1988; *Vampire's Kiss* 1988; *Sons* 1989; *Docteur M.* 1990.

Beard, John • Production designer • Born London. Began his career as an assistant art director on Nicholas Roeg's *Bad Timing* (1980) and soon graduated to full-fledged production designer. Beard has contributed to such visually stylized films as Roeg's *Eureka* (1983), Terry Gilliam's *Brazil* (1985) and Julien Temple's *Absolute Beginners* (1986), as well as Martin Scorsese's *The Last Temptation of Christ* (1988). • *Bad Timing* 1980 (asst.art d); *The Wildcats of St. Trinian's* 1980 (art d); *An Unsuitable Job For a Woman* 1981 (art d); *Digital Dreams* 1983 (art d); *Eureka* 1983 (art d); *Brazil* 1985 (art d); *Absolute Beginners* 1986 (pd); *Siesta* 1987 (pd); *The Last Temptation of Christ* 1988 (pd); *Erik the Viking* 1989 (pd).

Beatty, Ned • Actor • Born Louisville, KY, July 6, 1937. Chubby, sympathetic character player (even when playing bad guys) who moved into films after John Boorman saw him on Broadway in *The Great White Hope* and signed him for *Deliverance* (1972). Memorably as Gene Hackman's henchman, Otis, in the *Superman* movies (1978 and 1980). • *Deliverance* 1972; *The Life and Times of Judge Roy Bean* 1972; *The Last American Hero* 1973; *The Thief Who Came to Dinner* 1973; *White Lightning* 1973; *W.W. and the Dixie Dancekings* 1974; *Nashville* 1975; *All the President's Men* 1976; *The Big Bus* 1976; *Mikey and Nicky* 1976; *Network* 1976 **(AANBSA)**; *Silver Streak* 1976; *Exorcist II: The Heretic* 1977; *Gray Lady Down* 1977; *Shenanigans* 1977; *Alambrista!* 1978; *Superman* 1978; *1941* 1979; *American Success Company* 1979; *Promises in the Dark* 1979; *Wise Blood* 1979; *Hopscotch* 1980; *Superman II* 1980; *The Incredible Shrinking Woman* 1981; *The Toy* 1982; *The Ballad of Gregorio Cortez* 1983; *Stroker Ace* 1983; *Touched* 1983; *Restless Natives* 1985; *Back to School* 1986; *The Big Easy* 1986; *The Fourth Protocol* 1987; *Rolling Vengeance* 1987; *The Trouble With Spies* 1987; *After the Rain* 1988; *Midnight Crossing* 1988; *Physical Evidence* 1988; *Purple People Eater* 1988; *Shadows in the Storm* 1988; *Switching Channels* 1988; *The Unholy* 1988; *Ministry of Vengeance* 1989; *Time Trackers* 1989; *Twist of Fate* 1989; *Big Bad John* 1990; *Captain America* 1990; *Chattahoochee* 1990; *A Cry in the Wild* 1990; *Repossessed* 1990.

Beatty, Warren • Actor, producer; also director, screenwriter. • Born Henry Warren Beaty, Richmond, VA, March 30, 1937. *Educ.* Northwestern University. Intense, charismatic leading man who made an impressive screen debut in Elia Kazan's *Splendor in the Grass* (1961) and initiated his behind-the-camera career as producer of *Bonnie and Clyde* (1967), in which he also starred. Beatty has since divided his time among acting, directing and producing.

Politically active (he played a visible role in McGovern's 1972 presidential campaign and served as an unofficial advisor in Gary Hart's ill-fated 1988 bid), Beatty appeared in two of the more socially astute films of the 1970s: *The Parallax View* (1974), about an organization of political conspirators, and *Shampoo* (1975), tangentially a satire of the amorality of the Nixon administration.

Beatty's acting, directing, screenwriting and producing efforts reached a peak with *Reds* (1981), a churning love story set against the Russian revolution and based on the life of journalist John Reed. His subsequent output has been sporadic, although he successfully masterminded and starred in the larger-than-life comic-strip hit, *Dick Tracy* (1990). Beatty's name has been romantically linked to a number of screen personalities, notably co-stars Julie Christie, Diane Keaton and Madonna. He is the brother of Shirley MacLaine. • *The Roman Spring of Mrs. Stone* 1961 (a); *Splendor in the Grass* 1961 (a); *All Fall Down* 1962 (a); *Lilith* 1964 (a); *Mickey One* 1965 (a); *Kaleidoscope* 1966 (a); *Promise Her Anything* 1966 (a); *Bonnie and Clyde* 1967 (a,p) **(AANBA,AANBP)**; *The Only Game in Town* 1970 (a); *$* 1971 (a); *McCabe & Mrs. Miller* 1971 (a); *The Parallax View* 1974 (a); *The Fortune* 1975 (a); *Shampoo* 1975 (a,p,sc) **(AANBSC)**; *Heaven Can Wait* 1978 (a,d,p,sc) **(AANBA, AANBD,AANBP,AANBSC)**; *Reds* 1981 (a,d,p,sc) **(AANBA,AANBP,AANBSC, AABD)**; *Ishtar* 1987 (a,m,songs,p); *The Pick-Up Artist* 1978 (exec.p); *Dick Tracy* 1990 (a,d,p).

Beaudine, William • Director • Born New York, NY, January 15, 1892; died 1970. Began his career as a prop boy for D.W. Griffith in 1909 and worked his way up to the director's chair six years later. Handling features from 1922, Beaudine was a prolific craftsman rather than an auteur; he worked dependably across a wide range of genres and did on occasion turn out noteworthy films such as the Mary Pickford vehicle, *Sparrows* (1926).

From 1934 to 1937 Beaudine piloted over ten features in Great Britain and, after returning to the US, continued his prolific output, working for various low-budget producers and directing a number of the "Bowery Boys" movies. From the early 1950s he worked increasingly in TV, directing some 200 shows including over 80 episodes of "Lassie" and over 50 installments of the "Walt Disney" series. • *Catch My Smoke* 1922; *Heroes of the Street* 1922; *Watch Your Step* 1922; *Boy of Mine* 1923; *The Country Kid* 1923; *Her Fatal Millions* 1923; *Penrod and Sam* 1923; *The Printer's Devil* 1923; *Cornered* 1924; *Daring Youth* 1924; *Daughters of Pleasure* 1924; *The Narrow Street* 1924; *A Self-Made Failure* 1924; *Wandering Husbands* 1924; *A Broadway Butterfly* 1925; *How Baxter Butted in* 1925; *Little Annie Rooney* 1925; *The Canadian* 1926; *Hold That Lion* 1926; *The Social Highwayman* 1926; *Sparrows* 1926; *That's My Baby* 1926; *Frisco Sally Levy* 1927; *The Irresistible Lover* 1927; *The Life of Riley* 1927; *The Cohens and the Kellys in Paris* 1928; *Do Your Duty* 1928; *Give and Take* 1928; *Heart to Heart* 1928; *Home James* 1928; *Fugitives* 1929; *The Girl From Woolworth's* 1929; *Hard to Get* 1929; *Two Weeks Off* 1929; *Wedding Rings* 1929; *Road to Paradise* 1930; *Those Who Dance* 1930; *Father's Son* 1931; *The Lady Who Dared* 1931; *The Mad Parade* 1931; *Men in Her Life* 1931; *Misbehaving Ladies* 1931; *Penrod and Sam* 1931; *Make Me a Star* 1932; *Three Wise Girls* 1932; *The Crime of the Century* 1933; *Her Bodyguard* 1933; *The Old-Fashioned Way* 1934; *Boys Will Be Boys* 1935; *Dandy Dick* 1935 (d,sc); *Get Off My Foot* 1935; *Mr. Cohen Takes a Walk* 1935; *So You Won't Talk!* 1935; *Two Hearts in Harmony* 1935; *Educated Evans* 1936; *Good Morning, Boys* 1936 (d,sc); *It's in the Bag* 1936; *Windbag the Sailor* 1936; *Feather Your Nest* 1937; *Said O'Reilly to McNab* 1937; *Transatlantic Trouble* 1937; *Torchy Gets Her Man* 1938; *Torchy Blane in Chinatown* 1939; *Up Jumped the Devil* 1939; *Misbehaving Husbands* 1940; *Mr. Washington Goes to Town* 1940; *Blonde Comet* 1941; *Desperate Cargo* 1941; *Emergency Landing* 1941; *Federal Fugitives* 1941; *The Miracle Kid* 1941; *Mr. Celebrity* 1941; *The Warden's Daughter* 1941; *Broadway Big Shot* 1942; *Duke of the Navy* 1942 (d,sc,story); *Foreign Agent* 1942; *Gallant Lady* 1942; *The Living Ghost* 1942; *Men of San Quentin* 1942; *One Thrilling Night* 1942; *The Panther's Claw* 1942; *Phantom Killer* 1942; *Professor Creeps* 1942; *The Ape Man* 1943; *Clancy Street Boys* 1943; *Ghosts on the Loose* 1943; *Here Comes Kelly* 1943; *Mr. Muggs Steps Out* 1943; *The Mystery of the 13th Guest* 1943; *Spotlight Scandals* 1943; *What a Man!* 1943; *Adventures of Kitty O'Day* 1944; *Bowery Champs* 1944; *Crazy Knights* 1944; *Detective Kitty O'Day* 1944; *Follow the Leader* 1944; *Hot Rhythm* 1944; *Leave It to the Irish* 1944; *Mom and Dad* 1944; *Oh, What a Night!* 1944; *Shadow of Suspicion* 1944; *Voodoo Man* 1944; *Black Market Babies* 1945; *Come Out Fighting* 1945; *Fashion Model* 1945; *Swingin' on a Rainbow* 1945; *Below the Deadline* 1946; *Blonde Ransom* 1946; *Don't Gamble With*

Strangers 1946; *Face of Marble* 1946; *Girl on the Spot* 1946; *Mr. Hex* 1946; *One Exciting Week* 1946; *Spook Busters* 1946; *Bowery Buckaroos* 1947; *The Chinese Ring* 1947; *Gas House Kids Go West* 1947; *Hard Boiled Money* 1947; *Killer at Large* 1947; *News Hounds* 1947; *Philo Vance Returns* 1947; *Too Many Winners* 1947; *Angels Alley* 1948; *The Feathered Serpent* 1948; *Incident* 1948; *Jiggs and Maggie in Court* 1948; *Jinx Money* 1948; *Kidnapped* 1948; *The Mystery of the Golden Eye* 1948; *The Shanghai Chest* 1948; *Smugglers Cove* 1948; *Blonde Dynamite* 1949; *Blue Grass of Kentucky* 1949; *Forgotten Women* 1949; *Jiggs and Maggie in Jackpot Jitters* 1949; *The Lawton Story* 1949; *Tough Assignment* 1949; *Tuna Clipper* 1949; *Blues Busters* 1950; *County Fair* 1950; *Ghost Chasers* 1950; *Jiggs and Maggie Out West* 1950; *Lucky Losers* 1950; *Second Chance* 1950; *Bowery Battalion* 1951; *The Congregation* 1951; *Crazy Over Horses* 1951; *Cuban Fireball* 1951; *Havana Rose* 1951; *Let's Go Navy* 1951; *Rodeo* 1951; *A Wonderful Life* 1951; *Bela Lugosi Meets a Brooklyn Gorilla* 1952; *Feudin' Fool* 1952; *Here Come the Marines* 1952; *Hold That Line* 1952; *Jet Job* 1952; *No Holds Barred* 1952; *The Rose Bowl Story* 1952; *Born to the Saddle* 1953; *For Every Heart* 1953; *The Hidden Heart* 1953; *Jalopy* 1953; *Murder Without Tears* 1953; *Roar of the Crowd* 1953; *City Story (short)* 1954; *Highway Dragnet* 1954 (ad); *More For Peace* 1954; *Paris Playboys* 1954; *Pride of the Blue Grass* 1954; *Stryker's Progress* 1954; *Yukon Vengeance* 1954; *High Society* 1955; *Jail Busters* 1955; *Westward Ho the Wagons!* 1956; *Up in Smoke* 1957; *In the Money* 1958; *Ten Who Dared* 1960; *Lassie's Great Adventure* 1963; *Billy the Kid vs. Dracula* 1966; *Jesse James Meets Frankenstein's Daughter* 1966.

Beavers, Louise • Actress • Born Cincinnati, OH, March 8, 1902; died 1962. In films from the early 1920s, Beavers most often played the subservient but jovial black maid, as in the original *Imitation of Life* (1934). She later succeeded Hattie McDaniel as TV's third "Beulah" (1952-53). • *The Glad Rag Doll* 1929; *Nix on Dames* 1929; *Wall Street* 1929; *Back Pay* 1930; *Safety in Numbers* 1930; *She Couldn't Say No* 1930; *Wide Open* 1930; *Annabelle's Affairs* 1931; *Girls About Town* 1931; *Good Sport* 1931; *Ladies of the Big House* 1931; *Sundown Trail* 1931; *Divorce in the Family* 1932; *The Expert* 1932; *It's Tough to Be Famous* 1932; *Street of Women* 1932; *Too Busy to Work* 1932; *Unashamed* 1932; *What Price Hollywood?* 1932; *Wild Girl* 1932; *Young America* 1932; *Blonde Bombshell* 1933; *Girl Missing* 1933; *Her Bodyguard* 1933; *Her Splendid Folly* 1933; *In the Money* 1933; *Notorious But Nice* 1933; *Pick Up* 1933; *She Done Him Wrong* 1933; *A Shriek in the Night* 1933; *What Price Innocence?* 1933; *Bedside* 1934; *Cheaters* 1934; *Glamour* 1934; *Hat, Coat, and Glove* 1934; *I've Got Your Number* 1934; *Imitation of Life* 1934; *The Merry Frinks* 1934; *West of the Pecos* 1934; *Annapolis Farewell* 1935; *Bullets or Ballots* 1936; *General Spanky* 1936; *Rainbow on the River* 1936; *Wives Never Know* 1936; *The Last Gangster* 1937; *Love in a Bungalow* 1937; *Make Way For Tomorrow* 1937; *Wings Over Honolulu* 1937; *Brother Rat* 1938; *The Headleys at Home* 1938; *Peck's Bad Boy With the Circus* 1938; *Scandal Street* 1938; *The Lady's From Kentucky* 1939; *Made For Each Other* 1939; *Reform School* 1939; *I Want a Divorce* 1940; *No Time For Comedy* 1940; *Parole Fixer* 1940; *Women Without Names* 1940; *Belle Starr* 1941; *Kisses For Breakfast* 1941; *Shadow of the Thin Man* 1941; *Sign of the Wolf* 1941; *The Vanishing Virginian* 1941; *Virginia* 1941; *The Big Street* 1942; *Holiday Inn* 1942; *Reap the Wild Wind* 1942; *Seven Sweethearts* 1942; *Young America* 1942; *All By Myself* 1943; *Du Barry Was a Lady* 1943; *Jack London* 1943; *Barbary Coast Gent* 1944; *Dixie Jamboree* 1944; *Follow the Boys* 1944; *South of Dixie* 1944; *Delightfully Dangerous* 1945; *Lover Come Back* 1946; *Banjo* 1947; *For the Love of Mary* 1948; *Good Sam* 1948; *Mr. Blandings Builds His Dream House* 1948; *Tell It to the Judge* 1949; *Girls' School* 1950; *The Jackie Robinson Story* 1950; *My Blue Heaven* 1950; *Colorado Sundown* 1952; *I Dream of Jeanie* 1952; *Never Wave at a Wac* 1952; *Good-Bye, My Lady* 1956; *Teenage Rebel* 1956; *You Can't Run Away From It* 1956; *Tammy and the Bachelor* 1957; *The Goddess* 1958; *All the Fine Young Cannibals* 1960; *The Facts of Life* 1960.

Becker, Harold • Director • Born New York, NY. *Educ.* Pratt Institute, Brooklyn, NY (art). Talented filmmaker who began his career in still photography, moved into TV commercials and garnered praise for a number of short documentaries. Becker made a superb, if overlooked debut feature with *The Ragman's Daughter* (1972), shot in Britain, and gained attention with a cool, gripping adaptation of Joseph Wambaugh's *The Onion Field* (1979).

Becker's command of atmosphere and suspense is evident in such varied films as the tense cadet drama, *Taps* (1981), the intelligent juvenile romance, *Vision Quest* (1985) and the charged New York cop thriller, *Sea of Love* (1989). • *Interview With Bruce Gordon (short)* 1964; *The Ragman's Daughter* 1972 (d,p); *The Black Marble* 1979; *The Onion Field* 1979; *Taps* 1981; *Vision Quest* 1985; *The Boost* 1988; *Sea of Love* 1989.

Becker, Jacques • Director; also screenwriter. • Born Paris, September 15, 1906; died February 21, 1960, Paris. Former assistant to Jean Renoir who began directing his own features in the early 1940s. Becker directed only 13 films and has been largely neglected by critics, though he was celebrated by the auteurs of the New Wave for *Casque d'Or* (1952), a spirited tour of France's turn-of-the-century underworld, and *Touchez pas au Grisbi* (1953), a gangster melodrama starring Jean Gabin and Jeanne Moreau. Becker was married to actress Françoise Fabian and his son Jean Becker (b. 1933) is also a director. • *Le Bled* 1929 (a); *Boudu Sauve des Eaux* 1932 (a,ad); *Chotard et Compagnie* 1932 (ad); *La Nuit du carrefour* 1932 (ad); *Madame Bovary* 1934 (ad); *Toni* 1934 (ad); *Le Commissaire est bon enfant (short)* 1935 (a,d,sc,story); *Tête de turc (short)* 1935 (d,sc); *Les Bas-Fonds/The Lower Depths* 1936 (a,ad); *Un Partie de Campagne/A Day in the Country* 1936 (a,ad); *La Vie est à nous* 1936 (a,ad); *La Grande Illusion/Grand Illusion* 1937 (a,ad); *La Bête Humaine* 1938 (ad); *Communist Party Congress Documentary at Arles* 1938 (d); *La Marseillaise* 1938 (ad); *L'Or de Cristobal* 1939 (d); *La Règle du jeu/Rules of the Game* 1939 (ad); *Dernier Atout* 1942 (d,p,sc); *Goupi Mains rouges* 1943 (d,sc); *Falbalas* 1945 (d,sc); *Antoine and Antoinette* 1947 (d,sc); *Rendez-vous de Juillet* 1948 (d,sc,story,dial); *Edouard et Caroline* 1951 (d,sc); *Casque d'or* 1952 (d,sc,dial); *Rue de l'Estrapade* 1953 (d,dial); *Touchez Pas au Grisbi* 1953 (d,sc); *Ali-Baba et les quarante voleurs* 1954 (d,sc,story); *Les Aventures d'Arsène Lupin* 1956 (a,d,sc); *Montparnasse 19* 1958 (d,sc); *Le Trou* 1959 (d,sc,dial).

Bedelia, Bonnie • Actress • Born New York, NY, March 25, 1952. *Educ.* School of the American Ballet, New York; Hunter College, New York. Talented leading lady who, as a juvenile performer, racked up numerous credits on TV and Broadway and danced in four productions of the New York City Ballet. In films from 1969, Bedelia first gained widespread critical acclaim playing real-life race car driver Shirley Muldowney in *Heart Like a Wheel* (1982). She enjoyed renewed attention for her appearances in the popular summer releases *Die Hard* (1988), *Die Hard 2* and *Presumed Innocent* (both 1990). • *The Gypsy Moths* 1969; *They Shoot Horses, Don't They?* 1969; *Lovers and Other Strangers* 1970; *The Strange Vengeance* 1972; *Get Back* 1973; *The Big Fix* 1978; *Heart Like a Wheel* 1982; *Death of an Angel* 1985; *The Boy Who Could Fly* 1986; *Violets Are Blue* 1986; *The Stranger* 1987; *Die Hard* 1988; *The Prince of Pennsylvania* 1988; *Fat Man and Little Boy* 1989; *Die Hard 2: Die Harder* 1990; *Presumed Innocent* 1990.

Beery, Noah • Actor • Born Kansas City, MO, January 17, 1884; died 1946. One of screendom's most venerable villains, in films from 1917. His son, Noah Beery, Jr., started in films at the age of seven (appearing with his father in *The Mark of Zorro* 1920) and later became a routine character player. Elder half-brother of Wallace Beery. • *The Hostage* 1917; *A Mormon Maid* 1917; *Believe Me Xantippe* 1918; *Hidden Pearls* 1918; *His Robe of Honor* 1918; *Less Than Kin* 1918; *The Source* 1918; *The Squaw Man* 1918; *Too Many Millions* 1918; *The Whispering Chorus* 1918; *The White Man's Law* 1918; *Everywoman* 1919; *The Red Lantern* 1919; *The Valley of the Giants* 1919; *The Fighting Shepherdess* 1920; *Go and Get It* 1920; *The Mark of Zorro* 1920; *The Sea Wolf* 1920; *Beach of Dreams* 1921; *Bits of Life* 1921; *Bob Hampton of Placer* 1921; *The Call of the North* 1921; *Lotus Blossom* 1921; *The Scoffer* 1921; *Belle of Alaska* 1922; *The Crossroads of New York* 1922; *Ebb Tide* 1922; *Flesh and Blood* 1922; *Good Men and True* 1922; *The Heart Specialist* 1922; *I Am the Law* 1922; *The Lying Truth* 1922; *Omar the Tentmaker* 1922; *Penrod* 1922; *The Power of Love* 1922; *Tillie* 1922; *Wild Honey* 1922; *Youth to Youth* 1922; *The Call of the Canyon* 1923; *Dangerous Trails* 1923; *The Destroying Angel* 1923; *His Last Race* 1923; *Hollywood* 1923; *Main Street* 1923; *Quicksands* 1923; *The Soul of the Beast* 1923; *The Spider and the Rose* 1923; *The Spoilers* 1923; *Stephen Steps Out* 1923; *Stormswept* 1923; *Tipped Off* 1923; *To the Last Man* 1923; *Wandering Daughters* 1923; *The Female* 1924; *The Fighting Coward* 1924; *Lily of the Dust* 1924; *North of 36* 1924; *Wanderer of the Wastleland* 1924; *Welcome Stranger* 1924; *The Coming of Amos* 1925; *Contraband* 1925; *East of Suez* 1925; *The Light of Western Stars* 1925; *Lord Jim* 1925; *Old Shoes* 1925; *The Spaniard* 1925; *The Thundering Herd* 1925; *The Vanishing American* 1925; *Beau Geste* 1926; *The Crown of Lies* 1926; *The Enchanted Hill* 1926; *Padlocked* 1926; *Paradise* 1926; *The Dove* 1927; *Evening Clothes* 1927; *The Love Mart* 1927; *The Rough Riders* 1927; *Beau Sabreur* 1928; *Hell-Ship Bronson* 1928; *The Passion Song* 1928; *Two Lovers* 1928; *Careers* 1929; *False Fathers* 1929; *The Four Feathers* 1929; *Glorifying the American Girl* 1929; *The Godless Girl* 1929; *Linda* 1929; *Love in the Desert* 1929; *Noah's Ark* 1929; *The Show of Shows* 1929; *Two O'Clock in the Morning* 1929; *Big Boy* 1930; *Bright Lights* 1930; *Golden Dawn* 1930; *Isle of Escape* 1930; *The Love Trader* 1930; *Mammy* 1930; *Murder Will Out* 1930; *Oh! Sailor, Behave!* 1930; *Renegades* 1930; *A Soldier's Plaything* 1930; *Song of the Flame* 1930; *Tol'able David* 1930; *Under a Texas Moon* 1930; *The Way of All Men* 1930; *The Homicide Squad* 1931; *Honeymoon Lane* 1931; *In Line of Duty* 1931; *The Millionaire* 1931; *Riders of the Purple Sage* 1931; *Shanghaied Love* 1931; *The Big Stampede* 1932; *Cornered* 1932; *The Devil Horse* 1932; *The Drifter* 1932; *The Kid From Spain* 1932; *No Living Witness* 1932; *Out of Singapore* 1932; *The Stoker* 1932; *Stranger in Town* 1932; *Easy Millions* 1933; *Fighting With Kit Carson* 1933; *The Flaming Signal* 1933; *Laughing at Life* 1933; *Man of the Forest* 1933; *She Done Him Wrong* 1933; *Sunset Pass* 1933; *The Thundering Herd* 1933; *To the Last Man* 1933; *The Woman I Stole* 1933; *Caravan* 1934; *Cockeyed Cavaliers* 1934; *David Harum* 1934; *Happy Landing* 1934; *Kentucky Kernels* 1934; *Madame Spy* 1934; *Mystery Liner* 1934; *The Trail Beyond* 1934; *Sweet Adeline* 1935; *Someone at the Door* 1936; *Zorro Rides Again* 1937; *The Bad Man of Brimstone* 1938; *The Girl of the Golden West* 1938; *Panamint's Bad Man* 1938; *Mexicali Rose* 1939; *Mutiny on the Blackhawk* 1939; *Adventures of Red Ryder* 1940; *Grandpa Goes to Town* 1940; *Pioneers of the West* 1940; *The Tulsa Kid* 1940; *The Missouri Outlaw* 1941; *The Devil's Trail* 1942; *Outlaws of Pine Ridge* 1942; *Overland Mail* 1942; *Tennessee Johnson* 1942; *Carson City Cyclone* 1943; *Clancy Street Boys* 1943; *Salute to the Marines* 1943; *Barbary Coast Gent* 1944; *Block Busters* 1944; *Million Dollar Kid* 1944; *Sing Me a Song of Texas* 1945; *This Man's Navy* 1945.

Beery, Wallace • Actor • Born Kansas City, MO, April 1, 1885; died April 15, 1949, Beverly Hills, CA. Burly, barrel-chested heavy of the silent era who emerged as a stolid but endearing presence with the advent of sound, enlivening such films as *The Champ* (1931) and *Grand Hotel* (1932). Despite his bearish frame and none-too-handsome looks he was married to silent screen diva Gloria Swanson from 1916 to 1918. Half-brother of Noah Beery. • *Teddy at the Throttle* 1916; *Timothy Dobbs, That's Me* 1916 (d,p); *The Little American* 1917; *Johanna Enlists* 1918; *Behind the Door* 1919; *The Life Line* 1919; *The Love Burglar* 1919; *Soldiers of Fortune* 1919; *The Unpardonable Sin* 1919; *Victory* 1919; *813* 1920; *The Last of the Mohicans* 1920; *The Mollycoddle* 1920; *The Round-Up* 1920; *The Virgin of Stamboul* 1920; *The Four Horsemen of the Apocalypse* 1921; *The Golden Snare* 1921; *The Last Trail* 1921; *Patsy* 1921; *The Rookie's Return* 1921; *A Tale of Two Worlds* 1921; *Hurricane's Gal* 1922; *I Am the Law* 1922; *The Man From Hell's River* 1922; *Only a Shop Girl* 1922; *Robin Hood* 1922; *The Rosary* 1922; *The Sagebrush Trail* 1922; *Trouble* 1922; *Wild Honey* 1922; *Ashes of Vengeance* 1923; *Bavu* 1923; *Drifting* 1923; *The Eternal Struggle* 1923; *The Flame of Life* 1923; *Richard, the Lion-Hearted* 1923; *The Spanish Dancer* 1923; *Stormswept* 1923; *The Three Ages* 1923; *White Tiger* 1923; *Another Man's Wife* 1924; *The Drums of Jeopardy* 1924; *Dynamite Smith* 1924; *Madonna of the Streets* 1924; *The Red Lily* 1924; *The Sea Hawk* 1924; *The Signal Tower* 1924; *So Big* 1924; *Unseen Hands* 1924; *Adventure* 1925; *Coming Through* 1925; *The Devil's Cargo* 1925; *The Great Divide* 1925; *In the Name of Love* 1925; *Let Women Alone* 1925; *The Lost World* 1925; *The Night Club* 1925; *The Pony Express* 1925; *Rugged Water* 1925; *Behind the Front* 1926; *Old Ironsides* 1926; *Volcano* 1926; *The Wanderer* 1926; *We're in the Navy Now* 1926; *Casey at the Bat* 1927; *Fireman, Save My Child* 1927; *Now We're in the Air* 1927; *Beggars of Life* 1928; *The Big Killing* 1928; *Partners in Crime* 1928; *Wife Savers* 1928; *Chinatown Nights* 1929; *River of Romance* 1929; *Stairs of Sand* 1929; *The Big House* 1930 **(AANBA)**; *Billy the Kid* 1930; *A Lady's Morals* 1930; *Min and Bill* 1930; *Way For a Sailor* 1930; *The Champ* 1931 **(AABA)**; *Hell Divers* 1931; *The Secret Six* 1931; *Flesh* 1932; *Grand Hotel* 1932; *The Bowery* 1933; *Dinner at Eight* 1933; *Tugboat Annie* 1933; *The Mighty Barnum* 1934; *Treasure Island* 1934; *Viva Villa* 1934; *Ah, Wilderness!* 1935; *China Seas* 1935; *O'Shaughnessy's Boy* 1935; *A Message to Garcia* 1936; *Old Hutch* 1936; *The Good Old Soak* 1937; *Slave Ship* 1937; *The Bad Man of Brimstone* 1938; *Port of Seven Seas* 1938; *Stablemates* 1938; *Sergeant Madden* 1939; *Stand Up and Fight* 1939; *Thunder Afloat* 1939; *The Man From Dakota* 1940; *Twenty Mule Team* 1940; *Wyoming* 1940; *The Bad Man* 1941; *Barnacle Bill* 1941; *The Bugle Sounds* 1941; *Jackass Mail* 1942; *Salute to the Marines* 1943; *Barbary Coast Gent* 1944; *Rationing* 1944; *This Man's Navy* 1945; *Bad Bascomb* 1946; *Mighty McGurk* 1946; *Alias a Gentleman* 1947; *Big Jack* 1948; *A Date With Judy* 1948.

Begley, Ed • Actor • Born Edward James Begley, Hartford, CT, March 25, 1901; died 1970. Veteran character player, effective as sneering, insidious types in films like *Twelve Angry Men* (1957) and *Sweet Bird of Youth* (1962). Father of actor Ed Begley, Jr. • *Boomerang* 1947; *Deep Waters* 1948; *Sitting Pretty* 1948; *Sorry, Wrong Number* 1948; *The Street With No Name* 1948; *The Great Gatsby* 1949; *It Happens Every Spring* 1949; *Tulsa* 1949; *Backfire* 1950; *Convicted* 1950; *Dark City* 1950; *Saddle Tramp* 1950; *Stars in My Crown* 1950; *Wyoming Mail* 1950; *The Lady From Texas* 1951; *On Dangerous Ground* 1951; *U.S.S. Tea Kettle* 1951; *Boots Malone* 1952; *Deadline U.S.A.* 1952; *Lone Star* 1952; *The Turning Point* 1952; *Patterns* 1955; *Twelve Angry Men* 1957; *Odds Against Tomorrow* 1959; *Sweet Bird of Youth* 1962 **(AABSA)**; *The Unsinkable Molly Brown* 1964; *The Oscar* 1966; *Billion Dollar Brain* 1967; *Firecreek* 1968; *Hang 'Em High* 1968; *A Time to Sing* 1968; *The Monitors* 1969; *The Violent Enemy* 1969; *The Dunwich Horror* 1970.

Begley, Ed, Jr. • Actor; also comedian. • Born Los Angeles, CA, September 16, 1949. *Educ.* Valley College, Hollywood, CA. Tall, fair-haired performer who began his career in the early 1970s and is best in offbeat comic parts. Begley earned six successive Emmy nominations for his role as Dr. Vincent Ehrlich on TV's "St. Elsewhere" (1982-88). Son of actor Ed Begley. • *Charley and the Angel* 1972; *Now You See Him, Now You Don't* 1972; *Showdown* 1973; *Cockfighter* 1974; *Stay Hungry* 1975; *Citizens Band* 1977; *Record City* 1977; *Battlestar Galactica* 1978; *Blue Collar* 1978; *Goin' South* 1978; *The One and Only* 1978; *The Concorde—Airport '79* 1979; *Hardcore* 1979; *The In-Laws* 1979; *Private Lessons* 1980; *Buddy Buddy* 1981; *Cat People* 1982; *Eating Raoul* 1982; *The Entity* 1982; *An Officer and a Gentleman* 1982; *Get Crazy* 1983; *Protocol* 1984; *Streets of Fire* 1984; *This Is Spinal Tap* 1984; *Transylvania 6-5000* 1985; *Amazon Women on the Moon* 1987; *The Accidental Tourist* 1988; *Scenes From the Class Struggle in Beverly Hills* 1989; *She-Devil* 1989; *Meet the Applegates* 1991.

Beineix, Jean-Jacques • Director; also producer, screenwriter. • Born Paris, 1946. Won deserved international acclaim for his sleek, accomplished debut, *Diva* (1980). Beineix's subsequent films have been long on style but short on substance. • *L'Animal* 1977 (ad); *French Postcards* 1979 (ad); *Diva* 1980 (d,sc,dial); *La Lune dans le caniveau/The Moon in the Gutter* 1983 (d,sc); *37.2 Le Matin/Betty Blue* 1986 (d,p,sc); *Le Grand cirque* 1989 (a,p); *Roselyne et les lions* 1989 (d,p,sc).

Belafonte, Harry • Singer; also producer, actor. • Born Harold George Belafonte, Jr., New York, NY, March 1, 1927. *Educ.* Actors Studio; Dramatic Workshop of the New School for Social Research, New York; American Negro Theatre. Handsome singer who popularized calypso music in America in the 1950s. Although he has appeared in relatively few films, Belafonte turned in fine perfomances in Otto Preminger's *Carmen Jones* (1954), the taut crime thriller *Odds Against Tomorrow* (1959, his debut as a producer) and as a contrite black angel in Jan Kadar's affecting *The Angel Levine* (1970). Daughter Shari Belafonte is a highly successful model with some acting experience. • *Bright Road* 1953 (a); *Carmen Jones* 1954 (a); *Island in the Sun* 1957 (a); *Odds Against Tomorrow* 1959 (a,exec.p); *The World, the Flesh and the Devil* 1959 (a,song); *The Angel Levine* 1970 (a); *King: A Filmed Record... Montgomery to Memphis* 1970 (a); *Buck and the Preacher* 1972 (a); *Uptown Saturday Night* 1974 (a); *Beat Street* 1984 (add.m,m.prod,p); *First Look* 1984 (a); *Beetlejuice* 1988 (song).

Bellamy, Ralph • Actor • Born Chicago, IL, June 17, 1904. Engaging performer who made his mark as the luckless nice guy in several screwball comedies beginning with *The Awful Truth* (1937). A prolific character player, Bellamy has appeared in over 100 films; he contributed an excellent turn as a manipulative Wall Street mogul in the amusing social comedy *Trading Places* (1983). • *The Magnificent Lie* 1931; *The Secret Six* 1931; *Surrender* 1931; *West of Broadway* 1931; *Air Mail* 1932; *Almost Married* 1932; *Disorderly Conduct* 1932; *Forbidden* 1932; *Rebecca of Sunnybrook Farm* 1932; *Wild Girl* 1932; *The Woman in Room 13* 1932; *Young America* 1932; *Ace of Aces* 1933; *Before Midnight* 1933; *Below the Sea* 1933; *Blind Adventure* 1933; *Destination Unknown* 1933; *Ever in My Heart* 1933; *Flying Devils* 1933; *Headline Shooter* 1933; *The Narrow Corner* 1933; *Parole Girl* 1933; *Picture Snatcher* 1933; *Second Hand Wife* 1933; *The Crime of Helen Stanley* 1934; *Girl in Danger* 1934; *Helldorado* 1934; *Once to Every Woman* 1934; *One Is Guilty* 1934; *Spitfire* 1934; *This Man Is Mine* 1934; *Woman in the Dark* 1934; *Air Hawks* 1935; *Eight Bells* 1935; *Gigolette* 1935; *Hands Across the Table* 1935; *The Healer* 1935; *Navy Wife* 1935; *Rendezvous at Midnight* 1935; *The Wedding Night* 1935; *Counterfeit Lady* 1936; *Dangerous Intrigue* 1936; *The Final Hour* 1936; *The Man Who Lived Twice* 1936; *Roaming Lady* 1936; *Straight From the Shoulder* 1936; *Wild Brian Kent* 1936; *The Awful Truth* 1937 (**AANBSA**); *It Can't Last Forever* 1937; *Let's Get Married* 1937; *Boy Meets Girl* 1938; *Carefree* 1938; *The Crime of Dr. Hallett* 1938; *Fools for Scandal* 1938; *Girl's School* 1938; *Trade Winds* 1938; *Blind Alley* 1939; *Coast Guard* 1939; *Let Us Live* 1939; *Smashing the Spy Ring* 1939; *Brother Orchid* 1940; *Dance, Girl, Dance* 1940; *Ellery Queen, Master Detective* 1940; *Flight Angels* 1940; *His Girl Friday* 1940; *Meet the Wildcat* 1940; *Public Deb No. 1* 1940; *Queen of the Mob* 1940; *Affectionately Yours* 1941; *Dive Bomber* 1941; *Ellery Queen and the Murder Ring* 1941; *Ellery Queen and the Perfect Crime* 1941; *Ellery Queen's Penthouse Mystery* 1941; *Footsteps in the Dark* 1941; *The Wolf Man* 1941; *The Ghost of Frankenstein* 1942; *The Great Impersonation* 1942; *Lady in a Jam* 1942; *Men of Texas* 1942; *Stage Door Canteen* 1943; *Guest in the House* 1944; *Delightfully Dangerous* 1945; *Lady on a Train* 1945; *The Court Martial of Billy Mitchell* 1955; *Sunrise at Campobello* 1960; *The Professionals* 1966; *Rosemary's Baby* 1968; *Doctors' Wives* 1970; *Cancel My Reservation* 1972; *Oh, God!* 1977; *Trading Places* 1983; *Amazon Women on the Moon* 1987; *Disorderlies* 1987; *Coming to America* 1988; *The Good Mother* 1988; *Pretty Woman* 1990.

Bellocchio, Marco • Director; also screenwriter, actor. • Born Piacenza, Italy, November 9, 1939. *Educ.* University of the Sacred Heart, Milan (literature, philosophy); School of Dramatic Arts, Milan; Centro Sperimentale di Cinematografia, Rome (acting, directing); Slade School of Fine Arts, London (film). Iconoclastic director whose feature debut, *Fist in His Pocket* (1965), was a scathing political allegory about a family of bourgeois epileptics. The film, along with Bernardo Bertolucci's *Before the Revolution* (1964), was heralded as the beginning of a new era in Italian cinema.

Bellocchio's subsequent films, notably the antic satire of Italian politics, *China Is Near* (1967), and the surreal, biting memoir of a Jesuit education, *In the Name of the Father* (1971), have continued to criticize traditional social institutions, though they have generated less critical enthusiasm than his debut. His 1986 film *The Devil in the Flesh* was an uneven update of the 1946 classic adapted from the novel by Raymond Radiguet. Dedicated to Bellochio's analyst, it stirred some controversy for its explicit sex. • *I Pugni in Tasca/Fist in His Pocket* 1965 (d,sc); *Amore e rabbia* 1967 (d); *La Cina è vicina/China Is Near* 1967 (d,sc,story); *In Nome del Padre/In the Name of the Father* 1971 (d,sc); *Sbatti Il Mostro In Prima Pagina* 1972 (d); *La Marche Triomphale* 1975 (d,sc); *Matti da slegare* 1975 (d); *Salo o le Centiventi Giornate di Sodoma/Salo or the 120 Days of Sodom* 1975 (a); *Il Gabbiano* 1977 (d,sc.adapt); *Salto Nel Vuoto* 1980 (d,sc); *Vacanze in Val Trebbia* 1980 (a,d,sc); *Gli Occhi, la Bocca* 1982 (d,sc,story); *Enrico IV/Henry IV* 1984 (d,sc); *Il Diavolo in Corpo/The Devil in the Flesh* 1986 (d,sc); *La Visione del Sabba* 1988 (d,sc).

Bellon, Yannick • Director; also screenwriter. • Born France, 1924. Responsible for several noted documentaries on feminist issues before turning to fiction features in the early 1970s. Bellon has continued to address issues of sexual politics and is best known in the US for the penetrating study of rape, *Rape of Love/Violated Love* (1978). • *Colette* 1951 (d); *Die Windrose* 1956 (d); *Le Bureau des mariages* 1962 (d); *Quelque part, quelqu'un* 1972 (d,sc); *La Femme de Jean* 1973 (d,sc); *Jamais plus toujours* 1975 (d,sc); *L'Amour violé/Rape of Love/Violated Love* 1978 (d,sc,song); *La Triche* 1984 (d,sc); *Les Enfants du désordre* 1989 (d,p,sc,story).

Belmondo, Jean-Paul • Actor; also producer. • Born Neuilly-sur-Seine, France, April 9, 1933. *Educ.* Paris Conservatoire. Became part of cinema history with his performance as Michel Poiccard, the antihero of Jean-Luc Godard's groundbreaking New Wave feature *Breathless* (1959). Belmondo developed into one of the key actors of the New Wave and was a major international star by the early 1970s.

With the looks of a boxer rather than a movie star, Belmondo has project a simultaneously tough, yet thoughtful image in such films as Philippe De Broca's *That Man From Rio* (1964), Godard's *Pierrot le fou* (1965), Francois Truffaut's *Mississippi Mermaid* (1968), Jacques Deray's *Borsalino* (1970) and Alain Resnais and Jorge Semprun's *Stavisky* (1973). • *Charlotte et son Jules (short)* 1958 (a); *A bout de souffle/Breathless* 1959 (a); *A Double Tour* 1959 (a); *Ein Engel auf Erden* 1959 (a); *La Ciociara* 1960 (a); *Classe tous risques* 1960 (a); *Une Femme est une femme/A Woman Is a Woman* 1961 (a); *Cartouche* 1962 (a); *Un Coeur gros comme ça!* 1962 (a); *L'Aine des Ferchaux* 1963 (a); *Le Doulos* 1963 (a); *Dragées au Poivre* 1963 (a); *Echappement libre* 1964 (a); *L'Homme de Rio/That Man From Rio* 1964 (a); *Peau de banane* 1964 (a); *Pierrot le Fou* 1965 (a); *Casino Royale* 1967 (a); *Le Voleur* 1967 (a); *La Sirène du Mississipi/Mississippi Mermaid* 1968 (a); *Le Cerveau* 1969 (a); *Borsalino* 1970 (a); *Les Mariés de l'an Deux* 1970 (a); *Le Casse* 1971 (a); *Les Mariés de l'an II* 1971 (a); *Docteur Popaul* 1972 (a); *L'Héritier* 1972 (a); *La Scoumoune* 1972 (a); *Stavisky* 1973 (a); *Le Magnifique* 1974 (a); *L'Incorrigible* 1975 (a); *Peur sur la Ville* 1975 (a); *L'Alpagueur* 1976 (a); *Le Corps de Mon Ennemi* 1976 (a); *L'Animal* 1977 (a); *Flic ou voyou* 1979 (a); *L'As des As* 1982 (a); *Le Marginal* 1983 (a); *Les Morfalous* 1983 (a); *Joyeuses Paques* 1984 (a,p); *Hold-Up* 1985 (a); *Le Solitaire* 1987 (a); *Itinéraire d'un enfant gate* 1988 (a,p).

Belson, Jerry • American screenwriter, producer; also director. • Emmy-winning TV writer ("The Dick Van Dyke Show") and producer ("The Odd Couple") who crossed over to film in 1968, writing and producing the Debbie Reynolds vehicle *How Sweet It Is* (1968) with partner Garry Marshall. Perhaps his finest work as a screenwriter came with *Smile* (1975), a marvelously pointed satire of the California beauty pageant scene.

Belson made a disappointing directorial debut with *Jekyll & Hyde...Together Again* (1982) and fared only slightly better with the light romance, *Surrender* (1987). • *How Sweet It Is* 1968 (p,sc); *The Grasshopper* 1970 (p,sc); *Smile* 1975 (sc); *Fun With Dick and Jane* 1976 (sc); *Semi-Tough* 1977 (a); *The End* 1978 (sc); *Smokey and the Bandit II* 1980 (sc); *Student Bodies* 1981 (exec.p); *Jekyll and Hyde...Together Again* 1982 (d,sc); *Broadcast News* 1987 (assistance); *Surrender* 1987 (d,sc); *The Couch Trip* 1988 (a); *For Keeps* 1988 (p); *Always* 1989 (sc).

Belushi, James • Actor • Born Chicago, IL, June 15, 1954. *Educ.* DuPage College, IL (speech, theater); Southern Illinois University, Carbondale (speech, theater); University of Illinois (speech, theater). Talented, versatile second lead of the middle and late 1980s. Brother of John Belushi. • *Thief* 1981 (a); *Trading Places* 1983 (a); *The Man With One Red Shoe* 1985 (a); *About Last Night* 1986 (a); *Jumpin' Jack Flash* 1986 (a); *Little Shop of Horrors* 1986 (a); *Number One With a Bullet* 1986 (sc); *Salvador* 1986 (a); *The Principal* 1987 (a); *Real Men* 1987 (a); *Red Heat* 1988 (a); *Homer and Eddie* 1989 (a); *K-9* 1989 (a); *Dimenticare Palermo* 1990 (a); *Mr. Destiny* 1990 (a); *Taking Care of Business* 1990 (a); *Only the Lonely* 1991 (a).

Belushi, John • Actor, comedian • Born Chicago, IL, 1949; died March 5, 1982. Bearish, maniacal comic actor and star of NBC's *Saturday Night Live* (1975-79) who wreaked memorable havoc in the 1978 collegiate romp *Animal House.* On several occasions during his all-too-brief film career, Belushi teamed up with fellow "Saturday Night" alumnus Dan Aykroyd, notably as *The Blues Brothers* (1980).

Belushi's high-octane life—and death, aged 33, from a drug overdose—was the subject of a controversial 1989 biopic, *Wired,* based on the book by Robert Woodward. Brother is actor James Belushi. • *La Honte de la jungle* 1975 (a); *Goin' South* 1978 (a); *National Lampoon's Animal House* 1978 (a,song); *Old Boyfriends* 1978 (a); *1941* 1979 (a); *The Blues Brothers* 1980 (a); *Continental Divide* 1981 (a); *Neighbors* 1981 (a).

Bendix, William • Actor • Born New York, NY, January 4, 1906; died 1964. Burly supporting player, often as a likable tough guy. A former minor-league baseball player, Bendix landed one of his few leading roles in *The Babe Ruth Story* (1948). He was also memorable as Chester A. Riley in the radio and TV series, as well as the 1949 film version of, *The Life of Riley.* • *Brooklyn Orchid* 1942; *The Glass Key* 1942; *The McGuerins From Brooklyn* 1942; *Wake Island* 1942 (**AANBSA**); *Who Done It?* 1942; *Woman of the Year* 1942; *China* 1943; *The Crystal Ball* 1943; *Guadalcanal Diary* 1943; *Hostages* 1943; *Taxi, Mister* 1943; *Abroad With Two Yanks* 1944; *Greenwich Village* 1944; *The Hairy Ape* 1944; *Lifeboat* 1944; *A Bell For Adano* 1945; *Don Juan Quilligan* 1945; *It's in the Bag* 1945; *The Blue Dahlia* 1946; *The Dark Corner* 1946; *Sentimental Journey* 1946; *Two Years Before the Mast* 1946; *White Tie and Tails* 1946; *Blaze of Noon* 1947; *Calcutta* 1947; *I'll Be Yours* 1947; *Variety Girl* 1947; *The Web* 1947; *Where There's Life* 1947; *The Babe Ruth Story* 1948; *Race Street* 1948; *The Time of Your Life* 1948; *The Big Steal* 1949; *A Connecticut Yankee in King Arthur's Court* 1949; *Cover-Up* 1949; *Johnny Holiday* 1949; *The Life of Riley* 1949; *Streets of Laredo* 1949; *Gambling House* 1950; *Kill the Umpire* 1950; *Detective Story* 1951; *Submarine Command* 1951; *Blackbeard the Pirate* 1952; *A Girl in Every Port* 1952; *Macao* 1952; *Dangerous Mission* 1954; *Battle Stations* 1955; *Crashout* 1955; *The Deep Six* 1957; *The Rough and the Smooth* 1959; *Boys' Night Out* 1962; *For Love or Money* 1963; *The Young and the Brave* 1963; *Law of the Lawless* 1964; *Young Fury* 1965.

Benedek, Laslo • Director; also producer. • Born Laszlo Benedek, Budapest, Hungary, March 5, 1907. *Educ.* University of Vienna (psychiatry). Began his career at UFA and, after brief stints in France and England, arrived in the US in 1937. Benedek made his directorial debut a decade later with the Frank Sinatra vehicle *The Kissing Bandit* (1948) and teamed up with producer Stanley Kramer twice, for a faithful adaptation of *Death of a Salesman* (1951) and *The Wild One* (1953). *The Wild One* remains a signature film of the 1950s, largely thanks to the charismatic presence of Marlon Brando as the silent, rebel biker. From the mid-1950s Benedek worked primarily in TV. • *A Little Bit of Heaven* 1940 (ed); *The Kissing Bandit* 1948 (d); *Port of New York* 1949 (d); *Death of a Salesman* 1951 (d); *Storm Over Tibet* 1952 (p); *The Wild One* 1953 (d); *Bengal Brigade* 1954 (d); *Kinder, Mutter und ein General* 1955 (d,sc); *Affair in Havana* 1957 (d); *Moment of Danger* 1960 (d); *Recours en Grace* 1960 (d); *Namu, the Killer Whale* 1966 (d,p); *The Daring Game* 1968 (d); *The Night Visitor* 1971 (d); *Assault On Agathon* 1976 (d); *King Kongs Faust* 1985 (a).

Benigni, Roberto • Italian actor, comedian, screenwriter; also director. • Established Italian comedian who earned cult recognition in the US for his role as the comically maladjusted foreigner in Jim Jarmusch's *Down By Law* (1986). Benigni has directed, scripted and starred in three feature films, including *Il Piccolo Diavolo* (1988), opposite Walter Matthau. • *Letti Selvaggi* 1978 (a); *Tigers in Lipstick* 1978 (a); *Chiedo Asilo* 1979 (a); *Clair de Femme* 1979 (a); *I Giorni Cantati* 1979 (a); *La Luna* 1979 (a); *Il Minestrone* 1980 (a); *Il Pap'Occhio* 1981 (a); *FFSS Cioe: "Che mi hai portato a fare sopra a posillipo se non mi vuoi più bene?"* 1983 (a); *Lieto Fine* 1983 (a); *Tu Mi Turbi* 1983 (a,d,sc); *Non ci resta che piangere* 1984 (a,d,sc); *Tuttobenigni* 1985 (a); *Coffee and Cigarettes (short)* 1986 (a,sc); *Down By Law* 1986 (a); *Il Piccolo Diavolo* 1988 (a,d,sc,story); *Le Voce della Luna* 1990 (a).

Benjamin, Richard • Actor, director • Born New York, NY, May 22, 1938. *Educ.* High School of Performing Arts, New York; Northwestern University (drama). Best known for his characterizations of two Philip Roth characters, in *Goodbye Columbus* (1969) and *Portnoy's Complaint* (1972). Benjamin had walk-on juvenile parts in some 1950s films and first earned adult recognition on Broadway, starring in Neil Simon's *Star-Spangled Girl* (1966)—he had directed *Barefoot in the Park* in London the previous year. Other off-beat acting highlights include *Catch-22* (1970) and *The Sunshine Boys* (1975).

Benjamin made his directorial debut with *My Favorite Year* (1982), a comic look at the early days of TV starring Peter O'Toole; most of his subsequent work as a director has been disappointing. Married to actress Paula Prentiss, his co-star on the TV series "He and She" (1967-68), since 1961. • *Goodbye, Columbus* 1969 (a); *Catch-22* 1970 (a); *Diary of a Mad Housewife* 1970 (a); *The Marriage of a Young Stockbroker* 1971 (a); *The Steagle* 1971 (a); *Portnoy's Complaint* 1972 (a); *The Last of Sheila* 1973 (a); *Westworld* 1973 (a); *The Sunshine Boys* 1975 (a); *House Calls* 1978 (a); *Witches' Brew* 1978 (a); *The Last Married Couple in America* 1979 (a); *Love at First Bite* 1979 (a); *Scavenger Hunt* 1979 (a); *First Family* 1980 (a); *How to Beat the High Cost of Living* 1980 (a); *Saturday the 14th* 1981 (a); *My Favorite Year* 1982 (d); *City Heat* 1984 (d); *Racing With the Moon* 1984 (d); *The Money Pit* 1986 (d); *Little Nikita* 1988 (d); *My Stepmother Is an Alien* 1988 (d); *Downtown* 1990 (d); *Mermaids* 1990 (d).

Bennett, Alan • Playwright; also screenwriter, actor. • Born Leeds, England, May 9, 1934. *Educ.* Oxford. Began his career writing for and appearing in the "Beyond the Fringe" revue with Jonathan Miller, Peter Cook and Dudley Moore. An accomplished playwright and actor, Bennett's screenwriting credits include the penetrating study of spy Guy Burgess, *An Englishman Abroad* (1983), and the telling portrait of playwright Joe Orton, *Prick Up Your Ears* (1987). • *Pleasure at Her Majesty's* 1976 (a); *Long Shot* 1978 (a); *The Secret Policeman's Other Ball* 1981 (a); *An Englishman Abroad* 1983 (sc); *Return of the Jedi* 1983 (a); *A Private Function* 1984 (sc,story); *Dreamchild* 1985 (a); *The Insurance Man* 1985 (sc); *Prick Up Your Ears* 1987 (sc); *Little Dorrit* 1988 (a); *102 Boulevard Haussmann* 1990 (sc).

Bennett, Charles • Screenwriter; also director, playwright. • Born Shoreham-by-Sea, England, August 2, 1899. Playwright whose first film writing credit was as co-adaptor—with director Alfred Hitchcock—of his own play, *Blackmail* (1929), which also happened to be the first sound film produced in England. Bennett's knack for tense adventure stories fuelled such subsequent Hitchcock outings as *The 39 Steps* (1935) and *Foreign Correspondent* (1940). He also scripted the first screen version of the classic adventure yarn *King Solomon's Mines* (1937) and, in the mid-1950s, began a multi-film association with producer-director Irwin Allen (e.g. *Voyage to the Bottom of the Sea* 1961, *Five Weeks in a Balloon* 1962). Bennett himself directed several features and from the early 1950s began working extensively in TV. • *Tillie's Punctured Romance* 1914 (a); *The Adventures of Ruth* 1919 (a); *The Top of New York* 1922 (a); *America* 1924 (a); *Blackmail* 1929 (sc,from play); *The Man Who Knew Too Much* 1934 (story); *Treasure Island* 1934 (a); *The 39 Steps* 1935 (sc,adapt); *Blue Smoke* 1935 (story); *Sabotage* 1936 (sc); *Secret Agent* 1936 (sc); *King Solomon's Mines* 1937 (sc); *Young and Innocent* 1937 (sc); *The Young in Heart* 1938 (adapt); *Balalaika* 1939 (sc); *Foreign Correspondent* 1940 (sc,story) **(AANBSC)**; *They Dare Not Love* 1941 (sc); *Joan of Paris* 1942 (sc); *Reap the Wild Wind* 1942 (sc); *Forever and a Day* 1943 (sc); *The Story of Dr. Wassell* 1944 (sc); *Ivy* 1947 (sc); *Unconquered* 1947 (sc); *The Sign of the Ram* 1948 (sc); *Black Magic* 1949 (sc); *Madness of the Heart* 1949 (d); *Mystery Submarine* 1950 (ad); *Where Danger Lives* 1950 (sc); *The Green Glove* 1951 (sc,story); *Kind Lady* 1951 (sc); *No Escape* 1953 (d,sc); *Dangerous Mission* 1954 (sc); *The Man Who Knew Too Much* 1956 (story); *The Story of Mankind* 1957 (sc); *Curse of the Demon* 1958 (sc); *The Big Circus* 1959 (sc); *The Lost World* 1960 (sc); *Voyage to the Bottom of the Sea* 1961 (sc); *Five Weeks in a Balloon* 1962 (sc); *War Gods of the Deep* 1965 (sc).

Bennett, Compton • Director; also screenwriter. • Born Robert Compton-Bennett, Tunbridge Wells, Kent, England, January 15, 1900; died 1974. Entered film in 1932 as an editor for Alexander Korda and Sydney Box and worked on propaganda and training films for the British army between 1939 and 1941. Bennett made a strong impression with his debut feature, *The Seventh Veil* (1945), a superior psychological thriller that helped make James Mason a star. His only other well-known film, co-directed with Andrew Marton during a brief spell in Hollywood, is the second screen version of *King Solomon's Mines* (1950). • *Find, Fix and Strike (short)* 1941 (d); *Men of Rochdale* 1944 (d); *The Seventh Veil* 1945 (d); *Julius Caesar (short)* 1946 (d); *The Years Between* 1946 (d); *Daybreak* 1947 (d); *My Own True Love* 1949 (d); *That Forsyte Woman* 1949 (d); *King Solomon's Mines* 1950 (d); *It Started in Paradise* 1952 (d); *So Little Time* 1952 (d); *Desperate Moment* 1953 (d); *The Gift Horse* 1953 (d); *After the Ball* 1957 (d); *The Flying Scot* 1957 (d); *That Woman Opposite* 1957 (d,sc); *Beyond the Curtain* 1960 (d); *First Past Aden (short)* 1961 (d); *How to Undress in Public Without Undue Embarrassment* 1966 (d).

Bennett, Constance • Actress • Born New York, NY, October 22, 1905; died 1965. Entered film at age 17 and became a leading lady of Hollywood silents. Bennett's marriage to a well-heeled member of the international set resulted in a three-year absence from the screen, but she regained her star status with *This Thing Called Love* (1929) and went on to specialize in polished, witty comedies.

Bennett made her stage debut in Noel Coward's *Easy Virtue* in 1940 and acted primarily in the theater from the early 1950s. Her final film, *Madame X* (1966), was released posthumously after her death from a cerebral hemorrhage. Daughter of actor Richard Bennett and sister of actresses Joan and Barbara Bennett, and married to Hollywood "Latin lover" Gilbert Roland from 1941 to 1945. • *Evidence* 1922 (a); *Reckless Youth* 1922 (a); *What's Wrong With Women* 1922 (a); *Cytherea* 1924 (a); *Into the Net* 1924 (a); *Wandering Fires* 1924 (a); *Code of the West* 1925 (a); *The Goose Hangs High* 1925 (a); *The Goose Woman* 1925 (a); *Married?* 1925 (a); *My Son* 1925 (a); *My Wife and I* 1925 (a); *The Pinch Hitter* 1925 (a); *Sally, Irene and Mary* 1925 (a); *Rich People* 1929 (a); *This Thing Called Love* 1929 (a); *Common Clay* 1930 (a); *Sin Takes a Holiday* 1930 (a); *Son of the Gods* 1930 (a); *Three Faces East* 1930 (a); *Born to Love* 1931 (a); *Bought* 1931 (a); *The Common Law* 1931 (a); *The Easiest Way* 1931 (a); *Lady With a Past* 1932 (a); *Rockabye* 1932 (a); *Two Against the World* 1932 (a); *What Price Hollywood?* 1932 (a); *After Tonight* 1933 (a); *Bed of Roses* 1933 (a); *Our Betters* 1933 (a); *The Affairs of Cellini* 1934 (a); *Moulin Rouge* 1934 (a); *Outcast Lady* 1934 (a); *After Office Hours* 1935 (a); *Ladies in Love* 1936 (a); *Topper* 1937 (a); *Merrily We Live* 1938 (a); *Service De Luxe* 1938 (a); *Tail Spin* 1939 (a); *Topper Takes a Trip* 1939 (a); *Escape to Glory* 1940 (a); *Law of the Tropics* 1941 (a); *Two-Faced Woman* 1941 (a); *Wild Bill Hickok Rides* 1941 (a); *Madame Spy* 1942 (a); *Sin Town* 1942 (a); *Paris Underground* 1945 (a,p); *Centennial Summer* 1946 (a); *The Unsuspected* 1947 (a); *Angel on the Amazon* 1948 (a); *Smart Woman* 1948 (a); *As Young As You Feel* 1951 (a); *It Should Happen to You* 1954 (a); *Madame X* 1966 (a).

Bennett, Joan • Actress • Born Palisades, NJ, February 27, 1910; died December 7, 1990, Scarsdale, NY. Began her film career as a blonde ingenue (e.g. in *Little Women* 1933) but developed into a sultry, brunette femme fatale and proved outstanding in several 1940s films noirs, including a quartet of Fritz Lang thrillers—*Man Hunt* (1941), *The Woman in the Window* (1944), *Scarlet Street* (1945) and *Secret Beyond the Door* (1948). Bennett shifted to the role of witty and nurturing mother in

Vincente Minnelli's *Father of the Bride* (1950) and *Father's Little Dividend* (1951).

Her career was short-circuited in 1951 after her husband, producer Walter Wanger, shot her agent, Jennings Lang, accusing the latter of being a "homewrecker." She was offered few film roles after that, though she returned to the stage in several national tours.

Sister of actresses Constance and Barbara Bennett, and married to Wanger (her second husband) from 1940 to 1965. • *Power* 1928; *Bulldog Drummond* 1929; *Disraeli* 1929; *The Mississippi Gambler* 1929; *Three Live Ghosts* 1929; *Crazy That Way* 1930; *Maybe It's Love* 1930; *Moby Dick* 1930; *Puttin' on the Ritz* 1930; *Scotland Yard* 1930; *Doctors' Wives* 1931; *Hush Money* 1931; *Many a Slip* 1931; *The Careless Lady* 1932; *Me and My Gal* 1932; *She Wanted a Millionaire* 1932; *The Trial of Vivienne Ware* 1932; *Week-Ends Only* 1932; *Wild Girl* 1932; *Arizona to Broadway* 1933; *Little Women* 1933; *The Man Who Reclaimed His Head* 1934; *The Pursuit of Happiness* 1934; *The Man Who Broke the Bank at Monte Carlo* 1935; *Mississippi* 1935; *Private Worlds* 1935; *She Couldn't Take It* 1935; *Two For Tonight* 1935; *13 Hours By Air* 1936; *Big Brown Eyes* 1936; *Two in a Crowd* 1936; *Wedding Present* 1936; *Vogues of 1938* 1937; *Artists and Models Abroad* 1938; *I Met My Love Again* 1938; *The Texans* 1938; *Trade Winds* 1938; *The Housekeeper's Daughter* 1939; *The Man in the Iron Mask* 1939; *Green Hell* 1940; *The House Across the Bay* 1940; *The Man I Married* 1940; *The Son of Monte Cristo* 1940; *Confirm or Deny* 1941; *Man Hunt* 1941; *She Knew All the Answers* 1941; *Wild Geese Calling* 1941; *Girl Trouble* 1942; *Twin Beds* 1942; *The Wife Takes a Flyer* 1942; *Margin For Error* 1943; *The Woman in the Window* 1944; *Colonel Effingham's Raid* 1945; *Nob Hill* 1945; *Scarlet Street* 1945; *The Macomber Affair* 1947; *The Woman on the Beach* 1947; *Hollow Triumph* 1948; *Secret Beyond the Door* 1948; *The Reckless Moment* 1949; *Father of the Bride* 1950; *For Heaven's Sake* 1950; *Father's Little Dividend* 1951; *The Guy Who Came Back* 1951; *Highway Dragnet* 1954; *We're No Angels* 1955; *Navy Wife* 1956; *There's Always Tomorrow* 1956; *Desire in the Dust* 1960; *House of Dark Shadows* 1970; *Suspiria* 1976.

Bennett, Richard Rodney • Composer • Born Broadstairs, Kent, England, March 29, 1936. *Educ.* Royal Academy of Music, London. Deft, versatile composer who entered movies at age 20 and quickly established himself as one of the finest talents in the field. Bennett has often contributed to the films of John Schlesinger, scoring *Billy Liar* (1963), *Darling* (1965), *Far From the Madding Crowd* (1967) and *Yanks* (1979). He has worked mostly in TV since the early 1980s. • *Face in the Night* 1956 (m); *The Safecracker* 1957 (m); *Indiscreet* 1958 (m); *The Man Inside* 1958 (m); *The Angry Hills* 1959 (m); *Blind Date* 1959 (m); *The Devil's Disciple* 1959 (m); *The Man Who Could Cheat Death* 1959 (m); *The Mark* 1961 (m); *Satan Never Sleeps* 1962 (m); *Billy Liar* 1963 (m); *One Way Pendulum* 1964 (m); *Darling* 1965 (m); *The Nanny* 1965 (m); *Billion Dollar Brain* 1967 (m,m.cond); *Far From the Madding Crowd* 1967 (m) **(AANBM)**; *Secret Ceremony* 1968 (m); *The Buttercup Chain* 1970 (m); *The Go-Between* 1971 (m); *Nicholas and Alexandra* 1971 (m) **(AANBM)**; *Lady Caroline Lamb* 1972 (m); *Murder on the Orient Express* 1974 (m) **(AANBM)**; *Permission to Kill* 1975 (m); *Equus* 1977 (m); *L'Imprecateur* 1977 (m); *The Brink's Job* 1978 (m); *Yanks* 1979 (m); *The Jazz Singer* 1980 (song); *The Return of the Soldier* 1982 (m).

Benson, Robby • Actor; also director, screenwriter, composer, producer. • Born Robert Segal, Dallas, TX, January 21, 1956. Teen star of the 1970s who has since worked primarily behind the camera. Benson co-wrote one of his better efforts as an actor, *One on One* (1977), about a young college basketball star who falls for Annette O'Toole and drugs. He scored his first film in 1979—*Walk Proud*—and turned to producing the following year with *Die Laughing*. Benson's directorial debut, *White Hot* (1988), failed to achieve national release, but is historically notable as the first American film shot directly onto High Definition Video (HDTV). Married to singer-actress Karla DeVito. • *Jeremy* 1973 (a); *Jory* 1973 (a); *Lucky Lady* 1975 (a); *Ode to Billy Joe* 1975 (a); *One on One* 1977 (a,sc); *The End* 1978 (a); *Ice Castles* 1978 (a); *Walk Proud* 1979 (a,m); *Die Laughing* 1980 (a,m,p,sc,m); *Tribute* 1980 (a); *The Chosen* 1981 (a); *National Lampoon Goes to the Movies* 1982 (a); *Running Brave* 1983 (a); *Harry & Son* 1984 (a); *The Breakfast Club* 1985 (song); *City Limits* 1985 (a); *Rent-A-Cop* 1988 (a); *White Hot* 1988 (a,d,songs); *Modern Love* 1990 (song,a,d,p,sc).

Benton, Robert • Director, screenwriter; also producer. • Born Waxahachie, TX, September 29, 1932. *Educ.* University of Texas; Columbia. Benton began writing screenplays with colleague David Newman while a contributing editor at *Esquire* magazine. They scored a huge success with their first effort, *Bonnie and Clyde* (1962), which director Arthur Penn put into production after it had been rejected by over a dozen producers.

Benton was encouraged to move into directing in 1972 by Stanley Jaffe, then president of Paramount, and has subsequently enjoyed substantial critical and popular success. • *Bonnie and Clyde* 1967 (sc) **(AANBSC)**; *There Was a Crooked Man* 1970 (sc); *Bad Company* 1972 (d,sc); *Oh! Calcutta!* 1972 (sc); *What's Up, Doc?* 1972 (sc); *The Late Show* 1977 (d,sc) **(AANBSC)**; *Superman* 1978 (sc); *Kramer vs. Kramer* 1979 (d,sc) **(AABD,AABSC)**; *Still of the Night* 1982 (d,sc,story); *Places in the Heart* 1984 (d,sc) **(AANBD,AABSC)**; *Nadine* 1987 (d,sc); *The House on Carroll Street* 1988 (exec.p).

Berenger, Tom • Actor • Born Chicago, IL, May 31, 1950. *Educ.* University of Missouri (journalism, education, drama). Ruggedly handsome, blue-eyed lead of the 80s, often in brooding, aggressive roles, who came to attention as the self-effacing TV star in *The Big Chill* (1983) and received acclaim for his performance as the battle-hardened sergeant in *Platoon* (1986). Berenger began his career with studies at the Herbert Berghof Studio in New York and moved into films after doing time on the daytime soap "One Life to Live" and performing in several off-Broadway productions. • *In Praise of Older Women* 1977; *Looking For Mr. Goodbar* 1977; *The Sentinel* 1977; *Butch and Sundance: The Early Days* 1979; *The Dogs of War* 1980; *Oltre la Porta* 1982; *The Big Chill* 1983; *Eddie and the Cruisers* 1983; *Fear City* 1985; *Rustler's Rhapsody* 1985; *Platoon* 1986 **(AANBSA)**; *Dear America* 1987; *Someone to Watch Over Me* 1987; *Betrayed* 1988; *Last Rites* 1988; *Shoot to Kill* 1988; *Born on the Fourth of July* 1989; *Major League* 1989; *The Field* 1990; *Love at Large* 1990; *Shattered* 1991.

Berenson, Marisa • Actress • Born New York, NY, February 15, 1947. Former model who appeared in some prestigious international films of the 1970s. Granddaughter of fashion designer Elsa Schiaparelli. • *Morte a Venezia/Death in Venice* 1971; *Cabaret* 1972; *Barry Lyndon* 1975; *Casanova & Co.* 1977; *Killer Fish* 1979; *S.O.B.* 1981; *L'Arbalete* 1984; *The Secret Diary of Sigmund Freud* 1984; *La Tête dans le Sac* 1984; *Flagrant Désir* 1986; *Monte Napoleone* 1987; *Perfume of the Cyclone* 1990; *White Hunter, Black Heart* 1990.

Beresford, Bruce • Director; also screenwriter, producer. • Born Sydney, Australia, August 16, 1940. *Educ.* Sydney University (philosophy). Leading Australian director whose contributions to his country's film renaissance of the 1970s include the internationally praised *Breaker Morant* (1980), a powerful account of a true incident during the Boer War. Beresford's reputation for finely etched character studies made him an ideal choice for *Tender Mercies* (1982), a subtle, superbly realized drama that marked his US debut.

Beresford has subsequently alternated between Australia and the US, turning out a couple of inferior Hollywood films (such as *King David* 1985), but regaining his earlier form with the Oscar-winning adaptation of the Pulitzer Prize-winning play *Driving Miss Daisy* (1989), a sensitive portrait of an aging Jewish woman and her gently wise black chauffeur. • *The Adventures of Barry McKenzie* 1972 (d,sc); *Side By Side* 1975 (d,sc); *Don's Party* 1976 (d); *The Getting of Wisdom* 1977 (d); *Blue Fin* 1978 (uncred.asst.); *Money Movers* 1978 (d,sc); *Breaker Morant* 1980 (d,sc) **(AANBSC)**; *The Club* 1980 (d); *Fortress* 1981 (d); *Puberty Blues* 1981 (d); *Tender Mercies* 1982 (d) **(AANBD)**; *Barry McKenzie Holds His Own* 1984 (d,p,sc); *The Fringe Dwellers* 1985 (d,p,sc); *King David* 1985 (d); *Crimes of the Heart* 1986 (d); *Aria* 1987 (d,sc—"Die Tote Stadt"); *Driving Miss Daisy* 1989 (d); *Her Alibi* 1989 (d); *Mister Johnson* 1991 (d,sc).

Bergen, Candice • Actress; also photographer. • Born Beverly Hills, CA, May 8, 1946. *Educ.* University of Pennsylvania; University of Switzerland. Elegant, poised star of the 1960s and 70s who came to attention with her first film, playing the lesbian member of *The Group* (1966). One of Bergen's few subsequent roles of note came with a superb performance in Mike Nichols's *Carnal Knowledge* (1971), as the co-ed who gets involved with roommates Jack Nicholson and Art Garfunkel.

Bergen revived her flagging career in the late 1980s, playing the acerbically witty title character of the popular sitcom, "Murphy Brown" (1988-). Bergen's father was ventriloquist Edgar Bergen and she has been married to director Louis Malle since 1980. • *The Group* 1966 (a); *The Sand Pebbles* 1966 (a); *Vivre pour vivre* 1967 (a); *The Magus* 1968 (a); *Getting Straight* 1970 (a); *Soldier Blue* 1970 (a); *Carnal Knowledge* 1971 (a); *The Hunting Party* 1971 (a); *T. R. Baskin* 1971 (a); *11 Harrowhouse* 1974 (a); *Bite the Bullet* 1975 (a); *The Wind and the Lion* 1975 (a); *The Domino Killings* 1977 (a); *The End of the World in Our Usual Bed in a Night Full of Rain* 1977 (a); *Oliver's Story* 1978 (a); *Starting Over* 1979 (a,song) **(AANBSA)**; *Rich and Famous* 1981 (a); *Gandhi* 1982 (a); *Stick* 1985 (a).

Berger, Helmut • Actor • Born Helmut Steinberger, Salzburg, Austria, May 29, 1944. *Educ.* University of Perugia, Italy (drama). Blond, blue-eyed, high-cheekboned lead who first gained attention in Luchino Visconti's *The Damned* (1969), playing the disturbed heir of a prominent German industrial family caught up in the rise of fascism. Berger went on to become an international star, often playing tortured or twisted characters in films such as *Ludwig* (1972, again directed by Visconti) and *The Romantic Englishmwoman* (1975). Most of his roles in the 1980s were in German productions. • *Le Streghe/The Witches* 1968 (a); *La Caduta degli dei/The Damned* 1969 (a); *Un Beau Monstre* 1970 (a); *Il Giardino del Finzi-Continis/The Garden of the Finzi-Continis* 1971 (a); *Ludwig* 1972 (a); *Les Voraces* 1972 (a); *Ash Wednesday* 1973 (a); *El Clan de los Inmorales* 1973 (a); *Gruppo di famiglia in un interno/Conversation Piece* 1975 (a); *Madam Kitty* 1975 (a); *The Romantic Englishwoman* 1975 (a); *Das Fünfte Gebot* 1979 (a); *Le Rose di Danzica* 1979 (a); *Eroina* 1980 (a); *Femmes* 1983 (a); *Tunnel* 1983 (a); *Victoria* 1983 (a); *Code Name: Emerald* 1985 (a); *Der Gläserne Himmel* 1987 (a); *Les Predateurs de la nuit* 1987 (a); *Die Verlockung* 1987 (a); *Er-Sie-Es* 1989 (a); *Nie Im Leben* 1990 (a,d,sc).

Bergman, Alan • Songwriter, lyricist • Born Brooklyn, NY, September 11, 1925. *Educ.* University of North Carolina; UCLA. With wife Marilyn, one of the more successful songwriting teams of the past 20 years. • *Any Wednesday* 1966 (lyrics); *Stop the World—I Want to Get Off* 1966 (add.material); *The Thomas Crown Affair* 1968 (lyrics) **(AABS)**; *Gaily, Gaily* 1969 (song); *The Happy Ending* 1969 (song) **(AANBS)**; *John and Mary* 1969 (song); *Doctors' Wives* 1970 (lyrics); *Pieces of Dreams* 1970 (lyrics) **(AANBS)**; *The African Elephant* 1971 (lyrics); *Le Mans* 1971 (lyrics); *Sometimes a Great Notion* 1971 (lyrics) **(AANBS)**; *The Life and Times of Judge Roy Bean* 1972 (song) **(AANBS)**; *Molly and Lawless John* 1972 (lyrics); *40 Carats* 1973 (lyrics); *Breezy* 1973 (lyrics); *The Way We Were* 1973 (lyrics) **(AABS)**; *99 and 44/100% Dead* 1974 (lyrics); *Ode to Billy Joe* 1975 (lyrics); *From Noon Till Three* 1976 (a,lyrics); *Harry and Walter Go to New York* 1976 (lyrics); *A Star Is Born* 1976 (lyrics); *The One and Only* 1978 (lyrics); *Same Time, Next Year* 1978 (lyrics) **(AANBS)**; *And Justice For All* 1979 (lyrics); *The Promise* 1979 (lyrics) **(AANBS)**; *Starting Over* 1979 (lyrics); *A Change of Seasons* 1980 (lyrics); *Back Roads* 1981 (lyrics); *Author! Author!* 1982 (lyrics); *Best Friends* 1982 (m) **(AANBS)**; *Tootsie* 1982 (lyrics) **(AANBS)**; *Yes, Giorgio* 1982 (lyrics) **(AANBS)**; *The Man Who Loved Women* 1983 (lyrics); *Never Say Never Again* 1983 (lyrics); *Yentl* 1983 (lyrics) **(AABM,AANBS)**; *Micki & Maude* 1984 (song); *Shy People* 1987 (song); *Big* 1988 (song); *The January Man* 1988 (lyrics); *Major League* 1989 (lyrics); *Shirley Valentine* 1989 (lyrics) **(AANBS)**; *Welcome Home* 1989 (song).

Bergman, Andrew • Screenwriter, director; also producer. • Born Queens, NY, 1945. *Educ.* Harpur College, Binghamton, NY; University of Wisconsin (history). Former publicist and author of a book on depression-era cinema who co-wrote (with Richard Pryor and director Mel Brooks) the hilarious western parody *Blazing Saddles* (1974). Bergman scripted several other, often wacky comedies before making his directorial debut with *So Fine* (1981), about a professor who conquers the garment industry with an idea for see-through jeans.

Bergman began a profitable production partnership with Michael Lobell in the mid-1980s and landed his second directing assignment with *The Freshman* (1990), an engaging comedy starring Marlon Brando and Matthew Broderick. • *Blazing Saddles* 1974 (sc,story); *The In-Laws* 1979 (sc); *So Fine* 1981 (d,sc); *Oh, God! You Devil* 1984 (sc); *Big Trouble* 1985 (uncred. p,uncred.sc); *Fletch* 1985 (sc); *The Freshman* 1990 (d,sc,parody lyrics); *White Fang* 1991 (exec.p).

Bergman, Ingmar • Director, screenwriter • Born Ernst Ingmar Bergman, Uppsala, Sweden, July 14, 1918. *Educ.* University of Stockholm (literature, art history). Universally regarded as one of the great masters of modern cinema, Bergman has often concerned himself with spiritual and psychological conflicts. His work has evolved in distinct stages over four decades, while his visual style—intense, intimate, complex—has explored the vicissitudes of passion with a mesmerizing cinematic rhetoric. His prolific output tends to return to and elaborate upon recurrent images, subjects and techniques. Like the Baroque composers, Bergman works on a small scale, finding invention in theme and variation.

Bergman works primarily in the chamber cinema genre, although there are exceptions, such as the journey narrative of *Wild Strawberries* (1957) and the family epic of *Fanny and Alexander* (1982). Chamber cinema encloses space and time, permitting the director to focus on *mise-en-scène* and to pay careful attention to metaphoric detail and visual rhythm. Perhaps his most expressive technique is his use of the facial close-up. For Bergman, the face, along with the hand, allows the camera to reveal the inner aspects of human emotion. His fascination with the female face can be seen most strikingly in *Persona* (1966) and *Cries and Whispers* (1972). In his autobiography, Bergman claimed that he was always trying to generate his mother's face; hence, a psychological and aesthetic need are realized in this cinematic signature.

Of the early period, *Wild Strawberries* stands out for its narrative invention in a fluid manipulation of flashbacks, reveries and dream sequences. Its penetrating psychological investigation of the closing of the life cycle established Bergman's preoccupation with the relationship between desire, loss and guilt and compassion, restitution and celebration. *Naked Night* (1953), more allegorical than *Wild Strawberries*, is likewise designed around a journey motif of existential crisis. In contrast, the Mozartian *Smiles of a Summer Night* (1955) displays Bergman's romantic, comic sensibility. The early period concludes with two symbolic works, *The Seventh Seal* (1957) and *The Virgin Spring* (1960), both set in the Middle Ages. The extreme long shot in *The Seventh Seal* of Death leading the peasants in silhouette across the horizon now forms part of the iconography of modern cinema.

The second stage of Bergman's cinematic evolution shifts to the chamber style. Intense spiritual and psychological themes are explored in the "Silence" trilogy (*Through a Glass Darkly* 1961, *Winter Light* 1963, *The Silence* 1963), and in *The Shame* (1968), *The Hour of the Wolf* (1968) and *The Passion of Anna* (1969), three films all set on the island of Faro. With its dialectical editing and expressive compositions, *The Silence* is considered one of Bergman's most artfully structured films. *The Passion of Anna*, with its innovative application of red motifs, marked Bergman's first use of color photography.

Between these two trilogies came *Persona*, a work many critics consider Bergman's masterpiece. *Persona* shares a similar look and ambience with the Faro trilogy, and has direct links with *The Silence* in its focus on the antagonistic relationship between two women. Yet, with its distinctly avant-garde style and rhythm, it stands apart from any other of Bergman's films. Ostensibly concerned with identity crisis and the role reversal of a nurse and her mentally ill patient, the subtext of the film explores the nature of the cinematic apparatus itself. The narrative is framed by opening and closing shots of a film strip, projector, and light, which lead into and out of the figure of a young boy. With his directorial hand, the boy conjures up a gigantic close-up of the female face. In a now celebrated sequence, the two faces of the female protagonists dissolve into one. (The figure of the precocious, "magical" child, previously seen in *The Silence*, would later reappear in the autobiographical *Fanny and Alexander*.)

Sadomasochistic behavior, along with problems of role reversal and denied maternity, form the tortured core of both *Persona* and *Cries and Whispers*, the masterwork of the late period. In contrast to the spare decor, sharp black-and-white photography and disjunctive editing of *Persona*, *Cries and Whispers* is a 19th-century Gothic period-piece featuring rich colors, draped, theatrical decor and muted dissolve editing. The film revolves around three sisters, one of whom, Agnes, is dying, and their maid, Anna. Bergman evokes religious iconography, with each of the three sisters representing various theological concepts. The dying Agnes, set in cruciform position, returns as a resurrected savior/prophet. The exquisite Pieta/birth shot of Agnes and the Maid, as well as the revolutionary dissolve red-outs, are highlights in this brutal and beautiful film.

Even the minor films of Bergman's later period, such as *Face to Face* (1976), *Autumn Sonata* (1978) and *From the Life of the Marionettes* (1980) continue to explore and refine recurrent themes and techniques. In the underrated *The Touch* (1971), Bergman examines the theme of marriage, with an inventive subtext of the Persephone myth, in a visually expansive way that distinguishes it from the more conventional *Scenes from a Marriage* (1974). The cycle of Bergman's work appropriately concludes with *Fanny and Alexander*, an epic of family romance, touched with elements of fairy tale, horror and ghost story. All the preoccupations of Bergman's extraordinary career flow through the imagery, action and stylization of the film.

As an artist, Bergman pays homage to music and theater in general, to Bach, Mozart, and Strindberg in particular. His work seems a synthesis of the internalized Swedish sensibility and harsh Scandinavian landscape, yet he speaks to a universal vision of human passion. Although apparently not influenced by other filmmakers, with the possible exception of Carl Dreyer, Bergman himself has had a wide-ranging influence on a generation of filmmakers. A unique and powerful presence, his genius has made an extraordinary contribution to the art of the cinema. DMB • *Hets/Torment* 1944 (sc,ad); *Kris* 1945 (d,sc); *Det regnar pa var kärlek/It Rains on Our Love* 1946 (d,sc); *Kvinna utan ansikte/Woman Without a Face* 1947 (sc); *Skepp till India land/A Ship Bound For India* 1947 (d,sc); *Eva* 1948 (sc,story); *Hamnstad/Port of Call* 1948 (d,sc,adapt,add.dial); *Musik i mörker/Night Is My Future* 1948 (d); *Fängelse/The Devil's Wanton* 1949 (d,sc); *Till Glädje/To Joy* 1949 (a,d,sc); *Törst/Three Strange Loves* 1949 (a,d); *Medan Staden Sover* 1950 (idea); *Sant Händer Inte Här* 1950 (d); *Franskild* 1951 (sc,story); *Sommarlek/Summer Interlude* 1951 (d,sc); *Kvinnors Väntan/Secrets of Women* 1952 (a,d,sc); *Sommaren Med Monika/Monika* 1952 (d,sc); *Gycklarnas Afton/Sawdust and Tinsel/The Naked Night* 1953 (d,sc); *En Lektion i Karlek/A Lesson in Love* 1954 (a,d,sc); *Kvinnodröm/Dreams* 1955 (a,d,sc); *Sommarnattens Leende/Smiles of a Summer Night* 1955 (d,sc,lyrics); *Sista Paret Ut* 1956 (sc); *Det Sjunde Inseglet* 1957 (d,sc,from play *Tramalning*); *Smultronstället/Wild Strawberries* 1957 (d,sc) **(AANBSC)**; *Ansiktet/The Magician/The Face* 1958 (d,sc,lyrics); *Nära Livet/Brink of Life* 1958 (d); *L'Eau à la bouche* 1959 (from film *Sommarnattens Leende/Smiles of a Summer Night*); *Brollopsdagen* 1960 (story); *Djavulens Oga/The Devil's Eye* 1960 (d,sc); *Jungfrukällan/The Virgin Spring* 1960 (d); *Lustgarden* 1961 (sc); *Sasom i en Spegel/Through a Glass Darkly* 1961 (d,sc) **(AABSC)**; *Nattvardsgästerna/Winter Light* 1963 (d,sc); *Tystnaden/The Silence* 1963 (d,sc); *För att Inte Tala om Alla Dessa Kvinnor/All These Women* 1964 (d,sc); *Persona* 1966 (d,p,sc); *Stimulantia* 1967 (d,sc,ph); *Skammen/The Shame* 1968 (d,sc); *Vargtimmen/The Hour of the Wolf* 1968 (d,sc); *En Passion/The Passion of Anna* 1969 (d,sc); *Riten* 1969 (d,sc); *Farodokument* 1970 (d,p,sc); *Beröringen/The Touch* 1971 (d,p,sc); *Cries and Whispers* 1972 (d,p,sc) **(AANBD,AANBP,AANBSC)**; *Ingmar Bergman* 1972 (a); *Scenes From a Marriage* 1974 (d,p,sc); *Trollflojten/The Magic Flute* 1975 (d,sc,adapt); *Ansikte mot ansikte/Face to Face* 1976 (d,p,sc) **(AANBD)**; *A Little Night Music* 1977 (from film *Smiles of a Summer Night*); *Paradistorg* 1977 (p); *Das Schlangenei/The Serpent's Egg* 1977 (d,sc,story); *Hostsonaten/Autumn Sonata* 1978 (d,p,sc,prod.sup) **(AANBSC)**; *Farödokument 1979/Faro Document 1979* 1979 (a,d,sc); *Min Alskade* 1979 (exec.p); *Aus dem Leben der Marionetten/From the Life of the Marionettes* 1980 (d,p,sc); *Sally och friheten* 1981 (p); *Fanny och Alexander/Fanny and Alexander* 1982 (d,sc) **(AANBSC,AANBD)**; *Karins Ansikte/Karin's Face (short)* 1983 (d,p,sc); *After the Rehearsal* 1984 (d,sc); *Dokument Fanny och Alexander/Document: Fanny and Alexander* 1986 (d).

Bergman, Ingrid • Actress • Born Stockholm, Sweden, August 29, 1915; died August 29, 1982. *Educ.* Royal Dramatic Theater School, Stockholm. A highly popular actress known for her fresh, radiant beauty, Ingrid Bergman was a natural for virtuous roles but equally adept at playing notorious women. In 1933, fresh out of high school, she enrolled in the Royal Dramatic Theater and made her film debut the following year, soon becoming Sweden's most promising young actress. Her breakthrough film was Gustaf Molander's *Intermezzo* (1936), in which she played a pianist who has a love affair with a celebrated—and married—violinist. The film garnered the attention of American producer David O. Selznick, who invited her to Hollywood to do a remake. In 1939 she co-starred with Leslie Howard in that film, which the public loved, leading to a seven-year contract with Selznick.

Selznick promoted Bergman's wholesomeness from the beginning. He loaned her to other studios for *Adam Had Four Sons*, *Rage in Heaven* and *Dr. Jekyll and Mr. Hyde* (all 1941). In the latter film Bergman's insistence on playing the role of the prostitute rather than the good fiancée proved a shrewd move. She then starred with Humphrey Bogart in *Casablanca* (1942), perhaps her most popular film, and was also featured with Gary Cooper in *For Whom the Bell Tolls*

(1943). She won her first Oscar for her portrayal of a wife nearly driven mad by Charles Boyer in *Gaslight* (1944).

The following year, Bergman had starring roles as a New Orleans vixen with Cooper in *Saratoga Trunk*, a psychiatrist opposite Gregory Peck in Alfred Hitchcock's *Spellbound* and a nun opposite Bing Crosby's priest in *The Bells of St. Mary's*. Bergman's last picture under contract to Selznick, and probably her finest work, was Hitchcock's *Notorious* (1946), an emotionally complex espionage film in which she played a woman bent on self-destruction until redeemed by the love of a federal agent, played by Cary Grant.

Bergman then went freelance, first playing a prostitute in *Arch of Triumph* and then the contrasting *Joan of Arc* (both 1948), a role she had played to great acclaim on Broadway in 1946. Her final film for Hitchcock was the 1949 period piece, *Under Capricorn*.

Bergman's personal and professional life went into a tailspin in 1949 after she left her husband, Dr. Peter Lindstrom, for Italian director Roberto Rossellini. She married Rossellini, a union which produced three children and six films of varying artistic merit, beginning with *Stromboli* (1949). The international scandal tarnished her innocent image and, extraordinarily, led to her being barred from American films for 7 years.

Bergman's career began to recover with her appearance in Jean Renoir's *Paris Does Strange Things* (1956). She made a triumphant return to Hollywood with *Anastasia* (1956), for which she won her second Academy Award, a sign that her sins had been officially forgiven. In 1958 her marriage to Rossellini was annulled and she married theatrical producer Lars Schmidt.

Thereafter, Bergman began branching out into TV and stage roles. The films of this later period of her career were of varying quality. She received a third Academy Award for her supporting role in *Murder on the Orient Express* (1974) and won acclaim for her co-starring role with Liv Ullmann in Ingmar Bergman's *Autumn Sonata* (1978), an intense drama about a pianist and her daughter.

Bergman's health began to fail in the late 1970s, though she fought off cancer long enough to complete a TV movie, *A Woman Called Golda* (1982), in which she portrayed Israeli Prime Minister Golda Meir. The performance earned her an Emmy, her final honor. VMC • *Branningar* 1935; *Munkbrogreven* 1935; *Swedenhielms* 1935; *Valborgsmassoafton* 1935; *Intermezzo* 1936; *Pa solsidan* 1936; *Die 4 Gesellen* 1938; *Dollar* 1938; *En enda natt* 1938; *En kvinnas ansikte* 1938; *Juninatten* 1938; *Intermezzo* 1939; *Adam Had Four Sons* 1941; *Dr. Jekyll and Mr. Hyde* 1941; *Rage in Heaven* 1941; *Casablanca* 1942; *For Whom the Bell Tolls* 1943 **(AANBA)**; *Gaslight* 1944 **(AABA)**; *Swedes in America (short)* 1944; *The Bells of St. Mary's* 1945 **(AANBA)**; *Saratoga Trunk* 1945; *Spellbound* 1945; *Notorious* 1946; *Arch of Triumph* 1948; *Joan of Arc* 1948 **(AANBA)**; *Stromboli* 1949; *Under Capricorn* 1949; *Europa '51/The Greatest Love* 1951; *Siamo Donne/We, the Women* 1953; *Viaggio in Italia/Voyage to Italy* 1953; *Giovanna d'Arco al Rogo* 1954; *Die Angst/Fear* 1955; *Anastasia* 1956 **(AABA)**; *Elena et les hommes/ Paris Does Strange things/Elena and Her Men* 1956; *Indiscreet* 1958; *The Inn of the Sixth Happiness* 1958; *Goodbye Again/Aimez-vous Brahms?* 1961; *Der Besuch* 1964; *The Yellow Rolls-Royce* 1964; *Stimulantia* 1967; *Cactus Flower* 1969; *Langlois (short)* 1970; *A Walk in the Spring Rain* 1970; *From The Mixed-Up Files of Mrs. Basil E. Frankweiler* 1973; *Murder on the Orient Express* 1974 **(AABSA)**; *A Matter of Time* 1976; *Hostsonaten/Autumn Sonata* 1978 **(AANBA)**.

Bergman, Marilyn • Songwriter, lyricist • Born Marilyn Keith, New York, NY, November 10, 1929. *Educ.* NYU. See Bergman, Alan.

Bergner, Elisabeth • Actress • Born Elisabeth Ettel, Vienna, Austria, August 22, 1900; died May 12, 1986, London. *Educ.* Vienna Conservatory. International stage and screen star who rose to prominence in 1924 playing the title role in Max Reinhardt's Berlin production of G.B. Shaw's *Saint Joan*. Married to director Paul Czinner from 1933, Bergner made several films in England and France, including *Catherine the Great* (1934), which was banned in Nazi Germany for featuring "emigré Jews." • *Der Evangelimann* 1923; *Nju* 1924; *Liebe* 1926; *Dona Juana* 1927; *Königin Luise* 1927; *Fräulein Else* 1929; *Ariane* 1931; *Mélo* 1932; *Catherine the Great* 1934; *Escape Me Never* 1935 **(AANBA)**; *As You Like It* 1936; *Dreaming Lips* 1937; *Stolen Life* 1939; *Paris Calling* 1942; *Die Glückliche Jahre der Thorwalds* 1962; *Cry of the Banshee* 1970; *The Pedestrian* 1974; *Der Pfingstausflug* 1978.

Berkeley, Busby • Director, choreographer • Born William Berkeley Enos, Los Angeles, CA, November 29, 1895; died March 14, 1976. Busby Berkeley is known primarily as an innovative choreographer who freed dance in the cinema from the constraints of theatrical space. In Berkeley's musical numbers, the confining proscenium of the stage gives way to the fluid frame of the motion picture image, and dances are choreographed for the ideal, changing point of view of a film spectator, rather than for the static position of a traditional theatergoer.

After enlisting in the army during WWI, Berkeley found himself conducting trick parade drills for as many as 1200 men and training as an aerial observer—two experiences that clearly shaped his approach to dance on film.

After the war Berkeley worked in the theater, acting in and choreographing some numbers for touring musicals. His reputation grew steadily, and in 1928 he choreographed five Broadway shows, a considerable accomplishment for a man who had seriously studied neither choreography nor dance.

Berkeley's substantial success on Broadway led in 1930 to the opportunity to work in Hollywood on the newest movie genre, the film musical, then in its first flush of popularity after the recent arrival of sound. Sam Goldwyn hired him to direct the musical sequences of *Whoopee!* (1930), starring Eddie Cantor. In one sequence, Berkeley filmed the Goldwyn Girls, deployed in symmetrical fashion, from overhead—a technique that would become perhaps his most famous trademark.

Berkeley worked on several other musicals for MGM before settling in at Warner Bros. for seven years in 1933. His most famous Warner films included *42nd Street* (1933), *Gold Diggers of 1933* (1933) and *Dames* (1934). When he returned to MGM in 1939, Berkeley demonstrated that good musicals could be made with smaller budgets, but the development of the integrated dramatic musical left little room for his bravura approach. Berkeley doubled as director and choreographer on some of his films, and even directed the occasional dramatic feature, as with *They Made Me a Criminal* (1939), starring John Garfield.

The plots of Berkeley's musicals usually serve as little more than narrative pretexts for the the dance numbers, in which the camera soars through space, achieving a variety of startling surrealist effects. He choreographed dancing skyscrapers in *42nd Street* and 56 white pianos in *Gold Diggers of 1935*. In *Small Town Girl* (1953) only the arms and instruments of an orchestra are visible through the floors and walls.

Berkeley's choreography is also notable for its humorous and voyeuristic eroticism. *Golddiggers of 1933* opens with chorines, including a young Ginger Rogers, singing "We're in the Money" clad in nothing but large coins—a striking image of women as objects of exchange within a patriarchal society, and thus a metaphorical reinforcement of the film's central theme. The "Pettin' in the Park" number from the same movie features Dick Powell using a can opener to gain access to Ruby Keeler's metal-clad body. The famous sequence from *The Gang's All Here* (1943), featuring Carmen Miranda ("The Lady in the Tutti-Frutti Hat") and a line of chorus girls waving giant bananas, may be the essential Berkeley sequence; it combines his surreal visual style with an overblown Freudian symbolism that prefigures the sensibility of Camp.

There is an almost cubist element to Berkeley's penchant for breaking up the physical world into aesthetically pleasing, abstract visual patterns—as in the giant jigsaw puzzle of Ruby Keeler's face carried by the chorines in the "I Only Have Eyes for You" number in *Dames*. Berkeley's greatest achievement was that, in an era dominated by the illusionist style of the classical Hollywood film, he attempted to free the camera from the mere recording of surface reality. BKG • *Whoopee* 1930 (chor); *Palmy Days* 1931 (chor); *Bird of Paradise* 1932 (chor); *The Kid From Spain* 1932 (chor); *42nd Street* 1933 (chor); *Footlight Parade* 1933 (chor); *Gold Diggers of 1933* 1933 (chor); *Roman Scandals* 1933 (chor); *She Had to Say Yes* 1933 (d); *Dames* 1934 (chor); *Bright Lights* 1935 (d); *Gold Diggers of 1935* 1935 (chor,d) **(AANDANCE DIRECTION)**; *I Live For Love* 1935 (d); *In Caliente* 1935 (chor); *Stars Over Broadway* 1935 (chor); *Gold Diggers of 1937* 1936 (chor) **(AANDANCE DIRECTION)**; *Stage Struck* 1936 (d); *The Go Getter* 1937 (d); *Hollywood Hotel* 1937 (d); *The Singing Marine* 1937 (chor); *Varsity Show* 1937 (chor) **(AANDANCE DIRECTION)**; *Comet Over Broadway* 1938 (d); *Garden of the Moon* 1938 (d); *Gold Diggers in Paris* 1938 (chor); *Men Are Such Fools* 1938 (d); *Babes in Arms* 1939 (d); *Fast and Furious* 1939 (d); *They Made Me a Criminal* 1939 (d); *Forty Little Mothers* 1940 (d); *Strike Up the Band* 1940 (d); *Babes on Broadway* 1941 (d); *Blonde Inspiration* 1941 (d); *For Me and My Gal* 1942 (d); *The Gang's All Here* 1943 (d); *Cinderella Jones* 1946 (d); *Take Me Out to the Ball Game* 1949 (d); *Million Dollar Mermaid* 1952 (chor); *Easy to Love* 1953 (chor); *Small Town Girl* 1953 (chor); *Rose Marie* 1954 (chor); *Billy Rose's Jumbo* 1962 (chor).

Berkoff, Steven • Actor; also playwright. • Born London, 1937. Socially committed stage writer and director who subsidizes his strikingly original London theater work with (usually) villainous film and TV roles.

Berkoff made his screen debut in Stanley Kubrick's *A Clockwork Orange* (1971) and began making regular movie appearances in the 1980s. Best known as the arch-villain of *Beverly Hills Cop* (1984), as Adolf Hitler in the TV epic *War and Remembrance* (1988) and as the rival gangster who gets it between the eyes in *The Krays* (1990). • *A Clockwork Orange* 1971 (a); *Nicholas and Alexandra* 1971 (a); *Barry Lyndon* 1975 (a); *Outland* 1981 (a); *Octopussy* 1983 (a); *Beverly Hills Cop* 1984 (a); *Rambo: First Blood Part II* 1985 (a); *Revolution* 1985 (a); *Absolute Beginners* 1986 (a); *Under the Cherry Moon* 1986 (a); *Underworld* 1986 (a); *Prisoner of Rio* 1988 (a); *Streets of Yesterday* 1989 (a); *The Krays* 1990 (a).

Berlanga, Luis Garcia • Director, screenwriter • Born Luis Garcia Berlanga Marti, Valencia, Spain, June 12, 1921. *Educ.* Valencia University (philosophy); Instituto de Investigaciones y Experiencias Cinematograficas, Madrid. Along with Juan Antonio Bardem, the only significant figure in domestic Spanish film production of the 1950s. Berlanga first achieved international acclaim as the director of *Welcome Mr. Marshall* (1952), a comedy about the reaction of a small Spanish village to the Marshall Plan, which lifted Spanish cinema out of a 15-year doldrum. Berlanga's biggest commercial success came with *The National Shotgun* (1978), the first in a trilogy of films about the farcical effects of the post-Franco democracy on an aristocratic family. • *Esa Pareja Felíz/That Happy Pair* 1951 (s,sc); *Bienvenido Mr. Marshall/Welcome Mr. Marshall* 1952 (d); *Nóvio a la Vista* 1953 (d); *Los Gancheros* 1955 (d); *Calabuch/The Rocket From Calabuch* 1956 (d,sc); *Los Jueves Milagro* 1957 (d,sc,from story—"Arrivederci Dimas"); *Plácido* 1961 (d,sc); *Les Quatre Vérités* 1962 (d—"El Lenadór y la Muerte"); *El Verdugo/Not on Your Life* 1963 (d); *Las Pirañas* 1967 (d); *Vívan los Nóvios!* 1970 (d); *Life Size/Love Doll* 1977 (d,sc); *La Escopeta nacionál/The National Shotgun* 1978 (d,sc); *Moros y Cristianos* 1987 (d,sc).

Berlin, Irving • Composer, songwriter; also screenwriter. • Born Israel Isidore Baline, Temun, Siberia, Russia, May 11, 1888; died September 22, 1989, New York, NY. Celebrated popular composer who dominated American musical films and plays of the 1930s, 40s and 50s. Berlin wrote the first song ever to be used in a film—"Blue Skies," performed by Al Jolson in *The Jazz Singer* (1927). • *Stop, Look and Listen* 1926 (from story); *The Jazz Singer* 1927 (songs); *The Cocoanuts* 1929 (from play,songs); *Hallelujah* 1929 (song); *Mammy* 1930 (from play *Mr. Bones*,song); *Reaching For the Moon* 1931 (story,song); *Top Hat* 1935 (songs) **(AANBS)**; *Follow the Fleet* 1936 (songs); *On the Avenue* 1937 (songs); *Alexander's Ragtime Band* 1938 (songs) **(AANBS,AANBST)**; *Carefree* 1938 (songs) **(AANBS)**; *Second Fiddle* 1939 (song) **(AANBS)**; *Louisiana Purchase* 1941 (songs); *Holiday Inn* 1942 (story,songs) **(AANBST,AABS)**; *This Is the Army* 1943 (a,story,songs); *Christmas Holiday* 1944 (song); *Blue Skies* 1946 (story,songs) **(AANBS)**; *Easter Parade* 1948 (songs); *Annie Get Your Gun* 1950 (from play,songs); *Call Me Madam* 1953 (m); *There's No Business Like Show Business* 1954 (m,songs); *White Christmas* 1954 (songs) **(AANBS)**; *Sayonara* 1957 (song).

Berman, Pandro S. • Producer • Born Pittsburgh, PA, March 28, 1905. Distinguished and prolific producer who entered film as an assistant director at Universal (where his father, Harry M. Berman, was an executive) and then moved on to editing at RKO. Producing from 1931, he worked almost exclusively for RKO and then for MGM.

Berman's huge output contained a number of entertaining, high-quality productions ranging from superb literary adaptations such as *The Hunchback of Notre Dame* (1939) and *Sweet Bird of Youth* (1962) to the Astaire/Rogers classics *The Gay Divorcee* (1934) and *Top Hat* (1935). He made an atypical foray into socially conscious filmmaking with Richard Brooks's then-searing drama *Blackboard Jungle* (1955). • *Beyond London Lights* 1928 (ed); *Fangs of the Wild* 1928 (ed); *Phantom of the Range* 1928 (ed); *Stocks and Blondes* 1928 (ed); *Taxi 13* 1928 (ed); *The Texas Tornado* 1928 (ed); *Trial Marriage* 1929 (ed); *Bad Company* 1931 (p); *The Age of Consent* 1932 (assoc.p); *Aggie Appleby, Maker of Men* 1933 (p); *Ann Vickers* 1933 (p); *Bed of Roses* 1933 (assoc.p); *Morning Glory* 1933 (p); *One Man's Journey* 1933 (p); *The Age of Innocence* 1934 (p); *By Your Leave* 1934 (p); *The Fountain* 1934 (p); *The Gay Divorcee* 1934 (p); *Gridiron Flash* 1934 (p); *Hat, Coat, and Glove* 1934 (exec.p); *The Life of Vergie Winters* 1934 (p); *The Little Minister* 1934 (p); *Man of Two Worlds* 1934 (p); *Of Human Bondage* 1934 (p); *The Richest Girl in the World* 1934 (p); *Romance in Manhattan* 1934 (p); *Spitfire* 1934 (p); *Stingaree* 1934 (p); *This Man Is Mine* 1934 (p); *Alice Adams* 1935 (p); *Break of Hearts* 1935 (p); *Freckles* 1935 (p); *I Dream Too Much* 1935 (p); *In Person* 1935 (p); *Laddie* 1935 (p); *Roberta* 1935 (p); *Star of Midnight* 1935 (p); *Sylvia Scarlett* 1935 (p); *Top Hat* 1935 (p); *The Big Game* 1936 (p); *Follow the Fleet* 1936 (p); *Mary of Scotland* 1936 (p); *Muss 'Em Up* 1936 (p); *Swing Time* 1936 (p); *That Girl From Paris* 1936 (p); *Winterset* 1936 (p); *A Woman Rebels* 1936 (p); *A Damsel in Distress* 1937 (p); *Quality Street* 1937 (p); *Shall We Dance* 1937 (p); *The Soldier and the Lady* 1937 (p); *Stage Door* 1937 (p); *Carefree* 1938 (p); *Having Wonderful Time* 1938 (p); *The Mad Miss Manton* 1938 (p); *Mother Carey's Chickens* 1938 (p); *Room Service* 1938 (p); *The Flying Irishman* 1939 (p); *The Hunchback of Notre Dame* 1939 (p); *The Story of Vernon and Irene Castle* 1939 (p); *Honky Tonk* 1941 (p); *Love Crazy* 1941 (p); *Ziegfeld Girl* 1941 (p); *Rio Rita* 1942 (p); *Somewhere I'll Find You* 1942 (p); *Slightly Dangerous* 1943 (p); *Dragon Seed* 1944 (p); *Marriage Is a Private Affair* 1944 (p); *National Velvet* 1944 (p); *The Seventh Cross* 1944 (p); *The Picture of Dorian Gray* 1945 (p); *Undercurrent* 1946 (p); *If Winter Comes* 1947 (p); *Living in a Big Way* 1947 (p); *Sea of Grass* 1947 (p); *The Three Musketeers* 1948 (p); *The Bribe* 1949 (p); *The Doctor and the Girl* 1949 (p); *Madame Bovary* 1949 (p); *Father of the Bride* 1950 (p); *Father's Little Dividend* 1951 (p); *The Light Touch* 1951 (p); *Soldiers*

Three 1951 (p); *Ivanhoe* 1952 (p) **(AANBP)**; *The Prisoner of Zenda* 1952 (p); *All the Brothers Were Valiant* 1953 (p); *Battle Circus* 1953 (p); *Knights of the Round Table* 1953 (p); *The Long, Long Trailer* 1954 (p); *Blackboard Jungle* 1955 (p); *Quentin Durward* 1955 (p); *Bhowani Junction* 1956 (p); *Tea and Sympathy* 1956 (p); *Jailhouse Rock* 1957 (p); *Something of Value* 1957 (p); *The Brothers Karamazov* 1958 (p); *The Reluctant Debutante* 1958 (p); *All the Fine Young Cannibals* 1960 (p); *Butterfield 8* 1960 (p); *Sweet Bird of Youth* 1962 (p); *The Prize* 1963 (p); *Honeymoon Hotel* 1964 (p); *A Patch of Blue* 1965 (p); *Justine* 1969 (p); *Move* 1970 (p); *George Stevens: A Filmmaker's Journey* 1985 (a).

Bernhard, Sandra • Actress, comedian • Born Flint, MI, June 6, 1955. Aggressive, unusual-looking stand-up comic who made an impressive appearance as one of the psychopathic fans in Martin Scorsese's *The King of Comedy* (1983). Bernhard's eclectic, confrontational one-woman stage show, *Without You I'm Nothing*, was adapted to the screen in 1990. • *Cheech & Chong's Nice Dreams* 1981 (a); *The King of Comedy* 1983 (a); *Sesame Street Presents: Follow That Bird* 1985 (a); *The Whoopee Boys* 1986 (a); *Track 29* 1987 (a); *Heavy Petting* 1988 (a); *Without You I'm Nothing* 1990 (a,sc,from stage show,m.prod,song); *Hudson Hawk* 1991 (a).

Bernsen, Corbin • Actor • Born North Hollywood, CA, September 7, 1954. *Educ.* UCLA (theater arts, playwriting). Sturdy, handsome blond performer who first gained wide recognition as the manipulative attorney Arnie Becker in the popular TV series "L.A. Law" (1986-). Son of lead and supporting player Jeanne Cooper (*Plunder Road* 1957, *The Intruder* 1961, etc.) and married to actress Amanda Pays (*Oxford Blues* 1984, *Leviathan* 1989). • *Three the Hard Way* 1974; *Eat My Dust* 1976; *Hello, Again* 1987; *Mace* 1987; *Bert Rigby, You're a Fool* 1989; *Disorganized Crime* 1989; *Major League* 1989; *Shattered* 1991.

Bernstein, Elmer • Composer, conductor • Born New York, NY, April 4, 1922. *Educ.* Juilliard (music); NYU. Leading writer of film scores since the mid-1950s, when his work on *The Man With the Golden Arm* (1955) and *The Ten Commandments* (1956) pushed him into the front rank of Hollywood composers. Noted for his strong use of solo instruments and his facility with the jazz idiom. • *Never Wave at a Wac* 1952 (m); *Sudden Fear* 1952 (m); *Miss Robin Crusoe* 1953 (m); *Cat Women of the Moon* 1954 (m); *Make Haste To Live* 1954 (m); *Silent Raiders* 1954 (m,song); *The Eternal Sea* 1955 (m); *It's a Dog's Life* 1955 (m); *The Man With the Golden Arm* 1955 (m) **(AANBM)**; *Storm Fear* 1955 (m); *The View From Pompey's Head* 1955 (m); *Fear Strikes Out* 1956 (m); *Men in War* 1956 (m); *The Ten Commandments* 1956 (m); *Desire Under the Elms* 1957 (m); *Drango* 1957 (m); *The Naked Eye* 1957 (m); *Sweet Smell of Success* 1957 (m); *The Tin Star* 1957 (m); *Anna Lucasta* 1958 (m,song); *The Buccaneer* 1958 (m); *God's Little Acre* 1958 (m,m.cond); *Kings Go Forth* 1958 (m); *Some Came Running* 1958 (m); *The Miracle* 1959 (m); *The Story on Page One* 1959 (m); *From the Terrace* 1960 (m); *The Magnificent Seven* 1960 (m) **(AANBM)**; *The Rat Race* 1960 (m); *By Love Possessed* 1961 (m); *The Comancheros* 1961 (m); *Summer and Smoke* 1961 (m) **(AANBM)**; *The Young Doctors* 1961 (m); *Birdman of Alcatraz* 1962 (m); *A Girl Named Tamiko* 1962 (m); *Walk on the Wild Side* 1962 (m) **(AANBS)**; *The Caretakers* 1963 (m); *The Great Escape* 1963 (m); *Hud* 1963 (m); *Kings of the Sun* 1963 (m); *Love With the Proper Stranger* 1963 (m); *Rampage* 1963 (m); *The Carpetbaggers* 1964 (m); *Four Days in November* 1964 (m); *The World of Henry Orient* 1964 (m); *Baby, the Rain Must Fall* 1965 (m,song); *The Hallelujah Trail* 1965 (m); *The Reward* 1965 (m); *Seven Women* 1965 (m); *The Sons of Katie Elder* 1965 (m); *Cast a Giant Shadow* 1966 (m); *Hawaii* 1966 (m) **(AANBM,AANBS)**; *Return of the Seven* 1966 (m) **(AANBM)**; *The Silencers* 1966 (m); *Thoroughly Modern Millie* 1967 (m) **(AABM)**; *I Love You, Alice B. Toklas* 1968 (m,song); *The Scalphunters* 1968 (m); *The Gypsy Moths* 1969 (m); *A Run on Gold* 1969 (m,song); *True Grit* 1969 (m,song) **(AANBS)**; *Where's Jack?* 1969 (m,song); *Cannon For Cordoba* 1970 (m); *Doctors' Wives* 1970 (m); *The Liberation of L.B. Jones* 1970 (m); *A Walk in the Spring Rain* 1970 (m,song); *Big Jake* 1971 (m); *See No Evil* 1971 (m,m.cond); *The Magnificent Seven Ride* 1972 (m); *Nightmare Honeymoon* 1972 (m); *Cahill, United States Marshal* 1973 (m); *Gold* 1974 (m) **(AANBS)**; *McQ* 1974 (m); *The Trial of Billy Jack* 1974 (m); *Mr. Quilp* 1975 (m.sup); *Report to the Commissioner* 1975 (m); *Billy Jack Goes to Washington* 1976 (m); *From Noon Till Three* 1976 (a,m); *The Incredible Sarah* 1976 (m); *The Shootist* 1976 (m); *Slap Shot* 1977 (m.sup); *Bloodbrothers* 1978 (m); *Casey's Shadow* 1978 (m); *National Lampoon's Animal House* 1978 (m); *The Great Santini* 1979 (m); *Meatballs* 1979 (m,song); *Moonraker* 1979 (song); *Zulu Dawn* 1979 (m); *Airplane!* 1980 (m); *The Blues Brothers* 1980 (m); *Saturn 3* 1980 (m); *An American Werewolf in London* 1981 (m); *The Chosen* 1981 (m); *Genocide* 1981 (m); *Going Ape!* 1981 (m); *Heavy Metal* 1981 (m,m.dir); *Honky Tonk Freeway* 1981 (m,song); *Stripes* 1981 (m); *Airplane II: The Sequel* 1982 (m); *Five Days One Summer* 1982 (m); *Class* 1983 (m); *Making Michael Jackson's Thriller* 1983 (m); *Spacehunter: Adventures in the Forbidden Zone* 1983 (m); *Trading Places* 1983 (m) **(AANBS)**; *Bolero* 1984 (m,m.dir,m.sup); *Ghostbusters* 1984 (m); *Prince Jack* 1984 (m); *The Black Cauldron* 1985 (m); *Marie Ward* 1985 (m); *The Color of Money* 1986 (song); *Three Amigos!* 1986 (m); *Amazing Grace and Chuck* 1987 (m); *Leonard, Part 6* 1987 (m); *Da* 1988 (m); *Funny Farm* 1988 (m); *The Good Mother* 1988 (m); *Life Is Cheap...But Toilet Paper Is Expensive* 1989 (m); *My Left Foot* 1989 (m,m.cond); *Slipstream* 1989 (m); *The Field* 1990 (m); *The Grifters* 1990 (m); *A Rage in Harlem* 1991 (m).

Bernstein, Leonard • Composer, conductor; also pianist. • Born Lawrence, MA, August 25, 1918; died October 14, 1990, New York, NY. *Educ.* Harvard (music); Curtis Institute of Music. Brilliant, protean musical talent whose ouptut ranged from symphonies and ballets ("Fancy Free" 1943) to hit Broadway musicals (*On the Town* 1944, *West Side Story* 1957) and popular songs ("Maria," "New York, New York, A Helluva Town"). Bernstein's film work was occasional but distinguished, notably his contributions to *On the Town* (1949), *On the Waterfront* (1954) and *West Side Story* (1961). • *On the Town* 1949 (song); *On the Waterfront* 1954 (m) **(AANBM)**; *Satchmo the Great* 1957 (a); *West Side Story* 1961 (m,m,song); *To Kill a Mockingbird* 1962 (m) **(AANBM)**; *A Journey to Jerusalem* 1969 (a); *Heaven's Gate* 1980 (m); *A Midsummer Night's Sex Comedy* 1982 (m); *Terms of Endearment* 1983 (song); *Another Woman* 1988 (m); *Hollywood Mavericks* 1990 (m).

Bernstein, Walter • Screenwriter; also director, producer. • Born Brooklyn, NY, August 20, 1919. *Educ.* Dartmouth. Former writer for *The New Yorker* who wrote many distinguished scripts for live TV in the late 1940s. Bernstein earned one feature credit, for *Kiss the Blood Off My Hands* (1948), before being blacklisted in 1950. He returned to film work nine years later, scripting such fine films as Sidney Lumet's *Fail Safe*, John Frankenheimer's *The Train* (both 1964) with Franklin Coen and Frank Davis, and Martin Ritt's *The Molly Maguires* (1970), which he co-produced. His screenplay for *The Front* (1976) was a poignant, embittered portrait of the travails of a circle of screenwriters during the blacklist. Bernstein made his directing debut in 1980 with a rather bland remake of *Little Miss Marker*. • *Kiss the Blood Off My Hands* 1948 (adapt); *That Kind of Woman* 1959 (sc); *A Breath of Scandal* 1960 (sc); *Heller in Pink Tights* 1960 (sc); *Paris Blues* 1961 (sc); *Fail Safe* 1964 (sc); *The Train* 1964 (sc); *The Money Trap* 1966 (sc); *The Molly Maguires* 1970 (p,sc); *The Front* 1976 (sc) **(AANBSC)**; *Hollywood on Trial* 1976 (a); *Annie Hall* 1977 (a); *Semi-Tough* 1977 (sc); *The Betsy* 1978 (sc); *An Almost Perfect Affair* 1979 (sc); *Yanks*

1979 (sc); *Little Miss Marker* 1980 (d,sc); *The Legend of Billie Jean* 1985 (sc); *The House on Carroll Street* 1988 (sc).

Berri, Claude • Director, screenwriter, producer, distributor; also actor. • Born Claude Langman, Paris, July 1, 1934. Multi-faceted maverick of contemporary French cinema. Berri began his career as an actor and moved behind the camera in the early 1960s, earning critical praise for short films like *Le Poulet* (1964).

Since the formation of his production company Renn in 1968, Berri has been involved with an impressive array of quality films, directed by Claude Zidi, Bertrand Blier and Maurice Pialat, among others. In 1973 he developed a distribution arm, AMLF, which has since handled over 150 films.

As a director-writer, Berri's output has ranged from the lush pointlessness of *Le Sex Shop* (1972) to the lyrical power of *Jean de Florette* (1986). • *Les Bonnes Femmes* 1960 (a); *Les Sept péchés capitaux/The Seven Deadly Sins* 1962 (a); *Les Baisers* 1963 (d); *Behold a Pale Horse* 1964 (a); *Le Poulet (short)* 1964 (d) **(AABSF)**; *Mazel Tov ou le Mariage/Marry Me! Marry Me!* 1968 (a,d,p,sc); *L'Oeuf* 1971 (p); *Taking Off* 1971 (p); *Les Fous Du Stade* 1972 (p); *Le Sex Shop* 1972 (a,d,p,sc); *Je sais rien mais je dirai tout* 1973 (p); *Pleure pas la bouche pleine* 1973 (exec.p); *Je T'Aime Moi Non Plus* 1975 (p); *Le Male du Siècle* 1975 (a,d,sc); *Un Sac de Billes* 1975 (p); *La Première Fois* 1976 (d,sc); *Un Moment d'Egarement* 1977 (d,sc); *Tess* 1979 (p) **(AANBP)**; *Inspecteur la Bavure* 1980 (p); *Je vous aime* 1980 (d,p,sc); *Deux heures moins le quart avant Jèsus Christ* 1982 (p); *L'Africain* 1983 (p); *Banzai* 1983 (p); *Garçon!* 1983 (p); *L'Homme blessé* 1983 (a,p); *Tchao Pantin* 1983 (d,p,sc); *Blame It on Rio* 1984 (from screenplay *Un Moment d'Egarement*); *Le Vengeance du serpent à plumes* 1984 (p); *Scemo di Guerra* 1985 (p); *Jean de Florette* 1986 (d,sc); *Manon des sources* 1986 (d,p,sc); *Hôtel de France* 1987 (p); *A Gauche en sortant de l'ascenseur* 1988 (exec.p); *L'Ours/The Bear* 1988 (p); *Trois places pour le 26* 1988 (p); *Valmont* 1989 (p); *Stan the Flasher* 1990 (a); *Uranus* 1990 (d,p,sc).

Berry, John • Director; also screenwriter. • Born New York, NY, 1917. Began his career with Orson Welles's Mercury Theater in the late 1930s and made his directorial debut in 1945. Berry was noted for his ability to coax fine performances from his actors and earned a reputation as a visual stylist. As a result of the Hollywood blacklist he resettled in France, where he has done most of his work since the 1950s. Berry made his acting debut as the bartender in *'Round Midnight* (1986), Bertrand Tavernier's bittersweet ode to 1950s jazz. • *Too Much Johnson (short)* 1938 (a,prod.asst); *Double Indemnity* 1944 (3rd asst.d,uncred.a); *Miss Susie Slagle's* 1945 (d); *Tuesday in November (short)* 1945 (d); *Cross My Heart* 1946 (d); *From This Day Forward* 1946 (d); *Casbah* 1948 (d); *Caught* 1949 (d); *Tension* 1949 (d,uncred.sc); *The Hollywood Ten* 1950 (d); *Atoll K/Utopia* 1951 (d); *He Ran All the Way* 1951 (d); *C'est arrivé à Paris* 1953 (d); *Ça Va Barder* 1954 (d,sc,story); *Je Suis un Sentimental* 1955 (d,sc,story); *Pantaloons* 1956 (d,sc); *Tamango* 1957 (d,sc,adapt); *Oh, Que Mambo!* 1959 (d); *Maya* 1966 (d); *A tout casser* 1968 (d,sc); *Claudine* 1974 (d); *Comment Yukong Deplaça les Montagnes* 1976 (English version); *F comme Fairbanks* 1976 (a); *Thieves* 1977 (d); *The Bad News Bears Go to Japan* 1978 (d); *Le Voyage à Paimpol* 1985 (d,sc); *Autour de Minuit/'Round Midnight* 1986 (a); *Golden Eighties* 1986 (a); *Un Homme amoureux/A Man in Love* 1987 (a); *Blancs Cassés* 1988 (a); *Il y a maldonné* 1988 (d,sc).

Berto, Juliet • Actress; also director, screenwriter. • Born Grenoble, France, January 16, 1947; died January 10, 1990, Paris. Began her career with a bang, featuring in a series of films by Jean-Luc Godard, most notably *La Chinoise*, *Weekend* (both 1967) and *Le Gai Savoir* (1968). Later films of note include Jacques Rivette's *Celine and Julie Go Boating* (1973), which she also cowrote, and Alain Tanner's *The Middle of the World* (1974). Berto directed three features before dying from cancer one week before her 43rd birthday. • *Deux ou trois choses que je sais d'elle/Two or Three Things I Know About Her* 1966 (a); *La Chinoise, ou plutôt à la Chinoise* 1967 (a); *Weekend* 1967 (a); *Le Gai Savoir* 1968 (a); *Camarades* 1970 (a); *L'Escardon Volapuk* 1970 (a); *Un Eté sauvage* 1970 (a); *Vladimir et Rosa* 1970 (a); *La Cavale* 1971 (a); *Out 1: Noli Me Tangere* 1971 (a); *The Big Shots* 1972 (a); *Out 1: Spectre* 1972 a); *Le Retour d'Afrique* 1972 (a); *Le Sex Shop* 1972 (a); *Céline et Julie vont en bateau/Céline and Julie Go Boating* 1973 (a,sc); *Défense de savoir* 1973 (a); *Le Milieu du Monde/The Middle of the World* 1974 (a); *Le Protecteur* 1974 (a); *Summer Run* 1974 (a); *Le Male du Siècle* 1975 (a); *Duelle* 1976 (a); *Mr. Klein* 1976 (a); *L'Argent des autres* 1978 (a); *Roberte* 1978 (a); *Bastien, Bastienne* 1979 (a); *Guns* 1980 (a); *Neige* 1981 (a,d,sc); *Cap Canaille* 1983 (a,d); *La Vie de Famille* 1984 (a); *Gazl el Banat* 1985 (a); *Havre* 1986 (d,sc); *Un Amour à Paris* 1987 (a); *Hôtel du Paradis* 1987 (a); *Les Ministères de l'art* 1988 (a); *Une Vie suspendue* 1988 (a).

Bertolucci, Bernardo • Director, screenwriter • Born Parma, Italy, March 16, 1940. *Educ.* Rome University (modern literature). At the age of 24, Bernardo Bertolucci established himself at the forefront of international cinema with *Before the Revolution* (1964). Its operatic sensibility, coupled with a precocious facility for visual style, set the standard for the director's later works. Likewise, its focus on family romance and psychological crisis, framed by a sharply defined political and social context, staked out central concerns in Bertolucci's vision.

Influenced by writers and artists as diverse as Freud, Marx and Verdi, Bertolucci always shapes a set of rich associations in his cinematic texts, although never at the expense of visual style, which remains primary. In *Partner* (1968), which pays homage to the French New Wave and particularly Jean-Luc Godard, Bertolucci began to explore his fascination with the figure of the psychological double. The doubling theme reappears in *The Spider's Stratagem* (1970), which traces a son's search for his father through a surrealistic, complex narrative that incorporates Verdi's *Rigoletto* and the work of Borges and Magritte. A later film, *Tragedy of a Ridiculous Man* (1981), reverses that narrative premise, following a father's search for his son.

In *The Conformist* (1970), considered by many critics Bertolucci's masterpiece, lighting, decor, costume and music shape a stylized backdrop of Fascist Italy against which the hero attempts to resolve his own sexual and political conflicts. The classic sequence in which the two central women characters perform a tango is a Bertolucci signature: the dance as metaphor. The dance also appears at the center of his controversial *Last Tango in Paris* (1972). Considered obscene by some viewers, *Last Tango* was for others a breakthrough in the depiction of sexual politics in its presentation of the passionate, conflicted relationship between an older man and a younger woman in the enclosed psychological space of chamber cinema. As with *The Conformist*, the visual style and themes of *Last Tango* were to influence a generation of filmmakers.

Controversy also surrounded *La Luna* (1979) because of its graphic portrayal of mother/son incest. The mythic subtext of the film focuses once again on the search for a father: both the Italian sire of the young American boy and the artistic father (Verdi) of his opera-singer mother.

Bertolucci returned to his northern Italian roots in the sweeping epic *1900* (1976). The film charts 45 years of social history and class struggle through the friendship—and political enmity—of two men born, on different sides of the social fence, at the turn of the century. Bertolucci again demonstrated his adeptness with the epic form in *The Last Emperor* (1987), winner of nine Academy Awards including best director and best picture. The film follows the shifting fortunes of Pu Yi, who begins his life as the last emperor of China and ends it as a gardener in post-revolutionary Pekin. Recurrent themes of sexual and political identity are explored within the perverse ambience of the Chinese court and during Pu Yi's subsequent political exile, imprisonment and political "rehabilitation."

Bertolucci's much-anticipated adaptation of Paul Bowles's cult favorite *The Sheltering Sky* (1990), starring John Malkovich and Debra Winger, proved a critical and financial disappointment.

Romantic and sensuous, Bertolucci's work is characterized by expressive *mise-en-scène*, rhythmic editing, fluid camera movement and complex narration, typically backed by an evocative musical score. He is at once heir to a generation of great Italian filmmakers and a dominant force in international cinema today. DMB • *Accattone* 1961 (ad); *La Commare Secca/The Grim Reaper* 1962 (d,sc); *Prima Della Rivoluzione/Before the Revolution* 1964 (d,sc); *Amore e rabbia* 1967 (d); *Partner* 1968 (d,sc); *C'era una Volta il West/Once Upon a Time in the West* 1969 (story); *Il Conformista/The Conformist* 1970 (d,sc) **(AANBSC)**; *La Strategia del Ragno/The Spider's Strategem* 1970 (d,sc); *Last Tango in Paris* 1972 (d,sc) **(AANBD)**; *Novecento/1900* 1976 (d,sc); *La Luna* 1979 (d,sc,story); *La Tragedia di un Uomo Ridicolo/The Tragedy of a Ridiculous Man* 1981 (d,sc); *Sconcerto Rock* 1982 (p); *Io con te non ci sto più* 1983 (p); *The Last Emperor* 1987 (d,sc) **(AABD,AABSC)**; *The Sheltering Sky* 1990 (d,sc).

Bessie, Alvah • Screenwriter, author • Born New York, NY, June 4, 1904; died July 21, 1985, Terra Linda, CA. *Educ.* Columbia. Warner Bros. screenwriter whose career was ended when he was named one of the "Hollywood Ten." Bessie was sentenced to one year in prison and, unlike most of his fellow victims, never worked in the US film industry again. His son Dan wrote and directed the feature film, *Hard Traveling* (1986), adapted from Bessie's book *Bread and a Stone*. • *Northern Pursuit* 1943 (sc); *The Very Thought of You* 1944 (sc); *Hotel Berlin* 1945 (sc); *Objective Burma!* 1945 (story) **(AANBST)**; *Smart Woman* 1948 (sc); *Hollywood on Trial* 1976 (a); *Hard Traveling* 1986 (from novel *Bread and a Stone*).

Besson, Luc • Director, screenwriter; also producer. • Born Paris, March 18, 1959. *Educ.* Began film career as second assistant director. Stylish young talent who made an impressive debut at age 24 with *Le Dernier Combat* (1983), an apocalyptic drama noted for its striking black-and-white photography and bold lack of dialogue. Besson's subsequent films have been French box-office hits, more popular for their exhilarating visuals than for their fantasy-adventure storylines. He is best known for the underwater epic *The Big Blue* (1988), a huge commercial success at home but a failure in the international marketplace. • *Le Dernier Combat* 1983 (d,p,sc); *Le Grand Carnaval* 1983 (2u d); *Subway* 1985 (d,p,sc,dial); *Kamikaze* 1986 (p,sc); *Taxi Boy* 1986 (tech.ad); *Le Grand bleu/The Big Blue* 1988 (d,sc,idea,cam.op submarine crew,lyrics); *Nikita/La Femme Nikita* 1990 (d,sc,song).

Biberman, Herbert J. • *aka* Herbert Biberman • Director; also screenwriter, producer. • Born Philadelphia, PA, March 4, 1900; died June, 1971. *Educ.* University of Pennsylvania, Philadelphia (economics); Yale (drama). Stage actor and director who joined Columbia in 1935 and directed three films before being victimized as one of the "Hollywood Ten" in 1947. After serving a six-month jail term for contempt of Congress, Biberman made *Salt of the Earth* (1954), a potent socialist drama about striking New Mexico mineworkers. The film earned critical acclaim in Europe but, due to continued blacklisting, did not enjoy general US release until 1965. Biberman was married to actress Gale Sondergaard from 1930. • *One Way Ticket* 1935 (d); *Meet Nero Wolfe* 1936 (d); *King of Chinatown* 1939 (story); *Action in Arabia* 1944 (sc); *The Master Race* 1944 (d,sc,story); *Together Again* 1944 (story); *New Orleans* 1947 (story); *Salt of the Earth* 1954 (d); *Slaves* 1969 (d,sc).

Biehn, Michael • Actor • Born Anniston, AL, 1957. *Educ.* University of Arizona (drama). Athletic supporting player, mostly in action/adventure movies who came to prominence with major roles in the James Cameron films, *The Terminator* (1984), *Aliens* (1986) and *The Abyss* (1989). • *Coach* 1978; *Hog Wild* 1980; *The Fan* 1981; *The Lords of Discipline* 1983; *The Terminator* 1984; *Aliens* 1986; *Rampage* 1987; *In a Shallow Grave* 1988; *The Seventh Sign* 1988; *The Abyss* 1989; *Navy Seals* 1990.

Bigelow, Kathryn • Director; also screenwriter. • Born United States, c. 1951. *Educ.* San Francisco Art Institute; Whitney Museum, New York (independent study program); Columbia (film). Graduated to filmmaking from painting, and earned critical acclaim for her first short film, *Set-Up* (1978), and her first feature, *The Loveless* (1981), starring Willem Dafoe. Bigelow became a cult figure with the release of *Near Dark* (1987), a stylish, atmospheric tale of modern-day vampires which prompted New York's Museum of Modern Art to mount a retrospective of her brief career. Married to director James Cameron. • *Union City* 1980 (script supervisor); *The Loveless* 1981 (d,sc); *Born in Flames* 1982 (a); *Near Dark* 1987 (d,sc); *Blue Steel* 1989 (d,sc).

Bill, Tony • Producer, director; also actor. • Born San Diego, CA, August 23, 1940. *Educ.* Notre Dame (English, art). Began his career as an actor, first appearing on screen as Frank Sinatra's ingenuous younger brother in *Come Blow Your Horn* (1963). Bill then moved into production, co-founding Bill/Phillips Productions with Julia and Michael Phillips in 1971; his first producing credit was for the Jane Fonda/Donald Sutherland vehicle, *Steelyard Blues* (1973). In the same year he formed his own company, Tony Bill Productions, and scored a huge success with *The Sting*, starring Paul Newman and Robert Redford.

Bill's output as a director has ranged from the engaging teen comedy *My Bodyguard* (1980), to the flawed but finely acted *Five Corners* (1987), to Dudley Moore vehicles like *Crazy People* (1990). • *Come Blow Your Horn* 1963 (a); *Soldier in the Rain* 1963 (a); *Marriage on the Rocks* 1965 (a); *None But the Brave* 1965 (a); *How to Steal the World* 1968 (a); *Ice Station Zebra* 1968 (a); *Never a Dull Moment* 1968 (a); *Castle Keep* 1969 (a); *Flap* 1970 (a); *Steelyard Blues* 1973 (p); *The Sting* 1973 (p) **(AABP)**; *Hearts of the West* 1975 (exec.p); *Shampoo* 1975 (a); *Harry and Walter Go to New York* 1976 (exec.p); *Boulevard Nights* 1979 (exec.p); *Going in Style* 1979 (p); *Heart Beat* 1979 (a); *The Little Dragons* 1980 (a,exec.p); *My Bodyguard* 1980 (d); *Deadhead Miles* 1982 (p); *Six Weeks* 1982 (d); *Pee-wee's Big Adventure* 1985 (a); *Five Corners* 1987 (d,p); *Less Than Zero* 1987 (a); *Crazy People* 1990 (d).

Binder, Maurice • Title designer; also executive producer. • Born New York, NY, 1925. Best known for the erotic title sequences of the James Bond films, but also responsible for the haunting, vertiginous opening of Roman Polanski's *Repulsion* (1964) and the main title design for *The Last Emperor* (1987). Binder has worked primarily in Europe. • *Cry Danger* 1951 (prod.asst); *Damn Yankees* 1958 (title design); *The Mouse That Roared* 1959 (title design); *The Young Philadelphians* 1959 (title design); *Of Human Bondage* 1964 (graphic design); *Repulsion* 1964 (title design); *La Ronde* 1964 (title design); *After the Fox* 1966 (title design); *Arabesque* 1966 (title design); *The Chase* 1966 (main title design); *Kaleidoscope* 1966 (main title design); *Promise Her Anything* 1966 (main title design); *The Taming of the Shrew* 1967 (main title design); *Two For the Road* 1967 (title design); *The Magus* 1968 (title design); *Battle of Britain* 1969 (main title design); *Wuthering Heights* 1970 (main title design); *Young Winston* 1972 (title design); *E'Lollipop* 1975 (title design); *Shout at the Devil* 1976 (title design); *A Little Night Music* 1977 (graphic design); *The Spy Who Loved Me* 1977 (title design); *Brass Target* 1978 (title design); *Dracula* 1979 (visual consultant); *Moonraker* 1979 (title design); *The Passage* 1979 (exec.p); *The Awakening* 1980 (title design); *The Final Countdown* 1980 (fx—storm sequence); *The Sea Wolves* 1980 (title design,graphic design); *For Your Eyes Only* 1981 (main title design); *Green Ice* 1981 (main title design); *Who Dares Wins* 1982 (graphics); *Octopussy* 1983 (main title design); *Oxford Blues* 1984 (graphics design); *King David* 1985 (graphic design); *A View to a Kill* 1985 (main title design); *Max mon amour* 1986 (titles); *Shanghai Surprise* 1986 (main title design); *The Last Emperor* 1987 (main title design); *The Living Daylights* 1987 (main title design); *The Deceivers* 1988 (title design); *Licence to Kill* 1989 (main title design); *Return to the River Kwai* 1989 (graphics).

Binoche, Juliette • Actress • Born Paris. Appealing, promising lead of international films, best known as Tereza (the one without the hat) in *The Unbearable Lightness of Being* (1988). Binoche also appeared in Leos Carax's stylish 1986 feature, *Bad Blood.* • *Les Nanas* 1984; *La Vie de Famille/Family Life* 1984; *Je vous salue, Marie/Hail, Mary* 1985; *Mon beau-frère a tué ma soeur* 1985; *Rendez-vous* 1985; *Mauvais sang/Bad Blood* 1986; *Un Tour de manège* 1988; *The Unbearable Lightness of Being* 1988.

Birkin, Jane • Actress; also singer. • Born London, December 14, 1946. Landed several lightweight movie roles in the 1960s, when her looks seemed to symbolize the swinging spirit of the times (she played one of the schoolgirl/models in Antonioni's 1966 *Blow-Up*) and subsequently resurfaced as a respected talent in France. Birkin was the subject of a documentary by Agnes Varda, *Jane B. par Agnes V.* (1988) and gave an affecting performance opposite Dirk Bogarde in Bertrand Tavernier's *Daddy Nostalgia* (1990). Her daughter Charlotte Gainsbourg, by composer-director Serge Gainsbourg, is also an actress and her brother is writer-director Andrew Birkin (*Burning Secret* 1988). • *Blow-Up* 1966 (a); *Kaleidoscope* 1966 (a); *Wonderwall* 1968 (a); *Les Chemins de Katmandou* 1969 (a); *La Piscine* 1969 (a); *Cannabis* 1970 (a); *Romance of a Horse Thief* 1971 (a); *Trop jolies pour être honnêtes* 1972 (a); *Dark Places* 1973 (a); *Projection Privée* 1973 (a); *La Moutarde me monte au nez* 1974 (a); *Le Mouton Enragé* 1974 (a); *7 Morts sur Ordonnance* 1975 (a); *Catherine et Cie* 1975 (a); *La Course à l'echalote* 1975 (a); *Je T'Aime Moi Non Plus* 1975 (a); *Sérieux comme le plaisir* 1975 (a); *Le Diable au Coeur* 1976 (a); *L'Animal* 1977 (a); *Death on the Nile* 1978 (a); *The Rise and Fall of Ivor Dickie* 1978 (song); *Au bout du bout du banc* 1979 (a); *Mélancolie Baby* 1979 (a); *La Miel* 1979 (a); *La Fille Prodigue* 1981 (a); *Evil Under the Sun* 1982 (a); *L'Ami de Vincent* 1983 (a); *Circulez y'a rien à voir* 1983 (a); *L'Amour par terre/Love on the Ground* 1984 (a); *Le Garde du Corps* 1984 (a); *La Pirate* 1984 (a); *Beethoven's Nephew* 1985 (a); *Dust* 1985 (a); *Leave All Fair* 1985 (a); *La Femme de ma vie* 1986 (a); *Comedie!* 1987 (a,song); *Kung Fu Master!/La Petit Amour* 1987 (a,story); *Soigne ta droite* 1987 (a); *Jane B. par Agnes V.* 1988 (a); *Daddy Nostalgie/Daddy Nostalgia* 1990 (a,song); *Thick As Thieves* 1991 (song).

Biro, Lajos • *aka* Lajos Biros • Screenwriter • Born Nagyvarad, Hungary, 1880; died 1948. *Educ.* Royal University of Budapest. Austro-Hungarian playwright whose stage works served as the basis for a number of Hollywood films, notably Billy Wilder's *Five Graves to Cairo* (1943). Biro began writing directly for the screen with *The Way of All Flesh* (1927) and relocated to England in 1932 to work for Alexander Korda, often in collaboration with Arthur Wimperis. Outstanding credits include *The Scarlet Pimpernel* (1935) and *Knight Without Armour* (1937). • *Eve's Secret* 1925 (from play *Moonflower*); *The Silent Lover* 1926 (from play *Der Legioner*); *The Heart Thief* 1927 (from play *The Highwayman*); *Hotel Imperial* 1927 (from play); *The Way of All Flesh* 1927 (adapt); *Adoration* 1928 (story); *The Haunted House* 1928 (sc); *The Last Command* 1928 (story) (**AANBST**); *The Night Watch* 1928 (sc); *The Yellow Lily* 1928 (story); *Women Everywhere* 1930 (sc); *The Ghost Train* 1931 (sc); *The Private Life of Henry VIII* 1933 (sc,dial,story); *Strange Evidence* 1933 (story); *Sanders of the River* 1935 (sc); *The Scarlet Pimpernel* 1935 (sc,dial,cont); *The Man Who Could Work Miracles* 1936 (sc); *Dark Journey* 1937 (sc); *Knight Without Armour* 1937 (sc); *Over the Moon* 1937 (story); *The Divorce of Lady X* 1938 (sc,story); *Drums* 1938 (sc); *Hotel Imperial* 1939 (from play); *The Thief of Bagdad* 1940 (sc); *Five Graves to Cairo* 1943 (from play *Hotel Imperial*); *A Royal Scandal* 1945 (from play *The Czarina*); *The Epic That Never Was (I, Claudius)* 1965 (sc—"I, Claudius").

Biroc, Joseph • Director of photography • Born New York, NY, February 12, 1903. Worked his way up from studio office boy to become an assistant to cinematographer George Folsey and co-photographed his first feature, *It's a Wonderful Life,* in 1946. Biroc often collaborated with Samuel Fuller and Robert Aldrich and did extensive work in TV. He photographed one of the first TV programs to be shot on film, rather than using the kinescope process—1951's "The Honeymoon Is Over"—and won an Emmy for *Brian's Song* (1971). In 1989 Biroc was honored with a lifetime achievement award from the American Society of Cinematographers. • *It's a Wonderful Life* 1946 (ph); *Magic Town* 1947 (ph); *A Miracle Can Happen* 1948 (ph); *My Dear Secretary* 1948 (ph); *Johnny Allegro* 1949 (ph); *Mrs. Mike* 1949 (ph); *Roughshod* 1949 (ph); *The Killer That Stalked New York* 1950 (ph); *All That I Have* 1951 (ph); *The Bushwackers* 1952 (ph); *Bwana Devil* 1952 (ph); *Red Planet Mars* 1952 (ph); *Without Warning* 1952 (ph); *Appointment in Honduras* 1953 (ph); *Donovan's Brain* 1953 (ph); *The Glass Wall* 1953 (ph); *The Twonky* 1953 (ph); *Vice Squad* 1953 (ph); *Down Three Dark Streets* 1954 (ph); *World For Ransom* 1954 (ph); *Bengazi* 1955 (ph); *Attack!* 1956 (ph); *The Black Whip* 1956 (ph); *Ghost Town* 1956 (ph); *Nightmare* 1956 (ph); *Quincannon, Frontier Scout* 1956 (ph); *Tension at Table Rock* 1956 (ph); *The Amazing Colossal Man* 1957 (ph); *China Gate* 1957 (ph); *Forty Guns* 1957 (ph); *The Garment Jungle* 1957 (ph); *The Ride Back* 1957 (ph); *Run of the Arrow* 1957 (ph); *Underwater Warrior* 1957 (ph); *The Unknown Terror* 1957 (ph); *The Bat* 1959 (ph); *Born Reckless* 1959 (ph); *The F.B.I. Story* 1959 (ph); *Verboten!* 1959 (ph); *13 Ghosts* 1960 (ph); *Ice Palace* 1960 (ph); *The Devil at 4 O'Clock* 1961 (ph); *Gold of the Seven Saints* 1961 (ph); *Operation Eichmann* 1961 (ph); *Sail a Crooked Ship* 1961 (ph); *Confessions of an Opium Eater* 1962 (ph); *Convicts Four* 1962 (ph); *Hitler* 1962 (ph); *Bye Bye Birdie* 1963 (ph); *Toys in the Attic* 1963 (ph); *Under the Yum Yum Tree* 1963 (ph); *Bullet For a Badman* 1964 (ph); *Gunfight at Comanche Creek* 1964 (ph); *Hush ... Hush, Sweet Charlotte* 1964 (ph) (**AANBPH**); *Kitten With a Whip* 1964 (ph); *Ride the Wild Surf* 1964 (ph); *Viva Las Vegas* 1964 (ph); *The Young Lovers* 1964 (ph); *The Flight of the Phoenix* 1965 (ph); *I Saw What You Did* 1965 (ph); *Enter Laughing* 1966 (ph); *The Russians Are Coming, the Russians Are Coming* 1966 (ph); *The Swinger* 1966 (ph); *Fitzwilly* 1967 (ph); *Tony Rome* 1967 (ph); *Who's Minding the Mint?* 1967 (ph); *The Detective* 1968 (ph); *The Killing of Sister George* 1968 (ph); *Lady in Cement* 1968 (ph); *The Legend of Lylah Clare* 1968 (ph); *Whatever Happened to Aunt Alice?* 1969 (ph); *Too Late the Hero* 1970 (ph); *Escape From the Planet of the Apes* 1971 (ph); *The Grissom Gang* 1971 (ph); *The Organization* 1971 (ph); *Ulzana's Raid* 1972 (ph); *Cahill, United States Marshal* 1973 (ph); *Blazing Saddles* 1974 (ph); *The Longest Yard* 1974 (ph); *Shanks* 1974 (ph); *The Towering Inferno* 1974 (cam.op) (**AABPH**); *Hustle* 1975 (ph); *The Duchess and the Dirtwater Fox* 1976 (ph); *The Choirboys* 1977 (ph); *Beyond the Poseidon Adventure* 1979 (ph); *Airplane!* 1980 (ph); *All the Marbles* 1981 (ph); *Airplane II: The Sequel* 1982 (ph); *Hammett* 1982 (ph).

Bisset, Jacqueline • *aka* Jackie Bisset • Actress • Born Jacqueline Fraser-Bisset, Weybridge, Surrey, England, September 13, 1944. Former model whose striking looks have highlighted a number of glossy features from the 1960s through the 80s. Though often used for decoration, Bisset has proved herself a talented actress when given the chance, particularly in François Truffaut's *Day For Night* (1973), as an actress recovering from a nervous breakdown, and John Huston's *Under the Volcano* (1984), opposite Albert Finney. • *The Knack...and How to Get It* 1965; *Cul-de-Sac* 1966; *The Cape Town Affair* 1967; *Casino Royale* 1967; *Two For the Road* 1967; *Bullitt* 1968; *The Detective* 1968; *The Sweet Ride* 1968; *The First Time* 1969; *Airport* 1970; *The Grasshopper* 1970; *The Mephisto Waltz* 1970; *Believe in Me* 1971; *Secrets* 1971; *The Life and Times of Judge Roy Bean* 1972; *Stand Up and Be Counted* 1972; *La Nuit Américaine/Day For Night* 1973; *The Thief Who Came to Dinner* 1973; *Le Magnifique* 1974; *Murder on the Orient Express* 1974; *Der Richter und Sein Henker* 1975; *La Donna Della Domenica* 1976; *St. Ives* 1976; *The Deep* 1977; *The Greek Tycoon* 1978; *Who Is Killing the Great Chefs of Europe?* 1978; *Amo Non Amo* 1979; *When Time Ran Out* 1980; *Rich and Famous* 1981; *Inchon* 1982; *Class* 1983; *Notes From Under the Volcano* 1984; *Observations Under the Volcano* 1984; *Under the Volcano* 1984; *High Season* 1987; *La Maison de Jade* 1988; *Scenes From the Class Struggle in Beverly Hills* 1989; *Wild Orchid* 1989; *The Maid* 1990.

Bitzer, Billy • *aka* George William Bitzer • Director of photography • Born Johann Gottlob Wilhelm Bitzer, Roxbury, MA, April 21, 1872; died 1944, Hollywood, CA. *Educ.* Cooper Union Institute, New York (electrical engineering). G.W. "Billy" Bitzer, the cinematographer for most of D.W. Griffith's films, entered motion pictures at their start, 14 years before Griffith.

Initially trained as a silversmith, Bitzer took night classes in electrical engineering at the Cooper Union Institute in New York. In 1894 he joined the Magic Introduction Company, which later changed its name to the American Mutoscope and Biograph Company. There he helped former Edison inventor W.K.L. Dickson design the Mutoscope machine, a device which used the "flicker book" principle to create an illusion of motion. He also perfected the Biograph camera, adding an air compressor to reduce friction. Between 1896 and 1908 Bitzer photographed numerous newsreels, his assignments including President William McKinley's inauguration, the Spanish-American War in Cuba, and the Jim Jeffries-Jim Sharkey championship fight—possibly the first film to use artificial light.

Several innovations associated with Griffith were in fact developed much earlier by Bitzer. His 1896 short of famed actor Joseph Jefferson doing scenes from *Rip Van Winkle* used—for perhaps the first time—close-ups for dramatic effect. By 1904 Bitzer had become a master of the filmed chase, and was regularly shooting sequences in which establishing shots of actors were immediately followed by close-ups. By 1908 he had pioneered the matte shot, in which a pre-photographed background is combined with a live-action scene, as well as various kinds of effects lighting.

In 1908, Bitzer teamed up with Griffith on *A Calamitous Elopement*, beginning a collaboration that would last sixteen years. Griffith made the fullest use of Bitzer's innovations, encouraging him to perfect existing techniques (such as the fade and the dissolve) and to invent new ones for Griffith's increasingly complex narratives. Some of the Bitzer-Griffith innovations, such as the flashback, extreme long shot, traveling shot, split-screen shot, matte shot and various lighting effects, were planned in advance; others, however—such as backlighting, the iris shot, and the soft-focus shot—were the fortuitous result of mistakes Bitzer made during shooting.

By the time Bitzer and Griffith left Biograph for the Mutual Film Corporation in late 1913, they had developed the basic grammar for narrative cinema. Their next films, *Birth of a Nation* (1915) and *Intolerance* (1916), brought together the entire film grammar for the first time, and represent both men's artistic and financial apogees. Bitzer, who contributed his life savings of $7,000 to help meet the $60,000 production cost of *Birth*, recouped his investment four times over.

In the 1920s new cameras like the Bell & Howell, as well as the influx of German cinematographers to Hollywood and the advent of sound, changed the nature of cinematography. Bitzer now found himself ridiculed when he appeared on set with the Pathé camera he had used since *Birth of a Nation*. Rather than scorn the camera he loved so much, Bitzer began to work less frequently, shooting just five films after 1920. Sixteen years as an around-the-clock "camera fiend," however, had also taken their toll; Bitzer's alcoholism and domestic problems made him unreliable, eventually forcing Griffith to turn to the younger cinematographers who had once assisted his partner.

In 1926 Bitzer founded the International Photographers of the Motion Picture Industries society, for which he served two terms as president. In the late 1930s he returned to New York, where he worked in a photographic shop until 1939, when the Museum of Modern Art hired him to work on their film archives. There Bitzer repaired old cameras, restored film prints and annotated documents. He also began writing his autobiography, *Billy Bitzer: His Story*, which was eventually published in 1973. In 1943 Bitzer's health forced him to return to California, where he died, forgotten by the industry he had helped establish. CAN • *Interior New York Subway, 14th Street to 42nd Street* 1905 (ph); *The Black Hand* 1906 (ph); *The Hold Up of the Rocky Mountain Express* 1906 (ph); *Terrible Ted* 1907 (ph); *The Black Viper (short)* 1908 (cam.op); *A Calamitous Elopement* 1908 (ph); *The Usurer* 1910 (ph); *The Informer* 1912 (ph); *The Old Actor* 1912 (ph); *One Is Business, the Other Crime* 1912 (ph); *Judith of Bethulia* 1913 (ph); *The Avenging Conscience* 1914 (ph); *The Battle of the Sexes* 1914 (ph); *The Escape* 1914 (ph); *Home, Sweet Home* 1914 (ph); *Birth of a Nation* 1915 (ph); *Intolerance* 1916 (ph); *Hearts of the World* 1917 (ph); *The Great Love* 1918 (ph); *The Greatest Thing in Life* 1918 (ph); *Broken Blossoms* 1919 (ph); *The Girl Who Stayed at Home* 1919 (ph); *The Greatest Question* 1919 (ph); *A Romance of Happy Valley* 1919 (ph); *Scarlet Days* 1919 (ph); *True Heart Susie* 1919 (ph); *The Idol Dancer* 1920 (ph); *The Love Flower* 1920 (ph); *Way Down East* 1920 (ph); *Orphans of the Storm* 1921 (ph); *Sure Fire Flint* 1922 (ph); *The White Rose* 1923 (ph); *America* 1924 (ph); *The Midnight Girl* 1925 (ph); *The Battle of the Sexes* 1928 (ph); *Drums of Love* 1928 (ph); *Lady of the Pavements* 1929 (ph); *Hotel Variety* 1933 (ph).

Biziou, Peter • Director of photography • First made his mark with *Bugsy Malone* (1976), the first of a series of collaborations with director Alan Parker, and has since established himself as an accomplished visual stylist. Among Biziou's films are Terry Gilliam's *Time Bandits* (1981), Parker's *Pink Floyd The Wall* (1982) and Adrian Lyne's *9 1/2 Weeks* (1986). • *Mini-Midi (Hier, Aujourd'hui, Demain)* 1968; *Bugsy Malone* 1976; *Monty Python's Life of Brian* 1979; *Time Bandits* 1981; *Pink Floyd The Wall* 1982; *Another Country* 1984; *9 1/2 Weeks* 1986; *Mississippi Burning* 1988 **(AABPH)**; *A World Apart* 1988.

Björnstrand, Gunnar • Actor • Born Stockholm, Sweden, November 13, 1909; died May 24, 1986, Stockholm, Sweden. *Educ.* Royal Dramatic Theater School, Stockholm. Understated lead and character player in films by virtually every major postwar Swedish director, particularly Ingmar Bergman. Björnstrand appeared in more than 15 Bergman films between *It Rains On Our Love* (1946) and *Fanny and Alexander* (1982); the collaboration peaked in the mid-1950s with Bjornstrand playing elder gentlemen opposite various younger women in *Secrets of Woman* (1952), *Dreams* and *Smiles of a Summer Night* (both 1955). He was a classmate of Ingrid Bergman at Stockholm's famed Royal Dramatic Theater School. • *Det Regnar pa Var Kärlek/It Rains on Our Love* 1946 *Musik i mörker/Night Is My Future* 1948; *Kvinnors Väntan/Secrets of Women* 1952; *Gycklarnas Afton/Sawdust and Tinsel/The Naked Night* 1953; *En Lektion i Karlek/A Lesson in Love* 1954; *Kvinnodröm/Dreams* 1955; *Sommarnattens Leende/Smiles of a Sum-*

mer Night 1955; *Det Sjunde Inseglet/The Seventh Seal* 1957; *Smultronstället/Wild Strawberries* 1957; *Ansiktet/The Magician/The Face* 1958; *Djavulens Oga/The Devil's Eye* 1960; *Sasom i en Spegel/Through a Glass Darkly* 1961; *Nattvardsgästerna/Winter Light* 1963; *Alksande Par/Loving Couples* 1964; *Har Har Du Ditt Liv* 1966; *Persona* 1966; *Trafracken* 1966; *Den Rode Kappe* 1967; *Flickorna* 1968; *Skammen/The Shame* 1968; *Riten/The Ritual* 1969; *Pistolen* 1973; *Ansikte mot ansikte/Face to Face* 1976; *Tabu* 1976; *Hostsonaten/Autumn Sonata* 1978; *Charlotte Lowenskold* 1979; *Fanny och Alexander/Fanny and Alexander* 1982; *Avskedet* 1983.

Black, Karen • Actress • Born Karen Blanche Ziegler, Park Ridge, IL, July 1, 1942. *Educ.* Northwestern University; Actors Studio. Key female performer of the American film renaissance of the early 1970s. After earning praise as the smalltown waitress who falls for upper-class drifter Jack Nicholson in *Five Easy Pieces* (1970), Black lent her versatility and unconventional beauty to a number of both offbeat and mainstream films, including Nicholson's *Drive, He Said* (1971), Robert Altman's *Nashville* (1975) and Alfred Hitchcock's swan song, *Family Plot* (1976). Her son by screenwriter-actor L.M. Kit Carson is actor Hunter Carson, with whom she appeared in *Invaders From Mars* (1986). • *You're a Big Boy Now* 1967; *Easy Rider* 1969; *Hard Contract* 1969; *Five Easy Pieces* 1970 (**AANBSA**); *Born to Win* 1971; *Cisco Pike* 1971; *Drive, He Said* 1971; *A Gunfight* 1971; *Portnoy's Complaint* 1972; *Rhinoceros* 1972; *The Outfit* 1973; *The Pyx* 1973 (a,songs); *The Great Gatsby* 1974; *Law and Disorder* 1974; *Airport 1975* 1975; *The Day of the Locust* 1975; *Nashville* 1975 (a,songs); *Burnt Offerings* 1976; *Crime and Passion* 1976; *Family Plot* 1976; *In Praise of Older Women* 1977; *Capricorn One* 1978; *Killer Fish* 1979; *The Last Word* 1979; *Separate Ways* 1979; *The Squeeze* 1980; *Chanel Solitaire* 1981; *The Grass Is Singing* 1981; *Miss Right* 1981; *Come Back to the 5 & Dime Jimmy Dean, Jimmy Dean* 1982; *Can She Bake a Cherry Pie?* 1983 (a,m,songs); *Martin's Day* 1983; *Growing Pains* 1984; *The Blue Man* 1985; *Savage Dawn* 1985; *Cut and Run* 1986; *Flight of the Spruce Goose* 1986; *Invaders From Mars* 1986; *Hostage* 1987; *It's Alive III: Island of the Alive* 1987; *Dixie Lanes* 1988; *The Invisible Kid* 1988; *Homer and Eddie* 1989; *Out of the Dark* 1989; *The Children* 1990; *Mirror, Mirror* 1990; *Night Angel* 1990; *Overexposed* 1990; *Twisted Justice* 1990; *Zapped Again* 1990.

Blades, Ruben • Actor, musician, composer • Born Panama City, Panama, July 16, 1948. *Educ.* University of Panama (law, political science); Harvard Law School. Leading contemporary salsa musician who began scoring and writing songs for movies in the 1980s. In 1985 Blades gained widespread recognition as co-writer and star of *Crossover Dreams* (1985), playing a character loosely based on himself; he has subsequently turned in several assured movie performances. • *The Last Fight* 1983 (a,song); *When the Mountains Tremble* 1983 (m); *Beat Street* 1984 (add.m,m.perf); *Crossover Dreams* 1985 (a,sc,m,songs); *The Return of Ruben Blades* 1985 (m,m,a); *The Believers* 1987 (song); *Critical Condition* 1987 (a); *Fatal Beauty* 1987 (a); *El Hijo de Pedro Navajas* 1987 (song); *Por los Caminos Verdes* 1987 (m); *Coverup: Behind the Iran-Contra Affair* 1988 (songs); *Homeboy* 1988 (a); *The Milagro Beanfield War* 1988 (a); *Oliver & Company* 1988 (songs); *Romance de Empregada* 1988 (m); *Chances Are* 1989 (songs); *Disorganized Crime* 1989 (a); *Do the Right Thing* 1989 (songs); *The Lemon Sisters* 1989 (a); *True Believer* 1989 (songs); *The Heart of the Deal* 1990 (a); *Mo' Better Blues* 1990 (a); *Predator 2* 1990 (a); *Q&A* 1990 (m); *The Two Jakes* 1990 (a).

Blain, Gérard • Actor; also director, screenwriter. • Born Paris, October 23, 1930. Boyish-looking lead of two early Claude Chabrol classics, *Le Beau Serge* (1958) and *Les Cousins* (1959). Blain made a creditable transition to writing and directing in the early 1970s. • *Crime et Chatiment* 1956 (a); *Le Beau Serge* 1958 (a); *Charlotte et son Jules (short)* 1958 (a); *Giovani Mariti* 1958 (a); *Les Mistons* 1958 (a); *Les Cousins* 1959 (a); *Hatari!* 1962 (a); *La Bonne Soupe* 1964 (a); *Negresco***—Eine todliche Affaire* 1967 (a); *Cain de nulle part* 1970 (a); *Les Amis* 1971 (d,sc); *Le Pelican* 1973 (a,d,sc); *Der Amerikanische Freund/The American Friend* 1977 (a); *Un Enfant dans la foule* 1977 (d); *La Machine* 1977 (a); *Un Second Souffle* 1978 (d,sc,dial); *Utopia* 1978 (a); *Le Rebelle* 1980 (d); *La Derelitta* 1983 (a); *Poussière d'ange* 1986 (a); *La Presqu'ile* 1986 (a); *Pierre et Djemila* 1987 (d,sc); *Jour après jour* 1988 (a); *Natalia* 1988 (a); *L'Enfant de l'hiver* 1989 (a).

Blair, Linda • Actress • Born Westport, CT, January 22, 1959. Former child model who moved into TV films after a fiery performance as the sweet, but possessed, teenager in *The Exorcist* (1973). Blair has since returned to the big screen, mostly in exploitation films. • *The Way We Live Now* 1970 (a); *The Sporting Club* 1971 (a); *The Exorcist* 1973 (a) (**AANBSA**); *Airport 1975* 1975 (a); *Exorcist II: The Heretic* 1977 (a); *Summer of Fear* 1978 (a); *Roller Boogie* 1979 (a); *Wild Horse Hank* 1979 (a); *Hell Night* 1981 (a); *Chained Heat* 1983 (a); *Night Patrol* 1984 (a); *Savage Streets* 1984 (a); *Rote Hitze* 1985 (a); *Savage Island* 1985 (a); *Nightforce* 1987 (a,song); *Grotesque* 1988 (a,assoc.p); *Silent Assassins* 1988 (a); *Up Your Alley* 1988 (a); *Bad Blood* 1989 (a); *Witchcraft* 1989 (a); *A Woman Obsessed* 1989 (a); *Bail Out* 1990 (a); *Bedroom Eyes II* 1990 (a); *Moving Target* 1990 (a); *Repossessed* 1990 (a); *Zapped Again* 1990 (a).

Blakely, Colin • Actor • Born Bangor, Northern Ireland, September 23, 1930; died May 7, 1987, London. Respected character player who specialized at portraying the hero's best mate in numerous British "angry young man" films of the 1960s. Blakely also played Dr. Watson in Billy Wilder's *The Private Life of Sherlock Holmes* (1970). • *Saturday Night and Sunday Morning* 1960; *The Hellions* 1961; *The Password Is Courage* 1962; *This Sporting Life* 1963; *The Long Ships* 1964; *A Man For All Seasons* 1966; *The Spy With a Cold Nose* 1966; *Charlie Bubbles* 1967; *Decline and Fall... of a Bird Watcher* 1968; *The Vengeance of She* 1968; *Alfred the Great* 1969; *The Private Life of Sherlock Holmes* 1970; *Something to Hide* 1971; *Young Winston* 1972; *The National Health* 1973; *Galileo* 1974; *Murder on the Orient Express* 1974; *It Shouldn't Happen to a Vet* 1975; *The Pink Panther Strikes Again* 1976; *Equus* 1977; *All Things Bright And Beautiful* 1978; *The Big Sleep* 1978; *Meetings With Remarkable Men* 1979; *The Dogs of War* 1980; *Nijinsky* 1980; *Loophole* 1981; *Evil Under the Sun* 1982; *Red Monarch* 1983.

Blakely, Susan • Actress • Born Frankfurt, West Germany, September 7, 1950. *Educ.* University of Texas; Neighborhood Playhouse. Born in Germany, where her father was stationed with the US army. A top model, Blakely made her screen debut in 1972 and has since alternated between film and TV. She turned in noteworthy roles in *The Lords of Flatbush* (1974), as Julie Prescott in the TV miniseries *Rich Man, Poor Man* (1976), and as Frances Farmer in the TV film, *Will There Really Be a Morning* (1983). Divorced from screenwriter Todd Merer and married since 1982 to producer Steve Jaffe. • *Savages* 1972; *The Way We Were* 1973; *The Lords of Flatbush* 1974; *The Towering Inferno* 1974; *Capone* 1975; *Report to the Commissioner* 1975; *The Concorde—Airport '79* 1979; *Dreamer* 1979; *Over the Top* 1987; *The Survivalist* 1987; *My Mom's a Werewolf* 1989; *Out of Sight, Out of Mind* 1990.

Blanc, Mel • Actor, voice specialist • Born Melvin Jerome Blanc, San Francisco, CA, May 30, 1908; died July 10, 1989, Los Angeles, CA. The voice of Bugs Bunny, Woody Woodpecker, Daffy Duck, Porky Pig, Tweety Pie, Sylvester, the Road Runner and many others. Educated in Portland, Oregon, Blanc began his career as a musician and made his radio acting debut in 1933. He moved to Hollywood two years later and was hired by Leon Schlesinger productions, a cartoon workshop that went on to develop Warner Bros.' "Looney Tunes" and

"Merrie Melodies." Blanc provided the voices for nearly 3,000 animated cartoons during his 60-year career. • *Neptune's Daughter* 1949 (a); *Champagne For Caesar* 1950 (a); *Gay Purr-ee* 1962 (a); *Kiss Me, Stupid* 1964 (a); *Buck Rogers in the 25th Century* 1979 (a); *Great American Bugs Bunny - Road Runner Chase* 1979 (a); *Looney Looney Looney Bugs Bunny Movie* 1981 (a); *Daffy Duck's Movie: Fantastic Island* 1983 (a); *Strange Brew* 1983 (a); *Heathcliff: The Movie* 1986 (a); *Howard the Duck* 1986 (a); *Porky Pig in Hollywood* 1986 (a); *Daffy Duck's Quackbusters* 1988 (a); *Night of the Living Duck (short)* 1988 (a); *Who Framed Roger Rabbit?* 1988 (a); *Entertaining the Troops* 1989 (a); *Jetsons: The Movie* 1990 (a).

Blank, Les • Filmmaker, producer • Born Tampa, FL, November 27, 1935. *Educ.* Tulane University, New Orleans, LA (English, theater); USC, Los Angeles (communications). Highly acclaimed, maverick auteur of off-beat documentaries ranging from *Garlic Is as Good as Ten Mothers* (1980, a cultural-folk history of the magic herb), to *In Heaven There Is no Beer?* (1983, on Polish polka dancing), to *Werner Herzog Eats His Shoe* (1980, the result of the eponymous German director's losing a bet with his former assistant, Errol Morris).

Blank's best known work is the feature-length *Burden of Dreams* (1982), an extraordinary account of the production of Herzog's *Fitzcarraldo* (1982). His career has been the subject of major retrospectives at the Museum of Modern Art in New York (1979), the National Film Theatre in London (1982) and the Cinémathèque Française in Paris (1986). In 1990 the American Film Institute honored Blank with the Maya Deren award for outstanding lifetime achievement by an independent filmmaker.

Combining obsessions with music and food, Blank gives his movies a taste and feel that few commercial filmmakers can match. He's not above cooking up a mess of red beans and rice behind the screen to enhance the experience. He reminds us that movies are meant to celebrate life. • *Dizzy Gillespie* 1965 (d,idea,p); *The Blues Accordin' to Lightnin' Hopkins* 1968 (d,idea,p); *God Respects Us When We Work But Loves Us When We Dance* 1968 (d,idea,p); *Spend It All* 1971 (d,idea,p); *A Well Spent Life* 1971 (d,idea,p); *Dry Wood* 1973 (d,idea,p); *Hot Pepper* 1973 (d,idea,p); *Chulas Fronteras* 1976 (d,idea,p); *Always For Pleasure* 1978 (d,p,ph,ed); *Del Mero Corazon* 1979 (d,idea,p); *Poto and Cabengo* 1979 (ph); *Chicken Real* 1980 (d,idea); *Garlic Is as Good as Ten Mothers* 1980 (d); *Werner Herzog Eats His Shoe* 1980 (d); *Burden of Dreams* 1982 (d,p,ph); *In Heaven There Is No Beer?* 1983 (d,p,ph); *Sprout Wings and Fly* 1983 (d,ph); *Turumba* 1983 (p); *In the Land of the Owl Turds* 1987 (p); *J'ai été au bal* 1989 (d,p,sc,ph); *Yum, Yum, Yum! A Taste of Cajun & Creole Cooking* 1990 (d).

Blasetti, Alessandro • Director • Born Rome, July 3, 1900; died February 2, 1987, Rome. Leading Italian director of the 1930s and 40s whose *Four Steps in the Clouds* (1942) was considered a precursor of the Neorealist movement. • *Sole* 1928 (d,sc); *Nerone* 1930 (d); *Resurrectio* 1930 (d,sc); *Terra Madre* 1931 (d,sc); *Assisi* 1932 (d,sc); *Palio* 1932 (d); *La Tavola dei Poveri* 1932 (d,sc); *Il Caso Haller* 1933 (d); *Gesuzza la Sposa Garibaldina* 1933 (d,sc); *L'Impiegata di Papa* 1933 (d,sc); *Vecchia Guardia* 1934 (d,sc); *Aldebaran* 1935 (a,d,sc); *La Contessa di Parma* 1937 (d,sc); *Caccia alla Volpe* 1938 (d); *Ettore Fieramosca* 1938 (d,sc); *Abuna Messias* 1939 (d); *Un Avventura di Salvator Rosa* 1939 (d,sc); *Dora Nelson* 1939 (d); *Retroscena* 1939 (d,sc); *La Corona di Ferro* 1940 (d,sc); *La Cena delle Beffe* 1941 (d); *Quattro Passi fra la Nuvole/Four Steps in the Clouds* 1942 (a,p,sc); *Quelli della Montagna* 1942 (sc,prod.sup); *Nessuno torna indietro* 1943 (d); *Castel Sant'Angelo (short)* 1945 (commentary,d); *Sulla Cupola di San Pietro (short)* 1945 (d); *Il Testimone* 1945 (prod.sup); *La Gemma Orientale dei Papi* 1946 (d); *Una Giorno nella Vita* 1946 (d); *Il Duomo di Milano* 1947 (d); *Fabiola* 1948 (d); *Ippodromi all'Alba (short)* 1950 (d); *Prima Communione* 1950 (d,sc); *Bellissima* 1951 (a); *Quelli che Soffrono per noi (short)* 1951 (d); *Altri Tempi* 1952 (d,sc—"The Hand of Providence," "The Amorous Bus Driver"); *La Fiammata* 1952 (d); *Miracolo a Firenze (short)* 1953 (d); *Peccato che sia una canaglia* 1955 (d); *La Fortuna di essere Donna* 1956 (d,sc); *Amore e Chiacchiere* 1957 (d,sc); *Europa di Notte* 1958 (d); *Storie d'Amore Proibite* 1959 (sc); *Io amo, Tu ami* 1960 (d,sc); *Una Vita Dificile* 1961 (a); *Les Quatre Verites* 1962 (d,sc); *Liola* 1964 (d,sc); *Io, Io, Io...e gli Altri* 1965 (d,sc); *La Ragazza del Bersagliere* 1966 (d,sc); *Simon Bolivar* 1968 (d).

Blatty, William Peter • American novelist, screenwriter; also producer. • Born 1928. Horrormeister who successfully adapted his demonic novel *The Exorcist* for the screen in 1973. Blatty made his directorial debut with another adaptation of one of his own books, *The Ninth Configuration* (1979); he also directed *The Exorcist III* (1990). • *The Man From the Diner's Club* 1963 (sc,story); *John Goldfarb, Please Come Home* 1964 (sc); *A Shot in the Dark* 1964 (sc); *Promise Her Anything* 1966 (sc,story); *What Did You Do in the War, Daddy?* 1966 (sc); *Gunn* 1967 (sc); *The Great Bank Robbery* 1969 (sc); *Darling Lili* 1970 (sc); *The Exorcist* 1973 (p,sc,from novel *The Exorcist*) (**AANBP**); *Exorcist II: The Heretic* 1977 (from characters); *The Ninth Configuration* 1979 (d,sc,from novel); *Twinkle, Twinkle, "Killer" Kane* 1979 (sc,from novel,d,p); *William Peter Blatty's The Exorcist III* 1990 (d,sc,from novel *Legion*).

Blaustein, Julian C. • *aka* Julian Blaustein • Producer • Born New York, NY, May 30, 1913. *Educ.* Harvard. Chief of the story departments at Paramount and Selznick who graduated to producer status with Fox in the late 1940s. Responsible for films including *The Day the Earth Stood Still* (1951) and Peter Hall's *Three Into Two Won't Go* (1969). • *For Love or Money* 1939 (story); *The Noose Hangs High* 1948 (story); *Broken Arrow* 1950 (p); *Mister 880* 1950 (p); *The Day the Earth Stood Still* 1951 (p); *The Guy Who Came Back* 1951 (p); *Half Angel* 1951 (p); *Take Care of My Little Girl* 1951 (p); *Don't Bother to Knock* 1952 (p); *The Outcasts of Poker Flat* 1952 (p); *Desiree* 1954 (p); *The Racers* 1955 (p); *Storm Center* 1956 (p); *Bell, Book and Candle* 1958 (p); *Cowboy* 1958 (p); *The Wreck of the Mary Deare* 1959 (p); *Two Loves* 1961 (p); *The Four Horsemen of the Apocalypse* 1962 (p); *Khartoum* 1966 (p); *Three Into Two Won't Go* 1969 (p).

Blier, Bernard • Actor • Born Buenos Aires, January 11, 1916; died March 29, 1989, Paris. *Educ.* Paris Conservatoire. Prolific leading man of the 1950s turned venerable French character player. His later films include *Buffet Froid* (1979), directed by son Bertrand Blier. • *Gribouille* 1937; *Altitude 3.200* 1938; *Entrée des Artistes* 1938; *Hôtel du Nord* 1938; *L'Enfer des Anges* 1939; *Le Jour Se Lève/Daybreak* 1939; *Nuit de Decembre* 1939; *L'Assassinat du Père Noël?* 1941; *La Symphonie Fantastique* 1942; *Carmen* 1945; *Seuls dans la Nuit* 1945; *Messieurs Ludovic* 1946; *Quai des Orfèvres* 1947; *D'Homme a Hommes* 1948; *Dedée* 1948; *Les Casse-Pieds* 1949; *L'Ecole buissonnière* 1949; *Monseigneur* 1949; *Manèges* 1950; *La Souricière* 1950; *Sans Laisser d'Adresse* 1951; *Agence matrimoniale* 1952; *Avant le Déluge* 1954; *Secrets d'Alcove* 1954; *Le Dossier noir* 1955; *Crime et Châtiment* 1956; *L'Homme à l'Impérmeable* 1957; *Les Misérables* 1957; *Retour de Manivelle* 1957; *Les Grandes Familles* 1958; *Sans Famille* 1958; *Archimède le Clochard* 1959; *La Chatte* 1959; *La Grande Guerra* 1959; *Marie-Octobre* 1959; *Crimen* 1960; *Il Gobbo* 1960; *Arrêtez les Tambours* 1961; *Le Cave se rebiffe* 1961; *Le Président* 1961; *Le Septième Juror* 1962; *I Compagni* 1963; *Germinal* 1963; *Alta Infedeltà/High Infidelity* 1964; *Les Barbouzes* 1964 (uncred.); *La Bonne Soupe* 1964; *Cent mille Dollars au Soleil* 1964 (uncred.); *La Chasse à l'Homme* 1964; *Il Magnifico Cornuto* 1964; *Casanova '70* 1965; *Lo Straniero* 1967; *Mon Oncle Benjamin* 1969 (uncred.); *Appellez-moi Mathilde* 1970; *Elle boit pas, elle fume pas, elle drague pas...mais elle cause!* 1970; *Laisse Aller, c'est une valse*

1970; *Catch Me a Spy* 1971; *Le Cri du Cormoran le Soir Au-Dessus des Jonques* 1971; *Homo Eroticus* 1971; *Jo* 1971; *Le Tueur* 1971; *Elle cause plus...elle flingue* 1972; *Le Grand Blond avec une Chaussure Noire/The Tall blond Man with One Black Shoe* 1972; *Moi y'en a vouloir des Sous* 1972; *Tout le monde il est beau, tout le monde il est gentil* 1972; *Les Chinois à Paris* 1973; *Je sais rien mais je dirai tout* 1973; *La Main à Couper...* 1973; *Par le sang des autres* 1973; *Bon Baisers à Lundi* 1974; *Il Piatto Piange* 1974; *Amici Miei* 1975; *C'est dur pour tout le Monde* 1975; *Calmos* 1975; *Ce Cher Victor* 1975; *Le Faux-Cul* 1975; *Le Corps de Mon Ennemi* 1976; *Nuit d'or* 1976; *Le Compromis* 1978 (uncred.); *Buffet Froid* 1979; *Il Malato Immaginario* 1979; *Serie Noire* 1979; *Eugenio* 1980; *Passione d'amore* 1981; *Pétrole, Pétrole* 1981; *Ça n'arrive qu'à Moi* 1984; *Cuore* 1984; *Le Due vite di Mattia Pascal* 1985; *Scemo di Guerra* 1985; *Je hais les acteurs* 1986; *Pourvu que ce soit une fille* 1986; *Twist Again à Moscou* 1986; *I Picari* 1987; *Les Possédés* 1987; *Sotto il Ristorante Cinese* 1987; *Ada dans la Jungle* 1988; *Les Fanfarons* 1988; *Mangeclous* 1988; *Migrations* 1988; *Paganini* 1989.

Blier, Bertrand • Director, screenwriter • Born Paris, March 14, 1939. Undeniably gifted director whose blackly humorous, often surrealistic and sometimes misogynistic films have divided critics.

Blier began his career as an assistant to John Berry, Jean Delannoy and Christian-Jacque before making a series of cinéma vérité-style documentaries which culminated with *Hitler?...Connais Pas!* (1962), a feature-length study of disaffected teenagers. His first fiction feature was *Breakdown/If I Were a Spy* in 1967, but he hit the international spotlight with 1974's *Going Places/Getting It Up/Making It.* A kind of French *Clockwork Orange*, the film depicted the picaresque and primarily sexual escapades of two amoral, petty thugs (they are not above sniffing a young girl's underwear in an attempt to determine her age). By turns offensive, disturbing and hilarious, the film launched not only Blier, but then-unknown actors Gérard Depardieu, Patrick Dewaere and Miou-Miou.

After being vilified for the misogynism of *Calmos* (1975), Blier earned international acclaim for *Get Out Your Handkerchiefs* (1977), a ribald comedy, again starring Depardieu and Dewaere, which took the Oscar for best foreign film. *Buffet Froid* (1979) marked the director's incursion into surrealist territory, a farcical study in the psychology of murder pitting Depardieu, as a suspected serial killer, against Blier's father, Bernard, as an aging police inspector.

Blier continued to offend, alienate and entertain his audience with *Beau Père* (1981), a reworking of *Lolita* in which a widower (Dewaere) is left in charge of his adolescent stepdaughter, and *Ménage/Tenue de Soirée/Evening Dress* (1986), about a convivial gay burglar (Depardieu) who wreaks havoc within a bankrupt, heterosexual household. *Too Beautiful For You* (1989) saw a successful car dealer (Depardieu) abandoning his beautiful wife (Carole Bouquet) for a plain mistress (Josiane Balasko); Blier's disjunctive, non-linear narrative style served more to defuse the film's emotional impact than to explore new stylistic or psychological territory. JDP • *Laisse Aller, c'est une valse* 1970 (sc); *Les Valseuses* 1974 (d,sc,from book); *Calmos* 1975 (a,d,sc); *Preparez vos mouchoirs/Get Out Your Handkerchiefs* 1977 (d,p,sc,dial); *Buffet Froid* 1979 (d,sc); *Beau Père* 1981 (d,sc,from book); *Debout les Crabes la Mer Monte!* 1983 (idea); *La Femme de mon pote* 1983 (d,sc); *Notre Histoire* 1984 (d,sc); *Reveillon Chez Bob* 1984 (idea); *Femmes Fatales* 1985 (d); *Ménage/Tenue de Soirée/Evening Dress* 1986 (d,sc,dial); *Trop belle pour toi/Too Beautiful For You* 1989 (d,sc).

Blondell, Joan • Actress • Born New York, NY, August 30, 1909; died 1979. Unconventionally beautiful, gifted performer who appeared in over 80 films while maintaining a successful stage career. Blondell played a number of leads, secondary leads and, later, character parts, often as brassy but warm-hearted types; among her best known films are *Nightmare Alley* (1947) and *The Cincinatti Kid* (1965). She was married to cinematographer George Barnes (1933-35), actor Dick Powell (1936-45) and producer Mike Todd (1947-50). • *The Office Wife* 1930; *Sinner's Holiday* 1930; *Big Business Girl* 1931; *Blonde Crazy* 1931; *God's Gift to Women* 1931; *Illicit* 1931; *Millie* 1931; *My Past* 1931; *Night Nurse* 1931; *Other Men's Women* 1931; *The Public Enemy* 1931; *The Reckless Hour* 1931; *Big City Blues* 1932; *Central Park* 1932; *The Crowd Roars* 1932; *The Famous Ferguson Case* 1932; *The Greeks Had a Word For Them* 1932; *Lawyer Man* 1932; *Make Me a Star* 1932; *Miss Pinkerton* 1932; *Three on a Match* 1932; *Union Depot* 1932; *Blondie Johnson* 1933; *Broadway Bad* 1933; *Convention City* 1933; *Footlight Parade* 1933; *Gold Diggers of 1933* 1933; *Goodbye Again* 1933; *Havana Widows* 1933; *Dames* 1934; *He Was Her Man* 1934; *I've Got Your Number* 1934; *The Kansas City Princess* 1934; *Smarty* 1934; *Broadway Gondolier* 1935; *Miss Pacific Fleet* 1935; *Traveling Saleslady* 1935; *We're in the Money* 1935; *Bullets or Ballots* 1936; *Colleen* 1936; *Gold Diggers of 1937* 1936; *Sons O' Guns* 1936; *Stage Struck* 1936; *Three Men on a Horse* 1936; *Back in Circulation* 1937; *The King and the Chorus Girl* 1937; *The Perfect Specimen* 1937; *Stand-In* 1937; *There's Always a Woman* 1938; *The Amazing Mr. Williams* 1939; *East Side of Heaven* 1939; *Good Girls Go to Paris* 1939; *The Kid From Kokomo* 1939; *Off the Record* 1939; *I Want a Divorce* 1940; *Two Girls on Broadway* 1940; *Lady For a Night* 1941; *Model Wife* 1941; *Three Girls About Town* 1941; *Topper Returns* 1941; *Cry Havoc* 1943; *Adventure* 1945; *Don Juan Quilligan* 1945; *A Tree Grows in Brooklyn* 1945; *Christmas Eve* 1947; *The Corpse Came C.O.D.* 1947; *Nightmare Alley* 1947; *Sinner's Holiday* 1947; *For Heaven's Sake* 1950; *The Blue Veil* 1951 **(AABSC,AANBSA)**; *Lizzie* 1956; *The Opposite Sex* 1956; *Desk Set* 1957; *This Could Be the Night* 1957; *Will Success Spoil Rock Hunter?* 1957; *Angel Baby* 1961; *Advance to the Rear* 1963; *The Cincinnati Kid* 1965; *Ride Beyond Vengeance* 1966; *Waterhole Number 3* 1967; *Kona Coast* 1968; *Stay Away, Joe* 1968; *Big Daddy* 1969; *The Phynx* 1970; *Support Your Local Gunfighter* 1971; *The Glove* 1976; *Opening Night* 1977; *Grease* 1978; *The Champ* 1979; *The Woman Inside* 1981.

Bloom, Claire • Actress • Born London, February 15, 1931. *Educ.* Guildhall School of Music and Drama, London; Central School of Speech and Drama, London. Elegant, classically trained leading lady whose cool good looks and exceptional talent have kept her in demand for nearly four decades. Bloom received international notice in her second film, Charlie Chaplin's *Limelight* (1952), and, though her output was limited, distinguished herself in such excellent adaptations as Laurence Olivier's *Richard III* (1955), Tony Richardson's *Look Back in Anger* (1959) and Dick Clement's *A Severed Head* (1970). More recently she turned in fine supporting roles in *Sammy and Rosie Get Laid* (1987) and Woody Allen's *Crimes and Misdemeanors* (1989). Married to actor Rod Steiger from 1959 to 1969 and to novelist Philip Roth since 1990. • *Limelight* 1952; *Innocents in Paris* 1953; *The Man Between* 1953; *Richard III* 1955; *Alexander the Great* 1956; *The Brothers Karamazov* 1958; *The Buccaneer* 1958; *Look Back in Anger* 1959; *Die Schachnovelle* 1960; *The Chapman Report* 1962; *The Wonderful World of the Brothers Grimm* 1962; *The Haunting* 1963; *The Outrage* 1964; *The Spy Who Came in From the Cold* 1965; *Charly* 1968; *The Illustrated Man* 1969; *Three Into Two Won't Go* 1969; *A Severed Head* 1970; *Red Sky at Morning* 1971; *A Doll's House* 1973; *Islands in the Stream* 1976; *Clash of the Titans* 1981; *Déjà Vu* 1984; *Sammy and Rosie Get Laid* 1987; *Crimes and Misdemeanors* 1989.

Bluth, Don • Animation director; also producer, production designer. • Born El Paso, TX, September 13, 1938. *Educ.* Brigham Young University, Provo, UT (English). Leading figure in contemporary animation who worked for the Disney studios from 1972 until 1979. Bluth was lured to Ireland by that country's lower production costs and government incentives for the arts. • *Robin Hood* 1973 (character animation); *Pete's Dragon* 1977 (anim.d); *The Rescuers* 1977 (anim.d); *Xanadu* 1980 (anim); *The Secret of Nimh* 1982 (d,p,sc,anim.d,layout artist); *An American Tail* 1986 (d,p,pd,storyboard artist,title design); *The Land Before Time* 1988 (d,p,pd,storyboard artist); *All Dogs Go to Heaven* 1989 (d,p,story,pd,storyboard artist).

Blyth, Ann • Actress; also singer. • Born Ann Marie Blyth, Mt. Kisco, NY, August 16, 1928. *Educ.* New Wayburn's Dramatic School. Began her performing career at the age of five and arrived in Hollywood at age 15, earning recocnition as Joan Crawford's competitive daughter in the searing melodrama *Mildred Pierce* (1945). Blyth went on to appear in a wide range of films, including several musicals which exploited her schooled singing voice. • *Babes on Swing Street* 1944 (a); *Bowery to Broadway* 1944 (a); *Chip Off the Old Block* 1944 (a); *The Merry Monahans* 1944 (a); *Mildred Pierce* 1945 (a) **(AANBSA)**; *Swell Guy* 1946 (a); *Brute Force* 1947 (a); *Killer McCoy* 1947 (a); *Another Part of the Forest* 1948 (a); *Mr. Peabody and the Mermaid* 1948 (a); *A Woman's Vengeance* 1948 (a); *Free For All* 1949 (a); *Once More, My Darling* 1949 (a); *Red Canyon* 1949 (a); *Top O' the Morning* 1949 (a); *Our Very Own* 1950 (a); *The Golden Horde* 1951 (a); *The Great Caruso* 1951 (a); *I'll Never Forget You* 1951 (a); *Katie Did It* 1951 (a); *Thunder on the Hill* 1951 (a); *One Minute to Zero* 1952 (a); *Sally and Saint Anne* 1952 (a); *The World in His Arms* 1952 (a); *All the Brothers Were Valiant* 1953 (a); *Rose Marie* 1954 (a); *The Student Prince* 1954 (a); *The King's Thief* 1955 (a); *Kismet* 1955 (a); *Slander* 1956 (a); *The Buster Keaton Story* 1957 (a); *The Helen Morgan Story* 1957 (a).

Boam, Jeffrey • Screenwriter • Born Rochester, NY. *Educ.* Sacramento State College; UCLA (film). Commercially successful writer who scripted David Cronenberg's fine adaptation of Stephen King's *The Dead Zone* (1983) and has recently specialized in action/adventure blockbusters. • *Straight Time* 1978 (ad); *The Dead Zone* 1983 (assoc.p,sc); *Innerspace* 1987 (a,sc); *The Lost Boys* 1987 (sc); *Funny Farm* 1988 (sc); *Indiana Jones and the Last Crusade* 1989 (sc); *Lethal Weapon 2* 1989 (sc).

Bochner, Hart • Actor • Born Toronto, Ontario, Canada, December 3, 1956. *Educ.* University of California, San Diego (English). Capable lead who made his screen debut opposite George C. Scott in *Islands in the Stream* (1976) and gained recognition in his second film, the charming *Breaking Away* (1979); perhaps most widely known as the snivelling executive in *Die Hard* (1988). Son of actor Lloyd Bochner. • *Islands in the Stream* 1976; *Breaking Away* 1979; *Terror Train* 1980; *Rich and Famous* 1981; *Supergirl* 1984; *The Wild Life* 1984; *Making Mr. Right* 1987; *Apartment Zero* 1988; *Die Hard* 1988; *Teach 109 (short)* 1988; *Fellow Traveller* 1990; *Mr. Destiny* 1990.

Bode, Ralf D. • Director of photography • Born Berlin. *Educ.* University of Vermont; Yale School of Drama. German-born cinematographer, in the US since 1954, who first studied photography in the Army Signal Corps. Noted for his work on *Saturday Night Fever* (1977), *Coal Miner's Daughter* (1980) and *The Accused* (1988). • *Foreplay* 1974 (ph); *Saturday Night at the Baths* 1974 (ph); *There Is No 13* 1974 (ph); *S.O.S.* 1975 (ph); *Saturday Night Fever* 1977 (ph); *Moment By Moment* 1978 (tech.ad); *Slow Dancing in the Big City* 1978 (ph); *Somebody Killed Her Husband* 1978 (ph); *Rich Kids* 1979 (ph); *Coal Miner's Daughter* 1980 (ph) **(AANBPH)**; *Dressed to Kill* 1980 (ph); *A Little Sex* 1981 (ph); *Raggedy Man* 1981 (ph); *Gorky Park* 1983 (ph); *Firstborn* 1984 (ph); *Bring on the Night* 1985 (ph); *Violets Are Blue* 1986 (ph); *The Whoopee Boys* 1986 (ph); *The Big Town* 1987 (ph); *Critical Condition* 1987 (ph); *The Accused* 1988 (ph); *Distant Thunder* 1988 (ph); *Cousins* 1989 (ph); *The Long Way Home* 1989 (ph); *Uncle Buck* 1989 (ph); *One Good Cop* 1991 (ph).

Bodeen, DeWitt • Screenwriter • Born Fresno, CA, July 25, 1908; died March 12, 1988, Woodland Hills, CA. *Educ.* UCLA. Stage actor and playwright turned screenwriter, responsible for such fine thrillers as *Cat People* (1942) and *The Seventh Victim* (1943); Bodeen also won praise for the highly regarded drama *I Remember Mama* (1948), which he adapted from the play by John Van Druten. He frequently wrote on film, contributing to journals and penning several books including *From Hollywood*, an examination of the William Desmond Taylor murder case. • *Cat People* 1942 (sc); *The Seventh Victim* 1943 (sc); *The Curse of the Cat People* 1944 (sc); *The Yellow Canary* 1944 (sc); *The Enchanted Cottage* 1945 (sc); *Night Song* 1947 (adapt); *I Remember Mama* 1948 (sc); *Mrs. Mike* 1949 (sc); *The Girl in the Kremlin* 1957 (story); *Twelve to the Moon* 1960 (sc); *Billy Budd* 1962 (sc); *Cat People* 1982 (from film).

Boehm, Karlheinz • Actor • Born Karlheinz Böhm, Darmstadt, Germany, March 16, 1927. *Educ.* University of Graz, Austria (philosophy). Handsome, mannered performer who played the demented protagonist of Michael Powell's unforgettable *Peeping Tom* (1960); later in several R.W. Fassbinder films. Boehm's father was the world-famous conductor Karl Böhm. • *Alraune* 1952; *Haus des Lebens* 1952; *Salto Mortale* 1953; *Die Goldene Pest* 1954; *Die Hexe* 1954; *Sissi* 1956; *Sissi—die jung Kaiserin* 1957; *Das Dreimäderlhaus* 1958; *Le Passager clandestin* 1958; *Sissi—Schicksalsjahre einer Kaiserin* 1958; *Kriegsgericht* 1959; *La Paloma* 1959; *Peeping Tom* 1960; *Too Hot to Handle* 1960; *Come Fly With Me* 1962; *La Croix des Vivants* 1962; *Forever My Love* 1962; *The Four Horsemen of the Apocalypse* 1962; *The Magnificent Rebel* 1962; *The Wonderful World of the Brothers Grimm* 1962; *Rififi à Tokyo* 1963; *The Venetian Affair* 1967; *Fontane Effi Briest* 1974; *Martha* 1974; *Faustrecht der Freiheit/Fox and His Friends* 1975; *Mother Kusters Goes to Heaven* 1975; *Die Tannerhütte* 1976.

Boetticher, Budd • Director; also screenwriter, author. • Born Oscar Boetticher, Jr., Chicago, IL, July 29, 1916. *Educ.* Ohio State University, Columbus. Former bullfighter who began his film career as a technical consultant on Rouben Mamoulian's *Blood and Sand* (1941). Boetticher went on to make a string of well-received, male-oriented dramas, including several gritty, small-budget westerns starring Randolph Scott. His career was sidetracked by a seven-year attempt to realize a documentary on bullfighter Carlos Aruzza, the story of which is told in Boetticher's book *When in Disgrace*.

Boetticher attempted a comeback with the barely seen *A Time for Dying* (produced 1969, released 1971), a collaboration with Audie Murphy, and has since made only one film, the documentary *My Kingdom For...* (1985). • *Blood and Sand* 1941 (ad); *The Desperadoes* 1943 (ad); *Destroyer* 1943 (ad); *The More the Merrier* 1943 (ad); *Cover Girl* 1944 (ad); *The Girl in the Case* 1944 (ad); *The Missing Juror* 1944 (d); *One Mysterious Night* 1944 (d); *Escape in the Fog* 1945 (d); *The Fleet That Came to Stay (short)* 1945 (a); *Guy, a Gal and a Pal, A* 1945 (d); *Youth on Trial* 1945 (d); *Assigned to Danger* 1948 (d); *Behind Locked Doors* 1948 (d); *Black Midnight* 1949 (d); *The Wolf Hunters* 1949 (d); *Killer Shark* 1950 (d); *Bullfighter and the Lady* 1951 (d,story) **(AANBST)**; *The Cimarron Kid* 1951 (d); *Bronco Buster* 1952 (d); *Horizons West* 1952 (d); *Red Ball Express* 1952 (d); *City Beneath the Sea* 1953 (d); *East of Sumatra* 1953 (d); *The Man From the Alamo* 1953 (d); *Seminole* 1953 (d); *Wings of the Hawk* 1953 (d); *The Killer Is Loose* 1955 (d); *The Magnificent Matador* 1955 (d,story); *Seven Men From Now* 1956 (d); *Decision at Sundown* 1957 (d); *The Tall T* 1957 (d); *Buchanan Rides Alone* 1958 (d); *Ride Lonesome* 1959 (d,p); *Westbound* 1959 (d); *Comanche Station* 1960 (d,p); *The Rise and Fall of Legs Diamond* 1960 (d); *Two Mules For Sister Sara* 1970 (story); *Arruza* 1971 (d,p,sc); *A Time For Dying* 1971 (d,sc); *My Kingdom For...* 1985 (d,sc); *Tequila Sunrise* 1988 (a).

Bogarde, Dirk • *aka* Dirk Van den Bogaerde • Actor; also author. • Born Derek Niven Van den Bogaerde, Hampstead, London, England, March 28, 1921. *Educ.* Allen Glens College, Glasgow; University College, London; Chelsea Polytechnic School of Art; Royal College of Art, London. Celebrated English actor of Belgian and Scotch descent. Bogarde appeared in mostly routine light comedies and melodramas through the 1950s but began attracting serious attention in the following decade with his roles as a blackmailed homosexual lawyer in Basil Dearden's *Victim* (1961), and a corrupt valet who comes to dominate his "master" in Joseph Losey's *The Servant* (1963). He gave superb performances in the first two films of Luchino Visconti's "German decadence" trilogy: as the doomed head of the powerful Essenbeck munitions company in *The Damned* (1969); and as Gustav von Aschenbach, the stricken writer at the center of *Death in Venice* (1971). Bogarde recently attracted attention for an engaging role in Bertrand Tavernier's *Daddy Nostalgia* (1990). • *Come on George* 1939; *Dancing With Crime* 1947; *Esther Waters* 1948; *Once a Jolly Swagman* 1948; *Quartet* 1948; *Boys in Brown* 1949; *Dear Mr. Prohack* 1949; *The Blue Lamp* 1950; *So Long at the Fair* 1950; *The Woman in Question* 1950; *Blackmailed* 1951; *The Gentle Gunman* 1952; *Hunted* 1952; *Penny Princess* 1952; *Appointment in London* 1953; *Desperate Moment* 1953; *Doctor in the House* 1954; *For Better For Worse* 1954; *The Sea Shall Not Have Them* 1954; *The Sleeping Tiger* 1954; *They Who Dare* 1954; *Cast a Dark Shadow* 1955; *Doctor at Sea* 1955; *Simba* 1955; *The Spanish Gardener* 1956; *Doctor at Large* 1957; *Ill Met By Moonlight* 1957; *Campbell's Kingdom* 1958; *The Doctor's Dilemma* 1958; *A Tale of Two Cities* 1958; *The Wind Cannot Read* 1958; *Libel* 1959; *The Angel Wore Red* 1960; *The Singer Not the Song* 1960; *Song Without End* 1960; *Victim* 1961; *H.M.S. Defiant* 1962; *The Password Is Courage* 1962; *We Joined the Navy* 1962; *Doctor in Distress* 1963; *I Could Go on Singing* 1963; *The Mind Benders* 1963; *The Servant* 1963; *Agent 8 3/4* 1964; *King and Country* 1964; *Darling* 1965; *The High Bright Sun* 1965; *Modesty Blaise* 1966; *Accident* 1967; *Our Mother's House* 1967; *The Fixer* 1968; *Return to Lochaver (short)* 1968 (a,narrative text); *Sebastian* 1968; *La Caduta degli dei/The Damned* 1969; *Justine* 1969; *Oh! What a Lovely War* 1969; *Upon This Rock* 1970; *Morte a Venezia/Death in Venice* 1971; *Le Serpent* 1973; *The Night Porter* 1974; *Permission to Kill* 1975; *A Bridge Too Far* 1977; *Providence* 1977; *Despair* 1978; *The Vision* 1987; *Daddy Nostalgie/Daddy Nostalgia* 1990.

Bogart, Humphrey • Actor • Born Humphrey DeForest Bogart, New York, NY, January 23, 1899; died 1957. Born in 1899 to a prominent New York family, Humphrey Bogart emerged from a minor theatrical career in the 1920s to become one of Hollywood's most distinctive leading men of the 40s and 50s, principally through his often-revived appearances in *The Maltese Falcon* (1941), *Casablanca* (1942) and his Oscar-winning *The African Queen* (1951).

Though initially typecast as one of Warner Bros. tough guy/gangsters in the 30s, during and after WWII the "Bogie" persona grew into more fully developed anti-hero and reluctant hero personifications. Although he continually played men with criminal pasts, Bogart created a rich and complex screen image that stood as a visual and cultural icon for the "noir" side of Hollywood: his hangdog expression, perennial five-o'clock shadow, and dangling cigarette came to signify the world-weary cynic, the staid, self-reliant individualist who was at heart a moral, even sentimental human being. Whether portraying ex-con, war hero, detective or more offbeat characters, this combination of traits ultimately gave Bogart a romantic appeal of immense proportions, an appeal that has remained powerful with subsequent generations of moviegoers while other box office star images of the golden age have faded.

After military service in WWI, Bogart embarked on a theatrical career, first as a manager, then as an actor who worked his way to Broadway. Like many of his colleagues he traveled to Hollywood in the early 30s looking for employment in early sound films. From his earliest movie appearances Bogart portrayed gritty characters with criminal connection, as in *Up the River* (1930), a prison film starring Spencer Tracy. After signing a contract with Warner Bros.—the studio most closely associated with the tough guy image via its stars Edward G. Robinson and Jimmy Cagney—that reputation was only enhanced. Working simultaneously on Broadway and in film, Bogart appeared in ten minor movie roles before his breakthrough performance in *The Petrified Forest* (1935). Reprising the Broadway success of Robert Sherwood's play, Bogart portrayed Duke Mantee, an escaped convict/gangster who holds several people hostage in an Arizona diner. The tough but intelligent performance brought him popularity and a featured player contract with Warner Bros. for $550 a week.

Over the next five years Bogart appeared in 28 Warner Bros. features, almost always as an underworld figure. On occasion he played uncharacteristic supporting roles (a district attorney in Bette Davis's *Marked Woman* 1937, the miscast Irish stable master in *Dark Victory* 1939 or the bizarrely conceived zombie in *The Return of Dr. X.* 1939), but rose to prominence through a number of memorable supporting roles in urban crime films.

From the less distinguished gangster programmer *Bullets or Ballots* (1936), Bogart moved into an effective series of typically downbeat Warner films with urban, lower-class settings, including *Dead End* (1937), *Crime School* (1938) and *They Drive by Night* (1940), as well as the prison genre films *San Quentin* (1937) and the quintessential, *Angels With Dirty Faces* (1938). His reliable, unaffected performances won him both increasing box-office recognition and a doubling of salary in 1938. The following year he returned with two other gangster films, *King of the Underworld* (1939) and, more memorably, opposite Jimmy Cagney in *The Roaring Twenties* (1939), an episodic saga about war-veterans-turned-racketeers that summed up the studio's decade of mythmaking about the American gangster.

As Cagney and Robinson phased out their Warner Bros. stereotypes, the studio turned increasingly to Bogart. Although George Raft had been the heir to Cagney's top spot, he turned down a series of roles (in *High Sierra 1941*, *The Maltese Falcon* and *Casablanca*) that subsequently fell to Bogart, who needed them to make himself a star of major proportions. As Roy "Mad Dog" Earle in *High Sierra* Bogart proved himself more than just a fast-talking, unidimensional bad guy. With the aid of John Huston's screenwriting he created a sympathetic portrait of a criminal with a gentle heart and delivered a performance far more subdued than any seen in Cagney's maniac sociopaths. Later in the following year, Bogart received his first top-billing in John Huston's directorial debut *The Maltese Falcon*, a low-budget surprise hit that launched the actor into greater stardom as detective Sam Spade.

In 1942, Bogart signed a new seven-year contract for $2750 a week and embarked on an acclaimed series of wartime pictures, beginning with his now legendary portrayal of Rick Blaine in *Casablanca* (1942). Once again his character was a man with a past, but was now also capable of both romance and moral action. His reluctant-hero persona also contributed to Hollywood's war effort in Huston's *Across the Pacific* (1942), *Action in the North Atlantic* (1943), *Passage to Marseille* (1944) and Howard Hawks's *To Have and Have Not* (1944). The love scenes in *To Have and Have Not*, however, outshone the action sequences as Bogie and his young costar, Lauren Bacall, fell in love off-screen and married. Their on-screen collaboration proved instantly popular and the Bogie-Bacall pairing continued successfully in *The Big Sleep* (1946), *Dark Passage* (1947) and Huston's *Key Largo*

(1948). (The couple were also in the public eye when they participated in the Committee for the First Amendment, a group opposed to the HUAC harrassment of Hollywood liberals.)

The postwar years also saw the Bogie persona transformed into a "film noir" icon, beginning with his portrayal of Raymond Chandler's detective Philip Marlowe in *The Big Sleep* and continuing through a series of dark anti-hero roles, including *Dead Reckoning* (1947) and Nicholas Ray's *In a Lonely Place* (1950; an existential love story which many consider his finest performance).

As Hollywood's studio system and star contracts changed drastically heading into the 1950s, Bogart's career altered as well. In 1947 he signed a contract with Warner Bros. that not only paid him $200,000 per year and gave him approval of roles, directors and scripts, but also set him up with his own independent production company, Santana Pictures. He continued to work (and carouse) with friend John Huston (in *Treasure of the Sierra Madre* 1948, *The African Queen* 1951, *Beat the Devil* 1953), but his acting roles moved into greater variety, not only in the sometimes quirky Huston films, but also in lighter fare, such as Billy Wilder's *Sabrina* (1954).

Ultimately, however, it was the cynical, shady but psychologically complex characterizations to which Bogart returned at the end of his career. Most notably, he portrayed a manipulative film director opposite Ava Gardner in *The Barefoot Contessa*, the marble-rattling Capt. Queeg in *The Caine Mutiny* (both 1954), another escaped convict in *The Desperate Hours* (1955), and finally a sardonic sports writer/agent for the "noir" world of boxing in *The Harder They Fall* (1956). It proved to be Bogart's final screen appearance; he died of cancer the following year. DGS • *A Devil With Women* 1930; *Up the River* 1930; *Bad Sister* 1931; *Body and Soul* 1931; *A Holy Terror* 1931; *Women of All Nations* 1931; *Big City Blues* 1932; *Love Affair* 1932; *Three on a Match* 1932; *Midnight* 1934; *The Petrified Forest* 1935; *Black Legion* 1936; *Bullets or Ballots* 1936; *China Clipper* 1936; *Isle of Fury* 1936; *Two Against the World* 1936; *Dead End* 1937; *The Great O'Malley* 1937; *Kid Galahad* 1937; *Marked Woman* 1937; *San Quentin* 1937; *Stand-In* 1937; *The Amazing Dr. Clitterhouse* 1938; *Angels With Dirty Faces* 1938; *Crime School* 1938; *Men Are Such Fools* 1938; *Racket Busters* 1938; *Swing Your Lady* 1938; *Dark Victory* 1939; *King of the Underworld* 1939; *The Oklahoma Kid* 1939; *The Return of Dr. X* 1939; *The Roaring Twenties* 1939; *You Can't Get Away With Murder* 1939; *Brother Orchid* 1940; *Invisible Stripes* 1940; *It All Came True* 1940; *They Drive By Night* 1940; *Virginia City* 1940; *High Sierra* 1941; *The Maltese Falcon* 1941; *The Wagons Roll at Night* 1941; *Across the Pacific* 1942; *All Through the Night* 1942; *The Big Shot* 1942; *Casablanca* 1942 **(AANBA)**; *Action in the North Atlantic* 1943; *Sahara* 1943; *Thank Your Lucky Stars* 1943; *Passage to Marseilles* 1944; *To Have and Have Not* 1944; *Conflict* 1945; *The Two Mrs. Carrolls* 1945; *The Big Sleep* 1946; *Two Guys From Milwaukee* 1946; *Dark Passage* 1947; *Dead Reckoning* 1947; *Key Largo* 1948; *The Treasure of the Sierra Madre* 1948; *Knock on Any Door* 1949; *Tokyo Joe* 1949; *Chain Lightning* 1950; *In a Lonely Place* 1950; *The African Queen* 1951 **(AABA)**; *The Enforcer* 1951; *Sirocco* 1951; *Deadline U.S.A.* 1952; *Battle Circus* 1953; *Beat the Devil* 1953; *The Barefoot Contessa* 1954; *The Caine Mutiny* 1954 **(AANBA)**; *Sabrina* 1954; *The Desperate Hours* 1955; *The Left Hand of God* 1955; *We're No Angels* 1955; *The Harder They Fall* 1956; *Going Hollywood: The War Years* 1988 (archival footage); *Entertaining the Troops* 1989 (archival footage).

Bogdanovich, Peter • *aka* Derek Thomas • Director; also screenwriter, producer, critic, actor. • Born Kingston, NY, July 30, 1939. *Educ.* Stella Adler Theater School, New York. Former film critic (for such magazines as *Film Culture, Movie* and *Esquire*) who published a series of book-length studies on directors including Howard Hawks, Orson Welles and Alfred Hitchcock before entering film production under the aegis of Roger Corman.

After two pedestrian writing assignments Bogdanovich was allowed to direct his first film, *Targets* (1968), the first in a series of critical and financial successes that proved his mastery of a wide range of genres. Highlights were 1971's *The Last Picture Show* (still considered his masterpiece), the screwball comedy, *What's Up, Doc?* (1972) and the Depression-era comedy/drama, *Paper Moon* (1973).

Bogdanovich's fortunes began to flag with the ill-conceived costume drama *Daisy Miller* (1974). His subsequent output has been somewhat uneven, and not without its outright flops (*Illegally Yours* 1988). In 1990 *Texasville*, a sequel to *The Last Picture Show*, was released to mixed reviews.

Bogdanovich was formerly married to production designer Polly Platt. Subsequent companions included Cybill Shepherd and murdered *Playboy* model Dorothy Stratten; his current wife is Stratten's half-sister, Louise Hoogstraten. • *Voyage to the Planet of Prehistoric Women* 1965 (add.sequences d); *Targets* 1968 (a,d,p,sc,story); *Directed By John Ford* 1971 (d,sc,idea); *The Last Picture Show* 1971 (d,sc) **(AANBSC,AANBD)**; *What's Up, Doc?* 1972 (d,p,story); *Paper Moon* 1973 (d,p); *Vérités et Mensonges/F For Fake* 1973 (a); *Daisy Miller* 1974 (d,p); *At Long Last Love* 1975 (d,p,sc); *Diaries, Notes & Sketches—Volume 1, Reels 1-6: Lost Lost Lost* 1975 (a); *Nickelodeon* 1976 (d,sc); *Opening Night* 1977 (a); *Saint Jack* 1979 (a,d,sc); *They All Laughed* 1981 (d,sc,song); *The City Girl* 1983 (exec.p); *Mask* 1985 (d); *Illegally Yours* 1988 (d,p); *Hollywood Mavericks* 1990 (a); *Texasville* 1990 (d,p,sc).

Bogosian, Eric • Actor, playwright, monologuist • Born Woburn, MA, 1953. *Educ.* University of Chicago; Oberlin College, Ohio (drama). Protean "downtown" performance artist whose acclaimed one-man shows established him as one of the wittiest, most incisive chroniclers of the bloat and sleaze of the 1980s. Bogosian made his film debut in 1982's *Born in Flames* and is most widely known as the combative deejay Barry Champlain in *Talk Radio* (1988), which he adapted from his stage play with director Oliver Stone. • *Born in Flames* 1982 (a); *Special Effects* 1985 (a); *Arena Brains (short)* 1987 (a,sc); *Talk Radio* 1988 (a,sc,from play,creative collaboration); *Suffering Bastards* 1989 (a); *Sex, Drugs, Rock & Roll* 1991 (a,sc,from play).

Bohringer, Richard • Actor; also screenwriter. • Born Paris, 1941. Melancholic performer who first gained attention outside France as the eccentric zen-master in Jean-Jacques Beineix's *Diva* (1981); Bohringer subsequently won plaudits for his role as the relentlessly deceitful prison guard in *L'Addition* (1984) and was quietly effective as the epicurean title character of Peter Greenaway's art-house success *The Cook, the Thief, His Wife and Her Lover* (1989). • *Beau Masque* 1972 (sc); *L'Italien des Roses* 1972 (a); *La Punition* 1973 (sc); *Il pleut toujours ou c'est mouillé* 1974 (sc); *Les Conquistadores* 1975 (a); *Martin et Léa* 1978 (a); *Le Dernier Métro/The Last Metro* 1980 (a); *Diva* 1981 (a); *Le Grand Pardon* 1981 (a); *Les Uns et les autres/Bolero* 1981 (a); *J'ai Epousé Une Ombre* 1982 (a); *La Bête Noire* 1983 (a); *Cap Canaille* 1983 (a); *Debout les Crabes la Mer Monte!* 1983 (a); *Le Destin de Juliette* 1983 (a); *El Diablo y la Dama* 1983 (a); *Transit* 1983 (a); *L'Addition* 1984 (a); *Le Juge* 1984 (a); *Péril en la Demeure* 1984 (a); *Du Sel sur la Peau* 1984 (a); *Cent Francs l'Amour* 1985 (a); *Diesel* 1985 (a); *L'Intruse* 1985 (a); *Le Pactole* 1985 (a); *Subway* 1985 (a); *L'Inconnu de Vienne* 1986 (a); *Kamikaze* 1986 (a); *Le Paltoquet* 1986 (a); *Ubac* 1986 (a); *Agent Trouble* 1987 (a); *Flag* 1987 (a); *Folie Suisse* 1987 (a); *Le Grand Chemin/The Grand Highway* 1987 (a); *Les Saisons du plaisir* 1987 (a); *A Gauche en sortant de l'ascenseur* 1988 (a); *Ada dans la Jungle* 1988 (a); *La Nuit de l'océan* 1988 (a); *La Soule* 1988 (a); *The Cook, the Thief, His Wife and Her Lover* 1989 (a); *Marat* 1989 (a); *Dames Galantes* 1990 (a); *Stan the Flasher* 1990 (a).

Boisset, Yves • Director; also screenwriter, critic. • Born Paris, March 14, 1939. *Educ.* IDHEC, Paris. Former film critic who established himself in the 1970s with a series of fast-paced, often politically oriented thrillers, notably *L'Attentat* (1972). • *Coplan sauve sa Peau* 1968 (d,sc); *Un Condé* 1970 (d,sc); *Cran d'arrêt* 1970 (d,sc); *Le Saut de l'ange* 1971 (d,sc); *L'Attentat* 1972 (d); *R.A.S.* 1973 (d,sc); *Dupont Lajoie* 1975 (d,sc); *Folle à Tuer* 1975 (d); *Le Juge Fayard dit le "sheriff"* 1977 (d,sc); *Un Taxi mauve* 1977 (d,sc); *La Clé Sur la Porte* 1978 (d,sc); *La Femme Flic* 1980 (d,sc); *Le Prix du Danger* 1983 (d,sc); *Canicule* 1984 (d,sc); *Bleu Comme l'enfer* 1985 (d,sc); *Radio Corbeau* 1988 (d,sc,adapt); *La Travéstie* 1988 (d,sc); *Double Identity* 1991 (d); *La Tribu* 1991 (adapt,d).

Bolger, Ray • Actor • Born Raymond Wallace Bolger, Dorchester, MA, January 10, 1904; died January 15, 1987, Los Angeles, CA. Song-and-dance man best remembered for his role as the Scarecrow in *The Wizard of Oz* (1939). • *The Great Ziegfeld* 1936; *Rosalie* 1937; *Sweethearts* 1938; *The Wizard of Oz* 1939; *Four Jacks and a Jill* 1941; *Sunny* 1941; *Stage Door Canteen* 1943; *The Harvey Girls* 1946; *Look For the Silver Lining* 1949; *Make Mine Laughs* 1949; *April in Paris* 1952; *Where's Charley?* 1952; *Babes in Toyland* 1961; *The Daydreamer* 1966; *Just You and Me, Kid* 1979; *The Runner Stumbles* 1979; *That's Dancing!* 1985.

Bologna, Joseph • Actor; also screenwriter, playwright. • Born Brooklyn, NY, December 30, 1938. *Educ.* Brown University, Providence, RI (art history). Character player of the 1970s and 80s, usually in comic roles; outstanding as the manic host of an old-time TV variety show in the hilarious *My Favorite Year* (1982). Bologna writes for theater and TV with his wife, Renee Taylor; the duo co-adapted (from their own play) and co-directed the 1989 feature, *It Had to Be You*. • *Lovers and Other Strangers* 1970 (sc,from play) **(AANBSC)**; *Made For Each Other* 1971 (a,sc); *Cops and Robbers* 1973 (a); *Mixed Company* 1974 (a); *The Big Bus* 1976 (a); *Chapter Two* 1979 (a); *My Favorite Year* 1982 (a); *Blame It on Rio* 1984 (a); *The Woman in Red* 1984 (a); *Transylvania 6-5000* 1985 (a); *It Had to Be You* 1989 (a,d,sc,from play); *Coupe De Ville* 1990 (a).

Bolt, Robert • Screenwriter, playwright • Born Sayles, Manchester, England, August 15, 1924. *Educ.* University of Manchester (history); Exeter University. Despite his assertion that the "film writer is regarded as a technician, like an electrician," Bolt's writing has enjoyed a degree of respect in the movie world usually found only in the theater. He has won two best screenplay Oscars, one for his collaboration with David Lean, *Dr. Zhivago* (1965), and one for Fred Zinnemann's *A Man For All Seasons* (1966). The critics took less kindly to his sole directorial effort, *Lady Caroline Lamb* (1972). Remarried to actress Sarah Miles. Son is director Ben Bolt (*The Big Town* 1987). • *Lawrence of Arabia* 1962 (sc) **(AANBSC)**; *Doctor Zhivago* 1965 (sc) **(AABSC)**; *A Man For All Seasons* 1966 (sc,from play) **(AABSC)**; *Ryan's Daughter* 1970 (sc); *Lady Caroline Lamb* 1972 (d,sc); *The Bounty* 1984 (sc); *The Mission* 1986 (sc).

Bond, Ward • Actor • Born Denver, CO, April 9, 1903; died 1960. *Educ.* USC, Los Angeles. One of the most prolific of Hollywood character actors. Bond began his career in the late 1920s and was a key member of John Ford's stock company, playing the parson/Texas Ranger in *The Searchers* (1956) and fictional film director John Dodge in *The Wings of Eagles* (1956). He starred in the TV series, "Wagon Train." • *Salute* 1929; *Words and Music* 1929; *The Big Trail* 1930; *Born Reckless* 1930; *Hello, Trouble* 1932; *High Speed* 1932; *Rackety Rax* 1932; *Virtue* 1932; *White Eagle* 1932; *Heroes For Sale* 1933; *Obey the Law* 1933; *Police Car 17* 1933; *The Sundown Rider* 1933; *Unknown Valley* 1933; *When Strangers Marry* 1933; *Wild Boys of the Road* 1933; *The Wrecker* 1933; *Against the Law* 1934; *The Crime of Helen Stanley* 1934; *The Defense Rests* 1934; *The Fighting Code* 1934; *The Fighting Ranger* 1934; *Frontier Marshal* 1934; *Girl in Danger* 1934; *Here Comes the Groom* 1934; *The Human Side* 1934; *It Happened One Night* 1934; *A Man's Game* 1934; *Men of the Night* 1934; *Most Precious Thing in Life* 1934; *The Poor Rich* 1934; *Straightaway* 1934; *Voice in the Night* 1934; *Whirlpool* 1934; *Black Fury* 1935; *The Crimson Trail* 1935; *Devil Dogs of the Air* 1935; *Fighting Shadows* 1935; *Guard That Girl* 1935; *The Headline Woman* 1935; *His Night Out* 1935; *Little Big Shot* 1935; *Murder in the Fleet* 1935; *She Gets Her Man* 1935; *Too Tough to Kill* 1935; *Waterfront Lady* 1935; *Western Courage* 1935; *Avenging Waters* 1936; *The Bride Walks Out* 1936; *The Cattle Thief* 1936; *Conflict* 1936; *Crash Donovan* 1936; *The Leathernecks Have Landed* 1936; *Legion of Terror* 1936; *The Man Who Lived Twice* 1936; *Muss 'Em Up* 1936; *Pride of the Marines* 1936; *Second Wife* 1936; *They Met in a Taxi* 1936; *Without Orders* 1936; *23 1/2 Hours Leave* 1937; *Dead End* 1937; *Devil's Playground* 1937; *Escape By Night* 1937; *A Fight to the Finish* 1937; *Night Key* 1937; *Park Avenue Logger* 1937; *The Wildcatter* 1937; *You Only Live Once* 1937; *The Amazing Dr. Clitterhouse* 1938; *Born to Be Wild* 1938; *Gun Law* 1938; *The Law West of Tombstone* 1938; *Mr. Moto's Gamble* 1938; *Numbered Woman* 1938; *Over the Wall* 1938; *Prison Break* 1938; *Professor Beware* 1938; *Reformatory* 1938; *Submarine Patrol* 1938; *The Cisco Kid and the Lady* 1939; *Dodge City* 1939; *Drums Along the Mohawk* 1939; *Frontier Marshal* 1939; *The Girl From Mexico* 1939; *Gone With the Wind* 1939; *Heaven With a Barbed Wire Fence* 1939; *Made For Each Other* 1939; *The Oklahoma Kid* 1939; *Pardon Our Nerve* 1939; *They Made Me a Criminal* 1939; *Trouble in Sundown* 1939; *Waterfront* 1939; *Young Mr. Lincoln* 1939; *Buck Benny Rides Again* 1940; *The Grapes of Wrath* 1940; *Kit Carson* 1940; *Little Old New York* 1940; *The Long Voyage Home* 1940; *The Mortal Storm* 1940; *The Santa Fe Trail* 1940; *Doctors Don't Tell* 1941; *The Maltese Falcon* 1941; *Manpower* 1941; *Sergeant York* 1941; *The Shepherd of the Hills* 1941; *Swamp Water* 1941; *Tobacco Road* 1941; *Wild Bill Hickok Rides* 1941; *The Falcon Takes Over* 1942; *Gentleman Jim* 1942; *Hitler - Dead or Alive* 1942; *Sin Town* 1942; *Ten Gentlemen From West Point* 1942; *Adventures of the Flying Cadets* 1943; *A Guy Named Joe* 1943; *Hello, Frisco, Hello* 1943; *Slightly Dangerous* 1943; *They Came to Blow Up America* 1943; *Home in Indiana* 1944; *The Sullivans* 1944; *Tall in the Saddle* 1944; *Dakota* 1945; *They Were Expendable* 1945; *Canyon Passage* 1946; *It's a Wonderful Life* 1946; *My Darling Clementine* 1946; *The Fugitive* 1947; *Unconquered* 1947; *Fort Apache* 1948; *Joan of Arc* 1948; *Tap Roots* 1948; *The Time of Your Life* 1948; *Three Godfathers* 1949; *Kiss Tomorrow Goodbye* 1950; *Riding High* 1950; *Singing Guns* 1950; *Wagonmaster* 1950; *The Great Missouri Raid* 1951; *On Dangerous Ground* 1951; *Only the Valiant* 1951; *Operation Pacific* 1951; *Hellgate* 1952; *The Quiet Man* 1952; *Thunderbirds* 1952; *Blowing Wild* 1953; *Hondo* 1953; *The Moonlighter* 1953; *The Bob Mathias Story* 1954; *Gypsy Colt* 1954; *Johnny Guitar* 1954; *The Long Gray Line* 1955; *A Man Alone* 1955; *Mister Roberts* 1955; *Dakota Incident* 1956; *The Halliday Brand* 1956; *Pillars of the Sky* 1956; *The Searchers* 1956; *The Wings of Eagles* 1956; *China Doll* 1958; *Alias Jesse James* 1959; *Rio Bravo* 1959.

Bondarchuk, Sergei • Actor, director; also screenwriter. • Born Sergei Fyodorovich Bondarchuk, Belozersk, Ukraine, USSR, September 25, 1920. *Educ.* Rostov Theatrical College, Rostov-on-Don; VGIK, Moscow. Leading post-WWII actor who later turned to directing with epic results. While studying under Sergei Gerasimov, Bondarchuk was cast with other students in the director's *Young Guard* (1948) and later took lead roles in such noted Soviet films as *Taras Shevchenko* (1951) and *Othello* (1955), excelling at tragic, heroic parts.

He made his directing debut with the audacious *Destiny of a Man* (1959), in which he stars as an ordinary, unheroic soldier struggling to survive in a German

POW camp. Bondarchuk's compelling performance helped the film win the top prize at that year's Moscow Film Festival and earned international acclaim for the director.

After being cast as a Russian POW who escapes from a German camp in Roberto Rossellini's *Era Notte a Roma* (1960), Bondarchuk took on the job of directing the Soviet Union's grandest film production, and the world's most expensive (estimated at $100,000,000)—Tolstoy's *War and Peace.*

The eight-hour-long resulting film was originally released in three parts, one part per year from 1965 to 1967. Shot in 70mm wide-screen and color, it is a truly epic achievement, with Bondarchuk starring as Pierre and creating a brilliant visual correlative to Tolstoy's prose. *War and Peace* earned the 1968 Academy Award for best foreign film and is considered one of the finest literary adaptations in cinema history.

In 1970 Bondarchuk began teaching drama at VGIK while continuing to direct and act. His subsequent films, including the epics *Waterloo* (1970) and *Boris Godunov* (1986), have not lived up to his earlier achievements, though they bear the stamp of a mature, accomplished artist. Bondarchuk is married to Irina Skobtseva, who starred opposite him in *Othello*, and father of Natalia Bondarchuk, who starred in Andrei Tarkovsky's *Solaris* (1972). • *Michurin* 1948 (a); *Molodaya gvardiya/Young Guard* 1948 (a); *Povest o nastoyashchem cheloveke* 1948 (a); *The Path of Glory* 1949 (a); *Kavaler zulotoi zvezdi/Cavalier of the Golden Star* 1950 (a); *Taras Shevchenko* 1951 (a); *Admiral Ushakov* 1953 (a); *Korabli Shturmuyut bastiony/The Ships From the Bastion* 1953 (a); *Ob etom zabyvat nelzya/This Must Not Be Forgotten* 1954 (a); *Neokonchennaya povest* 1955 (a); *Othello* 1955 (a); *Poprigunya* 1955 (a); *Ivan Franko* 1956 (a); *Dvoe iz odnovo kvartala/Two From the Housing Block* 1957 (a); *Stranitsi iz rasskuzu/Pages From a Story* 1958 (a); *Shli soldati/The Soldiers Marched On* 1959 (a); *Sudba cheloveka/Destiny of a Man* 1959 (a,d); *Era Notte a Roma* 1960 (a); *Seriozha* 1960 (a); *Voina i Mir/War and Peace* 1965-67 (a,d,sc); *Bitka na Neretvi* 1968 (a); *Waterloo* 1970 (d,sc); *Dyadya Vanya/Uncle Vanya* 1971 (a); *Oni Srajalis Za Rodinou* 1975 (a,d,sc); *Vrhovi Zelengore* 1976 (a); *Otietz Sergii* 1978 (a); *The Steppe* 1978 (a,d,sc); *Red Bells: I've Seen the Birth of the New World* 1983 (d,sc); *Boris Godunov* 1986 (a,d,sc).

Bondi, Beulah • Actress • Born Beulah Bondy, Chicago, IL, May 3, 1892; died 1981. Stock and Broadway actress who began her Hollywood career in 1931, recreating her stage role as the gossipy, unsympathetic woman in *Street Scene*. Bondi was Oscar-nominated for her performances in *The Gorgeous Hussy* (1936) and *Of Human Hearts* (1938) and, in 1977, earned an Emmy for a guest appearance on "The Waltons" TV series. • *Arrowsmith* 1931; *Street Scene* 1931; *Rain* 1932; *Christopher Bean* 1933; *The Stranger's Return* 1933; *Finishing School* 1934; *Ready For Love* 1934; *Registered Nurse* 1934; *Two Alone* 1934; *Bad Boy* 1935; *The Good Fairy* 1935; *The Case Against Mrs. Ames* 1936; *The Gorgeous Hussy* 1936 **(AANBSA)**; *Hearts Divided* 1936; *The Invisible Ray* 1936; *The Moon's Our Home* 1936; *The Trail of the Lonesome Pine* 1936; *Maid of Salem* 1937; *Make Way For Tomorrow* 1937; *Of Human Hearts* 1938 **(AANBSA)**; *The Sisters* 1938; *Vivacious Lady* 1938; *Mr. Smith Goes to Washington* 1939; *On Borrowed Time* 1939; *The Captain Is a Lady* 1940; *Our Town* 1940; *Remember the Night* 1940; *One Foot in Heaven* 1941; *Penny Serenade* 1941; *The Shepherd of the Hills* 1941; *Tonight We Raid Calais* 1943; *Watch on the Rhine* 1943; *And Now Tomorrow* 1944; *I Love a Soldier* 1944; *Our Hearts Were Young and Gay* 1944; *She's a Soldier Too* 1944; *The Very Thought of You* 1944; *Back to Bataan* 1945; *Breakfast in Hollywood* 1945; *The Southerner* 1945; *It's a Wonderful Life* 1946; *Sister Kenny* 1946; *High Conquest* 1947; *The Sainted Sisters* 1948; *The Snake Pit* 1948; *So Dear to My Heart* 1948; *The Life of Riley* 1949; *Mr. Soft Touch* 1949; *Reign of Terror* 1949; *The Baron of Arizona* 1950; *The Furies* 1950; *Lone Star* 1952; *Latin Lovers* 1953; *Track of the Cat* 1954; *Back From Eternity* 1956; *The Unholy Wife* 1957; *The Big Fisherman* 1959; *A Summer Place* 1959; *Tammy Tell Me True* 1961; *The Wonderful World of the Brothers Grimm* 1962; *Tammy and the Doctor* 1963.

Bonham Carter, Helena • Actress • Born London, May 26, 1966. Cherubic leading lady of aristocratic descent; great-uncle was director Anthony Asquith. • *A Pattern of Roses* 1983; *Lady Jane* 1986; *A Room With a View* 1986; *Maurice* 1987; *The Vision* 1987; *La Maschera* 1988; *Francesco* 1989; *Getting It Right* 1989; *Hamlet* 1990; *Where Angels Fear to Tread* 1991.

Bonnaire, Sandrine • Actress • Born Clermont-Ferrand, France, 1967. Promising French actress who garnered acclaim for her very first screen performance, in Maurice Pialat's *À nos amours* (1983). Bonnaire won a best actress César for her role as the aimless vagrant in Agnès Varda's haunting *Vagabond* (1985) and turned in sterling performances in Pialat's *Under Satan's Sun* (1987) and Patrice Leconte's stylish thriller *Monsieur Hire* (1989). • *À nos amours* 1983; *La Meilleur de la Vie* 1984; *Tir à Vue* 1984; *Blanche et Marie* 1985; *Police* 1985; *Sans toit ni loi/Vagabond* 1985; *La Puritaine* 1986; *Les Innocents* 1987; *Jaune revolver* 1987; *Sous le soleil de Satan/Under Satan's Sun* 1987; *Peaux de vachés* 1988; *Quelques jours avec moi* 1988; *Monsieur Hire* 1989; *La Révolution Française* 1989; *La Captive du désert/Captive of the Desert* 1990; *Verso Sera* 1990.

Bonnot, Françoise • Editor • Born Bois-Colombés, France, August 17, 1939. Frequent collaborator with director Constantin Costa-Gavras; Bonnot earned an Oscar for *Z* (1969) and a British Academy award for *Missing* (1982). Her mother, Monique Bonnot, cut several films for Jean-Pierre Melville and her brother, Alain Bonnot, is an assistant director. • *Guns For San Sebastian* 1968; *L'Armée des ombres* 1969; *Z* 1969 **(AABED)**; *L'Aveu/The Confession* 1970; *Beau Masque* 1972; *Etat de siège/State of Siege* 1973; *Massacre in Rome* 1973; *Bon Baisers à Lundi* 1974; *Grandeur Nature* 1974; *1=2?* 1975; *Section Spéciale* 1975; *Le Locataire/The Tenant* 1976; *La Victoire en chantant/Black and White and in Color* 1976; *Black Out* 1977; *The Cassandra Crossing* 1977; *Le Passé Simple* 1977; *Le Dernier Amant Romantique* 1978; *Judith Therpauve* 1978; *Clair de Femme* 1979; *Chère Inconnue/I Sent a Letter to My Love* 1980; *Missing* 1982; *Hannah K* 1983; *Un Amour de Swann/Swann in Love* 1984; *Liste Noire* 1984; *Harem* 1985; *Year of the Dragon* 1985; *The Sicilian* 1987; *Le Palanquin des larmes* 1988; *Fat Man and Little Boy* 1989.

Boorman, John • Director; also screenwriter, producer. • Born Shepperton, Middlesex, England, January 18, 1933. Left the dry cleaning business to become first a film critic and then an assistant film editor for Britain's Independent Television, before going on to produce documentaries for Southern Television. In 1962, while heading the BBC's Bristol Film Unit, he experimented with a dramatic documentary style, resulting in the series "Citizen 63" and "The Newcomers."

Boorman's first feature, *Having a Wild Weekend* (1965), was a competent, exuberant 1960s musical featuring the Dave Clark Five which attempted, unsuccessfully, to duplicate the success of the Beatles/Richard Lester ground-breaker *A Hard Day's Night* (1964). After *The Great Director* (1966), a documentary on D.W. Griffith for the BBC, Boorman moved to the US and made the genre-bending *Point Blank* (1967). A taut, violent thriller starring Angie Dickinson and Lee Marvin and marked by a complex flashback narrative structure, the film went virtually unnoticed at the time but has since earned considerable critical acclaim.

Boorman's subsequent films, through *Zardoz* (1974), show off his impressive visual style, his gift for superior plotting and pace, and his recurrent concern with the themes of the hunt and survival. Among his greatest achievements is *Deliv-*

erance (1972), in which four Atlanta businessmen take off on a weekend canoe trip which turns into a nightmare. Adapted from the novel by James Dickey (who plays the sheriff in the film), *Deliverance* was noted for its masterful handling of the civilization vs. nature theme, for an unforgettably gruesome scene in which one of the travelers is raped by a backwoodsman, and for outstanding cinematography, including extremely long takes, by Vilmos Zsigmond. The son of one of the men was played by the director's son Charley Boorman, who later starred in *The Emerald Forest* (1985) as a white child who is raised for ten years by a primitive Amazon tribe.

After the ill-conceived and overambitious *Exorcist II: The Heretic* (1977), Boorman returned to form with *Excalibur* (1981), continuing to explore the mythic, quest themes of his earlier films. The delightful, semi-autobiographical *Hope and Glory* (1987) was a humorous account of a boy growing up in Blitz-torn London. • *Having a Wild Weekend* 1965 (d); *The Great Director* 1966 (d); *Point Blank* 1967 (d); *Hell in the Pacific* 1968 (d); *Leo the Last* 1970 (d,sc); *Deliverance* 1972 (d,p) **(AANBD)**; *Zardoz* 1974 (d,p,sc); *Exorcist II: The Heretic* 1977 (d,p); *Long Shot* 1978 (a); *Excalibur* 1981 (d,exec.p,sc); *Angel* 1982 (exec.p); *Nemo* 1983 (p); *The Emerald Forest* 1985 (d,p); *Hope and Glory* 1987 (a,d,p,sc) **(AANBP,AANBD)**; *Where the Heart Is* 1990 (d,p,sc).

Booth, Margaret • *aka* Maggie Booth • American editor • At MGM in the 1920s and 30s, helped develop the seamless, unobtrusive cutting style that came to be known as "classical" Hollywood editing. Booth became MGM's supervising film editor in 1939 and held the post for 29 years before resuming "hands-on" work in 1970. • *Husbands and Lovers* 1924 (ed); *Fine Clothes* 1925 (ed); *The Gay Deceiver* 1926 (ed); *Memory Lane* 1926 (ed); *In Old Kentucky* 1927 (ed); *Lovers?* 1927 (ed); *Bringing Up Father* 1928 (ed); *The Enemy* 1928 (ed); *A Lady of Chance* 1928 (ed); *The Mysterious Lady* 1928 (ed); *Telling the World* 1928 (ed); *The Bridge of San Luis Rey* 1929 (ed); *Wise Girls* 1929 (ed,titles); *The Lady of Scandal* 1930 (ed); *A Lady's Morals* 1930 (ed); *New Moon* 1930 (ed); *Redemption* 1930 (ed); *The Rogue Song* 1930 (ed); *Strictly Unconventional* 1930 (ed); *The Cuban Love Song* 1931 (ed); *Five and Ten* 1931 (ed); *It's a Wise Child* 1931 (ed); *The Prodigal* 1931 (ed); *Susan Lenox, Her Fall and Rise* 1931 (ed); *Lovers Courageous* 1932 (ed); *Smilin' Through* 1932 (ed); *Society Girl* 1932 (ed); *The Son-Daughter* 1932 (ed); *Strange Interlude* 1932 (ed); *The Blonde Bombshell* 1933 (ed); *Dancing Lady* 1933 (ed); *Peg o' My Heart* 1933 (ed); *Storm at Daybreak* 1933 (ed); *The White Sister* 1933 (ed); *The Barretts of Wimpole Street* 1934 (ed); *Riptide* 1934 (ed); *Mutiny on the Bounty* 1935 (ed) **(AANBED)**; *Reckless* 1935 (ed); *Romeo and Juliet* 1936 (ed); *Camille* 1937 (ed); *A Yank at Oxford* 1938 (ed); *The V.I.P.s* 1963 (prod.ad); *The Owl and the Pussycat* 1970 (ed); *Fat City* 1972 (ed); *To Find a Man* 1972 (ed); *The Way We Were* 1973 (ed); *The Black Bird* 1975 (ed); *The Sunshine Boys* 1975 (ed); *Murder By Death* 1976 (ed); *The Goodbye Girl* 1977 (ed); *California Suite* 1978 (ed); *The Cheap Detective* 1978 (assoc.p); *Chapter Two* 1979 (assoc.p,ed); *Seems Like Old Times* 1980 (assoc.p,ed); *Annie* 1982 (exec.asst.to p,ed); *The Toy* 1982 (assoc.p); *The Slugger's Wife* 1985 (exec.p).

Borden, Lizzie • Director; also producer. • Born Linda Elizabeth Borden, Detorit, MI, February 3, 1954. *Educ.* Wellesley College, MA (fine arts). Made her name as an independent New York filmmaker with the acclaimed feature *Born in Flames* (1982), shot on a budget of approximately $30,000. Borden has gone on to shape a cinema primarily concerned with the representation of women in contemporary society; she received widespread attention for *Working Girls* (1986), an incisive, witty probe of workaday life in a well-appointed brothel. • *Born in Flames* 1982 (d,p,sc,add.ph); *King Blank* 1982 (ed.asst); *Working Girls* 1986 (d,p,sc,ed); *Mankillers* 1987 (a); *Calling the Shots* 1988 (a); *Love Crimes* 1991 (d,p).

Borgnine, Ernest • Actor • Born Ermes Effron Borgnine, Hamden, CT, January 24, 1917. *Educ.* Randall School of Dramatic Arts, Hartford, CT. Stout, unglamorous character player who was critically noted for his fine performance as the lovelorn butcher in Delbert Mann's *Marty* (1955). Borgnine was also excellent as the menacing outlaw in *The Wild Bunch* (1969) but is best known as the mischievous, fun-seeking captain on TV's "McHale's Navy" (1962-66). • *China Corsair* 1951; *The Mob* 1951; *The Whistle at Eaton Falls* 1951; *From Here to Eternity* 1953; *The Stranger Wore a Gun* 1953; *Bad Day at Black Rock* 1954; *The Bounty Hunter* 1954; *Demetrius and the Gladiators* 1954; *Johnny Guitar* 1954; *Run For Cover* 1954; *Vera Cruz* 1954; *Violent Saturday* 1954; *The Last Command* 1955; *Marty* 1955 **(AABA)**; *The Square Jungle* 1955; *The Best Things in Life Are Free* 1956; *The Catered Affair* 1956; *Jubal* 1956; *Three Brave Men* 1956; *The Badlanders* 1958; *Torpedo Run* 1958; *The Vikings* 1958; *The Rabbit Trap* 1959; *Man on a String* 1960; *Pay or Die* 1960; *Summer of the Seventeenth Doll* 1960; *Go Naked in the World* 1961; *Barabbas* 1962; *McHale's Navy* 1964; *The Flight of the Phoenix* 1965; *The Oscar* 1966; *Chuka* 1967; *The Dirty Dozen* 1967; *Ice Station Zebra* 1968; *The Legend of Lylah Clare* 1968; *The Split* 1968; *The Wild Bunch* 1969; *A Bullet For Sandoval* 1970; *Suppose They Gave a War and Nobody Came?* 1970; *Bunny O'Hare* 1971; *Hannie Caulder* 1971; *Rain For a Dusty Summer* 1971; *Willard* 1971; *Film Portrait* 1972 (collaboration); *The Poseidon Adventure* 1972; *The Revengers* 1972; *The Emperor of the North Pole* 1973; *The Neptune Factor* 1973; *Law and Disorder* 1974; *The Devil's Rain* 1975; *Hustle* 1975; *Shoot* 1976; *Crossed Swords* 1977; *The Greatest* 1977; *Convoy* 1978; *The Black Hole* 1979; *The Double McGuffin* 1979; *Ravagers* 1979; *When Time Ran Out* 1980; *Deadly Blessing* 1981; *Escape From New York* 1981; *High Risk* 1981; *Supersnooper* 1981; *Young Warriors* 1983; *Geheimcode Wildganse* 1984; *The Manhunt* 1984; *Skeleton Coast* 1988; *Spike of Bensonhurst* 1988; *Gummibarchen kusst man nicht* 1989; *Laser Mission* 1989; *Qualcuno paghera* 1989; *Turnaround* 1989; *Any Man's Death* 1990; *Moving Target* 1990.

Borowczyk, Walerian • Animator, director; also screenwriter, painter. • Born Kwilcz, Poland, October 21, 1923. *Educ.* Academy of Fine Arts, Cracow (painting, lithography). Best known in Poland—and in France, where he emigrated in 1958—for his nightmarish animated shorts. His live-action films frequently feature his wife Ligia Brancie and, though equally surreal, are slightly less despairing than his animated work. • *Once Upon a Time (short)* 1957 (d); *Striptease (short)* 1957 (d); *Dom (short)* 1958 (d); *School (short)* 1958 (d); *Les Astronautes (short)* 1959 (d,sc); *Le Magicien (short)* 1959 (d); *Terra Incognita (short)* 1959 (d); *Boîte à Musique (short)* 1961 (d); *Solitude (short)* 1961 (d); *Le Concert de Monsieur et Madame Kabal (short)* 1962 (d); *L'Enclyclopédie de Grand'maman en 13 Volumes (short)* 1963 (d); *Holy Smoke (short)* 1963 (d); *Le Théâtre de Monsieur et Madame Kabal* 1967 (sc,story,anim,pd,sound mixer,a,d); *Mazepa* 1968 (d); *Goto, l'île d'amour* 1969 (d,sc); *Le Phonographe (short)* 1969 (d); *Blanche* 1971 (d,sc); *Contes Immoraux* 1974 (d,sc,dial,ed,art d); *La Bête* 1975 (d,sc,ed); *Dzieje Grzechu* 1976 (d,sc); *La Marge* 1976 (d,sc); *L'Interno di un Convento* 1978 (d,sc,dial,ed); *Collections Privées* 1979 (d,sc,adapt,dial—"L'armoire"); *Les Héroïnes du Mal* 1979 (d,sc,adapt,dial); *Lulu* 1980 (d,sc,pd); *Docteur Jekyll et les femmes* 1981 (d,sc,sets); *L'Art d'Aimer* 1983 (d,sc); *Emmanuelle 5* 1986 (d,sc); *Cérémonie d'amour* 1988 (d,sc).

Borzage, Frank • Director; also actor. • Born Salt Lake City, UT, April 23, 1893; died 1962. Borzage switched from acting to directing in 1916, bringing to the screen a dedication to romanticism that became his trademark. Although considered light and superficial, his films, especially from *Humoresque* (1920) through *Moonrise* (1948), were undeniably popular. Borzage was a pioneer in the use of techniques, such as soft focus, that have become standards of romantic filmmaking. He was the first ever recipient of a best director Oscar, for *Seventh Heaven* (1927); he won the award again for *Bad Girl* (1931). • *The Typhoon* 1914 (a); *The Wrath of the Gods* 1914 (a); *The Cup of Life* 1915 (a); *The Code of Honor* 1916 (a,d); *Dollars of Dross* 1916 (d,sc); *Enchantment* 1916 (a,d,sc); *The Forgotten Prayer* 1916 (a,d); *Immediate Lee* 1916 (a,d); *Land O' Lizards* 1916 (a,d); *Life's Harmony* 1916 (a,d); *Nell Dale's Men Folks* 1916 (a,d); *Pride and the Man* 1916 (a,d,sc); *The Silken Spider* 1916 (a,d); *That Girl of Burke's* 1916 (a,d); *Flying Colors* 1917 (d); *A Mormon Maid* 1917 (a); *Until They Get Me* 1917 (d); *Wee Lady Betty* 1917 (a,d); *The Atom* 1918 (a); *The Curse of Iku* 1918 (a,d); *The Ghost Flower* 1918 (d); *the Gun Woman* 1918 (a,d); *An Honest Man* 1918 (d); *Innocent's Progress* 1918 (d); *Shoes That Danced* 1918 (d); *Society For Sale* 1918 (d); *Who Is to Blame?* 1918 (d); *Ashes of Desire* 1919 (d); *Prudence of Broadway* 1919 (d); *Toton* 1919 (d); *Whom the Gods Destroy* 1919 (d); *Humoresque* 1920 (d); *The Duke of Chimney Butte* 1921 (d); *Get-Rich-Quick Wallingford* 1921 (d); *Back Pay* 1922 (d); *Billy Jim* 1922 (d); *The Good Provider* 1922 (d); *The Pride of Palomar* 1922 (d); *The Valley of Silent Men* 1922 (d); *The Age of Desire* 1923 (d); *Children of Dust* 1923 (d); *Nth Commandment* 1923 (d); *Secrets* 1924 (d); *The Circle* 1925 (d); *Daddy's Gone A-Hunting* 1925 (d); *The Lady* 1925 (d); *Lazybones* 1925 (d); *Wages For Wives* 1925 (d); *The Dixie Merchant* 1926 (d); *Early to Wed* 1926 (d); *The First Year* 1926 (d); *Marriage License?* 1926 (d); *Seventh Heaven* 1927 (d) **(AABD)**; *Street Angel* 1928 (d); *Lucky Star* 1929 (d); *The River* 1929 (d); *They Had to See Paris* 1929 (d); *Liliom* 1930 (d); *Song O' My Heart* 1930 (d); *Bad Girl* 1931 (d) **(AABD)**; *Doctors' Wives* 1931 (d); *Young As You Feel* 1931 (d); *After Tomorrow* 1932 (d); *A Farewell to Arms* 1932 (d); *Young America* 1932 (d); *A Man's Castle* 1933 (d); *Secrets* 1933 (d); *Flirtation Walk* 1934 (d); *Little Man, What Now?* 1934 (d); *Living on Velvet* 1934 (d); *No Greater Glory* 1934 (d); *Shipmates Forever* 1935 (d); *Stranded* 1935 (d); *Desire* 1936 (d); *Hearts Divided* 1936 (d); *The Big City* 1937 (d); *Green Light* 1937 (d); *History Is Made at Night* 1937 (d); *Mannequin* 1938 (d); *The Shining Hour* 1938 (d); *Three Comrades* 1938 (d); *Disputed Passage* 1939 (d); *Flight Command* 1940 (d); *The Mortal Storm* 1940 (d); *Strange Cargo* 1940 (d); *Smilin' Through* 1941 (d); *The Vanishing Virginian* 1941 (d); *Seven Sweethearts* 1942 (d); *His Butler's Sister* 1943 (d); *Stage Door Canteen* 1943 (d); *Till We Meet Again* 1944 (d); *The Spanish Main* 1945 (d); *I've Always Loved You* 1946 (d,p); *Magnificent Doll* 1946 (d); *That's My Man* 1947 (d,p); *Moonrise* 1948 (d); *China Doll* 1958 (d,p); *The Big Fisherman* 1959 (d).

Bosco, Philip • Actor • Born Jersey City, NJ, September 26, 1930. *Educ.* Catholic University, Washington, DC (drama). Avuncular character player who made his film debut in *Requiem For a Heavyweight* (1962) and usually plays sympathetic figures of authority. An acclaimed New York stage actor, Bosco has emerged as one of the finest contemporary interpreters of the work of George Bernard Shaw. • *Requiem For a Heavyweight* 1962; *A Lovely Way to Die* 1968; *Trading Places* 1983; *The Pope of Greenwich Village* 1984; *Flanagan* 1985; *Heaven Help Us* 1985; *Children of a Lesser God* 1986; *The Money Pit* 1986; *Suspect* 1987; *Three Men and a Baby* 1987; *Another Woman* 1988; *Working Girl* 1988; *Blue Steel* 1989; *The Dream Team* 1989; *The Luckiest Man in the World* 1989; *Quick Change* 1990; *F/X 2* 1991; *True Colors* 1991.

Bost, Pierre • Screenwriter • Born Lasalle, France, September 5, 1901. See Aurenche, Jean. • *La Symphonie Pastorale* 1946 (sc); *Le Diable au corps/Devil in the Flesh* 1947 (adapt); *La Mura di Malapaga/The Walls of Malapaga* 1949 (sc.adapt); *L'Auberge Rouge/The Red Inn* 1951 (adapt); *Jeux interdits/Forbidden Games* 1952 (sc); *Les Sept péchés capitaux/The Seven Deadly Sins* 1952 (sc—"Lust"); *Les Orgueilleux* 1953 (sc); *Le Blé en Herbe* 1954 (sc); *Rouge et Noir* 1954 (sc); *Gervaise* 1955 (sc); *La Traversée de Paris* 1956 (sc); *En cas de malheur/Love Is My Profession* 1958 (sc); *L'Horloger de St Paul/The Watchmaker* 1973 (sc); *Le Juge et l'assassin/The Judge and the Assassin* 1976 (sc); *Un Dimanche à la Campagne/A Sunday in the Country* 1984.

Botelho, Joao • Director; also screenwriter, producer, critic. • Born Lamego, Portugal, May 11, 1949. *Educ.* National Conservatory School of Cinema, Portugal. Leading figure in the contemporary Portugese film industry and founder of the critical and theoretical journal, *M.* Botelho's 1988 feature, *Hard Times*, was a highly stylized adaptation of the Dickens novel which attempted to recapture the visual purity of the early silent cinema. • *Um Adeus Português/A Portuguese Goodbye* 1985 (d,p,sc,dial,ed); *Tempos Dificeis/Hard Times* 1988 (d,p,sc,ed).

Bottoms, Timothy • Actor • Born Santa Barbara, CA, August 30, 1951. Sensitive actor who made a big splash in 1971 in Dalton Trumbo's *Johnny Got His Gun* and Peter Bogdanovich's *The Last Picture Show*, but has largely failed to live up to his early promise. Younger brothers Joseph and Sam are also actors. • *Johnny Got His Gun* 1971; *The Last Picture Show* 1971; *Liebe, Schmerz und das danze Verdammte Zeug* 1973; *The Paper Chase* 1973; *The Crazy World of Julius Vrooder* 1974; *The White Dawn* 1974; *Operation Daybreak* 1975; *A Small Town in Texas* 1976; *The Other Side of the Mountain—Part 2* 1977; *Rollercoaster* 1977; *Hurricane* 1979; *The High Country* 1981; *Secrets of the Phantom Caverns* 1983; *Tin Man* 1983; *The Census Taker* 1984; *Hambone and Hillie* 1984; *In the Shadow of Kilimanjaro* 1984; *The Sea Serpent* 1984; *The Fantasist* 1986; *Invaders From Mars* 1986; *Mio min Mio/Mio in the Land of Faraway* 1987; *The Drifter* 1988; *Husbands, Wives, Money and Murder* 1989; *Return to the River Kwai* 1989; *Istanbul: Keep Your Eyes Open* 1990; *Texasville* 1990.

Boulanger, Daniel • Screenwriter; also actor, author. • Born Campiegne, France, 1922. Mainstay of the New Wave who has played supporting roles in films by Jean-Luc Godard (as the hot-tempered police inspector in *Breathless*), Claude Chabrol and François Truffaut. Boulanger has written novels, short stories and plays as well as screenplays, mostly for Philippe De Broca. • *A bout de souffle/Breathless* 1959 (a); *Le Jeux de l'Amour/The Love Game* 1960 (sc); *Tirez Sur le Pianiste/Shoot the Piano Player* 1960 (a); *L'Amant de Cinq Jours* 1961 (sc); *Cartouche* 1962 (sc,dial); *Le Farceur* 1962 (sc); *L'Oeil du Malin/The Third Lover* 1962 (a); *La Récréation* 1962 (sc); *Les Sept péchés capitaux/The Seven Deadly Sins* 1962 (sc—"Gluttony"); *Echappement libre* 1964 (sc,dial,adapt); *L'Homme de Rio/That Man From Rio* 1964 (sc,dial) **(AANBSC)**; *Peau de banane* 1964 (sc); *Marie-Chantal Contre le Docteur Kha* 1965 (dial); *Monnaie de Singe* 1965 (dial); *Les Tribulations d'un Chinois en Chine* 1965 (sc); *Le Roi de Coeur/King of Hearts* 1966 (a,sc); *Tendre Voyou* 1966 (sc); *La Vie de Château* 1966 (dial); *Un Homme de trop* 1967 (dial); *La Route de Corinthe* 1967 (sc,dial); *Le Voleur/The Thief of Paris* 1967 (sc); *Histoires Extraordinaires/Spirits of the Dead* 1968 (sc); *La Mariée était en noir/The Bride Wore Black* 1968 (a); *Le Diable par la Queue* 1969 (dial); *Caprices de Marie* 1970 (sc); *Domicile conjugal/Bed and Board* 1970 (a); *La Maison Sous les Arbres* 1971 (sc); *Les Pétroleuses* 1971 (sc); *L'Affaire Dominici* 1972 (sc); *Pas folle la guêpe* 1972 (sc); *Toute une vie* 1974 (a); *Police Python.357* 1975 (sc); *Une Femme Fidèle* 1976 (dial,sc); *La Menace* 1977 (sc,dial); *La Zizanie* 1978 (a); *Le Cheval d'orgueil* 1979 (sc); *Ils sont grands ces petits* 1979 (sc,sc,dial); *Chouans!* 1988 (sc); *Marat* 1989 (sc); *La Révolution Française* 1989 (sc,French dial).

Boulting, John • Director; also screenwriter, producer. • Born Bray, England, November 21, 1913; died June 17, 1985, Sunningdale, Berkshire, England. *Educ.* McGill University, Montreal. With his twin brother Roy, a leading figure of the post-WWII British film industry. Though they alternated producing and directing chores, the brothers' individual filming styles were virtually indistinguishable. They formed Charter Films in 1937 and were responsible for gritty dramas such as *Thunder Rock* (1942) and *Brighton Rock* (1947) in the 40s. The team concentrated, during the next decade, on mildly anarchic comedies like *Private's Progress* (1956) and *I'm All Right Jack* (1959), a satire of British trade unions.

During the Spanish Civil War John had fought with the Republicans and, though he later eschewed left-wing politics, all his films carry a degree of social comment. In WWII he made films for the Royal Air Force while Roy directed for the Army Film Unit. In 1971 Roy married actress Hayley Mills (over thirty years his junior), from whom he was later divorced. • *Trunk Crime* 1939 (p); *Inquest* 1940 (p); *Thunder Rock* 1942 (p); *Desert Victory* 1943 (p); *Burma Victory* 1945 (p); *Journey Together* 1945 (d); *Brighton Rock* 1947 (d); *Fame Is the Spur* 1947 (p); *The Guinea Pig* 1948 (p); *Seven Days to Noon* 1950 (d); *High Treason* 1951 (p); *The Magic Box* 1951 (d); *Singlehanded* 1951 (p); *Crest of the Wave* 1954 (d,p); *Josephine and Men* 1955 (p); *Brothers in Law* 1956 (p); *Private's Progress* 1956 (d,sc); *Run For the Sun* 1956 (p); *Lucky Jim* 1957 (d); *Happy Is the Bride* 1958 (p); *Carlton-Browne of the F.O.* 1959 (p); *I'm All Right Jack* 1959 (d,sc); *A French Mistress* 1960 (p); *The Risk* 1960 (d,p); *Heaven's Above!* 1963 (d,sc); *Rotten to the Core* 1965 (d); *The Family Way* 1966 (p); *Twisted Nerve* 1968 (exec.p); *There's a Girl in My Soup* 1970 (p); *Undercovers Hero* 1975 (p); *The Number* 1979 (p).

Boulting, Roy • Director; also producer. • Born Bray, England, November 21, 1913. *Educ.* McGill University, Montreal. See Boulting, John. • *Trunk Crime* 1939 (d); *Inquest* 1940 (d); *Thunder Rock* 1942 (d); *Desert Victory* 1943 (d); *Tunisian Victory* 1943 (d); *Burma Victory* 1945 (d); *Brighton Rock* 1947 (p); *Fame Is the Spur* 1947 (d); *The Guinea Pig* 1948 (d,sc); *Seven Days to Noon* 1950 (d); *High Treason* 1951 (d,sc); *The Magic Box* 1951 (p); *Singlehanded* 1951 (d); *Crest of the Wave* 1954 (d,p,sc); *Josephine and Men* 1955 (d); *Brothers in Law* 1956 (d,sc); *Private's Progress* 1956 (p); *Run For the Sun* 1956 (d,sc); *Lucky Jim* 1957 (p); *Happy Is the Bride* 1958 (d,sc); *Carlton-Browne of the F.O.* 1959 (d,sc); *I'm All Right Jack* 1959 (p); *A French Mistress* 1960 (d,sc); *The Risk* 1960 (d,p); *Heaven's Above!* 1963 (p); *Rotten to the Core* 1965 (p); *The Family Way* 1966 (adapt,d); *Twisted Nerve* 1968 (d,sc); *There's a Girl in My Soup* 1970 (d); *Undercovers Hero* 1975 (d,sc); *The Last Word* 1979 (d); *The Number* 1979 (d).

Bouquet, Carole • Actress • Born Neuilly-sur-Seine, France, August 18, 1957. *Educ.* Sorbonne, Paris (philosophy); Paris Conservatoire. Made an arresting film debut, while still a teenager, sharing the title role of Luis Buñuel's *That Obscure Object of Desire* (1977) with Angela Molina. Subsequently in few films of note until Bertrand Blier's *Too Beautiful for You* (1989), which ironically cast her as an undesired, though extremely alluring, wife. Bouquet is also known internationally as the model for Chanel No.5 perfume. • *Cet obscur objet du désir/That Obscure Object of Desire* 1977; *Buffet Froid* 1979; *Il Cappotto di Astrakan* 1980; *For Your Eyes Only* 1981; *Bingo Bongo* 1983; *Mystère* 1983; *Némo* 1983; *Le Bon Roi Dagobert* 1984; *Rive Droite, Rive Gauche* 1984; *Special Police* 1985; *Double Messieurs* 1986; *Le Mal d'aimer* 1986; *Jenatsch* 1987; *Bunker Palace Hotel* 1989; *New York Stories* 1989; *Trop belle pour toi/Too Beautiful For You* 1989.

Bourgoin, Jean • *aka* Yves Bourgoin • Director of photography • Born Jean-Serge Bourgoin, Paris, March 4, 1913. Former apprentice to Christian Matras and Jean Bachelet who contributed to such visually powerful works as *Une Partie de Compagne* (1936), *Dédée* (1948), *Black Orpheus* (1959) and *The Longest Day* (1962). Son Georges Bourgoin is also a cinematographer. • *Une Partie de Campagne* 1936 (cam.op); *La Vie est à nous* 1936 (ph); *La Marseillaise* 1938 (ph); *Goupi Mains rouges* 1943 (ph); *Voyage surprise* 1946 (ph); *Dédée* 1948 (ph); *Justice est faite* 1950 (ph); *Manèges* 1950 (ph); *Nous sommes tous des Assassins* 1952 (ph); *Avant le Déluge* 1954 (ph); *Mr. Arkadin* 1955 (ph); *Mon Oncle* 1958 (ph); *Orfeu Negro/Black Orpheus* 1959 (ph); *The Counterfeit Traitor* 1962 (ph); *Gigot* 1962 (ph); *The Longest Day* 1962 (ph) **(AABPH)**; *Germinal* 1963 (ph); *Pas Question le Samedi* 1965 (ph); *Qui?* 1970 (ph); *La Chambre Rouge* 1972 (ph).

Bourne, Mel • Production designer • Born Chicago, IL. *Educ.* Yale School of Drama. Best known for his impeccable collaborations with Woody Allen, beginning with *Annie Hall* (1977). Bourne excels at urban settings and has worked with Michael Mann (*Thief* 1981), Robert Benton (*Still of the Night* 1982) and Barbet Schroeder (*Reversal of Fortune* 1990). • *The Miracle Worker* 1962 (asst.art d); *Annie Hall* 1977 (art d); *Nunzio* 1977 (pd); *The Greek Tycoon* 1978 (art d—US); *Interiors* 1978 (pd) **(AANBAD)**; *Manhattan* 1979 (pd); *Stardust Memories* 1980 (pd); *Windows* 1980 (pd); *Thief* 1981 (pd); *A Midsummer Night's Sex Comedy* 1982 (pd); *Still of the Night* 1982 (pd); *Zelig* 1983 (pd); *Broadway Danny Rose* 1984 (pd); *The Natural* 1984 (pd—New York) **(AANBAD)**; *F/X* 1986 (pd); *Manhunter* 1986 (pd); *Fatal Attraction* 1987 (pd); *The Accused* 1988 (pd consultant); *Cocktail* 1988 (pd); *Rude Awakening* 1989 (pd); *Reversal of Fortune* 1990 (pd).

Bow, Clara • Actress • Born Brooklyn, NY, August 25, 1905; died 1965. Won a beauty contest that took her to California at age 16 and a few years later, with the help of the Hollywood publicity machine, was a star. Bow achieved her greatest notoriety with the lead role in *It* (1927), which earned her the tag of the "It" girl—a quintessential jazz-age term which suggested modernity, independence and sexual liberation. At the height of her fame, Bow was linked to several scandals which eventually drove her from Hollywood. In 1931 she married actor/cowboy Rex Bell and in 1933, after an unsuccessful comeback, left the movies for good. • *Beyond the Rainbow* 1922; *Down to the Sea in Ships* 1922; *the Daring Years* 1923; *Maytime* 1923; *Black Lightning* 1924; *Black Oxen* 1924; *Daughters of Pleasure* 1924; *Empty Hearts* 1924; *Grit* 1924; *Poisoned Paradise* 1924; *This Woman* 1924; *Wine* 1924; *The Adventurous Sex* 1925; *The Ancient Mariner* 1925; *Capital Punishment* 1925; *Eve's Lover* 1925; *Free to Love* 1925; *The Keeper of the Bees* 1925; *Kiss Me Again* 1925; *Lawful Cheaters* 1925; *My Lady of Whims* 1925; *My Lady's Lips* 1925; *Parisian Love* 1925; *The Plastic Age* 1925; *The Primrose Path* 1925; *The Scarlet West* 1925; *Dancing Mothers* 1926; *Fascinating Youth* 1926; *Kid Boots* 1926; *Mantrap* 1926; *The Runaway* 1926; *The Shadow of the Law* 1926; *Two Can Play* 1926; *Children of Divorce* 1927; *Get Your Man* 1927; *Hula* 1927; *It* 1927; *Rough House Rosie* 1927; *Wings* 1927; *The Fleet's in* 1928; *Ladies of the Mob* 1928; *Red Hair* 1928; *Three Week-Ends* 1928; *Dangerous Curves* 1929; *The Saturday Night Kid* 1929; *The Wild Party* 1929; *Her Wedding Night* 1930; *Love Among the Millionaires* 1930; *Paramount on Parade* 1930; *True to the Navy* 1930; *Kick In* 1931; *No Limit* 1931; *Call Her Savage* 1932; *Hoopla* 1933.

Bowie, David • Singer, songwriter; also actor. • Born David Robert Jones, London, January 8, 1947. Mercurial and highly influential rock performer who has also turned in some impressive screen appearances. Bowie first attracted notice as the alien visitor—a role well suited to his deftly cultivated public image—in *The Man Who Fell to Earth* (1976) and made his Broadway debut in the early 1980s, playing John Merrick in *The Elephant Man*. Many of his songs have been used for feature soundtracks and he has contributed original music to several films. • *Ziggy Stardust and the Spiders From Mars* 1973 (a,m,song); *James Dean, the First American Teenager* 1975 (m); *The Man Who Fell to Earth* 1976 (a); *Jane Bleibt Jane* 1977 (m); *Radio On* 1979 (songs); *Schöner Gigolo—Armer Gigolo/Just a Gigolo*

1979 (a,song); *Christiane F wir Kinder vom Bahnhof Zoo/Christiane F* 1981 (songs,a); *Cat People* 1982 (lyrics,song); *Merry Christmas, Mr. Lawrence* 1982 (a); *Party, Party* 1982 (songs); *Hero* 1983 (m); *The Hunger* 1983 (a,song); *Yellowbeard* 1983 (a); *Into the Night* 1985 (a); *Absolute Beginners* 1986 (a,songs); *Labyrinth* 1986 (a,songs); *When the Wind Blows* 1986 (songs); *Imagine: John Lennon* 1988 (a); *The Last Temptation of Christ* 1988 (a).

Bowie, Les • Special effects artist • Born United Kingdom, 1913; died 1979. Matte shot specialist whose work spans several generations of special effects technology, beginning in the mid-1940s. • *Great Expectations* 1946 (fx); *The Red Shoes* 1948 (fx); *The Haunted Strangler* 1958 (fx ph); *One Million Years B.C.* 1966 (prologue designer); *The Quiller Memorandum* 1966 (fx); *Mosquito Squadron* 1968 (fx); *The Assassination Bureau* 1969 (fx); *Dracula A.D. 1972* 1972 (fx); *Call Him Mr. Shatter* 1975 (fx); *Dracula and the 7 Golden Vampires* 1975 (fx); *The Human Factor* 1975 (fx); *The Lifetaker* 1975 (fx); *To the Devil, a Daughter* 1976 (fx); *Star Wars* 1977 (fx); *Superman* 1978 (fx) **(AASPECIAL ACHIEVEMENT)**.

Box, Betty E. • Producer • Born Beckenham, Kent, England, 1920. Began her career as the producer of some 200 propaganda and training films during WWII and went on to shepherd several fine features before assuming charge of production at Islington Studios. Sister of producer Sydney Box and married to producer Peter Rogers. • *The Seventh Veil* 1945 (assoc.p); *The Years Between* 1946 (assoc.p); *Dear Murderer* 1947 (assoc.p); *So Long at the Fair* 1950 (p); *Appointment With Venus* 1951 (p); *The Venetian Bird* 1952 (p); *A Day to Remember* 1953 (p); *Doctor in the House* 1954 (p); *Doctor at Sea* 1955 (p); *Checkpoint* 1956 (p); *Doctor at Large* 1957 (p); *Campbell's Kingdom* 1958 (p); *A Tale of Two Cities* 1958 (p); *The 39 Steps* 1959 (p); *Conspiracy of Hearts* 1960 (p); *No Love For Johnnie* 1961 (p); *No, My Darling Daughter* 1961 (p); *The Wild and the Willing* 1962 (p); *Agent 8 3/4* 1964 (p); *Deadlier Than the Male* 1966 (p); *Doctor in Clover* 1966 (p); *The High Commissioner* 1968 (p); *Nobody Runs Forever* 1968 (p); *Some Girls Do* 1969 (p); *Doctor in Trouble* 1970 (p); *Percy* 1970 (p); *It's Not the Size That Counts* 1974 (p).

Box, John • Production designer • Born London, January 27, 1920. *Educ.* London School of Architecture. Chiefly known for his collaborations with David Lean, beginning with his Oscar-winning work on *Lawrence of Arabia* (1962). • *Zarak* 1956 (art d); *High Flight* 1957 (art d); *The Inn of the Sixth Happiness* 1958 (art d); *No Time to Die* 1958 (art d); *Our Man in Havana* 1959 (art d); *The World of Susie Wong* 1959 (art d); *Lawrence of Arabia* 1962 (pd) **(AABAD)**; *Of Human Bondage* 1964 (pd); *Doctor Zhivago* 1965 (pd) **(AABAD)**; *A Man For All Seasons* 1966 (pd); *Oliver!* 1968 (pd) **(AABAD)**; *The Looking Glass War* 1970 (p); *Nicholas and Alexandra* 1971 (pd,2u d) **(AABAD)**; *Travels With My Aunt* 1972 (pd) **(AANBAD)**; *The Great Gatsby* 1974 (pd); *Rollerball* 1975 (pd); *Sorcerer* 1977 (pd); *The Keep* 1983 (pd); *A Passage to India* 1984 (pd) **(AANBAD)**.

Box, Muriel • Screenwriter; also director, producer. • Born Muriel Baker, Tolworth, England, 1905. With husband Sydney, to whom she was married from 1935 to 1969, wrote several British films including the classy melodramas, *The Seventh Veil* (1945) and *The Brothers* (1947). Muriel Box began her directing career in 1952 with the Ealing-style comedy, *The Happy Family.* • *Alibi Inn* 1935 (sc); *The Seventh Veil* 1945 (sc,story) **(AABSC)**; *The Years Between* 1946 (sc); *The Brothers* 1947 (sc); *Daybreak* 1947 (sc); *Dear Murderer* 1947 (p,sc); *Holiday Camp* 1947 (sc); *The Man Within* 1947 (p,sc); *The Blind Goddess* 1948 (sc); *Easy Money* 1948 (sc); *Portait From Life* 1948 (sc); *Christopher Columbus* 1949 (sc); *The Astonished Heart* 1950 (sc); *So Long at the Fair* 1950 (sc); *The Happy Family* 1952 (d,sc); *Street Corner* 1953 (d,sc); *The Beachcomber* 1954 (d); *To Dorothy a Son* 1954 (d); *Simon and Laura* 1955 (d); *Eyewitness* 1956 (d); *The Passionate Stranger* 1957 (d,sc); *The Truth About Women* 1958 (d,p,sc); *Subway in the Sky* 1959 (d); *This Other Eden* 1959 (d); *Too Young to Love* 1960 (d); *The Piper's Tune* 1962 (d); *Rattle of a Simple Man* 1964 (d).

Box, Sydney • Screenwriter; also producer. • Born Beckenham, England, April 29, 1907; died May 25, 1983, Perth, Australia. See Box, Muriel. • *The Seventh Veil* 1945 (p,sc,story) **(AABSC)**; *The Years Between* 1946 (p,sc); *The Brothers* 1947 (p,sc); *Daybreak* 1947 (p,sc); *Dear Murderer* 1947 (p,sc); *Holiday Camp* 1947 (p,sc); *The Man Within* 1947 (p,sc); *The Blind Goddess* 1948 (sc); *Easy Money* 1948 (sc); *Portait From Life* 1948 (sc); *Quartet* 1948 (p); *Christopher Columbus* 1949 (sc); *So Long at the Fair* 1950 (sc); *Trio* 1950 (p); *The Beachcomber* 1954 (sc); *The Prisoner* 1955 (exec.p); *The Passionate Stranger* 1957 (sc); *Floods of Fear* 1958 (p); *The Truth About Women* 1958 (p,sc); *Rattle of a Simple Man* 1964 (p); *Deadlier Than the Male* 1966 (p).

Boyer, Charles • Actor • Born Figeac, France, August 28, 1897; died August 26, 1978. *Educ.* Sorbonne, Paris (philosophy); Paris Conservatoire. Romantic French lead whose second stay in Hollywood (the first was from 1929-1931) established him as a major star and the personification of Gallic charm. Boyer played opposite some of Hollywood's greatest leading ladies and starred in three classics of unrequited love: *All This, and Heaven Too* (1940, opposite Bette Davis), *Back Street* (1941, opposite Margaret Sullavan) and *Hold Back the Dawn* (1941, opposite Olivia de Havilland). He played masterfully against type to drive Ingrid Bergman to insanity in *Gaslight* (1944).

After the war, Boyer continued to appear on Broadway and TV, in French films and on the London stage. His career lasted longer than that of any other romantic male of his era, earning him the title "the last of the cinema's great lovers." He was married from 1934 to British-born actress Pat Patterson; soon after she died, Boyer followed her by swallowing an overdose of barbiturates. • *Le Capitaine Fracasse* 1929; *The Magnificent Lie* 1931; *The Man From Yesterday* 1932; *Red-Headed Woman* 1932; *The Battle* 1934; *Caravan* 1934; *Liliom* 1934; *Break of Hearts* 1935; *Private Worlds* 1935; *Shanghai* 1935; *The Garden of Allah* 1936; *Mayerling* 1936; *Conquest* 1937 **(AANBA)**; *History Is Made at Night* 1937; *Tovarich* 1937; *Algiers* 1938 **(AANBA)**; *Love Affair* 1939; *When Tomorrow Comes* 1939; *All This, and Heaven Too* 1940; *Appointment for Love* 1941; *Back Street* 1941; *Hold Back the Dawn* 1941; *Tales of Manhattan* 1942; *The Constant Nymph* 1943; *Flesh and Fantasy* 1943 (a,p); *Gaslight* 1944 **(AANBA)**; *Together Again* 1944; *Confidential Agent* 1945; *Cluny Brown* 1946; *Arch of Triumph* 1948; *A Woman's Vengeance* 1948; *The 13th Letter* 1951; *The First Legion* 1951; *The Happy Time* 1952; *Thunder in the East* 1952; *The Earrings of Madame De...* 1953; *The Cobweb* 1955; *Around the World in 80 Days* 1956; *Paris Palace Hotel* 1956; *Une Parisienne* 1957; *The Buccaneer* 1958; *Maxime* 1958; *Fanny* 1961 **(AANBA)**; *Les Démons de Minuit* 1962; *The Four Horsemen of the Apocalypse* 1962; *Julia, du bist zauberhaft* 1962; *Love Is a Ball* 1963; *A Very Special Favor* 1965; *How to Steal a Million* 1966; *Paris brûle-t-il?/Is Paris Burning?* 1966; *Barefoot in the Park* 1967; *Casino Royale* 1967; *The April Fools* 1969; *The Madwoman of Chaillot* 1969; *Lost Horizon* 1973; *Stavisky* 1973; *A Matter of Time* 1976.

Boyle, Peter • Actor • Born Philadelphia, PA, October 18, 1933. *Educ.* LaSalle College, Philadelphia. Former monk in the Christian Brothers order who became a member of the Second City comedy troupe and began playing character roles in film and TV in the late 1960s. An imposing and volatile screen presence, Boyle gained attention as the reactionary title character of *Joe* (1970). He was excellent as the cynical campaign manager in *The Candidate* (1972) and the monster in *Young Frankenstein* (1974), but is also capable of quieter, more sympathetic characterizations. • *The Virgin President* 1968; *Medium Cool* 1969; *Diary of a Mad Housewife* 1970; *Joe* 1970; *T. R. Baskin* 1971; *The Candidate* 1972; *Crazy Joe* 1973; *The Friends of Eddie Coyle* 1973; *Ghost in the Noonday Sun* 1973; *Kid Blue* 1973; *Slither* 1973; *Steelyard Blues* 1973; *Young Frankenstein* 1974; *Swashbuckler* 1976; *Taxi Driver* 1976; *The Brink's Job* 1978; *F.I.S.T.* 1978; *Beyond the Poseidon Adventure* 1979; *Hardcore* 1979; *In God We Trust* 1980; *Where the Buffalo Roam* 1980; *Outland* 1981; *Hammett* 1982; *Yellowbeard* 1983; *Johnny Dangerously* 1984; *Turk 182* 1985; *The In Crowd* 1987; *Surrender* 1987; *Walker* 1987; *Funny* 1988; *Red Heat* 1988; *The Dream Team* 1989; *Speed Zone* 1989; *Men of Respect* 1990; *Solar Crisis* 1990; *Shadow of the Wolf: Kickboxer II* 1991.

Brabourne, Lord John • Producer • Born John Brabourne, United Kingdom, 1924. Responsible for such fine productions as *Othello* (1965), starring an ebony Laurence Olivier, *Romeo and Juliet* (1968), courtesy of Franco Zeffirelli, and several lively Agatha Christie adaptations. Brabourne also engineered the commercially risky (due to its length), superbly realized interpretation of the Dickens novel, *Little Dorrit* (1988). • *Raising a Riot* 1955 (prod.man); *The Seven Thunders* 1957 (assoc.p); *Harry Black and the Tiger* 1958 (p); *Othello* 1965 (p); *The Dance of Death* 1968 (p); *Romeo and Juliet* 1968 (p) **(AANBP)**; *Tales of Beatrix Potter* 1971 (p); *Murder on the Orient Express* 1974 (p); *The 'Copter Kids* 1976 (exec.p); *Death on the Nile* 1978 (p); *Stories From a Flying Trunk* 1979 (p); *The Mirror Crack'd* 1980 (p); *Evil Under the Sun* 1982 (p); *A Passage to India* 1984 (p) **(AANBP)**; *Little Dorrit* 1988 (p).

Bracco, Lorraine • Actress • Born Brooklyn, NY, 1955. Feisty, intelligent leading lady of the 1980s who formerly worked as a model and a deejay for Europe's Radio Luxembourg. Bracco made an isolated screen debut in the French production *Duos sur Canape* (1979), but her acting career did not take off until she returned to the US. She excels at playing tough, resilient working-class women, as in *Someone to Watch Over Me* (1987)—in which she delivers an effective upper-cut to the jaw of philandering husband Tom Berenger—and *Goodfellas* (1990), for which her portrayal of mob wife Karen Hill earned her a best supporting actress award from the Los Angeles film critics. Married to actor Harvey Keitel. • *Duos sur Canape* 1979; *Un Complicato Intrigo di Donne, Vicoli e Delitti* 1985; *The Pick-Up Artist* 1987; *Someone to Watch Over Me* 1987; *The Dream Team* 1989; *In una notte di chiaro di luna* 1989; *Sing* 1989; *Goodfellas* 1990; *Switch* 1991; *Talent For the Game* 1991.

Brach, Gérard • Screenwriter; also director. • Born Paris, 1927. Distinguished writer who earned his first screenplay credit for Roman Polanski's "Amsterdam" segment of the omnibus feature, *Les Plus belles escroqueries du monde* (1964). Brach is known as a regular collaborator with Polanski (from *Repulsion* 1965 through *Frantic* 1988), Jean-Jacques Annaud (*Quest For Fire* 1981, *The Name of the Rose* 1986, *The Bear* 1988) and Andrei Konchalovsky (*Maria's Lovers* 1985, *Shy People* 1987). • *Les Plus belles escroqueries du monde* 1964 (sc—"Amsterdam"); *Repulsion* 1965 (sc); *Cul-de-Sac* 1966 (sc); *The Fearless Vampire Killers* 1967 (sc,story); *Wonderwall* 1968 (story); *Cinéma Différent 3* 1970 (sc—"La rivière de diamants"); *Le Bateau sur l'herbe* 1971 (d,sc); *Le Locataire/The Tenant* 1976 (sc); *Le Point de mire* 1977 (sc,dial); *Rève de Singe* 1978 (sc); *Chiedo Asilo* 1979 (sc); *Tess* 1979 (sc); *Chère Inconnue/I Sent a Letter to My Love* 1980 (sc); *Le Coeur à l'Envers* 1980 (sc); *Quest For Fire* 1981 (sc); *Identificazione di una donna/Identification of a Woman* 1982 (sc); *L'Africain* 1983 (sc); *La Femme de mon pôte* 1983 (sc); *Une Pierre dans la bouche* 1983 (sc); *Le Bon Roi Dagobert* 1984 (sc); *Les Enragés* 1984 (sc); *Les Favoris de la Lune* 1984 (sc); *La Meilleur de la Vie* 1984 (sc); *Gazl el Banat* 1985 (sc); *Maria's Lovers* 1985 (sc); *Jean de Florette* 1986 (sc); *Manon des sources/Manon of the Spring* 1986 (sc); *The Name of the Rose* 1986 (sc); *Pirates* 1986 (sc); *Fuegos* 1987 (sc); *Ou que tu sois* 1987 (sc); *Shy People* 1987 (sc); *Domino* 1988 (sc); *Frantic* 1988 (sc); *L'Ours/The Bear* 1988 (sc); *Une Vie suspendué* 1988 (sc); *Divertimenti nella casa privata* 1990 (sc).

Bracken, Eddie • Actor • Born Edward Vincent Bracken, Queens, NY, February 7, 1920. *Educ.* Professional Children's School, New York; Began vaudeville career before age 10. Former vaudevillian whose screen humor was of the fast, physical and furious kind. Beginning his career with Paramount in 1940, Bracken was at his frenzied best in two Preston Sturges films: *The Miracle of Morgan's Creek* and *Hail The Conquering Hero* (both 1944). • *Too Many Girls* 1940; *Caught in the Draft* 1941; *Life With Henry* 1941; *Reaching For the Sun* 1941; *The Fleet's In* 1942; *Star Spangled Rhythm* 1942; *Sweater Girl* 1942; *Happy Go Lucky* 1943; *Young and Willing* 1943; *Hail the Conquering Hero* 1944; *The Miracle of Morgan's Creek* 1944; *Rainbow Island* 1944; *Bring on the Girls* 1945; *Duffy's Tavern* 1945; *Hold That Blonde* 1945; *Out of This World* 1945; *Fun on a Weekend* 1947; *Ladies' Man* 1947; *The Girl From Jones Beach* 1949; *Summer Stock* 1950; *Two Tickets to Broadway* 1951; *About Face* 1952; *We're Not Married* 1952; *A Slight Case of Larceny* 1953; *Una Domenica d'Estate* 1961; *Wild Wild World* 1961; *Shinbone Alley* 1971; *National Lampoon's Vacation* 1983; *Oscar* 1991.

Brackett, Charles • Screenwriter; also producer, author. • Born Saratoga Springs, NY, November 26, 1892; died 1969. *Educ.* Williams College, Williamstown, MA; Harvard School of Law. A drama critic for *The New Yorker* with several published novels to his name, Brackett signed on as staff writer with Paramount Pictures in 1935. His screenplays were generally unexceptional until he teamed up with Billy Wilder in 1938. The effective combination of Brackett producing, Wilder directing and the two sharing the screenplay credit generated a string of acclaimed films including multiple Oscar-winners *The Lost Weekend* (1945) and *Sunset Boulevard* (1950). • *Tomorrow's Love* 1925 (from story "Interlocutory"); *Risky Business* 1926 (from story "Pearls Before Cecily"); *Pointed Heels* 1929 (story); *Secrets of a Secretary* 1931 (story); *College Scandal* 1935 (sc); *Enter Madame* 1935 (sc); *The Last Outpost* 1935 (adapt); *Without Regret* 1935 (sc); *Piccadilly Jim* 1936 (sc); *Rose of the Rancho* 1936 (sc); *Woman Trap* 1936 (story); *Live, Love and Learn* 1937 (sc); *Bluebeard's Eighth Wife* 1938 (sc); *That Certain Age* 1938 (sc); *Midnight* 1939 (sc); *Ninotchka* 1939 (sc) **(AANBSC)**; *What a Life* 1939 (sc); *Arise, My Love* 1940 (sc); *Ball of Fire* 1941 (sc); *Hold Back the Dawn* 1941 (sc) **(AANBSC)**; *The Major and the Minor* 1942 (sc); *Five Graves to Cairo* 1943 (sc); *The Lost Weekend* 1945 (p,sc) **(AABSC)**; *To Each His Own* 1946 (p,sc,story) **(AANBST)**; *The Emperor Waltz* 1948 (p,sc,story); *A Foreign Affair* 1948 (p,sc) **(AANBSC)**; *Miss Tatlock's Millions* 1948 (p,sc); *The Mating Season* 1950 (p,sc); *Sunset Boulevard* 1950 (p,sc) **(AABSC)**; *The Model and the Marriage Broker* 1951 (p,sc); *Niagara* 1953 (p,sc); *Titanic* 1953 (p,sc,story) **(AABSC)**; *Garden of Evil* 1954 (p); *Woman's World* 1954 (p); *The Girl in the Red Velvet Swing* 1955 (p,sc); *The Virgin Queen* 1955 (p); *D-Day the Sixth of June* 1956 (p); *The King and I* 1956 (p) **(AANBP)**; *Teenage Rebel* 1956 (p,sc); *The Wayward Bus* 1957 (p); *The Gift of Love* 1958 (p); *The Remarkable Mr. Pennypacker* 1958 (p); *Ten North Frederick* 1958 (p); *Blue Denim* 1959 (p); *Journey to the Center of the Earth* 1959 (p,sc); *High Time* 1960 (p); *State Fair* 1962 (p).

Brackett, Leigh • Screenwriter; also novelist. • Born Los Angeles, CA, 1915; died 1978. Imaginative female writer of mostly male-oriented films. Brackett collaborated often with Howard Hawks, notably on *The Big Sleep* (1946) and the cycle of excellent westerns which began with *Rio Bravo* (1959) and ended with *Rio Lobo* (1970). • *The Vampire's Ghost* 1945 (sc,story); *The Big Sleep* 1946 (sc); *Crime Doctor's Manhunt* 1946 (sc); *Rio Bravo* 1958 (sc); *Gold of the Seven Saints* 1961 (sc); *13 West Street* 1962 (from story "The Tiger Among Us"); *Hatari!* 1962 (sc); *El Dorado* 1967 (sc); *Rio Lobo* 1970 (sc); *The Long Goodbye* 1973 (sc); *The Empire Strikes Back* 1980 (sc).

Braga, Sonia • Actress • Born Maringa, Parana, Brazil, 1951. Sensuous Brazilian performer who began her career on live TV at the age of 14 and debuted on the stage at 17, later becoming one of her country's top actresses. Braga first received international attention as the title character of Bruno Barreto's *Doña Flor and Her Two Husbands* (1977) and made a memorable English-language debut with her enigmatic, femme fatale role in *Kiss of the Spiderwoman* (1985). • *Doña Flor e Seus Dois Maridos/Doña Flor and Her Two Husbands* 1977; *Gabriela* 1983; *Kiss of the Spider Woman* 1985; *The Milagro Beanfield War* 1988; *Moon Over Parador* 1988; *The Rookie* 1990.

Brakhage, Stan • Filmmaker • Born Kansas City, MO, 1933. *Educ.* Institute of Fine Art, San Francisco (photography). Since 1952, and his first film, *Interim*, Brakhage has been engaged in an effort to reshape our habits of seeing. In his book, *Metaphors on Vision*, he wrote, "Imagine an eye unruled by man-made laws of perspective, an eye unprejudiced by compositional logic, an eye which does not repond to the name of everything but which must know each object encountered in life through an adventure of perception..." Brakhage has made over 200 films, ranging in length from less than a minute to more than four hours. Though the style of his filmmaking has been consistent over four decades—shallow focus, a rich and sensual use of color, rhythmic cutting, little or no soundtrack—Brakhage has dealt with a variety of themes. In *Scenes From Under Childhood* (1967-70) he sought to reconstruct the primal adventure of perception; in *Dog Star Man* (1959-64) he created a visual symphony that compares the ascent of a mountain to our passage into life; in *Mothlight* (1963) and a dozen other films made over the next 20-odd years, he pasted organic materials or painted, inked, or dyed images directly onto film stock, making streams of coherent images without the use of a camera.

The origin of Brakhage's cinema lies in the non-narrative realms of music, painting and poetry. Oliver Messiaen's music was a formative influence on *Scenes From Under Childhood;* poet Robert Creeley has been a commentator for and colleague of Brakhage for decades. In the 1960s Brakhage was celebrated for his subjective vision and his nonconformism; in the 70s he alienated many friends with his "Pittsburgh documents," especially the harrowing *Act of Seeing With One's Own Eyes* (1971), set in a morgue, as well as the sync-sound *The Stars Are Beautiful* (1974) and *The Governor* (1977), which tracked the chief executive of the State of Colorado. Simultaneously, Brakhage was producing the autobiographical "Sincerity/Duplicity" series (1973-80), a project which he may resume. In the 1980s he produced what he called his first "abstract" films: the *Roman Numeral Series* (1979-81), nine films titled only with roman numerals; and the *Arabics* (1980-82), 19 more works of "envisioned music"—which was as far as he would go in discussing the content of these brief, jewel-like bursts of light.

In 1988, commenting on his new film, *Marilyn's Window*, Brakhage spoke of how a "stream-of-visual-consciousness could be nothing less than the pathway of the soul," suggesting that his films speak to human senses that are vital but dormant, eyes that can grasp more than we have imagined. Parallel to his filmmaking, Brakhage has been a teacher and writer whose books include *Metaphors on Vision* (1963) and *Brakhage Scrapbook* (1982); *Film Biographies* (1977) and *Film At Wit's End* (1989), collections of essays on other filmmakers; and *I...Sleeping*, a dream journal from 1975, published in 1988. RAH • *Interim* 1952 (d); *The Wonder Ring (short)* 1955 (d); *Anticipation of the Night* 1958 (d,idea,p); *Window Water Baby Moving* 1959 (d,idea,p); *Mothlight* 1963 (d); *The Art of Vision* 1964 (a,d,p,sc,ph,ed); *Dog Star Man* 1964 (d,idea,p); *Lovemaking* 1968 (d,idea,p); *Scenes From Under Childhood* 1970 (d,idea,ed,p); *The Weir-Falcon Saga* 1970 (d,idea,ed,p); *The Act of Seeing With One's Own Eyes* 1971 (d,idea,ph,ed,p); *Eyes* 1971 (d,idea,p); *The Stars Are Beautiful* 1974 (d); *Star Garden* 1974 (d,p); *The Text of Light* 1974 (d,p); *Tragoedia* 1976 (d,p); *The Governor* 1977 (d,idea,ph,ed,p); *23rd Psalm Branch* 1978 (d,p); *Roman Numeral Series* 1979-81 (d); *Arabics* 1980-82 (d); *Sincerity* 1980 (d,p); *Songs 1-14* 1980 (d,p); *Tortured Dust* 1984 (d,p,sc,ph,ed); *Invocation Maya Deren* 1987 (a); *I...Dreaming* 1988 (d); *Marilyn's Window* 1988 (d).

Branagh, Kenneth • Actor; also director, playwright. • Born Belfast, Northern Ireland, December 10, 1960. *Educ.* RADA, London. Shining young star of the British stage who co-founded (with David Parfitt) the Renaissance Company, under whose banner Branagh successfully played *Hamlet*, staged his original play *Public Enemy* and mounted an acclaimed interpretation of *King Lear*.

Branagh gained international recognition as director and star of the 1989 screen version of *Henry V*. He has worked often opposite theater, film and TV performer Emma Thompson, whom he married in 1989. • *High Season* 1987 (a); *A Month in the Country* 1987 (a); *Henry V* 1989 (a,adapt,d) (**AANBA,AANBD**).

Brandauer, Klaus Maria • Actor; also director. • Born Bad Aussee, Austria, June 22, 1944. *Educ.* Academy of Music and Dramatic Arts, Stuttgart, West Germany. One of few contemporary German-speaking actors to have established himself as an international star. Brandauer first came to prominence for his compelling performance as Hendrik Hofgen, an ambitious young actor adopted by the Nazi party in 1930s Germany, in István Szabó's *Mephisto* (1981). • *The Salzburg Connection* 1972; *Die Babenberger in Osterreich* 1976; *Ein Sonntag im Oktober* 1979; *Mephisto* 1981; *Der Weg ins Freie* 1982; *Detskij Sad* 1983; *Never Say Never Again* 1983; *The Lightship* 1985; *Out of Africa* 1985 (**AANBD,AANBSA**); *Redl Ezredes/Colonel Redl* 1985; *Streets of Gold* 1986; *Burning Secret* 1988; *Hanussen* 1988; *Quo Vadis* 1988; *La Révolution Française* 1989; *Seven Minutes* 1989 (a,d); *Das Spinnennetz* 1989; *The Russia House* 1990; *White Fang* 1991.

Brando, Marlon • Actor; also producer, director. • Born Marlon Brando, Jr., Omaha, NB, April 3, 1924. *Educ.* Dramatic Workshop of the New School for Social Research, New York; Actors Studio. Marlon Brando first made his name as an exponent of "the method," an acting style based on the teachings of Constantin Stanislavsky. Method acting rejected the traditional techniques of stagecraft in favor of an emotional expressiveness ideally suited to the angst-ridden atmosphere of postwar American society. Brando studied the Stanislavsky technique in the 1940s, first at the New School and later at the Actors Studio.

Under the influence of Lee Strasberg and Stella Adler, Brando became the exemplar of the method, influencing American film actors from James Dean to Robert De Niro. As the unappointed spokesman for his generation, the young Brando became identified with a character in revolt against something he could not comprehend. When asked in *The Wild One* (1953), "What are you rebelling against?" he replies, "Whaddaya got?" Although Brando's rebels conveyed a strong sense of danger, the actor also lent a pathos to their stance, leaving his characters both menacing and vulnerable. Once he had became synonymous with the vulnerable rebel, Brando spent most of his career trying to purge himself and his audience of this initial identification.

Brando's first Broadway roles were in the sentimental hit *I Remember Mama* (1944), *Truckline Cafe* (1946) and *Candida* (1946). But his breakthrough came with his searing portrayal of Stanley Kowalski in Tennessee Williams's *A*

Streetcar Named Desire (1947). The role established a new order of acting intensity which soon led Brando to Hollywood.

Brando's first film was *The Men* (1950), in which he portrayed a paraplegic war veteran struggling for his dignity. Rather than play the role for its inherent pathos, however, Brando etched a portrait of an embittered, incoherent man-child. The film version of *Streetcar* (1951) followed, forever stamping the Brando image in the public imagination. But it wasn't until *The Wild One*, a motorcycle melodrama, that Brando had his first star-making vehicle. The Stanley Kowalski brute was now removed from Tennessee Williams's confining New Orleans ghetto, his anger directed scattershot against society at large.

With his Oscar-winning performance in *On the Waterfront* (1954), Brando became a full-fledged Hollywood power. He played against type in a number of subsequent roles—from the ill-tempered Napoleon of *Désirée* (1954) to the heel-clicking song and dance man of *Guys and Dolls* (1955) to the effete Fletcher Christian of *Mutiny on the Bounty* (1962)—but his rebel persona had nevertheless become a cliche by the end of the decade. (Actor-impressionist Frank Gorshin performed a devastating send-up of it in 1960's *Bells Are Ringing*.)

Brando finally purged his rebel image in the 1960s, playing a figure of authority in *The Ugly American* (1963) and parodying himself in *Bedtime Story* (1964). But despite complex performances in *Reflections in a Golden Eye* (1967) and *Burn!* (1969) his audience had largely abandoned him by the beginning of the 1970s.

It wasn't until *The Godfather* (1972) and his sensitive character role as Don Corleone that Brando regained his following. He gave perhaps his crowning performance, as a self-destructive American in Paris, in Bertolucci's disturbing *Last Tango in Paris* (1972). Since *Last Tango* Brando has appeared in few films, and has more than once announced his retirement from acting, most recently in September 1989. He lent a bizarre comic presence to *The Missouri Breaks* (1976) and *The Formula* (1980), stamped his moniker on such varied projects as *Superman* (1978) and *Apocalypse Now* (1979) and earned an Oscar nomination for his engaging performance as a crusty South African civil rights lawyer in *A Dry White Season* (1989). PB • *The Men* 1950; *A Streetcar Named Desire* 1951 **(AANBA)**; *Viva Zapata!* 1952 **(AANBA)**; *Julius Caesar* 1953 **(AANBA)**; *The Wild One* 1953; *Désirée* 1954; *On the Waterfront* 1954 **(AABA)**; *Guys and Dolls* 1955; *The Teahouse of the August Moon* 1956; *Sayonara* 1957 **(AANBA)**; *The Young Lions* 1958; *The Fugitive Kind* 1960; *One-Eyed Jacks* 1961 (a,d); *Mutiny on the Bounty* 1962; *The Ugly American* 1963; *Bedtime Story* 1964; *Morituri* 1965; *The Appaloosa* 1966; *The Chase* 1966; *Meet Marlon Brando* 1966; *A Countess From Hong Kong* 1967; *Reflections in a Golden Eye* 1967; *Candy* 1968; *The Night of the Following Day* 1968; *Quemada!/Burn!* 1969; *The Nightcomers* 1971; *The Godfather* 1972 **(AABA)**; *Last Tango in Paris* 1972 **(AANBA)**; *The Missouri Breaks* 1976; *Superman* 1978; *Apocalypse Now* 1979; *Raoni: The Fight For the Amazon* 1979; *The Formula* 1980; *A Dry White Season* 1989 **(AANBSA)**; *The Freshman* 1990.

Brasseur, Claude • Actor • Born Paris, June 15, 1936. *Educ.* Paris Conservatoire. Son of performers Pierre Brasseur and Odette Joyeux who concentrated on film after a serious accident suspended his professional bobsledding career in 1963. Brasseur has appeared in works by such directors as Jean-Luc Godard (*Band of Outsiders* 1964), Costa-Gavras (*Shock Troops* 1967) and Francis Girod (*The Savage State* 1977, *Descent Into Hell* 1986). • *Le Pays d'où Je viens* 1956 (a); *Rue des Prairies* 1959 (a); *Les Yeux sans Visage/Eyes Without a Face* 1959 (a); *Pierrot la Tendresse* 1960 (a); *La Bride sur le Cou* 1961 (a); *Les Menteurs* 1961 (a); *Les Enemies* 1962 (a); *Les Sept péchés capitaux/The Seven Deadly Sins* 1962 (a); *Dragées au Poivre* 1963 (a); *Germinal* 1963 (a); *Bande a Part/Band of Outsiders* 1964 (a); *Peau de banane* 1964 (a); *Du Rififi à Paname* 1966 (a); *Un Homme de trop/Shock Troops* 1967 (a); *Le Portrait de Marianne* 1970 (a); *Une Belle fille come moi/Such a Gorgeous Kid Like Me* 1972 (a); *Un Cave* 1972 (a); *Gli Eroi* 1972 (a); *Le Viager* 1972 (a); *Bel Ordure* 1973 (a); *L'Agression* 1974 (a); *Les Seins de Glace* 1974 (a); *Attention Les Yeux* 1975 (a); *Le Guepier* 1975 (a); *Il faut vivre Dangereusement* 1975 (a); *Barocco* 1976 (a); *Pardon Mon Affaire* 1976 (a); *L'Etat sauvage/The Savage State* 1977 (a); *Le Grand Escogriffe* 1977 (a); *Monsieur Papa* 1977 (a); *Nous irons tous au paradis* 1977 (a); *L'Argent des autres* 1978 (a); *Une Histoire simple* 1978 (a); *Au revoir, à lundi* 1979 (a); *La Guerre des Policiers* 1979 (a); *Ils sont grands ces petits* 1979 (a); *La Banquière* 1980 (a); *La Boum* 1980 (a); *Une Affaire d'Hommes* 1981 (a); *Josepha* 1981 (a); *L'Ombre Rouge* 1981 (a); *Une Robe noire pour un tueur* 1981 (a); *La Boum 2* 1982 (a); *Guy De Maupassant* 1982 (a); *La Crime* 1983 (a); *Le Léopard* 1983 (a); *Signes Extérieurs de Richesse* 1983 (a); *T'es heureuse? Moi toujours...* 1983 (a); *Palace* 1984 (a); *Souvenirs, Souvenirs* 1984 (a); *Détective* 1985 (a); *La Gitane* 1985 (a); *Les Loups entre eux* 1985 (a); *Descente aux enfers/Descent Into Hell* 1986 (a); *Taxi Boy* 1986 (a); *La Guerre Oubliée* 1987 (cam.op); *Dandin* 1988 (a); *Radio Corbeau* 1988 (a); *L'Orchestre Rouge* 1989 (a); *L'Union sacrée* 1989 (a); *Dancing Machine* 1990 (a).

Brault, Michel • Director of photography; also director. • Born Montreal, Quebec, Canada, 1928. *Educ.* University of Montreal (philosophy). Principle figure of Quebeçois cinema who established himself as a leading cinéma vérité cinematographer and director in the late 1950s. Brault is noted for his acclaimed collaborations with Jean Rouch (who called him the "greatest cameraman in the world") and countryman Claude Jutra. • *Chronique d'un été/Chronicle of a Summer* 1960 (ph); *Regard Sur la Folie* 1961 (ph); *La Punition* 1962 (ph); *Seul ou avec d'Autres (short)* 1962 (technical adviser); *A tout prendre* 1963 (ph); *La Fleur de l'age, ou les adoléscentes* 1964 (d); *Jusqu'au cou* 1964 (ph); *Ce soir-la, Gilles Vigneault* 1967 (ph); *Entre la mer et l'eau douce* 1967 (d,sc,dial,ph,ed); *Entre Tu Et Vous* 1969 (ph); *Eldridge Cleaver* 1970 (ph); *Festival Panafricain d'Alger* 1970 (ph); *Pays sans bon sens, ou Wake up, mes bons amis!!!, Un* 1970 (ph); *L'Acadie, l'Acadie* 1971 (d,ph); *Faut Aller Parmi le Monde pour l'Savior* 1971 (ph); *Mon Oncle Antoine* 1971 (ph); *Eliza's Horoscope* 1972 (ph); *Le Temps d'Une Chasse* 1972 (ph); *Kamouraska* 1973 (ph); *Les Ordres* 1974 (d,sc,ph); *Le Temps de l'avant* 1976 (ph); *La Tête de Normande St.-Onge* 1976 (ph); *Jules le magnifique* 1977 (ph); *Mourir à Tue-Tête* 1979 (ph); *Threshold* 1981 (ph); *La Quarantaine* 1982 (ph); *Louisiane* 1984 (ph); *The Great Land of Small* 1986 (ph); *Half a Lifetime* 1986 (ph); *No Mercy* 1986 (ph); *Hello Actors Studio* 1987 (ph); *Le Lys cassè* 1987 (p); *The Tadpole and the Whale* 1987 (ph—Florida); *Salut Victor!* 1989 (ph).

Braunberger, Pierre • Producer; also actor. • Born Paris, July 29, 1905; died November 16, 1990. Began his film career as an actor but had moved behind the camera by the age of 20, producing René Clair's avant-garde short *Entr'acte* in 1924. Braunberger's first feature as a producer was *La fille de l'eau* (1925), the first of several collaborations with Jean Renoir. Braunberger is remarkable not simply for the length and productivity of his career, but for the imagination and daring he showed in backing projects such as Luis Buñuel's banned surrealist classic *L'Age d'or* (1930) and early New Wave films by Chris Marker, Alain Resnais and Jean-Luc Godard. He was awarded an honorary César (the French Oscar) in 1980. • *Entr'acte (short)* 1924 (p); *La fille de l'eau* 1925 (p); *Nana* 1926 (a,p); *Rien que les heures* 1926 (p); *Voyage au Congo* 1926 (p); *Un Chien Andalou (short)* 1928 (p); *Tiré-au-Flanc* 1928 (p); *L'Age d'or* 1930 (p); *La Chienne* 1931 (exec.p); *Un Partie de Campagne* 1936 (p); *Paris 1900* 1948 (p); *Van Gogh (short)* 1948 (p); *Gauguin (short)* 1950 (p); *Guernica (short)* 1950 (p); *Bullfight* 1951 (d,p,sc); *La Course de Taureaux* 1951 (d); *Le Coup du Berger (short)* 1956 (p); *Toute la Mémoire du*

Monde 1956 (p); *Tous les Garçons s'appéllent Patrick/All Boys Are Called Patrick (short)* 1957 (p); *Le Chant du Styrène (short)* 1958 (p); *Une Histoire d'Eau (short)* 1958 (p); *Moi un Noir* 1958 (p); *L'Eau à la bouche* 1959 (p); *Ein Engel auf Erden* 1959 (p); *Tirez Sur le Pianiste/Shoot the Piano Player* 1960 (p); *Le Temps du Ghetto* 1961 (p); *Un Coeur gros comme ça!* 1962 (p); *La Dénonciation* 1962 (p); *Vivre sa Vie/My Life to Live* 1962 (p); *La Chasse au Lion à l'arc* 1965 (p); *De l'amour* 1965 (p); *Un Homme et une femme/A Man and a Woman* 1966 (p); *L'Astragale* 1968 (artist d,p); *Erotissimo* 1969 (p); *Trois hommes sur un cheval* 1970 (p); *Catch Me a Spy* 1971 (p); *La Cavale* 1971 (p); *Fantasia Chez Les Ploucs* 1971 (p); *On n'arrète pas le printemps* 1971 (p); *Elle Court, Elle Court la Banlieue* 1972 (p); *Collections Privées* 1979 (p); *Les Héroïnes du Mal* 1979 (p); *Dionysos* 1984 (p); *Kusameikyu (short)* 1984 (p); *Les Chévaliers de la table ronde* 1990 (p).

Brazzi, Rossano • Actor; also director. • Born Bologna, Italy, September 18, 1916. *Educ.* San Marco University, Florence; University of Florence. Popular Italian romantic lead who worked with resistance groups in Rome during WWII and moved to Hollywood in 1949. Brazzi was memorable as Katharine Hepburn's sensitive pursuer in David Lean's sumptuous *Summertime* (1955). • *Ritorno* 1939; *La Forza Bruta* 1940; *Kean* 1940; *Processo e Morte di Socrate* 1940; *Il Re si Diverte* 1941; *La Tosca* 1941; *I Due Foscari* 1942; *La Gorgona* 1942; *Noi Vivi/We the Living* 1942; *Una Signora dell'Ouest* 1942; *I Dieci Comandamenti* 1945; *Malia* 1945; *La Resa di Titi* 1945; *Aquila Nera* 1946; *Furia* 1946; *La Grande Aurora* 1946; *Eleanora Duse* 1947; *Il Passatore* 1947; *Little Women* 1949; *Romanzo d'Amore* 1950; *Vulcano* 1950; *La Vendetta di Aquila Nera* 1951; *L'Inguista Condanna* 1952; *La Chair et le Diable/The Flesh and the Devil* 1953; *The Barefoot Contessa* 1954; *Three Coins in the Fountain* 1954; *Angela* 1955; *La Castiglione* 1955; *Summertime* 1955; *Gli Ultimi Cinque Minuti* 1955; *Loser Takes All* 1956; *Interlude* 1957; *Legend of the Lost* 1957; *The Story of Esther Costello* 1957; *A Certain Smile* 1958; *South Pacific* 1958; *Count Your Blessings* 1959; *L'Assedio di Siracusa* 1960; *Austerlitz* 1960; *Light in the Piazza* 1962; *Les Quatre Verites* 1962; *Rome Adventure* 1962; *Dark Purpose* 1964; *The Battle of the Villa Fiorita* 1965; *Ragazza in Prestito* 1965; *The Christmas That Almost Wasn't* 1966 (a,d); *The Bobo* 1967; *Rey de Africa* 1967; *Woman Times Seven* 1967; *The Italian Job* 1969; *Krakatoa, East of Java* 1969; *The Adventurers* 1970; *Salvare la Faccia* 1970 (a,d); *Detrás de esa Puerta* 1972; *The Great Waltz* 1972; *Castello della Paura* 1973; *I Telefoni bianchi* 1976; *I Tempo degli Assassini* 1976; *Io e Caterina* 1980; *The Final Conflict* 1981; *La Voce* 1982; *Fear City* 1985; *Final Justice* 1985; *Formula For Murder* 1986; *Russicum* 1989.

Bregman, Martin • Producer • Born New York, NY, May 18, 1931. *Educ.* Indiana University; NYU. Successful producer of the 1970s and 80s who engineered a number of excellent Al Pacino vehicles, from *Serpico* (1973) through *Sea of Love* (1989). Bregman was formerly a personal manager for Hollywood stars including Barbra Streisand, Faye Dunaway and Woody Allen. In 1974 he co-founded the New York Advisory Council for Motion Pictures, Radio and TV, of which he is currently chairman. Married to actress Cornelia Sharpe. • *Serpico* 1973 (p); *Dog Day Afternoon* 1975 (p) **(AANBP)**; *The Next Man* 1976 (a,p,story); *The Seduction of Joe Tynan* 1979 (p); *Simon* 1980 (p); *The Four Seasons* 1981 (p); *Venom* 1981 (p); *Eddie Macon's Run* 1982 (p); *Scarface* 1983 (p); *Sweet Liberty* 1986 (p); *Real Men* 1987 (p); *A New Life* 1988 (p); *Sea of Love* 1989 (p); *Betsy's Wedding* 1990 (p).

Breillat, Catherine • Director, screenwriter; also author. • Born Bressuire, France, July 13, 1948. An occasional actress (she appeared in a couple of films with sister Marie-Hélène Breillat), she is best known for her varied and effective work as a screenwriter, notably of Maurice Pialat's introspective cop movie *Police* (1985). Breillat directed her first film in 1977 and gained some international attention with *36 Fillete* (1988), an uncompromising, finely observed coming-of-age study adapted from her own novel. • *Last Tango in Paris* 1972 (a); *Catherine et Cie* 1975 (sc); *Dracula Père et Fils* 1976 (a); *Bilitis* 1977 (sc.adapt); *Une Vraie jeune fille* 1977 (d,sc,from novel *La Soupirail*); *Tapage Nocturne* 1979 (d,sc); *E la nave Va/And the Ship Sails On* 1983 (sc—English version); *Police* 1985 (sc,story); *36 Fillette* 1988 (d,sc,from novel); *Milan Noir* 1988 (sc.adapt,dial); *La Nuit de l'ocean* 1988 (sc); *Zanzibar* 1989 (sc).

Brennan, Walter • Actor • Born Swampscott, MA, July 25, 1894; died 1974. Celebrated veteran of over 100 films, beginning in the late 1920s. Brennan became one of Hollywood's favorite wizened old codgers, particularly in westerns, and was the first performer to accumulate three Academy Awards—for *Come and Get It* (1936), *Kentucky* (1938) and *The Westerner* (1940), all in the best supporting actor category. He played Grandpa on TV's "The Real McCoys" (1957-63). • *Tearin' Into Trouble* 1927; *The Ballyhoo Buster* 1928; *The Lariat Kid* 1929; *The Long, Long Trail* 1929; *One Hysterical Night* 1929; *The Shannons of Broadway* 1929; *Smilin' Guns* 1929; *King of Jazz* 1930; *Dancing Dynamite* 1931; *Neck and Neck* 1931; *The Air Mail Mystery* 1932; *The All American* 1932; *Fighting For Justice* 1932; *Law and Order* 1932; *Texas Cyclone* 1932; *Two Fisted Law* 1932; *Man of Action* 1933; *One Year Later* 1933; *The Phantom of the Air* 1933; *Silent Men* 1933; *Sing, Sinner, Sing* 1933; *Good Dame* 1934; *Half a Sinner* 1934; *Barbary Coast* 1935; *Bride of Frankenstein* 1935; *Lady Tubbs* 1935; *Law Beyond the Range* 1935; *Man on the Flying Trapeze* 1935; *Northern Frontier* 1935; *Seven Keys to Baldpate* 1935; *The Wedding Night* 1935; *Banjo on My Knee* 1936; *Come and Get It* 1936 **(AABSA)**; *Fury* 1936; *The Moon's Our Home* 1936; *The Prescott Kid* 1936; *These Three* 1936; *The Three Godfathers* 1936; *Affairs of Cappy Ricks* 1937; *She's Dangerous* 1937; *When Love Is Young* 1937; *Wild and Woolly* 1937; *The Adventures of Tom Sawyer* 1938; *The Buccaneer* 1938; *The Cowboy and the Lady* 1938; *Kentucky* 1938 **(AABSA)**; *Mother Carey's Chickens* 1938; *The Texans* 1938; *Joe and Ethel Turp Call on the President* 1939; *Stanley and Livingstone* 1939; *The Story of Vernon and Irene Castle* 1939; *They Shall Have Music* 1939; *Maryland* 1940; *Northwest Passage* 1940; *The Westerner* 1940 **(AABSA)**; *Meet John Doe* 1941; *Nice Girl?* 1941; *Rise and Shine* 1941; *Sergeant York* 1941 **(AANBSA)**; *Swamp Water* 1941; *This Woman Is Mine* 1941; *The Pride of the Yankees* 1942; *Stand By For Action* 1942; *Hangmen Also Die* 1943; *The North Star* 1943; *Slightly Dangerous* 1943; *Home in Indiana* 1944; *The Princess and the Pirate* 1944; *To Have and Have Not* 1944; *Dakota* 1945; *Centennial Summer* 1946; *My Darling Clementine* 1946; *Nobody Lives Forever* 1946; *A Stolen Life* 1946; *Driftwood* 1947; *Blood on the Moon* 1948; *Red River* 1948; *Scudda-Hoo! Scudda-Hay!* 1948; *Brimstone* 1949; *The Green Promise* 1949; *Task Force* 1949; *Curtain Call At Cactus Creek* 1950; *The Showdown* 1950; *Singing Guns* 1950; *Surrender* 1950; *A Ticket to Tomahawk* 1950; *Along the Great Divide* 1951; *Best of the Badmen* 1951; *The Wild Blue Yonder* 1951; *Lure of the Wilderness* 1952; *Return of the Texan* 1952; *Sea of Lost Ships* 1953; *Bad Day at Black Rock* 1954; *Drums Across the River* 1954; *Four Guns to the Border* 1954; *At Gunpoint* 1955; *Come Next Spring* 1955; *The Far Country* 1955; *Glory* 1955; *Good-Bye, My Lady* 1956; *The Proud Ones* 1956; *God Is My Partner* 1957; *Tammy and the Bachelor* 1957; *The Way to the Gold* 1957; *Rio Bravo* 1959; *How the West Was Won* 1962; *Shoot Out at Big Sag* 1962; *Those Calloways* 1964; *The Oscar* 1966; *The Gnome-Mobile* 1967; *Who's Minding the Mint?* 1967; *The One and Only, Genuine, Original Family Band* 1968; *Support Your Local Sheriff* 1969; *Smoke in the Wind* 1971.

Brent, George • Actor • Born George Brendan Nolan, Shannonsbridge, Ireland, March 15, 1904; died 1979. Gentlemanly Broadway lead who made his screen debut in *Under Suspicion* (1930). Brent proved an effective romantic foil to stars such as Ruby Keeler (*42nd Street* 1933), Greta Garbo (*The Painted Veil* 1934) and, particularly, Bette Davis (*Jezebel* 1938, *Dark Victory* 1939, etc.). Brent came out of retirement for 1978's *Born Again*. • *Under Suspicion* 1930; *Charlie Chan Carries On* 1931; *Ex-Bad Boy* 1931; *Fair Warning* 1931; *The Lightning Warrior* 1931; *Once a Sinner* 1931; *The Crash* 1932; *Miss Pinkerton* 1932; *The Purchase Price* 1932; *The Rich Are Always With Us* 1932; *So Big* 1932; *They Call It Sin* 1932; *Week-End Marriage* 1932; *42nd Street* 1933; *Baby Face* 1933; *Female* 1933; *From Headquarters* 1933; *The Keyhole* 1933; *Lilly Turner* 1933; *Luxury Liner* 1933; *Desirable* 1934; *Housewife* 1934; *Living on Velvet* 1934; *The Painted Veil* 1934; *Stamboul Quest* 1934; *Front Page Woman* 1935; *The Goose and the Gander* 1935; *The Right to Live* 1935; *Special Agent* 1935; *Stranded* 1935; *The Case Against Mrs. Ames* 1936; *Give Me Your Heart* 1936; *God's Country and the Woman* 1936; *The Golden Arrow* 1936; *More Than a Secretary* 1936; *Snowed Under* 1936; *The Go Getter* 1937; *Mountain Justice* 1937; *Submarine D-1* 1937; *Gold Is Where You Find It* 1938; *Jezebel* 1938; *Racket Busters* 1938; *Secrets of an Actress* 1938; *Dark Victory* 1939; *The Old Maid* 1939; *The Rains Came* 1939; *Wings of the Navy* 1939; *'Til We Meet Again* 1940; *Adventure in Diamonds* 1940; *The Fighting 69th* 1940; *The Man Who Talked Too Much* 1940; *South of Suez* 1940; *The Great Lie* 1941; *Honeymoon For Three* 1941; *International Lady* 1941; *They Dare Not Love* 1941; *The Gay Sisters* 1942; *In This Our Life* 1942; *Silver Queen* 1942; *Twin Beds* 1942; *You Can't Escape Forever* 1942; *Experiment Perilous* 1944; *The Affairs of Susan* 1945; *Lover Come Back* 1946; *My Reputation* 1946; *The Spiral Staircase* 1946; *Temptation* 1946; *Tomorrow Is Forever* 1946; *Christmas Eve* 1947; *The Corpse Came C.O.D.* 1947; *Out of the Blue* 1947; *Sinner's Holiday* 1947; *Slave Girl* 1947; *Angel on the Amazon* 1948; *Luxury Liner* 1948; *Bride For Sale* 1949; *Illegal Entry* 1949; *The Kid From Cleveland* 1949; *Red Canyon* 1949; *F.B.I. Girl* 1951; *Montana Belle* 1952; *Mexican Manhunt* 1953; *Tangier Incident* 1953; *Born Again* 1978.

Bresson, Robert • Director; also screenwriter. • Born Bromont-Lamothe, Puy-de-Dome, France, September 25, 1907. Bresson originally pursued a career as a painter but turned to film in the early 1930s, gaining his first experience as a script consultant on *C'était un musicien* (1933), directed by Frédéric Zelnick and Maurice Gleize. In between other, unexceptional assignments as a screenwriter, he made a medium-length film, the long-lost *Les Affaires publiques*, in 1934. During WWII, Bresson was a prisoner of war from June 1940 to April 1941—an experience which profoundly marked his subsequent work in the cinema.

Bresson made a stunning feature debut with *Les Anges du péché* (1943), scripted by him and with dialogue by Jean Giraudoux. A melodramatic tale of a convent novice who sacrifices her life to save the soul of a murderer, it nevertheless defined the thematic territory of grace and redemption which Bresson would continue to explore. Like *Les Anges*, *Les Dames du Bois de Boulogne* (1945) featured dramatic cinematography, atmospheric music and professional actors—all elements which Bresson would later shun in his quest to forge a purer cinematic art.

Bresson's next three films marked the development of his own personal, mature style. *Diary of a Country Priest* (1950) is an account, adapted from the 1936 novel by Georges Bernanos, of an awkward young priest who saves the souls of others while he himself is dying of stomach cancer. *A Man Escaped* (1956) is based on the real-life experiences of André Devigny, a French resistance fighter imprisoned by the Nazis. *Pickpocket* (1959) tells of a lonely young thief who finds redemption in love.

All three films are narrated in the first person and bear what are now known as the hallmarks of Bresson's work: a spare, abstract visual style which concentrates on objective details to create a sense of timelessness; natural sounds in place of mood-creating music; elliptical narrative structures which preclude suspense and invoke spiritual isolation; an absence of character psychology; and nonprofessional actors giving flat, expressionless "performances." ("What I am seeking is not so much expression by means of gesture, speech, mimicry, but expression by means of the rhythm and combination of images, by position, relation and number," Bresson explained.)

Perhaps the ultimate expression of Bresson's unique cinematic voice is *The Trial of Joan of Arc* (1962) which, with his films of the late 1950s, was much admired by the filmmakers of the New Wave. In the austere documenting of Joan's imprisonment and trial, physical objects—chains, stones, walls, windows—become metaphors for her spiritual isolation and sounds—the scratching of a pen during her hearing—contribute to the minimalist musicality of the experience.

In *Balthazar* and *Mouchette* (both 1966), a mule and a young girl, respectively, endure the indignities, cruelty and callousness of existence. Balthazar is exploited and mistreated by a series of owners before finding peace in a memorable death sequence, on a hillside surrounded by sheep. Mouchette drowns herself to escape the abuse and humiliation she suffers at the hands of her parents. (The film was Bresson's second to be adapted from the work of Bernanos.)

Une Femme douce (1969) tracks the failure of a marriage between an inquisitive, self-educated wife interested in the arts and archeology and a husband who values money and security. The wife takes her own life, marking the director's increasing concern with suicide; he went on to articulate the theme in such color films as *Four Nights of a Dreamer* (1971).

In *Lancelot du Lac* (1974), Bresson found his most fitting subject matter since *Joan of Arc*. Lancelot and the Knights of King Arthur undertake a fruitless search for the Holy Grail in an age of chivalry defined by clumsy, episodic bloodshed, cumbersome armor and jealous in-fighting. At the film's conclusion Lancelot's horse, an arrow impaled in its neck, surveys the human carnage, as if recognizing a futility and horror to which the humans are blind.

Bresson's last masterpiece was *L'Argent* (1983). Chance events lead to the arrest of Yvon, an oil delivery man, for using counterfeit bills palmed off on him by a store clerk (perjury and a bribe protect the guilty). Now unemployable, Yvon commits a crime. While in jail his daughter dies, his wife abandons him and he unsuccessfuly attempts suicide. Upon release Yvon kills the family of an old lady who shelters him in a horrific ax-murder, for which Bresson refuses to provide a motivation.

No filmmaker has had a darker vision of man's inhumanity to man, nor has portrayed it with such consistent and remarkable style. In 1975, Bresson published *Notes on Cinematography*, an apologia for his singular cinematic vision which argues that film is a blend of music and painting rather than—as traditionally understood—theater and photography. • *C'était un musicien* 1933 (sc,dial); *Les Affaires publiques (short)* 1934 (d,sc,ph,ed); *Courrier Sud* 1936 (sc,adapt); *Les Jumeaux de Brighton* 1936 (sc); *Les Anges du péché* 1943 (d,sc); *Les Dames du Bois de Boulogne* 1945 (d,sc,adapt); *Le Journal d'un Curée de Campagne/Diary of a Country Priest* 1950 (d,sc); *Un Condamné à mort s'est echappé/A Man Escaped* 1956 (d,sc,adapt,dial); *Pickpocket* 1959 (d,sc); *Le Procés de Jeanne d'Arc/The Trial of Joan of Arc* 1962 (d,sc); *Au Hasard, Balthazar/Balthazar* 1966 (d,sc); *Mouchette* 1966 (d,sc); *Une Femme douce* 1969 (d,sc); *Quatre nuits d'un rêveur/Four Nights of a Dreamer* 1971 (d,sc,English subtitles); *Lancelot du Lac* 1974 (d,sc); *Le Diable Probablement* 1977 (d,sc,dial); *L'Argent* 1983 (d,sc); *De Weg Naar Bresson* 1984 (a).

Brest, Martin • Director; also producer, screenwriter. • Born Bronx, NY, 1951. *Educ.* NYU (film); AFI, Los Angeles. After making an award-winning short while a student at NYU (*Hot Dogs for Gaugin* starring Danny DeVito), Brest wrote and directed his first feature, *Hot Tomorrows* (1977), during a fellowship program at the American Film Institute. Brest has proved a master of the comedy/adventure genre, scoring at the box-office with the Eddie Murphy vehicle *Beverly Hills Cop* (1984) and directing Robert De Niro in one of his first effective light-hearted roles, opposite Charles Grodin in *Midnight Run* (1988). • *Hot Tomorrows* 1977 (d,p,sc,ed); *Going in Style* 1979 (d,sc); *Fast Times at Ridgemont High* 1982 (a); *Beverly Hills Cop* 1984 (d); *Spies Like Us* 1985 (a); *Midnight Run* 1988 (d,p).

Brialy, Jean-Claude • Actor; also director, screenwriter. • Born Aumale, Algeria, March 30, 1933. *Educ.* Strasbourg University (philosophy); Strasbourg Conservatoire. Escaped a military career forced on him by his officer father thanks to a chance meeting, while still enlisted, with future director Philippe de Broca. Brialy went on to became a central actor of the French New Wave, appearing in films by Eric Rohmer, Jean-Luc Godard, Jacques Rivette and, particularly, Claude Chabrol; he turned in a masterful performance as the cynically demonic urbanite opposite Gérard Blain's country bumpkin in Chabrol's *The Cousins* (1959). Brialy's directorial efforts, beginning in 1971 with *Eglantine*, have proved competent but unexceptional. • *Le Coup du Berger (short)* 1956; *Tous les Garçons s'appèllent Patrick/Are Boys Are Called Patrick (short)* 1957; *Le Beau Serge* 1958; *Une Histoire d'Eau (short)* 1958; *Les Cousins/The Cousins* 1959; *Les Quatre cents coups/The 400 Blows* 1959; *Les Godelureaux* 1960; *Paris Nous Appartient/Paris Belongs to Us* 1960; *Une Femme est une femme/A Woman Is a Woman* 1961; *Das Brennende Gericht* 1962; *Cléo de 5 à 7/Cleo From 5 to 7* 1962; *Les Sept péchés capitaux/The Seven Deadly Sins* 1962; *Château en Suéde* 1963; *La Bonne Soupe* 1964; *La Ronde* 1964; *La Mandragola* 1966; *La Mariée était en noir/The Bride Wore Black* 1968; *Le Genou de Claire/Claire's Knee* 1970; *Eglantine* 1971 (d,sc); *Un Meurtre est un Meurtre* 1972; *Les Volets Clos* 1972 (d,sc); *L'Oiseau Rare* 1973 (a,d,sc); *Un Amour de pluie* 1974 (d,sc); *Comme un pot des fraises!* 1974; *Le Fantôme de la Liberté/The Phantom of Liberty* 1974; *Catherine et Cie/Catherine and Co.* 1975; *Les Oeufs Brouillés* 1975; *Les Onze Mille Vèrges* 1975; *L'Année Sainte* 1976; *Barocco* 1976; *Le Juge et l'assassin/The Judge and the Assassin* 1976; *Doppio Delitto* 1977; *Julie pot de colle* 1977; *Le Point de mire* 1977; *Robert et Robert* 1978; *Bobo Jacco* 1979; *Le Maître-Nageur* 1979; *L'Oeil du Maître* 1979; *La Banquière* 1980; *Les Uns et les autres/Bolero* 1981; *Edith et Marcel* 1982; *La Nuit de Varennes* 1982; *Un Bon petit diable* 1983 (d,sc); *Cap Canaille* 1983; *La Crime* 1983; *Le Démon dans L'Isle* 1983; *Papy Fait de la Résistance* 1983; *La Ragazza di Trieste* 1983; *Sarah* 1983; *Stella* 1983; *Pinot, Simple Flic* 1984; *Le Téléphone sonne toujours deux fois!!* 1984; *L'Effrontée* 1985; *Le Mariage du Siècle* 1985; *Le Quatrième Pouvoir* 1985; *Suivez mon regard* 1985; *Le Débutant* 1986; *Grand Guignol* 1986; *Inspector Lavardin* 1986; *Levy et Goliath* 1986; *Les Innocents* 1987; *Maladie d'amour* 1987; *Maschenka* 1987; *Le Moustachu* 1987; *Comédie d'été* 1989; *C'era un castello con 40 cani* 1990; *Faux et usage de faux* 1990; *La Femme fardée* 1990; *Ripoux Contre Ripoux* 1990; *S'en fout la mort* 1990.

Brickman, Marshall • Screenwriter, director; also producer. • Born Rio de Janeiro, Brazil, August 25, 1941. *Educ.* University of Wisconsin. Wrote for TV's "Candid Camera" (1966) and "The Tonight Show" (1966-70) before beginning his highly successful association with Woody Allen. Brickman co-wrote two of Allen's best-loved films, *Annie Hall* (1977) and *Manhattan* (1979), before branching out on his own with the overlooked, cynical comedy *Simon* (1980) and the thoughtful anti-nuclear thriller *The Manhattan Project* (1986). • *Sleeper* 1973 (sc); *Annie Hall* 1977 (sc) (**AABSC**); *Manhattan* 1979 (sc) (**AANBSC**); *Simon* 1980 (d,sc); *Lovesick* 1983 (d,sc); *The Manhattan Project* 1986 (d,p,sc); *Funny* 1988 (a,assistance); *That's Adequate* 1989 (a).

Brickman, Paul • Screenwriter, director; also producer. • Born Chicago, IL. *Educ.* Claremont Men's College, CA. Scenarist with a gift for small, offbeat films, notably Jonathan Demme's *Handle With Care/Citizens Band* (1977). Brickman made his directing debut, from his own script, with the slick summer hit *Risky Business* (1983) and followed it seven years later with a finely observed familial comedy-drama, *Men Don't Leave* (1990), based on the French film *La vie continue* (1982). • *The Bad News Bears in Breaking Training* 1977 (sc); *Handle With Care/Citizens Band* 1977 (assoc.p,sc); *Deal of the Century* 1983 (exec.p,sc); *Risky Business* 1983 (d,sc); *Men Don't Leave* 1990 (d,p,sc).

Bridges, Alan • Director • Born Liverpool, England, September 28, 1927. *Educ.* RADA, London. Filmmaker who has brought a stage director's feel for actors and a sophisticated understanding of the English class structure to bear on finely observed dramas like *The Hireling* (1973), which took the Palme d'Or at Cannes, and *The Shooting Party* (1984). Bridges originally made his name as one of Britian's foremost TV directors during the 1960s. • *Act of Murder* 1965 (d); *Invasion* 1966 (d); *The Hireling* 1973 (d); *Out of Season* 1975 (d); *Age of Innocence* 1977 (d); *La Petite fille en velours bleu* 1978 (d,sc); *The Return of the Soldier* 1982 (d); *The Shooting Party* 1984 (d).

Bridges, Beau • Actor • Born Lloyd Vernet Bridges III, Hollywood, CA, December 9, 1941. *Educ.* UCLA (theater arts); University of Hawaii. The eldest son of actor Lloyd Bridges, he played small juvenile roles in films including *Force of Evil* (1948) and contemplated a career in basketball while in college. Bridges appeared on several TV shows, including his father's "Sea Hunt" series, in the early 1960s and began landing film roles toward the end of the decade.

Although he proved himself a capable romantic lead, particularly in *The Landlord* (1970), it is in his more recent character roles that Bridges has really excelled. He gave an impeccable performance as a low-rent, polyester-clad nightclub entertainer opposite his brother Jeff—who is now the leading man of the family—in Steve Kloves's engaging 1989 drama, *The Fabulous Baker Boys*. Bridges directed the 1987 film *The Wild Pair*, in which he appeared opposite his father and his two sons, Casey and Dylan. • *Force of Evil* 1948; *No Minor Vices* 1948; *The Red Pony* 1949; *Zamba* 1949; *The Explosive Generation* 1961; *Village of the Giants* 1965; *The Incident* 1967; *For Love of Ivy* 1968; *Gaily, Gaily* 1969; *Adam's Woman* 1970; *The Landlord* 1970; *The Christian Licorice Store* 1971; *Child's Play* 1972; *Hammersmith Is Out* 1972; *Your Three Minutes Are Up* 1973; *Lovin' Molly* 1974; *The Other Side of the Mountain* 1974; *Dragonfly* 1975; *Swashbuckler* 1976; *Two-Minute Warning* 1976; *Greased Lightning* 1977; *Norma Rae* 1978; *The 5th Musketeer* 1979; *The Runner Stumbles* 1979; *Silver Dream Racer* 1980; *Honky Tonk Freeway* 1981; *Night Crossing* 1981; *Heart Like a Wheel* 1982; *Love Child* 1982; *The Hotel New Hampshire* 1984; *The Killing Time* 1987; *The Wild Pair* 1987 (a,d); *Seven Hours to Judgment* 1988 (a,d); *The Fabulous Baker Boys* 1989; *The Iron Triangle* 1989; *Signs of Life* 1989; *The Wizard* 1989; *Daddy's Dyin'...Who's Got the Will?* 1990.

Bridges, James • Director, screenwriter; also playwright, actor. • Born Paris, AR, February 3, 1936. *Educ.* Arkansas Teachers College; USC, Los Angeles. Began his career as an actor in the late 1950s, wrote numerous shows for TV (including over 15 episodes of "The Alfred Hitchcock Hour") and received his first feature writing credit in 1966, as co-writer of *The Appaloosa*. Bridges made his directing debut with *The Baby Maker* (1970), a finely observed film about a middle-class couple who hire a hippy to bear their child after the wife discovers she is infertile.

Bridges has since directed a number of superior pictures and is probably best known for *The China Syndrome* (1979), a powerful indictment of both the nuclear power industry and the electronic media starring Jane Fonda.

• *The Appaloosa* 1966 (sc); *Faces* 1968 (a); *The Baby Maker* 1970 (d,sc); *Colossus: The Forbin Project* 1970 (sc); *Women in Limbo* 1972 (sc); *The Paper Chase* 1973 (d,sc) **(AANBSC)**; *9/30/55* 1977 (d,sc); *The China Syndrome* 1979 (d,sc) **(AANBSC)**; *Urban Cowboy* 1980 (d,sc); *Mike's Murder* 1982 (d,sc); *Fire and Ice* 1983 (a); *Perfect* 1985 (d,p,sc); *Bright Lights, Big City* 1988 (d); *White Hunter, Black Heart* 1990 (sc).

Bridges, Jeff • Actor • Born Los Angeles, CA, December 4, 1949. *Educ.* Herbert Berghof Studio, New York. Made his first screen appearance at the age of four months, playing the infant in Jane Greer's arms in *The Company She Keeps* (1950). He appeared on TV's "Sea Hunt" with his father Lloyd Bridges eight years later and was an occasional performer, with his brother Beau, on "The Lloyd Bridges Show" in 1962.

Bridges emerged as a boyishly charming lead in the 1970s, earning an Oscar nomination for his engaging performance in *The Last Picture Show* (1971). He is primarily known for his alienated, disaffected characterizations—a struggling boxer in *Fat City* (1972), a middle-class drifter in *Cutter's Way* (1981)—though he was highly convincing as an optimistic, indomitable, all-American entrepreneur in Francis Ford Coppola's *Tucker: The Man and His Dream* (1988). In 1990 Bridges reprised his role as Duane Jackson in Peter Bogdanovich's disappointing sequel to *Picture Show, Texasville*. • *Halls of Anger* 1970; *The Last Picture Show* 1971 **(AANBSA)**; *Bad Company* 1972; *Fat City* 1972; *The Iceman Cometh* 1973; *The Last American Hero* 1973; *Lolly-Madonna XXX* 1973; *Rancho Deluxe* 1974; *Thunderbolt And Lightfoot* 1974 **(AANBSA)**; *Hearts of the West* 1975; *Stay Hungry* 1975; *King Kong* 1976; *Somebody Killed Her Husband* 1978; *American Success Company* 1979; *Winter Kills* 1979; *Heaven's Gate* 1980; *Cutter's Way* 1981; *Kiss Me Goodbye* 1982; *The Last Unicorn* 1982; *Tron* 1982; *Against All Odds* 1983; *Starman* 1984 **(AANBA)**; *Jagged Edge* 1985; *8 Million Ways to Die* 1986; *The Morning After* 1986; *Nadine* 1987; *Tucker: The Man and His Dream* 1988; *The Fabulous Baker Boys* 1989; *See You in the Morning* 1989; *Texasville* 1990; *The Fisher King* 1991.

Bridges, Lloyd • Actor • Born Lloyd Vernet Bridges, San Leandro, CA, January 15, 1913. *Educ.* UCLA (political science). Lanky performer, mostly in supporting roles in westerns and assorted action films. Bridges is best known for the TV series "Sea Hunt" (1957-61) and "The Lloyd Bridges Show" (1962-63). Father of actors Beau and Jeff Bridges. • *Harmon of Michigan* 1941; *The Lone Wolf Takes a Chance* 1941; *The Royal Mounted Patrol* 1941; *Two Latins From Manhattan* 1941; *Alias Boston Blackie* 1942; *Atlantic Convoy* 1942; *Blondie Goes to College* 1942; *Canal Zone* 1942; *Commandos Strike at Dawn* 1942; *Flight Lieutenant* 1942; *North of the Rockies* 1942; *Pardon My Gun* 1942; *Riders of the Northland* 1942; *Shut My Big Mouth* 1942; *The Spirit of Stanford* 1942; *The Crime Doctor's Strangest Case* 1943; *Hail to the Rangers* 1943; *The Heat's on* 1943; *Passport to Suez* 1943; *Sahara* 1943; *Louisiana Hayride* 1944; *The Master Race* 1944; *Saddle Leather Law* 1944; *She's a Soldier Too* 1944; *Miss Susie Slagle's* 1945; *Secret Agent X-9* 1945; *Strange Confession* 1945; *A Walk in the Sun* 1945; *Abilene Town* 1946; *Canyon Passage* 1946; *Ramrod* 1947; *The Trouble With Women* 1947; *Unconquered* 1947; *16 Fathoms Deep* 1948; *Moonrise* 1948; *Secret Service Investigator* 1948; *Calamity Jane and Sam Bass* 1949; *Hideout* 1949; *Home of the Brave* 1949; *Red Canyon* 1949; *Trapped* 1949; *Colt .45* 1950; *Rocket Ship X-M* 1950; *The Sound of Fury* 1950; *The White Tower* 1950; *Little Big Horn* 1951; *Three Steps North* 1951; *The Whistle at Eaton Falls* 1951; *High Noon* 1952; *Last of the Comanches* 1952; *Plymouth Adventure* 1952; *City of Bad Men* 1953; *The Kid From Left Field* 1953; *The Limping Man* 1953; *The Tall Texan* 1953; *Deadly Game* 1954; *Pride of the Blue Grass* 1954; *Apache Woman* 1955; *Wichita* 1955; *The Rainmaker* 1956; *Wetbacks* 1956; *Ride Out For Revenge* 1957; *The Goddess* 1958; *Around the World Under the Sea* 1966; *Attack on the Iron Coast* 1968; *The Daring Game* 1968; *The Happy Ending* 1969; *To Find a Man* 1972; *Deliver Us From Evil* 1975; *The 5th Musketeer* 1979; *Bear Island* 1979; *Mission Galactica: The Cylon Attack* 1979; *Airplane!* 1980; *Airplane II: The Sequel* 1982; *Weekend Warriors* 1986; *Tucker: The Man and His Dream* 1988; *Cousins* 1989; *Joe Versus the Volcano* 1990.

Brimley, Wilford • Actor • Born Salt Lake City, UT, September 27, 1934. Stout, bespectacled actor who specializes in endearing curmudgeons. • *The China Syndrome* 1979; *The Electric Horseman* 1979; *Borderline* 1980; *Brubaker* 1980; *Absence of Malice* 1981; *Death Valley* 1981; *Tender Mercies* 1982; *The Thing* 1982; *Tough Enough* 1982; *10 to Midnight* 1983; *High Road to China* 1983; *The Stone Boy* 1983; *Country* 1984; *Harry & Son* 1984; *The Hotel New Hampshire* 1984; *The Natural* 1984; *Cocoon* 1985; *Remo Williams: The Adventure Begins...* 1985; *American Justice* 1986; *End of the Line* 1987; *Shadows on the Wall* 1987; *Cocoon: The Return* 1988.

Broca, Philippe de • Director; also screenwriter, producer. • Born Paris, March 15, 1933. *Educ.* Ecole Technique de Photographie et de Cinématographie, Paris. An assistant to New Wave directors François Truffaut and Claude Chabrol before making his directorial debut in 1960 with *The Love Game*. De Broca's best known film remains *King of Hearts* (1966), a whimsical fable about a WWI soldier (Alan Bates) in a French town populated exclusively by former inmates of the insane asylum. *Hearts* was the first of De Broca's films to be produced under his own Fildebroc production banner. • *Le Beau Serge* 1958 (a,ad); *A bout de souffle/Breathless* 1959 (a); *Les Cousins* 1959 (ad); *A Double Tour/Web of Passion* 1959 (ad); *Le Jeux de l'Amour/The Love Game* 1960 (d,sc); *L'Amant de Cinq Jours* 1961 (d,sc); *Cartouche* 1962 (a,d,sc); *Le Farceur* 1962 (d,sc); *Les Sept péchés capitaux/The Seven Deadly Sins* 1962 (d); *Les Veinards* 1962 (d,sc—"La Vedette"); *L'Homme de Rio/That Man From Rio* 1964 (d,sc); *Un Monsieur de Compagnie* 1964 (d,sc); *Les Tribulations d'un Chinois en Chine* 1965 (d,sc); *Le Roi de Coeur/King of Hearts* 1966 (d,p); *Le Plus vieux métier du monde* 1967 (d); *Le Diable par la Queue* 1969 (d,sc); *Caprices de Marie* 1970 (d,sc); *La Poudre d'escampette* 1971 (d,sc); *Chère Louise* 1972 (d); *Le Magnifique* 1974 (d); *L'Incorrigible* 1975 (d,sc); *Julie pot de colle* 1977 (d); *Tendre Poulet/Dear Inspector* 1977 (d,sc); *Le Cavaleur* 1978 (d,sc); *On a volé la cuisse de Jupiter/Jupiter's Thigh* 1979 (d,sc); *Psy* 1981 (d); *L'Africain* 1983 (d,sc); *Louisiane* 1984 (d); *La Gitane* 1985 (d,sc,dial); *Chouans!* 1988 (d,sc); *Sheherazade* 1990 (d,sc).

Broccoli, Albert R. • Producer • Born Long Island, NY, April 5, 1909. *Educ.* CCNY. Former agronomist; moved to London in 1951 where, ten years later, he co-produced the first of the "James Bond" films with Harry Saltzman. • *The Red Beret* 1953 (p); *The Black Knight* 1954 (p); *Hell Below Zero* 1954 (p); *The Cockleshell Heroes* 1955 (p); *Prize of Gold* 1955 (p); *Odongo* 1956 (exec.p); *Safari* 1956 (exec.p); *Zarak* 1956 (p); *Fire Down Below* 1957 (p); *High Flight* 1957 (p); *Interpol* 1957 (p); *The Man Inside* 1958 (p); *No Time to Die* 1958 (p); *The Bandit of Zhobe* 1959 (p); *Killers of Kilimanjaro* 1960 (p); *Dr. No* 1962 (p); *Call Me Bwana* 1963 (p); *From Russia With Love* 1963 (p); *Goldfinger* 1964 (p); *Thunderball* 1965 (p); *You Only Live Twice* 1967 (p); *Chitty Chitty Bang Bang* 1968 (p); *On Her Majesty's Secret Service* 1969 (p); *Diamonds Are Forever* 1971 (p); *Live and Let Die* 1973 (p); *The Man With the Golden Gun* 1974 (p); *The Spy Who Loved Me* 1977 (p); *Moonraker* 1979 (p); *For Your Eyes Only* 1981 (p); *Octopussy* 1983 (p); *A View to a Kill* 1985 (p); *The Living Daylights* 1987 (p); *Licence to Kill* 1989 (p).

Brocka, Lino • Director • Born San Jose, Nueva Ecija, Philippines, 1940. *Educ.* University of the Philippines. The best known of all Filipino filmmakers, Lino Brocka has made some 50 movies in a career spanning 20 years. He has used his standing as a successful commercial director as a platform from which to make the more personal and political films which are closest to his heart. Brocka's career can be divided into three phases, with the director establishing a foothold in the industry 1970-72, struggling for independence 1974-76 and coexisting with the commercial system (1977 to the present).

Brocka started his creer as a script supervisor on Eddie Romero's Filipino/American co-productions. He made a successful directorial debut with *Wanted: Perfect Mother* (1970), based on a "komiks" novel (a popular story released in illustrated, serialized form). Brocka and his producers, Lea Productions, followed this up over the next two years with eight more adaptations of "komiks" material that Brocka attempted to translate into touching, if not meaningful, melodrama. Having established a reputation as a reliable commercial director, Brocka then decided he was through with Lea Productions. After a self-imposed "retreat" of almost two years, he returned to the industry in 1974 at the helm of his own production company, CineManila.

Brocka's status as an important Filipino director was secured with *Maynila, Sa Mga Kuko Ng Liwanag/Manila, in the Claws of Light* (1975). The film was made for Cinema Artists, a company set up by Mike de Leon, who would later be a leading filmmaker in his own right. Ostensibly the story of two lovers, Julio and Ligaya, *Maynila* is also a powerful critique of exploitation; although Julio experiences injustice while searching for Ligaya on the streets of Manila, he is only capable of perceiving it as a personal problem. His tragedy lies in his failure to realize that "his" problems are symptomatic of the social, political and economic ills of the country at large. Julio finally takes vengeance into his own hands, not realizing that collective action (suggested by a political street demonstration) is a more effective weapon in the struggle against exploitation.

Brocka was able to exercise considerable freedom in choosing material for his mid-70s films: *Tinimbang Ka ngunit Kulang/You Are Weighed in the Balance But Are Found Wanting*; *Tatlo, Dalawa, Isa/Three, Two, One* (both 1974); *Lunes, Martes, Miyerkules, Huwebes, Biyernes, Sabado, Linggo/Monday, Tuesday, Wednesday, Thursday, Friday, Saturday, Sunday*; and *Insiang* (both 1976). *Insiang*, a story of passion, vengeance and crime in the slums, introduced Brocka to an international audience at the 1978 Cannes Film Festival.

Brocka's relative independence from commercial constraints was short-lived. CineManila ended in financial disaster when its 1976 production, *Mortal* (directed by Brocka screenwriter Mario O'Hara), got embroiled in a court case and mortally wounded the company. The third phase of Brocka's career has been characterized by an uneasy co-existence with the commerical system. For every film he cherishes making, Brocka always admits with resignation that he has to make three to five highly commercial ones.

Several of Brocka's more ambitious features have revisited the theme of exploitation he explored so intensely in *Maynila*. *Jaguar* (1980) deals with a worker's subservience to his boss; *Bona* (1981) documents the irrational and slavish submission of a fan to her idol; *Bayan Ko* (1984) dramatizes the exploitation of factory workers, as *Macho Dancer* (1988) does that of gay bar dancers. Like Julio in *Maynila*, these characters attempt to confront their problems individually and they tend to resort to violence as the ultimate solution. Brocka, however, shows the futility of the individual acting alone: Julio in *Maynila* is lynched by a mob; Poldo in *Jaguar* is jailed; Bona, we presume, will be punished; Turing in *Bayan Ko* is shot to death; and while Pol, in *Macho Dancer*, gets away with killing one police officer, another soon takes over the territory. Brocka has also shown the madness of violence in the hands of the military and vigilantes, as in *Ora Pro Nobis/Fight for Us/Les Insoumis* (1989). What he has not yet made clear is his position on revolutionary violence. The leftist movement and the National People's Army are only weakly alluded to in several of his films.

Brocka tapped foreign sources for production funds on *Bayan Ko* and *Fight for Us*, and there is some hope that a stronger financial base and a wider international market might mean a new phase in his prolific career—ideally, one that is less bounded by the constraints of the commercial Filipino industry. CDM • *Wanted: Perfect Mother* 1970 (d); *Tatlo, Dalawa, Isa/ Three, Two, One* 1974 (d); *Tinimbang ka ngunit kulang/You Are Weighed in the Balance But Are Found Wanting* 1974 (d); *Maynila, Sa Mga Kuko Ng Liwanag/Manila, in the Claws of Light* 1975 (d); *Insiang* 1976 (d); *Lunes, Martes Miyerkules, Huwebes, Biyernes, Sabado, Linggo/Monday, Tuesday, Wednesday, Thursday, Friday, Saturday, Sunday* 1976 (d); *Maynila: Jaguar/Jaguar* 1980 (d); *Bona* 1981 (d); *Bayan Ko-Kapit Sa Patalim* 1984 (d); *Signed, Lino Brocka* 1987 (a); *Macho Dancer* 1988 (d); *Ora Pro Nobis/Fight For Us/Les Insoumis* 1989 (d).

Broderick, Matthew • Actor • Born New York, NY, August 21, 1962. Talented, stage-trained young lead of the 1980s who has demonstrated a gift for both comedy and drama, scoring successes as the computer wiz caught up in nuclear intrigue in *WarGames* (1983), as Neil Simon's alter ego in *Biloxi Blues* (1988) and as a doomed Union commander in the fine Civil War drama *Glory* (1989). Son of late actor James Broderick. • *Max Dugan Returns* 1982; *WarGames* 1983; *1918* 1985; *Ladyhawke* 1985; *Ferris Bueller's Day Off* 1986; *On Valentine's Day* 1986; *Project X* 1987; *Biloxi Blues* 1988; *Torch Song Trilogy* 1988; *Family Business* 1989; *Glory* 1989; *The Freshman* 1990.

Bronson, Charles • *aka* Charles Buchinski, Charles Buchinsky • Actor • Born Charles Bunchinsky, Ehrenfield, PA, November 3, 1921. *Educ.* Pasadena Playhouse. Leathery, stoical leading man, often in action pictures directed by J. Lee Thompson. Bronson was memorable as the taciturn gunslinger in Sergio Leone's epic *Once Upon a Time in the West* (1969), although he is best known as the vengeance-seeking vigilante in the "Death Wish" series. Married to actress Jill Ireland until her death in May 1990. • *U.S.S. Tea Kettle* 1951; *Bloodhounds of Broadway* 1952; *Diplomatic Courier* 1952; *My Six Convicts* 1952; *Pat and Mike* 1952; *Red Skies of Montana* 1952; *Miss Sadie Thompson* 1953; *Apache* 1954; *Crime Wave* 1954; *Drum Beat* 1954; *Riding Shotgun* 1954; *Tennessee Champ* 1954; *Vera Cruz* 1954; *Big House, U.S.A.* 1955; *Target Zero* 1955; *Jubal* 1956; *Run of the Arrow* 1957; *Gang War* 1958; *Machine Gun Kelly* 1958; *Showdown at Boot Hill* 1958; *When Hell Broke Loose* 1958; *Never So Few* 1959; *The Magnificent Seven* 1960; *Master of the World* 1961; *A Thunder of Drums* 1961; *X—15* 1961; *Kid Galahad* 1962; *Four For Texas* 1963; *The Great Escape* 1963; *Battle of the Bulge* 1965; *The Sandpiper* 1965; *This Property Is Condemned* 1966; *The Dirty Dozen* 1967; *Guns For San Sebastian* 1968; *Villa Rides* 1968; *C'era una Volta il West/Once Upon a Time in the West* 1969; *Le Passager de la Pluie/Rider on the Rain* 1970; *Twinky* 1970; *Violent City* 1970; *De la Part des Copains/Cold Sweat* 1971; *Quelq'un derrière la porte/Someone Behind the Door* 1971; *Soleil Rouge/Red Sun* 1971; *Chato's Land* 1972; *The Mechanic* 1972; *Valachi Papers* 1972; *The Stone Killer* 1973; *Valdez il Mezzosangue* 1973; *Death Wish* 1974; *Mr. Majestyk* 1974; *Breakheart Pass* 1975; *Breakout* 1975; *Hard Times* 1975; *From Noon Till Three* 1976; *St. Ives* 1976; *Telefon* 1977; *The White Buffalo* 1977; *Love and Bullets* 1979; *Borderline* 1980; *Caboblanco* 1980; *Death Hunt* 1981; *Death Wish II* 1981; *10 to Midnight* 1983; *The Evil That Men Do* 1984; *Death Wish 3* 1985; *Murphy's Law* 1986; *Assassination* 1987; *Death Wish 4: The Crackdown* 1987; *Messenger of Death* 1988; *Kinjite* 1989.

Brook, Clive • Actor • Born Clifford Hardman Brook, London, June 1, 1887; died 1974. Distinguished English lead who began his acting career on the London stage after having been invalided out of the rifle corps during WWI. Brook was in Hollywood from 1924 to 1934 and is probably best known to US audiences for his performance as a world-weary doctor opposite Marlene Dietrich in *Shanghai Express* (1932). His daughter Faith, by actress Mildred Evelyn, is an actress. • *Christine of the Hungry Heart* 1924; *Human Desires* 1924; *The Mirage* 1924; *The Recoil* 1924; *Compromise* 1925; *Declassée* 1925; *Enticement* 1925; *The Home Maker* 1925; *If Marriage Fails* 1925; *Playing With Souls* 1925; *The Pleasure Buyers* 1925; *Seven Sinners* 1925; *The Woman Hater* 1925; *For Alimony Only* 1926; *The Popular Sin* 1926; *Three Faces East* 1926; *When Love Grows Cold* 1926; *Why Girls Go Back Home* 1926; *You Never Know Women* 1926; *Afraid to Love* 1927; *Barbed Wire* 1927; *The Devil Danger* 1927; *French Dressing* 1927; *Hula* 1927; *Underworld* 1927; *Forgotten Faces* 1928; *Midnight Madness* 1928; *The Perfect Crime* 1928; *The Yellow Lily* 1928; *Charming Sinners* 1929; *A Dangerous Woman* 1929; *The Four Feathers* 1929; *Interference* 1929; *The Laughing Lady* 1929; *Anybody's Woman* 1930; *Paramount on Parade* 1930; *Slightly Scarlet* 1930; *Sweethearts and Wives* 1930; *24 Hours* 1931; *East Lynne* 1931; *Husband's Holiday* 1931; *The Lawyer's Secret* 1931; *Scandal Sheet* 1931; *Silence* 1931; *Tarnished Lady* 1931; *The Man From Yesterday* 1932; *The Night of June 13* 1932; *Shanghai Express* 1932; *Sherlock Holmes* 1932; *Cavalcade* 1933; *If I Were Free* 1933; *Midnight Club* 1933; *Gallant Lady* 1934; *Let's Try Again* 1934; *Where Sinners Meet* 1934; *Dressed to Thrill* 1935; *The Lonely Road* 1936; *Love in Exile* 1936; *Action For Slander* 1937; *The Ware Case* 1938; *Return to Yesterday* 1940; *The List of Adrian Messenger* 1963.

Brook, Sir Peter • Director; also screenwriter. • Born Peter Brook, London, March 21, 1925. *Educ.* Magdalen College, Oxford. Renowned stage director whose provocative adaptations from theater and literature—from *Marat/Sade* (1966) to *King Lear* (1971) to an economical version of the Sanskrit epic *The Mahabarata* (1989)—have been critically acclaimed on both sides of the Atlantic.

Brook made an amateur feature-length film, *The Sentimental Journey*, in 1943 and crafted training films for the British Army in the last years of WWII; his first professional assignment as a screen director came with an energetic adaptation of *The Beggar's Opera* (1953), starring Laurence Olivier. • *The Sentimental Journey* 1943 (d); *The Beggar's Opera* 1953 (d); *Moderato Cantabile* 1960 (d); *Lord of the Flies* 1963 (d,sc,ed); *The Persecution and Assassination of Jean-Paul Marat As Performed By the Inmates of the Asylum of Charenton Under the Direction of the Marquis de Sade/Marat/Sade* 1966 (d); *Tell Me Lies* 1967 (d); *King Lear* 1971 (d,sc); *Meetings With Remarkable Men* 1979 (d,sc); *La Tragédie de Carmen* 1983 (d,sc); *Un Amour de Swann/Swann in Love* 1984 (sc); *Jean-Louis Barrault—A Man of the Theater* 1984 (a); *Mama's Pushcart: Ellen Stewart and 25 Years of La Mama Etc.* 1988 (a); *The Mahabharata* 1989 (adapt,d).

Brooks, Albert • Actor, director; also screenwriter. • Born Albert Einstein, Los Angeles, CA, July 22, 1947. *Educ.* Carnegie Institute of Technology, Pittsburgh, PA. Son of comedian Harry Einstein, and considered one of the wittiest, most incisive performers in movies today.

Brooks made his comic debut with the satiric parody LP, *A Star Is Bought* (1976), a catalogue of radio modes, from contemporary call-in shows to 1940s, Jack Benny-style comedy. Playing most of the roles himself, he quickly earned the sobriquet "comedian's comedian."

As a director, Brooks's films strike an effective balance between humor and social criticism, as evidenced in *Lost in America* (1985), a meticulously observed satire about disillusioned yuppies who take to the road in an ill-fated attempt to "find themselves." He is probably best known, however, as the talented but luckless TV journalist in James L. Brooks's *Broadcast News* (1987). • *Taxi Driver* 1976 (a); *Real Life* 1978 (a,d,sc); *Private Benjamin* 1980 (a); *Modern Romance* 1981 (a,d,sc); *Twilight Zone—the Movie* 1983 (a); *Unfaithfully Yours* 1983 (a); *Lost in America* 1985 (a,d,sc); *Broadcast News* 1987 (a) **(AANBSA)**; *Defending Your Life* 1991 (a,d,sc).

Brooks, James L. • Director, producer; also screenwriter. • Born North Bergen, NJ, May 9, 1940. *Educ.* NYU. Created such acclaimed series as "Room 222" (1969-74), "The Mary Tyler Moore Show" (1970-77) and "Taxi" (1978-83) before making his feature directorial debut with the Oscar-winning *Terms of Endearment* (1983), which he also wrote and produced. Brooks's neatly dovetailed storylines and clearly defined characters, the hallmarks of his TV background, have earned him popular and critical acclaim on the big screen. • *Real Life* 1978 (a); *Starting Over* 1979 (p,sc); *Modern Romance* 1981 (a); *Terms of Endearment* 1983 (d,p,sc) **(AABP,AABD,AABSC)**; *Broadcast News* 1987 (d,p,sc) **(AANBP,AANBSC)**; *Big* 1988 (p); *Say Anything* 1989 (exec.p); *The War of the Roses* 1989 (p).

Brooks, Louise • Actress; also author, critic. • Born Cherryvale, KS, November 14, 1906; died August 8, 1985, Rochester, NY. After stints as a Denishawn dancer (1922-24) and a glorified showgirl in both the *George White Scandals* (1924) and *Ziegfeld Follies* (1925), the alluring, precocious Brooks eased into films and quickly distinguished herself as one of the screen's great beauties.

When a series of lackluster roles failed to establish her as a major star however, Brooks—whose highly publicized social life was distinctly at odds with her penchant for reading Schopenhauer between takes—left Hollywood and, at the invitation of G.W. Pabst, headed for Germany.

It was under Pabst's guidance, in the twilight of the silent era, that Brooks gave two performances which helped redefine the art of screen acting: as the amoral Lulu in *Pandora's Box* and shortly thereafter as Thymiane in *The Diary of a Lost Girl* (both 1929). Both films flopped in the US, however, and Brooks, whose increasingly sporadic film career was over by 1940, began a gradual, tragic slide into oblivion.

The critical rediscovery of Brooks's work began during the "60 Ans de Cinéma" exhibition at the Musée National d'Art Moderne in 1955, when Henri Langlois issued the memorable rallying cry: "There is no Garbo! There is no Dietrich! There is only Louise Brooks!"

With the help of figures such as film historian James Card and former lover William S. Paley, the destitute Brooks was relocated to Rochester, New York, where her second career, as an acerbic, perceptive film essayist, began in earnest.

The two greatest boosts to the enduring cult of Louise Brooks were the appearance of Kenneth Tynan's celebrated *New Yorker* profile, "The Girl in the Black Helmet," in 1979, followed by the publication, to lavish praise, of Brooks's collected writings, *Lulu in Hollywood*, in 1982. JMM • *The Street of Forgotten Men* 1925; *The American Venus* 1926; *It's the Old Army Game* 1926; *Just Another Blonde* 1926; *Love 'Em and Leave 'Em* 1926; *The Show-Off* 1926; *A Social Celebrity* 1926; *The City Gone Wild* 1927; *Evening Clothes* 1927; *Now We're in the Air* 1927; *Rolled Stockings* 1927; *Beggars of Life* 1928; *Buchse der Pandora/Pandora's Box* 1928; *A Girl in Every Port* 1928; *The Canary Murder Case* 1929; *Das Tagebuch einer Verlorenen/The Diary of a Lost Girl* 1929; *Prix de Beauté* 1930; *Windy Riley Goes to Hollywood (short)* 1930; *God's Gift to Women* 1931; *It Pays to Advertise* 1931; *The Public Enemy* 1931; *The Steel Highway* 1931; *Empty Saddles* 1936; *King of Gamblers* 1937; *When You're in Love* 1937; *Overland Stage Raiders* 1938.

Brooks, Mel • Director; also actor, screenwriter, producer. • Born Melvin Kaminsky, Brooklyn, NY, June 28, 1926. Former stand-up comic who, together with Woody Allen and Bill Cosby, set the stage in the 1960s for the entire post-vaudeville, TV generation of comedians. While Allen was personal and self-deprecating and Cosby eschewed shtick in favor of witty commentary, Brooks—often working with Carl Reiner—embraced the craziness at the root of all ethnic vaudeville and reshaped it for decades to come. He was a saner Lenny Bruce, bringing high anxiety down to earth, where we could deal with it.

Brooks graduated from TV writer ("Your Show of Shows") to successful series creator ("Get Smart") before breaking into features with *The Producers* (1967), which set the zany, comedic tone of all his subsequent films. His two greatest successes, *Blazing Saddles* and *Young Frankenstein* (both 1974), were broad send-ups of the western and horror genres, respectively. As with all great comic filmmakers—Chaplin, Keaton, Lloyd, Tati, Allen—the persona surpasses the mise-en-scène, no matter how inventive it is.

His production company, BrooksFilms, Ltd. formed in 1979, has been responsible for such diverse works as David Lynch's *The Elephant Man* (1980), Graeme Clifford's *Frances* (1982) and David Cronenberg's *The Fly* (1986). Brooks has been married since 1964 to actress Anne Bancroft, opposite whom he starred in *To Be or Not to Be* (1983). • *New Faces* 1954 (sc,sketches); *The Producers* 1967 (d,sc) **(AABSC)**; *Putney Swope* 1969 (a); *The Twelve Chairs* 1970 (a,d,sc); *Shinbone Alley* 1971 (from book); *Blazing Saddles* 1974 (a,d,sc,song) **(AANBS)**; *Young Frankenstein* 1974 (d,sc) **(AANBSC)**; *Silent Movie* 1976 (a,d,sc); *High Anxiety* 1977 (a,d,p,sc,songs); *The Muppet Movie* 1979 (a); *The Elephant Man* 1980 (p); *The Nude Bomb* 1980 (from characters "Get Smart"); *History of the World Part I* 1981 (a,d,p,sc,songs); *Frances* 1982 (p); *To Be or Not to Be* 1983 (a,p,songs); *Sunset People* 1984 (a); *The Doctor and the Devils* 1985 (exec.p); *84 Charing Cross Road* 1986 (exec.p); *The Fly* 1986 (exec.p); *Solarbabies* 1986 (exec.p); *Spaceballs* 1987 (a,d,p,sc,song); *Look Who's Talking Too* 1990 (a); *Life Stinks* 1991 (a,d,p,sc,story).

Brooks, Richard • Director, screenwriter; also producer. • Born Philadelphia, PA, May 18, 1912. *Educ.* Temple University, Philadelphia. Former radio journalist and screenwriter who made his directorial debut in 1950 with the political thriller, *Crisis*. Brooks turned out a number of taut, male-oriented features before landing in the spotlight with the violent schoolroom drama, *Blackboard Jungle* (1955). He consolidated his position in the front rank of Hollywood directors with several fine literary adaptations, including his superb versions of the Tennessee Williams plays, *Cat on a Hot Tin Roof* (1958) and *Sweet Bird of Youth* (1962), and a suitably noirish treatment of Truman Capote's *In Cold Blood* (1967). Brooks's career tailed off in the 1970s, though *Looking For Mr. Goodbar* (1977) was praised for a bravura central performance by Diane Keaton. • *White Savage* 1943 (sc); *Cobra Woman* 1944 (sc); *My Best Gal* 1944 (story); *Swell Guy* 1946 (sc); *Brute Force* 1947 (sc); *Crossfire* 1947 (from novel *The Brick Foxhole*); *Key Largo* 1948 (sc); *To the Victor* 1948 (sc,story); *Any Number Can Play* 1949 (sc); *Crisis* 1950 (d,sc); *Mystery Street* 1950 (sc); *The Light Touch* 1951 (d,sc); *Storm Warning* 1951 (sc,story); *Deadline U.S.A.* 1952 (d,sc,story); *Battle Circus* 1953 (d,sc); *Take the High Ground* 1953 (d); *Flame and the Flesh* 1954 (d); *The Last Time I Saw Paris* 1954 (d,sc); *Blackboard Jungle* 1955 (d,sc) **(AANBSC)**; *The Last Hunt* 1955 (d,sc); *The Catered Affair* 1956 (d); *Something of Value* 1957 (d,sc); *The Brothers Karamazov* 1958 (d,sc); *Cat on a Hot Tin Roof* 1958 (d,sc) **(AANBD,AANBSC)**; *Elmer Gantry* 1960 (d,sc) **(AABSC)**; *Sweet Bird of Youth* 1962 (d,sc); *Lord Jim* 1965 (d,sc); *The Professionals* 1966 (d,p,sc) **(AANBD,AANBSC)**; *In Cold Blood* 1967 (d,sc) **(AANBD,AANBSC)**; *The Happy Ending* 1969 (d,p,sc); *$* 1971 (d,sc); *Bite the Bullet* 1975 (d,p,sc); *Looking For Mr. Goodbar* 1977 (d,sc); *Wrong Is Right* 1982 (d,p,sc); *Fever Pitch* 1985 (d,sc); *50 Years of Action!* 1986 (a); *Listen Up* 1990 (a).

Brown, Blair • Actress • Born Washington, DC, 1948. *Educ.* National Theater School of Canada. Attractive leading lady who began her stage career with the Canadian Stratford Shakespeare Festival and was an established actress in New York City when she made her screen debut in Robert Aldrich's *The Choirboys* (1977). Although her screen roles have been sporadic, Brown has enjoyed substantial success on TV as the title character of the popular series, "The Days and Nights of Molly Dodd" (1987-91). Divorced from actor Richard Jordan. • *The Choirboys* 1977; *Altered States* 1980; *One-Trick Pony* 1980; *Continental Divide* 1981; *A Flash of Green* 1985; *Stealing Home* 1988; *Strapless* 1989.

Brown, Bryan • Actor • Born Sydney, 1947. Rugged, commanding Australian lead who first received widespread acclaim for his performance in *Breaker Morant* (1980). Brown enjoyed mainstream American success with *F/X* (1986) and the TV miniseries "The Thorn Birds." Married to actress Rachel Ward. • *The Love Letters From Teralba Road* 1977; *The Chant of Jimmie Blacksmith* 1978; *The Irishman* 1978; *Money Movers* 1978; *Newsfront* 1978; *Cathy's Child* 1979; *The Odd Angry Shot* 1979; *Palm Beach* 1979; *Blood Money* 1980; *Breaker Morant* 1980; *Stir* 1980; *The Winter of Our Dreams* 1981; *Far East* 1982; *Give My Regards to Broad Street* 1983; *Parker* 1984; *The Empty Beach* 1985; *Rebel* 1985; *F/X* 1986; *The Good Wife* 1986; *Tai-Pan* 1986; *Cocktail* 1988; *Gorillas in the Mist* 1988; *Blood Oath* 1990; *F/X 2* 1991; *Sweet Talker* 1991 (a,p).

Brown, Clarence • Director; also producer. • Born Clinton, MA, May 10, 1890; died August 17 1987, Santa Monica, CA. *Educ.* University of Tennessee (engineering). Distinguished figure whose good taste and style characterized MGM's output from the late 1920s until his retirement in 1953; Greta Garbo's preferred director. • *The Great Redeemer* 1920 (d); *The Last of the Mohicans* 1920 (d); *The Foolish Matrons* 1921 (d); *The Light in the Dark* 1922 (d,sc); *The Acquittal* 1923 (d); *Don't Marry For Money* 1923 (d); *Butterfly* 1924 (d); *The Signal Tower* 1924 (a,d); *Smouldering Fires* 1924 (d); *The Eagle* 1925 (d); *The Goose Woman* 1925 (d); *Kiki* 1926 (d); *Flesh and the Devil* 1927 (d); *The Trail of '98* 1928 (d,p); *A Woman of Affairs* 1928 (d); *Navy Blues* 1929 (d); *Wonder of Women* 1929 (d,p); *Anna Christie* 1930 (d,p) **(AANBD)**; *Romance* 1930 (d) **(AANBD)**; *A Free Soul* 1931 (d,p) **(AANBD)**; *Inspiration* 1931 (d,p); *The Possessed* 1931 (d,p); *Emma* 1932 (d,p); *Letty Lynton* 1932 (d,p); *The Son-Daughter* 1932 (d); *Looking Forward* 1933 (d,p); *Night Flight* 1933 (d); *Chained* 1934 (d); *Fifteen Wives* 1934 (a); *Sadie McKee* 1934 (d); *Ah, Wilderness!* 1935 (d); *Anna Karenina* 1935 (d,p); *The Gorgeous Hussy* 1936 (d); *Wife vs. Secretary* 1936 (d); *Conquest* 1937 (d); *Of Human Hearts* 1938 (d); *Idiot's Delight* 1939 (d); *The Rains Came* 1939 (d); *Edison, the Man* 1940 (d); *Come Live With Me* 1941 (d,p); *They Met in Bombay* 1941 (d); *The Human Comedy* 1943 (d,p) **(AANBD)**; *National Velvet* 1944 (d) **(AANBD)**; *The White Cliffs of Dover* 1944 (d); *The Yearling* 1946 (d) **(AANBD)**; *Song of Love* 1947 (d,p); *Intruder in the Dust* 1949 (d,p); *The Secret Garden* 1949 (p); *To Please a Lady* 1950 (d,p); *Angels in the Outfield* 1951 (d,p); *It's a Big Country* 1951 (d); *Plymouth Adventure* 1952 (d); *When in Rome* 1952 (d,p); *Never Let Me Go* 1953 (p).

Brown, David • Executive, producer • Born New York, NY, July 28, 1916. *Educ.* Stanford; Columbia School of Journalism. With Darryl F. Zanuck's son Richard, founded the successful Zanuck-Brown production company in 1972. Married to *Cosmopolitan* editor Helen Gurley Brown. • *Sssssss* 1973 (exec.p); *The Sting* 1973 (p); *The Black Windmill* 1974 (exec.p); *The Girl From Petrovka* 1974 (p); *The Sugarland Express* 1974 (p); *Willie Dynamite* 1974 (p); *The Eiger Sanction* 1975 (exec.p); *Jaws* 1975 (p) **(AANBP)**; *MacArthur the Rebel General* 1977 (exec.p); *Jaws 2* 1978 (p); *The Island* 1980 (p); *Neighbors* 1981 (p); *The Verdict* 1982 (p) **(AANBP)**; *Cocoon* 1985 (p); *Target* 1985 (p); *Cocoon: The Return* 1988 (p); *Driving Miss Daisy* 1989 (exec.p).

Brown, Nacio Herb • American composer • Born February 22, 1896; died 1964. Made an initial splash with the screen's very first musical, *The Broad-*

way Melody (1929), and continued his successful union with MGM and lyricist Arthur Freed for many years thereafter. • *The Broadway Melody* 1929 (song); *The Hollywood Revue of 1929* 1929 (song); *The Pagan* 1929 (song); *The Show of Shows* 1929 (m); *Good News* 1930 (song); *Montana Moon* 1930 (song); *Whoopee* 1930 (song); *A Woman Commands* 1932 (m); *The Barbarian* 1933 (song); *Going Hollywood* 1933 (song); *Take a Chance* 1933 (from play); *Hollywood Party* 1934 (song); *Student Tour* 1934 (song); *A Night at the Opera* 1935 (song); *Broadway Melody of 1936* 1936 (song); *San Francisco* 1936 (song); *Thoroughbreds Don't Cry* 1937 (song); *Broadway Melody of 1938* 1938 (song); *Babes in Arms* 1939 (song); *Ziegfeld Girl* 1941 (song); *Wintertime* 1943 (song); *Greenwich Village* 1944 (song); *Holiday in Mexico* 1946 (song); *The Kissing Bandit* 1948 (song); *The Bribe* 1949 (song); *Pagan Love Song* 1950 (song); *Singin' in the Rain* 1952 (song).

Browne, Roscoe Lee • Actor; also author. • Born Woodbury, NJ, 1925. *Educ.* Lincoln University, PA; Middlebury College, VT (comparative literature, French); Columbia. A former international track star and professor of French and comparative literature, Browne made his stage debut in *Julius Caesar* in 1956 and began appearing onscreen in the early 1960s. He has gone on to become one of America's most distinguished black character players. • *The Connection* 1962; *Black Like Me* 1964; *The Comedians* 1967; *Uptight* 1968; *Topaz* 1969; *The Liberation of L.B. Jones* 1970; *Cisco Pike* 1971; *The Cowboys* 1971; *The Ra Expeditions* 1971; *The World's Greatest Athlete* 1972; *Superfly TNT* 1973; *Uptown Saturday Night* 1974; *Logan's Run* 1976; *Twilight's Last Gleaming* 1977; *Nothing Personal* 1979; *Jumpin' Jack Flash* 1986; *Legal Eagles* 1986; *Oliver & Company* 1988; *Open Window (short)* 1988.

Browning, Tod • Director; also screenwriter, actor. • Born Charles Albert Browning, Louisville, KY, July 12, 1882; died 1962, Santa Monica, CA. Browning turned to directing after working in the circus, vaudeville and as a film actor. His early films, for Metro and Universal, have been described as routine melodramas and did little to advance his career. It was Browning's collaborations with Lon Chaney that pulled him from the rank and file to a position as one of Hollywood's bankable directors.

Much of Browning's reputation as one of the top directors of horror films rests on the Chaney silents. However, these films remain largely inaccessible (*The Unholy Three* 1925, *The Road to Mandalay* 1926, *The Unknown* 1927, etc.) or completely lost (*London After Midnight* 1927). Little doubt remains that the creative force behind the films was Chaney himself, with his expressive makeup and physical contortions.

Dracula (1931), originally planned as a Chaney vehicle before his untimely death, is another film that succeeds largely because of a performance; Bela Lugosi's distant, stylized portrayal of the vampire conveys an elegance that Browning's use of the camera fails to match. Although the film's early scenes set in Transylvania have a degree of atmosphere, the shift of the setting to England brings with it a plodding, static quality, reflecting the screenplay's debt to the stage adaptation of *Dracula*. Though the ponderous script is largely to blame, Browning must bear some responsibility for *Dracula*'s anemic style; instead of showing action the director is content to let characters describe it. Similarly, *Freaks* (1932) achieved its early infamy and current cult status through its use of real circus "freaks," who command a voyeuristic appeal, rather than through strong plotting or directorial flourish. Browning's camera again remains static; much of the film is shot in tableaux, and technically it appears to be from an earlier period. Only in the final sequence, as the freaks chase the trapeze artist through the mud and rain to revenge one of their own, do shot selection and editing begin to correspond to the bizarre quality of the story.

Browning's two best directorial efforts in sound horror film are usually obscured by the reputations of *Dracula* and *Freaks*. *Mark of the Vampire* (1935), a remake of *London After Midnight*, maintains a consistently eerie atmosphere and contains several understated scenes of chilling beauty featuring Lugosi and the ethereal Carol Borland as a "vampire" couple. Despite the fact that the film's supernatural elements give way by the conclusion to a standard mystery story, Browning here displays more control and visual polish than in either *Dracula* or *Freaks*. *The Devil-Doll* (1936), in which Devil's Island escapee Lionel Barrymore shrinks the partners who framed him for embezzlement to the size of toys, is in many ways a standard revenge melodrama. But the director makes inventive use of a wide variety of cinematic tools—canted shots, a moving camera, montages—to enhance the suspense and charge of the science fiction trappings. Only a protracted denouement mars what is certainly Browning's best film.

While Browning's movies have certainly provided audiences with a few shudders, he is no longer considered "the Edgar Allan Poe of the cinema." Critical opinion in the past twenty years has found his work to be infused with a curious indifference; something which would seem to be corroborated by his decision to retire from directing in 1939 to concentrate on his real estate holdings. ES • *The Deadly Glass of Beer (short)* 1916 (d); *Intolerance* 1916 (a); *Jim Bludso* 1917 (d); *The Jury of Fate* 1917 (d); *A Love Sublime* 1917 (d); *Peggy, The Will o' the Wisp* 1917 (d); *The Brazen Beauty* 1918 (d); *The Deciding Kiss* 1918 (d); *The Eyes of Mystery* 1918 (d); *The Legion of Death* 1918 (d); *Revenge* 1918 (d); *Set Free* 1918 (d,sc); *Which Woman* 1918 (d); *Bonnie, Bonnie Lassie* 1919 (d,sc); *The Exquisite Thief* 1919 (d); *A Petal on the Current* 1919 (d); *The Unpainted Woman* 1919 (d); *The Wicked Darling* 1919 (d); *The Virgin of Stamboul* 1920 (d,sc); *No Woman Knows* 1921 (d,sc); *Outside the Law* 1921 (d,sc,story); *Man Under Cover* 1922 (d); *Under Two Flags* 1922 (adapt,d); *The Wise Kid* 1922 (d); *Day of Faith* 1923 (d); *Drifting* 1923 (d,sc); *White Tiger* 1923 (d,sc,story); *The Dangerous Flirt* 1924 (d); *Silk Stocking Sal* 1924 (d); *Dollar Down* 1925 (d); *The Mystic* 1925 (d,story); *The Unholy Three* 1925 (d,p); *The Black Bird* 1926 (d,story); *The Road to Mandalay* 1926 (d,story); *London After Midnight* 1927 (d,story); *The Show* 1927 (d); *The Unknown* 1927 (d,story); *The Big City* 1928 (d,p,story); *West of Zanzibar* 1928 (d); *The Thirteenth Chair* 1929 (d,p); *Where East Is East* 1929 (d,p,story); *Outside the Law* 1930 (d,sc); *Dracula* 1931 (d); *The Iron Man* 1931 (d,p); *Freaks* 1932 (d,p); *Fast Workers* 1933 (d,p); *Mark of the Vampire* 1935 (d,from short story—"The Hypnotist"); *The Devil-Doll* 1936 (d,sc); *Miracles For Sale* 1939 (d); *Inside Job* 1946 (story).

Bruckheimer, Jerry • Producer • Born Detroit, MI. *Educ.* University of Arizona (psychology). Former advertising executive who moved into film production in the early 1970s. Together with Don Simpson, with whom he formed Simpson-Bruckheimer Productions in 1983, Bruckheimer set the trend for the big-budget, action/adventure films which dominated Hollywood's output throughout the decade. Their joint ventures include *Beverly Hills Cop* (1984) and *Top Gun* (1986), both among the 20 highest-grossing features of all time and both produced via the company's long-term deal with Paramount Pictures.

The ending of that deal by "mutual agreement" at the end of 1990 was taken by many as the sign of a changing Hollywood mindset, with studios starting to put less emphasis on "blockbuster" productions and more on lower-budget films with "smaller" subjects. Simpson and Bruckheimer signed a non-exclusive, five-year deal with Disney subsidiary Hollywood Pictures in early 1991. The team are known to each other as "Mr. Inside" (Simpson worked his way up through the Hollywood corporate structure) and "Mr. Outside" (Bruckheimer drew on a background of hands-on experience with the nuts and bolts of filmmaking). • *Farewell, My Lovely* 1975 (p); *March or Die* 1977 (p); *American Gigolo* 1980 (p); *Defiance* 1980 (p); *Thief* 1981 (p); *Cat People* 1982 (exec.p); *Young Doctors in Love* 1982 (p); *Flashdance* 1983 (p); *Bev-*

erly Hills Cop 1984 (p); *Thief of Hearts* 1984 (p); *Top Gun* 1986 (p); *Beverly Hills Cop II* 1987 (p); *Days of Thunder* 1990 (p).

Brynner, Yul • *aka* Youl Bryner • Actor; also TV director. • Born Taidje Khan, Sakhalin Island (off coast of Siberia), July 12, 1915; died October 10, 1985, New York. Took up acting after a serious accident curtailed his career as a circus acrobat. Brynner moved to America in 1940, failed a screen test at Universal in 1947 because he looked "too oriental" and gave the first of 4,625 performances as the King of Siam in *The King and I* in 1951. Trading on his unidentifiably exotic looks and somewhat imperious manner, Brynner played a succession of royals, secret agents and gunslingers, notably in *The Magnificent Seven* (1960) and *Westworld* (1973). • *Port of New York* 1949; *Anastasia* 1956; *The King and I* 1956 **(AABA)**; *The Ten Commandments* 1956; *The Brothers Karamazov* 1958; *The Buccaneer* 1958; *The Sound and the Fury* 1958; *The Journey* 1959; *Solomon and Sheba* 1959; *Le Testament d'Orphée/The Testament of Orpheus* 1959; *The Magnificent Seven* 1960; *Once More, With Feeling* 1960; *Surprise Package* 1960; *Escape From Zahrain* 1962; *Taras Bulba* 1962; *Kings of the Sun* 1963; *Flight From Ashiya* 1964; *Invitation to a Gunfighter* 1964; *Morituri* 1965; *Cast a Giant Shadow* 1966; *The Poppy Is Also a Flower* 1966; *Return of the Seven* 1966; *Triple Cross* 1966; *The Double Man* 1967; *The Long Duel* 1967; *Bitka na Neretvi* 1968; *Villa Rides* 1968; *The File of the Golden Goose* 1969; *The Madwoman of Chaillot* 1969; *The Magic Christian* 1970; *Adios Sabata* 1971; *Catlow* 1971; *The Light at the Edge of the World* 1971; *Romance of a Horse Thief* 1971; *Fuzz* 1972; *Le Serpent* 1973; *Westworld* 1973; *The Ultimate Warrior* 1975; *Futureworld* 1976; *Gli Indesiderabili* 1976; *It's Showtime* 1976.

Buchman, Sidney • Screenwriter; also producer, executive. • Born Duluth, MN, March 27, 1902; died 1975. *Educ.* University of Minnesota; Columbia. Screenwriter at Columbia Pictures who did sparkling work for directors including Frank Capra, Leo McCarey, George Cukor and Joseph Mankiewicz. Buchman had begun a successful climb up the studio's corporate ladder when, in 1951, he was called to testify before HUAC. He admitted to having once been a member of the Communist Party but refused to "name names" and was blacklisted. Buchman moved to France in the 1960s. • *Matinee Ladies* 1927 (story); *The Beloved Bachelor* 1931 (dial); *Daughter of the Dragon* 1931 (dial); *If I Had a Million* 1932 (sc); *No One Man* 1932 (sc); *The Sign of the Cross* 1932 (sc); *Thunder Below* 1932 (sc); *From Hell to Heaven* 1933 (sc); *The Right to Romance* 1933 (sc); *All of Me* 1934 (sc); *Broadway Bill* 1934 (uncred.sc); *His Greatest Gamble* 1934 (sc); *Whom the Gods Destroy* 1934 (sc); *I'll Love You Always* 1935 (sc); *Love Me Forever* 1935 (sc); *She Married Her Boss* 1935 (sc); *Adventure in Manhattan* 1936 (sc); *The King Steps Out* 1936 (sc); *The Music Goes 'Round* 1936 (story); *Theodora Goes Wild* 1936 (sc); *The Awful Truth* 1937 (uncred.sc); *Lost Horizon* 1937 (uncred.sc); *Holiday* 1938 (sc); *She Married an Artist* 1938 (p); *Mr. Smith Goes to Washington* 1939 (sc) **(AANBSC)**; *The Howards of Virginia* 1940 (sc); *Here Comes Mr. Jordan* 1941 (sc) **(AABSC)**; *Talk of the Town* 1942 (sc) **(AANBSC)**; *Sahara* 1943 (uncred.sc); *Over 21* 1945 (p,sc); *A Song to Remember* 1945 (sc); *The Jolson Story* 1946 (uncred.from story); *To the Ends of the Earth* 1948 (p); *Jolson Sings Again* 1949 (p,sc) **(AANBSC)**; *Saturday's Hero* 1951 (sc); *Boots Malone* 1952 (p); *The Mark* 1961 (p,sc); *Cleopatra* 1963 (sc); *The Group* 1966 (p,sc); *La Maison Sous les Arbres* 1971 (assoc.p,sc); *Billy Jack Goes to Washington* 1976 (from sc—"Mr. Smith Goes to Washington").

Bujold, Geneviève • Actress • Born Montreal, Quebec, Canada, July 1, 1942. *Educ.* Quebec Conservatory of Drama. Began her career on the French-Canadian stage and established herself as a thoughtful, mature screen lead in the 1960s. Bujold, who first came to attention in Phillipe de Broca's cult classic *King of Hearts* (1966), became an international star with *Anne of the Thousand Days* (1969) but proceeded to appear in a string of run-of-the-mill movies before returning to form in the 1980s. She became a member of Alan Rudolph's informal stock company, giving suitably cryptic performances opposite Keith Carradine in *Choose Me* (1984), *Trouble in Mind* (1985) and *The Moderns* (1988). Bujold was also memorable opposite dueling Jeremy Ironses in David Cronenberg's *Dead Ringers* (1988). Married from 1967 to 1973 to Paul Almond, who directed her in four films. • *La Fleur de l'age, ou les adolescentes* 1964; *La Guerre est finie* 1966; *Le Roi de Coeur/King of Hearts* 1966; *Isabel* 1967; *Le Voleur/The Thief of Paris* 1967; *Anne of the Thousand Days* 1969 **(AANBA)**; *Act of the Heart* 1970; *The Trojan Women* 1971; *Journey* 1972; *Kamouraska* 1973; *Earthquake* 1974; *L'Incorrigible* 1975; *Alex & the Gypsy* 1976; *Obsession* 1976; *Swashbuckler* 1976; *Another Man, Another Chance* 1977; *Coma* 1978; *Murder By Decree* 1979; *Final Assignment* 1980; *The Last Flight of Noah's Ark* 1980; *Monsignor* 1982; *Choose Me* 1984; *Tightrope* 1984; *Trouble in Mind* 1985; *Dead Ringers* 1988; *The Moderns* 1988; *False Identity* 1990; *Les Noces de papier/A Paper Wedding* 1990; *Rue du Bac* 1991.

Bumstead, Henry • American production designer • Veteran production designer whose credits range from the classic Hitchcock thrillers *The Man Who Knew Too Much* (1956) and *Vertigo* (1958) to Clint Eastwood's *High Plains Drifter* (1973) and George Roy Hill's *The World According to Garp* (1982). Bumstead won Oscars for his work on *To Kill a Mockingbird* (1962) and *The Sting* (1973). • *The Man Who Knew Too Much* 1956 (art d); *As Young As We Are* 1958 (art d); *I Married a Monster From Outer Space* 1958 (art d); *Vertigo* 1958 (art d) **(AANBAD)**; *The Hangman* 1959 (art d); *The Trap* 1959 (art d); *The Great Impostor* 1960 (art d); *To Kill a Mockingbird* 1962 (art d) **(AABAD)**; *The Brass Bottle* 1964 (art d); *Father Goose* 1964 (art d); *Banning* 1967 (art d); *A Man Called Gannon* 1969 (art d); *Tell Them Willie Boy Is Here* 1969 (art d); *Topaz* 1969 (art d); *One More Train to Rob* 1971 (art d); *Raid on Rommel* 1971 (art d); *Slaughterhouse-Five* 1971 (pd); *Joe Kidd* 1972 (art d); *High Plains Drifter* 1973 (art d); *Showdown* 1973 (art d); *The Sting* 1973 (art d) **(AABAD)**; *The Front Page* 1974 (art d); *The Great Waldo Pepper* 1975 (art d); *Family Plot* 1976 (pd); *Rollercoaster* 1977 (pd); *Slap Shot* 1977 (art d); *House Calls* 1978 (pd); *Same Time, Next Year* 1978 (pd); *The Concorde - Airport '79* 1979 (pd); *A Little Romance* 1979 (pd); *Smokey and the Bandit II* 1980 (pd); *The World According to Garp* 1982 (pd); *Harry & Son* 1984 (pd); *The Little Drummer Girl* 1984 (pd); *Warning Sign* 1985 (pd); *Psycho III* 1986 (pd); *Funny Farm* 1988 (pd); *A Time of Destiny* 1988 (a,pd); *Her Alibi* 1989 (pd); *Almost an Angel* 1990 (pd); *Ghost Dad* 1990 (pd).

Buñuel, Luis • Director; also screenwriter, producer, actor. • Born Calanda, Spain, February 22, 1900; died July 29, 1983, Mexico City. *Educ.* Colegio del Salvador (religion, entomology, zoology); Instituto Nacional de Enseñanza Media; University of Madrid (agricultural engineering, natural sciences, history); Académie du Cinéma, Paris. The founder of surrealist cinema, Luis Buñuel enjoyed a career as diverse and contradictory as his films: he was a master of both silent and sound cinema, of documentaries as well as features; his greatest work was produced in the two decades after his 60th year, a time when most directors have either retired or gone into decline; and although frequently characterized as a surrealist, many of his films were dramas and farces in the realist or neo-realist mode. Yet despite all the innovations and permutations of his work, Buñuel remained suprisingly consistent and limited in the targets of his social satire: the Catholic Church, bourgeois culture, and Fascism. As he once commented, "Religious education and Surrealism have marked me for life."

Buñuel described his childhood in Calanda, a village in the Spanish province of Aragon, as having "slipped by in an almost medieval atmosphere." Between the ages of six and fifteen he attended Jesuit school, where a strict educational program, unchanged since the 18th century, instilled in him a lifelong rebellion against religion.

In 1917 Buñuel enrolled in the University of Madrid and soon became involved in the political and literary peñas, or clubs, that met in the city's cafes. His friends included several of Spain's future great artists and writers, including Salvador Dalí, Federico García Lorca and Rafael Albertini. Within a few years the avant-garde movement had reached the peñas and spawned its Spanish variants, *creacionismo* and *ultraísmo*. Although influenced by these, Buñuel was often critical of the Spanish avant-garde for its allegiance to traditional forms.

In 1925 Buñuel left Madrid for Paris, with no clear idea of what he would do. When he saw Fritz Lang's *Destiny* (1921), however, he realized where his vocation lay. He approached the renowned French director, Jean Epstein, who hired him as an assistant. Buñuel began to learn the techniques of filmmaking but was fired when he refused to work with Epstein's own mentor, Abel Gance, whose films he did not like. In a prophetic statement, Epstein warned Buñuel about his "surrealistic tendencies."

In 1928, with financial support from his mother, Buñuel collaborated with Dali on *Un Chien Andalou*, a "surrealist weapon" designed to shock the bourgeois as well as criticize the avant-garde. As in his earlier book of poems, *Un Perro Andaluz*, Buñuel rejected the avant-garde's emphasis on form, or camera "tricks," over content. Instead, his influences were commercial neo-realism, horror films and American comedies.

Buñuel's three early films established him as a master of surrealist cinema, whose goal was to treat all human experience—dreams, madness or "normal" waking states—on the same level. The critical success of *L'Age d'or* (1930), secured Buñuel a contract with MGM, which he turned down after a visit to Hollywood in 1930. His next film, *Las Hurdes: Tierra Sin Pan* (1932) was a documentary financed with money won in a lottery and shot with a camera borrowed from Yves Allégret. Ostensibly an objective study of a remote, impoverished region in western Spain, the film constituted such a militant critique of both church and state that it was banned in Spain. The stage had been set, however, for Buñuel's later work, in which realism—with its preestablished mass appeal—provided an accessible context for his surreal aesthetic and moral code.

After *Las Hurdes*, Buñuel would not direct another film until 1947. Although still critical of commercial cinema, he spent the next 14 years within the industry, learning all aspects of film production. From 1933 to 1935 he dubbed dialogue for Paramount in Paris and then Warner Bros. in Spain; between 1935 and the outbreak of the Spanish Civil War in 1936 he produced popular musical comedies in Spain; during the Civil War he served the Republican government, compiling newsreel material into a documentary about the war, *España leal en armas* (1937). In 1938, while he was in Hollywood supervising two other documentaries, the Fascists assumed power at home. Unable to return to Spain, Buñuel went to work for the Museum of Modern Art in New York, reediting and dubbing documentaries for distribution in Latin America. He was forced to resign in 1942, however, because of his suspected communist background—a suspicion which he later claimed had been aroused by Dalí. In order to survive, Buñuel narrated documentaries for the Army Corps of Engineers until 1944, when Warner Bros. hired him to produce Spanish versions of their films.

In 1946 Buñuel moved to Mexico, where many of Spain's intellectuals and artists had emigrated after the Civil War. He would live there for the rest of his life, becoming a citizen in 1949 and directing 20 films by 1964. This period is often described as an "apprenticeship" in which Buñuel was forced to shoot low-budget commercial films in between a handful of surreal "classics." Indeed, Buñuel's supposed indifference to style—his minimal use of non-diegetic music, close-ups or camera movement—is often judged to be largely the result of the limited resources available to him. Yet his Mexican films can more accurately be seen as a refinement of the unobstrusive aesthetic style that had been evident since *Un Chien Andalou*. As Buñuel himself insisted, "I never made a single scene that compromised my convictions or my personal morality."

Buñuel's third Mexican film, *Los Olvidados* (1950), brought him to international attention once again. Although hailed as a surrealist film, it owes much to postwar neorealism in its unsentimental depiction of Mexico's slum children. As in his other Mexican films before *Nazarin* (1958), dream sequences and surreal images are introduced at strategic moments into an otherwise realist narrative. (Contributing to the relative neglect of these films has been their unavailability outside Mexico, and perhaps their proletarian and "ethnic" focus.)

In 1955 Buñuel began to direct international—and more openly political—coproductions in Europe. In 1961 he was invited to Spain to film *Viridiana*. The completed film was a direct assault on Spanish Catholicism and Fascism and was banned by its unwitting patron; a *succès de scandale*, it won the Palm d'Or at Cannes and secured long overdue international acclaim for its director. After *Viridiana*, Buñuel worked mostly in France. The growth of his new international (and consequently educated and middle-class) audience coincided with his return to a surrealist aesthetic. *The Exterminating Angel* (1962), *The Discreet Charm of the Bourgeoisie* (1972) and *The Phantom of Liberty* (1974) depict a bourgeoisie trapped within their own conventions, if not—in the latter film's metaphorical conceit—their own homes. *Belle de jour* (1967), *Tristana* (1970) and *That Obscure Object of Desire* (1977) explore sexual obsessions and preoccupations. And *The Milky Way* (1969) launches a frontal assault on the Church, in a summation of Buñuel's lifelong contempt for that institution.

In 1980 Buñuel collaborated with Jean-Claude Carrière, his screenwriter since *Diary of a Chambermaid* (1963), on his autobiography, *My Last Sigh*.
CAN • *Mauprat* 1926 (a,ad); *La Sirène des tropiques* 1927 (ad); *Un Chien Andalou* 1928 (a,d,p,sc,ed,m); *La Chute de la maison Usher/The Fall of the House of Usher* 1928 (ad); *L'Age d'or/The Golden Age* 1930 (d,p,sc,ed); *Las Hurdes/Land Without Bread* 1932 (d,sc); *Don Quintin el amargao* 1935 (exec.p,prod.sup); *La Hija de Juan Simon* 1935 (a,exec.p,prod.sup); *Centinela alerta!* 1936 (a,exec.p,prod.sup); *Quién me quiere a mí?* 1936 (exec.p,prod.sup); *España leal en armas (short)* 1937 (ed,commentary,m); *Gran Casino* 1947 (d); *El Gran Calavera* 1949 (d); *Los Olvidados* 1950 (d,sc); *Si usted no puede, yo si* 1950 (story); *La Hija Del Engaño* 1951 (d); *Una Mujer Sín Amor* 1951 (d); *Susana* 1951 (d); *Adventures of Robinson Crusoe* 1952 (d,sc,dial); *El Bruto* 1952 (d,sc); *El/This Strange Passion* 1952 (d,sc); *Subida Al Cielo/Mexican Bus Ride* 1952 (d,sc); *Abismos de Pasión/Wuthering Heights* 1954 (d,sc); *La Ilusión Viaja En Tranvia/Illusion Travels By Streetcar* 1954 (d); *El Río y la Muerte/The River and Death* 1954 (d,sc); *Ensayo De Un Crimen/The Criminal Life of Archibaldo de La Cruz* 1955 (d,sc); *Cela s'appèlle l'aurore* 1956 (d,sc); *La Mort en ce jardin/Death in the Jungle* 1956 (d,sc); *Nazarin* 1958 (d,sc); *La Fièvre Monte à El Pao/Fever Mounts at El Pao* 1959 (d,sc); *The Young One* 1960 (d,sc); *Viridiana* 1961 (d,sc); *El Angel Exterminadór/The Exterminating Angel* 1962 (d,sc,from scenario *Los Naufragos de la calle de la Providencia*,dial); *Le Journal d'une femme de chambre/Diary of a Chambermaid* 1963 (d,sc); *Simón del Desierto/Simon of the Desert* 1965 (d,sc,dial); *Belle de Jour* 1967 (d,sc); *La Voie Lactée/The Milky Way* 1969 (d,sc,m); *Tristana* 1970 (d,sc); *Le Charme Discret de la Bourgeoisie/The Discreet Charm of the Bourgeoisie* 1972 (d,sc) **(AANBSC)**; *Le Moine* 1973 (sc); *Le Fantôme de la Liberté/Phantom of Liberty* 1974 (d,sc,special sound effects); *Cet obscur objet du désir/That Obscure Object of Desire* 1977 (d,sc,adapt,dial) **(AANBSC)**.

Burel, Leonce-Henri • *aka* Leonce-Henry Burel • Director of photography; also director. • Born Indret, France, November 23, 1892. *Educ.* Ecole des Beaux-

Arts, Paris; Nantes University (art). Cinematographer on several classic French films, from Abel Gance's *Napoleon* (1927) to Robert Bresson's *Diary of a Country Priest* (1950) and *The Trial of Joan of Arc* (1962). • *La Floraison (short)* 1913 (d); *L'Industrie du verre (short)* 1913 (d); *La Pousse des plantes (short)* 1913 (d); *Les Rapaces diurnes et Nocturnes (short)* 1913 (d); *Alsace* 1915 (ph); *Barbe-Rousse* 1916 (ph); *Ce que les flots racontent* 1916 (ph); *L'Enigme de 10 heures* 1916 (ph); *La Femme inconnue* 1916 (ph); *Fioritures* 1916 (ph); *La Fleur des Ruines* 1916 (ph); *Le Fou de la falaise* 1916 (ph); *Les Gaz Mortels* 1916 (ph); *L'Héroïsme de Paddy* 1916 (ph); *Les Mouettes* 1916 (ph); *Le Droit à la vie* 1917 (ph); *Mater Dolorosa* 1917 (ph); *La Zone de la mort* 1917 (ph); *La Dixième symphonie* 1918 (ph); *J'Accuse* 1918 (ph); *L'Hirondelle et la mésange* 1921 (uncred.ph); *Mademoiselle de la seiglière* 1921 (ph); *L'Arlésienne* 1922 (ph); *La Conquête des Gaules* 1922 (d); *Crainquebille* 1923 (ph); *La Roue* 1923 (ph); *Visages d'enfants* 1924 (ph); *Das Bildnis* 1925 (ph); *Michel Strogoff* 1926 (ph); *Casanova* 1927 (ph); *La Danseuse orchidée* 1927 (ph); *Morgane la Sirène* 1927 (ph); *Napoleon* 1927 (ph); *L'Equipage* 1928 (ph); *The Three Passions* 1928 (ph); *L'Evadée* 1929 (d); *Nuits de princes* 1929 (ph); *Le Mystère de la chambre jaune* 1930 (ph); *Le Parfum de la dame en noir* 1930 (ph); *L'Aiglon* 1931 (ph); *Baroud* 1932 (ph); *Danton* 1932 (ph); *La Fada* 1932 (d); *Coralie et Cie* 1933 (ph); *Un Homme en or* 1934 (ph); *Toboggan (short)* 1934 (ph); *L'Homme à l'oreille cassée* 1935 (ph); *Son autre amour* 1935 (ph); *La Dernière valse* 1936 (ph); *Hélène* 1936 (ph); *Les Petites alliées* 1936 (ph); *Abus de confiance* 1937 (ph); *Mademoiselle ma mère* 1937 (ph); *Mirages* 1937 (ph); *La Mort du cygne* 1937 (ph); *Carrefour* 1938 (ph); *Les Filles du Rhone* 1938 (ph); *Retour à l'aube* 1938 (ph); *Le Club des soupirants* 1939 (ph); *L'Homme du Niger* 1939 (ph); *La Vénus aveugle* 1940 (ph); *Une Femme dans la Nuit* 1941 (ph); *Ne le criez pas sur les toits* 1941 (ph); *La Belle aventure* 1942 (d); *Feu sacré* 1942 (ph); *Les Mystères de Paris* 1943 (ph); *Estrange destin* 1945 (ph); *La Route du Bagne* 1945 (ph); *La Colore des dieux* 1946 (ph); *Dernier Refuge* 1946 (ph); *Le Fugitif* 1946 (ph); *La Revanche de Baccarat* 1946 (ph); *Rocambole* 1946 (ph); *Carrefour du crime* 1947 (ph); *Métier de fous* 1947 (ph); *Le Mystère Barton* 1948 (ph); *Suzanne et ses brigands* 1948 (ph); *Tous les deux* 1948 (ph); *Les Casse-Pieds* 1949 (ph); *La Ronde des heures* 1949 (ph); *Les Valse brillante* 1949 (ph); *Banco de prince* 1950 (ph); *Bille de clown* 1950 (ph); *Le Journal d'un Curé de Campagne/Diary of a Country Priest* 1950 (ph); *La Vie chantée* 1950 (ph); *La Demoiselle et son revenant* 1951 (ph); *Vérité sur Bébé Donge* 1951 (ph); *Mon gosse de père* 1952 (ph); *L'Envers du paradis* 1953 (ph); *L'Etrange désir de Monsieur Bard* 1953 (ph); *La Route Napoléon* 1953 (ph); *Secrets d'Alcove* 1954 (ph—"Riviera Express"); *Bonjour sourire* 1955 (ph); *La Madone des sleepings* 1955 (ph); *Marianne de ma jeunesse* 1955 (ph); *Tant qu'il y aura des femmes* 1955 (ph); *Toute la ville accuse* 1955 (ph); *Vous pigez?* 1955 (ph); *Un Condamné à mort s'est echappé/A Man Escaped* 1956 (ph); *Mon curé chez les pauvres* 1956 (ph); *Les Fanatiques* 1957 (ph); *Quand sonnera midi* 1957 (ph); *Cette nuit-la* 1958 (ph); *Pickpocket* 1959 (ph); *Un Soir sur la plage* 1961 (ph); *Le Procés de Jeanne d'Arc/The Trial of Joan of Arc* 1962 (ph); *Chair de Poule* 1963 (ph); *Un Drole de paroissien* 1963 (ph); *Dernier tierce* 1964 (ph); *Les Compagnons de la marguerite* 1966 (ph).

Burke, Billie • Actress • Born Mary William Ethelbert Appleton Burke, Washington, DC, August 7, 1885; died 1970. Glamorous light comedienne who, in the midst of a successful Broadway career, entered films at the behest of Thomas Ince in 1916. Perhaps best known as Glinda, the Good Witch of the East, in the timeless *The Wizard of Oz* (1939), Burke enjoyed great popularity as a featured player, often playing dithery, aristocratic types. Married to impresario Florenz Ziegfeld from 1914 until his death in 1932. • *Gloria's Romance* 1916; *Arms and the Girl* 1917; *The Land of Promise* 1917; *The Mysterious Miss Terry* 1917; *Eve's Daughter* 1918; *In Pursuit of Polly* 1918; *Let's Get a Divorce* 1918; *The Make-Believe Wife* 1918; *Good Gracious Annabelle* 1919; *The Misleading Widow* 1919; *Wanted - A Husband* 1919; *Away Goes Prudence* 1920; *The Frisky Mrs. Johnson* 1920; *The Education of Elizabeth* 1921; *A Bill of Divorcement* 1932; *Christopher Strong* 1933; *Dinner at Eight* 1933; *Only Yesterday* 1933; *Finishing School* 1934; *Forsaking All Others* 1934; *We're Rich Again* 1934; *Where Sinners Meet* 1934; *After Office Hours* 1935; *Becky Sharp* 1935; *Doubting Thomas* 1935; *A Feather in Her Hat* 1935; *Only Eight Hours* 1935; *She Couldn't Take It* 1935; *Splendor* 1935; *Craig's Wife* 1936; *My American Wife* 1936; *Piccadilly Jim* 1936; *The Bride Wore Red* 1937; *Navy, Blue and Gold* 1937; *Parnell* 1937; *Topper* 1937; *Everybody Sing* 1938; *Merrily We Live* 1938 **(AANBSA)**; *The Young in Heart* 1938; *Bridal Suite* 1939; *Eternally Yours* 1939; *Remember?* 1939; *Topper Takes a Trip* 1939; *The Wizard of Oz* 1939; *Zenobia* 1939; *And One Was Beautiful* 1940; *The Captain Is a Lady* 1940; *Dulcy* 1940; *The Ghost Comes Home* 1940; *Hullabaloo* 1940; *Irene* 1940; *The Man Who Came to Dinner* 1941; *One Night in Lisbon* 1941; *Topper Returns* 1941; *The Wild Man of Borneo* 1941; *Girl Trouble* 1942; *They All Kissed the Bride* 1942; *What's Cooking?* 1942; *Gildersleeve on Broadway* 1943; *Hi, Diddle Diddle* 1943; *So's Your Uncle* 1943; *You're a Lucky Fellow, Mr. Smith* 1943; *Breakfast in Hollywood* 1945; *The Cheaters* 1945; *Swing Out, Sister* 1945; *The Bachelor's Daughters* 1946; *And Baby Makes Three* 1949; *The Barkleys of Broadway* 1949; *Boy From Indiana* 1950; *Father of the Bride* 1950; *Three Husbands* 1950; *Father's Little Dividend* 1951; *Small Town Girl* 1953; *The Young Philadelphians* 1959; *Pepe* 1960; *Sergeant Rutledge* 1960.

Burks, Robert • Director of photography • Born Newport Beach, CA, 1910; died 1968. Proficient in virtually every genre and equally at home with black-and-white or color. Burks shot a string of 12 Hitchcock films, from *Strangers on a Train* (1951) through *Marnie* (1964). • *Escape in the Desert* 1945 (ph); *The Verdict* 1946 (fx ph); *Beyond the Forest* 1949 (ph); *The Fountainhead* 1949 (ph); *Close to My Heart* 1951 (ph); *Come Fill the Cup* 1951 (ph); *The Enforcer* 1951 (ph); *Strangers on a Train* 1951 (ph) **(AANBPH)**; *Tomorrow Is Another Day* 1951 (ph); *Mara Maru* 1952 (ph); *The Desert Song* 1953 (ph); *Hondo* 1953 (ph); *I Confess* 1953 (ph); *The Boy From Oklahoma* 1954 (ph); *Dial M For Murder* 1954 (ph); *Rear Window* 1954 (ph) **(AANBPH)**; *To Catch a Thief* 1955 (ph) **(AABPH)**; *The Trouble With Harry* 1955 (ph); *The Man Who Knew Too Much* 1956 (ph); *The Vagabond King* 1956 (ph); *The Wrong Man* 1956 (ph); *The Spirit of St. Louis* 1957 (ph); *The Black Orchid* 1958 (ph); *Vertigo* 1958 (ph); *But Not For Me* 1959 (ph); *North By Northwest* 1959 (ph); *The Great Impostor* 1960 (ph); *The Rat Race* 1960 (ph); *The Pleasure of His Company* 1961 (ph); *The Music Man* 1962 (ph); *The Birds* 1963 (ph); *Marnie* 1964 (ph); *Once a Thief* 1965 (ph); *A Patch of Blue* 1965 (ph) **(AANBPH)**; *A Covenant With Death* 1967 (ph); *Waterhole Number 3* 1967 (ph).

Burnett, Charles • Director • Born Vicksburg, MS, 1944. *Educ.* Los Angeles City College (electronics); UCLA (theater arts, film; also writing, languages). Highly acclaimed independent filmmaker whose *Killer of Sheep* (produced 1973, first seen 1977), about the emotional and behavioral effects of his job on a Los Angeles slaughter-house worker, won multiple awards; though it never received commercial release, the film was added to the National Film Registry by the Library of Congress in 1990.

Burnett's first theatrical release, *To Sleep With Anger* (1990), was completed on a budget of less than $1.5 million. It concerns a tightly-knit, middle-class black Los Angeles family that begins to unravel upon the return of a long-absent relative (Danny Glover). • *Killer of Sheep* 1977 (d,p,sc,ph,ed); *My Brother's Wedding* 1983 (d,p,sc,ph); *Bless Their Lit-*

tle Hearts 1984 (sc,ph); *Guests of Hotel Astoria* 1989 (ph); *To Sleep With Anger* 1990 (d,sc).

Burnett, W. R. • Screenwriter; also novelist. • Born William Riley Burnett, Springfield, OH, November 25, 1899; died 1982. *Educ.* Miami Military Institute; Ohio State University, Columbus. Author whose novels provided the basis for several films, notably crime and gangster features such as *Little Caesar* (1930). Burnett also adapted his own work for film (e.g. *High Sierra* 1941) and wrote original screenplays, both alone and in collaboration (e.g. *This Gun For Hire* 1942, *The Great Escape* 1963). • *Little Caesar* 1930 (from novel); *The Finger Points* 1931 (story); *The Iron Man* 1931 (from novel); *The Beast of the City* 1932 (story); *Law and Order* 1932 (from novel *Saint Johnson*); *Scarface* 1932 (adapt,dial); *Dark Hazard* 1934 (from novel); *Dr. Socrates* 1935 (story); *The Whole Town's Talking* 1935 (story); *36 Hours to Kill* 1936 (story); *Some Blondes Are Dangerous* 1937 (from story "Iron Man"); *Wild West Days* 1937 (from novel *Saint Johnson*); *Wine, Women, and Horses* 1937 (from novel); *King of the Underworld* 1939 (story); *Dark Command* 1940 (from novel); *Law and Order* 1940 (from novel *Saint Johnson*); *Dance Hall* 1941 (from novel); *The Get-Away* 1941 (sc); *High Sierra* 1941 (sc,from novel); *This Gun For Hire* 1942 (sc); *Wake Island* 1942 (sc) **(AANBSC)**; *Background to Danger* 1943 (sc); *Crash Dive* 1943 (story); *San Antonio* 1945 (sc); *Nobody Lives Forever* 1946 (sc); *Belle Starr's Daughter* 1948 (sc); *Yellow Sky* 1948 (story); *The Asphalt Jungle* 1950 (from novel); *Vendetta* 1950 (sc); *The Iron Man* 1951 (story); *The Racket* 1951 (sc); *Arrowhead* 1953 (story); *Law and Order* 1953 (from novel *Saint Johnson*); *Dangerous Mission* 1954 (sc); *Captain Lightfoot* 1955 (sc,adapt,story); *I Died a Thousand Times* 1955 (sc,from novel *High Sierra*); *Illegal* 1955 (sc); *Accused of Murder* 1956 (sc,from novel *Vanity Row*); *Short Cut to Hell* 1957 (sc); *The Badlanders* 1958 (from novel); *September Storm* 1960 (sc); *The Lawbreakers* 1961 (sc); *Sergeants 3* 1962 (sc); *Cairo* 1963 (from book *The Asphalt Jungle*); *The Great Escape* 1963 (sc); *Cool Breeze* 1972 (from novel *The Asphalt Jungle*).

Burns, George • *aka* Eddie DeLight, Jed Jackson • Actor; also comedian. • Born Nathan Birnbaum, New York, NY, January 20, 1896. After several unsuccessful attempts at a vaudeville career, Burns's luck changed in 1922, when he formed the Burns and Allen duo with young comic Gracie Allen (they wed in 1926). Gracie at first played the "straight man," but her wacky descriptions of her large family managed to garner all the laughs and the team wisely reversed roles. Having become vaudeville stars, the team appeared in several short films, made their feature debut with *The Big Broadcast* (1932) and played in several, mostly forgettable, movies during the 1930s and 40s.

With their low-keyed comic banter, Burns and Allen became a successful radio team and then starred in their own TV series from 1950 until Allen's retirement in 1958 (she died six years later).

Burns continued his career as a solo comedian and made an outstanding film comeback in 1975 with his award-winning performance as a cantankerous old vaudevillian in *The Sunshine Boys*. He has since appeared in several features, notably as the omniscient title character of Carl Reiner's *Oh, God!* (1977), and continues to smoke his trademark cigars and joke about his ageless virility. • *The Big Broadcast* 1932; *College Humor* 1933; *International House* 1933; *Many Happy Returns* 1934; *Six of a Kind* 1934; *We're Not Dressing* 1934; *The Big Broadcast of 1936* 1935; *Here Comes Cookie* 1935; *Love in Bloom* 1935; *The Big Broadcast of 1937* 1936; *College Holiday* 1936; *A Damsel in Distress* 1937; *College Swing* 1938; *Honolulu* 1939; *The Solid Gold Cadillac* 1956; *The Sunshine Boys* 1975 **(AABSA)**; *Oh, God!* 1977; *Movie Movie* 1978; *Sgt. Pepper's Lonely Hearts Club Band* 1978; *Going in Style* 1979; *Just You and Me, Kid* 1979; *Oh, God! Book II* 1980; *Oh, God! You Devil* 1984; *18 Again!* 1988.

Burr, Raymond • Actor • Born New Westminster, British Columbia, Canada, May 21, 1917. *Educ.* Stanford; Columbia; University of California; University of Chungking. Heavy-set character player, usually in bad-guy roles like that of the murderer in Hitchcock's *Rear Window* (1954). Burr later switched gears to star as TV's heroic lawyer "Perry Mason" (1957-66) and as the wheelchair-bound detective "Ironside" (1967-75). • *San Quentin* 1946; *Code of the West* 1947; *Desperate* 1947; *I Love Trouble* 1947; *Adventures of Don Juan* 1948; *Pitfall* 1948; *Raw Deal* 1948; *Ruthless* 1948; *Sleep, My Love* 1948; *Station West* 1948; *Walk a Crooked Mile* 1948; *Abandoned* 1949; *Black Magic* 1949; *Borderline* 1949; *Bride of Vengeance* 1949; *Love Happy* 1949; *Red Light* 1949; *Key to the City* 1950; *Unmasked* 1950; *Bride of the Gorilla* 1951; *F.B.I. Girl* 1951; *His Kind of Woman* 1951; *M* 1951; *The Magic Carpet* 1951; *The Man He Found* 1951; *New Mexico* 1951; *A Place in the Sun* 1951; *Horizons West* 1952; *Mara Maru* 1952; *Meet Danny Wilson* 1952; *The Bandits of Corsica* 1953; *The Blue Gardenia* 1953; *Fort Algiers* 1953; *Serpent of the Nile* 1953; *Tarzan and the She-Devil* 1953; *Casanova's Big Night* 1954; *Gorilla at Large* 1954; *Khyber Patrol* 1954; *Passion* 1954; *Rear Window* 1954; *They Were So Young* 1954; *Thunder Pass* 1954; *Count Three and Pray* 1955; *A Man Alone* 1955; *You're Never Too Young* 1955; *The Brass Legend* 1956; *A Cry in the Night* 1956; *Gojira* 1956; *Great Day in the Morning* 1956; *Please Murder Me* 1956; *Ride the High Iron* 1956; *Secret of Treasure Mountain* 1956; *Affair in Havana* 1957; *Crime of Passion* 1957; *Desire in the Dust* 1960; *P.J.* 1968; *Tomorrow Never Comes* 1978; *Out of the Blue* 1980; *Airplane II: The Sequel* 1982; *Gojira* 1985.

Burstyn, Ellen • *aka* Edna Rae, Keri Flynn, Erica Dean, Ellen McRae • Actress • Born Edna Rae Gillooly, Detroit, MI, December 7, 1932. *Educ.* Actors Studio. Went through several stage names and an assortment of odd jobs before making her Broadway debut in *Fair Game* in 1957. Burstyn earned Oscar nominations for her roles in *The Last Picture Show* (1971) and *The Exorcist* (1973); she anchored the latter film, with her fully believable performance as a resilient, middle-aged woman who against impossible odds refuses to yield and acts as a counterpoint to the more fantastical elements of the plot. Burstyn then won the best actress Oscar for another superb performance in *Alice Doesn't Live Here Anymore* (1974), a project which she herself packaged and got off the ground.

Unfortunately, though steadily employed in other media, Burstyn was given few opportunities to expand her body of film work during the 1980s. She acted as the first female president of Actor's Equity from 1982 to 1985 and as co-artistic director, with Al Pacino, of the Actors Studio from 1982 to 1988. She is thrice married and divorced, the second time to director Paul Roberts and the third to actor Neil Burstyn. • *For Those Who Think Young* 1964; *Goodbye, Charlie* 1964; *Pit Stop* 1969; *Alex in Wonderland* 1970; *Tropic of Cancer* 1970; *The Last Picture Show* 1971 **(AANBSA)**; *The King of Marvin Gardens* 1972; *The Exorcist* 1973 **(AANBA)**; *Alice Doesn't Live Here Anymore* 1974 **(AABA)**; *Harry and Tonto* 1974; *Providence* 1977; *A Dream of Passion* 1978; *Same Time, Next Year* 1978 **(AANBA)**; *Resurrection* 1980 **(AANBA)**; *Acting: Lee Strasberg and The Actors Studio* 1981; *Silence of the North* 1981; *The Ambassador* 1984; *In Our Hands* 1984; *Twice in a Lifetime* 1985; *Dear America* 1987; *Hello Actors Studio* 1987; *Hanna's War* 1988.

Burton, Richard • Actor • Born Richard Walter Jenkins, Jr., Pontrhydfen, South Wales, November 10, 1925; died August 5, 1984, Celigny, Switzerland. *Educ.* Oxford. Through much of his early career Richard Burton was dogged by the label "promising actor." Several brilliant performances, particularly in British stage productions of Shakespeare, seemed to confirm that promise. But during most of the rest of his life, critics complained the promise went unfulfilled. One thing everyone agreed on, however, was the extraordinary quality of his voice.

Burton was a miner's son and the 12th of 13 children. In secondary school he came under the influence of teacher Phillip Burton, who helped the young man lose his Welsh accent and get into Oxford at age 16. Burton also made his stage debut at this time in Emlyn William's *Druid's Rest* (1943), taking on the surname of his mentor. With his performance in Christopher Fry's play *The Lady's Not for Burning* (1949), Burton had his big breakthrough. A series of minor films followed, of which the first, *The Last Days of Dolwyn* (1949), written and directed by Emlyn Williams, was the best.

Burton made his film breakthrough in 1952 with the Hollywood production, *My Cousin Rachel.* A financial and critical success, it earned him his first of six Oscar nominations (though Burton never won an Academy Award). His screen career continued to build with *The Desert Rats* (1953) and *The Robe* (1953), the first Cinemascope feature. The films that followed were not successful, although many feel his performance as the seething Jimmy Porter in John Osborne's *Look Back in Anger* (1959) was one of Burton's best.

Burton's career revived in 1960 with a triumphant return to the stage as King Arthur in the Lerner & Loewe Broadway hit, *Camelot.* While the musical was still running, he made the fateful decision to play Mark Antony in 20th Century-Fox's spectacular production of *Cleopatra* (1963). The film launched him to international stardom, as well as marking the beginning of his tempestuous, highly publicized relationship with costar Elizabeth Taylor. Burton divorced his first wife, Welsh actress Sybil Williams, to marry Taylor in 1963; the couple were divorced, re-married and divorced for a second time in the 1970s.

Unfortunately, the off-screen chemistry between the two rarely showed up in the films they made together. With the exception of *Who's Afraid of Virginia Woolf?* (1966) and *The Taming of the Shrew* (1967), these tended to range from the lackluster (*Doctor Faustus, The Comedians* both 1967) to the downright soapy (*The Sandpiper* 1965, *Boom!* 1968). Burton appeared in three fine films without Taylor during this decade—*Beckett, The Night of the Iguana* (both 1964) and *The Spy Who Came in From the Cold* (1965)—as well as making American theatrical history in 1964 by playing the longest consecutive run of *Hamlet*.

When Burton's film career hit another low ebb, he returned to Broadway in 1976 to take over the role of Dr. Dysart in *Equus*. The 1977 screen version garnered him another Oscar nomination but was not a box office hit. He never did a much-awaited production of *King Lear* but toured a revival of *Camelot* in 1980 and 1981. With Taylor, he appeared in a 1983 stage production of *Private Lives* which was soundly trounced by the critics. His last film role was as O'Brien in a remake of George Orwell's *1984* (1984).

When Burton died he left four ex-wives and the legend of a great talent wasted. It was, however, a life fully lived and not without its share of real triumphs. Daughter Kate Burton is a respected stage actress. DLY • *The Last Days of Dolwyn* 1949; *Now Barabbas Was a Robber* 1949; *Waterfront* 1950; *The Woman With No Name* 1950; *Green Grow the Rushes* 1951; *My Cousin Rachel* 1952 **(AANBSA)**; *The Desert Rats* 1953; *The Robe* 1953 **(AANBA)**; *Thursday's Children* 1953; *Demetrius and the Gladiators* 1954; *Prince of Players* 1955; *The Rains of Ranchipur* 1955; *Alexander the Great* 1956; *Sea Wife* 1957; *Bitter Victory* 1958; *Look Back in Anger* 1959; *The Bramble Bush* 1960; *Ice Palace* 1960; *The Longest Day* 1962; *The Caretaker* 1963 (funding); *Cleopatra* 1963; *The V.I.P.s* 1963; *Zulu* 1963; *Becket* 1964 **(AANBA)**; *Hamlet* 1964; *The Night of the Iguana* 1964; *The Sandpiper* 1965; *The Spy Who Came in From the Cold* 1965 **(AANBA)**; *Who's Afraid of Virginia Woolf?* 1966 **(AANBA)**; *The Comedians in Africa (short)* 1967; *The Comedians* 1967; *Doctor Faustus* 1967 (a,d,p); *The Taming of the Shrew* 1967 (a,p); *Boom!* 1968; *Candy* 1968; *Where Eagles Dare* 1968; *Anne of the Thousand Days* 1969 **(AANBA)**; *Staircase* 1969; *Raid on Rommel* 1971; *Under Milk Wood* 1971; *Villain* 1971; *The Assassination of Trotsky* 1972; *Bluebeard* 1972; *Hammersmith Is Out* 1972; *Massacre in Rome* 1973; *Sutjeska* 1973; *The Klansman* 1974; *Il Viaggio* 1974; *Volcano: An Inquiry Into the Life and Death of Malcolm Lowry* 1976; *Equus* 1977 **(AANBA)**; *Exorcist II: The Heretic* 1977; *The Medusa Touch* 1978; *The Wild Geese* 1978; *Absolution* 1979; *Teil Steiner - Das Eiserne Kreuz 2* 1979; *Circle of Two* 1980; *Wagner* 1983; *1984* 1984.

Burton, Tim • Director • Born US, 1960. *Educ.* California Institute of the Arts (animation). Young director known for his comic-strip visual sensibility (rooted in his early apprenticeship as a Disney animator) and black, surreal humor.

During his stint with Disney, Burton made a six-minute animated short, *Vincent*, narrated by Vincent Price. The film used the skewed perspectives of German expressionism to portray the dual life of a tortured but seemingly normal suburban child; it won a number of awards and was released commercially in 1982. His next venture, the 29-minute live-action feature *Frankenweenie*, was considered unsuitable for release but landed Burton his first feature directing assignment—at the tender age of 25—on *Pee Wee's Big Adventure* (1985).

Next came *Beetlejuice*, an inventive, campy ghost story, with outstanding special effects, which became one of the biggest sleeper hits of 1988; its live-action cartoon style made Burton a good choice to direct *Batman* (1989), an enormously successful feature high on dark, brooding atmosphere and stylish visuals but marred by somewhat wooden action sequences.

Burton consolidated his position as Hollywood wunderkind of the early 1990s with *Edward Scissorhands* (1990), a suburban fable of a youth with scissor shears instead of hands. The role of the "inventor" responsible for the title character's bizarre deformity was played by Vincent Price, whom Burton cites as an important influence on his directorial sensibility. • *Pee-wee's Big Adventure* 1985 (d); *Beetlejuice* 1988 (d); *Batman* 1989 (d); *Edward Scissorhands* 1990 (d,p,story).

Buscemi, Steve • Actor; also performance artist. • Born Brooklyn, NY, 1958. Graduate of New York's downtown theater scene, most notably in collaboration with Mark Boone Jr., who made his film debut in 1984 and has subsequently appeared in a number of interesting, off-beat productions. Married to performance artist/choreographer Jo Andres. • *The Way It Is or Eurydice in the Avenues* 1984; *No Picnic* 1986; *Parting Glances* 1986; *Sleepwalk* 1986; *Force of Circumstance* 1987; *Heart* 1987; *Kiss Daddy Good Night* 1987; *Call Me* 1988; *Coffee and Cigarettes Part Two (short)* 1988; *Heart of Midnight* 1988; *Vibes* 1988; *Bloodhounds of Broadway* 1989; *Borders* 1989; *Mystery Train* 1989; *New York Stories* 1989; *Slaves of New York* 1989; *King of New York* 1990; *Miller's Crossing* 1990; *Tales From the Darkside: The Movie* 1990; *Zandalee* 1991.

Busey, Gary • Actor • Born Goose Creek, TX, June 29, 1944. *Educ.* Kansas State College (theater); Oklahoma State University (theater). Fresh-faced former drummer who first appeared on TV in "The High Chapparal" in 1970 and gave a winning film performance as the title character of *The Buddy Holly Story* (1978). Later in character roles, often as a heavy. • *Angels Hard As They Come* 1971 (a); *Dirty Little Billy* 1972 (a); *Hex* 1972 (a); *The Last American Hero* 1973 (a); *Lolly-Madonna XXX* 1973 (a); *Thunderbolt And Lightfoot* 1974 (a); *You and Me* 1975 (a); *The Gumball Rally* 1976 (a); *A Star Is Born* 1976 (a); *Big Wednesday* 1978 (a); *The Buddy Holly Story* 1978 (a,song) **(AANBA)**; *Straight Time* 1978 (a); *Foolin' Around* 1979 (a); *Carny* 1980 (a); *Barbarosa* 1982 (a); *D.C. Cab* 1983 (a,songs); *The Bear* 1984 (a); *Insignificance* 1985 (a); *Silver Bullet* 1985 (a); *Eye of the Tiger* 1986 (a); *Half a Lifetime* 1986 (a); *Let's Get Harry* 1987 (a); *Lethal Weapon* 1987 (a); *Act of Piracy* 1988 (a); *Bulletproof* 1988 (a);

Hider in the House 1989 (a); *Predator 2* 1990 (a); *My Heroes Have Always Been Cowboys* 1991 (a).

Bushman, Francis X. • Actor • Born Francis Xavier Bushman, Norfolk, VA, January 10, 1883; died 1966. Enormously popular, handsome romantic lead of the 1910s, best known for starring in *Romeo and Juliet* (1916) and playing Messala in *Ben Hur* (1925). • *Graustark* 1915; *Pennington's Choice* 1915; *The Silent Voice* 1915; *In the Diplomatic Service* 1916 (a,d,sc); *Man and His Soul* 1916; *A Million a Minute* 1916; *Romeo and Juliet* 1916; *The Wall Between* 1916; *The Adopted Son* 1917; *The Great Secret* 1917; *Red, White and Blue Blood* 1917; *Their Compact* 1917; *The Voice of Conscience* 1917; *The Brass Check* 1918; *Cyclone Higgins, D D* 1918; *A Pair of Cupids* 1918; *The Poor Rich Man* 1918; *Social Quicksands* 1918; *Under Suspicion* 1918; *With Neatness and Dispatch* 1918; *Daring Hearts* 1919; *God's Outlaw* 1919; *Smiling All the Way* 1920; *Modern Marriage* 1923; *Ben Hur, A Tale of the Christ* 1925; *The Masked Bride* 1925; *The Marriage Clause* 1926; *The Lady in Ermine* 1927; *The Thirteenth Juror* 1927; *The Charge of the Gauchos* 1928; *The Grip of the Yukon* 1928; *Man Higher Up* 1928; *Midnight Life* 1928; *Say It With Sables* 1928; *The Call of the Circus* 1930; *The Dude Wrangler* 1930; *Once a Gentleman* 1930; *The Galloping Ghost* 1931; *Hollywood Boulevard* 1936; *Dick Tracy* 1937; *Mr. Celebrity* 1941; *Peer Gynt* 1941; *Wilson* 1944; *David and Bathsheba* 1951; *Apache Country* 1952; *Sabrina* 1954; *The Story of Mankind* 1957; *The Phantom Planet* 1961; *The Ghost in the Invisible Bikini* 1966.

Byrne, David • Composer, musician; also director, actor. • Born Dumbarton, Scotland, May 14, 1952. *Educ.* Rhode Island School of Design, Providence (photography, performance, video); Maryland Institute College of Art, Baltimore. Leader of the influential rock group Talking Heads whose eclectic, trans-cultural borrowings have made him one of the most celebrated popular musicians in the world. Clad in a hugely over-sized suit, Byrne gave a magnetic performance in Jonathan Demme's hypnotic concert film *Stop Making Sense* (1984). An accomplished video artist, he moved into feature filmmaking with the quirky, well-received *True Stories* (1986), a quizzical look at the American midwest. Byrne has also contributed songs to a number of features and shared an Oscar with Ryuichi Sakamoto and Cong Su for his scoring of Bernardo Bertolucci's *The Last Emperor* (1987). • *Times Square* 1980 (song); *The Animals Film* 1981 (song); *America Is Waiting (short)* 1982 (songs); *The King of Comedy* 1983 (song); *Stop Making Sense* 1984 (a,stage conception,stage lighting,sound rerecording mixer,song); *Dead End Kids* 1986 (m); *Something Wild* 1986 (songs); *True Stories* 1986 (a,d,sc,m,2u director ("Wild Wild Life," "Love For Sale"),m); *The Last Emperor* 1987 (m) **(AABM)**; *Wall Street* 1987 (song); *April 16th 1989 (short)* 1988 (d); *Checking Out* 1988 (a); *Completely Pogued* 1988 (a); *Heavy Petting* 1988 (a); *Married to the Mob* 1988 (m); *A Rustling of Leaves: Inside the Philippine Revolution* 1988 (m,m.perf); *Magicians of the Earth* 1989 (m); *Umbabarauma (short)* 1989 (exec.p).

Byrne, Gabriel • Actor • Born Dublin, Ireland, 1950. *Educ.* University College, Dublin. Brooding, handsome actor, in international films since 1978. Byrne proved himself a capable lead in the taut political thriller *Defence of the Realm* (1985) and is best known to American audiences as the star of the Coen brothers' stylish gangster drama, *Miller's Crossing* (1990). Married to actress Ellen Barkin, opposite whom he starred—less memorably—in *Siesta* (1987). • *On a Paving Stone Mounted* 1978; *The Outsider* 1979; *Excalibur* 1981; *Hannah K* 1983; *The Keep* 1983; *Reflections* 1983; *Defence of the Realm* 1985; *Gothic* 1986; *The Courier* 1987; *Hello, Again* 1987; *Julia and Julia* 1987; *Lionheart* 1987; *Siesta* 1987; *A Soldier's Tale* 1988; *Diamond Skulls* 1989; *Hakon Hakonsen* 1990; *Miller's Crossing* 1990.

Caan, James • Actor; also director. • Born Queens, NY, March 26, 1939. *Educ.* Michigan State University, East Lansing; Hofstra University, Hempstead, NY; Neighborhood Playhouse, New York. After some stage experience, began his film career with an uncredited bit part in *Irma La Douce* (1963). Caan gained prominence in the early 1970s with two powerful performances: as the cancer-stricken football player in the made-for-TV *Brian's Song* (1971) and the hot-tempered eldest son in Francis Ford Coppola's *The Godfather* (1972). His sole directing effort was the smoothly handled drama *Hide in Plain Sight* (1980). • *Lady in a Cage* 1964; *The Glory Guys* 1965; *Red Line 7000* 1965; *El Dorado* 1967; *Games* 1967; *Submarine X-1* 1967; *Countdown* 1968; *Journey to Shiloh* 1968; *The Rain People* 1969; *Rabbit, Run* 1970; *T. R. Baskin* 1971; *The Godfather* 1972 **(AANBSA)**; *Cinderella Liberty* 1973; *Slither* 1973; *Freebie and the Bean* 1974; *The Gambler* 1974; *The Godfather, Part II* 1974; *Funny Lady* 1975; *The Killer Elite* 1975; *Rollerball* 1975; *Harry and Walter Go to New York* 1976; *Another Man, Another Chance* 1977; *A Bridge Too Far* 1977; *Comes a Horseman* 1978; *Little Moon & Jud McGraw* 1978; *Chapter Two* 1979; *Hide in Plain Sight* 1980 (a,d); *Thief* 1981; *Les Uns et les autres* 1981; *Kiss Me Goodbye* 1982; *Gardens of Stone* 1987; *Alien Nation* 1988; *Dick Tracy* 1990; *Misery* 1990.

Cabanne, Christy • *aka* W. Christy Cabanne • Director; also screenwriter. • Born William Christy Cabanne, St. Louis, MO, April 16, 1888; died 1950. *Educ.* US Naval Academy, Annapolis, MD. Entered films as an actor for D.W. Griffith before turning to directing in 1913. Cabanne remained popular and successful until the late 1920s, when he was reduced to directing low-budget features. • *The Adopted Brother* 1913 (d); *The Blue or the Gray* 1913 (d); *The Conscience of Hassan Bey* 1913 (d); *Judith of Bethulia* 1913 (ad); *The Suffragette Minstrels* 1913 (d); *The Vengeance of Galora* 1913 (d); *Arms and the Gringo* 1914 (d); *The Better Way* 1914 (d); *The Gangsters of New York (short)* 1914 (d); *Granny* 1914 (d); *The Hunchback* 1914 (d); *A Lesson in Mechanics* 1914 (d); *A Question of Courage* 1914 (d); *The Quicksands* 1914 (d); *The Rebellion of Kitty Belle* 1914 (d); *The Saving Grace* 1914 (d); *The Sisters* 1914 (d); *The Suffragette Battle of Nuttyville* 1914 (d); *Double Trouble* 1915 (d,sc); *Enoch Arden* 1915 (d); *The Lamb* 1915 (d,sc); *The Lost House* 1915 (d); *The Martyrs of the Alamo* 1915 (d,sc); *Daphne and the Pirate* 1916 (d); *Diane of the Follies* 1916 (d); *Flirting With Fate* 1916 (d); *The Flying Torpedo* 1916 (d); *Reggie Mixes It* 1916 (d); *Sold For Marriage* 1916 (d); *Draft 258* 1917 (d); *The Great Secret* 1917 (d,p,sc); *Miss Robinson Crusoe* 1917 (d,story); *One of Many* 1917 (d,p,sc); *The Slacker* 1917 (d,sc); *Cyclone Higgins, D D* 1918 (d,sc); *Beloved Cheater* 1919 (d); *Fighting Through* 1919 (d); *God's Outlaw* 1919 (d,sc); *The Mayor of Filbert* 1919 (d); *The Pest* 1919 (d); *Regular Fellow* 1919 (d); *The Triflers* 1919 (d); *Burnt Wings* 1920 (d,sc); *Life's Twist* 1920 (d); *The Notorious Mrs. Sands* 1920 (d); *The Stealers* 1920 (d,story); *At the Stage Door* 1921 (d,sc); *The Barricade* 1921 (d); *Live and Let Live* 1921 (d,story); *What's a Wife Worth?* 1921 (d,sc); *Beyond the Rainbow* 1922 (d); *Till We Meet Again* 1922 (d); *The Average Woman* 1924 (d); *Is Love Everything?* 1924 (d,story); *Lend Me Your Husband* 1924 (d); *The Sixth Commandment* 1924 (d,p); *The Spitfire* 1924 (d); *Youth For Sale* 1924 (d); *Ben Hur, A Tale of the Christ* 1925 (d); *The Masked Bride* 1925 (d); *The Midshipman*

1925 (d); *Altars of Desire* 1926 (d); *Monte Carlo* 1926 (d); *Annapolis* 1928 (d); *Driftwood* 1928 (d); *Nameless Men* 1928 (d); *Restless Youth* 1929 (d); *Conspiracy* 1930 (d); *The Dawn Trail* 1930 (d); *Convicted* 1931 (d); *Graft* 1931 (d); *Sky Raiders* 1931 (d); *Hearts of Humanity* 1932 (d); *Hotel Continental* 1932 (d); *The Midnight Patrol* 1932 (d); *The Red Haired Alibi* 1932 (d); *The Unwritten Law* 1932 (d); *Western Limited* 1932 (d); *Daring Daughters* 1933 (d); *Midshipman Jack* 1933 (d); *The World Gone Mad* 1933 (d); *A Girl of the Limberlost* 1934 (d); *Jane Eyre* 1934 (d); *Money Means Nothing* 1934 (d); *When Strangers Meet* 1934 (d); *Another Face* 1935 (d); *Behind the Green Lights* 1935 (d); *The Keeper of the Bees* 1935 (d); *One Frightened Night* 1935 (d); *Rendezvous at Midnight* 1935 (d); *Storm Over The Andes* 1935 (d); *It's Up to You* 1936 (d); *The Last Outlaw* 1936 (d); *Annapolis Salute* 1937 (d,story); *Criminal Lawyer* 1937 (d); *Don't Tell the Wife* 1937 (d); *The Outcasts of Poker Flat* 1937 (d); *We Who Are About to Die* 1937 (d); *The Westland Case* 1937 (d); *You Can't Beat Love* 1937 (d); *Everybody's Doing It* 1938 (d); *Night Spot* 1938 (d); *This Marriage Business* 1938 (d); *Alas Sobre El Chaco* 1939 (d); *Legion of Lost Flyers* 1939 (d); *Man From Montreal* 1939 (d); *Mutiny on the Blackhawk* 1939 (d); *Smashing the Spy Ring* 1939 (d); *Tropic Fury* 1939 (d); *Alias the Deacon* 1940 (d); *Black Diamonds* 1940 (d); *Danger on Wheels* 1940 (d); *The Devil's Pipeline* 1940 (d); *Hot Steel* 1940 (d); *The Mummy's Hand* 1940 (d); *Scattergood Baines* 1941 (d); *Scattergood Meets Broadway* 1941 (d); *Scattergood Pulls the Strings* 1941 (d,sc); *Drums of the Congo* 1942 (d); *Scattergood Rides High* 1942 (d); *Scattergood Survives a Murder* 1942 (d); *Timber* 1942 (d); *Top Sergeant* 1942 (d); *Cinderella Swings It* 1943 (d); *Keep 'Em Slugging* 1943 (d); *Dixie Jamboree* 1944 (d); *The Man Who Walked Alone* 1945 (d,story); *Sensation Hunters* 1945 (d); *King of the Bandits* 1947 (d,story); *Robin Hood of Monterey* 1947 (d); *Scared to Death* 1947 (d); *Back Trail* 1948 (d); *Silver Trails* 1948 (d).

Cacoyannis, Michael • Director, screenwriter; also editor, producer. • Born Mikhalis Kakogiannis, Limassol, Cyprus, June 11, 1922. Studied law and acting in England before returning to Greece to direct his first feature, *Windfall in Athens* (1953). After several critically acclaimed films, including the much-lauded adaptation of *Electra* (1961), Cacoyannis achieved international fame with 1964's US-produced *Zorba the Greek*. Although *Zorba* remains his biggest success, Cacoyannis is generally more at home with epic, theatrically-derived material. • *Windfall in Athens* 1953 (d,sc); *Stella* 1955 (d,sc); *To Koritsi Me Ta Mara* 1956 (d,sc); *To telefteo psema/A Matter of Dignity* 1957 (d,sc); *Our Last Spring* 1959 (d,sc); *Eroica* 1960 (d,sc); *Electra* 1961 (d,sc); *Il Relitto* 1961 (d,sc); *Zorba the Greek* 1964 (d,p,sc,ed) **(AANBD)**; *The Day the Fish Came Out* 1967 (d,sc); *The Trojan Women* 1971 (d,p,sc); *Attila 74* 1975 (a,d,p,ed); *Iphigenia* 1977 (d,sc,ed); *Sweet Country* 1986 (d,p,sc,ed).

Cage, Nicolas • Actor • Born Nicholas Coppola, Long Beach, CA, January 7, 1964. *Educ.* American Conservatory Theatre (acting). Nephew of director Francis Coppola who graduated from teen roles in *Valley Girl* (1983) and *Rumble Fish* (1983) to off-beat leading roles in Alan Parker's *Birdy* (1984), Coppola's romantic comedy *Peggy Sue Got Married* (1986) and David Lynch's *Wild at Heart* (1990). • *Rumble Fish* 1983; *Valley Girl* 1983; *Birdy* 1984; *The Cotton Club* 1984; *Racing With the Moon* 1984; *The Boy in Blue* 1986; *Peggy Sue Got Married* 1986; *Moonstruck* 1987; *Raising Arizona* 1987; *Vampire's Kiss* 1988; *Never on Tuesday* 1989; *Tempo di Uccidere* 1989; *Fire Birds* 1990; *Wild at Heart* 1990; *Zandalee* 1991.

Cagney, James • Actor; also producer. • Born James Francis Cagney, Jr., New York, NY, July 17, 1899; died March 30, 1986, Stanfordville, NY. *Educ.* Columbia (German). The American gangster film, and the output of Warner Bros. in its most influential decade, would be unimaginable without the contributions of James Cagney. One of talking pictures' first generation of actors, Cagney forever romanticized the figures of the criminal and the con artist with his jittery physical dynamism and breakneck staccato vocal patterns.

Raised in New York City's tough Yorkville neighborhood, Cagney was a veteran of settlement house revues, vaudeville and five years of Broadway when he came to Warner Bros. in 1930. Cagney, Bette Davis and Edward G. Robinson, all signed to long-term contracts during this period, became the core of the studio's stock company, which also included character and supporting players such as Alan Jenkins and Frank McHugh. After playing several featured roles Cagney attained instant and lasting fame with his role as vicious gunman Tom Powers in William Wellman's *The Public Enemy* (1931).

The Public Enemy's story of a wisecracking hood who seemed to delight in violence indelibly stamped the gangster genre. Along with *Little Caesar* (1931) and *I Am a Fugitive From a Chain Gang* (1932), the picture cemented Warner Bros.' position as a major studio. Between 1930 and 1941, Cagney made 38 films at Warner Bros. While most were crime and action dramas or comedies, quickly produced on modest budgets and featuring few other box office "names," many have become genre classics. Several, including *Angels With Dirty Faces* (1938) and *The Roaring Twenties* (1939), remain seminal works in American film history. Cagney reached a creative peak with *Yankee Doodle Dandy* (1942), a biopic based on the life of composer George M. Cohan. A sentimental masterpiece, the film drew on Cagney's prodigious singing and dancing talents, previously unexploited at Warner Bros., and brought him the Academy Award for best actor.

A series of well-publicized salary disputes at Warner Bros. led to Cagney's forming an independent production company, Cagney Productions. Headed by James and his brother William, a former actor, the firm was based on terms developed in James's last Warner Bros. contract and gave him unprecedented leeway in choosing vehicles and participating in profits. It proved a failure, releasing only three films through United Artists, but was nevertheless a pathbreaking model which many others in the industry would soon follow.

In 1949 Cagney made an explosive return to Warner Bros. in the Raoul Walsh-directed *White Heat*, playing Cody Jarrett, a violent, Freudianized update of the Tom Powers character in *The Public Enemy*. Like the earlier film, *White Heat* was both profitable and enormously influential.

Throughout the 1950s Cagney played sardonic and often villainous characters for several studios, in films occasionally produced by Cagney Productions. The decade also saw his only directing assignment, *Short Cut To Hell* (1957), and his last musical, the delightful *Never Steal Anything Small* (1959).

After a bravura performance in Billy Wilder's ironic farce *One, Two, Three* (1961), Cagney retired. The following years saw him receive many honors, including the 1974 Life Achievement Award of the American Film Institute—the second such award ever given. His good friend and neighbor, director Milos Forman, lured him from retirement for *Ragtime* (1981), but Cagney's own desires to perform again were hampered by increasing ill health. He made only one more appearance before his death, the made-for-TV movie *Terrible Joe Moran* (1984). KJH • *The Doorway to Hell* 1930; *Sinner's Holiday* 1930; *Blonde Crazy* 1931; *Little Caesar* 1931; *The Millionaire* 1931; *Other Men's Women* 1931; *The Public Enemy* 1931; *Smart Money* 1931; *The Crowd Roars* 1932; *I Am a Fugitive From a Chain Gang* 1932; *Taxi* 1932; *Winner Take All* 1932; *Footlight Parade* 1933; *Hard to Handle* 1933; *Lady Killer* 1933; *The Mayor of Hell* 1933; *Picture Snatcher* 1933; *He Was Her Man* 1934; *Here Comes the Navy* 1934; *Jimmy the Gent* 1934; *The St. Louis Kid* 1934; *Ceiling Zero* 1935; *Devil Dogs of the Air* 1935; *Frisco Kid* 1935; *G-Men* 1935; *The Irish in Us* 1935; *A Midsummer Night's Dream* 1935; *Great Guy* 1936; *Something to Sing About* 1937; *Angels With Dirty*

Faces 1938 (**AANBA**); *Boy Meets Girl* 1938; *Each Dawn I Die* 1939; *The Oklahoma Kid* 1939; *The Roaring Twenties* 1939; *City For Conquest* 1940; *The Fighting 69th* 1940; *Torrid Zone* 1940; *The Bride Came C.O.D.* 1941; *The Strawberry Blonde* 1941; *Captains of the Clouds* 1942; *Yankee Doodle Dandy* 1942 (**AABA**); *Johnny Come Lately* 1943; *Blood on the Sun* 1945; *13 Rue Madeleine* 1947; *The Time of Your Life* 1948; *White Heat* 1949; *Kiss Tomorrow Goodbye* 1950; *The West Point Story* 1950; *Come Fill the Cup* 1951; *Starlift* 1951; *What Price Glory* 1952; *A Lion Is in the Streets* 1953; *Run For Cover* 1954; *Love Me or Leave Me* 1955 (**AANBA**); *Mister Roberts* 1955; *The Seven Little Foys* 1955; *Tribute to a Bad Man* 1955; *These Wilder Years* 1956; *Man of a Thousand Faces* 1957; *Short Cut to Hell* 1957 (a,d); *Never Steal Anything Small* 1959 (a,song); *Shake Hands With the Devil* 1959; *The Gallant Hours* 1960; *One, Two, Three* 1961; *Arizona Bushwhackers* 1968; *It's Showtime* 1976; *Ragtime* 1981; *Going Hollywood: The War Years* 1988 (archival footage); *Entertaining the Troops* 1989 (archival footage).

Caine, Michael • Actor • Born Maurice Joseph Micklewhite, Bermondsey, England, March 14, 1933. Commanding, prolific, cockney-voiced leading man who became a household name with the success of *Alfie* (1966) and a trilogy of films (*Ipcress File* 1965, *Funeral in Berlin* 1966, *Billion Dollar Brain* 1967) based on Len Deighton spy thrillers. Caine's movies range from the routine to the award-winning but his performances are consistently capable and often outstanding. He allegedly changed his name after seeing the marquee for *The Caine Mutiny* (1954). • *A Hill in Korea* 1956; *How to Murder a Rich Uncle* 1957; *Blind Spot* 1958; *The Key* 1958; *The Two-Headed Spy* 1958; *The Bulldog Breed* 1960; *Foxhole in Cairo* 1960; *The Day the Earth Caught Fire* 1961; *Solo For Sparrow* 1962; *The Wrong Arm of the Law* 1962; *Zulu* 1963; *The Ipcress File* 1965; *Alfie* 1966 (**AANBA**); *Funeral in Berlin* 1966; *Gambit* 1966; *The Wrong Box* 1966; *Billion Dollar Brain* 1967; *Hurry Sundown* 1967; *Tonite Let's All Make Love in London* 1967; *Woman Times Seven* 1967; *Deadfall* 1968; *The Magus* 1968; *Play Dirty* 1968; *Battle of Britain* 1969; *The Italian Job* 1969; *Too Late the Hero* 1970; *Get Carter* 1971; *Kidnapped* 1971; *The Last Valley* 1971; *Pulp* 1972; *Sleuth* 1972 (**AANBA**); *X Y & Zee* 1972; *The Black Windmill* 1974; *The Destructors* 1974; *The Man Who Would Be King* 1975; *Peeper* 1975; *The Romantic Englishwoman* 1975; *The Wilby Conspiracy* 1975; *The Eagle Has Landed* 1976; *Harry and Walter Go to New York* 1976; *A Bridge Too Far* 1977; *Silver Bears* 1977; *California Suite* 1978; *The Swarm* 1978; *Ashanti* 1979; *Beyond the Poseidon Adventure* 1979; *Dressed to Kill* 1980; *The Island* 1980; *Escape to Victory* 1981; *The Hand* 1981; *Deathtrap* 1982; *Beyond the Limit* 1983; *Educating Rita* 1983 (**AANBA**); *Blame It on Rio* 1984; *The Jigsaw Man* 1984; *Water* 1984; *The Holcroft Covenant* 1985; *Half Moon Street* 1986; *Hannah and Her Sisters* 1986 (**AABSA**); *Mona Lisa* 1986; *Sweet Liberty* 1986; *The Fourth Protocol* 1987 (a,exec.p); *Jaws: The Revenge* 1987; *Surrender* 1987; *The Whistle Blower* 1987; *Dirty Rotten Scoundrels* 1988; *John Huston* 1988; *Without a Clue* 1988; *Bullseye!* 1990; *Mr. Destiny* 1990; *A Shock to the System* 1990.

Calhern, Louis • Actor • Born Carl Henry Vogt, New York, NY, February 16, 1895; died 1956, Tokyo. In silent films as a young man but best remembered for his elderly roles of the 1950s, notably in the title role of *Julius Caesar* (1953) and as Oliver Wendell Holmes in John Sturges's *The Magnificent Yankee* (1950). Married to actresses Ilka Chase, Julia Hoyt, Natalie Schaefer and Marianne Stewart. • *The Blot* 1921; *Too Wise Wives* 1921; *What's Worth While?* 1921; *Woman, Wake Up!* 1922; *The Last Moment* 1923; *Blonde Crazy* 1931; *The Road to Singapore* 1931; *Stolen Heaven* 1931; *Afraid to Talk* 1932; *Night After Night* 1932; *Okay America* 1932; *They Call It Sin* 1932; *20,000 Years in Sing Sing* 1933; *Diplomaniacs* 1933; *Duck Soup* 1933; *Frisco Jenny* 1933; *Strictly Personal* 1933; *The Woman Accused* 1933; *The World Gone Mad* 1933; *The Affairs of Cellini* 1934; *The Count of Monte Cristo* 1934; *The Man With Two Faces* 1934; *The Arizonian* 1935; *The Last Days of Pompeii* 1935; *Sweet Adeline* 1935; *Woman Wanted* 1935; *The Gorgeous Hussy* 1936; *Her Husband Lies* 1937; *The Life of Emile Zola* 1937; *Fast Company* 1938; *Charlie McCarthy, Detective* 1939; *Fifth Avenue Girl* 1939; *Juarez* 1939; *Dr. Ehrlich's Magic Bullet* 1940; *I Take This Woman* 1940; *Heaven Can Wait* 1943; *Nobody's Darling* 1943; *The Bridge of San Luis Rey* 1944; *Up in Arms* 1944; *Notorious* 1946; *Arch of Triumph* 1948; *The Red Danube* 1949; *The Red Pony* 1949; *Annie Get Your Gun* 1950; *The Asphalt Jungle* 1950; *Devil's Doorway* 1950; *A Life of Her Own* 1950; *The Magnificent Yankee* 1950 (**AANBA**); *Nancy Goes to Rio* 1950; *Two Weeks With Love* 1950; *The Man With a Cloak* 1951; *Invitation* 1952; *The Prisoner of Zenda* 1952; *Washington Story* 1952; *We're Not Married* 1952; *Confidentially Connie* 1953; *Julius Caesar* 1953; *Latin Lovers* 1953; *Main Street to Broadway* 1953; *Remains to Be Seen* 1953; *Athena* 1954; *Betrayed* 1954; *Executive Suite* 1954; *Men of the Fighting Lady* 1954; *Rhapsody* 1954; *The Student Prince* 1954; *Blackboard Jungle* 1955; *The Prodigal* 1955; *Forever, Darling* 1956; *High Society* 1956.

Cambridge, Godfrey • Actor • Born New York, NY, February 26, 1933; died November 29, 1976, Hollywood, CA. *Educ.* CCNY. Heavyset (sometimes overweight), black player who began his career off-Broadway in *Take a Giant Step* (1956) and won acclaim, and an Obie Award, for his performance in the all-star production of Jean Genet's *The Blacks* (1961) in which he played a black man who is transformed into an aged white woman. Adept at both ironic comedy and serious drama, Cambridge often starred in films with racial themes including the satirical *Watermelon Man* (1970) as a white bigot who wakes up to find himself suddenly turned into a black man. Cambridge, who was also memorable in *The President's Analyst* (1967) and *Cotton Comes to Harlem* (1970), died of a heart attack on the set of a TV movie in which he was playing Idi Amin Dada. • *The Last Angry Man* 1959; *Gone Are the Days* 1963; *The Troublemaker* 1964; *The Busy Body* 1967; *The President's Analyst* 1967; *The Biggest Bundle of Them All* 1968; *Bye Bye Braverman* 1968; *Cotton Comes to Harlem* 1970; *Watermelon Man* 1970; *Beware the Blob* 1972; *The Biscuit Eater* 1972; *Come Back Charleston Blue* 1972; *Five on the Black Hand Side* 1973; *Friday Foster* 1975; *Whiffs* 1975; *Scott Joplin* 1977.

Cameron, James • Director; also screenwriter, producer. • Born Kapuskasing, Ontario, Canada, August 16, 1954. *Educ.* California State University (physics). Began his career designing sets for Roger Corman and has since established himself as a premier director of action films. Cameron is divorced from his sometime producer Gale Ann Hurd, and since 1989, married to director Kathryn Bigelow. • *Battle Beyond the Stars* 1980 (art d); *Happy Birthday, Gemini* 1980 (set dresser asst); *Galaxy of Terror* 1981 (pd,2u d); *Piranha II: Flying Killers* 1981 (d); *The Terminator* 1984 (d,sc); *Rambo: First Blood Part II* 1985 (sc); *Aliens* 1986 (d,sc,story); *The Abyss* 1989 (d,sc); *Terminator 2: Judgment Day* 1991 (d,p,sc).

Camp, Colleen • Actress; also singer. • Born San Francisco, CA, 1953. Versatile, chameleon-like character actress, equally adept at sexy or priggish parts. Has played in three Martha Coolidge films and served as associate producer of her 1983 film, *The City Girl.* • *The Swinging Cheerleaders* 1974; *Smile* 1975; *Death Game* 1976; *Love and the Midnight Auto Supply* 1977; *Apocalypse Now* 1979; *Cloud Dancer* 1979; *Game of Death* 1979 (a,songs); *Who Fell Asleep?* 1979; *The Seduction* 1981; *They All Laughed* 1981 (a,song); *The City Girl* 1983 (a,assoc.p,song); *Loose Ends* 1983; *Smokey and the Bandit—Part 3* 1983; *Valley Girl* 1983; *Joy of Sex* 1984; *Clue* 1985; *D.A.R.Y.L.* 1985; *Doin' Time* 1985; *Police Academy 2: Their First Assignment* 1985; *The Rosebud Beach*

Hotel 1985; *Police Academy 4: Citizens on Patrol* 1987; *Track 29* 1987; *Walk Like a Man* 1987; *Illegally Yours* 1988 (a,song); *Wicked Stepmother* 1989; *My Blue Heaven* 1990.

Campion, Jane • Director; also screenwriter. • Born Waikanae, New Zealand, c. 1954. *Educ.* Australian Film, Television and Radio School. After receiving the Palme d'Or at Cannes in 1986 for a much-admired program of short films, Campion directed *Two Friends* (1985), an award-winning television movie, before making a darkly stylish feature debut with *Sweetie* (1989), a disturbing study of familial tensions and mental breakdown.

Campion consolidated her reputation as a major talent with *An Angel at My Table* (1990), based on writer Janet Frame's three autobiographical novels. The film was originally broadcast as a mini-series on New Zealand television, and subsequently released theatrically to international acclaim. • *Peel (short)* 1982 (d,sc,ed); *A Girl's Own Story (short)* 1983 (d,sc,song); *Passionless Moments (short)* 1984 (d,p,sc,ph,cam.op); *Sweetie* 1989 (d,sc,idea,casting); *An Angel at My Table* 1990 (d).

Camus, Marcel • Director • Born Chappes, France, April 21, 1912; died 1982. The work of Marcel Camus is characterized by a lyricism which, although central to his fine films of the 1950s and 60s—*Fugitive in Saigon* (1957), *Black Orpheus* (1959) and *Vivre la nuit* (1968)—later deteriorated into superficial sentimentality.

Camus was a professor of painting and sculpture before breaking into film as an assistant to Alexandre Astruc, Georges Rouquier and Jacques Becker, among others. During this period he made his first film, a short documentary called *Renaissance du Havre* (1950).

Like many French filmmakers whose first chance to direct a feature came in the postwar era, Camus chose to deal explicitly with the issue of personal sacrifice in the context of war. But unlike most of his colleagues who quite naturally dealt with WWII, Camus took as his subject the war in Indochina. Based on a novel by Jean Hougron, *Fugitive in Saigon* depicts a village caught between two fronts. Its only possibility of survival involves the destruction of a dam on which it depends.

Camus then embarked on three films in collaboration with scenarist Jacques Viot. The first, *Black Orpheus*, brought him international acclaim. Winner of the 1959 grand prize at Cannes and an Academy Award as best foreign language film, this exotic modern adaptation of the Greek legend portrays its Orpheus (Breno Mello) as a streetcar conductor who meets his Eurydice (Marpessa Dawn) and lives out his legendary destiny during the Carnival in Rio de Janeiro.

The next two Camus-Viot collaborations, *Os Bandeirantes* (1960) and *Dragon Sky* (1962), were generally well received, but neither lived up to the expectations created by *Black Orpheus*. *Vivre la nuit* (1968), an affecting portrait of nocturnal Paris, proved successful, but *Un été savage* (1970) was generally recognized as an inauthentic and superficial evocation of young people on vacation in Saint-Tropez.

Camus then returned to the subject of war, this time with a gentle comedy about a Normandy restaurant owner who becomes a hero of the Resistance in spite of himself. *Le Mur de l'Atlantique* (1970) offered a rich role for comic actor Bourvil, but was essentially a routine commercial product. This unfortunate trend continued with *Otalia de Bahia* (1977), a spaghetti western titled *Trinita voit rouge* (1975) and some unexceptional work for French TV. RDH • *Cela s'appèlle l'aurore* 1956 (ad); *Morte en Fraude/Fugitive in Saigon* 1957 (d,sc); *Orfeu Negro/Black Orpheus* 1959 (adapt,dial,d); *Os Bandeirantes* 1960 (d,sc); *L'Oiseau de Paradis/Dragon Sky* 1962 (d,sc); *Le Chant du Monde* 1965 (d,sc); *L'Homme de New York* 1967 (d,sc); *Vivre la nuit* 1968 (d,sc); *Un été sauvage* 1970 (d,sc); *Le Mur de l'Atlantique* 1970 (d,sc); *Trinita voit rouge* 1975 (d); *Os Pastores da Noite/Otalia de Bahia* 1977 (d,sc,dial).

Candy, John • Actor • Born John Franklin Candy, Toronto, Ontario, Canada, October 31, 1950. *Educ.* Centennial Community College, Toronto (journalism). Popular chubby supporting comedian. Candy began his career in 1972 with Chicago's Second City comedy troupe, co-founded its Canadian offshoot and came to attention as a performer and award-winning writer with the resulting "SCTV" television show. After appearing in several features with Second City alumni such as John Belushi and Bill Murray, he assayed his first starring role in *Summer Rental* (1985) and has carried many comedies playing bumbling schemers or overbearing wiseguys. • *It Seemed Like a Good Idea at the Time* 1975; *The Clown Murders* 1976; *The Silent Partner* 1978; *1941* 1979; *Lost and Found* 1979; *The Blues Brothers* 1980; *Heavy Metal* 1981; *Stripes* 1981; *It Came From Hollywood* 1982; *Going Berserk* 1983; *National Lampoon's Vacation* 1983; *Splash* 1984; *Brewster's Millions* 1985; *Sesame Street Presents: Follow That Bird* 1985; *Summer Rental* 1985; *Volunteers* 1985; *Armed and Dangerous* 1986; *The Canadian Conspiracy* 1986; *Little Shop of Horrors* 1986; *Planes, Trains and Automobiles* 1987; *Spaceballs* 1987; *The Great Outdoors* 1988; *Hot to Trot* 1988; *Speed Zone* 1989; *Uncle Buck* 1989; *Who's Harry Crumb?* 1989 (a,exec.p); *Home Alone* 1990; *The Rescuers Down Under* 1990; *Masters of Menace* 1991; *Nothing But Trouble* 1991; *Only the Lonely* 1991.

Cannon, Dyan • *aka* Dianne Cannon • Actress • Born Samille Diane Friesen, Tacoma, WA, January 4, 1937. *Educ.* University of Washington (anthropology). Sexy, zany and spirited blonde who, after some TV work and minor features, sparkled as a deft comedienne in several trendy films of the 1970s and 80s. Cannon had a stormy marriage (1965-68) to actor Cary Grant, 35 years her senior. In 1976 she directed, wrote, produced, edited and scored the AFI sponsored, Oscar-nominated live-action short, *Growing Pains: Number One* about children's natural curiosity about their bodies and the adult values that stifle them, and made her feature directing and writing debut with the semi-autobiographical, *The End of Innocence* (1990). • *The Rise and Fall of Legs Diamond* 1960 (a); *This Rebel Breed* 1960 (a); *Bob & Carol & Ted & Alice* 1969 (a) **(AANBSA)**; *Doctors' Wives* 1970 (a); *The Anderson Tapes* 1971 (a); *Le Casse* 1971 (a); *The Love Machine* 1971 (a); *Such Good Friends* 1971 (a); *Shamus* 1972 (a); *The Last of Sheila* 1973 (a); *Child Under a Leaf* 1974 (a); *Growing Pains: Number One* (short) 1976 (d,p,sc); *Heaven Can Wait* 1978 (a) **(AANBSA)**; *Revenge of the Pink Panther* 1978 (a); *Coast to Coast* 1980 (a); *Honeysuckle Rose* 1980 (a); *Author! Author!* 1982 (a); *Deathtrap* 1982 (a); *Caddyshack II* 1988 (a); *The End of Innocence* 1990 (a,d,sc).

Canonero, Milena • Costume designer • Versatile designer, exceptional with films set in the past (*Chariots of Fire* 1981, *Out of Africa* 1985), present (*Barfly* 1987, *The Godfather Part III* 1990) and future (*A Clockwork Orange* 1971). Has collaborated on three of Stanley Kubrick's visually meticulous masterpieces and three of Coppola's. • *A Clockwork Orange* 1971 (cost); *Barry Lyndon* 1975 (cost) **(AABCD)**; *Midnight Express* 1978 (cost); *The Shining* 1980 (cost); *Chariots of Fire* 1981 (cost) **(AABCD)**; *Give My Regards to Broad Street* 1983 (cost); *The Hunger* 1983 (cost); *The Cotton Club* 1984 (cost); *Out of Africa* 1985 (cost) **(AANBCD)**; *Good Morning Babylon* 1986 (assoc.p); *Barfly* 1987 (visual consult,cost); *Haunted Summer* 1988 (cost); *Mamba* 1988 (assoc.p,cost consult); *Tucker: The Man and His Dream* 1988 (cost) **(AANBCD)**; *Lost Angels* 1989 (cost.consult); *Dick Tracy* 1990 (cost) **(AANBCD)**; *The Godfather Part III* 1990 (cost); *Naked Tango* 1990 (p); *Reversal of Fortune* 1990 (cost.consult).

Cantinflas • *aka* Mario Moreno • Clown; also actor. • Born Mario Moreno Reyes, Mexico City, August 11, 1911. Renowned performer of the Spanish-speaking world, in films from 1936.

Best known in the US as Passepartout in the star-studded *Around the World in 80 Days* (1956). • *No te engañes Corazón* 1936 (a); *El Circo* 1942 (a); *Romeo y Julieta* 1943 (a); *Los Tres Mosqueteros* 1943 (a); *Gran Hotel* 1944 (a); *El Mago* 1949 (a); *El Bombero atomico* 1951 (a); *Arriba el Telón* 1954 (a); *Around the World in 80 Days* 1956 (a); *Pepe* 1960 (a); *Un Quijote Sin Mancha* 1970 (a,sc); *Ministro y Yo* 1976 (a,story); *El Patrullero 777* 1978 (a).

Cantor, Eddie • Comedian; also actor, singer. • Born Edward Israel Iskowitz, New York, NY, January 31, 1892; died 1964. Energetic vaudeville performer, in Hollywood from 1926. Cantor was extremely popular in the 1930s on the radio, and in mostly routine movies that showcased his inimitable, infectious style of song, dance and comedy. He has a small part in the meager 1954 biopic *The Eddie Cantor Story*, starring Keefe Brasselle. • *Kid Boots* 1926 (a); *Special Delivery* 1927 (a,story); *Glorifying the American Girl* 1929 (a); *Whoopee* 1930 (a); *Mr. Lemon of Orange* 1931 (sc); *Palmy Days* 1931 (a,sc,story); *The Kid From Spain* 1932 (a); *Roman Scandals* 1933 (a); *Kid Millions* 1934 (a); *Strike Me Pink* 1936 (a); *Ali Baba Goes to Town* 1937 (a); *Forty Little Mothers* 1940 (a); *Thank Your Lucky Stars* 1943 (a); *Hollywood Canteen* 1944 (a); *Show Business* 1944 (a,p); *If You Knew Susie* 1948 (a,p); *The Story of Will Rogers* 1952 (a); *The Eddie Cantor Story* 1954 (a); *The Good Fight: The Abraham Lincoln Brigade in the Spanish Civil War* 1984 (song); *Entertaining the Troops* 1989 (archival footage); *Gremlins 2: The New Batch* 1990 (song).

Canutt, Yakima • Actor; also director • Born Enos Edward Canutt, Colfax, WA, November 29, 1895; died May 24, 1986, North Hollywood, CA. Five-time world champion rodeo rider from 1917 to 1923 and legendary Hollywood stuntman who became an important second unit director. Canutt also acted (usually as a villain) in many of the western and action films for which he did the stunt work and served as a double for such stars as John Wayne, Clark Gable and Gene Autry. From the late 1930s he also worked as a second unit director of action sequences, most notably on *Stagecoach* (1939), the chariot race in *Ben-Hur* (1959) and *Spartacus* (1960). In the mid-40s he directed four B westerns. Canutt earned a special Oscar in 1966 for "achievements as a stuntman and for developing safety devices to protect stuntmen everywhere." • *The Heart of a Texan* 1922; *Branded a Bandit* 1924; *The Days of '49* 1924; *The Desert Hawk* 1924; *Ridin' Mad* 1924; *Romance and Rustlers* 1924; *The Cactus Cure* 1925; *The Human Tornado* 1925; *The Ridin' Comet* 1925; *Scar Hanan* 1925 (a,story); *Sell 'Em Cowboy* 1925; *The Strange Rider* 1925; *A Two-Fisted Sheriff* 1925; *White Thunder* 1925; *Wolves of the Road* 1925; *Desert Greed* 1926; *The Devil Horse* 1926; *The Fighting Stallion* 1926; *Hellhounds of the Plains* 1926; *The Outlaw Breaker* 1926; *Iron Rider* 1927; *The Vanishing West* 1928; *Bad Men's Money* 1929; *Captain Cowboy* 1929; *Riders of the Storm* 1929; *The Three Outcasts* 1929; *Bar-L Ranch* 1930; *Canyon Hawks* 1930; *Firebrand Jordan* 1930; *The Lonesome Trail* 1930; *Ridin' Law* 1930; *Westward Bound* 1930; *Battling With Buffalo Bill* 1931; *Hurricane Horseman* 1931; *Pueblo Terror* 1931; *The Vanishing Legion* 1931; *Cheyenne Cyclone* 1932; *Guns For Hire* 1932; *The Last Frontier* 1932; *The Last of the Mohicans* 1932; *Riders of the Golden Gulch* 1932 (a,story); *The Shadow of the Eagle* 1932; *Two Fisted Justice* 1932; *Wyoming Whirlwind* 1932; *The Fighting Texans* 1933; *Law and Lawless* 1933; *Sagebrush Trail* 1933; *The Telegraph Trail* 1933; *Via Pony Express* 1933; *'Neath the Arizona Skies* 1934; *Blue Steel* 1934; *Fighting Through* 1934; *The Lucky Texan* 1934; *Man From Hell* 1934; *The Man From Utah* 1934; *Randy Rides Alone* 1934; *The Star Packer* 1934; *Texas Tornado* 1934; *West of the Divide* 1934; *Branded a Coward* 1935; *Circle of Death* 1935; *Cyclone of the Saddle* 1935; *The Dawn Rider* 1935; *The Lawless Frontier* 1935; *Lawless Range* 1935; *Pals of the Range* 1935; *Paradise Canyon* 1935; *Rough Riding Ranger* 1935; *Texas Terror* 1935; *Westward Ho* 1935; *The Black Coin* 1936; *The Clutching Hand* 1936; *Ghost Town Gold* 1936; *King of the Pecos* 1936; *The Lonely Trail* 1936; *The Oregon Trail* 1936; *The Vigilantes Are Coming* 1936; *Wildcat Trooper* 1936; *Winds of the Wasteland* 1936; *Come on Cowboys* 1937; *Gunsmoke Ranch* 1937; *Heart of the Rockies* 1937; *Hit the Saddle* 1937; *The Painted Stallion* 1937; *Prairie Thunder* 1937; *Range Defenders* 1937; *Riders of the Rockies* 1937; *Riders of the Whistling Skull* 1937; *Roarin' Lead* 1937; *Trouble in Texas* 1937; *The Mysterious Pilot* 1938; *The Secret of Treasure Island* 1938; *Cowboys From Texas* 1939; *Gone With the Wind* 1939; *The Kansas Terrors* 1939; *Stagecoach* 1939 (2u d,a); *Dark Command* 1940 (2u d,a); *Frontier Vengeance* 1940; *Ghost Valley Raiders* 1940; *The Great Train Robbery* 1940; *Pioneers of the West* 1940; *The Ranger and the Lady* 1940; *Under Texas Skies* 1940; *Gauchos of Eldorado* 1941; *Prairie Pioneers* 1941; *Shadows on the Sage* 1942; *In Old Oklahoma* 1943 (2u d,a); *Hidden Valley Outlaws* 1944; *Pride of the Plains* 1944; *Federal Operator 99* 1945 (d); *Manhunt of Mystery Island* 1945 (d); *Sheriff of Cimarron* 1945 (d); *Angel and the Badman* 1947 (2u d); *G-Men Never Forget* 1947 (d); *Wyoming* 1947 (2u d); *Adventures of Frank and Jesse James* 1948 (d); *Carson City Raiders* 1948 (d); *Dangers of the Canadian Mounted* 1948 (d); *Oklahoma Badlands* 1948 (d); *Sons of Adventure* 1948 (d); *The Doolins of Oklahoma* 1949 (2u d); *Rocky Mountain* 1950; *The Showdown* 1950; *Ivanhoe* 1952 (2u d); *Knights of the Round Table* 1953 (2u d); *The Lawless Rider* 1954 (d); *The Far Horizons* 1955; *Helen of Troy* 1956 (2u d); *Zarak* 1956 (assoc.d); *Old Yeller* 1958 (2u d); *Ben-Hur* 1959 (2u d); *Spartacus* 1960 (2u d); *The Swiss Family Robinson* 1960 (scene staging,stunt staging); *El Cid* 1961 (2u d); *How the West Was Won* 1962 (2u d); *The Fall of the Roman Empire* 1964 (2u d); *Cat Ballou* 1965 (2u d); *Khartoum* 1966 (2u d); *The Flim-Flam Man* 1967 (2u d); *Where Eagles Dare* 1968 (2u d); *A Man Called Horse* 1970 (2u d); *Rio Lobo* 1970 (2u d); *Song of Norway* 1970 (2u d); *Breakheart Pass* 1975 (2u d,stunt coordinator); *Equus* 1977 (tech.consultant—horses); *High on the Range* 1985.

Capra, Frank • *aka* Frank R. Capra • Director; also producer, screenwriter. • Born Bisaquino, Sicily, Italy, May 18, 1897. *Educ.* California Institute of Technology, Pasadena (chemical engineering). Although his critical reputation has fluctuated wildly, writer-producer-director Frank Capra remains, alongside John Ford, and perhaps Howard Hawks, a preeminent filmmaker of the prewar Hollywood cinema. Conventional wisdom has tended to pigeonhole Capra as a director of maudlin social comedies, but his 40-year career included a much more diverse body of work.

In fact, Capra's first 21 features, made between 1926 and 1932, bear almost none of the trademarks of his better-known films of the middle and late 30s. Capra's film career began in 1922 when, as an unemployed chemical engineer and WWI vet, he talked his way into directing an independently produced short, *Fultah Fisher's Boarding House*. For the next several years he apprenticed his way up the production ladder, eventually becoming a comedy writer for both Hal Roach (on some of the early "Our Gang" shorts) and Mack Sennett.

Between 1926 and 1927, Capra made his feature directorial debut with three successful vehicles for the popular silent comic Harry Langdon, but was fired when Langdon decided to direct himself.

The following year, a struggling Columbia Pictures made Capra a company director. Over the next ten years he would direct 25 films for that studio, including nine features in his first 12 months alone. But before carving out his niche as a maker of comic fables with a message, Capra became known as a reliable craftsman of efficient and profitable productions, regardless of genre. His early Columbia work included military/action dramas (*Submarine* 1928, *Flight* 1929, *Dirigible* 1931); newspaper stories (*The Power of the Press* 1928); Barbara Stanwyck melodramas (*Ladies of*

Leisure 1930, *The Miracle Woman* 1931, *Forbidden* 1932); and tearjerkers (*The Younger Generation* 1929).

But it was the sassy comedy *Platinum Blonde* (1931) that marked a turning point in the young director's career. The film's dialogue writer, Robert Riskin, became Capra's collaborator on seven of his next ten projects, a successful string of Depression-era comedies in which they perfected the "Capriskin formula": the individual idealist vs. a corrupt institution.

The first Capra-Riskin production, *American Madness* (1932), introduced the team's signature theme and idealistic hero: a dedicated community banker (Walter Huston) forestalls a bank run by rallying faithful depositors against the machinations of nefarious big businessmen. But Capra's transformation from house director to New Deal auteur was not immediate. His next film, the remarkably lush and atmospheric *The Bitter Tea of General Yen* (also 1932), departed from his all-American milieu, featuring Barbara Stanwyck as a missionary whose ideals are overwhelmed by her desire for a Chinese warlord. When Capra's "art film" drew little attention, he returned to work with Riskin on what he deemed a more blatantly commercial project. The result, the snappy comedy *It Happened One Night* (1934), swept the major Academy Awards (much to Capra's surprise) and proved to be a prototype for the screwball genre.

Capra's Oscars elevated him to a new level of prestige in the industry, and he began to produce as well as direct all of his projects. Arguably it was his role as producer that enabled Capra to create the string of celebrated films—*Mr Deeds Goes to Town* (1936), *Lost Horizon* (1937), *You Can't Take It With You* (1938), *Mr. Smith Goes to Washington* (1939), *Meet John Doe* (1941) and, quintessentially, *It's a Wonderful Life* (1946)—most closely associated with his name. However, the director himself recounts that these films of raw idealism and evangelical faith in the common man were the direct result of a personal conversion that followed a prolonged illness in 1935. Whether or not one believes that an anonymous visitor convinced Capra that he was to transform the silver screen into a pulpit committed to a love-thy-neighbor philosophy, the fact remains that these films consistently delivered that unabashed message, often in Oscar-winning fashion.

Capra successfully adapted existing properties to fit his utopian vision of the world: the popular novel *Lost Horizon* became a lavish film spectacle, with Ronald Colman as the idealistic diplomat who dreams of a warless world, while the freewheeling stage comedies *You Can't Take It With You* and *Arsenic and Old Lace* (1944) were transformed into paeans to democratic individualism. But Capra's message was memorably portrayed in original material, specifically in his trilogy of films—*Mr. Deeds/Mr. Smith/John Doe*—depicting small-town eccentrics as saviors of such "lost causes" as Christian charity, honesty and community. These celebrations of traditional values in the milieu of everyday life struck responsive chords in prewar America.

In the years since, Capra's harshest critics have found his images of the "wonderful life" to be naive, simplistic and overly sentimental. Paradoxically, "Capracorn" seems to argue for both extreme individualism (his heroes are nonconformists, like the pixilated tuba player Longfellow Deeds) and for conformity (resolution is attained only when individuals are in harmony with the community, as in the Christmas Eve reunion of *It's a Wonderful Life*). Such conflicting impulses have led to a variety of political readings of Capra. His films have been alternately seen as fascistic and libertarian, conservative and liberal, reactionary and progressive.

Finally, although the director's five post-*Wonderful Life* features lack the commitment and power of his earlier social comedies, Capra's film career must also be remembered for its landmark contributions to the field of documentary production. Under his supervision, the US government's *Why We Fight* propaganda films of WWII proved as emotionally powerful as any of Capra's Depression-era hits, and were exempla of found-footage montage. Though much less known, the series of educational science documentaries produced, directed and written by Capra for the Bell System between 1952 and 1957 all exhibit this same skill at manipulating banal images into an inspirationally charged, utopian vision of human life. DGS • *Fultah Fisher's Boarding House (short)* 1922 (d); *The Strong Man* 1926 (d); *Tramp, Tramp, Tramp* 1926 (assoc.p,d,sc,story); *For the Love of Mike* 1927 (d); *His First Flame* 1927 (sc); *Long Pants* 1927 (d); *The Matinee Idol* 1928 (d); *The Power of the Press* 1928 (d); *Say It With Sables* 1928 (d,story); *So This Is Love* 1928 (d); *Submarine* 1928 (d); *That Certain Thing* 1928 (d); *The Way of the Strong* 1928 (d); *The Donovan Affair* 1929 (d); *Flight* 1929 (d,dial); *The Younger Generation* 1929 (d); *Ladies of Leisure* 1930 (d); *Rain or Shine* 1930 (d); *Dirigible* 1931 (d); *The Miracle Woman* 1931 (d); *Platinum Blonde* 1931 (d); *American Madness* 1932 (d); *The Bitter Tea of General Yen* 1932 (d); *Forbidden* 1932 (d,story); *Lady For a Day* 1933 (d) **(AANBD)**; *Broadway Bill* 1934 (d); *It Happened One Night* 1934 (d) **(AABD)**; *Mr. Deeds Goes to Town* 1936 (d,p) **(AABD)**; *Lost Horizon* 1937 (d,p); *You Can't Take It With You* 1938 (d,p) **(AABD)**; *Mr. Smith Goes to Washington* 1939 (d,p) **(AANBD)**; *Meet John Doe* 1941 (d,p); *Why We Fight* 1942 (d,p—"Battle of Russia," "War Comes to America"); *Tunisian Victory* 1943 (d,p); *Arsenic and Old Lace* 1944 (d,p); *The Negro Soldier* 1944 (d,p); *Know Your Enemy: Japan* 1945 (d,p); *It's a Wonderful Life* 1946 (d,p,sc) **(AANBD)**; *State of the Union* 1948 (d,p); *Riding High* 1950 (d,p); *Here Comes the Groom* 1951 (d,p); *Westward the Women* 1951 (story); *A Hole in the Head* 1959 (d,p); *A Pocketful of Miracles* 1961 (d,p); *George Stevens: A Filmmaker's Journey* 1985 (archival footage); *Arriva Frank Capra* 1987 (archival footage).

Capshaw, Kate • Actress • Born Kathleen Sue Nail, Fort Worth, TX, 1953. *Educ.* University of Missouri (education). Frizzy-haired, slim blonde lead, best known as Harrison Ford's skittish heroine in *Indiana Jones and the Temple of Doom* (1984) and the dragon-lady nightclub owner in *Black Rain* (1989). • *A Little Sex* 1981; *Best Defense* 1984; *Dreamscape* 1984; *Indiana Jones and the Temple of Doom* 1984; *Windy City* 1984; *Power* 1986; *SpaceCamp* 1986; *Ti Presento un'Amica* 1988; *Black Rain* 1989; *Love at Large* 1990; *My Heroes Have Always Been Cowboys* 1991.

Capucine • Actress • Born Germaine Lefébvre, Toulon, France, January 6, 1933; died March 17, 1990, Lausanne, Switzerland. Former model who studied acting and made her screen debut in the US. Later an international star in films by Federico Fellini and Joseph Mankiewicz. • *North to Alaska* 1960; *Song Without End* 1960; *The Lion* 1962; *Walk on the Wild Side* 1962; *The 7th Dawn* 1964; *The Pink Panther* 1964; *What's New, Pussycat?* 1965; *Le Fate* 1966; *The Honey Pot* 1967; *Fräulein Doktor* 1968; *Satyricon/Fellini Satyricon* 1969; *Las Crueles* 1971; *Soleil Rouge/Red Sun* 1971; *L'Incorrigible* 1975; *Per Amore* 1976; *Ritratto di Borghesia in Nero* 1978; *Arabian Adventure* 1979; *Da Dunkerque alla Vittoria* 1979; *De l'enfer à la Victoire* 1979; *Jaguar Lives!* 1979; *Trail of the Pink Panther* 1982; *Balles Perdues* 1983; *Curse of the Pink Panther* 1983; *Le Foto di Gioia* 1987; *I Miei Primi Quarant'Anni* 1987; *Blue Blood* 1988.

Carax, Leos • French director, screenwriter • Born 1962. Gifted enfant terrible of the contemporary French cinema whose stylistic and thematic derivations from the original New Wave (particularly the work of Jean-Luc Godard) have made him the self-appointed heir to that tradition.

After writing film criticism, Carax made his feature debut at the age of 22 with the widely acclaimed *Boy Meets Girl* (1984), a velvety black-and-white canvas, small on plot (as the title suggests) but big on atmosphere.

His second feature, *Bad Blood* (1986), again starring the acrobatic Denis Lavant, and again strikingly composed (this time in color), involves a convoluted plot weaving together an AIDS-like virus (contracted by those who make love but are not really in love), gangsters and their molls (Michel Piccoli and Juliette Binoche), and an intricate heist. Though an equally impressive effort, the film proved an economic flop and received only luke-warm critical praise. Carax also played the Fool in Godard's *King Lear* (1987). • *Boy Meets Girl* 1984 (d,sc); *Mauvais sang/Bad Blood* 1986 (d,sc); *King Lear* 1987 (a); *Les Ministères de l'art* 1988 (a).

Cardiff, Jack • Director of photography; also director, actor. • Born Yarmouth, Norfolk, England, September 18, 1914. A child actor in the silent years, he later trained at Technicolor in the US and became one of England's first and most outstanding color cinematographers. Cardiff's work as a director has been less celebrated, although his 1960 adaptation of D.H. Lawrence's *Sons and Lovers* earned considerable acclaim. • *As You Like It* 1936 (ph); *Knight Without Armour* 1937 (cam.op); *Wings of the Morning* 1937 (ph); *Western Approaches* 1944 (ph); *Caesar and Cleopatra* 1945 (ph); *A Matter of Life and Death* 1946 (ph); *Black Narcissus* 1947 (ph) **(AABPH)**; *The Red Shoes* 1948 (ph); *Under Capricorn* 1949 (ph); *The Black Rose* 1950 (ph); *The African Queen* 1951 (ph); *The Magic Box* 1951 (ph); *Pandora and the Flying Dutchman* 1951 (ph); *The Master of Ballantrae* 1953 (ph); *The Barefoot Contessa* 1954 (ph); *The Brave One* 1956 (ph); *War and Peace* 1956 (ph) **(AANBPH)**; *Legend of the Lost* 1957 (ph); *The Prince and the Showgirl* 1957 (ph); *The Big Money* 1958 (cam.op); *Intent to Kill* 1958 (d); *The Vikings* 1958 (ph); *Beyond This Place* 1959 (d); *The Diary of Anne Frank* 1959 (location photography); *Scent of Mystery* 1960 (d); *Sons and Lovers* 1960 (d,ph) **(AANBD)**; *Fanny* 1961 (ph) **(AANBPH)**; *The Lion* 1962 (d); *My Geisha* 1962 (d); *Satan Never Sleeps* 1962 (d); *The Long Ships* 1964 (d); *Young Cassidy* 1965 (d); *The Liquidator* 1966 (d); *The Mercenaries* 1968 (d); *La Motocyclette* 1968 (d); *Naked Under Leather* 1968 (d); *Scalawag* 1973 (ph); *The Mutation* 1974 (d); *Ride a Wild Pony* 1975 (ph); *Crossed Swords* 1977 (ph); *Death on the Nile* 1978 (ph); *The 5th Musketeer* 1979 (ph); *Avalanche Express* 1979 (ph); *Man, a Woman and a Bank, A* 1979 (ph); *The Awakening* 1980 (ph); *The Dogs of War* 1980 (ph,add.ph); *Ghost Story* 1981 (ph); *The Wicked Lady* 1983 (ph); *Conan the Destroyer* 1984 (ph); *Scandalous* 1984 (ph); *Rambo: First Blood Part II* 1985 (ph); *Stephen King's Cat's Eye* 1985 (ph); *Tai-Pan* 1986 (ph,cam.op); *Million Dollar Mystery* 1987 (ph); *Call From Space* 1989 (ph).

Cardinale, Claudia • Actress • Born Tunis, Tunisia, April 15, 1939. *Educ.* Centro Sperimentale di Cinematografia, Rome (acting). Much-admired international leading lady who got her start in films after winning a beauty contest. Formerly married to producer Franco Cristaldi. • *I Soliti Ignoti/The Big Deal on Madonna Street* 1958; *Un Maledetto Imbroglio* 1959; *Les Noces Venetienne* 1959; *Upstairs and Downstairs* 1959; *Il Bell'Antonio* 1960; *Rocco e i suoi Fratelli/Rocco and His Brothers* 1960; *La Ragazza con la Valigia* 1961; *La Viaccia* 1961; *Cartouche* 1962; *Senilità* 1962; *Il Gattopardo/The Leopard* 1963; *Otto e Mezzo/8 1/2* 1963; *La Ragazza di Bube* 1963; *Circus World* 1964; *Gli Indifferenti/Time of Indifference* 1964; *Il Magnifico Cornuto/The Magnificent Cuckold* 1964; *The Pink Panther* 1964; *Vaghe stelle dell'orsa/Sandra* 1965; *Blindfold* 1966; *Le Fate* 1966; *Lost Command* 1966; *The Professionals* 1966; *Una Rosa per Tutti* 1966; *Don't Make Waves* 1967; *Il Giorno della Civetta* 1968; *The Hell With Heroes* 1968; *C'era una Volta il West/Once Upon a Time in the West* 1969; *Ruba al Prossimo Tuo* 1969; *The Adventures of Gerard* 1970; *Popsy Pop* 1970; *La Tenda rossa/The Red Tent* 1970; *Bello Onesto Emigrato Australia Sposerebbe Compaesan Illibata* 1971; *Les Pétroleuses* 1971; *L'Udienza* 1971; *La Scoumoune* 1972; *Il Giorno del Furore* 1973; *Libera, Amore Mio* 1974; *Gruppo di famiglia in un interno/Conversation Piece* 1975; *A Mezzanotte va la ronda del Piacere* 1975; *Qui comincia l'avventura* 1976; *Il Prefetto di Ferro* 1977; *L'Arma* 1978; *Corleone* 1978; *La Part du feu* 1978; *La Petite fille en velours bleu* 1978; *Escape to Athena* 1979; *La Pelle* 1981; *The Salamander* 1981; *Burden of Dreams* 1982; *Le Cadeau/The Gift* 1982; *Fitzcarraldo* 1982; *Le Ruffian* 1983; *Stelle Emigranti* 1983; *Enrico IV/Henry IV* 1984; *L'Eté Prochain* 1984; *La Donna Delle Meraviglie* 1985; *La Storia/History* 1986; *Un Homme amoureux/A Man in Love* 1987; *Naso di Cane* 1987; *Blu Elettrico* 1988; *Hiver 54, l'abbe Pierre* 1989; *La Révolution Française* 1989; *Atto di Dolore* 1990; *La Batalla de los Tres Reyes* 1990.

Carey, Harry • Actor • Born Henry DeWitt Carey II, Bronx, NY, January 16, 1878; died September 21, 1947, Brentwood, CA. *Educ.* NYU; NYU Law School. After trying his hand as a playwright, began his film career at Biograph, appearing in numerous D.W. Griffith films until the 1920s when he became a star of westerns. Carey was an Eastener like John Ford with whom he collaborated on (writing, and often directing and producing) the Cheyenne Harry films. After *Trader Horn* (1931) Carey made the transition to solid, versatile character actor usually playing stoic or authority figures. All told he acted in some 25 John Ford films. Married to actress Olive Deering and father of Harry Carey, Jr.

• *The Informer* 1912; *Judith of Bethulia* 1913; *Graft* 1916; *Love's Lariat* 1916 (p); *The Three Godfathers* 1916; *Bucking Broadway* 1917 (a,p); *The Fighting Gringo* 1917; *A Marked Man* 1917; *The Secret Man* 1917; *Straight Shooting* 1917; *Hell Bent* 1918 (a,sc,story); *The Phantom Riders* 1918; *The Scarlet Drop* 1918; *Thieves' Gold* 1918; *Three Mounted Men* 1918; *Wild Women* 1918 (a,p); *A Woman's Fool* 1918; *The Ace of the Saddle* 1919; *Bare Fists* 1919; *A Fight for Love* 1919; *A Gun Fightin' Gentleman* 1919 (a,story); *The Outcasts of Poker Flat* 1919; *The Rider of the Law* 1919; *Riders of Vengeance* 1919 (a,story); *Roped* 1919; *Blue Streak McCoy* 1920; *Bullet Proof* 1920; *Hearts Up!* 1920 (a,story); *Human Stuff* 1920 (a,sc); *Marked Men* 1920; *Overland Red* 1920; *Sundown Slim* 1920; *West Is West* 1920; *Desperate Trails* 1921; *The Fox* 1921 (a,story); *The Freeze Out* 1921; *If Only Jim* 1921; *The Wallop* 1921; *Good Men and True* 1922; *The Kick Back* 1922 (a,story); *Man to Man* 1922; *The Canyon of the Fools* 1923; *Crashin' Thru* 1923; *Desert Driven* 1923; *The Miracle Baby* 1923; *The Flaming Forties* 1924; *The Lightning Rider* 1924; *The Man From Texas* 1924; *The Night Hawk* 1924; *Roaring Rails* 1924; *Tiger Thompson* 1924; *The Bad Lands* 1925; *Beyond the Border* 1925; *The Man From Red Gulch* 1925; *The Prairie Pirate* 1925; *Silent Sanderson* 1925; *Soft Shoes* 1925 (a,story); *The Texas Trail* 1925; *Driftin' Thru* 1926; *The Frontier Trail* 1926; *Satan Town* 1926; *The Seventh Bandit* 1926; *A Little Journey* 1927; *Slide, Kelly, Slide* 1927; *The Border Patrol* 1928; *Burning Bridges* 1928; *The Trail of '98* 1928; *Bad Company* 1931; *Cavalier of the West* 1931; *Trader Horn* 1931; *The Vanishing Legion* 1931; *Border Devils* 1932; *The Devil Horse* 1932; *The Last of the Mohicans* 1932; *Law and Order* 1932; *Night Rider* 1932; *Without Honors* 1932; *Man of the Forest* 1933; *Sunset Pass* 1933; *The Thundering Herd* 1933; *Barbary Coast* 1935; *The Last of the Clintons* 1935; *Powdersmoke Range* 1935; *Rustlers' Paradise* 1935; *The Wagon Trail* 1935; *Wild Mustang* 1935; *The Accusing Finger* 1936; *Aces Wild* 1936; *Ghost Town* 1936; *The Last Outlaw* 1936; *Little Miss Nobody* 1936; *The Prisoner of Shark Island* 1936; *Sutter's Gold* 1936; *Valiant Is the Word For Carrie* 1936; *Annapolis Salute* 1937; *Border Cafe* 1937; *Born Reckless* 1937; *Danger Patrol* 1937; *Kid Galahad* 1937; *Souls at Sea* 1937; *Gateway* 1938; *King of Alcatraz* 1938; *The Law West of Tombstone* 1938; *Port of Missing Girls* 1938; *Sky Giant* 1938; *You and Me* 1938; *Burn 'Em Up O'Connor* 1939; *Code of the Streets* 1939; *El Diablo Rides* 1939; *Inside Information* 1939; *Mr. Smith Goes to Washington* 1939 **(AANBSA)**; *My Son Is Guilty* 1939; *Street of Missing Men* 1939; *Beyond Tomorrow* 1940; *Outside the 3-Mile Limit* 1940; *They Knew*

What They Wanted 1940; *Among the Living* 1941; *Parachute Battalion* 1941; *The Shepherd of the Hills* 1941; *Sundown* 1941; *The Spoilers* 1942; *Air Force* 1943; *Happy Land* 1943; *The Great Moment* 1944; *China's Little Devils* 1945; *Angel and the Badman* 1947; *Duel in the Sun* 1947; *Sea of Grass* 1947; *So Dear to My Heart* 1948.

Carey, Harry, Jr. • Actor • Born Saugus, CA, May 16, 1921. *Educ.* Black Fox Military Academy, Hollywood. Veteran character player who like his father, Harry Carey, has appeared mostly in westerns, many by John Ford and Andrew V. McLaglen. • *Rolling Home* 1946; *Pursued* 1947; *Moonrise* 1948; *Red River* 1948; *She Wore a Yellow Ribbon* 1949; *Three Godfathers* 1949; *Copper Canyon* 1950; *Rio Grande* 1950; *Wagonmaster* 1950; *The Wild Blue Yonder* 1951; *Beneath the 12 Mile Reef* 1953; *Island in the Sky* 1953; *Niagara* 1953; *San Antone* 1953; *Sweethearts on Parade* 1953; *The Outcast* 1954; *Silver Lode* 1954; *House of Bamboo* 1955; *The Long Gray Line* 1955; *Mister Roberts* 1955; *The Great Locomotive Chase* 1956; *Gun the Man Down* 1956; *The Searchers* 1956; *Seventh Cavalry* 1956; *Kiss Them For Me* 1957; *The River's Edge* 1957; *From Hell to Texas* 1958; *Escort West* 1959; *Rio Bravo* 1959; *The Great Impostor* 1960; *Noose For a Gunman* 1960; *Two Rode Together* 1961; *A Public Affair* 1962; *The Raiders* 1963; *Taggart* 1964; *Shenandoah* 1965; *Alvarez Kelly* 1966; *Billy the Kid vs. Dracula* 1966; *The Rare Breed* 1966; *The Ballad of Josie* 1967; *The Way West* 1967; *Bandolero!* 1968; *The Devil's Brigade* 1968; *Death of a Gunfighter* 1969; *The Undefeated* 1969; *Dirty Dingus Magee* 1970; *The Moonshine War* 1970; *Big Jake* 1971; *Continuavano A Chiamarlo Trinita* 1971; *E Poi lo Chiamarono il Magnifico* 1971; *One More Train to Rob* 1971; *Something Big* 1971; *Cahill, United States Marshal* 1973; *Take a Hard Ride* 1975; *Nickelodeon* 1976; *The Long Riders* 1980; *Endangered Species* 1982; *Gremlins* 1984; *Mask* 1985; *Crossroads* 1986; *The Whales of August* 1987; *Cherry 2000* 1988; *Illegally Yours* 1988; *Bad Jim* 1989; *Breaking In* 1989; *Back to the Future III* 1990; *William Peter Blatty's The Exorcist III* 1990.

Carfagno, Edward C. • *aka* Edward Carfagno • American production designer • Established himself in the 1950s with such films as Vincente Minnelli's *The Bad and the Beautiful* (1952), Joseph Mankiewicz's *Julius Caesar* (1953) and William Wyler's *Ben-Hur* (1959). Carfagno has since worked consistently on a variety of films, including five collaborations with director Clint Eastwood. • *Quo Vadis* 1951 (art d) **(AANBAD)**; *The Bad and the Beautiful* 1952 (art d) **(AABAD)**; *Julius Caesar* 1953 (art d,cost) **(AABAD)**; *The Story of Three Loves* 1953 (art d) **(AANBAD)**; *Executive Suite* 1954 (art d) **(AANBAD)**; *Ben-Hur* 1959 (art d) **(AABAD)**; *Ada* 1961 (art d); *Period of Adjustment* 1962 (art d) **(AANBAD)**; *The Wonderful World of the Brothers Grimm* 1962 (art d) **(AANBAD)**; *The Shoes of the Fisherman* 1968 (art d) **(AANBAD)**; *The Extraordinary Seaman* 1969 (art d); *The Trouble With Girls* 1969 (art d); *The Traveling Executioner* 1970 (art d); *Melinda* 1972 (pd); *Skyjacked* 1972 (pd); *The Man Who Loved Cat Dancing* 1973 (pd); *Soylent Green* 1973 (pd); *The Hindenburg* 1975 (pd) **(AANBAD)**; *Gable and Lombard* 1976 (pd); *The Last Hard Men* 1976 (art d); *Demon Seed* 1977 (pd); *Looking For Mr. Goodbar* 1977 (art d); *The One and Only* 1978 (pd); *Meteor* 1979 (pd); *Time After Time* 1979 (pd); *Little Miss Marker* 1980 (pd); *Honkytonk Man* 1982 (pd); *The Sting II* 1982 (pd); *Wrong Is Right* 1982 (pd); *Sudden Impact* 1983 (pd); *All of Me* 1984 (pd); *City Heat* 1984 (pd); *Tightrope* 1984 (pd); *Pale Rider* 1985 (pd); *Heartbreak Ridge* 1986 (pd); *Ratboy* 1986 (pd); *Bird* 1988 (pd); *The Dead Pool* 1988 (pd); *Pink Cadillac* 1989 (pd).

Carlino, Lewis John • Screenwriter; also director, playwright. • Born New York, NY, January 1, 1932. *Educ.* El Camino College; USC, Los Angeles. Smoothly efficient scenarist, especially adept at making the bizarre or metaphysical believable, as with *Seconds* (1966) and *Resurrection* (1980). Carlino tried his hand at directing with an effective adaptation of Yukio Mishima's *The Sailor Who Fell From Grace with the Sea* (1975). • *Seconds* 1966 (sc); *The Fox* 1967 (sc); *The Brotherhood* 1968 (sc,tech.sup); *A Reflection of Fear* 1971 (sc); *The Mechanic* 1972 (p,sc); *Crazy Joe* 1973 (sc); *The Sailor Who Fell From Grace With the Sea* 1975 (d,sc); *I Never Promised You a Rose Garden* 1977 (sc) **(AANBSC)**; *The Great Santini* 1979 (d,sc); *Resurrection* 1980 (sc); *Class* 1983 (d); *Haunted Summer* 1988 (sc).

Carlsen, Henning • Director; also producer, screenwriter, editor. • Born Aalborg, Jutland, Denmark, June 4, 1927. Former cinéma vérité filmmaker whose first feature was the quasi-documentary *Dilemma* (1962), shot clandestinely in South Africa and based on Nadine Gordimer's novel *A World of Strangers*. Carlsen then gained international attention with his fourth full-length film, *Hunger* (1966), featuring an award-winning performance by Per Oscarsson.

Carlsen has since established himself as the preeminent Danish director of his day, at his best with biopics like *Wolf at the Door* (1986) or literary-based material like *Did Somebody Laugh?* (1978), from the novel by Eigel Jensen. • *Dilemma* 1962 (d,sc); *How About Us?* 1963 (d); *Kattorna* 1965 (d,sc); *Sult/Hunger* 1966 (d,p,sc); *Mennesker Moedes Og Soed Musik Opstaar I Hjertet* 1967 (d,p,sc); *Klabautermanden* 1969 (d,p,sc); *Er I Bange?* 1970 (d,sc); *I Din Fars Lomme* 1972 (p); *Man sku vaere noget ved musikken* 1972 (d,p,sc,story); *Da Svante forsvandt* 1975 (d,p); *Un Divorce Heureux* 1975 (d,sc); *Hoer, Var Der Ikke En, Som Lo?/Did Somebody Laugh?* 1978 (d,sc,ed); *A Street Under the Snow* 1978 (d,p,sc); *Arven* 1979 (ed); *Pengene Eller Livet* 1982 (d,sc); *Elise* 1985 (post-production assistant); *Wolf at the Door* 1986 (d,p,sc,story).

Carmichael, Hoagy • Composer; also actor. • Born Hoagland Howard Carmichael, Bloomington, IN, November 22, 1899; died 1981. *Educ.* Indiana University, Bloomington (law). Tin Pan Alley legend who began composing for films in 1936 and won an Academy Award for "In the Cool Cool Cool of the Evening" in 1951. As an actor he usually played himself, sitting at a piano, smoking a cigarette and singing a song. • *Anything Goes* 1936 (song); *Topper* 1937 (song); *College Swing* 1938 (song); *Every Day's a Holiday* 1938 (song); *Sing, You Sinners* 1938 (song); *Thanks For the Memory* 1938 (song); *Road Show* 1941 (song); *True to Life* 1943 (song); *To Have and Have Not* 1944 (a,song); *Johnny Angel* 1945 (a,song); *The Stork Club* 1945 (song); *The Best Years of Our Lives* 1946 (a,song); *Canyon Passage* 1946 (a,song) **(AANBS)**; *Night Song* 1947 (a,song); *Johnny Holiday* 1949 (a,song); *Young Man With a Horn* 1950 (a); *Here Comes the Groom* 1951 (song) **(AABS)**; *Belles on Their Toes* 1952 (a,song); *The Las Vegas Story* 1952 (a,song); *Gentlemen Prefer Blondes* 1953 (song); *Three For the Show* 1954 (song); *Timberjack* 1955 (a,song); *Hey Boy! Hey Girl!* 1959 (song); *Hatari!* 1962 (song); *The Big T.N.T. Show* 1966 (song).

Carné, Marcel • *aka* Albert Cranche • Director; also screenwriter. • Born Paris, August 18, 1909. Marcel Carné is best known for his collaborations with screenwriter Jacques Prévert. By the time the team broke up in 1947 they had forever marked French cinema, leaving behind such undisputed masterpieces as *Le Quai des Brumes* (1938), *Le Jour Se Lève* (1939), *Les Enfants du Paradis* (1945) and *Les Portes de la nuit* (1946). For ten years their work dominated the industry and their style, termed "poetic realism," had an international influence.

After working as an assistant cameraman for Jacques Feyder on *Les Nouveaux Messieurs* (1928), Carné made a short (*Nogent—Eldorado du dimanche* 1929) which so impressed René Clair that he hired Carné as his assistant on *Sous les Toits de Paris* (1930). Carné then worked as assistant to Feyder on *Pension Mimosas* (1934) and *La Kermesse Héroïque* (1935). During this period he also made publicity shorts and wrote film criticism, sometimes under the pseudonym Albert Cranche. Then, thanks to Feyder's intervention, Carné was allowed to direct his first feature, a routine melodrama called *Jenny* (1936), scripted by Jacques Prévert.

A poet whose broad appeal dervied from a unique combination of humor, sentimentality and social satire, Prévert had been associated with the surrealists as well as the Popular Front. In the best studio tradition, he and Carné gathered together a team of professionals, including set designer Alexandre Trauner and composer Maurice Jaubert (replaced on his death by Joseph Kosma).

The poetic realist style flowered as French society plunged from the euphoria of the Popular Front to the despair of the Occupation. Typically, Carné-Prévert collaborations were marked by a tension between gritty realism and the suggestion of a metaphysical dimension beyond that represented on the screen. They are noted for their lyrical language and pessimistic atmosphere, for their meticulous recreations of concrete social milieux, and for truly remarkable performances by, among others, Jean Gabin, Arletty, Michèle Morgan, Michel Simon and Jules Berry.

Though their films were banned during the Occupation, Carné and Prévert were allowed to continue working together, with the clandestine assistance of Trauner and Kosma (both of whom were Jewish). Unable to portray contemporary events, the team turned instead to historical subjects. *Les Visiteurs du soir* (1942), a medieval allegory of love and death, was a considerable success in its time; its wooden performances and heavy-handed treatment, however, have aged badly. Their next film remains one of the most celebrated in cinema history. *Les Enfants du Paradis*, shot during the Occupation but not released until after the Liberation, was an ambitious tale of love and theater life set in a dazzlingly recreated 19th-century Paris and featuring outstanding performances by Arletty, Jean-Louis Barrault and Maria Casarès, among others.

With the war over, Carné and Prévert revived poetic realism in *Les Portes de la nuit*, but the film met with a poor reception from the public. When their next feature, *La Fleur de l'age*, was cancelled in mid-production, the two ended their working relationship.

Carné's later career, despite his willingness to work with younger actors and new subject matter, is relatively unremarkable. Carné excelled at studio production, where reality could be recreated within the controllable confines of the sound stage, and the trend in France, encouraged by the young turks of the *nouvelle vague*, was to take film out of the studio and into the streets. Although he became a symbol of the New Wave filmmakers' scorn for the "tradition of quality" in French cinema, Carné left behind a body of films which have stood the test of time. RDH

• *Les Nouveaux messieurs* 1928 (cam.asst); *Cagliostro* 1929 (cam.asst); *Nogent—Eldorado du Dimanche (short)* 1929 (d,sc); *Sous les toits de Paris* 1930 (ad); *Le Grand jeu* 1933 (ad); *Pension Mimosas* 1934 (ad); *La Kermesse Héroïque/Carnival in Flanders* 1935 (ad,prod.man); *Jenny* 1936 (d); *Drôle de Drame/Bizarre Bizarre* 1937 (d); *Hôtel du Nord* 1938 (d,sc,adapt); *Le Quai des Brumes/Port of Shadows* 1938 (d); *Le Jour Se Lève/Daybreak* 1939 (d); *Les Visiteurs du soir/The Devil's Envoys* 1942 (d); *Les Enfants du Paradis/Children of Paradise* 1945 (d); *Les Portes de la nuit/Gates of the Night* 1946 (d); *La Marie du Port* 1950 (d,sc); *Juliette ou la clef des Songes* 1951 (d,sc); *Thérèse Raquin* 1953 (d,sc,dial); *L'Air de Paris* 1954 (d,sc); *Le Pays d'où Je viens* 1956 (d,sc); *Le Tricheurs* 1958 (d,sc); *Terrain vague* 1960 (d,sc); *Du Mouron pour les Petits Oiseaux* 1963 (d,sc); *Trois Chambres à Manhattan* 1965 (d,sc); *Les Jeunes Loups* 1966 (d,sc); *Les Assasins de L'Ordre* 1971 (d,sc); *La Merveilleuse visite* 1974 (d,sc); *Carné: l'Homme à la Camera* 1980 (a); *La Bible* 1984 (d,sc).

Carney, Art • Actor • Born Arthur William Matthew Carney, Mount Vernon, NY, November 4, 1918. Brilliant comic performer best known as Jackie Gleason's goofy sidekick Ed Norton on the popular 1950s TV comedy series, "The Jackie Gleason Show/The Honeymooners." Carney also displayed his versatility during this period, appearing on numberous dramatic TV specials ("Playhouse 90," "Our Town") during the 1950s and 60s and originating the role of Felix Unger in the Broadway production of *The Odd Couple* (1965) opposite Walter Matthau. His film acting career took off after his award-winning performance in *Harry and Tonto* (1974) and he has been much in demand as cantankerous old codgers in both drama and comedy. His most finely etched film performance, however, may be as the aging detective hired by, and reluctantly partnered with, the flaky Lily Tomlin in Robert Benton's off-beat whodunit, *The Late Show* (1977).

• *Pot o' Gold* 1941; *The Yellow Rolls-Royce* 1964; *A Guide For the Married Man* 1967; *Harry and Tonto* 1974 **(AABA)**; *W. W. and the Dixie Dancekings* 1974; *Won Ton Ton, the Dog Who Saved Hollywood* 1976; *The Late Show* 1977; *Scott Joplin* 1977; *House Calls* 1978; *Movie Movie* 1978; *Going in Style* 1979; *Ravagers* 1979; *Sunburn* 1979; *Defiance* 1980; *Roadie* 1980; *Steel* 1980; *St. Helens* 1981; *Take This Job and Shove It* 1981; *Better Late Than Never* 1983; *Firestarter* 1984; *The Muppets Take Manhattan* 1984; *The Naked Face* 1985; *Night Friend* 1988.

Carol, Martine • *aka* Maryse Arley • Actress • Born Maryse Mourer, Biarritz, France, May 16, 1922; died 1967. Popular, tantalizing leading lady of the 1950s. In several films by her husband Christian-Jaque but most engaging in the title role of Max Ophuls's *Lola Montès* (1955). • *La Ferme aux Loups* 1943; *Les Amants de Vérone* 1948; *Caroline Chérie* 1950; *Méfiez-vous des Blondes* 1950; *Nous irons à Paris* 1950; *Adorables Créatures* 1952; *Les Belles de Nuit* 1952; *Le Désir et l'amour* 1952; *Un Caprice de Caroline Chérie* 1953; *Lucrèce Borgia* 1953; *La Spiaggia* 1953; *Destinées* 1954; *Madame du Barry* 1954; *Secrets d'Alcôve/The Bed* 1954; *Lola Montès* 1955; *Nana* 1955; *Around the World in 80 Days* 1956; *Les Carnets du Major Thompson/The French, They Are a Funny Race* 1956; *Difendo il Mio Amore* 1956; *Action of the Tiger* 1957; *Nathalie Agent Secret* 1957; *Prima Notte* 1958; *Ten Seconds to Hell* 1959; *Austerlitz* 1960; *La Française et l'amour/Love and the Frenchwoman* 1960; *Le Cave se rebiffe* 1961; *Vanina Vanini* 1961; *Hell Is Empty* 1967.

Caron, Leslie • Actress; also dancer. • Born Boulogne-sur-Seine, France, July 1, 1931. *Educ.* Paris Conservatoire (dance). Endearing French leading lady who, after being discovered by Gene Kelly for *An American in Paris* (1951), starred successfully in several other English-language movies. • *An American in Paris* 1951; *The Man With a Cloak* 1951; *Glory Alley* 1952; *Lili* 1953 **(AANBA)**; *The Story of Three Loves* 1953; *The Glass Slipper* 1954; *Daddy Long Legs* 1955; *Gaby* 1956; *The Doctor's Dilemma* 1958; *Gigi* 1958; *The Man Who Understood Women* 1959; *The Subterraneans* 1960; *Fanny* 1961; *The L-Shaped Room* 1962 **(AANBA)**; *The Caretaker* 1963 (funding); *Father Goose* 1964; *A Very Special Favor* 1965; *Promise Her Anything* 1966; *Madron* 1970; *Chandler* 1971; *Serail* 1976; *L'Homme qui aimait les femmes/The Man Who Loved Women* 1977; *Valentino* 1977; *Goldengirl* 1979; *Contract* 1980; *Tous Vedettes* 1980; *Imperativ* 1982; *Die Unerreichbare* 1982; *La Diagonale du Fou/Dangerous Moves* 1984; *Courage Mountain* 1989; *Guerriers et captives* 1989.

Carpenter, John • Director; also screenwriter, producer, composer. • Born Bowling Green, KY, January 16, 1948. *Educ.* Western Kentucky University; USC, Los Angeles (film). John Carpenter is known primarily for his handling of slick action sequences, which has established him as one of Hollywood's most skillful directors of violence and suspense. He decided to become a director after seeing movies such as *It Came From Outer Space* and *Forbidden Planet*, and most of his work to date has been in the horror and science fiction genres. Carpenter also works on the scripts, special effects photography and electronic music for his films.

While a graduate student Carpenter made several short films, including *The Resurrection of Bronco Billy*, which won an Academy Award in 1970, and, with classmate Dan O'Bannon, the science fiction story *Dark Star*, which he expanded into his first feature in 1974. Shot on a budget of only $60,000, the feature offers a blackly comic alternative to Stanley Kubrick's *2001: A Space Odyssey* in its vision of man in space overwhelmed by technology. *Dark Star*, along with the follow-up, *Assault on Precinct 13* (1976)—a clever blend of Howard Hawks's western *Rio Bravo* and George Romero's horror classic *Night of the Living Dead*—established the director with European cinéastes fond of "masculine" American auteurs.

Carpenter's commercial breakthrough came in 1978 with the low-budget thriller *Halloween*. The film's success launched a series of sequels (directed by others), as well as Carpenter's entry into mainstream Hollywood production.

Carpenter's approach rests firmly in the American tradition of action filmmaking embodied by directors like John Ford, Raoul Walsh, Alfred Hitchcock and Howard Hawks. His greatest skill is an uncluttered depiction of action in a way that almost transcends narrative constraints. Sequences such as the famous lengthy point-of-view shot that opens *Halloween*, or the astronaut's chase of a mischievous alien creature through the ship's elevator shaft in *Dark Star*, show the director's undeniable command of action and suspense. His stylistic trademark is a driving pace, enforced by a powerful sense of montage and insistent electronic music.

Thematically, Carpenter's films are concerned with issues of communication and isolation. In *Dark Star*, as the men on the ship grow apart through boredom and indifference, outer space becomes a metaphor for the vast distance of inner space. The final images of *The Thing* (1982) show two survivors warily sitting opposite each other, separated by the wide-screen image, their mutual distrust and the iciness of their environment. *They Live* (1988), a noble but unsuccessful combination of action with a progressive critique of the "culture industry," seeks to expose mass communications and popular culture as carrying subliminal, insidiously seductive subtexts. Love and mutual understanding, however, can overcome our isolation and distrust, as they do for the alien and the earthwoman in *Starman* (1984).

Unfortunately, since moving into bigger-budget productions, Carpenter's thematic interests have been smothered by an excess of production values. In *The Thing* (the first film over which he did not have contractual control), Rob Bottin's impressive special effects steal the spotlight from an ostensibly humanist theme. Similarly, *Escape From New York* (1981) drops its intriguing premise to settle for the conventional heroics required by the plot. *Christine* (1983) begins as a promising exploration of America's automobile fetish only to dissolve into a spectacle of the eponymous car's several physical metamorphoses. Whether Carpenter can rediscover his strengths in a commercial cinema that encourages the presentation of action as overblown visual spectacle, and return to the themes that animated his earlier work, remains to be seen. BG • *Dark Star* 1974 (d,p,sc,m,m.dir,song); *Assault on Precinct 13* 1976 (d,sc,m,song); *Eyes of Laura Mars* 1978 (sc,story); *Halloween* 1978 (d,sc,m); *The Fog* 1980 (a,d,sc,story,m); *Escape From New York* 1981 (d,sc,m); *Halloween II* 1981 (p,sc,m); *Halloween III: Season of the Witch* 1982 (m,p); *The Thing* 1982 (d); *Christine* 1983 (d,m); *The Philadelphia Experiment* 1984 (exec.p); *Starman* 1984 (d); *Big Trouble in Little China* 1986 (d,m,song); *Black Moon Rising* 1986 (sc,story); *The Boy Who Could Fly* 1986 (a); *Prince of Darkness* 1987 (d,m); *Halloween 4: The Return of Michael Myers* 1988 (m); *The House on Carroll Street* 1988 (a); *They Live* 1988 (d,m,sc); *Halloween 5: The Revenge of Michael Meyers* 1989 (m).

Carradine, David • Actor; also director, singer, songwriter. • Born John Arthur Carradine, Hollywood, CA, December 8, 1936. *Educ.* San Francisco State College. Elder half-brother of Keith and Robert Carradine, chiefly known for starring in the TV show "Kung Fu" (1972-74). His best performance was as folk hero Woody Guthrie, in Arthur Penn's *Bound For Glory* (1976). • *Taggart* 1964; *Bus Riley's Back in Town* 1965; *The Violent Ones* 1967; *The Good Guys and the Bad Guys* 1969; *Heaven With a Gun* 1969; *Young Billy Young* 1969; *Macho Callahan* 1970; *The McMasters* 1970; *Boxcar Bertha* 1972; *The Long Goodbye* 1973; *Mean Streets* 1973; *Death Race 2000* 1975; *You and Me* 1975 (a,d); *Bound For Glory* 1976; *Cannonball* 1976; *Gray Lady Down* 1977; *Das Schlangenei* 1977; *Thunder and Lightning* 1977; *Deathsport* 1978; *Fast Charlie - The Moonbeam Rider* 1978; *Roger Corman: Hollywood's Wild Angel* 1978; *The Silent Flute* 1978; *Cloud Dancer* 1979 (a,song); *The Long Riders* 1980; *Safari 3000* 1980; *Americana* 1981 (a,d,m,ed,song,p); *Lone Wolf McQuade* 1982; *Q* 1982; *Trick or Treats* 1982; *A Distant Scream* 1983; *The Warrior and the Sorceress* 1983; *Rio Abajo* 1984; *Armed Response* 1986; *The Misfit Brigade* 1986; *P.O.W. the Escape* 1986; *Maniac Cop* 1988 (song); *Crime Zone* 1989; *Future Force* 1989; *Night Children* 1989; *Nowhere to Run* 1989; *Sauf votre respect* 1989; *Sundown, the Vampire in Retreat* 1989; *Tropical Snow* 1989; *Wizards of the Lost Kingdom II* 1989; *Bird on a Wire* 1990; *Fatal Secret* 1990; *Future Zone* 1990; *Sonny Boy* 1990 (a,song); *Think Big* 1990; *Dune Warriors* 1991.

Carradine, John • *aka* John Peter Richmond • Actor • Born Richmond Reed Carradine, New York, NY, February 5, 1906; died November 27, 1988, Milan, Italy. *Educ.* Philadelphia Graphics Art School. Celebrated Hollywood supporting player who appeared in ten John Ford films, including the 1940 classic *The Grapes of Wrath*. Carradine was also a keen Shakespearean stage actor, and his habit of reciting soliloquies while walking in public earned him the nickname "Bard of the Boulevard." Father of four acting Carradines: David, Robert, Keith and Bruce. • *Forgotten Commandments* 1932; *The Sign of the Cross* 1932; *Les Miserables* 1935; *Daniel Boone* 1936; *Dimples* 1936; *The Garden of Allah* 1936; *Laughing at Trouble* 1936; *Mary of Scotland* 1936; *The Prisoner of Shark Island* 1936; *Ramona* 1936; *Under Two Flags* 1936; *White Fang* 1936; *Winterset* 1936; *Ali Baba Goes to Town* 1937; *Captains Courageous* 1937; *Danger—Love at Work* 1937; *Hurricane* 1937; *The Last Gangster* 1937; *Love Under Fire* 1937; *Nancy Steele Is Missing* 1937; *Thank You, Mr. Moto* 1937; *This Is My Affair* 1937; *Alexander's Ragtime Band* 1938; *Four Men and a Prayer* 1938; *Gateway* 1938; *I'll Give a Million* 1938; *International Settlement* 1938; *Kentucky Moonshine* 1938; *Kidnapped* 1938; *Of Human Hearts* 1938; *Submarine Patrol* 1938; *Captain Fury* 1939; *Drums Along the Mohawk* 1939; *Five Came Back* 1939; *Frontier Marshal* 1939; *The Hound of the Baskervilles* 1939; *Jesse James* 1939; *Mr. Moto's Last Warning* 1939; *Stagecoach* 1939; *The Three Musketeers* 1939; *Brigham Young, Frontiersman* 1940; *Chad Hanna* 1940; *The Grapes of Wrath* 1940; *The Return of Frank James* 1940; *Blood and Sand* 1941; *Man Hunt* 1941; *Swamp Water* 1941; *Western Union* 1941; *Northwest Rangers* 1942; *Reunion in France* 1942; *Son of Fury* 1942; *Whispering Ghosts* 1942; *Captive Wild Woman* 1943; *Gangway For Tomorrow* 1943; *Hitler's Hangman* 1943; *I Escaped From the Gestapo* 1943; *Isle of Forgotten Sins* 1943; *Revenge of the Zombies* 1943; *Silver Spurs* 1943; *The Adventures of Mark Twain* 1944; *Alaska* 1944; *Barbary Coast Gent* 1944; *The Black Parachute* 1944; *Bluebeard* 1944; *House of Frankenstein* 1944; *The Invisible Man's Revenge* 1944; *The Mummy's Ghost* 1944; *Return of the Ape Man* 1944; *Voodoo Man* 1944; *Waterfront* 1944; *Captain Kidd* 1945; *Fallen Angel* 1945; *House of Dracula* 1945; *It's in the Bag* 1945; *Down Missouri Way* 1946; *Face of Marble* 1946; *C-Man* 1949; *Casanova's Big Night* 1954; *The Egyptian* 1954; *Johnny Guitar* 1954; *Stranger on Horseback* 1954; *Thunder Pass* 1954; *Desert Sands* 1955; *Hidden Guns* 1955; *The Kentuckian* 1955; *Around the World in 80 Days* 1956; *The Black Sleep* 1956; *The Court Jester* 1956; *Female Jungle* 1956; *The Ten Commandments* 1956; *Hell Ship Mutiny* 1957; *Jujin Yukiotoko* 1957; *The Story of Mankind* 1957; *The*

True Story of Jesse James 1957; *The Unearthly* 1957; *The Cosmic Man* 1958; *The Incredible Petrified World* 1958; *The Last Hurrah* 1958; *Proud Rebel* 1958; *Showdown at Boot Hill* 1958; *Curse of the Stone Hand* 1959; *Invisible Invaders* 1959; *The Oregon Trail* 1959; *The Adventures of Huckleberry Finn* 1960; *Sex Kittens Go to College* 1960; *Tarzan the Magnificent* 1960; *Cheyenne Autumn* 1964; *The Patsy* 1964; *The Wizard of Mars* 1964; *House of the Black Death* 1965; *Billy the Kid vs. Dracula* 1966; *The Hostage* 1966; *Munster, Go Home* 1966; *Night Train to Mundo Fine* 1966; *Dr. Terror's Gallery of Horrors* 1967; *The Helicopter Spies* 1967; *Hillbillys in a Haunted House* 1967; *The Astro-Zombies* 1968; *Blood of Dracula's Castle* 1968; *The Good Guys and the Bad Guys* 1969; *The Lonely Man* 1969; *They Ran For Their Lives* 1969; *The Trouble With Girls* 1969; *Bigfoot* 1970; *Cain's Way* 1970; *Horror of the Blood Monsters* 1970; *Myra Breckinridge* 1970; *The Seven Minutes* 1971; *Shinbone Alley* 1971; *Boxcar Bertha* 1972; *Everything You Always Wanted To Know About Sex* (*but were afraid to ask)* 1972; *Richard* 1972; *Bad Charleston Charlie* 1973; *Big Foot* 1973; *The Gatling Gun* 1973; *Silent Night, Bloody Night* 1973; *Terror in the Wax Museum* 1973; *The House of Seven Corpses* 1974; *Moon Child* 1974; *Death Corps* 1975; *Mary, Mary, Bloody Mary* 1975; *The Killer Inside Me* 1976; *The Last Tycoon* 1976; *The Shootist* 1976; *Crash* 1977; *Golden Rendezvous* 1977; *The Mouse and His Child* 1977; *Satan's Cheerleaders* 1977; *The Sentinel* 1977; *The White Buffalo* 1977; *The Bees* 1978; *Nocturna* 1978; *Sunset Cove* 1978; *The Vampire Hookers* 1978; *The Boogeyman* 1980; *The Howling* 1980; *The Monster Club* 1981; *The Nesting* 1981; *Boogeyman II* 1982; *House of the Long Shadows* 1982; *Satan's Mistress* 1982; *The Scarecrow* 1982; *The Secret of Nimh* 1982; *The Vals* 1982; *Monster in the Closet* 1983; *The Ice Pirates* 1984; *Prison Ship* 1984; *Evils of the Night* 1985; *Peggy Sue Got Married* 1986; *Revenge* 1986; *The Tomb* 1986; *Evil Spawn* 1987; *Star Slammer, the Escape* 1988; *Buried Alive* 1990.

Carradine, Keith • Actor; also singer, songwriter. • Born Keith Ian Carradine, San Mateo, CA, August 8, 1949. *Educ.* Colorado State University, Fort Collins (theater arts). Lean, cool, laconic leading man who dropped out of college and appeared on Broadway in the counter-culture musical *Hair* (1969-70) before moving to Los Angeles. At the age of 21 Carradine appeared in his first two films, *A Gunfight* and Robert Altman's *McCabe & Mrs. Miller* (both 1971). In 1975 Carradine co-starred as a country and western singer in Altman's masterpiece, *Nashville*, winning a best song Oscar for his ballad, "I'm Easy." More recently, he starred in a series of stylish, intriguing films by Altman's former protégé Alan Rudolph, including *Choose Me* (1984) and *The Moderns* (1988). Son of the late John Carradine, brother of Robert Carradine, half-brother of David Carradine and father, by Shelly Plimpton, of actress Martha Plimpton. • *A Gunfight* 1971; *McCabe & Mrs. Miller* 1971; *Hex* 1972; *Antoine et Sebastien* 1973; *The Emperor of the North Pole* 1973; *Idaho Transfer* 1973; *Thieves Like Us* 1974; *Lumière* 1975; *Nashville* 1975 (a,songs) **(AABS)**; *You and Me* 1975; *Welcome to L.A.* 1976 (a,song); *The Duellists* 1977; *Old Boyfriends* 1978; *Pretty Baby* 1978; *Sgt. Pepper's Lonely Hearts Club Band* 1978; *An Almost Perfect Affair* 1979; *The Long Riders* 1980; *Southern Comfort* 1981; *Choose Me* 1984; *Maria's Lovers* 1985 (a,songs); *Trouble in Mind* 1985; *Half a Lifetime* 1986; *Backfire* 1987; *L'Inchiesta/The Inquiry* 1987; *The Moderns* 1988 (a,artist); *Sans espoir de retour* 1988; *Cold Feet* 1989; *Daddy's Dyin'...Who's Got the Will?* 1990; *The Ballad of the Sad Cafe* 1991.

Carrière, Jean-Claude • Screenwriter; also novelist, actor. • Born Colombière, France, 1931. Highly accomplished European scenarist who began his career writing novelizations of Jacques Tati movies, and then turning out several screenplays for Pierre Etaix. Although best known for his many collaborations with Luis Buñuel, Carrière is adept at a variety of genres and excels at literary adaptations. He was worked with Jacques Deray, England's Peter Brook, Germany's Volker Schlöndorff and Poland's Andrzej Wajda, among others. • *Le Journal d'une femme de chambre/Diary of a Chambermaid* 1963 (a,sc); *Le Soupirant* 1963 (sc); *Víva María* 1965 (sc); *Yoyo* 1965 (sc); *Hotel Paradiso* 1966 (sc); *Belle de Jour* 1967 (sc); *Le Voleur/The Thief of Paris* 1967 (sc); *La Pince à ongles (short)* 1968 (d); *La Piscine* 1969 (sc,dial); *La Voie Lactée/The Milky Way* 1969 (a,sc); *L'Alliance* 1970 (a,sc,from novel); *Borsalino* 1970 (sc); *La Cagna* 1971 (sc); *Un Peu de soleil dans l'eau froide* 1971 (sc); *Taking Off* 1971 (sc); *Le Charme Discret de la Bourgeoisie/The Discreet Charm of the Bourgeoisie* 1972 (sc) **(AANBSC)**; *Dorothea's Rache* 1973 (sc); *Un Homme Est Mort/The Outside Man* 1973 (sc); *Le Moine* 1973 (sc); *Un Amour de pluie* 1974 (sc); *La Chair de l'orchidée* 1974 (sc); *Le Fantôme de la Liberté/The Phantom of Liberty* 1974 (sc); *France Société Anonyme* 1974 (sc); *La Faille* 1975 (sc); *Léonor* 1975 (sc); *Les Oeufs Brouillés* 1975 (sc); *Sérieux comme le plaisir* 1975 (a,sc); *Le Jardin des Supplices* 1976 (a); *Cet obscur objet du désir/That Obscure Object of Desire* 1977 (sc,adapt,dial) **(AANBSC)**; *Le Diable dans la boîte* 1977 (sc); *Le Gang* 1977 (sc); *Julie pot de colle* 1977 (sc); *Photo Souvenir* 1977 (a,sc); *Chaussette Surprise* 1978 (sc,dial); *Un Papillon sur l'Epaule* 1978 (sc); *L'Associé* 1979 (sc); *Die Blechtrommel/The Tin Drum* 1979 (sc); *L'Homme en colère* 1979 (sc); *Ils sont grands ces petits* 1979 (a,sc); *Retour à la Bien-Aimée* 1979 (sc,dial); *Sauve qui peut (la vie)/Every Man For Himself* 1980 (sc); *Die Falschung/Circle of Deceit* 1981 (sc); *Antonieta* 1982 (sc); *Danton* 1982 (sc); *Itinéraire Bis* 1982 (sc); *Le Retour de Martin Guerre/The Return of Martin Guerre* 1982 (sc); *Le Général de l'Armée Morte* 1983 (sc); *La Tragédie de Carmen* 1983 (sc); *Un Amour de Swann/Swann in Love* 1984 (sc); *La Jeune fille et l'enfer* 1984 (sc); *L'Unique* 1985 (d,sc); *Max mon amour* 1986 (sc,from original idea); *Wolf at the Door* 1986 (story); *Les Exploits d'un jeune Don Juan* 1987 (sc); *Les Possedes/The Possessed* 1987 (sc); *La Nuit Bengali* 1988 (sc); *The Unbearable Lightness of Being* 1988 (sc) **(AANBSC)**; *Hard to Be a God* 1989 (sc); *J'écris dans l'espace* 1989 (sc); *Jeniec Europy* 1989 (sc—translations); *The Mahabharata* 1989 (sc); *Valmont* 1989 (sc); *Cyrano de Bergerac* 1990 (sc,adapt); *Milou en mai/May Fools* 1990 (sc).

Carrière, Mathieu • Actor; also director. • Born Hanover, West Germany, August 2, 1950. Handsome European leading man who began his career while still a teen, starring in the Thomas Mann adaptation *Tonio Kröger* (1964) and Volker Schlöndorff's *Young Torless* (1966). Carrière has since played in films by the likes of Marguerite Duras, Krzysztof Zanussi and Paul Morrissey, and made his feature directing debut with *Fool's Mate* (1989). • *Tonio Kröger* 1964; *Der Junge Törless/Young Torless* 1966; *Gates to Paradise* 1967; *Lo Stato d'Assedio* 1969; *Le Petit Matin* 1971; *Rendez-Vous a Bray* 1971; *Bluebeard* 1972; *L'Homme Au Cerveau Greffe* 1972; *Il n'y a pas de Fumée sans Feu* 1972; *Malpertuis: Histoire d'une maison Maudite* 1972; *Don Juan 1973 ou si Don Juan était une femme* 1973; *Giordano Bruno* 1973; *Isabelle devant le désir* 1974; *La Jeune Fille assassinée* 1974; *Blondy* 1975; *India Song* 1975; *Police Python.357* 1975; *Der Fangschuss* 1976; *Bilitis* 1977; *Les Indiens sont encore loin* 1977; *L'Associé* 1979; *Le Navire Night* 1979; *Pareil Pas Pareil* 1979; *Wege in der Nacht* 1979; *La Femme de l'aviateur/The Aviator's Wife* 1980; *Anima—Symphonie Phantastique* 1981; *Benvenuta* 1983; *Die Flambierte Frau/A Woman in Flames* 1983; *Freiwild* 1983; *L'Amour en Douce* 1984; *Angelan Sota/Angelas Krig* 1984; *Bay Boy* 1984; *Flügel und Felleln* 1984; *Yerma* 1984; *Beethoven's Nephew* 1985 (a,sc); *Bras de Fer* 1985; *Marie Ward* 1985; *Johann Strauss le roi sans couronne* 1987; *El Placer de Matar/The Pleasure of Killing* 1987; *Cérémonie d'amour* 1988; *L'Oeuvre au noir/The Abyss* 1988; *Sanguines* 1988; *Zugzwang/Fool's Mate* 1989 (a,d,sc); *Malina* 1991.

Carroll, Diahann • Actress; also singer. • Born Carol Diahann Johnson, Bronx, NY, July 17, 1935. *Educ.* New York High School of Music and Art; NYU (sociology). Accomplished stage and film entertainer who first came to prominence in Otto Preminger's *Carmen Jones* (1954) and was featured as Clara in his *Porgy and Bess* (1959). Star of the Broadway musicals, *House of Flowers* (1954) and *No Strings* (1962) which was written for her by Richard Rodgers, Carroll has played everything from a middle-class working woman on the landmark TV series, "Julia" (1968-71), to a welfare mother in the warm-hearted romantic comedy-drama, *Claudine* (1974) and, from 1984 to 1987, a glamorous, scheming businesswoman on the prime-time serial, "Dynasty" (1980-89). • *Carmen Jones* 1954; *Porgy and Bess* 1959; *Goodbye Again* 1961; *Paris Blues* 1961; *Hurry Sundown* 1967; *The Split* 1968; *Claudine* 1974 (**AANBA**); *The Five Heartbeats* 1991.

Carroll, Leo G. • Actor • Born Weedon, England, 1892; died 1972. Tall, dignified character actor popular on the London and New York stages before turning to Hollywood in 1934. Carroll appeared in more Hitchcock films then anyone other than the director himself, most notably as the insidious Dr. Murchison in *Spellbound* (1945). • *The Barretts of Wimpole Street* 1934; *Outcast Lady* 1934; *Sadie McKee* 1934; *The Casino Murder Case* 1935; *Clive of India* 1935; *Murder on a Honeymoon* 1935; *The Right to Live* 1935; *London By Night* 1937; *A Christmas Carol* 1938; *Bulldog Drummond's Secret Police* 1939; *Charlie Chan in City in Darkness* 1939; *The Private Lives of Elizabeth and Essex* 1939; *Tower of London* 1939; *Wuthering Heights* 1939; *Charlie Chan's Murder Cruise* 1940; *Rebecca* 1940; *Waterloo Bridge* 1940; *Bahama Passage* 1941; *Scotland Yard* 1941; *Suspicion* 1941; *This Woman Is Mine* 1941; *The House on 92nd Street* 1945; *Spellbound* 1945; *Forever Amber* 1947; *The Paradine Case* 1947; *Song of Love* 1947; *Time Out of Mind* 1947; *Enchantment* 1948; *So Evil My Love* 1948; *Father of the Bride* 1950; *The Happy Years* 1950; *The Desert Fox* 1951; *The First Legion* 1951; *Strangers on a Train* 1951; *The Bad and the Beautiful* 1952; *Rogue's March* 1952; *The Snows of Kilimanjaro* 1952; *Treasure of the Golden Condor* 1953; *Young Bess* 1953; *Tarantula* 1955; *We're No Angels* 1955; *The Swan* 1956; *North By Northwest* 1959; *1 + 1—Exploring the Kinsey Reports* 1961; *The Parent Trap* 1961; *The Prize* 1963; *That Funny Feeling* 1965; *The Double Affair* 1966; *One Spy Too Many* 1966; *The Spy in the Green Hat* 1966; *The Helicopter Spies* 1967; *The Karate Killers* 1967; *How to Steal the World* 1968; *From Nashville With Music* 1969.

Carroll, Madeleine • Actress • Born Marie-Madeleine Bernadette O'Carroll, West Bromwich, Staffordshire, England, February 26, 1906; died October 2, 1987, Marbella, Spain. *Educ.* Birmingham University (French). Perhaps the most beautiful of Britain's exports to Hollywood, Carroll began her career in England in 1928 and was signed to a 20th Century-Fox contract in 1936. She is best remembered as Hitchock's prototypical frosty blonde handcuffed to Robert Donat in *The 39 Steps* (1935) and as John Gielgud's co-spy in *Secret Agent* (1936). Other smooth, aristocratic performances followed, including *The Prisoner of Zenda* (1937), perfectly matched with Ronald Colman, and kidding her image as *My Favorite Blonde* (1942). Carroll distinguished herself working with the Red Cross during WWII and later did a notable amount of stage work. One of her four husbands was actor Sterling Hayden. • *The First Born* 1928; *The Guns of Loos* 1928; *What Money Can Buy* 1928; *The American Prisoner* 1929; *Atlantic* 1929; *The Crooked Billet* 1929; *L'Instinct* 1929; *Escape* 1930; *Fascination* 1930; *French Leave* 1930; *Madame Guillotine* 1930; *School For Scandal* 1930; *The W Plan* 1930; *Young Woodley* 1930; *The Kissing Cup Race* 1931; *The Written Law* 1931; *I Was a Spy* 1933; *Sleeping Car* 1933; *The World Moves On* 1934; *The 39 Steps* 1935; *The Dictator* 1935; *The Case Against Mrs. Ames* 1936; *The General Died at Dawn* 1936; *Lloyd's of London* 1936; *Secret Agent* 1936; *It's All Yours* 1937; *On the Avenue* 1937; *The Prisoner of Zenda* 1937; *Blockade* 1938; *Cafe Society* 1939; *Honeymoon in Bali* 1939; *My Son, My Son* 1940; *North West Mounted Police* 1940; *Safari* 1940; *Bahama Passage* 1941; *One Night in Lisbon* 1941; *Virginia* 1941; *My Favorite Blonde* 1942; *White Cradle Inn* 1946; *Don't Trust Your Husband* 1948; *The Fan* 1949.

Carson, Jack • Actor • Born John Elmer Carson, Carmen, Manitoba, Canada, October 27, 1910; died 1963. *Educ.* Carleton College, Ottawa, Ontario. Competent character player, married to actress Lola Albright from 1952 to 1958. • *Circle of Death* 1935; *High Flyers* 1937; *Stage Door* 1937; *Stand-In* 1937; *Too Many Wives* 1937; *You Only Live Once* 1937; *Bringing Up Baby* 1938; *Carefree* 1938; *Crashing Hollywood* 1938; *Go Chase Yourself* 1938; *Having Wonderful Time* 1938; *Night Spot* 1938; *Quick Money* 1938; *The Saint in New York* 1938; *She's Got Everything* 1938; *This Marriage Business* 1938; *Vivacious Lady* 1938; *Destry Rides Again* 1939; *The Honeymoon's Over* 1939; *The Kid From Texas* 1939; *Legion of Lost Flyers* 1939; *Mr. Smith Goes to Washington* 1939; *Alias the Deacon* 1940; *Enemy Agent* 1940; *Girl in 313* 1940; *I Take This Woman* 1940; *The Jones Family in Young As You Feel* 1940; *Love Thy Neighbor* 1940; *Lucky Partners* 1940; *Parole Fixer* 1940; *Queen of the Mob* 1940; *Sandy Gets Her Man* 1940; *Shooting High* 1940; *Typhoon* 1940; *Blues in the Night* 1941; *The Bride Came C.O.D.* 1941; *Love Crazy* 1941; *Mr. & Mrs. Smith* 1941; *Navy Blues* 1941; *The Strawberry Blonde* 1941; *Gentleman Jim* 1942; *The Hard Way* 1942; *Larceny, Inc.* 1942; *The Male Animal* 1942; *Wings For the Eagle* 1942; *Princess O'Rourke* 1943; *Thank Your Lucky Stars* 1943; *Arsenic and Old Lace* 1944; *The Doughgirls* 1944; *Hollywood Canteen* 1944; *Make Your Own Bed* 1944; *Shine on Harvest Moon* 1944; *Mildred Pierce* 1945; *Roughly Speaking* 1945; *One More Tomorrow* 1946; *Time, the Place and the Girl, The* 1946; *Two Guys From Milwaukee* 1946; *Love and Learn* 1947; *April Showers* 1948; *Romance on the High Seas* 1948; *Two Guys From Texas* 1948; *It's a Great Feeling* 1949; *John Loves Mary* 1949; *My Dream Is Yours* 1949; *Bright Leaf* 1950; *The Good Humor Man* 1950; *The Groom Wore Spurs* 1951; *Mr. Universe* 1951; *Dangerous When Wet* 1953; *Phffft* 1954; *Red Garters* 1954; *A Star Is Born* 1954; *Ain't Misbehavin'* 1955; *The Bottom of the Bottle* 1956; *Magnificent Roughnecks* 1956; *The Tattered Dress* 1957; *Cat on a Hot Tin Roof* 1958; *Rally Round the Flag, Boys!* 1958; *The Tarnished Angels* 1958; *The Bramble Bush* 1960; *King of the Roaring 20's - The Story of Arnold Rothstein* 1961.

Carson, L. M. Kit • Screenwriter; also actor, director. • Born Dallas, TX. *Educ.* NYU (film). With director Jim McBride, made the ingenious mid-1960s gem *David Holzman's Diary* (1967). Carson's later work as a scenarist has produced mostly middling fare, though his collaboration on Wim Wender's much-lauded *Paris, Texas* (1984) earned him renewed praise. Son Hunter Carson, by actress Karen Black, made a memorable screen debut in *Paris, Texas.* • *David Holzman's Diary* 1967 (a,sc); *The Lexington Experience* 1970 (sc); *The American Dreamer* 1971 (d,sc); *The Last Word* 1979 (sc); *Breathless* 1983 (sc); *Chinese Boxes* 1984 (a,sc); *Paris, Texas* 1984 (story adaptation); *The Texas Chainsaw Massacre Part 2* 1986 (assoc.p,sc,song); *Running on Empty* 1988 (a).

Cartwright, Veronica • Actress • Born Bristol, England, 1949. Former child star who developed into a highly accomplished character actress during the 1970s and 80s. Sister of actress Angela Cartwright. • *In Love and War* 1958; *The Children's Hour* 1961; *The Birds* 1963; *Spencer's Mountain* 1963; *One Man's Way* 1964; *Inserts* 1975; *Goin' South* 1978; *Invasion of the Body Snatchers* 1978; *Alien* 1979; *Nightmares* 1983; *The Right Stuff* 1983; *My Man Adam* 1985; *Flight of the Navigator* 1986; *Wis-*

dom 1986; *The Witches of Eastwick* 1987; *Valentino Returns* 1989; *False Identity* 1990.

Casarés, Maria • Actress • Born Maria Casarés Quiroga, La Coruña, Spain, November 21, 1922. *Educ.* Paris Conservatoire. Stage actress whose film appearances have been minimal but memorable, as in Jean Cocteau's *Orpheus* (1950). Casares's highly distinctive voice has narrated numerous documentaries. • *Les Dames du Bois de Boulogne* 1945; *Les Enfants du Paradis/Children of Paradise* 1945; *L'Amour autour de la Maison* 1946; *La Revenche de Roger la Honte* 1946; *Roger la Honte* 1946; *La Septième Porte* 1946; *Baggares* 1948; *La Chartreuse de Parme* 1948; *L'Homme qui revient de Loin* 1949; *Guernica* (short) 1950; *Orphée/Orpheus* 1950; *Ombre et Lumière* 1951; *Le Testament d'Orphée/The Testament of Orpheus* 1959; *La Reine verte* 1964; *Blanche et Marie* 1985; *De sable et de sang* 1988; *La Lectrice* 1988; *Les Chevaliers de la table ronde* 1990.

Casey, Bernie • Actor • Born Wyco, WV, June 8, 1939. Imposing, dignified former pro football star (for the 49ers and Rams) who played the lead in several black exploitation movies of the 1970s. Casey has also proved himself an effective supporting actor in less heroic roles, in such films as *The Man Who Fell to Earth* (1975) and *Sharkey's Machine* (1981), and parodied his earlier roles in Keenan Ivory Wayan's hilarious send-up of "blaxploitation" movies, *I'm Gonna Git You Sucka* (1989). In 1979 he starred in the short-lived "Harris and Company," one of TV's first attempts to portray black family life on a dramatic series. • *Guns of the Magnificent Seven* 1969; *Tick, Tick, Tick* 1970; *Black Chariot* 1971; *Black Gunn* 1972; *Boxcar Bertha* 1972; *Hit Man* 1972; *Cleopatra Jones* 1973; *Maurie* 1973; *Cornbread, Earl & Me* 1975; *Dr. Black, Mr. Hyde* 1975; *The Man Who Fell to Earth* 1976; *Brothers* 1977; *The Watts Monster* 1979; *Sharky's Machine* 1981; *Never Say Never Again* 1983; *Revenge of the Nerds* 1984; *Spies Like Us* 1985; *Backfire* 1987; *Steele Justice* 1987; *I'm Gonna Git You Sucka* 1988; *Rent-A-Cop* 1988; *Bill and Ted's Excellent Adventure* 1989; *Another 48 Hrs.* 1990; *Chains of Gold* 1990.

Cash, Rosalind • Actress • Born Atlantic City, NJ, December 31, 1938. Black leading lady of the 1970s. • *The Omega Man* 1971; *Hickey and Boggs* 1972; *Melinda* 1972; *The New Centurions* 1972; *The All-American Boy* 1973; *Amazing Grace* 1974; *Uptown Saturday Night* 1974; *Cornbread, Earl & Me* 1975; *Dr. Black, Mr. Hyde* 1975; *The Monkey Hustle* 1976; *The Class of Miss MacMichael* 1978; *The Watts Monster* 1979; *Wrong Is Right* 1982; *The Adventures of Buckaroo Banzai: Across the 8th Dimension* 1984; *Go Tell It on the Mountain* 1984; *The Offspring* 1987; *Forced March* 1989.

Cassavetes, John • Director, actor; also screenwriter, producer, playwright. • Born New York, NY, December 9, 1929; died February 3, 1989, Los Angeles, CA. *Educ.* Mohawk Valley Community College, Utica, NY (English); Colgate University, Hamilton, NY (English); AADA, New York. For 35 years, John Cassavetes held a unique position in American film, maintaining dual careers as a highly regarded actor in popular movies and as a director of independent films which themselves explored the art of acting. Like Orson Welles, he fused the roles in a truly remarkable way.

From 1953 through 1956 the "Golden Age" of TV afforded Cassavetes a unique opportunity to experiment as an actor; he essayed more than 80 roles during this three-year period. He began almost immediately to take on more filmmaking responsibilities, writing the teleplays for *The Night Holds Terror* (1955) and *Crime in the Streets* (1956). Shortly after performing opposite Sidney Poitier in Martin Ritt's *Edge of the City* (1957), a ground-breaking portrait of interracial bonding, Cassavetes began work on his own first feature, *Shadows*—also an interracial story, but with a profoundly different style.

Shot in 16-mm black-and-white on location in the streets of New York, *Shadows* (1960) began a new era in American film. As an actor turning to directing, Cassavetes displayed many of the same concerns that characterized the approach of the film critics-turned-auteurs who were revolutionizing French cinema. In a way, Cassavetes was the American New Wave, but with a difference. Instead of a critic's perspective, he brought an actor's understanding to the director's chair. Cassavetes's work is often mistaken as improvisational, or even as cinéma vérité. In fact, his films are thoughtful celebrations of the art of acting and, in most cases, are shot from precise scripts (even if those scripts are based on extensive improvisational exercises).

Shadows, according to Cassavetes, "emanates from characters" thoroughly analyzed by the actors before improvisation. It is a family drama: jazz musician Hugh, the older brother, is dark-skinned; his younger brother Ben and sister Lelia are light-skinned. Hugh must confront racial tensions while Ben and Lelia can pass as whites, avoiding them. Hugh struggles with Lelia and Ben over their denial of color in a racist society, avoiding any comfortable resolution to a sensitive issue.

Despite its underground quality, *Shadows* was successful enough to gain the attention of Hollywood studio executives. *Too Late Blues* (1961) and *A Child Is Waiting* (1962), both studio productions, frustrated Cassavetes. He returned to acting to finance has next film, the independently produced *Faces* (1968).

Faces, like most Cassavetes films, focuses intently on family and friends—on both sides of the camera—as the director tracks the breakdown of a marriage. Like *Shadows*, it was an underground hit. (Throughout his career, Cassavetes was able to garner a much wider audience for his independent films than one might expect.) The late 60s witnessed some of his most memorable commercial film roles, in *The Dirty Dozen* (1967) and *Rosemary's Baby* (1968).

By 1970, the pattern was established, with fees for acting jobs paying for the occasional independent production. *Husbands* (1970), *Minnie and Moskowitz* (1971), *A Woman Under the Influence* (1974), *Opening Night* (1977), *Gloria* (1980) and *Love Streams* (1984) each celebrate relationships—mostly middle-aged—from different perspectives, and usually with the same group of acting family and friends collaborating.

For Gus (Cassavetes), Archie (Peter Falk) and Harry (Ben Gazzara), *Husbands* is a chance to explore their own lives as well as their chosen professions. These three suburbanites react to a friend's death by flying off to London for a drunken weekend. Along the way, they get to do some tour-de-force ensemble acting.

Having provided a vehicle for himself in *Husbands*, Cassavetes offered a couple to his wife, Gena Rowlands, in *Minnie and Moskowitz* and *A Woman Under the Influence*. *Minnie and Moskowitz* is a romantic duet between Rowlands, who works in a museum, and Seymour Cassel, a garage attendant. *A Woman Under the Influence* is a tragic duet between Rowlands and Peter Falk, who plays her husband, and remains an insightful essay on sexual politics. As Rowlands delicately crosses the line of sanity it becomes apparent that imposed social roles are the cause.

The Killing of a Chinese Bookie (1976) stars old friend and collaborator Ben Gazzara as Cosmo, a loner up against the mob. *Opening Night* (1977) is more directly about the job and art of acting. Rowlands, as star, superbly limns the complex relationships between actor and character, actor and collaborators. *Gloria*, like *Bookie*, is one of the more accessible Cassavetes works, featuring a relatively strong storyline. It also encourages audience identification with a tough, independent woman (Rowlands again), who learns to love a child that she is obliged to protect from the mob. *Love Streams* is a free-form, off-beat look at the emotional interdependence of a brother and sister.

Throughout his career, Cassavetes as a filmmaker was absorbed with the work he did as an actor. His style and concerns are so powerful they often come through just as strongly in his acting vehicles as in the films he wrote and directed. Elaine May's *Mikey and Nicky* (1976) stars Cassavetes and Falk in what looks like a sequel to *Husbands* with a bit of *Bookie* thrown in. And Paul Mazursky's *Tempest* (1982) stars Cassavetes as the Prospero figure in this reworking of Shakespeare's highly personal play about the life of the stage. Gradually, Cassavetes, the actor-director, overwhelms colleague Mazursky, the director-actor. No one in contemporary cinema has so eloquently illuminated the relationships of the stage, the bonds between the family of players. JM • *Fourteen Hours* 1951 (a); *Taxi* 1953 (a); *The Night Holds Terror* 1955 (a); *Crime in the Streets* 1956 (a); *Affair in Havana* 1957 (a); *Edge of the City* 1957 (a); *Saddle the Wind* 1958 (a); *Virgin Island* 1958 (a); *Shadows* 1960 (d,sc); *Too Late Blues* 1961 (d,p,sc); *A Child Is Waiting* 1962 (d); *The Webster Boy* 1962 (a); *The Killers* 1964 (a); *Devil's Angels* 1967 (a); *The Dirty Dozen* 1967 (a) **(AANBSA)**; *Faces* 1968 (d,sc) **(AANBSC)**; *Roma Come Chicago* 1968 (a); *Rosemary's Baby* 1968 (a); *If It's Tuesday, This Must Be Belgium* 1969 (a); *Gli Intoccabili* 1969 (a); *Husbands* 1970 (a,d,sc); *Minnie and Moskowitz* 1971 (a,d,sc); *A Woman Under the Influence* 1974 (d,sc) **(AANBD)**; *Capone* 1975 (a); *The Killing of a Chinese Bookie* 1976 (d,sc); *Mikey and Nicky* 1976 (a); *Two-Minute Warning* 1976 (a); *Opening Night* 1977 (a,d,sc,story); *Brass Target* 1978 (a); *The Fury* 1978 (a); *Gloria* 1980 (d,p,sc); *Whose Life Is It Anyway?* 1981 (a); *The Haircut (short)* 1982 (a); *The Incubus* 1982 (a); *Tempest* 1982 (a); *"I'm Almost Not Crazy..." John Cassavetes: The Man and His Work* 1983 (a); *Marvin and Tige* 1983 (a); *Love Streams* 1984 (a,d,sc,song); *Big Trouble* 1985 (d,sc); *Hollywood Mavericks* 1990 (archival footage).

Cassel, Jean-Pierre • Actor • Born Jean-Pierre Crochon, Paris, October 27, 1932. Attractive Gallic leading man who worked as an extra and nightclub dancer before being "discovered" by Gene Kelly. Subsequently popular in a number of English-language, as well as continental, productions, including a series of Philippe de Broca films, Cassel also played the dinner host in Buñuel's *The Discreet Charm of the Bourgeoisie* (1971) and co-starred in *Is Paris Burning?* (1966) and *Murder on the Orient Express* (1974). • *Candide, ou l'optimisme au XX siècle* 1960; *Le Jeux de l'Amour* 1960; *L'Amant de Cinq Jours* 1961; *Arsène Lupin contre Arsène Lupin* 1962; *Le Caporal épingle* 1962; *Le Farceur* 1962; *Les Sept péchés capitaux/The Seven Deadly Sins* 1962; *Cyrano et d'Artagnan* 1963; *Alta Infedeltà/High Infidelity* 1964; *Un Monsieur de Compagnie* 1964; *Les Plus belles escroqueries du monde* 1964; *La Ronde* 1964; *Les Fêtes Gallantes* 1965; *Those Magnificent Men in Their Flying Machines* 1965; *Paris brûle-t-il?/Is Paris Burning?* 1966; *Le Dolci signore* 1967; *Jeu de massacre/Comic Strip Hero* 1967; *L'Armée des ombres* 1969; *Oh! What a Lovely War* 1969; *L'Ours et la poupée* 1970; *La Rupture* 1970; *Baxter* 1972; *Le Charme Discret de la Bourgeoisie/The Discreet Charm of the Bourgeoisie* 1972; *Malpertuis: Histoire d'une maison Maudite* 1972; *The Three Musketeers* 1973; *Le Mouton Enragé* 1974; *Murder on the Orient Express* 1974; *Docteur Françoise Gailland* 1975; *The Four Musketeers* 1975; *That Lucky Touch* 1975; *Folies bourgeoises* 1976; *Grandison* 1978; *Les Rendez-Vous d'Anna* 1978; *Who Is Killing the Great Chefs of Europe?* 1978; *Da Dunkerque alla Vittoria* 1979; *De l'enfer à la Victoire* 1979; *La Giacca Verde* 1979; *Je te tiens, tu me tiens par la Barbichette* 1979; *Le Soleil en face* 1979; *La Ville des Silences* 1979; *5% de Risque* 1980; *La Vie Continue* 1981; *Ehrengard* 1982; *La Truite/The Trout* 1982; *Vive la Sociale!* 1983; *Tranches de Vie* 1984; *Chouans!* 1988; *Mangeclous* 1988; *Migrations* 1988; *Vado a riprendermi il gatto* 1989; *Mister Frost* 1990.

Cassel, Seymour • Actor • Born Detroit, MI, January 22, 1932. *Educ.* American Theater Wing, New York; Actors Studio. Blonde, often mustachioed, and scruffy character player best known as part of John Cassavetes's informal clan of actors. After studying at an acting workshop taught by Cassavetes, Cassel served as associate producer on his directorial debut, *Shadows* (1960) and then acted under Cassavetes's direction in *Too Late Blues* (1961) and in almost all of his films, starring as Moskowitz, opposite Gena Rowlands, in *Minnie and Moskowitz* (1971). Cassel has also been featured as a supporting actor in numerous other films including Barry Levinson's *Tin Men* (1987) and as Sam Catchem in *Dick Tracy* (1990). • *Murder, Inc.* 1960; *Shadows* 1960 (assoc.p); *Too Late Blues* 1961; *The Webster Boy* 1962; *The Hanged Man* 1964; *The Killers* 1964; *Coogan's Bluff* 1968; *Faces* 1968**(AANBSA)**; *The Sweet Ride* 1968; *The Revolutionary* 1970; *Minnie and Moskowitz* 1971; *Black Oak Conspiracy* 1976; *Death Game* 1976; *The Killing of a Chinese Bookie* 1976; *The Last Tycoon* 1976; *Opening Night* 1977; *Scott Joplin* 1977; *Valentino* 1977; *Convoy* 1978; *California Dreaming* 1979; *Ravagers* 1979; *Sunburn* 1979; *The Mountain Men* 1980; *King of the Mountain* 1981; *"I'm Almost Not Crazy..." John Cassavetes: The Man and His Work* 1983; *Love Streams* 1984; *Eye of the Tiger* 1986; *Survival Game* 1987; *Tin Men* 1987; *Track 29* 1987; *Colors* 1988; *Johnny Be Good* 1988; *Plain Clothes* 1988; *Wicked Stepmother* 1989; *Cold Dog Soup* 1990; *Dick Tracy* 1990; *White Fang* 1991.

Cassidy, Joanna • Actress • Born Joanna Virginia Caskey, Camden, NJ, August 2, 1944. *Educ.* Syracuse University, NY (art). Statuesque brunette who appeared in a number of first-rate films including *The Stepford Wives*, *Stay Hungry* (both 1975) and *Blade Runner* (1982). After a lag in the mid-80s, Cassidy revived her career with a critically praised role opposite Dabney Coleman in the TV series, "Buffalo Bill" (1983-84). • *Bullitt* 1968; *Fools* 1970; *The Laughing Policeman* 1973; *The Outfit* 1973; *Bank Shot* 1974; *Stay Hungry* 1975; *The Stepford Wives* 1975; *The Glove* 1976; *The Late Show* 1977; *Stunts* 1977; *Our Winning Season* 1978; *Night Games* 1979; *Blade Runner* 1982; *Under Fire* 1983; *Club Paradise* 1986; *The Fourth Protocol* 1987; *1969* 1988; *Who Framed Roger Rabbit* 1988; *The Package* 1989; *May Wine* 1990; *Where the Heart Is* 1990.

Castle, Nick • Director; also screenwriter. • Born Nick Castle, Jr., Los Angeles, CA, September 21, 1947. *Educ.* Santa Monica College, CA; USC, Los Angeles (film). Son of Hollywood choreographer Nick Castle, Sr., who has written and/or directed a variety of popular entertainments. Castle's best works are his sly screenplay for John Carpenter's *Escape From New York* (1983), his own *The Boy Who Could Fly* (1986), a slightly flawed, but well-intentioned, "small movie," and his old-fashioned homage to black dancers, *Tap* (1989). • *Artists and Models* 1955 (a); *Halloween* 1978 (a); *Skatetown, USA* 1979 (sc,story); *Escape From New York* 1981 (sc); *Tag* 1982 (d); *The Last Starfighter* 1984 (d); *The Boy Who Could Fly* 1986 (a,d,sc,songs); *Tap* 1989 (d,sc).

Castle, William • Director; also producer, actor. • Born William Schloss, New York, NY, April 24, 1914; died May 31, 1977, Beverly Hills, CA. Eccentric director of routine low-budget horror films, with a flair for self-promotion. Castle's standout efforts include the B thriller, *When Strangers Marry* (1944), with Robert Mitchum in his first important role and the camp gem, *House on Haunted Hill* (1958). Like a latter-day P.T. Barnum, upon whom he modeled himself, Castle lured audiences to his chillers by appearing in their trailers and psyching the audience up to be scared. Most of his films included outrageous gimmicks such as an insurance policy against death by fright for *Macabre* (1958), skeletons that whistled over the audience in a process called "Emergo" during critical scenes in *House on Haunted Hill* and his most audacious stunt, "Percepto," which literally shocked the audience by wiring selected seats in the theater with electricity and administering mild jolts during moments in *The Tingler* (1959). Castle is also noted as the producer of the psychological thriller, *Rosemary's Baby* (1968).

• *He Stayed For Breakfast* 1940 (a); *North to the Klondike* 1942 (story); *The Chance of a Lifetime* 1943 (d); *Klondike Kate* 1943 (d); *The Mark of the Whistler* 1944 (d); *She's a Soldier Too* 1944 (d); *When Strangers Marry* 1944 (d); *The Whistler* 1944 (d); *The Crime Doctor's Warning* 1945 (d); *Voice of the Whistler* 1945 (d,sc); *Crime Doctor's Manhunt* 1946 (d); *Just Before Dawn* 1946 (d); *The Mysterious Intruder* 1946 (d); *The Return of Rusty* 1946 (d); *The Crime Doctor's Gamble* 1947 (d); *The Gentleman From Nowhere* 1948 (d); *The Lady From Shanghai* 1948 (assoc.p); *Texas, Brooklyn and Heaven* 1948 (d); *Johnny Stool Pigeon* 1949 (d); *Undertow* 1949 (d); *It's a Small World* 1950 (d,sc,story); *Cave of Outlaws* 1951 (d); *The Fat Man* 1951 (d); *Hollywood Story* 1951 (d); *Conquest of Cochise* 1953 (d); *Fort Ti* 1953 (d); *Serpent of the Nile* 1953 (d); *Slaves of Babylon* 1953 (d); *Battle of Rogue River* 1954 (d); *Charge of the Lancers* 1954 (d); *Drums of Tahiti* 1954 (d); *The Iron Glove* 1954 (d); *Jesse James vs. the Daltons* 1954 (d); *The Law vs. Billy the Kid* 1954 (d); *Masterson of Kansas* 1954 (d); *New Orleans Uncensored* 1954 (d); *The Saracen Blade* 1954 (d); *The Americano* 1955 (d); *Duel on the Mississippi* 1955 (d); *The Gun That Won the West* 1955 (d); *The Houston Story* 1956 (d); *Uranium Boom* 1956 (d); *House on Haunted Hill* 1958 (d,p); *Macabre* 1958 (d,p); *The Tingler* 1959 (d,p); *13 Ghosts* 1960 (d,p); *Homicidal* 1961 (a,d,p); *Mr. Sardonicus* 1961 (d,p); *Zotz* 1962 (d,p); *13 Frightened Girls* 1963 (d,p); *The Old Dark House* 1963 (d,p); *The Night Walker* 1964 (d,p); *Strait-Jacket* 1964 (d,p); *I Saw What You Did* 1965 (d,p); *Let's Kill Uncle* 1966 (d,p); *The Busy Body* 1967 (d,p); *The Spirit Is Willing* 1967 (d,p); *Project X* 1968 (d,p); *Riot* 1968 (p); *Rosemary's Baby* 1968 (a,p); *Shanks* 1974 (a,d,exec.p); *Bug* 1975 (p,sc); *The Day of the Locust* 1975 (a); *Shampoo* 1975 (a).

Cates, Phoebe • Actress • Born New York, NY, 1963. *Educ.* Juilliard (dance); Professional Children's School, New York. Top teen model of the late 1970s and romantic lead of the 80s, with some stage experience, who first appeared in films aimed at the teen market: *Paradise* and *Fast Times at Ridgemont High* (both 1982) and *Private School* (1983). Cates won attention as Zach Galligan's girlfriend in *Gremlins* (1984) and in the TV movies, *Lace* (1984) and *Lace II* (1985). Daughter of producer-director Joseph Cates and niece of director Gilbert Cates, she is married to actor Kevin Kline. • *Fast Times at Ridgemont High* 1982; *Paradise* 1982; *Private School* 1983; *Gremlins* 1984; *Date With an Angel* 1987; *Bright Lights, Big City* 1988; *Shag* 1988; *Heart of Dixie* 1989; *Gremlins 2: The New Batch* 1990; *Drop Dead Fred* 1991.

Cattrall, Kim • Actress • Born Liverpool, England, August 21, 1956. *Educ.* LAMDA, London; Banff School of Fine Arts, Alberta; AADA, New York. Attractive, versatile supporting player and occasional lead, who won attention as the sex-starved coach in the surprise hit teen comedy *Porky's* (1981), and was excellent opposite Rob Lowe, in Bob Swaim's stylish thriller *Masquerade* (1988). • *Rosebud* 1975; *Tribute* 1980; *Porky's* 1981; *Ticket to Heaven* 1981; *Police Academy* 1984; *City Limits* 1985; *Hold-Up* 1985; *Turk 182* 1985; *Big Trouble in Little China* 1986; *Mannequin* 1987; *Masquerade* 1988; *Midnight Crossing* 1988; *Palais Royale* 1988; *Brown Bread Sandwiches* 1989; *The Return of the Musketeers* 1989; *Bonfire of the Vanities* 1990; *Honeymoon Academy* 1990.

Cavalcanti, Alberto • Director; also producer, screenwriter, production designer. • Born Alberto De Almeida-Cavalcanti, Rio de Janeiro, Brazil, February 6, 1897; died 1982. Designed sets for French experimental filmmakers in the 1920s and directed his first film in 1926. Cavalcanti moved to England in 1934, making documentaries and, later, documentary-influenced features at Ealing Studios before returning to Brazil in 1949. While there he helped set up and headed Vera Cruz Studios. Cavalcanti's attempt to forge a new Brazilian Cinema, free of American dominance, was sabotaged when he was denounced as a communist. Despite losing his job he managed to make several films, most impressively the bitter and lyrical *Song of the Sea* (1953). Upon returning to Europe he directed the highly regarded *Herr Puntilla und sein Knecht Matti* (1955), co-written with Bertolt Brecht.

Though Cavalcanti's was a significant contribution to world cinema, the diversity of his interests diluted the impact of his career as a whole. • *Feu Mathias Pascal* 1925 (art d); *Rien que les heures* 1926 (d,p,sc); *Le Train sans yeux* 1925 (d); *En Rade* 1927 (d,sc); *Yvette* 1927 (d,sc); *Le Capitaine Fracasse* 1929 (d,sc); *La Jalousie du Barbouille* (short) 1929 (d,sc); *La P'tite Lilie* (short) 1929 (d); *Le Petit chaperon rouge* 1929 (d,sc); *Vous verrez la semaine prochaine* 1929 (d); *Toute sa vie* 1930 (d); *Dans une île perdue* 1931 (d); *A Mi-chemin du ciel* 1931 (d); *Les Vacances du diable* 1931 (d); *En lisant le journal* (short) 1932 (d); *Le Jour du frotteur* (short) 1932 (d,sc); *Nous ne ferons jamais le cinéma* (short) 1932 (d); *Revue Montmartroise* (short) 1932 (d); *Tour de Chant* (short) 1932 (d,sc); *Coralie et Cie* 1933 (d); *Le Mari Garçon* 1933 (d); *Plaisirs défendus* (short) 1933 (d); *New Rates* (short) 1934 (d); *Pett and Pott (short)* 1934 (d,sc); *SOS Radio Service* (short) 1934 (d,sc); *Coal Face* (short) 1935 (d,sc); *Message From Geneva* (short) 1936 (d,sc); *The Line to Tschierva Hut* (short) 1937 (d); *We Live in Two Worlds* (short) 1937 (d); *Who Writes to Switzerland (short)* 1937 (d,sc); *Four Barriers* (short) 1938 (d,sc); *Men of the Alps* (short) 1939 (d); *Midsummer Day's Work* (short) 1939 (d,sc); *Yellow Caesar* (short) 1941 (d); *Young Veteran (short)* 1941 (d); *Alice in Switzerland (short)* 1942 (d); *Film and Reality* 1942 (d); *Greek Testament* 1942 (p); *Went the Day Well?/48 Hours* 1942 (d); *Watertight* (short) 1943 (d); *Champagne Charlie* 1944 (d); *Dead of Night* 1945 (d); *Nicholas Nickleby* 1947 (d); *They Made Me a Fugitive/I Became a Criminal* 1947 (d); *The First Gentleman/Affairs of a Rogue* 1948 (d); *For Them That Trespass* 1949 (d); *Simão o Caolho* 1952 (d,p); *O Canto do Mar/Song of the Sea* 1953 (d,p,sc); *Mulher de Verdade* 1954 (d,p); *Herr Puntila und sein Knecht Matti* 1955 (d,sc); *Castle in the Carpathians* 1957 (d); *La Prima Notte* 1958 (d); *The Monster of Highgate Pond* 1960 (d); *Thus Spake Theodor Herzl* 1967 (d,sc).

Cavalier, Alain • Director; also screenwriter. • Born Alain Fraisse, Vendôme, France, September 14, 1931. *Educ.* Faculté des Lettres, Paris; IDHEC, Paris. Former assistant to Louis Malle and Edouard Molinaro who came of age with the New Wave, directing *Le Combat dans l'île* (1962). Best known for *La Chamade* (1968), a smoothly handled romance written in collaboration with Francoise Sagan (whose novel it is based on), and *Thérèse* (1986), a well-acted and nuanced portrait of 19th-century Carmelite convent life. • *Le Combat dans l'île* 1962 (d,story); *L'Insoumis* 1964 (d,sc); *Mise à Sac* 1967 (d,sc,story); *La Chamade* 1968 (d,sc); *Le Plein de Super* 1976 (d,sc); *Martin et Lea* 1978 (d,sc,dial); *Ce Répondeur Ne Prend Pas de Messages* 1979 (a,d,sc); *Thérèse* 1986 (d,sc,dial); *Portraits d'Alain Cavalier* 1988 (d).

Cavani, Liliana • Director; also screenwriter. • Born Carpi, Italy, January 12, 1936. *Educ.* University of Bologna (classics); Centro Sperimentale di Cinematografia, Rome (directing). Best known for *The Night Porter* (1974) which, like many of her films, boldly and effectively deals with socio-political and sexual themes. • *Galileo* 1968 (d,sc); *I Cannibali* 1970 (d,sc,story); *L'Ospite* 1971 (d,sc,ed); *Milarepa* 1974 (d,sc); *The Night Porter* 1974 (d,sc,story); *Al di la del bene e del male* 1977 (d,sc); *La Pelle* 1981 (d,sc); *Oltre la Porta* 1982 (d,sc); *Interno Berlinese* 1985 (d,sc); *Francesco/St. Francis of Assissi* 1989 (d,sc,story).

Cayatte, André • Director; also screenwriter. • Born Carcassonne, France, February 3, 1909; died February 5, 1989, Paris. Former lawyer who turned to filmmaking as a means of criticizing the French legal system, as with *We Are All Murderers* (1952).

• *La Fausse Maîtresse* 1942 (d); *Au Bonheur des Dames* 1943 (d); *Pierre et Jean* 1943 (d); *Le Dernier Sou* 1945 (d); *Sérénade aux Nuages* 1945 (d); *Roger la Honte* 1946 (d); *Le Chanteur inconnu* 1947 (d); *Les Dessous des Cartes* 1947 (d); *Les Amants de Vérone* 1948 (d); *Retour à la vie* 1949 (d); *Justice est faite/Justice Is Done* 1950 (d); *Nous sommes tous des Assassins/We Are All Murderers* 1952 (d); *Avant le Déluge* 1954 (d); *Le Dossier noir* 1955 (d); *Oeil pour Oeil* 1957 (d); *The Mirror Has Two Faces* 1958 (d,sc,story); *Le Passage du Rhin* 1960 (d); *Le Glaive et la Balance* 1963 (d); *La Vie Conjugale: My Days With Jean-Marc* 1964 (d,sc,story,adapt); *La Vie conjugale: My Nights With Françoise* 1964 (d,sc,story,adapt); *Piège pour Cendrillon* 1965 (d); *Les Risques du Métier* 1967 (d); *Les Chemins de Katmandou* 1969 (d,sc); *Mourir d'aimer/To Die of Love* 1970 (d,sc); *Il n'y a pas de Fumée sans Feu* 1972 (d,sc); *Le Testament* 1974 (d,sc,ed); *A chacun son enfer* 1976 (d,sc,adapt); *L'Amour en Question* 1978 (d,sc); *La Raison d'état* 1978 (d,sc).

Cazale, John • Actor • Born Boston, MA, 1936; died March 12, 1978, New York. *Educ.* Oberlin College, OH; Boston University (drama). Fiery, gifted character actor, adept at playing hysterics and losers, whose impressive career was cut short by cancer. After winning two Obie awards for his performances off-Broadway in Israel Horovitz's *The Indian Wants the Bronx* (1968; opposite his frequent co-star Al Pacino) and *Line* (1971), Cazale was memorable in his screen debut as the Don Corleone's weak, high-living son Fredo, in *The Godfather* (1972) and as Al Pacino's nervous heist partner in *Dog Day Afternoon* (1975). • *The Godfather* 1972; *The Conversation* 1974; *The Godfather, Part II* 1974; *Dog Day Afternoon* 1975; *The Deer Hunter* 1978.

Cecchi D'Amico, Suso • *aka* Suso Cecchi D'Amico • Screenwriter • Born Giovanna Cecchi, Rome, July 21, 1914. Leading scenarist who has worked with nearly every major postwar Italian director (most notably with Visconti, Antonioni, and De Sica); usually writes in collaboration. • *Mio Figlio Professore* 1946 (sc); *Vivere in Pace* 1946 (sc); *Il Delitto di Giovanni Episcopo* 1947 (sc); *L'Onorevole Angelina* 1947 (sc); *Fabiola* 1948 (sc); *Ladri di Biciclette/The Bicycle Thief* 1948 (sc); *Proibito Rubare* 1948 (sc); *E Primaera* 1949 (sc); *La Mura di Malapaga/The Walls of Malapaga* 1949 (sc,story); *Miracolo a Milano/Miracle in Milan* 1950 (sc); *Bellissima* 1951 (sc); *Altri Tempi* 1952 (sc—"The Baby"/"Il Pupo"); *Buongiorno Elefante!* 1952 (from subject,scenes); *Processo alla Città* 1952 (sc); *I Vinti* 1952 (sc,story); *Siamo Donne* 1953 (sc); *La Signora Senza Camelie/Camille Without Camelias* 1953 (sc); *Senso/The Wanton Contessa* 1954 (sc); *Le Amiche/The Girlfriends* 1955 (sc); *Peccato che sia una canaglia* 1955 (sc); *Difendo il Mio Amore* 1956 (sc,story); *Le Notti Bianche/White Nights* 1957 (sc); *I Soliti Ignoti/Big Deal on Madonna Street* 1958 (sc); *Nella città l'inferno* 1958 (dial,adapt); *Estate Violena* 1959 (sc); *It Started in Naples* 1960 (sc); *Risate di Gioia* 1960 (sc); *Rocco e i suoi Fratelli/Rocco and His Brothers* 1960 (sc,idea); *I Due Nemici* 1961 (sc); *Il Relitto* 1961 (sc); *Boccaccio '70* 1962 (sc—"Il lavoro"); *Salvatore Giuliano* 1962 (sc); *Il Gattopardo/The Leopard* 1963 (sc); *Gli Indifferenti/Time of Indifference* 1964 (sc); *Casanova '70* 1965 (sc) **(AANBSC)**; *Vaghe stelle dell'orsa/Sandra* 1965 (sc); *Lo Straniero/The Stranger* 1967 (sc); *The Taming of the Shrew* 1967 (sc); *Metello* 1970 (sc); *Ludwig* 1972 (sc); *La Mortadella* 1972 (sc); *Brother Sun, Sister Moon* 1973 (sc); *Amore Amaro* 1974 (sc); *Gruppo di famiglia in un interno/Conversation Piece* 1975 (sc); *Caro Michele* 1976 (sc); *L'Innocente/The Innocent* 1976 (sc); *Les Mots pour le dire* 1983 (sc); *Bertoldo, Bertoldino e Cacasenno* 1984 (sc); *Crackers* 1984 (from film—*I Soliti Ignoti/Big Deal on Madonna Street*); *Cuore* 1984 (sc); *Uno Scandalo Perbene* 1984 (sc); *Le Due vite di Mattia Pascal/The Two Lives of Mattia Pascal* 1985 (sc); *I Soliti Ignoti...Vent'Anni Dopo/Big Deal on Madonna Street...Twenty Years Later* 1986 (sc); *Pourvu que ce soit une fille* 1986 (sc); *La Storia/History* 1986 (sc); *Oci Ciornie/Dark Eyes* 1987 (sc); *I Picari* 1987 (sc); *Ti Presento un'Amica* 1988 (sc); *Stradivari* 1989 (sc); *Il Male Oscuro* 1990 (sc).

Celi, Adolfo • Actor • Born Sicily, Italy, July 27, 1922; died February 19, 1986, Siena, Italy. *Educ.* Rome Academy. Played the heavy in numerous international films. • *Natale al Campo* 1948; *Proibito Rubare* 1948; *L'Homme de Rio/That Man From Rio* 1964; *Un Monsieur de Compagnie* 1964; *The Agony and the Ecstasy* 1965; *E Venne un uomo* 1965; *Thunderball* 1965; *Von Ryan's Express* 1965; *El Greco* 1966; *Das Geheimnis der Gelben Mönche* 1966; *Grand Prix* 1966; *Le Roi de Coeur/King of Hearts* 1966; *Adogni Costo* 1967; *The Bobo* 1967; *The Honey Pot* 1967; *Diabolik* 1968; *Dirty Heroes* 1968; *Il Padre di Famiglia* 1968; *L'Alibi* 1969 (a,d,sc); *Detective Belli* 1969; *Io, Emmanuelle* 1969; *A Run on Gold* 1969; *Brancaleone Alle Crociate* 1970; *Fragment of Fear* 1970; *In Search of Gregory* 1970; *Chi l'ha Vista Morire?* 1971; *Hanno Cambiate Faccia* 1971; *Murders in the Rue Morgue* 1971; *Ragazza Tutta Nuda Assassinata nel Parco* 1971; *The Italian Connection* 1972; *Brother Sun, Sister Moon* 1973; *Hitler: The Last Ten Days* 1973; *Le Metaf* 1973; *Il Sorriso del Grande Tentatore* 1973; *La Villeggiatura* 1973; *Le Fantôme de la Liberté/The Phantom of Liberty* 1974; *Libera, Amore Mio* 1974; *Amici Miei* 1975; *And Then There Were None* 1975; *La Moglie di mio padre* 1976; *Signore e Signori, Buonanotte* 1976; *Uomini si nasce poliziotti si muore* 1976; *Le Grand Escogriffe* 1977; *Les Passagers* 1977; *La Soldatessa Alle Grandi Manovre* 1978; *Café Express* 1980; *Cenerentola '80* 1980; *Monsignor* 1982; *Amici miei atto II* 1983; *Amici Miei Atto III* 1986.

Chabrol, Claude • Director, screenwriter; also critic, producer, actor. • Born Paris, June 24, 1930. *Educ.* Sorbonne, Paris (pharmacy, literature). Upstart critic for *Cahiers du cinéma* in the 1950s, financial force behind early New Wave films in the early 60s and himself a key director of the movement, Chabrol's filmmaking career spans nearly 35 years and some 45 films. They range from uninspired commercial projects (1964's *Marie-Chantal Contre le Docteur Kha*), to costly financial flops (1962's *Bluebeard*), to some of the darkest and most penetrating studies of obsession and, especially, murder ever to reach the screen.

Chabrol had just co-written, with Eric Rohmer, his celebrated monograph on *Hitchcock* (1957) and was working as a critic for *Cahiers du Cinéma* when money from his wife's inheritance allowed him to leave the magazine and make his first film, *Le Beau Serge/Bitter Reunion* (1958). A tragic, rural drama shot in black-and-white, *Le Beau Serge* helped define the New Wave of filmmaking that would posit the "auteur," or director, as key creator of his or her cinematic work.

Chabrol immediately followed *Le Beau Serge* with the equally dark and cruelly ironic *Les Cousins/The Cousins* (1959), a decadent tale of Parisian student bohemians. Again Chabrol served up the New Wave hallmarks of realism and intimacy, informal style and bold content. Jean-Claude Brialy starred as the cousin who is as evil as he is appealing; the Brialy character was the first of many ambiguous Chabrol creations who would subvert traditional concepts of the "bad guy."

The financial success of *Les Cousins* allowed Chabrol to set up AJYM, his own production company which financed the first films of Rohmer, Philippe De Broca and Jacques Rivette. Chabrol's own next films as a director, however, did not fare well at the box-office.

The highly stylized *A Double Tour/Leda* (1959) and *Les Bonnes Femmes* (1960) dealt with psychopaths and underlined the director's fascination with murder. The commercial disappointment of the expensive *Landru/Bluebeard* (1962), based on a true-life murderer, made it difficult for Chabrol to find backing for his own projects. In the Hollywood tradition, he became a director-for-hire, crafting a number of lightweight films which included several spy spoofs.

Chabrol enjoyed his "golden era" in the late 60s, triumphing with a string of highly successful thrillers: *La Femme infidèle/Unfaithful Wife* (1968); *Que la Bête Meure/This Man Must Die!* (1969); and *Le Boucher* (1969). Both *Les Biches/The Girlfriends* (1967) and *La Rupture/The Breakup* (1970), though not strictly thrillers, explored the director's signature themes of obsession and compulsion. Ironically, one of Chabrol's biggest commercial successes of the 60s was one of his least favorite films—*La Ligne de Démarcation* (1966), a drama about French Resistance heroes which he deemed "naive."

It was also during this period that Chabrol cemented long-standing professional relationships, including those with cinematographer Jean Rabier, actress Stéphane Audran (who had appeared in *Les Cousins* and whom Chabrol married in 1964), leading man Michel Bouquet, character players Attal and Zidi, composer Pierre Jansen and screenwriter Paul Gegauff, who co-scripted *Les Cousins.* The celebrated Chabrol/Gegauff collaborations often reflected a cynical view of relationships and of bourgeois values that fostered hypocrisy and violence. (Ironically and tragically, Gegauff was brutally murdered by his second wife in 1983.)

After a number of professional frustrations and disappointments in the 70s, Chabrol turned to TV work. He resumed his theatrical career toward the end of the decade with the stunning features, *Violette* (1977)—another real-life tale of murder—and *The Horse of Pride* (1979), a poetic look at Breton peasant life.

From 1984 to 1987, Chabrol teamed with producer Marin Karmitz to make a trio of Hitchcockian thrillers, *Poulet au vinaigre/Cop Au Vin* (1985), *Inspector Lavardin* (1986) and *Masques* (1987). The two collaborated again in 1988 on the critically acclaimed *Story of Women*, a bleak tale of a woman (Isabelle Huppert) who performs illegal abortions in order to support herself during the Nazi occupation of France.

With a typically Gallic zest for life and moral inquiry, Chabrol is a quintessential Frenchman who has largely worked within his native land and language. His films have taken him to the far corners of his own country—Brittany, Provence, Alsace, etc.—as much, it is said, for the fine cuisine as the fine locations. He has also directed several films in English including *Ten Days Wonder* (1972), *The Twist* (1976) and the 1983 HBO made-for-cable feature, *The Blood of Others*. DT • *Le Coup du Berger (short)* 1956 (p,sc); *Le Beau Serge/Bitter Reunion* 1958 (a,d,p,sc,dial); *A bout de souffle/Breathless* 1959 (art sup.,tech.consult); *Les Cousins/The Cousins* 1959 (d,p,sc); *A Double Tour/Web of Passion/Leda* 1959 (d); *Les Bonnes Femmes* 1960 (d); *Les Godelureaux* 1960 (d,sc); *Paris Nous Appartient/Paris Belongs to Us* 1960 (a,p); *Landru/Bluebeard* 1962 (d); *L'Oeil du Malin/The Third Lover* 1962 (d,sc); *Ophélia* 1962 (d); *Les Sept péchés capitaux/The Seven Deadly Sins* 1962 (d); *Les Plus belles escroqueries du monde* 1964 (d); *Le Tigre Aime la Chair Fraîche* 1964 (d); *Marie-Chantal Contre le Docteur Kha* 1965 (a,d,sc); *Paris Vu Par.../Six in Paris* 1965 (a,d,sc—"La Muette"); *Le Tigre se parfume à la dynamite* 1965 (a,d); *La Ligne de Démarcation* 1966 (d,sc); *Le Scandale* 1966 (d); *Les Biches/The Girlfriends* 1967 (a,d,sc); *La Route de Corinthe* 1967 (a,d); *La Femme Infidèle/The Unfaithful Wife* 1968 (d,sc); *Le Boucher* 1969 (d,sc,adapt,dial); *Que la Bête Meure/This Man Must Die!* 1969 (d); *La Rupture/The Break Up* 1970 (d,sc); *La Décade Prodigieuse/Ten Days' Wonder* 1971 (d); *Juste avant la nuit/Just Before Nightfall* 1971 (d,sc); *Docteur Popaul/High Heels!* 1972 (d,lyrics); *Les Noces Rouges/Wedding in Blood* 1973 (d,sc); *The Bench of Desolation (short)* 1974 (d); *Nada* 1974 (d,sc); *Une Partie de Plaisir* 1974 (d); *Les Innocents aux mains Sales* 1975 (d,sc); *Les Magiciens* 1975 (d,sc); *Alice ou la dernière Fugue* 1976 (d,sc); *Folies bourgeoises/The Twist* 1976 (a,d,sc); *L'Animal* 1977 (a); *Les Liens de sang* 1977 (d,sc); *Violette Nozière/Violette* 1977 (d); *Le Cheval d'orgueil/The Horse of Pride* 1979 (d,sc); *Les Folies d'Elodie* 1981 (a); *Les Fantômes du Chapelier* 1982 (d,sc); *Polar* 1982 (a); *Le Sang des Autres/The Blood of Others* 1984 (d); *Les Voleurs de la nuit* 1984 (a); *Poulet au Vinaigre/Cop au Vin* 1985 (d,sc); *Suivez mon regard* 1985 (a); *Inspector Lavardin* 1986 (d,sc); *Je hais les acteurs* 1986 (a); *Le Bonheur se porte large* 1987 (consultant); *Le Cri du hibou* 1987 (d,sc); *Jeux d'artifices* 1987 (a); *L'été en pente douce* 1987 (a); *Masques* 1987 (d,sc); *Sale destin!* 1987 (a); *Une Affaire de femmes/Story of Women* 1988 (d,sc); *Alouette, je te plumerai* 1988 (a); *Docteur M.* 1989 (d,sc); *Jours tranquilles à Clichy/Quiet Days in Clichy* 1990 (d,sc).

Chahine, Youssef • Director; also screenwriter, producer, actor. • Born Alexandria, Egypt, January 25, 1926. *Educ.* Alexandria University (engineering); Pasadena Playhouse (acting). Preeminent Egyptian filmmaker whose output is in striking contrast to the light musicals which dominate his national industry. Chahine first gained a reputation for his incisive critiques of contemporary Arab society, such as *Son of the Nile* (1951) and *The Blazing Sky* (1952), but has subsequently shown a command of the medium which ranges across all genres. He is equally adept at dealing with the personal and lyrical (*An Egyptian Story* 1982) as with the overtly political (*The Sparrow* 1973). • *Son of the Nile* 1951 (d); *The Blazing Sky* 1952 (d); *An-Nasr Salah ad-Din* 1963 (d,sc); *The Sparrow* 1973 (d); *Iskindiria...Leh?* 1978 (d,p,sc); *Death of a Princess* 1980 (prod.services—Egypt); *An Egyptian Story* 1982 (d); *Al-Wedaa Ya Bonaparte* 1985 (d,sc); *Le Sixième Jour* 1986 (d,sc); *Sarikat Sayfeya* 1988 (p); *Iskindiriah Kaman Oue Kaman* 1990 (a,d,sc).

Challis, Christopher • Director of photography • Born London, March 18, 1919. Outstanding color cinematographer who established himself after WWII with a series of Michael Powell/Emeric Pressburger films, notably the black-and-white *Small Back Room* (1948) and the lushly colorful *The Red Shoes* (1948) and *Tales of Hoffman* (1951). • *The Red Shoes* 1948; *The Small Back Room* 1948; *The Elusive Pimpernel* 1950; *Gone to Earth* 1950; *Tales of Hoffmann* 1951; *24 Hours of a Woman's Life* 1952; *Genevieve* 1953; *The Story of Gilbert and Sullivan* 1953; *Flame and the Flesh* 1954; *Malaga* 1954; *Saadia* 1954; *Footsteps in the Fog* 1955; *Oh Rosalinda* 1955; *Quentin Durward* 1955; *Raising a Riot* 1955; *Battle of the River Plate* 1956; *The Spanish Gardener* 1956; *Ill Met By Moonlight* 1957; *Windom's Way* 1957; *Floods of Fear* 1958; *Rooney* 1958; *Blind Date* 1959; *The Grass Is Greener* 1960; *Surprise Package* 1960; *H.M.S. Defiant* 1962; *An Evening With the Royal Ballet* 1963; *The Victors* 1963; *The Americanization of Emily* 1964 (add.ph); *The Long Ships* 1964; *A Shot in the Dark* 1964; *Return From the Ashes* 1965; *Those Magnificent Men in Their Flying Machines* 1965; *Arabesque* 1966; *Kaleidoscope* 1966; *Two For the Road* 1967; *Chitty Chitty Bang Bang* 1968; *A Dandy in Aspic* 1968; *Staircase* 1969; *The Private Life of Sherlock Holmes* 1970; *Catch Me a Spy* 1971; *Mary, Queen of Scots* 1971; *Villain* 1971; *Follow Me!* 1972; *The Little Prince* 1974; *Mr. Quilp* 1975; *The Incredible Sarah* 1976; *The Deep* 1977; *White Rock* 1977; *Force 10 From Navarone* 1978; *The Riddle of the Sands* 1979; *Why Not Stay For Breakfast?* 1979; *The Mirror Crack'd* 1980; *Evil Under the Sun* 1982; *Secrets* 1982; *Top Secret!* 1984; *Steaming* 1985.

Chamberlain, Richard • Actor; also singer. • Born George Richard Chamberlain, Beverly Hills, CA, March 31, 1935. *Educ.* Pomona College, CA (art); Los Angeles Conservatory of Music (voice). Blond, clean-cut and perenially boyish matinee idol who attained heartthrob status as TV's young physician, "Dr. Kildare" from 1961 to 1966 before his role as Tchaikovsky in Ken Russell's *The Music Lovers* (1971) established him as a serious dramatic actor. Chamberlain went to England in 1970 to study acting and star in a repertory production of *Hamlet*. Although his film career waned in the late 1970s and he was relegated to pretty-boy or swashbuckling roles, Chamberlain returned to international star status with his forceful dramatic performances in prestige TV specials and mini-series such as *The Man in the Iron Mask* (1978), *Centennial* (1978), *Shogun* (1980) and *The Thorn Birds* (1983), which have earned him four Emmy nominations. • *The Secret of the Purple Reef* 1960; *A Thunder of Drums* 1961; *Twilight of Honor* 1963; *Joy in the Morning* 1965; *Petulia* 1968; *The Madwoman of Chaillot* 1969; *Julius Caesar* 1970; *The Music Lovers* 1971; *Lady Caroline Lamb* 1972; *The Three Musketeers* 1973; *The Towering Inferno* 1974; *The Four Musketeers* 1975; *The Slipper and the Rose* 1976; *The Last Wave* 1977; *The Swarm* 1978; *Murder By Phone* 1983; *King Solomon's Mines* 1985; *Allan Quatermain and the Lost City of Gold* 1987; *The Return of the Musketeers* 1989.

Chandler, Jeff • Actor • Born Ira Grossel, Brooklyn, NY, December 15, 1918; died June 17, 1961, Culver City, CA. *Educ.* Feagin School of Dramatic Art, New York. Tough, virile lead with prematurely steel grey, wavy hair and a muscular physique who starred in action films of the late 1940s and 50s, often as American Indians (three times as Cochise), gangsters and cavalrymen. Not a docile star, Chandler rebelled against Universal's mediocre action projects and was suspended several times. Chandler's career was cut short by his premature death—due to blood poisoning after routine spinal surgery for a slipped disc—at age 42. • *The Invisible Wall* 1947; *Johnny O'Clock* 1947; *Roses Are Red* 1947; *Abandoned* 1949; *Mr. Belvedere Goes to College* 1949; *Sword in the Desert* 1949; *Broken Arrow* 1950 **(AANBSA)**; *Deported* 1950; *Two Flags West* 1950; *Bird of Paradise* 1951; *Flame of Araby* 1951; *The Iron Man* 1951; *Smuggler's Island* 1951; *The Battle at Apache Pass* 1952; *Because of You* 1952; *Red Ball Express* 1952; *Yankee Buccaneer* 1952; *East of Sumatra* 1953; *The Great Sioux Uprising* 1953; *Sign of the Pagan* 1954; *Taza, Son of Cochise* 1954; *War Arrow* 1954; *Yankee Pasha* 1954; *Female on the Beach* 1955; *Foxfire* 1955; *The Spoilers* 1955; *Away All Boats* 1956; *Pillars of the Sky* 1956; *Toy Tiger* 1956; *Drango* 1957; *Jeanne Eagels* 1957; *The Lady Takes a Flyer* 1957; *Man in the Shadow* 1957; *The Tattered Dress* 1957; *Raw Wind in Eden* 1958; *The Jayhawkers* 1959; *Stranger in My Arms* 1959; *Ten Seconds to Hell* 1959; *Thunder in the Sun* 1959; *The Plunderers* 1960; *Return to Peyton Place* 1961; *Merrill's Marauders* 1962.

Chandler, Raymond • Novelist; also screenwriter. • Born Raymond Thornton Chandler, Chicago, IL, July 22, 1888; died 1959. Intelligent, hard-hitting crime writer whose highly cinematic novels had a direct influence on the emergence of film noir. Though often written in collaboration, Chandler's screenplays bear all the trademarks of his books, from lightning-quick dialogue to labyrinthine plots. *The Big Sleep* (published 1939) was filmed in 1946, and *Farewell, My Lovely* (published 1940) was filmed as *The Falcon Takes Over* (1942) and *Murder, My Sweet* (1944) before being brought to the screen in 1975 with its title intact. Chandler's private eye Philip Marlowe has been portrayed on the screen by actors as diverse as Robert Mitchum, Dick Powell, Elliott Gould and, most definitively, Humphrey Bogart in the noir masterpiece *The Big Sleep*. • *The Falcon Takes Over* 1942 (from novel *Farewell My Lovely*); *Time to Kill* 1942 (from novel); *And Now Tomorrow* 1944 (sc); *Double Indemnity* 1944 (sc) **(AANBSC)**; *Murder, My Sweet* 1944 (from novel *Farewell My Lovely*); *The Unseen* 1945 (sc); *The Big Sleep* 1946 (from novel); *The Blue Dahlia* 1946 (sc,story) **(AANBSC)**; *Lady in the Lake* 1946 (from novel); *The Brasher Doubloon* 1947 (from novel *The High Window*); *Strangers on a Train* 1951 (sc); *Marlowe* 1969 (from novel *The Little Sister*); *The Long Goodbye* 1973 (from novel); *Farewell, My Lovely* 1975 (from novel); *The Big Sleep* 1978 (from novel); *The Man Who Envied Women* 1985 (from writings); *Proini Peripolos* 1987 (from writings).

Chaney, Lon • Actor • Born Alonso Chaney, Colorado Springs, CO, April 1, 1883; died August 26, 1930. Dubbed "the Man of a Thousand Faces" and the first great master of horror before it became a formalized genre in the 1930s. The child of deaf-mute parents, Chaney learned the expressive use of pantomime to communicate, and developed a remarkable sensitivity to the pain of the outsider which added humanity and pathos to the gallery of grotesque and deformed characters which he created.

After a brief career in theater as a comic, dancer and stage hand, he went to Hollywood in 1912 and appeared in numerous shorts and features (some by Allan Dwan) as western villains and "exotics" (often as more than one character in a film). He starred in his first of many collaborations with horror master Tod Browning, *The Wicked Darling*, and won recognition in his first major role, as a bogus cripple in *The Miracle Man* (both 1919).

Chaney was renowned for his artistry with makeup and the great, almost masochistic, lengths he would go to to create the grotesque bodies that hid the tortured, often sensitive and injured souls of his characters. Chaney bound his legs behind him and walked on his knees in *The Penalty* (1920), strapped his arms tightly to his body to play the part of an armless knife thrower in *The Unknown* (1927), and wore enormous, painful teeth to create a vampire in *London After Midnight* (1927; he also played a detective). In *The Hunchback of Notre Dame* (1923) he wore a 40 pound hunch in a 30 pound harness strapped to his back, covered his eyeball with an eggshell membrane to look sightless, and contorted his body in a straightjacket. (When he appeared in *Tell It to the Marines* in 1926 without any makeup, one critic wrote that he didn't look quite natural.) More than merely a master of disguise and horror, Chaney's genius was in communicating the man behind the monster: the hunger for acceptance, the unrequited love and sexual frustration, and the pain caused by society's cruelty that fuels his monsters' desire for revenge, which is most eloquently conveyed in his definitive *Phantom of the Opera* (1925).

His son Creighton, a novice in films when his father died, changed his name to Lon Chaney, Jr. and worked mainly in B horror films. It was James Cagney who played Chaney Sr. in his film biography, *The Man of 1,000 Faces* (1957). • *Richelieu* 1914; *Father and the Boys* 1915; *Bobbie of the Ballet* 1916; *The Gilded Spider* 1916; *The Grasp of Greed* 1916; *The Grip of Jealousy* 1916; *If My Country Should Call* 1916; *The Mark of Cain* 1916; *The Piper's Price* 1916; *The Place Beyond the Winds* 1916; *The Price of Silence* 1916; *Tangled Hearts* 1916; *Anything Once* 1917; *A Doll's House* 1917; *Fires of Rebellion* 1917; *The Flashlight* 1917; *The Girl in the Checkered Coat* 1917; *Pay Me* 1917; *The Rescue* 1917; *The Scarlet Car* 1917; *Triumph* 1917; *The Vengeance of the West* 1917; *Broadway Love* 1918; *A Broadway Scandal* 1918; *Danger, Go Slow* 1918; *The False Faces* 1918; *Fast Company* 1918; *The Grand Passion* 1918; *The Kaiser, the Beast of Berlin* 1918; *Riddle Gawne* 1918; *The Talk of the Town* 1918; *That Devil Bateese* 1918; *A Man's Country* 1919; *The Miracle Man* 1919; *Paid in Advance* 1919; *The Trap* 1919; *Victory* 1919; *When Bearcat Went Dry* 1919; *The Wicked Darling* 1919; *Daredevil Jack* 1920; *The Gift Supreme* 1920; *Nomads of the North* 1920; *The Penalty* 1920; *Treasure Island* 1920; *While Paris Sleeps* 1920; *The Ace of Hearts* 1921; *Bits of Life* 1921; *For Those We Love* 1921; *Outside the Law* 1921; *Voices of the City* 1921; *A Blind Bargain* 1922; *Flesh and Blood* 1922; *The Light in the Dark* 1922; *Oliver Twist* 1922; *Quincy Adams Sawyer* 1922; *Shadows* 1922; *The Trap* 1922; *All the Brothers Were Valiant* 1923; *The Hunchback of Notre Dame* 1923; *The Shock* 1923; *He Who Gets Slapped* 1924; *The Next Corner* 1924; *The Monster* 1925; *Phantom of the Opera* 1925; *The Tower of Lies* 1925; *The Unholy Three* 1925; *The Black Bird* 1926; *The Road to Mandalay* 1926; *Tell It to the Marines* 1926; *London After Midnight* 1927; *Mockery* 1927; *Mr. Wu* 1927; *The Unknown* 1927; *The Big City* 1928; *Laugh, Clown, Laugh* 1928; *West of Zanzibar* 1928; *While the City Sleeps* 1928; *Thunder* 1929; *Where East Is East* 1929; *The Unholy Three* 1930.

Chaney, Lon, Jr. • Actor • Born Creighton Chaney, Oklahoma City, OK, February 10, 1906; died July 12, 1973, San Clemente, CA. Heavy-set character actor, mostly in horror films or westerns whose most famous role was as *The Wolf Man* in numerous films beginning in 1941. Chaney also appeared out of monster makeup in support of Bob Hope in *My Favorite Brunette* (1947) and as the arthritic marshall in *High Noon* (1952), but his finest starring role was as the slow-witted Lennie in Steinbeck's *Of Mice and Men* (1939). • *The Phantom of the Opera* 1925; *Bird of Paradise* 1932; *The Last Frontier* 1932; *Lucky Devils* 1933; *Scarlet River* 1933; *Son of the Border* 1933; *The Three Musketeers* 1933; *Girl o' My Dreams* 1934; *The Life of Vergie Winters* 1934; *Sixteen Fathoms Deep* 1934; *Accent on Youth* 1935; *Captain Hurricane* 1935; *The Marriage Bargain* 1935; *Ace Drummond* 1936; *The Singing Cowboy* 1936; *Undersea Kingdom* 1936; *Angel's Holiday* 1937; *Cheyenne Rides Again* 1937; *Midnight Taxi* 1937; *The Old Corral* 1937; *Wife, Doctor, and Nurse* 1937; *Wild and Woolly* 1937; *Mr. Moto's Gamble* 1938; *Passport Husband* 1938; *Road Demon* 1938; *Charlie Chan in City in Darkness* 1939; *Frontier Marshal* 1939; *Jesse James* 1939; *Of Mice and Men* 1939; *North West Mounted Police* 1940; *One Million B.C.* 1940; *Badlands of Dakota* 1941; *Billy the Kid* 1941; *Man-Made Monster* 1941; *Riders of Death Valley* 1941; *San Antonio Rose* 1941; *Too Many Blondes* 1941; *The Wolf Man* 1941; *Eyes of the Underworld* 1942; *The Ghost of Frankenstein* 1942; *Mummy's Tomb* 1942; *North to the Klondike* 1942; *Overland Mail* 1942; *Calling Dr. Death* 1943; *Crazy House* 1943; *Frankenstein Meets the Wolf Man* 1943; *Frontier Badmen* 1943; *Son of Dracula* 1943; *Cobra Woman* 1944; *Dead Man's Eyes* 1944; *Follow the Boys* 1944; *Ghost Catchers* 1944; *House of Frankenstein* 1944; *The Mummy's Curse* 1944; *The Mummy's Ghost* 1944; *Weird Woman* 1944; *The Daltons Ride Again* 1945; *The Frozen Ghost* 1945; *Here Come the Co-eds* 1945; *House of Dracula* 1945; *Pillow of Death* 1945; *Strange Confession* 1945; *Albuquerque* 1947; *My Favorite Brunette* 1947; *16 Fathoms Deep* 1948; *Abbott and Costello Meet Frankenstein* 1948; *The Counterfeiters* 1948; *There's a Girl in My Heart* 1949; *Captain China* 1950; *Once a Thief* 1950; *Behave Yourself* 1951; *Bride of the Gorilla* 1951; *Flame of Araby* 1951; *Inside Straight* 1951; *Only the Valiant* 1951; *The Battles of Chief Pontiac* 1952; *The Black Castle* 1952; *The Bushwackers* 1952; *High Noon* 1952; *Springfield Rifle* 1952; *Thief of Damascus* 1952; *Jack London's Tales of Adventure* 1953; *A Lion Is in the Streets* 1953; *Raiders of the Seven Seas* 1953; *The Big Chase* 1954; *The Black Pirates* 1954; *The Boy From Oklahoma* 1954; *Casanova's Big Night* 1954; *Jivaro* 1954; *Passion* 1954; *Big House, U.S.A.* 1955; *I Died a Thousand Times* 1955; *The Indestructible Man* 1955; *The Indian Fighter* 1955; *Manfish* 1955; *Not As a Stranger* 1955; *The Silver Star* 1955; *The Black Sleep* 1956; *Daniel Boone, Trail Blazer* 1956; *Pardners* 1956; *Cyclops* 1957; *The Defiant Ones* 1958; *Money, Women and Guns* 1958; *The Alligator People* 1959; *Night of the Ghouls* 1959; *The Devil's Messenger* 1961; *The Haunted Palace* 1963; *Law of the Lawless* 1964; *Spider Baby* 1964 (a,song); *Stage to Thunder Rock* 1964; *Black Spurs* 1965; *House of the Black Death* 1965; *Town Tamer* 1965; *Young Fury* 1965; *Apache Uprising* 1966; *Johnny Reno* 1966; *Dr. Terror's Gallery of Horrors* 1967; *Hillbillys in a Haunted House* 1967; *Welcome to Hard Times* 1967; *Buckskin* 1968; *Dracula Vs. Frankenstein* 1971; *The Female Bunch* 1971.

Channing, Stockard • Actress • Born Susan Stockard, New York, NY, February 13, 1944. *Educ.* Radcliffe College, Cambridge, MA. Gifted, award-winning stage performer, in occasional films. • *The Hospital* 1971; *Up the Sandbox* 1972; *The Fortune* 1975; *The Big Bus* 1976; *Dandy, the All American Girl* 1976; *The Cheap Detective* 1978; *Grease* 1978; *The Fish That Saved Pittsburgh* 1979; *Safari 3000* 1980; *Without a Trace* 1983; *Heartburn* 1986; *The Men's Club* 1986; *A Time of Destiny* 1988; *Staying Together* 1989; *Meet the Applegates* 1991.

Chaplin, Sir Charles • *aka* Charlie Chaplin • Actor, director, screenwriter; also producer, composer. • Born Charles Spencer Chaplin, London, April 16, 1889; died December 25, 1977. James Agee wrote that "the finest pantomime, the deepest emotion, the richest and most poignant poetry were in Chaplin's work." Andrew Sarris calls Chaplin "the single most important artist produced by the cinema, certainly its most extrordinary performer, and probably still its most universal icon." In a career spanning half a century, the soaring flicker of the Chaplin myth has been immense, enveloping both the cinema and world culture in its glow.

Chaplin's childhood was marked by wretched poverty, hunger, cruelty and loneliness—subjects which became major themes in his silent comedies. Born in London to music hall entertainers, the young Chaplin saw his father die of alcoholism and his mother go insane, forcing him and his brother Sydney into a succession of workhouses. His escape from grueling poverty was through the theater, where by the age of 16 he was playing the featured role of Billy in William Gillette's West End production of *Sherlock Holmes* (1905). At the prompting of his brother, Chaplin secured a spot in Fred Karno's music hall revue, appearing as a drunk in "A Night in the English Music Hall" and in the sketches "Mummingbirds" and "Harlequinade in Black and White." While the Karno troupe was touring the US, Chaplin was spotted by film producer Mack Sennett and signed to his Keystone Company.

Chaplin's performances drew on the pantomime traditions of the French and British music halls—a style decisively out of place in the mechanized world of Sennett, who ran his studio with production-line efficiency, churning out two films a week and allowing no more than ten camera setups per film. For an actor used to refining a set character night after night with the Karno company, the Sennett style was a loud slap in the face.

In his first film for Sennett, *Making a Living* (1914), Chaplin played a boulevard roué in the finicky Max Linder manner. But in *Kid Auto Races at Venice* (1914) and *Mabel's Strange Predicament* (1914), Chaplin emerged in his emblematic costume (influenced by Dan Leno and Fred Kitchen from his Karno days) of baggy pants, decrepit shoes on the wrong feet, carefully trimmed moustache, cane and dirty derby hat, moving with a gait and manner contrary to his slovenly appearance.

Kid Auto Races demonstrated Chaplin's uncanny ability to communicate with his audience. As Sennett's comic buffoons mugged on the sidelines of a kiddie car race, Chaplin held the camera with his gaze. By his thirteenth film, *Caught in the Rain* (1914), Chaplin had begun to direct himself, and the fissure between the Sennett and Chaplin styles was beginning to widen. Chaplin began to move the camera closer than Sennett permitted, allowing his costume to function as an extension of character rather than a simple jester's emblem. Chaplin brought to the frenetic Keystone world a comedy of emotions, an ability to convey thoughts and feelings more in line with a Lillian Gish than a Ford Sterling or Ben Turpin. He also slowed the breakneck Keystone pace, reducing the number of gags per film and increasing the time devoted to each.

Within a year, Chaplin had revolutionized film comedy, transforming it from the rag-tag knockabout farces of Sennett into an art form by introducing characterization, mime and slapstick pathos. As a director, Chaplin rebelled against the montage technique of Griffith; he introduced, in André Bazin's words, a "comedy of space" in which the Tramp interacted with other objects in the *mise-en-scène* and reconstructed them through his presence. Chaplin's subtle and reflective acting techniques also radically changed the notion of film performance, allowing action to be motivated through character rather than through some exterior force. Thanks to Chaplin, comedy began to be centered on the performer as opposed to the events which befall him or her—an emphasis on character which paved the way for the subsequent achievements of Buster Keaton, Harold Lloyd, Harold Langdon and Stan Laurel.

But it was the public, most of all, who transformed Chaplin from a star into a mythic figure. By 1915 he was a household word. Cartoons, poems and comic strips under the Chaplin name appeared in newspapers. Chaplin dolls, toys and books were manufactured. While the public eagerly awaited the release of the next Chaplin production, pretenders to the throne raced in, comics like Lloyd, Billy West, Billy Ritchie and even someone who billed himself as Charlie Alpin.

Chaplin took advantage of his fame to consolidate control over his career and Tramp character. The years 1915-25 not only marked the period of his greatest popularity, but the time in which Chaplin, bucking the newly formed studio system, held his own as an independent filmmaker. His spiraling salaries reflected both his popularity and his artistic freedom. After leaving Sennett, where he had begun at $150 a week, Chaplin signed with Essanay at a salary of $1250 per week. By 1918, Chaplin's fame led to film's first million-dollar contract, with First National, which also agreed to build a studio for him.

At Essanay Chaplin began to assemble his stock company and, with the emergence of Edna Purviance as his leading lady, introduced an element of sentimentality and gentlemanly respect into his films. The Sennett knockabout factor was still a dominant ingredient, but it was tempered with humanity and the gags featured a degree of experimentation. With *The Bank* and *The Tramp* (both 1915), Chaplin introduced a new comic twist—the unhappy ending. In *The Tramp*, Chaplin for the first time exits the film alone, with a kick of the feet and a twirl of the cane, down a deserted road.

Chaplin's twelve Mutual films of 1916 and 1917 rank among his greatest achievements. *One A.M.* (1916), *The Pawnshop* (1916), *Behind the Screen* (1916), *The Rink* (1916), *Easy Street* (1917), *The Cure* (1917), *The Immigrant* (1917) and *The Adventurer* (1917) all revealed a master at work, with mime and satire, sentimentality and slapstick all stitched into a seamless whole.

In such First National films as *A Dog's Life* (1918), *Shoulder Arms* (1918) and *The Pilgrim* (1923), Chaplin took his first serious steps toward feature-length comedy. *The Kid* (1921), expanded from a planned three-reeler, proved that the Chaplin persona could sustain his comic appeal for the duration of a feature-length film, broadening the parameters of screen comedy and paving the way for the works of Lloyd and Keaton.

In 1919, Chaplin (along with fellow stars Douglas Fairbanks and Mary Pickford and director D.W. Griffith) formed United Artists as a vehicle for distributing their films without studio interference. Chaplin's first United Artists production was the atypical *A Woman of Paris* (1923), a comedy of manners and the swan song for Chaplin's costar Edna Purviance. He appeared in the film only in a cameo role and it was his first financial failure (although it proved to be an influence on Ernst Lubitsch, who adapted its understatement and ellipses for his 1924 film *The Marriage Circle*).

With *The Gold Rush* (1925), Chaplin basked once again in the public's adulation. By this time, however, his output had begun to slow as he assiduously refined his art, subjecting his comic persona to an increasingly microscopic scrutiny. *The Circus* (1928) investigates the nature of comedy and audience acceptance. *City Lights* (1931) is a chamber study musing on the fine line between comedy and tragedy, as well as a deification of the Tramp character. In *Modern Times* (1936) Chaplin bid farewell to the Tramp, leaving society in satirical ruins and again walking into the sunrise, but this time with a street urchin in tow.

The look of Chaplin's films also changed during this period. In what may have been a response to a series of emotionally draining scandals, Chaplin had increasingly restricted his productions to the studio; the settings consequently took on an otherworldly look in a kind of retreat from the reality of 1930s America. His sentimentality had also become laced with dark strains of cynicism and hopelessness. ("An old tramp is not funny," he once explained.)

The startling transformation of Chaplin into the murderous *Monsieur Verdoux* (1947) turned his once adoring public against him. Finally, in 1952, amid an atmosphere of Red-baiting hysteria, Chaplin, who had never become an American citizen, found his re-entry permit to the US revoked after he had attended the London premiere of *Limelight.* Public reaction against Chaplin was so rabid that *A King in New York* (1957), a gentle satire on American consumerism and political paranoia, remained unreleased in the United States until 1976. Chaplin's last film, *A Countess From Hong Kong* (1967), proved to be a sadly anachronistic farce more appropriate to the 1930s and totally out of place in a cinematic era that included *Weekend*, *Bonnie and Clyde* and *The Graduate.* PB • *Between Showers (short)* 1914 (uncred.a,uncred.sc); *A Busy Day (short)* 1914 (a,d,sc); *Caught in a Cabaret* 1914 (a,d,sc); *Caught in the Rain (short)* 1914 (a,d,sc); *Cruel, Cruel Love (short)* 1914 (uncred.a,uncred.sc); *Dough and Dynamite (short)* 1914 (a,d); *The Face on the Barroom Floor* 1914 (uncred.a,a,d,sc); *The Fatal Mallet (short)* 1914 (a,d,sc); *A Film Johnnie (short)* 1914 (uncred.a,uncred.sc); *Gentlemen of Nerve (short)* 1914 (a,d,sc); *Getting Acquainted (short)* 1914 (a,d,sc); *Her Friend the Bandit (short)* 1914 (a,d,sc); *His Favorite Pastime (short)* 1914 (uncred.a,uncred.sc); *His Musical Career (short)* 1914 (a,d,sc); *His New Profession (short)* 1914 (a,d,sc); *His Prehistoric Past* 1914 (a,d,sc); *His Trysting Place* 1914 (a,d,sc); *Kid Auto Races at Venice* 1914 (uncred.a,uncred.sc); *The Knockout* 1914 (uncred.a,uncred.sc); *Laughing Gas* 1914 (a,d,sc); *Mabel at the Wheel (short)* 1914 (uncred.a,uncred.sc); *Mabel's Busy Day* 1914 (a,d,sc); *Mabel's Married Life* 1914 (a,d,sc); *Mabel's Strange Predicament (short)* 1914 (uncred.a,uncred.sc); *Making a Living (short)* 1914 (a,uncred.sc); *The Masquerader (short)* 1914 (a,d,sc); *The New Janitor (short)* 1914 (a,d,sc); *The Property Man* 1914 (a,d,sc); *Recreation (short)* 1914 (a,d,sc); *The Rounders (short)* 1914 (a,d,sc); *The Star Boarder (short)* 1914 (uncred.a,uncred.sc); *Tango Tangles (short)* 1914 (uncred.a,uncred.sc); *Those Love Pangs (short)* 1914 (a,d,sc); *Tillie's Punctured Romance* 1914 (a); *Twenty Minutes of Love (short)* 1914 (uncred.a,uncred.sc); *The Bank* 1915 (a,d,sc); *By the Sea (short)* 1915 (a,d,sc); *The Champion* 1915 (a,d,sc); *His New Job* 1915 (a,d,sc); *His Regeneration (short)* 1915 (uncred.a); *In the Park (short)* 1915 (a,d,sc); *A Jitney Elopement* 1915 (a,d,sc); *A Night Out* 1915 (a,d,sc); *A Night in the Show (short)* 1915 (a,d,sc); *Shanghaied (short)* 1915 (a,d,sc); *The Tramp* 1915 (a,d,sc); *A Woman (short)* 1915 (a,d,sc); *Work* 1915 (a,d,sc); *Behind the Screen* 1916 (a,d,p,sc); *Charlie Chaplin's Burlesque on Carmen* 1916 (a,d,sc); *The Count* 1916 (a,d,sc); *The Fireman* 1916 (a,d,sc); *The Floorwalker* 1916 (a,d,sc); *One A.M. (short)* 1916 (a,d,p,sc); *The Pawnshop (short)* 1916 (a,d,p,sc); *Police!* 1916 (a,d,sc); *The Rink (short)* 1916 (a,d,p,sc); *The Vagabond* 1916 (a,d,sc); *The Adventurer* 1917 (a,d,sc); *The Cure* 1917 (a,d,sc); *Easy Street* 1917 (a,d,sc); *The Immigrant* 1917 (a,d,sc); *The Bond (short)* 1918 (a,d,sc); *A Dog's Life* 1918 (a,d,sc); *Shoulder Arms* 1918 (a,d,sc); *A Day's Pleasure (short)* 1919 (a,d,p,sc); *Sunnyside* 1919 (a,d,p,sc); *The Idle Class* 1921 (a,d,p,sc); *The Kid* 1921 (a,d,p,sc); *The Nut* 1921 (a); *Nice and Friendly (short)* 1922 (a,d,sc); *Pay Day* 1922 (a,d,p,sc); *The Pilgrim* 1923 (a,d,p,sc); *Souls For Sale* 1923 (a); *A Woman of Paris* 1923 (a,d,p,sc,m); *The Gold Rush* 1925 (a,d,p,sc); *A Woman of the Sea* 1926 (idea,p); *The Circus* 1928 (a,d,p,sc,ed) **(AANBA,AANBD)**; *Show People* 1928 (a); *City Lights* 1931 (a,d,p,sc,m,ed); *Modern Times* 1936 (a,d,p,sc,m); *The Great Dictator* 1940 (a,d,p,sc) **(AANBA,AANBSC,AANBP)**; *Monsieur Verdoux* 1947 (a,d,p,sc,m) **(AANBSC)**; *Limelight* 1952 (a,d,p,sc,story,m,chor) **(AABM)**; *A King in New York* 1957 (a,d,p,sc,m); *A Countess From Hong*

Kong 1967 (sc,m,song,a,d,exec.p); *Chaplinesque, My Life and Hard Times* 1972 (a); *Smile* 1975 (m); *It's Showtime* 1976 (a); *Mauvais sang/Bad Blood* 1986 (song).

Chaplin, Geraldine • Actress • Born Santa Monica, CA, July 31, 1944. *Educ.* Royal Ballet School, London. Introverted, gaunt leading lady and former dancer with the English Royal Ballet, in a number of films by long-term companion Carlos Saura, notably *Peppermint Frappé* (1967). Chaplin has also been associated with the work of Robert Altman (as the confused British journalist in *Nashville* 1975, *Buffalo Bill and the Indians* 1976, *A Wedding* 1978) and his protégé Alan Rudolph (*Welcome to L.A.* 1976, *Remember My Name* 1978, and *The Moderns* 1988). Chaplin made her debut in *Limelight* (1951) directed by her father Charles Chaplin who also directed her in *A Countess from Hong Kong* (1967). Granddaughter of playwright Eugene O'Neill. • *Limelight* 1952; *Doctor Zhivago* 1965; *A Countess From Hong Kong* 1967; *J'ai tué Raspoutine* 1967; *Peppermint Frappé* 1967; *Stranger in the House* 1967; *La Madriguera* 1969 (a,sc); *The Hawaiians* 1970; *La Casa Sin Fronteras* 1971; *Sur un Arbre Perché* 1971; *Innocent Bystanders* 1972; *Z.P.G.* 1972; *Ana Y Los Lobos* 1973; *Le Mariage à la Mode* 1973; *The Three Musketeers* 1973; *La Banda de Jaider* 1974; *Verflucht dies Amerika!* 1974; *The Four Musketeers* 1975; *Nashville* 1975; *Buffalo Bill and the Indians, or Sitting Bull's History Lesson* 1976; *Cría Cuervos/Cría* 1976; *Noroit* 1976; *Welcome to L.A.* 1976; *Elisa, Vida Mía* 1977; *In Memorium* 1977; *Une Page d'Amour* 1977; *Roseland* 1977; *Adoption* 1978; *Los Ojos Vendados* 1978; *Remember My Name* 1978; *A Wedding* 1978; *Mais où et donc ornicar* 1979; *Mama Cumple 100 Anos/Mama Turns 100* 1979; *Le Voyage en Douce* 1979; *The Mirror Crack'd* 1980; *Les Uns et les autres/Bolero* 1981; *La Vie est un roman/Life Is a Bed of Roses* 1983; *L'Amour par terre/Love on the Ground* 1984; *Buried Alive* 1984; *Gentile Alouette* 1985; *White Mischief* 1987; *The Moderns* 1988; *Je veux rentrer à la maison* 1989; *The Return of the Musketeers* 1989; *The Children* 1990.

Chaplin, Saul • Composer, songwriter; also arranger, producer. • Born Saul Kaplan, Brooklyn, NY, February 19, 1912. *Educ.* NYU (accounting). Oscar-winning musical director and arranger of *An American in Paris* (1951) and *Seven Brides For Seven Brothers* (1954) in films from 1930. Chaplin scored a number of lush-sounding classic musicals between *Summer Stock* (1950) and *West Side Story* (1961), for which he won a third Oscar. Chaplin has subsequently concentrated his efforts on producing. • *Manhattan Merry-Go-Round* 1937 (m); *Argentine Nights* 1940 (m); *Honolulu Lu* 1941 (song); *Rookies on Parade* 1941 (story); *Time Out For Rhythm* 1941 (song); *Two Latins From Manhattan* 1941 (song); *Blondie Goes to College* 1942 (song); *Crazy House* 1943 (m); *Meet Me on Broadway* 1946 (m); *The Countess of Monte Cristo* 1948 (m); *Jolson Sings Again* 1949 (m.dir); *On the Town* 1949 (vocal arranger); *Summer Stock* 1950 (m); *An American in Paris* 1951 (m,m.dir,orch) **(AABM)**; *Lovely to Look At* 1952 (m.dir); *Give a Girl a Break* 1953 (m); *Kiss Me Kate* 1953 (m) **(AANBM)**; *Seven Brides For Seven Brothers* 1954 (m.dir,orch) **(AABM)**; *High Society* 1956 (m) **(AANBM)**; *The Teahouse of the August Moon* 1956 (m); *Les Girls* 1957 (assoc.p); *Merry Andrew* 1958 (assoc.p,m,song); *Can-Can* 1960 (assoc.p); *West Side Story* 1961 (assoc.p) **(AABM)**; *The Sound of Music* 1965 (assoc.p); *Star!* 1968 (p); *L'Uomo della Mancha/Man of La Mancha* 1972 (assoc.p); *That's Entertainment Part 2* 1976 (p,lyrics); *Le Dernier Métro/The Last Metro* 1980 (m).

Chapman, Graham • Actor, screenwriter • Born Leicester, England, January 8, 1941; died October 4, 1989, England. *Educ.* Emmanuel College, Cambridge (medicine); St. Bartholomew's Hospital, London (medicine). Member of the famed "Monty Python" comedy team. A veteran of the "Cambridge Circus" student revue, Chapman was drawn to scriptwriting and performing as an alternative to the routine of a physician's rounds in a London hospital. He joined the Pythons after working on British TV's "The Frost Report." Chapman died of throat cancer at age 48. • *Doctor in Trouble* 1970 (a); *The Magic Christian* 1970 (a,add.material); *The Rise and Rise of Michael Rimmer* 1970 (a,sc); *The Statue* 1970 (a); *And Now For Something Completely Different* 1971 (a,sc,idea); *Monty Python and the Holy Grail* 1975 (a,sc); *Pleasure at Her Majesty's* 1976 (a); *The Odd Job* 1978 (a,p,sc); *Monty Python's Life of Brian* 1979 (a,sc); *The Secret Policeman's Other Ball* 1981 (a); *Monty Python Live at the Hollywood Bowl* 1982 (a,sc); *Monty Python's The Meaning of Life* 1983 (sc,m,song,a); *Yellowbeard* 1983 (a,sc).

Chapman, Michael • Director of photography; also director. • Born New York, NY, November 21, 1935. Former camera operator and assistant to cinematographer Gordon Willis who has worked several times with Philip Kaufman. Chapman's crisp, powerful images proved integral to several Martin Scorsese pictures, most notably the gritty black-and-white of *Raging Bull* (1980) and the atmospheric, intense neon color of nighttime New York in *Taxi Driver* (1976). As a director, Chapman has been less effective, though *All the Right Moves* (1983) enjoyed some success. Married to editor-director-screenwriter, Amy Jones (*Love Letters* 1983, *Maid to Order* 1987). • *The End of the Road* 1970 (cam.op); *The Landlord* 1970 (cam.op); *Klute* 1971 (cam.op); *The Godfather* 1972 (cam.op); *The Last Detail* 1973 (a,ph); *The White Dawn* 1974 (ph); *Jaws* 1975 (cam.op); *The Front* 1976 (ph); *The Next Man* 1976 (ph); *Taxi Driver* 1976 (ph); *American Boy* 1977 (ph,p.asst); *Fingers* 1977 (ph); *Invasion of the Body Snatchers* 1978 (ph); *The Last Waltz* 1978 (ph); *Hardcore* 1979 (ph); *The Wanderers* 1979 (ph); *Raging Bull* 1980 (ph) **(AANBPH)**; *Dead Men Don't Wear Plaid* 1982 (ph); *Personal Best* 1982 (ph); *All the Right Moves* 1983 (d); *The Man With Two Brains* 1983 (ph); *The Clan of the Cave Bear* 1986 (d); *The Lost Boys* 1987 (ph); *Scrooged* 1988 (ph); *Shoot to Kill* 1988 (a,ph); *Ghostbusters II* 1989 (ph); *Kindergarten Cop* 1990 (ph); *Quick Change* 1990 (a,ph).

Charisse, Cyd • *aka* Lily Norwood • Dancer; also actress. • Born Tula Ellice Finklea, Amarillo, TX, March 8, 1921. Alluring, statuesque dancer who reached her peak enlivening several MGM musicals of the 1950s. Charisse appeared opposite such luminaries as Gene Kelly and Fred Astaire. • *Mission to Moscow* 1943; *Something to Shout About* 1943; *The Harvey Girls* 1946; *Three Wise Fools* 1946; *Till the Clouds Roll By* 1946; *Ziegfeld Follies* 1946; *Fiesta* 1947; *The Unfinished Dance* 1947; *The Kissing Bandit* 1948; *On an Island With You* 1948; *Words and Music* 1948; *East Side, West Side* 1949; *Tension* 1949; *Mark of the Renegade* 1951; *Singin' in the Rain* 1952; *The Wild North* 1952; *The Band Wagon* 1953; *Easy to Love* 1953; *Sombrero* 1953; *Brigadoon* 1954; *Deep in My Heart* 1954; *It's Always Fair Weather* 1955; *Invitation to the Dance* 1956; *Meet Me in Las Vegas* 1956; *Silk Stockings* 1957; *Party Girl* 1958; *Twilight For the Gods* 1958; *Un, deux, trois, quatre!* 1960; *Cinque Ore in Contanti* 1961; *Two Weeks in Another Town* 1962; *Assassinio Made in Italy* 1963; *The Silencers* 1966; *Maroc 7* 1967; *Film Portrait* 1972 (collaboration); *Warlords of Atlantis* 1978; *Visioni Privati* 1990.

Chartoff, Robert • Producer • Born New York, NY, August 26, 1933. *Educ.* Union College; Columbia School of Law. Formed Chartoff-Winkler Productions with Irwin Winkler in the mid-1960s and subsequently turned out both commercial blockbusters (all the "Rocky" films beginning in 1976) as well as intelligent, critical successes (*They Shoot Horses, Don't They?* 1969, *Raging Bull* 1980, *The Right Stuff* 1983). The partnership dissolved in 1985. • *Point Blank* 1967 (p); *The Split* 1968 (p); *They Shoot Horses, Don't They?* 1969 (p); *Leo the Last* 1970 (p); *The Strawberry Statement* 1970 (p); *Believe in Me* 1971 (p); *The Gang That Couldn't Shoot Straight* 1971 (p); *The*

Mechanic 1972 (p); *The New Centurions* 1972 (p); *Thumb Tripping* 1972 (p); *Up the Sandbox* 1972 (p); *Busting* 1973 (p); *The Gambler* 1974 (p); *Spys* 1974 (p); *Breakout* 1975 (p); *Peeper* 1975 (p); *Nickelodeon* 1976 (p); *Rocky* 1976 (p) **(AABP)**; *New York, New York* 1977 (p); *Valentino* 1977 (p); *Comes a Horseman* 1978 (exec.p); *Uncle Joe Shannon* 1978 (p); *Rocky II* 1979 (p); *Raging Bull* 1980 (p) **(AANBP)**; *True Confessions* 1981 (p); *Rocky III* 1982 (p); *The Right Stuff* 1983 (p) **(AANBP)**; *Beer* 1985 (p); *Rocky IV* 1985 (p); *Rocky V* 1990 (p).

Chase, Borden • Screenwriter, author • Born Frank Fowler, New York, NY, January 11, 1900; died 1971. Allegedly getting the inspiraton for his name from Borden Milk and Chase-Manhattan Bank, he went through an assortment of jobs including the building of New York's Holland Tunnel before turning first to short stories and novels and then to screenwriting with *Under Pressure* (1935), based on his Holland Tunnel experience. Chase provided the story for Anthony Mann's first film, *Dr. Broadway* (1942), but his screenplays for the director's 1950s westerns (*Winchester '73* 1950, *Bend of the River* 1952 and *The Far Country* 1955) are his crowning achievments. • *Under Pressure* 1935 (sc,story); *Midnight Taxi* 1937 (story); *The Devil's Party* 1938 (from novel *Hell's Kitchen Has a Pantry*); *Trouble Wagon* 1938 (sc); *Blue, White and Perfect* 1941 (story); *Dr. Broadway* 1942 (story); *The Navy Comes Through* 1942 (from story "Pay to Learn"); *Destroyer* 1943 (sc); *Harrigan's Kid* 1943 (story); *The Fighting Seabees* 1944 (sc,story); *Flame of the Barbary Coast* 1945 (sc); *This Man's Navy* 1945 (sc); *I've Always Loved You* 1946 (sc,story); *Tycoon* 1947 (sc); *The Man From Colorado* 1948 (story); *Red River* 1948 (sc) **(AANBST)**; *The Great Jewel Robber* 1950 (sc); *Montana* 1950 (sc); *Winchester '73* 1950 (sc); *The Iron Man* 1951 (sc); *Bend of the River* 1952 (sc); *Lone Star* 1952 (sc,story); *The World in His Arms* 1952 (sc); *His Majesty O'Keefe* 1953 (sc); *Sea Devils* 1953 (sc,story); *Man Without a Star* 1954 (sc); *Vera Cruz* 1954 (story); *The Far Country* 1955 (sc,story); *The Far Horizons* 1955 (uncred.a); *Backlash* 1956 (sc); *Night Passage* 1957 (sc); *Ride a Crooked Trail* 1958 (sc); *Mutiny on the Bounty* 1962 (uncred.sc); *Monstrosity* 1964 (uncred.a); *Los Pistoleros de Casa Grande* 1965 (sc,story); *Backtrack* 1969 (sc); *A Man Called Gannon* 1969 (sc); *Self Serve* 1990 (a).

Chase, Chevy • Actor • Born Cornelius Crane Chase, New York, NY, October 8, 1944. *Educ.* Bard College, Annandale-on-Hudson, NY (English); MIT; CCS Institute (audio research). Gifted comic performer, particulaly adept at deadpan humor. Chase began writing comedy material for an off-Broadway revue which later became the basis of his film debut, *The Groove Tube* (1974). An original member of TV's "Saturday Night Live," he has subsequently appeared in mostly mediocre films. At his comedic best in *Foul Play* (1978) and the "Fletch" movies. • *The Groove Tube* 1974; *Tunnelvision* 1976; *Foul Play* 1978; *Caddyshack* 1980; *Oh Heavenly Dog* 1980; *Seems Like Old Times* 1980; *Modern Problems* 1981; *Under the Rainbow* 1981; *Deal of the Century* 1983; *National Lampoon's Vacation* 1983; *Fletch* 1985; *National Lampoon's European Vacation* 1985; *Sesame Street Presents: Follow That Bird* 1985; *Spies Like Us* 1985; *Three Amigos!* 1986 (a,song); *Caddyshack II* 1988; *The Couch Trip* 1988; *Funny Farm* 1988 (a,p); *Fletch Lives* 1989; *National Lampoon's Christmas Vacation* 1989; *L.A. Story* 1991 (uncred.a); *Nothing But Trouble* 1991.

Chatterton, Ruth • Actress; also playwright, novelist. • Born New York, NY, December 24, 1893; died 1961. Respected stage actress who made her screen debut in *Sins of the Fathers* (1928), but is most memorable as Walter Huston's wife in *Dodsworth* (1936). Chatterton wrote a Broadway play in 1930 (*Monsieur Brotonneau*) and after retiring from films eight years later, published several popular novels in the 1950s. Married to actors Ralph Forbes, George Brent and Barry Thomson. • *Sins of the Fathers* 1928 (a); *Charming Sinners* 1929 (uncred.a); *The Doctor's Secret* 1929 (uncred.a); *The Dummy* 1929 (a); *The Laughing Lady* 1929 (a); *Madame X* 1929 (a) **(AANBA)**; *Anybody's Woman* 1930 (uncred.a); *The Lady of Scandal* 1930 (a); *Paramount on Parade* 1930 (a); *The Right to Love* 1930 (a); *Sarah and Son* 1930 (a) **(AANBA)**; *The Magnificent Lie* 1931 (a); *Once a Lady* 1931 (a); *Unfaithful* 1931 (a); *The Crash* 1932 (uncred.a); *The Rich Are Always With Us* 1932 (a); *Tomorrow and Tomorrow* 1932 (a); *Female* 1933 (a); *Frisco Jenny* 1933 (a); *Lilly Turner* 1933 (a); *Journal of a Crime* 1934 (a); *Dodsworth* 1936 (a); *Girls' Dormitory* 1936 (a); *Lady of Secrets* 1936 (a); *The Rat* 1937 (a); *A Royal Divorce* 1938 (a).

Chayefsky, Paddy • *aka* Sidney Aaron • Screenwriter, playwright; also novelist. • Born Sidney Aaron Chayefsky, Bronx, NY, January 29, 1923; died August 1, 1981, New York, NY. *Educ.* CCNY. Passionate, perceptive American scenarist and playwright (*The Tenth Man, Gideon, The Latent Heterosexual*) who first gained recognition during the Golden Age of Television in the early 1950s. Chayefsky's early naturalistic dramas for both TV and film, best exemplified by the award-winning feature, *Marty* (1955, adapted from one of his TV scripts), demonstrated an informed respect for common people and their everyday problems. His later bitingly satirical work, however, such as the Oscar-winning *The Hospital* (1971) and *Network* (1976), took on a bitter, critical edge rarely equalled in American films. Though he wrote the novel, *Altered States*, his screenplay for the 1980 film of the same name was so altered by director Ken Russell that Chayefsky took credit under the pseudonym Sidney Aaron. • *A Double Life* 1947 (a); *As Young As You Feel* 1951 (story); *Marty* 1955 (sc,from teleplay *Marty*) **(AABSC)**; *The Catered Affair* 1956 (from teleplay); *The Bachelor Party* 1957 (assoc.p,sc,from teleplay); *The Goddess* 1958 (sc,story) **(AANBSC)**; *Middle of the Night* 1959 (sc,from play); *The Americanization of Emily* 1964 (sc); *Paint Your Wagon* 1969 (sc,adapt); *The Hospital* 1971 (sc,story) **(AABSC)**; *Network* 1976 (sc) **(AABSC)**; *Altered States* 1980 (sc,from novel).

Cheech and Chong • See Marin, Cheech, and Chong, Thomas.

Cher • *aka* Cherilyn Sarkisian La Piere, Cher Bono • Actress, singer • Born Cherilyn Sarkisian, El Centro, CA, May 20, 1946. First made her name as half of the "Sonny and Cher" pop duo, opposite then-husband Sonny Bono. Their soft rock sound, daring psychedelic wardrobe, irreverent delivery and natural rapport with the audience aptly captured the mood of the times and their summer replacement TV series, "The Sonny and Cher Comedy Hour" (1971-74) became a major hit.

Cher made her film debut in 1965's *Wild on the Beach* but began earning serious acclaim for her acting in the 1980s, with an Academy Award nomination as best supporting actress for *Silkwood* (1983), the best actress award at Cannes for *Mask* (1985) and the corresponding Oscar for *Moonstruck* (1987). Cher has a daughter, Chastity, by Bono and a son, Elijah, by second husband, rock performer Greg Allman, from whom she is divorced. • *Wild on the Beach* 1965; *Good Times* 1967; *Chastity* 1969; *Come Back to the 5 & Dime Jimmy Dean, Jimmy Dean* 1982; *Silkwood* 1983 **(AANBSA)**; *Mask* 1985; *Moonstruck* 1987 **(AABA)**; *Suspect* 1987; *The Witches of Eastwick* 1987; *Mermaids* 1990.

Cherkassov, Nikolai • *aka* Nikolai Cherkasov • Actor • Born Nikolai Konstantinovich Cherkassov, St. Petersburg, Russia, July 27, 1903; died 1966. *Educ.* Leningrad Theater Institute. Forceful star of the Soviet stage and screen, best known in the West for his subdued but powerful performances in the title roles of three Eisenstein films: *Alexander Nevsky* (1938), *Ivan the Terrible Part I* (1945) and *Ivan the Terrible Part II* (1946). Cherkassov's autobiography, *Notes of a Soviet Film Actor*, was published in 1953. • *Czar's Poet* 1927; *Hectic Days* 1935; *The Baltic Deputy* 1937; *Peter the First, Part I* 1937; *Aleksandr Nevski/Alexander Nevsky* 1938; *Captain*

Grant's Children 1938; *Friends* 1938; *The Man With the Gun* 1938; *Conquests of Peter the Great* 1939; *Lenin in 1918* 1939; *His Name Is Sukhe-Bator* 1942; *Ivan Grozny Part I/Ivan the Terrible Part I* 1945; *Ivan Grozny Part II/Ivan the Terrible Part II* 1946; *Pirogov* 1947; *Spring* 1947; *Vo imya zhizni* 1947; *Akademik Ivan Pavlov* 1949; *Mussorgsky* 1950; *Stalingradskaya bitva* 1950; *Rimsky-Korsakov* 1953; *Don Kikhot/Don Quijote* 1957.

Chevalier, Maurice • Actor; also singer. • Born Paris, September 12, 1888; died 1972. Celebrated French music-hall entertainer, in films from 1908. Though awarded the Croix de Guerre after being wounded and captured by the Germans during WWI, Chevalier was accused of collaboration in WWII. Later exonerated, he emerged more popular than ever to sing, to appear in international films and to "thank heaven for little girls." • *Trop Crédule* 1908; *Un Marie qui se fait attendre* 1911; *La Mariée recalcitrante* 1911; *Par Habitude* 1911; *Une Soirée mondaine* 1917; *La Valse renversante* 1917; *Le Match Criqui-Ledoux* 1922; *Le Mauvais Garçon* 1922; *Affaire de la Rue de Lourcine* 1923; *Gonzague* 1923; *Jim Bougne Boxeur* 1923; *Par Habitude* 1924; *Bonjour New York* 1928; *Innocents of Paris* 1929; *The Love Parade* 1929 **(AANBA)**; *The Big Pond* 1930 **(AANBA)**; *Paramount on Parade* 1930; *Playboy of Paris* 1930; *El Cliente Seductor* 1931; *The Smiling Lieutenant* 1931; *The Stolen Jools* 1931; *Love Me Tonight* 1932; *Make Me a Star* 1932; *One Hour With You* 1932; *A Bedtime Story* 1933; *The Way to Love* 1933; *The Merry Widow* 1934; *Toboggan (short)* 1934; *Folies Bergère* 1935; *Beloved Vagabond* 1936; *Avec le Sourire* 1937; *L'Homme du Jour* 1937; *Break the News* 1938; *Pièges* 1939; *Le Silence est d'or* 1947; *Paris 1900* 1948; *Ma Pomme* 1950; *Le Roi* 1950; *Schlägerparade* 1953; *Cento Anni d'Amore* 1954; *J'avais sept filles* 1954; *The Happy Road* 1956 (song); *Rendez-vous avec Maurice Chevalier* 1956; *Love in the Afternoon* 1957; *Gigi* 1958 (a,song); *Count Your Blessings* 1959; *A Breath of Scandal* 1960; *Can-Can* 1960; *Pepe* 1960; *Un, deux, trois, quatre!/Black Tights* 1960; *Fanny* 1961; *Jessica* 1961; *In Search of the Castaways* 1962; *A New Kind of Love* 1963; *I'd Rather Be Rich* 1964; *Panic Button* 1964; *Monkeys, Go Home!* 1967; *The Aristocats* 1970 (song); *Le Bal* 1983 (song); *Coup de Foudre/Entre Nous* 1983 (song).

Chong, Rae Dawn • Actress • Born Vancouver, British Columbia, Canada, 1962. First earned attention with her role as an ice age woman in Jean-Jacques Annaud's prehistoric epic, *Quest For Fire* (1981). Chong won a Génie (the Canadian Oscar) for her performance, which involved speaking a special language devised by novelist Anthony Burgess. She has since displayed a gift for wise-cracking, off-beat characterizations in more contemporary settings. Daughter of comedian Thomas Chong and wife, since 1989, of actor C. Thomas Howell. • *Stony Island* 1978; *Quest For Fire* 1981; *Beat Street* 1984; *Cheech & Chong's the Corsican Brothers* 1984; *Choose Me* 1984; *American Flyers* 1985; *City Limits* 1985; *The Color Purple* 1985; *Commando* 1985; *Fear City* 1985; *Running Out of Luck* 1985; *Soul Man* 1986; *The Principal* 1987; *The Squeeze* 1987; *Walking After Midnight* 1988; *Far Out, Man!* 1990; *Tales From the Darkside: The Movie* 1990; *Amazon* 1991.

Chong, Thomas • *aka* Chong, Tommy Chong • Actor; also director, screenwriter. • Born Edmonton, Alberta, Canada, May 24, 1938. Former rhythm and blues guitar player who moved into films after forming a comedy/improvisation team with Cheech Marin. Father of actress Rae Dawn Chong. • *Cheech & Chong's Up in Smoke* 1978 (a,sc,song); *Cheech & Chong's Next Movie* 1980 (a,d,sc); *Cheech & Chong's Nice Dreams* 1981 (a,d,sc,song); *It Came From Hollywood* 1982 (a); *Things Are Tough All Over* 1982 (sc); *Cheech & Chong's Still Smokin'* 1983 (a,d,sc); *Yellowbeard* 1983 (a); *Cheech & Chong's the Corsican Brothers* 1984 (a,d,sc); *After Hours* 1985 (a).

Chopra, Joyce • American director; also producer. • Born 1938. *Educ.* Brandeis University, Waltham, MA (comparative literature); Neighborhood Playhouse, New York. Former documentary filmmaker who made a polished and powerful dramatic feature debut with *Smooth Talk* (1985), a disturbing tale about a teenage girl's sexual awakening and intense mother-daughter conflict which boasted a fine central performance by Laura Dern. Chopra was replaced by James Bridges on her next picture, *Bright Lights, Big City* (1988), and received mixed reviews for the ensemble piece, *The Lemon Sisters* (1989), starring Diane Keaton, Carol Kane and Kathryn Grody. • *Martha Clarke, Light and Dark* 1981 (d,ed,p); *Smooth Talk* 1985 (d); *The Lemon Sisters* 1989 (d).

Chow, Raymond • Producer • Born Hong Kong. *Educ.* St. John's University, Shanghai. Former manager of Shaw Brothers, the dominant force in Asian film production and distribution from the 1940s through the early 70s. Known as the "Hollywood of the East," the Shaw Empire went into decline following Chow's departure from the company in 1970 to form the rival Golden Harvest group. Chow turned to producing English-language films in 1977. • *Fist of Fury* 1972 (p); *Deep Thrust—The Hand of Death* 1973 (p); *Enter the Dragon* 1973 (p); *Return of the Dragon* 1973 (p); *The Man From Hong Kong* 1974 (p); *S.T.A.B.* 1976 (exec.p); *The Amsterdam Kill* 1977 (exec.p); *The Boys in Company C* 1977 (exec.p); *Game of Death* 1979 (p); *Night Games* 1979 (exec.p); *The Big Brawl* 1980 (exec.p); *The Cannonball Run* 1980 (exec.p); *The Happenings* 1980 (p); *Death Hunt* 1981 (exec.p); *Megaforce* 1982 (exec.p); *Zu* 1982 (p); *Better Late Than Never* 1983 (exec.p); *Cannonball Run II* 1983 (exec.p); *High Road to China* 1983 (exec.p); *Lassiter* 1984 (exec.p); *Wheels on Meals* 1984 (exec.p); *Happy Din Don* 1985 (exec.p); *Jingcha Gushi/Jackie Chan's Police Story* 1985 (exec.p); *The Millionaire's Express* 1985 (exec.p); *The Protector* 1985 (exec.p); *Chocolate Inspector* 1986 (exec.p); *K'ung-pu fen-tzu* 1986 (p); *Long Xiong Hu Di* 1986 (exec.p); *A Jihua Xuji* 1987 (exec.p); *The Association* 1987 (p); *Eastern Condors* 1987 (p); *My Lucky Stars* 1987 (p); *The Reincarnation of Golden Lotus* 1989 (exec.p); *Wan-ch'un ch'ing-shih* 1989 (exec.p); *A Show of Force* 1990 (exec.p); *Teenage Mutant Ninja Turtles* 1990 (exec.p); *Teenage Mutant Ninja Turtles II: The Secret of the Ooze* 1991 (exec.p).

Christensen, Benjamin • *aka* Benjamin Christianson, Benjamin Christiansen • Director; also actor, screenwriter. • Born Viborg, Denmark, September 28, 1879; died 1959. *Educ.* University of Copenhagen (medicine); Royal Theater Academy, Copenhagen. Major European director of the silent era. Christensen's early grasp of sophisticated cinematic techniques (which may predate those of both D.W. Griffith and Louis Feuillade) should have assured him a more prominent place in film history, but prints of many of his films remain lost. In Hollywood from 1925 to 1929 as Benjamin Christiansen. • *The Mysterious X* 1913 (d,sc,uncred.a); *Night of Vengeance* 1915 (a,d,sc); *Haxan/Witchcraft Through the Ages* 1922 (a,d,sc); *Seine Frau die Unbekannte* 1923 (d,sc); *Unter Juden* 1923 (d); *Mikael* 1924 (a); *Die Frau mit dem schlechten Ruf* 1925 (d); *The Devil's Circus* 1926 (d,sc,story); *Mockery* 1927 (d,story); *The Haunted House* 1928 (d); *The Hawk's Nest* 1928 (d); *The House of Horror* 1929 (d); *The Mysterious Island* 1929 (d); *Seven Footprints to Satan* 1929 (d); *Children of Divorce* 1939 (d,sc); *The Child* 1940 (d,sc); *Come Home With Me* 1941 (d); *The Lady With the Light Gloves* 1943 (d).

Christian-Jaque • Director • Born Christian Maudet, Paris, September 4, 1904. *Educ.* Collège Rollin, Paris; Ecole des Beaux-Arts, Paris; Ecole des Arts Decoratifs (architecture). Former film critic (for *Cinégraf* magazine), poster artist and art director. His prolific output as a director, beginning in 1932 with the medium-length feature, *Le Bidon d'or*, has been generally light and undistinguished with the exception of his highly regarded spoof of swashbuckling movies, *Fanfan la Tulipe/Fanfan the Tulip*

(1952). From 1950 until 1961, Christian-Jaque was one of France's most commericially successful directors, concocting quite popular, elaborate costume extravaganzas and period romances, filmed in lush color, and featuring voluptuous international actresses. Three of his five marriages were to actresses: Simone Renat, Renée Faure and Martine Carol. • *Le Bidon d'or* 1932 (d); *Adhemar Lampiot* 1933 (d); *La Boeuf sur la Langue* 1933 (d); *Ça Colle* 1933 (d); *L'Hôtel du Libre-Echange* 1933 (d); *Le Tendron d'Achille* 1933 (d); *Compartiment des Dames seules* 1935 (d); *La Famille Pont-Biquet* 1935 (d); *Le Père Lampion* 1935 (d); *Sacré Léonce* 1935 (d); *La Sonnette d'Alarme* 1935 (d); *Sous la griffe* 1935 (d); *Voyage d'Agrément* 1935 (d); *L'Ecole des Journalistes* 1936 (d); *Josette* 1936 (d); *Monsieur Personne* 1936 (d); *On ne roule pas Antoinette* 1936 (d); *Rigolboche* 1936 (d); *Un de la Legion* 1936 (d); *Degourdis de la Onzième* 1937 (d); *François Ier* 1937 (d); *La Maison d'en face* 1937 (d); *Les Perles de la Couronne* 1937 (d); *A Venise une nuit* 1937 (d); *Les Disparus de Saint-Agil* 1938 (d); *Ernest le Rebelle* 1938 (d); *Les Pirates du Rail* 1938 (d); *C'était moi* 1939 (d); *L'Enfer des Anges* 1939 (d); *Raphael le Tatoué* 1939 (d); *Le Grand Elan* 1940 (d); *L'Assassinat du Père Noël?* 1941 (d); *Première Bal* 1941 (d); *La Symphonie Fantastique* 1942 (d); *Voyage sans espoir* 1943 (d); *Boule de Suif* 1945 (d,sc.adapt); *Carmen* 1945 (d,sc); *Sortilèges* 1945 (d); *Un Revenant* 1946 (d,sc.adapt); *La Chartreuse de Parme* 1948 (d,sc); *D'Homme à Hommes* 1948 (d,sc); *Le Singoalla* 1950 (d,sc); *Souvenirs perdus* 1950 (d,sc); *Barbe-Bleue* 1951 (d,sc,adapt); *Adorables Créatures* 1952 (d,sc,adapt); *Fanfan la Tulipe/Fanfan the Tulip* 1952 (d,p,sc.adapt); *Lucrèce Borgia* 1953 (d,sc); *Destinées* 1954 (d); *Madame du Barry* 1954 (d,sc); *Nana* 1955 (d,sc); *Si Tous les Gars du Monde...* 1956 (adapt,dial,d); *Nathalie Agent Secret* 1957 (adapt,d,p); *La Loi c'est la loi* 1958 (adapt,d); *Babette s'en va-t-en Guerre* 1959 (d); *La Française et l'amour/Love and the Frenchwoman* 1960 (d); *Madame Sans-Gène* 1961 (d,sc); *Les Bonnes Causes* 1963 (d,sc); *La Tulipe Noir* 1963 (d); *Le Repas des Fauves* 1964 (d); *La Fabuleuse aventure de Marco Polo* 1965 (d); *Le Gentleman de Cocody* 1965 (d,sc); *La Guerre secrète* 1965 (d,sc); *Le Saint prend l'Affut* 1966 (d); *La Seconde verite* 1966 (d); *Deux billets pour Mexico* 1967 (d,sc); *Les Amours de Lady Hamilton/Lady Hamilton/The Making of a Lady* 1968 (d,sc); *Les Pétroleuses* 1971 (d); *Docteur Justice* 1975 (d); *La Vie Parisienne* 1978 (d,sc); *Carné: l'Homme à la Camera* 1980 (d).

Christie, Julie • Actress • Born Julie Frances Christie, Chukua, Assam, India, April 14, 1941. *Educ.* Brighton Technical College (art); Central School of Speech and Drama, London. Combining radiant, striking beauty and genuine talent, Christie emerged as one of the more engaging female leads of the 1960s and 70s. She got her break as star of British TV's *A For Andromeda* (1960) and had small parts in two Ken Annakin films before achieving big-screen success with leading roles in John Schlesinger's *Billy Liar* (1963) and in the tailor-made *Darling* (1965). Although usually exemplifying the sexually liberated, contemporary woman, Christie also starred as the object of desire in lavish period films: David Lean's *Doctor Zhivago* (1965), John Schlesinger's *Far From the Madding Crowd* (1967) and Joseph Losey's *The Go-Between* (1971).

Since the 1980s Christie has chosen fewer, and lower profile, projects, while continuing to turn in exemplary performances, as in *Heat and Dust* (1983), *Miss Mary* (1986) and as the ravishingly beautiful, alcoholic widow in the otherwise disappointing *Fools of Fortune* (1990). • *Crooks Anonymous* 1962; *The Fast Lady* 1962; *Billy Liar* 1963; *Darling* 1965 **(AABA)**; *Doctor Zhivago* 1965; *Young Cassidy* 1965; *Fahrenheit 451* 1966; *Far From the Madding Crowd* 1967; *Tonite Let's All Make Love in London* 1967; *Petulia* 1968; *In Search of Gregory* 1970; *The Go-Between* 1971; *McCabe & Mrs. Miller* 1971 **(AANBA)**; *Don't Look Now* 1973; *Nashville* 1975; *Shampoo* 1975; *Demon Seed* 1977; *Heaven Can Wait* 1978; *The Animals Film* 1981; *Memoirs of a Survivor* 1981; *The Return of the Soldier* 1982; *The Gold Diggers* 1983; *Heat and Dust* 1983; *Miss Mary* 1986; *Power* 1986; *Yilmaz Guney: His Life, His Films* 1987; *La Memoire tatouee/Secret Obsession* 1988; *Fools of Fortune* 1990.

Chukhrai, Grigori • Director • Born Melitopol, Ukraine, USSR, 1921. *Educ.* VGIK, Moscow. Prominent Soviet director whose early works *The Forty-First* (1956)—a remake of Yakov Protazanov's silent film of the same name—and *Ballad of a Soldier* (1959), regained international acclaim and acceptance for the Soviet Cinema. Chukhrai's films broke from the socialist realism of the Stalinist era, largely due to their sincerity, romanticism and humor. • *Nazar Srodolia* 1955 (d); *Sorok pervyi/The Forty-First* 1956 (d); *Ballada o soldatye/Ballad of a Soldier* 1959 (d,sc) **(AANBSC)**; *Chistoye nebo/Clear Skies* 1961 (d); *There Was an Old Couple* 1965 (d); *People!* 1966 (d); *Nachalo Nevedomogo Veka* 1967 (p); *Pamyat* 1971 (d,sc); *Netepichnaja Istoria* 1978 (d,sc); *La Vita è bella* 1982 (d,sc); *Mikhail Romm: Ispoved Kinorezhisera* 1986 (a).

Chytilová, Véra • Director; also screenwriter. • Born Ostrava, Czechoslovakia, February 2, 1929. *Educ.* FAMU, Prague. Véra Chytilová grew up amid the feverish experimentalism of the Prague arts world of the 1930s, and had survived both the war and Stalinism by the time she joined the avant-garde of feminist directors in the 1960s. At Charles University she studied philosophy and architecture, but her beauty opened up another career as a model, which in turn led to contact with the cinema world and enrollment in the Czech Film Academy (FAMU). Her graduation film from FAMU, *Ceiling* (1962), was a witheringly funny look at men's exploitation of women as models. The film's disgust with consumerism and fantastical imagery foreshadowed her future work.

Something Different (1963), Chytilová's first feature, used parallel narratives and a *cinéma vérité* style to contrast the lives of a gymnast and a housewife. Though unconventional, it only hinted at the kinds of experimentation that would make her next film, *Daisies* (1966), a triumph of anarchy. The two heroines of *Daisies*, Marie I and Marie II, entertain themselves and us with a series of irresponsibile pranks that culminate in their wantonly trashing a table of food and swinging from a chandelier. The only guideline to their outrageous behavior is their exchange, prior to each episode: "It matters?" "It doesn't matter." Too funny to be nihilistic, *Daisies* remains Chytilová's best loved work.

Fruit of Paradise (1970) carried Chytilová's attack on the male establishment farther, with its elegant dissection of a triangular relationship between a couple and a serpentine man.

After the Soviet invasion of 1968, Chytilová was idle until 1976, when *The Apple Game* marked a turn toward a more conventional storyline and character development. This trend was continued in *Story from a Housing Estate* (1979) and *Calamity* (1982), both of which reflect the norms of anti-bureaucratic thinking. However, with *The Very Late Afternoon of a Fawn* (1984), *Wolf's Lair* (1986) and *The Jester and the Queen* (1988), Chytilová reclaimed her position as the most stylish and provocative director in Czechoslavakia. *Tainted Horseplay* (1989) flaunted Western sympathies in a tragicomedy about AIDS.

Fellow Czech surrealist Juraj Jakubisko, who has worked with Chytilová, once described her approach to filmmaking: "She makes a film as if she were buying a hat: a magnificent ceremony, full of elegance and feminine cleverness. And all the while she is suffering. In a little while, the hat she bought doesn't appeal to her anymore, and right there a style of storytelling emerges." Chytilová's signature remains a vertiginous camera technique and disjunctive editing style that keeps the viewer constantly aware of the director's wry stance toward her subjects. KJ • *Villa in the Suburbs (short)* 1959 (d,sc); *Mr. K—Green Street (short)* 1960 (d,sc); *Academy Newsreel (short)* 1961 (d,sc); *A Bagful of Fleas* 1962 (d,sc); *Ceiling* 1962 (d,sc); *Something Different* 1963 (d,sc);

Perlicky Na Dne/Pearls of the Deep 1965 (d "At the World Cafeteria"); *Sedmikrasky/Daisies* 1966 (d,sc,story); *Fruit of Paradise* 1970 (d,sc); *Hra o jablko/The Apple Game* 1977 (d,sc,story); *Prefab Story/Story From a Housing Estate* 1979 (d,sc); *Calamity* 1982 (d); *The Very Late Afternoon of a Faun* 1984 (d,sc); *Prague* 1985 (d,sc); *Vlci Bouda/Wolf's Lair* 1986 (d,sc); *Sasek a Kralovna/The Jester and the Queen* 1988 (d,sc); *Kopytem sem, Kopytem tam/Tainted Horseplay* 1989 (d,sc).

Cilento, Diane • Actress; also novelist. • Born Brisbane, Queensland, Australia, October 5, 1933. *Educ.* AADA, New York; RADA, London. Talented blonde beauty with a sly, seductive smile, successful on stage but in few substantial films. Her most memorable film performances include the enticing Molly in *Tom Jones* (1963), which won her an Oscar nomination, and the tart with a heart of gold in *Rattle of a Simple Man* (1964). Cilento turned to writing in the late 1960s, publishing her first novel, *The Manipulator*, in 1969. Married to Sean Connery from 1962 to 1973, their son Jason is also an actor. • *Wings of Danger* 1952; *The Passing Stranger* 1954; *The Angel Who Pawned Her Harp* 1956; *The Admirable Crichton* 1957; *The Truth About Women* 1958; *Jet Storm* 1959; *The Full Treatment* 1961; *The Naked Edge* 1961; *I Thank a Fool* 1962; *Tom Jones* 1963 **(AANBSA)**; *Rattle of a Simple Man* 1964; *The Third Secret* 1964; *The Agony and the Ecstasy* 1965; *Hombre* 1967; *Negatives* 1968; *Z.P.G.* 1972; *Hitler: The Last Ten Days* 1973; *The Wicker Man* 1973; *The Tiger Lily* 1975; *Partners* 1981; *The Boy Who Had Everything* 1985; *For the Term of His Natural Life* 1985.

Cimino, Michael • Director; also screenwriter. • Born New York, NY, 1943. *Educ.* Yale (painting). Former protégé of Clint Eastwood who was as much lauded for his award-winning *The Deer Hunter* (1978) as he was reviled for the financially disastrous *Heaven's Gate* (1980), which helped topple the troubled United Artists. Cimino's excessive tendencies have since continued to overwhelm his obvious directorial talent. • *Silent Running* 1971 (sc); *Magnum Force* 1973 (sc); *Thunderbolt And Lightfoot* 1974 (d,sc); *The Deer Hunter* 1978 (d,p,story) **(AANBSC,AABD,AABP)**; *Heaven's Gate* 1980 (d,sc); *Year of the Dragon* 1985 (d,sc); *50 Years of Action!* 1986 (a); *The Sicilian* 1987 (d,p); *Desperate Hours* 1990 (d,p).

Clair, René • Director; also screenwriter, actor. • Born René-Lucien Chomette, Paris, November 11, 1898; died March 15, 1981, Neuilly, France. René Clair almost single-handedly revived French film comedy after WWI, adapting the pre-war comic tradition to sound technology and the realities of the postwar era. Though he eventually broadened his range of material and faltered toward the end of his career, he will always be remembered as France's first great director of comedies.

After short stints as a journalist, an actor under Feuillade and Protozanov and an assistant to Baroncelli, Clair made an engaging satire of French society, *Paris qui dort*, in 1924. In this science fiction fantasy, an angry scientist invents a ray gun which paralyzes the French capital. Those few who escape the ray wander throughout Paris poking fun at various people they encounter, though they end up reenacting the very gestures and attitudes they initially mocked. With its flat sets, rudimentary animation and stock character types recalling both American slapstick and the work of Georges Méliès, *Paris qui dort* combined social satire with a witty exploration of film's ability to manipulate time and motion. Clair followed with the deliciously outrageous dada masterpiece, *Entr'acte* (1924), based on notes by Francis Picabia. With music by Erik Satie and starring Marcel Duchamp and Man Ray, *Entr'acte* was made for the Ballet suédois production of Picabia's *Relâche* (literally, "performance canceled"). The opening sequence is virtually plotless, structured along graphic and rhythmic principles and including a number of comic gags, while the second half shows a crowd of mourners chasing a camel-drawn hearse through the streets of Paris.

Clair next made a series of fantasy works *à la Méliès*, including *Le Voyage imaginaire* (1925) and *Le Fantôme du Moulin-Rouge* (1926). He established an international reputation with *The Italian Straw Hat* (1927), a brilliant updating of Labiche-Michel's play. An early and vocal opponent of sound film, Clair nonetheless proved its capacity for eloquence with *Under the Roofs of Paris* (1930) and two other masterpieces, *Le million* (1931) and *A nous la liberté* (1932), in which he perfected his command of comic timing and gift for almost musical plot structure.

Following the unexpected failure of *Le dernier milliardaire* (1934), Clair moved to England. There he made two films, including *The Ghost Goes West* (1935), in which an American (Robert Donat) transports a castle back to the States, only to discover that it's haunted. With the coming of WWII Clair himself headed west. Unlike other French exiles such as Jean Renoir, Clair fared rather well in Hollywood, making the successful comedy-fantasies *The Flame of New Orleans* (1941) with Marlene Dietrich and *I Married a Witch* (1942) with Fredric March and Veronica Lake (a feud between these two made for lively filming). In *It Happened Tomorrow* (1944) Dick Powell plays a reporter who can predict the future, a journalistic advantage which leads to unexpected complications when he learns of his own death. Clair completed his US stay with a highly suspenseful Agatha Christie adaptation, *And Then There Were None* (1945).

Clair's post-war return to France coincided with a turn to more demanding subject matter. *Man About Town* (1947) is a nostalgic reflection on the silent film era which also condemns totalitarianism and the irresponsible use of science. It was followed by a free adaptation of the Faust legend, *Beauty and the Devil* (1950), starring Michel Simon (as Mephisto) and Gerard Philipe. Philipe returned in *Beauties of the Night* (1952), a comic fantasy in several timeframes based on D.W. Griffith's *Intolerance*, and *The Grand Maneuver* (1956). Neither film was particularly successful, and *Gates of Paris* (1957) continued Clair's undeniable decline.

Although elected in 1960 to the Académie Française, Clair found that his last few films had badly tainted his reputation. Nevertheless, he is now regarded as one of the preeminent French filmmakers, the man whose wit, irony and delicate sense of timing inspired both Chaplin and the Marx Brothers. RDH • *Entr'acte* 1924 (d,sc); *Paris qui dort* 1924 (d,sc); *Le Fantôme du Moulin Rouge* 1925 (d,sc); *Le Voyage imaginaire* 1926 (d,sc); *Un Chapeau de Paille d'Italie/The Italian Straw Hat* 1927 (d,sc); *La Proie du Vent* 1927 (d,sc); *Les Deux Timides* 1928 (d,sc); *La Tour (short)* 1928 (d,sc); *Sous les toits de Paris/Under the Roofs of Paris* 1930 (d,sc,dial); *Le Million* 1931 (d,sc,lyrics); *A Nous la Liberté* 1932 (d,sc,dial); *Quatorze Juillet* 1933 (d,sc); *Le Dernier Milliardaire* 1934 (d,sc); *The Ghost Goes West* 1935 (d); *Un Village dans Paris: Montmartre* 1935 (p); *Break the News* 1938 (d,p); *The Flame of New Orleans* 1941 (d); *I Married a Witch* 1942 (d,p); *Forever and a Day* 1943 (d,p); *It Happened Tomorrow* 1944 (d,sc); *And Then There Were None* 1945 (d,p); *Le Silence est d'or/Man About Town* 1947 (d,sc); *La Beauté du Diable/Beauty and the Devil* 1950 (d,sc); *Les Belles de nuit/Beauties of the Night* 1952 (d,sc); *Les Grandes Maneuvres/The Grand Maneuver* 1956 (d,p,sc,adapt,dial); *Porte de Lilas/Gates of Paris* 1957 (d,sc); *La Française et l'amour/Love and the Frenchwoman* 1960 (d); *Tout l'Or du Monde* 1961 (d,sc); *Les Quatre Verités* 1962 (d,sc); *Les Fêtes galantes* 1965 (d,sc); *Ladies & Gentlemen* 1984 (from sc *It Happened Tomorrow*).

Clark, Bob • *aka* Benjamin Clark • Director; also producer. • Born New Orleans, LA, August 5, 1941. *Educ.* Catawba College; Hillsdale College; University of Miami (drama). Entered films via low-budget horror pictures, *Dead of Night*, *Deathdream* (both 1972) and *Children Shouldn't Play With Dead Things* (1974), before branching out as a competent helmer of a wide variety of genres, mostly from his own original stories. His films include the atmospheric, imaginative period thriller, *Murder By Decree* (1979) in which Sherlock Holmes and Dr. Watson solve the mystery of Jack the Ripper, the film version of the sentimental father-son stage drama, *Tribute* (1980) and the semi-autobiographical, smarmy but high grossing hit comedies, *Porky's* (1981) and *Porky's II—The Next Day* (1983). • *Dead of Night* 1972 (d,p); *Deathdream* 1972 (d); *Black Christmas* 1974 (d,p); *Children Shouldn't Play With Dead Things* 1974 (d); *Breaking Point* 1976 (d,p); *Murder By Decree* 1979 (d,p); *Tribute* 1980 (d); *Porky's* 1981 (d,p,sc); *A Christmas Story* 1983 (d,p); *Porky's II: The Next Day* 1983 (d,p,sc); *Rhinestone* 1984 (d); *Porky's Revenge* 1985 (from characters); *Turk 182* 1985 (d); *From the Hip* 1987 (d,p,sc); *Loose Cannons* 1989 (d,sc).

Clark, Candy • Actress • Born Norman, OK, June 20, 1947. Unusual, dynamic model-turned-actress who followed her film debut in John Huston's *Fat City* (1972) with a memorable, Oscar-nominated performance in George Lucas's seminal coming-of-age film, *American Graffiti* (1973). Clark's subsequent career, however, has not lived up to her fine work of the 1970s (*The Man Who Fell to Earth* 1976, *When You Comin' Back, Red Ryder?* 1979), or her country turns in the TV films (*Amateur Night at the Dixie Bar and Grill* 1979, *Rodeo Girl* 1980). • *Fat City* 1972; *American Graffiti* 1973 **(AANBSA)**; *I Will...I Will...For Now* 1975; *The Man Who Fell to Earth* 1976; *Citizens Band* 1977; *The Big Sleep* 1978; *More American Graffiti* 1979; *When You Comin' Back, Red Ryder?* 1979; *National Lampoon Goes to the Movies* 1982; *Q* 1982; *Amityville 3-D* 1983; *Blue Thunder* 1983; *Hambone and Hillie* 1984; *Stephen King's Cat's Eye* 1985; *At Close Range* 1986; *Blind Curve (short)* 1988; *The Blob* 1988.

Clarke, Charles G. • *aka* Charles Clarke • Director of photography; also actor. • Born Charles Galloway Clarke, Potter Valley, CA, March 18, 1899; died July 1, 1983, Beverly Hills, CA. Began his career as a portrait photographer in 1912. Clarke designed a battery-run camera motor which became the industry standard during the silent era, was a pioneer of matte photography techniques and developed a reputation for location work under difficult conditions. He was nominated four times for an Academy Award. • *Half Breed* 1922; *The Light That Failed* 1923; *The Dawn of a Tomorrow* 1924; *Flaming Barriers* 1924; *Tiger Love* 1924; *Friendly Enemies* 1925; *Without Mercy* 1925; *Going Crooked* 1926; *One Minute to Play* 1926; *Rocking Moon* 1926; *Whispering Smith* 1926; *Ham and Eggs at the Front* 1927; *A Racing Romeo* 1927; *Singed* 1927; *Upstream* 1927; *Plastered in Paris* 1928; *The Red Dance* 1928; *Riley the Cop* 1928; *Sharp Shooters* 1928; *The Exalted Flapper* 1929; *Masquerade* 1929; *Nix on Dames* 1929; *Not Quite Decent* 1929; *The Sin Sister* 1929; *A Song of Kentucky* 1929; *The Veiled Woman* 1929; *Words and Music* 1929; *Men on Call* 1930; *Oh, For a Man!* 1930; *So This Is London* 1930; *Temple Tower* 1930; *Annabelle's Affairs* 1931; *Girls Demand Excitement* 1931; *Good Sport* 1931; *Too Busy to Work* 1932; *Hot Pepper* 1933; *Second Hand Wife* 1933; *The Cat and the Fiddle* 1934; *Evelyn Prentice* 1934; *Tarzan and His Mate* 1934; *Víva Villa* 1934; *The Casino Murder Case* 1935; *The Perfect Gentleman* 1935; *Pursuit* 1935; *Shadow of Doubt* 1935; *The Winning Ticket* 1935; *Woman Wanted* 1935; *All American Chump* 1936; *The Garden Murder Case* 1936; *Moonlight Murder* 1936; *Trouble For Two* 1936; *Stand-In* 1937; *The Thirteenth Chair* 1937; *Under Cover of Night* 1937; *Charlie Chan in Honolulu* 1938; *Safety in Numbers* 1938; *Frontier Marshal* 1939; *Mr. Moto Takes a Vacation* 1939; *Pardon Our Nerve* 1939; *The Return of the Cisco Kid* 1939; *The Jones Family in Young As You Feel* 1940; *Street of Memories* 1940; *Viva Cisco Kid* 1940; *Yesterday's Heroes* 1940; *Accent on Love* 1941; *The Bride Wore Crutches* 1941; *Cadet Girl* 1941; *The Cowboy and the Blonde* 1941; *Dead Men Tell* 1941; *For Beauty's Sake* 1941; *The Last of the Duanes* 1941; *Marry the Boss's Daughter* 1941; *Murder Among Friends* 1941; *The Perfect Snob* 1941; *Romance of the Rio Grande* 1941; *Careful, Soft Shoulder* 1942; *A Gentleman at Heart* 1942; *It Happened in Flatbush* 1942; *Moontide* 1942 **(AANBPH)**; *Through Different Eyes* 1942; *Time to Kill* 1942; *Guadalcanal Diary* 1943; *Hello, Frisco, Hello* 1943 **(AANBPH)**; *Ladies of Washington* 1944; *Tampico* 1944; *Junior Miss* 1945; *Molly and Me* 1945; *Thunderhead* 1945; *Smoky* 1946; *Captain From Castile* 1947; *Thunder in the Valley* 1947; *The Iron Curtain* 1948; *Green Grass of Wyoming* 1948 **(AANBPH)**; *That Wonderful Urge* 1948; *Sand* 1949 **(AANBPH)**; *Slattery's Hurricane* 1949; *The Big Lift* 1950; *I'll Get By* 1950; *Golden Girl* 1951; *Kangaroo* 1952; *Red Skies of Montana* 1952; *Stars and Stripes Forever* 1952; *City of Bad Men* 1953; *Destination Gobi* 1953; *Black Widow* 1954; *Night People* 1954; *Suddenly* 1954; *Violent Saturday* 1954; *The Bridges at Toko-Ri* 1955; *The Man in the Gray Flannel Suit* 1955; *Prince of Players* 1955; *The Virgin Queen* 1955; *Carousel* 1956; *Oh, Men! Oh, Women!* 1956; *Three Brave Men* 1956; *Stopover Tokyo* 1957; *The Wayward Bus* 1957; *The Barbarian and the Geisha* 1958; *The Hunters* 1958; *The Sound and the Fury* 1958; *Holiday For Lovers* 1959; *Hound Dog Man* 1959; *A Private's Affair* 1959; *These Thousand Hills* 1959; *Flaming Star* 1960; *Return to Peyton Place* 1961; *Madison Avenue* 1962.

Clarke, Shirley • Filmmaker • Born Shirley Brimberg, New York, NY, 1925. *Educ.* Stephens College; Johns Hopkins Univerity; Bennington School of Dance, VT; University of North Carolina. Former dancer, choreographer and head of the National Dance Association who began making short films in 1953 with *Dance in the Sun*. After developing a searing cinéma verité style in her experimental shorts and documentaries, she graduated to features with *The Connection* (1962), based on Jack Gelber's play about heroin junkies being filmed by a documentarist, and *Portrait of Jason* (1967), an interview with a black male hustler. While alienating her from Hollywood, Clarke's provocative subject matter made her a major influence on American underground film culture. (With Jonas Mekas she co-founded New York's Filmmaker's Cooperative in 1962.) In Agnes Varda's *Lions Love* (1969), she appropriately plays "Shirley Clarke," a character trying to interest a producer in a film project. • *Dance in the Sun (short)* 1953 (d,p,ph,ed); *In Paris Parks (short)* 1954 (d,p,ph,ed); *Bullfight (short)* 1955 (d,p,ph,ed); *Moment in Love (short)* 1957 (d,p,ph,ed); *Loops (short)* 1958 (d,p,ph,ed); *The Skyscraper (short)* 1958 (d,ed,p); *Bridges-Go-Round (short)* 1959 (d,p,ph,ed); *A Scary Time (short)* 1960 (d,ph,ed); *The Connection* 1962 (d,ed,p); *The Cool World* 1963 (d,sc); *Robert Frost: A Lover's Quarrel With the World* 1963 (d); *Portrait of Jason* 1967 (d,ed,p); *Lions Love* 1969 (a); *Diaries, Notes & Sketches - Volume 1, Reels 1-6: Lost Lost Lost* 1975 (a); *The March on Paris 1914* 1977 (ed); *He Stands in a Desert Counting the Seconds of His Life* 1985 (a); *Ornette: Made in America* 1985 (d,ed).

Clarke, T. E. B. • Screenwriter • Born Thomas Ernest Bennett Clarke, Watford, Hertfordshire, England, June 7, 1907; died February 11, 1989, Surrey, England. *Educ.* Cambridge (law). Former journalist and novelist who, while under contract to Ealing from 1943 to 1957, wrote several of the studio's classic comedies, notably *The Lavender Hill Mob* (1951) for which he won an Academy Award. After leaving Ealing, Clarke collaborated on the excellent screenplay for *Sons and Lovers* (1960). • *Champagne Charlie* 1944 (sc); *Dead of Night* 1945 (sc—"The Linking Story"); *Johnny Frenchman* 1945 (sc); *Hue and Cry* 1947 (sc); *Against the Wind* 1948 (sc); *Passport to Pimlico* 1949 (sc) **(AANBSC)**; *The Blue Lamp* 1950 (sc); *The Magnet* 1950 (sc); *Encore* 1951 (sc—"The Ant and the Grasshopper"); *The Lavender Hill Mob* 1952 (sc,from story) **(AABSC)**; *The Titfield Thunderbolt* 1953 (sc); *Law and Disorder* 1956 (sc); *All at Sea* 1957 (sc); *Gideon's Day* 1958 (sc); *A Tale of Two Cities* 1958 (sc); *Sons and Lovers* 1960 (sc) **(AANBSC)**; *The Horse With-*

out a Head 1963 (sc); *A Man Could Get Killed* 1966 (sc); *A Hitch in Time* 1979 (sc); *High Rise Donkey* 1980 (sc).

Clavell, James • Screenwriter; also director, producer, novelist. • Born Charles Edmund DuMaresq de Clavelle, Sydney, New South Wales, Australia, October 10, 1924. *Educ.* Birmingham University, England; University of Maryland. Best-selling author of epic, historical novels (*Tai Pan*, *Shogun*, *Noble House*), who has worked as a screenwriter and director in the US since 1953, though his best film as director is the British-produced, *To Sir With Love* (1967). Clavell's novel *King Rat*, based on his experiences in a WWII Japanese prison camp, was effectively brought to the screen in 1965 by another versatile talent, Bryan Forbes, and most of his other novels have been filmed or made into TV mini-series. • *The Fly* 1958 (sc); *Five Gates to Hell* 1959 (d,p,sc); *Watusi* 1959 (sc); *Walk Like a Dragon* 1960 (d,p,sc); *The Sweet and the Bitter* 1962 (d,p,sc); *The Great Escape* 1963 (sc); *633 Squadron* 1964 (sc); *King Rat* 1965 (from novel); *The Satan Bug* 1965 (sc); *To Sir With Love* 1967 (d,p,sc); *Where's Jack?* 1969 (d); *The Last Valley* 1971 (d,p,sc,adapt); *Tai-Pan* 1986 (from novel).

Clayburgh, Jill • Actress • Born New York, NY, April 30, 1944. *Educ.* Sarah Lawrence College, Bronxville, NY (philosophy, drama). Sincere, comely Broadway lead and musical comedy performer (*The Rothschilds* 1970, *Pippin* 1972) who came to film prominence after the successful comedy-romance-adventure, *Silver Streak* (1976) and after winning the best actress prize at Cannes for *An Unmarried Woman* (1978). As a contemporary everywoman, Clayburgh has played vulnerable yet strong women emblematic of the sexual and social confusion of the liberated 1970s and 80s. Powerful in highly emotional drama (*I'm Dancing As Fast As I Can* 1982), she is equally warm and appealing in light romantic comedy (*Semi-Tough* 1977, *Starting Over* 1979). Married since 1979 to playwright David Rabe. • *The Wedding Party* 1969; *The Telephone Book* 1971; *Portnoy's Complaint* 1972; *The Thief Who Came to Dinner* 1973; *The Terminal Man* 1974; *Gable and Lombard* 1976; *Silver Streak* 1976; *Semi-Tough* 1977; *An Unmarried Woman* 1978 **(AANBA)**; *La Luna/Luna* 1979; *Starting Over* 1979 **(AANBA)**; *It's My Turn* 1980; *First Monday in October* 1981; *I'm Dancing As Fast As I Can* 1982; *Hannah K* 1983; *In Our Hands* 1984; *Where Are the Children?* 1986; *Shy People* 1987; *Beyond the Ocean* 1990.

Clayton, Jack • Director; also producer. • Born Brighton, Sussex, England, March 1, 1921. Solid, professional craftsman who from 1935 worked his way up from third assistant director to editor with Alexander Korda's London Films before directing the medium-length film, *The Bespoke Overcoat* (1955), which won a short-subject Oscar and a prize at the Venice Film Festival. Clayton then served as producer on several routine pictures before directing his first feature, the powerful, class-conscious drama, *Room at the Top* (1959), which inaugurated a new kind of kitchen-sink realism and frank sensuality in the British cinema.

Working once again in black and white with cinematographer Freddie Francis, Clayton followed with *The Innocents* (1961), the chilling, atmospheric retelling of Henry James's classic ghost story "The Turn of the Screw," which perfectly exemplified the recurring theme in the majority of his films—*Room*, *The Great Gatsby* (1974), *Something Wicked This Way Comes* (1983)—the clash of innocence and corruption often involving a child's loss of innocence and the power of the supernatural.

After a four-year absence from film, Clayton returned in 1987 to direct the critically acclaimed, heartbreakingly bleak, *The Lonely Passion of Judith Hearne*, once again demonstrating his skill with actors, eliciting sensitive performances from Maggie Smith and Bob Hoskins. • *An Ideal Husband* 1947 (prod.man); *The Queen of Spades* 1948 (assoc.p); *Flesh and Blood* 1951 (assoc.p); *Moulin Rouge* 1952 (assoc.p); *Beat the Devil* 1953 (assoc.p); *The Good Die Young* 1954 (assoc.p); *The Bespoke Overcoat (short)* 1955 (d,p); *I Am a Camera* 1955 (assoc.p); *Dry Rot* 1956 (p); *Sailor Beware!* 1956 (p); *Three Men in a Boat* 1956 (p); *The Story of Esther Costello* 1957 (p); *Room at the Top* 1959 (d) **(AANBD)**; *The Whole Truth* 1958 (p); *The Innocents* 1961 (d,p); *The Pumpkin Eater* 1964 (d); *Our Mother's House* 1967 (d,p); *The Great Gatsby* 1974 (d); *Something Wicked This Way Comes* 1983 (d); *The Lonely Passion of Judith Hearne* 1987 (d).

Cleese, John • Actor, screenwriter; also producer. • Born John Marwood Cleese, Weston-Super-Mare, England, October 27, 1939. *Educ.* Downing College, Cambridge (law). Tall and jut-jawed, Cleese began his comedy career with the "Cambridge Circus," and met both Connie Booth (whom he would later marry) and Terry Gilliam (a future co-member of "Monty Python's Flying Circus") while on tour with the student revue group in the US. On returning to England, Cleese landed a job writing for TV's "The Frost Report" before becoming a member of the Monty Python team. Possibly the best-known of the Pythons, he also enjoyed considerable success with the TV series "Fawlty Towers," co-written by Booth. Cleese is also founder of Video Arts Ltd., a company specializing in witty training films. • *The Bliss of Mrs. Blossom* 1968 (a); *The Magic Christian* 1970 (a,add.material); *The Rise and Rise of Michael Rimmer* 1970 (a,sc); *The Statue* 1970 (a); *And Now For Something Completely Different* 1971 (a,sc,idea); *Monty Python and the Holy Grail* 1975 (a,sc); *Pleasure at Her Majesty's* 1976 (a); *Monty Python's Life of Brian* 1979 (a,sc); *The Secret Policeman's Ball* 1979 (a,stage d,sc); *The Great Muppet Caper* 1981 (a); *The Secret Policeman's Other Ball* 1981 (a,stage show ad); *Time Bandits* 1981 (a); *Monty Python Live at the Hollywood Bowl* 1982 (a,sc); *Privates on Parade* 1982 (a); *Monty Python's The Meaning of Life* 1983 (a,sc,song); *Yellowbeard* 1983 (a); *Silverado* 1985 (a); *Clockwise* 1986 (a); *The Secret Policeman's Third Ball* 1987 (a); *A Fish Called Wanda* 1988 (a,exec.p,sc,story) **(AANBSC)**; *The Big Picture* 1989 (a); *Erik the Viking* 1989 (a); *Bullseye!* 1990 (a).

Clément, Aurore • French actress • Made a remarkable screen debut as the young Jewish woman in Louis Malle's solemn, atmospheric *Lacombe, Lucien* (1973), and has steadily continued turning in impressive performances. Clement has appeared in three Chantal Akerman films, notably as the title character of *Les Rendez-Vous d'Anna* (1978). Married to production designer Dean Tavoularis. • *Lacombe, Lucien* 1973 (a); *Caro Michele* 1976 (a); *Le Crabe-Tambour* 1977 (a); *Le Juge Fayard dit le "sheriff"* 1977 (a); *Les Rendez-Vous d'Anna* 1978 (a); *Travels With Anita* 1978 (a); *Buone Notizie* 1979 (a); *Caro Papa* 1979 (a); *5% de Risque* 1980 (a); *Soweit das Auge reicht* 1980 (a); *L'Amour des Femmes* 1981 (a); *Les Fantômes du Chapelier* 1982 (a); *Toute une nuit/All Night Long* 1982 (a); *Les Années 80* 1983 (a); *El Sur* 1983 (a); *Paris, Texas* 1984 (a); *Festa di Laurea* 1985 (a); *Je vous salue, Marie/Hail Mary* 1985 (a—*The Book of Mary*); *El Suizo—Un Amour En Espagne* 1985 (a); *Mosca Addio* 1987 (a); *Der Einbruch* 1988 (uncred.); *Gemini: The Twin Stars* 1988 (a); *Comédie d'amour* 1989 (a); *Stan the Flasher* 1990 (a).

Clément, René • Director; also screenwriter. • Born Bordeaux, France, March 18, 1913. *Educ.* Ecole des Beaux Arts, Paris (architecture). Versatile, gifted director whose early documentary experience was effectively employed for the making of *Battle of the Rails* (1945), a painstaking chronicle of the French Resistance movement. Clement also made the superior thriller *Les Maudits* (1947), but his greatest effort was the touching, yet unsentimental *Forbidden Games* (1952), about a child adrift in war-torn France. Since the mid-1960s his work has lacked the spark of earlier years. • *Soigne ton Gauche (short)* 1936 (d,sc); *L'Arabie interdite (short)* 1937 (d,sc,ph); *La Grande Chartreuse (short)* 1938 (d,sc,ph); *La Bièvre (short)* 1939 (d,sc,ph); *La Triage (short)* 1940 (d,sc,ph); *Ceux du Rail (short)* 1942 (d,sc,ph); *La Grande Pastorale (short)*

1943 (d,sc,ph); *Chefs de Demain (short)* 1944 (d,sc,ph); *La Belle et la Bête* 1945 (technical assistant); *La Bataille du Rail/Battle of the Rails* 1945 (d,sc); *Le Père Tranquille* 1946 (d); *Les Maudits* 1947 (d,sc,adapt); *La Mura di Malapaga/The Walls of Malapaga* 1949 (d); *Le Château de Verre* 1950 (d,sc); *Jeux interdits/Forbidden Games* 1952 (d,sc); *Monsieur Ripois* 1954 (d,sc); *Gervaise* 1955 (d); *Barrage contre le Pacifique* 1957 (d,sc); *Plein soleil/Purple Noon* 1959 (d,sc); *Quelle Joie de vivre* 1961 (d,sc); *Jour et l'heure* 1963 (d,sc); *Les Félins* 1964 (d); *Paris brûle-t-il?/Is Paris Burning?* 1966 (d); *Le Passager de la Pluie/Rider on the Rain* 1970 (d); *La Maison Sous les Arbres* 1971 (d,sc); *La Course du lièvre à travers les champs* 1972 (d); *Baby Sitter—Un maledetto pasticcio* 1975 (d,sc).

Clémenti, Pierre • Actor • Born Paris, 1942. Stage-trained European leading man of the 1970s with dark, striking, androgynous features who entered films in 1960. Clémenti came to attention with Luis Buñuel's *Belle de Jour* (1967) and appeared in a host of international films by such bold filmmakers as Liliana Cavani (*I Cannibali/The Cannibals* 1970), Bernardo Bertolucci (*The Conformist* 1970) and Philippe Garrel (*La Cicatrice Intérieure/Inner Scar* 1972). Clementi was arrested on a drug charge in 1972, served 17 months in prison before the charge was dropped for insuffient evidence and then wrote a book about his experiences. • *Il Gattopardo/The Leopard* 1963 (a); *Belle de Jour* 1967 (a); *Un Homme de trop/Shock Troops* 1967 (a); *Benjamin, ou les memoires d'un puceau* 1968 (a); *Partner* 1968 (a); *Scusi, Facciamo l'amore?* 1968 (a); *Porcile/Pigpen* 1969 (a); *La Voie Lactée/The Milky Way* 1969 (a); *Antenna* 1970 (a); *I Cannibali/The Cannibals* 1970 (a); *Il Conformista/The Cannibals* 1970 (a); *Nini Tirabuscle* 1970 (a); *La Pacifista* 1971 (a); *La Cicatrice Intérieure/The Inner Scar* 1972 (a); *Crush Proof* 1972 (a); *L'Ironie du Sort* 1974 (a); *Steppenwolf* 1974 (a); *Sweet Movie* 1974 (a); *Le Fils d'Amr est Mort* 1975 (a); *L'Affiche Rouge* 1976 (a); *Les Apprentis Sorciers* 1977 (a); *Le Manque* 1977 (a); *La Chanson de Roland* 1978 (a); *Zoo-Zero* 1978 (a); *Cauchemars* 1980 (a); *L'Amour des Femmes* 1981 (a); *Le Pont du Nord* 1981 (a); *Quartet* 1981 (a); *Exposed* 1983 (a); *Canicule* 1984 (a); *Clash* 1984 (a); *Le Rapt* 1984 (a); *44 ou les recits de la nuit* 1985 (a); *A l'ombre de la canaille bleue* 1986 (a,d,p,sc,ph,ed); *L'Austrichienne* 1989 (a); *Hard to Be a God* 1989 (a).

Clifford, Graeme • Australian director; also editor. • *Educ.* Sydney University (medicine). After working as an editor for the BBC and CBC-TV, joined Robert Altman in Canada as assistant editor and second assistant director on *That Cold Day in the Park* (1969) and continued as casting director and assistant director on Altman's *McCabe and Mrs. Miller* (1971) and editor of *Images* (1972). Clifford then edited Nicolas Roeg's eerie psychological thriller *Don't Look Now* (1973), and *The Man Who Fell to Earth* (1976) and cut the cult classic *The Rocky Horror Picture Show* (1975) before making his directorial debut with *Frances* (1982), a biopic of atress-rebel Frances Farmer. • *McCabe & Mrs. Miller* 1971 (casting); *Images* 1972 (ed); *Don't Look Now* 1973 (ed); *The Rocky Horror Picture Show* 1975 (ed); *The Man Who Fell to Earth* 1976 (ed); *Convoy* 1978 (ed); *F.I.S.T.* 1978 (ed); *The Postman Always Rings Twice* 1981 (ed); *Frances* 1982 (d); *Burke & Wills* 1985 (d,p,sc); *Gleaming the Cube* 1988 (d).

Clift, Montgomery • Actor • Born Edward Montgomery Clift, Omaha, NB, October 17, 1920; died July 23, 1966, New York, NY. Moody, boyishly handsome and elegantly charming (on and off screen) romantic lead. Along with Marlon Brando, Clift was the first of America's new breed of brooding, nonconformist young stars of the late 1940s and 50s whose naturalistic acting style and independence from Hollywood studio-stardom shaped the next crop of actors including James Dean. Clift began acting at the age of 12, first in amateur and stock productions and by 14 was a promising young Broadway talent, appearing in 13 productions during the 1940s including *There Shall Be No Night* opposite Alfred Lunt and Lynn Fontanne, *The Skin of Our Teeth* with Tallulah Bankhead, the 1944 revival of *Our Town* and Tennessee Williams's *You Touched Me* (1945).

Courted by Hollywood because of his growing theatrical reputation and matinee-idol good looks, he shot his first film, Howard Hawks's western, *Red River* opposite John Wayne in 1946. Due to a law suit by Howard Hughes which delayed release, however, his debut film became Fred Zinnemann's *The Search* (1948).

With his expressive, pale grey eyes (in an otherwise deadpan but classically beautiful face) and his air of vulnerability and sexual ambivalence, Clift excelled at playing sensitive loners and idealists and gave his characters a jittery, contemporary psychological edge rarely seen in Hollywood. He embarked on an impressive career of 17 films and four Academy Award nominations over the next 18 years before his death.

In 1948 he signed a unique three-film contract with Paramount that gave him script approval, promised he would only work in films directed by Billy Wilder, George Stevens or Norman Krasna, and gave him freedom to work at another studio. He followed with strong, Oscar-nominated performances in Stevens's *A Place in the Sun* (1951) and Fred Zinnemann's *From Here to Eternity* (1953).

During the filming of *Raintree County* (1957), Clift was involved in a near-fatal car accident which disfigured his almost too beautiful face, leaving it half-paralyzed and him in almost continual pain and dependent on drugs. Although he made several strong films, including his fourth Oscar-nominated role in Stanley Kramer's *Judgment at Nuremberg* (1961; a 7-minute performance for which he took no salary), his life and career never recovered: His concentration as an actor was gone, his features thickened and his drinking became a problem on the set. Cast in "Reflections in a Golden Eye," once again opposite his long-time friend, Elizabeth Taylor, Clift died of a heart attack at 45 before the film began shooting. • *Red River* 1948 (a); *The Search* 1948 (a) **(AANBA)**; *The Heiress* 1949 (a); *The Big Lift* 1950 (a); *A Place in the Sun* 1951 (a) **(AANBA)**; *From Here to Eternity* 1953 (a) **(AANBA)**; *I Confess* 1953 (a); *Indiscretion of an American Wife* 1953 (a); *Raintree County* 1957 (a); *Lonelyhearts* 1958 (a); *The Young Lions* 1958 (a); *Suddenly, Last Summer* 1959 (a); *Wild River* 1960 (a); *Judgment at Nuremberg* 1961 (a) **(AANBSA)**; *The Misfits* 1961 (a); *Freud* 1962 (a); *The Defector* 1966 (a); *George Stevens: A Filmmaker's Journey* 1985 (archival footage).

Cline, Eddie • *aka* Edward Cline • Director, screenwriter; also actor. • Born Edward F. Cline, Kenosha WS, November 7, 1892; died 1961. In films from 1913 as a Keystone Cop, and from 1916 as a director of several Mack Sennett "bathing beauties" shorts. In 1920 Cline co-directed *One Week* with Buster Keaton, and went on to work on several of Keaton's early gems, including *Cops* (1922) and *The Three Ages* (1923). Though Cline made numerous comedies over the next two decades, only his collaborations with W.C. Fields stand out. • *His Busted Trust (short)* 1916 (d,sc); *Sunshine (short)* 1916 (d,sc); *The Winning Punch (short)* 1916 (d,sc); *A Bedroom Blunder (short)* 1917 (d,sc); *Dog Catcher's Love (short)* 1917 (d,sc); *The Pawnbroker's Heart (short)* 1917 (d,sc); *That Night (short)* 1917 (d,sc); *Hide and Seek Detectives (short)* 1918 (d,sc); *His Smothered Love (short)* 1918 (d,sc); *The Kitchen Lady (short)* 1918 (d,sc); *The Summer Girls (short)* 1918 (d,sc); *Those Athletic Girls (short)* 1918 (d,sc); *Whose Little Wife Are You? (short)* 1918 (d,sc); *Cupid's Day Off (short)* 1919 (d,sc); *East Lynne With Variations (short)* 1919 (d,sc); *Hearts and Flowers (short)* 1919 (d,sc); *When Love Is Blind (short)* 1919 (d,sc); *Convict 13 (short)* 1920 (d,sc); *Neighbors (short)* 1920 (d,sc); *One Week (short)* 1920 (d,sc); *The Scarecrow (short)* 1920 (d,sc); *The Boat (short)* 1921 (d,sc); *Hard Luck (short)* 1921 (d,sc); *The Haunted House (short)* 1921 (d,sc); *The High Sign (short)* 1921 (d,sc); *The Pale-*

face (short) 1921 (d,sc); *The Playhouse (short)* 1921 (d,sc); *Cops (short)* 1922 (d); *Day Dreams (short)* 1922 (d,sc); *The Electric House (short)* 1922 (d,sc); *The Frozen North (short)* 1922 (d,sc); *My Wife's Relations (short)* 1922 (d,sc); *The Balloonatic (short)* 1923 (d,sc); *Circus Days* 1923 (d,sc); *The Love Nest (short)* 1923 (d,sc); *The Meanest Man in the World* 1923 (d); *The Three Ages* 1923 (d,sc); *Along Came Ruth* 1924 (d); *Captain January* 1924 (d); *The Good Bad Boy* 1924 (d); *Little Robinson Crusoe* 1924 (d); *The Plumber* 1924 (d); *When a Man's a Man* 1924 (d); *Bashful Jim* 1925 (d); *Cold Turkey* 1925 (d); *Dangerous Curves Behind* 1925 (d); *Love and Kisses* 1925 (d); *Old Clothes* 1925 (d); *The Rag Man* 1925 (d); *Tee For Two* 1925 (d); *A Blonde's Revenge* 1926 (d); *Flirty Four-Flushers* 1926 (d); *The Ghost of Folly* 1926 (d); *Gooseland* 1926 (d); *The Gosh-Darn Mortgage* 1926 (d); *A Harem Knight* 1926 (d); *A Love Sundae* 1926 (d); *Puppy Lovetime* 1926 (d); *Smith's Baby* 1926 (d); *Spanking Breezes* 1926 (d); *When a Man's a Prince* 1926 (d); *The Bullfighters* 1927 (d); *The Girl From Everywhere* 1927 (d); *The Jolly Jilter* 1927 (d); *Let It Rain* 1927 (d); *Soft Cushions* 1927 (d); *The Crash* 1928 (d); *The Head Man* 1928 (d); *Hold That Pose* 1928 (d); *Ladies' Night in a Turkish Bath* 1928 (d); *Love at Fist Sight* 1928 (d); *Man Crazy* 1928 (d); *Vamping Venus* 1928 (d); *Broadway Fever* 1929 (d); *The Forward Pass* 1929 (d); *His Lucky Day* 1929 (d); *Hook, Line and Sinker* 1930 (d); *In the Next Room* 1930 (d); *Leathernecking* 1930 (d); *Sweet Mama* 1930 (d); *The Widow From Chicago* 1930 (d); *Cracked Nuts* 1931 (d); *The Girl Habit* 1931 (d); *Mlle. Irene the Great (short)* 1931 (d); *The Naughty Flirt* 1931 (d); *His Week-End (short)* 1932 (d); *Million Dollar Legs* 1932 (d); *Parole Girl* 1933 (d); *So This Is Africa* 1933 (d); *The Dude Ranger* 1934 (d); *Fighting to Live* 1934 (d); *Peck's Bad Boy* 1934 (d); *The Cowboy Millionaire* 1935 (d); *When a Man's a Man* 1935 (d); *F-Man* 1936 (d); *It's a Great Life* 1936 (d); *Forty Naughty Girls* 1937 (d); *High Flyers* 1937 (d); *On Again - Off Again* 1937 (d); *Breaking the Ice* 1938 (d); *Go Chase Yourself* 1938 (d); *Hawaii Calls* 1938 (d); *Peck's Bad Boy With the Circus* 1938 (d); *The Bank Dick* 1940 (d); *My Little Chickadee* 1940 (d); *The Villain Still Pursued Her* 1940 (d); *Cracked Nuts* 1941 (d); *Hello, Sucker* 1941 (d); *Meet the Chump* 1941 (d); *Never Give a Sucker an Even Break* 1941 (d); *Behind the Eight Ball* 1942 (d); *Give Out, Sisters* 1942 (d); *Private Buckaroo* 1942 (d); *Snuffy Smith, Yard Bird* 1942 (d); *What's Cooking?* 1942 (d); *Crazy House* 1943 (d); *He's My Guy* 1943 (d); *Ghost Catchers* 1944 (d); *Hat Check Honey* 1944 (d); *Moonlight and Cactus* 1944 (d); *Night Club Girl* 1944 (d); *Slightly Terrific* 1944 (d); *Swingtime Johnny* 1944 (d); *Penthouse Rhythm* 1945 (d); *See My Lawyer* 1945 (d); *Bringing Up Father* 1946 (d,story); *Jiggs and Maggie in Court* 1948 (d,sc); *Jiggs and Maggie in Society* 1948 (d,sc); *Jiggs and Maggie in Jackpot Jitters* 1949 (sc); *Jiggs and Maggie Out West* 1950 (story); *The Story of Will Rogers* 1952 (a).

Clive, Colin • Actor • Born Clive Greig, St. Malo, France, January 20, 1898; died 1937. In films and the US from 1930; best known for his portrayals of Frankenstein. • *Journey's End* 1930; *Frankenstein* 1931; *The Stronger Sex* 1931; *Lily Christine* 1932; *Christopher Strong* 1933; *Looking Forward* 1933; *Jane Eyre* 1934; *The Key* 1934; *One More River* 1934; *Bride of Frankenstein* 1935; *Clive of India* 1935; *The Girl From 10th Avenue* 1935; *Mad Love* 1935; *The Man Who Broke the Bank at Monte Carlo* 1935; *The Right to Live* 1935; *The Widow From Monte Carlo* 1936; *History Is Made at Night* 1937; *The Woman I Love* 1937.

Cloquet, Ghislain • Director of photography • Born Ghislain Pierre Cloquet, Antwerp, Belgium, 1924; died 1982. *Educ.* Ecole Nationale de Photographie et Cinématographie, Paris; IDHEC, Paris. After shooting several of Alain Resnais's 1950s documentaries, established himself in the 60s as one of the world's top cinematographers of both black-and-white (e.g. Arthur Penn's *Mickey One* 1965) and color (e.g. Jacques Demy's *The Young Girls of Rochefort* 1967). • *Les Statues Meurent Aussi* (short) 1953 (ph); *Nuit et Brouillard/Night and Fog* 1955 (ph); *Toute la Mémoire du Monde* (short) 1956 (ph); *Le Mystère de l'atelier Quinze* (short) 1957 (ph); *Classe tous risques* 1960 (ph); *La Belle Américaine* 1961 (ph); *Vive le Tour!* (short) 1962 (ph); *Le Feu Follet/The Fire Within* 1963 (ph); *Mickey One* 1965 (ph); *Au Hasard, Balthazar* 1966 (ph); *L'Homme au Crane rasé/The Man Who Had His Hair Cut Short* 1966 (ph); *Mouchette* 1966 (ph); *Loin du Viêtnam/Far From Vietnam* 1967 (collaboration); *Benjamin, ou les mémoires d'un puceau* 1968 (ph); *Mazel Tov ou le Mariage* 1968 (ph); *Une Femme douce* 1969 (ph); *Peau d'âne/Donkey Skin* 1970 (ph); *Faustine et le bel été* 1971 (ph); *Pouce* 1971 (ph); *Quatre nuits d'un rêveur/Four Nights of a Dreamer* 1971 (add.footage); *Rendez-Vous à Bray* 1971 (ph); *Au Rendez-Vous de la mort joyeuse* 1972 (ph); *Nathalie Granger* 1972 (ph); *Belle* 1973 (ph); *L'Histoire très bonne et très joyeuse de Colinot Trousse chemise* 1973 (ph); *La Boucher, la Star et l'Orphéline* 1974 (ph); *Dites-Le avec des fleurs* 1974 (ph); *Love and Death* 1975 (ph); *Monsieur Albert* 1975 (ph); *The Secret Life of Plants* 1978 (ph); *Tess* 1979 (ph) **(AABPH)**; *Chère Inconnue/I Sent a Letter to My Love* 1980 (ph); *Four Friends* 1981 (ph); *Sans Soleil/Sunless* 1982 (a).

Close, Glenn • Actress • Born Greenwich, CT, March 19, 1947. *Educ.* College of William and Mary, Williamsburg, VA (anthropology, acting). Critically acclaimed, cooly aristocratic blonde lead who began her stage career in 1974 with New York's Phoenix Theatre Company and her film career when director George Roy Hill spotted her in the Broadway musical, *Barnum* and signed her for *The World According to Garp* (1982). Close has since established herself as a major Hollywood presence with a succession of strong performances: as Kevin Kline's warmly wise doctor-wife in *The Big Chill* (1983), as the romantically entangled lawyer in the thriller, *Jagged Edge* (1985) and as the revengeful, rejected lover in Adrian Lyne's disturbingly misogynistic *Fatal Attraction* (1987). She displayed her immense versatility as another monster of sexual manipulation in *Dangerous Liaisons* (1988) and brought a surprising sympathy to the role of pathetic, frivolous society woman, Sunny von Bulow in *Reversal of Fortune* (1990).

As well as her five Oscar nominations, Close has received a Tony Award for Tom Stoppard's *The Real Thing* (1984) and an Emmy nomination for the 1984 TV movie *Something About Amelia*. • *The World According to Garp* 1982 **(AANBSA)**; *The Big Chill* 1983 **(AANBSA)**; *The Stone Boy* 1983; *Greystoke: The Legend of Tarzan, Lord of the Apes* 1984; *The Natural* 1984 **(AANBSA)**; *Jagged Edge* 1985; *Maxie* 1985; *Fatal Attraction* 1987 **(AANBA)**; *Dangerous Liaisons* 1988 **(AANBA)**; *Light Years* 1988; *Immediate Family* 1989; *Hamlet* 1990; *Reversal of Fortune* 1990.

Clothier, William H. • *aka* William Clothier • Director of photography • Born Decatur, IL, 1903. Noted cinematographer, especially of westerns. • *Sofia* 1948 (ph); *Once a Thief* 1950 (ph); *Confidence Girl* 1952 (ph); *Phantom From Space* 1953 (ph); *The High and the Mighty* 1954 (aerial ph); *Killers From Space* 1954 (ph); *Track of the Cat* 1954 (ph); *Gang-Busters* 1955 (p,ph); *The Sea Chase* 1955 (ph); *Sincerely Yours* 1955 (ph); *Good-Bye, My Lady* 1956 (ph); *Gun the Man Down* 1956 (ph); *Man in the Vault* 1956 (ph); *Seven Men From Now* 1956 (ph); *Dragoon Wells Massacre* 1957 (ph); *China Doll* 1958 (ph); *Darby's Rangers* 1958 (ph); *Fort Dobbs* 1958 (ph); *Lafayette Escadrille* 1958 (ph); *Escort West* 1959 (ph); *The Horse Soldiers* 1959 (ph); *The Alamo* 1960 (ph) **(AANBPH)**; *The Comancheros* 1961 (ph); *The Deadly Companions* 1961 (ph); *Ring of Fire* 1961 (ph); *Tomboy and the Champ* 1961 (ph); *The Man Who Shot Liberty Valance* 1962 (ph); *Merrill's Marauders* 1962 (ph); *Donovan's Reef* 1963 (ph); *McLintock!* 1963 (ph); *Cheyenne Autumn* 1964 (ph) **(AANBPH)**; *A Distant Trumpet* 1964 (ph); *Shenandoah*

1965 (ph); *The Rare Breed* 1966 (ph); *Stagecoach* 1966 (ph); *Way...Way Out* 1966 (ph); *The War Wagon* 1967 (ph); *The Way West* 1967 (ph); *Bandolero!* 1968 (ph); *The Devil's Brigade* 1968 (ph); *Firecreek* 1968 (ph); *The Undefeated* 1969 (ph); *The Cheyenne Social Club* 1970 (ph); *Chisum* 1970 (ph); *Rio Lobo* 1970 (ph); *Big Jake* 1971 (ph); *The Train Robbers* 1973 (ph).

Clouzot, Henri-Georges • Director, screenwriter • Born Niort, France, November 20, 1907; died January 12, 1977. Plagued by ill health for most of his life, Clouzot broke into films as a writer and assistant director in the early 1930s. He made his first feature, *L'Assassin habité au 21* in 1941, but it was his second film, *The Raven* (1943), that gained him both fame and notoriety. A mature suspense picture concerning the effects of a rash of poison-pen letters on a provincial town, it introduced a new talent. Its bleak view of French country life, however, combined with the fact that it was financed by a German company, led to Clouzot's being briefly banned from filmmaking after the war.

He resumed his career in 1947 earning the reputation as the French master of suspense (or the French Hitchcock) with a number of adroitly handled thrillers including the brilliant, suspenseful and pessimistic character study, *The Wages of Fear* (1953) and the equally bleak and shocking *Diabolique* (1955), both starring his wife Vera Clouzot (born Amado, 1921). Clouzot also made the invaluable and highly entertaining document of the painter at work, *The Mystery of Picasso* (1956). • *La Terreur de Batignolles (short)* 1931 (d,sc); *Ein Lied für dich* 1933 (d); *L'Assassin habité au 21* 1941 (d,sc); *Le Corbeau/The Raven* 1943 (d,sc); *Quai des Orfèvres* 1947 (d,sc); *Manon* 1949 (d,sc); *Retour à la vie* 1949 (d,sc—*La Retour de Jean*); *Miquette et sa Mère* 1950 (d,sc); *The 13th Letter* 1951 (from story "Le Corbeau"); *Le Salaire de la Peur/The Wages of Fear* 1953 (d,p); *Les Diabolique/Diabolique* 1955 (d,p,sc,dial); *Le Mystère Picasso/The Mystery of Picasso* 1956 (d,p,sc); *Si Tous les Gars du Monde...* 1956 (adapt,dial); *Les Espions* 1957 (d,sc); *La Vérité/The Truth* 1960 (d,sc); *L'Enfer* 1964 (d,sc); *La Prisonnière* 1968 (d,sc).

Cluzet, Francois • French actor • Amiable young lead, best known as the overly supportive, puppy-dog-like jazz fan in Bertrand Tavernier's *'Round Midnight* (1986) and the betrayed husband in Bertrand Blier's *Trop belle pour toi/Too Beautiful for You* (1989). Cluzet has also appeared in three Claude Chabrol films: *Le Cheval d'orgueil/The Horse of Pride* (1979), *Les Fantômes du Chapelier/The Hatter's Ghosts* (1981) and *Story of Women* (1988). • *Le Cheval d'orgueil/The Horse of Pride* 1979; *Cocktail Molotov* 1979; *L'Eté meurtrier/One Deadly Summer* 1982; *Les Fantômes du Chapelier/The Hatter's Ghosts* 1982; *Coup de Foudre/Entre Nous* 1983; *Vive la Sociale!* 1983; *Les Enragés* 1984; *Elsa, Elsa!* 1985; *Association de Malfaiteurs* 1986; *Autour de Minuit/'Round Midnight* 1986; *Etats d'âme* 1986; *Rue du départ* 1986; *Jaune revolver* 1987; *Une Affaire de femmes/Story of Women* 1988; *Chocolat* 1988; *Deux* 1988; *Un Tour de manège* 1988; *Force Majeure* 1989; *La Révolution Française* 1989; *Trop belle pour toi/Too Beautiful For You* 1989.

Coates, Anne V. • Editor • Born Reigate, Surrey, England, 1925. *Educ.* Bartrum Gables College. Talented, prolific editor of the 1960s, 70s and 80s. Coates won an Oscar for her work on David Lean's 1962 classic *Lawrence of Arabia* and also acted as a consultant on the restoration of the film in 1990. Son Anthony Hickox is a director. • *The Pickwick Papers* 1952; *The Horse's Mouth* 1958; *The Truth About Women* 1958; *Tunes of Glory* 1960; *Don't Bother to Knock* 1961; *Lawrence of Arabia* 1962 **(AABED)**; *Becket* 1964 **(AANBED)**; *Those Magnificent Men in Their Flying Machines* 1965; *Young Cassidy* 1965; *The Bofors Gun* 1968; *Great Catherine* 1968; *The Adventurers* 1970; *Friends* 1971; *Follow Me!* 1972; *The Nelson Affair* 1973; *11 Harrowhouse* 1974; *Murder on the Orient Express* 1974; *Man Friday* 1975; *Aces High* 1976; *The Eagle Has Landed* 1976; *The Medusa Touch* 1978 (ed,p); *The Legacy* 1979; *The Elephant Man* 1980 **(AANBED)**; *The Bushido Blade* 1981 (ed cons); *Ragtime* 1981; *The Pirates of Penzance* 1982; *Greystoke: The Legend of Tarzan, Lord of the Apes* 1984; *Lady Jane* 1986; *Raw Deal* 1986; *Masters of the Universe* 1987; *Farewell to the King* 1989; *Listen to Me* 1989; *I Love You to Death* 1990; *Isabelle Eberhardt* 1991; *What About Bob?* 1991.

Cobb, Lee J. • Actor • Born Leo Jacob, New York, NY, December 8, 1911; died 1976. *Educ.* CCNY (accounting). Powerhouse actor of both stage and screen. Cobb joined the Group Theater in 1935, appearing in Clifford Odets's *Waiting for Lefty* and *Golden Boy* before making his screen debut in 1937. He often played boorish characters or heavies, most memorably as the corrupt boss in *On The Waterfront* (1954) and the intransigent bigot in *Twelve Angry Men* (1957). • *Ali Baba Goes to Town* 1937; *North of the Rio Grande* 1937; *Rustlers' Valley* 1937; *Danger on the Air* 1938; *Golden Boy* 1939; *The Phantom Creeps* 1939; *Men of Boys Town* 1941; *This Thing Called Love* 1941; *Paris Calling* 1942; *Buckskin Frontier* 1943; *The Moon Is Down* 1943; *The Song of Bernadette* 1943; *Tonight We Raid Calais* 1943; *Winged Victory* 1944; *Anna and the King of Siam* 1946; *Boomerang* 1947; *Captain From Castile* 1947; *Johnny O'Clock* 1947; *Call Northside 777* 1948; *The Dark Past* 1948; *The Luck of the Irish* 1948; *The Miracle of the Bells* 1948; *Thieves' Highway* 1949; *The Man Who Cheated Himself* 1950; *The Family Secret* 1951; *Sirocco* 1951; *The Fighter* 1952; *The Tall Texan* 1953; *Day of Triumph* 1954; *Gorilla at Large* 1954; *On the Waterfront* 1954 **(AANBSA)**; *Yankee Pasha* 1954; *The Left Hand of God* 1955; *The Man in the Gray Flannel Suit* 1955; *The Racers* 1955; *The Road to Denver* 1955; *Miami Expose* 1956; *The Garment Jungle* 1957; *The Three Faces of Eve* 1957; *Twelve Angry Men* 1957; *The Brothers Karamazov* 1958 **(AANBSA)**; *Man of the West* 1958; *Party Girl* 1958; *But Not For Me* 1959; *Green Mansions* 1959; *The Trap* 1959; *Exodus* 1960; *The Four Horsemen of the Apocalypse* 1962; *How the West Was Won* 1962; *Come Blow Your Horn* 1963; *Our Man Flint* 1966; *In Like Flint* 1967; *Coogan's Bluff* 1968; *Il Giorno della Civetta* 1968; *Las Vegas 500 Milliones* 1968; *MacKenna's Gold* 1969; *The Liberation of L.B. Jones* 1970; *Macho Callahan* 1970; *Lawman* 1971; *The Exorcist* 1973; *The Man Who Loved Cat Dancing* 1973; *Blood Sweat and Fear* 1975; *The Nark* 1975; *That Lucky Touch* 1975; *Ultimatum* 1975; *La Legge violenta della squadra anticrimine* 1976; *Arthur Miller on Home Ground* 1979.

Coburn, Charles • Actor • Born Savannah, GA, June 19, 1877; died 1961. A stage star before entering films in his sixties with the title roll in *Boss Tweed* (1933). Coburn subsequently became one of Hollywood's most beloved character actors. • *Boss Tweed* 1933; *Lord Jeff* 1938; *Of Human Hearts* 1938; *Vivacious Lady* 1938; *Yellow Jack* 1938; *Bachelor Mother* 1939; *Idiot's Delight* 1939; *In Name Only* 1939; *Made For Each Other* 1939; *Stanley and Livingstone* 1939; *The Story of Alexander Graham Bell* 1939; *The Captain Is a Lady* 1940; *Edison, the Man* 1940; *Florian* 1940; *Road to Singapore* 1940; *Three Faces West* 1940; *The Devil and Miss Jones* 1941 **(AANBSA)**; *H. M. Pulham, Esq.* 1941; *King's Row* 1941; *The Lady Eve* 1941; *Our Wife* 1941; *Unexpected Uncle* 1941; *George Washington Slept Here* 1942; *In This Our Life* 1942; *The Constant Nymph* 1943; *Heaven Can Wait* 1943; *The More the Merrier* 1943 **(AABSA)**; *My Kingdom For a Cook* 1943; *Princess O'Rourke* 1943; *The Impatient Years* 1944; *Knickerbocker Holiday* 1944; *Together Again* 1944; *Wilson* 1944; *Colonel Effingham's Raid* 1945; *Over 21* 1945; *Rhapsody in Blue* 1945; *A Royal Scandal* 1945; *Shady Lady* 1945; *The Green Years* 1946 **(AANBSA)**; *B.F.'s Daughter* 1947; *Lured* 1947; *The Paradine Case* 1947; *Green Grass of Wyoming* 1948; *The Doctor and the Girl* 1949; *Everybody Does It* 1949; *The Gal Who Took the West* 1949; *Impact* 1949; *Yes, Sir, That's My Baby* 1949; *Louisa* 1950; *Mr. Music* 1950; *Peggy* 1950; *The Highway-*

man 1951; *Has Anybody Seen My Gal?* 1952 (a,song); *Monkey Business* 1952; *Gentlemen Prefer Blondes* 1953; *Trouble Along the Way* 1953; *The Long Wait* 1954; *Rocket Man* 1954; *How to Be Very, Very Popular* 1955; *Around the World in 80 Days* 1956; *The Power and the Prize* 1956; *The Story of Mankind* 1957; *The Remarkable Mr. Pennypacker* 1958; *John Paul Jones* 1959; *Stranger in My Arms* 1959; *Pepe* 1960.

Coburn, James • Actor • Born Laurel, NB, August 31, 1928. *Educ.* Los Angeles City College (acting); USC, Los Angeles (drama). Capable, rough-hewn leading man whose toothy grin and lanky build made him the perfect tough-guy villain in numerous westerns and action films. Coburn came to wider prominence with the lead in the popular spy spoof *Our Man Flint* (1966) and its 1967 sequel, *In Like Flint*. He produced and starred in the comedy-thriller, *The President's Analyst* (1967). • *Face of a Fugitive* 1959; *Ride Lonesome* 1959; *The Magnificent Seven* 1960; *The Murder Men* 1961; *Hell Is For Heroes* 1962; *Charade* 1963; *The Great Escape* 1963; *The Americanization of Emily* 1964; *The Man From Galveston* 1964; *A High Wind in Jamaica* 1965; *The Loved One* 1965; *Major Dundee* 1965; *Dead Heat on a Merry-Go-Round* 1966; *Our Man Flint* 1966; *What Did You Do in the War, Daddy?* 1966; *In Like Flint* 1967; *The President's Analyst* 1967 (a,p); *Waterhole Number 3* 1967; *Candy* 1968; *Duffy* 1968; *Hard Contract* 1969; *Last of the Mobile Hot-Shots* 1969; *The Honkers* 1971; *The Carey Treatment* 1972; *Duck, You Sucker* 1972; *Harry in Your Pocket* 1973; *The Last of Sheila* 1973; *Pat Garrett and Billy the Kid* 1973; *The Internecine Project* 1974; *Una Ragione Per Morire* 1974; *Bite the Bullet* 1975; *Hard Times* 1975; *Battle of Midway* 1976; *The Last Hard Men* 1976; *Sky Riders* 1976; *Cross of Iron* 1977; *White Rock* 1977; *The Silent Flute* 1978 (story); *Firepower* 1979; *Goldengirl* 1979; *The Muppet Movie* 1979; *The Baltimore Bullet* 1980; *Loving Couples* 1980; *Mr. Patman* 1980; *High Risk* 1981; *Looker* 1981; *Martin's Day* 1983; *Screwballs* 1983; *The Leonski Incident* 1985; *The Lion's Roar* 1985; *Death of a Soldier* 1986; *Walking After Midnight* 1988; *Call From Space* 1989; *Tag till himlen* 1989; *Young Guns II* 1990; *Hudson Hawk* 1991.

Coco, James • Actor • Born New York, NY, March 21, 1929; died February 25, 1987, New York, NY. Rotund, comic supporting actor who has worked onstage and in films with Neil Simon and Elaine May. Best roles in *A New Leaf* (1971) and *Only When I Laugh* (1981). • *Ensign Pulver* 1964; *Generation* 1969; *The End of the Road* 1970; *The Strawberry Statement* 1970; *Tell Me That You Love Me, Junie Moon* 1970; *A New Leaf* 1971; *Such Good Friends* 1971; *L'Uomo della Mancha/Man of La Mancha* 1972; *The Wild Party* 1975; *Murder By Death* 1976; *Charleston* 1978; *The Cheap Detective* 1978; *Rêve de Singe* 1978; *Scavenger Hunt* 1979; *Wholly Moses!* 1980; *Only When I Laugh* 1981 **(AANBSA)**; *The Muppets Take Manhattan* 1984; *The Bradbury Trilogy* 1985; *Hunk* 1987; *The Chair* 1988; *That's Adequate* 1989.

Cocteau, Jean • Director, screenwriter; also poet, playwright, novelist. • Born Jean Maurice Eugène Clément Cocteau, Maisons-Lafitte, France, July 5, 1889; died October 11, 1963. Jean Cocteau is a preeminent figure in 20th century French culture. A major contributor to the history of the cinema, he is also noted for his work as a novelist, poet, painter, sculptor and playwright.

Cocteau wrote, directed, narrated, edited and performed in his first film, *The Blood of a Poet*, shot in 1930. Privately financed by the Vicomte de Noailles, the film's release was delayed for two years due to the scandal that surrounded another 1930 Noailles production, Dalí and Buñuel's *L'Age d'or*, which was denounced as "sacrilegious" when first screened.

Blood of a Poet was certainly influenced by the work of Dalí and Buñuel, as well as other surrealist films by Man Ray and René Clair. But in its unprecedented use of sync-sound dialogue, narration and music (by the prolific and accomplished Georges Auric), juxtaposed with free-form episodic imagery, Cocteau's debut marked a watershed in non-narrative, personal filmmaking. Bracketing the beginning and end of the work with a shot of a factory chimney collapsing (to show that the events represented actually take place in an instant of "real time"), Cocteau designed the piece as a series of disparate sections, each centering on the adventures of a young poet/artist condemned to walk the halls of the "Hotel of Dramatic Follies" for his crime of having brought a statue to life. Perhaps the most famous of the film's striking images is the sequence in which the young man, having created a drawing with a moving mouth, wipes the mouth onto his hand in an effort to erase it from the picture; whereupon the mouth takes on a life of its own, begging for air and later drinking from a bowl of water. Another memorable—and much-imitated—conceit is that of the poet passing through a mirror which turns into a pool of water.

Cocteau worked only intermittently in film for the next 15 years, one reason being his recurring addiction to opium. His return to directing in 1945, with *Beauty and the Beast*, was partly due to the efforts of his favorite actor and close associate Jean Marais, who played the Beast in the film.

Relentlessly romantic, beautifully mounted (despite the problems attendant on film production in post-war France) and flawlessly acted, *Beauty and the Beast* marked a triumphant return to the screen for Cocteau. With its linear narrative and familiar mythic structure, the film was less experimental than *Blood of a Poet*. Yet Marais's unforgettable performance, the beast's (pre-prosthetic) make-up and Cocteau's inspired visual conceits (the beast's fingers smoking after a kill, human hands used as candelabras in his castle), made the film one of the director's most memorable—and most enduringly popular—works.

Cocteau directed two films adapted from his own plays, *The Eagle with Two Heads* and *The Storm Within* (both 1948). *Eagle* is a rather ordinary palace romance which the director later claimed he had created solely to please Marais. *The Storm Within*, on the other hand, is perhaps the finest of all Cocteau's narrative films. At the center of the work is the magnetic performance of Yvonne de Bray as Marais's violently possessive, drug-addicted mother, who kills herself when her son decides to marry. Shot almost entirely in one apartment, *The Storm Within* achieves an unparalled sense of claustrophobic melancholy, highlighted by brilliant camera movement within the confines of the small, cramped flat.

In 1950 Cocteau made the film for which he is perhaps best known, *Orpheus*, again starring Marais, this time as a young poet beset by artistic and romantic rivals. When his wife dies, Orpheus descends to Hell to rescue her, only to be brought before a tribunal where his final fate is determined. Once again, Cocteau makes considerable use of liquid mirrors through which his protagonists enter and leave rooms. Attacked in some quarters as being too mannered and occasionally pretentious (a charge that followed Cocteau throughout his career), the film is on the whole a successful blend of the real and the fantastic, "a realistic document of unrealistic events," as Cocteau had termed *Blood of a Poet* many years earlier.

Over the next ten years Cocteau worked on several projects, providing dialogue and/or off-screen narration for a number of features by other directors and contributing to several short films. His one-act, one-person play *The Human Voice* was made into an excellent short film (*L'Amore*) in 1948 by Roberto Rossellini and also provided the inspiration for Pedro Almadovar's 1988 farce, *Women on the Verge of a Nervous Breakdown*. Cocteau also adapted his novel *Les Enfants Terribles* into the screenplay for Jean-Pierre Mélville's 1950 film of the same name. Like Jean Delannoy's *L'Eternel Retour* (1943), the work bears Cocteau's stamp far more than that of its nominal director.

In 1959, with private financing (part of it coming from François Truffaut), Cocteau made his last film as a director, *The Testament of Orpheus*. A rather elaborate home movie starring its director, the work features cameos from numerous celebrities including Pablo Picasso, Yul Brynner and Jean-Pierre Léaud. A nostalgic return to the legend of Orpheus in the manner and style of *The Blood of a Poet*, the film lacks the earlier work's imagination and intensity. WWD • *Jean Cocteau fait du cinéma (short)* 1925 (d,sc,ph,ed); *Le Sang d'un poète/The Blood of a Poet* (prod. 1930, rel. 1932) (a,d,sc,ed,sets); *La Comédie du bonheur* 1940 (sc,adapt,dial); *Le Baron fantôme* 1943 (a,dial); *L'Eternel Retour* 1943 (sc); *La Malibran* 1943 (a); *Tennis (short)* 1944 (a,comm); *La Belle et la bête/Beauty and the Beast* 1945 (d,sc,voice); *Les Dames du Bois de Boulogne* 1945 (dial); *L'Amitié noir (short)* 1946 (a,comm); *Ruy Blas* 1947 (sc,dial); *L'Aigle à deux têtes/The Eagle With Two Heads* 1948 (a,d,sc,from play); *L'Amore* 1948 (from play *La voix humaine*); *La Leggenda di Sant'Orsola (short)* 1948 (a,comm—French-language version); *Les Noces de Sable* 1948 (a,comm); *Les Parents Terribles/The Storm Within* 1948 (a,d,sc,from play); *Romantici a Venezia (short)* 1948 (a,comm—French-language version); *Ce siècle a cinquante ans* 1949 (sc—"1914"); *Désordre (short)* 1949 (a); *The Emperor's Nightingale* 1949 (a,comm—French-language version); *Coriolan (short)* 1950 (a,d,sc,story,ed,sets); *Les Enfants Terribles* 1950 (a,sc,dial,from novel); *Goya (short)* 1950 (a,comm—French-language version); *Orphée/Orpheus* 1950 (a,d,sc,from play); *Colette* 1951 (a); *La Corona Negra* 1952 (sc); *Intimate Relations* 1952 (from play *Les Parents terribles*); *Le Rouge est mis (short)* 1952 (a,comm); *La Villa Santo-Sospir (short)* 1952 (a,d,p,sc,story,ed,sets); *Gustave Doré* 1953 (foreword); *Le Jeune homme et la mort (short)* 1953 (from ballet); *Jigo Kumen* 1953 (foreword—French-language version); *Pantomimes (short)* 1954 (foreword); *A l'Aube du Monde (short)* 1955 (a,comm); *8 x 8* 1956 (a,sc,from story "Queening of the Pawn"); *Le Bel Indifférent (short)* 1957 (from play); *Django Reinhardt (short)* 1958 (preface); *Le Musée Grevin (short)* 1958 (a,dial); *Le Testament d'Orphée/The Testament of Orpheus* 1959 (a,d,sc,story); *La Princesse de Cléves* 1960 (adapt,dial); *Anna la Bonne (short)* 1962 (m,lyrics); *Egypte o Egypte* 1962 (a,comm—"Dans ce jardin atroce"); *Le Pauvre matelot (short)* 1962 (from play); *Thomas l'Imposteur/Thomas the Imposter* 1965 (sc,from novel); *Le Jeune homme et la mort (short)* 1967 (from ballet); *Peau d'ane* 1970 (from poem); *La Voix humaine (short)* 1970 (from play); *La Voix du large (short)* 1971 (from play *La voix humaine*); *Il Mistro di Oberwald* 1980 (from play *L'Aigle à deux tetes*); *Jeux d'artifices* 1987 (from novel *Les enfants terribles*).

Coen, Ethan • Producer; also screenwriter. • Born St. Louis Park, MN, 1958. *Educ.* Princeton (philosophy). With his director brother Joel, one of the most imaginative talents on the contemporary American scene. Each of the team's three films to date have paid homage to, and revivified, a classic cinematic genre with a knowing quality born of many hours spent in darkened screening rooms. The Coen brothers have watched a lot of movies, and it shows.

Both brothers started writing screenplays soon after graduation, with Joel also editing some low-budget features for directors including Sam Raimi (who makes a cameo appearance in 1990's *Miller's Crossing*). They have co-written all their features, beginning with *Blood Simple* (1984), a masterful tribute to the *film noir* genre starring John Getz, Frances McDormand and, in an indelible portrayal of a seedy Texan private eye, M. Emmet Walsh. From the opening shot of a rain-spattered windshield through a stomach-tighteningly tense (and artfully composed) finale, *Blood Simple* created an atmosphere of suspense and mutual suspicion to match any film of its kind. It was followed, in a bravura display of technical and artistic versatility, by *Raising Arizona* (1987), a screwball comedy about a childless couple (Nicolas Cage and Holly Hunter) who decide to kidnap a quintuplet. Superb performances, (appropriately) flashy camera pyrotechnics and some brilliantly conceived scenes—John Goodman literally bursting up out of the earth during a rainstorm—helped create a world as far removed from that of *Blood Simple* as was possible.

With *Miller's Crossing*, the Coens tried to do for the gangster genre what they had succeeded in doing with film noir and screwball comedy. Loosely based on Dashiel Hammett's *The Glass Key*, the film stars Albert Finney as a mob boss and Gabriel Byrne as the advisor from whom he becomes estranged during a period of inter-gang conflict. Though it was again well received, some critics felt the film suffered from an excess of style—that the brothers were too concerned with showing off their familiarity with earlier, landmark gangster films to successfully forge their own contribution to the genre. It nevertheless confirmed the team as one of the most creative pairings in American cinema of the 1980s, and a force to watch through the 90s. JDP • *Blood Simple* 1984 (p,sc); *Crimewave* 1985 (sc); *Raising Arizona* 1987 (p,sc); *Miller's Crossing* 1990 (p,sc).

Coen, Joel • Director; also screenwriter. • Born St. Louis Park, MN, 1955. *Educ.* Simon's Rock College, MA; NYU Institute of Film and TV. See Coen, Ethan. • *The Evil Dead* 1980 (editor assistant); *Fear No Evil* 1980 (asst.ed); *Blood Simple* 1984 (d,sc); *Crimewave* 1985 (sc); *Spies Like Us* 1985 (a); *Raising Arizona* 1987 (d,sc); *Miller's Crossing* 1990 (d,sc).

Cohen, Larry • Director, screenwriter; also producer. • Born New York, NY, July 15, 1941. *Educ.* CCNY Film Institute. Throughout the 1970s, engineered a series of schlocky but thoroughly entertaining films, including the blaxploitation installment *Black Caesar* (1972), the cult horror film about a man-eating baby, *It's Alive* (1974)—followed by two sequels—and the biopic *The Private Files of J. Edgar Hoover* (1977). In the 1980s, Cohen continued to develop his cinematic prowess, turning out a new series of low-budget, self-conscious pictures, most notably the sci-fi/cop thriller *Q* (1982). • *I Deal in Danger* 1966 (sc); *Return of the Seven* 1966 (sc); *Daddy's Gone A-Hunting* 1969 (sc,story); *El Condor* 1970 (sc); *Black Caesar* 1972 (d,p,sc); *Bone* 1972 (d,p,sc); *Hell Up in Harlem* 1973 (d,p,sc); *It's Alive* 1974 (d,p,sc); *God Told Me To* 1976 (d,p,sc); *The Private Files of J. Edgar Hoover* 1977 (d,p,sc); *It's Alive 2* 1978 (d,p,sc); *American Success Company* 1979 (sc,story); *Full Moon High* 1981 (d,p,sc); *I, the Jury* 1981 (sc); *Q* 1982 (d,p,sc); *Perfect Strangers* 1983 (d,p,sc); *Scandalous* 1984 (story); *Special Effects* 1985 (d,sc); *Spies Like Us* 1985 (a); *The Stuff* 1985 (d,exec.p,sc); *Best Seller* 1987 (sc); *Deadly Illusion* 1987 (d,sc); *It's Alive III: Island of the Alive* 1987 (d,exec.p,sc); *A Return to Salem's Lot* 1987 (d,exec.p,sc,story); *Maniac Cop* 1988 (p,sc); *Wicked Stepmother* 1989 (d,exec.p,sc); *The Ambulance* 1990 (d,sc); *Maniac Cop 2* 1990 (p,sc).

Cohen, Rob • Producer; also director. • Born Cornwall-on-Hudson, NY, March 12, 1949. *Educ.* Harvard. Began producing films for the Motown corporation at the age of 24. Cohen was later head of Keith Barish Productions before branching out on his own. • *Mahogany* 1975 (p); *The Bingo Long Traveling All-Stars and Motor Kings* 1976 (p); *Almost Summer* 1977 (p); *Scott Joplin* 1977 (exec.p); *Thank God It's Friday* 1978 (p); *The Wiz* 1978 (p); *A Small Circle of Friends* 1980 (d); *The Razor's Edge* 1984 (exec.p); *Scandalous* 1984 (d,sc,story); *The Legend of Billie Jean* 1985 (p); *Ironweed* 1987 (exec.p); *Light of Day* 1987 (p); *The Monster Squad* 1987 (exec.p); *The Running Man* 1987 (exec.p); *The Witches of Eastwick* 1987 (exec.p); *The Serpent and the Rainbow* 1988 (2u d,exec.p); *Disorganized Crime* 1989 (exec.p); *Bird on a Wire* 1990 (2u d,p); *The Hard Way* 1991 (p).

Cohn, Arthur • Swiss producer • Born 1928. Responsible for several acclaimed European productions including most of Vittorio De Sica's later features. Cohn produced four Oscar-winning films: the documentary, *Sky Above and Mud Below* (1961); De Sica's *The Garden of the*

Finzi-Continis (1971); Jean-Jacques Annaud's *Black and White in Color* (1976) and *Dangerous Moves* (1984). • *Le Ciel et la boue/Sky Above and Mud Below* 1961 (p) **(AABDOC)**; *Woman Times Seven* 1967 (p); *Gli Amanti* 1969 (p); *I Girasoli* 1969 (p); *Maedchen mit Gewalt* 1970 (p); *Il Giardino del Finzi-Continis/The Garden of the Finzi-Continis* 1971 (p) **(AABFLP)**; *Lo Chiameremo Andrea* 1972 (p); *Una Breve Vacanza* 1973 (p); *La Victoire en chantant/Black and White and in Color* 1976 (p) **(AABFLP)**; *The Final Solution* 1983 (p); *L'Amour par terre* 1984 (exec.p); *La Diagonale du Fou/Dangerous Moves* 1984 (p) **(AABFLP)**; *American Dream* 1990 (p) **(AANBDOC)**.

Cohn, Harry • Executive • Born New York, NY, July 23, 1891; died 1958, Phoenix, AZ. After numerous jobs ranging from vaudevillian to fur salesman, Cohn became personal secretary to Universal Studios head Carl Laemmle in 1918. Two years later, with brother Jack and friend Joe Brandt, he formed the CBC Film Sales Company, which formally changed its name to Columbia in 1924. When Brandt left the company, Harry became president of West Coast production and in 1932, after his brother's failure to oust him, took effective control of the studio.

With unscrupulous flair, Cohn turned Columbia into one of Hollywood's most profitable studios; his ruthless tactics also caused a great many stars, directors and screenwriters to despise him (he was nicknamed the "White Fang" by Ben Hecht). A noteworthy biography by Bob Thomas, entitled *King Cohn*, was published in 1967.

Colbert, Claudette • Actress • Born Claudette Lily Chauchoin, Paris, September 13, 1905. *Educ.* Art Students League, New York. Moved to New York City in 1910 and appeared on Broadway in 1925 before making her film debut in Frank Capra's *For the Love of Mike* (1927). Ingenuous, beautiful and with a natural aptitude for both drama and sophisticated comedy, Colbert was one of Hollywood's brightest talents during the 1930s and 40s. • *For the Love of Mike* 1927 (a); *A Hole in the Wall* 1929 (a); *The Lady Lies* 1929 (a); *The Big Pond* 1930 (a); *L'Enigmatique M. Parkes* 1930 (archival footage); *Manslaughter* 1930 (a); *Young Man of Manhattan* 1930 (a); *His Woman* 1931 (a); *Honor Among Lovers* 1931 (a); *Secrets of a Secretary* 1931 (a); *The Smiling Lieutenant* 1931 (a); *The Man From Yesterday* 1932 (a); *The Misleading Lady* 1932 (a); *The Phantom President* 1932 (a); *The Sign of the Cross* 1932 (a); *The Wiser Sex* 1932 (a); *I Cover the Waterfront* 1933 (a); *Three Cornered Moon* 1933 (a); *Tonight Is Ours* 1933 (a); *Torch Singer* 1933 (a); *Cleopatra* 1934 (a); *Four Frightened People* 1934 (a); *Imitation of Life* 1934 (a); *It Happened One Night* 1934 (a) **(AABA)**; *The Gilded Lily* 1935 (a); *Private Worlds* 1935 (a) **(AANBA)**; *She Married Her Boss* 1935 (a); *The Bride Comes Home* 1936 (a); *Under Two Flags* 1936 (a); *I Met Him in Paris* 1937 (a); *Maid of Salem* 1937 (a); *Tovarich* 1937 (a); *Bluebeard's Eighth Wife* 1938 (a); *Drums Along the Mohawk* 1939 (a); *It's a Wonderful World* 1939 (a); *Midnight* 1939 (a); *Zaza* 1939 (a); *Arise, My Love* 1940 (a); *Boom Town* 1940 (a); *Remember the Day* 1941 (a); *Skylark* 1941 (a); *The Palm Beach Story* 1942 (a); *No Time For Love* 1943 (a); *So Proudly We Hail* 1943 (a); *Practically Yours* 1944 (a); *Since You Went Away* 1944 (a) **(AANBA)**; *Guest Wife* 1945 (a); *The Secret Heart* 1946 (a); *Tomorrow Is Forever* 1946 (a); *Without Reservations* 1946 (a); *The Egg and I* 1947 (a); *Family Honeymoon* 1948 (a); *Sleep, My Love* 1948 (a); *Bride For Sale* 1949 (a); *The Secret Fury* 1950 (a); *Three Came Home* 1950 (a); *Let's Make It Legal* 1951 (a); *Thunder on the Hill* 1951 (a); *The Planter's Wife* 1952 (a); *Daughters of Destiny* 1953 (a); *Si Versailles m'était conté/Royal Affairs in Versailles* 1954 (archival footage); *Texas Lady* 1955 (a); *Parrish* 1961 (a); *Going Hollywood: The War Years* 1988 (archival footage).

Cole, Lester • *aka* Lewis Copley • Screenwriter; also playwright. • Born New York, NY, June 19, 1904; died August 15, 1985, San Francisco, CA. One of the original ten blacklisted by Hollywood, Cole began his writing career in 1932 with *If I Had a Million.* His autobiography was aptly titled *Hollywood Red.* • *Painted Faces* 1929 (a); *Love at First Sight* 1930 (a); *If I Had a Million* 1932 (sc); *Charlie Chan's Greatest Case* 1933 (sc); *Pursued* 1934 (sc—English-language version); *Sleepers East* 1934 (sc); *Wild Gold* 1934 (sc); *Hitch Hike Lady* 1935 (sc); *Too Tough to Kill* 1935 (sc); *Under Pressure* 1935 (sc); *Follow Your Heart* 1936 (sc); *The President's Mystery* 1936 (sc); *Affairs of Cappy Ricks* 1937 (sc); *The Man in Blue* 1937 (sc); *Some Blondes Are Dangerous* 1937 (sc); *The Crime of Dr. Hallett* 1938 (sc,story); *The Jury's Secret* 1938 (sc,story); *Midnight Intruder* 1938 (sc); *Secrets of a Nurse* 1938 (sc); *Sinners in Paradise* 1938 (sc); *The Big Guy* 1939 (sc); *I Stole a Million* 1939 (story); *Pirates of the Skies* 1939 (from story "Sky Police"); *Winter Carnival* 1939 (sc); *The House of the Seven Gables* 1940 (sc); *The Invisible Man Returns* 1940 (sc); *When the Daltons Rode* 1940 (sc); *Among the Living* 1941 (sc,story); *Footsteps in the Dark* 1941 (sc); *Midnight Angel* 1941 (sc); *Pacific Blackout* 1942 (sc); *Hostages* 1943 (sc); *Night Plane From Chungking* 1943 (sc); *None Shall Escape* 1944 (sc); *South of Dixie* 1944 (a); *Blood on the Sun* 1945 (sc); *Men in Her Diary* 1945 (adapt); *Objective Burma!* 1945 (sc); *Strange Conquest* 1946 (story); *Fiesta* 1947 (sc,story); *High Wall* 1947 (sc); *The Romance of Rosy Ridge* 1947 (sc); *Hollywood on Trial* 1976 (a).

Coleman, Dabney • Actor • Born Austin, TX, January 3, 1932. *Educ.* University of Texas (law); Neighborhood Playhouse, New York. Popular character player of the 1980s, especially as obnoxious-yet-likeable types. Best known for his roles in *9 to 5* (1980) and *On Golden Pond* (1981) and on TV's "Mary Hartman, Mary Hartman" (1976-77) and "Buffalo Bill" (1983-84). • *The Slender Thread* 1965; *This Property Is Condemned* 1966; *The Scalphunters* 1968; *Downhill Racer* 1969; *The Trouble With Girls* 1969; *I Love My Wife* 1970; *The Dove* 1974; *The Other Side of the Mountain* 1974; *Bite the Bullet* 1975; *Bogard* 1975; *The Black Street Fighter* 1976; *Rolling Thunder* 1977; *Viva Knievel!* 1977; *North Dallas Forty* 1979; *Nothing Personal* 1979; *9 to 5* 1980; *How to Beat the High Cost of Living* 1980; *Melvin and Howard* 1980; *Modern Problems* 1981; *On Golden Pond* 1981; *Tootsie* 1982; *Young Doctors in Love* 1982; *WarGames* 1983; *Cloak and Dagger* 1984; *The Muppets Take Manhattan* 1984; *The Man With One Red Shoe* 1985; *Dragnet* 1987; *Hot to Trot* 1988; *Short Time* 1990; *Where the Heart Is* 1990; *Clifford* 1991; *Meet the Applegates* 1991.

Collins, Joan • Actress • Born London, May 23, 1933. *Educ.* RADA, London. One-note performer whose career blossomed when she starred as the conniving Alexis Carrington on TV's "Dynasty" (1981-89). Collins had begun her film career in the early 1950s, frequently playing wayward young girls in mostly forgettable features, but began appearing to better effect on TV in the early 1960s. Married (1963-71) to Anthony Newley. Sister of novelist Jackie Collins, two of whose works—*The Stud* (1978) and *The Bitch* (1979)—have been made into films starring Joan. • *I Believe in You* 1951; *The Adventures of Sadie* 1953; *Cosh Boy* 1953; *Decameron Nights* 1953; *Our Girl Friday* 1953; *The Square Ring* 1953; *Turn the Key Softly* 1953; *The Good Die Young* 1954; *The Woman's Angle* 1954; *The Girl in the Red Velvet Swing* 1955; *Land of the Pharaohs* 1955; *The Virgin Queen* 1955; *The Opposite Sex* 1956; *Island in the Sun* 1957; *Sea Wife* 1957; *Stopover Tokyo* 1957; *The Wayward Bus* 1957; *The Bravados* 1958; *Rally Round the Flag, Boys!* 1958; *Esther and the King* 1960; *Seven Thieves* 1960; *The Road to Hong Kong* 1962; *Warning Shot* 1967; *Can Heironymus Merkin Ever Forget Mercy Humppe and Find True Happiness?* 1969; *If It's Tuesday, This Must Be Belgium* 1969; *Lo Stato d'Assedio* 1969; *Subterfuge* 1969; *The Executioner* 1970; *Up in the Cellar* 1970; *Quest For Love* 1971; *Revenge* 1971; *Fear in the Night* 1972; *Tales From The Crypt* 1972; *Dark Places* 1973;

Tales That Witness Madness 1973; *Alfie Darling* 1974; *The Bawdy Adventures of Tom Jones* 1976; *The Devil Within Her* 1976; *Empire of the Ants* 1977; *The Big Sleep* 1978; *The Stud* 1978; *Zero to Sixty* 1978; *The Bitch* 1979; *Game For Vultures* 1979; *Sunburn* 1979; *Homework* 1982; *Nutcracker* 1982.

Colman, Ronald • Actor • Born Richmond, Surrey, England, February 9, 1891; died 1958, Santa Barbara, CA. After some stage and film experience in England, moved to the US in 1920. Though a formidable romantic lead in the silent era, it was with the sound film that Colman best asserted himself. His suave good looks, coupled with his engaging, well-modulated voice, made him the perfect hero of many adventure movies, though he was also adept at comedy and drama. • *Sheba* 1918; *Snow in the Desert* 1919; *A Son of David* 1919; *The Toilers* 1919; *Anna the Adventuress* 1920; *The Black Spider* 1920; *Handcuffs or Kisses* 1921; *The White Sister* 1923; *$20 a Week* 1924; *Her Night of Romance* 1924; *Romola* 1924; *Tarnish* 1924; *The Dark Angel* 1925; *Her Sister From Paris* 1925; *His Supreme Moment* 1925; *Lady Windemere's Fan* 1925; *The Sporting Venus* 1925; *Stella Dallas* 1925; *A Thief in Paradise* 1925; *Beau Geste* 1926; *Kiki* 1926; *The Winning of Barbara Worth* 1926; *Magic Flame* 1927; *The Night of Love* 1927; *Two Lovers* 1928; *Bulldog Drummond* 1929 **(AANBA)**; *Condemned* 1929 **(AANBA)**; *The Rescue* 1929; *Raffles* 1930; *Arrowsmith* 1931; *The Devil to Pay* 1931; *The Unholy Garden* 1931; *Cynara* 1932; *The Masquerader* 1933; *Bulldog Drummond Strikes Back* 1934; *Clive of India* 1935; *The Man Who Broke the Bank at Monte Carlo* 1935; *A Tale of Two Cities* 1935; *Under Two Flags* 1936; *Lost Horizon* 1937; *The Prisoner of Zenda* 1937; *If I Were King* 1938; *The Light That Failed* 1939; *Lucky Partners* 1940; *My Life With Caroline* 1941; *Random Harvest* 1942 **(AANBA)**; *Talk of the Town* 1942; *Kismet* 1944; *A Double Life* 1947 **(AABA)**; *The Late George Apley* 1947; *Champagne For Caesar* 1950; *Around the World in 80 Days* 1956; *The Story of Mankind* 1957.

Coltrane, Robbie • Actor • Born Rutherglen, Scotland, 1950. *Educ.* Glasgow School of Art (drawing, painting, film). Burly supporting player known for his aggressive stare and thick Scottish brogue. Coltrane began his career with Edinburgh's celebrated Traverse Theatre and achieved cult status in the UK as a member of TV's "Comic Strip" team. • *La Mort en Direct* 1979; *Flash Gordon* 1980; *Subway Riders* 1981; *Britannia Hospital* 1982; *Scrubbers* 1982; *Ghost Dance* 1983; *Krull* 1983; *Loose Connections* 1983; *Chinese Boxes* 1984; *Defence of the Realm* 1985; *Revolution* 1985; *The Supergrass* 1985; *Absolute Beginners* 1986; *Caravaggio* 1986; *Mona Lisa* 1986; *Eat the Rich* 1987; *The Secret Policeman's Third Ball* 1987; *The Strike* 1987; *The Fruit Machine* 1988; *Midnight Breaks* 1988; *Bert Rigby, You're a Fool* 1989; *Henry V* 1989; *Lenny Live* 1989; *Let It Ride* 1989; *Nuns on the Run* 1990; *Perfectly Normal* 1990; *The Pope Must Die* 1991.

Coluche • *aka* Michel Coluche • Actor; also director, screenwriter. • Born Michel Colucci, France, October 28, 1944; died June 19, 1986, France. Bitingly humorous, much-loved French star, best remembered in the US for *Tchao Pantin* (1983). Coluche was also known for his political, and especially anti-racist, activism. He died in a motorcycle accident at age 41. • *L'Aile et la Cuisse* 1976 (a); *Drôles de zébres* 1977 (a); *Vous n'aurez pas l'Alsace et la Lorraine* 1977 (a,d,sc); *Inspecteur la Bavure* 1980 (a); *Deux heures moins le quart avant Jésus Christ* 1982 (a); *Banzai* 1983 (a); *La Femme de mon pôte/My Best Friend's Girl* 1983 (a); *Tchao Pantin* 1983 (a); *Le Bon Roi Dagobert* 1984 (a); *Les Rois du Gag* 1984 (a); *Le Véngeance du serpent a plumes* 1984 (a); *Sac de Noeuds/All Mixed Up* 1985 (a); *Scemo di Guerra* 1985 (a).

Columbus, Chris • Screenwriter; also director. • Born Christopher Columbus, Spangler, PA, 1959. *Educ.* NYU (film). Combines a sensitivity to the world of children with a knack for adventure yarns. Columbus sold his first script while still at college and wrote four highly imaginative and commercially popular films for producer Steven Spielberg before making a competent directorial debut with *Adventures in Babysitting* (1987). He also directed the runaway hit of 1990-91, *Home Alone*, John Hughes's sentimental Christmas adventure told from a child's vantage point. • *Gremlins* 1984 (sc); *Reckless* 1984 (sc); *The Goonies* 1985 (sc); *Young Sherlock Holmes* 1985 (sc); *Adventures in Babysitting* 1987 (d); *Heartbreak Hotel* 1988 (d,sc); *Gremlins 2: The New Batch* 1990 (from characters); *Home Alone* 1990 (d); *Only the Lonely* 1991 (d,sc).

Comden, Betty • Playwright; also lyricist, screenwriter. • Born Elizabeth Cohen, Brooklyn, NY, May 3, 1916. *Educ.* NYU. With partner Adolph Green wrote memorable songs and musicals for stage and screen. Their fast-paced scenarios and impeccable lyrics gave birth to hit after hit, including what many consider the greatest movie musical of all time, *Singin' in the Rain* (1952). • *Greenwich Village* 1944 (a); *Good News* 1947 (sc,song); *The Barkleys of Broadway* 1949 (sc); *On the Town* 1949 (sc,from play,lyrics); *Singin' in the Rain* 1952 (sc,story); *The Band Wagon* 1953 (sc) **(AANBSC)**; *It's Always Fair Weather* 1955 (sc,lyrics) **(AANBSC)**; *Auntie Mame* 1958 (sc); *Bells Are Ringing* 1960 (sc,from play); *What a Way to Go!* 1964 (sc); *Blue Sunshine* 1977 (song); *Frances* 1982 (song); *The Return of Captain Invincible* 1982 (song); *Garbo Talks* 1984 (a).

Comencini, Luigi • Director, screenwriter • Born Salo, Italy, June 8, 1916. Although his early career was influenced by neorealism, Comencini built a reputation in the mid-1950s as a competent director of light, popular comedies, such as *Bread, Love and Dreams* (1953) and *Bread, Love and Jealousy* (1954), both starring Gina Lollobrigida and Vittorio De Sica. He also co-founded, with director Alberto Lattuada, the Cineteca Italiana film archive in Milan. • *Proibito Rubare* 1948 (d,sc); *L'Imperatore di Capri* 1949 (d); *Persiane chiuse* 1950 (d); *Heidi* 1952 (d); *La Tratta delle Bianche* 1952 (d); *Pane, Amore, e Fantasia/Bread, Love and Dreams* 1953 (d,sc); *La Valigia dei Sogni* 1953 (d); *Pane, Amore e gelosia/Bread, Love and Jealousy* 1954 (d,story); *La Bella di Roma* 1955 (d,sc); *La Finestra sul Luna Park* 1956 (d,sc); *Mariti in Città* 1957 (d,sc); *Mogli pericolose* 1958 (d,sc,story); *Le Sorprese dell'Amore* 1959 (d); *Und das am Montagmorgen* 1959 (d); *Tutti a Casa* 1960 (d,sc); *A Cavallo della Tigre* 1961 (d,sc); *Il Commissario* 1962 (d); *La Ragazza di Bube* 1963 (d,sc); *Tre Notti d'Amore* 1964 (d); *Le Bambole/The Dolls* 1965 (d); *La Bugiarda* 1965 (d,sc); *Il Compagno Don Camillo* 1965 (d); *La Mia Signorina* 1965 (d,sc—"Eritrea"); *Incompresso* 1966 (d); *Italian Secret Service* 1968 (d,sc,story); *Infanzia Vocazione e Prime Esperienze di Giacomo Casanova—Veneziano* 1969 (d,sc); *Senza Sapere nulla di Lei* 1969 (d,sc); *Lo Scopone Scientifico* 1972 (d); *Delitto d'Amore* 1974 (d,sc); *Mio Dio, come sono Caduta in Basso* 1974 (d,sc); *Basta che non si sappia in giro!* 1976 (d); *La Donna Della Domenica* 1976 (d); *La Goduria* 1976 (d,sc); *Quelle Strane Occasioni* 1976 (d); *Signore e Signori, Buonanotte* 1976 (d,sc); *Tra Moglie e Marito* 1977 (d); *Il Gatto* 1978 (d); *Le Grand embouteillage* 1979 (d,sc); *Voltati Andrea* 1979 (d); *Eugenio* 1980 (d,sc,art d,cost); *Cercasi Gesu* 1982 (d); *Il Matrimonio di Caterina* 1982 (d); *Till Marriage Do Us Part* 1982 (d,sc); *Cuore* 1984 (d,sc); *La Storia* 1986 (d,sc); *La Bohème* 1987 (adapt,d,p); *Un Ragazzo di Calabria* 1987 (d,sc); *Buon Natale, Buon Anno* 1989 (d,sc).

Conklin, Chester • Actor • Born Oskaloosa, IA, January 11, 1888; died 1971. Walrus-mustachioed vaudevillian and clown who debuted (as did Charlie Chaplin) in the Mack Sennett comedy, *Making a Living* (1914). Conklin is best remembered for his numerous appearances in the early Chaplin vehicles. • *The Anglers* 1914; *Between Showers (short)* 1914; *Caught in a Cabaret* 1914; *Cruel, Cruel Love (short)* 1914; *Dough and Dynamite (short)* 1914; *The Face on the Barroom Floor* 1914; *Mabel's Strange Predicament (short)* 1914; *Mak-*

ing a Living (short) 1914; *The Masquerader (short)* 1914; *Tango Tangles (short)* 1914; *Tillie's Punctured Romance* 1914; *Twenty Minutes of Love (short)* 1914; *Ambrose's Sour Grapes* 1915; *The Best of Enemies* 1915; *The Cannon Ball* 1915; *Love Speed and Thrills* 1915; *A One Night Stand* 1915; *Cinders of Love* 1916; *Dizzy Heights and Daring Hearts* 1916; *A Tugboat Romeo* 1916; *A Clever Dummy* 1917; *An International Sneak* 1917; *The Pullman Bride* 1917; *It Pays to Exercise* 1918; *Ladies First* 1918; *The Village Chestnut* 1918; *Yankee Doodle in Berlin* 1919; *Chicken a la Cabaret* 1920; *Married Life* 1920; *Skirts* 1921; *Anna Christie* 1923; *Desire* 1923; *Souls For Sale* 1923; *Tea—With a Kick* 1923; *Another Man's Wife* 1924; *Battling Bunyan* 1924; *The Fire Patrol* 1924; *Galloping Fish* 1924; *North of Nevada* 1924; *The Great Jewel Robbery* 1925; *The Great Love* 1925; *Greed* 1925; *The Masked Bride* 1925; *My Neighbor's Wife* 1925; *One Year to Live* 1925; *The Phantom of the Opera* 1925; *The Pleasure Buyers* 1925; *Under the Rouge* 1925; *Where Was I?* 1925; *The Winding Stair* 1925; *A Woman of the World* 1925; *Behind the Front* 1926; *The Duchess of Buffalo* 1926; *Fascinating Youth* 1926; *The Lady of the Harem* 1926; *Midnight Lovers* 1926; *The Nervous Wreck* 1926; *Say It Again* 1926; *A Social Celebrity* 1926; *We're in the Navy Now* 1926; *The Wilderness Woman* 1926; *Cabaret* 1927; *Kiss in a Taxi* 1927; *McFadden's Flats* 1927; *Rubber Heels* 1927; *Tell It to Sweeney* 1927; *Two Flaming Youths* 1927; *The Big Noise* 1928; *Fools For Luck* 1928; *Gentlemen Prefer Blondes* 1928; *The Haunted House* 1928; *Taxi 13* 1928; *Tillie's Punctured Romance* 1928; *Varsity* 1928; *Fast Company* 1929; *The House of Horror* 1929; *Marquis Preferred* 1929; *The Show of Shows* 1929; *Stairs of Sand* 1929; *The Studio Murder Mystery* 1929; *Sunset Pass* 1929; *The Virginian* 1929; *The Love Trader* 1930; *Swing High* 1930; *Her Majesty, Love* 1931; *Hallelujah, I'm a Bum* 1933; *Call of the Prairie* 1936; *Modern Times* 1936; *The Preview Murder Case* 1936; *Hotel Haywire* 1937; *Every Day's a Holiday* 1938; *Hollywood Cavalcade* 1939; *Zenobia* 1939; *The Great Dictator* 1940; *Harmon of Michigan* 1941; *Goodnight, Sweetheart* 1944; *Hail the Conquering Hero* 1944; *Knickerbocker Holiday* 1944; *Fear* 1946; *The Perils of Pauline* 1947; *Song of the Wasteland* 1947; *Springtime in the Sierras* 1947; *The Beautiful Blonde From Bashful Bend* 1949; *The Golden Stallion* 1949; *Jiggs and Maggie in Jackpot Jitters* 1949; *Joe Palooka in Humphrey Takes a Chance* 1950; *Apache Woman* 1955; *Beast With 1,000,000 Eyes* 1955; *Paradise Alley* 1962; *A Big Hand For the Little Lady* 1966; *Chaplinesque, My Life and Hard Times* 1972.

Conner, Bruce • Filmmaker • Born McPherson, KS, 1933. *Educ.* University of Nebraska. Leading figure in the American avant-garde of the 1960s. His short experimental works rely on rhythmic editing, often of "found" footage, to create both humorous and politically challenging statements, as with *A Movie* (1958), *Cosmic Ray* (1961)—in which Ray Charles' "What'd I Say" accompanies a semi-nude go-go dancer—and *Report* (1965), which repeatedly shows the assassination of John F. Kennedy. • *A Movie (short)* 1958 (d,ed,p); *Cosmic Ray* (short) 1961 (d,ed,p);*Report (short)* 1965 (d,ed,p); *Marilyn Times Five (short)* 1974 (d,ed,p); *Mongoloid (short)* 1978 (d,ed,p); *Valse Triste (short)* 1978 (d,ed,p); *America Is Waiting (short)* 1982 (d,ed,p).

Connery, Sean • Actor • Born Thomas Sean Connery, Edinburgh, Scotland, August 25, 1930. Former bodybuilder, model and chorus boy who went on to repertory, TV and film work in the 1950s. Connery was chosen by a London Daily Express readers' poll to play Ian Fleming's superspy James Bond in *Dr. No* (1962), which catapulted him to stardom. The only star of the series to successfully transcend its casting limitations, he starred in four Sidney Lumet films during his tenure as Bond and has since made a smooth shift to older, fatherly roles, as in *The Name of the Rose* (1986), *The Untouchables* (1987), *Indiana Jones and the Last Crusade* (1989) and *The Hunt For Red October* (1990).

An enduring presence harking back to the stars of the Hollywood studio system, he has achieved impressive subtleties of characterization within a narrowly defined range of roles. Connery was married to actress Diane Cilento from 1962 to 1973 and their son Jason is also an actor. • *No Road Back* 1956; *Action of the Tiger* 1957; *Hell Divers* 1957; *Time Lock* 1957; *Another Time, Another Place* 1958; *Darby O'Gill and the Little People* 1959 (a,song); *Tarzan's Greatest Adventure* 1959; *The Frightened City* 1961; *On the Fiddle* 1961; *Dr. No* 1962; *The Longest Day* 1962; *From Russia With Love* 1963; *Goldfinger* 1964; *Marnie* 1964; *Woman of Straw* 1964; *The Hill* 1965; *Thunderball* 1965; *A Fine Madness* 1966; *You Only Live Twice* 1967; *Shalako* 1968; *The Molly Maguires* 1970; *La Tenda rossa* 1970; *The Anderson Tapes* 1971; *Diamonds Are Forever* 1971; *The Offence* 1973; *Murder on the Orient Express* 1974; *Ransom* 1974; *Zardoz* 1974; *The Man Who Would Be King* 1975; *The Wind and the Lion* 1975; *The Next Man* 1976; *Robin and Marian* 1976; *A Bridge Too Far* 1977; *Cuba* 1979; *The First Great Train Robbery* 1979; *Meteor* 1979; *Outland* 1981; *Time Bandits* 1981; *Five Days One Summer* 1982; *G'Ole* 1982; *Wrong Is Right* 1982; *Never Say Never Again* 1983; *Sword of the Valiant—The Legend of Gawain and the Green Knight* 1984; *Highlander* 1986; *The Name of the Rose* 1986; *The Untouchables* 1987 **(AABSA)**; *Memories of Me* 1988; *The Presidio* 1988; *Family Business* 1989; *Indiana Jones and the Last Crusade* 1989; *The Hunt For Red October* 1990; *The Russia House* 1990; *Highlander II—the Quickening* 1991; *Robin Hood: Prince of Thieves* 1991.

Constantine, Eddie • Actor; also singer. • Born Los Angeles, CA, October 29, 1917. Constantine first achieved fame in Paris, where he launched a successful career as a popular singer under the tutelage of Edith Piaf. On screen from 1953, his tough guy manner was put to good use in French imitations of Bogart films, several of which featured Peter Cheyney's no-nonsense, hard-hitting private detective, Lemmy Caution. In 1965 Godard appropriated both Constantine and the Caution character for *Alphaville* (1965) the director's futuristic, parodic homage to the detective genre. • *Cet Homme est dangereux* 1953 (a); *La Môme vert de gris* 1953 (a); *Avanzi di galera* 1954 (a); *Ça va barder* 1954 (a); *Les Femmes s'en balancent* 1954 (a); *Je suis un sentimental* 1955 (a); *Les Truands* 1956 (a); *Folies-Bergère* 1957 (a); *Le Grand bluff* 1957 (a); *L'Homme et l'enfant* 1957 (a); *Ces Dames preférent le mambo* 1958 (a); *Incognito* 1958 (a); *Du Rififi chez les Femmes/Riff Raff Girls* 1959 (a); *Passport to Shame* 1959 (a); *S.O.S. Pacific* 1959 (a); *The Treasure of San Teresa* 1959 (a); *Bomben auf Monte Carlo* 1960 (a); *La Chien de pique* 1960 (a); *Lemmy pour les dames* 1961 (a); *Mani in Alto* 1961 (a); *Cléo de 5 à 7/Cleo From 5 to 7* 1962 (a); *L'Empire de la nuit* 1962 (a); *Les Sept péchés capitaux/The Seven Deadly Sins* 1962 (a); *Lucky Jo* 1964 (a); *Alphaville* 1965 (a); *Je vous salue Mafia* 1965 (a); *Lions Love* 1969 (a); *Malatesta* 1970 (a); *Warnung Vor Einer Heiligen Nutte/Beware of a Holy Whore* 1971 (a); *Souvenir de Gibraltar* 1975 (a); *Bloedverwanten* 1977 (a); *Le Couple témoin* 1977 (a); *It's Alive 2* 1978 (a); *Bildnis einer Trinkerin* 1979 (a); *Die Dritte Generation* 1979 (a); *The Long Good Friday* 1980 (a); *Tango Durch Deutschland* 1980 (a); *Freak Orlando* 1981 (a); *Boxoffice* 1982 (a); *La Bête noire* 1983 (a); *Fluchtpunk Berlin/Flight to Berlin* 1983 (a); *Paul Chevrolet en de ultieme hallucinatie* 1985 (a); *Der Schnuffler* 1985 (a); *Seifenblasen* 1985 (a); *Makaroni Blues* 1986 (a); *Helsinki Napoli All Night Long* 1988 (a); *Europa, abends* 1989 (a).

Conte, Richard • Actor • Born Nicholas Peter Conte, Jersey City, NJ, March 24, 1914; died 1975. *Educ.* Neighborhood Playhouse, New York. Brooding Italian-American leading man who starred in several quality films from the mid-1940 through the 50s usually as a criminal or lover, before his career went into decline. Later memorable as the scheming Don Barzini in *The Godfather* (1972). • *Heaven With a Barbed Wire Fence* 1939; *Guadalcanal Diary* 1943; *The Purple Heart* 1944; *A Bell For Adano* 1945; *Captain Eddie* 1945; *The Spider* 1945; *A Walk in the Sun* 1945; *Backfire* 1946; *13 Rue Madeleine* 1947; *The Other Love* 1947; *Big Jack* 1948; *Call Northside 777* 1948; *Cry of the City* 1948; *House of Strangers* 1949; *Thieves' Highway* 1949; *Whirlpool* 1949; *The Sleeping City* 1950; *Under the Gun* 1950; *Hollywood Story* 1951; *The Raging Tide* 1951; *The Fighter* 1952; *The Raiders* 1952; *The Blue Gardenia* 1953; *Desert Legion* 1953; *Slaves of Babylon* 1953; *Highway Dragnet* 1954; *Mask of Dust* 1954; *Bengazi* 1955; *The Big Combo* 1955; *The Big Tip Off* 1955; *I'll Cry Tomorrow* 1955; *Little Red Monkey* 1955; *New York Confidential* 1955; *Target Zero* 1955; *Barrage contre le Pacifique* 1957; *The Brothers Rico* 1957; *Full of Life* 1957; *They Came to Cordura* 1959; *Ocean's Eleven* 1960; *Pepe* 1960; *The Eyes of Annie Jones* 1963; *Who's Been Sleeping in My Bed?* 1963; *Circus World* 1964; *The Greatest Story Ever Told* 1965; *Synanon* 1965; *Assault on a Queen* 1966; *Hotel* 1967; *Sentenza di morte* 1967; *Tony Rome* 1967; *Lady in Cement* 1968; *Explosion* 1969; *Operation Cross Eagles* 1969 (a,d); *The Godfather* 1972; *Anastasia mio fratello ovvero il presunto capo dell'aninima assassini* 1973; *Anna quel particolare piacere* 1973; *Big Guns* 1973; *Il Boss* 1973; *Milano trema: La Polizia vuole giustizia* 1973; *Piazza Pulita* 1973; *Il Poliziotto è marcio* 1974.

Conti, Bill • Composer • Born Providence, RI, April 13, 1943. *Educ.* Louisiana State University, Baton Rouge (music); Juilliard (music). Prolific composer of the 1970s and 80s who gained attention with the infectious score for the surprise 1976 hit, *Rocky*, and won an Oscar for his lyrical, inspirational work on *The Right Stuff* (1983). • *Blume in Love* 1973 (m.sup); *Pacific Challenge* 1973 (m); *Harry and Tonto* 1974 (m); *Next Stop, Greenwich Village* 1976 (m); *Rocky* 1976 (m,song) **(AANBS)**; *Citizens Band* 1977 (m,song); *Five Days From Home* 1977 (m); *The Big Fix* 1978 (m); *F.I.S.T.* 1978 (m); *Paradise Alley* 1978 (m,song); *Slow Dancing in the Big City* 1978 (a,m); *Uncle Joe Shannon* 1978 (m); *An Unmarried Woman* 1978 (m); *Dreamer* 1979 (m,song); *Goldengirl* 1979 (m,song); *A Man, a Woman and a Bank* 1979 (m,song); *Rocky II* 1979 (m); *The Seduction of Joe Tynan* 1979 (m); *The Formula* 1980 (m); *Gloria* 1980 (m); *Private Benjamin* 1980 (m); *Carbon Copy* 1981 (m,song); *Escape to Victory* 1981 (m); *For Your Eyes Only* 1981 (m,song) **(AANBS)**; *I, the Jury* 1981 (m); *Neighbors* 1981 (m); *Rocky III* 1982 (m,song); *Split Image* 1982 (m,song); *That Championship Season* 1982 (m); *Bad Boys* 1983 (m); *The Right Stuff* 1983 (m) **(AABM)**; *Unfaithfully Yours* 1983 (m); *The Bear* 1984 (m); *The Karate Kid* 1984 (m,song); *Mass Appeal* 1984 (m); *Beer* 1985 (m); *Big Trouble* 1985 (m); *The Coolangatta Gold* 1985 (m); *Gotcha!* 1985 (m); *Nomads* 1985 (m); *Rocky IV* 1985 (m); *Weird Science* 1985 (songs); *50 Years of Action!* 1986 (m); *The Boss' Wife* 1986 (m); *F/X* 1986 (m); *The Karate Kid Part II* 1986 (m,song); *Baby Boom* 1987 (m,song); *Broadcast News* 1987 (m); *Happy New Year* 1987 (m,m.cond); *I Love N.Y.* 1987 (m); *Masters of the Universe* 1987 (m); *A Prayer For the Dying* 1987 (m); *Betrayed* 1988 (m); *Cohen and Tate* 1988 (m); *For Keeps* 1988 (m); *A Night in the Life of Jimmy Reardon* 1988 (m); *The Karate Kid Part III* 1989 (m); *Lean on Me* 1989 (m); *Lock Up* 1989 (m); *Backstreet Dreams* 1990 (m); *The Fourth War* 1990 (m); *Ghost Dad* 1990 (m); *Rocky V* 1990 (m).

Conti, Tom • Actor • Born Paisley, Scotland, November 22, 1941. *Educ.* Royal Scottish Academy of Music, Glasgow. Gifted, stage-trained comedic player who has been cast in a variety of ethnic roles. Conti won a Tony for his Broadway performance in *Whose Life Is It Anyway?* and acclaim for his film work as the title character, a boozy Scottish poet, in *Reuben, Reuben* (1983); as the only bilingual prisoner and title character in Nagisa Oshima's harrowing Japanese POW camp drama, *Merry Christmas, Mr. Lawrence* (1982); as the hilariously neurotic psychiatrist in Robert Altman's *Beyond Therapy* (1987); and as the archetypal Greek lothario in *Shirley Valentine* (1989). Married to actress Kara Wilson. • *Flame* 1974; *Galileo* 1974; *Eclipse* 1976; *The Duellists* 1977; *Full Circle* 1977; *Merry Christmas, Mr. Lawrence* 1982; *Reuben, Reuben* 1983 **(AANBA)**; *American Dreamer* 1984; *Miracles* 1984; *Heavenly Pursuits* 1986; *Saving Grace* 1986; *Beyond Therapy* 1987; *Shirley Valentine* 1989; *That Summer of White Roses* 1989.

Coogan, Jackie • Actor • Born Jack Leslie Coogan, Los Angeles, CA, October 26, 1914; died March 1, 1984, Santa Monica, CA. *Educ.* Villanova University, PA; USC, Los Angeles. Child star who charmed audiences in Charlie Chaplin's 1921 classic *The Kid*. By the mid-1930s his career had slowed considerably and in 1938 he attempted to win back his $4 million childhood earnings from his mother and step-father. By the time the case was settled the amount had dropped to approximately $250,000, of which Coogan received only a portion. The case resulted in the Coogan Act, or Child Actors Bill, set up to protect the assets of child stars. After WWII most of Coogan's work was on TV, where he gained success as Uncle Fester on "The Addams Family." Married to Betty Grable from 1937 to 1940. • *Skinner's Baby* 1917; *A Day's Pleasure (short)* 1919; *The Kid* 1921; *Peck's Bad Boy* 1921; *My Boy* 1922; *Oliver Twist* 1922; *Trouble* 1922; *Circus Days* 1923; *Daddy* 1923; *Long Live the King* 1923; *A Boy of Flanders* 1924; *Little Robinson Crusoe* 1924; *Old Clothes* 1925; *The Rag Man* 1925; *The Bugle Call* 1927; *Buttons* 1927; *Johnny Get Your Hair Cut* 1927; *Free and Easy* 1930; *Tom Sawyer* 1930; *Huckleberry Finn* 1931; *Home on the Range* 1935; *College Swing* 1938; *Million Dollar Legs* 1939; *Sky Patrol* 1939; *French Leave* 1947; *Kilroy Was Here* 1947; *Skipalong Rosenbloom* 1951; *Varieties on Parade* 1951; *Mesa of Lost Women* 1952; *Outlaw Women* 1952; *The Proud Ones* 1956; *The Buster Keaton Story* 1957; *Eighteen and Anxious* 1957; *The Joker Is Wild* 1957; *High School Confidential* 1958; *Lonelyhearts* 1958; *Night of the Quarter Moon* 1958; *No Place to Land* 1958; *The Space Children* 1958; *The Beat Generation* 1959 (a,dial.coach); *The Big Operator* 1959; *Sex Kittens Go to College* 1960; *John Goldfarb, Please Come Home* 1964; *Girl Happy* 1965; *A Fine Madness* 1966; *The Shakiest Gun in the West* 1968; *Marlowe* 1969; *Cahill, United States Marshal* 1973; *The Manchu Eagle Murder Caper Mystery* 1975; *Dr. Heckyl & Mr. Hype* 1980; *Human Experiments* 1980; *The Prey* 1980; *The Escape Artist* 1982.

Cook, Jr., Elisha • Actor • Born San Francisco, CA, December 26, 1906. *Educ.* Chicago Academy of Dramatic Art. Diminutive, wiry character player memorable for his numerous roles as cowardly villians and neurotics. Originally from vaudeville and Broadway, Cook—who briefly entered film in 1929 before returning to the stage—made a strong impression with his definitive sniveling gunsel in *The Maltese Falcon* (1941). He followed up with similar roles as weaklings or sadistic loser-hoods, such as Harry Jones in *The Big Sleep* (1946) or George Peatty in Kubrick's *The Killing* (1956), over a more than 50-year career. • *Her Unborn Child* 1929; *Pigskin Parade* 1936; *Two in a Crowd* 1936; *Danger—Love at Work* 1937; *The Devil Is Driving* 1937; *Life Begins in College* 1937; *Love Is News* 1937; *They Won't Forget* 1937; *Wife, Doctor, and Nurse* 1937; *My Lucky Star* 1938; *Submarine Patrol* 1938; *Grand Jury Secrets* 1939; *Newsboy's Home* 1939; *He Married His Wife* 1940; *Public Deb No. 1* 1940; *Stranger on the Third Floor* 1940; *Tin Pan Alley* 1940; *I Wake Up Screaming* 1941; *Love Crazy* 1941; *The Maltese Falcon* 1941; *Man at Large* 1941; *A-Haunting We Will Go* 1942; *A Gentleman at Heart* 1942; *Manila Calling* 1942; *Sleepytime Gal* 1942; *Wildcat* 1942; *Dark Mountain* 1944; *Dark Waters* 1944; *Phantom Lady* 1944; *Up in Arms* 1944; *Dillinger* 1945; *Why Girls Leave Home* 1945; *The Big Sleep* 1946; *Blonde Alibi* 1946; *Cinderella Jones* 1946; *The*

Falcon's Alibi 1946; *Joe Palooka, Champ* 1946; *Two Smart People* 1946; *Born to Kill* 1947; *Fall Guy* 1947; *The Gangster* 1947; *The Long Night* 1947; *Flaxy Martin* 1949; *The Great Gatsby* 1949; *Behave Yourself* 1951; *Don't Bother to Knock* 1952; *I, the Jury* 1953; *Shane* 1953; *Thunder Over the Plains* 1953; *Drum Beat* 1954; *The Outlaw's Daughter* 1954; *The Indian Fighter* 1955; *Timberjack* 1955; *Accused of Murder* 1956; *The Killing* 1956; *Baby Face Nelson* 1957; *Chicago Confidential* 1957; *The Lonely Man* 1957; *Plunder Road* 1957; *Voodoo Island* 1957; *Day of the Outlaw* 1959; *College Confidential* 1960; *Platinum High School* 1960; *One-Eyed Jacks* 1961; *Black Zoo* 1963; *The Haunted Palace* 1963; *Johnny Cool* 1963; *Papa's Delicate Condition* 1963; *Blood on the Arrow* 1964; *The Glass Cage* 1964; *The Spy in the Green Hat* 1966; *Welcome to Hard Times* 1967; *Rosemary's Baby* 1968; *The Great Bank Robbery* 1969; *El Condor* 1970; *The Great Northfield Minnesota Raid* 1972; *Electra Glide in Blue* 1973; *The Emperor of the North Pole* 1973; *The Outfit* 1973; *Pat Garrett and Billy the Kid* 1973; *The Black Bird* 1975; *Messiah of Evil* 1975; *Winterhawk* 1975; *St. Ives* 1976; *1941* 1979; *The Champ* 1979; *Carny* 1980; *Harry's War* 1981; *Hammett* 1982; *National Lampoon Goes to the Movies* 1982.

Cook, Peter • Actor; also screenwriter. • Born Torquay, England, November 17, 1937. Gained fame with the "Beyond The Fringe" comedy group before he and sometime-partner Dudley Moore turned to TV and films. Publisher of England's long-running satirical magazine *Private Eye*. • *The Wrong Box* 1966 (a); *Bedazzled* 1967 (a,sc,story); *A Dandy in Aspic* 1968 (a); *The Bed Sitting Room* 1969 (a); *Monte Carlo or Bust!* 1969 (a); *The Rise and Rise of Michael Rimmer* 1970 (a,sc); *The Adventures of Barry McKenzie* 1972 (a); *Pleasure at Her Majesty's* 1976 (a); *The Hound of the Baskervilles* 1978 (a,sc); *The Secret Policeman's Ball* 1979 (a,sc); *Beaubourg* 1980 (a); *Derek and Clive Get the Horn* 1980 (a,exec.p); *The Secret Policeman's Other Ball* 1981 (a); *Yellowbeard* 1983 (a,sc); *Supergirl* 1984 (a); *Whoops Apocalypse* 1986 (a); *Mr. Jolly Lives Next Door* 1987 (a); *The Princess Bride* 1987 (a); *Without a Clue* 1988 (a); *Getting It Right* 1989 (a); *Great Balls of Fire* 1989 (a); *Kokoda Crescent* 1989 (sc).

Coolidge, Martha • Director; also screenwriter, producer. • Born New Haven, CT, August 17, 1946. *Educ.* Rhode Island School of Design, Providence (animation); School of Visual Arts, New York NY; Columbia; NYU Institute of Film and TV. A key figure in the formation of the Association of Independent Video and Filmmakers, Coolidge began her career writing, producing and directing documentaries. Several of these, including the semi-autobiographical docudrama about rape, *Not a Pretty Picture* (1975), won festival awards. After working in Canadian TV, in 1983 Coolidge made two superb, low-budget fiction features: *The City Girl*, a realistic study of a woman photographer's professional and personal life; and the engaging teen picture, *Valley Girl*. Her subsequent studio features, *Joy of Sex* (1984), *Real Genius* (1985) and *Plain Clothes* (1988), have been less effective. • *Old Fashioned Woman* 1974 (d,p,sc,ed); *Not a Pretty Picture* 1975 (a,d,p,sc,ed,song); *The Omega Connection* 1979 (story); *The City Girl* 1983 (d,p,story); *Valley Girl* 1983 (d); *Joy of Sex* 1984 (d); *Real Genius* 1985 (d); *50 Years of Action!* 1986 (a); *Calling the Shots* 1988 (a); *Plain Clothes* 1988 (d); *That's Adequate* 1989 (a).

Coop, Denys • Director of photography • Born Reading, Berkshire, England, July 20, 1920; died 1981. Began career at age 16 assisting cinematographer Freddie Young. Coop graduated to full-fledged director of photography in the 1960s and shot several classic black-and-white British films of the decade, including the early John Schlesinger films, *A Kind of Loving* (1962) and *Billy Liar* (1963), Lindsay Anderson's *This Sporting Life* (1963), Joseph Losey's *King and Country* (1964) and Otto Preminger's *Bunny Lake is Missing* (1965). In 1978 he shared a special achievement Oscar for the special visual effects of *Superman*. • *A Kind of Loving* 1962; *Billy Liar* 1963; *The Mind Benders* 1963; *This Sporting Life* 1963; *King and Country* 1964; *Of Human Bondage* 1964 (add.ph); *One Way Pendulum* 1964; *Bunny Lake Is Missing* 1965; *Arrivederci, Baby!* 1966; *The Double Man* 1967; *The Birthday Party* 1968; *Goodbye, Mr. Chips* 1969 (cam.op); *My Side of the Mountain* 1969; *10 Rillington Place* 1970; *The Executioner* 1970; *Ryan's Daughter* 1970 (2u ph); *Asylum* 1972; *The Darwin Adventure* 1972; *The Little Ark* 1972; *And Now the Screaming Starts* 1973; *The Vault of Horror* 1973; *Inserts* 1975; *Rosebud* 1975; *Superman* 1978 (fx) **(AASPECIAL ACHIEVEMENT)**; *Superman II* 1980 (aerial ph); *Venom* 1981.

Cooper, Gary • Actor • Born Frank James Cooper, Helena, MT, May 7, 1901; died May 13, 1961. *Educ.* Wesleyan College, Bozeman, MT; Grinnell College, Iowa. Tall, commanding leading man and one of the greatest stars Hollywood has known. After failing as a newspaper cartoonist, "Coop" began appearing as an extra in westerns in 1925. His big break came in 1926 with *The Winning of Barbara Worth*, playing the supporting lead to Ronald Coleman and Vilma Banky. By the mid-1930s his good looks and slow, thoughtful delivery had endeared him to film fans the world over. He epitomized the powerful, quiet American and, though he starred in numerous comedies and dramas, he is best recognized for his many westerns, from *The Virginian* (1929) to the taut, mythic *High Noon* (1952). In 1960, dying of cancer, he received a special Academy Award for his lifetime contribution to the cinema. • *The Eagle* 1925; *The Thundering Herd* 1925; *Wild Horse Mesa* 1925; *The Enchanted Hill* 1926; *The Winning of Barbara Worth* 1926; *Arizona Bound* 1927; *Children of Divorce* 1927; *It* 1927; *The Last Outlaw* 1927; *Nevada* 1927; *Wings* 1927; *Beau Sabreur* 1928; *Doomsday* 1928; *The First Kiss* 1928; *Half a Bride* 1928; *The Legion of the Condemned* 1928; *Lilac Time* 1928; *Betrayal* 1929; *The Shopworn Angel* 1929; *The Virginian* 1929; *Wolf Song* 1929; *A Man From Wyoming* 1930; *Morocco* 1930; *Only the Brave* 1930; *Paramount on Parade* 1930; *Seven Days Leave* 1930; *The Spoilers* 1930; *The Texan* 1930; *City Streets* 1931; *Fighting Caravans* 1931; *His Woman* 1931; *I Take This Woman* 1931; *The Devil and the Deep* 1932; *A Farewell to Arms* 1932; *If I Had a Million* 1932; *Make Me a Star* 1932; *Alice in Wonderland* 1933; *Design For Living* 1933; *One Sunday Afternoon* 1933; *Operator 13* 1933; *Today We Live* 1933; *Now and Forever* 1934; *The Lives of a Bengal Lancer* 1935; *Peter Ibbetson* 1935; *The Wedding Night* 1935; *Desire* 1936; *The General Died at Dawn* 1936; *Hollywood Boulevard* 1936; *Mr. Deeds Goes to Town* 1936 **(AANBA)**; *The Plainsman* 1937; *Souls at Sea* 1937; *The Adventures of Marco Polo* 1938; *Bluebeard's Eighth Wife* 1938; *The Cowboy and the Lady* 1938; *Beau Geste* 1939; *The Real Glory* 1939; *North West Mounted Police* 1940; *The Westerner* 1940; *Ball of Fire* 1941; *Meet John Doe* 1941; *Sergeant York* 1941 **(AABA)**; *The Pride of the Yankees* 1942 **(AANBA)**; *For Whom the Bell Tolls* 1943 **(AANBA)**; *Casanova Brown* 1944; *The Story of Dr. Wassell* 1944; *Along Came Jones* 1945 (a,p); *Saratoga Trunk* 1945; *Cloak and Dagger* 1946; *Unconquered* 1947; *Variety Girl* 1947; *Good Sam* 1948; *The Fountainhead* 1949; *It's a Great Feeling* 1949; *Task Force* 1949; *Bright Leaf* 1950; *Dallas* 1950; *Distant Drums* 1951; *It's a Big Country* 1951; *Starlift* 1951; *U.S.S. Tea Kettle* 1951; *High Noon* 1952 **(AABA)**; *Springfield Rifle* 1952; *Blowing Wild* 1953; *Return to Paradise* 1953; *Garden of Evil* 1954; *Vera Cruz* 1954; *The Court Martial of Billy Mitchell* 1955; *Friendly Persuasion* 1956; *Love in the Afternoon* 1957; *Man of the West* 1958; *Ten North Frederick* 1958; *Alias Jesse James* 1959; *The Hanging Tree* 1959; *They Came to Cordura* 1959; *The Wreck of the Mary Deare* 1959; *The Naked Edge* 1961; *Hollywood on Trial* 1976 (archival footage).

Cooper, Jackie • Actor; also director. • Born John Cooper, Jr., Los Angeles, CA, September 15, 1921. Cute, popular child star of the 1930s; later successful as a TV actor, director and producer. • *Fox Movietone Follies of 1929* 1929; *Sunny Side Up* 1929; *The Champ* 1931; *Skippy* 1931 **(AANBA)**; *Sooky* 1931; *Young Donovan's Kid* 1931; *Divorce in the Family* 1932; *When a Feller Needs a Friend* 1932; *The Bowery* 1933; *Broadway to Hollywood* 1933; *Lone Cowboy* 1933; *Peck's Bad Boy* 1934; *Treasure Island* 1934; *Dinky* 1935; *O'Shaughnessy's Boy* 1935; *Devil Is a Sissy* 1936; *Tough Guy* 1936; *Boy of the Streets* 1937; *Gangster's Boy* 1938; *That Certain Age* 1938; *White Banners* 1938; *The Big Guy* 1939; *Newsboy's Home* 1939; *Scouts to the Rescue* 1939; *Spirit of Culver* 1939; *Streets of New York* 1939; *Two Bright Boys* 1939; *What a Life* 1939; *Gallant Sons* 1940; *The Return of Frank James* 1940; *Seventeen* 1940; *Glamour Boy* 1941; *Her First Beau* 1941; *Life With Henry* 1941; *Ziegfeld Girl* 1941; *Men of Texas* 1942; *The Navy Comes Through* 1942; *Syncopation* 1942; *Where Are Your Children?* 1944; *French Leave* 1947; *Kilroy Was Here* 1947; *Stork Bites Man* 1947; *Everything's Ducky* 1961; *The Love Machine* 1971; *Stand Up and Be Counted* 1972 (d); *Chosen Survivors* 1974; *The Pink Panther Strikes Again* 1976; *Superman* 1978; *Superman II* 1980; *Superman III* 1983; *Superman IV: The Quest For Peace* 1987; *Surrender* 1987; *Going Hollywood: The War Years* 1988.

Cooper, Merian C. • Producer; also director. • Born Merian Caldwell Cooper, Jacksonville, FL, October 24, 1893; died 1973. *Educ.* US Naval Academy, Annapolis, MD; Georgia School of Technology. Director, with Ernest Schoedsack, of exotic adventure films in the 1920s and 30s, most notably *King Kong* (1933). Cooper subsequently concentrated on producing, often in collaboration with John Ford, and received a Special Academy Award in 1952 for his "many innovations and contributions to the art of motion pictures." • *The Lost Empire* 1924 (title writer,ed); *Grass* 1925 (d,p,ph); *Chang* 1927 (d,p); *Gow the Headhunter* 1928 (d,p,ph); *The Four Feathers* 1929 (d,p,ph); *The Most Dangerous Game* 1932 (p); *The Phantom of Crestwood* 1932 (p); *Roar of the Dragon* 1932 (story); *Ace of Aces* 1933 (exec.p); *Ann Vickers* 1933 (p); *Bed of Roses* 1933 (p); *Flying Down to Rio* 1933 (p); *King Kong* 1933 (d,p,sc,story); *Little Women* 1933 (p); *Lucky Devils* 1933 (p); *Morning Glory* 1933 (exec.p); *No Marriage Ties* 1933 (exec.p); *Son of Kong* 1933 (p); *The Crime Doctor* 1934 (p); *The Lost Patrol* 1934 (exec.p); *The Last Days of Pompeii* 1935 (p); *She* 1935 (p); *The Toy Wife* 1938 (p); *The Fugitive* 1947 (p); *Fort Apache* 1948 (p); *Mighty Joe Young* 1949 (p,story); *She Wore a Yellow Ribbon* 1949 (p); *Three Godfathers* 1949 (p); *Rio Grande* 1950 (p); *Wagonmaster* 1950 (p); *The Quiet Man* 1952 (p) **(AANBP)**; *This Is Cinerama* 1952 (p); *The Sun Shines Bright* 1953 (p); *The Searchers* 1956 (exec.p); *The Best of Cinerama* 1963 (p).

Copland, Aaron • Composer; also pianist, conductor. • Born Brooklyn, NY, November 14, 1900; died December 2, 1990, North Tarrytown, NY. *Educ.* Fontainebleau School of Music, France. Distinguished 20th-century composer who brought a melodic, richly textured sophistication to film scoring. Like the Soviet composer Prokofiev, his work had a distinctly national flavor, perhaps best exemplified in *Of Mice and Men* (1939), *Our Town* (1940) and *The Red Pony* (1949). • *The City* 1939 (m); *Of Mice and Men* 1939 (m) **(AANBM)**; *Our Town* 1940 (m) **(AANBM)**; *The North Star* 1943 (m) **(AANBM)**; *Fiesta* 1947 (m); *The Heiress* 1949 (m) **(AABM)**; *Idlers That Work* 1949 (m); *The Red Pony* 1949 (m); *Three Installations* 1952 (m); *Something Wild* 1961 (m); *Love & Money* 1980 (m); *Riding High* 1980 (song); *Conversations With Willard Van Dyke* 1981 (m); *Miles From Home* 1988 (m).

Coppola, Carmine • Composer; also conductor. • Born New York, NY, June 11, 1910. *Educ.* Juilliard (flute, composition); Manhattan School of Music (flute, composition). Former flautist under Arturo Toscanini with the NBC Symphony Orchestra. Coppola has scored several films directed by his son Francis. He is portrayed, as a young boy, by Oreste Baldini in *The Godfather Saga* (1977), the TV movie which combined the first two "Godfather" films with extra footage not used in the original versions. Coppola also composed the music for the restored version of Abel Gance's classic silent film, *Napoléon*. He is the father of actress Talia Shire. • *Tonight For Sure* 1962 (m); *The Godfather, Part II* 1974 (m,m.cond) **(AABM)**; *Mustang...The House that Joe Built* 1975 (m,songs); *Harry and Walter Go to New York* 1976 (a); *Apocalypse Now* 1979 (m); *The Black Stallion* 1979 (m); *One From the Heart* 1982 (a); *The Outsiders* 1983 (m,song); *Children of a Lesser God* 1986 (song); *Gardens of Stone* 1987 (m); *Tucker: The Man and His Dream* 1988 (m); *Blood Red* 1989 (m,m.cond); *New York Stories* 1989 (a,m); *The Freshman* 1990 (songs); *The Godfather, Part III* 1990 (m,m.cond,song).

Coppola, Francis Ford • Director; also producer, screenwriter. • Born Detroit, MI, April 7, 1939. *Educ.* Hofstra College (now University); UCLA Film School. Francis Ford Coppola is one of America's most erratic, energetic and controversial filmmakers. Known primarily for his successful "Godfather" trilogy—*The Godfather* (1972), *The Godfather, Part II* (1974) and *The Godfather, Part III* (1990)—Coppola has had a life and career of both stunning triumphs and tragic setbacks.

He has won five Academy Awards, received ten Oscar nominations and is winner of two Cannes Film Festival Palme d'Or Awards. But throughout the 1980s Coppola's financial setbacks (including out-of-control budgets, costly box-office flops and problems at his cherished Zoetrope Studios) were well-publicized. Personal tragedy hit in 1986 when his son Gio died in a boating accident.

Coppola's films, over which he usually enjoys total control, vary considerably in style, genre and content. With the exception of more personal works (the "Godfather" series and 1979's war-themed *Apocalypse Now*), and films which reflect his fascination with technology (*The Conversation* 1974 and *One From the Heart* 1982), Coppola's oeuvre suggests not so much an auteur's unique distinction as a gifted director's complete command of his craft.

A fiercely driven Hollywood outsider, Coppola was raised in suburban New York in a creative, supportive Italian-American family (Coppola's father Carmine is the composer/musician; his mother Italia had been an actress). He studied theater at Hofstra University, where he staged the school's first all-student production.

In 1960, Coppola entered UCLA film school, eventually earning a Masters Degree. Learning both in the classroom and in the field, Coppola's years at UCLA were highly productive: he worked in various capacities on several soft-core porn films as well as projects for low-budget king Roger Corman; he wrote the Samuel Goldwyn Award-winning script *Pilma, Pilma* (which was never filmed); and he directed his first feature, the Corman-produced *Dementia 13*, while in Ireland in the summer of 1963.

Coppola's 1966 UCLA thesis project was *You're a Big Boy Now*, a goofy Richard Lesteresque comedy which was distributed theatrically by Warner Bros.

In 1968, Coppola received his first studio directorial assignment, the big-budget box-office disappointment *Finian's Rainbow*. Shortly thereafter he wrote and directed *The Rain People* (1969), a small, personal film starring Shirley Knight as a distressed housewife who takes to the road.

During the 1960s, Coppola wrote or collaborated on over a dozen screenplays including the adaptation of *This Property is Condemned* (1966). He co-wrote with Gore Vidal the screenplay for *Is Paris Burning?* (1966) and, at age 31, capped off a prolific decade with his first Oscar, for the screenplay of *Patton* (1970, co-written with Edmund H. North).

In 1972, Coppola struck box-office gold and assured himself a lengthy chapter in film history with the monumental *Godfather*, which he directed for Paramount. The film, co-adapted with Mario

Puzo from the latter's bestseller, became one of the highest-grossing films in movie history and brought Coppola another Oscar for best screenplay adaptation. The film also earned the Oscar for best picture and a best director nomination for Coppola.

Starring Marlon Brando as Mafia Don Vito Corleone, Al Pacino as the favored son who takes over Vito's empire, Diane Keaton as Michael's beleaguered WASP wife, Robert Duvall as his trusted *consigliere* and Coppola's sister, Talia Shire, as the Don's daughter, *The Godfather* has become a classic of American cinema, spawning two sequels.

Following work on the screenplay for *The Great Gatsby* (1974), Coppola returned to directing in 1974 with *The Conversation*, from his own script about a lonely surveillance expert (Gene Hackman) whose obsessive eavesdropping leads to tragedy. The film, which brought Coppola two Oscar nominations and won the Palme d'Or at Cannes, features the high-tech gadgetry (here highlighted in the superb soundtrack, designed by Walter Murch) which was to fascinate Coppola throughout his career.

That same year, Coppola directed and co-wrote with Puzo the hugely successful *The Godfather Part II*, winner of six Oscars, including three for Coppola as producer, director and writer. This sequel, starring Robert De Niro, daringly intercuts the story of young Vito's rise to power (a prelude to the first film) with the parallel, contrasting story of his son Michael's ascendance 30 years later. (Both parts of *The Godfather* were later recut in chronological sequence for a nine-part TV series.)

Coppola followed with the wildly over-budget, long-delayed and catastrophe-prone *Apocalypse Now* (1979). Loosely based on Joseph Conrad's *Heart of Darkness*, the film tracks a CIA operative (Martin Sheen) who travels up a Cambodian river during the Vietnam War in search of Colonel Kurtz (Marlon Brando), a legendary figure who has established a bizarre empire deep in the jungle. Production of the film was so problematic that, Coppola said, "little by little we went crazy." After many months of difficult jungle shooting and strenuous editing, the long-awaited, $30 million production enjoyed an emotional premiere at the Cannes Film Festival, where it won the Palme d'Or. A year later, the film took two Oscars.

Apocalypse Now was followed by 11 years of box-office disappointments, with Coppola's films often suffering as a result of the director's egocentric tendencies. The $26 million production of *One From the Heart* (1982) was a major financial and critical disappointment, due largely to Coppola's preoccupation with costly high-tech gadgets and experimental computer and video techniques at the expense of basic storytelling values.

In 1983 Coppola invested his own money in two adaptations of teenage-themed novels by S.E. Hinton. *The Outsiders* and *Rumble Fish* were both criticized as over-stylized and lacking in strong narrative impact and both lost money. Nevertheless, they captured the writer's world, as Coppola had intended, and provided screen introductions for an astonishing number of young actors who would, within a few years, come to dominate the Hollywood scene. Their casts include Matt Dillon, Mickey Rourke, Nicolas Cage, C. Thomas Howell, Ralph Macchio, Patrick Swayze, Rob Lowe, Emilio Estevez, Tom Cruise and Christopher Penn, as well as Diane Lane, Tom Waits, and Dennis Hopper.

Showing considerable tenacity, Coppola next turned to *The Cotton Club* (1984), an ambitious musical set in the famous Harlem jazz club of the 1920s. He put the script through nearly 40 drafts before the trouble-plagued production began. During the filming of the $48 million extravaganza, Coppola reportedly spent most of his time in his customized high-tech trailer, the "Silverfish," a state-of-the-art audio/video fortress bristling with cameras, monitors, decks and computers.

Following the financial failure of *The Cotton Club*, Coppola became a director-for-hire on the light time-travel comedy, *Peggy Sue Got Married* (1986). With the facility, audacity and vision which have marked all his best films, he produced a haunting elegy for times past which had great appeal for Peggy Sue's contemporaries in the audience, then in their forties. He captured the look and feel, the colors and emotions of high school in the 1950s as no one else had. Rather quickly, *Peggy Sue* became something of a perennial on videotape and TV, a proper companion piece to colleague and protégé George Lucas's *American Graffiti* (1973), which deals with a slightly later period in our collective past. The film solidified Kathleen Turner's reputation and made a star of Coppola's nephew, Nicolas Cage.

Coppola's 1987 *Gardens of Stone*, a well acted Vietnam War-era drama played out on the home front, pleased some critics but not audiences. The far more impressive *Tucker: The Man and His Dream* (1988) starred Jeff Bridges in the role of the real-life 1940s auto-industry visionary. Coppola had been planning to make this film since the early 70s, when he had become fascinated with the story of Tucker, the brash but intelligent entrepreneur who dared to challenge the Detroit establishment. The story is not without parallels to Coppola's own career in Hollywood but, more importantly, *Tucker* focuses attention on entrepreneurship and innovation at a time in American history when those qualities are sorely lacking. Like *Peggy Sue, Tucker* also reveals a striking sense of period. Because Coppola uses the cinematic conventions of the 1940s to capture the look and feel of the time, *Tucker* is as much about his (and our) memory of the period as it is about the period itself. If you weren't alive during that time, this is as close as you'll get.

In 1989, Coppola directed the *Life Without Zoe* segment (co-written by his daughter Sofia) of *New York Stories* and received the weakest reviews of the three participating directors (Martin Scorsese and Woody Allen were the others).

Throughout his career, shaky business ventures have magnified the problems of Coppola's box-office flops. In the 1960s, he poured profits from screenwriting into an ill-faited venture called Scopitone, a device which showed short movies on a juke box; the world was not yet ready for music videos. In the 70s, the San Francisco-based *City Magazine* failed soon after he took it over. American Zoetrope went through several incarnations, first in San Francisco, where Coppola had settled early on, then in Los Angeles after he bought the Goldwyn Studios with visions of creating a studio controlled by artists. Reeling from the failure of *One From the Heart*, he was pushed to the brink of bankruptcy as his debts vaulted to a staggering $30 million. In January 1990, just as Coppola began shooting *The Godfather Part III*, Zoetrope Studios finally filed for Chapter 11 bankruptcy.

Coppola was working in Rome when the opportunity arose to direct *Godfather III*. On the verge of financial ruin and in need of a hit—just as he had been in 1971 when the first Godfather project was handed to him—Coppola acceded to Paramount chairman Frank Mancuso's pleas for a third installment. Bargaining for full artistic control over the project, he began what was to become a $55 million dollar, rumor-bound production in November 1989. *The Godfather Part III* reunited screenwriters Coppola and Puzo and stars Al Pacino, Diane Keaton and sister Talia Shire, this time joined by his daughter Sofia.

Whatever Coppola does in the future, the "Godfather" series will remain the monument of his career. The first two installments alone earned more than $800 million at the international box-office. Audiences may have come for the mafia gangster drama but they stayed for the family saga. The conflict that gives the trilogy its demonstrated mythic power is not the gangster-film tension of good guys versus bad guys (where are the good guys?). It's the all-too-familiar tension between professional and personal commitments—gangster or filmmaker, you're still torn between home and office.

It is a conflict, to be sure, close to Coppola's heart. Practicing in real life the pervasive "Godfather" theme of the sanctity of the family, Coppola has consistently made members of his own family, including father Carmine, sister Talia

Shire, nephew Nicolas Cage and daughter Sofia, key contributors to his films. He's not unique in this—Cassavetes, Scorsese and Mazursky have done the same. Sofia's co-starring role in *The Godfather Part III*, however, was widely cited as the most serious of the film's flaws.

Besides his family, Coppola has been a kind of "godfather" to other directors, executive-producing for the likes of Paul Schrader, Wim Wenders and Akira Kurosawa and playing an important part in the restoration of Abel Gance's classic silent film, *Napoléon*. Coppola has also indulged his love of technology in a version of the *Rip Van Winkle* story for cable TV and in the high-tech Michael Jackson fantasy short, *Captain Eo* (1986). DT, JM • *Tonight For Sure* 1962 (d,p,sc); *Tower of London* 1962 (dial.d); *Dementia 13* 1963 (d,sc); *Battle Beyond the Sun* 1963 (d, as "Thomas Colchart"; dubbed, reedited version of Russian film *Nebo zovyot*); *The Terror* 1963 (ad); *Is Paris Burning?* 1966 (sc); *This Property Is Condemned* 1966 (sc); *You're a Big Boy Now* 1966 (d,sc); *Finian's Rainbow* 1968 (d); *The Rain People* 1969 (d,sc); *Patton* 1970 (sc) **(AABSC)**; *THX 1138* 1971 (exec.p); *The Godfather* 1972 (d,sc) **(AANBD,AABSC)**; *American Graffiti* 1973 (p) **(AANBP)**; *The Conversation* 1974 (d,p,sc) **(AANBP,AANBSC)**; *The Godfather, Part II* 1974 (d,p,sc) **(AABD,AABP,AABSC)**; *The Great Gatsby* 1974 (sc); *Apocalypse Now* 1979 (a,d,p,sc,m) **(AANBP)**; *The Black Stallion* 1979 (exec.p); *The Escape Artist* 1982 (exec.p); *Hammett* 1982 (exec.p); *One From the Heart* 1982 (d,sc); *The Black Stallion Returns* 1983 (exec.p); *The Outsiders* 1983 (d,p); *Rumble Fish* 1983 (d,exec.p); *The Cotton Club* 1984 (d,sc,story); *Mishima: A Life in Four Chapters* 1985 (exec.p); *Captain Eo* 1986 (d); *Peggy Sue Got Married* 1986 (d); *Gardens of Stone* 1987 (d,p); *Lionheart* 1987 (exec.p); *Tough Guys Don't Dance* 1987 (exec.p); *Powaqqatsi* 1988 (p); *Tucker: The Man and His Dream* 1988 (d); *New York Stories* 1989 (d,sc—"Life Without Zoe"); *The Godfather Part III* 1990 (d,p,sc); *Hollywood Mavericks* 1990 (a).

Corey, Wendell • Actor • Born Dracut, MA, March 20, 1914; died Novemeber 11, 1968, Woodland Hills, CA. Dependable lead and supporting actor who usually played solid, sober characters. After scoring a triumph on Broadway in Elmer Rice's *Dream Girl* (1945), Corey was signed by producer Hal Wallis and, over the next two decades, appeared as a servant/henchman to gambler John Hodiak in *Desert Fury* (1947, his debut), as a homicide detective opposite Loretta Young in the thriller, *The Accused* (1948), as an exhausted mobster in *Any Number Can Play* (1949) and as Frank James in *The Great Missouri Raid* (1951). Corey later moved into politics, serving as president of the Academy of Motion Picture Arts and Sciences and the Screen Actors Guild and, later, as a member of the Santa Monica, CA, City Council. • *Desert Fury* 1947; *I Walk Alone* 1947; *The Accused* 1948; *Man-Eater of Kumaon* 1948; *The Search* 1948; *Sorry, Wrong Number* 1948; *Any Number Can Play* 1949; *The File on Thelma Jordan* 1949; *Holiday Affair* 1949; *The Furies* 1950; *No Sad Songs For Me* 1950; *The Great Missouri Raid* 1951; *Rich, Young and Pretty* 1951; *The Wild Blue Yonder* 1951; *Carbine Williams* 1952; *My Man and I* 1952; *The Wild North* 1952; *Jamaica Run* 1953; *Laughing Anne* 1953; *Hell's Half Acre* 1954; *Rear Window* 1954; *The Big Knife* 1955; *The Bold and the Brave* 1955; *The Killer Is Loose* 1955; *The Rack* 1956; *The Rainmaker* 1956; *Loving You* 1957; *The Light in the Forest* 1958; *Alias Jesse James* 1959; *Blood on the Arrow* 1964; *Agent For H.A.R.M.* 1966; *Cyborg 2087* 1966; *Picture Mommy Dead* 1966; *Waco* 1966; *Women of the Prehistoric Planet* 1966; *Red Tomahawk* 1967; *The Astro-Zombies* 1968; *Buckskin* 1968.

Corliss, Richard • Critic • Born US. Long-time critic for *Time* magazine and editor of *Film Comment*, one of the longest-surviving serious US film journals. Corliss was instrumental in the 1970s in the development of the new film culture in the US. His book *Talking Pictures: Screenwriters in the American Cinema 1927-1973* (1974) emphasized, quite convincingly, the primacy of the writer at a time when most film scholars were under the thrall of the auteur theory.

Corman, Roger • Director, producer; also screenwriter. • Born Los Angeles, CA, April 5, 1926. *Educ.* Stanford (engineering); Balliol College, Oxford (English). Roger Corman is known primarily for his low budget, highly profitable films, but also for providing in-house training to young filmmakers who went on to become masters of the Hollywood cinema. Working outside the studio system, Corman has established a record as one of the most commercially successful filmmakers in Hollywood history, with over 200 films to his credit, 90% of which have turned a profit.

After graduating from Stanford in 1947, Corman broke into the film business, first as a messenger boy and later as a story analyst and screenwriter. After his first script (*Highway Dragnet* 1954) was altered by a studio, he decided to make his own movies, beginning with *Monster from the Ocean Floor* in 1954. American Releasing Corporation, which later became known as American International Pictures, distributed Corman's second film, *The Fast and the Furious* (1954), as part of an unusual deal: ARP advanced the filmmaker cash to make additional movies. Corman later employed this arrangement with other distributors such as Allied Artists.

By 1955, when he made his directorial debut, the Corman formula was in place: quirky characters; offbeat plots laced with social commentary; clever use of special effects, sets and cinematography; employment of fresh talent; and above all, miniscule budgets (under $100,000) and breakneck shooting schedules (5-10 days). Corman titles from the 1950s and 60s include such genre films as *Swamp Women* (1956), *Machine Gun Kelly* (1958), *Little Shop of Horrors* (1961), *The Wild Angels* (1966) and *The Trip* (1967). His films based on the stories and poems of Edgar Allan Poe (*The Pit and the Pendulum* 1961, *Tales of Terror* 1962, *The Raven* 1963, *Masque of the Red Death* 1964) were typically shot in three weeks on extremely low budgets, yet have become classics of the horror genre.

Dissatisfied with increasing studio and AIP interference in both the content and budgets of his films, Corman decided to start his own company in order to exert total control over his product. In 1970 he formed New World Pictures, which produced and distributed, not only exploitation movies such as *Death Race 2000* (1975), but also sophisticated European art films by celebrated directors such as Truffaut, Bergman and Fellini. Corman once again demonstrated his Midas touch; New World became the largest independent production and distribution company in the US and in January 1983 he sold it for $16.5 million.

In 1983 Corman founded Concorde/New Horizons, a production company which continues to be both prolific (over 20 films annually) and commercially prodigious (1987 gross earnings: $94 million). Taking full advantage of "ancillary" markets (videocassete, pay TV and foreign sales), Corman continues his lucrative practice of releasing successful, cut-rate exploitation films such as *Not of this Earth* (1988), *Nightfall* (1988) and *The Lawless Land* (1989).

Corman's legendary success is attributed to the fact that he operates outside the usual Hollywood constraints. He does not shrink from hiring unconventional actors such as pornography film stars like Traci Lords; he was one of the first producers to recognize the financial advantages of shooting in Europe; and he has even used sets discarded from other lavish, expensive movies for his own films.

In addition to his successful business innovations, Corman is recognized for his sponsorship of new talent. His ability to locate, and then provide a training ground for young filmmakers has produced an impressive roster of directors and performers. Francis Ford Coppola, Peter Bogdanovich, Martin Scorsese, John Sayles, Robert Towne, Jack Nicholson, Robert De Niro, Dennis Hopper and Charles Bronson are but a few of the names associated with Corman films early in their careers. TKB • *The Fast and the Furious* 1954 (p,sc); *Highway Dragnet* 1954 (story); *Monster From the Ocean Floor* 1954 (p); *Apache Woman* 1955 (d,p); *Five Guns West* 1955 (d,p); *The Day the World Ended* 1956 (d,p); *The Gunslinger* 1956 (d,p); *It Conquered the World* 1956 (d,p); *The Oklahoma Woman* 1956 (d,p); *Swamp Women* 1956 (d); *Attack of the Crab Monsters* 1957 (d,p); *Carnival Rock* 1957 (d); *Naked Paradise* 1957 (d,p); *Not of This Earth* 1957 (d,p); *Rock All Night* 1957 (d); *Sorority Girl* 1957 (d,p); *Teenage Doll* 1957 (d,p); *The Undead* 1957 (d,p); *Viking Women and the Sea Serpent* 1957 (d,p); *Cry Baby Killer* 1958 (p); *Hot Car Girl* 1958 (exec.p); *Machine Gun Kelly* 1958 (d,p); *Night of the Blood Beast* 1958 (exec.p); *She Gods of Shark Reef* 1958 (d); *Teenage Caveman* 1958 (d,p); *War of the Satellites* 1958 (d,p); *A Bucket of Blood* 1959 (d,p); *I Mobster* 1959 (d,p); *Nebo zovyot* 1959 (exec.p—American version); *Atlas* 1960 (d); *Attack of the Giant Leeches* 1960 (exec.p); *Creature From the Haunted Sea* 1960 (d,p); *House of Usher* 1960 (d,p); *The Last Woman on Earth* 1960 (d,p); *Ski Troop Attack* 1960 (d); *The Wasp Woman* 1960 (d,p); *Little Shop of Horrors* 1961 (d,p); *The Pit and the Pendulum* 1961 (d,p); *The Intruder* 1962 (d,p); *The Premature Burial* 1962 (d,p); *Tales of Terror* 1962 (d,p); *Tower of London* 1962 (d); *Dementia 13* 1963 (exec.p); *The Haunted Palace* 1963 (d,p); *The Raven* 1963 (d,p); *The Terror* 1963 (d,p); *X* 1963 (d,p); *The Young Racers* 1963 (d,p); *The Masque of the Red Death* 1964 (d,p); *The Secret Invasion* 1964 (d); *The Tomb of Ligeia* 1965 (d,p); *The Wild Angels* 1966 (d,p); *The St. Valentine's Day Massacre* 1967 (d,p); *The Trip* 1967 (d,p); *Das Ausschweifende Leben des Marquis De Sade* 1969 (d); *How to Make It* 1969 (a,d); *Bloody Mama* 1970 (d,p); *The Dunwich Horror* 1970 (exec.p); *Gas-s-s-s!* 1970 (d,p); *The Student Nurses* 1970 (exec.p); *Von Richthofen and Brown* 1971 (d); *Boxcar Bertha* 1972 (p); *The Unholy Rollers* 1972 (p); *I Escaped From Devil's Island* 1973 (p); *Big Bad Mama* 1974 (p); *Cockfighter* 1974 (p); *The Godfather, Part II* 1974 (a); *Capone* 1975 (p); *Death Race 2000* 1975 (p); *Lumiere* 1975 (p); *Cannonball* 1976 (a); *Eat My Dust* 1976 (p); *Fighting Mad* 1976 (p); *Jackson County Jail* 1976 (exec.p); *Moving Violation* 1976 (exec.p); *Grand Theft Auto* 1977 (exec.p); *I Never Promised You a Rose Garden* 1977 (exec.p); *Thunder and Lightning* 1977 (p); *Avalanche* 1978 (p); *Deathsport* 1978 (p); *Fast Charlie—The Moonbeam Rider* 1978 (p); *Outside Chance* 1978 (p); *Piranha* 1978 (exec.p); *Roger Corman: Hollywood's Wild Angel* 1978 (a); *Rock 'n' Roll High School* 1979 (exec.p); *Saint Jack* 1979 (p); *Battle Beyond the Stars* 1980 (exec.p); *The Howling* 1980 (a); *Galaxy of Terror* 1981 (p); *Smokey Bites the Dust* 1981 (p); *The Territory* 1981 (exec.p); *Forbidden World* 1982 (p); *Der Stand der Dinge* 1982 (a); *Love Letters* 1983 (p); *Space Raiders* 1983 (p); *Suburbia* 1983 (exec.p); *The Warrior and the Sorceress* 1983 (exec.p); *Deathstalker* 1984 (exec.p); *Swing Shift* 1984 (a); *Streetwalkin'* 1985 (exec.p); *Amazons* 1987 (p); *Hour of the Assassin* 1987 (exec.p); *Munchies* 1987 (p); *Slumber Party Massacre II* 1987 (p); *Stripped to Kill* 1987 (exec.p); *Sweet Revenge* 1987 (exec.p); *Big Bad Mama II* 1988 (p); *Daddy's Boys* 1988 (p); *Dangerous Love* 1988 (exec.p); *The Drifter* 1988 (exec.p); *Nightfall* 1988 (p); *Not of this Earth* 1988 (exec.p); *Watchers* 1988 (exec.p); *Andy Colby's Incredibly Awesome Adventure* 1989 (exec.p); *Bloodfist* 1989 (p); *Crime Zone* 1989 (exec.p); *Dance of the Damned* 1989 (exec.p); *Heroes Stand Alone* 1989 (exec.p); *The Lawless Land* 1989 (exec.p); *Lords of the Deep* 1989 (p); *The Masque of the Red Death* 1989 (p); *Stripped to Kill II* 1989 (exec.p); *The Terror Within* 1989 (p); *Time Trackers* 1989 (p); *Two to Tango* 1989 (p); *Wizards of the Lost Kingdom II* 1989 (p); *Back to Back* 1990 (exec.p); *Bloodfist II* 1990 (p); *A Cry in the Wild* 1990 (exec.p); *Full Fathom Five* 1990 (exec.p); *The Haunting of Morella* 1990 (p); *Overexposed* 1990 (p); *Primary Target* 1990 (p); *Roger Corman's Frankenstein Unbound* 1990 (d,p,sc); *Silk 2* 1990 (p); *Streets* 1990 (exec.p); *Transylvania Twist* 1990 (exec.p); *Watchers II* 1990 (p); *Welcome to Oblivion* 1990 (exec.p); *Hollywood Boulevard II* 1991 (exec.p); *The Silence of the Lambs* 1991 (a); *The Terror Within II* 1991 (exec.p).

Cornelius, Henry • Director; also producer, screenwriter. • Born South Africa, August 18, 1913; died 1958. *Educ.* Sorbonne, Paris. Studied under Max Reinhardt and worked with René Clair and Alexander Korda before returning in 1940 to South Africa, where he produced several films for General Smuts's pro-British propaganda campaign. • *The Ghost Goes West* 1935 (asst.ed); *Passport to Pimlico* 1949 (d); *The Galloping Major* 1951 (d,sc); *Genevieve* 1953 (d,p); *I Am a Camera* 1955 (d); *Next to No Time* 1958 (d,sc).

Cort, Bud • Actor • Born Walter Edward Cox, New Rochelle, NY, March 29, 1950. *Educ.* NYU. After appearing in five films in 1970, Cort enjoyed his greatest success as the death-fixated young adult who falls in love with a 79-year-old woman (Ruth Gordon) in Hal Ashby's hilarious *Harold and Maude* (1971). • *Brewster McCloud* 1970; *Gas-s-s-s!* 1970; *M*A*S*H* 1970; *The Strawberry Statement* 1970; *The Traveling Executioner* 1970; *Harold and Maude* 1971; *Why Shoot the Teacher?* 1976; *Die Laughing* 1980; *She Dances Alone* 1981; *Hysterical* 1983; *Love Letters* 1983; *Electric Dreams* 1984; *The Secret Diary of Sigmund Freud* 1984; *Maria's Lovers* 1985; *Invaders From Mars* 1986; *Love at Stake* 1987; *The Chocolate War* 1988; *Out of the Dark* 1989; *Brain Dead* 1990.

Cortese, Valentina • *aka* Valentina Cortesa • Actress • Born Milan, Italy, January 1, 1925. *Educ.* Academy of Arts, Rome. European leading lady, in English language films from 1948 with *The Glass Mountain*. Married *House on Telegraph Hill* (1951) co-star Richard Basehart in 1951. • *Orizzonte dipinto* 1940; *Il Bravo de Venezia* 1941; *La Cena delle Beffe* 1941; *Primo Amore* 1941; *La Regina di Navarra* 1941; *L'Angelo bianco* 1942; *Giorni felici* 1942; *Orizzonte di sangue* 1942; *Una Signora dell'Ouest* 1942; *Soltana un bacio* 1942; *Chi l'ha visto?* 1943; *Nessuno torna indietro* 1943; *Quarta Pagina* 1943; *Quattro ragazze sognano* 1943; *I Dieci Comandamenti* 1945; *Roma citta libera* 1946; *A Yank in Rome* 1946; *Il Corriere del Re* 1947; *L'Ebreo errante* 1947; *I Miserabili: La caccia all'uomo* 1947; *I Miserabili: Tempesta su Parigi* 1947; *Il Passatore* 1947; *Gli Uomini sono nemici* 1947; *Le Carrefour des passions* 1948; *The Glass Mountain* 1948; *Black Magic* 1949; *Donne Senza Nome* 1949; *Malaya* 1949; *Thieves' Highway* 1949; *Shadow of the Eagle* 1950; *The House on Telegraph Hill* 1951; *The Secret People* 1951; *Lulu* 1952; *Addio, mia bella signora!* 1953; *Donne Proibite* 1953; *Il Matrimonio* 1953; *La Passeggiata* 1953; *Avanzi di Galera* 1954; *The Barefoot Contessa* 1954; *Adriana Lecouvreur* 1955; *Le Amiche* 1955; *IL Conte Aquila* 1955; *Faccia da mascalzone* 1955; *Calabuch* 1956; *Dimentica il mio passata* 1956; *Magic Fire* 1956; *Amore e guai* 1959; *Nasilje na trgu* 1961; *Axel Munthe, der Arzt von San Michele* 1962; *Barabbas* 1962; *La Ragazza che sapeva troppo* 1962; *Der Besuch* 1964; *La Donna del lago* 1965; *Giulietta degli Spiriti* 1965; *Soleil noir* 1966; *The Legend of Lylah Clare* 1968; *Scusi, facciamo l'amore* 1968; *The Secret of Santa Vittoria* 1969; *Toh, e morta la nonna!* 1969; *Caprices de Marie* 1970; *First Love* 1970; *Madly* 1970; *Le Bateau sur l'herbe* 1971; *Imputazione di omicidio per uno studente* 1971; *The Assassination of Trotsky* 1972; *L'Iguana dalla lingua di fuoco* 1972; *Il Bacio* 1973; *Brother Sun, Sister Moon* 1973; *Franco Zeffirelli: A Florentine Artist* 1973; *La Nuit Américaine/Day For Night* 1973 **(AABSA)**; *Amore mio non farmi male* 1974; *Appassionata* 1974; *Tendre Dracula* 1974; *Le Grand Escogriffe* 1977; *Widows' Nest* 1977; *Nido de Viudas* 1978; *When Time Ran Out* 1980; *Monte Napoleone* 1987; *The Adventures of Baron Munchausen* 1988; *Il Giovane Toscanini/Young Toscanini* 1988.

Cortez, Stanley • *aka* Stanislaus Kranze • Director of photography • Born Stanislaus Krantz, New York, NY, November 4, 1908. *Educ.* NYU. Master of chiaroscuro cinematography who described himself as "always chosen to shoot weird things." Often employed on independent, low-budget productions which tended to allow more room for visual experimentation. Brother of actor/director Ricardo Cortez (1899-1977). • *Armored Car* 1937 (ph); *Four Days' Wonder* 1937 (ph); *The Wildcatter* 1937 (ph); *The Black Doll* 1938 (ph); *Danger on the Air* 1938 (ph); *The Lady in the Morgue* 1938 (ph); *Personal Secretary* 1938 (ph); *For Love or Money* 1939 (ph); *The Forgotten Woman* 1939 (ph); *Hawaiian Nights* 1939 (ph); *Laugh It Off* 1939 (ph); *They Asked For It* 1939 (ph); *Alias the Deacon* 1940 (ph); *The Leather Pushers* 1940 (ph); *Love, Honor, and Oh, Baby!* 1940 (ph); *Margie* 1940 (ph); *Meet the Wildcat* 1940 (ph); *Badlands of Dakota* 1941 (ph); *The Black Cat* 1941 (ph); *A Dangerous Game* 1941 (ph); *Moonlight in Hawaii* 1941 (ph); *San Antonio Rose* 1941 (ph); *Sealed Lips* 1941 (ph); *Bombay Clipper* 1942 (ph); *Eagle Squadron* 1942 (ph); *The Magnificent Ambersons* 1942 (ph) **(AANBPH)**; *Flesh and Fantasy* 1943 (ph); *Since You Went Away* 1944 (ph) **(AANBPH)**; *Let There Be Light* 1945 (ph); *Smash-Up, the Story of a Woman* 1947 (ph); *Secret Beyond the Door* 1948 (ph); *Smart Woman* 1948 (ph); *The Man on the Eiffel Tower* 1949 (ph); *The Admiral Was a Lady* 1950 (ph); *The Underworld Story* 1950 (ph); *The Basketball Fix* 1951 (ph); *Fort Defiance* 1951 (ph); *Abbott and Costello Meet Captain Kidd* 1952 (ph); *Models, Inc.* 1952 (ph); *Stronghold* 1952 (ph); *The Diamond Queen* 1953 (ph); *Dragon's Gold* 1953 (ph); *The Neanderthal Man* 1953 (ph); *Shark River* 1953 (ph); *Black Tuesday* 1954 (ph); *Riders to the Stars* 1954 (ph); *The Night of the Hunter* 1955 (ph); *Man From Del Rio* 1956 (ph); *The Three Faces of Eve* 1957 (ph); *Top Secret Affair* 1957 (ph); *The Angry Red Planet* 1959 (ph); *Thunder in the Sun* 1959 (ph); *Dinosaurus!* 1960 (ph); *Back Street* 1961 (ph); *Shock Corridor* 1963 (ph); *Madmen of Mandoras* 1964 (ph); *The Naked Kiss* 1964 (ph); *Nightmare in the Sun* 1965 (ph); *Young Dillinger* 1965 (ph); *The Ghost in the Invisible Bikini* 1966 (ph); *The Navy Vs. the Night Monsters* 1966 (ph); *Blue* 1968 (ph); *The Bridge at Remagen* 1969 (ph); *Tell Me That You Love Me, Junie Moon* 1970 (ph—title sequence); *The Date* 1971 (ph); *Another Man, Another Chance* 1977 (ph); *Damien—Omen II* 1978 (ph—miniatures); *When Time Ran Out* 1980 (ph—miniatures).

Corti, Axel • Director • Born Paris, 1933. Multi-award-winning director of French and Austrian theater, TV and radio, who began making films (both for TV and theatrical release) in the early 1960s. Corti gained well-deserved international recognition for his black-and-white "Where To and Back" trilogy, based on the autobiographical screenplays by Georg Stefan Troller: *God Does Not Believe in Us Anymore, Santa Fe* (both 1985) and *Welcome in Vienna* (1986). Shot in a neo-documentary style but not lacking in narrative drive, the trilogy constitutes a gripping social and political history of Vienna just before, during and immediately after WWII. • *Der Verweigerung/The Refusal* 1972 (d); *Totstellen/The Condemned* 1975 (d); *Donauwalzer/Waltzes of the Danube* 1984 (a); *A Woman's Pale Blue Handwriting* 1984 (d,sc); *An uns glaubt Gott nicht mehr/God Does Not Believe in Us Anymore* 1985 (d); *Santa Fe* 1985 (d); *Welcome in Vienna* 1986 (d,sc); *The King's Whore* 1990 (d,sc).

Cosby, Bill • Actor; also comedian, author. • Born William H. Cosby, Jr., Philadelphia, PA, July 12, 1937. *Educ.* Temple University, Philadelphia; University of Massachusetts (education). One of the most highly paid TV personalities in the US and an icon of contemporary American culture: Emmy-winning co-star of the series *I Spy* (1965-1969), narrator of the cartoon *Fat Albert* (1972-79), salesman of Jell-O and Coca-Cola, and creator, producer and star of the phenomenally successful *The Cosby Show* (1984-). Cosby has been less successful on the big screen, though in the 1970s he starred in three popular films (*Uptown Saturday Night* 1974, *Let's Do It Again* 1975, *A Piece of the Action* 1977) with director-actor Sidney Poitier.

Quietly, Cosby has done as much as anyone in entertainment to advance the role of African-Americans. As a stand-up comic in the 1960s, he refused to "go the chitlin route," eschewing racial comedy and commenting instead on universal family situations. As co-star of "I Spy" with Robert Culp, he set a model for black actors and black characters, playing a role devoid of racial overtones. In the 70s, he returned to school to complete a doctorate in education and has since been active in educational circles. "The Cosby Show" was the top-rated TV program through most of the late 80s.

Despite all these socially conscious and uplifting career moves, an element of anger and impatience lurks never far beneath the surface, especially in Cosby's stand-up performances. It gives an added dimension to his work and reminds us that we still have a long way to go. JM • *Man and Boy* 1971 (a,exec.p); *Hickey and Boggs* 1972 (a); *Uptown Saturday Night* 1974 (a); *Let's Do It Again* 1975 (a); *Mother, Jugs & Speed* 1976 (a); *A Piece of the Action* 1977 (a); *California Suite* 1978 (a); *The Devil and Max Devlin* 1981 (a); *Bill Cosby—"Himself"* 1983 (a,d,p,sc); *Leonard, Part 6* 1987 (a,p,story); *Ghost Dad* 1990 (a).

Cosmatos, George Pan • Director; also screenwriter. • Born Tuscany, Italy, January 4, 1941. *Educ.* London University (international law); National Film School, London. Talented director who first gained attention with *Massacre in Rome* (1973), starring Richard Burton and Marcello Mastroianni, and is probably best known in the US for *Rambo: First Blood Part II* (1985). Cosmatos specializes in action pictures and, fluent in five languages, has directed in at least as many countries. • *Exodus* 1960 (ad); *Zorba the Greek* 1964 (ad); *The Beloved* 1971 (d); *Massacre in Rome* 1973 (d,sc); *The Cassandra Crossing* 1977 (d,sc); *Escape to Athena* 1979 (d,story); *Of Unknown Origin* 1982 (d); *Rambo: First Blood Part II* 1985 (d); *Cobra* 1986 (d); *Leviathan* 1989 (d).

Costa-Gavras • *aka* Constantin Costa-Gavras, Costi Costa-Gavras • Director • Born Konstantinos Gavras, Klivia, Greece, 1933. *Educ.* Sorbonne, Paris (comparative literature); IDHEC, Paris (producing, directing). Constantin Costa-Gavras is the preeminent figure in the development of the political thriller during the past two decades. Several of his films (*State of Siege* 1973, *Missing* 1982) are archetypes of the genre and *Z* (1969) is a crucial fictional account of political repression in the 20th century.

Born to a Russian father and a Greek mother, Costa-Gavras was mesmerized as a boy by the energy and movement of the many American films he saw. Because of his father's activities in the Greek resistance during WWII, Costa-Gavras's educational and occupational opportunities were stifled when the rightist Greek government blacklisted him. When he failed to obtain a visa to the US Costa-Gavras went to Paris, where he studied at the Sorbonne. Like other young cineastes such as François Truffaut and Jean-Luc Godard, he haunted the Cinémathèque Française and the Left Bank repertory film theaters. In November 1954 he enrolled in IDHEC, the French national film school.

After completing his formal training in 1958 Costa-Gavras started work as a directorial trainee, receiving valuable mentorship from, among others, René Clement, René Clair and Jacques Demy. His first film, *The Sleeping Car Murder* (1965), a detective thriller starring Yves Montand and Simone Signoret, was followed by the overtly political *Shock Troops*, a tale of the French Maquis starring Michel Piccoli. Shown at the Moscow Film Festival in 1967, *Shock Troops* was re-edited and given a happy ending by United Artists prior to its American release in 1969.

While preparing another project, Costa-Gavras discovered Vassilis Vassilikos's novel *Z*, based on the events surrounding the assassination of Greek reformer Grigoris Lambrakis in 1963. His film version, starring Yves Montand,

Irene Papas and Jean-Louis Trintignant, was released as a French/Algerian coproduction in 1969 and touched the consciousness of young cineastes, critics and political activists around the world. *Z* won the jury and best actor prizes at Cannes as well as the Oscar for best foreign film. It also spawned a host of imitations in France and the US. The film deals with the themes which have remained central to Costa-Gavras's work: the mechanics and repercussions of tyranny and the subtle varieties of guilt. Hugely successful in France and abroad (but banned in Greece), it remains a landmark of recent cinema.

The Confession (1970) followed, again based on a true incident in which a spurious confession was tortured out of a Czech Communist Party functionary (Yves Montand) and used in a sham trial. With *State of Siege*, Costa-Gavras completed an intensely creative period. Another fictionalized treatment of an actual event, the film tells the story of a clandestine American intelligence agent (Montand) assassinated by Uraguayan political terrorists. *State of Siege* also witnessed the maturation of Costa-Gavras' working method: beginning with a novelistic retelling of a single event and working in close collaboration with his screenwriter, the director meticulously researches the details of the incident, which is then brought to the screen via a highly disciplined but visually eclectic shooting style.

Special Section (1975) reunited Costa-Gavras with Jorge Semprun, the screenwriter of *Z*, on a project devoted to the activities of the French Vichy government. Roundly criticized by French patriots who had hoped for a melodramatic rewriting of wartime events, *Special Section* is a meditative and even-handed study of one of the most painful periods of French history. *Clair de femme*, an emphatically apolitical film starring Montand and Romy Schneider, was released in 1979.

The American focus of *State of Siege* and the director's own fascination with American political culture have been developed in his most recent films. *Missing* (1982), with Jack Lemmon and Sissy Spacek, told of the kidnapping and death-squad murder of Charles Horman, a leftist American journalist, in Chile in 1973. The film attracted criticism (as have all Costa-Gavras's films since *Z*) from doctrinaire Marxists for its use of dramatic devices to invoke sympathy for an individual victim of political repression. Yet *Missing* was well calibrated for its American audience, which responded enthusiastically to the most significant political thriller made in the US since *The Manchurian Candidate*.

Betrayed (1988), starring Tom Berenger and Debra Winger, explores the underworld of racist politics in rural America. *The Music Box* (1989) relates the trial of an alleged Hungarian war criminal (Armin Mueller-Stahl) who has been a US citizen for 40 years; he is defended in court by his daughter (Jessica Lange). Costa-Gavras's recent work has amply demonstrated his understanding of the American character, as well as his ability to introduce dramatic tensions into politically themed films.

In 1982 Costa-Gavras took over the directorship of the Cinémathèque Française, then badly in disarray. During his tenure, he proved a tireless champion of both film preservation and artistic freedom, furthering the institution's international renown even as he continued to work on his own films. Costa-Gavras remains a passionate cinephile, a tireless researcher and a storyteller of profound skill and integrity. KJH • *L'Ambitieuse* 1959 (ad); *Robinson et le triporteur* 1959 (ad); *Cresus* 1960 (ad); *L'Homme à femmes* 1960 (ad); *Tout l'Or du Monde* 1961 (ad); *Un Singe en hiver* 1962 (ad); *La Baie des anges* 1963 (ad); *Jour et l'heure* 1963 (ad); *Echappement libre/Backfire* 1964 (ad); *Les Felins* 1964 (ad); *Peau de banane/Banana Peel* 1964 (ad); *Compartiment tueurs/The Sleeping Car Murder* 1965 (d,sc); *Un Homme de trop/Shock Troops* 1967 (d,sc); *Z* 1969 (d,sc); *L'Aveu/The Confession* 1970 (d); *Etat de siège/State of Siege* 1973 (d,sc); *Les Deux Mémoires* 1974 (voice); *Section Spéciale/Special Section* 1975 (d,sc); *Madame Rosa* 1977 (a); *Clair de femme/Womanlight* 1979 (d,sc); *Missing* 1982 (d,sc); *Hannah K* 1983 (d,p,sc); *Spies Like Us* 1985 (a); *Le Thé au harem d'Archimède* 1985 (p); *Conseil de Famille* 1986 (d,sc,dial); *Betrayed* 1988 (d); *Music Box* 1989 (d).

Costello, Lou • Actor; also vaudevillian. • Born Louis Francis Cristillo, Paterson, NJ, March 6, 1906; died 1959. See Abbott, Bud.

Costner, Kevin • Actor; also director, producer. • Born Los Angeles, CA, January 18, 1955. *Educ.* California State University, Fullerton (marketing). Handsome, amiable leading man who emerged as a major Hollywood star in the late 1980s. Cast by Lawrence Kasdan as the dead friend Alex, to be fondly remembered in flashbacks in *The Big Chill* (1983), Costner ended up on the cutting-room floor. In recompense Kasdan gave him a more prominent role in *Silverado* (1985), and the actor went on to earn critical and popular success in films like *The Untouchables* (1987), as Eliot Ness, and *Bull Durham* (1988), as minor-league baseball veteran "Crash" Davis. Costner made an auspicious directorial debut with *Dances with Wolves* (1990), in which he also starred. • *Shadows Run Black* 1981; *Night Shift* 1982; *Stacy's Knights* 1982; *The Gunrunner* 1983; *Table For Five* 1983; *Testament* 1983; *American Flyers* 1985; *Fandango* 1985; *Silverado* 1985; *Sizzle Beach, U.S.A.* 1986; *No Way Out* 1987; *The Untouchables* 1987; *Bull Durham* 1988; *Chasing Dreams* 1989; *Field of Dreams* 1989; *Dances With Wolves* 1990 (a,d,p); *Revenge* 1990 (a,exec.p); *Robin Hood: Prince of Thieves* 1991.

Cotten, Joseph • Actor • Born Joseph Cheshire Cotten, Petersburg, VA, May 15, 1905. *Educ.* Robert Nugent Hickman School of Expression, Washington DC. Member of Orson Welles's Mercury Theater who went to Hollywood with the director to make *Citizen Kane* (1941) and stayed to enjoy considerable success in *The Magnificent Ambersons* (1942), *Journey into Fear* (1942, opposite Welles) and Carol Reed's *The Third Man* (1949); Cotten also appeared, unbilled, as the drunken coroner in Welles's *Touch of Evil* (1958). Other outstanding credits include Hitchcock's *Shadow of a Doubt* (1943), *Since You Went Away* (1944), *Love Letters* (1945) and William Dieterle's *Portrait of Jennie* (1948), for which Cotten was named best actor at the Venice Film Festival. He married actress Patricia Medina in 1960. • *Citizen Kane* 1941; *Lydia* 1941; *Journey Into Fear* 1942 (a,sc); *The Magnificent Ambersons* 1942; *Hers to Hold* 1943; *Shadow of a Doubt* 1943; *Gaslight* 1944; *I'll Be Seeing You* 1944; *Since You Went Away* 1944; *Love Letters* 1945; *Duel in the Sun* 1947; *The Farmer's Daughter* 1947; *Portrait of Jennie* 1948; *Beyond the Forest* 1949; *The Third Man* 1949; *Under Capricorn* 1949; *Two Flags West* 1950; *Walk Softly, Stranger* 1950; *Half Angel* 1951; *The Man With a Cloak* 1951; *Peking Express* 1951; *September Affair* 1951; *The Steel Trap* 1952; *Untamed Frontier* 1952; *A Blueprint For Murder* 1953; *Niagara* 1953; *The Killer Is Loose* 1955; *Special Delivery* 1955; *The Bottom of the Bottle* 1956; *The Halliday Brand* 1956; *From the Earth to the Moon* 1958; *Touch of Evil* 1958; *The Angel Wore Red* 1960; *The Last Sunset* 1961; *Hush...Hush, Sweet Charlotte* 1964; *Comanche Blanco* 1965; *The Great Sioux Massacre* 1965; *I Crudeli* 1966; *The Money Trap* 1966; *The Oscar* 1966; *Gli Uomini del Passo Pesanti* 1966; *Brighty of the Grand Canyon* 1967; *Jack of Diamonds* 1967; *Some May Live* 1967; *Un Giorno di Fuoco* 1968; *Petulia* 1968; *Ido Zero Daisakusen* 1969; *Vene l'Ora della Vendetta, E* 1969; *The Grasshopper* 1970; *Tora! Tora! Tora!* 1970; *The Abominable Doctor Phibes* 1971; *La Figlia di Frankenstein* 1971; *Doomsday Voyage* 1972; *Gli Orrori del Castello di Norimberga* 1972; *Lo Scopone Scientifico* 1972; *A Delicate Balance* 1973; *Soylent Green* 1973; *Timber Tramps* 1973; *F Is For Fake* 1973; *Airport 77* 1977; *Sussuri Nel Buio* 1977; *Twilight's Last Gleaming* 1977; *Caravans* 1978; *L'Ordre et la sécurite du monde* 1978; *The Fish Men* 1979; *Guyana: Cult of the Damned* 1979; *L'Isola degli uomini Pesce* 1979; *The Hearse* 1980; *Heaven's Gate* 1980; *The House Where Death Lives* 1980; *The*

Survivor 1981; *Rambo Sfida la Citta* 1982; *Hitchcock, Il Brivido del Genio* (doc) 1985.

Courant, Curt • *aka* Kurt Courant • Director of photography • Born Curtis Courant, Germany, c. 1895. One of Europe's most distinguished cinematograhers who shot films for Marcel Carné, Alfred Hitchcock, Jean Renoir and Charlie Chaplin (*Monsieur Verdoux* 1947). Of Jewish descent, Courant worked with Fritz Lang before leaving Germany in 1933. His son, Willy Kurant, is also a cinematographer and has collaborated with Jean-Luc Godard (*Masculin-Feminin* 1966), Orson Welles (*The Immortal Story* 1968) and Maurice Pialat (*Under Satan's Sun* 1987). • *Hilde Warren und der Tod* 1917; *Hamlet* 1920; *Peter der Grosse/Peter the Great* 1922; *Quo Vadis?* 1924; *Ich Liebe Dich* 1926; *Das Brennende Herz/Burning Heart* 1929; *Die Frau Nach der Man Sich Sehnt* 1929; *Die Frau im Mond/The Woman in the Moon* 1929; *Der Weisse Teufel/The White Devil* 1930; *Coeur de Lilas* 1931; *Der Mann, der Den Mord Beging* 1931; *Rasputin* 1932; *Cette Vieille Canaille/The Old Devil* 1933; *Ciboulette* 1933; *Perfect Understanding* 1933; *Amok* 1934; *The Man Who Knew Too Much* 1934; *Le Voleur* 1934; *The Iron Duke* 1935; *Broken Blossoms* 1936; *Dusty Ermine* 1936; *Le Puritain* 1937; *La Bête Humaine/The Human Beast* 1938; *Louise* 1938; *Le Jour se lève/Daybreak* 1939; *De Mayerling à Sarajevo* 1940; *Monsieur Verdoux* 1947; *It Happened in Athens* 1962.

Courtenay, Tom • Actor • Born Hull, Yorkshire, England, February 25, 1937. *Educ.* London University (English); RADA, London. Innocent-looking, gaunt leading man who came of age with Alan Bates, Albert Finney and the British film renaissance of the early 1960s. Courtenay turned in superb performances as diffident or sullen anti-heroes in films like the bleak borstal drama, *The Loneliness of the Long Distance Runner* (1962), *Billy Liar* (1963), as a dreamy, Walter Mitty-like character, Joseph Losey's *King and Country* (1964), as a WWI soldier on trial for desertion, and Bryan Forbes's POW drama, *King Rat* (1965). Since 1971 he has concentrated almost exclusively on his stage career, making a strong return to film in 1983 by recreating his acclaimed London and Broadway stage performance as *The Dresser*. • *The Loneliness of the Long Distance Runner* 1962; *Private Potter* 1962; *Billy Liar* 1963; *King and Country* 1964; *Doctor Zhivago* 1965 **(AANBSA)**; *King Rat* 1965; *Operation Crossbow* 1965; *The Night of the Generals* 1966; *The Day the Fish Came Out* 1967; *A Dandy in Aspic* 1968; *Otley* 1968; *Catch Me a Spy* 1971; *One Day in the Life of Ivan Denisovich* 1971; *The Dresser* 1983 **(AANBA)**; *Happy New Year* 1987; *Le Dernier papillon* 1991.

Coutard, Raoul • Director of photography; also director. • Born Paris, September 16, 1924. Largely due to his ability to work fast, with minimal (often natural) lighting and hand-held cameras, Coutard was the most popular cinematographer among New Wave directors. Though he shot 14 films with Godard over a highly experimental eight-year period, he was also known for his ability to adapt himself to numerous directorial styles. Stand-outs of his 1960s work include the richly textured black-and-white of Truffaut's *Jules and Jim* (1961), the bleak grays of *Alphaville* (1965), the saturated color of *Contempt* (1963)—in which he appears—and the crisp brilliance of *Pierrot le fou* (1965). Coutard won praise for his feature directing debut, *Hoa-binh* (1970), though his subsequent efforts have been less impressive. • *Paradiso terrestre* 1956 (ph); *La Passe du diable* 1957 (ph); *Ramuntcho* 1958 (ph); *A bout de souffle/Breathless* 1959 (ph); *Pecheur d'islande* 1959 (ph); *Chronique d'un été* 1960 (ph); *Les Grandes personnes* 1960 (ph); *Le Petit Soldat* 1960 (ph); *Tirez Sur le Pianiste/Shoot the Piano Player* 1960 (ph); *Une Femme est une femme/A Woman Is a Woman* 1961 (ph); *Jules et Jim/Jules and Jim* 1961 (ph); *Lola* 1961 (ph); *Tire au flanc 62* 1961 (ph); *L'Amour à vingt ans/Love at Twenty* 1962 (ph—"Paris: Antoine et Colette"); *Et Satan conduit le bal* 1962 (ph); *La Poupée* 1962 (ph); *Vacances portugaises* 1962 (ph); *Vivre sa Vie/My Life to Live* 1962 (ph); *Als twee druppels water* 1963 (ph); *Les Baisers* 1963 (ph); *Les Carabiniers* 1963 (ph); *Difficulté d'être infidèle* 1963 (ph); *Le Mépris/Contempt* 1963 (a,ph); *La 317ème section* 1964 (ph); *Bande à part/Band of Outsiders* 1964 (ph); *Une Femme mariée* 1964 (ph); *Un Monsieur de compagnie* 1964 (ph); *La Peau Douce/The Soft Skin* 1964 (ph); *Les Plus belles escroqueries du monde* 1964 (ph—"Le grand escroc"); *Alphaville* 1965 (ph); *Je vous salue, Mafia* 1965 (ph); *Pierrot le Fou* 1965 (ph); *Scruggs* 1965 (ph); *Les Voix d'Orly* 1965 (ph); *The Defector* 1966 (ph); *Deux ou trois choses que je sais d'elle/Two or Three Things I Know About Her* 1966 (ph); *L'Horizon* 1966 (ph); *La Chinoise, ou plûtot à la Chinoise* 1967 (ph); *The Sailor From Gibraltar* 1967 (ph); *Weekend* 1967 (ph); *L'Etoile du sud* 1968 (ph); *La Mariée était en noir/The Bride Wore Black* 1968 (ph); *Rocky Road to Dublin* 1968 (ph); *Z* 1969 (a,ph); *L'Aveu* 1970 (a,ph); *Etes-vous fiancée à un marin grec ou à un pilote de ligne?* 1970 (ph); *Hoa-Binh* 1970 (d,sc); *La Liberté en croupe* 1970 (ph); *Les Aveux les plus doux* 1971 (ph); *Embassy* 1971 (ph); *L'Explosion* 1971 (ph); *The Jerusalem File* 1971 (ph); *Le Gang des Otages* 1972 (ph); *Le Trêfle à cinq feuilles* 1972 (ph); *Comme un pot des fraises!* 1974 (ph); *Le Crabe-Tambour* 1977 (ph); *La Legion saute sur kolwezi* 1979 (d); *Passion* 1982 (ph); *SAS à San Salvador* 1982 (d); *Prénom Carmen/First Name: Carmen* 1983 (ph); *La Diagonale du Fou* 1984 (ph); *La Garce* 1984 (ph); *Du Sel sur la Peau* 1984 (ph); *Max, mon amour* 1986 (ph); *Fuegos* 1987 (ph); *Blanc de chine* 1988 (ph); *Brennende Betten/Burning Beds* 1988 (ph); *Ne réveillez pas un flic qui dort* 1988 (ph); *Peaux de vaches* 1988 (ph); *Bethune: The Making of a Hero* 1990 (ph); *La Femme fardée* 1990 (ph); *Il gêle en enfer* 1990 (ph).

Coward, Sir Noel • Playwright; also screenwriter, actor. • Born Noel Pierce Coward, Teddington, Middlesex, England, December 16, 1899; died 1973. The epitome of English suavity, elegance and wit, many of whose plays formed the basis for successful, sophisticated films. Coward made his movie debut with a bit part in D.W. Griffith's *Hearts of the World* (1917) and won a special Academy Award for *In Which We Serve* (1942), co-directed with David Lean. • *Hearts of the World* 1918 (a); *Easy Virtue* 1927 (from play); *The Queen Was in the Parlor* 1927 (sc); *The Vortex* 1927 (from play); *Private Lives* 1931 (from play); *Bitter Sweet* 1933 (from play); *Cavalcade* 1933 (from play); *Design For Living* 1933 (from play); *Tonight Is Ours* 1933 (from play); *The Scoundrel* 1935 (a); *Bitter Sweet* 1940 (from play); *In Which We Serve* 1942 (p,d,m,a); *We Were Dancing* 1942 (from play *Tonight at 8:30*); *This Happy Breed* 1944 (p,from play); *Blithe Spirit* 1945 (p,sc,from play); *Brief Encounter* 1945 (p,sc,from play); *The Astonished Heart* 1950 (sc,from play,m,a); *Meet Me Tonight/Tonight at 8:30* 1952 (from play); *Our Man in Havana* 1960 (a); *Surprise Package* 1960 (a); *Paris When it Sizzles* 1964 (a); *Bunny Lake Is Missing* 1965 (a); *Pretty Polly/A Matter of Innocence* 1967 (from story); *Boom!* 1968 (a); *The Italian Job* 1969 (a).

Cox, Alex • Director; also screenwriter. • Born Liverpool, England, December 15, 1954. *Educ.* Oxford (law); Bristol University (film); UCLA Film School. Hip, intelligent young director, each of whose films—with the exception of *Straight to Hell* (1987), an ill-conceived spaghetti western starring a bunch of English pop stars—seems guaranteed to earn instant cult status. *Repo Man* (1984), ostensibly a science fiction thriller, took a winning, wacky look at the underside of Los Angeles "culture"; *Sid and Nancy* (1986), a genuine contemporary tragedy, combined a moving love story (between punk performer Sid Vicious and former groupie Nancy Spungeon) with a harrowing portrayal of heroin addiction; *Walker* (1987) was an ambitious biopic of William Walker, would-be American dictator of Nicaragua in the 1850s, which drew some heavy-handed parallels with American foreign policy of the 1980s.

• *Repo Man* 1984 (a,d,sc); *Scarred* 1984 (a,ad,story cons); *Sid and Nancy* 1986 (d,sc); *Straight to Hell* 1987 (d,sc); *Walker* 1987 (d,ed).

Cox, Paul • Director, screenwriter; also producer. • Born Paulus Henriqus Benedictus Cox, Venlo, Netherlands, April 16, 1940. *Educ.* Melbourne University. Cerebral Dutch-born filmmaker, in Australia from the mid-1960s. Cox first gained international recognition with his offbeat romance, *Lonely Hearts* (1981), continued to garner attention with *Man of Flowers* (1983) and received considerable critical acclaim for *Vincent* (1987), a documentary portrait of Van Gogh based on the artist's letters. • *Illuminations* 1975 (d,sc,ed); *Inside Looking Out* 1977 (d,p,sc,ph,ed); *Kostas* 1979 (d,idea); *Lonely Hearts* 1981 (d,sc); *Last Night at the Alamo* 1983 (m,songs); *Man of Flowers* 1983 (d,p,sc); *My First Wife* 1984 (d,p,sc); *Wo die grunen Ameisen traumen/Where the Green Ants Dream* 1984 (a); *Death and Destiny* 1985 (d,sc,ed); *Cactus* 1986 (d,p,sc,story); *Vincent—The Life and Death of Vincent Van Gogh* 1987 (d,sc,ph,ed); *Island* 1989 (d,p,sc); *The Golden Braid* 1990 (a,d,p,sc).

Cox, Ronny • Actor • Born Cloudcroft, NM, August 23, 1938. *Educ.* Georgetown University, Washington DC (drama); Eastern New Mexico University. Cool, efficient character player from the stage who made his debut as the intellectual, introspectve member of the rafting party in *Deliverance* (1972). In the 1980s Cox specialized in authority figures, businessmen and bureaucrats in such films as *Beverly Hills Cop* (1984), *Robocop* (1987) and *Total Recall* (1990). • *Deliverance* 1972; *The Happiness Cage* 1972; *Hugo the Hippo* 1975; *Bound For Glory* 1976; *The Car* 1977; *Gray Lady Down* 1977; *Harper Valley P.T.A.* 1978; *The Onion Field* 1979; *The Beast Within* 1981 (a,m,m.perf); *Taps* 1981; *Some Kind of Hero* 1982; *Beverly Hills Cop* 1984; *Courage* 1984 (a,p,sc); *Vision Quest* 1985; *Hollywood Vice Squad* 1986; *Beverly Hills Cop II* 1987; *Robocop* 1987; *Steele Justice* 1987; *Loose Cannons* 1989; *One Man Force* 1989; *Captain America* 1990; *Total Recall* 1990.

Coyote, Peter • Actor • Born Peter Cohon, New York, NY, 1942. *Educ.* San Francisco State University (writing); San Francisco Actors Workshop. Intense, driven supporting player from the San Francisco stage, occasionally in leading roles (*A Man in Love* 1987, etc.). Coyote was memorable as the government scientist on the trail of *E.T.* (1982) and as the tenacious prosecuting attorney in *Jagged Edge* (1985). • *Sgt. Pepper's Lonely Hearts Club Band* 1978; *Die Laughing* 1980; *Tell Me a Riddle* 1980; *The Pursuit of D.B. Cooper* 1981; *Southern Comfort* 1981; *E.T., the Extra-Terrestrial* 1982; *Endangered Species* 1982; *Out* 1982; *Timerider: The Adventure of Lyle Swann* 1982; *Cross Creek* 1983; *Stranger's Kiss* 1983; *Heartbreakers* 1984; *Slayground* 1984; *Contrary Warriors: The Story of the Crow Tribe* 1985; *Jagged Edge* 1985; *The Legend of Billie Jean* 1985; *Troupers* 1985; *Un Homme amoureux/A Man in Love* 1987; *Outrageous Fortune* 1987; *Stacking* 1987; *Heart of Midnight* 1988; *The Man Inside* 1990; *Crooked Hearts* 1991.

Crain, Jeanne • Actress • Born Barstow, CA, May 25, 1925. *Educ.* UCLA (drama, art). Sweet, fresh-faced former beauty queen who entered film as a 20th Century-Fox starlet in 1943, before the age of 20. Crain played wholesome girl-next-door characters in a series of light entertainments (*State Fair* 1945, *Centennial Summer* 1946, etc.) until she was cast against type in Elia Kazan's racial drama *Pinky* (1949), as a young black woman passing for white. In the 1950s Crain attempted to develop a more glamourous image and to appear in more sophisticated fare, but met with only limited success. • *The Gang's All Here* 1943; *Home in Indiana* 1944; *In the Meantime, Darling* 1944; *Winged Victory* 1944; *Leave Her to Heaven* 1945; *State Fair* 1945; *Centennial Summer* 1946; *Margie* 1946; *Apartment For Peggy* 1948; *A Letter to Three Wives* 1948; *You Were Meant For Me* 1948; *The Fan* 1949; *Pinky* 1949 **(AANBA)**; *Cheaper By the Dozen* 1950; *I'll Get By* 1950; *The Model and the Marriage Broker* 1951; *People Will Talk* 1951; *Take Care of My Little Girl* 1951; *Belles on Their Toes* 1952; *O. Henry's Full House* 1952; *City of Bad Men* 1953; *Dangerous Crossing* 1953; *Vicki* 1953; *Duel in the Jungle* 1954; *Man Without a Star* 1954; *Gentlemen Marry Brunettes* 1955; *The Second Greatest Sex* 1955; *The Fastest Gun Alive* 1956; *The Joker Is Wild* 1957; *The Tattered Dress* 1957; *Guns of the Timberland* 1960; *Ponzia Pilato* 1961; *Twenty Plus Two* 1961; *Col Ferro e col Fuoco* 1962; *Madison Avenue* 1962; *Nefertite Regina del Nilo* 1962; *Hot Rods to Hell* 1967; *Skyjacked* 1972; *The Night God Screamed* 1974.

Craven, Wes • Director, producer; also screenwriter. • Born Wesley Earl Craven, Cleveland, OH, August 2, 1939. *Educ.* Wheaton College, IL (English, psychology); Johns Hopkins University, Baltimore MD (writing, philosophy). Former humanities professor turned master of the macabre. Craven began his film career as an editor and assistant producer to Sean Cunningham and is best known for inaugurating the commercially successful "Nightmare on Elm Street" series, in which the horrific Freddy Krueger haunts the dreamscapes of small-town America. An element of self-parody has crept into the director's later work, while devotees of the horror genre tend to prefer his earlier, less fanciful efforts (e.g. *The Hills Have Eyes* 1977). • *Together* 1971 (asst.prod); *You've Got to Walk It Like You Talk It or You'll Lose That Beat* 1971 (ed); *It Happened in Hollywood* 1972 (ed); *Last House on the Left* 1972 (d,sc); *The Hills Have Eyes* 1977 (d,sc,ed); *Summer of Fear* 1978 (d); *Deadly Blessing* 1981 (d,sc); *Swamp Thing* 1982 (d,sc); *A Nightmare on Elm Street* 1984 (d,sc); *The Hills Have Eyes Part II* 1985 (d,sc); *Deadly Friend* 1986 (d); *Flowers in the Attic* 1987 (sc); *A Nightmare on Elm Street Part III: Dream Warriors* 1987 (exec.p,sc,story); *The Serpent and the Rainbow* 1988 (d); *Shocker* 1989 (a,d,exec.p,sc); *Bloodfist II* 1990 (adviser).

Crawford, Broderick • Actor • Born William Broderick Crawford, Philadelphia, PA, December 9, 1911; died April 26, 1986, Rancho Mirage, CA. *Educ.* Harvard. Burly, gruff-voiced supporting player of the 1940s and 50s and son of popular stage and film comedienne Helen Broderick and vaudevillian Lester Crawford. After a brief stab at Hollywood, Crawford returned to Broadway and won acclaim for his performance as Lennie in the stage adaptation of John Steinbeck's *Of Mice and Men* (1937) before returning to film. Because of his thug-like mug he was relegated to playing gangsters and villainous cowboys in mostly forgettable fare until 1949, when he won an Oscar for his portrayal of political demogogue Willie Stark in Robert Rossen's *All The King's Men*. The following year, in *Born Yesterday*, he played a coarse, bullying junk dealer (reputedly parodying Columbia studio head Harry Cohn) who gets his comeuppance from Judy Holliday. After these two gems, Crawford reverted to character roles. Highlights of Crawford's later career were *The Mob* (1951), Fellini's *Il Bidone/The Swindle* (1955), in which he played a struggling con-man, and a starring role in the popular syndicated police series, "Highway Patrol" (1955-59). • *Submarine D-1* 1937; *Woman Chases Man* 1937; *Start Cheering* 1938; *Ambush* 1939; *Beau Geste* 1939; *Eternally Yours* 1939; *Island of Lost Men* 1939; *The Real Glory* 1939; *Undercover Doctor* 1939; *I Can't Give You Anything But Love, Baby* 1940; *Seven Sinners* 1940; *Slightly Honorable* 1940; *Trail of the Vigilantes* 1940; *When the Daltons Rode* 1940; *Badlands of Dakota* 1941; *The Black Cat* 1941; *South of Tahiti* 1941; *Texas Rangers Ride Again* 1941; *Tight Shoes* 1941; *Broadway* 1942; *Butch Minds the Baby* 1942; *Larceny, Inc.* 1942; *Men of Texas* 1942; *North to the Klondike* 1942; *Sin Town* 1942; *Black Angel* 1946; *The Runaround* 1946; *The Flame* 1947; *Slave Girl* 1947; *Bad Men of Tombstone* 1948; *Sealed Verdict* 1948; *The Time of Your Life* 1948; *All the King's Men* 1949 **(AABA)**; *Anna Lucasta* 1949; *A Kiss in the Dark* 1949; *Night Unto Night* 1949; *Born Yesterday* 1950; *Cargo to Capetown* 1950; *Convicted* 1950; *The Mob* 1951;

Last of the Comanches 1952; *Lone Star* 1952; *Scandal Sheet* 1952; *Stop, You're Killing Me* 1952; *The Last Posse* 1953; *Down Three Dark Streets* 1954; *Human Desire* 1954; *Night People* 1954; *Il Bidone* 1955; *Big House, U.S.A.* 1955; *New York Confidential* 1955; *Not As a Stranger* 1955; *Between Heaven and Hell* 1956; *The Fastest Gun Alive* 1956; *The Decks Ran Red* 1958; *Convicts Four* 1962; *El Valle de las espadas* 1963; *A House Is Not a Home* 1964; *Up From the Beach* 1965; *Kid Rodelo* 1966; *The Oscar* 1966; *Texas Kid* 1966; *Red Tomahawk* 1967; *Wie Kommt ein So Reizendes Maedchen zu Diesem Gewerbe?* 1970; *Embassy* 1971; *Terror in the Wax Museum* 1973; *The Private Files of J. Edgar Hoover* 1977; *A Little Romance* 1979; *There Goes the Bride* 1979; *Harlequin* 1980; *Den Tuchtigen Gehort Die Welt* 1981; *Liar's Moon* 1982.

Crawford, Joan • *aka* Billie Cassin • Actress • Born Lucille Fay Le Sueur, San Antonio, TX, March 23, 1904; died May 10, 1977, New York, NY. Joan Crawford's extraordinary career encompassed 45 years and some 80 films. Spotted in a chorus line by MGM and signed in 1925, her portrayal of a "flapper" in her 21st film, *Our Dancing Daughters* (1928), made her a star. Crawford maintained this status throughout the remainder of her career, but not without setbacks. Her films of the 1930s, though lavish and stylish, were mostly routine and superficial. Despite a mature and impressive performance in *The Women* (1939), Crawford continued to be given less-than-challenging roles by the studio.

In 1942 Crawford left MGM and her career took a decided upward turn after she signed with Warner Bros. the following year. In numerous Warner Bros. melodramas and *films noirs*, a new Crawford persona emerged: intelligent, often neurotic, powerful and sometimes ruthless, but also vulnerable and dependent. Memorable roles in *Mildred Pierce* (1945), *Humoresque* (1946) and *Possessed* (1947) restored and consolidated her popularity. In her nine *films noirs* for Warner Bros. and other studios, as well in most of her non-*noir* features (such as *Harriet Craig*, 1950), Crawford gave expert and fully realized interpretations.

After this brief period of success, Crawford's career declined once again, and in 1951 she left Warners. She worked for various studios, most memorably for RKO in *Sudden Fear* (1952), a performance which earned her an Oscar nomination. With the exception of *Whatever Happened to Baby Jane?* (1962), Crawford's performances of the 60s were mostly self-caricatures in second-rate horror films (*Berserk!* 1967, *Trog* 1970). Although these later features were poor vehicles for her talents, she was a resilient and consummate professional who continued to impose the highest standards of performance upon herself. Crawford was married to actors Douglas Fairbanks, Jr., and Franchot Tone and was portrayed as a cruel and calculating mother by Faye Dunaway in the 1981 film, *Mommie Dearest*, based on a biography by her adopted daughter Christina. LPM • *Lady of the Night* 1925; *Old Clothes* 1925; *The Only Thing* 1925; *Pretty Ladies* 1925; *Proud Flesh* 1925; *Sally, Irene and Mary* 1925; *The Boob* 1926; *Paris* 1926; *Tramp, Tramp, Tramp* 1926; *Spring Fever* 1927; *The Taxi Dancer* 1927; *Twelve Miles Out* 1927; *The Understanding Heart* 1927; *The Unknown* 1927; *Winners of the Wilderness* 1927; *Across to Singapore* 1928; *Dream of Love* 1928; *Four Walls* 1928; *The Law of the Range* 1928; *Our Dancing Daughters* 1928; *Rose Marie* 1928; *West Point* 1928; *The Duke Steps Out* 1929; *The Hollywood Revue of 1929* 1929; *Our Modern Maidens* 1929; *Untamed* 1929; *Montana Moon* 1930; *Our Blushing Brides* 1930; *Paid* 1930; *Dance, Fools, Dance* 1931; *Laughing Sinners* 1931; *Possessed* 1931; *This Modern Age* 1931; *The Stolen Jools (short)* 1931; *Grand Hotel* 1932; *Letty Lynton* 1932; *Rain* 1932; *Dancing Lady* 1933; *Today We Live* 1933; *Chained* 1934; *Forsaking All Others* 1934; *Sadie McKee* 1934; *I Live My Life* 1935; *No More Ladies* 1935; *The Gorgeous Hussy* 1936; *Love on the Run* 1936; *The Bride Wore Red* 1937; *The Last of Mrs. Cheyney* 1937; *Mannequin* 1938; *The Shining Hour* 1938; *Ice Follies* 1939; *The Women* 1939; *Strange Cargo* 1940; *Susan and God* 1940; *When Ladies Meet* 1941; *A Woman's Face* 1941; *Reunion in France* 1942; *They All Kissed the Bride* 1942; *Above Suspicion* 1943; *Hollywood Canteen* 1944; *Mildred Pierce* 1945 **(AABA)**; *Humoresque* 1946; *Daisy Kenyon* 1947; *Possessed* 1947 **(AANBA)**; *Flamingo Road* 1949; *It's a Great Feeling* 1949; *The Damned Don't Cry* 1950; *Harriet Craig* 1950; *Goodbye, My Fancy* 1951; *Sudden Fear* 1952 **(AANBA)**; *This Woman Is Dangerous* 1952; *Torch Song* 1953; *Johnny Guitar* 1954; *Female on the Beach* 1955; *Queen Bee* 1955; *Autumn Leaves* 1956; *The Story of Esther Costello* 1957; *The Best of Everything* 1959; *What Ever Happened to Baby Jane?* 1962; *The Caretakers* 1963; *Strait-Jacket* 1964; *I Saw What You Did* 1965; *Berserk!* 1967; *The Karate Killers* 1967; *Trog* 1970; *Birch Interval* 1975; *Going Hollywood: The War Years* 1988 (archival footage).

Crenna, Richard • Actor • Born Los Angeles, CA, November 30, 1927. *Educ.* USC, Los Angeles. Lead and character player who first gained attention as a squeaky-voiced juvenile on radio serials. Although Crenna made several pictures throughout the 50s, his first notable adult roles came as the star of such TV series as "The Real McCoys" (1957-63) and "Slattery's People" (1964-65).

On the big screen regularly since the mid-60s, Crenna has appeared in such diverse roles as the gang boss in Jean-Pierre Mélville's swan song, *Un flic* (1972), and as the beach club big-shot, opposite a young Matt Dillon, in Garry Marshall's coming-of-age drama, *The Flamingo Kid* (1984). • *It Grows on Trees* 1952; *The Pride of St. Louis* 1952; *Red Skies of Montana* 1952; *Over-Exposed* 1955; *Our Miss Brooks* 1956; *John Goldfarb, Please Come Home* 1964; *Made in Paris* 1966; *The Sand Pebbles* 1966; *Wait Until Dark* 1967; *Star!* 1968; *Marooned* 1969; *A Run on Gold* 1969; *Doctors' Wives* 1970; *Catlow* 1971; *Red Sky at Morning* 1971; *La Spina Dorsale del Diavola* 1971; *Un Flic* 1972; *Jonathan Livingston Seagull* 1973; *The Man Called Noon* 1973; *Breakheart Pass* 1975; *The Evil* 1977; *Death Ship* 1979; *Hard Ride to Rantan* 1979; *Stone Cold Dead* 1979; *Wild Horse Hank* 1979; *Body Heat* 1981; *First Blood* 1982; *Table For Five* 1983; *The Flamingo Kid* 1984; *Rambo: First Blood Part II* 1985; *Summer Rental* 1985; *50 Years of Action!* 1986; *Rambo III* 1988; *Leviathan* 1989.

Crichton, Charles • Director; also producer. • Born Wallasey, Cheshire, England, August 6, 1910. *Educ.* Oxford. Edited several noted British productions from 1935 to 1944—including Zoltan Korda's *Sanders of the River* (1935)—before moving over to Ealing Studios in 1940 and making his feature directing debut with *For Those in Peril* (1944). *Hue and Cry* (1947), followed by *The Lavender Hill Mob* (1951) and *The Titfield Thunderbolt* (1953), established Crichton as a key architect of the Ealing comedy style, with a knack for eliciting fine performances from his actors. After the closing of Ealing in 1959, he made fewer features, working in British TV on series such as "Danger Man" and "The Avengers." In 1988 he scored a comeback hit with *A Fish Called Wanda*, an energetic farce reminiscent of the classic Ealing style. • *Sanders of the River* 1935 (ed); *Things to Come* 1936 (ed); *21 Days* 1937 (ed); *Elephant Boy* 1937 (ed); *Prison Without Bars* 1938 (ed); *Old Bill and Son* 1940 (ed); *The Thief of Bagdad* 1940 (ed); *The Big Blockade* 1941 (ed); *Yellow Caesar* 1941 (ed); *Greek Testament* 1942 (assoc.p); *For Those in Peril* 1944 (d); *Dead of Night* 1945 (d); *Painted Boats* 1945 (d); *Hue and Cry* 1947 (d); *Against the Wind* 1948 (d); *Another Shore* 1948 (d); *Train of Events* 1949 (d); *Dance Hall* 1950 (d); *Hunted* 1952 (d); *The Lavender Hill Mob* 1951 (d); *The Love Lottery* 1953 (d); *The Titfield Thunderbolt* 1953 (d); *The Divided Heart* 1954 (d); *Law and Disorder* 1956 (d); *The Man in the Sky* 1956 (d); *Floods of Fear* 1958 (d,sc); *The Battle of the Sexes* 1959 (d); *The Boy Who Stole a Million* 1960 (d,sc); *The Third Secret* 1964 (d); *He Who Rides a Tiger* 1965 (d); *Tomorrow's Island (short)* 1968 (d,sc); *A Fish Called Wanda* 1988 (d,story) **(AANBD,AANBSC)**.

Crichton, Michael • Novelist; also screenwriter, director. • Born John Michael Crichton, Chicago, IL, October 23, 1942. *Educ.* Harvard University; Harvard Medical School; Salk Institute for Biological Sciences, La Jolla. Medical student who turned out several novels under various pseudonyms (usually "John Lange") before hitting the jackpot under his own name with *The Andromeda Strain* (1969). Filmed by Robert Wise in 1971, it paved the way for Crichton to make his own directorial debut with the robot thriller, *Westworld* (1973). He has since been responsible for several well-made thrillers, usually adapted from his own science fiction or medically-based best sellers. • *The Andromeda Strain* 1971 (from novel); *Dealing: Or the Berkeley-to-Boston Forty-Brick Lost-Bag Blues* 1972 (from novel); *Extreme Close-Up* 1973 (sc); *Westworld* 1973 (d,sc); *The Terminal Man* 1974 (from novel) *Coma* 1978 (d,sc); *The First Great Train Robbery* 1979 (d,sc,from novel) *Looker* 1981 (d,sc); *Runaway* 1984 (d,sc); *Physical Evidence* 1988 (d).

Crisp, Donald • Actor, director • Born Aberfeldy, Perthshire, Scotland, July 27, 1880; died May 25, 1974, Van Nuys, CA. *Educ.* Oxford. In the US from 1906, Crisp enjoyed a long and varied career as an actor and, until 1930, a director; he later featured as a fatherly character performer in some 400 movies through the early 1960s. At the Biograph studios, Crisp appeared in numerous D.W. Griffith films—portraying General Grant in *Birth of a Nation* (1915), playing Lillian Gish's brutal father in *Broken Blossoms* (1919) and serving as Griffith's assistant director on both. He also directed a good number of silents including *Don Q, Son of Zorro* (1925), starring Douglas Fairbanks; *The Navigator* (1924) was co-directed with Buster Keaton.

As a supporting actor, Crisp fought alongside Errol Flynn in *The Charge of the Light Brigade*, was a stuffy military man opposite Kay Francis in *The White Angel* (both 1936) and played a judge in *The Oklahoma Kid* (1939). After winning a supporting actor Oscar as the head of a Welsh mining family in John Ford's *How Green Was My Valley* (1941), Crisp was typecast as white-haired, crusty but good-hearted fathers or men of the cloth in a slew of sentimental classics (*Lassie Come Home* 1943, *National Velvet* 1944). He was married to screenwriter Jane Murfin from 1932 to 1944. • *The Availing Prayer* 1914 (d); *Down the Hill to Creditville* 1914 (d); *The Escape* 1914 (a); *Her Father's Silent Partner* 1914 (d); *Her Mother's Necklace* 1914 (d); *Home, Sweet Home* 1914 (a); *The Mysterious Shot* 1914 (d); *The Newer Woman* 1914 (d); *Sands of Fate* 1914 (d); *The Tavern of Tragedy* 1914 (d); *Their First Acquaintance* 1914 (d); *The Warning* 1914 (d); *Birth of a Nation* 1915 (a); *An Old-Fashioned Girl* 1915 (d); *Ramona* 1916 (d); *The Bond Between* 1917 (d); *The Clever Mrs. Carfax* 1917 (d); *The Cook of Canyon Camp* 1917 (d,sc,story); *The Countess Charming* 1917 (d); *Eyes of the World* 1917 (d); *His Sweetheart* 1917 (d); *Lost in Transit* 1917 (d); *The Marcellini Millions* 1917 (d); *A Roadside Impresario* 1917 (d); *Believe Me Xantippe* 1918 (d); *The Firefly of France* 1918 (d); *The Goat* 1918 (d); *The House of Silence* 1918 (d); *Jules of the Strong Heart* 1918 (d); *Less Than Kin* 1918 (d); *Rimrock Jones* 1918 (d); *Under the Top* 1918 (d); *The Way of a Man With a Maid* 1918 (d); *Broken Blossoms* 1919 (a); *It Pays to Advertise* 1919 (d); *Johnny Get Your Gun* 1919 (d); *Love Insurance* 1919 (d); *Poor Boob* 1919 (d); *Putting It Over* 1919 (d); *Something to Do* 1919 (d); *Venus in the East* 1919 (d); *A Very Good Young Man* 1919 (d); *Why Smith Left Home* 1919 (d); *The Barbarian* 1920 (d); *Held By the Enemy* 1920 (d); *Miss Hobbs* 1920 (d); *The Six Best Cellars* 1920 (d); *Too Much Johnson* 1920 (d); *Appearances* 1921 (d); *The Bonnie Brier Bush* 1921 (a,d); *The Princess of New York* 1921 (d); *Tell Your Children* 1922 (d); *Ponjola* 1923 (d); *The Navigator* 1924 (d); *Don Q, Son of Zorro* 1925 (a,d); *The Black Pirate* 1926 (a); *Man Bait* 1926 (d); *Sunny Side Up* 1926 (d); *Young April* 1926 (d); *Dress Parade* 1927 (d); *The Fighting Eagle* 1927 (d); *Nobody's Widow* 1927 (d); *Vanity* 1927 (d,p); *The Cop* 1928 (d); *The River Pirate* 1928 (a); *Stand and Deliver* 1928 (d,p); *The Pagan* 1929 (a); *Trent's Last Case* 1929 (a); *The Viking* 1929 (a); *The Runaway Bride* 1930 (d); *Scotland Yard* 1930 (a); *Kick In* 1931 (a); *Svengali* 1931 (a); *A Passport to Hell* 1932 (a); *Red Dust* 1932 (a); *Broadway Bad* 1933 (a); *The Crime Doctor* 1934 (a); *The Life of Vergie Winters* 1934 (a); *The Little Minister* 1934 (a); *What Every Woman Knows* 1934 (a); *Laddie* 1935 (a); *Mutiny on the Bounty* 1935 (a); *Oil For the Lamps of China* 1935 (a); *Vanessa, Her Love Story* 1935 (a); *Beloved Enemy* 1936 (a); *The Charge of the Light Brigade* 1936 (a); *Mary of Scotland* 1936 (a); *The White Angel* 1936 (a); *A Woman Rebels* 1936 (a); *Confession* 1937 (a); *The Great O'Malley* 1937 (a); *The Life of Emile Zola* 1937 (a); *Parnell* 1937 (a); *That Certain Woman* 1937 (a); *The Amazing Dr. Clitterhouse* 1938 (a); *The Beloved Brat* 1938 (a); *Comet Over Broadway* 1938 (a); *The Dawn Patrol* 1938 (a); *Jezebel* 1938 (a); *Sergeant Murphy* 1938 (a); *The Sisters* 1938 (a); *Valley of the Giants* 1938 (a); *Daughters Courageous* 1939 (a); *Juarez* 1939 (a); *The Oklahoma Kid* 1939 (a); *The Old Maid* 1939 (a); *The Private Lives of Elizabeth and Essex* 1939 (a); *Wuthering Heights* 1939 (a); *Brother Orchid* 1940 (a); *City For Conquest* 1940 (a); *Dr. Ehrlich's Magic Bullet* 1940 (a); *Knute Rockne - All American* 1940 (a); *The Sea Hawk* 1940 (a); *Dr. Jekyll and Mr. Hyde* 1941 (a); *How Green Was My Valley* 1941 (a) **(AABSA)**; *Shining Victory* 1941 (a); *The Gay Sisters* 1942 (a); *Forever and a Day* 1943 (a); *Lassie Come Home* 1943 (a); *The Adventures of Mark Twain* 1944 (a); *National Velvet* 1944 (a); *The Uninvited* 1944 (a); *Son of Lassie* 1945 (a); *The Valley of Decision* 1945 (a); *Ramrod* 1947 (a); *Hills of Home* 1948 (a); *Challenge to Lassie* 1949 (a); *Whispering Smith* 1949 (a); *Bright Leaf* 1950 (a); *Home Town Story* 1951 (a); *Prince Valiant* 1954 (a); *The Long Gray Line* 1955 (a); *The Man From Laramie* 1955 (a); *Drango* 1957 (a); *The Last Hurrah* 1958 (a); *Saddle the Wind* 1958 (a); *A Dog of Flanders* 1959 (a); *Pollyanna* 1960 (a); *Spencer's Mountain* 1963 (a).

Cristaldi, Franco • Producer • Born Turin, Italy, October 3, 1924. *Educ.* Turin University (law). Respected European producer who has backed films by most of the major post-war Italian directors, including Luchino Visconti (*White Nights* 1957), Mario Monicelli (*The Big Deal on Madonna Street* 1958), Marco Bellocchio, Francesco Rosi and Federico Fellini (*Amarcord* 1974, *And the Ship Sails On* 1983). Formerly married to actress Claudia Cardinale. • *Kean* 1940 (p); *La Pattuglia Sperduta* 1953 (p); *Il Seduttore Camilla* 1954 (p); *Mio Figlio Nerone* 1956 (p); *Le Notti Bianche/White Nights* 1957 (p); *The Big Deal on Madonna Street* 1958 (p); *Kapo* 1960 (p); *L'Assassino* 1961 (p); *Divorzio All'Italiano/Divorce—Italian Style* 1961 (p); *Salvatore Giuliano* 1962 (p); *I Compagni/The Organizer* 1963 (p); *La Ragazza di Bube* 1963 (p); *Gli Indifferenti* 1964 (p); *Sedotta e Abbandonata/Seduced and Abandoned* 1964 (p); *Vaghe stelle dell'orsa* 1965 (p); *Una Rosa per Tutti* 1966 (p); *La Cina e vicina* 1967 (p); *Ruba al Prossimo Tuo* 1969 (exec.p); *La Tenda rossa/The Red Tent* 1970 (p); *In Nome del Padre/In the Name of the Father* 1971 (p); *L'Udienza* 1971 (p); *Il Caso Mattei* 1972 (p); *Lady Caroline Lamb* 1972 (exec.p); *Amarcord* 1974 (p); *Re: Lucky Luciano* 1973 (p); *Beato Loro* 1975 (p); *Qui comincia l'avventura* 1976 (p); *Mogliamante* 1977 (p); *Cristo si e Fermato a Eboli/Christ Stopped at Eboli* 1978 (p); *Ogro* 1979 (p); *Ratataplan* 1979 (p); *Cafe Express* 1980 (p); *Il Cappotto di Astrakan* 1980 (p); *Ho Fatto Splash* 1980 (p); *Domani Si Balla* 1982 (p); *Arrivano i miei* 1983 (p); *E la nave Va/And the Ship Sails On* 1983 (p); *Garibaldi - the General* 1986 (p); *The Name of the Rose* 1986 (p); *Nuovo Cinema Paradiso/Cinema Paradiso* 1988 (p); *Vanille Fraise* 1989 (p); *C'era un castello con 40 cani* 1990 (p).

Cromwell, John • Director • Born Elwood Dagger Cromwell, Toledo, OH, December 23, 1888; died September 26, 1979, Santa Barbara, CA. Theater success (as actor, director, producer) who went to Hollywood in the late 1920s at the age of 40 and proved a capable craftsman of polished studio fare. Cromwell displayed a gift for eliciting surprisingly solid performances from even mediocre actors.

Initially with Paramount, he moved to RKO in 1933, before branching out to work for various producers, most notably the autocratic David O. Selznick. Among Cromwell's better efforts are *Of Human Bondage* (1934), which made Bette Davis a star; *Abe Lincoln in Illinois* (1940), a popular slice of Americana which owes much of its success to Robert Sherwood's play basis; *Since You Went Away* (1944)—mostly the vision of producer Selznick; the sensitive, but not sentimental, romantic fantasy *The Enchanted Cottage* (1945); and the visually rewarding *Anna and the King of Siam* (1946), which won Oscars for its cinematographer and production designer.

After leaving Selznick in the postwar period and being blacklisted in the early 1950s, Cromwell brought a grittier, more realistic edge to such films as *Dead Reckoning* (1947); the women's prison expose, *Caged* (1950); and *The Goddess* (1958), based by screenwriter Paddy Chayefsky on the life of Marilyn Monroe. Cromwell appeared in character parts in Robert Altman's *Three Women* (1977) and as the semi-senile priest in *A Wedding* (1978). Married to actresses Alice Indahl, Marie Goff, Kay Johnson and Ruth Nelson and father of actor James (Jamie) Cromwell. • *Close Harmony* 1929 (d); *The Dance of Life* 1929 (d,uncred.a); *The Dummy* 1929 (uncred.a); *The Mighty* 1929 (d,uncred.a); *For the Defense* 1930 (d,uncred.a); *Seven Days Leave* 1930 (ad); *Street of Chance* 1930 (a,d); *The Texan* 1930 (d); *Tom Sawyer* 1930 (d); *Rich Man's Folly* 1931 (d); *Scandal Sheet* 1931 (d); *Unfaithful* 1931 (d); *The Vice Squad* 1931 (d); *The World and the Flesh* 1932 (d); *Ann Vickers* 1933 (d); *Double Harness* 1933 (d); *The Silver Cord* 1933 (d); *Sweepings* 1933 (d); *The Fountain* 1934 (d); *Of Human Bondage* 1934 (d); *Spitfire* 1934 (d); *This Man Is Mine* 1934 (d); *I Dream Too Much* 1935 (d); *Jalna* 1935 (d); *Village Tale* 1935 (d); *Banjo on My Knee* 1936 (d); *Little Lord Fauntleroy* 1936 (d); *To Mary—With Love* 1936 (d); *The Prisoner of Zenda* 1937 (d); *Algiers* 1938 (d); *In Name Only* 1939 (d); *Made For Each Other* 1939 (d); *Abe Lincoln in Illinois* 1940 (d); *Victory* 1940 (d); *So Ends Our Night* 1941 (d); *Son of Fury* 1942 (d); *Since You Went Away* 1944 (d); *The Enchanted Cottage* 1945 (d); *Anna and the King of Siam* 1946 (d); *Dead Reckoning* 1947 (d); *Night Song* 1947 (d); *Adventure in Baltimore* 1948 (d); *Caged* 1950 (d); *The Company She Keeps* 1950 (d); *The Racket* 1951 (d); *Top Secret Affair* 1957 (a); *The Goddess* 1958 (d); *The Scavengers* 1959 (d); *A Matter of Morals* 1960 (d); *Three Women* 1977 (a); *A Wedding* 1978 (a).

Cronenberg, David • Director, screenwriter • Born Toronto, Ontario, Canada, March 15, 1943. *Educ.* University of Toronto (English, science). One of the best of the new generation of horror film directors, Cronenberg's explorations of biological terror and sexual dread have provided a strikingly original approach to the genre. Because he has worked so often in the horror genre, Cronenberg was until recently labeled an exploitation director; his recent films, however, have moved away from graphic and revolting special effects to concentrate instead on theme and character.

While at university, Cronenberg made two experimental science fiction shorts, *Stereo* (1969) and *Crimes of the Future* (1970), before beginning his work in features. Both films demonstrated Cronenberg's penchant for stylistic experimentation and his ability to use architectural space for expressive purposes. His first feature was the effective shocker, *They Came From Within/Shivers/The Parasite Murders* (1975), which was coproduced by fellow Canadian Ivan Reitman. In its depiction of an artificially created parasite that releases uncontrollable sexual desire, Cronenberg fashioned a wry commentary on the sexual liberation of the time. Playing on the same theme, *Rabid* (1977) cleverly cast Marilyn Chambers, former Ivory Snow Girl and porn star, as the unfortunate victim of an operation that leaves her with a vampiric appetite for blood. A murderous phallic spike that protrudes from her armpit makes her embrace literally deadly.

The Brood (1979), another exercise in biological horror, showed Cronenberg reaching for some measure of respectability. For the first time he used established actors, Oliver Reed and Samantha Eggar. Even though he placed them within a gruesome tale in which biological mutation is identified as a metaphor for emotional rage, he handled his performers with surprising skill. But it was with *The Dead Zone* (1983) that Cronenberg truly rose above the level of horror exploitation. The film is adapted from a Stephen King novel about a man able to predict future events in people's lives simply by touching them (and thus marks Cronenberg's first non-original screenplay). Here, atmosphere and acting—especially a fine central performance by Christopher Walken—take precedence over special effects.

Videodrome (1983) is a self-reflexive, McLuhanesque horror tale about the effects of TV on its viewers. The film tells the story of an opportunistic TV producer, played by James Woods, who grows obsessed with a sadistic-erotic program emanating from a mysterious pirate station. His fantasies, stimulated by the show, grow increasingly out of control and seem to represent the consciousness of the typical male TV viewer shaped by that medium's emphasis on violence, sex and spectacle. *Videodrome* is a formal tour de force in which fantasy merges with reality to the point where the viewer of the film, like the protagonist himself, cannot separate the two. It drives home the degree to which we are all "programmed" by the media—a theme strikingly visualized by the image of a newly evolved orifice in the producer's stomach for receiving video software.

Cronenberg has had to struggle for the critical recognition his work deserves, largely because of the nature of his material. Early response in his native Canada ranged from MPs in Parliament railing about government funding for a "disgusting" movie like *Shivers*, to critic Robert Fulford's review entitled *You Should Know How Bad This Film Is. After All, You Paid For It.* Robin Wood's influential 1979 essay *An Introduction to the American Horror Film*, which set the terms for discussion of the genre in the 80s, identified Cronenberg as a prime example of the horror film's "Reactionary Wing." Many have followed Wood in viewing Cronenberg's work as motivated by sexual disgust.

Cronenberg's 1986 remake of *The Fly* would seem to endorse such a view. The hero, a scientist whose atomic structure has been confused with that of a housefly, undergoes a gradual physical disintegration that has been read as a metaphor for AIDS. Yet his most recent film, *Dead Ringers* (1988), a resounding critical and commercial success, would seem to refute this interpretation. In this impressively accomplished work, Cronenberg's biological horror is almost entirely submerged within the psychological exploration of character and the director's precise command of color, decor and camera movement. A bravura performance by Jeremy Irons makes this grisly story of twin gynecologists who descend into drugs, madness and, finally, suicide, a chilling examination of masculine sexual dread and a powerful critique of the patriarchal control of the medical profession.

In retrospect, much of Cronenberg's earlier work can be seen as an ironic critique of the fears and repression that inform our apparently liberated society, rather than a visualization of the director's personal obsessions. BKG • *Stereo (short)* 1969 (d,p,sc,ph,ed); *Crimes of the Future (short)* 1970 (d,p,sc,ph,ed); *The Parasite Murders* 1975 (d,sc); *Rabid* 1977 (d,sc); *The Brood* 1979 (d,sc); *Fast Company* 1979 (d,sc); *Scanners* 1981 (d,sc); *The Dead Zone* 1983 (d); *Videodrome* 1983 (d,sc); *Into the Night* 1985 (a); *The Fly* 1986 (a,d,sc); *Dead Ringers* 1988 (d,p,sc); *Nightbreed* 1990 (a).

Cronenweth, Jordan • American director of photography • Made his debut as a cinematographer on Robert Altman's *Brewster McCloud* (1970) and has since tended to work on independent or non-mainstream productions such as Frank Perry's *Play It as It Lays* (1972), Ken Russell's *Altered States* (1980), Ivan Passer's *Cutter's Way* (1981) and films by Jonathan Demme, Francis Coppola and Phil Joanou. • *Brewster McCloud* 1970; *Count Your Bullets* 1972; *Face to the Wind* 1972; *Play It As It Lays* 1972; *The Front Page* 1974; *The Touch of Satan* 1974; *Zandy's Bride* 1974; *The Nickel Ride* 1975; *Gable and Lombard* 1976; *Citizens Band* 1977; *Rolling Thunder* 1977; *Altered States* 1980; *Cutter's Way* 1981; *Best Friends* 1982; *Blade Runner* 1982; *Stop Making Sense* 1984; *Just Between Friends* 1986; *Peggy Sue Got Married* 1986 **(AANBPH)**; *Gardens of Stone* 1987; *U2 Rattle and Hum* 1988 (ph—color); *State of Grace* 1990.

Cronyn, Hume • Actor; also screenwriter. • Born London, Ontario, Canada, July 18, 1911. *Educ.* Ridley College; McGill University, Montreal (pre-law); AADA, New York; Mozarteum, Salzburg, Austria (acting). Wiry, short and enormously versatile triple-threat talent who has successfully conducted simultaneous careers on stage and screen. A much-lauded Broadway presence (as actor, director, producer and writer) since the 1930s, Cronyn made his screen debut as the literal-minded, snooping, armchair detective-neighbor in Hitchcock's understated thriller, *Shadow of a Doubt* (1943); he also collaborated on the screenplays for the director's *Rope* (1948) and *Under Capricorn* (1949) and appeared as the ship's radio operator in *Lifeboat* (1944).

Initially cast as ruthless, coolly intelligent villains such as the Nazi collaborator in *The Cross of Lorraine* (1943) and the sadistic warden in *Brute Force* (1947), Cronyn has since played everything from a jealous physician, in *People Will Talk* (1951), to Roosevelt's gruff counselor, Louis Howe, in *Sunrise at Campobello* (1960).

Teamed with actress Jessica Tandy, whom he married in 1942, Cronyn has starred on Broadway (*The Fourposter, A Delicate Balance, The Gin Game, Foxfire*), in numerous tours, on a TV series (*The Marriage* 1954) and, more recently, on screen, in a series of cantankerous-old-codger roles in *Cocoon* (1985), its 1988 sequel and *Batteries Not Included* (1987). • *The Cross of Lorraine* 1943; *The Phantom of the Opera* 1943; *Shadow of a Doubt* 1943; *Blonde Fever* 1944; *Lifeboat* 1944; *Main Street After Dark* 1944; *The Seventh Cross* 1944 **(AANBSA)**; *The Sailor Takes a Wife* 1945; *The Beginning or the End* 1946; *The Green Years* 1946; *A Letter For Evie* 1946; *The Postman Always Rings Twice* 1946; *The Secret Heart* 1946 (voice); *Ziegfeld Follies* 1946; *Brute Force* 1947; *The Bride Goes Wild* 1948; *Rope* 1948 (adapt); *Top O' the Morning* 1949; *Under Capricorn* 1949 (adapt); *People Will Talk* 1951; *Crowded Paradise* 1955; *Sunrise at Campobello* 1960; *Cleopatra* 1963; *Hamlet* 1964; *The Arrangement* 1969; *Gaily, Gaily* 1969; *There Was a Crooked Man* 1970; *Conrack* 1973; *The Parallax View* 1974; *Honky Tonk Freeway* 1981; *Rollover* 1981; *The World According to Garp* 1982; *Impulse* 1984; *Brewster's Millions* 1985; *Cocoon* 1985; *Hitchcock, Il Brivido del Genio* 1985; *Batteries Not Included* 1987; *Cocoon: The Return* 1988.

Crosby, Bing • Singer, actor • Born Harry Lillis Crosby, Tacoma, WA, May 2, 1904; died October 14, 1977, outside Madrid, Spain. *Educ.* Gonzaga University, Spokane (law). Popular crooner and box-office star of the 1940s and 50s who amassed one of the entertainment world's largest fortunes. Crosby made his screen debut as a band singer in *King of Jazz* (1930), but his most successful films were the "Road" movies of the 1940s with Bob Hope and Dorothy Lamour.

Crosby's effortless, mellow singing style, easy-going charm and escapist material—songs with a "Sunny Side of the Street/Pennies From Heaven" philosophy and sentimental films like *Holiday Inn* (1942), *Going My Way* (1944), *White Christmas* (1954) and *High Society* (1956)—helped audiences forget WWII and its aftermath and made him enormously popular. Although he refused to play screen heavies, in the 1950s Crosby proved his skill as dramatic actor with his complex performance as a washed-up, alcoholic singer in *The Country Girl* (1954); he played another alcoholic, this time a doctor, in the 1966 remake of *Stagecoach*. Crosby co-authored an autobiography, *Call Me Lucky*, in 1952, but his son Gary's scathing portrait of his father in *Going My Own Way* (1983) reveals a stern, unloving disciplinarian in stark contrast to Crosby's easy-going public image. • *King of Jazz* 1930; *The Big Broadcast* 1932; *College Humor* 1933; *Going Hollywood* 1933; *Too Much Harmony* 1933; *Here Is My Heart* 1934; *She Loves Me Not* 1934; *We're Not Dressing* 1934; *The Big Broadcast of 1936* 1935; *Mississippi* 1935; *Two For Tonight* 1935; *Anything Goes* 1936; *Pennies From Heaven* 1936; *Rhythm on the Range* 1936; *Double or Nothing* 1937; *Waikiki Wedding* 1937; *Doctor Rhythm* 1938; *Sing, You Sinners* 1938; *East Side of Heaven* 1939; *Paris Honeymoon* 1939; *The Star Maker* 1939; *If I Had My Way* 1940; *Rhythm on the River* 1940; *Road to Singapore* 1940; *Birth of the Blues* 1941; *Road to Zanzibar* 1941; *Holiday Inn* 1942; *Road to Morocco* 1942; *Star Spangled Rhythm* 1942; *Dixie* 1943; *Going My Way* 1944 **(AABA)**; *Here Come the Waves* 1944; *The Bells of St. Mary's* 1945 **(AANBA)**; *Duffy's Tavern* 1945; *Blue Skies* 1946; *The Road to Utopia* 1946; *Road to Rio* 1947; *Variety Girl* 1947; *Welcome Stranger* 1947; *The Emperor Waltz* 1948; *A Connecticut Yankee in King Arthur's Court* 1949; *Down Memory Lane* 1949; *Top o'the Morning* 1949; *Mr. Music* 1950; *Riding High* 1950; *Here Comes the Groom* 1951; *Just For You* 1952; *Road to Bali* 1952; *Little Boy Lost* 1953; *The Country Girl* 1954 **(AANBA)**; *White Christmas* 1954; *Anything Goes* 1956; *High Society* 1956; *Man on Fire* 1957; *Alias Jesse James* 1959; *Say One For Me* 1959; *High Time* 1960; *Let's Make Love* 1960; *Pepe* 1960; *The Road to Hong Kong* 1962; *Robin and the Seven Hoods* 1964; *Stagecoach* 1966; *Ben* 1972 (p); *That's Entertainment!* 1974; *It's Showtime* 1976.

Crosby, Floyd • Director of photography • Born Floyd Delafield Crosby, New York, NY, December 12, 1899; died September 30, 1985, Ojai, CA. *Educ.* New York Institute of Photography. Master documentary cinematographer who shot films for both Robert Flaherty and Joris Ivens before turning to narrative features. After a couple of Hollywood pictures, most notably *High Noon* (1952), Crosby began a long-time collaboration with producer-director Roger Corman. Son is rock 'n' roll performer David Crosby. • *Tabu* 1931 **(AABPH)**; *Matto Grosso* 1932 (d); *The Fight For Life* 1940; *My Father's House* 1947; *Of Men and Music* 1951; *The Fighter* 1952 (add.ph); *High Noon* 1952; *Man Crazy* 1953; *Man in the Dark* 1953; *The Steel Lady* 1953; *Monster From the Ocean Floor* 1954; *Stormy, the Thoroughbred* 1954; *Apache Woman* 1955; *Five Guns West* 1955; *Hell's Horizon* 1955; *The Naked Street* 1955; *Shack Out on 101* 1955; *Attack of the Crab Monsters* 1957; *Hell Canyon Outlaws* 1957; *Reform School Girl* 1957; *Ride Out For Revenge* 1957; *Teenage Doll* 1957; *Cry Baby Killer* 1958; *Hot Rod Gang* 1958; *Machine Gun Kelly* 1958; *The Old Man and the Sea* 1958 (add.ph); *She Gods of Shark Reef* 1958; *Suicide Battalion* 1958; *Teenage Caveman* 1958; *War of the Satellites* 1958; *Wolf Larsen* 1958; *Blood and Steel* 1959; *Crime and Punishment* 1959; *I Mobster* 1959; *The Miracle of the Hills* 1959; *The Rookie* 1959; *The Wonderful Country* 1959; *Freckles* 1960; *The High-Powered Rifle* 1960; *House of Usher* 1960; *Twelve Hours to Kill* 1960; *Walk Tall* 1960; *A Cold Wind in August* 1961; *The Explosive Generation* 1961; *The Gambler Wore a Gun* 1961; *The Little Shepherd of Kingdom Come* 1961; *Operation Bottleneck* 1961; *The Pit and the Pendulum* 1961; *The Purple Hills* 1961; *Seven Women From Hell* 1961; *The Two Little Bears* 1961; *The Broken Land* 1962; *The Firebrand* 1962; *Hand of Death* 1962; *The Premature Burial* 1962; *Tales of Terror* 1962; *Woman Hunt* 1962; *Black Zoo* 1963; *The Haunted Palace* 1963; *The*

Raven 1963; *X* 1963; *The Yellow Canary* 1963; *The Young Racers* 1963; *The Comedy of Terrors* 1964; *Pajama Party* 1964; *Sallah Shabati* 1964; *Sex and the College Girl* 1964; *Beach Blanket Bingo* 1965; *How to Stuff a Wild Bikini* 1965; *Raiders From Beneath the Sea* 1965; *Sergeant Deadhead* 1965; *Fireball 500* 1966; *The Cool Ones* 1967; *The Arousers* 1973.

Crosland, Alan • Director; also screenwriter • Born New York, NY, August 10, 1894; died 1936. Best known for directing two sound barrier-breaking films: *Don Juan* (1926), with synchronized music; and *The Jazz Singer* (1927), the first "talkie." Married to silent screen lead Elaine Hammerstein, whom he directed in several films, and father of director-editor Alan Crosland, Jr. • *The Apple-Tree Girl* 1917 (d,sc); *Kidnapped* 1917 (d); *Light in Darkness* 1917 (d,sc); *The Unbeliever* 1918 (d); *The Whirlpool* 1918 (d); *The Country Cousin* 1919 (d); *Broadway and Home* 1920 (d); *The Flapper* 1920 (d); *Greater Than Fame* 1920 (d); *The Point of View* 1920 (d); *Youthful Folly* 1920 (d); *Is Life Worth Living?* 1921 (d); *Room and Board* 1921 (d); *Worlds Apart* 1921 (d,p); *The Face in the Fog* 1922 (d); *The Prophet's Paradise* 1922 (d); *Shadows of the Seas* 1922 (d); *Slim Shoulders* 1922 (d); *The Snitching Hour* 1922 (d); *Why Announce Your Marriage?* 1922 (d,p,sc,story); *The Enemies of Women* 1923 (d); *Under the Red Robe* 1923 (d); *Miami* 1924 (d,p); *Sinners in Heaven* 1924 (d); *Three Weeks* 1924 (d); *Unguarded Women* 1924 (d); *Bobbed Hair* 1925 (d); *Compromise* 1925 (d); *Contraband* 1925 (d); *Don Juan* 1926 (d); *The Beloved Rogue* 1927 (d); *The Jazz Singer* 1927 (d); *Old San Francisco* 1927 (d); *When a Man Loves* 1927 (d); *Glorious Betsy* 1928 (d); *The Scarlet Lady* 1928 (d); *General Crack* 1929 (d); *On With the Show* 1929 (d); *Big Boy* 1930 (d); *Captain Thunder* 1930 (d); *The Furies* 1930 (d); *Song of the Flame* 1930 (d); *Viennese Nights* 1930 (d); *Children of Dreams* 1931 (d); *The Silver Lining* 1932 (d,p); *Week-Ends Only* 1932 (d); *The Case of the Howling Dog* 1934 (d); *Massacre* 1934 (d); *Midnight Alibi* 1934 (d); *The Personality Kid* 1934 (d); *The Great Impersonation* 1935 (d); *It Happened in New York* 1935 (d); *King Solomon of Broadway* 1935 (d); *Lady Tubbs* 1935 (d); *Mr. Dynamite* 1935 (d); *The White Cockatoo* 1935 (d).

Crothers, Scatman • Actor • Born Benjamin Sherman Crothers, Terre Haute, IN, May 23, 1910; died November 26, 1986, Van Nuys, CA. Bald, wide-eyed character player whose career reached its peak in the 1970s with several memorable screen roles and the popular TV show *Chico and the Man* (1974-1978). • *Meet Me at the Fair* 1952 (a,songs); *East of Sumatra* 1953; *Walking My Baby Back Home* 1953; *Between Heaven and Hell* 1956; *The Sins of Rachel Cade* 1961; *Lady in a Cage* 1964; *The Patsy* 1964; *The Aristocats* 1970; *Bloody Mama* 1970; *The Great White Hope* 1970; *Chandler* 1971; *The King of Marvin Gardens* 1972; *Lady Sings the Blues* 1972; *Black Belt Jones* 1973; *Detroit 9000* 1973; *Truck Turner* 1974; *Chesty Anderson—U.S. Navy* 1975; *Coonskin* 1975; *Friday Foster* 1975; *One Flew Over the Cuckoo's Nest* 1975; *Stay Hungry* 1975; *The Shootist* 1976; *Silver Streak* 1976; *The Cheap Detective* 1978; *Mean Dog Blues* 1978; *Scavenger Hunt* 1979; *Bronco Billy* 1980; *The Shining* 1980; *The Rats* 1982; *Zapped!* 1982; *Twilight Zone—the Movie* 1983; *Two of a Kind* 1983; *The Journey of Natty Gann* 1985; *Transformers—The Movie* 1986.

Crouse, Lindsay • Actress • Born Lindsay Ann Crouse, New York, NY, May 12, 1948. *Educ.* Radcliffe College, Cambridge MA. Promising character actress of the 1970s and 80s who played a cool, impressive lead in *House of Games* (1987), written and directed by then-husband David Mamet. Daughter of musical playwright Russel Crouse. • *All the President's Men* 1976; *Between the Lines* 1977; *Slap Shot* 1977; *Prince of the City* 1981; *The Verdict* 1982; *Daniel* 1983; *Iceman* 1984; *Places in the Heart* 1984 **(AANBSA)**; *House of Games* 1987; *Communion, A True Story* 1989; *Desperate Hours* 1990.

Crowe, Cameron • Screenwriter, director • Born Palm Springs, CA, July 13, 1957. *Educ.* California State University, San Diego. Precocious music journalist (Crowe was writing for *Rolling Stone* by the age of 15) who made an "undercover" return to high school to research his book on teen life, *Fast Times at Ridgemont High*. The book was optioned by Universal Studios before it reached the stores and Crowe himself adapted it for the 1982 film version, directed by Amy Heckerling and starring future Hollyood luminaries Sean Penn and Jennifer Jason Leigh. *Fast Times* remains one of the most honest and entertaining evocations of suburban high school culture, far superior to the slew of films which followed in its wake.

Crowe made his directorial debut with *Say Anything* (1989), another winning, insightful study of teen angst finely acted by John Cusack, Ione Skye and John Mahoney, as a seemingly perfect father whose exposure as a crook shatters his daughter's world. Married to Nancy Wilson, singer-guitarist with rock supergroup Heart. • *American Hot Wax* 1978 (a); *Fast Times at Ridgemont High* 1982 (sc,from book); *The Wild Life* 1984 (p,sc); *Say Anything* 1989 (d,sc).

Cruise, Tom • Actor • Born Thomas Cruise Mapother IV, Syracuse, NY, July 3, 1962. Hollywood's biggest male box-office attraction of the late 1980s. After achieving popular acclaim for a succession of competent teen roles, Cruise proved himself more than a pretty face opposite Paul Newman in Martin Scorsese's *The Color of Money* (1986). He has since consolidated his serious dramatic credentials with *Rain Man* (1988), opposite Oscar-winner Dustin Hoffman, and *Born on the Fourth of July* (1989), for which his portrayal of crippled Vietnam veteran Ron Kovic earned him a best actor Oscar nomination. Divorced from actress Mimi Rogers and married to promising Australian lead Nicole Kidman (*Dead Calm* 1989), his costar in 1990's *Days of Thunder*. • *Endless Love* 1981; *Taps* 1981; *All the Right Moves* 1983; *Losin' It* 1983; *The Outsiders* 1983; *Risky Business* 1983; *Legend* 1985; *The Color of Money* 1986; *Top Gun* 1986; *Cocktail* 1988; *Rain Man* 1988; *Born on the Fourth of July* 1989 **(AANBA)**; *Days of Thunder* 1990 (a,story).

Cruze, James • Director; also actor, producer. • Born Jens Cruze Bosen, Five Points, UT, March 27, 1884; died August 3, 1942. *Educ.* "Colonel" F. Cooke Caldwell Dramatic School. Born to Danish immigrant parents, he became first an actor and then, as a result of breaking his leg, a director. During the 1920s Cruze proved one of Hollywood's more varied and prolific filmmakers (in 1927 he was also the highest paid, earning $7,000 a week). His lavishly produced historical epics *The Covered Wagon* (1923) and *Old Ironsides* (1926) were noted for their almost documentary-like visuals; Cruze is also remembered for *One Glorious Day* (1922) and *Beggar on Horseback* (1925). Married to silent screen star Betty Compson from 1924 to 1930. • *The Million Dollar Mystery* 1914 (a); *Armstrong's Wife* 1915 (a); *Zudora* 1915 (a); *The Call of the East* 1917 (a); *Her Temptation* 1917 (a); *Nan of Music Mountain* 1917 (a); *What Money Can't Buy* 1917 (a); *Believe Me Xantippe* 1918 (a); *The City of Dim Faces* 1918 (a); *The Dub* 1918 (d); *Hidden Pearls* 1918 (a); *Less Than Kin* 1918 (a); *The Source* 1918 (a); *Too Many Millions* 1918 (d); *Wild Youth* 1918 (a); *An Adventure in Hearts* 1919 (d); *Alias Mike Moran* 1919 (d); *Hawthorne of the U.S.A.* 1919 (d); *The Lottery Man* 1919 (d); *The Love Burglar* 1919 (d); *The Roaring Road* 1919 (d); *The Valley of the Giants* 1919 (d); *You're Fired* 1919 (d); *Always Audacious* 1920 (d); *Food for Scandal* 1920 (d); *A Full House* 1920 (d); *Mrs. Temple's Telegram* 1920 (d); *The Sins of St. Anthony* 1920 (d); *Terror Island* 1920 (d); *What Happened to Jones* 1920 (d); *The Charm School* 1921 (d); *Crazy to Marry* 1921 (d); *The Dollar-a-Year Man* 1921 (d); *The Fast Freight* 1921 (d); *Gasoline Gus* 1921 (d); *Leap Year* 1921 (d); *The Dictator* 1922 (d); *Is Matrimony a Failure?* 1922 (d); *The Old Homestead* 1922 (d); *One Glorious Day* 1922 (d); *Thirty Days* 1922 (d); *The Covered Wagon* 1923 (d,p); *Hollywood* 1923 (d); *Ruggles of Red Gap* 1923 (d); *To the*

Ladies 1923 (d,p); *The City That Never Sleeps* 1924 (d); *The Enemy Sex* 1924 (d); *The Fighting Coward* 1924 (d); *The Garden of Weeds* 1924 (d); *Merton of the Movies* 1924 (d,p); *Beggar on Horseback* 1925 (d,p); *The Goose Hangs High* 1925 (d); *Marry Me* 1925 (d); *The Pony Express* 1925 (d); *Waking Up the Town* 1925 (d,story); *Welcome Home* 1925 (d); *Mannequin* 1926 (d); *Old Ironsides* 1926 (d); *The Waiter From the Ritz* 1926 (d); *The City Gone Wild* 1927 (d); *On to Reno* 1927 (d); *We're All Gamblers* 1927 (d,p); *Excess Baggage* 1928 (d); *The Mating Call* 1928 (d); *The Red Mark* 1928 (d); *Wife Savers* 1928 (p); *The Duke Steps Out* 1929 (d); *The Great Gabbo* 1929 (d); *A Man's Man* 1929 (d); *The Costello Case* 1930 (p); *Once a Gentleman* 1930 (d,p); *She Got What She Wanted* 1930 (d); *The Command Performance* 1931 (p); *Salvation Nell* 1931 (d); *If I Had a Million* 1932 (d); *Washington Merry-Go-Round* 1932 (d); *I Cover the Waterfront* 1933 (d); *Mr. Skitch* 1933 (d); *Racetrack* 1933 (d); *Sailor Be Good* 1933 (d); *David Harum* 1934 (d); *Helldorado* 1934 (d); *Their Big Moment* 1934 (d); *Two Fisted* 1935 (d); *Sutter's Gold* 1936 (d); *The Wrong Road* 1937 (d); *Come on Leathernecks* 1938 (d); *Gangs of New York* 1938 (d); *Prison Nurse* 1938 (d).

Crystal, Billy • Actor; also comedian. • Born Long Beach, NY, March 14, 1947. *Educ.* Marshall University; Nassau Community College (theater); NYU. Successful, personable and multi-talented stand-up comic who, after making the comedy club rounds, appeared on the landmark sitcom, "Soap" (1977-81), as TV's first openly gay character. Crystal made his film debut playing the world's first pregnant man in *Rabbit Test* (1978), directed by Joan Rivers. He was a superb foil for Danny De Vito in the latter's directorial debut, *Throw Momma From the Train* (1987), and proved a credible romantic hero in Rob Reiner's *When Harry Met Sally* (1989). Crystal is a fine mimic and his outrageous caricatures have been widely showcased on TV, especially during his season on "Saturday Night Live" (1984-85), on numerous specials and as a popular host of the Academy Awards. • *Rabbit Test* 1978 (a); *Animalympics* 1979 (a); *This Is Spinal Tap* 1984 (a); *Running Scared* 1986 (a); *The Princess Bride* 1987 (a); *Throw Momma From the Train* 1987 (a); *Memories of Me* 1988 (a,p,sc); *When Harry Met Sally...* 1989 (a); *City Slickers* 1991 (a,exec.p).

Cukor, George • Director • Born George Dewey Cukor, New York, NY, July 7, 1899; died 1983. In the historically male-dominated field of motion picture directing, George Cukor's reputation as a "woman's director" was not one he relished. Yet in the 50 films he directed between 1931 and 1981, Cukor's sensitivity to women is amply evident, particularly in portraying strong, intelligent female characters. Also typical of a Cukor film is a combination of glamour, fantasy and illusion, and a seamless quality that shows no visible sign of "direction."

The young Cukor pursued a career in the theater, initially as a stage manager, and eventually became one of the leading directors on Broadway in the mid-1920s. With the advent of the "talkies," Cukor was invited to Hollywood in 1929 to serve as a dialogue coach. After co-directing three films, he got solo credit for the first time on *Tarnished Lady* (1931), with Tallulah Bankhead. Through the 30s Cukor's stature grew, partly thanks to his personal style but also as a result of his collaborative capacities; Cukor truly embraced the collective nature of theater and film, actively fostering enthusiasm and mutual respect among actors, writers and technicians alike. He also worked with the strengths, and around the drawbacks of, the studio system. Cukor was particularly skillful in bringing classic costume novels and stage plays to the screen while respecting the integrity of the originals.

In 1933 he directed Katharine Hepburn in Louisa May Alcott's *Little Women* and an all-star MGM cast, including Jean Harlow and Marie Dressler, in George S. Kaufman's *Dinner At Eight*. The former brought Cukor the first of five Oscar nominations for best director. *David Copperfield* followed two years later and was nominated for Best Picture. In 1937 Cukor directed Greta Garbo in *Camille*, perhaps her most memorable role. The film is emblematic of Cukor's work; a flawlessly crafted costume piece which underscores his respect and affection for the cultural dichotomy women must endure. Style and substance would take a humorous turn the following year in *Holiday*, one of the classic examples of screwball comedy so popular with Depression-era movie audiences.

Cukor's successes were rewarded when David O. Selznick hired him to direct *Gone With The Wind*; soon after shooting began, however, he was replaced by Victor Fleming. (Ironically, Fleming had just finished *The Wizard of Oz*, which Cukor had turned down, in part because he was eager to prepare for the filming of the Margaret Mitchell bestseller.) Although Cukor declined comment at the time, he later admitted that his firing had something to do with Clark Gable's fear that Cukor's favored status among actresses might diminish Gable's performance in the role of Rhett Butler. Cukor's impact on *GWTW* was significant, in that virtually all of the footage shot under his direction made it to the final cut. Additionally, actresses Vivien Leigh and Olivia de Havilland continued to receive private coaching from Cukor long after he left the picture.

Of all Cukor's films, none embrace his trademark of glamour and feminine awareness more than *The Women* (1939), which MGM offered him following his firing from "GWTW." In 1940 he renewed his working relationship with Hepburn in *The Philadelphia Story*.

The 40s brought major changes to the studio system but, unlike other directors, Cukor adapted. In 1947 he commenced a successful collaboration with Garson Kanin and Ruth Gordon, the husband-and-wife writing team. During these years Cukor directed a string of critical and commercial successes that included *Adam's Rib* (1949), with Hepburn and Spencer Tracy, and *Born Yesterday* (1950), with Oscar-winner Judy Holiday and William Holden. Cukor's knack for handling difficult actresses was put to the test while directing Judy Garland in a musical remake of *A Star Is Born* (1954), Cukor's second musical and his first film in color. His next musical was *My Fair Lady*, released in 1964. Although a box-office disappointment, the film earned Oscars for best picture and director, the latter Cukor's first after five nominations.

Cukor continue to work for the next 15 years in both film and TV; his final collaboration with Katharine Hepburn was the TV movie, *Love Among the Ruins* (1975), which earned him an Emmy. In 1981 he made his 50th and final picture as a director, *Rich And Famous*. KG • *Grumpy* 1930; *The Royal Family of Broadway* 1930; *The Virtuous Sin* 1930; *Girls About Town* 1931; *Tarnished Lady* 1931; *A Bill of Divorcement* 1932; *Rockabye* 1932; *What Price Hollywood?* 1932; *Dinner at Eight* 1933; *Little Women* 1933 **(AANBD)**; *Our Betters* 1933; *David Copperfield* 1935; *Sylvia Scarlett* 1935; *Romeo and Juliet* 1936; *Camille* 1937; *Holiday* 1938; *The Women* 1939; *Zaza* 1939; *The Philadelphia Story* 1940 **(AANBD)**; *Susan and God* 1940; *Two-Faced Woman* 1941; *A Woman's Face* 1941; *Her Cardboard Lover* 1942; *Keeper of the Flame* 1942; *Gaslight* 1944; *Winged Victory* 1944; *Desire Me* 1947; *A Double Life* 1947 **(AANBD)**; *Edward, My Son* 1948; *Adam's Rib* 1949; *Born Yesterday* 1950 **(AANBD)**; *A Life of Her Own* 1950; *The Model and the Marriage Broker* 1951; *The Marrying Kind* 1952; *Pat and Mike* 1952; *The Actress* 1953; *It Should Happen to You* 1954; *A Star Is Born* 1954; *Bhowani Junction* 1956; *Les Girls* 1957; *Wild Is the Wind* 1957; *Heller in Pink Tights* 1960; *Let's Make Love* 1960; *Song Without End* 1960; *The Chapman Report* 1962; *My Fair Lady* 1964 **(AABD)**; *Justine* 1969; *Ne Men... Alla* 1972 (exec.p); *Travels With My Aunt* 1972 (d,exec.p); *The Blue Bird* 1976; *Rich and Famous* 1981.

Cummings, Robert • *aka* Blade Stanhope Conway, Brice Hutchens • Actor • Born Charles Clarence Robert Orville Cummings, Joplin, MO, June 9, 1908; died December 1, 1990, Woodland Hills, CA. *Educ.* Drury College, Springfield MO; Carnegie Institute of Technology, Pittsburgh PA; AADA, New York. Amiable leading man who hit his peak in the early 1940s. Perennially youthful, Cummings started his film career in light comedies but proved his dramatic talents with starring roles in two Hitchcock films—*Saboteur* (1942), as the naive, innocent aircraft worker, and *Dial M For Murder* (1954)—as well as Sam Wood's *King's Row* (1942) and Martin Gabel's *The Lost Moment* (1947).

Although he appeared in dramatic roles on many of the anthology series of early TV and won an Emmy for his starring performance in Reginald Rose's drama, *12 Angry Men* (1954), Cummings was best known on the small screen as the playboy photographer in his popular series, "The Bob Cummings Show/Love That Bob" (1955-59). • *Camille* 1916; *The Convict's Code* 1930; *Millions in the Air* 1935; *So Red the Rose* 1935; *The Virginia Judge* 1935; *The Accusing Finger* 1936; *Arizona Mahoney* 1936; *Border Flight* 1936; *Desert Gold* 1936; *Forgotten Faces* 1936; *Hideaway Girl* 1936; *Hollywood Boulevard* 1936; *Three Cheers For Love* 1936; *The Last Train From Madrid* 1937; *Souls at Sea* 1937; *Wells Fargo* 1937; *College Swing* 1938; *I Stand Accused* 1938; *The Texans* 1938; *Touchdown Army* 1938; *You and Me* 1938; *Charlie McCarthy, Detective* 1939; *Everything Happens at Night* 1939; *Rio* 1939; *Three Smart Girls Grow Up* 1939; *The Under-Pup* 1939; *And One Was Beautiful* 1940; *One Night in the Tropics* 1940; *Private Affairs* 1940; *Spring Parade* 1940; *The Devil and Miss Jones* 1941; *Free and Easy* 1941; *It Started With Eve* 1941; *Moon Over Miami* 1941; *Between Us Girls* 1942; *King's Row* 1942; *Saboteur* 1942; *Flesh and Fantasy* 1943; *Forever and a Day* 1943; *Princess O'Rourke* 1943; *You Came Along* 1945; *The Bride Wore Boots* 1946; *The Chase* 1946; *Heaven Only Knows* 1947; *The Lost Moment* 1947; *The Accused* 1948; *Let's Live a Little* 1948 (a,p); *Sleep, My Love* 1948; *Free For All* 1949; *Paid in Full* 1949; *Reign of Terror* 1949; *Tell It to the Judge* 1949; *For Heaven's Sake* 1950; *The Petty Girl* 1950; *The Barefoot Mailman* 1951; *The First Time* 1952; *Dial M For Murder* 1954; *Lucky Me* 1954; *Marry Me Again* 1954; *How to Be Very, Very Popular* 1955; *My Geisha* 1962; *Beach Party* 1963; *The Carpetbaggers* 1964; *What a Way to Go!* 1964; *Promise Her Anything* 1966; *Stagecoach* 1966.

Curry, Tim • Actor; also singer. • Born Cheshire, England, April 19, 1946. *Educ.* Birmingham University (drama, English). Versatile, gifted performer of stage, TV and, occasionally, films. Curry originated the character of Frank N. Furter in the 1973 London production of *The Rocky Horror Show*, a role which he reprised in the 1975 film adaptation. He also played Mozart in the 1981 Broadway production of *Amadeus*. Curry turned in an enjoyably demonic performance—complete with prosthetic horns—in Ridley Scott's *Legend* (1985). • *The Rocky Horror Picture Show* 1975; *The Shout* 1978; *Times Square* 1980; *Annie* 1982; *The Ploughman's Lunch* 1983; *Blue Money* 1984; *Clue* 1985; *Legend* 1985; *Pass the Ammo* 1987; *The Hunt For Red October* 1990; *Oscar* 1991.

Curtis, Jamie Lee • Actress • Born Los Angeles, CA, November 22, 1958. *Educ.* University of the Pacific, Stockton CA (law, drama). Attractive, capable leading lady who played the heroine in numerous horror films before moving into more prestigious terrain, notably opposite John Cleese in *A Fish Called Wanda* (1988) and, as a policewoman who gets romantically involved with a psychotic killer, in Kathryn Bigelow's *Blue Steel* (1990). Daughter of Janet Leigh and Tony Curtis, and married to actor Christopher Guest. • *Halloween* 1978; *Fog,The* 1980; *Prom Night* 1980; *Terror Train* 1980; *Halloween II* 1981; *Road Games* 1981; *Love Letters* 1983; *Trading Places* 1983; *The Adventures of Buckaroo Banzai: Across the 8th Dimension* 1984; *Grandview, U.S.A.* 1984; *Perfect* 1985; *Amazing Grace and Chuck* 1987; *Un Homme amoureux* 1987; *Dominick and Eugene* 1988; *A Fish Called Wanda* 1988; *Blue Steel* 1989; *Queens Logic* 1991.

Curtis, Tony • Actor • Born Bernard Schwartz, Bronx, NY, June 3, 1925. *Educ.* CCNY; Dramatic Workshop of the New School for Social Research, New York. Curtis began his career at Universal, where he appeared in mainly pretty-boy roles for a decade. His performance as the seedy, ruthless Sidney Falco in *Sweet Smell of Success* (1957) led to more substantial parts, most notably in *The Defiant Ones* (1958), opposite Sidney Poitier, and *Some Like It Hot* (1959), as a musician who goes on the run from a Chicago mob—in drag—and tries to win the heart of Marilyn Monroe en route. Married to actresses Janet Leigh (1951-1962) and Christine Kaufman (1963-1967). Daughter, with Leigh, is Jamie Lee Curtis. • *Criss Cross* 1948; *City Across the River* 1949; *Francis* 1949; *Johnny Stool Pigeon* 1949; *The Lady Gambles* 1949; *I Was a Shoplifter* 1950; *Kansas Raiders* 1950; *Sierra* 1950; *Winchester '73* 1950; *The Prince Who Was a Thief* 1951; *Flesh and Fury* 1952; *Meet Danny Wilson* 1952; *No Room For the Groom* 1952; *Son of Ali Baba* 1952; *The All American* 1953; *Forbidden* 1953; *Houdini* 1953; *Beachhead* 1954; *The Black Shield of Falworth* 1954; *Johnny Dark* 1954; *Six Bridges to Cross* 1954; *So This Is Paris* 1954; *The Purple Mask* 1955; *The Square Jungle* 1955; *The Rawhide Years* 1956; *Trapeze* 1956; *The Midnight Story* 1957; *Mister Cory* 1957; *Sweet Smell of Success* 1957; *The Defiant Ones* 1958 **(AANBA)**; *Kings Go Forth* 1958; *The Vikings* 1958; *Operation Petticoat* 1959; *The Perfect Furlough* 1959; *Some Like It Hot* 1959; *The Great Impostor* 1960; *The Rat Race* 1960; *Spartacus* 1960; *Who Was That Lady?* 1960; *The Outsider* 1961; *40 Pounds of Trouble* 1962; *Taras Bulba* 1962; *The List of Adrian Messenger* 1963; *Paris When It Sizzles* 1963; *Captain Newman, M.D.* 1964; *Goodbye, Charlie* 1964; *Sex and the Single Girl* 1964; *Wild and Wonderful* 1964; *Boeing Boeing* 1965; *The Great Race* 1965; *Arrivederci, Baby!* 1966; *Not With My Wife, You Don't* 1966; *La Cintura di Castita* 1967; *Don't Make Waves* 1967; *The Boston Strangler* 1968; *Rosemary's Baby* 1968; *Eye of the Cat* 1969 (p); *Monte Carlo or Bust!* 1969; *Suppose They Gave a War and Nobody Came?* 1970; *Jennifer on My Mind* 1971 (p); *That Man Bolt* 1973 (p); *Bucktown* 1975 (p); *Lepke* 1975; *Trackdown* 1975 (p); *The Last Tycoon* 1976; *Casanova & Co.* 1977; *The Manitou* 1977; *The Bad News Bears Go to Japan* 1978; *Sextette* 1978; *Title Shot* 1979; *Coal Miner's Daughter* 1980 (p); *Little Miss Marker* 1980; *The Mirror Crack'd* 1980; *Road Games* 1981 (exec.p); *Balboa* 1982; *BrainWaves* 1982; *Othello* 1982; *Psycho II* 1983 (exec.p); *Where Is Parsifal?* 1984; *Club Life* 1985; *Insignificance* 1985; *St. Elmo's Fire* 1985 (exec.p); *Sweet Dreams* 1985 (p); *The Fantasy Film World of George Pal* 1986; *The Last of Philip Banter* 1986; *Midnight* 1988; *Welcome to Germany* 1988; *Lobster Man From Mars* 1989; *Walter & Carlo I Amerika* 1989.

Curtiz, Michael • *aka* Michael Kertesz, Michael Courtice • Director • Born Mihaly Kertesz, Budapest, Hungary, December 24, 1888; died 1962. *Educ.* Markoszy University, Budapest; Royal Academy of Theater and Art, Budapest. Made his stage debut in 1906 and his screen acting and directing debuts in 1912. After assisting both Victor Sjöstrom and Maurtiz Stiller in Scandinavia, Curtiz directed over 30 films in Hungary between 1914 and 1919, after which he branched out to Germany, France, Austria and Italy. *Moon of Israel* (1924), produced by Sandor (later Alexander) Korda and seen by Jack Warner, led to his move to America. By the time he left Europe, Curtiz had directed over 60 films; he would turn out approximately 100 more in the US, making him one of the world's most prolific feature directors.

While his European work was influenced by Swedish naturalism in its use of outdoor locations, in the US Curtiz would become an extraordinary studio director, using the back lots of Hollywood to transport his audiences to exotic foreign lands. He remained with Warners until the early 1950s, turning out routine films as well as memorable pictures starring Errol Flynn (*Captain Blood* 1935), Humphrey Bogart (*Passage to Marseille* 1944) and Bette Davis (*20,000 Years in Sing Sing* 1933).

Although many critics have labeled Curtiz a superior craftsman rather than an auteur, he left behind an undeniably impressive body of work: the noir melodrama *Mildred Pierce* (1945) and the wartime love story *Casablanca* (1942), in particular, are among the most successful Hollywood films of all time. • *Ma es Holnap* 1912; *Rablelek* 1913; *As Ejszaka* 1914 (a,d); *Bank Ban* 1914; *Akit Ketten Szeretnek* 1915 (a,d); *A Farkus* 1916; *A Magyar Fold Ereje* 1916; *A Medikus* 1916 (a,d); *Doktor Ur* 1916; *Makkhetes* 1916; *A Fold Embere* 1917; *Ezredes, Az* 1917; *Tatarjaras* 1917; *Alraune* 1918; *Judas* 1918; *Kilencvenkilenc* 1918; *Lulu* 1918; *Die Dame mit dem schwarzen Handschuh* 1919; *Die Göttesgeissel* 1919; *Liliom* 1919; *Boccaccio* 1920; *Die Dame mit den Sonnenblumen* 1920; *Herzogin Satanella* 1920; *Miss Tutti Frutti* 1920; *Der Stern von Damaskus* 1920; *Cherchez la Femme* 1921; *Frau Dorothys Bekenntnis* 1921; *Wege des Schreckens* 1921; *Der Junge Medardus* 1923; *Die Lawine* 1923; *Namenlos* 1923; *Samson und Dalila* 1923 (prod.sup); *Sodom und Gomorrah* 1923; *Harun al Raschid* 1924; *Die Sklavenkönigin/Moon of Israel* 1924; *Eine Spiel ums Leben* 1924; *Celimene—la poupée de Montmartre* 1925; *Fiaker Nr. 13* 1926; *Der Goldene Schmetterling* 1926; *The Desired Woman* 1927; *Good Time Charley* 1927; *A Million Bid* 1927; *The Third Degree* 1927; *Tenderloin* 1928; *The Gamblers* 1929; *The Glad Rag Doll* 1929; *Hearts in Exile* 1929; *The Madonna of Avenue A* 1929; *Noah's Ark* 1929; *Bright Lights* 1930; *Mammy* 1930; *The Matrimonial Bed* 1930; *Moby Dick* 1930; *River's End* 1930; *A Soldier's Plaything* 1930; *Under a Texas Moon* 1930; *God's Gift to Women* 1931; *The Mad Genius* 1931; *Alias the Doctor* 1932; *The Cabin in the Cotton* 1932; *Doctor X* 1932; *The Strange Love of Molly Louvain* 1932; *The Woman From Monte Carlo* 1932; *20,000 Years in Sing Sing* 1933; *Female* 1933; *Goodbye Again* 1933; *The Kennel Murder Case* 1933; *The Keyhole* 1933; *The Mystery of the Wax Museum* 1933; *Private Detective 62* 1933; *British Agent* 1934; *Jimmy the Gent* 1934; *The Key* 1934; *Mandalay* 1934; *Black Fury* 1935; *Captain Blood* 1935; *The Case of the Curious Bride* 1935; *Front Page Woman* 1935; *Little Big Shot* 1935; *The Charge of the Light Brigade* 1936; *Stolen Holiday* 1936; *The Walking Dead* 1936; *Kid Galahad* 1937; *Mountain Justice* 1937; *The Perfect Specimen* 1937; *Angels With Dirty Faces* 1938 **(AANBD)**; *Four Daughters* 1938 **(AANBD)**; *Four's a Crowd* 1938; *Gold Is Where You Find It* 1938; *Robin Hood* 1938; *Daughters Courageous* 1939; *Dodge City* 1939; *Four Wives* 1939; *The Private Lives of Elizabeth and Essex* 1939; *Sons of Liberty (short)* 1939; *The Santa Fe Trail* 1940; *The Sea Hawk* 1940; *Virginia City* 1940; *Dive Bomber* 1941; *The Sea Wolf* 1941; *Captains of the Clouds* 1942; *Casablanca* 1942 **(AABD)**; *Yankee Doodle Dandy* 1942 **(AANBD)**; *Mission to Moscow* 1943; *This Is the Army* 1943; *Janie* 1944; *Passage to Marseille* 1944; *Mildred Pierce* 1945; *Roughly Speaking* 1945; *Night and Day* 1946; *Life With Father* 1947; *The Unsuspected* 1947; *Romance on the High Seas* 1948; *Flamingo Road* 1949; *The Lady Takes a Sailor* 1949; *My Dream Is Yours* 1949 (d,p); *The Breaking Point* 1950; *Bright Leaf* 1950; *Young Man With a Horn* 1950; *Force of Arms* 1951; *Jim Thorpe—All American* 1951; *I'll See You in My Dreams* 1952; *The Story of Will Rogers* 1952; *The Jazz Singer* 1953; *Trouble Along the Way* 1953; *The Boy From Oklahoma* 1954; *The Egyptian* 1954; *White Christmas* 1954; *The Scarlet Hour* 1955 (d,p); *We're No Angels* 1955; *The Best Things in Life Are Free* 1956; *The Vagabond King* 1956; *The Helen Morgan Story* 1957; *King Creole* 1958; *Proud Rebel* 1958; *The Hangman* 1959; *The Man in the Net* 1959; *The Adventures of Huckleberry Finn* 1960; *A Breath of Scandal* 1960; *The Comancheros* 1961; *Francis of Assisi* 1961.

Cusack, Cyril • Actor • Born Durban, Natal, South Africa, November 26, 1910. *Educ.* National University of Ireland, Dublin. Talented Irish stage performer who made his film debut in *Knocknagow* (1917) but did not come into his own as a screen actor until 1947, with Carol Reed's *Odd Man Out*. With an elfin face that can register both melancholy and stern disapproval, Cusack has played everything from clerics (*My Left Foot* 1989) to spies (*The Spy Who Came in from the Cold* 1965); he was memorable in Truffaut's *Fahrenheit 451* (1966), as the book-burning fire chief. Father of actresses Sinead, Niamh and Sorcha Cusack, with all of whom he co-starred in the 1990 production of *The Three Sisters* at Dublin's Gate Theater. • *Knocknagow* 1917; *Odd Man Out* 1947; *Escape* 1948; *The Small Back Room* 1948; *The Blue Lagoon* 1949; *The Elusive Pimpernel* 1950; *Gone to Earth* 1950; *The Blue Veil* 1951; *The Secret of Convict Lake* 1951; *Soldiers Three* 1951; *Saadia* 1954; *The Man Who Never Was* 1955; *The Spanish Gardener* 1956; *Ill Met By Moonlight* 1957; *Rising of the Moon* 1957; *Floods of Fear* 1958; *Gideon's Day* 1958; *Shake Hands With the Devil* 1959; *A Terrible Beauty* 1960; *I Thank a Fool* 1962; *Waltz of the Toreadors* 1962; *The Spy Who Came in From the Cold* 1965; *Where the Spies Are* 1965; *Fahrenheit 451* 1966; *I Was Happy Here* 1966; *The Taming of the Shrew* 1967; *Galileo* 1968; *Oedipus the King* 1968; *Country Dance* 1970; *David Copperfield* 1970; *Sacco and Venzetti* 1970; *Harold and Maude* 1971; *King Lear* 1971; *Tam Lin* 1971; *... Piu forte ragazzi* 1972; *The Italian Connection* 1972; *La Polizia Ringrazia* 1972; *The Day of the Jackal* 1973; *The Homecoming* 1973; *The Abdication* 1974; *Children of Rage* 1974; *Poitin* 1978; *True Confessions* 1981; *The Outcasts* 1983; *1984* 1984; *Dr. Fischer of Geneva* 1984; *Little Dorrit* 1988; *My Left Foot* 1989; *The Fool* 1990.

Cusack, Joan • Actress • Born Evanston, IL, October 11, 1962. *Educ.* Piven Theater Workshop, Evanston; University of Wisconsin, Madison. Ex-"Saturday Night Live" performer (1985-86), in films since the age of 16. Cusack excels at off-beat comedic roles and was outstanding as the harried production assistant in *Broadcast News* (1987) and as Melanie Griffith's secretarial sidekick in *Working Girl* (1988). Sister of actor John Cusack. • *My Bodyguard* 1980; *Class* 1983; *Grandview, U.S.A.* 1984; *Sixteen Candles* 1984; *The Allnighter* 1987; *Broadcast News* 1987; *Married to the Mob* 1988; *Stars and Bars* 1988; *Working Girl* 1988 **(AANBSA)**; *Men Don't Leave* 1990; *My Blue Heaven* 1990; *The Cabinet of Dr. Ramirez* 1991.

Cusack, John • Actor • Born Evanston, IL, June 28, 1966. *Educ.* Piven Theatre Workshop, Evanston. Popular, promising young lead of the late 1980s who rose above the schlock teen material of his early career. Cusack has turned in fine performances in more engaging movies, including John Sayles's *Eight Men Out* (1988), Cameron Crowe's affecting, bittersweet love story *Say Anything* (1989) and Stephen Frears's contemporary film noir *The Grifters* (1990). Like sister Joan Cusack, with whom he has appeared in four films, he remains active in the theater. • *Class* 1983; *Grandview, U.S.A.* 1984; *Sixteen Candles* 1984; *Better Off Dead* 1985; *The Journey of Natty Gann* 1985; *The Sure Thing* 1985; *One Crazy Summer* 1986; *Stand By Me* 1986; *Broadcast News* 1987; *Hot Pursuit* 1987; *Eight Men Out* 1988; *Tapeheads* 1988 (a,song); *Fat Man and Little Boy* 1989; *Say Anything* 1989; *The Grifters* 1990; *True Colors* 1991.

Cushing, Peter • Actor • Born Kenley, Surrey, England, May 26, 1913. *Educ.* Guildhall School of Music and Drama. Made his screen debut in the US with a supporting part in *The Man in the Iron Mask* (1939) before playing in his first British film, Laurence Olivier's *Hamlet* (1948). Cushing is known for his numerous horror films, often produced by Hammer Studios. • *The Man in the Iron Mask* 1939; *A Chump at Oxford* 1940; *Laddie* 1940; *Vigil in the Night* 1940; *They Dare Not Love* 1941; *Hamlet* 1948; *Moulin Rouge* 1952; *The Black Knight*

1954; *The End of the Affair* 1955; *Alexander the Great* 1956; *Magic Fire* 1956; *The Abominable Snowman* 1957; *The Curse of Frankenstein* 1957; *Time Without Pity* 1957; *Horror of Dracula* 1958; *The Revenge of Frankenstein* 1958; *The Hound of the Baskervilles* 1959; *John Paul Jones* 1959; *The Mummy* 1959; *The Brides of Dracula* 1960; *Cone of Silence* 1960; *The Flesh and the Fiends* 1960; *The Risk* 1960; *Sword of Sherwood Forest* 1960; *Cash on Demand* 1961; *The Naked Edge* 1961; *Captain Clegg* 1962; *The Man Who Finally Died* 1963; *Dr. Terror's House of Horrors* 1964; *The Evil of Frankenstein* 1964; *The Gorgon* 1964; *She* 1965; *The Skull* 1965; *Dr. Who and the Daleks* 1966; *Island of Terror* 1966; *The Skull* 1966; *Frankenstein Created Woman* 1967; *Blood Beast Terror* 1968; *Corruption* 1968; *Torture Garden* 1968; *Frankenstein Must Be Destroyed* 1969; *The House That Dripped Blood* 1970; *Scream and Scream Again* 1970; *The Vampire Lovers* 1970; *I Monster* 1971; *Twins of Evil* 1971; *Asylum* 1972; *The Creeping Flesh* 1972; *Doctor Phibes Rises Again* 1972; *Dracula A.D. 1972* 1972; *Frankenstein and the Monster From Hell* 1972; *Panico en el Transiberiano* 1972; *Tales From The Crypt* 1972; *And Now the Screaming Starts* 1973; *The Beast Must Die* 1974; *La Grande Trouille* 1974; *Madhouse* 1974; *Call Him Mr. Shatter* 1975; *Death Corps* 1975; *Dirty Knights' Work* 1975; *Dracula and the 7 Golden Vampires* 1975; *From Beyond the Grave* 1975; *The Ghoul* 1975; *At the Earth's Core* 1976; *A Choice of Weapons* 1976; *Die Standarte* 1977; *Star Wars* 1977; *The Uncanny* 1977; *The Satanic Rites of Dracula* 1978; *Arabian Adventure* 1979; *Monster Island* 1981; *House of the Long Shadows* 1982; *Sword of the Valiant—The Legend of Gawain and the Green Knight* 1984; *Top Secret!* 1984; *Biggles* 1986.

Cybulski, Zbigniew • Actor • Born Kniaze, Ukraine, USSR, November 3, 1927; died 1967, Poland. *Educ.* Academy of Commerce and Journalism, Cracow, Poland; Theater School, Cracow, Poland. Known as "The Polish James Dean," he made his film debut—as did Roman Polanski—with a small part in Andrzej Wajda's *A Generation* (1954). Cybulski subsequently became one of Poland's brightest young stars, equally adept in comic as well as brooding dramatic roles. He is best known in the West as the conflicted resistance fighter in Wajda's *Ashes and Diamonds* (1958). The year after Cybulski was killed in a train accident, Wajda made a pseudo-fictional tribute to the actor, *Everything For Sale* (1968). • *Pokolenie/A Generation* 1954 (a); *Trzy starty/Three Stars* 1955 (a); *Tajemnica dzikiego szybu/Secret of the Old Pit* 1956 (a); *Koniec nocy/End of the Night* 1957 (a); *Wraki/Wrecks* 1957 (a); *Der Achte Wochentag/The Eighth Day of the Week* 1958 (a); *Popiol i Diament/Ashes and Diamonds* 1958 (a); *Krzyz walecznych/The Cross of Valor* 1959 (a); *Pociag/Baltic Express* 1959 (a); *Do widzenia do jutra/See You Tomorrow* 1960 (a,sc); *Niewinni Czarodzieje/Innocent Sorcerors* 1960 (a); *Rozstanie/Partings* 1961 (a); *L'Amour à vingt ans/Love at Twenty* 1962 (a); *La Poupée* 1962 (a); *Spoznieni przechodnie/Those Who Are Late* 1962 (a); *Ich dzien powszedni/Their Everyday Life* 1963 (a); *Jak byc kochana/How To Be Loved* 1963 (a); *Milczenie/Silence* 1963 (a); *Rozwodow nie bedzie/No More Divorces* 1963 (a); *Zbrodniarz i panna/The Murderer and the Girl* 1963 (a); *Att Alska/To Love* 1964 (a); *Giuseppe w Warszawie/An Italian in Warsaw* 1964 (a); *Rekopis znaleziony w Saragossie/The Saragossa Manuscript* 1964 (a); *Jutro Meksyk/Tomorrow Mexico* 1965 (a); *Pingwin/Penguin* 1965 (a); *Salto/Jump* 1965 (a); *Sam posrod miasta/Alone in a City* 1965 (a); *Cala naprzod/Full Ahead* 1966 (a); *Przedswiateczny wieczor/Christmas Eve* 1966 (a); *Szyfry/The Code* 1966 (a); *Jowita/Yovita* 1967 (a); *Morderca zostawia slad/The Murderer Leaves a Clue* 1967 (a).

Czinner, Paul • Director; also producer. • Born Budapest, Hungary, 1890; died 1972. A child prodigy on the violin, Czinner was active in the theater before making his film directing debut in Vienna in 1919. He earned international acclaim with *Husbands or Lovers* (1924), starring his future wife Elisabeth Bergner, but fled Germany in 1933.

Czinner continued directing films and plays in both England and the US, later experimenting with multiple cameras to film ballets and operas. • *Homo immanis* 1919 (d); *Inferno* 1920 (d); *Nju/Husbands or Lovers* 1924 (d,sc); *Liebe* 1926 (d,sc); *Dona Juana* 1927 (d,sc); *Fräulein Else* 1929 (d,sc); *The Woman He Scorned* 1930 (d,sc); *Ariane* 1931 (d,sc); *Mélo* 1932 (d,sc); *Catherine the Great* 1934 (d,sc); *Escape Me Never* 1935 (d); *As You Like It* 1936 (d,p); *Dreaming Lips* 1937 (d,sc); *Stolen Life* 1939 (d,sc); *Die Träumende Mund* 1953 (sc); *Don Giovanni* 1955 (d); *The Bolshoi Ballet* 1957 (d); *The Royal Ballet* 1959 (d); *Der Rosenkavalier* 1962 (d); *Romeo and Juliet* 1966 (d).

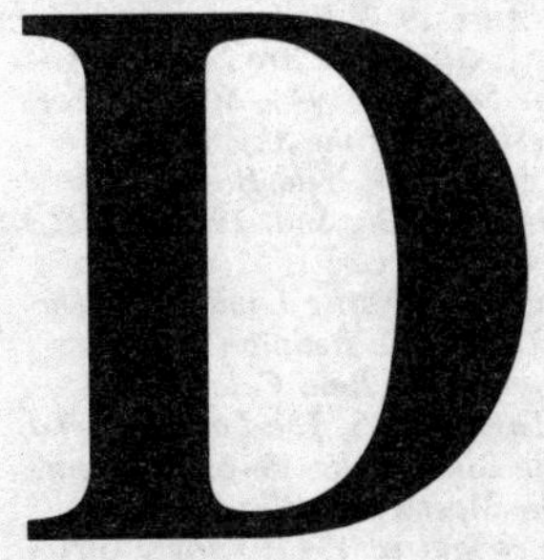

D'Amico, Suso Cecchi • See Cecchi D'Amico, Suso.

D'Angelo, Beverly • Actress • Born Columbus, OH, November 15, 1954. Feisty blonde performer who was a rock singer and cartoonist for Hanna-Barbera before moving onto Broadway (*Rockabye Hamlet*) and then into films. D'Angelo first gained wide attention as Sheila in Miloš Forman's *Hair* (1979) and was nominated for a best supporting actress Oscar for her canny portrayal of Patsy Cline in *Coal Miner's Daughter* (1980). • *Annie Hall* 1977; *First Love* 1977; *The Sentinel* 1977; *Every Which Way But Loose* 1978; *Hair* 1979; *Highpoint* 1979; *Coal Miner's Daughter* 1980 **(AANBSA)**; *Honky Tonk Freeway* 1981; *Paternity* 1981; *National Lampoon's Vacation* 1983; *Finders Keepers* 1984; *Big Trouble* 1985; *National Lampoon's European Vacation* 1985; *Aria* 1987; *In the Mood* 1987; *Maid to Order* 1987; *High Spirits* 1988; *Trading Hearts* 1988; *Cold Front* 1989; *National Lampoon's Christmas Vacation* 1989; *Daddy's Dyin'... Who's Got the Will?* 1990 (a,song); *Pacific Heights* 1990; *The Miracle* 1991; *The Pope Must Die* 1991.

D'Onofrio, Vincent Phillip • Actor • Born Brooklyn, NY. Husky-voiced young supporting player who made a strong impression as the dangerously unstable Private Pyle in Stanley Kubrick's *Full Metal Jacket* (1987) and played Lili Taylor's lovable hunk in the bittersweet *Mystic Pizza* (1988). • *The First Turn-On!!* 1984; *Adventures in Babysitting* 1987; *Full Metal Jacket* 1987; *Mystic Pizza* 1988; *The Blood of Heroes* 1989; *Signs of Life* 1989; *Naked Tango* 1990.

Da Silva, Howard • Actor • Born Harold Silverblatt, Cleveland, OH, May 4, 1909; died February 16, 1986, Ossining, NY. *Educ.* Carnegie Institute of Technology, Pittsburgh PA. Character player, often in sinister roles, who was blacklisted in the 1950s. Da Silva worked in theater before resuming his screen career in the early 60s, turning in fine performances in both film and TV, particularly as Louis B. Mayer in *Mommie Dearest* (1981). • *Abe Lincoln in Illinois* 1940;

I'm Still Alive 1940; *Bad Men of Missouri* 1941; *Nine Lives Are Not Enough* 1941; *The Sea Wolf* 1941; *Sergeant York* 1941; *Steel Against the Sky* 1941; *Strange Alibi* 1941; *Wild Bill Hickok Rides* 1941; *The Big Shot* 1942; *Bullet Scars* 1942; *Juke Girl* 1942; *Keeper of the Flame* 1942; *Native Land* 1942; *The Omaha Trail* 1942; *Reunion in France* 1942; *Tonight We Raid Calais* 1943; *Duffy's Tavern* 1945; *The Lost Weekend* 1945; *The Blue Dahlia* 1946; *Two Years Before the Mast* 1946; *Blaze of Noon* 1947; *Unconquered* 1947; *Variety Girl* 1947; *They Live By Night* 1948; *Border Incident* 1949; *The Great Gatsby* 1949; *Three Husbands* 1950; *Tripoli* 1950; *The Underworld Story* 1950; *Wyoming Mail* 1950; *Fourteen Hours* 1951; *M* 1951; *David and Lisa* 1962; *The Outrage* 1964; *Nevada Smith* 1966; *1776* 1972; *The Great Gatsby* 1974; *I'm a Stranger Here Myself* 1974; *Hollywood on Trial* 1976; *The Private Files of J. Edgar Hoover* 1977; *Mommie Dearest* 1981; *Garbo Talks* 1984.

Dafoe, Willem • Actor • Born Appleton, WI, July 22, 1955. A member of New York's acclaimed experimental theater company the Wooster Group, Dafoe achieved instant star status as Sgt. Elias in *Platoon* (1986). His sharp facial features originally landed him in villainous roles but he has proved his versatility with *Mississippi Burning* (1988), as a by-the-book FBI man, and in the demanding title role of *The Last Temptation of Christ* (1988). • *The Loveless* 1981; *New York Nights* 1982; *The Hunger* 1983; *The Communists Are Comfortable (And Three Other Stories)* 1984; *Roadhouse 66* 1984; *Streets of Fire* 1984; *To Live and Die in L.A.* 1985; *Platoon* 1986 **(AANBSA)**; *Dear America* 1987; *The Last Temptation of Christ* 1988; *Mississippi Burning* 1988; *Off Limits* 1988; *Born on the Fourth of July* 1989; *Triumph of the Spirit* 1989; *Cry-Baby* 1990; *Wild at Heart* 1990; *Flight of the Intruder* 1991; *The Doors* 1991.

Dahlbeck, Eva • Actress; also screenwriter. • Born Saltsjo-Duvnas, Sweden, March 8, 1920. *Educ.* Royal Dramatic Theater School, Stockholm. In films by Gustaf Molander and others from 1942, but best known outside Sweden for her collaborations with Ingmar Bergman. Dahlbeck has also written plays, screenplays, novels and a volume of poetry, *Genom Fonstren* (1963), under the nom-de-plume Lis Edvardson. • *Rid i natt/Ride Tonight* 1942 (a); *Black Roses* 1945 (a); *Eva* 1948 (a); *Only a Mother* 1949 (a); *Kvinnors Vantan/Secrets of Women* 1952 (a); *The Village* 1952 (a); *Defiance* 1953 (a); *En Lektion i Karlek/A Lesson in Love* 1954 (a); *Kvinnodrom/Dreams/Journey Into Autumn* 1955 (a); *Sommarnattens Leende/Smiles of a Summer Night* 1955 (a); *Sista Paret Ut* 1956 (a); *Nara Livet/Brink of Life* 1958 (a); *A Matter of Morals* 1960 (a); *Barabbas* 1962 (a); *The Counterfeit Traitor* 1962 (a); *Alksande Par/Loving Couples* 1964 (a); *For att Inte Tala om Alla Dessa Kvinnor/All These Women* 1964 (a); *Les Creatures* 1965 (a); *Kattorna/The Cats* 1965 (a); *Morianna* 1965 (a); *Yngsjomordet* 1966 (sc); *Mennesker Moedes Og Soed Musik Opstaar I Hjertet* 1967 (a); *Den Rode Kappe* 1967 (a).

Dalle, Beatrice • Actress • Born Le Mans, France, December 19, 1964. Popular French box-office attraction who came to international prominence as the enticing, impulsive title character of *Betty Blue* (1986). Dalle also starred in Marco Bellocchio's 1988 study of witchcraft, *The Witches' Sabbath*. • *37.2 Le Matin/Betty Blue* 1986; *On a Volé Charlie Spencer!* 1986; *La Visione del Sabba/The Witches' Sabbath* 1988; *Les Bois noirs* 1989; *Chimère* 1989; *La Vengeance d'une femme/A Woman's Revenge* 1990.

Dallesandro, Joe • Actor • Born US, 1948. Tall, androgynous leading man who made his name in several of director Paul Morrissey's collaborations with Andy Warhol. • *The Loves of Ondine* 1967; *Flesh* 1968; *Lonesome Cowboys* 1968; *Trash* 1970; *Heat* 1972; *Andy Warhol's Frankenstein* 1973; *Blood For Dracula* 1974; *Donna e Bello* 1974; *The Gardener* 1974; *Black Moon* 1975; *Je T'Aime Moi Non Plus* 1975; *La Marge* 1976; *Un Cuore Semplice* 1978; *Tapage Nocturne* 1979; *Seeds of Evil* 1980; *Merry Go Round* 1983; *The Cotton Club* 1984; *Critical Condition* 1987; *Sunset* 1988; *Private War* 1989; *Cry-Baby* 1990; *Double Revenge* 1990.

Dalton, Timothy • Actor • Born Colwyn Bay, Clywd, Wales, March 21, 1944. *Educ.* RADA, London; National Youth Theatre, England. Handsome leading man who began his career on the stage and proved his range with two contrasting character studies in English costume dramas: *The Lion in Winter* (1968), as a model of effete venom, and *Wuthering Heights* (1970), as a sensually charged Heathcliff. Dalton assured his cult status by playing the lead opposite an octogenarian Mae West in *Sextette* (1978) and earned international stardom as the fourth actor to play James Bond, beginning with *The Living Daylights* (1987). He has brought a more contemporary, cynical edge to the Bond character. • *The Lion in Winter* 1968; *Cromwell* 1970; *Wuthering Heights* 1970; *Mary, Queen of Scots* 1971; *Permission to Kill* 1975; *El Hombre Que Supo Amar* 1976; *Sextette* 1978; *Agatha* 1979; *Flash Gordon* 1980; *Chanel Solitaire* 1981; *The Doctor and the Devils* 1985; *The Living Daylights* 1987; *Hawks* 1988; *Brenda Starr* 1989; *Licence to Kill* 1989; *The King's Whore* 1990; *The Rocketeer* 1991.

Damiani, Damiano • Director; also screenwriter, actor. • Born Pasiano, Italy, July 23, 1922. *Educ.* Academia di Belle Arti, Milan; Brera Academy, Milan (fine arts). Competent director who favors socially conscious, and often mafia-related, thrillers. Made numerous shorts from 1946 before his first feature, *Lipstick* (1960), took a prize at the San Sebastian Film Festival. • *Head of a Tyrant* 1960 (sc); *Il Rosetto/Lipstick* 1960 (d,sc); *Il Sepolcro dei re* 1961 (sc); *Il Sicario* 1961 (d,sc); *L'Isola di Arturo* 1962 (d,sc); *La Noia/The Empty Canvas* 1963 (d,sc); *La Rimpatriata* 1963 (d,sc); *La Strega in Amore* 1966 (d,sc); *Quien Sabe?/A Bullet for the General* 1967 (a,d); *Il Giorno della Civetta/Mafia* 1968 (d,sc); *Una Ragazza Piuttosto Complicata* 1969 (d,sc,art d); *La Moglie piu Bella* 1970 (d,sc,story); *Confessione di un Commissario di Polizia al Procuratore Della Repubblica* 1971 (d,sc); *L'Istruttoria e chiusa: Dimentichi!* 1971 (a,d,sc); *Girolimoni, Il Mostro di Roma* 1972 (d,sc); *Il Delitto Matteotti/The Assassination of Matteotti* 1973 (a); *Il Sorriso del Grande Tentatore/The Devil is a Woman* 1973 (d,sc); *Perche si uccide un Magistrato* 1974 (a,d,sc); *Genio, Due Compari, Un Pollo, Un* 1975 (d,sc); *I Am Afraid* 1977 (d,sc); *Goodbye and Amen* 1978 (d,sc); *L'Ultimo nome* 1979 (d,sc); *Amityville II: The Possession* 1982 (d); *Attacco alla Piovra* 1984 (d,sc); *L'Inchiesta/The Investigation* 1987 (d,sc); *Giocodi Massacro* 1990 (d,sc,from play); *Il Sole Buio/The Dark Sun* 1990 (d,sc,story).

Damiano, Gerard • American director, screenwriter; also actor, producer. • Best known for *Deep Throat* (1972) and *The Devil in Miss Jones* (1973), two pornographic movies which added a veneer of respectability to the genre by paying increased attention to narrative and incorporating a degree of irony. • *Deep Throat* 1972 (d,sc,ed); *The Devil in Miss Jones* 1973 (a,d,p,sc,ed); *Memories Within Miss Aggie* 1973 (d,sc); *The Story of Joanna* 1975 (a,d,p,sc,ed,song); *Let My Puppets Come* 1977 (d,p); *Odyssey* 1977 (d,p,sc); *Waterpower* 1978 (d); *For Richer For Poorer* 1980 (d,p,sc,ed); *Throat—12 Years After* 1984 (d,p,sc).

Dance, Charles • Actor • Born Plymouth, England, October 10, 1946. *Educ.* Leicester College of Art (graphic design). Distinguished-looking lead who first established himself in the highly acclaimed English TV series *The Jewel in the Crown*. • *For Your Eyes Only* 1981; *The McGuffin* 1985; *Plenty* 1985; *The Golden Child* 1986; *Good Morning Babylon* 1986; *Hidden City* 1987; *White Mischief* 1987; *Pascali's Island* 1988.

Dandridge, Dorothy • Actress • Born Cleveland, OH, November 9, 1923; died 1965. Child performer who went on to become one of Hollywood's first black female stars with title roles in two exceptional musicals, *Carmen Jones* (1954) and *Porgy and Bess* (1959). Dandridge died from a drug overdose at age 41. • *A Day at the Races* 1937; *Bahama Passage* 1941; *Lady From Louisiana* 1941; *Sun Valley Serenade* 1941; *Sundown* 1941; *Drums of the Congo* 1942; *Hit Parade of 1943* 1943; *Atlantic City* 1944; *Since You Went Away* 1944; *The Harlem Globetrotters* 1951; *Tarzan's Peril* 1951; *Bright Road* 1953; *Remains to Be Seen* 1953; *Carmen Jones* 1954 **(AANBA)**; *Island in the Sun* 1957; *Tamango* 1957; *The Decks Ran Red* 1958; *Porgy and Bess* 1959; *Moment of Danger* 1960; *The Murder Men* 1961.

Dangerfield, Rodney • Actor, screenwriter • Born Babylon, NY, 1921. Nightclub performer (as Jack Roy) who became a comedian in middle age and enjoyed a series of screen successes in the 1980s. • *The Projectionist* 1971 (a); *Caddyshack* 1980 (a); *Easy Money* 1983 (a,sc); *Back to School* 1986 (a,sc,story,song); *Moving* 1988 (a).

Daniels, Jeff • Actor • Born Georgia, 1955. *Educ.* Central Michigan University, Mt. Pleasant (English). Leading man of the 1980s with a flair for playing perplexed characters overtaken by unusual circumstances. Memorable in Woody Allen's *The Purple Rose of Cairo* (1985), as a movie hero who steps off the silver screen and into the arms of a downtrodden, Depression-era housewife (Mia Farrow). Daniels won an Obie award in 1982 for a one-man show adapted from Dalton Trumbo's *Johnny Got His Gun*. • *Ragtime* 1981; *Terms of Endearment* 1983; *Marie* 1985; *The Purple Rose of Cairo* 1985; *Heartburn* 1986; *Something Wild* 1986; *Radio Days* 1987; *Checking Out* 1988; *The House on Carroll Street* 1988; *Sweet Hearts Dance* 1988; *Arachnophobia* 1990; *Love Hurts* 1990; *Welcome Home, Roxy Carmichael* 1990.

Daniels, William H. • Director of photography • Born Cleveland, OH, 1895; died 1970. *Educ.* USC, Los Angeles. Eminent and prolific cinematographer who created the appropriately harsh look of Erich von Stroheim's realist masterpiece *Greed* (1925). Daniels subsequently became known as Greta Garbo's preferred cameraman shooting 20 of her Hollywood pictures. (He allegedly earned the distinction as much for his personal tact as for his technical prowess.) In the 1950s and 60s Daniels worked frequently, and successfully, with director Anthony Mann and actor Frank Sinatra. Brother of theater and TV director Jack Daniels. • *Blind Husbands* 1919; *The Devil's Passkey* 1920; *Foolish Wives* 1922; *Merry-Go-Round* 1923; *Helen's Babies* 1924; *Greed* 1925; *The Merry Widow* 1925; *Women and Gold* 1925; *Altars of Desire* 1926; *Bardelys the Magnificent* 1926; *The Boob* 1926; *Dance Madness* 1926; *Money Talks* 1926; *Monte Carlo* 1926; *The Temptress* 1926; *The Torrent* 1926; *Captain Salvation* 1927; *Flesh and the Devil* 1927; *Love* 1927; *On Ze Boulevard* 1927; *Tillie the Toiler* 1927; *The Actress* 1928; *Bringing Up Father* 1928; *Dream of Love* 1928; *A Lady of Chance* 1928; *The Latest From Paris* 1928; *The Mysterious Lady* 1928; *Telling the World* 1928; *A Woman of Affairs* 1928; *The Kiss* 1929; *The Last of Mrs. Cheyney* 1929; *Their Own Desire* 1929; *The Trial of Mary Dugan* 1929; *Wild Orchids* 1929; *Wise Girls* 1929; *Anna Christie* 1930 **(AANBPH)**; *Montana Moon* 1930; *Romance* 1930; *Strictly Unconventional* 1930; *A Free Soul* 1931; *The Great Meadow* 1931; *Inspiration* 1931; *Strangers May Kiss* 1931; *Susan Lenox, Her Fall and Rise* 1931; *As You Desire Me* 1932; *Grand Hotel* 1932; *Lovers Courageous* 1932; *Mata Hari* 1932; *Rasputin and the Empress* 1932; *Skyscraper Souls* 1932; *Broadway to Hollywood* 1933; *Christopher Bean* 1933; *Dinner at Eight* 1933; *Queen Christina* 1933; *The Stranger's Return* 1933; *The White Sister* 1933; *The Barretts of Wimpole Street* 1934; *The Painted Veil* 1934; *Anna Karenina* 1935; *Naughty Marietta* 1935; *The Rendezvous* 1935; *Romeo and Juliet* 1936; *Rose Marie* 1936; *Beg, Borrow, or Steal* 1937; *Camille* 1937; *Double Wedding* 1937; *The Last Gangster* 1937; *Personal Property* 1937; *Broadway Melody of 1938* 1938; *Dramatic School* 1938; *Marie Antoinette* 1938; *Three Loves Has Nancy* 1938; *Another Thin Man* 1939; *Idiot's Delight* 1939; *Ninotchka* 1939; *Stronger Than Desire* 1939; *The Mortal Storm* 1940; *New Moon* 1940; *The Shop Around the Corner* 1940; *Back Street* 1941; *Design For Scandal* 1941; *Dr. Kildare's Victory* 1941; *So Ends Our Night* 1941; *They Met in Bombay* 1941; *For Me and My Gal* 1942; *Keeper of the Flame* 1942; *Girl Crazy* 1943; *Brute Force* 1947; *Lured* 1947; *Family Honeymoon* 1948; *For the Love of Mary* 1948; *The Naked City* 1948 **(AABPH)**; *Abandoned* 1949; *The Gal Who Took the West* 1949; *Illegal Entry* 1949; *The Life of Riley* 1949; *Deported* 1950; *Harvey* 1950; *Winchester '73* 1950; *Woman in Hiding* 1950; *Bright Victory* 1951; *The Lady Pays Off* 1951; *Thunder on the Hill* 1951; *Glory Alley* 1952; *Never Wave at a Wac* 1952; *Pat and Mike* 1952; *Plymouth Adventure* 1952; *When in Rome* 1952; *Forbidden* 1953; *Thunder Bay* 1953; *The Glenn Miller Story* 1954; *Six Bridges to Cross* 1954; *War Arrow* 1954; *The Benny Goodman Story* 1955; *The Far Country* 1955; *Foxfire* 1955; *The Girl Rush* 1955; *The Shrike* 1955; *Strategic Air Command* 1955; *Away All Boats* 1956; *The Unguarded Moment* 1956; *Interlude* 1957; *Istanbul* 1957; *My Man Godfrey* 1957; *Night Passage* 1957; *Cat on a Hot Tin Roof* 1958 **(AANBPH)**; *Some Came Running* 1958; *Voice in the Mirror* 1958; *A Hole in the Head* 1959; *Never So Few* 1959; *Stranger in My Arms* 1959; *All the Fine Young Cannibals* 1960; *Can-Can* 1960; *Ocean's Eleven* 1960; *Come September* 1961; *Billy Rose's Jumbo* 1962; *How the West Was Won* 1962 **(AANBPH)**; *Come Blow Your Horn* 1963; *The Prize* 1963; *Robin and the Seven Hoods* 1964 (assoc.p,ph); *Marriage on the Rocks* 1965 (p,ph); *None But the Brave* 1965 (assoc.p); *Von Ryan's Express* 1965; *Assault on a Queen* 1966 (assoc.p,ph); *In Like Flint* 1967; *Valley of the Dolls* 1967; *The Impossible Years* 1968; *The Maltese Bippy* 1969; *Marlowe* 1969; *Move* 1970.

Dankworth, John • Composer; also conductor. • Born Woodford, Essex, England, 1927. *Educ.* Royal Academy of Music, London. Songwriter and performer whose jazz-oriented scores enhanced several British films of the 1960s. Frequent collaborator with directors Karel Reisz and Joseph Losey. Married to singer-actress Cleo Laine. • *We Are the Lambeth Boys* 1958 (m); *The Whole Truth* 1958 (m.perf); *Sapphire* 1959 (m.perf); *The Criminal/The Concrete Jungle* 1960 (m); *Saturday Night and Sunday Morning* 1960 (m,m.cond); *Hamilton in the Music Festival (short)* 1961 (m); *Hamilton the Musical Elephant (short)* 1961 (m); *A Taste of Honey* 1961 (song); *All Night Long* 1962 (a); *The Servant* 1963 (m,m.cond); *Top Flight (short)* 1964 (m); *Darling* 1965 (m); *Return From the Ashes* 1965 (m,m.cond); *Sands of the Kalahari* 1965 (m); *Scruggs* 1965 (m); *The World at Three (short)* 1965 (m); *The Idol* 1966 (m); *Modesty Blaise* 1966 (m); *Morgan—A Suitable Case For Treatment* 1966 (m); *Accident* 1967 (m); *Fathom* 1967 (m); *The Last Safari* 1967 (m,m.dir); *Boom!* 1968 (song); *I Love You, I Hate You* 1968 (m); *The Magus* 1968 (m,m.cond); *Salt and Pepper* 1968 (m); *10 Rillington Place* 1970 (m,m.cond); *The Engagement* 1970 (m); *The Last Grenade* 1970 (m,m.dir); *Perfect Friday* 1970 (m,m.dir); *Pianorama (short)* 1973 (m); *Strike It Rich* 1989 (m).

Danner, Blythe • Actress • Born Philadelphia, PA, February 3, 1943. *Educ.* Bard College, Annandale-on-Hudson NY. Acclaimed Broadway performer (*Butterflies Are Free, Betrayal*), occasionally in films and often on TV. Married since 1969 to executive TV producer Bruce Paltrow ("The White Shadow," "St. Elsewhere"). • *1776* 1972; *To Kill a Clown* 1972; *Lovin' Molly* 1974; *Hearts of the West* 1975; *Futureworld* 1976; *The Great Santini* 1979; *Man, Woman and Child* 1982; *Brighton Beach Memoirs* 1986; *One Art* 1987; *Another Woman* 1988; *Alice* 1990; *Mr. & Mrs. Bridge* 1990.

Danson, Ted • Actor • Born Flagstaff, AZ, December 29, 1947. *Educ.* Stanford; Carnegie-Mellon University, Pittsburgh, PA (drama); Actors Institute. Tall, handsome star of the popular TV sitcom

"Cheers," seen increasingly in films during the 1980s. Notable as the cynical DA in *Body Heat* (1981). • *The Onion Field* 1979; *Spider-Man The Dragon's Challenge* 1980; *Body Heat* 1981; *Creepshow* 1982; *Little Treasure* 1985; *A Fine Mess* 1986; *Just Between Friends* 1986; *Three Men and a Baby* 1987; *Cousins* 1989; *Dad* 1989; *Three Men and a Little Lady* 1990.

Dante, Joe • Director • Born Morristown, NJ. Former Roger Corman protégé who has directed several films produced under the auspices of Steven Spielberg. Best known for the enjoyably satiric "Gremlins" movies. • *The Arena* 1974 (ed); *Hollywood Boulevard* 1976 (d,ed); *Grand Theft Auto* 1977 (ed); *Piranha* 1978 (d,ed); *Roger Corman: Hollywood's Wild Angel* 1978 (a); *Rock 'n' Roll High School* 1979 (story); *The Howling* 1980 (d,ed); *The Slumber Party Massacre* 1981 (a); *Twilight Zone—the Movie* 1983 (d); *Gremlins* 1984 (d); *Explorers* 1985 (d); *The Fantasy Film World of George Pal* 1986 (a,assistance); *The Puppetoon Movie* 1986 (assistance); *Amazon Women on the Moon* 1987 (d); *Innerspace* 1987 (d); *The Burbs* 1989 (d); *Gremlins 2: The New Batch* 1990 (d).

Darnell, Linda • Actress • Born Monetta Eloyse Darnell, Dallas, TX, October 16, 1921; died April 1965. Sultry brunette who developed into one of Fox's biggest stars of the 1940s and proved herself capable of a wide range of dramatic roles. Darnell played a hopeful Hollywood ingenue in *Stardust* (1940), the Virgin Mary in *The Song of Bernadette* (1943), a classic spitfire in Ford's *My Darling Clementine* (1946) and an opportunistic broad from the wrong side of the tracks in *A Letter to Three Wives* (1948). Darnell was married to cinematographer J. Peverell Marley from 1943 to 1952. She died during a house fire at age 43. • *Day-Time Wife* 1939; *Hotel For Women* 1939; *Brigham Young, Frontiersman* 1940; *Chad Hanna* 1940; *The Mark of Zorro* 1940; *Stardust* 1940; *Blood and Sand* 1941; *Rise and Shine* 1941; *The Loves of Edgar Allan Poe* 1942; *City Without Men* 1943; *The Song of Bernadette* 1943; *Buffalo Bill* 1944; *It Happened Tomorrow* 1944; *Summer Storm* 1944; *Sweet and Low Down* 1944; *Fallen Angel* 1945; *The Great John L.* 1945; *Hangover Square* 1945; *Anna and the King of Siam* 1946; *Centennial Summer* 1946; *My Darling Clementine* 1946; *Forever Amber* 1947; *A Letter to Three Wives* 1948; *Unfaithfully Yours* 1948; *The Walls of Jericho* 1948; *Everybody Does It* 1949; *Slattery's Hurricane* 1949; *No Way Out* 1950; *Two Flags West* 1950; *The 13th Letter* 1951; *The Guy Who Came Back* 1951; *The Lady Pays Off* 1951; *Blackbeard the Pirate* 1952; *Night Without Sleep* 1952; *Saturday Island* 1952; *Donne Proibite/Angels of Darkness* 1953; *Second Chance* 1953; *This Is My Love* 1954; *Gli Ultimi Cinque Minuti* 1955; *Dakota Incident* 1956; *Zero Hour!* 1957; *El Valle de las espadas* 1963; *Black Spurs* 1965.

Darrieux, Danielle • Actress • Born Bordeaux, France, May 1, 1917. *Educ.* Paris Conservatoire (music). Enduringly beautiful, international leading lady, in films from 1931. Darrieux progressed from playing pouty teens to worldy sophisticates, hitting a creative peak in the early 1950s with her appearances in three Max Ophuls films. She was married to director Henri Decoin from 1935 to 1941 and starred in several of his movies into the 1950s. • *Le Bal* 1931; *Château de Rêve* 1933; *La Crise Est Finie* 1934; *Dédé* 1934; *Mauvaise Graine* 1934; *L'Or dans la rue* 1934; *Volga en Flammes* 1934; *Le Domino Vert* 1935; *Quelle drôle de Gosse!* 1935; *Club de Femmes* 1936; *Mademoiselle Mozart* 1936; *Mayerling* 1936; *Port Arthur* 1936; *Tarass Boulba* 1936; *Abus de confiance* 1937; *Mademoiselle ma mère* 1937; *Katia* 1938; *The Rage of Paris* 1938; *Retour à l'Aube* 1938; *Battements de Coeur* 1939; *Caprices* 1941; *Premier rendez-vous* 1941; *Adieu Chérie* 1946; *Au Petit Bonheur* 1946; *Ruy Blas* 1947; *Jean de la Lune* 1948; *Occupe-toi d'Amélie* 1949; *La Ronde* 1950; *La Maison Bonnadieu* 1951; *Le Plaisir* 1951; *Rich, Young and Pretty* 1951; *Vérite sur Bébé Donge* 1951; *Adorables Creatures* 1952; *Five Fingers* 1952; *Le Bon Dieu sans Confession* 1953; *The Earrings of Madame De...* 1953; *Napoléon* 1954; *Rouge et Noir* 1954; *L'Amant de Lady Chatterley* 1955; *Bonnes à tuer* 1955; *Alexander the Great* 1956; *Typhon sur Nagasaki* 1956; *Pot Bouille* 1957; *Le Désordre et la nuit* 1958; *Un Drôle de Dimanche* 1958; *Marie-Octobre* 1959; *Les Yeux de l'Amour* 1959; *The Greengage Summer* 1961; *Landru/Bluebeard* 1962; *Patate* 1964; *Le Coup de Grace* 1965; *Le Dimanche de la Vie* 1965; *Les Demoiselles de Rochefort* 1967; *Les Oiseaux vont mourir au Pérou* 1968; *Vingt-Quatre heures de la vie d'une Femme* 1968; *La Maison de Campagne* 1969; *Divine* 1975; *Roses rouges et Piments verts* 1975; *L'Année Sainte* 1976; *Le Cavaleur* 1978; *Une Chambre en Ville* 1982; *En Haut des Marches* 1983; *Corps et biens* 1986; *Le Lieu du Crime/Scene of the Crime* 1986; *Quelques jours avec moi/A Few Days With Me* 1988; *Bille en Tête* 1989.

Dassin, Jules • *aka* Perlo Vita • Director; also producer, screenwriter, actor. • Born Julius Dassin, Middletown, CT, December 18, 1911. Gained experience in theater and radio in New York before going to work in Hollywood in 1940, first with RKO (as assistant director) and then with MGM. Dassin hit his stride in the late 1940s with such dynamic (and still well-regarded) film noir melodramas as *Brute Force* (1947) and *The Naked City* (1948). After being blacklisted he moved to Europe, where he scored his greatest international successes with the French-produced *Rififi* (1955) and the then-scandalous *Never on Sunday* (1959), starring his second wife Melina Mercouri. For the most part, his later films—like *Uptight* (1968), an ill-conceived black remake of John Ford's 1935 classic *The Informer*—have been disappointing and inconclusive. Dassin's daughter, Julie, is an actress. • *The Tell-Tale Heart (short)* 1941 (d,sc); *The Affairs of Martha* 1942 (d); *Nazi Agent* 1942 (d); *Reunion in France* 1942 (d); *Young Ideas* 1943 (d); *The Canterville Ghost* 1944 (d); *A Letter For Evie* 1946 (d); *Two Smart People* 1946 (d); *Brute Force* 1947 (d); *The Naked City* 1948 (d); *Thieves' Highway* 1949 (d); *Night and the City* 1950 (d); *The Trio: Rubinstein, Heifetz and Piatigorsky (short)* 1952 (d,sc); *Rififi* 1955 (a,d,sc,adapt); *Celui Qui Doit Mourir* 1957 (d,sc); *La Loi/Where the Hot Wind Blows* 1958 (d,sc); *Pote Tin Kyriaki/Never on Sunday* 1959 (a,d,sc) **(AANBD)**; *Phaedra* 1962 (a,d,p,sc); *Topkapi* 1964 (d,p); *10:30 P.M. Summer* 1966 (d,p,sc); *Survival 1967* 1968 (d,p); *Uptight* 1968 (d,p,sc); *La Promesse de l'aube* 1970 (a,d,p,sc); *The Rehearsal* 1974 (d); *A Dream of Passion* 1978 (d,p,sc); *Circle of Two* 1980 (d); *Keine Zufallige Geschichte* 1983 (a).

Dauman, Anatole • Producer • Born Warsaw, Poland, 1925. Pioneering producer of the French New Wave who has since been responsible for some of the finest international co-productions of recent years, including Nagisa Oshima's *Empire of the Senses* (1976), Volker Schlöndorff's *The Tin Drum* (1979), Wim Wenders's *Paris, Texas* (1984) and *Wings of Desire* (1987) and Andrei Tarkovski's *The Sacrifice* (1986). Former wife Pascale Dauman produced Peter Greenaway's recent film, *The Cook, the Thief, His Wife and Her Lover* (1989). • *Nuit et Brouillard/Night and Fog* 1955 (p); *Letter From Siberia (short)* 1957 (p); *Les Hommes de la baleine (short)* 1958 (p); *La Premiere nuit (short)* 1958 (p); *Hiroshima, mon amour* 1959 (p); *Chronique d'un été/Chronicle of a Summer* 1960 (p); *L'Année dernière à Marienbad/Last Year at Marienbad* 1961 (p); *La Jetée (short)* 1962 (p); *Muriel* 1963 (p); *Au Hasard, Balthazar* 1966 (p); *Deux ou trois choses que je sais d'elle/Two or Three Things I Know About Her* 1966 (p); *Masculin-Feminin* 1966 (p); *Mouchette* 1966 (p); *Les Rendezvous en Foret* 1971 (p); *Contes Immoraux* 1974 (p); *La Bête* 1975 (p); *L'Empire des sens/Empire of the Senses* 1976 (p); *Der Fangschuss* 1976 (p); *L'Empire de la Passion* 1978 (p); *Die Blechtrommel/The Tin Drum* 1979 (exec.p); *Die Falschung/Circle of Deceit* 1981 (p); *Les Fruits de la Passion* 1981 (p—France); *La Belle Captive* 1982 (p); *Sans Soleil/Sunless* 1982 (p); *Paris,*

Texas 1984 (p); *Offret-Sacrificatio/The Sacrifice* 1986 (p); *Der Himmel uber Berlin/Wings of Desire* 1987 (p).

Davenport, Nigel • Actor • Born Shelford Cambridge, England, May 23, 1928. *Educ.* Trinity College, Oxford. Veteran British character actor who, by his own estimate, has played "two kings, two dukes, a lot of lords and the odd private soldier." Best known as the Duke of Norfolk opposite Paul Scofield's Sir Thomas More in *A Man for All Seasons* (1966). • *Look Back in Anger* 1959; *Peeping Tom* 1960; *In the Cool of the Day* 1963; *The Third Secret* 1964; *A High Wind in Jamaica* 1965; *Life at the Top* 1965; *Sands of the Kalahari* 1965; *Where the Spies Are* 1965; *A Man For All Seasons* 1966; *Play Dirty* 1968; *Sebastian* 1968; *The Strange Affair* 1968; *The Royal Hunt of the Sun* 1969; *Sinful Davey* 1969; *The Virgin Soldiers* 1969; *The Mind of Mr. Soames* 1970; *No Blade of Grass* 1970; *The Last Valley* 1971; *Mary, Queen of Scots* 1971; *Villain* 1971; *Charley-One-Eye* 1972; *Living Free* 1972; *Phase IV* 1974; *La Regenta* 1974; *The Island of Dr. Moreau* 1977; *Stand Up Virgin Soldiers* 1977; *The Omega Connection* 1979; *Zulu Dawn* 1979; *Chariots of Fire* 1981; *Den Tuchtigen Gehort Die Welt* 1981; *Nighthawks* 1981; *Strata* 1982; *Greystoke: The Legend of Tarzan, Lord of the Apes* 1984; *Caravaggio* 1986; *Without a Clue* 1988.

Daves, Delmer • Director; also screenwriter, producer, actor. • Born San Francisco, CA, July 24, 1904; died 1977. *Educ.* Stanford (law). Accomplished visual stylist who often wrote his own imaginative, and genre-defying, screenplays; his films are always technically proficient but sometimes lack substance. As a teenager Daves lived for a time with native American Indians, an experience which informed his 1950 film *Broken Arrow*, one of the first sympathetic treatments of American Indians to reach the screen. • *Christmas Memories* 1915 (a); *Zander the Great* 1925 (a); *On to Reno* 1927 (props); *Excess Baggage* 1928 (a,props); *The Night Flyer* 1928 (a,props); *The Red Mark* 1928 (a,props); *Three Sinners* 1928 (a,props); *The Duke Steps Out* 1929 (a); *A Man's Man* 1929 (a,props); *So This Is College* 1929 (a,sc,story); *The Bishop Murder Case* 1930 (a); *Good News* 1930 (a); *Shipmates* 1931 (a,adapt,dial); *Divorce in the Family* 1932 (a,sc,story); *Clear All Wires* 1933 (sc,cont); *Dames* 1934 (sc,story); *Flirtation Walk* 1934 (sc,story); *No More Women* 1934 (sc,story); *Page Miss Glory* 1935 (sc); *The Petrified Forest* 1935 (sc); *Shipmates Forever* 1935 (sc,story); *Stranded* 1935 (sc); *The Go Getter* 1937 (sc); *The Singing Marine* 1937 (sc,story); *Slim* 1937 (sc,story); *Professor Beware* 1938 (sc); *She Married an Artist* 1938 (sc); *$1,000 a Touchdown* 1939 (sc); *Love Affair* 1939 (sc); *The Farmer's Daughter* 1940 (story); *Safari* 1940 (sc); *Young America Flies (short)* 1940 (sc); *The Night of January 16th* 1941 (sc); *Unexpected Uncle* 1941 (sc); *You Were Never Lovelier* 1942 (sc); *Destination Tokyo* 1943 (d,sc); *Stage Door Canteen* 1943 (sc); *Hollywood Canteen* 1944 (d,sc); *The Very Thought of You* 1944 (d,sc); *Pride of the Marines* 1945 (d); *Dark Passage* 1947 (d,sc); *The Red House* 1947 (d,sc); *To the Victor* 1948 (d); *A Kiss in the Dark* 1949 (d); *Task Force* 1949 (d,sc,story); *Broken Arrow* 1950 (d); *Bird of Paradise* 1951 (d,p,sc); *Return of the Texan* 1952 (d); *Never Let Me Go* 1953 (d); *Treasure of the Golden Condor* 1953 (d,sc); *Demetrius and the Gladiators* 1954 (d); *Drum Beat* 1954 (d,p,sc,story); *White Feather* 1955 (sc); *An Affair to Remember* 1956 (sc); *Jubal* 1956 (d,sc); *The Last Wagon* 1956 (d,sc); *3:10 to Yuma* 1957 (d); *Cowboy* 1958 (d); *Kings Go Forth* 1958 (d); *The Hanging Tree* 1959 (d); *A Summer Place* 1959 (d,p,sc); *Parrish* 1961 (d,p,sc); *Susan Slade* 1961 (d,p,sc); *Rome Adventure* 1962 (d,p,sc); *Spencer's Mountain* 1963 (d,p,sc); *Youngblood Hawke* 1964 (d,p,sc); *The Battle of the Villa Fiorita* 1965 (d,p,sc).

Davi, Robert • Actor • Born US, c. 1953. *Educ.* Hofstra University, Hempstead, NY (drama); Actors Studio. Character player, typically as an exotic villain. • *City Heat* 1984; *The Goonies* 1985; *Raw Deal* 1986; *Wild Thing* 1987; *Action Jackson* 1988; *Die Hard* 1988; *Traxx* 1988; *Licence to Kill* 1989; *Maniac Cop 2* 1990; *Peacemaker* 1990; *Predator 2* 1990; *Amazon* 1991; *The Taking of Beverly Hills* 1991.

Daviau, Allen • American director of photography • Shot promotional films for artists including Jimi Hendrix and The Who in the mid-1960s and worked in TV before earning his first feature film credit, for additional photography on the special edition of Steven Spielberg's *Close Encounters of the Third Kind* (1980). Daviau has subsequently photographed several Spielberg films, including *E.T.* (1982) and *Empire of the Sun* (1987). • *Close Encounters of the Third Kind* (special edition) 1980 (add. ph); *Harry Tracy* 1981 (ph); *E.T., the Extra-Terrestrial* 1982 (ph) **(AANBPH)**; *Twilight Zone—the Movie* 1983 (ph—"Kick the Can," "Nightmare at 20,000 Feet"); *Indiana Jones and the Temple of Doom* 1984 (2u ph); *The Color Purple* 1985 (ph) **(AANBPH)**; *The Falcon and the Snowman* 1985 (ph); *Empire of the Sun* 1987 (ph) **(AANBPH)**; *Harry and the Hendersons* 1987 (ph); *Avalon* 1990 (ph) **(AANBPH)**; *Defending Your Life* 1991.

Davies, Marion • Actress; also producer. • Born Marion Cecilia Douras, Brooklyn, NY, January 3, 1897; died 1961. Best known for her long association with newspaper magnate William Randolph Hearst, who vowed to make the 19 year-old Davies into a great Hollywood star. Hearst's multi-million dollar efforts—including a production company devoted solely to Davies films—were unsuccessful, and were hampered by his insistence on casting her in traditional romantic roles rather than the comic parts to which she was better suited. • *Runaway Romany* 1917 (a,sc,story); *The Burden of Proof* 1918; *Cecilia of the Pink Roses* 1918; *The Belle of New York* 1919; *The Cinema Murder* 1919; *The Dark Star* 1919; *Getting Mary Married* 1919; *April Folly* 1920; *The Restless Sex* 1920; *The Bride's Play* 1921; *Buried Treasure* 1921; *Enchantment* 1921; *Beauty's Worth* 1922; *When Knighthood Was in Flower* 1922; *The Young Diana* 1922; *Adam and Eva* 1923; *Little Old New York* 1923; *Janice Meredith* 1924; *Yolanda* 1924; *Lights of Old Broadway* 1925; *Zander the Great* 1925; *Beverly of Graustark* 1926; *The Fair Co-ed* 1927; *The Patsy* 1927; *Quality Street* 1927; *The Red Mill* 1927; *Tillie the Toiler* 1927; *Cardboard Lover* 1928; *Show People* 1928 (a,p); *The Hollywood Revue of 1929* 1929; *Marianne* 1929; *The Floradora Girl* 1930; *Not So Dumb* 1930; *The Bachelor Father* 1931 (a,p); *Five and Ten* 1931 (a,p); *It's a Wise Child* 1931 (a,p); *Blondie of the Follies* 1932 (a,p); *Polly of the Circus* 1932; *Going Hollywood* 1933; *Operator 13* 1933; *Peg o' My Heart* 1933; *Page Miss Glory* 1935; *Cain and Mabel* 1936; *Hearts Divided* 1936; *Ever Since Eve* 1937.

Davis, Andrew • Director; also director of photography, screenwriter. • Born Chicago, IL. *Educ.* University of Illinois (communications). Capable director with a knack for evocative use of urban locations, particularly Chicago. Davis began his career as a cinematographer, wrote and directed the critically acclaimed independent production *Stony Island* (1978) and scored a huge commercial success with *Above the Law* (1988), starring Steven Seagal. • *Cool Breeze* 1972 (ph); *Hit Man* 1972 (ph); *Private Parts* 1972 (ph); *The Slams* 1973 (ph); *Lepke* 1975 (ph); *The Terror of Dr. Chancey* 1975 (ph); *Stony Island* 1978 (d,p,sc); *Over the Edge* 1979 (ph); *The Final Terror* 1981 (d); *Angel* 1983 (ph); *Code of Silence* 1985 (d); *Above the Law* 1988 (d,p,story,sc,ph—Vietnam sequence); *The Package* 1989 (d,p); *Schweitzer* 1990 (a).

Davis, Bette • Actress • Born Ruth Elizabeth Davis, Lowell, MA, April 5, 1908; died October 6, 1989, Neuilly-sur-Seine, France. *Educ.* Mariarden School of Dancing; John Murray Anderson's Drama School, New York. Bette Davis was a strong-willed, independent personality and a unique, powerful star. Large eyes, clipped New England diction, and distinctive mannerisms—including extravagant cigarette smoking—engendered frequent imitation. She made some 100 films, for which she received 10 Academy Award nominations, winning best actress twice.

Davis's parents divorced when she was 7 and she was raised by her mother, who encouraged her interest in acting by taking her to New York in 1928. Rejected for Eva Le Gallienne's acting classes, Davis joined a stock company in Rochester, New York, where after a few months she was dismissed by director George Cukor. She made her New York acting debut in 1929 at the Provincetown Playhouse, in Virgil Geddes's *The Earth Between.* Her excellent reviews led to parts in other successes, including her first Broadway hit, *Broken Dishes*, at the age of 21.

Universal Pictures signed her to a contract and in 1930 Davis and her mother went to Hollywood. Her first film was *Bad Sister* (1931), which also featured Humphrey Bogart. Appearances in five more lackluster films discouraged the young actress, until George Arliss, who was to remain her mentor, persuaded Warner Bros. to hire her to play opposite him in *The Man Who Played God* (1932). It proved to be her breakthrough film. Warner Bros. then signed her to a long-term contract, beginning her stormy relationship with a studio more accustomed to promoting its tough male stars.

Over the next three years, Davis made 14 more films for Warner Bros., most of them forgettable. But her career took a dramatic turn in 1934 when she was lent to RKO to play the slatternly Mildred opposite Leslie Howard in *Of Human Bondage.* This unsympathetic role gave Davis an opportunity to cut loose and her riveting performance garnered much critical acclaim. Now Warner Bros. took notice of her, and she began to get better parts. The following year, she made *Dangerous* (1935), for which she won her first Oscar, and in 1936 she and Howard reteamed in *The Petrified Forest.*

That same year, Davis's long-standing resentment against the strictures of the studio contract system came to a head when she defied Warner Bros. and went to London to make pictures with a British company. After Warner Bros. successfully sued her, she returned to Hollywood, where she was treated with new-found respect: Warner Bros. signed her to a new contract and offered her even better roles. Thus began the peak period of her career, a series of memorable roles that started with her fiery Southern belle in *Jezebel* (1938), for which she won her second Oscar. 1939 alone saw Davis appearing in four classic films: *Dark Victory, Juarez, The Old Maid* and *The Private Lives of Elizabeth and Essex.*

As she perfected her acting techniques and developed her famous mannerisms, Davis achieved a new level of artistic maturity. Filmgoers, especially women, loved her portrayals of fiercely independent characters who also suffered nobly. The early 40s saw Davis's popularity continue to grow with such films as *All This and Heaven Too, The Letter* (both 1940), and *The Little Foxes* (1941), plus her roles as a timid spinster who blossoms into a vital woman of the world in *Now, Voyager* (1942) and a vain society woman in *Mr. Skeffington* (1944).

By the end of the decade, however, Davis's career had begun to sag under the weight of weaker pictures, but she bounced back in 1950 with a stunning performance as Margo Channing, a tempestuous Broadway star (based on Tallulah Bankhead), in Joseph Mankiewicz's *All About Eve.* The film's wittily savage view of theater people offered Davis—here with her almost self-parodying grand gestures, and the now-famous line, "Fasten your seat belts, it's going to be a bumpy night!"—the role of a lifetime.

In the 50s, her career began to falter seriously, but she again came back in the popular black comedy, *Whatever Happened to Baby Jane?* (1962), in which she and Joan Crawford squared off as a pair of nutty sisters, show-biz has-beens, living in a decaying Hollywood mansion. Davis found a new outlet for her talents in horror films and continued to work steadily on the big screen as well as in theater and on TV.

A survivor of four unhappy marriages and estrangement from her daughter B.D., Davis found her greatest satisfaction in working and continued to do so until the end, with her last significant film appearance in *The Whales of August* (1987) opposite Lillian Gish. Despite her extraordinary talent, audiences flocked to see the spitfire as much as the genius. Davis herself once said, "I adore playing bitches... there's a little bit of bitch in every woman; and a little bit of bitch in every man." She died much-loved, admired for her scraps with studio bigwigs, her uncompromising view of self and her savage grasp of hard work. In 1977, she was the first woman to receive the American Film Institute Life Achievement Award. VMC • *Bad Sister* 1931; *Seed* 1931; *Waterloo Bridge* 1931; *The Cabin in the Cotton* 1932; *The Dark Horse* 1932; *Hell's House* 1932; *The Man Who Played God* 1932; *The Menace* 1932; *The Rich Are Always With Us* 1932; *So Big* 1932; *Three on a Match* 1932; *Way Back Home* 1932; *20,000 Years in Sing Sing* 1933; *The Adopted Father* 1933; *Bureau of Missing Persons* 1933; *Ex-Lady* 1933; *The Parachute Jumper* 1933; *The Big Shakedown* 1934; *Bordertown* 1934; *Fashions of 1934* 1934; *Fog Over Frisco* 1934; *Housewife* 1934; *Jimmy the Gent* 1934; *Of Human Bondage* 1934; *Dangerous* 1935 **(AABA)**; *Front Page Woman* 1935; *The Girl From 10th Avenue* 1935; *Special Agent* 1935; *The Golden Arrow* 1936; *The Petrified Forest* 1936; *Satan Met a Lady* 1936; *It's Love I'm After* 1937; *Kid Galahad* 1937; *Marked Woman* 1937; *That Certain Woman* 1937; *Jezebel* 1938 **(AABA)**; *The Sisters* 1938; *Dark Victory* 1939 **(AANBA)**; *Juarez* 1939; *The Old Maid* 1939; *The Private Lives of Elizabeth and Essex* 1939; *All This and Heaven Too* 1940; *The Letter* 1940 **(AANBA)**; *The Bride Came C.O.D.* 1941; *The Great Lie* 1941; *The Little Foxes* 1941 **(AANBA)**; *The Man Who Came to Dinner* 1941; *Shining Victory* 1941; *In This Our Life* 1942; *Now, Voyager* 1942 **(AANBA)**; *Old Acquaintance* 1943; *Thank Your Lucky Stars* 1943; *Watch on the Rhine* 1943; *Hollywood Canteen* 1944; *Mr. Skeffington* 1944 **(AANBA)**; *The Corn Is Green* 1945; *Deception* 1946; *A Stolen Life* 1946 (a,p); *June Bride* 1948; *Winter Meeting* 1948; *Beyond the Forest* 1949; *All About Eve* 1950 **(AANBA)**; *Payment on Demand* 1951; *Another Man's Poison* 1952; *Phone Call From a Stranger* 1952; *The Star* 1952 **(AANBA)**; *The Virgin Queen* 1955; *The Catered Affair* 1956; *Storm Center* 1956; *John Paul Jones* 1959; *The Scapegoat* 1959; *A Pocketful of Miracles* 1961; *What Ever Happened to Baby Jane?* 1962 **(AANBA)**; *La Noia/The Empty Canvas* 1963; *Dead Ringer* 1964; *Hush...Hush, Sweet Charlotte* 1964; *Where Love Has Gone* 1964; *The Anniversary* 1967; *Connecting Rooms* 1969; *Bunny O'Hare* 1971; *Lo Scopone Scientifico* 1972; *Burnt Offerings* 1976; *Death on the Nile* 1978; *Return From Witch Mountain* 1978; *Watcher in the Woods* 1980; *Directed By William Wyler* 1986; *The Whales of August* 1987; *Going Hollywood: The War Years* 1988 (archival footage); *Wicked Stepmother* 1989.

Davis, Brad • Actor • Born Florida, November 6, 1949. Versatile male lead who made a compelling film debut as an incarcerated drug-smuggler in Alan Parker's *Midnight Express* (1978). Davis's relatively sparse screen credits include off-beat gems such as *Chariots of Fire* (1981), Fassbinder's *Querelle* (1982) and Percy Adlon's *Rosalie Goes Shopping* (1989). • *Midnight Express* 1978; *A Small Circle of Friends* 1980; *Chariots of Fire* 1981; *Querelly—ein Pakt mit dem Teufel/Querelle* 1982; *Cold Steel* 1987; *Heart* 1987; *Rosalie Goes Shopping* 1989; *Hangfire* 1991.

Davis, Geena • Actress • Born Virginia Davis, Wareham, MA, January 21, 1957. *Educ.* Boston University (acting). Former model with a knack for quirky comedy. Davis made her feature debut as the soap-opera actress who shares a dressing room with Dustin Hoffman in *Tootsie* (1982). She soon graduated to leading roles, notably in *The Fly* (1986) and *Earth Girls Are Easy* (1989), both opposite Jeff Goldblum (the two were married in 1987 and separated in 1990). Davis won a best supporting actress Oscar for her role as the kooky dog-trainer who wins the heart of William Hurt in *The Accidental Tourist* (1988).

• *Tootsie* 1982; *Fletch* 1985; *Transylvania 6-5000* 1985; *The Fly* 1986; *The Accidental Tourist* 1988 **(AABSA)**; *Beetlejuice* 1988; *Earth Girls Are Easy* 1989; *Quick Change* 1990; *Thelma and Louise* 1991.

Davis, George W. • art director • Born Kokomo, IN, April 17, 1914. *Educ.* USC, Los Angeles. Celebrated designer who began his career at 20th Century-Fox and won Oscars for his work on *The Robe* (1953) and *The Diary of Anne Frank* (1959). Davis also worked extensively in TV. • *All About Eve* 1950 **(AANAD)**; *David and Bathsheba* 1951 **(AANAD)**; *Rawhide* 1951; *The Robe* 1953 **(AABAD)**; *The Egyptian* 1954; *Love Is a Many Splendored Thing* 1955 **(AANBAD)**; *Funny Face* 1957 **(AANBAD)**; *Girl Most Likely* 1958; *In Love and War* 1958; *The Diary of Anne Frank* 1959 **(AABAD)**; *This Earth Is Mine* 1959; *Cimarron* 1960 **(AANBAD)**; *Ada* 1961; *Atlantis, the Lost Continent* 1961; *Bachelor in Paradise* 1961; *All Fall Down* 1962; *How the West Was Won* 1962 **(AANBAD)**; *Mutiny on the Bounty* 1962 **(AANBAD)**; *Period of Adjustment* 1962 **(AANBAD)**; *Ride the High Country* 1962; *The Wonderful World of the Brothers Grimm* 1962 **(AANBAD)**; *Advance to the Rear* 1963; *The Courtship of Eddie's Father* 1963; *The Prize* 1963; *Twilight of Honor* 1963 **(AANBAD)**; *The Americanization of Emily* 1964 **(AANBAD)**; *The Unsinkable Molly Brown* 1964 **(AANBAD)**; *Clarence, the Cross-Eyed Lion* 1965; *Harum Scarum* 1965; *Mister Buddwing* 1965 **(AANBAD)**; *A Patch of Blue* 1965 **(AANBAD)**; *Point Blank* 1967; *Welcome to Hard Times* 1967; *The Shoes of the Fisherman* 1968 **(AANBAD)**; *Stay Away, Joe* 1968; *The Extraordinary Seaman* 1969; *Heaven With a Gun* 1969; *Marlowe* 1969; *The Trouble With Girls* 1969; *The Strawberry Statement* 1970; *Tick, Tick, Tick* 1970; *The Traveling Executioner* 1970; *Pretty Maids All in a Row* 1971; *Wild Rovers* 1971.

Davis, Judy • Actress • Born Australia, 1956. *Educ.* Western Australia Institute of Technology; National Institute of Dramatic Art. Sensitive, likeable leading lady who dropped out of convent school to sing in a rock band. Davis first gained international recognition in Gillian Armstrong's *My Brilliant Career* (1979). She gave complex, memorable performances opposite husband Colin Friels in *Kangaroo* (1986) and *High Tide* (1987). • *High Rolling* 1977; *My Brilliant Career* 1979; *Heatwave* 1981; *Hoodwink* 1981; *The Winter of Our Dreams* 1981; *Who Dares Wins* 1982; *A Passage to India* 1984 **(AANBA)**; *Kangaroo* 1986; *High Tide* 1987; *Georgia* 1988; *Alice* 1990; *Impromptu* 1991; *Where Angels Fear to Tread* 1991.

Davis, Ossie • Actor; also director, screenwriter. • Born Cogdell, GA, December 18, 1917. *Educ.* Howard University, Washington DC. Black character player who can be both amiable and imposing. Davis began his career acting and writing for the theater and made his film directorial debut in 1970 with an adaptation of Chester Himes's classic novel, *Cotton Comes to Harlem*. Married to actress Ruby Dee. • *No Way Out* 1950; *The Cardinal* 1963; *Gone Are the Days* 1963 (a,sc,from play *Purlie Victorious*); *Shock Treatment* 1964; *The Hill* 1965; *A Man Called Adam* 1966; *The Scalphunters* 1968; *Sam Whiskey* 1969; *Slaves* 1969; *Cotton Comes to Harlem* 1970 (d,sc,song); *Kongi's Harvest* 1971 (d); *Black Girl* 1972 (d); *Malcolm X* 1972; *Gordon's War* 1973 (d); *Let's Do It Again* 1975; *Countdown at Kusini* 1976 (a,d,sc); *Hot Stuff* 1979; *The House of God* 1979; *Harry & Son* 1984; *Avenging Angel* 1985; *School Daze* 1988; *Do the Right Thing* 1989; *Making "Do the Right Thing"* 1989; *Route One/U.S.A.* 1989; *Joe Versus the Volcano* 1990.

Davis, Sammi • Actress • Born Kidderminster, Hereford and Worcester, England, June 21, 1964. *Educ.* Kidderminster College of Further Education (English, drama). Diminutive, feisty blonde performer who played a heroin addict in Neil Jordan's *Mona Lisa* (1986) and has been noted for her work in John Boorman's *Hope and Glory* (1987) and as the lead of Ken Russell's *The Rainbow* (1989). • *Mona Lisa* 1986; *Hope and Glory* 1987; *Lionheart* 1987; *A Prayer For the Dying* 1987; *Consuming Passions* 1988; *The Lair of the White Worm* 1988; *The Rainbow* 1989; *The Horseplayer* 1990; *Shadow of China* 1990.

Davison, Bruce • Actor • Born Philadelphia, PA, June 28, 1946. *Educ.* Pennsylvania State University (art); NYU. Blond, boyish lead of the 1970s who made an auspicious debut in Frank Perry's sensitive teen film, *Last Summer* (1969), opposite Richard Thomas and Barbara Hershey. Davison has since accepted challenging and controversial roles, such as the child-molesting title character of Robert M. Young's prison drama *Short Eyes* (1977) and a man who cares for his AIDS-victim lover in *Longtime Companion* (1990); the latter performance earned him a best supporting actor award from the New York Film Critics Circle. Davison continues to appear on stage (*Streamers*, *The Normal Heart*). • *Last Summer* 1969; *The Strawberry Statement* 1970; *Been Down So Long It Looks Like Up to Me* 1971; *The Jerusalem File* 1971; *Willard* 1971; *Ulzana's Raid* 1972; *Mother, Jugs & Speed* 1976; *Grand Jury* 1977; *Short Eyes* 1977; *Brass Target* 1978; *French Quarter* 1978; *The Lathe of Heaven* 1979; *High Risk* 1981; *Lies* 1983; *Crimes of Passion* 1984; *Spies Like Us* 1985; *The Ladies Club* 1986; *The Misfit Brigade* 1986; *Longtime Companion* 1990; *Steel and Lace* 1991; *Oscar* 1991.

Dawson, Anthony M. • See Margheriti, Antonio.

Day, Doris • Actress, singer • Born Doris von Kappelhoff, Cincinnati, OH, April 3, 1924. Entered film in 1948 after a brief but successful career as a band singer and for the next two decades virtually defined the wholesome, girl-next-door type in musicals, dramas and innocent sex farces. Day, after a lengthy reign as America's number one box-office attraction, left films in the late 60s to star in the popular TV sitcom "The Doris Day Show" (1968-73). • *Romance on the High Seas* 1948; *It's a Great Feeling* 1949; *My Dream Is Yours* 1949; *Tea For Two* 1950; *The West Point Story* 1950; *Young Man With a Horn* 1950; *The Lullaby of Broadway* 1951; *On Moonlight Bay* 1951; *Starlift* 1951; *Storm Warning* 1951; *April in Paris* 1952; *I'll See You in My Dreams* 1952; *The Winning Team* 1952; *By the Light of the Silvery Moon* 1953; *Calamity Jane* 1953; *Lucky Me* 1954; *Love Me or Leave Me* 1955; *Young at Heart* 1955; *Julie* 1956; *The Man Who Knew Too Much* 1956; *The Pajama Game* 1957; *Teacher's Pet* 1958; *The Tunnel of Love* 1958; *It Happened to Jane* 1959; *Pillow Talk* 1959 **(AANBA)**; *Midnight Lace* 1960; *Please Don't Eat the Daisies* 1960; *Billy Rose's Jumbo* 1962; *Lover Come Back* 1962; *That Touch of Mink* 1962; *Move Over, Darling* 1963; *The Thrill of It All* 1963; *Send Me No Flowers* 1964; *Do Not Disturb* 1965; *The Glass Bottom Boat* 1966; *The Ballad of Josie* 1967; *Caprice* 1967; *Where Were You When the Lights Went Out?* 1968; *With Six You Get Eggroll* 1968.

Day, Richard • art director • Born Victoria, British Columbia, Canada, May 9, 1896; died 1972. One of Hollywood's most distinguished art directors, with MGM from 1923 to 1930 and 20th Century-Fox (as head of the art department) from 1939 to 1943. During his collaboration with Erich von Stroheim in the 1920s Day developed a distinctive, realist style which he put to outstanding use in numerous subsequent films. • *Foolish Wives* 1922 (art d); *Merry-Go-Round* 1923 (art d); *Greed* 1925 (art d); *The Merry Widow* 1925 (art d,cost); *Bardelys the Magnificent* 1926 (art d); *Beverly of Graustark* 1926 (art d); *The Show* 1927 (art d); *The Student Prince in Old Heidelberg* 1927 (art d); *The Unknown* 1927 (art d); *The Enemy* 1928 (art d); *Queen Kelly* 1928 (art d); *The Wedding March* 1928 (art d); *Anna Christie* 1930 (art d); *Whoopee* 1930 (art d) **(AANBAD)**; *Arrowsmith* 1931 (art d) **(AANBAD)**; *The Front Page* 1931 (art d); *Indiscreet* 1931 (art d); *Street Scene* 1931 (art d); *Rain* 1932 (art d); *The Bowery* 1933 (art d); *Hallelujah, I'm a Bum* 1933 (art d);

Roman Scandals 1933 (art d); *The Affairs of Cellini* 1934 (art d) **(AANBAD)**; *Bulldog Drummond Strikes Back* 1934 (art d); *The House of Rothschild* 1934 (art d); *Looking For Trouble* 1934 (art d); *The Mighty Barnum* 1934 (art d); *Nana* 1934 (art d); *We Live Again* 1934 (art d); *Barbary Coast* 1935 (art d); *The Call of the Wild* 1935 (art d); *Cardinal Richelieu* 1935 (art d); *Clive of India* 1935 (art d); *The Dark Angel* 1935 (art d) **(AABAD)**; *Folies Bergere* 1935 (art d); *Les Miserables* 1935 (art d); *Splendor* 1935 (art d); *The Wedding Night* 1935 (art d); *Come and Get It* 1936 (art d); *Dodsworth* 1936 (art d) **(AABAD)**; *The Gay Desperado* 1936 (art d); *These Three* 1936 (art d); *Dead End* 1937 (art d) **(AANBAD)**; *Hurricane* 1937 (art d); *Stella Dallas* 1937 (art d); *Woman Chases Man* 1937 (art d); *The Adventures of Marco Polo* 1938 (art d); *The Cowboy and the Lady* 1938 (art d); *The Goldwyn Follies* 1938 (art d) **(AANBAD)**; *Drums Along the Mohawk* 1939 (art d); *Frontier Marshal* 1939 (art d); *The Gorilla* 1939 (art d); *Hollywood Cavalcade* 1939 (art d); *The Hound of the Baskervilles* 1939 (art d); *Rose of Washington Square* 1939 (art d); *Swanee River* 1939 (art d); *Young Mr. Lincoln* 1939 (art d); *Chad Hanna* 1940 (art d); *Down Argentine Way* 1940 (art d) **(AANBAD)**; *Four Sons* 1940 (art d); *The Grapes of Wrath* 1940 (art d); *I Was an Adventuress* 1940 (art d); *Johnny Apollo* 1940 (art d); *Lillian Russell* 1940 (art d) **(AANBAD)**; *The Mark of Zorro* 1940 (art d); *The Return of Frank James* 1940 (art d); *Young People* 1940 (art d); *Blood and Sand* 1941 (art d) **(AANBAD)**; *Charley's Aunt* 1941 (art d); *The Great American Broadcast* 1941 (art d); *How Green Was My Valley* 1941 (art d) **(AABAD)**; *Man Hunt* 1941 (art d); *Rise and Shine* 1941 (art d); *Swamp Water* 1941 (art d); *Tobacco Road* 1941 (art d); *Western Union* 1941 (art d); *A Yank in the R.A.F.* 1941 (art d); *The Black Swan* 1942 (art d); *China Girl* 1942 (art d); *Moontide* 1942 (art d); *My Gal Sal* 1942 (art d) **(AABAD)**; *Orchestra Wives* 1942 (art d); *Rings on Her Fingers* 1942 (art d); *Roxie Hart* 1942 (art d); *Son of Fury* 1942 (art d); *Tales of Manhattan* 1942 (art d); *This Above All* 1942 (art d) **(AABAD)**; *Thunder Birds* 1942 (art d); *Crash Dive* 1943 (art d); *Margin For Error* 1943 (art d); *The Ox-Bow Incident* 1943 (art d); *Up in Arms* 1944 (technical adviser); *The Razor's Edge* 1946 (art d) **(AANBAD)**; *Boomerang* 1947 (art d); *Captain From Castile* 1947 (art d); *The Ghost and Mrs. Muir* 1947 (art d); *I Wonder Who's Kissing Her Now* 1947 (art d); *Miracle on 34th Street* 1947 (art d); *Moss Rose* 1947 (art d); *Mother Wore Tights* 1947 (art d); *Force of Evil* 1948 (art d); *Joan of Arc* 1948 (art d) **(AANBAD)**; *Edge of Doom* 1950 (art d); *My Foolish Heart* 1950 (art d); *Our Very Own* 1950 (art d); *Cry Danger* 1951 (art d); *I Want You* 1951 (art d); *A Streetcar Named Desire* 1951 (art d) **(AABAD)**; *Hans Christian Andersen* 1952 (art d) **(AANBAD)**; *On the Waterfront* 1954 (art d) **(AABAD)**; *Solomon and Sheba* 1959 (art d); *Exodus* 1960 (art d); *Something Wild* 1961 (art d); *Cheyenne Autumn* 1964 (art d); *Goodbye, Charlie* 1964 (art d); *The Greatest Story Ever Told* 1965 (art d) **(AANBAD)**; *The Chase* 1966 (pd); *The Happening* 1967 (pd); *Valley of the Dolls* 1967 (art d); *The Boston Strangler* 1968 (art d); *The Sweet Ride* 1968 (art d); *Tora! Tora! Tora!* 1970 (art d) **(AANBAD)**.

Day-Lewis, Daniel • Actor • Born London, 1958. *Educ.* Bristol Old Vic; Bristol Arts Centre. Versatile leading man who first came to prominence with his roles in Stephen Frears's *My Beautiful Laundrette* (1985) and the Merchant/Ivory production, *A Room With a View* (1986). Day-Lewis won a best actor Oscar for his bravura performance as quadruplegic writer Christy Brown in *My Left Foot* (1989). Son of writer C. Day Lewis and actress Jill Balcon. • *Gandhi* 1982; *The Bounty* 1984; *The Insurance Man* 1985; *My Beautiful Laundrette* 1985; *A Room With a View* 1986; *Nanou* 1987; *Stars and Bars* 1988; *The Unbearable Lightness of Being* 1988; *Eversmile, New Jersey* 1989; *My Left Foot* 1989 **(AABA)**.

De Antonio, Emile • Filmmaker • Born Scranton, PA, 1920; died December 16, 1989, New York, NY. *Educ.* Harvard. Leftist documentary filmmaker who attended Harvard in the same class as John F. Kennedy and described himself as a "Marxist among capitalists." De Antonio worked primarily with pre-existing footage, relying solely on editing (he disdained narration as "inherently fascist") to create his stinging, often riveting critiques of the American establishment. He continually ran afoul of the government and the FBI and on one occasion, during the making of a film about the radical Weather Underground movement, received support in his battle for artistic freedom from a number of Hollywood figures including Warren Beatty, Hal Ashby, Mel Brooks and Jack Nicholson. • *Point of Order* 1964 (d,ed,p); *Rush to Judgment* 1967 (d,p); *America Is Hard to See* 1968 (d); *In the Year of the Pig* 1969 (d) **(AANBDOC)**; *Millhouse: A White Comedy* 1971 (d,p); *Painters Painting* 1973 (d,p,sc); *Underground* 1976 (a,d,p); *The Trials of Alger Hiss* 1979 (technical consultant); *In the King of Prussia* 1982 (d,p,sc); *Poetry in Motion* 1982 (prod.cons); *Comic Book Confidential* 1988 (cons); *Mr. Hoover and I* 1989 (a,d,p,sc); *Resident Alien* 1990 (a).

De Beauregard, Georges • Producer • Born Edgar Denys Nau De Beauregard, Marseilles, France, December 23, 1920; died September 10, 1984, Paris. Major force behind the French New Wave who began his career in Spain, working with director Juan Antonio Bardem. Awarded an honorary Cesar (the French Oscar) in 1984. • *Muerte de un Ciclista/Death of a Cyclist* 1955 (p); *Calle Mayor* 1956 (p); *A bout de souffle/Breathless* 1959 (p); *Le Petit Soldat* 1960 (a,p); *Une Femme est une femme/A Woman Is a Woman* 1961 (p); *Leon Morin, Prêtre* 1961 (p); *Lola* 1961 (p); *Cléo de 5 à 7* 1962 (p); *Landru/Bluebeard* 1962 (p); *L'Oeil du Malin/The Third Lover* 1962 (p); *Les Carabiniers* 1963 (p); *Le Doulos* 1963 (p); *Le Mépris/Contempt* 1963 (p); *Pierrot le Fou* 1965 (p); *Suzanne Simonin, la Religieuse de Denis Diderot/The Nun* 1965 (p); *La Collectionneuse* 1966 (p); *La Ligne de Démarcation* 1966 (p); *Made in U.S.A.* 1966 (p); *L'Amour Fou* 1968 (p); *Numéro Deux* 1975 (assoc.p); *Le Crabe-Tambour* 1977 (p); *Le Cheval d'orgueil* 1979 (p); *La Legion saute sur kolwezi* 1979 (p); *Tout depend des filles* 1980 (p).

de Broca, Philippe • See Broca, Philippe de.

De Cuir, John • Production designer • Born San Francisco, CA, June 4, 1918. Veteran, multi-award-winning designer; son John De Cuir, Jr., (b. 1941) is also an art director. • *Casbah* 1948 (art d); *The Naked City* 1948 (art d); *The House on Telegraph Hill* 1951 (art d) **(AANAD)**; *Diplomatic Courier* 1952 (art d); *My Cousin Rachel* 1952 (art d) **(AANBAD)**; *The Snows of Kilimanjaro* 1952 (art d) **(AANBAD)**; *Call Me Madam* 1953 (art d); *There's No Business Like Show Business* 1954 (art d); *Three Coins in the Fountain* 1954 (art d); *Daddy Long Legs* 1955 (art d) **(AANBAD)**; *The King and I* 1956 (art d) **(AABAD)**; *Island in the Sun* 1957 (art d); *A Certain Smile* 1958 (art d) **(AANBAD)**; *South Pacific* 1958 (art d); *The Big Fisherman* 1959 (pd) **(AANBAD)**; *Seven Thieves* 1960 (art d); *Cleopatra* 1963 (pd) **(AABAD)**; *Circus World* 1964 (pd); *The Agony and the Ecstasy* 1965 (pd) **(AANBAD)**; *A Man Could Get Killed* 1966 (art d); *Doctor Faustus* 1967 (pd); *The Taming of the Shrew* 1967 (assoc.pd) **(AANBAD)**; *Hello, Dolly!* 1969 (pd) **(AABAD)**; *The Great White Hope* 1970 (pd); *On a Clear Day You Can See Forever* 1970 (art d); *Once Is Not Enough* 1975 (pd); *That's Entertainment Part 2* 1976 (pd); *The Other Side of Midnight* 1977 (pd); *Love and Bullets* 1979 (pd); *Raise the Titanic* 1980 (pd); *Monsignor* 1982 (pd); *Ghostbusters* 1984 (pd); *Jo Jo Dancer, Your Life Is Calling* 1986 (pd); *Legal Eagles* 1986 (pd).

De Havilland, Olivia • Actress • Born Olivia Mary De Havilland, Tokyo, July 1, 1916. *Educ.* Mills College, Oakland CA. Born to British parents in the Orient, raised in California and discovered by Max Reinhardt. De Havilland was often cast as the forgiving, passive woman opposite swashbuckling men like Errol Flynn, first proving her serious dramatic ability as the long-suffering Melanie in *Gone with the Wind* (1939). In a celebrated court case of the 1940s she successfully sued Warner Bros. for refusing to release her at the end of a seven-year contract. (Warners had suspended her for six months for demanding better roles and claimed that she had to make up the extra time at the end of the seven-year period.) De Havilland's victory marked a breakthrough in players' rights, with studio contracts subsequently being limited to a total of seven years. Sister of actress Joan Fontaine. • *Alibi Ike* 1935; *Captain Blood* 1935; *The Irish in Us* 1935; *A Midsummer Night's Dream* 1935; *Anthony Adverse* 1936; *The Charge of the Light Brigade* 1936; *Call It a Day* 1937; *The Great Garrick* 1937; *It's Love I'm After* 1937; *Four's a Crowd* 1938; *Gold Is Where You Find It* 1938; *Hard to Get* 1938; *Robin Hood* 1938; *Dodge City* 1939; *Gone With the Wind* 1939 **(AANBSA)**; *The Private Lives of Elizabeth and Essex* 1939; *Wings of the Navy* 1939; *My Love Came Back* 1940; *Raffles* 1940; *The Santa Fe Trail* 1940; *Hold Back the Dawn* 1941 **(AANBA)**; *The Strawberry Blonde* 1941; *They Died With Their Boots On* 1941; *In This Our Life* 1942; *The Male Animal* 1942; *Government Girl* 1943; *Princess O'Rourke* 1943; *Thank Your Lucky Stars* 1943; *The Dark Mirror* 1946; *Devotion* 1946; *To Each His Own* 1946 **(AABA)**; *The Well-Groomed Bride* 1946; *The Snake Pit* 1948 **(AANBA)**; *The Heiress* 1949 **(AABA)**; *My Cousin Rachel* 1952; *Not As a Stranger* 1955; *That Lady* 1955; *The Ambassador's Daughter* 1956; *Proud Rebel* 1958; *Libel* 1959; *Light in the Piazza* 1962; *Hush...Hush, Sweet Charlotte* 1964; *Lady in a Cage* 1964; *The Adventurers* 1970; *Pope Joan* 1972; *Airport 77* 1977; *The Swarm* 1978; *The 5th Musketeer* 1979.

De Laurentiis, Dino • Producer • Born Torre Annunciata, Italy, August 8, 1918. *Educ.* Centro Sperimentale di Cinematografia, Rome. Produced several prestigious Italian films in collaboration with Carlo Ponti in the 1950s, before turning to grandiose international productions. After the failure of his massive Dinocitta studio De Laurentiis moved to the US. His taste for overblown spectacle has led to some expensive failures (*Hurricane* 1979, *Tai-Pan* 1986), though he was also behind such critically lauded productions as *Ragtime* (1981) and *Blue Velvet* (1986).

In 1984 De Laurentiis unveiled the DEG (DeLaurentiis Entarainment Group) Film Studios in Wilmington, NC, but the venture was a failure and its founder bowed out in 1988. Rafaella De Laurentiis, the second of his four children with actress Silvana Mangano, is a Hollywood-based producer who formed her own company in 1987. • *L'Amore canta* 1941 (p); *Il Bandito* 1946 (p); *La Figlia del capitano* 1947 (p); *Il Lupo della sila* 1949 (p); *Molti Sogni per le Strade* 1949 (p); *Riso Amaro/Bitter Rice* 1949 (p); *Il Brigante Musolino* 1950 (p); *Anna* 1951 (p); *Guardie Ladri* 1951 (p); *Ulysses* 1953 (p); *La Lupa* 1954 (p); *Mambo* 1954 (p); *L'Oro di Napoli/The Gold of Naples* 1954 (p); *La Strada* 1954 (p) **(AABP)**; *Attila* 1955 (p); *La Bella Mugnaia* 1955 (p); *Guendalina* 1955 (p); *Outlaw Girl* 1955 (p); *Le Notti di Cabiria/Nights of Cabiria* 1956 (p); *War and Peace* 1956 (p); *Barrage contre le Pacifique* 1957 (exec.p); *La Tempesta* 1958 (p); *La Grande Guerra* 1959 (p); *Crimen* 1960 (p); *Five Branded Women* 1960 (p); *Sotto dieci bandiere* 1960 (p); *Tutti a Casa* 1960 (p); *I Due Nemici* 1961 (p); *Barabbas* 1962 (p); *Il Mafioso* 1962 (p); *Pierrot le Fou* 1965 (p); *Le Tigre se parfume à la dynamite* 1965 (p); *I Tre Volti/Three Faces of a Woman* 1965 (a,p); *La Bibbia/The Bible* 1966 (p); *Se Tutte le Donne Del Mondo* 1967 (p); *Lo Straniero/The Stranger* 1967 (p); *Anzio* 1968 (p); *Barbarella* 1968 (p); *Diabolik* 1968 (p); *Fräulein Doktor* 1968 (p); *La Mariée était en noir/The Bride Wore Black* 1968 (p); *Romeo and Juliet* 1968 (p); *Le Streghe/The Witches* 1968 (p); *Monte Carlo or Bust!* 1969 (p); *A Man Called Sledge* 1970 (p); *Waterloo* 1970 (p); *Valachi Papers* 1972 (p); *Crazy Joe* 1973 (p); *Serpico* 1973 (p); *Three Tough Guys* 1973 (p); *Death Wish* 1974 (exec.p); *Porgi l'Altra Guancia* 1974 (p); *Mandingo* 1975 (p); *Three Days of the Condor* 1975 (exec.p); *Il Casanova di Federico Fellini/Fellini's Casanova* 1976 (p); *Drum* 1976 (p); *King Kong* 1976 (p); *Lipstick* 1976 (exec.p); *The Shootist* 1976 (p); *Das Schlangenei/The Serpent's Egg* 1977 (p); *The White Buffalo* 1977 (exec.p); *The Brink's Job* 1978 (exec.p); *King of the Gypsies* 1978 (p); *Hurricane* 1979 (p); *Flash Gordon* 1980 (p); *Ragtime* 1981 (p); *The Dead Zone* 1983 (exec.p); *The Bounty* 1984 (exec.p); *Conan the Destroyer* 1984 (p); *Dune* 1985 (exec.p); *Year of the Dragon* 1985 (p); *Tai-Pan* 1986 (exec.p); *Desperate Hours* 1990 (p).

De Luise, Dom • Actor • Born Brooklyn, NY, August 1, 1933. *Educ.* High School for the Performing Arts, New York; Tufts University, Medford MA. Portly comic who moved from the New York stage to become a fixture of TV shows and specials in the 1960s and 70s. In films De Luise has worked most often with Mel Brooks, Burt Reynolds and Gene Wilder; he made a commendable directorial debut with *Hot Stuff* (1979). Son Peter De Luise is also an actor. • *Fail Safe* 1964; *The Glass Bottom Boat* 1966; *The Busy Body* 1967; *What's So Bad About Feeling Good?* 1968; *Norwood* 1970; *The Twelve Chairs* 1970; *Who Is Harry Kellerman, and Why Is He Saying Those Terrible Things About Me?* 1971; *Every Little Crook and Nanny* 1972; *Blazing Saddles* 1974; *The Adventures of Sherlock Holmes' Smarter Brother* 1975; *Silent Movie* 1976; *The World's Greatest Lover* 1977; *The Cheap Detective* 1978; *The End* 1978; *Sextette* 1978; *Fatso* 1979; *Hot Stuff* 1979 (a,d); *The Last Married Couple in America* 1979; *The Muppet Movie* 1979; *The Cannonball Run* 1980; *Smokey and the Bandit II* 1980; *Wholly Moses!* 1980; *History of the World Part I* 1981; *The Best Little Whorehouse in Texas* 1982; *The Secret of Nimh* 1982; *Cannonball Run II* 1983; *Johnny Dangerously* 1984; *An American Tail* 1986; *Haunted Honeymoon* 1986; *Going Bananas* 1987; *Spaceballs* 1987; *Un Tassinaro à New York* 1987; *Oliver & Company* 1988; *All Dogs Go to Heaven* 1989; *Loose Cannons* 1989; *Happily Ever After* 1990; *Driving Me Crazy* 1991.

De Mornay, Rebecca • Actress • Born Los Angeles, CA, August 29, 1961. *Educ.* Lee Strasberg Institute, Los Angeles. Born in California but raised in Europe, DeMornay made her film debut in Francis Ford Coppola's *One from the Heart* (1982) and achieved leading lady status opposite Tom Cruise in *Risky Business* (1983). Her strongest performance to date has been in *The Trip to Bountiful* (1986), with Geraldine Page. • *One From the Heart* 1982; *Risky Business* 1983; *Testament* 1983; *Runaway Train* 1985; *The Slugger's Wife* 1985; *The Trip to Bountiful* 1986; *Beauty and the Beast* 1987; *And God Created Woman* 1988; *Feds* 1988; *Dealers* 1989.

De Niro, Robert • Actor • Born New York, NY, August 17, 1943. *Educ.* Stella Adler Conservatory, New York; American Workshop. One of the most gifted actors of the post-Brando generation and often regarded as Brando's heir, Robert De Niro combines the qualities of exceptional movie actors—danger, unpredictability, magnetism—with a distinctive touch of nihilism. The son of abstract expressionist artist Robert De Niro and painter Virginia Admiral, he studied drama with Stella Adler and Lee Strasberg and appeared in several Off-Broadway productions early in his career. De Niro's first screen appearances came in films directed by Brian De Palma; his roles in *Greetings* (1968), *The Wedding Party* (1969) and *Hi, Mom!* (1970) displayed signs of the defiance and irreverence which typified his later work. Other glimpses of what would become signature De Niro characteristics were visible in his portrayals of a moody, drug-addicted criminal in *Bloody Mama* (1970) and a charmingly roguish small-time thief in *The Gang That Couldn't Shoot Straight* (1971).

De Niro's breakthrough role was that of the slow-witted, dying baseball player in *Bang the Drum Slowly* (1973), which won him the New York Film Critics best actor award. Next came a small gem of a performance in *Mean Streets* (1973), as the irresponsible—and irrepressible—Johnny Boy. In *The Godfather, Part II* (1974), De Niro faced the challenge of depicting a young version of one of the most familiar characters in all of sound cinema—Marlon Brando's inspired portrayal of Don Vito Corleone. De Niro's performance, which won him a best supporting actor Academy Award, was a masterpiece of nuanced gestures, glances and speech patterns that captured the pride and inner reserve of Brando's mature "Godfather." An equally astonishing portrayal was his enigmatic steelworker-turned-Green Beret in *The Deer Hunter* (1978), a compelling central performance that held the entire film together.

The collaboration with director Martin Scorese that began with *Mean Streets* produced some of De Niro's most memorable performances—the deranged Travis Bickle in *Taxi Driver* (1976), jazz saxophonist Jimmy Doyle in *New York, New York* (1977), boxer Jake La Motta in *Raging Bull* (1980, a tour de force which won him a best actor Oscar), frustrated comic Rupert Pupkin in *The King of Comedy* (1983) and small-time mobster Jimmy Conway in *GoodFellas* (1990). Remarkably, De Niro recorded the reprehensible qualities of these characters without losing sight of their humanity. Travis Bickle's crazed in-the-mirror monologue ("You talkin' to me?") is so chilling because it is so recognizably human.

De Niro is at his best when he can suggest a man on the edge, struggling with his demons, as he did with the caring but mercurial Vietnam veteran in *Jacknife* (1989) and the obsessed but kindhearted bounty hunter in *Midnight Run* (1988). Just the suggestion of this struggle made his looney rebel cameo in *Brazil* (1985) memorable and allowed him to create effective characters in films that were otherwise less than entirely successful—his ambitious monsignor in *True Confessions* (1981), his reflective gangster in *Once Upon a Time in America* (1984) and his militant Jesuit priest in *The Mission* (1986). His attempts at playing unambiguously evil characters (*Angel Heart* 1987, *The Untouchables* 1987) have been less fruitful, as have his portrayals of passive figures (*The Last Tycoon* 1976, *1900* 1976, *Falling in Love* 1984, *Stanley and Iris* 1990). But regardless of a particular film's merits, De Niro consistently finds ways to create extraordinary characters who allow us to see deeper into ourselves.

De Niro is known as a champion of New York film production and his Tribeca Film Center, in which his own Tribeca Films company is based, has become a hub of the city's production community. CRB • *Greetings* 1968; *Sam's Song* 1969; *The Wedding Party* 1969; *Bloody Mama* 1970; *Hi, Mom!* 1970; *Born to Win* 1971; *The Gang That Couldn't Shoot Straight* 1971; *Bang the Drum Slowly* 1973; *Mean Streets* 1973; *The Godfather, Part II* 1974 **(AABSA)**; *The Last Tycoon* 1976; *Novecento/1900* 1976; *Taxi Driver* 1976 **(AANBA)**; *New York, New York* 1977; *The Deer Hunter* 1978 **(AANBA)**; *Raging Bull* 1980 **(AABA)**; *The Swap* 1980; *Acting: Lee Strasberg and The Actors Studio* 1981; *True Confessions* 1981; *The King of Comedy* 1983; *Falling in Love* 1984; *Once Upon a Time in America* 1984; *Brazil* 1985; *The Mission* 1986; *Angel Heart* 1987; *Dear America* 1987; *Hello Actors Studio* 1987; *The Untouchables* 1987; *Midnight Run* 1988; *Jacknife* 1989; *We're No Angels* 1989 (a,exec.p); *Awakenings* 1990; *GoodFellas* 1990; *Hollywood Mavericks* 1990; *Stanley and Iris* 1990; *Guilty By Suspicion* 1991.

De Palma, Brian • Director, screenwriter; also producer. • Born Brian Russell De Palma, Newark, NJ, September 11, 1940. *Educ.* Columbia (fine arts, physics); Sarah Lawrence College, Bronxville, NY. Master of the psychological thriller, De Palma has consistently demonstrated a fluent, inventive cinematic style. Sometimes criticized as a mere imitation of Alfred Hitchcock, De Palma's work, though it pays homage to Hitchcock, differs strikingly in subject matter and technique. Similarly criticized for portraying graphic violence, De Palma responds that he is incorporating Eisenstein's theory of montage as conflict, that "film 'is' violence." Stylization acts to aesthetically distance De Palma's violence so that it becomes a visual effect rather than a naturalistic detail.

De Palma began making films as a student, first at Columbia, later at Sarah Lawrence. In the early 60s, a short, *Wotan's Wake* (1962), won him several awards. His first feature films, *The Wedding Party* (produced 1966, released 1969), *Greetings* (1968) and *Hi, Mom* (1970), were low-budget affairs, now best-known for early screen appearances by Robert De Niro and Jill Clayburgh.

Beginning with his commercial breakthrough, *Carrie* (1976), De Palma's work began to deal with recurrent themes and narrative patterns. The narrative frame of the dream/nightmare brackets both *Dressed to Kill* (1980) and *Casualties of War* (1989). Many of his films portray a failed attempt to rescue a female character, as most tragically portrayed in *Blow Out* (1981). De Palma's fascination with the dual role of the gifted young person as a heroic ideal and outsider is illustrated in *Carrie* and *The Fury* (1978).

A subtext of family romance and oedipal conflict underlies the psychological power of De Palma's vision. Such elements as the search for the father, repressed incestual desire and sibling rivalry appear in several of his films. The complex narrative structures of *Obsession* (1976) and *The Fury* examine these themes with particular force. De Palma also explores the dynamics of sadomasochism and voyeurism in *Body Double* (1984), *Dressed to Kill* and *Blow Out.*

In addition, De Palma explores social and ethical tensions that deconstruct the American mythos. Paranoid conspiracy and power politics shape the ethical dilemmas of the young heroes in such works as *Blow Out* and *Casualties of War.* While De Palma may peripherally examine larger social issues of institutional, professional and political corruption, as in *Scarface* (1983), *The Untouchables* (1987) and *Bonfire of the Vanities* (1990), the director regards himself as an artist and not a polemicist. Even *Carrie,* which explores the social conformity and cruelty of teenage bonding, essentially parodies itself through De Palma's characteristic black humor.

Although De Palma works primarily in the genre of the psychological thriller, elements of romance, horror and gangster melodramas are explored as well. Adept at urban location shooting, De Palma has brought to the screen the visual ambience of such cities as Chicago, New York, Philadelphia, New Orleans and Florence. Even *Casualties of War,* an anomaly in genre and location, nevertheless begins and ends on a San Francisco train.

De Palma's most important contributions to contemporary cinema lie in his inventive, visually dynamic style. He frequently employs such techniques as the stalking, searching camera; the "God's eye" point of view; and an expressively detailed *mise-en-scène*. A master of rhythmic editing, he often opens his films with an extended, viscerally composed sequence. The now-classic prom sequence in *Carrie,* with its use of the split screen, slow-motion and cross-cutting, typifies the rich versatility of De Palma's craft. DMB • *Wotan's Wake (short)* 1962 (d); *Greetings* 1968 (d,sc,ed); *Murder à la Mod* 1968 (d,sc,ed); *The Wedding Party* 1969 (d,p,sc,ed); *Dionysus in 69* 1970 (d,ph,ed); *Hi, Mom!* 1970 (d,sc,story); *Get to Know Your Rabbit* 1972 (d); *Sisters* 1973 (d,sc,story); *Phantom of the Paradise* 1974 (d,sc); *Carrie* 1976 (d); *Obsession* 1976 (d,story); *The Fury* 1978 (d); *Home Movies* 1979 (d,p,story); *Dressed to Kill* 1980 (d,sc); *Blow Out* 1981 (d,sc); *The First Time* 1982 (creative consultant); *Scarface* 1983 (d); *Body Double* 1984 (d,p,sc,story); *Wise Guys* 1986 (d); *The Untouchables* 1987 (d); *The Great O'Grady* 1988 (a); *Casualties of War* 1989 (d); *Bonfire of the Vanities* 1990 (d,p,uncred.a).

De Rochemont, Louis • Producer; also director. • Born Chelsea, MA, January 13, 1899; died 1978. *Educ.* MIT; Harvard. Documentary filmmaker who created the highly respected "March of Time" newsreel series with Roy E. Larsen in 1934. Some of the postwar narrative features produced by De Rochement, like *The House on 92nd Street* (1945) and *Lost Boundaries* (1949), displayed stylistic affinities with the Italian neorealist movement. • *The First World War* 1934 (d,p); *Metropolitan Opera* 1934 (p); *The Great Depression* 1935 (exec.p); *American Lifestyles* 1939 (exec.p); *The Ramparts We Watch* 1940 (d); *We Are the Marines* 1942 (d,p); *The Fighting Lady* 1944 (ed,p); *The House on 92nd Street* 1945 (p); *Postwar Problems and Solutions* 1946 (exec.p); *13 Rue Madeleine* 1947 (p); *Boomerang* 1947 (p); *Lost Boundaries* 1949 (p); *The Whistle at Eaton Falls* 1951 (p); *Walk East on Beacon* 1952 (p); *The Great Adventure* 1953 (p); *Martin Luther* 1953 (p); *Animal Farm* 1954 (p); *Cinerama Holiday* 1955 (p,sc); *Ni Liv* 1957 (p); *Der Veruntreute Himmel* 1958 (p); *Windjammer* 1958 (d,p); *Man on a String* 1960 (p); *Question 7* 1961 (p); *The Roman Spring of Mrs. Stone* 1961 (p); *The Fight* 1970 (p).

De Santis, Giuseppe • Director; also screenwriter. • Born Fondi, Italy, February 11, 1917. *Educ.* Centro Sperimentale di Cinematografia, Rome. Film critic and early advocate of Italian neorealism who turned to directing after co-writing several films, notably Luchino Visconti's first feature *Ossessione* (1942). *Bitter Rice* (1949) remains De Santis's best known work, a somber but sexy study of female rice pickers in the Po Valley starring Silvana Mangano. • *Ossessione* 1942 (sc,adapt,ad); *Giorni di Gloria* 1945 (prod.coord.); *Caccia tragica* 1947 (d); *Riso Amaro/Bitter Rice* 1949 (d) **(AANBST)**; *Non c'e Pace tra gli Ulivi* 1950 (d,sc); *Roma Ore 11* 1952 (d,sc); *Marito per Anna Zaccheo* 1953 (d,sc); *Giorni d'Amore* 1954 (d,sc); *Uomini e Lupi* 1956 (d,sc); *L'Uomo senza Domenica* 1957 (d,sc); *La Strada lunga un Anno* 1958 (d,sc); *La Garconniere* 1960 (d,sc); *Italiani brava Gente* 1964 (d,sc); *Un Apprezzato Professionista di Sicuro Avvenire* 1971 (d,sc).

De Santis, Pasqualino • Director of photography • Born Pasquale De Santis, Italy. Leading cinematographer who has often worked with Francesco Rosi, Luchino Visconti and Robert Bresson. • *La Strada lunga un Anno* 1958 (ph); *La Notte/The Night* 1961 (cam.op); *L'Eclisse/The Eclipse* 1962 (cam.op); *Otto e Mezzo/8 1/2* 1963 (cam.op); *C'era una Volta.../More Than a Miracle/Cinderella—Italian Style* 1967 (ph); *Romeo and Juliet* 1968 (ph) **(AABPH)**; *Gli Amanti* 1969 (ph); *La Caduta degli dei/The Damned* 1969 (ph); *Uomini Contro* 1970 (ph); *Morte a Venezia/Death in Venice* 1971 (ph); *The Assassination of Trotsky* 1972 (ph); *Il Caso Mattei* 1972 (ph); *Guernica* 1972 (ph); *Re: Lucky Luciano* 1973 (ph); *Lancelot du Lac* 1974 (ph); *Gruppo di famiglia in un interno/Conversation Piece* 1975 (ph); *A Mezzanotte va la ronda del Piacere* 1975 (ph); *Cadaveri Eccellenti/Illustrious Corpses* 1976 (ph); *L'Innocente/The Innocent* 1976 (ph); *Le Diable Probablement* 1977 (ph); *Una Giornata Particolare/A Special Day* 1977 (ph); *Nene* 1977 (ph); *Cristo si e Fermato a Eboli/Christ Stopped at Eboli* 1978 (ph); *La Terrazza* 1979 (ph); *I Tre fratelli/Three Brothers* 1980 (ph); *L'Argent* 1983 (ph); *Bizet's Carmen* 1984 (ph); *Misunderstood* 1984 (ph); *Sheena* 1984 (ph); *Harem* 1985 (ph); *I Soliti Ignoti...Vent'Anni Dopo* 1986 (ph); *Salome* 1986 (ph); *Cronaca di una morte annunciata/Chronicle of a Death Foretold* 1987 (ph); *High-Frequency* 1988 (ph); *Musica per Vecchi Animali* 1989 (ph); *Dimenticare Palermo* 1990 (ph).

De Sica, Vittorio • Director, actor; also screenwriter, producer. • Born Sora, Italy, July 7, 1902; died 1974. Italian director Vittorio De Sica was also a notable actor who appeared in over 100 films, to which he brought the same charm and brightness which infused his work behind the camera.

By 1918, at the age of 16, De Sica had already begun to dabble in stage work and in 1923 he joined Tatiana Pavlova's theater company. His good looks and breezy manner made him an overnight matinee idol in Italy with the release of his first sound picture, *La Vecchia Signora* (1931). De Sica turned to directing during WWII, with his first efforts typical of the light entertainments of the time. It was with *The Children are Watching Us* (1942) that he began to use non-professional actors and socially conscious subject matter. The film was also his first of many collaborations with scenarist Cesare Zavattini, a combination which shaped the postwar Italian Neorealist movement.

With the end of the war, De Sica's films began to express the personal as well as collective struggle to deal with the social problems of post-Mussolini Italy. *Shoeshine* (1946), *Bicycle Thieves* (1948) and *Umberto D* (1952) combined classic neorealist traits—working-class settings, anti-authoritarianism, emotional sincerity—with technical and compositional sophistication and touches of poignant humor.

De Sica continued his career as an actor with sufficient success to finance some of his directorial projects, playing a host of twinkling-eyed fathers and Chaplinesque figures in films such as *Pane, amore e gelosia* (1954). His later directorial career was highlighted by his work with Sophia Loren and Marcello Mastroianni in *Yesterday, Today & Tomorrow* (1963), which won the Oscar as best foreign film. After a period of decline in which he came to be perceived as a slick, rather tasteless master of burlesque, De Sica resurfaced with *The Garden of the Finzi-Continis* (1971), a baroque political romance which won him another Oscar for best foreign film.

Active to the end, De Sica appeared as himself in Ettore Scola's *We All Loved Each Other So Much* (1975), which was released after his death. T • *The Clemenceau Affair* 1918 (a); *La Compagnia dei Matti* 1928 (a); *La Vecchia Signora* 1931 (a); *Gli Uomini che Mascalzoni* 1932 (a); *Passa l'Amore* 1933 (a); *La Canzone del Sole* 1934 (a); *Amo te Sola* 1935 (a); *Daro un Milione* 1935 (a); *Tempe Massimo* 1935 (a); *Lohengrin* 1936 (a); *Napoli d'Altri Tempi* 1937 (a); *Il Signor Max* 1937 (a); *Le Due Madri* 1938 (a); *La Mazurka di Papa* 1938 (a); *Castelli in Aria* 1939 (a); *I Grandi Magazzini* 1939 (a); *Manon Lescaut* 1940 (a); *La Peccatrice* 1940 (a); *Rose Scarlatte, Melodie Eterne* 1940 (a,d,sc); *Maddalena Zero in Condotta* 1941 (a,d,sc); *Teresa Venerdi* 1941 (a,d,sc); *I Bambini Ci Guardano/The Children Are Watching Us* 1942 (d,sc); *Un Garibaldino al Convento* 1942 (a,d,sc); *I Nostri sogni* 1942 (a); *Dieci Minuti di Vita* 1943 (a); *Porta del Cielo* 1945 (d,sc); *Roma Città Libera* 1946 (a); *Sciuscia/Shoeshine* 1946 (d); *Ladri di Biciclette/The Bicycle Thief/Bicycle Thieves* 1948 (d,p); *Natale al Campo* 1948 (p); *Domani e troppo Tardi* 1950 (a); *Miracolo a Milano/Miracle in Milan* 1950 (d,p,sc); *Altri Tempi* 1952 (a); *Buongiorno Elefante!* 1952 (a,idea,p); *Umberto D* 1952 (d,p,sc); *The Earrings of Madame De...* 1953 (a); *Indiscretion of an American Wife* 1953 (d,p); *Pane, Amore, e Fantasia/Bread, Love and Dreams* 1953 (a); *Villa Borghese* 1953 (a); *L'Oro di Napoli/The Gold of Naples* 1954 (a,d,sc); *Pane, Amore e gelosia/Bread, Love and Jealousy* 1954 (a); *Secrets d'Alcove* 1954 (a); *La Bella Mugnaia* 1955 (a); *Il Bigamo* 1955 (a); *Peccato che sia una canaglia* 1955 (a); *Il Segno di Venere* 1955 (a); *Mio Figlio Nerone* 1956 (a); *Pane, Amore e...* 1956 (a); *Amore e Chiacchiere* 1957 (a); *A Farewell to Arms* 1957 (a) **(AANBSA)**; *The Monte Carlo Story* 1957 (a); *Padri e Figli* 1957 (a); *Souvenir D'Italie* 1957 (a); *Il Tetto* 1957 (d,p); *Vacanze ad Ischia* 1957 (a); *Ballerina e buon Dio* 1958 (a); *Fast and Sexy* 1958 (a,m); *Il Generale Della Rovere* 1959 (a); *Il Moralista* 1959 (a); *The Angel Wore Red* 1960 (a); *Austerlitz* 1960 (a); *La Ciociara/Two Women* 1960 (d,sc); *It Started in Naples* 1960 (a); *The Millionairess* 1960 (a); *Il Giudizio Universale* 1961 (a,d,sc); *The Wonders of Aladdin* 1961 (a); *Boccaccio '70* 1962 (d); *Eva* 1962 (a); *Lafayette* 1962 (a); *I Sequestrati di Altona/The Condemned of Altona* 1962 (d); *Il Boom* 1963 (d,sc); *Ieri, Oggi, Domani/Yesterday, Today and Tomorrow* 1963 (d,sc); *Matrimonio all'italiana/Marriage Italian Style* 1964 (d); *The Amorous Adventures of Moll Flanders* 1965 (a); *After the Fox* 1966 (a,d); *Un Monde Nouveau* 1966 (d,sc); *Woman Times Seven* 1967 (d); *The Biggest Bundle of Them All* 1968 (a); *The Shoes of the Fisherman* 1968 (a); *Le*

Streghe/The Witches 1968 (d,sc—"A Night Like Any Other"); *Gli Amanti* 1969 (d,sc); *I Girasoli/Sunflower* 1969 (d); *If It's Tuesday, This Must Be Belgium* 1969 (a); *Il Giardino del Finzi-Continis/The Garden of the Finzi-Continis* 1971 (d); *Snow Job* 1971 (a); *Lo Chiameremo Andrea* 1972 (d); *Trastevere* 1972 (a); *Una Breve Vacanza/A Brief Vacation* 1973 (d); *Il Delitto Matteotti* 1973 (a); *Blood For Dracula* 1974 (a); *C'eravamo tanto amati/We All Loved Each Other So Much* 1974 (a); *Il Viaggio/The Voyage* 1974 (d).

De Toth, André • *aka* Endre Toth, Andreas Toth, Andre DeToth • Director; also producer, screenwriter. • Born Sasvrai Farkasfawi Tothfalusi Toth Endre Antai Mihaly, Mako, Hungary, May 15, 1913. *Educ.* Hungarian Royal University, Budapest (law). One-eyed director who nonetheless made one of the first 3-D movies, *House of Wax* (1953). De Toth directed six Hungarian films before arriving in the US in 1942, where he turned out mostly tough, violent crime and western pictures. He was married to actress Veronica Lake from 1944 to 1952 and has worked primarily in Europe since the late 1950s. • *Balalaika* 1939 (d); *Hat Het Buldogsag* 1939 (d); *Ket Lany Az Utcan* 1939 (d); *Ot Ora 40* 1939 (d); *Semmelweis* 1939 (d); *Toprini Nasz* 1939 (d); *The Thief of Bagdad* 1940 (2u d); *Jungle Boy* 1942 (2u d); *Passport to Suez* 1943 (d); *Dark Waters* 1944 (d); *None Shall Escape* 1944 (d); *The Other Love* 1947 (d); *Ramrod* 1947 (d); *Pitfall* 1948 (d); *Slattery's Hurricane* 1949 (d); *The Gunfighter* 1950 (story) **(AANBST)**; *Man in the Saddle* 1951 (d); *Carson City* 1952 (d); *Last of the Comanches* 1952 (d); *Springfield Rifle* 1952 (d); *House of Wax* 1953 (d); *The Stranger Wore a Gun* 1953 (d); *Thunder Over the Plains* 1953 (d); *The Bounty Hunter* 1954 (d); *Crime Wave* 1954 (d); *Riding Shotgun* 1954 (d); *Tanganyika* 1954 (d); *The Indian Fighter* 1955 (d); *Hidden Fear* 1957 (d,sc,story); *Monkey on My Back* 1957 (d); *The Two-Headed Spy* 1958 (d); *Day of the Outlaw* 1959 (d); *Man on a String* 1960 (d); *I Mongoli* 1960 (d); *Morgan Il Pirata* 1960 (d,sc); *Oro Per I Cesari* 1962 (d); *Billion Dollar Brain* 1967 (exec.p); *Play Dirty* 1968 (d,exec.p); *El Condor* 1970 (p); *Gangland* 1987 (assistance); *Spontaneous Combustion* 1989 (a).

De Vito, Danny • Actor; also director. • Born Asbury Park, NJ, November 17, 1944. *Educ.* Wilfred Academy of Hair and Beauty Culture; AADA, New York. Short, chubby character player with a flair for the demonically comic. De Vito reprised an earlier stage role for his memorable performance in *One Flew Over the Cuckoo's Nest* (1975) and enjoyed success on the hit TV comedy series *Taxi* (1978-1982) before rejuvenating his big screen career in *Romancing the Stone* (1984). He made his directorial debut with *Throw Momma from the Train* (1987), a fast-moving comedy starring De Vito and Billy Crystal and influenced by Hitchcock's *Strangers on a Train.* Married to actress Rhea Perlman of TV's "Cheers." • *Dreams of Glass* 1968 (a); *La Mortadella* 1972 (a); *Hurry Up, or I'll Be 30* 1973 (a); *Scalawag* 1973 (a); *One Flew Over the Cuckoo's Nest* 1975 (a); *The Van* 1977 (a); *The World's Greatest Lover* 1977 (a); *Goin' South* 1978 (a); *Going Ape!* 1981 (a); *Terms of Endearment* 1983 (a); *Johnny Dangerously* 1984 (a); *Romancing the Stone* 1984 (a); *The Jewel of the Nile* 1985 (a); *Head Office* 1986 (a); *My Little Pony* 1986 (a); *Ruthless People* 1986 (a); *Wise Guys* 1986 (a); *Throw Momma From the Train* 1987 (a,d); *Tin Men* 1987 (a); *Twins* 1988 (a); *The War of the Roses* 1989 (a,d).

Deakins, Roger • Director of photography • Born Torquay, Devon, England, May 24, 1949. *Educ.* National Film School, London. Deakins shot short films, documentaries and even a softcore vehicle for Koo Stark before emerging as one of England's leading cinematographers of the 1980s. His crisp, controlled color work ranges from the bleak canvases of *1984* (1984) and *Sid and Nancy* (1986) to the warm hues of *Pascali's Island* (1988). Since 1989 Deakins has worked mostly in the US. • *Empty Hand (short)* 1976 (ph); *Welcome to Britain* 1976 (ph); *Before Hindsight* 1977 (ph); *Cruel Passion* 1977 (ph); *Blue Suede Shoes* 1979 (ph); *The Animals Film* 1981 (ph); *Memoirs of a Survivor* 1981 (2u ph); *Van Morrison in Ireland* 1981 (ph); *Alan Bush: A Life* 1983 (ph); *Another Time, Another Place* 1983 (ph); *Return to Waterloo* 1983 (ph); *1984* 1984 (ph); *The Innocent* 1984 (ph); *Defence of the Realm* 1985 (ph); *Shadey* 1985 (ph); *Sid and Nancy* 1986 (ph); *The Kitchen Toto* 1987 (ph); *Personal Services* 1987 (ph); *White Mischief* 1987 (ph); *Pascali's Island* 1988 (ph); *Stormy Monday* 1988 (ph); *Air America* 1990 (cam.op,ph); *The Long Walk Home* 1990 (ph); *Mountains of the Moon* 1990 (cam.op,ph).

Dean, James • Actor • Born James Byron Dean, Marion, IN, February 8, 1931; died September 30, 1955. *Educ.* Santa Monica Junior College, CA; UCLA. Dean appeared in TV commercials and in several films as a bit player before moving to New York, where he was in two plays on Broadway. After returning to the west coast Dean played three lead roles in just over a year, displaying the versatility and force of a gifted new star, but died in a car crash after the release of only one of his major features. He became widely associated with the phrase "rebel without a cause" after starring in the movie of the same name and his hypnotic, angst-ridden performances struck a chord with teenagers the world over. • *Fixed Bayonets* 1951 (a); *Has Anybody Seen My Gal?* 1952 (a); *East of Eden* 1955 (a) **(AANBA)**; *Rebel Without a Cause* 1955 (a); *Giant* 1956 (a) **(AANBA)**; *George Stevens: A Filmmaker's Journey* 1985 (archival footage).

Dearden, Basil • Director; also producer, screenwriter. • Born Basil Dear, Westcliffe, England, January 1, 1911; died 1971. Capable, intelligent filmmaker who co-directed his first films with English comedian Will Hay. Father of writer-director James Dearden. • *It's in the Air* 1938 (ad); *Penny Paradise* 1938 (ad); *This Man Is News* 1938 (sc); *Come on George* 1939 (ad); *Let George Do It* 1940 (sc); *Spare a Copper* 1940 (p); *The Black Sheep of Whitehall* 1941 (d); *Turned Out Nice Again* 1941 (assoc.p); *Young Veterans (short)* 1941 (ad); *The Goose Steps Out* 1942 (d); *Bells Go Down* 1943 (d); *My Learned Friend* 1943 (d); *The Halfway House* 1944 (d); *They Came to a City* 1944 (d); *Dead of Night* 1945 (d—"Hearse Driver"); *The Captive Heart* 1946 (d); *Frieda* 1947 (d); *Saraband For Dead Lovers* 1948 (d); *Train of Events* 1949 (d); *The Blue Lamp* 1950 (d); *Cage of Gold* 1950 (d); *Pool of London* 1950 (d); *I Believe in You* 1951 (d,p,sc); *The Gentle Gunman* 1952 (d,p); *The Square Ring* 1953 (d,p); *Out of the Clouds* 1954 (d,p); *The Rainbow Jacket* 1954 (d,p); *The Ship That Died of Shame* 1955 (d,p,sc); *Who Done It?* 1955 (d,p); *The Green Man* 1956 (prod.sup); *Davy* 1957 (p); *Smallest Show on Earth* 1957 (d,p); *Rockets Galore* 1958 (p); *Violent Playground* 1958 (d); *Desert Mice* 1959 (p); *Sapphire* 1959 (d,p); *The League of Gentlemen* 1960 (d); *Man in the Moon* 1960 (d,p); *The Secret Partner* 1960 (d); *Victim* 1961 (d,p); *All Night Long* 1962 (d,p); *Life For Ruth* 1962 (d); *The Mind Benders* 1963 (d); *A Place to Go* 1963 (d); *Woman of Straw* 1964 (d,p); *Masquerade* 1965 (d); *Khartoum* 1966 (d); *Only When I Larf* 1968 (d); *The Assassination Bureau* 1969 (d); *The Man Who Haunted Himself* 1970 (d,sc).

Dearden, James • Director; also screenwriter. • Born London, September 14, 1949. *Educ.* New College, Oxford. First made his name with the screenplay for *Fatal Attraction* (1987), which was itself based on a 47-minute film he had written and directed in Britain (*Diversion* 1980). Dearden made a capable directorial debut with *Pascali's Island* (1988), a meditative spy thriller set in pre-WWI Greece. Son of director Basil Dearden. • *Fatal Attraction* 1987 (sc) **(AANBSC)**; *Pascali's Island* 1988 (d,sc); *A Kiss Before Dying* 1991 (d,sc).

Decaë, Henri • Director of photography; also director. • Born Saint-Denis, France, July 31, 1915; died March 7, 1987, Paris. After Raoul Coutard, the most distinguished cinematographer to have come to prominence with the

French New Wave. Decaë directed several short films through the 1940s before becoming the regular cinematographer for Jean-Pierre Mélville (*Bob le Flambeur* 1955, etc.). He shot the debut features of both Claude Chabrol (*Le Beau Serge* 1958) and François Truffaut (*The 400 Blows* 1959) and also worked frequently for Louis Malle (*Elevator to the Gallows* 1957, etc.). Decaë began shooting international productions in the late 1960s and remained active until a few years before his death. He demonstrated a special flair for atmospheric nighttime sequences. • *Le Charcutier de Machonville* 1946 (cam.op); *Le Silence de la mer* 1948 (ph,ed,sound); *Les Enfants Terribles* 1949 (ph); *Bertrand, coeur de Lion* 1950 (ph); *Cher vieux Paris! (short)* 1950 (ph); *Au coeur de la Casbah* 1951 (ph); *Le Carnaval sacre (short)* 1951 (d); *La Course de Taureaux* 1951 (ph); *Faits d'hiver (short)* 1951 (d); *Le Garde-chasse (short)* 1951 (d,ph); *Visite au Haras (short)* 1951 (d,ph); *Crève-Coeur* 1954 (ph); *Bob le Flambeur* 1955 (a,ph); *S.O.S. Noronha* 1956 (ph); *Ascenseur pour l'echafaud/Elevator to the Gallows* 1957 (ph); *Le Désir mène les hommes* 1957 (ph); *L'A.F.P. nous communique* 1958 (ph); *Les Amants/The Lovers* 1958 (ph); *Le Beau Serge/Handsome Serge* 1958 (ph); *Un Témoin dans la ville* 1958 (ph); *Les Cousins* 1959 (ph); *A Double Tour/Web of Passion/Leda* 1959 (ph); *Plein soleil* 1959 (ph); *Les Quatre cents coups/The Four Hundred Blows* 1959 (ph); *La Sentence* 1959 (ph); *Les Bonnes Femmes* 1960 (ph); *Les Dimanches de Ville d'Avray* 1961 (ph); *Leon Morin, Prêtre* 1961 (ph); *Quelle Joie de vivre* 1961 (ph); *Vie Privée* 1961 (ph); *Eva* 1962 (ph—Venice sequence); *Les Sept péchés capitaux/The Seven Deadly Sins* 1962 (ph—"Lust," "Laziness," "Pride"); *L'Aine des Ferchaux* 1963 (ph); *Dragées au Poivre* 1963 (ph); *Jour et l'heure* 1963 (ph); *La Porteuse de pain* 1963 (ph); *La Tulipe Noir* 1963 (ph); *La Ronde* 1964 (ph); *Week-End à Zuydcoote* 1964 (ph); *Viva Maria* 1965 (ph); *Hotel Paradiso* 1966 (ph); *The Night of the Generals* 1966 (ph); *The Comedians* 1967 (ph); *Diaboliquement Votre* 1967 (ph); *Le Samourai* 1967 (ph); *Le Voleur/The Thief of Paris* 1967 (ph); *Castle Keep* 1969 (ph); *Le Clan des Siciliens/The Sicilian Clan* 1969 (ph); *Le Cercle rouge* 1970 (ph); *Hello-Goodbye* 1970 (ph); *The Only Game in Town* 1970 (ph); *La Folie des grandeurs* 1971 (ph); *Jo* 1971 (ph); *The Light at the Edge of the World* 1971 (ph); *Le Droit d'aimer* 1972 (ph); *Les Aventures de Rabbi Jacob* 1973 (ph); *Don Juan 1973 ou si Don Juan était une femme* 1973 (ph); *Two People* 1973 (ph); *Isabelle devant le desir* 1974 (ph); *La Moutarde me monte au nez* 1974 (ph); *La Course à l'echalote* 1975 (ph); *Operation Daybreak* 1975 (ph); *Seven Nights in Japan* 1976 (ph); *Bobby Deerfield* 1977 (ph); *Mort d'un pourri* 1977 (ph); *Le Point de mire* 1977 (ph); *The Boys From Brazil* 1978 (ph); *Ils sont fous ces sorciers* 1978 (ph); *An Almost Perfect Affair* 1979 (ph); *Flic ou voyou* 1979 (ph); *Le Coup du Parapluie* 1980 (ph); *Est-ce bien raisonnable?* 1980 (ph); *Inspecteur la Bavure* 1980 (ph); *The Island* 1980 (ph); *Attention! Une femme peut en cacher une autre* 1983 (ph); *L'Eté de nos quinze ans* 1983 (ph); *Exposed* 1983 (ph); *Les Parents ne sont pas simples cette année* 1984 (ph); *Le Vengeance du serpent à plumes* 1984 (ph).

Dehn, Paul • Screenwriter; also lyricist. • Born Manchester, England, November 5, 1912; died 1976. *Educ.* Oxford. Critic turned playwright who entered film in 1950, sharing a best original story Oscar with James Bernard for *Seven Days to Noon*. Through the 1960s Dehn scripted several superior espionage films, notably *Goldfinger* (1964), *The Spy Who Came in from the Cold* (1965) and *The Deadly Affair* (1967). • *Seven Days to Noon* 1950 (story) **(AABST)**; *Moulin Rouge* 1952 (lyrics); *I Am a Camera* 1955 (lyrics,song); *Orders to Kill* 1958 (sc); *The Innocents* 1961 (lyrics); *Goldfinger* 1964 (sc); *The Spy Who Came in From the Cold* 1965 (sc); *The Night of the Generals* 1966 (sc); *The Deadly Affair* 1967 (sc); *The Taming of the Shrew* 1967 (sc); *Beneath the Planet of the Apes* 1970 (sc,story); *Fragment of Fear* 1970 (assoc.p,sc); *Escape From the Planet of the Apes* 1971 (sc); *Conquest of the Planet of the Apes* 1972 (sc); *Battle For the Planet of the Apes* 1973 (story); *Murder on the Orient Express* 1974 (sc) **(AANBSC)**.

Del Ruth, Roy • Director • Born Philadelphia, PA, October 18, 1895; died 1961. Capable studio director who, though never a front-rank figure, did much to shape the output of Warner Bros. in the 1930s and 40s. Del Ruth worked in TV from 1955 to 1961. Brother of screenwriter-director Hampton Del Ruth and father of cinematographer Thomas Del Ruth. • *Eve's Lover* 1925 (d); *Hogan's Alley* 1925 (d); *Across the Pacific* 1926 (d); *Footloose Widows* 1926 (d); *The Little Irish Girl* 1926 (d); *The Man Upstairs* 1926 (d); *Three Weeks in Paris* 1926 (d); *The First Auto* 1927 (d); *Ham and Eggs at the Front* 1927 (d); *If I Were Single* 1927 (d); *Wolf's Clothing* 1927 (d); *Beware of Bachelors* 1928 (d); *Conquest* 1928 (d); *Five and Ten Cent Annie* 1928 (d); *Powder My Back* 1928 (d); *The Terror* 1928 (d); *The Aviator* 1929 (d); *The Desert Song* 1929 (d); *Gold Diggers of Broadway* 1929 (d); *The Hottentot* 1929 (d); *Divorce Among Friends* 1930 (d); *Hold Everything* 1930 (d); *The Life of the Party* 1930 (d); *The Second Floor Mystery* 1930 (d); *Three Faces East* 1930 (d); *Blonde Crazy* 1931 (d); *The Maltese Falcon* 1931 (d); *My Past* 1931 (d); *Side Show* 1931 (d); *Beauty and the Boss* 1932 (d); *Blessed Event* 1932 (d); *Taxi* 1932 (d); *Winner Take All* 1932 (d); *Bureau of Missing Persons* 1933 (d); *Captured* 1933 (d); *Employees' Entrance* 1933 (d); *Lady Killer* 1933 (d); *The Little Giant* 1933 (d); *The Mind Reader* 1933 (d); *Bulldog Drummond Strikes Back* 1934 (d); *Kid Millions* 1934 (d); *Upperworld* 1934 (d); *Folies Bergere* 1935 (d); *Thanks a Million* 1935 (d); *Born to Dance* 1936 (d); *Broadway Melody of 1936* 1936 (d); *It Had to Happen* 1936 (d); *Private Number* 1936 (d); *On the Avenue* 1937 (d); *Broadway Melody of 1938* 1938 (d); *Happy Landing* 1938 (d); *My Lucky Star* 1938 (d); *Here I Am a Stranger* 1939 (d); *The Star Maker* 1939 (d); *Tail Spin* 1939 (d); *He Married His Wife* 1940 (d); *The Chocolate Soldier* 1941 (d); *Topper Returns* 1941 (d); *Maisie Gets Her Man* 1942 (d); *Du Barry Was a Lady* 1943 (d); *Barbary Coast Gent* 1944 (d); *Broadway Rhythm* 1944 (d); *It Happened on Fifth Avenue* 1947 (d,p); *The Babe Ruth Story* 1948 (d,p); *Always Leave Them Laughing* 1949 (d); *Red Light* 1949 (d,p); *The West Point Story* 1950 (d); *On Moonlight Bay* 1951 (d); *Starlift* 1951 (d); *About Face* 1952 (d); *Stop, You're Killing Me* 1952 (d); *Three Sailors and a Girl* 1953 (d); *Phantom of the Rue Morgue* 1954 (d); *The Alligator People* 1959 (d); *Why Must I Die?* 1960 (d).

Delannoy, Jean • Director; also screenwriter. • Born Noisy-le-Sec, France, January 12, 1908. *Educ.* University of Paris (literature); Lille University. Appeared in small film roles while a student at the University of Paris and worked briefly for the French Army Film Unit before becoming an editor at Paramount's Joinville studios in 1932. Delannoy directed several sensitive, well-crafted films in the 1930s and 40s before turning to less substantial thrillers and period dramas in the following decades. He was made president of IDHEC, the French film school, in 1975. Brother of silent film actress Henriette Delannoy. • *La Belle Marinière* 1932 (ed); *Paris-Deauville* 1935 (d); *La Venus de l'or* 1938 (d,sc); *Le Diamant noir* 1940 (d); *Macao, l'enfer du jeu* 1940 (d); *Fièvres* 1941 (d); *L'Assassin a peur la nuit* 1942 (d); *Pontacarral Colonel d'Empire* 1942 (d); *L'Eternel Retour/The Eternal Return* 1943 (d); *Le Bossu* 1944 (d); *La Part de l'ombre* 1945 (d,sc); *La Symphonie Pastorale* 1946 (d,sc,adapt); *Les Jeux sont faits* 1947 (d,sc); *Aux yeux du souvenir* 1948 (d,sc); *Le Secret de Mayerling* 1949 (d,sc); *Dieu a besoin des Hommes* 1950 (d); *Le Garçon sauvage* 1951 (d); *La Minute de Vérité* 1952 (d,sc,adapt); *La Route Napoleon* 1953 (d); *Déstinées* 1954 (d,sc—"Joan of Arc"); *Obsession* 1954 (d,sc); *Secrets d'Alcove* 1954 (d,sc—"Pompadour Bed"); *Chiens perdus sans Collier* 1955 (d,sc); *Marie Antoinette* 1955 (d); *Maigret Tend un Piège/Maigret Sets a Trap* 1957 (d,sc,adapt); *Notre-Dame de Paris/The Hunchback of Notre Dame* 1957 (d); *Guinguette* 1959 (d,sc);

Maigret et l'Affaire Saint-Fiacre 1959 (d,sc); *Le Baron de l'Ecluse* 1960 (d,sc); *La Française et l'amour/Love and the Frenchwoman* 1960 (d); *La Princesse de Clèves* 1960 (d); *Le Rendez-vous* 1961 (d,sc); *Vénus impériale* 1962 (d); *Les Amitiés particulières* 1964 (d); *Le Lit à deux Places* 1965 (d); *Le Majordome* 1965 (d); *Les Sultans* 1966 (d,sc); *Le Soleil des voyous* 1967 (d,sc); *La Peau de Torpedo* 1970 (d,sc); *Pas folle la guepe* 1972 (d,sc); *Bernadette* 1988 (d,sc).

Delerue, Georges • Composer; also conductor. • Born Roubaix, France, March 12, 1925. *Educ.* Paris Conservatoire. Acclaimed international composer who first gained prominence with the emergence of the French New Wave. Delerue's prolific output includes ballets, operas, chamber pieces, orchestral works, a series of vocal melodies for the poems of Paul Eluard, and music for TV and plays.

In the 1950s Delerue scored over 20 short films, including some documentaries directed by Alain Resnais. He moved into features with Pierre Kast's *Un amour de poche* (1957) and contributed memorable, evocative scores to New Wave features like *Hiroshima, Mon Amour* (1959) and *Jules et Jim* (1961). Delerue's first US film was John Huston's *A Walk with Love and Death* (1969) and highlights of his prolific international career include *A Man for All Seasons* (1966), *Women in Love* (1969) and *Julia* (1977).

Delerue's gift for interpreting and embellishing character and atmosphere have made him one of contemporary cinema's most respected and sought-after composers. His most frequent collaborators have been François Truffaut and Philippe De Broca. • *Un Amour de Poche/Nude in His Pocket* 1957 (m); *Le Mystère de l'atelier Quinze* 1957 (m.dir); *Le Chant du Syrène* (short) 1958 (m.dir); *Hiroshima, mon amour* 1959 (m); *Classe tous risques* 1960 (m); *Tirez Sur le Pianiste/Shoot the Piano Player* 1960 (m); *L'Amant de Cinq Jours* 1961 (m); *Une Aussi longue Absence* 1961 (m); *Jules et Jim* 1961 (m); *L'Amour à vingt ans/Love at 20* 1962 (m); *Cartouche* 1962 (m); *Un Coeur gros comme ca!* 1962 (add.m); *Le Farceur* 1962 (m); *Vive le Tour!* 1962 (m); *L'Aine des Ferchaux* 1963 (m); *Le Mépris/Contempt* 1963 (m); *L'Homme de Rio/That Man From Rio* 1964 (m); *Un Monsieur de Compagnie* 1964 (m); *La Peau Douce/The Soft Skin* 1964 (m); *The Pumpkin Eater* 1964 (m); *Le Corniaud* 1965 (m); *Rapture* 1965 (m,m.cond); *Viva Maria* 1965 (m); *A Man For All Seasons* 1966 (m,m.cond); *Le Roi de Coeur/King of Hearts* 1966 (m); *Le Vieil homme et l'enfant* 1967 (m); *Anne of the Thousand Days* 1969 (m) **(AANBM)**; *Le Cerveau* 1969 (m); *A Walk With Love and Death* 1969 (m,m.dir); *Women in Love* 1969 (m,m.cond); *Alex in Wonderland* 1970 (song); *Il Conformista/The Conformist* 1970 (m); *Mira* 1970 (m); *La Promesse de l'aube* 1970 (m); *Les Deux Anglaises et le Continent/Two English Girls* 1971 (m); *The Horsemen* 1971 (m); *Une Belle fille comme moi/Such a Gorgeous Kid Like Me* 1972 (m); *Chère Louise* 1972 (m); *Malpertuis: Histoire d'une maison maudite* 1972 (m); *Quelque part, quelqu'un* 1972 (m); *Angela* 1973 (m); *The Day of the Dolphin* 1973 (m,m.cond) **(AANBM)**; *The Day of the Jackal* 1973 (m); *La Nuit Américaine/Day for Night* 1973 (m); *La Gifle/The Slap* 1974 (m); *Calmos* 1975 (m); *L'Important c'est d'aimer* 1975 (m); *L'Incorrigible* 1975 (m); *Police Python.357* 1975 (m); *Le Grand Escogriffe* 1977 (m); *Julia* 1977 (m) **(AANBM)**; *Julie pot de colle* 1977 (m); *Photo Souvenir* 1977 (m); *Le Point de mire* 1977 (m); *Préparez vos mouchoirs/Get Out Your Handkerchiefs* 1977 (m); *Tendre Poulet/Dear Inspector* 1977 (m); *Le Cavaleur* 1978 (m); *La Petite fille en velours bleu* 1978 (m); *Va voir Maman, Papa travaille* 1978 (m); *An Almost Perfect Affair* 1979 (m); *L'Amour en Fuite/Love on the Run* 1979 (m); *A Little Romance* 1979 (m,m.dir) **(AABM)**; *Mijn Vriend* 1979 (m); *Le Mouton Noir* 1979 (m); *Premier Voyage* 1979 (m); *Carné: l'Homme à la Camera* 1980 (m); *Le Dernier Métro/The Last Metro* 1980 (m); *Richard's Things* 1980 (m); *Willie & Phil* 1980 (m); *All Night Long* 1981 (m); *Broken English* 1981 (m); *La Femme d'à côté/The Woman Next Door* 1981 (m); *Garde à Vue* 1981 (m); *Josepha* 1981 (m); *A Little Sex* 1981 (m); *Rich and Famous* 1981 (m); *True Confessions* 1981 (m); *La Vie Continue* 1981 (m); *The Escape Artist* 1982 (m); *L'Eté meurtrier/One Deadly Summer* 1982 (m,song); *Guy De Maupassant* 1982 (m); *Man, Woman and Child* 1982 (m,m.dir,song); *Partners* 1982 (m); *Simone de Beauvoir* 1982 (m); *Vivement Dimanche/Confidentially Yours* 1982 (m); *L'Africain* 1983 (m); *The Black Stallion Returns* 1983 (m); *Le Bon Plaisir* 1983 (m); *Exposed* 1983 (m,m.dir); *Femmes de personne* 1983 (m); *Liberty Belle* 1983 (m); *Les Morfalous* 1983 (m); *Silkwood* 1983 (m,m.dir); *Partir Revenir* 1984 (m); *Agnes of God* 1985 (m) **(AANBM)**; *Maxie* 1985 (m); *Conseil de Famille* 1986 (m); *Crimes of the Heart* 1986 (m); *Déscente aux enfers* 1986 (m); *Mesmerized* 1986 (m); *Platoon* 1986 (m,m.arr,m); *Salvador* 1986 (m,m.dir); *Un Homme amoureux/A Man in Love* 1987 (m); *The Lonely Passion of Judith Hearne* 1987 (m); *Maid to Order* 1987 (m); *The Pick-Up Artist* 1987 (m); *Summer Heat* 1987 (m); *Beaches* 1988 (m); *Biloxi Blues* 1988 (m); *Chouans!* 1988 (m); *Heartbreak Hotel* 1988 (m); *The House on Carroll Street* 1988 (m); *Memories of Me* 1988 (m); *Paris By Night* 1988 (m); *Popielusko* 1988 (m); *A Summer Story* 1988 (m); *Twins* 1988 (m); *Der Aten* 1989 (m); *Hard to Be a God* 1989 (m); *Her Alibi* 1989 (m); *La Révolution Française* 1989 (m); *Seven Minutes* 1989 (m); *Steel Magnolias* 1989 (m); *Strapless* 1989 (m); *Cadence* 1990 (m); *Joe Versus the Volcano* 1990 (m,song); *A Show of Force* 1990 (m); *Mister Johnson* (m) 1991.

Delli Colli, Tonino • Director of photography • Born Antonio Delli Colli, Rome, November 20, 1923. Versatile cinematographer, equally distinguished for his gritty, urban, black-and-white images (*Accatone* 1961) as for his brilliantly hued color landscapes (*Lacombe, Lucien* 1973). Delli Colli shot Italy's first color film, *Toto a Colori* (1951), and collaborated frequently with directors Pier Paolo Pasolini and Sergio Leone. • *Il Paese senza Pace* 1942 (ph); *La Strada Buia* 1951 (ph); *Toto a Colori* 1951 (ph); *Il Sacco di Roma* 1953 (ph); *Amori di Mezzo Secolo* 1954 (ph); *Le Rouge et le Noir* 1954 (ph); *Povere ma Belli* 1956 (ph); *Seven Hills of Rome* 1957 (ph); *Primo Amore* 1958 (ph); *Morgan Il Pirata/Morgan the Pirate* 1960 (ph); *Accattone* 1961 (ph); *Il Ladro di Bagdad/Thief of Bagdad* 1961 (ph); *The Wonders of Aladdin* 1961 (ph); *Mamma Roma* 1962 (ph); *RoGoPag* 1962 (ph—"La Ricotta"); *El Verdugo* 1963 (ph); *Comizi d'Amore* 1964 (ph); *Liola* 1964 (ph); *Les Plus belles escroqueries du monde* 1964 (ph—"Naples"); *Il Vangelo Secondo Matteo/The Gospel According to St. Matthew* 1964 (ph); *Il Buono, il Brutto, il Cattivo/The Good, the Bad, and the Ugly* 1966 (ph); *La Mandragola* 1966 (ph); *Uccellacci e Uccellini/The Hawks and the Sparrows* 1966 (ph); *La Cina è vicina/China Is Near* 1967 (ph); *Il Giorno della Civetta* 1968 (ph); *Niente Rose per OSS 117* 1968 (ph); *C'era una Volta il West/Once Upon a Time in the West* 1969 (ph); *Metti, una Sera a Cena* 1969 (ph); *Porcile/Pigsty* 1969 (ph); *Pussycat, Pussycat, I Love You* 1970 (ph); *Cometogether* 1971 (ph); *Il Decamerone/The Decameron* 1971 (ph); *Homo Eroticus* 1971 (ph); *Pilgrimage* 1972 (ph); *I Racconti di Canterbury/The Canterbury Tales* 1972 (ph); *Un Uomo da Rispettare* 1972 (ph); *Deaf Smith and Johnny Ears* 1973 (ph); *Lacombe, Lucien* 1973 (ph); *Paolo Il Caldo* 1973 (ph); *Storie Scellerate* 1973 (ph); *Lovers and Other Relatives* 1974 (ph); *Mio Dio, come sono Caduta in Basso* 1974 (ph); *Pasqualino Settebellezze/Seven Beauties* 1975 (ph); *Salo o le Centiventi Giornate di Sodoma/Salo, or The 120 Days of Sodom* 1975 (ph); *Anima Persa* 1976 (ph); *Caro Michele* 1976 (ph); *Il Casotto* 1977 (ph); *I Nuovi Mostri* 1977 (ph); *Un Taxi mauve* 1977 (ph); *Fatto di sangue fra due uomini per causa di una vedova. Si sospettano moventi politici/Revenge/Blood Feud* 1978 (ph); *Primo Amore* 1978 (ph); *Travels With Anita* 1978 (ph); *Caro Papa* 1979 (ph); *Sono Fotogenico* 1980 (ph); *Sunday Lovers* 1980 (ph—Italian segment); *Fantasma* *d'Amore* 1981 (ph); *Storie di Ordinaria Follia/Tales of Ordinary Madness* 1981 (ph); *Till Marriage Do Us Part* 1982 (ph); *Trenchcoat* 1982 (ph); *Il Futuro e Donna/The Future Is Woman* 1984 (ph); *Once Upon a Time in America* 1984 (ph); *Ginger et Fred* 1986 (ph); *The Name of the Rose* 1986 (ph); *Stradivari* 1989 (ph); *L'Africana* 1990 (ph); *Le Voce della Luna/The Voices of the Moon* 1990 (ph).

Delluc, Louis • Director; also screenwriter, critic, theorist. • Born Louis-Jean-Rene Delluc, Cadouin, France, October 14, 1890; died 1924. Influential early film enthusiast who wrote for and edited various journals and helped start the French ciné-club movement. Delluc made several well-regarded films including *Le Silence* (1920) and the highly atmospheric *Fièvre* (1921), both starring his Belgian wife Eve Francis, and was a key figure of the Impressionist school which also included Jean Epstein and Germaine Dulac. He was equally distinguished for his books on the cinema, including *Charlot/Charlie Chaplin* (1921) and *Photogénie* (1920). Delluc died of tuberculosis at the age of 33. The Prix Louis Delluc is awarded annually to an outstanding French feature film. • *La Fête Espagnole* 1919 (sc); *Fumée noire* 1920 (d,sc); *Le Silence* 1920 (d,sc); *Le Chemin d'Ernoa* 1921 (d,sc); *Fièvre* 1921 (d,sc); *Prométhée Banquier* 1921 (a); *Le Tonnerre* 1921 (d,sc); *La Femme de nulle part* 1922 (d,sc); *L'Inondation* 1924 (d,sc); *Le Train sans yeux* 1925 (from novel).

Delon, Alain • Actor; also producer, director, screenwriter. • Born Sceaux, France, November 8, 1935. With Jean-Paul Belmondo, one of France's biggest screen attractions of the 1960s and 70s. Adept at macho, action roles, as in *Borsalino* (1970), as well as with more chillingly subdued characters, as in Jean-Pierre Mélville's *Le Samourai* (1967). Delon became responsible for several of his own vehicles after launching a successful producing career in 1964. Married to actress-director Nathalie Delon (née Berthelmy, 1938) from 1964 to 1969. • *Quand la femme s'en mêle* 1957 (a); *Christine* 1958 (a); *Sois belle et tais-toi* 1958 (a); *Faibles Femmes* 1959 (a); *Plein soleil* 1959 (a); *Rocco e i suoi Fratelli/Rocco and His Brothers* 1960 (a); *Amours célèbres* 1961 (a); *Quelle Joie de vivre* 1961 (a); *Carambolages* 1962 (a); *Le Diable et les Dix Commandements* 1962 (a); *L'Eclisse/The Eclipse* 1962 (a); *Mélodie en sous-sol* 1962 (a); *Il Gattopardo/The Leopard* 1963 (a); *La Tulipe Noir* 1963 (a); *Amour à la mer* 1964 (a); *Les Félins* 1964 (a); *L'Insoumis* 1964 (a,p); *The Yellow Rolls-Royce* 1964 (a); *Once a Thief* 1965 (a); *Lost Command* 1966 (a); *Paris brûle-t-il?/Is Paris Burning?* 1966 (a); *Texas Across the River* 1966 (a); *Les Aventuriers* 1967 (a); *Diaboliquement Votre* 1967 (a); *Le Samourai* 1967 (a); *Adieu l'ami* 1968 (a); *Histoires Extraordinaires/Spirits of the Dead* 1968 (a); *La Motorcyclette* 1968 (a); *Le Clan des Siciliens/The Sicilian Clan* 1969 (a); *Jeff* 1969 (a,p); *La Piscine* 1969 (a); *Borsalino* 1970 (a,p); *Le Cercle rouge* 1970 (a); *Madly* 1970 (a,p); *Sortie de secours* 1970 (a,p); *Doucement Les Basses!* 1971 (a); *Il Etait une fois un flic* 1971 (a); *Fantasia Chez Les Ploucs* 1971 (a); *Soleil Rouge* 1971 (a); *La Veuve Couderc* 1971 (a); *The Assassination of Trotsky* 1972 (a); *Un Flic/Dirty Money* 1972 (a); *La Prima Notte di Quiete* 1972 (a,p); *Traitement de choc* 1972 (a); *Big Guns* 1973 (a); *Deux hommes dans la ville* 1973 (a); *Les Granges Brulées* 1973 (a); *La Race des "Seigneurs"* 1973 (a); *Scorpio* 1973 (a); *Borsalino and Co.* 1974 (a,p); *Creezy* 1974 (a); *La Gifle* 1974 (a); *Les Seins de Glace* 1974 (a); *Flic Story* 1975 (a); *Le Gitan* 1975 (a); *Zorro* 1975 (a); *Comme Un Boomerang* 1976 (a,p,sc); *Mr. Klein* 1976 (a,p); *Armaguedon* 1977 (a); *Le Gang* 1977 (a,exec.p); *L'Homme pressé* 1977 (a); *Mort d'un pourri* 1977 (a,sc); *Attention, les enfants regardent* 1978 (a); *The Concorde—Airport '79* 1979 (a); *Harmonie* 1979 (a); *Le Toubib* 1979 (a); *Trois Hommes à Abattre* 1980 (a,p); *Pour la peau d'un flic* 1981 (a,d,p,sc); *Teheran '43* 1981 (a); *Le Choc* 1982 (a,sc); *Le Battant* 1983 (a,d,p,sc); *Un Amour de Swann/Swann in Love* 1984 (a); *Notre Histoire* 1984 (a); *Parole de Flic* 1985 (a,exec.p,sc,song); *Le Passage* 1986 (a,p); *Ne réveillez pas un flic qui dort* 1988 (a,p,sc); *Dancing Machine* 1990 (a,exec.p); *Nouvelle Vague/New Wave* 1990 (a).

Delvaux, André • Director, screenwriter • Born Heverle, Brabant, Belgium, March 21, 1926. *Educ.* Free University of Brussels (German philology, law); Royal Conservatory of Brussels (piano, composition). Film and TV director who began his career providing piano accompaniment for silent films shown at the Belgian Cinémathèque. Delvaux's feature films rely on tightly controlled rhythms and a precise use of visual counterpoint to create a highly distinctive blend of fantasy and reality. • *L'Homme au Crane rasé/The Man Who Had His Hair Cut Short* 1966 (d,sc,song); *Un Soir un Train* 1968 (d,sc); *Rendez-Vous à Bray/Appointment in Bray* 1971 (d,sc); *Belle* 1973 (d,sc); *Een Vrouw Tussen Hond en Wolf* 1979 (d,sc); *To Woody Allen, From Europe With Love* 1980 (d,idea); *Benvenuta* 1983 (d,sc); *Babel Opera* 1985 (d,sc); *L'Oeuvre au noir* 1988 (d,sc).

DeMille, Cecil B. • Director; also producer, screenwriter. • Born Cecil Blount de Mille, Ashfield, MA, August 12, 1881; died January 21, 1959. *Educ.* AADA, New York. As the ace director in the mid-1910s for Famous Players-Lasky, a company he had a hand in creating, DeMille was a crucial figure in the early development of the classic Hollywood narrative filmmaking style. Although less critically revered than D.W. Griffith, DeMille actually played a more important role in shaping the structure of the Hollywood system.

One of DeMille's most influential films of the 1910s was *The Cheat*. Released the same year (1915) as *The Birth of a Nation*, *The Cheat* was instrumental in developing the rules of classic Hollywood filmmaking. This melodrama is the story of a society woman, Mrs. Richard Hardy, who attempts to save her husband from financial ruin by borrowing needed funds from a wealthy Japanese acquaintance. When the man demands sexual favors in return, Mrs. Hardy returns the money, but this enrages him and he brands her on the shoulder with a red-hot iron. When Richard Hardy attacks the Japanese man, (his nationality was changed to Burmese in later prints to increase foreign export potential), he is put on trial. In a final courtroom sequence, he is about to be judged guilty when his wife reveals the wound on her shoulder. DeMille worked wonders with what could have been a hackneyed melodrama by giving it a unique visual style, featuring complex lighting and patterns of shadow suggestive of jail bars. Characters are surrounded by smoke, silhouetted behind screens and appear from nowhere amidst pitch black. In DeMille's hands, *The Cheat* became an intricate study of individual responsibility, handled with subtlety and sophistication. The film is entirely free of sentimentality and the acting of stars Fanny Ward and Sessue Hayakawa is remarkably modern, direct but without sweeping gestures. With this extremely profitable feature, DeMille proved his mastery of film narrative. Over the next eight years, his output would include comedies and dramas that captured American society in transition.

DeMille's initial works brought famous plays and novels to the screen for Famous Players—*Joan the Woman* (1917), *Old Wives for New* (1918) and *Male and Female* (1919). These and other films of the period starred such proven players as James O'Neil, from Broadway, and Geraldine Farrar, from the operatic stage. In the postwar period came a series of comedies, unlike *The Cheat* in story form, but very similar in faithfulness to the newly established Hollywood rules: *We Can't Have Everything* (1918), *Why Change Your Wife?* (1920) and *Saturday Night* (1922). Ernst Lubitsch, much more famous for his comedies of manners, has singled out the DeMille films from this era as a major influence.

DeMille the innovator became DeMille the moneymaker with *The Ten Commandments* (1923). Budgeted at more than a million dollars, the film proved immensely profitable for Paramount. By the middle of the decade DeMille, with his Germanic swagger, boots and riding crop, had come to represent the archetypal director to the movie-going public. Chafing under the strictures of the studio system, he quit Paramount in 1925 to set up his own studio, buying the old Ince Studios to form Cinema Corporation of America. Later the company merged with the Keith vaudeville chain, then into Pathe.

The independent DeMille's greatest film was *King of Kings* (1927), a two-million-dollar rendering of the life of Christ. However, the company's lack of other such successes forced DeMille to sign with MGM in 1928. The contrast could not have been greater; he went from autonomy to the strict control of Louis B. Mayer and Nicholas M. Schenck. In 1932 DeMille returned to Paramount, where he would stay for the remainder of his remarkable career.

During the 1930s and 1940s DeMille was Paramount's most bankable director, turning out such hits as *The Sign of the Cross* (1932), *The Plainsman* (1937), *The Buccaneer* (1938), *Union Pacific* (1939), *Northwest Mounted Police* (1940), *Reap the Wild Wind* (1942), *The Story of Dr. Wassell* (1944), *Unconquered* (1947) and *Samson and Delilah* (1949). He was at his best with historical costume epics such as *Cleopatra* (1934) and *The Crusades* (1935). Under president Barney Balaban and studio boss Y. Frank Freeman, DeMille helped make Paramount the most profitable of the studios during Hollywood's Golden Age.

DeMille also directed and hosted a successful radio show, "Lux Radio Theatre," on CBS from 1936 until 1945, when he refused to join the radio union and quit the program instead. In the late 40s and early 50s, he would become a leader of the Hollywood right wing and the anti-communist witch hunt. His directorial career ended with his spectacular remake of *The Ten Commandments* (1956). Most of his later directorial efforts were forgettable, save for the charming *The Greatest Show on Earth* (1952), a film with an untypically contemporary—though hardly realistic—setting.

In the final analysis, DeMille's big-budget spectacles, made at Paramount from 1932 through 1956, emerge as less significant than those films he made in the pioneering days of the Hollywood studio system. If his early partner Adolph Zukor taught the world how to use movies to fashion a corporate empire, the Cecil B. DeMille of the 1910s must take credit as a key shaper of the classic Hollywood narrative film—a filmmaking form which remains dominant to this day. DG • *Brewster's Millions* 1914 (d); *The Call of the North* 1914 (d,p,sc); *Cameo Kirby* 1914 (sc); *The Circus Man* 1914 (sc); *The Making of Bobby Burnit* 1914 (prod.sup); *The Man From Home* 1914 (d,p,sc,ed); *The Man on the Box* 1914 (d,p); *The Only Son* 1914 (d,sc); *Ready Money* 1914 (sc); *Rose of the Rancho* 1914 (d,p,sc,from play,ed); *The Squaw Man* 1914 (d,sc); *The Virginian* 1914 (d,p,sc,ed); *What's His Name* 1914 (d,p,sc,ed); *After Five* 1915 (from play); *The Arab* 1915 (d,p,sc,ed); *The Captive* 1915 (d,p,sc,story,ed); *Carmen* 1915 (d,p); *The Cheat* 1915 (d,ed,p); *Chimmie Fadden* 1915 (d,p,sc,ed); *Chimmie Fadden Out West* 1915 (d,p,sc,ed); *The Country Boy* 1915 (sc); *A Gentleman of Leisure* 1915 (sc); *The Girl of the Golden West* 1915 (d,p,sc,ed); *The Golden Chance* 1915 (d,p,sc,story,ed); *The Goose Girl* 1915 (d,sc); *The Governor's Lady* 1915 (sc); *Kindling* 1915 (d,p,sc); *The Puppet Crown* 1915 (sup.); *Snobs* 1915 (sc); *The Unafraid* 1915 (d,p,sc,ed); *The Warrens of Virginia* 1915 (d,ed,p); *The Wild Goose Chase* 1915 (d,p); *Young Romance* 1915 (sc); *The Dream Girl* 1916 (d,ed,p); *The Heart of Nora Flynn* 1916 (d,ed,p); *Joan the Woman* 1916 (d,ed,p); *The Love Mask* 1916 (sc); *Maria Rosa* 1916 (d,ed,p); *Temptation* 1916 (d,ed,p); *The Trail of the Lonesome Pine* 1916 (d,p,sc,ed); *The Devil Stone* 1917 (d,ed,p); *Joan the Woman* 1917 (d,ed,p); *The Little American* 1917 (d,p,sc,ed); *A Romance of the Redwoods* 1917 (d,p,sc,story,ed); *The Woman God Forgot* 1917 (d,ed,p); *Old Wives For New* 1918 (d,ed,p); *The Squaw Man* 1918 (d,p); *Till I Come Back to You* 1918 (d,p); *We Can't Have Everything* 1918 (d,ed,p); *The Whispering Chorus* 1918 (d,ed,p); *Don't Change Your Husband* 1919 (d,p); *For Better, For Worse* 1919 (d,p); *Male and Female* 1919 (d,p); *Something to Think About* 1920 (d,p); *Why Change Your Wife?* 1920 (d,p); *The Affairs of Anatol* 1921 (d,p); *Fool's Paradise* 1921 (d,p); *Forbidden Fruit* 1921 (d,p); *Manslaughter* 1922 (d); *Saturday Night* 1922 (d,p); *Adam's Rib* 1923 (d,p); *Hollywood* 1923 (a); *The Ten Commandments* 1923 (d,p) **(AANBP)**; *Feet of Clay* 1924 (d,p); *Triumph* 1924 (d,p); *The Golden Bed* 1925 (d,p); *The Night Club* 1925 (from play *After Five*); *The Road to Yesterday* 1925 (d,p); *The Volga Boatman* 1926 (d,p); *The Forbidden Woman* 1927 (p); *A Harp in the Hock* 1927 (p); *King of Kings* 1927 (d,p); *The Little Adventuress* 1927 (p); *Dynamite* 1929 (d,p); *The Godless Girl* 1929 (d); *Free and Easy* 1930 (a); *Madam Satan* 1930 (d,p); *The Squaw Man* 1931 (d,p); *The Sign of the Cross* 1932 (d,p); *This Day and Age* 1933 (d,p); *Cleopatra* 1934 (d,p); *Four Frightened People* 1934 (d); *The Crusades* 1935 (d,p); *The Plainsman* 1937 (d,p); *The Buccaneer* 1938 (d,p); *Land of Liberty* 1939 (ed); *Union Pacific* 1939 (d,p); *North West Mounted Police* 1940 (d,p); *Reap the Wild Wind* 1942 (d,p); *Star Spangled Rhythm* 1942 (a); *The Story of Dr. Wassell* 1944 (d,p); *Unconquered* 1947 (d,p); *Variety Girl* 1947 (a); *California's Golden Beginning* 1948 (d); *Samson and Delilah* 1949 (d,p); *Sunset Boulevard* 1950 (a); *The Greatest Show on Earth* 1952 (d,p) **(AANBD,AABP)**; *The Ten Commandments* 1956 (d,p) **(AANBP)**; *The Buccaneer* 1958 (a,prod.sup).

Demme, Jonathan • Director; also producer, screenwriter. • Born Baldwin, NY, February 22, 1944. *Educ.* University of Florida (chemistry). Jonathan Demme graduated from B movies, where he began as a member of Roger Corman's stable of writers in the 1970s. He developed his craft through a series of lyrical sketches of rural Americana and is now best known for his fast-paced, urban style.

After a few semesters at the University of Florida marked by his success as a film reviewer for the college newspaper, Demme moved to New York, where from 1966 to 1968 he was a publicist at Embassy Pictures. During this period he also wrote movie reviews for *Film Daily* and rock reviews for *Fusion* and produced the 16mm short film, *Good Morning, Steve.*

During a brief stint as a producer of TV commercials in 1969, Demme earned his first feature film credit, as music coordinator on the Irving Allen-produced *Eyewitness/Sudden Terror* (1970). A meeting with producer Roger Corman led to Demme's first feature as co-producer and co-screenwriter (with director Joe Viola), *Angels Hard as They Come* (1971), for Corman's recently-formed New World Pictures. Demme worked on four more features under Corman's auspices, making his directorial debut in 1974 with *Caged Heat,* before branching out on his own.

Citizen's Band (1977), later retitled *Handle With Care,* is a series of vignettes, ranging from the mundane to the whimsical to the disturbing, concerning CB radio operators who are dominated by their radio personae. The film, which wavers between glorifying, lampooning, and seriously questioning the implications of the CB craze, earned critical acclaim but generated little box office enthusiasm.

Melvin and Howard (1980) is a relaxed yet revealing examination of American values via an unlikely encounter between a working-class Everyman (gas station owner Melvin Dummar) and an eccentric millionaire (Howard Hughes, whom Dummar claimed named him sole heir to his fortune). Named best picture by the National Society of Film Critics, this satiric but tolerant look at the American class structure also won Demme the New York Film Critics Society's best director award.

Swing Shift (1984) had the potential to be a probing look at women factory workers during WWII, but the film suffered from disagreements between Demme and star-producer Goldie Hawn over plot development and editing. Demme tried to focus on female camaraderie and endurance in the face of domineering male employers; Hawn chose to dwell on the doomed love affair between a married woman and her supervisor. Disjointed and awkward, the film lacks Demme's typical balance and polish.

An enthusiastic contemporary music fan, Demme compiled footage from three concerts by rock group Talking Heads into the riveting, energetic *Stop Making Sense* (1984). His appreciation for rock music is also apparent in *Something Wild* (1986), a screwball comedy/film noir that examines contemporary America through the metaphoric relationship between a spontaneous *gamine* and a staid stockbroker. Rapid editing, sharp camera angles, a breakneck pace and a raucous soundtrack make for a breathless, dizzying movie experience. The film's claustrophobic urban sensibility marked a notable departure for Demme, whose work earlier in the decade had celebrated open American landscapes and traditional community values.

In *Married to the Mob* (1988), the law enforcement community and gangster society commingle in New York and Miami thanks to the ironic, romantic entanglement of a gangster's widow and a young FBI agent. Popular music punctuates the soundtrack, contributing to the movie's success with audiences and critics alike.

Demme achieved his greatest critical and commercial success with *The Silence of the Lambs* (1991), superbly adapted from the novel by Thomas Harris. A genuinely terrifying thriller, the film centers on an FBI trainee (Jodie Foster) who enlists the help of one psychopath (Anthony Hopkins) in order to track down another (Ted Levine). Despite the grisly nature of the story—one killer who eats his victims, another who skins them, etc.—Demme resisted the possibilities for exploitation and instead fashioned a compelling psychological drama with a courageous, independent female protagonist. He also elicited landmark performances from both Foster and Hopkins.

Of his work, Demme has said, "There's nothing I'd rather do than direct because directing combines three of my favorite things in life: people, imagery, and sound—not just music, but the sounds of life." CSE • *Angels Hard As They Come* 1971 (p,sc); *Black Mama, White Mama* 1972 (story); *The Hot Box* 1972 (p,sc); *Caged Heat* 1974 (d,sc); *Crazy Mama* 1975 (d); *Fighting Mad* 1976 (d,sc); *Citizens Band/Handle With Care* 1977 (d); *The Incredible Melting Man* 1977 (a); *Roger Corman: Hollywood's Wild Angel* 1978 (a); *Last Embrace* 1979 (d); *Melvin and Howard* 1980 (d); *Ladies and Gentlemen, the Fabulous Stains* 1982 (sc); *Stop Making Sense* 1984 (d,sound); *Swing Shift* 1984 (d,sc); *Into the Night* 1985 (a); *Perfect Kiss (short)* 1985 (d,sc); *Something Wild* 1986 (d,p); *Swimming to Cambodia* 1987 (d); *Haiti Dreams of Democracy* 1988 (d,p,sc); *Married to the Mob* 1988 (d); *Miami Blues* 1990 (p); *The Silence of the Lambs* 1991 (d).

Dempsey, Patrick • Actor • Born Lewiston, ME, 1966. Boyishly handsome young lead, notably as Sonny Wisecarver in Phil Alden Robinson's subdued comedy *In the Mood* (1987). • *Heaven Help Us* 1985; *Meatballs III* 1986; *Can't Buy Me Love* 1987; *In the Mood* 1987; *Il Giovane toscanini* 1988; *In a Shallow Grave* 1988; *Some Girls* 1988; *Happy Together* 1989; *Loverboy* 1989; *Coupe De Ville* 1990; *Run* 1991.

Demy, Jacques • Director; also screenwriter. • Born Pont-Château, France, June 5, 1931; died October 27, 1990. *Educ.* Ecole des Beaux-Arts, Nantes; Ecole Technique de Photographie et de Cinématographie, Paris. Versatile director whose films, such as *Lola* (1961), are generally noted for their stylish, bittersweet romanticism. Demy made several musicals, including *The Umbrellas of Cherbourg* (1964)—in which all the dialogue was sung—and worked often with actress Catherine Deneuve and composer Michel Legrand. He married director Agnès Varda in 1962. • *Les Quatre cents coups/The 400 Blows* 1959 (a); *Paris Nous Appartient/Paris Belongs to Us* 1960 (a); *Lola* 1961 (d); *Les Sept péchés capitaux/The Seven Deadly Sins* 1962 (d,sc—"Lust"); *La Baie des anges* 1963 (d,sc); *Les Parapluies de Cherbourg/The Umbrellas of Cherbourg* 1964 (d,sc,lyrics); *Les Demoiselles de Rochefort/The Young Girls of Rochefort* 1967 (d,sc); *Model Shop* 1968 (d,p,sc); *Peau d'ane/Donkey Skin* 1970 (d,sc); *The Pied Piper* 1972 (d,sc); *L'Evènement le plus important depuis que l'homme a marché sur la lune/A Slightly Pregnant Man* 1973 (d,sc); *Lady Oscar* 1979 (d); *Une Chambre en Ville* 1982 (d,sc); *Parking* 1985 (d,sc,lyrics); *La Table tournante* 1988 (d,sc); *Trois places pour le 26* 1988 (d,sc).

Dench, Dame Judi • Actress • Born Judi Dench, York, England, 1934. *Educ.* Central School of Speech and Drama, London. Distinguished English actress, primarily on stage. Dench was bestowed a Damehood in 1987. • *A Midsummer Night's Dream* 1968; *Luther* 1974; *Nela* 1980; *Saigon—Year of the Cat* 1983; *Angelic Conversations* 1985; *Wetherby* 1985; *84 Charing Cross Road* 1986; *A Room With a View* 1986; *A Handful of Dust* 1988; *Henry V* 1989.

Deneuve, Catherine • Actress • Born Catherine Dorléac, Paris, October 22, 1943. Entered film as a teenager using her actress mother's maiden name and appeared in several routine movies such as *Les Portes Claquent* (1960), with elder sister Françoise Dorléac. Deneuve first attracted attention in Jacques Demy's musical *The Umbrellas of Cherbourg* (1964) and went on to become a leading international star, with her icy charm put to brilliant use by Roman Polanski (*Repulsion* 1965) and Luis Buñuel (*Belle de Jour* 1967, *Tristana* 1970). She continued to turn in impressive work in the 1980s (*The Last Metro* 1980), though some of her roles have been ill-advised (*The Hunger* 1983, *A Strange Place to Meet* 1988).

The daughter of veteran French actor Maurice Dorléac, Deneuve was formerly married to photographer David Bailey and has children by director Roger Vadim and actor Marcello Mastroianni. • *Les Collégiennes* 1956; *Les Petits chats* 1959; *L'Homme à femmes* 1960; *Les Parisiennes* 1960; *Les Portes claquent* 1960; *Et Satan conduit le bal* 1962; *Le Vice et la vertu* 1962; *Vacances Portugaises* 1963; *La Chasse à l'Homme* 1964; *Constanza della Ragione* 1964; *Un Monsieur de Compagnie* 1964; *Les Parapluies de Cherbourg/The Umbrellas of Cherbourg* 1964; *Les Plus belles escroqueries du monde* 1964; *Le Chant du Monde* 1965; *Les Créatures* 1965; *Liebes Karusell* 1965; *Repulsion* 1965; *La Vie de Chateau* 1966; *Belle de Jour* 1967; *Les Demoiselles de Rochefort/The Young Girls of Rochefort* 1967; *Manon 70* 1967; *Benjamin, ou les mémoires d'un puceau* 1968; *La Chamade* 1968; *Mayerling* 1968; *La Sirène du Mississippi/Mississippi Mermaid* 1968; *The April Fools* 1969; *Peau d'ane/Donkey Skin* 1970; *Tristana* 1970; *Ça n'arrive qu'aux autres* 1971; *La Cagna* 1971; *Un Flic/Dirty Money* 1972; *L'Evenement le plus important depuis que l'homme a marche sur la lune/A Slightly Pregnant Man* 1973; *Touche pas à la femme blanche!* 1973; *L'Agression* 1974; *La Femme aux Bottes Rouges* 1974; *Zig-Zig* 1974; *Fatti di Gente Perbene* 1975; *Hustle* 1975; *Le Sauvage* 1975; *Anima Persa* 1976; *Si c'était à refaire* 1976; *March or Die* 1977; *L'Argent des autres* 1978; *Ecoute Voir* 1978; *A nous deux* 1979; *Courage Fuyons* 1979 (a,song); *Ils sont grands ces petits* 1979; *Le Dernier Métro/The Last Metro* 1980; *Je vous aime* 1980; *Le Choix des armes/Choice of Arms* 1981; *Le Choc* 1982; *Hôtel des Amériques* 1982; *L'Africain* 1983; *Le Bon Plaisir* 1983; *The Hunger* 1983; *Fort Saganne* 1984; *Paroles et Musique/Love Songs* 1984; *Le Lieu du Crime/Scene of the Crime* 1986; *Pourvu que ce soit une fille* 1986; *Agent Trouble* 1987; *Drôle d'endroit pour une rencontre/A Strange Place to Meet* 1988 (a,p); *Fréquence meurtre* 1988: *Helmut Newton: Frames From the Edge* 1989.

Dennehy, Brian • Actor • Born Bridgeport, CT, July 9, 1939. *Educ.* Columbia (history). Burly supporting player who made his screen debut in *Semi-Tough* (1977) and has distinguished himself playing smooth villains and average Joes, as well as the occasional lead. Dennehy was named best actor at the Chicago

Film Festival for his performance in Peter Greenaway's *The Belly of an Architect* (1987). • *Looking For Mr. Goodbar* 1977; *Semi-Tough* 1977; *F.I.S.T.* 1978; *Foul Play* 1978; *10* 1979; *Butch and Sundance: The Early Days* 1979; *Little Miss Marker* 1980; *First Blood* 1982; *Split Image* 1982; *Gorky Park* 1983; *Never Cry Wolf* 1983; *Finders Keepers* 1984; *The River Rat* 1984; *Cocoon* 1985; *Silverado* 1985; *Twice in a Lifetime* 1985; *The Check Is in the Mail* 1986; *F/X* 1986; *Legal Eagles* 1986; *The Belly of an Architect* 1987; *Best Seller* 1987; *Dear America* 1987; *Cocoon: the Return* 1988; *Miles From Home* 1988; *Return to Snowy River Part II* 1988; *Indio* 1989; *The Last of the Finest* 1989; *Seven Minutes* 1989; *Presumed Innocent* 1990; *F/X 2* 1991.

Denner, Charles • Actor • Born Tarnow, Poland, May 29, 1926. Stage-experienced French performer (he emigrated from Poland at the age of four) whose first star billing came in the title role of Claude Chabrol's *Bluebeard* (1962). • *La Meilleure part* 1956; *Ascenseur pour l'échafaud/Elevator to the Gallows* 1957; *Landru/Bluebeard* 1962; *Les Plus belles escroqueries du monde* 1964; *La Vie à l'Envers/Life Upside Down* 1964; *Compartiment tueurs/The Sleeping Car Murders* 1965; *Marie-Chantal Contre le Docteur Kha* 1965; *Le Vieil homme et l'enfant* 1967; *Le Voleur/The Thief of Paris* 1967; *La Mariée était en noir/The Bride Wore Black* 1968; *La Trève* 1968; *Z* 1969; *Le Voyou* 1970; *Les Assasins de L'Ordre* 1971; *L'Aventure c'est l'aventure* 1972; *Une belle fille come moi/Such a Gorgeous Kid Like Me* 1972; *L'Héritier* 1972; *Défense de savoir* 1973; *Les Gaspards* 1973; *Un Officier de Police sans Importance* 1973; *Toute une vie* 1974; *Peur sur la Ville* 1975; *Mado* 1976; *La Première fois* 1976; *Si c'était à refaire* 1976; *L'Homme qui amait les femmes/The Man Who Loved Women* 1977; *Robert et Robert* 1978; *La Verdad sobre el Caso Savolta* 1979; *Le Coeur à l'Envers* 1980; *La Préferé* 1983; *Stella* 1983; *L'Unique* 1985; *Golden Eighties* 1986.

Dennis, Sandy • Actress • Born Sandra Dale Dennis, Hastings, NB, April 27, 1937. *Educ.* Actors Studio. Method-trained lead of the 1960s who first made her name on Broadway. Dennis's high-pitched, neurotic style lent itself to quirky, eccentric roles in films such as *Splendor in the Grass* (1961, her debut), *Who's Afraid of Virginia Woolf* (1966), which earned her an Oscar for best supporting actress, and *Up the Down Staircase* (1967). She has turned in some fine middle-aged performances in more recent films, notably *Come Back to the Five and Dime, Jimmy Dean, Jimmy Dean* (1982) and, in a hilarious cameo, Bob Balaban's overlooked *Parents* (1989). • *Splendor in the Grass* 1961; *The Three Sisters* 1964; *Who's Afraid of virginia Woolf?* 1966 (**AABSA**); *The Fox* 1967; *Up the Down Staircase* 1967; *Sweet November* 1968; *That Cold Day in the Park* 1969; *The Out-of-Towners* 1970; *Mr. Sycamore* 1974; *God Told Me To* 1976; *Nasty Habits* 1976; *The Animals Film* 1981; *The Four Seasons* 1981; *Come Back to the Five and Dime, Jimmy Dean, Jimmy Dean* 1982; *976-EVIL* 1988; *Another Woman* 1988; *Parents* 1989.

Depardieu, Gérard • Actor • Born Chateauroux, France, December 27, 1948. *Educ.* Théâtre National Populaire, Paris. Burly, highly talented leading man and one of Europe's most prolific screen performers of the 1970s and 80s. Depardieu brings to his portrayals an intensity and attention to detail that endows all his characters with a sense of urgency. Landmark films include *Going Places* (1974), as a nihilistic but somehow lovable petty thug; *Get Out Your Handkerchiefs* (1977), as a man who tries to cheer up his wife by finding her a lover; *The Return of Martin Guerre* (1982), as a 16th-century peasant who may not be what he claims; *Jean de Florette* (1986), as a naive, inexperienced farmer; and *Cyrano de Bergerac* (1990), in the title role of Jean-Paul Rappeneau's adaptation. Depardieu is probably best known to American audiences as the star of *Green Card* (1990), Peter Weir's popular romantic comedy. He directed 1984's *Le Tartuffe* and co-produced *A Strange Place to Meet* (1988) and the Satyajit Ray-directed *Shakha Proshaka/Branches of the Tree* (1991). Depardieu's actress wife Elisabeth (née Guignot) has appeared opposite him several times, as in *Jean de Florette*. • *Le Cri du Cormoran le Soir Au-Dessus des Jonques* 1971; *Un Peu de soleil dans l'eau froide* 1971; *Le Tueur* 1971; *L'Affaire dominici* 1972; *Au Rendez-Vous de la mort joyeuse* 1972; *Nathalie Granger* 1972; *La Scoumoune* 1972; *Le Viager* 1972; *Deux hommes dans la ville* 1973; *Les Gaspards* 1973; *Rude journee pour la reine* 1973; *Stavisky* 1973; *La Femme du Gange* 1974; *Pas si mechant que ça...* 1974; *Les Valseuses/Going Places* 1974; *Vincent, François Paul...et les Autres/Vincent, François, Paul...and the Others* 1974; *7 Morts sur Ordonnance* 1975; *Je T'Aime Moi Non Plus* 1975; *Maîtresse* 1975; *Barocco* 1976; *La Dernière Femme/The Last Woman* 1976; *Novecento/1900* 1976; *La Nuit tous les chat sont gris* 1976; *René la Canne* 1976; *Violanta* 1976; *Baxter, Vera, Baxter* 1977; *Le Camion* 1977; *Dites-lui que je l'aime* 1977; *Die Linkshändige Frau/The Left-Handed Woman* 1977; *Preparez vos mouchoirs/Get Out Your Handkerchiefs* 1977; *Les Chiens* 1978; *Rêve de Singe* 1978; *Le Sucre* 1978; *Buffet Froid* 1979; *Le Grand embouteillage/Traffic Jam* 1979; *Loulou* 1979; *Mon oncle d'Amérique* 1979; *Rosy la Bourrasque* 1979; *Le Dernier Métro/The Last Metro* 1980; *Inspecteur la Bavure* 1980; *Je vous aime* 1980; *Le Choix des armes/Choice of Arms* 1981; *La femme d'à côté/The Woman Next Door* 1981; *La Chévre* 1982; *Danton* 1982; *Le Grand Frère* 1982; *Le Retour de Martin Guerre/The Return of Martin Guerre* 1982; *Les Compères* 1983; *La Lune dans le caniveau/The Moon in the Gutter* 1983; *Fort saganne* 1984; *Rive Droite, Rive Gauche* 1984; *Le Tartuffe* 1984 (a,adapt,d); *Une Femme ou deux/One Woman or Two* 1985; *Police* 1985; *Les Fugitifs* 1986; *Jean de Florette* 1986; *Ménage* 1986; *Rue du départ* 1986; *Sous le soleil de Satan/Under Satan's Sun* 1987; *Camille Claudel* 1988; *Deux* 1988; *Drôle d'endroit pour une rencontre/A Strange Place to Meet* 1988 (a,p); *Henry V* 1989; *Je veux rentrer à la maison* 1989; *Trop belle pour toi/Too Beautiful For You* 1989; *Cyrano de Bergerac* 1990; *Green Card* 1990; *Uranus* 1990; *Merci, la vie* 1991; *Shakha Proshaka/Branches of the Tree* 1991 (p).

Deray, Jacques • Director; also screenwriter. • Born Jacques Deray-Desrayaud, Lyon, France, February 19, 1929. Competent, entertaining director whose earlier films, particularly *Rififi à Tokyo* and *Symphonie pour un massacre* (both 1963), showed occasional flourishes of brilliance. Between 1968 and 1980 Deray directed seven features for producer-star Alain Delon, most notably *Borsalino* (1970). • *Çela s'appelle l'aurore* 1956 (ad); *Le Gigolo* 1960 (d,sc); *Rififi à Tokyo* 1963 (d,sc); *Symphonie pour un massacre* 1963 (d,sc); *Par un beau matin d'été* 1964 (d,sc); *That Man George!* 1966 (d,sc); *Avec la peau des autres* 1967 (d,sc); *La Piscine* 1969 (d,sc,dial); *Borsalino* 1970 (d,sc); *Doucement les basses!* 1971 (d); *Un peu de soleil dans l'eau froide* 1971 (d); *Un Homme est mort* 1973 (d,sc); *Borsalino and Co.* 1974 (d,sc); *Flic Story* 1975 (d); *Le Gang* 1977 (d,sc); *Un Papillon sur l'épaule* 1978 (d,sc); *Trois Hommes à abattre* 1980 (d,sc); *Le Marginal* 1983 (d,sc); *On ne meurt que 2 Fois* 1985 (d,sc); *Maladie d'amour* 1987 (d); *Le Solitaire* 1987 (d,sc); *Les Bois noirs* 1989 (d,sc); *Netchaiev est de retour* 1991 (d).

Derek, John • Actor; also producer, director, director of photography, screenwriter. • born Derek Harris, Hollywood, CA, August 12, 1926. Handsome young lead who turned from acting to still photography and then to directing. The son of writer-director Lawson Harris and actress Dolores Johnson, Derek was formerly married to actresses Ursula Andress and Linda Evans and is currently wed to Bo Derek. • *I'll Be Seeing You* 1944 (a); *Since You Went Away* 1944 (a); *A Double Life* 1947 (a); *All the King's Men* 1949 (a); *Knock on any Door* 1949 (a); *Rogues of Sherwood Forest* 1950 (a); *The Family Secret* 1951 (a); *The Mask of the Avenger 1951 (a);* *Saturday's Hero* (a); *Scandal Sheet* 1952 (a); *Thunderbirds* 1952 (a); *Ambush at Tomahawk Gap* 1953 (a); *The Last Posse* 1953 (a); *Mission Over Korea* 1953 (a); *Prince of Pirates* 1953 (a); *Sea of Lost Ships* 1953 (a); *The Adventures of Hajji Baba* 1954 (a); *The Outcast* 1954 (a); *Run For Cover* 1954 (a); *An Annapolis Story* 1955 (a); *Prince of Players* 1955 (a); *The Leather Saint* 1956 (a); *The Ten Commandments* 1956 (a); *Fury at Showdown* 1957 (a); *High Hell* 1957 (a); *Omar Khayyam* 1957 (a); *I Battellieri del Volga* 1959 (a); *Exodus* 1960 (a); *Nightmare in the Sun* 1965 (a,p); *Once Before I Die* 1965 (a,d,p); *A Boy...a Girl* 1969 (d,sc,ph); *Childish Things* 1969 (d,ph); *Fantasies* 1973 (d,sc,ph); *Tarzan, The Ape Man* 1981 (d,ph); *Bolero* 1984 (d,sc,ph,uncred.ed); *Ghosts Can't Do It* 1990 (d,p,sc,ph).

Deren, Maya • *aka* Eleanora Deren • Filmmaker, theorist • Born Eleanora Derenkowsky, Kiev, Ukraine, April 29, 1917; died October 13, 1961. *Educ.* Syracuse University, NY (journalism, political science); NYU; Smith College, Northampton, MA (English). Leading American avant-garde director sometimes referred to as the "mother of the underground film." In the US from the mid-1920s, Deren turned from poetry to film when she met Czech documentarist Alexander Hammid, who in 1942 became her second husband. Her first film, the surrealistic *Meshes of the Afternoon* (1943, 18 minutes) was co-directed with Hammid. In her next work, *At Land* (1944, 15 minutes), Deren brought to the fore her concern with the manipulation of space and time, a recurrent preoccupation which resurfaced in *Ritual in Transfigured Time* (1946, 16 minutes), a formally daring exploration of dance and ritual.

Deren also lectured extensively and helped establish New York's "underground" film circuit, setting up avant-garde screening venues which gave birth to independent distribution houses such as Amos Vogel's Cinema 16. An insightful and articulate writer, she authored *The Divine Horseman: the Living God of Haiti* (1953), the result of a trip to Haiti which was to be the basis of a film, and the seminal *An Anagram of Ideas on Art, Form and Film* (1946). • *Meshes of the Afternoon* 1943 (a,d,p,sc,ph,ed); *At Land* 1944 (a,d,p,sc,ed); *A Study in Choreography For Camera* 1945 (d,p,sc,ph,ed); *Ritual in Transfigured Time* 1946 (a,d,p,sc,ed); *Meditation on Violence* 1948 (d,p,sc,ph,ed,m,sound); *The Very Eye of Night* 1958 (ph,ed,d,p); *Witch's Cradle* 1961 (d,p,sc,ph,ed); *Out-Takes From Maya Deren's Study in choreography For Camera* 1975 (d,p,sc,ph).

Dern, Bruce • Actor • Born Winnetka, IL, June 4, 1936. *Educ.* University of Pennsylvania, Philadelphia; Actors Studio. Character player since the 1960s who has oten been typecast in psychotic roles. dern has occasionally proved himself an engaging lead, particularly in Douglas Trumbull's poignant science-fiction fable, *Silent Running* (1971). formerly married to actress Diane Ladd and father of actress Laura Dern. • *Wild River* 1960; *Hush...Hush, Sweet Charlotte* 1964; *Marnie* 1964; *The Wild Angels* 1966; *The St. Valentine's Day Massacre* 1967; *The Trip* 1967; *The War Wagon* 1967; *Waterhole Number 3* 1967; *Hang 'Em High* 1968; *Psych-Out* 1968; *Will Penny* 1968; *Castle Keep* 1969; *Number One* 1969; *Support Your Local Sheriff* 1969; *They Shoot Horses, Don't They?* 1969; *Bloody Mama* 1970; *Cycle Savages* 1970; *Rebel Rousers* 1970; *The Cowboys* 1971; *Drive, He Said* 1971; *The Incredible Two-Headed Transplant* 1971; *Silent Running* 1971; *The King of Marvin Gardens* 1972; *Thumb Tripping* 1972; *The Laughing Policeman* 1973; *The Great Gatsby* 1974; *Posse* 1975; *Smile* 1975; *Family Plot* 1976; *Folies bourgeoises* 1976; *Won Ton Ton, the Dog Who Saved Hollywood* 1976; *Black Sunday* 1977; *Coming Home* 1977 **(AANBSA)**; *The Driver* 1978; *Middle Age Crazy* 1980; *Harry Tracy* 1981; *Tattoo* 1981; *That Championship Season* 1982; *On the Edge* 1985; *The Big Town* 1987; *1969* 1988; *World Gone Wild* 1988; *The Burbs* 1989; *After Dark, My Sweet* 1990.

Dern, Laura • Actress • Born Santa Monica, CA, 1966. *Educ.* Lee Strasberg Institute; RADA, London. Young lead whose innocent good looks have been well used in films exploring the darker side of small-town life (*Smooth Talk* 1985, *Blue Velvet* 1986). The daughter of actors Bruce Dern and Diane Ladd, Dern demonstrated her wider range with a brassy performance as Lula, Nicolas Cage's uninhibited traveling companion, in David Lynch's *Wild at Heart* (1990). • *Foxes* 1980; *Ladies and Gentlemen, the Fabulous Stains* 1982; *Teachers* 1984; *Mask* 1985; *Smooth Talk* 1985; *Blue Velvet* 1986; *Haunted Summer* 1988; *Fat Man and Little Boy* 1989; *Wild at Heart* 1990.

Deschanel, Caleb • Director of photography; also director. • Born Philadelphia, PA, September 21, 1941. *Educ.* Johns Hopkins University, Baltimore, MD. Superior color cinematographer whose directorial career, beginning in 1982 with the flawed but interesting *The Escape Artist*, has been disappointing. Wife Mary Jo is an actress. • *A Woman Under the Influence* 1974 (ph); *Being There* 1979 (ph); *The Black Stallion* 1979 (ph); *More American Graffiti* 1979 (ph); *The Escape Artist* 1982 (d); *Let's Spend the Night Together* 1982 (ph); *The Black Stallion Returns* 1983 (add.ph); *The Right Stuff* 1983 (ph) **(AANBPH)**; *The Natural* 1984 (ph) **(AANBPH)**; *The Slugger's Wife* 1985 (ph); *50 Years of Action!* 1986 (ph); *Crusoe* 1988 (d).

Deutch, Howard • Director • Born New York, NY. *Educ.* Ohio State University, Columbus. Former music video director who has competently helmed three features for producer-screenwriter John Hughes. • *Pretty in Pink* 1986; *Some Kind of Wonderful* 1987; *The Great Outdoors* 1988.

Deville, Michel • Director; also screenwriter, producer. • Born Boulogne-sur-Seine, France, April 13, 1931. French director who eschewed the stylistic advances of the New Wave in favor of traditional technical proficiency and lightweight, commercial subject matter. Exceptions to his mostly routine output include the taut political thriller *Dossier 51* (1978) and the mildly surreal *La Lectrice* (1988), starring Miou-Miou. • *Une Belle dans le Canon* 1958 (d); *Ce Soir ou jamais* 1960 (d,p,sc); *Adorable Menteuse* 1961 (d,p,sc); *A cause à cause d'une femme* 1962 (d,p,sc); *L'Appartement des filles* 1963 (d,sc); *Lucky Jo* 1964 (d,story); *On a volé la Joconde* 1965 (d,story); *Martin Soldat* (d,story); *Tendres Requins* 1967 (d); *Benjamin, ou les mémoires d'un puceau* 1968 (d,story); *Bye Bye Barbara* 1969 (d,sc); *L'Ours et la poupée* 1970 (d,sc); *Raphaël, ou le Débauché* 1971 (d); *La Femme en Bleu* 1973 (d,sc); *Le Mouton Enragé* 1974 (d); *L'Apprenti salaud* 1977 (d,sc,dial); *Le dossier 51/Dossier 51* 1978 (d,sc,dial); *Le Voyage en Douce* 1979 (d,sc); *Eaux Profondes* 1981 (d,sc); *La Petite Bande* 1983 (d,sc); *Péril en la Demeure* 1984 (d,sc,adapt); *Le Paltoquet* 1986 (d,exec.p,sc); *La Lectrice* 1988 (d,p,sc,adapt,dial); *Nuit d'été en ville* 1990 (d).

Dewaere, Patrick • Actor • Born Sain-Brieuc, France, January 26, 1947; died July 16, 1982. Short-lived, popular leading man with a flair for comedy, who made an arresting film debut as Gérard Depardieu's temporarily impotent sidekick in Bertrand Blier's *Going Places* (1974). Dewaere was also memorable in Jean-Jacques Annaud's darkly comic *Hot Head* (1979) and Blier's *Beau Père* (1981). Dewaere appeared in over 20 films before he died in 1982, allegedly after shooting himself in the head. • *Lily Aime-Moi* 1974; *Les Valseuses/Going Places* 1974; *Adieu Poulet* 1975; *Catherine et Cie/Catherine & Co.* 1975; *La Marche Triomphale* 1975; *La meilleure façon de marcher* 1975; *F comme Fairbanks* 1976; *Le Juge Fayard dit le sheriff* 1977; *Préparez vos mouchoirs/Get Out Your Handkerchiefs* 1977; *La Stanza del Vescovo* 1977; *La Clé sur la Porte* 1978; *Coup de Tête/Hot Head* 1979; *Le Grand embouteillage/Traffic Jam* 1979; *Paco the Infallible* 1979; *Série noire* 1979; *The Best Way* 1980; *Un Mauvais Fils* 1980; *Plein Sud/Heat of Desire* 1980; *Beau Pére* 1981; *Psy* 1981; *Hôtel des Amériques* 1982; *Paradis pour tous* 1982.

Dewhurst, Colleen • Actress • Born Montreal, Quebec, Canada, June 3, 1926. *Educ.* Downer College For Young Ladies, Milwaukee, WI; AADA, New York. Award-winning stage and TV performer, in relatively few films. Twice married to, and divorced from, actor George C. Scott. • *The Nun's Story* 1959; *Man on a String* 1960; *A Fine Madness* 1966; *The Cowboys* 1971; *The Last Run* 1971; *McQ* 1974; *Annie Hall* 1977; *Ice Castles* 1978; *Arthur Miller on Home Ground* 1979; *When a Stranger Calls* 1979; *Final Assignment* 1980; *Tribute* 1980; *The Dead Zone* 1983; *The Good Fight: The Abraham Lincoln Brigade in the Spanish Civil War* 1984; *The Boy Who Could Fly* 1986; *Termini Station* 1989.

Di Palma, Carlo • Director of photography; also director. • Born Rome, April 17, 1925. First gained prominence for his striking color photography on Michelangelo Antonioni's *Red Desert* (1964) and *Blow-Up* (1966). Di Palma's other notable redits include Elio Petri's debut feature *The Assissin* (1961) and, more recently, several films directed by Woody Allen. He made his directing debut with *Teresa la ladra* (1973), photographed by his nephew, Dario Di Palma (*The Clowns* 1970, *The Seduction of Mimi* 1972). • *Ivan* 1954 (ph); *La Lunga Notte del '43* 1960 (ph); *L'Assassino/The Assassin/The Lady Killer of Rome* 1961 (ph); *Omicron* 1963 (ph); *Deserto Rosso/Red Desert* 1964 (ph); *Liola* 1964 (ph); *I Tre Volti/Three Faces of a Woman* 1965 (ph); *Blow-up* 1966 (ph); *La Cintura di Castita* 1967 (ph); *The Appointment* 1969 (ph); *Drama della Gelosia* 1970 (ph); *Nini Tirabuscle* 1970 (ph); *Gli Ordini Sono Ordini* 1971 (ph); *La Pacifista* 1971 (ph); *Teresa la Ladra* 1973 (ph); *Qui comincia l'avventura* 1976 (ph); *Amo Non Amo* 1979 (ph); *La Tragedia di un Uomo Ridiculo/The Tragedy of a Ridiculous Man* 1981 (ph); *Identificazione di una donna/Identification of a woman* 1982 (ph); *The Black Stallion Returns* 1983 (ph); *Gabriela* 1983 (ph); *Hannah and Her Sisters* 1986 (ph); *Off Beat* 1986 (ph); *Radio Days* 1987 (ph); *The Secret of My Success* 1987 (ph); *September* 1987 (ph); *Alice* 1990 (ph).

Di Venanzo, Gianni • Director of photography • Born Teramo, Italy, December 18, 1920; died 1966. One of Italy's leading cinematographers, Di Venanzo shot films for Antonioni, Fellini, and Francesco Rossi. • *Achtung Banditi!* 1951 (ph); *Amore in Citta/Love in the City* 1953 (ph—"Un Agenzia Matrimoniale"); *Cronache di Poveri Amanti* 1954 (ph); *Le Amichi/The Girlfriends* 1955 (ph); *Il Grido/The Outcry* 1957 (ph); *La Sfida* 1957 (ph); *Suor Letizia* 1957 (ph); *I Solti ignoti/Big Deal on Madonna Street* 1958 (ph); *La Loi c'est la loi* 1958 (ph); *Crimen* 1960 (ph); *I Delfini* 1960 (ph); *La Notte/The Night* 1961 (ph); *L'Eclisse/The Eclipse* 1962 (ph); *Eva* 1962 (ph); *Salvatore Giuliano* 1962 (ph); *Le Mani sulla Citta/Hands Over the City* 1963 (ph); *Otto e Mezzo/8 1/2* 1963 (ph); *La Ragazza di Bube* 1963 (ph); *Gli indiferrenti/A Time of Indifference* 1964 (ph); *La Decima Vittima/The Tenth Victim* 1965 (ph); *Giuletta degli Spiriti/Juliet of the Spirits* 1965 (ph); *Il Momento della Verita* 1965 (ph); *The Honey Pot* 1967 (ph).

Diamond, I.A.L. • *aka* Isadore A. L. Diamond, Izzy Diamond • Screenwriter; also producer. • Born Itek Dommnici, Ungeny, Rumania, June 27, 1920; died April 21, 1988, Beverly Hills, CA. Immigrated to the US (Brooklyn) at age 9, adding the decorative initials to his name some time later. Diamond moved to Hollywood in 1941, working on mostly unexceptional films before teaming up with Billy Wilder for *Love in the Afternoon* (1957). He became Wilder's co-writer of choice (taking the place of Charles Brackett), with the team turning out consistently incisive, outstanding comedies through the director's most recent film, *Buddy, Buddy* (1981). • *Murder in the Blue Room* 1944 (sc); *Never Say Goodbye* 1946 (sc); *Two Guys From Milwaukee* 1946 (sc,story); *Always Together* 1947 (dial); *Romance on the High Seas* 1948 (dial); *Two Guys From Texas* 1948 (sc); *The Girl From Jones Beach* 1949 (sc); *It's a Great Feeling* 1949 (story); *Let's Make It Legal* 1951 (sc); *Love Nest* 1951 (sc); *Monkey Business* 1952 (sc); *Something For the Birds* 1952 (sc); *That Certain Feeling* 1956 (sc); *Love in the Afternoon* 1957 (sc); *Merry Andrew* 1958 (sc); *Some Like It Hot* 1959 (sc) **(AANBSC)**; *The Apartment* 1960 (sc) **(AABSC)**; *One, Two, Three* 1961 (sc); *Irma la Douce* 1963 (sc); *Kiss Me, Stupid* 1964 (sc); *The Fortune Cookie* 1966 (sc) **(AANBSC)**; *Cactus Flower* 1969 (sc); *The Private Life of Sherlock Holmes* 1970 (sc); *Avanti!* 1972 (sc); *The Front Page* 1974 (sc); *Fedora* 1978 (sc, assoc.p); *Buddy, Buddy* 1981 (sc).

Dickinson, Angie • Actress • Born Angeline Brown, Kulm, ND, September 30, 1931. *Educ.* Heart College; Glendale College, CA. Wholesome former beauty queen who began appearing in films in the mid-1950s. Most of Dickinson's movies used her for ornamental purposes, though she displayed talent when given the chance (*Rio Bravo* 1959, *The Chase* 1966, *Dressed to Kill* 1980). She has often starred on TV, most notably as "Police Woman" (1975-78). Divorced from composer Burt Bacharach. • *Lucky Me* 1954; *Hidden Guns* 1955; *Man Without a Gun* 1955; *The Return of Jack Slade* 1955; *The Black Whip* 1956; *Gun the Man Down* 1956; *Tension at Table Rock* 1956; *Calypso Joe* 1957; *China Gate* 1957; *I Married a Woman* 1957; *Shoot-Out at Medicine Band* 1957; *Cry Terror!* 1958; *Rio Bravo* 1959; *The Bramble Bush* 1960; *Ocean's Eleven* 1960; *A Fever in the Blood* 1961; *Jessica* 1961; *The Sins of Rachel Cade* 1961; *Rome Adventure* 1962; *Captain Newman, M.D.* 1964; *The Killers* 1964; *The Art of Love* 1965; *Cast a Giant Shadow* 1966; *The Chase* 1966; *The Poppy Is Also a Flower* 1966; *The Last Challenge* 1967; *Point Blank* 1967; *Sam Whiskey* 1969; *Some Kind of a Nut* 1969; *Young Billy Young* 1969; *Pretty Maids All in a Row* 1971; *The Resurrection of Zachary Wheeler* 1971; *Un Homme est mort* 1973; *Big Bad Mama* 1974; *L'Homme en colore* 1979; *Jack London's Klondike Fever* 1979; *Dressed to Kill* 1980; *Charlie Chan and the Curse of the Dragon Queen* 1981; *Death Hunt* 1981; *Big Bad Mama II* 1988.

Dickson, William Kennedy Laurie • Inventor; also director. • Born Minihic-sur-Ranse, France, 1860; died 1935, Twickenham, Middlesex, England. Began working for Thomas Edison in 1883, and between 1887 and 1891 invented the Kinetograph camera and Kinetoscope viewer, both key developments in motion picture technology. Dickson produced and directed hundreds of the short films which supplied Edison's Kinetoscope parlors, and designed the glass-built "Black Maria," considered the world's first movie studio.

In 1895 Dickson co-founded the KMCD syndicate (later the American Mutoscope Company and finally the American Biograph Company). Sidestepping Edison's patents on his own inventions, Dickson created the Mutograph camera and Mutoscope viewer, which provided the only serious competition to the Edison Company in the early days of peepshow cinema.

Dickson and his group were also responsible for the camera and projector system known as the Biograph which, due to its larger film, produced a superior image to the Edison-owned Vitascope, but nonetheless failed to become the industry standard. Dickson returned to England in 1897.

Diegues, Carlos • Director; also screenwriter, producer. • Born Maceio, Alagoas, Brazil, 1940. Former poet, journalist and film critic who turned to directing in the early days of the Cinema Nôvo movement. All of Diegue's films have focused on Brazilian life, whether indicating early slave-traders (*Ganga Zumba* 1963) or examining the contemporary hinterland through the eyes of traveling side-show entertainers (*Bye Bye Brazil* 1980). At his best, as in *Quilombo* (1984), Diegues successfully blends social and historical concerns with an engaging feel for character and plot. • *Cinco vezes favela* 1961 (d,sc,story); *Ganga Zumba* 1963 (d,p,sc,adapt); *Deus e o Diabo na Terra do Sol/Black God, White Devil* 1964 (ad); *A Grande Cidade* 1966 (d,p,sc,story); *Terra em Transe/Land in Anguish* 1967 (assoc.p); *Adoravel* *trapalhao* 1968 (story); *Capitu* 1968 (assoc.p); *Os Herdeiros/The Inheritors* 1969 (d,p,sc,story,adapt); *Pobre principe encantado* 1969 (sc); *Quando o carnaval chegar* 1972 (assoc.p,d,sc,story); *Les Soleils de Lîle de Paques* 1972 (a); *Joanna Francesca* 1973 (d,sc,story); *A Estrela sobe* 1974 (sc); *Xica da Silva/Xica* 1975 (d,sc,story); *Na Boca de Mundo* 1978 (from book); *A Summer Rain* 1979 (d,sc); *Bye Bye Brazil* 1980 (d,sc); *Joana Francesa* 1981 (d,sc); *Quilombo* 1984 (d,sc); *Um Trem para as estrelas/Subway to the Stars* 1987 (d,sc); *Dede Mamata* 1988 (p); *Dias Melhores Virao* 1990 (d,p,sc).

Dieterle, William • Director; also actor, producer. • Born Wilhelm Dieterle, Ludwigshafen, Rheinpfalz, Germany, July 15, 1893; died December 9, 1972. Joined Max Reinhardt's theater company in Berlin after WWI and began appearing in, and directing, silent films in the early 1920s. Dieterle starred in many of his own features, including 1923's *Der Mensch am Wege*, opposite Marlene Dietrich in her debut leading role.

Dieterle moved to Hollywood in 1930, working for Warner Bros. for a decade and proving himself particularly adept at biopics (*The Story of Louis Pasteur* 1936, *The Life of Emile Zola* 1937, *Juarez* 1939). From 1942 to 1957 he worked for numerous studios before briefly returning to Europe to make several films. Dieterle's wife, Charlotte Hagenbruch, scripted several of his early German productions. • *Der Mensch Am Wege* 1923 (a,d); *Faust* 1926 (a); *Qualen der Nacht* 1926 (a); *Das Geheimnis des Abbe X* 1927 (a,d,sc,story); *Geschlect in Fesseln* 1928 (a,d); *Die Heilige und Ihr Narr* 1928 (a,d); *Frühlingsrauschen* 1929 (a,d); *Ich Lebe Für Dich* 1929 (a,d); *Ludwig der Zweite, Koenig von Bayern* 1929 (a,d); *Das Schweigen im Walde* 1929 (a,d); *Eine Stunde Glück* 1929 (a,d); *Kismet* 1930 (d); *Der Tans Geht Weiter* 1930 (a,d); *Those Who Dance* 1930 (d); *The Way of All Men* 1930 (d); *Her Majesty, Love* 1931 (d); *The Last Flight* 1931 (d); *The Crash* 1932 (d); *Jewel Robbery* 1932 (d); *Lawyer Man* 1932 (d); *Man Wanted* 1932 (d); *Scarlet Dawn* 1932 (d); *Six Hours to Live* 1932 (d); *Adorable* 1933 (d); *The Devil's in Love* 1933 (d); *Female* 1933 (d); *From Headquarters* 1933 (d); *Grand Slam* 1933 (d); *Fashions of 1934* 1934 (d); *The Firebird* 1934 (d); *Fog Over Frisco* 1934 (d); *Madame Du Barry* 1934 (d); *Dr. Socrates* 1935 (d); *A Midsummer Night's Dream* 1935 (d); *The Secret Bride* 1935 (d); *Satan Met a Lady* 1936 (d); *The Story of Louis Pasteur* 1936 (d); *The White Angel* 1936 (d); *Another Dawn* 1937 (d); *The Great O'Malley* 1937 (d); *The Life of Emile Zola* 1937 (d) **(AANBD)**; *Blockade* 1938 (d); *The Hunchback of Notre Dame* 1939 (d); *Juarez* 1939 (d); *A Dispatch From Reuters* 1940 (d); *Dr. Ehrlich's Magic Bullet* 1940 (d); *The Devil and Daniel Webster* 1941 (d,p); *Syncopation* 1942 (d,p); *Tennessee Johnson* 1942 (d); *I'll Be Seeing You* 1944 (d); *Kismet* 1944 (d); *Love Letters* 1945 (d); *This Love of Ours* 1945 (d); *The Searching Wind* 1946 (d); *The Accused* 1948 (d); *Portrait of Jennie* 1948 (d); *Paid in Full* 1949 (d); *Rope of Sand* 1949 (d); *Dark City* 1950 (d); *Vulcano* 1950 (d,p); *Peking Express* 1951 (d); *Red Mountain* 1951 (d); *September Affair* 1951 (d); *Boots Malone* 1952 (d); *The Turning Point* 1952 (d); *Salome* 1953 (d); *Elephant Walk* 1954 (d); *Magic Fire* 1956 (d,p); *Omar Khayyam* 1957 (d); *Il Vindicatore* 1959 (a,d); *Die Fastnachtsbeichte* 1960 (d); *Herrin der Welt* 1960 (d); *Quick, Let's Get Married* 1964 (d).

Dietrich, Marlene • *aka* Maria Magdalena Von Losch • Actress; also singer. • Born Maria Magdalene Dietrich, Berlin, December 27, 1901. *Educ.* Hochschüle fur Musik, Berlin (violin); Max Reinhardt's Deutsche Theaterschüle. There are only a handful of actors in the history of film whose personalities far extend the film frame, and Marlene Dietrich is one of these. More than just an actress, Dietrich has become one of the most recognizable figures of the 20th century—a Hollywood star who never imagined her profession to be more important than it was.

After studying acting under the renowned Max Reinhardt, Dietrich's film career began in 1923 with *The Little Napoleon*. She made over a dozen German films, including *Tragödie der Liebe* (1923), Alexander Korda's *A Modern Du Barry* and *Madame Wants No Children* (both 1926), and Maurice Tourneur's *The Ship of Lost Men* (1929), before being discovered by American director Josef von Sternberg, who was in Germany to cast the female lead in *The Blue Angel* (1930). The character of Lola Lola, a dance-hall girl who could drive a professor to the most extreme humiliations in the name of love, was perfect for Dietrich. With her sultry version of "Falling in Love Again," the entire world fell in love, for the first time, with Marlene Dietrich.

Over the next five years at Paramount Pictures, Dietrich and von Sternberg sustained one of film's greatest creative collaborations through six films (*Morocco* 1930, *Dishonored* 1931, *Shanghai Express* 1932, *Blonde Venus* 1932, *The Scarlet Empress* 1934 and *The Devil is a Woman* 1935), each one considerably more abstract and less commercially successful than *The Blue Angel*. After the failure of *The Devil Is a Woman*, Dietrich and von Sternberg parted ways.

In the ensuing decades Dietrich would act for some of the greatest directors—Ernst Lubitsch, René Clair, Raoul Walsh, Billy Wilder, Alfred Hitchcock, Fritz Lang and Orson Welles—and co-star with some of the greatest actors—Charles Boyer, James Stewart, John Wayne, Edward G. Robinson, Jean Gabin, Ray Milland, Charles Laughton, Spencer Tracy and Burt Lancaster. During the early 1940s, her on-screen accomplishments were often overshadowed by her contributions to the war effort. After turning down a lucrative offer from Hitler to make films for her Nazi homeland, the anti-Fascist Dietrich retaliated by raising the spirits of American servicemen in numerous USO appearances.

In the early 1960s Dietrich decided to bid farewell to the screen, deciding that her advancing years would be less obvious as a concert singer than as an actress. Her last film appearance, in *Just a Gigolo* (1979) opposite David Bowie, was only a brief one. More recently, she has become increasingly and obsessively reclusive, refusing to be photographed. Though she was the subject of the 1984 documentary *Marlene*, which she commissioned Maximillian Schell to direct, Dietrich refused to appear on camera. DC • *Der Kleine Napoleon* 1923; *Der Mensch Am Wege* 1923; *Tragödie der Liebe* 1923; *Der Sprung ins Leben* 1924; *Die Freudlose gasse/The Joyless Street* 1925; *Eine DuBarry von heute/A Modern Du Barry* 1926; *Der Juxbaron* 1926; *Kopf Hoch, Charly!* 1926; *Madame wönscht keine Kinder/Madame Wants No Children* 1926; *Manon Lescaut* 1926; *Cafe Electric* 1927; *Sein Grösster Bluff* 1927; *Ich küsse ihre Hand, Madame* 1928; *Prinzessin Olala* 1928; *Die Frau Nach der Man Sich Sehnt* 1929; *Gefahren der Brautzeit* 1929; *Das Schiff der verlorenen Menschen/The Ship of Lost Men* 1929; *Der Blaue Engel/The Blue Angel* 1930 (a,song); *Morocco* 1930 **(AANBA)**; *Dishonored* 1931; *Blonde Venus* 1932 (a,song); *Shanghai Express* 1932; *Song of Songs* 1933; *The Scarlet Empress* 1934; *The Devil Is a Woman* 1935; *Desire* 1936 (a,song); *The Garden of Allah* 1936; *I Loved a Soldier* 1936; *Angel* 1937; *Knight Without Armour* 1937; *Destry Rides Again* 1939; *Seven Sinners* 1940; *The Flame of New Orleans* 1941; *Manpower* 1941; *The Lady Is Willing* 1942; *Pittsburgh* 1942; *The Spoilers* 1942; *Follow the Boys* 1944; *Kismet* 1944; *Martin Roumagnac* 1946; *Golden Earrings* 1947; *A Foreign Affair* 1948; *Jigsaw* 1949; *Stage Fright* 1950; *No Highway* 1951; *Rancho Notorious* 1952; *Around the World in 80 Days* 1956; *The Monte Carlo Story* 1957; *Witness For the Prosecution* 1957; *Touch of Evil* 1958; *Judgment at Nuremberg* 1961; *The Black Fox* 1962; *Paris When It Sizzles* 1963; *La Jeune Fille assassinée* 1974 (song); *Schöner Gigolo—Armer Gigolo/Just a Gigolo* 1979 (a,song); *Marlene* 1984; *Going Hollywood: The War Years* 1988 (archival footage); *Entertaining the Troops* 1989 (archival footage).

Dilley, Leslie • Production designer • Born Rhondda, Mid Glamorgan, Wales. *Educ.* Willesden Technical College, England. Innovative, multi award-winning art director who began his career on TV's "The Saint." • *The Last Remake of Beau Geste* 1977 (art d); *Star Wars* 1977 (art d) **(AABAD)**; *Superman* 1978 (art d); *Alien* 1979 (art d); *The Empire Strikes Back* 1980 (art d) **(AANBAD)**; *An American Werewolf in London* 1981 (art d); *Raiders of the Lost Ark* 1981 (art d) **(AABAD)**; *Eureka* 1983 (art d); *Never Say Never Again* 1983 (art d); *Bad Medicine* 1985 (pd); *Legend* 1985 (asst.art d); *Invaders From Mars* 1986 (pd); *Allan Quatermain and the Lost City of Gold* 1987 (pd—Los Angeles); *Stars and Bars* 1988 (pd); *The Abyss* 1989 (pd) **(AANBAD)**; *William Peter Blatty's The Exorcist III* 1990 (pd); *Guilty By Suspicion* 1991 (pd); *What About Bob?* 1991 (pd).

Dillman, Bradford • Actor • Born San Francisco, CA, April 14, 1930. *Educ.* Yale. Contemplative lead and supporting player who made his name on Broaday in the mid-1950s with *Long Day's Journey Into Night* and gained international attention with *Compulsion* (1959), sharing best actor honors at Cannes with co-stars Dean Stockwell and Orson Welles. Dillman has worked extensively on TV. • *A Certain Smile* 1958; *In Love and War* 1958; *Compulsion* 1959; *Crack in the Mirror* 1960; *Circle of Deception* 1961; *Francis of Assisi* 1961; *Sanctuary* 1961; *Sergeant Ryker* 1963; *A Rage to Live* 1965; *The Plainsman* 1966; *The Helicopter Spies* 1967; *Jigsaw* 1968; *The Bridge at Remagen* 1969; *Brother John* 1970; *The Mephisto Waltz* 1970; *Suppose They Gave a War and Nobody Came?* 1970; *Escape From the Planet of the Apes* 1971; *The Resurrection of Zachary Wheeler* 1971; *The Iceman Cometh* 1973; *The Way We Were* 1973; *99 and 44/100% Dead* 1974; *Chosen Survivors* 1974; *Gold* 1974; *Bug* 1975; *The Enforcer* 1976; *Mastermind* 1976; *The Amsterdam Kill* 1977; *The Lincoln Conspiracy* 1977; *Piranha* 1978; *The Swarm* 1978; *Guyana: Cult of the Damned* 1979; *Love and Bullets* 1979; *Sudden Impact* 1983; *El Tesoro del Amazones* 1985; *Hot Pursuit* 1987; *Man Outside* 1987; *Heroes Stand Alone* 1989; *Lords of the Deep* 1989.

Dillon, Kevin • Actor • Born Mamaroneck, NY, 1965. Younger brother of actor Matt Dillon. • *Heaven Help Us* 1985; *Platoon* 1986; *Dear America* 1987; *The Blob* 1988; *Remote Control* 1988; *The Rescue* 1988; *War Party* 1988; *Immediate Family* 1989; *The Doors* 1991.

Dillon, Matt • Actor • Born New Rochelle, NY, February 18, 1964. Moody teenage lead of several films of the 1980s, including Francis Ford Coppola's cult hit *Rumble Fish* (1983). Dillon gave an impressively mature performance as an outlaw heroin addict in Gus Van Sant's acclaimed *Drugstore Cowboy* (1989). • *Over the Edge* 1979; *Little Darlings* 1980; *My Bodyguard* 1980; *Liar's Moon* 1982; *Tex* 1982; *The Outsiders* 1983; *Rumble Fish* 1983; *The Flamingo Kid* 1984; *Rebel* 1985; *Target* 1985; *Native Son* 1986; *The Big Town* 1987; *Dear America* 1987; *Kansas* 1988; *Bloodhounds of Broadway* 1989; *Drugstore Cowboy* 1989; *A Kiss Before Dying* 1991.

Dillon, Melinda • Actress • Born Hope, AZ, October 13, 1939. *Educ.* Goodman Theater School of Drama, Chicago. Blonde leading lady who made her Broadway debut as Honey in the original Broadway production of *Who's Afraid of Virginia Woolf?* in 1962. Dillon's feature film credits include *Bound for Glory* (1976), *Close Encounters of the Third Kind* (1977), as one of the "touched" earthlings, and *Absence of Malice* (1981). • *The April Fools* 1969; *Bound For Glory* 1976; *Close Encounters of the Third Kind* 1977 **(AANBSA)**; *Slap Shot* 1977; *F.I.S.T.* 1978; *Absence of Malice* 1981 **(AANBSA)**; *A Christmas Story* 1983; *Songwriter* 1984; *Harry and the Hendersons* 1987; *Spontaneous Combustion* 1989; *Staying Together* 1989; *Captain America* 1990.

Disney, Walt • Producer, animation director, executive. • Born Walter Elias Disney, Chicago, IL, December 5, 1901; died December 15, 1966, California. *Educ.* Kansas City Art Institute. World-renowned figure who began his career making animated commercials. An innovator and a perfectionist, Disney was responsible for the first cartoon to feature synchronized sound (1928's *Steamboat Willie*, starring Mickey Mouse) as well as the first American feature-length cartoon, *Snow White and the Seven Dwarfs* (1937), and went on to dominate American screen animation for over two decades with his superior craftsmanship, prolific output and memorable characters including Mickey and Minnie Mouse, Donald Duck and Goofy. • *The Gallopin' Gaucho* 1928 (d); *Plane Crazy* 1928 (d); *Steamboat Willie* 1928 (d); *The Barn Dance* 1929 (d); *The Barnyard Battle* 1929 (d); *The Cat's Away* 1929 (d); *The Haunted House* 1929 (d); *The Jazz Fool* 1929 (d); *Jungle Rhythm* 1929 (d); *The Karnival Kid* 1929 (d); *Mickey's Choo-Choo* 1929 (d); *The Opry House* 1929 (d); *The Plow Boy* 1929 (d); *The Skeleton Dance* 1929 (d); *El Terrible Toreador* 1929 (d); *Snow White and the Seven Dwarfs* 1937 (p) **(AAHON)**; *Fantasia* 1940 (p) **(AAHON)**; *Pinocchio* 1940 (p); *Dumbo* 1941 (p); *The Reluctant Dragon* 1941 (p); *Bambi* 1942 (p); *Saludos* 1942 (d,p); *Victory Through Air Power* 1943 (p); *The Three Caballeros* 1944 (p); *Make Mine Music* 1946 (p); *Song of the South* 1946 (p); *Fun and Fancy Free* 1947 (p); *Melody Time* 1948 (p); *So Dear to My Heart* 1948 (p); *Ichabod and Mr. Toad* 1949 (p); *Cinderella* 1950 (p); *Treasure Island* 1950 (p); *Alice in Wonderland* 1951 (p); *The Story of Robin Hood* 1952 (p); *The Living Desert* 1953 (p); *Peter Pan* 1953 (p); *Rob Roy, the Highland Rogue* 1953 (p); *The Sword and the Rose* 1953 (p); *20,000 Leagues Under the Sea* 1954 (p); *The Vanishing Prairie* 1954 (p); *The African Lion* 1955 (p); *Davy Crockett, King of the Wild Frontier* 1955 (exec.p); *Lady and the Tramp* 1955 (p); *The Littlest Outlaw* 1955 (p); *Davy Crockett and the River Pirates* 1956 (p); *The Great Locomotive Chase* 1956 (p); *Secrets of Life* 1956 (exec.p); *Westward Ho the Wagons!* 1956 (exec.p); *Johnny Tremain* 1957 (p); *Perri* 1957 (p); *The Light in the Forest* 1958 (p); *Old Yeller* 1958 (p); *Tonka* 1958 (p); *White Wilderness* 1958 (p); *Darby O'Gill and the Little People* 1959 (p); *The Shaggy Dog* 1959 (p); *Sleeping Beauty* 1959 (p); *Third Man on the Mountain* 1959 (p); *The Absent-Minded Professor* 1960 (p); *Kidnapped* 1960 (p); *Pollyanna* 1960 (p); *The Sign of Zorro* 1960 (p); *The Swiss Family Robinson* 1960 (p); *Ten Who Dared* 1960 (p); *Toby Tyler* 1960 (p); *Babes in Toyland* 1961 (p); *Greyfriars Bobby* 1961 (p); *Nikki - Wild Dog of the North* 1961 (p); *One Hundred and One Dalmatians* 1961 (p); *The Parent Trap* 1961 (p); *Almost Angels* 1962 (p); *Big Red* 1962 (p); *In Search of the Castaways* 1962 (p); *The Legend of Lobo* 1962 (p); *Moon Pilot* 1962 (p); *The Incredible Journey* 1963 (p); *Miracle of the Wild Stallions* 1963 (p); *Savage Sam* 1963 (p); *Son of Flubber* 1963 (p); *Summer Magic* 1963 (p); *The Sword in the Stone* 1963 (p); *The Three Lives of Thomasina* 1963 (p); *Emil and the Detectives* 1964 (p); *Mary Poppins* 1964 (p) **(AANBP)**; *The Misadventures of Merlin Jones* 1964 (p); *The Moon-Spinners* 1964 (p); *Those Calloways* 1964 (p); *A Tiger Walks* 1964 (p); *The Monkey's Uncle* 1965 (p); *That Darn Cat* 1965 (p); *The Fighting Prince of Donegal* 1966 (p); *Follow Me, Boys!* 1966 (p); *Lt. Robin Crusoe, U.S.N.* 1966 (p); *Run, Appaloosa, Run* 1966 (p); *The Ugly Dachsund* 1966 (p); *The Adventures of Bullwhip Griffin* 1967 (p); *The Gnome-Mobile* 1967 (p); *Happiest Millionaire* 1967 (p); *The Jungle Book* 1967 (exec.p); *Monkeys Go Home!* 1967 (p); *Blackbeard's Ghost* 1968 (p); *Hollywood on Trial* 1976 (a).

Divine • Actor • Born Harris Glenn Milstead, US, c. 1947; died March 7, 1989, Hollywood, CA. Much loved, oversized female impersonator who starred in six films directed by high-school friend John Waters. Divine achieved cult status with Waters's *Pink Flamingos* (1972). • *Mondo Trasho* 1970; *Multiple Maniacs* 1971; *Pink Flamingos* 1972; *Female Trouble* 1975 (a,song); *Underground and Emigrants* 1976; *Tally Brown, N.Y.* 1979; *The Alternative Miss World* 1980;

Polyester 1981; *Lust in the Dust* 1984; *Trouble in Mind* 1985; *Hairspray* 1988; *Out of the Dark* 1989.

Dmytryk, Edward • Director; also producer. • Born Grand Forks, British Columbia, Canada, September 4, 1908. *Educ.* California Institute of Technology, Pasadena. Former projectionist and editor at Paramount who directed his first film, *The Hawk*, in 1935. Concentrating on directing from 1939, Dmytryk made several socially and politically oriented films such as *Hitler's Children* (1943) and *Crossfire* (1947) before fellow director Sam Wood gave his name to the House Committee on Un-American Activities. One of the "Hollywood Ten" cited for contempt of Congress after refusing to testify, Dmytryk was fired by RKO and spent some time in England, where he made several movies.

Forced to return to the US in 1951 to renew his passport, he was arrested and sentenced to six months in jail. Dmytryk then appeared before HUAC a second time, recanting his earlier statements and himself "naming names," and was removed from the blacklist. He went on to direct several films, most notably *The Sniper* (1952) for producer Stanley Kramer, and worked on a number of prestigious, big-budget productions, most of which lacked the edge of his earlier, more modest works. In the 1980s, Dmytryk published a series of books on film, including *On Directing* (1984) and *Cinema: Concept and Practice.* • *Only Saps Work* 1930 (ed); *The Royal Family of Broadway* 1930 (ed); *College Rhythm* 1934 (ed); *The Hawk* 1935 (d); *Easy to Take* 1936 (ed); *Three Cheers For Love* 1936 (ed); *Too Many Parents* 1936 (ed); *Double or Nothing* 1937 (ed); *Hold Em' Navy* 1937 (ed); *Murder Goes to College* 1937 (ed); *Turn Off the Moon* 1937 (ed); *Bulldog Drummond's Peril* 1938 (ed); *Prison Farm* 1938 (ed); *Love Affair* 1939 (ed); *Some Like It Hot* 1939 (ed); *Television Spy* 1939 (d); *Zaza* 1939 (ed); *Emergency Squad* 1940 (d); *Golden Gloves* 1940 (d); *Her First Romance* 1940 (d); *Mystery Sea Raider* 1940 (d); *The Blonde From Singapore* 1941 (d); *Confessions of Boston Blackie* 1941 (d); *The Devil Commands* 1941 (d); *Secrets of the Lone Wolf* 1941 (d); *Sweetheart of the Campus* 1941 (d); *Under Age* 1941 (d); *Counter-Espionage* 1942 (d); *Seven Miles From Alcatraz* 1942 (d); *Behind the Rising Sun* 1943 (d); *Captive Wild Woman* 1943 (d); *The Falcon Strikes Back* 1943 (d); *Hitler's Children* 1943 (d); *Tender Comrade* 1943 (d); *Murder, My Sweet* 1944 (d); *Back to Bataan* 1945 (d); *Cornered* 1945 (d); *Till the End of Time* 1946 (d); *Crossfire* 1947 (d) **(AANBD)**; *So Well Remembered* 1947 (d); *Give Us This Day* 1949 (d); *Obsession* 1949 (d); *Eight Iron Men* 1952 (d); *Mutiny* 1952 (d); *The Sniper* 1952 (d); *The Juggler* 1953 (d); *Broken Lance* 1954 (d); *The Caine Mutiny* 1954 (d); *The End of the Affair* 1955 (d); *The Left Hand of God* 1955 (d); *Soldier of Fortune* 1955 (d); *The Mountain* 1956 (d,p); *Raintree County* 1957 (d); *The Young Lions* 1958 (d); *The Blue Angel* 1959 (d); *Warlock* 1959 (d,p); *The Reluctant Saint* 1962 (d,p); *Walk on the Wild Side* 1962 (d); *The Carpetbaggers* 1964 (d); *Where Love Has Gone* 1964 (d); *Mirage* 1965 (d); *Alvarez Kelly* 1966 (d); *Anzio* 1968 (d); *Shalako* 1968 (d); *Bluebeard* 1972 (d,sc,story); *The Human Factor* 1975 (d); *He Is My Brother* 1976 (d); *Hollywood on Trial* 1976 (a); *50 Years of Action!* 1986 (a).

Donaggio, Pino • Italian composer; also songwriter. • Versatile and highly prolific composer of the 1970s and 80s who has scored five films for director Brian De Palma. • *Don't Look Now* 1973 (m); *Carrie* 1976 (m,song); *Piranha* 1978 (m); *Home Movies* 1979 (m); *Senza Buccia* 1979 (m,song); *Tourist Trap* 1979 (m); *Augh! Augh!* 1980 (m); *The Black Cat* 1980 (m); *Desideria, La Vita Interiore* 1980 (m); *Dressed to Kill* 1980 (m); *The Howling* 1980 (m); *Blow Out* 1981 (m); *The Fan* 1981 (m); *Morte in Vaticano* 1982 (m); *Oltre la Porta* 1982 (m); *Target Eagle* 1982 (song); *Tex* 1982 (m); *Via degli Specchi* 1982 (m); *Baby, It's You* 1983 (song); *Hercules* 1983 (m); *Hercules II* 1983 (m); *Over the Brooklyn Bridge* 1983 (m,song); *Body Double* 1984 (m); *Déjà vu* 1984 (m); *Non ci resta che piangere* 1984 (m); *L'Attenzione* 1985 (m); *Interno Berlinese* 1985 (m); *Sotto il Vestito Niente* 1985 (m); *7 Chili in 7 Giorni* 1986 (m); *Il Caso Moro* 1986 (m); *Hotel Colonial* 1986 (m); *The Barbarians* 1987 (m); *Dancers* 1987 (m); *Going Bananas* 1987 (m); *Jenatsch* 1987 (m); *La Monaca di Monza* 1987 (m); *Scirocco* 1987 (m); *Appointment With Death* 1988 (m); *Catacombs* 1988 (m); *High-Frequency* 1988 (m); *Kansas* 1988 (m); *Phantom of Death* 1988 (m); *Sacrilege* 1988 (m); *Zelly and Me* 1988 (m); *Indio* 1989 (m); *Night Games* 1989 (m); *Meridian—Kiss of the Beast* 1990 (m); *Rito d'amore* 1990 (m); *Two Evil Eyes* 1990 (m).

Donaldson, Roger • Director; also producer. • Born Ballarat, Australia, November 15, 1945. Has worked in New Zealand—where he emigrated at age 19—Australia and the US, and is best for political thrillers like his feature debut *Sleeping Dogs* (1977) and 1987's *No Way Out.* • *Sleeping Dogs* 1977 (d,p); *Smash Palace* 1981 (d,p,sc); *The Bounty* 1984 (d); *Marie* 1985 (d); *No Way Out* 1987 (d); *Cocktail* 1988 (d); *Cadillac Man* 1990 (d,p).

Donat, Robert • Actor • Born Withington, Manchester, England, March 18, 1905; died 1958. Highly gifted, handsome British lead who worked in theater from 1921 and continued appearing on the stage throughout most of his film career. Donat gained instant, international fame for his role in Alexander Korda's *The Private Life of Henry VIII* (1933), moving Charles Laughton to dub him "the most graceful actor of our time." He made only one US film, *The Count of Monte Cristo* (1934); thereafter he shunned Hollywood, restricting his film roles to prestigious British productions which took advantage of his beautiful, highly expressive voice.

Donat gave superb performances in Hitchcock's *The 39 Steps* (1935), Vidor's *The Citadel* (1938) and Carol Reed's *The Young Mr. Pitt* (1942) and *The Winslow Boy* (1948). For a time his popularity and prestige exceeded that of Olivier and Leslie Howard; his career went into a decline, however, partly due to his depressive character and chronic asthma. (Illness sometimes lent his performances an ethereal edge, as in 1939's *Goodbye, Mr. Chips*, for which Donat beat Clark Gable—*Gone With the Wind*—out of an Oscar.) His death at the age of 53 was hastened by the illness.

Donat was married to actress Renee Asherson from 1953 until their separation in 1956. He was the uncle of actor Peter Donat. • *Men of Tomorrow* 1932 (a); *That Night in London* 1932 (a); *Cash* 1933 (a); *The Private Life of Henry VIII* 1933 (a); *The Count of Monte Cristo* 1934 (a); *The 39 Steps* 1935 (a); *The Ghost Goes West* 1935 (a); *Knight Without Armour* 1937 (a); *The Citadel* 1938 (a) **(AANBA)**; *Goodbye, Mr. Chips* 1939 (a) **(AABA)**; *The Young Mr. Pitt* 1942 (a); *The Adventures of Tartu* 1943 (a); *Vacation From Marriage* 1945 (a); *Captain Boycott* 1947 (a); *The Winslow Boy* 1948 (a); *The Cure For Love* 1949 (a,d,p,sc); *The Magic Box* 1951 (a); *Royal Heritage (short)* 1952 (a); *Lease of Life* 1954 (a); *The Stained Glass at Fairford (short)* 1956 (a); *The Inn of the Sixth Happiness* 1958 (a).

Donen, Stanley • Director, producer; also choreographer. • Born Columbia, SC, April 13, 1924. *Educ.* University of South Carolina, Columbia. Former Broadway dancer turned acclaimed director of musicals. Donen's first job as a choreographer was on the stage version of *Best Foot Forward* (1941), as Gene Kelly's assistant, and he made his film directing debut as Kelly's full-fledged collaborator with the energetic *On the Town* (1949). Donen became a star director of musicals in the 1950s with films such as *Singin' in the Rain* (1952, again with Kelly), *Seven Brides for Seven Brothers* (1954) and his spirited George Abbott collaborations, *The Pajama Game* (1957) and *Damn Yankees* (1958).

In 1958 Donen began working in England, turning out sophisticated fare like the comic thriller, *Charade* (1963), and the stylish romantic drama, *Two for the Road* (1966). His later films have met with lukewarm critical response. Married to dancer Jeannie Coyne (who later wed Gene Kelly) from 1948 to 1949, Donen married actress Yvette Mimieux in 1972. • *On the Town* 1949 (d); *Take Me Out to the Ball Game* 1949 (d,story); *Royal Wedding* 1951 (d); *Fearless Fagan* 1952 (d); *Love Is Better Than Ever* 1952 (d); *Singin' in the Rain* 1952 (chor,d); *Give a Girl a Break* 1953 (chor,d); *Deep in My Heart* 1954 (d); *Seven Brides For Seven Brothers* 1954 (d); *It's Always Fair Weather* 1955 (chor,d); *Funny Face* 1957 (d); *Kiss Them For Me* 1957 (d); *The Pajama Game* 1957 (d,p); *Damn Yankees* 1958 (d,p); *Indiscreet* 1958 (d,p); *The Grass Is Greener* 1960 (d,p); *Once More, With Feeling* 1960 (d,p); *Surprise Package* 1960 (d,p); *Charade* 1963 (d,p); *Arabesque* 1966 (d,p); *Bedazzled* 1967 (d,p); *Two For the Road* 1967 (d,p); *Staircase* 1969 (d,p); *The Little Prince* 1974 (d,p); *Lucky Lady* 1975 (d); *Movie Movie* 1978 (d,p); *Saturn 3* 1980 (d,p); *Blame It on Rio* 1984 (d,p).

Donlevy, Brian • Actor • Born Portadown, Ireland, February 9, 1899; died 1972. Durable Irish-American character player, often cast as a fast-talking tough guy with a heart of gold. Donlevy's only leading role was in Preston Sturges's directing debut, *The Great McGinty* (1940), but he made memorable appearances in *Beau Geste* (1939, as the villainous sergeant), *Destry Rides Again* (1939), *The Glass Key* (1942) and *An American Romance* (1944). Second wife was actress Marjorie Lane. • *Damaged Hearts* 1924; *School For Wives* 1925; *A Man of Quality* 1926; *Mother's Boy* 1929; *Another Face* 1935; *Barbary Coast* 1935; *Mary Burns, Fugitive* 1935; *13 Hours By Air* 1936; *36 Hours to Kill* 1936; *Crack-Up* 1936; *Half Angel* 1936; *High Tension* 1936; *Human Cargo* 1936; *Strike Me Pink* 1936; *Born Reckless* 1937; *Midnight Taxi* 1937; *This Is My Affair* 1937; *The Battle of Broadway* 1938; *In Old Chicago* 1938; *Sharpshooters* 1938; *Allegheny Uprising* 1939; *Beau Geste* 1939 **(AANBSA)**; *Behind Prison Gates* 1939; *Destry Rides Again* 1939; *Jesse James* 1939; *Union Pacific* 1939; *Brigham Young, Frontiersman* 1940; *The Great McGinty* 1940; *When the Daltons Rode* 1940; *Billy the Kid* 1941; *Birth of the Blues* 1941; *Hold Back the Dawn* 1941; *I Wanted Wings* 1941; *South of Tahiti* 1941; *A Gentleman After Dark* 1942; *The Glass Key* 1942; *The Great Man's Lady* 1942; *Nightmare* 1942; *The Remarkable Andrew* 1942; *Stand By For Action* 1942; *Two Yanks in Trinidad* 1942; *Wake Island* 1942; *Hangmen Also Die* 1943; *An American Romance* 1944; *The Miracle of Morgan's Creek* 1944; *Duffy's Tavern* 1945; *The Beginning or the End* 1946; *Canyon Passage* 1946; *Our Hearts Were Growing Up* 1946; *Two Years Before the Mast* 1946; *The Virginian* 1946; *Heaven Only Knows* 1947; *Killer McCoy* 1947; *The Kiss of Death* 1947; *The Song of Scheherazade* 1947; *The Trouble With Women* 1947; *Command Decision* 1948; *A Southern Yankee* 1948; *Impact* 1949; *The Lucky Stiff* 1949; *Kansas Raiders* 1950; *Shakedown* 1950; *Fighting Coast Guard* 1951; *Slaughter Trail* 1951; *Hoodlum Empire* 1952; *Ride the Man Down* 1952; *The Woman They Almost Lynched* 1953; *The Big Combo* 1955; *A Cry in the Night* 1956; *Escape From Red Rock* 1957; *The Quatermass Experiment* 1957; *Cowboy* 1958; *Juke Box Rhythm* 1959; *Never So Few* 1959; *The Errand Boy* 1961; *The Girl in Room 13* 1961; *The Pigeon That Took Rome* 1962; *The Curse of the Fly* 1965; *How to Stuff a Wild Bikini* 1965; *The Fat Spy* 1966; *Waco* 1966; *Hostile Guns* 1967; *Arizona Bushwhackers* 1968; *Rogue's Gallery* 1968; *Pit Stop* 1969.

Donner, Clive • Director • Born London, January 21, 1926. Former editor who made several admirable, visually polished films in the 1960s, notably *Nothing but the Best* (1964), before turning mostly to TV work. • *A Christmas Carol* 1951 (ed); *The Promoter* 1952 (ed); *Genevieve* 1953 (ed); *The Purple Plain* 1954 (ed); *I Am a Camera* 1955 (ed); *The Secret Place* 1957 (d); *Heart of a Child* 1958 (d); *Marriage of Convenience* 1961 (d); *The Sinister Man* 1961 (d); *Some People* 1962 (d); *The Caretaker* 1963 (d); *Nothing But the Best* 1964 (d); *What's New, Pussycat?* 1965 (d); *Here We Go 'Round the Mulberry Bush* 1968 (d,p); *Alfred the Great* 1969 (d); *Old Dracula* 1975 (d); *The Thief of Bagdad* 1978 (d); *The Nude Bomb* 1980 (d); *Charlie Chan and the Curse of the Dragon Queen* 1981 (d); *Stealing Heaven* 1988 (d).

Donner, Jörn • Director, screenwriter; also producer, actor, author. • Born Jörn Johan Donner, Helsinki, Finland, February 5, 1933. *Educ.* Helsinki University (political science, Swedish literature). Leading figure of the Finnish cinema ever since the release of his first feature as a director, *A Sunday in September* (1963). Donner's films range from documentaries to melodramas with, for the most part, his more "serious" work being made in Sweden and his more commercial work in Finland. He is the author of *The Personal Vision of Ingmar Bergman* (1964) as well as numerous novels and political works. A member of the Finnish parliament, Donner is married to Harriet Andersson, who has appeared in a number of his films. • *A Sunday in September* 1963 (d); *Att Alska* 1964 (d,sc); *Adventure Starts Here* 1965 (d); *Rooftree* 1967 (d,ed); *Stimulantia* 1967 (d); *Teenage Rebellion* 1967 (d); *Black on White* 1968 (a,d,ed,exec.p); *69* 1969 (a,d,exec.p); *Anna* 1970 (d,p,sc); *Portraits of Women* 1970 (a,d,ed,exec.p); *Perkele!/Fuck Off!—Images of Finland* 1971 (d,exec.p); *Marja Pieni* 1972 (p); *Tenderness* 1972 (d,exec.p); *Baksmalla* 1973 (a,d,sc); *Maa on Syntinen laulu* 1974 (p); *Tre Scener Med Ingmar Bergman/Three Scenes With Ingmar Bergman* 1975 (d,p,sc); *Drommen om Amerika* 1976 (exec.p); *Langt borta och nara* 1976 (p); *Tabu* 1976 (p); *Bluff Stop* 1977 (p); *Hemat i Natten* 1977 (exec.p); *Frigetens Murar* 1978 (exec.p); *Man kan inte Valdtas* 1978 (d,p,sc); *Mannen i skuggan* 1978 (exec.p); *Slumrande toner* 1978 (p); *Fanny och Alexander/Fanny and Alexander* 1982 (exec.p); *Ingenjor Andrees Luftfard* 1982 (p); *Yhdeksan Tapaa Lahestya Helsinkia* 1982 (d,p,sc,ed,commentary text); *Eishockey-Fieber* 1983 (a); *Regina Ja Miehet* 1983 (a); *After the Rehearsal* 1984 (p); *Angelan Sota/Angelas Krig* 1984 (a,exec.p,from novel); *Dirty Story* 1984 (d,p,sc); *Riisuminen* 1986 (p); *Brev Fran Sverige* 1987 (d,p,sc,ed); *Paradise America* 1990 (p).

Donner, Richard • Director; also producer. • Born New York, NY, 1939. Former actor who directed numerous episodes of the classic TV series "The Twilight Zone" and "The Fugitive" before moving into feature work in 1961. Donner scored some notable commercial successes in the 1970s and 80s, notably with *The Omen* (1976) and *Lethal Weapon* (1987). • *X—15* 1961 (d); *Salt and Pepper* 1968 (d); *Twinky* 1970 (d); *The Omen* 1976 (d); *Superman* 1978 (d); *Inside Moves* 1980 (d); *The Final Conflict* 1981 (exec.p); *The Toy* 1982 (d); *The Goonies* 1985 (d,p); *Ladyhawke* 1985 (d,p); *Lethal Weapon* 1987 (d,p); *The Lost Boys* 1987 (exec.p); *Scrooged* 1988 (d,p); *Lethal Weapon 2* 1989 (d,p).

Donohoe, Amanda • English actress • *Educ.* Central School of Speech and Drama, London. Attractive leading lady who turned in a deliciously campy performance as a snakewoman in *The Lair of the White Worm* (1988), Ken Russell's slice of contemporary Gothic ham. Also known to American audiences for TV's *LA Law*. • *Castaway* 1986; *Foreign Body* 1986; *The Lair of the White Worm* 1988; *Diamond Skulls* 1989; *The Rainbow* 1989; *Tank Malling* 1989; *Paper Mask* 1990.

Donskoy, Mark • Director; also screenwriter, playwright. • Born Odessa, Russia, March 12, 1897; died 1980. *Educ.* GIK, Moscow. Major Soviet filmmaker who studied under Eisenstein and is best known for his "Gorky" trilogy (*The Childhood of Maxim Gorky* 1938, *My Apprenticeship/Out in the World/Among People* 1939, *My Universities/University of Life* 1940), based on the early life of his celebrated writer friend. After a brief period of government harassment, Donskoy returned to filmmaking with a remake of Vsevolod Pudovkin's silent classic *Mother* (1956) which, like most of his films through the following decade, was somewhat lackluster. He returned to form with two films on Soviet leader V. I. Lenin, *Heart of a Mother* and *A Mother's Devotion* (both 1967), which were acclaimed for their brilliant evocation of pre-Soviet Russia. • *Prostitutka* 1926 (a); *Yevo Prevosoditelstvo* 1927 (ed); *V bolshom gorode* 1928 (d,sc); *Tsena cheloveka* 1929 (d); *Chuzoi bereg* 1930 (d); *Pizhon* 1930 (d); *Ogon* 1931 (d); *Pesnya o schastye* 1934 (d); *Dyetstvo Gorkovo/The Childhood of Maxim Gorky* 1938 (d,sc); *V Lyudyakh/My Apprenticeship* 1939 (d,sc); *Brat Geroya* 1940 (art d); *Moi Universiteti/My Universities* 1940 (d,sc); *Romantiki* 1941 (d,sc); *Boevoi Kinosbornik 9* 1942 (d,sc); *Kak Zakalyalas Stal* 1942 (d,sc); *Raduga* 1944 (d,sc); *Nepokorenniye* 1945 (d,sc); *Selskaya uchitelnitsa* 1947 (d); *Alitet ukhodit v gory* 1949 (d,sc,from novel); *Mat* 1956 (d,sc); *Dorogoi tsenoi* 1958 (d); *Foma Gordeyev* 1959 (d,sc); *Zdravstvuitye deti* 1962 (d,sc); *Serdtze Materi/Heart of a Mother* 1967 (d,p); *Vernost materi/A Mother's Devotion* 1967 (d); *Chaliapin* 1969 (d).

Dooley, Paul • Actor • Born Parkersburg, WV, February 22, 1928. *Educ.* West Virginia University, Morgantown (speech). Excels at fatherly roles, as in *A Wedding* (1978) and *Breaking Away* (1979), in both of which his son is played by Dennis Christopher. Dooley has appeared in five films by Robert Altman, with whom he collaborated on the screenplay for *Health* (1980). He is also head of All Over Creations, which produces industrial films and radio commercials. • *What's So Bad About Feeling Good?* 1968; *The Out-of-Towners* 1970; *Death Wish* 1974; *The Gravy Train* 1974; *Raggedy Ann & Andy* 1976; *Slap Shot* 1977; *A Wedding* 1978; *Breaking Away* 1979; *A Perfect Couple* 1979; *Rich Kids* 1979; *Health* 1980 (a,sc); *Popeye* 1980; *Paternity* 1981; *Endangered Species* 1982; *Kiss Me Goodbye* 1982; *Going Berserk* 1983; *Monster in the Closet* 1983; *Strange Brew* 1983; *Sixteen Candles* 1984; *Big Trouble* 1985; *O.C. and Stiggs* 1987; *Last Rites* 1988; *Flashback* 1990.

Dörrie, Doris • Director; also screenwriter. • Born Hanover, West Germany, 1955. *Educ.* Hochschüle für Film und Fernsehen, Munich. Dörrie had made documentaries and a fine medium-length fiction film, *The First Waltz* (1978), before directing her first feature, the highly assured *Straight Through the Heart*, in 1983. A witty psychodrama involving an insecure young woman and an equally insecure older man, it was followed two years later by the international success *Men*, another—though more lighthearted—look at male-female role playing.

Dörrie's first English-language film, *Me and Him* (1988), was based on Alberto Moravia's story about a man whose penis begins talking to him; interesting but flawed, it failed to achieve theatrical release in the US. • *Der Hauptdarsteller* 1977 (a); *Der Erste Walzer/The First Waltz* 1978 (d,sc); *Mitten Ins Herz/Straight Through the Heart* 1983 (d); *Im Innern des Wals* 1985 (d,sc); *King Kongs Faust* 1985 (a); *Männer/Men* 1985 (d,sc); *Paradies* 1986 (d,sc); *Wann—Wenn Nicht Jetzt?* 1987 (sc); *Me and Him* 1988 (d,sc); *Geld* 1989 (d,sc).

Dors, Diana • Actress • Born Diana Fluck, Swindon, England, October 23, 1931; died May 4, 1984, Windsor, England. *Educ.* LAMDA, London. Blonde leading lady of British films of the 1950s and 60s who once described herself as "the only sex symbol Britain [had] produced since Lady Godiva." • *The Shop at Sly Corner* 1946; *Holiday Camp* 1947; *Good Time Girl* 1948; *Here Come the Huggetts* 1948; *Oliver Twist* 1948; *Diamond City* 1949; *Dance Hall* 1950; *Lady Godiva Rides Again* 1951; *The Saint's Return* 1953; *A Kid For Two Farthings* 1954; *The Weak and the Wicked* 1954; *An Alligator Named Daisy* 1955; *As Long As They're Happy* 1955; *Value For Money* 1955; *Blonde Sinner* 1956; *I Married a Woman* 1957; *La Ragazza del Palio* 1957; *The Unholy Wife* 1957; *The Long Haul* 1958; *Tread Softly Stranger* 1958; *Passport to Shame* 1959; *Scent of Mystery* 1960; *King of the Roaring 20's—The Story of Arnold Rothstein* 1961; *On the Double* 1961; *Allez France* 1964; *The Sandwich Man* 1966; *Berserk* 1967; *Danger Route* 1967; *Hammerhead* 1968; *Baby Love* 1969; *Deep End* 1970; *There's a Girl in My Soup* 1970; *Hannie Caulder* 1971; *The Pied Piper* 1972; *Craze* 1973; *Theatre of Blood* 1973; *From Beyond the Grave* 1975; *Keep It Up Downstairs* 1976; *Adventures of a Private Eye* 1977; *The Groove Room* 1977; *Confessions From the David Galaxy Affair* 1979; *Steaming* 1985.

Dos Santos, Nelson Pereira • Director; also writer, editor, producer. • Born São Paulo, Brazil, October 26, 1928. *Educ.* IDHEC, Paris (film). As an adolescent and young man, dos Santos worked as a journalist, studied law, participated in amateur theatrical ventures and was active in the cultural and political activities of the Communist Party. The young dos Santos was a film aficionado and an avid reader of leading Brazilian writers of the time such as Jorge Amado and Graciliano Ramos.

Dos Santos broke into the Brazilian motion picture industry as an assistant director in the early 1950s, after having taught himself the basics of 16mm production. Although he is primarily known as a director, he has also worked as an actor, editor, producer, and scriptwriter—he generally scripts the films that he directs. Because he has successfully undertaken a wide range of styles and themes, dos Santos has proven himself one of the most innovative directors in the rich history of Brazilian film.

Dos Santos adopted a neorealist style for his first feature, *Rio, 40 Graus/Rio, 40 Degrees* (1954). The film is a landmark in the history of Brazilian cinema, the first feature to realistically and critically examine the issue of poverty. In addition, the film's shoe-string financing and low-cost mode of production proved that artistically and socially ambitious works could be made outside the studio system.

In his political allegories *Fome de Amor* and *Azyllo Muito Louco*, the director abandoned neorealist precepts in favor of artistic experimentation with non-naturalistic styles. Perhaps the best known of his allegorical films is the anthropological fiction feature *Como Era Gostoso o Meu Frances/How Tasty Was My Little Frenchman* (1971), an offbeat depiction of the conquest and colonization of Brazil in which the Tupinamba Indians figuratively and literally cannibalize their European enemies.

In the 1970s and 80s, dos Santos made four features in an attempt to create a "popular cinema" that would be an authentic reflection of Brazilian popular culture. *O Amuleto de Ogum/The Amulet of Ogum* (1975) tells a story of criminal gangs that operate under the magic spell of 'umbanda,' an Afro-Brazilian religion. Dos Santos explores racial themes in *Tenda dos Milagres* (1975) and *Jubiaba* (1985), which are adapted from the Jorge Amado novels of the same names. The commercially successful *Estrada da Vida* recounts the real-life and imagined adventures of a popular "country" singing duo.

Dos Santos's adaptations of two books by author Graciliano Ramos, *Vidas Secas/Barren Lives* (1963) and *Memórias do Cárcere/Memories of Prison* (1984), have been hailed as masterpieces. *Vidas Secas*, a landmark of the *cinema nôvo* movement, is a powerful depiction of a landless family's struggle to survive in the Northeastern backlands in the face of drought and an oppresive socioeconomic system. In *Memorias do Carcere/Memories of Prison*, dos Santos traces the effort of Ramos himself to write about prison life while coping with his own unjust incarceration.

Dos Santos is highly regarded in Brazilian film circles for his affable personality and spirited defense and promotion of his nation's cinema. He has at times filmed with student crews in an effort to introduce young people to hands-on production; and he has participated actively in different organizations, such as an exhibition cooperative, designed to enhance the status of Brazilian cinema. DW • *Youth (short)* 1950 (d); *Rio, 40 Graus/Rio, 40 Degrees* 1954 (d); *Rio, Zone Norte/Rio, Northern Zone* 1957 (d); *Barravento/The Turning Wind* 1962 (ed); *Vidas Secas/Barren Lives* 1963 (d,sc); *O Alienista* 1970 (d,sc); *Como Era Gostoso o Meu Frances/How Tasty Was My Little Frenchman* 1971 (d,sc); *Quem e Beta?/Where is Beta?* 1973 (d,sc); *O Amuleto de Ogum/The Amulet of Ogum* 1975 (d,sc); *Tenda da Milagres* 1975 (d,sc); *Memórias do Cárcere/Memories of Prison* 1984 (d,sc); *Jubiaba* 1985 (d,sc).

Douglas, Kirk • *aka* Isidore Demsky • Actor; also producer, director. • Born Issur Danielovitch, Amsterdam, NY, December 9, 1916. *Educ.* St. Lawrence University; AADA, New York. Along with Burt Lancaster, Douglas was the top male Hollywood star of the post-WWII era. A singularly unrelaxed performer, he brought relentless drive as well as talent to his screen roles, which were often as cynical, egotistical types.

Douglas made his screen debut as a jaded weakling in *The Strange Love of Martha Ivers* (1946), achieved stardom as the ruthless boxer in Stanley Kramer's *Champion* (1949) and was memorable as Vincent van Gogh in Vincente Minnelli's biopic, *Lust for Life* (1956). He played classic heels in Billy Wilder's *The Big Carnival/Ace in the Hole* and William Wyler's *Detective Story* (both 1951) and more sympathetic characters in *Out of the Past* (1947), *Gunfight at the O.K. Corral* (1957, as Doc Holliday), *Paths of Glory* (1957) and *The List of Adrian Messenger* (1963).

Douglas turned to producing in the late 1950s and his public announcement that blacklisted writer Dalton Trumbo would script *Spartacus* (1960) was a key move in Hollywood's reacceptance of allegedly communist figures. Douglas is the father of actor-director-producer Michael and TV producer Joel (with his first wife, actress Diana Dill) and of producer Peter and actor Eric (with his second wife and former publicity agent, Anne Buydens). • *The Strange Love of Martha Ivers* 1946; *I Walk Alone* 1947; *Mourning Becomes Electra* 1947; *Out of the Past* 1947; *A Letter to Three Wives* 1948; *My Dear Secretary* 1948; *The Walls of Jericho* 1948; *Champion* 1949 **(AANBA)**; *The Glass Menagerie* 1950; *Young Man With a Horn* 1950; *Along the Great Divide* 1951; *The Big Carnival* 1951; *Detective Story* 1951; *The Bad and the Beautiful* 1952 **(AANBA)**; *The Big Sky* 1952; *The Big Trees* 1952; *Act of Love* 1953; *The Juggler* 1953; *The Story of Three Loves* 1953; *Ulysses* 1953; *20,000 Leagues Under the Sea* 1954; *Man Without a Star* 1954; *The Indian Fighter* 1955; *The Racers* 1955; *Lust For Life* 1956 **(AANBA)**; *Gunfight at the O.K. Corral* 1957; *Paths of Glory* 1957; *Top Secret Affair* 1957; *The Vikings* 1958 (a,exec.p); *The Devil's Disciple* 1959 (a,exec.p); *Last Train From Gun Hill* 1959; *Spartacus* 1960 (a,exec.p); *Strangers When We Meet* 1960; *The Last Sunset* 1961; *Town Without Pity* 1961; *Lonely Are the Brave* 1962; *Two Weeks in Another Town* 1962; *For Love or Money* 1963; *The Hook* 1963; *The List of Adrian Messenger* 1963; *The Long Ships* 1964; *Seven Days in May* 1964; *The Heroes of Telemark* 1965; *In Harm's Way* 1965; *Cast a Giant Shadow* 1966; *Paris brule-t-il?* 1966; *The War Wagon* 1967; *The Way West* 1967; *The Brotherhood* 1968 (a,p); *A Lovely Way to Die* 1968; *The Arrangement* 1969; *There Was a Crooked Man* 1970; *Catch Me a Spy* 1971; *A Gunfight* 1971; *The Light at the Edge of the World* 1971; *Summertree* 1971 (p); *Un Uomo da Rispettare* 1972; *Scalawag* 1973 (a,d); *Once Is Not Enough* 1975; *Posse* 1975 (a,d,p); *Holocaust 2000* 1977; *The Chosen* 1978; *The Fury* 1978; *Home Movies* 1979; *The Villain* 1979; *The Final Countdown* 1980; *Saturn 3* 1980; *Eddie Macon's Run* 1982; *The Man From Snowy River* 1982; *Tough Guys* 1986 (a,prod.cons); *Oscar* 1991.

Douglas, Melvyn • Actor • Born Melvyn Edouard Hesselberg, Macon, GA, April 5, 1901. Broadway star, in Hollywood from 1931. Douglas often played the suave sophisticate in pursuit of a beautiful woman, as in Ernst Lubitsch's classic *Ninotchka* (1939), opposite Greta Garbo. Douglas began appearing in supporting roles in the early 1960s and turned in an Oscar-winning performance in *Hud* (1963). Married to actress turned US Representative Helen Gahagan. • *Tonight or Never* 1931; *As You Desire Me* 1932; *The Broken Wing* 1932; *The Old Dark House* 1932; *Prestige* 1932; *The Wiser Sex* 1932; *Counsellor at Law* 1933; *Nagana* 1933; *The Vampire Bat* 1933; *Dangerous Corner* 1934; *Woman in the Dark* 1934; *Annie Oakley* 1935; *Mary Burns, Fugitive* 1935; *The People's Enemy* 1935; *She Married Her Boss* 1935; *And So They Were Married* 1936; *The Gorgeous Hussy* 1936; *The Lone Wolf Returns* 1936; *Theodora Goes Wild* 1936; *Angel* 1937; *Captains Courageous* 1937; *I Met Him in Paris* 1937; *I'll Take Romance* 1937; *Women of Glamour* 1937; *Arsene Lupin Returns* 1938; *Fast Company* 1938; *The Shining Hour* 1938; *That Certain Age* 1938; *There's Always a Woman* 1938; *There's That Woman Again* 1938; *The Toy Wife* 1938; *The Amazing Mr. Williams* 1939; *Good Girls Go to Paris* 1939; *Ninotchka* 1939; *Tell No Tales* 1939; *He Stayed For Breakfast* 1940; *Third Finger, Left Hand* 1940; *Too Many Husbands* 1940; *Our Wife* 1941; *That Uncertain Feeling* 1941; *This Thing Called Love* 1941; *Two-Faced Woman* 1941; *A Woman's Face* 1941; *They All Kissed the Bride* 1942; *We Were Dancing* 1942; *Three Hearts For Julia* 1943; *The Guilt of Janet Ames* 1947; *Sea of Grass* 1947; *Mr. Blandings Builds His Dream House* 1948; *The Great Sinner* 1949; *My Own True Love* 1949; *A Woman's Secret* 1949; *My Forbidden Past* 1951; *On the Loose* 1951; *Billy Budd* 1962; *Advance to the Rear* 1963; *Hud* 1963 **(AABSA)**; *The Americanization of Emily* 1964; *Rapture* 1965; *Hotel* 1967; *I Never Sang For My Father* 1970 **(AANBA)**; *The Candidate* 1972; *One Is a Lonely Number* 1972; *Le Locataire* 1976; *Twilight's Last Gleaming* 1977; *Being There* 1979 **(AABSA)**; *The Changeling* 1979; *The Seduction of Joe Tynan* 1979; *Tell Me a Riddle* 1980; *Ghost Story* 1981; *Hot Touch* 1982.

Douglas, Michael • Actor, producer • Born New Brunswick, NJ, September 25, 1944. *Educ.* University of California, Santa Barbara (drama); Neighborhood Playhouse, New York; American Place Theatre, New York. Began his career as assistant director on several of father Kirk Douglas's mid-1960s films. Douglas co-starred with Karl Malden in, and directed some episodes of, the TV series *The Streets of San Francisco* (1972-77) and made an auspicious feature producing debut with *One Flew Over the Cuckoo's Nest* (1975). Until *Romancing the Stone* (1984) he was known more for his producing than for his acting, but he has subsequently merged the two careers to achieve both critical and commercial success. Douglas won a best actor Oscar for his portrayal of ruthless stockbroker Gordon Gekko in Oliver Stone's *Wall Street* (1987). • *Hail, Hero!* 1969 (a); *Adam at 6 A.M.* 1970 (a); *Summertree* 1971 (a); *Napoleon and Samantha* 1972 (a); *One Flew Over the Cuckoo's Nest* 1975 (p) **(AABP)**; *Coma* 1978 (a); *The China Syndrome* 1979 (a,p); *Running* 1979 (a,exec.p); *It's My Turn* 1980 (a); *The Star Chamber* 1983 (a); *Romancing the Stone* 1984 (a,p); *Starman* 1984 (exec.p); *A Chorus Line* 1985 (a); *The Jewel of the Nile* 1985 (a,p); *Fatal Attraction* 1987 (a); *Wall Street* 1987 (a) **(AABA)**; *Black Rain* 1989 (a); *The War of the Roses* 1989 (a); *Flatliners* 1990 (p).

Dourif, Brad • Actor • Born Huntington, WV, March 18, 1950. *Educ.* University of Huntington, WV. Excels at playing frail or tormented characters, notably as Billy Bibbitt in *One Flew Over the Cuckoo's Nest* (1975) and as deranged preacher Hazel Motes in John Huston's cult hit *Wise Blood* (1979). • *W. W. and the Dixie Dancekings* 1974; *One Flew Over the Cuckoo's Nest* 1975 **(AANBSA)**; *Gruppenbild Mit Dame* 1977; *Eyes of Laura Mars* 1978; *Wise Blood* 1979; *Heaven's Gate* 1980; *Ragtime* 1981; *Dune* 1985; *Blue Velvet* 1986; *Impure Thoughts* 1986; *Fatal Beauty* 1987; *Child's Play* 1988; *Mississippi Burning* 1988; *Split* 1988; *Medium Rare* 1989; *Spontaneous Combustion* 1989; *Child's Play 2* 1990; *Grim Prairie Tales* 1990; *Hidden Agenda* 1990; *The Horseplayer* 1990; *Sonny Boy* 1990; *Stephen King's Graveyard Shift* 1990; *William Peter Blatty's The Exorcist III* 1990.

Dovzhenko, Alexander • Director; also screenwriter, actor. • Born Alexander Petrovich Dovzhenko, Sosnitsa, Chernigov, Ukraine, Russia, September 12, 1894; died 1956. *Educ.* Teachers Institute, Glukhov (science, athletics); Commercial Institute, Kiev (economics, technology); Academy of Fine Arts, Kiev. Born to illiterate, impoverished peasants who were descendants of Cossacks, Alexander Dovzhenko completed his education and left the Desna River Valley to become a school teacher. His aspirations in the arts led to involvement in literary circles after the Communist Revolution of 1917, a revolution he embraced as the first step toward Ukrainian national independence. He joined the army and later studied art in Berlin. In 1923, he returned to his beloved Ukraine to launch a career as an illustrator. His painter's eye was expressed in detailed political cartoons and book illustrations which supported the "People's Republic." His films would express his strong ties to Ukrainian culture, particularly in the romantically nationalistic *Zvenyhora* (1928) and *Arsenal* (1929), considered his most complete and masterful works.

With no formal training and little knowledge of how a film is made, Dovzhenko, having explored the potential of writing, painting and architecture, turned suddenly to what he considered a perfectly political medium by assuming an apprenticeship at the film studios at Odessa. His first film, *Vasya the Reformer* (1926), was a laughable attempt at comedy.

Dovzhenko's enduring contribution to world cinema is found in the poetic vision of *Arsenal* (1929) and *Earth* (1930), contemplative, rhythmically edited works that one critic called "biological, pantheistic conception(s)."

Stylistically, Dovzhenko's work, as exemplified by *Earth*, is a montage of associations and impressions. The film has very little camera movement or movement within the frame. Narrative flow is the product of editing and composition, with each shot composed and framed according to the director's painterly vision.

After serving as a war correspondent for *Red Army* and *Izvestia* during WWII, Dovzhenko assumed writing and producing chores at Mosfilm studios. But for years he complained of creative suffocation in Stalin's political bureaucracy, which caused several Dovzhenko projects to be shelved.

Although his final output was relatively modest, it was the young Dovzhenko, along with his contemporaries V.I. Pudovkin and Sergei Eisenstein, who best combined the principle of montage with a realistic appreciation for the natural landscape. TZ • *Vasya reformator/Vasya the Reformer* 1926 (d,sc); *Love's Berries* 1926 (d,sc); *The Diplomatic Pouch* 1927 (a,adapt,d); *Zvenyhora* 1928 (d); *Arsenal* 1929 (d,sc); *Zemlya/Earth* 1930 (d,sc); *Ivan* 1932 (d,sc); *Aerograd* 1935 (d,sc); *Shchors* 1939 (d,sc); *Osvobozhdenie/Liberation* 1940 (d,sc,ed); *Aleksandr Parkhomenko* 1941 (prod.sup); *Bogdan Khmelnitskii* 1941 (prod.sup); *Strana rodnaya* 1945 (commentary,ed,d); *Michurin* 1948 (d,p,sc,from play); *Poema o morye/Poem of the Sea* 1958 (sc); *Povest plamennikh let/Chronicle of Flaming Years* 1960 (sc).

Downey, Robert • American director; also actor, producer, screenwriter. • Born June 1936. Irreverent, mordantly humorous director who formerly worked in advertising. Downey's best known film remains *Putney Swope* (1969), about the hilarious changes made by a token black member of an ad agency after he is accidentally elected Chairman of the Board. Son, actor Robert Downey, Jr., has appeared in five of his films. • *Babo 73* 1964 (d,p,sc); *Chafed Elbows* 1965 (d,p,sc); *No More Excuses* 1968 (a,d); *Putney Swope* 1969 (d,sc); *Pound* 1970 (d,sc); *Is There Sex After Death?* 1971 (a); *You've Got to Walk It Like You Talk It or You'll Lose That Beat* 1971 (a); *Greaser's Palace* 1972 (d,p,sc); *Two Tons of Turquoise to Taos Tonight* 1976 (a); *Jive* 1979 (sc); *The Gong Show Movie* 1980 (sc); *Up the Academy* 1980 (d); *America* 1982 (d,sc); *To Live and Die in L.A.* 1985 (a); *Johnny Be Good* 1988 (a); *Rented Lips* 1988 (d); *Too Much Sun* 1991 (d,sc).

Downey, Robert, Jr. • Actor • Born New York, NY, April 4, 1965. Gifted young actor who made his first screen appearance at age five, playing a puppy (!) in *Pound* (1970), directed by father Robert Downey. He landed his breakthrough role as the dissipated cocaine addict, Julian, in *Less Than Zero* (1987) and has since turned in mature performances as a young, idealistic lawyer opposite James Woods in *True Believer* and as the confused romantic hero of *Chances Are* (both 1989). • *America* 1982; *Baby, It's You* 1983; *Firstborn* 1984; *Tuff Turf* 1985; *Weird Science* 1985; *Back to School* 1986; *Dear America* 1987; *Less Than Zero* 1987; *The Pick-Up Artist* 1987; *1969* 1988; *Johnny Be Good* 1988; *Rented Lips* 1988; *Chances Are* 1989; *That's Adequate* 1989; *True Believer* 1989; *Air America* 1990; *Too Much Sun* 1991.

Dreier, Hans • Production designer • Born Bremen, Germany, August 21, 1885; died 1966. *Educ.* Munich University (engineering, architecture). Began his film career with UFA in 1919 and came to the US four years later. Dreier was skilled at creating foreign locales on the studio lot, a talent frequently drawn on by European directors such as Josef von Sternberg, Rouben Mamoulian and Ernst Lubitsch. He was head of Paramount's design department from 1928 to 1951 and created the sets for 11 Cecil B. DeMille films between 1933 and 1949. • *Danton* 1921; *Forbidden Paradise* 1924; *Underworld* 1927; *The Docks of New York* 1928; *The Dragnet* 1928; *The Last Command* 1928; *The Patriot* 1928 **(AANBAD)**; *The Street of Sin* 1928; *Betrayal* 1929; *The Case of Lena Smith* 1929; *The Love Parade* 1929 **(AANBAD)**; *Thunderbolt* 1929; *Morocco* 1930 **(AANBAD)**; *The Vagabond King* 1930 **(AANBAD)**; *An American Tragedy* 1931; *Dishonored* 1931; *The Smiling Lieutenant* 1931; *Broken Lullaby* 1932; *Dr. Jekyll and Mr. Hyde* 1932; *Love Me Tonight* 1932; *One Hour With You* 1932; *Shanghai Express* 1932; *Trouble in Paradise* 1932; *Design For Living* 1933; *I'm No Angel* 1933; *Song of Songs* 1933; *Cleopatra* 1934; *Death Takes a Holiday* 1934; *The Scarlet Empress* 1934; *The Crusades* 1935; *The Devil Is a Woman* 1935; *The Lives of a Bengal Lancer* 1935 **(AANBAD)**; *Ruggles of Red Gap* 1935; *Desire* 1936; *The General Died at Dawn* 1936; *The Texas Rangers* 1936; *Angel* 1937; *High, Wide, And Handsome* 1937; *Maid of Salem* 1937; *Make Way For Tomorrow* 1937; *The Plainsman* 1937; *Souls at Sea* 1937 **(AANBAD)**; *Wells Fargo* 1937; *Bluebeard's Eighth Wife* 1938; *If I Were King* 1938 **(AANBAD)**; *You and Me* 1938; *Beau Geste* 1939 **(AANBAD)**; *Union Pacific* 1939; *Arise, My Love* 1940 **(AANBAD)**; *Dr. Cyclops* 1940; *North West Mounted Police* 1940 **(AANBAD)**; *Road to Singapore* 1940; *Typhoon* 1940; *Hold Back the Dawn* 1941 **(AANBAD)**; *I Wanted Wings* 1941; *The Glass Key* 1942; *The Major and the Minor* 1942; *The Palm Beach Story* 1942; *Reap the Wild Wind* 1942; *Take a Letter, Darling* 1942 **(AANBAD)**; *Five Graves to Cairo* 1943 **(AANBAD)**; *For Whom the Bell Tolls* 1943 **(AANBAD)**; *No Time For Love* 1943 **(AANBAD)**; *Double Indemnity* 1944; *Frenchman's Creek* 1944 **(AABAD)**; *Going My Way* 1944; *Lady in the Dark* 1944 **(AANBAD)**; *Ministry of Fear* 1944; *The Story of Dr. Wassell* 1944; *Hold That Blonde* 1945; *Love Letters* 1945 **(AANBAD)**; *The Unseen* 1945; *The Blue Dahlia* 1946; *Blue Skies* 1946; *Kitty* 1946 **(AANBAD)**; *The Virginian* 1946; *Calcutta* 1947; *Road to Rio* 1947; *Unconquered* 1947; *The Accused* 1948; *The Big Clock* 1948; *The Emperor Waltz* 1948; *So Evil My Love* 1948; *Sorry, Wrong Number* 1948; *Chicago Deadline* 1949; *The File on Thelma Jordan* 1949; *The Great Gatsby* 1949; *Samson and Delilah* 1949 **(AABAD)**; *Dark City* 1950; *Sunset Boulevard* 1950 **(AABAD)**; *Appointment With Danger* 1951; *A Place in the Sun* 1951; *A Farewell to Arms* 1957 **(AANBAD)**.

Dressler, Marie • *aka* Leila Marie Koerber • Actress • Born Coburg, Ontario, Canada, November 9, 1869; died 1934, Beverly Hills, CA. Made her film debut in Mack Sennett's screen version of her popular stage hit *Tillie's Punctured Romance* (1914), co-starring Charles Chaplin. Dressler gained immense popularity with several commanding performances in the early 1930s. • *Tillie's Punctured Romance* 1914; *Tillie's Tomato Surprise* 1915; *The Scrublady* 1917; *Tillie Wakes Up* 1917; *The Agonies of Agnes* 1918; *The Cross Red Nurse*

1918; *Breakfast at Sunrise* 1927; *The Callahans and the Murphys* 1927; *The Joy Girl* 1927; *The Patsy* 1927; *Bringing Up Father* 1928; *The Divine Lady* 1929; *The Hollywood Revue of 1929* 1929; *The Vagabond Lover* 1929; *Anna Christie* 1930; *Caught Short* 1930; *Chasing Rainbows* 1930; *The Girl Said No* 1930; *Let Us Be Gay* 1930; *Min and Bill* 1930 **(AABA)**; *One Romantic Night* 1930; *Politics* 1931; *Reducing* 1931; *Emma* 1932 **(AANBA)**; *Prosperity* 1932; *Christopher Bean* 1933; *Dinner at Eight* 1933; *Tugboat Annie* 1933.

Dreyer, Carl Theodor • Director; also screenwriter. • Born Copenhagen, Denmark, February 3, 1889; died March 20, 1968. Carl Theodor Dreyer was born the illegitimate son of a Danish farmer father and a Swedish mother; when he was a young boy his mother died and he was adopted by a Danish family named Dreyer. He embarked upon several careers before becoming a journalist in 1909. In this position, he wrote a series of articles profiling Danish celebrities which put Dreyer in touch with the world of film and theater. In the tradition of other Scandinavian directors, he began his film career by writing scripts; he joined the Danish state studio, Nordisk Films, in 1913 and became a full time screenwriter two years later, scouting for and adapting literary material, writing intertitles and editing film.

With 23 scripts to his credit, Dreyer was given a film to direct in 1919, beginning a career that would virtually span the history of cinema. *The President*, like each of Dreyer's subsequent films, was based on a literary work that Dreyer himself had selected. Adaptation was essential to his aesthetic, in which film was envisioned as an extension of literature and theater, and narrative and psychological truth were paramount. *The President* is memorable for its simple sets, carefully created to reflect each character's personality. Perhaps most significantly, Dreyer believed that it was a personal work of art, unlike the assembly-line product of the day.

Leaves from Satan's Book/Blade at Satan's Bog (1919) solidified Dreyer's reputation as a director with an uncompromising personal vision. This elaborate project, which Dreyer had been planning for years, faced numerous production difficulties and was altered without the director's permission when it was shown. Even so, *Leaves* was praised for its sophisticated composition and for the subtlety of its character portrayals; it also raised controversy for its treatment of socialism and its depiction of Christ.

Dreyer left Nordisk and made *The Parson's Widow* (1920) for the Swedish company, Svensk Filmindustri, before filming *Love One Another* in Berlin in 1921. The latter film employed Russian émigré actors from Stanislavsky's troupe as well as some of Max Reinhardt's performers. At this time Dreyer began his lifelong habit of collecting and studying prints and photographs to get ideas for sets. Although he returned to Denmark to make *Once Upon a Time* (1922), a beloved operetta filmed with theatrical actors, he would spend the rest of his career as a free-lance director, working for any film company that would offer him artistic freedom.

In Berlin, Dreyer made *Mikael* (1924) for UFA, a film known for its ambitious and scrupulously designed sets, which Dreyer helped to dress with items bought throughout the city. Unhappy that the film's ending was changed without his consent, Dreyer returned to Denmark to make *The Master of the House* (1925). For this film, which established Dreyer's reputation in France, a fully functioning two-room apartment was built in the studio to provide the actors with a realistic space in which to perform. *The Bride of Glomdal* (1925) was made in Norway with the mere outline of a script and much improvisation.

During the 1920s and 1930s, when many of Europe's great directors emigrated to Hollywood, Dreyer remained in Europe. Under contract to the French firm Société Générale des Films, Dreyer was given a seven-million franc budget to make *The Passion of Joan of Arc* (1927). He rejected the original script, based on Joseph Delteil's biography of the heroine, in favor of the actual trial records. Preparations for the eight-month production included the construction of a vast concrete recreation of Rouen castle, complete with sliding walls to facilitate shooting. The realism of the sets extended to every aspect of the production; actors were cast according to facial type; makeup was rejected; and the film was shot in exact sequence. On the unusually silent and intense set, the actors—ruled by Dreyer's belief that the face was the mirror of the soul—were left alone to find the essence of their character, which was then captured in closeup. The film remains one of the most closely examined, and highly acclaimed, in the history of cinema.

With the Danish film industry in financial ruins, Dreyer turned to private financing from Baron Nicholas de Gunzburg to make *Vampyr* (1932), an hypnotically photographed supernatural tale with an elliptical narrative which blends fantasy and reality. After abandoning *Mudundu*, an African project that was completed by another director, Dreyer returned to Denmark to work as a journalist.

After the Nazi invasion of Denmark and the subsequent ban on film imports, Danish films were once again in demand. Dreyer worked on a number of documentary shorts for the government before embarking on *Day of Wrath* (1943), a somber, slowly-paced account of a woman who is wrongly burned as a witch.

Over the next decade Dreyer assumed the job of managing a film theater. He also wrote a script for a film about Mary, Queen of Scots, with his son and started research for a film about Christ which would preoccupy him for the rest of his life.

In 1954, Dreyer made the award-winning *Ordet/The Word*, based on the Kaj Munk play. It is noteworthy for its unusually long takes, shot with the continual smooth camera movement that Dreyer believed to be characteristic of modern film technique, as opposed to the short scenes and quick cutting of silent cinema.

After a ten-year silence, the much-anticipated *Gertrud* (1964) appeared, only to face a disastrous reception. Dreyer used silence and softly-spoken dialogue to portray the failure of communication in this story of a middle-aged woman who leaves her home and husband to live alone in Paris. 25 years later, the film still divides critics. Dreyer's last years were spent researching *Jesus*, as he scouted locations in Israel, learned Hebrew and collected crates of photographs and notes. Although financial backing finally came through in 1967, Dreyer died before he could start the film.

Dreyer's transcendental aesthetic, his search for a spiritual truth beyond the surface of everyday life, marks him as a quintessentially Romantic artist. Yet, as critics have pointed out, his later films are among the most modern ever made, conveying the tension between a conservative vision and an experimental style. The integrity of his vision, combined with his consummate grasp of the film medium, make him one of the greatest directors in the history of cinema. RJB • *Bryggerens datter* 1912 (sc,story); *Balloneksplosionen* 1913 (sc,story); *Chatollets hemmelighed* 1913 (story,sc); *Hans og Grethe* 1913 (sc,story); *Krigskorrespondent* 1913 (sc,story); *Ned med vabnene* 1914 (sc); *Pavillionens hemmelighed* 1914 (sc); *Penge* 1914 (sc); *En forbryders liv og levned* 1915 (sc); *Guldets Gift* 1915 (sc); *Den Hvide djaevel* 1915 (sc); *Juvelerernes skraek* 1915 (sc,story); *Rovedderkoppen* 1915 (sc); *Den Skonne Evelyn* 1915 (sc); *Fange Nr. 113* 1916 (sc); *Gillekop* 1916 (sc); *Glaedens dag* 1916 (sc,story); *Hans rigtige kone* 1916 (sc,story); *Lydia* 1916 (sc); *Den Mystiske selskabsdame* 1916 (sc); *Hotel Paradis* 1917 (sc); *Grevindens aere* 1918 (sc); *Praesidenten/The President* 1919 (d,sc,art d); *Blade Af Satans Bog/Leaves From Satan's Book* 1919 (d,sc,art d); *Prastankan/The Parson's Widow* 1920 (d,sc); *Die Gezeichneten/Love One Another* 1921 (d,sc); *Der Var Engang/Once Upon a Time* 1922 (d,sc,ed); *Mikael* 1924 (d,sc); *Glomdalsbruden/The Bride of Glomdal* 1925 (d,sc,art d); *Du Skal Aere din Hustru/The Master of the House* 1925 (d,sc,art d); *La Passion de Jeanne d'Arc/The Passion of Joan of Arc* 1927 (d,sc); *Vampyr* 1932 (d,p,sc,ed); *Jungla nera* 1936 (sc); *Vredens Dag/Day of Wrath* 1943 (d,sc); *Tva Maniksor/Two People* 1945 (d,sc,ed); *Ordet* 1954 (d,sc); *Gertrud* 1964 (d,sc); *Carl Theodor Dreyer* 1966 (a); *Diaries, Notes and Sketches* 1969 (a).

Dreyfuss, Richard • Actor • Born Brooklyn, NY, October 29, 1947. *Educ.* San Fernando Valley State College, CA. American leading man who has played his fair share of irritating pests. Dreyfuss worked his way up through bit parts (*The Graduate* 1967, etc.) and TV before coming to prominence with *American Graffiti* (1973) and in the title role of *The Apprenticeship of Duddy Kravitz* (1974). The second half of the 1970s saw him established as a major star, playing lead roles in *Jaws* (1975) and *Close Encounters of the Third Kind* (1977) and winning an Oscar for *The Goodbye Girl* (1977). Dreyfuss also produced and starred in the entertaining private eye movie *The Big Fix* (1978).

After a lull in the early 1980s, Dreyfuss re-established himself as one of Hollywood's more engaging leads, in such films as Paul Mazursky's *Down and Out in Beverly Hills* (1986), Barry Levinson's *Tin Men* (1987) and Spielberg's *Always* (1989). He has also remained active in the theater. • *The Graduate* 1967; *Valley of the Dolls* 1967; *The Young Runaways* 1968; *Hello Down There* 1969; *American Graffiti* 1973; *Dillinger* 1973; *The Apprenticeship of Duddy Kravitz* 1974; *The Second Coming of Suzanne* 1974; *Inserts* 1975; *Jaws* 1975; *Close Encounters of the Third Kind* 1977; *The Goodbye Girl* 1977 **(AABA)**; *The Big Fix* 1978 (a,p); *The Competition* 1980; *Whose Life Is It Anyway?* 1981; *The Buddy System* 1984; *Down and Out in Beverly Hills* 1986; *Stand By Me* 1986; *Nuts* 1987; *Stakeout* 1987; *Tin Men* 1987; *Moon Over Parador* 1988; *Always* 1989; *Let It Ride* 1989; *Postcards From the Edge* 1990; *Rosencrantz & Guildenstern Are Dead* 1990; *Once Around* 1991; *What About Bob?* 1991.

Duff, Howard • Actor • Born Bremerton, WA, August 24, 1913; died July 8, 1990, Santa Barbara, CA. *Educ.* Seattle Repertory Playhouse, WA. Tough supporting player who starred in several B pictures. Married to actress-director Ida Lupino from 1951 to 1973. • *Brute Force* 1947; *All My Sons* 1948; *The Naked City* 1948; *Calamity Jane and Sam Bass* 1949; *Illegal Entry* 1949; *Johnny Stool Pigeon* 1949; *Red Canyon* 1949; *Shakedown* 1950; *Spy Hunt* 1950; *Woman in Hiding* 1950; *The Lady From Texas* 1951; *Steel Town* 1951; *Models, Inc.* 1952; *Jennifer* 1953; *Roar of the Crowd* 1953; *Private Hell 36* 1954; *Tanganyika* 1954; *The Yellow Mountain* 1954; *Women's Prison* 1955; *Blackjack Ketchum, Desperado* 1956; *The Broken Star* 1956; *Flame of the Islands* 1956; *While The City Sleeps* 1956; *Sierra Stranger* 1957; *Boys' Night Out* 1962; *Panic in the City* 1968; *The Late Show* 1977; *A Wedding* 1978; *Kramer vs. Kramer* 1979; *Double Negative* 1980; *Oh, God! Book II* 1980; *Monster in the Closet* 1983; *No Way Out* 1987; *Too Much Sun* 1991.

Dukakis, Olympia • Actress • Born Lowell, MA, June 20, 1931. *Educ.* Boston University (theater arts). Prolific stage performer whose screen career was boosted by a best supporting actress Oscar for *Moonstruck* (1987). Cousin of 1988 Democratic presedential candidate Michael Dukakis. Married to Louis Zorich. • *Lilith* 1964; *Twice a Man* 1964; *John and Mary* 1969; *Made For Each Other* 1971; *Death Wish* 1974; *Rich Kids* 1979; *The Wanderers* 1979; *The Idolmaker* 1980; *National Lampoon Goes to the Movies* 1982; *Flanagan* 1985; *Moonstruck* 1987 **(AABSA)**; *Working Girl* 1988; *Dad* 1989; *Look Who's Talking* 1989; *Steel Magnolias* 1989; *In the Spirit* 1990; *Look Who's Talking Too* 1990.

Dulac, Germaine • Filmmaker; also theorist. • Born Charlotte-Elizabeth-Germaine Saisset-Schneider, Amiens, France, November 17, 1882; died 1942, Paris. Early female director of the Impressionist school, with a background in theater and journalism. Dulac began making experimental films as early as 1915 but is best known for *The Smiling Madame Beudet* (1923) and the Antonin Artaud-scripted *The Seashell and the Clergyman* (1927). Dulac also wrote on the cinema as a critic and theorist, championing film as a medium distinct from the other visual arts. From 1930 she supervised the production of newsreel documentaries for Pathé-Journal, France Actualités-Gaumont and Le Cinéma au Service de l'Histoire. • *Les Soeurs Ennemies* 1915 (d); *Dans l'Ouragan de la Vie* 1916 (d); *Geo le Mysterieux* 1916 (d); *Venus Victrix* 1916 (d); *Ames de Fous* 1917 (d,sc); *Le Bonheur des autres* 1918 (d); *La Cigarette* 1919 (d,sc); *La Fête Espagnole* 1919 (d); *La Belle Dame sans Merci* 1920 (d); *Malencontre* 1920 (d); *La Mort du Soleil* 1921 (d); *Werther* 1922 (d); *Gossette* 1923 (d); *La Souriante Madame Beudet/The Smiling Madame Beudet* 1923 (d); *Le Diable dans la Ville* 1924 (d); *Ame d'Artiste* 1925 (d,sc); *La Folie des Vaillants* 1925 (d); *Antoinette Sabrier* 1926 (d); *Le Cinéma au Service de l'Histoire* 1927 (d); *La Coquille et le Clergyman/The Seashell and the Clergyman* 1927 (d); *L'Invitation au Voyage* 1927 (d); *Disque 927* 1928 (d); *Germination d'un haricot* 1928 (d); *La Princesse Mandane* 1928 (d); *Thèmes et Variations* 1928 (d); *Etude Cinégraphique sur une Arabesque* 1929 (d).

Dullea, Keir • Actor • Born Cleveland, OH, May 30, 1936. *Educ.* Rutgers University, New Brunswick, NJ; San Francisco State College. Offbeat, attractive leading man, excellent as the disturbed David in Frank Perry's *David and Lisa* (1962) but best known as astronaut David Bowman in Stanley Kubrick's *2001: A Space Odyssey* (1968). • *The Hoodlum Priest* 1961; *David and Lisa* 1962; *Mail Order Bride* 1964; *The Thin Red Line* 1964; *Bunny Lake Is Missing* 1965; *Madame X* 1966; *The Fox* 1967; *2001: A Space Odyssey* 1968; *Das Ausschweifende Leben des Marquis De Sade* 1969; *Pope Joan* 1972; *Paperback Hero* 1973; *Black Christmas* 1974; *Paul et Michelle* 1974; *Full Circle* 1977; *Welcome to Blood City* 1977; *Leopard in the Snow* 1978; *BrainWaves* 1982; *2010* 1984; *Blind Date* 1984; *The Next One* 1984.

Dunaway, Faye • Actress • Born Bascom, FL, January 14, 1941. *Educ.* University of Florida; Boston University School of Fine and Applied Arts (theater arts). Theater-trained, classically beautiful star of the 1960s, 70s and 80s. Dunaway made her screen debut in Otto Preminger's *Hurry Sundown* (1967) and went on to turn in a series of superb performances in films such as *Bonnie and Clyde* (1967), with Warren Beatty, *Chinatown* (1974), opposite Jack Nicholson, and *Network* (1976), with Peter Finch.

Dunaway was acclaimed for her portrayal of movie star and abusive mother Joan Crawford in the uneven *Mommie Dearest* (1981), but her subsequent appearances (*The Wicked Lady* 1983, *Supergirl* 1984) seemed to tend increasingly toward self-parody of her "grande dame" image. In 1987 she boosted her flagging critical reputation with a bold performance as wealthy boozer Wanda Wilcox in *Barfly*, opposite Mickey Rourke. Dunaway produced the 1990 TV movie, *Cold Sassy Tree*, in which she starred with Richard Widmark. • *Bonnie and Clyde* 1967 **(AANBA)**; *The Happening* 1967; *Hurry Sundown* 1967; *The Thomas Crown Affair* 1968; *Gli Amanti/A Place For Lovers* 1969; *The Arrangement* 1969; *The Extraordinary Seaman* 1969; *Little Big Man* 1970; *Puzzle of a Downfall Child* 1970; *Doc* 1971; *La Maison Sous les Arbres/The Deadly Trap* 1971; *Oklahoma Crude* 1973; *The Three Musketeers* 1973; *Chinatown* 1974 **(AANBA)**; *The Towering Inferno* 1974; *The Four Musketeers* 1975; *Three Days of the Condor* 1975; *Network* 1976 **(AABA)**; *Voyage of the Damned* 1976; *Eyes of Laura Mars* 1978; *Arthur Miller on Home Ground* 1979; *The Champ* 1979; *First Deadly Sin* 1980; *Mommie Dearest* 1981; *The Wicked Lady* 1983; *Supergirl* 1984; *Ordeal By Innocence* 1985; *Barfly* 1987; *Burning Secret* 1988; *Midnight Crossing* 1988; *La Partita/The Gamble* 1988; *The Handmaid's Tale* 1989; *Helmut Newton: Frames From the Edge* 1989; *In una notte di chiaro di luna/Crystal or Ash, Fire or Wind, as Long as it's Love* 1989; *Wait Until Spring, Bandini* 1989.

Dunne, Griffin • Actor, producer • Born New York, NY, June 8, 1955. *Educ.* Neighborhood Playhouse, New York. Amiable, unassuming leading man who also runs the New York-based production company Double Play with partner Amy Robinson. Dunne produced the Martin Scorsese-directed *After Hours* (1985), in which he also starrred. He is the son of writer Dominick Dunne and brother of the late actress Dominique Dunne. Married to model-turned-actress Carey Lowell since 1989. • *The Other Side of the Mountain* 1974 (a); *Head Over Heels* 1979 (a,p); *An American Werewolf in London* 1981 (a); *The Fan* 1981 (a); *Baby, It's You* 1983 (p); *Cold Feet* 1983 (a); *Almost You* 1984 (a); *Johnny Dangerously* 1984 (a); *After Hours* 1985 (a,p); *Amazon Women on the Moon* 1987 (a); *Who's That Girl* 1987 (a); *Le Grand bleu/The Big Blue* 1988 (a); *Me and Him* 1988 (a); *Running on Empty* 1988 (p); *White Palace* 1990 (p); *Once Around* 1991 (a,p).

Dunne, Irene • Actress • Born Irene Marie Dunn, Louisville, KY, December 20, 1901; died September 4, 1990, Hollywood, CA. *Educ.* Chicago Musical College. Patrician, sympathetic leading lady, in films from 1930 after a successful stage career. Hugely popular for two decades, Dunne was equally at home in screwball comedies, musicals and romantic dramas. • *Leathernecking* 1930; *Bachelor Apartment* 1931; *Cimarron* 1931 **(AANBA)**; *Consolation Marriage* 1931; *The Great Lover* 1931; *The Stolen Jools (short)* 1931; *Back Street* 1932; *Symphony of Six Million* 1932; *Thirteen Women* 1932; *Ann Vickers* 1933; *If I Were Free* 1933; *No Other Woman* 1933; *The Secret of Madame Blanche* 1933; *The Silver Cord* 1933; *The Age of Innocence* 1934; *Stingaree* 1934; *This Man Is Mine* 1934; *Magnificent Obsession* 1935; *Roberta* 1935; *Sweet Adeline* 1935; *Show Boat* 1936; *Theodora Goes Wild* 1936 **(AANBA)**; *The Awful Truth* 1937 **(AANBA)**; *High, Wide, And Handsome* 1937; *Joy of Living* 1938; *Invitation to Happiness* 1939; *Love Affair* 1939 **(AANBA)**; *When Tomorrow Comes* 1939; *My Favorite Wife* 1940; *Penny Serenade* 1941; *Unfinished Business* 1941; *Lady in a Jam* 1942; *A Guy Named Joe* 1943; *Together Again* 1944; *The White Cliffs of Dover* 1944; *Over 21* 1945; *Anna and the King of Siam* 1946; *Life With Father* 1947; *I Remember Mama* 1948 **(AANBA)**; *The Mudlark* 1950; *Never a Dull Moment* 1950; *It Grows on Trees* 1952; *It's Showtime* 1976.

Dunne, Philip • Director, screenwriter; also producer. • Born New York, NY, February 11, 1908. *Educ.* Harvard. Began his Hollywood career as a scenarist in the wid-30s and scripted a number of first-rate productions incuding *How Green Was My Valley* (1941), *The Ghost and Mrs. Muir* (1947) and *The Robe* (1953).

Directing from 1954, Dunne turned out a series of smoothly crafted, finely acted dramas, notably *Hilda Crane* (1956), *Blue Denim* (1959) and the suspenseful *Lisa* (1962). Dunne also served as a speech writer on the presidential campaigns of Adlai Stevenson and John F. Kennedy. • *The Count of Monte Cristo* 1934 (sc); *Helldorado* 1934 (sc); *Student Tour* 1934 (sc); *The Melody Lingers On* 1935 (sc); *Under Pressure* 1935 (sc); *The Last of the Mohicans* 1936 (sc); *Breezing Home* 1937 (story); *The Lancer Spy* 1937 (sc); *Suez* 1938 (sc); *The Rains Came* 1939 (sc); *Stanley and Livingstone* 1939 (sc); *Swanee River* 1939 (sc,story); *Johnny Apollo* 1940 (sc); *How Green Was My Valley* 1941 (sc) **(AANBSC)**; *Son of Fury* 1942 (sc); *A Salute to France* 1944 (p); *The Town* 1944 (p); *Forever Amber* 1947 (sc); *The Ghost and Mrs. Muir* 1947 (sc); *The Late George Apley* 1947 (sc); *Escape* 1948 (sc); *The Luck of the Irish* 1948 (sc); *Pinky* 1949 (sc); *Anne of the Indies* 1951 (sc); *David and Bathsheba* 1951 (sc) **(AANBSC)**; *Lydia Bailey* 1952 (sc); *Way of a Gaucho* 1952 (p,sc); *The Robe* 1953 (sc); *Demetrius and the Gladiators* 1954 (sc); *The Egyptian* 1954 (sc); *Prince of Players* 1955 (d,p); *The View From Pompey's Head* 1955 (d,p,sc); *Hilda Crane* 1956 (d,sc); *Three Brave Men* 1956 (d,sc); *In Love and War* 1958 (d); *Ten North Frederick* 1958 (d,sc); *Blue Denim* 1959 (d,sc); *Wild in the Country* 1961 (d); *Forbid Them Not* 1962 (a); *Lisa* 1962 (d); *The Agony and the Ecstasy* 1965 (sc,story); *Blindfold* 1966 (d,sc).

Duras, Marguerite • Director, novelist, screenwriter; also playwright. • Born Marguerite Donnadieu, Giadinh, French Indochina, April 4, 1914. *Educ.* Sorbonne, Paris (law, mathematics, political science). Influential novelist who has had several of her works brought to the screen by others, contributed the haunting script for Alain Resnais's *Hiroshima, Mon Amour* (1959), and began her own career as a film writer-director in the mid-1960s.

Associated with the "nouveau roman" school, Duras generally eschews action and plot in favor of stylized meditations on themes such as memory, subjectivity and the nature of human relationships. • *Barrage contre le Pacifique/The Sea Wall* 1957 (from novel); *Hiroshima, mon amour* 1959 (sc) **(AANBSC)**; *Moderato Cantabile* 1960 (dial,adapt,from novel); *Une Aussi longue Absence/The Long Absence* 1961 (sc); *10:30 P.M. Summer* 1966 (sc,from novel *Dix heures et demie du soir en été*); *La Musica* 1966 (d,sc,from play); *La Voleuse* 1966 (dial); *The Sailor From Gibraltar* 1967 (from novel); *Détruire, Dit-Elle* 1969 (d,sc); *Jaune le soleil* 1971 (d,p,sc,from novel *Abahn Sabana David*); *Nathalie Granger* 1972 (d,sc,m); *La Femmes du Gange* 1974 (d,sc); *India Song* 1975 (a,d,sc,adapt); *Des Journées Entières dans les Arbres/Entire Days in the Trees* 1976 (d,sc,from play); *Baxter, Vera Baxter* 1977 (d,sc); *Le Camion/The Truck* 1977 (a,d,sc); *Le Navire Night* 1979 (d,sc,song); *Sauve qui peut la vie/Every Man for Himself* 1980 (a); *Les Enfants/The Children* 1984 (d,sc); *Das Mal des Todes* 1985 (from novel); *The Death of a Father—A Conspiracy of Silence* 1986 (from writings).

Durbin, Deanna • Actress • Born Edna Mae Durbin, Winnipeg, Manitoba, Canada, December 4, 1921. Wholesome teen lead of the late 1930s and 40s who shared a Special Academy Award with Mickey Rooney in 1938 "for bringing to the screen the spirit and personification of youth." She retired in 1948, partially due to weight problems. • *One Hundred Men and a Girl* 1937; *Three Smart Girls* 1937; *Mad About Music* 1938; *That Certain Age* 1938; *First Love* 1939; *Three Smart Girls Grow Up* 1939; *It's a Date* 1940; *Spring Parade* 1940; *It Started With Eve* 1941; *Nice Girl?* 1941; *The Amazing Mrs Holliday* 1943; *Hers to Hold* 1943; *His Butler's Sister* 1943; *Can't Help Singing* 1944; *Christmas Holiday* 1944; *Lady on a Train* 1945; *Because of Him* 1946; *I'll Be Yours* 1947; *Something in the Wind* 1947; *For the Love of Mary* 1948; *Up in Central Park* 1948.

Durning, Charles • Actor • Born Highland Falls, NY, February 28, 1933. *Educ.* NYU. Heavy-set character player who has achieved near-star status. Durning began in burlesque, worked as a ballroom dancer for a decade and acted prolifically on the New York stage before making his big-screen mark as Lieutenant Snyder in *The Sting* (1973). Standout performances include *The Front Page* (1974), *Dog Day Afternoon* (1975), *The Best Little Whorehouse in Texas* and *Tootsie* (both 1982). • *Harvey Middleman, Fireman* 1965; *I Walk the Line* 1970; *The Pursuit of Happiness* 1971; *Dealing: Or the Berkeley-to-Boston Forty-Brick Lost-Bag Blues* 1972; *Sisters* 1973; *The Sting* 1973; *The Front Page* 1974; *Breakheart Pass* 1975; *Dog Day Afternoon* 1975; *The Hindenburg* 1975; *Harry and Walter Go to New York* 1976; *The Choirboys* 1977; *Twilight's Last Gleaming* 1977; *An Enemy of the People* 1978; *The Fury* 1978; *The Greek Tycoon* 1978; *The Muppet Movie* 1979; *North Dallas Forty* 1979; *Starting Over* 1979; *Tilt* 1979; *When a Stranger Calls* 1979; *Die Laughing* 1980; *The Final Countdown* 1980; *Sharky's Machine* 1981; *True Confessions* 1981; *The Best Little Whorehouse in Texas* 1982 **(AANBSA)**; *Deadhead Miles* 1982; *Tootsie* 1982; *To Be or Not to Be* 1983 **(AANBSA)**; *Two of a Kind* 1983; *Mass Appeal* 1984; *Big Trouble* 1985; *The Man With One Red Shoe* 1985; *Stand Alone* 1985; *Stick* 1985; *Solarbabies* 1986; *Tough Guys* 1986; *Where the River Runs Black* 1986; *Happy New Year* 1987; *The Rosary Mur-*

ders 1987; *A Tiger's Tale* 1987; *Cop* 1988; *Far North* 1988; *Brenda Starr* 1989; *Cat Chaser* 1989; *Etoile* 1989; *Dick Tracy* 1990; *Fatal Sky* 1990; *Project: Alien* 1990.

Duryea, Dan • Actor • Born White Plains, NY, January 23, 1907; died 1968. *Educ.* Cornell University, Ithaca NY. Character player who excelled at playing weak, whining villains; memorable in several Fritz Lang movies, including *Ministry of Fear* (1944) and *Scarlet Street* (1945). • *Ball of Fire* 1941; *The Little Foxes* 1941; *The Pride of the Yankees* 1942; *That Other Woman* 1942; *Sahara* 1943; *Main Street After Dark* 1944; *Man From Frisco* 1944; *Ministry of Fear* 1944; *Mrs. Parkington* 1944; *None But the Lonely Heart* 1944; *The Woman in the Window* 1944; *Along Came Jones* 1945; *The Great Flamarion* 1945; *Lady on a Train* 1945; *Scarlet Street* 1945; *The Valley of Decision* 1945; *Black Angel* 1946; *White Tie and Tails* 1946; *Another Part of the Forest* 1948; *Black Bart* 1948; *Criss Cross* 1948; *Larceny* 1948; *River Lady* 1948; *Johnny Stool Pigeon* 1949; *Manhandled* 1949; *Too Late For Tears* 1949; *One Way Street* 1950; *The Underworld Story* 1950; *Winchester '73* 1950; *Al Jennings of Oklahoma* 1951; *Chicago Calling* 1951; *Sky Commando* 1953; *Thirty-Six Hours* 1953; *Thunder Bay* 1953; *Rails Into Laramie* 1954; *Ride Clear of Diablo* 1954; *Silver Lode* 1954; *This Is My Love* 1954; *World For Ransom* 1954; *Foxfire* 1955; *The Marauders* 1955; *Storm Fear* 1955; *Battle Hymn* 1956; *The Burglar* 1957; *Night Passage* 1957; *Slaughter on Tenth Avenue* 1957; *Kathy O'* 1958; *Platinum High School* 1960; *Six Black Horses* 1962; *Do You Know This Voice?* 1963; *Un Fiume di dollari* 1963; *Walk a Tightrope* 1963; *He Rides Tall* 1964; *Taggart* 1964; *The Bounty Killer* 1965; *The Flight of the Phoenix* 1965; *Incident at Phantom Hill* 1966; *Five Golden Dragons* 1967; *The Bamboo Saucer* 1968.

Duvall, Robert • Actor; also director, producer. • Born San Diego, CA, January 5, 1931. *Educ.* Principia College, Elsah IL (drama, history, government); Neighborhood Playhouse, New York. Cool, versatile performer who moved from supporting to leading roles in the 1970s. Duvall is equally adept with menacing, authoritarian figures (the "surfing colonel" in *Apocalypse Now* 1979) or sympathetic characters (faded country singer Mac Sledge in *Tender Mercies* 1982). A prolific actor, he has appeared in a high proportion of quality productions, including such modern classics as *M*A*S*H* (1970), the first two "Godfather" films and *Network* (1976).

Duvall has been nominated for four Oscars (he won for *Tender Mercies*) and earned an Emmy nomination for his flawless performance as Texas Ranger Gus McCrae in the TV adaptation of Larry McMurtry's *Lonesome Dove* (1989).

In 1975 Duvall completed an award-winning documentary, *We're Not the Jet Set*, about a Nebraska rodeo family, and made his narrative feature directing debut with the engaging, well-received portrait of New York Gypsy life, *Angelo, My Love* (1983). • *To Kill a Mockingbird* 1962; *Captain Newman, M.D.* 1964; *Nightmare in the Sun* 1965; *The Chase* 1966; *Bullitt* 1968; *Countdown* 1968; *The Detective* 1968; *The Rain People* 1969; *True Grit* 1969; *M*A*S*H* 1970; *The Revolutionary* 1970; *Lawman* 1971; *THX 1138* 1971; *Tomorrow* 1971; *The Godfather* 1972 **(AANBSA)**; *The Great Northfield Minnesota Raid* 1972; *Joe Kidd* 1972; *Badge 373* 1973; *Lady Ice* 1973; *The Outfit* 1973; *The Conversation* 1974; *The Godfather, Part II* 1974; *Breakout* 1975; *The Killer Elite* 1975; *We're Not the Jet Set* (doc) 1975 (d); *The Eagle Has Landed* 1976; *Network* 1976; *The Seven Per-Cent Solution* 1976; *The Greatest* 1977; *The Betsy* 1978; *Invasion of the Body Snatchers* 1978; *Apocalypse Now* 1979 (a,song) **(AANBSA)**; *The Great Santini* 1979 **(AANBA)**; *The Pursuit of D.B. Cooper* 1981; *True Confessions* 1981; *Angelo, My Love* 1982 (d,p,sc); *Tender Mercies* 1982 (a,assoc.p,songs) **(AABA)**; *The Stone Boy* 1983; *The Natural* 1984; *1918* 1985 (song); *Belizaire the Cajun* 1985 (a,creative consultant); *The Lightship* 1985; *Hotel Colonial* 1986; *Let's Get Harry* 1987; *Colors* 1988; *The Handmaid's Tale* 1989; *Days of Thunder* 1990; *A Show of Force* 1990.

Duvall, Shelley • Actress, producer • Born Houston, TX, 1950. Gifted, gangly leading lady of the 1970s and 80s, discovered by Robert Altman while hosting an art exhibition. Brilliant in Altman's *Three Women* (1977), for which she was cited best actress at Cannes, Duvall is particularly adept at playing characters for whom everything goes wrong, as in Stanley Kubrick's *The Shining* (1980).

Since the formation of Platypus Productions in 1982, followed by Think Entertainment, Duvall has emerged as a major force in cable TV production, with such notable programs as "Faerie Tale Theatre," "Shelley Duvall's Tall Tales & Legends" and "Nightmare Classics" to her credit. • *Brewster McCloud* 1970; *McCabe & Mrs. Miller* 1971; *Un Homme Qui Dort* 1974; *Thieves Like Us* 1974; *Nashville* 1975; *Buffalo Bill and the Indians, or Sitting Bull's History Lesson* 1976; *Annie Hall* 1977; *Three Women* 1977; *Popeye* 1980; *The Shining* 1980; *Time Bandits* 1981; *Roxanne* 1987; *Suburban Commando* 1991.

Duvivier, Julien • Director, screenwriter • Born Lille, France, October 8, 1896; died 1967. Prolific, competent craftsman whose career lasted almost five decades; best remembered for the film noir precursor *Pépé le Moko* (1936) and the superb slice of poetic realism *Un Carnet de Bal* (1937). Duvivier made occasional American movies as well as the British *Anna Karenina* (1948, with Vivien Leigh). • *Haceldama* 1919 (d,sc); *La Réincarnation de Serge Renaudier* 1920 (d,sc); *L'Ouragan sur la Montagne* 1922 (d,sc); *Les Roquevillard* 1922 (d,sc); *Der Unheimliche Gast* 1922 (d,sc); *Reflet de Claude Mercoeur* 1923 (d,sc); *Coeurs Farouches* 1924 (d,sc); *Credo ou la Tragédie de Lourdes* 1924 (d,sc); *La Machine à refaire la vie* 1924 (d,sc); *L'Oeuvre immortelle* 1924 (d,sc); *L'Abbé Constantin* 1925 (d,sc); *Poil de Carotte* 1925 (d,sc); *L'Agonie de Jerusalem* 1926 (d,sc); *L'Homme à l'Hispano* 1926 (d,sc); *Le Mariage de Mademoiselle Beulemans* 1927 (d,sc); *Le Mystère de la Tour Eiffel* 1927 (d,sc); *Le Tourbillon de Paris* 1928 (d,sc); *La Divine Croisière* 1929 (d,sc); *Maman Colibri* 1929 (d,sc); *La Vie miraculeuse de Thérèse Martin* 1929 (d,sc); *Au Bonheur des Dames* 1930 (d,sc); *David Golder* 1930 (d,sc); *Allo Berlin? Ici Paris!* 1932 (d,sc); *Les Cinq Gentlemen maudits* 1932 (d,sc); *Poil de Carotte* 1932 (d,sc); *La Venus du collège* 1932 (d,sc); *La Machine à refaire la vie* 1933 (d,sc); *Le Petit Roi* 1933 (d,sc); *La Tête d'un Homme* 1933 (d,sc); *La Bandera* 1934 (d,sc); *Maria Chapdelaine/The Naked Heart* 1934 (d,sc); *La Paquebot 'Tenacity'* 1934 (d,sc); *Golgotha* 1935 (d,sc); *La Belle Equipe* 1936 (d,sc); *Der Golem* 1936 (d,sc,story); *Pépé Le Moko* 1936 (d,sc); *Un Carnet de Bal* 1937 (d); *L'Homme du Jour* 1937 (d,sc); *The Great Waltz* 1938 (d); *La Charrette Fantôme* 1939 (d,sc); *La Fin du Jour/The End of the Day* 1939 (d,sc); *Untel père et fils* 1940 (d,sc); *Lydia* 1941 (d,story); *Tales of Manhattan* 1942 (d); *Flesh and Fantasy* 1943 (d,p); *The Impostor* 1944 (d,p,sc,story); *Panique* 1946 (d,sc); *Anna Karenina* 1948 (d,sc); *Au royaume des cieux/The Sinners* 1949 (d,sc); *Black Jack* 1950 (d,p,sc); *Le Petit Monde de Don Camillo* 1951 (d,sc); *Sous le Ciel de Paris* 1951 (d,sc); *La Fête à Henriette/Holiday for Henrietta* 1952 (d,sc); *L'Affaire Maurizius/On Trial* 1953 (d,sc); *Retour de Don Camillo* 1953 (sc,dial); *Marianne de ma jeunesse* 1955 (d,sc); *Voici le temps des assassins/Deadlier than the Male* 1956 (d,sc); *L'Homme à l'impermeable/The Man in the Raincoat* 1957 (d,sc,dial,lyrics); *Pot Bouille* 1957 (d); *La Femme et le Pantin* 1959 (d,sc); *Marie Octobre* 1959 (d,sc); *Boulevard* 1960 (d,sc); *La Grande Vie* 1960 (d,sc); *Das Brennende Gericht/The Burning Court* 1962 (d,sc); *Le Diable et les dix commandements/The Devil and the Ten Commandments* 1962 (d,sc); *Chair de Poule/Highway Pickup* 1963 (d); *Paris When It Sizzles* 1963 (from story *Holiday for Henrietta*); *Diaboliquement Votre/Diabolically Yours* 1967 (d,sc).

Dwan, Allan • Director; also screenwriter, producer. • Born Joseph Aloysius Dwan, Toronto, Ontario, Canada, April 3, 1885; died 1981. *Educ.* Notre Dame. Dwan's first job was as a lighting engineer for the Peter Cooper Hewitt Company, where he helped develop a forerunner of the neon tube known as the mercury vapor arc. He became intrigued by "those silly things called movies" while supervising the installation of some arcs at Essanay studios, asked about the stories the filmmakers used, and proceeded to sell them 15 he had written at college. Essanay then offered him a job as scenario editor.

Dwan's career spanned the history of American motion pictures, from the days of silent one-reelers to modern Technicolor features that utilized some of the cinematic techniques whose use he had pioneered. By his own estimate, Dwan participated in the making of 1,850 films, some 400 of these as a director. (Only a few of his works remain extant.)

In 1911 he moved to the American Film Company, where he got the opportunity to direct when the person originally given the assignment was discovered drunk. Dwan made more than 250 films there, mostly one-reel westerns, which he later recalled "the actors showed me how to direct."

It was Dwan's engineering skills that were particularly useful to him: he is credited with mounting a camera on a car and inventing the dolly shot. He proposed the construction of a rail system on the set of Griffith's *Intolerance* and years later developed techniques for on-set sound recording.

In 1913 Dwan joined Universal, where he worked with Lon Chaney and met his first wife, Pauline Bush. Later that decade he began making films with Douglas Fairbanks and Gloria Swanson.

Although he made a successful transition to sound, Dwan was relegated for a number of years to the directing of programmers at Fox. Despite his commercial success with several Shirley Temple films, most of his work was confined to the grind of B pictures. He may have been comfortable with this, as he later remarked: "If you get your head up above the mob, they try to knock it off. If you stay down, you last forever."

Dwan later went to work at Republic, where his *The Sands of Iwo Jima* (1949) helped make John Wayne the mythic American war-hero. Dwan described the old Hollywood this way: "Years ago we had no supervision. We made pictures our own way. We pleased nobody but ourselves and the public." • *Maiden and Men* 1912 (d); *The County Chairman* 1914 (d,sc); *Richelieu* 1914 (d,sc); *The Dancing Girl* 1915 (d); *David Harum* 1915 (d); *The Foundling* 1915 (d); *Jordan Is a Hard Road* 1915 (d,sc); *The Pretty Sister of Jose* 1915 (d); *Betty of Greystone* 1916 (d); *Fifty-Fifty* 1916 (d,story); *The Good Bad Man* 1916 (d); *The Habit of Happiness* 1916 (d,story); *The Half-Breed* 1916 (d); *An Innocent Magdalene* 1916 (d); *Manhattan Madness* 1916 (d); *Fighting Odds* 1917 (d); *A Modern Musketeer* 1917 (d,sc); *Panthea* 1917 (d,sc); *Until They Get Me* 1917 (p); *Bound in Morocco* 1918 (d,sc,story); *He Comes Up Smiling* 1918 (d); *Headin' South* 1918 (story); *An Honest Man* 1918 (p); *Innocent's Progress* 1918 (p); *Mr. Fix-It* 1918 (d,sc); *Shoes That Danced* 1918 (p); *Society For Sale* 1918 (p); *Cheating Cheaters* 1919 (d); *The Dark Star* 1919 (d); *Getting Mary Married* 1919 (d); *Sahara* 1919 (p); *Soldiers of Fortune* 1919 (d); *The Forbidden Thing* 1920 (d); *In the Heart of a Fool* 1920 (d,p); *The Luck of the Irish* 1920 (d); *A Splendid Hazard* 1920 (p); *A Broken Doll* 1921 (d); *A Perfect Crime* 1921 (d,sc); *The Scoffer* 1921 (d,p); *The Sin of Martha Queed* 1921 (d,sc); *The Hidden Woman* 1922 (d,p); *Robin Hood* 1922 (d); *Superstition* 1922 (d); *Big Brother* 1923 (d,p); *The Glimpses of the Moon* 1923 (d); *Lawful Larceny* 1923 (d); *Zaza* 1923 (d,p); *Argentine Love* 1924 (d,p); *Her Love Story* 1924 (d); *Manhandled* 1924 (d); *A Society Scandal* 1924 (d,p); *Wages of Virtue* 1924 (d,p); *The Coast of Folly* 1925 (d); *Fifty-Fifty* 1925 (story); *Night Life of New York* 1925 (d); *Stage Struck* 1925 (d,p); *Padlocked* 1926 (d); *Sea Horses* 1926 (d); *Summer Bachelors* 1926 (d); *Tin Gods* 1926 (d); *East Side, West Side* 1927 (d,sc); *French Dressing* 1927 (d,p); *The Joy Girl* 1927 (d); *The Music Master* 1927 (d); *The Big Noise* 1928 (d,p); *Harold Teen* 1928 (p); *Mad Hour* 1928 (p); *The Whip Woman* 1928 (p); *The Far Call* 1929 (d); *Frozen Justice* 1929 (d); *The Iron Mask* 1929 (d); *South Sea Rose* 1929 (d); *Tide of Empire* 1929 (d); *Man to Man* 1930 (d); *What a Widow!* 1930 (d,p); *Chances* 1931 (d); *Wicked* 1931 (d); *Her First Affair* 1932 (d); *While Paris Sleeps* 1932 (d); *Counsel's Opinion* 1933 (d); *I Spy* 1933 (d,sc); *Hollywood Party* 1934 (d); *Black Sheep* 1935 (d,story); *Navy Wife* 1935 (d); *15 Maiden Lane* 1936 (d); *High Tension* 1936 (d); *Human Cargo* 1936 (d); *The Song and Dance Man* 1936 (d); *Heidi* 1937 (d); *One Mile From Heaven* 1937 (d); *That I May Live* 1937 (d); *Woman-Wise* 1937 (d); *Josette* 1938 (d); *Rebecca of Sunnybrook Farm* 1938 (d); *Suez* 1938 (d); *Frontier Marshal* 1939 (d); *The Gorilla* 1939 (d); *The Three Musketeers* 1939 (d); *Sailor's Lady* 1940 (d); *Trail of the Vigilantes* 1940 (d); *Young People* 1940 (d); *Look Who's Laughing* 1941 (d,p); *Rise and Shine* 1941 (d); *Friendly Enemies* 1942 (d); *Here We Go Again* 1942 (d,p); *Around the World* 1943 (d,p); *Abroad With Two Yanks* 1944 (d); *Up in Mabel's Room* 1944 (d); *Brewster's Millions* 1945 (d); *Getting Gertie's Garter* 1945 (d,sc); *Calendar Girl* 1946 (d); *Rendezvous With Annie* 1946 (d); *Driftwood* 1947 (d); *Northwest Outpost* 1947 (d); *Angel in Exile* 1948 (d); *The Inside Story* 1948 (d); *Sands of Iwo Jima* 1949 (d); *Surrender* 1950 (d); *Belle le Grand* 1951 (d); *The Wild Blue Yonder* 1951 (d); *I Dream of Jeanie* 1952 (d); *Montana Belle* 1952 (d); *Sweethearts on Parade* 1953 (d); *The Woman They Almost Lynched* 1953 (d); *Cattle Queen of Montana* 1954 (d); *Escape to Burma* 1954 (d); *Flight Nurse* 1954 (d); *Passion* 1954 (d); *Silver Lode* 1954 (d); *Pearl of the South Pacific* 1955 (d); *Tennessee's Partner* 1955 (d); *Hold Back the Night* 1956 (d); *Slightly Scarlet* 1956 (d); *The Restless Breed* 1957 (d); *The River's Edge* 1957 (d); *Enchanted Island* 1958 (d); *The Most Dangerous Man Alive* 1961 (d).

Eastman, George • Inventor, photographic pioneer • Born Waterville, NY, July 12, 1854; died 1932. Former amateur photographer responsible for several key developments in photographic technology. Eastman founded the Eastman Kodak company in 1880, developing paper roll film in 1884 and perforated celluloid film in 1889.

Eastwood, Clint • Actor, director; also producer. • Born Clinton Eastwood, Jr., San Francisco, CA, May 31, 1930. *Educ.* Los Angeles City College (business). Clint Eastwood rose out of semi-obscurity to become the number-one box-office star in the world, subsequently earning critical acclaim as a director. His production company, Malpaso, puts out low-budget, high-profit movies, with an occasional quality film to satisfy Eastwood's interest in jazz. Eastwood is not part of the Hollywood establishment; his business is run out of Carmel, California, on the Monterey Peninsula, where he has served as mayor and run a restaurant.

Eastwood grew up in Depression-era California, where his parents were itinerant workers. After high school, he worked as a lumberjack in Oregon, played honky-tonk piano and was a swimming instructor in the US Army. On the G.I. Bill, he studied at Los Angeles City College. Signed by Universal, one of his first experiences with the indignity actors must suffer was in a "Francis the Talking Mule" movie, *Francis in the Navy* (1955). Many B-movies later, he moved to New York and gained recognition as the trail boss Rowdy Yates in the successful TV series "Rawhide" (1959-66).

Tight TV schedules and good training helped him develop the minimalist acting style for which he is famous; it was first appreciated in Europe where he starred in a trilogy of spaghetti westerns directed by Sergio Leone in Spain. Sinewy and lethal, he embodied to Europeans the maverick, unpredictably violent American, whose philosophy in *A Fistful of Dollars* (1964) was "everybody gets rich or dead." *For a Few Dollars More* (1965) and *The Good, the Bad, and the Ugly* (1966) became classics of nihilism and made Eastwood a cult star. "My characters," he has said, "are usually calloused men with a sensitive spot for right and wrong." He has also noted that "My movies add up to a morality, not a politics." His friendship with Ronald Reagan has attracted criticism from some, but Eastwood's concern for the environment, he claims, would make him befriend any President and his Department of the Interior.

Eastwood's second famed screen incarnation was Harry Callahan, the cop of Don Siegel's *Dirty Harry* (1971) who found it easier to shoot suspects than interrogate them. Hence Harry's immortal line in *Sudden Impact* (1983) when a crook threatens him, "Go ahead—make my day," snarled from the responsible end of a massive handgun. One unique feature in Eastwood's cop movies has been their female characters, who come off more like real people than the fantasy objects customary to the genre. These and other Eastwood films have explored sexual violence in a way that has distinguished him as a controversial and complex filmmker.

His portraits of tormented men with intense inner lives and little ability to communicate with others found an apogee in *Bird* (1988), his moody portrait of jazz musician Charlie Parker. Virtual "auteurist" control has enabled him to make mystical westerns (*High Plains Drifter* 1973; *Pale Rider* 1985) and cop movies exploring feminist concerns (*Sudden Impact 1983*; *Tightrope* 1984). He has even entrusted himself to first-time directors, such as Michael Cimino, although they are assumed to be "yes-men." Eastwood's control is so thorough that it begs the question of what his directors do. "A director's job," he once said, "is to make the set a comfortable place for the actors." If directors can be considered the equivalent of the talk-show host, then Eastwood has set himself apart by not talking. KJ • *Francis in the Navy* 1955 (a); *Lady Godiva* 1955 (a); *Never Say Goodbye* 1955 (a); *Revenge of the Creature* 1955 (a); *Tarantula* 1955 (a); *The First Traveling Saleslady* 1956 (a); *Star in the Dust* 1956 (a); *Escapade in Japan* 1957 (a); *Ambush at Cimarron Pass* 1958 (a); *Lafayette Escadrille* 1958 (a); *Per un Pugno di Dollari/A Fistful of Dollars* 1964 (a); *Per qualche dollaro in piu/For a Few Dollars More* 1965 (a); *Il Buono, il Brutto, il Cattivo/The Good, the Bad, and the Ugly* 1966 (a); *Coogan's Bluff* 1968 (a); *Hang 'Em High* 1968 (a); *Le Streghe/The Witches* 1968 (a); *Where Eagles Dare* 1968 (a); *Paint Your Wagon* 1969 (a); *Kelly's Heroes* 1970 (a); *Two Mules For Sister Sara* 1970 (a); *The Beguiled* 1971 (a); *Dirty Harry* 1971 (a); *Play Misty For Me* 1971 (a,d); *Joe Kidd* 1972 (a); *Breezy* 1973 (d); *High Plains Drifter* 1973 (a,d); *Magnum Force* 1973 (a); *Thunderbolt and Lightfoot* 1974 (a); *The Eiger Sanction* 1975 (a,d); *The Outlaw Josey Wales* 1975 (a,d); *The Enforcer* 1976 (a); *The Gauntlet* 1977 (a,d); *Every Which Way But Loose* 1978 (a); *Escape From Alcatraz* 1979 (a); *Any Which Way You Can* 1980 (a,song); *Bronco Billy* 1980 (a,d,song); *Firefox* 1982 (a,d,p); *Honkytonk Man* 1982 (a,d,p); *Sudden Impact* 1983 (a,d,p); *City Heat* 1984 (a,song); *Tightrope* 1984 (a,p); *Pale Rider* 1985 (a,d,p); *Heartbreak Ridge* 1986 (a,d,p,song); *Bird* 1988 (d,p); *The Dead Pool* 1988 (a,p); *Thelonious Monk: Straight, No Chaser* 1988 (exec.p); *Pink Cadillac* 1989 (a); *The Rookie* 1990 (a,d); *White Hunter, Black Heart* 1990 (a,d,p).

Eberhardt, Thom • Director; also screenwriter. • Born Thomas Eberhardt, Los Angeles, CA. Award-winning maker of social-issue documentaries for public TV before moving into motion pictures. • *Night of the Comet* 1984 (d,sc); *Sole Survivor* 1984 (d,sc,ed); *The Night Before* 1988 (d,sc); *Without a Clue* 1988 (d); *Gross Anatomy* 1989 (d).

Ebert, Roger • Critic; also author. • Born Illinois. *Educ.* University of Illinois. The first-ever recipient of a Pulitzer Prize for film criticism (in 1975), Ebert is best known for his TV work opposite critic-colleague Gene Siskel on "Siskel and Ebert" (they were formerly hosts of PBS's "At the Movies"). He is the author of several books on the cinema, including *A Kiss Is Still A Kiss* (1984), and has also written screenplays, most notably for Russ Meyer's cult classic, *Beyond the Valley of the Dolls* (1970).

Eddy, Nelson • Singer; also actor. • Born Providence, RI, June 29, 1901; died March 6, 1967, Miami Beach, FL. Successful opera baritone with a wholesome masculinity who starred opposite Jeanette McDonald in a series of enormously popular MGM operettas in the 1930s. • *Broadway to Hollywood* 1933; *Dancing Lady* 1933; *Student Tour* 1934; *Naughty Marietta* 1935; *Rose Marie* 1936; *Maytime* 1937; *Rosalie* 1937; *The Girl of the Golden West* 1938; *Sweethearts* 1938; *Balalaika* 1939; *Let Freedom Ring* 1939; *Bitter Sweet* 1940; *New Moon* 1940; *The Chocolate Soldier* 1941; *I Married an Angel* 1942; *The Phantom of the Opera* 1943; *Knickerbocker Holiday* 1944; *Make Mine Music* 1946; *Northwest Outpost* 1947.

Edeson, Arthur • Director of photography • Born New York, NY, October 24, 1891; died 1970. *Educ.* CCNY. Former actor and portrait photographer who began a highly influential cinematographic career in 1914. Edeson shot many of Douglas Fairbanks's adventures from 1917 through the 1920's and showed off his command of the moving camera in the early sound film *All Quiet on the Western Front* (1930). He made a significant contribution to the output of Warner Bros. from 1936 to 1947, photographing such classics as *The Maltese Falcon* (1941) and *Casablanca* (1942), before retiring in 1949. • *The Dollar Mark* 1914; *Hearts in Exile* 1915; *Wildfire* 1915; *Bought and Paid For* 1916; *The Deep Purple* 1916; *The Devil's Toy* 1916; *The Gilded Cage* 1916; *Miss Petticoats* 1916; *Baby Mine* 1917; *In Again, Out Again* 1917; *The Master Hand* 1917 (ph,ad); *Nearly Married* 1917; *The Page Mystery* 1917; *The Price of Pride* 1917; *Reaching For the Moon* 1917; *Souls Adrift* 1917; *A Square Deal* 1917; *The Stolen Paradise* 1917; *Wild and Woolly* 1917; *A Woman Alone* 1917; *Jack Spurlock, Prodigal* 1918; *The Road Through the Dark* 1918; *The Savage Woman* 1918; *The Better Wife* 1919; *Cheating Cheaters* 1919; *The Eyes of Youth* 1919; *The Hushed Hour* 1919; *For the Soul of Rafael* 1920; *The Forbidden Woman* 1920; *Good Women* 1921; *Hush* 1921; *Mid-Channel* 1921; *The Three Musketeers* 1921; *Robin Hood* 1922; *The Worldly Madonna* 1922; *The End of the World* 1924; *Inez From Hollywood* 1924; *The Thief of Bagdad* 1924; *Her Sister From Paris* 1925; *The Lost World* 1925; *One Way Street* 1925; *Stella Dallas* 1925; *The Talker* 1925; *Waking Up the Town* 1925; *The Bat* 1926; *Just Another Blonde* 1926; *Partners Again* 1926; *Subway Sadie* 1926; *Sweet Daddies* 1926; *The Drop Kick* 1927; *The Gorilla* 1927; *McFadden's Flats* 1927; *The Patent Leather Kid* 1927; *Me, Gangster* 1928; *A Thief in the Dark* 1928; *The Cockeyed World* 1929; *Girls Gone Wild* 1929; *In Old Arizona* 1929 (**AANBPH**); *Romance of the Rio Grande* 1929; *All Quiet on the Western Front* 1930 (**AANBPH**); *The Big Trail* 1930 (ph—70mm); *Always Goodbye* 1931; *Doctors' Wives* 1931; *Frankenstein* 1931; *The Man Who Came Back* 1931; *Waterloo Bridge* 1931; *Fast Companions* 1932; *Flesh* 1932; *The Impatient Maiden* 1932; *The Last Mile* 1932; *The Old Dark House* 1932; *Strangers of the Evening* 1932; *Those We Love* 1932; *The Big Brain* 1933; *The Constant Woman* 1933; *His Double Life* 1933; *The Invisible Man* 1933; *The Life of Jimmy Dolan* 1933; *A Study in Scarlet* 1933; *Here Comes the Navy* 1934; *The Merry Frinks* 1934; *Palooka* 1934; *Ceiling Zero* 1935; *Devil Dogs of the Air* 1935; *Dinky*

1935; *Going Highbrow* 1935; *Maybe It's Love* 1935; *Mutiny on the Bounty* 1935; *While the Patient Slept* 1935; *China Clipper* 1936; *Gold Diggers of 1937* 1936; *The Golden Arrow* 1936; *Hot Money* 1936; *Satan Met a Lady* 1936; *The Footloose Heiress* 1937; *The Go Getter* 1937; *The Kid Comes Back* 1937; *Mr. Dodd Takes the Air* 1937; *Submarine D-1* 1937; *They Won't Forget* 1937; *Boy Meets Girl* 1938; *Cowboy From Brooklyn* 1938; *Mr. Chump* 1938; *Racket Busters* 1938; *Swing Your Lady* 1938; *Each Dawn I Die* 1939; *Kid Nightingale* 1939; *Nancy Drew - Reporter* 1939; *No Place to Go* 1939; *Sweepstakes Winner* 1939; *Wings of the Navy* 1939; *Castle on the Hudson* 1940; *Lady With Red Hair* 1940; *They Drive By Night* 1940; *Tugboat Annie Sails Again* 1940; *Kisses For Breakfast* 1941; *The Maltese Falcon* 1941; *Sergeant York* 1941 (add.ph—war sequences); *Across the Pacific* 1942; *Casablanca* 1942 **(AANBPH)**; *The Male Animal* 1942; *Old Acquaintance* 1943 (uncred.ph); *Thank Your Lucky Stars* 1943; *The Conspirators* 1944; *The Mask of Dimitrios* 1944; *Shine on Harvest Moon* 1944; *Never Say Goodbye* 1946; *Nobody Lives Forever* 1946; *Three Strangers* 1946; *The Time, the Place and the Girl* 1946; *Two Guys From Milwaukee* 1946; *My Wild Irish Rose* 1947; *Stallion Road* 1947; *Two Guys From Texas* 1948; *The Fighting O'Flynn* 1949.

Edison, Thomas Alva • Inventor • Born Milan, OH, February 11, 1847; died 1931. Dubbed the "Wizard of Menlo Park" during his own lifetime, and considered by some the "ancestral deity" of General Electric, Edison was a major contributor to the age of electronics. Renowned for his work on the incandescent light bulb and phonograph, his ingenuity also touched devices such as the stock ticker, mimeograph machine and telephone transmitter. Edison's New Jersey labs in Newark, Menlo Park and West Orange were think tanks extraordinaire, where creative minds worked together on key developments in early motion picture technology.

Edison had already made a number of significant inventions, primarily in the field of telegraphic systems, and established himself in West Orange, the third and largest of his New Jersey laboratories, when he wrote on October 8, 1888, "I am experimenting upon an instrument which does for the Eye what the phonograph does for the Ear." This instrument was developed by Edison's assistant, amateur photographer W.K.L. Dickson. Dickson followed the experiments of European photographers Etienne-Jules Marey and Eadweard Muybridge, who had been working with the notion of "persistence of vision"—whereby a quickly moving series of pictures gives the illusion of movement. Dickson improved on the European "zoetrope" or "magic lantern," which was constructed of separate glass plates mounted on a turning cylinder, by using strips of John Corbutt's (and later John Eastman's) newly invented flexible celluloid film. Rather than Marey's "photographic rifle," or Muybridge's closely spaced cameras going off in rapid succession, Dickson devised an electrically controlled camera called the "Kinetograph." November 1890 saw the production of Dickson's debut film, *Monkeyshines*, featuring the antics of Fred Ott, another Edison assistant.

At first, Edison rejected the notion of projected film. Instead, he had Dickson perfect the "Kinetoscope," a small cabinet with a peephole, suitable for solitary viewing. The first nickelodeon "parlor," a storefront of ten Kinetoscopes with each viewing costing a nickel, opened April 14, 1894, at 1155 Broadway, in New York. It was soon followed by others in major cities in the US and Europe.

Early movies were 60 to 90 second action shorts with titles such as *Barber Shop, Barroom, Wrestling, Highland Dance, Trapeze* and so on. These were produced in the West Orange "Black Maria" studio, a black tar-papered building on a pivot so that it could be turned to follow the path of the sun through its one skylight giving natural light. "Documentaries" of activities on Valley Road outside the lab were also filmed. Because he had failed to patent the Kinetoscope properly, however, Edison's developments were much copied. Although the 1894 prize fight between Mike Leonard and Jack Cushing, fought in the "Black Maria," proved a financial coup, he did not in general make much profit from his motion picture devices.

This situation changed in 1895, when Edison joined forces with Thomas Armat, who was working on a "Vitascope" projector. Projected films, with the potential to reach large audiences, premiered on April 23, 1896, at Koster and Bial's Music Hall, at 34th and Broadway, in New York, sharing the bill with vaudeville acts.

Classics such as Edwin S. Porter's *The Life of an American Fireman* and *The Great Train Robbery* (both 1903) were filmed at the "Black Maria" before the construction, in 1905, of a large glass studio in the Bronx, New York. In 1909 Edison, along with several other fledgling movie producers, formed the Motion Picture Patents Company to try to impede independent film production. In 1917, however, this monopoly was broken and Edison retired from the film business.

MGM immortalized "the Wizard" in two 1940 movies, *Young Tom Edison* and *Edison the Man*. CSE

Edlund, Richard • American special effects artist • *Educ.* USC, Los Angeles (film). Leading contemporary figure in the world of visual effects, largely thanks to his work on the "Star Wars" trilogy. Edlund founded the highly successful Industrial Light & Magic company for George Lucas in 1975 and created his own Boss Film Corp. eight years later. • *Star Wars* 1977 (miniature ph,fx) **(AABFX)**; *Battlestar Galactica* 1978 (fx ph); *The China Syndrome* 1979 (miniature ph); *The Empire Strikes Back* 1980 (fx) **(AASPECIAL ACHIEVEMENT)**; *Raiders of the Lost Ark* 1981 (fx) **(AABFX)**; *Poltergeist* 1982 (fx) **(AANBFX)**; *Return of the Jedi* 1983 (fx) **(AASPECIAL ACHIEVEMENT)**; *2010* 1984 (fx) **(AANBFX)**; *Ghostbusters* 1984 (fx) **(AANBFX)**; *Fright Night* 1985 (fx prod); *Big Trouble in Little China* 1986 (fx prod); *The Boy Who Could Fly* 1986 (fx); *Legal Eagles* 1986 (fx); *Poltergeist II: The Other Side* 1986 (fx) **(AANBFX)**; *Solarbabies* 1986 (fx prod); *Date With an Angel* 1987 (fx prod); *Leonard, Part 6* 1987 (fx prod); *Masters of the Universe* 1987 (fx); *The Monster Squad* 1987 (fx prod); *Big Top Pee-Wee* 198/8 (fx); *Die Hard* 1988 (fx prod) **(AANBFX)**; *Elvira, Mistress of the Dark* 1988 (fx); *Vibes* 1988 (fx prod); *Farewell to the King* 1989 (ph—special water unit); *Ghost* 1990 (fx); *Solar Crisis* 1990 (fx,p).

Edson, Richard • Actor; also musician. • Born New York, NY. Former musician whose quirky, understated debut in Jim Jarmusch's *Stranger Than Paradise* (1984) has led to several supporting roles in both Hollywood and New York, most notably as Danny Aiello's less volatile son in *Do the Right Thing* (1989). • *Vortex* 1982 (m); *Stranger Than Paradise* 1984; *Desperately Seeking Susan* 1985; *Ferris Bueller's Day Off* 1986; *Howard the Duck* 1986; *Platoon* 1986; *Good Morning, Vietnam* 1987; *Walker* 1987; *The Chair* 1988; *China Lake* 1988; *Eight Men Out* 1988; *Tougher Than Leather* 1988; *Bloodhounds of Broadway* 1989; *Do the Right Thing* 1989; *Let It Ride* 1989; *Making "Do the Right Thing"* 1989.

Edwards, Anthony • Actor • Born Santa Barbara, CA, July 19, 1963. *Educ.* Royal Academy of Arts, London; USC, Los Angeles (drama). Promising young lead, memorable in the title role of *Mr. North* (1988) and as the perplexed college student caught up in European espionage in the spy thriller *Gotcha!* (1985). • *Fast Times at Ridgemont High* 1982; *Heart Like a Wheel* 1982; *Revenge of the Nerds* 1984; *Gotcha!* 1985; *The Sure Thing* 1985; *Top Gun* 1986; *Revenge of the Nerds II* 1987; *Summer Heat* 1987; *Hawks* 1988; *Miracle Mile* 1988; *Mr. North* 1988; *How I Got Into College* 1989; *Downtown* 1990.

Edwards, Blake • Director; also producer, screenwriter, actor. • Born William Blake McEdwards, Tulsa, OK, July 26, 1922. Accomplished director, best known for his "Pink Panther" comedies starring Peter Sellers as the bumbling Inspector Clouseau.

The grandson of silent director J. Gordon Edwards, he began acting in films in 1942 and writing screenplays in 1948, making his directing debut with *Bring Your Smile Along* (1955). Although primarily associated with comedies, Edwards has also been responsible for some fine thrillers, including the taut, strikingly photographed *Experiment in Terror* (1962).

Continual disputes with the Hollywood establishment led Edwards to spend five years in Europe in the 1970s, and his critical reputation has since fluctuated. Son Geoffrey is a screenwriter, daughter Jennifer is an actress and second wife, actress-singer Julie Andrews, has starred in several of his recent films (*S.O.B.* 1981, *Victor/Victoria* 1982, *That's Life* 1986). • *Ten Gentlemen From West Point* 1942 (a); *In the Meantime, Darling* 1944 (a); *Marshal of Reno* 1944 (a); *Strangler of the Swamp* 1945 (a); *Tokyo Rose* 1945 (a); *Panhandle* 1948 (a,p,sc); *Stampede* 1949 (p,sc); *Rainbow 'Round My Shoulder* 1952 (sc); *Sound Off* 1952 (sc,story); *All Ashore* 1953 (sc,story); *Cruisin' Down the River* 1953 (sc,story); *The Atomic Kid* 1954 (story); *Drive a Crooked Road* 1954 (sc); *Bring Your Smile Along* 1955 (d,sc,story,song); *My Sister Eileen* 1955 (sc); *He Laughed Last* 1956 (d,sc,story); *Mister Cory* 1957 (d,sc); *Operation Mad Ball* 1957 (sc); *This Happy Feeling* 1958 (d,sc); *Operation Petticoat* 1959 (d); *The Perfect Furlough* 1959 (d); *High Time* 1960 (d); *Breakfast at Tiffany's* 1961 (d); *The Couch* 1962 (story); *Days of Wine and Roses* 1962 (d); *Experiment in Terror* 1962 (d,p); *The Notorious Landlady* 1962 (sc); *Soldier in the Rain* 1963 (sc); *The Pink Panther* 1964 (d,sc); *A Shot in the Dark* 1964 (d,p,sc); *The Great Race* 1965 (d,story); *What Did You Do in the War, Daddy?* 1966 (d,p,story); *Gunn* 1967 (d,sc,story); *The Party* 1968 (d,p,sc,story); *Darling Lili* 1970 (d,p,sc); *Wild Rovers* 1971 (d,p,sc); *The Carey Treatment* 1972 (d); *The Tamarind Seed* 1974 (d,sc); *The Return of the Pink Panther* 1975 (d,p,sc); *The Pink Panther Strikes Again* 1976 (d,p,sc); *Revenge of the Pink Panther* 1978 (d,p,sc,story); *10* 1979 (d,p,sc); *S.O.B.* 1981 (d,exec.p,sc); *Trail of the Pink Panther* 1982 (d,p,sc,story); *Victor/Victoria* 1982 (d,p,sc) **(AANBSC)**; *Curse of the Pink Panther* 1983 (d,p,sc); *The Man Who Loved Women* 1983 (d,p,sc); *City Heat* 1984 (sc,story); *Micki & Maude* 1984 (d); *A Fine Mess* 1986 (d,sc); *That's Life!* 1986 (d,sc); *Blind Date* 1987 (d); *Sunset* 1988 (d,sc); *Skin Deep* 1989 (d,sc); *Switch* 1991 (d,sc).

Eggar, Samantha • Actress • Born Victoria Louise Samantha Eggar, London, March 5, 1939. Striking, fresh-faced redhead who first made her mark as the object of Terence Stamp's obsessive desire in William Wyler's haunting *The Collector* (1965), a role which earned her a best actress award at Cannes. Subsequently in international films and numerous TV movies and miniseries. • *The Wild and the Willing* 1962; *Doctor in Distress* 1963; *Dr. Crippen* 1963; *Psyche '59* 1964; *The Collector* 1965 **(AANBA)**; *Return From the Ashes* 1965; *Walk, Don't Run* 1966; *Doctor Dolittle* 1967; *La Dame dans l'auto avec des lunettes et un fusil* 1970; *The Molly Maguires* 1970; *The Walking Stick* 1970; *The Light at the Edge of the World* 1971; *The Dead Are Alive* 1972; *The Seven Per-Cent Solution* 1976; *Why Shoot the Teacher* 1976; *The Uncanny* 1977; *Welcome to Blood City* 1977; *The Brood* 1979; *The Exterminator* 1980; *Curtains* 1982; *Hot Touch* 1982; *For the Term of His Natural Life* 1985; *Directed By William Wyler* 1986; *Ragin' Cajun* 1990.

Egoyan, Atom • Canadian director, screenwriter; also producer, editor. • *Educ.* University of Toronto. Stylish and highly assured young filmmaker whose work combines self-reflexive meditations on the nature of film and video with a darkly ironic sense of humor. Director Wim Wenders was so impressed with Egoyan's *Family Viewing* (1987) that, when awarded the Prix Alcan for *Wings of Desire* at the 1987 Montreal New Cinema Festival, he publicly turned the prize over to the younger filmmaker. • *Next of Kin* 1984 (d,m,p,sc,ed); *Family Viewing* 1987 (d,p,sc,ed); *La Boite à Soleil* 1988 (a); *Speaking Parts* 1989 (d,p,sc,ed).

Eichhorn, Lisa • Actress • Born Reading, PA, February 4, 1952. *Educ.* Queen's University, Kingston, Canada; Oxford; RADA, London. Talented leading lady who divides her time among stage and film roles in both England and the US. • *The Europeans* 1979; *Yanks* 1979; *Why Would I Lie?* 1980; *Cutter's Way* 1981; *The Weather in the Streets* 1983; *Wildrose* 1984; *Opposing Force* 1986; *Grim Prairie Tales* 1990; *Nocturne* 1990.

Eisenstein, Sergei • Director, theoretician; also screenwriter, editor. • Born Sergei Mikhailovich Eisenstein, Riga, Latvia, January 23, 1898; died February 10, 1948, Moscow. *Educ.* School of Fine Arts, Riga; Institute of Civil Engineering, Petrograd (architecture); Officers Engineering School (engineering); General Staff Academy, Moscow (Oriental languages); State School for Stage Direction. As a youth, Sergei Eisenstein attended the science-oriented Realschule, to prepare himself for engineering school. However, he did find time for vigorous reading in Russian, German, English and French, as well as drawing cartoons and performing in a children's theater troupe which he founded. In 1915, he moved to Petrograd to continue his studies at the Institute of Civil Engineering, his father's alma mater. On his own, he also studied Renaissance art and attended avant-garde theater productions of Meyerhold and Yevreinov.

After the February 1917 Revolution, he sold his first political cartoons, signed Sir Gay, to several magazines in Petrograd. He also served in the volunteer militia and in the engineering corps of the Russian army. Although there is little record that Eisenstein was immediately affected by the events of October 1917, in the spring of 1918 he did volunteer for the Red Army. His father joined the Whites and subsequently emigrated. While in the military, Eisenstein again managed to combine his service as a technician with study of theater, philosophy, psychology and linguistics. He staged and performed in several productions, for which he also designed sets and costumes.

In 1920 Eisenstein left the army for the General Staff Academy in Moscow where he joined the First Workers' Theater of Proletcult as a scenic and costume designer. After he gained fame from his innovative work on a production of *The Mexican*, adapted from a Jack London story, Eisenstein enrolled in his idol Meyerhold's experimental theater workshop and collaborated with several avant-garde theater groups, all of whom shared a mistrust of traditional art forms and "high" culture in general. The new theater's contribution to the revolutionary cause was to destroy the old art entirely and create a new, democratic one. The young Soviet artists resorted to "low" culture—circus, music hall, sports, fair performances—to educate the largely illiterate Russian masses in a "true" communist spirit.

Eisenstein's studies of *commedia dell'arte* paid off in his 1923 staging of *The Sage*, a huge success not only as propaganda but also as sheer entertainment. For that production he made a short comic film, *Glumov's Diary* (1923), a parody of newsreels whose hero's grotesque metamorphoses anticipated the metaphors of *Strike* (1925), Eisenstein's first feature. But even more important for his career as a filmmaker was the structure of *The Sage*. Eisenstein took an old Ostrovsky play and reassembled it as a series of effective, circus-like attractions. The assemblage of such shocking scenes, as he claimed in his 1923 manifesto, *The Montage of Attractions*, would lead the public's attention in a direction planned by the "montageur."

Having studied the films of Griffith, Lev Kuleshov's montage experiments and Esfir Shub's re-editing techniques, Eisenstein became convinced that in cinema one could manipulate time and space to create new meanings, epecially if the images were not to be merely linked, as Kuleshov suggested, but juxtaposed. Because at that time he believed that his duty as an artist was to contribute to the forging of the new life for his country, Eisenstein eagerly embraced the film medium as the most efficient tool of communist propaganda. However, as much as *Strike* was a condemnation of czarism, it was also an innovative work of art. With this film, an inexperienced director immediately caught up with the work of Soviet, German and French avant-garde filmmakers. *Strike* is filled with expressionistic camera angles, mirror reflections and visual metaphors. In a story of police spies, the camera itself turns into a spy, a voyeur, a trickster. The film was the first full display of Eisenstein's bold new cinematic grammar, a montage of conflicting shots that served as words and sentences endowed with the maximum power of persuasion. Although his command of this new technique was shaky—some sequences did not convey the intended message—*Strike* was a ground-breaking accomplishment.

As Eisenstein's second film, the enormously successful and influential *Battleship Potemkin* (1925), demonstrated, his art could be even more powerful when it achieved a balance between experimental and traditional narrative forms. If *Strike* was an agitated visual poem arousing emotions within a receptive audience, *Potemkin*, the fictionalized story of one of the tragic episodes of the 1905 Russian revolution, was a work of prose, highly emotional but clear in its logical, public speech. The close-ups of suffering human faces and the soldiers' boots in the now legendary "Odessa steps" sequence carried such impact that some screenings of the film outside the USSR provoked clashes with police when audiences were convinced they were watching a newsreel.

Later in his career Eisenstein would compare the film director's art with the craft of a shaman. But in the 20s he was trying hard to find a rational basis for it: in Bekhterv's reflexology, in Russian formalist literary theory, in Marxist dialectics. As his films became more complex, they raised the ire of the new breed of ideologues who called for art accessible to the masses and flexible enough to illustrate the latest party line. However, Eisenstein was too deeply involved with his personal research to follow everyday politics. Thus, *October*, commissioned for the tenth anniversary of the October revolution of 1917 was not released until 1928; for one thing, all sequences featuring Trotsky, one of the leaders of the revolt, had to be deleted. Then too, the authorities were disappointed with Eisenstein, for while the edited *October* was considered ideologically correct, its confusing structure and abundance of abstract metaphors diminished it propagandistic message, and it did not carry the same impact as *Potemkin*. Attacking him for the "sins of formalism," critics claimed that he "lost his way in the corridors of the Winter Palace" and pointed to the more intelligible anniversary films shot by his colleagues on more modest budgets and in less time. In a way, the critics were correct; in none of his other films was Eisenstein's search for the new cinematic language so radical.

After *October*, Eisenstein was able to resume work that had been interrupted on *The General Line* (1929), a film meant to demonstrate the advantages of collective labor in the village. However, during the production of *October*, the party policy toward peasantry had drastically changed from persuasion to coercion, and the film's surrealistic imagery and sophisticated montage, which anticipated Godard, were considered inappropriate. Stalin summoned Eisenstein and his co-director Grigori Alexandrov and ordered them to make radical changes. They made a few cuts and immediately embarked on a trip abroad to investigate the new sound technology. With Eisenstein out of the country, the film was released under the neutral title *Old and New* to vicious attacks. His claim that the film was an experiment which could be understood by the millions was ridiculed as wishful thinking; according to one of his critics, the public needed "simple, realistic pictures with clear plot."

Meanwhile, Eisenstein's reception in Europe nurtured his opinion that he could be both avant-garde artist and creator of popular and ideologically "correct" films. In every country he visited he was hailed by radical students and intellectuals. He met with Joyce, Cocteau, Abel Gance, Marinetti, Einstein, Le Corbusier, Gertrude Stein, all of whom seemed excited about his work. In May 1930 Eisenstein arrived in the United States, where he lectured at several Ivy League schools before moving on to Hollywood, where he hoped to make a film for Paramount. Although he was welcomed by leading Hollywood figures, including Fairbanks, von Sternberg, Disney and especially Chaplin, who became his close friend, his proposal for an adaptation of *An American Tragedy* was rejected as too complicated, as were several other highly original projects.

Just before he left America, Eisenstein was encouraged by Robert Flaherty and Diego Rivera to make a film about Mexico, and in December 1930, with funding from writer Upton Sinclair, he began work on *Que Viva Mexico*. This project, which promised to become Eisenstein's most daring, took a tragic turn when Sinclair, caving in to pressures from his family, who cited financial reasons, and Stalin, who was afraid that Eisenstein might defect, cancelled the film with shooting almost finished. Although Eisenstein was told the footage would be sent to Moscow for editing, he was never to see it again.

Upset over the loss of his footage and shocked at the differences in the political and cultural climate that he noticed after three years abroad, he suffered a nervous breakdown. One after another, his ideas for projects were bluntly rejected, and he became the target of intense hostility from Boris Shumyatsky, the Soviet film industry chief whose objective was to create a Stalinist Hollywood. With his bitter memories of commercial filmmaking and strong ties to European modernism, Eisenstein could not make the switch to directing cheerful *agitkas* and was thus perceived as a threat. He took an appointment to head the Direction Department at the Moscow film school and became a devoted teacher and scholar. In January 1935, he was villified at the All-Union Conference of Cinema Workers but eventually was allowed to start working on his first sound film, *Bezhin Meadow*.

On this notorious project Eisenstein tried to create a universal tragedy out of the true story of a young communist vigilante who informed on his father and was murdered in retaliation by the victim's relatives. The authorities wanted to demonstrate that family ties should not be an obstacle to carrying out one's duty—a theme common to Soviet and German cinema of the time. Why Eisenstein agreed to deal with such dubious subject matter is not clear, but what has been saved from the allegedly destroyed film suggests that he once again confounded the Soviet authorities' expectations. After *Bezhin Meadow* was banned, Eisenstein had to repent for his new "sins of formalism." As one Soviet film scholar put it, "Eisenstein was apologizing for being Eisenstein."

As if to save his life, Eisenstein next made *Alexander Nevsky* (1938), a film about a 13th-century Russian prince's successful battle against invading German hordes. This monumental costume epic starring familiar character actors was a striking departure from Eisenstein's principles of montage and "typage" (casting non-professionals in leading roles). *Nevsky* was a deliberate step back, in the direction of old theater or, even worse, opera productions which Eisenstein has been fiercely opposed to in the 20s. Still, the film demonstrated Eisenstein in top form in several sequences, such as the famous battle scene on the ice. Also significant were his attempts to achieve synthesis between the plastic elements of picture and music with the film's memorable score by Prokofiev, possibly reflecting Eisenstein's prolonged admiration for the cartoons of Walt Disney.

Nevsky was a huge success both in the USSR and abroad, partially due to growing anti-German sentiment, and Eisenstein was able to secure a position in the Soviet cinema at a time when many of his friends were being arrested. On February 1, 1939, he was awarded the Order of Lenin for *Nevsky* and shortly thereafter embarked on a new project, *The Great Fergana Canal*, hoping to create an epic on a scale of his aborted Mexican film. Yet after intense pre-production work the project was cancelled, and following the signing of the non-aggression treaty between the USSR and Germany, *Nevsky* was quietly shelved as well. In February 1940, in a Radio Moscow broadcast to Germany, Eisenstein suggested that the pact provided a solid basis for cultural cooperation. At that time he was commissioned to stage Wagner's opera *Die Walküre* at the Bolshoi theater. At the November 21, 1940, premiere, the German diplomats in Moscow, not unlike Stalin's henchman before them, were dismayed by Eisenstein's artistry. They accused him of "deliberate Jewish tricks." Yet when the Nazis attacked Russia less than a year later, it was *Die Walküre*'s turn to be banned while *Nevsky* could once again be screened.

In 1941 Eisenstein was commissioned to do an even larger scale historic epic, a three-part film glorifying the psychopathic and murderous 16th-century Russian czar, Ivan the Terrible. However, Part I of *Ivan the Terrible* (1945) was an enormous success and Eisenstein was awarded the Stalin Prize. But *Ivan the Terrible Part II* (1946) showed a different Ivan: a bloodthirsty tyrant, the unmistakable predecessor of Stalin. Naturally, *Part II* was banned and the footage of *Part III* destroyed. Eisenstein was hospitalized with a heart attack, but he recovered and petitioned Stalin to be allowed to revise *Part II* as the bureaucracy wanted, only to be dismissed. In fact, Eisenstein was too weak to resume shooting, and he died in 1948, surrounded by unfinished theoretical works and plans for new films. *Ivan the Terrible Part II* was first shown in 1958 on the 60th anniversary of Eisenstein's birth. In 1988, at the international symposium at Oxford marking Eisenstein's 90th anniversary, Naum Kleiman, the director of the Eisenstein Museum in Moscow, showed a scene that survived from *Part III*. In it, Ivan is interrogating a foreign mercenary in a manner resembling one of Stalin's secret police. With the abundance of literature on Stalin's crimes now available even in the USSR, the significance of *Ivan the Terrible Part II* as a document of its tragic time has diminished, but as a work of art it is still significant. In his last completed film, Eisenstein achieved what he had dreamt of since 1928, when he saw a Japanese Kabuki troupe performance: the synthesis of gesture, sound, costume, sets and color into one powerful, polyphonic experience. Both *Nevsky* and *Walküre* were steps in that direction, but only the celebrated danse macabre of Ivan's henchmen comes close to the synthesis of the arts which has haunted artists for ages.

Eisenstein's death prevented him from summing up his theoretical views in the areas of the psychology of creativity, the anthropology of art and semiotics. Although not many filmmakers have followed Eisenstein the director, his essays on the nature of film art have been translated into several languages and studied by scholars of many nations. Soviet scholars published a six-volume set of his selected works in the 60s. 1988 saw the publication of a new English-language edition of his writings. AB • *Kinodnevik Glumova/Glumov's Diary* 1923 (a,d,sc,ed); *Bronenosets Potyomkin/Battleship Potemkin* 1925 (d,sc,ed); *Stachka/Strike* 1925 (d,sc,story,ed); *Oktyabar/October/Ten Days That Shook the World* 1928 (d,sc); *Staroye i novoye/The General Line* 1929 (d,sc,ed); *Sturm uber la Sarraz (short)* 1929 (a,d); *Romance sentimentale (short)* 1930 (d); *Que Viva Mexico* 1932 (d,sc); *Bezhin Lug/Bezhin Meadow* 1937 (d); *Aleksandr Nevski/Alexander Nevsky* 1938 (d,sc,sets,cost,ed); *Ferghana Canal* 1939 (d,sc); *An Appeal to the Jews of the World* 1941 (a); *Seeds of Freedom* 1943 (d); *Ivan the Terrible Part I* 1945 (d,p,sc,dial,ed,decor sketches,costume sketches); *Ivan the Terrible Part II* 1946 (d,p,sc,dial,ed,decor sketches,costume sketches); *Ivan the Terrible Part III* 1947 (d,sc); *The Secret Life of Sergei Eisenstein* 1985 (archival footage).

Eisler, Hanns • Composer • Born Leipzig, Germany, July 6, 1898; died 1962. *Educ.* Vienna Conservatory. Former student of Schönberg and collaborator with Bertolt Brecht who left Germany in 1933 and worked in Holland, England, France and the USSR with European filmmakers including Joris Ivens and Jacques Feyder before moving to the US in 1936. A Marxist and a modernist, Eisler worked with several noted directors including Fritz Lang and Jean Renoir before being deported in 1948 as an unfriendly witness to the HUAC hearings. Settling in East Germany, he wrote the new state's national anthem, composed music for several films (including an outstanding score for Alain Resnais's *Night and Fog* 1955) and co-authored a scathing book on movie music, *Composing for the Films* (1947), with philosopher Theodor W. Adorno. • *Das Lied vom Leben/Song of Life* 1930 (m); *Niemandsland/No Man's Land* 1931 (m); *Kuhle Wampe oder Wem gehört die Welt?* 1932 (m); *Pesn o geroyazh/Song of Heroes* 1932 (m); *Dans les rues* 1933 (m); *Le Grand jeu* 1933 (m); *Nieuwe gronden/New Earth* (short) 1933 (m); *Abdul the Damned* 1935 (m); *Pagliacci* 1936 (m.dir); *La Vie est à nous/The People of France* 1936 (song); *The 400 Million* 1938 (m); *White Flood* 1940 (m); *A Child Went Forth (short)* 1941 (m); *The Forgotten Village* 1941 (m); *Our Russian Front* 1941 (m); *China Fights* 1942 (m); *Hangmen Also Die* 1943 (m) **(AANBM)**; *None But the Lonely Heart* 1944 (m) **(AANBM)**; *Jealousy* 1945 (m); *The Spanish Main* 1945 (m); *Deadline at Dawn* 1946 (m); *Thieves' Holiday* 1946 (m,m.dir); *So Well Remembered* 1947 (m); *The Woman on the Beach* 1947 (m); *Krizova trojka* 1948 (m); *Unser täglich Brot/Our Daily Bread* 1949 (m); *Der Rat der Götter* 1950 (m); *Das Leben unseres Präsidenten* 1951 (m); *Frauenschicksale* 1952 (m); *Schicksal am Lenkrad* 1953 (m); *Bel Ami* 1954 (m); *Gasparone* 1955 (m.adapt,librettist); *Herr Puntila und sein Knecht Matti* 1955 (m); *Nuit et Brouillard/Night and Fog* 1955 (m); *Fidelio* 1956 (m.adapt,librettist); *Les Sorcières de Salem/The Witches of Salem* 1956 (m—German vers. only); *Katzgraben* 1957 (m); *Geschwader Fledermaus* 1958 (m); *Die Mutter* 1958 (m); *Trübe Wasser* 1959 (m); *Aktion J* 1961 (m); *Unbändiges Spanien* 1962 (m).

Eisner, Lotte • Historian, critic • Born Berlin, 1896; died November 25, 1983, France. Author of *The Haunted Screen* (1952), a definitive study of early German cinema, as well as critical books on F.W. Murnau and Fritz Lang. Eisner was the subject of a 1979 documentary, *Die Langen Ferien der Lotte H. Eisner*.

Eisner, Michael D. • Executive • Born Mt. Kisco, NY, March 7, 1942. *Educ.* Denison University, Granville OH. Former TV executive who became president of Paramount Pictures in 1976 and, as chairman and CEO of Walt Disney Productions from 1984, revitalized the corporation together with Jeffrey Katzenberg (chairman of The Walt Disney Studios during the same period). The team's policy involved using then-waning stars (Bette Midler, Richard Dreyfuss) in mainstream comedies with strictly controlled budgets, in an era when other studios were paying escalating fees for the services of top box-office draws. The Eisner/Katzenberg strategy also encompassed a diversification into more adult fare, via Disney's Touchstone Pictures and Hollywood Pictures divisions. Video sales of the company's classic animated features, as well as the annual release of a new feature-length animated film, have also contributed to Disney's enormous fiscal success over the last half-decade.

Ekberg, Anita • Actress • Born Malmö, Sweden, September 29, 1931. Statuesque former "Miss Sweden," in Hollywood from 1953. Memorable as an archetypal screen sex symbol in Fellini's *La Dolce Vita* (1959). Married to actors Anthony Steel (1956-1962) and Rik Van Nutter (1963-1975). • *The Golden Blade* 1953; *The Mississippi Gambler* 1953; *Artists and Models* 1955; *Blood Alley* 1955; *Back From Eternity* 1956; *Hollywood or Bust* 1956; *Man in the Vault* 1956; *War and Peace* 1956; *Zarak* 1956; *Interpol* 1957; *Valerie* 1957; *The Man Inside* 1958; *Paris Holiday* 1958; *Screaming Mimi* 1958; *La Dolce Vita* 1959; *Nel Segno di Roma* 1959; *I Mongoli* 1960; *Boccaccio '70* 1962; *Call Me Bwana* 1963; *Four For Texas* 1963; *The Alphabet Murders* 1966; *Way... Way Out* 1966;

Il Cobra 1967; *The Glass Sphinx* 1967; *Woman Times Seven* 1967; *If It's Tuesday, This Must Be Belgium* 1969; *I Clowns/The Clowns* 1970; *Fangs of the Living Dead* 1973; *Cicciabomba* 1983; *Dolce Pella di Angela* 1987; *Federico Fellini's Intervista* 1987.

Elam, Jack • Actor • Born Miami, AZ, November 13, 1916. *Educ.* Santa Monica Junior College, CA; Modesto Junior College. Veteran Hollywood player whose crookedly menacing face and sightless left eye helped him carve a niche as a villain in numerous westerns and crime dramas from the 1950s onward. • *Wild Weed* 1949; *An American Guerrilla in the Philippines* 1950; *High Lonesome* 1950; *One Way Street* 1950; *The Sundowners* 1950; *Bird of Paradise* 1951; *Rawhide* 1951; *The Battle at Apache Pass* 1952; *The Bushwackers* 1952; *High Noon* 1952; *Kansas City Confidential* 1952; *Lure of the Wilderness* 1952; *Montana Territory* 1952; *My Man and I* 1952; *Rancho Notorious* 1952; *The Ring* 1952; *Appointment in Honduras* 1953; *Count the Hours* 1953; *Gun Belt* 1953; *The Moonlighter* 1953; *Ride, Vaquero* 1953; *Cattle Queen of Montana* 1954; *Jubilee Trail* 1954; *Man Without a Star* 1954; *Princess of the Nile* 1954; *Ride Clear of Diablo* 1954; *Tarzan's Hidden Jungle* 1954; *Vera Cruz* 1954; *Artists and Models* 1955; *The Far Country* 1955; *Kismet* 1955; *Kiss Me Deadly* 1955; *The Man From Laramie* 1955; *Moonfleet* 1955; *Wichita* 1955; *Jubal* 1956; *Pardners* 1956; *Thunder Over Arizona* 1956; *Baby Face Nelson* 1957; *Dragoon Wells Massacre* 1957; *Gunfight at the O.K. Corral* 1957; *Lure of the Swamp* 1957; *Night Passage* 1957; *The Gun Runners* 1958; *Edge of Eternity* 1959; *The Comancheros* 1961; *The Last Sunset* 1961; *A Pocketful of Miracles* 1961; *Four For Texas* 1963; *The Night of the Grizzly* 1966; *The Rare Breed* 1966; *The Last Challenge* 1967; *The Way West* 1967; *Firecreek* 1968; *Never a Dull Moment* 1968; *C'era una Volta il West/Once Upon a Time in the West* 1969; *Support Your Local Sheriff* 1969; *The Cockeyed Cowboys of Calico County* 1970; *Dirty Dingus Magee* 1970; *Rio Lobo* 1970; *The Wild Country* 1970; *Hannie Caulder* 1971; *Last Rebel* 1971; *Support Your Local Gunfighter* 1971; *Pat Garrett and Billy the Kid* 1973; *A Knife For the Ladies* 1974; *The Creature From Black Lake* 1976; *Hawmps* 1976; *Pony Express Rider* 1976; *The Winds of Autumn* 1976; *Grayeagle* 1977; *Hot Lead and Cold Feet* 1978; *The Norseman* 1978; *The Apple Dumpling Gang Rides Again* 1979; *The Villain* 1979; *The Cannonball Run* 1980; *Jinxed!* 1982; *Cannonball Run II* 1983; *The Aurora Encounter* 1986; *Hawken's Breed* 1989; *Big Bad John* 1990.

Elfand, Martin • Executive; also producer. • Born Los Angeles, CA, 1937. Former talent agent who joined AEC (American Entertainment Complex) as a producer in 1972 and was made head of production at Warner Bros. in 1977. • *Kansas City Bomber* 1972 (p); *Dog Day Afternoon* 1975 (p) **(AANBP)**; *It's My Turn* 1980 (p); *An Officer and a Gentleman* 1982 (p); *King David* 1985 (p); *Clara's Heart* 1988 (p); *Her Alibi* 1989 (exec.p); *A Talent For the Game* 1991 (p).

Elfman, Danny • Composer, musician, singer • Born Los Angeles, CA, 1954. Singer-songwriter with rock band Oingo Boingo (since 1980) who has become one of the hottest film composers of recent years. Elfman's first feature score, for 1985's *Pee-wee's Big Adventure*, began a fruitful association with then-novice director Tim Burton. Since then he has created playful, impish and even lushly romantic synthesizer-based scores, adding a dimension of mischievous wit and dark sensuality to such Burton films as *Beetlejuice* (1988), *Batman* (1989) and *Edward Scissorhands* (1990). Elfman also scored Warren Beatty's *Dick Tracy* and Sam Raimi's *Darkman* (both 1990) and composed the theme for TV's "The Simpsons." • *Forbidden Zone* 1979 (m); *Urgh! A Music War* 1981 (song); *Fast Times at Ridgemont High* 1982 (song); *The Tempest* 1982 (song); *Bachelor Party* 1983 (songs); *Surf II* 1984 (songs); *Pee-wee's Big Adventure* 1985 (m); *Weird Science* 1985 (song); *Something Wild* 1986 (song); *Back to School* 1986 (song); *The Texas Chainsaw Massacre Part 2* 1986 (song); *Wisdom* 1986 (m,song); *Summer School* 1987 (m); *Beetlejuice* 1988 (m); *My Best Friend Is a Vampire* 1988 (song); *Midnight Run* 1988 (m); *Big Top Pee-wee* 1988 (m); *Scrooged* 1988 (m); *Batman* 1989 (m); *She's Out of Control* 1989 (song); *Ghostbusters II* 1989 (song); *Dick Tracy* 1990 (m); *Darkman* 1990 (m); *Edward Scissorhands* 1990 (m).

Elliott, Denholm • Actor • Born London, May 31, 1922. *Educ.* Malvern College; RADA, London. Consummate character player who began his screen career playing earnest, dependable young men, as in *The Cruel Sea* (1953). By the time of *Nothing But the Best* (1964), Elliott had perfected the seedy, rumpled and usually boozy persona which he used to portray a succession of conmen, journalists, and assorted shabby types. He has won two British Film Awards, for his roles in *A Private Function* (1984) and *Defence of the Realm* (1985), and was nominated for an Oscar for his performance as the professor father of Julian Sands in *A Room With a View* (1986). Married to first wife, actress Virginia McKenna, from 1954 to 1956. • *Dear Mr. Prohack* 1949; *The Holly and the Ivy* 1952; *The Ringer* 1952; *The Sound Barrier* 1952; *The Cruel Sea* 1953; *The Heart of the Matter* 1953; *Lease of Life* 1954; *The Man Who Loved Redheads* 1954; *They Who Dare* 1954; *The Night My Number Came Up* 1955; *Scent of Mystery* 1960; *Station Six Sahara* 1962; *Nothing But the Best* 1964; *The High Bright Sun* 1965; *King Rat* 1965; *Alfie* 1966; *The Spy With a Cold Nose* 1966; *Maroc 7* 1967; *Here We Go 'Round the Mulberry Bush* 1968; *The Night They Raided Minsky's* 1968; *The Sea Gull* 1968; *The House That Dripped Blood* 1970; *Percy* 1970; *The Rise and Rise of Michael Rimmer* 1970; *Too Late the Hero* 1970; *Quest For Love* 1971; *A Doll's House* 1973; *The Vault of Horror* 1973; *The Apprenticeship of Duddy Kravitz* 1974; *It's Not the Size That Counts* 1974; *Russian Roulette* 1975; *Partners* 1976; *Robin and Marian* 1976; *To the Devil, a Daughter* 1976; *Voyage of the Damned* 1976; *A Bridge Too Far* 1977; *The Boys From Brazil* 1978; *The Hound of the Baskervilles* 1978; *La Petite fille en velours bleu* 1978; *Sweeney 2* 1978; *Watership Down* 1978; *Cuba* 1979; *Game For Vultures* 1979; *Saint Jack* 1979; *Zulu Dawn* 1979; *Bad Timing* 1980; *Rising Damp* 1980; *Sunday Lovers* 1980; *The Missionary* 1981; *Raiders of the Lost Ark* 1981; *Brimstone and Treacle* 1982; *The Hound of the Baskervilles* 1983; *Trading Places* 1983; *The Wicked Lady* 1983; *A Private Function* 1984; *The Razor's Edge* 1984; *Defence of the Realm* 1985; *Past Caring* 1985; *The Happy Valley* 1986; *A Room With a View* 1986 **(AANBSA)**; *Underworld* 1986; *The Whoopee Boys* 1986; *Maurice* 1987; *September* 1987; *Over Indulgence* 1988; *Stealing Heaven* 1988; *Indiana Jones and the Last Crusade* 1989; *Killing Dad* 1989; *Return to the River Kwai* 1989; *Toy Soldiers* 1991.

Elliott, Sam • Actor • Born Sacramento, CA, August 9, 1944. *Educ.* University of Oregon. Rugged leading man who first gained attention in Daniel Petrie's 1976 film, *Lifeguard*. Married to actress Katharine Ross. • *Butch Cassidy and the Sundance Kid* 1969; *The Games* 1970; *Frogs* 1972; *Molly and Lawless John* 1972; *Lifeguard* 1976; *The Legacy* 1979; *Mask* 1985; *Fatal Beauty* 1987; *Shakedown* 1988; *Prancer* 1989; *Road House* 1989; *Sibling Rivalry* 1990.

Elmes, Frederick • American director of photography • *Educ.* Rochester Institute of Technology, NY (photography); NYU Institute of Film and TV; AFI, Los Angeles CA (cinematography). Frequent collaborator with former AFI co-student David Lynch. • *A Woman Under the Influence* 1974 (add.cam.op); *The Killing of a Chinese Bookie* 1976 (ph); *Breakfast in Bed* 1977 (ph); *Eraserhead* 1977 (ph,fx ph); *Opening Night* 1977 (ph); *Real Life* 1978 (add.ph); *A Force of One* 1979 (cam.op); *Citizen: The Political Life of Allard K. Lowenstein* 1982 (ph); *Valley Girl* 1983 (ph); *Red Dawn* 1984 (cam.op); *Broken Rainbow* 1985 (ph); *Dune* 1985 (2u d,add.unit sup,add.ph sup); *Real Genius* 1985 (2u ph); *Blue Vel-*

vet 1986 (ph); *Allan Quatermain and the Lost City of Gold* 1987 (2u ph—Los Angeles); *Aria* 1987 (ph "Tristan und Isolde"); *Heaven* 1987 (ph); *River's Edge* 1987 (ph); *Moonwalker* 1988 (ph—anthology segments); *Permanent Record* 1988 (ph); *Cold Dog Soup* 1990 (ph); *Hollywood Mavericks* 1990 (cam.op); *Wild at Heart* 1990 (ph).

Elwes, Cary • Actor • Born London, October 26, 1962. *Educ.* Sarah Lawrence College, Bronxville NY (acting); Actors Studio. Young English lead who made his screen debut in *Another Country* (1984). Son of painter Dominic Elwes and stepson of producer Elliott Kastner. • *Another Country* 1984; *Oxford Blues* 1984; *The Bride* 1985; *Lady Jane* 1986; *Maschenka* 1987; *The Princess Bride* 1987; *Glory* 1989; *Never on Tuesday* 1989; *Days of Thunder* 1990.

Endfield, Cy • *aka* C. Raker, Cyril Endfield, Hugh Raker, C. Raker Endfield • Director; also screenwriter. • Born Cyril Raker Endfield, South Africa, November 1914; died 1983. *Educ.* Yale; New Theater School, New York. Made several socially aware thrillers such as *The Sound of Fury* (1950) before being blacklisted. Endfield continued to work in the UK, notably on the spectacular African siege drama *Zulu* (1964). • *Gentleman Joe Palooka* 1946 (d,sc); *Joe Palooka, Champ* 1946 (sc); *Mr. Hex* 1946 (sc); *Hard Boiled Money* 1947 (sc); *Stork Bites Man* 1947 (d,sc); *The Argyle Secrets* 1948 (d,sc,story); *Joe Palooka in the Big Fight* 1949 (adapt,d); *Joe Palooka in the Counterpunch* 1949 (story); *The Sound of Fury* 1950 (a,d); *The Underworld Story* 1950 (d); *Tarzan's Savage Fury* 1952 (d); *The Limping Man* 1953 (d,lyrics "I Couldn't Care Less"); *The Master Plan* 1954 (d,sc); *Impulse* 1955 (d); *The Secret* 1955 (d,sc); *Child in the House* 1956 (d,sc); *Hell Divers* 1957 (d,sc); *Curse of the Demon* 1958 (uncred.sc); *Sea Fury* 1958 (d,sc); *Jet Storm* 1959 (d,sc); *Mysterious Island* 1961 (d); *Zulu* 1963 (d,p,sc); *Hide and Seek* 1964 (d); *Sands of the Kalahari* 1965 (d,p,sc); *Das Ausschweifende Leben des Marquis De Sade* 1969 (d); *Universal Soldier* 1971 (d); *Zulu Dawn* 1979 (sc,story).

Englund, Robert • Actor • Born Los Angeles, CA, June 6, 1949. *Educ.* California State University, Northridge (acting); UCLA (acting); RADA (American school), Rochester MI. Began studying acting at the age of 12 and achieved cult status in the 1980s as Freddy Krueger, the pernicious king of the dream world in the *Nightmare on Elm Street* movies. • *Buster and Billie* 1974; *Hustle* 1975; *Stay Hungry* 1975; *The Great Smokey Roadblock* 1976; *St. Ives* 1976; *A Star Is Born* 1976; *Eaten Alive* 1977; *Big Wednesday* 1978; *Bloodbrothers* 1978; *The Fifth Floor* 1979; *Dead and Buried* 1981; *Don't Cry, It's Only Thunder* 1981; *Galaxy of Terror* 1981; *A Nightmare on Elm Street* 1984; *A Nightmare on Elm Street, Part 2: Freddy's Revenge* 1985; *Never Too Young to Die* 1986; *A Nightmare on Elm Street 3: Dream Warriors* 1987; *976-EVIL* 1988 (d); *A Nightmare on Elm Street 4: The Dream Master* 1988; *A Nightmare on Elm Street 5: The Dream Child* 1989; *The Phantom of the Opera* 1989; *The Adventures of Ford Fairlane* 1990.

Ephron, Nora • Screenwriter, novelist; also producer. • Born New York, NY, May 19, 1941. *Educ.* Wellesley College, MA. Acclaimed essayist (*Crazy Salad* 1975) and novelist who has written screenplays for several popular films, all featuring strong female characters such as anti-nuclear activist Karen Silkwood and aspiring mobster "Cookie" Voltecki.

Ephron is the daughter of stage and screen writing team Henry and Phoebe Ephron, whose works include *Carousel* (1956), *The Desk Set* (1957) and *Take Her, She's Mine*, based on letters their daughter wrote them from college. Formerly married to novelist Dan Greenberg and investigative journalist Carl Bernstein, Ephron is now wed to crime writer Nicholas Pileggi. • *Silkwood* 1983 (sc) **(AANBSC)**; *Heartburn* 1986 (sc,from novel); *Cookie* 1989 (exec.p,sc); *Crimes and Misdemeanors* 1989 (a); *When Harry Met Sally...* 1989 (assoc.p,sc) **(AANBSC)**; *My Blue Heaven* 1990 (exec.p,sc).

Epstein, Jean • Director; also theoretician, producer, screenwriter. • Born Warsaw, Poland, March 25, 1897; died April 3, 1953, Paris. *Educ.* University of Lyons, France (medicine). Key figure of the Impressionist school who arrived on the film scene with the 1921 publication of *Bonjour Cinema*, a collection of essays celebrating the medium in lyrical, poetic style. Epstein made his directing debut with *Pasteur* (1922) and then signed a ten-year contract with Pathé. After several films including the Balzac adaptation *L'Auberge rouge* (1923) and the exceptional, photographically sophisticated *The Faithful Heart* (1923) he dissolved the contract, forming his own production company, Les Films Jean Epstein, in 1926. Epstein is perhaps best known for his inspired adaptation of Poe's *The Fall of the House of Usher* (1928). His sister Marie (born 1899) worked closely with him as well as directing several films of her own. • *Le Tonnerre* 1921 (ad); *Pasteur (short)* 1922 (d); *Les Vendanges* 1922 (d); *L'Auberge rouge* 1923 (d,sc); *La Belle Nivernaise* 1923 (d,sc); *Coeur fidéle/The Faithful Heart* 1923 (d,sc); *La Montagne infidéle* 1923 (d); *L'Affiche* 1924 (d,sc); *La Goute de Sang* 1924 (d); *Le Lion des Mogols* 1924 (adapt,d); *Les Aventures de Robert Macaire* 1925 (d); *Le Double Amour* 1925 (d); *Au Pays de George Sand* 1926 (d); *Mauprat* 1926 (d); *Le Glace à Trois Faces* 1927 (d,p); *Six et Demi-Onze* 1927 (d,p); *La Chute de la maison Usher/The Fall of the House of Usher* 1928 (d,p); *Finis Terrae* 1929 (d,sc); *Sa Tête (short)* 1929 (d,sc); *Mor'Vran (short)* 1930 (d,sc); *Le Pas de la Mule (short)* 1930 (d); *Le Chanson des Peupliers (short)* 1931 (d); *Le Cor (short)* 1931 (d); *Notre Dame de Paris (short)* 1931 (d); *Les Berceaux (short)* 1932 (d); *L'Or des Mers* 1932 (d,sc); *Le Vieux Chaland (short)* 1932 (d); *La Villanelle des Rubans (short)* 1932 (d); *Chanson d'Armor (short)* 1933 (adapt,d); *Le Châtelaine du Liban* 1933 (d,sc); *L'Homme à l'Hispano* 1933 (d,sc); *La Vie d'un Grand Journal (short)* 1934 (d); *Marius et Olive a Paris (short)* 1935 (d); *La Bourgogne (short)* 1936 (d); *La Bretagne (short)* 1936 (d); *Cuor di vagabondo* 1936 (adapt,d); *La Femme du Bout du Monde* 1937 (d,sc); *Vive la Vie (short)* 1937 (d); *Les Bâtisseurs (short)* 1938 (d); *Eau Vive (short)* 1938 (d,sc); *La Relève* 1938 (d); *Artères de France (short)* 1939 (d); *La Charrette Fantôme* 1939 (fx); *Le Tempestaire (short)* 1947 (d,sc); *Les Feux de la Mer (short)* 1948 (d).

Epstein, Julius J. • Screenwriter; also playwright. • Born New York, NY, August 22, 1909. *Educ.* Penn State University. Under contract with Warner Bros. for over 17 years, during which time, often in collaboration with brother Philip G. Epstein, he wrote several outstanding films including the much-lauded *Casablanca* (1942) and *The Brothers Karamazov* (1958). Julius concentrated on writing solo screenplays from 1955. Philip's son is novelist Leslie Epstein. • *Living on Velvet* 1934 (sc,story); *The Big Broadcast of 1936* 1935 (uncred.sc); *Broadway Gondolier* 1935 (sc); *I Live For Love* 1935 (sc,story); *In Caliente* 1935 (sc); *Little Big Shot* 1935 (sc); *Stars Over Broadway* 1935 (sc); *Sons O' Guns* 1936 (sc); *Confession* 1937 (sc); *Four Daughters* 1938 (sc) **(AANBSC)**; *Secrets of an Actress* 1938 (sc,story); *Daughters Courageous* 1939 (sc); *Four Wives* 1939 (sc); *No Time For Comedy* 1940 (sc); *Saturday's Children* 1940 (sc); *The Bride Came C.O.D.* 1941 (sc); *Honeymoon For Three* 1941 (sc); *The Man Who Came to Dinner* 1941 (sc); *The Strawberry Blonde* 1941 (sc); *Casablanca* 1942 (sc) **(AABSC)**; *The Male Animal* 1942 (sc); *Yankee Doodle Dandy* 1942 (sc); *Arsenic and Old Lace* 1944 (sc); *Mr. Skeffington* 1945 (p,sc); *Chicken Every Sunday* 1948 (from play); *Romance on the High Seas* 1948 (sc); *Born Yesterday* 1950 (uncred.sc); *My Foolish Heart* 1950 (sc); *Take Care of My Little Girl* 1951 (sc); *Forever Female* 1953 (sc); *The Last Time I Saw Paris* 1954 (sc); *The Tender Trap* 1955 (sc); *Young at Heart* 1955 (sc); *Kiss Them For Me* 1957 (sc); *The Brothers Karamazov* 1958 (adapt); *Take a Giant Step* 1959 (p,sc); *Tall Story* 1960 (sc); *Fanny* 1961 (sc); *Light in the Piazza* 1962 (sc); *Send Me No Flowers* 1964 (sc); *Return From the Ashes* 1965 (sc); *Any Wednesday* 1966 (p,sc); *Pete 'n' Tillie* 1972 (p,sc,adapt) (**AANBSC**); *Once Is Not Enough* 1975 (sc); *Cross of Iron* 1977 (sc); *House Calls* 1978 (sc,story); *Reuben, Reuben* 1983 (p,sc) (**AANBSC**).

Epstein, Philip G. • Screenwriter • Born New York, NY, August 22, 1909; died 1952. See Epstein, Julius J. • *Gift of Gab* 1934 (story); *The Bride Walks Out* 1936 (sc); *Grand Jury* 1936 (sc); *Love on a Bet* 1936 (sc); *Mummy's Boys* 1936 (sc); *New Faces of 1937* 1937 (sc); *The Mad Miss Manton* 1938 (sc); *There's That Woman Again* 1938 (sc); *Daughters Courageous* 1939 (sc); *Four Wives* 1939 (sc); *No Time For Comedy* 1940 (sc); *Saturday's Children* 1940 (sc); *The Bride Came C.O.D.* 1941 (sc); *Honeymoon For Three* 1941 (sc); *The Man Who Came to Dinner* 1941 (sc); *The Strawberry Blonde* 1941 (sc); *Casablanca* 1942 (sc) (**AABSC**); *The Male Animal* 1942 (sc); *Yankee Doodle Dandy* 1942 (sc); *Arsenic and Old Lace* 1944 (sc); *Mr. Skeffington* 1945 (p,sc); *Chicken Every Sunday* 1948 (from play); *Romance on the High Seas* 1948 (sc); *My Foolish Heart* 1950 (sc); *Take Care of My Little Girl* 1951 (sc); *Forever Female* 1953 (sc); *The Last Time I Saw Paris* 1954 (sc); *The Brothers Karamazov* 1958 (adapt).

Erice, Victor • Director; also screenwriter. • Born Victor Erice Aras, San Sebastian, Spain, 1940. *Educ.* Escuela Oficial de Cinematografia. Former critic who made a number of short films before graduating to features with his highly assured evocation of childhood, *The Spirit of the Beehive* (1973), followed ten years later by the equally absorbing recollection *El Sur* (1983). • *En la Terraza (short)* 1961 (d,sc); *Paginas de un Diario (short)* 1962 (d,sc); *Los Dias Perdidos (short)* 1963 (d,sc); *El Proximo otono* 1964 (sc); *Entre vias (short)* 1966 (d); *Oscuros suenos de Agosto* 1968 (sc); *Los Desafios* 1969 (d,sc); *El Espiritu de la Colmena/The Spirit of the Beehive* 1973 (d,sc); *El Sur* 1983 (d,sc).

Estevez, Emilio • Actor; also director, screenwriter. • Born New York, NY, May 12, 1962. Charismatic young lead of the 1980s who first made his name in Alex Cox's cult hit *Repo Man* (1984). By the end of the decade Estevez had moved behind the camera, writing three screenplays and directing two of them, to middling results. He is the eldest son of actor Martin Sheen (he adopted his father's birthname) and the brother of actors Charlie and Ramon Sheen, and actress Renee Estevez. • *Tex* 1982 (a); *Nightmares* 1983 (a); *The Outsiders* 1983 (a); *Repo Man* 1984 (a); *The Breakfast Club* 1985 (a); *St. Elmo's Fire* 1985 (a); *That Was Then... This Is Now* 1985 (a,sc); *Maximum Overdrive* 1986 (a); *Wisdom* 1986 (a,d,sc); *Stakeout* 1987 (a); *Young Guns* 1988 (a); *Never on Tuesday* 1989 (a); *Men at Work* 1990 (a,d,sc); *Young Guns II* 1990 (a).

Eszterhas, Joe • American screenwriter; also novelist. • Versatile scenarist who in late 1989 was at the center of a highly publicized struggle with Michael Ovitz, head of the Creative Artists Agency, concerning the degree of influence exercised over an artist by his or her representative. The controversy highlighted a growing concern within the Hollywood community about the power wielded by a small group of influential "superagents." Eszterhas left CAA and subsequently sold a "spec" screenplay, "Basic Instinct," for an unprecedented $3,000,000. • *F.I.S.T.* 1978 (sc,story); *Flashdance* 1983 (sc); *Jagged Edge* 1985 (sc); *Big Shots* 1987 (sc); *Hearts of Fire* 1987 (sc); *Betrayed* 1988 (exec.p,sc); *Checking Out* 1988 (sc); *Music Box* 1989 (exec.p,sc).

Evans, Dame Edith • Actress • Born Edith Evans, London, England, February 8, 1888; died October 14, 1976, Cranbrook, Kent, England. Legendary stage performer, acclaimed for her precise diction, ironic delivery and forthright acting style, who won renown for her performances in the works of Shakespeare, Shaw and Wilde and in several Restoration comedies. After appearing in two early silent films, Evans did not return to the screen until 1948. Her definitive portrayal of Wilde's Lady Bracknell in *The Importance of Being Earnest* was captured on screen in 1952, and in her seventies and eighties she created a bevy of memorable characters in such films as *Tom Jones* (1963) and *The Whisperers* (1967). • *A Welsh Singer* 1915; *East Is East* 1916; *The Queen of Spades* 1948; *The Last Days of Dolwyn* 1949; *The Importance of Being Earnest* 1952; *Look Back in Anger* 1959; *The Nun's Story* 1959; *Tom Jones* 1963 (**AANBSA**); *The Chalk Garden* 1964 (**AANBSA**); *Young Cassidy* 1965; *Fitzwilly* 1967; *The Whisperers* 1967 (**AANBA**); *Prudence and the Pill* 1968; *Crooks and Coronets* 1969; *The Madwoman of Chaillot* 1969; *David Copperfield* 1970; *Scrooge* 1970; *Upon This Rock* 1970; *Craze* 1973; *A Doll's House* 1973; *Nasty Habits* 1976; *The Slipper and the Rose* 1976.

Evans, Robert • *aka* Bob Evans • Producer; also actor. • Born Robert Shapera, New York, NY, June 29, 1930. Former child actor who at age 21 became a successful clothing manufacturer before returning to the screen to play Irving G. Thalberg in *Man of a Thousand Faces* (1957). Evans moved into production in the 1960s, becoming vice president in charge of production at Paramount Pictures in 1966 and acting as executive vice president, worldwide production, from 1971-75. He supervised such box-office hits as *Barefoot in the Park* (1967), *Rosemary's Baby* (1968), *Goodbye, Columbus* (1969), *Love Story* (1970) and the first two installments of the "Godfather" saga before becoming an independent producer in 1974. Former married to actresses Sharon Hugueny, Camilla Sparv, Ali MacGraw and TV sports commentator Phyllis George. Son (by MacGraw) is actor Josh Evans. • *Hey, Rookie* 1944 (a); *Lydia Bailey* 1952 (a); *Man of a Thousand Faces* 1957 (a); *The Sun Also Rises* 1957 (a); *The Fiend Who Walked the West* 1958 (a); *The Best of Everything* 1959 (a); *Too Soon to Love* 1960 (a); *Chinatown* 1974 (p) (**AANBP**); *Marathon Man* 1976 (p); *Black Sunday* 1977 (p); *Players* 1979 (p); *Popeye* 1980 (p); *Taboo (the Single and the LP)* 1980 (p); *Urban Cowboy* 1980 (p); *The Cotton Club* 1984 (p); *Desperate Hours* 1990 (a); *The Two Jakes* 1990 (p).

Evein, Bernard • Production designer; also costume designer. • Born Saint-Nazaire, France, January 5, 1929. *Educ.* Ecole des Beaux-Arts, Nantes; IDHEC, Paris (set design). Key New Wave art director who has effectively adapted himself to a wide range of directorial styles. Evein created menacing interiors for Claude Chabrol (*Les Cousins* and *A Double Tour*, both 1959) as well as the bold, open vistas of Jacques Demy's *Lola* (1961). Other outstanding works include Godard's vivacious color debut *A Woman Is a Woman* (1961) and Louis Malle's melancholic *The Fire Within* (1963). • *La Danseuse nue* 1952 (asst.art d); *Douze heures de bonheur* 1952 (asst.art d); *On ne badine pas avec l'amour* 1952 (art d,cost); *Le Bel Indifferent (short)* 1957 (art d); *Les Amants* 1958 (art d); *Les Cousins* 1959 (art d); *A Double Tour* 1959 (art d); *Les Quatre cents coups/The 400 Blows* 1959 (art d); *La Sentence* 1959 (art d); *Les Grandes personnes* 1960 (art d); *Le Jeux de l'Amour* 1960 (art d); *Les Scelerats* 1960 (art d); *Zazie dans le metro* 1960 (art d); *L' Amant de Cinq Jours* 1961 (art d); *L'Année dernière a Marienbad/Last Year at Marienbad* 1961 (cost—Delphine Seyrig's feather dresses); *Les Dimanches de Ville d'Avray/Sundays and Cybele* 1961 (art d); *Une Femme est une femme/A Woman Is a Woman* 1961 (art d); *Les Fiancés du Pont Macdonald (short)* 1961 (art d,cost); *Lola* 1961 (art d,cost); *Rendez-vous de minuit* 1961 (art d); *Vie Privée* 1961 (art d); *Cleo de 5 à 7/Cleo From 5 to 7* 1962 (art d,cost); *Le Combat dans l'ile* 1962 (art d); *Les Sept péchés capitaux/The Seven Deadly Sins* 1962 (art d—"Lust"); *La Baie des anges* 1963 (art d); *Le Feu Follet/The Fire Within* 1963 (art d); *Jour et l'heure* 1963 (art d); *Aimez-vous les femmes?* 1964 (art d); *Comment epouser un premier ministre* 1964 (art d); *L'Insoumis* 1964 (art d); *Les Parapluies de Cherbourg/The Umbrellas of Cherbourg* 1964 (art d); *Viva Maria* 1965 (art d); *Qui êtes-vous, Polly Maggoo?* 1966 (art d); *Les Demoi-*

selles de Rochefort 1967 (art d); *Le Plus vieux metier du monde* 1967 (art d—"Mademoiselle Mimi"); *Woman Times Seven* 1967 (art d); *Adolphe ou l'Age Tendre* 1968 (art d); *Tendres Chasseurs* 1969 (art d,sets); *L'Aveu* 1970 (art d); *Le Bateau sur l'herbe* 1971 (art d); *L'Evènement le plus important depuis que l'homme a marché sur la lune* 1973 (art d); *The Grand Bazar* 1973 (art d); *Le Hasard Et La Violence* 1973 (art d); *La Merveilleuse visite* 1974 (art d); *L'Alpagueur* 1976 (art d); *Le Jouet* 1976 (art d); *Néa* 1976 (art d); *Madame Rosa* 1977 (art d); *Lady Oscar* 1979 (art d); *Chère Inconnue* 1980 (art d); *Tous Vedettes* 1980 (art d); *Notre Histoire* 1984 (art d); *La Rumba* 1986 (art d); *Thérèse* 1986 (art d,sets); *Trois places pour le 26* 1988 (art d).

Everett, Rupert • Actor • Born Norfolk, England, 1959. *Educ.* Central School of Speech & Drama, London. Handsome young lead of the 1980s, especially in upper-class or aristocratic roles. • *Real Life* 1983 (a); *Another Country* 1984 (a); *Dance With a Stranger* 1985 (a); *Duet For One* 1986 (a); *The Right Hand Man* 1986 (a); *Cronaca di una morte annunciata/Chronicle of a Death Foretold* 1987 (a); *Hearts of Fire* 1987 (a); *Gli Occhiali d'Oro* 1987 (a); *Tolerance* 1989 (a); *The Comfort of Strangers* 1990 (a).

Everson, William K. • Born London, 1929. Long-time independent film curator, impresario of old movies and prolific historian of the silent film.

Growing up outside of London near the film studios, William K. Everson was addicted to cinema before he could read. At the age of 21 he emigrated to the US and, like most immigrants, was struck breathless by the new land. It wasn't the Statue of Liberty, the skyscrapers, or the waving fields of wheat, however, that impressed him: "As soon as I got off the boat, I was confronted by 42nd Street!," he explained years later. "Row upon row of marquees! And the first marquee I saw had Chaplin's *City Lights* and von Sternberg's *The Scarlet Empress*, neither of which I'd seen in England, so I was off like a shot!"

Almost immediately, Everson began collecting films. He was in the right place at the right time. The studios were lax in preserving films from the 20s and 30s that they thought had no value, and TV had not yet discovered the treasure trove of the studio libraries. Working in the industry as a sometime publicist, he would often hear that some reels of an old film were about to be destroyed simply because a distributor's contract had run out. He'd offer to buy them; sometimes legal barriers required that he "liberate" them. Answering to a higher authority, he did so.

Gradually the hobby became an obsession. It wasn't enough to own a representative set of John Fords, for example; he had to have them all. Moreover, at the same time that he was passionately collecting, Hollywood was dispassionately destroying "useless" old movies.

What Everson and other private collectors were doing on their own in the US, governments were sponsoring in Europe. Compare Everson's experience in New York to that of Henri Langlois in Paris. A similarly obsessed collector, Langlois was able to found the Cinémathèque Française, an official, funded organization. In 1970, when the American Film Institute was founded, some of the pressure was taken off Everson.

By the mid-70s Everson's collection had grown to more than 4,000 titles, nearly all of which were stored in his West Side New York apartment. From the beginning he had had been showing prints from his collection in his living room to a small circle of aficionados. In 1966 he began a long-running series of screenings at New York's New School for Social Research, where thousands of filmgoers and scores of filmmakers have been exposed to an important part of film history that would, without Everson, have been lost. JM

Ewell, Tom • *aka* S. Yewell Tompkins • Actor • Born Yewell Tompkins, Owensboro, KY, April 29, 1909. *Educ.* University of Wisconsin. Comic performer with stage experience who had his first featured role playing a philanderer in *Adam's Rib* (1949) and went on to specialize in portraying inept woman-chasers and harried ordinary men. Ewell had the good fortune to co-star with two of Hollywood's biggest leading ladies of the mid-1950s: Marilyn Monroe in *The Seven Year Itch* (1955) and Jayne Mansfield in *The Girl Can't Help It* (1956). • *They Knew What They Wanted* 1940; *Desert Bandit* 1941; *Adam's Rib* 1949; *An American Guerrilla in the Philippines* 1950; *A Life of Her Own* 1950; *Mr. Music* 1950; *Finders Keepers* 1951; *Up Front* 1951; *Back at the Front* 1952; *Lost in Alaska* 1952; *The Lieutenant Wore Skirts* 1955; *The Seven Year Itch* 1955; *The Girl Can't Help It* 1956; *The Great American Pastime* 1956; *A Nice Little Bank That Should Be Robbed* 1958; *State Fair* 1962; *Tender Is the Night* 1962; *Suppose They Gave a War and Nobody Came?* 1970; *They Only Kill Their Masters* 1972; *To Find a Man* 1972; *The Great Gatsby* 1974; *Easy Money* 1983.

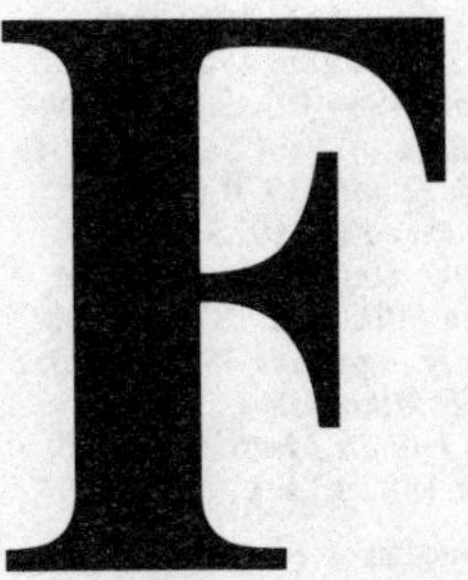

Fabian, Françoise • Actress • Born Michèle Cortès De Leon y Fabianera, Hussein Dey, Algeria, May 10, 1932. *Educ.* Conservatory of Dramatic Arts, Algeria; Paris Conservatoire. Memorable in the title role of *My Night at Maud's* (1969) as the beautiful divorcee whose charms Jean-Louis Trintignant finally succeeds in resisting. Fabian was married to director Jacques Becker from 1958 until his death in 1960. • *Mémoires d'un flic* 1955; *Cette Sacrée Gamine* 1956; *Le Courturier de Ces Dames* 1956; *Les Fanatiques* 1957; *Le Feux aux Poudres* 1957; *Michel Strogoff* 1957; *Les Violents* 1958; *Brune que voilà* 1961; *Maigret voit Rouge* 1963; *La Jeune Morte* 1965; *Belle de Jour* 1967; *Le Voleur* 1967; *L'Américain* 1969; *Ma nuit chez Maud/My Night at Maud's* 1969; *Un Condé* 1970; *Out 1: Noli Me Tangere* 1971; *Raphaël, ou le Débauché* 1971; *Au Rendez-Vous de la mort joyeuse* 1972; *L'Amour, l'apres-midi/Chloe in the Afternoon* 1972; *Out 1: Spectre* 1972; *Les Voraces* 1972; *La Bonne Année* 1973; *Projection Privée* 1973; *Salut l'artiste* 1973; *Per Amare Ofelia* 1974; *Perche si uccide un Magistrato* 1974; *Per le Antiche Scale* 1975; *Les Fougères Bleues* 1977; *Madame Claude* 1977; *Deux heures moins le quart avant Jesus Christ* 1982; *L'Ami de Vincent* 1983; *Benvenuta* 1983; *Le Cercle des Passions* 1983; *Partir Revenir* 1984; *Faubourg Saint-Martin* 1986; *Quo Vadis* 1988; *Trois places pour le 26* 1988; *Réunion* 1989.

Fábri, Zoltán • Director; also screenwriter, production designer. • Born Budapest, Hungary, 1917. *Educ.* Academy of Fine Arts, Budapest (painting, set design); Academy for Theater and Film Art, Budapest. Former theater director who found his form with the emergence of the Hungarian New Wave in the 1950s. Fábri's films usually explore anti-Fascist themes and he is best remembered for *Merry-Go-Round* (1955) and *Professor Hannibal* (1956); later work, with the exception of some intelligently made films on social issues in the 60s, proved largely disappointing. • *The Storm* 1952 (d); *Fourteen Lives* 1954 (d); *Kohrinta/Merry-Go-Round* 1955 (d,sc,ed,art d); *Professor Hannibal* 1956 (d,sc); *Summer Clouds* 1957 (art d,d); *Anna* 1958 (d,sc,art d); *The Brute* 1959 (d,sc,art d); *The Last Goal* 1961 (art d,d); *Darkness in Daytime* 1963 (d,sc,art d); *Twenty Hours* 1964 (d); *Late Season* 1967 (d); *The Boys of Paul Street* 1969 (d,sc); *The Toth Family* 1970 (d); *One Day More One Day Less* 1973 (d); *141 Minutes From the Unfinished Sentence* 1975 (d,sc); *The Fifth Seal* 1977 (d,sc); *Magyarok/The Hungarians* 1978 (d,sc); *Fabian Balint Talalkozasa Istennel/Balint Fabian Meets God* 1980 (d,sc); *Requiem* 1982 (d,sc).

Fairbanks, Douglas • *aka* Elton Banks, Elton Thomas • Actor; also producer, screenwriter. • Born Douglas Elton Ulman, Denver, CO, May 23, 1883; died December 12, 1939, Santa Monica, CA. *Educ.* Colorado School of Mines; Harvard. Douglas Fairbanks wrote: "Indeed it is possible to stand with one foot on the inevitable banana peel of life with both eyes peering into the Great Beyond, and still be happy, comfortable, and serene—if we will even so much as smile." Between 1915 and 1934, Fairbanks brought this simplistic philosophy, bolstered by a natural zest for life, to over 40 films in which he portrayed a character of incredible athletic exuberance and unbounded energy possessed of an almost unshakable faith in American values. He jumped, swung, leaped and, most importantly, smiled his way across American movie screens of the 1910s to become the popular philosopher of American vitality and zip. By the 20s, he had become reigning Hollywood royalty, entertaining lavishly at his mansion Pickfair with his ruling queen Mary Pickford, producing (sometimes writing) and starring in high-budgeted swashbuckling adventures and presiding over the operation of United Artists, the studio which he founded with Pickford, D.W. Griffith and Charlie Chaplin in 1919.

Fairbanks had come to films after a successful theatrical career, playing the leads in such 1914 Broadway successes as *He Comes Up Smiling* and *The Show Shop.* In 1915, Fairbanks signed with Triangle Films at a salary of $2,000 per week and found himself under the wing of D.W. Griffith. With his Victorian sensibilities, the director had no feel for Fairbanks's 20th-century dynamism and the star's first films, *The Lamb* and *Double Trouble* (both 1915), traded on his Broadway successes rather than the Fairbanks charm. When Griffith delegated to others the task of molding Fairbanks's screen persona, Fairbanks sought more compatible collaborators. With *His Picture in the Papers* (1916), director-writer John Emerson and writer Anita Loos joined the Fairbanks camp and immediately hit on the right approach. The Loos/Emerson combination created a peppy satire featuring the up-and-at-'em Fairbanks athleticism, a response to the increasing industrialization and encroaching commercialization of the American landscape. The trio continued to mock commercial faddism and celebrity pretensions, with Fairbanks often playing an upper-class dynamo who shows up his fellow aristocrats in such films as *The Half Breed* (1916), *American Aristocracy* (1916), *Manhattan Madness* (1916), *The Matrimaniac* (1916), *The Americano* (1917), *In Again, Out Again* (1917), *Wild and Woolly* (1917), *Down to Earth* (1917) and *Reaching for the Moon* (1917). With *The Habit of Happiness* (1916) another Fairbanks stalwart, director Alan Dwan, came into the fold; it was also the first film in which Fairbanks revealed his penchant for aphoristic philosophy: "To be happy, you must be enthusiastic; to be enthusiastic, you must be healthy; to be healthy, you must keep your mind and body active."

WWI not only interrupted Fairbanks's career—he sold Liberty Bonds with his future wife, Mary Pickford—but its sobering aftermath left Fairbanks feeling that audiences would no longer identify with the anachronistic persona of a carefree aristocrat. In *The Nut* (1921) and *When the Clouds Roll By* (1919), Fairbanks introduced elements of the fantastic to contemporary stories. In this way, he was preparing his audience for a shift of scene: the 20s found Fairbanks starring in a series of lavish costume films which placed his pre-war optimist into historical and fairy-tale settings. *The Mark of Zorro* (1920) showed the way with innovative special effects and transcendent production design. In film after film, from *The Three Musketeers* (1921) to *Robin Hood* (1922), *Don Q, Son of Zorro* (1925), *The Black Pirate* (1926) and the summit of Fairbanks fantasy, *The Thief of Bagdad* (1924), he continued to proclaim his optimism ("Happiness must be earned" is the motto in *Thief*). At the same time, Harold Lloyd was making millions in his comedies, which relocated the Fairbanks character from the heights of the aristocracy to the more realistic level of the booming middle class of 20s America. With the stock market crash of 1929, optimism was dealt a death blow, but in his final film, *The Private Life of Don Juan* (1934), Fairbanks still traded on his old style. In a nation sinking ever deeper into depression, he had become a king with no subjects to follow him.

Fairbanks was married to his second wife, Lady Sylvia Ashley, from 1936 until his death. PB • *Double Trouble* 1915 (a); *The Lamb* 1915 (a); *American Aristocracy* 1916 (a); *Flirting With Fate* 1916 (a); *The Good Bad Man* 1916 (a,sc); *The Habit of Happiness* 1916 (a); *The Half-Breed* 1916 (a); *His Picture in the Papers* 1916 (a); *Intolerance* 1916 (a); *Manhattan Madness* 1916 (a); *The Matrimoniac* 1916 (a); *Mystery of the Leaping Fish* 1916 (a); *Reggie Mixes It* 1916 (a); *The Americano* 1917 (a); *Down to Earth* 1917 (a,story); *In Again, Out Again* 1917 (a); *The Man From Painted Post* 1917 (a,sc); *A Modern Musketeer* 1917 (a); *Reaching For the Moon* 1917 (a); *War Relief* 1917 (a); *Wild and Woolly* 1917 (a); *Arizona* 1918 (a,sc); *Bound in Morocco* 1918 (a); *Fire the Kaiser* 1918 (a); *He Comes Up Smiling* 1918 (a,p); *Headin' South* 1918 (a,p); *Mr. Fix-It* 1918 (a); *Say! Young Fellow* 1918 (a); *Sic 'em Sam!* 1918 (a); *His Majesty, the American* 1919 (a); *The Knickerbocker Buckaroo* 1919 (a,sc); *Private Film For the Duke of Sutherland* 1919 (a); *When the Clouds Roll By* 1919 (a,sc,story); *The Mark of Zorro* 1920 (a,sc); *The Mollycoddle* 1920 (a); *The Nut* 1921 (a,p); *The Three Musketeers* 1921 (a); *Robin Hood* 1922 (a,p,story); *The Thief of Bagdad* 1924 (a,p,sc,story); *Don Q, Son of Zorro* 1925 (a); *The Black Pirate* 1926 (a,story); *The Gaucho* 1928 (a,p,story); *Show People* 1928 (a); *The Iron Mask* 1929 (a,adapt,p); *The Taming of the Shrew* 1929 (a); *Around the World in 80 Minutes With Douglas Fairbanks* 1931 (a,d,sc); *Reaching For the Moon* 1931 (a); *Mr. Robinson Crusoe* 1932 (a,story); *The Private Life of Don Juan* 1934 (a).

Fairbanks, Douglas, Jr. • Actor; also producer. • Born Douglas Elton Ulman Fairbanks, New York, NY, December 9, 1909. *Educ.* Pasadena Polytechnic, CA; Harvard Military Academy, Los Angeles; Bovee Art School, NY; Collegiate Military Academy, NY. Dashing, versatile leading man who entered films as a juvenile lead at the age of 13. Fairbanks became a full-fledged star in the late 1920s, proving himself adept both in swashbuckling adventures such as *Gunga Din* (1939) and *The Exile* (1947) and—thanks to his suave, cultured presence—comedies like *The Rage of Paris* (1938) and *Joy of Living* (1938). Since *Catherine the Great* (1934) he has spent much time in the UK, and in 1949 became an Honorary Knight of the British Empire. The son of Douglas Fairbanks and actress Anna Beth Sully, he was married to actress Joan Crawford from 1929 to 1933. • *Stephen Steps Out* 1923; *The Thief of Bagdad* 1924; *The Air Mail* 1925; *Stella Dallas* 1925; *Wild Horse Mesa* 1925; *The American Venus* 1926; *Broken Hearts of Hollywood* 1926; *Man Bait* 1926; *Padlocked* 1926; *Is Zat So?* 1927; *A Texas Steer* 1927; *Women Love Diamonds* 1927; *The Barker* 1928; *Dead Man's Curve* 1928; *Modern Mothers* 1928; *The Power of the Press* 1928; *The Toilers* 1928; *A Woman of Affairs* 1928; *The Careless Age* 1929; *Fast Life* 1929; *The Forward Pass* 1929; *The Iron Mask* 1929; *The Jazz Age* 1929; *Our Modern Maidens* 1929; *The Show of Shows* 1929; *The Dawn Patrol* 1930; *Going Wild* 1930; *The Little Accident* 1930; *Little Caesar* 1930; *Loose Ankles* 1930; *One Night at Susie's* 1930; *Outward Bound*

1930; *Party Girl* 1930; *The Way of All Men* 1930; *Chances* 1931; *I Like Your Nerve* 1931; *Local Boy Makes Good* 1931; *It's Tough to Be Famous* 1932; *Love Is a Racket* 1932; *Scarlet Dawn* 1932; *Union Depot* 1932; *Captured* 1933; *The Life of Jimmy Dolan* 1933; *Morning Glory* 1933; *The Narrow Corner* 1933; *The Parachute Jumper* 1933; *Catherine the Great* 1934; *Success at Any Price* 1934; *Man of the Moment* 1935; *Mimi* 1935; *Accused* 1936; *The Amateur Gentleman* 1936; *Jump For Glory* 1937 (a,p); *The Prisoner of Zenda* 1937; *Having Wonderful Time* 1938; *Joy of Living* 1938; *The Rage of Paris* 1938; *The Young in Heart* 1938; *Gunga Din* 1939; *Rulers of the Sea* 1939; *Angels Over Broadway* 1940; *Green Hell* 1940; *Safari* 1940; *The Corsican Brothers* 1941; *The Exile* 1947 (a,p,sc); *Sinbad the Sailor* 1947; *That Lady in Ermine* 1948; *The Fighting O'Flynn* 1949 (a,p,sc); *State Secret* 1950; *Mister Drake's Duck* 1951; *Another Man's Poison* 1952 (p); *Police Dog* 1955 (p); *Chase a Crooked Shadow* 1958 (p); *Moment of Danger* 1960 (p); *The Funniest Man in the World* 1969; *Red and Blue* 1967; *Churchill the Man* 1973; *Ghost Story* 1981; *George Stevens: A Filmmaker's Journey* 1985; *Going Hollywood: The War Years* 1988.

Falk, Peter • Actor • Born New York, NY, September 16, 1927. *Educ.* Hamilton College, Clinton NY; New School For Social Research, New York NY (political science); Maxwell School of Syracuse University, NY (public administration). Gifted as both a comic and dramatic player, and best known, from 1971 to 1977, as scrubby, deceptively bumbling Lieutenant Columbo on TV's "NBC Sunday Mystery Movie." Falk appeared in three John Cassavetes films in the 1970s and gave a memorable performance, as himself, in Wim Wenders's art-house success *Wings of Desire* (1987). • *Wind Across the Everglades* 1958; *The Bloody Brood* 1959; *Murder, Inc.* 1960 (**AANBSA**); *Pretty Boy Floyd* 1960; *The Secret of the Purple Reef* 1960; *A Pocketful of Miracles* 1961 (**AANBSA**); *Pressure Point* 1962; *The Balcony* 1963; *It's a Mad, Mad, Mad, Mad World* 1963; *Italiani brava Gente* 1964; *Robin and the Seven Hoods* 1964; *The Great Race* 1965; *Penelope* 1966; *Luv* 1967; *Anzio* 1968; *Castle Keep* 1969; *Gli Intoccabili* 1969; *Rosolino paterno, Soldato* 1969; *Husbands* 1970; *The Politics Film (short)* 1972; *A Woman Under the Influence* 1974; *Mikey and Nicky* 1976; *Murder By Death* 1976; *Opening Night* 1977; *The Brink's Job* 1978; *The Cheap Detective* 1978; *The In-Laws* 1979; *All the Marbles* 1981; *The Great Muppet Caper* 1981; *Big Trouble* 1985; *Happy New Year* 1987; *Der Himmel uber Berlin/Wings of Desire* 1987; *The Princess Bride* 1987; *Vibes* 1988; *Cookie* 1989; *In the Spirit* 1990; *Motion and Emotion* 1990; *Tune in Tomorrow* 1990.

Farmer, Frances • Actress • Born Seattle, WA, September 19, 1913; died August 1, 1970. *Educ.* University of Washington. Intelligent leading lady of the late 1930s whose promising career was curtailed by her reputation as a rebellious and exacting actress, her left-wing politics and, most importantly, alcoholism. After suffering a nervous breakdown in 1944, Farmer spent much of the that decade in mental institutions. Her life story was told in the feature film *Frances* (1983), starring Jessica Lange, and in a made-for-TV movie starring Susan Blakely based on Farmer's posthumously-published autobiography, *Will There Really Be a Morning?*. Farmer was married to actor Leif Erickson from 1934 to 1942 and died of cancer at the age of 56. • *Border Flight* 1936; *Come and Get It* 1936; *Rhythm on the Range* 1936; *Too Many Parents* 1936; *Ebb Tide* 1937; *Exclusive* 1937; *The Toast of New York* 1937; *Ride a Crooked Mile* 1938; *Flowing Gold* 1940; *South of Pago-Pago* 1940; *Among the Living* 1941; *Badlands of Dakota* 1941; *World Premiere* 1941; *Son of Fury* 1942; *The Party Crashers* 1958.

Farrell, Charles • Actor • Born Onset Bay, MA, August 9, 1901; died May 6, 1990, Palm Springs, CA. *Educ.* Boston University. Enjoyed a successful screen partnership with Janet Gaynor in a series of popular romantic films of the late 1920s and early 30s. Farrell was later mayor of Palm Springs and played Gale Storm's dapper father on the popular series "My Little Margie." • *The Cheat* 1923; *The Hunchback of Notre Dame* 1923; *Rosita* 1923; *The Ten Commandments* 1923; *Clash of the Wolves* 1925; *The Freshman* 1925; *The Love Hour* 1925; *Wings of Youth* 1925; *Old Ironsides* 1926; *Sandy* 1926; *A Trip to Chinatown* 1926; *The Rough Riders* 1927; *Seventh Heaven* 1927; *Fazil* 1928; *The Red Dance* 1928; *Street Angel* 1928; *Happy Days* 1929; *Lucky Star* 1929; *The River* 1929; *Sunny Side Up* 1929; *City Girl* 1930; *High Society Blues* 1930; *Liliom* 1930; *The Princess and the Plummer* 1930; *Body and Soul* 1931; *Delicious* 1931; *Heartbreak* 1931; *The Man Who Came Back* 1931; *Merely Mary Ann* 1931; *After Tomorrow* 1932; *The First Year* 1932; *Tess of the Storm Country* 1932; *Wild Girl* 1932; *Aggie Appleby, Maker of Men* 1933; *Girl Without a Room* 1933; *The Big Shakedown* 1934; *Change of Heart* 1934; *Falling in Love* 1934; *Fighting Youth* 1935; *Forbidden Heaven* 1935; *The Flying Doctor* 1937; *Midnight Menace* 1937; *Moonlight Sonata* 1937; *Flight to Fame* 1938; *Just Around the Corner* 1938; *Tail Spin* 1939; *The Deadly Game* 1941.

Farrow, John V. • Director; also screenwriter, author. • Born John Villiers Farrow, Sydney, Australia, February 10, 1904; died 1963. *Educ.* Newington College, Australia; Winchester College, Great Britain; Royal Naval Academy. Former naval officer, in Hollywood from 1927 as a scriptwriter. Farrow turned out several well-crafted entertainments often marked by the imaginative use of locations, such as the huge skyscraper in which his 1948 thriller *The Big Clock* is largely set. He also pursued careers as a historian and novelist, and married Maureen O'Sullivan in 1936; daughters Mia and Tisa are both actresses. • *White Gold* 1927 (titles); *The Wreck of the Hesperus* 1927 (story); *The Blue Danube* 1928 (story); *The First Kiss* 1928 (sc); *Ladies of the Mob* 1928 (sc); *The Showdown* 1928 (titles); *Three Week-Ends* 1928 (adapt); *The Woman From Moscow* 1928 (sc); *A Dangerous Woman* 1929 (sc); *The Four Feathers* 1929 (titles); *The Wheel of Life* 1929 (sc); *Wolf Song* 1929 (sc); *The Bad One* 1930 (story); *Inside the Lines* 1930 (dial); *Seven Days Leave* 1930 (sc); *Shadow of the Law* 1930 (sc); *The Common Law* 1931 (sc); *A Woman of Experience* 1931 (sc,from play "The Registered Woman"); *The Impassive Footman* 1932 (sc); *Don Quichotte* 1933 (sc—English-language version); *The Spectacle Maker (short)* 1934 (d,sc); *War Lord (short)* 1934 (d,sc); *Last of the Pagans* 1935 (sc,story); *Tarzan Escapes* 1936 (sc); *Men in Exile* 1937 (d); *West of Shanghai* 1937 (d); *Broadway Musketeers* 1938 (d); *The Invisible Menace* 1938 (d); *Little Miss Thoroughbred* 1938 (d); *My Bill* 1938 (d); *She Loved a Fireman* 1938 (d); *Five Came Back* 1939 (d); *Full Confession* 1939 (d); *Reno* 1939 (d); *The Saint Strikes Back* 1939 (d); *Sorority House* 1939 (d); *Women in the Wind* 1939 (d); *A Bill of Divorcement* 1940 (d); *Married and in Love* 1940 (d); *Commandos Strike at Dawn* 1942 (d); *Wake Island* 1942 (d) (**AANBD**); *China* 1943 (d); *The Hitler Gang* 1944 (d); *You Came Along* 1945 (d); *Two Years Before the Mast* 1946 (d); *Blaze of Noon* 1947 (d); *Calcutta* 1947 (d); *California* 1947 (d); *Easy Come, Easy Go* 1947 (d); *Alias Nick Beal* 1948 (d); *Beyond Glory* 1948 (d); *The Big Clock* 1948 (d); *The Night Has a Thousand Eyes* 1948 (d); *Red, Hot and Blue* 1949 (d,sc); *Copper Canyon* 1950 (d); *Where Danger Lives* 1950 (d); *His Kind of Woman* 1951 (d,p); *Red Mountain* 1951 (d); *Submarine Command* 1951 (d,p); *Botany Bay* 1953 (d); *Hondo* 1953 (d); *Plunder of the Sun* 1953 (d); *Ride, Vaquero* 1953 (d); *A Bullet Is Waiting* 1954 (d); *King of the Khyber Rifles* 1954 (a); *The Sea Chase* 1955 (d,p); *Around the World in 80 Days* 1956 (d,sc) (**AANBD,AABSC**); *Back From Eternity* 1956 (d,p); *The Unholy Wife* 1957 (d,p); *Forbidden Island* 1959 (a); *John Paul Jones* 1959 (d,sc).

Farrow, Mia • Actress • Born Maria de Lourdes Villiers Farrow, Hollywood, CA, February 9, 1945. Delicately beautiful lead who shot to stardom as the alluring Allison Mackenzie on TV's "Peyton Place" and whose ability to project vulnerability, best exemplified in Roman Polanski's chilling *Rosemary's Baby* (1968), has been the cornerstone of her acting career. Farrow successfully played against type as a tough mafia moll in *Broadway Danny Rose* (1984), one of her more than ten film collaborations with companion Woody Allen. Farrow was married to singer Frank Sinatra from 1966 to 1968 and to conductor André Previn from 1970 to 1979. She is the daughter of actress Maureen O'Sullivan and director John Farrow, in whose *John Paul Jones* (1959) she made her first screen appearance. • *John Paul Jones* 1959; *The Age of Curiosity (short)* 1963; *Guns at Batasi* 1964; *A Dandy in Aspic* 1968; *Rosemary's Baby* 1968; *Secret Ceremony* 1968; *John and Mary* 1969; *See No Evil* 1971; *Docteur Popaul* 1972; *Follow Me!* 1972; *The Great Gatsby* 1974; *Full Circle* 1977; *Avalanche* 1978; *Death on the Nile* 1978; *A Wedding* 1978; *Hurricane* 1979; *The Last Unicorn* 1982; *A Midsummer Night's Sex Comedy* 1982; *Sarah* 1982; *Zelig* 1983; *Broadway Danny Rose* 1984; *Supergirl* 1984; *The Purple Rose of Cairo* 1985; *Hannah and Her Sisters* 1986; *Radio Days* 1987; *September* 1987; *Another Woman* 1988; *Crimes and Misdemeanors* 1989; *New York Stories* 1989; *Alice* 1990.

Fassbinder, Rainer Werner • *aka* Franz Fassbinder, Franz Walsch • Director, screenwriter; also actor, producer, playwright. • Born Bad Wörishofen, Bavaria, Germany, May 31, 1945; died June 10, 1982, Munich. By far the best-known director of the New German Cinema, Fassbinder has also been called the most important filmmaker of the post-WWII generation. Exceptionally versatile and prolific, he directed over 40 films between 1969 and 1982; in addition, he wrote most of his scripts, produced and edited many of his films and wrote plays and songs, as well as acting on stage, in his own films and in the films of others. Although he worked in a variety of genres—the gangster film, comedy, science fiction, literary adaptations—most of his stories employed elements of Hollywood melodrama from the 1950s overlayed with social criticism and avant-garde techniques. Fassbinder's expressed desire was to make films that were both popular and critical successes, but assessment of the results has been decidedly mixed: his critics contend that he became so infatuated with the Hollywood forms he tried to appropriate that the political impact of his films is indistinguishable from conventional melodrama, while his admirers argue that he was a post-modernist filmmaker whose films satisfy audience expectations while simultaneously subverting them.

Fassbinder often described his early years as lonely and lacking in love and affection. His father, a physician, and his mother, a translator, were divorced in 1951, and Fassbinder had little contact with his father after that. From around the age of seven, Fassbinder would be sent by his mother to the cinema so that she could work on her translation projects. He would later claim that during this period of his life he went to the movies almost every day, sometimes two or three times a day. He attended private and public schools at Augsburg and Munich but left before graduating in 1964 to enroll in a private drama school.

In the summer of 1967 Fassbinder joined the Action Theater, modeled on American Julian Beck's Living Theater. Two months later, he had become the company's co-director, and when it reorganized under the name "anti-theater," he emerged as its leader. The group lived together and staged a number of controversial and politically radical plays in 1968 and 1969, including some of Fassbinder's original works and adaptations.

Fassbinder's work in the theater, however, was primarily a means toward his goal of making films. He had applied in 1965 to the Berlin Film and Television Academy but failed the entrance exam. In the same year he wrote and directed his first film, a ten-minute short entitled *The City Tramp.* During his "anti-theater" period he made ten feature films, including *Love is Colder Than Death* (1969), *Katzelmacher* (1969), and *Beware of a Holy Whore* (1971). Influenced by Jean-Luc Godard, Jean-Marie Straub and the theories of Bertolt Brecht, these film are austere and minimalist in style, and although praised by many critics, they proved too demanding and inaccessible for a mass audience. It was during this time, however, that Fassbinder developed his rapid working methods. Using actors and technicians from the "anti-theater" group, he was able to complete films ahead of schedule and often under budget and thus compete successfully for government subsidies.

In search of a wider, more sympathetic audience, Fassbinder turned for a model to Hollywood melodrama, particulary the films of German-trained Douglas Sirk, who made *All That Heaven Allows, Magnificent Obsession* and *Imitation of Life* for Universal Pictures during the 1950s. Fassbinder was attracted to these films not only because of their entertainment value but also for their depiction of various kinds of repression and exploitation. This mixture of melodrama and politics is evident in Fassbinder's first commercially successful film, *The Merchant of Four Seasons* (1972). But the film that brought him international acclaim was *Ali: Fear Eats the Soul* (1974), which won the International Critics Prize at Cannes in 1974.

Ali relates a love story between a German cleaning woman in her fifties and a young Moroccan immigrant worker. The two are drawn to each other out of mutual loneliness. As their relationship becomes known, they experience various forms of hostility and public rejection. Fassbinder makes it apparent that social and economic factors constrain the couple, through his favorite techniques of double-framing shots and extremely long takes of characters looking with objectifying gazes. At the end, Fassbinder withholds a "happy solution" and directs our attention to the ongoing problems of migrant workers. The overall effect of the film is to foreground the tenuous boundaries between public and private life and to stimulate the audience to find a solution to the couple's problems.

Enthusiasm for Fassbinder's films grew quickly after *Ali.* Vincent Canby paid tribute to Fassbinder as "the most original talent since Godard," and in 1977, Manhattan's New Yorker Theater held a Fassbinder Festival. That same year saw the release of *Despair.* Shot in English on a budget that nearly equalled the cost of his first fifteen films, *Despair* was based on a novel by Vladimir Nabokov, adapted by Tom Stoppard, and starred Dirk Bogarde. Favorable comparisons with such revered directors as Ingmar Bergman, Luis Buñuel, and Luchino Visconti soon followed.

But even as enthusiasm for Fassbinder grew outside of Germany, his films seemed to make little impression on German audiences. At home, he was better known for his work in television (*Eight Hours Are Not a Day,* 1972 and the 15 1/2 hour *Berlin Alexanderplatz* 1980) and for a certain notoriety surrounding his lifestyle and open homosexuality. Coupled with the controversial issues that his films took up—terrorism, state violence, racial intolerance, sexual politics—it seemed that everything Fassbinder did provoked or offended someone. Charges leveled against him included anti-Semitism, anti-Communism, and anti-feminism.

With *The Marriage of Maria Braun* (1978) Fassbinder finally attained the popular acceptance he sought, even with German audiences. The film recounts and assesses postwar German history as embodied in the rise and fall of the main character, played by Hanna Schygulla. Its story of manipulation and betrayal exposes Germany's spectacular postwar economic recovery in terms of its cost in human values. In the years following *Maria Braun,* Fassbinder made "private" films like *In a Year with Thirteen Moons* (1978) and *The Third Generation* (1979), stories that translated personal experiences and attitudes, as well as big budget spectacles like *Lili Marleen* and *Lola* (both 1981). By the time he made his last film, *Querelle* (1982), heavy doses of drugs and alcohol had apparently become necessary to sustain his unrelenting work habits. When Fassbinder was found dead in a Munich apartment on June 10, 1982, the cause of death was reported as heart failure resulting from interaction between sleeping pills and cocaine. The script for his next film, *Rosa Luxemburg*, was found next to him. He had wanted Romy Schneider to play the lead. PR • *Der Stadtstreicher (short)* 1965 (a,d,sc); *Das Kleine Chaos (short)* 1966 (a,d,sc); *Tonys Freunde* 1967 (a); *Der Brautigam, die Komödiantin und der Zuhälter* 1968 (a); *Al Capone im deutschen Wald* 1969 (a); *Alarm* 1969 (a); *Baal* 1969 (a); *Fernes Jamaica* 1969 (sc); *Frei bis zum nächsten Mal* 1969 (a); *Götter der Pest* 1969 (a,d,p,sc,ed); *Katzelmacher* 1969 (a,d,sc,ed,pd); *Liebe Ist Kälter als der Tod/Love Is Colder Than Death* 1969 (a,d,p,sc,ed,art d); *Der Amerikanische Soldat* 1970 (a,d,p,sc,art d,song); *Das Kaffeehaus* 1970 (d,sc,from stage production); *Matthias Kneissl* 1970 (a); *Die Niklashauser Fahrt* 1970 (a,d,sc,ed); *Pioniere in Ingolstadt* 1970 (d,sc); *Der Plötzliche Reichtum der armen Leute von Kombach* 1970 (a); *Rio das Mortes* 1970 (a,d,sc); *Warum Laüft Herr R. Amok?* 1970 (d,sc,ed); *Whity* 1970 (a,d,sc,ed); *Warnung Vor Einer Heiligen Nutte/Beware of a Holy Whore* 1971 (a,d,p,sc,ed); *Acht Stunden sind kein Tag Eine Familienserie/Eight Hours Are Not a Day* 1972 (d); *Die Bitteren Tränen der Petra von Kant/The Bitter Tears of Petra von Kant* 1972 (sc,from play,pd,d,exec.p); *Bremer Freiheit* 1972 (a,d,sc); *Der Handler der vier Jahreszeiten/The Merchant of Four Seasons* 1972 (a,d,p,sc,ed); *Wildwechsel* 1972 (d,sc); *Nora Helmer* 1973 (d,sc); *Welt am Draht* 1973 (d,sc); *Zärtlichkeit der Wolfe* 1973 (a,p); *1 Berlin Harlem* 1974 (a); *Angst Essen Seele Auf/Ali: Fear Eats the Soul* 1974 (a,d,exec.p,sc,art d); *Fontane Effi Briest* 1974 (a,d,sc); *Martha* 1974 (d,sc); *Angst vor der Angst* 1975 (d,sc); *Faustrecht der Freiheit* 1975 (a,d,p,sc); *Mütter Kusters Fahrt Zum Himmel/Mother Kusters Goes to Heaven* 1975 (d,sc); *Wie ein Vogel auf dem Draht* 1975 (d,sc); *Chinesiches Roulette* 1976 (d,p,sc); *Ich will doch nur, dass Ihr mich liebt* 1976 (d,sc); *Satansbraten* 1976 (d,sc); *Schatten Der Engel* 1976 (a,sc,from play *Der Mull die Stadt und der Tod oder Frankenstein am Main*); *Frauen in New York* 1977 (d); *Bolwieser/The Stationmaster's Wife* 1978 (d,sc); *Despair* 1978 (d); *Deutschland im Herbst* 1978 (a,d,sc); *Die Ehe der Maria Braun/The Marriage of Maria Braun* 1978 (a,d,idea,dial,ed); *Der Kleine Godard* 1978 (a); *Die Dritte Generation/The Third Generation* 1979 (d,p,sc,ph); *In Einem Jahr Mit 13 Monden/In a Year With Thirteen Moons* 1979 (d,p,sc,ph,ed,art d); *Berlin Alexanderplatz* 1980 (d,sc); *Lili Marleen* 1981 (a,d,sc,add.dial,ed); *Lola* 1981 (d,exec.p,sc,ed); *Chambre 666* 1982 (a); *Kamikaze '89* 1982 (a); *Querelly - ein Pakt mit dem Teufel/Querelle—a Pact With the Devil* 1982 (d,sc,ed); *Veronika Voss* 1982 (a,d,sc); *The Wizard of Babylon* 1982 (a).

Faye, Alice • Actress; also dancer, singer. • Born Alice Jeanne Leppert, New York, NY, May 5, 1912. Personable blonde mainstay of 20th Century-Fox musicals during the late 1930s and 40s whose natural, youthful charm and rich, velvety contralto voice made her a popular favorite. A former nightclub and Broadway chorus dancer and singer with Rudy Vallee's band, Faye went to Hollywood to appear with Vallee in a small role in *George White's Scandals* (1934) and, in true movie musical tradition, was elevated to the lead when star Lilian Harvey walked off the set. In a series of handsomely produced box-office hits—backstage musicals, costume romances and then south-of-the-border, "Good Neighbor" musicals—she usually played jilted, but perservering, women who get their man (often Don Ameche or Tyrone Power) by the last reel.

After retiring from films in 1945, Faye hosted a successful radio program with second husband, bandleader Phil Harris, made appearances in the remake of *State Fair* (1964) and *The Magic of Lassie* (1978) and starred in a 1973 Broadway revival of *Good News* opposite John Payne. She was married to Tony Martin from 1936-40. JDK • *George White's Scandals* 1934; *Now I'll Tell* 1934; *She Learned About Sailors* 1934; *365 Nights in Hollywood* 1934; *Every Night at Eight* 1935; *George White's 1935 Scandals* 1935; *King of Burlesque* 1935; *Music Is Magic* 1936; *Sing, Baby, Sing* 1936; *Stowaway* 1936; *On the Avenue* 1937; *Wake Up and Live* 1937; *You Can't Have Everything* 1937; *You're a Sweetheart* 1937; *Alexander's Ragtime Band* 1938; *In Old Chicago* 1938; *Sally, Irene and Mary* 1938; *Barricade* 1939; *Hollywood Cavalcade* 1939; *Rose of Washington Square* 1939; *Tail Spin* 1939; *Little Old New York* 1940; *Lillian Russell* 1940; *Tin Pan Alley* 1940; *The Great American Broadcast* 1941; *That Night in Rio* 1941; *Week-End in Havana* 1941; *Four Jills in a Jeep* 1943; *The Gang's All Here* 1943; *Hello, Frisco, Hello* 1943; *Fallen Angel* 1945; *State Fair* 1962; *The Magic of Lassie* 1978.

Feldman, Corey • Actor • Born Reseda, CA, July 16, 1971. Juvenile performer, notable as the easily excited Teddy Duchamp in *Stand By Me* (1986). • *Time After Time* 1979; *The Fox and the Hound* 1981; *Friday the 13th - The Final Chapter* 1983; *Gremlins* 1984; *Friday the 13th, Part V: A New Beginning* 1985; *The Goonies* 1985; *Stand By Me* 1986; *The Lost Boys* 1987; *License to Drive* 1988; *The Burbs* 1989; *Dream a Little Dream* 1989; *Teenage Mutant Ninja Turtles* 1990.

Feldman, Marty • Actor; also screenwriter, director. • Born London, 1933; died December 2, 1982, Mexico City. Diminutive, pop-eyed TV comedian and writer; memorable as a variety of manic characters in Mel Brooks and Gene Wilder films, especially as Igor in Brooks's *Young Frankenstein* (1974). Feldman made his directorial debut with the Foreign Legion spoof, *The Last Remake of Beau Geste* (1977). • *The Bed Sitting Room* 1969 (a); *Every Home Should Have One* 1970 (a,sc); *Young Frankenstein* 1974 (a); *40 gradi soto il lenzuolo* 1975 (a); *The Adventure of Sherlock Holmes' Smarter Brother* 1975 (a); *Silent Movie* 1976 (a); *The Last Remake of Beau Geste* 1977 (a,d,sc,story,subtitles); *In God We Trust* 1980 (a,d,sc); *Yellowbeard* 1983 (a); *Slapstick of Another Kind* 1984 (a).

Fellini, Federico • Director, screenwriter; also actor. • Born Rimini, Italy, January 20, 1920. Italian humanist director Federico Fellini is among the most intensely autobiographical film directors the cinema has known. "If I were to make a film about the life of a sole," said Fellini, "it would end up being about me." Born in Rimini, a resort city on the Adriatic, Fellini was fascinated by the circuses and vaudeville performers that his town attracted. His education in Catholic schools also profoundly affected his later work, which, while critical of the Church, is infused with a strong spiritual dimension. After jobs as a crime reporter and artist specializing in caricature, Fellini began his film career as a gag writer for actor Aldo Fabrizi.

In 1943, Fellini met and married actress Giulietta Masina, who has appeared in several of his films and whom Fellini has called the greatest influence on his work. In 1945, he got his first important break in film, when he was invited to collaborate on the script of *Open City*, Roberto Rossellini's seminal work of the neorealist movement. In 1948, Rossellini directed *L'Amore*, one part of which was based on Fellini's original story "Il Miracolo/The Miracle" about a peasant woman (Anna Magnani) who thinks that a tramp (Fellini) who has impregnated her is St. Joseph and that she is about to give birth to Christ.

Variety Lights (1950) was Fellini's directorial debut, in collaboration with Alberto Lattuada. *The White Sheik* (1952) and *I Vitelloni* (1953) followed; the former was a comedy about a woman's affair with a comic strip hero, the latter a comedy-drama about the aimless lives of a group of young men.

Fellini's international breakthrough came with *La Strada* (1954). One of the most memorable and moving films of world cinema, it is the story of an innocent, simple young woman (Masina) who is sold by her family to a brutish strongman in a traveling circus. Because Fellini infused his film with surreal scenes, he was accused of violating the precepts of neorealism. Ultimately, *La Strada*, Fellini's first unquestioned masterpiece, is a poetic and expressive parable of two unlikely souls journeying toward salvation. The film's impact is bolstered immeasurably by Nino Rota's unforgettable music, marking the beginning of a collaboration between the two men which would end only with Rota's death in 1979. A luminous performance by Masina, and the moving Jungian imagery of earth, air, fire and water, are also memorable elements of *La Strada*.

After two strong but relatively minor works—*Il Bidone* (1955) and *Nights of Cabiria* (1956), the latter providing Masina with a hallmark role as the hapless prostitute—Fellini directed his two most influential masterworks: *La Dolce Vita* (1959) and *8 1/2* (1963). *La Dolce Vita* was a three-hour, panoramic view of contemporary Italian society as seen from the perspective of a journalist, played by Fellini's alter ego, actor Marcello Mastroianni. A savage, if subtle satire which exposes the worthless hedonism of Italian society, *La Dolce Vita* provides a wealth of unforgettable images, from its opening—a parody of the Ascension as a helicopter transports a suspended statue of Christ over rooftops with sunbathing women in bikinis—to its signature scene of bosomy Anita Ekberg bathing in the Trevi Fountain. The film was a scandalous success, a worldwide box-office hit that was condemned by both the Catholic Church for its casual depiction of suicide and sexual themes and by the Italian government for its scathing criticism of Italy.

Celebrated as a brilliant social critic, Fellini now found himself under careful scrutiny by the international community, which anxiously awaited his next film. *8 1/2* represented a brilliant gamble: as a filmmaker who did not know what film to make next, Fellini decided to make a film about an internationally acclaimed director who does not know what film to make next, thus confronting his personal confusions head-on; Mastroianni again played the director's alter ego. Having directed seven features and one segment of *Boccaccio '70* (1962), Fellini chose *8 1/2* as his title. For the first time, surreal dream imagery clearly dominated, with no clear demarcation between fantasy and reality in this groundbreaking and exceptionally influential film.

Fellini's next film, *Juliet of the Spirits* (1965), was his first in color. Again starring Masina, *Juliet* applied the methods of his previous two films to examine the psyche of an upper-class housewife. For the first time, the voices of those critics who attacked Fellini for self-indulgence were louder than those who praised him for his perceptive vision. A feminist film ahead of its time, *Juliet of the Spirits* seems today even stronger than when released, and one sequence—Juliet's memory of a religious pageant of school girls directed by unknowingly sadistic nuns—certainly stands among the most memorable and terrifying sequences in world cinema.

Many critics called Fellini's next film his "ne plus ultra." *Fellini Satyricon* (1969), loosely based on extant parts of Petronius's *Satyricon*, is the most phantasmagorical of all Fellini's work, following the bawdy adventures of bisexual characters in the pre-Christian world. Fellini has himself described the film as science fiction of the past; and indeed the whole film moves with the logic of a dream: fragmentary, at times incomprehensible, and ending, literally, in the middle of a sentence. *Fellini Satyricon* is unusually sensuous, more so than his other works; there is a constant tension between the film's sense-pleasing surface and its often disturbing elements, which include sex and nudity, dwarves, an earthquake, a hermaphrodite, a decapitation, an erotic feast and orgy, suicides, mythological creatures, violence and hundreds of the most grotesque extras ever assembled. *Satyricon* polarized critics: some attacked the film as proof that Fellini's self-indulgence had run amuck, and others praised it as a great fountainhead of a new kind of non-linear cinema, a head-trip (not unlike Stanley Kubrick's *2001: A Space Odyssey*) representing the aesthetic culmination of the 1960s and the ultimate comment, through an examination of the imaginary past, on the present.

Fellini's work since *Satyricon* has been less focused, his international acclaim less consistent. Retreating from the splendid excess of *Satyricon*, he has created several very fine, more modest films, all marked by striking imagery, which diminished the distinctions between fiction film and documentary: *The Clowns* (1970), which deals with Fellini's life-long love of circuses; *Fellini's Roma* (1972), about his infatuation with the Eternal City; and *Orchestra Rehearsal* (1978), portraying the orchestra as a metaphor for Italian politics. Perhaps Fellini's most acclaimed post-*Satyricon* film is *Amarcord* (1973), an accessible work which can be seen as a summation of his autobiographical impulse (the title means "I remember"). Lovingly describing his Rimini boyhood, *Amarcord* organizes its images through a strong emphasis on the natural cycle and a coherent narrative. Other more recent films, such as *Fellini's Casanova* (1976), *And the Ship Sails On* (1983), *Ginger and Fred* (1984) and *Intervista* (1987) seem less significant. CD • *Lo Vedi come soi... lo vedi come sei?!* 1939 (gags); *Non me lo dire!* 1940 (gags); *Il Pirata sono io!* 1940 (gags); *Documento Z 3* 1941 (uncred.sc); *Avanti c'è posto...* 1942 (uncred.sc); *Apparizione* 1943 (uncred.sc); *Campo de' Fiori* 1943 (adapt); *Chi l'ha visto?* 1943 (sc,story); *Quarta Pagina* 1943 (sc,story); *L'Ultima carrozzella* 1943 (sc); *Roma, città aperta/Open City/Rome, Open City* 1945 (sc,ad) **(AANBSC)**; *Paisan* 1946 (sc,story,uncred.ad) **(AANBSC)**; *Il Delitto di Giovanni Episcopo* 1947 (sc); *L'Ebreo errante* 1947 (sc); *Fumeria d'oppio* 1947 (sc); *Senza Pietà* 1947 (sc,story); *L'Amore* 1948 (a,story,ad—"Il Miracolo"); *La Città dolente* 1948 (sc); *In nome delle legge* 1948 (sc); *Il Mulino del Po* 1949 (sc); *Il Cammino della speranza* 1950 (sc,story); *Francesco Giullare di Dio* 1950 (sc); *Luci del Varietà/Variety Lights* 1950 (d,p,sc,story); *Persiane chiuse* 1950 (sc,story); *Cameriera bella presenza offresi* 1951 (sc); *La Città si difende* 1951 (sc,story); *Europa '51* 1951 (uncred.sc); *Il Brigante di Tacca del Lupo* 1952 (story); *Lo Sceicco Bianco/The White Sheik* 1952 (d,sc,story); *Amore in Città/Love in the City* 1953 (d,sc—"Un Agenzia Matrimoniale"); *I Vitelloni* 1953 (d,sc,story) **(AANBSC)**; *La Strada* 1954 (d,sc,story) **(AANBSC)**; *Il Bidone* 1955 (d,sc,story); *Le Notti di Cabiria/Nights of Cabiria* 1956 (d,sc,story); *Fortunella* 1957 (sc,story); *La Dolce Vita* 1959 (d,sc,story) **(AANBD,AANBSC)**; *Boccaccio '70* 1962 (d,sc—"Le tentazioni del dottor Antonio/The Temptation of Doctor Antonio"); *Otto e Mezzo/8 1/2* 1963 (d,sc,story) **(AANBD,AANBSC)**; *Giulietta degli Spiriti/Juliet of the Spirits* 1965 (d,sc,story,idea); *Histoires Extraordinaires/Spirits of the Dead* 1968 (d,sc—"Il ne faut pas parier sa tête contre le diable"/"Toby Dammit"); *Satyricon* 1969 (d,sc,story,scenery sketches) **(AANBD)**; *Sweet Charity* 1969 (from story "Le Notti di Cabiria"); *Alex in Wonderland* 1970 (a); *Ciao, Federico!* 1970 (a); *I Clowns/The Clowns* 1970 (a,d,p,sc); *Roma/Fellini's Roma* 1972 (a,d,sc,story); *Amarcord/Fellini's Amarcord* 1973 (d,sc) **(AANBD, AANBSC)**; *C'eravamo tanto amati/We All Loved Each Other So Much* 1974 (a); *Il Casanova di Federico Fellini/Fellini's Casanova* 1976 (d,sc,pd) **(AANBSC)**; *Prova d'Orchestra/Orchestra Rehearsal* 1978 (a,d,sc); *La Città Delle Donne/City of Women* 1980 (d,sc,story); *E la nave Va/And the Ship Sails On* 1983 (d,sc,story,idea); *Il Tassinaro* 1983 (a); *Ginger et Fred/Ginger and Fred* 1986 (d,sc,story); *Federico Fellini's Intervista* 1987 (a,d,sc); *Le Voce della Luna/Voices of the Moon* 1990 (d,sc).

Fenton, George • British composer • Acclaimed composer who has also worked in theater and TV, most notably on the award-winning series "The Jewel in the Crown." • *Private Road* 1971 (m); *Bloody Kids* 1979 (m); *Hussy* 1979 (m,m.dir); *Gandhi* 1982 (orch,add.m,m.dir) **(AANBM)**; *Loving Walter* 1983 (m); *Runners* 1983 (m,m.dir); *Saigon - Year of the Cat* 1983 (m); *Billy the Kid and the Green Baize Vampire* 1985 (m,m.cond,pianist); *The Company of Wolves* 1985 (m); *Past Caring* 1985 (m); *84 Charing Cross Road* 1986 (m,m.dir); *Clockwise* 1986 (m); *Cry Freedom* 1987 (m,m.dir,m.arr) **(AANBM,AANBS)**; *White Mischief* 1987 (m); *White of the Eye* 1987 (m.dir,m); *Dangerous Liaisons* 1988 (m) **(AANBM)**; *The Dressmaker* 1988 (m); *A Handful of Dust* 1988 (m); *High Spirits* 1988 (m,m.cond,orch); *We're No Angels* 1989 (m,m.cond,orch); *102 Boulevard Haussmann* 1990 (m); *The Long Walk Home* 1990 (m); *Memphis Belle* 1990 (m,orch); *White Palace* 1990 (m).

Fernandel • Actor • Born Fernand Joseph Désiré Contandin, Marseille, France, May 8, 1903; died February 26, 1971, Paris. Popular, prolific long-faced French comedian with an enormous horsey grin who, through the expressive use of his hands, homely face and voice, became one of the most beloved film stars in France and appeared, often as innocent peasant characters, in almost 150 movies. Although he first gained screen popularity with a serious role in Bernard Deschamps's *Le Rosier de Madame Husson* (1932), Fernandel was best known for his numerous comic portrayals, especially as the title character, an irascible Italian village priest, in the "Don Camillo" series. • *Le Blanc et le Noir* 1931; *Coeur de Lilas* 1931; *Paris-Beguin* 1931; *Les Gaietés de l'Escadron* 1932; *Le Rosier de Madame Husson* 1932; *L'Ordonnance* 1933; *Adéma ï Aviateur* 1934; *Angele* 1934; *La Porteuse de pain* 1934; *Ferndinand le Noceur* 1935; *Un De la Legion* 1936; *Josette* 1936; *Un Carnet de Bal* 1937; *Le Dégourdis de lo Onzième* 1937; *Francois I* 1937; *Hercule* 1937; *Igance* 1937; *Regain* 1937; *Le Roi du Sport* 1937; *Le Schpountz* 1938; *Fric-Frac* 1939; *Un Chapeau de Paille d'Italie/The Italian Straw Hat* 1940; *La Fille du Puisatier* 1940; *Simplet* 1942 (a,d); *Adrien* 1943 (a,d); *Naïs* 1945; *Les Gueux au Paradis* 1946; *Pétrus* 1946; *L'Armoire volante* 1949; *Botta e Riposta* 1949; *Emile l'Africain* 1949; *Meurtres* 1950; *Topaze* 1950; *Adhémar* 1951 (a,d); *L'Auberge Rouge* 1951; *L'Ennemi Public No. 1* 1951 (a,d); *Le Petit Monde de Don Camillo/The Little World of Don Camillo* 1951; *Coiffeur pour Dames* 1952; *Le Fruit défendu* 1952; *La Table aux Crevés* 1952; *Retour de Don Camillo* 1953; *Ali Baba* 1954; *Mam'zelle Nitouche* 1954; *Le Mouton à cinq pattes/The Sheep Has Five Legs* 1954; *Around the World in 80 Days* 1956; *Le Courturier de Ces Dames* 1956; *Pantaloons* 1956; *The Wild Oat* 1956; *L'Homme à l'Imperméable* 1957; *Three Feet in Bed* 1957; *The Virtuous Bigamist* 1957; *La Loi c'est la loi* 1958; *Paris Holiday* 1958; *Senéchal Le Magnifique* 1958; *Le Grand Chef* 1959; *La Vache et le Prisonnier* 1959; *Le Caid* 1960; *Crésus* 1960; *Cocagne* 1961; *Don Camillo Monseigneur* 1961; *Dynamite Jack* 1961; *Le Diable et les Dix Commandements* 1962; *La Cuisine au Beurre* 1963; *L'Age Ingrat* 1964 (a,p); *Don Camillo à Moscou* 1965; *Le Voyage du Père* 1966; *L'Homme à la Buick* 1967; *Heureux qui comme Ulysse* 1970.

Fernandez, Emilio • Director, screenwriter; also actor. • Born El Seco, Coahuila, Mexico, March 26, 1904; died August 6, 1986, Mexico City. Emilio "El Indio" Fernandez is not only the most famous figure in the history of the Mexican film industry, he was for many decades a national symbol. Fernandez's legendary on-and-off screen persona incarnates a type of Mexican "machismo" that grew out of the Mexican Revolution of 1910-17: the temperamental, at times violent, man committed to the defense of cultural nationalism—those ideals and values perceived as authentically Mexican. Fernandez was born to an Indian mother in the Mexican state of Coahuila. As a young man he participated in the revolutionary struggles, and after the defeat of his faction he sought exile in the United States. In Hollywood in the late 1920s and early 30s Fernandez worked as an extra and bit player while he learned about filmmaking.

In 1933 Fernandez was able to return to Mexico and the following year he commenced his long career in the Mexican motion picture industry, first as a screenwriter and actor. He had his first lead role, as an Indian, in the drama *Janitzio* (1934). El Indio's athletic physique and his strikingly Indian countenance made him much in demand to play revolutionaries, bandits and "charros" (Mexican cowboys). By the 1960s, Fernandez's off-screen reputation as a violent man had led to his typecasting as brutal villains in many Mexican and American films such as Sam Peckinpah's *The Wild Bunch* (1969), in which he played the sadistic military leader Mapache.

However, acting and screenwriting were lesser concerns for Fernandez, who became Mexico's most famous director in the 1940s, the so-called golden age of Mexican cinema. Two of El Indio's finest films were *Flor silvestre* and *Maria Candelaria* (both 1943). *Flor silvestre* is a rural melodrama-love-story-adventure set during the Mexican Revolution; *Maria Candelaria* tells the tragic tale of the suffering and love of an Indian peasant couple in Xochimilco, a picturesque area of gardens and waterways. Both these films and Fernandez's other important works from the 1940s—*Enamorada* (1946), *Rio Escondido* (1947) and *Pueblerina* (1949)—were co-scripted by the director and photographed by the prominent cinematographer Gabriel Figueroa. In these films, the Fernandez-Figueroa team developed a beautiful poetic-epic visual style evidently influenced by Sergei Eisenstein's unfinished *Que viva Mexico* and Paul Strand's photography for *Redes/The Wave* (1936). This style glorifies the beauty of the Mexican landscape through meticulously composed, stationary-camera long shots that highlight "typically Mexican" motifs: the prickly pear cactus and the maguey, the towering poplar trees along the waterways of Xochimilco, baroque churches, rolling clouds in boundless skies.

Fernandez continued directing films in Mexico until the mid-1970s, but his creativity started to decline in the 1950s. Today the director is best remembered for his distinctive visual style and his private notoriety—he was convicted of manslaughter in 1976 for fatally shooting a farm laborer, he claimed, in self-defense. DW • *The Land of Missing Men* 1930 (a); *Oklahoma Cyclone* 1930 (a); *The Western Code* 1932 (a); *La Buena Ventura* 1934 (a); *Janitzio* 1934 (a); *Isla de la Passion* 1941 (d,sc); *Soy Puro Mexicano* 1942 (d,sc); *Flor Silvestre* 1943 (a,d,sc); *Maria Candelaria* 1943 (d,sc); *Las Abandonadas* 1945 (d,sc); *Bugambilia* 1945 (d,sc); *Pepita Jimenez* 1945 (d,sc); *Enamorada* 1946 (d,sc); *La Perla* 1946 (a,d,sc); *Rio Escondido* 1947 (d,sc); *Maclovia* 1948 (d,sc); *Salon Mexico* 1948 (d,sc); *Duelo en las Montanas* 1949 (d,sc); *La Malquerida* 1949 (d,sc); *Pueblerina* 1949 (d,sc); *Un Dia de Vida* 1950 (d,sc); *The Torch* 1950 (d,sc); *Victimas del Pecado* 1950 (d,sc); *Acapulco* 1951 (d,sc); *La Bien amada* 1951 (d,sc); *Islas Marias* 1951 (d,sc); *Siempre Tuya* 1951 (d,sc); *Soave Patria* 1951 (d,sc); *Cuando levanta la Niebla* 1952 (d,sc); *El Mar y Tu* 1952 (d,sc); *El Rapto* 1953 (d,sc); *La Red* 1953 (d,sc); *El Reportaje* 1953 (d,sc); *Nostros Dos* 1954 (d,sc); *La Rebellion de los Colgados* 1954 (d,sc); *La Rosa Blanca* 1954 (d,sc); *La Tierra del Fuego se Apaga* 1955 (d,sc); *Una Cita de Amor* 1956 (d,sc); *El Imposter* 1957 (d,sc); *Pueblito* 1962 (d,sc); *The Night of the Iguana* 1964 (assoc.d); *The Reward* 1965 (a); *The Appaloosa* 1966 (a); *A Loyal Soldier of Pancho Villa* 1966 (d,sc); *Return of the Seven* 1966 (a); *A Covenant With Death* 1967 (a); *The War Wagon* 1967 (a); *The Wild Bunch* 1969 (a); *Detras de esa Puerta* 1972 (a); *Pat Garrett and Billy the Kid* 1973 (a); *Bring Me the Head of Alfredo Garcia* 1974 (a); *La Choca* 1974 (d); *El Rincon de las Virgenes* 1974 (a); *Lucky Lady* 1975 (a); *Zona Roja* 1976 (d,sc); *Las Amantes del Senor de la Noche* 1983 (a); *Observations Under the Volcano* 1984 (a); *Under the Volcano* 1984 (a); *El Tesoro del Amazones* 1985 (a); *Pirates* 1986 (a).

Ferrara, Abel • Director; also songwriter • Born US. Known for his highly atmospheric, stylized portraits of an ultraviolent, crime-ridden New York City. Ferrara's first feature was the exploitation flic *Driller Killer* (1979), on which he also served as editor and songwriter under the pseudonym Jimmy Laine. His best works are the cult hit *Ms. 45* (1980), about a vengeance-seeking rape victim, *China Girl* (1988), about interracial love and violence in Chinatown, and *King of New York* (1990), starring Christopher Walken as an ex-con crime lord out to regain his turf. Ferrara also directed the TV series "Crime Story" (1986-88). • *The Driller Killer* 1979 (a,d,ed,song); *Ms. 45* 1980 (a,d); *Fear City* 1985 (d); *China Girl* 1987 (d,songs); *Cat Chaser* 1989 (d); *King of New York* 1990 (d).

Ferrer, José • Actor; also director. • Born José Vincente Ferrer De Otero y Cintron, Santurce, Puerto Rico, January 8, 1912. *Educ.* Princeton (architecture, music composition). Distinguished Broadway actor-director-producer who made his Hollywood debut in *Joan of Arc* (1948) and proved his versatility in films including *Whirlpool* (1949), *Cyrano de Bergerac* (1950) and *Lawrence of Arabia* (1962). Ferrer's work as a director was generally undistinguished, one exception being his scathing look at the TV industry, *The Great Man* (1956). • *Joan of Arc* 1948 **(AANBSA)**; *Whirlpool* 1949; *Crisis* 1950; *Cyrano de Bergerac* 1950 **(AABA)**; *Anything Can Happen* 1952; *Moulin Rouge* 1952 **(AANBA)**; *Miss Sadie Thompson* 1953; *The Beautiful Stranger* 1954 (song); *The Caine Mutiny* 1954; *Deep in My Heart* 1954; *The Cockleshell Heroes* 1955 (a,d); *The Shrike* 1955 (a,d); *The Great Man* 1956 (a,d,sc); *I Accuse!* 1957 (a,d); *Mayerling* 1957; *The High Cost of Loving* 1958 (a,d); *Return to Peyton Place* 1961 (d); *Forbid Them Not* 1962; *Lawrence of Arabia* 1962; *State Fair* 1962 (d); *Cyrano et d'Artagnan* 1963; *Nine Hours to Rama* 1963; *The Greatest Story Ever Told* 1965; *Ship of Fools* 1965; *Enter Laughing* 1966; *Cervantes* 1967; *The Little Drummer Boy (short)* 1969; *El Clan de los Inmorales* 1973; *E'Lollipop* 1975; *Paco* 1975; *The Big Bus* 1976; *Voyage of the Damned* 1976; *Crash* 1977; *Dracula's Dog* 1977; *The Private Files of J. Edgar Hoover* 1977; *The Sentinel* 1977; *Who Has Seen the Wind* 1977; *The Amazing Captain Nemo* 1978; *Fedora* 1978; *The Swarm* 1978; *The 5th Musketeer* 1979; *Natural Enemies* 1979; *The Big Brawl* 1980; *Bloody Birthday* 1980; *Blood Tide* 1982; *A Midsummer Night's Sex Comedy* 1982; *The Being* 1983; *To Be or Not to Be* 1983; *The Evil That Men Do* 1984; *Dune* 1985; *Ingrid* 1985; *El Sol y la Luna* 1987; *Samson and Delilah* 1988; *A Life of Sin* 1990; *Old Explorers* 1990.

Ferrer, Mel • Actor; also director, producer. • Born Melchior Gaston Ferrer, Elberon, NJ, August 25, 1917. *Educ.* Princeton. Gaunt, lanky and graceful player who, after a successful career as a radio producer-director and a Broadway dancer-actor, moved into film, first as a director and then as a reserved, sensitive and usually romantic leading man. Married to Audrey Hepburn from 1954 to 1968, Ferrer co-starred with her in *War and Peace* (1956), directed her in *Green Mansions* (1959) and produced the tense thriller, *Wait Until Dark* (1967), in which she starred. • *The Girl of the Limberlost* 1945 (d); *The Fugitive* 1947 (ad); *Lost Boundaries* 1949; *Born to Be Bad* 1950; *The Secret Fury* 1950 (d); *Vendetta* 1950 (d); *The Brave Bulls* 1951; *Rancho Notorious* 1952; *Scaramouche* 1952; *Knights of the Round Table* 1953; *Lili* 1953; *Saadia* 1954; *Elena et les hommes/Paris Does Strange Things* 1956; *War and Peace* 1956; *The Sun Also Rises* 1957; *The Vintage* 1957; *Fraulein* 1958; *Green Mansions* 1959 (d); *The World, the Flesh and the Devil* 1959; *...Et mourir de plaisir/Blood and Roses* 1960; *Le Diable et les Dix Commandements/The Devil and the 10 Commandments* 1962; *The Longest Day* 1962; *Paris When It Sizzles* 1963 (uncred.a); *The Fall of the Roman Empire* 1964; *Sex and the Single Girl* 1964; *Cabriola/Every Day Is a Holiday* 1965 (d,exec.p,sc,story); *El Greco* 1966 (a,m,p); *Wait Until Dark* 1967 (p); *Embassy* 1971 (p); *The Night Visitor* 1971 (p); *A Time For Loving/Paris Was Made For Lovers* 1971 (a,p); *W* 1974 (p); *Brannigan* 1975; *Das Netz* 1975; *Il Corsaro Nero* 1976; *Eaten Alive* 1977; *La Ragazza del Piagiame Gialle* 1977; *The Amazing Captain Nemo* 1978; *L'Anti Cristo/The Tempter* 1978; *The Hi-Riders* 1978; *The Norseman* 1978; *Zwischengleis* 1978; *The Fifth Floor* 1979; *Guyana: Cult of the Damned* 1979; *L'Isola degli uomini Pesce* 1979; *The Visitor* 1979; *City of the Walking Dead* 1980; *Mangiati vivi dai Cannibali* 1980; *Lili Marleen* 1981.

Ferreri, Marco • Director; also screenwriter, producer, actor. • Born Milan, Italy, May 11, 1928. *Educ.* Milan University (veterinary studies). Former production manager on Italian films of the early 1950s who began his directing career in Spain. Ferreri's films are characterized by an absurd, misanthropic sense of humor as exemplified in his award-winning *The Wheelchair* (1959), in which a grandfather torments his family until they buy him an electric wheelchair for which he has no need. His exposés of contemporary middle-class mores, and especially sexual relations, continued through the 1960s and 70s with films such as *The Conjugal Bed* (1963), *Dillinger Is Dead* (1968)—considered his masterpiece by most critics—and the notorious *La Grande Bouffe* (1973), in which a group of bored people literally eat themselves to death. Ferreri gave a memorable performance as the deaf, murderous art collector in Mario Monicelli's *Casanova '70* (1965). • *Il Principe ribelle* 1950 (a); *Il Cappotto* 1951 (prod.man); *Amore in Citta* 1953 (prod.man); *Appunti su un fatto di Cronaca* 1953 (p); *La Spiaggia* 1953 (a,prod.man); *Donne e soldati* 1954 (a,sc,prod.man); *Fiesta Brava* 1956 (prod.man); *El Pisito* 1958 (a,d,sc); *Los Chicos* 1959 (d,sc); *El Cochecito/The Wheelchair* 1959 (d,sc); *El Secreto de Los Hombres Azules* 1960 (d—begun by Ferreri, completed by Edmon Agabra); *Le Italiane e l'amore* 1961 (d,sc); *Il Mafioso* 1962 (sc); *Una Storia moderna/The Conjugal Bed* 1963 (d,sc); *Contro Sesso* 1964 (a,d,sc); *La Donna Scimmia/The Ape Woman* 1964 (d,sc); *Oggi, domani e dopodomani* 1964 (a,d,sc—"L'uomo dei cinque palloni"); *Casanova '70* 1965 (a); *Marcia nuziale* 1966 (d,sc); *Break-Up* 1967 (a,d,sc); *Il Fischio al nasio* 1967 (a); *L'Harem* 1967 (d,sc,story); *Dillinger è Morto/Dillinger Is Dead* 1968 (d,sc,story); *Porcile/Pigpen* 1969 (a); *Il Seme dell'uomo* 1969 (a,d,sc,story); *Le Vent d'est* 1969 (a); *Ciao Gulliver* 1970 (a); *Sortilegio* 1970 (a); *12 dicembre* 1971 (collaboration); *La Cagna* 1971 (d,sc); *Lui per lei* 1971 (a); *L'Udienza* 1971 (d,sc,story,adapt); *La Grande Bouffe* 1973 (d,sc); *Touche pas à la femme blanche!* 1973 (d,sc); *La Dernière Femme* 1976 (d,sc,story); *Rève de Singe* 1978 (d,sc,story); *Chiedo Asilo* 1979 (d); *Storie di Ordinaria Follia/Tales of Ordinary Madness* 1981 (d,sc,story); *Storia di Piera* 1982 (d,sc); *Il Futuro è Donna* 1984 (d,sc); *I Love You* 1986 (d,sc); *Y'a bon les blancs* 1987 (d,sc,art d); *Le Voce della Luna* 1990 (prod.man); *La Casa del Sorriso/House of Smiles* 1991 (d,sc).

Ferretti, Dante • Italian production designer • Leading art director who designed most of Pasolini's films of the 1970s and has been a consistent collaborator with Fellini since *Orchestra Rehearsal* (1978). Ferretti's later credits include Jean-Jacques Annaud's 13th-century mystery *The Name of the Rose* (1986) and Terry Gilliam's visual extravaganza *The Adventures of Baron Munchausen* (1988). • *Anzio* 1968 (asst.art d); *Medea* 1970 (pd); *Il Decamerone/The Decameron* 1971 (pd); *La Classe Operaia Va In Paradise/The Working Class Goes to Heaven* 1972 (pd); *I Racconti di Canterbury/The Canterbury Tales* 1972 (pd); *Sbatti Il Mostro In Prima Pagina* 1972 (pd); *Storie Scellerate* 1973 (pd); *Delitto d'Amore* 1974 (pd); *Il Fiore Delle Mille e Una Notte/The Arabian Nights* 1974 (pd); *Mio Dio, come sono Caduta in Basso* 1974 (pd); *Salò o le Centiventi Giornate di Sodoma/Salo or the 120 Days of Sodom* 1975 (pd); *Todo Modo* 1976 (pd); *Eutanasia di un amore* 1978 (pd); *Il Gatto* 1978 (pd); *Prova d'Orchestra/Orchestra Rehearsal* 1978 (pd); *Rêve de singe/Bye Bye Monkey* 1978 (pd); *La Città Delle Donne/City of Women* 1980 (pd); *Il Minestrone* 1980 (pd); *La Pelle* 1981 (pd); *Storie di Ordinaria Follia/Tales of Ordinary Madness* 1981 (pd); *La Nuit de Varennes* 1982 (pd); *Oltre la Porta* 1982 (pd); *Till Marriage Do Us Part* 1982 (pd); *E la nave Va/And the Ship Sails On* 1983 (pd); *Le Bon Roi Dagobert* 1984 (pd); *Il Futuro è Donna/The Future Is Woman* 1984 (pd); *Pianoforte* 1984 (pd); *Ginger et Fred/Ginger and Fred* 1986 (sets,art d); *The Name of the Rose* 1986 (pd); *The Adventures of Baron Munchausen* 1988 (pd)

(AANBAD); *Lo Zio Indegno* 1989 (pd); *Docteur M.* 1990 (pd); *Hamlet* 1990 (pd); *Le Voce della Luna/Voices of the Moon* 1990 (art d,sets).

Feuillade, Louis • Director, screenwriter; also producer. • Born Lunel, France, February 19, 1873; died February 25, 1925, Paris. Prolific director of over 700 films, most of them short or medium-length. Feuillade began his career with Gaumont where, as well as directing his own features, he was appointed artistic director in charge of production in 1907. Feuillade's work was largely comprised of film series; his first series, begun in 1910 and numbering 15 episodes, was *Le Film Esthétique*, a financially unsuccessful attempt at "highbrow" cinema. More popular was *Life As It Is* (1911-13), which moved from the costume pageantry of his earlier work to a more realistic, if somewhat melodramatic, depiction of contemporary life. Feuillade also directed scores of short films featuring the characters "Bébé" and "Bout-de-zan."

Feuillade's most successful feature-length serials were *Fantômas* (1913-14), which chronicled the diabolical exploits of the "emperor of crime," and *Les Vampires* (1915-16), which trailed a criminal gang led by Irma Vep (Musidora) and was noted for its imaginative use of locations and lyrical, almost surreal style. • *Fantômas* 1913 (d,sc); *Juve contre Fantômas* 1913 (d,sc); *Le Mort qui tue* 1913 (d,sc); *Fantômas contre Fantômas* 1914 (d,sc); *Le Faux magistrat* 1914 (d,sc); *Les Vampires* 1915 (d,sc); *L'Aventure des millions* 1916 (d,sc); *Judex* 1916 (d,sc); *Un Mariage de raison* 1916 (d,sc); *Notre pauvre coeur* 1916 (d,sc); *La Deserteuse* 1917 (d,sc); *La Nouvelle mission de Judex* 1917 (d,sc); *Le Passe de Monique* 1917 (d,sc); *Les Petites marionnettes* 1918 (d,sc); *Tih Minh* 1918 (d,sc); *Vendemiaire* 1918 (d,sc); *Barrabas* 1919 (d,sc); *L'Engrenage* 1919 (d,sc); *L'Homme sans visage* 1919 (d,sc); *Les Deux gamines* 1920 (d,sc); *L'Orpheline* 1921 (d,sc); *Parisette* 1921 (d,sc); *Le Fils du filibustier* 1922 (d,sc); *Le Gamin de Paris* 1923 (d,sc); *La Gosseline* 1923 (d,sc); *L'Orphelin de Paris* 1923 (d,sc); *Vindicta* 1923 (d,sc); *La Fille bien gardée* 1924 (d,sc); *Lucette* 1924 (d,sc); *Pierrot, Pierrette* 1924 (d,sc); *Le Stigmate* 1924 (d,sc); *Judex 34* 1933 (from orig.sc); *Les Deux gamines* 1935 (from orig.sc); *Judex* 1963 (from orig.sc).

Feyder, Jacques • Director; also screenwriter. • Born Jacques Frédérix, Ixelles, Belgium, July 21, 1885; died May 25, 1948, Rive de Praugins, Switzerland. In films as an actor from 1913 and director from 1916. Feyder's lyrical handling of realistic subject-matter created some of the finest French films of the 1920s, including *Crainquebille* (1923), *Visage d'enfants* (1924) and the celebrated Zola adaptation, *Thérèse Raquin* (1928). After a brief sojourn in Hollywood, he assured his place as a key figure of "poetic realism" with a series of films starring his wife Françoise Rosay and co-written by Charles Spaak. Feyder's assistant during this period was future director Marcel Carné. • *Protea* 1913 (a); *Autour d'une bague* 1914 (a); *Quand minuit sonna* 1914 (a); *Les Vampires* 1915 (a); *Le Bluff* 1916 (d,sc); *Un Conseil d'ami* 1916 (d,sc); *Le Frère de lait* 1916 (d,sc); *L'Homme de compagnie* 1916 (adapt,d); *L'Instinct est maître* 1916 (d,sc); *Monsieur Pinson, policier* 1916 (a,ad); *Le Pied qui étreint* 1916 (d,sc); *Têtes de femmes, femmes de tête* 1916 (d,sc); *Tiens, vous êtes à Poitiers?* 1916 (d,sc); *Abrégeons les formalités!* 1917 (d,sc); *Le Billard cassé* 1917 (d,sc); *Le Pardessus de demi-saison* 1917 (d,sc); *Le Ravin sans fond* 1917 (adapt,d); *La Trouvaille de Buchu* 1917 (d,sc); *Les Vieilles femmes de l'hospice* 1917 (adapt,d); *La Faute d'orthographe* 1919 (d,sc); *L'Atlantide* 1921 (d,sc); *Crainquebille* 1923 (d,sc,art d); *Visages d'enfants* 1924 (d,sc,art d); *Das Bildnis* 1925 (a,d,sc,titles); *Gribiche* 1925 (d,sc); *Poil de Carotte* 1925 (sc); *Carmen* 1926 (d,sc,ed); *Au pays du roi lépreux* 1927 (d,sc); *Les Nouveaux messieurs* 1928 (d); *Thérèse Raquin* 1928 (d,sc,adapt,titles); *Gardiens de phare* 1929 (sc); *His Glorious Night* 1929 (d); *The Kiss* 1929 (d,sc); *The Unholy Night* 1929 (d); *Anna Christie* 1930 (d); *Daybreak* 1931 (d); *Son of India* 1931 (d); *Le Grand jeu* 1933 (d,sc); *Pension Mimosas* 1934 (d,sc); *La Kermesse heroique/Carnival in Flanders* 1935 (d,sc); *Fahrendes Volk* 1937 (d,sc); *Knight Without Armour* 1937 (d); *La Loi du nord* 1939 (d,sc); *Femme disparaît* 1941 (d,p,sc); *Matura reise* 1942 (prod.sup); *Macadam* 1946 (artistic director); *Jacques Feyder et son chef d'oeuvre* 1974 (archival footage).

Fiedel, Brad • Composer • Born New York, NY. Began his career as a keyboard performer with Hall and Oates and worked primarily in the horror and action genres before composing for such mainstream films as *The Big Easy* (1986) and *The Accused* (1988). • *Apple Pie* 1975 (m); *Deadly Hero* 1976 (m); *Looking Up* 1977 (m); *The Astrologer* 1978 (m); *Terror Eyes* 1981 (m); *Hit and Run* 1982 (m); *Eyes of Fire* 1984 (m); *The Terminator* 1984 (m); *Compromising Positions* 1985 (m); *Fraternity Vacation* 1985 (m); *Fright Night* 1985 (m); *The Big Easy* 1986 (m); *Desert Bloom* 1986 (m); *Let's Get Harry* 1987 (m); *Nowhere to Hide* 1987 (m); *The Accused* 1988 (m,song,orch); *Fright Night, Part II* 1988 (m); *Mystic Pizza* 1988 (song); *The Serpent and the Rainbow* 1988 (m); *Immediate Family* 1989 (m); *True Believer* 1989 (m).

Field, Sally • Actress; also producer. • Born Pasadena, CA, November 6, 1946. *Educ.* Actors Studio. Youthful, wholesome lead of TV's "Gidget" (1965-66) and "The Flying Nun" (1967-70), in films from 1967. Field first earned critical attention with her Emmy Award-winning role as *Sybil* (1976) and cemented her reputation with two Oscar-winning performances: as union organizer *Norma Rae* (1979) and as a resilient widow in *Places in the Heart* (1984). • *The Way West* 1967; *Stay Hungry* 1975; *Heroes* 1977; *Smokey and the Bandit* 1977; *The End* 1978; *Hooper* 1978; *Norma Rae* 1978 **(AABA)**; *Beyond the Poseidon Adventure* 1979; *Smokey and the Bandit II* 1980; *Absence of Malice* 1981; *Back Roads* 1981; *Kiss Me Goodbye* 1982; *Places in the Heart* 1984 **(AABA)**; *Murphy's Romance* 1985; *Surrender* 1987; *Punchline* 1988 (a,p); *Steel Magnolias* 1989; *Not Without My Daughter* 1991.

Field, Shirley Anne • *aka* Shirley Ann Field • Actress • Born London, June 27, 1938. Attractive, brunette former model who appeared in several important English films of the early 1960s, notably *Saturday Night and Sunday Morning* (1960) and *Alfie* (1966); Field's career petered out in the late 70s but she has lately carved a niche as a character actress. • *It's Never Too Late* 1956; *The Good Companions* 1957; *The Silken Affair* 1957; *Horrors of the Black Museum* 1959; *Upstairs and Downstairs* 1959; *Beat Girl* 1960; *The Entertainer* 1960; *Man in the Moon* 1960; *Once More, With Feeling* 1960; *Peeping Tom* 1960; *Saturday Night and Sunday Morning* 1960; *These Are the Damned* 1962; *The War Lover* 1962; *Kings of the Sun* 1963; *Alfie* 1966; *Doctor in Clover* 1966; *Hell Is Empty* 1967; *With Love in Mind* 1969; *Doctor Maniac* 1973; *My Beautiful Laundrette* 1985; *Shag* 1988; *Getting It Right* 1989; *The Rachel Papers* 1989.

Fielding, Jerry • Composer • Born Pittsburgh, PA, June 17, 1922. *Educ.* Carnegie Institute of Technology, Pittsburgh PA. Frequent collaborator with directors Sam Peckinpah and Michael Winner. Fielding has also worked extensively in TV ("Hogan's Heroes," "McMillan and Wife"). • *Advise and Consent* 1962 (m,song); *The Nun and the Sergeant* 1962 (m); *For Those Who Think Young* 1964 (m); *McHale's Navy* 1964 (m); *McHale's Navy Joins the Air Force* 1965 (m); *Mission Impossible Vs. the Mob* 1969 (m,m.dir); *The Wild Bunch* 1969 (m) **(AANBM)**; *Suppose They Gave a War and Nobody Came?* 1970 (m,song); *Johnny Got His Gun* 1971 (m); *Lawman* 1971 (m); *The Nightcomers* 1971 (m); *Straw Dogs* 1971 (m) **(AANBM)**; *Chato's Land* 1972 (m); *Junior Bonner* 1972 (m); *The Mechanic* 1972 (m); *The Outfit* 1973 (m); *Scorpio* 1973 (m); *The Super Cops* 1973 (m); *Bring Me the Head of Alfredo Garcia* 1974 (m); *The Gambler* 1974 (m); *The Black Bird* 1975 (m); *The Killer Elite* 1975 (m,m.dir); *The Outlaw Josey Wales* 1975 (m) **(AANBM)**; *The Bad News*

Bears 1976 (m); *The Enforcer* 1976 (m); *Demon Seed* 1977 (m,m.dir); *The Gauntlet* 1977 (m); *Gray Lady Down* 1977 (m); *Semi-Tough* 1977 (m,m.dir); *The Big Sleep* 1978 (m); *Beyond the Poseidon Adventure* 1979 (m); *Escape From Alcatraz* 1979 (m); *Below the Belt* 1980 (m,lyrics); *Cries in the Night* 1981 (m).

Fields, W. C. • *aka* Charles Bogle, Mahatma Kane Jeeves, Otis Criblecoblis • Actor; also screenwriter. • Born William Claude Dukenfield, Philadelphia, PA, February 10, 1879; died December 25, 1946, Pasadena, CA. Former juggler, vaudevillian and stage performer whose propensity for caustic wisecracks made him an international star. Fields began making regular film appearances in 1924, partly propelled by his successful starring role as Eustace McGargle in the Broadway musical *Poppy*. His innovatively abrasive humor—which included a professed hatred for animals and babies as well as numerous jokes about his love of liquor—came into its own with the arrival of sound. In the 1930s and 40s, often with a story or screenplay provided by himself under a pseudonym, Fields did battle with authority figures and henpecking wives, one-lining his way through such classics as *It's a Gift* (1934), *You Can't Cheat an Honest Man* (1939), *The Bank Dick* (1940), *My Little Chickadee* (1940) and the almost surrealistically incoherent *Never Give a Sucker an Even Break* (1941). Though misanthropic, his comic persona was nonetheless popular and sympathetic, earning him a place as one of the greatest screen comics of all time. • *His Lordship's Dilemma* 1915 (a); *Pool Sharks* 1915 (a); *Janice Meredith* 1924 (a); *Sally of the Sawdust* 1925 (a); *That Royle Girl* 1925 (a); *It's the Old Army Game* 1926 (a); *So's Your Old Man* 1926 (a); *The Potters* 1927 (a); *Running Wild* 1927 (a); *Two Flaming Youths* 1927 (a); *Fools For Luck* 1928 (a); *Tillie's Punctured Romance* 1928 (a); *The Golf Specialist (short)* 1930 (uncred.story,a); *Her Majesty, Love* 1931 (a); *The Dentist (short)* 1932 (uncred.story,uncred.a); *If I Had a Million* 1932 (a); *Million Dollar Legs* 1932 (a); *Alice in Wonderland* 1933 (a); *The Barber Shop (short)* 1933 (a,story); *The Fatal Glass of Bear (short)* 1933 (uncred.story,uncred.a); *Hip Action* 1933 (a); *International House* 1933 (a); *The Pharmacist (short)* 1933 (story,uncred.a); *Tillie and Gus* 1933 (a); *It's a Gift* 1934 (a,story); *Mrs. Wiggs of the Cabbage Patch* 1934 (a); *The Old-Fashioned Way* 1934 (a,story); *Six of a Kind* 1934 (a); *You're Telling Me* 1934 (a); *David Copperfield* 1935 (a); *Man on the Flying Trapeze* 1935 (a,story); *Mississippi* 1935 (a); *Poppy* 1936 (a); *The Big Broadcast of 1938* 1938 (a); *You Can't Cheat an Honest Man* 1939 (a,story); *The Bank Dick* 1940 (a,sc); *My Little Chickadee* 1940 (a,sc); *Never Give a Sucker an Even Break* 1941 (a,story); *Tales of Manhattan* 1942 (a); *Follow the Boys* 1944 (a); *Song of the Open Road* 1944 (a); *Sensations of 1945* 1945 (a); *Down Memory Lane* 1949 (archival footage).

Figgis, Mike • Director; also screenwriter, composer, actor. • Born Michael Figgis, Kenya, c. 1949. Began his career as a musician with rock band, The Gas Board (which also featured Bryan Ferry), and spent nearly ten years touring with the experimental theater group, The People Show, in the 1970s. After an unsuccessful application to London's National Film School in 1976, Figgis made his mark with a TV movie, *The House*, which attracted the attention of producer David Puttnam. He has since proved himself an adept handler of moody thrillers. • *Stormy Monday* 1988 (d,sc,m); *Internal Affairs* 1990 (a,d,m); *Liebestraum* 1991 (p,d,sc).

Figueroa, Gabriel • Director of photography • Born Mexico City, April 24, 1907. *Educ.* Conservatorio Nacional (design, violin). Preeminent, immensely prolific Mexican cinematographer whose mastery of chiaroscuro earned him international acclaim in the 1940s and 50s. Figueroa appenticed in Hollywood under Gregg Toland and, after returning to Mexico, worked extensively with both Emilio Fernandez—for whom he shot *María Candelaria* (1943) and *Maclovia* (1948) among many others—and Luis Buñuel, with whom his collaborations include *Los Olvidados* (1950) and *Nazarín* (1958). John Ford's *The Fugitive* (1947) and John Huston's *Night of the Iguana* (1964) and *Under the Volcano* (1984) benefitted from Figueroa's brilliant compositions of his native Mexico. • *Almas Encontradas* 1934 (stills); *El Escándolo* 1934; *María Elena* 1935; *El Primo Brasílio* 1935; *Allá en el Rancho Grande* 1936; *Vámonos con Pancho Villa* 1936; *Bajo el Cielo de México* 1937; *Jalisco nunca pierde* 1937; *Las Mujeres mándan* 1937; *La Adelita* 1938; *Canción del alma* 1938; *La Casa del ogro* 1938; *Mi candidato* 1938; *Miéntras México duerme* 1938; *Los Millones de Chaflán* 1938; *Refugiados en Madríd* 1938; *La Béstia negra* 1939; *La Noche de los mayas* 1939; *Papacito lindo* 1939; *Allá en el trópico* 1940; *La Canción del milagro* 1940; *Con su amable permiso* 1940; *El Jefe máximo* 1940; *Los de Abajo* 1940; *El Monje loco* 1940; *Que viene mi marido!* 1940; *Áy, que tiempos, señor Don Simón!* 1941; *La Casa del rencór* 1941; *Creo en Díos* 1941; *La Gallina clueca* 1941; *El Gendarme desconocido* 1941; *Mi viuda alegre* 1941; *Ní sangre ní arena* 1941; *El Rápido de las 9:15* 1941; *Cuando viajan las estrellas* 1942; *História de un grán amór* 1942; *El Verdugo de Sevilla* 1942; *Vírgen de medianoche* 1942; *La Vírgen que forjó una pátria* 1942; *El Círco* 1943; *Distinto amanecér* 1943; *El Espectro de la nóvia* 1943; *Flór Silvestre* 1943; *María Candelaria* 1943; *Los Trés Mosqueteros* 1943; *Adíos, Mariquita Linda* 1944; *El As Negro* 1944; *El Corosario Negro* 1944; *La Fuga* 1944; *El Intruso* 1944; *La Mujér sín cabeza* 1944; *Las Abandonadas* 1945; *Bugambilia* 1945; *Cantaclaro* 1945; *Un Día con el diablo* 1945; *Más allá del amór* 1945; *Enamorada* 1946; *Su última aventura* 1946; *La Casa colorada* 1947; *The Fugitive* 1947; *Río Escondído* 1947; *Dueña y señora* 1948; *Maclovia* 1948; *María de la 0* 1948; *Salón México* 1948; *Tarzan and the Mermaids* 1948; *Un Cuerpo de mujér* 1949; *Duelo en las Montañas* 1949; *El Embajadór* 1949; *La Malquerída* 1949; *Medianoche* 1949; *Ópio* 1949; *Pueblerina* 1949; *Un Día de Vída* 1950; *El Gavilán pollero* 1950; *Nuestras Vídas* 1950; *Los Olvidados* 1950; *Prisión de sueños* 1950; *The Torch* 1950; *La Bién amada* 1951; *El Bombero atómico* 1951; *Islas Marías* 1951; *Pecado* 1951; *Los Pobres van al cielo* 1951; *Siempre Tuya* 1951; *Ahí viene Martín Corona* 1952; *Ansiedád* 1952; *Cuando levanta la Niebla* 1952; *Dos Típos de cuidado* 1952; *Él/This Strange Passion* 1952; *El Enamorado* 1952; *Un Gallo en corrál ajeno* 1952; *Hay un niño en su futuro* 1952; *La Histerica* 1952; *El Már y Tú* 1952; *Ní pobres ní rícos* 1952; *El Ribozo de Soledád* 1952; *El Señor fotografo* 1952; *Camelia* 1953; *Llévame en tus brazos* 1953; *El Niño y la niebla* 1953; *Estafa de amór* 1954; *El Mónstruo de la sombra* 1954; *La Mujér X* 1954; *La Rebelión de los Colgados* 1954; *La Rosa Blanca* 1954; *Cautiva del recuerdo* 1955; *La Doncella de piedra* 1955; *La Escondida* 1955; *La Tierra del Fuego se Apaga* 1955; *El Bolero de Raquel* 1956; *Canasta de cuentos Mexicanos* 1956; *Una Cita de Amór* 1956; *Flór de Mayo* 1957; *La Sonrisa de la Vírgen* 1957; *La Cucaracha* 1958; *Estrella vácia* 1958; *Maricrúz* 1958; *Nazarín* 1958; *El Puño del amo* 1958; *La Fièvre Monte à El Pao* 1959; *Macarío* 1959; *Sonatas* 1959 (ph—Mexico); *Juana Gallo* 1960; *La Muchacha* 1960; *The Young One* 1960; *Ánimas Trujano, el hombre importante* 1961; *Los Hermanos del hierro* 1961; *La Rosa Blanca* 1961; *El Tejedór de Milagros* 1961; *El Ángel Exterminadór/The Exterminating Angel* 1962; *La Bandida* 1963; *El Hombre de papél* 1963; *El Gallo de óro* 1964; *The Night of the Iguana* 1964 **(AANBPH)**; *Amór, Amór, Amór* 1965; *Los Bienamados* 1965; *Simón del Desierto/Simon of the Desert* 1965; *Pedro Paramo* 1966; *Mariana* 1967; *Corazón salvaje* 1968; *Pax?* 1968; *La Puerta (short)* 1968; *The Big Cube* 1969; *Kelly's Heroes* 1970; *Two Mules For Sister Sara* 1970; *El Señor de Osanto* 1972; *Interval* 1973; *El Monasterio de los buitres* 1973; *Once Upon a Scoundrel* 1973; *Presagio* 1974; *La Vida Cambia* 1976; *The Children of Sánchez* 1978; *El Corazón de la Noche* 1983; *Observations Under the Volcano* 1984 (a); *Under the Volcano* 1984; *El Maleficio II* 1986 (p).

Finch, Peter • Actor • Born William Mitchell, London, September 28, 1916; died January 14, 1977, Los Angeles, CA. Rugged, intelligent leading man who lived in Australia from age 10, appearing in Australian films from the mid-1930s and enjoying some success as a radio actor. Finch's screen career took off after he was spotted by Laurence Olivier, who invited him to London in 1949. He was outstanding as the homosexual doctor in *Sunday Bloody Sunday* (1971) and as the raving news commentator in his swan song, *Network* (1976), for which he won a posthumous Oscar. Son Charles Finch is a director and screenwriter. • *Dave and Dad Come to Town* 1938; *Mr. Chedworth Steps Out* 1938; *Ants in His Pants* 1939; *The Power and the Glory* 1942; *Red Sky at Morning* 1943; *The Rats of Tobruk* 1944; 1946; *A Son Is Born* 1946; *Eureka Stockade* 1948 (a,ad,casting d); *Train of Events* 1949; *The Miniver Story* 1950; *The Wooden Horse* 1950; *The Story of Robin Hood* 1952; *The Heart of the Matter* 1953; *The Story of Gilbert and Sullivan* 1953; *Elephant Walk* 1954; *Father Brown* 1954; *Make Me an Offer* 1954; *Josephine and Men* 1955; *Passage Home* 1955; *Simon and Laura* 1955; *The Warriors* 1955; *Battle of the River Plate* 1956; *A Town Like Alice* 1956; *Robbery Under Arms* 1957; *The Shiralee* 1957; *Windom's Way* 1957; *The Nun's Story* 1959; *Operation Amsterdam* 1959; *Kidnapped* 1960; *The Trials of Oscar Wilde* 1960; *No Love For Johnnie* 1961; *The Sins of Rachel Cade* 1961; *I Thank a Fool* 1962; *Girl With Green Eyes* 1963; *In the Cool of the Day* 1963; *First Men in the Moon* 1964; *The Pumpkin Eater* 1964; *The Flight of the Phoenix* 1965; *10:30 P.M. Summer* 1966; *Judith* 1966; *Far From the Madding Crowd* 1967; *The Legend of Lylah Clare* 1968; *La Tenda rossa/The Red Tent* 1970; *Something to Hide* 1971; *Sunday, Bloody Sunday* 1971 **(AANBA)**; *England Made Me* 1973; *Lost Horizon* 1973; *The Nelson Affair* 1973; *The Abdication* 1974; *Network* 1976 **(AABA)**.

Finney, Albert • Actor • Born Salford, Lancashire, England, May 9, 1936. *Educ.* RADA, London. Dynamic stage and film star who first made his mark on the London stage in *Billy Liar* (1960) and in film as a dissatisfied working-class lothario in Karel Reisz's classic of the British Free Cinema movement, *Saturday Night and Sunday Morning* (1960). After quitting the starring role in David Lean's *Lawrence of Arabia*, to avoid being tied to a long-term film contract, Finney cemented his film stardom as the rakish, startlingly handsome hero of Tony Richardson's lavish, bawdy *Tom Jones* (1963).

Selective of his film roles, Finney's first love seems to be the stage, where he has won acclaim in John Osborne's *Luther* (1961), Peter Nichols's *A Day in the Death of Joe Egg* (1968) and numerous Shakespearean and contemporary plays as both an actor and director. In 1965 with actor Michael Medwin he founded Memorial Enterprises Productions, which was responsible for several outstanding features including his own directorial debut, *Charlie Bubbles* (1967).

In recent years Finney has eschewed romantic roles in favor of juicier character leads, camouflaging his ruddy good looks under wigs, putty noses and other highly theatrical makeup and his rich voice under a variety of accents. Memorable turns include Hercule Poirot in *Murder on the Orient Express* (1974), Daddy Warbucks in *Annie* (1982), a peevish actor-manager in *The Dresser* (1984) and a lovestruck Irish mob boss in the Coen Brothers' *Miller's Crossing* (1990). In a rare contemporary role, Finney gave an explosive, sexually-charged performance as the estranged husband in Alan Parker's harrowing *Shoot the Moon* (1981). Married to second wife, actress Anouk Aimee, from 1970 to 1978. JDK • *The Entertainer* 1960; *Saturday Night and Sunday Morning* 1960; *Tom Jones* 1963 **(AANBA)**; *The Victors* 1963; *Night Must Fall* 1964 (a,p); *Charlie Bubbles* 1967 (a,d); *Two For the Road* 1967; *The Picasso Summer* 1970; *Scrooge* 1970; *Gumshoe* 1971; *Alpha Beta* 1973; *Murder on the Orient Express* 1974 **(AANBA)**; *The Adventures of Sherlock Holmes' Smarter Brother* 1975 (uncred.a); *The Duellists* 1977; *Looker* 1981; *Loophole* 1981; *Shoot the Moon* 1981; *Wolfen* 1981; *Annie* 1982; *The Dresser* 1983 **(AANBA)**; *Notes From Under the Volcano* 1984; *Observations Under the Volcano* 1984; *Under the Volcano* 1984 **(AANBA)**; *Orphans* 1987; *Miller's Crossing* 1990.

Fiorentino, Linda • Actress • Born Clorinda Fiorentino, Philadelphia, PA. *Educ.* Rosemont College, PA (political science); Circle in the Square, New York. Dark, slender, beautiful leading lady, memorable as an off-beat sculptress in *After Hours*, an espionage agent in *Gotcha!* (both 1985) and an art appreciator in *The Moderns* (1988). • *After Hours* 1985; *Vision Quest* 1985; *Gotcha!* 1985; *The Moderns* 1988; *Wildfire* 1988; *Queens Logic* 1991.

Firth, Colin • Actor • Born Hampshire, England, c. 1961. *Educ.* Drama Centre, London. Made his London stage debut in Julian Mitchell's *Another Country*, replacing Rupert Everett in the leading role of upper class spy-in-the-making Guy Bennett, and went on to make his screen debut in the 1984 film version. • *1919* 1984; *Another Country* 1984; *A Month in the Country* 1987; *Apartment Zero* 1988; *Valmont* 1989; *Wings of Fame* 1990.

Firth, Peter • Actor • Born Bradford, Yorkshire, England, October 27, 1953. Former child TV performer who first gained attention as the disturbed Alan Strang in Peter Shaffer's play *Equus* (1973), a role he reprised in Sidney Lumet's 1977 screen adaptation. • *Brother Sun, Sister Moon* 1973; *Aces High* 1976; *Joseph Andrews* 1976; *Equus* 1977 **(AANBSA)**; *Tess* 1979; *When You Comin' Back, Red Ryder?* 1979; *Tristan Und Isolde* 1981; *The Aerodrome* 1983; *White Elephant* 1984; *A Letter to Brezhnev* 1985; *Lifeforce* 1985; *A State of Emergency* 1986; *Born of Fire* 1987; *Prisoner of Rio* 1988; *Deadly Triangle* 1989; *Tree of Hands* 1989; *Burndown* 1990; *The Hunt For Red October* 1990; *The Rescuers Down Under* 1990.

Fischer, Gunnar • Director of photography • Born Ljungby, Sweden, November 18, 1910. Distinguished cinematographer, best known for his work on the early films of Ingmar Bergman. Fischer's sometimes subdued, sometimes stark, black-and-white photography produced some of the most impressive images of the 1950s, in films like *Smiles of a Summer Night* (1955), *The Seventh Seal* and *Wild Strawberries* (both 1957). Son Peter Fischer is also a cinematographer. • *Det Ar min musik* 1942; *Natt i hamn* 1943 (sc,ph); *Blajackor* 1945; *Tant Grun, Tant Brun och Tant Gredelin* 1945; *Tva Maniksor* 1945; *Krigsmans erinran* 1947; *Tappa inte sugen* 1947; *Hamnstad/Port of Call* 1948; *Soldat Bom* 1948; *Till Gladje/To Joy* 1949; *Torst/Three Strange Loves* 1949; *Sant Hander Inte Har* 1950; *Sommarlek/Summer Interlude* 1951; *I dimma dold* 1952; *Kvinnors Vantan/Secrets of Women* 1952; *Sommaren Med Monika/Summer With Monica* 1952; *Vi tre debutera* 1953; *Gabrielle* 1954; *Seger i morker* 1954; *Egen ingang* 1955; *Den Harda leken* 1955; *Sommarnattens Leende/Smiles of a Summer Night* 1955; *Stampen* 1955; *Lek pa regnbagen* 1957; *Moten i skymningen* 1957; *Det Sjunde Inseglet* 1957; *Smultronstallet/Wild Strawberries* 1957; *Ansiktet/The Magician* 1958; *Du ar mitt aventyr* 1958; *Det Svanger pa slottet* 1959; *Djavulens Oga* 1960; *Pojken i tradet* 1960; *Een blandt mange* 1961; *Lustgarden* 1961; *Kort ar sommaren* 1962; *Siska* 1962; *Two Living, One Dead* 1962; *491* 1963; *For vanskaps skull* 1963; *Min kara ar en ros* 1963; *Juninatt* 1965; *Ojojoj eller Sangen om den eldroda hummern* 1965; *Adamson i Sverige* 1966; *Ola och Julia* 1967; *Stimulantia* 1967; *Made in Sweden* 1968; *Svarta palmkronor* 1968; *Miss and Mrs. Sweden* 1969; *Beroringen/The Touch* 1971 (title ph); *Parade* 1974.

Fishburne, Larry • Actor • Born Larry Fishburne III, US, 1963. Black supporting player, often in films by Francis Ford Coppola. Fishburne made his film debut at age 12 as the star of *Cornbread, Earl & Me* (1975). • *Cornbread, Earl & Me* 1975; *Apocalypse Now* 1979; *Willie & Phil* 1980; *Death Wish II* 1981; *Rumble Fish* 1983; *The Cotton Club* 1984;

The Color Purple 1985; *Band of the Hand* 1986; *Quicksilver* 1986; *Gardens of Stone* 1987; *A Nightmare on Elm Street 3: Dream Warriors* 1987; *Red Heat* 1988; *School Daze* 1988; *King of New York* 1990; *Class Action* 1991.

Fisher, Carrie • Actress; also novelist, screenwriter. • Born Los Angeles, CA, October 21, 1956. *Educ.* Central School of Speech and Drama, London. Daughter of Eddie Fisher and Debbie Reynolds who first gained fame with her leading role as the feisty Princess Leia in the *Star Wars* trilogy. Most of Fisher's subsequent film appearances have been as a witty, wisecracking best-friend-of-the-lead supporting player, but she gained renewed attention in 1990 with her screenplay for *Postcards From the Edge*, adapted from her best-selling semi-autobiographical novel about an actress dealing with both drug rehabilitation and an alcoholic, attention-hungry mother. Her second novel, *Surrender the Pink* (1990), is a fictional account of her relationship with ex-husband, singer-songwriter Paul Simon. • *Shampoo* 1975; *Star Wars* 1977; *Mr. Mike's Mondo Video* 1979; *The Blues Brothers* 1980; *The Empire Strikes Back* 1980; *Under the Rainbow* 1981; *Return of the Jedi* 1983; *Garbo Talks* 1984; *The Man With One Red Shoe* 1985; *Hannah and Her Sisters* 1986; *Hollywood Vice Squad* 1986; *Amazon Women on the Moon* 1987; *The Time Guardian* 1987; *Appointment With Death* 1988; *The Burbs* 1989; *Loverboy* 1989; *She's Back* 1989; *When Harry Met Sally...* 1989; *Postcards From the Edge* 1990 (sc,from novel); *Sibling Rivalry* 1990; *Drop Dead Fred* 1991.

Fisher, Terence • *aka* T. R. Fisher • Director; also editor. • Born February 23, London, 1904; died June 18, 1980. Leading British horror director of the 1950s and 60s who began his career as an editor. Fisher joined Hammer Studios in 1952 and first hit his stride in 1957 with *Curse of Frankenstein*. His subsequent output of low-budget remakes of Universal horror classics, including proficient low-budget chillers like *Horror of Dracula* (1958) and *The Devil Rides Out* (1968), is noted for its brash colors, liberal use of blood and for the casting of has-been American stars. • *Falling For You* 1933 (ed); *Brown on Resolution* 1935 (asst.ed); *Everybody Dance* 1936 (ed); *Good Morning, Boys* 1936 (ed); *Jack of All Trades* 1936 (ed); *Tudor Rose* 1936 (ed); *Windbag the Sailor* 1936 (ed); *Mr. Satan* 1938 (ed); *On the Night of the Fire* 1939 (ed); *George and Margaret* 1940 (ed); *Atlantic Ferry* 1941 (ed); *The Seventh Survivor* 1941 (ed); *The Flying Fortress* 1942 (ed); *Night Invader* 1942 (ed); *The Peterville Diamond* 1942 (ed); *Tomorrow We Live* 1942 (ed); *The Dark Tower* 1943 (ed); *Flight From Folly* 1944 (ed); *The Hundred Pound Window* 1944 (prod.sup); *One Exciting Night* 1944 (ed); *The Wicked Lady* 1945 (ed); *The Master of Bankdam* 1947 (ed); *Colonel Bogey* 1948 (d); *Portait From Life* 1948 (d); *A Song For Tomorrow* 1948 (d); *To the Public Danger (short)* 1948 (d); *Marry Me* 1949 (d); *The Astonished Heart* 1950 (d); *So Long at the Fair* 1950 (d); *Home to Danger* 1951 (d); *Distant Trumpet* 1952 (d); *The Last Page* 1952 (d); *Stolen Face* 1952 (d); *Wings of Danger* 1952 (d); *Blood Orange* 1953 (d); *Four Sided Triangle* 1953 (d,sc); *Mantrap* 1953 (d,sc); *Spaceways* 1953 (d); *Black Glove* 1954 (d); *Children Galore* 1954 (d); *Final Appointment* 1954 (d); *Mask of Dust* 1954 (d); *The Stranger Came Home* 1954 (d); *The Flaw* 1955 (d); *Murder By Proxy* 1955 (d); *Stolen Assignment* 1955 (d); *The Gelignite Gang* 1956 (d); *The Last Man to Hang* 1956 (d); *The Curse of Frankenstein* 1957 (d); *Kill Me Tomorrow* 1957 (d); *Horror of Dracula* 1958 (d); *The Revenge of Frankenstein* 1958 (d); *The Hound of the Baskervilles* 1959 (d); *The Man Who Could Cheat Death* 1959 (d); *The Mummy* 1959 (d); *The Stranglers of Bombay* 1959 (d); *The Brides of Dracula* 1960 (d); *Sword of Sherwood Forest* 1960 (d); *The Two Faces of Dr. Jekyll* 1960 (d); *The Curse of the Werewolf* 1961 (d); *The Phantom of the Opera* 1962 (d); *Sherlock Holmes und der Halsband des Todes/Sherlock Holmes and the Deadly Necklace* 1962 (d); *The Earth Dies Screaming* 1964 (d); *The Gorgon* 1964 (d); *The Horror of It All* 1964 (d); *Dracula—Prince of Darkness* 1965 (d); *Island of Terror* 1966 (d); *Frankenstein Created Woman* 1967 (d); *Night of the Big Heat* 1967 (d); *The Devil Rides Out* 1968 (d); *Frankenstein Must Be Destroyed* 1969 (d); *Frankenstein and the Monster From Hell* 1972 (d).

Fisk, Jack • Production designer; also director. • Born Ipava, IL, December 19, 1934. *Educ.* Cooper Union, New York; Pennsylvania Academy of Fine Arts. After reaping acclaim for the barren, rural landscape of Terence Malick's *Badlands* (1973), the futuristic environment of Brian DePalma's rock fable, *Phantom of the Paradise* (1974), and the heightened teen world of DePalma's *Carrie* (1976), Fisk turned to directing with *Raggedy Man* (1981), starring Sissy Spacek, his wife since 1974. • *Angels Hard As They Come* 1971 (pd); *Cool Breeze* 1972 (pd); *Badlands* 1973 (pd); *The Slams* 1973 (pd); *Phantom of the Paradise* 1974 (pd); *Darktown Strutters* 1975 (pd); *Messiah of Evil* 1975 (pd); *Vigilante Force* 1975 (pd); *Carrie* 1976 (pd); *Days of Heaven* 1978 (pd); *Movie Movie* 1978 (pd); *Heart Beat* 1979 (pd); *Raggedy Man* 1981 (d); *Violets Are Blue* 1986 (d); *Daddy's Dyin'... Who's Got the Will?* 1990 (d).

Fitzgerald, Geraldine • Actress; also stage director • Born Dublin, Ireland, November 24, 1914. *Educ.* Dublin Art School. Classic beauty from the Dublin stage who had appeared in several British films before making her Broadway debut in the 1938 Mercury Theater production of *Heartbreak House* and her Hollywood debut in *Dark Victory* (1939). Perhaps best remembered for her Oscar-nominated performance in *Wuthering Heights* (1939), Fitzgerald played strong-willed women throughout the 1940s but, after being put on suspension for protesting her studio-chosen roles, found her career at a virtual standstill by the end of the decade.

In the 1970s she made a triumphant return to the stage as an actress (*Long Day's Journey Into Night* 1971), director (*Mass Appeal* 1980) and street performer (with her own Everyman Street Theatre, founded in 1968). Son is director Michael Lindsay-Hogg. • *Blind Justice* 1934; *Open All Night* 1934; *Department Store* 1935; *The Lad* 1935; *Lieutenant Daring R.N.* 1935; *Three Witnesses* 1935; *Turn of the Tide* 1935; *Cafe Mascot* 1936; *Debt of Honor* 1936; *The Mill on the Floss* 1937; *Dark Victory* 1939; *Wuthering Heights* 1939 **(AANBSA)**; *'Til We Meet Again* 1940; *A Child Is Born* 1940; *Flight From Destiny* 1941; *Shining Victory* 1941; *The Gay Sisters* 1942; *Watch on the Rhine* 1943; *Ladies Courageous* 1944; *Wilson* 1944; *The Strange Affair of Uncle Harry* 1945; *Nobody Lives Forever* 1946; *O.S.S.* 1946; *Three Strangers* 1946; *So Evil My Love* 1948; *The Late Edwina Blake* 1951; *Ten North Frederick* 1958; *The Fiercest Heart* 1961; *The Pawnbroker* 1965; *Rachel, Rachel* 1968; *The Last American Hero* 1973; *Harry and Tonto* 1974; *Echoes of a Summer* 1976; *The Mango Tree* 1977; *Rêve de Singe* 1978; *Arthur* 1981; *Easy Money* 1983; *The Link* 1985; *Poltergeist II: The Other Side* 1986.

Flaherty, Robert J. • Filmmaker • Born Robert Joseph Flaherty, Iron Mountain, MI, February 16, 1884; died July 23, 1951, Vermont. *Educ.* Upper Canada College, Toronto; Michigan College of Mines. Mineralogist and explorer turned pioneering documentarist. Flaherty shot material for his first film, a study of the Belcher Islands, in 1917 but the footage was accidentally destroyed by a cigarette fire in his editing room. Undeterred, he planned another film, on Eskimo life, and received backing from the Revillon Frères fur company to make *Nanook of the North* (1922). An engaging chronicle of the day-to-day struggle for survival of one family, *Nanook* became an international success despite initial skepticism on the part of distributors. It also represented a landmark in the development of the documentary, thanks to its use of elements associated with narrative film: Flaherty structured the work around a storyline, directed the Eskimos in scenes "staged" for the benefit of the camera and made sophisticated use of techniques including close-ups, tilts and pans. The success of *Nanook* earned Flaherty studio backing from Paramount to make the lyrical Polynesian documentary *Moana* (1926), which was praised by critics but justly attacked by anthropologists as a poetic fantasy rather than an accurate representation of island life.

Flaherty went on to co-direct the narrative feature *White Shadows in the South Seas* (1928) with W.S. Van Dyke and to collaborate with F.W. Murnau on *Tabu* (1931), though he withdrew from both projects before completion. In 1931 he immigrated to England, where he exerted a significant influence on John Grierson and the British "social documentary" movement of the 1930s. Flaherty's best-known British film was *Man of Aran* (1934), a lyrical study of an Irish fisherman and his daily struggle for survival.

Flaherty later returned to the US and made two more highly acclaimed documentaries, *The Land* (1942), for the US Information Service, and *Louisiana Story* (1948), for Standard Oil. • *Untitled Film From the Far North* 1916 (d,sc,ed); *Nanook of the North* 1922 (d,sc,ph,ed,titles); *The Pottery Maker* 1925 (d,p,sc,ph,ed); *Moana* 1926 (d,sc,ph,ed,titles); *The Twenty-Four Dollar Island* 1927 (d,p,sc,ph,ed); *White Shadows in the South Seas* 1928 (d,sc,ph); *Country Comes to Town (short)* 1931 (technical adviser); *Industrial Britain (short)* 1931 (d,sc,ph); *Tabu* 1931 (d); *The English Potter* 1933 (d,ph); *The Glassmakers of England* 1933 (d,ph); *Man of Aran* 1934 (d,sc,ph); *Elephant Boy* 1937 (d); *The Titan* 1940 (ed—English-language version); *It's All True* 1942 (story—"Bonito the Bull"/"My Friend Bonito"); *The Land* 1942 (a,d,sc,ph); *What's Happening Sugar? (short)* 1945 (p); *Louisiana Story* 1948 (d,p,sc); *Matthaus Passion* 1949 (a,comm,ed—English-language version); *Green Mountain Land (short)* 1950 (p); *An Investment in Human Welfare (short)* 1951 (a); *Studies For Louisiana Story* 1967 (d,sc,ph).

Fleischer, Max • Animator; also producer. • Born Vienna, Austria, July 17, 1883; died 1972, Woodland Hills, CA. *Educ.* Art Students League, New York; Cooper Union, New York; Mechanics and Tradesmen's School, New York. Walt Disney's main screen animation competitor and the creator, with brother Dave (1894-1979), of cartoon luminaries such as Betty Boop and Popeye. The brothers also made animated features such as *Gulliver's Travels* (1939) and instructional films like *The Einstein Theory of Relativity* (1923) and *Darwin's Theory of Evolution* (1925). Fleischer made a significant contribution to animation technology with the Rotoscope, a machine which projects live-action film in such a way that animated characters may be traced directly from real-life figures. Son Richard is a director and daughter Ruth an actress. • *Out of the Inkwell* 1915 (d,p,sc,anim); *How to Read an Army Map (short)* 1918 (d); *The Einstein Theory of Relativity* 1923 (anim,d); *Darwin's Theory of Evolution* 1925 (anim,d); *Gulliver's Travels* 1939 (p); *Mr. Bug Goes to Town* 1941 (p); *Rudolph, the Red-Nosed Reindeer (short)* 1948 (d).

Fleischer, Richard • Director • Born Richard O. Fleischer, Brooklyn, NY, December 8, 1916. *Educ.* Brown University, Providence, RI (psychology); Yale School of Drama. Veteran director with a knack for action and suspense; his *The Narrow Margin* (1952) is regarded by many critics as one of the finest film noirs ever made. A rapid, efficient director who has often filmed real life crime stories such as *The Girl in the Red Velvet Swing* (1955), *Compulsion* (1959), *The Boston Strangler* (1968) and *10 Rillington Place* (1970), Fleischer has also helmed such big-budget epics and extravaganzas as *The Vikings* (1958), *Doctor Doolittle* (1967) and the disastrous *Tora! Tora! Tora!* (1970) as well as the comtemptible *Mandingo* (1975). Son of animator Max Fleischer. • *Air Crew (short)* 1943 (sc); *Memo For Joe (short)* 1944 (d); *Child of Divorce* 1946 (d); *Banjo* 1947 (d); *Bodyguard* 1948 (d); *Design For Death* 1948 (d,p) **(AABDOC)**; *So This Is New York* 1948 (d); *The Clay Pigeon* 1949 (d); *Follow Me Quietly* 1949 (d); *Make Mine Laughs* 1949 (d); *Trapped* 1949 (d); *Armored Car Robbery* 1950 (d); *The Happy Time* 1952 (d); *The Narrow Margin* 1952 (d); *Arena* 1953 (d); *20,000 Leagues Under the Sea* 1954 (d); *Violent Saturday* 1954 (d); *The Girl in the Red Velvet Swing* 1955 (d); *Bandido* 1956 (d); *Between Heaven and Hell* 1956 (d); *The Vikings* 1958 (d); *Compulsion* 1959 (d); *These Thousand Hills* 1959 (d); *Crack in the Mirror* 1960 (d); *North to Alaska* 1960 (pre-production manager); *The Big Gamble* 1961 (d); *Barabbas* 1962 (d); *Fantastic Voyage* 1966 (d); *Doctor Dolittle* 1967 (d); *The Boston Strangler* 1968 (d); *Che!* 1969 (d); *10 Rillington Place* 1970 (d); *Tora! Tora! Tora!* 1970 (d); *The Last Run* 1971 (d); *See No Evil* 1971 (d); *The New Centurions* 1972 (d); *The Don Is Dead* 1973 (d); *Soylent Green* 1973 (d); *Mr. Majestyk* 1974 (d); *The Spikes Gang* 1974 (d); *Mandingo* 1975 (d); *The Incredible Sarah* 1976 (d); *Crossed Swords* 1977 (d); *Ashanti* 1979 (d); *The Jazz Singer* 1980 (d); *Tough Enough* 1982 (d); *Amityville 3-D* 1983 (d); *Conan the Destroyer* 1984 (d); *Red Sonja* 1985 (d); *Million Dollar Mystery* 1987 (d); *Call From Space* 1989 (d).

Fleming, Victor • Director; also director of photography, producer. • Born Pasadena, CA, February 23, 1883; died January 6, 1949, Cottonwood, AZ. Former race car driver who began his film career as a cinematographer, working with Allan Dwan, Douglas Fairbanks and D.W. Griffith before graduating to directing in 1919. Fleming's talent for spectacular action and his ability to elicit strong performances from leading stars made him one of the most popular directors of the 1930s. He is most widely known for *The Wizard of Oz* (1939) and for taking over the direction of *Gone with the Wind* (1939) from George Cukor. • *American Aristocracy* 1916 (ph); *Betty of Greystone* 1916 (ph); *Fifty-Fifty* 1916 (ph); *The Good Bad Man* 1916 (ph); *The Habit of Happiness* 1916 (ph); *The Half-Breed* 1916 (ph); *His Picture in the Papers* 1916 (ph); *An Innocent Magdalene* 1916 (ph); *Little Meena's Romance* 1916 (ph); *Macbeth* 1916 (ph); *Manhattan Madness* 1916 (ph); *The Matrimaniac* 1916 (ph); *Mystery of the Leaping Fish* 1916 (ph); *The Social Secretary* 1916 (ph); *The Americano* 1917 (ph); *Down to Earth* 1917 (ph); *The Man From Painted Post* 1917 (ph); *A Modern Musketeer* 1917 (ph); *Reaching For the Moon* 1917 (ph); *His Majesty, the American* 1919 (ph); *Private Film For the Duke of Sutherland* 1919 (d); *When the Clouds Roll By* 1919 (d); *The Mollycoddle* 1920 (d); *Mama's Affair* 1921 (d); *Woman's Place* 1921 (d); *Anna Ascends* 1922 (d); *The Lane That Had No Turning* 1922 (d); *Red Hot Romance* 1922 (d); *The Call of the Canyon* 1923 (d); *Dark Secrets* 1923 (d); *The Law of the Lawless* 1923 (d); *To the Last Man* 1923 (d); *The Code of the Sea* 1924 (d); *Empty Hands* 1924 (d); *Adventure* 1925 (d,p); *The Devil's Cargo* 1925 (d); *Lord Jim* 1925 (d); *A Son of His Father* 1925 (d); *The Blind Goddess* 1926 (d); *Mantrap* 1926 (d); *Hula* 1927 (d); *The Rough Riders* 1927 (d); *The Way of All Flesh* 1927 (d); *The Awakening* 1928 (d); *Abie's Irish Rose* 1929 (d,p); *The Virginian* 1929 (d); *Wolf Song* 1929 (d,p); *Common Clay* 1930 (d); *Renegades* 1930 (d); *Around the World in 80 Minutes With Douglas Fairbanks* 1931 (d); *Red Dust* 1932 (d,p); *The Wet Parade* 1932 (d,p); *The Blonde Bombshell* 1933 (d,p); *The White Sister* 1933 (d,p); *Treasure Island* 1934 (d); *The Farmer Takes a Wife* 1935 (d); *Reckless* 1935 (d); *Captains Courageous* 1937 (d); *The Good Earth* 1937 (d); *A Star Is Born* 1937 (d); *The Crowd Roars* 1938 (d); *The Great Waltz* 1938 (d); *Test Pilot* 1938 (d); *Too Hot to Handle* 1938 (d); *Gone With the Wind* 1939 (d) **(AABD)**; *The Wizard of Oz* 1939 (d); *Dr. Jekyll and Mr. Hyde* 1941 (d,p); *Tortilla Flat* 1942 (d); *A Guy Named Joe* 1943 (d); *Adventure* 1945 (d); *Joan of Arc* 1948 (d).

Fletcher, Louise • Actress • Born Birmingham, AL, July, 1934. *Educ.* University of North Carolina. Exceptional supporting player, best remembered as the dictatorial Nurse Ratched in *One Flew Over the Cuckoo's Nest* (1975). • *Thieves Like Us* 1974; *One Flew Over the Cuckoo's Nest* 1975 **(AABA)**; *Russian Roulette* 1975; *Exorcist II: The Heretic* 1977; *The Cheap Detective* 1978; *The Lady in Red* 1979; *The Magician of Lublin* 1979; *Natural Enemies* 1979; *The Lucky Star* 1980; *Mamma Dracula* 1980;

Dead Kids 1981; *Talk to Me* 1982; *Brainstorm* 1983; *Strange Invaders* 1983; *Firestarter* 1984; *The Boy Who Could Fly* 1986; *Invaders From Mars* 1986; *Nobody's Fool* 1986; *Flowers in the Attic* 1987; *Mama Dracula* 1988; *Two Moon Junction* 1988; *Best of the Best* 1989; *Blue Steel* 1989; *Shadowzone* 1990.

Florey, Robert • Director; also screenwriter, author. • Born Paris, September 14, 1900; died 1979. French screenwriter, director of short films and actor who moved to Hollywood in 1921. Florey worked as assistant director to Josef von Sternberg, Frank Borzage and Victor Fleming before making his feature directing debut in 1926. He turned out more than 50 movies over the next 23 years, ranging from the first Marx brothers vehicle, *The Cocoanuts* (1929), to low-budget crime programmers like *The Crooked Way* (1949). Notable films include the experimental short *Life and Death of 9413, A Hollywood Extra* (1927) and *The Beast with Five Fingers* (1946).

Florey was one of the first seasoned feature directors to turn to TV in the 1950s, working in the new medium for over a decade. He also wrote a number of books including *Pola Negri, Charlie Chaplin* (both 1927), *Hollywood d'hier et d'aujord'hui* (1948), *La Lanterne magique* (1966) and *Hollywood annee zero* (1972). • *Heureuse intervention (short)* 1919 (d,sc); *Isidore à la déveine (short)* 1919 (d,sc); *Isidore sur le lac (short)* 1919 (d,sc); *L'Orpheline* 1921 (a,ad); *Saturnin ou Le bon allumeur* 1921 (a); *Monte Cristo* 1922 (technical adviser); *Robin Hood* 1922 (French subtitles); *Fifty-Fifty (short)* 1923 (d,sc); *Valentino en Angleterre (short)* 1923 (d,sc); *Wine* 1924 (ad); *The Masked Bride* 1925 (ad); *Parisian Nights* 1925 (ad,technical adviser); *Time, the Comedian* 1925 (ad); *Bardelys the Magnificent* 1926 (ad); *La Boheme* 1926 (ad); *Dance Madness* 1926 (ad); *The Exquisite Sinner* 1926 (ad); *The Gay Deceiver* 1926 (ad); *Monte Carlo* 1926 (ad); *Paris* 1926 (ad); *That Model From Paris* 1926 (d,sc); *The Coffin Maker (short)* 1927 (d,sc); *Face Value* 1927 (d); *Heaven on Earth* 1927 (ad); *Life and Death of 9413, a Hollywood Extra (short)* 1927 (d,sc); *The Love of Zero (short)* 1927 (d,sc); *Magic Flame* 1927 (ad); *One Hour of Love* 1927 (d); *The Romantic Age* 1927 (d); *Bonjour New York! (short)* 1928 (d,sc); *The Cohens and the Kellys in Paris* 1928 (2u d); *Skyscraper Symphony (short)* 1928 (d,sc,ph); *The Woman Disputed* 1928 (ad); *The Battle of Paris* 1929 (d); *The Cocoanuts* 1929 (d); *A Hole in the Wall* 1929 (d); *Lillian Roth and Her Piano Boys (short)* 1929 (d); *Night Club (short)* 1929 (d); *Pusher-in-the-Face (short)* 1929 (d); *L'Amour Chante* 1930 (d,sc); *Anna Christie* 1930 (d); *La Route est belle* 1930 (d); *Le Blanc et le Noir* 1931 (d); *Frankenstein* 1931 (uncred.sc); *The Man Called Back* 1932 (d); *Murders in the Rue Morgue* 1932 (adapt,d); *Those We Love* 1932 (d); *Ex-Lady* 1933 (d); *Girl Missing* 1933 (d); *The House on 56th Street* 1933 (d); *A Study in Scarlet* 1933 (sc); *Bedside* 1934 (d); *I Sell Anything* 1934 (d); *Registered Nurse* 1934 (d); *Smarty* 1934 (d); *Don't Bet on Blondes* 1935 (d); *The Florentine Dagger* 1935 (d); *Go Into Your Dance* 1935 (d); *Going Highbrow* 1935 (d); *I Am a Thief* 1935 (d); *Oil For the Lamps of China* 1935 (uncred.ad); *The Pay-Off* 1935 (d); *Ship Cafe* 1935 (d); *The Woman in Red* 1935 (d); *Hollywood Boulevard* 1936 (d,sc); *The Preview Murder Case* 1936 (d); *Rose of the Rancho* 1936 (d); *Till We Meet Again* 1936 (d); *Daughter of Shanghai* 1937 (d); *King of Gamblers* 1937 (d); *Mountain Music* 1937 (d); *Outcast* 1937 (d); *This Way Please* 1937 (d); *Dangerous to Know* 1938 (d); *King of Alcatraz* 1938 (d); *Death of a Champion* 1939 (d); *Disbarred* 1939 (d); *Hotel Imperial* 1939 (d); *The Magnificent Fraud* 1939 (d); *Parole Fixer* 1940 (d); *Women Without Names* 1940 (d); *Dangerously They Live* 1941 (d); *The Face Behind the Mask* 1941 (d); *Meet Boston Blackie* 1941 (d); *Two in a Taxi* 1941 (d); *Lady Gangster* 1942 (d); *Bomber's Moon* 1943 (d); *The Desert Song* 1943 (d); *Man From Frisco* 1944 (d); *Roger Touhy, Gangster* 1944 (d); *Danger Signal* 1945 (d); *Escape in the Desert* 1945 (d); *God Is My Co-Pilot* 1945 (d); *The Beast With Five Fingers* 1946 (d); *Monsieur Verdoux* 1947 (assoc.d); *Adventures of Don Juan* 1948 (uncred.sc); *Rogue's Regiment* 1948 (d,story); *Tarzan and the Mermaids* 1948 (d); *The Crooked Way* 1949 (d); *Johnny One-Eye* 1949 (d); *Outpost in Morocco* 1949 (d); *The Vicious Years* 1950 (d).

Flynn, Errol • Actor • Born Errol Leslie Thomson Flynn, Hobart, Tasmania, June 20, 1909; died October 14, 1959, Vancouver, British Columbia, Canada. *Educ.* University of Tasmania. Swashbuckling adventure hero of the 1930s and 40s who made his screen debut as Fletcher Christian in the Australian film *In the Wake of the Bounty* (1932). In Hollywood from 1935, Flynn quickly established himself as a leading adventure star and male sex symbol, appearing in such classics as *Captain Blood* (1935) and *Robin Hood* (1938).

As well known for his dissipated lifestyle as for his movie roles, Flynn was at the center of a controversy in 1942 when he was tried (unsuccessfully) for statutory rape of two teenage girls. His career went into decline, largely due to alcohol and drug abuse, in the late 1940s, although he salvaged a battered critical reputation with roles as middle-aged drunkards in the 1950s. His autobiography, *My Wicked, Wicked Ways*, was published posthumously in 1959. • *In the Wake of the Bounty* 1932; *Murder at Monte Carlo* 1934; *Captain Blood* 1935; *The Case of the Curious Bride* 1935; *Don't Bet on Blondes* 1935; *The Charge of the Light Brigade* 1936; *Pirate Party on Catalina Isle (short)* 1936; *Another Dawn* 1937; *Green Light* 1937; *The Perfect Specimen* 1937; *The Prince and the Pauper* 1937; *The Dawn Patrol* 1938; *Four's a Crowd* 1938; *Robin Hood* 1938; *The Sisters* 1938; *Dodge City* 1939; *The Private Lives of Elizabeth and Essex* 1939; *The Santa Fe Trail* 1940; *The Sea Hawk* 1940; *Virginia City* 1940; *Dive Bomber* 1941; *Footsteps in the Dark* 1941; *They Died With Their Boots On* 1941; *Desperate Journey* 1942; *Gentleman Jim* 1942; *Edge of Darkness* 1943; *Northern Pursuit* 1943; *Thank Your Lucky Stars* 1943; *Uncertain Glory* 1944; *Objective Burma!* 1945; *San Antonio* 1945; *Never Say Goodbye* 1946; *Always Together* 1947; *Cry Wolf* 1947; *Escape Me Never* 1947; *Adventures of Don Juan* 1948; *Silver River* 1948; *It's a Great Feeling* 1949; *That Forsyte Woman* 1949; *Kim* 1950; *Montana* 1950; *Rocky Mountain* 1950; *Adventures of Captain Fabian* 1951 (a,sc); *Hello God* 1951; *Against All Flags* 1952; *Cruise of the Zaca (short)* 1952 (a,d); *Deep Sea Fishing (short)* 1952 (a,d); *Mara Maru* 1952; *The Master of Ballantrae* 1953; *William Tell* 1953 (a,p); *Let's Make Up* 1954; *Il Maestro di Don Giovanni* 1954; *King's Rhapsody* 1955; *The Warriors* 1955; *The Big Boodle* 1957; *Istanbul* 1957; *The Sun Also Rises* 1957; *The Roots of Heaven* 1958; *Too Much, Too Soon* 1958; *Cuban Rebel Girls* 1959 (a,sc); *It's Showtime* 1976 (archival footage).

Folsey, George • Director of photography • Born New York, NY, 1898; died November 1, 1988, Santa Monica, CA. Veteran cinematographer, long with MGM, who produced outstanding work in collaboration with Frank Borzage and Vincente Minnelli, among others. Son George Folsey, Jr. (born 1939) is an editor and producer. • *The Incorrigible Dukane* 1915 (a,asst.cam.op); *The Fear Market* 1919; *His Bridal Night* 1919; *The Frisky Mrs. Johnson* 1920; *Sinners* 1920; *The Stolen Kiss* 1920; *The Case of Becky* 1921; *The Education of Elizabeth* 1921; *A Heart to Let* 1921; *The Price of Possession* 1921; *The Road to London* 1921 (a); *Room and Board* 1921; *Sheltered Daughters* 1921; *The Game Chicken* 1922; *Mars* 1922; *Nancy From Nowhere* 1922; *Slim Shoulders* 1922; *What's Wrong With Women* 1922; *The Bright Shawl* 1923; *The Fighting Blade* 1923; *Radio-Mania* 1923; *Twenty-One* 1923; *Born Rich* 1924; *The Enchanted Cottage* 1924; *The Half-Way Girl* 1925; *The Necessary Evil* 1925; *The Scarlet Saint* 1925; *Ladies at Play* 1926; *The Savage* 1926; *Too Much Money* 1926; *American Beauty* 1927; *Her Wild Oat* 1927; *Naughty But Nice* 1927; *No Place to Go* 1927; *Orchids and Ermine* 1927; *See You in Jail* 1927; *The Butter and Egg Man* 1928; *Lady Be Good* 1928; *Applause* 1929; *The Cocoanuts* 1929; *Gentlemen of* *the Press* 1929; *Glorifying the American Girl* 1929; *A Hole in the Wall* 1929; *The Laughing Lady* 1929; *The Letter* 1929; *Night Club (short)* 1929; *Pusher-in-the-Face (short)* 1929; *Animal Crackers* 1930; *The Big Pond* 1930; *Dangerous Nan McGrew* 1930; *Laughter* 1930; *The Royal Family of Broadway* 1930; *The Cheat* 1931; *Honor Among Lovers* 1931; *My Sin* 1931; *Secrets of a Secretary* 1931; *The Smiling Lieutenant* 1931; *Stolen Heaven* 1931; *The Big Broadcast* 1932; *The Misleading Lady* 1932; *The Wiser Sex* 1932; *Going Hollywood* 1933; *Men Must Fight* 1933; *Operator 13* 1933 **(AANBPH)**; *Reunion in Vienna* 1933; *Stage Mother* 1933; *Storm at Daybreak* 1933; *Chained* 1934; *Forsaking All Others* 1934; *Men in White* 1934; *I Live My Life* 1935; *Kind Lady* 1935; *Page Miss Glory* 1935; *Reckless* 1935; *The Gorgeous Hussy* 1936 **(AANBPH)**; *The Great Ziegfeld* 1936; *Hearts Divided* 1936; *The Bride Wore Red* 1937; *The Last of Mrs. Cheyney* 1937; *Parnell* 1937 (uncred.ph); *Arsene Lupin Returns* 1938; *Hold That Kiss* 1938; *Mannequin* 1938; *The Shining Hour* 1938; *Fast and Loose* 1939; *Lady of the Tropics* 1939; *Remember?* 1939; *Society Lawyer* 1939; *Third Finger, Left Hand* 1940; *Two Girls on Broadway* 1940; *Come Live With Me* 1941; *Dr. Kildare's Wedding Day* 1941; *Free and Easy* 1941; *Lady Be Good* 1941; *Married Bachelor* 1941; *The Trial of Mary Dugan* 1941; *Andy Hardy's Double Life* 1942; *Dr. Gillespie's New Assistant* 1942; *Grand Central Murder* 1942; *Panama Hattie* 1942; *Rio Rita* 1942; *Seven Sweethearts* 1942; *A Guy Named Joe* 1943; *Thousands Cheer* 1943 **(AANBPH)**; *Three Hearts For Julia* 1943; *Meet Me in St. Louis* 1944 **(AANBPH)**; *The White Cliffs of Dover* 1944 **(AANBPH)**; *The Clock* 1945; *The Green Years* 1946 **(AANBPH)**; *The Harvey Girls* 1946; *The Secret Heart* 1946; *Till the Clouds Roll By* 1946; *Ziegfeld Follies* 1946; *Green Dolphin Street* 1947 **(AANBPH)**; *If Winter Comes* 1947; *State of the Union* 1948; *Adam's Rib* 1949; *The Great Sinner* 1949; *Malaya* 1949; *Take Me Out to the Ball Game* 1949; *The Big Hangover* 1950; *A Life of Her Own* 1950; *The Law and the Lady* 1951; *The Man With a Cloak* 1951; *Mr. Imperium* 1951; *Night Into Morning* 1951; *Shadow in the Sky* 1951; *Lovely to Look At* 1952; *All the Brothers Were Valiant* 1953 **(AANBPH)**; *The Band Wagon* 1953 (uncred.ph); *Deep in My Heart* 1954; *Executive Suite* 1954 **(AANBPH)**; *Men of the Fighting Lady* 1954; *Seven Brides For Seven Brothers* 1954 **(AANBPH)**; *Tennessee Champ* 1954; *The Battle of Gettysburg (short)* 1955; *The Cobweb* 1955; *Hit the Deck* 1955; *The Fastest Gun Alive* 1956; *Forbidden Planet* 1956; *The Power and the Prize* 1956; *These Wilder Years* 1956; *House of Numbers* 1957; *The Seventh Sin* 1957; *Tip on a Dead Jockey* 1957; *Cash McCall* 1959; *I Passed For White* 1960; *Protection For People (short)* 1962; *The Balcony* 1963 **(AANBPH)**; *Glass Houses* 1971.

Fonda, Bridget • Actress • Born United States, 1964. *Educ.* NYU (theater); Lee Strasburg Institute, New York. Promising, vivacious young lead of the late 1980s. Granddaughter of Henry Fonda and daughter of Peter Fonda. • *Aria* 1987; *Light Years* 1988; *Shag* 1988; *You Can't Hurry Love* 1988; *Scandal* 1989; *Strapless* 1989; *The Godfather Part III* 1990; *Roger Corman's Frankenstein Unbound* 1990; *Drop Dead Fred* 1991.

Fonda, Henry • Actor • Born Henry Jaynes Fonda, Grand Island, NB, May 16, 1905; died 1982. *Educ.* University of Minnesota (journalism). Beloved, enduring screen star who began his acting career with the Omaha Community Playhouse, working his way to Broadway in 1929 and Hollywood in 1934. Fonda's benign, paternal presence landed him roles ranging from conscientious US presidents, in *Young Mr. Lincoln* (1939) and *Fail Safe* (1964), to the patient juror who saves an innocent man's life in *Twelve Angry Men* (1957). He continued both his stage and screen careers through the 1970s, winning the best actor Oscar for his swansong performance in *On Golden Pond* (1981). The first of his five marriages was to actress Margaret Sullavan. Children Jane and Peter Fonda, by second wife Frances Seymour Brokaw, are both actors. • *The Farmer Takes a Wife* 1935; *I Dream Too Much* 1935; *Way Down East* 1935; *The Moon's Our Home* 1936; *Spendthrift* 1936; *The Trail of the Lonesome Pine* 1936; *Slim* 1937; *That Certain Woman* 1937; *Wings of the Morning* 1937; *You Only Live Once* 1937; *Blockade* 1938; *I Met My Love Again* 1938; *Jezebel* 1938; *The Mad Miss Manton* 1938; *Spawn of the North* 1938; *Drums Along the Mohawk* 1939; *Jesse James* 1939; *Let Us Live* 1939; *The Story of Alexander Graham Bell* 1939; *Young Mr. Lincoln* 1939; *Chad Hanna* 1940; *The Grapes of Wrath* 1940 **(AANBA)**; *Lillian Russell* 1940; *The Return of Frank James* 1940; *The Lady Eve* 1941; *Wild Geese Calling* 1941; *You Belong to Me* 1941; *The Big Street* 1942; *The Magnificent Dope* 1942; *The Male Animal* 1942; *Rings on Her Fingers* 1942; *Tales of Manhattan* 1942; *Immortal Sergeant* 1943; *The Ox-Bow Incident* 1943; *My Darling Clementine* 1946; *Daisy Kenyon* 1947; *The Fugitive* 1947; *The Long Night* 1947; *Fort Apache* 1948; *A Miracle Can Happen* 1948; *Jigsaw* 1949; *Grant Wood (short)* 1950; *Home of the Homeless (short)* 1950; *Benjy (short)* 1951; *Growing Years (short)* 1951; *The Impressionable Years (short)* 1952; *Mister Roberts* 1955; *War and Peace* 1956; *The Wrong Man* 1956; *The Tin Star* 1957; *Twelve Angry Men* 1957 (a,p) **(AANBP)**; *Reach for Tomorrow (short)* 1958; *Stage Struck* 1958; *The Man Who Understood Women* 1959; *Warlock* 1959; *Advise and Consent* 1962; *How the West Was Won* 1962; *The Longest Day* 1962; *Rangers of Yellowstone (short)* 1963; *Spencer's Mountain* 1963; *The Best Man* 1964; *Fail Safe* 1964; *Sex and the Single Girl* 1964; *Battle of the Bulge* 1965; *La Guerre secrète/The Dirty Game* 1965; *In Harm's Way* 1965; *The Rounders* 1965; *A Big Hand For the Little Lady* 1966; *All About People (short)* 1967; *The Golden Flame (short)* 1967; *The Really Big Family* 1967; *Welcome to Hard Times* 1967; *Born to Buck (short)* 1968; *The Boston Strangler* 1968; *Firecreek* 1968; *An Impression of John Steinbeck—Writer (short)* 1968; *Madigan* 1968; *Yours, Mine and Ours* 1968; *C'era una Volta il West/Once Upon a Time in the West* 1969; *The Cheyenne Social Club* 1970; *There Was a Crooked Man* 1970; *Too Late the Hero* 1970; *Directed By John Ford* 1971; *Sometimes a Great Notion* 1971; *Alcohol Abuse: The Early Signs (short)* 1973; *Ash Wednesday* 1973; *Il Mio nome e Nessuno/My Name Is Nobody* 1973; *Le Serpent/The Serpent* 1973; *Mussolini: Ultimo Atto* 1974; *Battle of Midway* 1976; *The Great Smokey Roadblock* 1976; *Il Grande attacco* 1977; *Rollercoaster* 1977; *Tentacoli/Tentacles* 1977; *Big Yellow Schooner to Byzantium (short)* 1978; *Fedora* 1978; *The Swarm* 1978; *City on Fire* 1979; *Meteor* 1979; *Wanda Nevada* 1979; *On Golden Pond* 1981 **(AABA)**.

Fonda, Jane • Actress; also producer. • Born Jane Seymour Fonda, New York, NY, December 21, 1937. *Educ.* Vassar College, Poughkeepsie NY; Art Students League, New York; Actors Studio; Harvard. Leading Hollywood star whose adherence to radical political causes stirred some controversy in the 1960s and 70s. The daughter of Henry Fonda and sister of Peter, she made her film debut in *Tall Story* (1960) and, over the next two decades, appeared in several roles which have come to seem emblematic of their times: she played a psychedelic science-fiction heroine in *Barbarella* (1968), an independent-yet-vulnerable middle-class call girl in *Klute* (1971) and an American journalist involved in a French factory occupation in *Tout va bien* (1972).

In the 1980s, again in keeping with the spirit of the times, Fonda espoused the less radical cause of the body beautiful, producing and appearing in an extremely lucrative series of excercise videotapes. She also gave forceful performances in a string of quality commerical films such as *9 to 5* (1980), *On Golden Pond* (1981) and *The Morning After* (1986). Fonda married French director Roger Vadim in 1965, and political activist Tom Hayden—from whom she is now divorced—in 1973. • *Tall Story* 1960; *The Chapman Report* 1962; *Period of Adjustment* 1962; *Walk on the Wild Side* 1962; *In the Cool of the Day* 1963; *Sunday in New York* 1963; *La Ronde* 1964; *Cat Ballou* 1965; *Any Wednesday* 1966;

The Chase 1966; *Barefoot in the Park* 1967; *Hurry Sundown* 1967; *Barbarella* 1968; *Histoires Extraordinaires/Spirits of the Dead* 1968; *They Shoot Horses, Don't They?* 1969 **(AANBA)**; *Klute* 1971 **(AABA)**; *FTA* 1972 (a,p,sc—FTA Show,song); *Tout va bien* 1972; *A Doll's House* 1973; *Steelyard Blues* 1973; *Introduction to the Enemy* 1974 (a,d); *The Blue Bird* 1976; *Fun With Dick and Jane* 1976; *Coming Home* 1977 **(AABA)**; *Julia* 1977 **(AANBA)**; *California Suite* 1978; *Comes a Horseman* 1978; *The China Syndrome* 1979 **(AANBA)**; *The Electric Horseman* 1979; *9 to 5* 1980; *No Nukes* 1980; *Acting: Lee Strasberg and The Actors Studio* 1981; *On Golden Pond* 1981 **(AANBSA)**; *Rollover* 1981; *Montgomery Clift* 1982; *Agnes of God* 1985; *The Morning After* 1986 **(AANBA)**; *Leonard, Part 6* 1987; *Old Gringo* 1989 (a,p); *Stanley and Iris* 1990.

Fonda, Peter • Actor; also producer, screenwriter, director. • Born New York, NY, February 23, 1939. *Educ.* University of Omaha, Nebraska. Progressed from playing boy-next-door roles to rebel biker types (*The Wild Angels* 1966, *Easy Rider* 1969) in the 1960s; subsequently appeared in mostly inferior productions. Fonda directed the terse, finely acted western *The Hired Hand* in 1971. Son of Henry, brother of Jane and father of Bridget. • *Tammy and the Doctor* 1963; *The Victors* 1963; *Lilith* 1964; *The Young Lovers* 1964; *The Rounders* 1965; *The Wild Angels* 1966; *The Trip* 1967; *Histoires Extraordinaires/Spirits of the Dead* 1968; *Easy Rider* 1969 (a,p,sc) **(AANBSC)**; *The Hired Hand* 1971 (a,d); *The Last Movie* 1971; *Idaho Transfer* 1973 (d); *Two People* 1973; *Dirty Mary, Crazy Larry* 1974; *Open Season* 1974; *92 in the Shade* 1975; *The Diamond Mercenaries* 1975; *Race With the Devil* 1975; *Fighting Mad* 1976; *Futureworld* 1976; *Outlaw Blues* 1977 (a,song); *High-ballin'* 1978; *Roger Corman: Hollywood's Wild Angel* 1978; *Wanda Nevada* 1979 (a,d); *The Cannonball Run* 1980; *Spasms* 1982; *Split Image* 1982; *Daijoobu, Mai Furrendo* 1983; *Peppermint Frieden* 1983; *Certain Fury* 1984; *Freedom Fighter* 1988; *Hawken's Breed* 1989; *The Rose Garden* 1989; *Fatal Mission* 1990 (a,sc).

Fong, Allen • *aka* Fong Yu-ping, Fong Yuk-ping • Director • Born Hong Kong, July 10, 1947. *Educ.* Hong Kong Baptist College (communications); USC, Los Angeles (film). Leading Hong Kong director who made his mark in TV before joining the leftist Feng Huang Motion Picture Company. Fong made his feature debut with *Father and Son* (1981), a refreshing autobiographical tale of a young would-be director who returns from the US with a film degree, but whose father sees a different future for him. • *Father and Son* 1981 (d); *Meiguo xin/Just Like the Weather* 1986 (a,d); *Aiqing Qiangfeng Xunhao/Working Title* 1986 (d); *Life Is Cheap... But Toilet Paper Is Expensive* 1989 (a); *Dancing Bull* 1990 (d,p).

Fontaine, Joan • *aka* Joan Burfield • Actress • Born Joan De Beauvoir De Havilland, Tokyo, October 22, 1917. Delicately beautiful leading lady, born to British parents in the Orient. In the US from 1919, Fontaine made her screen debut with a bit part in *No More Ladies* (1935). She achieved stardom in the early 1940s with memorable roles in Alfred Hitchcock's *Rebecca* (1940), opposite Laurence Olivier, and *Suspicion* (1941), opposite Cary Grant. Her subsequent roles, though capably played, failed to make the best use of her talents. The younger sister of Olivia De Havilland, Fontaine was married to actor Brian Aherne from 1939 to 1945, producer William Dozier from 1949 to 1951 and producer Collier Young from 1952 to 1961. • *No More Ladies* 1935; *A Damsel in Distress* 1937; *The Man Who Found Himself* 1937; *Music For Madame* 1937; *Quality Street* 1937; *You Can't Beat Love* 1937; *Blond Cheat* 1938; *Maid's Night Out* 1938; *Sky Giant* 1938; *The Duke of West Point* 1939; *Gunga Din* 1939; *Man of Conquest* 1939; *The Women* 1939; *Rebecca* 1940 **(AANBA)**; *Suspicion* 1941 **(AABA)**; *This Above All* 1942; *The Constant Nymph* 1943 **(AANBA)**; *Frenchman's Creek* 1944; *Jane Eyre* 1944; *The Affairs of Susan* 1945; *From This Day Forward* 1946; *Ivy* 1947; *The Emperor Waltz* 1948; *Kiss the Blood Off My Hands* 1948; *Letter From an Unknown Woman* 1948; *You Gotta Stay Happy* 1948; *Born to Be Bad* 1950; *Darling, How Could You* 1951; *September Affair* 1951; *Ivanhoe* 1952; *Othello* 1952; *Something to Live For* 1952; *The Bigamist* 1953; *Decameron Nights* 1953; *Flight to Tangier* 1953; *Casanova's Big Night* 1954; *Serenade* 1955; *Beyond a Reasonable Doubt* 1956; *Island in the Sun* 1957; *Until They Sail* 1957; *A Certain Smile* 1958; *Voyage to the Bottom of the Sea* 1961; *Tender Is the Night* 1962; *The Witches* 1966; *Hitchcock, Il Brivido del Genio* 1985.

Foote, Horton • Playwright, screenwriter; also producer. • Born Wharton, TX. Acclaimed for his poignant evocations of rural America. Foote has written a number of successful screenplays and teleplays as well as directing many of his own works for the stage. Children Hallie and Horton Foote, Jr. both act. • *Storm Fear* 1955 (sc); *To Kill a Mockingbird* 1962 (sc) **(AABSC)**; *Baby, the Rain Must Fall* 1965 (sc,from story "The Traveling Lady"); *The Chase* 1966 (from story and play); *Hurry Sundown* 1967 (sc); *Tomorrow* 1971 (sc); *Tender Mercies* 1982 (assoc.p,sc) **(AABSC)**; *1918* 1985 (sc,from play); *Courtship* 1986 (sc,from play); *On Valentine's Day* 1986 (sc,from play); *The Trip to Bountiful* 1986 (p,sc,from play) **(AANBSC)**.

Forbes, Bryan • Director; also screenwriter, producer, actor, novelist. • Born John Theobald Clarke, Stratford-atte-Bow, London, July 22, 1926. *Educ.* RADA, London. Began his career as an actor, formed the Beaver Films production company with Richard Attenborough in 1959, and proved himself as a director in the 1960s with sensitive studies of everyday life such as *Whistle Down the Wind* (1961) and *The L-Shaped Room* (1962). In 1969 Forbes was appointed head of production at London's Elstree Studios, but resigned the post after two years in order to concentrate on writing (he went on to produce several best-selling novels). Wife Nanette Newman has appeared in many of his films. • *The Small Back Room* 1948 (a); *All Over the Town* 1949 (a); *Dear Mr. Prohack* 1949 (a); *Saturday Night (short)* 1950 (a); *The Wooden Horse* 1950 (a); *Green Grow the Rushes* 1951 (uncred.a); *The World in His Arms* 1952 (a); *Appointment in London* 1953 (a); *The Man With a Million* 1953 (uncred.a); *Sea Devils* 1953 (a); *Wheel of Fate* 1953 (a); *The Black Knight* 1954 (uncred.add.ph); *The Colditz Story* 1954 (a); *An Inspector Calls* 1954 (a); *Up to His Neck* 1954 (a); *An Alligator Named Daisy* 1955 (uncred.sc); *The Cockleshell Heroes* 1955 (sc); *Now and Forever* 1955 (a); *Passage Home* 1955 (a); *Quatermass 2* 1955 (a); *The Baby and the Battleship* 1956 (a,add.ph); *The Black Tent* 1956 (sc); *The Extra Day* 1956 (a); *House of Secrets* 1956 (sc); *It's Great to Be Young* 1956 (a); *The Last Man to Hang* 1956 (uncred.a); *Satellite in the Sky* 1956 (a); *The Captain's Table* 1958 (sc); *Danger Within* 1958 (sc); *I Was Monty's Double* 1958 (a,sc); *The Key* 1958 (a); *The Angry Silence* 1959 (a,p,sc) **(AANBSC)**; *Yesterday's Enemy* 1959 (a); *The League of Gentlemen* 1960 (a,sc); *Man in the Moon* 1960 (sc); *The Guns of Navarone* 1961 (a); *Only Two Can Play* 1961 (sc); *Whistle Down the Wind* 1961 (d); *The L-Shaped Room* 1962 (a,d,sc); *Station Six Sahara* 1962 (sc); *The Wrong Arm of the Law* 1962 (uncred.sc); *Of Human Bondage* 1964 (a,sc,add.d); *Seance on a Wet Afternoon* 1964 (d,p,sc); *A Shot in the Dark* 1964 (a); *The High Bright Sun* 1965 (uncred.sc); *King Rat* 1965 (d,sc); *The Wrong Box* 1966 (d,sc); *The Whisperers* 1967 (d,sc); *Deadfall* 1968 (d,sc); *The Madwoman of Chaillot* 1969 (d); *The Raging Moon* 1970 (a,d,sc); *I Am a Dancer* 1972 (a); *The Stepford Wives* 1975 (a,d); *The Slipper and the Rose* 1976 (a,d,sc); *International Velvet* 1978 (a,d,p,sc); *Hopscotch* 1980 (sc); *Sunday Lovers* 1980 (d); *Better Late Than Never* 1983 (d,sc); *The Naked Face* 1985 (d,sc); *Restless Natives* 1985 (a).

Ford, Aleksander • Director • Born, Lódz, Poland, November 24, 1908; died April 29, 1980. *Educ.* Warsaw University (art history). Key figure of the Polish cinema who established himself in the

1930s with films such as *Legion of the Streets* (1932) and the documentary *Street of the Young* (1936), banned for its controversial depiction of poor and impoverished Poles and Jews. After the end of WWII Ford headed the newly formed state film organization, Film Polski, and continued to direct films of note such as *Border Street* (1948) and *Five From Barska Street* (1953). As well as helping to establish the reputation of Polish cinema abroad, Ford exerted an important influence on the early career of Andrzej Wajda. He emigrated to Israel in the late 1960s. • *At Dawn (short)* 1929 (d); *Lódz—the Polish Manchester (short)* 1929 (d); *The Mascot* 1930 (d); *Legion of the Streets* 1932 (d); *Probuzeni* 1934 (d); *Sabra* 1934 (d); *Forward Cooperation* 1935 (d); *Street of the Young* 1936 (d); *People of the Vistula* 1937 (d); *Maidanek (short)* 1944 (d); *The Battle of Kolberg (short)* 1945 (d); *Border Street* 1948 (d,sc); *Young Chopin* 1952 (d,sc); *Piatka z ulicy Barskiej/Five From Barska Street* 1953 (d,sc); *Der Achte Wochentag* 1958 (d,sc); *Kryzacy* 1960 (d,sc); *The First Day of Freedom* 1964 (d); *Der Arzt stellt fest* 1966 (d); *Good Morning Poland* 1970 (d); *The First Circle* 1972 (d,sc); *Sie sind freid, Dr. Korczak!* 1974 (d).

Ford, Glenn • Actor • Born Gwyllyn Samuel Newton, Quebec, Canada, May 1, 1916. Dependable, solidly built leading man who took his stage name from Glenford, a town in Canada. Ford entered films in 1939 after some experience on Broadway and first made his name in *Gilda* (1946), opposite Rita Hayworth. He excelled at playing well-meaning, ordinary men confronted by unusual or threatening situations, as in *Young Man With Ideas* (1952), *The Big Heat* (1953) and *Blackboard Jungle* (1955). Married to actress-dancer Eleanor Powell from 1943 to 1959. • *Heaven With a Barbed Wire Fence* 1939; *My Son Is Guilty* 1939; *Babies For Sale* 1940; *Blondie Plays Cupid* 1940; *Convicted Woman* 1940; *The Lady in Question* 1940; *Men Without Souls* 1940; *Go West, Young Lady* 1941; *So Ends Our Night* 1941; *Texas* 1941; *The Adventures of Martin Eden* 1942; *Flight Lieutenant* 1942; *The Desperadoes* 1943; *Destroyer* 1943; *Hollywood in Uniform (short)* 1943; *Gallant Journey* 1946; *Gilda* 1946; *A Stolen Life* 1946; *Framed* 1947; *The Loves of Carmen* 1948; *Make It Real (short)* 1948; *The Man From Colorado* 1948; *The Mating of Millie* 1948; *The Return of October* 1948; *The Doctor and the Girl* 1949; *Hollywood Goes to Church (short)* 1949; *Lust For Gold* 1949; *Mr. Soft Touch* 1949; *Undercover Man* 1949; *Convicted* 1950; *The Flying Missile* 1950; *The Redhead and the Cowboy* 1950; *The White Tower* 1950; *Follow the Sun* 1951; *The Green Glove* 1951; *The Secret of Convict Lake* 1951; *Affair in Trinidad* 1952; *Young Man With Ideas* 1952; *Appointment in Honduras* 1953; *The Big Heat* 1953; *The Man From the Alamo* 1953; *Plunder of the Sun* 1953; *Terror on a Train* 1953; *City Story (short)* 1954; *Human Desire* 1954; *The Violent Men* 1954; *The Americano* 1955; *Blackboard Jungle* 1955; *Interrupted Melody* 1955; *Trial* 1955; *The Fastest Gun Alive* 1956; *Jubal* 1956; *Ransom* 1956; *The Teahouse of the August Moon* 1956; *3:10 to Yuma* 1957; *Don't Go Near the Water* 1957; *Cowboy* 1958; *Imitation General* 1958; *The Sheepman* 1958; *Torpedo Run* 1958; *It Started With a Kiss* 1959; *Cimarron* 1960; *The Gazebo* 1960; *Cry For Happy* 1961; *A Pocketful of Miracles* 1961; *Experiment in Terror* 1962; *The Four Horsemen of the Apocalypse* 1962; *Advance to the Rear* 1963; *The Courtship of Eddie's Father* 1963; *Love Is a Ball* 1963; *Dear Heart* 1964; *Fate Is the Hunter* 1964; *The Rounders* 1965; *Seapower (short)* 1965; *The Money Trap* 1966; *Paris brûle-t-il?/Is Paris Burning?* 1966; *Rage* 1966; *The Last Challenge* 1967; *The Long Ride Home* 1967; *Day of the Evil Gun* 1968; *Heaven With a Gun* 1969; *Smith* 1969; *Santee* 1973; *Battle of Midway* 1976; *Superman* 1978; *The Visitor* 1979; *Fukkatsu no hi/Virus* 1980; *Happy Birthday to Me* 1980; *Border Shootout* 1990; *Casablanca Express* 1990.

Ford, Harrison • Actor • Born Chicago, IL, July 13, 1942. *Educ.* Ripon College, WI. Leading man whose craggy features and powerful physical presence enhanced some of Hollywood's most successful "blockbusters" of the 1970s and 80s. Ford shot to fame as arrogant space pilot Han Solo in the first installment of George Lucas's *Star Wars* series, and established himself as a leading international star with his role as the archeologist hero of Steven Spielberg's *Indiana Jones* chronicles. He earned a place in the hearts of cult movie audiences playing the cynical, robot-killing cop in *Blade Runner* (1982) and proved capable of a wider emotional range with fine performances in *Witness* (1985) and *Presumed Innocent* (1990). • *Dead Heat on a Merry-Go-Round* 1966; *The Long Ride Home* 1967; *Journey to Shiloh* 1968; *Getting Straight* 1970; *American Graffiti* 1973; *The Conversation* 1974; *Heroes* 1977; *Star Wars* 1977; *Force 10 From Navarone* 1978; *Apocalypse Now* 1979; *The Frisco Kid* 1979; *Hanover Street* 1979; *The Empire Strikes Back* 1980; *Raiders of the Lost Ark* 1981; *Blade Runner* 1982; *Return of the Jedi* 1983; *Indiana Jones and the Temple of Doom* 1984; *Witness* 1985 **(AANBA)**; *The Mosquito Coast* 1986; *Frantic* 1988; *Working Girl* 1988; *Indiana Jones and the Last Crusade* 1989; *Presumed Innocent* 1990; *Regarding Henry* 1991.

Ford, John • *aka* Sean Aloysius O'Feeney, Jack Ford, Sean O'Feeney • Director; also producer, screenwriter. • Born Sean Aloysius O'Fearna, Cape Elizabeth, ME, February 1, 1895; died August 31, 1973. John Ford grew up with the American cinema. In the early days of filmmaking, his older brother Francis moved to Hollywood to work for Universal Pictures and John joined him in 1914, forging his apprenticeship as a moviemaker during the formative period of the classical Hollywood cinema. By 1917 he had been promoted to contract director, fashioning westerns which often starred Harry Carey, Sr. Ford moved to the Fox studio in 1921 and established his reputation with such films as the western spectacular *The Iron Horse* (1924). In his silent films, Ford composed images with a formality and a symmetry that valued order; even at this stage, he had acquired the mantle of a Hollywood master.

Although best known for his westerns such as the landmark *Stagecoach* (1939), Ford worked in many other genres through his long career. Early in the 1930s, he led Fox's top comedy star, Will Rogers, through *Doctor Bull* (1933), *Judge Priest* (1934) and *Steamboat 'Round the Bend* (1935). Ford also set a number of his films in his parents' native Ireland. *The Informer* (1935), a drama of the Irish rebellion, won him the first of four Academy Awards for his direction. In retrospect, the film seems stylistically stodgy and thematically preachy, especially next to the vitality of *The Quiet Man* (1952), an unpretentious film about an Irish-American returning to settle in his native land. Ford also dealt with American history in *The Prisoner of Shark Island* (1936), *Young Mr. Lincoln* (1939), *Drums Along the Mohawk* (1939) and *The Grapes of Wrath* (1940).

After WWII Ford fashioned some of the best westerns ever to come out of Hollywood, including *She Wore a Yellow Ribbon* (1949), *Wagonmaster* (1950), *The Searchers* (1956) and *The Man Who Shot Liberty Valance* (1962). In creating the archetype for the genre in *My Darling Clementine* (1946), Ford focused on the classic cinematic shoot-out, the famous final gunfight at OK Corral, where Wyatt Earp (Henry Fonda) and his brothers avenge the murder of their youngest brother. Against the harsh background of the buttes and desert of Monument Valley, Ford had the Earps ally with Easterner Doc Holiday (Victor Mature) to rid Tombstone of the evil Clantons and bring civilization to the town. In reshaping these familiar elements, Ford demonstrated that Hollywood genre films could be transformed into complex artifacts of popular culture and history.

Ford's postwar westerns examined all facets of the settling of the West. He began with a shared optimism in *My Darling Clementine* and *She Wore a Yellow Ribbon* and ended with a close examination of the dark side of manifest destiny in *The Man Who Shot Liberty Valance.*

Possibly his most underrated film, *She Wore a Yellow Ribbon*, should be singled out for its brilliant use of color: rich and muted hues blended into an often somber aura. In this transitional work, part of a trilogy (including *Fort Apache* 1948 and *Rio Grande* 1950) about life in the United States cavalry, Ford praises the work of the military in settling the West, while undercutting the role of war in settling disputes. *The Searchers*, now highly regarded by critics, historians, and such contemporary directors as Steven Spielberg, Martin Scorsese and George Lucas, presents not only a rousing adventure tale, but also a melancholy examination of the contradictions of settling the old West. At the center of the film stands Ethan Edwards (John Wayne), a bitter, ruthless and frustrated veteran of the Civil War who engages in an epic quest to retrieve an orphaned niece abducted by a Comanche raiding party. This neurotic man belongs neither to the civilized world of settlers hanging on at the edge of Monument Valley nor to the proud but doomed Native Americans he doggedly pursues. Torn between his respect for, but racist hatred of, Indians, Edwards speaks their language and is at home with their customs but is not deterred from seeking revenge for his murdered sister-in-law and her daughter. In *The Searchers* the wilderness never seemed so brutal nor civilization so tenuous and threatened. There are no towns, only outposts and isolated homesteads. The towering buttes of Monument Valley, in vivid Technicolor, are stunning but seem terribly threatening at the same time. After years of searching, Ethan gently lifts his niece in his arms to take her home, back to a family which is long dead, a homestead long deserted. The western myth persists above all.

If the latter film is one of the most beautiful color films ever made, *The Man Who Shot Liberty Valance*, in black & white, is surely one of the most bleak and barren. This dark vision of a West of deceit and lying, abandons the stunning Technicolor vistas of the buttes of Monument Valley for the rickety buildings of a ramshackle town continually cast in shadow. The heroic shooting by Ranson Stoddard (James Stewart) of evil Liberty Valance (Lee Marvin), revealed in flashback, is shown by the end of the film to be a lie and a sham. Still, society hails Stoddard as a hero and elevates him to a position of power as a United States Senator. The true Western hero, Tom Doniphon (John Wayne), dies a pauper, unknown, save to his closest friends.

Although his final film was *Seven Women* (1965), *Cheyenne Autumn*, released in 1964 and his final film shot in Monument Valley, seems a more fitting cap to a career begun some fifty years earlier. Ford made many of the best films ever to come out of Hollywood, even as he managed to make a few of the worst. By focusing on the aforementioned works, one overlooks the wretched excess of *Wings of Eagles* (1957). How he could make this film just after his masterpiece, *The Searchers*, is a paradox that suggests a great deal about working in Hollywood. DG • *Lucille Love, Girl of Mystery* 1914 (a,props); *The Mysterious Rose (short)* 1914 (a); *The Broken Coin* 1915 (a); *The Doorway of Destruction (short)* 1915 (a,ad); *The Hidden City (short)* 1915 (a); *Three Bad Men and a Girl* 1915 (a); *The Bandit's Wager (short)* 1916 (a); *Chicken-Hearted Jim (short)* 1916 (a); *The Lumber Yard Gang (short)* 1916 (a); *Bucking Broadway* 1917 (d); *Cheyenne's Pal* 1917 (d,story); *A Marked Man* 1917 (d); *The Scrapper* 1917 (a,d,sc); *The Secret Man* 1917 (d); *The Soul Herder* 1917 (d); *Straight Shooting* 1917 (d); *The Tornado* 1917 (a,d,sc); *The Trail of Hate* 1917 (a,d,sc); *Delirium* 1918 (d,sc,story); *Hell Bent* 1918 (d,sc,story); *The Phantom Riders* 1918 (d); *The Scarlet Drop* 1918 (d,story); *Thieves' Gold* 1918 (d); *Three Mounted Men* 1918 (d,p); *Wild Women* 1918 (d); *A Woman's Fool* 1918 (d); *The Ace of the Saddle* 1919 (d); *Bare Fists* 1919 (d); *By Indian Posts (short)* 1919 (d); *A Fight for Love* 1919 (d); *The Fighting Brothers (short)* 1919 (d); *A Gun Fightin' Gentleman* 1919 (d,story); *Gun Law (short)* 1919 (d); *The Gun Pusher* 1919 (d,story); *The Last Outlaw (short)* 1919 (d); *The Outcasts of Poker Flat* 1919 (d); *The Rider of the Law* 1919 (d); *Riders of Vengeance* 1919 (d,story); *Roped* 1919 (d); *The Rustlers* 1919 (d); *The Big Punch* 1920 (d,sc); *The Girl in Number 29* 1920 (d); *Hitchin' Posts* 1920 (d); *Just Pals* 1920 (d); *Marked Men* 1920 (d); *The Prince of Avenue A* 1920 (d); *Under Sentence* 1920 (story); *Action* 1921 (d,d); *Desperate Trails* 1921 (d); *The Freeze Out* 1921 (d); *Jackie* 1921 (d); *Sure Fire* 1921 (d,p); *The Wallop* 1921 (d,p); *Little Miss Smiles* 1922 (d); *Nero* 1922 (d); *Silver Wings* 1922 (d); *The Village Blacksmith* 1922 (d); *Cameo Kirby* 1923 (d); *The Face on the Barroom Floor* 1923 (d); *Hoodman Blind* 1923 (d); *North of Hudson Bay* 1923 (d); *Three Jumps Ahead* 1923 (d,sc); *Hearts of Oak* 1924 (d); *The Iron Horse* 1924 (d); *The Fighting Heart* 1925 (d); *Kentucky Pride* 1925 (d); *Lightnin'* 1925 (d); *Thank You* 1925 (d); *The Blue Eagle* 1926 (d); *The Shamrock Handicap* 1926 (d); *Three Bad Men* 1926 (d); *What Price Glory* 1926 (d); *Seventh Heaven* 1927 (d); *Upstream* 1927 (d); *Four Sons* 1928 (d); *Hangman's House* 1928 (d); *Mother Machree* 1928 (d); *Napoleon's Barber* 1928 (d); *Riley the Cop* 1928 (d); *Big Time* 1929 (a); *The Black Watch* 1929 (d); *Salute* 1929 (d); *Strong Boy* 1929 (d); *Born Reckless* 1930 (d); *Men Without Women* 1930 (d,story); *Up the River* 1930 (d); *Arrowsmith* 1931 (d); *The Brat* 1931 (d); *Seas Beneath* 1931 (d); *Air Mail* 1932 (d); *Flesh* 1932 (d,p); *Doctor Bull* 1933 (d); *Pilgrimage* 1933 (d); *Judge Priest* 1934 (d); *The Lost Patrol* 1934 (d); *The World Moves On* 1934 (d); *The Informer* 1935 (d) **(AABD)**; *Steamboat 'Round the Bend* 1935 (d); *The Whole Town's Talking* 1935 (d); *The Last Outlaw* 1936 (story); *Mary of Scotland* 1936 (d); *The Plough and the Stars* 1936 (d); *The Prisoner of Shark Island* 1936 (d); *Hurricane* 1937 (d); *Wee Willie Winkie* 1937 (d); *The Adventures of Marco Polo* 1938 (d); *Four Men and a Prayer* 1938 (d); *Submarine Patrol* 1938 (d); *Drums Along the Mohawk* 1939 (d); *Stagecoach* 1939 (d) **(AANBD)**; *Young Mr. Lincoln* 1939 (d); *The Grapes of Wrath* 1940 (d) **(AABD)**; *The Long Voyage Home* 1940 (d); *How Green Was My Valley* 1941 (d) **(AABD)**; *Sex Hygiene (short)* 1941 (d); *Tobacco Road* 1941 (d); *The Battle of Midway (short)* 1942 (commentary,ph,ed,d); *Torpedo Squadron (short)* 1942 (d); *December 7th (short)* 1943 (d); *We Sail at Midnight (short)* 1943 (d); *They Were Expendable* 1945 (d,p); *My Darling Clementine* 1946 (d); *The Fugitive* 1947 (d,p); *Fort Apache* 1948 (d,p); *Everybody Does It* 1949 (a); *Mighty Joe Young* 1949 (p); *Pinky* 1949 (d); *She Wore a Yellow Ribbon* 1949 (d,p); *Three Godfathers* 1949 (d); *Rio Grande* 1950 (d,p); *Wagonmaster* 1950 (d,p); *When Willie Comes Marching Home* 1950 (d); *Bullfighter and the Lady* 1951 (uncred.ed); *This Is Korea* 1951 (d); *The Quiet Man* 1952 (d,p) **(AABD)**; *What Price Glory* 1952 (d); *Hondo* 1953 (2u d); *Mogambo* 1953 (d); *The Sun Shines Bright* 1953 (d,p); *The Long Gray Line* 1955 (d); *Mister Roberts* 1955 (d); *The Red, White and Blue Line (short)* 1955 (d); *The Searchers* 1956 (d); *The Wings of Eagles* 1956 (d); *The Growler Story (short)* 1957 (d); *The Lady Takes a Flyer* 1957 (technical adviser); *Rising of the Moon* 1957 (d); *Gideon's Day* 1958 (d,p); *The Last Hurrah* 1958 (d,p); *So Alone (short)* 1958 (d); *The Horse Soldiers* 1959 (d); *Korea (short)* 1959 (d,p); *Sergeant Rutledge* 1960 (d); *Two Rode Together* 1961 (d); *How the West Was Won* 1962 (d); *The Man Who Shot Liberty Valance* 1962 (d); *Donovan's Reef* 1963 (d,p); *Cheyenne Autumn* 1964 (d); *Seven Women* 1965 (d); *Young Cassidy* 1965 (d); *Directed By John Ford* 1971 (a); *Vietnam! Vietnam!* 1971 (exec.p); *Hollywood Mavericks* 1990 (archival footage).

Foreman, Carl • Screenwriter; also producer, director. • Born Chicago, IL, July 23, 1914; died June 26, 1984, Beverly Hills, CA. *Educ.* University of Illinois; Northwestern University. Wrote several outstanding screenplays for producer Stanley Kramer, including *Home of the Brave* (1949) and *The Men* (1950), before refusing to cooperate with the House Committee on Un-American Activities in the early 1950s. Subsequently blacklisted, Foreman went to England and worked uncredited on *The Bridge on the River Kwai* (1957), before beginning his producing career in 1959. His sole directorial effort was *The Victors* (1963), an admirable WWII drama. • *Bowery Blitzkrieg* 1941 (sc); *Spooks Run Wild* 1941 (sc,story); *Rhythm Parade* 1942 (sc,story); *Dakota* 1945 (story); *Know Your Enemy: Japan* 1945 (commentary); *Let's Go to the Movies (short)* 1948 (story); *So This Is New York* 1948 (sc); *Champion* 1949 (sc) **(AANBSC)**; *The Clay Pigeon* 1949 (sc,story); *Home of the Brave* 1949 (sc); *Cyrano De Bergerac* 1950 (sc); *The Men* 1950 (sc,story) **(AANBSC)**; *Young Man With a Horn* 1950 (sc); *High Noon* 1952 (uncred.p,sc) **(AANBSC)**; *The Constant Husband* 1954 (sc consult.); *The Man Who Loved Redheads* 1954 (sc consult); *The Deep Blue Sea* 1955 (sc consult.); *Richard III* 1955 (sc consult.); *Storm Over the Nile* 1955 (sc consult.); *Summertime* 1955 (sc consult.); *The Bridge on the River Kwai* 1957 (uncred.sc); *The Key* 1958 (exec.p,sc); *Smiley Gets a Gun* 1958 (sc consult.); *The Mouse That Roared* 1959 (exec.p); *The Guns of Navarone* 1961 (exec.p,sc) **(AANBSC)**; *The Directors (short)* 1963 (a); *The Victors* 1963 (d,p,sc); *Born Free* 1966 (exec.p); *Monsieur Lecoq* 1968 (exec.p); *Otley* 1968 (exec.p); *MacKenna's Gold* 1969 (p,sc); *The Virgin Soldiers* 1969 (exec.p); *Living Free* 1972 (exec.p); *Young Winston* 1972 (p,sc) **(AANBSC)**; *Force 10 From Navarone* 1978 (exec.p,story); *When Time Ran Out* 1980 (sc); *Remembrance* 1981 (song).

Forman, Milos • *aka* Tomas Jan • Director; also screenwriter, producer. • Born Cáslav, Czechoslovakia, February 18, 1932. *Educ.* University of Prague (film); FAMU, Prague. Miloš Forman stands as one of the few established foreign directors to find consistent success within the American film industry. Like Fritz Lang, Forman was an influential filmmaker in his homeland who went on to achieve equal influence in Hollywood. Forman's Czechoslovakian films, including *Loves of a Blonde* (1965) and *The Fireman's Ball* (1967), marked a distinct thematic and stylistic break with the prior generation of filmmaking in that country, and they played a major role in shaping the Czech New Wave of the 60s. These films were characterized by an ironic humor and detailed observation of character for which Forman has become well known.

Forman came to the United States in 1968, following the Soviet invasion of his homeland. *Taking Off* (1971), his first American feature, was a critical if not commercial success, but it was with *One Flew Over the Cuckoo's Nest* (1975) that Forman solidified his stature in this country. *Cuckoo's Nest* was a box-office smash which became only the second film in history to sweep the top five Academy Awards, winning for best director, picture, screenplay adaptation (Bo Goldman), actor (Jack Nicholson) and actress (Louise Fletcher). Forman followed this breakthrough with a series of screen triumphs that included *Hair* (1979), *Ragtime* (1981) and *Amadeus* (1984).

A persistent theme in Forman's work is generational conflict, particularly as it is played out within a family context. Some critics have suggested that Forman's preoccupation with parent-child relationships stems from the loss of his own parents in Nazi concentration camps when he was eight years old. In Forman's first two features, *Black Peter* (1963) and *Loves of a Blonde*, he deals with the theme in a gentle and humanistic manner, using it for subtle criticism of the socio-political climate in Czechoslovakia of the mid-60s. The political content of Forman's Czech films is rarely overt, but rather suggested through the harshly authentic depiction of a bleak environment and inflexible social order. To achieve this authenticity, Forman routinely used non-professional actors who were often instructed to improvise their dialogue to achieve a sense of spontaneity. The political implications of Forman's realism are complemented by his narratives, which, as in *Loves of a Blonde*, often tell the story of young people struggling to find happiness and meaning within an established social order that has not provided for their personal and emotional fulfillment. In all his Czechoslovakian films, the political critique is gently ironic and the humanism abundant.

Forman's first two American films bear strong thematic and stylistic resemblance to his Czechoslovakian work; *Taking Off* developed the generation gap theme and *One Flew Over the Cuckoo's Nest* explored the struggle of the individual against the establishment. Though his subsequent American films explore new genres—the musical (*Hair*) and the historical drama (*Ragtime* and *Amadeus*)—they still exhibit Forman's humanistic concern for the individual. JFK • *Nechte to na mne* 1955 (sc); *Dedecek automobil* 1956 (a,ad); *Štenata* 1957 (sc,story,ad); *Tam za lesem/Beyond the Forest* 1962 (a,ad); *Kdyby ty muziky nebyly (short)* 1963 (d,sc,adapt); *Konkurs (short)* 1963 (d,sc,adapt); *Cerny Petr/Black Peter* 1964 (d,sc); *Lásky Jedné Plavovlásky/Loves of a Blonde* 1965 (d,sc); *Hoří, Má Panenko/The Fireman's Ball* 1967 (d,sc); *La Pince à ongles (short)* 1968 (sc); *Meeting Milos Forman (short)* 1971 (a); *Taking Off* 1971 (d,sc); *Visions of Eight* 1973 (d); *Le Mâle du Siècle* 1975 (story); *One Flew Over the Cuckoo's Nest* 1975 (d) **(AABD)**; *Hair* 1979 (d); *Ragtime* 1981 (d); *Before the Nickelodeon: The Early Cinema Of Edwin S. Porter* 1982 (a); *Chytilova vs. Forman* 1983 (a); *Amadeus* 1984 (d) **(AABD)**; *50 Years of Action!* 1986 (a); *Heartburn* 1986 (a); *New Year's Day* 1989 (a); *Valmont* 1989 (d,sc).

Forrest, Frederic • Actor • Born Waxahachie, TX, December 23, 1936. *Educ.* University of Oklahoma; University of Colorado; Texas Christian University, Fort Worth; Actors Studio. Leading man of the 1970s and 80s, in several films by Francis Coppola; memorable in the title role of *Hammett* (1982), Wim Wenders's moody, cerebral essay in film noir. • *When the Legends Die* 1972; *The Don Is Dead* 1973; *The Conversation* 1974; *The Gravy Train* 1974; *Permission to Kill* 1975; *The Missouri Breaks* 1976; *It's Alive 2* 1978; *Apocalypse Now* 1979; *The Rose* 1979 **(AANBSA)**; *Hammett* 1982; *One From the Heart* 1982; *Saigon—Year of the Cat* 1983; *The Stone Boy* 1983; *Valley Girl* 1983; *Return* 1985; *Where Are the Children?* 1986; *Stacking* 1987; *Quo Vadis* 1988; *Tucker: The Man and His Dream* 1988; *Cat Chaser* 1989; *Music Box* 1989; *Valentino Returns* 1989; *The Two Jakes* 1990.

Forsyth, Bill • Director, screenwriter • Born William David Forsyth, Glasgow, Scotland, July 29, 1946. *Educ.* National Film School, London. This droll filmmaker blends quirky but incisive comedy with bracing moral underpinnings. At 17 Forsyth was hired as the sole assistant to a documentary filmmaker and gradually learned all aspects of production. After a brief stint in the late 1960s at London's National Film School and at the BBC as an assistant editor, he returned to Glasgow. Forsyth ended his partnership in a sponsored film company when he wearied of the documentary's impersonal form. A subsequent collaboration with an amateur theater group of mostly young players led to his first feature, *That Sinking Feeling* (1979), shot for $10,000.

Forsyth's characters are often cases of blithely arrested development; indeed, he believes that "adolescence is a kind of permanent terminal state." He has described *That Sinking Feeling*, whose destitute teens survive by stealing kitchen fixtures, as "a fairy tale for the workless." *Gregory's Girl* (1981), whose initial idea was, according to Forsyth, inspired by Jack Kerouac's novel, *Maggie Cassidy*, observes a young man's infatuation with love. The burglar duo of *Breaking In* (1989) risk all on comradely night-time capers.

Local Hero (1983), his first US feature, brings an American oil company executive to the Scottish seaside on a financial mission. *Comfort and Joy* (1984), a more personal project, returned to his beloved Glasgow to tell the story of Dickie Bird, a lovelorn d.j. who is drawn into a civil war between factions of an Italian clan ("the Scotia Nostra") over the rights to Glasgow's ice cream market. Both films, produced by David Puttnam and exquisitely photographed by Chris Menges, are poignant observations of a lonely man's search for peace of mind. The eccentric free spirit of *Housekeeping* (1987), who moves in to care for her orphaned nieces in the Pacific Northwest, affirms Forsyth's affinity for the peculiar but universal wisdom of non-conformist souls. MDM • *Mackintosh* 1970 (ed); *That Sinking Feeling* 1979 (d,p,sc); *Gregory's Girl* 1981 (d,sc); *Local Hero* 1983 (d,sc); *Comfort and Joy* 1984 (d,sc); *Housekeeping* 1987 (d,sc); *Breaking In* 1989 (d).

Fosse, Bob • Director, choreographer; also screenwriter, actor. • Born Robert Louis Fosse, Chicago, IL, June 23, 1927; died 1987. *Educ.* American Theater Wing. Highly influential choreographer with a distinctive, jazz-influenced style. Fosse began his career in vaudeville and worked as an actor and dancer on stage and in films before choreographing his first Broadway show, *The Pajama Game*, in 1954. *Game* earned him the first of eight Tonys for best choreography, and the screen version in 1957 brought him his first chance to choreograph for film. He directed a string of successful Broadway musicals beginning in 1959 and made his screen directing debut ten years later.

A supreme stylist, Fosse often employed a loose narrative structure, shifting seamlessly between past, present and future to create his striking portraits. Besides *Cabaret* (1972), which won eight Academy Awards, he made stark, uncompromising biopics of Lenny Bruce (*Lenny* 1974) and slain Playboy Playmate Dorothy Stratten (*Star 80* 1983). *All That Jazz* (1979) was a semi-autobiographical, Felliniesque portrait of a workaholic, womanizing genius. • *The Affairs of Dobie Gillis* 1953 (a); *Give a Girl a Break* 1953 (a); *Kiss Me Kate* 1953 (a); *My Sister Eileen* 1955 (chor); *The Pajama Game* 1957 (chor); *Damn Yankees* 1958 (a,chor,song); *How to Succeed in Business Without Really Trying* 1967 (chor); *Sweet Charity* 1969 (d,chor); *Cabaret* 1972 (d) **(AABD)**; *Lenny* 1974 (d) **(AANBD)**; *The Little Prince* 1974 (a,chor—"Snake in the Grass"); *Thieves* 1977 (a); *All That Jazz* 1979 (d,sc,chor) **(AANBD,AANBSC)**; *Star 80* 1983 (d,sc).

Foster, Jodie • Actress; also director. • Born Alicia Christian Foster, Los Angeles, CA, November 19, 1962. *Educ.* Lycée Français, CA; Yale. Exceptionally mature, talented child star of the 1970s who made an indelible impression with her controversial appearance in *Taxi Driver* (1976), playing the teenage prostitute who inspires Robert De Niro's deranged personal crusade. After completing a BA at Yale, Foster turned in some equally impressive adult performances, capping her success with an Oscar-winning role in *The Accused* (1988) and a landmark performance opposite Anthony Hopkins in Jonathan Demme's *The Silence of the Lambs* (1991). Foster made her feature directorial debut in 1991 with *Little Man Tate*, an intimate portrait of the difficulties faced by a working-class single mother whose child happens to be a prodigy. • *Kansas City Bomber* 1972; *Napoleon and Samantha* 1972; *One Little Indian* 1973; *Tom Sawyer* 1973; *Alice Doesn't Live Here Anymore* 1974; *Bugsy Malone* 1976; *Echoes of a Summer* 1976; *Freaky Friday* 1976; *Taxi Driver* 1976 **(AANBSA)**; *Candleshoe* 1977; *Il Casotto* 1977; *The Little Girl Who Lives Down the Lane* 1977; *Moi, Fleur Bleue* 1977; *Movies Are My Life* 1978; *Carny* 1980; *Foxes* 1980; *O'Hara's Wife* 1982; *The Hotel New Hampshire* 1984; *Le Sang des Autres/The Blood of Others* 1984; *Mesmerized* 1986 (a,p); *Five Corners* 1987; *Siesta* 1987; *The Accused* 1988 **(AABA)**; *Stealing Home* 1988; *Backtrack* 1990; *Little Man Tate* 1991 (d,a); *The Silence of the Lambs* 1991.

Fox, Edward • Actor • Born London, April 13, 1937. Tall, blonde lead, memorable as the menacing assassin in *The Day of the Jackal* (1973). Brother of actor James Fox. • *The Mind Benders* 1963; *The Frozen Dead* 1967; *I'll Never Forget What's 'Is Name* 1967; *The Naked Runner* 1967; *Battle of Britain* 1969; *Oh! What a Lovely War* 1969; *Skullduggery* 1970; *The Go-Between* 1971; *The Day of the Jackal* 1973; *A Doll's House* 1973; *Galileo* 1974; *A Bridge Too Far* 1977; *The Duellists* 1977; *The Squeeze* 1977; *The Big Sleep* 1978; *Force 10 From Navarone* 1978; *The Cat and the Canary* 1979; *Soldier of Orange* 1979; *The Mirror Crack'd* 1980; *Nighthawks* 1981; *Gandhi* 1982; *The Dresser* 1983; *Never Say Never Again* 1983; *The Bounty* 1984; *The Shooting Party* 1984; *Wild Geese II* 1985; *Return to the River Kwai* 1989; *They Never Slept* 1990.

Fox, James • Actor • Born London, May 19, 1939. British leading man of the 1960s who gave up acting for religion in 1972 but returned to the screen ten years later. Son of influential talent agent Robin Fox and brother of actor Edward. • *The Magnet* 1950; *The Loneliness of the Long Distance Runner* 1962; *The Servant* 1963; *Tamahine* 1963; *King Rat* 1965; *Those Magnificent Men in Their Flying Machines* 1965; *The Chase* 1966; *Arabella* 1967; *Thoroughly Modern Millie* 1967; *Duffy* 1968; *Isadora* 1968; *Performance* 1970; *No Longer Alone* 1978; *Country* 1981; *Pavlova* 1983; *Runners* 1983; *Greystoke: The Legend of Tarzan, Lord of the Apes* 1984; *A Passage to India* 1984; *Absolute Beginners* 1986; *New World* 1986; *Comrades* 1987; *High Season* 1987; *The Whistle Blower* 1987; *Boys in the Island* 1989; *Farewell to the King* 1989; *She's Been Away* 1989; *The Russia House* 1990.

Fox, Michael J. • Actor • Born Edmonton, Alberta, Canada, June 9, 1961. Made his name playing quintessential yuppie Alex P. Keaton on the successful TV series "Family Ties" and time-traveling boy-next-door Marty McFly in *Back to the Future* (1985). Fox has more recently attempted more serious roles, most notably in Brian De Palma's *Casualties of War* (1989). Married to actress Tracey Pollan. • *Midnight Madness* 1980; *Class of 1984* 1982; *Back to the Future* 1985; *Teen Wolf* 1985; *Dear America* 1987; *Light of Day* 1987 (a,songs); *The Secret of My Success* 1987; *Bright Lights, Big City* 1988; *Back to the Future II* 1989; *Casualties of War* 1989; *Back to the Future III* 1990; *The Hard Way* 1991.

Fox, William • Executive; also distributor, exhibitor. • Born Wilhelm Fried, Tulchva, Hungary, January 1, 1879; died 1952, New York. In the US from infancy, Fox began his career in the garment trade and moved into the penny arcade business in 1904. He went on to develop successful film exhibition, distribution and production operations, merging all three interests with the formation, in 1915, of the Fox Film Corporation. By the end of the 1920s the company had accumulated several top stars and directors and produced a number of prestigious films; the stock market crash of 1929, however, forced the overextended Fox to sell his shares in the corporation. He filed for bankruptcy in 1936 and was briefly imprisoned after allegedly attempting to bribe a judge. Fox subsequently lived off the earnings from various sound patents that he had acquired earlier in his career. • *The Silent Lie* 1917 (p); *Should a Husband Forgive?* 1919 (p); *The Strongest* 1920 (p); *The Road to Glory* 1925 (p); *The River* 1929 (p).

Fraker, William A. • Director of photography; also director. • Born Los Angeles, CA, 1923. *Educ.* USC, Los Angeles (film). Distinguished, versatile cinematographer who began his career in TV. Fraker made his directing debut with the melancholy western *Monte Walsh* (1970). • *Forbid Them Not* 1962 (ph); *Father Goose* 1964 (cam.op); *Morituri* 1965 (cam.op); *Wild Seed* 1965 (cam.op); *The Fox* 1967 (ph); *Games* 1967 (ph); *The President's Analyst* 1967 (ph); *Bullitt* 1968 (ph); *Rosemary's Baby* 1968 (ph); *Paint Your Wagon* 1969 (ph); *Monte Walsh* 1970 (d); *Dusty and Sweets McGee* 1971 (a,ph); *A Reflection of Fear* 1971 (d); *The Day of the Dolphin* 1973 (ph); *Rancho Deluxe* 1974 (ph); *Aloha, Bobby and Rose* 1975 (ph); *Coonskin* 1975 (ph); *One Flew Over the Cuckoo's Nest* 1975 (ph); *Gator* 1976 (ph); *The Killer Inside Me* 1976 (ph); *Lipstick* 1976 (ph); *Close Encounters of the Third Kind* 1977 (add.ph—American scenes); *Exorcist II: The Heretic* 1977 (ph); *Looking For Mr. Goodbar* 1977 (ph) **(AANBPH)**; *American Hot Wax* 1978 (ph); *Heaven Can Wait* 1978 (ph) **(AANBPH)**; *Old Boyfriends* 1978 (ph); *1941* 1979 (ph) **(AANBFX,AANBPH)**; *Close Encounters of the Third Kind: Special Edition* 1980 (add.ph—American sequences); *Divine Madness* 1980 (ph); *The Hollywood Knights* 1980 (ph); *The Legend of the Lone Ranger* 1981 (d); *Sharky's Machine* 1981 (ph); *The Best Little Whorehouse in Texas* 1982 (ph); *WarGames* 1983 (ph) **(AANBPH)**; *Irreconcilable Differences* 1984 (ph); *Protocol* 1984 (ph); *Fever Pitch* 1985 (ph); *Murphy's Romance* 1985 (ph) **(AANBPH)**; *SpaceCamp* 1986 (ph); *Baby Boom* 1987 (ph); *Burglar* 1987 (ph); *Chances Are* 1989 (ph); *An Innocent Man* 1989 (ph); *The Freshman* 1990 (ph).

Franciosa, Anthony • *aka* Tony Franciosa • Actor • Born Anthony Papaleo, New York, NY, October 28, 1928. Handsome, forceful leading man. Married to actress Shelly Winters from 1957 to 1960. • *A Face in the Crowd* 1957; *A Hatful of Rain* 1957 **(AANBA)**; *This Could Be the Night* 1957; *Wild Is the Wind* 1957; *The Long, Hot Summer* 1958; *Career* 1959; *The Naked Maja* 1959; *The Story on Page One* 1959; *Go Naked in the World* 1961; *Period of Adjustment* 1962; *Senilita* 1962; *The Pleasure Seekers* 1964; *Rio Conchos* 1964; *Assault on a Queen* 1966; *A Man Could Get Killed* 1966; *The Swinger* 1966; *Fathom* 1967; *In Enemy Country* 1968; *The Sweet Ride* 1968; *A Man Called Gannon* 1969; *Across 110th Street* 1972; *Ghost in the Noonday Sun* 1973; *The Drowning Pool* 1975; *Firepower* 1979; *The World Is Full of Married Men* 1979; *Aiutami a sognare* 1981; *Death Wish II* 1981; *Sotto gli occhi dell'Assassino* 1982; *Ghost Writer* 1989; *Backstreet Dreams* 1990; *La Morte e di moda* 1990.

Francis, Freddie • Director, director of photography; also producer. • Born Frederick Francis, Islington, London, 1917. Former camera operator for Alexander Korda whose highly acclaimed work as a cinematographer ranges from the gritty urban landscapes of *Room at the Top* (1959) to the lush colors of *Glory* (1989). Francis's work as a director has been primarily in the horror genre. • *A Hill in Korea* 1956 (ph); *Moby Dick* 1956 (2u ph); *The Scamp* 1957 (ph); *Time Without Pity* 1957 (ph); *Next to No Time* 1958 (ph); *Virgin Island* 1958 (ph); *The Battle of the Sexes* 1959 (ph); *Room at the Top* 1959 (ph); *Never Take Sweets From a Stranger* 1960 (ph); *Saturday Night and Sunday Morning* 1960 (ph); *Sons and Lovers* 1960 (ph); *The Horsemasters* 1961 (ph); *The Innocents* 1961 (ph); *2 and 2 make 6* 1962 (d); *The Day of the Triffids* 1962 (d); *Paranoiac* 1962 (d); *Vengeance* 1962 (d); *Nightmare* 1963 (d); *Dr. Terror's House of Horrors* 1964 (d); *The Evil of Frankenstein* 1964 (d); *Hysteria* 1964 (d); *Night Must Fall* 1964 (ph); *The Psychopath* 1964 (d); *The Skull* 1965 (d); *Traitor's Gate* 1965 (d); *The Deadly Bees* 1967 (d); *They Came From Beyond Space* 1967 (d); *Dracula Has Risen From the Grave* 1968 (d); *Intrepid Mr. Twigg (short)* 1968 (d); *Torture Garden* 1968 (d); *Mumsy, Nanny, Sonny & Girly* 1970 (d); *Trog* 1970 (d); *Gebissen wird nur nachts-Happening der Vampire* 1971 (d); *The Creeping Flesh* 1972 (d); *Tales From The Crypt* 1972 (d); *Craze* 1973 (d); *Tales That Witness Madness* 1973 (d); *Son of Dracula* 1974 (d); *The Ghoul* 1975 (d); *Legend of the Werewolf* 1975 (d); *Golden Rendezvous* 1977 (d); *The Elephant Man* 1980 (ph); *The French Lieutenant's Woman* 1981 (ph); *Memed My Hawk* 1983 (ph); *The Jigsaw Man* 1984 (ph); *Code Name: Emerald* 1985 (ph); *The Doctor and the Devils* 1985 (d); *Dune* 1985 (ph); *Clara's Heart* 1988 (ph); *Dark Tower* 1989 (d); *Glory* 1989 (ph) **(AABPH)**; *Her Alibi* 1989 (ph).

Francis, Kay • Actress • Born Katherine Edwina Gibbs, Oklahoma City, OK, January 13, 1903; died 1968. Broadway leading lady who made her screen debut in 1929 and became one of Hollywood's leading stars of the 1930s. After WWII Francis co-produced three of her own films before retiring from the screen. • *The Cocoanuts* 1929; *Dangerous Curves* 1929; *Gentlemen of the Press* 1929; *Illusion* 1929; *The Marriage Playground* 1929; *Behind the Make-Up* 1930; *For the Defense* 1930; *Let's Go Native* 1930; *A Notorious Affair* 1930; *Paramount on Parade* 1930; *Passion Flower* 1930; *Raffles* 1930; *Street of Chance* 1930; *The Virtuous Sin* 1930; *24 Hours* 1931; *The False Madonna* 1931; *Girls About Town* 1931; *Guilty Hands* 1931; *Ladies' Man* 1931; *Scandal Sheet* 1931; *Transgression* 1931; *The Vice Squad* 1931; *Cynara* 1932; *Jewel Robbery* 1932; *Man Wanted* 1932; *One Way Passage* 1932; *Strangers in Love* 1932; *Street of Women* 1932; *Trouble in Paradise* 1932; *The House on 56th Street* 1933; *I Loved a Woman* 1933; *The Keyhole* 1933; *Mary Stevens, M.D.* 1933; *Storm at Daybreak* 1933; *British Agent* 1934; *Dr. Monica* 1934; *Living on Velvet* 1934; *Mandalay* 1934; *Wonder Bar* 1934; *The Goose and the Gander* 1935; *I Found Stella Parish* 1935; *Stranded* 1935; *Give Me Your Heart* 1936; *Stolen Holiday* 1936; *The White Angel* 1936; *Another Dawn* 1937; *Confession* 1937; *First Lady* 1937; *Women Are Like That* 1937; *Comet Over Broadway* 1938; *My Bill* 1938; *Secrets of an Actress* 1938; *In Name Only* 1939; *King of the Underworld* 1939; *Women in the Wind* 1939; *It's a Date* 1940; *Little Men* 1940; *When the Daltons Rode* 1940; *Charley's Aunt* 1941; *The Feminine Touch* 1941; *The Man Who Lost Himself* 1941; *Play Girl* 1941; *Always in My Heart* 1942; *Between Us Girls* 1942; *Four Jills in a Jeep* 1943; *Allotment Wives* 1945 (a,p); *Divorce* 1945 (a,p); *Wife Wanted* 1946 (a,p).

Franju, Georges • Director; also screenwriter, archivist. • Born Fougères, France, April 12, 1912; died November 5, 1987. Former set designer who in 1937 co-founded the renowned Cinématheque Française film archive with Henri Langlois. Franju made several gripping documentaries including *Le Sang des Bêtes* (1949) and *Hôtel des Invalides* (1951), noted for their distinctive blending of the lyrical with the horrific; he later carried the style over into feature films such as *La Tête contre les Murs* (1958) and *Eyes Without a Face* (1959). Major influences on Franju include Louis Feuillade, whose "Judex" serial he respectfully remade in 1963, and Jean Cocteau, whose novel *Thomas the Imposter* Franju filmed in 1965. • *Le Métro (short)* 1935 (d,sc); *Le Sang des Bêtes/The Blood of the Beasts (short)* 1949 (d,sc); *En passant par La Lorraine* 1950 (d,sc,commentary); *Hôtel des Invalides (short)* 1951 (d,sc,commentary); *Le Grand Méliès* 1952 (d,sc,commentary); *Monsieur et Madame Curie (short)* 1953 (d,sc,commentary); *Navigation marchande* 1954 (commentary,d); *Les Poussières (short)* 1954 (d,sc,commentary); *A propos d'une rivière (short)* 1955 (d,sc,commentary); *Mon Chien (short)* 1955 (d,sc); *Décembre, mois des enfants (short)* 1956 (sc); *Sur le pont d'Avignon (short)* 1956 (d,sc,commentary); *Le Théatre National Populaire (short)* 1956 (d,sc,commentary); *La Déroute (short)* 1957 (artistic consultant); *Notre Dame, cathédrale de Paris (short)* 1957 (d,sc); *La Première nuit (short)* 1958 (d); *La Tête contre les murs* 1958 (d); *Les Yeux sans Visage/Eyes Without a Face* 1959 (d); *Pleins feux sur l'assassin* 1961 (d); *Thérèse Desqueyroux* 1962 (d,sc); *Judex* 1963 (d); *Les Rideaux Blancs (short)* 1965 (d); *Thomas l'Imposteur* 1965 (d,sc); *La Faute de l'Abbé Mouret* 1970 (d,sc,adapt); *Nuits rouges* 1973 (d,m); *Un Homme Qui Dort* 1974 (assistance); *Le Dernier Mélodrame* 1980 (d).

Frank, Melvin • Director; also screenwriter, producer. • Born Chicago, IL, August 13, 1913; died October 13, 1988, Los Angeles, CA. *Educ.* University of Chicago (engineering). Began his career, with partner Norman Panama, as a writer for the Bob Hope radio show. The pair graduated to feature film writing in 1942, subsequently collaborating on the Hope/Bing Crosby "Road" movies as well as a number of noted romantic comedies including *Mr. Blandings Builds His Dream House* (1948), which they also produced. From 1949 onward Frank and Panama alternated directing and producing duties on several films, including the Danny Kaye vehicles *Knock on Wood* (1954) and *The Court Jester* (1956), before amicably dissolving the partnership in 1960. Each subsequently pursued a successful solo career. • *My Favorite Blonde* 1942 (story); *Star Spangled Rhythm* 1942 (sketches); *Happy Go Lucky* 1943 (sc); *Thank Your Lucky Stars* 1943 (sc); *And the Angels Sing* 1944 (sc); *Duffy's Tavern* 1945 (sc); *Monsieur Beaucaire* 1946 (sc); *Our Hearts Were Growing Up* 1946 (sc); *The Road to Utopia* 1946 (sc) **(AANBSC)**; *It Had *to Be You* 1947 (sc); *Mr. Blandings Builds His Dream House* 1948 (sc); *The Return of October* 1948 (sc); *A Southern Yankee* 1948 (story); *The Reformer and the Redhead* 1950 (d,p,sc); *Callaway Went Thataway* 1951 (d,p,sc,story); *Strictly Dishonorable* 1951 (d,p,sc); *Above and Beyond* 1952 (d,p,sc); *Knock on Wood* 1954 (d,p,sc) **(AANBSC)**; *White Christmas* 1954 (sc); *The Court Jester* 1956 (d,p,sc); *That Certain Feeling* 1956 (d,p,sc); *The Jayhawkers* 1959 (d,p,sc); *Li'l Abner* 1959 (d,p,sc,from play); *The Trap* 1959 (p); *The Facts of Life* 1960 (d,sc) **(AANBSC)**; *The Road to Hong Kong* 1962 (p,sc); *Strange Bedfellows* 1965 (d,p,sc,story); *A Funny Thing Happened on the Way to the Forum* 1966 (p,sc); *Not With My Wife, You Don't* 1966 (story); *Buona Sera, Mrs. Campbell* 1968 (d,p,sc,song); *A Touch of Class* 1973 (d,p,sc) **(AANBP,AANBSC)**; *The Prisoner of Second Avenue* 1974 (d,p); *The Duchess and the Dirtwater Fox* 1976 (d,p,sc,lyrics); *Lost and Found* 1979 (d,p,sc); *Walk Like a Man* 1987 (d).

Frank, Robert • Filmmaker; also photographer. • Born Zurich, Switzerland, 1924. Independent filmmaker, in the US from 1947. Frank was a magazine photographer before publishing *The Americans*, a collection of his own work, in 1958. The next year he made his best-known excursion into cinema with *Pull My Daisy*, a short, free adaptation of a portion of Jack Kerouac's play *The Beat Generation*. He was subsequently labeled a member of the American "underground," though this applies more to the availability of his films than to their form or content. *Me and My Brother* (1969) is a sensitive, semi-documentary study of catatonic schizophrenia; *Candy Mountain* (1986, co-directed with Rudy Wurlitzer) is an intriguing tale of a down-and-out rocker who traverses North America in search of an elusive guitar-maker. • *Pull My Daisy (short)* 1959 (adaptation from *The Beat Generation*,ph,ed,d,p); *Sin of Jesus (short)* 1961 (d,ed); *O.K. End Here* 1963 (d); *Chappaqua* 1966 (ph); *Life-Raft Earth* 1969 (d); *Me and My Brother* 1969 (d,sc,ph,ed); *About Me: A Musical* 1971 (d); *Conversations in Vermont (short)* 1971 (d,ph); *CS Blues* 1972 (d); *Let the Good Times Roll* 1973 (stills); *Sunseed* 1973 (ph); *No Second Chances (short)* 1974 (ph); *Diaries, Notes & Sketches—Volume 1, Reels 1-6: Lost Lost Lost* 1975 (a); *Keep Busy* 1975 (d); *Energy and How to Get It* 1980 (d); *Life Dances On...* 1980 (d); *This Song For Jack* 1983 (d); *Candy Mountain* 1987 (d); *I Will Not Make Any More Boring Art* 1988 (a); *Herzliche Wilkommen* 1989 (a); *UHF* 1989 (a).

Frankenheimer, John • Director; also producer. • Born Malba, NY, February 19, 1930. *Educ.* Williams College, Williamstown, MA (English). Major American director of the 1960s who began his career in TV. Frankenheimer learned filmmaking while in the Air Force, graduated to assistant directing jobs at CBS and made his directing debut with *The Plot Against King Solomon*, an episode of Sidney Lumet's highly regarded dramatic series "You Are There" (1953-57). Frankenheimer's first feature, *The Young Stranger* (1957), was a remake of a TV episode he had directed called *Deal a Blow* (1955). Though the film was well received, Frankenheimer was unsettled by the experience and returned to working in TV. When he finally left the medium in 1960 he was regarded, along with Sidney Lumet and Arthur Penn, as one of America's most promising young directors.

Frankenheimer's second feature was the taut, visually striking *The Young Savages* (1961), starring Burt Lancaster as an idealistic prosecutor out to save the lives of three innocent gang members. The theme of a lone male up against "the system" recurs in much of the director's best work, including *The Manchurian Candidate* (1962), *Seconds* (1966) and *52 Pick-Up* (1986). Frankenheimer's superb visual sense is equally effective in thrillers like *The Train* (1964) or *Black Sunday* (1977) and in more dramatic pieces such as *The Fixer* (1968) and *The Gypsy Moths* (1969). • *The Young Stranger* 1957 (d); *The Young Savages* 1961 (d); *All Fall Down* 1962 (d); *Birdman of Alcatraz* 1962 (d); *The Manchurian Candidate* 1962 (d,p,sc); *Seven Days in May* 1964 (d); *The Train* 1964 (d); *Grand Prix* 1966 (d); *Seconds* 1966 (d); *The Fixer* 1968 (d); *The Extraordinary Seaman* 1969 (d); *The Gypsy Moths* 1969 (d); *I Walk the Line* 1970 (d); *The Horsemen* 1971 (d,p); *The Iceman Cometh* 1973 (d); *Impossible Object* 1973 (d); *99 and 44/100% Dead* 1974 (d); *French Connection II* 1975 (d); *Black Sunday* 1977 (a,d); *Prophecy* 1979 (d); *The Challenge* 1982 (d); *The Holcroft Covenant* 1985 (d); *52 Pick-Up* 1986 (d); *Dead-Bang* 1989 (d); *The Fourth War* 1990 (d).

Franklin, Sidney • Director, producer • Born Sidney Arnold Franklin, San Francisco, CA, March 21, 1893; died 1972. In films from 1914, often sharing credit with his brother Chester. Franklin developed into a skilled, sensitive director in the 1930s with films such as *The Guardsman* (1931) and *The Barretts of Wimpole Street* (1934) and began producing for MGM in 1939. He won the best picture Oscar for *Mrs. Miniver* (1942) and was responsible for Clarence Brown's *The Yearling* (1946) as well as four Mervyn LeRoy movies. Franklin remade two of his own films, *The Barretts* (1934 and 1956) and *Smilin' Through* (1922 and 1932). • *Burning Daylight* 1914 (ad); *An Odyssey of the North* 1914 (ad); *A Ten-Cent Adventure (short)* 1914 (d); *Smoke Bellew* 1915 (ad); *The Children in the House* 1916 (d); *Going Straight* 1916 (d); *Gretchen, the Greenhorn* 1916 (d); *Let Katie Do It* 1916 (d); *The Little School Ma'am* 1916 (d); *Martha's Vindication* 1916 (d); *A Sister of Six* 1916 (d); *Aladdin and the Wonderful Lamp* 1917 (d); *The Babes in the Woods* 1917 (d); *Jack and the Beanstalk* 1917 (d,sc); *Treasure Island* 1917 (d); *Ali Baba and the Forty Thieves* 1918 (d); *The Bride of Fear* 1918 (d,sc); *Confession* 1918 (d,sc,story); *Fan Fan* 1918 (d); *Forbidden City* 1918 (d); *The Heart of Wetona* 1918 (d); *Her Only Way* 1918 (d,from story "What Might Have Been"); *The Safety Curtain* 1918 (d,sc); *Six Shooter Andy* 1918 (d); *Heart O' the Hills* 1919 (d); *The Hoodlum* 1919 (d); *The Probation Wife* 1919 (d); *Two Weeks* 1920 (d); *Courage* 1921 (d,exec.p); *Not Guilty* 1921 (d); *Unseen Forces* 1921 (d,p); *East Is West* 1922 (d); *The Primitive Lover* 1922 (d); *Smilin' Through* 1922 (d,sc); *Brass* 1923 (d); *Dulcy* 1923 (d); *Tiger Rose* 1923 (d,p); *Her Night of Romance* 1924 (d); *Her Sister From Paris* 1925 (d); *Learning to Love* 1925 (d); *Beverly of Graustark* 1926 (d); *The Duchess of Buffalo* 1926 (d); *Quality Street* 1927 (d); *The Actress* 1928 (d); *Devil May Care* 1929 (d); *The Last of Mrs. Cheyney* 1929 (d); *Wild Orchids* 1929 (d); *The Lady of Scandal* 1930 (d); *A Lady's Morals* 1930 (d); *The Guardsman* 1931 (d); *Private Lives* 1931 (d); *Smilin' Through* 1932 (d); *Reunion in Vienna* 1933 (d); *The Barretts of Wimpole Street* 1934 (d); *The Dark Angel* 1935 (d); *The Good Earth* 1937 (d) **(AANBD)**; *Marie Antoinette* 1938 (pre-prod.planning); *On Borrowed Time* 1939 (p); *The Women* 1939 (uncred.sc); *Waterloo Bridge* 1940 (p); *Mrs. Miniver* 1942 (p) **(AABP)**; *Random Harvest* 1942 (p); *Madame Curie* 1943 (p); *The White Cliffs of Dover* 1944 (p); *The Yearling* 1946 (p); *Command Decision* 1948 (p); *Homecoming* 1948 (p); *The Miniver Story* 1950 (p); *The Story of Three Loves* 1953 (p); *Young Bess* 1953 (p); *The Barretts of Wimpole Street* 1956 (d); *The Seventh Sin* 1957 (uncred.p).

Frears, Stephen • Director • Born Leicester, England, 1941. *Educ.* Cambridge (law). Armed with a keen visual awareness and compelling ability to tell a story, Stephen Frears has established himself as a leading director in the British cinema of the 1980s. After studying law at Cambridge, Frears became interested in the stage and joined London's Royal Court Theater. He did not become involved in film until 1966 when Karel Reisz offered an unemployed Frears a job as assistant director on *Morgan*. Frears continued working as an assistant director for Reisz, Lindsay Anderson and Albert Finney before he had the opportunity to direct his first feature. *Gumshoe* (1971) was a satire on American detective films with Finney as a romantic dreamer who envisions himself a private eye.

It was not until 1984 that Frears would work on another project intended specifically for theatrical release. During this interval, he worked continously in television, refining his craft while developing a reputation for workmanlike efforts and an ability to get along with both writers and actors. Frears returned to feature filmmaking with *The Hit* (1984), a taut, well-crafted thriller which, like *Gumshoe*, provided an interesting twist to the crime genre. Terence Stamp plays an informer living out his days in Spain, with John Hurt as a hard-boiled hit man hired to take him back to Paris to receive his come-uppance from the crime boss he had snitched on. This downbeat film regards its characters and their predicaments with a biting sense of humor, a quality which has marked all of Frears's films.

With *My Beautiful Launderette* (1985), shot in 16mm for only $900,000 for British television, Frears had his breakthrough picture. Working with writer Hanif Kureishi, Frears portrays the effects of racism and underemployment on working-class London through the eyes of a young Pakistani attempting to carve his own place in the world. The next Kureshi/Frears effort, *Sammy and Rosie Get Laid* (1987), dealt with these same themes in a multilayered look at the social relations revolving around a liberal, educated, mixed-race couple (Pakistani and upper-middle-class British) living in a poor section of London. Though the themes are not explored to their fullest, the rich visuals and good performances make this an entertaining film that exposes many of the inequities of British society.

Between these two efforts Frears adapted John Lahr's biography of playwright Joe Orton, who was brutally murdered at the height of his fame by his longtime lover and roommate Ken Halliwell. Rather than a standard biography, *Prick Up Your Ears* (1987) concentrates mainly on the relationship of these two men as a study of marriage gone tragically sour. In 1988 Frears fulfilled his longtime wish to work in the Hollywood system, a move he hoped would broaden his potential while providing greater financial rewards. *Dangerous Liaisons*, an adaptation of Christopher Hampton's play (which itself was based on Choderlos de Laclos's 18th-century novel), displayed the customary Frears trademarks: good performances and witty dialogue. But it was also his most glossy, stylized film, lacking the conviction and compellingness of his earlier efforts.

As if in response to this, Frears's next Hollywood outing, *The Grifters* (1990), retained the stylization (a timeless Southern California floating somewhere between the 1950s and the 1980s), but added the grittiness that had informed his British features. Adapted from the novel by Jim Thompson and starring John Cusack, Annette Bening, and Anjelica Huston, the film was critically acclaimed and confirmed Frears's bankable status in Hollywood. PP • *Morgan* 1966 (ad); *The Burning (short)* 1967 (d); *Charlie Bubbles* 1967 (ad); *If...* 1968 (asst to Lindsay Anderson); *Gumshoe* 1971 (d); *The Lifetaker* 1975 (ad); *Long Shot* 1978 (a); *Bloody Kids* 1979 (d); *Loving Walter* 1983 (d); *Saigon-Year of the Cat* 1983 (d); *The Hit* 1984 (d); *My Beautiful Laundrette* 1985 (d); *Mr. Jolly Lives Next Door* 1987 (d); *Prick Up Your Ears* 1987 (d); *Sammy and Rosie Get Laid* 1987 (d); *Dangerous Liaisons* 1988 (d); *The Grifters* 1990 (d).

Freed, Arthur • Producer; also lyricist. • Born Arthur Grossman, Charleston, SC, September 9, 1894; died 1973. Popular songwriter—notably in collaboration with Nacio Herb Brown—who joined MGM with the advent of sound and produced virtually every great Hollywood musical of the 1940s and 50s. Freed gathered around him such luminaries as Vincente Minnelli, Gene Kelly, Syd Charisse and Judy Garland, and produced classic films including the all-black *Cabin in the Sky* (1943), *Meet Me in St. Louis* (1944), *On The Town* (1949), *Singin' in the Rain* (1952) and *Silk Stockings* (1957). • *Around the World via Graf Zeppelin* 1929 (lyrics); *The Broadway Melody* 1929 (lyrics); *The Hollywood Revue of 1929* 1929 (lyrics); *Marianne* 1929 (lyrics); *The Pagan* 1929 (lyrics); *The Show of Shows* 1929 (lyrics"You Were Meant For Me"); *Good News* 1930 (lyrics "If You're Not Kissing Me," "Football"); *A Lady's Morals* 1930 (lyrics); *Lord Byron of Broadway* 1930 (lyrics); *Montana Moon* 1930 (lyrics); *Those Three French Girls* 1930 (story,lyrics); *Laughing Sinners* 1931 (lyrics); *Never the Twain Shall Meet* 1931 (lyrics); *The Big Broadcast* 1932 (lyrics); *Blondie of the Follies* 1932 (lyrics); *The Barbarian* 1933 (lyrics); *College Coach* 1933 (lyrics); *Dancing Lady* 1933 (lyrics); *Going Hollywood* 1933 (lyrics); *Hold Your Man* 1933 (lyrics); *Peg o' My Heart* 1933 (lyrics); *Stage Mother* 1933 (lyrics); *Hide-Out* 1934 (lyrics); *Hollywood Party* 1934 (lyrics); *Riptide* 1934 (lyrics); *Sadie McKee* 1934 (lyrics); *Sequoia* 1934 (lyrics); *Student Tour* 1934 (lyrics); *China Seas* 1935 (lyrics); *A Night at the Opera* 1935 (lyrics); *After the Thin Man* 1936 (lyrics); *Broadway Melody of 1936* 1936 (lyrics); *Devil Is a Sissy* 1936 (lyrics); *San Francisco* 1936 (lyrics); *Thoroughbreds Don't Cry* 1937 (lyrics); *Wells Fargo* 1937 (lyrics); *Broadway Melody of 1938* 1938 (lyrics); *Babes in Arms* 1939 (lyrics,p); *Honolulu* 1939 (lyrics); *Ice Follies* 1939 (lyrics); *The Wizard of Oz* 1939 (uncred.assoc.p); *Broadway Melody of 1940* 1940 (lyrics); *Little Nellie Kelly* 1940 (lyrics,p); *Strike Up the Band* 1940 (lyrics,p) **(AANBS)**; *Two Girls on Broadway* 1940 (lyrics); *Babes on Broadway* 1941 (p); *Lady Be Good* 1941 (lyrics,p); *Penny Serenade* 1941 (lyrics); *Born to Sing* 1942 (lyrics); *For Me and My Gal* 1942 (p); *Panama Hattie* 1942 (p); *Best Foot Forward* 1943 (p); *Cabin in the Sky* 1943 (p); *Du Barry Was a Lady* 1943 (p); *Girl Crazy* 1943 (p); *Hi, Beautiful!* 1944 (lyrics); *Meet Me in St. Louis* 1944 (lyrics,p; also dubbed Leon Ames's singing voice); *Night Club Girl* 1944 (lyrics); *The Clock* 1945 (a,lyrics,p); *The Southerner* 1945 (lyrics); *Yolanda and the Thief* 1945 (lyrics,p); *The Harvey Girls* 1946 (p); *Till the Clouds Roll By* 1946 (p); *Undercurrent* 1946 (lyrics); *Ziegfeld Follies* 1946 (lyrics,p); *Good News* 1947 (lyrics,p); *Easter Parade* 1948 (p); *The Pirate* 1948 (p); *Summer Holiday* 1948 (p); *Words and Music* 1948 (p); *You Were Meant For Me* 1948 (lyrics); *Any Number Can Play* 1949 (lyrics,p); *The Barkleys of Broadway* 1949 (p); *On the Town* 1949 (p); *Take Me Out to the Ball Game* 1949 (p); *Annie Get Your Gun* 1950 (p); *Crisis* 1950 (p); *Pagan Love Song* 1950 (lyrics,p); *An American in Paris* 1951 (p) **(AABP)**; *Royal Wedding* 1951 (lyrics,p); *Show Boat* 1951 (p); *The Belle of New York* 1952 (p); *Singin' in the Rain* 1952 (from lyrics,p); *The Affairs of Dobie Gillis* 1953 (lyrics); *The Band Wagon* 1953 (p); *Brigadoon* 1954 (p); *It's Always Fair Weather* 1955 (p); *Kismet* 1955 (p); *Love Me or Leave Me* 1955 (lyrics); *Invitation to the Dance* 1956 (p); *Silk Stockings* 1957 (p); *Gigi* 1958 (p) **(AABP)**; *Bells Are Ringing* 1960 (p); *The Subterraneans* 1960 (lyrics,p); *Light in the Piazza* 1962 (p); *Doctor, You've Got to Be Kidding* 1967 (lyrics).

Freeman, Morgan • Actor • Born Memphis, TN, June 1, 1937. *Educ.* Los Angeles Community College, CA; Pasadena Playhouse. First gained recognition as Easy Reader on the childrens' TV show "The Electric Company," subsequently distinguishing himself in a host of roles off and on Broadway. Freeman attracted critical acclaim playing volatile pimp Fast Black in *Street Smart* (1987) and with a reprisal of his off-Broadway role as a chauffeur in the South in *Driving Miss Daisy* (1989). • *Who Says I Can't Ride a Rainbow* 1971; *Brubaker* 1980; *Eyewitness* 1980; *Harry & Son* 1984; *Teachers* 1984; *Marie* 1985; *That Was Then...This Is Now* 1985; *Street Smart* 1987 **(AANBSA)**; *Clean and Sober* 1988; *Driving Miss Daisy* 1989 **(AANBA)**; *Glory* 1989; *Johnny Handsome* 1989; *Lean on Me* 1989; *Bonfire of the Vanities* 1990; *Robin Hood: Prince of Thieves* 1991.

Freleng, Friz • *aka* I. Freleng • Director, animator; also producer. • Born Isadore Freleng, Kansas City, MO, c. 1900. Directed some of Warner Bros.' greatest cartoons of the 1940s and 50s, featuring such memorable characters as

Bugs Bunny, Speedy Gonzales, Road Runner, Sylvester and Tweetie Pie. When Warner Bros. shut down their animation department in 1963, Freleng formed the highly successful DePatie-Freleng Enterprises with David H. DePatie and produced several animated TV series, most notably "The Pink Panther." He also designed the title sequences for some of the live-action "Panther" films starring Peter Sellers. • *Bugs Bunny and the Three Bears* 1944 (anim,d); *Rhapsody Rabbit* 1946 (anim,d); *Sam the Pirate* 1946 (anim,d); *Tweety Pie and Sylvester* 1947 (anim,d); *Bugs Bunny Rides Again* 1948 (anim,d); *Two Guys From Texas* 1948 (anim.sequences d); *My Dream Is Yours* 1949 (anim.sequences d); *Canary Row* 1951 (anim,d); *Dog Pounded* 1953 (anim,d); *Bugs and Thugs* 1954 (anim,d); *By Word of Mouse* 1954 (anim,d); *Captain Hareblower* 1954 (anim,d); *Pizzicato Pussycat* 1955 (anim,d); *Red Riding Hoodwinked* 1955 (anim,d); *Sandy Claws* 1955 (anim,d); *Speedy Gonzalez* 1955 (anim,d); *Tweety's Circus* 1955 (anim,d); *Rabbitson Crusoe* 1956 (anim,d); *Tugboat Granny* 1956 (anim,d); *Tweet and Sour* 1956 (anim,d); *Birds Anonymous* 1957 (anim,d); *Show Biz Bugs* 1957 (anim,d); *Knightly Knight Bugs* 1958 (anim,d); *A Pizza Tweety-Pie* 1958 (anim,d); *Pied Piper of Guadalupe* 1961 (anim,p) **(AANBASF)**; *Rebel Without Claws* 1961 (anim,d); *Philbert (short)* 1963 (story,anim.d); *The Pink Panther* 1964 (title design); *The Pink Phink* 1964 (anim,p) **(AABASF)**; *The Pink Blueprint* 1966 (anim,p) **(AANBASF)**; *Looney Looney Looney Bugs Bunny Movie* 1981 (d,p); *Uncensored Cartoons* 1981 (d); *Bugs Bunny's 3rd Movie: 1001 Rabbit Tales* 1982 (p); *Curse of the Pink Panther* 1983 (from characters); *Daffy Duck's Movie: Fantastic Island* 1983 (d,p,sc); *Porky Pig in Hollywood* 1986 (d); *Daffy Duck's Quackbusters* 1988 (sequences d).

Freund, Karl • Director of photography; also director. • Born Koeniginhof, Bohemia, January 16, 1890; died 1969. At the age of 15, Karl Freund began his long, illustrious career in motion pictures as a projectionist. Within two years, he had graduated to camera operator and received a variety of assignments, including newsreels and shorts. In the 1920s, Freund worked at the Ufa studios during what has become known as the Golden Age of German cinema. Collaborating with such film artists as Fritz Lang, F.W. Murnau, Paul Wegener and E.A. Dupont, Freund helped to create some of the most beautiful and highly regarded films of the silent era. In 1924, he worked on *The Last Laugh* with Murnau and screenwriter Carl Mayer. Mayer collaborated closely with Freund to write a script exploiting the potentials of a moving camera. The camera became an integral part of the narrative, interpreting and visualizing the central character's state of mind. To film one scene where the main character is intoxicated, Freund strapped the camera to his chest, batteries to his back for balance, and stumbled about like a drunken man.

In 1925, Freund worked on *Variety*, directed by E.A. Dupont. Once again, Freund's expressive camerawork drew a great deal of praise. Faced with numerous inquiries about the innovative camerawork, Dupont wrote an article for the *New York Times* explaining the "photographer's ingenuity" in making the film. In 1927, Freund worked with Walter Ruttman on *Berlin—The Symphony of a Great City*. To achieve greater flexibility in difficult shooting situations, Freund developed a special high-speed film stock. The entire documentary was reportedly shot without a single person spotting the camera.

In 1929, Freund came to the United States to work on an experimental color process for Technicolor. Shortly thereafter, he went to work for Universal Studios, shooting *Dracula* (1931) and *Murders in the Rue Morgue* (1932). While under contract at Universal, he directed several films, including *The Mummy* (1932). He went on to work at MGM and Warner Brothers, receiving an Academy Award for his cinematography for *The Good Earth* (1937). Freund's work in the United States, including such diverse films as *Key Largo* (1948) and *Pride and Prejudice* (1940), reflected his tremendous range and versatility.

In 1944, Freund founded the Photo Research Corporation in California. In the early 1950s, he went to work in the television industry. His TV work includes the "I Love Lucy" show, where he designed an innovative way to film the live program using three 35mm cameras simultaneously. In 1954, he was given a technical award by the Academy of Motion Pictures Arts and Sciences for the design and development of a direct-reading brightness meter. The following year, he represented the US at the International Conference on Illumination in Zurich. Freund devoted his last years to his Photo Research Corporation, where he continued to experiment with and develop new photographic techniques. DFD • *Engelein* 1913; *Die Filmprimadonna* 1913; *Eine Venezianische Nacht* 1914; *Abseits vom Gluck* 1916; *Frau Eva* 1916; *Geloste Ketten* 1916; *Die Ehe der Luise Rohrbach* 1917; *Gefangene Seele* 1917; *Hartungen Christa* 1917; *Die Prinzessin von Neutralien* 1917; *Das Geschlecht derer von Ringwall* 1918; *Die Arche* 1919; *Die Letzten Menschen* 1919; *Rausch* 1919; *Satanas* 1919; *Der Bucklige und die Tänzerin* 1920; *Der Golem, wie er in die Welt kam* 1920; *Der Januskopf* 1920; *Katharina die Grosse* 1920; *Die Spinnen/The Spiders* 1920 (ph "Das Brillantenschiff/The Diamond Ship"); *Der Verlorene Schatten* 1920; *Kinder der Finsternis 1: Der Mann aus Neapel* 1921; *Kinder der Finsternis 2: Kampfende Welten* 1921; *Louise de Lavallière* 1921; *Marizza, gennant die Schmugglermadonna* 1921; *Die Ratten* 1921; *Der Roman der Christine von Herre* 1921; *Der Schwur des Peter Hergatz* 1921; *Verlogene Moral* 1921; *Die Brennende Acker* 1922; *Herzog Ferrantes Ende* 1922; *Lucrezia Borgia* 1922; *Die Austreibung—die Macht der zweiten Frau* 1923; *Die Finanzen des Grossherzogs* 1923; *Der Letzte Mann/The Last Laugh* 1924; *Mikaël* 1924 (a,ph—interiors); *Tartuff* 1925; *Varieté/Variety* 1925; *Faust* 1926 (pre-prod.ph); *Madame Wunscht keine Kinder* 1926 (prod.sup); *Manon Lescaut* 1926; *Metropolis* 1926; *Die Abenteuer eines Zehnmarkscheinen* 1927 (prod.sup); *Berlin—Die Sinfonie einer Gross Stadt/Berlin—Symphony of a Great City* 1927; *Doña Juana* 1927; *Der Sohn der Hagar* 1927 (prod.sup); *A Knight in London* 1928; *Fraülein Else* 1929; *All Quiet on the Western Front* 1930 (ph—butterfly sequence); *The Boudoir Diplomat* 1930; *Bad Sister* 1931; *Dracula* 1931; *Personal Maid* 1931; *Strictly Dishonorable* 1931; *Up For Murder* 1931; *Afraid to Talk* 1932; *Air Mail* 1932; *Back Street* 1932; *The Mummy* 1932 (d); *Murders in the Rue Morgue* 1932; *Scandal For Sale* 1932; *The Kiss Before the Mirror* 1933; *Moonlight and Pretzels* 1933 (d); *The Countess of Monte Cristo* 1934 (d); *Gift of Gab* 1934 (d); *I Give My Love* 1934 (d); *Madame Spy* 1934 (d); *Uncertain Lady* 1934 (d); *Mad Love* 1935 (d); *The Great Ziegfeld* 1936 (ph—roof sequences); *Camille* 1937; *Conquest* 1937; *The Good Earth* 1937 **(AABPH)**; *Parnell* 1937; *Letter of Introduction* 1938; *Man-Proof* 1938; *Port of Seven Seas* 1938; *Three Comrades* 1938 (uncred.ph); *Balalaika* 1939; *Barricade* 1939; *Golden Boy* 1939; *Rose of Washington Square* 1939; *Tail Spin* 1939; *Comrade X* 1940 (uncred.ph); *The Earl of Chicago* 1940 (uncred.ph); *Florian* 1940; *Green Hell* 1940; *Keeping Company* 1940; *Pride and Prejudice* 1940; *We Who Are Young* 1940; *Blossoms in the Dust* 1941 **(AANBPH)**; *The Chocolate Soldier* 1941 **(AANBPH)**; *Tortilla Flat* 1942; *The War Against Mrs. Hadley* 1942; *A Yank at Eton* 1942; *The Cross of Lorraine* 1943 (uncred.ph); *Cry Havoc* 1943; *Du Barry Was a Lady* 1943; *A Guy Named Joe* 1943; *The Seventh Cross* 1944; *The Thin Man Goes Home* 1944; *Dangerous Partners* 1945; *Without Love* 1945; *A Letter For Evie* 1946; *Two Smart People* 1946; *Undercurrent* 1946; *That Hagen Girl* 1947; *This Time For Keeps* 1947; *The Decision of Christopher Blake* 1948; *Key Largo* 1948; *Wallflower* 1948; *South of St. Louis* 1949; *Bright Leaf* 1950; *Montana* 1950.

Friedkin, William • Director; also screenwriter, producer. • Born Chicago, IL, August 29, 1939. Began his career as a director with a local Chicago TV station, and had allegedly worked on over 2,000 shows before graduating to features in the late 1960s. Friedkin joined the front rank of American directors with three adroitly handled and very different films: the finely acted adaptation of Mart Crowley's play *The Boys in the Band* (1970); the hard hitting Academy Award-winner *The French Connection* (1971); and the trendsetting horror masterpiece *The Exorcist* (1973). He excels at action scenes, particularly the renowned car chases in *The French Connection* and *To Live and Die in L.A.* (1985). Friedkin married actress-director Jeanne Moreau in 1977. • *Good Times* 1967 (d); *The Birthday Party* 1968 (d); *The Night They Raided Minsky's* 1968 (d); *The Boys in the Band* 1970 (d); *The French Connection* 1971 (d) **(AABD)**; *The Exorcist* 1973 (d) **(AANBD)**; *Sorcerer* 1977 (d,p); *The Brink's Job* 1978 (d); *Cruising* 1980 (d,sc); *Deal of the Century* 1983 (d); *To Live and Die in L.A.* 1985 (d,sc); *Stalking Danger* 1986 (d,p); *Rampage* 1987 (d,sc); *The Guardian* 1990 (d,sc).

Friels, Colin • Actor • Born Australia. *Educ.* Australian Institute of Dramatic Arts. Handsome young leading man. Married to actress Judy Davis. • *Monkey Grip* 1981; *Buddies* 1983; *Prisoners* 1983; *The Coolangatta Gold* 1985; *For the Term of His Natural Life* 1985; *Kangaroo* 1986; *Malcolm* 1986; *High Tide* 1987; *Warm Nights on a Slow Moving Train* 1987; *Grievous Bodily Harm* 1988; *Ground Zero* 1988; *Darkman* 1990; *Weekend With Kate* 1990.

Fujimoto, Tak • Director of photography • *Educ.* London Film School. Began his career in 1969, working on commercials as an assistant to Haskell Wexler. • *Badlands* 1973; *Bootleggers* 1974; *Caged Heat* 1974; *Crazy Mama* 1975 (2u ph); *Death Race 2000* 1975; *Dr. Black, Mr. Hyde* 1975; *Cannonball* 1976; *Chatter Box* 1977; *Star Wars* 1977 (cam.op); *Remember My Name* 1978; *Stony Island* 1978; *Last Embrace* 1979; *The Watts Monster* 1979; *Borderline* 1980; *Melvin and Howard* 1980; *Where the Buffalo Roam* 1980; *Heart Like a Wheel* 1982; *National Lampoon Goes to the Movies* 1982 (ph—"Success Wanters," "Growing Yourself"); *Swing Shift* 1984; *Ferris Bueller's Day Off* 1986; *Pretty in Pink* 1986; *Something Wild* 1986; *Backfire* 1987; *Cocoon: The Return* 1988; *Married to the Mob* 1988; *Sweet Hearts Dance* 1988; *84 Charlie Mopic* 1989 (assistance); *Miami Blues* 1990; *The Silence of the Lambs* 1991.

Fuller, Samuel • Director, screenwriter, producer; also novelist, actor. • Born Samuel Michael Fuller, Worcester, MA, August 12, 1911. Sam Fuller has always been Hollywood's bad boy. A director with a wide streak of independence, strangely contradictory politics and a pugnacious visual style, he has often been described as a cinematic primitive. Fuller worked as a newspaperman and a crime reporter for many years before turning in the late 1930s to screenwriting. (Even after he began directing, Fuller continued to write most of his own scripts.) During WWII he enlisted in the army, serving with the First Infantry Division throughout the European theater, earning numerous decorations. Fuller's experiences in the newsroom and on the front lines would mold his film work.

Fuller's first film as a director was *I Shot Jesse James* (1949), a low-budget reworking of the James legend concentrating on Bob Ford, the bandit's murderer, and characterized by a startling use of closeups. However, the fundamentally dull cast and lack of action hinder the overall effect. The film did well enough to establish Fuller and was followed by another western, *The Baron of Arizona* (1950). His first war film, *The Steel Helmet* (1951), was rushed into production to capitalize on the outbreak of hostilities in Korea, and became his first box-office hit. It was succeeded by *Fixed Bayonets* (also 1951), another gritty Korean War film about a corporal forced to take command of a rear guard action as his superiors are killed off. *Park Row* (1952), a period newspaper story, was a successful blend of history, action, and romance.

Pickup on South Street (1953) remains Fuller's best film. Richard Widmark stars as a pickpocket who accidentally steals a roll of microfilm intended for communist agents. He soon finds himself caught between the FBI and the communists before finally shirking off his cynicism to help defeat the foreign agents. The film features numerous Fuller touches: a shrill anti-communist line, a protagonist who is a borderline psychopath, "film noir" sensibilities, bursts of graphic violence, unapologetic sentimentality, and fluid, almost athletic, camerawork. It also benefits from a more polished look than many of his previous, independently produced films.

Fuller's concern with identity, whether racial or national, is the underlying focus of many of his films. His sympathetic treatment of Indians in *Run of the Arrow*, the Eurasian heroine in *China Gate* (both 1957), and the Japanese-American cop in *The Crimson Kimono* (1959) seem at odds with his anti-communist, gung-ho American attitudes. Yet such treatments are fully in keeping with Fuller's respect for the myth of the great American melting pot. Such thematic concerns, however, are always secondary to Fuller's primary impulse as a storyteller with pulp sensibilities. This trait is best displayed in such primal melodramas as *Forty Guns* (1957), a horse opera in the truest sense of the term, with Barbara Stanwyck as a black-clad woman with a whip, and in the crime expose *Underworld U.S.A.* (1961).

Fuller's tabloid style was most evident in *Shock Corridor* (1963) and *The Naked Kiss* (1964). Revealing a darker take on American life, the former followed a self-serving reporter who has himself confined to an asylum to uncover a murder so he can win the Pulitzer Prize. The asylum is revealed as a microcosm of contemporary society, and the reporter is eventually sucked into its maelstrom, losing his mind. In *The Naked Kiss*, a reformed prostitute moves to a small town to take a job working with hospitalized children. She becomes engaged to one of the community's leading citizens, only to discover that he is a child molester. In both movies Fuller plays the cinematic bully, confronting us with unpleasant characters and situations—and yet both films are oddly compelling. Critics most often split on Fuller over these films, one camp hailing him as an unpolished genius, the other dubbing him a sensationalist hack.

With the exception of *The Big Red One* (1980), an episodic paean to his WWII squadron, Fuller's output since the mid-1960s has been uneven, sporadic, and in some cases virtually unreleased. During this period Fuller has taken cameo roles in several films, notably as an American film director in Paris in Jean-Luc Godard's *Pierrot le fou* (1965), a gangster in Wim Wenders's *The American Friend* (1977), and as an aged cinematographer in Wenders's *The State of Things* (1982). ES • *Hats Off* 1936 (sc,story); *It Happened in Hollywood* 1937 (sc); *Adventure in Sahara* 1938 (story); *Federal Man Hunt* 1938 (story); *Gangs of New York* 1938 (sc,story); *Bowery Boy* 1940 (story); *Confirm or Deny* 1941 (story); *Power of the Press* 1943 (story); *Gangs of the Waterfront* 1945 (story); *I Shot Jesse James* 1949 (d,sc); *Shockproof* 1949 (sc,story); *The Baron of Arizona* 1950 (d,sc,story); *Fixed Bayonets* 1951 (d,sc); *The Steel Helmet* 1951 (d,p,sc,story); *The Tanks Are Coming* 1951 (story); *Park Row* 1952 (d,p,sc); *Scandal Sheet* 1952 (from novel *The Dark Page*); *Pickup on South Street* 1953 (d,sc); *The Command* 1954 (adapt); *Hell and High Water* 1954 (d,sc); *House of Bamboo* 1955 (d,sc,dial,uncred.a); *Prince of Players* 1955 (uncred.sc); *China Gate* 1957 (d,p,sc); *Forty Guns* 1957 (d,p,sc); *Run of the Arrow* 1957 (d,p,sc); *The Story of Esther Costello* 1957 (uncred.sc); *The Crimson Kimono* 1959 (d,p,sc); *Verboten!* 1959 (d,p,sc); *Underworld, U.S.A.* 1961 (d,p,sc); *Merrill's Marauders* 1962 (d,sc); *Shock Corridor* 1963 (d,p,sc,story,ph—16mm); *The Naked Kiss* 1964 (d,p,sc,ph—16mm); *Brigitte et Brigitte* 1965 (a); *Pierrot le Fou* 1965 (a); *The Cape Town Affair* 1967 (from sc

Pickup on South Street); *Shark* 1969 (d,sc); *The Last Movie* 1971 (a); *Dead Pigeon on Beethoven Street* 1972 (a,d,sc); *The Deadly Trackers* 1973 (from story "Riata"); *The Young Nurses* 1973 (a); *The Klansman* 1974 (sc); *Der Amerikanische Freund/The American Friend* 1977 (a); *Scott Joplin* 1977 (a); *1941* 1979 (a); *Samuel Fuller & The Big Red One* 1979 (a); *The Big Red One* 1980 (d,sc); *Hammett* 1982 (a); *Der Stand der Dinge/The State of Things* 1982 (a); *White Dog* 1982 (a,d,sc); *El-Lanaa* 1984 (from film *Shock Corridor*); *Slapstick of Another Kind* 1984 (a); *Les Voleurs de la nuit* 1984 (a,d,sc); *Let's Get Harry* 1987 (story); *A Return to Salem's Lot* 1987 (a); *Falkenau, The Impossible* 1988 (a,sc); *Helsinki Napoli All Night Long* 1988 (a); *Sans espoir de retour* 1988 (a,d,sc,ed); *Scorpion (short)* 1989 (a); *Sons* 1989 (a); *Tell Me Sam* 1989 (a); *Hollywood Mavericks* 1990 (a).

Furie, Sidney J. • Director; also producer, screenwriter. • Born Toronto, Ontario, Canada, February 28, 1933. *Educ.* Carnegie Institute of Technology, Pittsburgh, PA (theater). Successful young director of the late 1950s and early 60s whose later work has never quite lived up to his early promise. Furie began his career in Canada and moved in 1960 to Great Britain, where he put his flashy camera style to good use in *The Young Ones* (1961) and *The Ipcress File* (1965), starring Michael Caine. Furie moved to the US in 1966. • *A Dangerous Age* 1957 (d,p,sc); *A Cool Sound From Hell* 1959 (d,p,sc); *Doctor Blood's Coffin* 1960 (d); *During One Night* 1960 (d,p,sc); *The Snake Woman* 1960 (d); *Three on a Spree* 1961 (d); *The Young Ones* 1961 (d); *The Boys* 1962 (d,p); *The Leather Boys* 1963 (d); *Wonderful Life* 1964 (d); *The Ipcress File* 1965 (d); *The Appaloosa* 1966 (d); *The Naked Runner* 1967 (d); *The Lawyer* 1968 (d,sc); *Little Fauss and Big Halsy* 1970 (d); *Lady Sings the Blues* 1972 (d); *Hit* 1973 (d); *Sheila Levine Is Dead and Living in New York* 1975 (d); *Gable and Lombard* 1976 (d); *The Boys in Company C* 1977 (d,sc); *The Entity* 1982 (d); *Purple Hearts* 1984 (d,p,sc); *Iron Eagle* 1986 (d,sc); *Superman IV: The Quest For Peace* 1987 (d); *Iron Eagle II* 1988 (d,sc,from characters); *The Taking of Beverly Hills* 1991 (d,story).

Furst, Anton • British production designer • *Educ.* Royal College of Art, London. Gained initial attention for his work on *The Company of Wolves* (1985), Neil Jordan's revisionist version of "Little Red Riding Hood," before designing Stanley Kubrick's Vietnam opus *Full Metal Jacket* (1987) and the baroque, comic-book Gotham City of *Batman* (1989). • *Lady Chatterley's Lover* 1981; *An Unsuitable Job For a Woman* 1981; *The Company of Wolves* 1985; *The Frog Prince* 1985; *Full Metal Jacket* 1987; *High Spirits* 1988; *Batman* 1989 (**AABAD**); *Awakenings* 1990.

Furthman, Jules • *aka* Stephen Fox • Screenwriter • Born Julius Grinnell Furthmann, Chicago, IL, March 5, 1888; died 1960. *Educ.* Northwestern University. Began selling stories in 1915 and writing screenplays two years later. Furthman produced outstanding work in virtually every genre and proved himself compatible with a wide range of directing styles. He wrote or co-wrote eight scripts for Josef Von Sternberg (including *Morocco* 1930 and *Shanghai Express* 1932) and five for Howard Hawks (including *Only Angels Have Wings* 1939 and *The Big Sleep* 1946). He directed three films in the early 1920s. Brother Charles Furthman (1884-1936) was also a screenwriter. • *The Frame-Up* 1917 (sc,story); *All the World to Nothing* 1918 (sc); *The Camouflage Kiss* 1918 (sc,story); *Hearts or Diamonds* 1918 (sc); *Hobbs in a Hurry* 1918 (sc); *A Japanese Nightingale* 1918 (sc); *The Mantle of Charity* 1918 (sc); *More Trouble* 1918 (sc); *When a Man Rides Alone* 1918 (sc,story); *Wives and Other Wives* 1918 (sc,story); *Brass Buttons* 1919 (sc,story); *The Lincoln Highwayman* 1919 (adapt); *Six Feet Four* 1919 (sc); *Some Liar* 1919 (sc); *A Sporting Chance* 1919 (story); *This Hero Stuff* 1919 (story); *Victory* 1919 (sc); *Where the West Begins* 1919 (sc,story); *The Big Punch* 1920 (sc,story); *The Great Redeemer* 1920 (adapt); *The Iron Rider* 1920 (sc); *Leave It to Me* 1920 (sc); *The Man Who Dared* 1920 (sc,story); *A Sister to Salome* 1920 (sc,story); *The Skywayman* 1920 (sc,story); *The Texan* 1920 (sc); *Treasure Island* 1920 (sc); *The Twins of Suffering Creek* 1920 (sc); *The Valley of Tomorrow* 1920 (story); *The White Circle* 1920 (sc); *Would You Forgive?* 1920 (sc,story); *The Blushing Bride* 1921 (d,sc,story); *The Cheater Reformed* 1921 (sc,story); *Colorado Pluck* 1921 (d,sc); *The Land of Jazz* 1921 (d,sc,adapt); *The Last Trail* 1921 (sc); *The Roof Tree* 1921 (sc); *Singing River* 1921 (sc); *Arabian Love* 1922 (sc,story); *A California Romance* 1922 (story); *Calvert's Valley* 1922 (sc); *The Love Gambler* 1922 (sc); *Pawn Ticket 210* 1922 (sc); *The Ragged Heiress* 1922 (sc,story); *Strange Idols* 1922 (sc); *The Yellow Stain* 1922 (sc,story); *The Acquittal* 1923 (sc,cont); *Condemned* 1923 (sc,story); *Lovebound* 1923 (sc); *North of Hudson Bay* 1923 (sc,story); *The Call of the Mate* 1924 (sc); *Try and Get It* 1924 (sc); *Any Woman* 1925 (sc); *Before Midnight* 1925 (sc,story); *Big Pal* 1925 (sc,story); *Sackcloth and Scarlet* 1925 (sc); *The Wise Guy* 1926 (story); *You'd Be Surprised* 1926 (sc,story); *Barbed Wire* 1927 (sc,adapt); *Casey at the Bat* 1927 (sc); *The City Gone Wild* 1927 (sc,story); *Fashions For Women* 1927 (adapt); *Hotel Imperial* 1927 (sc); *The Way of All Flesh* 1927 (sc); *The Docks of New York* 1928 (sc); *The Dragnet* 1928 (sc,adapt); *Abie's Irish Rose* 1929 (sc); *The Case of Lena Smith* 1929 (sc); *New York Nights* 1929 (sc); *Thunderbolt* 1929 (sc,story); *Common Clay* 1930 (sc); *Ladron de Amor* 1930 (from screenplay *The Love Gambler*); *Morocco* 1930 (sc); *Renegades* 1930 (sc); *Body and Soul* 1931 (sc); *Merely Mary Ann* 1931 (sc); *Over the Hill* 1931 (sc); *The Yellow Ticket* 1931 (sc); *Blonde Venus* 1932 (sc); *Shanghai Express* 1932 (sc); *The Blonde Bombshell* 1933 (sc); *The Girl in 419* 1933 (story); *China Seas* 1935 (sc); *Mutiny on the Bounty* 1935 (sc) (**AANBSC**); *Come and Get It* 1936 (sc); *The Good Earth* 1937 (uncred.sc); *Spawn of the North* 1938 (sc); *Only Angels Have Wings* 1939 (sc); *Northwest Passage* 1940 (uncred.sc); *The Way of All Flesh* 1940 (story); *Man Hunt* 1941 (uncred.adapt); *The Shanghai Gesture* 1941 (sc); *The Outlaw* 1943 (sc); *To Have and Have Not* 1944 (sc); *The Big Sleep* 1946 (sc); *Moss Rose* 1947 (sc); *Nightmare Alley* 1947 (sc); *Pretty Baby* 1950 (from story "Gay Deception"); *Peking Express* 1951 (adapt); *Jet Pilot* 1957 (p,sc); *Rio Bravo* 1959 (sc).

Fusco, Giovanni • Composer • Born Sant'Agata dei Goti, Italy, October 10, 1906; died 1968. *Educ.* Accademia di Santa Cecilia, Rome (piano, composition). Prolific composer whose sparsely orchestrated scores were particularly suited to Michelangelo Antonioni's studies in contemporary alienation. Fusco also scored Alain Resnais's *Hiroshima, mon amour* (1959) and *La Guerre est finie* (1966). • *Il Cammino degli eroi* 1936; *Joe il Rosso* 1936; *La Contessa di Parma* 1937; *Il Dottor Antonio* 1937; *Il Peccato di Rogelia Sanchez* 1939; *Pazza di gioia* 1940; *Due cuori sotto sequestro* 1941; *L'Uomo venuto dal mare* 1941; *Soltana un bacio* 1942 (song); *Il Sole di Montecassino* 1945); *Uno Tra la folla* 1946; *Follie per l'opera* 1947 (song); *Ti ritrovero* 1948; *Gente Cosi* 1949; *Cronaca di un Amore/Story of a Love Affair* 1950; *Il Tenente Craig, mio marito* 1950; *Ha fatto tredici!* 1951; *Il Mercante di Venezia* 1952; *I Vinti* 1952; *Canzoni a due voci* 1953; *I Misteri Della Giungla Nera* 1953; *La Signora Senza Camelie/Camille Without Camelias* 1953; *Traviata '53* 1953; *La Vergine del Roncador* 1953; *Avanzi di Galera* 1954; *Miseria e nobilta* 1954; *L'Orfana del ghetto* 1954; *Le Amiche/The Girlfriends* 1955; *I Quattro del getto tonante* 1955; *Sbandati, Glue* 1955; *Il Grido/The Outcry* 1957; *Avventure nell'arcipelago* 1958; *L'Avventura* 1959; *I Cosacchi* 1959; *Un Eroe del nostro tempo* 1959; *Hiroshima, mon amour* 1959; *I Delfini* 1960; *La Donna dei Faraoni* 1960; *Il Rosetto/Lipstick* 1960; *Climats* 1961; *Mann Nennt Es Amore* 1961; *L'Oro di Roma* 1961; *Col Ferro e col Fuoco* 1962; *Dulcinea* 1962; *L'Eclisse/The Eclipse* 1962; *La Leggenda di Enea* 1962; *Il Mare* 1962;

La Monaca di Monza 1962; *Rocambole* 1962; *Lo Sceicco rosso* 1962; *Violenza Segreta* 1962; *La Corruzione* 1963; *I Fuorilegge del matrimonio* 1963; *Gli Indifferenti* 1963; *Milano Nera* 1963; *Sandokan, la tigre di Mompracem* 1963; *Storie sulla sabbia* 1963; *Deserto Rosso/Red Desert* 1964; *I Pirati della malesia* 1964; *Tre Notti d'Amore* 1964; *I Tre sergenti del Bengala* 1965; *La Guerre est finie* 1966; *Il Nostro agente a Casablanca* 1966; *Amore e rabbia* 1967; *Domani non siamo più qui* 1967; *Encrucijada para una monja* 1967; *Sovversivi* 1967; *Giarrettiera Colt* 1968; *Il Giorno della Civetta* 1968; *La Morte non ha sesso* 1968; *Il Sesso degli angeli* 1968; *La Battaglia del Sinai* 1969.

Gabin, Jean • Actor • Born Jean-Alexis Gabin Moncorgé, Paris, May 17, 1904; died 1976. Commanding French star who began his career with the Folies Bergère in the 1920s and made his screen debut in *Chacun sa chance* (1930). By the end of the decade Gabin was France's leading screen idol, thanks to films like *Maria Chapdelaine* (1934), *Pépé le Moko* (1936), *La Grande Illusion* (1937), *La Bête Humaine* (1938) and *Daybreak* (1939). His heroic, working-class persona made him the perfect foil for sundry femmes fatales including Simone Simon and Mireille Balin.

After spending WWII in Hollywood, Gabin restored his popularity in France, appearing in films through the 1970s and forming the Gafer production company with fellow actor Fernandel. Married to actress Gaby Basset from 1925 to 1933. • *Chacun sa chance* 1930 (a); *Méphisto* 1930 (a); *Coeur de Lilas* 1931 (a); *Coeur joyeux* 1931 (a); *Gloria* 1931 (a); *Paris-Beguin* 1931 (a); *Pour un soir* 1931 (a); *Tout ça ne vaut pas l'amour* 1931 (a); *La Belle Marinière* 1932 (a); *The Crowd Roars* 1932 (a); *Les Gaietés de l'Escadron* 1932 (a); *Du Haut en bas* 1933 (a); *Die Schönen Tagen von Aranjuez* 1933 (a); *L'étoile de Valencia* 1933 (a); *Der Tunnel* 1933 (a); *La Bandera* 1934 (a); *Maria Chapdelaine* 1934 (a); *Zouzou* 1934 (a); *Golgotha* 1935 (a); *Variétés* 1935 (a); *Les Bas-Fonds/The Lower Depths* 1936 (a); *La Belle Equipe* 1936 (a); *Pépé Le Moko* 1936 (a); *La Grande Illusion/Grand Illusion* 1937 (a); *Gueule d'amour* 1937 (a); *Le Messager* 1937 (a); *La Bête Humaine* 1938 (a); *Le Quai des Brumes/Port of Shadows* 1938 (a); *Le Jour Se Lève/Daybreak* 1939 (a); *Le Recif de corail* 1939 (a); *Remorques/Stormy Waters* 1941 (a); *Moontide* 1942 (a); *The Impostor* 1944 (a); *Martin Roumagnac* 1946 (a); *Miroir* 1947 (a); *La Mura di Malapaga/The Walls of Malapaga* 1949 (a); *E Più facile che un cammello* 1950 (a); *La Marie du Port* 1950 (a); *La Nuit est mon royaume* 1951 (a); *Le Plaisir* 1951 (a); *Vérité sur Bébé Donge* 1951 (a); *Victor* 1951 (a); *Bufére* 1952 (a); *La Minute de Vérité* 1952 (a); *Leur dernière nuit* 1953 (a); *Touchez Pas au Grisbi* 1953 (a); *La Vièrge du Rhin* 1953 (a); *L'Air de Paris* 1954 (a); *French Can-Can* 1954 (a); *Napoléon* 1954 (a); *Le Port de Désir* 1954 (a); *Razzia* 1954 (a); *Chiens perdus sans Collier* 1955 (a); *Des gens sans importance* 1955 (a); *Gas-Oil* 1955 (a); *Le Sang à la tête* 1955 (a); *Voici le temps des assassins* 1955 (a); *Le Cas du Dr. Laurent* 1956 (a); *Crime et Châtiment/Crime and Punishment* 1956 (a); *La Traversée de Paris* 1956 (a); *Maigret Tend un Piège* 1957 (a); *Les Misérables* 1957 (a); *Le Rouge est mis* 1957 (a); *Désordre et la nuit* 1958 (a); *En cas de malheur* 1958 (a); *Les Grandes Familles* 1958 (a); *Archiméde le Clochard* 1959 (a,idea); *Maigret et l'Affaire Saint-Fiacre* 1959 (a); *Rue des Prairies* 1959 (a); *Les Vieux de la vieille* 1959 (a); *Le Baron de l'Ecluse* 1960 (a); *Le Cave se rebiffe* 1961 (a); *Le Président* 1961 (a); *Le Gentleman d'Epsom* 1962 (a); *Mélodie en sous-sol* 1962 (a); *Un Singe en hiver* 1962 (a); *Maigret voit Rouge* 1963 (a); *L'Age Ingrat* 1964 (a); *Monsieur* 1964 (a); *Le Tonnerre de Dieu* 1965 (a); *Du Rififi à Paname* 1966 (a); *Jardinier d'Argenteuil* 1966 (a); *Le Soleil des voyous* 1967 (a); *La Pacha* 1968 (a); *Le Tatoue* 1968 (a); *Le Clan des Siciliens/The Sicilian Clan* 1969 (a); *Sous le signe du taureau* 1969 (a); *La Horse* 1970 (a); *Le Chat* 1971 (a); *Le Drapeau Noir Flotte Sur La Marmite* 1971 (a); *Le Tueur* 1971 (a); *L'Affaire Dominici* 1972 (a); *Deux hommes dans la ville* 1973 (a); *Le Testament/The Verdict* 1974 (a); *L'Année Sainte* 1976 (a).

Gable, Clark • Actor • Born William Clark Gable, Cadiz, OH, February 1, 1901; died November 16, 1960. The former blue-collar worker from Ohio became the "King of Hollywood," a title based on his being the leading male box office attraction throughout the 1930s. The dashing, mustachioed image of Rhett Butler in *Gone with the Wind* (1939) remains indelibly associated with the name Clark Gable, but before his "I don't give a damn" made screen history Gable (with the aid of his MGM publicist Howard Strickland) had already established a distinctive screen persona as the virile, lovable rogue whose gruff facade only thinly masked a natural charm and goodness.

Following his marriage to actress Josephine Dillon, Gable played bit parts in several silent Hollywood features (e.g., *The Merry Widow*, 1925) but he first achieved fame as a leading man on Broadway in the late 20s. With the flourishing of sound films, Gable joined the new generation of movie actors who made the move from New York to Hollywood in the early 30s. On the advice of director/actor Lionel Barrymore MGM granted him a screen test and, after a talkie debut in a Pathé western (*The Painted Desert* 1931), Gable signed a contract with the prestigious Metro studio, where he remained until 1954. In his first year alone, Gable appeared in a dozen features, quickly rising from supporting player to romantic lead. He was teamed with all of MGM's leading ladies, most notably opposite Norma Shearer in *A Free Soul* (1931), Greta Garbo in *Susan Lenox, Her Fall and Rise* (1931) and Joan Crawford in *The Possessed* (1931)—though he proved equally adept in male-oriented action sagas (*The Secret Six*, *Sporting Blood*, *Hell Divers*, all 1931).

Despite his rising popularity, Gable balked at having to play gangsters and overly callous characters. In a now legendary act of studio disciplining, Louis B. Mayer "punished" Gable by loaning him out to lowly Columbia for a role in a minor romantic comedy. The project, Frank Capra's *It Happened One Night* (1934), unexpectedly became the first film to sweep the five major Oscars (for best actor, actress, director, writer, and picture) and vaulted Gable to new prominence in the industry. His sensational appearance *sans* undershirt in the film's bedroom scene went down in Hollywood legend as the event that caused American males to make fewer trips to the haberdasher. While its effect on undershirt purchases may be purely apochryphal, the publicity from the event no doubt led to Gable's next major role, that of the bare-chested Fletcher Christian in MGM's *Mutiny on the Bounty* (1935), another Oscar-winner for Best Picture.

With such success under his belt, Gable commanded even greater star treatment at Metro and began appearing in fewer films each year, although his range of genre vehicle expanded. He continued his string of romantic comedies with Jean Harlow (*Red Dust* 1932, *Hold Your Man* 1933, *China Seas* 1935, *Wife vs. Secretary* 1936, and *Saratoga* 1937), but also made off-beat musical appearances (*San Francisco*, *Cain and Mabel*, both 1936; *Idiot's Delight* 1939, in which he sang "Puttin' on the Ritz"), action dramas (*The Call of the Wild* 1935, *Test Pilot* 1938) and romances (*Love on the Run* 1936). With MGM even promoting his image in its other feature films (Judy Garland singing "Dear Mr. Gable—You

Made Me Love You" in *Broadway Melody of 1938* and Mickey Rooney doing Gable impressions in *Babes in Arms* 1939) Clark Gable remained King of the Hollywood box office throughout the decade, culminating in his highly publicized and memorable performance in *Gone With the Wind*. Only his ill-conceived biopic *Parnell* (1937) interrupted a string of popular successes.

Gable's reign at the top of Hollywood stardom in 1939 was enhanced by his storybook romance and marriage to actress Carole Lombard. Her untimely death in a plane crash in January 1942 marked a tragic downturn in Gable's life. He turned his back on his film career and enlisted in the Army Air Corps. After two years of decorated combat service, Gable returned to the screen in 1945 with his macho hero's image only further amplified. But despite much studio publicity for his return in *Adventure* ("Gable's Back and Garson's Got Him") and some box office success, Gable's post-war film career consisted mostly of routine, undistinguished vehicles. He consistently starred in one film a year, but never regained his status of 30s. Still, there were no pretenders to the throne. When MGM remade *Red Dust* in 1953 as *Mogambo*, Ava Gardner was in for Harlow, Grace Kelly played the Mary Astor role, and Gable's part? Only Gable could fill Gable's shoes, even twenty-one years later.

After a short-lived marriage (Lady Sylvia Ashley) and an unsuccessful attempt at independent production in the 1950s, Gable proved himself the King one last time, romancing the fragile Marilyn Monroe in John Huston's *The Misfits* (1961). His performance was greatly praised, but Gable had insisted on performing his own stunts, including breaking a horse. Doctors had warned him about an already weakened heart and the exertion proved too much (this would be Monroe's last completed film as well). He widowed his fifth wife, the former Kay Spreckles, in 1960, shortly before she gave birth to John Clark Gable, the son Gable had always longed for. DGS • *Forbidden Paradise* 1924; *White Man* 1924; *Déclassée* 1925; *The Merry Widow* 1925; *North Star* 1925; *The Plastic Age* 1925; *The Johnstown Flood* 1926; *Dance, Fools, Dance* 1931; *The Easiest Way* 1931; *The Finger Points* 1931; *A Free Soul* 1931; *Hell Divers* 1931; *Laughing Sinners* 1931; *Night Nurse* 1931; *The Painted Desert* 1931; *The Possessed* 1931; *The Secret Six* 1931; *Sporting Blood* 1931; *Susan Lenox, Her Fall and Rise* 1931; *Polly of the Circus* 1932; *Red Dust* 1932; *Strange Interlude* 1932; *Dancing Lady* 1933; *Hold Your Man* 1933; *Night Flight* 1933; *No Man of Her Own* 1933; *The White Sister* 1933; *Chained* 1934; *Forsaking All Others* 1934; *It Happened One Night* 1934 **(AABA)**; *Manhattan Melodrama* 1934; *Men in White* 1934; *After Office Hours* 1935; *The Call of the Wild* 1935; *China Seas* 1935; *Mutiny on the Bounty* 1935 **(AANBA)**; *Cain and Mabel* 1936; *Love on the Run* 1936; *San Francisco* 1936; *Wife vs. Secretary* 1936; *Parnell* 1937; *Saratoga* 1937; *Test Pilot* 1938; *Too Hot to Handle* 1938; *Gone With the Wind* 1939 **(AANBA)**; *Idiot's Delight* 1939; *Boom Town* 1940; *Comrade X* 1940; *Strange Cargo* 1940; *Honky Tonk* 1941; *They Met in Bombay* 1941; *Somewhere I'll Find You* 1942; *Adventure* 1945; *The Hucksters* 1947; *Command Decision* 1948; *Homecoming* 1948; *Any Number Can Play* 1949; *Key to the City* 1950; *To Please a Lady* 1950; *Across the Wide Missouri* 1951; *Callaway Went Thataway* 1951; *Lone Star* 1952; *Mogambo* 1953; *Never Let Me Go* 1953; *Betrayed* 1954; *Soldier of Fortune* 1955; *The Tall Men* 1955; *The King and Four Queens* 1956; *Band of Angels* 1957; *Run Silent, Run Deep* 1958; *Teacher's Pet* 1958; *But Not For Me* 1959; *It Started in Naples* 1960; *The Misfits* 1961; *Going Hollywood: The War Years* 1988 (archival footage).

Gábor, Pál • Director • Born Budapest, Hungary, 1932; died October 21, 1987, Rome. *Educ.* University of Budapest; Academy for Theater and Film Art, Budapest. Directed his first feature film in 1968 and gained the attention of international audiences ten years later with *Angi Vera*, the award-winning story of a naive nursing aide who becomes an adept student of Stalinist politics. • *Tiltott Terulet* 1968 (d); *Horizont* 1971 (d,sc); *Utazas Jakabbal* 1973 (d,sc); *Jarvany* 1975 (d,sc); *Angi Vera* 1978 (d,sc); *Kettevalt Mennyezet* 1982 (d); *The Long Ride* 1984 (d,story); *La Sposa Era Bellissima* 1987 (d,sc).

Gambon, Michael • Actor • Born Dublin, Ireland, October 19, 1940. Accomplished leading man who gave an excellent performance as *The Singing Detective* in Dennis Potter's highly acclaimed 1986 British TV drama (released theatrically in the US in 1988). Also memorable as the boorish central character of Peter Greenaway's controversial—and highly successful—*The Cook, the Thief, His Wife and Her Lover* (1989). • *The Beast Must Die* 1974; *Turtle Diary* 1985; *The Singing Detective* 1988; *Paris By Night* 1988; *The Cook, the Thief, His Wife and Her Lover* 1989; *A Dry White Season* 1989; *Missing Link* 1989; *The Rachel Papers* 1989.

Gance, Abel • Director; also screenwriter, playwright, actor. • Born Abel Perethon, Paris, October 25, 1889; died November 10, 1981, Paris. Abel Gance is universally recognized as one of the greatest directors in history. Often compared with Erich von Stroheim for his talent, extravagence, imagination and ego, his experiments in camera movement, editing, and cinematography exceeded anything being done by his contemporaries and redefined the parameters of film discourse. But he often provoked animosity promoting his own genius and aggravated producers by running over budget on ever-expanding projects. Finally, like von Stroheim, the advent of sound prevented Gance from realizing his ambitions.

Initially drawn to the theater, Gance began writing scripts purely to support himself. According to historian Keven Brownlow, Gance had little regard for film at this time: "I thought they were infantile and stupid... of no artistic value." In 1910 he contracted tuberculosis but managed to overcome it, returning to Paris in good health but also in poverty. In 1911 he directed his first film, *La Digue* and founded a production company, Le Film Francais, going bankrupt after only four films. In 1914, he submitted his play *La Victoire de Samothrace* to Sarah Bernhardt. She would have appeared in it but the war broke out, closing theaters and ending Gance's theatrical career.

The war over, Gance quickly emerged as the most promising young director in France. After writing and directing several routine scripts, Gance made in 1915 the short, *La Folie du Dr. Tube* (the earliest existing work of Gance's) whose numerous optical effects—including shooting through distorting mirrors to suggest mental confusion—made the producer reluctant to release it. Between 1916 and 1919 he made a dozen films including *Les Gaz mortels* and *Barberouse* (both 1916), but it was *Mater Dolorosa* (1917) which first brought him commercial success. Despite a routine plot involving a love triangle, Gance's direction—which again emphasized the central characters' mental states—attracted much attention. Pretentious but successful, *La Dixième Symphonie* (1918) recounted the life of a suffering, misunderstood composer. And then came *J'accuse!* (1918), a film for which Gance received international acclaim. Intended as a recruiting film, *J'accuse!* was made with the cooperaton of the French army. When the war ended before its completion, Gance transformed it into an anti-war drama which was released shortly after the Armistice. In its most celebrated sequence, thousands of dead soldiers rise from the battlefield and march through the countryside to see if their sacrifice was warranted.

These last two films established Gance as the leading French director of his day. His next two features suggest he may have been the greatest director in Europe. *La Roue*'s (1922) story concerns a railroad engineer named Sisif (combining Sisyphus, Oedipus and Lear), the incestuous passion he shared with his son for his adopted daughter, and his desperate attempts to repress that passion. Like Gance's previous work, *La Roue* was unabashedly melodramatic and pompous, the title referring to train wheels, the wheel of fortune and a Victor Hugo quote which preceded the story. But the level of technical daring was so breathtaking that Jean Epstein called *La Roue* "the formidable cinematic monument in whose shadow all French cinematic art lives and believes." Gance spent six months on the script and an entire year shooting on location. Then came tragedy: Gance's wife died of tuberculosis the day he finished shooting. He mourned in the US where he met D.W. Griffith at the New York premiere of *J'accuse!*. Griffith was so impressed he invited Gance to his studio. As a result of this encounter, Gance spent an additional year reediting *La Roue.* Filled with contradictions, it also contains sensational climaxes and truly lyrical moments. Among the innovations: rhetorical figuring; dramatic lighting effects; sophisticated editing used for inserts, flashbacks, and parallel action; and dazzling rhythmic montage so extraordinary that when Russian directors Eisenstein and Pudovkin visited France they thanked Gance for having taught them editing.

After directing his friend Max Linder in a short, *Au secours!* (1923), Gance undertook his most ambitious project. *Napoléon vu par Abel Gance* (1927) is a landmark film, as ambitious and daring as the man it portrays. Gance initially conceived a six-part epic presenting all major events of Bonaparte's life filmed at their original locations. The final film (originally six hours) amounts to only the first section, focusing on Napoléon's early years. Curiously, Gance juxtaposed explicit historical references to fictitious characters and events; the overall impression is that Napoléon was the fulfillment of the French Revolution. Nevertheless, a superb cast including Albert Dieudonné (Napoléon), Antonin Artaud (Marat), Peirre Batcheff (Hoche) and Gance (Saint-Just) delivered magisterial performances and there are numerous extraordinary moments, among them: the snowball fight at Brienne College; the introduction of the *Marsaillaise*; the twin storms—Napoléon sailing back to France intercut with the "political storm" at the Convention; the triumphant entry of his army into Italy. This final sequence demonstrates a revolutionary technique, Gance's own Polyvision—the screen converts into a triptych, sometimes revealing one widescreen image, at other times juxtaposing three separate images. Yet this is only the most notable of a whole series of spectacular technical achievements: the use of rapid montage, lighting effects, masking, tinting, superimpositions, handheld camerawork, cameras mounted to anything moving (horses, a pendulum, a toboggan, cameramen). In short, Gance experimented with virtually every aspect of the medium. Hailed as a true masterpiece, *Napoléon* disappeared from circulation within a year of its release, in part because the French film industry was unwilling to support the necessary special screening facilities.

In 1930 Gance made *La Fin du monde* about a comet hurtling toward the earth. Conceived as a silent film to showcase Polyvision, it was instead post-synchronized, taken out of Gance's hands and ruined. Its disastrous reception shattered Gance's career. The freedom Gance enjoyed during the 1920s, when the disorganized state of film production allowed certain individuals to develop projects in relatively unrestricted conditions, was over. Studios tightened production control to offset the cost of sound technology and generally shifted to smaller, more politically engaged projects. Gance's grandiose melodramas were no longer possible and he was obliged to make uninspired commercial productions. He remained active, alternating between sound remakes of his own works (*Mater Dolorosa* 1932, *Napoléon Bonaparte* 1934, *J'accuse!* 1937) and adaptations of popular plays and novels (*La Dame aux Camélias* 1934; *Roman d'un jeune homme pauvre* 1935). In the mid-30s Gance again focused on romantic heros in *Lucréce Borgia* (1935) and *Un grand amour de Beethoven* (1936). Then came the embarrassing *Vénus aveugle* (1940), followed by the more tolerable *Capitaine Fracasse* (1942). But when he left France for Spain in 1943 to escape the Nazis, his career abruptly ended. Twelve years passed before his next completed feature, *La Tour de Nèsle* (1954). Though unremarkable, its release renewed interest in Gance's work, notably from then-critic François Truffaut. *Austerlitz* (1960) and *Cyrano et d'Artagnon* (1963), his last two films, were enjoyable if uninspired historical dramas. Gance spent much of his later years reworking *Napoléon* and unsuccessfully promoting a project on Christopher Columbus.

For years Gance has been undervalued because he focused his attention on style rather than narrative, because of his predilection for melodramas, and because of the deplorable state of available prints. His work is often pretentious, lacks rigor and represents the antithesis of narrative modernity. But thanks in large part to Brownlow (along with Francis Coppola and others), *Napoléon* and Gance's reputation have been restored to their proper places in film history. Having taken film further technologically and esthetically than any of his contemporaries, Gance has finally been recognized as the major figure in French film of the 1920s. RDH. • *La Digue* (short) 1911 (d,sc,p); *Drame au château d'Acre ou les Morts reviennent-ils?* (short) 1915 (d,sc); *La Folie du Dr. Tube* (short) 1915 (d,sc); *Barbe-Rousse* 1916 (d,sc); *Ce que les flots racontent* 1916 (d,sc); *L'Enigme de 10 heures* 1916 (d,sc); *La Femme inconnue* 1916 (d,sc); *Fioritures* 1916 (d,sc); *La Fleur des Ruines* 1916 (d,sc); *Le Fou de la falaise* 1916 (d,sc); *Les Gaz Mortels* 1916 (d,sc); *L'Héroisme de Paddy* 1916 (d,sc); *Le Périscope* 1916 (d,sc); *Strass et Cie* 1916 (d,sc); *Le Droit à la vie* 1917 (d,sc); *Mater Dolorosa* 1917 (d,sc); *La Zone de la mort* 1917 (d,sc); *La Dixième symphonie* 1918 (d,sc,ed); *Ecce Homo* 1918 (d,sc); *J'Accuse* 1918 (d,sc,ed); *La Roue* 1922 (d,sc,ed); *Au secours!* (short) 1923 (d,p,sc); *Napoléon* 1927 (a,d,sc,dial,ed); *Napoléon auf St. Helena* 1929 (sc); *La Fin du monde* 1930 (a,adapt,d); *Mater Dolorosa* 1932 (d,sc,dial); *Le Maître de forges* 1933 (sc,prod.sup); *La Dame aux camélies* 1934 (sc); *Napoléon Bonaparte* 1934 (a,d,sc,dial,ed); *Poliche* 1934 (d); *Jérôme Perreau, héros des barricades* 1935 (d); *Lucréce Borgia* 1935 (d); *Le Roman d'un jeune homme pauvre* 1935 (d); *Un Grand amour de Beethoven* 1936 (d,sc,ed); *Ladro di donne* 1936 (d); *J'Accuse* 1937 (d,sc,adapt); *Louise* 1938 (d); *Le Paradis perdu* 1938 (d); *Christophe Colomb* 1939 (d); *La Vénus aveugle* 1940 (d,sc,adapt); *Le Capitaine Fracasse* 1942 (d,sc,adapt,dial); *Manolete* 1944 (d); *Lumière et l'invention du cinématographe* 1953 (a,commentary); *La Reine Margot* 1954 (sc); *La Tour de Nèsle* 1954 (d,sc,dial); *La Roue* 1956 (from sc); *Austerlitz* 1960 (d,sc,dial); *Cyrano et d'Artagnan* 1963 (d,sc,dial,ed).

Ganz, Bruno • Actor • Born Zurich, Switzerland, 1941. Engaging performer who helped found Berlin's experimental theater company Schaubühne with director Peter Stein in 1970. Ganz's screen acting career began with Eric Rohmer's *The Marquise of O...* (1976) and has continued through films by some of Europe's best directors, including Wim Wenders, Claude Goretta and Alain Tanner. Best known as Damiel, the angel longing to be human, in Wenders's *Wings of Desire* (1987). • *Rece Do Gory* 1967 (a); *Lumière* 1975 (a); *Sommergaeste* 1975 (a); *La Marquise d'O.../The Marquise of O...* 1976 (a); *Die Wildente* 1976 (a); *Der Amerikanische Freund/The American Friend* 1977 (a); *Die Linkshändige Frau/The Left-Handed Woman* 1977 (a); *The Boys From Brazil* 1978 (a); *Messer im Kopf/Knife in the Head* 1978 (a); *Nosferatu, Phantom der Nacht* 1978 (a); *Schwarz und Weiss Wie Tage und Nächte* 1978 (a); *Retour à la Bien-Aimée* 1979 (a); *5% de Risque* 1980 (a); *Der Erfinder* 1980 (a); *Oggetti Smarriti* 1980 (a); *Polenta* 1980 (a); *La Provinciale/A Girl From Lorraine* 1980 (a); *Die Falschung/Circle of Deceit* 1981 (a); *Vera Storia Della Signora Delle Camelie* 1981 (a); *Dans la ville blanche/In the White City* 1982 (a); *Gedächtnis* 1982 (d); *Killer Aus Florida* 1983 (a); *System Ohne Schatten* 1983 (a); *De Ijssalon* 1985 (a); *Der Pendler* 1986 (a); *El Río de Oro* 1986 (a); *Der Himmel über Berlin/Wings of Desire* 1987 (a); *Bankomatt* 1989 (a); *Noch ein Wunsch* 1989 (a); *Strapless* 1989 (a).

Garbo, Greta • Actress • Born Greta Lovisa Gustafsson, Stockholm, Sweden, September 18, 1905; died April 15, 1990, New York, NY. *Educ.* Royal Dramatic Theater School, Stockholm. Greta Garbo is arguably the quintessential embodiment of the Hollywood star system. Her glamourous, Sphinx-like image—carefully cultivated by her employer, Metro-Goldwyn-Mayer—captivated American and European viewers of both the silent screen of the 20s and sound films of the 30s. Garbo's personal decision to leave her film career in 1941 and maintain a notoriously private, reclusive lifestyle has only further enhanced her mystique.

As a young model, she made her first screen appearances in Swedish advertising films and as an extra in features as early as 1921. While attending the Royal Dramatic Theater School, she was chosen by noted film director Mauritz Stiller to play the lead in *The Atonement of Gösta Berling* (1924) and he renamed his protégée "Garbo." After she gained further acclaim co-starring with the legendary tragedienne Asta Nielsen in G.W. Pabst's *The Joyless Street* (1925), she followed Stiller to Hollywood (and MGM) in 1925.

Metro was primarily interested in the services of Stiller, but at his request they gave Garbo a modest featured player's contract. She first appeared in two Latin love stories drawn from Blasco-Ibáñez novels. As a Spanish peasant girl in *The Torrent* (1926) and a vamp in *The Temptress* (1926), Garbo received favorable reviews, but she seemed indistinguishable from any number of other Hollywood actresses of the time. However, her breakthrough came when MGM paired her with the silent screen's most popular leading man, John Gilbert, in the unrestrained romance *Flesh and the Devil* (1927). By all accounts, the two developed an instant and intense romantic rapport that carried over on-screen and encouraged the publicity and gossip about her off-screen life that has followed Garbo ever since. Following the success of *Flesh and the Devil*, Garbo demanded a raise in her salary, from $600 to $5,000 per week. MGM at first refused her terms, so she sailed to Sweden and remained there for nearly a year until the studio's executives arrived with a new contract. Her indifference to stardom served only to fuel her legend even more.

Upon returning to Hollywood, Garbo was given the ultimate star treatment. She worked only with leading directors, most notably Clarence Brown (seven times), but also Sidney Franklin, fellow Swede Victor Sjöström, Jacques Feyder, Edmund Goulding, George Cukor and Rouben Mamoulian. More important, MGM captured the expressive, enigmatic nuances of her now-famous face by employing her favorite (and the studio's best) cinematographer, William Daniels, on almost all of her films. While conceding to working conditions dictated by the star (including closed sets and no overtime), Metro fashioned Garbo's public image until it was the epitome of the studio's glamorous excess.

It was during this time that Garbo developed the repertoire of roles that defined her as an actress. Although MGM avoided ruthless typecasting, the parts developed for its leading female star almost invariably presented her in period costume as a melancholy exotic who sacrifices her happiness for an unattainable love. She returned to the screen as the tragic Anna Karenina (again opposite John Gilbert), in *Love* (1927) a role she would reprise for Clarence Brown in 1935. In her six remaining silent features Garbo co-starred with Gilbert once (*A Woman of Affairs* 1928), but she continued to shine opposite other leading men (Nils Asther, Conrad Nagel) as the woman who must pay for her extramarital affairs, as in her three 1929 films, the lush *Wild Orchids, The Single Standard* and Hollywood's last major silent, *The Kiss.*

Finally, MGM permitted the last of its silent stars to speak on the screen, releasing Clarence Brown's version of Eugene O'Neill's *Anna Christie* (1930) with the famous ad line "Garbo Talks!" American audiences and critics responded favorably to her husky voice, even though Garbo despised her performance. (She was much more pleased with the German and Swedish versions of the film that Jacques Feyder directed for MGM's European release.) After the success of *Anna Christie,* Garbo appeared in a string of banal dramas which critics found redemeed only by her charismatic presence. But her career was again bolstered by the acclaimed *Grand Hotel* (1932), in which she uttered her trademark line, "I want to be alone," and *Queen Christina* (1933). In the latter, opposite John Gilbert for the last time, Garbo received her best notices, though she was essentially reprising her familiar role as the tragic diva who sacrifices for her lover. Over the next three years, MGM built three other expensive costume dramas around Garbo in this role—*Anna Karenina* (1935), *Camille* and *Conquest* (both 1937)—but none quite duplicated the radiance of her 1933 performance.

Having made ten silent and a dozen sound films at MGM, all tragic dramas, Garbo concluded her career with a pair of comedies. Her winning performance as a Russian spy in Ernst Lubitsch's *Ninotchka* (1939) elevated her to a surprising new level of acclaim. But the disastrous attempt to present Garbo as a domesticated American in George Cukor's *Two-Faced Woman* (1941) slowed her resurgence. Then the divine Duse-figure whose image had captured the public imagination for two decades retired suddenly and permanently. That she shunned publicity ever afterward merely encouraged the mythos which prompted critic Roland Barthes to write, "Garbo still belongs to that moment in cinema when capturing the human face still plunged audiences into the deepest ecstacy...where the flesh gives rise to mystical feelings of perditon." DGS • *En Lyckoriddare* 1921; *Luffar-Petter/Peter the Tramp* 1922; *Gösta Berlings Saga/The Atonement of Gösta Berling* 1924; *Die Freudlose gasse/Joyless Street* 1925; *The Temptress* 1926; *The Torrent* 1926; *Flesh and the Devil* 1927; *Love* 1927; *The Divine Woman* 1928; *The Mysterious Lady* 1928; *A Woman of Affairs* 1928; *The Kiss* 1929; *A Man's Man* 1929; *The Single Standard* 1929; *Wild Orchids* 1929; *Anna Christie* 1930 **(AANBA)**; *Romance* 1930 **(AANBA)**; *Inspiration* 1931; *Susan Lenox, Her Fall and Rise* 1931; *As You Desire Me* 1932; *Grand Hotel* 1932; *Mata Hari* 1932; *Queen Christina* 1933; *The Painted Veil* 1934; *Anna Karenina* 1935; *Camille* 1937 **(AANBA)**; *Conquest* 1937; *Ninotchka* 1939 **(AANBA)**; *Two-Faced Woman* 1941.

Garcia, Andy • Actor • Born Andres Arturo Garci-Menendez, Havana, Cuba, 1956. *Educ.* Florida International University, Miami (theater). Handsome, engaging lead who achieved star status in 1990, playing the good cop in Mike Figgis's sleek thriller, *Internal Affairs,* and the not-so-nice illegitimate nephew of Don Corleone in the third installment of Francis Coppola's "Godfather" saga.

In Florida from the early 1960s, Garcia worked in regional theater before entering films. Capable of projecting both toughness and sensitivity, he turned in a supremely villainous performance in *8 Million Ways to Die* (1986) before earning widespread recognition as an earnest, sharp-shooting FBI agent in Brian De Palma's *The Untouchables* (1987); he played another morally upright policeman in *Black Rain* (1989) and an equally just Board of Education official in *Stand and Deliver* (1988). • *Blue Skies Again* 1983; *The Mean Season* 1985; *8 Million Ways to Die* 1986; *The Untouchables* 1987; *American Roulette* 1988; *Stand and Deliver* 1988; *Black Rain* 1989; *The Godfather Part III* 1990; *Internal Affairs* 1990; *A Show of Force* 1990.

Gardenia, Vincent • Actor • Born Vincente Scognamiglio, Naples, Italy, January 7, 1922. Short, stocky character player who has earned critical praise for his work on both stage and screen. • *Cop Hater* 1958; *Murder, Inc.* 1960; *The Hustler* 1961; *Mad Dog Coll* 1961; *A View From the Bridge* 1962; *The Third Day* 1965; *Jenny* 1969; *Mission Impossible vs. the Mob* 1969; *Cold Turkey* 1971; *Little Murders* 1971; *Hickey and Boggs* 1972; *Bang the Drum Slowly* 1973 **(AANBSA)**; *Re: Lucky Luciano* 1973; *Death Wish* 1974; *The Front Page* 1974; *The Manchu Eagle Murder Caper Mys-*

tery 1975; *Fire Sale* 1977; *Greased Lightning* 1977; *Heaven Can Wait* 1978; *Firepower* 1979; *Home Movies* 1979; *The Last Flight of Noah's Ark* 1980; *Death Wish II* 1981; *Movers & Shakers* 1985; *Little Shop of Horrors* 1986; *Moonstruck* 1987 **(AANBSA)**; *Cavalli Si Nasce* 1989; *Skin Deep* 1989.

Gardner, Ava • Actress • Born Ava Lavinia Gardner, Grabton, NC, December 24, 1922; died January 25, 1990, London. *Educ.* Atlantic Christian College, Wilson, NC (secretarial studies). Green-eyed, brown-haired beauty, with MGM from 1941 to 1958, who landed her first featured role in the Dr. Gillespie movie *Three Men in White* (1944). Gardner achieved stardom playing femme fatale Kitty Collins opposite Burt Lancaster in *The Killers* (1946), with her earthy charm and magnetic beauty combining to make her one of Hollywood's reigning sex symbols through the next decade. Much to her chagrin, her private life, which included three marriages (Mickey Rooney, Artie Shaw and Frank Sinatra) and some notorious escapades, was well documented in the press. She moved to Spain in the mid-1950s and then to England, where she resided until her death. • *Calling Dr. Gillespie* 1942; *Joe Smith, American* 1942; *Kid Glove Killer* 1942; *Reunion in France* 1942; *Sunday Punch* 1942; *This Time For Keeps* 1942; *We Were Dancing* 1942; *Du Barry Was a Lady* 1943; *Ghosts on the Loose* 1943; *Hitler's Hangman* 1943; *Lost Angel* 1943; *Pilot No. 5* 1943; *Swing Fever* 1943; *Young Ideas* 1943; *Blonde Fever* 1944; *Maisie Goes to Reno* 1944; *Music For Millions* 1944; *Three Men in White* 1944; *Two Girls and a Sailor* 1944; *She Went to the Races* 1945; *The Killers* 1946 (a,song); *Whistle Stop* 1946; *The Hucksters* 1947; *Singapore* 1947; *One Touch of Venus* 1948; *The Bribe* 1949; *East Side, West Side* 1949; *The Great Sinner* 1949; *My Forbidden Past* 1951; *Pandora and the Flying Dutchman* 1951; *Show Boat* 1951; *Lone Star* 1952; *The Snows of Kilimanjaro* 1952; *The Band Wagon* 1953; *Knights of the Round Table* 1953; *Mogambo* 1953 **(AANBA)**; *Ride, Vaquero* 1953; *The Barefoot Contessa* 1954; *Bhowani Junction* 1956; *The Little Hut* 1957; *The Sun Also Rises* 1957; *The Naked Maja* 1959; *On the Beach* 1959; *The Angel Wore Red* 1960; *55 Days at Peking* 1963; *The Night of the Iguana* 1964; *Seven Days in May* 1964; *La Bibbia/The Bible* 1966; *Mayerling* 1968; *Tam Lin* 1971; *The Life and Times of Judge Roy Bean* 1972; *Earthquake* 1974; *Permission to Kill* 1975; *The Blue Bird* 1976; *The Cassandra Crossing* 1977; *The Sentinel* 1977; *City on Fire* 1979; *The Kidnapping of the President* 1980; *Priest of Love* 1980.

Garfield, Allen • Actor • Born Allen Goorwitz, Newark, NJ, November 22, 1939. *Educ.* Actors Studio. Chubby supporting player with a knack for portraying pushy, powerful characters such as Louis B. Mayer in *Gable and Lombard* (1976) and the film producer in Wim Wenders's *The State of Things* (1982). • *Greetings* 1968; *Putney Swope* 1969; *Cry Uncle* 1970; *Hi, Mom!* 1970; *The Owl and the Pussycat* 1970; *Bananas* 1971; *Believe in Me* 1971; *The Organization* 1971; *Roommates* 1971; *Taking Off* 1971; *You've Got to Walk It Like You Talk It or You'll Lose That Beat* 1971; *The Candidate* 1972; *Get to Know Your Rabbit* 1972; *Top Of The Heap* 1972; *Busting* 1973; *Slither* 1973; *The Conversation* 1974; *The Front Page* 1974; *The Commitment* 1975; *Nashville* 1975; *Paco* 1975; *Gable and Lombard* 1976; *Growing Pains: Number One* 1976; *Mother, Jugs & Speed* 1976; *The Brink's Job* 1978; *Skateboard* 1978; *One-Trick Pony* 1980; *The Stunt Man* 1980; *Continental Divide* 1981; *Deadhead Miles* 1982; *One From the Heart* 1982; *Der Stand der Dinge/The State of Things* 1982 (a,songs); *The Black Stallion Returns* 1983; *Get Crazy* 1983; *The Cotton Club* 1984; *Irreconcilable Differences* 1984; *Teachers* 1984; *Desert Bloom* 1986; *Beverly Hills Cop II* 1987; *Chief Zabu* 1988; *Let It Ride* 1989; *Night Visitor* 1989; *Dick Tracy* 1990.

Garfield, John • Actor • Born Jacob Julius Garfinkel, New York, NY, March 4, 1913; died 1952. *Educ.* Ouspenskaya Drama School, New York. Member of the Group Theater who entered films in 1938 and brought a fiery intensity to a number of memorable roles over the next 15 years. Garfield's background as a slum-raised immigrant helped contribute to his image as an anti-hero, and he excelled at playing tough urban figures in socially conscious dramas such as *Body and Soul* (1947) and *Force of Evil* (1948). Both of these films were produced by Enterprise Productions, which Garfield co-founded in 1949 in an attempt to encourage work by left-leaning artists. The heart attack which caused his death was considered to have been partially triggered by his blacklisting in the 1950s. • *Four Daughters* 1938 **(AANBSA)**; *Blackwell's Island* 1939; *Daughters Courageous* 1939; *Dust Be My Destiny* 1939; *Four Wives* 1939; *Juarez* 1939; *They Made Me a Criminal* 1939; *Castle on the Hudson* 1940; *East of the River* 1940; *Flowing Gold* 1940; *Saturday's Children* 1940; *Dangerously They Live* 1941; *Out of the Fog* 1941; *The Sea Wolf* 1941; *Tortilla Flat* 1942; *Air Force* 1943; *Destination Tokyo* 1943; *The Fallen Sparrow* 1943; *Thank Your Lucky Stars* 1943 (a,song); *Between Two Worlds* 1944; *Hollywood Canteen* 1944; *Pride of the Marines* 1945; *Humoresque* 1946; *Nobody Lives Forever* 1946; *The Postman Always Rings Twice* 1946; *Anni Difficili* 1947; *Body and Soul* 1947 **(AANBA)**; *Gentleman's Agreement* 1947; *Force of Evil* 1948; *Jigsaw* 1949; *We Were Strangers* 1949; *The Breaking Point* 1950; *Under My Skin* 1950; *He Ran All the Way* 1951; *Going Hollywood: The War Years* 1988 (archival footage).

Garland, Judy • Actress; also singer. • Born Frances Ethel Gumm, Grand Rapids, MN, June 10, 1922; died June 22, 1969, London. Much-loved entertainer who made her stage debut at age three and went on to charm audiences the world over in the *The Wizard of Oz* (1939).

Blessed with considerable charm and an outstanding singing voice, Garland appeared in a host of juvenile parts, many opposite the young Mickey Rooney, before blossoming into an adult lead. She starred in several celebrated musicals including *Meet Me in St. Louis* (1944) and *The Pirate* (1948), both directed by second husband Vincente Minnelli.

In the 1950s Garland's success began to give way to personal problems, and her outstanding dramatic performances in *A Star Is Born* (1954) and *A Child Is Waiting* (1962) seemed partially to reflect her troubled private life, which featured drugs, lawsuits, separations and suicide attempts. She made her last screen appearance in 1963. Garland's two daughters are Liza Minnelli and (by third husband Sidney Luft) singer Lorna Luft. • *Pigskin Parade* 1936; *Thoroughbreds Don't Cry* 1937; *Broadway Melody of 1938* 1938; *Everybody Sing* 1938; *Listen, Darling* 1938; *Love Finds Andy Hardy* 1938; *Babes in Arms* 1939; *The Wizard of Oz* 1939 **(AAHON)**; *Andy Hardy Meets a Debutante* 1940; *Little Nellie Kelly* 1940; *Strike Up the Band* 1940; *Babes on Broadway* 1941; *Life Begins For Andy Hardy* 1941; *Ziegfeld Girl* 1941; *For Me and My Gal* 1942; *Girl Crazy* 1943; *Presenting Lily Mars* 1943; *Thousands Cheer* 1943; *Meet Me in St. Louis* 1944; *The Clock* 1945; *The Harvey Girls* 1946; *Till the Clouds Roll By* 1946; *Ziegfeld Follies* 1946; *Easter Parade* 1948; *The Pirate* 1948; *Words and Music* 1948; *In the Good Old Summertime* 1949; *Summer Stock* 1950; *A Star Is Born* 1954 **(AANBA)**; *Pepe* 1960; *Judgment at Nuremberg* 1961 **(AANBSA)**; *A Child Is Waiting* 1962; *Gay Purr-ee* 1962; *I Could Go on Singing* 1963.

Garmes, Lee • Director of photography; also director. • Born Peoria, IL, May 27, 1898; died 1978. Celebrated cinematographer, in Hollywood from 1916. Garmes shot his first feature in 1924 and subsequently proved himself adept at romantic, exotic subjects, photographing several Josef von Sternberg films in the early 1930s. Outstanding achievements include *Zoo in Budapest* (1933), *China Girl* (1942) and Max Ophuls's *Caught* (1949). • *The Hope Chest* 1918 (cam.op); *I'll Get Him Yet* 1919 (cam.op); *Nobody Home* 1919 (cam.op); *Nugget Nell* 1919 (cam.op); *Find Your*

Man 1924 (ph); *Crack O'Dawn* 1925 (ph); *The Goat Getter* 1925 (ph); *Keep Smiling* 1925 (ph); *The Carnival Girl* 1926 (ph); *The Grand Duchess and the Waiter* 1926 (ph); *The Palm Beach Girl* 1926 (ph); *The Popular Sin* 1926 (ph); *The Show-Off* 1926 (ph); *A Social Celebrity* 1926 (ph); *The Garden of Allah* 1927 (ph); *The Love Mart* 1927 (ph); *The Private Life of Helen of Troy* 1927 (ph); *Rose of the Golden West* 1927 (ph); *The Barker* 1928 (ph); *The Little Shepherd of Kingdom Come* 1928 (ph); *Waterfront* 1928 (ph); *The Yellow Lily* 1928 (ph); *Disraeli* 1929 (ph); *The Great Divide* 1929 (ph); *His Captive Woman* 1929 (ph); *Love and the Devil* 1929 (ph); *Prisoners* 1929 (ph); *Say It With Songs* 1929 (ph); *Bright Lights* 1930 (ph); *Lilies of the Field* 1930 (ph); *Morocco* 1930 (ph) **(AANBPH)**; *The Other Tomorrow* 1930 (ph); *Song of the Flame* 1930 (ph); *Spring Is Here* 1930 (ph); *Whoopee!* 1930 (ph); *An American Tragedy* 1931 (ph); *City Streets* 1931 (ph); *Confessions of a Co-ed* 1931 (ph); *Dishonored* 1931 (ph); *Fighting Caravans* 1931 (ph); *Kiss Me Again* 1931 (ph); *Call Her Savage* 1932 (ph); *Scarface* 1932 (ph); *Shanghai Express* 1932 (ph) **(AABPH)**; *Smilin' Through* 1932 (ph); *Strange Interlude* 1932 (ph); *The Face in the Sky* 1933 (ph); *I Am Suzanne* 1933 (ph); *My Lips Betray* 1933 (ph); *Shanghai Madness* 1933 (ph); *Zoo in Budapest* 1933 (ph); *Crime Without Passion* 1934 (ph,assoc.d); *George White's Scandals* 1934 (ph); *Once in a Blue Moon* 1935 (ph,assoc.d); *The Scoundrel* 1935 (ph,assoc.d); *Miss Bracegirdle Does Her Duty (short)* 1936 (d); *Dreaming Lips* 1937 (d,ph,tech.sup); *The Lilac Domino* 1937 (assoc.p); *The Sky's the Limit* 1937 (d); *Gone With the Wind* 1939 (uncred.ph); *Angels Over Broadway* 1940 (d,ph); *Beyond Tomorrow* 1940 (p); *The Conquest of the Air* 1940 (uncred.ph); *Lydia* 1941 (assoc.p,ph); *China Girl* 1942 (ph); *Footlight Serenade* 1942 (ph); *The Jungle Book* 1942 (assoc.p,ph); *Flight For Freedom* 1943 (ph); *Forever and a Day* 1943 (ph); *Jack London* 1943 (uncred.ph); *Stormy Weather* 1943 (uncred.ph); *Guest in the House* 1944 (ph); *None Shall Escape* 1944 (ph); *Since You Went Away* 1944 (ph) **(AANBPH)**; *Love Letters* 1945 (ph); *Paris Underground* 1945 (ph); *The Searching Wind* 1946 (ph); *Specter of the Rose* 1946 (p,ph); *Young Widow* 1946 (ph); *Duel in the Sun* 1947 (ph); *Nightmare Alley* 1947 (ph); *The Paradine Case* 1947 (ph); *The Secret Life of Walter Mitty* 1947 (ph); *Caught* 1949 (ph); *The Fighting Kentuckian* 1949 (ph); *Roseanna McCoy* 1949 (ph); *My Foolish Heart* 1950 (ph); *My Friend Irma Goes West* 1950 (ph); *Our Very Own* 1950 (ph); *Detective Story* 1951 (ph); *Saturday's Hero* 1951 (ph); *That's My Boy* 1951 (ph); *Actors and Sin* 1952 (ph); *The Captive City* 1952 (ph); *The Lusty Men* 1952 (ph); *Thunder in the East* 1952 (ph); *Outlaw Territory* 1953 (d,p,sc); *The Desperate Hours* 1955 (ph); *Land of the Pharaohs* 1955 (ph); *Man Without a Gun* 1955 (ph); *D-Day the Sixth of June* 1956 (ph); *The Sharkfighters* 1956 (ph); *The Big Boodle* 1957 (ph); *Never Love a Stranger* 1958 (ph); *The Big Fisherman* 1959 (ph) **(AANBPH)**; *Happy Anniversary* 1959 (ph); *Misty* 1961 (ph); *Adventures of a Young Man* 1962 (ph); *Ten Girls Ago* 1962 (ph); *Lady in a Cage* 1964 (ph); *A Big Hand For the Little Lady* 1966 (ph); *How to Save a Marriage and Ruin Your Life* 1968 (ph); *Why?* 1972 (ph).

Garner, James • Actor • Born James Scott Baumgarner, Norman, OK, April 7, 1928. *Educ.* University of Oklahoma; Berghof School, New York. Handsome, likable leading man whose macho charm and light comic touch were put to good use in films such as *The Americanization of Emily* (1964), *Support Your Local Sheriff* (1969) and *Skin Game* (1971). Garner starred as private investigator Jim Rockford on the long-running TV series "The Rockford Files" (1974-80) and picked up a best actor Oscar nomination for *Murphy's Romance* (1985). • *The Girl He Left Behind* 1956; *Toward the Unknown* 1956; *Sayonara* 1957; *Shoot-Out at Medicine Bend* 1957; *Darby's Rangers* 1958; *Cash McCall* 1959; *Up Periscope* 1959; *The Children's Hour* 1961; *Boys' Night Out* 1962; *The Great Escape* 1963; *Move Over, Darling* 1963; *The Thrill of It All* 1963; *The Wheeler Dealers* 1963; *36 Hours* 1964; *The Americanization of Emily* 1964; *The Art of Love* 1965; *Mister Buddwing* 1965; *Duel at Diablo* 1966; *Grand Prix* 1966; *A Man Could Get Killed* 1966; *Hour of the Gun* 1967; *How Sweet It Is* 1968; *The Pink Jungle* 1968; *Marlowe* 1969; *Support Your Local Sheriff* 1969; *A Man Called Sledge* 1970; *Skin Game* 1971; *Support Your Local Gunfighter* 1971; *They Only Kill Their Masters* 1972; *One Little Indian* 1973; *The Castaway Cowboy* 1974; *Health* 1980; *The Fan* 1981; *Victor/Victoria* 1982; *Tank* 1984; *Murphy's Romance* 1985 **(AANBA)**; *Sunset* 1988.

Garnett, Tay • Director; also screenwriter. • Born William Taylor Garnett, Los Angeles, CA, June 13, 1898; died 1977. *Educ.* MIT. Prolific director of adventure films, westerns and other hard-hitting fare; in films from 1922 as a writer. • *Broken Chains* 1922 (uncred.sc); *The Hottentot* 1922 (sc); *Who's Your Friend* 1925 (sc,cont); *The Cruise of the Jasper B* 1926 (sc); *The Strong Man* 1926 (uncred.sc); *That's My Baby* 1926 (uncred.sc); *There You Are!* 1926 (uncred.sc); *Up in Mabel's Room* 1926 (sc); *Getting Gertie's Garter* 1927 (uncred.sc); *Long Pants* 1927 (uncred.sc); *No Control* 1927 (sc); *Rubber Tires* 1927 (sc); *Turkish Delight* 1927 (sc); *White Gold* 1927 (sc); *The Wise Wife* 1927 (sc); *Celebrity* 1928 (d,sc); *The Cop* 1928 (sc); *Power* 1928 (sc,story); *Skyscraper* 1928 (sc); *The Spieler* 1928 (adapt,d); *The Flying Fool* 1929 (d,sc,story); *Oh, Yeah!* 1929 (d,sc,lyrics); *Her Man* 1930 (d,story); *Officer O'Brien* 1930 (d); *Bad Company* 1931 (d,sc); *Okay America* 1932 (d); *One Way Passage* 1932 (d); *Prestige* 1932 (adapt,d); *Destination Unknown* 1933 (d); *S.O.S. Eisberg* 1933 (d); *China Seas* 1935 (d); *Professional Soldier* 1935 (d); *She Couldn't Take It* 1935 (d); *Love Is News* 1937 (d); *Slave Ship* 1937 (d); *Stand-In* 1937 (d); *Joy of Living* 1938 (d); *Trade Winds* 1938 (d,story); *Cafe Hostess* 1939 (story); *Eternally Yours* 1939 (a,d); *Seven Sinners* 1940 (d); *Slightly Honorable* 1940 (d,p); *Cheers For Miss Bishop* 1941 (d); *Unexpected Uncle* 1941 (p); *Week-End For Three* 1941 (p); *My Favorite Spy* 1942 (d); *Bataan* 1943 (d); *The Cross of Lorraine* 1943 (d); *Mrs. Parkington* 1944 (d); *See Here, Private Hargrove* 1944 (d); *The Valley of Decision* 1945 (d); *The Postman Always Rings Twice* 1946 (d); *Wild Harvest* 1947 (d); *A Connecticut Yankee in King Arthur's Court* 1949 (d); *The Fireball* 1950 (d,sc,story); *Cause For Alarm* 1951 (d); *Soldiers Three* 1951 (d); *One Minute to Zero* 1952 (d); *Main Street to Broadway* 1953 (d); *The Black Knight* 1954 (d); *Seven Wonders of the World* 1956 (d); *A Terrible Beauty* 1960 (d); *Cattle King* 1963 (d); *The Delta Factor* 1970 (d,sc); *Challenge to Be Free* 1972 (a,d); *The Mad Trapper* 1972 (d,sc); *Timber Tramps* 1973 (d).

Garr, Teri • Actress • Born Lakewood, OH, December 11, 1949. *Educ.* California State University, Northridge (speech, dance); Actors Studio. Successful, offbeat character actress of the 1970s and 80s. Garr first gained attention on "The Sonny and Cher Comedy Hour" and costarred in both *Mr. Mom* (1983) and *Firstborn* (1984). • *Head* 1968; *The Moonshine War* 1970; *The Conversation* 1974; *Young Frankenstein* 1974; *Won Ton Ton, the Dog Who Saved Hollywood* 1976; *Close Encounters of the Third Kind* 1977; *Oh, God!* 1977; *Witches' Brew* 1978; *The Black Stallion* 1979; *Mr. Mike's Mondo Video* 1979; *Close Encounters of the Third Kind: Special Edition* 1980; *Honky Tonk Freeway* 1981; *The Escape Artist* 1982; *One From the Heart* 1982; *The Sting II* 1982; *Tootsie* 1982 **(AANBSA)**; *The Black Stallion Returns* 1983; *Mr. Mom* 1983; *Firstborn* 1984; *Miracles* 1984; *After Hours* 1985; *Full Moon in Blue Water* 1988; *Out Cold* 1988; *Let It Ride* 1989; *Short Time* 1990; *Waiting For the Light* 1990.

Garson, Greer • Actress • Born County Down, Nothern Ireland, September 29, 1908. *Educ.* University of London; University of Grenoble, France. Former stage actress in films from 1939, mostly with MGM. Garson was one of Hollywood's biggest stars of the 1940s and often starred opposite Walter Pidgeon, as in her Oscar-winning performance as *Mrs. Miniver* (1942). Married to actor Richard Ney from 1943 to 1947. • *Goodbye, Mr. Chips* 1939 **(AANBA)**; *Remember?* 1939; *Pride and Prejudice* 1940; *Blossoms in the Dust* 1941 **(AANBA)**; *When Ladies Meet* 1941; *Mrs. Miniver* 1942 **(AABA)**; *Random Harvest* 1942; *Madame Curie* 1943 **(AANBA)**; *The Youngest Profession* 1943; *Mrs. Parkington* 1944 **(AANBA)**; *Adventure* 1945; *The Valley of Decision* 1945 **(AANBA)**; *Desire Me* 1947; *Julia Misbehaves* 1948; *That Forsyte Woman* 1949; *The Miniver Story* 1950; *The Law and the Lady* 1951; *Julius Caesar* 1953; *Scandal at Scourie* 1953; *Her Twelve Men* 1954; *Strange Lady in Town* 1954; *Pepe* 1960; *Sunrise at Campobello* 1960 **(AANBA)**; *The Singing Nun* 1966; *Happiest Millionaire* 1967; *Directed By William Wyler* 1986.

Garwood, Norman • British production designer • Outstanding artist whose eclectic and elaborate designs for Terry Gilliam's *Brazil* (1985) earned him an Oscar nomination (he won a second for 1989's *Glory*) and a British Academy Award. • *The Missionary* 1981 (art d); *Time Bandits* 1981 (art d); *Brimstone and Treacle* 1982 (art d); *Bullshot* 1983 (pd); *Red Monarch* 1983 (pd); *Water* 1984 (pd); *Brazil* 1985 (pd) **(AANBAD)**; *Shadey* 1985 (pd); *Link* 1986 (pd); *The Princess Bride* 1987 (pd); *Glory* 1989 (pd) **(AANBAD)**; *Misery* 1990 (pd).

Gassman, Vittorio • Actor; also director. • Born Genoa, Italy, September 1, 1922. *Educ.* Accademia Nazionale di Arte Drammatica, Rome. Popular Italian stage and screen performer who spent a few unremarkable years in Hollywood in the mid-1950s. After returning to Europe Gassman directed his first feature film, *Kean* (1956) and became one of Italy's most successful screen actors of the 1960s. In the late 70s Gassman again began appearing in US films, notably Robert Altman's *A Wedding* (1978) and *Quintet* (1979). Married to actress Shelley Winters from 1952 to 1955. • *Daniele Cortis* 1946; *Preludio d'amore* 1946; *Le Avventure di Pinocchio* 1947; *L'Ebreo errante* 1947; *La Figlia del capitano* 1947; *Il Cavaliere misterioso* 1948; *I Fuorilegge* 1949; *Ho Sognato il paradiso* 1949; *Il Lupo della sila* 1949; *Riso Amaro/Bitter Rice* 1949; *Lo Sparviero del Nilo* 1949; *Una voce nel tuo cuore* 1949; *Il Leone di Amalfi* 1950; *Anna* 1951; *Il Sogno di Zorro* 1951; *Il Tradimento* 1951; *La Corona Negra* 1952; *La Tratta delle Bianche* 1952; *Cry of the Hunted* 1953; *The Glass Wall* 1953; *Sombrero* 1953; *Mambo* 1954; *Rhapsody* 1954; *La Donna più bella del mondo* 1955; *Difendo il Mio Amore* 1956; *Giovanni delle bande nere* 1956; *Kean* 1956 (a,d,sc); *War and Peace* 1956; *La Ragazza del Palio* 1957; *Big Deal on Madonna Street* 1958; *La Tempesta/Tempest* 1958; *Audace colpo dei soliti* 1959; *La Cambiale* 1959; *La Grande Guerra* 1959; *Il Mattatore* 1959; *The Miracle* 1959; *Le Sorprese dell'Amore* 1959; *Crimen* 1960; *Fantasmi a Roma* 1960; *I Briganti italiani* 1961; *Il Giudizio Universale* 1961; *Una Vita Dificile* 1961; *L'Amore difficile* 1962; *Anima nera* 1962; *Barabbas* 1962; *La Marcia su Roma* 1962; *La Smania addosso* 1962; *Il Sorpasso* 1962; *Frenesia dell'estate* 1963; *I Mostri* 1963; *Il Successo* 1963; *La Congiuntura* 1964; *Il Gaucho* 1964; *Se Permettete parliamo di donna* 1964; *La Guerre secrète/The Dirty Game* 1965; *Slalom* 1965; *Una Vergine per il principe* 1965; *L'Armata Brancaleone* 1966; *Le Piacevoli notti* 1966; *Il Profeta* 1967; *Questi Fantasmi* 1967; *Lo Scatenato* 1967; *Il Tigre/The Tiger and the Pussycat* 1967; *Woman Times Seven* 1967; *L'Alibi* 1969 (a,d,sc); *L'Arcangelo* 1969; *Dove vai tutta nuda?* 1969; *La Pecora nera* 1969; *Una su tredici* 1969; *Brancaleone Alle Crociate* 1970; *Contestazione generale* 1970; *Il Divorzio* 1970; *In Nome del Popolo Italiano* 1971; *L'Udienza* 1971; *Che c'entriamo noi con la rivoluzione?* 1972; *Senza Famiglia Nullatenenti Cercano Affetto* 1972 (a,d,sc,story); *La Tosca* 1973; *C'eravamo tanto amati/We All Loved Each Other So Much* 1974; *Profumo di donna* 1974; *A Mezzanotte va la ronda del Piacere* 1975; *Anima Persa* 1976; *Come una rosa al naso* 1976; *Le Desert des tartares* 1976; *Signore e Signori, Buonanotte* 1976; *I Telefoni bianchi* 1976; *I Nuovi Mostri* 1977; *A Wedding* 1978; *Caro Papa* 1979; *Due pezzi di Pane* 1979; *Quintet* 1979 (a,dubbing sup—Italian version); *La Terrazza* 1979; *The Nude Bomb* 1980; *Sono Fotogenico* 1980; *Sharky's Machine* 1981; *Il Conte Tacchia* 1982; *Tempest* 1982; *Benvenuta* 1983; *Di Padre in Figlio* 1983 (a,d,sc,story); *La Vie est un roman* 1983; *Le Pouvoir du Mal* 1985; *I Soliti Ignoti...Vent'Anni Dopo/Big Deal on Madonna Street...Twenty Years Later* 1986; *La Famiglia/The Family* 1987; *I Picari* 1987; *Lo Zio Indegno/The Sleazy Uncle* 1989; *Dimenticare Palermo* 1990; *Divertimenti nella casa privata* 1990; *Sheherazade* 1990.

Gaumont, Leon • Inventor, executive; also producer. • Born Paris, May 10, 1864; died 1946. Pioneering entrepeneur who, with Charles Pathé, was the dominant figure in French film of the silent era. Gaumont began his career manufacturing film equipment but soon turned to production, with Alice Guy-Blache and later Louis Feuillade and Jacques Feyder as his key directors. Their success, combined with his continuing innovations and an expansion into exhibition, led Gaumont to open branches in England, Germany, the US and elsewhere. His inventions included a camera-projector apparatus, the Chronotographe (1895), and an early synchronized sound system, the Chronophone (1902). Gaumont retired in 1929.

Gaynor, Janet • Actress • Born Laura Gainor, Philadelphia, PA, October 6, 1906; died September 14, 1984, Palm Springs, CA. *Educ.* Hollywood Secretarial School. Wholesome silent screen star who won the best actress award at the first Oscar ceremony on May 16, 1929, for her combined work on *Sunrise*, *Seventh Heaven* (both 1927) and *Street Angel* (1928). • *The Blue Eagle* 1926; *The Johnstown Flood* 1926; *The Midnight Kiss* 1926; *The Return of Peter Grimm* 1926; *The Shamrock Handicap* 1926; *Seventh Heaven* 1927 **(AABA)**; *Sunrise* 1927 **(AABA)**; *Two Girls Wanted* 1927; *Four Devils* 1928; *Street Angel* 1928 **(AABA)**; *Christina* 1929; *Happy Days* 1929; *Lucky Star* 1929; *Sunny Side Up* 1929; *High Society Blues* 1930; *Daddy Long Legs* 1931; *Delicious* 1931; *The Man Who Came Back* 1931; *Merely Mary Ann* 1931; *The First Year* 1932; *Tess of the Storm Country* 1932; *Adorable* 1933; *Paddy the Next Best Thing* 1933; *State Fair* 1933; *Carolina* 1934; *Change of Heart* 1934; *La Ciudad de Carton* 1934; *Servant's Entrance* 1934; *The Farmer Takes a Wife* 1935; *One More Spring* 1935; *Ladies in Love* 1936; *Small Town Girl* 1936; *A Star Is Born* 1937 **(AANBA)**; *Three Loves Has Nancy* 1938; *The Young in Heart* 1938; *Bernardine* 1957.

Gazzara, Ben • Actor; also director. • Born Biagio Anthony Gazzara, New York, NY, August 28, 1930. *Educ.* CCNY (engineering); Dramatic Workshop of the New School for Social Research, New York; Actors Studio. Leading man whose ability to combine toughness with sensitivity enhanced several of his early films, especially *Anatomy of a Murder* (1959) and *Convicts Four* (1962). Gazzara was featured in three John Cassavetes films, notably *Husbands* (1970), but is primarily known for his TV appearances ("Run For Your Life" 1965-68). He has worked often in Italy, where in 1990 he made his directing debut with *Beyond the Ocean* (1990). Formerly married to actress Janice Rule. • *The Strange One* 1957; *Anatomy of a Murder* 1959; *Risate di Gioia* 1960; *The Young Doctors* 1961; *Città Prigioniera* 1962; *Convicts Four* 1962; *A Rage to Live* 1965; *The Big Mouth* 1967; *The Bridge at Remagen* 1969; *If It's Tuesday, This Must Be Belgium* 1969; *Husbands* 1970; *King: A Filmed Record... Montgomery to Memphis* 1970; *The Sicilian Connection* 1972; *The Neptune Factor* 1973; *Capone* 1975; *The Killing of a Chinese Bookie* 1976; *Voyage of the Damned* 1976; *High Velocity* 1977; *Opening Night* 1977; *Bloodline* 1979; *Saint Jack* 1979; *Storie di Ordinaria Follia/Tales of Ordinary Madness* 1981; *They All Laughed* 1981; *Inchon* 1982; *La Ragazza di Trieste* 1983; *Uno Scandalo Perbene* 1984; *La Donna Delle Meraviglie* 1985; *Figlio Mio Infinitamente Caro* 1985; *Il Camorrista/The Professor* 1986; *Il*

Giorno Prima 1987; *La Mémoire tatouée* 1988; *Quicker Than the Eye* 1988; *Road House* 1989; *Beyond the Ocean* 1990 (a,d,sc,story).

Gélin, Daniel • Actor; also director. • Born Angers, France, May 19, 1921. *Educ.* Paris Conservatoire. Handsome, sensitive star of a series of light romances of the 1950s; also memorable as the heavily disguised Arab spy in Hitchcock's *The Man Who Knew Too Much* (1956). Gélin was married to actress Daniélle Delorme from 1945 to 1954 and is the father of producer Xavier Gelin and actress Maria Schneider. He has published several collections of poems. • *Les Surprises de la radio* 1939; *Miquette et sa mère* 1940; *Soyez les bienvenus* 1940; *L'Assassin habite au 21* 1941; *Les Cadets de l'ocean* 1941; *Premier rendez-vous* 1941; *Les Petites du Quai aux Fleurs* 1944; *Un Ami viendra ce soir* 1945; *La Tentation de Barbizon* 1945; *La Femme en rouge* 1946; *Martin Roumagnac* 1946; *La Nuit de Sybille* 1946; *Le Mannequin assassiné* 1947; *Miroir* 1947; *Le Paradis des pilotes* 1948; *Rendez-vous de Juillet* 1948; *Dieu a besoin des Hommes* 1950; *La Ronde* 1950; *Edouard et Caroline* 1951; *Une Histoire d'amour* 1951; *Les Mains Sales* 1951; *Le Plaisir* 1951; *Adorables Créatures* 1952; *Les Dents longues* 1952 (a,d); *La Maison du silence* 1952; *L'Affaire Maurizius* 1953; *L'Esclave* 1953; *Opinione pubblica* 1953; *Rue de l'Estrapade* 1953; *Sang et lumières* 1953; *Si Versailles m'était conté* 1953; *L'Allegro squadrone* 1954; *Napoléon* 1954; *La Romana* 1954; *The Snow Was Black* 1954; *Les Amants du Tage* 1955; *Paris canaille* 1955; *En effeuillant la Marguerite* 1956; *Je eviendrai à Kandara* 1956; *The Man Who Knew Too Much* 1956; *Charmants garçons* 1957; *Maid in Paris* 1957; *Morte en Fraude* 1957; *Retour de Manivelle* 1957; *Trois jours à vivre* 1957; *Ce Corps tant desiré* 1958; *La Fille de Hambourg* 1958; *Suivez-moi, jeune homme* 1958; *Cartagine in fiamme* 1959; *Julie la Rouse* 1959; *Le Testament d'Orphée/The Testament of Orpheus* 1959; *Les Trois etc...du colonel* 1959; *Austerlitz* 1960; *La Morte-saison des amours* 1960; *La Proie pour l'ombre* 1960; *Reveille-toi, cherie* 1960; *Les Petits matins* 1961; *Réglements de comptes* 1962; *Vacances portugaises* 1962; *Tre piger i Paris* 1963; *La Bonne Soupe* 1964; *El Niño y el muro* 1964; *Compartiment tueurs/The Sleeping Car Murders* 1965; *Gorge trave* 1965; *Zwei Girls vom Roten Stern* 1965; *A Belles dents* 1966; *La Ligne de Demarcation* 1966; *Paris brule-t-il?/Is Paris Burning?* 1966; *Soleil noir* 1966; *Les Sultans* 1966; *Bruegel* 1967; *Le Mois le plus beau* 1968; *La Treve* 1968; *Détruire, Dit-Elle* 1969; *Hallucinations sadiques* 1969; *La Servante* 1969; *Slogan* 1969; *Christa* 1971; *Le Souffle au coeur/Murmur of the Heart* 1971; *Far From Dallas* 1972; *La Gueule de l'emploi* 1973; *La Polizia è al servizio del cittadino* 1973; *Dialogue d'exiles* 1974; *Un Linceul n'a pas de poches* 1974; *Trop c'est Trop* 1975; *Qu'il est joli garçon, l'assassin de papa* 1976; *Arrête de Ramer, T'Attaques la Falaise* 1977; *Nous irons tous au paradis* 1977; *La Vocation Suspendue* 1977; *L'Honorable Societé* 1978; *L'Oeil du Maître* 1979; *Guy De Maupassant* 1982; *La Nuit de Varennes* 1982; *Un Delitto* 1984; *Les Enfants* 1984; *Hitchcock, Il Brivido del Genio* 1985; *Killing Cars* 1985; *Sécurité publique* 1987; *La Vie est un long fleuve tranquille/Life Is a Long Quiet River* 1987; *Dandin* 1988; *Itinéraire d'un enfant gâté* 1988; *Mister Frost* 1990; *Mauvaise Fille* 1991.

George, Susan • Actress; also producer. • Born Surbiton, Surrey, England, July 26, 1950. *Educ.* Corona Stage Academy, London. Attractive, youthful star of the 1960s, in mostly inferior vehicles since the mid-70s. • *Come Fly With Me* 1962; *Cup Fever* 1965; *Davey Jones' Locker* 1965; *Billion Dollar Brain* 1967; *The Sorcerers* 1967; *Up the Junction* 1967; *The Strange Affair* 1968; *All Neat in Black Stockings* 1969; *Die Screaming Marianne* 1970; *Eyewitness* 1970; *The Looking Glass War* 1970; *Spring and Port Wine* 1970; *Twinky* 1970; *Fright* 1971; *Straw Dogs* 1971; *Sonny & Jed* 1972; *Dirty Mary, Crazy Larry* 1974; *Mandingo* 1975; *Out of Season* 1975; *A Small Town in Texas* 1976; *Tintorera* 1977; *Tomorrow Never Comes* 1978; *Enter the Ninja* 1981; *Venom* 1981; *The House Where Evil Dwells* 1982; *Czech Mate* 1983; *The Jigsaw Man* 1984; *Lightning—The White Stallion* 1986; *Stealing Heaven* 1988 (exec.p); *That Summer of White Roses* 1989 (a,exec.p).

Gerasimov, Sergei • Director; also actor, screenwriter. • Born Zlatoust, Ural Mountains, Russia, 1906; died November 28, 1985. *Educ.* Institute of Stage Art, Leningrad. Former member of the experimental Factory of the Eccentric Actor (FEX) who turned to directing in the early 1930s. Gerasimov's films eschewed his earlier avant-garde leanings and tended to conform with the prevailing dicta of socialist realism. He is best known for *The Young Guard* (1948) and his epic adaptation of Mikhail Sholokov's *And Quiet Flows the Don* (1957). • *22 Misfortunes* 1930 (d,sc); *The Heart of Solomon* 1932 (d); *The Deserter* 1933 (a); *Do I Love You?* 1934 (d,sc); *Seven Brave Men* 1936 (d,sc); *Komsomolsk* 1938 (d,sc); *The New Teacher* 1939 (d,sc); *Boevoi kinosbornik 1* 1941 (d); *Masquerade* 1941 (a,d,sc); *The Old Guard* 1941 (d); *Kinokontsert k 25-letiyu Krasnoy Armii* 1943 (d); *Nepobedimye* 1943 (d); *The Big Land* 1944 (d,sc); *Molodaya gvardiya/Young Guard* 1948 (d,sc); *The New China* 1950 (d); *The Country Doctor* 1952 (d); *Nadezhda* 1955 (d,sc); *Die Windrose* 1956 (d); *Tikhi Don/And Quiet Flows the Don* 1957 (d,sc); *Men and Beasts* 1962 (d,sc); *Zhurnalist* 1966 (a,d,sc); *By the Lake* 1970 (d,sc); *Leo Tolstoy* 1984 (a,d).

Gere, Richard • Actor • Born Philadelphia, PA, August 29, 1949. *Educ.* University of Massachusetts (philosophy, drama). One of Hollywood's biggest male screen attractions of the late 1970s and early 80s. Gere appeared on Broadway in *Grease* and other plays before making his film debut in 1975, landing his first starring role in Terrence Malick's highly acclaimed *Days of Heaven* (1978). After a string of commercial flops, Gere reasserted himself as a bankable star in 1990 with roles in the sophisticated thriller, *Internal Affairs*, and the huge box-office success, *Pretty Woman*. • *Baby Blue Marine* 1975; *Report to the Commissioner* 1975; *Looking For Mr. Goodbar* 1977; *Bloodbrothers* 1978; *Days of Heaven* 1978; *Yanks* 1979; *American Gigolo* 1980; *An Officer and a Gentleman* 1982; *Beyond the Limit* 1983; *Breathless* 1983; *The Cotton Club* 1984 (a,m); *King David* 1985; *No Mercy* 1986; *Power* 1986; *Miles From Home* 1988; *Internal Affairs* 1990; *Pretty Woman* 1990 (a,m,song); *Rhapsody in August* 1991.

Germi, Pietro • Director; also screenwriter, actor. • Born Genoa, Italy, September 14, 1914; died 1974. *Educ.* Centro Sperimentale di Cinematografia, Rome (acting, directing). Prolific director whose career was primarily divided between neorealist dramas and vicious satires. Of the former group, *The Railroad Man* (1955), in which he also starred, stands out. In 1961 Germi made *Divorce Italian Style*, the first of a series of dark, biting comedies which included *Seduced and Abandoned* (1963) and *The Birds, the Bees and the Italians* (1966). • *Retroscena* 1939 (sc,ad); *Nessuno torna indietro* 1943 (ad); *I Dieci Comandamenti* 1945 (sc); *Il Testimone* 1945 (d,sc,story); *Monte Cassino* 1946 (a); *Gioventù Perduta* 1947 (d,sc,story); *Fuga in Francia* 1948 (a); *In nome delle legge* 1948 (d,sc); *Il Cammino della speranza* 1950 (d,story,adapt); *La Città si difende* 1951 (d,sc,adapt); *Il Brigante di Tacca del Lupo* 1952 (d); *La Presidentessa* 1952 (d); *Black 13* 1953 (from sc "Gioventu perduta"); *Gelosia* 1953 (d,sc); *Amori di Mezzo Secolo* 1954 (d); *Il Ferroviere* 1955 (a,d,sc); *L'Uomo di paglia* 1957 (a,d,sc,story); *Un Maledetto Imbroglio* 1959 (a,d,sc); *Five Branded Women* 1960 (a); *Il Rosetto/Lipstick* 1960 (a); *Divorzio All'Italiano/Divorce Italian Style* 1961 (d,sc,story) **(AANBD,AABSC)**; *Il Sicario* 1961 (a); *La Viaccia* 1961 (a); *Sedotta e Abbandonata/Seduced and Abandoned* 1963 (d,sc,story); *Signore e signori/The Birds, the Bees and the Italians* 1966 (d,p,sc,story); *L'Immorale* 1967 (d,p,sc,story); *Serafino* 1968 (d,p,sc,story); *Le Castagne Sone Buone* 1970 (d,p,sc,story); *Alfredo, Alfredo* 1973 (d,p,sc,story); *Amici Miei* 1975 (sc,story).

Gershwin, George • Composer • Born Jacob Gershvin, Brooklyn, NY, September 26, 1898; died 1937. Celebrated writer of songs and scores whose music continues to feature in countless films. See also Gershwin, Ira. • *The Sunshine Trail* 1923 (m); *Life and Death of 9413, a Hollywood Extra (short)* 1927 (song); *Lady Be Good* 1928 (m); *King of Jazz* 1930 (m); *Song of the Flame* 1930 (m); *Delicious* 1931 (m,orchestral sequence); *Girl Crazy* 1932 (m); *The World Moves On* 1934 (song); *Komposition in Blau (short)* 1935 (m); *The Great Ziegfeld* 1936 (song); *The Singing Kid* 1936 (song); *A Damsel in Distress* 1937 (m); *Shall We Dance* 1937 (m) **(AANBS)**; *The Goldwyn Follies* 1938 (m); *Strike Up the Band* 1940 (song); *Lady Be Good* 1941 (song); *Girl Crazy* 1943 (m); *Rhapsody in Blue* 1945 (m); *Where Do We Go From Here?* 1945 (m); *An American in Paris* 1951 (m); *Funny Face* 1957 (m); *Porgy and Bess* 1959 (m).

Gershwin, Ira • *aka* Arthur Francis • Lyricist; also composer. • Born Israel Gershvin, New York, NY, December 6, 1896; died August 17, 1983, Beverly Hills, CA. *Educ.* CCNY; Columbia. With composer-brother George, formed one of America's most prestigious songwriting teams of the 1920s and 30s. Early Broadway classics include *Strike Up The Band* (1927) and the Pulitzer Prize-winning *Of Thee I Sing* (1932). The brothers had several of their stage hits adapted for film and composed original scores for such movies as 1937's *Shall We Dance* and *A Damsel in Distress*. (Their first work directly for the screen came in 1931 with *Delicious*.)

After George's death in 1937 Ira continued to write for stage and screen, teaming up with such luminaries as Kurt Weill, Aaron Copeland and Jerome Kern. • *Fascination* 1922 (song); *The Sunshine Trail* 1923 (lyics); *Life and Death of 9413, a Hollywood Extra (short)* 1927 (lyrics); *Song of the Flame* 1930 (lyrics); *Delicious* 1931 (lyrics); *Girl Crazy* 1932 (lyrics); *That's a Good Girl* 1933 (lyrics); *A Damsel in Distress* 1937 (lyrics); *Shall We Dance* 1937 (lyrics) **(AANBS)**; *The Goldwyn Follies* 1938 (lyrics); *Dancing Co-ed* 1939 (lyrics); *Strike Up the Band* 1940 (lyrics); *Lady Be Good* 1941 (lyrics); *Girl Crazy* 1943 (lyrics); *The North Star* 1943 (lyrics); *Princess O'Rourke* 1943 (lyrics); *So's Your Uncle* 1943 (lyrics); *Cover Girl* 1944 (song) **(AANBS)**; *Lady in the Dark* 1944 (lyrics); *George White's Scandals* 1945 (lyrics); *Where Do We Go From Here?* 1945 (lyrics); *The Jolson Story* 1946 (lyrics); *The Man I Love* 1946 (lyrics); *Till the Clouds Roll By* 1946 (lyrics); *Ziegfeld Follies* 1946 (lyrics); *Dark Passage* 1947 (lyrics); *The Shocking Miss Pilgrim* 1947 (lyrics,m.arr); *The Unsuspected* 1947 (lyrics); *Always Leave Them Laughing* 1949 (lyrics); *The Barkleys of Broadway* 1949 (lyrics); *Ce siecle a cinquante ans* 1949 (lyrics); *I'll Get By* 1950 (lyrics); *Nancy Goes to Rio* 1950 (lyrics); *Tea For Two* 1950 (lyrics); *Young Man With a Horn* 1950 (lyrics); *An American in Paris* 1951 (lyrics); *Starlift* 1951 (lyrics); *Fearless Fagan* 1952 (lyrics); *Meet Danny Wilson* 1952 (lyrics); *Somebody Loves Me* 1952 (lyrics); *With a Song in My Heart* 1952 (lyrics); *Give a Girl a Break* 1953 (song); *The Country Girl* 1954 (song); *A Star Is Born* 1954 (song) **(AANBS)**; *Three For the Show* 1954 (lyrics); *Funny Face* 1957 (lyrics); *Porgy and Bess* 1959 (lyrics).

Gertz, Jami • American actress • *Educ.* NYU (drama). Young lead of the 1980s who first made her mark on TV's "Square Pegs" opposite fellow newcomers Sarah Jessica Parker and Tracy Nelson. • *Endless Love* 1981; *Alphabet City* 1984; *Sixteen Candles* 1984; *Mischief* 1985; *Crossroads* 1986; *Quicksilver* 1986; *Solarbabies* 1986; *Less Than Zero* 1987; *The Lost Boys* 1987; *Listen to Me* 1989; *Renegades* 1989; *Zwei Frauen/Silence Like Glass* 1989; *Don't Tell Her It's Me* 1990.

Gherardi, Piero • Art director; also costume designer. • Born Poppi, Italy, November 20, 1909; died 1971. Made a smooth transition from the neorealism of post-WWII Italian cinema to the more flamboyant styles of the 1960s, as with Fellini's *8 1/2* (1963) and many films by Mario Monicelli. • *Notte di tempesta* 1945 (sets); *Daniele Cortis* 1946 (art d); *Eugenia Grandet* 1946 (sets); *Amanti senzi amore* 1947 (art d); *Senza Pietà* 1947 (art d); *Fuga in Francia* 1948 (art d); *Proibito Rubare* 1948 (art d); *Campane a martello* 1949 (art d); *Napoli milionaria* 1949 (art d); *Her Favourite Husband* 1950 (art d); *Romanzo d'Amore* 1950 (art d); *Camicie Rosse* 1951 (art d); *Buongiorno Elefante!* 1952 (art d); *Iolanda la figlia del corsaro nero* 1952 (sets); *Sensualita* 1952 (art d); *Anni facili* 1953 (art d); *Cinema d'altri tempi* 1953 (cost,sets); *Proibito* 1954 (art d,cost); *Le Notti di Cabiria/Nights of Cabiria* 1956 (art d); *War and Peace* 1956 (sets); *La Grande strada azzurra* 1957 (art d); *Il Medico e lo stregone* 1957 (art d,sets,cost); *Padri e Figli/Fathers and Sons* 1957 (art d); *Big Deal on Madonna Street* 1958 (art d,cost); *La Dolce Vita* 1959 (art d,cost) **(AANBAD,AABCD)**; *Crimen* 1960 (art d); *Il Gobbo* 1960 (cost); *Kapò* 1960 (art d); *Risate di Gioia* 1960 (art d); *Sotto dieci bandiere/Under Ten Flags* 1960 (art d); *Il Carabiniere a cavallo* 1961 (art d); *Il Re di Poggioreale* 1961 (art d); *Boccaccio '70* 1962 (art d—"Renzo e Luciana"); *Violenza Segreta* 1962 (cost); *Otto e Mezzo/8 1/2* 1963 (art d,cost) **(AANBAD,AABCD)**; *La Ragazza di Bube* 1963 (art d); *Alta Infedelta* 1964 (art d—"Peccato nel Pomeriggio"); *Tre Notti d'Amore* 1964 (art d,cost—"Fatebenefratelli"); *Le Bambole* 1965 (cost); *La Fuga* 1965 (art d,cost); *Giulietta degli Spiriti/Juliet of the Spirits* 1965 (art d,cost) **(AANBAD,AANBCD)**; *Madamigella di Maupin* 1965 (art d); *L'Armata Brancaleone* 1966 (art d,cost); *Le Fate* 1966 (art d—"Fata Armenia"); *Se Tutte le Donne Del Mondo/Kiss the Girls and Make Them Die* 1967 (cost—Dorothy Provine); *Diabolik* 1968 (cost); *Roma Come Chicago* 1968 (cost); *The Appointment* 1969 (art d,cost); *Infanzia Vocazione è Prime Esperienze di Giacomo Casanova—Veneziano* 1969 (art d,cost); *Quemada!/Burn!* 1969 (art d,cost); *Brancaleone Alle Crociate* 1970 (art d,cost).

Giannini, Giancarlo • Actor; also director and producer. • Born Spezia, Italy, August 1, 1942. *Educ.* Accademia Nazionale di Arti Drammatica, Rome. Charming, melancholic star of the 1970s who appeared in a string of Lina Wertmuller films including *Love and Anarchy* (1973) and *Seven Beauties* (1975). • *Rita la Zanzara* 1966; *Arabella* 1967; *Non Stuzzicate la Zanzara* 1967; *Anzio* 1968; *Fräulein Doktor* 1968; *The Secret of Santa Vittoria* 1969; *Le Sorelle* 1969; *Drama della Gelosia* 1970; *Prostituta al Servizio del Pubblico* 1970; *Mio Padre Monsignore* 1971; *Ettore lo Fusto* 1972; *Mimi Metallurgico Ferito Nell'Onore/The Seduction of Mimi* 1972; *La Prima Notte di Quiete* 1972; *Sono Stato Io* 1972; *La Tarantola dal Ventre Nero* 1972; *Film d'Amore e d'Anarchia/Love and Anarchy* 1973; *Paolo Il Caldo* 1973; *Sessomatto* 1973; *Il Bestione* 1974; *Travolti da un insolito destino nell'azzuro mare d'Agosto/Swept Away...By an Unusual Destiny In the Blue Sea of August* 1974; *Tutto a Posto e Niente In Ordine/All Screwed Up* 1974; *Fatti di Gente Perbene* 1975; *A Mezzanotte va la ronda del Piacere* 1975; *Pasqualino Settebellezze/Seven Beauties* 1975 (a,p) **(AANBA)**; *L'Innocente/The Innocent* 1976; *The End of the World in Our Usual Bed in a Night Full of Rain* 1977; *I Nuovi Mostri* 1977; *Fatto di sangue fra due uomini per causa di una vedova. Si sospettano moventi politici/Blood Feud* 1978; *Travels With Anita* 1978; *Buone Notizie* 1979 (a,p); *Lili Marleen* 1981; *Bello Mio Bellezza Mia* 1982; *La Vita è bella* 1982; *American Dreamer* 1984; *Mi Manda Picone* 1984; *Fever Pitch* 1985; *Saving Grace* 1986; *Ternosecco* 1986 (a,d); *I Picari* 1987; *Snack Bar Budapest* 1988; *Blood Red* 1989; *Brown Bread Sandwiches* 1989; *New York Stories* 1989; *O Re* 1989; *Tempo di Uccidere* 1989; *Lo Zio Indegno/The Sleazy Uncle* 1989; *Divertimenti nella casa privata* 1990; *Il Male Oscuro* 1990; *Nel giardino delle rose* 1990.

Gibbons, Cedric • Art director • Born New York, NY, March 23, 1893; died 1960, Westwood, CA. Gibbons was appointed head of the art department at the newly formed MGM in 1924, following short stints with Thomas Edison and the independent Goldwyn company. He was a key figure in the creation of the MGM "look," working as either art supervisor or art director for the next 30 years. He is also credited with designing the Oscar statuette, which he himself won 11 times for design and once (in 1950) "for consistent excellence." Married to actress Delores del Rio from 1930 to 1941. • *He Who Gets Slapped* 1924 (art d); *Ben Hur, A Tale of the Christ* 1925 (art d); *The Mystic* 1925 (art d); *The Unholy Three* 1925 (art d); *The Black Bird* 1926 (art d); *The Road to Mandalay* 1926 (art d); *London After Midnight* 1927 (art d); *The Show* 1927 (art d); *The Unknown* 1927 (art d); *The Big City* 1928 (art d); *West of Zanzibar* 1928 (art d); *The Bridge of San Luis Rey* 1929 (art d) **(AABAD)**; *The Hollywood Revue of 1929* 1929 (art d) **(AANBAD)**; *The Thirteenth Chair* 1929 (art d); *Where East Is East* 1929 (art d); *Anna Christie* 1930 (art d); *The Unholy Three* 1930 (art d); *The Champ* 1931 (art d); *Red Dust* 1932 (art d); *Fast Workers* 1933 (art d); *When Ladies Meet* 1933 (art d) **(AANBAD)**; *The Merry Widow* 1934 (art d) **(AABAD)**; *Tarzan and His Mate* 1934 (d); *Treasure Island* 1934 (art d); *Mad Love* 1935 (art d); *Mark of the Vampire* 1935 (art d); *Fury* 1936 (art d); *The Great Ziegfeld* 1936 (art d) **(AANBAD)**; *Romeo and Juliet* 1936 (art d) **(AANBAD)**; *Conquest* 1937 (art d) **(AANBAD)**; *Marie Antoinette* 1938 (art d) **(AANBAD)**; *Miracles For Sale* 1939 (art d); *Sergeant Madden* 1939 (art d); *The Wizard of Oz* 1939 (art d) **(AANBAD)**; *Bitter Sweet* 1940 (art d) **(AANBAD)**; *I Take This Woman* 1940 (art d); *Pride and Prejudice* 1940 (art d) **(AABAD)**; *Blossoms in the Dust* 1941 (art d) **(AABAD)**; *When Ladies Meet* 1941 (art d) **(AANBAD)**; *Random Harvest* 1942 (art d) **(AANBAD)**; *Madame Curie* 1943 (art d) **(AANBAD)**; *Thousands Cheer* 1943 (art d) **(AANBAD)**; *Gaslight* 1944 (art d) **(AABAD)**; *Kismet* 1944 (art d) **(AANBAD)**; *National Velvet* 1944 (art d) **(AANBAD)**; *The Picture of Dorian Gray* 1945 (art d) **(AANBAD)**; *The Postman Always Rings Twice* 1946 (art d); *The Yearling* 1946 (art d) **(AABAD)**; *Sea of Grass* 1947 (art d); *Act of Violence* 1948 (art d); *Border Incident* 1949 (art d); *The Bribe* 1949 (art d); *Little Women* 1949 (art d) **(AABAD)**; *Madame Bovary* 1949 (art d) **(AANBAD)**; *The Red Danube* 1949 (art d) **(AANBAD)**; *Annie Get Your Gun* 1950 (art d) **(AANBAD)**; *The Asphalt Jungle* 1950 (art d); *An American in Paris* 1951 (art d) **(AABAD)**; *Cause For Alarm* 1951 (art d); *Quo Vadis* 1951 (art d) **(AANBAD)**; *Too Young to Kiss* 1951 (art d) **(AANBAD)**; *The Bad and the Beautiful* 1952 (art d) **(AABAD)**; *The Merry Widow* 1952 (art d) **(AABAD)**; *Big Leaguer* 1953 (art d); *Julius Caesar* 1953 (art d,cost) **(AABAD)**; *Lili* 1953 (art d) **(AANBAD)**; *The Story of Three Loves* 1953 (art d) **(AANBAD)**; *Young Bess* 1953 (art d) **(AANBAD)**; *Brigadoon* 1954 (art d) **(AANBAD)**; *Executive Suite* 1954 (art d) **(AANBAD)**; *Blackboard Jungle* 1955 (art d) **(AANBAD)**; *I'll Cry Tomorrow* 1955 (art d) **(AANBAD)**; *Moonfleet* 1955 (art d); *Forbidden Planet* 1956 (art d); *Lust For Life* 1956 (art d) **(AANBAD)**; *Somebody Up There Likes Me* 1956 (art d) **(AABAD)**.

Gibson, Mel • Actor • Born Peekskill, NY, January 3, 1956. *Educ.* National Institute of Dramatic Art, Sydney. Ruggedly handsome lead who was born in the US and emigrated to Australia in 1968. Gibson came to screen prominence toward the end of the following decade playing both the embodiment of futuristic machismo in George Miller's *Mad Max* (1979) and a retarded handyman in love with an older woman in Michael Pate's *Tim* (1979). His versatility and good looks propelled him into the front rank of Hollywood stars upon his return to the US, where he hit the box-office jackpot as hard-hitting cop Martin Riggs in the *Lethal Weapon* movies. • *Summer City* 1977; *Mad Max* 1979; *Tim* 1979; *Attack Force Z* 1981; *Gallipoli* 1981; *The Road Warrior* 1981; *The Year of Living Dangerously* 1982; *The Bounty* 1984; *Mrs. Soffel* 1984; *The River* 1984; *Mad Max Beyond Thunderdome* 1985 (a,stunts); *Lethal Weapon* 1987; *Tequila Sunrise* 1988; *Lethal Weapon 2* 1989; *Air America* 1990; *Bird on a Wire* 1990; *Hamlet* 1990.

Gielgud, Sir John • Actor; also author. • Born Arthur John Gielgud, London, April 14, 1904. *Educ.* Lady Benson's Acting School; RADA, London. Highly distinguished and prolific performer who is considered, with Laurence Olivier, one of the finest actors of his generation. Gielgud played his first Hamlet in 1930 and quickly established himself as a superlative Shakespearean actor and respected director. He made his screen debut in 1924 and appeared in Hitchcock's *Secret Agent* (1936) as well as several stage adaptations like *Julius Caesar* (1953) and Olivier's *Richard III* (1955). Increasingly in character roles since the late 1960s. • *Who Is the Man?* 1924; *The Clue of the New Pin* 1929; *Insult* 1932; *The Good Companions* 1933; *Secret Agent* 1936; *The Prime Minister* 1941; *Julius Caesar* 1953; *Romeo and Juliet* 1954; *Richard III* 1955; *Around the World in 80 Days* 1956; *The Barretts of Wimpole Street* 1956; *Saint Joan* 1957; *The Immortal Land* 1958; *Mourir a Madrid/To Die in Madrid* 1963; *Becket* 1964 **(AANBSA)**; *Hamlet* 1964 (a,d,staging); *The Loved One* 1965; *Campanidas a Medianoche/Chimes at Midnight/Falstaff* 1966; *Révolution d'Octobre* 1967; *Assignment to Kill* 1968; *The Charge of the Light Brigade* 1968; *Sebastian* 1968; *The Shoes of the Fisherman* 1968; *Oh! What a Lovely War* 1969; *Julius Caesar* 1970; *Eagle in a Cage* 1971; *Lost Horizon* 1973; *11 Harrowhouse* 1974; *Galileo* 1974; *Gold* 1974; *Murder on the Orient Express* 1974; *Aces High* 1976; *Joseph Andrews* 1976; *A Portrait of the Artist As a Young Man* 1977; *Providence* 1977; *Caligula* 1979; *The Human Factor* 1979; *Murder By Decree* 1979; *Dyrygent* 1980; *The Elephant Man* 1980; *The Formula* 1980; *Lion of the Desert* 1980; *Priest of Love* 1980; *Sphinx* 1980; *Arthur* 1981 **(AABSA)**; *Chariots of Fire* 1981; *Gandhi* 1982; *Invitation to the Wedding* 1983; *Wagner* 1983; *The Wicked Lady* 1983; *Scandalous* 1984; *The Shooting Party* 1984; *Ingrid* 1985; *Leave All Fair* 1985; *Plenty* 1985; *Time After Time* 1985; *Barbablu Barbablu* 1987; *The Whistle Blower* 1987; *Appointment With Death* 1988; *Arthur 2 on the Rocks* 1988; *Getting It Right* 1989; *Strike It Rich* 1989; *A TV Dante* 1989; *Prospero's Books* 1991.

Gilbert, John • *aka* Jack Gilbert • Actor; also screenwriter. • Born John Pringle, Logan, UT, July 10, 1895; died 1936. Handsome, romantic lead of silent films who reached his peak in the late 1920s, starring opposite Greta Garbo in several features including *Flesh and the Devil* and *Love* (both 1927). Gilbert's career tailed off after the advent of sound. He died of a heart attack at age 41. • *The Apostle of Vengeance* 1916; *Bullets and Brown Eyes* 1916; *The Eye of the Night* 1916; *Hell's Hinges* 1916; *The Phantom* 1916; *Shell 43* 1916; *The Dark Road* 1917; *Devil Dodger* 1917;*Doing Her Bit* 1917; *Golden Rule Kate* 1917; *Happiness* 1917; *Hater of Men* 1917; *The Millionaire Vagrant* 1917; *The Mother Instinct* 1917; *Princess of the Dark* 1917; *The Dawn of Understanding* 1918; *The Mask of Riches* 1918; *More Trouble* 1918; *Nancy Comes Home* 1918; *Shackled* 1918; *Sons of Men* 1918; *Three X Gordon* 1918; *Wedlock* 1918; *The Busher* 1919; *Heart O' the Hills* 1919; *The Man Beneath* 1919; *The Red Viper* 1919; *The White Heather* 1919; *Widow By Proxy* 1919; *Deep Waters* 1920 (a,sc); *The Great Redeemer* 1920 (a,adapt); *The Servant in the House* 1920; *Should a Woman Tell?* 1920; *While Paris Sleeps* 1920; *The White Circle* 1920 (a,sc); *The Bait* 1921 (sc); *Ladies Must Live* 1921; *Love's Penalty* 1921 (d,sc); *Shame* 1921; *Arabian Love* 1922; *A California Romance* 1922; *Calvert's Valley* 1922; *Gleam o'Dawn* 1922; *Honor First* 1922; *The Love Gambler* 1922; *Monte Cristo* 1922; *The Yellow Stain* 1922; *Cameo Kirby* 1923; *The Exiles* 1923; *Madness of Youth* 1923; *St. Elmo* 1923; *Truxton King* 1923; *Black Lightning* 1924; *He Who Gets Slapped* 1924; *His Hour* 1924; *Just Off Broadway* 1924; *The Lone Chance* 1924; *A Man's Mate* 1924; *Married Flirts* 1924; *Romance Ranch* 1924; *The Snob* 1924; *Wife of the Centaur* 1924; *The Wolf Man* 1924; *The Big Parade* 1925; *His Greatest Battle* 1925; *The Merry Widow* 1925; *Bardelys the Magnifi-*

cent 1926; *La Bohème* 1926; *Flesh and the Devil* 1927; *Love* 1927; *Man, Woman, and Sin* 1927; *The Show* 1927; *Twelve Miles Out* 1927; *The Cossacks* 1928; *Four Walls* 1928; *The Masks of the Devil* 1928; *Show People* 1928; *A Woman of Affairs* 1928; *Desert Nights* 1929; *His Glorious Night* 1929; *The Hollywood Revue of 1929* 1929; *A Man's Man* 1929; *Redemption* 1930; *Way For a Sailor* 1930; *Gentleman's Fate* 1931; *The Phantom of Paris* 1931; *West of Broadway* 1931; *Downstairs* 1932 (a,story); *Fast Workers* 1933; *Queen Christina* 1933; *The Captain Hates the Sea* 1934.

Gilbert, Lewis • Director; also screenwriter, producer, actor. • Born London, March 6, 1920. Former juvenile performer who turned to directing in the 1940s and made his name with patriotic war films such as *Albert R.N.* (1953) and *Reach for the Sky* (1956). Gilbert's best work has revealed a wry, if sentimental understanding of English social mores, from *The Greengage Summer* (1961) to *Alfie* (1966) to *Shirley Valentine* (1989). His three "James Bond" outings were among the least satisfying of the series. Son John is a producer and Steve an actor. • *Dick Turpin* 1933 (a); *Over the Moon* 1937 (a); *The Divorce of Lady X* 1938 (a); *Goodbye, Mr. Chips* 1939 (a); *Room For Two* 1940 (a); *Target For Today* 1944 (ad); *The Little Ballerina* 1949 (d,sc); *Marry Me* 1949 (sc); *The Golden Age* 1950 (p); *Once a Sinner* 1950 (d); *Scarlet Thread* 1951 (d); *There Is Another Sun* 1951 (d); *Emergency Call* 1952 (d,sc); *Johnny on the Run* 1952 (d,p); *Time Gentlemen Please!* 1952 (d); *Albert R.N.* 1953 (d); *Cosh Boy* 1953 (d); *The Good Die Young* 1954 (d,sc); *The Sea Shall Not Have Them* 1954 (d,sc); *Cast a Dark Shadow* 1955 (d); *Reach for the Sky* 1956 (d,sc); *The Admirable Crichton* 1957 (adapt,d); *Carve Her Name With Pride* 1958 (d,sc); *A Cry From the Streets* 1958 (d,p); *Ferry to Hong Kong* 1959 (d,sc); *Light Up the Sky!* 1960 (d,p); *Sink the Bismarck!* 1960 (d); *The Greengage Summer* 1961 (d); *Spare the Rod* 1961 (uncred.p); *Emergency* 1962 (story); *H.M.S. Defiant* 1962 (d); *The 7th Dawn* 1964 (d); *Alfie* 1966 (a,d,p) **(AANBP)**; *You Only Live Twice* 1967 (d); *The Adventurers* 1970 (d,p,sc); *Friends* 1971 (d,p,story); *Paul et Michele* 1974 (d,p,story); *Operation Daybreak* 1975 (d); *Seven Nights in Japan* 1976 (d,p); *The Spy Who Loved Me* 1977 (d); *Moonraker* 1979 (d); *The World of Gilbert & George* 1981 (d,sc); *Educating Rita* 1983 (d,p); *Not Quite Jerusalem* 1984 (d,p); *Shirley Valentine* 1989 (d,p); *Stepping Out* 1991 (d,p).

Gilliam, Terry • Director; also screenwriter, animator, actor. • Born Minneapolis, MN, November 22, 1940. *Educ.* Occidental College, CA (political science). Successful cartoonist who met John Cleese while working on the magazine *Help!* and subsequently became the resident animator with Monty Python's Flying Circus. Gilliam made his solo directing debut with *Jabberwocky* (1976), a grisly medieval interpretation of the Lewis Carroll poem, and scored a popular success with the delightfully "adult" childrens' feature, *Time Bandits* (1981).

Gilliam's greatest success came when he moved away from Pythonesque humor to direct *Brazil* (1985), a visually stunning, Orwellian look into a totalitarian future. After he fought and won an extended battle with Universal to gain "final cut" on the picture, it was released to considerable critical acclaim and hailed by many as one of the best films of the 1980s. Gilliam's next feature, *The Adventures of Baron Munchausen* (1988), was an expensive, visually sumptuous commercial flop which failed to reach the kind of crossover audience that had patronized *Time Bandits*. • *And Now For Something Completely Different* 1971 (a,sc,idea,anim); *Monty Python and the Holy Grail* 1975 (a,anim,d,sc); *Jabberwocky* 1976 (d,sc); *Pleasure at Her Majesty's* 1976 (a); *Monty Python's Life of Brian* 1979 (a,sc,pd,anim); *Time Bandits* 1981 (d,p,sc); *Monty Python Live at the Hollywood Bowl* 1982 (a,sc); *Monty Python's The Meaning of Life* 1983 (a,sc,special sequence d,anim.d); *Brazil* 1985 (d,sc) **(AANBSC)**; *Spies Like Us* 1985 (a); *The Adventures of Baron Munchausen* 1988 (d,sc); *The Fisher King* 1991 (d).

Gilliat, Sidney • Director; also screenwriter, producer. • Born Edgeley, Cheshire, England, February 15, 1908. *Educ.* London University (English, history). Began his career writing intertitles for silent films, graduating to screenplays in the 1930s before eventually turning to directing. Working often with partner Frank Launder, Gilliat made a series of outstanding British comedies and suspense pictures from the mid-30s into the 60s; among the team's screenwriting credits are *The Lady Vanishes* (1938) and *Night Train to Munich* (1940). Launder and Gilliat became known for thrillers with a comic element, such as *I See a Dark Stranger*, *Green For Danger* (both 1946) and *State Secret* (1950). *The Belles of St. Trinian's* (1954) is one of their best-known outright comedies. Brother of producer Leslie Gilliat. • *Adam's Apple* 1928 (uncred.titles); *Champagne* 1928 (uncred.titles); *Toni* 1928 (uncred.titles); *Week-End Wives* 1928 (uncred.titles); *The Manxman* 1929 (uncred.research); *Under the Greenwood Tree* 1929 (tech.literary adv,uncred.cost); *Would You Believe It?* 1929 (a,ad,uncred.add.gags); *Bed and Breakfast* 1930 (uncred.sc); *The Last Hour* 1930 (ad,uncred.sound fx); *Lord Richard in the Pantry* 1930 (uncred.sc); *Red Pearls* 1930 (uncred.sc,ad); *You'd Be Surprised!* 1930 (ad,sound fx,uncred.add. gags,uncred.a); *A Gentleman of Paris* 1931 (sc); *The Ghost Train* 1931 (uncred.add.dial); *The Happy Ending* 1931 (uncred.sc); *A Night in Marseilles* 1931 (sc); *The Ringer* 1931 (uncred.add.dial); *Third Time Lucky* 1931 (uncred.add.dial); *Two-Way Street* 1931 (uncred.sc); *Lord Babs* 1932 (uncred.add.material); *Rome Express* 1932 (sc,add.dial); *Face the Music* 1933 (story); *Falling For You* 1933 (story); *Friday the Thirteenth* 1933 (story); *Orders Is Orders* 1933 (sc); *Chu-Chin-Chow* 1934 (sc,uncred.add.lyrics); *Jack Ahoy!* 1934 (sc); *My Heart Is Calling* 1934 (adapt,dial—English-language version); *Bulldog Jack* 1935 (sc); *King of the Damned* 1935 (sc); *Everybody Dance* 1936 (uncred.assoc.p); *Good Morning, Boys* 1936 (p,sc,story); *The Man Who Lived Again* 1936 (uncred.assoc.p,sc); *Seven Sinners* 1936 (sc); *Strangers on Honeymoon* 1936 (sc); *Tudor Rose* 1936 (uncred.assoc.p); *Twelve Good Men* 1936 (sc); *Take My Tip* 1937 (sc); *The Gaunt Stranger* 1938 (sc); *The Lady Vanishes* 1938 (sc); *Strange Boarders* 1938 (sc); *A Yank at Oxford* 1938 (story); *Ask a Policeman* 1939 (story); *Inspector Hornleigh* 1939 (sc); *Jamaica Inn* 1939 (sc,dial); *Crooks' Tour* 1940 (from radio series); *The Girl in the News* 1940 (sc); *Night Train to Munich* 1940 (sc); *They Came By Night* 1940 (sc); *The Ghost Train* 1941 (uncred.add.dial); *Kipps* 1941 (sc); *Uncensored* 1942 (uncred.sc); *Unpublished Story* 1942 (uncred.sc); *The Young Mr. Pitt* 1942 (sc); *Millions Like Us* 1943 (d,sc); *Waterloo Road* 1944 (d,sc); *The Rake's Progress* 1945 (d); *Green For Danger* 1946 (d,p,sc); *I See a Dark Stranger* 1946 (p,sc,story); *Captain Boycott* 1947 (p); *London Belongs to Me* 1948 (d,sc); *The Blue Lagoon* 1949 (p); *The Happiest Days of Your Life* 1950 (p); *State Secret* 1950 (d,p,sc,story); *Lady Godiva Rides Again* 1951 (p); *Folly to Be Wise* 1952 (p); *La Minuit de Vérité/The Moment of Truth* 1952 (p); *The Story of Gilbert and Sullivan* 1953 (d,p); *The Belles of St. Trinian's* 1954 (p,sc); *The Constant Husband* 1954 (d,p,sc); *Wee Geordie* 1955 (p,sc); *The Green Man* 1956 (p,sc,from play *Meet a Body*); *Blue Murder at St. Trinian's* 1957 (p,sc); *Smallest Show on Earth* 1957 (p); *Fortune Is a Woman* 1958 (d,sc); *The Bridal Path* 1959 (p); *Left, Right and Centre* 1959 (a,d,p,sc,story); *Pure Hell of St. Trinian's* 1960 (p,sc); *Two-Way Stretch* 1960 (uncred.exec.p); *Only Two Can Play* 1961 (d,p); *Ring of Spies* 1963 (uncred.p); *The Great St. Trinian's Train Robbery* 1966 (d,exec.p,story); *Endless Night* 1972 (d,exec.p,sc); *Ooh... You Are Awful* 1972 (exec.p); *The Lady Vanishes* 1979 (from sc); *The Wildcats of St. Trinian's* 1980 (p.cons).

Girardot, Annie • Actress • Born Paris, October 25, 1931. *Educ.* Paris Conservatoire. Popular European leading lady with a flair for comedy. Girardot first gained international attention with Luchino Visconti's *Rocco and His Broth-*

ers (1960) and has appeared opposite Philippe Noiret in several charming comedies including *La Vieille fille* (1971) and *Tendre Poulet* (1977). • *Treize à table* 1955; *L'Homme aux clefs d'or* 1956; *Reproduction Interdite* 1956; *L'Amour est en jeu* 1957; *Le Desert de Pigalle* 1957; *Maigret Tend un Piege* 1957; *Le Rouge est mis* 1957; *La Corde raide* 1959; *La Française et l'amour* 1960; *La Proie pour l'ombre* 1960; *Recours en Grace* 1960; *Rocco e i suoi Fratelli/Rocco and His Brothers* 1960; *Amours célèbres* 1961; *Le Rendez-vous* 1961; *Le Bateau d'Emile* 1962; *Le Crime ne paie pas* 1962; *Pourquoi Paris?* 1962; *Smog* 1962; *Le Vice et la vertu* 1962; *I Compagni/The Organizer* 1963; *I Fuorilegge del matrimonio* 1963; *Il Giorno più corto* 1963; *L'Autre femme* 1964; *Le Belle famiglie* 1964; *La Bonne Soupe* 1964; *La Donna Scimmia/The Ape Woman* 1964; *Un Monsieur de Compagnie* 1964; *Declic et des claques* 1965; *La Guerre secréte/The Dirty Game* 1965; *Ragazza in Prestito* 1965; *Trois Chambres à Manhattan* 1965; *L'Or du Duc* 1966; *Una Voglia da morire* 1966; *Zhurnalist* 1966; *Les Anarchistes ou la bande à Bonnot* 1967; *Vivre pour vivre* 1967; *Bice Skoro propast sveta* 1968; *Dillinger è Morto/Dillinger Is Dead* 1968; *Les Gauloises bleues* 1968; *Le Streghe* 1968; *La Vie, l'amour, la mort* 1968; *Erotissimo* 1969; *Un Homme qui me plaît* 1969; *Metti, una Sera a Cena* 1969; *Il Seme dell'uomo* 1969; *Le Clair de terre* 1970; *Elle boit pas, elle fume pas, elle drague pas...mais elle cause!* 1970; *Mourir d'aimer* 1970; *Les Novices* 1970;*Storia di una Donna* 1970; *Les Feux de la Chandeleur* 1971; *La Mandarine* 1971; *Le Vieille Fille* 1971; *Elle cause plus...elle flingue* 1972; *Il n'y a pas de Fumée sans Feu* 1972; *Traitement de choc* 1972; *Juliette et Juliette* 1973; *Ursule et Grelu* 1973 (a,p); *La Gifle/The Slap* 1974; *D'amour et d'eau fraîche* 1975; *Docteur Françoise Gailland* 1975; *Le Gitan* 1975; *Il Pleut sur Santiago* 1975; *Il faut vivre Dangereusement* 1975; *Il Sospetto* 1975; *A chacun son enfer* 1976; *Cours après moi que je t'attrape* 1976; *Le Dernier Baiser* 1977; *Jambon d'Ardenne* 1977; *Le Point de mire* 1977; *Tendre Poulet/Dear Inspector* 1977; *L'Amour en Question* 1978; *Le Cavaleur* 1978 (uncred.a); *La Clé Sur la Porte* 1978; *Vas-y Maman* 1978; *La Zizanie* 1978; *Bobo Jacco/Jacko & Lise* 1979; *Cause toujours...tu m'interesses!* 1979; *Le Grand embouteillage/Traffic Jam* 1979 (uncred.a); *On à volé la cuisse de Jupiter/Jupiter's Thigh* 1979; *Le Coeur à l'Envers* 1980; *All Night Long* 1981; *Une Robe noire pour un tueur* 1981; *La Vie Continue* 1981; *Liste Noire* 1984; *Partir Revenir* 1984; *Souvenirs, Souvenirs* 1984; *Adieu Blaireau* 1985; *Cinq jours en juin* 1989; *Comédie d'amour* 1989.

Gish, Annabeth • Actress • Born Alberquerque, NM, c. 1972. Juvenile actress who gave a fine performance as a young girl caught between bomb testings and family feuds in the 1986 "sleeper" hit, *Desert Bloom*. • *Desert Bloom* 1986; *Hiding Out* 1987; *Mystic Pizza* 1988; *Shag* 1988; *Coupe De Ville* 1990.

Gish, Dorothy • Actress • Born Dorothy Elizabeth Gish, Dayton, OH, March 11, 1898; died June 4, 1968, Rapallo, Italy. Talented leading lady of silent films. Gish is best remembered as a comic player but proved equally at home in dramatic parts, as in D.W. Griffith's *Orphans of the Storm* (1921), where she plays a blind woman opposite her sister Lillian. Though eclipsed by Lillian in popularity, Dorothy's output during the silent years was greater, with starring roles in numerous light comedies such as *Remodeling Her Husband* (1920, directed by her sister), and *Nell Gwyn* (1926). After the emergence of sound she made only five screen appearances but remained active on the stage. Gish was married to *Remodeling* co-star James Rennie from 1920 to 1935. • *A Cry For Help* 1912; *Gold and Glitter* 1912; *The Informer* 1912; *The Musketeers of Pig Alley* 1912; *My Hero* 1912; *The New York Hat* 1912; *An Unseen Enemy* 1912; *The Adopted Brother* 1913; *Almost a Wild Man* 1913; *The Blue or the Gray* 1913; *A Cure For Suffragettes* 1913; *A Fallen Hero* 1913; *For the Son of the House* 1913; *Her Mother's Oath* 1913; *The House of Discord* 1913; *Judith of Bethulia* 1913; *Just Gold* 1913; *The Lady and the Mouse* 1913; *Oil and Water* 1913; *Pa Says* 1913; *The Perfidy of Mary* 1913; *The Suffragette Minstrels* 1913; *Those Little Flowers* 1913; *The Vengeance of Galora* 1913; *The Widow's Kids* 1913; *Arms and the Gringo* 1914; *The Availing Prayer* 1914; *Back to the Kitchen* 1914; *The Better Way* 1914; *Down the Hill to Creditville* 1914; *A Fair Rebel* 1914; *The Floor Above* 1914; *Granny* 1914; *Her Father's Silent Partner* 1914; *Her Mother's Necklace* 1914; *Her Old Teacher* 1914; *Home, Sweet Home* 1914; *A Lesson in Mechanics* 1914; *Man's Enemy* 1914; *The Mountain Rat* 1914; *The Mysterious Shot* 1914; *The Newer Woman* 1914; *The Painted Lady* 1914; *A Question of Courage* 1914; *Sands of Fate* 1914; *The Saving Grace* 1914; *Silent Sandy* 1914; *The Sisters* 1914; *The Suffragette Battle of Nuttyville* 1914; *The Tavern of Tragedy* 1914; *Their First Acquaintance* 1914; *The Warning* 1914; *Bred in the Bone* 1915; *Her Grandparents* 1915; *Her Mother's Daughter* 1915; *How Hazel Got Even* 1915; *Jordan Is a Hard Road* 1915; *The Little Catamount* 1915; *The Lost Lord Lovell* 1915; *Minerva's Mission* 1915; *The Mountain Girl* 1915;*Old Heidelberg* 1915; *An Old-Fashioned Girl* 1915; *Out of Bondage* 1915; *Victorine* 1915; *Atta Boy's Last Race* 1916; *Betty of Greystone* 1916; *Children of the Feud* 1916; *Gretchen, the Greenhorn* 1916; *Little Meena's Romance* 1916; *The Little School Ma'am* 1916; *Susan Rocks the Boat* 1916; *Hearts of the World* 1917; *Her Official Fathers* 1917; *The Little Yank* 1917; *Stage Struck* 1917; *Battling Jane* 1918; *The Hope Chest* 1918; *The Hun Within* 1918; *Boots* 1919; *I'll Get Him Yet* 1919; *Nugget Nell* 1919; *Out of Luck* 1919; *Peppy Polly* 1919; *Turning the Tables* 1919; *Flying Pat* 1920; *Little Miss Rebellion* 1920; *Mary Ellen Comes to Town* 1920; *Remodeling Her Husband* 1920 (a,sc,story); *The Ghost in the Garret* 1921; *Orphans of the Storm* 1921; *The Country Flapper* 1922; *The Bright Shawl* 1923; *Fury* 1923; *Romola* 1924; *The Beautiful City* 1925; *Clothes Make the Pirate* 1925; *Night Life of New York* 1925; *London* 1926; *Nell Gwyn* 1926; *Madame Pompadour* 1927; *Tiptoes* 1927; *Wolves* 1930; • *Our Hearts Were Young and Gay* 1944; *Centennial Summer* 1946; *The Whistle at Eaton Falls* 1951; *The Cardinal* 1963.

Gish, Lillian • *aka* Dorothy Elizabeth Carter • Actress; also director. • Born Lillian Diana Gish, Springfield, OH, October 14, 1896. Lillian Gish virtually invented screen acting. Entering films at a time when most "serious" thespians regarded motion pictures as a rather base form of employment, Gish brought to her roles a sense of craft substantially different from that practiced by her theatrical colleagues. In time, her sensitive performances elevated not only her stature as an actress, but also the reputation of movies as an art form.

Both Lillian and her younger sister Dorothy were introduced to stage work at an early age. In 1912 the girls travelled to New York to pay a courtesy call on their friend Gladys Smith, who came to be more widely known as Mary Pickford. Smith was acting at the time in films for the Biograph Company. At the studio the Gish sisters were introduced to Biograph's top director, D.W. Griffith, who was smitten with the girls' innocent charm and cast them immediately in his current production. Lillian and Dorothy soon gave up their theatrical ambitions and signed with Griffith's unit.

Griffith's contributions to the cinema have been well-documented, but his association with Lillian Gish was one of those rare times when two visions combine to revolutionize an art form. Gish was a firm believer in art as a higher ideal; she did not consider acting to be a mere profession. She soon came to share her director's opinion that film was a legitimate medium which inherently possessed more potential for artistic expression than the stage. The pictures Griffith and Gish made together over nine years bear witness to this conviction.

There was a certain symbiotic nature to the Gish-Griffith collaborations. Gish's angelic beauty was emblematic of

Griffith's Victorian notions of womanhood, but her manner also served an important narrative purpose. In most Griffith films tension is created when an innocent young girl is imperiled by the capriciousness of a cruel world. The climax of these films is often a rescue scene which requires the actress to look suitably distraught. Gish excelled at playing the victim in the early two-reelers, but as Griffith began experimenting with longer pictures her roles assumed a different function. Rather than the object of endangerment, Gish and her tremendous acting ability were required to help sustain the story. As the films became more complex, so did her characterizations. For example, in *The Mothering Heart* (1913), Gish plays a pregnant wife deserted by her husband. She gives birth alone, the baby dies, and she wanders out into the garden and thrashes the blossoms off a rose bush. This moment of tragedy could have easily become maudlin, but Gish handles the scene with such restraint that we only feel the young woman's grief. The strategy of controlling emotion —particularly in close-ups— became a hallmark of Gish's technique. Unlike the arm-waving, eyelid-fluttering histrionics engaged in by other actresses (a method carried over from stage productions), Gish practiced the art of the small yet meaningful gesture.

Gish perfected her skills in such memorable films as *The Birth of a Nation* (1915), *Hearts of the World* (1917) and *True Heart Susie* (1919), but her greatest work with Griffith was in *Broken Blossoms* (1919), in which she portrayed Lucy, the wharf rat daughter of a cockney fighter. Brutalized at home, she is adored by an Oriental shopkeeper, but when her father discovers this strange relationship he beats the girl to death. Gish's performance allows her to display a variety of emotions, from childish delight to utter panic. Her death scene is particularly discomforting: as her father administers the fatal beating, she cowers in a closet like a caged animal, twisting hysterically to ward off his blows. In her autobiography Gish recalled that when the sequence was completed Griffith said, "My God, why didn't you warn me you were going to do that?"

She made several more movies with Griffith, most notably *Way Down East* (1920) and *Orphans of the Storm* (1921), before assuming control of her career. At this point, her reputation was such that she was able to wield great power within the industry. She made two films for Inspiration Pictures before signing a five-picture deal with MGM in 1925. Because Gish's star image was intimately linked to her capabilities as a serious actress, MGM placed her in a series of literary adaptations. In *La Bohème* (1926) she played the consumptive Mimi; in *The Scarlet Letter* (1926) she was the adulterous Hester Prynne. Unfortunately, with her prestigious stature came rising production costs, which cut into into the profit margins of her pictures.

Her best MGM film was *The Wind* (1928), a harrowing story of a genteel woman who is brutalized by a stranger in West Texas before shooting him and going mad. It was not only Gish's last great performance in silent pictures, it was also her last successful starring role. By the end of the 20s a new type of modern heroine, exemplified by Greta Garbo, Joan Crawford, and Clara Bow, was in vogue; Gish's appeal was somewhat more nostalgic.

She accepted her decline gracefully, directing her attentions towards Broadway, while acting in an occasional film. She achieved screen prominence again with roles on *Duel in the Sun* (1947), *The Night of the Hunter* (1955) and a television production of Horton Foote's *A Trip to Bountiful* (1953). Despite advancing age, she has remained active, becoming a forceful advocate for film preservation. At the age of 90 she made *The Whales of August* (1987) with Bette Davis, displaying all of the craft that has made her one of the most respected performers in the history of motion pictures. KMM • *The Burglar's Dilemma* 1912; *A Cry For Help* 1912; *Gold and Glitter* 1912; *In the Aisles of the Wild* 1912; *The Musketeers of Pig Alley* 1912; *My Baby* 1912; *The New York Hat* 1912; *The One She Loved* 1912; *Two Daughters of Eve* 1912; *An Unseen Enemy* 1912; *The Battle at Elderbush Gulch* 1913; *The Blue or the Gray* 1913; *The Conscience of Hassan Bey* 1913; *During the Round Up* 1913; *The House of Darkness* 1913; *An Indian's Loyalty* 1913; *Judith of Bethulia* 1913; *Just Gold* 1913; *Just Kids* 1913; *The Lady and the Mouse* 1913; *The Left-Handed Man* 1913; *The Madonna of the Storm* 1913; *A Misunderstood Boy* 1913; *A Modest Hero* 1913; *The Mothering Heart* 1913; *Oil and Water* 1913; *So Runs the Way* 1913; *The Stolen Bride* 1913; *A Timely Interception* 1913; *The Unwelcome Guest* 1913; *A Woman in the Ultimate* 1913; *The Angel of Contention* 1914; *The Battle of the Sexes* 1914; *The Escape* 1914; *The Folly of Anne* 1914; *The Green-Eyed Devil* 1914; *Home, Sweet Home* 1914; *The Hunchback* 1914; *Lord Chumley* 1914; *Man's Enemy* 1914; *The Quicksands* 1914; *The Rebellion of Kitty Belle* 1914; *Silent Sandy* 1914; *The Sisters* 1914; *The Tear That Burned* 1914; *The Birth of a Nation* 1915;*Captain Macklin* 1915; *Enoch Arden* 1915; *The Lily and the Rose* 1915; *The Lost House* 1915; *Souls Triumphant* 1915; *The Children Pay* 1916; *Daphne and the Pirate* 1916; *Diane of the Follies* 1916; *Flirting With Fate* 1916; *An Innocent Magdalene* 1916; *Intolerance* 1916; *Pathways of Life* 1916; *Sold For Marriage* 1916; *Hearts of the World* 1917; *The House Built Upon Sand* 1917; *The Great Love* 1918; *The Greatest Thing in Life* 1918; *Broken Blossoms* 1919; *The Greatest Question* 1919; *A Romance of Happy Valley* 1919; *True Heart Susie* 1919; *Remodeling Her Husband* 1920 (d); *Way Down East* 1920; *Orphans of the Storm* 1921; *The White Sister* 1923; *Romola* 1924; *La Bohème* 1926; *The Scarlet Letter* 1926; *Annie Laurie* 1927; *The Enemy* 1928; *The Wind* 1928; *One Romantic Night* 1930; *His Double Life* 1933; *Commandos Strike at Dawn* 1942; *Top Man* 1943; *Miss Susie Slagle's* 1945; *Duel in the Sun* 1947 **(AANBSA)**; *Portrait of Jennie* 1948; *The Cobweb* 1955; *The Night of the Hunter* 1955; *Orders to Kill* 1958; *The Unforgiven* 1960; *Follow Me, Boys!* 1966; *The Comedians* 1967; *Warning Shot* 1967; *Langlois (short)* 1970; *A Wedding* 1978; *Hambone and Hillie* 1984; *Lillian Gish* 1984; *Sweet Liberty* 1986; *The Whales of August* 1987.

Glass, Philip • Composer • Born Baltimore, MD, 1937. *Educ.* University of Chicago; Juilliard (music). Celebrated avant-garde composer known for his repetitive, minimalist style and ambitous contemporary operas such as *Einstein on the Beach* (1976). Glass's feature-length scores brilliantly complemented the fluid, poetic images of Godfrey Reggio's *Koyaanisqatsi* (1982) and *Powaqqatsi* (1988). • *North Star: Mark Disuvero* 1978 (m); *Koyaanisqatsi* 1982 (m,m.dir); *Breathless* 1983 (songs); *Modern American Composers I* 1984 (a); *Mishima: A Life in Four Chapters* 1985 (m,m.arr); *A Composer's Notes: Philip Glass and the Making of an Opera* 1986 (a,opera "Akhnaten"); *Dead End Kids* 1986 (m); *Dialogue (short)* 1986 (m); *Hamburger Hill* 1987 (m); *Robert Wilson and the Civil Wars* 1987 (a); *Powaqqatsi* 1988 (m,dramaturge consult); *The Thin Blue Line* 1988 (m); *Mindwalk* 1990 (m).

Gleason, Jackie • Actor • Born Herbert John Gleason, Brooklyn, NY, February 26, 1916; died June 24, 1987, Fort Lauderdale, FL. In several films through the 1940s, but best remembered as the grouchy, overweight Ralph Kramden in TV's "The Honeymooners" (1949-54). Gleason never matched his TV success after returning to the screen, though he was outstanding as billiards wizard Minnesota Fats in *The Hustler* (1961). • *Navy Blues* 1941; *All Through the Night* 1942; *Escape From Crime* 1942; *Lady Gangster* 1942; *Larceny, Inc.* 1942; *Orchestra Wives* 1942; *Springtime in the Rockies* 1942; *Tramp, Tramp, Tramp* 1942; *The Desert Hawk* 1950; *The Hustler* 1961 **(AANBSA)**; *Gigot* 1962 (a,story,m); *Requiem For a Heavyweight* 1962; *Papa's Delicate Condition* 1963; *Soldier in the Rain* 1963; *Skidoo* 1968; *Don't Drink the Water* 1969; *How to Commit Marriage* 1969; *How Do I Love Thee?* 1970; *Mr. Billion* 1977; *Smokey and the Bandit* 1977; *Smokey and the Bandit II* 1980; *The Sting II* 1982; *The Toy* 1982; *Smokey and the Bandit Part 3* 1983; *Nothing in Common* 1986.

Glen, John • Director • Born Sunbury-on-Thames, England, May 15, 1932. Former editor who specializes in action pictures, notably the "James Bond" series. • *Baby Love* 1969 (ed); *On Her Majesty's Secret Service* 1969 (2u d,ed); *Murphy's War* 1970 (ed); *Catlow* 1971 (ed,2u d); *Sitting Target* 1972 (ed); *A Doll's House* 1973 (ed); *Gold* 1974 (ed,2u d); *Conduct Unbecoming* 1975 (ed); *Seven Nights in Japan* 1976 (ed); *Shout at the Devil* 1976 (2u d); *The Spy Who Loved Me* 1977 (ed,2u d); *Superman* 1978 (2u d); *The Wild Geese* 1978 (2u d,ed); *Moonraker* 1979 (ed,2u d); *The Sea Wolves* 1980 (ed); *For Your Eyes Only* 1981 (d); *Octopussy* 1983 (d); *A View to a Kill* 1985 (d); *The Living Daylights* 1987 (d); *Licence to Kill* 1989 (d).

Glenn, Scott • Actor • Born Pittsburgh, PA, January 26, 1942. *Educ.* College of William and Mary, Williamsburg, VA; Actors Studio. Leading man of the 1980s whose weathered features have been put to good use by directors including James Bridges (*Urban Cowboy* 1980) and Philip Kaufman (*The Right Stuff* 1983). • *The Baby Maker* 1970; *Angels Hard As They Come* 1971; *Hex* 1972; *Nashville* 1975; *Fighting Mad* 1976; *Apocalypse Now* 1979; *More American Graffiti* 1979; *She Came to the Valley* 1979; *Urban Cowboy* 1980; *Cattle Annie and Little Britches* 1981; *The Challenge* 1982 (a,song); *Personal Best* 1982; *The Keep* 1983; *The Right Stuff* 1983; *The River* 1984; *Silverado* 1985; *Wild Geese II* 1985; *Gangland* 1987; *Man on Fire* 1987; *Off Limits* 1988; *Miss Firecracker* 1989; *The Hunt For Red October* 1990; *My Heroes Have Always Been Cowboys* 1991; *The Silence of the Lambs* 1991.

Glennon, Bert • Director of photography; also director. • Born Bert Lawrence Glennon, Anaconda, MT, November 19, 1895; died 1967. *Educ.* Stanford. Distinguished cinematographer noted for his work on several Josef von Sternberg films, including *The Last Command* (1928) and *Blonde Venus* (1932), and his numerous collaborations with John Ford. Son James Glennon is also a director of photography. • *Ramona* 1916 (ph); *Eyes of the World* 1917 (ph); *The Kentucky Colonel* 1920 (ph); *Cheated Love* 1921 (ph); *The Dangerous Moment* 1921 (ph); *A Daughter of the Law* 1921 (ph); *The Kiss* 1921 (ph); *Moonlight Follies* 1921 (ph); *Nobody's Fool* 1921 (ph); *Parted Curtains* 1921 (ph); *The Torrent* 1921 (ph); *Burning Sands* 1922 (ph); *Ebb Tide* 1922 (ph); *The Woman Who Walked Alone* 1922 (ph); *Java Head* 1923 (ph); *Salomy Jane* 1923 (ph); *The Ten Commandments* 1923 (ph); *You Can't Fool Your Wife* 1923 (ph); *Changing Husbands* 1924 (ph); *Open All Night* 1924 (ph); *Triumph* 1924 (ph); *Worldly Goods* 1924 (ph); *Are Parents People?* 1925 (ph); *The Dressmaker From Paris* 1925 (ph); *Flower of Night* 1925 (ph); *Grounds For Divorce* 1925 (ph); *Tomorrow's Love* 1925 (ph); *Wild Horse Mesa* 1925 (ph); *A Woman of the World* 1925 (ph); *The Crown of Lies* 1926 (ph); *Good and Naughty* 1926 (ph); *Barbed Wire* 1927 (ph); *The City Gone Wild* 1927 (ph); *Hotel Imperial* 1927 (ph); *Underworld* 1927 (ph); *We're All Gamblers* 1927 (ph); *The Woman on Trial* 1927 (ph); *Gang War* 1928 (d); *The Last Command* 1928 (ph); *The Patriot* 1928 (ph); *The Perfect Crime* 1928 (d); *The Street of Sin* 1928 (ph); *The Air Legion* 1929 (d); *Syncopation* 1929 (d); *Around the Corner* 1930(d); *Girl of the Port* 1930 (d); *Paradise Island* 1930 (d); *Second Wife* 1930 (sc); *In Line of Duty* 1931 (d); *Blonde Venus* 1932 (ph); *Half Naked Truth* 1932 (ph); *South of Santa Fe* 1932 (d); *Alice in Wonderland* 1933 (ph); *Christopher Strong* 1933 (ph); *Gabriel Over the White House* 1933 (ph); *Melody Cruise* 1933 (ph); *Morning Glory* 1933 (ph); *Grand Canary* 1934 (ph); *Hell in the Heavens* 1934 (ph); *The Scarlet Empress* 1934 (ph); *She Was a Lady* 1934 (ph); *Bad Boy* 1935 (ph); *Ginger* 1935 (ph); *The Lottery Lover* 1935 (ph); *Show Them No Mercy* 1935 (ph); *Thunder in the Night* 1935 (ph); *Can This Be Dixie?* 1936 (ph); *Dimples* 1936 (ph); *Half Angel* 1936 (ph); *Little Miss Nobody* 1936 (ph); *Lloyd's of London* 1936 (ph); *The Prisoner of Shark Island* 1936 (ph); *Hurricane* 1937 (ph); *Drums Along the Mohawk* 1939 (ph); *Stagecoach* 1939 (ph) (**AANBPH**); *Swanee River* 1939 (ph); *Young Mr. Lincoln* 1939 (ph); *The Howards of Virginia* 1940 (ph); *Our Town* 1940 (ph); *Dive Bomber* 1941 (ph) (**AANBPH**); *One Night in Lisbon* 1941 (ph); *The Reluctant Dragon* 1941 (ph); *They Died With Their Boots On* 1941 (ph); *Virginia* 1941 (ph); *Desperate Journey* 1942 (ph); *Juke Girl* 1942 (ph); *The Desert Song* 1943 (ph); *Destination Tokyo* 1943 (ph); *Mission to Moscow* 1943 (ph); *This Is the Army* 1943 (ph); *Hollywood Canteen* 1944 (ph); *The Very Thought of You* 1944 (ph); *San Antonio* 1945 (ph); *One More Tomorrow* 1946 (ph); *Shadow of a Woman* 1946 (ph); *Copacabana* 1947 (ph); *Mr. District Attorney* 1947 (ph); *The Red House* 1947 (ph); *Ruthless* 1948 (ph); *Red Light* 1949 (ph); *Rio Grande* 1950 (ph); *Wagonmaster* 1950 (ph); *Operation Pacific* 1951 (ph); *The Sea Hornet* 1951 (ph); *About Face* 1952 (ph); *The Big Trees* 1952 (ph); *The Man Behind the Gun* 1952 (ph); *House of Wax* 1953 (ph); *The Moonlighter* 1953 (ph); *Thunder Over the Plains* 1953 (ph); *Crime Wave* 1954 (ph); *The Mad Magician* 1954 (ph); *Riding Shotgun* 1954 (ph); *Davy Crockett and the River Pirates* 1956 (ph); *Sergeant Rutledge* 1960 (ph); *Lad: A Dog* 1962 (ph); *The Man From Galveston* 1964 (ph).

Globus, Yoram • Producer, executive • Born Tiberias, Israel. See Golan, Menahem. • *El Coleccionista de Cadaveres* 1968 (exec.p); *Guess What We Learned in School Today?* 1970 (exec.p); *Joe* 1970 (exec.p); *Malkat Hakvish* 1970 (p); *Jump* 1971 (exec.p); *Habricha el Hashemesh* 1972 (asst.p); *Abu el Banat* 1973 (p); *The House on Chelouche Street* 1973 (exec.p); *Kazablan* 1973 (p); *Diamonds* 1975 (p); *Lepke* 1975 (exec.p); *The No Mercy Man* 1975 (p); *The Four Deuces* 1976 (p); *The Jaws of Death* 1976 (exec.p); *Entebbe: Operation Thunderbolt* 1977 (p); *Kid Vengeance* 1977 (exec.p); *Cheerleaders' Beach Party* 1978 (p); *The Alaska Wilderness Adventure* 1979 (p); *Imi Hageneralit* 1979 (p); *Incoming Freshmen* 1979 (exec.p); *The Magician of Lublin* 1979 (p); *Nissuim Nosach Tel Aviv* 1979 (p); *Yotz im'kavua* 1979 (p); *The Apple* 1980 (p); *Dr. Heckyl & Mr. Hype* 1980 (p); *The Godsend* 1980 (exec.p); *The Happy Hooker Goes Hollywood* 1980 (p); *Hospital Massacre* 1980 (p); *New Year's Evil* 1980 (p); *Schizoid* 1980 (p); *Seed of Innocence* 1980 (p); *The Swap* 1980 (exec.p); *Body and Soul* 1981 (p); *Death Wish II* 1981 (p); *Enter the Ninja* 1981 (p); *Lady Chatterley's Lover* 1981 (exec.p); *Shifshuf Naim* 1981 (p); *House of the Long Shadows* 1982 (p); *The Last American Virgin* 1982 (p); *Nana* 1982 (p); *Sapiches* 1982 (p); *The Seven Magnificent Gladiators* 1982 (exec.p); *El Tesora de las Cuatro Coronas/Treasure of the Four Crowns* 1982 (exec.p); *That Championship Season* 1982 (p); *"I'm Almost Not Crazy..." John Cassavetes: The Man and His Work* 1983 (p); *10 to Midnight* 1983 (exec.p); *Hercules* 1983 (p); *Over the Brooklyn Bridge* 1983 (p); *Revenge of the Ninja* 1983 (p); *Roman Zair* 1983 (p); *The Wicked Lady* 1983 (p); *The Ambassador* 1984 (p); *Bolero* 1984 (exec.p); *Breakin'* 1984 (exec.p); *Breakin' 2 Electric Boogaloo* 1984 (p); *Déjà Vu* 1984 (p); *Exterminator 2* 1984 (exec.p); *Love Streams* 1984 (p); *Making the Grade* 1984 (exec.p); *Missing in Action* 1984 (p); *Ninja III-The Domination* 1984 (exec.p); *Sahara* 1984 (p); *Sword of the Valiant-The Legend of Gawain and the Green Knight* 1984 (p); *American Ninja* 1985 (p); *The Assisi Underground* 1985 (p); *Un Complicato Intrigo di Donne, Vicoli e Delitti* 1985 (p); *Death Wish 3* 1985 (p); *Fool For Love* 1985 (p); *Grace Quigley* 1985 (p); *Hame'ahev* 1985 (p); *Hareemu Ohgen* 1985 (p); *Hot Chili* 1985 (p); *Hot Resort* 1985 (p); *Interno Berlinese* 1985 (p); *Invasion U.S.A.* 1985 (p); *King Solomon's Mines* 1985 (p); *Lifeforce* 1985 (p); *Maria's Lovers* 1985 (exec.p); *Mata Hari* 1985 (exec.p); *Missing in Action 2-The Beginning* 1985 (p); *The Naked Face* 1985 (p); *Ordeal By Innocence* 1985 (exec.p); *Rappin'* 1985 (p); *Runaway Train* 1985 (p); *Le Soulier de Satin* 1985 (p); *Thunder Alley* 1985 (exec.p); *War and Love* 1985 (exec.p); *52 Pick-Up* 1986 (p); *America 3000* 1986 (p); *Avenging Force* 1986 (p); *Cobra* 1986 (p); *Dangerously Close* 1986 (exec.p); *The Delta Force* 1986 (p); *Duet*

For One 1986 (p); *Dumb Dicks* 1986 (p); *Field of Honor* 1986 (p); *Firewalker* 1986 (p); *Hashigaon Hagadol* 1986 (p); *Invaders From Mars* 1986 (p); *Journey to the Center of the Earth* 1986 (p); *K'Fafoth* 1986 (exec.p); *Lightning-The White Stallion* 1986 (exec.p); *Malkat Hakita* 1986 (p); *Murphy's Law* 1986 (exec.p); *The Naked Cage* 1986 (exec.p); *Number One With a Bullet* 1986 (p); *Otello* 1986 (p); *P.O.W. the Escape* 1986 (p); *Salome* 1986 (exec.p); *The Texas Chainsaw Massacre 2* 1986 (p); *Allan Quatermain and the Lost City of Gold* 1987 (p); *American Ninja 2* 1987 (p); *Assassination* 1987 (exec.p); *The Barbarians* 1987 (p); *Barfly* 1987 (exec.p); *Beauty and the Beast* 1987 (p); *Business As Usual* 1987 (exec.p); *Dancers* 1987 (p); *Death Wish 4: The Crackdown* 1987 (exec.p); *Down Twisted* 1987 (p); *Dutch Treat* 1987 (p); *The Emperor's New Clothes* 1987 (p); *Going Bananas* 1987 (p); *Gor* 1987 (exec.p); *Hansel and Gretel* 1987 (p); *King Lear* 1987 (p); *The Kitchen Toto* 1987 (exec.p); *Mascara* 1987 (exec.p); *Masters of the Universe* 1987 (p); *Over the Top* 1987 (p); *Red Riding Hood* 1987 (p); *Rumpelstiltskin* 1987 (p); *Shy People* 1987 (p); *Sleeping Beauty* 1987 (p); *Snow White* 1987 (p); *Street Smart* 1987 (p); *Superman IV: The Quest For Peace* 1987 (p); *Surrender* 1987 (exec.p); *Too Much* 1987 (p); *Tough Guys Don't Dance* 1987 (p); *Under Cover* 1987 (p); *Alien From L.A.* 1988 (p); *Appointment With Death* 1988 (exec.p); *Bloodsport* 1988 (exec.p); *Braddock: Missing in Action III* 1988 (p); *A Cry in the Dark* 1988 (exec.p); *Doin' Time on Planet Earth* 1988 (exec.p); *Freedom Fighter* 1988 (p); *Hanna's War* 1988 (p); *Haunted Summer* 1988 (exec.p); *Hero and the Terror* 1988 (exec.p); *Manifesto* 1988 (p); *Messenger of Death* 1988 (exec.p); *Powaqqatsi* 1988 (exec.p); *Puss in Boots* 1988 (p); *Salsa* 1988 (p); *Cyborg* 1989 (p); *Kinjite* 1989 (exec.p); *Rockula* 1989 (exec.p); *Sinbad of the Seven Seas* 1989 (p); *Young Love: Lemon Popsicle VII* 1989 (exec.p); *Delta Force II* 1990 (p); *A Man Called Sarge* 1990 (exec.p).

Glover, Crispin • Actor • Born Los Angeles, CA. First gained popularity as nerdy teenager George McFly in *Back to the Future* (1985) and has subsequently specialized in playing alienated, misfit youths, most successfully in Tim Hunter's haunting *River's Edge* (1987). Son of actor Bruce Glover. • *My Tutor* 1982; *Friday the 13th—The Final Chapter* 1983; *Racing With the Moon* 1984; *Teachers* 1984; *Back to the Future* 1985; *At Close Range* 1986; *River's Edge* 1987; *Twister* 1989; *Where the Heart Is* 1990; *Wild at Heart* 1990; *The Doors* 1991; *Little Noises* 1991.

Glover, Danny • Actor • Born San Francisco, CA, 1947. *Educ.* San Francisco State University; Black Actors' Workshop of the American Conservatory Theatre. Commanding black performer, memorable as the domineering husband in *The Color Purple* (1985) and as Mel Gibson's buddy/partner in the "Lethal Weapon" movies. • *Escape From Alcatraz* 1979; *Chu Chu and the Philly Flash* 1981; *Out* 1982; *Iceman* 1984; *Places in the Heart* 1984; *The Stand-In* 1984; *The Color Purple* 1985; *Silverado* 1985; *Witness* 1985; *Lethal Weapon* 1987; *BAT 21* 1988; *Lethal Weapon 2* 1989; *Predator 2* 1990; *To Sleep With Anger* 1990 (a,exec.p); *Flight of the Intruder* 1991; *A Rage in Harlem* 1991.

Glover, John • Actor • Born Salisbury, MD, August 7, 1944. *Educ.* Towson State College, Baltimore, MD. Prolific character actor of stage, screen and TV with a knack for playing villains, notably in *52 Pick-Up* (1986). Made an indelible impression as the actor boyfriend of Diane Keaton who wants her to touch his heart—with her foot, in *Annie Hall* (1977). • *Shamus* 1972; *Annie Hall* 1977; *Julia* 1977; *Somebody Killed Her Husband* 1978; *American Success Company* 1979; *Last Embrace* 1979; *Brubaker* 1980; *Melvin and Howard* 1980; *The Mountain Men* 1980; *The Incredible Shrinking Woman* 1981; *A Little Sex* 1981; *The Evil That Men Do* 1984; *A Flash of Green* 1985; *White Nights* 1985; *52 Pick-Up* 1986; *I Was a Teenage Boy* 1986; *A Killing Affair* 1986; *My Sister's Keeper* 1986; *The Chocolate War* 1988; *Masquerade* 1988; *Rocket Gibraltar* 1988; *Scrooged* 1988; *Home (short)* 1989; *Meet the Hollowheads* 1989; *Gremlins 2: The New Batch* 1990; *Robocop 2* 1990.

Glover, Julian • Actor • Born London, March 27, 1935. *Educ.* RADA, London. Popular character player of stage, screen and TV, primarily in villainous roles (*For Your Eyes Only* 1981, *Indiana Jones and the Last Crusade* 1989). • *Tom Jones* 1963; *The Alphabet Murders* 1966; *Blood Fiend* 1967; *The Magus* 1968; *The Adding Machine* 1969; *Alfred the Great* 1969; *Antony and Cleopatra* 1970; *The Last Grenade* 1970; *The Rise and Rise of Michael Rimmer* 1970; *Wuthering Heights* 1970; *Nicholas and Alexandra* 1971; *Hitler: The Last Ten Days* 1973; *The Internecine Project* 1974; *Juggernaut* 1974; *Luther* 1974; *Gulliver's Travels* 1977; *The Empire Strikes Back* 1980; *For Your Eyes Only* 1981; *Heat and Dust* 1983; *Cry Freedom* 1987; *The Fourth Protocol* 1987; *Hearts of Fire* 1987; *Indiana Jones and the Last Crusade* 1989; *Tusks* 1990; *King Ralph* 1991.

Godard, Jean-Luc • *aka* Hans Lucas • Director, screenwriter, critic; also producer, actor. • Born Paris, December 3, 1930. *Educ.* Sorbonne, Paris (ethnology). Few filmmakers have had so profound an effect on the development of the art as Jean-Luc Godard. From his early days as a critic and thinker in the pages of *Cahiers du Cinéma* and elsewhere, through the great age of the New Wave in the 1960s, continuing (with a lesser impact) in the 70s and 80s, Godard has redefined the way we look at film. An essayist and poet of the cinema, he makes the language of film a real part of his narratives.

With a prodigious sense of exploration, Godard has worked his way through no less than four artistic periods since his days as a critic in the 50s: The "New Wave" Godard (still the most influential) lasted from *Breathless* (1959) to *Weekend* (1967). The "Revolutionary" Godard stretched from *Le Gai savoir* (1968) to *Tout va bien* (1972), encompassing the "Dziga-Vertov" period. Godard the "Vidéoaste" lasted from the formation of the Sonimage production company with Anne-Marie Miéville in Grenoble through 1978. Finally, the "Contemplative" Godard began with *Sauve qui peut (la vie)* in 1980 and has extended through *Nouvelle Vague* (1990).

Godard's critical examination of international film masters, American auteurs and American genre films in the 50s was paralleled by his own early incursions into the medium. He acted in and produced early short films by fellow critics Eric Rohmer and Jacques Rivette and himself directed a series of shorts: from the documentary *Operation Beton* (1954), through the whimsical *All Boys Are Called Patrick* (1957), to the editing exercise, *Une histoire d'eau* (1958), shot by Truffaut but handed over to Godard after the former had given up on the material. These reciprocal forces, the back-and-forth from production to criticism, led to a series of homages, reinventions and variations which helped us all to understand what film had been—and what it was to become.

In *Breathless*, Godard broke with established narrative conventions, spontaneously mixing elements from the detective, comedy and suspense genres. *A Woman Is a Woman* (1961) applied this critical intelligence to the musical genre, as *Alphaville* (1965) did to science fiction. For the first time, a director was making films that were "about" other films (as well as about themselves). At the same time, Godard was developing the essay form as he began to speak more directly to his audiences in such films as *My Life to Live* (1962), *The Married Woman* (1964) and *Masculin-Féminin* (1966).

With the exception of *A Woman Is a Woman* (his lovesong to then-wife Anna Karina), the subject matter of these films is downbeat and darkly modernist. Godard's couples are alienated both from each other and from their environment; driven by uncertainty and mistrust, they act arbitrarily, often with tragic results. Fleeing the disorder of the city for refuge in nature, as in *Pierrot le fou* (1965), characters still cannot escape death. Language, inherently ambiguous, serves as a barrier to communication and precludes love. Even body language fails: in *Contempt* (1963), a husband's insecurity makes him suspect his wife's every facial gesture. Prostitution becomes the incessant metaphor.

Godard himself, however, was capable of broader understanding: if his characters couldn't communicate, he himself was getting better at it with every film. He best expressed this positive aspect in "Anticipation," his episode of the portmanteau film *Le Plus vieux métier du monde* (1967). In this parable, a soldier of the Sovietoamerican army of the future (Jean-Pierre Léaud) is sent to receive treatment from a "spiritual" prostitute (Anna Karina). Together, they reinvent the kiss (using the one part of the body that can both speak and make love). The authorities declare them dangerous, because "they are making love, progress, and conversation—all at the same time!"

In *Two or Three Things I Know About Her* (1967), Godard himself, the filmmaker/narrator, is a major character, commenting on the dysfunctional universe he depicts. By *Weekend*, the alienation has become absurd: the married couple openly cheat on each other in a disintegrating world. Human dignity and respect are absent from this savage vision of middle-class barbarians and murderous, aimless revolutionaries who become cannibals.

By this time, deciding that there was something fundamentally wrong with the way we lead our modern lives, Godard was ready—like so many of his contemporaries—to turn to political action as a solution. Politics had often been part of the background of the earlier films: *Le Petit soldat* (1960), his second film, was actually banned by the government for several years because it dealt with the Algerian situation. *Les Carabiniers* (1963) discussed the politics of war in absurdist terms, with a screenplay co-scripted by one of Godard's key influences, Roberto Rossellini; *Made in USA* (1966) was an attempt at a political suspense film (with references to the Ben Barka affair); *La Chinoise* (1967) was a collage portrait, in colorful, pop-art strokes, of the French new left student movement one year before the "events" of May '68. Now it was time to act.

Rejoining his colleagues from *Cahiers du Cinéma*, Godard participated in the 1968 demonstrations over the dismissal of Henri Langlois as head of the *Cinémathèque Française* which led to the "Events of May." Then, from 1968 through 1972 Godard made 11 films, over half in collaboration with Jean-Pierre Gorin (whose involvement varied from project to project), and most released as signed by the "Dziga-Vertov Group." Godard and Gorin were, they said, "making political films politically." Although they claimed, "we have no answers, only questions," these films appear to address and support militant issues. Yet, in the end, it's clear Godard and Gorin have more concern with the process of filmmaking than with the process of revolution. Throughout their collaboration, they are obsessed with the job of turning theory into practice. *British Sounds* (1969) is perhaps the most successful of Godard's "revolutionary" experiments, a collection of images and sounds meant to incite discussion about workers, about women, about students, about revolution. Godard and Gorin went on tour with their films, trying to directly engage their audiences in the dialogue.

The Dziga-Vertov period culminated with two films: *Tout va bien* and *A Letter to Jane* (1972). *Tout va bien*, with Yves Montand and Jane Fonda, was meant to summarize something of what the group had learned from their experiments in a commercial movie, complete with international stars. As if in reaction, *Letter to Jane* is an essay about an image of Jane Fonda in Vietnam which had appeared in the magazine *L'Express*. A 45-minute monologue by Godard/Gorin, *Letter to Jane* explains a lot about their theories of images and sounds and how they might relate to politics.

The Dziga-Vertov Group disbanded in 1973. Gorin moved to California to teach, later turning out a number of bold, engaging films, notably 1979's *Poto and Cahengo*); Godard moved to video, both because it was a better medium for the essays and experimentation he had in mind and because TV had by this time become the best way to communicate with the largest number of people. In 1975, he left Paris for Grenoble, and collaboration with Anne-Marie Miéville, his third wife.

In an alternate life, Godard might have "gone Hollywood." It wasn't for want of trying. Robert Benton and David Newman had approached him in the mid-60s about directing *Bonnie & Clyde.* Godard couldn't make a deal with the producers. A while later, again with Benton and Newman, he was set to direct *The Technique of a Political Murder*, about Trotsky, for producer Raoul Levy. Levy died unexpectedly. Godard was considered as director for Jules Feiffer's *Little Murders* until Elliott Gould realized Godard didn't want to make that movie, he wanted to make a movie about making that movie. In the early 80s he attempted to get an elaborate American production about Bugsy Siegel off the ground. It would have starred Diane Keaton. It didn't come to pass.

The main productions of the video period were the two series, "Six Fois Deux/Sur et sous la communication" (1976, ten hours), and "France-Tour-Detour-Deux-Enfants" (1978, six hours). Godard starts with the premise that "video is for those who do not see." These series comprise essays on commonplace, everyday subjects—including family, love, work, communication, and relationships—all as they are presented by the media for mass consumption. With some success, Godard challenges the passivity of TV viewers and their unquestioning acceptance of media messages.

Individual segments of the "Six Fois Deux" series examine the mass media's approach to such subjects as unemployment, farming, the language of images, photonews, relationships, math, madness and society, and filmmaking. In separate segments, real people with direct knowledge of each area of inquiry—including a farmer, a filmmaker and a mathematician—personally discuss these topics and their representation in the media. "France-Tour-Detour-Deux-Enfants" juxtaposes philosophical interviews with two children from the same family (ages 9 and 12) about the meaning of daily activities against images of everyday life with their parents, including watching TV. For the first time, in these projects for the small screen, Godard takes on the role of teacher to share with a much larger audience his understanding of the complex language of film and TV.

In 1975, Godard had released two films—*Numéro Deux* and *Comment Ça Va*—which indicated the direction for the future. For the first time here he contemplated his own cinematic history. Starting in 1980, Godard continued the reinvestigation of concerns and themes he had first developed in the 60s. *Sauve qui peut (la vie)* and *Passion* (1982) give us portraits of emotional confusion mixed with commentary on the problems of filmmaking—a fusion of the 60s and early 70s.

With his next three films, Godard hit his stride again. *First Name: Carmen* (1983) imaginatively retold the old story. *Détéctive* (1985), a comic homage to the genre (dedicated "to John Cassavetes, Edgar G. Ulmer, and Clint Eastwood") brought Godard back with pleasure to his first cinematic love. But it was *Hail Mary* (1985) which really marked Godard's return to theatrical prominence. This modern nativity tale—placing the story of Joseph and Mary in modernist society, rampant with jealousy, loneliness, and divorce—was actually condemned by the Vatican. At the age of 55, Jean-Luc Godard was once again the enfant terrible. *Hail Mary* evinces the same sort of fresh, exciting—and often infuriating—narrative innovation that made the films of Jean-Luc Godard required viewing for anyone who cared about film in the 60s.

In 1987, the ever-prolific and experimental Godard turned out three more films: his segment of the omnibus feature *Aria* was one of the bolder, funnier exercises, setting Jean-Baptiste Lully's *Armide* in a gymnasium with brooding, nude female workers contemplating the murder of muscle-bound males; *Soigne ta droite* was a docu-essay on French pop group Les Rita Mitsouko, drawing comparisons to his earlier *One Plus One* (1968), which had intercut the Rolling Stones recording "Sympathy for the Devil" with fragments of contemporary English life; *King Lear* marked Godard's English-language and, in some sense, Hollywood debut. (It was shot for Cannon films in Geneva, with Molly Ringwald as Cordelia, Burgess Meredith as Lear and stage director Peter Sellars as a bewildered "Will Shakespeare V.")

While not a cause célèbre, *New Wave* (1990), about big business machinations on a Swiss estate, continues Godard's very personal quest to understand the nature and meaning of the movies. RCB, JM • *Quadrille (short)* 1950 (a,p); *Opération Béton (short)* 1954 (d,p,sc,ed); *Une Femme Coquette (short)* 1955 (a,d,p,sc,ph,ed); *Le Coup du Berger (short)* 1956 (a); *La Sonate à Kreutzer* 1956 (p); *Tous les Garçons s'appèllent Patrick/All Boys Are Called Patrick* 1957 (d); *Charlotte et son Jules (short)* 1958 (a,d,sc,ed); *Une Histoire d'Eau (short)* 1958 (a,d,sc,ed); *A bout de souffle/Breathless* 1959 (a,d,sc); *Paris Nous Appartient/Paris Belongs to Us* 1960 (a); *Le Petit Soldat* 1960 (a,d,sc,story); *Le Signe du lion* 1960 (a); *Une Femme est une femme/A Woman Is a Woman* 1961 (d,sc,song); *Les Fiancés du Pont Macdonald (short)* 1961 (a); *Lola* 1961 (prod.cons); *Le Soleil dans l'oeil* 1961 (a); *Cléo de 5 à 7* 1962 (a); *RoGoPag* 1962 (a,d,sc,story—"Le Nouveau Monde"); *Les Sept péchés capitaux/The Seven Deadly Sins* 1962 (d,sc—"La Paresse/Laziness"); *Sheherazade* 1962 (a); *Vivre sa Vie/My Life to Live* 1962 (a,d,sc,story); *Les Carabiniers* 1963 (d,sc); *The Directors (short)* 1963 (a); *Le Mépris/Contempt* 1963 (a,d,sc); *Bande à Part/Band of Outsiders* 1964 (a,d,sc); *Begegnung mit Fritz Lang (short)* 1964 (a); *Une Femme mariée/A Married Woman* 1964 (d,sc,story); *Paparazzi (short)* 1964 (a); *Petit jour (short)* 1964 (a); *Les Plus belles escroqueries du monde* 1964 (a,d,sc,from story—"Le grand escroc"); *Reportage sur Orly (short)* 1964 (d); *Statues (short)* 1964 (a,commentary); *Temoignage sur Bardot-Godard ou Le parti des choses (short)* 1964 (a); *Alphaville* 1965 (d,sc,story); *Paris Vu Par.../Six in Paris* 1965 (d,sc—"Montparnasse et Levallois"); *Pierrot le Fou* 1965 (d,sc); *The Defector* 1966 (a); *Deux ou trois choses que je sais d'elle/Two or Three Things I Know About Her* 1966 (a,d,sc); *Made in U.S.A.* 1966 (a,d,sc); *Masculin-Féminin/Masculine Feminine* 1966 (d,sc); *Amore e rabbia* 1967 (d,sc,story—"L'amore"); *La Chinoise, ou plutôt à la Chinoise* 1967 (d,sc,story); *Loin du Viêtnam/Far From Vietnam* 1967 (a,d,sc); *Les Mauvaises frequentations* 1967 (p—"La Père Noël a les yeux bleus"/Santa Clause Has Blue Eyes"); *Le Plus vieux métier du monde* 1967 (d,sc, story—"Anticipation"); *Weekend* 1967 (sc,story); *Un Film comme les autres* 1968 (a,d,sc); *Le Gai Savoir* 1968 (d,sc,story); *One Plus One/Sympathy For the Devil* 1968 (a,d,sc,story); *Two American Audiences* 1968 (a); *Voices* 1968 (a); *British Sounds* 1969(d,sc); *Lotte in Italia* 1969 (d); *Pravda* 1969 (d); *Le Vent d'est/Wind From the East* 1969 (d,sc,ed); *Jusqu'à la Victoire/'Til Victory* 1970 (d,documentation); *Vladimir et Rosa* 1970 (a,d,p); *One American Movie/1 A.M.* 1971 (a,d,sc); *Letter to Jane* 1972 (a,d,p,sc); *La Longue marche de Jean-Luc Godard* 1972 (a); *Tout va bien* 1972 (d,p,sc); *Comment ça va* 1975 (d,sc); *Ici et ailleurs* 1975 (d,sc); *Numéro Deux* 1975 (a,d,p,sc); *Der Kleine Godard* 1978 (a); *Sauve qui peut (la vie)/Every Man For Himself (Slow Motion)* 1980 (d,p,sc,dial,ed); *Chambre 666* 1982 (a); *Passion* 1982 (d,sc,ed); *Breathless* 1983 (from sc *A bout de souffle*); *Prénom Carmen/First Name: Carmen* 1983 (a,d,sc,ed); *Détective* 1985 (d,sc); *Je vous salue, Marie/Hail, Mary* 1985 (d,sc,ed); *Grandeur et décadence d'un petit commerce de cinéma* 1986 (d,sc); *Aria* 1987 (d,sc,ed—"Armide"); *King Lear* 1987 (a,d,sc,ed); *Soigne ta droite* 1987 (a,d,sc,ed); *Nouvelle Vague/New Wave* 1990 (d,sc,ed).

Goddard, Paulette • *aka* Marion Levy • Actress • Born Pauline Marion Goddard Levee, Long Island, NY, June 3, 1911; died April 23, 1990, Switzerland. Amiable, effervescent leading lady, in Hollywood from 1929 but virtually unknown until she played opposite second husband Charles Chaplin in *Modern Times* (1936). A popular star through the 1940s, Goddard appeared in several films with third husband Burgess Meredith, including Jean Renoir's *The Diary of a Chambermaid* (1946). She wed her last husband, novelist Erich María Remarque, in 1958. • *The Locked Door* 1929; *City Streets* 1931; *The Girl Habit* 1931; *The Kid From Spain* 1932; *The Mouthpiece* 1932; *Pack Up Your Troubles* 1932; *Roman Scandals* 1933; *Kid Millions* 1934; *Modern Times* 1936; *Dramatic School* 1938; *The Young in Heart* 1938; *The Cat and the Canary* 1939; *The Women* 1939; *The Ghost Breakers* 1940; *The Great Dictator* 1940; *North West Mounted Police* 1940; *Second Chorus* 1940; *Hold Back the Dawn* 1941; *Nothing But the Truth* 1941; *Pot o' Gold* 1941; *The Forest Rangers* 1942; *The Lady Has Plans* 1942; *Reap the Wild Wind* 1942; *Star Spangled Rhythm* 1942; *The Crystal Ball* 1943; *So Proudly We Hail* 1943 (**AANBSA**); *I Love a Soldier* 1944; *Standing Room Only* 1944; *Duffy's Tavern* 1945; *The Diary of a Chambermaid* 1946; *Kitty* 1946; *An Ideal Husband* 1947; *Suddenly It's Spring* 1947; *Unconquered* 1947; *Variety Girl* 1947; *Hazard* 1948; *A Miracle Can Happen* 1948; *Anna Lucasta* 1949;*Bride of Vengeance* 1949; *The Torch* 1950; *Babes in Baghdad* 1952; *Paris Model* 1953; *Sins of Jezebel* 1953; *Vice Squad* 1953; *Charge of the Lancers* 1954; *Stranger Came Home* 1954; *Gli Indifferenti* 1964.

Golan, Menahem • Producer, executive; also director, screenwriter. • Born Tiberias, Israel, May 31, 1929. *Educ.* Habimah Theater, Tel Aviv; Old Vic, London (theater directing); LAMDA, London; CCNY (film production). Energetic, prolific figure who with cousin Yoram Globus has produced over 150 movies in a partnership dating back to the early 1960s.

After directing for the stage in Israel, Golan found his way to the US as one of Roger Corman's many young protégés. Upon his return to Israel he and Globus helped build that country's film industry, producing, and sometimes directing, several prestige productions such as *Sallah Shabati* (1964).

In 1979 the team moved to Hollywood, taking control of the Cannon group. In the following decade they turned out art-house productions such as John Cassavetes' *Love Streams* (1984) and Jean-Luc Godard's *King Lear* (1987), critical hits like *Barfly* (1987) and—primarily—formula action thrillers such as *The Delta Force* (1986) and *Over the Top* (1987), both directed by Golan.

The partnership dissolved in 1989 with Golan resigning from Cannon to head the 21st Century Film Corporation and Globus becoming CEO of Pathé International. • *Sallah Shabati/Sallah* 1964 (p); *El Coleccionista de Cadaveres* 1968 (exec.p); *Guess What We Learned in School Today?* 1970 (exec.p); *Joe* 1970 (exec.p); *Malkat Hakvish* 1970 (d,sc); *999-Aliza the Policeman* 1971 (d,p,sc); *Jump* 1971 (exec.p); *Ani Obev Otach Rosa* 1972 (p); *Habricha el Hashemesh* 1972 (d,p,sc); *Abu el Banat* 1973 (p); *The House on Chelouche Street* 1973 (p); *Kazablan* 1973 (d,p,sc); *Diamonds* 1975 (d,p,sc,story); *Lepke* 1975 (d,p); *The No Mercy Man* 1975 (p); *The Jaws of Death* 1976 (exec.p); *The Passover Plot* 1976 (exec.p); *Entebbe: Operation Thunderbolt* 1977 (d,p); *Kid Vengeance* 1977 (p); *Agenten kennen keine Tranen* 1978 (d); *Cheerleaders' Beach Party* 1978 (p); *The Alaska Wilderness Adventure* 1979 (p); *Imi Hageneralit* 1979 (p); *Incoming Freshmen* 1979 (exec.p); *The Magician of Lublin* 1979 (d,p,sc); *Nissuim Nosach Tel Aviv* 1979 (p); *Yotz im'kavua* 1979 (p); *The Apple* 1980 (d,p,sc); *Dr. Heckyl & Mr. Hype* 1980 (p); *The Godsend* 1980 (exec.p); *The Happy Hooker Goes Hollywood* 1980 (p); *Hospital Massacre* 1980 (p); *New Year's Evil* 1980 (p); *Schizoid* 1980 (p); *Seed of Innocence* 1980 (p); *The Swap* 1980 (exec.p); *Body and Soul* 1981 (p); *Death Wish II* 1981 (p); *Enter the Ninja* 1981 (d); *Lady Chatterley's Lover* 1981 (exec.p); *Shifshuf Naim* 1981 (p); *House of the Long Shadows* 1982 (p); *The Last American Virgin* 1982 (p); *Nana* 1982 (p); *Sapiches* 1982 (p); *The*

Seven Magnificent Gladiators 1982 (exec.p); *El Tesora de las Cuatro Coronas* 1982 (exec.p); *That Championship Season* 1982 (p); *"I'm Almost Not Crazy..." John Cassavetes: The Man and His Work* 1983 (a,p); *10 to Midnight* 1983 (exec.p); *Hercules* 1983 (p); *Over the Brooklyn Bridge* 1983 (d,p); *Revenge of the Ninja* 1983 (p); *Roman Zair* 1983 (p); *The Wicked Lady* 1983 (p); *The Ambassador* 1984 (p); *Bolero* 1984 (exec.p); *Breakin'* 1984 (exec.p); *Breakin' 2 Electric Boogaloo* 1984 (p); *Déjà Vu* 1984 (p); *Exterminator 2* 1984 (exec.p); *Love Streams* 1984 (p); *Making the Grade* 1984 (exec.p); *Missing in Action* 1984 (p); *Ninja III-The Domination* 1984 (exec.p); *Sahara* 1984 (p,story); *Sword of the Valiant-The Legend of Gawain and the Green Knight* 1984 (p); *American Ninja* 1985 (p); *The Assisi Underground* 1985 (p); *Un Complicato Intrigo di Donne, Vicoli e Delitti* 1985 (p); *Death Wish 3* 1985(p); *Fool For Love* 1985 (p); *Grace Quigley* 1985 (p); *Hame'ahev* 1985 (p); *Hareemu Ohgen* 1985 (p); *Hot Chili* 1985 (p); *Hot Resort* 1985 (p); *Interno Berlinese* 1985 (p); *Invasion U.S.A.* 1985 (p); *King Solomon's Mines* 1985 (p); *Lifeforce* 1985 (p); *Maria's Lovers* 1985 (exec.p); *Mata Hari* 1985 (exec.p); *Missing in Action 2-The Beginning* 1985 (p); *The Naked Face* 1985 (p); *Ordeal By Innocence* 1985 (exec.p); *Rappin'* 1985 (p); *Runaway Train* 1985 (p); *Le Soulier de Satin* 1985 (p); *Thunder Alley* 1985 (exec.p); *War and Love* 1985 (exec.p); *52 Pick-Up* 1986 (p); *America 3000* 1986 (p); *Avenging Force* 1986 (p); *Cobra* 1986 (p); *Dangerously Close* 1986 (exec.p); *The Delta Force* 1986 (d,p,sc); *Duet For One* 1986 (p); *Dumb Dicks* 1986 (p); *Field of Honor* 1986 (p); *Firewalker* 1986 (p); *Hashigaon Hagadol* 1986 (p,sc); *Invaders From Mars* 1986 (p); *Journey to the Center of the Earth* 1986 (p); *K'Fafoth* 1986 (exec.p); *Lightning-The White Stallion* 1986 (exec.p); *Malkat Hakita* 1986 (p); *Murphy's Law* 1986 (exec.p); *The Naked Cage* 1986 (exec.p); *Number One With a Bullet* 1986 (p); *Otello* 1986 (p); *P.O.W. the Escape* 1986 (p); *Salome* 1986 (exec.p); *The Texas Chainsaw Massacre 2* 1986 (p); *Allan Quatermain and the Lost City of Gold* 1987 (p); *American Ninja 2* 1987 (p); *Assassination* 1987 (exec.p); *The Barbarians* 1987 (p); *Barfly* 1987 (exec.p); *Beauty and the Beast* 1987 (p); *Business As Usual* 1987 (exec.p); *Dancers* 1987 (p); *Death Wish 4: The Crackdown* 1987 (exec.p); *Down Twisted* 1987 (p); *Dutch Treat* 1987 (p); *The Emperor's New Clothes* 1987 (p); *Going Bananas* 1987 (p,sc); *Gor* 1987 (exec.p); *The Hanoi Hilton* 1987 (p); *Hansel and Gretel* 1987 (p); *King Lear* 1987 (p); *The Kitchen Toto* 1987 (exec.p); *Mascara* 1987 (exec.p); *Masters of the Universe* 1987 (p); *Over the Top* 1987 (d,p); *Die Papierene Brucke* 1987 (a); *Red Riding Hood* 1987 (p); *Rumpelstiltskin* 1987 (p); *Shy People* 1987 (p); *Sleeping Beauty* 1987 (p); *Snow White* 1987 (p); *Street Smart* 1987 (p); *Superman IV: The Quest For Peace* 1987 (p); *Surrender* 1987 (exec.p); *Too Much* 1987 (p); *Tough Guys Don't Dance* 1987 (p); *Under Cover* 1987 (p); *Alien From L.A.* 1988 (p); *Appointment With Death* 1988 (exec.p); *Bloodsport* 1988 (exec.p); *Braddock: Missing in Action III* 1988 (p); *A Cry in the Dark* 1988 (exec.p); *Doin' Time on Planet Earth* 1988 (exec.p); *Freedom Fighter* 1988 (p); *Hanna's War* 1988 (d,p,sc); *Haunted Summer* 1988 (exec.p); *Hero and the Terror* 1988 (exec.p); *Manifesto* 1988 (p); *Messenger of Death* 1988 (exec.p); *Powaqqatsi* 1988 (exec.p); *Puss in Boots* 1988 (p); *Salsa* 1988 (p); *Bad Jim* 1989 (exec.p); *Cyborg* 1989 (p); *Kinjite* 1989 (exec.p); *Mack the Knife* 1989 (d,exec.p,sc); *The Phantom of the Opera* 1989 (exec.p); *The Rose Garden* 1989 (p); *Sinbad of the Seven Seas* 1989 (p); *Young Love: Lemon Popsicle VII* 1989 (exec.p); *Bullseye!* 1990 (exec.p); *Captain America* 1990 (p); *Delta Force II* 1990 (story,from characters); *The Fifth Monkey* 1990 (p); *The Forbidden Dance* 1990 (exec.p); *Night of the Living Dead* 1990 (exec.p); *Street Hunter* 1990 (exec.p).

Gold, Jack • Director • Born London, June 28, 1930. Made his name with *The Bofors Gun* (1968), a grim look at British army camp life in post-war Germany, and *The Naked Civil Servant* (1975), a sensitive TV movie portrait of Quentin Crisp starring John Hurt. • *Living Jazz* 1960 (d); *The Bofors Gun* 1968 (d); *The Reckoning* 1969 (d); *The National Health* 1973 (d); *Who?* 1974 (d); *Man Friday* 1975 (d); *Aces High* 1976 (d); *The Medusa Touch* 1978 (d,p,sc); *The Sailor's Return* 1978 (d); *Praying Mantis* 1982 (d); *Good and Bad at Games* 1983 (d); *Red Monarch* 1983 (d); *The Chain* 1985 (d); *Ball-Trap on the Cote Sauvage* 1989 (d).

Goldberg, Whoopi • Actress, comedienne • Born New York, NY, November 13, 1949. Versatile stand-up comedienne whose critically acclaimed one-woman Broadway show brought her to the attention of Hollywood. Goldberg made an affecting debut in *The Color Purple* (1985), but her considerable talents were subsequently wasted in a series of uninspired vehicles until her featured performance as a reluctant clairvoyant in the smash *Ghost* (1990). Married to cinematographer David Calessen. • *The Color Purple* 1985; *Jumpin' Jack Flash* 1986; *Burglar* 1987; *Fatal Beauty* 1987; *Clara's Heart* 1988; *The Telephone* 1988; *Beverly Hills Brats* 1989; *Homer and Eddie* 1989; *Ghost* 1990; *The Long Walk Home* 1990.

Goldblum, Jeff • Actor • Born Pittsburgh, PA, October 22, 1952. *Educ.* Neighborhood Playhouse, New York. Tall, gangly, stage-trained actor who first gained attention as the inquisitive journalist in *The Big Chill* (1983). Goldblum's dark intensity has served him well in roles ranging from the cardshark in *Silverado* (1985) to the scientist-turned-insect in *The Fly* (1986). • *Nashville* 1975; *Next Stop, Greenwich Village* 1976; *Special Delivery* 1976; *Annie Hall* 1977; *Between the Lines* 1977; *The Sentinel* 1977; *Invasion of the Body Snatchers* 1978; *Remember My Name* 1978; *Thank God It's Friday* 1978; *Threshold* 1981; *The Big Chill* 1983; *The Right Stuff* 1983; *The Adventures of Buckaroo Banzai: Across the 8th Dimension* 1984; *Into the Night* 1985; *Silverado* 1985; *Transylvania 6-5000* 1985; *The Fly* 1986; *Beyond Therapy* 1987; *Vibes* 1988; *Earth Girls Are Easy* 1989; *El Mono Loco/The Mad Monkey* 1989; *The Tall Guy* 1989; *Mister Frost* 1990.

Goldman, William • Screenwriter, author • Born Chicago, IL, 1931. *Educ.* Oberlin College,OH; Columbia. Bestselling novelist and Oscar-winning screenwriter whose first film credit came with *Soldier in the Rain* (1963), based on his 1960 story of the same name. Goldman is effective in a wide range of genres and is also known for his 1983 book, *Adventures in the Screen Trade*, a lighthearted, insider's look at the film business. • *Soldier in the Rain* 1963 (story); *Masquerade* 1965 (sc); *Harper* 1966 (sc); *No Way to Treat a Lady* 1968 (story); *Butch Cassidy and the Sundance Kid* 1969 (sc) **(AABSC)**; *The Hot Rock* 1972 (sc); *The Great Waldo Pepper* 1975 (sc); *The Stepford Wives* 1975 (sc); *All the President's Men* 1976 (sc) **(AABSC)**; *Marathon Man* 1976 (sc,from novel); *A Bridge Too Far* 1977 (sc); *Magic* 1978 (sc,from novel); *Butch and Sundance: The Early Days* 1979 (idea); *Heat* 1987 (sc,from novel); *The Princess Bride* 1987 (sc,from novel); *Misery* 1990 (sc).

Goldsmith, Jerry • Composer; also musician, conductor. • Born Jerrald Goldsmith, Los Angeles, CA, 1929. *Educ.* Los Angeles City College (piano); UCLA (film music); USC, Los Angeles. Prolific composer who started in radio and went on to score a number of TV shows, notably "Gunsmoke" and "The Man From U.N.C.L.E." Memorable film credits include *Freud* (1962), *Chinatown* (1974) and *The Omen* (1976), for which he won an Academy Award. Goldsmith's work in the 1980s was primarily in the action/adventure genre. • *Black Patch* 1957 (m); *City of Fear* 1958 (m,m.cond); *Face of a Fugitive* 1959 (m,m.cond); *Studs Lonigan* 1960 (m); *Freud* 1962 (m) **(AANBM)**; *Lonely Are the Brave* 1962 (m); *The Spiral Road* 1962 (m); *A Gathering of Eagles* 1963 (m); *Lilies of the Field* 1963 (m); *The List of Adrian Messenger* 1963 (m); *The Prize* 1963 (m); *The Stripper* 1963 (m); *Take Her, She's Mine* 1963 (m); *Fate Is the Hunter* 1964 (m); *Rio Conchos* 1964 (m); *Seven Days in May* 1964 (m); *Shock Treatment* 1964 (m); *The Agony and the Ecstasy* 1965 (add.m); *In Harm's Way* 1965 (m); *Morituri* 1965 (m); *A Patch of Blue* 1965 (m) **(AANBM)**; *The Satan Bug* 1965 (m); *Von Ryan's Express* 1965 (m); *The Blue Max* 1966 (m,m.cond); *Our Man Flint* 1966 (m); *The Sand Pebbles* 1966 (m) **(AANBM)**; *Seconds* 1966 (m); *Stagecoach* 1966 (m); *The Trouble With Angels* 1966 (m); *The Flim-Flam Man* 1967 (m); *Hour of the Gun* 1967 (m); *In Like Flint* 1967 (m); *Bandolero!* 1968 (m); *The Detective* 1968 (m); *Planet of the Apes* 1968 (m) **(AANBM)**; *Sebastian* 1968 (m,m.cond,song); *100 Rifles* 1969 (m); *The Chairman* 1969 (m,m.dir); *The Illustrated Man* 1969 (m); *Justine* 1969 (m); *The Ballad of Cable Hogue* 1970 (m,song); *The Magic Garden of Stanley Sweetheart* 1970 (song); *The Mephisto Waltz* 1970 (m); *Patton* 1970 (m) **(AANBM)**; *Rio Lobo* 1970 (m); *Tora! Tora! Tora!* 1970 (m); *The Traveling Executioner* 1970 (m); *Escape From the Planet of the Apes* 1971 (m); *The Last Run* 1971 (m); *Wild Rovers* 1971 (m); *The Culpepper Cattle Co.* 1972 (m); *The Man* 1972 (m); *The Other* 1972 (m); *Shamus* 1972 (m); *Ace Eli and Rodger of the Skies* 1973 (m); *The Don Is Dead* 1973 (m); *One Little Indian* 1973 (m); *Papillon* 1973 (m) **(AANBM)**; *Chinatown* 1974 (m) **(AANBM)**; *Ransom* 1974 (m); *Spys* 1974 (m); *Breakheart Pass* 1975 (m); *Breakout* 1975 (m); *The Reincarnation of Peter Proud* 1975 (m); *Take a Hard Ride* 1975 (m); *The Wind and the Lion* 1975 (m) **(AANBM)**; *Islands in the Stream* 1976 (m); *The Last Hard Men* 1976 (m); *Logan's Run* 1976 (m); *The Omen* 1976 (m) **(AANBS,AABM)**; *The Cassandra Crossing* 1977 (m); *Damnation Alley* 1977 (m); *High Velocity* 1977 (m); *MacArthur the Rebel General* 1977 (m); *Twilight's Last Gleaming* 1977 (m); *The Boys From Brazil* 1978 (m,song) **(AANBM)**; *Capricorn One* 1978 (m); *Coma* 1978 (m); *Damien: Omen II* 1978 (m); *Magic* 1978 (m); *The Swarm* 1978 (m); *Alien* 1979 (m); *The First Great Train Robbery* 1979 (m); *Players* 1979 (m); *Star Trek: The Motion Picture* 1979 (m) **(AANBM)**; *Caboblanco* 1980 (m); *The Final Conflict* 1981 (m); *Night Crossing* 1981 (m); *Outland* 1981 (m); *Raggedy Man* 1981 (m); *The Salamander* 1981 (m); *The Challenge* 1982 (m,m.dir); *First Blood* 1982 (m,song); *Inchon* 1982 (m); *Poltergeist* 1982 (m) **(AANBM)**; *The Secret of Nimh* 1982 (m,song); *Psycho II* 1983 (m); *Twilight Zone—the Movie* 1983 (m); *Under Fire* 1983 (m) **(AANBM)**; *Gremlins* 1984 (m); *The Lonely Guy* 1984 (m,song); *Runaway* 1984 (m); *Supergirl* 1984 (m,m.dir); *Baby: The Secret of the Lost Legend* 1985 (m); *Explorers* 1985 (m); *King Solomon's Mines* 1985 (m); *Legend* 1985 (m); *Rambo: First Blood Part II* 1985 (m); *Hoosiers* 1986 (m) **(AANBM)**; *Link* 1986 (m); *Poltergeist II: The Other Side* 1986 (m); *Allan Quatermain and the Lost City of Gold* 1987 (uncred.m); *Extreme Prejudice* 1987 (m); *Innerspace* 1987 (m); *Lionheart* 1987 (m); *Criminal Law* 1988 (m); *Rambo III* 1988 (m); *Rent-A-Cop* 1988 (m); *The Burbs* 1989 (m); *Leviathan* 1989 (m); *Star Trek V: The Final Frontier* 1989 (m,song); *Warlock* 1989 (m,m.cond); *Gremlins 2: The New Batch* 1990 (a,m); *The Russia House* 1990 (m); *Total Recall* 1990 (m); *Not Without My Daughter* 1991 (m); *Sleeping With the Enemy* (m).

Goldwyn, Samuel • aka Samuel Goldfish • Producer, executive • Born Schmuel Gelbfisz, Warsaw, Poland, August 27, 1882; died 1974. Penniless immigrant turned successful glove salesman who entered films in 1912, persuading his father-in-law, impressario Jesse Lasky, to establish a production and distribution company. Together with C.B. DeMille as director, they formed the Jesse L. Lasky Feature Play Company and scored a huge success with their first film, *The Squaw Man* (1914). In 1916 they merged with Adolph Zukor's Famous Players, but infighting inspired Goldwyn to leave and start afresh, forming the Goldwyn Pictures Corporation with Edgar Selwyn and others. Goldwyn's policy of enlisting only the best available talent and turning out only the finest product would become his legacy, a standard of excellence dubbed "the Goldwyn touch."

Two years after Goldwyn was forced out of power in 1922 his former company merged with Metro Pictures and Louis B. Mayer Productions to form MGM. Undaunted, Goldwyn founded his own corporation, Samuel Goldwyn Inc., and this time steered a completely independent path, appointing neither studio bosses nor a board of directors.

Notorious for his idosyncratic use—or misuse—of the English language ("Include me out," etc.), Goldwyn had a knack for finding the right property and talent. Among the stars he sought out and worked with were Ronald Colman, Vilma Banky, Gary Cooper, Anna Sten, Will Rogers, David Niven and Merle Oberon. Goldwyn also recruited some of the finest writers in the business, including Sinclair Lewis, Ben Hecht, Lillian Hellman and Sidney Kingsley. He enjoyed his most fruitful relationship with William Wyler, who directed Goldwyn's most glittering productions, notably *The Best Years of Our Lives* (1946). • *The Squaw Man* 1914 (p); *Jubilo* 1919 (p); *The Highest Bidder* 1921 (p); *The Eternal City* 1923 (p); *Potash and Perlmutter* 1923 (p); *Cytherea* 1924 (p); *In Hollywood With Potash and Perlmutter* 1924 (p); *Tarnish* 1924 (p); *Ben Hur, A Tale of the Christ* 1925 (exec.p); *The Dark Angel* 1925 (p); *His Supreme Moment* 1925 (p); *Stella Dallas* 1925 (p); *A Thief in Paradise* 1925 (p); *The Winning of Barbara Worth* 1926 (p); *The Devil Dancer* 1927 (p); *Magic Flame* 1927 (p); *The Night of Love* 1927 (p); *The Awakening* 1928 (p); *Two Lovers* 1928 (p); *Bulldog Drummond* 1929 (p); *Condemned* 1929 (p); *The Rescue* 1929 (p); *This Is Heaven* 1929 (p); *One Heavenly Night* 1930 (p); *Raffles* 1930 (p); *Whoopee* 1930 (p); *Arrowsmith* 1931 (p); *The Devil to Pay* 1931 (p); *Palmy Days* 1931 (p); *Street Scene* 1931 (p); *Tonight or Never* 1931 (p); *The Unholy Garden* 1931 (p); *Cynara* 1932 (p); *The Greeks Had a Word For Them* 1932 (p); *The Kid From Spain* 1932 (p); *The Masquerader* 1933 (p); *Roman Scandals* 1933 (p); *Kid Millions* 1934 (p); *Nana* 1934 (p); *We Live Again* 1934 (p); *Barbary Coast* 1935 (p); *The Dark Angel* 1935 (p); *Splendor* 1935 (p); *The Wedding Night* 1935 (p); *Beloved Enemy* 1936 (p); *Come and Get It* 1936 (p); *Dodsworth* 1936 (p); *Strike Me Pink* 1936 (p); *These Three* 1936 (p); *Dead End* 1937 (p); *Hurricane* 1937 (p); *Stella Dallas* 1937 (p); *Woman Chases Man* 1937 (p); *The Adventures of Marco Polo* 1938 (p); *The Cowboy and the Lady* 1938 (p); *The Goldwyn Follies* 1938 (p); *The Real Glory* 1939 (p); *They Shall Have Music* 1939 (p); *Wuthering Heights* 1939 (p) **(AANBP)**; *Raffles* 1940 (p); *The Westerner* 1940 (p); *Ball of Fire* 1941 (p); *The Little Foxes* 1941 (p); *The Pride of the Yankees* 1942 (p); *The North Star* 1943 (p); *They Got Me Covered* 1943 (p); *The Princess and the Pirate* 1944 (p); *Up in Arms* 1944 (p); *The Wonder Man* 1945 (p); *The Best Years of Our Lives* 1946 (p) **(AABP)**; *The Kid From Brooklyn* 1946 (p); *The Bishop's Wife* 1947 (p); *The Secret Life of Walter Mitty* 1947 (p); *Enchantment* 1948 (p); *A Song Is Born* 1948 (p); *Roseanna McCoy* 1949 (p); *Edge of Doom* 1950 (p); *My Foolish Heart* 1950 (p); *Our Very Own* 1950 (p); *I Want You* 1951 (p); *Hans Christian Andersen* 1952 (p); *Guys and Dolls* 1955 (p); *Porgy and Bess* 1959 (p).

Golino, Valeria • Actress • Pretty actress, of Greek and Italian descent, who made her film debut at 17 in Lina Wertmuller's *A Joke of Destiny* (1983). Best known to American audiences for her performance as Tom Cruise's girlfriend in *Rain Man* (1988). • *Scherzo del Destino in Agguato Dietro L'Angolo Come un Brigante di Strada/A Joke of Destiny Lying in Wait Around the Corner Like a Robber* 1983; *Blind Date* 1984; *Figlio Mio Infinitamente Caro/My Dearest Son* 1985; *Piccoli Fuochi/Little Fires* 1985; *Asilo di Polizia/Dumb Dicks* 1986; *Storia d'Amore/Love Story* 1986; *L'été dernier à Tanger/Last Summer in Tangiers* 1987; *Gli Occhiali d'Oro/The Gold-Rimmed Glasses* 1987; *Big Top Pee-Wee* 1988; *Paura e Amore/Three Sisters* 1988; *Rain Man* 1988; *Torrents of Spring* 1989; *Il y a des jours... et des lunes* 1990; *The King's Whore* 1990; *Tracce di una vita amorosa/Traces of an Amorous Life* 1990.

Golitzen, Alexander • *aka* Alexander Golizen • Art director • Born Moscow, February 28, 1907. Hollywood veteran who began his career at United Artists in the mid-1930s. From 1944 most of Golitzen's work was for Universal, where he was made supervising art director in 1960. • *The Call of the Wild* 1935 (art d); *Hurricane* 1937 (art d); *Foreign Correspondent* 1940 (art d) **(AANBAD)**; *Sundown* 1941 (art d) **(AANBAD)**; *That Uncertain Feeling* 1941 (art d); *Arabian Nights* 1942 (art d) **(AANBAD)**; *The Phantom of the Opera* 1943 (art d) **(AABAD)**; *The Climax* 1944 (art d) **(AANBAD)**; *Salome—Where She Danced* 1945 (p); *Scarlet Street* 1945 (art d); *Magnificent Doll* 1946 (art d); *Smash-Up, the Story of a Woman* 1947 (art d); *Letter From an Unknown Woman* 1948 (art d); *Duel at Silver Creek* 1952 (art d); *The World in His Arms* 1952 (art d); *All I Desire* 1953 (art d); *City Beneath the Sea* 1953 (art d); *The Man From the Alamo* 1953 (art d); *The Mississippi Gambler* 1953 (art d); *Seminole* 1953 (art d); *Take Me to Town* 1953 (art d); *Thunder Bay* 1953 (art d); *The Black Shield of Falworth* 1954 (art d); *The Glenn Miller Story* 1954 (art d); *Man Without a Star* 1954 (art d); *Sign of the Pagan* 1954 (art d); *So This Is Paris* 1954 (art d); *Captain Lightfoot* 1955 (art d); *The Far Country* 1955 (art d); *Red Sundown* 1955 (art d); *Tarantula* 1955 (art d); *This Island Earth* 1955 (art d); *All That Heaven Allows* 1956 (art d); *Away All Boats* 1956 (art d); *Battle Hymn* 1956 (art d); *The Rawhide Years* 1956 (art d); *There's Always Tomorrow* 1956 (art d); *Written on the Wind* 1956 (art d); *Damn Citizen!* 1957 (art d); *Day of the Badman* 1957 (art d); *Flood Tide* 1957 (art d); *The Incredible Shrinking Man* 1957 (art d); *Interlude* 1957 (art d); *The Lady Takes a Flyer* 1957 (art d); *Man in the Shadow* 1957 (art d); *Mister Cory* 1957 (art d); *The Tattered Dress* 1957 (art d); *Appointment With a Shadow* 1958 (art d); *The Big Beat* 1958 (art d); *The Female Animal* 1958 (art d); *Girls on the Loose* 1958 (art d); *Kathy O'* 1958 (art d); *The Last of the Fast Guns* 1958 (art d); *Live Fast, Die Young* 1958 (art d); *Money, Women and Guns* 1958 (art d); *Monster on the Campus* 1958 (art d); *Once Upon a Horse* 1958 (art d); *Raw Wind in Eden* 1958 (art d); *The Restless Years* 1958 (art d); *Ride a Crooked Trail* 1958 (art d); *The Saga of Hemp Brown* 1958 (art d); *Showdown at Boot Hill* 1958 (art d); *Summer Love* 1958 (art d); *The Thing That Couldn't Die* 1958 (art d); *This Happy Feeling* 1958 (art d); *A Time to Love and a Time to Die* 1958 (art d); *Touch of Evil* 1958 (art d); *Twilight For the Gods* 1958 (art d); *Voice in the Mirror* 1958 (art d); *Wild Heritage* 1958 (art d); *Curse of the Undead* 1959 (art d); *Imitation of Life* 1959 (art d); *Never Steal Anything Small* 1959 (art d); *No Name on the Bullet* 1959 (art d); *Operation Petticoat* 1959 (art d); *The Perfect Furlough* 1959 (art d); *Pillow Talk* 1959 (art d); *Step Down to Terror* 1959 (art d); *Stranger in My Arms* 1959 (art d); *This Earth Is Mine* 1959 (art d); *The Wild and the Innocent* 1959 (art d); *The Great Impostor* 1960 (art d); *Spartacus* 1960 (art d) **(AABAD)**; *Back Street* 1961 (art d); *Flower Drum Song* 1961 (art d) **(AANBAD)**; *The Last Sunset* 1961 (art d); *Tammy Tell Me True* 1961 (art d); *Cape Fear* 1962 (art d); *Lover Come Back* 1962 (art d); *That Touch of Mink* 1962 (art d) **(AANBAD)**; *To Kill a Mockingbird* 1962 (art d) **(AABAD)**; *The List of Adrian Messenger* 1963 (art d); *The Thrill of It All* 1963 (art d); *The Ugly American* 1963 (art d); *Bedtime Story* 1964 (art d); *The Brass Bottle* 1964 (art d); *Father Goose* 1964 (art d); *Man's Favorite Sport?* 1964 (art d); *The Art of Love* 1965 (art d); *Mirage* 1965 (art d); *Shenandoah* 1965 (art d); *And Now Miguel* 1966 (art d); *The Appaloosa* 1966 (art d); *Gambit* 1966 (art d) **(AANBAD)**; *Moment to Moment* 1966 (art d); *The Ballad of Josie* 1967 (art d); *Banning* 1967 (art d); *Don't Just Stand There!* 1967 (art d); *Games* 1967 (art d); *King's Pirate* 1967 (art d); *Thoroughly Modern Millie* 1967 (art d) **(AANBAD)**; *Angel in My Pocket* 1968 (art d); *Coogan's Bluff* 1968 (art d); *The Hell With Heroes* 1968 (art d); *Madigan* 1968 (art d); *The Lost Man* 1969 (art d); *The Love God?* 1969 (art d); *A Man Called Gannon* 1969 (art d); *Sweet Charity* 1969 (art d) **(AANBAD)**; *Tell Them Willie Boy Is Here* 1969 (art d); *Winning* 1969 (art d); *Airport* 1970 (art d) **(AANBAD)**; *Colossus: The Forbin Project* 1970 (art d); *How to Frame a Figg* 1970 (art d); *Storia di una Donna* 1970 (art d); *The Beguiled* 1971 (art d); *One More Train to Rob* 1971 (art d); *Play Misty For Me* 1971 (art d); *Raid on Rommel* 1971 (art d); *Red Sky at Morning* 1971 (art d); *Shoot Out* 1971 (art d); *Slaughterhouse-Five* 1971 (art d); *The Great Northfield Minnesota Raid* 1972 (art d); *Joe Kidd* 1972 (art d); *Breezy* 1973 (art d); *Showdown* 1973 (art d); *That Man Bolt* 1973 (art d); *Earthquake* 1974 (art d) **(AANBAD)**.

Goodman, John • Actor • Born St Louis, MO, c. 1952. *Educ.* Southwest Missouri State University. Burly, endearing character player whose mud-soaked entrance was one of the high points of the Coen Brothers' 1987 comic gem, *Raising Arizona*. Goodman achieved national fame as the forthright blue-collar husband on the TV series "Roseanne" and became a highly sought-after Hollywood actor in the late 1980s. • *C.H.U.D.* 1984; *Revenge of the Nerds* 1984; *Maria's Lovers* 1985; *Sweet Dreams* 1985; *The Big Easy* 1986; *True Stories* 1986; *Burglar* 1987; *Raising Arizona* 1987; *Everybody's All-American* 1988; *Punchline* 1988; *The Wrong Guys* 1988; *Always* 1989; *Sea of Love* 1989; *Arachnophobia* 1990; *Stella* 1990; *King Ralph* 1991.

Goodrich, Frances • Screenwriter, playwright; also actress. • Born Belleville, NJ, 1891; died January 29, 1984, Manhattan, NY. With husband Albert Hackett, wrote several Hollywood classics including *It's a Wonderful Life* (1946), in collaboration with director Frank Capra. • *Up Pops the Devil* 1931 (from play); *Penthouse* 1933 (sc); *The Secret of Madame Blanche* 1933 (sc); *Chained* 1934 (uncred.sc); *Fugitive Lovers* 1934 (sc); *Hide-Out* 1934 (sc); *The Thin Man* 1934 (sc) **(AANBSC)**; *Ah, Wilderness!* 1935 (sc); *Naughty Marietta* 1935 (sc); *After the Thin Man* 1936 (sc) **(AANBSC)**; *Rose Marie* 1936 (sc); *Small Town Girl* 1936 (sc); *The Firefly* 1937 (sc); *Thanks For the Memory* 1938 (from play); *Another Thin Man* 1939 (sc); *Society Lawyer* 1939 (sc); *The Hitler Gang* 1944 (sc); *Lady in the Dark* 1944 (sc); *It's a Wonderful Life* 1946 (sc); *The Virginian* 1946 (sc); *California* 1947 (uncred.sc); *Dear Ruth* 1947 (uncred.sc); *Easter Parade* 1948 (sc,story); *The Pirate* 1948 (sc); *Summer Holiday* 1948 (sc); *In the Good Old Summertime* 1949 (adapt); *Father of the Bride* 1950 (sc) **(AANBSC)**; *Father's Little Dividend* 1951 (sc); *Too Young to Kiss* 1951 (sc); *Give a Girl a Break* 1953 (sc); *The Long, Long Trailer* 1954 (sc); *Seven Brides For Seven Brothers* 1954 (sc) **(AANBSC)**; *Gaby* 1956 (sc); *A Certain Smile* 1958 (sc); *The Diary of Anne Frank* 1959 (sc,from play); *Five Finger Exercise* 1962 (sc).

Gordon, Lawrence • Producer; also executive. • Born Belzoni, MS, March 25, 1936. *Educ.* Tulane University, New Orleans, LA (business administration). Commercially successful producer of both independent and studio-based films; president of 20th Century-Fox from 1984 to 1986. Gordon, whose brother Charles is also a producer, began his career as an assistant to Aaron Spelling. • *Dillinger* 1973 (exec.p); *It's Not the Size That Counts* 1974 (exec.p); *Hard Times* 1975 (p); *Rolling Thunder* 1977 (exec.p); *The Driver* 1978 (p); *The End* 1978 (p); *Hooper* 1978 (exec.p); *The Warriors* 1979 (p); *Xanadu* 1980 (p); *Paternity* 1981 (p); *48 Hrs.* 1982 (p); *Jekyll and Hyde...Together Again* 1982 (p); *Streets of Fire* 1984 (p); *Brewster's Millions* 1985 (p); *Jumpin' Jack Flash* 1986 (p); *Lucas* 1986 (p); *Predator* 1987 (p); *The Couch Trip* 1988 (p); *Die Hard* 1988 (p); *The Wrong Guys* 1988 (exec.p); *Family Business* 1989 (p); *Field of Dreams* 1989 (p) **(AANBP)**; *K-9* 1989 (p); *Leviathan* 1989 (exec.p); *Lock Up* 1989 (p); *Another 48 Hrs.* 1990 (p); *Die Hard 2: Die Harder* 1990 (p); *Predator 2* 1990 (p).

Gordon, Ruth • Actress; also playwright, screenwriter. • Born Ruth Gordon Jones, Wollaston, MA, October 30, 1896; died August 28, 1985, Martha's Vineyard. *Educ.* AADA, New York. A distinguished stage actress through much of the first half of the century, Gordon was also a prolific playwright and screenwriter. Married to writer-director Garson Kanin in 1942, she collaborated with him on several George Cukor films, including the Tracy-Hepburn classics *Adam's Rib* (1949) and *Pat and Mike* (1952).

Though relatively inactive in the 1950s and 60s, her career picked up again in 1968 after her infamously diabolical role as Minnie Castavets in *Rosemary's Baby*. Gordon is perhaps best remembered as the octogenarian partner of 20-year-old Bud Cort in Hal Ashby's *Harold and Maude* (1971). • *The Whirl of Life* 1915; *Camille* 1916; *Abe Lincoln in Illinois* 1940; *Dr. Ehrlich's Magic Bullet* 1940; *Two-Faced Woman* 1941; *Action in the North Atlantic* 1943; *Edge of Darkness* 1943; *Over 21* 1945 (from play); *A Double Life* 1947 (sc) **(AANBSC)**; *Adam's Rib* 1949 (sc) **(AANBSC)**; *The Marrying Kind* 1952 (sc,story); *Pat and Mike* 1952 (sc) **(AANBSC)**; *The Actress* 1953 (sc,from play "Years Ago"); *Inside Daisy Clover* 1965 **(AANBSA)**; *Lord Love a Duck* 1966; *Rosie* 1967 (adapt from play "A Very Rich Woman"); *Rosemary's Baby* 1968 **(AABSA)**; *Whatever Happened to Aunt Alice?* 1969; *Where's Poppa?* 1970; *Harold and Maude* 1971; *The Big Bus* 1976; *Every Which Way But Loose* 1978; *Boardwalk* 1979; *Any Which Way You Can* 1980; *My Bodyguard* 1980; *Jimmy the Kid* 1982; *Delta Pi* 1985; *Maxie* 1985; *Voyage of the Rock Aliens* 1985.

Goretta, Claude • Director • Born Geneva, Switzerland, June 23, 1929. *Educ.* University of Geneva (law); British Film Institute. Began his career collaborating on a short film, *Nice Time* (1957), with friend and compatriot Alain Tanner. Goretta then directed documentaries and adapted plays for Swiss TV before making his feature directorial debut in 1970 with *Le Fou*, which he also wrote. His work is characterized by nonlinear narratives focusing on the humdrum details of everyday life and he is best known for *The Lacemaker* (1977), a harrowing depiction of a young woman's descent into madness. • *Le Fou* 1970 (d,sc); *L'Invitation* 1973 (d,sc); *Pas si méchant que ça...* 1974 (d,sc); *La Dentellière/The Lacemaker* 1977 (d,sc); *The Epistomology of Jean Piaget* 1977 (d); *Les Chemins de l'exil, ou les dernières années de Jean-Jacques Rousseau* 1978 (d,sc); *Bonheur toi-même* 1980 (d); *La Provinciale/A Girl From Lorraine* 1980 (d,sc,adapt,dial); *La Mort de Mario Ricci* 1983 (d,sc); *Orfeo* 1985 (d,sc); *Si le soleil ne revenait pas* 1987 (d,sc); *Les Ennemis de la mafia* 1988 (d,sc).

Gosho, Heinosuke • Director; also producer, screenwriter. • Born Tokyo, February 1, 1902; died 1981. *Educ.* Tokyo University. Early master of Japanese cinema whose more than 100 features include the country's first sound film, *The Neighbor's Wife and Mine* (1931). Many of Gosho's works, through the mid-1930s and again after WWII, deal with common, everyday subjects; these are treated with a mixture of wry wit and sentimentality, and Gosho displays an honest, if simplistic understanding of his (mostly working-class) characters. *An Inn at Osaka* (1954) and *Growing Up Twice* (1955) are the prime examples of his work to have reached the West.

From the 60s Gosho's old-style humanism, like that of contemporaries such as Yasujiro Ozu, seemed increasingly dated and his films generated little commercial interest. • *Hatsukoi* 1925 (d,sc); *Nanto no haru* 1925 (d,sc); *Otoko gokoro* 1925 (d,sc); *Seishun* 1925 (d,sc); *Sora wa haretari* 1925 (d); *Tosei Tamatebako* 1925 (d); *Haha-yo koishi* 1926 (d); *Honryu* 1926 (d); *Itoshino wagako* 1926 (d,sc); *Kaeranu sasabue* 1926 (d); *Kanojo* 1926 (d,sc); *Machi no Hitobito* 1926 (d); *Musume* 1926 (d,sc); *Hazukashii Yume* 1927 (d); *Karakuri musume* 1927 (d,sc); *Okame* 1927 (d,sc); *Sabishiki ranbomono* 1927 (d); *Shojo no shi* 1927 (d,sc); *Doraku goshinan* 1928 (d,sc); *Gaito no kishi* 1928 (d); *Hito no yo sugata* 1928 (d); *Kami eno michi* 1928 (d); *Mura no hanayome* 1928 (d); *Suki nareba koso* 1928 (d,sc); *Jonetsu no ichiya* 1929 (d,sc); *Oyaji to sonoko* 1929 (d); *Shin joseikan* 1929 (d); *Ukiyo buro* 1929 (d,sc); *Yoru no meneko* 1929 (d); *Aiyuko no yoru* 1930 (d); *Dai-Tokyo no ikkaku* 1930 (add.dial,d); *Dokushinsha goyojin* 1930 (d,sc); *Hohoemo jinsei* 1930 (d); *Kinuyo monogatari* 1930 (d); *Onna-yo kimi no na o kegasu nakare* 1930 (d); *Shojo nyuyo* 1930 (d); *Gutei kenkei* 1931 (add.dial,d); *Jokyu aishi* 1931 (d); *Madamu to byobo/The Neighbor's Wife and Mine* 1931 (d); *Shima no ratai jiken* 1931 (add.dial,d); *Wakaki hi no kangeki* 1931 (d); *Yoru hiraku* 1931 (d); *Ginza no yanagi* 1932 (d); *Hototogisu* 1932 (d); *Koi no Tokyo* 1932 (d); *Niisan no baka* 1932 (d); *Satsueijo romansu, renai annai* 1932 (d); *Tengoku ni musube koi* 1932 (d); *Aibu/Caress* 1933 (d); *Hanayome no negoto/The Bride Talks in Her Sleep* 1933 (d); *Izu no odoriko* 1933 (d); *Juku no haru* 1933 (d); *Shojo-yo sayonara* 1933 (d); *Ikitoshi ikerumono* 1934 (d); *Onna to umareta karanya* 1934 (d); *Sakura ondo* 1934 (d); *Akogare* 1935 (d); *Fukeyo koikaze* 1935 (d); *Hanamuko no negoto/The Bridegroom Talks in His Sleep* 1935 (d); *Hidari uchiwa* 1935 (d); *Jinsei no onimotsu* 1935 (d); *Oboroyo no onna* 1936 (d); *Okusama shakuyosho* 1936 (d); *Shindo* 1936 (d); *Hana-kago no uta* 1937 (adapt,d); *Mokuseki* 1940 (d); *Shinsetsu* 1942 (d); *Goju no to* 1944 (d); *Ima hitotabi no* 1945 (d); *Izu no musumetachi* 1945 (d); *Omokage* 1948 (d); *Wakare-gumo* 1951 (d,sc); *Asa no hamon* 1952 (d); *Entotsu no mieru basho/Where Chimneys Are Seen* 1953 (d); *Ai to shi no tanima* 1954 (d); *Niwatorio wa futatabi naku* 1954 (d); *Osaka no yado/An Inn at Osaka* 1954 (d,sc); *Takekurabe/Growing Up Twice* 1955 (d); *Aru yo futatabi* 1956 (d,sc); *Banka* 1957 (d); *Kiiroi karasu/Yellow Crow* 1957 (d); *Ari no machi no Maria* 1958 (d); *Hotarubi/Firefly Light* 1958 (d); *Yoku* 1958 (d); *Karatachi nikki* 1959 (d); *Waga ai* 1959 (d); *Shiroi kiba* 1960 (d); *Aijo no keifu* 1961 (d,p); *Kumo ga chigieru toki* 1961 (d,p); *Ryoju/Hunting Rifle* 1961 (d); *Kaachan kekkon shiroyo* 1962 (d,sc); *Hyakumannin no musumetachi* 1963 (d,sc); *Osorezan no onna/The Innocent Witch* 1965 (d); *Kaachan to juichi-nin no kodomo* 1966 (d); *Utage* 1967 (d); *Meiji haru aki* 1968 (d); *Onna to misoshiru* 1968 (d).

Gossett, Louis, Jr. • *aka* Louis Gossett • Actor • Born Brooklyn, NY, May 27, 1936. Charismatic black actor with a flair for projecting quiet authority. Gosset's career took off with his performance in the stage and film versions of *A Raisin in the Sun* (1961); he has latterly worked in both TV and film, notably in *An Officer and a Gentleman* (1982). • *A Raisin in the Sun* 1961; *The Bushbaby* 1970; *The Landlord* 1970; *Skin Game* 1971; *Travels With My Aunt* 1972; *The Laughing Policeman* 1973; *The White Dawn* 1974; *The River Niger* 1975; *J.D.'s Revenge* 1976; *The Choirboys* 1977; *The Deep* 1977; *An Officer and a Gentleman* 1982 **(AABSA)**; *Jaws 3-D* 1983; *Finders Keepers* 1984; *Enemy Mine* 1985; *Firewalker* 1986; *Iron Eagle* 1986; *The Principal* 1987; *Iron Eagle II* 1988; *The Punisher* 1989; *Toy Soldiers* 1991.

Gould, Elliott • Actor • Born Elliott Goldstein, Brooklyn, NY, August 29, 1938. Tall, curly-haired actor who came to personify the angst of the young, upwardly mobile middle class during the late 1960s and early 70s. Appeared in relatively few films in the (relatively angst-free) 80s. • *Quick, Let's Get Married* 1964; *The Night They Raided Minsky's* 1968; *Bob & Carol & Ted & Alice* 1969 **(AANBSA)**; *Getting Straight* 1970; *I Love My Wife* 1970; *M*A*S*H* 1970; *Move* 1970; *Beroringen* 1971; *Little Murders* 1971; *Ingmar Bergman* 1972; *Busting* 1973; *The Long Goodbye* 1973; *California Split* 1974; *Spys* 1974; *Who?* 1974; *I Will...I Will...For Now* 1975; *Nashville* 1975; *Whiffs* 1975; *Harry and Walter Go to New York* 1976; *Mean Johnny Barrows* 1976; *A Bridge Too Far* 1977; *Capricorn One* 1978; *Matilda* 1978; *The Silent Partner* 1978; *Escape to Athena* 1979; *The Lady Vanishes* 1979; *The Muppet Movie* 1979; *Falling in Love Again* 1980; *The Last Flight of Noah's*

Ark 1980; *The Devil and Max Devlin* 1981; *Dirty Tricks* 1981; *Over the Brooklyn Bridge* 1983; *Strawanzer* 1983; *The Muppets Take Manhattan* 1984; *The Naked Face* 1985; *Inside Out* 1986; *I Miei Primi Quarant'Anni* 1987; *Der Joker* 1987; *Dangerous Love* 1988; *The Telephone* 1988; *The Lemon Sisters* 1989; *Night Visitor* 1989; *Scandalo Segreto* 1989; *Dead Men Don't Die* 1990; *Giocodi Massacro* 1990.

Goulding, Edmund • Director; also screenwriter, playwright, novelist. • Born London, March 20, 1891; died 1959. In the US from 1919. Although his films lack a distinctive stamp, he is noted for his deft handling of actors and is probably best remembered for the swank, star-studded *Grand Hotel* (1932). Goulding also enjoyed a fruitful association with Bette Davis, directing *Dark Victory* (1939), *The Old Maid* (1939) and *The Great Lie* (1941). • *Henry VIII* 1911 (a); *Life of a London Shopgirl* 1914 (a); *Quest of Life* 1916 (from play "Ellen Young"); *The Silent Partner* 1917 (story); *The Ordeal of Rosetta* 1918 (story); *The Glorious Lady* 1919 (sc,story); *The Perfect Love* 1919 (sc); *A Regular Girl* 1919 (story); *Sealed Hearts* 1919 (story); *The Dangerous Paradise* 1920 (story); *A Daughter of Two Worlds* 1920 (sc); *The Imp* 1920 (story); *The Sin That Was His* 1920 (sc); *The Devil* 1921 (sc,story); *Don't Leave Your Husband* 1921 (story); *The Man of Stone* 1921 (story); *Tol'able David* 1921 (sc); *Broadway Rose* 1922 (sc,story); *Fascination* 1922 (sc,story); *Heroes of the Street* 1922 (sc); *Peacock Alley* 1922 (sc); *The Seventh Day* 1922 (sc); *Three Live Ghosts* 1922 (a); *Till We Meet Again* 1922 (sc); *Bright Lights of Broadway* 1923 (sc); *The Bright Shawl* 1923 (sc); *Dark Secrets* 1923 (sc,story); *Fury* 1923 (sc,from novel); *Jazzmania* 1923 (sc,story); *Tiger Rose* 1923 (sc); *Dante's Inferno* 1924 (sc); *Gerald Cranston's Lady* 1924 (sc); *The Man Who Came Back* 1924 (sc); *The Beautiful City* 1925 (sc,story); *The Dancers* 1925 (sc); *The Fool* 1925 (sc); *Havoc* 1925 (sc); *Sally, Irene and Mary* 1925 (d,p,sc); *The Scarlet Honeymoon* 1925 (story); *Sun-Up* 1925 (d,p,sc); *Dancing Mothers* 1926 (from play); *Paris* 1926 (d,sc,story); *Annie Laurie* 1927 (uncred.sc); *Love* 1927 (d,p,uncred.adapt); *Women Love Diamonds* 1927 (d,p,story); *Happiness Ahead* 1928 (story); *A Lady of Chance* 1928 (adapt); *The Broadway Melody* 1929 (story); *The Trespasser* 1929 (d,p,sc,story,song); *The Devil's Holiday* 1930 (d,sc,m); *The Grand Parade* 1930 (p,sc,song); *Paramount on Parade* 1930 (a,d); *The Night Angel* 1931 (d,sc,song); *Reaching For the Moon* 1931 (d,sc); *Blondie of the Follies* 1932 (a,d,lyrics); *Flesh* 1932 (story); *Grand Hotel* 1932 (d); *No Man of Her Own* 1933 (story); *Hollywood Party* 1934 (d); *Riptide* 1934 (d,sc,story); *The Flame Within* 1935 (d,p,sc,story); *That Certain Woman* 1937 (d,sc,story); *The Dawn Patrol* 1938 (d); *White Banners* 1938 (d); *Dark Victory* 1939 (d,song); *The Old Maid* 1939 (d); *We Are Not Alone* 1939 (d); *'Til We Meet Again* 1940 (d); *Two Girls on Broadway* 1940 (story); *The Great Lie* 1941 (d); *Claudia* 1943 (d); *The Constant Nymph* 1943 (d); *Forever and a Day* 1943 (d,p); *Flight From Folly* 1944 (story); *Of Human Bondage* 1946 (d); *The Razor's Edge* 1946 (d); *Nightmare Alley* 1947 (d); *The Shocking Miss Pilgrim* 1947 (d); *Everybody Does It* 1949 (d); *Mister 880* 1950 (d); *We're Not Married* 1952 (d); *Down Among the Sheltering Palms* 1953 (d); *Teenage Rebel* 1956 (d,song); *Mardi Gras* 1958 (d).

Grable, Betty • *aka* Frances Dean • Actress • Born Elizabeth Ruth Grable, St Louis, MO, December 18, 1916; died 1973. *Educ.* Hollywood Professional School. Best known as WWII's most pinned up pin-up. Grable's luxurious legs (insured by Lloyd's of London) and surprisingly wholesome appeal brightened a number of successful light musicals and dramas in the 1940s. Married to actor Jackie Coogan from 1937 to 1940. • *Happy Days* 1929; *Let's Go Places* 1930; *Whoopee* 1930; *Kiki* 1931; *Palmy Days* 1931; *The Greeks Had a Word For Them* 1932; *Hold 'Em Jail* 1932; *The Kid From Spain* 1932; *Probation* 1932; *Cavalcade* 1933; *Child of Manhattan* 1933; *Melody Cruise* 1933; *The Sweetheart of Sigma Chi* 1933; *What Price Innocence?* 1933; *By Your Leave* 1934; *The Gay Divorcee* 1934; *Hips, Hips, Hooray!* 1934; *Student Tour* 1934; *The Nitwits* 1935; *Old Man Rhythm* 1935; *Collegiate* 1936; *Don't Turn 'Em Loose* 1936; *Follow the Fleet* 1936; *Pigskin Parade* 1936; *This Way Please* 1937; *Thrill of a Lifetime* 1937; *Campus Confessions* 1938; *College Swing* 1938; *Give Me a Sailor* 1938; *The Day the Bookies Wept* 1939; *Man About Town* 1939; *Million Dollar Legs* 1939; *Down Argentine Way* 1940; *Tin Pan Alley* 1940; *I Wake Up Screaming* 1941; *Moon Over Miami* 1941; *A Yank in the R.A.F.* 1941; *Footlight Serenade* 1942; *Song of the Islands* 1942; *Springtime in the Rockies* 1942; *Coney Island* 1943; *Four Jills in a Jeep* 1943; *Sweet Rosie O'Grady* 1943; *Pin-Up Girl* 1944; *Diamond Horseshoe* 1945; *The Dolly Sisters* 1945; *Do You Love Me?* 1946; *Hollywood Bound (short)* 1947 (adapt); *Mother Wore Tights* 1947; *The Shocking Miss Pilgrim* 1947; *That Lady in Ermine* 1948; *When My Baby Smiles at Me* 1948; *The Beautiful Blonde From Bashful Bend* 1949; *My Blue Heaven* 1950; *Wabash Avenue* 1950; *Call Me Mister* 1951; *Meet Me After the Show* 1951; *The Farmer Takes a Wife* 1953; *How to Marry a Millionaire* 1953; *Three For the Show* 1954; *How to Be Very, Very Popular* 1955; *Going Hollywood: The War Years* 1988 (archival footage).

Grahame, Gloria • *aka* Gloria Hallward • Actress • Born Gloria Grahame Hallward, Los Angeles, CA, November 28, 1925; died 1981. Leading lady often cast as a seductress or unfaithful wife. Grahame's career peaked in 1952 with an Oscar-winning role in *The Bad and the Beautiful.* Married to actor Stanley Clements (1945-48), director Nicholas Ray (1948-52), writer-director Cy Howard (1954-57) and, from 1961, actor Anthony Ray—Nicholas Ray's son by a previous marriage. • *Blonde Fever* 1944; *Without Love* 1945; *It's a Wonderful Life* 1946; *Crossfire* 1947 (**AANBSA**); *It Happened in Brooklyn* 1947; *Merton of the Movies* 1947; *Song of the Thin Man* 1947; *Roughshod* 1949; *A Woman's Secret* 1949; *In a Lonely Place* 1950; *The Bad and the Beautiful* 1952 (**AABSA**); *The Greatest Show on Earth* 1952; *Macao* 1952; *Sudden Fear* 1952; *The Big Heat* 1953; *The Glass Wall* 1953; *Man on a Tightrope* 1953; *Prisoners of the Casbah* 1953; *The Good Die Young* 1954; *Human Desire* 1954; *Naked Alibi* 1954; *The Cobweb* 1955; *The Man Who Never Was* 1955; *Not As a Stranger* 1955; *Oklahoma!* 1955; *Ride Out For Revenge* 1957; *Odds Against Tomorrow* 1959; *Ride Beyond Vengeance* 1966; *Blood and Lace* 1971; *Chandler* 1971; *The Loners* 1971; *The Todd Killings* 1971; *Tarots* 1972; *The Terror of Dr. Chancey* 1975; *Head Over Heels/Chilly Scenes of Winter* 1979; *Melvin and Howard* 1980; *The Nesting* 1981.

Granger, Farley • Actor • Born San Jose, CA, July 1, 1925. Discovered by Samuel Goldwyn while still a high school student. Granger's soulful good looks were exploited in a string of "man with a secret" roles in the late 1940s and early 50s, but his Hollywood career never quite lived up to early expectations. Memorable in Hitchcock's *Rope* (1948) and *Strangers on a Train* (1951), as well as Luchino Visconti's *Senso* (1954). • *The North Star* 1943; *The Purple Heart* 1944; *Enchantment* 1948; *Rope* 1948; *They Live By Night* 1948; *Roseanna McCoy* 1949; *Edge of Doom* 1950; *Our Very Own* 1950; *Side Street* 1950; *Behave Yourself* 1951; *I Want You* 1951; *Strangers on a Train* 1951; *Hans Christian Andersen* 1952; *O. Henry's Full House* 1952; *Small Town Girl* 1953; *The Story of Three Loves* 1953; *Senso/The Wanton Contessa* 1954; *The Girl in the Red Velvet Swing* 1955; *The Naked Street* 1955; *Rogue's Gallery* 1968; *Lo Chiamarano Trinita* 1971; *Arnold* 1973; *The Man Called Noon* 1973; *Le Serpent* 1973; *La Polizia Chiede Aiuto* 1975; *The Prowler* 1981; *Deathmask* 1983; *Very Close Quarters* 1983; *Hitchcock, Il Brivido del Genio* 1985; *The Imagemaker* 1985; *The Whoopee Boys* 1986.

Granger, Stewart • Actor • Born London, May 6, 1913. *Educ.* Webber-Douglas School of Dramatic Art. One of the premier leading men of British film in the 1940s. Granger signed in 1950 with MGM, where for the next seven years he tended to play virile types in stylish adventure features. Married to actress Jean Simmons from 1950 to 1960. • *A Southern Maid* 1933; *Give Her a Ring* 1934; *So This Is London* 1939; *Convoy* 1940; *Secret Mission* 1942; *The Lamp Still Burns* 1943; *The Man in Gray* 1943; *Thursday's Child* 1943; *Fanny By Gaslight* 1944; *Love Story* 1944; *Madonna of the Seven Moons* 1944; *Waterloo Road* 1944; *Caesar and Cleopatra* 1945; *Caravan* 1946; *The Magic Box* 1946; *Blanche Fury* 1947; *Captain Boycott* 1947; *Saraband For Dead Lovers* 1948; *Woman Hater* 1948; *Adam and Evelyn* 1949; *King Solomon's Mines* 1950; *The Light Touch* 1951; *Soldiers Three* 1951; *The Prisoner of Zenda* 1952; *Scaramouche* 1952; *The Wild North* 1952; *All the Brothers Were Valiant* 1953; *Salome* 1953; *Young Bess* 1953; *Beau Brummell* 1954; *Green Fire* 1954; *Footsteps in the Fog* 1955; *The Last Hunt* 1955; *Moonfleet* 1955; *Bhowani Junction* 1956; *Gun Glory* 1957; *The Little Hut* 1957; *Harry Black and the Tiger* 1958; *The Whole Truth* 1958; *North to Alaska* 1960; *The Secret Partner* 1960; *Marcia o crepa* 1962; *Sodoma e Gomorra/Sodom and Gomorrah* 1962; *Lo Spadaccino di Siena* 1962; *Il Giorno piu corto* 1963; *The Crooked Road* 1964; *The Secret Invasion* 1964; *Unter Geiern* 1964; *Das Geheimnis der drei Dschunken* 1965; *Old Surehand 1.Teil* 1965; *Der Olprinz* 1965; *Spie contro il mondo* 1965; *Das Geheimnis der Gelben Mönche* 1966; *The Trygon Factor* 1966; *The Last Safari* 1967; *Requiem per un agento segreto* 1967; *The Wild Geese* 1978; *Hell Hunters* 1988.

Grant, Cary • Actor • Born Archibald Alexander Leach, Bristol, England, January 18, 1904; died November 29, 1986, Davenport, IA. Cary Grant once described his screen persona as "a combination of Jack Buchanan, Noel Coward and Rex Harrison. I pretended to be somebody I wanted to be, and, finally, I became that person. Or he became me." In fact, in the process of constructing his cool, sophisticated movie star persona, Grant became not only the illusory presence he would have liked to be but the perfect, debonair Hollywood star. In *Charade* (1963), Audrey Hepburn poses a question to her costar and then answers it herself: "Do you know what's wrong with you? Nothing." Cary Grant was the true iconic movie star, his suave outward style and external sheen masking an inner reserve and aloofness. And in that reserve and seeming unconcern lies the Grant mystique. The plots of most Grant films revolve around this mystique and the efforts of a female—a short list includes such disparate types as Irene Dunne, Jean Arthur, Ingrid Bergman, Katharine Hepburn, Eva Marie Saint, Leslie Caron and Grace Kelly—to break it. And the audience can only guess at Grant's seeming abandonment and surrender to these women, whether it's symbolized by the door slamming shut at the end of *The Awful Truth* (1937) or the train racing into a tunnel at the end of *North By Northwest* (1959). Whatever the final outcome, Cary Grant did not show passion. That was left to other, more demonstrative actors. His acting was subtle and seamless, transcending performance altogether. It could be said that Cary Grant became a state of mind.

Grant's early life belied his on-screen personality. Born Archibald Alexander Leach, he was the only child of impoverished parents. At the age of nine he lost his mother when she was institutionalized. Around that time, he developed a love for the English music hall and began working at odd jobs at the Hippodrome and Empire theaters. At 14, he joined the Bob Pender comedy troupe and honed his dancing, acrobatic, stilt-walking and pantomime skills. The troupe performed in small towns throughout England; in 1920 they sailed to the United States for a successful two-year tour, at the end of which young Archie decided to try it on his own in New York City. For five years, Leach eked out a living in jobs as varied as placard walker and society escort. In 1927, he made his first stage appearance in the musical *Golden Dawn*, followed by appearances in *Boom Boom* (1929), *A Wonderful Night* (1929) and *Nikki* (1931). In 1931, Leach appeared in his first film, a ten-minute short entitled *Singapore Sue.* By now, he felt the time was right to try his hand at the movies, and he traveled to Los Angeles, where he made a successful screen test for Paramount executive B.P. Schulberg. The studio offered him a five-year contract, suggesting he change his name to Cary Lockwood; Leach haggled with them, and they settled on the name Cary Grant.

Grant's feature debut was in *This Is the Night* (1932). He soon found himself playing colorless characters opposite such top Paramount female stars as Nancy Carroll, Sylvia Sidney, Marlene Dietrich and Mae West (though he said he learned more about acting and comic timing from her than anyone else he ever worked with). It was on a studio loan-out to RKO in 1935, when Grant appeared with Katharine Hepburn in *Sylvia Scarlett*, that he began to find his form and spark, playing a Cockney entertainer in a traveling troupe, a role for which he could draw on his experiences with the Pender company. When his Paramount contract expired in 1937, Grant bolted, choosing not to sign with another studio. Instead, he selected his own films, scripts and directors.

Once he left Paramount, Grant put his personal stamp on the screwball comedy genre. As sophisticated as his characters seemed, they were never above a pratfall, setting Grant apart from other leading men of the time and making him the perfect foil for the comic hijinks initiated by screwball comedy's wacky heroines. Grant and his female costars operated on the same plane, neither quite gaining the upper hand; he converted screwball comedy into a two-character, upper-class, adult slapstick parlor game.

Grant's first hit was *Topper* but it was *The Awful Truth* (both 1937) that made him a star. For the next three years, Grant appeared in a succession of hits, each of which honed his image to a fine gloss: *Bringing up Baby*, *Holiday* (both 1938), *Gunga Din*, *Only Angels Have Wings* (both 1939), *His Girl Friday*, *My Favorite Wife* and *The Philadephia Story* (all 1940). By 1940, Cary Grant had become an archetype.

After this amazing string, his career faltered. The films were either atrocious mistakes (*Once Upon a Honeymoon* 1942), bland fantasies (*The Bishop's Wife* 1947), or wholesome pap (*Room For One More* 1951). When Grant tried something different, something closer to his roots, as the poor East End drifter in *None But the Lonely Heart* (1944), he was working against a persona that was so implanted and perfected that his characterization seemed ineffective and forced.

Grant had become so much of an ideal that to play a normal person on the screen seemed impossible. Instead, Grant's best roles resulted in his playing off his film image, exposing it and exploiting it—particularly in his work with Alfred Hitchcock on *Suspicion* (1941), *Notorious* (1946), *To Catch a Thief* (1955) and *North by Northwest* (1959), as well as Stanley Donen's Hitchcock-esque *Charade.*

In 1966, Grant decided to retire from the screen. With his age beginning to show, his exit from the screen left the Grant image untarnished and alive. At the same time, his retirement seemed to signal a farewell to classic Hollywood glamour and sophistication. That Grant could find a place in the late-60s film world of Dennis Hopper, Jack Nicholson and Dustin Hoffman was unlikely. He belonged to a more innocent American film past. As Pauline Kael has written: "He embodies what seems a happier time—a time when we had a simpler relationship to a performer. We could admire him for his timing and nonchalance; we didn't expect emotional revelations from Cary Grant... He appeared before us in his radiantly shallow perfection and that is all we wanted of him.... We didn't want depth from him; we asked only that he be handsome and silky and make us laugh." PB • *Blonde Venus* 1932; *The Devil and the Deep* 1932; *Hot Saturday* 1932; *Madame Butterfly* 1932; *Merrily We Go to Hell* 1932; *Sinners in the Sun* 1932; *This Is the Night* 1932; *Alice in Wonderland* 1933; *The Eagle and the Hawk* 1933; *Gambling Ship* 1933; *I'm No Angel* 1933; *She Done Him Wrong*

1933; *The Woman Accused* 1933; *Born to Be Bad* 1934; *Kiss and Make Up* 1934; *Ladies Should Listen* 1934; *Thirty Day Princess* 1934; *Enter Madame* 1935; *The Last Outpost* 1935; *Sylvia Scarlett* 1935; *Wings in the Dark* 1935; *Big Brown Eyes* 1936; *Pirate Party on Catalina Isle (short)* 1936; *Suzy* 1936; *Wedding Present* 1936; *The Awful Truth* 1937; *Romance and Riches* 1937; *The Toast of New York* 1937; *Topper* 1937; *When You're in Love* 1937; *Bringing Up Baby* 1938; *Holiday* 1938; *Gunga Din* 1939; *In Name Only* 1939; *Only Angels Have Wings* 1939; *His Girl Friday* 1940; *The Howards of Virginia* 1940; *My Favorite Wife* 1940; *The Philadelphia Story* 1940; *Penny Serenade* 1941 **(AANBA)**; *Suspicion* 1941; *Once Upon a Honeymoon* 1942; *Talk of the Town* 1942; *Destination Tokyo* 1943; *Mr. Lucky* 1943; *Arsenic and Old Lace* 1944; *None But the Lonely Heart* 1944 **(AANBA)**; *Once Upon a Time* 1944; *Night and Day* 1946; *Notorious* 1946; *Without Reservations* 1946; *The Bachelor and the Bobby Soxer* 1947; *The Bishop's Wife* 1947; *Every Girl Should Be Married* 1948; *Mr. Blandings Builds His Dream House* 1948; *I Was a Male War Bride* 1949; *Crisis* 1950; *People Will Talk* 1951; *Monkey Business* 1952; *Room For One More* 1952; *Dream Wife* 1953; *To Catch a Thief* 1955; *An Affair to Remember* 1956; *Kiss Them For Me* 1957; *The Pride and the Passion* 1957; *Houseboat* 1958; *Indiscreet* 1958; *North By Northwest* 1959; *Operation Petticoat* 1959 (a,exec.p); *The Grass Is Greener* 1960; *That Touch of Mink* 1962; *Charade* 1963; *Father Goose* 1964; *Walk, Don't Run* 1966; *Elvis That's the Way It Is* 1970; *It's Showtime* 1976; *George Stevens: A Filmmaker's Journey* 1985.

Grant, Hugh • Actor • Born London. *Educ.* New College, Oxford. Handsome young English lead, often in aristocratic roles. • *Maurice* 1987; *White Mischief* 1987; *The Dawning* 1988; *The Lair of the White Worm* 1988; *La Nuit Bengali* 1988; *Remando al Viento* 1988; *The Big Man* 1990; *Impromptu* 1991.

Grant, Lee • Actress, director. • Born Lyova Haskell Rosenthal, New York, NY, October 31, 1927. *Educ.* Juilliard (music); Neighborhood Playhouse, New York. Made a stunning screen debut as the shoplifter in *Detective Story* (1951) but was blacklisted shortly afterward for failing to testify against her already blacklisted husband, playwright Arnold Manoff. Following 12 years of near inactivity Grant resurfaced in the 60s, appearing in numerous character parts. She has since turned her hand to both feature and TV directing, gaining acclaim with her 1985 documentary, *Down and Out in America,* winning an Oscar for best documentary. • *Detective Story* 1951 **(AANBSA)**; *Storm Fear* 1955; *Middle of the Night* 1959; *An Affair of the Skin* 1963; *The Balcony* 1963; *Pie in the Sky* 1963; *Terror in the City* 1965; *Divorce American Style* 1967; *In the Heat of the Night* 1967; *Valley of the Dolls* 1967; *Buona Sera, Mrs. Campbell* 1968; *The Big Bounce* 1969; *Marooned* 1969; *The Landlord* 1970 **(AANBSA)**; *There Was a Crooked Man* 1970; *Plaza Suite* 1971; *Portnoy's Complaint* 1972; *The Internecine Project* 1974; *Shampoo* 1975 **(AABSA)**; *The Stronger (short)* 1976 (d,sc,adapt); *Voyage of the Damned* 1976 **(AANBSA)**; *Airport 77* 1977; *Damien: Omen II* 1978; *The Mafu Cage* 1978; *The Swarm* 1978; *When You Comin' Back, Red Ryder?* 1979; *Little Miss Marker* 1980; *Tell Me a Riddle* 1980 (d); *Charlie Chan and the Curse of the Dragon Queen* 1981; *Visiting Hours* 1981; *The Wilmar 8* 1981 (a,d); *Constance* 1984; *Teachers* 1984; *Trial Run* 1984; *Down and Out in America* 1985 (d); *Arriving Tuesday* 1986; *The Big Town* 1987; *Hello Actors Studio* 1987; *Calling the Shots* 1988; *Staying Together* 1989 (d); *Defending Your Life* 1991.

Grant, Richard E. • Actor • Born Mbabane, Swaziland, May 5, 1957. *Educ.* University of Cape Town, South Africa. Impressive English lead who emerged in the late 1980s and has demonstrated a particular flair for delivering bitter diatribes; memorable as a "resting" 60s actor in Bruce Robinson's *Withnail & I* (1986) and as a crazed ad executive in the same director's *How To Get Ahead In Advertising* (1988). • *Honest, Decent and True* 1985; *Withnail & I* 1986; *Hidden City* 1987; *How to Get Ahead in Advertising* 1988; *Killing Dad* 1989; *Warlock* 1989; *Henry & June* 1990; *Mountains of the Moon* 1990; *Hudson Hawk* 1991; *L.A. Story* 1991.

Graves, Rupert • British actor • Conveys a combination of strength and fragility; often in upper-class roles. • *A Room With a View* 1986; *Maurice* 1987; *A Handful of Dust* 1988; *The Children* 1990; *Where Angels Fear to Tread* 1991.

Gray, Spalding • Actor • Born Barrington, RI, 1941. *Educ.* Emerson College, Boston, MA (theater). Co-founder in 1977 of the Wooster Group, New York's acclaimed experimental theater company. Gray subsequently won international critical acclaim for his performance pieces built around autobiographical monologues. His experience as a bit player in *The Killing Fields* (1984) was translated into an Obie-award winning one-person show, and then into the film *Swimming to Cambodia* (1987), directed by Jonathan Demme. • *Variety* 1983; *Almost You* 1984; *The Communists Are Comfortable (And Three Other Stories)* 1984; *Hard Choices* 1984; *The Killing Fields* 1984; *True Stories* 1986; *Swimming to Cambodia* 1987 (a,sc,from performance piece); *Beaches* 1988; *Clara's Heart* 1988; *Heavy Petting* 1988; *Stars and Bars* 1988.

Green, Adolph • Playwright; also lyricist. • Born Bronx, NY, December 2, 1918. See Comden, Betty. • *Greenwich Village* 1944 (a); *Good News* 1947 (sc,song); *The Barkleys of Broadway* 1949 (sc); *On the Town* 1949 (sc,from play,lyrics); *Singin' in the Rain* 1952 (sc,story); *The Band Wagon* 1953 (sc) **(AANBSC)**; *It's Always Fair Weather* 1955 (sc,lyrics) **(AANBSC)**; *Auntie Mame* 1958 (sc); *Bells Are Ringing* 1960 (sc,from play); *What a Way to Go!* 1964 (sc); *Blue Sunshine* 1977 (song); *Simon* 1980 (a); *Frances* 1982 (song); *My Favorite Year* 1982 (a); *The Return of Captain Invincible* 1982 (song); *Garbo Talks* 1984 (a); *Jatszani Kell* 1985 (a); *Funny* 1988 (a); *Bert Rigby, You're a Fool* 1989 (song); *Je veux rentrer à la maison/I Want to Go Home* 1989 (a).

Green, Guy • Director; also director of photography. • Born Somerset, England, 1913. Successful director of photography, notably in collaboration with David Lean, who began his own directing career in 1954. On the basis of his two finest efforts, *The Angry Silence* (1959) and *The Mark* (1961), Green was wooed and won by Hollywood, where he cranked out one mawkish, over-blown project after another. • *Song of the Plough* 1933 (asst.cam.op); *Breakers Ahead* 1935 (cam.op); *The Immortal Swan* 1935 (ph); *Hi, Gang!* 1941 (cam.op); *Pimpernel Smith* 1941 (uncred.cam.op); *In Which We Serve* 1942 (cam.op); *One of Our Aircraft Is Missing* 1942 (cam.op); *Escape to Danger* 1943 (ph); *This Happy Breed* 1944 (cam.op); *The Way Ahead* 1944 (ph); *The Way to the Stars* 1945 (2u ph); *Carnival* 1946 (sc,ph); *Great Expectations* 1946 (ph) **(AABPH)**; *Blanche Fury* 1947 (ph); *Take My Life* 1947 (ph); *Oliver Twist* 1948 (ph); *Adam and Evelyn* 1949 (ph); *The Passionate Friends* 1949 (ph); *Madeleine* 1950 (ph); *Captain Horatio Hornblower* 1951 (ph); *Night Without Stars* 1951 (ph); *The Hour of 13* 1952 (ph); *The Story of Robin Hood* 1952 (ph); *The Beggar's Opera* 1953 (ph); *Decameron Nights* 1953 (ph); *Rob Roy, the Highland Rogue* 1953 (ph); *For Better For Worse* 1954 (ph); *River Beat* 1954 (d); *Souls in Conflict* 1954 (ph); *I Am a Camera* 1955 (ph); *Lost* 1955 (d); *Portrait of Alison* 1955 (d,sc); *The Warriors* 1955 (ph); *House of Secrets* 1956 (d); *Sea of Sand* 1958 (d); *The Snorkel* 1958 (d); *The Angry Silence* 1959 (d); *S.O.S. Pacific* 1959 (d); *The Mark* 1961 (d); *Diamond Head* 1962 (d); *Light in the Piazza* 1962 (d); *A Patch of Blue* 1965 (d,sc); *Pretty Polly* 1967 (d); *The Magus* 1968 (d); *A Walk in the Spring Rain* 1970 (d); *Luther* 1974 (d); *Once Is Not Enough* 1975 (d); *Des Teufels Advokat/The Devil's Advocate* 1977 (d).

Green, Johnny • *aka* John Green • Composer; also conductor, arranger, songwriter. • Born John W. Green, New York, NY, October 10, 1908; died May 15, 1989, Beverly Hills, CA. *Educ.* Harvard (economics). Former bandleader and arranger, hired by MGM in 1942 as staff conductor and composer. Green went on to become the studio's general music director in the same year, and over the next decade supervised such productions as *Summer Stock* (1950) and *Brigadoon* (1954). He composed the scores for *They Shoot Horses, Don't They?* (1969) and won Academy Awards for his collaborations on *Easter Parade* (1948), *An American in Paris* (1951), *West Side Story* (1961) and *Oliver!* (1968). • *Animal Crackers* 1930 (m); *The Big Pond* 1930 (m.arr); *Queen High* 1930 (m.arr); *The Sap From Syracuse* 1930 (song); *Start Cheering* 1938 (a,m); *Bathing Beauty* 1944 (m.dir); *Broadway Rhythm* 1944 (m.dir); *The Sailor Takes a Wife* 1945 (m); *Weekend at the Waldorf* 1945 (m.dir); *Easy to Wed* 1946 (m); *Beat the Band* 1947 (m); *Body and Soul* 1947 (song); *Fiesta* 1947 (m) **(AANBM)**; *It Happened in Brooklyn* 1947 (m.dir); *Something in the Wind* 1947 (m); *Easter Parade* 1948 (m.dir) **(AABM)**; *Up in Central Park* 1948 (m.dir); *The Inspector General* 1949 (m.dir); *Summer Stock* 1950 (m.dir); *An American in Paris* 1951 (m.dir) **(AABM)**; *The Great Caruso* 1951 (m.sup) **(AANBM)**; *Mr. Imperium* 1951 (m.dir); *Royal Wedding* 1951 (m); *Because You're Mine* 1952 (m.dir); *The Merry Wives of Windsor Overture (short)* 1953 (p) **(AABSF)**; *Brigadoon* 1954 (m.dir); *The Strauss Fantasy (short)* 1954 (p) **(AANBSF)**; *High Society* 1956 (m.dir) **(AANBM)**; *Invitation to the Dance* 1956 (m.dir); *Meet Me in Las Vegas* 1956 (m) **(AANBM)**; *Raintree County* 1957 (m) **(AANBM)**; *The Five Pennies* 1959 (song); *Pepe* 1960 (m.sup) **(AANBM)**; *West Side Story* 1961 (m.cond) **(AABM)**; *Bye Bye Birdie* 1963 (m.dir) **(AANBM)**; *Twilight of Honor* 1963 (m); *Alvarez Kelly* 1966 (m,song); *The Busy Body* 1967 (song); *Oliver!* 1968 (m.sup,m.arr,orch,choral arr,m.cond) **(AABM)**; *They Shoot Horses, Don't They?* 1969 (assoc.p,m,song) **(AANBM)**; *The Last Tycoon* 1976 (song); *Vengeance of the Barbarians* 1977 (m.sup).

Greenaway, Peter • Director, screenwiter • Born London, April 5, 1942. One of Britain's leading auteurs, Greenaway trained as a painter before spending 11 years, beginning in 1965, as a film editor. During this period he began making short, highly formalist films influenced by structuralist philosophy. After his medium-length works such as *Vertical Features Remake* (short) and the humorous *A Walk Through H* (both 1978) had attracted attention on the international festival circuit, Greenaway hit the limelight in 1982 with the release of his first feature, *The Draughtsman's Contract.* An acclaimed study of 18th-century sexual intrigue set in an English country house, *Contract* staked out its directors's central concerns with formal symmetries and parallels; each element of the plot was mirrored and repeated several times in order to create an elaborate, baroque structure which proved popular with both critics and (art-house) audiences.

Although *Contract* put the English art film back on the map, Greenaway's next two features did not meet with comparable success; both *A Zed and Two Noughts* (1985) and *The Belly of an Architect* (1987) are undermined by their rigid formalism, though they remain intriguing and visually absorbing. The director returned to success with *The Cook, the Thief, His Wife and Her Lover* (1989), a visceral study of haute cuisine, adultery and murder centered on a riveting performance by Michael Gambon as a sadistic, foul-mouthed gangster. Thanks to its relatively conventional narrative, *The Cook* proved more accessible to English audiences and brought Greenaway his first substantial recognition in the US. JDP • *Train (short)* 1966 (d); *Tree (short)* 1966 (d); *Five Postcards From Capital Cities (short)* 1967 (d); *Revolution (short)* 1967 (d); *Intervals (short)* 1969 (d); *Erosion (short)* 1971 (d); *Water (short)* 1975 (d); *Water Wrackets (short)* 1975 (d); *Windows (short)* 1975 (d); *Goole By Numbers (short)* 1976 (d); *Dear Phone (short)* 1977 (d); *1-100 (short)* 1978 (d); *Vertical Features Remake* 1978 (d,p,sc,ph,ed); *A Walk Through H (short)* 1978 (d,sc,ed,pd,maps); *The Falls* 1980 (d,ed,sc); *Act of God (short)* 1981 (d); *Zandra Rhodes (short)* 1981 (d); *The Draughtsman's Contract* 1982 (d,sc); *Making a Splash (short)* 1984 (d); *Modern American Composers I* 1984 (d); *A TV Dante—Canto 5 (short)* 1984 (d); *Inside Rooms—The Bathroom (short)* 1985 (d); *A Zed and Two Noughts* 1985 (d,sc); *The Belly of an Architect* 1987 (d,sc); *Drowning By Numbers* 1988 (d,sc); *The Cook, the Theif, His Wife and Her Lover* 1989 (d,sc); *Death in the Seine* (short) 1989 (d,sc); *A TV Dante* 1989 (d); *Prospero's Books* (d) 1991.

Greenberg, Jerry • *aka* Gerald Greenberg • American editor • Top New York-based editor whose facility with taut action scenes was dazzlingly displayed in a trilogy of urban crime pictures: *The French Connection* (1971); *The Seven Ups* (1973); and *The Taking of Pelham 1,2,3* (1974). Greenberg cut most of Brian DePalma's films in the 1980s. • *The Subject Was Roses* 1968 (ed); *Alice's Restaurant* 1969 (assoc.ed); *The Boys in the Band* 1970 (ed); *The French Connection* 1971 (ed) **(AABED)**; *They Might Be Giants* 1971 (ed); *Come Back Charleston Blue* 1972 (ed); *The Stoolie* 1972 (ed); *Electra Glide in Blue* 1973 (ed); *The Seven Ups* 1973 (ed); *The Taking of Pelham 1,2,3* 1974 (ed); *The Happy Hooker* 1975 (ed); *The Missouri Breaks* 1976 (ed); *Apocalypse Now* 1979 (ed); *Kramer vs. Kramer* 1979 (ed) **(AANBED)**; *Dressed to Kill* 1980 (ed); *Heaven's Gate* 1980 (ed); *Reds* 1981 (add.ed); *Still of the Night* 1982 (ed); *Scarface* 1983 (ed); *Body Double* 1984 (ed); *Savage Dawn* 1985 (ed); *No Mercy* 1986 (ed); *Wise Guys* 1986 (ed); *The Untouchables* 1987 (ed); *The Accused* 1988 (ed); *National Lampoon's Christmas Vacation* 1989 (ed); *Awakenings* 1990 (ed); *Collision Course* 1990 (ed).

Greene, Ellen • Actress • Born Brooklyn, NY. *Educ.* Ryder College. Stage and screen actress best known for her performance in *Little Shop of Horrors* (1986). • *Next Stop, Greenwich Village* 1976; *I'm Dancing As Fast As I Can* 1981; *Little Shop of Horrors* 1986; *Me and Him* 1988; *Talk Radio* 1988; *Little Feet (short)* 1990; *Pump Up the Volume* 1990; *Rock-A-Doodle* 1991; *Stepping Out* 1991.

Greenstreet, Sydney • Actor • Born Sandwich, England, December 27, 1879; died 1954. Portly English actor who made a sensational screen debut as the cunning Kaspar Guttman in John Huston's *The Maltese Falcon* (1941). Greenstreet subsequently appeared in numerous films as a brilliant schemer and shrewd architect of villainy. • *The Maltese Falcon* 1941 **(AANBSA)**; *They Died With Their Boots On* 1941; *Across the Pacific* 1942; *Casablanca* 1942; *Background to Danger* 1943; *Between Two Worlds* 1944; *The Conspirators* 1944; *Hollywood Canteen* 1944; *The Mask of Dimitrios* 1944; *Passage to Marseille* 1944; *Christmas in Connecticut* 1945; *Conflict* 1945; *Pillow to Post* 1945; *Devotion* 1946; *Three Strangers* 1946; *The Verdict* 1946; *The Hucksters* 1947; *That Way With Women* 1947; *Ruthless* 1948; *The Velvet Touch* 1948; *The Woman in White* 1948; *Flamingo Road* 1949; *It's a Great Feeling* 1949; *Malaya* 1949.

Greenwood, Joan • Actress • Born London, March 4, 1921; died February 28, 1987, London. *Educ.* RADA, London. Appeared in several classic British comedies of the 1940s and 50s, including *Kind Hearts and Coronets* (1949), *The Man in the White Suit* (1951) and the screen version of Oscar Wilde's *The Importance of Being Earnest* (1952). • *John Smith Wakes Up* 1940; *He Found a Star* 1941; *My Wife's Family* 1941; *The Gentle Sex* 1943; *Latin Quarter* 1945; *They Knew Mr. Knight* 1945; *A Girl in a Million* 1946; *The Man Within* 1947; *The October Man* 1947; *The White Unicorn* 1947; *Saraband For Dead Lovers* 1948; *The Bad Lord Byron* 1949; *Kind Hearts and Coronets* 1949; *Whisky Galore!* 1949; *Garou-Garou, le passe-muraille* 1950; *Flesh and Blood* 1951; *The Man in the White Suit* 1951; *Young Wives' Tale* 1951; *The Importance of Being Earnest* 1952; *Father Brown* 1954; *Monsieur Ripois* 1954; *Moonfleet* 1955; *Stage Struck* 1958; *Hest pa sommerferie* 1959; *Mysterious Island* 1961; *The Amorous Prawn* 1962; *Tom Jones* 1963; *The*

Moon-Spinners 1964; *Girl Stroke Boy* 1971; *The Uncanny* 1977; *The Hound of the Baskervilles* 1978; *The Water Babies* 1979; *Country* 1981; *Past Caring* 1985; *Little Dorrit* 1988.

Greer, Jane • Actress • Born Bettejane Greer, Washington, DC, September 9, 1924. Versatile actress who played everything from society ladies to femmes fatales. Greer began her career at RKO, where she played a series of leads through the early 1950s before transferring to MGM. • *Dick Tracy* 1945; *George White's Scandals* 1945; *Pan-Americana* 1945; *Two O'Clock Courage* 1945; *The Bamboo Blonde* 1946; *The Falcon's Alibi* 1946; *Sunset Pass* 1946; *Out of the Past* 1947; *Sinbad the Sailor* 1947; *They Won't Believe Me* 1947; *Station West* 1948; *The Big Steal* 1949; *The Company She Keeps* 1950; *U.S.S. Tea Kettle* 1951; *Desperate Search* 1952; *The Prisoner of Zenda* 1952; *You For Me* 1952; *The Clown* 1953; *Down Among the Sheltering Palms* 1953; *Run For the Sun* 1956; *Man of a Thousand Faces* 1957; *Where Love Has Gone* 1964; *Billie* 1965; *The Outfit* 1973; *Against All Odds* 1983; *Just Between Friends* 1986; *Immediate Family* 1989.

Gregory, Andre • American actor; also stage director. • Avant-garde theater director who earned widespread recognition for his thoughtful, witty performance in Louis Malle's *My Dinner With Andre* (1981), co-written by Gregory and actor-playwright Wallace Shawn. • *My Dinner With Andre* 1981 (a,sc); *Author! Author!* 1982; *Protocol* 1984; *Always* 1985; *The Mosquito Coast* 1986; *Street Smart* 1987; *The Last Temptation of Christ* 1988; *Some Girls* 1988.

Greist, Kim • Actress • Born Stamford, CT, May 12, 1958. *Educ.* New School for Social Research, New York. Stage actress chosen by director Terry Gilliam to play the enigmatic heroine of *Brazil* (1985). • *C.H.U.D.* 1984; *Brazil* 1985; *Manhunter* 1986; *Throw Momma From the Train* 1987; *Punchline* 1988; *Un Plan d'enfer* 1989.

Grémillon, Jean • Director; also composer. • Born Bayeux, France, October 3, 1901; died 1959. *Educ.* Schola Cantorum, Paris (music). Made short documentaries and experimental films before directing his first feature in 1927. Gremillon earned critical acclaim but little box-office success with films such as *Maldone* (1927) and *La Petite Lise* (1930), subsequently working in Spain and Germany. After returning to France he produced some of his finest work during WWII—including *Lumière d'été* (1943), a Jacques Prevert-penned study of the decadent French aristocracy. Gremillon returned to making documentaries after the war and was president of the Cinémathèque Française from 1943 to 1958. • *Chartres (short)* 1923 (d,ed); *La Bière* 1924 (d,ed); *Du fil à l'aiguille* 1924 (d,ed); *La Croisière de l'Atalante* 1926 (d,ed); *La Vie des travailleurs Italiens en France* 1926 (d,ed); *Maldone* 1927 (d,m,uncred.ed); *Gardiens de phare* 1929 (d,ed); *La Petite Lise* 1930 (d,uncred.ed); *Dainah la métisse* 1931 (d); *Le Petit babouin* 1932 (d,ed,m); *Pour un sou d'amour* 1932 (d,uncred.ed); *Gonzague ou l'accordeur* 1933 (d,sc,dial); *La Dolorosa* 1934 (d); *Königswalzer* 1935 (d); *Centinela alerta!* 1936 (d); *Pattes de mouche* 1936 (d,sc); *Gueule d'amour* 1937 (d); *L'Etrange Monsieur Victor* 1938 (d); *Remorques/Storm Waters* 1941 (d); *Le Ciel est à vous* 1943 (d); *Lumière d'été* 1943 (d); *Le 6 juin, à l'aube* 1945 (d,sc,commentary,m); *Journal de la résistance (short)* 1945 (d); *Pattes Blanches* 1949 (d,dial); *L'Etrange Madame X* 1951 (d); *L'Astrologie ou Le miroir de la vie* 1952 (d,sc,narration,m); *L'Amour d'une femme* 1953 (d,sc,adapt,dial,dubbing—Paola Stoppa).

Grey, Joel • Actor; also singer, dancer. • Born Joel Katz, Cleveland, OH, April 11, 1932. Dynamic, pixie-like singer and dancer, best known for his performance as the unctuous emcee in *Cabaret* (1972). Daughter Jennifer Grey is an actress (*Dirty Dancing* 1987). • *About Face* 1952; *Calypso Heat Wave* 1957; *Come September* 1961; *Cabaret* 1972 **(AABSA)**; *Man on a Swing* 1974; *Buffalo Bill and the Indians, or Sitting Bull's History Lesson* 1976; *The Seven Per-Cent Solution* 1976; *Remo Williams: The Adventure Begins...* 1985.

Griem, Helmut • Actor • Born Germany, 1940. *Educ.* Hamburg University. German actor in scores of international films. • *La Caduta degli dei/The Damned* 1969; *The McKenzie Break* 1970; *Die Moral der Ruth Halbfass* 1971; *Cabaret* 1972; *Ludwig* 1972; *Children of Rage* 1974; *Ansichten Eines Clowns/The Clown* 1975; *Le Desert des tartares* 1976; *Voyage of the Damned* 1976; *Deutschland im Herbst/Germany in Autumn* 1978; *Die Glaeserne Zelle* 1978; *Mannen i skuggan* 1978; *Les Rendez-Vous d'Anna* 1978; *Die Hamburger Krankheit* 1979; *Steiner—Das Eiserne Kreuz, 2 Teil* 1979; *Berlin Alexanderplatz* 1980; *Kaltgestellt* 1980; *Malou* 1980; *La Passante* 1983; *The Second Victory* 1986; *Caspar David Friedrich* 1987; *Faust* 1989; *A Proposito di Quella Strana Ragazza* 1989; *Hard Days, Hard Nights* 1990.

Grier, Pam • Actress • Born Pamela Grier, US, 1949. Black leading lady of the 1970s and 80s. • *The Big Doll House* 1971; *The Big Bird Cage* 1972; *Black Mama, White Mama* 1972; *Hit Man* 1972; *Women in Cages* 1972; *Coffy* 1973; *Scream Blacula Scream* 1973; *Twilight People* 1973; *The Arena* 1974; *Foxy Brown* 1974; *Bucktown* 1975; *Friday Foster* 1975; *Sheba Baby* 1975; *Drum* 1976; *Greased Lightning* 1977; *Fort Apache, the Bronx* 1981; *Tough Enough* 1982; *Something Wicked This Way Comes* 1983; *The Vindicator* 1984; *On the Edge* 1985; *Stand Alone* 1985; *The Allnighter* 1987; *Above the Law* 1988; *The Package* 1989; *Class of 1999* 1990.

Grierson, John • Producer; also director. • Born Deanston, Scotland, April 25, 1898; died 1972. *Educ.* Glasgow University (philosophy). A pioneering figure in nonfiction filmmaking, Grierson was the first to use the term "documentary," in a review of Robert Flaherty's *Moana* (1926). Returing to Britain in 1927 after a stint in the US, Grierson petitioned the Empire Marketing Board to investigate the propaganda potential of film and was commissioned to form a unit within the organization. Inspired by the success of his first effort, *Drifters* (1929), a study of North Sea fishermen, he amassed a talented group of protégés whose work he encouraged and supervised. When the EMB was dissolved in 1933 Grierson's unit moved to the General Post Office (GPO), where their work included the outstanding *Nightmail* (1936). In 1937 Grierson established the Film Centre consultancy, serving as an advisor on, among other projects, the European editions of the US series, *The March of Time*. He also set up supervisory film panels in Canada, New Zealand, Australia and Scotland. Although Grierson would only direct one more film, *The Fishing Banks of Skye* (1935), he remained a driving force behind documentary movements worldwide. • *Bronenosets "Potyomkin"/Potemkin* 1925 (English titles); *Drifters* 1929 (d,ed,p); *Conquest* 1930 (d); *Scottish Poultry* 1930 (d); *Turksib* 1930 (English titles); *Australian Wine* 1931 (d); *Burma Teak* 1931 (d); *The Country Comes to Town* 1931 (d,p); *Empire Timber* 1931 (d); *Home Plums* 1931 (d); *Industrial Britain (short)* 1931 (commentary,assembly sup); *Lumber* 1931 (p); *National Mark Eggs* 1931 (d); *Scottish Tomatoes* 1931 (d); *Shadow on the Mountain: An Experiment in the Welsh Hills* 1931 (p); *Upstream* 1931 (p); *Aero Engine* 1932 (p); *The New Generation* 1932 (p); *O'er Hill and Dale* 1932 (p); *Voice of the World* 1932 (p); *6.30 Collection* 1933 (p); *Cable Ship* 1933 (p); *Cargo From Jamaica* 1933 (p); *The Coming of the Dial* 1933 (p); *The English Potter* 1933 (p); *Eskimo Village* 1933 (p); *The Fens* 1933 (p); *The Glassmakers of England* 1933 (p); *Granton Trawler* 1933 (a,commentary,ph,d,p); *Liner Cruising South* 1933 (p); *London Town* 1933 (p); *The New Operator* 1933 (p); *The Norfolk Bittern* 1933 (p); *Spring Comes to England* 1933 (p); *Spring on the Farm* 1933 (p); *Uncharted Waters* 1933 (p); *Windmill in Barbados* 1933 (p); *B.B.C.—Droitwich* 1934 (p); *Introducing the Dial* 1934 (p); *Lancashire at Work and Play* 1934 (p); *Pett and Pott (short)* 1934 (p); *Post-Haste (short)* 1934 (p); *Telephone Workers* 1934 (p); *Weather Forecast* 1934 (p);

B.B.C.—The Voice of Britain 1935 (p); *Banking For Millions* 1935 (p); *Coal Face* 1935 (p); *A Colour Box* 1935 (p); *The Fishing Banks of Skye* 1935 (commentary,d,p); *Song of Ceylon* 1935 (p,sc); *Children at School* 1936 (p); *Message From Geneva* 1936 (p); *Nightmail* 1936 (a,p); *A Job in a Million* 1937 (p); *The Line to Tschierva Hut* 1937 (p); *The Saving of Bill Blewitt* 1937 (p); *Trade Tattoo* 1937 (p); *We Live in Two Worlds* 1937 (p); *Who Writes to Switzerland (short)* 1937 (p); *The Face of Scotland* 1938 (p); *The Londoners* 1939 (p); *Men of the Alps* 1939 (p); *Action Stations* 1943 (p); *Brandy For the Parson* 1951 (exec.p); *Judgment Deferred* 1951 (exec.p); *The Brave Don't Cry* 1952 (exec.p); *Miss Robin Hood* 1952 (exec.p); *The Oracle* 1952 (exec.p); *You're Only Young Twice!* 1952 (exec.p); *Background* 1953 (exec.p); *Laxdale Hall* 1953 (p); *Man of Africa* 1953 (p); *Child's Play* 1954 (exec.p); *Devil on Horseback* 1954 (p); *John Grierson at the National Film Theatre (short)* 1959 (a); *Rivers at Work* 1960 (a,narrative text,commentary); *Seawards the Great Ships* 1960 (treatment); *The Heart of Scotland* 1961 (treatment); *I Remember, I Remember* 1968 (a); *Grierson* 1972 (a).

Griffith, D. W. • *aka* Lawrence Griffith, M. Gaston De Trolignac, Granville Warwick, Captain Victor Marier, Marquis De Trolignac, Irene Sinclair, Roy Sinclair • Director, producer, screenwriter; also actor. • Born David Lewelyn Wark Griffith, Oldham County, KY, January 22, 1875; died July 23, 1948, Hollywood, CA. David Wark Griffith's achievement is two-fold: he developed for Americans a syntax for expression in the movies, and he showed how the feature film could be a significant commercial and cultural element of American culture. The first achievement is less understood but more important than the second.

Griffith did not enter film with a record as a successful artist. He was a failure as a playwright, with but one of his plays actually produced. But because he approached film with the attitude that it was a temporary job, he saw it as an opportunity to experiment, to break the conventions of his era, to develop new means of relating narratives for the screen.

In 1907, when Griffith tried to sell a story to movie producer Edwin S. Porter who signed him on as an actor instead, American movies all too often consisted of series of scenes (originally called views) of events usually taken from the popular press or the stage. Static cameras recorded scenes connected by titles and little else. Four years earlier in *The Great Train Robbery,* Porter had stumbled onto more eloquent means of expression—shorter scenes, multiple locations, use of natural landscapes with actors moving through them, even the close-up—but he declined to develop these techniques. In fact when Griffith played the lead in Porter's *Rescued From an Eagle's Next* (1907), the young actor was so carelessly filmed that he was obscured by the edge of the frame. Later that year, Griffith got his chance to direct and he showed an immediate talent for creative use of the frame, as well as developing rhythmic editing to build dramatic tension. Griffith also sought out younger performers who were less bound to the broad style of stage acting and more open to the nuances required for acting for a camera.

From 1907 to 1913, Griffith averaged 2 1/2 films a week, most of them for Biograph, using overlapping schedules and a stock company of actors who rapidly moved from one film to the next, sometimes in the same day. Griffith paid special attention to his actresses, developing a number of important women performers, including Lillian and Dorothy Gish, Mary Pickford, Blanche Sweet and Mae Marsh.

In the midst of this whirlwind of production Griffith was developing new ways of telling stories that were uniquely suited to film. Editing became as important an element as cinematography, most notably in his use of cross-cutting between parallel story lines. This offered opportunities to contrast behavior or social circumstance, as in *A Corner in Wheat*, or to develop suspense with a rising tempo of action, as in *The Lonely Villa* (both 1909). Griffith's collaborators in this adventure of inventing film language included not only his cameraman, Billy Bitzer, but also the actors themselves, who were encouraged to suggest mannerisms to enrich their performances.

At this time, filmmakers in other countries, especially France and Denmark, were making comparable discoveries about the importance of editing; often their films were shown in the United States, just as Griffith's Biograph productions were exported to Europe. This ongoing dialogue has made it nearly impossible to clearly define sources of innovation and influences which many historians have consigned solely to Griffith.

In 1913 Griffith broke with the Biograph Company when it declined to let him make feature-length films and the following year he began production on his first feature, *Birth of a Nation* (1915). Its release brought Griffith enormous acclaim and infamy. Audiences were dazzled by the film's sweep and epic power, as well as its intimate moments of pain and joy, but Griffith's embrace of the Ku Klux Klan and his insensitive depiction of black characters stirred up a storm of controversy. Previously relegated to the status of an amusement on the fringes of culture, movies were catapulted by Griffith and his film into social and financial prominence.

Griffith won financial independence with *Birth of a Nation* and almost immediately moved on to another epic, an elaboration on the notion of parallel historical developments, which he would present through cross-cutting across time rather than geography. *Intolerance* (1916) was a quartet of stories of man's inhumanity to man which some historians charge was Griffith's compensation for the accusations of racism made against him after *Birth of a Nation.* Enormously expensive to produce, the film was nearly as big a box-office flop as *Birth* had been a hit. Its reputation over the years has in some ways surpassed its predecessor, and its influence is apparent in the works of Carl Dreyer, Sergei Eisenstein, Fritz Lang and many other directors.

As great an artistic achievement as *Intolerance* was, it also left Griffith on a permanent financial treadmill, as he sought to pay off his debts with proceeds from future productions. From 1916 to 1931, he made over two dozen more features. At least five of these—*Broken Blossoms* (1919), *Way Down East* (1920), *Orphans of the Storm* (1921), *The White Rose* (1923) and *Isn't Life Wonderful* (1924)—were either commercial or critical successes, but the financial dividends went to Griffith's creditors or producers. On one film, *The Sorrows of Satan* (1926), Griffith's producers inflated the cost of the production by pressuring Griffith to film material he did not need and then recut the film after he had completed it. By the end of the silent era, Griffith was saddled with a reputation for extravagance, which was undeserved, and sentimentality, which was an integral part of his personality, although a steadily less compelling component of his films.

Griffith made two sound films, the starched and safe *Abraham Lincoln* (1930) and *The Struggle* (1931). *The Struggle* is a haunting final work, full of melancholy and dread of alcoholism, but also distinguished by superb sequences photographed on New York City streets and an inventive use of sound in factory sequences which revealed Griffith still seeking new ways to narrate stories on film.

Ignored by the industry he played such an important role in creating, Griffith retreated to over a decade of isolation at Hollywood's Knickerbocker Hotel, where he died in 1948. For years, the scurrilous content of *Birth of a Nation* and the unabashed sentiment of many of the other features consigned Griffith to the status of irrelevancy, but in the mid-1960s, a Griffith revival began, with re-appraisal of his early works and acknowlegements of his immense contributions. RAH • Shorts: *Rescued From an Eagle's Nest* 1907 (a); *The Adventures of Dollie* 1908 (d); *After Many Years* 1908 (d); *The Awful Moment* 1908 (d,sc); *Balked at the Alter*

1908 (a,d,sc); *The Bandit's Waterloo* 1908 (d,sc); *The Barbarian Ingomar* 1908 (d,sc); *Behind the Scenes: Where All Is Not Gold That Glitters* 1908 (d,sc); *Betrayed By a Hand Print* 1908 (d,sc); *The Black Viper* 1908 (a,d); *A Calamitous Elopement* 1908 (a,d,sc); *The Call of the Wild* 1908 (d); *The Christmas Burglars* 1908 (d,sc); *The Clubman and the Tramp* 1908 (d,sc); *Concealing a Burglar* 1908 (d,sc); *The Devil* 1908 (a,d,sc); *The Fatal Hour* 1908 (d,sc); *Father Gets in the Game* 1908 (d,sc); *The Feud and the Turkey* 1908 (d,sc); *For Love of Gold* 1908 (d,sc); *For a Wife's Honor* 1908 (d,sc); *The Girl and the Outlaw* 1908 (d,sc); *The Greaser's Gauntlet* 1908 (d,sc); *The Guerrilla* 1908 (d,sc); *Heart of O Yama* 1908 (a,d,sc); *The Helping Hand* 1908 (d,sc); *The Ingrate* 1908 (d,sc); *The Man and the Woman* 1908 (d,sc); *Money Mad* 1908 (d,sc); *Mr. Jones at the Ball* 1908 (d,sc); *Mrs. Jones Entertains* 1908 (d,sc); *The Pirate's Gold* 1908 (d,sc); *The Planter's Wife* 1908 (d,sc); *The Reckoning* 1908 (d,sc); *The Red Girl* 1908 (d,sc); *The Redman and the Child* 1908 (d,sc); *Romance of a Jewess* 1908 (d,sc); *A Smoked Husband* 1908 (d,sc); *The Song of the Shirt* 1908 (d,sc); *The Stolen Jewels* 1908 (d,sc); *Taming of the Shrew* 1908 (d,sc); *The Tavern Keeper's Daughter* 1908 (d); *The Test of Friendship* 1908 (d,sc); *The Valet's Wife* 1908 (d,sc); *The Vaquero's Vow* 1908 (d,sc); *Where the Breakers Roar* 1908 (d,sc); *A Woman's Way* 1908 (d,sc);*The Zulu's Heart* 1908 (d,sc); *1776* 1909 (a,d,sc); *And a Little Child Shall Lead Them* 1909 (d,sc); *At the Altar* 1909 (a,d,sc); *The Awakening* 1909 (d); *A Baby's Shoe* 1909 (d,sc); *The Better Way* 1909 (d); *The Brahma Diamond* 1909 (d,sc); *The Broken Locket* 1909 (d,sc); *A Burglar's Mistake* 1909 (d,sc); *The Cardinal's Conspiracy* 1909 (d); *A Change of Heart* 1909 (d); *The Children's Friend* 1909 (d); *Comata, the Sioux* 1909 (d); *Confidence* 1909 (d,sc); *A Convict's Sacrifice* 1909 (d,sc); *The Cord of Life* 1909 (d,sc); *A Corner in Wheat* 1909 (d,sc); *The Country Doctor* 1909 (d,sc); *The Cricket on the Hearth* 1909 (d); *The Criminal Hypnotist* 1909 (d,sc); *The Curtain Pole* 1909 (d,sc); *The Death Disk* 1909 (d); *The Deception* 1909 (d); *Drive For a Life* 1909 (d,sc); *Drunkard's Reformation* 1909 (d,sc); *The Eavesdropper* 1909 (d,sc); *Edgar Allen Poe* 1909 (d,sc); *Eloping With Aunty* 1909 (d,sc); *Eradicating Aunty* 1909 (d,sc); *The Expiation* 1909 (d,sc); *The Faded Lilies* 1909 (d,sc); *A Fair Exchange* 1909 (d); *The Fascinating Mrs. Francis* 1909 (d,sc); *A Fool's Revenge* 1909 (d,sc); *Fools of Fate* 1909 (d); *The French Duel* 1909 (d,sc); *The Friend of the Family* 1909 (d,sc); *Getting Even* 1909 (d,sc); *The Gibson Goddess* 1909 (d,sc); *The Girls and Daddy* 1909 (a,d,sc); *The Golden Louis* 1909 (d,sc); *Her First Biscuits* 1909 (d,sc); *The Hindoo Dagger* 1909 (d,sc); *His Duty* 1909 (d); *His Lost Love* 1909 (d,sc); *His Ward's Love* 1909 (d,sc); *His Wife's Mother* 1909 (d,sc); *His Wife's Visitor* 1909 (d,sc); *The Honor of Thieves* 1909 (d,sc); *I Did It, Mama* 1909 (d,sc); *In Little Italy* 1909 (d); *In Old Kentucky* 1909 (d); *In a Hempen Bag* 1909 (d,sc); *In the Watches of the Night* 1909 (d,sc); *In the Window Recess* 1909 (d); *The Indian Runner's Romance* 1909 (d); *Jealousy and the Man* 1909 (d,sc); *The Jilt* 1909 (d,sc); *Jones and His New Neighbors* 1909 (d,sc); *Jones and the Lady Book Agent* 1909 (d,sc); *Jones' Burglar* 1909 (d,sc); *The Joneses Have Amateur Theatricals* 1909 (d,sc); *Lady Helen's Escapade* 1909 (d); *Leather Stocking* 1909 (d); *The Light That Came* 1909 (d,sc); *Lines of White on a Sullen Sea* 1909 (d,sc); *The Little Darling* 1909 (d,sc); *The Little Teacher* 1909 (d); *The Lonely Villa* 1909 (d); *Love Finds a Way* 1909 (d,sc); *Lucky Jim* 1909 (d); *The Lure of the Gown* 1909 (d,sc); *The Maniac Cook* 1909 (d,sc); *The Medicine Bottle* 1909 (d,sc); *The Mended Lute* 1909 (d); *The Message* 1909 (d); *Mexican Sweethearts* 1909 (d,sc); *A Midnight Adventure* 1909 (d,sc); *The Mills of the Gods* 1909 (d,sc); *The Mountaineer's Honor* 1909 (d,sc); *Mr. Jones Has a Card Party* 1909 (d,sc); *Mrs. Jones' Lover* 1909 (d,sc); *The Necklace* 1909 (d); *A New Trick* 1909 (d,sc); *The Note in the Shoe* 1909 (d,sc); *Nursing a Viper* 1909 (d,sc); *Oh, Uncle!* 1909 (d,sc); *One Busy Hour* 1909 (d,sc); *One Touch of Nature* 1909 (d); *The Open Gate* 1909 (d,sc); *The Peachbasket Hat* 1909 (d,sc); *Pippa Passes* 1909 (d,sc); *The Politician's Love Story* 1909 (d,sc); *Pranks* 1909 (d); *The Prussian Spy* 1909 (d,sc); *The Redman's View* 1909 (d); *The Renunciation* 1909 (d,sc); *The Restoration* 1909 (d,sc); *Resurrection* 1909 (d); *The Road to the Heart* 1909 (d,sc); *The Rocky Road* 1909 (d); *Roue's Heart* 1909 (d,sc);*The Rude Hostess* 1909(d,sc); *A Rural Elopement* 1909 (d,sc); *The Sacrifice* 1909 (d,sc); *The Salvation Army Lass* 1909 (d,sc); *Schneider's Anti-Noise Crusade* 1909 (d,sc); *Sealed Room* 1909 (d); *The Seventh Day* 1909 (d,sc); *The Slave* 1909 (d,sc); *The Son's Return* 1909 (d,sc); *A Sound Sleeper* 1909 (d,sc); *A Strange Meeting* 1909 (d,sc); *The Suicide Club* 1909 (d); *Sweet Revenge* 1909 (d,sc); *Sweet and Twenty* 1909 (d); *Tender Hearts* 1909 (d,sc); *The Test* 1909 (d,sc); *They Would Elope* 1909 (d); *Those Awful Hats* 1909 (d,sc); *Those Boys!* 1909 (d,sc); *Through the Breakers* 1909 (d); *'Tis an Ill Wind That Blows No Good* 1909 (d,sc); *To Save Her Soul* 1909 (d,sc); *Tragic Love* 1909 (d,sc); *A Trap for Santa Claus* 1909 (d,sc); *The Trick That Failed* 1909 (d); *A Troublesome Satchel* 1909 (d); *Trying to Get Arrested* 1909 (d,sc); *Twin Brothers* 1909 (d); *Two Memories* 1909 (d,sc); *Two Women and a Man* 1909 (d,sc); *The Violin Maker of Cremona* 1909 (d); *The Voice of the Violin* 1909 (d,sc); *Wanted: A Child* 1909 (d,sc); *Was Justice Served?* 1909 (d,sc); *The Way of Man* 1909 (d,sc); *The Welcome Burglar* 1909 (d,sc); *What Drink Did* 1909 (d,sc); *What's Your Hurry?* 1909 (d,sc); *The Winning Coat* 1909 (d,sc); *With Her Card* 1909 (d,sc); *The Wooden Leg* 1909 (d,sc); *A Wreath in Time* 1909 (d,sc); *An Arcadian Maid* 1910 (d); *As It Is in Life* 1910 (d); *As the Bells Rang Out* 1910 (d); *The Banker's Daughters* 1910 (d); *The Broken Doll* 1910 (d); *The Call to Arms* 1910 (d); *The Call* 1910 (d,sc); *A Child of the Ghetto* 1910 (d); *A Child's Faith* 1910 (d); *A Child's Impulse* 1910 (d); *A Child's Stratagem* 1910 (d); *The Chink at Golden Gulch* 1910 (d); *Choosing a Husband* 1910(d,sc); *The Cloister's Touch* 1910 (d); *The Converts* 1910 (d); *The Course of True Love* 1910 (d); *The Dancing Girl of Butte* 1910 (d,sc); *The Duke's Plan* 1910 (d,sc); *The Englishman and the Girl* 1910 (d,sc); *Examination Day at School* 1910 (d); *The Face at the Window* 1910 (d); *Faithful* 1910 (d); *The Final Settlement* 1910 (d); *A Flash of Light* 1910 (d); *The Fugitive* 1910 (d); *Gold Is Not All* 1910 (d); *A Gold Necklace* 1910 (d); *The Gold Seekers* 1910 (d); *The Golden Supper* 1910 (d); *Her Father's Pride* 1910 (d); *Her Terrible Ordeal* 1910 (d,sc); *His Last Burglary* 1910 (d); *His Last Dollar* 1910 (d); *His Sister-in-Law* 1910 (d); *The Honor of His Family* 1910 (d); *The House With Closed Shutters* 1910 (d); *The Iconoclast* 1910 (d); *The Impalement* 1910 (d); *In Life's Cycle* 1910 (d); *In Old California* 1910 (d); *In the Border States* 1910 (d); *In the Season of the Buds* 1910 (d); *A Knot in the Plot* 1910 (d); *The Last Deal* 1910 (d,sc); *The Lesson* 1910 (d); *Little Angels of Luck* 1910 (d); *Love Among the Roses* 1910 (d); *The Man* 1910 (d); *The Marked Time-Table* 1910 (d); *May and December* 1910 (d); *The Message of the Violin* 1910 (d,sc); *A Midnight Cupid* 1910 (d); *A Mohawk's Way* 1910 (d); *Mugsy Becomes a Hero* 1910 (d); *Mugsy's First Sweetheart* 1910 (d); *Never Again* 1910 (d,sc); *The Newlyweds* 1910 (d,sc); *Not So Bad As He Seemed* 1910 (d); *The Oath and the Man* 1910 (d); *On the Reef* 1910 (d,sc); *One Night and Then* 1910 (d,sc); *Over Silent Paths* 1910 (d); *A Plain Song* 1910 (d); *The Purgation* 1910 (d); *Ramona* 1910 (d,sc); *A Rich Revenge* 1910 (d); *A Romance of the Western Hills* 1910 (d); *Rose O' Salem Town* 1910 (d); *Serious Sixteen* 1910 (d); *Simple Charity* 1910 (d); *The Smoker* 1910 (d); *The Song of the Wildwood Flute* 1910 (d); *The Sorrows of the Unfaithful* 1910 (d); *A Summer Idyll* 1910 (d); *A Summer Tragedy* 1910 (d); *Sunshine Sue* 1910 (d); *Taming a Husband* 1910 (d); *Thou Shalt Not* 1910 (d); *The Thread of Destiny* 1910 (d,story); *The Twisted Trail* 1910 (d); *The Two Brothers* 1910 (d); *Two Little Waifs: A Modern Fairy Tale* 1910 (d); *The Unchanging Sea* 1910 (d,sc); *Unexpected Help* 1910 (d); *The Usurer* 1910 (d,sc); *A Victim of Jealousy* 1910 (d); *Waiter No.*

5 1910 (d); *The Way of the World* 1910 (d); *What the Daisy Said* 1910 (d); *When We Were in Our Teens* 1910 (d); *White Roses* 1910 (d); *Wilful Peggy* 1910 (d); *Winning Back His Love* 1910 (d); *The Woman From Mellon's* 1910 (d,sc); *The Adventures of Billy* 1911 (a,d); *As in a Looking Glass* 1911 (d); *The Battle* 1911 (d); *The Blind Princess and the Poet* 1911 (d); *Bobby the Coward* 1911 (d); *The Broken Cross* 1911 (d); *The Chief's Daughter* 1911 (d); *Conscience* 1911 (d); *A Country Cupid* 1911 (d); *Dan, the Daddy* 1911 (d); *A Decree of Destiny* 1911 (d); *The Diamond Star* 1911 (d); *Enoch Arden* 1911 (d); *The Failure* 1911 (d); *Fate's Turning* 1911 (d); *Fighting Blood* 1911 (d); *Fisher Folks* 1911 (d); *For His Son* 1911 (d); *The Heart of a Savage* 1911 (d); *Heartbeats of Long Ago* 1911 (d); *Her Awakening* 1911 (d); *Her Sacrifice* 1911 (d); *His Daughter* 1911 (d); *His Mother's Scarf* 1911 (d); *His Trust* 1911 (d); *His Trust Fulfilled* 1911 (d); *How She Triumphed* 1911 (d); *In the Days of '49* 1911 (d); *The Indian Brothers* 1911 (d); *The Italian Barber* 1911 (d,sc); *Italian Blood* 1911 (d); *A Knight of the Road* 1911 (d); *The Last Drop of Water* 1911 (d); *The Lily of the Tenements* 1911 (d); *The Lonedale Operator* 1911 (d); *The Long Road* 1911 (d); *Love in the Hills* 1911 (d); *Madame Hex* 1911 (d); *The Making of a Man* 1911 (d); *The Miser's Heart* 1911 (d); *The New Dress* 1911 (d); *The Old Bookkeeper* 1911 (d); *The Old Confectioner's Mistake* 1911 (d); *Out from the Shadow* 1911 (d); *Paradise Lost* 1911 (d); *The Poor Sick Men* 1911 (d); *The Primal Call* 1911 (d); *The Revenue Man and the Girl* 1911 (d); *A Romany Tragedy* 1911 (d); *The Rose of Kentucky* 1911 (d); *The Ruling Passion* 1911 (d); *Saved From Himself* 1911 (d); *A Smile of a Child* 1911 (d); *A Sorrowful Example* 1911 (d); *The Spanish Gypsy* 1911 (d); *The Squaw's Love* 1911 (d); *Sunshine Through the Dark* 1911 (d); *Swords and Hearts* 1911 (d); *A Terrible Discovery* 1911 (d); *The Thief and the Girl* 1911 (d); *Three Sisters* 1911 (d); *Through Darkened Vales* 1911 (d); *The Trail of Books* 1911 (d); *The Two Paths* 1911 (d); *The Two Sides* 1911 (d); *The Unveiling* 1911 (d); *The Voice of the Child* 1911 (d); *Was He a Coward?* 1911 (d); *What Shall We Do With Our Old?* 1911 (d); *When a Man Loves* 1911 (d); *The White Rose of the Wilde* 1911 (d); *A Woman Scorned* 1911 (d); *The Burglar's Dilemma* 1912 (d); *A Cry For Help* 1912 (d); *The Eternal Mother* 1912 (d,sc); *In the Aisles of the Wild* 1912 (d); *The Informer* 1912 (d); *The Musketeers of Pig Alley* 1912 (d); *My Hero* 1912 (d); *The New York Hat* 1912 (d); *The Old Actor* 1912 (d); *One Is Business, the Other Crime* 1912 (d); *The One She Loved* 1912 (d); *A Tale of the Wilderness* 1912 (d); *The Telephone Girl and the Lady* 1912 (d); *Two Daughters of Eve* 1912 (d); *An Unseen Enemy* 1912 (d); *The Battle at Elderbush Gulch* 1913 (d); *During the Round Up* 1913 (d); *Her Mother's Oath* 1913 (d); *The House of Darkness* 1913 (d); *Just Gold* 1913 (d); *Just Kids* 1913 (d); *The Lady and the Mouse* 1913 (d,d); *The Left-Handed Man* 1913 (d); *The Madonna of the Storm* 1913 (d); *The Mistake* 1913 (d); *A Misunderstood Boy* 1913 (d); *A Modest Hero* 1913 (d); *The Mothering Heart* 1913 (d); *Oil and Water* 1913 (d); *The Perfidy of Mary* 1913 (d); *So Runs the Way* 1913 (d); *A Timely Interception* 1913 (d); *The Unwelcome Guest* 1913 (d); *A Woman in the Ultimate* 1913 (d). Features: *Judith of Bethulia* 1913 (d); *The Avenging Conscience* 1914 (d,sc); *The Battle of the Sexes* 1914 (d,sc); *The Escape* 1914 (d,sc,d); *Home, Sweet Home* 1914 (d,sc); *Birth of a Nation* 1915 (d,sc); *Enoch Arden* 1915 (a); *Jordan Is a Hard Road* 1915 (p); *The Lamb* 1915 (from novel *The Man and the Test*); *The Lily and the Rose* 1915 (from novel *Mrs Billie*); *Betty of Greystone* 1916 (p); *Daphne and the Pirate* 1916 (sc); *Fifty-Fifty* 1916 (p); *The Good Bad Man* 1916 (p); *The Habit of Happiness* 1916 (p); *Hoodoo Ann* 1916 (sc); *An Innocent Magdalene* 1916 (p,story); *Intolerance* 1916 (d,sc); *Let Katie Do It* 1916 (from novel); *Manhattan Madness* 1916 (p); *The Missing Links* 1916 (from novel); *Hearts of the World* 1917 (d,p,sc,English trans,m,m.arr); *The Great Love* 1918 (d,p); *The Greatest Thing in Life* 1918 (d,p); *The Hun Within* 1918 (sc); *Broken Blossoms* 1919 (d,p,sc); *The Girl Who Stayed at Home* 1919 (d,p); *The Greatest Question* 1919 (d); *A Romance of Happy Valley* 1919 (d,p,sc); *Scarlet Days* 1919 (d,p); *True Heart Susie* 1919 (d,p); *The Idol Dancer* 1920 (d); *The Love Flower* 1920 (d,sc); *Way Down East* 1920 (d,p,sc); *Dream Street* 1921 (d,sc); *Orphans of the Storm* 1921 (d,p); *One Exciting Night* 1922 (d,p,sc,story); *The White Rose* 1923 (d,sc,story); *America* 1924 (d,p); *Isn't Life Wonderful?* 1924 (d,p,sc); *Sally of the Sawdust* 1925 (d,p); *That Royle Girl* 1925 (d,p); *The Sorrows of Satan* 1926 (d); *The Battle of the Sexes* 1928 (d); *Drums of Love* 1928 (d,p); *Lady of the Pavements* 1929 (d); *Abraham Lincoln* 1930 (d); *The Struggle* 1931 (d,sc); *One Million B.C.* 1940 (uncred.tech.adv).

Griffith, Melanie • Actress • Born New York, NY, August 9, 1957. *Educ.* Hollywood Professional School, CA. Attractive, vivacious performer, capable both in her early supporting parts and as a leading lady in films such as *Something Wild* (1986) and *Working Girl* (1988). Married to actor Don Johnson and daughter of actress Tippi Hedren. • *The Drowning Pool* 1975; *Night Moves* 1975; *Smile* 1975; *Joyride* 1977; *One on One* 1977; *Roar* 1981; *Body Double* 1984; *Fear City* 1985; *Something Wild* 1986; *Cherry 2000* 1988; *The Milagro Beanfield War* 1988; *Stormy Monday* 1988; *Working Girl* 1988 **(AANBA)**; *Bonfire of the Vanities* 1990; *In the Spirit* 1990; *Pacific Heights* 1990.

Grimaldi, Alberto • Producer • Born Naples, Italy, 1926. Established himself as a producer of spaghetti westerns directed by Sergio Leone before moving on to films by Federico Fellini, Bernardo Bertolucci and Pier Paolo Pasolini, among others. • *Per qualche dollaro in più/For a Few Dollars More* 1965 (p); *Il Buono, il Brutto, il Cattivo/The Good, the Bad, and the Ugly* 1966 (p); *La Resa dei Conti* 1966 (p); *Faccia a Faccia* 1967 (p); *Un Tranquillo Posto di Campagna* 1968 (p); *Quemada!/Burn!* 1969 (p); *Satyricon/Fellini's Satyricon* 1969 (p); *Ehi Amico...c'e Sabata* 1970 (p); *The Mercenary* 1970 (p); *Adios Sabata* 1971 (p); *Il Decamerone/The Decameron* 1971 (p); *E Poi lo Chiamarono il Magnifico* 1971 (p); *Oceano* 1971 (p); *Last Tango in Paris* 1972 (p); *I Racconti di Canterbury/The Canterbury Tales* 1972 (p); *Trastevere* 1972 (p); *L'Uomo della Mancha/Man of La Mancha* 1972 (exec.p); *Storie Scellerate* 1973 (p); *Il Fiore Delle Mille e Una Notte/The Arabian Nights* 1974 (p); *Salò o le Centiventi Giornate di Sodoma/Salò or the 120 Days of Sodom* 1975 (p); *Cadaveri Eccellenti* 1976 (p); *Il Casanova di Federico Fellini/Fellini's Casanova* 1976 (p); *Novecento/1900* 1976 (p); *Ginger et Fred/Ginger and Fred* 1986 (p).

Grodin, Charles • Actor; also playwright, stage director. • Born Pittsburgh, PA, April 21, 1935. *Educ.* Pittsburgh Playhouse; University of Miami. Dryly humorous figure who made his Broadway acting debut in 1962 and began his stage directing career, as an assistant to Gene Saks, in 1965. Grodin was memorable in Warren Beatty's *Heaven Can Wait* (1978) and, in a superbly tongue-in-cheek role opposite Robert De Niro, *Midnight Run* (1988). • *Sex and the College Girl* 1964; *Rosemary's Baby* 1968; *Catch-22* 1970; *The Heartbreak Kid* 1972; *11 Harrowhouse* 1974 (a,adapt); *King Kong* 1976; *Thieves* 1977; *Heaven Can Wait* 1978; *Real Life* 1978; *Sunburn* 1979; *It's My Turn* 1980; *Seems Like Old Times* 1980; *The Great Muppet Caper* 1981; *The Incredible Shrinking Woman* 1981; *The Lonely Guy* 1984; *The Woman in Red* 1984; *Movers & Shakers* 1985 (a,p,sc); *Last Resort* 1986; *Ishtar* 1987; *The Couch Trip* 1988; *Midnight Run* 1988; *You Can't Hurry Love* 1988; *Taking Care of Business* 1990; *Clifford* 1991.

Grosbard, Ulu • Director • Born Antwerp, Belgium, January 9, 1929. *Educ.* University of Chicago; Yale (drama). Renowned stage director who worked on a number of film productions before directing his first feature, *The Subject Was Roses*, in 1968. • *Splendor in the Grass* 1961 (ad—New York sequences); *The Pawnbroker* 1965 (prod.man); *The Sub-*

ject Was Roses 1968 (d); *Who Is Harry Kellerman, and Why Is He Saying Those Terrible Things About Me?* 1971 (d,p); *Straight Time* 1978 (d); *True Confessions* 1981 (d); *Falling in Love* 1984 (d).

Grot, Anton F. • Art director • Born Antocz Franziszek Grozewski, Kelbasin, Poland, 1884; died 1974. Prolific, distinguished art director, in the US from c. 1905. After some notable work in the silent era, Grot's career flowered in the 1930s. He designed films across a wide range of genres, notably for fellow European emigrés Michael Curtiz and William Dieterle. • *The Seven Pearls* 1917 (sets); *Sylvia of the Secret Service* 1917 (sets); *The Naulahka* 1918 (sets); *Bound and Gagged* 1919 (sets); *Pirate Gold* 1920 (sets); *The Velvet Fingers* 1921 (sets); *Robin Hood* 1922 (sets); *Tess of the Storm Country* 1922 (sets); *Dorothy Vernon of Haddon Hall* 1924 (sets); *The Thief of Bagdad* 1924 (assoc.art); *Don Q, Son of Zorro* 1925 (sets); *The Road to Yesterday* 1925 (sets); *A Thief in Paradise* 1925 (sets); *Silence* 1926 (sets); *The Volga Boatman* 1926 (sets); *Young April* 1926 (sets); *The Country Doctor* 1927 (sets); *King of Kings* 1927 (sets); *The Little Adventuress* 1927 (sets); *Vanity* 1927 (sets); *White Gold* 1927 (sets); *The Barker* 1928 (sets); *The Blue Danube* 1928 (sets); *Hold 'Em Yale* 1928 (sets); *A Ship Comes In* 1928 (sets); *Show Girl* 1928 (sets); *Stand and Deliver* 1928 (sets); *Walking Back* 1928 (sets); *Footlights and Fools* 1929 (sets); *The Godless Girl* 1929 (sets); *Her Private Life* 1929 (sets); *The Man and the Moment* 1929 (sets); *Noah's Ark* 1929 (sets); *Smiling Irish Eyes* 1929 (sets); *Why Be Good?* 1929 (sets); *Bright Lights* 1930 (sets); *Lilies of the Field* 1930 (sets); *Little Caesar* 1930 (art d); *No, No, Nanette* 1930 (sets); *A Notorious Affair* 1930 (sets); *Outward Bound* 1930 (sets); *Playing Around* 1930 (sets); *Song of the Flame* 1930 (sets); *Top Speed* 1930 (sets); *Body and Soul* 1931 (art d); *Heartbreak* 1931 (sets); *Honor of the Family* 1931 (sets); *The Mad Genius* 1931 (art d); *Surrender* 1931 (art d); *Svengali* 1931 (sets) **(AANBAD)**; *Alias the Doctor* 1932 (art d); *Big City Blues* 1932 (art d); *Doctor X* 1932 (art d); *The Hatchet Man* 1932 (art d); *Lawyer Man* 1932 (art d); *The Match King* 1932 (art d); *One Way Passage* 1932 (sets); *Scarlet Dawn* 1932 (art d); *Two Seconds* 1932 (art d); *20,000 Years in Sing Sing* 1933 (art d); *Baby Face* 1933 (art d); *Ever in My Heart* 1933 (art d); *Footlight Parade* 1933 (art d); *From Headquarters* 1933 (art d); *Gold Diggers of 1933* 1933 (art d); *Grand Slam* 1933 (art d); *The King's Vacation* 1933 (sets); *The Mystery of the Wax Museum* 1933 (art d); *Son of a Sailor* 1933 (art d); *British Agent* 1934 (art d); *Dr. Monica* 1934 (art d); *Easy to Love* 1934 (art d); *The Firebird* 1934 (art d); *Gambling Lady* 1934 (art d); *He Was Her Man* 1934 (art d); *Mandalay* 1934 (art d); *Side Streets* 1934 (art d); *Six Day Bike Rider* 1934 (art d); *Upperworld* 1934 (art d); *Bright Lights* 1935 (art d); *Broadway Gondolier* 1935 (art d); *Captain Blood* 1935 (art d); *The Case of the Curious Bride* 1935 (art d); *Dr. Socrates* 1935 (art d); *The Florentine Dagger* 1935 (art d); *Gold Diggers of 1935* 1935 (art d); *A Midsummer Night's Dream* 1935 (art d); *Red Hot Tires* 1935 (art d); *The Secret Bride* 1935 (art d); *Stranded* 1935 (art d); *Traveling Saleslady* 1935 (art d); *Anthony Adverse* 1936 (art d) **(AANBAD)**; *The Golden Arrow* 1936 (art d); *Sing Me a Love Song* 1936 (art d); *Stolen Holiday* 1936 (art d); *The White Angel* 1936 (art d); *Confession* 1937 (art d); *The Great Garrick* 1937 (art d); *The Life of Emile Zola* 1937 (art d) **(AANBAD)**; *Tovarich* 1937 (art d); *Fools for Scandal* 1938 (art d); *Hard to Get* 1938 (art d); *Juarez* 1939 (art d); *The Private Lives of Elizabeth and Essex* 1939 (art d) **(AANBAD)**; *They Made Me a Criminal* 1939 (art d); *A Dispatch From Reuters* 1940 (art d); *The Sea Hawk* 1940 (art d) **(AANBAD)**; *Affectionately Yours* 1941 (art d); *The Sea Wolf* 1941 (art d); *Thank Your Lucky Stars* 1943 (art d); *The Conspirators* 1944 (art d); *Mildred Pierce* 1945 (art d); *Rhapsody in Blue* 1945 (art d); *The Two Mrs. Carrolls* 1945 (art d); *Backfire* 1946 (art d); *Deception* 1946 (art d); *My Reputation* 1946 (art d); *Never Say Goodbye* 1946 (art d); *One More Tomorrow* 1946 (art d); *Nora Prentiss* 1947 (art d); *Possessed* 1947 (art d); *The Unsuspected* 1947 (art d); *June Bride* 1948 (art d); *One Sunday Afternoon* 1948 (art d); *Romance on the High Seas* 1948 (art d).

Gruault, Jean • Screenwriter • Born Fontenay-sous-Bois, France, 1924. Leading writer associated with the French New Wave; began his career in agit-prop theater. • *Paris Nous Appartient/Paris Belongs to Us* 1960 (sc); *Jules et Jim/Jules and Jim* 1961 (sc); *Vanina Vanini* 1961 (a,sc); *Les Carabiniers* 1963 (a,sc); *Suzanne Simonin, la Religieuse de Denis Diderot/The Nun* 1965 (sc,adapt); *La Prise de pouvoir par Louis XIV/The Rise of Louis XIV* 1966 (sc); *L'Enfant sauvage/The Wild Child* 1970 (sc); *Les Deux Anglaises et le Continent/Two English Girls* 1971 (sc); *L'Histoire d'Adèle H./The Story of Adèle H.* 1975 (sc); *La Chambre Verte/The Green Room* 1978 (sc); *Il Messia/The Messiah* 1978 (adapt); *Les Soeurs Brontë/The Brontë Sisters* 1978 (sc); *Mon oncle d'Amérique* 1979 (sc) **(AANBSC)**; *Via degli Specchi* 1982 (sc); *Les Années 80* 1983 (sc); *La Vie est un roman/Life Is a Bed of Roses* 1983 (sc); *L'Amour à mort* 1984 (sc); *Mystère Alexina* 1985 (sc); *Golden Eighties* 1986 (sc); *Australia* 1989 (sc).

Grusin, Dave • Composer; also conductor, performer. • Born David Grusin, Littleton, CO, 1934. Has contributed scores to films by directors including Mike Nichols, Warren Beatty and (five times) Sydney Pollack. Grusin's jazz-fusion style has highlighted several TV shows ("Good Times," "St. Elsewhere") and he has arranged albums by artists including Quincy Jones and Paul Simon. Grusin founded his own record label with partner Larry Rosen in 1983. • *Divorce American Style* 1967 (m); *The Graduate* 1967 (add.m); *Waterhole Number 3* 1967 (m); *Candy* 1968 (m,m.cond,song); *The Heart Is a Lonely Hunter* 1968 (m,m.dir); *Where Were You When the Lights Went Out?* 1968 (m); *Generation* 1969 (m); *The Mad Room* 1969 (m); *A Man Called Gannon* 1969 (m); *Tell Them Willie Boy Is Here* 1969 (m); *Winning* 1969 (m); *Adam at 6 A.M.* 1970 (m); *Halls of Anger* 1970 (m); *The Gang That Couldn't Shoot Straight* 1971 (m); *The Pursuit of Happiness* 1971 (m); *Shoot Out* 1971 (m); *Fuzz* 1972 (m); *The Great Northfield Minnesota Raid* 1972 (m); *The Friends of Eddie Coyle* 1973 (m); *The Midnight Man* 1974 (m); *W. W. and the Dixie Dancekings* 1974 (m); *The Nickel Ride* 1975 (m); *Three Days of the Condor* 1975 (m); *The Yakuza* 1975 (m); *The Front* 1976 (m); *Murder By Death* 1976 (m); *Bobby Deerfield* 1977 (m); *Fire Sale* 1977 (m); *The Goodbye Girl* 1977 (m); *Mr. Billion* 1977 (m); *Heaven Can Wait* 1978 (m) **(AANBM)**; *And Justice For All* 1979 (m,song); *The Champ* 1979 (m) **(AANBM)**; *The Electric Horseman* 1979 (m); *My Bodyguard* 1980 (m); *Absence of Malice* 1981 (m); *All Night Long* 1981 (song); *On Golden Pond* 1981 (m) **(AANBM)**; *Reds* 1981 (add.m); *Author! Author!* 1982 (m,song); *Tootsie* 1982 (m,song) **(AANBS)**; *Falling in Love* 1984 (m); *The Little Drummer Girl* 1984 (m); *The Pope of Greenwich Village* 1984 (m); *Racing With the Moon* 1984 (m); *Scandalous* 1984 (m,song); *The Goonies* 1985 (m); *Lucas* 1986 (m); *Casual Sex?* 1988 (songs); *Clara's Heart* 1988 (m); *The Milagro Beanfield War* 1988 (m) **(AABM)**; *Tequila Sunrise* 1988 (m); *A Dry White Season* 1989 (m); *The Fabulous Baker Boys* 1989 (m,pianist,song) **(AANBM)**; *Bonfire of the Vanities* 1990 (m); *Havana* 1990 (m); *Look Who's Talking Too* 1990 (m).

Guarnieri, Ennio • Director of photography • Born Rome, 1930. Has worked regularly with Lina Wertmuller and Franco Zefferelli, as well as on the final films of Vittorio De Sica. • *I Giorni contati* 1961 (ph); *Luciano, una vita bruciata* 1962 (ph); *Il Mare* 1962 (ph); *Una Storia moderna/The Conjugal Bed* 1963 (ph); *Un Tentativo sentimentale* 1963 (ph); *Alta Infedeltà* 1964 (ph—"Scandaloso," "Peccato nel pomeriggio," "La Sospirosa"); *Contro Sesso* 1964 (ph—"Una Donna d'Affari"); *Ecco... il finimondo* 1964 (ph); *I Malamondo* 1964 (ph); *Le Voci bianche* 1964 (ph); *Le Bambole* 1965 (ph—"The Telephone Call"/"La Telefonata"); *I Complessi* 1965 (ph—"Il complesso della schiava nubiana"); *La Costanza della ragione* 1965 (ph); *Made in Italy* 1965 (ph); *Nudi per vivere* 1965 (ph); *Questa volta parliamo di uomini/Let's Talk About Men* 1965 (ph); *Sette uomini di'oro* 1965 (ph); *Le Fate* 1966 (ph—"Fata Sabina"); *Il Grande colpo dei sette uomini di'oro* 1966 (ph); *Le Dolci signore* 1967 (ph); *Non Stuzzicate la Zanzara* 1967 (ph); *La Ragazza e il Generale* 1967 (ph); *Top Crak* 1967 (ph); *Il Medico della mutua* 1968 (ph); *Meglio Vedova* 1968 (ph); *Tenderly* 1968 (ph); *L'Assoluto Naturale* 1969 (ph); *Camille 2000* 1969 (ph); *Una Estate in quattro* 1969 (ph); *Gott mit uns* 1970 (ph); *L'Invasion* 1970 (ph); *Medea* 1970 (ph); *Metello* 1970 (ph); *Il Giardino del Finzi-Continis/The Garden of the Finzi-Continis* 1971 (ph); *Marta* 1971 (ph); *Lo Chiameremo Andrea* 1972 (ph); *L'Uccello migratore* 1972 (ph); *Ash Wednesday* 1973 (ph); *Una Breve Vacanza/A Brief Vacation* 1973 (ph); *Brother Sun, Sister Moon* 1973 (ph); *Daniele e Maria* 1973 (ph); *Hitler: The Last Ten Days* 1973 (ph); *That's Entertainment!* 1974 (ph); *Travolti da un insolito destino nell'azzuro mare d'Agosto/Swept Away...By an Unusual Destiny in the Blue Sea of August* 1974 (ph); *Il Viaggio/The Voyage* 1974 (ph); *Fatti di Gente Perbene/La Grande Bourgeoise* 1975 (ph); *Gente di rispetto* 1975 (ph); *L'Infermiera* 1975 (ph); *Per le Antiche Scale* 1975 (ph); *Der Richter und Sein Henker* 1975 (ph); *A chacun son enfer* 1976 (ph); *Al piacere di rivederla* 1976 (ph); *Cours apres moi que je t'attrape* 1976 (ph); *Eredita' Ferramonti* 1976 (ph); *Il Bel Paese* 1977 (ph); *The Cassandra Crossing* 1977 (ph); *Le Dernier Baiser* 1977 (ph); *Mogliamante/Wifemistress* 1977 (ph); *L'Enfant de la nuit* 1978 (ph); *Il Gatto* 1978 (ph); *Il Giocattolo* 1978 (ph); *Un Uomo in ginocchio* 1978 (ph); *Le Grand embouteillage/Traffic Jam* 1979 (ph); *Un Sacco Bello* 1979 (ph); *The Visitor* 1979 (ph); *Il Cappotto di Astrakan* 1980 (ph); *Les Ailes de la Colombe* 1981 (ph); *Borotalco* 1981 (ph); *Vera Storia Della Signora Delle Camelie* 1981 (ph); *Storia di Piera* 1982 (ph); *La Traviata* 1983 (ph); *Ginger et Fred* 1986 (ph); *Otello* 1986 (ph); *Dancers* 1987 (ph); *Mosca Addio* 1987 (ph); *Francesco* 1989 (ph—Perugia sequences); *L'Homme au masque d'or* 1990 (ph).

Guber, Peter • Producer • Born US, 1939. *Educ.* Syracuse University; University of Florence, Italy; NYU (law, business). Guber was recruited directly from college by Columbia Pictures in 1968 and began a successful career as an independent producer in 1976. In 1982 he joined with Jon Peters to form the Guber-Peters company, one of Hollywood's most effective producing teams of the 1980s with blockbusters such as *Flashdance* (1983) and *Batman* (1989). Guber and Peters were appointed joint heads of Columbia after the Sony corporation's costly purchase of the studio in 1989. • *The Deep* 1977 (p); *Midnight Express* 1978 (exec.p); *An American Werewolf in London* 1981 (exec.p); *Missing* 1982 (exec.p); *Six Weeks* 1982 (p); *D.C. Cab* 1983 (exec.p); *Flashdance* 1983 (exec.p); *Clue* 1985 (exec.p); *The Color Purple* 1985 (exec.p); *The Legend of Billie Jean* 1985 (exec.p); *Vision Quest* 1985 (p); *The Clan of the Cave Bear* 1986 (exec.p); *Head Office* 1986 (exec.p); *Youngblood* 1986 (exec.p); *Innerspace* 1987 (exec.p); *Who's That Girl* 1987 (exec.p); *The Witches of Eastwick* 1987 (p); *Caddyshack II* 1988 (p); *Gorillas in the Mist* 1988 (exec.p); *High Spirits* 1988 (assistance); *Rain Man* 1988 (exec.p); *Batman* 1989 (p); *Missing Link* 1989 (exec.p); *Tango and Cash* 1989 (p); *Bonfire of the Vanities* 1990 (exec.p).

Guerra, Ruy • Director, screenwriter; also producer, editor, actor. • Ruy Guerra was born in Lourenco Marques, Mozambique, which was at that time a Portuguese colony, in 1931. As a teenager and young man, Guerra published film criticism, short stories and essays, and he taught himself 8mm film production. Guerra was politically active, participating in anti-racist and pro-independence movements before leaving his country at age nineteen.

From 1952 to 1954, Guerra studied filmmaking in Paris at IDHEC; he broke into film production in France as an assistant cameraman and assistant director. Though best known as a director, Guerra has also worked as an editor, cinematographer, producer and actor (he played a Spanish "conquistador" in Werner Herzog's *Aquirre, Wrath of God* 1972). Guerra generally scripts or co-scripts the films that he directs. Although he has experimented with a wide range of styles, his strongest films show a similiar thrust: they are politically sophisticated, aesthetically innovative explorations of socioeconomic oppression and exploitation.

Though he has made films in several countries, Guerra is primarily associated with Brazilian cinema as a leading figure in that country's important Cinema Novo movement in the 1960s and early 70s. His first feature, *Os Cafajestes* (1962), was one of the few commercial successses of Cinema Novo. This controversial film, influenced stylistically by the French New Wave, ignited a scandal in Brazil for its powerful depiction of sexual violence and the immoral lifestyle of hustlers ("cafajestes") in Rio de Janeiro. Two of Guerra's features, *Os Fuzis* (1964) and *Os Deuses e os Mortos* (1970), are regarded as masterpieces of Cinema Novo. In *Os Fuzis*, the director blends fiction and documentary techniques within the framework of a realist aesthetic to portray political oppression afflicting starving peasants in the impoverished Northeast region of Brazil. *Os Deuses e os mortos* is a visually stylized political allegory in which Guerra draws on ritual, magic, and the symbolic use of color to explore the violent history and the economics of a cacao-growing region. *A Queda* (1978), co-directed with actor Nelson Xavier, is a provocative stylistic experiment that examines the job-related and personal problems of the protagonists of *Os Fuzis* years later, when they have become members of the exploited working class in Rio de Janeiro.

In the late 1970s, after Mozambique had gained its independence, Guerra returned to his native country to advise the newly formed national film institute. At that time, Guerra made Mozambique's first feature-length film, *Mueda* (1979). The film records a "people's theater" recreation of a massacre perpetrated by Portuguese soldiers in the 1960s.

In the mid and late 1980s, Guerra abandoned the radical treatment of political themes and made two beautifully photographed and edited features that offered broader commercial appeal. *Opera do Malandro* (1986), a Brazilian *Threepenny Opera*, touches on serious economic and social issues such as racism and American cultural influences in Brazil at the time of WWII while masquerading as entertaining musical comedy. *Fabula de la bella palomera* (1988) is a lush period piece and love story based on an original story by Nobel laureate Gabriél García Márquez.

Guerra has not confined his talents to filmmaking. In Brazil he has directed plays, worked as a playwright and collaborated as a lyricist with leading pop musicians. DW • *Chiens perdus sans Collier* 1955 (ad); *S.O.S. Noronha* 1956 (a); *Le Tout pour le tout* 1958 (ad); *Os Cafajestes/The Unscrupulous Ones* 1962 (d,sc); *Os Fuzis* 1964 (d,ed,sc,story); *Loin du Viêtnam* 1967 (d); *Benito Cereno* 1969 (a); *Tendres Chasseurs/Sweet Hunters* 1969 (d,sc,story,song); *Os Deuses e os mortos/Gods and the Dead* 1970 (d,sc,story,ed); *Le Maître du temps* 1970 (a); *Le Mur* 1970 (a); *Aquirre, der Zorn Göttes/Aguirre, the Wrath of God* 1972 (a); *A Queda/The Fall* 1978 (d,sc,ed,m); *Mueda memória e massacre* 1979 (d,ed,ph); *Erendira* 1982 (d); *Opera do Malandro* 1986 (d,p,sc); *Fabula de la Bella Palomera* 1988 (d,sc); *Kuarup* 1989 (d,p,sc).

Guerra, Tonino • Screenwriter; also novelist. • Born Antonio Guerra, Santarcangelo, Romagna, Italy, 1920. Has written material for leading Italian directors including Vittorio De Sica, Francesco Rosi, Elio Petri and—most frequently—Michelangelo Antonioni. • *Uomini e Lupi* 1956 (story); *Un Ettaro di cielo* 1957 (sc); *La Strada lunga un*

Anno 1958 (sc); *L'Avventura* 1959 (sc); *Il Carro armato dell'8 settembre* 1960 (sc); *Le Signore* 1960 (sc); *L'Assassino/The Lady Killer of Rome* 1961 (sc,story); *I Giorni contati* 1961 (sc,story); *La Notte* 1961 (sc); *L'Eclisse/The Eclipse* 1962 (sc,story); *La Noia/The Empty Canvas* 1963 (sc); *Contro Sesso* 1964 (sc,story—"Una Donna d'Affari"); *Deserto Rosso/Red Desert* 1964 (sc,story); *La Donna è una cosa meravigliosa* 1964 (sc,story—"Una donna dolce, dolce"); *Matrimonio all'italiana/Marriage Italian Style* 1964 (sc); *Le Ore nude* 1964 (sc); *Saul e David* 1964 (sc); *Casanova '70* 1965 (story) **(AANBSC)**; *La Decima Vittima/The Tenth Victim* 1965 (sc); *I Grandi condottieri* 1965 (sc,story); *Blow-Up* 1966 (sc) **(AANBSC)**; *Le Fate* 1966 (sc,story—"Fata Armenia"); *C'era una Volta.../More Than a Miracle/Cinderella Italian Style* 1967 (sc); *Lo Scatenato* 1967 (sc); *Partner* 1968 (a); *Sissignore* 1968 (sc,story); *Un Tranquillo Posto di Campagna* 1968 (story); *Gli Amanti* 1969 (sc); *I Girasoli* 1969 (sc); *L'Invitee* 1969 (sc); *Giochi particolari* 1970 (sc); *In Search of Gregory* 1970 (sc); *Tre nel mille* 1970 (sc,story); *Uomini Contro* 1970 (sc); *Zabriskie Point* 1970 (sc); *Bianco, Rosso e...* 1971 (sc,story); *Gli Ordini Sono Ordini* 1971 (sc); *La Supertestimone* 1971 (sc); *Il Caso Mattei* 1972 (sc); *Amarcord* 1973 (sc) **(AANBSC)**; *Andy Warhol's Frankenstein* 1973 (sc); *Re: Lucky Luciano* 1973 (sc); *Dites-Le avec des fleurs* 1974 (sc); *40 gradi soto il lenzuolo* 1975 (sc); *Cadaveri Eccellenti/Illustrious Corpses* 1976 (sc); *Caro Michele* 1976 (sc); *Il Casanova di Federico Fellini/Fellini's Casanova* 1976 (poem "The Great Miuna"); *Cristo si à Fermato a Eboli/Christ Stopped at Eboli* 1978 (sc,adapt); *Letti Selvaggi* 1978 (sc); *Un Papillon sur l'Epaule* 1978 (sc); *Tigers in Lipstick* 1978 (sc); *Il Mistero di Oberwald* 1980 (sc); *I Tre fratelli/Three Brothers* 1980 (sc); *La Notte di San Lorenzo/The Night of the Shooting Stars* 1981 (sc); *Identificazione di una donna/Identification of a Woman* 1982 (sc); *E la nave Va/And the Ship Sails On* 1983 (sc,story,idea); *Nostalghia/Nostalgia* 1983 (sc); *Bizet's Carmen* 1984 (sc); *Enrico IV/Henry IV* 1984 (sc); *Kaos/Chaos* 1984 (sc); *Taxidi stin Kythera* 1984 (sc,story); *Ginger et Fred* 1986 (sc,story); *Good Morning Babylon* 1986 (sc); *O Melissokomos/The Beekeeper* 1986 (sc); *Cronaca di una morte annunciata/Chronicle of a Death Foretold* 1987 (sc,adapt); *La Femme de mes amours* 1988 (sc,story); *Topio Stin Omichli/Landscape in the Mist* 1988 (sc); *Burro* 1989 (sc,story); *Dimenticare Palermo* 1990 (sc); *Il Male Oscuro* 1990 (sc); *Il Sole anche di notte/Night Sun* 1990 (sc); *Stanno Tutti Bene* 1990 (sc); *Viaggio d'amore* 1990 (sc,story).

Guest, Christopher • Actor; also director, screenwriter. • Born New York, NY, February 5, 1948. Effective as one of the fading rock stars in Rob Reiner's *This Is Spinal Tap* (1984), which he also co-wrote. Guest made his directing debut with *The Big Picture* (1989). Married to actress Jamie Lee Curtis. • *La Honte de la jungle* 1975; *Girlfriends* 1978; *The Last Word* 1979; *The Long Riders* 1980; *The Missing Link* 1980; *Heartbeeps* 1981; *This Is Spinal Tap* 1984 (a,sc,m,m.perf,lyrics,songs); *Little Shop of Horrors* 1986; *Beyond Therapy* 1987; *The Princess Bride* 1987; *Sticky Fingers* 1988; *The Big Picture* 1989 (d,sc,story,song).

Guffey, Burnett • Director of photography • Born Del Riod, TN, May 26, 1905. Leading Hollywood cinematographer of the 1950s and 60s, primarily at Columbia. • *The Courtship of Miles Standish* 1923 (cam.asst); *The Iron Horse* 1924 (cam.asst); *The Yankee Clipper* 1927 (cam.asst); *Love Over Night* 1928 (cam.asst); *Clive of India* 1935 (cam.op); *The Informer* 1935 (cam.op); *Foreign Correspondent* 1940 (cam.op); *Framed* 1940 (cam.op); *That Hamilton Woman* 1941 (cam.op); *Cover Girl* 1944 (cam.op); *Kansas City Kitty* 1944 (ph); *Sailor's Holiday* 1944 (ph); *The Soul of a Monster* 1944 (ph); *Tahiti Nights* 1944 (ph); *U-Boat Prisoner* 1944 (ph); *The Unwritten Code* 1944 (ph); *Blonde From Brooklyn* 1945 (ph); *Eadie Was a Lady* 1945 (ph); *Eve Knew Her Apples* 1945 (ph); *The Fighting Guardsman* 1945 (ph); *The Girl of the Limberlost* 1945 (ph); *I Love a Mystery* 1945 (ph); *My Name Is Julia Ross* 1945 (ph); *A Close Call For Boston Blackie* 1946 (ph); *Gallant Journey* 1946 (ph); *The Gay Senorita* 1946 (ph); *Meet Me on Broadway* 1946 (ph); *Night Editor* 1946 (ph); *The Notorious Lone Wolf* 1946 (ph); *So Dark the Night* 1946 (ph); *Framed* 1947 (ph); *Johnny O'Clock* 1947 (ph); *The Gallant Blade* 1948 (ph); *The Sign of the Ram* 1948 (ph); *To the Ends of the Earth* 1948 (ph); *All the King's Men* 1949 (ph); *And Baby Makes Three* 1949 (ph); *Knock on Any Door* 1949 (ph); *The Reckless Moment* 1949 (ph); *Undercover Man* 1949 (ph); *Convicted* 1950 (ph); *Emergency Wedding* 1950 (ph); *Father Is a Bachelor* 1950 (ph); *In a Lonely Place* 1950 (ph); *The Family Secret* 1951 (ph); *Sirocco* 1951 (ph); *Two of a Kind* 1951 (ph); *Assignment-Paris* 1952 (ph); *Boots Malone* 1952 (2u ph); *Scandal Sheet* 1952 (ph); *The Sniper* 1952 (ph); *From Here to Eternity* 1953 (ph) **(AABPH)**; *The Last Posse* 1953 (ph); *The Bamboo Prison* 1954 (ph); *Human Desire* 1954 (ph); *Private Hell 36* 1954 (ph); *The Violent Men* 1954 (ph); *Battle Stations* 1955 (ph); *Count Three and Pray* 1955 (ph); *Three Stripes in the Sun* 1955 (ph); *Tight Spot* 1955 (ph); *The Harder They Fall* 1956 (ph) **(AANBPH)**; *Nightfall* 1956 (ph); *Storm Center* 1956 (ph); *The Brothers Rico* 1957 (ph); *Decision at Sundown* 1957 (ph); *The Strange One* 1957 (ph); *The True Story of Lynn Stuart* 1957 (ph); *Me and the Colonel* 1958 (ph); *Screaming Mimi* 1958 (ph); *Edge of Eternity* 1959 (ph); *Gidget* 1959 (ph); *They Came to Cordura* 1959 (ph); *Hell to Eternity* 1960 (ph); *Let No Man Write My Epitaph* 1960 (ph); *The Mountain Road* 1960 (ph); *Cry For Happy* 1961 (ph); *Homicidal* 1961 (ph); *Mr. Sardonicus* 1961 (ph); *Birdman of Alcatraz* 1962 (ph) **(AANBPH)**; *Kid Galahad* 1962 (ph); *Four For Texas* 1963 (2u ph); *Flight From Ashiya* 1964 (ph); *Good Neighbor Sam* 1964 (ph); *King Rat* 1965 (ph) **(AANBPH)**; *The Silencers* 1966 (ph); *The Ambushers* 1967 (ph); *Bonnie and Clyde* 1967 (ph) **(AABPH)**; *How to Succeed in Business Without Really Trying* 1967 (ph); *The Split* 1968 (ph); *The Learning Tree* 1969 (ph); *The Madwoman of Chaillot* 1969 (ph); *Some Kind of a Nut* 1969 (ph); *Where It's At* 1969 (ph); *The Great White Hope* 1970 (ph); *Halls of Anger* 1970 (ph); *Suppose They Gave a War and Nobody Came?* 1970 (ph); *The Steagle* 1971 (ph).

Guffroy, Pierre • Production designer • Born France, 1926. *Educ.* IDHEC, Paris. Has worked with an august roster of directors including Cocteau, Bunuel, Godard, Bresson, Truffaut, Oshima and Polanski. • *L'Affaire Maurizius* 1953 (asst.art d); *Le Port de Désir* 1954 (asst.art d); *La Reine Margot* 1954 (asst.art d); *Chantage* 1955 (asst.art d); *Tant qu'il y aura des femmes* 1955 (asst.art d); *Les Aventures d'Arsène Lupin* 1956 (asst.art d); *La Châtelaine du Liban* 1956 (asst.art d); *Trapèze* 1956 (asst.art d); *Ascenseur pour l'échafaud/Elevator to the Gallows* 1957 (asst.art d); *Cigarettes, Whisky et p'tites pépées* 1958 (asst.art d); *The Quiet American* 1958 (asst.art d); *Sérénade au Texas* 1958 (asst.art d); *Tabarin* 1958 (asst.art d); *Bobosse* 1959 (asst.art d); *Le Bossu* 1959 (asst.art d); *Le Gendarme de Champignol* 1959 (asst.art d); *Pickpocket* 1959 (asst.art d); *Le Testament d'Orphée/The Testament of Orpheus* 1959 (art d); *Le Bois des Amants* 1960 (asst.art d); *Le Capitan* 1960 (asst.art d); *La Millième fenêtre* 1960 (asst.art d); *Adorable Menteuse* 1961 (asst.art d); *La Famille Fenouillard* 1961 (asst.art d); *A cause d'une Femme* 1962 (asst.art d); *Carambolages* 1962 (asst.art d); *La Dénonciation* 1962 (art d); *Mandrin, bandit gentilhomme* 1962 (art d); *Les Miracle des loups* 1962 (asst.art d); *Le Procès de Jeanne d'Arc/The Trial of Joan of Arc* 1962 (asst.art d); *OSS 117 se déchaîne* 1963 (art d); *Behold a Pale Horse* 1964 (asst.art d); *Un Gosse de la Butte* 1964 (art d); *The Train* 1964 (asst.art d); *La Loutre* 1965 (art d); *Pierrot le Fou* 1965 (art d); *Trois Chambres Manhattan* 1965 (asst.art d); *Le Vampire de Düsseldorf* 1965 (art d); *The Defector* 1966 (art d); *Mouchette* 1966 (art d); *The Night of the*

Generals 1966 (asst.art d); *Paris brûle-t-il?/Is Paris Burning?* 1966 (art d) **(AANBAD)**; *Le Grand Dadais* 1967 (art d); *A tout casser* 1968 (art d); *La Mariée etait en noir/The Bride Wore Black* 1968 (art d); *L'Invitée* 1969 (art d); *La Voie Lactée/The Milky Way* 1969 (art d); *Le Bal du Comte d'Orgel* 1970 (art d); *Un Beau Monstre* 1970 (art d); *Max et les Ferrailleurs* 1970 (art d); *Le Mur de l'Atlantique* 1970 (art d); *Le Passager de la Pluie/Rider on the Rain* 1970 (art d); *Bof! L'Anatomie d'un livreur* 1971 (art d); *César et Rosalie/César and Rosalie* 1972 (art d); *Le Charme Discret de la Bourgeoisie/The Discreet Charm of the Bourgeoisie* 1972 (art d); *La Course du lièvre à travers les champs* 1972 (art d); *Les Granges Brulées* 1973 (art d); *La Race des "Seigneurs"* 1973 (art d); *Le Fantôme de la Liberté/The Phantom of Liberty* 1974 (art d); *La Gifle/The Slap* 1974 (art d); *Paul et Michelle* 1974 (art d); *Que la fête commence.../Let Joy Reign Supreme...* 1974 (art d); *Les Mal Partis* 1975 (art d); *Le Locataire/The Tenant* 1976 (art d); *Mado* 1976 (art d); *Cet obscur objet du désir/That Obscure Object of Desire* 1977 (art d); *Tess* 1979 (pd,art d) **(AABAD)**; *Je vous aime* 1980 (art d); *L'Argent* 1983 (art d); *Hannah K* 1983 (pd); *Max mon amour* 1986 (pd); *Pirates* 1986 (pd); *Twist Again à Moscou* 1986 (art d); *Frantic* 1988 (pd); *The Unbearable Lightness of Being* 1988 (pd); *Valmont* 1989 (pd).

Guillemot, Agnès • Editor • Born Agnès Perché, Roubaix, France, 1931. *Educ.* IDHEC, Paris. Influential editor noted for her work with François Truffaut and, primarily, Jean-Luc Godard. Married to director Claude Guillemot. • *Le Petit Soldat* 1960 (ed); *Une Femme est une femme/A Woman Is a Woman* 1961 (ed); *RoGoPag* 1962 (ed—"Le Nouveau Monde"); *Vivre sa Vie/My Life to Live* 1962 (ed); *Les Carabiniers* 1963 (ed); *Le Mépris/Contempt* 1963 (ed); *Bande à Part/Band of Outsiders* 1964 (ed); *Une Femme mariée/A Married Woman* 1964 (ed); *Les Plus belles escroqueries du monde* 1964 (ed—"Le grand escroc"); *Alphaville* 1965 (ed); *Made in U.S.A.* 1966 (ed); *Masculin-Féminin/Masculine Feminine* 1966 (ed); *La Chinoise, ou plutôt à la Chinoise* 1967 (ed); *Weekend* 1967 (ed); *Baisers volés/Stolen Kisses* 1968 (ed); *La Sirène du Mississipi/Mississippi Mermaid* 1968 (ed); *La Trêve* 1968 (ed); *Domicile conjugal/Bed and Board* 1970 (ed); *L'Enfant sauvage/The Wild Child* 1970 (ed); *Cousin, Cousine* 1975 (ed); *Un Type comme moi ne devrait jamais mourir* 1976 (ed); *Le Pays Bleu* 1977 (ed); *Il y a longtemps que j'taime* 1979 (ed); *Croque la Vie* 1981 (ed); *La Diagonale du Fou* 1984 (ed); *Escalier C* 1985 (ed); *La Brute* 1987 (ed); *Fuegos* 1987 (ed); *La Lumière du lac* 1988 (ed); *Un Week-end sur deux* 1990 (ed).

Guillermin, John • Director • Born London, November 11, 1925. *Educ.* Cambridge. Former documentarist turned director of Hollywood blockbusters such as *The Towering Inferno* (1974) and *King Kong* (1976). • *Torment* 1949 (d,p,sc); *Four Days* 1951 (d); *Smart Alec* 1951 (d); *Two on the Tiles* 1951 (d); *Miss Robin Hood* 1952 (d); *Song of Paris* 1952 (d); *Operation Diplomat* 1953 (d,sc); *Strange Stories* 1953 (d); *Adventure in the Hopfields* 1954 (d); *The Crowded Day* 1954 (d); *Dust and Gold* 1955 (d); *Thunderstorm* 1956 (d); *Town on Trial* 1956 (d); *I Was Monty's Double* 1958 (d); *The Whole Truth* 1958 (d); *Tarzan's Greatest Adventure* 1959 (d,sc); *Never Let Go* 1960 (d,story); *The Day They Robbed the Bank of England* 1960 (d); *Tarzan Goes to India* 1962 (d,sc); *Waltz of the Toreadors* 1962 (d); *Guns at Batasi* 1964 (d); *Rapture* 1965 (d); *The Blue Max* 1966 (d); *House of Cards* 1968 (d); *P.J.* 1968 (d); *The Bridge at Remagen* 1969 (d); *El Condor* 1970 (d); *Skyjacked* 1972 (d); *Shaft in Africa* 1973 (d); *The Towering Inferno* 1974 (d); *King Kong* 1976 (d); *Death on the Nile* 1978 (d); *Mr. Patman* 1980 (d); *Sheena* 1984 (d); *King Kong Lives* 1986 (d).

Guinness, Sir Alec • Actor • Born London, April 2, 1914. *Educ.* Fay Compton Studio of Dramatic Art. Considered one of the most versatile performers of the century. Guinness first made his name as a screen actor in a brace of Ealing comedies, most notably with his tour-de-force performance playing eight roles in *Kind Hearts and Coronets* (1949). He went on to grace every genre (from drama in *The Bridge on the River Kwai* 1957, to science fiction in *Star Wars* 1977), adopting an international medley of accents including Indian (*A Passage to India* 1984), Arabic (*Lawrence of Arabia* 1962) and Scottish (*Tunes of Glory* 1960) along the way. Ranked with Laurence Olivier and John Gielgud as one of the finest talents of his generation, Guinness has imparted an air of cool intelligence and a stamp of authority to every role he has played. • *Evensong* 1934; *Great Expectations* 1946; *Oliver Twist* 1948; *Kind Hearts and Coronets* 1949; *A Run For Your Money* 1949; *Last Holiday* 1950; *The Mudlark* 1950; *The Man in the White Suit* 1951; *The Lavender Hill Mob* 1952 **(AANBA)**; *The Promoter* 1952; *Captain's Paradise* 1953; *Malta Story* 1953; *The Square Mile (short)* 1953; *Father Brown* 1954; *The Stratford Adventure* 1954; *The Ladykillers* 1955; *The Prisoner* 1955; *Rowlandson's England (short)* 1955; *To Paris With Love* 1955; *The Swan* 1956; *All at Sea* 1957; *The Bridge on the River Kwai* 1957 **(AABA)**; *The Horse's Mouth* 1958 (a,sc) **(AANBSC)**; *Our Man in Havana* 1959; *The Scapegoat* 1959; *Tunes of Glory* 1960; *A Majority of One* 1961; *H.M.S. Defiant* 1962; *Lawrence of Arabia* 1962; *The Fall of the Roman Empire* 1964; *Doctor Zhivago* 1965; *Situation Hopeless—But Not Serious* 1965; *Hotel Paradiso* 1966; *The Quiller Memorandum* 1966; *The Comedians in Africa (short)* 1967; *The Comedians* 1967; *Cromwell* 1970; *Scrooge* 1970; *Brother Sun, Sister Moon* 1973; *Hitler: The Last Ten Days* 1973; *Murder By Death* 1976; *Star Wars* 1977 **(AANBSA)**; *The Empire Strikes Back* 1980; *Raise the Titanic* 1980; *Lovesick* 1983; *Return of the Jedi* 1983; *A Passage to India* 1984; *A Handful of Dust* 1988; *Little Dorrit* 1988 **(AANBSA)**.

Guitry, Sacha • Playwright; also director, screenwriter, actor. • Born Alexander Guitry, St. Petersburg, Russia, February 21, 1885; died 1957. Turned his attention to film as a means of bringing his witty, inventive theatrical work to a wider audience. Although Guitry's films tended to be stagey, they evinced a subtle cinematic technique most evident in his masterpiece, *The Story of a Cheat* (1936). • *Ceux de chez nous (short)* 1915 (a,d,sc); *Un Roman d'amour... et d'aventures* 1918 (a); *Une Petite main qui se place (short)* 1922 (a,d,sc); *The Lover of Camille* 1924 (from play *Deburau*); *Sleeping Partners* 1930 (from play *Faisons un rêve*); *Le Blanc et le Noir* 1931 (sc,dial,from play); *Les Deux couverts* 1934 (from play); *Bonne Chance* 1935 (a,d,sc,dial); *Pasteur* 1935 (a,d,sc,dial,from play); *Mon père avait raison* 1936 (a,d,sc,dial,from play); *Le Mot de Cambronne* 1936 (a,d,sc,dial,from play); *Le Nouveau testament* 1936 (a,d,sc,dial,from play); *Le Roman d'un tricheur/The Story of a Cheat* 1936 (a,d,sc,dial,from novel *Le mémoires d'un tricheur*); *Desire* 1937 (a,d,sc,dial,from play); *Faisons un rêve* 1937 (a,d,sc,dial,from play); *Les Perles de la Couronne* 1937 (a,d,sc,dial); *Quadrille* 1937 (a,d,sc,dial,from play); *L'Accroche-coeur* 1938 (sc,dial,from play,prod.sup); *Bluebeard's Eighth Wife* 1938 (a); *Remontons les Champs-Elysées* 1938 (a,d,sc,dial); *Ils Etaient neuf célébataires* 1939 (a,d,sc,dial); *Lucky Partners* 1940 (from story "Bonne Chance"); *Le Destin fabuleux de Desiree Clary* 1941 (a,d,sc,dial); *La Loi du 21 juin 1907 (short)* 1942 (d,sc,dial); *Donne-moi tes yeux* 1943 (a,d,sc,dial); *La Malibran* 1943 (a,d,dial); *Le Comédien* 1947 (a,d,sc,dial,from play); *Le Diable boiteux* 1948 (a,d,sc,dial,from play); *Aux Deux Colombes* 1949 (a,d,sc,dial,from play); *Toa* 1949 (a,d,sc,dial,from play); *Le Trésor de Cantenac* 1949 (a,d,sc,dial); *Deburau* 1950 (a,d,sc,dial,from play); *Tu m'as sauvé la vie* 1950 (a,d,sc,dial,from play); *Adhemar* 1951 (sc,dial,lyrics); *Intimités (short)* 1951 (a); *La Poison* 1951 (a,d,sc,dial); *Je l'ai été trois fois* 1952 (a,d,sc,dial); *La Vie d'un honnête homme* 1952 (a,d,sc,dial,lyrics); *Si Versailles m'était conté/Royal Affairs in Versailles* 1953 (a,d,sc,dial); *Napoléon* 1954 (a,d,sc,dial); *Si Paris nous etait conté*

1955 (a,d,sc,dial); *Assassins et Voleurs* 1956 (d,sc,dial); *Les Trois font la paire* 1957 (a,d,sc,dial); *La Vie à deux* 1958 (sc,dial,from plays *Désiré, L'illusionniste, Françoise, Le blanc et le noir*); *Au voleur!* 1960 (sc,dial).

Güney, Yilmaz • *aka* Yilmaz Pütün • Filmmaker, actor • Born Adana, Turkey, 1937; died September 9, 1984, Paris. *Educ.* Ankara University (law); Istanbul University (economics). Güney and his work were almost entirely unknown outside of his Turkish homeland until his 1981 escape from imprisonment in Turkey and his "discovery" the following year at the Cannes Film Festival for his autobiographical screenplay for *Yol*, the festival's grand prize winner. Born in 1937 in a village near the southern city of Adana, Güney studied law and economics at the universities in Ankara and Istanbul, but by the age of 21 he found himself actively involved in filmmaking. As Yesilcam, the Turkish studio system, grew in strength, a handful of directors, including Atif Yilmaz, began to use the cinema as a means of addressing the problems of the people. Only state-sanctioned melodramas, war films and play adaptations had previously played in Turkish theaters, but these new filmmakers began to fill the screens with more artistic, personal and relevant pictures of Turkish life. The most popular name to emerge from the Young Turkish Cinema was that of Yilmaz Güney.

Güney was a gruff-looking young actor who earned the monicker "Cirkin Kral," or "the Ugly King." After apprenticing as a screenwriter for and assistant to Atif Yilmaz, Güney soon began appearing in as many as 20 films a year and became Turkey's most popular actor. More than a screen idol, Güney was a Turk who believed in the Turkish people and their way of life, as well as being personally committed to social change. Although the early 1960s brought some political reform to Turkey, Güney was imprisoned in 1961 for 18 months for publishing a "communist" novel. The country's political situation and Güney's relationship with the authorities only became more tense in the ensuing years. Not content with his star status atop the Turkish film industry, Güney began directing his own pictures in 1965 and, by 1968, had formed his own production company, Güney Filmcilik. Over the next few years, the titles of his films mirrored the feelings of the Turkish people: *Umut/Hope* (1970); *Agit/Elegy* (1971); *Aci/Pain* (1971); *Umutsuzlar/The Hopeless Ones*, (1971).

After 1972, however, Güney would spend most of his life in prison. Arrested for harboring anarchist students, Güney was jailed during preproduction on *Zavallilar/The Suffering Ones* (completed in 1975), and before completing *Endise/Anxiety*, which was finished in 1974 by Güney's assistant, Serif Goren. This was a cherished role that Goren would repeat over the next dozen years, directing several scripts that Güney wrote laboriously while behind bars. Released from prison in 1974 as part of a general amnesty, Güney was re-arrested that same year for shooting a judge. During this stretch of incarceration, his most successful screenplays were *Suru/The Herd* 1978) and *Dusman/The Enemy* 1979), both directed by Zeki Okten. After escaping from prison in 1981 and fleeing to France, Güney was greeted at the Cannes Film Festival with a Palm d'Or for *Yol*, again directed by Goren. It was not until 1983 that Güney resumed directing, telling a brutal tale of imprisoned children in his final film, *Le Mur/The Wall*, made in France with the cooperation of the French government. At that point, Güney's name was unspeakable in his homeland; 11 of the films he directed or appeared in were confiscated and reportedly burned to ashes; even so much as writing about Güney was forbidden. Despite the great international success of *Yol* and *The Wall*, Güney was ultimately a Turkish director for the Turkish people; his final separation from his home audience must have been even more painful to endure than his years of imprisonment. DC • *Umut/Hope* 1970 (d); *Aci/Pain* 1971 (d); *Umutsuzlar/The Hopeless Ones* 1971 (d,sc); *Agit/Elegy* 1972 (a,d,sc); *Endise/Anxiety* 1974 (d,sc); *Zavallilar/The Suffering Ones* 1975 (d,sc); *Dusman/The Enemy* 1979 (sc); *Suru/The Herd* 1979 (p,sc); *Chambre 666* 1982 (a); *Yol* 1982 (sc,ed,sound ed.dir—dubbing); *Autour du Mur* 1983 (a); *Le Mur/The Wall* 1983 (d,sc); *Yilmaz Guney: His Life, His Films* 1987 (archival footage).

Gunn, Bill • Director, screenwriter; also novelist, playwright. • Born Philadelphia, PA, c. 1930; died April 5, 1989, Nyack, NY. Trailblazing black artist whose plays and films are noted for their subtle insights into the nature of racial relationships and their angry irony. Gunn achieved his greatest success with the independently-produced *Ganja and Hess* (1973), which began as a genre vampire movie and ended up an eloquent and disturbing mix of passions, class and African mythology. Although a success at Cannes that year, the film was widely ignored in the US, having been recut by its producers. Two prints of Gunn's cut survived, however, and throughout the 70s its underground reputation grew through occasional screenings at the Museum of Modern Art and elsewhere. It is now regarded as one of the landmarks of the decade.

Gunn began his career as an actor on the New York stage in the 50s and found some work in TV series of the sixties ("Route 66," "The Fugitive") before scripting Harry Belafonte's production of *The Angel Levine* (1970) and Hal Ashby's *The Landlord* (1970). He wrote and directed his first feature, *STOP*, in 1970. He received an Emmy for writing *Johannas* (NBC, 1972). After *Ganja and Hess*, Gunn returned to the theater: *Black Picture Show* was a notable New York Shakespeare Festival production in 1975. He spent several years in the late 70s and early 80s working on "Personal Problems," an intended TV series dealing with the lives of everyday black characters; four hours of the project were shot. He also wrote and directed the five-hour series "The Alberta Hunter Story" (BBC, 1982). Gunn's novel *Rhinestone Sharecropping* is, like *Black Picture Show*, an indictment of the tenuous position of the black artist in a white industry. No matter which medium he worked in, Bill Gunn developed a sophisticated understanding of blacks in white America unmatched by any other artist. JM

Gunn, Moses • Actor • Born St. Louis, MO, October 2, 1929. *Educ.* Tennessee State University; University of Kansas. Authoritative black character actor, notably in *Ragtime* (1981) and as the African chief Kintango in TV's "Roots." • *The Great White Hope* 1970; *WUSA* 1970; *Eagle in a Cage* 1971; *Shaft* 1971; *Wild Rovers* 1971; *The Hot Rock* 1972; *Shaft's Big Score* 1972; *The Iceman Cometh* 1973; *Amazing Grace* 1974; *Aaron Loves Angela* 1975; *Cornbread, Earl & Me* 1975; *Rollerball* 1975; *Remember My Name* 1978; *Twinkle, Twinkle, "Killer" Kane* 1979; *Ragtime* 1981; *Amityville II: The Possession* 1982; *Certain Fury* 1984; *Firestarter* 1984; *The Neverending Story* 1984; *Heartbreak Ridge* 1986; *Leonard, Part 6* 1987; *Dixie Lanes* 1988; *The Luckiest Man in the World* 1989.

Guttenberg, Steve • Actor • Born US, 1958. Lanky second lead who, after a promising start in the late 1970s, has become a fixture in mediocre fare such as *Three Men and a Baby* (1987) and the never-ending "Police Academy" series. • *The Chicken Chronicles* 1977; *The Boys From Brazil* 1978; *Players* 1979; *Can't Stop the Music* 1980; *Diner* 1982; *The Man Who Wasn't There* 1983; *Police Academy* 1984; *Bad Medicine* 1985; *Cocoon* 1985; *Police Academy 2: Their First Assignment* 1985; *Police Academy 3: Back in Training* 1986; *Short Circuit* 1986; *Amazon Women on the Moon* 1987; *The Bedroom Window* 1987; *Police Academy 4: Citizens on Patrol* 1987 (a,prod.assoc); *Surrender* 1987; *Three Men and a Baby* 1987; *Cocoon: The Return* 1988; *High Spirits* 1988; *Don't Tell Her It's Me* 1990; *Three Men and a Little Lady* 1990.

Guy-Blaché, Alice • *aka* Alice Blaché • Director; also producer, screenplay. • Born Alice Guy, Paris, July 1, 1873; died 1968, Mahwah, NJ. Without doubt the first female director in the history of cinema. Whether Guy-Blaché is also the first fiction director remains debatable.

Somewhere between 1896 and 1900—the same years Georges Méliès is generally credited with directing the first narrative movies—she made *La Fée aux Choux*, an adaptation of a popular fairy tale.

Guy-Blaché joined Gaumont as a secretary in 1896 and became its primary director when the company began producing films. In 1907 she and her husband, cameraman Herbert Blache, moved to the US, first running Gaumont's American office and later setting up an independent production company, Solax. Her films, though not distinctive, were generally of a high quality.

In 1922, divorced from her husband and outdistanced by the growing American film industry, Guy-Blaché returned to France but was unsuccessful in her attempts to continue directing. Her contributions to cinema were finally recognized when she was awarded the Legion of Honor by the French government in 1953. • *Les Dangers de l'Alcoholisme* 1896 (d); *La Fée aux Choux* c. 1896 (d); *Au bal de Flore* 1900 (d); *La Danse des Saisons* 1900 (d); *Hussards et Grisettes* 1901 (d); *Le Pommier* 1902 (d); *Le Voleur sacrilège* 1903 (d); *Le Courrier de Lyon* 1904 (d); *Le Crime de la Rue du Temple* 1904 (d); *Paris la nuit* 1904 (d); *La Esmeralda* 1905 (d); *Réhabilitation* 1905 (d); *La Fée Printemps* 1906 (d); *Mireille* 1906 (d); *La Vie du Christ* 1906 (d); *Fanfan la Tulipe* 1907 (d); *The Doll* 1911 (d); *Rose of the Circus* 1911 (d); *The Violin Maker of Nuremberg* 1911 (d); *Algie the Miner (short)* 1912 (d); *The Blood Stain* 1912 (d); *Canned Harmony (short)* 1912 (d); *Dick Whittington and His Cat* 1912 (d,sc); *The Face at the Window* 1912 (d); *Falling Leaves* 1912 (d); *Fra Diavolo* 1912 (d); *In the Year 2000* 1912 (d); *Mignon* 1912 (d); *Phantom Paradise* 1912 (d); *Playing Trumps* 1912 (d); *The Sewer* 1912 (p); *Beasts of the Jungle* 1913 (p,sc); *The Girl in the Armchair (short)* 1913 (d); *A House Divided* 1913 (d,p); *The Little Hunchback* 1913 (d); *Matrimony's Speed Limit (short)* 1913 (d); *The Pit and the Pendulum* 1913 (d); *Rogues of Paris* 1913 (d); *The Star of India* 1913 (d); *A Terrible Night* 1913 (d); *Beneath the Czar* 1914 (d,sc); *The Dream Woman* 1914 (d,sc); *The Lure* 1914 (d,sc); *The Monster and the Girl* 1914 (d); *Shadows of the Moulin Rouge* 1914 (d,sc); *The Woman of Mystery* 1914 (d,sc); *The Heart of a Painted Woman* 1915 (d); *My Madonna* 1915 (d,sc); *What Will People Say?* 1915 (d); *The Girl With the Green Eyes* 1916 (d); *The Adventurer* 1917 (d); *Behind the Mask* 1917 (d); *The Empress* 1917 (d,sc); *The Great Adventure* 1918 (d); *Soul Adrift* 1919 (d); *Tarnished Reputations* 1920 (d); *Vampire* 1920 (d).

Gwenn, Edmund • Actor • Born Glamorgan, Wales, September 26, 1875; died 1959. In films from 1916, he made his mark in the 1940s as one of Hollywood's most endearing character actors. • *The Real Thing at Last* 1916; *The Skin Game* 1920; *Unmarried* 1920; *Hindle Wakes* 1931; *How He Lied to Her Husband* 1931; *The Skin Game* 1931; *Condemned to Death* 1932; *Frail Women* 1932; *The Good Companion* 1932; *Love on Wheels* 1932; *Money For Nothing* 1932; *Tell Me Tonight* 1932; *Cash* 1933; *Channel Crossing* 1933; *Early to Bed* 1933; *Friday the 13th* 1933; *I Was a Spy* 1933; *Marooned* 1933; *Smithy* 1933; *The Admiral's Secret* 1934; *Father and Son* 1934; *Java Head* 1934; *Passing Shadows* 1934; *Spring in the Air* 1934; *Waltzes From Vienna* 1934; *Warn London* 1934; *The Bishop Misbehaves* 1935; *Sylvia Scarlett* 1935; *All American Chump* 1936; *Anthony Adverse* 1936; *Laburnum Grove* 1936; *Mad Holiday* 1936; *The Walking Dead* 1936; *Parnell* 1937; *Penny Paradise* 1938; *South Riding* 1938; *A Yank at Oxford* 1938; *Cheer Boys Cheer* 1939; *An Englishman's Home* 1939; *The Doctor Takes a Wife* 1940; *The Earl of Chicago* 1940; *Foreign Correspondent* 1940; *Mad Men of Europe* 1940; *Pride and Prejudice* 1940; *Charley's Aunt* 1941; *Cheers For Miss Bishop* 1941; *The Devil and Miss Jones* 1941; *One Night in Lisbon* 1941; *Scotland Yard* 1941; *A Yank at Eton* 1942; *Forever and a Day* 1943; *Lassie Come Home* 1943; *The Meanest Man in the World* 1943; *Between Two Worlds* 1944; *Bewitched* 1945; *Dangerous Partners* 1945; *The Keys of the Kingdom* 1945; *She Went to the Races* 1945; *Of Human Bondage* 1946; *Undercurrent* 1946; *Green Dolphin Street* 1947; *Life With Father* 1947; *Miracle on 34th Street* 1947 **(AABSA)**; *Thunder in the Valley* 1947; *Apartment For Peggy* 1948; *Hills of Home* 1948; *Challenge to Lassie* 1949; *For Heaven's Sake* 1950; *Louisa* 1950; *Mister 880* 1950 **(AANBSA)**; *Pretty Baby* 1950; *A Woman of Distinction* 1950; *Peking Express* 1951; *Bonzo Goes to College* 1952; *Les Miserables* 1952; *Sally and Saint Anne* 1952; *Something For the Birds* 1952; *The Bigamist* 1953; *Mister Scoutmaster* 1953; *The Student Prince* 1954; *Them* 1954; *It's a Dog's Life* 1955; *The Trouble With Harry* 1955; *Calabuch* 1956.

Gwynne, Fred • Actor • Born New York, July 10, 1926. *Educ.* Harvard. Tall, distinctive comic actor best known for the TV series "Car 54, Where Are You?" (1961-63) and "The Munsters" (1964-66). His dour looks and deep voice have been exploited in a number of authoritarian roles of late. • *On the Waterfront* 1954; *Munster, Go Home* 1966; *La Luna* 1979; *Simon* 1980; *So Fine* 1981; *The Cotton Club* 1984; *Water* 1984; *The Boy Who Could Fly* 1986; *Off Beat* 1986; *Fatal Attraction* 1987; *Ironweed* 1987; *The Secret of My Success* 1987; *Disorganized Crime* 1989; *Pet Sematary* 1989.

Haas, Lukas • Actor • Born US, c. 1976. Gifted juvenile performer best known as the young Amish boy in *Witness* (1985); also impressive in *The Wizard of Loneliness* (1988). • *Testament* 1983; *Witness* 1985; *Solarbabies* 1986; *Lady in White* 1988; *Peacemaker (short)* 1988; *The Wizard of Loneliness* 1988; *Music Box* 1989; *See You in the Morning* 1989.

Hackford, Taylor • Director, producer • Born US, December 3, 1944. *Educ.* USC, Los Angeles (international relations). Won an Oscar for his 1978 short film, *Teenage Father*, and made an auspicious feature debut with *The Idolmaker* (1980), a slickly cynical look at the pop music industry. Hackford has continued to show an interest in popular music (he co-produced the 1987 Richie Valens biopic, *La Bamba*), with three of his directorial efforts spinning off hit songs. He is chairman of the successful independent production company, New Visions Entertainment Inc. • *Teenage Father (short)* 1978 (d,p) **(AABSF)**; *The Idolmaker* 1980 (d); *An Officer and a Gentleman* 1982 (d); *Against All Odds* 1983 (d,p); *White Nights* 1985 (d,p); *Hail! Hail! Rock 'n' Roll!* 1987 (d); *La Bamba* 1987 (p); *Everybody's All-American* 1988 (d,p); *Rooftops* 1989 (exec.p); *The Long Walk Home* 1990 (exec.p); *Mortal Thoughts* 1991 (exec.p); *Queens Logic* 1991 (exec.p); *Sweet Talker* 1991 (exec.p).

Hackman, Gene • Actor • Born Eugene Alden Hackman, San Bernardino, CA, January 30, 1930. *Educ.* University of Illinois (journalism, TV production); School of Radio Technique, New York; Pasadena Playhouse (drama). Formidable American character actor turned leading man whose performances are consistently natural and who often plays ordinary men caught up in moments of unexpected crisis.

Hackman quit high school to join the Marines and decided to pursue a serious career in acting at the age of 30, after years of wandering through a succession of odd jobs. His first important film appearance was in *Lilith* (1964) and his breakthrough came three years later, opposite Warren Beatty in *Bonnie and Clyde,* a role which earned him his first Oscar nomination.

In *The French Connection* (1971), Hackman etched an indelible portrait of the tough narcotics cop, Popeye Doyle, and won an Academy Award in the process. But he was capable of far more than bluster and rage, as evidenced by his roles in *The Conversation* (1974) and *Hoosiers* (1986), which revealed a gentler side and certified him as an actor of great range. Hackman earned another Oscar nomination for his role as a wily FBI veteran opposite Willem Dafoe in Alan Parker's *Mississippi Burning* (1988). • *Lilith* 1964; *Hawaii* 1966; *Banning* 1967; *Bonnie and Clyde* 1967 **(AANBSA)**; *A Covenant With Death* 1967; *First to Fight* 1967; *Riot* 1968; *The Split* 1968; *Downhill Racer* 1969; *The Gypsy Moths* 1969; *Marooned* 1969; *Doctors' Wives* 1970; *I Never Sang For My Father* 1970 **(AANBSA)**; *Cisco Pike* 1971; *The French Connection* 1971 **(AABA)**; *The Hunting Party* 1971; *The Poseidon Adventure* 1972; *Prime Cut* 1972; *Scarecrow* 1973; *The Conversation* 1974; *Young Frankenstein* 1974; *Zandy's Bride* 1974; *Bite the Bullet* 1975; *French Connection II* 1975; *Lucky Lady* 1975; *Night Moves* 1975; *A Bridge Too Far* 1977; *The Domino Killings* 1977; *March or Die* 1977; *Superman* 1978; *Superman II* 1980; *All Night Long* 1981; *Reds* 1981; *Eureka* 1983; *Two of a Kind* 1983; *Uncommon Valor* 1983; *Under Fire* 1983; *Misunderstood* 1984; *Target* 1985; *Twice in a Lifetime* 1985; *Hoosiers* 1986; *Power* 1986; *No Way Out* 1987; *Superman IV: The Quest For Peace* 1987; *Another Woman* 1988; *BAT 21* 1988; *Full Moon in Blue Water* 1988; *Mississippi Burning* 1988 **(AANBA)**; *Split Decisions* 1988; *Loose Cannons* 1989; *The Package* 1989; *Narrow Margin* 1990; *Postcards From the Edge* 1990; *Class Action* 1991.

Hagerty, Julie • Actress • Born Cincinnati, OH, c. 1954. Quirky, off-beat performer, at her best in *Airplane!* (1980) and *Lost in America* (1985). • *Airplane!* 1980; *Airplane II: The Sequel* 1982; *A Midsummer Night's Sex Comedy* 1982; *Bad Medicine* 1985; *Goodbye New York* 1985; *Lost in America* 1985; *Aria* 1987; *Beyond Therapy* 1987; *Bloodhounds of Broadway* 1989; *Rude Awakening* 1989; *Reversal of Fortune* 1990; *What About Bob?* 1991.

Haim, Corey • Actor • Born Toronto, Canada, 1972. Precocious juvenile performer, effective as a lovelorn 14-year-old in the title role of *Lucas* (1986). • *Firstborn* 1984; *Murphy's Romance* 1985; *Secret Admirer* 1985; *Silver Bullet* 1985; *Lucas* 1986; *The Lost Boys* 1987; *License to Drive* 1988; *Watchers* 1988; *Dream a Little Dream* 1989; *Fast Getaway* 1991.

Hall, Anthony Michael • Actor • Born Boston, MA, 1968. Former child performer on stage and TV who first gained attention as the likable "geek" in John Hughes's *Sixteen Candles* (1984). • *Six Pack* 1982; *National Lampoon's Vacation* 1983; *Sixteen Candles* 1984; *The Breakfast Club* 1985; *Weird Science* 1985; *Out of Bounds*1986; *Johnny Be Good* 1988; *Edward Scissorhands* 1990.

Hall, Conrad L. • *aka* Conrad Hall • Director of photography • Born Papeete, Tahiti, 1926. *Educ.* USC, Los Angeles (journalism, film). Exceptional American cinematographer who hit his peak in the late 1960s and 70s; equally at home with the bitter monochrome of *In Cold Blood* (1967) as with the warm, romantic hues of *Butch Cassidy and the Sundance Kid* (1969). • *Running Target* 1956 (sc); *Edge of Fury* 1958 (ph); *Incubus* 1965 (ph); *Morituri* 1965 (ph) **(AANBPH)**; *Wild Seed* 1965 (ph); *Harper* 1966 (ph); *The Professionals* 1966 (ph) **(AANBPH)**; *Cool Hand Luke* 1967 (ph); *Divorce American Style* 1967 (ph); *In Cold Blood* 1967 (ph) **(AANBPH)**; *Hell in the Pacific* 1968 (ph); *Butch Cassidy and the Sundance Kid* 1969 (ph) **(AABPH)**; *The Happy Ending* 1969 (ph); *Tell Them Willie Boy Is Here* 1969 (ph); *Fat City* 1972 (ph); *Catch My Soul* 1973 (ph); *Electra Glide in Blue* 1973 (ph); *The Day of the Locust* 1975 (ph) **(AANBPH)**; *Smile* 1975 (ph); *Marathon Man* 1976 (ph); *The Rose* 1979 (add.ph); *Black Widow* 1987 (ph); *Tequila Sunrise* 1988 (ph) **(AANBPH)**; *Class Action* 1991 (ph).

Hall, Sir Peter • Director; also producer. • Born Bury St. Edmunds, Suffolk, England, November 22, 1930. *Educ.* Cambridge. Acclaimed theater director whose occasional forays into film—usually stage adaptations—have met with varying degrees of success. Knighted in 1977. • *The Caretaker* 1963 (funding); *A Midsummer Night's Dream* 1968 (d); *Work Is a Four-Letter Word* 1968 (d); *Three Into Two Won't Go* 1969 (d); *Perfect Friday* 1970 (d); *The Homecoming* 1973 (d); *Akenfield* 1974 (d,p); *The Pedestrian* 1974 (a).

Haller, Ernest • Director of photography; also actor. • Born Los Angeles, CA, May 31, 1896; died 1970. Actor who moved behind the camera in the 1920s and worked on some of Hollywood's finest films of the next 40 years. Outstanding achievements include *Gone With the Wind* (1939), *The Roaring Twenties* (1939) and *Rebel Without a Cause* (1955), as well as several Bette Davis vehicles. • *The Hazards of Helen* 1914 (ph); *Wolves of the Rail* 1918 (ph); *Yes or No* 1920 (ph); *The Gilded Lily* 1921 (ph); *The Iron Trail* 1921 (ph); *The Road to Arcady* 1921 (ph); *Salvation Nell* 1921 (ph); *Such a Little Queen* 1921 (ph); *Wife Against Wife* 1921 (ph); *Homeward Bound* 1923 (ph); *The Ne'er-Do-Well* 1923 (ph); *Woman-Proof* 1923 (ph); *Empty Hearts* 1924 (ph); *Pied Piper Malone* 1924 (ph); *Rough Ridin'* 1924 (ph); *Any Woman* 1925 (ph); *The New Commandment* 1925 (ph); *Parisian Nights* 1925 (ph); *Three Keys* 1925 (ph); *The Dancer of Paris* 1926 (ph); *The Great Deception* 1926 (ph); *The Prince of Tempters* 1926 (ph); *The Reckless Lady* 1926 (ph); *Stacked Cards* 1926 (ph); *The Wilderness Woman* 1926 (ph); *Broadway Nights* 1927 (ph); *Convoy* 1927 (ph); *Dance Magic* 1927 (ph); *For the Love of Mike* 1927 (ph); *French Dressing* 1927 (ph);*Harold Teen* 1928 (ph); *Mad Hour* 1928 (ph); *Out of the Ruins* 1928 (ph); *Wheel of Chance* 1928 (ph); *The Whip Woman* 1928 (ph); *Dark Streets* 1929 (ph); *The Girl in the Glass Cage* 1929 (ph); *The House of Horror* 1929 (ph); *Naughty Baby* 1929 (ph); *Wedding Rings* 1929 (ph); *Young Nowheres* 1929 (ph); *The Dawn Patrol* 1930 (ph); *The Lash* 1930 (ph); *A Notorious Affair* 1930 (ph); *One Night at Susie's* 1930 (ph); *Son of the Gods* 1930 (ph); *Sunny* 1930 (ph); *24 Hours* 1931 (ph); *Chances* 1931 (ph); *Compromised* 1931 (ph); *The Finger Points* 1931 (ph); *Girls About Town* 1931 (ph); *Honor of the Family* 1931 (ph); *I Like Your Nerve* 1931 (ph); *Millie* 1931 (ph); *Mother's Millions* 1931 (ph); *Ten Cents a Dance* 1931 (ph); *The Crash* 1932 (ph); *Night After Night* 1932 (ph); *The Rich Are Always With Us* 1932 (ph); *Scarlet Dawn* 1932 (ph); *Street of Women* 1932 (ph); *The Woman From Monte Carlo* 1932 (ph); *The Emperor Jones* 1933 (ph); *The House on 56th Street* 1933 (ph); *International House* 1933 (ph); *King of the Jungle* 1933 (ph); *Murders in the Zoo* 1933 (ph); *British Agent* 1934 (ph); *Desirable* 1934 (ph); *Easy to Love* 1934 (ph); *The Firebird* 1934 (ph); *Journal of a Crime* 1934 (ph); *The Key* 1934 (ph); *Merry Wives of Reno* 1934 (ph); *Age of Indiscretion* 1935 (ph); *Dangerous* 1935 (ph); *Escapade* 1935 (ph); *Mary Jane's Pa* 1935 (ph); *The Captain's Kid* 1936 (ph); *Petticoat Fever* 1936 (ph); *Public Enemy's Wife* 1936 (ph); *The Voice of Bugle Ann* 1936 (ph); *Call It a Day* 1937 (ph); *The Great Garrick* 1937 (ph); *The Great O'Malley* 1937 (ph); *Mountain Justice* 1937 (ph); *That Certain Woman* 1937 (ph); *Brother Rat* 1938 (ph); *Four Daughters* 1938 (ph); *Four's a Crowd* 1938 (ph); *Jezebel* 1938 (ph) **(AANBPH)**; *Dark Victory* 1939 (ph); *Gone With the Wind* 1939 (ph) **(AABPH)**; *The Roaring Twenties* 1939 (ph); *All This, and Heaven Too* 1940 (ph) **(AANBPH)**; *Invisible Stripes* 1940 (ph); *It All Came True* 1940 (ph); *No Time For Comedy* 1940 (ph); *Blues in the Night* 1941 (ph); *The Bride Came C.O.D.* 1941 (ph); *Footsteps in the Dark* 1941 (ph); *Honeymoon For Three* 1941 (ph); *Manpower* 1941 (ph); *Outlaws of the Cherokee Trail* 1941 (ph); *George Washington Slept Here* 1942 (ph); *In This Our Life* 1942 (ph); *Princess O'Rourke* 1943 (ph); *The Doughgirls* 1944 (ph); *Mildred Pierce* 1945 (ph) **(AANBPH)**; *Mr.*

Skeffington 1945 (ph); *Saratoga Trunk* 1945 (ph); *Deception* 1946 (ph); *Devotion* 1946 (ph); *Humoresque* 1946 (ph); *A Stolen Life* 1946 (ph); *The Verdict* 1946 (ph); *The Unfaithful* 1947 (ph); *My Girl Tisa* 1948 (ph); *Winter Meeting* 1948 (ph); *Always Leave Them Laughing* 1949 (ph); *My Dream Is Yours* 1949 (ph); *Chain Lightning* 1950 (ph); *Dallas* 1950 (ph); *The Flame and the Arrow* 1950 (ph) **(AANBPH)**; *Jim Thorpe—All American* 1951 (ph); *On Moonlight Bay* 1951 (ph); *Monsoon* 1952 (ph); *Carnival Story* 1954 (ph); *Rummelplatz Der Liebe* 1954 (ph); *The Come On* 1955 (ph); *Rebel Without a Cause* 1955 (ph); *The Cruel Tower* 1956 (ph); *Dakota Incident* 1956 (ph); *Magic Fire* 1956 (ph); *Men in War* 1956 (ph); *Strange Intruder* 1956 (ph); *Back From the Dead* 1957 (ph); *Hell on Devil's Island* 1957 (ph); *Hell's Five Hours* 1957 (ph); *Plunder Road* 1957 (ph); *The Young Don't Cry* 1957 (ph); *God's Little Acre* 1958 (ph); *Man of the West* 1958 (ph); *Speed Crazy* 1958 (ph); *The Miracle* 1959 (ph); *The Boy and the Pirates* 1960 (ph); *The Third Voice* 1960 (ph); *Armored Command* 1961 (ph); *Pressure Point* 1962 (ph); *What Ever Happened to Baby Jane?* 1962 (ph) **(AANBPH)**; *Lilies of the Field* 1963 (ph) **(AANBPH)**; *Dead Ringer* 1964 (ph).

Halliwell, Leslie • Critic, author • Born England, 1929; died January 21, 1989. *Educ.* Cambridge. Author of the top-selling reference books *Halliwell's Film Guide*, comprising key credits and synopses of thousands of films, and *Halliwell's Filmgoer's Companion*, with filmographies and profiles of major and minor figures in world film history. Halliwell had a much-loved disregard for received critical opinion, giving terse, opinionated—and often highly entertaining—capsule assessments of both careers and films: Fassbinder is a "fashionable German director of the seventies, usually with something despairing to say"; *La Dolce Vita* is "a marathon self-indulgent wallow with a wagging finger never far away."

Hallstrom, Lasse • Director • Born Sweden, 1946. One of Sweden's most popular directors of comedy, Hallstrom began making 8mm films as a child and sold his first 16mm effort to TV while still in high school. He is best known in the US for *My Life As a Dog* (1985), a bittersweet evocation of provincial childhood. • *Tva killar och en tjej* 1983 (d,sc,ed); *Mitt liv som Hund/My Life as a Dog* 1985 (d,sc) **(AANBD)**; *Alla vi barn i Bullerby* 1986 (d); *Mer om oss barn i Bullerbyn* 1987 (d); *Once Around* 1991 (d,sc).

Hamill, Mark • Actor • Born Oakland, CA, September 25, 1952. *Educ.* Los Angeles City College (drama). Boyish leading man who came to prominence as Luke Skywalker in *Star Wars* (1977). • *Star Wars* 1977; *Wizards* 1977; *Corvette Summer* 1978; *The Big Red One* 1980; *The Empire Strikes Back* 1980; *The Night the Lights Went Out in Georgia* 1981; *Britannia Hospital* 1982; *Return of the Jedi* 1983; *Slipstream* 1989.

Hamilton, Guy • Director • Born Paris, France, 1922. *Educ.* Haileybury College. Competent craftsman, best at spy movies such as the underrated *Funeral in Berlin* (1966) and his four "James Bond" pictures. • *The Ringer* 1952 (d); *The Intruder* 1953 (d); *The Colditz Story* 1954 (d,sc); *An Inspector Calls* 1954 (d); *Charley Moon* 1956 (d); *Manuela* 1957 (d,sc); *The Devil's Disciple* 1959 (d); *A Touch of Larceny* 1960 (d,sc); *I Due Nemici* 1961 (d); *Goldfinger* 1964 (d); *The Man in the Middle* 1964 (d); *The Party's Over* 1965 (d); *Funeral in Berlin* 1966 (d); *Battle of Britain* 1969 (d); *Diamonds Are Forever* 1971 (d); *Live and Let Die* 1973 (d); *The Man With the Golden Gun* 1974 (d); *Force 10 From Navarone* 1978 (d); *The Mirror Crack'd* 1980 (d); *Evil Under the Sun* 1982 (d); *Remo Williams: The Adventure Begins...* 1985 (d); *Sauf votre respect* 1989 (d,sc).

Hamlisch, Marvin • Composer; also pianist. • Born New York, NY, June 2, 1944. *Educ.* Juilliard (music); Queens College, NY. Began scoring films in 1968 and, within five years, had won three Oscars for his work on *The Way We Were* (1973) and *The Sting* (1973). Though capable in a number of idioms, Hamlisch is particularly adept at incorporating a pop sensibility into his compositions. He scored Broadway's *A Chorus Line* and *They're Playing Our Song*, and other notable film contributions include *Bananas* (1971), *The Spy Who Loved Me* (1977) and *Sophie's Choice* (1982). Hamlisch has won a Tony award and a Pulitzer prize (both for 1976's *A Chorus Line*) and four Grammys, and was named to the National Council on the Arts in 1988. • *Ski Party* 1965 (song); *The Swimmer* 1968 (m); *The April Fools* 1969 (m); *Take the Money and Run* 1969 (m); *Flap* 1970 (m); *Move* 1970 (m); *Bananas* 1971 (m,song); *Kotch* 1971 (m,song) **(AANBS)**; *Something Big* 1971 (m); *Fat City* 1972 (m.sup); *The War Between Men and Women* 1972 (m); *The World's Greatest Athlete* 1972 (m); *Save the Tiger* 1973 (m); *The Sting* 1973 (m.adapt,song) **(AABSS)**; *The Way We Were* 1973 (m,song) **(AABM,AABS)**; *The Prisoner of Second Avenue* 1974 (m); *The Spy Who Loved Me* 1977 (m,song) **(AANBM,AANBS)**; *Ice Castles* 1978 (m,song) **(AANBS)**; *Same Time, Next Year* 1978 (m,song) **(AANBS)**; *Chapter Two* 1979 (m); *Starting Over* 1979 (song); *Ordinary People* 1980 (m.adapt); *Seems Like Old Times* 1980 (m); *The Devil and Max Devlin* 1981 (song); *The Fan* 1981 (song); *I Ought to Be in Pictures* 1981 (m); *Pennies From Heaven* 1981 (m,m.dir,m.arr); *Sophie's Choice* 1982 (m) **(AANBM)**; *Romantic Comedy* 1983 (m,song); *A Chorus Line* 1985 (m,song) **(AANBS)**; *D.A.R.Y.L.* 1985 (m,song); *Shy People* 1987 (song); *Three Men and a Baby* 1987 (m,song); *Big* 1988 (song); *The January Man* 1988 (m,song); *Little Nikita* 1988 (m); *The Experts* 1989 (m); *Shirley Valentine* 1989 (song) **(AANBS)**; *Troop Beverly Hills* 1989 (song).

Hammett, Dashiell • Novelist; also screenwriter. • Born St. Mary's County, MD, May 27, 1894; died 1961. Novelist who parlayed his experience as a Pinkerton operative into a series of taut, precisely observed detective fictions that revolutionized the genre. Hammet's novel *The Thin Man* was developed into a popular movie series of the 1930s and 40s starring William Powell and Myrna Loy, and his tightly plotted *Maltese Falcon* formed the basis of John Huston's 1941 classic. In 1931 Hammett was engaged by Paramount to write original screenplays. In 1951, he refused to testify before the HUAC and was jailed for six months. His long-term relationship with playwright Lillian Hellman was sensitively portrayed in the 1977 film *Julia*. • *City Streets* 1931 (story); *The Maltese Falcon* 1931 (from novel); *The Thin Man* 1934 (from novel); *Woman in the Dark* 1934 (story); *The Glass Key* 1935(from novel); *Mr. Dynamite* 1935 (from story "On the Make"); *After the Thin Man* 1936 (story); *Satan Met a Lady* 1936 (from novel *The Maltese Falcon*); *Another Thin Man* 1939 (story); *The Maltese Falcon* 1941 (from novel); *The Glass Key* 1942 (from novel); *Watch on the Rhine* 1943 (sc) **(AANBSC)**; *The Black Bird* 1975 (from characters *The Maltese Falcon*).

Hampton, Christopher • *aka* Chris Hampton • creenwriter, playwright • Born Christopher James Hampton, Fayal, Azores, January 26, 1946. *Educ.* Lancing College; Oxford (French, German). Leading figure of the English theater world, best known for his award-winning stage and screen adaptations of Choderlos de Laclos's *Dangerous Liaisons* (1988). • *A Doll's House* 1973 (sc); *Geschichten aus dem Wienerwald* 1978 (sc); *Beyond the Limit* 1983 (sc); *The Good Father* 1986 (sc); *The Wolf at the Door* 1986 (sc); *Dangerous Liaisons* 1988 (p,sc, from play *Les Liaisons Dangereuses)* **(AABSC)**.

Hancock, Herbie • Composer, musician • Born Herbert Hancock, Chicago, IL. Hancock was a pioneer in the fusion of jazz techniques with electronic instrumentation —a combination which fuelled several best-selling records as well as opening up a new film scoring idiom. He has provided the music for films including *Blow-Up* (1966), *A Soldier's Story* (1984) and *Colors* (1988), as well as for TV's "Fat Albert." Appropriately, Hancock scored Bertrand Tavernier's *'Round Midnight* (1986), a tribute to 1950s jazz greats Bud Powell and Lester Young, as well as playing a small part in the film. • *Blow-Up* 1966 (m); *The Spook Who Sat By the Door* 1973 (m);

Death Wish 1974 (m); *The Bitch* 1979 (songs); *Sunburn* 1979 (songs); *American Pop* 1981 (songs); *A Soldier's Story* 1984 (m); *Fast Forward* 1985 (song); *L'Homme aux yeux d'argent* 1985 (m.perf); *Autour de Minuit/'Round Midnight* 1986 (a,m,m.arr, m.dir,song) **(AABM)**; *Jo Jo Dancer, Your Life Is Calling* 1986 (m); *Back to the Beach* 1987 (song); *Action Jackson* 1988 (m); *Colors* 1988 (m); *Harlem Nights* 1989 (m); *Listen Up* 1990 (a).

Hancock, John • Director • Born LaPorte, IN, February 12, 1939. *Educ.* Harvard; AFI, Los Angeles. Theater director whose sporadic forays into film have produced some languorous, well-acted character studies. Hancock's most assured works are *Bang the Drum Slowly* (1973), a poignant portrait of a dying baseball player, and the neo-beach movie *California Dreaming* (1979). • *Sticky My Fingers...Fleet My Feet (short)* 1970 (p); *Let's Scare Jessica to Death* 1971 (d); *Bang the Drum Slowly* 1973 (d); *Baby Blue Marine* 1975 (d); *California Dreaming* 1979 (d); *Weeds* 1987 (d,p,sc); *Prancer* 1989 (d).

Handke, Peter • Novelist, screenwriter; also director, playwright. • Born Austria, 1942. Key contemporary German-language writer who entered films in 1972, co-adapting (with first-time director Wim Wenders) his novel *The Goalie's Anxiety at the Penalty Kick*. Handke made an assured directing debut with *The Left-Handed Woman* (1977), a perceptive study of alienation and ennui produced by Wenders and again adapted from his own novel. • *Die Angst des Tormanns beim Elfmeter/The Goalie's Anxiety at the Penalty Kick* 1972 (dial,from novel); *Falsche Bewegung/Wrong Move* 1975 (sc); *Die Linkshändige Frau/The Left–Handed Woman* 1977 (d,sc,from novel); *Das Mal des Todes* 1985 (a,d,sc); *Der Himmel über Berlin/Wings of Desire* 1987 (sc); *Ville Etrangère* 1988 (from story "A Moment of True Feeling").

Hanks, Tom • *aka* Thom Hanks • Actor • Born Thomas J. Hanks, Concord, CA, July 9, 1956. *Educ.* California State University, Sacramento. Dropped out of college in 1977 to pursue his acting career and turned in a number of intelligent, energetic film roles before hitting the jackpot with *Big* (1988), playing a boy in a man's body. Hanks has a son and daughter by actress-producer Samantha Lewes (divorced 1985) and married actress Rita Wilson in 1988. • *He Knows You're Alone* 1980; *Bachelor Party* 1983; *Splash* 1984; *The Man With One Red Shoe* 1985; *Volunteers* 1985; *Everytime We Say Goodbye* 1986; *The Money Pit* 1986; *Nothing in Common* 1986; *Dragnet* 1987; *Big* 1988 **(AANBA)**; *Punchline* 1988; *The Burbs* 1989; *Turner and Hooch* 1989; *Bonfire of the Vanities* 1990; *Joe Versus the Volcano* 1990.

Hanna, William • Animator; also executive. • Born Melrose, NM, July 14, 1910. See Barbera, Joseph.

Hannah, Daryl • Actress • Born Chicago, IL, 1960. *Educ.* Goodman Theater School of Drama, Chicago (acting); USC, Los Angeles. Niece of distinguished cinematographer Haskell Wexler. Hannah's striking features have been the cornerstone of her career —she was perfect as a beautiful android in Ridley Scott's *Blade Runner* (1982)—though she has recently proved herself capable of non-glamorous roles, as in *Steel Magnolias* (1989). Sister Page is also an actress. • *The Fury* 1978; *The Final Terror* 1981; *Hard Country* 1981; *Blade Runner* 1982; *Summer Lovers* 1982; *The Pope of Greenwich Village* 1984; *Reckless* 1984; *Splash* 1984; *The Clan of the Cave Bear* 1986; *Legal Eagles* 1986; *Roxanne* 1987; *Wall Street* 1987; *High Spirits* 1988; *Crimes and Misdemeanors* 1989; *Steel Magnolias* 1989.

Hardy, Oliver • *aka* Oliver Norvell Hardy, Babe Hardy • Actor, comedian • Born Norvell Hardy, Harlem, GA, January 18, 1892; died 1957. *Educ.* Georgia Military College; Atlanta Conservatory of Music. Mr. Laurel and Mr. Hardy, one a lank, childlike innocent with a penchant for anarchy, the other a rotund, bossy incompetent with a naive pomposity, arrived on the film scenelate in the silent era. Their brand of comedy served as a link between the era of silent character comedy, with its emphasis on aspirations to success and happiness, and the chaotic comedies of the 1930s, with its complete bedlam created by the characters' consistent failures. Laurel and Hardy slowed down the pace of silent slapstick, adjusting its gag structure for the more mundane pacing of sound film comedy. In the process, the duo became two of the most recognized faces in the film world.

Before their pairing in 1927, Laurel and Hardy had separate film careers, Stan's dating back to 1917 and Ollie's to 1913. As a teenager, Laurel joined Fred Karno's British music hall troupe, understudying Charlie Chaplin. During the Karno troupe's first tour of the United States, he quit the company in 1911, seeking success on the American vaudeville stage. He would later rejoin Karno, only to quit a final time. Although he did meet with limited success in American vaudeville, he made his first film appearance in *Nuts in May* (1917), a slapdash slapstick chaser. He then signed with Universal to make a series of shorts as the character Hickory Hiram. In 1919, Laurel appeared in a modestly successful group of comedies that parodied contemporary film hits. Despite two stints with the successful producer Hal Roach, by the mid-20s, Laurel had practically given up the hope of being a successful comic performer; he signed once again with Roach in 1926, this time as a writer and gagman.

As a young man, Oliver Hardy liked to sneak out of college and music school to go on the road singing with theater quartets and minstrel shows. At 18, he managed the first movie theater in Milledgeville, Georgia, but in 1913, he abandoned theatrical management for a film career, joining the Lubin Company as a character player and general assistant. After three years with Lubin, Hardy appeared through the late teens and early 20s in the Frank Baum "Oz" series and as a comic foil for various silent film comedians such as Billy West, Earl Williams, Jimmy Aubrey and Larry Semon. By the mid-20s, Hardy, like Laurel, had signed with Roach.

At that point, Roach was frantically seeking to regain the commercial success he had enjoyed with Harold Lloyd, who had left him for feature film stardom. In an act of desperation, Roach formed the Hal Roach Comedy All-Stars, into which he thrust his stock company of James Finlayson, Max Davidson, Clyde Cook, Eugene Palette, Edgar Kennedy, Noah Young, Mae Busch, Anita Garvin and Stan Laurel and Oliver Hardy.

It was only a matter of time before Roach's shuffling of his players would deal Laurel and Hardy into the same film. *Slipping Wives* (1927), however, found Laurel supporting Hardy. It was *Putting Pants on Philip* (1927) in which the Laurel and Hardy team first flowered. The famous mannerisms appeared, in Hardy's pomposity and Southern courtliness and Laurel's squeaky, squashed-faced cries. Previously known for his frenetic slapstickpace, Laurel slowed down and instead of a catalyst of action became a reactor to the destruction raining down upon Hardy's head.

In their methodical style, Laurel and Hardy transformed silent comedy and conducted a scientific investigation of gag structures. The jokes became rituals in which a gag is dissected, studied and explained in a process of passionless stateliness. In this emotionless artifice, the characters paused to await their fate. One character would stand by as his partner clipped off his tie with a pair of garden shears. Equally detached, the second character would watch as the tie-less gentleman clasps the shears and hurls them through the second character's car windshield. In the world of Laurel and Hardy, there are continually disapassionate shifts between victims and victimizers, resulting in mammoth destruction of hundreds of pies, a traffic jam of dozens of cars or the gutting of an entire residential neighborhood.

Over the next several years, Laurel and Hardy refined their pace in such shorts as *Leave 'em Laughing* (1928), *From Soup to Nuts* (1928), *Big Business* (1929) and *The Battle of the Century* (1927). The pair easily made the transition to sound, their slapstick style perfectly suited to its reality-bound pacing. From 1930 to 1935, Laurel and Hardy made several dozen shorts containing their best screen work, highlighted by the Academy Award-winning *The Music Box* (1932).

But the popularity of sound animated cartoons forced Laurel and Hardy into features, which either encased the team in cumbersome operettas or expanded their short-subject comic routines into clumsy assemblages. For every success—*Sons of the Desert* (1933) or *Way Out West* (1937)—there were several stumbles—*Babes in Toyland* (1934), *Pack Up Your Troubles* (1932) or *Saps at Sea* (1940). The end came when Laurel and Hardy signed on with the big Hollywood studios (RKO, Fox, MGM), who emasculated the darker aspects of their comedy and forced them into hackneyed formula films that denied them the creative freedom permitted by Roach. By the time their last film, *Atoll K/Utopia*, was released in 1951, the team was bedraggled and gutted, Laurel looking seriously ill and Hardy shocked and embarrassed.

But in their early films of 1927-35, Laurel and Hardy created brilliant comic structures and developed two characters who perfectly complemented one another in a poetic, primordial relationship that shifted from the realm of the comic into something broader which found its ultimate reflection in the barren landscapes of Samuel Beckett. PB • *A Lucky Dog (short)* 1917; *Nuts in May* 1917; *Fortune's Mask* 1922; *Little Wildcat* 1922; *One Stolen Night* 1923; *The Three Ages* 1923; *The Girl in the Limousine* 1924; *The King of the Wild Horses* 1924; *Enough to Do (short)* 1925; *The Perfect Clown* 1925; *The Wizard of Oz* 1925; *Yes,Yes, Nanette (short)* 1925; *45 Minutes From Hollywood (short)* 1926; *The Gentle Cyclone* 1926; *Madame Mystery (short)* 1926; *Stop, Look and Listen* 1926 (ad,a); *The Battle of the Century (short)* 1927; *Call of the Cuckoo (short)* 1927; *Do Detectives Think? (short)* 1927; *Duck Soup (short)* 1927; *Flying Elephants (short)* 1927; *Hats Off (short)* 1927; *Love 'em and Weep (short)* 1927; *No Man's Law* 1927; *Putting Pants on Philip (short)* 1927; *Sailors, Beware! (short)* 1927; *The Second Hundred Years (short)* 1927; *Should Tall Men Marry? (short)* 1927; *Slipping Wives (short)* 1927; *Sugar Daddies (short)* 1927; *Why Girls Love Sailors (short)* 1927; *With Love and Hisses (short)* 1927; *Early to Bed (short)* 1928; *The Finishing Touch (short)* 1928; *From Soup to Nuts (short)* 1928; *Habeas Corpus (short)* 1928; *Leave 'em Laughing (short)* 1928; *Should Married Men Go Home (short)* 1928; *Their Purple Moment (short)* 1928; *Two Tars* 1928; *We Faw Down (short)* 1928; *You're Darn Tootin' (short)* 1928; *Angora Love (short)* 1929; *Bacon Grabbers (short)* 1929; *Berth Marks (short)* 1929; *Big Business (short)* 1929; *Double Whoopee (short)* 1929; *The Hollywood Revue of 1929* 1929; *The Hoose-Gow (short)* 1929; *Liberty (short)* 1929; *Man O' War (short)* 1929; *Perfect Day (short)* 1929; *That's My Wife (short)* 1929; *They Go Boom (short)* 1929; *Unaccustomed As We Are (short)* 1929; *Wrong Again (short)* 1929; *Another Fine Mess (short)* 1930; *Below Zero (short)* 1930; *Blotto (short)* 1930; *Brats (short)* 1930; *Hog Wild (short)* 1930; *The Laurel-Hardy Murder Case (short)* 1930; *The Night Owls (short)* 1930; *The Rogue Song* 1930; *Beau Hunks (short)* 1931; *Chicken Come Home* 1931; *The Chiselers (short)* 1931; *Come Clean (short)* 1931; *Helpmates (short)* 1931; *Laughing Gravy (short)* 1931; *On the Loose (short)* 1931; *One Good Turn (short)* 1931; *Our Wife (short)* 1931; *Pardon Us* 1931; *Any Old Port (short)* 1932; *The Chimp* 1932; *County Hospital (short)* 1932; *The Music Box (short)* 1932; *Pack Up Your Troubles* 1932; *Scram! (short)* 1932; *Their First Mistake (short)* 1932; *Towed in a Hole (short)* 1932; *Busy Bodies (short)* 1933; *The Devil's Brother* 1933; *Dirty Work (short)* 1933; *Me and My Pal (short)* 1933; *The Midnight Patrol (short)* 1933; *Sons of the Desert* 1933; *Twice Two (short)* 1933; *Wild Poses (short)* 1933; *Babes in Toyland* 1934; *Going Bye-Bye! (short)* 1934; *Hollywood Party* 1934; *The Live Ghost (short)* 1934; *Oliver the Eighth* 1934; *Them Thar Hills (short)* 1934; *The Fixer Uppers (short)* 1935; *Heroes of the Regiment* 1935; *Thicker Than Water (short)* 1935; *Tit For Tat (short)* 1935; *The Bohemian Girl* 1936; *On the Wrong Trek (short)* 1936; *Our Relations* 1936; *Way Out West* 1937; *Block-Heads* 1938; *Swiss Miss* 1938; *The Flying Deuces* 1939; *Zenobia* 1939; *A Chump at Oxford* 1940; *Saps at Sea* 1940; *Great Guns* 1941; *A-Haunting We Will Go* 1942; *The Tree in a Test Tube (short)* 1942; *Air Raid Wardens* 1943; *The Dancing Masters* 1943; *Jitterbugs* 1943; *The Big Noise* 1944; *Nothing But Trouble* 1944; *The Bullfighters* 1945; *The Fighting Kentuckian* 1949; *Riding High* 1950; *Atoll K/Utopia* 1951; *Golden Age of Comedy* 1957 (archival footage); *The Crazy World of Laurel and Hardy* 1964(archival footage); *Laurel and Hardy's Laughing 20's* 1965 (archival footage); *The Further Perils of Laurel and Hardy* 1967 (archival footage); *Four Clowns* 1969 (archival footage); *The Best of Laurel and Hardy* 1971 (archival footage).

Hare, David • Director, screenwriter, playwright • Born Sussex, England, 1947. *Educ.* Lancing College; Jesus College, Cambridge. Left-leaning playwright whose excursions into film direction have yielded interesting and increasingly polished results. Hare's *Wetherby* (1985), a grim, obliquely told story of suicide in a northern English town, won the Golden Bear at the Berlin Film Festival. • *Licking Hitler* 1977 (d,sc); *Saigon—Year of the Cat* 1983 (sc); *Plenty* 1985 (sc,from play); *Wetherby* 1985 (d,sc); *Paris By Night* 1988 (d,sc); *Strapless* 1989 (d,sc).

Harewood, Dorian • Actor • Born Dayton, OH. *Educ.* University of Cincinnati. Former musical theater star encouraged to pursue a dramatic career by Bette Davis. Married to actress Ann McCurry. • *Sparkle* 1976; *Gray Lady Down* 1977; *Looker* 1981; *Against All Odds* 1983; *Tank* 1984; *The Falcon and the Snowman* 1985; *Full Metal Jacket* 1987; *Pacific Heights* 1990; *Solar Crisis* 1990.

Hark, Tsui • *aka* Xu Ke • Director, producer, actor; also screenwriter, production designer. • Born Vietnam, January 2, 1951. *Educ.* University of Texas (film). Leading figure of the Hong Kong film scene and head of his own production company, Film Workshop. Hark specializes in kaleidoscopic dramas characterized by frenzied action and a decidedly tongue-in-cheek tone. He is best known in the US for *Peking Opera Blues* (1986). • *Die Bian* 1979 (d); *The Butterfly Murders* 1979 (d,story); *We're Going to Eat You* 1980 (d,sc); *All the Wrong Spies* 1982 (a,pd); *Zu* 1982 (d); *The Perfect Wife* 1983 (pd); *Working Class* 1985 (a,d); *A Better Tomorrow* 1986 (exec.p); *Do ma dan/Peking Opera Blues* 1986 (d,p,pd); *A Better Tomorrow II* 1987 (p,sc); *Qian nu youhun/A Chinese Ghost Story* 1987 (p); *Die xue shuang xiong* 1989 (p); *A Better Tomorrow III* 1990 (p); *Sinnui Yauman II/A Chinese Ghost Story II* 1990 (exec.p); *The Swordsman* 1990 (d,exec.p); *The Terra-Cotta Warrior* 1990 (fx).

Harlan, Russell • *aka* Russ Harlan, Russell B. Harlan • Director of photography • Born Los Angeles, CA, September 16, 1903; died 1974. Outstanding cinematographer whose visual flair bolstered numerous routine westerns before he shot Lewis Milestone's *A Walk in the Sun* (1945), the first in a series of more distinguished productions for directors such as Howard Hawks (*Red River* 1948) and Richard Mulligan (*To Kill a Mockingbird* 1962). Harlan's long, hand-held shot from the back of a car during the bank hold-up in *Gun Crazy/Deadly Is the Female* (1949) was a remarkable precursor of the New Wave style which would emerge ten years later. • *Bar 20 Rides Again* 1935; *Hopalong Rides Again* 1937; *North of the Rio Grande* 1937; *Partners of the Plains* 1937; *Rustlers' Valley* 1937; *Texas Trail* 1937; *Bar 20 Justice* 1938; *Cassidy of Bar 20* 1938; *The Frontiersman* 1938; *Heart of Arizona* 1938; *In Old Mexico* 1938; *The Mysterious Rider* 1938; *Pride of the West* 1938; *Heritage of the Desert* 1939; *Law of the Pampas* 1939; *The Llano Kid* 1939; *Range War* 1939; *The Renegade Trail* 1939; *Silver on the Sage* 1939; *Cherokee Strip* 1940; *Hidden Gold* 1940; *Knights of the Range* 1940; *The Light of Western Stars* 1940; *Santa Fe Marshal* 1940; *The Showdown* 1940; *Stagecoach War* 1940; *Three Men From Texas* 1940; *Border Vigilantes* 1941; *Doomed Caravan* 1941; *In*

Old Colorado 1941; *Outlaws of the Desert* 1941; *The Parson of Panamint* 1941; *Pirates on Horseback* 1941; *Riders of the Timberline* 1941; *The Round-Up* 1941; *Secrets of the Wasteland* 1941; *Stick to Your Guns* 1941; *Twilight on the Trail* 1941; *Wide Open Town* 1941; *American Empire* 1942; *Lost Canyon* 1942; *Silver Queen* 1942; *Tombstone, the Town Too Tough to Die* 1942; *Undercover Man* 1942; *Bar 20* 1943; *Border Patrol* 1943; *Buckskin Frontier* 1943; *Colt Comrades* 1943; *False Colors* 1943; *Hoppy Serves a Writ* 1943; *The Kansan* 1943; *The Leather Burners* 1943; *Riders of the Deadline* 1943; *Tarzan's Desert Mystery* 1943; *The Woman of the Town* 1943; *Forty Thieves* 1944; *Lumberjack* 1944; *Mystery Man* 1944; *Texas Masquerade* 1944; *A Walk in the Sun* 1945; *Ramrod* 1947; *Bad Men of Tombstone* 1948; *Four Faces West* 1948; *Red River* 1948; Gun Crazy/*Deadly Is the Female* 1949; *The Man Who Cheated Himself* 1950; *Southside 1-1000* 1950; *Tarzan and the Slave Girl* 1950; *The Thing* 1951; *The Big Sky* 1952 **(AANBPH)**; *The Ring* 1952; *Ruby* 1952; *Riot in Cell Block 11* 1954; *Blackboard Jungle* 1955 **(AANBPH)**; *Land of the Pharaohs* 1955; *The Last Hunt* 1955; *Lust For Life* 1956; *Something of Value* 1957; *This Could Be the Night* 1957; *Witness For the Prosecution* 1957; *King Creole* 1958; *Run Silent, Run Deep* 1958; *Day of the Outlaw* 1959; *Operation Petticoat* 1959; *Rio Bravo* 1959; *Pollyanna* 1960; *Hatari!* 1962 **(AANBPH)**; *The Spiral Road* 1962; *To Kill a Mockingbird* 1962 **(AANBPH)**; *A Gathering of Eagles* 1963; *Dear Heart* 1964; *Man's Favorite Sport?* 1964; *Quick, Before It Melts* 1964; *The Great Race* 1965 **(AANBPH)**; *Hawaii* 1966 **(AANBPH)**; *Tobruk* 1967; *Darling Lili* 1970.

Harlin, Renny • Director; also screenwriter. • Born Finland, c. 1959. Began his career making shorts and documentaries in his native Finland and moved to the US in the mid-1980s. Harlin first attracted attention with the military action film, *Born American* (1986), and joined the Hollywood mainstream with two high-profile 1990 releases, *Die Hard 2* and *The Adventures of Ford Fairlane*. • *Born American* 1986 (d,sc); *A Nightmare on Elm Street 4: The Dream Master* 1988 (d); *Prison* 1988 (d); *The Adventures of Ford Fairlane* 1990 (d); *Die Hard 2: Die Harder* 1990 (d).

Harlow, Jean • Actress • Born Harlean Carpenter, Kansas City, MO, March 3, 1911; died June 7, 1937. The original platinum blonde who, despite the brevity of her career, became one of Hollywood's legendary stars. From the Howard Hughes spectacle *Hell's Angels* (1930)—in which she purrs, "Do you mind if I slip into something more comfortable?"—through the comedy classic *Libeled Lady* (1936), Harlow's image shifted from that of an unrefined sexual bombshell to a sophisticated comic talent. Part of the change was due to the newly implemented Hays Code, and to Harlow's leaving Hughes for MGM in 1932. At MGM her wisecracking demeanor proved the perfect foil to Clark Gable's tough sexuality in films like *Red Dust* (1932) and *Hold Your Man* (1933).

Harlow's personal life was a far cry from her screen success. Her director-husband Paul Bern, a close associate of Irving Thalberg, killed himself in 1932, just two months after their marriage. She was subsequently married to, and divorced from, director of photography Harold Rosson and later became involved with actor William Powell. Harlow died at 26 of cerebral edema, during the filming of *Saratoga* (1937). • *The Saturday Night Kid* 1929; *Hell's Angels* 1930; *Goldie* 1931; *The Iron Man* 1931; *Platinum Blonde* 1931; *The Public Enemy* 1931; *The Secret Six* 1931; *The Beast of the City* 1932; *Red Dust* 1932; *Red-Headed Woman* 1932; *Three Wise Girls* 1932; *The Blonde Bombshell* 1933; *Dinner at Eight* 1933; *Hold Your Man* 1933; *The Girl From Missouri* 1934; *China Seas* 1935; *Reckless* 1935; *Riffraff* 1935; *Libeled Lady* 1936; *Suzy* 1936; *Wife vs. Secretary* 1936; *Personal Property* 1937; *Saratoga* 1937; *Golden Age of Comedy* 1957 (archival footage).

Harmon, Mark • Actor • Born Burbank, CA, September 2, 1951. *Educ.* UCLA. Handsome leading man of the 1980s. Married to actress Pam Dawber and son of the late football star-sportscaster Tom Harmon. • *Comes a Horseman* 1978; *Beyond the Poseidon Adventure* 1979; *Dear America* 1987; *Let's Get Harry* 1987; *Summer School* 1987; *The Presidio* 1988; *Stealing Home* 1988; *Worth Winning* 1989.

Harper, Tess • Actress • Born Mammoth Springs, AR. *Educ.* Southwest Missouri State College, Springfield. Made an impressive debut opposite Robert Duvall in *Tender Mercies* (1982) and earned an Oscar nomination for her role as a nosy neighbor in *Crimes of the Heart* (1986). • *Tender Mercies* 1982; *Amityville 3-D* 1983; *Silkwood* 1983; *Flashpoint* 1984; *Crimes of the Heart* 1986 **(AANBSA)**; *Ishtar* 1987; *Criminal Law* 1988; *Far North* 1988; *Her Alibi* 1989; *Daddy's Dyin'... Who's Got the Will?* 1990.

Harris, Ed • Actor • Born Tenafly, NJ, November 28, 1950. *Educ.* Columbia; Oklahoma State University (acting); California Institute of the Arts. Award-winning stage performer and a capable, engaging leading man in several films of the 1980s. Harris has given fine performances in two roles based on real–life figures: astronaut John Glenn, in Philip Kaufman's *The Right Stuff* (1983); and crazed, would-be dictator William *Walker* in Alex Cox's 1987 historical allegory. Married to actress Amy Madigan. • *Coma* 1978; *Borderline* 1980; *Knightriders* 1981; *Creepshow* 1982; *The Right Stuff* 1983; *Under Fire* 1983; *Places in the Heart* 1984; *Swing Shift* 1984; *Alamo Bay* 1985; *Code Name: Emerald* 1985; *A Flash of Green* 1985 (a,sc consult); *Sweet Dreams* 1985; *Walker* 1987; *Popielusko* 1988; *The Abyss* 1989; *Jacknife* 1989; *State of Grace* 1990.

Harris, Richard • Actor; also singer. • Born Limerick, Ireland, October 1, 1930. *Educ.* LAMDA, London. Ruggedly handsome leading man who came to prominence playing the angry young rugby player in *This Sporting Life* (1963) and was equally effective in *Red Desert* (1964) and *A Man Called Horse* (1970). Harris also appeared in several inferior period movies, such as *Cromwell* (1970), and is known as a recording artist for the syrupy hit song, "MacArthur Park." Son Damian is a director. • *Alive and Kicking* 1959; *Shake Hands With the Devil* 1959; *The Wreck of the Mary Deare* 1959; *A Terrible Beauty* 1960; *The Guns of Navarone* 1961; *The Long and the Short and the Tall* 1961; *Mutiny on the Bounty* 1962; *This Sporting Life* 1963 **(AANBA)**; *Deserto Rosso/Red Desert* 1964; *The Heroes of Telemark* 1965; *Major Dundee* 1965; *I Tre Volti* 1965; *La Bibbia* 1966; *Hawaii* 1966; *Camelot* 1967; *Caprice* 1967; *Cromwell* 1970; *La Dame dans l'auto avec des lunettes et un fusil* 1970 (sc); *A Man Called Horse* 1970; *The Molly Maguires* 1970; *Bloomfield* 1971 (a,add.material,d); *Man in the Wilderness* 1971; *The Deadly Trackers* 1973; *99 and 44/100% Dead* 1974; *Juggernaut*1974; *Echoes of a Summer* 1976 (a,exec.p,songs); *The Return of a Man Called Horse* 1976 (a,exec.p); *Robin and Marian* 1976; *The Cassandra Crossing* 1977; *Golden Rendezvous* 1977; *Gulliver's Travels* 1977; *Orca... Killer Whale* 1977; *The Wild Geese* 1978; *Game For Vultures* 1979; *Highpoint* 1979; *The Last Word* 1979; *Ravagers* 1979; *Tarzan, The Ape Man* 1981; *El Triunfo de un Hombre Llamado Caballo* 1982; *Martin's Day* 1983; *Mack the Knife* 1989; *The Field* 1990; *King of the Wind* 1990; *Ruby Dreams* 1990.

Harrison, Rex • Actor • Born Reginald Carey Harrison, Huyton, Lancashire, England, March 5, 1908; died June 2, 1990, New York, NY. *Educ.* Liverpool College. Suave leading man best remembered for his patrician roles of the 1960s, especially in *My Fair Lady* (1964). Harrison's earlier career was built on a flair for sophisticated comedy, best displayed in the Preston Sturges classic *Unfaithfully Yours* (1948). Four of his six wives were actresses: Lilli Palmer, Kay Kendall, Rachel Roberts and Elizabeth Harris. • *The Great Game* 1930; *School For Scandal* 1930; *Get Your Man* 1934; *Leave It to Blanche* 1934; *All at Sea* 1935; *Men Are Not Gods* 1936; *Over the Moon* 1937; *School For Husbands* 1937; *Storm in a Teacup* 1937; *The Citadel* 1938;

St. Martin's Lane W.C.2 1938; *The Silent Battle* 1939; *Ten Days in Paris* 1939; *Night Train to Munich* 1940; *Major Barbara* 1941; *Blithe Spirit* 1945; *I Live in Grosvenor Square* 1945; *The Rake's Progress* 1945; *Anna and the King of Siam* 1946; *The Foxes of Harrow* 1947; *The Ghost and Mrs. Muir* 1947; *Escape* 1948; *Unfaithfully Yours* 1948; *The Long Dark Hall* 1951; *The Four Poster* 1952; *Main Street to Broadway* 1953; *The Constant Husband* 1954; *King Richard and the Crusaders* 1954; *The Reluctant Debutante* 1958; *Midnight Lace* 1960; *The Happy Thieves* 1962; *Cleopatra* 1963 **(AANBA)**; *My Fair Lady* 1964 **(AABA)**; *The Yellow Rolls-Royce* 1964; *The Agony and the Ecstasy* 1965; *Doctor Dolittle* 1967; *The Honey Pot* 1967; *A Flea in Her Ear* 1968; *Staircase* 1969; *Crossed Swords* 1977; *The 5th Musketeer* 1979; *Ashanti* 1979; *A Time to Die* 1979.

Harry, Debbie • Actress, singer • Born Deborah Harry, Miami, FL. *Educ.* Centenary College. Photogenic former singer for pop group Blondie who demonstrated a degree of acting talent in *Union City* (1980) and David Cronenberg's *Videodrome* (1983). Harry has also performed the theme songs for several films. • *The Foreigner* 1977 (a); *Mr. Mike's Mondo Video* 1979 (a); *Just Before Dawn* 1980 (song); *Little Darlings* 1980 (song); *Roadie* 1980 (a); *Union City* 1980 (a); *Endless Love* 1981 (song); *Polyester* 1981 (song); *The Last American Virgin* 1982 (song); *Partners* 1982 (song); *Party, Party* 1982 (song); *Rock Rule* 1982 (songs); *Wild Style* 1982 (song); *Scarface* 1983 (songs); *Videodrome* 1983 (a); *Forever, Lulu* 1986 (a); *The Money Pit* 1986 (songs); *Heaven* 1987 (assistance); *Hairspray* 1988 (a); *Married to the Mob* 1988 (song); *My Best Friend Is a Vampire* 1988 (song); *A Nightmare on Elm Street 4: The Dream Master* 1988 (song); *Satisfaction* 1988 (a); *New York Stories* 1989 (a); *Tales From the Darkside, The Movie* 1990 (a).

Harryhausen, Ray • Animator, special effects artist; also producer. • Born Los Angeles, CA, 1920. *Educ.* Los Angeles City College. Renowned for his work in model and puppet animation. Harryhausen enlived numerous horror and fantasy films of the 1950s through the 80s, creating rampaging behemoths for *Mighty Joe Young* (1949), battling skeleton armies for *Jason and the Argonauts* (1963) and Raquel Welch-threatening prehistoric beasts for *One Million Years B.C.* (1966). • *Mighty Joe Young* 1949 (fx); *The Animal World* 1956 (anim); *Twenty Million Miles to Earth* 1957 (story); *The 7th Voyage of Sinbad* 1958 (fx); *Jason and the Argonauts* 1963 (assoc.p, fx); *One Million Years B.C.* 1966 (fx); *The Golden Voyage of Sinbad* 1973 (fx,p); *Sinbad and the Eye of the Tiger* 1977 (p,story,fx); *Clash of the Titans* 1981 (fx,p); *Spies Like Us* 1985 (a); *The Fantasy Film World of George Pal* 1986 (a); *The Puppetoon Movie* 1986 (Puppetoon creative artist—USA).

Hart, William S. • Actor; also director, producer. • Born William Surrey Hart, Newburgh, NY, December 6, 1870; died 1946. Serious-looking hero of silent westerns and the genre's first bona fide star. Beginning in 1914, Hart helped define the genre, insisting on authentic recreations of the "old west" and often leaning more toward character development than adventure. By the early 1920s his style had been superseded by more action-oriented westerns and his popularity began to decline. Hart later turned to writing, authoring several western novels and an autobiography, *My Life—East and West* (1929). • *The Bargain* 1914 (a); *His Hour of Manhood* 1914 (a); *Jim Cameron's Wife* 1914 (a); *The Passing of Two-Gun Hicks* 1914 (a,d); *The Bad Buck of Santa Ynez* 1915 (a,d); *Cash Parrish's Pal* 1915 (a,d); *The Conversion of Frosty Blake* 1915 (a,d); *The Darkening Trail* 1915 (a,d); *The Disciple* 1915 (a,d); *The Grudge* 1915 (a,d); *Keno Bates, Liar* 1915 (a,d); *Knight of the Trails* 1915 (a,d); *The Man From Nowhere* 1915 (a,d); *Mr. Silent Haskins I915 (a,d); On the Night Stage* 1915 (a); *Pinto Ben* 1915 (a,d,story,from poem); *The Roughneck* 1915 (a,d); *The Ruse* 1915 (a,d); *Scourge of the Desert* 1915 (a,d); *The Sheriff's Streak of Yellow* 1915 (a,d); *The Taking of Luke McVane* 1915 (a,d); *Tools of Providence* 1915 (a,d); *The Apostle of Vengeance* 1916 (a,d); *The Aryan* 1916 (a,d); *Between Men* 1916 (a,d); *The Captive God* 1916 (a); *The Dawn Maker* 1916 (a,d); *The Devil's Double* 1916 (a,d); *The Gun Fighter* 1916 (a,d); *Hell's Hinges* 1916 (a,d); *The Patriot* 1916 (a,d); *The Primal Lure* 1916 (a,d); *The Return of Draw Egan* 1916 (a,d); *The Sheriff* 1916 (a); *Wolf Lowry* 1916 (a,d); *The Cold Deck* 1917 (a,d); *The Desert Man* 1917 (a,d); *The Narrow Trail* 1917 (a,d,sc); *The Silent Man* 1917 (a,d); *The Square Deal Man* 1917 (a,d); *Truthful Tulliver* 1917 (a,d); *Blue Blazes Rawden* 1918 (a,d); *The Border Wireless* 1918(a,d); *Branding Broadway* 1918 (a,d); *Riddle Gawne* 1918 (a,d); *Selfish Yates* 1918 (a,d); *Shark Monroe* 1918 (a,d); *The Tiger Man* 1918 (a,d); *Wolves of the Rail* 1918 (a,d); *Breed of Men* 1919 (a); *John Petticoats* 1919 (a); *The Money Corral* 1919 (a,sc,story); *The Poppy Girl's Husband* 1919 (a,d); *Square Deal Sanderson* 1919 (a); *Wagon Tracks* 1919 (a); *The Cradle of Courage* 1920 (a); *Sand* 1920 (a); *The Testing Block* 1920 (a,story); *The Toll Gate* 1920 (a,p,story); *The Whirlwind* 1920 (a,p); *O'Malley of the Mounted* 1921 (a,p,story); *Three Word Brand* 1921 (a,p); *The Whistle* 1921 (a); *White Oak* 1921 (a,p,story); *Travelin' On* 1922 (a,p,story); *Hollywood* 1923 (a); *Wild Bill Hickok* 1923 (a,p,story); *Singer Jim McKee* 1924 (a,p,story); *Tumbleweeds* 1925 (a,p); *Show People* 1928 (a); *O'Malley of the Mounted* 1936 (story).

Harvey, Laurence • aka Laruschka Mischa Skikne • Actor; also director • Born Hirsch Skikne, Yomishkis, Lithuania, October 1, 1928; died 1973. *Educ.* RADA, London. Harvey moved to England in 1946 after a spell in South Africa and made his film debut two years later. He went on to establish himself as a leading talent of the 1950s and 60s, noted for his cool charm and confidence. Harvey's role as the womanizing social climber in the 1958 classic *Room at the Top* led to parts in prestigious Hollywood films, including *Butterfield 8* (1960) opposite Elizabeth Taylor and *The Manchurian Candidate* (1962) with Frank Sinatra. He also directed two films. Harvey died of cancer at age 45. • *House of Darkness* 1948; *Landfall* 1949; *The Man From Yesterday* 1949; *Man on the Run* 1949; *The Black Rose* 1950; *Cairo Road* 1950; *I Believe in You* 1951; *Scarlet Thread* 1951; *There Is Another Sun* 1951; *A Killer Walks* 1952; *Women of Twilight* 1952; *Innocents in Paris* 1953; *The Good Die Young* 1954; *King Richard and the Crusaders* 1954; *Romeo and Juliet* 1954; *I Am a Camera* 1955; *Storm Over the Nile* 1955; *Three Men in a Boat* 1956; *After the Ball* 1957; *Room at the Top* 1958 **(AANBA)**; *The Silent Enemy* 1958; *The Truth About Women* 1958; *Expresso Bongo* 1959; *The Alamo* 1960; *Butterfield 8* 1960; *The Long and the Short and the Tall* 1961; *Summer and Smoke* 1961; *Two Loves* 1961; *A Girl Named Tamiko* 1962; *The Manchurian Candidate* 1962; *Walk on the Wild Side* 1962; *The Wonderful World of the Brothers Grimm* 1962; *The Ceremony* 1963 (a,add.dial,d,p); *The Running Man* 1963; *Of Human Bondage* 1964; *The Outrage* 1964; *Darling* 1965; *Life at the Top* 1965; *The Spy With a Cold Nose* 1966; *The Winter's Tale* 1966; *A Dandy in Aspic* 1968 (a,d); *Kampf um Rom* 1968; *Rebus* 1968; *L'Assoluto Naturale* 1969 (a,p); *Kampf um Rom II: Der Verrat* 1969; *The 43 Magic Christian* 1970; *Tchaikovsky* 1970; *WUSA* 1970; *Habricha el Hashemesh* 1972; *Night Watch* 1973; *Vérités et Mensonges/"F" For Fake* 1973; *Welcome to Arrow Beach* 1974 (a,d).

Hathaway, Henry • Director; also producer. • Born Henri Leopold de Fiennes, Sacramento, CA, March 13, 1898; died February 11,1985, Los Angeles, CA. The archetypal studio professional, Hathaway began working in films before the industry had settled in Hollywood. During his 40-year career he directed over 60 features (including Paramount's first Technicolor picture, 1936's *The Trail of the Lonesome Pine*), became a pioneer of location shooting, and developed a reputation as a technically accomplished, reliable entertainer. (He later bemoaned the familiar tag of "genial hack" which he had earned, he said, because of his reluctance to indulge in personal promotion.)

Hathaway began his career in San Diego,

as a child actor in one-reelers directed by Allan Dwan, before moving to Hollywood with his actress mother. Both worked for T.H. Ince, and then for Universal, where Hathaway returned after WWI. His first shot at directing came at Paramount in the early 1930s, where he remade eight Zane Grey stories that had been shot as silent films, often using footage from the originals. All but one of these starred Randolph Scott, and Hathaway went on to direct Gary Cooper, Marlene Dietrich and Mae West before moving in 1940 to 20th Century-Fox, where he worked almost exclusively for the next 20 years. His *The House on 92nd Street* (1945) marked the beginning of the semi-documentary filmmaking style popular in Hollywood after WWII. • *Damon and Pythias* 1914 (props); *The Dumb Girl of Portici* 1916 (props); *The Storm Boy* 1917 (a); *Blind Husbands* 1919 (props); *Foolish Wives* 1922 (props); *The Spoilers* 1923 (ad); *To the Last Man* 1923 (ad); *The Border Legion* 1924 (ad); *The Heritage of the Desert* 1924 (ad); *Ben Hur, A Tale of the Christ* 1925 (prod.asst); *The Thundering Herd* 1925 (ad); *Wild Horse Mesa* 1925 (ad); *Bachelor Brides* 1926 (ad); *Man of the Forest* 1926 (ad); *Mantrap* 1926 (ad); *Hula* 1927 (ad); *The Rough Riders* 1927 (ad); *Underworld* 1927 (ad); *The Last Command* 1928 (ad); *Under the Tonto Rim* 1928 (ad); *Redskin* 1929 (ad); *The Shopworn Angel* 1929 (ad); *Sunset Pass* 1929 (ad); *Thunderbolt* 1929 (ad); *The Virginian* 1929 (ad); *Wolf Song* 1929 (ad); *Morocco* 1930 (ad); *Seven Days Leave* 1930 (ad); *The Texan* 1930 (ad); *Dishonored* 1931 (ad); *Heritage of the Desert* 1932 (d); *Shanghai Express* 1932 (ad); *Wild Horse Mesa* 1932 (d); *Man of the Forest* 1933 (d); *Sunset Pass* 1933 (d); *The Thundering Herd* 1933 (d); *To the Last Man* 1933 (d); *Under the Tonto Rim* 1933 (d); *Come on Marines* 1934 (d); *The Last Round-Up* 1934 (d); *Now and Forever* 1934 (d); *The Witching Hour* 1934 (d); *The Lives of a Bengal Lancer* 1935 (d) **(AANBD)**; *Peter Ibbetson* 1935 (d); *Go West, Young Man* 1936 (d); *I Loved a Soldier* 1936 (d); *The Trail of the Lonesome Pine* 1936 (d); *Souls at Sea* 1937 (d,p); *Spawn of the North* 1938 (d); *The Real Glory* 1939 (d); *Brigham Young, Frontiersman* 1940 (d); *Johnny Apollo* 1940 (d); *The Shepherd of the Hills* 1941 (d); *Sundown* 1941 (d); *China Girl* 1942 (d); *Ten Gentlemen From West Point* 1942 (d); *Home in Indiana* 1944 (d); *Wing and a Prayer* 1944 (d); *The House on 92nd Street* 1945 (d); *Nob Hill* 1945 (d); *The Dark Corner* 1946 (d); *13 Rue Madeleine* 1947 (d); *The Kiss of Death* 1947 (d); *Call Northside777* 1948 (d); *Down to the Sea in Ships* 1949 (d); *The Black Rose* 1950 (d); *The Desert Fox* 1951 (d); *Fourteen Hours* 1951 (d); *Rawhide* 1951 (d); *U.S.S. Tea Kettle* 1951 (d); *Diplomatic Courier* 1952 (d); *0. Henry's Full House* 1952 (d); *Red Skies of Montana* 1952 (d); *Niagara* 1953 (d); *White Witch Doctor* 1953 (d); *Garden of Evil* 1954 (d); *Prince Valiant* 1954 (d); *The Racers* 1955 (d); *23 Paces to Baker Street* 1956 (d); *The Bottom of the Bottle* 1956 (d); *Legend of the Lost* 1957 (d,p); *The Wayward Bus* 1957 (d); *From Hell to Texas* 1958 (d); *Woman Obsessed* 1959 (d); *North to Alaska* 1960 (d,p); *Seven Thieves* 1960 (d); *How the West Was Won* 1962 (d); *Rampage* 1963 (d); *Circus World* 1964 (d); *Of Human Bondage* 1964 (d); *The Sons of Katie Elder* 1965 (d); *Nevada Smith* 1966 (d,p); *The Last Safari* 1967 (d,p); *5 Card Stud* 1968 (d); *True Grit* 1969 (d); *Airport* 1970 (add seq.d); *Raid on Rommel* 1971 (d); *Shoot Out* 1971 (d); *75 Years of Cinema Museum* 1972 (a); *Hangup* 1973 (d).

Hatton, Maurice • Director, screenwriter; also producer. • Born Britain. Once called "the most incorruptibly independent" of British filmmakers, Maurice Hatton has managed to combine politics, humor—and even, on occasion, minor commercial success—in a remarkable career. After a series of well-received documentaries in the 60s made with then-partner John Irvin, Hatton burst upon the scene with his first feature, *Praise Marx and Pass the Ammunition* (1968), combining sophisticated political analysis with a ripe and urgent sense of humor in a unique way. The story of Dom, a revolutionary with a reactionary personality, the film dares to satirize the avant-garde politicos of the 60s at the same time that it shares their passionate commitment. It showed us then—and continues to show us now—where we went wrong. It remains a landmark, 20 years ahead of its time. Almost alone among contemporary British filmmakers, Hatton has been able keep the satiric flame burning on the big screen.

During most of the 70s and 80s, Hatton kept himself busy with TV: *The Bouncing Boy* (1972), *Bitter Harvest* (1973, about Cesar Chavez and the California migrant workers) and *Nelly's Version* (1983) stand out. Occasionally during the last 20 years Hatton has been able to raise the necessary funds for a feature. *Long Shot* (1978) satirized the film industry on a minuscule budget. *American Roulette* (1988) starred Andy Garcia and did well on the festival circuit. As Hatton says, "the thing about the independent area is that films go from production to retrospective without the intervening stage of distribution." JM • *Praise Marx and Pass the Ammunition* 1968 (d,p,sc); *Long Shot* 1978 (d,p,ph, story); *Nelly's Version* 1983 (d,sc); *The Rewards of Virtue* 1983 (d,sc); *American Roulette/Latin Roulette* 1988 (d,sc).

Hauer, Rutger • Actor • Born Breukelen, Netherlands, January 23, 1944. Strikingly handsome, powerfully built leading man who made his screen debut in Paul Verhoeven's international erotic success, *Turkish Delight* (1973). Hauer's villainous roles have attracted more attention than his heroic ones, though he was superb as one of the aristocratic resistance fighters in Verhoeven's *Soldier of Orange* (1979). The intensity of his performances has contributed to the cult success of films such as *Blade Runner* (1982) and *The Hitcher* (1986). • *Turkish Delight* 1973; *Pusteblume* 1974; *Keetje Tippel* 1975; *The Wilby Conspiracy* 1975; *Max Havelaar* 1976; *Mysteries* 1978; *Soldier of Orange* 1979; *Een Vrouw Tussen Hond en Wolf* 1979; *Spetters* 1980; *Chanel Solitaire* 1981; *Nighthawks* 1981; *Blade Runner* 1982; *Eureka* 1983; *Grijpstra & De Gier* 1983; *The Osterman Weekend* 1983; *A Breed Apart* 1984; *Flesh + Blood* 1985; *Ladyhawke* 1985; *The Hitcher* 1986; *Wanted Dead or Alive* 1986; *La Leggenda del Santo Bevitore* 1988; *Blind Fury* 1989; *The Blood of Heroes* 1989; *Bloodhounds of Broadway* 1989; *In una notte di chiaro di luna* 1989 (a,dial).

Hawkins, Jack • Actor • Born John Edward Hawkins, London, September 1, 1910; died 1973. *Educ.* Italia Conti School of Acting. Best remembered for his numerous portrayals of military men, from the indomitable Major Warden in *The Bridge on the River Kwai* (1957) to the officer-turned-criminal mastermind in Basil Dearden's humorous *The League of Gentlemen* (1960). Although he lost his voice after an operation for cancer of the larynx in 1966, Hawkins continued to perform, with other actors dubbing his lines. He was married to actress Jessica Tandy from 1932 to 1942. • *Birds of Prey* 1930; *The Lodger* 1932; *The Good Companions* 1933; *I Lived With You* 1933; *The Jewel* 1933; *The Lost Chord* 1933; *A Shot in the Dark* 1933; *Autumn Crocus* 1934; *Death at Broadcasting House* 1934; *Peg of Old Drury* 1935; *Beauty and the Barge* 1937; *The Frog* 1937; *A Royal Divorce* 1938; *Who Goes Next?* 1938; *Murder Will Out* 1939; *The Flying Squad* 1940; *Next of Kin* 1942; *Bonnie Prince Charlie* 1948; *Fallen Idol* 1948; *The Small Back Room* 1948; *The Black Rose* 1950; *The Elusive Pimpernel* 1950; *State Secret* 1950; *The Adventurers* 1951; *Home at Seven* 1951; *No Highway* 1951; *Angels One Five* 1952; *Mandy* 1952; *The Planter's Wife* 1952; *The Cruel Sea* 1953; *The Intruder* 1953; *Malta Story* 1953; *Twice Upon a Time* 1953; *Front Page Story* 1954; *The Seekers* 1954; *Land of the Pharaohs* 1955; *The Prisoner* 1955; *Touch and Go* 1955; *The Long Arm* 1956; *The Man in the Sky* 1956; *The Bridge on the River Kwai* 1957; *Fortune Is a Woman* 1958; *Gideon's Day* 1958; *The Two-Headed Spy* 1958; *Ben-Hur* 1959; *The League of Gentlemen* 1960; *Two Loves* 1961; *Five Finger Exercise* 1962; *Lafayette* 1962; *Lawrence of Arabia* 1962; *Rampage* 1963; *Zulu* 1963; *Guns at Batasi* 1964; *The Third Secret* 1964; *Lord Jim* 1965; *Masquerade* 1965; *The Party's Over* 1965 (exec.p); *Judith* 1966; *The Poppy Is*

Also a Flower 1966; *Great Catherine* 1968; *Shalako* 1968; *Goodbye, Mr. Chips* 1969 (uncred exec.p); *Monte Carlo or Bust!* 1969; *Oh! What a Lovely War* 1969; *The Adventures of Gerard* 1970; *Twinky* 1970; *Waterloo* 1970; *The Beloved* 1971; *Kidnapped* 1971; *Nicholas and Alexandra* 1971; *When Eight Bells Toll* 1971; *Habricha el Hashemesh* 1972; *The Ruling Class* 1972 (p); *Young Winston* 1972; *The Last Lion* 1973; *Tales That Witness Madness* 1973; *Theatre of Blood* 1973.

Hawks, Howard • Director; also producer, screenwriter. • Born Howard Winchester Hawks, Goshen, IN, May 30, 1896; died December 26, 1977, Palm Springs, CA. *Educ.* Cornell (mechanical engineering). Widely acknowledged as one of the greatest American filmmakers, Hawks' career virtually spans the Hollywood studio era. In the summers of 1916 and 1917 Hawks had his first experiences with the movies, working in the props department of Famous Players–Lasky during his college vacations. After serving in the armed forces during WWI, Hawks worked as a racecar driver, aviator, and a designer in an aircraft factory—experiences that would later inform both his choice of subjects and his style as a director. He independently produced several films for director Allan Dwan and took a job with the script department of Famous Players-Lasky, where he worked, mostly uncredited, on the scripts of dozens of movies. (He also worked uncredited on the screenplays of all the films he directed.) Hawks wrote his first screenplay, *Tiger Love*, in 1924 and directed his first film, *The Road to Glory*, in 1925.

Although he made eight films during the silent era, it was with the coming of sound that Hawks began to hit his stride. He used sound expressively, his characters frequently delivering their lines at an unnaturally rapid pace. Indeed, Hawks was one of the few Hollywood directors to employ overlapping sound; as a result, dialogue in many of his films is delivered with the rhythm of machine-gun fire. These staccato bursts of speech reveal a fascination with the American language (made explicit in *Ball of Fire* 1941, with its conflict between Barbara Stanwyck's street slang and Gary Cooper's educated diction) and sustain the breakneck tempo of his comedies (perhaps best exemplified by Cary Grant's performance in *His Girl Friday* 1940).

Hawks worked well with actors, preferring to let his camera dwell on them rather than to impose his presence through visual style. Katharine Hepburn, Rosalind Russell and Ann Sheridan gave some of their best performances in Hawks comedies, and Lauren Bacall and Paula Prentiss established their careers under his direction. Cary Grant and John Wayne each enjoyed five of their best roles in Hawks films, with Wayne giving a great performance as the aging yet stubborn rancher Tom Dunson in *Red River* (1948). Hawks once defined a good director as "someone who doesn't annoy you." Consequently, his camerawork is generally more functional than florid. (The repeated motif of the cross in the early *Scarface* [1930, released 1932] is an example of the kind of editorial device that Hawks would soon abandon.) He preferred to position his camera at eye level, where it could best capture the crucial bits of physical business performed by his actors. In Hawks' movies, gestures—as in the way people roll, light and pass cigarettes—become important signifiers of character. According to Andrew Sarris, few other filmmakers have explored the implications of gesture as fully as Hawks. Similarly, with the exception of the labyrinthine whodunit *The Big Sleep* (1946), the narrative structure of Hawks' films is relatively straightforward. It has often been remarked that in all of his features, not once is there a flashback.

Hawks worked in virtually every genre. He made gangster films (*The Criminal Code* 1930, *Scarface* 1932), war films (*The Dawn Patrol* 1930, *Air Force* 1943), westerns (*Red River* 1948, *Rio Bravo* 1959), films noir (*The Big Sleep*), musicals (*Gentlemen Prefer Blondes* 1953), epics (*Land of the Pharaohs* 1955) and science fiction films (*The Thing* 1951, which he produced and, uncredited, partly directed). He is well known for both his sprawling action films (*The Crowd Roars* 1932, *Only Angels Have Wings* 1939) and for his screwball comedies (*Bringing Up Baby* 1938, *Monkey Business* 1952), a genre which some claim begins with his *Twentieth Century* (1934).

Across this generic range, Hawks consistently examined the nature and responsibilities of professionalism—defined as a cluster of values that includes honor, self–esteem and an unswerving devotion to getting a job done in the face of adversity. Hawks' view of such "masculine" professionalism is similar to the idea of "grace under pressure" explored in fiction by his close friend, Ernest Hemingway. Frequently in Hawks' films, a group of men are isolated from civilization, both physically and spiritually, and must fight against both nature and themselves to achieve their goal. In *Only Angels Have Wings*, the men fly mail planes in and out of the Andes; in *Air Force* they work as a unit on a B–17 bomber; in *Red River* the cowhands attempt to drive cattle along the Chisholm Trail; in *The Thing* the soldiers destroy a hostile alien in their isolated post at the North Pole. Removed from civilization, the group defines itself existentially, its purpose only to survive and to succeed. In most of these films conflict arises when a woman—embodying an emotional quality that threatens the stoic nature of Hawksian professionalism—intervenes; inevitably, she must be won over to the masculine point of view.

Hawks' movies would be of minimal interest if their vision were limited to the narrow notions of masculine professionalism offered in the action films. However, as several critics have observed, the moral thrust of the action films is inverted in the comedies, which offer a "feminine" counterweight to their celebration of masculine professionalism. As phrased in Robin Wood's influential study of Hawks, the "Self–Respect and Responsibility" of the action films is undermined by "The Lure of Irresponsibility" in the comedies. In these movies, the female characters are depicted as representing a joyous release and freedom from the constricting and dull responsibilities of professional life. Here, such values as warmth, openness and a sense of humor are celebrated. Perhaps the clearest expression of this alternative view is the end of *Bringing Up Baby*, in which Katharine Hepburn's uninhibited, madcap nature causes the ossified world view of paleontologist Cary Grant—symbolized by his reconstructed dinosaur skeleton—to collapse.

This relationship between the comedies and the action films makes Hawks one of the most interesting of directors from the perspective of classical auteurism. The meaning of any of the films individually is enhanced by the knowledge of alternatives offered elsewhere in his work. It is no coincidence that in the first issue of *Movie*, the influential auteurist journal from Great Britain, dated May 1962, only Hawks and Alfred Hitchcock were honored with the designation of "Great" directors. The significance of Hawks' films is indeed greater, more complex, than their individual meanings. Critical opinion does remain divided: for some, Hawks' films express a male adolescent vision of escape from relationships and responsibility that, as Leslie Fiedler and D.H. Lawrence have shown, is so pronounced in classic American fiction; for others, his work explores the cultural neurosis that gives rise to the excesses of machismo. While issues of gender, sexual difference and sexual politics continue to dominate cultural criticism, Hawks' work will remain central. BKG • *A Little Princess* 1917 (props); *Quicksands* 1923 (p,story); *Tiger Love* 1924 (sc); *The Dressmaker From Paris* 1925 (story); *The Road to Glory* 1925 (d,story); *Fig Leaves* 1926 (d,story); *Honesty—The Best Policy* 1926 (story); *The Cradle Snatchers* 1927 (d); *Paid to Love* 1927 (d); *Underworld* 1927 (uncred.sc,casting); *The Air Circus* 1928 (d); *Fazil* 1928 (d); *A Girl in Every Port* 1928 (d,sc,story); *Trent's Last Case* 1929 (d); *Criminal Code* 1930 (d); *The Dawn Patrol* 1930 (d,sc); *The Crowd Roars* 1932 (d,story); *Red Dust* 1932 (uncred.sc); *Scarface* 1932 (a,d,p); *Tiger Shark* 1932 (d); *Today We Live* 1933 (d,p); *Twentieth Century* 1934 (d,p); *Viva Villa*

1934 (d); *Barbary Coast* 1935 (d); *Ceiling Zero* 1935 (d); *Come and Get It* 1936 (d); *The Road to Glory* 1936 (d); *Sutter's Gold* 1936 (uncred.sc); *Captains Courageous* 1937 (uncred.sc); *Bringing Up Baby* 1938 (d,p); *Test Pilot* 1938 (uncred.sc); *Gone With the Wind* 1939 (uncred.sc); *Gunga Din* 1939 (uncred.sc); *Indianapolis Speedway* 1939 (story); *Only Angels Have Wings* 1939 (d,p,story); *His Girl Friday* 1940 (d,p); *Ball of Fire* 1941 (d); *Sergeant York* 1941 (d) **(AANBD)**; *Air Force* 1943 (d); *Corvette K-225* 1943 (p); *The Outlaw* 1943 (d); *To Have and Have Not* 1944 (d,p); *The Big Sleep* 1946 (d,p); *Red River* 1948 (d,p); *A Song Is Born* 1948 (d); *I Was a Male War Bride* 1949 (d); *The Thing* 1951 (p); *The Big Sky* 1952 (d,p); *Monkey Business* 1952 (d); *0.Henry's Full House* 1952 (d); *Gentlemen Prefer Blondes* 1953 (d); *Land of the Pharaohs* 1955 (d,p); *Rio Bravo* 1959 (d,p); *Hatari!* 1962 (d,p); *Man's Favorite Sport?* 1964 (d,p); *Red Line 7000* 1965 (d,p,story); *El Dorado* 1967 (d,p); *Rio Lobo* 1970 (d,p).

Hawn, Goldie • Actress, producer • Born Goldie Jean Hawn, Washington, DC, November 21, 1945. *Educ.* American University, Washington, DC (drama). Feisty former dancer whose gift for comedy helped her make the transition from TV to film via two stage adaptations: *Cactus Flower* (1969) and *There's a Girl in My Soup* (1970). Hawn subsequently established herself as one of Hollywood's most popular stars, appearing in several above-average films in the 1970s and surviving a string of mediocre movies in the 80s. Hawn was formerly married to director Gus Trikonis and comedian Bill Hudson, by whom she has two children; she also has a son by actor Kurt Russell. • *The One and Only, Genuine, Original Family Band* 1968; *Cactus Flower* 1969 **(AABSA)**; *There's a Girl in My Soup* 1970; *$* 1971; *Butterflies Are Free* 1972; *The Girl From Petrovka* 1974; *The Sugarland Express* 1974; *Shampoo* 1975; *The Duchess and the Dirtwater Fox* 1976; *Foul Play* 1978; *Travels With Anita* 1978; *Private Benjamin* 1980 (a,exec.p) **(AANBA)**; *Seems Like Old Times* 1980; *Best Friends* 1982; *Protocol* 1984 (a,exec.p); *Swing Shift* 1984; *Wildcats* 1986 (a,exec.p); *Overboard* 1987; *Bird on a Wire* 1990; *My Blue Heaven* 1990 (exec.p).

Hayden, Sterling • Actor • Born Sterling Relyea Walter, Montclair, NJ, March 26, 1916; died May 23, 1986, Sausalito, CA. Handsome, virile star of the late 1940s and 50s. Hayden spent several years at sea before signing with Paramount in 1940, appearing in two films with future wife Madeleine Carroll before he broke contract to join the Marines. He joined the Communist party in 1946 (he left after six months), and resumed his acting career the following year. Shortly after his superb performance in *The Asphalt Jungle* (1950), Hayden was blacklisted and was unable to work in Hollywood for six months. He then privately called on the FBI to make a statement concerning his former Communist affiliations, but was subpoenaed by HUAC in 1951 and obliged to testify in public. Hayden was then allowed to continue working, though he expressed his guilt over having "named names" in his 1966 autobiography, *Wanderer.* Ironically, in Stanley Kubrick's classic comedy *Dr. Strangelove* (1964), Hayden played the deranged General Jack D. Ripper, whose over-zealous desire to stop the "Communist threat" sets WWIII in motion. • *Bahama Passage* 1941; *Virginia* 1941; *Blaze of Noon* 1947; *Variety Girl* 1947; *El Paso* 1948; *Manhandled* 1949; *The Asphalt Jungle* 1950; *Flaming Feather* 1951; *Journey Into Light* 1951; *The Denver and Rio Grande* 1952; *Flat Top* 1952; *The Golden Hawk* 1952; *Hellgate* 1952; *The Star* 1952; *Fighter Attack* 1953; *Kansas Pacific* 1953; *So Big* 1953;*Take Me to Town* 1953; *Arrow in the Dust* 1954; *Crime Wave* 1954; *Johnny Guitar* 1954; *Naked Alibi* 1954; *Prince Valiant* 1954; *Suddenly* 1954; *Battle Taxi* 1955; *The Come On* 1955; *The Eternal Sea* 1955; *The Last Command* 1955; *Shotgun* 1955; *Timberjack* 1955; *Top Gun* 1955; *Five Steps to Danger* 1956; *The Killing* 1956; *Crime of Passion* 1957; *Gun Battle at Monterey* 1957; *The Iron Sheriff* 1957; *Valerie* 1957; *Zero Hour!* 1957; *Ten Days to Tulara* 1958; *Terror in a Texas Town* 1958; *Dr. Strangelove; or, How I Learned to Stop Worrying and Love the Bomb* 1964; *Hard Contract* 1969; *Tendres Chasseurs* 1969; *Loving* 1970; *Le Saut de l'ange* 1971; *The Godfather* 1972; *Le Grand Départ* 1972; *The Last Days of Man on Earth* 1973; *The Long Goodbye* 1973; *Novecento/1900* 1976; *King of the Gypsies* 1978; *The Outsider* 1979; *Winter Kills* 1979; *9 to 5* 1980; *Gas* 1981; *Venom* 1981; *Leuchtturm des Chaos* 1982; *Der Havarist* 1984 (from book *Wanderer*).

Hayward, Susan • Actress • Born Edythe Marrener, Brooklyn, NY, June 30, 1918; died 1975. Pretty, exuberant leading lady who began her Hollywood career in 1937 as a bit player and was a star by the mid-1940s. Often cast as the defiant heroine, as in *I Want to Live!* (1958), where she plays a woman wrongly sentenced to death. • *Girls on Probation* 1938; *$1,000 a Touchdown* 1939; *Beau Geste* 1939; *Our Leading Citizen* 1939; *Adam Had Four Sons* 1941; *Among the Living* 1941; *Sis Hopkins* 1941; *The Forest Rangers* 1942; *I Married a Witch* 1942; *Reap the Wild Wind* 1942; *Star Spangled Rhythm* 1942; *Hit Parade of 1943* 1943; *Jack London* 1943; *Young and Willing* 1943; *And Now Tomorrow* 1944; *The Fighting Seabees* 1944; *The Hairy Ape* 1944; *Canyon Passage* 1946; *Deadline at Dawn* 1946; *The Lost Moment* 1947; *Smash-Up, the Story of a Woman* 1947 **(AANBA)**; *They Won't Believe Me* 1947; *The Saxon Charm* 1948; *Tap Roots* 1948; *House of Strangers* 1949; *Tulsa* 1949; *My Foolish Heart* 1950 **(AANBA)**; *David and Bathsheba* 1951; *I Can Get It For You Wholesale* 1951; *I'd Climb the Highest Mountain* 1951; *Rawhide* 1951; *The Lusty Men* 1952; *The Snows of Kilimanjaro* 1952; *With a Song in My Heart* 1952 **(AANBA)**; *The President's Lady* 1953; *White Witch Doctor* 1953; *Demetrius and the Gladiators* 1954; *Garden of Evil* 1954; *I'll Cry Tomorrow* 1955 **(AANBA)**; *Soldier of Fortune* 1955; *Untamed* 1955; *The Conqueror* 1956; *Top Secret Affair* 1957; *I Want to Live!* 1958 **(AABA)**; *Thunder in the Sun* 1959; *Woman Obsessed* 1959; *The Marriage-Go-Round* 1960; *Ada* 1961; *Back Street* 1961; *I Thank a Fool* 1962; *Stolen Hours* 1963; *Where Love Has Gone* 1964; *The Honey Pot* 1967; *Valley of the Dolls* 1967; *The Revengers* 1972.

Hayworth, Rita • *aka* Rita Cansino • Actress; also dancer. • Born Margarita Carmen Cansino, Brooklyn, NY, October 17, 1918; died May 14, 1987. Immensely popular red-haired beauty of the 1940s. Dancing professionally with her father from childhood, Hayworth was "discovered" in 1935 and made her Hollywood debut the same year. She appeared in mostly small parts in some 25 films before giving her first substantial performance in Howard Hawks' *Only Angels Have Wings* (1939). In the following decade she became one of Hollywood's greatest stars, a genuinely talented actress and dancer as well as a celebrated WWII pinup.

Hayworth played a vulnerable femme fatale in *Gilda* (1946) and delivered a superbly ruthless variation on the same theme in second husband Orson Welles's *The Lady From Shanghai* (1948), with her trademark long red hair cut short and dyed blonde. Most of her later films were unexceptional, though both *Pal Joey* (1957) and particularly *Separate Tables* (1958) demonstrated a mature talent.

Hayworth died of Alzheimer's disease at age 68 and for the last six years of her life had been cared for by Princess Yasmin Aga Khan, her daughter by third husband, international playboy, Prince Aly Khan. • *Cruz diablo* 1934; *Charlie Chan in Egypt* 1935; *Dante's Inferno* 1935; *In Caliente* 1935; *Paddy O'Day* 1935; *Under the Pampas Moon* 1935; *Human Cargo* 1936; *Meet Nero Wolfe* 1936; *Rebellion* 1936; *Criminals of the Air* 1937; *The Game That Kills* 1937; *Girls Can Play* 1937; *Hit the Saddle* 1937; *Old Louisiana* 1937; *Paid to Dance* 1937; *The Shadow* 1937; *Trouble in Texas* 1937; *Convicted* 1938; *Homicide Bureau* 1938; *Juvenile Court* 1938; *Special Inspector* 1938; *Who Killed Gail Preston?* 1938; *The Lone Wolf Spy Hunt* 1939; *Only Angels Have Wings* 1939; *The Renegade Ranger* 1939; *Angels Over Broadway* 1940; *Blondie on a Budget* 1940; *The Lady in Question* 1940; *Music in My Heart* 1940; *Susan and God* 1940; *Affectionately Yours* 1941; *Blood and Sand* 1941; *The Strawberry Blonde* 1941; *You'll Never Get*

Rich 1941; *My Gal Sal* 1942; *Tales of Manhattan* 1942; *You Were Never Lovelier* 1942; *Cover Girl* 1944; *Tonight and Every Night* 1945; *Gilda* 1946; *Down to Earth* 1947; *The Lady From Shanghai* 1948; *The Loves of Carmen* 1948; *Affair in Trinidad* 1952; *Miss Sadie Thompson* 1953; *Salome* 1953; *Fire Down Below* 1957; *Pal Joey* 1957; *Separate Tables* 1958; *The Story on Page One* 1959; *They Came to Cordura* 1959; *The Happy Thieves* 1962; *Circus World* 1964; *The Money Trap* 1966; *The Poppy Is Also a Flower* 1966; *L'Avventuriero* 1967; *I Bastardi* 1969; *The Naked Zoo* 1970; *La Route de Salina* 1970; *The Wrath of God* 1972; *Circle* 1976; *Going Hollywood: The War Years* 1988 (archival footage).

Head, Edith • Costume designer • Born Los Angeles, CA, October 28, 1907; died 1981. *Educ.* UCLA; Stanford. With 35 Academy Award nominations, 8-time Oscar winner Edith Head emerged from Hollywood's fitting rooms to become a household name. One of the film industry's first professional women, she became a major American fashion force, designing for Vogue patterns and airlines as well. Her ability to shape each gown to a character or image made her as popular with film directors as with the glamour girls she dressed in both their private lives and screen roles. Yet the image she devoted the most work to was her own. Her friendly frankness led to regular appearances on Art Linkletter's daytime television show in the 1950s, offering advice to the unchic.

Born in California, Head studied at Stanford and was teaching French in 1923 at the Hollywood School for Girls when she bluffed her way into Paramount's wardrobe department. The workload might have overwhelmed anyone, but this feisty careerist used the volume and pace of designing for a healthy studio system to hone her style. Although she had a penchant for Mexican designs, Head's own appearance was deliberately severe, neutral and unsensuous, with cropped hair and her signature tinted eyeglasses. Yet she could turn other women into screen sirens.

In the 1920s, her designs transformed Clara Bow's squat body into an object of desire. Head then allowed Jean Harlow to display her best assets with an unforgettable bias-cut slip-dress. Head simplified the fin de siècle raunchiness of Mae West and learned to deal with the censors by covering her up—with skin-tight clothes. In the 1930s, when bare midriffs were the rage, Head learned how to get around the cinema censors' horror of the female navel. For the Biblical epic, *Samson and Delilah* (1949), Head created a famous peacock cape for Hedy Lamarr, extravagant even by Head's standards. She made Dorothy Lamour's sarong, Barbara Stanwyck's Latin American wardrobe for *The Lady Eve* (1941), the definitive tailored suit for Marlene Dietrich, the wasp-waisted gowns of Mary Martin, Veronica Lake, Bette Davis and Elizabeth Taylor, and, for Ingrid Bergman, men's clothes (*For Whom the Bell Tolls* 1943), a nun's habit (*The Bells of St. Mary's* 1945) and subtle espionage gear (*Notorious* 1946). Her talents were trumpeted by studio publicity departments determined to seize on fashion in films as a way of diverting attention from Paris and making Hollywood the arbiter of taste.

The "look" that stands out in Head's spectrum of styles is best exemplified in her designs for Hitchcock's blondes, particularly Grace Kelly's discreet sexiness, which she adapted for Audrey Hepburn and Natalie Wood.

In 1967, Head's contract at Paramount expired and was not renewed, despited 44 years of service. She moved her operation to Universal Studios and continued her workaholic pattern until her final film, *Dead Men Don't Wear Plaid* (1982), for which she adapted her own original designs for Steve Martin. Another of Head's male sartorial achievements was *The Sting* (1973), which launched one of many Head-inspired trends. In some 750 films through six decades, Head shaped the industry in the shape of its stars. KJ • *She Done Him Wrong* 1933 (cost); *Poppy* 1936 (cost); *The Lady Eve* 1941 (cost); *I Married a Witch* 1942 (cost); *For Whom the Bell Tolls* 1943 (cost); *The Bells of St. Mary's* 1945 (cost); *The Blue Dahlia* 1946 (cost); *Notorious* 1946 (cost); *The Accused* 1948 (cost); *The Big Clock* 1948 (cost); *The Emperor Waltz* 1948 (cost) **(AANBCD)**; *Beyond the Forest* 1949 (cost); *The File on Thelma Jordan* 1949 (cost); *The Heiress* 1949 (cost) **(AABCD)**; *Samson and Delilah* 1949 (cost) **(AABCD)**; *All About Eve* 1950 (cost) **(AABCD)**; *Dark City* 1950 (cost); *Detective Story* 1951 (cost); *A Place in the Sun* 1951 (cost) **(AABCD)**; *Carrie* 1952 (cost) **(AANBCD)**; *The Greatest Show on Earth* 1952 (cost) **(AANBCD)**; *Roman Holiday* 1953 (cost) **(AABCD)**; *Rear Window* 1954 (cost); *Run For Cover* 1954 (cost); *Sabrina* 1954 (cost) **(AABCD)**; *Artists and Models* 1955 (cost); *The Desperate Hours* 1955 (cost); *The Far Horizons* 1955 (cost); *The Girl Rush* 1955 (cost); *Hell's Island* 1955 (cost); *Lucy Gallant* 1955 (a,cost); *The Rose Tattoo* 1955 (cost) **(AANBCD)**; *The Scarlet Hour* 1955 (cost); *The Seven Little Foys* 1955 (cost); *Strategic Air Command* 1955 (cost); *To Catch a Thief* 1955 (cost) **(AANBCD)**; *The Trouble With Harry* 1955 (cost); *You're Never Too Young* 1955 (gowns); *Anything Goes* 1956 (cost); *The Birds and the Bees* 1956 (cost); *The Court Jester* 1956 (cost); *Fear Strikes Out* 1956 (cost); *Hollywood or Bust* 1956 (cost); *The Leather Saint* 1956 (cost); *The Man Who Knew Too Much* 1956 (cost); *The Mountain* 1956 (cost); *Pardners* 1956 (cost); *The Proud and the Profane* 1956 (cost) **(AANBCD)**; *The Rainmaker* 1956 (cost); *The Search For Bridey Murphy* 1956 (cost); *The Ten Commandments* 1956 (cost) **(AANBCD)**; *That Certain Feeling* 1956 (cost); *Three Violent People* 1956 (cost); *Beau James* 1957 (cost); *The Buster Keaton Story* 1957 (cost); *The Delicate Delinquent* 1957 (cost); *Funny Face* 1957 (cost) **(AANBCD)**; *Gunfight at the O.K. Corral* 1957 (cost); *The Joker Is Wild* 1957 (cost); *The Sad Sack* 1957 (cost); *The Tin Star* 1957 (cost); *Wild Is the Wind* 1957 (cost); *As Young As We Are* 1958 (cost); *The Black Orchid* 1958 (cost); *The Buccaneer* 1958 (cost) **(AANBCD)**; *The Geisha Boy* 1958 (cost); *Hot Spell* 1958 (cost); *Houseboat* 1958 (cost); *King Creole* 1958 (cost); *Maracaibo* 1958 (cost); *The Matchmaker* 1958 (cost); *The Party Crashers* 1958 (cost); *Rock-a-Bye Baby* 1958 (cost); *Separate Tables* 1958 (gowns—Rita Hayworth); *St Louis Blues* 1958 (cost); *Teacher's Pet* 1958 (cost); *Vertigo* 1958 (cost); *Alias Jesse James* 1959 (cost); *But Not For Me* 1959 (cost); *Career* 1959 (cost) **(AANBCD)**; *Don't Give Up the Ship* 1959 (cost); *The Five Pennies* 1959 (cost) **(AANBCD)**; *A Hole in the Head* 1959 (cost); *The Jayhawkers* 1959 (cost); *The Trap* 1959 (cost); *The Facts of Life* 1960 (cost) **(AABCD)**; *Pepe* 1960 (cost) **(AANBCD)**; *All in a Night's Work* 1961 (cost); *A Pocketful of Miracles* 1961 (cost) **(AANBCD)**; *Hatari!* 1962 (cost); *The Man Who Shot Liberty Valance* 1962 (cost) **(AANBCD)**; *My Geisha* 1962 (cost) **(AANBCD)**; *The Birds* 1963 (cost—Tippi Hedren); *Hud* 1963 (cost); *Love With the Proper Stranger* 1963 (cost) **(AANBCD)**; *A New Kind of Love* 1963 (cost) **(AANBCD)**; *Wives and Lovers* 1963 (cost) **(AANBCD)**; *A House Is Not a Home* 1964 (cost) **(AANBCD)**; *Man's Favorite Sport?* 1964 (cost); *Marnie* 1964 (cost—Tippi Hedren/Diane Baker); *What a Way to Go!* 1964 (cost) **(AANBCD)**; *The Family Jewels* 1965 (cost); *The Great Race* 1965 (cost); *Inside Daisy Clover* 1965 (cost) **(AANBCD)**; *Red Line 7000* 1965 (cost); *The Slender Thread* 1965 (cost) **(AANBCD)**; *The Sons of Katie Elder* 1965 (cost); *Assault on a Queen* 1966 (cost—Virna Lisi); *The Oscar* 1966 (a) **(AANBCD)**; *Torn Curtain* 1966 (cost—Julie Andrews); *Barefoot in the Park* 1967 (cost); *El Dorado* 1967 (cost); *Butch Cassidy and the Sundance Kid* 1969 (cost); *The Lost Man* 1969 (cost); *Sweet Charity* 1969 (cost) **(AANBCD)**; *Topaz* 1969 (cost); *Winning* 1969 (cost); *Airport* 1970 (cost) **(AANBCD)**; *Storia di una Donna* 1970 (cost); *Hammersmith Is Out* 1972 (cost—Elizabeth Taylor); *A Doll's House* 1973 (cost—Jane Fonda); *The Don Is Dead* 1973 (cost); *The Sting* 1973 (cost) **(AABCD)**; *Airport 1975* 1975 (cost); *The Great Waldo Pepper* 1975 (cost); *The Man Who Would Be King* 1975 (cost) **(AANBCD)**; *Family Plot* 1976 (cost); *Airport 77* 1977 (cost,cost) **(AANBCD)**; *The Big Fix* 1978 (cost); *A Matter of Love* 1978 (cost); *The Last Married Couple in America* 1979 (cost); *Dead Men Don't Wear Plaid* 1982 (cost).

Headly, Glenne • Actress • Born New London, CT, March 13, 1955. *Educ.* High School for the Performing Arts, New York; Herbert Berghof Studio, New York; American College of Switzerland. Capable lead and supporting actress of the 1980s, with extensive stage experience. Separated from actor John Malkovich. • *Four Friends* 1981; *Eleni* 1985; *Fandango* 1985; *Seize the Day* 1986; *Making Mr. Right* 1987; *Nadine* 1987; *Dirty Rotten Scoundrels* 1988; *Paperhouse* 1988; *Stars and Bars* 1988; *Dick Tracy* 1990; *Mortal Thoughts* 1991.

Heard, John • Actor • Born US, March 7, 1946. Versatile, stage-trained lead and supporting player of the 1980s, particularly charming in *Head Over Heels* (1979). Married to actress Margot Kidder. • *Between the Lines* 1977; *First Love* 1977; *On the Yard* 1978; *Head Over Heels* 1979; *Heart Beat* 1979; *Cutter's Way* 1981; *Cat People* 1982; *Too Scared to Scream* 1982; *Best Revenge* 1984; *C.H.U.D.* 1984; *Violated* 1984; *After Hours* 1985; *Heaven Help Us* 1985; *The Trip to Bountiful* 1986; *Dear America* 1987; *Beaches* 1988; *Betrayed* 1988; *Big* 1988; *The Milagro Beanfield War* 1988; *The Seventh Sign* 1988; *The Telephone* 1988; *The Package* 1989; *Awakenings* 1990; *The End of Innocence* 1990; *Home Alone* 1990; *Mindwalk* 1990.

Hecht, Ben • Screenwriter, playwright; also director, producer, novelist. • Born New York, NY, February 28, 1893; died 1964. Former journalist who entered films in 1927. Alone or in collaboration (often with Charles MacArthur), Hecht wrote some of Hollywood's most acclaimed films of the 1930s and 40s. His credits include the cynical comedy classic *Nothing Sacred* (1937), the superb adaptation of Emily Bronte's *Wuthering Heights* (1939) and Hitchcock's *Notorious* (1946), which has at its center one of filmdom's most compelling villains.

Hecht also worked uncredited on numerous scripts and directed a number of films, none of which were particularly successful. In the late 1940s, due to his outspoken criticism of English policy in Palestine, his name was removed from any of his films shown in British theaters. • *Underworld* 1927 (story) **(AABST)**; *The Big Noise* 1928 (story); *The Great Gabbo* 1929 (story); *The Unholy Night* 1929 (story); *Roadhouse Nights* 1930 (story); *The Front Page* 1931 (from play); *The Unholy Garden* 1931 (sc); *Scarface* 1932 (sc); *Design For Living* 1933 (sc); *Hallelujah, I'm a Bum* 1933 (story); *Turn Back the Clock* 1933 (sc); *Crime Without Passion* 1934 (d,p,sc); *Shoot the Works* 1934 (from play *The Great Magoo*); *Twentieth Century* 1934 (sc,from play); *Upperworld* 1934 (story); *Viva Villa* 1934 (sc) **(AANBSC)**; *Barbary Coast* 1935 (sc,story); *The Florentine Dagger* 1935 (from novel); *Once in a Blue Moon* 1935 (d,p,sc); *The Scoundrel* 1935 (d,p,sc,story) **(AABST)**; *Spring Tonic* 1935 (from play *Man-Eating Tiger*); *Soak the Rich* 1936 (d,p,sc,from play); *Nothing Sacred*1937 (sc); *The Goldwyn Follies* 1938 (sc,story); *Gunga Din* 1939 (adapt); *It's a Wonderful World* 1939 (sc,story); *Lady of the Tropics* 1939 (sc); *Let Freedom Ring* 1939 (sc,story); *Some Like It Hot* 1939 (from play); *Wuthering Heights* 1939 (sc) **(AANBSC)**; *Angels Over Broadway* 1940 (d,p,sc) **(AANBSC)**; *Comrade X* 1940 (sc); *His Girl Friday* 1940 (from play *The Front Page*); *Lydia* 1941 (sc); *The Black Swan* 1942 (sc); *China Girl* 1942 (p,sc); *Tales of Manhattan* 1942 (sc,story); *Spellbound* 1945 (sc); *Notorious* 1946 (sc) **(AANBSC)**; *Specter of the Rose* 1946 (d,sc); *Her Husband's Affairs* 1947 (sc); *The Kiss of Death* 1947 (sc); *Ride the Pink Horse* 1947 (sc); *The Miracle of the Bells* 1948 (sc); *Whirlpool* 1949 (sc); *Edge of Doom* 1950 (sc,narrative text—prologue and epilogue); *Perfect Strangers* 1950 (from play *Ladies and Gentleman*); *Where the Sidewalk Ends* 1950 (sc); *Actors and Sin* 1952 (d,p,sc,from stories *Woman of Sin* and *Actor's Blood*); *Monkey Business* 1952 (sc); *Ulysses* 1953 (sc); *Living It Up* 1954 (m); *The Indian Fighter* 1955 (sc); *Miracle in the Rain* 1956 (sc,from novel); *A Farewell to Arms* 1957 (sc); *Legend of the Lost* 1957 (sc); *The Fiend Who Walked the West* 1958 (from screenplay *Kiss of Death*); *Queen of Outer Space* 1958 (story); *Billy Rose's Jumbo* 1962 (story); *Mutiny on the Bounty* 1962 (uncred.sc); *Circus World* 1964 (sc); *Gaily, Gaily* 1969 (from novel); *The Front Page* 1974 (from play); *Je hais les acteurs* 1986 (from novel *I Hate Actors*); *Switching Channels* 1988 (from play *The Front Page*).

Hecht, Harold • Producer • Born New York, NY, June 1, 1907; died May 26, 1985, Beverly Hills, CA. *Educ.* American Laboratory Theater. With partner Burt Lancaster, one of the first Hollywood producers to break away from the traditional studio system and to handle every aspect of film production on an independent basis. Hecht came to Hollywood as a dance director, having previously performed on the New York stage, with the Metropolitan Opera Co. and with the Martha Graham company. He then became a literary agent, formed Norma Productions with Lancaster shortly after WWII, and went on to enjoy sustained critical and commercial success with films such as *Marty* (1955), *Separate Tables* (1958) and *Cat Ballou* (1965). • *Kiss the Blood Off My Hands* 1948 (exec.p); *The Flame and the Arrow* 1950 (p); *Ten Tall Men* 1951 (p); *The Crimson Pirate* 1952 (p); *The First Time* 1952 (p); *His Majesty O'Keefe* 1953 (p); *Apache* 1954 (p); *Vera Cruz* 1954 (p); *The Kentuckian* 1955 (p); *Marty* 1955 (p) **(AABP)**; *Trapeze* 1956 (p); *The Bachelor Party* 1957 (p); *Sweet Smell of Success* 1957 (exec.p); *Run Silent, Run Deep* 1958 (p); *Separate Tables* 1958 (p) **(AANBP)**; *The Devil's Disciple* 1959 (p); *The Unforgiven* 1960 (p); *The Young Savages* 1961 (exec.p); *Birdman of Alcatraz* 1962 (exec.p); *Taras Bulba* 1962 (p); *Flight From Ashiya* 1964 (p); *Wild and Wonderful* 1964 (p); *Cat Ballou* 1965 (p); *The Way West* 1967 (p).

Heckerling, Amy • Director; also screenwriter. • Born New York, NY, May 7, 1954. *Educ.* NYU Institute of Film and TV; AFI, Los Angeles (directing). One of the few women directors to be regularly working in Hollywood. Heckerling began her career as a TV editor and enjoyed an unexpected box-office success with the 1987 "sleeper" hit, *Look Who's Talking*. Married to writer Neal Israel. • *Fast Times at Ridgemont High* 1982 (d); *Johnny Dangerously* 1984 (d); *Into the Night* 1985 (a); *National Lampoon's European Vacation* 1985 (d); *Look Who's Talking* 1989 (d,sc); *Look Who's Talking Too* 1990 (d,sc,from characters).

Hedren, Tippi • Actress • Born Nathalie Hedren, Lafayette, MN, 1935. Icy blonde known for her leading roles in two Hitchcock films. Mother of actress Melanie Griffith. • *The Birds* 1963; *Marnie* 1964; *A Countess From Hong Kong* 1967; *Satan's Harvest* 1970; *Tiger by the Tail* 1970; *The Harrad Experiment* 1973; *Roar* 1981 (a,p); *Hitchcock, Il Brivido del Genio* 1985; *Deadly Spygames* 1989; *Pacific Heights* 1990.

Heflin, Van • Actor • Born Emmett Evan Heflin, Jr., Walters, OK, December 13, 1910; died 1971, Hollywood, CA. *Educ.* Long Beach Polytechnic, CA; University of Oklahoma; Yale School of Drama. Competent leading man with a flair for playing charming, opportunistic types. *The Prowler* (1951) and *3:10 to Yuma* (1957) show him at two extremes: as a crooked, ruthless cop and an honest, innocent farmer out to help the law. • *A Woman Rebels* 1936; *Annapolis Salute* 1937; *Flight From Glory* 1937; *The Outcasts of Poker Flat* 1937; *Saturday's Heroes* 1937; *Back Door to Heaven* 1939; *The Santa Fe Trail* 1940; *The Feminine Touch* 1941; *H. M. Pulham, Esq.* 1941; *Johnny Eager* 1941 **(AABSA)**; *Grand Central Murder* 1942; *Kid Glove Killer* 1942; *Seven Sweethearts* 1942; *Tennessee Johnson* 1942; *Presenting Lily Mars* 1943; *The Strange Love of Martha Ivers* 1946; *Till the Clouds Roll By* 1946; *B.F.'s Daughter* 1947; *Green Dolphin Street* 1947; *Possessed* 1947; *Act of Violence* 1948; *Tap Roots* 1948; *The Three Musketeers* 1948; *East Side, West Side* 1949; *Madame Bovary* 1949; *The Prowler* 1951; *Tomahawk* 1951; *Weekend With Father* 1951; *My Son John* 1952; *Shane* 1953; *Wings of the Hawk* 1953; *Battle Cry* 1954; *Black Widow* 1954; *The Raid* 1954; *South of Algiers* 1954; *Tanganyika* 1954;

Woman's World 1954; *Count Three and Pray* 1955; *Patterns* 1955; *3:10 to Yuma* 1957; *Gunman's Walk* 1958; *La Tempesta/The Tempest* 1958; *They Came to Cordura* 1959; *Five Branded Women* 1960; *Sotto dieci bandiere/Under Ten Flags* 1960; *Il Relitto* 1961; *Cry of Battle* 1963; *The Greatest Story Ever Told* 1965; *Once a Thief* 1965; *Stagecoach* 1966; *Ognuno Per Se* 1968; *The Big Bounce* 1969; *Airport* 1970.

Hellman, Lillian • Playwright, screenwriter, author • Born New Orleans, LA, June 20, 1905; died June 30, 1984, Martha's Vineyard, MA. *Educ.* NYU; Columbia. Leading American dramatist whose tough, socially conscious dramas achieved critical and commercial success in the 1930s and 40s. Hellman was blacklisted in 1952 for refusing to identify former leftist associates to HUAC with the now-famous declaration that "I cannot and will not cut my conscience to fit this year's fashions." She was portrayed by Jane Fonda in the successful 1977 film *Julia*, based on one of her short stories. • *The Dark Angel* 1935 (sc); *These Three* 1936 (sc,from play *The Children's Hour*); *Dead End* 1937 (sc); *The Little Foxes* 1941 (sc,from play) **(AANBSC)**; *The North Star* 1943 (sc,story) **(AANBSC)**; *Watch on the Rhine* 1943 (add.scenes,dial,from play); *The Searching Wind* 1946 (sc,from play); *Another Part of the Forest* 1948 (from play); *The Children's Hour* 1961 (adapt,from play); *Toys in the Attic* 1963 (from play); *The Chase* 1966 (sc); *Julia* 1977 (from book *Pentimento*); *Directed By William Wyler* 1986 (a).

Hellman, Monte • Director • Born New York, NY, 1932. *Educ.* Stanford (drama); UCLA (film). Hellman began his career under the guidance of Roger Corman and showed considerable promise with his off-beat 1960s westerns and his Warren Oates vehicles of the 70s, particularly *Two-Lane Blacktop* (1971). Lack of commercial success subsequently stymied his directing career. • *Beast From Haunted Cave* 1959 (d); *Creature From the Haunted Sea* 1960 (d); *The LastWoman on Earth* 1960 (2u d); *Ski Troop Attack* 1960 (2u d); *The Terror* 1963 (2u d); *Back Door to Hell* 1964 (d); *Bus Riley's Back in Town* 1965 (asst.ed); *Flight to Fury* 1966 (d,story); *Ride in the Whirlwind* 1966 (d,ed,p); *The Wild Angels* 1966 (ed); *The Long Ride Home* 1967 (ed); *The Shooting* 1967 (d,ed,p); *The St. Valentine's Day Massacre* 1967 (dialogue director); *How to Make It* 1969 (ed); *The Christian Licorice Store* 1971 (a); *Two-Lane Blacktop* 1971 (d,ed); *Cockfighter* 1974 (d); *Call Him Mr. Shatter* 1975 (d); *The Killer Elite* 1975 (ed); *China 9, Liberty 37* 1978 (d,p,sc); *Iguana* 1988 (d,sc,ed); *Silent Night, Deadly Night III: Better Watch Out!* 1989 (d,story).

Hemingway, Mariel • Actress • Born US, November 22, 1961. Beautiful granddaughter of Ernest Hemingway whose abilities were best displayed in *Manhattan* (1979), *Personal Best* (1982) and *Star 80* (1983). Sister Margaux is an actress and successful model. • *Lipstick* 1976; *Manhattan* 1979 **(AANBSA)**; *Personal Best* 1982; *Star 80* 1983; *Creator* 1985; *The Mean Season* 1985; *The Suicide Club* 1987 (a,p); *Superman IV: The Quest For Peace* 1987; *Sunset* 1988; *Fire, Ice and Dynamite* 1990.

Hemmings, David • Actor; also director, producer. • Born Guildford, Surrey, England, November 18, 1941. *Educ.* Epsom School of Art. Hemmings was a professional singer by the age of 9 and an exhibited painter at 15. He entered films in 1950 and is best known for his first starring role, as the photographer in Michelangelo Antonioni's classic portrait of "swinging London," *Blow-Up* (1966). The following year he co-founded the Hemdale Corporation with his business manager John Daly (Hemmings left the company in 1970). He has also directed several films, including *Just a Gigolo* (1979). Hemmings is divorced from actress Gayle Hunnicutt. • *Night and the City* 1950; *The Rainbow Jacket* 1954; *Five Clues to Fortune* 1957; *The Heart Within* 1957; *Saint Joan* 1957; *In the Wake of a Stranger* 1959; *No Trees in the Street* 1959; *The Painted Smile* 1961; *The Wind of Change* 1961; *Play It Cool* 1962; *Some People* 1962; *Live It Up* 1963; *Two Left Feet* 1963; *West 11* 1963; *The System* 1964; *Be My Guest* 1965; *Blow-Up* 1966; *Eye of the Devil* 1966; *Camelot* 1967; *Barbarella* 1968; *The Charge of the Light Brigade* 1968; *Only When I Larf* 1968; *Alfred the Great* 1969; *The Best House in London* 1969; *Fragment of Fear* 1970; *S.W.A.L.K. Melody* 1970 (p); *The Walking Stick* 1970; *The Love Machine* 1971; *Unman, Wittering and Zigo* 1971; *Autobiography* 1972; *Running Scared* 1972 (d,sc); *The 14* 1973 (d); *Voices* 1973; *Juggernaut* 1974; *Mr. Quilp* 1975; *Profondo Rosso* 1975; *Islands in the Stream* 1976; *Crossed Swords* 1977; *Disappearance* 1977 (a,p); *Les Liens de sang* 1977; *The Squeeze* 1977; *Power Play* 1978 (a,p); *Murder By Decree* 1979; *Schöner Gigolo—Armer Gigolo/Just a Gigolo* 1979 (a,d,song); *Thirst* 1979; *Beyond Reasonable Doubt* 1980; *Harlequin* 1980; *Dead Kids* 1981 (exec.p); *Race For the Yankee Zephyr* 1981 (2u d,d,p); *The Survivor* 1981 (d); *Turkey Shoot* 1981 (exec.p); *Man, Woman and Child* 1982; *Prisoners* 1983; *The Rainbow* 1989.

Henley, Beth • Playwright, screenwriter • Born Jackson, MS. *Educ.* Southern Methodist University, Dallas, TX (theater); University of Illinois (theater). Won a Pulitzer prize for her first play, *Crimes of the Heart*, and an Oscar nomination for its screen adaptation five years later. • *Swing Shift* 1984 (a); *Crimes of the Heart* 1986 (sc,from play) **(AANBSC)**; *Nobody's Fool* 1986 (sc,story); *True Stories* 1986 (sc); *Miss Firecracker* 1989 (sc,from play *The Miss Firecracker Contest*).

Henreid, Paul • Actor; also director. • Born Paul George Julius von Henreid, Trieste, Austria-Hungary, January 10, 1908. *Educ.* Institute of Graphic Arts, Vienna. Henreid began his acting career with Max Reinhardt's theater in Vienna, moving to Great Britain and then, in 1940, the US. The epitome of continental charm, he is best remembered as Ingrid Bergman's resistance leader-husband in *Casablanca* (1942). • *Hohe Schule* 1934; *...Nur ein Komödiant* 1935; *Eva* 1935; *Victoria the Great* 1937; *An Englishman's Home* 1939; *Under Your Hat* 1940; *Casablanca* 1942; *Joan of Paris* 1942; *Now, Voyager* 1942; *Between Two Worlds* 1944; *The Conspirators* 1944; *Hollywood Canteen* 1944; *In Our Time* 1944; *The Spanish Main* 1945; *Deception* 1946; *Devotion* 1946; *Of Human Bondage* 1946; *Song of Love* 1947; *Hollow Triumph* 1948 (a,p); *Rope of Sand* 1949; *Last of the Buccaneers* 1950; *So Young, So Bad* 1950; *For Men Only* 1951 (a,d,p); *Pardon My French* 1951; *Stolen Face* 1952; *Thief of Damascus* 1952; *Mantrap* 1953; *Siren of Bagdad* 1953; *Deep in My Heart* 1954; *Kabarett* 1954; *Pirates of Tripoli* 1954; *Meet Me in Las Vegas* 1956; *Ten Thousand Bedrooms* 1956; *A Woman's Devotion* 1956 (a,d); *Girls on the Loose* 1958 (d); *Live Fast, Die Young* 1958 (d); *Holiday For Lovers* 1959; *Never So Few* 1959; *The Four Horsemen of the Apocalypse* 1962; *Dead Ringer* 1964 (d); *Operation Crossbow* 1965; *Blues For Lovers* 1966 (d,story); *Peking Remembered* 1967; *The Madwoman of Chaillot* 1969; *Exorcist II: The Heretic* 1977; *On the Road to Hollywood* 1984 (collaboration).

Henriksen, Lance • Actor • Born New York, NY. *Educ.* Actors Studio. Stage and film actor best known as astronaut Wally Schirra in *The Right Stuff* (1983) and the android, Bishop, in *Aliens* (1986). • *It Ain't Easy* 1972; *Dog Day Afternoon* 1975; *The Terror of Dr. Chancey* 1975; *The Next Man* 1976; *Close Encounters of the Third Kind* 1977; *Damien: Omen II* 1978; *The Visitor* 1979; *Close Encounters of the Third Kind: Special Edition* 1980; *The Dark End of the Street* 1981; *Piranha II: Flying Killers* 1981; *Prince of the City* 1981; *Nightmares* 1983; *The Right Stuff* 1983; *The Terminator* 1984 (a,sc); *Jagged Edge* 1985; *Savage Dawn* 1985; *Aliens* 1986; *Choke Canyon* 1986; *Near Dark* 1987; *Deadly Intent* 1988; *Pumpkinhead* 1988; *Hit List* 1989; *The Horror Show* 1989; *Johnny Handsome* 1989; *Survival Quest* 1989.

Henry, Buck • Screenwriter, actor; also director. • Born Buck Henry Zuckerman, New York, NY, 1930. *Educ.* Choate, Wallingford, CT; Dartmouth. Former stage actor and TV writer ("Get Smart") who turned to film in the mid-1960s, bringing with him a peculiarly humorous perspective on all things American. His outstanding adaptations include *The Graduate* (1967) and *Catch 22* (1970), and his performances in both of these as well as in Milos Forman's *Taking Off* (1971) are memorable. • *The Troublemaker* 1964 (a,sc,story); *The Graduate* 1967 (a,sc) **(AANBSC)**; *Candy* 1968 (sc); *The Secret War of Harry Frigg* 1968 (a); *Catch-22* 1970 (a,sc); *The Owl and the Pussycat* 1970 (a,sc); *Is There Sex After Death* 1971 (a); *Taking Off* 1971 (a); *What's Up, Doc?* 1972 (sc); *The Day of the Dolphin* 1973 (sc); *The Man Who Fell to Earth* 1976 (a); *Heaven Can Wait* 1978 (a,p) **(AANBD)**; *Old Boyfriends* 1978 (a); *First Family* 1980 (a,d,sc); *Gloria* 1980 (a); *The Nude Bomb* 1980 (from characters "Get Smart"); *Eating Raoul* 1982 (a); *Protocol* 1984 (sc); *Aria* 1987 (a); *I Love N.Y.* 1987 (sc); *Dark Before Dawn* 1988 (a); *Rude Awakening* 1989 (a); *Tune in Tomorrow* 1990 (a); *Defending Your Life* 1991 (a).

Henson, Jim • Producer; also screenwriter, director. • Born James Muary Henson, Greenville, MS, September 24, 1936; died May 16, 1990, New York, NY. *Educ.* University of Maryland (theater arts). Henson invented the irresistibly cute Muppets as a teenager, appearing with them on numerous shows before the advent of "Sesame Street" in 1969, which made them household names. In 1976 came "The Muppet Show" which gained worldwide popularity and generated several feature films, notably *The Muppets Take Manhattan* (1984). Henson was involved in several other fantasy-related film and TV ventures through his successful Henson Associates. He began proceedings to merge his corporation with the Walt Disney Company in 1989, shortly before his untimely death from pneumonia; the merger attempt was finally abandoned in 1991.

More than any other writer or filmmaker—even George Lucas or Steven Spielberg—Henson was responsible for creating the culture our children have grown up in since 1970. The world of *The Muppets*, *Sesame Street* and *Fraggle Rock* is sophisticated and realistically complex at the same time that it is childlike and refreshingly entertaining. Where Disney gave an earlier generation simplistic cartoon figures and reworked 19th–century myths, Henson and associates created fresh myths to encompass new realities. JM • *Time Piece (short)* 1965 (p); *The Muppet Movie* 1979 (a,p,song) **(AANBS)**; *An American Werewolf in London* 1981 (a); *The Great Muppet Caper* 1981 (Muppet performer,a,d,song) **(AANBS)**; *The Dark Crystal* 1982 (a,d,p,story); *The Muppets Take Manhattan*1984 (a,chor,exec.p); *Into the Night* 1985 (a); *Sesame Street Presents: Follow That Bird* 1985 (a); *Labyrinth* 1986 (d,story); *Hey, You're As Funny As Fozzie Bear!* 1988 (d,p,sc); *Mother Goose Stories* 1988 (d); *Neat Stuff...To Know and to Do* 1988 (d); *Peek-a-Boo* 1988 (d); *Sing-Along, Dance-Along, Do-Along* 1988 (d); *Wow You're a Cartoonist!* 1988 (d).

Hepburn, Audrey • Actress • Born Edda van Heemstra Hepburn-Ruston, Brussels, Belgium, May 4, 1929. *Educ.* Arnhem Conservatory (ballet). Graceful former model, in films from 1951. After small parts in European productions, Hepburn gained immediate prominence in the US with *Roman Holiday* (1953), which was followed by similarly enchanting performances in films such as *Funny Face* (1957) and, as Holly Golightly, *Breakfast at Tiffany's* (1961). She proved a beautiful, elegant foil to fatherly older men Gary Cooper, Humphrey Bogart and Fred Astaire, as well as young leads George Peppard and Albert Finney.

After a nine-year absence from the screen Hepburn turned in an impressive "middle-aged" performance in *Robin and Marian* (1976) and has continued to make occasional appearances, most recently in Steven Spielberg's *Always* (1989). She was married to actor Mel Ferrer from 1954 to 1968. • *Laughter in Paradise* 1951; *Nous irons! Monte Carlo* 1951; *One Wild Oat* 1951; *The Secret People* 1951; *Young Wives' Tale* 1951; *The Lavender Hill Mob* 1952; *Roman Holiday* 1953 **(AABA)**; *Sabrina* 1954 **(AANBA)**; *War and Peace* 1956; *Funny Face* 1957; *Love in the Afternoon* 1957; *Green Mansions* 1959; *The Nun's Story* 1959 **(AANBA)**; *The Unforgiven* 1960; *Breakfast at Tiffany's* 1961 **(AANBA)**; *The Children's Hour* 1961; *Charade* 1963; *Paris When It Sizzles* 1963; *My Fair Lady* 1964; *How to Steal a Million* 1966; *Two For the Road* 1967; *Wait Until Dark* 1967 **(AANBA)**; *Robin and Marian* 1976; *Bloodline* 1979; *They All Laughed* 1981; *Directed By William Wyler* 1986; *Always* 1989.

Hepburn, Katharine • Actress • Born Katharine Houghton Hepburn, Hartford, CT, November 9, 1907. *Educ.* Bryn Mawr (drama). Katharine Hepburn was born to a prominent New England family; her father was a famous surgeon, her mother an early crusader for women's rights. After graduating from Bryn Mawr College in 1928, she embarked on a career as a theatrical actress, training diligently with drama and voice coaches. She appeared in numerous summer stock and Broadway productions, gathering a reputation for flinty independence. Her 1932 Broadway appearance in *The Warrior's Husband* led to a film contract with RKO. Hepburn's film debut in *A Bill of Divorcement* (1932) was a propitious one, for it teamed her with director George Cukor, with whom Hepburn would collaborate on some of her best features. In Hepburn's early films she often portrayed strong female characters, anticipating feminist concerns in such works as *Little Women* (1933) and *Stage Door* (1937), which depict women in mutually supportive relationships. *Sylvia Scarlett* (1935), which first picks up the thread of androgyny that runs through Hepburn's career, was a ground-breaking film for its undermining of socially constructed norms of femininity and masculinity.

Hepburn won the first of her four Academy Awards (she has been nominated a record 12 times) for *Morning Glory* (1933), but five years later she was forced to buy out her contract from RKO rather than appear in a woefully unsuitable film, *Mother Cary's Chickens.* Hepburn, an intelligent, individualistic woman who knew her own strengths and weaknesses, often refused inappropriate casting, publicity and the superficialities of Hollywood fashion and society. In 1938, she returned to Broadway to do *The Philadelphia Story,* a play written expressly for her by Philip Barry. After the play was a smash, Hepburn, who owned the movie rights, returned to Hollywood and chose Cukor to direct her in the film version opposite Cary Grant and James Stewart. The 1940 feature is a showcase for her remarkable charm and vitality, even as it attributes her famed rebelliousness to the acts of a spoiled socialite who is eventually punished and tamed.

In this film and other comedy classics such as *Bringing Up Baby* and *Holiday* (both 1938), Hepburn's strength and self-assertion in the face of male domination appealed to female audiences. In many films her vigorous persona, with its vocal eccentricities and powerful physical presence, was exaggerated to the point that she seemed more male than female—as "one of the boys" she was less threatening. It was her pairing with Spencer Tracy in a series of successful films that made her rebelliousness most acceptable. Tracy, the most solidly masculine of all Hollywood actors, could act securely as a foil to Hepburn's feminist struggles, and, in spite of role reversals such as those in *Woman of the Year* (1942), dominate in the end. The Hepburn-Tracy films may end on a conventional note, but they are full of scenes depicting Tracy's admiration for Hepburn's intelligence or natural athletic ability (as in *Pat and Mike* 1952), and they are sparked by the charged dynamism of a relationship between equals that is rare in most Hollywood product of the 1940s and 50s.

With *The African Queen* (1951), Hepburn began a series of roles as perverse or odd spinsters or women in need of a man, even as they maintained a certain aloofness and independence. She found success and Academy Award nominations in several of these films, including *Summertime* (1955), *The Rainmaker* (1956) and *Suddenly, Last Summer* (1959).

Hepburn continued to act in both film and theater through the 1980s. She made a memorable Mary Tyrone in the film version of O'Neill's *Long Day's Journey Into Night (1962)* and won three more Academy Awards, for *Guess Who's Coming to Dinner?* (1967, her final appearance with Tracy, who died shortly after production was completed), *The Lion in Winter* (1968) and *On Golden Pond* (1981). Many consider her best work of this later period to be the TV films she made with George Cukor, *Love Among the Ruins* (1975) and *The Corn Is Green* (1979). Throughout her life, Hepburn continued to exert a firm control over her career and to maintain her dignity and extraordinary vitality. RJB • *A Bill of Divorcement* 1932 (a); *Christopher Strong* 1933 (a); *Little Women* 1933 (a); *Morning Glory* 1933 (a) **(AABA)**; *The Little Minister* 1934 (a); *Spitfire* 1934 (a); *Alice Adams* 1935 (a) **(AANBA)**; *Break of Hearts* 1935 (a); *Sylvia Scarlett* 1935 (a); *Mary of Scotland* 1936 (a); *A Woman Rebels* 1936 (a); *Quality Street* 1937 (a); *Stage Door* 1937 (a); *Bringing Up Baby* 1938 (a); *Holiday* 1938 (a); *The Philadelphia Story* 1940 (a) **(AANBA)**; *Keeper of the Flame* 1942 (a); *Woman of the Year* 1942 (a) **(AANBA)**; *Stage Door Canteen* 1943 (a); *Dragon Seed* 1944 (a); *Without Love* 1945 (a); *Undercurrent* 1946 (a); *Sea of Grass* 1947 (a); *Song of Love* 1947 (a); *State of the Union* 1948 (a); *Adam's Rib* 1949 (a); *The African Queen* 1951 (a) **(AANBA)**; *Pat and Mike* 1952 (a); *Summertime* 1955 (a) **(AANBA)**; *The Iron Petticoat* 1956 (a); *The Rainmaker* 1956 (a) **(AANBA)**; *Desk Set* 1957 (a); *Suddenly, Last Summer* 1959 (a) **(AANBA)**; *Long Day's Journey Into Night* 1962 (a) **(AANBA)**; *Guess Who's Coming to Dinner?* 1967 (a) **(AABA)**; *The Lion in Winter* 1968 (a) **(AABA)**; *The Madwoman of Chaillot* 1969 (a); *The Trojan Women* 1971 (a); *A Delicate Balance* 1973 (a); *Rooster Cogburn* 1975 (a); *Olly, Olly, Oxen Free* 1978 (a); *On Golden Pond* 1981 (a) **(AABA)**; *Grace Quigley* 1985 (a); *Going Hollywood: The War Years* 1988 (archival footage).

Hepworth, Cecil • Director, producer; also inventor. • Born Cecil Milton Hepworth, Lambeth, London, 1874; died 1953, Greenford, Middlesex, England. Pioneering British filmmaker who patented several inventions and published one of the first books on film, *Animated Photography, or the ABC of the Cinematograph* (1897). Hepworth set up a studio and laboratory and made several documentaries as well as the remarkably advanced narrative short, *Rescued By Rover* (1905). He was a major figure in British cinema until the end of WWI, primarily as a producer.

The postwar slump that disabled the entire British film industry forced Hepworth out of business in the early 1920s. He later lectured on the history of cinema and made trailers and advertising shorts. • *Express Train in a Railway Cutting* 1899 (d,p,ph); *The Eccentric Dancer* 1900 (d,p,ph); *The Explosion of a Motor Car* 1900 (d,p,ph); *How It Feels to Be Run Over* 1900 (d,p,ph); *The Kiss* 1900 (d,p,ph); *Coronation of King Edward VII* 1901 (d,p,ph); *Funeral of Queen Victoria* 1901 (d,p,ph); *The Glutton's Nightmare* 1901 (d,p,ph); *How the Burglar Tricked the Bobby* 1901 (d,p,ph); *The Call to Arms* 1902 (d,p,ph); *How to Stop a Motor Car* 1902 (d,p,ph); *Alice in Wonderland* 1903 (d,p,ph); *Firemen to the Rescue* 1903 (d,p,ph); *The Jonah Man* 1904 (d,p,ph); *The Alien's Invasion* 1905 (d,p,ph); *A Den of Thieves* 1905 (d,p,ph); *Falsely Accused* 1905 (d,p,ph); *Rescued By Rover* 1905(a,d,p); *A Seaside Girl* 1907 (d,p,ph); *John Gilpin's Ride* 1908 (d,p,ph); *Tilly the Tomboy* 1909 (d,p,ph); *Rachel's Sin* 1911 (d,p,ph); *The Basilisk* 1915 (d,p); *The Battle* 1915 (d,p); *The Canker of Jealousy* 1915 (d,p); *Iris* 1915 (d,p); *The Man Who Stayed at Home* 1915 (d,p); *The Outrage* 1915 (d,p); *Sweet Lavender* 1915 (d,p); *Time the Great Healer* 1915 (d,p); *Annie Laurie* 1916 (d,p); *The Cobweb* 1916 (d,p); *Comin' Thro' the Rye* 1916 (d,p); *Sowing the Wind* 1916 (d,p); *The American Heiress* 1917 (d,p); *Nearer My God to Thee* 1917 (d,p); *The Blindness of Fortune* 1918 (d,p); *Boundary House* 1918 (d,p); *The Forest on the Hill* 1919 (d,p); *The Nature of the Beast* 1919 (d,p); *Sheba* 1919 (d,p); *Alf's Button* 1920 (d,p); *Anna the Adventuress* 1920 (d,p); *Helen of Four Gates* 1920 (d,p); *Narrow Valley* 1921 (d,p); *Tinted Venus* 1921 (d,p); *Wild Heather* 1921 (d,p); *Comin' Thro' the Rye* 1922 (d,p); *Mist in the Valley* 1922 (d,p); *Pipes of Pan* 1922 (d,p); *The House of Marney* 1927 (d,p).

Herman, Pee-wee • *aka* Paul Reubens • Actor; also TV host. • Born Paul Rubenfield, Sarasota, FL, July, 1952. Comic persona whose androgynous sexuality, unabashed materialism, obsessive neatness and sly anti-authoritarian pose have earned him cult status among children and impressionable adults. Star of TV's popular "Pee-wee's Playhouse." • *The Blues Brothers* 1980 (a); *Cheech & Chong's Next Movie* 1980 (a); *Cheech & Chong's Nice Dreams* 1981 (a); *Pandemonium* 1981 (a); *Meatballs Part II* 1984 (a); *Pee-wee's Big Adventure* 1985 (a,sc); *Flight of the Navigator* 1986 (a); *Back to the Beach* 1987 (a); *Big Top Pee-Wee* 1988 (a,p).

Herrmann, Bernard • Composer; also conductor. • Born New York, NY, June 29, 1911; died December 24, 1975. *Educ.* NYU; Juilliard (music). Preeminent film composer brought to Hollywood by Orson Welles and subsequently renowned for his collaborations with Alfred Hitchcock. Herrmann had scored many of Welles's radio shows before making the move west for *Citizen Kane* (1941), and immediately joined the front rank of film composers. In contrast to the prevailing Hollywood style, Herrmann's scores moved away from full, lush arrangements to smaller, often unorthodox orchestration. Equally innovative was his use of brief, easily recognizable themes in place of lengthier melodies.

Of Herrmann's many collaborations with Hitchcock, *The Man Who Knew Too Much* (1956)—in which he appears as the conductor—*Vertigo* (1958) and *Psycho* (1960) stand out. His other outstanding credits include *The Devil and Daniel Webster* (1941)—which beat out his "Kane" score for the Oscar—*The Seventh Voyage of Sinbad* (1958), Francois Truffaut's *The Bride Wore Black* (1968) and Martin Scorsese's *Taxi Driver* (1976). • *Citizen Kane* 1941 (m) **(AANBM)**; *The Devil and Daniel Webster* 1941 (m) **(AABM)**; *The Magnificent Ambersons* 1942 (m); *Jane Eyre* 1944 (m.dir); *Hangover Square* 1945 (m); *Anna and the King of Siam* 1946 (m) **(AANBM)**; *The Ghost and Mrs. Muir* 1947 (m); *The Day the Earth Stood Still* 1951 (m); *On Dangerous Ground* 1951 (m); *Five Fingers* 1952 (m); *The Snows of Kilimanjaro* 1952 (m); *Beneath the 12 Mile Reef* 1953 (m); *Le Salaire de la Peur/The Wages of Fear* 1953 (m); *White Witch Doctor* 1953 (m); *The Egyptian* 1954 (m); *Garden of Evil* 1954 (m); *King of the Khyber Rifles* 1954 (m); *The Kentuckian* 1955 (m); *The Man in the Gray Flannel Suit* 1955 (m); *Prince of Players* 1955 (m); *The Trouble With Harry* 1955 (m); *The Man Who Knew Too Much* 1956 (m); *The Wrong Man* 1956 (m); *A Hatful of Rain* 1957 (m); *Williamsburg: The Story of a Patriot* 1957 (m); *The 7th Voyage of Sinbad* 1958 (m); *The Fiend Who Walked the West* 1958 (m); *The Naked and the Dead* 1958 (m); *The Seventh Voyage of Sinbad* 1958 (m); *Vertigo* 1958 (m); *Blue Denim* 1959 (m); *Journey to the Center of the Earth* 1959 (m); *North By Northwest* 1959 (m); *Psycho* 1960 (m); *The Three Worlds of Gulliver* 1960 (m); *Mysterious Island* 1961 (m); *Cape Fear* 1962 (m); *Tender Is the Night* 1962 (m); *The Birds* 1963 (sound construction); *Jason and the Argonauts* 1963 (m); *Marnie* 1964 (m); *Joy in the Morning* 1965 (m); *Fahrenheit 451* 1966 (m); *Bitka na Neretvi* 1968 (m); *La Mariée)tait en noir/The Bride Wore Black* 1968 (m); *Twisted Nerve* 1968 (m,m.dir); *Bezeten—het gat in de muur* 1969 (m); *The Night Digger* 1971 (m); *Endless Night* 1972 (m); *Sisters* 1973 (m); *It's Alive* 1974 (m); *Obsession* 1976 (m) **(AANBM)**; *Taxi Driver* 1976 (m,song) **(AANBM)**; *It's Alive 2* 1978 (m); *It's Alive III: Island of the Alive* 1987 (m).

Herrmann, Edward • Actor • Born Washington, DC, July 31, 1943. *Educ.* Bucknell University, Lewisburg PA; LAMDA, London. Tall, bespectacled actor with stage and TV experience. Often cast as conservative or executive types, and memorable for his TV portrayals of Franklin Delano Roosevelt. • *The Day of the Dolphin* 1973 (a); *The Paper Chase*

1973 (a); *The Great Gatsby* 1974 (a); *The Great Waldo Pepper* 1975 (a); *The Betsy* 1978 (a); *Brass Target* 1978 (a); *Take Down* 1978 (a); *The North Avenue Irregulars* 1979 (a); *Death Valley* 1981 (a); *Harry's War* 1981 (a); *A Little Sex* 1981 (a); *Reds* 1981 (a); *Annie* 1982 (a,song); *Mrs. Soffel* 1984 (a); *Compromising Positions* 1985 (a); *The Man With One Red Shoe* 1985 (a); *The Purple Rose of Cairo* 1985 (a); *The Lost Boys* 1987 (a); *Overboard* 1987 (a); *Big Business* 1988 (a).

Hershey, Barbara • *aka* Barbara Seagull • Actress • Born Barbara Herzstein, Hollywood, CA, February 5, 1948. Hershey tended to be typecast in "love child" roles until she won rave reviews for her performance opposite Peter O'Toole in *The Stunt Man* (1980). She went on to star in numerous superior films of the 1980s and was the first person to win two consecutive best actress awards at the Cannes Film Festival: for Andrei Konchalovsky's *Shy People* (1987) and Chris Menges's *A World Apart* (1988). • *With Six You Get Eggroll* 1968 (a); *Heaven With a Gun*1969 (a); *Last Summer* 1969 (a); *The Baby Maker* 1970 (a); *The Liberation of L.B. Jones* 1970 (a); *The Pursuit of Happiness* 1971 (a); *Boxcar Bertha* 1972 (a); *Dealing: Or the Berkeley-to-Boston Forty-Brick Lost-Bag Blues* 1972 (a); *Angela* 1973 (a); *The Crazy World of Julius Vrooder* 1974 (a); *Diamonds* 1975 (a); *You and Me* 1975 (a); *A Choice of Weapons* 1976 (a); *The Last Hard Men* 1976 (a); *The Stunt Man* 1980 (a); *Americana* 1981 (a); *Take This Job and Shove It* 1981 (a); *The Entity* 1982 (a); *The Right Stuff* 1983 (a); *The Natural* 1984 (a); *Hannah and Her Sisters* 1986 (a); *Hoosiers* 1986 (a); *Shy People* 1987 (a); *Tin Men* 1987 (a); *Beaches* 1988 (a,song); *The Last Temptation of Christ* 1988 (a); *A World Apart* 1988 (a); *Tune in Tomorrow* 1990 (a).

Herzog, Werner • Director, screenwriter, producer • Born Werner Stipetic, Sachrang, Germany, September 5, 1942. *Educ.* Munich University; University of Pittsburgh, PA. One of the most eccentric figures in the New German Cinema, Werner Herzog has been characterized as the "romantic visionary" of the movement as well as its most notorious self-promoter who possesses an almost legendary need to confront danger in making his films. His well-documented production difficulties—dragging a ship over a mountain, attempting to film the eruption of a volcano, hypnotizing an entire cast—may well be extra-filmic means of establishing the authenticity of his films, but in Herzog's case they threaten to become the real event of which the actual film is merely a record. "Film," Herzog insists, "is not the art of scholars, but of illiterates," and it is not surprising that his work has aroused contradictory responses. Those who are fascinated by his awe-inspiring landscapes and enigmatic heroes see him as a poet whose work is haunting, sublime and mysterious; others see him as a mystic—or worse, as a mystifier—whose films are regressive, self-indulgent and naively romantic.

Like many of his documentaries, Herzog's biography appears to be a mixture of fact and fantasy. His legal name is Stipetic and he grew up in a remote Bavarian village. At 15, he wrote his first script, and at 17 tried to make his first film. His association with cantankerous star Klaus Kinski started when Herzog's family moved to Munich and shared a house with the actor. To earn money for filmmaking, Herzog worked in factories, as a parking lot attendant and—so he claims—as a rodeo rider. Supposedly while on a Fulbright scholarship at the University of Pittsburgh, he studied film and TV for a brief period. For a time he allegedly made his living smuggling TV sets across the Mexican border. In 1964 he won the Carl Mayer Prize for the screenplay that was to become his first feature film, *Signs of Life* (1968).

Among Herzog's most popular films, though not an immediate success, is *Aguirre, the Wrath of God* (1972). Shot in the jungles of Peru against formidable difficulties, *Aguirre* tells the story of a maniacal conquistador played by Klaus Kinski, who, through intimidation and murder, gains control of his expedition party, declares himself the "wrath of God" and sets off to find El Dorado. Floating downstream on a raft, the crew is attacked by Indians and battered by rapids as disease and starvation gradually take their toll. At the end, a crazed Aguirre remains alone on the raft overrun by monkeys.

Visually, *Aguirre* is one of Herzog's most beautiful and haunting films. The opening sequence is breathtaking, as we see in an extreme long-shot the heavily burdened expedition carefully making its way down the side of a mountain. (The film was shot with a cast and crew of 500.) The closing shot is equally impressive as the camera circles around the raft, reinforcing a sense of entrapment and doom. Although the film can be read as an allegory of the fascist personality, the stunning images leave us with a sense of awe and wonder, even admiration, for the heroic madman.

As this brief summary indicates, sublime landscapes, astounding images, and haunting music are the hallmark of Herzog's films. This is certainly true of other features like *The Mystery of Kaspar Hauser* (1974), based on the true story of a strange man found wandering the streets of Nuremberg in 1820 and regarded by many as his best film; *Nosferatu The Vampyre* (1978), an homage to Murnau's classic version of the Dracula legend; and *Fitzcarraldo* (1982), which Herzog completed against seemingly insurmountable odds, as documented in Les Blank's documentary, *Burden of Dreams* (1982). Given Herzog's obsession with quasi-mystical images and landscapes, it is not surprising that many consider his "documentaries" to be his best work. As is the case with a number of other directors of the New German Cinema, the reception of Herzog's films has been more favorable in France, England and the United States than in his own country. PR • *Herakles (short)* 1962 (d,p,sc,ed,sound); *Spiel im Sand (short)* 1964 (d,p,sc,ed,sound); *Die Beispiellose Verteidigung der Festung Deutschkreutz (short)* 1967 (d,p,sc,ed); *Letzte Worte (short)* 1967 (d,p,sc); *Lebenszeichen/Signs of Life* 1968 (a,d,p,sc); *Fata Morgana* 1969 (d,p,sc,sound); *Die Fliegenden Arzte von Ostafrika* 1969 (d,p,sc,sound); *Massnahmen Gegen Fanatiker* 1969 (d,p,sc,sound); *Auch Zwerge Haben Klein Angefangen/Even Dwarfs Started Small* 1970 (d,p,sc,m.adapt); *Behinderte Zukunft* 1970 (d,p,sc,sound); *Land des Schweigens und der Dunkelheit* 1971 (d,p,sc,sound); *Aguirre, der Zorn Gottes/Aguirre, the Wrath of God* 1972 (d,p,sc,sound); *Die Grosse Ekstase des Bildschnitzers Steiner* 1974 (d,p,sc); *Jeder für sich und Gott gegen alle/Every Man For Himself and God Against All/The Mystery of Kaspar Hauser* 1974 (d,p,sc); *Herz aus Glas/Heart of Glass* 1976 (a,d,p,sc); *How Much Wood Would a Woodchuck Chuck* 1976 (d,p,sc,sound); *Mit mir will keiner spielen (short)* 1976 (d,p,sc); *La Soufrière* 1977 (English narrative text,sound,d,p); *Stroszek* 1977 (d,p,sc); *Nosferatu, Phantom der Nacht/Nosferatu the Vampire* 1978 (a,d,p,sc); *Was Ich Bin, Sind Meine Filme* 1978 (a); *Woyzeck* 1979 (d,p,sc); *Glaube und Wahrung* 1980 (d,sc); *Huie's Predigt* 1980 (d,p,sc); *Burden of Dreams* 1982 (a); *Chambre 666* 1982 (a); *Fitzcarraldo* 1982 (d,p,sc); *Man of Flowers* 1983 (a); *Ballade vom kleinen Soldaten* 1984 (a,d,p,sc); *Wo die grünen Ameisen traumen/Where the Green Ants Dream* 1984 (d,sc); *Gasherbrum—Der leuchtende Berg* 1985 (d,p,sc); *Tokyo-Ga* 1985 (a); *Cobra Verde/Slave Coast* 1988 (d,sc); *Herdsmen of the Sun* 1988 (d); *Lightning Over Braddock: A Rustbowl Fantasy* 1988 (a); *Gekauftes Glück* 1989 (a); *Hard to Be a God* 1989 (a); *Echos Aus Einem Düsteren Reich* 1990 (d,p).

Heston, Charlton • Actor; also director. • Born Charles Carter, St. Helen, MI, October 4, 1924. *Educ.* Northwestern University (speech, drama). Commanding male lead, on Broadway from 1947 and in Hollywood from 1950. (He had previously appeared in two 16mm films directed by fellow Northwestern student David Bradley.) Heston's righteous, imposing screen presence, mixed with evident intelligence, made him the appropriate star of several biblical epics, most notably *The Ten Commandments* (1956) and *Ben-Hur* (1959). He first went behind the camera in 1972 and has starred in all the films he has directed.

A six-term president of the Screen Actors Guild, Heston has remained active in politics and earned a reputation as a staunch Republican, serving as co-chairman of Ronald Reagan's Task Force on the Arts and Humanities. Son Fraser Clarke Heston is a director, screenwriter and producer. • *Peer Gynt* 1941 (a); *Julius Caesar* 1949 (a); *Dark City* 1950 (a); *The Greatest Show on Earth* 1952 (a); *Ruby* 1952 (a); *The Savage* 1952 (a); *Arrowhead* 1953 (a); *Pony Express* 1953 (a); *The President's Lady* 1953 (a); *Bad For Each Other* 1954 (a); *The Naked Jungle* 1954 (a); *Secret of the Incas* 1954 (a); *The Far Horizons* 1955 (a); *Lucy Gallant* 1955 (a); *The Private War of Major Benson* 1955 (a); *The Ten Commandments* 1956 (a); *Three Violent People* 1956 (a); *The Big Country* 1958 (a); *The Buccaneer* 1958 (a); *Touch of Evil* 1958 (a); *Ben-Hur* 1959 (a) **(AABA)**; *The Wreck of the Mary Deare* 1959 (a); *El Cid* 1961 (a); *Diamond Head* 1962 (a); *The Pigeon That Took Rome* 1962 (a); *55 Days at Peking* 1963 (a); *The Agony and the Ecstasy* 1965 (a); *The Greatest Story Ever Told* 1965 (a); *Major Dundee* 1965 (a); *The War Lord* 1965 (a); *Khartoum* 1966 (a); *All About People (short)* 1967 (a); *Counterpoint* 1967 (a); *Planet of the Apes* 1968 (a); *Will Penny* 1968 (a); *The Festival Game* 1969 (a); *Number One* 1969 (a); *Antony and Cleopatra* 1970 (a,d,sc.adapt); *Beneath the Planet of the Apes* 1970 (a); *The Hawaiians* 1970 (a); *Julius Caesar* 1970 (a); *King: A Filmed Record... Montgomery to Memphis* 1970 (a); *The Omega Man* 1971 (a); *Vietnam! Vietnam!* 1971 (a); *Call of the Wild* 1972 (a); *Skyjacked* 1972 (a); *Soylent Green* 1973 (a); *The Three Musketeers* 1973 (a); *Earthquake* 1974 (a); *Airport 1975* 1975 (a); *The Four Musketeers* 1975 (a); *America atthe Movies* 1976 (a); *Battle of Midway* 1976 (a); *The Last Hard Men* 1976 (a); *Two-Minute Warning* 1976 (a); *Crossed Swords* 1977 (a); *Gray Lady Down* 1977 (a); *The Awakening* 1980 (a); *The Mountain Men* 1980 (a); *Mother Lode* 1982 (a,d); *Directed By William Wyler* 1986 (a); *The Fantasy Film World of George Pal* 1986 (a); *Call From Space* 1989 (a); *Almost an Angel* 1990 (a); *Solar Crisis* 1990 (a).

Hickey, William • American actor • Craggy-faced veteran of the Broadway stage who made his screen debut in *A Hatful of Rain* (1957) and has since carved a niche as a character player; memorable as a mafia Don in John Huston's *Prizzi's Honor* (1985). • *A Hatful of Rain* 1957 (a); *Operation Mad Ball* 1957 (a); *The Producers* 1967 (a); *The Boston Strangler* 1968 (a); *Little Big Man* 1970 (a); *Happy Birthday, Wanda June* 1971 (a); *A New Leaf* 1971 (a); *The Telephone Book* 1971 (a); *Between Time and Timbuktu* 1972 (a); *92 in the Shade* 1975 (a); *Mikey and Nicky* 1976 (a); *The Sentinel* 1977 (a); *Wise Blood* 1979 (a); *Flanagan* 1985 (a); *Prizzi's Honor* 1985 (a) **(AANBSA)**; *Remo Williams: The Adventure Begins...* 1985 (a); *The Name of the Rose* 1986 (a); *One Crazy Summer* 1986 (a); *Seize the Day* 1986 (a); *Bright Lights, Big City* 1988 (a); *Da* 1988 (a); *It Had to Be You* 1989 (a); *National Lampoon's Christmas Vacation* 1989 (a); *Pink Cadillac* 1989 (a); *Puppet Master* 1989 (a); *Sea of Love* 1989 (a); *Sons* 1989 (a); *Any Man's Death* 1990 (a); *Mob Boss* 1990 (a); *My Blue Heaven* 1990 (a); *Tales From the Darkside, The Movie* 1990 (a).

Hickox, Sidney • *aka* Sid Hickox • Director of photography • Born New York, NY, July 15, 1895. Long associated with Warner Bros.; noted for his contributions to the films of Howard Hawks and Raoul Walsh, among others. • *Gloria's Romance* 1916 (ph); *School Days* 1921 (ph); *Your Best Friend* 1922 (ph); *Marriage Morals* 1923 (ph); *The Little Giant* 1925 (ph); *The Private Life of Helen of Troy* 1927 (ph); *Happiness Ahead* 1928 (ph); *Lilac Time* 1928 (ph); *Oh, Kay!* 1928 (ph); *Sailor's Wives* 1928 (ph); *Synthetic Sin* 1928 (ph); *Footlights and Fools* 1929 (ph); *Hot Stuff* 1929 (ph); *The Love Racket* 1929 (ph); *Smiling Irish Eyes* 1929 (ph); *Two Weeks Off* 1929 (ph); *Why Be Good?* 1929 (ph); *The Flirting Widow* 1930 (ph); *The Gorilla* 1930 (ph); *Kismet* 1930 (ph); *Moby Dick* 1930 (ph—German-language version); *Strictly Modern* 1930 (ph); *Sweet Mama* 1930 (ph); *Those Who Dance* 1930 (ph); *Top Speed* 1930 (ph); *The Way of All Men* 1930 (ph); *Blonde Crazy* 1931 (ph); *Broad-Minded* 1931 (ph); *Convicted* 1931 (ph); *The Last Flight* 1931 (ph); *The Naughty Flirt* 1931 (ph); *Party Husbands* 1931 (ph); *Safe in Hell* 1931 (ph); *Sea Ghost* 1931 (ph); *Too Young to Marry* 1931 (ph); *Under Eighteen* 1931 (ph); *A Bill of Divorcement* 1932 (ph); *Central Park* 1932 (ph); *The Crowd Roars* 1932 (ph); *The Hatchet Man* 1932 (ph); *Love Is a Racket* 1932 (ph); *Pleasure* 1932 (ph); *The Purchase Price* 1932 (ph); *So Big* 1932 (ph); *The Adopted Father* 1933 (ph); *The Avenger* 1933 (ph);*Central Airport* 1933 (ph); *Christopher Strong* 1933 (uncred.ph); *Female* 1933 (ph); *Frisco Jenny* 1933 (ph); *Grand Slam* 1933 (ph); *Lilly Turner* 1933 (ph); *The Little Giant* 1933 (ph); *Mary Stevens, M.D.* 1933 (ph); *Sensation Hunters* 1933 (ph); *Bedside* 1934 (ph); *The Big Shakedown* 1934 (ph); *The Circus Clown* 1934 (ph); *Dames* 1934 (ph); *Heat Lightning* 1934 (ph); *I Sell Anything* 1934 (ph); *Living on Velvet* 1934 (ph); *A Lost Lady* 1934 (ph); *Registered Nurse* 1934 (ph); *The St. Louis Kid* 1934 (ph); *Twenty Million Sweethearts* 1934 (ph); *Bright Lights* 1935 (ph); *The Goose and the Gander* 1935 (ph); *I Am a Thief* 1935 (ph); *The Right to Live* 1935 (ph); *Special Agent* 1935 (ph); *Stranded* 1935 (ph); *Brides Are Like That* 1936 (ph); *The Case of the Velvet Claws* 1936 (ph); *Freshman Love* 1936 (ph); *Give Me Your Heart* 1936 (ph); *The Law in Her Hands* 1936 (ph); *Stolen Holiday* 1936 (ph); *Trailin' West* 1936 (ph); *Two Against the World* 1936 (ph); *Confession* 1937 (ph); *First Lady* 1937 (ph); *Missing Witnesses* 1937 (ph); *San Quentin* 1937 (ph); *The Singing Marine* 1937 (ph); *Slim* 1937 (ph); *Women Are Like That* 1937 (ph); *Men Are Such Fools* 1938 (ph); *My Bill* 1938 (ph); *Secrets of an Actress* 1938 (ph); *A Slight Case of Murder* 1938 (ph); *Everybody's Hobby* 1939 (ph); *Indianapolis Speedway* 1939 (ph); *The Kid From Kokomo* 1939 (ph); *King of the Underworld* 1939 (ph); *The Return of Dr. X* 1939 (ph); *Women in the Wind* 1939 (ph); *British Intelligence* 1940 (ph); *The Doctor Takes a Wife* 1940 (ph); *East of the River* 1940 (ph); *Flowing Gold* 1940 (ph); *King of the Lumberjacks* 1940 (ph); *The Man Who Talked Too Much* 1940 (ph); *Tear Gas Squad* 1940 (ph); *Law of the Tropics* 1941 (ph); *Thieves Fall Out* 1941 (ph); *Underground* 1941 (ph); *The Wagons Roll at Night* 1941 (ph); *All Through the Night* 1942 (ph); *Always in My Heart* 1942 (ph); *The Big Shot* 1942 (ph); *Gentleman Jim* 1942 (ph); *Edge of Darkness* 1943 (ph); *Northern Pursuit* 1943 (ph); *To Have and Have Not* 1944 (ph); *Uncertain Glory* 1944 (ph); *God Is My Co-Pilot* 1945 (ph); *The Horn Blows at Midnight* 1945 (ph); *The Big Sleep* 1946 (ph); *The Man I Love* 1946 (ph); *Cheyenne* 1947 (ph); *Dark Passage* 1947 (ph); *Fighter Squadron* 1948 (ph); *One Sunday Afternoon* 1948 (ph); *Silver River* 1948 (ph); *Colorado Territory* 1949 (ph); *White Heat* 1949 (ph); *The Great Jewel Robber* 1950 (ph); *Three Secrets* 1950 (ph); *The West Point Story* 1950 (2u ph); *Along the Great Divide* 1951 (ph); *Distant Drums* 1951 (ph); *Forth Worth* 1951 (ph); *Lightning Strikes Twice* 1951 (ph); *April in Paris* 1952 (2u ph); *The Winning Team* 1952 (ph); *Blowing Wild* 1953 (ph); *Battle Cry* 1954 (ph); *Drum Beat* 1954 (2u ph); *Lucky Me* 1954 (background ph—Miami); *Them* 1954 (ph); *Helen of Troy* 1956 (2u ph).

Higgins, Colin • Screenwriter; also director, producer, actor. • Born Noumea, New Caledonia, July 28, 1941; died August 5, 1988, Beverly Hills, CA. *Educ.* Actors Studio; Stanford; Sorbonne, Paris; UCLA. Best remembered for writing the Hal Ashby-directed black comedy, *Harold and Maude* (1971), and for directing the Dolly Parton vehicles, *9 to 5* (1980) and *The Best Little Whorehouse in Texas* (1982). • *Harold and Maude* 1971 (p,sc); *Silver Streak* 1976 (sc); *Foul Play* 1978 (d,sc); *The Shout* 1978 (a); *That Summer* 1979 (a); *9 to 5* 1980 (d,sc); *The Best Little Whorehouse in Texas* 1982 (d); *E la nave Va/And the Ship Sailed On* 1983 (a); *Into the Night* 1985 (a); *Hope and Glory* 1987 (a).

Hill, Bernard • Actor • Born Manchester, England, December 17, 1944. *Educ.* Manchester Art College (drama); Everyman Theatre, Liverpool. Acclaimed stage, TV and film performer who has proved his versatility in roles ranging from the reticent, reluctant hero of *Bellman & True* (1987) to the boorish husband of *Shirley Valentine* (1989). • *It Could Happen to You* 1975; *A Choice of Weapons* 1976; *The Black Stuff* 1978; *The Sailor's Return* 1978; *Gandhi* 1982; *Runners* 1983; *Squaring the Circle* 1983; *The Bounty* 1984; *The Chain* 1985; *Restless Natives* 1985; *Milwr Bychan* 1986; *New World* 1986; *No Surrender* 1986; *Bellman & True* 1987; *Drowning By Numbers* 1988; *Shirley Valentine* 1989; *Mountains of the Moon* 1990.

Hill, Debra • Producer; also screenwriter. • Born Haddonfield, NJ. Initiated a five-film collaboration with director John Carpenter on *Halloween* (1978) and has recently branched out into other popular genres. • *Halloween* 1978 (p,sc); *The Fog* 1980 (p,sc,story); *Escape From New York* 1981 (p); *Halloween II* 1981 (p,sc); *Halloween III: Season of the Witch* 1982 (p); *The Dead Zone* 1983 (p); *Clue* 1985 (p); *Head Office* 1986 (p); *Adventures in Babysitting* 1987 (p); *Big Top Pee-Wee* 1988 (p); *Heartbreak Hotel* 1988 (p); *Gross Anatomy* 1989 (p); *The Fisher King* 1991 (p).

Hill, George Roy • Director; also actor. • Born Minneapolis, MN, December 20, 1922. *Educ.* Yale (music); Trinity College, Dublin (music). Former actor with Cyril Cusack's company at the Abbey Theatre in Dublin who began writing and directing for American TV in the 1950s. Hill's first Broadway success as a director came with *Look Homeward Angel* in 1957 and his first two films were based on stage plays he had directed. He made his name with two fluid, lightly handled vehicles for the superstar team of Paul Newman and Robert Redford: *Butch Cassidy and the Sundance Kid* (1969) and *The Sting* (1973), which earned Hill an Oscar for best direction. • *Walk East on Beacon* 1952 (a); *Period of Adjustment* 1962 (d); *Toys in the Attic* 1963 (d); *The World of Henry Orient* 1964 (d); *Hawaii* 1966 (d); *Thoroughly Modern Millie* 1967 (d); *Butch Cassidy and the Sundance Kid* 1969 (d) **(AANBD)**; *Slaughterhouse-Five* 1971 (d); *The Sting* 1973 (d) **(AABD)**; *The Great Waldo Pepper* 1975 (d,p,story); *Slap Shot* 1977 (d); *A Little Romance* 1979 (d,dial); *The World According to Garp* 1982 (d,p); *The Little Drummer Girl* 1984 (d); *Funny Farm* 1988 (d).

Hill, Walter • Screenwriter, director • Born Long Beach, CA, January 10, 1942. *Educ.* Michigan State University. Made his directorial debut with the hard-boiled Depression-era saga, *Hard Times* (1975), and went on to establish himself as one of Hollywood's premier writers and directors of action films. Hill's efforts encompass science fiction, a western and one of the most successful of urban "buddy" films, *48 Hrs.* (1982). • *The Thomas Crown Affair* 1968 (ad); *Take the Money and Run* 1969 (ad); *The Getaway* 1972 (sc); *Hickey and Boggs* 1972 (sc); *The Mackintosh Man* 1973 (sc); *The Thief Who Came to Dinner* 1973 (sc); *The Drowning Pool* 1975 (sc); *Hard Times* 1975 (d,sc); *The Driver* 1978 (d,sc); *Alien* 1979 (p); *The Warriors* 1979 (d,sc); *The Long Riders* 1980 (d); *Southern Comfort* 1981 (d,sc); *48 Hrs.* 1982 (d,sc); *Streets of Fire* 1984 (d,sc); *Brewster's Millions* 1985 (d); *Aliens* 1986 (exec.p,story); *Blue City* 1986 (p,sc); *Crossroads* 1986 (d); *Extreme Prejudice* 1987 (d); *Red Heat* 1988 (d,p,sc,story); *Johnny Handsome* 1989 (d); *Another 48 Hrs.* 1990 (d,from characters).

Hiller, Arthur • Director • Born Edmonton, Alberta, Canada, November 22, 1923. *Educ.* University of Alberta, Edmonton; University of Toronto (psychology); University of British Columbia (law). Although he has worked in a variety of genres, from the dramatic (*The Man in the Glass Booth* 1974) to the romantic (*Love Story* 1970), Hiller is on surest ground with light comedy, perhaps a reflection of his background in TV. *Silver Streak* (1976) and *The In-Laws* (1979) are two of his more inspired comic efforts. • *The Careless Years* 1957 (d); *Miracle of the White Stallions* 1963 (d); *The Wheeler Dealers* 1963 (d); *The Americanization of Emily* 1964 (d); *Eye of the Devil* 1966 (d); *Penelope* 1966 (d); *Promise Her Anything* 1966 (d); *The Tiger Makes Out* 1967 (d); *Tobruk* 1967 (d); *Popi* 1969 (d); *Love Story* 1970 (d) **(AANBD)**; *The Out-of-Towners* 1970 (d); *The Hospital* 1971 (d); *Plaza Suite* 1971 (d); *Raid on Rommel* 1971 (action sequences d); *L'Uomo della Mancha/Man of La Mancha* 1972 (d,p); *The Crazy World of Julius Vrooder* 1974 (d,p); *The Man in the Glass Booth* 1974 (d); *Silver Streak* 1976 (d); *W.C. Fields and Me* 1976 (d); *The In-Laws* 1979 (d,p); *Nightwing* 1979 (d); *Author! Author!* 1982 (d); *Making Love* 1982 (d); *Romantic Comedy* 1983 (d); *The Lonely Guy* 1984 (d,p); *Teachers* 1984 (d); *Outrageous Fortune* 1987 (d); *See No Evil, Hear No Evil* 1989 (d); *Taking Care of Business* 1990 (d).

Hillyer, Lambert • Director; also actor, screenwriter. • Born South Bend, IN, July 8, 1889. Newspaperman, short-story writer, vaudevillian and stock actor who broke into film in the early teens and directed scores of low-budget productions over the next three decades. Hillyer cranked out a host of silent westerns for stars such as William S. Hart and Tom Mix before moving onto romantic dramas, crime melodramas and thrillers. He spent the last part of his career at Monogram in the 1940s. • *The Desert Man* 1917 (sc); *The Even Break* 1917 (d,sc); *The Mother Instinct* 1917 (d); *The Narrow Trail* 1917 (d); *Unfaithful* 1918 (sc); *Breed of Men* 1919 (d); *John Petticoats* 1919 (d); *The Money Corral* 1919 (d,sc); *Square Deal Sanderson* 1919 (d); *Wagon Tracks* 1919 (d); *The Cradle of Courage* 1920 (d,sc); *Sand* 1920 (d,sc); *The Testing Block* 1920 (d,sc); *The Toll Gate* 1920 (d,sc,story); *The Man From Lost River* 1921 (sc); *O'Malley of the Mounted* 1921 (d,sc); *Three Word Brand* 1921 (d,sc); *The Whistle* 1921 (d,sc); *White Oak* 1921 (d); *The Altar Stairs* 1922 (d); *Caught Bluffing* 1922 (d); *Skin Deep* 1922 (d); *The Super-Sex* 1922 (d,sc); *Travelin' On* 1922 (d,sc); *White Hands* 1922 (d,sc); *Eyes of the Forest* 1923 (d); *The Lone Star Ranger* 1923 (d,sc); *Mile-a-Minute Romeo* 1923 (d); *Scars of Jealousy* 1923 (d,sc); *The Shock* 1923 (d); *The Spoilers* 1923 (d); *Temporary Marriage* 1923 (d,sc); *Barbara Frietchie* 1924 (d,sc); *Idle Tongues* 1924 (d); *Those Who Dance* 1924 (d,sc); *I Want My Man* 1925 (d); *The Knockout* 1925 (d); *The Making of O'Malley* 1925 (d); *The Unguarded Hour* 1925 (d); *30 Below Zero* 1926 (d); *Her Second Chance* 1926 (d); *Miss Nobody* 1926 (d); *Chain Lightning* 1927 (d,sc); *Hills of Peril* 1927 (d); *The War Horse* 1927 (d,sc,story); *The Branded Sombrero* 1928 (d,sc); *Fleetwing* 1928 (d,story); *Beau Bandit* 1930 (d); *The Hide-Out* 1930 (sc,story); *The Deadline* 1932 (d,sc,story); *The Fighting Fool* 1932 (d); *Hello, Trouble* 1932 (d,p,sc,story); *One Man Law* 1932 (d,sc,story); *South of the Rio Grande* 1932 (d); *White Eagle* 1932 (d); *Before Midnight* 1933 (d); *The California Trail* 1933 (d,sc); *Dangerous Crossroads* 1933 (d); *Master of Men* 1933 (d); *Police Car 17* 1933 (d,sc,story); *State Trooper* 1933 (story); *The Sundown Rider* 1933 (d,sc); *Unknown Valley* 1933 (d,sc); *Against the Law* 1934 (d); *The Defense Rests* 1934 (d); *The Fighting Code* 1934 (d,sc); *The Man Trailer* 1934 (d,sc); *Men of the Night* 1934 (d,sc,story); *Most Precious Thing in Life* 1934 (d); *Once to Every Woman* 1934 (d); *One Is Guilty* 1934 (d); *Straightaway* 1934 (sc,story); *Awakening of Jim Burke* 1935 (d); *Behind the Evidence* 1935 (d); *Guard That Girl* 1935 (d,sc,story); *In Spite of Danger* 1935 (d); *Law Beyond the Range* 1935 (sc,story); *Men of the Hour* 1935 (d); *Superspeed* 1935 (d); *Dangerous Waters* 1936 (d); *Dracula's Daughter* 1936 (d); *The Forbidden Trail* 1936 (d); *The Invisible Ray* 1936 (d); *All American Sweetheart* 1937 (d); *Girls Can Play* 1937 (d,sc); *Speed to Spare* 1937 (d,sc,story); *Women in Prison* 1937 (d); *Extortion* 1938 (d); *Gang Bullets* 1938 (d); *Highway Patrol* 1938 (story); *My Old Kentucky Home* 1938 (d); *Convict's Code* 1939 (d); *The Girl From Rio* 1939 (d); *Parents on Trail* 1939 (sc); *Should a Girl Marry?* 1939 (d); *Beyond the Sacramento* 1940 (d); *The Durango Kid* 1940 (d); *Hands Across the Rockies* 1941 (d); *King of Dodge City* 1941 (d); *The Medico of Painted Springs* 1941 (d); *North From the Lone Star* 1941 (d); *The Officer and the Lady* 1941 (sc,story); *The Pinto Kid* 1941 (d); *Prairie Stranger* 1941 (d); *The Return of Daniel Boone* 1941 (d);*Roaring Frontiers* 1941 (d); *The Royal Mounted Patrol* 1941 (d); *The Son of Davy Crockett*

1941 (d,sc); *Thunder Over the Prairie* 1941 (d); *The Wildcat of Tucson* 1941 (d); *The Devil's Trail* 1942 (d); *Fighting Frontier* 1942 (d); *North of the Rockies* 1942 (d); *Prairie Gunsmoke* 1942 (d); *Vengeance of the West* 1942 (d); *Batman* 1943 (d); *Six-Gun Gospel* 1943 (d); *The Stranger From Pecos* 1943 (d); *The Texas Kid* 1943 (d); *Ghost Guns* 1944 (d); *Land of the Outlaws* 1944 (d); *Law Men* 1944 (d); *Partners of the Trail* 1944 (d); *Range Law* 1944 (d); *Smart Guy* 1944 (d); *West of the Rio Grande* 1944 (d); *Border Bandits* 1945 (d); *Flame of the West* 1945 (d); *Frontier Feud* 1945 (d); *The Lost Trail* 1945 (d); *South of the Rio Grande* 1945 (d); *Stranger From Santa Fe* 1945 (d); *The Gentleman From Texas* 1946 (d); *Shadows on the Range* 1946 (d); *Silver Range* 1946 (d); *Trigger Fingers* 1946 (d); *Under Arizona Skies* 1946 (d); *The Case of the Baby Sitter* 1947 (d); *Flashing Guns* 1947 (d); *Gun Talk* 1947 (d); *The Hat Box Mystery* 1947 (d); *Land of the Lawless* 1947 (d); *Prairie Express* 1947 (d); *Raiders of the South* 1947 (d); *Song of the Drifter* 1947 (d); *Trailing Danger* 1947 (d); *Valley of Fear* 1947 (d); *Crossed Trails* 1948 (d); *The Fighting Ranger* 1948 (d); *Frontier Agent* 1948 (d); *Oklahoma Blues* 1948 (d); *Outlaw Brand* 1948 (d); *Overland Trails* 1948 (d); *Partners of the Sunset* 1948 (d); *Range Renegades* 1948 (d); *The Sheriff of Medicine Bow* 1948 (d); *Sundown Riders* 1948 (d); *Gun Law Justice* 1949 (d); *Gun Runner* 1949 (d); *Haunted Trails* 1949 (d); *Range Land* 1949 (d); *Riders of the Dusk* 1949 (d); *Trail's End* 1949 (d).

Hines, Gregory • Actor, dancer • Born New York, NY, February 14, 1946. Black tap dancer extraordinaire who made his professional debut at the age of five with his brother Maurice and was appearing on Broadway three years later. Hines began landing both dancing and dramatic film roles in the 1980s, notably opposite Mikhail Baryshnikov in *White Nights* (1985). • *History of the World Part I* 1981 (a); *Wolfen* 1981 (a); *Deal of the Century* 1983 (a); *The Cotton Club* 1984 (a,chor); *The Muppets Take Manhattan* 1984 (a); *White Nights* 1985 (a,chor); *Running Scared* 1986 (a); *Off Limits* 1988 (a); *Tap* 1989 (a,chor); *Eve of Destruction* 1991 (a); *A Rage in Harlem* 1991 (a).

Hirszman, Leon • Director; also screenwriter. • Born Rio de Janeiro, Brazil, 1937; died September 15, 1987, Rio de Janeiro, Brazil. Leading filmmaker associated with Brazil's Cinema Novo movement. His best known works are *Sao Bernardo* (1970), considered a Brazilian classic, and *They Don't Wear Black Tie* (1981), which won an award at the Venice Film Festival. • *A Falecida* 1965 (d); *Sao Bernardo* 1970 (d); *Eles Nao Usam Black Tie/They Don't Wear Black Tie* 1981 (d); *Imagens do inconsciente* 1988 (d).

Hitchcock, Sir Alfred • Director; also screenwriter, producer. • Born Alfred Joseph Hitchcock, Leytonstone, England, August 13, 1899; died April 28, 1980. *Educ.* St.Ignatius College, London; School of Engineering and Navigation (mechanics, electricity, acoustics, navigation); University of London (art). The acknowledged master of the thriller genre he virtually invented, Alfred Hitchcock was also a brilliant technician who deftly blended sex, suspense and humor. He began his filmmaking career in 1919 illustrating title cards for silent films at Paramount's Famous Players-Lasky studio in London. There he learned scripting, editing and art direction, and rose to assistant director in 1922. That year he directed an unfinished film, *No. 13* or *Mrs. Peabody*. His first completed film as director was *The Pleasure Garden* (1925), an Anglo-German production filmed in Munich. This experience, plus a stint at Germany's UFA studios as an assistant director, help account for the Expressionistic character of his films, both in their visual schemes and thematic concerns. *The Lodger* (1926), his breakthrough film, was a prototypical example of the classic Hitchcock plot: an innocent protagonist is falsely accused of a crime and becomes involved in a web of intrigue.

An early example of Hitchcock's technical virtuosity was his creation of "subjective sound" for *Blackmail* (1929), his first sound film. In this story of a woman who stabs an artist to death when he tries to seduce her, Hitchcock emphasized the young woman's anxiety by gradually distorting all but one word—"knife"—of a neighbor's dialogue the morning after the killing. Here and in *Murder* (1930), Hitchcock first made explicit the link between sex and violence.

The Man Who Knew Too Much (1934), a commercial and critical success, established a favorite pattern: an investigation of family relationships within a suspenseful story. *The 39 Steps* (1935) showcases a mature Hitchcock; it is a stylish and efficiently told chase film brimming with exciting incidents and memorable characters. Despite their merits, both *The Secret Agent* and *Sabotage* (both 1936) exhibited flaws Hitchcock later acknowledged and learned from. According to his theory, suspense is developed by providing the audience with information denied endangered characters. But to be most effective and cathartic, no harm should come to the innocent—as it does in both of those films. *The Lady Vanishes* (1938), on the other hand, is sleek, exemplary Hitchcock: fast-paced, witty, and magnificently entertaining.

Hitchcock's last British film, *Jamaica Inn* (1939), and his first Hollywood effort, *Rebecca* (1940), were both handsomely mounted though somewhat uncharacteristic works based on novels by Daphne du Maurier. Despite its somewhat muddled narrative, *Foreign Correspondent* (1940) was the first Hollywood film in his recognizable style. *Suspicion* (1941), the story of a woman whothinks her husband is a murderer about to make her his next victim, was an exploration of family dynamics; its introduction of evil into the domestic arena foreshadowed *Shadow of a Doubt* (1943), Hitchcock's early Hollywood masterwork. One of his most disturbing films, *Shadow* was nominally the story of a young woman who learns that a favorite uncle is a murderer, but at heart it is a sobering look at the dark underpinnings of American middle-class life. Fully as horrifying as Uncle Charlie's attempts to murder his niece was her mother's tearful acknowledgment of her loss of identity in becoming a wife and mother. "You know how it is," she says, "you sort of forget you're you. You're your husband's wife." In Hitchcock, evil manifests itself not only in acts of physical violence, but also in the form of psychological, institutionalized and systemic cruelty.

Hitchcock would return to the feminine sacrifice-of-identity theme several times, most immediately with the masterful *Notorious* (1946), a perverse love story about an FBI agent who must send the woman he loves into the arms of a Nazi in order to uncover an espionage ring. Other psychological dramas of the late 1940s were *Spellbound* (1945), *The Paradine Case* (1947), and *Under Capricorn* (1949). Both *Lifeboat* (1944) and *Rope* (1948) were interesting technical excercises: in the former, the object was to tell a film story within the confines of a small boat; in *Rope*, Hitchcock sought to make a film that appeared to be a single, unedited shot. *Rope* shared with the more effective *Strangers on a Train* (1951) a villain intent on committing the perfect murder as well as a strong homoerotic undercurrent.

During his most inspired period, from 1950 to 1960, Hitchcock produced a cycle of memorable films which included minor works such as *I Confess* (1953), the sophisticated thrillers *Dial M for Murder* (1954) and *To Catch a Thief* (1955), a bland remake of *The Man Who Knew Too Much* (1956) and the black comedy *The Trouble with Harry* (1955). He also directed several top-drawer films like *Strangers on a Train* and the troubling early docudrama *The Wrong Man* (1956), a searing critique of the American justice system.

His three unalloyed masterpieces of the period were investigations into the very nature of watching cinema. *Rear Window* (1954) made viewers voyeurs, then had them pay for their pleasure. In its story of a photographer who happens to witness a murder, Hitchcock provocatively probed the relationship between the watcher and the watched, involving, by extension, the viewer of the film. *Vertigo* (1958), as haunting a movie as Hollywood has ever produced, took the lost-feminine-identity theme of *Shadow of a Doubt* and *Notorious* and identified its cause as male fetishism.

North by Northwest (1959) is perhaps Hitchcock's most fully realized film. From a script by Ernest Lehman, with a score (as usual) by Bernard Herrmann, and starring Cary Grant and Eva MarieSaint, this quintessential chase movie is full of all the things for which we remember Alfred Hitchcock: ingenious shots, subtle male–female relationships, dramatic score, bright technicolor, inside jokes, witty symbolism and—above all—masterfully orchestrated suspense.

Psycho (1960) is famed for its shower murder sequence—a classic model of shot selection and editing which was startling for its (apparent) nudity, graphic violence and its violation of the narrative convention that makes a protagonist invulnerable. Moreover, the progressive shots of eyes, beginning with an extreme close-up of the killer's peeping eye and ending with the open eye of the murder victim, subtly implied the presence of a third eye—the viewer's.

Later films offered intriguing amplifications of his main themes. *The Birds* (1963) presented evil as an environmental fact of life. *Marnie* (1964), a psychoanalytical thriller along the lines of *Spellbound,* showed how a violent, sexually tinged childhood episode turns a woman into a thief, once again associating criminality with violence and sex. Most notable about *Torn Curtain* (1966), an espionage story played against a cold war backdrop, was its extended fight-to-the death scene between the protagonist and a Communist agent in the kitchen of a farm house. In it Hitchcock reversed the movie convention of quick, easy deaths and showed how difficult—and how momentous—the act of killing really is.

Hitchcock's disappointing *Topaz* (1969), an unwieldy, unfocused story set during the Cuban missile crisis, was devoid of his typical narrative economy and wit. He returned to England to produce *Frenzy* (1972), a tale much more in the Hitchcock vein, about an innocent man suspected of being a serial killer. His final film, *Family Plot* (1976), pitted two couples against one another: a pair of professional thieves versus a female psychic and her working-class lover. It was a fitting end to a body of work that demonstrated the eternal symmetry of good and evil. CRB • (All films until 1923 as inter–titles designer): *Appearances* 1921; *The Bonnie Brier Bush* 1921; *The Call of Youth* 1921; *Dangerous Lies* 1921; *The Great Day* 1921; *The Mystery Road* 1921; *The Princess of New York* 1921; *Love's Boomerang* 1922; *The Man From Home* 1922; *The Spanish Jade* 1922; *Tell Your Children* 1922; *Three Live Ghosts* 1922; *The White Shadow* 1923 (ed,art d); *Woman to Woman* 1923 (sc,ed,art d,ad); *The Passionate Adventure* 1924 (sc,art d,ad); *The Prude's Fall* 1924 (sc,art d,ad); *The Blackguard* 1925 (sc,art d,ad); *The Pleasure Garden* 1925 (d); *The Lodger* 1926 (d,sc); *The Mountain Eagle* 1926 (d); *Downhill* 1927 (d); *Easy Virtue* 1927 (d); *The Ring* 1927 (d,sc,story); *Champagne* 1928 (d,sc,adapt); *The Farmer's Wife* 1928 (d,sc); *Blackmail* 1929 (d,sc,adapt); *The Manxman* 1929 (d); *Elstree Calling* 1930 (d); *Juno and the Paycock* 1930 (d,sc); *Murder* 1930 (adapt,d); *The Skin Game* 1931 (d,sc,adapt); *Number Seventeen* 1932 (d,sc); *Rich and Strange* 1932 (adapt,d); *The Man Who Knew Too Much* 1934 (d); *Waltzes From Vienna* 1934 (d); *The 39 Steps* 1935 (d); *Sabotage* 1936 (d); *Secret Agent* 1936 (d); *Young and Innocent* 1937 (d); *The Lady Vanishes* 1938 (d); *Jamaica Inn* 1939 (d); *Foreign Correspondent* 1940 (d); *The House Across the Bay* 1940 (add.d); *Rebecca* 1940 (d) **(AANBD)**; *Mr. & Mrs. Smith* 1941 (d); *Suspicion* 1941 (d); *Saboteur* 1942 (d); *Shadow of a Doubt* 1943 (d); *Lifeboat* 1944 (d) **(AANBD)**; *Spellbound* 1945 (d) **(AANBD)**; *Notorious* 1946 (d,p); *The Paradine Case* 1947 (d); *Rope* 1948 (d,p); *Under Capricorn* 1949 (d,p); *Stage Fright* 1950 (d,p); *Strangers on a Train* 1951 (d,p); *I Confess* 1953 (d,p); *Dial M For Murder* 1954 (d,p); *Rear Window* 1954 (d,p) **(AANBD)**; *To Catch a Thief* 1955 (d,p); *The Trouble With Harry* 1955 (d,p); *The Man Who Knew Too Much* 1956 (d,p); *The Wrong Man* 1956 (a,d,p); *Vertigo* 1958 (d,p); *North By Northwest* 1959 (d,p); *The Gazebo* 1960 (a); *Psycho* 1960 (d) **(AANBD)**; *The Birds* 1963 (d,p); *Marnie* 1964 (d,p); *Torn Curtain* 1966 (d,p); *Topaz* 1969 (d,p); *Frenzy* 1972 (d,p); *Family Plot* 1976 (d,p).

Hodges, Mike • Director • Born Michael Hodges, Bristol, England, 1932. *Educ.* Prior Park College, Bath (accounting). TV graduate whose film debut, *Get Carter* (1971), showed considerable promise. Hodges's interests continue to oscillate—with varying degrees of success—between pulp fiction and politics. • *Get Carter* 1971 (d,sc); *Pulp* 1972 (d,sc); *The Terminal Man* 1974 (d,p,sc); *Damien: Omen II* 1978 (sc); *Flash Gordon* 1980 (d); *E la nave Va/And the Ship Sails On* 1983 (d—English-language version); *Squaring the Circle* 1983 (d); *Buried Alive* 1984 (d,sc); *Morons From Outer Space* 1985 (d); *A Prayer For the Dying* 1987 (d); *Black Rainbow* 1989 (d,sc).

Hoffman, Dustin • Actor • Born Los Angeles, CA, August 8, 1937. *Educ.* Los Angeles Conservatory of Music; Santa Monica City College; Pasadena Playhouse. Dustin Hoffman burst upon the American cinema scene in 1967 in Mike Nichols's *The Graduate.* As Benjamin Braddock, Hoffman proved problematic for a generation of young people who strongly rejected the values of their parents but felt uncertain and confused about their future. Navigating that treacherous strait between satiric caricature and method drama, Hoffman delivered a hilarious yet profoundly moving performance. Somewhere between his comic seduction by Anne Bancroft's Mrs. Robinson and his anguish in the film's climactic wedding scene, Hoffman became a screen icon of unusual proportions. Although stardom for men in the American cinema had previously been reserved for the conventionally attractive or rugged, Hoffman succeeded in part *because* of his unconventional looks and short stature; he soon joined other less conventional looking performers like Barbra Streisand and Jack Nicholson as new stars for a new generation of moviegoers.

An Academy Award nomination for *The Graduate* was followed by another Oscar-nominated performance, as Ratso Rizzo in *Midnight Cowboy* (1969), an urban drama that was a landmark for new screen frankness in its depiction of the sordid world of street hustlers. Ratso was a wheezing, scruffy, dumb, tubercular loser; it was a case of an actor unafraid to immerse his already unconventional looks in a character even more physically unattractive. Notable too was Hoffman's willingness, after the huge success of *The Graduate,* to take essentially a subsidiary role to the lead character played by Jon Voight.

John and Mary (1969), though not a critical success, showed Hoffman's ability to play a more conventional role as a young man, opposite Mia Farrow, confronting contemporary courtship rituals. In *Lenny* (1974), Hoffman was nominated for an Academy Award, again for an unpleasant characterization: a complex, multi-dimensional portrait of the hard-driving social comedian Lenny Bruce. In *All the President's Men* (1976), he played Carl Bernstein, the aggressive reporter who helped expose Nixon's Watergate crimes. *Straight Time* (1978) failed to attract popular attention, but Hoffman's critically acclaimed performance as a hardcore criminal stands as a hallmark of his approach to performance, which eschews easy sentiment in favor of three-dimensional grit.

Hoffman scored a popular success in 1979 with his most accessible performance (and his first Academy Award), opposite Meryl Streep in *Kramer vs. Kramer,* as a father who must develop a relationship with his young son when his wife temporarily abandons them. If the subtext of *Kramer vs. Kramer* implied that a man could be a better mother than a woman, Hoffman's next film, *Tootsie* (1982) showed that a man could be a better woman than a woman. In this very funny comedy about role reversal, Hoffman plays an actor who masquerades as a woman in order to get a part on a soap opera and then promptly becomes a public role model as a liberated, feminist woman. Although *Tootsie* showed Hoffman's continuing interest in transforming his physical appearance, his performance is somewhat atypically (if appropriately) warm; on some level it seems a valentine to all underemployed actors, for whom Hoffman retains tremendous empathy.

His Broadway performance as Willy Loman in *Death of a Salesman,* filmed in 1985, was the subject of mixed reviews. Competing with the ghost of Lee J. Cobb's original stage performance and Hoffman's own iconic definition as Benjamin Braddock, some critics found Hoffman too slight and too young—ignoring the fact that Hoffman was almost a decade older than Cobb when Cobb first played the role on Broadway, and that Arthur Miller had described Loman as a small and "low" man.

After the failure of *Ishtar* (1987), Hoffman won a second Academy Award for his riveting portrayal of Ramond Babbit, an autistic savant in *Rain Man* (1988). Hoffman's performance is again notable not only for his physical transformation, but for his absolute unwillingness to become sentimental or maudlin; indeed, Raymond may be the most objective, unsentimental depiction of a handicapped person in the American cinema. *Rain Man* also suggests a transition point in screen history. Just as Hoffman came to prominence as the star for a 60s generation, his pairing in *Rain Man* opposite Tom Cruise suggests the passing of the mantle to a new star more accessible to the 80s generation of young filmgoers. CD. • *The Graduate* 1967 (a) **(AANBA)**; *The Tiger Makes Out* 1967 (a); *John and Mary* 1969 (a); *Madigan's Millions* 1969 (a); *Midnight Cowboy* 1969 (a) **(AANBA)**; *Little Big Man* 1970 (a); *Straw Dogs* 1971 (a); *Who Is Harry Kellerman, and Why Is He Saying Those Terrible Things About Me?* 1971 (a); *Alfredo, Alfredo* 1973 (a); *Papillon* 1973 (a); *Lenny* 1974 (a) **(AANBA)**; *All the President's Men* 1976 (a); *Marathon Man* 1976 (a); *Straight Time* 1978 (a); *Agatha* 1979 (a); *Kramer vs. Kramer* 1979 (a) **(AABA)**; *Tootsie* 1982 (a) **(AANBA)**; *Death of a Salesman* 1985 (a); *Private Conversations* 1985 (a); *Ishtar* 1987 (a,songs); *Rain Man* 1988 (a) **(AABA)**; *Family Business* 1989 (a); *Dick Tracy* 1990 (a).

Hogan, Paul • Actor; also producer, screenwriter, director. • Born Australia, 1942. Best known in the US for the hugely successful *Crocodile Dundee* (1986) and several TV commercials which also traded on the "beer'n'barbie" stereotype of Australian culture. Married to *Crocodile* co-star Linda Kozlowski. • *Anzacs* 1985 (a); *Crocodile Dundee* 1986 (a,sc,from original story) **(AANBSC)**; *Crocodile Dundee 2* 1988 (a,exec.p,sc); *The Humpty Dumpty Man* 1989 (d,sc); *Almost an Angel* 1990 (a,exec.p,sc).

Holden, William • Actor • Born William Franklin Beedle, Jr., O'Fallon, IL, April 17, 1918; died November 16, 1981. *Educ.* Pasedena Junior College, CA. Dependable leading man whose career peaked in the 1950s. The earnest quality of his early roles gradually yielded to cynicism in the later films, notably *Sunset Boulevard* (1950). Married to leading lady Brenda Marshall from 1941 to 1970. • *Prison Farm* 1938 (a); *Golden Boy* 1939 (a); *Million Dollar Legs* 1939 (a); *Arizona* 1940 (a); *Invisible Stripes* 1940 (a); *Our Town* 1940 (a); *Those Were The Days* 1940 (a); *I Wanted Wings* 1941 (a); *Texas* 1941 (a); *The Fleet's In* 1942 (a); *Meet the Stewarts* 1942 (a); *The Remarkable Andrew* 1942 (a); *Young and Willing* 1943 (a); *Blaze of Noon* 1947 (a); *Dear Ruth* 1947 (a); *Variety Girl* 1947 (a); *Apartment For Peggy* 1948 (a); *The Dark Past* 1948 (a); *The Man From Colorado* 1948 (a); *Rachel and the Stranger* 1948 (a); *Miss Grant Takes Richmond* 1949 (a); *Streets of Laredo* 1949 (a); *Born Yesterday* 1950 (a); *Dear Wife* 1950 (a); *Father Is a Bachelor* 1950 (a); *Sunset Boulevard* 1950 (a) **(AANBA)**; *Union Station* 1950 (a); *Force of Arms* 1951 (a); *Submarine Command* 1951 (a); *Boots Malone* 1952 (a); *The Turning Point* 1952 (a);*Escape From Fort Bravo* 1953 (a); *Forever Female* 1953 (a); *The Moon Is Blue* 1953 (a); *Stalag 17* 1953 (a) **(AABA)**; *The Country Girl* 1954 (a); *Executive Suite* 1954 (a); *Miyamoto Musashi* 1954 (a,ed); *Sabrina* 1954 (a); *The Bridges at Toko-Ri* 1955 (a); *Love Is a Many Splendored Thing* 1955 (a); *Picnic* 1956 (a); *The Proud and the Profane* 1956 (a); *Toward the Unknown* 1956 (a); *The Bridge on the River Kwai* 1957 (a); *The Key* 1958 (a); *The Horse Soldiers* 1959 (a); *The World of Suzie Wong* 1960 (a); *The Counterfeit Traitor* 1962 (a); *The Lion* 1962 (a); *Satan Never Sleeps* 1962 (a); *Paris When It Sizzles* 1963 (a); *The 7th Dawn* 1964 (a); *Alvarez Kelly* 1966 (a); *Casino Royale* 1967 (a); *The Devil's Brigade* 1968 (a); *L'Arbre de Noel* 1969 (a); *The Wild Bunch* 1969 (a); *Wild Rovers* 1971 (a); *The Revengers* 1972 (a); *Breezy* 1973 (a); *Open Season* 1974 (a); *The Towering Inferno* 1974 (a); *Network* 1976 (a) **(AANBA)**; *Damien: Omen II* 1978 (a); *Fedora* 1978 (a); *Ashanti* 1979 (a); *Escape to Athena* 1979 (a); *The Earthling* 1980 (a); *When Time Ran Out* 1980 (a); *S.O.B.* 1981 (a).

Holland, Agnieszka • Director, screenwriter • Born Warsaw, Poland, November 28, 1948. *Educ.* FAMU, Prague. Sometime screenwriter for Andrzej Wajda whose own films as a director have focused on the lives of the marginal and the doomed. Holland studied filmmaking in Czechoslovakia under Milos Forman and Ivan Passer, returning to Poland in 1972 after police harassment had culminated in a jail sentence. She made her co-directing debut in 1977 with *Screen Tests* and wrote her first screenplay for Wajda, *Without Anaesthesia*, in 1978. Two years later her solo feature directing debut, *Provincial Actors*, won the FIPRESCI (International Critics') prize at Cannes. After the imposition of martial law in 1981 Holland emigrated to Paris, where she still lives.

Holland's last Polish feature, *A Woman Alone* (1981), chronicles the grim plight of an unmarried mother employed as a letter-carrier. The 1985 West German film *Angry Harvest* reverted to a wartime theme, detailing the relations between a mildly prosperous farmer and the Jewish refugee woman he discovers and shelters. Holland married Czech director Laco Adamik, by whom she has one daughter, in 1968. • *Zdjecia Probne/Screen Tests* 1977 (d,sc); *Aktorzy prowincjonalni/Provincial Actors* 1979 (d,sc); *Bez Znieczulenia* 1979 (sc); *Goraczka* 1980 (d); *Kobieta samotna/A Woman Alone* 1981 (d,sc); *Danton* 1982 (sc); *Przesluchanie* 1982 (a); *Eine Liebe in Deutschland* 1983 (sc); *Bittere Ernte/Angry Harvest* 1985 (d,sc); *Anna* 1987 (sc,story); *Les Possédés* 1987 (sc); *La Amiga* 1988 (sc); *Popielusko* 1988 (d,sc); *Europa, Europa* 1990 (d,sc); *Korczak* 1990 (sc).

Holliday, Judy • Actress; also comedienne. • Born Judith Tuvim, New York, NY, June 21, 1922; died 1965. Spirited, intelligent actress who played variations on the "dumb blonde" role in a number of breezy comedies of the 1940s and 50s; memorable in *Adam's Rib* (1949). • *Greenwich Village* 1944 (a); *Something For the Boys* 1944 (a); *Winged Victory* 1944 (a); *Adam's Rib* 1949 (a); *Born Yesterday* 1950 (a) **(AABA)**; *The Marrying Kind* 1952 (a); *It Should Happen to You* 1954 (a); *Phfft* 1954 (a); *The Solid Gold Cadillac* 1956 (a); *Full of Life* 1957 (a); *Bells Are Ringing* 1960 (a).

Holm, Ian • Actor • Born Ian Holm Cuthbert, Goodmayes, England, September 12, 1931. *Educ.* RADA, London. Preeminent British character player who began his career with the Stratford (later Royal Shakespeare) Company in the mid-1950s and emerged as a solid film presence in the late 60s. Memorable as a calculating robot in *Alien* (1979) and a blandly evil bureaucrat in *Brazil* (1985). • *The Bofors Gun* 1968; *The Fixer* 1968; *A Midsummer Night's Dream* 1968; *Oh! What a Lovely War* 1969; *A Severed Head* 1970; *Mary, Queen of Scots* 1971; *Nicholas and Alexandra* 1971; *Young Winston* 1972; *The Homecoming* 1973; *Juggernaut* 1974; *Robin and Marian* 1976; *Shout at the Devil* 1976; *March or Die* 1977; *The Thief of Bagdad* 1978; *Alien* 1979; *Chariots of Fire* 1981 **(AANBSA)**; *Time Bandits* 1981; *Battle For the Falklands* 1982; *The Return of the Soldier* 1982; *Greystoke: The Legend of Tarzan, Lord of the Apes* 1984; *Laughterhouse* 1984; *Brazil* 1985; *Dance With a Stranger* 1985; *Dreamchild* 1985; *Wetherby* 1985; *Another Woman* 1988; *Henry V* 1989; *Hamlet* 1990.

Holt, Tim • Actor • Born Charles John Holt Jr., Beverly Hills, CA, February 5, 1918; died 1973. *Educ.* Culver Military Academy. Began his career as a child actor in silent films starring his father, Jack Holt, and graduated to juvenile parts in B productions of the 1930s. Holt landed significant roles in *The Magnificent Ambersons* (1942) and, opposite Humphrey Bogart, in *The Treasure of the Sierra Madre* (1948). Brother of B-movie actress Jennifer Holt (born 1920). • *The Vanishing Pioneer* 1928; *History Is Made at Night* 1937; *Stella Dallas* 1937; *Gold Is Where You Find It* 1938; *I Met My Love Again* 1938; *The Law West of Tombstone* 1938; *Sons of The Legion* 1938; *Fifth Avenue Girl* 1939; *The Girl and the Gambler* 1939; *The Renegade Ranger* 1939; *The Rookie Cop* 1939; *Spirit of Culver* 1939; *Stagecoach* 1939; *The Fargo Kid* 1940; *Laddie* 1940; *The Swiss Family Robinson* 1940; *Wagon Train* 1940; *Along the Rio Grande* 1941; *Back Street* 1941; *The Bandit Trail* 1941; *Come on Danger* 1941; *Cyclone on Horseback* 1941; *Dude Cowboy* 1941; *Land of the Open Range* 1941; *Riding the Wind* 1941; *Robbers of the Range* 1941; *Six-Gun Gold* 1941; *Thundering Hoofs* 1941; *Bandit Ranger* 1942; *Fighting Frontier* 1942; *The Magnificent Ambersons* 1942; *Pirates of the Prairie* 1942; *Red River Robin Hood* 1942; *The Avenging Rider* 1943; *Hitler's Children* 1943; *Sagebrush Law* 1943; *My Darling Clementine* 1946; *The Arizona Ranger* 1947; *Thunder Mountain* 1947; *Under the Tonto Rim* 1947; *Wild Horse Mesa* 1947; *Gun Smugglers* 1948; *Guns of Hate* 1948; *Indian Agent* 1948; *The Treasure of the Sierra Madre* 1948; *Western Heritage* 1948; *Brothers in the Saddle* 1949; *Masked Raiders* 1949; *The Mysterious Desperado* 1949; *Riders of the Range* 1949; *The Rustlers* 1949; *Stagecoach Kid* 1949; *Border Treasure* 1950; *Dynamite Pass* 1950; *Law of the Badlands* 1950; *Rider From Tucson* 1950; *Rio Grande Patrol* 1950; *Storm Over Wyoming* 1950; *Gunplay* 1951; *His Kind of Woman* 1951; *Hot Lead* 1951; *Overland Telegraph* 1951; *Pistol Harvest* 1951; *Saddle Legion* 1951; *Desert Passage* 1952; *Road Agent* 1952; *Target* 1952; *Trail Guide* 1952; *The Monster That Challenged the World* 1957; *This Stuff'll Kill Ya!* 1971.

Homolka, Oscar • *aka* Oskar Homolka • Actor • Born Vienna, Austria, August 12, 1898; died 1978. *Educ.* Royal Dramatic Academy, Vienna. Austrian actor whose broad "Brezhnevite" features and Slavic accent were exploited in both comic and villainous roles after he settled in the US in 1936. • *Schinderhannes* 1927; *Rhodes of Africa* 1935; *Sabotage* 1936; *Ebb Tide* 1937; *Comrade X* 1940; *Seven Sinners* 1940; *Ball of Fire* 1941; *The Invisible Woman* 1941; *Rage in Heaven* 1941; *Hostages* 1943; *Mission to Moscow* 1943; *I Remember Mama* 1948 (**AANBSA**); *Anna Lucasta* 1949; *The White Tower* 1950; *Top Secret* 1952; *Prisoner of War* 1954; *The Seven Year Itch* 1955; *War and Peace* 1956; *A Farewell to Arms* 1957; *The Key* 1958; *La Tempesta* 1958; *Mr. Sardonicus* 1961; *Boys' Night Out* 1962; *The Wonderful World of the Brothers Grimm* 1962; *Joy in the Morning* 1965; *Funeral in Berlin* 1966; *Billion Dollar Brain* 1967; *The Happening* 1967; *Assignment to Kill* 1968; *The Madwoman of Chaillot* 1969; *The Executioner* 1970; *Song of Norway* 1970; *The Tamarind Seed* 1974.

Hooper, Tobe • Director • Born Austin, TX, 1946. One of the foremost practitioners of the "splatter" horror genre, whose crowning achievement to date is the grisly cult classic, *The Texas Chainsaw Massacre* (1974). Made on a budget of approximately $350,000, the film has grossed in excess of $3 million. • *Eggshells* 1969 (d,p,sc); *The Windsplitter* 1971 (a); *The Texas Chainsaw Massacre* 1974 (d,p,sc,story,add.ph,m); *Eaten Alive* 1977 (d,story,m); *The Funhouse* 1981 (d); *Poltergeist* 1982 (d); *Lifeforce* 1985 (d); *Invaders From Mars* 1986 (d); *The Texas Chainsaw Massacre 2* 1986 (d,m,modelmaker,p); *Spontaneous Combustion* 1989 (d,sc); *Leatherface: The Texas Chainsaw Massacre III* 1990 (from characters).

Hope, Bob • Actor • Born Leslie Townes Hope, Eltham, England, May 29, 1903. In the US from age four, Hope drifted intovaudeville in the 1920s and made his Broadway musical debut in 1933. After appearing in short films and on radio he moved to Hollywood in 1938, first teaming up with Bing Crosby in *The Road to Singapore* (1940). Trading on his knack for rapid-fire wisecracking, Hope made seven "road" films with Crosby and Dorothy Lamour and went on to become a showbiz institution. His image as a tame tweaker of contemporary foibles has been bolstered by legions of gag writers through the years. • *The Big Broadcast of 1938* 1938 (a); *College Swing* 1938 (a); *Give Me a Sailor* 1938 (a); *Thanks For the Memory* 1938 (a); *The Cat and the Canary* 1939 (a); *Never Say Die* 1939 (a); *Some Like It Hot* 1939 (a); *The Ghost Breakers* 1940 (a); *Road to Singapore* 1940 (a); *Caught in the Draft* 1941 (a); *Louisiana Purchase* 1941 (a); *Nothing But the Truth* 1941 (a); *Road to Zanzibar* 1941 (a); *My Favorite Blonde* 1942 (a); *Road to Morocco* 1942 (a); *Star Spangled Rhythm* 1942 (a); *Let's Face It* 1943 (a); *They Got Me Covered* 1943 (a); *Welcome to Britain* 1943 (a); *The Princess and the Pirate* 1944 (a); *Duffy's Tavern* 1945 (a); *Monsieur Beaucaire* 1946 (a); *The Road to Utopia* 1946 (a); *My Favorite Brunette* 1947 (a); *Road to Rio* 1947 (a); *Variety Girl* 1947 (a); *Where There's Life* 1947 (a); *The Paleface* 1948 (a); *The Great Lover* 1949 (a); *Sorrowful Jones* 1949 (a); *Fancy Pants* 1950 (a); *The Lemon Drop Kid* 1951 (a); *My Favorite Spy* 1951 (a); *The Greatest Show on Earth* 1952 (a); *Road to Bali* 1952 (a); *Son of Paleface* 1952 (a); *Here Come the Girls* 1953 (a); *Off Limits* 1953 (a); *Casanova's Big Night* 1954 (a); *The Seven Little Foys* 1955 (a); *The Iron Petticoat* 1956 (a); *That Certain Feeling* 1956 (a); *Beau James* 1957 (a); *Paris Holiday* 1958 (a,p,story); *Alias Jesse James* 1959 (a,exec.p); *The Five Pennies* 1959 (a); *The Facts of Life* 1960 (a); *Bachelor in Paradise* 1961 (a); *The Road to Hong Kong* 1962 (a); *Call Me Bwana* 1963 (a); *Critic's Choice* 1963 (a); *A Global Affair* 1964 (a); *I'll Take Sweden* 1965 (a); *Boy, Did I Get a Wrong Number!* 1966 (a); *Not With My Wife, You Don't* 1966 (a); *The Oscar* 1966 (a); *Eight on the Lam* 1967 (a); *The Private Navy of Sgt. O'Farrell* 1968 (a); *How to Commit Marriage* 1969 (a,exec.p); *Cancel My Reservation* 1972 (a,exec.p); *Hearts and Minds* 1974 (archival footage); *It's Showtime* 1976 (a); *The Muppet Movie* 1979 (a); *Going Hollywood: The War Years* 1988 (archival footage); *The Best Show in Town* 1989 (a); *Entertaining the Troops* 1989 (a).

Hopkins, Anthony • Actor • Born Port Talbot, South Wales, December 31, 1937. *Educ.* Cardiff College of Drama, Wales; RADA, London. Celebrated British stage actor who has also done fine work in films such as *The Looking Glass War* (1970) and *84 Charing Cross Road* (1986). Hopkins made an indelible impression, and reached his widest audience to date, as Hannibal "The Cannibal" Lecter, the brilliant, cultivated serial killer at the center of Jonathan Demme's *The Silence of the Lambs* (1991). • *The White Bus (short)* 1967; *The Lion in Winter* 1968; *Hamlet* 1970; *The Looking Glass War* 1970; *When Eight Bells Toll* 1971; *Young Winston* 1972; *A Doll's House* 1973; *The Girl From Petrovka* 1974; *Juggernaut* 1974; *Audrey Rose* 1977; *A Bridge Too Far* 1977; *International Velvet* 1978; *Magic* 1978; *A Change of Seasons* 1980; *The Elephant Man* 1980; *The Bounty* 1984; *84 Charing Cross Road* 1986; *Blunt* 1986; *The Good Father* 1986; *The Dawning* 1988; *A Chorus of Disapproval* 1989; *Desperate Hours* 1990; *The Silence of the Lambs* 1991.

Hopkins, Miriam • Actress; also dancer. • Born Ellen Miriam Hopkins, Bainbridge, GA, October 18, 1902; died October 9, 1972, New York, NY. *Educ.* Goddard Seminary, Barre, VT; Syracuse University, NY (ballet). Broadway actress who signed with Paramount in 1930 and gained early attention for her roles in productions including *Trouble in Paradise* (1932) and *Becky Sharp* (1935). Hopkins returned to the stage in the 1940s and began playing film character parts in the 50s. Her third husband was director Anatole Litvak. • *Fast and Loose* 1930 (a); *24 Hours* 1931 (a); *The Smiling Lieutenant* 1931 (a); *Dancers in the Dark* 1932 (a); *Dr. Jekyll and Mr. Hyde* 1932 (a); *Trouble in Paradise* 1932 (a); *Two Kinds of Women* 1932 (a); *The World and the Flesh* 1932 (a); *The Story of Temple Drake* 1933 (a); *The Stranger's Return* 1933 (a); *All of Me* 1934 (a); *The Richest Girl in the World* 1934 (a); *She Loves Me Not* 1934 (a); *Barbary Coast*

1935 (a); *Becky Sharp* 1935 (a) **(AANBA)**; *Splendor* 1935 (a); *These Three* 1936 (a); *Wise Girl* 1937 (a); *Woman Chases Man* 1937 (a); *The Woman I Love* 1937 (a); *The Old Maid* 1939 (a); *Lady With Red Hair* 1940 (a); *Virginia City* 1940 (a); *A Gentleman After Dark* 1942 (a); *Old Acquaintance* 1943 (a); *The Heiress* 1949 (a); *The Mating Season* 1950 (a); *Carrie* 1952 (a); *The Outcasts of Poker Flat* 1952 (a); *The Children's Hour* 1961 (a); *Fanny Hill: Memoirs of a Woman of Pleasure* 1965 (a); *The Chase* 1966 (a).

Hopper, Dennis • Actor, director; also screenwriter, photographer. • Born Dodge City, KS, May 17, 1936. *Educ.* Old Globe Theatre, San Diego, CA; Actors Studio. Dennis Hopper's career has been a process of self-mythification since his first screen appearance in *Rebel Without a Cause* (1955). His search for a cause has preoccupied him ever since, through various phases as an actor, director, writer and photographer.

Because *Rebel* became a clarion call for a generation about to revolt against middle-class American respectability, Hopper himself came to symbolize that revolution, particularly as other actors associated with *Rebel* died. (By 1981, Hopper and Corey Allen were the lone survivors of the film's leading players.) His early acting career often cast him in secondary roles, playing sensitive young men, as in *Giant* (1956) and a spate of westerns. His intuitive, improvisatory approach was at odds with many old-time Hollywood professionals; during the making of *From Hell to Texas* (1958), director Henry Hathaway and Hopper reportedly battled through over 100 takes, an infamous incident that Hopper claimed relegated him to B-movie roles for years.

Hopper's anti-Establishment reputation took an ironic turn with his direction of *Easy Rider* (1969), a road movie on motorcycles through reactionary America, a trip in more than one sense—the film featured a notorious psychedelic sequence, shot in a cemetery in New Orleans. Hailed by critics, feted at the Cannes Film Festival as a major new filmmaker, Hopper also found success at home when the movie was a box-office smash.

The Hopper self-mythification ascended through a documentary self-portrait called *The American Dreamer* (1971) and reached a culmination of sorts in *The Last Movie* (1971), his free-form film, shot in Peru, about a movie crew making a western among natives who decide to ape them with real bullets. The film's pretensions were deemed ludicrous, and Hopper was virtually abandoned by critics and other filmmakers.

For the next 15 years Hopper acted mostly in films shot outside the US, where audiences remained loyal to his impervious, impenetrable American swagger. Among his credits were *Mad Dog* (1976), filmed in Australia; *Resurrection* (1979), in Spain; *The American Friend* (1977) and *White Star* (1981), in West Germany; *Couleur chair* (1977), *The Sorcerer's Apprentices* (1977) and *L'Ordre et la Sécurité du Monde* (1978) in France. While acting in *Out of the Blue* (1980), a Canadian film shot in the US, he took over direction of the film in mid-production. By the early 80s, his drug habits and erratic behavior had virtually sent him into exile, although he reveled in the role of the ugly American. His character in *Apocalypse Now* (1979)—a flipped-out, camera-obsessed journalist—only served to reinforce his reputation.

Hopper had in the meanwhile become an accomplished photographer, and he began showing his work in galleries. The breadth of his experience, combined with his bizarre point of view, made his work a unique record of an absurd popular culture, even as he became increasingly vocal about straightening out his personal life.

Hopper's comeback began with his unnerving appearance in *Blue Velvet* (1986). Director David Lynch vociferously defended Hopper's talent against accusations of typecasting, although a follow-up film, *River's Edge* (1987), again featured Hopper as an insane derelict. Still, his rehabilitation seemed complete with his successful direction of *Colors* (1988), a drama about L.A. gang wars, followed by *The Hot Spot* (1990). KJ • *I Died a Thousand Times* 1955 (a); *Rebel Without a Cause* 1955 (a); *Giant* 1956 (a); *Gunfight at the O.K. Corral* 1957 (a); *Sayonara* 1957 (a); *The Story of Mankind* 1957 (a); *From Hell to Texas* 1958 (a); *The Young Land* 1959 (a); *Key Witness* 1960 (a); *Night Tide* 1961 (a); *Tarzan and Jane Regained...Sort of* 1964 (a); *The Sons of Katie Elder* 1965 (a); *Queen of Blood* 1966 (a); *Cool Hand Luke* 1967 (a); *The Glory Stompers* 1967 (a); *The Trip* 1967 (a); *Hang 'Em High* 1968 (a); *Head* 1968 (a); *Panic in the City* 1968 (a); *Easy Rider* 1969 (a,d,sc) **(AANBSC)**; *The Festival Game* 1969 (a); *True Grit* 1969 (a); *The American Dreamer* 1971 (a,sc); *The Last Movie* 1971 (a,d,story,ed); *Crush Proof* 1972 (a); *Kid Blue* 1973 (a); *James Dean, the First American Teenager* 1975 (a); *Mad Dog* 1976 (a); *Tracks* 1976 (a); *Der Amerikanische Freund/The American Friend* 1977 (a); *Les Apprentis Sorciers/The Sorcerer's Apprentices* 1977 (a); *Couleur chair* 1977 (a); *L'Ordre et la Sécurité du Monde* 1978 (a); *Apocalypse Now* 1979 (a); *Resurrection* (1979) (a); *Out of the Blue* 1980 (a,d); *King of the Mountain* 1981 (a); *Renacida* 1981 (a); *White Star* (1981) (a); *Human Highway* 1982 (a); *The Osterman Weekend* 1983 (a); *Rumble Fish* 1983 (a); *Slagskampen* 1984 (a); *My Science Project* 1985 (a); *Running Out of Luck* 1985 (a); *The American Way* 1986 (a); *Blue Velvet* 1986 (a); *Hoosiers* 1986 (a) **(AANBSA)**; *The Texas Chainsaw Massacre 2* 1986 (a); *Black Widow* 1987 (a); *O.C. and Stiggs* 1987 (a); *The Pick-Up Artist* 1987 (a); *River's Edge* 1987 (a); *Straight to Hell* 1987 (a); *Colors* 1988 (d); *Blood Red* 1989 (a); *Backtrack* 1990 (a,uncred.d); *Chattahoochee* 1990 (a); *Flashback* 1990 (a); *Hollywood Mavericks* 1990 (a); *The Hot Spot* 1990 (d); *Motion and Emotion* 1990 (a); *Superstar: The Life and Times of Andy Warhol* 1990 (a,technical adviser).

Hordern, Sir Michael • Actor • Born Michael Murray Hordern, Berkhamsted, Hertfordshire, England, October 3, 1911. *Educ.* Brighton College. Distinguished, long-faced character player, often of rumpled establishment figures. A veteran of over 100 films, he was made Sir Michael Hordern in 1983. • *The Girl in the News* 1940; *A Girl in a Million* 1946; *School For Secrets* 1946; *The Years Between* 1946; *Mine Own Executioner* 1947; *Night Beat* 1947; *Good Time Girl* 1948; *Portait From Life* 1948; *Third Time Lucky* 1948; *Passport to Pimlico* 1949; *The Astonished Heart* 1950; *Highly Dangerous* 1950; *Trio* 1950; *A Christmas Carol* 1951; *Flesh and Blood* 1951; *The Magic Box* 1951; *Tom Brown's Schooldays* 1951; *The Hour of 13* 1952; *The Promoter* 1952; *The Story of Robin Hood* 1952; *Grand National Night* 1953; *The Heart of the Matter* 1953; *Personal Affair* 1953; *Street Corner* 1953; *The Beachcomber* 1954; *The Constant Husband* 1954; *Forbidden Cargo* 1954; *You Know What Sailors Are* 1954; *The Man Who Never Was* 1955; *The Night My Number Came Up* 1955; *Storm Over the Nile* 1955; *The Warriors* 1955; *Alexander the Great* 1956; *The Baby and the Battleship* 1956; *Pacific Destiny* 1956; *The Spanish Gardener* 1956; *I Accuse!* 1957; *Windom's Way* 1957; *Girls at Sea* 1958; *I Was Monty's Double* 1958; *The Spaniard's Curse* 1958; *Macbeth* 1960; *Man in the Moon* 1960; *Moment of Danger* 1960; *Sink the Bismarck!* 1960; *El Cid* 1961; *Cleopatra* 1963; *Dr. Syn—Alias the Scarecrow* 1963; *The V.I.P.s* 1963; *The Yellow Rolls-Royce* 1964; *Genghis Khan* 1965; *The Spy WhoCame in From the Cold* 1965; *Cast a Giant Shadow* 1966; *A Funny Thing Happened on the Way to the Forum* 1966; *Khartoum* 1966; *How I Won the War* 1967; *I'll Never Forget What's 'Is Name* 1967; *The Jokers* 1967; *The Taming of the Shrew* 1967; *Where Eagles Dare* 1968; *Anne of the Thousand Days* 1969; *The Bed Sitting Room* 1969; *Futtocks End* 1969; *Some Will, Some Won't* 1969; *Demons of the Mind* 1971; *Girl Stroke Boy* 1971; *Up Pompeii* 1971; *Alice's Adventures in Wonderland* 1972; *The Pied Piper* 1972; *The Possession of Joel Delaney* 1972; *England Made Me* 1973; *The Mackintosh Man* 1973; *Theatre of Blood* 1973; *Juggernaut* 1974; *Barry Lyndon* 1975; *Lucky Lady* 1975; *Mr. Quilp* 1975; *Royal Flash* 1975; *Joseph Andrews* 1976; *The Slipper and the Rose* 1976; *The Medusa Touch* 1978; *Watership Down* 1978; *The Wildcats of St. Trinian's* 1980; *The*

Missionary 1981; *Gandhi* 1982; *Yellowbeard* 1983; *Young Sherlock Holmes* 1985; *Labyrinth* 1986; *Lady Jane* 1986; *Comrades* 1987; *The Trouble With Spies* 1987; *Diamond Skulls* 1989; *The Fool* 1990.

Horne, Lena • *aka* Helena Horne • Actress, singer • Born Lena Calhoun Horne, Brooklyn, NY, June 30, 1917. Silky-voiced chanteuse who made her debut as a chorine at New York's Cotton Club in 1933. The first black performer to land a long-term contract with a major studio (MGM), Horne's career was nevertheless hampered by prevailing racial attitudes, with some exhibitors excising her scenes from films before showing them. Her daughter, actress Gail Jones, was formerly married to Sidney Lumet; Lumet directed Horne in *The Wiz* (1978) and her granddaughter, Jenny Lumet, in *Q&A* (1990). • *The Duke Is Tops* 1938 (a); *Harlem Hotshots (short)* 1940 (a); *Boogie Woogie Dream (short)* 1942 (a); *Harlem on Parade* 1942 (a); *Panama Hattie* 1942 (a); *Cabin in the Sky* 1943 (a); *I Dood It* 1943 (a); *Stormy Weather* 1943 (a); *Swing Fever* 1943 (a); *Thousands Cheer* 1943 (a); *Broadway Rhythm* 1944 (a); *Two Girls and a Sailor* 1944 (a); *Mantan Messes Up (short)* 1946 (a); *Till the Clouds Roll By* 1946 (a); *Ziegfeld Follies* 1946 (a); *Words and Music* 1948 (a); *Duchess of Idaho* 1950 (a); *Meet Me in Las Vegas* 1956 (a); *The Heart of Show Business (short)* 1957 (a); *Death of a Gunfighter* 1969 (a); *The Wiz* 1978 (a); *Entertaining the Troops* 1989 (a).

Horner, James • Composer • Born Los Angeles, CA. *Educ.* Royal College of Music, London; USC, Los Angeles; UCLA. Talented and prolific composer of the 1970s and 80s. • *The Lady in Red* 1979 (m,m.adapt); *Battle Beyond the Stars* 1980 (m); *Humanoids From the Deep* 1980 (m); *Deadly Blessing* 1981 (m); *The Hand* 1981 (m); *The Pursuit of D.B. Cooper* 1981 (m); *Wolfen* 1981 (m); *48 Hrs.* 1982 (m); *P.K. and the Kid* 1982 (m); *Star Trek II: The Wrath of Khan* 1982 (m); *Brainstorm* 1983 (m); *The Dresser* 1983 (m,m.cond); *Gorky Park* 1983 (m); *Krull* 1983 (m,m); *Something Wicked This Way Comes* 1983 (m); *Space Raiders* 1983 (m); *The Stone Boy* 1983 (m); *Testament* 1983 (m); *Uncommon Valor* 1983 (m); *Wizards of the Lost Kingdom* 1983 (m); *Star Trek III: The Search For Spock* 1984 (m,m.dir); *Barbarian Queen* 1985 (m); *Cocoon* 1985 (m); *Commando* 1985 (m,m.prod); *Heaven Help Us* 1985 (m); *In Her Own Time* 1985 (m); *The Journey of Natty Gann* 1985 (m); *Volunteers* 1985 (m); *Aliens* 1986 (m,m.cond,m.arr) (**AANBM**); *An American Tail* 1986 (m,song) (**AANBS**); *The Name of the Rose* 1986 (m); *Off Beat* 1986 (m); *Where the River Runs Black* 1986 (m); *Batteries Not Included* 1987 (m); *Project X* 1987 (m); *Cocoon: The Return* 1988 (m); *Driving Me Crazy* 1988 (song); *The Land Before Time* 1988 (m,song); *Red Heat* 1988 (m); *Vibes* 1988 (m); *Willow* 1988 (m); *Andy Colby's Incredibly Awesome Adventure* 1989 (m); *Dad* 1989 (m); *Field of Dreams* 1989 (m,instrumental soloist) (**AANBM**); *Glory* 1989 (m); *Honey, I Shrunk the Kids* 1989 (m); *In Country* 1989 (m); *Tummy Trouble* 1989 (m); *Another 48 Hrs* 1990 (m); *I Love You to Death* 1990 (m).

Hoskins, Bob • Actor; also director, screenwriter. • Born England, October 26, 1942. Stocky cockney actor who first won critical attention in TV's "Pennies from Heaven" and gave an outstanding performance as a doomed London mobster in *The Long Good Friday* (1980). Hoskins has gone on to establish himself as a leading international star, earning a British Academy best actor award for *Mona Lisa* (1986) and making his directorial debut in 1988 with *The Raggedy Rawney*. • *The National Health* 1973 (a); *Inserts* 1975 (a); *Zulu Dawn* 1979 (a); *The Long Good Friday* 1980 (a); *Pink Floyd The Wall* 1982 (a); *Beyond the Limit* 1983 (a); *The Cotton Club* 1984 (a); *Lassiter* 1984 (a); *Brazil* 1985 (a); *The Dunera Boys* 1985 (a); *The Woman Who Married Clark Gable (short)* 1985 (a); *Mona Lisa* 1986 (a) (**AANBA**); *Sweet Liberty* 1986 (a); *The Lonely Passion of Judith Hearne* 1987 (a); *A Prayer For the Dying* 1987 (a); *The Secret Policeman's Third Ball* 1987 (a); *The Raggedy Rawney* 1988 (a,d,sc); *Who Framed Roger Rabbit* 1988 (a); *Major League* 1989 (a); *Heart Condition* 1990 (a); *Mermaids* 1990 (a).

Hou Hsiao-Hsien • Director; also screenwriter, actor. • Born Meixian, Kuantung Province, China, 1947. *Educ.* National Taiwan Arts Academy (film). Of the ten films that Hou Hsiao-Hsien has directed between 1980 and 1989, seven received best film and/or best director awards from prestigious international films festivals in Venice, Berlin, Hawaii and the Festival of the Three Continents in Nantes. In a 1988 worldwide critics' poll, Hou was championed as "one of the three directors most crucial to the future of cinema."

Hou's birthplace, a county in Kuangtung Province, had been well known as an intellectual center in China. In 1948 his family moved to Taiwan and, like all children raised there, he went through an extremely demanding educational system. In 1969 he studied film at the National Taiwan Arts Academy. After graduation in 1972, he worked briefly as a salesman. Later he began his film career as a scriptwriter and assistant director.

Hou's cinema is often concerned with his experiences of growing up in rural Taiwan in the 1950s and 60s. The 50s marked a time in which refugee families from the mainland were painfully struggling for survival, while the 60s saw the beginning of the most significant social change in modern Taiwan. The economic boom of that period meant the beginning of Westernization and urbanization. The normal frustrations of growing up were aggravated by these complicated changes, and Hou's films are intimate expressions of those experiences.

His emotionally charged work is replete with highly nostalgic images and beautiful compositions; their power lies in his total identification with the past and the fate of families who suffered through difficult times. His stories, often written in collaboration with scriptwriters Chu Tien-wen and Wu Nien-chun, depict the complex intertwining of the different strands that shape the lives of individuals. In a poetic yet relaxed style, they reflect a deep sympathy and a profound humanism. JKWL • *The Sandwich Man* 1983 (d—"Son's Big Doll"); *A Summer at Grandpa's* 1984 (d,sc); *A Time to Live and a Time to Die* 1985 (d,sc); *Show* 1986 (a); *Daughter of the Nile* 1987 (d); *City of Sadness* 1989 (d); *Sunless Days* 1990 (a).

Houseman, John • Producer, actor; also screenwriter, author. • Born Jacques Haussmann, Bucharest, Romania, September 22, 1902; died October 31, 1988, Malibu, CA. Houseman co-founded the Mercury Theatre with Orson Welles in 1937 and helped write and produce some of their ground-breaking achievements, notably the stage production of *Julius Caesar* (1937), the controversial radio production of *War of the Worlds* (1938) and the landmark film *Citizen Kane* (1941). After an acrimonious dispute with Welles over the authorship of *Kane*, Houseman embarked on a fruitful period of film production, collaborating with the likes of Max Ophuls, Vincente Minnelli, Nicholas Ray and John Frankenheimer. Between 1945 and 1962 he produced 18 films for Paramount, Universal and MGM.

In the early 1970s Houseman established a second career as a character actor, developing a crusty elder statesman persona which he later reprised in several TV commercials. • *Too Much Johnson (short)* 1938 (a,p); *Citizen Kane* 1941 (script ed—uncred); *Saboteur* 1942 (uncred.sc); *Jane Eyre* 1944 (sc); *Miss Susie Slagle's* 1945 (assoc.p); *Tuesday in November (short)* 1945 (p); *The Unseen* 1945 (assoc.p); *The Blue Dahlia* 1946 (p); *Letter From an Unknown Woman* 1948 (p); *They Live By Night* 1948 (p); *The Company She Keeps* 1950 (p); *On Dangerous Ground* 1951 (p); *The Bad and the Beautiful* 1952 (p); *Holiday For Sinners* 1952 (p); *Julius Caesar* 1953 (p) (**AANBP**); *Executive Suite* 1954 (p); *Her Twelve Men* 1954 (p); *The Cobweb* 1955 (p); *Moonfleet* 1955 (p); *Lust For Life* 1956 (p); *All Fall Down* 1962 (p); *Two Weeks in Another Town* 1962 (p); *In the Cool of the Day* 1963 (p); *Seven Days in May* 1964 (uncred.a); *Voyage to America (short)* 1964 (p,sc); *This Property Is Condemned* 1966 (p); *The Paper Chase* 1973 (a) (**AABSA**); *I'm a Stranger Here Myself* 1974 (a); *Rollerball* 1975 (a); *Three*

Days of the Condor 1975 (a); *Circle* 1976 (a); *St. Ives* 1976 (a); *The Cheap Detective* 1978 (a); *Old Boyfriends* 1978 (a); *The Fog* 1980 (a); *My Bodyguard* 1980 (a); *Wholly Moses!* 1980 (a); *Ghost Story* 1981 (a); *Bells* 1982 (a); *Murder By Phone* 1983 (a); *The Good Fight: The Abraham Lincoln Brigade in the Spanish Civil War* 1984 (a); *Another Woman* 1988 (a); *The Naked Gun - From the Files of Police Squad!* 1988 (a); *Scrooged* 1988 (a).

Houston, Penelope • Critic; also author. • Born London. *Educ.* Somerville College, Oxford (history). Author of *The Contemporary Cinema* (1963), a seminal work in the development of the new film culture in late 1950s and early 60s, and a formidable, long-time (1956-1990) editor of the British Film Institute's journal, *Sight and Sound*, one of the most consistently intelligent and entertaining magazines of its kind.

Howard, Leslie • Actor; also director, producer. • Born Leslie Howard Stainer, London, April 24, 1893; died 1943. *Educ.* Dulwich College, London. Urbane English lead of the 1930s with a flair for projecting composure and quiet authority. Howard was memorable opposite Bette Davis in *Of Human Bondage* (1934), as the dashing title character in *The Scarlet Pimpernel* (1935) and as Professor Higgins in *Pygmalion* (1938). He also directed several films in the early 1940s before dying when a plane in which he was a passenger was shot down by German fighters. Brother of character player Arthur Howard and father of actor Ronald Howard. • *The Heroine of Mons (short)* 1914 (a); *The Happy Warrior* 1917 (a); *The Lackey and the Lady* 1919 (a); *Bookworms (short)* 1920 (a,p); *The Bump (short)* 1920 (p); *Five Pound Reward (short)* 1920 (a,p); *Twice Two (short)* 1920 (p); *The Temporary Lady (short)* 1921 (p); *Too Many Cooks (short)* 1921 (p); *Outward Bound* 1930 (a); *Devotion* 1931 (a); *Five and Ten* 1931 (a); *A Free Soul* 1931 (a); *Never the Twain Shall Meet* 1931 (a); *The Animal Kingdom* 1932 (a); *Service For Ladies* 1932 (a); *Smilin' Through* 1932 (a); *Berkeley Square* 1933 (a) **(AANBA)**; *Captured* 1933 (a); *Secrets* 1933 (a); *British Agent* 1934 (a); *The Lady Is Willing* 1934 (a); *Of Human Bondage* 1934 (a); *The Petrified Forest* 1935 (a); *The Scarlet Pimpernel* 1935 (a); *Romeo and Juliet* 1936 (a); *It's Love I'm After* 1937 (a); *Stand-In* 1937 (a); *Pygmalion* 1938 (a,d) **(AANBA)**; *Gone With the Wind* 1939 (a); *Intermezzo* 1939 (a,assoc.p); *Common Heritage (short)* 1940 (a); *49th Parallel* 1941 (a); *From the Four Corners (short)* 1941 (a); *Pimpernel Smith* 1941 (d); *The White Eagle (short)* 1941 (a); *The First of the Few* 1942 (a,d,p); *In Which We Serve* 1942 (a); *The Gentle Sex* 1943 (d); *The Lamp Still Burns* 1943 (p); *War in the Mediterranean* 1943 (a).

Howard, Ron • *aka* Ronny Howard • Director, producer; also actor, screenwriter. • Born Duncan, OK, March 1, 1954. *Educ.* University of Southern California. Son of actors Rance and Jean Howard who made his first professional appearance at 18 months, starred as a child on TV's "The Andy Griffith Show" (1960–68) and played the proverbial boy-next-door in "Happy Days" (1974–84). Howard made his mark as a director with his second venture, *Night Shift* (1982), and has proved capable at handling light comic material. He collaborates frequently with his former "Happy Days" writers, Lowell Ganz and Babaloo Mandel. • *The Journey* 1959 (a); *The Music Man* 1962 (a); *The Courtship of Eddie's Father* 1963 (a); *Village of the Giants* 1965 (a); *Smoke* 1970 (a); *The Wild Country* 1970 (a); *American Graffiti* 1973 (a); *Happy Mother's Day... Love, George* 1973 (a); *The Spikes Gang* 1974 (a); *The First Nudie Musical* 1975 (a); *Eat My Dust* 1976 (a); *The Shootist* 1976 (a); *Grand Theft Auto* 1977 (a,d,sc); *Roger Corman: Hollywood's Wild Angel* 1978 (a); *More American Graffiti* 1979 (a); *Leo and Loree* 1980 (exec.p); *Night Shift* 1982 (d); *Splash* 1984 (d); *Cocoon* 1985 (d); *Gung Ho* 1986 (d,exec.p); *No Man's Land* 1987 (exec.p); *Clean and Sober* 1988 (exec.p); *Just One Step: The Great Peace March* 1988 (a); *Vibes* 1988 (exec.p); *Willow* 1988 (d); *The Burbs* 1989 (p); *Parenthood* 1989 (d,story); *Backdraft* 1991 (d); *Closet Land* 1991 (exec.p).

Howard, Trevor • Actor • Born Cliftonville, England, September 29, 1916; died January 7, 1988, Bushey, England. *Educ.* Clifton College, England; RADA, London. One of the finest film actors of his generation. Howard began his career in the 1940s and excelled at playing debonair officers and gentlemen, carving a niche in his latter years as England's favorite screen autocrat. His understated performance opposite Celia Johnson in David Lean's *Brief Encounter* (1945) brought him to international attention and led to work with a distinguished roster of directors including Luchino Visconti, Joseph Losey and Tony Richardson. Howard enjoyed his most productive association with Carol Reed, memorably as the police major with an impeccably stiff upper lip in *The Third Man* (1949). • *The Way Ahead* 1944; *Brief Encounter* 1945; *Volga-Volga* 1945; *The Way to the Stars* 1945; *Green For Danger* 1946; *I See a Dark Stranger* 1946; *So Well Remembered* 1947; *They Made Me a Fugitive* 1947; *The Golden Salamander* 1949; *The Passionate Friends* 1949; *The Third Man* 1949; *The Clouded Yellow* 1950; *Odette* 1950; *Lady Godiva Rides Again* 1951; *Outcast of the Islands* 1951; *The Gift Horse* 1953; *The Heart of the Matter* 1953; *La Mano dello Straniero* 1953; *Les Amants du Tage* 1955; *The Cockleshell Heroes* 1955; *Around the World in 80 Days* 1956; *Run For the Sun* 1956; *Interpol* 1957; *Manuela* 1957; *The Key* 1958; *The Roots of Heaven* 1958; *Moment of Danger* 1960; *Sons and Lovers* 1960 **(AANBA)**; *The Lion* 1962; *Mutiny on the Bounty*1962; *Father Goose* 1964; *The Man in the Middle* 1964; *Morituri* 1965; *Operation Crossbow* 1965; *Von Ryan's Express* 1965; *The Liquidator* 1966; *The Poppy Is Also a Flower* 1966; *Triple Cross* 1966; *The Long Duel* 1967; *Pretty Polly* 1967; *The Charge of the Light Brigade* 1968; *Battle of Britain* 1969; *Ryan's Daughter* 1970; *Twinky* 1970; *Catch Me a Spy* 1971; *Kidnapped* 1971; *Mary, Queen of Scots* 1971; *The Night Visitor* 1971; *Ludwig* 1972; *Pope Joan* 1972; *Craze* 1973; *A Doll's House* 1973; *The Offence* 1973; *Persecution* 1973; *11 Harrowhouse* 1974; *Who?* 1974; *Conduct Unbecoming* 1975; *Hennessy* 1975; *Whispering Death* 1975; *Aces High* 1976; *The Bawdy Adventures of Tom Jones* 1976; *Eliza Fraser* 1976; *The Last Remake of Beau Geste* 1977; *Slavers* 1977; *Flashpoint Africa* 1978; *Stevie* 1978; *Superman* 1978; *Hurricane* 1979; *Meteor* 1979; *The Sea Wolves* 1980; *The Shillingbury Blowers* 1980; *Sir Henry at Rawlinson End* 1980; *Windwalker* 1980; *Les Années lumières* 1981; *The Missionary* 1981; *Gandhi* 1982; *Sherlock Holmes' The Sign of Four* 1983; *Sword of the Valiant—The Legend of Gawain and the Green Knight* 1984; *Dust* 1985; *Time After Time* 1985; *Foreign Body* 1986; *White Mischief* 1987; *The Dawning* 1988; *The Unholy* 1988.

Howard, William K. • Director • Born St. Mary's, OH, June 16, 1899; died 1954. *Educ.* Ohio State University (engineering, law). Versatile technician best known for *The Power and the Glory* (1933). The film employed an innovative "flashback" narrative style which predated a similar technique used in *Citizen Kane* by eight years. • *Get Your Man* 1921 (d); *The One-Man Trail* 1921 (sc); *Play Square* 1921 (d); *What Love Will Do* 1921 (d); *Captain Fly-By-Night* 1922 (d); *The Crusader* 1922 (sc); *Deserted at the Altar* 1922 (d); *Extra! Extra!* 1922 (d); *Lucky Dan* 1922 (d); *Trooper O'Neil* 1922 (sc); *Danger Ahead* 1923 (d); *The Fourth Musketeer* 1923 (d); *Let's Go* 1923 (d); *The Border Legion* 1924 (d); *East of Broadway* 1924 (d); *The Torrent* 1924 (d); *Code of the West* 1925 (d); *The Light of Western Stars* 1925 (d); *The Thundering Herd* 1925 (d); *Bachelor Brides* 1926 (d,p); *Gigolo* 1926 (d); *Red Dice* 1926 (d); *Volcano* 1926 (d,p); *The Main Event* 1927 (d); *White Gold* 1927 (d); *The River Pirate* 1928 (d); *A Ship Comes In* 1928 (d); *Christina* 1929 (d); *Love, Live and Laugh* 1929 (d); *Sin Town* 1929 (sc,story); *The Valiant* 1929 (d,p); *Good Intentions* 1930 (d,story); *Scotland Yard* 1930 (d); *Don't Bet on Women* 1931 (d); *Surrender* 1931 (d); *Transatlantic* 1931 (d); *The First Year* 1932 (d); *Sherlock Holmes* 1932 (d); *The Trial of Vivienne Ware* 1932 (d); *The Power and the Glory* 1933 (d); *The*

Cat and the Fiddle 1934 (d); *Evelyn Prentice* 1934 (d); *This Side of Heaven* 1934 (d); *Mary Burns, Fugitive* 1935 (d); *The Rendezvous* 1935 (d); *Vanessa, Her Love Story* 1935 (d); *Fire Over England* 1936 (d); *The Princess Comes Across* 1936 (d); *Over the Moon* 1937 (d); *The Squeaker* 1937 (d); *Back Door to Heaven* 1939 (d,p,story); *Money and the Woman* 1940 (d); *Bullets For O'Hara* 1941 (d); *Klondike Fury* 1942 (d); *Johnny Come Lately* 1943 (d); *When the Lights Go onAgain* 1944 (d); *A Guy Could Change* 1945 (d).

Howe, James Wong • Director of photography; also director. • Born Wong Tung Jim, Kwantung (Canton), China, August 28, 1899; died 1976. In the US from 1904, Howe worked his way up from the position of janitor at the Lasky Studios in 1917 to become one of the greatest, and most prolific, Hollywood cinematographers of all time. The list of directors with whom he worked reads like a history of American cinema, stretching from Victor Fleming and Allan Dwan in the 1920s to Sidney Lumet and John Frankenheimer in the 60s, with a number of landmark figures in between. Nicknamed "Low Key Hoe" for his unadorned style, Howe pioneered the use of deep-focus photography and of the hand-held camera; for Robert Rossen's matador feature *The Brave Bulls* (1951), he strapped cameras to the actors' waists to capture an unprecedented perspective on the action. Howe also directed several films and TV shows and formed three production companies during his career. He was married to novelist Sanora Babb. • *Male and Female* 1919 (ph.asst); *Puppy Love* 1919 (ph.asst); *Told in the Hills* 1919 (ph.asst); *Everything For Sale* 1921 (ph .asst); *Burning Sands* 1922 (2nd cam.op); *Ebb Tide* 1922 (2nd cam.op); *The Siren Call* 1922 (2nd cam.op); *The Woman Who Walked Alone* 1922 (2nd cam.op); *The Call of the Canyon* 1923 (ph); *Drums of Fate* 1923 (ph); *The Spanish Dancer* 1923 (ph); *To the Last Man* 1923 (ph); *The Trail of the Lonesome Pine* 1923 (ph); *The Woman With Four Faces* 1923 (ph); *The Alaskan* 1924 (ph); *The Breaking Point* 1924 (ph); *Peter Pan* 1924 (ph); *The Side Show of Life* 1924 (ph); *The Best People* 1925 (ph); *The Charmer* 1925 (ph); *The King on Main Street* 1925 (ph); *Not So Long Ago* 1925 (ph); *Mantrap* 1926 (ph); *Padlocked* 1926 (ph); *Sea Horses* 1926 (ph); *The Song and Dance Man* 1926 (ph); *The Rough Riders* 1927 (ph); *Sorrell and Son* 1927 (ph); *Four Walls* 1928 (ph); *Laugh, Clown, Laugh* 1928 (ph); *The Perfect Crime* 1928 (ph); *Desert Nights* 1929 (ph); *Criminal Code* 1930 (ph); *Today* 1930 (ph); *Untitled, Monrovia* 1930 (d); *Around the World in 80 Minutes With Douglas Fairbanks* 1931 (uncred.ph 2u); *The Spider* 1931 (ph); *Surrender* 1931 (ph); *Transatlantic* 1931 (ph); *The Yellow Ticket* 1931 (ph); *After Tomorrow* 1932 (ph); *Amateur Daddy* 1932 (ph); *Chandu the Magician* 1932 (ph); *Dance Team* 1932 (ph); *Man About Town* 1932 (ph); *Shanghai Express* 1932 (uncred ph 2u); *Walking Down Broadway* 1932 (ph); *Beauty For Sale* 1933 (ph); *The Power and the Glory* 1933 (ph); *Biography of a Bachelor Girl* 1934 (ph); *Have a Heart* 1934 (ph); *Hollywood Party* 1934 (ph); *Manhattan Melodrama* 1934 (ph); *The Show-Off* 1934 (ph); *Stamboul Quest* 1934 (ph); *The Thin Man* 1934 (ph); *Viva Villa* 1934 (ph); *The Flame Within* 1935 (ph); *Mark of the Vampire* 1935 (ph); *The Night Is Young* 1935 (ph); *O'Shaughnessy's Boy* 1935 (ph); *Three Live Ghosts* 1935 (ph); *Whipsaw* 1935 (ph); *Fire Over England* 1936 (ph); *Farewell Again* 1937 (ph); *The Prisoner of Zenda* 1937 (ph); *The Adventures of Tom Sawyer* 1938 (ph); *Algiers* 1938 (ph) **(AANBPH)**; *Comet Over Broadway* 1938 (ph); *Daughters Courageous* 1939 (ph); *Dust Be My Destiny* 1939 (ph); *The Oklahoma Kid* 1939 (ph); *On Your Toes* 1939 (ph); *They Made Me a Criminal* 1939 (ph); *Abe Lincoln in Illinois* 1940 (ph) **(AANBPH)**; *City For Conquest* 1940 (ph); *A Dispatch From Reuters* 1940 (ph); *Dr. Ehrlich's Magic Bullet* 1940 (ph); *Saturday's Children* 1940 (ph); *Torrid Zone* 1940 (ph); *King's Row* 1941 (ph) **(AANBPH)**; *Navy Blues* 1941 (ph); *Out of the Fog* 1941 (ph); *Shining Victory* 1941 (ph); *The Strawberry Blonde* 1941 (ph); *The Hard Way* 1942 (ph); *Yankee Doodle Dandy* 1942 (ph); *Air Force* 1943 (ph) **(AANBPH)**; *Hangmen Also Die* 1943 (ph); *The North Star* 1943 (ph) **(AANBPH)**; *Passage to Marseille* 1944 (ph); *Confidential Agent* 1945 (ph); *Counter-Attack* 1945 (ph); *Danger Signal* 1945 (ph); *Objective Burma!* 1945 (ph); *My Reputation* 1946 (ph); *Body and Soul* 1947 (ph); *Nora Prentiss* 1947 (ph); *Pursued* 1947 (ph); *Mr. Blandings Builds His Dream House* 1948 (ph); *The Time of Your Life* 1948 (ph); *The Baron of Arizona* 1950 (ph); *The Eagle and the Hawk* 1950 (ph); *Tripoli* 1950 (ph); *Behave Yourself* 1951 (ph); *The Brave Bulls* 1951 (ph); *He Ran All the Way* 1951 (ph); *The Lady Says No* 1951 (ph); *Come Back Little Sheba* 1952 (ph); *The Fighter* 1952 (ph); *Jennifer* 1953 (ph); *Main Street to Broadway* 1953 (ph); *Go, Man, Go!* 1954 (d); *On the Waterfront* 1954 (uncred.ph); *Dong Kingman (short)* 1955 (d,p); *The Rose Tattoo* 1955 (ph) **(AABPH)**; *Death of a Scoundrel* 1956 (ph); *Picnic* 1956 (ph); *Drango* 1957 (ph); *A Farewell to Arms* 1957 (uncred.ph); *Bell, Book and Candle* 1958 (ph); *Invisible Avenger* 1958 (d); *The Old Man and the Sea* 1958 (ph) **(AANBPH)**; *The Last Angry Man* 1959 (ph); *The Story on Page One* 1959 (ph); *Song Without End* 1960 (ph); *Tess of the Storm Country* 1960 (ph); *Hud* 1963 (ph) **(AABPH)**; *The Outrage* 1964 (ph); *The Glory Guys* 1965 (ph); *James Wong Howe (short)* 1965 (a); *Seconds* 1966 (ph) **(AANBPH)**; *This Property Is Condemned* 1966 (ph); *Hombre* 1967 (ph); *The Heart Is a Lonely Hunter* 1968 (ph); *Last of the Mobile Hot-Shots* 1969 (ph); *I Walk the Line* 1970 (pre-prod.man.); *The Molly Maguires* 1970 (ph); *James Wong Howe, A.S.C.: A Lesson in Light (short)* 1973 (a); *Funny Lady* 1975 (ph) **(AANBPH)**.

Howell, C. Thomas • Actor • Born Van Nuys, CA, December 7, 1966. Unexceptional young lead of the 1980s. Married to actress Rae Dawn Chong. • *The Outsiders* 1983; *Grandview, U.S.A.* 1984; *Red Dawn* 1984; *Tank* 1984; *Secret Admirer* 1985; *The Hitcher* 1986; *Soul Man* 1986; *A Tiger's Tale* 1987; *Il Giovane Toscanini* 1988; *The Return of the Musketeers* 1989; *Far Out, Man!* 1990; *The Kid* 1990; *Side Out* 1990.

Hudson, Hugh • Director • Born London, 1936. Prolific director of TV commercials who graduated to features in 1977 and has made his mark with lush period productions, notably *Chariots of Fire* (1981). • *Fangio* 1977 (d,sc); *12 Squadron Buccaneers (short)* 1978 (d); *Midnight Express* 1978 (2u d); *Chariots of Fire*1981 (d) **(AANBD)**; *Greystoke: The Legend of Tarzan, Lord of the Apes* 1984 (d,p); *Revolution* 1985 (d); *Lost Angels* 1989 (d).

Hudson, Rock • Actor • Born Roy Harold Scherer, Jr., Winnetka, IL, November 17, 1925; died October 2, 1985, Beverly Hills, CA. With extreme good looks but no acting experience, Rock Hudson was very much a studio creation, borrowing his screen name from the Rock of Gibraltar and the Hudson River and taking singing, dancing and acting lessons before he made his debut in *Fighter Squadron* (1948). He went on to become one of the leading male screen idols of the 1950s and 60s, displaying his first signs of real ability in *Giant* (1956) and a decided comic flair in a series of romantic comedies, often opposite Doris Day. Hudson was later popular on TV in the series "Macmillan and Wife" (1971–77). His death in 1985 was caused by complications resulting from AIDS. • *Fighter Squadron* 1948 (a); *Undertow* 1949 (a); *The Desert Hawk* 1950 (a); *I Was a Shoplifter* 1950 (a); *One Way Street* 1950 (a); *Peggy* 1950 (a); *Shakedown* 1950 (a); *Winchester '73* 1950 (a); *Air Cadet* 1951 (a); *Bright Victory* 1951 (a); *The Fat Man* 1951 (a); *The Iron Man* 1951 (a); *Tomahawk* 1951 (a); *Bend of the River* 1952 (a); *Has Anybody Seen My Gal?* 1952 (a); *Here Come the Nelsons* 1952 (a); *Horizons West* 1952 (a); *Scarlet Angel* 1952 (a); *Back to God's Country* 1953 (a); *The Golden Blade* 1953 (a); *Gun Fury* 1953 (a); *The Lawless Breed* 1953 (a); *Sea Devils* 1953 (a); *Seminole* 1953 (a); *Bengal Brigade* 1954 (a); *Magnificent Obsession* 1954 (a); *Taza, Son of Cochise* 1954 (a); *Captain Lightfoot* 1955 (a); *Never Say Goodbye* 1955 (a); *One Desire* 1955 (a); *All That Heaven Allows* 1956 (a); *Battle Hymn* 1956 (a); *Giant* 1956 (a) **(AANBA)**; *Written on* *the Wind* 1956 (a); *A Farewell to Arms* 1957 (a); *Something of Value* 1957 (a); *The Tarnished Angels* 1958 (a); *Twilight For the Gods* 1958 (a); *Pillow Talk* 1959 (a,song); *This Earth Is Mine* 1959 (a); *Come September* 1961 (a); *The Last Sunset* 1961 (a); *Lover Come Back* 1962 (a); *The Spiral Road* 1962 (a); *A Gathering of Eagles* 1963 (a); *Marilyn* 1963 (a); *Man's Favorite Sport?* 1964 (a); *Send Me No Flowers* 1964 (a); *Strange Bedfellows* 1965 (a); *A Very Special Favor* 1965 (a); *Blindfold* 1966 (a); *Seconds* 1966 (a); *Tobruk* 1967 (a); *Ice Station Zebra* 1968 (a); *Ruba al Prossimo Tuo* 1969 (a); *The Undefeated* 1969 (a); *Darling Lili* 1970 (a); *Hornet's Nest* 1970 (a); *Pretty Maids All in a Row* 1971 (a); *Showdown* 1973 (a); *Embryo* 1976 (a); *Avalanche* 1978 (a); *The Mirror Crack'd* 1980 (a); *The Ambassador* 1984 (a); *George Stevens: A Filmmaker's Journey* 1985 (a).

Hughes, Howard • Producer, director • Born Houston, TX, December 24, 1905; died 1976. *Educ.* Rice Institute; California Institute of Technology. Eccentric entrepreneur who turned to film production in the early 1920s. In 1930 Hughes launched the career of Jean Harlow—the first of many ingenues he would findand promote—with *Hell's Angels*, which he both produced and directed. Following a brief interruption in his film career (during which he embarked on a new trajectory as an airplane designer and pilot), Hughes sparked a furor with the appearance of *The Outlaw* (1943), initially withdrawn from theaters thanks to the conspicuous cleavage of Jane Russell.

In 1944 Hughes formed a production company with Preston Sturges and four years later he obtained a controlling interest in RKO, which he *mis*managed from a distance for nearly ten years. Despite the studio's loss of $20 million by 1953 and bankruptcy by 1957, he managed to sell it to a subsidiary of the General Tire Company for a $10 million dollar profit. Hughes was a recluse for the last ten years of his life, managing his business interests from a Las Vegas hotel.

Hughes was portrayed by Jason Robards in Jonathan Demme's engaging 1980 feature, *Melvin & Howard,* and by Dean Stockwell in Francis Ford Coppola's *Tucker* (1988); a Hughes–style character was also at the center of the 1964 Harold Robbins adaptation, *The Carpetbaggers*. • *Everybody's Acting* 1926 (p); *Swell Hogan* 1926 (p); *Two Arabian Knights* 1927 (p); *The Mating Call* 1928 (p); *The Racket* 1928 (p); *Hell's Angels* 1930 (d,p); *The Age For Love* 1931 (p); *The Front Page* 1931 (p); *Cock of the Air* 1932 (p); *Scarface* 1932 (p); *Sky Devils* 1932 (p); *The Outlaw* 1943 (d,p); *The Sin of Harold Diddlebock* 1947 (p); *Born to Be Bad* 1950 (p); *Experiment Alcatraz* 1950 (p); *Never a Dull Moment* 1950 (p); *Outrage* 1950 (p); *Vendetta* 1950 (p); *His Kind of Woman* 1951 (exec.p); *Two Tickets to Broadway* 1951 (p); *Angel Face* 1952 (p); *The Conqueror* 1956 (p); *F for Fake* 1973 (a).

Hughes, John • Director, screenwriter; also producer. • Born Chicago, IL, c. 1950. Educ. University of Arizona. John Hughes's films are set in the familiar mid-American landscape of well-lit shopping malls, neat two-story houses, and—most especially—locker-lined high school corridors. Peopled by the denizens of middle- and upper-middle-class suburbia, they focus on the discontented teenage children of baby boomers.

A writer and editor for *National Lampoon* magazine, Hughes started in films by writing scripts for two forgettable movies, *National Lampoon's Class Reunion* (1982) and *Nate and Hays* (1983). These were followed by two family comedy hits of 1983: *National Lampoon's Vacation*, which displayed his debt to the magazine's low comedy style, and *Mr. Mom,* which revealed his talent for capturing the comic absurdities of the suburban family. His first film as a writer and director, *Sixteen Candles* (1984), about the heartaches suffered by a young girl (Molly Ringwald) on her 16th birthday, firmly established his command of teenage comedy.

Weird Science (1985) was a Frankenstinian fantasy about two lonely high school "nerds" who create the perfect woman for themselves, only to realize that they are better off with girlstheir own age. *The Breakfast Club* (1985) charts the gradual self-discovery of five high school students serving time in a Saturday detention hall and clearly expresses Hughes's central concern with the perils of coming-of-age. In these early films, and again in the likeable *Ferris Bueller's Day Off* (1986), Hughes suggests, cheeringly if unconvincingly, that adolescent woes evaporate once teens recognize their self-worth; by means of a mediator (Ferris for his pal Cameron, Lisa for the two boys in *Weird Science*, the "Breakfast Clubbers" for one another), Hughes's high schoolers learn to "fit in" simply by being themselves.

Pretty in Pink (1986), written and produced by Hughes and directed by Howard Deutch, is a working-class version of *Sixteen Candles*, and the first Hughes film to look at the costs of assimilation rather than seeing it as an end in itself. For the first time, too, Hughes makes explicit the class tensions which had been implicit in his earlier films—tensions which become even more central in *Some Kind of Wonderful* (1987, also directed by Deutch for writer-producer Hughes), the culmination of his high school cycle. Here, the middle- to lower-middle-class characters achieve liberation by resisting the snares of the status quo; the rich kids, on the other hand, are trapped in a life of mean-spirited hedonism because of their blind allegiance to a system that fosters petty rivalries and inhumane expectations.

After *Ferris Bueller*, Hughes the writer-director tackled life beyond high school. *Planes, Trains and Automobiles* (1987) focuses on the misadventures of two traveling businessmen (Steve Martin and John Candy). *She's Having a Baby* (1988) is a vision of what might happen to the couple from *Sixteen Candles* after they get married. *Uncle Buck* (1989) effectively combines Hughes's comic exaggeration with his acute awareness of the problems hiding inside handsome suburban homes. *Home Alone* (1990, written and directed by Hughes, directed by Chris Columbus) took the Hughes focus down to the eight–year–old level and proved a scorching box–office success.

It is easy to dismiss Hughes as a mere "high school humanist." His characters do, however, ask themselves some tough questions, and they do come up with honest answers. "I realized that I took more than I gave," says the young husband at the end of *She's Having a Baby*, "that what I was looking for was not to be found but to be made." At his best, Hughes deftly blends comedy and drama, digging beneath the superficial tranquility of suburbia to examine the restive quality of modern American life. CRB • *National Lampoon's Class Reunion* 1982 (sc); *Mr. Mom* 1983 (sc); *Nate and Hayes* 1983 (sc); *National Lampoon's Vacation* 1983 (sc,song); *Sixteen Candles* 1984 (d,sc); *The Breakfast Club* 1985 (d,p,sc); *National Lampoon's European Vacation* 1985 (sc,story); *Weird Science* 1985 (d,sc); *Ferris Bueller's Day Off* 1986 (d,p,sc); *Pretty in Pink* 1986 (exec.p,sc;) *Planes, Trains and Automobiles* 1987 (d,p,sc,song); *Some Kind of Wonderful* 1987 (p,sc); *The Great Outdoors* 1988 (exec.p,sc); *She's Having a Baby* 1988 (d,p,sc); *National Lampoon's Christmas Vacation* 1989 (p,sc); *Uncle Buck* 1989 (d,p,sc); *Home Alone* 1990 (p,sc); *Career Opportunities* 1991 (exec.p,sc); *Only the Lonely* 1991 (p).

Hughes, Wendy • Actress • Born Australia, c. 1952. Found her stride as part of the "new Australian film" movement which attracted international critical acclaim in the late 1970s and 80s with such films as *My Brilliant Career* (1979). Hughes was central to the success of both *Lonely Hearts* (1982) and *Careful, He Might Hear You* (1983). Married to producer Patric Juillet. • *Petersen* 1974 (a); *Sidecar Racers* 1975 (a); *High Rolling* 1977 (a); *Newsfront* 1978 (a); *Kostas* 1979 (a); *My Brilliant Career* 1979 (a); *Touch and Go* 1980 (a); *Partners* 1981 (a); *A Dangerous Summer* 1982 (a); *Lonely Hearts* 1982 (a); *Careful, He Might Hear You* 1983 (a); *My First Wife* 1984 (a); *I Can't Get Started* 1985 (a); *An Indecent Obsession* 1985 (a); *Shadows of the Peacock* 1986 (a); *Happy New Year* 1987 (a); *Warm Nights on a Slow Moving Train* 1987 (a); *Boundaries of the Heart* 1988 (a,assoc.p); *Echoes of Paradise* 1988 (a).

Hui, Ann • *aka* Xu Anhua, Hsu An-hua • Director; also screenwriter. • Leading Hong Kong filmmaker whose best works, such as *Story of Woo Viet* and *Boat People* (both 1982), deal with contemporary social and political issues. • *The Secret* 1979 (d); *Hu-Yueh-Te Ku-Shih/Story of Woo Viet* 1982 (d); *T'ou-Pen Hu-Hai/Boat People* 1982 (d); *Shue gim yan shau luk* 1987 (d,sc); *Jinye Xingguang Canlan/Starry is the Night* 1989 (d); *Ke Tu Chiu Hen* 1990 (d); *The Swordsman* 1990 (d).

Hulce, Tom • Actor • Born Thomas Hulce, White Water, WI, December 6, 1953. *Educ.* North Carolina School of the Arts. Gifted stage actor whose bravura performance in the title role of *Amadeus* (1984) led to similarly challenging roles in smaller films, notably *Slam Dance* (1987) and *Dominick and Eugene* (1988). • *9/30/55* 1977; *National Lampoon's Animal House* 1978; *Those Lips Those Eyes* 1980; *Amadeus* 1984 **(AANBA)**; *Echo Park* 1985; *Slam Dance* 1987; *Dominick and Eugene* 1988; *Shadowman* 1988; *Black Rainbow* 1989; *Parenthood* 1989.

Hunt, Linda • Actress • Born Morristown, NJ, April 2, 1945. *Educ.* Interlochen Arts Academy, MI; Goodman Theater School of Drama, Chicago. Accomplished, diminutive stage actress whose occasional screen appearances, particularly in *The Year of Living Dangerously* (1982), have been impressive. • *Popeye* 1980; *The Year of Living Dangerously* 1982 **(AABSA)**; *The Bostonians* 1984; *Dune* 1985; *Eleni* 1985; *Silverado* 1985; *Waiting For the Moon* 1987; *She-Devil* 1989; *Kindergarten Cop* 1990; *If Looks Could Kill* 1991.

Hunter, Holly • Actress • Born Conyers, GA, February 2, 1958. *Educ.* Carnegie-Mellon University, Pittsburgh (drama). Fiery, diminutive performer who came to prominence in 1987 with lead roles in the Coen brothers' *Raising Arizona* and James Brooks's *Broadcast News*. • *The Burning* 1981; *Swing Shift* 1984; *Broadcast News* 1987 **(AANBA)**; *End of the Line* 1987; *Raising Arizona* 1987; *Always* 1989; *Animal Behavior* 1989; *Miss Firecracker* 1989; *Once Around* 1991.

Hunter, Kim • Actress • Born Janet Cole, Detroit, MI, November 12, 1922. Vivacious leading lady of the 1940s and early 50s who made an impressive screen debut in *The Seventh Victim* (1943) and is best remembered as Stella Kowalski in *A Streetcar Named Desire* (1951). Hunter was blacklisted in the early 1950s but returned to the screen later in the decade. • *The Seventh Victim* 1943; *Tender Comrade* 1943; *When Strangers Marry* 1944; *You Came Along* 1945; *A Matter of Life and Death* 1946; *A Streetcar Named Desire* 1951 **(AABSA)**; *Anything Can Happen* 1952; *Deadline U.S.A.* 1952; *Storm Center* 1956; *The Young Stranger* 1957; *Money, Women and Guns* 1958; *Lilith* 1964; *Planet of the Apes* 1968; *The Swimmer* 1968; *Beneath the Planet of the Apes* 1970; *Escape From the Planet of the Apes* 1971; *The Kindred* 1986.

Hunter, Tim • American director; also screenwriter. • *Educ.* Harvard; AFI, Los Angeles (directing, critical studies). Former professor at the University of California, Santa Cruz, who made his directorial debut with *Tex* (1982), adapted from the novel by S.E. Hinton. Hunter has a sure feel for adolescent angst and alienation, perhaps best displayed in *River's Edge* (1987), a brilliant study of how a teenage murder affects the loyalties and allegiances of a group of small-town high school students. Hunter also directed an episode of David Lynch's cult TV series, "Twin Peaks." He is the son of screenwriters Aileen Hamilton and Ian McLellan Hunter. • *Over the Edge* 1979 (sc); *Tex* 1982 (d,sc); *Sylvester* 1985 (d); *River's Edge* 1987 (d); *Paint It Black* 1990 (d).

Huppert, Isabelle • Actress • Born Paris, March 16, 1955. *Educ.* Versailles Conservatoire; Paris Conservatoire; Facult) de Clichy (Russian literature). Huppert made her screen debut at age 16 and had appeared in over 15 films by the age of 21. Her roles as the guileless main character of Claude Goretta's *The Lacemaker* (1977) and as the casual murderess *Violette Nozière* (1978) demonstrated an enviable dramatic range and propelled her into international stardom. In the early 1980s Huppert earned a reputation for using her influence to help uncommercial projects get off the ground; such films included Jean-Luc Godard's *EveryMan for Himself* (1980), Joseph Losey's *The Trout* (1982) and sister Caroline Huppert's *Signed, Charlotte* (1984). Huppert has continued to work with non-mainstream directors as well as established international figures. • *Faustine et le bel été* 1971; *Le Bar de la Fourche* 1972; *César et Rosalie* 1972; *L'Ampélopède* 1973; *Les Valseuses* 1974; *Aloise* 1975; *Docteur Françoise Gailland* 1975; *Dupont Lajoie* 1975; *Le Grand Délire* 1975; *Je Suis Pierre Rivière* 1975; *Le Petit Marcel* 1975; *Rosebud* 1975; *Sérieux comme le plaisir* 1975; *Le Juge et l'assassin* 1976; *La Dentellière/The Lacemaker* 1977; *Des Enfants Gâtés* 1977; *Les Indiens sont encore loin/Far From India* 1977; *Violette Nozière/Violette* 1977; *Les Soeurs Bronté)/The Bronté) Sisters* 1978; *Loulou* 1979; *Retour à la Bien-Aimée* 1979; *Heaven's Gate* 1980; *Orokseg* 1980; *Sauve qui peut la vie/Every Man For Himself* 1980; *Les Ailes de la Colombe/Wings of the Dove* 1981; *Coup de Torchon/Clean Slate* 1981; *Eaux Profondes* 1981; *Vera Storia Della Signora Delle Camelie* 1981; *Passion* 1982; *Storia di Piera* 1982; *La Truite/The Trout* 1982; *Coup de Foudre/Entre Nous* 1983; *La Femme de mon pote/My Best Friend's Girl* 1983; *La Garce* 1984; *Signé Charlotte/Signed, Charlotte* 1984; *Sac de Noeuds* 1985; *Cactus* 1986; *The Bedroom Window* 1987; *Les Possédés* 1987; *Une Affaire de femmes/Story of Women* 1988; *Migrations* 1988; *Milan Noir* 1988; *La Vengeance d'une femme* 1990; *Madame Bovary* 1991; *Malina* 1991.

Hurd, Gale Anne • Producer • Born Los Angeles, CA, October 25, 1955. *Educ.* Stanford (economics, communications). Hurd apprenticed with Roger Corman's New World Pictures and became one of Hollywood's leading independent producers after her successes with then-husband James Cameron's *The Terminator* (1984) and *Aliens* (1986). • *The Terminator* 1984 (p,sc); *Aliens* 1986 (p); *Alien Nation* 1988 (p); *Bad Dreams* 1988 (p); *The Abyss* 1989 (p); *Downtown* 1990 (exec.p); *Tremors* 1990 (exec.p); *Terminator 2: Judgment Day* 1991 (exec.p).

Hurt, John • Actor • Born Shirebrook, Derbyshire, England, January 22, 1940. *Educ.* St. Martin's School, London (art); RADA, London. One of Britain's most distinguished contemporary actors and one of the few who have also carved a successful career in European and Hollywood films. Hurt first appeared on stage in 1962 and has made some 50 movie appearances, first as fresh-faced characters like Richard Rich in *A Man For All Seasons* (1966) and more recently as weathered, quintessentially English types such as Stephen Ward in *Scandal* (1989). Hurt received a Golden Globe Award, a British Academy Award and an Oscar nomination for his role in *Midnight Express* (1978) and turned in landmark performances as Quentin Crisp in the 1975 TV movie, *The Naked Civil Servant*, and as John Merrick in David Lynch's *The Elephant Man* (1980). • *The Wild and the Willing* 1962; *This Is My Street* 1963; *A Man For All Seasons* 1966; *The Sailor From Gibraltar* 1967; *Before Winter Comes* 1968; *Sinful Davey* 1969; *10 Rillington Place* 1970; *In Search of Gregory* 1970; *Mr. Forbush and the Penguins* 1971; *The Pied Piper* 1972; *Little Malcolm and His Struggle Against the Eunuchs* 1974; *Do Yourself Some Good (short)* 1975; *The Ghoul* 1975; *East of Elephant Rock* 1976; *La Linea del fiume* 1976; *Shadows of Doubt (short)* 1976; *Disappearance* 1977; *The Lord of the Rings* 1978; *Midnight Express* 1978 **(AANBSA)**; *The Shout* 1978; *Watership Down* 1978; *Alien* 1979; *The Elephant Man* 1980 **(AANBA)**; *Heaven's Gate* 1980; *History of the World Part I* 1981; *Night Crossing* 1981; *Partners* 1982; *The Plague Dogs* 1982; *Champions* 1983; *The Osterman Weekend* 1983; *1984* 1984; *The Hit* 1984; *Observations Under the Volcano* 1984; *Success Is the Best Revenge* 1984; *Sunset People* 1984; *After Darkness* 1985; *The Black Cauldron* 1985; *Jake Speed* 1986; *Rocinante* 1986; *Aria* 1987; *From the Hip*

1987; *Spaceballs* 1987; *Vincent—The Life and Death of Vincent Van Gogh* 1987; *White Mischief* 1987; *Little Sweetheart* 1988; *La Nuit Bengali* 1988; *Deadline* 1989; *Scandal* 1989; *The Field* 1990; *Resident Alien* 1990; *Roger Corman's Frankenstein Unbound* 1990; *Romeo-Juliet* 1990; *Windprints* 1990; *King Ralph* 1991.

Hurt, Mary Beth • Actress • Born Marshalltown, IA, September 26, 1948. *Educ.* NYU. Versatile stage performer in occasional films, notably *Interiors* (1978) and *Head Over Heels* (1979). Formerly married to actor William Hurt, now married to director Paul Schrader. • *Interiors* 1978; *Head Over Heels* 1979; *A Change of Seasons* 1980; *The World According to Garp* 1982; *Compromising Positions* 1985; *D.A.R.Y.L.* 1985; *Parents* 1989; *Slaves of New York* 1989.

Hurt, William • Actor • Born Washington, DC, March 20, 1950. *Educ.* Tufts University, Medford, MA (theology, theater); Juilliard (drama). Consummately professional star of the 1980s and 1990s who has enjoyed an almost uninterrupted string of critically acclaimed performances in high–profile films. Hurt established himself with roles in *Altered States* (1980), as a scientist obsessed with out–of–body experiences, and in *Body Heat* (1981), as a gullible lawyer obsessed with Kathleen Turner; the latter film marked the beginning of a fruitful association with director Lawrence Kasdan, in whose *The Big Chill* Hurt also featured.

Hurt's bravura performance as the gay window dresser who shares a prison cell with Raul Ruiz in *Kiss of the Spider Woman* (1985) earned him best actor awards from the British Film Academy and the Cannes Film Festival as well as an Oscar. Two more Academy Award nominations followed, for *Children of a Lesser God* (1986) and *Broadcast News* (1987), in which he played a facile, manipulative TV anchor who nearly wins the heart of intelligent, principled journalist Holly Hunter. The Hurt/Turner/Kasdanteaming was repeated in 1988's *The Accidental Tourist*. • *Altered States* 1980; *Eyewitness* 1980; *Body Heat* 1981; *The Big Chill* 1983; *Gorky Park* 1983; *Kiss of the Spider Woman* 1985 **(AABA)**; *Children of a Lesser God* 1986 **(AANBA)**; *Broadcast News* 1987 **(AANBA)**; *The Accidental Tourist* 1988; *A Time of Destiny* 1988; *Alice* 1990; *I Love You to Death* 1990; *Jusqu'au bout du monde/Till the End of the World* 1991.

Huston, Anjelica • Actress • Born California, July 8, 1951. Raised in Ireland and London, Huston played her first starring role as a teenager in father John Huston's *A Walk with Love and Death* (1969). After the death of her mother, ballerina Enrica Soma, she relocated to New York where she pursued a successful career as a model. Huston returned to the screen in the mid-1970s and scored her first major breakthrough with an Oscar-winning performance in *Prizzi's Honor* (1985). She followed up with a series of virtuoso characterizations: in *The Dead* (1987), the last film to be directed by her father; in *Crimes and Misdemeanors* (1989), as a desperate, neglected mistress whose threats to "go public" cost her her life; in *Enemies, A Love Story* (1989), as a wife who returns as if from the dead to complicate the life of her re–married husband (Ron Silver); and in *The Grifters* (1990), as a hardened con–artist vying with a beautiful young woman (Annette Bening) for the loyalties of her estranged son (John Cusack).

Brother Tony Huston is a screenwriter and half-brother Danny is a director. • *Sinful Davey* 1969; *A Walk With Love and Death* 1969; *Hamlet* 1970; *The Last Tycoon* 1976; *Swashbuckler* 1976; *The Postman Always Rings Twice* 1981; *Frances* 1982; *The Ice Pirates* 1984; *This Is Spinal Tap* 1984; *Prizzi's Honor* 1985 **(AABSA)**; *Captain Eo* 1986; *Good to Go* 1986; *The Dead* 1987; *Gardens of Stone* 1987; *John Huston & The Dubliners* 1987; *The Cowboy and the Ballerina* 1988; *A Handful of Dust* 1988; *John Huston* 1988; *Mr. North* 1988; *Crimes and Misdemeanors* 1989; *Enemies, A Love Story* 1989 **(AANBSA)**; *The Grifters* 1990; *The Witches* 1990.

Huston, John • Director; also screenwriter, actor, producer. • Born Nevada, MO, August 5, 1906; died August 28, 1987, Middletown, RI. *Educ.* Smith School of Art, Los Angeles. In *The Man Who Would Be King* (1975), co-written and directed by John Huston, two rogues, Peachy Carnehan (Michael Caine) and Daniel Dravot (Sean Connery), desert their British army post in India in the 1880s to go adventuring. In a retrospective voice-over, Peachy fondly remembers their encounters with native tribesmen: "At night, we told them stories of our own devising, and they loved them, because we showed them that their dreams could come true."

In the years immediately preceding his death in 1987, John Huston's critical reputation as one of America's leading directors was reestablished with the twin success of *Prizzi's Honor* (1985) and *The Dead* (1987). But it is his earlier films, especially *The Treasure of the Sierra Madre* (1948), *The African Queen* (1951) and *The Maltese Falcon* (1941) which will ultimately be responsible for Huston's place in film history as a teller of imaginative tales of enchantment, quest and loss.

The son of noted stage and screen actor Walter Huston (who would win an Oscar for his role in his son's *The Treasure of the Sierra Madre*), John Huston was a juvenile actor on the vaudeville circuit, a champion boxer, a painter, a leading man on the legitimate stage, a writer and reporter and even a lieutenant in the Mexican calvary. After an abortive career as a screenwriter in the early 1930s, Huston returned to Hollywood later in the decade and achieved great renown with his contributions to six screenplays written under contract at Warner Bros., including *Jezebel* (1938), *High Sierra* (1941) and *Sergeant York* (1941). Even after he became a director, Huston would continue to contribute substantially to the screenplays of all his films.

Huston made a stunning debut as a director with *The Maltese Falcon.* One of the first examples of film noir, this stylistically assured feature revealed his interests in ironic comedy and the motif of the unresolved quest. *The Maltese Falcon* is one of the most influential and enjoyable of the cinema's masterworks.

Huston's wartime filmmaking experiences for the signal corps resulted in equally groundbreaking documentary work, including *The Battle of San Pietro* (1945) and *Let There Be Light* (1945), the latter an account of psychological dysfunction among American G.I.s which federal authorities withheld from release for many years.

Between 1948 and 1952, Huston produced a succession of important films. *The Treasure of the Sierra Madre* refined the Huston theme of the quest into an archetype and cemented his critical reputation, largely thanks to a series of reviews and articles by James Agee—who would later write the screenplay for *The African Queen. The Asphalt Jungle* (1950) proved Huston's ability to manipulate simultaneously a variety of characters and stories; the film's sharply drawn milieu and unusual symphathy for its criminal protagonists mark it as among Huston's most compelling works. *The Red Badge of Courage* (1951) began Huston's identification as an adaptor of literary classics. This film also marked the first of several visually stylized features which Huston based on specific visual sources. *The Red Badge* took its groupings of figures and sun-bleached tones from Mathew Brady's daguerrotypes of the Civil War; the compositions in *Moby Dick* (1956) emulate scrimshaw carvings from the whaling days it depicts; and *Moulin Rouge* (1952) utilizes a color scheme based on Toulouse-Lautrec's paintings, which are themselves an important part of the film's narrative. This period of maturity and experimentation also saw the production of *The African Queen,* an essentially two-character film which underscored Huston's deft control of actors.

Beginning with the disappointing reception accorded his offbeat comic thriller *Beat the Devil* (1953), Huston's reputation suffered a series of setbacks over the next 20 years. A tumultuous personal life mirrored this decline, but Huston continued his dedication to literary adpatations. In 1963, with Otto Preminger's *The Cardinal,* Huston began an acting career, appearing in his own and others' films. He provided narration for a multitude of TV shows and documentary films, and appearances in public service campaigns and his outspoken opposition to colorization gained him further public recognition. By the time of his death, Huston's craggy, beautifully ugly face and melodious baritone voice made him one of the few directors of his era as familiar to his public as any of his stars.

Fat City (1972), a sorrowful story of the ebbing fortunes of a washed-up boxer, marked the start of Huston's comeback in the critical community. *The Man Who Would Be King,* originally planned more than 20 years previous as a vehicle for Bogart and Gable, remains Huston's most fully realized quest narrative. *Wise Blood* (1979), a compelling piece of Southern Gothic based on Flannery O'Connor's novel, similarly represents one of Huston's greatest achievements as an adaptor of literature. After the disasters of *Victory* (1981) and *Annie* (1982), Huston scored another triumph with *Prizzi's Honor*, a grim but somehow hilarious and touching comedy of love among mobsters. The film won a supporting actress Oscar for Huston's daughter Anjelica, mirroring father Walter's win for *Treasure of the Sierra Madre.*

Huston's final completed film was *The Dead* (1987), another long-cherished literary adaptation, of James Joyce's short story. Huston's son Tony adapted the story and Anjelica was featured in the cast. At the time of his death, he was involved in the production of *Mr. North* (1988) as writer and producer, with his son Danny directing. KJH • *Hell's Heroes* 1929 (a); *The Shakedown* 1929 (a); *Two Americans (short)* 1929 (a); *The Storm* 1930 (a); *A House Divided* 1932 (dial); *Law and Order* 1932 (adapt); *Murders in the Rue Morgue* 1932 (dial); *Death Drives Through* 1935 (story); *The Amazing Dr. Clitterhouse* 1938 (sc); *Jezebel* 1938 (sc); *Juarez* 1939 (sc); *Dr. Ehrlich's Magic Bullet* 1940 (sc) **(AANBSC)**; *High Sierra* 1941 (sc); *The Maltese Falcon* 1941 (d,sc) **(AANBSC)**; *Sergeant York* 1941 (sc) **(AANBSC)**; *Across the Pacific* 1942 (d); *In This Our Life* 1942 (d); *Report From the Aleutians* 1943 (a,commentary,ph,ed,prod.sup,d); *The Battle of San Pietro* 1945 (a,d,sc,commentary); *Let There Be Light* 1945 (a,commentary,ph,d); *The Killers* 1946 (uncred.sc); *The Stranger* 1946 (uncred.sc); *Three Strangers* 1946 (sc,story); *Key Largo* 1948 (d,sc); *The Treasure of the Sierra Madre* 1948 (d,sc) **(AABD,AABSC)**; *We Were Strangers* 1949 (d,sc); *The Asphalt Jungle*1950 (d,p,sc) **(AANBD,AANBSC)**; *The African Queen* 1951 (d,sc) **(AANBD,AANBSC)**; *The Red Badge of Courage* 1951 (d,sc); *Moulin Rouge* 1952 (d,sc) **(AANBD)**; *Beat the Devil* 1953 (d,p,sc); *Moby Dick* 1956 (d,p,sc); *Heaven Knows, Mr. Allison* 1957 (d,sc) **(AANBSC)**; *The Barbarian and the Geisha* 1958 (d); *The Roots of Heaven* 1958 (d); *The Unforgiven* 1960 (d); *The Misfits* 1961 (d); *Freud* 1962 (d); *The Cardinal* 1963 (a) **(AANBSA)**; *The List of Adrian Messenger* 1963 (a,d); *The Night of the Iguana* 1964 (d,sc); *La Bibbia/The Bible* 1966 (a,d); *Casino Royale* 1967 (a,d); *Reflections in a Golden Eye* 1967 (d,p); *Candy* 1968 (a); *Das Ausschweifende Leben des Marquis De Sade* 1969 (a); *Sinful Davey* 1969 (d); *A Walk With Love and Death* 1969 (a,d,p); *The Bridge in the Jungle* 1970 (a); *The Kremlin Letter* 1970 (a,d,sc); *Myra Breckinridge* 1970 (a); *Man in the Wilderness* 1971 (a); *La Spina Dorsale del Diavola* 1971 (a); *Fat City* 1972 (d,p); *The Life and Times of Judge Roy Bean* 1972 (a,d); *Battle For the Planet of the Apes* 1973 (a); *The Mackintosh Man* 1973 (d); *Chinatown* 1974 (a); *Breakout* 1975 (a); *The Man Who Would Be King* 1975 (d,sc) **(AANBSC)**; *The Wind and the Lion* 1975 (a); *Hollywood on Trial* 1976 (a); *Independence* 1976 (d); *Tentacoli* 1977 (a); *Jaguar Lives!* 1979 (a); *The Visitor* 1979 (a); *Winter Kills* 1979 (a); *Wise Blood* 1979 (a,d); *Agee* 1980 (a); *Head On* 1980 (a); *Phobia* 1980 (d); *Victory* 1981 (d); *Annie* 1982 (d); *Cannery Row* 1982 (a); *Lovesick* 1983 (a); *Young Giants* 1983 (a); *Angela* 1984 (a); *Notes From Under the Volcano* 1984 (a); *Under the Volcano* 1984 (d); *The Black Cauldron* 1985 (a); *George Stevens: A Filmmaker's Journey* 1985 (a); *Prizzi's Honor* 1985 (d) **(AANBD)**; *50 Years of Action!* 1986 (a); *Directed By William Wyler* 1986 (a); *Momo* 1986 (a); *Mr. Corbett's Ghost* 1986 (a); *Rufino Tamayo: The Sources of His Art* 1986 (a); *The Dead* 1987 (d); *John Huston & The Dubliners* 1987 (a); *Mr. North* 1988 (exec.p,sc).

Huston, Walter • Actor • Born Walter Houghston, Toronto, Ontario, Canada, April 6, 1884; died 1950. *Educ.* Toronto College of Music (drama). Entered films in 1929 after some success in vaudeville and on Broadway. Huston played both lead and character parts and excelled at fatherly roles; he was outstanding in *Dodsworth* (1936), *The Devil and Daniel Webster* (1941) and son John Huston's *Treasure of the Sierra Madre* (1948). • *Gentlemen of the Press* 1929; *The Lady Lies* 1929; *The Virginian* 1929; *Abraham Lincoln* 1930; *The Bad Man* 1930; *Criminal Code* 1930; *The Virtuous Sin* 1930; *The Ruling Voice* 1931; *The Star Witness* 1931; *American Madness* 1932; *The Beast of the City* 1932; *A House Divided* 1932; *Kongo* 1932; *Law and Order* 1932; *Night Court* 1932; *Rain* 1932; *The Wet Parade* 1932; *The Woman From Monte Carlo* 1932; *Ann Vickers* 1933; *Gabriel Over the White House* 1933; *Hell Below* 1933; *The Prizefighter and the Lady* 1933; *Storm at Daybreak* 1933; *Keep 'Em Rolling* 1934; *Rhodes of Africa* 1935; *The Tunnel* 1935; *Dodsworth* 1936 **(AANBA)**; *Of Human Hearts* 1938; *The Light ThatFailed* 1939; *The Devil and Daniel Webster* 1941 **(AANBA)**; *The Maltese Falcon* 1941; *The Shanghai Gesture* 1941; *Swamp Water* 1941; *Always in My Heart* 1942; *In This Our Life* 1942; *Why We Fight* 1942; *Yankee Doodle Dandy* 1942 **(AANBSA)**; *Edge of Darkness* 1943; *Mission to Moscow* 1943; *The North Star* 1943; *The Outlaw* 1943; *Report From the Aleutians* 1943; *Dragon Seed* 1944; *And Then There Were None* 1945; *Dragonwyck* 1946; *Duel in the Sun* 1947; *Summer Holiday* 1948; *The Treasure of the Sierra Madre* 1948 **(AABSA)**; *The Great Sinner* 1949; *The Furies* 1950.

Hutton, Betty • Actress; also singer. • Born Betty June Thornburg, Battle Creek, MI, February 26, 1921. Effervescent performer who signed with Paramount in 1941; best remembered for her lead roles in *Annie Get Your Gun* (1950) and C.B. DeMille's *The Greatest Show on Earth* (1952). Hutton left Paramount after the studio refused to allow her husband, choreographer Charles Curran, to direct her films; her career subsequently went into a downward spiral. • *The Fleet's In* 1942 (a); *Star Spangled Rhythm* 1942 (a); *Happy Go Lucky* 1943 (a); *Let's Face It* 1943 (a); *And the Angels Sing* 1944 (a); *Here Come the Waves* 1944 (a); *The Miracle of Morgan's Creek* 1944 (a); *Duffy's Tavern* 1945 (a); *Incendiary Blonde* 1945 (a); *The Stork Club* 1945 (a); *Cross My Heart* 1946 (a); *The Perils of Pauline* 1947 (a); *Dream Girl* 1948 (a); *Red, Hot and Blue* 1949 (a); *Annie Get Your Gun* 1950 (a); *Let's Dance* 1950 (a); *Sailor Beware* 1951 (a); *The Greatest Show on Earth* 1952 (a); *Somebody Loves Me* 1952 (a); *Spring Reunion* 1957 (a); *Crimes and Misdemeanors* 1989 (song).

Hutton, Timothy • Actor • Born Malibu, CA, August 16, 1960. Gifted young lead of the 1980s who appeared on film at the age of five in *Never Too Late* (1965), featuring his father Jim Hutton. Hutton first gained attention for his work in TV movies, especially *Friendly Fire* (1979), which led to his being cast in the Oscar-winning role of Conrad Jarrett in Robert Redford's *Ordinary People* (1980). He is separated from actress Debra Winger, with whom he has a child. • *Never Too Late* 1965; *Ordinary People* 1980 **(AABSA)**; *Taps* 1981; *Daniel* 1983; *Iceman* 1984; *The Falcon and the Snowman* 1985; *Turk 182* 1985; *Made in Heaven* 1987; *Everybody's All-American* 1988; *A Time of Destiny* 1988; *Torrents of Spring* 1989; *Q&A* 1990.

Hyams, Peter • Director, screenwriter; also director of photography, producer. • Born New York, NY, July 26, 1943. *Educ.* Hunter College, New York; Syracuse University, NY. Competent craftsman whose action-oriented films are often distinguished by their lush cinematography. • *T. R. Baskin* 1971 (p,sc); *Busting* 1973 (d,sc); *Our Time* 1974 (d,sc); *Peeper* 1975 (d); *Telefon* 1977 (sc); *Capricorn One* 1978 (d,sc); *Hanover Street* 1979 (d,sc); *The Hunter* 1980 (sc); *Outland* 1981 (d,sc); *The Star Chamber* 1983 (d,sc); *2010* 1984 (d,p,sc,ph); *Running Scared* 1986 (d,exec.p,ph); *The Monster Squad* 1987 (exec.p); *The Presidio* 1988 (d,ph); *Narrow Margin* 1990 (d,sc,ph).

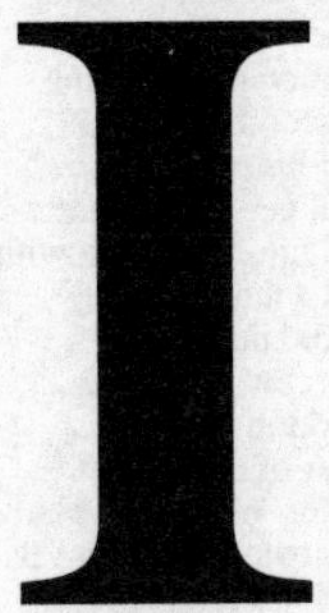

Ichikawa, Kon • Director; also producer. • Born Uji Yamada, Japan, November 20, 1915. *Educ.* Ichioka Commercial School, Osaka (animation). Influenced by artists as diverse as Walt Disney and Jean Renoir, Kon Ichikawa's films cover a wide spectrum of moods, from the comic to the overwhelmingly ironic and even the perverse. Ichikawa began his career as a cartoonist, and this influence is apparent in his skillful use of the widescreen, and in the strong, angular patterns seen in many of his compositions. He has also directed *Pu–san* (1953), a popular film based on Junichiro Yokoyama's "Mr. Pu" comic strip. At various points in his career, Ichikawa has shown that he is capable of appealing to a popular audience without compromising his artistry.

A great visual stylist and perfectionist, Ichikawa excels at screen adaptations of literary masterpieces, including Soseki Natsume's *The Heart* (1954), Yukio Mishima's *Conflagration* (1959), Junichiro Tanizaki's *Odd Obsession* (1959) and *I Am a Cat* (1975) and Toson Shimazaki's *The Outcast* (1961). He has also remade film classics, such as Yutaka Abe's *The Woman Who Touched Legs* (1952) and Teinosuke Kinugasa's *An Actor's Revenge* (1963), transposing them to contemporary settings.

The West was first introduced to Ichikawa when his *The Burmese Harp* (1956) won the San Giorgio Prize at the 1956 Venice Film Festival. His epic documentary on the 1964 Tokyo Olympiad (released the following year) and *Alone on the Pacific* (1963) explore, with dignity and imagination, the limits of human endurance. He has also worked in the thriller genre, with *The Pit* (1957), *The Inugamis* (1976) and *Island of Horrors* (1977).

Ichikawa tends to present strongly etched, complex characters: the stuttering acolyte who desires to preserve the "purity" of the Golden Pavilion (*Enjo*); the elderly husband who resorts to injections and voyeurism in order to remain sexually active (*Kagi*); the member of a pariah class who tries to deny his identity and to "pass" in regular society (*Hakai*). More recently, *Film Actress* (1987) is a tribute to the fiercely independent Japanese actress Kinuyo Tanaka, who starred in many of Kenji Mizoguchi's films and was herself a director in later life.

On the lighter side, Ichikawa's characters also include a 19th-century cat; a good-hearted, hapless teacher; and a baby who narrates how the world looks from his vantage point. He is especially adept at mixing comedy and tragedy within the same story. Until 1965, Ichikawa's close collaborator was his wife, screenwriter Natto Wada, with whose assistance he produced most of his finest films. LCE • *Musume Dojoji* 1946 (d,sc); *Toho senichi-ya* 1947 (d); *Hana hiraku* 1948 (d); *Sanbyaku rokujugo-ya* 1948 (d); *Hateshinaki jonetsu* 1949 (d); *Ningen moyo* 1949 (d); *Akatsuki no tsuiseki* 1950 (d); *Ginza Sanshiro* 1950 (d); *Netsudeichi* 1950 (d); *Bungawan Solo* 1951 (d,sc); *Ieraishan* 1951 (d,sc); *Kekkon Koshinkyoku* 1951 (d,sc); *Koibito* 1951 (d,sc); *Mukokuseki-sha* 1951 (d,sc); *Nusumareta koi* 1951 (d,sc); *Ano tekono te* 1952 (d,sc); *Ashi ni sawatta onna/The Woman Who Touched Legs* 1952 (d,sc); *Rakkii-san* 1952 (d); *Wakai hito* 1952 (d,sc); *Ai-jin* 1953 (d); *Aoiro kakumei* 1953 (d); *Pu-san* 1953 (d,sc); *Seishun Zenigata Heiji* 1953 (d,sc); *Josei ni kansuru juni sho* 1954 (d); *Kokoro/The Heart* 1954 (d); *Okuman choja* 1954 (d,sc); *Watashi no subete o* 1954 (d,sc); *Seishun kaidan* 1955 (d); *Biruma no Tategoto/The Burmese Harp* 1956 (d); *Nihonbashi* 1956 (d); *Shokei no heya* 1956 (d); *Ana/The Pit* 1957 (d,sc); *Manin densha* 1957 (d,sc); *Tohoku no zunmu-tachi* 1957 (d,sc); *Enjo/Fires on the Plain/Conflagration* 1959 (d); *Jokyo* 1959 (d); *Kagi/The Key/Odd Obsession* 1959 (d,sc); *Nobi* 1959 (d); *Sayonara, Konnichiwa* 1959 (d,sc); *Bonchi* 1960 (d,sc); *Ototo* 1960 (d); *Hakai/The Outcast* 1961 (d); *Kuroi junin no onna* 1961 (d); *Watashi wa nisai* 1962 (d); *Taiheiyo Hitoribotchi/Alone on the Pacific* 1963 (d); *Yukinojo henge/An Actor's Revenge* 1963 (d); *Zeni no odori* 1964 (d,sc); *Tokyo Orimpikku* 1965 (d,sc); *Toppo Jijo no botan senso* 1967 (d,sc); *Dodeskaden* 1970 (p); *Kyoto (short)* 1970 (d,sc); *Nihon to Nihonjin (short)* 1970 (d,sc); *Ai futatabi* 1971 (d); *Matatabi* 1973 (d,p,sc); *Visions of Eight* 1973 (d); *Wagahai wa neko de aru/I Am a Cat* 1975 (d); *Inugami-ke no ichizoku/The Inugamis* 1976 (d,sc); *Tsuma to onna no aida* 1976 (d); *Akuma no temariuta* 1977 (d,sc); *Gokumonto/Island of Horrors* 1977 (d,sc); *Jo-bachi* 1978 (d,sc); *Hi no tori* 1980 (d,sc); *Koto* 1980 (d,sc); *Kofuku* 1982 (d,sc); *Sasame Yuki* 1983 (d,sc); *Biruma no Tategoto* 1985 (d); *Ohan* 1985 (d,p,sc); *Koneko Monogatari* 1986 (assoc.d); *Rokumeikan* 1986 (d); *Eiga Joyu/Film Actress* 1987 (d,p,sc); *Taketori Monogatari* 1987 (d,sc).

Idle, Eric • Actor, screenwriter • Born South Shields, England, March 23, 1943. *Educ.* Pembroke College, Cambridge (English). Former president of Cambridge's renowned Footlights Revue. Idle worked for a number of British TV shows including "The Frost Report" before joining the "Monty Python's Flying Circus" team in 1969. • *And Now For Something Completely Different* 1971 (a,sc,idea); *Monty Python and the Holy Grail* 1975 (a,sc); *Monty Python's Life of Brian* 1979 (a,sc,songs); *Monty Python Live at the Hollywood Bowl* 1982 (a,sc); *Monty Python's The Meaning of Life* 1983 (a,sc,song); *Yellowbeard* 1983 (a); *National Lampoon's European Vacation* 1985 (a); *Transformers - The Movie* 1986 (a); *The Adventures of Baron Munchausen* 1988 (a,song); *Nuns on the Run* 1990 (a); *Too Much Sun* 1991 (a).

Imamura, Shohei • Director; also screenwriter. • Born Tokyo, Japan, 1926. Shohei Imamura's films dig beneath the surface of Japanese society to reveal a wellspring of sensual, often irrational, energy that lies beneath. Along with his colleagues Nagisa Oshima and Masahiro Shinoda, Imamura began his serious directorial career as a member of the New Wave movement in Japan. Reacting against the studio system, and particularly against the style of Yasujiro Ozu, the director he first assisted, Imamura moved away from the subtlety and understated nature of the classical masters to a celebration of the primitive and spontaneous aspects of Japanese life. To explore this level of Japanese consciousness, Imamura focuses on the lower classes, with characters who range from bovine housewives to shamans, and from producers of blue movies to troupes of third-rate traveling actors. He has proven himself unafraid to explore themes usually considered taboo, particularly those of incest and superstition.

Imamura himself was not born into the kind of lower-class society he depicts. The college-educated son of a physician, he was drawn toward film, and particularly toward the kinds of films he would eventually make, by his love of the avant-garde theater.

Imamura has worked as a documentarist, recording the statements of Japanese who remained in other parts of Asia after the end of WWII, and of the "karayuki-san"—Japanese women sent to accompany the army as prostitutes during the war period.

His heroines tend to be remarkably strong and resilient, able to outlast, and even to combat, the exploitative situations in which they find themselves. This is a stance that would have seemed impossible for the long-suffering heroines of classical Japanese films.

In 1983, Imamura won the Grand Prix at the Cannes Film Festival for *Narayama Bushiko/The Ballad of Narayama*, based on a Fukazawa novel about a village where the elderly are abandoned on a sacred mountaintop to die. Unlike director Keisuke Kinoshita's earlier version of the same story, Imamura's film, shot on location in a remote mountain village, highlights the more disturbing aspects of the tale through its harsh realism.

In his attempt to capture what is real in Japanese society, and what it means to be Japanese, Imamura used an actual 40-year-old former prostitute in his *Nippon Konchuki/The Insect Woman* (1963); a woman who was searching for her missing fiance in *Ningen johatsu/A Man Vanishes* (1967); and a non-actress bar hostess as the protagonist of his *Nippon Sengoshi: Madamu Onboro no seikatsu/History of Postwar Japan As Told By a Bar Hostess* (1974). Despite this anthropological bent, Imamura has cleverly mixed the real with the fictional, even within what seems to be a documentary. This is most notable in his *A Man Vanishes*, in which the fiancée becomes more interested in an actor playing in the film than with her missing lover. In a time when the word "Japanese" is often considered synonymous with "coldly efficient," Imamura's vision of a more robust and intuitive Japanese character adds an especially welcome cinematic dimension. LCE • *Bakushu/Early Summer* 1951 (ad); *Ochazuke No Aji/The Flavor of Green Tea Over Rice* 1952 (ad); *Tokyo Monogatari/Tokyo Story* 1953 (ad); *Kuroi ushio* 1954 (ad); *Tsukiwa noborinu* 1955 (ad); *Fusen* 1956 (sc); *Bakumatsu Taiyoden* 1958 (sc); *Hateshinaki yokubo* 1958 (d,sc); *Nishi-Ginza eki mae* 1958 (d,sc); *Nusumareta yokujo* 1958 (d); *Jigoku no magarikago* 1959 (sc); *Nianchan* 1959 (d,sc); *Buta To Gunkan* 1961 (d,sc); *Kyupora no aru machi* 1962 (sc); *Nippon Konchuki/The Insect Woman* 1963 (d,sc); *Samurai no ko* 1963 (sc); *Akai satsui* 1964 (d,sc); *Keirin shonin gyojoki* 1964 (sc); *Jinruigaku Nyumon: Erogotshi Yori/The Pornographers* 1966 (d,p,sc); *Neon taiheiki-keieigaku nyumon* 1967 (sc); *Ningen johatsu/A Man Vanishes* 1967 (a,d,p,sc); *Higashi Shinaki* 1968 (sc,story); *Kamigami No Fukaki Yokubo* 1968 (d,p,sc,story); *Nippon Sengoshi: Madam Onboro no seikatsu/History of Postwar Japan As Told By a Bar Hostess* 1974 (a,d,sc); *Fukushu Suruwa Ware ni Ari/Vengeance Is Mine* 1979 (d); *Eijanaika* 1980 (d,sc,story); *Narayama Bushiko/The Ballad of Narayama* 1983 (d,sc); *Yuki yukite shingun* 1987 (idea); *Zegen* 1987 (d,sc); *Black Rain* 1989 (d,exec.p,sc).

Ince, Thomas H. • *aka* T.H. Ince • Producer; also director, screenwriter, actor. • Born Thomas Harper Ince, Newport, RI, November 6, 1882; died November 19, 1924, aboard William Randolph Hearst's yacht. While critics of Thomas Harper Ince's films have described his stature as an artist as ranging from unimaginative hack to a "Rodin of the shadows" by all accounts Ince became one of the most important forces in early American cinema, enormously increasing film's industrial (if not its aesthetic) capacity. Usually considered the founder of the studio system of moviemaking, Thomas Ince defined the creative and industrial role of "producer," institutionalized the continuity script and as early as 1912 constructed the blueprint for departmentalized, factory-like studio filmmaking that would become the model for Hollywood.

Ince was raised in a theatrical family and from childhood traveled widely in stock, vaudeville and Broadway companies. Between 1906 and 1910 he made a handful of acting appearances in film, but was essentially an underemployed stage actor when he took his last bit part in a Biograph film of November 1910 (his wife Eleanor Alice Kershaw was a Biograph actress). A month later he was given a chance to direct for Carl Laemmle's Independent Motion Pictures (IMP), where his first film was *Little Nell's Tobacco* (1910). In 1911 Ince took a company of IMP players and technicians to Cuba where he and fellow fledgling director George Loene Tucker made several one-reelers featuring Mary Pickford. Before the year was out, however, he joined the New York Motion Picture Company (NYMP) as a director and in November was sent to Edendale, CA, to shoot westerns for the company's Bison brandname.

Other film companies had also set up small "studios" in Southern California when Ince arrived (including Mack Sennett's Keystone, which like Ince's Bison, was a subsidiary of Adam Kessel and Charles O. Bauman's NYMP), but Ince's operation led all others in the expansion of production facilities and the quality and quantity of films being manufactured. In 1912, Ince's company took an important step by acquiring the properties and services of the Miller Bros. 101 Ranch and Wild West Show. Not only did this give the "Bison 101" film company a stable of talented and authentic cowboy and Indian performers for its westerns, it also included the acquisition of made-to-order sets, costumes, props and, most important of all, 18,000 acres of land around Santa Monica and the Santa Ynez canyon. Under Ince's guidance, NYMP constructed a vast infrastructure for film production which soon became known as Inceville. The lot included administrative office buildings, multiple, glass-enclosed shooting stages, huge standing sets, laboratories, physical plant facilites, hundreds of dressing rooms, commissaries, property and wardrobe warehouses and so on. Others had built "movie factories" before, but Inceville dwarfed its predecessors.

The building of Inceville signified not only the increasing size of the nascent film industry but also institutionalized a new mode of production for films. Film production before 1912 (as practiced, for example, by the Motion Picture Patents Company units, or even IMP's company that Ince had taken to Cuba) usually centered on a director and his camera operator leading a small band of actors and craftspeople in the improvisatory shooting of one-reel narrative. Ince's new model, however, placed production power in the hands of a central producer. By mid-1912 Ince found the output of his company exceeding what he could personally direct, so he split his personnel into two units, with Francis Ford (brother of John) directing those films which Ince did not handle himself. Within the next few years, the number of directors working for Ince expanded, with a number of talents surpassing Ford, including William S. Hart, Frank Borzage, Jack Conway, Raymond B. West, Reginald Barker and Fred Niblo. In 1913, the need for greater control over the expanding production process invited other significant changes at Inceville. NYMP hired an accountant, George Stout, as "production manager" and allowed him to reorganize the Ince operation into systematically controlled departments with strict division of labor.

Ince became officially "director-general," an executive who directed, wrote and edited less and less himself, but exerted greater control over the conception and execution of film production. His principle mechanism for keeping films on budget and giving creative instructions was his insistence on detailed continuity scripts. Rather than merely provide directors with rough scenarios or let them work without any script (as D.W. Griffith did), Ince delivered a pre-planned, shot-for-shot blueprint of each film. A staff of scenario editors (Richard V. Spencer, William H. Clifford, C. Gardner Sullivan) assisted Ince in constructing each film on paper: scenes were numbered and broken down by shot and camera set-up, instructions on smaller details, such as camera speed, lighting effects, acting styles and post-production procedures like tinting, special effects and title cards, were also indicated specifically—or at least suggested with the caveat "Get Mr. Ince's opinion." Presenting his directors with such scripts weeks in advance of shooting allowed for greater efficiency, and the resulting profitability led the major companies which rose to prominence in the teens to adopt similar practices. By 1913 others were technically directing his company's films, but the label "Thomas H. Ince Presents" which appeared on the title cards remained accurate given the vast amount of personnel supervision the producer now gave to each film.

The Ince name became associated with well-constructed action dramas and consistent popular appeal. But whatever his contribution to the art of filmmaking, Ince's career remains more significant for its marked entrepreneurship and constant involvemnet in the shifts of power that took place as the American film industry made its transition from Patents Company domination in 1912 to vertically integrated Hollywood studios of the 1920s. During this decade in which companies merged, competed, diversified, invested and expanded, Thomas Ince remained one of the industry's chief power brokers.

In June 1912, for example, Ince saw his present and former employers, NYMP and IMP, combine to form Universal, a firm hoping to compete with the Patent Co.'s General Film distribution monopoly. The marriage was short-lived and Universal took the Bison 101 trademark as part of the legal split-up. Inces's California operation was diversified by NYMP into three new brands—Kay Bee, Broncho and Domino—which were distributed by newly-formed Mutual. With this diversification, Ince began to produce not only westerns and action dramas, but a variety of subjects, most notably a popular series of Japanese idylls (including *The Wrath of the Gods* and *The Typhoon,* both 1914; the latter made an instant film star of Sessue Hayakawa and his wife Tsuru Aoki), but also anti-German historical propoganda films, such as *The Despoiler (1915), Claws of the Hun* (1918) and *The Kaiser's Shadow* (1915). Significantly, he was also steadily increasing the length of his productions, as in the successful five-reel release of his epic *The Battle of Gettysburg* (1913), which helped speed the industry's move to feature-length films.

By 1915, Ince was recognized alongside D.W. Griffith as film's most prominent producer-director. With Griffith and associate Mack Sennett, Ince formed the three powerful elements of the Triangle Film Corporation, a major new production-distribution-exhibition company with capital holdings of $5,000,000. Mutual's Harry Aitken took on the role of president and attempted to create the nation's first completely vertically integrated film corporation (Ince and his former employers Bauman and Kessel were vice-presidents). To enhance production values, the original Inceville studio was sold and a new half-million–dollar facility was built in Culver City, CA. The new lot featured five (later eight) stages, some one thousand employees and expanded creative departments. Triangle's strategy was to offer prestige pictures of feature length and, through the strength of their producers' reputations, charge greater prices for their films. Ince responded with productions like *The Italian* (1915), William Hart's *Hell's Hinges* (1916) and his trademark expressive epics such as the Civil War drama *The Coward* (1915) and his most famous production, *Civilization* (1916).

Despite some impressive success from Ince, Triangle soon dissolved. Its distribution company had successfully recruited W.W. Hodkinson (the founder of the powerful Paramount distributorship who had been forced out by Adolf Zukor) and the company was in the process of leasing a chain of first class theaters. But internal mismanagement at Triangle, along with the huge losses incurred by Griffith's *Intolerance* (1916) and the huge salaries paid to theatrical stars who did not attract film audiences, added up to financial failure by 1918.

Even in the face of Triangle's major failure, Ince remained a strong force in film production. In 1918 he formed his own production company and, with financing from Harry Aitken again, moved to a second lot in Culver City (the first having been sold to Sam Goldwyn). His new production office was a white, colonial mansion modeled on Mount Vernon, which in later years became a familiar sight as the logo for David O. Selznick's films. (Selznick acquired the property in 1935, after Metro, DeMille, Pathé and RKO had all utilized it.) Although his films continued to make considerable profits, his output slowed to several features a year as he was forced to compete against vertically integrated studios.

In 1918-19, Ince briefly distributed through rival Paramount and then Metro. But he attempted to re-enter the top echelon of the industry by coordinating the founding of Associated Producers, Inc. in October 1919. Ince became president of this national distribution firm that had the partnership of several major producer-directors, including Mack Sennett, Allan Dwan, Maurice Tourneur, Marshall Nielan and George Loane Tucker. Associated Pictures failed to compete with Paramount and merged with another major, First National, in September 1922. The independent Ince production company released its features through First National through 1924.

By the early 1920s, the Ince company was being edged out of the studio system which was becoming known as "Hollywood." He attempted to compete on other levels: in 1921 he and other producers combined with banking interests to form the Cinematic Finance Corporation, an effort to make production loans available to producers with a proven track record; following the death-by-drug-overdose of film star Wallace Reid, Ince and Reid's widow produced *Human Wreckage* (1923), an exploitation exposé on the subject of drug addiction; and, in a bid to regain falling prestige, Ince bought the rights to Eugene O'Neill's *Anna Christie* and released a high-class adaptation starring Blanche Sweet in 1923.

Although the "big Ince machine" that had begun in 1912 with its "every minute efficiency" was surpassed by the grander-scaled, star-laden film studios of early Hollywood, Thomas Ince was still a major independent producer when his name once again received worldwide publicity. Already scandalized by the Fatty Arbuckle trial and other "sins of Hollywood" the film community was further traumatized when Thomas Ince fell fatally ill while on a yachting trip with newspaper baron William Randolph Hearst and his movie star mistress, Marion Davies. The nature of his death was never completely disclosed; Hollywood whispered that Hearst took a potshot at Charlie Chaplin for illicit relations with Davies. The bullet supposedly missed and felled Ince instead, clinching the career of struggling journalist Louella Parsons, aboard at the right time. The film industry closed its doors on the story, and the Ince name remained more closely associated with the Hollywood scandals of the 1920s than for Ince's notable contributions to the production practices of studio-style filmmaking. DGS •

Little Nell's Tobacco 1910 (d,sc); *The Dream* 1911 (d); *The Great Sacrifice* 1912 (p); *War on the Plains* 1912 (d); *The Battle of Gettysburg* 1913 (d); *Custer's Last Fight* 1913 (d); *Harvest of Sin* 1913 (p); *The Bargain* 1914 (p); *The Passing of Two-Gun Hicks* 1914 (p); *The Typhoon* 1914 (p); *The Wrath of the Gods* 1914 (p); *The Bad Buck of Santa Ynez* 1915 (p); *Cash Parrish's Pal* 1915 (p); *The Conversion of Frosty Blake* 1915 (p); *The Coward* 1915 (p,sc); *The Cup of Life* 1915 (p); *The Darkening Trail* 1915 (p); *The Despoiler (short)* 1915 (p,sc); *The Devil* 1915 (d); *The Disciple* 1915 (p,sc); *The Grudge* 1915 (p); *The Italian* 1915 (p); *Keno Bates, Liar* 1915 (p); *Knight of the Trails* 1915 (p); *The Man From Nowhere* 1915 (p); *The Mating* 1915 (p); *Mr. Silent Haskins* 1915 (p); *On the Night Stage* 1915 (p,sc); *Pinto Ben* 1915 (p); *The Reward* 1915 (p); *The Rouchneck* 1915 (p); *The Ruse* 1915 (p,sc); *Scourge of the Desert* 1915 (p); *The Sheriff's Streak of Yellow* 1915 (p); *The Sign of the Rose* 1915 (d); *The Taking of Luke McVane* 1915 (p); *Tools of Providence* 1915 (p); *The Apostle of Vengeance* 1916 (p); *The Aryan* 1916 (p); *Between Men* 1916 (p); *Civilization* 1916 (p); *Civilization's Child* 1916 (p); *The Dawn Maker* 1916 (p); *The Devil's Double* 1916 (p); *The Gun Fighter* 1916 (p); *Hell's Hinges* 1916 (p); *The Patriot* 1916 (p); *The Primal Lure* 1916 (p); *The Raiders* 1916 (p); *The Return of Draw Egan* 1916 (p); *Wolf Lowry* 1916 (p); *The Cold Deck* 1917 (p); *The Desert Man* 1917 (p); *Flying Colors* 1917 (p); *Princess of the Dark* 1917 (p); *The Silent Man* 1917 (p); *The Square Deal Man* 1917 (p); *Truthful Tulliver* 1917 (p); *Blue Blazes Rawden* 1918 (p); *Branding Broadway* 1918 (p); *The Claws of the Hun* 1918 (p); *Fuss and Feathers* 1918 (p); *The Kaiser's Shadow* 1918 (p); *The Marriage Ring* 1918 (p); *Riddle Gawne* 1918 (p); *Shark Monroe* 1918 (p); *The Tiger Man* 1918 (p); *When Do We Eat?* 1918 (p); *Wolves of the Rail* 1918 (p); *23 1/2 Hours Leave* 1919 (p); *Breed of Men* 1919 (p); *Happy Though Married* 1919 (p); *The Haunted Bedroom* 1919 (p); *John Petticoats* 1919 (p); *The Law of Men* 1919 (p); *The Money Corral* 1919 (p); *Partners Three* 1919 (p); *The Poppy Girl's Husband* 1919 (p); *Square Deal Sanderson* 1919 (p); *Stepping Out* 1919 (p); *The Virtuous Thief* 1919 (p); *Wagon Tracks* 1919 (p); *What Every Woman Learns* 1919 (p); *The False Road* 1920 (p); *Hairpins* 1920 (p); *The Jail-Bird* 1920 (p); *The Home Stretch* 1921 (p); *The Rookie's Return* 1921 (p); *Skin Deep* 1922 (p); *Anna Christie* 1923 (p); *Human Wreckage* 1923 (p); *Scars of Jealousy* 1923 (p); *The Soul of the Beast* 1923 (p); *Barbara Frietchie* 1924 (p); *Dynamite Smith* 1924 (p); *Idle Tongues* 1924 (p); *Those Who Dance* 1924 (p); *Enticement* 1925 (p); *Playing With Souls* 1925 (p); *Aloha* 1931 (story); *The Outlaw Deputy* 1935 (sc).

Ireland, Jill • Actress • Born London, April 24, 1936; died May 18, 1990, Malibu, CA. Professional dancer who made her screen debut in 1955. Ireland, who had formerly been married to actor David McCallum, often appeared in films opposite second husband Charles Bronson. Her autobiographical writings documented, among other things, Ireland's struggles with her adopted son's heroin addiction and her own, recurring cancer—ultimately the cause of her death. The second installment, *Lifelines*, was made into a 1991 TV movie starring Jill Clayburgh. • *Oh Rosalinda* 1955 (a); *Three Men in a Boat* 1956 (a); *Hell Divers* 1957 (a); *Robbery Under Arms* 1957 (a); *The Big Money* 1958 (a); *Carry On Nurse* 1959 (a); *Raising the Wind* 1961 (a); *Twice Round the Daffodils* 1962 (a); *The Karate Killers* 1967 (a); *Villa Rides* 1968 (a); *Le Passager de la Pluie* 1970 (a); *Violent City* 1970 (a); *De la Part des Copains* 1971 (a); *Quelqu'un derrière la porte* 1971 (a); *The Mechanic* 1972 (a); *Valachi Papers* 1972 (a); *Valdez il Mezzosangue* 1973 (a); *Breakheart Pass* 1975 (a); *Breakout* 1975 (a); *Hard Times* 1975 (a); *From Noon Till Three* 1976 (a); *Love and Bullets* 1979 (a); *Death Wish II* 1981 (a); *The Evil That Men Do* 1984 (assoc.p); *Murphy's Law* 1986 (p); *Assassination* 1987 (a); *Caught* 1987 (a).

Ireland, John Actor Born John Benjamin Ireland, Vancouver, Canada, January 30, 1914. Leading man of the 1940s, in several notable westerns including *My Darling Clementine* (1946) and *Red River* (1948); subsequently in supporting roles, often as a villain. Married to actresses Elaine Sheldon (1940-49), Joanne Dru (1949-58) and Daphne Cameron (from 1962). *Behind Green Lights* 1945 (a); *A Walk in the Sun* 1945 (a); *Backfire* 1946 (a); *It Shouldn't Happen to a Dog* 1946 (a); *My Darling Clementine* 1946 (a); *Wake Up and Dream* 1946 (a); *The Gangster* 1947 (a); *I Love Trouble* 1947 (a); *Railroaded* 1947 (a); *Repeat Performance* 1947 (a); *Joan of Arc* 1948 (a); *Open Secret* 1948 (a); *Raw Deal* 1948 (a); *Red River* 1948 (a); *A Southern Yankee* 1948 (a); *All the King's Men* 1949 (a) **(AANBSA)**; *Anna Lucasta* 1949 (a); *The Doolins of Oklahoma* 1949 (a); *I Shot Jesse James* 1949 (a); *Mr. Soft Touch* 1949 (a); *Roughshod* 1949 (a); *Undercover Man* 1949 (a); *The Walking Hills* 1949 (a); *Cargo to Capetown* 1950 (a); *The Return of Jesse James* 1950 (a); *The Scarf* 1950 (a); *The Basketball Fix* 1951 (a); *Little Big Horn* 1951 (a); *Red Mountain* 1951 (a); *This Is Korea* 1951 (a); *Vengeance Valley* 1951 (a); *The Bushwackers* 1952 (a); *Hurricane Smith* 1952 (a); *The 49th Man* 1953 (a); *Combat Squad* 1953 (a); *Outlaw Territory* 1953 (a,d,p,sc); *The Fast and the Furious* 1954 (a,d); *The Glass Cage* 1954 (a); *The Good Die Young* 1954 (a); *Security Risk* 1954 (a); *Southwest Passage* 1954 (a); *The Steel Cage* 1954 (a); *Hell's Horizon* 1955 (a); *Queen Bee* 1955 (a); *The Gunslinger* 1956 (a); *Gunfight at the O.K. Corral* 1957 (a); *No Place to Land* 1958 (a); *Party Girl* 1958 (a); *Black Tide* 1960 (a); *Faces in the Dark* 1960 (a); *Med Mord i Bagaget* 1960 (a); *Spartacus* 1960 (a); *Return of a Stranger* 1961 (a); *Wild in the Country* 1961 (a); *Brushfire!* 1962 (a); *55 Days at Peking* 1963 (a); *The Ceremony* 1963 (a); *The Fall of the Roman Empire* 1964 (a); *Day of the Nightmare* 1965 (a); *I Saw What You Did* 1965 (a); *Caxambu!* 1967 (a); *Fidarsi e Bene, Sparare e Meglio* 1967 (a); *Fort Utah* 1967 (a); *Odio Per Odio* 1967 (a); *El "Che" Guevara* 1968 (a); *Arizona Bushwhackers* 1968 (a); *Corri, Uomo, Corri* 1968 (a); *Dirty Heroes* 1968 (a); *Una Pistola Per Cento Bare* 1968 (a); *Quanto Costa Morire* 1968 (a); *Quel Caldo Maledetto Giorno di Fuoco* 1968 (a); *T'Ammazzo! Raccomandanti a Dio* 1968 (a); *Tutto Per Tutto* 1968 (a); *Villa Rides* 1968 (a); *Gli Insaziabili* 1969 (a); *Una sull'altra* 1969 (a); *Zenabel* 1969 (a); *The Adventurers* 1970 (a); *La Sfida Dei Mackenna* 1970 (a); *Habricha el Hashemesh* 1972 (a); *Der WGrger Kommt Auf Leisen Socken* 1972 (a); *Dieci Bianchi Uccidi da un Piccolo Indiano* 1974 (a); *The House of Seven Corpses* 1974 (a); *Welcome to Arrow Beach* 1974 (a); *Farewell, My Lovely* 1975 (a); *La Furie du D)sir* 1975 (a); *Il Letto in Piazza* 1975 (a); *Madam Kitty* 1975 (a); *Noi Non Siamo Angeli* 1975 (a); *The Swiss Conspiracy* 1975 (a); *On the Air Live With Captain Midnight* 1976 (a); *The Delta Fox* 1977 (a); *Kino, the Padre on Horseback* 1977 (a); *Love and the Midnight Auto Supply* 1977 (a); *Maniac* 1977 (a); *Quel Pomeriggio Maledetto* 1977 (a); *Satan'sCheerleaders* 1977 (a); *Tomorrow Never Comes* 1978 (a); *Bordello* 1979 (a); *Guyana: Cult of the Damned* 1979 (a); *The Shape of Things to Come* 1979 (a); *Garden of Venus* 1981 (a); *The Incubus* 1982 (a); *Martin's Day* 1983 (a); *El Tesoro del Amazones* 1985 (a); *Thunder Run* 1986 (a); *Messenger of Death* 1988 (a); *Sundown, the Vampire in Retreat* 1989 (a).

Irene • Costume designer • Born Irene Gibbons, Montana, 1901; died November 15, 1962, Los Angeles, CA. Worked for seven years, from 1942, as executive costume designer for MGM, succeeding Adrian. During that time Irene designed for over 50 films, as well as supervising the personal wardrobes of top stars. She became world-famous for her "soufflé creations," but is probably best remembered for Lana Turner's outfits in *The Postman Always Rings Twice* (1946), notably Turner's entrance costume of turban, midriff blouse and "hot pants" (the first time the latter had been worn on screeen).

Irene was married to screenwriter Eliot Gibbons, brother of Cedric Gibbons, the supervising art director of MGM (whose influence helped land Irene there after she had been discovered by Dolores Del Rio). When her contract with MGM ended, she opened her own fashion house and was the first leading costume designer to have boutiques inside department stores throughout the US. She committed suicide in 1962. • *Merrily We Live* 1938; *The Palm Beach Story* 1942; *Take a Letter Darling* 1942; *Gaslight* 1943; *Kismet* 1944; *Mrs. Parkington* 1944; *The Picture of Dorian Gray* 1945; *Without Love* 1945; *The Green Years* 1946; *The Postman Always Rings Twice* 1946; *Easter Parade* 1948; *State of the Union* 1948; *Summer Holiday* 1948; *Three Daring Daughters* 1948; *The Bribe* 1949; *The Great Sinner* 1949; *Neptune's Daughter* 1949; *Malaya* 1950; *Lover Come Back* 1962; *A Gathering of Eagles* 1963.

Irons, Jeremy • Actor • Born Cowes, Isle of Wight, England, September 19, 1948. *Educ.* Sherbourne School, Dorset; Bristol Old Vic Theatre School. Classically trained actor who first came to prominence in "Brideshead Revisited" (1981), the TV adaptation of Evelyn Waugh's classic novel. Irons specializes in playing haunted upper-class types, frequently in period roles, and has managed to achieve star status without compromising his reputation as a "serious" actor. He gave a bravura performance as the twin brother protagonists of David Cronenberg's *Dead Ringers* (1988) and was equally impressive as suspected murderer Claus Von Bulow in Barbet Schroeder's *Reversal of Fortune* (1990). Married to actress Sinead Cusack. • *Nijinsky* 1980; *The French Lieutenant's Woman* 1981; *The Masterbuilders* 1982; *Moonlighting* 1982; *The Wild Duck* 1982; *Betrayal* 1983; *Un Amour de Swann/Swann in Love* 1984; *The Mission* 1986; *Dead Ringers* 1988; *Australia* 1989; *A Chorus of Disapproval* 1989; *Reversal of Fortune* 1990.

Irvin, John • Director • Born Newcastle, England, May 7, 1940. *Educ.* London School of Film Technique. A competent technician whose work has ranged from military action features (*The Dogs of War* 1980) to finely observed character studies

(*Turtle Diary* 1985). Irvin began his career as an assistant director with British Transport Films. • *Gala Day (short)* 1963 (d,sc); *The Malakeen (short)* 1964 (d); *Carousella (short)* 1965 (d,sc); *Pedro Cays (short)* 1965 (d); *Bedtime (short)* 1967 (d,sc); *Mafia No! (short)* 1967 (d); *The Dogs of War* 1980 (d); *Ghost Story* 1981 (d); *Champions* 1983 (d); *Turtle Diary* 1985 (d); *Raw Deal* 1986 (d); *Hamburger Hill* 1987 (d); *Next of Kin* 1989 (d); *Eminent Domain* 1991 (d).

Irving, Amy • Actress • Born Palo Alto, CA, September 10, 1953. *Educ.* American Conservatory Theatre; LAMDA, London. Sympathetic, intelligent performer, mostly in supporting roles; played an effective lead in Joan Micklin Silver's *Crossing Delancey* (1988). Irving, an accomplished stage actress, is the daughter of Priscilla Pointer and the late Jules Irving, founder of San Francisco's Actor's Workshop and later artistic director of New York City's Repertory Theatre of Lincoln Center. She was married to director Steven Spielberg, with whom she has a child, from 1985 until their divorce in 1989 and also has a child with director Bruno Barreto. • *Carrie* 1976; *The Fury* 1978; *Voices* 1979; *The Competition* 1980; *Honeysuckle Rose* 1980; *Yentl* 1983 **(AANBSA)**; *Micki & Maude* 1984; *Rumpelstiltskin* 1987; *Crossing Delancey* 1988; *Who Framed Roger Rabbit?* 1988; *A Show of Force* 1990.

Itami, Juzo • *aka* Ichizu Itami • Director, screenwriter; also actor, essayist. • Born Kyoto, Japan, 1933. Itami entered films as an actor and made his directing debut with the assured black comedy, *The Funeral* (1985). He followed it with a series of impressive films—particularly the "noodle western" *Tampopo* (1986)—that have gained him international acclaim and a host of Japanese Academy Awards. His action comedies, *A Taxing Woman* (1987) and *A Taxing Woman's Return* (1988), have proved popular in the US, despite the fact that their heroine—played by Itami's gifted wife, Nobuko Miyamoto—is a tax inspector possessed of considerable detective powers. Itami is the son of film pioneer Mansaku Itami. • *The Big Wave* 1962 (a); *55 Days at Peking* 1963 (a); *Lord Jim* 1965 (a); *Nihon Shunka-Ko* 1967 (a); *Wagahai wa neko de aru/I Am a Cat* 1975 (a); *Collections Privées* 1979 (a); *Mo Hoozue Wa Tsukanai* 1980 (a); *Kazoku Game/Family Game* 1983 (a); *The Politician* 1983 (a); *Sasame Yuki/The Makioka Sisters* 1983 (a); *Kusameikyu (short)* 1984 (a); *MacArthur's Children* 1985 (a); *Ososhiki/The Funeral* 1985 (d,sc); *Tampopo* 1986 (d,p,sc); *Marusa no Onna/A Taxing Woman* 1987 (d,sc); *Marusa no Onna II/A Taxing Woman's Return* 1988 (d,sc); *Sweet Home* 1988 (exec.p); *A-Ge-Man* 1990 (d,p,sc).

Ivens, Joris • Filmmaker; also actor, writer. • Born Georg Henri Anton Ivens, Nijmegen, Netherlands, November 18, 1898; died June 28, 1989, Paris. *Educ.* Rotterdam College of Economics; University of Charlottenburg, Berlin (photochemistry). Joris Ivens's contributions to the development of documentary filmmaking are multitudinous. His editing style employed the principles of Russian montage editing, at the same time displaying an impressionistic lyricism, often focused on continuity of movement, which remains unsurpassed. His sound films often utilized a dialectical relationship between sound and image, and several times he enjoyed significant collaborations with literary artists. Although he has been faulted for using too many re-enactments in his documentaries, the ultimate force of his work overshadows such criticisms.

His formal education began in 1917 at the Rotterdam College of Economics. Military service intervened, and when he returnedto college, he became active in politics and trade union movements, already showing signs of his life-long passion for political causes. Later, he studied photochemistry at the University of Charlottenburg in Berlin and gained practical experience at the Ica and Ernemann camera factories. In 1926, he returned to Amsterdam, heading the technical department of CAPI, his father's photography equipment firm.

Ivens frequented the cafes where expressionist and avant-garde artists viewed the new cinema from Germany and Russia. In September 1926, Ivens and his colleagues founded the Dutch Film League (Filmliga) to develop constructive, original film criticism. The Filmliga proved a success, and major filmmakers began to preview their films in Amsterdam.

Ivens then turned to CAPI's resources to produce his own films. Helen van Dongen, a CAPI secretary, became Ivens's closest collaborator, a role which would continue for years to come. Ivens's earliest films experimented with the laws of continuity of movement. The first to receive international praise was *De Brug/The Bridge* (1928), a masterful composition documenting the contrasts, movements and rhythms of a bridge, and the film which is also credited with inaugurating the Dutch cinema.

Branding/Breakers (1929), his first fictional film, was unremarkable, although it did mark the beginning of Ivens's long association with John Ferhout (also known as Ferno), who was a 14-year-old assistant on the film and eventually became Ivens's principal cameraman.

Ivens next notable work was *Regen/Rain* (1929). Structured to resemble a single downpour, the film is actually a meticulously edited assemblage of four months' worth of raw footage depicting every kind of rainfall. Heralded as "pure cinema," *Regen* demonstrated an impressionistic style new to the documentary form.

The body of work which immediately followed was remarkable. *Nieuve Gronden/New Earth* (1933) begins as a lyrical montage of movement and music, only to shift in tone, creating a biting, satirical narrative. *New Earth* is considered to be one of the greatest of all documentaries. *The Spanish Earth* (1937), his next film, was made in collaboration with Ernest Hemingway, who wrote and narrated the commentary, indicting the Fascist cruelties during the Spanish Civil War. Proceeds from the film's box office were used to purchase ambulances for the Loyalist cause.

Outstanding among his later films was *Lied der Ströme/Song of the Rivers* (1954), a compilation film utilizing footage shot in 32 countries. Honored with several prizes, including the International Peace Prize of the World Peace Council, the film was eventually seen by approximately 250 million people worldwide.

La Seine a Rencontré Paris/The Seine Meets Paris (1957), counterposed with a poem by Jacques Prévert, was chosen best documentary at Cannes.

Ivens's distinguished career is so prolific that it can only be suggested in this brief space. A teacher, political activist and visual artist, as well as award-winning documentarist, he continued to remain active until his death at the age of 90. MCJ • *Zeedijk-filmstudie* 1927 (d,ph,ed); *Arm Drenthe* 1928 (d,ph); *De Brug/The Bridge* 1928 (d,sc,ph,ed); *Caissounbouw Rotterdam* 1928 (d,sc,ph,ed); *Etudes de mouvements* 1928 (d,sc,ph,ed); *Heien* 1928 (d,sc,ph,ed); *Nieuwe architectuur* 1928 (d,sc,ph,ed); *Zuid Limburg* 1928 (d,sc,ph,ed); *Branding/Breakers* 1929 (d,ph,ed); *Jeugddag* 1929 (ed); *NVV-Congres* 1929 (d,ph,ed); *Regen/Rain* (short) 1929 (d,ph,ed); *Wij Bouwen* 1929 (d,sc,ph,ed); *Demostratie van proletarische solidariteit* 1930 (d,ed); *Filmnotities uit de Sovjet-Unie* 1930 (d,ed); *Timmerfabriek* 1930 (d,ph,ed); *Creosoot* 1931 (d,sc,ed); *Philips-Radio* 1931 (d,ph,ed); *Pesn o geroyazh* 1932 (d,ed); *Misère au Borinage* 1933 (d,sc,ph,ed); *Nieuwe gronden/New Earth* (short) 1933 (a,d,sc,ph,commentary); *Zuiderzee* 1933 (d,sc,ph); *Bortsi* 1935 (sc); *The Spanish Earth* 1937 (d,p,sc,ph); *The 400 Million* 1938 (d,p,sc); *New Frontiers* 1940 (d,sc); *Power and the Land* 1940 (d); *Bip Goes to Town* 1941 (d); *Our Russian Front* 1941 (d); *Worst of Farm Disasters* 1941 (d); *Action Stations* 1943 (d,sc,ed); *The Flight of the Dragon* 1943 (m); *Know Your Enemy: Japan* 1945 (d); *The Story of G.I. Joe* 1945 (technical adviser); *Indonesia Calling (short)* 1946 (d,sc,ed); *Peirwsze lata* 1949 (d,ed); *Pokoj zwyciezy swiat* 1951 (d); *My za mir/We Are For Peace* 1952 (d); *Wyscig pokoju Warsawa-Berlin-Praga/Peace Tour 1952* 1952 (d,sc); *Lied der Ströme/Song of the Rivers* 1954 (d,sc); *Les Aventures de Till l'Espiègle* 1956 (d); *Mein Kind* 1956 (artistic supervisor); *Die Windrose* 1956 (prod.sup); *La*

Seine a rencontré Paris/The Seine Meets Paris 1957 (d,sc); *Early Spring* 1958 (d,sc,ed); *Carnet de viaje* 1960 (d,sc); *Demain à Nanguila* 1960 (d); *Pueblo Armado* 1961 (d,sc); *Marc Chagall* 1962 (ed); *El Circo mas pequeño del mundo* 1963 (d); ... *Valparaíso (short)* 1964 (d); *El Trén de la victoria* 1964 (d); *Le Ciél, la terre* 1965 (a,d); *Pour le mistral* 1965 (d,sc); *Rotterdam-Europoort* 1966 (d); *Loin du Viêtnam/Far From Vietnam* 1967 (d); *Agrippes à la terre* 1968 (d); *Determinés à vaincre* 1968 (d); *Dix-septième Parallel* 1968 (d); *L'Armée populaire arme le peuple* 1969 (d); *La Guerre Populaire au Laos* 1969 (d); *Le Peuple est invincible* 1969 (d); *Peuple et ses fusils* 1969 (d); *Le Peuple ne peut rien sans ses fusils* 1969 (d); *Le Peuple peut tout* 1969 (d); *Qui commande aux fusils* 1969 (d); *Rencontre avec le President Ho Chi Minh* 1969 (d); *Grierson* 1972 (a); *Les Artisans* 1976 (d); *Autour du pétrole: Taking* 1976 (d); *Une Caserne* 1976 (d); *Comment Yukong Déplaça les Montagnes* 1976 (d,idea); *Entraînement au Cirque de Pékin* 1976 (d); *Histoire d'un ballon: le lycée no. 31 à Pékin* 1976 (d); *Impressions d'une Ville: Shanghai* 1976 (d); *Pharmacie No. 3: Shanghai* 1976 (d); *Le Professeur Tsien* 1976 (d); *Une Répétition à l'Opéra de Pékin* 1976 (d); *Une Femme, une Famille* 1976 (d); *L'Usine de générateurs* 1976 (d); *Le Village de pêcheurs* 1976 (d); *Les Kazaks—minorité nationale—Sinkiang* 1977 (d); *Les Ouigours—minorité nationale—Sinkiang* 1977 (d); *Conversations With Willard Van Dyke* 1981 (a); *Havre* 1986 (a); *Une Histoire de vent* 1988 (a,d,sc).

Ives, Burl • Actor; also singer. • Born Hunt, IL, June 14, 1909. *Educ.* Charleston Teachers College, IL. Folk balladeer turned film actor whose trademark paunch and Mephistophelean beard were exploited in mainly villainous or Southern patrician roles. Probably best known as "Big Daddy" in Richard Brooks's screen version of *Cat On a Hot Tin Roof* (1958). • *Smoky* 1946 (a); *Green Grass of Wyoming* 1948 (a); *So Dear to My Heart* 1948 (a); *Station West* 1948 (a); *Sierra* 1950 (a); *East of Eden* 1955 (a); *The Power and the Prize* 1956 (a); *Desire Under the Elms* 1957 (a); *A Face in the Crowd* 1957 (a); *Gun Glory* 1957 (song); *The Big Country* 1958 (a) (**AABSA**); *Cat on a Hot Tin Roof* 1958 (a); *Wind Across the Everglades* 1958 (a); *Day of the Outlaw* 1959 (a); *Our Man in Havana* 1959 (a); *Let No Man Write My Epitaph* 1960 (a); *The Spiral Road* 1962 (a); *Summer Magic* 1963 (a); *The Brass Bottle* 1964 (a); *Ensign Pulver* 1964 (a); *Mediterranean Holiday* 1964 (a,song); *The Daydreamer* 1966 (a); *Jules Verne's Rocket to the Moon* 1967 (a); *The McMasters* 1970 (a); *Hugo the Hippo* 1975 (a); *Baker's Hawk* 1976 (a); *The Bermuda Depths* 1978 (a); *Just You and Me, Kid* 1979 (a); *Earthbound* 1980 (a); *White Dog* 1982 (a); *Uphill All the Way* 1984 (a); *Two Moon Junction* 1988 (a).

Ivey, Judith • Actress • Born El Paso, TX, September 4, 1951. *Educ.* Illinois State University. Acclaimed stage performer who began her career with the Goodman Theater in Chicago and entered films after gaining prominence on Broadway with Tony award-winning performances in *Steaming* (1982) and *Hurlyburly* (1984). • *Harry & Son* 1984; *The Lonely Guy* 1984; *The Woman in Red* 1984; *Compromising Positions* 1985; *Brighton Beach Memoirs* 1986; *Hello, Again* 1987; *Sister, Sister* 1987; *Miles From Home* 1988; *In Country* 1989; *Everybody Wins* 1990; *Love Hurts* 1990.

Ivory, James • director; also screenwriter • Born Berkely, CA, June 7, 1928. *Educ.* University of Oregon (fine arts); USC (film). Began his career as a documentary filmmaker before teaming up with producer Ismael Merchant to make *The Householder* (1963). Based on a novel by Ruth Prawer Jhabvala, the film marked the first of the trio's features centering on the people and culture of India. The team's second effort, *Shakespare Wallah* (1965), attracted international attention for its sensitive portrayal of a family of British touring actors and its insights into the legacy of colonialism. Merchant and Ivory went on to earn a reputation for quality films made on shoestring budgets, with their best work—heavily influenced by Satjayit Ray—examining the interplay between different cultures (*Bombay Talkie* 1970, *Heat and Dust* 1983). Merchant, Ivory and Jhabvala are also known for their adaptations of literary classics. *The Europeans* (1979) and *The Bostonians* (1984) are highly regarded translations of the works of Henry James; *A Room With a View* (1986), adapted from the novel by E.M. Forster, was a huge success with both critics and public, earning eight Oscar nominations and taking in approximately $20 million at the box-office. Ivory's shift to more contemporary ground, however, with an adaptation of Tama Janowitz's novel *Slaves of New York* (1989), was ill-conceived and unsatisfying. • *Four in the Morning (short)* 1953 (d,sc,ph,ed); *Venice: Theme and Variations* 1957 (d,p,sc,ph); *The Sword and the Flute* 1959 (d); *The Householder* 1963 (d); *The Delhi Way* 1964 (d); *Shakespeare Wallah* 1965 (d,sc); *The Guru* 1969 (d,sc); *Bombay Talkie* 1970 (d,sc); *Adventures of a Brown Man in Search of Civilization* 1972 (d,sc); *Helen, Queen of the Nautch Girls* 1972 (sc); *Savages* 1972 (d,p,sc,story); *Mahatma and the Mad Boy (short)* 1973 (p); *Autobiography of a Princess* 1975 (d); *The Wild Party* 1975 (d); *Sweet Sounds* 1976 (p); *Roseland* 1977 (d); *The Europeans* 1979 (a,d); *Hullabaloo Over Georgie and Bonnie's Pictures* 1979 (d); *Jane Austen in Manhattan* 1980 (d); *Quartet* 1981 (d); *The Courtesans of Bombay* 1982 (p,sc); *Heat and Dust* 1983 (d); *The Bostonians* 1984 (d); *A Room With a View* 1986 (d) (**AANBD**); *Maurice* 1987 (d,sc); *Slaves of New York* 1989 (d); *Mr. & Mrs. Bridge* 1990 (d).

Iwerks, Ub • Animator, director; also special effects artist. • Born Ubbe Ert Iwwerks, Kansas City, MO, March 24, 1901; died 1972. Animator who collaborated intermittently with Walt Disney after the pair met in 1919 while working in a Chicago art studio. Iwerks received on-screen credit ("drawn by") for early Disney cartoons and was instrumental in creating Mickey Mouse. He also supervised the special effects for Hitchcock's *The Birds* (1963). • *The Gallopin' Gaucho* 1928 (anim,d); *Plane Crazy* 1928 (a,uncred.); *Steamboat Willie* 1928 (anim,d); *Autumn* 1929 (anim,d); *The Barn Dance* 1929 (anim,d); *The Barnyard Battle* 1929 (anim,d); *The Cat's Away* 1929 (anim,d); *The Haunted House* 1929 (anim,d); *The Jazz Fool* 1929 (anim,d); *Jungle Rhythm* 1929 (anim,d); *The Karnival Kid* 1929 (anim,d); *Mickey's Choo-Choo* 1929 (anim,d); *Mickey's Follies* 1929 (anim,d); *The Opry House* 1929 (anim,d); *The Plow Boy* 1929 (anim,d); *The Skeleton Dance* 1929 (anim,d); *Springtime* 1929 (anim,d); *Summer* 1929 (anim,d); *El Terrible Toreador* 1929 (anim,d); *Cinderella* 1950 (fx); *Peter Pan* 1953 (fx); *Lady and the Tramp* 1955 (fx); *White Wilderness* 1958 (fx); *Sleeping Beauty* 1959 (fx); *The Birds* 1963 (tech.adviser—fx) (**AANBFX**); *The Three Lives of Thomasina* 1963 (fx).

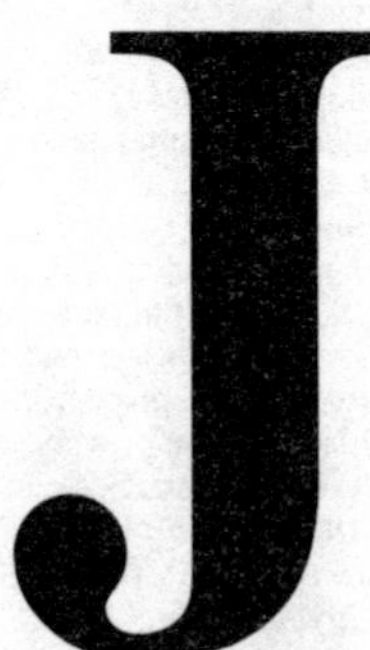

Jackson, Glenda • Actress • Born Birkenhead, Cheshire, England, May 9, 1936. *Educ.* RADA, London. Jackson made her screen debut with a small appearance in *This Sporting Life* (1963) but first attracted attention as a stage actress, notably as Charlotte Corday in the London and New York productions of Peter Brook's *Marat/Sade*. She reprised her role for the 1967 screen version and subsequently gave outstanding performances in films by directors including Ken Russell, John Schlesinger and Joseph Losey. Jackson has won two best actress Oscars, for her roles in Russell's D.H. Lawrence adaptation, *Women in Love* (1969), and Melvin Frank's *A Touch of Class* (1973). She has a peculiar flair for portraying strong-willed, independent women and made an assured switch to middle-aged roles in the mid-1970s, beginning with the Hepburn-Tracy style comedy, *House Calls* (1978), co-starring Walter Matthau. In March 1990 Jackson announced her decision to run for a seat in the British Parliament as a member of the Labour Party. • *This Sporting Life* 1963; *The Benefit of the Doubt* 1966; *The Persecution and Assassination of Jean Paul Marat as Performed by the Inmates of the Asylum of Charenton Under the Direction of the Marquis De Sade/Marat/Sade* 1966; *Tell Me Lies* 1967; *Negatives* 1968; *Women in Love* 1969 **(AABA)**; *The Boy Friend* 1971; *Mary, Queen of Scots* 1971; *The Music Lovers* 1971; *Sunday Bloody Sunday* 1971 **(AANBA)**; *The Nelson Affair* 1973; *Il Sorriso del Grande Tentatore* 1973; *A Touch of Class* 1973 **(AABA)**; *The Triple Echo* 1973; *The Maids* 1974; *Hedda* 1975 **(AANBA)**; *The Romantic Englishwoman* 1975; *The Incredible Sarah* 1976; *Nasty Habits* 1976; *The Class of Miss MacMichael* 1978; *House Calls* 1978; *Stevie* 1978; *Lost and Found* 1979; *Health* 1980; *Hopscotch* 1980; *And Nothing But the Truth* 1982; *Giro City* 1982; *The Return of the Soldier* 1982; *Turtle Diary* 1985; *Beyond Therapy* 1987; *Business As Usual* 1987; *Salome's Last Dance* 1988; *The Rainbow* 1989; *King of the Wind* 1990.

Jacobi, Derek • Actor • Born London, October 22, 1938. *Educ.* Cambridge. Celebrated stage actor, occasionally in films. Memorable in the title role of TV's "I, Claudius." • *Othello* 1965; *Three Sisters* 1970; *The Day of the Jackal* 1973; *The Odessa File* 1974; *The Medusa Touch* 1978; *The Human Factor* 1979; *Mannen som gick upp i rok* 1980; *Charlotte* 1981; *Enigma* 1982; *The Secret of Nimh* 1982; *Little Dorrit* 1988; *Henry V* 1989; *The Fool* 1990.

Jaffe, Stanley R. • Producer • Born New Rochelle, NY, July 1940. *Educ.* University of Pennsylvania Wharton School of Business. Jaffe produced *Goodbye Columbus* (1969) at the age of 28 and was appointed head of Paramount Studios two years later. He subsequently spent some time at Columbia before turning independent in 1979 with the Academy Award-winning *Kramer vs. Kramer*. Since *Racing With the Moon* (1984), Jaffe was worked in collaboration with former 20th Century-Fox president Sherry Lansing, through their Jaffe-Lansing Productions company. • *Goodbye, Columbus* 1969 (p); *I Start Counting* 1969 (exec.p); *Bad Company* 1972 (p); *The Bad News Bears* 1976 (p); *Kramer vs. Kramer* 1979 (p) **(AABP)**; *Taps* 1981 (p); *Without a Trace* 1983 (d,p); *Firstborn* 1984 (exec.p); *Racing With the Moon* 1984 (exec.p); *Fatal Attraction* 1987 (p) **(AANBP)**; *The Accused* 1988 (p); *Black Rain* 1989 (p).

Jaglom, Henry • Director; also screenwriter. • Born London, 1939. *Educ.* University of Pennsylvania, PA (acting, writing, directing); Actors Studio. Began his Hollywood career as an actor on TV shows including "Gidget" and "The Flying Nun" and became involved with the independent filmmaking scene in the late 1960s. Jaglom's films as a director work best when the strong ensemble acting which is his trademark is well grounded, as are *Sitting Ducks* (1979) and *Can She Bake a Cherry Pie?* (1983). • *Psych-Out* 1968 (a); *Easy Rider* 1969 (consultant); *Drive, He Said* 1971 (a); *The Last Movie* 1971 (a); *A Safe Place* 1971 (d,sc); *The Other Side of the Wind* 1972 (a); *Hearts and Minds* 1974 (p) **(AABDOC)**; *Lily Aime-Moi* 1974 (a); *Tracks* 1976 (d,sc); *Sitting Ducks* 1979 (a,d,sc); *National Lampoon Goes to the Movies* 1982 (d); *Can She Bake a Cherry Pie?* 1983 (a,d); *Always* 1985 (a,d,p,sc); *Someone to Love* 1987 (a,d,p,sc,ed); *New Year's Day* 1989 (a,d,p,sc,ed); *Eating* 1990 (d,sc,ed); *Little Noises* 1991 (exec.p).

Jakubowska, Wanda • Director • Born Warsaw, Poland, November 10, 1907. *Educ.* Warsaw University (art history). Founding member of Poland's Society of Devotees of the Artistic Film (START) in the 1920s. Jakubowska began her career making documentaries, notably *The Awakening* (1934), on which she collaborated with Aleksander Ford. The negative of her first feature, *On the River Niemen*, was destroyed during the burning of Warsaw in 1939 and Jakubowska herself was confined in both Auschwitz and Ravensbruck; she survived to become one of Poland's leading directors after the close of WWII. Several of her films drew on her experiences in the concentration camps, particularly the award-winning *The Last Stage* (1948), which helped attract international attention to the burgeoning Polish film industry. • *Probuzeni/The Awakening* 1934; *Nar Niemmem/On the Niemen River* 1939; *Ostatni etap/The Last Stage* 1948; *Zolnierz zwyciestwa* 1953; *Opowiesc atlantycka* 1954; *Pozegnanie z diablem* 1956; *Krol Macius I* 1957; *Historia wspolczesna* 1960; *Spotkanie w mroku* 1960; *Koniec naszego swista* 1964; *Goraca linia* 1965; *150 na Godzine* 1971; *Bialy mazur* 1973; *Ludwik Warynski* 1978.

Jancsó, Miklós • Director • Born Vac, Hungary, September 27, 1921. *Educ.* Kolozsvar University, Rumania (law); Academy for Theater and Film Art, Budapest. Hungarian director Miklós Jancsó gained international recognition in the late 1960s, when *The Round-up* (1966), *The Red and The White* (1967) and *The Confrontation* (1969) garnered numerous awards at a variety of international film festivals. Displaying evidence of a developing revolutionary vision and uniquely formalistic cinematic style, these films not only established Jancsó's reputation as an auteur, but also helped to serve notice to the world that Hungarian filmmaking had entered into a dynamic new era.

Jancsó's world-wide acclaim reached its peak with *Red Psalm* (1972), for which he was named best director at the Cannes Film Festival. *Red Psalm* stands as perhaps the most coherent expression of the director's desire to combine a revolutionary form of filmic language with the theme of the moral complexities of social revolution. Although he would receive a lifetime achievement award at Cannes in 1979, Jancsó's more recent films, such as *The Dawn* (1986) and *Season of Monsters* (1987), have not found the widespread approval granted to his films of the 60s and early 70s. His films are now criticized as experiments in purely abstract formalism, devoid of social relevance and lacking in human compassion. Ultimately, his most enduring contribution to cinema may well be the role he played during the 60s in liberating Hungarian filmmaking from the formal and thematic constraints of state-sanctioned realism.

From his first feature in 1958 (*The Bells Have Gone to Rome*), Jancsó demonstrated a preoccupation with history, particularly for its potential for providing scenarios of political conflict and social upheaval. By the late 60s, he had developed a remarkably consistent narrative model, in which historical situations are used to isolate specific political oppositions, which are then played out to their ultimate conclusion. In each film, the conflict is presented abstractly, with little explanation as to its origins or to individual character psychology or motivation. In *The Red and The White*, the setting is 1918 Russia during civil war, the action an ongoing military battle that occurs in an unspecified location. The red and the white armies engage in a series of struggles which leave first one side, and then the other, temporarily victorious. Each victory, however fleeting, precipitates the massacre of prisoners to solidify the gain. The outnumbered red army is eventually extinguished by what remains of the white forces. By decontextualizing the conflict and presenting it in abstract terms, Jancso encourages reflection on the larger theme of the nature of power and its relation to human brutality.

The abstract nature in which Jancsó develops his narratives is complemented by his highly original visual style, which serves to undercut normal narrative conventions. Jancsó's trademark is his masterful use of long takes, in which elaborate camera movements are utilized in tandem with highly choreographed movements of figures within the frame. Actors are often arranged into geometric patterns to match the topography of the rural landscapes the director favors. Dialogue is used sparingly, accompanied by an expressionless acting style which limits viewer identification with the characters. The overall effect of this visual design is to encourage contemplation and analysis of the complex ideas circulating through the films. Though Jancsó's style has been increasingly criticized as overly mechanical, it remains unmistakably his own, and for that reason his films will continue to make a distinct contribution to international cinema. JFK • *Kezunkbe vettuk a beke ugyet (short)* 1950 (d,sc); *A Maksimenko Brigad (short)* 1950 (story); *A Szovjet mezogazdasagai kuldottsek tanitasai (short)* 1951 (d,ph); *Ezerkilencszazotvenketto. 1952 Majus 1/A 8.szavad Majus 1 (short)* 1952 (d); *Arat az Oroshazi "Dozsa" (short)* 1953 (d); *Kozos Utan (short)* 1953 (d); *Egy kiallitas kepei (short)* 1954 (d); *Elteto Tisza-viz (short)* 1954 (d); *Emberek! Ne engedjetek! (short)* 1954 (d,sc); *Galga menten (short)* 1954 (d); *Osz Badacsonyban (short)* 1954 (d); *Angyalfoldi fiatalok (short)* 1955 (d); *Egy delutan Koppanymonostorban (short)* 1955 (d); *Emlekezz, ifjusag! (short)* 1955 (d); *Varsoi Vilagifjusagi Talalkozo I-III (short)* 1955 (d); *Zsigmond Moricz 1879-1942 (short)* 1956 (d); *A Varos Peremen (short)* 1957 (d); *Del Kina tajain (short)* 1957 (d); *Kina vendegei voltunk (short)* 1957 (d); *Peking palotai (short)* 1957 (d); *Szinfoltok Kinabol (short)* 1957 (d); *Derkovitz Gyula 1894-1934 (short)* 1958 (d); *A Harangok Romaba mentek/The Bells Have Gone to Rome* 1958 (d); *Halhatatlansag (short)* 1959 (d,sc,ph); *Izotopok a gyogyaszatban (short)* 1959 (d); *Eladas muveszete, Az (short)* 1960 (d,sc); *Harom csillag* 1960 (d); *Ido kereke, Az (short)* 1960 (d,sc); *Szerkezettervezes (short)* 1960 (d,sc); *Alkonyok es hajnalok (short)* 1961 (d,sc); *Indiantortenet (short)* 1961 (d,sc); *Oldas es kotes* 1962 (d,sc); *Hej, te eleven fa... (short)* 1963 (d,sc); *Igy jottem (short)* 1964 (d); *Jelenlet (short)* 1965 (d,sc); *Kozelrolia: A ver (short)* 1966 (d); *Szegenylegenyek/The Roundup* 1966 (d); *Csend es Kialtas* 1967 (d,sc); *Csillagosok, Katonak/The Red and the White* 1967 (d,sc); *Kameraval Kosztromaban* 1967 (a); *Voros Majus (short)* 1968 (d); *The Boys of Paul Street* 1969 (a); *Fenyes Szelek/The Confrontation* 1969 (d); *Sirokko* 1969 (d,sc); *Egi barany* 1970 (d,sc); *Fust (short)* 1970 (d); *Il Giovane Attila* 1971 (d,sc); *La Pacifista* 1971 (d,sc); *Meg Ker A Nep/The People Still Ask* 1972 (d); *Roma Rivuole Cesare* 1973 (d,sc); *Szerelmem, Elektra* 1975 (d); *Vizi Privati, Pubbliche Virtu* 1976 (d); *Difficile morire* 1977 (a); *Allegro Barbarao Magyar Rapszodia 2* 1979 (d,sc); *Eletunket es verunket* 1979 (d,sc); *A Zsarnok szive avagy Boccaccio Magyarorszagon* 1981 (d,sc); *Omega, Omega* 1982 (d); *Muzsika* 1984 (d,sc); *L'Aube* 1986 (d,sc); *Szornyek Evadja* 1987 (d,sc); *Jezus Krisztus Horoszkopia* 1989 (d).

Jannings, Emil • Actor • Born Theodor Friedrich Emil Janenz, Rorschach, Switzerland, July 23, 1884; died 1950. Imposing silent star who first gained prominence with Max Reinhardt's Berlin theater in the teens. Jannings appeared in several superior early German films, particularly those directed by Ernst Lubitsch, and was outstanding as the humiliated doorman in F.W. Murnau's *The Last Laugh* (1924). He moved to Hollywood in 1926 and won an Academy Award for his performances in *The Way of All Flesh* (1927) and Josef von Sternberg's *The Last Command* (1928), but after the advent of sound his inadequate English forced a return to Germany. There he turned in his most famous performance, as Professor Rath in von Sternberg's *The Blue Angel* (1930).

In 1938 Jannings accepted Goebbels's invitation to head the Tobis Film Company, which produced Nazi propaganda features such as Veidt Harlan's *Der Herrscher* (1937) and Hans Steinhoff's *Ohm Kruger* (1941). The Allied authorities refused to allow Jannings to work after the war, though a subsequent inquiry into his fascist affiliations cleared him of any serious involvement with the Nazi regime. • *Im Schutzengraben* 1914 (a); *Aus Mangel an Beweisen* 1916 (a); *Die Bettlerin von St. Marien* 1916 (a); *Frau Eva* 1916 (a); *Im Angesicht des Töten* 1916 (a); *Das Leben ein Traum* 1916 (a); *Nachte des Grauens* 1916 (a); *Passionels Tagebuch* 1916 (a); *Stein unter Steinen* 1916 (a); *Unheilbar* 1916 (a); *Der Zehnte Pavillon der Zitadelle* 1916 (a); *Die Ehe der Luise Rohrbach* 1917 (a); *Das Fidele Gefängnis* 1917 (a); *Das Geschaft* 1917 (a); *Lulu* 1917 (a); *Der Ring der Giuditta Foscari* 1917 (a); *Wenn vier dasselbe tun* 1917 (a); *Die Augen der Mummie Ma* 1918 (a); *Keimendes Leben 1. Teil* 1918 (a); *Nach Zwanzig Jahren* 1918 (a); *Keimendes Leben 2. Teil* 1919 (a); *Madame Du Barry* 1919 (a); *Der Mann der Tat* 1919 (a); *Rose Bernd* 1919 (a); *Der Töchter des Mehemed* 1919 (a); *Algol* 1920 (a); *Anne Boleyn* 1920 (a); *Die Brüder Karamasoff* 1920 (a); *Colombine* 1920 (a); *Die Grosse Licht* 1920 (a); *Kölhiesels Töchter* 1920 (a); *Der Schädel der Pharaonentochter* 1920 (a); *Danton* 1921 (a); *Die Ratten* 1921 (a); *Der Schwur des Peter Hergatz* 1921 (a); *Der Stier von Olivera* 1921 (a); *Vendetta* 1921 (a); *Othello* 1922 (a); *Peter der Grosse* 1922 (a); *Das Weib des Pharao* 1922 (a); *Alles für Geld* 1923 (a); *Liebe Macht Blind* 1923 (a); *Tragödie der Liebe* 1923 (a); *Der Letzte Mann/The Last Laugh* 1924 (a); *Nju* 1924 (a); *Quo Vadis?* 1924 (a); *Das Wachsfigurenkabinett* 1924 (a); *Tartuff* 1925 (a); *Variete* 1925 (a); *Faust* 1926 (a); *The Way of All Flesh* 1927 (a) **(AABA)**; *The Last Command* 1928 (a) **(AABA)**; *The Patriot* 1928 (a); *Sins of the Fathers* 1928 (a); *The Street of Sin* 1928 (a); *Betrayal* 1929 (a); *Der Blaue Engel/The Blue Angel* 1930 (a); *Liebling der Götter* 1930 (a); *Stürme der Leidenschaft* 1931 (a); *Die Abenteuer des Königs Pausole* 1933 (a); *Der Schwarze Walfisch* 1934 (a); *Der Alte und der junge König* 1935 (a); *Traumulus* 1936 (a); *Der Herrscher* 1937 (a,prod.sup); *Der Zerbrochene Krug* 1937 (a); *Robert Koch, der Bekämpfer des Todes* 1939 (a); *Ohm Krüger* 1941 (a,prod.sup); *Die Entlassung* 1942 (a,p); *Altes Herz wird weider jung* 1943 (a).

Jarman, Derek • Filmmaker • Born England, 1942. Avant-garde British director whose films focus, in an uncompromising and personal manner, on homosexuality. Jarman's art is influenced by Jean Cocteau, Kenneth Anger and Ken Russell, among others, and he has described himself as one of the last generation to remember the "countryside before mechanization intervened and destroyed everything."

Trained in the fine arts, Jarman made his first films (super-8 shorts) while working as a designer on Russell's *The Devils* (1971) and *Savage Messiah* (1972). His first feature was *Sebastiane* (1976), a lyrical, homoerotic portrait of the Christian saint. In *Jubilee* (1978), Queen Elizabeth I is conducted on a tour of a futuristic England in which violence and anarchy hold sway; the film became something of a beacon of the punk movement of the late 1970s. Jarman's *The Tempest* was a typically irreverent and somewhat rambling reworking of Shakespeare's play.

Jarman's most accessible film is *Caravaggio* (1986), a stylishly rendered biopic that dramatizes the conflicts between the painter's need for patronage, his religious beliefs and his sexuality. Noting that Caravaggio consistently painted Saint John as muscle-bound, Jarman suggests that the painter found sexual as well as aesthetic elation with a street thug he used as a model. The director also has fun creating filmic facsimiles of some of the painter's best known works. Curiously, though it undercuts narrative conventions by using heavy-handed anachronisms—typewriters, motorbikes, etc—the film nevertheless reiterates one of the oldest cliches of Hollywood biopics like *Lust for Life*: i.e. that art is little more than immediately recorded experience, "life" thrown directly onto the canvas; the *process* of artistic creation is completely glossed over.

Jarman returned to the super-8 medium and a non-narrative mode for his next film, *The Last of England* (1987), an angry, self-indulgent vision of Britain as an urban wasteland which intercuts shots of Jarman writing with excerpts from his own old home movies and images of surreal violence and degradation.

The WWI poems of Wilfred Owen, set to the music of Benjamin Britten, shaped *War Recquiem* (1988), a powerful essay on the wastes of wars past which also deals with the contemporary battle against AIDS.

A champion of film art and a dedicated experimentalist, Jarman has remained a critic of, and at odds with, what he sees as the stifling, repressive commercialism of mainstream cinema.

Always struggling for funds, his first seven features were produced for a combined cost of only $3 million. He published an autobiography, *Dancing Ledge*, in 1984. • *The Devils* 1971 (sets); *Broken English (short)* 1972 (d); *Savage Messiah* 1972 (sets); *Sebastian* 1976 (d,sc); *Jubilee* 1978 (d); *Nighthawks* 1978 (a); *The Tempest* 1979 (d,sc); *In the Shadow of the Sun* 1981 (uncred.p,d,ph,ed); *T.G.—Psychic Rally in Heaven (short)* 1981 (d); *The Dream Machine (short)* 1982 (d); *Waiting For Waiting For Godot (short)* 1982 (d); *Imagining October (short)* 1984 (d,p,sc,ph); *Angelic Conversations* 1985 (d,sc); *Caravaggio* 1986 (d,sc); *Aria* 1987 (d,sc "Louise"); *The Last of England* 1987 (d,ph,narrative text); *Ostia* 1987 (a); *Prick Up Your Ears* 1987 (a); *Cactus Land* 1988 (a); *Derek Jarman: You Know What I Mean* 1988 (a); *War Requiem* 1988 (d,sc); *The Garden* 1990 (d,sc,ph).

Jarmusch, Jim • Director, screenwriter; also actor, composer. • Born Akron, OH, 1953. *Educ.* Columbia; NYU Institute of Film and TV. Jim Jarmusch's hip, urban, comic jags arose from the same East Village-New York University explosion that nurtured the relentlessly contemporary films of Susan Seidelman and Spike Lee. Jarmusch offers lowlife reflections of post-modernist communication and mis-communication between characters sealed off from one another, their only connection the many-tentacled pop trash culture of America.

In 1971, Jarmusch enrolled at Columbia University in the English literature program. A few months before graduation, on a visit to Paris, Jarmusch discovered the rich treasures of the Cinémathèque Française and wound up staying in France for a year. Upon returning to New York City, he enrolled in the graduate film program at New York University, where he became a teaching assistant to director Nicholas Ray, then teaching at NYU. Through Ray's efforts, Jarmusch became a production assistant on Wim Wenders's tribute to Ray, *Lighting Over Water* (1980). Jarmusch completed his NYU film project, *Permanent Vacation* (1980), and began work on a short film, shot over one weekend, that eventually became *Stranger Than Paradise* two years later.

Stranger Than Paradise startled audiences with its gritty cool and fresh comic tone, winning the Camera d'Or at Cannes and the best film award from the National Society of Film Critics. Jarmusch has referred to his first three feature films as a trilogy. *Stranger Than Paradise*, along with *Down By Law* (1986) and *Mystery Train* (1989), take place in a blighted American cultural landscape—from the bleak, wintry moonscape of Ohio and the cracked seaminess of an over-ripe Florida in *Stranger Than Paradise* to the diffuse, cinema-reflected New Orleans in *Down By Law* and the tawdry, clapboard decay of Memphis's *Mystery Train*. In this world characters make connections by sharing TV dinners, chanting ice cream jingles and revering Elvis Presley. A Jarmusch film begins with characters who live a robot-like existence, unable to relate or communicate; a typical Jarmusch shot features a character staring offscreen until the screen fades to black or there is a cut to darkness. Into this stultifying atmosphere, a character with a different viewpoint and perspective enters, exposing the shallowness of the enmeshed character's existence. This foreign presence may be a Hungarian visitor (*Stranger Than Paradise*), an Italian tourist (*Down By Law*) or Japanese teenagers on a pilgrimage to Graceland (*Mystery Train*). As Jarmusch explains, "America's a kind of throwaway culture that's a mixture of different cultures. To make a film about America, it seems to me logical to have at least one perspective that's transplanted because ours is a collection of transplanted influences." In this clash lies the basis of Jarmusch's invigorating originality.

Through the course of his three films, Jarmusch's comic vision has become more despairing. At the end of *Stranger Than Paradise*, Eva and Eddie still have a hopeful chance of happiness. In *Down By Law*, however, Jack and Zack are still on the run as Roberto plans for a promising future. And in *Mystery Train*, the three sets of characters spend the film barely missing each other and, as dawn comes up in Memphis, all race off in different directions. In a world of declining values and lovelessness, the population in Jarmusch's films are all racing off in different directions, seeking their own personal shelters of comfort and familiarity, blanketed by the shrilly blaring music of Screamin' Jay Hawkins and Irma Thomas—recorded voices shouting into a void. PB • *Lightning Over Water* 1980 (prod.asst); *Underground U.S.A.* 1980 (sound); *Fräulein Berlin* 1982 (a); *Permanent Vacation* 1982 (d,p,sc,ed,m); *Burroughs* 1983 (sound); *Stranger Than Paradise* 1984 (d,sc,ed); *Coffee and Cigarettes (short)* 1986 (d,sc); *Down By Law* 1986 (d,sc); *Sleepwalk* 1986 (cam.op); *Candy Mountain* 1987 (a); *Straight to Hell* 1987 (a); *Coffee and Cigarettes Part Two (short)* 1988 (d,sc); *Helsinki Napoli All Night Long* 1988 (a); *Leningrad Cowboys Go America* 1989 (a); *Mystery Train* 1989 (d,sc); *The Golden Boat* 1990 (a).

Jarre, Maurice • Composer • Born Maurice Alexis Jarre, Lyon, France, September 13, 1924. *Educ.* University of Lyon; Sorbonne, Paris (engineering); Paris Conservatoire (composition, percussion). Jarre established himself as a serious composer and writer of theatrical scores in the 1950s and earned a reputation for feature film scoring in the following decade. He has demonstrated a particular flair for sweeping, epic spectacles, winning Oscars for his three collaborations with David Lean (*Lawrence of Arabia* 1962, *Doctor Zhivago* 1965, *A Passage to India* 1984). Jarre has latterly become a frequent collaborator with director Peter Weir. His son, Jean-Michel Jarre, is a successful composer of popular electronic music. • *Hôtel des Invalides (short)* 1951 (m); *Le Voyage d'Abdallah* 1953 (m); *L'Univers d'Utrillo (short)* 1954 (m); *Festival d'Avignon (short)* 1955 (m); *Le Grand Silence (short)* 1955 (m); *Sur le pont d'Avignon (short)* 1956 (m); *Le Théatre National Populaire (short)* 1956 (m); *Toute la Mémoire du Monde* 1956 (m); *Le Bel Indifférent (short)* 1957 (m); *Bravo Alpha (short)* 1957 (m); *Donne-moi la main* 1958 (m); *La Génération du désert (short)* 1958 (m); *La Tête contre les murs* 1958 (m); *La Bête à l'affût* 1959 (m); *Chronique provinciale (short)* 1959 (m); *La Corde raide* 1959 (m); *Les Dragueurs* 1959 (m); *Les Etoiles de midi* 1959 (m); *Le Main chaude* 1959 (m); *Vous n'avez rien à déclarer?* 1959 (m); *Les Yeux sans Visage/Eyes Without a Face* 1959 (m); *Crack in the Mirror* 1960 (m); *Malrif, aigle royal (short)* 1960 (m); *Le Puits aux trois vérités* 1960 (m); *Recours en Grace* 1960 (m); *Le Tapis volant (short)* 1960 (m); *Vel' d'hiv' (short)* 1960 (m); *Amours célèbres* 1961 (m); *The Big Gamble* 1961 (m,m.cond); *Les Dimanches de Ville d'Avray/Sundays and Cybele* 1961 (m) **(AANBM)**; *Pleins feux sur l'assassin* 1961 (m); *Le Président* 1961 (m); *Le Soleil dans l'oeil* 1961 (m); *Le Temps du Ghetto* 1961 (m); *Lawrence of Arabia* 1962 (m) **(AABM)**; *The Longest Day* 1962 (m); *L'Oiseau de Paradis* 1962 (m); *Les Oliviers de la justice* 1962 (m); *Présence d'Albert Camus (short)* 1962 (m); *Thérèse Desqueyroux* 1962 (m); *Ton ombre est la mienne* 1962 (m); *Les Animaux* 1963 (m); *Encore Paris (short)* 1963 (m); *Judex* 1963 (m); *Mort, où est ta victoire?* 1963 (m); *Mourir à Madrid/To Die in Madrid* 1963 (m); *Pour l'Espagne (short)* 1963 (m); *Un Roi sans divertisement* 1963 (m); *Le Travestis du diable (short)* 1963 (m); *Behold a Pale Horse* 1964 (m,m.cond); *The Train* 1964 (m,m.cond); *Week-End à Zuydcoote* 1964 (m); *The Collector* 1965 (m); *Doctor Zhivago* 1965 (m,m.cond) **(AABM)**; *Gambit* 1966 (m,m.cond,song); *Grand Prix* 1966 (m); *The Night of the Generals* 1966 (m); *Paris brûle-t-il?/Is Paris Burning?* 1966 (m); *The Professionals* 1966 (m); *La Guerre pour une paix (short)* 1967 (m); *5 Card Stud* 1968 (m,m.cond,song); *A Hollywood avec... (short)* 1968 (m); *Barbarella* 1968 (m); *The Fixer* 1968 (m,m.cond); *Isadora* 1968 (m); *Villa Rides* 1968 (m); *Broceliande (short)* 1969 (m); *La Caduta degli dei/The Damned* 1969 (m,m.dir); *The Extraordinary Seaman* 1969 (m,m.dir); *Topaz* 1969 (m,m.dir); *Airborn (short)* 1970 (m); *El Condor* 1970 (m,m.dir); *The Only Game in Town* 1970 (m,m.cond); *Ryan's Daughter* 1970 (m,m.cond); *Plaza Suite* 1971 (m); *Soleil Rouge* 1971 (m); *Una Stagione all'inferno* 1971 (m); *The Effect of Gamma Rays on Man-in-the-Moon Marigolds* 1972 (m); *The Life and Times of Judge Roy Bean* 1972 (m) **(AANBS)**; *Pope Joan* 1972 (m,m.cond); *Ash Wednesday* 1973 (m); *The Mackintosh Man* 1973 (m); *Mrs. Uschyck (short)* 1973 (m); *Grandeur Nature* 1974 (m); *The Island at the Top of the World* 1974 (m); *Mr. Sycamore* 1974 (m); *Great Expectations* 1975 (m); *The Man Who Would Be King* 1975 (m,m.dir); *Mandingo* 1975 (m); *Posse* 1975 (m); *The Last Tycoon* 1976 (m,m.cond); *Mohammad Messenger of God* 1976 (m) **(AANBM)**; *Shout at the Devil* 1976 (m,m.dir); *Crossed Swords* 1977 (m); *March or Die* 1977 (m,m.dir); *The Spy Who Loved Me* 1977 (m); *Mon Royaume Pour un Cheval* 1978 (m); *Two Solitudes* 1978 (m); *American Success Company* 1979 (m); *The Black Marble* 1979 (m); *Die Blechtrommel/The Tin Drum* 1979 (m); *The Magician of Lublin* 1979 (m,m.dir,song); *Winter Kills* 1979 (m); *The Last Flight of Noah's Ark* 1980 (m,m.dir,m); *Lion of the Desert* 1980 (m,m.dir); *Resurrection* 1980 (m,m.dir); *Don't Cry, It's Only Thunder* 1981 (m); *Die Falschung/Circle of Deceit* 1981 (m); *Taps* 1981 (m); *Firefox* 1982 (m); *Wrong Is Right* 1982 (m); *The Year of Living Dangerously* 1982 (m); *Young Doctors in Love* 1982 (m,m.dir); *Au nom de tous les Miens* 1983 (m); *Dreamscape* 1984 (m); *A Passage to India* 1984 (m,m.cond) **(AABM)**; *Top Secret!* 1984 (m,m.dir); *The Bride* 1985 (m); *Enemy Mine* 1985 (m,m.cond); *Mad Max Beyond Thunderdome* 1985 (m,m); *Witness* 1985 (m) **(AANBM)**; *The Mosquito Coast* 1986 (m,m.sup); *Solarbabies* 1986 (m); *Tai-Pan* 1986 (m,m.cond); *Fatal Attraction* 1987 (m,orch); *Gaby - A True Story* 1987 (m,m); *Julia and Julia* 1987 (m); *No Way Out* 1987 (m); *Shuto Shoshitsu* 1987 (m); *Buster* 1988 (m); *Distant Thunder* 1988 (m); *Gorillas in the Mist* 1988 (m) **(AANBM)**; *Moon Over Parador* 1988 (m,m.cond); *Le Palanquin des larmes* 1988 (m); *Wildfire* 1988 (m); *Chances Are* 1989 (m,m.cond); *Dead Poets Society* 1989 (m); *Enemies, A Love Story* 1989 (m); *Prancer* 1989 (m,m.cond); *After Dark, My Sweet* 1990 (m); *Almost an Angel* 1990 (m); *Ghost* 1990 (m,orch); *Jacob's Ladder* 1990 (m); *Solar Crisis* 1990 (m).

Jasny, Vojtech • Director; also screenwriter. • Born Kelc, Moravia, Czechoslovakia, November 30, 1925. • *Educ.* Charles University, Prague (philosophy, Russian); FAMU. Central figure of the Czech New Wave. Jasny entered the acclaimed Prague film school (FAMU) in its inaugural year, worked in documentaries with early collaborator Karel Kachyna and began turning out fiction features in the mid-1950s.

Jasny's first solo feature, *September Nights* (1957), is generally considered a seminal work of the New Wave, but it was his next film, *Desire* (1958), which propelled him into the international spotlight. *Desire* displayed a lyrical, poetic quality that found its greatest expression, three features later, in *The Cassandra Cat* (1963).

An infectious mixture of childrens' fairy tale and political satire, *Cat* whimsically chronicles the arrival in a small town of a magical cat, whose unshielded gaze turns people the color of their true character; thus lovers turn red, adulterers yellow, cheats and thieves grey, etc. The film won a Special Jury Prize at Cannes and remains the director's best known work in the West.

Just before the Soviet invasion of Prague in 1968, Jasny crafted another exceptional work, *All My Good Countrymen* (1968), a satirical take on life in a small town between 1945 and 1968. *Countrymen* won best director honors at Cannes in 1969 but also precipitated Jasny's departure from a now Soviet-controlled Czechoslovakia. He made a beautifully orchestrated "farewell to my homeland," the 20-minute *Czech Rhapsody* (1969), before landing in the West. Jasny's subsequent films (including a 1975 adaptation of Heinrich Böll's *The Clown*) have been sporadic and less highly regarded than his earlier, Czech works.

Jasny taught film in Prague, Germany and Austria and, since 1984, has been lecturing at Columbia University in New York, where his old pupil, Milos Forman, is co-chairman of the film department. SKK • *Everything Ends Tonight* 1954 (d); *September Nights* 1957 (d,sc); *Desire* 1958 (d,sc); *I Survived Certain Death* 1960 (d); *Pilgrimage to the Virgin Mary* 1961 (d); *The Cassandra Cat/That Cat* 1963 (d,sc); *Vsichni Dobri Rodaci/All My Good Countrymen* 1968 (d,sc); *Czech Rhapsody* 1969 (short) (d); *Ansichten Eines Clowns/The Clown* 1975 (d,sc); *Fluchtversuch* 1976 (d); *Ernst Fuchs* 1976 (d); *The Peanut Butter Solution/Tales For All (Part 2)* 1985 (sc); *The Great Land of Small/Tales For All (Part 5)* 1986 (d,sc).

Jaubert, Maurice • Composer • Born Nice, France, January 3, 1900; died 1940. *Educ.* Nice Conservatoire; Sorbonne, Paris (law). Leading French film composer of the 1930s whose subtle, intimate scores and sparse orchestration were in distinct contrast to the prevailing trend in Hollywood. Jaubert worked with René Clair, Marcel Carné and Julien Duvivier, among others, before being killed in combat shortly before the French surrender in WWII. Jaubert's work enjoyed a revival of interest in the 70s and 80s, with his music featuring on the soundtrack of several films, including four directed by François Truffaut. • *L'Hirondelle et la mésange* 1921 (add.m); *Le Petit chaperon rouge* 1929 (m); *Die Wunderbare Lüge der Nina Petrowna* 1929 (m); *Au pays du scalp* 1931 (m); *L'Affaire est dans le sac* 1932 (m); *Mélo* 1932 (m.cond); *Mirages de Paris* 1932 (m.cond); *Le Petit Roi* 1933 (m.cond); *Quatorze Juillet* 1933 (m); *Trois vies et une corde* 1933 (m); *Zéro de conduite* 1933 (m); *L'Atalante* 1934 (m,m.cond,song); *Le Dernier Milliardaire* 1934 (m.cond); *En Crète sans les dieux* 1934 (m); *Les Misérables* 1934 (m.cond); *Les Nuits Moscovites* 1934 (m.cond); *Obsession* 1934 (m); *Sans Famille* 1934 (m.cond); *Sapho* 1934 (m.cond); *L'Equipage* 1935 (m.cond); *Terre d'amour (short)* 1935 (m.cond); *La Vie Parisienne* 1935 (m.arr); *Un Village dans Paris: Montmartre* 1935 (m); *Mayerling* 1936 (m); *Un Carnet de Bal* 1937 (m); *Drôle de Drame/Bizarre Bizarre* 1937 (m); *Les Maisons de la misère* 1937 (m); *We Live in Two Worlds* 1937 (m); *Altitude 3.200* 1938 (m); *Ces Dames aux chapeaux verts* 1938 (m); *Eau Vive (short)* 1938 (m); *Les Filles du Rhône* 1938 (m); *Hôtel du Nord* 1938 (m); *Lumières de Paris* 1938 (a,uncred.m); *Le Quai des Brumes/Port of Shadows* 1938 (m); *L'Esclave blanche* 1939 (m); *La Fin du Jour* 1939 (m); *Le Jour Se Lève/Daybreak* 1939 (m); *Nuit de Décembre* 1939 (a); *Poil de Carotte* 1973 (m); *L'Argent de poche/Small Change* 1975 (m); *L'Histoire d'Adèle H./The Story of Adele H.* 1975 (m); *L'Homme qui aimait les femmes/The Man Who Loved Women* 1977 (m); *La Chambre Verte/Green Room* 1978 (m); *Le Temps Détruit: Lettres d'une guerre 1939-40* 1985 (m); *Cién Niños Esperando un Trén* 1988 (m).

Jenkins, George • Production designer • Born Baltimore, MD, November 19, 1911. *Educ.* University of Pennsylvania, PA. Versatile, prolific art director who has worked with directors including William Wyler (*The Best Years of Our Lives* 1946), Arthur Penn (*The Miracle Worker* 1962) and, especially, Alan Pakula (*Klute* 1971, *All the President's Men* 1976, *Sophie's Choice* 1982, *Presumed Innocent* 1990). • *The Best Years of Our Lives* 1946 (art d); *The Secret Life of Walter Mitty* 1947 (art d); *A Song Is Born* 1948 (art d); *Roseanna McCoy* 1949 (art d); *The Miracle Worker* 1962 (art d); *Mickey One* 1965 (pd); *Up the Down Staircase* 1967 (art d); *Wait Until Dark* 1967 (art d); *No Way to Treat a Lady* 1968 (art d); *The Subject Was Roses* 1968 (art d); *Me, Natalie* 1969 (art d);

The Angel Levine 1970 (pd); *Klute* 1971 (art d); *The Pursuit of Happiness* 1971 (art d); *1776* 1972 (art d); *The Paper Chase* 1973 (art d); *The Parallax View* 1974 (pd); *Funny Lady* 1975 (pd); *Night Moves* 1975 (pd); *All the President's Men* 1976 (pd) **(AABAD)**; *Comes a Horseman* 1978 (pd); *The China Syndrome* 1979 (pd) **(AANBAD)**; *Starting Over* 1979 (pd); *The Postman Always Rings Twice* 1981 (pd); *Rollover* 1981 (pd); *Sophie's Choice* 1982 (pd); *Dream Lover* 1986 (pd); *Orphans* 1987 (pd); *See You in the Morning* 1989 (pd); *Presumed Innocent* 1990 (pd).

Jennings, Humphrey • *aka* F. H. Jennings • Filmmaker • Born Frank Humphrey Sinkler Jennings, Walberswick, Suffolk, England, 1907; died 1950, Greece. *Educ.* Pembroke College, Cambridge (English). A poet, surrealist painter and theatrical set designer, Jennings began making documentaries in the 1930s after joining the renowned GPO Film Unit. He produced his best work during WWII, with his most notable achievements including: *Words For Battle* (1942), which matched passages of literature with footage of the Home Front; *Listen to Britain* (1942), which eschewed any narrative commentary in favor of "found" sound; and *Fires Were Started* (1943), his only feature film. Jennings's postwar output lacked the verve and lyricism of his earlier work, partly because he felt himself out of joint with what he saw as a fragmented society. Lindsay Anderson wrote that the director's "traditionalist spirit was unable to adjust itself to the changed circumstances of Britain after the war." Others have attributed the decline in the quality of his output to the cessation of his working relationship with editor and sometime co-director Stewart McAllister. Jennings died in a rock fall while scouting locations for a film on a Greek island. • *Locomotives (short)* 1934 (d); *Post-Haste (short)* 1934 (d); *Story of the Wheel (short)* 1935 (d); *Design For Spring (short)* 1938 (d); *English Harvest (short)* 1938 (d); *Penny Journey (short)* 1938 (d); *Speaking From America (short)* 1938 (d); *The First Days (short)* 1939 (d); *S.S. Ionian (short)* 1939 (d); *Spare Time (short)* 1939 (d); *London Can Take It! (short)* 1940 (d); *Spring Offensive (short)* 1940 (d); *Welfare of the Workers (short)* 1940 (d); *The Heart of Britain (short)* 1941 (d); *Listen to Britain (short)* 1942 (d,ed); *Words For Battle (short)* 1942 (d,sc); *Fires Were Started* 1943 (d,sc); *The Silent Village (short)* 1943 (d,p,sc); *The Eighty Days (short)* 1944 (d,p); *The True Story of Lili Marlene (short)* 1944 (a,d,p,sc); *A Diary For Timothy (short)* 1945 (d,sc); *Myra Hess (short)* 1945 (d,sc); *A Defeated People (short)* 1946 (d,sc); *The Cumberland Story (short)* 1947 (d,sc); *The Dim Little Island (short)* 1949 (d,p); *Family Portrait (short)* 1950 (d,sc).

Jessua, Alain • Director; also screenwriter, producer. • Born Paris, January 16, 1932. Former assistant to Max Ophuls and Marcel Carné who showed considerable directorial promise with his first two features. *Life Upside Down* (1964) was a wryly observed account of a man's withdrawal from reality into fantasy and *Comic Strip Hero* (1967) used trick photography to blend the real world with that of a strip cartoon; both were distinctive and imaginative films that presaged a bright career. In the following decades, however, Jessua's output has been minimal. His more recent works, like *En toute innocence* (1988), are accomplished, if unexceptional, entertainments. • *Casque d'or* 1952 (ad); *Chevalier de Menilmontant (short)* 1953 (ad); *The Earrings of Madame De...* 1953 (ad); *Métier de danseur (short)* 1953 (ad); *Mam'zelle Nitouche* 1954 (ad); *Lola Montès* 1955 (ad); *Oasis* 1955 (ad); *Léon la lune (short)* 1956 (d,sc); *Le Huitième jour* 1960 (ad); *Terrain vague* 1960 (ad); *La Vie à l'Envers/Life Upside Down* 1964 (d,sc); *Jeu de massacre/Comic Strip Hero* 1967 (a,d,sc); *Traitement de choc* 1972 (d,sc,adapt,m); *Armaguedon* 1977 (d,sc); *Les Chiens* 1978 (a,d,sc,idea,dial); *Paradis pour tous* 1982 (d,p,sc,idea); *Frankenstein 90* 1984 (d,p,sc); *En toute innocence* 1988 (d,p,sc,dial).

Jewison, Norman • Director; also producer. • Born Norman P. Jewison, Toronto, Ontario, Canada, July 21, 1926. *Educ.* Malvern Collegiate Institute, Toronto; Victoria College, University of Toronto. Highly skilled technician with a knack for eliciting fine performances from his casts. After working in TV as an actor, writer and director, Jewison turned to features in the 1960s and made his name with *The Cincinnati Kid* (1965) and *In the Heat of the Night* (1967), which won five Academy awards. He scored a sizeable box-office success in 1987 with *Moonstruck*, a deftly handled romantic comedy which won Oscars for best actress (Cher), best supporting actress (Olympia Dukakis) and best screenplay (John Patrick Shanley). • *40 Pounds of Trouble* 1962 (d); *The Thrill of It All* 1963 (d); *Send Me No Flowers* 1964 (d); *The Art of Love* 1965 (d); *The Cincinnati Kid* 1965 (d); *The Russians Are Coming, the Russians Are Coming* 1966 (d,p) **(AANBP)**; *In the Heat of the Night* 1967 (d) **(AANBD)**; *The Thomas Crown Affair* 1968 (d,p); *Gaily, Gaily* 1969 (d,p); *The Landlord* 1970 (p); *Fiddler on the Roof* 1971 (d,p) **(AANBD,AANBP)**; *Norman Jewison Film Maker* 1971 (a); *Billy Two Hats* 1973 (p); *Jesus Christ Superstar* 1973 (d,p,sc); *Rollerball* 1975 (d,p); *F.I.S.T.* 1978 (d,exec.p); *And Justice For All* 1979 (d,p); *The Dogs of War* 1980 (exec.p); *Best Friends* 1982 (d,p); *Fraülein Berlin* 1982 (a); *Iceman* 1984 (p); *A Soldier's Story* 1984 (d,p) **(AANBP)**; *Agnes of God* 1985 (d,p); *Moonstruck* 1987 (d,p) **(AANBD,AANBP)**; *The January Man* 1988 (p); *In Country* 1989 (d,p).

Jhabvala, Ruth Prawer • Novelist, screenwriter • Born Cologne, Germany, May 7, 1927. *Educ.* Queen Mary College, England; London University (English). In England from 1939, Jhabvala moved to India in 1959 and is best known for her collaborations with director James Ivory. Several Ivory/Jhabvala screenplays have been adapted from her own novels; *Heat and Dust*, published in 1975, became one of the team's finest screen achievements in 1983. • *The Householder* 1963 (sc,from novel); *Shakespeare Wallah* 1965 (sc); *The Guru* 1969 (sc); *Bombay Talkie* 1970 (sc); *Autobiography of a Princess* 1975 (sc); *Roseland* 1977 (sc); *The Europeans* 1979 (sc); *Hullabaloo Over Georgie and Bonnie's Pictures* 1979 (sc); *Jane Austen in Manhattan* 1980 (sc); *Quartet* 1981 (sc); *The Courtesans of Bombay* 1982 (p,sc); *Heat and Dust* 1983 (sc,from novel); *The Bostonians* 1984 (sc); *A Room With a View* 1986 (sc) **(AABSC)**; *Madame Sousatzka* 1988 (sc); *Mr. & Mrs. Bridge* 1990 (sc).

Joffe, Roland • Director • Born London, November 17, 1945. *Educ.* Manchester University. The youngest director ever to work at London's National Theatre, Joffe made his big-screen mark in the 1980s with two large-scale, politically oriented spectacles. *The Killing Fields* (1984) was based on the experiences of New York Times correspondent Sydney Schanberg and his Cambodian assistant, Dith Pran, before and after the fall of Phnom Penh to the Khmer Rouge in 1975; *The Mission* (1986) focused on political intrigue and exploitation in a Jesuit mission in Brazil in the late 18th century. Both films were visually sumptuous—they earned Chris Menges two Oscars for best cinematography—though the lushness and length of each was felt by some critics to lessen their dramatic impact. • *The Killing Fields* 1984 (d,p) **(AANBD)**; *The Mission* 1986 (d) **(AANBD)**; *Fat Man and Little Boy* 1989 (d,sc).

Johns, Glynis • Actress • Born Durban, South Africa, October 5, 1923. Husky-voiced daughter of actor Mervyn Johns who made her London stage bow in 1935 and her screen debut three years later. Her spirited personality has enlivened a number of comedies. • *Murder in the Family* 1938; *Prison Without Bars* 1938; *South Riding* 1938; *The Briggs Family* 1939; *On the Night of the Fire* 1939; *Under Your Hat* 1940; *49th Parallel* 1941; *The Prime Minister* 1941; *The Adventures of Tartu* 1943; *Half-Way House* 1945; *Vacation From Marriage* 1945; *This Man Is Mine* 1946; *Frieda* 1947; *An Ideal Husband* 1947; *Miranda* 1948; *Third Time Lucky* 1948; *Dear Mr. Prohack* 1949; *State Secret* 1950; *Appointment With Venus* 1951; *Encore* 1951;

Flesh and Blood 1951; *The Magic Box* 1951; *No Highway* 1951; *The Promoter* 1952; *Personal Affair* 1953; *Rob Roy, the Highland Rogue* 1953; *The Sword and the Rose* 1953; *The Beachcomber* 1954; *The Seekers* 1954; *The Weak and the Wicked* 1954; *Josephine and Men* 1955; *Around the World in 80 Days* 1956; *The Court Jester* 1956; *Loser Takes All* 1956; *All Mine to Give* 1957; *Another Time, Another Place* 1958; *Shake Hands With the Devil* 1959; *The Spider's Webb* 1960; *The Sundowners* 1960 **(AANBSA)**; *The Cabinet of Caligari* 1962; *The Chapman Report* 1962; *Papa's Delicate Condition* 1963; *Mary Poppins* 1964; *Dear Brigitte* 1965; *Don't Just Stand There!* 1967; *Lock Up Your Daughters!* 1969; *Under Milk Wood* 1971; *The Vault of Horror* 1973; *Zelly and Me* 1988; *Nukie* 1989.

Johnson, Don • Actor • Born Flatt Creek, MO, December 15, 1950. *Educ.* University of Kansas; American Conservatory Theatre, San Francisco. Handsome leading man of the 1980s, best known as one of the pastel-clad detectives on TV's "Miami Vice" (1984-89). Johnson married actress Melanie Griffith for the second time in 1989. • *The Magic Garden of Stanley Sweetheart* 1970 (a); *Zachariah* 1970 (a); *The Harrad Experiment* 1973 (a); *A Boy and His Dog* 1974 (a); *Return to Macon County* 1975 (a); *Melanie* 1981 (a); *Cease Fire* 1985 (a); *G.I. Joe: The Movie* 1987 (a); *Sweet Hearts Dance* 1988 (a); *Dead-Bang* 1989 (a); *The Hot Spot* 1990 (a).

Johnson, Nunnally • Screenwriter; also director, producer. • Born Columbus, GA, December 5, 1897; died 1977. Though not consistently successful, Johnson's overall output clearly marks him as one of the best scenarists to work within the Hollywood system. Prolific and versatile, he wrote or co-wrote impressive American portraits (*Jesse James* 1939, *The Grapes of Wrath* 1940), urban thrillers (*The Woman in the Window* 1944) and tough action capers (*Flaming Star* 1960, *The Dirty Dozen* 1967), as well as a host of memorable comedies. Johnson married actress Dorris Bowdon in 1940 and co-wrote the screenplay for *The World of Henry Orient* (1964) with his daughter Nora, author of the original novel. • *For the Love of Mike* 1927 (uncred.sc); *Rough House Rosie* 1927 (story); *It Ought to be a Crime* (short) 1931 (sc,story); *Mlle. Irene the Great (short)* 1931 (sc,story); *His Week-End* (short) 1932 (sc,story); *Twenty Horses (short)* 1932 (sc,story); *Wild Horse Mesa* 1932 (uncred.sc); *A Bedtime Story* 1933 (sc); *Mama Loves Papa* 1933 (sc); *Bulldog Drummond Strikes Back* 1934 (sc); *The House of Rothschild* 1934 (sc); *Kid Millions* 1934 (sc,story); *Moulin Rouge* 1934 (sc,story); *Baby Face Harrington* 1935 (sc); *Cardinal Richelieu* 1935 (uncred.sc); *The Man Who Broke the Bank at Monte Carlo* 1935 (assoc.p,sc); *Thanks a Million* 1935 (sc); *Banjo on My Knee* 1936 (assoc.p,sc); *The Country Doctor* 1936 (assoc.p); *Dimples* 1936 (assoc.p); *The Prisoner of Shark Island* 1936 (assoc.p,sc); *The Road to Glory* 1936 (assoc.p); *Cafe Metropole* 1937 (p); *Love Under Fire* 1937 (sc); *Nancy Steele Is Missing* 1937 (p); *Slave Ship* 1937 (assoc.p); *Jesse James* 1939 (assoc.p,sc,story); *Rose of Washington Square* 1939 (p,sc); *Wife, Husband, and Friend* 1939 (assoc.p,sc); *Chad Hanna* 1940 (assoc.p,sc); *The Grapes of Wrath* 1940 (assoc.p,sc) **(AANBSC)**; *I Was an Adventuress* 1940 (assoc.p); *Tobacco Road* 1941 (sc); *Life Begins at Eight-Thirty* 1942 (p,sc); *Moontide* 1942 (uncred.sc); *The Pied Piper* 1942 (p,sc); *Roxie Hart* 1942 (p,sc); *Holy Matrimony* 1943 (p,sc) **(AANBSC)**; *The Moon Is Down* 1943 (p,sc); *Casanova Brown* 1944 (p,sc); *The Woman in the Window* 1944 (p,sc); *Along Came Jones* 1945 (sc); *The Keys of the Kingdom* 1945 (sc); *The Southerner* 1945 (uncred.sc); *The Dark Mirror* 1946 (p,sc); *The Senator Was Indiscreet* 1947 (p); *Mr. Peabody and the Mermaid* 1948 (p,sc); *Everybody Does It* 1949 (p,sc); *The Gunfighter* 1950 (p,uncred.sc); *The Mudlark* 1950 (p,sc); *Three Came Home* 1950 (p,sc); *The Desert Fox* 1951 (p,sc); *The Long Dark Hall* 1951 (sc); *My Cousin Rachel* 1952 (p,sc); *O. Henry's Full House* 1952 (uncred.sc); *Phone Call From a Stranger* 1952 (p,sc); *We're Not Married* 1952 (p,sc); *How to Marry a Millionaire* 1953 (p,sc); *Black Widow* 1954 (d,p,sc); *Night People* 1954 (d,p,sc); *How to Be Very, Very Popular* 1955 (d,p,sc); *The Man in the Gray Flannel Suit* 1955 (d,sc); *Oh, Men! Oh, Women!* 1956 (d,p); *The Three Faces of Eve* 1957 (d,p,sc); *The True Story of Jesse James* 1957 (from screenplay); *The Man Who Understood Women* 1959 (d,p,sc); *The Angel Wore Red* 1960 (d,sc); *Flaming Star* 1960 (sc); *Mr. Hobbs Takes a Vacation* 1962 (sc); *Cleopatra* 1963 (script consult—original production); *Take Her, She's Mine* 1963 (sc); *The World of Henry Orient* 1964 (sc); *Dear Brigitte* 1965 (uncred.sc); *The Dirty Dozen* 1967 (sc).

Jolson, Al • Singer, actor • Born Asa Yoelson, Srednike, Lithuania, May 26, 1886; died 1950. Celebrated song-and-dance man who was a major Broadway attraction before gaining world-wide fame as the star of the first "talking picture," *The Jazz Singer* (1927). Jolson's fame declined in the 1930s but was revived with the 1946 biopic *The Jolson Story*, starring Larry Parks but with Jolson's voice dubbed in for the songs. His third wife was actress Ruby Keeler. • *The Jazz Singer* 1927 (a); *The Singing Fool* 1928 (a); *Say It With Songs* 1929 (a); *Sonny Boy* 1929 (a); *Big Boy* 1930 (a); *Mammy* 1930 (a); *Showgirl in Hollywood* 1930 (a); *Hallelujah, I'm a Bum* 1933 (a); *Wonder Bar* 1934 (a); *Go Into Your Dance* 1935 (a); *Kings of the Turf* 1935 (a); *The Singing Kid* 1936 (a); *Hollywood Cavalcade* 1939 (a); *Rose of Washington Square* 1939 (a); *Swanee River* 1939 (a); *Rhapsody in Blue* 1945 (a); *The Jolson Story* 1946 (voice dubbing); *You Are What You Eat* 1968 (song); *Twinkle, Twinkle, "Killer" Kane* 1979 (songs); *Phar Lap* 1983 (song); *Hannah and Her Sisters* 1986 (song).

Jones, Chuck • *aka* Chuck M. Jones, Charles M. Jones • Animation director; also producer. • Born Charles Martin Jones, Spokane, WA, September 1, 1912. *Educ.* Chouinard Art Institute, Los Angeles. Between 1938 and 1963 Jones worked almost exclusively at Warner Bros., where he established himself as a leading figure of the golden age of Hollywood animation. Among the characters he helped to create were Bugs Bunny, Daffy Duck and the existential coupling of the ever-pursuing Wile E. Coyote and the ever-escaping Road Runner. Jones also did four months of uncredited work on Walt Disney's *Sleeping Beauty*. He moved to MGM in the mid-1960s and also produced a number of "Tom and Jerry" cartoons. He was credited as Charles M. Jones until the mid-50s. • *Hell-Bent For Election* 1944 (d); *Sleeping Beauty* 1959 (uncred.anim); *Beep Prepared* 1961 (anim,p) **(AANBASF)**; *Nelly's Folly* 1961 (anim,p) **(AANBASF)**; *Gay Purr-ee* 1962 (sc); *The Dot and the Line* 1965 (anim,p) **(AABASF)**; *The Phantom Tollbooth* 1970 (d,p,sc); *Bugs Bunny Superstar* 1975 (anim); *1941* 1979 (uncred.creative asst); *Great American Bugs Bunny—Road Runner Chase* 1979 (d,p,sc); *Looney Looney Looney Bugs Bunny Movie* 1981 (anim); *Uncensored Cartoons* 1981 (d); *Bugs Bunny's 3rd Movie: 1001 Rabbit Tales* 1982 (anim); *Daffy Duck's Movie: Fantastic Island* 1983 (d); *Gremlins* 1984 (a); *Porky Pig in Hollywood* 1986 (anim,d); *Innerspace* 1987 (a); *Daffy Duck's Quackbusters* 1988 (sequences d); *Who Framed Roger Rabbit* 1988 (anim.consult); *Gremlins 2: The New Batch* 1990 (anim.writing,anim.d—Bugs Bunny and Daffy Duck).

Jones, James Earl • Actor • Born Arkabutla, MS, January 17, 1931. *Educ.* University of Michigan (drama); American Theatre Wing, New York. Distinguished black actor who gained initial prominence on the New York stage, particularly in *The Great White Hope* (1966)—a role which earned him an Oscar nomination when he reprised it for the screen in 1970. Jones lent his powerful, resonant voice to "Star Wars" villain Darth Vader. Son of boxer/actor Robert Earl Jones. • *Dr. Strangelove; or, How I Learned to Stop Worrying and Love the Bomb* 1964; *The Comedians* 1967; *The End of the Road* 1970; *The Great White Hope* 1970 **(AANBA)**; *King: A Filmed Record... Montgomery to Memphis* 1970; *Malcolm X* 1972; *The*

Man 1972; *Claudine* 1974; *The River Niger* 1975; *The Bingo Long Traveling All-Stars and Motor Kings* 1976; *Deadly Hero* 1976; *Swashbuckler* 1976; *Exorcist II: The Heretic* 1977; *The Greatest* 1977; *The Last Remake of Beau Geste* 1977; *A Piece of the Action* 1977; *Star Wars* 1977; *The Empire Strikes Back* 1980; *The Bushido Blade* 1981; *Blood Tide* 1982; *Conan the Barbarian* 1982; *Return of the Jedi* 1983; *City Limits* 1985; *My Little Girl* 1986; *Soul Man* 1986; *Allan Quatermain and the Lost City of Gold* 1987; *Gardens of Stone* 1987; *Matewan* 1987; *Pinocchio and the Emperor of the Night* 1987; *Coming to America* 1988; *Teach 109 (short)* 1988; *Best of the Best* 1989; *Field of Dreams* 1989; *Three Fugitives* 1989; *The Ambulance* 1990; *Grim Prairie Tales* 1990; *The Hunt For Red October* 1990.

Jones, Jennifer • Actress • Born Phylis Isley, Tulsa, OK, March 2, 1919. *Educ.* Monte Cassino Junior College, Tulsa, OK; Northwestern University; AADA, New York. Leading lady who became the protégé of producer David O. Selznick in the early 1940s, marrying him in 1949 after her divorce from actor Robert Walker. Selznick took control of her career and ensured her appearances in prestigious productions by leading directors: Jones starred as the visionary title character in *The Song of Bernadette* (1943), in the epic color western *Duel in the Sun* (1947) and as the enigmatic, inspirational subject of *Portrait of Jennie* (1948). Sons Robert Walker, Jr. and Michael Ross Walker are both actors. Married since 1971 to industrialist Norton Simon. • *Dick Tracy's G-Men* 1939; *The New Frontier* 1939; *The Song of Bernadette* 1943 **(AABA)**; *Since You Went Away* 1944 **(AANBSA)**; *Love Letters* 1945 **(AANBA)**; *The American Creed (short)* 1946; *Cluny Brown* 1946; *Duel in the Sun* 1947 **(AANBA)**; *Portrait of Jennie* 1948; *Madame Bovary* 1949; *We Were Strangers* 1949; *Gone to Earth* 1950; *Carrie* 1952; *Ruby* 1952; *Beat the Devil* 1953; *Stazione Termini/Indiscretion of an American Wife* 1953; *Good Morning, Miss Dove* 1955; *Love Is a Many Splendored Thing* 1955 **(AANBA)**; *The Man in the Gray Flannel Suit* 1955; *The Barretts of Wimpole Street* 1956; *A Farewell to Arms* 1957; *Tender Is the Night* 1962; *The Idol* 1966; *Angel, Angel Down We Go* 1969; *The Towering Inferno* 1974; *Patricia—einmal Himmel und zurück* 1980; *Going Hollywood: The War Years* 1988 (archival footage).

Jones, Quincy • Composer, arranger, producer • Born Quincy Delight Jones, Jr., Chicago, IL, March 14, 1935. *Educ.* Seattle University, WA; Berklee School of Music, Boston. Versatile, multi-award-winning artist whose prolific film work during the 1960s and 70s ran the gamut from the lightly comedic *Walk, Don't Run* (1966) to the chilling *In Cold Blood* (1967). Jones has enjoyed noted collaborations with Sidney Lumet, particularly on *The Pawnbroker* (1965) and *The Anderson Tapes* (1971), and his work encompasses discordant, atonal compositions as well as more conventional melodic scores. He is also one of the most successful contemporary pop songwriters and producers, due to the record-breaking sales of Michael Jackson's "Thriller" album and the charity benefit single, "We Are the World." • *Pojken i tradet* 1960 (m); *Mirage* 1965 (m); *The Pawnbroker* 1965 (m); *The Slender Thread* 1965 (m); *Enter Laughing* 1966 (m); *Made in Paris* 1966 (song); *Walk, Don't Run* 1966 (m); *Banning* 1967 (m,song) **(AANBS)**; *The Deadly Affair* 1967 (m); *In Cold Blood* 1967 (m) **(AANBM)**; *In the Heat of the Night* 1967 (m); *The Counterfeit Killer* 1968 (m); *A Dandy in Aspic* 1968 (m); *For Love of Ivy* 1968 (m) **(AANBS)**; *The Hell With Heroes* 1968 (m); *Jigsaw* 1968 (m); *The Split* 1968 (m,song); *Bob & Carol & Ted & Alice* 1969 (m,m); *Cactus Flower* 1969 (m,song); *The Italian Job* 1969 (m,song); *John and Mary* 1969 (m,song); *Last of the Mobile Hot-Shots* 1969 (m); *The Lost Man* 1969 (m,song); *MacKenna's Gold* 1969 (m); *Brother John* 1970 (m); *Eggs* 1970 (tm); *Of Men and Demons* 1970 (m); *The Out-of-Towners* 1970 (m); *They Call Me Mr. Tibbs* 1970 (m); *Up Your Teddy Bear* 1970 (m,song); *$* 1971 (m); *The Anderson Tapes* 1971 (m); *Honky* 1971 (m); *Man and Boy* 1971 (m.sup); *Come Back Charleston Blue* 1972 (m.sup,song); *The Getaway* 1972 (m); *The Hot Rock* 1972 (m); *The New Centurions* 1972 (m); *Save the Children* 1973 (a,trumpeter,keyboardist); *Toda Nudez Sera Castigada* 1973 (m); *Mother, Jugs & Speed* 1976 (song); *The Rise and Fall of Ivor Dickie* 1978 (song); *The Wiz* 1978 (m.adapt,m.sup, dance arranger,orch,songs) **(AANBM)**; *The Last American Virgin* 1982 (song); *Making Michael Jackson's Thriller* 1983 (m,song); *The Color Purple* 1985 (m,song,p) **(AANBM,AANBP)**; *Fast Forward* 1985 (m); *Fever Pitch* 1985 (m,songs); *Lost in America* 1985 (song); *The Slugger's Wife* 1985 (m); *Listen Up* 1990 (a,m).

Jones, Terry • Director, screenwriter; also actor, author. • Born Colwyn Bay, North Wales, February 1, 1942. *Educ.* St. Edmund Hall, Oxford (English). A former student of medieval literature, Terry Jones declined an academic life while maintaining an ironic link to the middle ages via his film and publishing career. He was a veteran of the Experimental Theatre Club and the Oxford Revue and had written for TV and radio when he joined the "Monty Python's Flying Circus" team in 1969. Jones has functioned as the sole director of two "Python" films as well as *Erik the Viking* (1989), adapted from his own children's book. • *And Now For Something Completely Different* 1971 (a,sc,idea); *Monty Python and the Holy Grail* 1975 (a,d,sc); *Jabberwocky* 1976 (a); *Pleasure at Her Majesty's* 1976 (a); *Monty Python's Life of Brian* 1979 (a,d,sc); *The Secret Policeman's Ball* 1979 (a,sc); *Monty Python Live at the Hollywood Bowl* 1982 (a,sc); *Monty Python's The Meaning of Life* 1983 (sc,song,a,d); *Labyrinth* 1986 (sc); *Personal Services* 1987 (d); *Consuming Passions* 1988 (from play *Secrets*); *Erik the Viking* 1989 (a,d,sc,from stories "The Saga of Erik the Viking").

Jones, Tommy Lee • Actor • Born San Saba, TX, September 15, 1946. *Educ.* Harvard (English). Leading man and supporting player, often in villainous roles. Jones won an Emmy for his portrayal of convicted murderer Gary Gilmore in TV's *The Executioner's Song* (1982). • *Eliza's Horoscope* 1972; *Jackson County Jail* 1976; *Rolling Thunder* 1977; *The Betsy* 1978; *Eyes of Laura Mars* 1978; *Coal Miner's Daughter* 1980; *Back Roads* 1981; *Nate and Hayes* 1983; *The River Rat* 1984; *Black Moon Rising* 1986; *The Big Town* 1987; *Stormy Monday* 1988; *The Package* 1989; *Fire Birds* 1990; *Blue Sky* 1991.

Jones, Trevor • Composer • Born Cape Town, South Africa, March 23, 1949. Noted film and TV composer of the 1980s. • *Alfred the Great* 1969 (a); *Brothers and Sisters* 1980 (m,m.dir); *The Dollar Bottom (short)* 1981 (m,m.dir); *Excalibur* 1981 (m,m.dir,m); *Time Bandits* 1981 (m,song); *The Dark Crystal* 1982 (m,synthesized electrical sound); *The Sender* 1982 (m); *Give My Regards to Broad Street* 1983 (a); *Nate and Hayes* 1983 (m,orch); *Return of the Jedi* 1983 (a); *Those Glory Glory Days* 1983 (m); *Aderyn Papur* 1984 (m); *Dr. Fischer of Geneva* 1984 (m); *Runaway Train* 1985 (m,m.cond); *Labyrinth* 1986 (m); *Angel Heart* 1987 (m); *Dominick and Eugene* 1988 (m,m.cond); *Just Ask For Diamond* 1988 (m,m.dir,song); *Mississippi Burning* 1988 (m); *A Private Life* 1989 (m); *Sea of Love* 1989 (m); *Sweet Lies* 1989 (m); *Arachnophobia* 1990 (m); *Bad Influence* 1990 (m).

Jordan, Neil • Director, screenwriter; also author. • Born County Sligo, Ireland, 1950. Gifted, versatile figure who entered films as a script consultant on John Boorman's *Excalibur* (1981) before directing three impressive British features in the early-to-mid 1980s. Jordan is best known for the last of these, *Mona Lisa* (1986), a gritty contemporary thriller boasting a fine central performance by Bob Hoskins. After a disappointing Hollywood foray, Jordan returned to impressive, fanciful form with *The Miracle* (1991). He has published two novels as well as an award-winning collection of short stories, *Night in Tunisia* (1978). • *Excalibur* 1981 (script consultant); *Traveller* 1981 (sc);

Angel 1982 (d,sc); *The Company of Wolves* 1985 (d,sc); *Mona Lisa* 1986 (d,sc); *The Courier* 1987 (exec.p); *High Spirits* 1988 (d,sc); *We're No Angels* 1989 (d); *The Miracle* 1991 (d,sc).

Josephson, Erland • Actor; also director, screenwriter. • Born Stockholm, Sweden, June 15, 1923. Long-time collaborator with Ingmar Bergman as an actor, scriptwriter and stage director. Josephson successfully branched out into international roles in the 1980s, in such films as Philip Kauffman's *The Unbearable Lightness of Being*, Istvan Szabo's *Hanussen* (both 1988) and notably as the anguished protagonist of Andrei Tarkovski's *The Sacrifice* (1986). • *Det regnar pa var karlek* 1946; *Till Gladje/To Joy* 1949; *Ansiktet/The Magician* 1958; *Nara Livet/Brink of Life/So Close To Life* 1958; *For att Inte Tala om Alla Dessa Kvinnor/All These Women* 1964 (sc); *Flickorna* 1968; *Vargtimmen/Hour of the Wolf* 1968; *En Passion/The Passion of Anna* 1969; *Cries and Whispers* 1972; *Scenes From a Marriage* 1974; *Monismanien 1995* 1975; *Ansikte mot ansikte/Face to Face* 1976; *Al di la del bene e del male/Beyond Good and Evil* 1977; *Den Allvarsamma Leken* 1977; *En och En* 1978 (a,d,p,sc); *Die Erste Polka* 1978; *Hostsonaten/Autumn Sonata* 1978; *Dimenticare Venezia* 1979; *Karleken* 1980; *Marmeladupproret* 1980 (a,d,p,sc); *Montenegro* 1981; *Bella Donna* 1982; *Fanny och Alexander/Fanny and Alexander* 1982; *Variola Vera* 1982; *La Casa del tappetto Giallo* 1983; *Nostalghia/Nostalgia* 1983; *After the Rehearsal* 1984; *Angelan Sota/Angelas Krig/Angela's War* 1984; *Bakom Jalusin* 1984; *Un Caso di Incoscienza* 1984; *Dirty Story* 1984; *The Flying Devils* 1985; *Amarosa* 1986; *Garibaldi—the General* 1986; *L'Ultima Mazurka* 1986; *Le Mal d'aimer* 1986; *Offret—Sacrificatio/The Sacrifice* 1986; *Saving Grace* 1986; *Il Giorno Prima* 1987; *Testament d'un poète juif assassiné* 1987; *Directed By Andrei Tarkovsky* 1988; *La Donna Spezzata* 1988; *Hanussen* 1988; *Migrations* 1988; *The Unbearable Lightness of Being* 1988; *God afton, Herr Wallenberg* 1990; *Il Sole Buio* 1990; *The Ox* 1991; *Prospero's Books* 1991; *Wicked* 1991.

Jost, Jon • Director, screenwriter, producer; also director of photography, editor, composer. • Born Chicago, IL, 1943. Leading independent who began making films in the early 1960s. Jost served a two-year jail term (beginning in 1965) for refusing to do military service and, following his release in 1967, has made numerous shorts and over ten features. His feature budgets range from less than $3,000 to—for *All the Vermeers in New York* (1990)—just under $0.25 million.

Jost's work examines issues such as the lasting effects of the Vietnam war, capitalism and consumerism, sex and class conflicts and, in his ten-part documentary series "Plain Talk and Common Sense (uncommon senses)" (1988), the US as myth and institution. An engaging, unconventional storyteller, he is noted for his long takes and improvised dialogue (he has rarely used scripts). In early 1991 Jost was the subject of a retrospective at New York's Museum of Modern Art. • *Speaking Directly: Some American Notes* 1973 (d,ed,m,p,ph,sc); *Angel City* 1977 (d,ed,p,ph,sc); *Last Chants For a Slow Dance* 1977 (d,ed,song,p,ph,sc); *Chameleon* 1978 (d,p,ph,sc); *Nightshift* 1982 (a,ph); *Slow Moves* 1984 (d,ed,m,p,ph,sc); *Bell Diamond* 1987 (d,ed,p,ph,sc); *Rembrandt Laughing* 1989 (art d,d,ed,p,ph,sc); *All the Vermeers in New York* 1990 (art d,d,ed,ph,sc); *Sure Fire* 1990 (d,ed,ph,sc).

Jourdan, Louis • Actor • Born Louis Gendre, Marseille, France, June 19, 1919. *Educ.* Ecole Dramatique, Paris (drama). Young, handsome lead of the 1940s and 50s, memorable in *Letter From an Unknown Woman* (1948) and *Gigi* (1958). Jourdan has more recently turned to playing eccentric villains, as in *Swamp Thing* (1982) and its 1989 sequel. • *Untel père et Fils* 1940 (a); *Premier rendez-vous* 1941 (a); *L'Arlésienne* 1942 (a); *Félicie Nanteuil* 1942 (a); *La Vie de Bohème* 1942 (a); *The Paradine Case* 1947 (a); *Letter From an Unknown Woman* 1948 (a); *No Minor Vices* 1948 (a); *Madame Bovary* 1949 (a); *Anne of the Indies* 1951 (a); *Bird of Paradise* 1951 (a); *The Happy Time* 1952 (a); *Decameron Nights* 1953 (a); *Rue de l'Estrapade* 1953 (a); *Three Coins in the Fountain* 1954 (a); *Julie* 1956 (a); *La Mariée est Trop Belle* 1956 (a); *The Swan* 1956 (a); *Dangerous Exile* 1958 (a); *Gigi* 1958 (a,song); *The Best of Everything* 1959 (a); *Can-Can* 1960 (a); *Le Comte de Monte Cristo* 1961 (a); *Les Vièrges de Rome* 1961 (a); *Il Disordine* 1962 (a); *The V.I.P.s* 1963 (a); *Made in Paris* 1966 (a); *Cervantes* 1967 (a); *Peau d'Espion* 1967 (a); *A Flea in Her Ear* 1968 (a); *Plus ça va, moins ça va* 1977 (a); *Silver Bears* 1977 (a); *Double Deal* 1981 (a); *Swamp Thing* 1982 (a); *Octopussy* 1983 (a); *Counterforce* 1989 (a); *The Return of Swamp Thing* 1989 (a).

Jouvet, Louis • Actor • Born Jules Eugène Louis Jouvet, Crozon, France, December 24, 1887; died 1951. Celebrated stage performer who appeared in a number of outstanding French films of the 1930s, particularly by Jean Renoir and Marcel Carné. • *Knock ou le triomphe de la médecine* 1933 (a,d); *Topaze* 1933 (a); *La Kermesse héroïque/Carnival in Flanders* 1935 (a); *Les Bas-Fonds* 1936 (a); *Mr. Flow* 1936 (a); *L'Alibi* 1937 (a); *Un Carnet de Bal* 1937 (a); *Le Drame de Shanghai* 1937 (a); *Drôle de Drame* 1937 (a); *Forfaiture* 1937 (a); *Mademoiselle Docteur* 1937 (a); *Ramuntcho* 1937 (a); *Education de Prince* 1938 (a); *Entrée des Artistes* 1938 (a); *Hôtel du Nord* 1938 (a); *La Maison du Maltais* 1938 (a); *La Marseillaise* 1938 (a); *La Charrette Fantôme* 1939 (a); *La Fin du Jour* 1939 (a); *Sérénade* 1939 (a); *Untel père et Fils* 1940 (a); *Volpone* 1940 (a); *Un Revenant* 1946 (a); *Copier Conforme* 1947 (a); *Quai des Orfèvres* 1947 (a); *Les Amoureux sont seuls au monde* 1948 (a); *Entre onze heures et minuit* 1948 (a); *Lady Paname* 1949 (a); *Miquette et sa mère* 1949 (a); *Retour à la Vie* 1949 (a); *Une Histoire d'amour* 1950 (a); *Knock ou le triomphe de la médecine* 1950 (a,art d); *Comédiens ambulantes (short)* 1951 (a).

Julia, Raul • Actor • Born San Juan, Puerto Rico, March 9, 1940. *Educ.* University of Puerto Rico (liberal arts). Urbane, cosmopolitan character player with extensive stage experience; outstanding in *Compromising Positions* and *Kiss of the Spider Woman* (both 1985). • *Been Down So Long It Looks Like Up to Me* 1971; *Panic in Needle Park* 1971; *The Gumball Rally* 1976; *Eyes of Laura Mars* 1978; *The Escape Artist* 1982; *One From the Heart* 1982; *Tempest* 1982; *Compromising Positions* 1985; *Kiss of the Spider Woman* 1985; *The Morning After* 1986; *La Gran Fiesta* 1987; *Moon Over Parador* 1988; *The Penitent* 1988; *Tango Bar* 1988; *Tequila Sunrise* 1988; *Trading Hearts* 1988; *Mack the Knife* 1989; *Romero* 1989; *A Life of Sin* 1990; *Presumed Innocent* 1990; *Roger Corman's Frankenstein Unbound* 1990; *The Rookie* 1990.

Junge, Alfred • Art director • Born Gorlitz, Germany, January 29, 1886; died 1964. Outstanding art director, in England from the late 1920s; frequent collaborator with director Michael Powell. • *Hintertreppe* 1921 (asst.art d); *Das Alte Gesetz* 1923 (art d); *Die Grüne Manuela* 1923 (art d); *Der Mann um Mitternacht* 1924 (art d); *Mensch gegen Mensch* 1924 (pd); *Das Wachsfigurenkabinett* 1924 (uncred.art d); *Athleten* 1925 (art d); *Der Kampf gegen Berlin* 1925 (art d); *Die Kleine aus der Konfektion* 1925 (art d); *Ein Lebenskünstler* 1925 (art d); *Sündenbabel* 1925 (art d); *Die Vertauschte Braut* 1925 (art d); *Brennende Grenze* 1926 (art d); *Liebeshändel* 1926 (art d); *Spitzen* 1926 (art d); *Da Halt die Welt den Atem an* 1927 (art d); *Mata Hari* 1927 (art d); *Regina, die Tragödie einer Frau* 1927 (art d); *Die Tragödie eines Verlorenen* 1927 (art d); *Die Carmen von St. Pauli* 1928 (art d); *Moulin Rouge* 1928 (art d); *Picadilly* 1928 (art d); *Die Drei um Edith* 1929 (art d); *Der Günstling von Schonbrunn* 1929 (art d); *Ich Lebe Fur Dich* 1929 (art d); *Cape Forlorn* 1930 (art d); *Two Worlds* 1930 (art d); *Marius* 1931 (art d); *Die Nacht von Port Said* 1931 (art d); *Salto Mortale* 1931 (art d); *8 Madels im Boot* 1932 (art d); *After the Ball* 1932 (art d); *The Midshipmaid* 1932 (art d); *Service For Ladies* 1932 (art d); *Teilnehmer antwortet nicht*

1932 (art d); *Brittania of Billingsgate* 1933 (art d); *Channel Crossing* 1933 (art d); *The Constant Nymph* 1933 (art d); *A Cuckoo in the Nest* 1933 (art d); *The Fire Raisers* 1933 (art d); *Friday the Thirteenth* 1933 (art d); *The Ghoul* 1933 (art d); *The Good Companions* 1933 (art d); *I Was a Spy* 1933 (art d); *Just Smith* 1933 (art d); *Orders Is Orders* 1933 (art d); *Sleeping Car* 1933 (art d); *Turkey Time* 1933 (art d); *Waltz Time* 1933 (art d); *A Cup of Kindness* 1934 (art d); *Dirty Work* 1934 (art d); *Evensong* 1934 (art d); *Evergreen* 1934 (art d); *Jack Ahoy!* 1934 (art d); *Jew Suss* 1934 (art d); *Lady in Danger* 1934 (art d); *Little Friend* 1934 (art d); *The Man Who Knew Too Much* 1934 (art d); *My Song For You* 1934 (art d); *The Night of the Party* 1934 (art d); *Red Ensign* 1934 (art d); *Road House* 1934 (art d); *Wild Boy* 1934 (art d); *Brown on Resolution* 1935 (art d); *Bulldog Jack* 1935 (art d); *Car of Dreams* 1935 (art d); *The Clairvoyant* 1935 (art d); *The Guv'nor* 1935 (art d); *The Iron Duke* 1935 (art d); *Me and Marlborough* 1935 (art d); *Everything Is Thunder* 1936 (art d); *His Lordship* 1936 (art d); *It's Love Again* 1936 (art d); *Gangway* 1937 (art d); *Head Over Heels* 1937 (art d); *King Solomon's Mines* 1937 (art d); *Young and Innocent* 1937 (art d); *The Citadel* 1938 (art d); *Climbing High* 1938 (art d); *Sailing Along* 1938 (art d); *Goodbye, Mr. Chips* 1939 (art d); *The Mind of Mr. Reeder* 1939 (art d); *Busman's Honeymoon* 1940 (art d); *Contraband* 1940 (art d); *Gaslight* 1940 (uncred.art d sup); *He Found a Star* 1941 (art d); *The Life and Death of Colonel Blimp* 1943 (pd); *The Silver Fleet* 1943 (pd); *The Volunteer (short)* 1943 (pd); *A Canterbury Tale* 1944 (pd); *I Know Where I'm Going* 1945 (pd); *A Matter of Life and Death* 1946 (pd); *Black Narcissus* 1947 (pd) **(AABAD)**; *Edward, My Son* 1948 (art d); *Conspirator* 1949 (art d); *The Miniver Story* 1950 (art d); *Calling Bulldog Drummond* 1951 (art d); *The Hour of 13* 1952 (art d); *Ivanhoe* 1952 (art d); *Knights of the Round Table* 1953 (art d) **(AANBAD)**; *Mogambo* 1953 (art d); *Never Let Me Go* 1953 (art d); *Terror on a Train* 1953 (art d); *Beau Brummell* 1954 (art d); *Bedevilled* 1954 (art d); *Betrayed* 1954 (art d); *Crest of the Wave* 1954 (art d); *Flame and the Flesh* 1954 (art d); *Quentin Durward* 1955 (art d); *That Lady* 1955 (uncred.art d); *The Barretts of Wimpole Street* 1956 (art d); *Invitation to the Dance* 1956 (art d); *A Farewell to Arms* 1957 (art d).

Kadár, Ján • Director; also screenwriter. • Born János Kadár, Budapest, Hungary, April 1, 1918; died 1979. *Educ.* Bratislava Film School, Czechoslovakia. Began his career after WWII making documentary shorts, then moved to Prague where he made one feature, *Katya* (1950), before teaming up with Elmar Klos in 1952. Despite wary Czech censors, the pair co-directed and co-wrote a number of socially oriented documentaries and features, achieving international recognition for their Oscar-winning film, *The Shop on Main Street* (1964). *Adrift*, begun in 1968 but interrupted by the Soviet invasion of Czechoslovakia, proved on its release in 1971 to be one of the most haunting depictions of mental breakdown in modern cinema. After his partnership with Klos dissolved in 1969, Kadár tried his hand in the US and Canada with varying degrees of success. • *Life Is Rising from the Ruins* 1945 (d); *Katka/Cathy* 1950 (d); *Unos* 1952 (d); *Hudba z Marsu* 1954 (d); *Tam na konecne* 1957 (d); *Tri prani* 1958 (d); *Spartakiade* 1960 (d); *Smrt si rika Engelchen/Death Is Called Engelchen* 1963 (d); *Obchod Na Korze/The Shop on Main Street* 1964 (d); *Obzalovny* 1964 (d); *The Angel Levine* 1970 (d); *Touha zvana Anada/Adrift* 1971 (d,sc); *Lies My Father Told Me* 1975 (d).

Kael, Pauline • Critic, author • Born Sonoma County, CA, June 19, 1919. *Educ.* University of California, Berkeley (philosophy). Prolific, enduring columnist for *The New Yorker* magazine, Pauline Kael remains the most influential American film critic of the last 50 years.

Kael settled in Berkeley after graduating, made some short films, and wound up managing movie theaters and broadcasting for the Pacifica radio station. She reached national attention in the 60s, first in a brief stint as critic for *The New Republic*, finally as a long-time fixture at *The New Yorker* (1968-1991). Along with Andrew Sarris and John Simon, she helped to shape the new film culture of the 60s and 70s. While Sarris championed the French "auteur" theory and Simon eloquently represented the conservative, literate tradition, Kael reminds us constantly of the personal, emotional, visceral excitement of movies. This is a quintessentially American approach to the art that continues the tradition established by Vachel Lindsay in the 20s. For Kael, movies are near-sexual experiences, as the titles of her critical anthologies suggest: *I Lost It at the Movies, Kiss Kiss Bang Bang, Going Steady, Deeper Into Movies, Reeling, When the Lights Go Down, Taking It All In, Movie Love.* Her general guidebook, *5001 Nights at the Movies*, was revised in 1991.

Kael's career has been almost as passionate and dramatic as her approach to movies. She was notorious in the 60s for her controversial opinions, especially in defense of gutsy American movies (like *Bonnie and Clyde*) versus intellectual European films (like *Blow-Up*). In 1971, her essay *Raising Kane*, critical of the received opinion of Orson Welles, created an historical controversy in the film community. In 1972, her rave review of *Last Tango in Paris* caused a public stir. In 1974, her angry—and much-discussed—essay *On the Future of Movies* sketched a cynical picture of the American film industry as a battleground between venal businessmen and pusillanimous (albeit talented) directors. A year later, she offended fellow critics by scooping them, reviewing Robert Altman's *Nashville* from a rough cut several months before it was released. (She hailed it as "an orgy for movie-lovers.") In a final affront to accepted critical mores, she jumped ship in 1979 to take a job at Paramount in Hollywood as "Executive Consultant." It was a measure of both her remarkable power and her engaging sense of life as a work of art. Five months later, she quit to return to the pages of *The New Yorker*, where she lived out the 80s—like the movies she had to write about—quietly, commercially, and without much controversy, as the focus of film criticism shifted from the sensuality of the printed page to the thumbs-up consumerism of TV. When she retired from *The New Yorker* in February, 1991, she told *The Hollywood Reporter*: "I was lucky enough to work in that great period of filmmaking between the 60s and the early 70s when filmmakers took chances," although she concluded that, when she began writing reviews, "films were as dull as they are now." In between, Pauline Kael contributed much to the excitement. JM

Kahn, Madeline • Actress; also singer. • Born Boston, MA, September 29, 1942. *Educ.* Hofstra University, Long Island, NY. Best remembered as Lili von Shtupp in Mel Brooks's *Blazing Saddles* (1974), a role which fully exploited Kahn's operatic training and zany personality. • *The Dove (short)* 1968 (a); *What's Up, Doc?* 1972 (a); *From The Mixed-Up Files of Mrs. Basil E. Frankweiler* 1973 (a); *Paper Moon* 1973 (a) **(AANBSA)**; *Blazing Saddles* 1974

(a) (**AANBSA**); *Young Frankenstein* 1974 (a); *The Adventure of Sherlock Holmes' Smarter Brother* 1975 (a); *At Long Last Love* 1975 (a); *Won Ton Ton, the Dog Who Saved Hollywood* 1976 (a); *High Anxiety* 1977 (a); *The Cheap Detective* 1978 (a); *The Muppet Movie* 1979 (a); *First Family* 1980 (a); *Happy Birthday, Gemini* 1980 (a); *Simon* 1980 (a); *Wholly Moses!* 1980 (a); *History of the World—Part I* 1981 (a); *Yellowbeard* 1983 (a); *City Heat* 1984 (a); *Slapstick of Another Kind* 1984 (a,song); *Clue* 1985 (a); *An American Tail* 1986 (a); *My Little Pony* 1986 (a); *Betsy's Wedding* 1990 (a).

Kahn, Michael • American editor • Former TV editor ("Hogan's Heroes," etc.) who has cut several films directed by Steven Spielberg, beginning with *Close Encounters of the Third Kind* (1977). *The Activist* 1969 (ed); *Black Jack* 1971 (ed); *Rage* 1972 (ed); *Trouble Man* 1972 (ed); *Black Belt Jones* 1973 (ed); *The Spook Who Sat By the Door* 1973 (ed); *Buster and Billie* 1974 (ed); *Golden Needles* 1974 (ed); *The Savage Is Loose* 1974 (ed); *Truck Turner* 1974 (ed); *The Devil's Rain* 1975 (ed); *The Ultimate Warrior* 1975 (ed); *The Return of a Man Called Horse* 1976 (ed); *Close Encounters of the Third Kind* 1977 (ed) (**AANBED**); *Eyes of Laura Mars* 1978 (ed); *Ice Castles* 1978 (ed); *1941* 1979 (assoc.p,ed); *Close Encounters of the Third Kind: Special Edition* 1980 (ed); *Used Cars* 1980 (ed); *Raiders of the Lost Ark* 1981 (ed) (**AABED**); *Poltergeist* 1982 (ed); *Table For Five* 1983 (ed); *Twilight Zone - the Movie* 1983 (ed—"Kick the Can"); *Falling in Love* 1984 (ed); *Indiana Jones and the Temple of Doom* 1984 (ed); *The Color Purple* 1985 (ed); *The Goonies* 1985 (ed); *Wisdom* 1986 (ed); *Empire of the Sun* 1987 (ed) (**AANBED**); *Fatal Attraction* 1987 (ed) (**AANBED**); *Arthur 2 on the Rocks* 1988 (ed); *Always* 1989 (ed); *Indiana Jones and the Last Crusade* 1989 (ed); *Arachnophobia* 1990 (ed).

Kaige, Chen • Chinese director • Born 1952. *Educ.* Beijing Film Institute. The son of a filmmaker from the earlier generation of Chinese socialist realism, Chen Kaige represents the Fifth Generation, filmmakers who attended Beijing Film Institute after the Cultural Revolution. After graduating in 1982, Chen and his classmates began a new wave in Chinese cinema by emphasizing the visual and aural qualities of film rather than traditional dramatic and literary elements. Their films have also been characterized by a strong political commitment which has led to objections from censors and has limited their domestic audience to students and intellectuals. Outside China, however, Chen Kaige and the other Fifth Generation filmmakers have drawn attention from film scholars and been awarded top festival prizes in Tokyo, Hawaii and Berlin.

Chen Kaige has directed three feature films. His first feature, *Huang Tudi/Yellow Earth*, was completed in 1984 at a small production unit in southern China. The deceptively simple plot concerns a soldier who comes to a remote village in the spring of 1939 to collect folk songs. Describing revolutionary change and extolling the virtues of communism, the soldier convinces the young bride of an arranged marriage to run away. The girl, however, disappears while crossing a river. Photographed by the famous cinematographer, Zhang Yimou, who shot *Red Sorghum* (1987), the film is notable for its exquisite visual imagery and expressive compositions as well as its challenging reexamination of Chinese culture, in this case the repressive ideology of feudalism.

Chen's second film, *Da Yuebing/The Big Parade*, was made in 1986 and reflects the Fifth Generation filmmakers' sense of history and their political attitude toward the Cultural Revolution. The film relates the experience of an army unit which is compelled to perform arduous exercises in preparation for a brief appearance in a meaningless parade. Chen has called the Cultural Revolution "China's biggest parade."

Kaige's *King of Children* (1988) draws heavily on his own life during the years between 1966 and 1976. The hero of the film, as were Chen and his classmates, is sent to work with the peasants. Unprepared for his assignment, he is nevertheless directed to teach Maoist ideology to the poor. The film concludes by showing the futility of rote learning whatever the context, be it during the Cultural Revolution or in the contemporary Chinese educational system.

Chen and the other Fifth Generation filmmakers have brought a new vitality to Chinese cinema that is recognized by film critics around the world. What effect this mounting international attention will have on the official government's assessment of China's new cinema artists remains to be seen. TKB • *Huang Tudi/Yellow Earth* 1984 (d); *Da Yuebing/The Big Parade* 1986 (d); *The Last Emperor* 1987 (a); *Haizi Wang/King of Children* 1988 (d,sc).

Kalatozov, Mikhail • Director; also director of photography. • Born Mikhail Konstantinovich Kalatozishvili, Tiflis (now Tbilisi), Georgia, Russia, December 23, 1903; died 1973. Began his career as an actor, editor and cameraman at the Tiflis studios. Kalatozov's second feature as a director, *The Salt of Svanetia* (1930), is considered a landmark of early Russian cinema, but his third, *The Nail in the Boot* (1932), was banned by the Soviet authorities for "negativism." His output was sporadic during the 1930s and 40s (partly due to his being consigned to a series of administrative posts) but he earned widespread international acclaim for *The Cranes Are Flying* (1957). A poignant WWII drama featuring a fine central performance from Tatiana Samoilova and some rather gymnastic camera techniques, *Cranes* was a co-winner of the best film award at the 1958 Cannes Film Festival. Kalatozov's subsequent output was relatively unexceptional. • *Dyelo Tariela Mklavadze* 1925 (a); *Parovoz No. 10006 (short)* 1926 (ph); *Giulli* 1927 (sc,ph); *Ikh tsartsvo* 1928 (d); *Tsiganskaya krov* 1928 (sc,ph); *Slepaya (short)* 1930 (d); *Sol Dla Svanetia/The Salt of Svanetia* 1930 (d,ph); *Gvozd v sapoge/The Nail in the Boot* 1932 (d); *Muzhestvo* 1939 (d); *Valeri Chkalov* 1941 (a,d); *Kinokontsert k 25-letiyu Krasnoy Armii* 1943 (d); *Nepobedimye* 1943 (d,uncred.); *Zagovor obrechyonnikh* 1950 (d); *Verniye druzya* 1954 (d); *Pervi eshelon* 1955 (d,sc); *Vikhri vrazhdebnye* 1956 (d); *Letyat zhuravli/The Cranes Are Flying* 1957 (d); *Dyelo "Pestrykh"* 1958 (prod.sup); *Neotpravlennoye pismo* 1960 (d); *Ya Cuba* 1963 (d); *La Tenda rossa/The Red Tent* 1970 (d).

Kamen, Michael • Composer; also conductor, arranger. • Born New York, NY. *Educ.* Juilliard (music). Successful film and TV composer who has also written several scores for the Joffrey Ballet and the La Scala Opera Company. Kamen has worked with directors David Cronenberg (*The Dead Zone* 1983), Neil Jordan (*Mona Lisa* 1986) and Terry Gilliam (*Brazil* 1985, *The Adventures of Baron Munchausen* 1988). • *Zachariah* 1970 (song); *The Next Man* 1976 (m,song); *Between the Lines* 1977 (add.m); *Stunts* 1977 (m,song); *Boardwalk* 1979 (m.arr); *Polyester* 1981 (m,keyboardist,oboist,songs); *Angelo, My Love* 1982 (m.dir); *Pink Floyd The Wall* 1982 (m.dir,m.arr); *The Dead Zone* 1983 (m); *Brazil* 1985 (m); *Lifeforce* 1985 (m); *Highlander* 1986 (m); *Mona Lisa* 1986 (m); *Rita, Sue and Bob Too* 1986 (m); *Shanghai Surprise* 1986 (m); *Shoot for the Sun* 1986 (m); *Adventures in Babysitting* 1987 (m); *Lethal Weapon* 1987 (m,m.perf,orch,m.cond); *Someone to Watch Over Me* 1987 (m,song); *Suspect* 1987 (m); *Action Jackson* 1988 (m); *The Adventures of Baron Munchausen* 1988 (m,orch,m.prod,m.cond,song); *Crusoe* 1988 (m,m.cond); *Die Hard* 1988 (m,m.cond); *For Queen & Country* 1988 (m); *Homeboy* 1988 (m,keyboardist); *The Raggedy Rawney* 1988 (m); *Dead-Bang* 1989 (add.m); *Lethal Weapon 2* 1989 (m,orch); *Licence to Kill* 1989 (m); *Renegades* 1989 (m); *Road House* 1989 (m,m.cond); *Rooftops* 1989 (m,song); *Cold Dog Soup* 1990 (m); *Die Hard 2: Die Harder* 1990 (orch,m.cond); *The Krays* 1990 (m).

Kane, Carol • Actress • Born Cleveland, OH, June 18, 1952. *Educ.* Professional Children's School, New York. Petite, frizzy-haired actress who gained prominence in the 1970s, starring in *Hester Street* (1975) and playing Woody

Allen's first wife in *Annie Hall* (1977). Kane, a veteran stage actress, has since turned in a number of effective character roles onscreen. • *Carnal Knowledge* 1971 (a); *Desperate Characters* 1971 (a); *Wedding in White* 1972 (a); *The Last Detail* 1973 (a); *Dog Day Afternoon* 1975 (a); *Hester Street* 1975 (a) **(AANBA)**; *Harry and Walter Go to New York* 1976 (a); *Annie Hall* 1977 (a); *The Mafu Cage* 1977 (a); *Valentino* 1977 (a); *The World's Greatest Lover* 1977 (a); *The Muppet Movie* 1979 (a); *La Sabina* 1979 (a); *When a Stranger Calls* 1979 (a); *Pandemonium* 1981 (a); *Norman Loves Rose* 1982 (a); *Can She Bake a Cherry Pie?* 1983 (a); *Over the Brooklyn Bridge* 1983 (a); *Racing With the Moon* 1984 (a); *The Secret Diary of Sigmund Freud* 1984 (a); *Transylvania 6-5000* 1985 (a); *Jumpin' Jack Flash* 1986 (a); *Ishtar* 1987 (a); *The Princess Bride* 1987 (a); *License to Drive* 1988 (a); *Scrooged* 1988 (a); *Sticky Fingers* 1988 (a); *Flashback* 1990 (a); *Joe Versus the Volcano* 1990 (a); *The Lemon Sisters* 1990 (a); *My Blue Heaven* 1990 (a).

Kanin, Garson • Screenwriter, director; also playwright and author. • Born Rochester, NY, November 24, 1912. *Educ.* AADA, New York. Leaving a successful Broadway career at Hollywood's invitation in 1938, Kanin directed several sparkling comedies during the next several years. In addition to the smash stage comedy *Born Yesterday*, which made Judy Holliday a star in 1946, Kanin is best remembered for his screenwriting partnership with actress Ruth Gordon, whom he married in 1942, notably on *A Double Life* (1948), *Adam's Rib* 1949) and *Pat and Mike* (1952). Brother Michael Kanin (b. 1910) was also a screenwriter. • *A Man to Remember* 1938 (d); *Next Time I Marry* 1938 (d); *Bachelor Mother* 1939 (a,d); *The Great Man Votes* 1939 (d); *They Made Her a Spy* 1939 (sc); *My Favorite Wife* 1940 (d); *They Knew What They Wanted* 1940 (d); *Tom, Dick and Harry* 1941 (d); *Fellow Americans* 1942 (d); *Night Shift (short)* 1942 (d); *Ring of Steel* 1942 (d); *A Lady Takes a Chance* 1943 (uncred.sc); *The More the Merrier* 1943 (uncred.sc); *Battle Stations (short)* 1944 (d); *A Salute to France* 1944 (d); *The True Glory* 1945 (p,d) **(AABDOC)**; *From This Day Forward* 1946 (adapt); *A Double Life* 1947 (sc) **(AANBSC)**; *Adam's Rib* 1949 (sc) **(AANBSC)**; *Born Yesterday* 1950 (adapt.play); *The Marrying Kind* 1952 (sc,story); *Pat and Mike* 1952 (sc) **(AANBSC)**; *It Should Happen to You* 1954 (sc,story); *The Girl Can't Help It* 1956 (from novella "Do Re Mi"); *High Time* 1960 (story); *The Rat Race* 1960 (sc,from play); *The Right Approach* 1961 (from play *The Live Wire*); *Dunku cocuk* 1965 (from play *Born Yesterday*); *Walk, Don't Run* 1966 (uncred. from sc *The More the Merrier*); *Some Kind of a Nut* 1969 (d,sc); *Where It's At* 1969 (d,sc).

Kaplan, Jonathan • Director; also actor. • Born Paris, November 25, 1947. *Educ.* University of Chicago; NYU Institute of Film and TV. The son of blacklisted composer Sol Kaplan and an early protégé of Roger Corman, Kaplan directed several competent action films in the 1970s before graduating to more character-driven features in the 80s. His best works include the underrated "troubled teen" movie, *Over the Edge* (1979), and 1982's *Heart Like a Wheel*, which boasted a fine central performance by Bonnie Bedelia. • *The Slams* 1973 (d); *The Student Teachers* 1973 (d); *Night Call Nurses* 1974 (d); *Truck Turner* 1974 (d); *White Line Fever* 1975 (d,sc); *Cannonball* 1976 (a); *Hollywood Boulevard* 1976 (a); *Mr. Billion* 1977 (d,sc); *Roger Corman: Hollywood's Wild Angel* 1978 (a); *Over the Edge* 1979 (d); *Heart Like a Wheel* 1982 (d); *Project X* 1987 (d); *The Accused* 1988 (d); *Immediate Family* 1989 (d).

Kaplan, Nelly • Director; also writer. • Born Buenos Aires, Argentina, 1931. *Educ.* University of Buenos Aires (economics). Worked as Abel Gance's assistant and collaborator from 1954, going on to direct shorts, an acclaimed medium length effort, *Le Regard Picasso* (1967), and feature films. Among her several books is *Le Sunlight d'Austerlitz*, on the making of Gance's *Austerlitz* (1960). Kaplan's work embraces paradox and contradiction and is driven by a feminist sensibility. • *La Tour de Nesle* 1954 (a); *Austerlitz* 1960 (a,ad); *Gustave Moreau (short)* 1961 (commentary,ed,d); *Rodolphe Bresdin 1825-1885 (short)* 1961 (commentary,ed,d); *Abel Gance, hier et demain (short)* 1963 (commentary,ph,ed,d); *Cyrano et d'Artagnan* 1963 (sc,ed,2u d); *La Prima Donna (short)* 1964 (a); *A la Source, la Femme Aimée (short)* 1966 (d,sc,ed); *Les Années 25 (short)* 1966 (d,sc,commentary,ed); *Dessins et merveilles (short)* 1966 (d,sc,dial,ed); *La Nouvelle Orangerie (short)* 1966 (d,sc,commentary,ed); *Le Regard Picasso (short)* 1967 (d,sc); *La Fiancée du pirate/A Very Private Affair* 1969 (d,sc,ed); *Papa les Petits Bateaux* 1971 (a,d,sc); *Au verre de l'amitié (short)* 1974 (adapt); *Il faut vivre Dangereusement* 1975 (p,sc); *Néa* 1976 (a,d,sc,adapt,dial); *Charles et Lucie* 1979 (a,adapt,dial,ed,d); *Abel Gance et Son Napoléon* 1984 (d,p,sc).

Kapoor, Shashi • Actor • Born March 18, 1938, Calcutta, India. Popular Indian star, best known to Western audiences for his roles in the films of Merchant/Ivory; he came to widespread attention with the first of these, *Shakespeare Wallah*, in 1965. Kapoor was recently seen in Stephen Frear's *Sammy and Rosie Get Laid* (1987). He is the son of actor-director-film statesman Prithviraj Kapoor (1906-1972) and the brother of Raj Kapoor (b. 1924), a director and popular, Chaplinesque actor. Kapoor was married to actress Jennifer Kendal, who died in 1985; he had met her when, during his early career as a stage actor, he performed with her "Shakespeariana" troupe. • *The Householder* 1963 (a); *Shakespeare Wallah* 1965 (a); *Pretty Polly/A Matter of Innocence* 1967 (a); *Bombay Talkie* 1970 (a); *Siddhartha* 1972 (a); *Junoon/Obsession* 1978 (a,p); *Heat and Dust* 1983 (a); *Vijeta/Conquest* 1983 (a,p); *Utsav/Festival* 1984 (a,p); *New Delhi Times* 1986 (a); *Sammy and Rosie Get Laid* 1987 (a); *The Deceivers* 1988 (a).

Karina, Anna • Actress; also screenwriter, director. • Born Hanna Karin Blarke Bayer, Copenhagen, Denmark, September 22, 1940. Slender, dark-haired actress who appeared in several films of the French New Wave, particularly those directed by first husband Jean-Luc Godard. Karina was outstanding as the lonely, lovelorn prostitite in *My Life to Live* (1962) and the effervescent petty criminal in *Band of Outsiders* (1964). She continues to appear in international features and directed the 1973 film, *Vivre Ensemble*. • *Pigen og skoene (short)* 1959 (a); *Ce Soir ou jamais* 1960 (a); *Le Petit Soldat* 1960 (a); *Une Femme est une femme/A Woman Is a Woman* 1961 (a); *Les Fiancés du Pont Macdonald (short)* 1961 (a); *Présentation ou Charlotte et son steack (short)* 1961 (a); *She'll Have to Go* 1961 (a); *Le Soleil dans l'oeil* 1961 (a); *Cléo de 5 à 7/Cleo From 5 to 7* 1962 (a); *Le Joli Mai* 1962 (a); *Les Quatre Vérités* 1962 (a); *Sheherazade* 1962 (a); *Vivre sa Vie/My Life to Live* 1962 (a); *Dragées au Poivre* 1963 (a); *Un Mari à prix fixe* 1963 (a); *Bande à Part/Band of Outsiders* 1964 (a); *De l'amour* 1964 (a); *Petit jour (short)* 1964 (a); *La Ronde* 1964 (a); *Le Voleur du Tibidabo* 1964 (a); *Alphaville* 1965 (a); *Pierrot le Fou* 1965 (a); *Le Soldatesse* 1965 (a); *Suzanne Simonin, la Religieuse de Denis Diderot/The Nun* 1965 (a); *Made in U.S.A.* 1966 (a); *Lamiel* 1967 (a); *Le Plus vieux Métier du Monde/The Oldest Profession* 1967 (a); *Lo Straniero* 1967 (a); *Tendres Réquins* 1967 (a); *Before Winter Comes* 1968 (a); *The Magus* 1968 (a); *Justine* 1969 (a); *Laughter in the Dark* 1969 (a); *Michael Kohlhaas - Der Rebell* 1969 (a); *Le Temps de mourir* 1969 (a); *L'Alliance* 1970 (a); *Rendez-Vous à Bray* 1971 (a); *The Salzburg Connection* 1972 (a); *Pane e Cioccolata/Bread and Chocolate* 1973 (a); *Vivre Ensemble* 1973 (a,d,p,sc); *L'Invenzione di Morel* 1974 (a); *L'Asassin Musicien* 1975 (a); *Les Oeufs Brouillés* 1975 (a); *Also es war so...* 1976 (a); *Chinesisches Roulette* 1976 (a); *Chaussette Surprise* 1978 (a); *Olyan mint otthon* 1978 (a); *Historien om en Moder* 1979 (a); *L'Ami de Vincent* 1983 (a); *Ave*

Maria 1984 (a); *L'Ile au Trésor* 1985 (a); *Cayenne-Palace* 1987 (a); *L'été dernier à Tanger* 1987 (a); *Last Song* 1987 (a,sc); *L'Oeuvre au noir/The Abyss* 1988 (a); *Man, Der Ville Vaere Skyldig* (a) (1990).

Karloff, Boris • Actor • Born William Henry Pratt, London, November 23, 1887; died 1969. *Educ.* King's College, London. In Hollywood from 1919 after extensive stage experience. Karloff was a regular player of heavies and villains in silent films, but did not make his breakthrough until the sound era, when his distinctive, slightly lisping voice proved ideal for the title roles of films such as *Frankenstein* (1931) and *The Mummy* (1932). Although he never shook the "monster" characterization, Karloff was a fine character player, and turned in a number of roles against type throughout his career. One of his last performances was in Peter Bogdonavich's *Targets* (1968), playing an aged horror film star. • *His Majesty, the American* 1919 (a); *The Prince and Betty* 1919 (a); *The Courage of Marge O'Doone* 1920 (a); *The Deadlier Sex* 1920 (a); *The Last of the Mohicans* 1920 (a); *The Notorious Miss Lisle* 1920 (a); *The Cave Girl* 1921 (a); *Cheated Hearts* 1921 (a); *The Hope Diamond Mystery* 1921 (a); *Without Benefit of Clergy* 1921 (a); *The Altar Stairs* 1922 (a); *The Infidel* 1922 (a); *The Man From Downing Street* 1922 (a); *Omar the Tentmaker* 1922 (a); *The Woman Conquers* 1922 (a); *The Gentleman From America* 1923 (a); *The Prisoner* 1923 (a); *Dynamite Dan* 1924 (a); *The Hellion* 1924 (a); *Forbidden Cargo* 1925 (a); *Lady Robinhood* 1925 (a); *Never the Twain Shall Meet* 1925 (a); *Parisian Nights* 1925 (a); *The Prairie Wife* 1925 (a); *The Bells* 1926 (a); *The Eagle of the Sea* 1926 (a); *Flames* 1926 (a); *Flaming Fury* 1926 (a); *The Golden Web* 1926 (a); *The Greater Glory* 1926 (a); *Her Honor the Governor* 1926 (a); *The Man in the Saddle* 1926 (a); *The Nickel Hopper (short)* 1926 (archival footage); *Old Ironsides* 1926 (a); *Let It Rain* 1927 (a); *The Love Mart* 1927 (a); *The Meddlin' Stranger* 1927 (a); *The Phantom Buster* 1927 (a); *The Princess from Hoboken* 1927 (a); *Soft Cushions* 1927 (a); *Tarzan and the Golden Lion* 1927 (a); *Two Arabian Knights* 1927 (a); *Valencia* 1927 (a); *Burning the Wind* 1928 (a); *The Little Wild Girl* 1928 (a); *Vultures of the Sea* 1928 (a); *Anne Against the World* 1929 (a); *Behind That Curtain* 1929 (a); *The Devil's Chaplain* 1929 (a); *The Fatal Warning* 1929 (a); *King of the Kongo* 1929 (a); *The Phantom of the North* 1929 (a); *Two Sisters* 1929 (a); *The Unholy Night* 1929 (a); *The Bad One* 1930 (a); *Criminal Code* 1930 (a); *Mother's Cry* 1930 (a); *The Sea Bat* 1930 (a); *The Utah Kid* 1930 (a); *Cracked Nuts* 1931 (a); *Five Star Final* 1931 (a); *Frankenstein* 1931 (a); *Graft* 1931 (a); *Guilty Generation* 1931 (a); *I Like Your Nerve* 1931 (a); *King of the Wild* 1931 (a); *The Mad Genius* 1931 (a); *The Public Defender* 1931 (a); *Smart Money* 1931 (a); *Tonight or Never* 1931 (a); *The Yellow Ticket* 1931 (a); *Young Donovan's Kid* 1931 (a); *Alias the Doctor* 1932 (a); *Behind the Mask* 1932 (a); *Business and Pleasure* 1932 (a); *The Cohens and Kellys in Hollywood* 1932 (a); *The Mask of Fu Manchu* 1932 (a); *The Miracle Man* 1932 (a); *The Mummy* 1932 (a); *Night World* 1932 (a); *The Old Dark House* 1932 (a); *Scarface* 1932 (a); *The Ghoul* 1933 (archival footage); *The Black Cat* 1934 (a); *Gift of Gab* 1934 (a); *The House of Rothschild* 1934 (a); *The Lost Patrol* 1934 (a); *The Black Room* 1935 (a); *Bride of Frankenstein* 1935 (a); *Hollywood Hobbies (short)* 1935 (archival footage); *The Raven* 1935 (a); *Charlie Chan at the Opera* 1936 (a); *The Invisible Ray* 1936 (a); *Juggernaut* 1936 (archival footage); *The Man Who Lived Again* 1936 (a); *The Walking Dead* 1936 (a); *Cinema Circus (short)* 1937 (archival footage); *Night Key* 1937 (a); *West of Shanghai* 1937 (a); *The Invisible Menace* 1938 (a); *Mr. Wong, Detective* 1938 (a); *Devil's Island* 1939 (a); *The Man They Could Not Hang* 1939 (a); *Mr. Wong in Chinatown* 1939 (a); *The Mystery of Mr. Wong* 1939 (a); *Son of Frankenstein* 1939 (a); *Tower of London* 1939 (a); *The Ape* 1940 (a); *Before I Hang* 1940 (a); *Black Friday* 1940 (a); *British Intelligence* 1940 (a); *Doomed to Die* 1940 (a); *The Fatal Hour* 1940 (a); *The Man With Nine Lives* 1940 (a); *You'll Find Out* 1940 (a); *The Devil Commands* 1941 (a); *Information Please No. 12 (short)* 1941 (archival footage); *Information Please No. 8 (short)* 1941 (archival footage); *The Boogie Man Will Get You* 1942 (a); *The Climax* 1944 (a); *House of Frankenstein* 1944 (a); *The Body Snatcher* 1945 (a); *Isle of the Dead* 1945 (a); *Bedlam* 1946 (a); *Dick Tracy Meets Gruesome* 1947 (a); *Lured* 1947 (a); *The Secret Life of Walter Mitty* 1947 (a); *Unconquered* 1947 (a); *Cisaruv Slavik* 1948 (a); *Tap Roots* 1948 (a); *Abbott and Costello Meet the Killer, Boris Karloff* 1949 (a); *The Strange Door* 1951 (a); *The Black Castle* 1952 (a); *Abbott and Costello Meet Dr. Jekyll and Mr. Hyde* 1953 (a); *Il Mostro dell'isola* 1953 (a); *Sabaka* 1953 (a); *The Juggler of Our Lady (short)* 1957 (a); *Voodoo Island* 1957 (a); *Frankenstein 1970* 1958 (a); *The Haunted Strangler* 1958 (a); *The Raven* 1963 (a); *The Terror* 1963 (a); *I Tre volti della paura* 1963 (a); *Bikini Beach* 1964 (a); *The Comedy of Terrors* 1964 (a); *Die Die, Monster* 1965 (a); *The Daydreamer* 1966 (a); *The Ghost in the Invisible Bikini* 1966 (a); *Mad Monster Party* 1967 (a); *Mondo balordo* 1967 (a); *The Sorcerers* 1967 (archival footage); *The Venetian Affair* 1967 (a); *La Camara del Terror* 1968 (a); *El Coleccionista de Cadaveres* 1968 (a); *Curse of the Crimson Altar* 1968 (a); *House of Evil* 1968 (a); *Invasion siniestra* 1968 (a); *La Muerte Viviente* 1968 (a); *Targets* 1968 (a); *Madhouse* 1974 (archival footage); *Transylvania Twist* 1990 (archival footage).

Karlson, Phil • Director; also producer. • Born Philip N. Karlstein, Chicago, IL, July 2, 1908; died December 12, 1985. *Educ.* Chicago Art Institute; Loyola University, Los Angeles (law). Former gagman (for Buster Keaton), propman, studio manager and assistant director who turned out his first feature-length film in 1944. Karlson hit his stride in the 1950s with a brace of gritty crime melodramas noted for their realistic detail and graphic violence. Foremost among these were *Scandal Sheet* (1952), *99 River Street* (1953) and three 1955 films: *Tight Spot, Five Against the House* and *The Phenix City Story* (in which the lead actor wore the actual clothes of the murder victim on whose story the film was based). Although he received a measure of critical attention and developed something of a cult following, Karlson remained a B director for the duration of his career. He scored a box-office success in 1973 with *Walking Tall.* • *Destry Rides Again* 1932 (ad,2u d); *The Fourth Horseman* 1932 (ad); *My Pal, the King* 1932 (ad,2u d); *The Rider of Death Valley* 1932 (ad,2u d); *Cheating Cheaters* 1934 (ad); *The Countess of Monte Cristo* 1934 (ad); *Embarassing Moments* 1934 (ad); *Great Expectations* 1934 (ad); *I Like It That Way* 1934 (ad); *The Affair of Susan* 1935 (ad); *Alias Mary Dow* 1935 (ad); *His Night Out* 1935 (ad); *Manhattan Moon* 1935 (ad); *Mystery of Edwin Drood* 1935 (ad); *She Gets Her Man* 1935 (ad); *Strange Wives* 1935 (ad); *Werewolf of London* 1935 (ad); *Love Before Breakfast* 1936 (ad); *Parole* 1936 (ad); *Postal Inspector* 1936 (ad); *The Last Express* 1938 (ad); *The Family Next Door* 1939 (ad); *The House of Fear* 1939 (ad); *Rio* 1939 (ad); *The Invisible Man Returns* 1940 (ad); *Margie* 1940 (ad); *Seven Sinners* 1940 (ad); *Slightly Tempted* 1940 (ad); *The Flame of New Orleans* 1941 (ad); *In the Navy* 1941 (ad); *It Started With Eve* 1941 (assoc.p); *Where Did You Get That Girl?* 1941 (ad); *Between Us Girls* 1942 (assoc.p); *G.I. Honeymoon* 1944 (d); *A Wave, a Wac and a Marine* 1944 (d); *The Shanghai Cobra* 1945 (d); *There Goes Kelly* 1945 (d); *Behind the Mask* 1946 (d); *Bowery Bombshell* 1946 (d); *Dark Alibi* 1946 (d); *Live Wires* 1946 (d); *The Missing Lady* 1946 (d); *Swing Parade of 1946* 1946 (d); *Wife Wanted* 1946 (d); *Adventures in Silverado* 1947 (d); *Black Gold* 1947 (d); *Kilroy Was Here* 1947 (d); *Louisiana* 1947 (d); *Rocky* 1948 (d); *Thunderhoof* 1948 (d); *The Big Cat* 1949 (d); *Down Memory Lane* 1949 (d); *Ladies of the Chorus* 1949 (d); *The Iroquois Trail* 1950 (d); *Lorna Doone* 1951 (d); *The Mask of the Avenger* 1951 (d); *The Texas Rangers* 1951 (d); *Assignment-Paris* 1952 (d); *The Brigand* 1952 (d); *Kansas City Confidential* 1952 (d); *Scan-*

dal Sheet 1952 (d); *99 River Street* 1953 (d); *They Rode West* 1954 (d); *Five Against the House* 1955 (d); *Hell's Island* 1955 (d); *The Phenix City Story* 1955 (d); *Tight Spot* 1955 (d); *The Brothers Rico* 1957 (d); *Gunman's Walk* 1958 (d); *Hell to Eternity* 1960 (d); *Key Witness* 1960 (d); *The Secret Ways* 1961 (d); *The Young Doctors* 1961 (d); *Kid Galahad* 1962 (d); *Rampage* 1963 (d); *The Silencers* 1966 (d); *The Long Ride Home* 1967 (d); *The Wrecking Crew* 1968 (d); *Hornet's Nest* 1970 (d); *Ben* 1972 (d); *Walking Tall* 1973 (d); *Framed* 1975 (d).

Karmitz, Marin • Producer; also director, exhibitor, distributor. • Born Bucharest, Romania, 1938. *Educ.* IDHEC, Paris (cinematography). In France from 1947, Karmitz entered films as an assistant to directors such as Jean-Luc Godard and Agnès Varda before setting up MK Productions in 1964. He made his directorial debut in 1967 with *Sept jours ailleurs* and followed it, much affected by the events of May '68, with the militantly leftist *Comrades* (1970) and *Blow For Blow* (1972).

Subsequently ostracized by the French film industry, Karmitz turned to exhibition and distribution, helping promote works by young, unknown directors including Wim Wenders and Marco Bellocchio. Under the MK2 banner he has produced an impressive list of films, including Godard's *Every Man for Himself* (1980), Louis Malle's *Au revoir, les enfants* (1987) and a series of features by Claude Chabrol. • *Cléo de 5 à 7/Cleo From 5 to 7* 1962 (ad); *Nuit noire, Calcutta (short)* 1964 (d); *Adolescence (short)* 1966 (p) **(AANBDOC)**; *Sept jours ailleurs* 1967 (d); *Camarades/Comrades* 1970 (d,sc); *Coup Pour Coup/Blow For Blow* 1972 (d); *Voyage en grande Tartarie* 1973 (p); *Viva Portugal* 1976 (p); *L'Amour violé* 1978 (p); *Salto Nel Vuoto* 1980 (p); *Sauve qui peut la vie/Every Man For Himself* 1980 (assoc.p); *Looks and Smiles* 1981 (p); *La Notte di San Lorenzo/The Night of the Shooting Stars* 1981 (p); *L'Ombre Rouge* 1981 (p); *Mourir à Trente Ans* 1982 (p); *Simone de Beauvoir* 1982 (p); *Autour du Mur* 1983 (p); *Le Bon Plaisir* 1983 (p); *La Java des ombres* 1983 (exec.p); *Le Mur* 1983 (p); *Kaos/Chaos* 1984 (p); *No Man's Land* 1985 (p); *Poulet au Vinaigre* 1985 (p); *Sans toit ni loi/Vagabond* 1985 (p); *La Tentation d'Isabelle* 1985 (exec.p); *Good Morning Babylon* 1986 (co-p); *Inspector Lavardin* 1986 (p); *O Melissokomos* 1986 (p); *Mélo* 1986 (p); *Opera do Malandro* 1986 (p); *Singing the Blues in Red* 1986 (p); *La Storia/History* 1986 (p); *Au revoir, les enfants* 1987 (p); *La Loi Sauvage* 1987 (p); *Masques* 1987 (p); *La Vallée fantôme* 1987 (exec.p); *La Vie est un long fleuve tranquille/Life Is a Long Quiet River* 1987 (p); *Une Affaire de femmes* 1988 (p); *Je veux rentrer à la maison* 1989 (p); *Korczak* 1990 (p); *Taxi Blues* 1990 (p); *Madame Bovary* 1991 (p).

Kasdan, Lawrence • Director, screenwriter • Born Miami, FL, January 14, 1949. *Educ.* University of Michigan, Ann Arbor (English, education); UCLA. After dropping out of his graduate screenwriting course at UCLA, Kasdan worked for five years as an advertising copywriter (picking up a Clio award along the way) before returning to screenwriting in 1980, when he collaborated with Irvin Kershner on *The Empire Strikes Back*. (He would go on to collaborate on the last entry in the Star Wars trilogy, *Return of the Jedi* 1983, and the first of the Indiana Jones adventures, *Raiders of the Lost Ark* 1981.)

Kasdan's initial effort as a director seemed to herald the arrival of a major talent. An updated version of Billy Wilder's noir classic *Double Indemnity*, *Body Heat* (1981) featured William Hurt and Kathleen Turner as the steamiest screen couple of the early 1980s. Peppered with intriguing dialogue and propelled by a tight plot, the film paid homage to the genre without being merely derivative. Along the way, Kasdan demonstrated a knack for subtle characterization, creating a cynical gem that belies his more optimistic work as a Spielberg-Lucas hired pen.

The follow-up, 1983's *The Big Chill*, proved more commercially successful, but less satisfying, than his promising debut. Instead of reaching back to the 40s, this time Kasdan covered ground explored by a contemporary film, John Sayles's low-budget *The Return of the Secaucus Seven* (1980). A group of "baby boomers" (played by, among others, Hurt, Glenn Close and Kevin Kline) spend a mournful weekend lamenting their lost innocence, but instead of Sayles's touching character study, Kasdan's film comes off as knee-jerk 60s nostalgia—complete with Motown soundtrack. The film's success paved the way for other Reagan-era films that would romanticize 60s ideals in order to reach that most desirable demographic, the disillusioned hippy.

Politics aside, the most disappointing thing about *The Big Chill* was the two-dimensionality of Kasdan's characters. Similar problems plagued his next feature, the western saga *Silverado* (1985). Kasdan's early strength, characterization, was now only a memory, as still more hip young actors in flat, underwritten roles paraded through a film that tried too hard to be a parody. Silverado suffered from an overly complex narrative, but its real downfall was the film's condescending tone: it ultimately ridicules, rather than satirizes, the western genre. In the process, Kasdan revealed that writing action pictures and directing them are two different things.

The Accidental Tourist (1988) returned Kasdan to his original form. Once again his characters were impeccably drawn, and this time his camera, making generous use of the close-up, worked to highlight the brilliant performances offered by Oscar-winner Geena Davis and the reunited Hurt and Turner. Poignant and well-observed, *The Accidental Tourist* is the kind of intelligent, well-crafted work that Kasdan proved himself so capable of producing with *Body Heat*. JCP • *The Empire Strikes Back* 1980 (sc); *Body Heat* 1981 (d,sc); *Continental Divide* 1981 (sc); *Raiders of the Lost Ark* 1981 (sc); *The Big Chill* 1983 (d,exec.p,sc) **(AANBSC)**; *Return of the Jedi* 1983 (sc); *Into the Night* 1985 (a); *Silverado* 1985 (d,p,sc); *Cross My Heart* 1987 (p); *The Accidental Tourist* 1988 (d,p,sc) **(AANBP,AANBSC)**; *Immediate Family* 1989 (exec.p); *I Love You to Death* 1990 (d).

Kastner, Elliott • Producer • Born New York, NY, 1930. *Educ.* University of Miami; Columbia. London-based producer of international films who began his career as a talent agent. Kastner's productions include a trio of Raymond Chandler-inspired works, *The Long Goodbye* (1973), *Farewell, My Lovely* (1975) and *The Big Sleep* (1978). • *Calcutta* 1960 (p); *Bus Riley's Back in Town* 1965 (p); *Harper* 1966 (p); *Kaleidoscope* 1966 (p); *The Bobo* 1967 (p); *The Night of the Following Day* 1968 (exec.p); *Sweet November* 1968 (p); *Where Eagles Dare* 1968 (p); *A Severed Head* 1970 (exec.p); *The Walking Stick* 1970 (p); *The Nightcomers* 1971 (p); *Tam Lin* 1971 (p); *Villain* 1971 (exec.p); *When Eight Bells Toll* 1971 (p); *Count Your Bullets* 1972 (exec.p); *Face to the Wind* 1972 (exec.p); *X Y & Zee* 1972 (exec.p); *Cops and Robbers* 1973 (p); *Jeremy* 1973 (exec.p); *The Long Goodbye* 1973 (exec.p); *11 Harrowhouse* 1974 (p); *Dogpound Shuffle* 1974 (exec.p); *Rancho Deluxe* 1974 (p); *92 in the Shade* 1975 (exec.p); *Breakheart Pass* 1975 (exec.p); *Farewell, My Lovely* 1975 (exec.p); *Russian Roulette* 1975 (exec.p); *The Missouri Breaks* 1976 (p); *Swashbuckler* 1976 (exec.p); *Black Joy* 1977 (p); *Equus* 1977 (p); *A Little Night Music* 1977 (p); *The Big Sleep* 1978 (p); *The Medusa Touch* 1978 (assoc.p); *The Stick Up* 1978 (exec.p); *Absolution* 1979 (p); *Goldengirl* 1979 (exec.p); *Yesterday's Hero* 1979 (exec.p); *First Deadly Sin* 1980 (exec.p); *ffolkes* 1980 (p); *Death Valley* 1981 (p); *Man, Woman and Child* 1982 (p); *Garbo Talks* 1984 (p); *Oxford Blues* 1984 (p); *Nomads* 1985 (exec.p); *Angel Heart* 1987 (p); *Gaby-A True Story* 1987 (assistance); *Heat* 1987 (p); *Zombie High* 1987 (p); *The Blob* 1988 (p); *Homeboy* 1988 (p); *Jack's Back* 1988 (exec.p); *A Chorus of Disapproval* 1989 (exec.p); *Never on Tuesday* 1989 (p).

Katz, Ephraim • Historian, author; also filmmaker • Born Tel Aviv, March 11, 1932. *Educ.* Hebrew University, Jerusalem (law, economics); Hunter College, New York (political science); NYU (cinema studies). Sole author of the monumental critical-historical study of world cinema, *The Film Encyclopedia* (1979). The one-volume work accounts for major and minor figures of US, European and Third World cinema and includes entries on technical terms, national film industries and important cinematic schools and movements. It remains a landmark in American film scholarship. Katz has also made numerous documentaries and educational and industrial films. His 1960 book *Minister of Death*, co-written with Quintin Reynolds, was an account of the hunt and capture of Nazi war criminal Adolf Eichmann.

Kaufman, Boris • Director of photography • Born Bialystock, Russia, 1906; died 1980. *Educ.* Sorbonne, Paris. Younger brother of Soviet filmmakers Dziga Vertov and Mikhail Kaufman who went to France in the mid-1920s and shot all of Jean Vigo's films, among others. In the US after WWII, he photographed a number of shorts and documentaries before being hired as cinematographer on Elia Kazan's *On the Waterfront* (1954).

For the next 15 years Kaufman remained independent from Hollywood and worked almost exclusively with left-oriented directors on a number of outstanding films shot in New York. He worked on seven Sidney Lumet features including *The Pawnbroker* (1965), a strikingly photographed black-and-white journey through the mind of a concentration camp survivor living in Harlem.

The re-release in 1990 of the restored *L'Atalante* brought posthumous acclaim for Kaufman's shimmering cinematography. • *24 heures en 30 minutes (short)* 1928 (ph); *Champs-Elysées (short)* 1928 (ph); *La Marche des machines (short)* 1928 (ph); *A propos de Nice (short)* 1929 (ph); *Les Halles (short)* 1929 (ph); *La Natation par Jean Taris champion de France (short)* 1931 (ph); *Le Mile de Jules Ladoumegue (short)* 1932 (ph); *Travaux du tunnel sous l'Escaut (short)* 1932 (ph); *La Vie d'un fleuve la Seine (short)* 1932 (ph); *Le Chemin du bonheur* 1933 (cam.op); *Zéro de conduite* 1933 (ph); *L'Atalante* 1934 (ph); *Zouzou* 1934 (cam.op); *Lucrèce Borgia* 1935 (ph); *Le Père Lampion* 1935 (ph); *L'Homme sans coeur* 1936 (ph); *Oeil-de-Lynx, détective (short)* 1936 (ph); *On ne roule pas Antoinette* 1936 (ph); *Quand minuit sonnera* 1936 (ph); *Cinderella* 1937 (ph); *Etes-vous jalouse?* 1937 (ph); *Les Hommes sans nom* 1937 (ph); *Fort-Dolores* 1938 (ph); *Les Gaietés de l'exposition* 1938 (ph); *Sérénade* 1939 (ph); *Le Veau gras* 1939 (ph); *Toscanini, Hymn of the Nations (short)* 1944 (ph); *A Better Tomorrow (short)* 1945 (ph); *Capital Story (short)* 1945 (ph); *The Southwest (short)* 1945 (ph); *Journey Into Medicine* 1946 (ph); *Osmosis (short)* 1948 (ph); *Terribly Talented (short)* 1948 (ph); *The Lambertville Story (short)* 1949 (ph); *Preface to a Life (short)* 1950 (ph); *The Tanglewood Story (short)* 1950 (ph); *The Gentleman in Room 6 (short)* 1951 (ph); *Leonardo da Vinci* 1952 (ph); *And the Earth Shall Give Back Life (short)* 1953 (ph); *Amazing What Color Can Do (short)* 1954 (ph); *Garden of Eden* 1954 (ph); *On the Waterfront* 1954 (ph) **(AABPH)**; *Within Man's Power (short)* 1954 (ph); *Crowded Paradise* 1955 (ph); *Patterns* 1955 (ph); *Baby Doll* 1956 (ph) **(AANBPH)**; *Twelve Angry Men* 1957 (ph); *That Kind of Woman* 1959 (ph); *The Fugitive Kind* 1960 (ph); *Splendor in the Grass* 1961 (ph); *Long Day's Journey Into Night* 1962 (ph); *All the Way Home* 1963 (ph); *Gone Are the Days* 1963 (ph); *The World of Henry Orient* 1964 (ph); *Film* 1965 (ph); *The Pawnbroker* 1965 (ph); *The Group* 1966 (ph); *The Brotherhood* 1968 (ph); *Bye Bye Braverman* 1968 (ph); *Uptight* 1968 (ph); *Tell Me That You Love Me, Junie Moon* 1970 (ph).

Kaufman, Philip • Director, screenwriter • Born Chicago, IL, October 23, 1936. *Educ.* University of Chicago; Harvard (history); Harvard Law School. First gained attention for the violent western, *The Outlaw Josey Wales* (1975), and *The Wanderers* (1979), a high school drama set in the 1960s. Kaufman scored critical successes in the 1980s with intelligent adaptations of books by Tom Wolfe (*The Right Stuff* 1983) and Milan Kundera (*The Unbearable Lightness of Being* 1988). • *Goldstein* 1965 (d,p,sc); *Fearless Frank* 1969 (d,p,sc); *The Great Northfield Minnesota Raid* 1972 (d,sc); *The White Dawn* 1974 (d); *The Outlaw Josey Wales* 1975 (sc); *Invasion of the Body Snatchers* 1978 (d); *The Wanderers* 1979 (d,sc); *Raiders of the Lost Ark* 1981 (story); *The Right Stuff* 1983 (d,sc); *The Unbearable Lightness of Being* 1988 (d,sc) **(AANBSC)**; *Henry & June* 1990 (d,p,sc).

Kaurismaki, Aki • Director; also screenwriter, producer. • Born Finland 1957. Inventive, prolific young director who began receiving international recognition in the late 1980s. Kaurismaki's output has ranged from wacky, comic-book style adventures (*Calamari Union* 1985, *Leningrad Cowboys Go America* 1989) to revisionist adaptations of literary classics (*Crime and Punishment* 1983, *Hamlet Goes Business* 1987), and he has proved himself adept at combining gritty, noirish realism with sly, sardonic humor (*Ariel* 1988).

With his brother Mika (*Rosso* 1985, *Helsinki Napoli All Night Long* 1988), and other directors including Pekka Parikka (*Plainlands* 1988, *The Winter War* 1989), Kaurismaki is at the forefront of a burgeoning new wave of Finnish cinema. • *Saimaa-Ilmio* 1982 (d); *Arvottomat* 1983 (sc,art d); *Rikos ja Rangaistus/Crime and Punishment* 1983 (d,sc); *Calamari Union* 1985 (d,p,sc,ed); *Klaani: Tarina Sammakoitten Suvusta* 1985 (sc); *Kuningas lahtee Ranskaan* 1986 (lighting); *Rocky VI (short)* 1986 (d); *Tilinteko* 1986 (p,sc); *Varjoja paratiisissa/Shadows in Paradise* 1986 (d,sc); *Hamlet Liikemaailmassa/Hamlet Goes Business* 1987 (d,p,sc); *Macbeth* 1987 (p); *Ariel* 1988 (d,p,sc); *Sirppi ja Kitara* 1988 (exec.p); *Leningrad Cowboys Go America* 1989 (d,p,sc,story); *Tulitikkutehtaan tytto/The Match Factory Girl* 1990 (d,p,sc,ed); *I Hired a Contract Killer* 1990 (d,p,sc).

Kaye, Danny • Actor • Born David Daniel Kominski, New York, NY, January 18, 1913; died March 3, 1987. Gifted comedic entertainer, few of whose feature films of the 1940s and 50s did justice to his talents. Best remembered for *The Secret Life of Walter Mitty* (1947), *The Inspector General* (1949), *Hans Christian Andersen* (1952) and *The Court Jester* (1956). Married composer-lyricist Sylvia Fine in 1940. • *Dime a Dance (short)* 1937 (a); *Cupid Takes a Holiday (short)* 1938 (a); *Getting an Eyeful (short)* 1938 (a); *Money on Your Life (short)* 1938 (a); *Night Shift (short)* 1942 (a); *The Birth of a Star* 1944 (a); *Up in Arms* 1944 (a); *The Wonder Man* 1945 (a); *The Kid From Brooklyn* 1946 (a); *The Secret Life of Walter Mitty* 1947 (a); *A Song Is Born* 1948 (a); *The Inspector General* 1949 (a); *It's a Great Feeling* 1949 (a); *On the Riviera* 1951 (a); *Hans Christian Andersen* 1952 (a); *Assignment Children* 1954 (a); *Hula From Hollywood (short)* 1954 (a); *Knock on Wood* 1954 (a); *White Christmas* 1954 (a); *The Court Jester* 1956 (a); *Me and the Colonel* 1958 (a); *Merry Andrew* 1958 (a); *The Five Pennies* 1959 (a,exec.p); *On the Double* 1961 (a); *The Man From the Diner's Club* 1963 (a); *The Madwoman of Chaillot* 1969 (a); *The Pied Piper* 1972 (a); *Entertaining the Troops* 1989 (a).

Kazan, Elia • Director; also screenwriter, producer, actor. • Born Elia Kazanjoglou, Kadi-Kev, Constantinople, Turkey, September 7, 1909. *Educ.* Williams College, Williamstown, MA; Yale School of Drama. One of the leading forces in both the American theater and Hollywood film, Elia Kazan was a Greek immigrant who arrived in New York in 1913 at the age of four under the name Elia Kazanjioglou. In 1932, he joined New York's influential Group Theatre as an actor, appearing in a number of important plays, including Clifford Odets's *Waiting for Lefty* and *Golden Boy*. Although he worked briefly during the 1930s in film, assisting Ralph Steiner and Frontier Films on short documentaries, Kazan first rose to prominence as one of the most sought-after stage directors in the US. Among his landmark Broadway productions were the debuts of *The Skin of Our Teeth* (1942), *A Streetcar Named Desire* (1947), *Death of a Salesman* (1949) and *Cat on a Hot Tin Roof* (1955).

Kazan became increasingly involved with filmmaking in the postwar years. He acted briefly in two Hollywood films (*City for Conquest* 1940 and *Blues in the Night* 1941), and the "boy genius of Broadway" was recruited as a director by several studios in 1944. Teaming with producer Darryl F. Zanuck at 20th Century-Fox, Kazan quickly established himself as a quality filmmaker whose work mirrored his theatrical reputation: an expert handler of actors and an artist dedicated to addressing contemporary social problems. His initial efforts, *A Tree Grows in Brooklyn* (1945) and *Boomerang* (1947), were solid, if somewhat stagey dramas. But with *Gentleman's Agreement* (1947) and *Pinky* (1949), Kazan broke new ground in Hollywood's cycle of postwar "problem pictures." *Gentleman's Agreement*, which won Oscars for best picture, director, and supporting actress, was one of the first Hollywood productions to deal directly with anti-semitism, while *Pinky* addressed problems of race.

Kazan won further acclaim as a film director for his memorable adaptation of *A Streetcar Named Desire* (1951), but his career was threatened when he became embroiled in the HUAC's search for Communist subversion in the filmmaking community. Like many of his Group Theatre colleagues, Kazan had been a member of the Communist Party of America (from 1934 to 1936), but he had left the CPA embittered. Kazan reversed his initial resistance to HUAC and in April 1952 "named names" for the committee. Criticized by many for caving in to the witch hunt, Kazan answered the snubs with *On the Waterfront* (1954), in which dock worker Terry Malloy (Marlon Brando) takes the unpopular action of testifying against corrupt labor leaders. Kazan later wrote: "When Brando, at the end, yells...'I'm glad what I done—you hear me?—glad what I done!' that was me saying with identical heat, that I was glad I'd testified as I had."

Whether *On the Waterfront* redeemed Kazan politically, the film marked another milestone in his career, garnering six Academy Awards, including best picture and best director. *Waterfront* marked a culmination of two of the defining characteristics of his 'oeuvre,' combining tenets of neorealism with strong, naturalistic acting performances. Kazan had used real locations to film *Panic in the Streets* (1950) and *Viva Zapata!* (1952), but with *On the Waterfront* he also cast real dockworkers in authentic locales. The director's real forte was his ability to elicit visceral performances from his stars. He and Lee Strasberg founded the famed Actor's Studio in 1947, and under Kazan's tutelage the Studio's star pupil, Marlon Brando, established himself as the American cinema's most charismatic leading man of the early 1950s, earning Oscar nominations under Kazan for his portrayals of Stanley Kowalski, Emiliano Zapata and Terry Malloy. Kazan also proved capable of getting stellar performances from less schooled actors, including James Dean (*East of Eden* 1955), Carroll Baker (*Baby Doll* 1956), Andy Griffith (*A Face in the Crowd* 1957) and Natalie Wood and Warren Beatty (*Splendor in the Grass* 1961). In all, Kazan directed 21 Oscar-nominated performances and nine winners.

In the 1960s, Elia Kazan completely abandoned his theater work, took up fiction writing, and focused his film career on much more personal, independently produced projects. *America, America* (1963) was a critically acclaimed adaptation of his own novel about his family's emigration to the US. His subsequent efforts, *The Arrangement* (1969, again from his own novel) and *The Visitors* (1972, shot at his home in 16mm), were resounding failures. Kazan made a successful though unexpected return to mainstream filmmaking with Harold Pinter's adaptation of F. Scott Fitzgerald's *The Last Tycoon* (1976). His autobiography, *A Life*, appeared in 1988. Screenwriter Nicholas Kazan (*Reversal of Fortune* 1990) is Kazan's son by his first wife, the late Molly Day Thatcher; he was also married to the late actress Barbara Loden. DGS • *Cafe Universal (short)* 1934 (a); *Pie in the Sky (short)* 1934 (a,d); *People of the Cumberland (short)* 1937 (ad); *City For Conquest* 1940 (a); *Blues in the Night* 1941 (a); *It's Up to You* 1941 (d); *A Tree Grows in Brooklyn* 1945 (d); *Boomerang* 1947 (d); *Gentleman's Agreement* 1947 (d) **(AAHON,AABD)**; *Sea of Grass* 1947 (d); *Pinky* 1949 (d); *Panic in the Streets* 1950 (d); *A Streetcar Named Desire* 1951 (d,sc) **(AANBD)**; *Viva Zapata!* 1952 (d); *Man on a Tightrope* 1953 (d); *On the Waterfront* 1954 (d) **(AABD)**; *East of Eden* 1955 (d,p) **(AANBD)**; *Baby Doll* 1956 (adapt,d,p); *A Face in the Crowd* 1957 (d,p); *Wild River* 1960 (d,original screenplay "Garth's Island"); *Splendor in the Grass* 1961 (d,p); *America, America* 1963 (d,p,sc,from novel, from unpublished story "Hama!" **(AANBP,AANBD,AANBSC)**; *The Directors (short)* 1963 (a); *The Arrangement* 1969 (d,p,sc, from novel); *The Visitors* 1972 (d); *The Fighters* 1974 (a); *The Last Tycoon* 1976 (d); *Acting: Lee Strasberg and The Actors Studio* 1981 (a); *He Stands in a Desert Counting the Seconds of His Life* 1985 (a); *50 Years of Action!* 1986 (a); *Hello Actors Studio* 1987 (a); *L'Héritage de la chouette* 1989 (a); *Sis* 1989 (a).

Keach, Stacy • Actor • Born Walter Stacy Keach, Jr., Savannah, GA, June 2, 1941. *Educ.* University of California, Berkeley; Yale School of Drama; LAMDA. In films from 1968, following extensive stage experience. After several starring roles in the 1970s he became well known as TV private eye Mike Hammer. Son of actor Stacy Keach, Sr., and brother of actor James Keach. • *The Heart Is a Lonely Hunter* 1968 (a); *Brewster McCloud* 1970 (a); *The End of the Road* 1970 (a); *The Traveling Executioner* 1970 (a); *Doc* 1971 (a); *The Repeater (short)* 1971 (a,d,p,sc,lyrics); *Fat City* 1972 (a); *The Life and Times of Judge Roy Bean* 1972 (a); *The New Centurions* 1972 (a); *The Gravy Train* 1974 (a); *Luther* 1974 (a); *One By One* 1974 (a); *Watched* 1974 (a); *Conduct Unbecoming* 1975 (a); *Hamburger Hamlet (short)* 1975 (a); *James Dean, the First American Teenager* 1975 (a); *The Killer Inside Me* 1976 (a); *Street People* 1976 (a); *The Duellists* 1977 (a); *Il Grande attacco* 1977 (a); *Gray Lady Down* 1977 (a); *The Squeeze* 1977 (a); *Cheech & Chong's Up in Smoke* 1978 (a); *La Montagna del dio Cannibale* 1978 (a); *Two Solitudes* 1978 (a); *The Search For Solutions* 1979 (a); *Twinkle, Twinkle, "Killer" Kane* 1979 (a); *The Long Riders* 1980 (a,exec.p,sc); *Butterfly* 1981 (a); *Cheech & Chong's Nice Dreams* 1981 (a); *Road Games* 1981 (a); *That Championship Season* 1982 (a); *The Class of 1999* 1990 (a); *False Identity* 1990 (a).

Keaton, Buster • Actor, director; also screenwriter. • Born Joseph Frank Keaton, Piqua, KS, October 4, 1895; died February 1, 1966. Buster Keaton's films enjoyed only moderate commercial success at the time of their release; it is with the passage of time that their subtle riches have been fully appreciated. Keaton's public signature was his stone face, which seemed never to betray his feelings. But this impassivity was belied by his body, a dynamo of movement and acrobatic grace that carried Buster through many a hostile situation. Trains, automobiles, hot air balloons, houses of all kinds (haunted, electric and build-it-yourself), ocean liners, river boats, row boats, herds of cattle, squads of police, armies of women—even the mechanism of cinema itself—all imperil Keaton as he seeks love, the promise of wealth or the comfort of his family. Unlike Fatty Arbuckle, the comedian who gave Keaton his start in films and who took savage glee in delivering vengeance to the pompous, Keaton sought a measure of serenity in a world where peace is hard to find.

Keaton set up his "style" of comedy in *One Week* (1920), a short about a man trying to assemble a build-it-yourself house. In collaboration with Eddie Cline as scenarist and director, Keaton followed with the surreal *Neighbors* (1920) and *The Boat* (1921), to cite two highlights from a prolific period. *The Baloonatic* and *The Love Nest* (both 1923) were next, and then he and producer Joseph M. Schenck (who was the brother of Keaton's wife, actress Natali Talmadge) expanded their horizons with the feature *The Three Ages* (1923). Thereafter Keaton devoted his primary attention to feature films, directing by himself.

Within 18 months, he came out with *Our Hospitality* (1923), *Sherlock, Jr.* (1924) and *The Navigator* (1924), a string of first features almost unmatched in film history. *Sherlock, Jr.* involves a projectionist stepping into and out of the movies he casts upon the screen, becoming subject to the plastic worlds of space and time that Keaton so deftly manipulated in all of his films. A sure sense of what was appropriate and possible on film is what ultimately animates his films for later generations. A few examples from *Seven Chances* (1925): Keaton wants to show the passage of time, so we see a montage of a puppy growing to become a huge dog; to move his character across town in an automobile, Keaton has him enter the car, dissolves the background to the new location, and the character promptly exits, a new form of shorthand uniquely appropriate to the movies, one that is thoroughly artificial, anything but realistic, but works consistently because Keaton uses his film audience as an "accomplice," and we appreciate it. Keaton took delight in exploring the properties of the medium as in *Seven Chances*, a silent film in which his character is trying to propose to a woman on a golf course; she is unable to "hear" what we have "seen" (thanks to the titles), and a crowd gathers around him, listening to the words we cannot "hear!"

Keaton continued for several years to make works of this high caliber, including his masterpiece, *The General* (1927), a Civil War romance. But his career came undone when Schenck persuaded him to abandon his own studio and join MGM. From 1928 on, Keaton's ability to improvise and develop his narratives was compromised by the studio production system, which eventually rejected him. Abandoned by his wife, retreating to alcohol, Keaton was reduced to work as a gag man and to bit parts until a 1962 retrospective at Paris's Cinémathèque Française sparked a revival of interest in his early films.

In 1965, he acted in two notable short films, *Film*, from a screenplay by Samuel Beckett, and *The Railrodder;* that September, he appeared at the Venice Film Festival to a tumultuous reception. Keaton's art and life were splendidly taken up by Kevin Brownlow and David Gill in their TV documentary series, "Buster Keaton: A Hard Act to Follow" (1987).RAH • *The Butcher Boy (short)* 1917 (a); *Coney Island (short)* 1917 (a); *A Country Hero (short)* 1917 (a); *His Wedding Night (short)* 1917 (a); *Oh, Doctor! (short)* 1917 (a); *A Reckless Romeo (short)* 1917 (a); *The Rough House (short)* 1917 (a); *The Bell Boy (short)* 1918 (a); *The Cook (short)* 1918 (a); *Good Night Nurse (short)* 1918 (a); *Moonshine (short)* 1918 (a); *Out West (short)* 1918 (a); *Back Stage (short)* 1919 (a); *The Garage (short)* 1919 (a); *The Hayseed (short)* 1919 (a); *Love (short)* 1919 (a); *The Round Up (short)* 1919 (a); *Convict 13 (short)* 1920 (a,d,sc); *Neighbors (short)* 1920 (d,sc); *One Week (short)* 1920 (a,d,sc); *The Saphead* 1920 (a,p); *The Scarecrow (short)* 1920 (a,d,sc); *The Boat (short)* 1921 (a,d,sc); *The Goat* 1921 (a,d,sc); *Hard Luck (short)* 1921 (a,d,sc); *The Haunted House (short)* 1921 (a,d,sc); *The High Sign (short)* 1921 (a,d,sc); *The Paleface (short)* 1921 (a,d,sc); *The Playhouse (short)* 1921 (a,d,sc); *The Blacksmith (short)* 1922 (a,d,sc); *Cops (short)* 1922 (a,d,sc); *Day Dreams (short)* 1922 (a,d,sc); *The Electric House (short)* 1922 (a,d,sc); *The Frozen North (short)* 1922 (a,d,sc); *My Wife's Relations (short)* 1922 (a,d,sc); *The Balloonatic (short)* 1923 (a,d,sc); *The Love Nest (short)* 1923 (a,d,sc); *Our Hospitality* 1923 (a,d); *The Three Ages* 1923 (d,sc,uncred.a); *The Navigator* 1924 (d,uncred.a); *Sherlock, Jr.* 1924 (d,uncred.a); *Go West* 1925 (a,d,story); *Seven Chances* 1925 (a,d); *Battling Butler* 1926 (d,uncred.a); *College* 1927 (a); *The General* 1927 (a,d,story); *The Cameraman* 1928 (a,p); *Steamboat Bill, Jr.* 1928 (p,uncred.a); *The Hollywood Revue of 1929* 1929 (uncred.a); *Spite Marriage* 1929 (a,p); *Doughboys* 1930 (p,uncred.a); *Free and Easy* 1930 (uncred.a); *Parlor, Bedroom and Bath* 1931 (a,p); *Sidewalks of New York* 1931 (p,uncred.a); *Splash (short)* 1931 (archival footage); *The Passionate Plumber* 1932 (a,p); *Speak Easily* 1932 (uncred.a); *What! No Beer?* 1933 (uncred.a); *Allez Oop (short)* 1934 (a); *The Gold Ghost (short)* 1934 (a); *Le Roi des Champs-Elysées* 1934 (a); *The E-Flat Man (short)* 1935 (a); *Hayseed Romance (short)* 1935 (a); *One-Run Elmer (short)* 1935 (a); *Palooka From Paducah (short)* 1935 (a); *Tars and Stripes (short)* 1935 (a); *The Timid Young Man (short)* 1935 (a); *Blue Blazes (short)* 1936 (a); *The Chemist (short)* 1936 (a); *La Fiesta de Santa Barbara (short)* 1936 (a); *Grand Slam Opera (short)* 1936 (a); *The Invader (short)* 1936 (a); *Jail Bait (short)* 1936 (a); *Mixed Magic (short)* 1936 (a); *Three on a Limb (short)* 1936 (a); *Ditto (short)* 1937 (a); *Love Nest on Wheels (short)* 1937 (a); *Hollywood Handicap (short)* 1938 (d); *Life in Sometown, USA (short)* 1938 (d); *Love Finds Andy Hardy* 1938 (uncred.tech.cons); *Streamlined Swing (short)* 1938 (d); *Too Hot to Handle* 1938 (uncred.gags); *At the Circus* 1939 (uncred.gags); *Hollywood Cavalcade* 1939 (uncred.a); *The Jones Family in Hollywood* 1939 (story); *The Jones Family in Quick Millions* 1939 (story); *Moochin' Through Georgia (short)* 1939 (a); *Nothing But Pleasure (short)* 1939 (a); *Pest From the West (short)* 1939 (a); *Comrade X* 1940 (uncred.gags); *Li'l Abner* 1940 (a); *New Moon* 1940 (archival footage); *Pardon My Berth Marks (short)* 1940 (archival footage); *The Spook Speaks* 1940 (archival footage); *The Taming of the Snood (short)* 1940 (a); *The Villain Still Pursued Her* 1940 (uncred.a); *General Nuisance (short)* 1941 (a); *His Ex Marks the Spot* 1941 (a); *She's Oil Mine (short)* 1941 (a); *So You Won't Squawk (short)* 1941 (a); *Tales of Manhattan* 1942 (uncred.gags); *Forever and a Day* 1943 (uncred.a); *I Dood It* 1943 (uncred.gags); *El Moderno Barba-Azul* 1943 (a); *Bathing Beauty* 1944 (uncred.gags); *Nothing But Trouble* 1944 (uncred.gags); *San Diego, I Love You* 1944 (a); *She Went to the Races* 1945 (uncred.gags); *That Night With You* 1945 (uncred.a); *That's the Spirit* 1945 (uncred.a); *Equestrian Quiz (What's Your I.Q.? No. 11) (short)* 1946 (uncred.gags); *God's Country* 1946 (a); *Cynthia* 1947 (uncred.sc); *It Happened in Brooklyn* 1947 (uncred.gags); *Merton of the Movies* 1947 (uncred.tech.adviser); *A Southern Yankee* 1948 (uncred.gags); *In the Good Old Summertime* 1949 (uncred.a); *The Lovable Cheat* 1949 (a); *Neptune's Daughter* 1949 (uncred.dial); *You're My Everything* 1949 (uncred.a); *Un Duel à mort* 1950 (a,sc); *Sunset Boulevard* 1950 (a); *Watch the Birdie* 1950 (uncred.gags); *Ça c'est du cinéma* 1951 (archival footage); *Excuse My Dust* 1951 (uncred.gags); *Paradise For Buster* 1951 (a); *Limelight* 1952 (a); *L'Incantevole nemica* 1953 (a); *Around the World in 80 Days* 1956 (a); *When Comedy Was King* 1957 (archival footage); *The Adventures of Huckleberry Finn* 1960 (a); *The Great Chase* 1962 (archival footage); *Ten Girls Ago* 1962 (uncred.a); *30 Years of Fun* 1963 (archival footage); *It's a Mad, Mad, Mad, Mad World* 1963 (a); *The Sound of Laughter* 1963 (archival footage); *Pajama Party* 1964 (a); *Beach Blanket Bingo* 1965 (a); *Buster Keaton Rides Again* 1965 (a); *Film (short)* 1965 (a); *How to Stuff a Wild Bikini* 1965 (uncred.a); *The Railrodder (short)* 1965 (a); *Sergeant Deadhead* 1965 (a); *Due Marines e un General* 1966 (a); *A Funny Thing Happened on the Way to the Forum* 1966 (a); *Four Clowns* 1969 (archival footage); *The Three Stooges Follies* 1974 (archival footage).

Keaton, Diane • Actress; also director, photographer. • Born Diane Hall, Los Angeles, CA, January 5, 1946. *Educ.* Santa Ana College, CA; Neighborhood Playhouse, New York. Gifted actress who proved her versatility in the 1970s, starring opposite then-partner Woody Allen in a series of comedies and playing the lone WASP in the "Godfather" films. The 80s saw Keaton turn in several fine performances as strong-willed, independent women in films of otherwise varying quality. She made her feature directing debut with the quirky, feature-length documentary *Heaven* (1987) and her television directing debut with episodes of the acclaimed series "China Beach" and "Twin Peaks." She has also published two volumes of photography. • *Lovers and Other Strangers* 1970 (a); *The Godfather* 1972 (a); *Play It Again, Sam* 1972 (a); *Sleeper* 1973 (a); *The Godfather, Part II* 1974 (a); *I Will...I Will...For Now* 1975 (a); *Love and Death* 1975 (a); *Harry and Walter Go to New York* 1976 (a); *Annie Hall* 1977 (a,song) **(AABA)**; *Looking For Mr. Goodbar* 1977 (a); *Interiors* 1978 (a); *Manhattan* 1979 (a); *Reds* 1981 (a) **(AANBA)**; *Shoot the Moon* 1981 (a); *The Little Drummer Girl* 1984 (a); *Mrs. Soffel* 1984 (a); *Crimes of the Heart* 1986 (a); *Baby Boom* 1987 (a); *Heaven* 1987 (d); *Radio Days* 1987 (a); *The Good Mother* 1988 (a); *The Lemon Sisters* 1990 (a); *The Godfather Part III* 1990 (a).

Keaton, Michael • Actor • Born Michael Douglas, Pittsburgh, PA, September 9, 1951. *Educ.* Kent State University, OH (speech). Comic star of the 1980s who made an impressive debut in *Night Shift* (1982) and scored at the box office as the caped crusader himself in Tim Burton's *Batman* (1989). • *Night Shift* 1982; *Mr. Mom* 1983; *Johnny Dangerously* 1984; *Gung Ho* 1986; *Touch and Go* 1986; *The Squeeze* 1987; *Beetlejuice* 1988; *Clean and Sober* 1988; *Batman* 1989; *The Dream Team* 1989; *Pacific Heights* 1990.

Keel, Howard • *aka* Harold Keel • Actor; also singer. • Born Harry Clifford Leek, Gillespie, IL, April 13, 1917. Gained instant stardom as Betty Hutton's singing cowboy love interest in *Annie Get Your Gun* (1950), appearing in a host of other musicals throughout the 1950s and several action pictures in the next decade. Began appearing on the TV show "Dallas" in 1981. • *The Small Voice* 1948 (a); *Annie Get Your Gun* 1950 (a); *Pagan Love Song* 1950 (a); *Across the Wide Missouri* 1951 (a); *Callaway Went Thataway* 1951 (a); *Show Boat* 1951 (a); *Texas Carnival* 1951 (a); *Three Guys Named Mike* 1951 (a); *Desperate Search* 1952 (a); *Lovely to Look At* 1952 (a); *Calamity Jane* 1953 (a); *Fast Company* 1953 (a); *Kiss Me Kate* 1953 (a); *Ride, Vaquero* 1953 (a); *Deep in My Heart* 1954 (a); *Rose Marie* 1954 (a); *Seven Brides For Seven Brothers* 1954 (a); *Jupiter's Darling* 1955 (a); *Kismet* 1955 (a); *Floods of Fear* 1958 (a); *The Big Fisherman* 1959 (a); *Armored Command* 1961 (a); *The Day of the Triffids* 1962 (a); *The Man From Button Willow* 1965 (a); *Waco* 1966 (a); *Red Tomahawk* 1967 (a); *The War Wagon* 1967 (a); *Arizona Bushwhackers* 1968 (a).

Keeler, Ruby • Actress; also singer. • Born Halifax, Canada, August 25, 1909. Former chorus girl and Broadway lead who began appearing in films in the 1930s. Keeler came to prominence as the good-natured star (usually opposite Dick Powell) of several spectacular Warner Bros. musicals distinguished by their elaborate, surrealistic, Busby Berkley-designed dance routines. She retired from the screen in the early 1940s and, after intermittent TV appearances in the 50s and 60s, re-appeared on Broadway in the 1970 revival of the musical *No No Nanette*. Keeler was married to Al Jolson from 1928 to 1940. • *42nd Street* 1933 (a); *Footlight Parade* 1933 (a); *Gold Diggers of 1933* 1933 (a); *Dames* 1934 (a); *Flirtation Walk* 1934 (a); *Go Into Your Dance* 1935 (a); *Shipmates Forever* 1935 (a); *Colleen* 1936 (a); *Ready, Willing and Able* 1937 (a); *Mother Carey's Chickens* 1938 (a); *Sweetheart of the Campus* 1941 (a); *The Phynx* 1970 (a).

Keitel, Harvey • Actor • Born New York, NY, 1941. *Educ.* Actors Studio. Keitel had worked in summer stock, repertory and little theater for ten years before coming to prominence in the early films of Martin Scorsese, particularly *Mean Streets* (1973) and *Taxi Driver* (1976). He has turned in impressive performances in films by some of America's leading directors and has also worked with European figures such as Bertrand Tavernier (*Death Watch* 1979), Nicolas Roeg (*Bad Timing* 1980) and Lina Wertmuller (*A Complicated Story of Streets* 1985). Married to actress Lorraine Bracco. • *Who's That Knocking at My Door?* 1968 (a); *Street Scenes 1970* 1970 (prod.asst,stills); *Mean Streets* 1973 (a); *Alice Doesn't Live Here Anymore* 1974 (a); *That's the Way of the World* 1975 (a); *Buffalo Bill and the Indians, or Sitting Bull's History Lesson* 1976 (a); *Mother, Jugs & Speed* 1976 (a); *Taxi Driver* 1976 (a); *Welcome to L.A.* 1976 (a); *The Duellists* 1977 (a); *Fingers* 1977 (a); *Blue Collar* 1978 (a); *Eagle's Wing* 1978 (a); *La Mort en Direct/Death Watch* 1979 (a); *Bad Timing* 1980 (a); *Saturn 3* 1980 (a); *The Border* 1981 (a); *La Nuit de Varennes* 1982 (a); *Copkiller* 1983 (a); *Exposed* 1983 (a); *Nemo* 1983 (a); *Une Pierre dans la bouche* 1983 (a); *Falling in Love* 1984 (a); *Un Complicato Intrigo di Donne, Vicoli e Delitti/A Complicated Story of Streets* 1985 (a); *Off Beat* 1985 (a); *El Caballero del Dragon* 1986 (a); *The Men's Club* 1986 (a); *Wise Guys* 1986 (a); *Blindside* 1987 (a); *Dear America* 1987 (a); *Hello Actors Studio* 1987 (a); *L'Inchiesta* 1987 (a); *The Pick-Up Artist* 1987 (a); *Caro Gorbaciov* 1988 (a); *The January Man* 1988 (a); *The Last Temptation of Christ* 1988 (a); *Two Evil Eyes* 1990 (a); *The Two Jakes* 1990 (a); *Mortal Thoughts* 1991 (a); *Thelma and Louise* 1991 (a).

Keller, Marthe • Actress • Born Basle, Switzerland, c. 1945. *Educ.* Croakslavsky School, Munich; Heidelberg repertory company. International leading lady who made her American debut opposite Dustin Hoffman in John Schlesinger's *Marathon Man* (1976). Keller has a son by director Philippe De Broca. • *Le Diable par la Queue* 1969; *Caprices de Marie* 1970; *Le Vieille Fille* 1971; *Un Cave* 1972; *Elle Court, Elle Court la Banlieue* 1972; *La Raison du plus fou* 1972; *La Chute D'Un Corps* 1973; *Toute une vie* 1974; *Die Antwort Kennt Nur der Wind* 1975; *Le Guepier* 1975; *Per le Antiche Scale* 1975; *Marathon Man* 1976; *Black Sunday* 1977; *Bobby Deerfield* 1977; *Fedora* 1978; *The Formula* 1980; *The Amateur* 1981; *Femmes de personne* 1983; *Wagner* 1983; *Joan Lui: Ma un Giorno ne Paese Arrivo io di Lunedi* 1985; *Rouge Baiser* 1985; *Oci Ciornie/Dark Eyes* 1987; *Seven Minutes* 1989.

Kellerman, Sally • Actress • Born Long Beach, CA, June 2, 1938. *Educ.* Los Angeles City College; Actors Studio. Came to prominence in the 1970s, notably as Major "Hot Lips" Houlihan in Robert Altman's *M*A*S*H* (1970). Married to Jonathan Krane, founder, chairman and C.E.O of the Management Company Entertainment Group. • *Reform School Girl* 1957 (a); *Hands of a Stranger* 1962 (a); *The Lollipop Cover* 1965 (song); *The Third Day* 1965 (a); *The Boston Strangler* 1968 (a); *The April Fools* 1969 (a); *Brewster McCloud* 1970 (a); *M*A*S*H* 1970 (a) **(AANBSA)**; *A Reflection of Fear* 1971 (a); *Last of the Red Hot Lovers* 1972 (a); *Lost Horizon* 1973 (a); *Slither* 1973 (a); *Rafferty and the Gold Dust Twins* 1974 (a); *The Big Bus* 1976 (a); *Welcome to L.A.* 1976 (a); *The Mouse and His Child* 1977 (a); *It Rained All Night the Day I Left* 1978 (a); *Magee and the Lady* 1978 (a); *A Little Romance* 1979 (a); *Foxes* 1980 (a); *Head On* 1980 (a); *Loving Couples* 1980 (a); *Serial* 1980 (a); *Lethal* 1985 (a); *Moving Violations* 1985 (a); *Sesame Street Presents: Follow That Bird* 1985 (a); *Back to School* 1986 (a); *Meatballs III* 1986 (a); *That's Life!* 1986 (a); *Someone to Love* 1987 (a); *Three For the Road* 1987 (a); *Paramedics* 1988 (a); *You Can't Hurry Love* 1988 (a); *All's Fair* 1989 (a); *Limit Up* 1989 (a); *Happily Ever After* 1990 (a).

Kelly, Gene • Actor, dancer, director, choreographer • Born Eugene Curran Kelly, Pittsburgh, PA, August 23, 1912. *Educ.* Pennsylvania State University (economics). Renowned dancer-choreographer and a key figure in shaping the golden age of the Hollywood musical. Kelly's first screen test, for RKO in 1935, was unsuccessful. Three years after moving to New York in 1938, however, he had established a reputation on Broadway strong enough for David Selznick to sign him to a seven-year contract. Kelly was loaned to MGM for his first film, *For Me and My Gal* (1942), opposite Judy Garland. The film was unexceptional, but Kelly's performance impressed MGM enough to buy out his contract. He went on to become a leading Hollywood star—a handsome, capable actor and a competent director, but a dancer and choreographer of incomparable grace and charm.

Kelly's greatest achievements came with a series of musicals, particularly *Singin' in the Rain* (1952), co-directed with Stanley Donen. In 1951 he received a Special Academy Award for his exceptional talents, "especially for his brilliant achievements in the art of choreography on film." He was married to actress Betsy Blair from 1940 to 1957 and to dancer Jeannie Coyne (Donen's former wife) from 1960 until her death in 1973. • *For Me and My Gal* 1942 (a); *The Cross of Lorraine* 1943 (a); *Du Barry Was a Lady* 1943 (a); *Pilot No. 5* 1943 (a); *Thousands Cheer* 1943 (a,chor,conception "Mop Dance"); *Christmas Holiday* 1944 (a); *Cover Girl* 1944 (a,chor,conception "Alter Ego"); *Anchors Aweigh* 1945 (a,chor) **(AANBA)**; *Ziegfeld Follies* 1946 (a); *Living in a Big Way* 1947 (a,chor); *The Pirate* 1948 (a,chor); *The Three Musketeers* 1948 (a); *Words and Music* 1948 (a,choreography "Slaughter on 10th Avenue"); *Black Hand* 1949 (a); *On the Town* 1949 (a,chor,d); *Take Me Out to the Ball Game* 1949 (a,d,story,chor); *Summer Stock* 1950 (a,chor); *An American in Paris* 1951 (a,chor); *It's a Big Country* 1951 (a); *The Devil Makes Three* 1952 (a); *Love Is Better Than Ever* 1952 (a); *Singin' in the Rain* 1952 (a,chor,d); *Brigadoon* 1954 (a,chor); *Crest of the Wave* 1954 (a); *Deep in My Heart* 1954 (a); *It's Always Fair Weather* 1955 (a,chor,d); *The Happy Road* 1956 (a,d,p); *Invitation to the Dance* 1956 (a,chor,d,sc); *Les Girls* 1957 (a,chor—finale); *Marjorie Morningstar* 1958 (a); *Something For the Girls (short)* 1958 (a); *The Tunnel of Love* 1958 (d); *Inherit the Wind* 1960 (a); *Let's Make Love* 1960 (a); *Gigot* 1962 (d); *What a Way to Go!* 1964 (a,chor); *A Guide For the Married Man* 1967 (a,d); *Hello, Dolly!* 1969 (d); *The Cheyenne Social Club* 1970 (a,d,p); *A Clockwork Orange* 1971 (song); *40 Carats* 1973 (a); *That's Entertainment!* 1974 (a); *It's Showtime* 1976 (a); *That's Entertainment Part 2* 1976 (a,d); *Viva Knievel!* 1977 (a); *Xanadu* 1980 (a,song); *Reporters* 1981 (archival footage); *One From the Heart* 1982 (m); *That's Dancing!* 1985 (a); *Going Hollywood: The War Years* 1988 (archival footage).

Kelly, Grace • *aka* Grace Grimaldi • Actress • Born Grace Patricia Kelly, Philadelphia, PA, November 12, 1928; died 1982. *Educ.* AADA, New York (acting); Neighborhood Playhouse, New York. Former model and stage actress who came to film prominence with *High Noon* (1952) and her Oscar-nominated role in *Mogambo* (1953). Kelly then starred in three consecutive films directed by Alfred Hitchcock, who made brilliant use of her signature combination of cool, elegant charm and smoldering sensuality. In 1956 she married Prince Rainier of Monaco, becoming Her Serene Highness, Princess Grace of Monaco, and retired from film (though she served on the board of directors of 20th Century-Fox from 1976 to 1981). Kelly died in a car accident in 1982. • *Fourteen Hours* 1951; *High Noon* 1952; *Mogambo* 1953 **(AANBSA)**; *The Country Girl* 1954 **(AABA)**; *Dial M For Murder* 1954; *Green Fire* 1954; *Rear Window* 1954; *The Bridges at Toko-Ri* 1955; *To Catch a Thief* 1955; *High Society* 1956; *The Swan* 1956; *Invitation to Monte Carlo* 1959; *The Poppy Is Also a Flower* 1966.

Kemper, Victor J. • Director of photography • Born Newark, NJ, April 14, 1927. *Educ.* Seton Hall University, NJ. Noted for his work on such stylistically disparate films as John Cassavetes's *Husbands* (1970), Sidney Lumet's *Dog Day Afternoon* (1975) and Elia Kazan's *The Last Tycoon* (1976). • *Husbands* 1970; *The Magic Garden of Stanley Sweetheart* 1970; *The Hospital* 1971; *They Might Be Giants* 1971; *Who Is Harry Kellerman, and Why Is He Saying Those Terrible Things About Me?* 1971; *The Candidate* 1972; *Last of the Red Hot Lovers* 1972; *Shamus* 1972; *The Friends of Eddie Coyle* 1973; *From The Mixed-Up Files of Mrs. Basil E. Frankweiler* 1973; *Gordon's War* 1973; *The Gambler* 1974; *Dog Day Afternoon* 1975; *The Reincarnation of Peter Proud* 1975; *Stay Hungry* 1975; *The Last Tycoon* 1976; *Mikey and Nicky* 1976; *Audrey Rose* 1977; *Oh, God!* 1977; *Slap Shot* 1977; *Coma* 1978; *Eyes of Laura Mars* 1978; *Magic* 1978; *The One and Only* 1978; *And Justice For All* 1979; *The Jerk* 1979; *The Final Countdown* 1980; *Night of the Juggler* 1980; *Xanadu* 1980; *Chu Chu and the Philly Flash* 1981; *The Four Seasons* 1981; *Author! Author!* 1982; *Partners* 1982; *Mr. Mom* 1983; *National Lampoon's Vacation* 1983; *Cloak and Dagger* 1984; *The Lonely Guy* 1984; *Clue* 1985; *Pee-wee's Big Adventure* 1985; *Secret Admirer* 1985; *Walk Like a Man* 1987; *Cohen and Tate* 1988; *Hot to Trot* 1988; *See No Evil, Hear No Evil* 1989; *Crazy People* 1990; *F/X II* 1991.

Kendall, Kay • Actress • Born Kay Justine Kendall McCarthy, Withernsea, Yorkshire, England, 1926; died 1959. Effervescent leading lady of the 1950s who first hit her stride with *Genevieve* (1953). Married to Rex Harrison from 1957 until her death (caused by leukemia) two years later. • *Champagne Charlie* 1944; *Dreaming* 1944; *Fiddlers Three* 1944; *Caesar and Cleopatra* 1945; *Waltz Time* 1945; *London Town* 1946; *Spring Song* 1946; *Dance Hall* 1950; *Happy Go Lovely* 1951; *Lady Godiva Rides Again* 1951; *Curtain Up* 1952; *It Started in Paradise* 1952; *Wings of Danger* 1952; *Genevieve* 1953; *Mantrap* 1953; *Meet Mr. Lucifer* 1953; *The Square Ring* 1953; *Street of Shadows* 1953; *The Constant Husband* 1954; *Doctor in the House* 1954; *Fast and Loose* 1954; *Abdullah the Great* 1955; *Quentin Durward* 1955; *Simon and Laura* 1955; *Les Girls* 1957; *The Reluctant Debutante* 1958; *Once More, With Feeling* 1960.

Kennedy, Arthur • Actor • Born John Arthur Kennedy, Worcester, MA, February 17, 1914; died January 5, 1990. *Educ.* Carnegie Institute of Technology, Pittsburgh PA (drama). Gifted supporting player and occasional leading man, discovered by James Cagney while perfoming on stage. Kennedy made his screen debut in *City For Conquest* (1940), playing Cagney's kid brother, and subsequently appeared in over 60 films through the late 1980s. His theater work included a Tony Award-winning performance as Biff in *Death of a Salesman* (1948). • *City For Conquest* 1940; *Bad Men of Missouri* 1941; *High Sierra* 1941; *Highway West* 1941; *Knockout* 1941; *Strange Alibi* 1941; *They Died With Their Boots On* 1941; *Desperate Journey* 1942; *Air Force* 1943; *It's Your America (short)* 1944 (narration); *Devotion* 1946; *Boomerang* 1947; *Cheyenne* 1947; *Champion* 1949 **(AANBSA)**; *Chicago Deadline* 1949; *Too Late For Tears* 1949; *The Walking Hills* 1949; *The Window* 1949; *The Glass Menagerie* 1950; *Bright Victory* 1951 **(AANBA)**; *Red Mountain* 1951; *Bend of the River* 1952; *The Girl in White* 1952; *The Lusty Men* 1952; *Rancho Notorious* 1952; *Crashout* 1955; *The Desperate Hours* 1955; *Impulse* 1955; *The Man From Laramie* 1955; *The Naked Dawn* 1955; *Trial* 1955 **(AANBSA)**; *The Rawhide Years* 1956; *Peyton Place* 1957 **(AANBSA)**; *Some Came Running* 1958 **(AANBSA)**; *Twilight For the Gods* 1958; *Home Is the Hero* 1959; *A Summer Place* 1959; *Elmer Gantry* 1960; *Claudelle Inglish* 1961; *Murder She Said* 1961; *Adventures of a Young Man* 1962; *Barabbas* 1962; *Lawrence of Arabia* 1962; *Cheyenne Autumn* 1964; *Italiani brava Gente* 1964; *Battle of the Bulge...the Brave Rifles* 1965; *Joaquin Murrieta* 1965; *Joy in the Morning* 1965; *La Chica del Lunes* 1966; *Fantastic Voyage* 1966; *Nevada Smith* 1966; *Un Minuto per pregare, un instante per morire* 1967; *Anzio* 1968; *Day of the Evil Gun* 1968; *Hail, Hero!* 1969; *Shark* 1969; *Glory Boy* 1971; *Baciamo le mani* 1972; *Ricco* 1973; *Fin de semana para los muertos* 1974; *La Polizia ha le mani legate* 1974; *Roma A Mano Armata* 1975; *Nove ospiti per un delitto* 1976; *La Spiaggia del desiderio* 1976; *Ab Morgen sind wir reich und ehrlich* 1977; *Ciclon* 1977; *The Sentinel* 1977; *Gli Ultimi angeli* 1977; *L'Anti Cristo* 1978; *Bermude: La Fossa Maledetta* 1978; *Sono stato un'agente CIA* 1978; *L'Umanoide* 1979; *My Old Man's Place* 1988; *Signs of Life* 1989.

Kennedy, George • Actor • Born New York, NY, February 18, 1925. Burly character actor of the 1960s, 70s and 80s. Equally effective as a hulking heavy or a reassuring, reliable good guy; perhaps at his best as Paul Newman's fellow convict in *Cool Hand Luke* (1967). • *The Little Shepherd of Kingdom Come* 1961; *Lonely Are the Brave* 1962; *The Silent Witness (short)* 1962; *Charade* 1963; *The Man From the Diner's Club* 1963; *Hush...Hush, Sweet Charlotte* 1964; *Island of the Blue Dolphins* 1964; *McHale's Navy* 1964; *Strait-Jacket* 1964; *The Flight of the Phoenix* 1965; *In Harm's Way* 1965; *Mirage* 1965; *Shenandoah* 1965; *The Sons of Katie Elder* 1965; *Three Songs (short)* 1965 (d,p); *The Ballad of Josie* 1967; *Cool Hand Luke* 1967 **(AABSA)**; *The Dirty Dozen* 1967; *Hurry Sundown* 1967; *Bandolero!* 1968; *The Boston Strangler* 1968; *The Legend of Lylah Clare* 1968; *The Pink Jungle* 1968; *Gaily, Gaily* 1969; *The Good Guys and the Bad Guys* 1969; *Guns of the Magnificent Seven* 1969; *Airport* 1970; *Dirty Dingus Magee* 1970; *Tick, Tick, Tick* 1970; *Zigzag* 1970; *Fools' Parade* 1971; *Cahill, United States Marshal* 1973; *Lost Horizon* 1973; *Earthquake* 1974; *Thunderbolt and Lightfoot* 1974; *Airport 1975* 1975; *The Eiger Sanction* 1975; *The Human Factor* 1975; *Airport 77* 1977; *Ningen no shomei* 1977; *Brass Target* 1978; *Death on the Nile* 1978; *Mean Dog Blues* 1978; *The Concorde—Airport '79* 1979; *Death Ship* 1979; *The Double McGuffin* 1979; *Hotwire* 1980; *Just Before Dawn* 1980; *Steel* 1980; *Virus* 1980; *Modern Romance* 1981; *A Rare Breed* 1981; *Search & Destroy* 1981; *The Jupiter Menace* 1982; *Wacko* 1983; *Bolero* 1984; *Chattanooga Choo Choo* 1984; *Rigged* 1985; *Savage Dawn* 1985; *The Delta Force* 1986; *Radioactive Dreams* 1986; *Creepshow 2* 1987; *Born to Race* 1988; *Demonwarp* 1988; *Esmeralda Bay* 1988; *The Naked Gun—From the Files of Police Squad!* 1988; *Nightmare at Noon* 1988; *Private Roads (No Trespassing)* 1988; *Uninvited* 1988; *Counterforce* 1989; *Ministry of Vengeance* 1989; *The Terror Within* 1989; *Brain Dead* 1990.

Kennedy, Kathleen • American producer • *Educ.* San Diego State University. Worked at local San Diego TV station KCST in various capacities (video editor, news production coordinator, etc.) before forming the highly successful Amblin Entertainment with Frank Marshall and Steven Spielberg in 1984. Kennedy has since had a hand in most of the company's films, as well as on every Spielberg-directed feature since *Raiders of the Lost Ark* (1982). • *1941* 1979 (prod.asst); *Raiders of the Lost Ark* 1981 (asst. to Steven Spielberg,assoc.p); *E.T., the Extra-Terrestrial* 1982 (p) **(AANBP)**; *Poltergeist* 1982 (p); *Twilight Zone - the Movie* 1983 (assoc.p); *Gremlins* 1984 (exec.p); *Indiana Jones and the Temple of Doom* 1984 (assoc.p); *Back to the Future* 1985 (exec.p); *The Color Purple* 1985 (p) **(AANBP)**; *Fandango* 1985 (exec.p); *The Goonies* 1985 (exec.p); *Young Sherlock Holmes* 1985 (exec.p); *An American Tail* 1986 (exec.p); *The Money Pit* 1986 (exec.p); *Batteries Not Included* 1987 (exec.p); *Empire of the Sun* 1987 (p); *Innerspace* 1987 (co-exec.p); *The Land Before Time* 1988 (co-exec.p); *U2 Rattle and Hum* 1988 (assistance); *Who Framed Roger Rabbit* 1988 (exec.p); *Always* 1989 (exec.p); *Back to the Future II* 1989 (exec.p); *Dad* 1989 (exec.p); *Indiana Jones and the Last Crusade* 1989 (prod.exec—USA); *Tummy Trouble* 1989 (exec.p); *Arachnophobia* 1990 (p); *Back to the Future III* 1990 (exec.p); *Gremlins 2: The New Batch* 1990 (exec.p); *Joe Versus the Volcano* 1990 (exec.p); *Rollercoaster Rabbit* 1990 (exec.p).

Kern, Jerome • Composer • Born Jerome David Kern, New York, NY, January 27, 1885; died 1945. Celebrated composer of songs (from 1902) and Broadway scores (from 1912). Kern is probably best remembered for *Show Boat*, which in fact ended a run of relatively unsuccessful stage works in 1927, and for the songs "Ol' Man River" and "Smoke Gets in Your Eyes." Although he was persuaded by actress Billie Burke to compose the accompaniment for *Gloria's Romance* (1916), Kern's next work directly for film was not until 1930. He settled in Hollywood in 1934, adapting his musicals for the screen as well as composing original scores and songs. • *Gloria's Romance* 1916 (m); *Sally* 1925 (from play,song); *Can't Help Loving Dat Man (short)* 1929 (song); *Ol' Man River (short)* 1929 (song); *Show Boat* 1929 (song); *Sally* 1930 (from play); *Sunny* 1930 (from play,song,m); *Three Sisters* 1930 (song); *Men of the Sky* 1931 (sc,story,song); *The Cat and the Fiddle* 1934 (from play); *Look For the Silver Lining (short)* 1934 (from play,m); *Music in the Air* 1934 (from play,song); *The Flame Within* 1935 (m); *I Dream Too Much* 1935 (song); *Reckless* 1935 (song); *Roberta* 1935 (from play, song) **(AANBS)**; *Sweet Adeline* 1935 (from play,song); *The Great Ziegfeld* 1936 (song); *Show Boat* 1936 (from play,song); *Swing Time* 1936 (song) **(AABS)**; *High, Wide, And Handsome* 1937 (song); *When You're in Love* 1937 (song); *Joy of Living* 1938 (song); *The Story of Vernon and Irene Castle* 1939 (song); *One Night in the Tropics* 1940 (song); *Lady Be Good* 1941 (song) **(AABS)**; *Sunny* 1941 (from play,m); *You Were Never Lovelier* 1942 (song) **(AANBS)**; *Song of Russia* 1943 (song); *Broadway Rhythm* 1944 (from play *Very Warm For May*,song); *Can't Help Singing* 1944 (m,song) **(AANBM,AANBS)**; *Cover Girl* 1944 (m) **(AANBS)**; *Centennial Summer* 1946 (song) **(AANBS)**; *The Man I Love* 1946 (song); *Till the Clouds Roll By* 1946 (song); *Show Boat* 1951 (from play); *Lovely to Look At* 1952 (from play *Roberta*,song).

Kerr, Deborah • Actress • Born Deborah Jane Kerr-Trimmer, Helensburgh, Scotland, September 30, 1921. *Educ.* Sadlers Wells Ballet School, London. Entered films in 1940 after some stage experience and went on to star in a series of superior British and American productions. Often cast in poised, upper-class roles. • *Hatter's Castle* 1941; *Love on the Dole* 1941; *Major Barbara* 1941; *Penn of Pennsylvania* 1941; *The Day Will Dawn* 1942; *The Life and Death of Colonel Blimp* 1943; *Vacation From Marriage* 1945; *I See a Dark Stranger* 1946; *Black Narcissus* 1947; *The Hucksters* 1947; *If Winter Comes* 1947; *Edward, My Son* 1948 **(AANBA)**; *King Solomon's Mines* 1950; *Please Believe Me* 1950; *Quo Vadis* 1951; *The Prisoner of Zenda* 1952; *Thunder in the East* 1952; *Dream Wife* 1953; *From Here to Eternity* 1953 **(AANBA)**; *Julius Caesar* 1953; *Young Bess* 1953; *The End of the Affair* 1955; *An Affair to Remember* 1956; *The King and I* 1956 **(AANBA)**; *The Proud and the Profane* 1956; *Tea and Sympathy* 1956; *Bonjour Tristesse* 1957; *Heaven Knows, Mr. Allison* 1957 **(AANBA)**; *Separate Tables* 1958 **(AANBA)**; *Beloved Infidel* 1959; *Count Your Blessings* 1959; *The Journey* 1959; *The Grass Is Greener* 1960; *The Sundowners* 1960 **(AANBA)**; *The Innocents* 1961; *The Naked Edge* 1961; *The Chalk Garden* 1964; *The Night of the Iguana* 1964; *Marriage on the Rocks* 1965; *Eye of the Devil* 1966; *Casino Royale* 1967; *Prudence and the Pill* 1968; *The Arrangement* 1969; *The Gypsy Moths* 1969; *The Assam Garden* 1985.

Kershner, Irvin • Director; also producer. • Born Philadelphia, PA, April 29, 1923. *Educ.* Drexel Institute of Technology, Philadelphia; Cambridge; Temple University Tyler School of Fine Arts, Philadelphia (graduated 1946); University of Southern California Art Center School, Los Angeles (photography, design). Began his career making films for the US Information Service in the Middle East. Kershner then worked in TV, directing the documentary segments of the 1955 series "Confidential File," which recreated the events behind contemporary news headlines. He first made his mark as a feature director in the early 1960s with modestly budgeted, finely acted dramas such as *The Young Captives* (1958), *The Hoodlum Priest* (1961) and *The Luck of Ginger Coffey* (1964). Kershner has since moved on to expensive mainstream ventures, most successfully with the middle segment of the "Star Wars" trilogy, *The Empire Strikes Back* (1980). • *Stakeout on Dope Street* 1958 (d,sc); *The Young Captives* 1958 (d); *The Hoodlum Priest* 1961 (d); *A Face in the Rain* 1963 (d); *The Luck of Ginger Coffey* 1964 (d); *A Fine Madness* 1966 (d); *The Flim-Flam Man* 1967 (d); *Loving* 1970 (d); *A Man Called Horse* 1970 (uncred.sc); *Up the Sandbox* 1972 (d); *Badlands* 1973 (assistance); *Spys* 1974 (d); *The Return of a Man Called Horse* 1976 (d); *Eyes of Laura Mars* 1978 (d); *The Empire Strikes Back* 1980 (d); *Never Say Never Again* 1983 (d); *Wildfire* 1988 (exec.p); *Robocop 2* 1990 (d).

Kidder, Margot • Actress • Born Margaret Ruth Kidder, Yellowknife, Northwest Territories, Canada, October 17, 1948. *Educ.* University of British Columbia. Dark-haired, deep-voiced leading lady who came to prominence in the early 1970s, notably in *Quackser Fortune Has a Cousin in the Bronx* (1970) and Brian DePalma's haunting *Sisters* (1973); best known as Lois Lane in the "Superman" movies. In 1975 Kidder wrote and directed a medium length film, *And Again*. She married third husband, director Philippe De Broca, in 1983, having previously been married to writer-director Thomas McGuane and to actor John Heard. • *Gaily, Gaily* 1969; *Quackser Fortune Has a Cousin in the Bronx* 1970; *A Quiet Day in Belfast* 1973; *Sisters* 1973; *Black Christmas* 1974; *The Gravy Train* 1974; *92 in the Shade* 1975; *And Again (short)* 1975 (d,sc); *The Great Waldo Pepper* 1975; *The Reincarnation of Peter Proud* 1975; *Superman* 1978 (a,song); *The Amityville Horror* 1979; *Mr. Mike's Mondo Video* 1979; *Superman II* 1980; *Willie & Phil* 1980; *Heartaches* 1981; *Miss Right* 1981; *Some Kind of Hero* 1982; *Trenchcoat* 1982; *Superman III* 1983; *Louisiane* 1984; *Little Treasure* 1985; *Speaking Our Peace* 1985; *The Canadian Conspiracy* 1986; *Gobots: Battle of the Rock Lords* 1986; *Keeping Track* 1987; *Superman IV: The Quest For Peace* 1987; *Mob Story* 1989; *The White Room* 1990.

Kieslowski, Krzysztof • Polish director; also screenwriter. • Born 1941. *Educ.* Lódz Film School. Leading Polish director whose films are most influenced by those of his countryman, Andrzej Wajda. Kieslowski began his career making documentaries which focused on the social and economic problems which sparked the emergence of the Solidarity movement. His award-winning 1979 feature, *Amator/Camera Buff*, was a slyly humorous look at life in a corrupt provincial factory. *Blind Chance*, made in 1981, was banned for five years before finally being released in 1987.

Kieslowski confirmed his status as a major contemporary director with *Decalogue* (1988), a series of ten hour-long films funded by Polish TV and based on the Ten Commandments. In the same year, he expanded segments five and six into two features, *A Short Film About Killing* and *A Short Film About Love*. Partially set, like the rest of the series, on a Warsaw housing estate, *A Short Film About Killing* is a grim and powerful tale drawing formal parallels between the act of murder and the workings of the criminal justice system. The film won the Cannes Festival Jury Award as well as the "Felix" for best picture (it was the first recipient of this pan-European award, inaugurated in 1988). • *From the City of Lodz* 1969 (d); *Personel* 1975 (d,sc); *Spokoj* 1976 (d); *Amator/Camera Buff* 1979 (d,sc,dial); *Dlugi Dzien Pracy* 1981 (d); *Przypadek/Blind Chance* 1981 (d,sc); *Bez Konca* 1984 (d,sc); *Dekalog 1/I Am the Lord Thy God* 1988 (d,sc); *Dekalog 2/Thou Shalt Not Take the Name of the Lord They God in Vain* 1988 (d,sc); *Dekalog 3/Honor the Sabbath Day* 1988 (d,sc); *Dekalog 4/Honor Thy Father and Thy Mother* 1988 (d,sc); *Dekalog 5/Krotki film o milosci/Thou Shalt Not Kill/A Short Film About Killing* 1988 (d,sc); *Dekalog 6/Krotki film o zabijaniu/Thou Shalt Not Commit Adultery/A Short Film About Love* 1988 (d,sc); *Dekalog 7/Thou Shalt Not Steal* 1988 (d,sc); *Dekalog 8/Thou Shalt Not Bear False Witness* 1988 (d,sc); *Dekalog 9/Thou Shalt Not Covet Thy Neighbor's Wife* 1988 (d,sc); *Dekalog 10/Thou Shalt Not Covet Thy Neighbor's Goods* 1988 (d,sc); *City Life* 1990 (d—"Seven Days a Week").

Kilmer, Val • Actor • Born Los Angeles, CA, December 31, 1959. *Educ.* Hollywood Professional School, CA; Juilliard (drama). Handsome, classically trained performer who made an exuberant screen debut as an Elvis-like singer in the freewheeling comedy *Top Secret!* (1984). Kilmer was justly praised, and thrust into the Hollywood spotlight, for his uncannily accurate portrayal—even doing his own vocals—of Jim Morrison in Oliver Stone's otherwise lackluster biopic, *The Doors* (1991). Married to British actress Joanne Whalley-Kilmer. • *Top Secret!* 1984; *Real Genius* 1985; *Top Gun* 1986; *Willow* 1988; *Kill Me Again* 1989; *The Doors* 1991.

King, Alan • Actor, comedian; also producer, author. • Born Irwin Alan Kinberg, Brooklyn, NY, December 26, 1927. "Borscht Belt" comedian who has appeared in occasional films, including three directed by Sidney Lumet (*Bye Bye Braverman* 1968, *The Anderson Tapes* 1971, *Just Tell Me What You Want* 1980). • *Hit the Deck* 1955 (a); *The Girl He Left Behind* 1956 (a); *Miracle in the Rain* 1956 (a); *The Helen Morgan Story* 1957 (a); *On the Fiddle* 1961 (a); *Bye Bye Braverman* 1968 (a); *The Anderson Tapes* 1971 (a); *Happy Birthday, Gemini* 1980 (exec.p); *Just Tell Me What You Want* 1980 (a); *Cattle Annie and Little Britches* 1981 (p); *I, the Jury* 1981 (a); *Wolfen* 1981 (exec.p); *Author! Author!* 1982 (a); *Lovesick* 1983 (a); *Stephen King's Cat's Eye* 1985 (a); *You Talkin' to Me?* 1987 (a); *Funny* 1988 (a); *Memories of Me* 1988 (a,p); *Pinocchio's Christmas* 1988 (a); *Enemies, A Love Story* 1989 (a); *Bonfire of the Vanities* 1990 (a).

King, Henry • Director; also actor. • Born Montgomery County, VA, June 24, 1886; died 1982. A film actor from 1913 and a director from 1915, King established himself as one of the great artists of the silent period with *Tol'able David* (1921), a poignant evocation of rural Americana. With Fox from 1930 to 1961, King proved himself one of Hollywood's most prolific and consistently commercial directors, though his sound films have generally drawn less critical praise than his early work. King's nostalgia for the America of boundless prairies and visionary pioneers resurfaced in numerous films, including *In Old Chicago* (1938) and *Jesse James* (1939). Brother of director Louis King (1898-1962). • *The Birth Mark (short)* 1913 (a); *A False Friend (short)* 1913 (a); *The Sea Wolf (short)* 1913 (a); *The Split Nugget (short)* 1913 (a); *For the Commonwealth* 1915 (a); *The Fruit of Folly* 1915 (a); *Houses of Glass* 1915 (a); *The Love Liar* 1915 (a); *The Pomp of Earth* 1915 (a); *The Price of Fame* 1915 (a); *The Pursuit of Pleasure* 1915 (a); *Should a Woman Forgive?* 1915 (d,sc); *Today and Tomorrow* 1915 (a); *Toil and Tyranny* 1915 (a); *Unto Herself Alone* 1915 (a); *When Justice Sleeps* 1915 (a); *Who Pays?* 1915 (a); *Faith's Reward* 1916 (a,d); *Joy and the Dragon* 1916 (a,d); *Little Mary Sunshine* 1916 (a,d); *The Oath of Hate* 1916 (a,d); *The Sand Lark* 1916 (a,d); *Shadows and Sunshine* 1916 (a,d); *The Bride's Silence* 1917 (d); *The Climber* 1917 (a,d); *The Devil's Bait* 1917 (a); *A Game of Wits* 1917 (d); *The Mate of the Sally Ann* 1917 (d); *Souls in Pawn* 1917 (d); *Southern Pride* 1917 (d); *Sunshine and Gold* 1917 (a,d); *Told at Twilight* 1917 (a,d); *Twin Kiddies* 1917 (a,d); *Vengeance of the Dead* 1917 (a); *All the World to Nothing* 1918 (a,d); *Beauty and the Rogue* 1918 (d); *Hearts or Diamonds* 1918 (a,d); *Hobbs in a Hurry* 1918 (d); *The Locked Heart* 1918 (a,d); *Powers That Prey* 1918 (d); *Social Briars* 1918 (d); *Up Romance Road* 1918 (a,d); *When a Man Rides Alone* 1918 (d); *23 1/2 Hours Leave* 1919 (d); *Brass Buttons* 1919 (d); *A Fugitive From Matrimony* 1919 (d); *Haunting Shadows* 1919 (d); *Six Feet Four* 1919 (d); *Some Liar* 1919 (d); *A Sporting Chance* 1919 (d); *This Hero Stuff* 1919 (d); *Where the West Begins* 1919 (d); *Dice of Destiny* 1920 (d); *Help Wanted - Male* 1920 (a,d); *A Live Wire Hick* 1920 (d); *One Hour Before Dawn* 1920 (d); *Peggy Rebels* 1920 (d); *Uncharted Channels* 1920 (d); *The White Dove* 1920 (d); *The Mistress of Shenstone* 1921 (d); *Salvage* 1921 (d); *The Sting of the Lash* 1921 (d); *Tol'able David* 1921 (d,sc,adapt); *When We Were Twenty-One* 1921 (d); *The Bond Boy* 1922 (d); *The Seventh Day* 1922 (d); *Sonny* 1922 (d,sc); *Fury* 1923 (d,prod.sup); *The White Sister* 1923 (d); *Romola* 1924 (d,p); *Any Woman* 1925 (d,p); *Sackcloth and Scarlet* 1925 (d); *Stella Dallas* 1925 (d,p); *Partners*

Again 1926 (d); *The Winning of Barbara Worth* 1926 (d); *Magic Flame* 1927 (d); *The Woman Disputed* 1928 (d,p); *She Goes to War* 1929 (d); *The Eyes of the World* 1930 (d); *Hell Harbor* 1930 (d); *Lightnin'* 1930 (d); *Merely Mary Ann* 1931 (d); *Over the Hill* 1931 (d); *The Woman in Room 13* 1932 (d); *I Loved You Wednesday* 1933 (d); *State Fair* 1933 (d); *Carolina* 1934 (d); *Marie Galante* 1934 (d); *One More Spring* 1935 (d); *Way Down East* 1935 (d); *The Country Doctor* 1936 (d); *Lloyd's of London* 1936 (d); *Ramona* 1936 (d); *Seventh Heaven* 1937 (d); *Alexander's Ragtime Band* 1938 (d); *In Old Chicago* 1938 (d); *Jesse James* 1939 (d); *Stanley and Livingstone* 1939 (d); *Chad Hanna* 1940 (d); *Little Old New York* 1940 (d); *Maryland* 1940 (d); *Remember the Day* 1941 (d); *A Yank in the R.A.F.* 1941 (d); *The Black Swan* 1942 (d); *The Song of Bernadette* 1943 (d) **(AANBD)**; *Spotlight Scandals* 1943 (a); *Wilson* 1944 (d) **(AANBD)**; *A Bell For Adano* 1945 (d); *Out of This World* 1945 (a); *Margie* 1946 (d); *Captain From Castile* 1947 (d); *Deep Waters* 1948 • (d); *Prince of Foxes* 1949 (d); *Twelve O'Clock High* 1949 (d); *The Gunfighter* 1950 (d); *David and Bathsheba* 1951 (d); *I'd Climb the Highest Mountain* 1951 (d); *O. Henry's Full House* 1952 (d); *The Snows of Kilimanjaro* 1952 (d); *Wait Till the Sun Shines, Nellie* 1952 (d); *King of the Khyber Rifles* 1954 (d); *Love Is a Many Splendored Thing* 1955 (d); *Untamed* 1955 (d); *Carousel* 1956 (d); *The Sun Also Rises* 1957 (d); *The Bravados* 1958 (d); *Beloved Infidel* 1959 (d); *This Earth Is Mine* 1959 (d); *Tender Is the Night* 1962 (d).

King, Stephen • *aka* Richard Bachman • American novelist; also screenwriter, director. • Born c. 1948. Best-selling author who has had several works adapted for the screen with varying degrees of success; Brian De Palma's *Carrie* (1976), Stanley Kubrick's *The Shining* (1980), David Cronenberg's *The Dead Zone* (1983) and Rob Reiner's *Stand By Me* (1986) and *Misery* (1990) stand out. King made a lackluster directorial debut with *Maximum Overdrive* (1986). • *Carrie* 1976 (from novel); *The Shining* 1980 (from novel); *Creepshow* 1982 (a,sc,from story "The Crate"); *Christine* 1983 (from novel); *Cujo* 1983 (from novel); *The Dead Zone* 1983 (from novel); *Firestarter* 1984 (from novel); *Stephen King's Children of the Corn* 1984 (from story); *Silver Bullet* 1985 (sc,from novelette "Cycle of the Werewolf"); *Stephen King's Cat's Eye* 1985 (sc,from stories "Quitters Inc," "The Ledge"); *Maximum Overdrive* 1986 (d,sc,from short story "Trucks" in anthology *Night Shift*); *Stand By Me* 1986 (from novella "The Body"); *Creepshow 2* 1987 (a,from stories "Old Chief Wood'n Head," "The Hitchhiker," "The Raft"); *A Return to Salem's Lot* 1987 (from characters,creative consultant); *The Running Man* 1987 (from novel); *Pet Sematary* 1989 • (a,sc,from novel); *Misery* 1990 (from novel); *Stephen King's Graveyard Shift* 1990 (from short story in anthology *Night Shift*); *Tales From the Darkside, The Movie* 1990 (from story "Cat From Hell").

Kingsley, Ben • Actor • Born Yorkshire, England, December 31, 1943. Meticulous and accomplished stage performer who first earned attention on film with the title role in *Gandhi* (1982). Dividing his time between the screen and stage, Kingsley has appeared in several highly polished, literate productions. He is among the foremost interpreters of the work of Harold Pinter, whether his plays (*Betrayal* 1983) or his screenplays (*Turtle Diary* 1985). • *Fear Is the Key* 1972; *Gandhi* 1982 **(AABA)**; *Betrayal* 1983; *Sleeps Six* 1984; *Harem* 1985; *Turtle Diary* 1985; *Maurice* 1987; *Testimony* 1987; *Pascali's Island* 1988; *Without a Clue* 1988; *Slipstream* 1989; *The Children* 1990; *The Fifth Monkey* 1990; *Una Vita Scellerata/A Violent Life* 1990.

Kinoshita, Keisuke • Director; also screenwriter. • Born Hamamatsu, Shizuoka, Japan, December 5, 1912. *Educ.* Oriental School of Photography. Accomplished in a wide range of genres, Kinoshita made satiric comedies, stirring social dramas and the visually compelling, Kabuki version of *The Ballad of Narayama* (1958). He is probably best known, however, for his numerous sentimental romances of the 1950s and 60s, such as *She Was Like a Wild Chrysanthemum* (1955). *Carmen Comes Home* (1951), about a big-city stripper who shakes up her home town during a short visit, was Japan's first film to be released in color and one of the director's best.

Kinoshita's brother Chuji scored a number of his films, as well as Masaki Kobayashi's epic, *The Human Condition* (1958-61); his brother-in-law Hiroyuki (Hiroshi) Kusuda was the cinematographer on many of his films. • *Gonin no kyodai* 1939 (sc); *Hana saku minato* 1943 (d); *Ikite iru Magoroku* 1943 (d,sc,story); *Kanko no machi* 1944 (d); *Rikugun* 1944 (d); *Osone-ke no asa* 1946 (d); *Waga koi seshi otome* 1946 (d,sc,story); *Fushicho* 1947 (d,sc); *Kekkon* 1947 (d,story); *Hakai* 1948 (d); *Onna* 1948 (d,sc,story); *Shozo* 1948 (d); *Ojosan kampai* 1949 (d); *Yabure-daiko* 1949 (d,sc,story); *Yotsuya kaidan* 1949 (d); *Konyaku yubiwa* 1950 (d,sc,story); *Zemma* 1950 (d,sc); *Karumen Kokyo Ni Kaeru/Carmen Comes Home* 1951 (d,sc,story); *Shonenki* 1951 (d,sc); *Umi no hanabi* 1951 (d,sc,story); *Karumenjunjosu* 1952 (d,sc,story); *Magokoro* 1953 (sc); *Nihon no higeki* 1953 (d,sc,story); *Nijushi no hitomi/Twenty Four Eyes* 1954 (d,sc); *Onna no sono* 1954 (d,sc); *Nogiku no gotokikimi nariki/She Was Like a Wild Chrysanthemum* 1955 (d,sc); *Toi kumo* 1955 (d,sc,story); *Taiyo to bara* 1956 (d,sc,story); *Yuyake-gumo* 1956 (d); *Fuzen no tomoshibi* 1957 (d,sc,story); *Yorokobi mo kanashimi no ikutoshitisuki* 1957 (d,sc,story); *Koni ten no niji* 1958 (d,sc,story); *Narayama-bushi ko/Ballad of Narayama* 1958 (d,sc); *Kazabana* 1959 (d,sc,story); *Kyo mo mata kakute ari nan* 1959 (d,sc,story); *Sekishun-cho* 1959 (d,sc,story); *Fuefukigawa* 1960 (d,sc); *Haru no yume* 1960 (d,sc,story); *Eien no hito* 1961 (d,sc,story); *Futari de aruita iku shunju* 1962 (d,sc); *Kotoshi no koi* 1962 (d,sc,story); *Shito no densetsu* 1963 (d,sc,story); *Utae wakado-tachi* 1963 (d); *Koge* 1964 (d,sc); *Akogare* 1966 (sc); *Natsukashiki fue ya taiko* 1967 (d,sc,story); *Sri Lanka no ai to wakare* 1976 (d,sc,story); *Shodo satsujin-musuko yo* 1979 (d,sc); *Kono Ko Wo Nokoshite* 1984 (d,sc); *Shin Yorokobimo Kanashimimo Ikutoshitsuki* 1986 (d,sc).

Kinski, Klaus • Actor • Born Nikolaus Gunther Nakszynski, Zoppot, Poland, 1926. Sinister-looking performer, in films from 1948. Kinski's piercing eyes and prominent features have led to his being typecast in crazed or obsessed roles, and he has not always resisted the temptation to ham them up. His critical reputation rests on his performances in films by New German Cinema director Werner Herzog, particularly in *Aguirre, The Wrath of God* (1972), *Nosferatu* (1978) and *Fitzcarraldo* (1982). Father of actresses Pola and Nastassja Kinski. • *Morituri* 1948 (a); *Decision Before Dawn* 1952 (a); *Hanussen* 1955 (a); *Kinder, Mutter und ein General* 1955 (a); *Ludwig II* 1955 (a); *Sarajewo* 1955 (a); *Waldwinter* 1956 (a); *Geliebte Corinna* 1958 (a); *A Time to Love and a Time to Die* 1958 (a); *Der Racher* 1960 (a); *Bankraub in der Rue Latour* 1961 (a); *Das Geheimnis der gelben Narzissen* 1961 (a); *Das Rätsel der roten Orchidée* 1961 (a); *Der Seltsame Gräfin* 1961 (a); *Die Toten Augen von London* 1961 (a); *The Counterfeit Traitor* 1962 (a); *Das Gasthaus an der Themse* 1962 (a); *Der Rote Rausch* 1962 (a); *Die Tür mit den sieben Schlossern* 1962 (a); *Das Geheimnis der schwarzen Witwe* 1963 (a); *Das Indische Tuch* 1963 (a); *Kali-Yug, la dea della vendetta* 1963 (a); *Il Mistero del tempio Indiano* 1963 (a); *Picadilly null Uhr zwölf* 1963 (a); *Der Schwarze Abt* 1963 (a); *Die Schwarze Kobra* 1963 (a); *Scotland Yard jägt Doktor Mabuse* 1963 (a); *The Zinker* 1963 (a); *Das Geheimnis der chinesischen Nelke* 1964 (a); *Die Gurft mit dem Rätselschloss* 1964 (a); *Der Letzte Ritt nach Santa Cruz* 1964 (a); *Wartezimmer zum Jenseits* 1964 (a); *Winnetou: II Teil* 1964 (a); *Doctor Zhivago* 1965 (a); *Estambul 65* 1965 (a); *La Guerre secréte* 1965 (a); *Neues vom Hexer* 1965 (a); *The Pleasure Girls* 1965 (a); *Spie contro il mondo* 1965 (a); *Traitor's Gate* 1965 (a);

Circus of Fear 1966 (a); *Das Geheimnis der Gelben Mönche* 1966 (a); *Our Man in Marrakesh* 1966 (a); *Per qualche dollaro in più/For a Few Dollars More* 1966 (a); *Ad ogni costo* 1967 (a); *Die Blaue Hand/Creature With the Blue Hand* 1967 (a); *Carmen, Baby* 1967 (a); *Five Golden Dragons* 1967 (a); *Mister Zehn Prozent-Miezen und Moneten* 1967 (a); *Quien Sabe?* 1967 (a); *Sumuru* 1967 (a); *L'Uomo, l'orgoglio, la vendetta* 1967 (a); *A qualsiasi prezzo* 1968 (a); *Cinque per l'inferno* 1968 (a); *Coplan sauve sa Peau* 1968 (a); *Due volte Giuda* 1968 (a); *Il Grande silenzio* 1968 (a); *Marquis de Sade: Justine* 1968 (a); *Ognuno Per Se* 1968 (a); *Sartana* 1968 (a); *I Bastardi* 1969 (a); *Il Dito nella piaga* 1969 (a); *Double Face* 1969 (a); *E Dio disse a Caino...* 1969 (a); *La Legge dei gangsters* 1969 (a); *Paroxismus* 1969 (a); *Sono Sartana, il vostro becchino* 1969 (a); *Appuntamente col disonore* 1970 (a); *La Belva* 1970 (a); *Count Dracula* 1970 (a); *Giu le mani... carogna* 1970 (a); *I Leopardi di Churchill* 1970 (a); *La Peau de Torpedo* 1970 (a); *Per una bara piena di dollari* 1970 (a); *Prega il morte e ammazza il vivo* 1970 (a); *Wie Kommt ein So Reizendes Mädchen zu Diesem Gewerbe?* 1970 (a); *La Bestia uccide a sangue freddo* 1971 (a); *Black Killer* 1971 (a); *Lo Chiamavano King...* 1971 (a); *La Mano Nascosta di Dio* 1971 (a); *Nella stretta morsa del ragno* 1971 (a); *L'Occhio del ragno* 1971 (a); *La Vendetta è un piatto che si serve freddo* 1971 (a); *Aquirre, der Zorn Gottes/Aguirre, the Wrath of God* 1972 (a); *Doppia taglia per Minnesota Stinky* 1972 (a); *Il Ritorno di Clint il solitario* 1972 (a); *Il Venditore di morte* 1972 (a); *Imperativo categorio: contro il crimine con rabbia* 1973 (a); *La Mano che nutre la morte* 1973 (a); *La Mano spietata della legge* 1973 (a); *Il Mio nome è Shanghai Joe* 1973 (a); *La Morte sorride all'assassino* 1973 (a); *Le Amanti del mostro* 1974 (a); *Le Orme* 1974 • (a); *Who Stole the Shah's Jewels?* 1974 (a); *Un Genio, Due Compari, Un Pollo* 1975 (a); *L'Important c'est d'aimer* 1975 (a); *Lifespan* 1975 (a); *Das Netz* 1975 (a); *Jack the Ripper* 1976 (a); *Nuit d'or* 1976 (a); *Entebbe: Operation Thunderbolt* 1977 (a); *Madame Claude* 1977 (a); *Mort d'un pourri* 1977 (a); *La Chanson de Roland* 1978 (a); *Nosferatu, Phantom der Nacht* 1978 (a); *Zoo-Zero* 1978 (a); *Haine* 1979 (a); *Woyzeck* 1979 (a); *La Femme-Enfant* 1980 (a); *Love & Money* 1980 (a); *Schizoid* 1980 (a); *Buddy Buddy* 1981 (a); *Les Fruits de la Passion* 1981 (a); *Venom* 1981 (a); *Android* 1982 (a); *Burden of Dreams* 1982 (a); *Fitzcarraldo* 1982 (a); *The Soldier* 1982 (a); *Geheimcode Wildganse* 1984 (a); *The Little Drummer Girl* 1984 (a); *The Secret Diary of Sigmund Freud* 1984 (a); *Creature* 1985 (a); *Kommando Leopard* 1985 (a); *El Caballero del Dragon* 1986 (a); *Crawlspace* 1986 (a); *Nosferatu a Venezia* 1987 (a); *Cobra Verde* 1988 (a); *Paganini* 1989 (a,d,sc).

Kinski, Nastassja • Actress • Born Berlin, January 24, 1960. Strikingly attractive lead, best known for her title role in Roman Polanski's sumptuous *Tess* (1979). Kinski has appeared in two films directed by Wim Wenders: *Wrong Move* (1975)—in which she says nothing—and *Paris, Texas* (1984), one of her most affecting performances to date. The daughter of Klaus Kinski and sister of actress Pola Kinski, she married producer M. Ibrahim Moussa in 1984. • *Falsche Bewegung/False Move* 1975; *To the Devil, a Daughter* 1975; *Così come sei* 1978; *Leidenschaftliche Blümchen* 1978; *Tess* 1979; *Cat People* 1982; *One From the Heart* 1982; *Reifezeugnis* 1982; *Exposed* 1983; *La Lune dans le caniveau/The Moon in the Gutter* 1983; *Unfaithfully Yours* 1983; *Frühlingssinfonie/Spring Symphony* 1984; *The Hotel New Hampshire* 1984; *Paris, Texas* 1984; *Harem* 1985; *Maria's Lovers* 1985; *Revolution* 1985; *Maladie d'amour* 1987; *Silent Night* 1988; *In una notte di chiaro di luna/Crystal or Ash, Fire or Wind, As Long As Its Love* 1989; *Torrents of Spring* 1989; *Il Segreto/The Secret* 1990; *Il Sole anche di notte/Night Sun* 1990; *The Insulted and the Injured* 1991.

Kinugasa, Teinosuke • Director; also actor, screenwriter. • Born Mie, Japan, January 1, 1896; died 1982. Former female impersonator who entered films in 1917 as an actor, turned to directing in 1922 and made some of the most formally brilliant Japanese films of the following decades. The few of Kinugasa's early works to have reached the West betray a highly mature, sophisticated talent. His best-known silent films are *A Crazy Page/Page of Madness* (1926), an old print of which was found by Kinugasa in his attic and re-released in the 1970s, and *Crossways* (1928). Both have been hailed for their inventive camera work, which has been compared to that of the celebrated German expressionist films being made during the same period. (It was not until 1929 that Kinugasa himself traveled abroad and encountered European directors and their films.)

In the 1950s and 60s Kinugasa made a number of period dramas noted for their sumptuous color and imaginative use of the wide screen; *Gate of Hell* (1953) was named best film at the 1954 Cannes Film Festival and won an Oscar for best foreign film. • *Hibana* 1922 (d,sc); *Niwa no kotori* 1922 (d,sc); *Choraku no kanata* 1923 (d,sc); *Hanasaka jijii* 1923 (d,sc); *Jinsei o mitsumete* 1923 (d,sc); *Konjiki yasha* 1923 (d,sc); *Ma no ike* 1923 (d,sc); *Onna-yo ayamaru nakare* 1923 (d,sc); *Jashumon no onna* 1924 (d,sc); *Kanojo to unmei* 1924 (d,sc); *Kiri no ame* 1924 (d,sc); *Kishin Yuri keiji* 1924 (d,sc); *Koi* 1924 (d); *Koi towa narinu* 1924 (d); *Kyoren no buto* 1924 (d,sc); *Sabishiki mura* 1924 (d); *Shohin - Shusoku* 1924 (d,sc); *Shohin—Shuto* 1924 (d,sc); *Tsuma no himitsu* 1924 (d); *Koi to bushi* 1925 (d,sc); *Nichirin* 1925 (d); *Shinju yoimachigusa* 1925 (d); *Tsukigata Hanpeita* 1925 (d); *Wakaki hi no Chuji* 1925 (d); *Kirinji* 1926 (d); *Kurutta Ippeiji/A Crazy Page/Page of Madness* 1926 (d); *Tenichibo to Iganosuke* 1926 (d); *Teru hi kumoru hi* 1926 (d,sc); *Akatsuki no yushi* 1927 (d); *Dochu sugoroku bune* 1927 (d); *Dochu sugoroku kago* 1927 (d); *Gekka no kyojin* 1927 (d); *Goyosen* 1927 (d); *Hikuidori* 1927 (d); *Kinnoi jidai* 1927 (d); *Meoto boshi* 1927 (d); *Ojo Kichiza* 1927 (d); *Oni azami* 1927 (d); *Benten kozo* 1928 (d); *Chokun yasha* 1928 (d); *Jujiro/Crossways* 1928 (d,sc); *Kaikokuki* 1928 (d); *Keiraku hicho* 1928 (d); *Reimei izen* 1931 (d,sc); *Tojin Okichi* 1931 (d); *Chushingura* 1932 (d,sc); *Ikinokotta Shinsengumi* 1932 (d,sc); *Futatsu doro* 1933 (d,sc); *Koina no Gimpei* 1933 (d,sc); *Tenichibo to Iganosuke* 1933 (d,sc); *Fyuki shinju* 1934 (d,sc); *Ippon gatana dohyoiri* 1934 (d,sc); *Kutsukate Tokijiro* 1934 (d,sc); *Nagurareta Kochiyama* 1934 (d,sc); *Kurayami no Ushimatsu* 1935 (d,sc); *Yukinojo henge* 1935 (d,sc); *Osaka natsu no jin* 1937 (d,sc); *Kuroda seichuroku* 1938 (d,sc); *Hebihigmesama* 1940 (d,sc); *Kawanakajima kassen* 1941 (d,sc); *Susume dokuritsuki* 1943 (d); *Umi no bara* 1945 (d); *Aru yo no tonosama* 1946 (d); *Joyu* 1947 (d,sc); *Yottsu no koi no monogatari* 1947 (d); *Kobanzame* 1949 (d,sc); *Koga yashiki* 1949 (d,sc); *Satsujinsha no kao* 1950 (d); *Beni komori* 1951 (d,sc); *Meigatsu somato* 1951 (d,sc); *Tsuki no wataridori* 1951 (d,sc); *Daibutsu kaigen* 1952 (d,sc); *Shurajo hibun* 1952 (d,sc); *Jigo Kumen/Gate of Hell* 1953 (d); *Hana no nagadosu* 1954 (d,sc); *Tekka bugyo* 1954 (d,sc); *Yuki no yo no ketto* 1954 (d,sc); *Bara ikutabi* 1955 (d,sc); *Kawa no aru shitamachi no hanashi* 1955 (d,sc); *Yushima no shiraume—onna keizu* 1955 (d,sc); *Hibana* 1956 (d,sc); *Tsukigata Hanpeita* 1956 (d,sc); *Yoshinaka o meguru sannin o onna* 1956 (d,sc); *Naruto hicho* 1957 (d,sc); *Ukifune* 1957 (d,sc); *The Barbarian and the Geisha* 1958 (script supervisor); *Haru koro no hana no en* 1958 (d,sc); *Osaka no onna* 1958 (d,sc); *Shirasagi* 1958 (d,sc); *Joen* 1959 (d,sc); *Kagero ezu* 1959 (d,sc); *Kao* 1960 (sc); *Shirokoya Komako* 1960 (sc); *Uta andon* 1960 (d,sc); *Midaregami* 1961 (d,sc); *Okoto to Sasuke* 1961 (d,sc); *Uso* 1963 (d,screenplay "San jotai"/"Women"/"Types of Women"); *Yoso* 1963 (d,sc); *Yukinojo henge* 1963 (sc); *Malenki beglyets* 1967 (d,sc); *75 Years of Cinema Museum* 1972 (a).

Kirby, Bruno • Actor • Born New York, NY. Versatile character player, remembered as the young Clemenza in *The Godfather Part II* (1974) and the humorless lieutenant Hauk in *Good Morning, Vietnam* (1987). Son of actor Bruce Kirby. • *The Harrad Experiment* 1973; *Superdad* 1973; *The Godfather, Part II* 1974; *Almost Summer* 1977; *Between the Lines* 1977; *Borderline* 1980; *Where the Buffalo Roam* 1980; *Modern Romance* 1981; *Birdy* 1984; *This Is Spinal Tap* 1984; *Flesh + Blood* 1985; *Good Morning, Vietnam* 1987; *The In Crowd* 1987; *Tin Men* 1987; *Bert Rigby, You're a Fool* 1989; *We're No Angels* 1989; *When Harry Met Sally...* 1989; *The Freshman* 1990; *City Slickers* 1991.

Kirkland, Sally • Actress • Born New York, NY, October 31, 1944. *Educ.* Actors Studio. Sometime associate of Andy Warhol who gained a degree of notoriety in the 1960s for her nude stage apearances and other experimental theatrics. Kirkland, a noted acting instructor, earned international recognition for her title role in *Anna* (1987). • *The Thirteen Most Beautiful Women* 1964; *Coming Apart* 1969; *Futz* 1969; *Brand X* 1970; *Going Home* 1971; *Cinderella Liberty* 1973; *The Sting* 1973; *The Way We Were* 1973; *The Young Nurses* 1973; *Big Bad Mama* 1974; *Candy Stripe Nurses* 1974; *Bite the Bullet* 1975; *Breakheart Pass* 1975; *Crazy Mama* 1975; *Pipe Dreams* 1976; *A Star Is Born* 1976; *Private Benjamin* 1980; *The Incredible Shrinking Woman* 1981; *Fatal Games* 1982; *Human Highway* 1982; *Talking Walls* 1982; *Love Letters* 1983; *Anna* 1987 **(AANBA)**; *White Hot* 1988; *Best of the Best* 1989; *Cold Feet* 1989; *High Stakes* 1989; *Paint It Black* 1990; *Revenge* 1990; *Superstar* 1990; *Two Evil Eyes* 1990.

Kirsanoff, Dimitri • *aka* Dimitri Kirsanov • Director • Born Dorpat, Estonia, Russia, March 6, 1899; died 1957. *Educ.* Ecole Normale de Musique, Paris. In France from 1923. Kirsanoff was at the forefront of Parisian avant-garde filmmaking thanks to works such as *Menilmontant* (1924), which combined Soviet-style montage with hand-held camerawork and lyrically composed static shots. Kirsanoff's early silent films, many starring first wife Nadia Sibirskaia, are considered his best works. With the coming of sound the quality of his output declined, though he continued to direct commercial ventures into the 1950s. His second marriage was to editor Monique Kirsanoff. • *L'Ironie du destin* 1923 (a,d,sc); *Menilmontant* 1924 (d,p,sc,ph); *Sables* 1927 (d); *Sylvie Destin* 1927 (d,sc); *Brumes d'Automne* 1929 (d,sc); *Die Nacht von Port Said* 1931 (d); *Rapt* 1934 (d); *Visages de France* 1936 (d); *Franco de Port* 1937 (d,sc); *L'Avion de minuit* 1938 (d,dial); *La Plus belle fille du monde* 1938 (d,sc); *Quartier sans Soleil* 1939 (d,sc); *Le Témoin de minuit* 1952 (d); *Le Craneur* 1955 (d); *Ce soir les Jupons volent* 1956 (d); *Miss Catastrophe* 1956 (d).

Kleiser, Randal • American director; also producer. • Born July 20, 1946. *Educ.* USC Film School, Los Angeles. Former TV director ("Marcus Welby, M.D.," "Starsky & Hutch") who struck lucky at the box-office with his first feature, *Grease* (1978). • *Street People* 1976 (sc); *Grease* 1978 (d); *The Blue Lagoon* 1980 (d,p); *Rich and Famous* 1981 (a); *Summer Lovers* 1982 (d,sc); *Grandview, U.S.A.* 1984 (d); *Flight of the Navigator* 1986 (d); *North Shore* 1987 (exec.p,story); *Big Top Pee-Wee* 1988 (d); *Getting It Right* 1989 (d); *White Fang* 1991 (d); *Return to the Blue Lagoon* 1991 (exec.p).

Klimov, Elem • Director; also executive. • Born Stalingrad, USSR, 1933. Soviet director noted for his documentary-style camerawork and often grotesque, unsympathetic characters. Klimov was the founding First Secretary of the Union of Soviet Filmmakers and earned worldwide acclaim with *Come and See* (1985), a stark, unrelenting account of a young boy's passage to manhood as a partisan in war-torn Byelorussia in the early 1940s. Klimov was married to the late director Larisa Shepitko (1938-1979), whose unrealized final project, *Farewell* (1981), he directed. • *Agonia/Agony* 1975 (d); *Proshchanie/Farewell* 1981 (d); *Idi i Smotri/Come and See* 1985 (d,sc).

Kline, Kevin • Actor; also stage director. • Born St. Louis, MO, October 24, 1947. *Educ.* Indiana University (music, drama, mime); Juilliard (drama). Gifted stage performer and a founding member of John Housman's Acting Company. Kline had won two Tony awards, for *On The Twentieth Century* and *The Pirates of Penzance*, before making an impressive screen debut opposite Meryl Streep in *Sophie's Choice* (1982). He has continued to make regular stage appearances, notably for the New York Shakespeare Festival, alongside his screen work. Married to actress Phoebe Cates. • *The Pirates of Penzance* 1982; *Sophie's Choice* 1982; *The Big Chill* 1983; *Silverado* 1985; *Violets Are Blue* 1986; *Cry Freedom* 1987; *A Fish Called Wanda* 1988 **(AABSA)**; *The January Man* 1988; *I Love You to Death* 1990.

Kline, Richard H. • American director of photography • Born 1926. Versatile, veteran cinematographer whose best work includes the semi-documentary *The Boston Strangler* (1968) and Lawrence Kasdan's film noir, *Body Heat* (1981). • *Chamber of Horrors* 1966 (ph); *Camelot* 1967 (ph) **(AANBPH)**; *The Boston Strangler* 1968 (ph); *Hang 'Em High* 1968 (ph); *Backtrack* 1969 (ph); *A Dream of Kings* 1969 (ph); *Gaily, Gaily* 1969 (ph); *The Moonshine War* 1970 (ph); *The Andromeda Strain* 1971 (ph); *Kotch* 1971 (ph); *Black Gunn* 1972 (ph); *Hammersmith Is Out* 1972 (ph); *The Mechanic* 1972 (ph); *When the Legends Die* 1972 (ph); *Battle for the Planet of the Apes* 1973 (ph); *The Don Is Dead* 1973 (ph); *The Harrad Experiment* 1973 (ph); *Soylent Green* 1973 (ph); *The Harrad Summer* 1974 (ph); *Mr. Majestyk* 1974 (ph); *The Terminal Man* 1974 (ph); *Mandingo* 1975 (ph); *King Kong* 1976 (ph) **(AANBPH)**; *Won Ton Ton, the Dog Who Saved Hollywood* 1976 (ph); *The Fury* 1978 (ph); *Who'll Stop the Rain?* 1978 (ph); *Firepower* 1979 (2u ph); *Star Trek: The Motion Picture* 1979 (ph); *Tilt* 1979 (ph); *Touched By Love* 1979 (ph); *The Competition* 1980 (ph); *Body Heat* 1981 (ph); *Death Wish II* 1981 (ph); *Man, Woman and Child* 1982 (ph); *Breathless* 1983 (ph); *Deal of the Century* 1983 (ph); *Hard to Hold* 1983 (ph); *All of Me* 1984 (ph); *The Man With One Red Shoe* 1985 (ph); *Howard the Duck* 1986 (ph); *Touch and Go* 1986 (ph); *My Stepmother Is an Alien* 1988 (ph); *Downtown* 1990 (ph).

Kluge, Alexander • Director; also screenwriter, producer, author. • Born Halbertstadt, Harz, Germany, 1932. *Educ.* University of Freiburg; University of Frankfurt; University of Marburg. Kluge is the "godfather" of New German Cinema. As one of the originators (some say the driving force) of the 1962 Oberhausen Manifesto, Kluge urged young filmmakers to rebel against the moribund German film establishment. Originally trained as a lawyer, he has written widely about aesthetic theory, film and economics, and as head of the Institut für Filmgestaltung in Ulm, he shaped the talents and consciousness of Wim Wenders and Edgar Reitz, among others. His own films, marked by an acerbic wit, satirize political incongruities through avant-garde editing and narrative techniques.

Kluge's first feature, *Abschied von Gestern/Yesterday Girl* (1966), took eight prizes at the 1966 Venice Film Festival, alerting the world of the imminent revival of the German cinema. The film observes the forces that shape Anita G., a larcenous young lady who's unlucky in love. Many of Kluge's most amusing characters are women facing a repressive sexist society, as with *Gelegenheitsarbeit einer sklavin/Occassional Work of a Female Slave* (1974), in which a girl sells sausages wrapped in political manifestos to workers. Kluge's films often stress the continuum between Germany's past and its present, illustrating the pitfalls of its abiding twin obsessions: materialism and militarism.

Kluge's films are not easily understood by American audiences, even though they often deal with Germany's dependency on America, such as in *Willi Tobler and the Decline of the Sixth Fleet* (1970). His exceedingly specific political satire can parody Marxism as well as capitalism but mystifies most viewers.

In Kluge's view, institutions retreat into their own authority until they cease to serve the purposes for which they were created. His outrage extends even to those who tolerate mediocrity and reinforce it from the bastions of their own institutional allegiances, as in *The Patriot* (1979) and *The Candidate* (1980).

"Society does not serve human beings' needs," Kluge has stated, "but it is so nonaggressive that it does not stimulate a direct struggle." Thus, his villains are as ineffective as his heroes: for example, Ferdinand, the fascistic boob in *Strongman Ferdinand* (1976). Kluge believes that by observing absurdity, human consciousness will aspire to rise above it, and to that end, his films have become increasingly absurdist, in a way that is not, however, inconsistent with German history. He has said, "I create historical characters in an ahistorical society." KJ • *Brutalität in Stein (short)* 1960 (d,p,sc); *Rennen (short)* 1961 (d,p); *Lehrer im Wandel (short)* 1963 (d,p,sc,ed); *Porträt einer Bewahrung (short)* 1963 (d,sc); *Protokoll einer Revolution (short)* 1963 (a,commentary,p); *Poker-Spiel (short)* 1965 (a,adapt,commentary); *Unendliche Fahrt: aber begrenzt (short)* 1965 (story); *Abschied von Gestern/Yesterday Girl* 1966 (a,d,p,sc,from story "Attendance List For a Funeral"); *Frau Blackburn, geb. 5. Jan, 1872, wird gefilmt (short)* 1967 (a,d,sc); *Mahlzeiten* 1967 (tech.adv—art); *Die Artisten in der Zirkuskuppel: Ratlos* 1968 (a,d,sc); *Feuerloscher E. A. Winterstein (short)* 1968 (d,sc); *Ein Arzt aus Halberstadt (short)* 1970 (d,sc); *Willi Tobler und der Untergang der 6. Flotte/Willi Tobler and the Decline of the 6th Fleet* 1970 (d,sc); *Der Grosse Verhau* 1971 (d,p,sc); *Wir verbauen 3 x 27 Milliarden Dollar in einen Angriffsschlachter (short)* 1971 (d,sc); *Besitzburgerin, Jahrgang 1908 (short)* 1973 (d,sc); *Die Reise nach Wien* 1973 (sc); *Gelegenheitsarbeit einer Sklavin/Occassional Work of a Female Slave* 1974 (d,sc); *In Gefahr Grösster Not Bringt der Mittelweg den Tod* 1975 (d,sc,art d); *Der Starke Ferdinand/Strongman Ferdinand* 1976 (a,d,sc); *Die Menschen, die die Staufer—ausstellung vorbereiten* 1977 (d,sc); *Nachrichten von der Staufern (short)* 1977 (d,sc); *Zu boser Schlacht schleich ich heut nacht so bang* 1977 (d,sc); *Deutschland im Herbst* 1978 (d,prod.sup); *Die Patriotin/The Patriot* 1979 (a,d,p,sc); *Der Kandidat/The Candidate* 1980 (d,sc); *Krieg und Frieden* 1982 (a,d,sc,conception); *Auf der Suche nach einer praktisch-realistischen Haltung (short)* 1983 (d,sc); *Die Macht der Gefühle* 1983 (a,d,p,sc); *Der Angriff der Gegenwart auf die ubrige Zeit* 1985 (d,sc); *Vermischte Nachrichten* 1986 (d,p,sc); *Schweinegeld, Ein Märchen der Gebrüder Nimm* 1989 (p).

Knieper, Jurgen • Composer • Born Karlsruhe, Germany. *Educ.* State High School of Music, Berlin. Knieper's sparse, haunting scores have been particularly favored by Wim Wenders. He has also scored several films by Helma Sanders-Brahms, notably *Germany, Pale Mother* (1979). • *Die Angst des Tormanns bein Elfmeter/The Goalie's Anxiety at the Penalty Kick* 1972; *Der Scharlachrote Buchstabe/The Scarlet Letter* 1972; *Falsche Bewegung/False Move* 1975; *Auf Biegen Oder Brechen* 1976; *Der Amerikanische Freund/The American Friend* 1977; *Eierdiebe* 1977; *Kalte Heimat* 1978; *Arabische Nachte* 1979; *Deutschland Bleiche Mutter/Germany, Pale Mother* 1979; *De Witte Van Sichem* 1980; *Christiane F wir Kinder vom Bahnhof Zoo* 1981; *Chambre 666* 1982; *Der Stand der Dinge/The State of Things* 1982; *Der Zauberberg* 1982; *Edith's Tagebuch* 1983; *Einmal Ku'Damm und Zurück* 1983; *Der Kleine Brüder* 1983; *Flugel und Felleln* 1984; *Die Verliebten* 1986; *Rocinante* 1986; *Devil's Paradise* 1987; *Der Himmel über Berlin/Wings of Desire* 1987; *River's Edge* 1987; *Geteilte Liebe* 1988; *Après la guerre* 1989; *Etoile* 1989; *The December Bride* 1990; *End of the Night* 1990; *Paint It Black* 1990.

Knight, Shirley • *aka* Shirley Knight-Hopkins • Actress • Born Shirley Enola Knight, Goessel, KS, July 5, 1937. *Educ.* Philipps University, Enid, OK; University of Wichita; University of California; Lake Forest College. Bright, gifted and outspoken leading lady who earned early critical acclaim in Hollywood for such films as *The Dark at the Top of the Stairs* (1960), but has remained dedicated to the theater. Married British playwright John Hopkins in 1970. • *Five Gates to Hell* 1959; *The Dark at the Top of the Stairs* 1960 **(AANBSA)**; *Ice Palace* 1960; *The Couch* 1962; *House of Women* 1962; *Sweet Bird of Youth* 1962 **(AANBSA)**; *Flight From Ashiya* 1964; *The Group* 1966; *The Dutchman* 1967; *The Counterfeit Killer* 1968; *Petulia* 1968; *The Rain People* 1969; *Secrets* 1971; *Juggernaut* 1974; *Beyond the Poseidon Adventure* 1979; *The Great British Striptease* 1980; *Endless Love* 1981; *The Sender* 1982; *Prisoners* 1983; *Sweet Scene of Death* 1983.

Kobayashi, Masaki • Director • Born Hokkaido, Japan, February 14, 1916. *Educ.* Waseda University, Tokyo (philosophy, Oriental art). Best known for his epic trilogy, *The Human Condition* (*No Greater Love* 1959, *Road to Eternity* 1959, *A Soldier's Prayer* 1961), which documents Japan's wartime atrocities as seen through the eyes of a young pacifist who eventually discovers that the Russians he dreams of reaching in a socialist paradise are indistinguishable from the Japanese militarists. Kobayashi's gift for grand widescreen compositions was also well used in his visually sumptuous and socially critical trilogy of period dramas—*Harakiri* (1962), *Kwaidan* (1964) and *Rebellion* (1967). • *Fushicho* 1947 (ad); *Hakai* 1948 (ad); *Onna* 1948 (ad); *Shozo* 1948 (ad); *Ojosan kampai* 1949 (ad); *Yabure-daiko* 1949 (ad); *Yotsuya kaidan* 1949 (ad); *Karumen Kokyo Ni Kaeru/Carmen Comes Home* 1951 (ad); *Karumenjunjosu* 1952 (ad); *Musuko no seishun* 1952 (d); *Magokoro* 1953 (d); *Nihon no higeki* 1953 (ad); *Kono hiroi sora no dokoka ni* 1954 (d); *Mittsu no ai* 1954 (d,sc,story); *Uruwashiki saigetsu* 1955 (d); *Anata kaimasu* 1956 (d); *Izumi* 1956 (d); *Kabe atsuki heya* 1956 (d); *Kuroi kawa* 1957 (d); *Ningen no joken I-II/The Human Condition/No Greater Love* 1959 (d,sc,dial); *Ningen no joken III-IV/The Human Condition 2/The Road to Eternity* 1959 (d,sc); *Ningen no joken V-VI/The Human Condition III/A Soldier's Prayer* 1961 (d,sc); *Harakiri* 1962 (d); *Karamiai* 1962 (d,p); *Kwaidan* 1964 (d); *Jiouchi* 1967 (d); *Joiuchi/Rebellion* 1967 (d); *Nihon no seishun* 1968 (d); *Dodes 'Ka-den* 1970 (p); *Inochi Bonifuro* 1971 (d); *Kaseki* 1974 (d); *Moeru aki* 1980 (d); *Shokutaku No Nai Ie* 1985 (sc); *Tokyo Saiban* 1985 (d,sc).

Koch, Howard • Screenwriter; also playwright. • Born New York, NY, December 12, 1902. *Educ.* St. Stephen's College, Annandale-on-Hudson NY; Columbia School of Law. Had several plays produced under the auspices of the Federal Theater Project before signing on to write radio shows for Orson Welles's Mercury Theater. Koch's best-known work for Welles was the notorious 1938 adaptation of *The War of the Worlds.* With Warner Bros. from 1940, he wrote several outstanding films, notably *The Letter* (1940) and *Letter from an Unknown Woman* (1948), as well as collaborating on *Casablanca* (1942) with the brothers Epstein.

Following his blacklisting in 1951, Koch used the pseudonym Peter Howard to write the British-produced *Finger of Guilt* (1956), directed by fellow exile Joseph Losey under the pseudonym Joseph Walton. • *The Letter* 1940 (sc); *The Sea Hawk* 1940 (sc); *Virginia City* 1940 (uncred.sc); *Sergeant York* 1941 (sc) **(AANBSC)**; *Shining Victory* 1941 (sc); *Casablanca* 1942 (sc) **(AABSC)**; *In This Our Life* 1942 (sc); *Mission to Moscow* 1943 (sc); *In Our Time* 1944 (sc); *Rhapsody in Blue* 1945 (sc); *Tuesday in November (short)* 1945 (sc); *The Best Years of Our Lives* 1946 (uncred.sc); *Three Strangers* 1946 (sc); *Letter From an Unknown Woman* 1948 (sc); *Border Incident* 1949 (ad); *No Sad Songs For Me* 1950 (sc); *The 13th Letter* 1951 (sc); *Fort Yuma* 1955 (p); *Finger of Guilt* 1956 (sc,from novel *Pay the Piper*); *The Greengage Summer* 1961 (sc); *The War Lover* 1962 (sc); *633 Squadron* 1964 (sc); *The Fox* 1967 (assoc.p,sc).

Koch, Howard W. • Producer, executive; also director. • Born New York, NY, April 11, 1916. Veteran Hollywood producer who began his career as an assistant cutter at 20th Century-Fox. Koch began turning out films in the 1950s, acted as a producer for Frank Sinatra Enterprises from 1961 to 1964 and has enjoyed a long-term association with Paramount Pictures, where he was vice president in charge of production from 1964 to 1966. Son Howard W. Koch, Jr. (born 1945) is also a producer (*Heaven Can Wait* 1978, *Gorky Park* 1983, etc.). • *War Paint* 1953 (p); *Beachhead* 1954 (p); *Shield For Murder* 1954 (d); *The Yellow Tomahawk* 1954 (p); *Big House, U.S.A.* 1955 (d); *Desert Sands* 1955 (p); *Three Bad Sisters* 1955 (p); *The Black Sleep* 1956 (p); *The Broken Star* 1956 (p); *Crime Against Joe* 1956 (p); *Emergency Hospital* 1956 (p); *Ghost Town* 1956 (p); *Hot Cars* 1956 (p); *Pharaoh's Curse* 1956 (p); *Quincannon, Frontier Scout* 1956 (p); *Rebel in Town* 1956 (p); *Bop Girl* 1957 (d); *The Girl in Black Stockings* 1957 (d); *Hell Bound* 1957 (p); *Jungle Heat* 1957 (d); *Outlaw's Son* 1957 (p); *Revolt at Fort Laramie* 1957 (p); *Tomahawk Trail* 1957 (p); *Untamed Youth* 1957 (d); *Voodoo Island* 1957 (p); *War Drums* 1957 (p); *Andy Hardy Comes Home* 1958 (d); *Fort Bowie* 1958 (d); *Frankenstein - 1970* 1958 (d); *Violent Road* 1958 (d); *Born Reckless* 1959 (d); *The Last Mile* 1959 (d); *The Manchurian Candidate* 1962 (exec.p); *Sergeants 3* 1962 (p); *Come Blow Your Horn* 1963 (exec.p); *Robin and the Seven Hoods* 1964 (exec.p); *None But the Brave* 1965 (exec.p); *The President's Analyst* 1967 (p); *The Odd Couple* 1968 (p); *On a Clear Day You Can See Forever* 1970 (p); *A New Leaf* 1971 (p); *Plaza Suite* 1971 (p); *Star Spangled Girl* 1971 (p); *Last of the Red Hot Lovers* 1972 (p); *Badge 373* 1973 (d,p); *Once Is Not Enough* 1975 (p); *Ghost* 1990 (exec.p).

Koenekamp, Fred J. • *aka* Fred Koenkamp • Director of photography • Born Los Angeles, CA, November 11, 1922. Began his career as a film loader at RKO after WWII and became a full-fledged cinematographer in 1966. Koenekamp has earned a reputation as a consistent, meticulous craftsman and has collaborated several times with director Franklin Schaffner. He shared an Oscar with Joseph Biroc for his work on *The Towering Inferno* (1974). Not to be confused with H.F. Koenekamp, Hollywood cinematographer of the silent era. • *Raintree County* 1957 (cam.asst); *Watusi* 1959 (cam.op); *The Four Horsemen of the Apocalypse* 1962 (cam.op); *The Hook* 1963 (cam.op); *One Spy Too Many* 1966 (ph); *The Spy in the Green Hat* 1966 (ph); *Doctor, You've Got to Be Kidding* 1967 (ph); *The Karate Killers* 1967 (ph); *Live a Little, Love a Little* 1968 (ph); *Sol Madrid* 1968 (ph); *Stay Away, Joe* 1968 (ph); *The Great Bank Robbery* 1969 (ph); *Heaven With a Gun* 1969 (ph); *Beyond the Valley of the Dolls* 1970 (ph); *Flap* 1970 (ph); *Patton* 1970 (ph); *Billy Jack* 1971 (ph); *Happy Birthday, Wanda June* 1971 (ph); *Skin Game* 1971 (ph); *Kansas City Bomber* 1972 (ph); *The Magnificent Seven Ride* 1972 (ph); *Rage* 1972 (ph); *Stand Up and Be Counted* 1972 (ph); *Harry in Your Pocket* 1973 (ph); *Papillon* 1973 (ph); *The Towering Inferno* 1974 (ph) **(AABPH)**; *Uptown Saturday Night* 1974 (ph); *Doc Savage, The Man of Bronze* 1975 (ph); *The McCullochs* 1975 (ph); *Posse* 1975 (ph); *White Line Fever* 1975 (ph); *Embryo* 1976 (ph); *Fun With Dick and Jane* 1976 (ph); *Islands in the Stream* 1976 (ph) **(AANBPH)**; *The Bad News Bears in Breaking Training* 1977 (ph); *The Domino Killings* 1977 (ph); *The Other Side of Midnight* 1977 (ph); *The Swarm* 1978 (ph); *The Amityville Horror* 1979 (ph); *The Champ* 1979 (ph); *Love and Bullets* 1979 (ph); *First Family* 1980 (ph); *The Hunter* 1980 (ph); *When Time Ran Out* 1980 (ph); *Carbon Copy* 1981 (ph); *First Monday in October* 1981 (ph); *It Came From Hollywood* 1982 (ph—new footage); *Wrong Is Right* 1982 (ph); *Yes, Giorgio* 1982 (ph); *Two of a Kind* 1983 (ph); *The Adventures of Buckaroo Banzai: Across the 8th Dimension* 1984 (ph); *Stick* 1985 (add.ph); *Stewardess School* 1986 (ph); *Listen to Me* 1989 (ph); *Welcome Home* 1989 (ph).

Konchalovsky, Andrei • Director; also screenwriter. • Born Andrei Mikhalkov-Konchalovsky, Moscow, August 20, 1937. *Educ.* Moscow Conservatory (music); VGIK (film). The son of two poets (his father wrote the Soviet national anthem), Konchalovsky originally studied as a concert pianist before moving on to filmmaking, writing scripts for acclaimed director Andrei Tarkovsky. His short thesis film, *The Boy and the Pigeon*, won first prize in its category at the 1962 Venice Film Festival and his feature debut, *The First Teacher* (1965), established his reputation for finely observed, well-acted character studies. *Asya's Happiness* (1967) was suppressed upon completion but released to critical acclaim in 1988.

In 1979 Konchalovsky's three-and-a-half-hour *Siberiade* was awarded the Special Jury Prize at Cannes, earning him international attention and leading—partly due to the efforts of actor Jon Voight—to his move to the US in 1980. Apart from the 1985 Voight-starrer *Runaway Train*, however, Konchalovsky's American output has been disappointing. Brother Nikita Mikhalkov is also a director and played the role of Alexei in *Siberiade*. • *The Steamroller and the Violin* 1960 (sc); *Malchik i golub/The Boy and the Pigeon (short)* 1961 (d,sc); *Pervyi uchitel/The First Teacher* 1965 (d,sc); *Andrei Rublyov* 1966 (sc); *Istoria Asi Klyachinoi, kotoraya lyubila, da nie vshla zamuzh/Asya's Happiness* 1967 (d,sc); *Dvoryanskoe gnezdo/A Nest of Gentlefolk* 1969 (d,sc); *Dyadya Vanya/Uncle Vanya* 1971 (d,sc); *Romans o vljublehhych/Romance for Lovers* 1974 (d,sc); *Siberiade* 1978 (d); *Maria's Lovers* 1985 (d,sc,song); *Runaway Train* 1985 (d); *Duet For One* 1986 (d,sc); *Shy People* 1987 (d,sc,story); *Homer and Eddie* 1989 (d); *Tango and Cash* 1989 (d).

Korda, Sir Alexander • *aka* Sandor Korda, Sursum Corda • Director, producer, executive • Born Sandor Laszlo Kellner, Turkeve, Hungary, September 16, 1893; died 1956. Korda helped found the Hungarian film industry and worked in the studios of Vienna, Berlin and Hollywood before becoming a naturalized and, in 1943, a knighted Englishman. Together with his brothers Vincent (a production designer) and Zoltan (a director), Korda helped define the cinematic image of the British Empire. (His taste for pomp and pageantry had become apparent as early as 1920, when he filmed an adaptation of Mark Twain's *The Prince and the Pauper* for an Austrian company.)

After a stay in Berlin Korda was invited to Hollywood in 1926, where he soon realized that the talents of his actress wife Maria were in greater demand than his own. He nevertheless acquired a reputation for historical costume dramas before returning to Europe in 1930.

In Paris, Korda collaborated with his brother Vincent on *Marius* (1931) before moving to England and establishing his own company, London Film Productions, in 1932. Within two years he was being hailed as the most important figure in British film, the man who had beaten Hollywood at its own game by directing and producing the lavish and successful spectacle, *The Private Life of Henry VIII* (1932). Although he was to direct several more films, including *Rembrandt* (1936), Korda became increasingly involved with production duties, handing over the directorial reigns to Zoltan.

Vincent completed the fraternal team, though the brothers' work together was punctuated by loud disagreements worked out on the studio floor in a mixture of Hungarian, German and English. One of their arguments concerned the glorification of the British Empire, a theme in *Sanders of the River* (1935), *Drums* (1938) and *The Four Feathers* (1939). Even a film set during the Russian Revolution and featuring Marlene Dietrich, *Knight Without Armour* (1937), emphasized the aplomb of a British intelligence agent, played by Robert Donat, and the public-schoolboy decency of a young Bolshevik sympathizer, as portrayed by John Clements.

In the late 1930s, Korda's patriotic feelings for his adopted country expressed themselves in filmed warnings of imminent threats from abroad: 1936's

...ome opened with a grimly re- ... raid on a city uncomfortably ...ndon; later films relayed a similar ...ge to other audiences, including a ...tral United States policy—with the ...panish Empire or Napoleon's fleet standing in for more contemporary expansionist forces. (Neither was Korda's patriotism limited to the celluloid realm; as well as pawning his life insurance agreement to finance a propaganda film about the Royal Air Force, he also, according to historians of espionage, made his North American offices available to members of Britain's intelligence organizations.)

Korda, whose second wife was actress Merle Oberon, helped launch the careers of Vivien Leigh, Charles Laughton and Robert Donat, among many. He played a significant part in earning a world reputation for British films, and in the process captured a heroic image of the British Empire on celluloid. LR • *A Becsapott ujsagiro* 1914 (d); *Lyon Lea* 1915 (d); *A Tiszti kardbojt* 1915 (d,sc); *Tutyu es Totyo* 1915 (d); *Ciklamen* 1916 (d); *Az Egymillio fontos banko* 1916 (d,sc); *Feher ejszakak* 1916 (d,sc); *A Ketszivu ferfi* 1916 (d); *Magnas Miska* 1916 (d); *Mesek az irogeprol* 1916 (d,sc); *A Nagymama* 1916 (d,sc); *A Nevto Szaszkia* 1916 (d); *Vergodo szivek* 1916 (d); *A Csikos* 1917 (p); *Faun* 1917 (d); *A Golyakalifa* 1917 (d); *Harrison es Barrison* 1917 (d); *A Ketlelku asszony* 1917 (p); *Magia* 1917 (d); *A Peleskei notarius* 1917 (p); *Piros bugyellaris* 1917 (p); *A Riporterkiraly* 1917 (p); *Szent Peter esernyoje* 1917 (d); *Aranyember, Az* 1918 (d); *Karoly Bakak* 1918 (p); *A Kis lord* 1918 (p); *Mary Ann* 1918 (d); *A Testor* 1918 (p); *A 111-es* 1919 (d); *Ave Caesar* 1919 (d); *Feher rozsa* 1919 (d); *Se ki, Se be* 1919 (d); *Yamata* 1919 (d); *Seine Majestät das Bettelkind/The Prince and the Pauper* 1920 (d); *Herren der Meere* 1922 (d); *Eine Versunkene Welt* 1922 (d); *Samson und Dalila* 1923 (d,p,sc); *Das Unbekannte Morgen* 1923 (d,sc); *Jedermanns Frau* 1924 (d); *Tragödie im Hause Hapsburg* 1924 (d); *Der Tanzer meiner Frau* 1925 (d,sc); *Verklungene Wiener Tage* 1925 (producer—"Tragödie im Hause Hapsburg"); *Eine Dubarry von Heute* 1926 (d); *Madame Wunscht keine Kinder* 1926 (d); *The Private Life of Helen of Troy* 1927 (d); *The Stolen Bride* 1927 (d); *The Night Watch* 1928 (d); *The Yellow Lily* 1928 (d); *Her Private Life* 1929 (d); *Love and the Devil* 1929 (d); *The Squall* 1929 (d); *Laughter* 1930 (d,p); *Lilies of the Field* 1930 (d); *The Princess and the Plummer* 1930 (d); *Women Everywhere* 1930 (d); *Marius* 1931 (d); *Men of Tomorrow* 1932 (p); *The Private Life of Henry VIII* 1932 (d,p); *Service For Ladies* 1932 (d); *That Night in London* 1932 (p); *Wedding Rehearsal* 1932 (d,p); *Cash* 1933 (p); *Counsel's Opinion* 1933 (p); *The Girl From Maxim's* 1933 (d,p); *Strange Evidence* 1933 (p); *Catherine the Great* 1934 (d,p); *The Private Life of Don Juan* 1934 (d,p); *The Private Life of the Gannets (short)* 1934 (p); *The Ghost Goes West* 1935 (p); *Moscow Nights* 1935 (p); *Sanders of the River* 1935 (p); *The Scarlet Pimpernel* 1935 (d,p); *Wharves & Strays (short)* 1935 (p); *Fire Over England* 1936 (p); *Forget-Me-Not* 1936 (p); *Fox Hunt (short)* 1936 (p); *Lobsters (short)* 1936 (p); *The Man Who Could Work Miracles* 1936 (p); *Men Are Not Gods* 1936 (p); *Miss Bracegirdle Does Her Duty (short)* 1936 (p); *Rembrandt* 1936 (d,p); *Things to Come* 1936 (p); *21 Days* 1937 (p); *Action For Slander* 1937 (p); *Dark Journey* 1937 (p); *Elephant Boy* 1937 (p); *Farewell Again* 1937 (p); *Knight Without Armour* 1937 (p); *Over the Moon* 1937 (p); *Paradise For Two* 1937 (p); *The Return of the Scarlet Pimpernel* 1937 (p); *The Squeaker* 1937 (p); *The Challenge* 1938 (p); *The Divorce of Lady X* 1938 (p); *Drums* 1938 (p); *Prison Without Bars* 1938 (p); *South Riding* 1938 (p); *Clouds Over Europe* 1939 (p); *The Four Feathers* 1939 (p); *The Lion Has Wings* 1939 (d,p); *The Rebel Son* 1939 (p); *The Spy in Black/U-Boat 29* 1939 (p); *The Conquest of the Air* 1940 (p); *Old Bill and Son* 1940 (p); *The Thief of Bagdad* 1940 (d,p); *Lydia* 1941 (p); *New Wine* 1941 (p); *That Hamilton Woman* 1941 (d,p); *The Jungle Book* 1942 (p); *To Be or Not to Be* 1942 (p); *The Biter Bit (short)* 1943 (p); *Vacation From Marriage* 1945 (d,p); *Panique* 1946 (p); *The Shop at Sly Corner* 1946 (p); *Les Dessous des Cartes* 1947 (p); *An Ideal Husband* 1947 (d,p); *A Man About the House* 1947 (p); *Mine Own Executioner* 1947 (p); *Night Beat* 1947 (p); *Anna Karenina* 1948 (p); *Bonnie Prince Charlie* 1948 (d,p); *Fallen Idol* 1948 (p); *The Small Back Room* 1948 (p); *The Winslow Boy* 1948 (p); *Au royaume des cieux* 1949 (p); *The Cure For Love* 1949 (p); *Interrupted Journey* 1949 (p); *The Last Days of Dolwyn* 1949 (p); *Saints and Sinners* 1949 (p); *That Dangerous Age* 1949 (p); *The Third Man* 1949 (p); *The Angel With the Trumpet* 1950 (p); *The Bridge of Time (short)* 1950 (p); *The Elusive Pimpernel* 1950 (p); *Gone to Earth* 1950 (exec.p); *The Happiest Days of Your Life* 1950 (p); *Miracolo a Milano/Miracle in Milan* 1950 (p); *My Daughter Joy* 1950 (p); *Seven Days to Noon* 1950 (p); *State Secret* 1950 (p); *The Wonder Kid* 1950 (p); *The Wooden Horse* 1950 (p); *Cry, the Beloved Country* 1951 (p); *Flesh and Blood* 1951 (p); *Home at Seven* 1951 (p); *Lady Godiva Rides Again* 1951 (p); *Mr. Denning Drives North* 1951 (p); *Outcast of the Islands* 1951 (p); *Sous le Ciel de Paris* 1951 (p); *Tales of Hoffmann* 1951 (p); *Edinburgh (short)* 1952 (p); *La Fête à Henriette* 1952 (p); *Folly to Be Wise* 1952 (p); *The Holly and the Ivy* 1952 (p); *The Lost Hours* 1952 (p); *The Ringer* 1952 (p); *The Road to Canterbury (short)* 1952 (p); *The Sound Barrier* 1952 (p); *Who Goes There!* 1952 (p); *Captain's Paradise* 1953 (p); *The Heart of the Matter* 1953 (p); *The Man Between* 1953 (p); *The Story of Gilbert and Sullivan* 1953 (p); *Three Cases of Murder* 1953 (p); *Twice Upon a Time* 1953 (p); *Aunt Clara* 1954 (p); *The Belles of St. Trinian's* 1954 (p); *The Constant Husband* 1954 (p); *Devil Girl From Mars* 1954 (p); *The Green Scarf* 1954 • (p); *Hobson's Choice* 1954 (p); *A Kid For Two Farthings* 1954 (p); *The Man Who Loved Redheads* 1954 (p); *The Teckman Mystery* 1954 (p); *The Deep Blue Sea* 1955 (p); *I Am a Camera* 1955 (p); *The Man Who Never Was* 1955 (p); *Marianne de ma jeunesse* 1955 (p); *Raising a Riot* 1955 (p); *Richard III* 1955 (p); *Storm Over the Nile* 1955 (p); *Summertime* 1955 (p); *Smiley* 1956 (p); *The Epic That Never Was* 1965 (producer—"I, Claudius").

Korda, Vincent • Production designer • Born Vincent Kellner, Turkeve, Hungary, 1897; died 1979. *Educ.* Academy of Art, Budapest. Distinguished art director who frequently collaborated with his brothers Alexander and Zoltan Korda. His work on William Cameron Menzies's ambitious science fiction tale, *Things to Come* (1936), was a landmark in feature film production design. • *Marius* 1931 (sets); *Men of Tomorrow* 1932 (sets); *The Private Life of Henry VIII* 1932 (sets); *Wedding Rehearsal* 1932 (sets); *The Girl From Maxim's* 1933 (sets); *Catherine the Great* 1934 (sets); *The Private Life of Don Juan* 1934 (sets); *The Ghost Goes West* 1935 (sets); *Moscow Nights* 1935 (sets); *Sanders of the River* 1935 (sets); *The Scarlet Pimpernel* 1935 (sets); *The Man Who Could Work Miracles* 1936 (sets); *Men Are Not Gods* 1936 (sets); *Rembrandt* 1936 (sets); *Things to Come* 1936 (sets); *21 Days* 1937 (sets); *Action For Slander* 1937 (art d); *Elephant Boy* 1937 (sets); *Over the Moon* 1937 (sets); *Paradise For Two* 1937 (art d); *The Squeaker* 1937 (sets); *The Challenge* 1938 (sets); *Drums* 1938 (sets); *Prison Without Bars* 1938 (art d); *Clouds Over Europe* 1939 (art d); *The Four Feathers* 1939 (sets); *The Lion Has Wings* 1939 (sets); *The Spy in Black* 1939 (art d); *The Conquest of the Air* 1940 (sets); *Old Bill and Son* 1940 (sets); *The Thief of Bagdad* 1940 (pd) **(AABAD)**; *Lydia* 1941 (pd); *Major Barbara* 1941 (pd); *That Hamilton Woman* 1941 (pd) **(AANBAD)**; *The Jungle Book* 1942 (pd) **(AANBAD)**; *To Be or Not to Be* 1942 (pd); *Vacation From Marriage* 1945 (sets); *An Ideal Husband* 1947 (sets); *Bonnie Prince Charlie* 1948 (sets); *Fallen Idol* 1948 (sets); *The Third Man* 1949 (sets); *Miracolo a Milano/Miracle in Milan* 1950 (art d); *Home at Seven* 1951 (sets); *Outcast of the Islands* 1951 (sets); *The Holly and the Ivy* 1952 (sets); *The Sound Barrier* 1952 (sets); *The Story of Gilbert and Sullivan* 1953 (assistance); *Malaga* 1954 (sets); *The Deep Blue Sea* 1955 (pd); *Summertime* 1955 (pd); *Scent of Mystery* 1960 (sets); *The Longest Day*

1962 (sets) **(AANBAD)**; *The Yellow Rolls-Royce* 1964 (art d—European sequences); *The Epic That Never Was* 1965 (art d—"I, Claudius"); *Nicholas and Alexandra* 1971 (art d).

Korda, Zoltan • Director • Born Zoltan Kellner, Turkeve, Hungary, May 3, 1895; died 1961. Followed his brother Alexander from Hungary to Vienna to England, where he became a British citizen in 1945. Korda made a number of entertaining, exotic adventure movies, first in Great Britain (*Sanders of the River* 1935, *The Four Feathers* 1939), and then in the US. His brother Vincent designed the sets for most of his films, and Alexander produced all of his British efforts. • *Karoly Bakak* 1918 (d); *Samson und Dalila* 1923 (uncred.ed); *A Csodagyerek* 1924 (d); *Die Elf Teufel* 1927 (d); *Women Everywhere* 1930 (story); *Men of Tomorrow* 1932 (d); *Cash* 1933 (d); *Sanders of the River* 1935 (d); *Forget-Me-Not* 1936 (d); *Elephant Boy* 1937 (d); *Drums* 1938 (d); *The Four Feathers* 1939 (d); *The Conquest of the Air* 1940 (d); *The Thief of Bagdad* 1940 (assoc.p,d); *The Jungle Book* 1942 (d); *Sahara* 1943 (d,sc); *Counter-Attack* 1945 (d); *The Macomber Affair* 1947 (d); *A Woman's Vengeance* 1948 (d,p); *Cry, the Beloved Country* 1951 (d,p); *Storm Over the Nile* 1955 (d,p).

Korngold, Erich Wolfgang • Composer; also conductor. • Born Brno, Moravia, Austria-Hungary, May 29, 1897; died 1957. Renowned musical prodigy who scored theatrical productions for Max Reinhardt before beginning his memorable film career. In the US from the late 1920s, Korngold worked almost exclusively for Warner Bros. His rich, intricate compositions for films such as *Anthony Adverse* (1936) and *King's Row* (1941) were an important influence on the development of the Hollywood score. • *Noah's Ark* 1929 (m); *Captain Blood* 1935 (m.adapt); *A Midsummer Night's Dream* 1935 (m.arr); *Anthony Adverse* 1936 (m) **(AABM)**; *Give Us This Night* 1936 (song); *The Green Pastures* 1936 (uncred. scored sequences—"The Creation" and "The Flood"); *Rose of the Rancho* 1936 (song); *Another Dawn* 1937 (m); *The Prince and the Pauper* 1937 (m); *Robin Hood* 1938 (m) **(AABM)**; *Juarez* 1939 (m); *The Private Lives of Elizabeth and Essex* 1939 (m) **(AANBM)**; *The Sea Hawk* 1940 (m) **(AANBM)**; *King's Row* 1941 (m); *The Sea Wolf* 1941 (m); *The Constant Nymph* 1943 (m); *Between Two Worlds* 1944 (m); *Deception* 1946 (m); *Devotion* 1946 (m); *Of Human Bondage* 1946 (m); *Escape Me Never* 1947 (m); *Magic Fire* 1956 (a,m.sup,m.adapt).

Kosma, Joseph • Composer • Born Jozsef Kozma, Budapest, Hungary, October 22, 1905; died 1969. *Educ.* Budapest Academy of Music. In France from 1933, Kosma distinguished himself with his scores for several films directed by Jean Renoir; he also co-wrote a number of memorable songs with Jacques Prévert, including "Les feuilles mortes/Autumn Leaves" for Marcel Carné's *Gates of the Night* (1946). During WWII, as a Jew in Nazi-controlled Paris, Kosma worked under the pseudonym Georges Mouque. • *Elet, halal, szerelem* 1929 (m); *La Pêche à la baleine (short)* 1934 (m); *La Marche de la faim (short)* 1935 (m); *Le Crime de Monsieur Lange* 1936 (song); *Jenny* 1936 (a,m); *Un Partie de Campagne* 1936 (m); *La Grande Illusion/Grand Illusion* 1937 (m); *Le Temps des cerises* 1937 (m); *La Bête Humaine* 1938 (m); *La Goualeuse* 1938 (m); *La Marseillaise* 1938 (m.arr); *La Règle du jeu/The Rules of the Game* 1939 (m.arr); *Une Femme dans la Nuit* 1941 (m); *Le Soleil a toujours raison* 1941 (song); *Les Visiteurs du soir* 1942 (song); *Adieu Léonard* 1943 (m); *Les Enfants du Paradis/Children of Paradise* 1945 (m,song); *L'Amour autour de la Maison* 1946 (m); *L'Arche de Noé* 1946 (m); *Aubervilliers (short)* 1946 (m); *Les Chouans* 1946 (m); *L'Homme (short)* 1946 (m); *Messieurs Ludovic* 1946 (m); *Petrus* 1946 (m); *Les Portes de la nuit/Gates of the Night* 1946 (m,song); *Voyage surprise* 1946 (m); *Bethsabée* 1947 (m); *La Dame d'onze heures* 1947 (m); *Le Petit Soldat (short)* 1947 (m); *Les Amants de Vérone* 1948 (m); *Bagarres* 1948 (m); *Le Carrefour des passions* 1948 (m); *D'Homme à Hommes* 1948 (m); *France, nouvelle patrie (short)* 1948 (m); *Le Paradis des pilotes* 1948 (m); *Au Grand Balcon* 1949 (m); *La Belle que voila* 1949 (m); *Désordre (short)* 1949 (m); *Les Eaux troublés* 1949 (m); *L'Ecole buissonnière* 1949 (m); *La Ferme des sept péchés* 1949 (m); *Le Grand rendez-vous* 1949 (m); *Hans le Marin* 1949 (m); *Le Jugement de Dieu* 1949 (m); *Le Sang des bêtes/The Blood of Beasts (short)* 1949 (m); *Black Jack* 1950 (m); *Champions juniors (short)* 1950 (m); *En passant par La Lorraine* 1950 (m); *L'Inconnue de Montréal* 1950 (m); *La Marie du Port* 1950 (m); *Souvenirs perdus* 1950 (m); *Trois télégrammes* 1950 (m); *Vendetta en Camargue* 1950 (m); *Les Anonymes du ciel (short)* 1951 (m); *Le Canard aux cerises (short)* 1951 (m); *Le Cap de l'Espérance* 1951 (m); *La Commune de Paris (short)* 1951 (m); *Dupont-Barbes* 1951 (m); *Festival arobatique (short)* 1951 (m); *Les Feuilles mortes (short)* 1951 (m); *Un Grand Patron* 1951 (m); *The Green Glove* 1951 (m); *Isabelle (short)* 1951 (m); *Juliette ou la clef des Songes* 1951 (m); *Les Loups chassent la nuit* 1951 (m); *Mon ami Pirre (short)* 1951 (m); *Ombre et Lumière* 1951 (m); *Pardon My French* 1951 (m); *Paris est toujours Paris* 1951 (song); *Sans Laisser d'Adresse* 1951 (m); *Si toutes les villes du monde... (short)* 1951 (m); *Agence matrimoniale* 1952 (m); *La Bergère et le ramoneur* 1952 (m); *Operation Magali* 1952 (m); *Le Rideau Rouge* 1952 (m); *Torticola contre Frankensberg* 1952 (m); *Alerte au Sud* 1953 (m); *La Cigale et la fourmi (short)* 1953 (m); *Les Enfants de l'amour* 1953 (m); *François le rhinocéros (short)* 1953 (m); *Les Fruits sauvages* 1953 (m); *Innocents in Paris* 1953 (m); *Le Loup et l'agneau (short)* 1953 (m); *Lumière et l'invention du cinématographe* 1953 (m); *A Paris... un jeudi (short)* 1954 (m); *Les Chiffonniers d'Emmaus* 1954 (m); *Les Evadés* 1954 (m); *Fantaisie d'un jour* 1954 (m); *Huis clos/No Exit* 1954 (m); *Ma Jeannette et mes copains (short)* 1954 (m); *Pas de souris dans le bizness* 1954 (m); *Le Port de Désir* 1954 (m); *Le Village Magique* 1954 (m); *L'Amant de Lady Chatterley* 1955 (m); *Chagall (short)* 1955 (m); *Des gens sans importance* 1955 (m); *Le Devoir de Zouzou* 1955 (m); *Goubbiah* 1955 (m); *Un Grain de bon sens (short)* 1955 (m); *Guillaume Appollinaire (short)* 1955 (m); *M'sieur la Caille* 1955 (m); *Maigret dirige l'enquête* 1955 (m); *Pas de pitié pour les caves* 1955 (m); *Le Sixième jour* 1955 (m); *La Tapisserie au XXe Siècle (short)* 1955 (m); *Tindous (short)* 1955 (m); *Le Trésor d'Ostende (short)* 1955 (m); *Zut, chien des rues (short)* 1955 (m); *Autumn Leaves* 1956 (song); *Calle Mayor* 1956 (m); *Le Cas du Dr. Laurent* 1956 (m); *Cela s'appelle l'aurore* 1956 (m); *Eléna et les hommes/Elena and Her Men/Paris Does Strange Things* 1956 (m); *L'Inspecteur aime la bagarre* 1956 (m); *Je reviendrai à Kandara* 1956 (m); *Le Long des Troittoirs* 1956 (m); *Le Quai des illusions (short)* 1956 (m); *Soupçons* 1956 (m); *Un Certain M. Jo* 1957 (m); *Les Louves* 1957 (m); *Tamango* 1957 (m); *Trois jours à vivre* 1957 (m); *The Doctor's Dilemma* 1958 (m); *G.S.O.* 1958 (m); *Le Grand Erg Oriental (short)* 1958 (m); *Magie du diamant (short)* 1958 (m); *La Chatte* 1959 (m); *La Cocotte d'azur (short)* 1959 (m); *Le Déjeuner sur l'herbe* 1959 (m); *Hey Boy! Hey Girl!* 1959 (song); *Le Testament du Dr. Cordelier* 1959 (m); *Crésus* 1960 (m); *La Française et l'amour/Love and the Frenchwoman* 1960 (m); *Le Huitième jour* 1960 (m); *Katia* 1960 (m); *Neuf étages tout acier (short)* 1960 (m); *Quand midi sonne sur la France (short)* 1960 (m); *Teiva, enfant des îles (short)* 1960 (m); *Accident (short)* 1961 (m); *Henri Matisse ou Le talent du bonheur (short)* 1961 (m); *Les Hommes Veulent vivre* 1961 (m); *Lemmy pour les Dames* 1961 (m); *Le Pavé de Paris* 1961 (m); *Snobs!* 1961 (m); *Le Trésor des hommes bleus* 1961 (m); *A Fleur de peau* 1962 (m); *Le Caporal épinglé* 1962 (m); *Le Poupée* 1962 (m); *La Salamandre d'or* 1962 (m); *A l'aube du troisième jour* 1963 (m); *A la Française* 1963 (m); *Un Drôle de paroissien* 1963 (m); *Fruits amers* 1966 (m); *Un Soir à Tiberiade* 1966 (m); *Le Désordre à vingt ans* 1967 (m); *Le Petit Théatre de Jean Renoir* 1969 (m); *The Virgin Soldiers* 1969 (m).

…ry • Director; also screen- … orn Hermann Kosterlitz, Ber- … 1, 1905; died September 21, … *Educ.* Academy of Fine Arts, Ber- … lexible studio talent who began his …eer as a critic, becoming a scenarist in 1926 and a director in 1932. Leaving Germany the year Hitler took power, Koster made several films in Europe before going to Hollywood. His US debut with *Three Smart Girls* (1937), the first in a series of Deanna Durbin vehicles, was a resounding success and helped bolster the straitened Universal studios.

Koster is perhaps best known for *Harvey* (1950), in which James Stewart played opposite an invisible six-foot rabbit; he also directed *The Robe* (1953), the first film to be shot in CinemaScope. • *Die Waise von Lowood* 1926 (sc); *Kinderseelen Klagen An* 1927 (sc); *Der Mann, der Den Mord Beging* 1931 (sc); *Das Abenteuer der Thea Roland* 1932 (d); *Das Hässliche Mädchen* 1933 (d); *Der Storch Hat Uns Getraut* 1933 (d); *Toto* 1933 (sc); *L'Or dans la rue* 1934 (sc); *Die Privatsekretärin Heiratet* 1935 (d); *Maria Baschkirtzeff* 1936 (d); *One Hundred Men and a Girl* 1937 (d); *Three Smart Girls* 1937 (d); *The Rage of Paris* 1938 (d); *First Love* 1939 (d); *Three Smart Girls Grow Up* 1939 (d); *Spring Parade* 1940 (d); *It Started With Eve* 1941 (d); *Between Us Girls* 1942 (d,p); *Music For Millions* 1944 (d); *Two Sisters From Boston* 1946 (d); *The Bishop's Wife* 1947 (d) **(AANBD)**; *The Unfinished Dance* 1947 (d); *The Luck of the Irish* 1948 (d); *Come to the Stable* 1949 (d); *The Inspector General* 1949 (d); *Harvey* 1950 (d); *My Blue Heaven* 1950 (d); *Wabash Avenue* 1950 (d); *Elopement* 1951 (d); *Mr. Belvedere Rings the Bell* 1951 (d); *No Highway* 1951 (d); *My Cousin Rachel* 1952 (d); *O. Henry's Full House* 1952 (d); *Stars and Stripes Forever* 1952 (d); *The Robe* 1953 (d); *Desiree* 1954 (d); *A Man Called Peter* 1954 (d); *Good Morning, Miss Dove* 1955 (d); *The Virgin Queen* 1955 (d); *D-Day the Sixth of June* 1956 (d); *The Power and the Prize* 1956 (d); *My Man Godfrey* 1957 (d); *Fraulein* 1958 (d); *The Naked Maja* 1959 (d); *The Story of Ruth* 1960 (d); *Flower Drum Song* 1961 (d); *Mr. Hobbs Takes a Vacation* 1962 (d); *Marilyn* 1963 (d); *Take Her, She's Mine* 1963 (d,p); *Dear Brigitte* 1965 (d,p); *The Singing Nun* 1966 (d).

Kotcheff, Ted • *aka* William T. Kotcheff • Director • Born William Theodore Kotcheff, Toronto, Ontario, Canada, April 7, 1931. Director of mostly routine features, with the notable exception of *The Apprenticeship of Duddy Kravitz* (1974), an inspired adaptation of Mordecai Richler's novel. • *Tiara Tahiti* 1962 (d); *Life at the Top* 1965 (d); *Two Gentlemen Sharing* 1969 (d); *Outback* 1971 (d); *Billy Two Hats* 1973 (d); *The Apprenticeship of Duddy Kravitz* 1974 (d); *Fun With Dick and Jane* 1976 (d); *Why Shoot the Teacher* 1976 (prod.cons); *Who Is Killing the Great Chefs of Europe?* 1978 (d); *North Dallas Forty* 1979 (d,sc); *First Blood* 1982 (d); *Split Image* 1982 (d,p); *Uncommon Valor* 1983 (d,exec.p); *Joshua Then and Now* 1985 (d); *The Check Is in the Mail* 1986 (p); *Switching Channels* 1988 (d); *Weekend at Bernie's* 1989 (a,d); *Winter People* 1989 (d).

Kotto, Yaphet • Actor; also director. • Born New York, NY, November 15, 1937. Stage-experienced performer in both supporting and occasional lead roles. Best known for *Live and Let Die* (1973) and *Alien* (1979). • *Nothing But a Man* 1964 (a); *5 Card Stud* 1968 (a); *The Thomas Crown Affair* 1968 (a); *The Liberation of L.B. Jones* 1970 (a); *Man and Boy* 1971 (a); *Across 110th Street* 1972 (a); *Bone* 1972 (a); *The Limit* 1972 (a,d,p,story); *Live and Let Die* 1973 (a); *Truck Turner* 1974 (a); *Friday Foster* 1975 (a); *Report to the Commissioner* 1975 (a); *Shark's Treasure* 1975 (a); *Drum* 1976 (a); *The Monkey Hustle* 1976 (a); *Blue Collar* 1978 (a); *Alien* 1979 (a); *Brubaker* 1980 (a); *Fighting Back* 1982 (a); *The Star Chamber* 1983 (a); *Warning Sign* 1985 (a); *Eye of the Tiger* 1986 (a); *PrettyKill* 1987 (a); *The Running Man* 1987 (a); *Terminal Entry* 1987 (a); *Midnight Run* 1988 (a); *Ministry of Vengeance* 1989 (a); *A Whisper to a Scream* 1989 (a); *Tripwire* 1990 (a).

Kovacs, Laszlo • *aka* Leslie Kovacs • Director of photography • Born Hungary, May 14, 1933. *Educ.* Academy for Theater and Film Art, Budapest. Distinguished cinematographer who has contributed to several notable American movies, from independent productions such as *Five Easy Pieces* (1970) and *The King of Marvin Gardens* (1972) to commercial blockbusters such as *Close Encounters of the Third Kind* (1977) and *Ghostbusters* (1984). • *Ungarn in Flammen* 1957 (ph); *Lullaby (short)* 1963 (ph); *The Nasty Rabbit* 1964 (a,asst.cam.op); *The Time Travelers* 1964 (cam.op); *The Notorious Daughter of Fanny Hill* 1965 (ph); *Hell's Angels on Wheels* 1967 (ph); *A Man Called Dagger* 1967 (ph); *Mondo Mod* 1967 (ph); *Blood of Dracula's Castle* 1968 (ph); *Hell's Bloody Devils* 1968 (ph); *Mantis in Lace* 1968 (ph); *Mark of the Gun* 1968 (ph); *Psych-Out* 1968 (ph); *The Savage Seven* 1968 (ph); *Single Room Furnished* 1968 (ph); *Targets* 1968 (ph); *A Day With the Boys (short)* 1969 (ph); *Easy Rider* 1969 (ph); *That Cold Day in the Park* 1969 (ph); *Alex in Wonderland* 1970 (ph); *Five Easy Pieces* 1970 (ph); *Getting Straight* 1970 (ph); *Rebel Rousers* 1970 (ph); *The American Dreamer* 1971 (a); *Directed By John Ford* 1971 (ph); *Dusty and Sweets McGee* 1971 (uncred.ph—Whiskey a-Go-Go sequence); *The Last Movie* 1971 (ph); *The Marriage of a Young Stockbroker* 1971 (ph); *A Reflection of Fear* 1971 (ph); *The King of Marvin Gardens* 1972 (ph); *Pocket Money* 1972 (ph); *What's Up, Doc?* 1972 (ph); *Paper Moon* 1973 (ph); *Slither* 1973 (ph); *Steelyard Blues* 1973 (ph); *For Pete's Sake* 1974 (ph); *Freebie and the Bean* 1974 (ph); *Huckleberry Finn* 1974 (ph); *At Long Last Love* 1975 (ph); *Baby Blue Marine* 1975 (ph); *Shampoo* 1975 (ph); *Harry and Walter Go to New York* 1976 (ph); *Nickelodeon* 1976 (ph); *Close Encounters of the Third Kind* 1977 (add.ph); *New York, New York* 1977 (ph); *F.I.S.T.* 1978 (ph); *The Last Waltz* 1978 (ph); *Paradise Alley* 1978 (ph); *Butch and Sundance: The Early Days* 1979 (ph); *Heart Beat* 1979 (ph); *The Rose* 1979 (add.ph—concert scenes); *The Runner Stumbles* 1979 (ph); *Close Encounters of the Third Kind: Special Edition* 1980 (add.ph); *Inside Moves* 1980 (ph); *Blow Out* 1981 (uncred.ph); *The Legend of the Lone Ranger* 1981 (ph); *Frances* 1982 (ph); *The Toy* 1982 (ph); *Crackers* 1984 (ph); *Ghostbusters* 1984 (ph); *Mask* 1985 (ph); *Legal Eagles* 1986 (ph); *Little Nikita* 1988 (ph); *Say Anything* 1989 (ph).

Kozintsev, Grigori • Director; also screenwriter. • Born Kiev, Russia, 1905; died 1973. *Educ.* Academy of Fine Arts, Leningrad. An important figure in post-revolutionary art circles, Kozintsev was one of several co-founders—including his future partner Leonid Trauberg—of the influential, experimental theater group, FEX (Factory of the Eccentric Actor). A few years after its foundation in 1921 FEX turned its attention to filmmaking, bringing its eclectic, bombastic style to the screen with the medium-length *The Adventures of Oktyabrina* (1924).

Kozintsev and Trauberg began co-directing feature films later in the decade, reaching their peak with the hugely popular "Maxim" trilogy (*The Youth of Maxim* 1935, *The Return of Maxim* 1937, *The Vyborg Side* 1938), an unromanticized portrait of the formation of a revolutionary. A number of subsequent projects failed to reach completion and the pair finally split, demoralized by the Stalinist suppression of *Plain People* (1945, released 1956). From 1947 on Kozintsev directed alone. His last three films were fine adaptions of literary classics, most notably *Hamlet* (1964); he was planning a version of *The Tempest* at the time of his death. • *Pokhozdeniya Oktyabrini/The Adventures of Oktyabrina* 1924 (d,sc); *Mishki protiv Yudenicha* 1925 (d,sc); *Chyortovo koleso* 1926 (d); *Shinel/The Overcoat* 1926 (d); *Bratishka* 1927 (d,sc); *Soyouz Velikovo Dela* 1927 (d); *Novyi Vavilon* 1929 (d,sc); *Odna* 1931 (d,sc); *Yunost Maksima/The Youth of Maxim* 1935 (d,sc); *Vozvrashchenie Maksima/The Return of Maxim* 1937 (d,sc); *Vyborgskaya storona/The Vyborg Side* 1938 (d,sc); *Boevoi kinosbornik 1* 1941 (sc—"Wstretscha s Maksimom"/"Meeting With Maxim"); *Boevoi kinosbornik 2*

1941 (d,sc—"Slutshai no telegrafe"/ "Incident at the Telegraph Office"); *Prostiye lyudi/Plain People* 1945 (d,sc); *Pirogov* 1947 (d); *Belinsky* 1953 (d); *Don Kikhot/Don Quixote* 1957 (d); *Hamlet* 1964 (d,sc); *King Lear* 1971 (d,sc).

Krabbe, Jeroen • Actor • Born Amsterdam, Netherlands, December 5, 1944. *Educ.* Academy of Dramatic Art, Amsterdam; Academy of Fine Arts. Prominent Dutch actor who first came to prominence in the films of Paul Verhoeven, particularly *Soldier of Orange* (1979) and the cult thriller, *The Fourth Man* (1982). Krabbe has since landed leading roles in a number of international films. Memorable in Joan Micklin Silver's *Crossing Delancey* (1988) as the manipulative, self-important author who unsuccessfully tries to seduce Amy Irving. • *The Little Ark* 1972; *Alicia* 1974; *Een Pak Slaag* 1979; *Soldier of Orange* 1979; *Spetters* 1980; *De Vierde Man/The Fourth Man* 1982; *In de Schaduw Van de Overwinning* 1985; *Turtle Diary* 1985; *Jumpin' Jack Flash* 1986; *No Mercy* 1986; *The Living Daylights* 1987; *Crossing Delancey* 1988; *Jan Cox, a Painter's Odyssey* 1988; *Shadowman* 1988; *A World Apart* 1988; *Melancholia* 1989; *The Punisher* 1989; *Scandal* 1989.

Kracauer, Siegfried • Theoretician, historian; also author. • Born Frankfurt am Main, Germany, 1889; died November 26, 1966. *Educ.* Berlin University. Former editor of the *Frankfurter Zeitung* who moved to the US in 1941. Kracauer is best known for *From Caligari to Hitler: A Psychological History of the German Film* (1947). A landmark in the sociological analysis of cinema, it argues that German films of the 1920s reflected, and even contributed to, a national psychosis that paved the way for fascism.

Kracauer's magnum opus, *Theory of Film* (1960), is a sprawling apologia for the realist film aesthetic. The book argues that, since film is "uniquely equipped to record and reveal" reality, it is therefore under a moral obligation to exploit this tendency; film should bring us back into communication with the real world, thus enabling us to better understand our material existence.

Kramer, Stanley • *aka* Stanley E. Kramer • Producer; also director, screenwriter. • Born Stanley Earl Kramer, New York, NY, September 23, 1913. *Educ.* NYU. Highly regarded producer responsible for several films dealing with social issues in the 1950s and 60s. Kramer began his career in the mid-30s in a variety of minor jobs and produced his first feature, the comedy *So This Is New York*, in 1948. Over the next seven years he worked with some of Hollywood's most gifted writers and directors, including Mark Robson and blacklistees Edward Dmytryk and Carl Foreman. Notable achievements of this period include *Champion* (1949), *The Men* (1950) and *Death of a Salesman* (1951). The year 1952 saw seven Kramer productions, including *The Sniper* and the classic western *High Noon*.

Kramer's career as a director began in 1955 with *Not As a Stranger* and, though uneven, was not without its triumphs. He earned best director Oscar nominations for *The Defiant Ones* (1958), a racial drama featuring one white and one black escapee from a chain gang; *Judgment at Nuremberg* (1961), a war crimes trial saga marred by its unrelieved solemnity and flashy camerawork; and *Guess Who's Coming to Dinner* (1967), in which sterling performances by Sidney Poitier, Spencer Tracy and Katharine Hepburn overcome a saccharine screenplay. • *So Ends Our Night* 1941 (prod.asst); *The Moon and Sixpence* 1942 (assoc.p); *So This Is New York* 1948 (p); *Champion* 1949 (p); *Home of the Brave* 1949 (p); *Cyrano De Bergerac* 1950 (p); *The Men* 1950 (p); *Death of a Salesman* 1951 (p); *Eight Iron Men* 1952 (p); *The Four Poster* 1952 (p); *The Happy Time* 1952 (p); *High Noon* 1952 (p) **(AANBP)**; *The Member of the Wedding* 1952 (p); *My Six Convicts* 1952 (p); *The Sniper* 1952 (p); *The 5,000 Fingers of Dr. T.* 1953 (p); *The Juggler* 1953 (p); *The Wild One* 1953 (p); *The Caine Mutiny* 1954 (p) **(AANBP)**; *Not As a Stranger* 1955 (d,p); *The Pride and the Passion* 1957 (d,p); *The Defiant Ones* 1958 (d,p) **(AANBD,AANBP)**; *On the Beach* 1959 (d,p); *Inherit the Wind* 1960 (d,p); *Judgment at Nuremberg* 1961 (d,p) **(AANBD,AANBP)**; *A Child Is Waiting* 1962 (p); *Pressure Point* 1962 (p); *It's a Mad, Mad, Mad, Mad World* 1963 (d,p); *Invitation to a Gunfighter* 1964 (p); *Ship of Fools* 1965 (d,p) **(AANBP)**; *Guess Who's Coming to Dinner* 1967 (d,p) **(AANBD,AANBP)**; *Journey Into Self* 1969 (a,tech.ad); *The Secret of Santa Vittoria* 1969 (d,p); *R.P.M.* 1970 (d,p); *Bless the Beasts & Children* 1971 (d,p); *Oklahoma Crude* 1973 (d,p); *The Domino Killings* 1977 (d,p); *The Runner Stumbles* 1979 (d,p).

Krasker, Robert • Director of photography • Born Perth, Australia, August 21, 1913; died 1981. *Educ.* Photohandler Schule, Dresden. Accomplished cinematographer who collaborated several times with Carol Reed and is best known for the director's shadow-ridden masterpiece, *The Third Man* (1949). • *Catherine the Great* 1934 (cam.asst); *The Private Life of Don Juan* 1934 (cam.asst); *Forget-Me-Not* 1936 (cam.asst); *The Man Who Could Work Miracles* 1936 (cam.op); *Men Are Not Gods* 1936 (cam.op); *Rembrandt* 1936 (cam.op); *Things to Come* 1936 (cam.asst); *Over the Moon* 1937 (ph—exteriors); *The Squeaker* 1937 (cam.op); *The Challenge* 1938 (cam.op); *Drums* 1938 (cam.op); *The Four Feathers* 1939 (cam.op); *The Thief of Bagdad* 1940 (cam.op); *Dangerous Moonlight* 1941 (cam.op); *One of Our Aircraft Is Missing* 1942 (add.ph); *Rose of Tralee* 1942 (cam.op); *The Gentle Sex* 1943 (ph); *The Lamp Still Burns* 1943 (ph); *The Saint Meets the Tiger* 1943 (ph); *Henry V* 1944 (ph); *Brief Encounter* 1945 (ph); *Caesar and Cleopatra* 1945 (ph); *Odd Man Out* 1947 (ph); *Uncle Silas* 1947 (ph); *Bonnie Prince Charlie* 1948 (ph); *The Third Man* 1949 (ph) **(AABPH)**; *The Angel With the Trumpet* 1950 (ph); *State Secret* 1950 (ph); *The Wonder Kid* 1950 (ph); *Cry, the Beloved Country* 1951 (ph); *Another Man's Poison* 1952 (ph); *Malta Story* 1953 (ph); *Never Let Me Go* 1953 (ph); *Romeo and Juliet* 1954 (ph); *Senso* 1954 (ph); *That Lady* 1955 (ph); *Alexander the Great* 1956 (ph); *Trapeze* 1956 (ph); *Rising of the Moon* 1957 (ph); *The Story of Esther Costello* 1957 (ph); *Behind the Mask* 1958 (ph); *The Doctor's Dilemma* 1958 (ph); *The Quiet American* 1958 (ph); *Libel* 1959 (ph); *The Criminal* 1960 (ph); *El Cid* 1961 (ph); *Romanoff and Juliet* 1961 (ph); *Billy Budd* 1962 (ph); *Birdman of Alcatraz* 1962 (uncred.ph); *Guns of Darkness* 1962 (ph); *The Running Man* 1963 (ph); *The Fall of the Roman Empire* 1964 (ph); *The Collector* 1965 (ph); *The Epic That Never Was* 1965 (cam. op—"I, Claudius"); *The Heroes of Telemark* 1965 (ph); *The Trap* 1966 (ph); *Red (short)* 1976 (ph); *Cry Wolf (short)* 1980 (ph).

Krasna, Norman • Playwright, screenwriter; also producer, director. • Born Queens, NY, November 7, 1909; died November 1, 1984. *Educ.* NYU; Columbia; St. John's University (law). Drama critic turned playwright who went to Hollywood in 1932 and wrote several delightful comedies including *Bachelor Mother* (1939) and *The Devil and Miss Jones* (1941). • *Hollywood Speaks* 1932 (sc,story); *That's My Boy* 1932 (sc); *Love, Honor, and Oh, Baby!* 1933 (sc,adapt); *Meet the Baron* 1933 (story); *Parole Girl* 1933 (sc,from story "Dance of the Millions"); *So This Is Africa* 1933 (sc,story); *The Richest Girl in the World* 1934 (sc,story) **(AANBST)**; *Romance in Manhattan* 1934 (story); *Four Hours to Kill* 1935 (sc,from play *Small Miracles*); *Hands Across the Table* 1935 (sc); *Fury* 1936 (story) **(AANBST)**; *Wife vs. Secretary* 1936 (sc); *As Good as Married* 1937 (story); *The Big City* 1937 (p,story); *The King and the Chorus Girl* 1937 (sc,from story "Grand Passion"); *The First Hundred Years* 1938 (p,story); *Three Loves Has Nancy* 1938 (p); *You and Me* 1938 (story); *Bachelor Mother* 1939 (sc); *It's a Date* 1940 (sc); *The Devil and Miss Jones* 1941 (sc) **(AANBSC)**; *The Flame of New Orleans* 1941 (sc); *It Started With Eve* 1941 (sc); *Mr. & Mrs. Smith* 1941 (sc,story); *Princess O'Rourke* 1943 (d,sc) **(AABSC)**; *Bride By Mistake* 1944 (story); *Practically Yours* 1944 (sc); *Dear*

; *John Loves Mary* ... *e Big Hangover* ... , *Dear Wife* 1950 ... in play *Dear Ruth*); *Be-* ... 951 (p); *The Blue Veil* ... *ar Brat* 1951 (from charac- ... *Dear Ruth*); *Clash By Night* ... , *The Lusty Men* 1952 (p); W... *Christmas* 1954 (sc); *The Ambassador's Daughter* 1956 (d,p,sc); *Bundle of Joy* 1956 (sc); *Indiscreet* 1958 (sc,from play *Kind Sir*); *Let's Make Love* 1960 (sc); *Who Was That Lady?* 1960 (p,sc,from play); *My Geisha* 1962 (sc); *Sunday in New York* 1963 (sc,from play); *I'd Rather Be Rich* 1964 (sc).

Krasner, Milton • Director of photography • Born Milton R. Krasner, Philadelphia, PA, 1901; died July 16, 1988. Began his film career at age 15 and graduated to director of photography in 1933. Although he had shot nearly 90 films before the end of WWII, it was in the postwar period that Krasner distinguished himself. He is best remembered for his neorealist-influenced, black-and-white work in the late 1940s and his glossy CinemaScope compositions—particularly his collaborations with Vincente Minnelli—in the mid-50s. • *70,000 Witnesses* 1932 (cam.op); *Is My Face Red?* 1932 (cam.op); *Ride Him Cowboy* 1932 (cam.op); *A Woman Commands* 1932 (cam.op); *Golden Harvest* 1933 (ph); *I Love That Man* 1933 (ph); *Sitting Pretty* 1933 (ph); *Strictly Personal* 1933 (ph); *Death on the Diamond* 1934 (ph); *The Great Flirtation* 1934 (ph); *Paris Interlude* 1934 (ph); *Private Scandal* 1934 (ph); *She Made Her Bed* 1934 (ph); *Cheers of the Crowd* 1935 (ph); *Forbidden Heaven* 1935 (ph); *Great God Gold* 1935 (ph); *The Great Impersonation* 1935 (ph); *Hold 'Em Yale* 1935 (ph); *Honeymoon Limited* 1935 (ph); *Murder in the Fleet* 1935 (ph); *The Virginia Judge* 1935 (ph); *Women Must Dress* 1935 (ph); *Crash Donovan* 1936 (ph); *The Girl on the Front Page* 1936 (ph); *Laughing Irish Eyes* 1936 (ph); *Love Letters of a Star* 1936 (ph); *Mr. Cinderella* 1936 (ph); *Yellowstone* 1936 (ph); *A Girl With Ideas* 1937 (ph); *The Lady Fights Back* 1937 (ph); *Love in a Bungalow* 1937 (ph); *Mysterious Crossing* 1937 (ph); *Oh, Doctor!* 1937 (ph); *Prescription For Romance* 1937 (ph); *She's Dangerous* 1937 (ph); *There Goes the Groom* 1937 (ph); *We Have Our Moments* 1937 (ph); *The Crime of Dr. Hallett* 1938 (ph); *The Devil's Party* 1938 (ph); *The Jury's Secret* 1938 (ph); *Midnight Intruder* 1938 (ph); *The Missing Guest* 1938 (ph); *Nurse From Brooklyn* 1938 (ph); *The Storm* 1938 (ph); *The Family Next Door* 1939 (ph); *The House of Fear* 1939 (ph); *I Stole a Million* 1939 (ph); *Little Accident* 1939 (ph); *Man From Montreal* 1939 (ph); *Missing Evidence* 1939 (ph); *Newsboy's Home* 1939 (ph); *You Can't Cheat an Honest Man* 1939 (ph); *The Bank Dick* 1940 (ph); *Diamond Frontier* 1940 (ph); *Hired Wife* 1940 (ph); *The House of the Seven Gables* 1940 (ph); *The Invisible Man Returns* 1940 (ph); *Oh, Johnny, How You Can Love!* 1940 (ph); *Private Affairs* 1940 (ph); *Sandy Is a Lady* 1940 (ph); *Ski Patrol* 1940 (ph); *Trail of the Vigilantes* 1940 (ph); *Zanzibar* 1940 (ph); *Bachelor Daddy* 1941 (ph); *Buck Privates* 1941 (ph); *The Lady From Cheyenne* 1941 (ph); *This Woman Is Mine* 1941 (ph); *Too Many Blondes* 1941 (ph); *Arabian Nights* 1942 (ph) **(AANBPH)**; *A Gentleman After Dark* 1942 (ph); *The Ghost of Frankenstein* 1942 (ph); *Men of Texas* 1942 (ph); *Pardon My Sarong* 1942 (ph); *Paris Calling* 1942 (ph); *The Spoilers* 1942 (ph); *Gung Ho!* 1943 (ph); *The Mad Ghoul* 1943 (ph); *So's Your Uncle* 1943 (ph); *Two Tickets to London* 1943 (ph); *We've Never Been Licked* 1943 (ph); *Hat Check Honey* 1944 (ph); *The Invisible Man's Revenge* 1944 (ph); *The Woman in the Window* 1944 (ph); *Along Came Jones* 1945 (ph); *Delightfully Dangerous* 1945 (ph); *Scarlet Street* 1945 (ph); *The Dark Mirror* 1946 (ph); *Without Reservations* 1946 (ph); *A Double Life* 1947 (ph); *The Egg and I* 1947 (ph); *The Farmer's Daughter* 1947 (ph); *Something in the Wind* 1947 (ph); *The Accused* 1948 (ph); *The Saxon Charm* 1948 (ph); *Up in Central Park* 1948 (ph); *Holiday Affair* 1949 (ph); *House of Strangers* 1949 (ph); *The Set-Up* 1949 (ph); *All About Eve* 1950 (ph) **(AANBPH)**; *No Way Out* 1950 (ph); *Three Came Home* 1950 (ph); *Half Angel* 1951 (ph); *I Can Get It For You Wholesale* 1951 (ph); *The Model and the Marriage Broker* 1951 (ph); *People Will Talk* 1951 (ph); *Rawhide* 1951 (ph); *Deadline U.S.A.* 1952 (ph); *Dreamboat* 1952 (ph); *Monkey Business* 1952 (ph); *O. Henry's Full House* 1952 (ph—"The Ransom of Red Chief"); *Phone Call From a Stranger* 1952 (ph); *Dream Wife* 1953 (ph); *Taxi* 1953 (ph); *Vicki* 1953 (ph); *Demetrius and the Gladiators* 1954 (ph); *Desiree* 1954 (ph); *Garden of Evil* 1954 (ph); *Three Coins in the Fountain* 1954 (ph) **(AABPH)**; *The Girl in the Red Velvet Swing* 1955 (ph); *How to Be Very, Very Popular* 1955 (ph); *The Rains of Ranchipur* 1955 (ph); *The Seven Year Itch* 1955 (ph); *23 Paces to Baker Street* 1956 (ph); *An Affair to Remember* 1956 (ph) **(AANBPH)**; *Boy on a Dolphin* 1956 (ph); *Bus Stop* 1956 (ph); *Kiss Them For Me* 1957 (ph); *A Certain Smile* 1958 (ph); *The Gift of Love* 1958 (ph); *The Remarkable Mr. Pennypacker* 1958 (ph); *Count Your Blessings* 1959 (ph); *The Man Who Understood Women* 1959 (ph); *Bells Are Ringing* 1960 (ph); *Home From the Hill* 1960 (ph); *Go Naked in the World* 1961 (ph); *King of Kings* 1961 (ph); *The Four Horsemen of the Apocalypse* 1962 (ph); *How the West Was Won* 1962 (ph—"The Outlaws") **(AANBPH)**; *Sweet Bird of Youth* 1962 (ph); *Two Weeks in Another Town* 1962 (ph); *Advance to the Rear* 1963 (ph); *The Courtship of Eddie's Father* 1963 (ph); *Love With the Proper Stranger* 1963 (ph) **(AANBPH)**; *A Ticklish Affair* 1963 (ph); *Fate Is the Hunter* 1964 (ph) **(AANBPH)**; *Goodbye, Charlie* 1964 (ph); *Looking For Love* 1964 (ph); *Red Line 7000* 1965 (ph); *The Sandpiper* 1965 (ph); *Made in Paris* 1966 (ph); *The Singing Nun* 1966 (ph); *The Ballad of Josie* 1967 (ph); *Don't Just Stand There!* 1967 (ph); *Hurry Sundown* 1967 (ph); *The St. Valentine's Day Massacre* 1967 (ph); *The Venetian Affair* 1967 (ph); *The Sterile Cuckoo* 1969 (ph); *Beneath the Planet of the Apes* 1970 (ph).

Krige, Alice • Actress • Born Upington, South Africa, June 28, 1954. *Educ.* Central School of Speech and Drama, London. Stage, TV and film actress, in the U.K. since the age of 22. • *Chariots of Fire* 1981; *Ghost Story* 1981; *King David* 1985; *Barfly* 1987; *Haunted Summer* 1988; *See You in the Morning* 1989.

Kristel, Sylvia • Actress • Born Utrecht, Netherlands, September 28, 1952. Became an erotic icon of the mid-1970s thanks to her title role in the softcore feature *Emmanuelle* (1974) and two of its several sequels. Kristel has also appeared in films by noted directors Fons Rademakers (*Because of the Cats* 1973), Alain Robbe-Grillet (*Le Jeu avec le feu* 1974) and Claude Chabrol (*Alice or the Last Escapade* 1976). • *Frank en Eva* 1973; *Naakt over de schutting* 1973; *Niet voor de poesen/Because of the Cats* 1973; *Emmanuelle* 1974; *Le Jeu avec le feu* 1974; *Un Linceul n'a pas de poches* 1974; *Der Lieberschuler* 1975; *Alice ou la derniére Fugue/Alice or the Last Escapade* 1976; *Emmanuelle l'anti-vièrge* 1976; *Une Femme Fidèle* 1976; *La Marge* 1976; *René la Canne* 1976; *Goodbye Emmanuelle* 1978; *Letti Selvaggi* 1978; *Mysteries* 1978; *Pastorale 1943* 1978; *Tigers in Lipstick* 1978; *The 5th Musketeer* 1979; *The Concorde-Airport '79* 1979; *Un Amore in prima classe* 1980; *The Nude Bomb* 1980; *Private Lessons* 1980; *Lady Chatterley's Lover* 1981; *Emmanuelle 4* 1983; *Private School* 1983; *Mata Hari* 1985; *Rote Hitze* 1985; *The Big Bet* 1986; *Dracula's Widow* 1988; *The Arrogant* 1989.

Kristofferson, Kris • *aka* Kris Karson • Singer, songwriter, actor • Born Brownsville, TX, June 22, 1936. *Educ.* Pomona College, CA (creative writing); Oxford. Former Rhodes scholar and English literature teacher at West Point who turned to songwriting and helped rejuvenate the country-and-western scene in the late 1960s and early 70s with songs such as "Sunday Morning Comin' Down," "Help Me Make It Through the Night" and "Me and Bobby McGee." Kristofferson made his film acting debut in 1971 with a bit part in *The Last Movie*, directed by Dennis Hopper. He has starred opposite actresses including Ellen Burstyn (*Alice Doesn't Live Here*

Anymore 1974) and Barbra Streisand (*A Star Is Born* 1976). Divorced from singer Rita Coolidge. • *Cisco Pike* 1971 (a,songs); *The Last Movie* 1971 (a,m); *Two-Lane Blacktop* 1971 (song); *Fat City* 1972 (songs); *The Gospel Road* 1972 (song); *Blume in Love* 1973 (a,song); *Pat Garrett and Billy the Kid* 1973 (a); *Alice Doesn't Live Here Anymore* 1974 (a); *Bring Me the Head of Alfredo Garcia* 1974 (a); *Janis* 1974 (song); *The Sailor Who Fell From Grace With the Sea* 1975 (a,song); *Vigilante Force* 1975 (a); *A Star Is Born* 1976 (a); *Semi-Tough* 1977 (a); *Convoy* 1978 (a); *Saint Jack* 1979 (song); *Beyond Reasonable Doubt* 1980 (song); *Heaven's Gate* 1980 (a); *Honeysuckle Rose* 1980 (song); *One-Trick Pony* 1980 (song); *Maeve* 1981 (song); *Rollover* 1981 (a); *Traveller* 1981 (song); *Flashpoint* 1984 (a); *Songwriter* 1984 (a,m,song) **(AANBSS)**; *Trouble in Mind* 1985 (a,song); *Something Wild* 1986 (song); *Mascara* 1987 (song); *Big Top Pee-Wee* 1988 (a); *Walking After Midnight* 1988 (m); *Millennium* 1989 (a); *Tennessee Nights* 1989 (m); *Welcome Home* 1989 (a); *Perfume of the Cyclone* 1990 (a).

Kubrick, Stanley • Director; also screenwriter, producer. • Born New York, NY, July 26, 1928. One of the most consistently interesting filmmakers of the last 30 years, Stanley Kubrick has seen his work praised and damned with equal vigor. Just as his singularly brilliant visual style has won him great acclaim, his unconventional sense of narrative has often elicited critical scorn. Above all, he has remained a unique artist in a medium dominated by repetition and imitation. If his ambitious vision has at times exceeded his capacity to satisfy the demands of mainstream filmmaking, this chink in his aesthetic armor only serves to highlight the distinctiveness of Kubrick's cinema.

After some success as a photographer for *Look* magazine in the late 1940s, the young Kubrick produced and sold several documentaries before attempting a pair of self-financed low-budget features—*Fear and Desire* (1953) and *Killer's Kiss* (1955). Little in these early efforts suggests the brilliance to come. Working with producer James B. Harris, Kubrick was able to graduate to professional cast and crew with his next effort, *The Killing* (1956), a well-paced, assured drama about a race track heist. At a time when independent filmmakers were rare, critics began to take notice.

Paths of Glory (1957) marked Kubrick's emergence as a major director. This WWI saga is a sharp and intelligent indictment of military practice and psychology. It is also a powerful piece of filmmaking, as Kubrick synthesizes the lessons he has learned about composition and camera movement. He proved that talent could be applied to Hollywood subject matter with *Spartacus* (1960), his first—and only—work-for-hire, a widescreen, technicolor epic typical of the 1950s.

Having proved he could succeed as a Hollywood director, Kubrick left the US for England in 1961. He has worked there ever since, developing and producing only seven films in 30 years, each meticulously crafted, each markedly different from the others.

Lolita (1962) is an adaptation of Vladimir Nabokov's controversial novel about a middle-aged man's infatuation with a 12-year-old girl. Though Kubrick has since complained that over-zealous censors kept him from exploring the story in appropriately lubricious detail (two years were even added to Lolita's age), the film stands today as a superb example of understated, double-entendre comedy.

The ironic touch he displayed in *Lolita* was blown up to cosmic proportions for his next film, *Dr. Strangelove or: How I Learned to Stop Worrying and Love the Bomb* (1964), perhaps the most deliciously satirical comedy of the last three decades. (Ironically, the project began as a serious thriller about the possibility of nuclear Armageddon.) Kubrick's dark laughter at man's penchant for destroying himself acquired him a reputation for coldness and inhumanity that has followed him to this day.

Despite some moral backlash, the successes of *Lolita* and *Strangelove*, along with his earlier work as a hired hand on *Spartacus*, earned Kubrick the freedom to choose his own subjects and, more importantly, to exert total control over the filmmaking process, a rare freedom for any filmmaker.

The first product of this arrangement was the science-fiction classic (and quintessential late 60s "head" movie), *2001: A Space Odyssey* (1968). Five years in the making, this film redefined the boundaries of the genre and established visual conventions, filmic metaphors and special-effects technology that have remained standards for the industry well into the 1990s. As visually hypnotic as it was narratively daring (little dialogue, no final explanations, a timespan of eons), *2001* made Kubrick a cultural hero. Despite mixed reviews at the time of its release, it has proven to be as stylistically influential as any film released in the last 25 years.

Further cementing his anti-establishment reputation, Kubrick followed *2001* with another futuristic work, *A Clockwork Orange* (1971), adapted from the novel by Anthony Burgess. No critic could take an uncommitted stance toward this film about a violent and amoral punk, Alex (Malcolm McDowell), whose ruthless behavior is reconditioned by the—equally diabolical—state. Kubrick's camera moved with an audacity unrivaled in contemporary cinema and his reputation as a filmmak[...] total control of his craft was firmly e[...]lished.

Barry Lyndon (1975) was a bold attempt to bring modern techniques to bear upon a narrative set in the 18th century. Kubrick spent as much technical effort and expertise recreating the lighting and imagery of Thackeray's novel as he had done inventing a future in his two previous films. The commercial failure of *Barry Lyndon* may have influenced Kubrick's recent choices for adaptation: Stephen King's horror novel *The Shining* (1980) and Gustav Hasford's tale of Vietnam combat, *Full Metal Jacket* (1987). While these films contain memorable sequences and reiterate Kubrick's previous themes of dehumanization and alienation in contemporary society, they failed to arouse the kind of excitement and controversy engendered by his earlier films. The peak Kubrick achieved from *Strangelove* to *A Clockwork Orange* may be beyond his (or anyone's) reach today. JCP, JM • *Day of the Fight* 1951 (d,ph,ed,sound); *Flying Padre* 1951 (d,ph,ed,sound); *The Seafarers (short)* 1952 (d,ph); *Fear and Desire* 1953 (d,p,sc,ph,ed); *Killer's Kiss* 1955 (d,p,sc,story,ph,ed); *The Killing* 1956 (d,sc); *Paths of Glory* 1957 (d,sc); *Spartacus* 1960 (d); *Lolita* 1962 (d); *Dr. Strangelove; or, How I Learned to Stop Worrying and Love the Bomb* 1964 (d,p,sc) **(AANBD,AANBP,AANBSC)**; *2001: A Space Odyssey* 1968 (sc,special photographic effects designer and director,d,p) **(AANBD,AANBSC,AABFX)**; *A Clockwork Orange* 1971 (d,p,sc,add.ph) **(AANBD,AANBP,AANBSC)**; *Barry Lyndon* 1975 (d,p,sc) **(AANBD,AANBP, AANBSC)**; *The Shining* 1980 (d,p,sc); *Full Metal Jacket* 1987 (d,p,sc) **(AANBSC)**.

Kuleshov, Lev • *aka* Leo Kuleshov • Director; also screenwriter, art director, film theoretician. • Born Lev Vladimovich Kuleshov, Tambov, Russia, January 14, 1899; died 1970. *Educ.* School of Art, Architecture and Sculpture, Moscow. Undeservedly overlooked by film historians, Lev Kuleshov was the first theorist of Soviet cinema whose experiments with juxtaposing the face of an actor and various other images revealed the impact of montage. Pudovkin and Eisenstein have often been credited with this discovery, although their own testimony shows they credited Kuleshov, who was their teacher.

In 1917, just before the Revolution, the 18-year-old Kuleshov made his first short film, *The Project of Engineer Prite*, and published his first articles which reflected an expressionistic vision, comparable to that of German filmmakers, and exceptionally advanced for the relatively primitive state of Russian cinema. His radical aesthetics suited the leaders of [illegible] as dispatched to [illegible] men on the [illegible]

[illegible] Moscow, Kuleshov [illegible] of the First State Film [illegible] be sent to the western [illegible] ment a Polish uprising. [illegible] riences informed *On the Red F*[illegible] 20), but the style of the film owe[illegible] great deal to American chase films and D.W. Griffith, whose *Intolerance* exerted a strong influence on Kuleshov and his teaching. These American enthusiasms would eventually cause Kuleshov political problems, particularly after *By the Law* (1926), adapted from a Jack London story about the Klondike gold rush.

Meanwhile, however, Kuleshov's famous "films without film" workshops, held from 1920 to 1923, prepared filmmakers for the days when they could obtain raw stock to put in their empty cameras. Kuleshov's next important work was *The Extraordinary Adventures of Mr. West in the Land of the Bolsheviks* (1924), a comedy about an American confused and exploited by Revolutionaries. A steady output of films, *The Death Ray* (1925), *By the Law*, *The Journalist* (1927), *The Gay Canary* (1929), *Two-Buldi-Two* (1929) and *Forty Hearts* (1931), paralleled his career as a gifted teacher, but his increasing emphasis on internationalism made him a target of Stalinists in the 30s and his filmmaking career was temporarily halted in 1933.

In 1940, he was allowed to make *The Siberians*, followed by *Incident on a Volcano* (1941), *Timour's Oath* (1942) and *We From the Urals* (1944), but these were films with no particular appeal beyond the USSR. Kuleshov's considerable importance to Soviet filmmaking, including the publication of his classic textbook on direction (*Fundamentals of Film Direction*, 1941) was not acknowledged until 1960, when film historian Jay Leyda published *Kino*, a reassessment of Soviet film history. With his significance now recognized even in the West, Kuleshov was invited to sit on juries of film festivals and attend retrospectives of his work. KJ • *Chernaia trex dnei* 1917 (art d); *Korol Parizha* 1917 (art d); *Nabat* 1917 (art d); *Teni liubvi* 1917 (art d); *Za schastem* 1917 (a,art d,d); *Zhizn trex dnei* 1917 (art d); *Miss Meri* 1918 (art d); *Pesn'liubvi nedopetaia* 1918 (a,art d,d); *Proekt inzhenera Praita/The Project of Engineer Prite* 1918 (art d,d); *Sliakot bulvarnaia* 1918 (art d); *Vdova* 1918 (art d); *Na Krasnom fronte/On the Red Front* 1920 (a,d,sc); *Neobychainye priklucheniya Mistera Vesta v stranya Bolshevikov/The Extraordinary Adventures of Mr. West in the Land of the Bolsheviks* 1924 (d,sc); *Luch smerti/The Death Ray* 1925 (a,d); *Parovoz No. 10006 (short)* 1926 (d); *Po zakonu/By the Law* 1926 (d); *Zhurnalista/Your Acquaintance* 1927 (d); *Veselaia kanaraika/The Gay Canary* 1929 (d); *Dva-buldi-dva* 1930 (d); *Sasha* 1930 (sc); *Sorokserdets/Forty Hearts (short)* 1931 (d); *Gorizont* 1932 (d,sc); *Velikii uteshitel* 1933 (d,sc,art d); *Dohunda* 1934 (d); *Theft of Sight* 1934 (prod.sup); *Sibiraki/Siberians* 1940 (d); *Sluchai v vulkane/Incident in a Volcano* 1941 (d); *Kliatva Timura/Timour's Oath* 1942 (d); *Boevoi kinosbornik 13* 1943 (d); *My s Urala/We From the Urals* 1944 (d).

Kurosawa, Akira • Director, screenwriter • Born Omori, Tokyo, March 23, 1910. *Educ.* Doshusha School of Western Painting. Akira Kurosawa is unquestionably the best known Japanese filmmaker in the West. This can perhaps be best explained by the fact that he is not so much a Japanese or a Western filmmaker, but that he is a "modern" filmmaker. Like postwar Japan itself, he combines the ancient traditions with a distinctly modern, Western twist. Kurosawa got his start in films following an education which included study of Western painting, literature and political philosophy. His early films were made under the stringent auspices of the militaristic government then in power and busily engaged in waging the Pacific war. While one can detect aspects of the prowar ideology in early works like *The Men Who Tread on the Tiger's Tail* (1945) or, more especially, *Sanshiro Sugata* (1943), these films are notable more for stylistic experimentation than prowar inspiration. Before he had a chance to mature under these conditions, Kurosawa, like all of Japan he experienced the American occupation. Under its auspices he produced pro-democracy films, the most appealing of which is *No Regrets for Our Youth* (1946), interestingly his only film which has a woman as its primary protaganist. His ability to make films that could please Japanese militarists or American occupiers should not be taken as either cultural schizophrenia or political fence-sitting, for at their best these early films have a minimal value as propaganda, and tend to reveal early glimpses of the major themes which would dominate his cinema. His style, too, is an amalgam, a deft dialectic of the great pictorial traditions of the silent cinema and the dynamism of the Soviet cinema and the Golden Age of Hollywood filmmaking.

Above all, Kurosawa is a modern filmmaker, portraying the ethical and metaphysical dilemmas characteristic of postwar culture, the world of the atomic bomb, which has rendered certainty and dogma absurd. The consistency at the heart of Kurosawa's work is his exploration of the concept of heroism. Whether portraying the world of the wandering swordsman, the intrepid policeman or the the civil servant, Kurosawa focuses on men faced with ethical and moral choices. The choice of action suggests that Kurosawa's heroes share the same dilemma as Camus' existential protagonists, but for Kurosawa the choice is to act morally, to work for the betterment of one's fellow men.

Perhaps because Kurosawa experienced the twin devastations of the great Kanto earthquake of 1923 and WWII, his cinema focuses on times of chaos. From the destruction of the glorious Heian court society that surrounds the world of *Rashomon* (1950) to the never-ending destruction of the civil war era of the 16th century that gives *The Seven Samurai* (1954) its dramatic impetus, to the savaged Tokyo in the wake of US bombing raids in *Drunken Angel* (1948), to the ravages of the modern bureaucratic mind-set that pervade *Ikiru* (1952) and *The Bad Sleep Well* (1960): Kurosawa's characters are situated in periods of metaphysical eruption, threatened equally by moral destruction and physical annihilation; in a world in which God is dead and nothing is certain. But it is his hero who, living in a world of moral chaos, in a vacuum of ethical and behavorial standards, nevertheless chooses to act for the public good.

Kurosawa was dubbed "Japan's most Western director" by critic Donald Richie at a time when few Westerners had seen many of the director's films and at a time when the director was in what should have been merely the middle of his career. Richie felt that Kurosawa was Western in the sense of being an original creator, as distinct from doing the more rigidly generic or formulaic work of most Japanese directors during the height of Kurosawa's creativity. And indeed some of the director's best work is completely "sui generis," drawing upon individual genius such as few filmmakers in the history of world cinema have. *Rashomon*, *Ikiru* and *Record of a Living Being* (1955) defy classification and are stunning in their originality of style, theme and setting. Furthermore, Kurosawa's attractions to the West were apparent in both content and form. His adaptations from Western literature, although not unique in Japanese cinema, are among his finest films, with *Throne of Blood* (1957, from *Macbeth*) and *Ran* (1985, from *King Lear*) standing among the finest versions of Shakespeare ever put on film. And if Western high culture obviously appealed to him, so did more popular, even pulp forms, as evinced by critically acclaimed adaptations of Dashiell Hammet's *Red Harvest* to fashion *Yojimbo* (1961) and Ed McBain's *King's Ransom* to create the masterful *High and Low* (1962).

Yet for all of the Western adaptations and the attraction to Hollywood and Soviet-style montage, Kurosawa's status as a Japanese filmmaker can never be doubted. If, as has often been remarked, his period films have similarities with Hollywood westerns, they are nevertheless accurately drawn from the turmoil of Japanese history. If he has been attracted to Shakespearean theater, he has equally been drawn to the rarefied world of Japanese Noh drama. And if Kurosawa is a master of dynamic montage, he is equally the master of the Japanese trademarks of the long take and gracefully mobile camera.

Thus to see Kurosawa as somehow a "Western" filmmaker is not only to ignore the traditional bases for much of his style and many of his themes, but to do a disservice to the nature of film style and culture across national boundaries. Kurosawa's cinema may be taken as paradigmatic of the nature of modern changing Japan, of how influences from abroad are adapted, transformed and made new by the genius of the Japanese national character, which remains distinctive yet ever-changing. And if Kurosawa tends to focus on an individual hero, a man forced to choose a mode of behavior and a pattern of action in the modern Western tradition of the loner-hero, it is only in recognition of global culture that increasingly centralizes, bureaucratizes and dehumanizes. DD. • *Senman choja* 1936 (ad); *Chakkiri Kinta* 1937 (ad); *Otto no teiso* 1937 (ad); *Sengoku gunto den* 1937 (ad); *Bikkuri jinsei* 1938 (ad); *Chinetsu* 1938 (ad); *Nadare* 1938 (ad); *Tojuro no koi* 1938 (ad); *Tsuzurikata kyoshitsu* 1938 (ad); *Chushingura* 1939 (ad); *Seishun no kiryu* 1941 (sc,ad); *Uma* 1941 (sc,ad,2u d,ed); *Tsubasa no gaika* 1942 (sc); *Sugata Sanshiro/Judo Saga* 1943 (d,sc,ed); *Dohyosai* 1944 (sc); *Ichiban Utsukushiku/The Most Beautiful* 1944 (d,sc,story); *Appare Isshin Tasuke* 1945 (sc); *Sanshiro Sugata Zoku/Judo Saga II* 1945 (d,sc); *Tora no O o Fumu Otokotachi/The Men Who Tread on the Tiger's Tail* 1945 (d,sc); *Asu o Tsukuru Hitobito* 1946 (d); *Waga Seishun ni Kuinashi/No Regrets For Our Youth* 1946 (d,sc); *Ginrei no hate* 1947 (sc); *Subarashiki Nichiyobi* 1947 (d,sc); *Yottsu no koi no monogatari* 1947 (sc—"Hatuskoi"/"First Love"); *Shozo* 1948 (sc); *Yoidore Tenshi/Drunken Angel* 1948 (d,sc); *Jakoman to Tetsu* 1949 (sc); *Jigoku no kifujin* 1949 (sc); *Nora Inu* 1949 (d,sc); *Shizukanaru naru ketto* 1949 (d,sc); *Akatsuki no dasso* 1950 (sc); *Jiruba Tetsu* 1950 (sc); *Rashomon* 1950 (d,sc); *Shuban* 1950 (d,sc,story); *Tateshi danpei* 1950 (sc); *Ai to nikushime no kanata* 1951 (sc); *Hakuchi/The Idiot* 1951 (d,sc); *Kedamono no yado* 1951 (sc); *Ketto kagiya no tsuji* 1951 (sc); *Ikiru* 1952 (d,sc,story); *Sengoku burai* 1952 (sc); *Shichinin no Samurai/The Seven Samurai* 1954 (d,sc,story); *Ikimono no Kiroku/Record of a Living Being* 1955 (d,sc,story); *Sugata Sanshiro* 1955 (sc); *Donzoko/The Lower Depths* 1957 (d,p,sc); *Kumonosu-jo/Throne of Blood* 1957 (d,p,sc); *Tekichu odan sanbyakuri* 1957 (sc); *Kakushi Toride no San-Akunin/The Hidden Fortress* 1958 (d,p,sc,story); *The Magnificent Seven* 1960 (from sc); *Sengoku gunto den* 1960 (adapt); *Warui yatsu hodo yoku nemuru/The Bad Sleep Well* 1960 (d,p,sc,story); *Yojimbo* 1961 (d,sc,story); *Tsubaki Sanjuro/Sanjuro* 1962 (d,sc); *The Directors (short)* 1963 (a); *Tengoku to Jigoku/High and Low* 1963 (d,sc); *Jakoman to Tetsu* 1964 (sc); *The Outrage* 1964 (from sc); *Per un Pugno di Dollari/For a Fistful of Dollars* 1964 (from sc); *Akahige/Red Beard* 1965 (d,sc); *Sugata Sanshiro* 1965 (sc); *The Savage Seven* 1968 (from sc); *Dodes 'Kaden* 1970 (d,p,sc); *75 Years of Cinema Museum* 1972 (a); *Dersu Uzala* 1975 (d,sc); *Battle Beyond the Stars* 1980 (from sc); *Kagemusha* 1980 (d,exec.p,sc); *Ran* 1985 (d,sc,ed); *Runaway Train* 1985 (from sc); *Akira Kurosawa's Dreams* 1990 (d,sc); *Rhapsody in August* 1991 (d,sc).

Kurtz, Swoosie • Actress • Born Omaha, NB, September 6, 1944. *Educ.* USC, Los Angeles; LAMDA, London. Multi award-winning performer of stage, film and TV. • *First Love* 1977; *Slap Shot* 1977; *Oliver's Story* 1978; *The World According to Garp* 1982; *Against All Odds* 1983; *True Stories* 1986; *Wildcats* 1986; *Bright Lights, Big City* 1988; *Dangerous Liaisons* 1988; *Vice Versa* 1988; *A Shock to the System* 1990; *Stanley and Iris* 1990.

Kurys, Diane • French director; also producer, screenwriter. • Born 1948. Former member of Jean-Louis Barrault's theater group who made her film directing debut with *Peppermint Soda* (1977), the first installment in an absorbing semi-autobiographical trilogy. *Peppermint Soda* was France's highest-grossing film of 1977 and won the Prix Louis Delluc as best picture of the year. *A Man in Love* (1987), Kurys's first film with a male protagonist, was a watery international melodrama which lacked the conviction of her earlier work. • *Diabolo Menthe/Peppermint Soda* 1977 (d,sc,dial); *Cocktail Molotov* 1979 (d,p,sc); *Le Coup de sirocco* 1979 (p); *Le Grand Pardon* 1981 (p); *Coup de Foudre/Entre Nous* 1983 (d,sc,from book,adapt); *Un Homme amoureux/A Man in Love* 1987 (d,sc,adapt); *La Baule les pins/C'est la vie* 1990 (d,sc).

Kusturica, Emir • Director; also screenwriter. • Born Sarajevo, Yugoslavia, 1955. *Educ.* FAMU, Prague (film direction). Began his career in TV and made an auspicious feature debut with *Do You Remember Dolly Bell?* (1981), a coming-of-age story set in Sarajevo in the early 1960s. *Dolly Bell* won the Golden Lion for best first film at the Venice Festival and was followed by *When Father Was Away on Business* (1985), also scripted by Muslim poet Abdulah Sidran. An absorbing portrait of provincial life and politics in 1950s Yugoslavia, partially seen through the eyes of a six-year-old child, *Father* confirmed Kusturica as an international director of note. It won the Palme d'Or at Cannes, five Golden Arena awards (the Yugoslavian Oscars) and an Academy Award nomination as best foreign film.

Kusturica's third feature, *Time of the Gypsies* (1988), was inspired by a newspaper article about the inter-European trade in young gypsy chidren. It employs an elliptical, fantastic style influenced by Latin American "magic realism" and features nonprofessional, gypsy actors delivering most of their dialogue in Romanian (a language the director barely understands). *Gypsies* brought further critical acclaim for Kusturica, earning him the best director award at the 1989 Cannes Film Festival; he was awarded the Roberto Rossellini prize for lifetime achievement in film the same year. Kusturica has also taught film directing at Columbia University since 1988. JDP • *Do You Remember Dolly Bell?* 1981 (d); *Otac Na Sluzbenom Putu/When Father Was Away On Business* 1985 (d); *Strategija svrake* 1987 (sc); *Zivot Radnika* 1987 (sc); *Dom Za Vesanje/Time of the Gypsies* 1988 (d,sc).

Kyo, Machiko • Actress • Born Osaka, Japan, March 25, 1924. Former dancer with the Tokyo Nippon Gekijo who joined the Daiei film company in the late 1940s and gained internatioal recognition with Akira Kurosawa's *Rashomon* (1950). Over the next two decades Kyo starred in numerous films by some of Japan's greatest directors, including Mizoguchi's *Ugetsu Monogatari* (1953), Kinugasa's *Gate of Hell* (1953), Ichikawa's *Odd Obsession* (1959) and Ozu's *Floating Weeds* (1959). Her sole US film was *The Teahouse of the August Moon* (1956), with Marlon Brando and Glenn Ford. • *Chijin no ai* 1949; *Chikagai no dankon* 1949; *Hanakurabe Tanuki Goten* 1949; *Hebihime dochu* 1949; *Mittsu no shinju* 1949; *Saigo no warau otoko* 1949; *Asakusa no hada* 1950; *Bibo no umi* 1950; *Fukkatsu* 1950; *Harukanari haha no kuni* 1950; *Hi no tori* 1950; *Rashomon* 1950; *Zoku hebihime dochu* 1950; *Bakuro ichidai* 1951; *Genji monogatari* 1951; *Itsuwareru seiso* 1951; *Jiyu gakko* 1951; *Joen no hatoba* 1951; *Koi no Orandazaka* 1951; *Mesu inu* 1951; *Asakusa kurenai-dan* 1952; *Bijo to tozoku* 1952; *Daibutsu kaigen* 1952; *Kanojo no tokudane* 1952; *Nagasaki no uta wa wasureji* 1952; *Taki no shiraito* 1952; *Ani imoto* 1953; *Jigo Kumen/Gate of Hell* 1953; *Kurohyo* 1953; *Ugetsu Monogatari/Tales of the Pale and Silvery Moon After the Rain* 1953; *Aizen katsura* 1954; *Aru onna* 1954; *Asakusa no yoru* 1954; *Bazoku geisha* 1954; *Haru no uzumaki* 1954; *Sen-Hime* 1954; *Shunkin monogatari* 1954; *Bara ikutabi* 1955; *Shin josei mondo* 1955; *Tojuro no koi* 1955; *Yokihi/The Princess Yang Kwei Fei* 1955; *Akasen Chitai/Street of Shame* 1956; *Niji Ikutabi* 1956; *The Teahouse of the August Moon* 1956; *Yoshinaka o meguru sannin o onna* 1956; *Ana* 1957; *Itohan* *monogatari* 1957; *Jigokubana* 1957; *Odoriko* 1957; *Onna no hada* 1957; *Yoru no cho* 1957; *Akasen no hi wa kiezu* 1958; *Chushingura* 1958; *Kanashimi wa onna dakeni* 1958; *Musume no boken* 1958; *Osaka no onna* 1958; *Yoru no sugao* 1958; *Yurakucho de aimasho* 1958; *Jirocho Fuji* 1959; *Jokyo* 1959; *Kagi/Odd Obsession* 1959; *Onna to kaizoku* 1959; *Sasame-yuki* 1959; *Sayonara, Konnichiwa* 1959; *Ukigusa/Floating Weeds* 1959; *Yoru no togyo* 1959; *Ashi ni sawatta onna* 1960; *Bonchi* 1960; *Kao* 1960; *Odeon jigoku* 1960; *Ruten no ohi* 1960; *San-nin no kaoyaku* 1960; *Kodachi o tsukao onna* 1961; *Konki* 1961; *Nuregami botan* 1961; *Onna no kunsho* 1961; *Shaka* 1961; *Kuro tokage* 1962; *Onna no issho* 1962; *Jokei kazoku* 1963; *Shin no shikotei* 1963; *Amai ase* 1964; *Gendai Inchiki monogatari* 1964; *Jinchoge* 1966; *Tanin no kao/The Face of Another* 1966; *Malenki beglyets* 1967; *Senbazuru/Thousand Cranes* 1969; *Kesho* 1985.

La Cava, Gregory • Director; also screenwriter, producer. • Born George Gregory La Cava, Towanda, PA, March 10, 1892; died 1952. Began his film career working with Walter Lantz as an animator and wrote and directed comedy shorts before graduating to features in 1922. La Cava displayed a flair for comedy laced with social observation and earned a reputation for coaxing fine ensemble performances from his actors. Perhaps at his best with *My Man Godfrey* (1936). • *His Nibs* 1922 (d); *The New School Teacher* 1924 (d); *Restless Wives* 1924 (d); *Womanhandled* 1925 (d); *Let's Get Married* 1926 (d); *Say It Again* 1926 (d); *So's Your Old Man* 1926 (d); *The Gay Defender* 1927 (d); *Paradise For Two* 1927 (d); *Running Wild* 1927 (d,story); *Tell It to Sweeney* 1927 (d,p); *Feel My Pulse* 1928 (d); *Half a Bride* 1928 (d); *Big News* 1929 (d); *His First Command* 1929 (d); *Saturday's Children* 1929 (d); *Laugh and Get Rich* 1931 (d,sc); *Smart Woman* 1931 (d); *The Age of Consent* 1932 (d); *Half Naked Truth* 1932 (d,sc); *Symphony of Six Million* 1932 (d); *Bed of Roses* 1933 (add.dial,d); *Gabriel Over the White House* 1933 (d); *The Affairs of Cellini* 1934 (d); *Gallant Lady* 1934 (d); *What Every Woman Knows* 1934 (d,p); *Private Worlds* 1935 (d,sc); *She Married Her Boss* 1935 (d); *My Man Godfrey* 1936 (d,p) **(AANBD)**; *Stage Door* 1937 (d) **(AANBD)**; *Fifth Avenue Girl* 1939 (d,p); *The Primrose Path* 1940 (d,p,sc); *Unfinished Business* 1941 (d,p); *Lady in a Jam* 1942 (d,p); *Living in a Big Way* 1947 (d,sc,story); *One Touch of Venus* 1948 (d).

La Shelle, Joseph • Director of photography • Born Los Angeles, CA, 1905; died August 20, 1989. Spent 14 years as a camera operator for Arthur Miller before graduating to director of photography in 1943. La Shelle excelled at sleazy, noirish compositions, doing outstanding work in the 1940s, with directors such as Otto Preminger and Henry King, and 60s, especially with Billy Wilder. He also shot several episodes of TV's "The Twilight Zone." • *The Flame of the Yukon* 1926 (2nd cam.op); *Rocking Moon* 1926 (2nd cam.op); *Whispering Smith* 1926 (2nd cam.op); *The Pagan* 1929 (cam.op); *The Painted Desert* 1931 (cam.op); *The White Parade* 1934 (cam.op); *It's a Small World* 1935 (cam.op); *The Little Colonel* 1935 (cam.op); *The Baroness and the Butler* 1938 (cam.op); *Brigham Young, Frontiersman* 1940 (cam.op); *How Green Was My Valley* 1941 (cam.op); *Tobacco Road* 1941 (cam.op); *Happy Land* 1943 (ph); *The Song of Bernadette* 1943 (cam.op); *Bermuda Mystery* 1944 (ph); *The Eve of St. Mark* 1944 (ph); *Laura* 1944 (ph) **(AABPH)**; *Take It or Leave It* 1944 (ph); *A Bell For Adano* 1945 (ph); *Doll Face* 1945 (ph); *Fallen Angel* 1945 (ph); *Claudia and David* 1946 (ph); *Cluny Brown* 1946 (ph); *The Foxes of Harrow* 1947 (ph); *The Late George Apley* 1947 (ph); *Deep Waters* 1948 (ph); *The Luck of the Irish* 1948 (ph); *Road House* 1948 (ph); *Come to the Stable* 1949 (ph) **(AANBPH)**; *Everybody Does It* 1949 (ph); *The Fan* 1949 (ph); *The Jackpot* 1950 (ph); *Mister 880* 1950 (ph); *Mother Didn't Tell Me* 1950 (ph); *Under My Skin* 1950 (ph); *Where the Sidewalk Ends* 1950 (ph); *The 13th Letter* 1951 (ph); *Elopement* 1951 (ph); *The Guy Who Came Back* 1951 (ph); *Mr. Belvedere Rings the Bell* 1951 (ph); *Les Miserables* 1952 (ph); *My Cousin Rachel* 1952 (ph) **(AANBPH)**; *The Outcasts of Poker Flat* 1952 (ph); *Something For the Birds* 1952 (ph); *Dangerous Crossing* 1953 (ph); *Mister Scoutmaster* 1953 (ph); *River of No Return* 1954 (ph); *Marty* 1955 (ph) **(AANBPH)**; *Storm Fear* 1955 (ph); *The Conqueror* 1956 (ph); *Our Miss Brooks* 1956 (ph); *Run For the Sun* 1956 (ph); *The Abductors* 1957 (ph); *The Bachelor Party* 1957 (ph); *Crime of Passion* 1957 (ph); *Fury at Showdown* 1957 (ph); *The Fuzzy Pink Nightgown* 1957 (ph); *I Was a Teenage Werewolf* 1957 (ph); *No Down Payment* 1957 (ph); *The Long, Hot Summer* 1958 (ph); *The Naked and the Dead* 1958 (ph); *Career* 1959 (ph) **(AANBPH)**; *The Apartment* 1960 (ph) **(AANBPH)**; *All in a Night's Work* 1961 (ph); *The Honeymoon Machine* 1961 (ph); *The Outsider* 1961 (ph); *A Child Is Waiing* 1962 (ph); *How the West Was Won* 1962 (ph—"The Civil War," "The Railroad") **(AANBPH)**; *Irma la Douce* 1963 (ph) **(AANBPH)**; *Kiss Me, Stupid* 1964 (ph); *Wild and Wonderful* 1964 (ph); *Seven Women* 1965 (ph); *The Chase* 1966 (ph); *The Fortune Cookie* 1966 (ph) **(AANBPH)**; *Barefoot in the Park* 1967 (ph); *Kona Coast* 1968 (ph); *Eighty Steps to Jonah* 1969 (ph).

Lachman, Ed • American director of photography • Born Edward Lachman, 1948. *Educ.* Ohio University, Athens. Former assistant to luminaries such as Robby Müller (*The American Friend* 1977), Sven Nykvist (*King of the Gypsies* 1978) and Vittorio Storaro (*La Luna* 1979) who photographed several notable independent productions of the 1980s. • *The Lords of Flatbush* 1974 (ph); *False Face* 1976 (ph); *How Much Wood Would a Woodchuck Chuck* 1976 (cam.op); *Der Amerikanische Freund/The American Friend* 1977 (cam.op); *La Soufrière* (short) 1977 (ph); *Stroszek* 1977 (ph,ad); *King of the Gypsies* 1978 (ph); *Hurricane* 1979 (cam.op); *Last Embrace* 1979 (add.ph); *La Luna* 1979 (cam.op); *Huie's Predigt* 1980 (cam.op); *Lightning Over Water* 1980 (a,ph); *No Nukes* 1980 (cam.op—Madison Square Garden); *Union City* 1980 (ph); *They All Laughed* 1981 (cam.op); *Say Amen, Somebody—The Good News Musical* 1982 (ph); *Body Rock* 1984 (add. ph—New York); *In Our Hands* 1984 (cam.op); *Desperately Seeking Susan* 1985 (ph); *Heart of the Garden* 1985 (ph); *I Played It For You* 1985 (ph); *Insignificance* 1985 (add. ph—New York); *The Look* 1985 (ph); *Mother Teresa* 1985 (ph); *Ornette: Made in America* 1985 (ph); *Stripper* 1985 (ph); *Tokyo-Ga* 1985 (ph); *El Dia Que Me Quieras* 1986 (ph); *True Stories* 1986 (ph); *Hail! Hail! Rock 'n' Roll!* 1987 (cam op-docu,ph—concert); *Less Than Zero* 1987 (ph); *Making Mr. Right* 1987 (ph); *Backtrack* 1990 (ph); *Mississippi Masala* 1991 (ph).

Ladd, Alan • Actor • Born Hot Springs, AR, September 3, 1913; died 1964. Diminutive, laconic performer who flourished in the 1940s after achieving his breakthrough in *This Gun For Hire* (1942). Ladd excelled at playing soft-spoken, understated tough guys who would only reluctantly resort to violence. Married to actress Sue Carol, who later became his manager, from 1942; father of film executive Alan Ladd, Jr., and actors David and Alana Ladd. • *Once in a Lifetime* 1932; *No Man of Her Own* 1933; *Saturday's Millions* 1933; *Pigskin Parade* 1936; *All Over Town* 1937; *Hold Em' Navy* 1937; *The Last Train From Madrid* 1937; *Rustlers' Valley* 1937; *Souls at Sea* 1937; *Come on Leathernecks* 1938; *Fresh-*

man Year 1938; *The Goldwyn Follies* 1938; *Hitler, Beast of Berlin* 1939; *Rulers of the Sea* 1939; *Brother Rat and a Baby* 1940; *Captain Caution* 1940; *Cross Country Romance* 1940; *Gangs of Chicago* 1940; *The Green Hornet* 1940; *Her First Romance* 1940; *The Howards of Virginia* 1940; *In Old Missouri* 1940; *The Light of Western Stars* 1940; *Meet the Missus* 1940; *Those Were The Days* 1940; *Wildcat Bus* 1940; *The Black Cat* 1941; *Cadet Girl* 1941; *Citizen Kane* 1941; *Great Guns* 1941; *Paper Bullets* 1941; *Petticoat Politics* 1941; *The Reluctant Dragon* 1941; *They Met in Bombay* 1941; *The Glass Key* 1942; *Joan of Paris* 1942; *Lucky Jordan* 1942; *Star Spangled Rhythm* 1942; *This Gun For Hire* 1942; *China* 1943; *And Now Tomorrow* 1944; *Duffy's Tavern* 1945; *Salty O'Rourke* 1945; *The Blue Dahlia* 1946; *O.S.S.* 1946; *Two Years Before the Mast* 1946; *Calcutta* 1947; *Variety Girl* 1947; *Wild Harvest* 1947; *Beyond Glory* 1948; *Saigon* 1948; *Chicago Deadline* 1949; *The Great Gatsby* 1949; *Whispering Smith* 1949; *Branded* 1950; *Captain Carey, U.S.A.* 1950; *Appointment With Danger* 1951; *Red Mountain* 1951; *The Iron Mistress* 1952; *Thunder in the East* 1952; *Botany Bay* 1953; *Desert Legion* 1953; *The Red Beret* 1953; *Shane* 1953; *The Black Knight* 1954; *Drum Beat* 1954; *Hell Below Zero* 1954; *Saskatchewan* 1954; *Hell on Frisco Bay* 1955; *The McConnell Story* 1955; *A Cry in the Night* 1956; *Santiago* 1956; *The Big Land* 1957; *Boy on a Dolphin* 1957; *The Deep Six* 1957; *The Badlanders* 1958; *Proud Rebel* 1958; *Island of Lost Women* 1959 (exec.p); *The Man in the Net* 1959 (a,exec.p); *All the Young Men* 1960; *Guns of the Timberland* 1960; *One Foot in Hell* 1960; *Orazi e Curiazi* 1961; *13 West Street* 1962; *The Carpetbaggers* 1964; *George Stevens: A Filmmaker's Journey* 1985 (archival footage).

Ladd, Diane • Actress • Born Rose Diane Ladner, Meridian, MS, November 29, 1939. *Educ.* St. Aloysius Academy. Character actress, in films since 1961; probably best known as Flo in *Alice Doesn't Live Here Anymore* (1974). Ladd's first husband was actor Bruce Dern and her daughter is actress Laura Dern. • *Something Wild* 1961; *The Wild Angels* 1966; *The Reivers* 1969; *Macho Callahan* 1970; *Rebel Rousers* 1970; *WUSA* 1970; *White Lightning* 1973; *Alice Doesn't Live Here Anymore* 1974 (**AANBSA**); *Chinatown* 1974; *Embryo* 1976; *The November Plan* 1976; *All Night Long* 1981; *Something Wicked This Way Comes* 1983; *Black Widow* 1987; *Plain Clothes* 1988; *National Lampoon's Christmas Vacation* 1989; *Wild at Heart* 1990; *A Kiss Before Dying* 1991.

Laemmle, Carl • Executive • Born Laupheim, Germany, January 17, 1867; died 1939. Clothing store manager who went into the nickelodeon business in 1906 and became one of the burgeoning film industry's leading distributors. In 1909 Laemmle resisted the monopolistic maneuverings of the Motion Picture Patents Company, not only defying their efforts to squash his distribution entity but also founding his own production operation, the Independent Motion Picture Company.

In 1912 Laemmle won a landmark court battle against the MPPC which spurred the trust's demise. The same year he merged with a number of smaller companies to form the Universal Film Manufacturing Company (later known as Universal). The spectacular success of their 1913 feature release, *Traffic in Souls* (an exposé of white slave traffic), convinced the industry of the profitability of feature-film making. Laemmle's reign at Universal (continued by proxy when he installed his son, Carl Laemmle, Jr., as his successor in 1929) came to an end in 1935 when mismanagement and the Depression conspired to force the sale of the company for $5 million.

Lafont, Bernadette • Actress; also dancer. • Born Nimes, France, October 26, 1938. Lead and character player of French and international features who made her cinematic debut—as did director François Truffaut—with the 1958 short, *Les Mistons*. Lafont has gone on to appear in nearly 100 films, notably several by director Claude Chabrol. • *Bal de nuit* 1958; *Le Beau Serge* 1958; *Giovani Mariti* 1958; *Les Mistons* (short) 1958; *A Double Tour/Web of Passion/Leda* 1959; *L'Eau à la bouche* 1959; *Les Bonnes Femmes* 1960; *Les Godelureaux* 1960; *Les Mordus* 1960; *Me faire ça a moi...* 1961; *Tire au flanc 62* 1961; *Un Clair de lune à Maubeuge* 1962; *Et Satan conduit le bal* 1962; *Jusqu'à plus soif* 1962; *Les Femmes d'abord* 1963; *L'Avatar botanique de Mlle. Flora (short)* 1964; *La Chasse à l'Homme* 1964; *Tous les enfants du monde* 1964; *Les Bons vivants* 1965; *Compartiment tueurs/The Sleeping Car Murders* 1965; *Pleins feux sur Stanislas* 1965; *Un Idiot à Paris* 1966; *Je ne sais pas (short)* 1966; *Lamiel* 1967; *Le Voleur/Thief of Paris* 1967; *L'Amour c'est gai, l'amour c'est triste* 1968; *Le Dernier voyage du Commandant Le Bihan (short)* 1968; *Falak* 1968; *Les Idoles* 1968; *Le Révélateur* 1968; *Elise ou La vraie vie* 1969; *La Fiancée du pirate/A Very Curious Girl* 1969; *Paul* 1969; *Sex Power* 1969; *Le Voleur de crimes* 1969; *Cain de nulle part* 1970; *Cinéma Different 3* 1970; *Les Stances à Sophie* 1970; *Valparaiso, Valparaiso!* 1970; *Catch Me a Spy* 1971; *Etoile aux dents* 1971; *La Famille* 1971; *Je, tu, elles...* 1971; *L'Oeuf* 1971; *Out 1: Noli Me Tangere* 1971; *Une Belle fille come moi/Such a Gorgeous Kid Like Me* 1972; *Out 1: Spectre* 1972; *Trop jolies pour être honnêtes* 1972; *What a Flash* 1972; *Défense de savoir* 1973; *Les Gants Blancs du Diable* 1973; *L'Histoire très bonne et tres joyeuse de Colinot Trousse chemise* 1973; *La Maman et la putain* 1973; *Une Baleine qui avait mal aux dents* 1974; *Permette signora che ami vostra figlia* 1974; *Zig-Zig* 1974; *Un Divorce Heureux* 1975; *La Ville bidon* 1975; *Vincent mit l'âne dans un pré* 1975; *Noroît* 1976; *L'Ordinateur des pompes funèbres* 1976; *Qu'il est joli garçon, l'assassin de papa* 1976; *Le Trouble-Fesses* 1976; *Un Type comme moi ne devrait jamais mourir* 1976; *Arrète de Ramer, t'Attaques la Falaise* 1977; *L'Irrévolution* 1977; *Strauberg Ist Da* 1977; *Violette Nozière/Violette* 1977; *Chaussette Surprise* 1978; *La Tortue sur le dos* 1978; *Certaines Nouvelles* 1979; *La Frisée aux lardons* 1979; *La Gueule de l'autre* 1979; *Il Ladrone* 1979; *Nous maigrirons ensemble* 1979; *Une Merveilleuse journée* 1980; *Retour en force* 1980; *Le Roi des cons* 1981; *Si ma gueule vous plaît...* 1981; *On n'est pas sorti de l'auberge* 1982; *La Bête Noire* 1983; *Un Bon petit diable* 1983; *Cap Canaille* 1983; *The Perils of Gwendoline in the Land of the Yik Yak* 1983; *Canicule* 1984; *L'Effrontée* 1985; *Le Pactole* 1985; *Inspector Lavardin* 1986; *Masques* 1987; *Les Saisons du plaisir* 1987; *Waiting For the Moon* 1987; *Une Nuit à l'assemblée nationale* 1988; *Prisonnières* 1988; *L'Air de Rien* 1989; *Boom Boom* 1990.

Lahr, Bert • Actor; also vaudevillian. • Born Irving Lahrheim, New York, NY, August 13, 1895; died 1967. Melancholic clown whose performance as the cowardly lion in *The Wizard of Oz* (1939) has become a part of American folklore. • *Flying High* 1931; *Mr. Broadway* 1933; *Love and Hisses* 1937; *Merry-Go-Round of 1938* 1937; *Josette* 1938; *Just Around the Corner* 1938; *The Wizard of Oz* 1939; *Zaza* 1939; *Ship Ahoy* 1942; *Sing Your Worries Away* 1942; *Meet the People* 1944; *Always Leave Them Laughing* 1949; *Mr. Universe* 1951; *Rose Marie* 1954; *The Second Greatest Sex* 1955; *Ten Girls Ago* 1962; *The Night They Raided Minsky's* 1968.

Lahti, Christine • Actress • Born Birmingham, MI, April 4, 1950. *Educ.* University of Michigan (drama); Florida State University (fine arts). Attractive, stage-trained performer whose impressive, off-beat characterizations have ranged from a highly eccentric aunt (*Housekeeping* 1987) to a long-suffering radical matriarch (*Running on Empty* 1988). Married to director Thomas Schlamme. • *And Justice For All* 1979; *Whose Life Is It Anyway?* 1981; *Ladies and Gentlemen, the Fabulous Stains* 1982; *Swing Shift* 1984 (**AANBSA**); *Just Between Friends* 1986; *Housekeeping* 1987; *Stacking* 1987; *Running on Empty* 1988; *Gross Anatomy* 1989; *Miss Firecracker* 1989; *Funny About Love* 1990.

Lai, Francis • Composer • Born France, 1932. Came to prominence with his music for Claude Lelouch's *A Man and a Woman* (1966) and has gone on to contribute lush scores to numerous French, English and American films. • *Un Homme et une femme/A Man and a Woman* 1966 (m); *Masculin-Féminin/Masculine-Feminine* 1966 (m); *The Bobo* 1967 (m); *I'll Never Forget What's 'is Name* 1967 (m); *Mon Amour, Mon Amour* 1967 (m); *Le Soleil des voyous* 1967 (m); *Vivre pour vivre* 1967 (m); *Hannibal Brooks* 1968 (m); *House of Cards* 1968 (m); *Mayerling* 1968 (m); *Treize Jours en France* 1968 (m,song); *La Vie, l'amour, la mort* 1968 (m); *Three Into Two Won't Go* 1969 (m); *With Love in Mind* 1969 (m,song); *The Games* 1970 (m); *Hello-Goodbye* 1970 (m); *Love Story* 1970 (m) **(AABM)**; *La Modification* 1970 (m); *Le Passager de la Pluie/Rider on the Rain* 1970 (m); *Le Petit Matin* 1971 (m); *Les Pétroleuses* 1971 (m); *Smic, Smac, Smoc* 1971 (a,m); *L'Aventure c'est l'aventure* 1972 (m); *La Course du lièvre à travers les champs* 1972 (m); *Le Petit Poucet* 1972 (m); *La Bonne Année* 1973 (m); *Un Homme Libre* 1973 (m); *Un Amour de pluie* 1974 (m); *Mariage* 1974 (m); *Par Le sang des autres/Bolero* 1974 (m); *Toute une vie* 1974 (m); *Visit to a Chief's Son* 1974 (m); *Baby Sitter-Un maledetto pasticcio* 1975 (m); *Le Bon et les mechants* 1975 (m); *Le Chat et la Souris* 1975 (m); *Hustle* 1975 (song); *Anima Persa* 1976 (m); *Le Corps de Mon Ennemi* 1976 (m); *Emmanuelle l'anti-vièrge* 1976 (m); *Si c'etait à refaire* 1976 (m); *Another Man, Another Chance* 1977 (m); *Bilitis* 1977 (m); *Widows' Nest* 1977 (m); *International Velvet* 1978 (m); *Leidenschaftliche Blümchen* 1978 (m); *Oliver's Story* 1978 (song); *Les Ringards* 1978 (m); *Robert et Robert* 1978 (m,song); *A nous deux* 1979 (m); *By the Blood of Others* 1980 (m); *Beyond the Reef* 1981 (m); *Madame Claude 2* 1981 (m,song); *Les Uns et les autres* 1981 (m); *Edith et Marcel* 1982 (m); *Canicule* 1984 (m); *J'ai Recontre le Pére Noël* 1984 (m); *AIDS-Gefähr Für die Liebe* 1985 (m); *MARIE* 1985 (m); *Les Ripoux/My New Partner* 1985 (m); *Association de Malfaiteurs* 1986 (m); *Un Homme et une femme: Vingt ans deja* 1986 (m); *Attention Bandits* 1987 (m); *Oci Ciornie/Dark Eyes* 1987 (m); *Bernadette* 1988 (m); *Itinéraire d'un enfant gaté* 1988 (m); *Les Pyramides bleues* 1988 (m); *Der Aten* 1989 (m); *Earth Girls Are Easy* 1989 (song); *Trop belle pour toi/Too Beautiful For You* 1989 (m); *Il y a des jours...et des lunes* 1990 (m); *Ripoux Contre Ripoux/My New Partner II* 1990 (m).

Lake, Veronica • *aka* Constance Keane • Actress • Born Constance Frances Marie Ockelman, Brooklyn, NY, November 14, 1919; died 1973. Blonde lead of the 1940s who built a career out of an aloof attitude and an eye-obscuring hairstyle. Lake's first husband, from 1944 to 1952, was director Andre De Toth. • *All Women Have Secrets* 1939; *Sorority House* 1939; *The Wrong Room (short)* 1939; *Forty Little Mothers* 1940; *The Jones Family in Young As You Feel* 1940; *Hold Back the Dawn* 1941; *I Wanted Wings* 1941; *Sullivan's Travels* 1941; *The Glass Key* 1942; *I Married a Witch* 1942; *Star Spangled Rhythm* 1942; *This Gun For Hire* 1942; *So Proudly We Hail* 1943; *The Hour Before the Dawn* 1944; *Bring on the Girls* 1945; *Duffy's Tavern* 1945; *Hold That Blonde* 1945; *Miss Susie Slagle's* 1945; *Out of This World* 1945; *The Blue Dahlia* 1946; *Ramrod* 1947; *Variety Girl* 1947; *Isn't It Romantic* 1948; *Saigon* 1948; *The Sainted Sisters* 1948; *Slattery's Hurricane* 1949; *Stronghold* 1952; *Footsteps in the Snow* 1966; *Flesh Feast* 1970.

Lamarr, Hedy • *aka* Hedy Kiesler • Austrian actress • Born Hedwig Eva Maria Kiesler, November 9, 1913. Alluring bit player in Austro-German films who caused a furor when she appeared nude in the 1932 Czech film *Ecstasy*. Lamarr arrived in Hollywood in 1938, where she contributed little but her exotic beauty to a host of productions, mostly at MGM. Lamarr's second husband was writer Gene Markey and her third, actor John Loder. • *Geld auf der Strasse (short)* 1930 (a,sc.sup); *Die Koffer des Herrn O.F.* 1931 (a); *Man braucht kein Geld* 1931 (a); *Stürm im Wasserglas* 1931 (a); *Extase/Ecstasy* 1932 (a); *Algiers* 1938 (a); *Lady of the Tropics* 1939 (a); *Boom Town* 1940 (a); *Comrade X* 1940 (a); *I Take This Woman* 1940 (a); *Come Live With Me* 1941 (a); *H. M. Pulham, Esq.* 1941 (a); *Ziegfeld Girl* 1941 (a); *Crossroads* 1942 (a); *Tortilla Flat* 1942 (a); *White Cargo* 1942 (a); *The Heavenly Body* 1943 (a); *The Conspirators* 1944 (a); *Experiment Perilous* 1944 (a); *Her Highness and the Bellboy* 1945 (a); *The Strange Woman* 1946 (a); *Dishonored Lady* 1947 (a); *Let's Live a Little* 1948 (a); *Samson and Delilah* 1949 (a); *Copper Canyon* 1950 (a); *A Lady Without Passport* 1950 (a); *My Favorite Spy* 1951 (a); *Eterna Femmina* 1954 (a); *The Story of Mankind* 1957 (a); *The Female Animal* 1958 (a); *Going Hollywood: The War Years* 1988 (archival footage); *Entertaining the Troops* 1989 (archival footage); *Instant Karma* 1990 (a).

Lambert, Christopher • *aka* Christophe Lambert • Actor • Born New York, NY, March 29, 1957. *Educ.* Paris Conservatoire. Tall, handsome lead of French and international films who made his screen debut in 1980. Lambert gave a commendable performance in the title role of Hugh Hudson's *Greystoke: The Legend of Tarzan, Lord of the Apes* (1984). Married to actress Diane Lane. • *Le Bar du Téléphone* 1980; *Legitimate Violence* 1980; *Greystoke: The Legend of Tarzan, Lord of the Apes* 1984; *Paroles et Musique/Love Songs* 1984; *Subway* 1985; *Highlander* 1986; *I Love You* 1986; *The Sicilian* 1987; *Love Dream* 1988; *Popielusko* 1988; *Un Plan d'enfer* 1989; *Highlander II—the Quickening* 1991.

Lamorisse, Albert • Filmmaker • Born Paris, January 13, 1922; died Iran, 1970. *Educ.* IDHEC, Paris. Maker of acclaimed short fantasy films, notably *The Red Balloon* (1956), who made an unsuccessful foray into features in the 1960s. Lamorisse also invented Helivision, an apparatus enabling filming from a helicopter; he was unfortunately killed in a helicopter crash while filming *The Lovers' Wind* in Iran in 1970. The film, completed by his widow and released eight years later, won an Oscar as best documentary. • *Djerba (short)* 1947 (d,sc,commentary); *Bim le petit ane (short)* 1949 (d); *Crin Blanc le cheval sauvage* 1952 (d,sc,commentary); *Le Ballon Rouge/The Red Balloon* (short) 1956 (d,p,sc) **(AABSC)**; *Le Voyage en ballon* 1960 (d,sc,aerial ph); *Fifi la plume* 1964 (d,p,sc); *Islande de flammes et d'eaux (short)* 1969 (d); *Paris jamais vu (short)* 1969 (d,sc,ph); *Versailles (short)* 1969 (d,sc); *Le Vent des amoureux/The Lovers' Wind* 1978 (d,p) **(AANBDOC)**.

Lamour, Dorothy • Actress • Born Mary Leta Dorothy Kaumeyer, New Orleans, LA, December 10, 1914. Engaging female lead, in films—mostly musicals and comedies—from the late 1930s. Best known as the romantic cornerstone of the Hope-Crosby "road" pictures. • *The Jungle Princess* 1936; *The Stars Can't Be Wrong (short)* 1936; *High, Wide, and Handsome* 1937; *Hurricane* 1937; *The Last Train From Madrid* 1937; *Swing High, Swing Low* 1937; *Thrill of a Lifetime* 1937; *The Big Broadcast of 1938* 1938; *Her Jungle Love* 1938; *Spawn of the North* 1938; *Tropic Holiday* 1938; *Disputed Passage* 1939; *Man About Town* 1939; *St. Louis Blues* 1939; *Chad Hanna* 1940; *Johnny Apollo* 1940; *Moon Over Burma* 1940; *Road to Singapore* 1940; *Typhoon* 1940; *Aloma of the South Seas* 1941; *Caught in the Draft* 1941; *Road to Zanzibar* 1941; *Beyond the Blue Horizon* 1942; *The Fleet's In* 1942; *Road to Morocco* 1942; *Star Spangled Rhythm* 1942; *Dixie* 1943; *Riding High* 1943; *They Got Me Covered* 1943; *And the Angels Sing* 1944; *Rainbow Island* 1944; *Duffy's Tavern* 1945; *Masquerade in Mexico* 1945; *A Medal For Benny* 1945; *The Road to Utopia* 1946; *My Favorite Brunette* 1947; *Road to Rio* 1947; *Variety Girl* 1947; *Wild Harvest* 1947; *The Girl From Manhattan* 1948; *Lulu Belle* 1948; *A Miracle Can Happen* 1948; *The Lucky Stiff* 1949; *Manhandled* 1949; *Slightly French* 1949; *Here Comes the Groom* 1951; *The Greatest Show on Earth* 1952; *Road to Bali* 1952; *The Road to Hong Kong* 1962; *Donovan's Reef* 1963; *Pa-*

jama Party 1964; *The Phynx* 1970; *Creepshow 2* 1987; *Entertaining the Troops* 1989.

Lancaster, Burt • Actor; also producer. • Born Burton Stephen Lancaster, New York, NY, November 2, 1913. *Educ.* NYU. Former circus performer who became a popular, athletic leading man in the 1940s. Lancaster formed the first of several independent production companies in 1948, joining forces with his agent Harold Hecht and, soon afterward, producer James Hill. He went on to star in a bevy of successful westerns, war films and dramas through the 1950s and 60s, giving a landmark performance as an Italian aristocrat in Visconti's *The Leopard* (1963). Lancaster has made a graceful transition to elderly roles, notably in Bertolucci's *1900* (1976) and, more recently, *Atlantic City* (1980) and *Local Hero* (1983), the former of which won him his fourth Oscar nomination as well as the New York Film Critics' best actor award. • *The Killers* 1946; *Brute Force* 1947; *Desert Fury* 1947; *I Walk Alone* 1947; *Variety Girl* 1947; *All My Sons* 1948; *Criss Cross* 1948; *Kiss the Blood Off My Hands* 1948; *Sorry, Wrong Number* 1948; *Rope of Sand* 1949; *The Flame and the Arrow* 1950; *Mister 880* 1950; *Jim Thorpe - All American* 1951; *Ten Tall Men* 1951; *Vengeance Valley* 1951; *Come Back Little Sheba* 1952; *The Crimson Pirate* 1952 (a,p); *The First Time* 1952 (p); *From Here to Eternity* 1953 **(AANBA)**; *His Majesty O'Keefe* 1953; *South Sea Woman* 1953; *Apache* 1954; *Vera Cruz* 1954; *The Kentuckian* 1955 (a,d); *Marty* 1955 (p); *The Rose Tattoo* 1955; *The Rainmaker* 1956; *Trapeze* 1956; *The Bachelor Party* 1957 (p); *Gunfight at the O.K. Corral* 1957; *Sweet Smell of Success* 1957; *Run Silent, Run Deep* 1958 (a,p); *Separate Tables* 1958; *The Devil's Disciple* 1959; *Take a Giant Step* 1959 (p); *Elmer Gantry* 1960 **(AABA)**; *Summer of the Seventeenth Doll* 1960 (p); *The Unforgiven* 1960; *Judgment at Nuremberg* 1961; *The Young Savages* 1961; *Birdman of Alcatraz* 1962 **(AANBA)**; *A Child Is Waiting* 1962; *Il Gattopardo/The Leopard* 1963; *The List of Adrian Messenger* 1963; *Seven Days in May* 1964; *The Train* 1964; *The Hallelujah Trail* 1965; *The Professionals* 1966; *The Scalphunters* 1968; *The Swimmer* 1968; *Castle Keep* 1969; *The Gypsy Moths* 1969; *Airport* 1970; *King: A Filmed Record...Montgomery to Memphis* 1970; *Lawman* 1971; *Valdez Is Coming* 1971; *Ulzana's Raid* 1972; *Executive Action* 1973; *Scorpio* 1973; *The Midnight Man* 1974 (a,d,p,sc); *Ali the Man: Ali the Fighter* 1975; *Gruppo di famiglia in un interno/Conversation Piece* 1975; *Buffalo Bill and the Indians, or Sitting Bull's History Lesson* 1976; *Novecento/1900* 1976; *The Cassandra Crossing* 1977; *The Island of Dr. Moreau* 1977; *Twilight's Last Gleaming* 1977; *Go Tell the Spartans* 1978; *Arthur Miller on Home Ground* 1979; *Zulu Dawn* 1979; *Atlantic City* 1980 **(AANBA)**; *Cattle Annie and Little Britches* 1981; *La Pelle* 1981; *Local Hero* 1983; *The Osterman Weekend* 1983; *Little Treasure* 1985; *Tough Guys* 1986; *Il Giorno Prima* 1987; *Dawn's Early Light: Ralph McGill and the Segregated South* 1988; *Rocket Gibraltar* 1988; *La Boutique de l'orfevre* 1989; *Field of Dreams* 1989.

Lanchester, Elsa • Actress; also revue comedienne, singer. • Born Elizabeth Sullivan, Lewisham, England, October 8, 1902; died December 26, 1986. *Educ.* Isadora Duncan's Bellevue School, Paris. Character actress, often in eccentric parts, in the US from 1934. Perhaps best remembered for her dual roles in *The Bride of Frankenstein* (1935), as both the monster's mate and his "creator," author Mary Shelley. Lanchester was married to actor Charles Laughton from 1929 until his death in 1962. • *The Scarlet Woman (short)* 1924; *One of the Best* 1927; *Bluebottles (short)* 1928; *The Constant Nymph* 1928; *Day-Dreams (short)* 1928; *The Tonic (short)* 1928; *Comets* 1929; *Mr. Smith Wakes Up (short)* 1929; *Ashes (short)* 1930; *The Love Habit* 1931; *Officer's Mess* 1931; *Potiphar's Wife* 1931; *The Stronger Sex* 1931; *The Private Life of Henry VIII* 1933; *The Private Life of Don Juan* 1934; *Bride of Frankenstein* 1935; *David Copperfield* 1935; *Frankie and Johnnie (short)* 1935; *The Ghost Goes West* 1935; *Naughty Marietta* 1935; *Miss Bracegirdle Does Her Duty (short)* 1936; *Rembrandt* 1936 (a,song); *Vessel of Wrath* 1938; *Ladies in Retirement* 1941; *Son of Fury* 1942; *Tales of Manhattan* 1942; *Forever and a Day* 1943; *Lassie Come Home* 1943; *Passport to Destiny* 1943; *Thumbs Up* 1943; *The Razor's Edge* 1946; *The Spiral Staircase* 1946; *The Bishop's Wife* 1947; *Northwest Outpost* 1947; *The Big Clock* 1948; *Come to the Stable* 1949 **(AANBSA)**; *The Inspector General* 1949; *The Secret Garden* 1949; *Buccaneer's Girl* 1950; *Frenchie* 1950; *Mystery Street* 1950; *The Petty Girl* 1950; *Androcles and the Lion* 1952; *Dreamboat* 1952; *Les Miserables* 1952; *The Girls of Pleasure Island* 1953; *The Glass Slipper* 1954; *Hell's Half Acre* 1954; *Three Ring Circus* 1954; *Witness For the Prosecution* 1957 **(AANBSA)**; *Bell, Book and Candle* 1958; *Honeymoon Hotel* 1964; *Mary Poppins* 1964; *Pajama Party* 1964; *That Darn Cat* 1965; *Easy Come, Easy Go* 1967; *Blackbeard's Ghost* 1968; *Me, Natalie* 1969; *My Dog, the Thief* 1969; *Rascal* 1969; *Willard* 1971; *Arnold* 1973; *Terror in the Wax Museum* 1973; *Murder By Death* 1976; *Die Laughing* 1986.

Lanci, Giuseppe • Italian director of photography • *Educ.* Centro Sperimentale di Cinematografia, Rome. Has worked with leading European directors including Paolo and Vittorio Taviani (*Chaos* 1984), Andrei Tarkovski (*Nostalgia* 1983) and Lina Wertmuller (*A Complex Plot About Women, Alleys and Crimes* 1985). Lanci has also collaborated on all of Marco Bellocchio's output since the late 1970s. • *La Cina e vicina/China Is Near* 1967 (asst.cam.op); *Maternale* 1978 (ph); *Starcrash* 1979 (add.ph); *Con Fusione* 1980 (ph); *Salto Nel Vuoto/Leap Into the Void* 1980 (ph); *Ehrengard* 1982 (ph); *Gli Occhi, la Bocca/The Eyes, the Mouth* 1982 (ph); *Nostalghia/Nostalgia* 1983 (ph); *Piso Pisello* 1983 (ph); *Stelle Emigranti* 1983 (ph); *Enrico IV/Henry IV* 1984 (ph); *Kaos/Chaos* 1984 (ph); *Blues Metropolitano* 1985 (ph); *Un Complicato Intrigo di Donne, Vicoli e Delitti/A Complex Plot About Women, Alleys and Crimes* 1985 (ph); *Il Diavolo in Corpo/Devil in the Flesh* 1986 (ph); *Everytime We Say Goodbye* 1986 (ph); *Good Morning Babylon* 1986 (ph); *Havinck* 1987 (ph); *Paura e Amore/Three Sisters* 1988 (ph); *La Visione del Sabba* 1988 (ph); *Zoo* 1988 (ph); *Francesco/St. Francis of Assissi* 1989 (ph); *Palombella Rossa* 1989 (ph); *Il Prete Bello* 1989 (ph); *La Baule les pins/C'est la vie* 1990 (ph); *I Tarassachi* 1990 (ph).

Landau, Martin • Actor • Born New York, NY, June 20, 1931. *Educ.* Pratt Institute, Brooklyn; Actors Studio. Has appeared in films by such directors as Alfred Hitchcock (*North by Northwest* 1959), George Stevens and Joseph Mankiewicz, but is probably best known as the makeup artist on the popular TV series "Mission Impossible" (1966-68). Following years of relative inactivity, Landau has been acclaimed for his recent character roles in Francis Ford Coppola's *Tucker* (1988) and Woody Allen's *Crimes and Misdemeanors* (1989). • *North By Northwest* 1959; *Pork Chop Hill* 1959; *Stagecoach to Dancer's Rock* 1962; *Cleopatra* 1963; *The Greatest Story Ever Told* 1965; *The Hallelujah Trail* 1965; *Nevada Smith* 1966; *Mission Impossible Vs. the Mob* 1969; *They Call Me Mr. Tibbs* 1970; *A Town Called Hell* 1971; *Black Gunn* 1972; *Strange Shadows in an Empty Room* 1976; *The Last Word* 1979; *Meteor* 1979; *Without Warning* 1980; *The Being* 1983; *L'île au Tresor* 1985; *Cyclone* 1987; *Empire State* 1987; *Sweet Revenge* 1987; *W.A.R. Women Against Rape* 1987; *Delta Fever* 1988; *Tucker: The Man and His Dream* 1988 **(AANBSA)**; *Crimes and Misdemeanors* 1989 **(AANBSA)**; *Paint It Black* 1990; *Real Bullets* 1990; *Eye of the Widow* 1991.

Landis, John • Director; also screenwriter, producer, actor. • Born Chicago, IL, August 3, 1950. Solid, sometimes inspired technician whose yen for broad physical comedy reflects his former life as a stuntman. Although Landis has proved adept at both social satire (*Trading Places* 1983) and sci-fi pyrotechnics (*The Twilight Zone* 1983), he seems most at home with the raucous goings-on of films such as *National Lampoon's Animal House* (1978) and *The Blues Brothers* (1980). His most widely viewed work is undoubtedly the promotional video for Michael Jackson's "Thriller" album. • *Kelly's Heroes* 1970 (uncred. prod.asst); *Battle For the Planet of the Apes* 1973 (a); *Schlock* 1973 (a,d,sc); *Death Race 2000* 1975 (a); *The Kentucky Fried Movie* 1977 (a,d); *National Lampoon's Animal House* 1978 (d); *1941* 1979 (a); *The Blues Brothers* 1980 (a,d,sc); *An American Werewolf in London* 1981 (a,d,sc); *Eating Raoul* 1982 (a,assistance); *Making Michael Jackson's Thriller* (short) 1983 (d,p,sc—part one); *Trading Places* 1983 (d); *Twilight Zone—The Movie* 1983 (d,p,sc—"Back There," "Prologue"); *The Muppets Take Manhattan* 1984 (a); *Clue* 1985 (exec.p,story); *Into the Night* 1985 (a,d); *Spies Like Us* 1985 (d); *Three Amigos!* 1986 (d); *Amazon Women on the Moon* 1987 (d,exec.p); *Coming to America* 1988 (d); *Spontaneous Combustion* 1989 (a); *Darkman* 1990 (a); *Oscar* 1991 (d).

Lane, Diane • Actress • Born New York, January, 1965. Appealing juvenile actress who has recently graduated to playing sultry femmes fatales. Married to actor Christopher Lambert. • *A Little Romance* 1979; *Touched By Love* 1979; *Cattle Annie and Little Britches* 1981; *Ladies and Gentlemen, the Fabulous Stains* 1982; *National Lampoon Goes to the Movies* 1982; *Six Pack* 1982; *The Outsiders* 1983; *Rumble Fish* 1983; *The Cotton Club* 1984; *Streets of Fire* 1984; *The Big Town* 1987; *Lady Beware* 1987; *Love Dream* 1988; *Vital Signs* 1990.

Lang, Charles B. • Director of photography • Born Charles Bryant Lang, Bluff, UT, March 27, 1902. *Educ.* USC, Los Angeles (law). Veteran cinematographer who has worked with several generations of distinguished Hollywood directors, from Dorothy Arzner (*Anybody's Woman* 1930) to Paul Mazursky (*Bob & Carol & Ted & Alice* 1969). Lang has produced outstanding work in both black-and-white (*A Farewell to Arms* 1932, *The Big Heat* 1953) and color (*Butterflies Are Free* 1972). • *Ritzy* 1927; *Half Way to Heaven* 1929; *Innocents of Paris* 1929; *The Shopworn Angel* 1929; *Anybody's Woman* 1930; *Behind the Make-Up* 1930; *For the Defense* 1930; *The Light of Western Stars* 1930; *The Right to Love* 1930; *Sarah and Son* 1930; *Seven Days Leave* 1930; *Shadow of the Law* 1930; *Street of Chance* 1930; *Tom Sawyer* 1930; *Caught* 1931; *The Magnificent Lie* 1931; *Newly Rich* 1931; *Once a Lady* 1931; *Unfaithful* 1931; *The Vice Squad* 1931; *The Devil and the Deep* 1932; *A Farewell to Arms* 1932; *He Learned About Women* 1932; *No One Man* 1932; *Thunder Below* 1932; *Tomorrow and Tomorrow* 1932; *A Bedtime Story* 1933; *Cradle Song* 1933; *Gambling Ship* 1933; *She Done Him Wrong* 1933; *The Way to Love* 1933; *Death Takes a Holiday* 1934; *Mrs. Wiggs of the Cabbage Patch* 1934; *She Loves Me Not* 1934; *We're Not Dressing* 1934; *The Lives of a Bengal Lancer* 1935; *Mississippi* 1935; *Peter Ibbetson* 1935; *Desire* 1936; *Angel* 1937; *Souls at Sea* 1937; *Tovarich* 1937; *Doctor Rhythm* 1938; *Spawn of the North* 1938; *You and Me* 1938; *The Cat and the Canary* 1939; *The Gracie Allen Murder Case* 1939; *Midnight* 1939; *Zaza* 1939; *Adventure in Diamonds* 1940; *Arise, My Love* 1940; *Buck Benny Rides Again* 1940; *Dancing on a Dime* 1940; *The Ghost Breakers* 1940; *Women Without Names* 1940; *Nothing But the Truth* 1941; *The Shepherd of the Hills* 1941; *Skylark* 1941; *Sundown* 1941; *Are Husbands Necessary?* 1942; *The Forest Rangers* 1942; *The Lady Has Plans* 1942; *No Time For Love* 1943; *So Proudly We Hail* 1943; *True to Life* 1943; *Frenchman's Creek* 1944 (uncred.ph); *Here Come the Waves* 1944; *I Love a Soldier* 1944; *Practically Yours* 1944; *Standing Room Only* 1944; *The Uninvited* 1944; *Miss Susie Slagle's* 1945; *The Stork Club* 1945; *Blue Skies* 1946; *Cross My Heart* 1946; *Desert Fury* 1947; *Desire Me* 1947 (uncred.ph); *The Ghost and Mrs. Muir* 1947; *Where There's Life* 1947; *A Foreign Affair* 1948; *Miss Tatlock's Millions* 1948; *The Great Lover* 1949; *My Own True Love* 1949; *Rope of Sand* 1949; *Branded* 1950; *Copper Canyon* 1950; *Fancy Pants* 1950; *The Mating Season* 1950; *The Big Carnival/Ace in the Hole* 1951; *Mr. Belvedere Rings the Bell* 1951; *Peking Express* 1951; *Red Mountain* 1951; *September Affair* 1951; *Aaron Slick From Punkin Crick* 1952; *The Atomic City* 1952; *Sudden Fear* 1952; *The Big Heat* 1953; *Salome* 1953; *It Should Happen to You* 1954; *Phfft* 1954; *Sabrina* 1954; *Female on the Beach* 1955; *The Man From Laramie* 1955; *Queen Bee* 1955; *Autumn Leaves* 1956; *The Rainmaker* 1956; *The Solid Gold Cadillac* 1956; *Gunfight at the O.K. Corral* 1957; *Loving You* 1957; *Wild Is the Wind* 1957; *The Matchmaker* 1958; *Separate Tables* 1958; *Last Train From Gun Hill* 1959; *Some Like It Hot* 1959; *The Facts of Life* 1960; *The Magnificent Seven* 1960; *Song Without End* 1960 (uncred.ph); *Strangers When We Meet* 1960; *Blue Hawaii* 1961; *One-Eyed Jacks* 1961; *Summer and Smoke* 1961; *A Girl Named Tamiko* 1962; *How the West Was Won* 1962; *Charade* 1963; *Critic's Choice* 1963; *Paris When It Sizzles* 1963; *The Wheeler Dealers* 1963; *Father Goose* 1964; *Sex and the Single Girl* 1964; *Inside Daisy Clover* 1965; *How to Steal a Million* 1966; *Not With My Wife, You Don't* 1966; *The Flim-Flam Man* 1967; *Hotel* 1967; *Wait Until Dark* 1967; *A Flea in Her Ear* 1968; *The Stalking Moon* 1968; *Bob & Carol & Ted & Alice* 1969 **(AANBPH)**; *How to Commit Marriage* 1969; *Doctors' Wives* 1970; *A Walk in the Spring Rain* 1970; *The Love Machine* 1971; *Butterflies Are Free* 1972 **(AANBPH)**; *40 Carats* 1973.

Lang, Fritz • Director, screenwriter; also producer. • Born Friedrich Christian Anton Lang, Vienna, Austria, December 5, 1890; died August 2, 1976. *Educ.* Technische Hochshule (architecture); Vienna Academy of Graphic Arts (art); School of Arts and Crafts, Munich (art); Academie Julien, Paris. *Human Desire* (1954), made during Fritz Lang's last decade as a film director, begins with an emblematic image: a locomotive rushes forward, swift and dynamic, but locked to the tracks, its path fixed, its destination visible. Like Lang's films the train and the tracks speak of a world of narrowly defined choices. The closing image is even more severe: survivor Glenn Ford departs, his locomotive passing a sign on a bridge. Ford does not see the sign, but we do; abbreviated by intervening beams we suddenly see "The world takes" just before the film ends.

This vision of a hostile universe, constraints on freedom and messages that are missed or misunderstood but always seen by someone, can be found in all of Fritz Lang's films. His work has a consistency and a richness that are unique in world cinema. In Germany, in France, in Hollywood, then in Germany again, Lang built genre worlds for producers and audiences and veiled meditations on human experience for himself.

Lang's vision is that of the outsider. James Baldwin, an outsider himself, catches Lang's "concern, or obsession...with the fact and effect of human loneliness, and the ways in which we are all responsible for the creation, and the fate, of the isolated..." Born an Austrian, Lang fled his training as an architect for a jaunt through the middle and far east, returned to Paris just in time for the beginning of WWI, then fought on the losing side of the war. Recovering from wounds which cost him the sight in his right eye, Lang wrote his first scenarios: a werewolf story which found no buyers, and *Wedding in the Eccentric Club* and *Hilde Warren and Death*, which were sold and eventually produced by Joe May. May's deviations from Lang's scripts motivated Lang to become a director himself; his first movie was *Halbblut/The Half-Caste* (1919), a still-lost film about the revenge of a half-Mexican mistress. Later that year he directed the first film of a two-part international thriller called *The Spiders* (1920). Part one, subtitled *The Golden Lake*, proved so popular that his producers insisted Lang immediately make part two, *The Diamond Ship*. He had been working on another script which he hoped to film, so he reluctantly gave up *The Cabinet of Dr. Caligari* (1919) to Robert Wiene. His contribution to that landmark film nevertheless was crucial: Lang thought up the framing device, in which it is revealed at the story's end that we have been watching a tale told by a madman, thus significantly undercutting the audience's perceptions of the story.

Lang's career in the 1920s was one of spectacular rise to fame. With each film, he became more assured, garnering critical acclaim as well as a popular following. *Dr. Mabuse the Gambler* (1922), *Die Nibelungen* (1924), *Metropolis* (1927), and *Spies* (1928) are among the greatest silent films produced anywhere. Lang also made a remarkable transtition to sound, with *M* (1931), but he ran afoul of Nazi authorities with *The Last Will of Dr. Mabuse* (1933), whose villains mouthed Nazi propaganda. When the film was banned and Lang was requested to make films for the cause of the Third Reich, he immediately fled Germany, leaving behind most of his personal possessions, as well as his wife, screenwriter Thea von Harbou (who had joined the Nazi party and become an official screenwriter).

Lang made one film in France, then moved on to Hollywood, where he spent the next 20 years working in a variety of genres, mainly thrillers (e.g. *Man Hunt* 1941, *Scarlet Street* 1945, *While the City Sleeps* 1956) and some outstanding westerns (*The Return of Frank James* 1940, *Rancho Notorious* 1952). Tired of warring with insensitive producers, Lang left the U.S. in the mid-1950s to make a film in India and then returned to Germany for his last set of films, including a final chapter in the Dr. Mabuse saga.

The disorienting frame in *Caligari* is an important part of Lang's distinctive vision. His films are punctuated by shifts of viewpoint and discoveries which transform the reactions of his characters—and of his audience. The most obvious of these shifts of viewpoint come in *Caligari* and *The Woman in the Window* (1944), in which the drama is suddenly revealed to be a dream. But they also occur in the *Mabuse* films; in *M*, with the policeman mistaken by a burglar for another thief; and in *House By the River* (1950), when a servant is strangled because another maid appears to be responding to her cries for help.

Lang's films are also about contingency, the recognition that extra-personal forces mold our lives, shape our destiny in ways we cannot predict and only somewhat modify. In the two-part film, *Die Nibelungen*, Kriemhild is transformed from a secondary figure in the first film (*Siegfried*) into a whirlwind of fury in the second (*Kriemhild's Revenge*). Even the characters in the film are shaken by these transformations. The king of the Huns is staggered by Kriemhild's thirst for death; the vengeful underworld in *M* that has captured and tried Peter Lorre is taken aback by Lorre's confession that he "must" rape and murder, that he is something of a spectator to his crimes.

These moments of perception are the foundation of Lang's importance and continuing strength as a filmmaker. They constitute a kind of morality that he never abandoned. In the script for *Liliom* (1934), his French film made after he fled the Nazis, Lang wrote, "If death settled everything it would be too easy...Where would justice be if death settled everything?" Thirty years later, playing himself in Jean-Luc Godard's *Contempt* (1963), Lang wrote for his character, "La mort n'est pas une solution." ("Death is no solution"). Nor does death erase human striving. In *Der Müde Tod/Destiny* (1921) the force of love survives, in *Fury* (1936) the cycle of vengeance is broken, in *Clash By Night* (1952) Barbara Stanwyck chooses reponsibility, in *The Big Heat* (1953) Glenn Ford finally turns to the police and ends his vendetta, and in *Human Desire* Ford again leaves the scene of the crime, choosing life over the locus of death. RAH • *Die Peitsche* 1916 (sc); *Hilde Warren und der Tod/Hilde Warren and Death* 1917 (a,d); *Die Hochzeit in Exzentric-Club/Wedding in the Eccentric Club* 1917 (uncred.sc); *Die Bettler-G.m.b.H.* 1918 (sc); *Die Rache Ist Mein* 1918 (sc); *Die Frau mit den Orchideen* 1919 (sc); *Halbblut/The Half Caste* 1919 (d,sc); *Harakiri* 1919 (d); *Der Herr der Liebe* 1919 (a,d); *Lilith und Ly* 1919 (sc); *Die Pest in Florenz* 1919 (sc); *Totentanz* 1919 (sc); *Wolkenbau und Flimmerstern* 1919 (sc); *Die Herrin der Welt* 1920 (ad); *Die Spinnen/The Spiders* 1920 (d,sc); *Das Wandernde Bild* 1920 (d,sc); *Das Indische Grabmal* 1921 (d); *Der Müde Tod/Destiny* 1921 (d,sc); *Vier um die Frau* 1921 (d,sc); *Dr. Mabuse der Spieler/Dr. Mabuse the Gambler* 1922 (d); *Die Nibelungen* 1924 (d,sc); *Metropolis* 1927 (d,sc); *Spione/Spies* 1928 (d,p,sc,story); *Die Frau im Mond* 1929 (d,p,sc); *M* 1931 (d); *Das Testament des Dr. Mabuse/The Last Will of Dr. Mabuse* 1933 (d); *Liliom* 1934 (d,sc); *Fury* 1936 (d,sc); *You Only Live Once* 1937 (d); *You and Me* 1938 (d,p); *The Return of Frank James* 1940 (d); *Man Hunt* 1941 (d); *Western Union* 1941 (d); *Hangmen Also Die* 1943 (d,p,story,adapt); *Ministry of Fear* 1944 (d); *The Woman in the Window* 1944 (d); *Scarlet Street* 1945 (d,p); *Cloak and Dagger* 1946 (d); *Secret Beyond the Door* 1948 (d,p); *An American Guerrilla in the Philippines* 1950 (d); *House By the River* 1950 (d); *M* 1951 (from original screenplay); *Clash By Night* 1952 (d); *Rancho Notorious* 1952 (d); *The Big Heat* 1953 (d); *The Blue Gardenia* 1953 (d); *Hollywood Goes a-Fishin' (short)* 1953 (a); *Human Desire* 1954 (d); *Moonfleet* 1955 (d); *Beyond a Reasonable Doubt* 1956 (d); *While The City Sleeps* 1956 (d); *Das Indische Grabmal* 1959 (d); *Die Tausend Augen des Dr. Mabuse/The Thousand Eyes of Dr. Mabuse* 1960 (d,p,sc); *Le Mépris/Contempt* 1963 (a); *Begegnung mit Fritz Lang (short)* 1964 (a); *75 Years of Cinema Museum* 1972 (a); *The Exiles* 1989 (archival footage).

Langdon, Harry • Actor • Born Council Bluffs, IA, June 15, 1884; died 1944. Harry Langdon emerged in the mid-1920s on the American comedy scene like a super nova burning startlingly bright, only to die down quickly to darkness. His cherubic little figure, dressed in a tiny, cloth hat, oversized coat, and broad, floppy shoes, arrived during a period of stagnation in the character comedies of Lloyd, Keaton, and Chaplin: Lloyd was repeating himself, Keaton was repeating Lloyd and Chaplin was inactive from 1925 to 1928. And into this breach came Langdon.

Langdon developed his character and some basic comic situations as a successful stage performer. Film producer Mack Sennett spotted him, signed him to a contract in 1923, and assigned Sennett staff members Arthur Ripley, Harry Edwards and Frank Capra to work with Langdon to translate his comic persona to film. His first film for Sennett, *Picking Peaches* (1924), showed little promise, but by the time Langdon made his final short for Sennett, *Saturday Afternoon* (1926), his character was in place.

The Langdon character possesses an imperishable optimism and a babylike innocence, characterized by a fleeting half-smile and a meek wave of greeting. In a bizarre twist, it happens that this waif-like creature is a grown man, a social being possessing a job and a family. But this man's childish nature is taken as a given and his purity is endowed by a primal religious faith protected by a higher power. As Capra once explained it, "His only ally was God. Langdon might be saved by a brick falling on a cop, but it was verboten that he in any way motivate the brick's fall."

Langdon's passivity and ambiguous presence was a refreshing tonic for audiences of the mid-20, giving them a new perspective. Walter Kerr called Langdon "a comma," a reference to his place among the other popular comedians of the day. Langdon gently rattled the overly familiar slapstick situations, in which some type of action is required; his inaction bared the comic structures to film audiences and at the same time kept them alive.

Langdon's rise to popularity was swift; in 1925, *Photoplay* would write: "Ask Harold Lloyd who gives him the biggest celluloid laugh. Ask any star. They will all say Langdon. In a year, he has taken up his comedy post right behind Keaton and Lloyd."

Inevitably, Langdon would expand into features. When he signed with Warner Bros. in 1926, he took Edwards, Ripley and Capra with him. His first three features (*Tramp, Tramp, Tramp* 1926; *The Strong Man* 1926; *Long Pants* 1927) were critical and popular successes. Then, according to Capra, Langdon began to fancy himself another Chaplin; he fired Capra and Edwards and began to direct himself.

Without a firm grasp on his screen character, the Langdon-directed films were mawkish, maudlin and repetitive. Langdon had allowed the thin ambiguity that kept his persona afloat to sink under him. After the triple disasters of *Three's A Crowd* (1927), *The Chaser* and *Heart Trouble* (both 1928), Langdon's career was in ruins. Like Keaton, Langdon found himself relegated to bit parts in features, low-budget comedy shorts and gag writing, with rare notable performances (*Hallelujah I'm a Bum* 1933; *Zenobia* 1939).

Langdon's legacy will always be the quiet flame of his unique silent character. Perhaps it was a balancing act that could not be substained for long, for it was too narrow, too reflective of the forms. But there was no denying the genius. As James Agee wrote, "Langdon had one queerly toned, unique little reed. But out of it he could get incredible melodies." PB • *All Night Long (short)* 1924 (a); *Boobs in the Wood (short)* 1924 (a); *The Cat's Meow (short)* 1924 (a); *Feet of Mud (short)* 1924 (a); *The First Hundred Years* 1924 (a); *Flickering Youth (short)* 1924 (a); *The Hansom Cabman (short)* 1924 (a); *His Marriage Wow (short)* 1924 (a); *His New Mamma (short)* 1924 (a); *Luck o' the Foolish (short)* 1924 (a); *Picking Peaches (short)* 1924 (a); *The Sea Squawk (short)* 1924 (a); *Shanghaied Lovers (short)* 1924 (a); *Smile Please (short)* 1924 (a); *Horace Greely, Jr. (short)* 1925 (a); *Lucky Stars (short)* 1925 (a); *Plain Clothes (short)* 1925 (a); *Remember When? (short)* 1925 (a); *There He Goes (short)* 1925 (a); *The White Wing's Bride (short)* 1925 (a); *Ella Cinders* 1926 (a); *Fiddlesticks (short)* 1926 (a); *Saturday Afternoon (short)* 1926 (a); *Soldier Man* 1926 (a); *The Strong Man* 1926 (a); *Tramp, Tramp, Tramp* 1926 (a,p); *His First Flame* 1927 (a); *Long Pants* 1927 (a); *Three's a Crowd* 1927 (a,d); *The Chaser* 1928 (a,d); *Heart Trouble* 1928 (a,d); *The Head Guy (short)* 1929 (a); *Hotter Than Hot (short)* 1929 (a); *Skirt Shy (short)* 1929 (a); *Sky Boy (short)* 1929 (a); *The Big Kick (short)* 1930 (a); *The Fighting Parson (short)* 1930 (a); *The King (short)* 1930 (a); *See America Thirsty* 1930 (a); *The Shrimp (short)* 1930 (a); *A Soldier's Plaything* 1930 (a); *The Big Flash (short)* 1932 (a); *Hallelujah, I'm a Bum* 1933 (a); *The Hitch Hiker (short)* 1933 (a); *Hooks and Jabs (short)* 1933 (a); *Knight Duty (short)* 1933 (a); *Marriage Humor (short)* 1933 (a); *My Weakness* 1933 (a); *On Ice (short)* 1933 (a); *A Roaming Romeo (short)* 1933 (a); *The Stage Hand (short)* 1933 (archival footage,d,story); *Tied For Life (short)* 1933 (a); *Tired Feet (short)* 1933 (a); *A Circus Hoodoo (short)* 1934 (a); *No Sleep on the Deep (short)* 1934 (a); *Petting Preferred (short)* 1934 (a); *Shivers (short)* 1934 (a); *Trimmed in Furs (short)* 1934 (a); *Atlantic Adventure* 1935 (a); *His Bridal Sweet (short)* 1935 (a); *His Marriage Mixup (short)* 1935 (a); *I Don't Remember (short)* 1935 (a); *The Leathernecker (short)* 1935 (a); *Wise Guys* 1937 (d); *Block-Heads* 1938 (sc,story); *A Doggone Mixup (short)* 1938 (a); *He Loved an Actress* 1938 (a); *Sue My Lawyer (short)* 1938 (a,story); *There Goes My Heart* 1938 (a); *Cold Turkey (short)* 1939 (a); *The Flying Deuces* 1939 (sc,story); *Goodness! A Ghost (short)* 1939 (a,sc); *Zenobia* 1939 (a); *A Chump at Oxford* 1940 (sc,story); *Misbehaving Husbands* 1940 (a); *Saps at Sea* 1940 (sc,story); *All American Co-Ed* 1941 (a); *Beautiful Clothes (Make Beautiful Girls) (short)* 1941 (a); *Double Trouble* 1941 (a); *Road Show* 1941 (sc); *Carry Harry (short)* 1942 (a); *House of Errors* 1942 (a,story); *Piano Mooner (short)* 1942 (a,sc,story); *Tireman, Spare My Tires (short)* 1942 (a); *What Makes Lizzy Dizzy (short)* 1942 (a); *A Blitz on the Fritz (short)* 1943 (a); *Blonde and Groom (short)* 1943 (a,sc,story); *Here Comes Mr. Zerk (short)* 1943 (a); *Spotlight Scandals* 1943 (a); *Block Busters* 1944 (a); *Bride By Mistake* 1944 (gags); *Defective Detectives (short)* 1944 (a); *Hot Rhythm* 1944 (a); *Mopey Dope (short)* 1944 (a); *To Heir Is Human (short)* 1944 (a); *Pistol Packin' Nitwits (short)* 1945 (a,story); *Snooper Service (short)* 1945 (a); *Swingin' on a Rainbow* 1945 (a); *Golden Age of Comedy* 1957 (archival footage); *30 Years of Fun* 1963 (archival footage); *The Sound of Laughter* 1963 (archival footage).

Lange, Jessica • Actress • Born Cloquet, MN, April 20, 1949. *Educ.* University of Minnesota. Successfully outgrew the image established by her screen debut—as the scantily clad playmate of *King Kong* (1976)—to emerge as one of the finest Hollywood actresses of the 1980s. Lange proved her versatility with two 1982 roles: as 30s actress Frances Farmer in *Frances* and as Dustin Hoffman's love interest in *Tootsie*; the first won her an Oscar nomination for best actress and the second, the award for best supporting actress. She has subsequently racked up three more nominations, most recently with a searching, intelligent performance as the unsuspecting daughter of a war criminal in Costa-Gavras's *Music Box* (1989). Lange has three children, one by Mikhail Baryshnikov and two by Sam Shepard. • *King Kong* 1976 (a); *All That Jazz* 1979 (a); *How to Beat the High Cost of Living* 1980 (a); *The Postman Always Rings Twice* 1981 (a); *Frances* 1982 (a) **(AANBA)**; *Tootsie* 1982 (a) **(AABSA)**; *Country* 1984 (a,p) **(AANBA)**; *Sweet Dreams* 1985 (a) **(AANBA)**; *Crimes of the Heart* 1986 (a); *Everybody's All-American* 1988 (a); *Far North* 1988 (a); *Music Box* 1989 (a) **(AANBA)**; *Men Don't Leave* 1990 (a); *Blue Sky* 1991 (a).

Langella, Frank • Actor • Born Bayonne, NJ, January 1, 1940. Tall, dark and handsome leading man of the 1970s; best known for his title role in *Dracula* (1979). • *Diary of a Mad Housewife* 1970; *The Twelve Chairs* 1970; *La Maison Sous les Arbres* 1971; *The Wrath of God* 1972; *Dracula* 1979; *Sphinx* 1980; *Those Lips Those Eyes* 1980; *The Men's Club* 1986; *Masters of the Universe* 1987; *And God Created Woman* 1988.

Langlois, Henri • Archivist, filmmaker • Born Smyrna, Turkey, November 13, 1914; died 1977. Co-founder, with Georges Franju and Jean Mitry, of the Cinémathèque Française film archive in 1936. Starting with only ten features, Langlois aggressively increased the Cinémathèque's collection to some 60,000 films during his tenure. (As well as preserving many silent films, Langlois and his colleagues concealed and thus saved potentially controversial works from the occupying German forces during WWII.) Langlois' shrine to cinema history influenced a whole generation of filmmakers, notably the future leading lights of the French New Wave. Although the archive was subsidized by the French government from 1945, a bitter dispute erupted in 1968 between Langlois and the Ministry of Culture, headed by André Malraux. Impatient with Langlois' unconventional working methods, Malraux sought to remove him from control of the Cinémathèque by halting governmental support. After street rallies in Paris and protests from leading international film figures, Langlois was reinstated, though the subsidy was not. • *Le Métro (short)* 1935 (d); *Marc Chagall* 1962 (d); *From Lumière to Langlois* 1970 (d); *75 Years of Cinema Museum* 1972 (a); *The Challenge* 1976 (archival footage); *He Stands in a Desert Counting the Seconds of His Life* 1985 (a).

Lansbury, Angela • Actress • Born London, October 16, 1925. *Educ.* Feagin School of Dramatic Arts, New York. Stage-trained actress whose early screen career was marked by a string of unsympathetic portraits, beginning with her acclaimed debut in *Gaslight* (1944); Lansbury was also memorable as Laurence Harvey's manipulative mother in *The Manchurian Candidate* (1962). Most of her subsequent work has been for stage and TV, most notably Tony award-winning roles in *Mame, Dear World, Gypsy* and *Sweeney Todd*, and the long-running TV series "Murder, She Wrote." • *Gaslight* 1944 (a) **(AANBSA)**; *National Velvet* 1944 (a); *The Picture of Dorian Gray* 1945 (a) **(AANBSA)**; *The Harvey Girls* 1946 (a); *The Hoodlum Saint* 1946 (a); *Till the Clouds Roll By* 1946 (a); *If Winter Comes* 1947 (a); *The Private Affairs of Bel Ami* 1947 (a); *State of the Union* 1948 (a); *Tenth Avenue Angel* 1948 (a); *The Three Musketeers* 1948 (a); *The Red Danube* 1949 (a); *Sam-*

son and Delilah 1949 (a); *Kind Lady* 1951 (a); *Mutiny* 1952 (a); *Remains to Be Seen* 1953 (a); *The Key Man* 1954 (a); *A Lawless Street* 1955 (a); *The Purple Mask* 1955 (a); *The Court Jester* 1956 (a); *Please Murder Me* 1956 (a); *The Long, Hot Summer* 1958 (a); *The Reluctant Debutante* 1958 (a); *A Breath of Scandal* 1960 (a); *The Dark at the Top of the Stairs* 1960 (a); *Summer of the Seventeenth Doll* 1960 (a); *Blue Hawaii* 1961 (a); *All Fall Down* 1962 (a); *The Four Horsemen of the Apocalypse* 1962 (voice dubbing—Ingrid Thulin); *The Manchurian Candidate* 1962 (a) **(AANBSA)**; *In the Cool of the Day* 1963 (a); *Dear Heart* 1964 (a); *The World of Henry Orient* 1964 (a); *The Amorous Adventures of Moll Flanders* 1965 (a); *The Greatest Story Ever Told* 1965 (a); *Harlow* 1965 (a); *Mister Buddwing* 1965 (a); *Something For Everyone* 1970 (a); *Bedknobs and Broomsticks* 1971 (a); *Death on the Nile* 1978 (a); *The Lady Vanishes* 1979 (a); *The Mirror Crack'd* 1980 (a); *The Last Unicorn* 1982 (a); *The Pirates of Penzance* 1982 (a); *The Company of Wolves* 1985 (a).

Lansing, Sherry • Producer, executive; also actress • Born Chicago, IL, July 31, 1944. *Educ.* Northwestern University (speech). Former school teacher, model and actress who worked her way up through the Hollywood heirarchy to be appointed president of 20th Century-Fox (the first time a woman had held such a position) in 1980. Lansing formed Jaffe-Lansing productions with producer Stanley R. Jaffe and since 1984 the team have been responsible for films such as *Fatal Attraction* (1987) and *The Accused* (1988). • *Loving* 1970 (a); *Rio Lobo* 1970 (a); *Firstborn* 1984 (exec.p); *Racing With the Moon* 1984 (exec.p); *Fatal Attraction* 1987 (p) **(AANBP)**; *The Accused* 1988 (p); *Calling the Shots* 1988 (a); *Black Rain* 1989 (p).

Lanza, Mario • Opera singer, actor • Born Alfredo Cocozza, Philadelphia, PA, January 31, 1921; died 1959. Opera singer turned romantic lead who appeared in a number of films manufactured to exploit his lush voice and latinate sex appeal. Lanza's short-lived career ran aground in the mid-1950s, partly due to drugs, alcohol and conspicuous weight problems. • *That Midnight Kiss* 1949 (a); *The Toast of New Orleans* 1950 (a); *The Great Caruso* 1951 (a); *Because You're Mine* 1952 (a); *The Student Prince* 1954 (m); *Serenade* 1955 (a); *Seven Hills of Rome* 1957 (a,song); *Serenade Einer Grossen Liebe* 1959 (a); *Bird* 1988 (m); *The Mario Lanza Story (short)* 1989 (m,m.perf); *Just Me and Mario* 1990 (song).

Lardner, Ring, Jr. • Screenwriter • Born Ringgold Wilmer Lardner, Jr., Chicago, IL, August 19, 1915. *Educ.* Princeton; Moscow University. Hollywood publicist turned script doctor who began having his own screenplays produced in the 1940s. Lardner's notable contributions include the acid satire, *Nothing Sacred* (1937), the effervescent comedy, *Woman of the Year* (1942) and the noir classic, *Laura* (1944). One of the "Hollywood Ten," Lardner served a term in prison before circumventing his blacklisting by using various pseudonyms. He resurfaced under his own name in the mid-60s with the excellent drama, *The Cincinnati Kid* (1965). Son of humorist Ring Lardner and brother of writers John, James and David Lardner. • *Nothing Sacred* 1937 (uncred.sc); *A Star Is Born* 1937 (uncred.sc); *Meet Dr. Christian* 1939 (sc); *The Courageous Dr. Christian* 1940 (sc,story); *Arkansas Judge* 1941 (adapt); *Woman of the Year* 1942 (sc,story) **(AABSC)**; *The Cross of Lorraine* 1943 (sc); *Laura* 1944 (uncred.sc); *Tomorrow the World* 1944 (sc); *Brotherhood of Man* 1946 (sc); *Cloak and Dagger* 1946 (sc); *Forever Amber* 1947 (sc); *Britannia Mews* 1949 (sc); *Swiss Tour* 1949 (dial); *The Hollywood Ten* 1950 (a,sc); *The Big Night* 1951 (uncred.sc); *Virgin Island* 1958 (sc); *A Breath of Scandal* 1960 (uncred.sc); *The Cardinal* 1963 (uncred.sc); *The Cincinnati Kid* 1965 (sc); *M*A*S*H* 1970 (sc) **(AABSC)**; *La Maison Sous les Arbres* 1971 (uncred.sc); *La Mortadella* 1972 (sc,adapt—English-language version); *Hollywood on Trial* 1976 (a); *The Greatest* 1977 (sc); *My Name Is Bertolt Brecht—Exile in U.S.A.* 1988 (a).

Lasky, Jesse L. • Executive; also producer. • Born San Francisco, September 13, 1880; died 1958. Impresario who formed the Jesse Lasky Feature Play Company with brother-in-law Samuel Goldfish (later Goldwyn) and Cecil B. DeMille in 1913. The success of their 1914 production, *Squaw Man*, put both the company and Hollywood on the map (it was the first feature shot in Southern California). Following a series of mergers, first with Adolph Zukor's company in 1916, the consolidated outfit was rechristened Paramount and went on to became a major Hollywood studio. In 1932, Lasky was forced out of the organization he had helped to found and embarked on a moderately successful career as an independent producer. Lasky's son, Jesse, Jr. (1908-1988), was an author and screenwriter (*Samson and Delilah* 1949, *The Ten Commandments* 1956). • *The Call of the North* 1914 (p); *Squaw Man* 1914 (p); *Brewster's Millions* 1921 (p); *The Sorrows of Satan* 1926 (p); *Zoo in Budapest* 1933 (p); *Helldorado* 1934 (p); *The Gay Deception* 1935 (p); *Here's to Romance* 1935 (p); *Redheads on Parade* 1935 (p); *The Gay Desperado* 1936 (p); *One Rainy Afternoon* 1936 (p); *Hitting a New High* 1937 (p); *Music For Madame* 1937 (p); *Sergeant York* 1941 (p); *The Adventures of Mark Twain* 1944 (p); *Rhapsody in Blue* 1945 (p); *Without Reservations* 1946 (p); *The Miracle of the Bells* 1948 (p).

Lassally, Walter • Director of photography; also producer, director. • Born Berlin, December 18, 1926. Award-winning cinematographer who found his stride with the emergence of the British Free Cinema movement. Like many of the directors with whom he worked—Lindsay Anderson, Karel Reisz, Tony Richardson—Lassally contributed to "alternative" journals such as *Film* in the 1950s, proving an articulate champion of personal, low-budget filmmaking. He has been involved in a series of independent production companies and has latterly worked on several Merchant/Ivory features. • *Dancing With Crime* 1947 (clapper loader); *Things Happen at Night* 1948 (cam.asst); *This Was a Woman* 1948 (cam.asst); *What's in a Number (short)* 1948 (cam.asst); *Every Five Minutes (short)* 1950 (ph); *Night and the City* 1950 (focus puller 2u); *Forward a Century (short)* 1951 (ph—South Bank); *From Plan Into Action (short)* 1951 (ph); *At Whose Door? (short)* 1952 (ph); *Festival (short)* 1952 (ph); *Three Installations* (short) 1952 (ph); *Wakefield Express* (short) 1952 (ph); *House of Blackmail* 1953 (asst.ed); *The Pleasure Garden* (short) 1953 (ph); *Strange Stories* 1953 (cam.asst); *Sunday By the Sea (short)* 1953 (ph); *Thursday's Children* (short) 1953 (ph); *The Passing Stranger* 1954 (ph); *The Children Upstairs (short)* 1955 (ph); *Continuous Observation (short)* 1955 (ph); *Foot and Mouth (short)* 1955 (ph); *Green and Pleasant Land (short)* 1955 (ph); *Henry (short)* 1955 (ph); *A Hundred Thousand Children (short)* 1955 (ph); *Momma Don't Allow (short)* 1956 (ph); *To Koritsi Me Ta Mara* 1956 (ph); *Together* 1956 (add.ph); *Every Day Except Christmas* (short) 1957 (ph); *To telefteo psema* 1957 (ph); *George Bernard Shaw* (short) 1958 (ph); *We Are the Lambeth Boys* (short) 1958 (ph); *Enquiry Into General Practice (short)* 1959 (ph); *Aliki sto naftiko* 1960 (ph); *Beat Girl* 1960 (ph); *Eroica* 1960 (ph); *Madalena* 1960 (ph); *Electra* 1961 (ph); *I Liza kai i alli* 1961 (ph); *A Taste of Honey* 1961 (ph); *The Loneliness of the Long Distance Runner* 1962 (ph); *Tom Jones* 1963 (ph); *The Peaches (short)* 1964 (ph); *Psyche '59* 1964 (ph); *Zorba the Greek* 1964 (ph) **(AABPH)**; *Assignment Skybolt* 1966 (ph); *The Day the Fish Came Out* 1967 (ph); *Anikiti epistoli* 1968 (ph); *Joanna* 1968 (ph); *Oedipus the King* 1968 (ph); *Olimpiada en Mexico* 1968 (ph); *The Adding Machine* 1969 (ph); *Three Into Two Won't Go* 1969 (ph); *Something For Everyone* 1970 (ph); *Twinky* 1970 (ph); *Can Horses Sing? (short)* 1971 (ph); *Le Mans* 1971 (uncred.ph—racetrack); *Savages* 1972 (ph); *To Kill a Clown* 1972 (ph); *Bilocation* 1973 (ph); *Happy Mother's Day...Love, George* 1973 (ph); *The Sea-*

weed Children 1973 (ph); *Visions of Eight* 1973 (ph—"The Highest"); *Aprés le vent des sables* 1974 (ph); *Carved in Ivory (short)* 1974 (ph); *W.S.P. (short)* 1974 (ph); *Ansichten Eines Clowns* 1975 (ph); *Autobiography of a Princess* 1975 (ph); *The Wild Party* 1975 (ph); *Ernst Fuchs* 1976 (ph); *Fluchtversuch* 1976 (ph); *Pleasantville* 1976 (ph); *Requiem For a Village* 1976 (add.ph); *Morgensterne* 1977 (ph); *Shenanigans* 1977 (ph); *Die Frau Gegenüber* 1978 (ph); *How the Myth Was Made: A Study of Robert Flaherty's Man of Aran* 1978 (a); *Hullabaloo Over Georgie and Bonnie's Pictures* 1979 (ph); *Something Short of Paradise* 1979 (ph); *The Blood of Hussain* 1980 (ph); *The Pilot* 1980 (ph); *Der Preis fürs Überleben* 1980 (ph); *Engel aus Eisen* 1981 (ph); *Memoirs of a Survivor* 1981 (ph); *Tuxedo Warrior* 1982 (ph); *The Case of Marcel Duchamp* 1983 (ph); *Heat and Dust* 1983 (ph); *Private School* 1983 (ph); *The Bostonians* 1984 (ph); *Indian Summer* 1987 (ph); *The Deceivers* 1988 (ph); *The Perfect Murder* 1988 (ph); *Fragments of Isabella* 1989 (ph); *Kamilla og tyven II* 1989 (ph); *The Ballad of the Sad Cafe* 1991 (ph).

Laszlo, Andrew • Director of photography • Born Sombor, Yugoslavia, January 12, 1926. Cinematographer noted for his work in the urban action genre. Laszlo moved with his family to Hungary as a child and emigrated to the US in 1947. He began his American career in TV ("The Phil Silvers Show," "Naked City"). • *One Potato, Two Potato* 1964 (ph); *You're a Big Boy Now* 1967 (ph); *The Night They Raided Minsky's* 1968 (ph); *Popi* 1969 (ph); *Lovers and Other Strangers* 1970 (ph); *The Out-of-Towners* 1970 (ph); *The Owl and the Pussycat* 1970 (ph); *Jennifer on My Mind* 1971 (ph); *To Find a Man* 1972 (ph); *Class of '44* 1973 (ph); *Countdown at Kusini* 1976 (ph); *Thieves* 1977 (ph); *Somebody Killed Her Husband* 1978 (ph); *Rockshow* 1979 (ph); *The Warriors* 1979 (ph); *The Funhouse* 1981 (ph); *I, the Jury* 1981 (ph); *Southern Comfort* 1981 (ph); *Comeback* 1982 (ph); *First Blood* 1982 (ph); *Streets of Fire* 1984 (ph); *Thief of Hearts* 1984 (ph); *Remo Williams: The Adventure Begins...* 1985 (ph); *That's Dancing!* 1985 (add.ph); *Poltergeist II: The Other Side* 1986 (ph); *Innerspace* 1987 (ph); *Star Trek V: The Final Frontier* 1989 (ph); *Ghost Dad* 1990 (ph).

Laszlo, Ernest • Director of photography • Born Budapest, Hungary, c. 1906; died January 6, 1984. Distinguished cinematographer, in Hollywood from 1926. An eight-time Oscar nominee, Laszlo won the award once, for *Ship of Fools* (1965). • *Tongues of Scandal* 1927 (cam.op); *Wings* 1927 (add.ph); *The Pace That Kills* 1928 (ph); *Linda* 1929 (ph); *Street Corners* 1929 (ph); *The White Outlaw* 1929 (ph); *Hell's Angels* 1930 (ph—Technicolor footage); *The Primrose Path* 1931 (ph); *Rich Man's Folly* 1931 (cam.op); *The Miracle Man* 1932 (cam.op); *The Phantom President* 1932 (cam.op); *The Case of the Curious Bride* 1935 (cam.op); *Hold Back the Dawn* 1941 (cam.op); *The Major and the Minor* 1942 (cam.op); *The Hitler Gang* 1944 (ph); *Two Years Before the Mast* 1946 (ph); *Dear Ruth* 1947 (ph); *Road to Rio* 1947 (ph); *The Girl From Manhattan* 1948 (ph); *Let's Live a Little* 1948 (ph); *Lulu Belle* 1948 (ph); *The Big Wheel* 1949 (ph); *Cover-Up* 1949 (ph); *Impact* 1949 (ph); *The Lucky Stiff* 1949 (ph); *Manhandled* 1949 (ph); *D.O.A.* 1950 (ph); *The Jackie Robinson Story* 1950 (ph); *Riding High* 1950 (ph); *M* 1951 (ph); *The Well* 1951 (ph); *When I Grow Up* 1951 (ph); *The First Time* 1952 (ph); *The Lady in the Iron Mask* 1952 (ph); *Mutiny* 1952 (ph); *The Star* 1952 (ph); *The Steel Trap* 1952 (ph); *Three For Bedroom C* 1952 (ph); *The Trio: Rubinstein, Heifetz and Piatigorsky (short)* 1952 (ph); *Houdini* 1953 (ph); *The Moon Is Blue* 1953 (ph); *Scared Stiff* 1953 (ph); *Stalag 17* 1953 (ph); *About Mrs. Leslie* 1954 (ph); *Apache* 1954 (ph); *The Naked Jungle* 1954 (ph); *Vera Cruz* 1954 (ph); *The Big Knife* 1955 (ph); *The Kentuckian* 1955 (ph); *Kiss Me Deadly* 1955 (ph); *Bandido* 1956 (ph); *While The City Sleeps* 1956 (ph); *Gunsight Ridge* 1957 (ph); *Omar Khayyam* 1957 (ph); *Valerie* 1957 (ph); *Attack of the Puppet People* 1958 (ph); *The Restless Years* 1958 (ph); *The Space Children* 1958 (ph); *On the Beach* 1959 (uncred.add.ph—deserted San Francisco sequence); *Ten Seconds to Hell* 1959 (ph); *Inherit the Wind* 1960 (ph) **(AANBPH)**; *Tormented* 1960 (ph); *Judgment at Nuremberg* 1961 (ph) **(AANBPH)**; *The Last Sunset* 1961 (ph); *Four For Texas* 1963 (ph); *It's a Mad, Mad, Mad, Mad World* 1963 (ph) **(AANBPH)**; *One Man's Way* 1964 (ph); *Baby, the Rain Must Fall* 1965 (ph); *Ship of Fools* 1965 (ph) **(AABPH)**; *Fantastic Voyage* 1966 (ph) **(AANBPH)**; *The Big Mouth* 1967 (ph); *Luv* 1967 (ph); *Star!* 1968 (ph) **(AANBPH)**; *Daddy's Gone A-Hunting* 1969 (ph); *The First Time* 1969 (ph); *Airport* 1970 (ph) **(AANBPH)**; *James Wong Howe, A.S.C.: A Lesson in Light (short)* 1973 (a); *Showdown* 1973 (ph); *That's Entertainment!* 1974 (add.ph); *Logan's Run* 1976 (ph) **(AANBPH)**; *The Domino Killings* 1977 (ph).

Lathrop, Philip H. • American director of photography • Born 1916. Began his career in 1934 as a camera loader and graduated to cinematographer in 1957. Lathrop proved himself a meticulous craftsman with films such as *The Cincinnati Kid* (1965) and *Point Blank* (1967) and shot several of the big-budget, spectacular "disaster" films favored by Hollywood in the 1970s. • *All My Sons* 1948 (cam.op); *Kiss the Blood Off My Hands* 1948 (cam.asst); *Mr. Peabody and the Mermaid* 1948 (cam.op); *The Lady Gambles* 1949 (cam.op); *Flame of Araby* 1951 (cam.op); *Little Egypt* 1951 (cam.op); *The Raging Tide* 1951 (cam.op); *Against All Flags* 1952 (cam.op); *Back at the Front* 1952 (cam.op); *Bronco Buster* 1952 (cam.op); *Scarlet Angel* 1952 (cam.op); *The Treasure of Lost Canyon* 1952 (cam.op); *Yankee Buccaneer* 1952 (cam.op); *It Happens Every Thursday* 1953 (cam.op); *The Man From the Alamo* 1953 (cam.op); *Seminole* 1953 (cam.op); *The Veils of Bagdad* 1953 (cam.op); *Man Afraid* 1957 (cam.op); *Girls on the Loose* 1958 (ph); *Live Fast, Die Young* 1958 (ph); *Money, Women and Guns* 1958 (ph); *The Saga of Hemp Brown* 1958 (ph); *Touch of Evil* 1958 (cam.op); *Wild Heritage* 1958 (ph); *Cry Tough* 1959 (ph); *The Monster of Piedras Blancas* 1959 (ph); *The Perfect Furlough* 1959 (ph); *The Private Lives of Adam and Eve* 1960 (ph); *Days of Wine and Roses* 1962 (ph); *Experiment in Terror* 1962 (ph); *Lonely Are the Brave* 1962 (ph); *Dime With a Halo* 1963 (cam.op); *Soldier in the Rain* 1963 (ph); *Twilight of Honor* 1963 (ph); *36 Hours* 1964 (ph); *The Americanization of Emily* 1964 (ph) **(AANBPH)**; *The Pink Panther* 1964 (ph); *The Cincinnati Kid* 1965 (ph); *Girl Happy* 1965 (ph); *In Harm's Way* 1965 (2u ph); *Never Too Late* 1965 (ph); *What Did You Do in the War, Daddy?* 1966 (ph); *Don't Make Waves* 1967 (ph); *Gunn* 1967 (ph); *The Happening* 1967 (ph); *Point Blank* 1967 (ph); *Finian's Rainbow* 1968 (ph); *I Love You, Alice B. Toklas* 1968 (ph); *The Gypsy Moths* 1969 (ph); *The Illustrated Man* 1969 (ph); *They Shoot Horses, Don't They?* 1969 (ph); *The Hawaiians* 1970 (ph); *Rabbit, Run* 1970 (ph); *The Traveling Executioner* 1970 (ph); *Wild Rovers* 1971 (ph); *Every Little Crook and Nanny* 1972 (ph); *Portnoy's Complaint* 1972 (ph); *The All-American Boy* 1973 (ph); *Lolly-Madonna XXX* 1973 (ph); *The Thief Who Came to Dinner* 1973 (ph); *Earthquake* 1974 (ph) **(AANBPH)**; *Mame* 1974 (ph); *The Prisoner of Second Avenue* 1974 (ph); *Together Brothers* 1974 (ph); *Airport 1975* 1975 (ph); *The Black Bird* 1975 (ph); *Hard Times* 1975 (ph); *The Killer Elite* 1975 (ph); *Swashbuckler* 1976 (ph); *Airport 77* 1977 (ph); *A Different Story* 1978 (ph); *The Driver* 1978 (ph); *Moment By Moment* 1978 (ph); *The Concorde—Airport '79* 1979 (ph); *Foolin' Around* 1979 (ph); *A Change of Seasons* 1980 (ph); *Little Miss Marker* 1980 (ph); *Loving Couples* 1980 (ph); *All Night Long* 1981 (ph); *Hammett* 1982 (ph); *Jekyll and Hyde... Together Again* 1982 (ph); *National Lampoon's Class Reunion* 1982 (ph); *Deadly Friend* 1986 (ph); *Ray's Male Heterosexual Dance Hall (short)* 1988 (ph).

Lattuada, Alberto • Director; also art director • Born Milan, Italy, November 13, 1914. *Educ.* Berchet School, Milan (architecture). Former writer and illustrator for anti-Fascist journals who began designing sets for films in the early 1930s and graduated to directing in 1942. Lattuada found his stride with the emergence of Italian neorealism, earning critical praise for *The Bandit* (1946) and—in collaboration with Federico Fellini—*Variety Lights* (1950). Lattuada's achievements were subsequently eclipsed by those of contemporaries such as Fellini and Antonioni, though he proved adept in a wide range of genres and achieved commercial success with films like *Anna* (1951), starring Silvana Mangano. Lattuada was a co-founder, in 1940, of the first Italian film archive, Milan's Cineteca Italiana. Son of composer Felice (1882-1962), who scored several of his films, and husband of actress Carla Del Poggio. • *Cuore rivelatore* 1933 (art d); *Il Museo dell'amore (short)* 1935 (color consult); *La Danza delle lancette* 1936 (ad); *1948 (short)* 1941 (art. consult); *Piccolo mondo antico* 1941 (sc,ad); *Sissignora* 1941 (adapt,ad); *Giacomo l'idealista* 1943 (d,sc); *La Freccia nel fianco* 1944 (d,sc); *La Nostra guerra (short)* 1944 (d); *Il Bandito/The Bandit* 1946 (d,sc,story); *Il Delitto di Giovanni Episcopo* 1947 (d,sc); *Senza Pieta* 1947 (sc); *Miss Italia* 1949 (story); *Il Mulino del Po* 1949 (adapt,d); *Luci del Varieta/Variety Lights* 1950 (assoc.p,d,sc); *Anna* 1951 (d); *Il Cappotto* 1951 (d,sc); *Amore in Citta/Love in the City* 1953 (d,sc); *La Spiaggia* 1953 (d,sc,story); *La Lupa* 1954 (d,sc); *Scuola elementare* 1954 (d,sc,story); *Un Eroe dei nostri tempi* 1955 (a); *Guendalina* 1955 (d,sc); *La Tempesta/The Tempest* 1958 (d,sc); *Dolci inganni* 1960 (d,story,adapt); *Lettere di una novizia* 1960 (d,sc); *L'Imprevu* 1961 (d); *Il Mafioso* 1962 (d,sc); *La Steppa* 1962 (d,sc); *La Mandragola* 1966 (d,sc); *Matchless* 1966 (d,sc); *Don Giovanni in Sicilia* 1967 (d,sc); *Fraülein Doktor* 1968 (d,sc); *L'Amica* 1969 (d,sc); *Venga a prendere il caffe...da noi* 1970 (a,d,sc); *Bianco, Rosso e...* 1971 (d,sc); *Sono Stato Io* 1972 (a,d,sc,story); *Le Faro da Padre* 1974 (a,d,sc); *Cuore Di Cane* 1975 (a,d,p,sc,adapt); *Oh, Serafina!* 1976 (a,d,sc); *Così come sei* 1978 (a,d,sc); *Il Corpo della ragassa* 1979 (adapt); *La Cicala* 1980 (d,sc); *Nudo di Donna* 1981 (d); *Una Spina nel Cuore* 1986 (d,sc).

Laughton, Charles • Actor • Born Scarborough, England, July 1, 1899; died 1962. *Educ.* Stonyhurst College; RADA, London. Portly English stage and screen actor who made his New York theater debut in 1931's *Payment Deferred* and began a successful Hollywood career the following year. Laughton became one of the most popular actors of the 1930s, playing everything from self-indulgent monarchs (*The Private Life of Henry VIII* 1933) to selfless butlers (*Ruggles of Red Gap* 1935) to *The Hunchback of Notre Dame* (1939). He displayed a propensity for eye-rolling ham in the later stages of his career, though he returned to earlier form with two superb performances in *Witness For the Prosecution* (1957) and *Advise and Consent* (1962).

Laughton's single directorial effort was 1955's *Night of the Hunter*; featuring a fine script by James Agee and a compellingly psychotic performance by Robert Mitchum, it was a dismal commercial failure upon its initial release but has since become a critical and cult favorite. Married to actress Elsa Lanchester from 1929 until his death. • *Bluebottles (short)* 1928 (a); *Day-Dreams (short)* 1928 (a); *Comets* 1929 (a); *Piccadilly* 1929 (a); *Wolves* 1930 (a); *Down River* 1931 (a); *The Devil and the Deep* 1932 (a); *If I Had a Million* 1932 (a); *The Old Dark House* 1932 (a); *Payment Deferred* 1932 (a); *The Sign of the Cross* 1932 (a); *Island of Lost Souls* 1933 (a); *The Private Life of Henry VIII* 1933 (a) **(AABA)**; *White Woman* 1933 (a); *The Barretts of Wimpole Street* 1934 (a); *Frankie and Johnnie (short)* 1935 (a); *Les Miserables* 1935 (a); *Mutiny on the Bounty* 1935 (a) **(AANBA)**; *Ruggles of Red Gap* 1935 (a); *Rembrandt* 1936 (a); *St. Martin's Lane W.C.2* 1938 (a); *Vessel of Wrath* 1938 (a,p); *The Hunchback of Notre Dame* 1939 (a); *Jamaica Inn* 1939 (a); *They Knew What They Wanted* 1940 (a); *It Started With Eve* 1941 (a); *Stand By For Action* 1942 (a); *Tales of Manhattan* 1942 (a); *The Tuttles of Tahiti* 1942 (a); *Forever and a Day* 1943 (a); *The Man From Down Under* 1943 (a); *This Land Is Mine* 1943 (a); *The Canterville Ghost* 1944 (a); *The Suspect* 1944 (a); *Captain Kidd* 1945 (a); *Because of Him* 1946 (a); *The Paradine Case* 1947 (a); *Arch of Triumph* 1948 (a); *The Big Clock* 1948 (a); *The Girl From Manhattan* 1948 (a); *The Bribe* 1949 (a); *The Man on the Eiffel Tower* 1949 (a,d); *The Blue Veil* 1951 (a); *The Strange Door* 1951 (a); *Abbott and Costello Meet Captain Kidd* 1952 (a); *O. Henry's Full House* 1952 (a); *Salome* 1953 (a); *Young Bess* 1953 (a); *Hobson's Choice* 1954 (a); *The Night of the Hunter* 1955 (d); *Witness For the Prosecution* 1957 (a) **(AANBA)**; *Sotto dieci bandiere* 1960 (a); *Spartacus* 1960 (a); *Advise and Consent* 1962 (a); *The Epic That Never Was (I, Claudius)* 1965 (a); *Galileo* 1974 (from translation); *Charles Laughton: A Difficult Actor* 1988 (archival footage).

Launder, Frank • Screenwriter; also director, producer. • Born Hitchin, England, 1907. See Gilliat, Sidney. • *Cocktails* 1928 (titles); *Under the Greenwood Tree* 1929 (sc); *Children of Chance* 1930 (sc); *The Compulsory Husband* 1930 (dial,dubbing sup); *Harmony Heaven* 1930 (add.dial); *The Middle Watch* 1930 (sc); *Song of Soho* 1930 (sc); *The W Plan* 1930 (add.dial); *The Woman Between* 1930 (sc); *Hobson's Choice* 1931 (sc); *How He Lied to Her Husband* 1931 (sc); *Keepers of Youth* 1931 (sc); *After Office Hours* 1932 (sc); *Arms and the Man* 1932 (uncred.sc); *For the Love of Mike* 1932 (uncred.sc); *Josser in the Army* 1932 (sc); *The Last Coupon* 1932 (sc); *Facing the Music* 1933 (sc,adapt); *Happy* 1933 (sc,dial,adapt); *Hawleys of High Street* 1933 (sc); *A Southern Maid* 1933 (sc,adapt,lyrics); *You Made Me Love You* 1933 (sc); *Those Were the Days* 1934 (sc,adapt); *Black Mask* 1935 (sc); *Emil and the Detectives* 1935 (sc); *Get Off My Foot* 1935 (sc); *I Give My Heart* 1935 (sc,adapt); *Mr. What's-His-Name* 1935 (sc); *Rolling Home* 1935 (sc); *So You Won't Talk!* 1935 (sc,dial); *Educated Evans* 1936 (sc); *Seven Sinners* 1936 (sc); *Twelve Good Men* 1936 (sc); *Where's Sally?* 1936 (sc); *Oh, Mr. Porter!* 1937 (story); *The Lady Vanishes* 1938 (sc); *A Girl Must Live* 1939 (sc); *Inspector Hornleigh* 1939 (sc); *Crooks' Tour* 1940 (from radio series); *Inspector Hornleigh Goes to It* 1940 (story); *Night Train to Munich* 1940 (sc); *They Came By Night* 1940 (sc); *Partners in Crime (short)* 1942 (story); *Uncensored* 1942 (uncred.sc); *The Young Mr. Pitt* 1942 (sc); *Millions Like Us* 1943 (d,sc); *We Dive at Dawn* 1943 (uncred.sc); *Soldier, Sailor* 1944 (sc); *Two Thousand Women* 1944 (d,sc); *The Rake's Progress* 1945 (p,sc); *Green For Danger* 1946 (p); *I See a Dark Stranger* 1946 (d,p,sc,story); *Captain Boycott* 1947 (d,p,sc); *London Belongs to Me* 1948 (p); *The Blue Lagoon* 1949 (d,p,sc); *The Happiest Days of Your Life* 1950 (d,p,sc); *State Secret* 1950 (p); *Lady Godiva Rides Again* 1951 (d,p,sc); *Folly to Be Wise* 1952 (d,p,sc); *La Minute de Vérité* 1952 (p); *The Story of Gilbert and Sullivan* 1953 (p); *The Belles of St. Trinian's* 1954 (d,p,sc); *The Constant Husband* 1954 (p); *Wee Geordie* 1955 (d,p,sc); *The Green Man* 1956 (p,sc,from play *Meet a Body*); *Blue Murder at St. Trinian's* 1957 (d,p,sc); *Fortune Is a Woman* 1958 (p,sc); *The Bridal Path* 1959 (d,p,sc); *Left, Right and Centre* 1959 (d,p); *Pure Hell of St. Trinian's* 1960 (d,p,sc); *Two-Way Stretch* 1960 (uncred.exec.p); *Ring of Spies* 1963 (sc); *Joey Boy* 1965 (d,sc); *The Great St. Trinian's Train Robbery* 1966 (d,sc,story); *The Lions Are Free* 1967 (uncred.sc); *An Elephant Called Slowly* 1969 (uncred.sc); *Endless Night* 1972 (exec.p); *Ooh... You Are Awful* 1972 (exec.p); *The Lady Vanishes* 1979 (from screenplay); *The Wildcats of St. Trinian's* 1980 (d,sc).

Laurel, Stan • Actor; also screenwriter, vaudevillian, producer. • Born Arthur Stanley Jefferson, Ulverston, Lanchashire, England, June 16, 1890; died 1965. See Hardy, Oliver. • *The Evolution of Fashion (short)* 1917 (a); *A Lucky Dog (short)* 1917 (a); *Nuts in May (short)* 1917 (a); *Bears and Bad Men (short)* 1918 (a); *Do You Love Your Wife? (short)* 1918 (a); *Frauds and Frenzies (short)* 1918 (a); *Hickory Hiram (short)* 1918 (a); *Huns and Hyphens (short)* 1918 (a); *Hustling For Health (short)* 1918 (a); *It's Great to Be Crazy (short)* 1918 (a); *Just Rambling Along* *(short)* 1918 (a); *No Place Like Jail (short)* 1918 (a); *Phoney Photos (short)* 1918 (a); *Whose Zoo? (short)* 1918 (a); *Hoot Mon (short)* 1919 (a); *The Rent Collector (short)* 1921 (a); *The Egg (short)* 1922 (a); *Mud and Sand* 1922 (a); *The Pest (short)* 1922 (a); *The Weak-End Party (short)* 1922 (a); *Collars and Cuffs (short)* 1923 (a); *Frozen Hearts (short)* 1923 (a); *Gas and Air (short)* 1923 (a); *The Handy Man (short)* 1923 (a); *Kill or Cure (short)* 1923 (a); *A Man About Town (short)* 1923 (a); *Mother's Joy (short)* 1923 (a); *Noon Whistle (short)* 1923 (a); *Oranges and Lemons (short)* 1923 (a); *Pick and Shovel (short)* 1923 (a); *Roughest Africa (short)* 1923 (a); *Save the Ship (short)* 1923 (a); *Scorching Sands (short)* 1923 (a); *Short Orders (short)* 1923 (a); *The Soilers (short)* 1923 (a); *Under Two Jags (short)* 1923 (a); *When Knights Were Cold (short)* 1923 (a); *White Wings (short)* 1923 (a); *The Whole Truth (short)* 1923 (a); *Brothers Under the Chin (short)* 1924 (a); *Detained (short)* 1924 (a); *Madam Mix-Up (short)* 1924 (a); *Monsieur Don't Care (short)* 1924 (a); *Near Dublin (short)* 1924 (a); *Postage Due (short)* 1924 (a); *Rupert of Hee-Haw (short)* 1924 (a); *Short Kilts (short)* 1924 (a); *Smithy (short)* 1924 (a); *West of Hot Dog (short)* 1924 (a); *Wide Open Spaces (short)* 1924 (a); *Zeb vs. Paprika (short)* 1924 (a); *Dr. Pyckle and Mr. Pride (short)* 1925 (a); *Enough to Do (short)* 1925 (a,d); *Half a Man (short)* 1925 (a); *Moonlight and Noses (short)* 1925 (a,d); *Navy Blue Days (short)* 1925 (a); *Pie-Eyed (short)* 1925 (a); *The Sleuth (short)* 1925 (a); *The Snow Hawk (short)* 1925 (a); *Somewhere in Wrong (short)* 1925 (a); *Twins (short)* 1925 (a); *Unfriendly Enemies (short)* 1925 (a,d); *Wandering Papas (short)* 1925 (a,d); *Yes, Yes, Nanette (short)* 1925 (a,d); *45 Minutes From Hollywood (short)* 1926 (a); *Atta Boy* 1926 (a); *Get 'em Young (short)* 1926 (a); *Madame Mystery (short)* 1926 (a,d); *The Merry Widower (short)* 1926 (a,d); *Never Too Old (short)* 1926 (a,d); *On the Front (short)* 1926 (a); *Raggedy Rose (short)* 1926 (a,d); *Wise Guys Prefer Brunettes (short)* 1926 (a,d); *The Battle of the Century (short)* 1927 (a); *Call of the Cuckoo (short)* 1927 (a); *Do Detectives Think? (short)* 1927 (a); *Duck Soup (short)* 1927 (a); *Eve's Love Letters (short)* 1927 (a); *Flying Elephants (short)* 1927 (a); *Hats Off (short)* 1927 (a); *Love 'em and Weep (short)* 1927 (a); *Now I'll Tell One (short)* 1927 (a); *Putting Pants on Philip (short)* 1927 (a); *Sailors, Beware! (short)* 1927 (a); *The Second Hundred Years (short)* 1927 (a); *Seeing the World (short)* 1927 (a); *Should Tall Men Marry? (short)* 1927 (a); *Slipping Wives (short)* 1927 (a); *Sugar Daddies (short)* 1927 (a); *Why Girls Love Sailors (short)* 1927 (a); *With Love and Hisses (short)* 1927 (a); *Early to Bed (short)* 1928 (a); *The Finishing Touch (short)* 1928 (a); *From Soup to Nuts (short)* 1928 (a); *Habeas Corpus (short)* 1928 (a); *Leave 'em Laughing (short)* 1928 (a); *Should Married Men Go Home (short)* 1928 (a); *Their Purple Moment (short)* 1928 (a); *Two Tars* 1928 (a); *We Faw Down (short)* 1928 (a); *You're Darn Tootin' (short)* 1928 (a); *Angora Love (short)* 1929 (a); *Bacon Grabbers (short)* 1929 (a); *Berth Marks (short)* 1929 (a); *Big Business (short)* 1929 (a); *Double Whoopee (short)* 1929 (a); *The Hollywood Revue of 1929* 1929 (a); *The Hoose-Gow (short)* 1929 (a); *Liberty (short)* 1929 (a); *Man O' War (short)* 1929 (a); *Perfect Day (short)* 1929 (a); *That's My Wife (short)* 1929 (a); *They Go Boom (short)* 1929 (a); *Unaccustomed As We Are (short)* 1929 (a); *Wrong Again (short)* 1929 (a); *Another Fine Mess (short)* 1930 (a); *Below Zero (short)* 1930 (a); *Blotto (short)* 1930 (a); *Brats (short)* 1930 (a); *Hog Wild (short)* 1930 (a); *The Laurel-Hardy Murder Case (short)* 1930 (a); *The Night Owls (short)* 1930 (a); *The Rogue Song* 1930 (a); *Beau Hunks (short)* 1931 (a); *Chicken Come Home* 1931 (a); *The Chiselers (short)* 1931 (a); *Come Clean (short)* 1931 (a); *Helpmates (short)* 1931 (a); *Laughing Gravy (short)* 1931 (a); *On the Loose (short)* 1931 (a); *One Good Turn (short)* 1931 (a); *Our Wife (short)* 1931 (a); *Pardon Us* 1931 (a); *The Stolen Jools* 1931 (a); *Any Old Port (short)* 1932 (a); *The Chimp* 1932 (a); *County Hospital (short)* 1932 (a); *The Music Box (short)* 1932 (a); *Pack Up Your Troubles* 1932 (a); *Scram! (short)* 1932 (a); *Their First Mistake (short)* 1932 (a); *Towed in a Hole (short)* 1932 (a); *Busy Bodies (short)* 1933 (a); *The Devil's Brother* 1933 (a); *Dirty Work (short)* 1933 (a); *Me and My Pal (short)* 1933 (a); *The Midnight Patrol (short)* 1933 (a); *Sons of the Desert* 1933 (a); *Twice Two (short)* 1933 (a); *Wild Poses (short)* 1933 (a); *Babes in Toyland* 1934 (a); *Going Bye-Bye! (short)* 1934 (a); *Hollywood Party* 1934 (a); *The Live Ghost (short)* 1934 (a); *Oliver the Eighth* 1934 (a); *Them Thar Hills (short)* 1934 (a); *The Fixer Uppers (short)* 1935 (a); *Heroes of the Regiment* 1935 (a); *Thicker Than Water (short)* 1935 (a); *Tit For Tat (short)* 1935 (a); *The Bohemian Girl* 1936 (a); *On the Wrong Trek (short)* 1936 (a); *Our Relations* 1936 (a,p); *Pick a Star* 1937 (a); *Way Out West* 1937 (a,p); *Block-Heads* 1938 (a); *Knight of the Plains* 1938 (p); *Songs and Bullets* 1938 (p); *Swiss Miss* 1938 (a); *Code of the Fearless* 1939 (p); *The Flying Deuces* 1939 (a); *In Old Montana* 1939 (p); *Two Gun Troubador* 1939 (p); *A Chump at Oxford* 1940 (a); *Saps at Sea* 1940 (a); *Great Guns* 1941 (a); *A-Haunting We Will Go* 1942 (a); *The Tree in a Test Tube (short)* 1942 (a); *Air Raid Wardens* 1943 (a); *The Dancing Masters* 1943 (a); *Jitterbugs* 1943 (a); *The Big Noise* 1944 (a); *Nothing But Trouble* 1944 (a); *The Bullfighters* 1945 (a); *Atoll K/Utopia* 1951 (a); *Golden Age of Comedy* 1957 (archival footage); *The Crazy World of Laurel and Hardy* 1964 (archival footage); *Laurel and Hardy's Laughing 20's* 1965 (archival footage); *The Further Perils of Laurel and Hardy* 1967 (archival footage); *Four Clowns* 1969 (archival footage); *The Best of Laurel and Hardy* 1971 (archival footage).

Laurie, Piper • Actress • Born Rosetta Jacobs, Detroit, MI, January 22, 1932. Perky, lightweight leading lady of the 1950s whose first substantial screen role, in Robert Rossen's *The Hustler* (1961), earned her an Oscar nomination. Laurie took a break from film to marry critic Joseph Morgenstern in 1962, but in recent years she's re-emerged as a distinctive character player (*Carrie* 1976, TV's "Twin Peaks," etc.). • *Louisa* 1950 (a); *The Milkman* 1950 (a); *Francis Goes to the Races* 1951 (a); *The Prince Who Was a Thief* 1951 (a); *Has Anybody Seen My Gal?* 1952 (a,song); *No Room For the Groom* 1952 (a); *Son of Ali Baba* 1952 (a); *The Golden Blade* 1953 (a); *The Mississippi Gambler* 1953 (a); *Dangerous Mission* 1954 (a); *Dawn at Socorro* 1954 (a); *Johnny Dark* 1954 (a); *Smoke Signal* 1954 (a); *Ain't Misbehavin'* 1955 (a); *Kelly and Me* 1956 (a); *Until They Sail* 1957 (a); *The Hustler* 1961 (a) **(AANBA)**; *Carrie* 1976 (a) **(AANBSA)**; *Ruby* 1977 (a); *The Boss' Son* 1978 (a); *Tim* 1979 (a); *Return to Oz* 1985 (a); *Children of a Lesser God* 1986 (a) **(AANBSA)**; *Distortions* 1987 (a); *Appointment With Death* 1988 (a); *Tiger Warsaw* 1988 (a); *Dream a Little Dream* 1989 (a); *Mother, Mother (short)* 1989 (a).

Lawford, Peter • Actor; also producer. • Born Peter Sidney Ernest Aylen Lawford, London, September 7, 1923; died December 24, 1984. Leading man in MGM comedies of the late 1940s and early 1950s; brother-in-law of President John F. Kennedy. • *Lord Jeff* 1938 (a); *Junior Army* 1942 (a); *A Yank at Eton* 1942 (a); *The Purple V* 1943 (a); *The West Side Kid* 1943 (a); *The Canterville Ghost* 1944 (a); *Mrs. Parkington* 1944 (a); *The White Cliffs of Dover* 1944 (a); *The Picture of Dorian Gray* 1945 (a); *Son of Lassie* 1945 (a); *Cluny Brown* 1946 (a); *My Brother Talks to Horses* 1946 (a); *Two Sisters From Boston* 1946 (a); *Good News* 1947 (a); *It Happened in Brooklyn* 1947 (a); *Easter Parade* 1948 (a); *Julia Misbehaves* 1948 (a); *On an Island With You* 1948 (a); *Little Women* 1949 (a); *The Red Danube* 1949 (a); *Please Believe Me* 1950 (a); *Royal Wedding* 1951 (a); *Just This Once* 1952 (a); *Kangaroo* 1952 (a); *Rogue's March* 1952 (a); *You For Me* 1952 (a); *It Should Happen to You* 1954 (a); *Never So Few* 1959 (a); *Exodus* 1960 (a); *Ocean's Eleven* 1960 (a); *Pepe* 1960 (a); *Advise and Consent* 1962 (a); *The Longest Day* 1962 (a); *Sergeants 3* 1962 (a); *Dead Ringer* 1964 (a); *Billie* 1965 (exec.p); *Harlow* 1965 (a); *Sylvia* 1965 (a); *A Man Called Adam* 1966 (a); *The Oscar* 1966 (a); *Buona Sera, Mrs Campbell* 1968 (a); *Hook, Line* *and Sinker* 1968 (a); *Salt and Pepper* 1968 (a); *Skidoo* 1968 (a); *The April Fools* 1969 (a); *One More Time* 1970 (a); *Clay Pigeon* 1971 (a); *They Only Kill Their Masters* 1972 (a); *That's Entertainment!* 1974 (a); *Rosebud* 1975 (a); *Body and Soul* 1981 (a); *Where Is Parsifal?* 1984 (a).

Lawrence, Florence • *aka* "The Biograph Girl," "The Imp Girl" • American actress • Born 1886; died 1938. Popular actress of the early silent era who was known as "the Biograph Girl" due to her affiliation with the studio and its foremost director, D.W. Griffith. Lawrence was lured away from Biograph in 1910 by Carl Laemmle, of the Independent Motion Picture Company of America, who renamed her the "IMP Girl." Thanks to one of Laemmle's canny publicity stunts, involving a newspaper story claiming that Lawrence was dead, she became the first film star whose real name was known to the public. Lawrence's career was effectively over by the mid-20s, though she remained on the MGM payroll through the 30s. • *Elusive Isabel* 1916; *The Unfoldment* 1921; *The Satin Girl* 1923; *Gambling Wives* 1924.

Lawson, John Howard • Screenwriter; also playwright. • Born New York, NY, September 25, 1894; died 1977. *Educ.* Williams College, Williamstown, MA. Left-leaning playwright who moved to Hollywood in 1928 and wrote several, mostly unremarkable films, some on political themes. Lawson served a year in prison because of his refusal to cooperate with the House Un-American Activities Committee and did little film work thereafter. • *Dream of Love* 1928 (titles); *Dynamite* 1929 (titles); *The Pagan* 1929 (titles); *Our Blushing Brides* 1930 (sc); *The Sea Bat* 1930 (sc); *The Ship From Shanghai* 1930 (sc); *Bachelor Apartment* 1931 (sc,story); *Goodbye Love* 1933 (sc,add.dial); *Success at Any Price* 1934 (sc,from play *Success Story*); *Party Wire* 1935 (sc); *Heart of Spain* 1937 (a); *Algiers* 1938 (sc); *Blockade* 1938 (sc,story) **(AANBST)**; *They Shall Have Music* 1939 (sc); *Earthbound* 1940 (sc); *Four Sons* 1940 (sc); *Action in the North Atlantic* 1943 (sc); *Sahara* 1943 (sc); *Counter-Attack* 1945 (sc); *The Jolson Story* 1946 (uncred.sc); *Smash-Up, the Story of a Woman* 1947 (sc); *The Hollywood Ten* 1950 (a,sc); *Cry, the Beloved Country* 1952 (uncred.sc); *Terror in a Texas Town* 1958 (uncred.sc).

Le Mat, Paul • Actor • Born New Jersey, 1952. *Educ.* Herbert Berghof Studio, New York. Beefy, laconic leading man of the 1970s. Best known for his performance as Melvin Dummar, an aimless blue-collar worker who enjoys a fortunate encounter with millionaire Howard Hughes, in Jonathan Demme's engaging, off-beat *Melvin and Howard* (1980). • *American Graffiti* 1973; *Aloha, Bobby and Rose* 1975; *Citizens Band* 1977; *More American Graffiti* 1979; *Melvin and Howard* 1980; *Death Valley* 1981; *Jimmy the Kid* 1982; *P.K. and the Kid* 1982; *Rock & Rule* 1982; *Strange Invaders* 1983; *The Hanoi Hilton* 1987; *Private Investigations* 1987; *Easy Wheels* 1989; *Puppet Master* 1989; *Veiled Threat* 1989; *Grave Secrets* 1990.

Leachman, Cloris • Actress • Born Des Moines, IA, April 30, 1926. *Educ.* Northwestern University (drama). Capable comic and dramatic actress who made her film debut as the seductive lead in *Kiss Me Deadly* (1955). Leachman was acclaimed for her performance as the lonely housewife in *The Last Picture Show* (1971) and has adorned several Mel Brooks films, notably *Young Frankenstein* (1974). Probably best known, from 1970 to 1975, as the daffy Phyllis on TV's "The Mary Tyler Moore Show" (1970-77); Leachman also starred in the spin-off series, "Phyllis" (1975-77). • *Kiss Me Deadly* 1955; *The Rack* 1956; *The Chapman Report* 1962; *Butch Cassidy and the Sundance Kid* 1969; *Lovers and Other Strangers* 1970; *The People Next Door* 1970; *WUSA* 1970; *The Last Picture Show* 1971 **(AABSA)**; *The Steagle* 1971; *Charley and the Angel* 1972; *Dillinger* 1973; *Happy Mother's Day... Love, George* 1973; *Daisy Miller* 1974; *Young Frankenstein* 1974; *Crazy Mama* 1975; *High Anxiety* 1977; *The Mouse and His Child* 1977; *Foolin' Around* 1979; *The Muppet Movie* 1979; *The North Avenue Irregulars* 1979; *Scavenger Hunt* 1979; *Yesterday* 1979; *Herbie Goes Bananas* 1980; *History of the World Part I* 1981; *My Little Pony* 1986; *Shadow Play* 1986; *Hansel and Gretel* 1987; *Walk Like a Man* 1987; *Prancer* 1989; *Love Hurts* 1990; *Texasville* 1990.

Leacock, Richard • *aka* Ricky Leacock • Filmmaker • Born Canary Islands, July 18, 1921. *Educ.* Harvard (physics). Began his film career working on Robert Flaherty's *Louisiana Story* (1948) and collaborated with several other noted documentarians before forming his own production company with Robert Drew in 1958. While at Drew Associates, Leacock turned out a number of TV documentaries, including the experimental "Living Camera" series, which established him as a pioneering figure of American "direct cinema" (a movement similar to, and concurrent with, France's "cinéma vérité"). Leacock has also worked with Albert Maysles and D.A. Pennebaker, with whom he formed a production company in 1963. Brother Philip Leacock is a director and producer of both film and television; son Robert is also a filmmaker. • *Louisiana Story* 1948 (assoc.p,ph); *To Hear Your Banjo Play (short)* 1948 (ph); *Mount Vernon (short)* 1949 (ph); *New Frontier (short)* 1950 (ph,ed); *Years of Change (short)* 1950 (ph); *Earthquake in Ecuador (short)* 1951 (ph); *Secure the Blessings (short)* 1951 (ph); *Another Light (short)* 1952 (ph); *Head of the House* 1952 (d,ed,p); *The Lonely Night* 1952 (ph); *New York University (short)* 1952 (ph); *American Frontier (short)* 1953 (ph); *Days to Remember (short)* 1954 (ed); *Jazz Dance (short)* 1954 (ph); *Jealousy (short)* 1954 (ed); *Recollections of Boyhood: An Interview With Joseph Welch (short)* 1954 (ph); *Who's Right (short)* 1954 (ed); *A Family Affair (short)* 1955 (ph); *Bitter Welcome (short)* 1958 (ph); *The Bright Side (short)* 1958 (ph); *Coulomb Force Constant (short)* 1959 (d); *Coulomb's Law (short)* 1959 (d); *Crystals (short)* 1959 (d); *Electric Fields (short)* 1959 (d); *Frames of Reference (short)* 1959 (d); *Primary* 1960 (d,ed); *Kenya, Africa* 1961 (d); *On the Road to Button Bay* 1962 (d); *Republicans—The New Breed* 1964 (d); *Timothy Leary's Wedding Day* 1964 (p); *Elizabeth and Mary* 1965 (p); *The Anatomy of Cindy Fink (short)* 1966 (p,ph); *Old Age: The Wasted Years (short)* 1966 (ph); *Don't Look Back* 1967 (p); *A Stravinsky Portrait* 1967 (d,ph,ed); *Dope (short)* 1968 (p); *French Lunch (short)* 1968 (ph); *Goin' to San Francisco (short)* 1968 (p); *Hickory Hill* 1968 (d,ph,ed); *Monterey Pop* 1968 (ph); *Chiefs* 1969 (d,ph); *A Journey to Jerusalem* 1969 (ph); *Maidstone* 1970 (ph); *Original Cast Album: Company (short)* 1970 (d,ph,sound); *Queen of Apollo* 1970 (d,ph,ed); *Sweet Toronto* 1970 (ph); *One American Movie/1 A.M.* 1971 (a,ph); *Tread* 1972 (d); *A Visit to Monica (short)* 1974 (d,ph); *Isabella Stewart Gardner* 1977 (d); *Centerbeam (short)* 1978 (d); *Murals Without Walls (short)* 1978 (d); *Elliott Carter* 1980 (ph); *Light Coming Through* 1980 (d); *Diaries* 1981 (a); *Rebuilding an Old Japanese House (short)* 1981 (d); *Lulu in Berlin* 1984 (d); *Dance Black America* 1985 (ph); *Directed By William Wyler* 1986 (ph); *Impressions de l'ile des Morts* 1986 (d,ph); *Sherman's March* 1986 (a); *Working Girls* 1986 (a); *Girltalk* 1988 (ph).

Lean, Sir David • Director; also producer, screenwriter. • Born Croydon, England, March 25, 1908. A consummate craftsman, David Lean's best films are the product of a creative tension between romantic style and realist content.

Working his way up from clapper-boy to editor's apprentice in the 1930s, Lean edited newsreels and then features. His first outing as a director, with Noel Coward, *In Which We Serve* (1942), was a moving study of wartime England that contrasted the duty to fight with the human sacrifice required to win. Lean's next three films came from Coward's pen: *This Happy Breed* (1944), the story of a London family from 1919 to 1939; the rousingly entertaining *Blithe Spirit* (1945); and the quietly effective *Brief Encounter* (1945), about a bored housewife (Celia Johnson) who almost has an affair with a doctor (Trevor Howard). These were followed by faithful adaptations of

Great Expectations (1946) and *Oliver Twist* (1948), justly regarded as exemplary translations of Dickens to the screen.

Of his next three films, the semi-documentary *The Sound Barrier* (1952), where he returned to the duty/sacrifice thematics of *In Which We Serve*, is most noteworthy. Lean's rollicking version of the stage comedy *Hobson's Choice* (1954), the story of a woman's emancipation from her overbearing father, featured the first in a series of strong, independent women characters that would include Lara (*Dr. Zhivago* 1965), Rosy Ryan (*Ryan's Daughter* 1970), and Miss Quested and Mrs. Moore (*A Passage to India* 1984). *Summertime* (1955), about the Venice affair of a lonely American spinster (Katharine Hepburn), saw the emergence of one of Lean's central themes: the journey as a quest for self-knowledge. This theme would provide the narrative backbone for several subsequent films.

Accordingly, the WWII adventure *The Bridge on the River Kwai* (1957) revolves around the self-delusion of Col. Nicholson (Alec Guinness), leader of the British contingent in a Burmese prisoner-of-war camp. Commercially and critically successful, winning seven Academy Awards including best picture and best director, *Bridge* initiated the cycle of big-budget spectacles that would characterize Lean's later work. It was also the first of two films expressing the director's increasingly jaundiced view of wartime heroics. While *Bridge* presents militarism as an insane but inevitable extension of the strutting male ego, *Lawrence of Arabia* (1962) investigates the psychology of heroism. Starting with a dashing, if eccentric and enigmatic hero (stunningly played by Peter O'Toole), the film gradually peels away the bravado to reveal the confused shell beneath.

Lean's next two films, also scripted by Robert Bolt, were love stories. The international success of the lushly rendered *Dr. Zhivago*, based on the Boris Pasternak novel, may have encouraged him to accentuate his romantic tendency, which he did with disastrous results in *Ryan's Daughter*. Partly due to the poor reception of this film, it would be 14 years before Lean would complete his next picture, a splendid adaptation of E.M. Forster's *A Passage to India*. Returning to the motif of the journey of self-discovery, and sharpening the ambiguities of the source novel, Lean succeeded in restoring the romantic/realist tension which had informed his best work.

At its most resonant, Lean's is an elegant style that questions elegance, using breathtaking cinematic technique to present biting social criticism: thus *The Bridge on the River Kwai* is a wide-screen anti-war statement; *A Passage to India* is a sumptuously photographed critique of colonialism; and *Lawrence of Arabia* is a perfectly made chronicle of human imperfection. CRB • *Escape Me Never* 1935 (ed); *As You Like It* 1936 (ed); *Pygmalion* 1938 (ed); *French Without Tears* 1939 (ed); *49th Parallel* 1941 (ed); *Major Barbara* 1941 (d,ed); *In Which We Serve* 1942 (d); *One of Our Aircraft Is Missing* 1942 (ed); *This Happy Breed* 1944 (adapt,d); *Blithe Spirit* 1945 (adapt,d); *Brief Encounter* 1945 (d,sc) **(AANBD,AANBSC)**; *Great Expectations* 1946 (d,sc) **(AANBD,AANBSC)**; *Oliver Twist* 1948 (d,sc); *The Passionate Friends* 1949 (adapt,d); *Madeleine* 1950 (d,p); *The Sound Barrier* 1952 (d,p); *Hobson's Choice* 1954 (d,p,sc); *Summertime* 1955 (d,sc) **(AANBD)**; *The Bridge on the River Kwai* 1957 (d) **(AABD)**; *Lawrence of Arabia* 1962 (d) **(AABD)**; *Doctor Zhivago* 1965 (d) **(AANBD)**; *Ryan's Daughter* 1970 (d); *A Passage to India* 1984 (d,sc,ed) **(AANBD,AANBSC)**.

Léaud, Jean-Pierre • Actor • Born Paris, May 5, 1944. Made an unforgettable impact as wayward adolescent Antoine Doinel in François Truffaut's autobiographical masterpiece, *The 400 Blows* (1959). Léaud has starred in a number of Truffaut films over the years, frequently as the Antoine Doinel character, and has also appeared in seven films by Jean-Luc Godard, notably *Masculin-Féminin* (1966). Son of writer and assistant director Pierre Léaud and actress Jacqueline Pierreux. • *La Tour, prends garde!* 1957 (a); *Les Quatre cents coups/The 400 Blows* 1959 (a); *Le Testament d'Orphée/The Testament of Orpheus* 1959 (a); *Boulevard* 1960 (a); *L'Amour à vingt ans/Love at Twenty* 1962 (a); *Une Femme mariée/A Married Woman* 1964 (ad); *Mata Hari, Agent H-21* 1964 (a,ad); *La Peau Douce/The Soft Skin* 1964 (ad); *Alphaville* 1965 (a,ad); *Pierrot le Fou* 1965 (a,ad); *Made in U.S.A.* 1966 (a,ad); *Masculin-Féminin/Masculine-Feminine* 1966 (a); *La Chinoise, ou plutôt à la Chinoise* 1967 (a); *Le Départ* 1967 (a); *Les Mauvaises fréquentations* 1967 (a); *Le Plus vieux métier du monde* 1967 (a); *Weekend* 1967 (a); *Baisers volés/Stolen Kisses* 1968 (a); *La Concentration* 1968 (a); *Dialog* 1968 (a); *Le Gai Savoir* 1968 (a); *Os Herdeiros/The Inheritors/* 1969 (a); *Paul* 1969 (a); *Porcile/Pigpen* 1969 (a); *Une Aventure de Billy le Kid* 1970 (a); *Domicile conjugal/Bed and Board* 1970 (a); *Der Leone Have Sept Cabecas* 1970 (a); *Les Deux Anglaises et le Continent/Two English Girls* 1971 (a); *Out 1: Noli Me Tangere* 1971 (a); *Last Tango in Paris* 1972 (a); *Out 1: Spectre* 1972 (a); *La Maman et la putain* 1973 (a); *La Nuit Américaine/Day For Night* 1973 (a); *Les Lolos de Lola* 1975 (a); *Umarmungen und andere Sachen* 1975 (a); *L'Amour en Fuite/Love on the Run* 1979 (a); *On a pas fini d'en parler* 1979 (a); *Aiutami a sognare* 1981 (a); *Parano* 1981 (a); *La Cassure* 1983 (a); *Rebelote* 1983 (a); *Csak Egy Mozi* 1984 (a); *L'Herbe rouge* 1984 (a); *Paris vu par...vingt ans Après* 1984 (a); *Détective* 1985 (a); *L'Ile au Trêsor* 1985 (a); *Vivement Truffaut!* 1985 (a); *Corps et biens* 1986 (a); *Grandeur et décadence d'un petit commerce de cinéma* 1986 (a); *Boran—Zeit Zum Zielen* 1987 (a); *Les Keufs* 1987 (a); *Ossegg-Oder die Wahrheit Uber Hänsel und Gretel* 1987 (a); *36 Fillette* 1988 (a); *La Couleur du vent* 1988 (a); *Jane B. par Agnes V.* 1988 (a); *Les Ministères de l'art* 1988 (a); *Bunker Palace Hotel* 1989 (a); *Femme de papier* 1989 (a); *I Hired a Contract Killer* 1990 (a).

Lederer, Charles • Screenwriter; also director. • Born Charles Davies Lederer, New York, NY, December 31, 1910; died 1976. *Educ.* University of California, Berkeley. Former journalist who turned to screenwriting in the early 1930s and often worked in collaboration with Ben Hecht (*His Girl Friday* 1940, *The Kiss of Death* 1947, etc). Lederer's scripts were noted for their sharp wit, though his few directorial efforts proved somewhat lackluster. The son of theater producer George W. Lederer and nephew of actress Marion Davies, Lederer married Orson Welles's former wife Virginia Nicholson in 1940 and actress Anne Shirley in 1949. • *The Front Page* 1931 (add.dial); *Cock of the Air* 1932 (sc,dial,story); *Topaze* 1933 (uncred.sc); *Baby Face Harrington* 1935 (add.dial); *Double or Nothing* 1937 (sc); *Mountain Music* 1937 (sc); *Broadway Serenade* 1939 (sc); *Within the Law* 1939 (sc); *Comrade X* 1940 (sc); *His Girl Friday* 1940 (sc); *I Love You Again* 1940 (sc); *Love Crazy* 1941 (sc); *Fingers at the Window* 1942 (d); *Slightly Dangerous* 1943 (sc); *The Youngest Profession* 1943 (sc); *Her Husband's Affairs* 1947 (sc); *The Kiss of Death* 1947 (sc); *Ride the Pink Horse* 1947 (sc); *Macbeth* 1948 (a); *I Was a Male War Bride* 1949 (sc); *Red, Hot and Blue* 1949 (from story "Broadway Story"); *Wabash Avenue* 1950 (sc); *On the Loose* 1951 (d); *The Thing* 1951 (sc); *Fearless Fagan* 1952 (sc); *Monkey Business* 1952 (sc); *Gentlemen Prefer Blondes* 1953 (sc); *Kismet* 1955 (sc,from play); *Gaby* 1956 (sc); *The Spirit of St. Louis* 1957 (adapt); *Tip on a Dead Jockey* 1957 (sc); *The Fiend Who Walked the West* 1958 (from screenplay); *It Started With a Kiss* 1959 (sc,song); *Never Steal Anything Small* 1959 (d,sc,story); *Can-Can* 1960 (sc); *Ocean's Eleven* 1960 (sc); *Follow That Dream* 1962 (sc); *Mutiny on the Bounty* 1962 (sc); *A Global Affair* 1964 (sc).

Lee, Bruce • Actor • Born San Francisco, CA, 1941; died 1973. *Educ.* University of Washington (philosophy). Diminutive martial arts dynamo whose flying fists and feet battled their way through a number of internationally successful, Hong Kong-produced action films. The mysterious circumstances surrounding Lee's premature death transformed him into a James Dean-style cult figure among millions of martial arts enthusiasts. *Game of Death* (1979) was completed after Lee's death by using footage from earlier films as well as the services of a Lee look-alike, Kim Tai Jong. • *The Wrecking Crew* 1968 (tech. ad—karate); *Marlowe* 1969 (a); *The Chinese Connection* 1972 (a); *Fist of Fury* 1972 (a); *Enter the Dragon* 1973 (a); *Return of the Dragon* 1973 (a,d,sc); *The Silent Flute* 1978 (story); *Game of Death* 1979 (a).

Lee, Christopher • Actor • Born Christopher Frank Carandini Lee, London, May 27, 1922. British actor whose "tall, dark and gruesome" persona (from the title of Lee's autobiography) has been exploited in scores of sinister roles, beginning in the early 1950s. Lee's gallery of villanous portraits includes his famed Dracula impersonations, a handful of outings as Fu Manchu and a memorable turn as *Rasputin the Mad Monk* (1964). He has been based in the US since the mid-70s and became a familiar TV presence in the 80s. • *Corridor of Mirrors* 1947 (a); *Hamlet* 1948 (a); *My Brother's Keeper* 1948 (a); *One Night With You* 1948 (a); *Penny and the Pownall Case* 1948 (a); *Scott of the Antarctic* 1948 (a); *A Song For Tomorrow* 1948 (a); *Trottie True* 1949 (a); *Prelude to Fame* 1950 (a); *They Were Not Divided* 1950 (a); *Captain Horatio Hornblower* 1951 (a); *Valley of the Eagles* 1951 (a); *Babes in Baghdad* 1952 (a); *The Crimson Pirate* 1952 (a); *Moulin Rouge* 1952 (a); *Paul Temple Returns* 1952 (a); *Top Secret* 1952 (a); *Innocents in Paris* 1953 (a); *Thought to Kill* 1953 (a); *The Triangle* 1953 (a); *The Death of Michael Turbin* 1954 (a); *Destination Milan* 1954 (a); *The Final Column* 1954 (a); *Alias John Preston* 1955 (a); *The Cockleshell Heroes* 1955 (a); *Man in Demand* 1955 (a); *Police Dog* 1955 (a); *Storm Over the Nile* 1955 (a); *That Lady* 1955 (a); *The Warriors* 1955 (a); *Battle of the River Plate* 1956 (a); *Port Afrique* 1956 (a); *Private's Progress* 1956 (a); *Beyond Mombasa* 1957 (a); *The Curse of Frankenstein* 1957 (a); *Ill Met By Moonlight* 1957 (a); *The Traitor* 1957 (a); *Battle of the V-1* 1958 (a); *Bitter Victory* 1958 (a); *Corridors of Blood* 1958 (a); *Fortune Is a Woman* 1958 (a); *Horror of Dracula* 1958 (a); *A Tale of Two Cities* 1958 (a); *The Truth About Women* 1958 (a); *The Hound of the Baskervilles* 1959 (a); *The Man Who Could Cheat Death* 1959 (a); *The Mummy* 1959 (a); *Tempi duri per i vampiri* 1959 (a); *The Treasure of San Teresa* 1959 (a); *Beat Girl* 1960 (a); *The City of the Dead* 1960 (a); *Ercole al centro della terra/Hercules in the Haunted World* 1960 (a); *Les Mains d'Orlac/The Hands of Orlac/Hands of the Strangler* 1960 (a); *The Terror of the Tongs* 1960 (a); *Too Hot to Handle* 1960 (a); *The Two Faces of Dr. Jekyll* 1960 (a); *Das Geheimnis der gelben Narzissen* 1961 (a); *The Pirates of Blood River* 1961 (a); *Das Rätsel der roten Orchidee/The Puzzle of the Red Orchid* 1961 (a); *Taste of Fear* 1961 (a); *In Namen des Teufels* 1962 (a); *Sherlock Holmes und das Halsband des Todes* 1962 (a); *The Devil-Ship Pirates* 1963 (a); *La Frusta e il corpo* 1963 (a); *Sfiela al diavolo* 1963 (a); *Il Castello dei morti vivi/Castle of the Living Dead* 1964 (a); *La Cripta e l'incubo* 1964 (a); *Dr. Terror's House of Horrors* 1964 (a); *The Gorgon* 1964 (a); *Rasputin the Mad Monk* 1964 (a); *La Vergine di Norimberga/The Castle of Terror* 1964 (a); *Dracula-Prince of Darkness* 1965 (a); *The Face of Fu Manchu* 1965 (a); *She* 1965 (a); *The Skull* 1965 (a); *The Brides of Fu Manchu* 1966 (a); *Blood Fiend* 1967 (a); *Five Golden Dragons* 1967 (a); *Night of the Big Heat* 1967 (a); *Die Schlangengrube und das Pendel/Torture Chamber of Dr. Sadism* 1967 (a); *The Vengeance of Fu Manchu* 1967 (a); *The Blood of Fu Manchu* 1968 (a); *Curse of the Crimson Altar* 1968 (a); *The Devil Rides Out* 1968 (a); *Dracula Has Risen From the Grave* 1968 (a); *The Face of Eve* 1968 (a); *Die Folterkammer des Doktor Fu Manchu/The Castle of Fu Manchu* 1968 (a); *Victims of Terror (short)* 1968 (a); *The Oblong Box* 1969 (a); *El Proceso de los brujas* 1969 (a); *Taste the Blood of Dracula* 1969 (a); *Count Dracula* 1970 (a); *Cuadecuc (Vampir)* 1970 (a); *Eugenie* 1970 (a); *The House That Dripped Blood* 1970 (a); *Julius Caesar* 1970 (a); *The Magic Christian* 1970 (a); *The Private Life of Sherlock Holmes* 1970 (a); *The Scars of Dracula* 1970 (a); *Scream and Scream Again* 1970 (a); *Umbracle* 1970 (a); *Hannie Caulder* 1971 (a); *I Monster* 1971 (a); *The Creeping Flesh* 1972 (a); *Dracula A.D. 1972* 1972 (a); *Nothing But the Night* 1972 (a); *Panico en el Transiberiano/Horror Express* 1972 (a); *Dark Places* 1973 (a); *Deathline* 1973 (uncred.); *The Three Musketeers* 1973 (a); *The Wicker Man* 1973 (a); *La Boucher, la Star et l'Orphéline* 1974 (a); *Diagnosis: Murder* 1974 (a); *The Man With the Golden Gun* 1974 (a); *The Diamond Mercenaries* 1975 (a); *The Four Musketeers* 1975 (a); *In Search of Dracula* 1975 (a); *The Keeper* 1975 (a); *Revenge of the Dead* 1975 (a); *Whispering Death* 1975 (a); *Dracula Père et Fils/Dracula and Son* 1976 (a); *To the Devil, a Daughter* 1976 (a); *Airport 77* 1977 (a); *End of the World* 1977 (a); *Starship Invasions* 1977 (a); *Caravans* 1978 (a); *Return From Witch Mountain* 1978 (a); *The Satanic Rites of Dracula* 1978 (a); *The Silent Flute* 1978 (a); *1941* 1979 (a); *Arabian Adventure* 1979 (a); *Bear Island* 1979 (a); *Jaguar Lives!* 1979 (a); *Nutcracker Fantasy* 1979 (a,song); *The Passage* 1979 (a); *Desperate Moves* 1980 (a); *Safari 3000* 1980 (a); *Serial* 1980 (a); *An Eye For an Eye* 1981 (a); *The Salamander* 1981 (a); *House of the Long Shadows* 1982 (a); *The Last Unicorn* 1982 (a); *The Return of Captain Invincible* 1982 (a); *The Howling II... Your Sister Is a Werewolf* 1985 (a); *The Rosebud Beach Hotel* 1985 (a); *The Girl* 1986 (a); *Jocks* 1986 (a); *Mio min Mio* 1987 (a); *Dark Mission* 1988 (a); *Mask of Murder* 1989 (a); *Murder Story* 1989 (a); *The Return of the Musketeers* 1989 (a); *La Révolution Française* 1989 (a); *L'Avaro* 1990 (a); *Gremlins 2: The New Batch* 1990 (a); *Honeymoon Academy* 1990 (a).

Lee, Spike • Director, screenwriter; also actor, producer. • Born Shelton Jackson Lee, Atlanta, GA, 1956. *Educ.* Morehouse College, Atlanta, GA (communications); NYU Institute of Film and TV. Director/writer/actor Spike Lee burst onto the movie scene in 1986, immediately establishing himself as one of the world's most important young filmmakers and a controversial figure in African-American culture.

A Brooklynite, a third-generation alumnus of Atlanta's Morehouse College and a graduate of New York University's film school, Lee won immediate acclaim for his commercial debut, *She's Gotta Have It* (1986). This independently produced, stylish, black-and-white (and partly color) feature did surprising box-office business and garnered critical acclaim at the Cannes Film Festival. Although the film's sharp, witty direction impressed critics, Lee's portrayal of the comic streetwise hustler Mars Blackmon (and his trademark litany, "please, baby, please, baby, please, baby, please, baby") proved to be the most compelling element of the production.

Between film projects Lee directed himself as Mars in an Anita Baker music video ("No One in the World"), a short made for "Saturday Night Live" (*Horn of Plenty*), and most notably, in two Nike Air Jordan television commercials ("Hangtime" and "Cover") in which Mars Blackmon appears with basketball star Michael Jordan.

Television work, in fact, has been a much more frequent outlet for Lee's creative energies, as he battles to make uncompromising yet commercial films about the black experience within Hollywood's white-dominated financing, production and distribution system. Following the success of *She's Gotta Have It*, a number of black musical artists—including Miles Davis, Brandford Marsalis, Steel Pulse and Grandmaster Flash—have sought Lee to direct their music videos. With a film production team that includes editor Barry Brown and the gifted cinematographer Ernest Dickerson, Lee completed not only a number of videos, but also five one-minute spots for MTV, another series of Nike commercials, and ads for Jesse Jackson's campaign in the 1988 New York Presidential primary.

These projects have all supplemented Spike Lee's driving ambition, the production of feature films for his company, 40 Acres and a Mule Filmworks. After the self-described "guerilla filmmaking" techniques employed to produce the low-budget *She's Gotta Have It*, as well as his earlier NYU thesis film, *Joe's Bed-Stuy Barber Shop: We Cut Heads* (1982), Lee's second feature, *School Daze* (1988), was partly financed by Columbia Pictures. Despite Columbia's underfinancing (Lee was given only a third of the usual Hollywood budget), *School Daze* remained true to his provocative vision. And despite the studio's poor promotion efforts and unenthusiastic reviews, the film grossed more than twice its cost. With an all-black ensemble cast, the film satirically addresses, in the form of a musical-comedy, class and color divisions within the student body at a black college: affluent, light-skinned "gammas" clash with underclass, dark-skinned "jigaboos." In the face of production problems (Morehouse, Lee's alma mater, refused cooperation just before shooting began), *School Daze* was a notable achievement on two counts. Spike Lee became perhaps the first black director given complete control by Hollywood over his film, and *School Daze*, as one critic wrote, established that a vehicle which "puts real African American people on the screen" could succeed—redeeming a history of stereotyped screen images by speaking and acting from authentic experience.

Lee's next film, *Do the Right Thing* (1989), enlarged upon his successes on several levels—commercially, artistically and thematically. Based on several real-life racially motivated acts of violence in New York City, Lee's politically charged and polemical drama stirred controversy even before its release. The finished film was widely praised for its exciting and flamboyant visual craftsmanship. Like his other films, *Do the Right Thing* presents a slice-of-life look at a predominantly black environment, in this case a block of Brooklyn's Bedford-Stuyvesant neighborhood. Lee's portrait is both celebratory and critical: the *mise-en-scène*, music and dialogue are rich in allusions to African-American cultural history (a deejay's litany of black musical stars mixes with the score written by the director's father, jazz bassist Bill Lee), and, as in *School Daze*, Lee also unflinchingly presents the divisions within the black community by centering the film on a photograph of Malcolm X and Martin Luther King and ending it with seemingly opposing quotations from both men. More importantly, *Do the Right Thing* focuses its tense drama on the interracial violence that occurs between Bed-Stuy's black underclass and the white family that runs the local pizzeria. Climaxing with the killing of a black youth at the hands of white policemen and a fiery street riot, Lee's film offers no resolution for the racial violence which has plagued the city.

In presenting both the inter- and intra-racial problems that have marked recent American history, Spike Lee's films collectively call for an awakening of consciousness. A sleeping character in *Joe's Bed-Stuy Barber Shop* is hailed with the line, "Wake up. The black man has been asleep for 400 years." *School Daze*'s problematic climax features warring factions greeting a sunrise with the cry, "Wake up!" *Do the Right Thing* continues the plea, as the same refrain introduces both the film and Lee's Mookie character. DGS • *Joe's Bed-Stuy Barbershop: We Cut Heads* 1982 (d,p,sc,ed); *She's Gotta Have It* 1986 (a,d,sc,ed); *School Daze* 1988 (a,d,p,sc); *Do the Right Thing* 1989 (a,d,p,sc,song) **(AANBS)**; *Making "Do the Right Thing"* 1989 (a); *Mo' Better Blues* 1990 (a,d,p,sc,song).

Legrand, Michel • Composer • Born Michel Jean Legrand, Paris, 1932. *Educ.* Paris Conservatoire. Legrand worked as a piano accompanist for singers including Juliette Greco and Bing Crosby and enjoyed success as a composer and singer of popular music before turning his attention to the screen in the mid-1950s. His richly melodic work graced the early films of New Wave directors such as Jean-Luc Godard and Agnès Varda and he has subsequently worked with international figures including Norman Jewison, Joseph Losey, Kon Ichikawa and Orson Welles. Legrand has also enjoyed a long and fruitful association with fellow-countryman Jacques Demy. He made his feature directing debut with *Five Days in June* (1989), an autobiographical drama set against the Normandy landings. • *Les Amants du Tage* 1955 (m); *Charmants garçons* 1957 (uncred.); *Rafles sur la Ville* 1958 (m); *La Chien de Pique* 1960 (m); *Les Portes claquent* 1960 (m); *Terrain vague* 1960 (m); *Le Cave se rebiffe* 1961 (m); *Une Femme est une femme/A Woman Is a Woman* 1961 (m,song); *Lola* 1961 (m); *Me faire ça à moi...* 1961 (m); *Der Traum von Lieschen Muller* 1961 (m.arr,m.dir); *Cléo de 5 à 7/Cleo From 5 to 7* 1962 (a,m,song); *Un Coeur gros comme ça!* 1962 (m); *Comme un poisson dans l'eau* 1962 (m); *L'Empire de la nuit* 1962 (m); *Eva* 1962 (m,song); *Le Gentleman d'Epsom* 1962 (m); *Une Grosse tête* 1962 (m); *Le Joli Mai* 1962 (m); *Les Sept péchés capitaux/The Seven Deadly Sins* 1962 (m); *Vivre sa Vie/My Life To Live* 1962 (m); *Les Amoureux du "France"* 1963 (m); *La Baie des anges* 1963 (m); *Love Is a Ball* 1963 (m); *Maigret voit Rouge* 1963 (m); *Bande à Part/Band of Outsiders* 1964 (m); *Fascinante Amazonie* 1964 (m); *Les Parapluies de Cherbourg/The Umbrellas of Cherbourg* 1964 (m,m.cond,song,voice dubbing) **(AANBM,AANBS)**; *Les Pieds-Nickelés 1964* 1964 (m); *Les Plus belles escroqueries du monde* 1964 (m); *Une Ravissante Idiote* 1964 (m); *La Route de Jérusalem (short)* 1964 (m); *Corrida pour un espion* 1965 (m); *Monnaie de Singe* 1965 (m); *L'Or et le plomb* 1965 (a,m); *Quand passent les faisans* 1965 (m); *Et la femme créa l'amour* 1966 (m); *The Plastic Dome of Norma Jean* 1966 (m); *Qui êtes-vous, Polly Maggoo?/Who Are You, Polly Maggoo?* 1966 (m); *Tendre Voyou* 1966 (m); *La Vie de Château* 1966 (m); *Les Demoiselles de Rochefort/The Young Girls of Rochefort* 1967 (m) **(AANBM)**; *L'Homme à la Buick* 1967 (m); *Le Plus vieux métier du monde* 1967 (m); *Pretty Polly* 1967 (m,m.cond,song); *How to Save a Marriage and Ruin Your Life* 1968 (m); *Ice Station Zebra* 1968 (m); *Play Dirty* 1968 (m); *Sweet November* 1968 (m); *The Thomas Crown Affair* 1968 (m,song) **(AANBM,AABS)**; *Castle Keep* 1969 (m,m.dir); *The Happy Ending* 1969 (m,m.dir,song) **(AANBS)**; *La Piscine* 1969 (m); *La Dame dans l'auto avec des lunettes et un fusil* 1970 (m); *The Magic Garden of Stanley Sweetheart* 1970 (m); *Peau d'ane/Donkey Skin* 1970 (a,m); *The Picasso Summer* 1970 (m); *Pieces of Dreams* 1970 (m) **(AANBS)**; *Wuthering Heights* 1970 (m,m.cond); *Les Feux de la Chandeleur* 1971 (m); *The Go-Between* 1971 (m); *Le Mans* 1971 (m); *Les Mariés de l'an II* 1971 (m); *Un Peu de soleil dans l'eau froide* 1971 (m); *La Poudre d'escampette* 1971 (m); *Summer of '42* 1971 (m) **(AABM)**; *Time For Loving* 1971 (a,m); *Le Vieille Fille* 1971 (m); *Le Gang des Otages* 1972 (m); *Lady Sings the Blues* 1972 (m); *One Is a Lonely Number* 1972 (m); *Pas folle la guêpe* 1972 (m); *Portnoy's Complaint* 1972 (m); *40 Carats* 1973 (m); *Breezy* 1973 (m); *Cops and Robbers* 1973 (m); *A Doll's House* 1973 (m); *L'Evènement le plus important depuis que l'homme a marché sur la lune* 1973 (m); *Un Homme Est Mort/The Outside Man* 1973 (m); *Impossible Object* 1973 (m); *The Nelson Affair* 1973 (m); *The Three Musketeers* 1973 (m); *Vérités et Mensonges/F For Fake* 1973 (m); *Our Time* 1974 (m); *Ode to Billy Joe* 1975 (m); *Le Sauvage* 1975 (m); *Section Spéciale* 1975 (m); *Sheila Levine Is Dead and Living in New York* 1975 (m); *The Smurfs and the Magic Flute* 1975 (m); *La Ville bidon* 1975 (m); *Gable and Lombard* 1976 (m); *Le Voyage de Noces* 1976 (m,song); *Black Joy* 1977 (song); *Gulliver's Travels* 1977 (m); *The Other Side of Midnight* 1977 (m); *Semi-Tough* 1977 (m); *Le Baratineur* 1978 (song); *La Belle emmerdeuse* 1978 (m); *Ça fait tilt!* 1978 (m); *Mon premier amour* 1978 (m); *On peut le dire sans se facher* 1978 (m); *Les Routes du Sud* 1978 (m); *Les Fabuleuses aventures du légendaire baron de Munchausen* 1979 (m); *Je vous ferai aimer la vie* 1979 (m); *Lady Oscar* 1979 (m); *Atlantic City* 1980 (m,m.dir); *Falling in Love Again* 1980 (m); *Hi no tori/The Phoenix* 1980 (m); *The Hunter*

1980 (m); *Melvin and Howard* 1980 (m,song); *The Mountain Men* 1980 (m); *Finishing Touch* 1981 (m); *Les Uns et les autres/Bolero* 1981 (m); *Best Friends* 1982 (m,song) **(AANBS)**; *Le Cadeau/The Gift* 1982 (m); *Friends of the Family (short)* 1982 (m); *Qu-est-ce qui fait courir David?/What Makes David Run?* 1982 (m,song); *Eine Liebe in Deutschland* 1983 (m); *Never Say Never Again* 1983 (m,song); *La Revanche des humanoides* 1983 (m); *Yentl* 1983 (m,m.dir,orch,song) **(AANBS,AABSS)**; *Micki & Maude* 1984 (song); *Palace* 1984 (m); *Paroles et Musique/Love Songs* 1984 (m,song); *Partir Revenir* 1984 (m); *Slapstick of Another Kind* 1984 (m,m); *Train d'Enfer* 1984 (m); *Parking* 1985 (m); *Secret Places* 1985 (m,m.dir,song); *Club de rencontres* 1987 (m); *Spirale* 1987 (m); *Switching Channels* 1988 (m,m); *Trois places pour le 26* 1988 (m); *Cinq jours en juin/Five Days in June* 1989 (d,sc,m); *Eternity* 1990 (m).

Lehman, Ernest • Screenwriter; also producer, director. • Born New York, NY, 1920. *Educ.* CCNY. Short story-writer and publicist who arrived in Hollywood in 1953 and went on to script a number of tightly plotted dramas (*North By Northwest* 1959) and musicals (*West Side Story* 1961). • *The Inside Story* 1948 (story); *Executive Suite* 1954 (sc); *Sabrina* 1954 (sc) **(AANBSC)**; *The King and I* 1956 (sc); *Somebody Up There Likes Me* 1956 (sc); *Trapeze* 1956 (uncred.sc); *Sweet Smell of Success* 1957 (sc,from novella); *North By Northwest* 1959 (sc) **(AANBSC)**; *From the Terrace* 1960 (sc); *West Side Story* 1961 (sc) **(AANBSC)**; *The Prize* 1963 (sc); *The Sound of Music* 1965 (sc); *Who's Afraid of Virginia Woolf?* 1966 (sc) **(AANBSC)**; *Hello, Dolly!* 1969 (p,sc) **(AANBP)**; *Portnoy's Complaint* 1972 (adapt,d,p); *Family Plot* 1976 (sc); *Black Sunday* 1977 (sc).

Leigh, Janet • Actress • Born Jeanette Helen Morrison, Merced, CA, July 6, 1927. *Educ.* College of the Pacific, Stockton, CA (music, psychology). Signed by MGM in 1946 after Norma Shearer "discovered" her via a photograph. Leigh (her new surname was chosen by Louis B. Mayer) evolved from a fetching ingenue into a competent leading lady, turning in creditable performances in *Touch of Evil* (1958) and *Pyscho* (1960). She was married to Tony Curtis from 1951 to 1962 and is the mother of Jamie Lee Curtis. • *If Winter Comes* 1947; *The Romance of Rosy Ridge* 1947; *Act of Violence* 1948; *Hills of Home* 1948; *Words and Music* 1948; *The Doctor and the Girl* 1949; *Holiday Affair* 1949; *Little Women* 1949; *The Red Danube* 1949; *That Forsyte Woman* 1949; *Angels in the Outfield* 1951; *It's a Big Country* 1951; *Strictly Dishonorable* 1951; *Two Tickets to Broadway* 1951; *Fearless Fagan* 1952; *Just This Once* 1952; *Scaramouche* 1952; *Confidentially Connie* 1953; *Houdini* 1953; *The Naked Spur* 1953; *Walking My Baby Back Home* 1953; *The Black Shield of Falworth* 1954; *Living It Up* 1954; *Prince Valiant* 1954; *Rogue Cop* 1954; *My Sister Eileen* 1955; *Pete Kelly's Blues* 1955; *Safari* 1956; *Jet Pilot* 1957; *Touch of Evil* 1958; *The Vikings* 1958; *The Perfect Furlough* 1959; *Pepe* 1960; *Psycho* 1960 **(AANBSA)**; *Who Was That Lady?* 1960; *The Manchurian Candidate* 1962; *Bye Bye Birdie* 1963; *Wives and Lovers* 1963; *An American Dream* 1966 (a,song); *Harper* 1966; *Kid Rodelo* 1966; *The Spy in the Green Hat* 1966; *Three on a Couch* 1966; *Ad ogni costo* 1967; *Hello Down There* 1969; *Night of the Lepus* 1972; *One Is a Lonely Number* 1972; *Boardwalk* 1979; *The Fog* 1980; *Hitchcock, Il Brivido del Genio* 1985; *The Fantasy Film World of George Pal* 1986.

Leigh, Jennifer Jason • Actress • Born Los Angeles, CA, 1958. *Educ.* Lee Strasberg Institute. First gained attention in Amy Heckerling's *Fast Times at Ridgemont High* (1982), playing a juvenile in a hurry to grow up. Leigh's acclaimed performances in *Last Exit to Brooklyn* (1989) and *Miami Blues* (1990) confirmed her status as one of the most affecting actresses of her generation. Daughter of actor Vic Morrow. • *Eyes of a Stranger* 1980; *Fast Times at Ridgemont High* 1982; *Wrong Is Right* 1982; *Easy Money* 1983; *Grandview, U.S.A.* 1984; *Flesh + Blood* 1985; *The Hitcher* 1986; *The Men's Club* 1986; *Sister, Sister* 1987; *Under Cover* 1987; *Heart of Midnight* 1988; *The Big Picture* 1989; *Last Exit to Brooklyn* 1989; *Miami Blues* 1990; *Crooked Hearts* 1991.

Leigh, Mike • Director; also screenwriter. • Born Salford, England, 1943. *Educ.* RADA, London; Camberwell Art School, London; Central School of Arts and Crafts, London; London Film School. Stage, TV and film director, primarily concerned with social and political issues. Leigh earned critical acclaim for his 1977 TV drama, *Abigail's Party*, and for the theatrical feature *High Hopes* (1988), a grim portrait of Thatcherite London. Married to actress Alison Steadman. • *Bleak Moments* 1972 (d,sc,from play,idea); *Meantime* 1983 (d,sc,idea); *Four Days in July* 1984 (d,sc,idea); *The Short and Curlies (short)* 1987 (d,sc); *High Hopes* 1988 (d,sc); *Life Is Sweet* 1991 (d,sc).

Leigh, Vivien • Actress • Born Vivian Mary Hartley, Darjeeling, India, November 5, 1913; died 1967. *Educ.* RADA, London. Stage-trained actress, born to a British military family stationed in India, whose delicate beauty first graced the screen in 1935. Leigh became an international celebrity with her role as Scarlett O'Hara in *Gone With the Wind* (1939) and married Laurence Olivier the following year. Also memorable as Blanche du Bois in the film version of *A Streetcar Named Desire* (1951). • *Look Up and Laugh* 1935; *Things Are Looking Up* 1935; *The Village Squire* 1935; *Fire Over England* 1936; *21 Days* 1937; *Dark Journey* 1937; *Gentleman's Agreement* 1937; *Storm in a Teacup* 1937; *St. Martin's Lane W.C.2* 1938; *A Yank at Oxford* 1938; *Blind Dogs (short)* 1939; *Gone With the Wind* 1939 **(AABA)**; *Waterloo Bridge* 1940; *That Hamilton Woman* 1941; *Caesar and Cleopatra* 1945; *Anna Karenina* 1948; *A Streetcar Named Desire* 1951 **(AABA)**; *The Deep Blue Sea* 1955; *The Roman Spring of Mrs. Stone* 1961; *Ship of Fools* 1965.

Leland, David • Director; also screenwriter, actor. • Born Cambridge, England, April 20, 1947. TV- and stage-experienced writer-director whose *Wish You Were Here* (1987) was well received, particularly for its fine central performance by newcomer Emily Lloyd. • *1917* 1968 (a); *Julius Caesar* 1970 (a); *One Brief Summer* 1970 (a); *The Missionary* 1981 (a); *Time Bandits* 1981 (a); *Mona Lisa* 1986 (sc); *Personal Services* 1987 (sc,a); *Wish You Were Here* 1987 (d,sc,lyrics "Lost in a Dream," "Gentle Wind"); *Checking Out* 1988 (d); *The Big Man* 1990 (d).

Lelouch, Claude • Director, screenwriter; also producer, director of photography. • Born Claude Barruck Lelouch, Paris, October 30, 1937. *Educ.* Collège Sainte-Barbe. French director who emerged in the 1960s, scoring a popular international success with the romantic melodrama, *A Man and a Woman* (1966). Despite an early reputation as an "outsider" who combined social criticism with a flashy visual technique, Lelouch rapidly became assimilated into the mainstream of commercial French cinema. • *Quand le rideau se lève (short)* 1957 (d,sc,ph,ed); *Elle conduit (short)* 1960 (d,sc); *Le Propre de l'homme* 1960 (a,d,sc,adapt,dial); *L'Amour avec des si...* 1963 (d,p,sc,adapt); *La Femme spectacle* 1964 (d,sc,adapt); *Une Fille et des fusils* 1964 (d,sc,ed,cam.op); *... Pour un maillot jaune (short)* 1965 (d,sc,ph,ed); *Les Grands moments* 1965 (d,sc,adapt,dial, ed,cam.op); *Jean Paul Belmondo (short)* 1965 (d); *Un Homme et une femme/A Man and a Woman* 1966 (d,sc,story,ph, ed) **(AABSC,AANBD)**; *Loin du Viêtnam/Far From Vietnam* 1967 (d); *Vivre pour vivre* 1967 (d,sc,ed,ph); *Treize Jours en France* 1968 (d,sc,ph,ed); *La Vie, l'amour, la mort* 1968 (d,sc,adapt, dial); *Un Homme qui me plaît* 1969 (d,p,sc,cam.op); *Le Voyou* 1970 (d,sc,ph); *Smic, Smac, Smoc* 1971 (d,sc,cam.op); *L'Aventure c'est l'aventure* 1972 (d,sc,ph); *La Bonne Année* 1973 (d,p,sc,ph); *Visions of Eight* 1973 (d,sc—"The Losers"); *Mariage* 1974 (d,sc,cam.op); *Toute une vie* 1974 (d,sc,cam.op) **(AANBSC)**; *Le Bon et les* *méchants* 1975 (d,sc,ph); *Le Chat et la Souris* 1975 (d,p,sc,ph); *Rendezvous (short)* 1976 (d,ph); *Si c'était à refaire* 1976 (d,p,sc); *Another Man, Another Chance* 1977 (d,sc); *Confidences pour confidences* 1978 (a); *Molière* 1978 (exec.p); *Robert et Robert* 1978 (d,exec.p,sc,cam.op); *A nous deux* 1979 (d,p,sc,cam.op); *Alors, Heureux?* 1979 (p); *Un Après-midi avec les moteurs (short)* 1979 (d); *Il A Besoin (short)* 1981 (d,sc); *Les Uns et les autres/Bolero* 1981 (d,p,sc,dial); *Edith et Marcel* 1982 (d,sc,dial); *Partir Revenir* 1984 (d,p,sc); *Viva la Vie!* 1984 (d,p,sc); *Un Homme et une femme: Vingt ans déjà/A Man and a Woman: 20 Years Later* 1986 (d,p,sc,); *Attention Bandits* 1987 (d,p,sc,story); *Happy New Year* 1987 (a,from film *La bonne année*); *Itineraire d'un enfant gâté* 1988 (d,p,sc); *Il y a des jours...et des lunes* 1990 (d,p,sc).

Lemmon, Jack • Actor • Born John Uhler Lemmon III, Boston, MA, February 8, 1925. *Educ.* Harvard. Began his career as a radio, theater and TV actor and first gained screen prominence with an Oscar-winning role as the opportunistic Ensign Pulver in *Mister Roberts* (1955). Lemmon went on to establish himself as one of America's finest comedic performers, particularly with his roles in two of Billy Wilder's comic masterpieces: in the delirious *Some Like It Hot* (1959) he played a nightclub musician who, together with Tony Curtis, dresses in drag in order to escape the clutches of a Chicago mob; and in *The Apartment* (1960) he portrayed a hapless insurance clerk who, in a bid for promotion, allows his superiors to conduct their extra-marital affairs in his city flat. The latter role, of a put-upon figure fighting a continual losing battle with life's daily frustrations and humiliations, became Lemmon's trademark. Alongside other comic triumphs such as *Irma la Douce* (1963) and *The Odd Couple* (1968), Lemmon has also proved a thoughtful and engaging dramatic player; his performances in two political thrillers—*The China Syndrome* (1979) and *Missing* (1982)—each earned him a best actor award at the Cannes Film Festival. Lemmon has directed one feature, *Kotch* (1971), and was awarded the American Film Institute Life Achievement Award in 1988. He was formerly married (1950-56) to actress Cynthia Stone and wed Felicia Farr in 1962; son Chris Lemmon (b. 1954) is also an actor (*Swing Shift* 1984, etc.). • *It Should Happen to You* 1954; *Phffft* 1954; *Three For the Show* 1954; *Mister Roberts* 1955 **(AABSA)**; *My Sister Eileen* 1955; *You Can't Run Away From It* 1956; *Fire Down Below* 1957 (a,harmonica theme); *Operation Mad Ball* 1957; *Bell, Book and Candle* 1958; *Cowboy* 1958; *It Happened to Jane* 1959; *Some Like It Hot* 1959 **(AANBA)**; *The Apartment* 1960 **(AANBA)**; *Pepe* 1960; *Le Voyage en ballon* 1960; *The Wackiest Ship in the Army* 1960; *Days of Wine and Roses* 1962 **(AANBA)**; *The Notorious Landlady* 1962; *Irma la Douce* 1963; *Under the Yum Yum Tree* 1963; *Good Neighbor Sam* 1964; *The Great Race* 1965; *How to Murder Your Wife* 1965; *The Fortune Cookie* 1966; *Luv* 1967; *The Odd Couple* 1968; *There Comes a Day (short)* 1968; *The April Fools* 1969; *The Out-of-Towners* 1970; *Kotch* 1971 (a,d); *Avanti!* 1972; *The War Between Men and Women* 1972; *Save the Tiger* 1973 **(AABA)**; *The Front Page* 1974; *The Prisoner of Second Avenue* 1974; *Alex & the Gypsy* 1976; *Gentleman Tramp* 1976; *Airport 77* 1977; *The China Syndrome* 1979 **(AANBA)**; *Ken Murray: Shooting Stars* 1979; *Portrait of a 60% Perfect Man* 1980 (narr); *Tribute* 1980 (a,song) **(AANBA)**; *Buddy Buddy* 1981; *Missing* 1982 **(AANBA)**; *Mass Appeal* 1984; *Macaroni* 1985; *That's Life!* 1986; *Dad* 1989.

Leone, Sergio • Director; also screenwriter. • Born Rome, 1921; died April 30, 1989. Began his career as an assistant on numerous Italian productions of the late 1940s and early 50s and came to prominence in the 1960s, when he revitalized the western genre with a series of gritty, semi-satirical hommages known as "spaghetti westerns." "The cowboy picture has got lost in psychology," he said. "The West was made by violent uncomplicated men, and it is this strength and simplicity that I try to recapture in my pictures."

Leone's gun-and-sun operas provided employment for a number of American actors, most notably Clint Eastwood, who starred as the laconic anti-hero of *For a Fistful of Dollars* (1964), *For a Few Dollars More* (1965) and *The Good, the Bad, and the Ugly* (1967). Leone's last major project was *Once Upon a Time in America* (1984), a bloody tribute to the American gangster film starring Robert De Niro. It was severely cut for US release to an extent which made it almost incomprehensible, though the version praised at the Cannes Film Festival and across Europe is now available in the US. Father Vincenzo Leone was a noted silent film director. • *Taxi...signore? (short)* 1957 (d); *Nel Segno di Roma* 1959 (sc); *Gli Ultimi giorni di Pompei* 1959 (sc,2u d); *El Coloso de Rodas* 1961 (d,sc); *Le Sette sfide* 1961 (sc); *Sodoma e Gomorra* 1962 (d); *Duel of the Titans* 1963 (sc,story); *Le Verdi bandiere di Allah* 1963 (sc); *Per un Pugno di Dollari/A Fistful of Dollars* 1964 (d,sc,story); *Per qualche dollaro in più/For a Few Dollars More* 1965 (d,sc,story); *Il Buono, il Brutto, il Cattivo/The Good, the Bad, and the Ugly* 1967 (d,sc,story); *C'era una Volta il West/Once Upon a Time in the West* 1969 (d,sc,story); *Duck, You Sucker/A Fistful of Dynamite* 1972 (d); *Il Mio nome è Nessuno/My Name Is Nobody* 1973 (idea); *Il Gatto* 1978 (exec.p); *Bianco Rosso e Verdone* 1981 (p); *Once Upon a Time in America* 1984 (d,sc); *Troppo Forte* 1985 (uncred.d).

Lerner, Alan Jay • Playwright; also lyricist, screenwriter. • Born New York, NY, August 31, 1918. *Educ.* Harvard; Juillard. Enjoyed a long and prosperous collaboration with composer Frederick Loewe (beginnining in 1943) which resulted in such musicals as *Brigadoon* (1954), *My Fair Lady* (1964) and *Camelot* (1967). Lerner also adapted a number of his plays for the screen and wrote several original film scripts. Two of his eight marriages have been to actresses: Nancy Olson (1950-57) and Liz Robertson (1981-). • *An American in Paris* 1951 (sc,story) **(AABSC)**; *Royal Wedding* 1951 (sc,story,lyrics) **(AANBS)**; *Brigadoon* 1954 (sc,m,lyrics); *Gigi* 1958 (sc,m,lyrics,song) **(AABS,AABSC)**; *The Adventures of Huckleberry Finn* 1960 (song); *My Fair Lady* 1964 (sc,m,lyrics,song) **(AANBSC)**; *Zvonyat, otkroitye dver* 1965 (song); *Camelot* 1967 (sc,from play,lyrics,song); *Paint Your Wagon* 1969 (m,p); *On a Clear Day You Can See Forever* 1970 (p,sc,from play,lyrics,song); *The Little Prince* 1974 (sc,lyrics) **(AANBS,AANBSS)**.

LeRoy, Mervyn • Director, producer; also actor. • Born San Francisco, CA, October 15, 1900; died September 13, 1987. Former actor and comedy writer who began a prolific directing career in 1927. LeRoy did his best work at Warner Bros. in the 1930s, turning out a string of grittily realistic films which reflected the hardships of Depression-era America. His 1930 gangster film, *Little Caesar*, launched Edward G. Robinson into stardom and inaugurated the genre with which Warner Bros. would make its name. In 1938 LeRoy switched to MGM and turned his hand to glossier and, for the most part, less satisfactory fare. His other achievements include producing *The Wizard of Oz* (1939), taking over the direction of *Mister Roberts* (1955) from an ailing John Ford and introducing Ronald Reagan to Nancy Davis. • *Double Speed* 1920 (uncred.a); *Too Much Speed* 1921 (a); *The Ghost Breaker* 1922 (a); *The Call of the Canyon* 1923 (a); *Going Up* 1923 (a); *Little Johnny Jones* 1923 (a); *Prodigal Daughters* 1923 (a); *Broadway After Dark* 1924 (a); *The Chorus Lady* 1924 (a); *In Hollywood With Potash and Perlmutter* 1924 (gags); *The Desert Flower* 1925 (gags); *Sally* 1925 (gags); *We Moderns* 1925 (gags); *Ella Cinders* 1926 (sc); *Irene* 1926 (gags); *It Must Be Love* 1926 (gags); *Twinkletoes* 1926 (gags); *Naughty But Nice* 1927 (gags); *No Place to Go* 1927 (d); *Orchids and Ermine* 1927 (gags); *Flying Romeos* 1928 (d); *Harold Teen* 1928 (d); *Oh, Kay!* 1928 (d); *Broadway Babies* 1929 (d); *Hot Stuff* 1929 (d); *Little Johnny Jones* 1929 (d); *Naughty Baby* 1929 (d); *Little Caesar* 1930 (d); *Num-*

bered Men 1930 (d); *Playing Around* 1930 (d); *Showgirl in Hollywood* 1930 (d); *Top Speed* 1930 (d); *Broad-Minded* 1931 (d); *Five Star Final* 1931 (d); *Gentleman's Fate* 1931 (d); *Local Boy Makes Good* 1931 (d); *Tonight or Never* 1931 (d); *Too Young to Marry* 1931 (d); *Big City Blues* 1932 (d); *The Dark Horse* 1932 (d); *The Heart of New York* 1932 (d); *High Pressure* 1932 (d); *I Am a Fugitive From a Chain Gang* 1932 (d); *Three on a Match* 1932 (d); *Two Seconds* 1932 (d); *42nd Street* 1933 (ad—production number); *Elmer the Great* 1933 (d); *Gold Diggers of 1933* 1933 (d); *Hard to Handle* 1933 (d); *Tugboat Annie* 1933 (d); *The World Changes* 1933 (d); *Happiness Ahead* 1934 (d); *Heat Lightning* 1934 (d); *Hi, Nellie!* 1934 (d); *I Found Stella Parish* 1935 (d); *Oil For the Lamps of China* 1935 (d); *Page Miss Glory* 1935 (d); *Sweet Adeline* 1935 (d); *Anthony Adverse* 1936 (d); *Three Men on a Horse* 1936 (d,p); *The Great Garrick* 1937 (prod.sup); *The King and the Chorus Girl* 1937 (d,p); *Mr. Dodd Takes the Air* 1937 (p); *They Won't Forget* 1937 (d,p); *Dramatic School* 1938 (p); *Fools for Scandal* 1938 (d,p); *At the Circus* 1939 (p); *Stand Up and Fight* 1939 (p); *The Wizard of Oz* 1939 (p); *Escape* 1940 (d,p); *Waterloo Bridge* 1940 (d); *Blossoms in the Dust* 1941 (d); *Johnny Eager* 1941 (d); *Unholy Partners* 1941 (d); *Random Harvest* 1942 (d) **(AANBD)**; *Madame Curie* 1943 (d); *Thirty Seconds Over Tokyo* 1944 (d); *The House I Live In (short)* 1945 (p); *Without Reservations* 1946 (d); *Desire Me* 1947 (d); *Homecoming* 1948 (d); *Any Number Can Play* 1949 (d); *East Side, West Side* 1949 (d); *Little Women* 1949 (d,p); *Quo Vadis* 1951 (d); *Lovely to Look At* 1952 (d); *Million Dollar Mermaid* 1952 (d); *Latin Lovers* 1953 (d); *Rose Marie* 1954 (d,p); *Strange Lady in Town* 1954 (d,p); *Mister Roberts* 1955 (d); *The Bad Seed* 1956 (d,p); *Toward the Unknown* 1956 (d,p); *Home Before Dark* 1958 (d,p); *No Time For Sergeants* 1958 (d,p); *The F.B.I. Story* 1959 (d,p); *Wake Me When It's Over* 1960 (d,p); *The Devil at 4 O'Clock* 1961 (d,p); *A Majority of One* 1961 (d,p); *Gypsy* 1962 (d,p); *Mary, Mary* 1963 (d,p); *Moment to Moment* 1966 (d,p); *The Green Berets* 1968 (uncred.assoc.d).

Lester, Richard • Director • Born Philadelphia, PA, January 19, 1932. *Educ.* University of Pennsylvania (clinical psychology). Young American TV director in the 1950s who took a break to travel around Europe, settled in England, and established a career directing some landmarks of 1960s cinema.

Lester's career began with a Peter Sellers collaboration, the short *The Running, Jumping, and Standing Still Film* (1959). He reached major prominence with the Beatles movies, *A Hard Day's Night* (1964) and *Help!* (1965), chronicling the fictional adventures of the pop group in appropriately zany, exuberant style. *The Knack* (1965), from the popular play by Ann Jellicoe, with Michael Crawford and Rita Tushingham, assured his reputation, not only as the chief chronicler of "swinging London" in the 60s, but also as a film stylist whose work has had a profound effect on contemporary film language. Even more than his New Wave contemporaries, Lester freed the camera to join the action, and freed filmmakers from conventions that had become tired and restrictive by that time.

While poorly received at the time, *A Funny Thing Happened On the Way to the Forum* (1966), from the rambunctious musical by Steven Sondheim and starring a gallery of classic *farceurs* from Zero Mostel to Buster Keaton, remains a classic translation of a rich stage musical—one of few that try to match the moviemaking to the music.

After attempting to apply the same freewheeling style to a more ambitious antiwar subject in *How I Won the War* (1967), Lester returned to America for *Petulia* (1968), an essay on life in these United States set against the background of the Vietnam war, which quickly became a connoisseur's favorite. The story of the breakdown of a marriage set in the hills of San Francisco captured the uneasiness of the times with a haunting metaphor. Back in London, Lester turned to apocalyptic farce with *The Bed-Sitting Room* (1969), a post-nuclear-war idyll which went straight over the heads of audiences the world over who had not yet discovered "Monty Python's Flying Circus" and couldn't remember "The Goon Show."

Lester sat out the next four years, busying himself with witty TV commercials. When he returned to the big screen with *The Three Musketeers* in 1973, the 60s were long past. His subsequent films, mainly big-budget serial blockbuster productions, have been witty but far more mainstream. But then, so have the times. The Richard Lester of the 60s remains one of the most influential filmmakers of the last 30 years as the anarchic techniques he pioneered have become staples of the contemporary pop video lexicon. JM • *The Running, Jumping and Standing Still Film (short)* 1959 (a,d,idea,ph,ed,m); *Mildred (short)* 1960 (sc); *It's Trad, Dad!* 1961 (d); *The Mouse on the Moon* 1963 (d); *A Hard Day's Night* 1964 (d); *Help!* 1965 (d); *The Knack... and How to Get It* 1965 (a,d); *A Funny Thing Happened on the Way to the Forum* 1966 (d); *How I Won the War* 1967 (d,p); *Teenage Rebellion* 1967 (d); *Petulia* 1968 (d); *The Bed Sitting Room* 1969 (d,p); *Richard Lester: The Running, Jumping, Standing Still Director (short)* 1971 (a); *The Three Musketeers* 1973 (d); *Juggernaut* 1974 (d); *The Four Musketeers* 1975 (d); *Royal Flash* 1975 (d); *The Ritz* 1976 (d); *Robin and Marian* 1976 (d); *Butch and Sundance: The Early Days* 1979 (a,d); *Cuba* 1979 (d); *Superman II* 1980 (d); *Superman III* 1983 (d); *Finders Keepers* 1984 (d,exec.p); *The Return of the Musketeers* 1989 (d).

Leven, Boris • Production designer • Born Moscow, 1900. *Educ.* USC, College of Architecture and Fine Arts; Beaux Arts Institute of Design, New York. Russian emigre who began his film career as a sketch artist at Paramount in 1933 and moved to Fox three years later. Leven has proved his mastery across a wide range of genres including westerns, science fiction films and musicals and has worked often with Martin Scorsese. • *Alexander's Ragtime Band* 1938 (art d) **(AANBAD)**; *Just Around the Corner* 1938 (art d); *Everybody's Baby* 1939 (art d); *The Flying Deuces* 1939 (art d); *Second Chorus* 1940 (art d); *The Shanghai Gesture* 1941 (art d) **(AANBAD)**; *Girl Trouble* 1942 (art d); *Life Begins at Eight-Thirty* 1942 (art d); *Tales of Manhattan* 1942 (art d); *Hello, Frisco, Hello* 1943 (art d); *Doll Face* 1945 (art d); *Home, Sweet Homicide* 1946 (art d); *Drummer Man (short)* 1947 (art d); *I Wonder Who's Kissing Her Now* 1947 (art d); *The Senator Was Indiscreet* 1947 (art d); *The Shocking Miss Pilgrim* 1947 (art d); *Criss Cross* 1948 (art d); *Mr. Peabody and the Mermaid* 1948 (art d); *The Lovable Cheat* 1949 (art d); *Search For Danger* 1949 (art d); *Dakota Lil* 1950 (art d); *Destination Murder* 1950 (art d); *Experiment Alcatraz* 1950 (art d); *House By the River* 1950 (art d); *The Jackie Robinson Story* 1950 (pd); *Once a Thief* 1950 (pd); *Quicksand* 1950 (art d); *Woman on the Run* 1950 (art d); *The Basketball Fix* 1951 (art d); *Chicago Calling* 1951 (art d); *A Millionaire For Christy* 1951 (art d); *The Prowler* 1951 (art d); *The Second Woman* 1951 (pd); *Two Dollar Bettor* 1951 (art d); *Rose of Cimarron* 1952 (art d); *The Star* 1952 (art d); *Sudden Fear* 1952 (art d); *Crazylegs* 1953 (art d); *Donovan's Brain* 1953 (pd); *Fort Algiers* 1953 (art d); *Invaders From Mars* 1953 (art d); *The Long Wait* 1954 (art d); *The Silver Chalice* 1954 (art d); *Giant* 1956 (pd) **(AANBAD)**; *Courage of Black Beauty* 1957 (art d); *My Gun Is Quick* 1957 (art d); *Zero Hour!* 1957 (pd); *Anatomy of a Murder* 1959 (pd); *John Paul Jones* 1959 (uncred.art d); *Thunder in the Sun* 1959 (pd); *September Storm* 1960 (art d); *West Side Story* 1961 (pd) **(AABAD)**; *Two For the Seesaw* 1962 (pd); *Strait-Jacket* 1964 (pd); *The Sound of Music* 1965 (pd) **(AANBAD)**; *The Sand Pebbles* 1966 (pd) **(AANBAD)**; *Star!* 1968 (pd) **(AANBAD)**; *A Dream of Kings* 1969 (pd); *The Andromeda Strain* 1971 (pd) **(AANBAD)**; *Happy Birthday, Wanda June* 1971 (pd); *The New Centurions* 1972 (pd); *Jonathan Livingston Seagull* 1973 (pd); *Shanks* 1974 (pd); *Mandingo* 1975 (pd); *New York, New York* 1977 (pd); *The Last Waltz* 1978 (pd); *Matilda* 1978 (pd); *The King of*

Comedy 1983 (pd); *Fletch* 1985 (pd); *The Color of Money* 1986 (pd) **(AANBAD)**; *Wildcats* 1986 (pd).

Levine, Joseph E. • Producer, distributor • Born Joseph Edward Levine, Boston, MA, September 9, 1905; died July 21, 1987. Self-proclaimed movie "mogul" who entered the film business as an exhibitor, specializing in importing foreign films. Alongside classics such as *Open City* (1945) and *The Bicycle Thief* (1948), Levin imported cheaply made entertainments such as *Godzilla* (1954) and *Hercules* (1959), a major commercial success which thrust him into the Hollywood big time. He then moved into production and had a significant hand in some major films of the 1960s including *8 1/2* (1963) and *The Graduate* (1967). The crass movie producer played by Jack Palance in Godard's *Contempt* (1963) was widely considered to be based on Levine—who produced the film! • *Attila* 1955 (exec.p); *La Ciociara/Two Women* 1960 (exec.p); *Le Mépris/Contempt* 1963 (p); *Otto e Mezzo/8 1/2* 1963 (p); *The Carpetbaggers* 1964 (p); *Matrimonio all'italiana/Marriage Italian Style* 1964 (exec.p); *Where Love Has Gone* 1964 (p); *Harlow* 1965 (p); *A Man Called Adam* 1966 (exec.p); *Nevada Smith* 1966 (exec.p); *The Graduate* 1967 (p); *Woman Times Seven* 1967 (exec.p); *The Lion in Winter* 1968 (exec.p); *I Girasoli* 1969 (exec.p); *La Piscine* 1969 (exec.p); *Stiletto* 1969 (exec.p); *The Adventurers* 1970 (p); *The Ski Bum* 1970 (p); *Carnal Knowledge* 1971 (exec.p); *Rivals* 1972 (exec.p); *Hurry Up, or I'll Be 30* 1973 (p); *Interval* 1973 (p); *Paper Tiger* 1975 (p); *A Bridge Too Far* 1977 (p); *Magic* 1978 (p); *Tattoo* 1981 (p).

Levinson, Barry • Director, screenwriter; also actor. • Born Baltimore, MD, 1932. *Educ.* American University, Washington DC (broadcast journalism). Levinson entered the entertainment business as a comic writer and performer, scripting several TV programs, including "The Carol Burnett Show," before graduating to film work. He co-scripted (with Mel Brooks) and appeared in both *Silent Movie* (1976) and *High Anxiety* (1977), providing a memorable turn as the maniacal bellhop in the latter.

Levinson made an auspicious directorial debut with *Diner* (1982), a semi-autobiographical coming-of-age tale set in late 1950s Baltimore. Alternately poignant and hilarious, the film played a large part in promoting the careers of its young stars Mickey Rourke, Steve Guttenberg, Daniel Stern, Kevin Bacon and Ellen Barkin. Levinson demonstrated an understated, non-intrusive style and an ear for ensemble dialogue that would serve him well in subsequent features.

The Natural (1984), adapted from Bernard Malamud's 1952 novel, starred Robert Redford as baseball pro Roy Hobbs; it received mixed reviews, with some critics finding it inconsistent and sentimental but many praising the cinematography (by Caleb Deschanel) and score (Randy Newman). *Young Sherlock Holmes* (1985) was a mildly charming Steven Spielberg-produced project that turned out to be long on special effects and short on narrative.

The year 1987 saw the release of two Levinson films: one returned to the autobiographical territory first explored in *Diner* and the other established the director's major-league box-office credentials. *Tin Men*, set in Baltimore in 1963—several years after the events of *Diner*—follows the misadventures of rival aluminum-siding salesmen. A rich character study, it maintains a fine balance between humor and melancholy and features some brilliantly funny dialogue, mostly traded between Richard Dreyfuss and Danny DeVito as the two protagonists. *Good Morning, Vietnam* was a commercially successful Robin Williams vehicle that gave its star the chance to deliver a series of highly effective comic monologues. It earned Williams an Oscar nomination, though it did not seem to exploit fully Levinson's talents for ensemble character studies.

Levinson's next feature was *Rain Man* (1988), a finely handled study of the relationship between an autistic "idiot savant" (Dustin Hoffman) and his opportunistic car-salesman brother (Tom Cruise). A huge success at the box-office, the film also earned four Oscars, for best picture, director, actor (Hoffman) and screenplay (Ronald Bass and Barry Morrow). While the central performances garnered most of the critical attention, the director's ability to handle the unorthodox subject-matter with sensitivity and style was central to the film's success. (The project had been through at least three other directors and countless script re-writes before Levinson finally brought it to fruition.)

Levinson again returned to Baltimore to make *Avalon* (1990), an epic saga tracing the history of his own family from the point when they first arrived in the US. Critics reacted with measured praise to a work that was felt to be overlong and lacking in direction, if ultimately rewarding. That such a personal and uncommercial project could even be produced in the Hollywood of the early 1990s bears witness to its director/producer's commitment, integrity and vision. JCP • *The Internecine Project* 1974 (sc); *Street Girls* 1974 (sc,asst.cam.op); *Silent Movie* 1976 (a,sc); *High Anxiety* 1977 (a,sc); *And Justice For All* 1979 (sc) **(AANBSC)**; *Inside Moves* 1980 (sc); *History of the World Part I* 1981 (a); *Best Friends* 1982 (sc); *Diner* 1982 (d,sc) **(AANBSC)**; *Unfaithfully Yours* 1983 (sc); *The Natural* 1984 (d); *Young Sherlock Holmes* 1985 (d); *Good Morning, Vietnam* 1987 (d); *Tin Men* 1987 (d,sc); *Rain Man* 1988 (a,d) **(AABD)**; *Avalon* 1990 (d,p,sc).

Lewis, Jerry • Actor; also director, producer, screenwriter. • Born Joseph Levitch, Newark, NJ, March 16, 1926. Stand-up comic whose floundering career was boosted when he paired with straight man Dean Martin in 1946. The pair's hit nightclub routine was first transferred to film in 1949, with Lewis and Martin going on to star in a total of 16 films, all based on the same formula: suave, good-natured Dino is undermined by the goofy antics of the impossibly nerdy Jerry. The team acrimoniously broke up in 1956, with Lewis going on to star in, and direct, his own vehicles. Since French cinéastes "unmasked" the comic genius lurking beneath his sophomoric antics, Lewis has cultivated his image as an auteur in books and on talk shows. Although his film roles have been intermittent of late, Lewis received crictal acclaim for his dramatic performance in Martin Scorsese's *The King of Comedy* (1983). • *My Friend Irma* 1949 (a); *At War With the Army* 1950 (a); *My Friend Irma Goes West* 1950 (a); *Sailor Beware* 1951 (a); *That's My Boy* 1951 (a); *Jumping Jacks* 1952 (a); *Road to Bali* 1952 (a); *The Stooge* 1952 (a); *The Caddy* 1953 (a); *Money From Home* 1953 (a,d); *Scared Stiff* 1953 (a); *Living It Up* 1954 (a); *Three Ring Circus* 1954 (a); *Artists and Models* 1955 (a); *You're Never Too Young* 1955 (a); *Hollywood or Bust* 1956 (a); *Pardners* 1956 (a); *The Delicate Delinquent* 1957 (a,p); *The Sad Sack* 1957 (a); *The Geisha Boy* 1958 (a,p); *Rock-a-Bye Baby* 1958 (a,p); *Don't Give Up the Ship* 1959 (a); *Li'l Abner* 1959 (a); *The Bellboy* 1960 (a,d,p,sc); *Cinderfella* 1960 (a,p); *Raymie* 1960 (song); *Visit to a Small Planet* 1960 (a); *The Errand Boy* 1961 (a,d,sc,lyrics,song); *The Ladies' Man* 1961 (a,d,p,sc,story); *It's Only Money* 1962 (a); *It's a Mad, Mad, Mad, Mad World* 1963 (a); *The Nutty Professor* 1963 (a,d,sc); *Who's Minding the Store?* 1963 (a); *The Disorderly Orderly* 1964 (a,exec.p); *The Patsy* 1964 (a,d,sc,story); *Boeing Boeing* 1965 (a); *The Family Jewels* 1965 (a,d,p,sc); *Three on a Couch* 1966 (a,d,lyrics,p); *Way... Way Out* 1966 (a); *The Big Mouth* 1967 (a,d,p,sc); *Don't Raise the Bridge, Lower the River* 1968 (a); *Hook, Line and Sinker* 1968 (a,p); *One More Time* 1970 (d); *Which Way to the Front?* 1970 (a,d,p); *Hardly Working* 1981 (a,d,sc); *The King of Comedy* 1983 (a); *Retenez moi... ou je fais un malheur* 1983 (a); *Smorgasbord* 1983 (a,d,sc); *Par ou t'es rentré? On t'as vu Sortir* 1984 (a); *Slapstick of Another Kind* 1984 (a); *Cookie* 1989 (a).

Lewton, Val • *aka* Carlos Keith, Cosmo Forbes • Producer; also screenwriter, novelist. • Born Vladimir Ivan Leventon, Yalta, Russia, May 7, 1904; died 1951. *Educ.* Columbia (journalism).

Versatile and prolific writer of novels, nonfiction and poetry who entered film as a protege of David O. Selznick in the early 1930s. Lewton went on to produce a number of stylish, low-budget horror films for RKO, notably the atmospheric *Cat People* (1942), the engagingly macabre *I Walked With A Zombie* (1943) and the chilling *Bedlam* (1946). • *No Man of Her Own* 1933 (from novel "No Bed of Her Own"); *A Tale of Two Cities* 1935 (prod.sup—revolutionary scenes); *Cat People* 1942 (p); *The Ghost Ship* 1943 (p); *I Walked With a Zombie* 1943 (p); *The Leopard Man* 1943 (p); *The Seventh Victim* 1943 (p); *The Curse of the Cat People* 1944 (p); *Mademoiselle Fifi* 1944 (p); *Youth Runs Wild* 1944 (p); *The Body Snatcher* 1945 (p,sc); *Isle of the Dead* 1945 (p); *Bedlam* 1946 (p,sc); *My Own True Love* 1949 (p); *Please Believe Me* 1950 (p); *Apache Drums* 1951 (p).

L'Herbier, Marcel • Director; also writer, composer. • Born Paris, April 23, 1888; died 1979. *Educ.* Ecole des Hautes Etudes Sociales, Paris. Avant-garde filmmaker of the late teens whose works incorporated the talents of renowned artists from other fields, including painter Fernand Leger and architect Mallet Stevens. L'Herbier's silent films and theoretical writing inspired a generation of cinéastes, such as directors Alberto Cavalcanti and Claude Autant-Lara, although his critical reputation ebbed with the advent of sound. He founded the noted film school, IDHEC, in 1943. • *Le Torrent* 1917 (sc); *Bouclette* 1917 (sc,a); *Phantasmes* 1918 (d,sc); *Rose-France* 1919 (d,sc); *Le Bércail* 1919 (d); *Le Carnaval des vérités* 1919 (d,sc); *L'Homme du large* 1920 (d,sc,a); *Prométhée Banquier* 1921 (d,p); *Villa Déstin* 1921 (d,adapt); *El Dorado* 1921 (d,sc); *Don Juan et Faust* 1922 (d,adapt); *Resurrection* 1923 (d,sc); *L'Inhumaine* 1923 (d,sc); *Le Marchand de plaisirs* 1923 (prod.sup); *La Galérie des monstres* 1924 (art.d); *Féu Mathias Pascal* 1925 (d,sc); *Le Vertige* 1926 (d,sc); *L'Argent* 1927 (d); *Le Diable au coeur* 1927 (d,sc); *Nuits de princes* 1929 (d,adapt); *Autour de l'argent* 1929 (a); *Le Mystère de la chambre jaune* 1930 (d,sc); *Le Parfum de la dame en noir* 1930 (d,sc); *L'Enfant de l'amour* 1930 (d,sc); *La Femme d'une nuit* 1930 (d); *Le Martyre de l'obèse* 1932 (prod.sup); *L'Epervier* 1933 (d); *Midi* 1933 (commentary); *Le Scandale* 1934 (d); *L'Aventurier* 1934 (d,sc); *La Bataille* 1934 (prod.sup); *La Route impériale* 1935 (d,sc); *Le Bonheur* 1935 (d,sc); *Veille d'armes* 1935 (d,sc); *Les Hommes nouveaux* 1936 (d,sc); *La Porte du large* 1936 (d,sc); *Nuits de feu* 1936 (d,sc); *Le Coin des enfants* 1936 (d,sc); *Forfaiture* 1937 (d); *La Citadelle du silence* 1937 (d); *La Mode rêvée* 1938 (d,sc); *Adrienne Lecouvreur* 1938 (d); *La Tragédie impériale* 1938 (d,sc); *Terre de feu* 1938 (d); *La Brigade sauvage* 1939 (uncred.d); *Entente Cordiale* 1939 (d); *La Comédie du Bonheur* 1940 (d,sc); *Histoire de rire* 1941 (d); *L'Honorable Catherine* 1941 (d); *La Vie de Bohème* 1942 (d); *La Nuit fantastique* 1942 (d,adapt); *Le Loup des Malveneur* 1943 (prod.sup); *Au Petit Bonheur* 1946 (d); *L'Affaire du collier de la reine* 1946 (d); *La Révoltée* 1948 (d,adapt); *Une Grande fille toute simple* 1948 (prod.sup); *Les Dernières jours de Pompéi* 1949 (d,adapt); *Le Père de Mademoiselle* 1953 (d,sc); *Homage à Debussy* 1963 (d); *Le Cinéma du diable* 1967 (d); *La Féerie des fantasmes* 1978 (d).

Lindblom, Gunnel • Actress; also director, screenwriter. • Born Göteborg, Sweden, December 18, 1931. Swedish leading lady, notably in several films directed by Ingmar Bergman. Lindblom made her debut as a director-screenwriter in 1977. • *Love* 1952 (a); *Girl in the Rain* 1956 (a); *Song of the Scarlet Flower* 1956 (a); *Det Sjunde Inseglet/The Seventh Seal* 1957 (a); *Smultronstallet/Wild Strawberries* 1957 (a); *Jungfrukallan/The Virgin Spring* 1960 (a); *My Love Is a Rose* 1963 (a); *Nattvardsgasterna/Winter Light* 1963 (a); *Tystnaden/The Silence* 1963 (a); *Loving Couples* 1964 (a); *Rapture* 1965 (a); *De Dans van de Reiger* 1966 (a); *Sult/Hunger* 1966 (a); *Yngsjomordet* 1966 (a); *Flickorna/The Girls* 1968 (a); *The Father* 1969 (a); *Broder Carl/Brother Carl* 1971 (a); *Scenes From a Marriage* 1974 (a); *Paradistorg/Summer Paradise/Paradise Place* 1977 (d,sc); *Bomsalva* 1978 (a); *Sally och friheten* 1981 (d); *Bakom Jalusin* 1984 (a); *Sommarkvallar pa jorden/Summer Nights* 1987 (d,sc).

Linder, Max • Actor, director; also screenwriter. • Born Gabriel-Maximilien Leuvielle, Caverne, France, December 16, 1883; died 1925. *Educ.* Bordeaux Conservatory (acting). French vaudevillian and stage actor who had became one of the screen's most popular comedians by 1910. Playing an impeccably mannered dandy in a number of Pathé slapstick films, Linder influenced a generation of silent clowns, most notably Charlie Chaplin. He went on to enjoy a fruitful writing and directing career which was interrupted by WWI, during the course of which he was exposed to mustard gas. Linder moved to Hollywood in 1917, but lingering illness had effectively ended his performing days by 1924. He and his wife died in a suicide pact the following year. • *Max amoureux de la teinturière (short)* 1911 (a,d,sc); *Max dans sa famille (short)* 1911 (a,d,sc); *Max en convalescence (short)* 1911 (a,d,sc); *Max et Jane en voyage de noces (short)* 1911 (a,d,sc); *Max et Jane font des crèpes (short)* 1911 (a,d,sc); *Max et son chien Dick (short)* 1911 (a,d,sc); *Max lance la mode (short)* 1911 (a,d,sc); *Max reprend sa liberté (short)* 1911 (a,d,sc); *Max veut faire du théatre (short)* 1911 (a,d,sc); *Voisin... voisine (short)* 1911 (a,d,sc); *Une Idylle à la ferme (short)* 1912 (a,d,sc); *Le Mal de mer (short)* 1912 (a,d,sc); *La Malle au mariage (short)* 1912 (a,d,sc); *Un Mariage au téléphone (short)* 1912 (a,d,sc); *Max cocher de fiacre (short)* 1912 (a,d,sc); *Max escamoteur (short)* 1912 (a,d,sc); *Max et l'Intente Cordiale (short)* 1912 (a,d,sc); *Max et les femmes (short)* 1912 (a,d,sc); *Max veut grandir (short)* 1912 (a,d,sc); *Un Nuit agitée (short)* 1912 (a,d,sc); *La Vengeance du domestique (short)* 1912 (a,d,sc); *Voyage de noces en Espagne (short)* 1912 (a,d,sc); *Comment Max fait le tour du monde (short)* 1913 (a,d,sc); *Le Duel de Max (short)* 1913 (a,d,sc); *Un Enlèvement en hydroplane (short)* 1913 (a,d,sc); *Le Hasard et l'amour (short)* 1913 (a,d,sc); *Un Mariage imprévu (short)* 1913 (a,d,sc); *Le Rivalité de Max (short)* 1913 (a,d,sc); *Max illusionniste (short)* 1914 (a,d,sc); *Max pédicure (short)* 1914 (a,d,sc); *Max devrait porter des bretelles (short)* 1915 (a,d,sc); *Max et l'espion (short)* 1915 (a,d,sc); *Max et le sac (short)* 1915 (a,d,sc); *Max entre deux feux (short)* 1916 (a,d,sc); *Max et la Main-qui-entreint (short)* 1916 (a,d,sc); *Max comes across (short)* 1917 (a,d,sc); *Max in a taxi (short)* 1917 (a,d,sc); *Max wants a divorce (short)* 1917 (a,d,sc); *Le Petit café* 1919 (a,sc); *Le Feu sacré* 1920 (a,sc); *Be My Wife* 1921 (a,d,p,sc); *Seven Years Bad Luck* 1921 (a,d,p,sc); *The Three Must-Get-Theres* 1922 (a,d,sc); *Au secours!* 1923 (a,sc,idea); *Clown aus Liebe* 1924 (a,d,sc); *En compagnie de Max Linder* 1963 (archival footage); *The Man in the Silk Hat* 1983 (archival footage).

Lindfors, Viveca • Actress • Born Elsa Viveca Torstensdotter Lindfors, Uppsala, Sweden, December 29, 1920. *Educ.* Royal Dramatic Theater School, Stockholm. Gifted, stage-trained star of Swedish films who arrived in Hollywood in 1946. Lindfors turned in fine supporting performances in several films of the late 1970s (*Welcome to L.A.* 1976, *Girlfriends* 1978) and is also memorable as the English teacher in *The Sure Thing* (1985). • *Adventures of Don Juan* 1948; *To the Victor* 1948; *Night Unto Night* 1949; *Backfire* 1950; *Dark City* 1950; *The Flying Missile* 1950; *No Sad Songs For Me* 1950; *This Side of the Law* 1950; *Gypsy Fury* 1951; *Journey Into Light* 1951; *No Time For Flowers* 1952; *The Raiders* 1952; *Run For Cover* 1954; *Moonfleet* 1955; *The Halliday Brand* 1956; *I Accuse!* 1957; *Weddings and Babies* 1958; *The Story of Ruth* 1960; *King of Kings* 1961; *Le Temps du Ghetto* 1961; *These Are the Damned* 1962; *An Affair of the Skin* 1963; *Brainstorm* 1965; *Sylvia* 1965; *El Coleccionista de Cadaveres* 1968; *Coming Apart* 1969; *Puzzle of a Downfall Child* 1970; *La Casa Sin Fronteras* 1971; *La Campana Del Infierno* 1973; *The Way We Were* 1973; *Tabu* 1976; *Welcome to L.A.* 1976;

Girlfriends 1978; *A Wedding* 1978; *Linus Eller Tegelhusets Hemlighet* 1979; *Natural Enemies* 1979; *Voices* 1979; *The Hand* 1981; *Creepshow* 1982; *Dies Rigorosen Leben* 1983; *Silent Madness* 1983; *Going Undercover* 1984; *The Sure Thing* 1985; *Unfinished Business...* 1986 (a,d,sc); *Lady Beware* 1987; *Rachel River* 1987; *Forced March* 1989; *Misplaced* 1989; *Goin' to Chicago* 1990; *Luba* 1990; *William Peter Blatty's The Exorcist III* 1990; *Zandalee* 1991.

Linson, Art • Producer; also director. • Born Chicago, IL, c. 1942. *Educ.* University of California, Berkeley; UCLA (law). Former rock group manager who has produced films by directors including Brian De Palma, Jonathan Demme and Amy Heckerling. • *Rafferty and the Gold Dust Twins* 1974 (p); *Car Wash* 1976 (p); *American Hot Wax* 1978 (p,sc); *Melvin and Howard* 1980 (p); *Where the Buffalo Roam* 1980 (d,p); *Fast Times at Ridgemont High* 1982 (p); *The Wild Life* 1984 (d,p); *The Untouchables* 1987 (p); *Scrooged* 1988 (p); *Casualties of War* 1989 (p); *We're No Angels* 1989 (p); *Dick Tracy* 1990 (exec.p).

Liotta, Ray • Actor • Born Union, NJ. *Educ.* University of Miami. Rising screen star who began his career on the NBC daytime soap, "Another World," and demonstrated his versatility with roles as a violent ex-convict (*Something Wild* 1986), a man who cares for his brain-damaged brother (*Dominick and Eugene* 1988) and a back-from-the-dead baseball great (*Field of Dreams* 1989). Liotta gave a commanding performance in Martin Scorsese's *Goodfellas* (1990), as a brutal yet sympathetic mobster destined by his Irish heritage to remain on the fringes of the "organization." • *The Lonely Lady* 1983; *Something Wild* 1986; *Arena Brains (short)* 1987; *Dominick and Eugene* 1988; *Field of Dreams* 1989; *Goodfellas* 1990.

Lisi, Virna • Actress • Born Virna Pieralisi, Ancona, Italy, September 8, 1937. Picturesque Italian blonde who appeared in a number of melodramas and costume extravaganzas before evolving into a glamorous international lead in the 1960s. Lisi made her American film debut opposite Jack Lemmon in *How to Murder Your Wife* (1965). • *... E Napoli canta* 1953; *Il Cardinale Lambertini* 1954; *La Corda d'acciaio* 1954; *Desiderio è sole* 1954; *Lettera Napoletana* 1954; *Piccola santa* 1954; *Ripudiata* 1954; *Violenza sul lago* 1954; *Le Diciottenni* 1955; *Les Hussards* 1955; *Luna nuova* 1955; *Il Vetturale del Moncenisio* 1955; *La Donna del giorno* 1956; *La Rossa* 1956; *Caterina Sforza, leonessa di Romagna* 1958; *Il Conte di Matera* 1958; *Toto, Peppino e le fanatiche* 1958; *Vite perdute* 1958; *Un Militare e mezzo* 1959; *Il Mondo dei miracoli* 1959; *Il Padrone delle ferriere* 1959; *Cinque marines per cento ragazze* 1961; *Lo Scapolo* 1961; *Sua Eccellenza di fermo a mangiare* 1961; *Eva* 1962; *Les Bonnes Causes* 1963; *Duel of the Titans* 1963; *Il Giorno più corto* 1963; *La Tulipe Noir* 1963; *Coplan prend des risques* 1964; *Oggi, domani e dopodomani* 1964; *Le Bambole* 1965; *Casanova '70* 1965; *La Donna del lago* 1965; *How to Murder Your Wife* 1965; *Made in Italy* 1965; *Una Vergine per il principe* 1965; *Assault on a Queen* 1966; *Not With My Wife, You Don't* 1966; *Signore e signori/The Birds, the Bees, and the Italians* 1966; *Le Dolci signore* 1967; *Arabella* 1967; *La Ragazza e il Generale* 1967; *La Vingt-cinquième heure* 1967; *Meglio Vedova* 1968; *Tenderly* 1968; *L'Arbre de Noël* 1969; *If It's Tuesday, This Must Be Belgium* 1969; *The Secret of Santa Vittoria* 1969; *Un Beau Monstre* 1970; *Giochi particolari* 1970; *The Statue* 1970; *Le Temps des Loups* 1970; *Les Galets d'Etretat* 1971; *Roma bene* 1971; *Bluebeard* 1972; *Le Serpent* 1973; *Il Ritorno di Zanna Bianca* 1974; *Zanna Bianca* 1974; *Al di la del bene e del male* 1977; *Ernesto* 1978; *Professione figlio* 1979; *La Cicala* 1980; *Miss Right* 1981; *Sapore Di Mare* 1983; *Stelle Emigranti* 1983; *Amarsi un po'* 1984; *I Love N.Y.* 1987; *Buon Natale, Buon Anno* 1989; *I Ragazzi di Via Panisperna* 1989.

Lithgow, John • Actor • Born Rochester, NY, October 19, 1945. *Educ.* Harvard; LAMDA, London. Versatile character player who divides his time among theater, film and TV. Lithgow earned Oscar nominations for his performance as a transsexual football player in 1982's *The World According to Garp* and his role in 1983's *Terms of Endearment.* • *Dealing: Or the Berkeley-to-Boston Forty-Brick Lost-Bag Blues* 1972; *Obsession* 1976; *The Big Fix* 1978; *All That Jazz* 1979; *Rich Kids* 1979; *Blow Out* 1981; *I'm Dancing As Fast As I Can* 1981; *The World According to Garp* 1982 **(AANBSA)**; *Terms of Endearment* 1983 **(AANBSA)**; *Twilight Zone—the Movie* 1983; *2010* 1984; *The Adventures of Buckaroo Banzai: Across the 8th Dimension* 1984; *Footloose* 1984; *Santa Claus: The Movie* 1985; *The Manhattan Project* 1986; *Mesmerized* 1986; *Harry and the Hendersons* 1987; *Distant Thunder* 1988; *Out Cold* 1988; *Memphis Belle* 1990; *L.A. Story* 1991.

Littleton, Carol • Editor • Born Oklahoma. *Educ.* University of Oklahoma. Successful Hollywood editor of the 1980s and 90s who began her career working on TV commercials. Littleton has cut four films directed by Lawrence Kasdan. • *Premonition* 1972 (asst.ed); *Legacy* 1975 (ed); *The Mafu Cage* 1978 (ed); *French Postcards* 1979 (ed); *Roadie* 1980 (ed); *Body Heat* 1981 (ed); *E.T., the Extra-Terrestrial* 1982 (ed) **(AANBED)**; *The Big Chill* 1983 (ed); *Places in the Heart* 1984 (ed); *Silverado* 1985 (ed); *Brighton Beach Memoirs* 1986 (ed); *Swimming to Cambodia* 1987 (ed); *The Accidental Tourist* 1988 (ed); *Vibes* 1988 (ed); *White Palace* 1990 (ed).

Litvak, Anatole • Director; also screenwriter. • Born Mikhail Anatol Litvak, Kiev, Russia, May 10, 1902; died 1974. *Educ.* University of St. Petersburg (philosophy); State Theater School. Began his film career at Leningrad's Nordkino studios in 1923, moved to Germany in 1925 and began directing for UFA in 1930. Following the international success of the French production, *Mayerling* (1936), Litvak moved to the US where he signed with Warner Bros. in 1937. He earned a reputation as a capable handler of urban dramas (*City For Conquest* 1940, *Blues in the Night* 1941, *Sorry, Wrong Number* 1948) and received critical acclaim for *The Snake Pit* (1948), a harrowing, realistic account of life in a mental institution. Litvak's post-1950s work—all European—consisted primarily of glossy, somewhat turgid star vehicles. He was married to actress Miriam Hopkins (1937-39) and costume designer Sophie Steur, who worked on some of his films. • *Tatiana* 1923 (d); *Serdtsi i dollari (short)* 1924 (d); *Die Freudlose gasse* 1925 (ed); *Samii yunii pioner* 1925 (sc); *Casanova* 1927 (ad); *Napoleon* 1927 (ad); *Dolly Macht Karriere* 1929 (d); *Sheherazade* 1929 (adapt,ad); *Der Weisse Teufel* 1930 (ad,u.man,dial.seq.sup.); *Coeur de Lilas* 1931 (d,sc); *Nie Wieder Liebe* 1931 (d,sc,adapt); *Tell Me Tonight* 1932 (d); *Cette Vieille Canaille* 1933 (d,sc,adapt); *Sleeping Car* 1933 (d); *L'Equipage* 1935 (d,sc); *Mayerling* 1936 (d); *Tovarich* 1937 (d); *The Woman I Love* 1937 (d); *The Amazing Dr. Clitterhouse* 1938 (d); *The Sisters* 1938 (d); *Confessions of a Nazi Spy* 1939 (d); *The Roaring Twenties* 1939 (d); *All This, and Heaven Too* 1940 (d); *Castle on the Hudson* 1940 (d); *City For Conquest* 1940 (d); *All This, and Heaven Too* 1940 (d); *Blues in the Night* 1941 (d); *Out of the Fog* 1941 (d); *This Above All* 1942 (d); *Why We Fight* 1942 (d,sc—"The Battle of Russia"); *The American People (short)* 1945 (a,d); *The Long Night* 1947 (d,p); *Meet Me at Dawn* 1947 (from play *Le tueur*); *The Snake Pit* 1948 (d,p) **(AANBD)**; *Sorry, Wrong Number* 1948 (d,p); *Decision Before Dawn* 1952 (d,p) **(AANBP)**; *Act of Love* 1953 (d,p); *The Deep Blue Sea* 1955 (d,p); *Anastasia* 1956 (d); *Behind the Screen* 1956 (a); *The Journey* 1959 (d,p); *Goodbye Again* 1961 (a,d,p); *I Don Giovanni della Costa Azzurra* 1962 (a); *Five Miles to Midnight* 1963 (d,p); *10:30 P.M. Summer* 1966 (p); *The Night of the Generals* 1966 (d); *La Dame dans l'auto avec des lunettes et un fusil* 1970 (d,p).

Livesey, Roger • Actor • Born Barry, South Wales, June 25, 1906; died 1976. Versatile English character player from the early 1920s, probably best known for his title role in *The Life and Death of Colonel Blimp* (1943). One of an acting dynasty which included father Sam Livesey (1873-1936), brothers Jack (1901-61) and Barry (born 1904) and wife Ursula Jeans. • *The Four Feathers* 1921; *Married Love* 1923; *East Lynne on the Western Front* 1931; *Blind Justice* 1934; *Lorna Doone* 1935; *Rembrandt* 1936; *Drums* 1938; *Keep Smiling* 1938; *Spies of the Air* 1939; *The Girl in the News* 1940; *The Life and Death of Colonel Blimp* 1943; *I Know Where I'm Going* 1945; *A Matter of Life and Death* 1946; *Vice Versa* 1948; *That Dangerous Age* 1949; *The Master of Ballantrae* 1953; *Es Geschah am 20.Juli* 1956; *Finger of Guilt* 1956; *The Entertainer* 1960; *The League of Gentlemen* 1960; *No, My Darling Daughter* 1961; *Of Human Bondage* 1964; *The Amorous Adventures of Moll Flanders* 1965; *Oedipus the King* 1968; *Futtocks End* 1969; *Hamlet* 1970.

Lloyd, Christopher • Actor • Born Stamford, CT, October 22, 1938. *Educ.* Neighborhood Playhouse, New York. Made an effective film debut as a mental hospital inmate in *One Flew Over the Cuckoo's Nest* (1975) and has developed his career around variations on the themes of madness and eccentricity. Lloyd won two Emmys for his role in the popular TV series, "Taxi", and is best known to movie audiences as the DeLorean-driving "Doc" Emmett Brown in the *Back to the Future* films. • *One Flew Over the Cuckoo's Nest* 1975; *Three Warriors* 1977; *Goin' South* 1978; *The Black Marble* 1979; *Butch and Sundance: The Early Days* 1979; *The Lady in Red* 1979; *The Onion Field* 1979; *Pilgrim, Farewell* 1980; *Schizoid* 1980; *The Legend of the Lone Ranger* 1981; *The Postman Always Rings Twice* 1981; *National Lampoon Goes to the Movies* 1982; *Mr. Mom* 1983; *To Be or Not to Be* 1983; *The Adventures of Buckaroo Banzai: Across the 8th Dimension* 1984; *Joy of Sex* 1984; *Miracles* 1984; *Star Trek III: The Search For Spock* 1984; *Back to the Future* 1985; *Clue* 1985; *Track 29* 1987; *Walk Like a Man* 1987; *The Cowboy and the Ballerina* 1988; *Eight Men Out* 1988; *Who Framed Roger Rabbit?* 1988; *Back to the Future II* 1989; *The Dream Team* 1989; *Un Plan d'enfer* 1989; *Back to the Future III* 1990; *DuckTales: The Movie* 1990.

Lloyd, Emily • Actress • Born London, 1970. *Educ.* Italia Conti School, London. Spirited young lead who earned widespread acclaim for her debut performance in *Wish You Were Here* (1987), based on the early life of future brothel madame Cynthia Payne. • *Wish You Were Here* 1987; *Cookie* 1989; *In Country* 1989; *Chicago Joe and the Showgirl* 1990.

Lloyd, Harold • Actor • Born Harold Clayton Lloyd, Burchard, NE, April 20, 1893; died 1971. Harold Lloyd brought a journeyman's precision and a craftsman's expertise to American comedy at a time when its style was rapidly headed towards the idiosyncratic. In the process, Lloyd created a bespectacled comic Everyman that tapped the pulse of flashy and brash 1920s America, making Lloyd one of the richest and most popular comic performer of that era.

In high school, Lloyd gave vent to his competitive energies as a boxer and debator, but the theater bug hit him and, after graduating, he obtained an acting spot in a traveling repertory company. When the company closed in Los Angeles, Lloyd began to make the rounds of the movie studios, seeking out a living as a movie extra. Another extra trying to scrape together a living was Hal Roach and the two became friends. When Roach inherited money and decided to make his own films, Lloyd went to work for him. Together they created the character of Willie Work in several shorts made from 1913 to 1915, but only the last one, *Just Nuts,* found its way to theatrical distribution. On the basis of that film, Mack Sennett hired Lloyd, but, after an unsuccessful year at Keystone, Lloyd came back to Roach, where he created another character, Lonesome Luke. With Luke, Lloyd joined the legion of Charlie Chaplin imitators so popular at the time. Restless and unhappy with this less-than-original creation, Lloyd was trapped by its success, and the film exchanges were reluctant to allow him to try something different. However, Lloyd was determined to find a new character, even if it meant forsaking his new-found success.

After seeing a play featuring a fighting priest who wore horn-rimmed glasses, Lloyd experimented with the concept of a more realistic looking character who also wore glasses, not an outsider (as Chaplin's tramp was), but rather a working member of society. Lloyd featured his new character in a series of shorts, starting with *Over the Fence* (1917), reducing his output from two-reelers to one-reelers to insure exposure of his new character in a new film once a week instead of twice a month. But it wasn't until *The City Slicker* (1918) that Lloyd finally developed the formula for this bespectacled character, a brash young go-getter whose single-mindededness leads him to succeed and get the girl by the story's end. In fact, what Lloyd had done was adapt the Douglas Fairbanks persona from the 1910s to his own talents, converting Fairbanks's aristocrat to a clean-cut Horatio Alger-type from the middle class. Lloyd's early films with this character were nothing more than remakes of old Fairbanks comedies: *Grandma's Boy* (1922) is a remade version of *The Mollycoddle* (1920); *Doctor Jack* (1922) is a remake of *Down to Earth* (1917); *Why Worry?* (1923) another version of *His Majesty the American* (1919). But in adapting the Fairbanks type to the middle class, Lloyd had hit on a national archetype, a character who celebrated the 20s boom and consumer consumption. There was no criticism of the social structure—in fact, according to Lloyd, the character reveled in it: "I think my character represented the white-collar middle class that felt frustrated but was always fighting to overcome its shortcomings. We had a big appeal for businessman."

A more realistic comic character emerged, giving rise to a more realistic comedy style which linked the energy and movement of the character clowns with the psychological realism of the dramatic tradition. Since the character was not essentially funny in himself, jokes had to be constructed around him, the gags more tightly controlled and used to propel the storyline. Each gag followed the next in a logical progression until the film's climactic vindication and triumph of the Lloyd hero.

Building the gags into a narrative line made it much easier for Lloyd to expand into feature production. Throughout the 20s Lloyd was a box-office draw, from *A Sailor-Made Man* (1921) to *Speedy* (1928). His steady output—two features a year—kept his public happy with such pictures as *Grandma's Boy,* (1922), and *Safety Last* (1923), *The Freshman* (1925), *The Kid Brother* (1927). But after the 1929 stock market crash, Lloyd's character became obsolete, his brashness coming off as abrasive.

And just as Lloyd had reworked the type from Fairbanks, the type was reworked again, transformed into the success-at-any-price gangsters of Paul Muni, Edward G. Robinson and James Cagney. The sociable character with glasses had become a murderous sociopath. By the late 1930s, Lloyd's character had become merely wholesome and *Newsweek* noted that Lloyd was "the leading representative of 100 per cent American purity." After *Professor Beware* (1938), Lloyd left films, only to resurface ten years later in an aborted comeback, *Mad Wednesday/The Sin of Harold Diddlebock*, a subversion of his 20s persona to fit the doom-laden 40s, a film that one critic called "a slapstick equivalent of *Death of a Salesman.*"

Although Lloyd's films seem mechanical today, he made important contributions, with detailed gag constructions and dramatic structure integrated with slapstick, to leave a lasting mark on the film comedy landscape. PB • *From Italy's Shores (short)* 1913; *His Heart, His Hand and His Sword (short)* 1914; *Samson* 1914; *Willie (short)* 1914; *A Foozle at the Tea Party (short)* 1915; *Into the Light (short)* 1915; *Just Nuts (short)* 1915; *Miss Fatty's Seaside Lovers (short)* 1915; *Lonesome Luke Leans to the Literary (short)* 1916; *Luke Lugs Luggage (short)* 1916; *Bliss (short)* 1917; *By the Sad Sea Waves (short)* 1917; *The Flirt (short)* 1917; *Luke's Busy Day (short)* 1917; *Luke's Lost Liberty (short)* 1917; *Over the Fence (short)* 1917; *Pinched (short)* 1917; *Rainbow Island (short)* 1917; *The Big Idea (short)* 1918; *The City Slicker* 1918; *It's a Wild Life (short)* 1918; *On the Jump* 1918; *Pipe the Whiskers (short)* 1918; *Spring Fever (short)* 1918; *Bumping Into Broadway (short)* 1919; *Captain Kidd's Kids (short)* 1919; *From Hand to Mouth (short)* 1919; *His Royal Slyness (short)* 1919; *An Eastern Westerner (short)* 1920; *Get Out and Get Under (short)* 1920; *Haunted Spooks (short)* 1920; *High and Dizzy (short)* 1920; *Number, Please (short)* 1920; *Among Those Present* 1921; *Be My Wife* 1921; *I Do* 1921; *Never Weaken* 1921; *Now or Never* 1921; *A Sailor-Made Man* 1921; *Back to the Woods* 1922; *Doctor Jack* 1922; *Grandma's Boy* 1922; *Safety Last* 1923 (a,sc); *Why Worry?* 1923; *Girl Shy* 1924; *Hot Water* 1924; *The Freshman* 1925; *For Heaven's Sake* 1926; *The Kid Brother* 1927; *Speedy* 1928; *Welcome Danger* 1929 (a,p); *Feet First* 1930; *Movie Crazy* 1932 (a,p); *The Cat's Paw* 1934; *The Milky Way* 1936; *Professor Beware* 1938 (a,p); *A Girl, a Guy and a Gob* 1941 (p); *My Favorite Spy* 1942 (p); *Mad Wednesday/The Sin of Harold Diddlebock* 1947.

Loach, Ken • Director • Born Kenneth Loach, Nuneaton, Warwickshire, June 17, 1936. *Educ.* Oxford (law). Revue performer who gravitated to TV direction in the 1960s, notably with the popular BBC police series, "Z-Cars." Loach's debut feature, *Poor Cow* (1967), incorporated the cinéma-vérité techniques and leftist principles that had informed some of his TV work (particularly the controversial "Wednesday Play" series) to paint a sordid picture of English working-class life. Together with producer Tony Garnett, Loach went on to turn out a number of stark, socially conscious films, often featuring non-professional actors; he enjoyed critical and commercial success with *Kes* (1969), a poignant study in the life of a neglected Yorkshire schoolboy. Loach's recent work includes the well-received drama, *Looks and Smiles* (1981), and the political thriller, *Singing the Blues in Red* (1986). • *Poor Cow* 1967 (d,sc); *Kes* 1969 (d,sc,adapt); *Family Life* 1971 (d); *Black Jack* 1979 (d,sc,adapt); *The Gamekeeper* 1980 (d,sc); *Looks and Smiles* 1981 (d); *Singing the Blues in Red* 1986 (d); *Hidden Agenda* 1990 (d).

Locke, Sondra • Actress; also director. • Born Shelbyville, TN, May 28, 1947. Resilient blonde lead who came to prominence in a number of films starring Clint Eastwood—her sometime partner—during the 1970s. • *The Heart Is a Lonely Hunter* 1968 (a) **(AANBSA)**; *Cover Me Babe* 1970 (a); *A Reflection of Fear* 1971 (a); *Willard* 1971 (a); *The Second Coming of Suzanne* 1974 (a); *The Outlaw Josey Wales* 1975 (a); *Death Game* 1976 (a); *The Gauntlet* 1977 (a); *Every Which Way But Loose* 1978 (a); *Wishbone Cutter* 1978 (a); *Any Which Way You Can* 1980 (a); *Bronco Billy* 1980 (a); *Sudden Impact* 1983 (a); *Ratboy* 1986 (a,d); *Impulse* 1990 (d).

Lockwood, Margaret • *aka* Margie Day • Actress • Born Margaret Mary Lockwood, Karachi, India (now Pakistan), September 15, 1916; died July 15, 1990. *Educ.* Italia Conti School, London; RADA, London. Popular British leading lady of the late 1930s and 40s. Trained on the stage, Lockwood made her film debut in 1935 and distinguished herself in productions such as Hitchcock's *The Lady Vanishes* (1938) and Carol Reed's mining-town drama, *The Stars Look Down* (1939); a brief Hollywood foray in 1939, however, proved unsuccessful. Lockwood retired in the mid-50s but resurfaced two decades later to play Cinderella's stepmother in *The Slipper and the Rose* (1976). Daughter Julia Lockwood is also an actress. • *The Case of Gabriel Perry* 1935; *Honours Easy* 1935; *Lorna Doone* 1935; *Man of the Moment* 1935; *Midshipman Easy* 1935; *Some Day* 1935; *The Amateur Gentleman* 1936; *Beloved Vagabond* 1936; *Irish For Luck* 1936; *Jury's Evidence* 1936; *Bank Holiday* 1937; *Doctor Syn* 1937; *Melody and Romance* 1937; *The Street Singer* 1937; *Who's Your Lady Friend?* 1937; *The Lady Vanishes* 1938; *Owd Bob* 1938; *A Girl Must Live* 1939; *Rulers of the Sea* 1939; *The Stars Look Down* 1939; *Susannah of the Mounties* 1939; *The Girl in the News* 1940; *Night Train to Munich* 1940; *Quiet Wedding* 1940; *The Alibi* 1943; *Dear Octopus* 1943; *The Man in Gray* 1943; *Give Us the Moon* 1944; *Love Story* 1944; *I'll Be Your Sweetheart* 1945; *A Place of One's Own* 1945; *The Wicked Lady* 1945; *Bedelia* 1946; *Hungry Hill* 1946; *Jassy* 1947; *The White Unicorn* 1947; *Cardboard Cavalier* 1948; *Look Before You Love* 1948; *Madness of the Heart* 1949; *Highly Dangerous* 1950; *Trent's Last Case* 1952; *Laughing Anne* 1953; *Trouble in the Glen* 1953; *Cast a Dark Shadow* 1955; *Futures Vedettes* 1955; *The Slipper and the Rose* 1976.

Loesser, Frank • Composer; also songwriter. • Born New York, NY, June 29, 1910; died 1969. Popular composer of such Broadway hits as *Guys and Dolls* who scored and contributed songs to many films, most notably *How to Suceed in Business Without Really Trying* (1967). • *Blossoms on Broadway* 1937 (song); *Fight For Your Lady* 1937 (song); *Hurricane* 1937 (song); *Vogues of 1938* 1937 (song); *College Swing* 1938 (song); *Sing, You Sinners* 1938 (song); *Spawn of the North* 1938 (song); *Thanks For the Memory* 1938 (song); *Destry Rides Again* 1939 (song); *Man About Town* 1939 (song); *Some Like It Hot* 1939 (song); *St. Louis Blues* 1939 (song); *Zaza* 1939 (song); *Buck Benny Rides Again* 1940 (song); *Johnny Apollo* 1940 (song); *Seven Sinners* 1940 (song); *Typhoon* 1940 (song); *Aloma of the South Seas* 1941 (song); *Kiss the Boys Goodbye* 1941 (song); *Las Vegas Nights* 1941 (song) **(AANBS)**; *Manpower* 1941 (song); *Sailors on Leave* 1941 (song); *Sis Hopkins* 1941 (song); *Beyond the Blue Horizon* 1942 (song); *Priorities on Parade* 1942 (sc,song); *Seven Days Leave* 1942 (song); *Sweater Girl* 1942 (song); *This Gun For Hire* 1942 (song); *Happy Go Lucky* 1943 (song); *Swing Your Partner* 1943 (song); *Thank Your Lucky Stars* 1943 (song) **(AANBS)**; *Christmas Holiday* 1944 (song); *Something For the Boys* 1944 (song); *The Perils of Pauline* 1947 (song) **(AANBS)**; *Variety Girl* 1947 (song); *Neptune's Daughter* 1949 (song) **(AABS)**; *Red, Hot and Blue* 1949 (a,song); *Roseanna McCoy* 1949 (song); *Dark City* 1950 (song); *Let's Dance* 1950 (song); *Hans Christian Andersen* 1952 (song) **(AANBS)**; *Where's Charley?* 1952 (m,song); *Money From Home* 1953 (song); *Guys and Dolls* 1955 (m); *How to Succeed in Business Without Really Trying* 1967 (from play,song).

Loew, Marcus • Executive; also exhibitor. • Born New York, NY, May 7, 1870; died 1927. Successful peep-show owner who began acquiring movie theaters in 1907 and by 1912 owned over 400 cinemas, in partnership with Adolph Zukor. In 1920, in order to guarantee a regular supply of films for his theaters, Loew bought Metro Pictures; in 1924, Metro merged with the Goldwyn company and Louis B. Mayer Pictures to form MGM, of which Loew's, Inc., was the parent company. Loew's twin sons both worked in the film business, Arthur as an executive for Loew's and David as an independent producer.

Loewe, Frederick • Composer • Born Vienna, June 10, 1904; died February 14, 1988. German composer who arrived in New York in 1924 and supported himself in a variety of odd jobs before breaking into Broadway songwriting in 1935. A chance encounter with Alan Lerner in 1942 marked the beginning of a long and fruitful collaboration that resulted in such popular stage productions as *Paint Your Wagon* and *My Fair Lady.* The 1958 release of *Gigi* marked the first of several highly successful musicals they adapted for the screen. See also Lerner, Alan Jay. • *Brigadoon* 1954 (m); *Gigi* 1958 (m,song) **(AABS)**; *My Fair Lady* 1964 (m,song); *Camelot* 1967 (from play,song); *Paint Your Wagon* 1969 (m,m); *The Little Prince* 1974 (m) **(AANBS,AANBSS)**.

Loggia, Robert • Actor • Born New York, NY. *Educ.* University of Missouri (journalism); Actors Studio. Rugged character actor in film since the late 1950s, often as a figure of authority. Loggia received an Oscar nomination for his role as a seedy private detective in Richard Marquand's thriller, *Jagged Edge* (1985). He has also directed for TV. • *Somebody Up There Likes Me* 1956; *The Gar-*

ment Jungle 1957; *Cop Hater* 1958; *The Lost Missile* 1958; *Cattle King* 1963; *The Three Sisters* 1964; *The Greatest Story Ever Told* 1965; *Che!* 1969; *First Love* 1977; *Speedtrap* 1977; *Revenge of the Pink Panther* 1978; *Twinkle, Twinkle, "Killer" Kane* 1979; *S.O.B.* 1981; *An Officer and a Gentleman* 1982; *Trail of the Pink Panther* 1982; *Curse of the Pink Panther* 1983; *Psycho II* 1983; *Scarface* 1983; *Jagged Edge* 1985 **(AANBSA)**; *Prizzi's Honor* 1985; *Armed and Dangerous* 1986; *That's Life!* 1986; *The Believers* 1987; *Gaby - A True Story* 1987; *Hot Pursuit* 1987; *Over the Top* 1987; *Big* 1988; *Oliver & Company* 1988; *Relentless* 1989; *Running Away* 1989; *Triumph of the Spirit* 1989; *Opportunity Knocks* 1990; *The Marrying Man* 1991.

Lohmann, Dietrich • German director of photography • Key cinematographer of the New German Cinema whose credits include several films directed by Rainer Werner Fassbinder. Lohmann also photographed the 32-hour US TV miniseries, *War and Remembrance* (1988). • *Letzte Worte (short)* 1967 (cam.asst); *Die Artisten in der Zirkuskuppel: Ratlos* 1968 (cam.asst); *Lebenszeichen* 1968 (cam.asst); *Neun Leben hat die Katze* 1968 (ph); *Cardillac* 1969 (ph); *Götter der Pest* 1969 (ph); *Katzelmacher* 1969 (ph); *Liebe Ist Kälter als der Tod* 1969 (ph); *Massnahmen Gegen Fanatiker* 1969 (ph); *Der Amerikanische Soldat* 1970 (ph); *Die Niklashauser Fahrt* 1970 (ph); *Pioniere in Ingolstadt* 1970 (ph); *Rio das Mortes* 1970 (ph); *Warum Lauft Herr R. Amok?* 1970 (ph); *Willi Tobler und der Untergang der 6. Flotte* 1970 (ph); *Ein Grosser Graublauer Vogal* 1971 (ph); *Acht Stunden sind kein Tag Eine Familienserie/Eight Hours Are Not a Day* 1972 (ph); *Bremer Freiheit* 1972 (d,sc,ph); *Der Händler der vier Jahreszeiten* 1972 (ph); *Harlis* 1972 (ph); *Ludwig—Requiem Fur einen jungfraulichen König/Ludwig—Requiem For a Virgin King* 1972 (ph); *Wildwechsel* 1972 (ph); *Fontane Effi Briest/Effi Briest* 1974 (ph); *Karl May* 1974 (ph); *Winifred Wagner und die Geschichte des Hauses Wahnfried 1914-1975/Confessions of Winifred Wagner* 1975 (ph); *Berlinger* 1976 (ph); *Bomber und Paganini* 1976 (ph); *Das Brot des Bäckers* 1976 (ph); *Der Letzte Schrei* 1976 (ph); *Vera Romeyke Ist Nicht Tragbar* 1976 (ph); *Hitler, Ein film aus Deutschland/Hitler, a Film From Germany* 1977 (ph); *Der Mädchenkrieg* 1977 (ph); *Das Schlangenei/The Serpent's Egg* 1977 (add.ph); *Zu böser Schlacht schleich' Ich heute nacht so bang* 1977 (ph); *Deutschland im Herbst* 1978 (ph,cam.op); *H-Moll Messe: Ana begegnet der Musik des Johann Sebastian Bach/Bach: B-Minor Mass* 1978 (ph); *Der Sturz* 1978 (ph); *Taugenichts* 1978 (ph); *Kassbach* 1979 (ph); *Milo Milo* 1979 (ph); *Der Schneider Von Ulm* 1979 (ph); *Kaltgestellt* 1980 (ph); *Die Reinheit des Herzens* 1980 (ph); *Soweit das Auge reicht* 1980 (ph); *Liebe Ist Kein Argument* 1983 (ph); *Strawanzer* 1983 (ph); *Unerreichbare Nähe* 1984 (ph); *Die Forstenbuben* 1985 (ph); *Der Joker* 1987 (ph); *Zwei Frauen* 1989 (ph); *The Lover* 1990 (ph).

Lollobrigida, Gina • *aka* Diana Loris • Actress; also photographer. • Born Luigina Lollobrigida, Subiaco, Italy, July 4, 1927. *Educ.* Rome Academy of Fine Arts (sculpture, painting). Voluptuous former beauty queen who began appearing in Italian films in the late 1940s. Lollobrigida moved to Hollywood in 1949 but was unable to work there for seven years after Howard Hughes declined to take up an option on a contract he had signed with her. She eventually featured in a number of US productions before retiring from the screen in the early 70s. • *Aquila Nera* 1946; *Elisir d'amore* 1946; *Lucia di Lammermoor* 1946; *Il Delitto di Giovanni Episcopo* 1947; *Follie per l'opera* 1947; *A Man About the House* 1947; *Il Segreto di Don Giovanni* 1947; *I Pagliacci* 1948; *Campane a martello* 1949; *Miss Italia* 1949; *La Sposa non puo attendere* 1949; *Storia di cinque città* 1949; *Alina* 1950; *Cuori senza frontiere* 1950; *Vita da cani* 1950; *Achtung Banditi!* 1951; *Amor non ho! pero...pero...* 1951; *La Città si difende* 1951; *Enrico Caruso, leggenda di una voce* 1951; *Altri Tempi* 1952; *Les Belles de nuit* 1952; *Fanfan la Tulipe* 1952; *Le Infedeli* 1952; *Moglie Per Una Notte* 1952; *Beat the Devil* 1953; *Le Grand Jeu* 1953; *Pane, Amore, e Fantasia* 1953; *La Provinciale* 1953; *Il Maestro di Don Giovanni* 1954; *Pane, Amore e gelosia* 1954; *La Romana* 1954; *La Donna più bella del mondo* 1955; *Trapeze* 1956; *Notre-Dame de Paris/The Hunchback of Notre Dame* 1957; *Fast and Sexy* 1958; *La Loi* 1958; *Never So Few* 1959; *Solomon and Sheba* 1959; *Come September* 1961; *Go Naked in the World* 1961; *La Bellezza di Ippolita* 1962; *Venere imperiale* 1962; *Mare Matto* 1963; *Woman of Straw* 1964; *Le Bambole* 1965; *Io, Io, Io...e gli Altri* 1965; *Strange Bedfellows* 1965; *Hotel Paradiso* 1966; *Le Piacevoli notti* 1966; *Les Sultans* 1966; *Cervantes* 1967; *La Morte ha fatto l'uovo* 1967; *Un Bellissimo Novembre* 1968; *Buona Sera, Mrs. Campbell* 1968; *The Private Navy of Sgt. O'Farrell* 1968; *Stuntman* 1968; *Bad Man's River* 1972; *Le Filippine* 1972 (a,d,p,sc); *King, Queen, Knave* 1972; *No encontre rosas para mi madre* 1972; *Ritratto di Fidel* 1975 (a,d,p,sc); *Vengeance of the Barbarians* 1977; *Stelle Emigranti* 1983.

Lombard, Carole • *aka* Carol Lombard • Actress • Born Jane Alice Peters, Fort Wayne, IN, October 6, 1908; died January 19, 1942. Beautiful, vivacious blonde who made her screen debut at age 12 in Alan Dwan's *A Perfect Crime* (1921) and entered film full-time in 1925. At first repeatedly cast in virginal ingenue roles, Lombard displayed an energetic comic talent in *Twentieth Century* (1934). She went on to become one of the screen's finest comediennes of the 1930s, showcasing her intelligence and charm in a number of screwball comedies, notably *My Man Godrey* (1936), *Nothing Sacred* (1937) and her swansong, *To Be or Not to Be* (1942). Lombard's glittering career was cut short that same year when she perished in a plane crash. Married to actors William Powell (1931-33) and Clark Gable (from 1939). • *A Perfect Crime* 1921; *Durand of the Bad Lands* 1925; *Hearts and Spurs* 1925; *Marriage in Transit* 1925; *The Divine Sinner* 1928; *Me, Gangster* 1928; *Ned McCobb's Daughter* 1928; *Power* 1928; *Show Folks* 1928; *Big News* 1929; *High Voltage* 1929; *The Racketeer* 1929; *The Arizona Kid* 1930; *Fast and Loose* 1930; *Safety in Numbers* 1930; *I Take This Woman* 1931; *It Pays to Advertise* 1931; *Ladies' Man* 1931; *Man of the World* 1931; *Up Pops the Devil* 1931; *No More Orchids* 1932; *No One Man* 1932; *Sinners in the Sun* 1932; *Virtue* 1932; *Brief Moment* 1933; *The Eagle and the Hawk* 1933; *From Hell to Heaven* 1933; *No Man of Her Own* 1933; *Supernatural* 1933; *White Woman* 1933; *Bolero* 1934; *The Gay Bride* 1934; *Lady By Choice* 1934; *Now and Forever* 1934; *Twentieth Century* 1934; *We're Not Dressing* 1934; *Hands Across the Table* 1935; *Rumba* 1935; *Love Before Breakfast* 1936; *My Man Godfrey* 1936 **(AANBA)**; *The Princess Comes Across* 1936; *Nothing Sacred* 1937; *Swing High, Swing Low* 1937; *True Confession* 1937; *Fools for Scandal* 1938 (uncred.a); *In Name Only* 1939; *Made For Each Other* 1939; *They Knew What They Wanted* 1940; *Vigil in the Night* 1940; *Mr. & Mrs. Smith* 1941; *To Be or Not to Be* 1942; *Golden Age of Comedy* 1957 (archival footage); *Entertaining the Troops* 1989 (archival footage).

Loncraine, Richard • English director • Born 1946. Competent British director, best known for *Brimstone and Treacle* (1982). • *Sunday Bloody Sunday* 1971 (a); *Flame* 1974 (d); *Full Circle* 1977 (d); *The Missionary* 1981 (d); *Brimstone and Treacle* 1982 (d); *Bellman & True* 1987 (d,sc).

Long, Shelley • Actress • Born Fort Wayne, IN, August 23, 1949. *Educ.* Northwestern University (drama). Former TV producer and host who entered films after a spell with Chicago's Second City theater company. Long's first noted big-screen role came opposite Henry Winkler and Michael Keaton in Ron Howard's *Night Shift* (1982) and she has subsequently appeared in a number of light film comedies. An attractive and intelligent comedienne, she is best known as barmaid Diane Chambers in TV's "Cheers." • *A Small Circle of Friends* 1980; *Caveman* 1981; *Night Shift* 1982;

Losin' It 1983; *Irreconcilable Differences* 1984; *The Money Pit* 1986; *Hello, Again* 1987; *Outrageous Fortune* 1987; *Troop Beverly Hills* 1989; *Don't Tell Her It's Me* 1990.

Lonsdale, Michel • *aka* Michael Lonsdale • Actor • Born Paris, 1931. French character player who divides his time between the screen and stage. Among the noted directors with whom Lonsdale has worked are Truffaut, Losey, Welles, Carné, Rivette and Guerra. • *C'est arrivé à Aden* 1956; *Une Balle dans le canon* 1958; *Le Main chaude* 1959; *Les Portes claquent* 1960; *Adorable Menteuse* 1961; *Nom d'une pipe (short)* 1961; *Rendez-vous de minuit* 1961; *Snobs!* 1961; *Le Bureau des mariages* 1962; *Le Crime ne paie pas* 1962; *La Dénonciation* 1962; *The Trial* 1962; *Behold a Pale Horse* 1964; *Les Copains* 1964; *Jaloux comme un tigre* 1964; *Le Loup et le chien (short)* 1964; *Tous les enfants du monde* 1964; *Je vous salue Maffia* 1965; *Le Mari (short)* 1965; *La Bourse et la vie* 1966; *Comédie (short)* 1966; *Les Compagnons de la marguérite* 1966; *Le Fer à repasser (short)* 1966; *Paris brûle-t-il?/Is Paris Burning?* 1966; *L'Authentique procés de Carl-Emmanuel Jung* 1967; *L'Homme à la Buick* 1967; *Le Judoka agent secret* 1967; *Meli-mélodrame (short)* 1967; *Baisers volés/Stolen Kisses* 1968; *La Grand Lessive(!)* 1968; *La Mariée était en noir/The Bride Wore Black* 1968; *La Pince à ongles (short)* 1968; *Animaux pièges (short)* 1969; *Détruire, Dit-Elle* 1969; *Hibernatus* 1969; *L'Hiver* 1969; *Le Jeu de la puce* 1969; *Projet Orfée (short)* 1969; *Demeures aquatiques (short)* 1970; *L'Etalon* 1970; *La Rose et le revolver* 1970; *Un Troisième (short)* 1970; *Les Années Lumière—1895-1900* 1971; *Les Assasins de L'Ordre* 1971; *Boris et Pierre (short)* 1971; *Il Etait une fois un flic* 1971; *Jaune le soleil* 1971; *Out 1: Noli Me Tangere* 1971; *Papa les Petits Bateaux* 1971; *La Poule (short)* 1971; *Le Printemps* 1971; *Le Souffle au coeur/Murmur of the Heart* 1971; *Station Service (short)* 1971; *Le Vieille Fille* 1971; *L'Automne* 1972; *Chut* 1972; *Film sur Hans Bellmer* 1972; *Les Musiciens du culte (short)* 1972; *Out 1: Spectre* 1972; *La Raison du plus fou* 1972; *The Day of the Jackal* 1973; *Duo (short)* 1973; *La Fille au violoncelle* 1973; *Glissements progressifs du plaisir* 1973; *Les Grands sentiments font les bons gueuletons* 1973; *Le Jeu des preuves (short)* 1973; *Stavisky* 1973; *Une Baleine qui avait mal aux dents* 1974; *Le Fantôme de la Liberté* 1974; *Galileo* 1974; *La Grande Paulette* 1974; *Un Linceul n'a pas de poches* 1974; *La Vérité sur l'imaginaire passion d'un inconnu* 1974; *Aloise* 1975; *La Choisie* 1975; *Le Droit à la ville (short)* 1975; *Folle à Tuer* 1975; *India Song* 1975; *NE* 1975; *Les Oeufs Brouillés* 1975; *Les Rideaux dechirés* 1975; *The Romantic Englishwoman* 1975; *Section Spéciale* 1975; *Sérieux comme le plaisir* 1975; *Le Téléphone Rose* 1975; *La Traque* 1975; *L'Eden Palace* 1976; *Mr. Klein* 1976; *L'Adieu nu* 1977; *Aurais du faire gaffe le choc est terrible* 1977; *Le Diable dans la boite* 1977; *L'Imprécateur* 1977; *Jacques Prevert (short)* 1977; *Die Linkshändige Frau* 1977; *Une Sale Histoire* 1977; *Bartleby* 1978; *La Dame à la licorne (short)* 1979; *Moonraker* 1979; *The Passage* 1979; *Samedi-Dimanche (short)* 1979; *Le Risque de Vivre* 1980; *Chariots of Fire* 1981; *Les Jeux de la Comtesse Dolingen de Gratz* 1981; *La Leçon de chant (short)* 1981; *Seuls* 1981; *Douce enquête sur la violence* 1982; *Enigma* 1982; *Erendira* 1982; *Chronopolis* 1983; *Une Jeunesse* 1983; *La Voix humaine* 1983 (d); *Le Bon Roi Dagobert* 1984; *Le Juge* 1984; *Billy-Ze-Kick* 1985; *Canevas la ville* 1985; *Cinécalligramme* 1985; *L'Eveille du Pont d'Alma* 1985; *The Holcroft Covenant* 1985; *The Name of the Rose* 1986; *Der Madonna Mann* 1987; *Souvenir* 1987; *Niezwykla Podroz Baltazara Kobera* 1988.

Loos, Anita • Screenwriter; also playwright, author. • Born Sissons (now Mount Shasta), CA, April 26, 1893. Actress and journalist turned teenage scenarist who landed a contract with Biograph in 1912. Loos earned a reputation for writing satirical intertitles and, during the sound era, breezily cynical dialogue. She enjoyed a fruitful association with D.W. Griffith and played a significant role in the early career of Douglas Fairbanks. Loos is best known for her 1925 comic novel, *Gentlemen Prefer Blondes*, which she adapted for stage and the screen. Her second husband was director John Emerson (1875-1956) and her third, writer-director Richard Sale. • *The New York Hat* 1912 (sc); *The Telephone Girl and the Lady (short)* 1912 (sc); *The Lady and the Mouse (short)* 1913 (sc); *The Mistake (short)* 1913 (sc); *Billy's Rival (short)* 1914 (sc); *The Gangsters of New York (short)* 1914 (sc); *The Hunchback* 1914 (sc); *A Lesson in Mechanics* 1914 (sc); *Lord Chumley* 1914 (sc); *The Saving Grace* 1914 (uncred.sc); *The Sisters (short)* 1914 (sc); *A Ten-Cent Adventure (short)* 1914 (sc); *When the Road Parts (short)* 1914 (sc); *Double Trouble* 1915 (sc); *The Lost House* 1915 (sc); *American Aristocracy* 1916 (sc,story); *A Corner in Cotton* 1916 (sc,story); *A Daughter of the Poor (short)* 1916 (sc); *The Deadly Glass of Beer (short)* 1916 (sc); *The Half-Breed* 1916 (sc); *His Picture in the Papers* 1916 (sc,story); *Intolerance* 1916 (inter-titles); *The Little Liar* 1916 (sc); *Macbeth* 1916 (inter-titles); *The Matrimoniac* 1916 (sc); *The Social Secretary* 1916 (sc,story); *Stranded (short)* 1916 (sc,story); *The Wharf Rat (short)* 1916 (sc,story); *A Wild Girl of the Sierras (short)* 1916 (sc,story); *The Americano* 1917 (sc,story); *Down to Earth* 1917 (sc); *In Again, Out Again* 1917 (sc,story); *Reaching For the Moon* 1917 (sc,story); *Wild and Woolly* 1917 (sc); *Come on In* 1918 (p,sc,story); *Goodbye, Bill* 1918 (p,sc,story); *Hit-the-Trail Holliday* 1918 (sc); *Let's Get a Divorce* 1918 (sc); *Under the Top* 1918 (story); *Getting Mary Married* 1919 (sc,story); *The Isle of Conquest* 1919 (sc); *Oh, You Women!* 1919 (sc,story); *A Temperamental Wife* 1919 (sc,from story *Information Please*,prod.sup); *The Virtuous Vamp* 1919 (p,sc); *The Branded Woman* 1920 (sc); *Dangerous Business* 1920 (p,sc,story); *In Search of a Sinner* 1920 (p,sc,adapt); *The Love Expert* 1920 (p,sc,story); *The Perfect Woman* 1920 (p,sc,story); *Two Weeks* 1920 (sc,adapt); *Mama's Affair* 1921 (sc,adapt); *Woman's Place* 1921 (p,sc,story); *Polly of the Follies* 1922 (p,sc,story); *Red Hot Romance* 1922 (p,sc,story); *Dulcy* 1923 (sc,adapt); *Three Miles Out* 1924 (sc); *Learning to Love* 1925 (sc,story); *The Whole Town's Talking* 1926 (from play); *Publicity Madness* 1927 (story); *Stranded* 1927 (story); *Gentlemen Prefer Blondes* 1928 (sc,from novel,titles); *The Fall of Eve* 1929 (story); *Ex-Bad Boy* 1931 (from play "The Whole Town's Talking"); *The Struggle* 1931 (sc,story,dial); *Blondie of the Follies* 1932 (dial); *Red-Headed Woman* 1932 (d,sc); *The Barbarian* 1933 (sc,dial); *Hold Your Man* 1933 (sc,story); *Midnight Mary* 1933 (story); *Biography of a Bachelor Girl* 1934 (sc); *The Girl From Missouri* 1934 (sc,story); *The Merry Widow* 1934 (uncred.sc); *The Social Register* 1934 (from play); *Riffraff* 1935 (sc); *San Francisco* 1936 (sc); *Mama Steps Out* 1937 (sc); *Saratoga* 1937 (sc,story); *The Cowboy and the Lady* 1938 (uncred.sc); *Babes in Arms* 1939 (uncred.sc); *The Women* 1939 (sc); *Susan and God* 1940 (sc); *Blossoms in the Dust* 1941 (sc); *They Met in Bombay* 1941 (sc); *When Ladies Meet* 1941 (sc); *I Married an Angel* 1942 (sc); *Gentlemen Prefer Blondes* 1953 (from novel); *Gentlemen Marry Brunettes* 1955 (from novel).

Loquasto, Santo • Production designer, costume designer • *Educ.* King's College, Cambridge; Yale (drama). Award-winning designer, equally at home with film, ballet or theater (Loquasto has won two Tony awards for his stage work). Frequent collaborator with Woody Allen. • *Sammy Stops the World* 1978 (sets,cost); *Simon* 1980 (cost); *Stardust Memories* 1980 (cost); *The Fan* 1981 (pd); *So Fine* 1981 (pd); *A Midsummer Night's Sex Comedy* 1982 (cost); *Zelig* 1983 (cost) **(AANBCD)**; *Falling in Love* 1984 (pd); *Desperately Seeking Susan* 1985 (pd); *Radio Days* 1987 (pd) **(AANBAD)**; *September* 1987 (pd); *Another Woman* 1988 (pd); *Big* 1988 (pd); *Bright Lights, Big City* 1988 (pd); *Crimes and Misdemeanors* 1989 (pd); *New York Stories* 1989 (pd—"Oedipus Wrecks"); *She-Devil* 1989 (pd); *Alice* 1990 (pd).

Loren, Sophia • *aka* Sofia Lazzaro • Actress • Born Sofia Scicolone, Rome, September 20, 1934. Loren was a struggling teenage model and bit player when she met producer and future husband Carlo Ponti, one of a panel of judges presiding over a beauty contest in which she was competing, in 1951. Under Ponti's guidance she became one of Italy's leading stars of the 1950s, an earthy, voluptuous figure in the style of Gina Lollobrigida. Over the next two decades, Loren demonstrated the talent and range necessary to transcend her pin-up status; she appeared in some noteworthy films after signing a contract with Paramount in 1957 (*The Black Orchid* 1958, *Heller in Pink Tights* 1960) and earned a Cannes Festival award as well as an Oscar for her memorable performance in De Sica's *Two Women* (1960). Loren, who made infrequent appearances during the 80s, received an honorary Oscar in 1991 from the Academy of Motion Picture Arts and Sciences in recognition of her lifetime achievement in film, citing her as "one of the genuine treasures of world cinema." • *Cuori sul mare* 1950; *Luci del Varieta/Variety Lights* 1950; *Le Sei mogli di Barbablu* 1950; *Toto Tarzan* 1950; *Il Voto* 1950; *Anna* 1951; *E' arrivato l'accordatore* 1951; *Era lui...si...si!* 1951; *Io sono il capataz* 1951; *Lebbra Bianca* 1951; *Il Mago per forza* 1951; *Milano Miliardaria* 1951; *Quo Vadis* 1951; *Il Sogno di Zorro* 1951; *Africa sotto i mari* 1952; *Altri Tempi* 1952; *La Favorita* 1952; *La Tratta delle Bianche* 1952; *Aida* 1953; *Ci troviamo in galleria* 1953; *La Domenica della buona gente* 1953; *Due notti con Cleopatra* 1953; *Un Giorno in pretura* 1953; *Il Paese dei Campanelli* 1953; *Carosello Napoletano* 1954; *La Donna del Fiume* 1954; *Miseria e nobilta* 1954; *L'Oro di Napoli/The Gold of Naples* 1954; *Pellegrini d'amore* 1954; *Attila* 1955; *La Bella Mugnaia* 1955; *Peccato che sia una canaglia* 1955; *Il Segno di Venere* 1955; *La Fortuna di essere Donna* 1956; *Pane, Amore e...* 1956; *Boy on a Dolphin* 1957; *Desire Under the Elms* 1957; *Legend of the Lost* 1957; *The Pride and the Passion* 1957; *The Black Orchid* 1958; *Houseboat* 1958; *The Key* 1958; *That Kind of Woman* 1959; *A Breath of Scandal* 1960; *La Ciociara/Two Women* 1960 **(AABA)**; *Heller in Pink Tights* 1960; *It Started in Naples* 1960; *The Millionairess* 1960; *El Cid* 1961; *Madame Sans-Gene* 1961; *Boccaccio '70* 1962; *I Sequestrati di Altona/The Condemned of Altona* 1962; *Showman* 1962; *Five Miles to Midnight* 1963; *Ieri, Oggi, Domani/Yesterday, Today and Tomorrow* 1963; *The Fall of the Roman Empire* 1964; *Matrimonio all'italiana/Marriage Italian Style* 1964 **(AANBA)**; *Lady L* 1965; *Operation Crossbow* 1965; *Arabesque* 1966; *Judith* 1966; *C'era una Volta...* 1967; *A Countess From Hong Kong* 1967; *Questi Fantasmi* 1967; *I Girasoli* 1969; *Bianco, Rosso e...* 1971; *La Moglie del Prete* 1971; *La Mortadella* 1972; *L'Uomo della Mancha/Man of La Mancha* 1972; *La Pupa del gangster* 1974; *Le Testament/The Verdict* 1974; *Il Viaggio* 1974; *The Cassandra Crossing* 1977; *Una Giornata Particolare/A Special Day* 1977; *Brass Target* 1978; *Fatto di sangue fra due uomini per causa di una vedova. Si sospettano moventi politici* 1978; *Firepower* 1979; *Angela* 1984; *Running Away* 1989; *Sabato, Domenica e Lunedi/Saturday, Sunday and Monday* 1990.

Lorentz, Pare • Filmmaker • Born Clarksburg, WV, December 11, 1905. *Educ.* West Virginia Wesleyan College; University of West Virginia. Journalist and critic turned filmmaker who produced two landmark documentaries while he served as film advisor to F.D. Roosevelt's US Resettlement Administration: *The Plow That Broke the Plains* (1936) and *The River* (1937). Despite Hollywood's resistance to Lorentz's subsidized films (the studios claimed unfair competition), his socially progressive work received widespread critical and popular support. In 1938 Lorentz founded the US Film Service, a unit responsible for producing some noteworthy documentaries before Congress withdrew its support in 1940. Lorentz subsequently produced short films for RKO and for the armed forces and occupied two more government posts before seting up shop as a New York-based producer of commercial and industrial films. • *The Plow That Broke the Plains (short)* 1936 (d,sc,ed); *The River (short)* 1937 (d,sc,ed); *The City* 1939 (from outline); *The Fight For Life* 1940 (d,p,sc,ed); *Power and the Land* 1940 (prod.man); *The Land* 1942 (prod.man); *Name, Age, Occupation (short)* 1942 (d,sc,ed); *Nürnberg* 1948 (from material,p).

Lorre, Peter • Actor • Born Ladislav Loewenstein, Rozsahegy, Hungary, June 26, 1904; died 1964. Both a skilled actor and a unique screen presence, Peter Lorre was one of the movies' most memorable personalities. Lorre appeared on the stage and had several small film roles in Europe before coming to international attention in 1931 in Fritz Lang's *M*. Lorre's performance as the child-murderer set the standard for all sexual psychopaths on film since. Initially, his cherubic face and protruding eyes project the perfect mask of innocence. But as the film progresses and the massed forces of the police and the underworld close in on him, that innocence collapses into a series of feral outbursts. Lorre's confession scene is a finely balanced mixture of self-loathing and uncontrollable passion that still produces a painful double blow of revulsion and pity in viewers. Peter Lorre's performance in *M* remains one of the greatest in the history of cinema.

Almost as quickly as he achieved world-wide fame, Lorre became typecast. In spite of his diminutive size, Lorre became synonymous with dread. Fleeing the Nazi machine, Lorre left Germany in 1933, landing in England, where Alfred Hitchcock exploited his image by casting him as the head of a ring of kidnappers who menace young Nova Pilbeam in *The Man Who Knew Too Much* (1934). Two years later Hitchcock cast him in a similar role in *Secret Agent.* For *Mad Love* (1935), his first American film and a rare foray into horror for MGM, Lorre's head was shaved, further emphasizing his bulging eyes and giving him a slick, reptilian appearance. In his second Hollywood outing he played yet another murderer—Raskolnikov in Sternberg's version of *Crime and Punishment* (1935)—an excellent performance in a rather disappointing film. Although obssesives and psychopaths were Lorre's stock-in-trade, he never gave the same performance twice. Each of his villains was a singular creation born out of distinctive character psychology and motivations.

Between 1937 and 1939 Lorre stepped into a more conventional role, playing the Japanese detective Mr. Moto in eight films for 20th Century-Fox. Always beneath the easy-going surface of Lorre's Moto was a threatening edge that made the character far more interesting than most of Hollywood's other series detectives. This ability to give subtle shading to his acting was a key to Lorre's success. All his villainous roles have a darkly humorous touch, while his light or comedic performances feature a sinister undertone. The slight twist in his performances gave them a tension that continues to tantalize audiences.

Most of Lorre's starring roles were in B features, where he was often teamed with Sydney Greenstreet, although a number of these films were better than typical Hollywood A product. For instance, Lorre added a judicious amount of pathos to his role as a vengeful, disfigured immigrant in *The Face Behind the Mask* (1941), turning the film into an eloquent statement about the failure of the American dream. Throughout the 1940s Lorre added color to movies in numerous supporting roles, notably in Warner Bros. films, as Joel Cairo in *The Maltese Falcon* (1941) and Ugarte, the obsequious black marketeer, in *Casablanca* (1942).

By the end of the decade, Lorre's face and silken voice had become so recognizable that he was caricatured in Warner Bros. cartoons and on Spike Jones records. He even successfully parodied his "image" in films like *Arsenic and Old Lace* (1944) and *My Favorite Brunette* (1947), yet he was never reduced to parodying himself.

During the 1950s, health problems forced Lorre to take fewer roles, although he did expand his repertoire with a musical, *Silk Stockings* (1957) and several comedies. His comedic talent was displayed in a 1960s series of comedy/horror films for American-International Pictures. His precise timing and droll delivery in *The Raven* (1963) suggested that Hollywood never fully explored Lorre's range as an actor. ES • *Bomben auf Monte Carlo* 1931; *Fünf von der Jazzband* 1931; *Die Koffer des Herrn O.F.* 1931; *M* 1931; *F.P.1 antwortet nicht* 1932; *Schuss im Morgengrauen* 1932; *Der Weisse Dämon* 1932; *Du Haut en bas* 1933; *Was Frauen traümen* 1933; *The Man Who Knew Too Much* 1934; *Crime and Punishment* 1935; *Mad Love* 1935; *Crack-Up* 1936; *Secret Agent* 1936; *The Lancer Spy* 1937; *Nancy Steele Is Missing* 1937; *Thank You, Mr. Moto* 1937; *Think Fast, Mr. Moto* 1937; *I'll Give a Million* 1938; *Mr. Moto Takes a Chance* 1938; *Mr. Moto's Gamble* 1938; *Mysterious Mr. Moto* 1938; *Mr. Moto Takes a Vacation* 1939; *Mr. Moto in Danger Island* 1939; *Mr. Moto's Last Warning* 1939; *I Was an Adventuress* 1940; *Island of Doomed Men* 1940; *Strange Cargo* 1940; *Stranger on the Third Floor* 1940; *You'll Find Out* 1940; *The Face Behind the Mask* 1941; *The Maltese Falcon* 1941; *Mr. District Attorney* 1941; *They Met in Bombay* 1941; *All Through the Night* 1942; *The Boogie Man Will Get You* 1942; *Casablanca* 1942; *Invisible Agent* 1942; *Background to Danger* 1943; *The Constant Nymph* 1943; *The Cross of Lorraine* 1943; *Arsenic and Old Lace* 1944; *The Conspirators* 1944; *Hollywood Canteen* 1944; *The Mask of Dimitrios* 1944; *Passage to Marseille* 1944; *Confidential Agent* 1945; *Hotel Berlin* 1945; *The Beast With Five Fingers* 1946; *Black Angel* 1946; *The Chase* 1946; *Three Strangers* 1946; *The Verdict* 1946; *My Favorite Brunette* 1947; *Casbah* 1948; *Rope of Sand* 1949; *Double Confession* 1950; *Quicksand* 1950; *Der Verlorene* 1951 (a,d,sc); *Beat the Devil* 1953; *20,000 Leagues Under the Sea* 1954; *Around the World in 80 Days* 1956; *Congo Crossing* 1956; *Meet Me in Las Vegas* 1956; *The Buster Keaton Story* 1957; *Hell Ship Mutiny* 1957; *The Sad Sack* 1957; *Silk Stockings* 1957; *The Story of Mankind* 1957; *The Big Circus* 1959; *Scent of Mystery* 1960; *Voyage to the Bottom of the Sea* 1961; *Five Weeks in a Balloon* 1962; *Tales of Terror* 1962; *The Raven* 1963; *The Comedy of Terrors* 1964; *Muscle Beach Party* 1964; *The Patsy* 1964.

Losey, Joseph • *aka* Andrea Forzano, Victor Hanbury, Joseph Walton • Director; also producer, critic. • Born Joseph Walton Losey III, La Crosse, WI, January 14, 1909; died June 22, 1984. *Educ.* Dartmouth College (medicine); Harvard (English literature). Joseph Losey, born to a family whose American roots predated the American Revolution, has been called the "most European of American directors." His influences include Bertolt Brecht and Harold Pinter as well as Italian neo-realism and German expressionism. In 1935, he even studied under Sergei Eisenstein in Moscow, where he also met Brecht. It was his blacklisting in 1951, however, that forced Losey to make Europe his home.

In 1930, after receiving his M.A. from Harvard, Losey moved to New York City to work in the theater; he directed his first play, Little Ol' Boy, three years later. Directing for both political theater groups and the WPA's "Living Newspaper" productions, Losey combined an anti-realist aesthetic with radical political views. In 1947 he directed the world premiere of Brecht's *Galileo Galilei*, a play he would film in 1975.

Losey began to work in film in 1938, making educational documentaries for the Rockefeller Foundation. He directed his first feature, *The Boy With Green Hair*, ten years later, and by 1951 had directed five films, the last being a remake of Fritz Lang's *M*. Although none of these films expressed Losey's radical views, recurrent themes such as manhunts and mass hysteria provided a timely commentary on the political paranoia of the day. Losey himself was blacklisted in 1951 when he refused to testify before the HUAC. Unable to work in Hollywood, he moved to England, where he worked under pseudonyms for several years.

In England, Losey's focus shifted from the public themes of his Hollywood films to private relationships within the rigid British class system. He brought a stern moral scrutiny to bear on the status quo, often using the figure of the disruptive intruder as a catalyst. Striving for an intellectual rather than an emotional engagement with his audience, he tended to contain the action of his films within tightly defined settings, and to pay minute attention to symbolic details of the mise-en-scène. All of these factors combined to give his work an allegorical quality which, together with Losey's didacticism and pessimistic world view, alienated popular audiences.

Losey's most successful films were his collaborations with playwright Harold Pinter: *The Servant* (1963), *Accident* (1967) and *The Go-Between* (1971). Losey and Pinter also attemped to film Marcel Proust's *Remembrance of Things Past*, but while Pinter's screenplay was published, their film never got made. Like Orson Welles, Losey is almost as well known for his numerous uncompleted or aborted projects as for his finished ones. (He was, in fact, set to direct *High Noon* shortly before he was blacklisted.)

In 1976 Losey relocated to France—where he is considered one of the great auteurs of cinema—and directed three films in French. His last feature, *Steaming*, released posthumously in 1985, was his first English-language film in almost a decade. In the early 1980s, Losey almost fulfilled his dream of making another film in the United States, but both of his planned projects fell through, one within days of shooting.

Losey resented his alienation from his country, but also acknowledged its positive aspects. Rather than end up a jaded Hollywood director, he was forced to be an outsider—a position that was to inspire, as well as frustrate, his work. CAN • *Dick Turpin (short)* 1933 (d); *A Child Went Forth (short)* 1941 (d,p,sc); *Pete Roleum and His Cousins (short)* 1941 (d,p,sc); *Youth Gets a Break (short)* 1941 (d,sc); *Hotel Reserve (short)* 1944 (d); *The Boy With Green Hair* 1948 (d); *The Lawless* 1950 (d); *Mystery Street* 1950 (uncred.sc); *The Big Night* 1951 (d,sc); *M* 1951 (d); *The Prowler* 1951 (d); *The Tall Target* 1951 (uncred.sc); *Imbarco a Mezzanotte* 1952 (d); *The Final Column* 1954 (uncred. sc.ed); *Pellegrini d'amore* 1954 (d); *River Beat* 1954 (p); *The Sleeping Tiger* 1954 (d); *A Man on the Beach (short)* 1955 (d); *Finger of Guilt* 1956 (d); *Time Without Pity* 1957 (d); *The Gypsy and the Gentleman* 1958 (d); *Blind Date* 1959 (d); *The Criminal* 1960 (d); *Eva* 1962 (a,d,lyrics); *These Are the Damned* 1962 (d); *The Servant* 1963 (d,p); *King and Country* 1964 (d,p); *Modesty Blaise* 1966 (d); *Accident* 1967 (d,p); *Boom!* 1968 (d); *Secret Ceremony* 1968 (d); *Figures in a Landscape* 1970 (d,sc); *The Go-Between* 1971 (d); *75 Years of Cinema Museum* 1972 (a); *The Assassination of Trotsky* 1972 (d,p); *A Doll's House* 1973 (d,exec.p); *Galileo* 1974 (d,sc,adapt); *The Romantic Englishwoman* 1975 (d); *Comment Yukong Déplaca les Montagnes* 1976 (prod.sup—English version); *Hollywood on Trial* 1976 (assistance); *Mr. Klein* 1976 (d); *Resistance* 1976 (a); *Les Routes du Sud* 1978 (d,sc); *Don Giovanni* 1979 (d,sc,adapt); *La Truite* 1982 (a,d,sc,adapt); *Steaming* 1985 (d).

Lowe, Rob • Actor • Born Virginia, March 17, 1964. First came to prominence as one of the "brat pack," the group of young actors who surfaced in films such as Francis Ford Coppola's *The Outsiders* (1983) and Joel Schumacher's *St. Elmo's Fire* (1985). Brother Chad Lowe is also an actor. • *Class* 1983; *The Outsiders* 1983; *The Hotel New Hampshire* 1984; *Oxford Blues* 1984; *St. Elmo's Fire* 1985; *About Last Night* 1986; *Youngblood* 1986; *Square Dance* 1987; *Illegally Yours* 1988; *Masquerade* 1988; *Bad Influence* 1990.

Loy, Myrna • Actress • Born Myrna Williams, Raidersburg, MT, August 2, 1905. Former dancer, in films as a bit player from the mid-1920s and primarily cast as mysterious, exotic types for the first ten years of her career. In 1934, W.S. Van Dyke cast Loy opposite William Powell in the first of the hugely successful *Thin Man* movies, making her an instant favorite with movie audiences around the country. Loy became one of

Hollywood's most popular actresses of the 30s and went on to star in a number of films opposite Clark Gable. Increasingly active in politics after her WWII service with the Red Cross (she was a founder member of the Committee of the First Amendment), Loy's postwar screen career was distinguished by a fine performance opposite Fredric March in *The Best Years of Our Lives* (1946). Loy, who was never nominated for an Oscar, received an honorary statuette in 1991 from the Academy of Motion Picture Arts and Sciences in recognition of her 55-year screen career. Her first husband was producer Arthur Hornblow, Jr. (married 1936-42) and her third, screenwriter-producer Gene Markey (married 1946-50). • *Ben Hur, A Tale of the Christ* 1925; *Pretty Ladies* 1925; *Satan in Sables* 1925; *Sporting Life* 1925; *Across the Pacific* 1926; *The Caveman* 1926; *Don Juan* 1926; *The Exquisite Sinner* 1926; *The Gilded Highway* 1926; *The Love Toy* 1926; *Millionaires* 1926; *So This Is Paris* 1926; *The Wanderer* 1926; *Why Girls Go Back Home* 1926; *Bitter Apples* 1927; *The Climbers* 1927; *Finger Prints* 1927; *The Girl From Chicago* 1927; *Ham and Eggs at the Front* 1927; *Heart of Maryland* 1927; *If I Were Single* 1927; *The Jazz Singer* 1927; *A Sailor's Sweetheart* 1927; *Simple Sis* 1927; *The Third Degree* 1927; *When a Man Loves* 1927; *Beware of Married Men* 1928; *The Crimson City* 1928; *A Girl in Every Port* 1928; *The Midnight Taxi* 1928; *Pay as You Enter* 1928; *State Street Sadie* 1928; *Turn Back the Hours* 1928; *What Price Beauty* 1928; *The Black Watch* 1929; *The Desert Song* 1929; *Evidence* 1929; *Fancy Baggage* 1929; *The Great Divide* 1929; *Hardboiled Rose* 1929; *Noah's Ark* 1929; *The Show of Shows* 1929; *The Squall* 1929; *Bride of the Regiment* 1930; *Cameo Kirby* 1930; *Cock O' the Walk* 1930; *Isle of Escape* 1930; *Jazz Cinderella* 1930; *Last of the Duanes* 1930; *Renegades* 1930; *Rogue of the Rio Grande* 1930; *The Truth About Youth* 1930; *Under a Texas Moon* 1930; *Arrowsmith* 1931; *Body and Soul* 1931; *Connecticut Yankee* 1931; *Consolation Marriage* 1931; *The Devil to Pay* 1931; *Hush Money* 1931; *The Naughty Flirt* 1931; *Rebound* 1931; *Skyline* 1931; *Transatlantic* 1931; *The Animal Kingdom* 1932; *Emma* 1932; *Love Me Tonight* 1932; *The Mask of Fu Manchu* 1932; *New Morals For Old* 1932; *Thirteen Women* 1932; *Vanity Fair* 1932; *The Wet Parade* 1932; *The Woman in Room 13* 1932; *The Barbarian* 1933; *Night Flight* 1933; *Penthouse* 1933; *The Prizefighter and the Lady* 1933; *Scarlet River* 1933; *Topaze* 1933; *When Ladies Meet* 1933; *Broadway Bill* 1934; *Evelyn Prentice* 1934; *Manhattan Melodrama* 1934; *Men in White* 1934; *Stamboul Quest* 1934; *The Thin Man* 1934; *Whipsaw* 1935; *Wings in the Dark* 1935; *After the Thin Man* 1936; *The Great Ziegfeld* 1936; *Libeled Lady* 1936; *Petticoat Fever* 1936; *To Mary - With Love* 1936; *Wife vs. Secretary* 1936; *Double Wedding* 1937; *Parnell* 1937; *Man-Proof* 1938; *Test Pilot* 1938; *Too Hot to Handle* 1938; *Another Thin Man* 1939; *Lucky Night* 1939; *The Rains Came* 1939; *Verdensberomtheder i Kobenhavn* 1939; *I Love You Again* 1940; *Third Finger, Left Hand* 1940; *Love Crazy* 1941; *Shadow of the Thin Man* 1941; *The Thin Man Goes Home* 1944; *The Best Years of Our Lives* 1946; *So Goes My Love* 1946; *The Bachelor and the Bobby Soxer* 1947; *The Senator Was Indiscreet* 1947; *Song of the Thin Man* 1947; *Mr. Blandings Builds His Dream House* 1948; *The Red Pony* 1949; *That Dangerous Age* 1949; *Cheaper By the Dozen* 1950; *Belles on Their Toes* 1952; *The Ambassador's Daughter* 1956; *Lonelyhearts* 1958; *From the Terrace* 1960; *Midnight Lace* 1960; *The April Fools* 1969; *Airport 1975* 1975; *It's Showtime* 1976; *The End* 1978; *Just Tell Me What You Want* 1980.

Lubitsch, Ernst • Director • Born Berlin, Germany, January 28, 1892; died 1947. Dubbed "a man of pure Cinema" by Alfred Hitchcock, "a prince" by François Truffaut and "a giant" by Orson Welles, Ernst Lubitsch is a preeminent figure in the history of cinema. More than a great director of actors and action, Lubitsch added his own personal signature, "the Lubitsch touch," to all his work, a sense of style and grace that rarely been matched on the screen.

Born the son of a draper, Lubitsch gained prominence at the age of 19 as a member of Max Reinhardt's troupe; by 21, he had begun to create the comic screen persona *"Meyer,"* a slapstick Jewish archetype who became a favorite of German audiences.

The following year, Lubitsch got his first chance to display his filmmaking skills, writing and directing a one-reeler called *Fräulein Seifenschaum/Miss Soapsuds* (1915). Eager to test his own range and gain acceptance as a dramatic actor, Lubitsch wrote and directed *Als ich tot War/When I Was Dead* (1916), but the film failed to stir the interest of an audience who loved "Meyer." Stereotyped as an actor, Lubitsch turned his full attention to directing and scored his first major success with *Schuhpalast Pinkus/Shoe Salon Pinkus* (1916).

The first Lubitsch picture to be shown in America was *Die Augen Der Mummie Ma/The Eyes of the Mummy* (1918), his first teaming of Pola Negri and Emil Jannings. It was their second film, however, with Lubitsch, *Madame Du Barry/Passion* (1919) which proved to be his first masterwork, as well as a crucial film for the German film industry, as it was the first success of the film's coproducers, the newly formed UFA. With *Madame Du Barry,* Lubitsch became known for an unerring ability to "humanize" sumptuous screen spectacles and costume dramas, to give them the warmth that would endear them to the public. In 1923, Lubitsch's career would enter a new phase when Mary Pickford invited him to Hollywood to direct *Rosita.*

It was with his next film, *The Marriage Circle* (1924), inspired by Chaplin's *A Woman of Paris,* that Lubitsch began to hone his famed "touch." With the arrival of sound, Lubitsch's ear for shimmering dialogue and exhilarating musical numbers only enhanced his talent. The director's greatest achievements would begin in 1932 with *Trouble in Paradise* and continue with such masterworks as *Design For Living* (1933), *The Merry Widow* (1934), *Angel* (1937), *Ninotchka* (1939), *The Shop Around the Corner* (1940), *To Be or Not to Be* (1942), *Heaven Can Wait* (1943) and *Cluny Brown* (1946).

In 1935, Lubitsch was named head of production at Parmount, but his real talent lay in producing and directing motion pictures, not studio administration, and he was relieved of his duties after a year. During production on *That Lady in Ermine* (1948), he died of a heart attack, and the film was completed by Otto Preminger. DC • *Die Ideale Gattin* 1913 (a); *Bedingung—kein Anhang!* 1914 (a); *Die Firma heiratet* 1914 (a); *Der Stolz der Firma* 1914 (a); *Arme Maria* 1915 (a); *Auf Eis geführt* 1915 (a,d); *Blindekuh* 1915 (a,d); *Fraulein Piccolo* 1915 (a); *Fräulein Seifenschaum/Miss Soapsuds* 1915 (a,d); *Der Kraftmeyer* 1915 (a,d); *Der Letzte Anzug* 1915 (a,d); *Robert und Bertram oder: Die lustigen Vagabunden* 1915 (a); *Der Schwarze Moritz* 1915 (a); *Sein einziger Patient* 1915 (a,d); *Ein Verliebter Racker* 1915 (a); *Zucker und Zimt* 1915 (a,d,sc,story); *Als ich tot war/When I Was Dead* 1916 (a,d); *Doktor Satansohn* 1916 (a); *Der G.m.b.H. Tenor* 1916 (a,d); *Der Gemischte Frauenchor* 1916 (a,d); *Käsekönig Hollander* 1916 (a,d,sc); *Die Neue Nase* 1916 (a,d); *Das Schönste Geschenk* 1916 (a,d); *Schuhpalast Pinkus/Shoe Salon Pinkus* 1916 (a,d); *Der Blusenkönig* 1917 (a,d,sc); *Das Fidele Gefängnis* 1917 (a,d,sc); *Hans Trutz im Schlaraffenland* 1917 (a); *Ossi's Tagebuch* 1917 (d); *Prinz Sami* 1917 (a,d,sc); *Wenn vier dasselbe tun* 1917 (d,sc); *Die Augen der Mummie Ma/The Eyes of the Mummy* 1918 (d); *Carmen* 1918 (d); *Der Fall Rosentopf* 1918 (a,d,sc); *Ich möchte kein Mann sein* 1918 (d,sc); *Das Mädel vom Ballett* 1918 (d); *Marionetten* 1918 (d); *Meyer aus Berlin* 1918 (a,d); *Der Rodelkavalier* 1918 (a,d,sc); *Die Austernprinzessin* 1919 (d,sc); *Der Lustige Ehemann* 1919 (sc); *Madame Du Barry/Passion* 1919 (d); *Meine Frau, die Filmschauspielerin* 1919 (d,sc); *Die Puppe* 1919 (d); *Rausch* 1919 (d); *Anne Boleyn* 1920 (d); *Kolhiesels Tochter* 1920 (d,sc); *Romeo und Julia im Schnee* 1920 (d,sc); *Sumurun* 1920 (a,d,sc); *Die Wohnungsnot* 1920 (sc); *Die Bergkatze* 1921 (d,sc); *Vendetta* 1921 (d); *Die Flamme* 1922 (d); *Das Weib des Pharao* 1922 (d); *Rosita* 1923 (d); *Forbidden Paradise* 1924 (d); *The Marriage Circle* 1924 (d); *Three Women* 1924 (d,story); *Kiss Me Again* 1925 (d); *Lady Windemere's Fan* 1925 (d); *So This Is Paris* 1926 (d); *The Student Prince in Old Heidelberg* 1927 (d); *The Last Command* 1928 (from incident); *The Patriot* 1928 (d,ed) **(AANBD)**; *Eternal Love* 1929 (d); *The Love Parade* 1929 (d,p) **(AANBD)**; *Monte Carlo* 1930 (d,p); *Paramount on Parade* 1930 (d); *The Smiling Lieutenant* 1931 (d,p); *Broken Lullaby* 1932 (d,p); *If I Had a Million* 1932 (d,sc); *One Hour With You* 1932 (d,p); *Trouble in Paradise* 1932 (d,p); *Design For Living* 1933 (d,p); *Mr. Broadway* 1933 (a); *The Merry Widow* 1934 (d); *Desire* 1936 (p); *I Loved a Soldier* 1936 (p); *Angel* 1937 (d,p); *Bluebeard's Eighth Wife* 1938 (d,p); *Ninotchka* 1939 (d,p); *The Shop Around the Corner* 1940 (d,p); *That Uncertain Feeling* 1941 (d,p); *To Be or Not to Be* 1942 (d,p,story); *Heaven Can Wait* 1943 (d,p) **(AANBD)**; *A Royal Scandal* 1945 (p); *Where Do We Go From Here?* 1945 (a); *Cluny Brown* 1946 (d,p); *Dragonwyck* 1946 (uncred.p); *That Lady in Ermine* 1948 (d,p); *The Fighting O'Flynn* 1949 (sc).

Lucas, George • Director, producer • Born George Walton Lucas Jr., Modesto, CA, May 14, 1944. *Educ.* University of Southern California (film). The supreme "anti-auteur," George Lucas has achieved a startling measure of commercial success and cultural influence with surprisingly few director's credits. Although he's not a critics' favorite—his work lacks "thematic weight"—he has enhanced popular culture with an irrepressible enthusiasm. Almost singlehandedly he established the 1960s as a proper subject of cinematic nostalgia in *American Graffiti* (1973), then gave the science fiction genre a new, broad appeal with the *Star Wars* trilogy, combining fantasy and nostalgia (perfectly embodied in the opening title of *Star Wars*, "Long ago in a galaxy far, far away") in a way which proved popular with young and adult audiences alike.

While a graduate student at the University of Southern California, Lucas served as an intern on Francis Ford Coppola's musical, *Finian's Rainbow* (1968). The two men quickly discovered their mutual love for the cinema and became close friends. It was Coppola who provided backing for Lucas's first feature, *THX 1138* (1971), an expansion of a 20-minute short made during Lucas's student days. An intelligent work of science fiction, the film demonstrated his keen understanding of the genre. The film draws heavily on classic dystopian visions like Huxley's *Brave New World* and Orwell's *1984*, and for many it remains Lucas's best to date, offering his most inventive imagery with a minimal reliance on special effects.

To Lucas's great dismay, Warner Bros. reedited the film and gave it only a limited release. *THX* consequently performed poorly at the box-office, although it would later achieve something of cult status. It also earned Lucas a reputation as an intellectual director of science fiction, so in conscious reaction he conceived the semi-autobiographical *American Graffiti* (1973), a story designed to appeal to a broader audience. Produced on a budget of only $750,000, again with help from Coppola, the film became one of the most profitable movies of the decade. *American Graffitti*'s rock-and-roll "oldies" soundtrack established the commercial potential of classic rock in the cinema, and the film's success allowed Lucas to produce his subsequent films independently.

Lucas's next, and to date his last, movie as director would change the history of the science fiction film. *Star Wars*, published as a novel in 1976 and released as a film the following year, is relatively standard "space opera" fare: fascist villains attempt to gain control of decent, democratic folk, who are forced to become heroes to defeat them. The characters are little more than the stock figures of the genre, but Lucas managed to present them with a freshness and exuberance that had been absent from the screen since the Flash Gordon and Buck Rogers serials of decades earlier, to which they pay homage.

Lucas claimed he wanted to restore the qualities of romance and vigor to the genre, which he felt had grown too intellectual. Thus *Star Wars* is distinguished by bravura action sequences, state-of-the-art special effects, carefully considered production design and a breathtaking pace, and avoids any serious thematic issues. At the heart of the film's popular appeal is the concept of "the Force": although never fully explained, and functioning as little more than a plot convenience, its primary function is to suggest a mythic union between life and science, biology and technology.

Lucas earned a fortune from the movie, the most successful science fiction film until Steven Spielberg's *E.T.: The Extraterrestrial* in 1982. Made for $10.5 million, it earned more than $400 million around the world, and sparked an unprecedented merchandising campaign of toys, lunch boxes, T-shirts, mugs and other memorabilia. The *Star Wars* myths have been a powerful staple of kid's culture since the late 70s, exceeded only by the world of Jim Henson's Muppets. With his profits from the film, Lucas established his own production facility, Lucasfilm Ltd., in Marin County, California.

Star Wars was an exhausting experience for Lucas, and he swore never to direct a "big" film again. He has likened the director's role on such a large production to that of a general and claims that he would rather be a filmmaker, creating more intimate, even avant-garde works. Since 1977 Lucas has indeed avoided directorial duties to concentrate on production. Two *Star Wars* sequels, *The Empire Strikes Back* (1980) and *Return of the Jedi* (1983), have reinforced the myth (Lucas originally planned an overly ambitious nine-film series). He has also produced movies in other genres with mixed success, from the profitable *Indiana Jones* adventures (in partnership with Steven Spielberg) to the disastrous *Howard the Duck* (1986). However, Lucas—now a kind of symbol for the commercial cinema—has yet to turn from such major, mainstream ventures to a more personal style of filmmaking. He seems content, instead, to continue to distill the stuff of 30s and 40s American popular movies, communicating the naive thrill of those heroic serial adventures to new generations of Saturday-morning children. BKG, JM • *Freiheit (short)* 1965 (d,sc); *Look at Life (short)* 1965 (d); *1:42:08: A Man and His Car (short)* 1966 (d,sc); *Herbie (short)* 1966 (d); *6-18-67 (short)* 1967 (d); *Anyone Lived in a Pretty How Town (short)* 1967 (d,sc); *The Emperor (short)* 1967 (d); *Marcello, I'm So Bored (short)* 1967 (ed); *The Rain People* 1969 (prod.assoc); *Gimme Shelter* 1970 (ph); *THX 1138* 1971 (d,sc,story,ed); *American Graffiti* 1973 (d,p,sc) **(AANBD,AANBSC)**; *Star Wars* 1977 (d,sc) **(AANBD,AANBSC)**; *More American Graffiti* 1979 (exec.p,from characters); *The Empire Strikes Back* 1980 (exec.p,sc,story); *Kagemusha* 1980 (exec.prod—international version); *Body Heat* 1981 (uncred.exec.p); *Raiders of the Lost Ark* 1981 (exec.p,story); *Return of the Jedi* 1983 (exec.p,sc,story); *Twice Upon a Time* 1983 (exec.p); *Beruchet dit la Boulie* 1984 (a); *Indiana Jones and the Temple of Doom* 1984 (exec.p,story); *Mishima: A Life in Four Chapters* 1985 (exec.p); *Return to Oz* 1985 (assistance); *Captain Eo* 1986 (exec.p); *Howard the Duck* 1986 (exec.p); *Labyrinth* 1986 (exec.p); *The Land Before Time* 1988 (exec.p); *Powaqqatsi* 1988 (p); *Tucker: The Man and His Dream* 1988 (exec.p); *Willow* 1988 (exec.p,story); *Indiana Jones and the Last Crusade* 1989 (exec.p,story).

Lugosi, Bela • *aka* Arisztid Olt • Actor • Born Béla Blasko, Lugos, Hungary, October 20, 1882; died August 1956. Lugosi trained on the Budapest stage and appeared in some German films before arriving in the US in 1921. He made his mark as "Dracula" in a popular New York stage production and successfully reprised the role in Tod Browning's 1931 film adaptation. His macabre appearance and Hungarian accent made him the very incarnation of evil in scores of horror films through the 1950s. Lugosi's will decreed that he be buried in his trademark Dracula cape. • *Alarcosbal* 1917; *Elet kiralya, Az* 1917; *Ezredes, Az* 1917; *A Leopard* 1917;

Naszdal 1917; *Tavaszi vihar* 1917; *Casanova* 1918; *Kilencvenkilenc* 1918; *Kuzdelem a letert* 1918; *Lulu* 1918; *Sklaven fremden Willens* 1919; *Die Frau im Delphin oder 30 Tage auf dem Meeresgrund* 1920; *Der Fruch der Menschheit 1. Teil: Die Tochter der Arbeit* 1920; *Der Fruch der Menschheit 2. Teil: Im Rausche der Milliarden* 1920; *Das Ganze Sein ist flammend Leid* 1920; *Der Januskopf* 1920; *Lederstrumpf 2. Teil: Der letzte Mohikaner* 1920; *Lederstrumpfs Abeteuer 1. Teil: Der Wildtoter* 1920; *Nat Pinkerton im Kampf 1. Teil: das Ende des Artisten Bartolini* 1920; *Der Tanz auf dem Vulkan 1. Teil: Sybil Joung* 1920; *Der Tanz auf dem Vulkan 2. Teil: Der Tod des Grossfursten* 1920; *Die Teufelsanbeter* 1920; *Die Todeskarawane* 1920; *The Silent Command* 1923; *The Rejected Woman* 1924; *Daughters Who Pay* 1925; *The Midnight Girl* 1925; *Puchinello (short)* 1925; *The Last Performance* 1927; *How to Handle Women* 1928; *Prisoners* 1929; *The Thirteenth Chair* 1929; *The Veiled Woman* 1929; *King of Jazz* 1930; *Oh, For a Man!* 1930; *Renegades* 1930; *Such Men Are Dangerous* 1930; *Viennese Nights* 1930; *Wild Company* 1930; *The Black Camel* 1931; *Broad-Minded* 1931; *Dracula* 1931; *Fifty Million Frenchmen* 1931; *Women of All Nations* 1931; *Chandu the Magician* 1932; *The Death Kiss* 1932; *Murders in the Rue Morgue* 1932; *White Zombie* 1932; *The Devil's in Love* 1933; *International House* 1933; *Island of Lost Souls* 1933; *Night of Terror* 1933; *Whispering Shadows* 1933; *The Black Cat* 1934; *Gift of Gab* 1934; *The Return of Chandu* 1934; *The Best Man Wins* 1935; *Mark of the Vampire* 1935; *Murder By Television* 1935; *The Mysterious Mr. Wong* 1935; *Mystery of the Marie Celeste* 1935; *The Raven* 1935; *The House of a Thousand Candles* 1936; *The Invisible Ray* 1936; *Postal Inspector* 1936; *Shadow of Chinatown* 1936; *S.O.S. Coast Guard* 1937; *Dark Eyes of London* 1939; *The Gorilla* 1939; *Ninotchka* 1939; *The Phantom Creeps* 1939; *Son of Frankenstein* 1939; *Black Friday* 1940; *Saint's Double Trouble* 1940; *You'll Find Out* 1940; *The Black Cat* 1941; *The Devil Bat* 1941; *The Invisible Ghost* 1941; *Spooks Run Wild* 1941; *The Wolf Man* 1941; *Black Dragons* 1942; *Bowery at Midnight* 1942; *The Corpse Vanishes* 1942; *The Ghost of Frankenstein* 1942; *Night Monster* 1942; *The Ape Man* 1943; *Frankenstein Meets the Wolf Man* 1943; *Ghosts on the Loose* 1943; *The Return of the Vampire* 1943; *One Body Too Many* 1944; *Return of the Ape Man* 1944; *Voodoo Man* 1944; *The Body Snatcher* 1945; *Zombies on Broadway* 1945; *Genius at Work* 1946; *Scared to Death* 1947; *Abbott and Costello Meet Frankenstein* 1948; *Bela Lugosi Meets a Brooklyn Gorilla* 1952; *Meet Bela Lugosi and Oliver Hardy (short)* 1952; *Mother Riley Meets the Vampire* 1952; *Glen or Glenda* 1954; *The Black Sleep* 1956; *The Bride of the Monster* 1956; *Plan 9 From Outer Space* 1958; *Lock Up Your Daughters* 1959 (archival footage).

Lumet, Sidney • Director; also actor, screenwriter, producer. • Born Philadelphia, PA, June 25, 1924. *Educ.* Columbia (dramatic literature); Actors Studio. When the history of American film since 1950 is written, the name of Sidney Lumet will loom large. In many ways a throwback to the Golden Age of Hollywood of the 30s and 40s, Lumet has demonstrated an ease with a variety of genres, producing a body of work that rivals in quantity and quality many of the most productive studio directors of this famed period. But unlike many of the house directors of the past, Lumet may considered the primary author of most of his works, a genuine auteur.

Whether working in intimate, intense dramas reflecting his experience in the golden age of TV drama (*Twelve Angry Men* 1957, *The Offence* 1973) or larger scale but equally intense urban dramas (*Prince of the City* 1981, *Dog Day Afternoon* 1975), police thrillers (*Serpico* 1973), musical extravaganzas (*The Wiz* 1978), literate comedies (*Just Tell Me What You Want* 1980, *Bye Bye Braverman* 1968), or stage adaptations (*Long Day's Journey Into Night* 1962), Lumet concentrates on similar themes and issues. And with his own background in acting and theater (he began appearing in Yiddish theater productions in the late 1920s and went on to work on Broadway), Lumet consistently manages to get powerful performances from powerful movie stars.

There are a handful of significant recurring subjects in Lumet's cinema. He is extremely concerned with family life, whether actual families, as in *Long Day's Journey* and *Daniel* (1983), or extended/substitute families, in *Dog Day Afternoon* and *Prince of the City.* Within these family groups individuals struggle to form their own identities while also struggling to preserve familial ties. Although family life is a common experience, the American cinema has been more often concerned with individuals, with images and ideals of the "self-made man," so Lumet's focus, even if it is broadly conceived at times, marks a significant variation.

Lumet is concerned with the struggles and joys of family life—how ethnic, regional or racial subcultures inform our lives and nation. He is equally focused on larger social questions: as few American directors have been, he is interested in understanding how our greater culture works, in the complex social structures that wield influence on our lives. In this respect, *Network* (1976), a ruthless portrait of the demeaning effects of television written by Paddy Chayevsky, is one of Lumet's most powerful films, as well as one of his most popular. This impulse toward larger issues can also be seen in *Fail Safe* (1964) and *Power* (1986). Lumet also deal with questions of social justice and how history affects and informs individual lives and the life of the nation.

All these impulses come together in one of Lumet's masterpieces, *The Pawnbroker* (1965). This story of a survivor of the Nazi Holocaust demonstrates the tragedy of the loss of family and the need to continue to reach out for new relationships and new families, how social injustice needs to be countered by all of us wherever it is found, and how history is forgotten at our individual and national peril. DD • *The 400 Million* 1938 (a); *One Third of a Nation* 1939 (a); *Twelve Angry Men* 1957 (d) **(AANBD)**; *Stage Struck* 1958 (d); *That Kind of Woman* 1959 (d); *The Fugitive Kind* 1960 (d); *Long Day's Journey Into Night* 1962 (d); *A View From the Bridge* 1962 (d); *Fail Safe* 1964 (d); *The Hill* 1965 (d); *The Pawnbroker* 1965 (d); *The Group* 1966 (d); *The Deadly Affair* 1967 (d,p); *Bye Bye Braverman* 1968 (d,p); *The Sea Gull* 1968 (d,p); *The Appointment* 1969 (d); *Last of the Mobile Hot-Shots* 1969 (d,p); *King: A Filmed Record... Montgomery to Memphis* 1970 (d); *The Anderson Tapes* 1971 (d); *Child's Play* 1972 (d); *The Offence* 1973 (d); *Serpico* 1973 (d); *Lovin' Molly* 1974 (d); *Murder on the Orient Express* 1974 (d); *Dog Day Afternoon* 1975 (d) **(AANBD)**; *Network* 1976 (d) **(AANBD)**; *Equus* 1977 (d); *The Wiz* 1978 (d); *Just Tell Me What You Want* 1980 (d,p); *Prince of the City* 1981 (d,sc) **(AANBSC)**; *Deathtrap* 1982 (d); *The Verdict* 1982 (d); *Daniel* 1983 (d,exec.p); *Garbo Talks* 1984 (d); *50 Years of Action!* 1986 (a); *The Morning After* 1986 (d); *Power* 1986 (d); *Funny* 1988 (a); *Running on Empty* 1988 (d); *Family Business* 1989 (d); *Listen Up* 1990 (a); *Q&A* 1990 (d,sc).

Lumière, Louis • Inventor; also director, producer. • Born Besançon, France, October 5, 1864; died 1948. The two flowing rivers of the birth of film are considered to be Thomas Edison and Louis and Auguste Lumière. Edison was the Grand Showman, recording music hall turns inside his barnlike studio with a monstrous, cumbersome camera. The Lumières were Grand Documentarians, taking to the Parisian streets with their cinématographe and photographing everyday occurences, displaying a joy in movement and commonplace realities, celebrating the mundane as a lifeforce.

From the first, the Lumières were technicians. Their father, Antoine, was a well-known portrait painter who gave up paint for financial rewards in the business of photographic supplies. Antoine sent his sons to technical school, but because of recurring headaches, Louis left the school early and began experimenting with his father's photographic apparatus. In the process, he discovered a new process for the preparation of photographic plates and a factory was built to manufacture them. By 1895, the Lumière factory was the leading European manufacturer of photographic products, employing over 300 workers. Like Edison, the Lumières had become successful inventor-businessmen.

An invitational demonstration of the Edison Kinetoscope, a parlor peephole machine, in Paris in 1894, sparked the Lumières' interest in motion pictures and the brothers set out to devise a machine that would combine motion picture movement with front projection. In 1895, Louis came up with such a device, and the cinématographe was patented in his name.

With the cinématographe, the emphasis of the nascent motion picture form was dramatically changed. Edison's bulky, stationary camera forced its subjects to display themselves in front of the camera as objects of a performance. The cinématographe, on the other hand, was not bulky but lightweight (about five kilograms), hand-cranked and not bound to a studio. The Lumière camera reduced the frames-per-second speed from Edison's 48 to 16, using less film and reducing the clatter and grinding of the Edison camera. The cinematographe was also unique in that the same housing functioned as a camera, projector and printer.

And, perhaps most importantly of all, the Lumières applied the principle of intermittent movement to film projection, allowing smooth-running projection through the film gate—a idea Edison had rejected as he struggled to perfect projection using continous movement past the film gate. The Lumières' technical innovations allowed the motion pictures to venture into the world outside of a studio, permitting any object in reality to become a subject of interest for the camera.

From their first film, *La Sortie des Usines/Workers Leaving the Lumiere Factory* (1895), the Lumières made everyday processes their subjects. In 1895, they recorded over 20 subjects, including *L'Arrivée d'un Train en Gare/Arrival of a Train, Le Repas de Bébé/Feeding the Baby, L'Arroseur Arrosée/Watering the Gardener, Demolition d'un Mur/The Falling Wall* and *Course en Sacs/The Sack Race.*

At first, the Lumières kept their invention a secret, only demonstrating the cinématographe at private screenings, first at a March 22, 1895, industrial meeting in Paris and later at a June 10 meeting of photographers at Lyon. These private exhibitions were met with great enthusiasm, and, on December 28, 1895, the Lumières held their first public screening at the Grand Café on the Boulevard des Capucines. The reaction was sensational and before long there were 20 showings a day to meet the tremendous public demand. The success spurred the Lumières to debut the cinématographe in England, Belgium, Holland, and Germany.

By 1897, the Lumières were a global success, training hundreds of operators and expanding their film catalog to over 750 titles. But after the Paris Exposition of 1900, during which they projected a film on a mammoth 99 x 79-foot screen, the brothers decided to curtail their film exhibitions and devote themselves to the manufacture and sale of their inventions.

As inventors and businessmen, the Lumières were perhaps uneasy shooting film subjects in an area that had begun to attract burgeoning film artists. While Edison stubbornly struggled to hold back the clock, forming a trust to quash up-and-coming filmmakers, the Lumières' withdrawal from the vanguard of filmmaking opened the door for others to advance the aesthetic side of film.

Nevertheless, during their brief careers in production, the Lumières brought filmmaking to five continents, demonstrated the beauty of movement in the mundane, and forever enshrined "cinema" as the art form of the 20th century. PB

Lundgren, Dolph • Actor • Born Stockholm, Sweden, 1959. *Educ.* Washington State University; MIT; Royal Institute of Technology, Stockholm. Former karate champion who made his film debut as the butt of Sylvester Stallone's anti-Soviet pummelling in *Rocky IV* (1985). • *Rocky IV* 1985; *A View to a Kill* 1985; *Masters of the Universe* 1987; *The Punisher* 1989; *Red Scorpion* 1989; *I Come in Peace* 1990.

Lupino, Ida • Actress; also director, screenwriter, producer. • Born Brixton, London, February 4, 1918. *Educ.* RADA, London. The daughter of British comedian Stanley Lupino and actress Connie Emerald, Lupino arrived in Hollywood in 1933 and was relegated to ingenue roles on the Paramount lot until coming into her own playing headstrong, grasping women in a string of Warner Bros. melodramas, most notably *High Sierra* (1941), *On Dangerous Ground* (1951) and *The Big Knife* (1955).

After forming a production company, The Filmakers, in 1949 with then-husband Collier Young, Lupino, already involved as writer and producer, took over the direction of *Not Wanted* (1949) when director Elmer Clifton took ill; she made her formal directorial debut with *Never Fear* (1950), emerging in the process as the only female director of the postwar era.

Although each of Lupino's directorial efforts was distinctive, the highlights are arguably *The Hitch-Hiker* (1953), a seminal, atmospheric thriller in which two complacent businessmen, returning from a business trip, discover that the man they've picked up is a homicidal psychopath, and *The Bigamist* (1953), the sensitive account of a travelling salesman's foolhardy decision to marry twice.

Lupino did most of her subsequent directing for TV, working extensively on such programs as "The Untouchables," "Have Gun-Will Travel" and "The Fugitive," and has made intermittent small-screen appearances. Also married to actors Louis Hayward (1938-45) and Howard Duff (1951-73). JMM • *Her First Affair* 1932 (a); *The Love Race* 1932 (a); *The Ghost Camera* 1933 (a); *High Finance* 1933 (a); *I Lived With You* 1933 (a); *Money For Speed* 1933 (a); *Prince of Arcadia* 1933 (a); *Come on Marines* 1934 (a); *Ready For Love* 1934 (a); *Search For Beauty* 1934 (a); *Paris in Spring* 1935 (a); *Peter Ibbetson* 1935 (a); *Smart Girl* 1935 (a); *Anything Goes* 1936 (a); *The Gay Desperado* 1936 (a); *One Rainy Afternoon* 1936 (a); *Yours For the Asking* 1936 (a); *Artists and Models* 1937 (a); *Fight For Your Lady* 1937 (a); *Let's Get Married* 1937 (a); *Sea Devils* 1937 (a); *The Adventures of Sherlock Holmes* 1939 (a); *The Lady and the Mob* 1939 (a); *The Light That Failed* 1939 (a); *The Lone Wolf Spy Hunt* 1939 (a); *They Drive By Night* 1940 (a); *High Sierra* 1941 (a); *Ladies in Retirement* 1941 (a); *Out of the Fog* 1941 (a); *The Sea Wolf* 1941 (a); *The Hard Way* 1942 (a); *Life Begins at Eight-Thirty* 1942 (a); *Moontide* 1942 (a); *Forever and a Day* 1943 (a); *Thank Your Lucky Stars* 1943 (a); *Hollywood Canteen* 1944 (a); *In Our Time* 1944 (a); *Pillow to Post* 1945 (a); *Devotion* 1946 (a); *The Man I Love* 1946 (a); *Young Widow* 1946 (uncred.p); *Deep Valley* 1947 (a); *Escape Me Never* 1947 (a); *Road House* 1948 (a); *Lust For Gold* 1949 (a); *Not Wanted* 1949 (p,sc,uncred.d); *Never Fear* 1950 (d,sc,story); *Outrage* 1950 (d,sc,story); *Woman in Hiding* 1950 (a); *Hard, Fast and Beautiful* 1951 (a,d); *On Dangerous Ground* 1951 (a); *Beware, My Lovely* 1952 (a); *The Bigamist* 1953 (a,d); *The Hitch-Hiker* 1953 (d,sc); *Jennifer* 1953 (a); *Private Hell 36* 1954 (a,sc); *The Big Knife* 1955 (a); *Women's Prison* 1955 (a); *Strange Intruder* 1956 (a); *While The City Sleeps* 1956 (a); *The Trouble With Angels* 1966 (d); *Backtrack* 1969 (a); *Junior Bonner* 1972 (a); *The Devil's Rain* 1975 (a); *The Food Of The Gods* 1975 (a); *My Boys Are Good Boys* 1978 (a); *Deadhead Miles* 1982 (a).

Lurie, John • American actor; also musician, composer. • Impossibly hip leading light of New York's downtown music scene, primarily with his group the Lounge Lizards. Lurie is best known for his deadpan performances in the films of Jim Jarmusch, to which he has also contributed distinctive scores. • *Permanent Vacation* 1980 (a,m,m.perf,saxophonist); *Underground U.S.A.* 1980 (a); *The Loveless* 1981 (add.m); *Subway Riders* 1981 (a,m,saxophonist); *Variety* 1983 (m); *Paris, Texas* 1984 (a); *Stranger Than Par-*

adise 1984 (a,m); *Desperately Seeking Susan* 1985 (a); *Down By Law* 1986 (a,m); *Slam Dance* 1987 (add.m); *The Last Temptation of Christ* 1988 (a); *Il Piccolo Diavolo* 1988 (a); *Mystery Train* 1989 (m,guitarist,harmonica player); *Wild at Heart* 1990 (a); *Jusqu'au bout du monde/Till the End of the World* 1991 (a).

Lye, Len • Animator; also painter, sculptor. • Born Christchurch, New Zealand, July 5, 1901; died 1980. *Educ.* Wellington Technical College; Canterbury College of Fine Arts, Christchurch. Painter and sculptor turned animator who served in John Greirson's GPO unit, where he made documentaries and publicity films. In 1934 Lye developed a new technique for applying paint directly to film, which he introduced in his animated short, *A Colour Box* (1935). He later experimented with techniques involving images scratched onto film stock and with what he called "kinetic sculpture." • *Tusalava* 1929 (anim,d); *Experimental Animation* 1933 (anim,d); *A Colour Box* 1935 (d); *Kaleidoscope* 1935 (anim,d); *The Birth of the Robot* 1936 (anim,d); *Rainbow Dance* 1936 (d); *Full Fathom Five* 1937 (anim,d); *Trade Tattoo* 1937 (d); *Colour Flight* 1938 (anim,d); *He Loved an Actress* 1938 (fx); *N. or N.W.* 1938 (d); *Musical Poster No. 1* 1940 (anim,d); *Swinging the Lambeth Walk* 1940 (anim,d); *Newspaper Train (short)* 1941 (d); *Wheatmeal Bread (short)* 1941 (d); *When the Pie Was Opened (short)* 1941 (d); *Work Party (short)* 1941 (d); *Collapsible Metal Tubes (short)* 1942 (d); *Factory Family (short)* 1943 (d); *Kill or Be Killed (short)* 1943 (d); *Planned Crops (short)* 1943 (d); *Basic English (short)* 1944 (d); *Cameramen at War (short)* 1944 (d); *Peace* 1950 (d); *Bells of Atlantis (short)* 1952 (sfx—color); *Color Cry* 1953 (d); *Free Radicals* 1958 (d); *Particles in Space* 1969 (d); *Tal Farlow* 1981 (d).

Lynch, David • Director, writer; also actor. • Born Missoula, MT, January 20, 1946. *Educ.* Corcoran School of Art, Washington DC (painting); Boston Museum School; Philadelphia Academy of Fine Arts; Center for Advanced Film Studies, Los Angeles. This Hollywood envoy of the avant-garde has had one of the more unlikely odysseys to film success. Lynch, a son of a Department of Agriculture tree scientist, was born in Montana and spent his youth in Idaho, Washington and Alexandria, Virginia. On the basis of *The Alphabet* (1968), a five-minute short combining live action and animation, Lynch received a grant from the American Film Institute to make a 34-minute film, *The Grandmother* (1970). Over a five-year period, working in and around the AFI's Center for Advanced Film Studies in Los Angeles, he created *Eraserhead* (1977), a perverse stream of sub-consciousness, a nightmarish vision packed with grotesque physical deformities and an unlikely quest for spiritual purity.

Mel Brooks saw *Eraserhead* and thought Lynch a kindred "madman" who would be the perfect director to film a script Brooks wanted to produce about John Merrick—a man whose exterior was as hideous as his soul was beautiful. Lynch's film about this real person, who was hideously deformed by disease, *The Elephant Man* (1980), was an elegy to the freakishness of the human condition disguised as a piece of Victorian morality theater. Exploring territory similar to *Eraserhead*, Lynch exposed undercurrents of metaphysical anguish and absurdist fear, but the accessible humanity within Merrick's tale made the film a box-office success and earned it eight Academy Award nominations, including one for best director.

Lynch was offered the third Star Wars film, *Return of the Jedi*, but opted to advance his script *Ronnie Rocket* at Francis Coppola's Zoetrope Studios. This project did not materialize, and Lynch waded into deep water with producer Dino DeLaurentiis, who owned the rights to Frank Herbert's byzantine, epic science fiction novel, *Dune*. Lynch once described *Dune* (1985), which was released in drastically shortened form, as "a garbage compactor. Things are supposed to be mysterious, not confusing." This striking, underrated, but nevertheless muddled production only partly revealed Lynch's concerns and was a box-office failure.

He was back in true form with *Blue Velvet* (1986), a quasiautobiographical transit through zones of Kafka, Bosch, Bunuel, Capra and Hitchcock that Lynch has described as "The Hardy Boys Go to Hell." In this scatological film noir, composed as if inspired by the ambience of a nightmarish asylum, collegiately handsome Kyle MacLachlan stumbles upon, and is subsumed in, a crucible of child abduction, drug wars, voyeurism, sexual abuse, small town corruption, and compulsive souls desperate to find truth in a dimension that seems to be devoid of meaningful questions. Sensuous details mix with a painterly neo-Gothic eye for the bizarre. All is the opposite of what it seems: Neat, placid surfaces cloak macabre "reality" and the outwardly horrible is ultimately the most benign. Malignant impulses fester deep within people and things. Dennis Hopper's manic performance as Frank catapults that character into the stratosphere of cinema psychos. The surreal conclusion gives us pause — where does the dream end and the temporal world begin?

Lynch's characters inhabit the outer fringes of society and mind. He is obsessed with texture and tension, sexual and biological functions (and dysfunctions), moods and sensation. Industrial images and sounds reinforce the machine metaphor of artificial reality. "Finding love in hell may be a theme in all my movies," he has said.

In 1990, Lynch ventured into television with "Twin Peaks," a more discreet cut of *Blue Velvet* fabric, and directed *Wild at Heart*, a "road" movie and unlikely paean to *The Wizard of Oz*. MDM • *The Alphabet* (short) 1968 (d,sc,ph,ed,anim,pd,sound,song); *The Grandmother* (short) 1970 (a,d,p,sc,ph,ed,anim,sound effects); *Eraserhead* 1977 (d,p,sc,ed,pd,fx,lyrics "In Heaven [Everything Is Fine]"); *The Elephant Man* 1980 (d,sc,sound design) **(AANBD,AANBSC)**; *Dune* 1985 (d,sc); *Blue Velvet* 1986 (d,lyrics "Blue Star"; "Mysteries of Love",sc,song) **(AANBD)**; *Weeds* 1987 (song); *Zelly and Me* 1988 (a); *Hollywood Mavericks* 1990 (a); *Wild at Heart* 1990 (d,sc,song); *The Cabinet of Dr. Ramirez* 1991 (exec.p).

Lynch, Kelly • American actress • Born c. 1959. Former model who began her acting career in TV and turned in several decorative film performances in the late 1980s. Lynch attracted serious critical attention with a moving, resolutely unglamorous performance as a heroin addict in Gus Van Sant's grim, picaresque *Drugstore Cowboy* (1989). • *Osa* 1985; *Bright Lights, Big City* 1988; *Cocktail* 1988; *Drugstore Cowboy* 1989; *Road House* 1989; *Warm Summer Rain* 1989; *Desperate Hours* 1990.

Lyne, Adrian • English director • Began his career, like contemporaries Tony and Ridley Scott and Alan Parker, directing the kind of glossy commercials which get screened at New York's Museum of Modern Art. Lyne first established himself on the international scene with *Flashdance* (1983) and scored a huge box-office hit with *Fatal Attraction* (1987). • *Foxes* 1980; *Flashdance* 1983; *9 1/2 Weeks* 1986; *Fatal Attraction* 1987 **(AANBD)**; *Jacob's Ladder* 1990.

MacArthur, Charles • Screenwriter; also director, playwright. • Born Scranton, PA, May 5, 1895; died 1956. Former Chicago journalist who teamed up with Ben Hecht to write several Broadway hits, including *The Front Page* (1928) and *Twentieth Century* (1932), before turning his attentions to Hollywood. MacArthur's best work as both writer (*Barbary Coast* 1935, *Wuthering Heights* 1939) and director (*Crime Without Passion* 1934, *The Scoundrel* 1935) was done in collaboration with Hecht. MacArthur married actress Helen Hayes in 1928 and their adopted son is actor James MacArthur. • *Billy the Kid* 1930 (add.dial); *The Girl Said No* 1930 (dial); *Paid* 1930 (sc); *Way For a Sailor* 1930 (add.dial,uncred.sc); *The Front Page* 1931 (from play); *New Adventures of Get Rich Quick Wallingford* 1931 (sc,adapt); *The Sin of Madelon Claudet* 1931 (sc,dial,cont); *The Unholy Garden* 1931 (sc); *Wallingford* 1931 (adapt); *Rasputin and the Empress* 1932 (sc) **(AANBST)**; *Crime Without Passion* 1934 (a,d,p,sc); *Twentieth Century* 1934 (sc,from play); *Barbary Coast* 1935 (sc,story); *Once in a Blue Moon* 1935 (d,p,sc); *The Scoundrel* 1935 (a,d,p,sc,story) **(AABST)**; *Soak the Rich* 1936 (d,p,sc,from play); *Gunga Din* 1939 (adapt,story); *Wuthering Heights* 1939 (sc) **(AANBSC)**; *His Girl Friday* 1940 (from play *The Front Page*); *I Take This Woman* 1940 (from play); *The Senator Was Indiscreet* 1947 (sc); *Lulu Belle* 1948 (from play); *Perfect Strangers* 1950 (from play *Ladies and Gentlemen*); *Billy Rose's Jumbo* 1962 (from play); *The Front Page* 1974 (from play); *Switching Channels* 1988 (from play *The Front Page*).

Macchio, Ralph • Actor • Born Long Island, NY, November 4, 1962. Young lead best known as *The Karate Kid* (1984); formerly on TV's "Eight Is Enough." • *Up the Academy* 1980; *The Outsiders* 1983; *The Karate Kid* 1984; *Teachers* 1984; *Crossroads* 1986; *The Karate Kid Part II* 1986; *Distant Thunder* 1988; *The Karate Kid Part III* 1989; *Too Much Sun* 1991.

MacCorkindale, Simon • Actor; also producer, screenwriter. • Born England, February 2, 1952. Young British leading man who emerged in the late 1970s in films such as *Death on the Nile* (1978) and formed his own production company, Amy International, in the late 80s. MacCorkindale has also worked extensively in TV. Married to actress Susan George. • *Death on the Nile* 1978 (a); *The Quatermass Conclusion* 1979 (a); *The Riddle of the Sands* 1979 (a); *Caboblanco* 1980 (a); *The Sword and the Sorcerer* 1982 (a); *Jaws 3-D* 1983 (a); *Sincerely, Violet* 1987 (a); *Stealing Heaven* 1988 (p); *That Summer of White Roses* 1989 (p,sc).

MacDonald, Jeanette • Actress; also singer. • Born Jeanette Anne MacDonald, Philadelphia, PA, June 18, 1901; died 1965. Broadway singer who entered films in 1929 under the auspices of Ernst Lubitsch and starred in a number of his films, often opposite Maurice Chevalier. In 1935 MacDonald made *Naughty Marietta*, the first in a series of films co-starring Nelson Eddy (and mostly directed by W.S. Van Dyke) that turned the couple into one of Hollywood's most popular singing teams. After WWII MacDonald turned to a successful concert hall career. She married actor Gene Raymond in 1937 and her sister was actress Marie Blake. • *The Love Parade* 1929; *Let's Go Native* 1930; *The Lottery Bride* 1930; *Monte Carlo* 1930; *Oh, For a Man!* 1930; *Paramount on Parade* 1930; *The Vagabond King* 1930; *Annabelle's Affairs* 1931; *Don't Bet on Women* 1931; *Love Me Tonight* 1932; *One Hour With You* 1932; *The Cat and the Fiddle* 1934; *The Merry Widow* 1934; *Naughty Marietta* 1935; *Rose Marie* 1936; *San Francisco* 1936; *The Firefly* 1937; *Maytime* 1937; *The Girl of the Golden West* 1938; *Sweethearts* 1938; *Broadway Serenade* 1939; *Bitter Sweet* 1940; *New Moon* 1940; *Smilin' Through* 1941; *Cairo* 1942; *I Married an Angel* 1942; *Follow the Boys* 1944; *Three Daring Daughters* 1948; *The Sun Comes Up* 1949.

MacDonald, Joseph P. • *aka* Joe MacDonald • Director of photography • Born Joseph Patrick MacDonald, Mexico City, December 15, 1906; died 1968. *Educ.* USC, Los Angeles (mining engineering). Black-and-white and color cinematographer, long with 20th Century-Fox. MacDonald worked often for Henry Hathaway (*Call Northside 777* 1948, *Niagara* 1953) and made notable contributions to films by Elia Kazan (*Viva Zapata!* 1952) and Samuel Fuller (*Pickup on South Street* 1953), among others. • *We Moderns* 1925 (cam.asst); *Hat Check Girl* 1932 (cam.op); *Rebecca of Sunnybrook Farm* 1932 (cam.op); *Marie Galante* 1934 (cam.op); *Rosa de Francia* 1935 (ph); *Charlie Chan in Rio* 1941 (ph); *Sun Valley Serenade* 1941 (cam.op); *Little Tokyo U.S.A.* 1942 (ph); *The Man Who Wouldn't Die* 1942 (ph); *The Postman Didn't Ring* 1942 (ph); *Quiet, Please, Murder* 1942 (ph); *That Other Woman* 1942 (ph); *Wintertime* 1943 (ph); *The Big Noise* 1944 (ph); *In the Meantime, Darling* 1944 (ph); *Sunday Dinner For a Soldier* 1944 (ph); *Behind Green Lights* 1945 (ph); *Captain Eddie* 1945 (ph); *The Dark Corner* 1946 (ph); *My Darling Clementine* 1946 (ph); *Shock* 1946 (ph); *Call Northside 777* 1948 (ph); *The Street With No Name* 1948 (ph); *Yellow Sky* 1948 (ph); *Down to the Sea in Ships* 1949 (ph); *It Happens Every Spring* 1949 (ph); *Pinky* 1949 (ph); *Panic in the Streets* 1950 (ph); *Stella* 1950 (ph); *As Young As You Feel* 1951 (ph); *Fourteen Hours* 1951 (ph); *U.S.S. Tea Kettle* 1951 (ph); *Diplomatic Courier* 1952 (2u ph); *O. Henry's Full House* 1952 (ph); *Viva Zapata!* 1952 (ph); *What Price Glory* 1952 (ph); *How to Marry a Millionaire* 1953 (ph); *Niagara* 1953 (ph); *Pickup on South Street* 1953 (ph); *Titanic* 1953 (ph); *White Witch Doctor* 1953 (uncred.ph); *Broken Lance* 1954 (ph); *Hell and High Water* 1954 (ph); *The New Venezuela (short)* 1954 (ph); *Woman's World* 1954 (ph); *House of Bamboo* 1955 (ph); *The Racers* 1955 (ph); *The View From Pompey's Head* 1955 (ph); *Bigger Than Life* 1956 (ph); *Hilda Crane* 1956 (ph); *On the Threshold of Space* 1956 (ph); *Teenage Rebel* 1956 (ph); *A Hatful of Rain* 1957 (ph); *The True Story of Jesse James* 1957 (ph); *Will Success Spoil Rock Hunter?* 1957 (ph); *The Fiend Who Walked the West* 1958 (ph); *Ten North Frederick* 1958 (ph); *The Young Lions* 1958 (ph) **(AANBPH)**; *Warlock* 1959 (ph); *The Gallant Hours* 1960 (ph); *Pepe* 1960 (ph) **(AANBPH)**; *The Last Time I Saw Archie* 1961 (ph); *40 Pounds of Trouble* 1962 (ph); *Taras Bulba* 1962 (ph); *Walk on the Wild Side* 1962 (ph); *Kings of the Sun* 1963 (ph); *The List of Adrian Messenger* 1963 (ph); *The Carpetbaggers* 1964 (ph); *Flight From Ashiya* 1964 (ph); *Invitation to a Gunfighter* 1964 (ph); *Rio Conchos* 1964 (ph); *Where Love Has Gone* 1964 (ph); *Mirage* 1965 (ph); *The Reward* 1965 (ph); *Alvarez Kelly* 1966 (ph); *Blindfold* 1966 (ph); *The Sand Pebbles* 1966 (ph) **(AANBPH)**; *A Guide For the Married Man* 1967 (ph); *MacKenna's Gold* 1969 (ph); *Gas-s-s-s!* 1970 (m); *'68* 1987 (song); *The Last Winter* 1989 (p); *The Old Believers* 1989 (p); *Moss Rose* 1947 (ph).

MacDonald, Richard • Production designer • Born Bristol, England, 1919. *Educ.* Royal College of Art, London. Acclaimed art director whose designs have contributed strongly to the ambience of such films as *The Servant* (1963), *A Severed Head* (1970) and *Plenty* (1985). A frequent collaborator with Joseph Losey, MacDonald made uncredited contributions to several of the blacklisted director's films in the 1950s. • *The Sleeping Tiger* 1954 (pd consultant); *A Man on the Beach (short)* 1955 (pd consultant); *Summertime* 1955 (titles painter); *Finger of Guilt* 1956 (pd consultant); *Time Without Pity* 1957 (pd consultant); *The Gypsy and the Gentleman* 1958 (pd consultant); *Blind Date* 1959 (pd consultant); *The Criminal* 1960 (pd); *Eva* 1962 (pd); *These Are the Damned* 1962 (pd consultant); *The Servant* 1963 (pd); *King and Country* 1964 (pd); *Modesty Blaise* 1966 (pd); *Far From the Madding Crowd* 1967 (pd); *Boom!* 1968 (pd); *Secret Ceremony* 1968 (pd); *A Severed Head* 1970 (pd); *Bloomfield* 1971 (pd); *The Go-Between* 1971 (titles); *The Assassination of Trotsky* 1972 (pd); *A Doll's House* 1973 (titles); *Jesus Christ Superstar* 1973 (pd); *Galileo* 1974 (pd); *The Day of the Locust* 1975 (pd); *The Romantic Englishwoman* 1975 (pd); *Marathon Man* 1976 (pd); *Exorcist II: The Heretic* 1977 (pd); *F.I.S.T.* 1978 (pd); *And Justice For All* 1979 (pd); *The Rose* 1979 (pd); *Altered States* 1980 (pd); *Cannery Row* 1982 (pd); *Something Wicked This Way Comes*

1983 (pd); *Crimes of Passion* 1984 (pd); *Electric Dreams* 1984 (pd); *Supergirl* 1984 (pd); *Teachers* 1984 (pd); *Plenty* 1985 (pd); *SpaceCamp* 1986 (pd); *Coming to America* 1988 (pd); *The Russia House* 1990 (pd).

MacDowell, Andie • Actress; also model. • Born Rose Anderson MacDowell, South Carolina. Successful model whose film debut opposite Christopher Lambert in *Greystoke: The Legend of Tarzan, Lord of the Apes* (1984) was notable primarily for the fact that her voice was dubbed by actress Glenn Close. MacDowell's breakthrough came with a critically praised performance as a repressed Southern wife in Steven Soderbergh's *sex, lies, and videotape* (1989). • *Greystoke: The Legend of Tarzan, Lord of the Apes* 1984; *St. Elmo's Fire* 1985; *sex, lies, and videotape* 1989; *Green Card* 1990; *Hudson Hawk* 1991; *The Object of Beauty* 1991.

MacGraw, Ali • Actress • Born Alice MacGraw, Pound Ridge, NY, April 1, 1938. *Educ.* Wellesley College, MA (art history). Former model who gained instant stardom with *Goodbye, Columbus* (1969) and *Love Story* (1970), but has since made only occasional screen appearances. Married first to studio executive Robert Evans, and then to actor Steve McQueen (1973-1978). Son Josh Evans is also an actor. • *Goodbye, Columbus* 1969; *Love Story* 1970 **(AANBA)**; *The Getaway* 1972; *Convoy* 1978; *Players* 1979; *Just Tell Me What You Want* 1980.

Mackendrick, Alexander • Director; also screenwriter. • Born Boston, MA, 1912. *Educ.* Glasgow School of Art. Gifted director whose films are marked by fine writing and acting; best known for his ingenious Ealing comedies of the 1950s. Born to Scottish parents in the US and raised in Scotland, Mackendrick worked in advertising and then made propaganda shorts during WWII. In 1946 he joined Ealing Studios, co-writing a number of Basil Dearden movies before making his directing debut with the comedy classic *Tight Little Island* (1949). It was followed by several sharply observed comedies, such as *The Man in the White Suit* (1951) and *The Ladykillers* (1955), both starring Alec Guiness and both superb examples of the Ealing style.

Mackendrick's ability to elicit outstanding performances from his actors, particularly children, is displayed in *Crash of Silence* (1952) and *A High Wind in Jamaica* (1965). He also directed Tony Curtis in two of his best performances, as the opportunistic press agent in the scathing *Sweet Smell of Success* (1957) and in the Southern Californian comedy *Don't Make Waves* (1967). In 1969 Mackendrick was appointed Dean of the Film and Video Department at the California Institute of the Arts, an institution with which he is still connected. • *Midnight Menace* 1937 (story); *Saraband For Dead Lovers* 1948 (sc); *Tight Little Island* 1949 (d); *Whisky Galore!* 1949 (d); *The Blue Lamp* 1950 (add.dial,uncred.2ud); *Dance Hall* 1950 (sc); *The Man in the White Suit* 1951 (d,sc) **(AANBSC)**; *Crash of Silence* 1952 (d); *Mandy* 1952 (d); *High and Dry* 1954 (d); *The Ladykillers* 1955 (d); *Sweet Smell of Success* 1957 (d); *Fanfare* 1958 (script assistance); *The Devil's Disciple* 1959 (d); *The Guns of Navarone* 1961 (d); *Sammy Going South* 1963 (d); *A High Wind in Jamaica* 1965 (d); *Don't Make Waves* 1967 (d); *Oh Dad, Poor Dad, Mamma's Hung You in the Closet and I'm Feelin' So Sad* 1967 (d).

Mackenzie, John • Director • Born Britain, 1932. Film and TV director who won critical acclaim for *The Long Good Friday* (1980), a ganster thriller noted for its fine central performances by Bob Hoskins and Helen Mirren. • *One Brief Summer* 1970; *Umman, Wittering and Zigo* 1971; *Made* 1972; *The Long Good Friday* 1980; *Beyond the Limit* 1983; *The Innocent* 1984; *A Sense of Freedom* 1985; *The Fourth Protocol* 1987; *The Last of the Finest* 1989.

MacLachlan, Kyle • Actor • Born U.S.A., 1960. Clean-cut young lead who has served as the protagonist of much of David Lynch's work, beginning with the sci-fi epic, *Dune* (1984). Maclachlan is best known for his deadpan performance as an ingenuous teenage sleuth in *Blue Velvet* (1986) and as the super-efficient FBI man with a weakness for non-sequiturs in Lynch's cult TV series, "Twin Peaks" (1990). • *Dune* 1984; *Blue Velvet* 1986; *The Hidden* 1987; *Don't Tell Her It's Me* 1990; *The Doors* 1991.

MacLaine, Shirley • Actress; also author. • Born Shirley MacLean Beaty, Richmond, VA, April 24, 1934. *Educ.* Washington School of the Ballet. Discovered by talent scouts after being pulled from the chorus to replace lead Carol Haney in the hit Broadway musical *Pajama Game* (1954), MacLaine made her screen debut in Alfred Hitchcock's whimsical *The Trouble With Harry* (1955) and gave memorable performances in such films as *Some Came Running* (1958), *The Apartment* (1960) and *Irma La Douce* (1963). MacLaine, who was earlier associated with the Hollywood "Rat Pack" (Frank Sinatra, Dean Martin, Sammy Davis Jr., etc.), displayed a more serious side of her character in the late 1960s when she became actively involved in liberal politics. She also began working extensively in TV and on stage and published the first of several best-selling autobiographical works, *Don't Fall Off the Mountain*, in 1970. MacLaine received renewed attention as a film actress in the 1980s, earning an Oscar for her role in James Brooks's 1983 tear-jerker, *Terms of Endearment*. Her continuing autobiographical installments (e.g, 1983's *Out on a Limb*) have provoked some amusement for their theories of "out-of-body" experiences and reincarnation. MacLaine is the sister of Warren Beatty and is divorced from producer Steve Parker. Her daughter Sachi Parker is an actress. • *Artists and Models* 1955; *The Trouble With Harry* 1955; *Around the World in 80 Days* 1956; *Hot Spell* 1958; *The Matchmaker* 1958; *The Sheepman* 1958; *Some Came Running* 1958 **(AANBA)**; *Ask Any Girl* 1959; *Career* 1959; *The Apartment* 1960 **(AANBA)**; *Can-Can* 1960; *Ocean's Eleven* 1960; *All in a Night's Work* 1961; *The Children's Hour* 1961; *Two Loves* 1961; *My Geisha* 1962; *Two For the Seesaw* 1962; *Irma la Douce* 1963 **(AANBA)**; *John Goldfarb, Please Come Home* 1964; *What a Way to Go!* 1964; *The Yellow Rolls-Royce* 1964; *Gambit* 1966; *Woman Times Seven* 1967; *The Bliss of Mrs. Blossom* 1968; *Sweet Charity* 1969; *Two Mules For Sister Sara* 1970; *Desperate Characters* 1971; *The Possession of Joel Delaney* 1972; *The Year of the Woman* 1973; *The Other Half of the Sky: A China Memoir* 1974 (a,d,exec.p,sc) **(AANBDOC)**; *Sois belle et tais-toi* 1977; *The Turning Point* 1977 **(AANBA)**; *Being There* 1979; *A Change of Seasons* 1980; *Loving Couples* 1980; *Cannonball Run II* 1983; *Terms of Endearment* 1983 **(AABA)**; *Madame Sousatzka* 1988; *Steel Magnolias* 1989; *Postcards From the Edge* 1990; *Waiting For the Light* 1990.

MacMurray, Fred • Actor • Born Fredrick Martin MacMurray, Kankakee, IL, August 30, 1908. *Educ.* Carroll College, Wisconsin. Started his career as a saxophonist and singer and began landing leading film roles in the 1930s, mostly in light comedies and dramas. MacMurray was primarily seen as a benign husband/father figure, despite a memorable performance as the murderous insurance man in *Double Indemnity* (1944) and hard-boiled roles in *The Caine Mutiny* and *Pushover* (both 1954), as well as several westerns. He starred as the father on the long-running TV show "My Three Sons" (1960-1971). McMurray married actress June Haver in 1954, after the death of his first wife Lillian Lamont. • *Girls Gone Wild* 1929; *Tiger Rose* 1929; *Alice Adams* 1935; *Car 99* 1935; *Grand Old Girl* 1935; *Hands Across the Table* 1935; *Men Without Names* 1935; *13 Hours By Air* 1936; *The Bride Comes Home* 1936; *The Princess Comes Across* 1936; *The Texas Rangers* 1936; *The Trail of the Lonesome Pine* 1936; *Champagne Waltz* 1937; *Exclusive* 1937; *Maid of Salem* 1937; *Swing High, Swing Low* 1937; *True Confession* 1937; *Cocoanut Grove* 1938; *Men With Wings* 1938; *Sing, You Sinners* 1938; *Cafe Society* 1939; *Honeymoon in Bali* 1939; *Invitation to Happiness* 1939; *Little Old New York* 1940; *Rangers of Fortune* 1940; *Re-*

member the Night 1940; *Too Many Husbands* 1940; *Dive Bomber* 1941; *New York Town* 1941; *One Night in Lisbon* 1941; *Virginia* 1941; *The Forest Rangers* 1942; *The Lady Is Willing* 1942; *Star Spangled Rhythm* 1942; *Take a Letter, Darling* 1942; *Above Suspicion* 1943; *Flight For Freedom* 1943; *The Last Will and Testament of Tom Smith (short)* 1943; *No Time For Love* 1943; *And the Angels Sing* 1944; *Double Indemnity* 1944; *Practically Yours* 1944; *Standing Room Only* 1944; *Captain Eddie* 1945; *Murder, He Says* 1945; *Pardon My Past* 1945; *Where Do We Go From Here?* 1945; *Smoky* 1946; *The Egg and I* 1947; *Singapore* 1947; *Suddenly It's Spring* 1947; *Don't Trust Your Husband* 1948; *Family Honeymoon* 1948; *A Miracle Can Happen* 1948; *The Miracle of the Bells* 1948; *Borderline* 1949; *Father Was a Fullback* 1949; *Never a Dull Moment* 1950; *Callaway Went Thataway* 1951; *A Millionaire For Christy* 1951; *Fair Wind to Java* 1953; *The Moonlighter* 1953; *The Caine Mutiny* 1954; *Pushover* 1954; *Woman's World* 1954; *At Gunpoint* 1955; *The Far Horizons* 1955; *The Rains of Ranchipur* 1955; *There's Always Tomorrow* 1956; *Day of the Badman* 1957; *A Gun For a Coward* 1957; *Quantez* 1957; *Good Day For a Hanging* 1958; *Face of a Fugitive* 1959; *The Oregon Trail* 1959; *The Shaggy Dog* 1959; *The Absent-Minded Professor* 1960; *The Apartment* 1960; *Bon Voyage!* 1962; *How to Get Where You Want to Go (short)* 1962; *Son of Flubber* 1963; *Kisses For My President* 1964; *Follow Me, Boys!* 1966; *Happiest Millionaire* 1967; *Charley and the Angel* 1972; *The Swarm* 1978; *George Stevens: A Filmmaker's Journey* 1985.

MacNicol, Peter • Actor • Born Dallas, TX, 1954. *Educ.* University of Minnesota. Diminutive stage actor who first made his big-screen mark as Stingo, the puppyish writer involved in a love triangle with Meryl Streep, in *Sophie's Choice* (1982). • *Dragonslayer* 1981; *Sophie's Choice* 1982; *Heat* 1987; *Fakebook* 1989; *Ghostbusters II* 1989.

Madigan, Amy • Actress • Born Chicago, IL, 1957. *Educ.* Chicago Conservatory (piano); Marquette University, Milwaukee, WI (philosophy); Lee Strasberg Institute, Los Angeles. Former rock musician turned lead and supporting player of stage, film and TV. Married actor Ed Harris in 1983, with whom she's appeared in Robert Benton's *Places in the Heart* (1984) and Louis Malle's *Alamo Bay* (1985). • *Love Child* 1982; *Love Letters* 1983; *Places in the Heart* 1984; *Streets of Fire* 1984; *Alamo Bay* 1985 (a,song); *Twice in a Lifetime* 1985 **(AANBSA)**; *Crossroads* 1986 (song); *Nowhere to Hide* 1987; *The Prince of Pennsylvania* 1988; *Field of Dreams* 1989; *Uncle Buck* 1989.

Madonna • Singer; also actress, songwriter. • Born Madonna Louise Ciccone, Detroit, MI, August 16, 1959. *Educ.* University of Michigan (dance). Pop-singing sensation of the 1980s who has turned in some less-than-sensational film performances. Madonna's best role was in *Desperately Seeking Susan* (1985), playing a character loosely based on herself. Divorced from actor Sean Penn. • *A Certain Sacrifice* 1983 (a); *Desperately Seeking Susan* 1985 (a,songs); *Vision Quest* 1985 (a,songs); *At Close Range* 1986 (songs); *Shanghai Surprise* 1986 (a); *Who's That Girl* 1987 (a,songs); *Bloodhounds of Broadway* 1989 (a); *Dick Tracy* 1990 (a); *Truth or Dare: On the Road, Behind the Scenes & in Bed With Madonna* 1991 (a,exec.p).

Madsen, Virginia • Actress • Born Winnetka, IL, 1963. *Educ.* Northwestern University (theater). Striking blonde lead who made her screen debut in the 1983 film, *Class*, and landed her first major role as Princess Irulian in David Lynch's overblown sci-fi epic, *Dune* (1984). Madsen gave a commendable performance opposite Anthony Edwards in *Mr. North* (1988), directed by husband Danny Huston. Brother Michael Madsen is also an actor. • *Class* 1983; *Electric Dreams* 1984; *Creator* 1985; *Dune* 1984; *Fire With Fire* 1986; *Modern Girls* 1986; *Slam Dance* 1987; *Zombie High* 1987; *Hot to Trot* 1988; *Mr. North* 1988; *Heart of Dixie* 1989; *The Hot Spot* 1990; *Highlander II - the Quickening* 1991.

Magnani, Anna • Actress • Born Rome, March 7, 1908; died 1973. *Educ.* Accademia d'Arte Drammatica, Rome. Volatile, commanding star of post-war Italian cinema who gained international attention for her performance in Roberto Rossellini's *Open City* (1945). Though her early career had encompassed repertory work, musical comedy and vaudeville, Magnani subsequently tended to land only earthy, maternal roles, as in *The Rose Tattoo* (1955). She was outstanding as the Commedia Dell'Arte actress in Jean Renoir's *The Golden Coach* (1952) and in Rossellini's *L'Amore* (1948). Magnani's marriage to director Goffredo Alessandrini was annulled in 1950 and she later had a child by actor Massimo Serrato. • *La Cieca di Sorrento/The Blind Woman of Sorrento* 1934; *Tempo massimo* 1934; *Cavalleria* 1936; *Trenta secondi d'amore* 1936; *La Principessa Tarakanova* 1938; *Una Lampada alla finestra* 1940; *Teresa Venerdi* 1941; *Finalmente soli* 1942; *La Fortuna viene dal cielo* 1942; *La Fuggitiva* 1942; *L'Avventura di Annabella* 1943; *Campo de'Fiori* 1943; *L'Ultima carrozzella* 1943; *La Vita e bella* 1943; *Il Fiore sotto gli occhi* 1944; *Abbasso la miseria!* 1945; *Quartetto pazzo* 1945; *Roma, citta aperta/Open City* 1945; *Abbasso la ricchezza!* 1946; *Il Bandito* 1946; *Davanti a lui tremava tutta Roma* 1946; *Un Uomo ritorna* 1946; *L' Onorevole Angelina* 1947; *L'Amore* 1948; *Lo Sconosciuto di San Marino* 1948; *Molti Sogni per le Strade* 1949; *Vulcano* 1950; *Bellissima* 1951; *Camicie Rosse* 1951; *La Carosse d'Or/The Golden Coach* 1952; *Siamo Donne* 1953; *Carosello di varieta* 1955; *The Rose Tattoo* 1955 **(AABA)**; *Suor Letizia* 1957; *Wild Is the Wind* 1957 **(AANBA)**; *Nella citta l'inferno* 1958; *Of Life and Love* 1958; *The Fugitive Kind* 1960; *Risate di Gioia* 1960; *Mamma Roma* 1962; *Made in Italy* 1965; *The Secret of Santa Vittoria* 1969; *...Correva l'anno di grazia 1870* 1972; *Roma* 1972; *Io Sono Anna Magnani* 1980 (archival footage).

Magnuson, Ann • Actress; also singer, writer. • Born West Virginia, 1956. *Educ.* Denison University, Ohio (theater). Popular New York performance artist who has gradually drifted into the mainstream, from her appearance opposite David Bowie in Tony Scott's *The Hunger* (1983) to her role as the incorrigibly chic magazine editor on TV's "Anything But Love." Magnuson is probably best known for starring opposite John Malkovich in Susan Seidelman's comedy, *Making Mr. Right* (1987). • *Vortex* 1982; *The Hunger* 1983; *Desperately Seeking Susan* 1985; *Sleepwalk* 1986; *The Critical Years (short)* 1987; *Making Mr. Right* 1987; *Checking Out* 1988; *Heavy Petting* 1988; *Mondo New York* 1988; *A Night in the Life of Jimmy Reardon* 1988; *Tequila Sunrise* 1988; *Love at Large* 1990.

Mahin, John Lee • Screenwriter; also actor. • Born Evanston, IL, 1902; died April 18, 1984, Santa Monica, CA. *Educ.* Harvard. Veteran Hollywood writer, mostly at MGM; instrumental in the formation of the Writers Guild. • *The Unholy Garden* 1931 (uncred.sc); *The Beast of the City* 1932 (sc,cont); *Red Dust* 1932 (sc); *Scarface* 1932 (adapt,dial,cont); *Tiger Shark* 1932 (uncred.sc); *The Wet Parade* 1932 (sc,adapt); *The Blonde Bombshell* 1933 (sc); *Eskimo* 1933 (sc); *Hell Below* 1933 (uncred.a); *The Prizefighter and the Lady* 1933 (sc); *Chained* 1934 (sc); *Laughing Boy* 1934 (sc); *Treasure Island* 1934 (sc); *China Seas* 1935 (uncred.sc); *Naughty Marietta* 1935 (sc); *Riffraff* 1935 (uncred.sc); *Devil Is a Sissy* 1936 (sc); *Love on the Run* 1936 (sc); *Small Town Girl* 1936 (sc); *Wife vs. Secretary* 1936 (sc); *Captains Courageous* 1937 (sc) **(AANBSC)**; *The Last Gangster* 1937 (sc); *A Star Is Born* 1937 (uncred.sc); *Test Pilot* 1938 (uncred.sc); *Too Hot to Handle* 1938 (sc); *Gone With the Wind* 1939 (uncred.sc); *The Wizard of Oz* 1939 (uncred.sc); *Boom Town* 1940 (sc); *Foreign Correspondent* 1940 (uncred.sc); *Dr. Jekyll and Mr. Hyde* 1941 (sc); *Johnny Eager* 1941 (sc); *Tortilla Flat* 1942 (sc); *Woman of the Year* 1942 (uncred.sc); *The Adventures of Tartu* 1943 (sc); *Adventure* 1945 (uncred.sc); *The*

Yearling 1946 (uncred.sc); *Down to the Sea in Ships* 1949 (sc); *Love That Brute* 1950 (sc,story); *Quo Vadis* 1951 (sc); *Show Boat* 1951 (sc); *My Son John* 1952 (uncred.sc); *Mogambo* 1953 (sc); *Elephant Walk* 1954 (sc); *Lucy Gallant* 1955 (sc); *The Bad Seed* 1956 (sc); *Heaven Knows, Mr. Allison* 1957 (sc) (**AANBSC**); *No Time For Sergeants* 1958 (sc); *The Horse Soldiers* 1959 (p,sc); *North to Alaska* 1960 (sc); *The Spiral Road* 1962 (sc); *Moment to Moment* 1966 (sc).

Mahoney, John • Actor • Born Manchester, England, June 20, 1940. *Educ.* Quincy College, IL; Western Illinois University (English). Versatile character player who gave up his job as editor of a medical journal at the age of 37 in order to pursue his acting career. Formerly with Chicago's Steppenwolf Theater, Mahoney is best known as the philandering communications professor who befriends Olympia Dukakis in *Moonstruck* (1987). • *Mission Hill* 1982; *Code of Silence* 1985; *The Manhattan Project* 1986; *Streets of Gold* 1986; *Moonstruck* 1987; *Suspect* 1987; *Tin Men* 1987; *Betrayed* 1988; *Eight Men Out* 1988; *Frantic* 1988; *Say Anything* 1989; *Love Hurts* 1990; *The Russia House* 1990.

Maibaum, Richard • Screenwriter; also producer, actor. • Born New York, NY, May 26, 1909; died January 4, 1991. *Educ.* NYU; University of Iowa. Stage actor who entered films in the mid-1930s as a writer and began to take on production duties after WWII. Maibaum is best known for writing or co-writing most of the "James Bond" screenplays. • *Gold Diggers of 1937* 1936 (from play "Sweet Mystery of Life"); *We Went to College* 1936 (sc); *Live, Love and Learn* 1937 (sc); *They Gave Him a Gun* 1937 (sc); *The Bad Man of Brimstone* 1938 (sc); *Stablemates* 1938 (sc); *The Amazing Mr. Williams* 1939 (sc); *Coast Guard* 1939 (sc); *The Lady and the Mob* 1939 (sc); *The Ghost Comes Home* 1940 (sc); *Twenty Mule Team* 1940 (sc); *I Wanted Wings* 1941 (sc); *Ten Gentlemen From West Point* 1942 (sc); *See My Lawyer* 1945 (from play); *O.S.S.* 1946 (p,sc); *The Big Clock* 1948 (p); *The Sainted Sisters* 1948 (p); *Bride of Vengeance* 1949 (p); *The Great Gatsby* 1949 (p,sc); *Song of Surrender* 1949 (p,sc); *Captain Carey, U.S.A.* 1950 (p); *Dear Wife* 1950 (p); *No Man of Her Own* 1950 (p); *The Red Beret* 1953 (sc); *Hell Below Zero* 1954 (adapt); *The Cockleshell Heroes* 1955 (sc); *Bigger Than Life* 1956 (sc); *Ransom* 1956 (sc,story); *Zarak* 1956 (sc); *No Time to Die* 1958 (sc,story); *The Bandit of Zhobe* 1959 (story); *The Day They Robbed the Bank of England* 1960 (adapt); *Killers of Kilimanjaro* 1960 (adapt); *Battle at Bloody Beach* 1961 (p,sc,story); *Dr. No* 1962 (sc); *From Russia With Love* 1963 (sc); *Goldfinger* 1964 (sc); *Thunderball* 1965 (sc); *Chitty Chitty Bang Bang* 1968 (add.dial); *On Her Majesty's Secret Service* 1969 (sc); *Diamonds Are Forever* 1971 (sc); *The Man With the Golden Gun* 1974 (sc); *The Spy Who Loved Me* 1977 (sc); *For Your Eyes Only* 1981 (sc); *Octopussy* 1983 (sc,story); *A View to a Kill* 1985 (sc); *The Living Daylights* 1987 (sc); *Licence to Kill* 1989 (sc,story).

Mailer, Norman • Novelist; also director, screenwriter. • Born Norman Kingsley Mailer, Long Branch, NJ, January 31, 1923. *Educ.* Harvard (aeronautical engineering); Sorbonne, Paris. Controversial, celebrated post-WWII American writer who first gained recognition at age 25 for his scathing anti-war novel, *The Naked and the Dead* (1948). Mailer directed three "underground" features in the late 1960s and has made appearances in works by avant-garde directors such as Kenneth Anger and Jonas Mekas. His books have been used as the basis for several studio-backed features, one of which, the forgettable, noirish *Tough Guys Don't Dance* (1987), he also directed. Son Michael Mailer is a film producer and daughter Kate is an actress. • *The Naked and the Dead* 1958 (from novel); *An American Dream* 1966 (from novel); *Beyond the Law* 1968 (a,d,ed,p); *Will the Real Norman Mailer Please Stand Up?* 1968 (a); *Diaries, Notes and Sketches* 1969 (a); *Wild 90* 1969 (a,d,p,story,ed); *Double Pisces, Scorpio Rising* 1970 (a); *Maidstone* 1970 (a,d,p,sc,ed); *The Year of the Woman* 1973 (a); *Diaries, Notes & Sketches—Volume 1, Reels 1-6: Lost Lost Lost* 1975 (a); *Town Bloody Hall* 1979 (a); *Ragtime* 1981 (a); *Hello Actors Studio* 1987 (a); *King Lear* 1987 (a); *Tough Guys Don't Dance* 1987 (d,sc—from novel,lyrics "You'll Come Back, You Always Do").

Mainwaring, Daniel • *aka* Geoffrey Homes • Screenwriter; also novelist. • Born Daniel Geoffrey Homes Mainwaring, Oakland, CA, February 27, 1902; died 1977. *Educ.* Fresno College, CA. Prolific scenarist who wrote most of his crime/action novels and screenplays under the name Geoffrey Homes. Perhaps best known for the noir standard, *Out of the Past* (1947), based on his 1946 book, *Build My Gallows High*. • *No Hands on the Clock* 1941 (from novel); *Secrets of the Underground* 1942 (sc,story); *Crime By Night* 1944 (from novel *Forty Whacks*); *Dangerous Passage* 1944 (sc,story); *Scared Stiff* 1945 (sc,story); *Tokyo Rose* 1945 (sc); *Hot Cargo* 1946 (sc); *Swamp Fire* 1946 (sc,story); *They Made Me a Killer* 1946 (sc); *Big Town* 1947 (sc,story); *Out of the Past* 1947 (sc,from novel *Build My Gallows High*); *The Big Steal* 1949 (sc); *Roughshod* 1949 (sc); *The Eagle and the Hawk* 1950 (sc); *The Lawless* 1950 (sc,from novel *The Voice of Stephen Wilder*); *The Last Outpost* 1951 (sc,story); *Roadblock* 1951 (story); *The Tall Target* 1951 (story); *Bugles in the Afternoon* 1952 (sc); *This Woman Is Dangerous* 1952 (sc); *The Hitch-Hiker* 1953 (uncred. from story); *Powder River* 1953 (sc); *Those Redheads From Seattle* 1953 (sc); *Alaska Seas* 1954 (sc); *Black Horse Canyon* 1954 (sc); *The Desperado* 1954 (sc); *Southwest Passage* 1954 (sc); *An Annapolis Story* 1955 (sc); *A Bullet For Joey* 1955 (sc); *The Phenix City Story* 1955 (sc); *Invasion of the Body Snatchers* 1956 (sc); *Thunderstorm* 1956 (sc); *Baby Face Nelson* 1957 (sc); *East of Kilimanjaro* 1957 (story); *Cole Younger, Gunfighter* 1958 (sc); *The Gun Runners* 1958 (sc); *Space Master X-7* 1958 (sc); *La Rivolta degli schiavi* 1960 (dial.,English-language version); *Teseo Contro il Minotauro* 1960 (sc.,English-language version); *Walk Like a Dragon* 1960 (sc); *Atlantis, the Lost Continent* 1961 (sc); *The George Raft Story* 1961 (sc); *Catacombs* 1964 (sc); *Convict Stage* 1965 (sc); *Against All Odds* 1983 (from novel *Build My Gallows High*).

Makavejev, Dusan • Director; also screenwriter. • Born Belgrade, Yugoslavia, October 13, 1932. *Educ.* Belgrade University (psychology); Academy of Theatre, Radio, Film and Television, Belgrade. Dušan Makavejev is the premier figure in Yugoslavian film history; his films are deeply rooted in his nation's painful postwar experiences and draw on important Yugoslavian cinematic and cultural models. Makavejev's work has violated many political and sexual taboos and invited censorship in dozens of nations.

In the 1950s, after studying psychology at Belgrade University, Makavejev became involved in the activities of various film societies and festivals and studied direction at the Academy for Radio, Television and Film. As early as 1953, he began making short films and documentaries and would work in various capacities at both the Zagreb and Avala studios during the late 50s and early 60s. The documentary impulse remains powerful in Makavejev's work, as does the tendency to intercut undigested segments from other films into longer works.

Makavejev enjoyed great critical success with his first three features, *Man Is Not a Bird* (1966), *Love Affair* (1967) and *Innocence Unprotected* (1968). Highly allegorical and relying on techniques derived from Brecht and influenced by Godard, these films were sardonic and anarchistic views of Eastern European state socialist milieux.

Much of Makavejev's work has been uncompromisingly experimental as well as politically outrageous; *W.R.: Mysteries of the Organism* (1971) is the best example of this combination and is the director's most influential work to date. Much of the film is composed of a documentary Makavejev researched in the late 1960s while in the US on a Ford Foundation grant and which was eventually financed by German TV. A witty, passionate, and often rambling account of pioneering psychoanalyst Wilhelm Reich and his American disciples, the material is intercut with a fictitious political-sexual allegory set in contemporary Belgrade. The film was instantly banned in Yugoslavia and made Makavejev persona non grata in his native country until the late 1980s.

Sweet Movie (1974) was made in Canadian exile, with some production resources furnished by the National Film Board of Canada. Also a disjointed, two-part narrative, it again focuses on radical techniques in sexual psychotherapy, here played out rather than verbalized. Intertwined is yet another acidic, allegorical fable of the decay of Yugoslavia's socialist legacy. Extremely violent and sexually explicit, *Sweet Movie* was dismissed (and censored) as pornography in many countries, and added to Makavejev's reputation as a "filmmaker maudit."

Montenegro (1981) has been Makavejev's greatest financial success to date. Political commentary and formal experimentation are subordinated to narrative drive in this story of a housewife (Susan Anspach) who grapples with sexual liberation and fails.

The Coca-Cola Kid (1985), Makavejev's second major international coproduction, was marred by on-set squabbles between actors, and the rejection of Makavejev's intriguing plan to use a long reel of multilingual Coca-Cola commercials as a narrative structuring device. What emerged was a genuinely erotic film which takes a quirky, satiric view both of its Australian setting and the international business world.

Makavejev's long exile from his homeland ended in 1988 with the release of *Manifesto*, a Ruritanian political farce mostly shot in Yugoslavia. Although the film marks the most disciplined, traditional storytelling of Makavejev's career, it has seen only limited bookings in the US. KJH • *Kiše zemlje moje/My Country's Rains* 1963 (a); *Covek Nije Tijka/Man Is Not a Bird* 1966 (d,sc); *Budenje pacova* 1967 (a); *Ljubavni Slucaj/Love Affair/Switchboard Operator* 1967 (d,sc); *Nevinost Bez Zastite/Innocence Unprotected* 1968 (d,sc,decorations); *W.R. Misterije Organizma/WR: Mysteries of the Organism* 1971 (d,p,sc); *I Miss Sonia Henie* 1972 (d); *Sweet Movie* 1974 (d,sc); *Wet Dreams* 1974 (d,sc,song); *Montenegro* 1981 (d,sc); *The Soldier's Tale* 1984 (a); *The Coca-Cola Kid* 1985 (d); *Manifesto* 1988 (d,sc).

Makk, Károly • Director • Born Hungary, 1925. *Educ.* Academy for Theatre and Film Art, Budapest. Key post-war Hungarian director who made several notable films in the 1950s, such as the powerful drama *The House Under the Rocks* (1958), but enjoyed little of the international acclaim showered on Hungarian cinema in the 60s. *Love* (1971), based upon the novel by Tibor Dery, revived Makk's reputation, winning a Special Jury Prize at the 1971 Cannes Film Festival. Like *Love*, Makk's subsequent films have been observant, finely acted works, ranging from *A Very Moral Night* (1977), a light comedy based in a brothel, to the astute, morally and politically charged *Another Way* (1982), about a doomed lesbian relationship in post-1956 Hungary. • *A Harag napja* 1953 (d); *Liliomfi* 1954 (d); *Simon Menyhut Szuletese* 1954 (d); *9-es korterem* 1955 (d); *Mese a 12 talalatrol* 1956 (d); *Haz a sziklak alatt/The House Under the Rocks* 1958 (d); *A 39-es dandar* 1959 (d); *Fure lepni szabad* 1960 (d); *Megszallottak* 1961 (d); *El Veszett paradicsom* 1962 (d); *Utolso elotti ember, Az* 1963 (d); *Mit csinatt felseged 3-tol 5-ig?* 1964 (d); *Bolondos vakacio* 1967 (d); *Isten es ember elott* 1968 (d); *Szerelem/Love* 1971 (d); *Macskajatek* 1974 (d,sc); *Egy Erkolcsos Ejszaka/A Very Moral Night* 1978 (d); *Ket tortenet a felmultbol (a teglafal mogott—Philemon es Baucis)* 1979 (d); *Olelkezo Tekintetek/Another Way* 1982 (d,sc); *Jatszani Kell* 1985 (d); *Utolso Kezirat, Az* 1986 (d,sc).

Malden, Karl • Actor • Born Karl Mladen Sekulovich, Chicago, IL, March 22, 1914. *Educ.* Goodman Theatre School of Drama, Chicago. Large-nosed (he broke it twice as a high school football player) supporting player who made his name in several outstanding movies of the 1950s and 60s. Malden was memorable in three films by Elia Kazan: *A Streetcar Named Desire* (1951), *On the Waterfront* (1954) and, as the bridegroom to Carroll Baker's child bride, *Baby Doll* (1956). He directed a highly effective wartime courtroom drama *Time Limit!* in 1957 and starred in the TV series "The Streets of San Francisco" (1972-77). President, since 1989, of the Academy of Motion Picture Arts and Sciences. • *They Knew What They Wanted* 1940; *Winged Victory* 1944; *13 Rue Madeleine* 1947; *Boomerang* 1947; *The Kiss of Death* 1947; *The Gunfighter* 1950; *Halls of Montezuma* 1950; *Where the Sidewalk Ends* 1950; *The Sellout* 1951; *A Streetcar Named Desire* 1951 **(AABSA)**; *Diplomatic Courier* 1952; *Operation Secret* 1952; *Ruby* 1952; *I Confess* 1953; *Take the High Ground* 1953; *On the Waterfront* 1954 **(AANBSA)**; *Phantom of the Rue Morgue* 1954; *Baby Doll* 1956; *Fear Strikes Out* 1956; *Bombers B-52* 1957; *Time Limit!* 1957 (d); *The Hanging Tree* 1959; *The Great Impostor* 1960; *Pollyanna* 1960; *One-Eyed Jacks* 1961; *Parrish* 1961; *All Fall Down* 1962; *Birdman of Alcatraz* 1962; *Come Fly With Me* 1962; *Gypsy* 1962; *How the West Was Won* 1962; *Cheyenne Autumn* 1964; *Dead Ringer* 1964; *The Cincinnati Kid* 1965; *Murderers' Row* 1966; *Nevada Smith* 1966; *The Adventures of Bullwhip Griffin* 1967; *Billion Dollar Brain* 1967; *Hotel* 1967; *Blue* 1968; *Hot Millions* 1968; *Patton* 1970; *Cat O' Nine Tails* 1971; *Wild Rovers* 1971; *The Summertime Killer* 1972; *Beyond the Poseidon Adventure* 1979; *Meteor* 1979; *The Sting II* 1982; *Suton* 1982; *Billy Galvin* 1986; *Nuts* 1987.

Malick, Terrence • Director; also screenwriter, producer. • Born Illinois, 1942. *Educ.* Harvard; Magdalen College, Oxford; AFI, Los Angeles. Former journalist and MIT philosophy professor who entered films in the early 1970s as a screenwriter. (Malick made uncredited contributions to Jack Nicholson's moody 1971 feature, *Drive, He Said*.) His output as a director has been minimal, yet his contribution to the art has been significant: both *Badlands* (1973) and *Days of Heaven* (1978) rank among the most poignant and richly photographed studies of the American midwest to have been captured on celluloid. • *Drive, He Said* 1971 (uncred.sc); *Pocket Money* 1972 (a,sc); *Badlands* 1973 (a,d,p,sc); *The Gravy Train* 1974 (sc); *Days of Heaven* 1978 (d,sc); *Deadhead Miles* 1982 (sc).

Malkovich, John • Actor • Born Benton, IL, December 9, 1953. *Educ.* Illinois State University. Exceptional stage performer and director who helped found, with Gary Sinise, Chicago's esteemed Steppenwolf Theatre Company before concentrating, since his 1984 film debut in *The Killing Fields*, on his screen career. Memorable as the Vicomte de Valmont, the high priest of seduction in the Stephen Frears/Christopher Hampton adaptation of Choderlos de Laclos's *Dangerous Liaisons* (1988). • *The Killing Fields* 1984; *Places in the Heart* 1984 **(AANBSA)**; *Eleni* 1985; *Private Conversations* 1985; *Empire of the Sun* 1987; *The Glass Menagerie* 1987; *Making Mr. Right* 1987; *The Accidental Tourist* 1988 (exec.p); *Dangerous Liaisons* 1988; *Miles From Home* 1988; *The Sheltering Sky* 1990; *The Object of Beauty* 1991; *Queens Logic* 1991.

Malle, Louis • Director; also producer, screenwriter. • Born Thumeries, France, October 30, 1932. *Educ.* Sorbonne, Paris (political science); IDHEC, Paris. One of the most consistently innovative filmmakers of his generation, Louis Malle has rarely received the critical attention his work deserves. Unlike the other directors most often associated with the French New Wave—Truffaut, Godard, Rohmer, Chabrol—Malle did not contribute criticism to *Cahiers du cinema;* unlike those filmmakers, he came from a privileged background, as an heir to the Beghin sugar fortune. His work is not easily evaluated according to the tenets of the auteur theory promoted by these critics-turned-filmmakers, who emphasized consistently recognizable stylistic or thematic traits in directors' work. From undersea documentaries to *films noirs*, from exposés on poverty to extended dinner conversations, Louis Malle's work could hardly be more diverse.

A graduate of IDHEC (the French government's prestigious filmmaking school), Malle began his career working with Jacques Cousteau on *Le Monde du silence* (1955) and assisting Robert Bresson on *A Condemned Man Escapes* (1956). His first feature was a stylish commercial thriller, *Elevator to the Gallows* (1957). International recognition came the next year with *The Lovers*, a study of upper-class ennui which featured a dazzling performance by Jeanne Moreau and which, due to its sexual frankness, was the first of Malle's films to generate scandal. Others include *Zazie dans le métro* (1960), the story of a foul-mouthed pre-teenager; *The Fire Within* (1963), a masterful study of mental disintegration; *Murmur of the Heart* (1971), a light, comic tale of incest; and *Lacombe Lucien* (1974), whose opportunistic protagonist sets out to become a hero of the Resistance but learns the fine art of political collaboration under the Nazis.

Malle has also produced an impressive body of documentary filmmaking, beginning with his collaboration with Cousteau. In 1969 he released *Calcutta*, an extended exposé of the city's incredible poverty and overpopulation; this was followed by a 6-hour series of documentary films, *Phantom India* (1969), shown originally on French TV. *Place de la République* (1973) featured confrontational remarks by passers-by at this Parisian intersection, and *Humain trop humain* (1973) explored, without recourse to narration, the dehumanizing effects of assembly-line manufacture.

In 1978 Malle returned to provocative fictional subjects with *Pretty Baby*, a tale of child prostitution in WWI-era New Orleans, starring Brooke Shields and Keith Carradine. Two outstanding American films followed: *Atlantic City* (1980) involving a has-been gangster (Burt Lancaster) and a city in transition, and *My Dinner with Andre* (1981), a lengthy conversation between playwright Wallace Shawn and director Andre Gregory.

Au revoir, les enfants (1987) marked Malle's professional return to France. An explicitly autobiographical work about boyhood friendships and betrayal during the German Occupation, it is perhaps his most successful film in terms of public and critical response. Married to actress Candice Bergen since 1980. RDH • *Le Monde du silence* 1955 (d,ph); *Un Condamné à mort s'est échappé/A Condemned Man Escapes* 1956 (prod.asst); *Ascenseur pour l'échafaud/Elevator to the Gallows* 1957 (d,sc,adapt); *Les Amants/The Lovers* 1958 (d,sc); *Calcutta* 1960 (English narration,ph,sc,a,d); *Zazie dans le métro* 1960 (d,sc); *Vie Privée* 1961 (a,d,sc); *Le Combat dans l'île* 1962 (art d.sup); *Vive le Tour!* 1962 (a,d,ph,sc); *Le Feu Follet/The Fire Within* 1963 (d,sc); *Viva Maria* 1965 (d,p,sc,dial,lyrics); *Der Junge Törless* 1966 (art d.sup); *Le Voleur/The Thief of Paris* 1967 (d,p,sc); *Histoires Extraordinaires* 1968 (d); *La Fiancée du pirate (short)* 1969 (a); *Calcutta* 1969 (d,narr,ph,sc); *L' Inde fantôme/Phantom India* 1969 (d,narr,ph); *La Voie Lactee/The Milky Way* 1969 (a); *Le Souffle au coeur/Murmur of the Heart* 1971 (d,sc) **(AANBSC)**; *The Godfather* 1972 (dubbing sup., French-language version); *Humain, trop humain* 1973 (d,p,ph); *Place de la Republique* 1973 (d,p,ph); *Lacôme Lucien* 1974 (d,p,sc); *Black Moon* 1975 (d,sc); *Mort d'un Guide* 1975 (ph); *Pretty Baby* 1978 (d,p,story); *Atlantic City* 1980 (d) **(AANBD)**; *My Dinner With Andre* 1981 (d); *Before the Nickelodeon: The Early Cinema Of Edwin S. Porter* 1982 (a); *Crackers* 1984 (d); *De Weg Naar Bresson* 1984 (a); *Alamo Bay* 1985 (d,p); *Au revoir, les enfants* 1987 (a,d,p,sc,adapt,dial) **(AANBSC)**; *Milou en mai/May Fools* 1990 (d,sc,story).

Malone, Dorothy • Actress • Born Dorothy Eloise Maloney, Chicago, IL, January 30, 1925. *Educ.* Southern Methodist University, Dallas, TX. Brunette (later blonde) leading lady, in films from 1943. Malone gained acclaim in the 1950s for her strong, sensual portrayals, notably in Douglas Sirk's *Written on the Wind* (1956) and *The Tarnished Angels* (1958). She also starred in the TV series "Peyton Place" (1964-1969). Married to actor Jacques Bergerac from 1959 to 1964. • *One Mysterious Night* 1944; *Too Young to Know* 1945; *The Big Sleep* 1946; *Janie Gets Married* 1946; *Night and Day* 1946; *One Sunday Afternoon* 1948; *To the Victor* 1948; *Two Guys From Texas* 1948; *Colorado Territory* 1949; *Flaxy Martin* 1949; *South of St. Louis* 1949; *Convicted* 1950; *The Killer That Stalked New York* 1950; *Mrs. O'Malley and Mr. Malone* 1950; *The Nevadan* 1950; *Saddle Legion* 1951; *The Bushwackers* 1952; *Jack Slade* 1953; *Law and Order* 1953; *Scared Stiff* 1953; *Torpedo Alley* 1953; *Battle Cry* 1954; *The Fast and the Furious* 1954; *The Lone Gun* 1954; *Loophole* 1954; *Private Hell 36* 1954; *Pushover* 1954; *Security Risk* 1954; *Artists and Models* 1955; *At Gunpoint* 1955; *Five Guns West* 1955; *Sincerely Yours* 1955; *Tall Man Riding* 1955; *Young at Heart* 1955; *Pillars of the Sky* 1956; *Tension at Table Rock* 1956; *Written on the Wind* 1956 **(AABSA)**; *Man of a Thousand Faces* 1957; *Quantez* 1957; *Tip on a Dead Jockey* 1957; *The Tarnished Angels* 1958; *Too Much, Too Soon* 1958; *Warlock* 1959; *The Last Voyage* 1960; *The Last Sunset* 1961; *Beach Party* 1963; *Gli Insaziabili* 1969; *Abduction* 1975; *The Man Who Would Not Die* 1975; *The November Plan* 1976; *Golden Rendezvous* 1977; *Good Luck, Miss Wyckoff* 1979; *Winter Kills* 1979; *The Day Time Ended* 1980; *The Being* 1983.

Maltin, Leonard • Critic; also historian • Born New York, NY, c. 1951. *Educ.* NYU (journalism). Popular TV film critic (most notably on "Entertainment Tonight") who began his career at the age of 15 as founder, publisher and editor of *Film Fan Monthly*. Maltin has authored numerous books on the cinema and, since 1969, has been the editor of the popular, annually updated reference book, *TV Movies and Video Guide* (formerly *TV Movies*). His 1971 book, *Behind the Camera*, was a study of motion picture cinematographers.

Maltz, Albert • Screenwriter; also playwright. • Born Brooklyn, NY, 1908; died 1985. *Educ.* Columbia (philosophy); Yale School of Drama. Award-winning author and short-story writer who scripted a number of effective propaganda films (both documentaries and features) during WWII. Maltz's career was curtailed by the activities of HUAC (he was jailed in 1950 as one of the Hollywood Ten), though he wrote several American films under pseudonyms while living in Mexico from 1952 to 1962. He worked uncredited on *The Robe* (1953). • *Afraid to Talk* 1932 (from play *Merry-Go-Round*); *Casablanca* 1942 (uncred.sc); *Razgrom nemetzkikh voisk pod Moskvoi* 1942 (commentary); *This Gun For Hire* 1942 (sc); *Destination Tokyo* 1943 (sc); *Seeds of Freedom* 1943 (dial,from story); *The Man in Half Moon Street* 1944 (uncred.sc); *The House I Live In (short)* 1945 (p,sc) **(AAHON)**; *Pride of the Marines* 1945 (sc) **(AANBSC)**; *Cloak and Dagger* 1946 (sc); *The Red House* 1947 (uncred.sc); *The Naked City* 1948 (sc); *The Hollywood Ten* 1950 (a); *The Robe* 1953 (uncred.sc); *Short Cut to Hell* 1957 (uncred. from sc); *Two Mules For Sister Sara* 1970 (sc); *The Beguiled* 1971 (sc); *The Possession of Joel Delaney* 1972 (sc); *Hangup* 1973 (sc); *Scalawag* 1973 (sc); *Hollywood on Trial* 1976 (a).

Mamet, David • Playwright, screenwriter, director • Born Chicago, IL, November 30, 1947. *Educ.* Goddard College (English); Neighborhood Playouse School of the Theater. Leading American playwright whose spare, gritty work reflects the rhythms of writer Harold Pinter and the attitudes of Mamet's native Chicago. Mamet's first produced screenplay was *The Postman Always Rings Twice* (1981), adapted from the novel by James M. Cain. He then turned out a number of meticulously crafted scripts before making his directorial debut with *House of Games* (1987), a slick, engrossing study of deceit and its various guises. Mamet also wrote and directed the whimsical comedy, *Things Change* (1988). • *The Postman Always Rings Twice* 1981 (sc); *The Verdict* 1982 (sc)

(AANBSC); *About Last Night* 1986 (from play *Sexual Perversity in Chicago*); *Black Widow* 1987 (a); *House of Games* 1987 (d,sc,story); *The Untouchables* 1987 (sc); *Things Change* 1988 (d,sc); *We're No Angels* 1989 (sc).

Mamoulian, Rouben • Director; also producer, writer. • Born Tiflis, Georgia, Russia, October 8, 1897; died December 4, 1987, Woodland Hills, CA. *Educ.* University of Moscow (law); Vakhtangov Studio, Moscow Art Theater; King's College; University of London (drama). Rouben Mamoulian, director of numerous theatrical productions and sixteen films, was known especially for his innovative use of the camera, sound and color. Mamoulian's work was guided by his creative instinct, informed intelligence and staunch independence, and emphasized stylization over naturalism.

Born in Russia to cultured Armenian parents, Mamoulian obtained a degree in criminal law from Moscow University but studied at night at the Moscow Art Theatre under Eugene Vakhtangov, a disciple of Stanislavsky. He founded a drama studio in Tiflis in 1918 and later toured England with the Russian Repertory Theatre. Mamoulian directed a hit play in London, *The Beating on the Door*, which led George Eastman to invite him to Rochester, New York, in 1923 to organize and direct the new American Opera Company. In 1926 he began teaching and directing at the Theatre Guild. Mamoulian's first Broadway show was the highly successful *Porgy* in 1927, a vivid production with an all-black cast; he would later use the play's inventive opening "symphony" of street noises in his film *Love Me Tonight* (1932).

Paramount invited Mamoulian to direct the film *Applause* at its Astoria, New York, studio in 1929. In the very early, awkward days of sound films, Mamoulian managed to liberate the camera from its sound-proof booth and also introduce the use of dual mikes and soundtracks, techniques which elevated this clichéd story of a fading burlesque queen (Helen Morgan) and her innocent daughter. In the gangster film, *City Streets* (1931), starring Gary Cooper, Mamoulian explored tracking shots and subjective sound. *Dr. Jekyll and Mr. Hyde* (1932) was striking in its use of subjective camera—the mystifying transformation of Fredric March was shown in one continous shot—and its emphasis on psychological tension. The witty and inventive musical *Love Me Tonight*, featuring Maurice Chevalier, Jeanette MacDonald and the music of Rodgers and Hart, was deliberately stylized, conceived in rhythmic terms.

Mamoulian next directed Marlene Dietrich in *Song of Songs* (1933) and Greta Garbo in *Queen Christina* (1933), the latter film particularly notable for its final, sustained close-up, where Garbo was instructed to remain expressionless so that each viewer could project onto her face whatever emotion he or she was feeling. Mamoulian's inventiveness took a new turn with his direction of the spirited Miriam Hopkins in the first three-color Technicolor feature, *Becky Sharp* (1935), in which he used color for dramatic rather than decorative effect. In *Blood and Sand* (1941), Mamoulian again used color in an original way, with images styled after paintings by the Spanish masters.

Mamoulian continued to make interesting films, but his independent nature did not always mix well with the restrictive Hollywood studio system; he was removed from several films, notably *Laura* (1944); *Porgy and Bess* (1959); and *Cleopatra* (1963). His final films included *Summer Holiday* (1948), a musical version of Eugene O'Neill's *Ah, Wilderness!* starring Mickey Rooney, and *Silk Stockings* (1957), a stylish musical remake of *Ninotchka* featuring Fred Astaire and Cyd Charisse.

In addition to his film work, Mamoulian also continued his distinguished career as a Broadway director, with such productions as *Porgy and Bess*, Gershwin's 1935 musical adaptation of *Porgy;* the immensely successful *Oklahoma!* (1943), the first musical to use song and dance expressly to advance the plot; *Carousel* (1945); and *Lost in the Stars* (1949). In his later years, Mamoulian occupied himself with writing; he adapted several plays, wrote a children's book, *Abigayil* (1964), and a drama textbook, *Hamlet Revised and Interpreted* (1965).

Rediscovery and new appreciation of Mamoulian's innovative work has been spurred by several retrospectives of his films, beginning in 1967 at the Museum of Modern Art, as well as the 1984 restoration of *Becky Sharp.* VMC • *Applause* 1929 (d); *City Streets* 1931 (d); *Dr. Jekyll and Mr. Hyde* 1932 (d,p); *Love Me Tonight* 1932 (d,p); *Queen Christina* 1933 (d); *Song of Songs* 1933 (d,p); *We Live Again* 1934 (d,p); *Becky Sharp* 1935 (d); *The Gay Desperado* 1936 (d); *High, Wide, And Handsome* 1937 (d); *Golden Boy* 1939 (d); *The Mark of Zorro* 1940 (d); *Blood and Sand* 1941 (d); *Rings on Her Fingers* 1942 (d); *Rhapsody in Blue* 1945 (a); *Summer Holiday* 1948 (d); *Gone to Earth* 1950 (d); *Silk Stockings* 1957 (d); *Never Steal Anything Small* 1959 (from play *Devil's Hornpipe*); *George Stevens: A Filmmaker's Journey* 1985; *50 Years of Action!* 1986.

Mancini, Henry • Composer; also songwriter, arranger. • Born Enrico Nicola Mancini, Cleveland, OH, April 16, 1924. *Educ.* Carnegie Institute of Technology, Pittsburgh PA (music); Juilliard (music). Multi award-winning composer whose numerous scores of the 1950s, 60s and 70s were sometimes better known than the films and TV shows they were written for. In 1958 Mancini provided both the hard-boiled theme for Blake Edward's "Peter Gunn" TV show and the latin-accented, percussive score for Orson Welles's classic *Touch of Evil.* Mancini's easy facility across a wide range of popular genres has enabled him to remain one of the leading artists in his field. He has collaborated most consistently with director Blake Edwards. • *Lost in Alaska* 1952 (m); *The Glenn Miller Story* 1954 (m.adapt,song) **(AANBM)**; *Six Bridges to Cross* 1954 (song); *The Benny Goodman Story* 1955 (add.m); *Foxfire* 1955 (song); *Four Girls in Town* 1956 (m.adapt); *Rock, Pretty Baby* 1956 (add.m); *The Unguarded Moment* 1956 (a); *Damn Citizen!* 1957 (m); *Flood Tide* 1957 (m); *Man Afraid* 1957 (m); *The Big Beat* 1958 (add.m); *Summer Love* 1958 (m); *Touch of Evil* 1958 (m); *Voice in the Mirror* 1958 (m); *Never Steal Anything Small* 1959 (m.adapt); *The Great Impostor* 1960 (m); *High Time* 1960 (m); *Bachelor in Paradise* 1961 (m,song) **(AANBS)**; *Breakfast at Tiffany's* 1961 (m,song) **(AABM,AABS)**; *The Second Time Around* 1961 (song); *Days of Wine and Roses* 1962 (m) **(AABS)**; *Experiment in Terror* 1962 (m); *Hatari!* 1962 (m); *Mr. Hobbs Takes a Vacation* 1962 (m); *Charade* 1963 (m) **(AANBS)**; *Soldier in the Rain* 1963 (m); *Dear Heart* 1964 (m) **(AANBS)**; *The Killers* 1964 (song); *Man's Favorite Sport?* 1964 (m,song); *The Pink Panther* 1964 (m) **(AANBM)**; *A Shot in the Dark* 1964 (m,song); *The Great Race* 1965 (m,song) **(AANBS)**; *Arabesque* 1966 (m); *Moment to Moment* 1966 (m); *Walk, Don't Run* 1966 (song); *What Did You Do in the War, Daddy?* 1966 (m); *Gunn* 1967 (m); *Two For the Road* 1967 (m); *Wait Until Dark* 1967 (m); *The Brotherhood* 1968 (song); *The Party* 1968 (m,song); *Downhill Racer* 1969 (song); *Gaily, Gaily* 1969 (m,song); *I Girasoli* 1969 (m) **(AANBM)**; *Me, Natalie* 1969 (m); *Darling Lili* 1970 (m,song) **(AANBS)**; *The Hawaiians* 1970 (m); *The Molly Maguires* 1970 (m); *The Night Visitor* 1971 (m); *Sometimes a Great Notion* 1971 (m) **(AANBS)**; *The Salzburg Connection* 1972 (song); *Oklahoma Crude* 1973 (m); *The Thief Who Came to Dinner* 1973 (m); *Visions of Eight* 1973 (m); *99 and 44/100% Dead* 1974 (m); *The Girl From Petrovka* 1974 (m); *The Parallax View* 1974 (song); *That's Entertainment!* 1974 (m.adapt); *The White Dawn* 1974 (m); *The Great Waldo Pepper* 1975 (m); *Once Is Not Enough* 1975 (m); *The Return of the Pink Panther* 1975 (m); *Alex & the Gypsy* 1976 (m); *The Big Bus* 1976 (song); *Lifeguard* 1976 (song); *The Pink Panther Strikes Again* 1976 (m,m.dir,song) **(AANBS)**; *Silver Streak* 1976 (m,m.cond); *W.C. Fields and Me* 1976 (m); *House Calls* 1978 (m); *Revenge of the Pink Panther* 1978 (m,song); *Who Is Killing the Great Chefs of Europe?* 1978 (m); *10* 1979 (m,song) **(AANBM,AANBS)**; *The Great Santini*

1979 (song); *More American Graffiti* 1979 (song); *Nightwing* 1979 (m); *Prisoner in the Street* 1979 (add.m); *The Prisoner of Zenda* 1979 (m); *A Change of Seasons* 1980 (m,song); *Little Miss Marker* 1980 (m); *Back Roads* 1981 (m,song); *Condorman* 1981 (m); *Mommie Dearest* 1981 (m); *S.O.B.* 1981 (m); *Class of 1984* 1982 (song); *Grease 2* 1982 (song); *An Officer and a Gentleman* 1982 (song); *Second Thoughts* 1982 (m); *Some Kind of Hero* 1982 (song); *Trail of the Pink Panther* 1982 (m); *Victor/Victoria* 1982 (m,song) **(AABM)**; *Young Doctors in Love* 1982 (song); *Better Late Than Never* 1983 (m); *Curse of the Pink Panther* 1983 (m,song); *The Lords of Discipline* 1983 (song); *The Man Who Loved Women* 1983 (m); *The Right Stuff* 1983 (m,song); *Angela* 1984 (m); *Best Defense* 1984 (songs); *Harry & Son* 1984 (m); *Fletch* 1985 (song); *Lifeforce* 1985 (m); *Porky's Revenge* 1985 (m); *Santa Claus: The Movie* 1985 (m,song); *That's Dancing!* 1985 (m); *A Fine Mess* 1986 (m,song); *The Great Mouse Detective* 1986 (m,song); *Off Beat* 1986 (song); *That's Life!* 1986 (m,song) **(AANBS)**; *Blind Date* 1987 (m,song); *The Glass Menagerie* 1987 (m); *Heaven* 1987 (songs); *No Man's Land* 1987 (song); *Heavy Petting* 1988 (m); *Permanent Record* 1988 (song); *Physical Evidence* 1988 (m); *The Presidio* 1988 (song); *Sunset* 1988 (m); *Without a Clue* 1988 (m); *Born on the Fourth of July* 1989 (song); *Mother, Mother (short)* 1989 (m); *Welcome Home* 1989 (m); *Days of Thunder* 1990 (song); *Ghost Dad* 1990 (m); *Switch* 1991 (m).

Mandel, Johnny • Composer • Born U.S.A., 1926. Has worked with Norman Jewison, Hal Ashby and Sidney Lumet, among others. • *I Want to Live!* 1958 (m,m.cond); *The Third Voice* 1960 (m); *Drums of Africa* 1963 (m); *The Americanization of Emily* 1964 (m,song); *The Sandpiper* 1965 (m,song) **(AABS)**; *An American Dream* 1966 (m,song) **(AANBS)**; *Harper* 1966 (m); *The Russians Are Coming, the Russians Are Coming* 1966 (m); *Point Blank* 1967 (m); *Pretty Poison* 1968 (m); *Heaven With a Gun* 1969 (m,song); *Some Kind of a Nut* 1969 (m); *That Cold Day in the Park* 1969 (m); *M*A*S*H* 1970 (m,song); *The Man Who Had Power Over Women* 1970 (m); *Journey Through Rosebud* 1972 (m); *Molly and Lawless John* 1972 (m); *The Last Detail* 1973 (m); *Summer Wishes, Winter Dreams* 1973 (m); *Escape to Witch Mountain* 1974 (m); *W* 1974 (m); *The Sailor Who Fell From Grace With the Sea* 1975 (m); *Freaky Friday* 1976 (m); *Agatha* 1979 (m); *Being There* 1979 (m); *The Baltimore Bullet* 1980 (m); *Caddyshack* 1980 (m); *Best Friends* 1982 (song); *Deathtrap* 1982 (m); *Lookin' to Get Out* 1982 (m,song); *Soup For One* 1982 (add.m); *The Verdict* 1982 (m); *Staying Alive* 1983 (add.m,m.adapt); *Brenda Starr* 1989 (m).

Mandel, Robert • American director • *Educ.* Columbia; AFI, Los Angeles (directing). Former stage and TV director best known for the engaging adventure yarn *F/X* (1986). • *Nights at O'Rear's* 1980 (d,p); *Independence Day* 1982 (d); *F/X* 1986 (d); *Touch and Go* 1986 (d); *Big Shots* 1987 (d).

Manfredi, Nino • Actor; also director, screenwriter. • Born Saturnino Manfredi, Castro dei Volsci, Italy, 1921. *Educ.* Accademia d'Arte Drammatica, Rome. Popular Italian leading man, equally adept at drama and comedy. Manfredi made his directorial debut with *Per grazia ricevuta* (1971), which won the Best First Film award at Cannes. • *Monastero di Santa Chiara* 1949; *Torna a Napoli* 1949; *Anema e core* 1951; *La Prigioniera della torre di fuoco* 1952; *C'era una volta Angelo Musco* 1953; *Canzoni, canzoni, canzoni!* 1953; *La Domenica della buona gente* 1953; *Ho scelto l'amore* 1953; *Viva il cinema!* 1953; *Ridere, ridere, ridere!* 1954; *Gli Inamorati* 1955; *Prigioniere del male* 1955; *La Scapolo* 1955; *Guardia, guardia scelta, brigadiere e maresciallo* 1956; *Non scherzare con le donne* 1956; *Tempo di villeggiatura* 1956; *Toto, Peppino e la malafemmina* 1956; *Adorabili e bugiarde* 1957; *Camping* 1957 (a,sc,story); *Femmine tre volte* 1957; *Susanna tutta panna* 1957; *Il Bacio del sole* 1958; *Caporale di giornata* 1958; *Carmela e una bambola* 1958; *Guardia, ladro e cameriera* 1958; *Kanonenserenade* 1958; *I Ragazzi dei Pariole* 1958; *Venezia, la luna e tu* 1958; *Audace colpo dei soliti* 1959; *L'Impiegato* 1959 (a,sc,story); *Crimen* 1960; *Le Pillole di Ercole* 1960; *A cavallo della tigre* 1961; *Il Carabiniere a cavallo* 1961; *Il Giudizio Universale* 1961; *L'Amore difficile/Of Wayward Love* 1962 (a,d,sc—"L'avventura di un soldato"); *Anni ruggenti* 1962; *I Motorizzati* 1962; *I Cuori infranti* 1963 (a,sc,story); *In Italia si chiama amore* 1963; *La Parmigiana* 1963; *El Verdugo* 1963; *Alta Infedelta* 1964; *Contro Sesso* 1964; *Il Gaucho* 1964; *Le Bambole* 1965; *I Complessi* 1965; *Io la conoscevo bene* 1965; *Io, Io, Io... e gli Altri* 1965; *Made in Italy* 1965; *Questa volta parliamo di uomini/Let's Talk About Men* 1965; *Thrilling* 1965; *Adulterio all'Italiana* 1966; *Operazione San Gennaro* 1966 (a,sc); *Una Rosa per Tutti* 1966 (a,sc); *Italian Secret Service* 1968; *Il Padre di Famiglia* 1968; *Riusciranno i nostri eroi a ritrovare l'amico misteriosamente scomparso in Africa?* 1968; *Straziami, ma di baci saziami* 1968; *Nell'anno del Signore* 1969; *Rosolino paterno, Soldato* 1969; *Vedo nudo* 1969; *Contestazione generale* 1970; *La Betia* 1971; *Per Grazia Ricevuta* 1971 (a,d,sc,story); *Roma bene* 1971; *Girolimoni, Il Mostro di Roma* 1972; *Lo Chiameremo Andrea* 1972; *Trastevere* 1972; *Pane e Cioccolata/Bread and Chocolate* 1973 (a,sc); *C'eravamo tanto amati/We All Loved Each Other So Much* 1974; *Attenti al Buffone* 1975; *Basta che non si sappia in giro!* 1976; *Brutti, Sporchi e Cattivi* 1976; *Quelle Strane Occasioni* 1976; *Signore e Signori, Buonanotte* 1976; *In Nome del Papa Re* 1977; *Il Giocattolo* 1978 (a,sc); *La Mazzetta* 1978; *Gros Calin* 1979; *Cafe Express* 1980 (a,sc); *Nudo di Donna* 1981 (a,d,sc,story); *Spaghetti House* 1982 (a,sc); *Testa O Croce* 1982 (a,sc); *Questo e Quello* 1983 (a,sc—"In the Red Beret"); *Grandi Magazzini* 1985; *Il Tenente dei Carabinieri* 1986; *I Picari* 1987; *Secondo Ponzio Pilato* 1987; *Helsinki Napoli All Night Long* 1988; *Alberto Express* 1990; *Mima* 1991.

Mangano, Silvana • Actress • Born Rome, April 21, 1930; died December 16, 1989, Madrid, Spain. *Educ.* Academy of Zhia Ruskaya, Rome (dance). Beautiful leading lady who came to international prominence as a struggling, scantily clad peasant in Giuseppe De Santis's neorealist drama, *Bitter Rice* (1949). Mangano later proved her ability in films by directors Vittorio De Sica (*Gold of Naples* 1954), Pier Paolo Pasolini (*Teorema* 1968) and Luchino Visconti (*Death in Venice* 1971). She married producer Dino DeLaurentiis in 1949 and appeared in a number of his films, as well as one—*Dune* (1984)—produced by their daughter, Raffaella DeLaurentiis. • *Elisir d'amore* 1946; *Il Delitto di Giovanni Episcopo* 1947; *Gli Uomini sono nemici* 1947; *Assunta Spina* 1948; *Black Magic* 1949; *Il Lupo della sila* 1949; *Riso Amaro/Bitter Rice* 1949; *Il Brigante Musolino* 1950; *Anna* 1951; *Ulysses* 1953; *Mambo* 1954; *L'Oro di Napoli/Gold of Naples* 1954; *Outlaw Girl* 1955; *Uomini e Lupi/The Wolves* 1956; *Barrage contre le Pacifique/The Sea Wall* 1957; *La Tempesta/The Tempest* 1958; *La Grande Guerra* 1959; *Crimen* 1960; *Five Branded Women* 1960; *Il Giudizio Universale* 1961; *Una Vita Dificile* 1961; *Barabbas* 1962; *Il Processo di Verona* 1962; *Il Disco Volante* 1964; *Io, Io, Io... e gli Altri* 1965; *La Mia Signorina* 1965; *Scusi, lei e' favorevole o contrario?* 1966; *Edipo Re/Oedipus Rex* 1967; *Le Streghe* 1968; *Teorema/Theorem* 1968; *Scipione detto anche l'Africano* 1970; *Il Decamerone/The Decamerone* 1971; *Morte a Venezia/Death in Venice* 1971; *D'Amore Si Muore* 1972; *Ludwig* 1972; *Lo Scopone Scientifico* 1972; *Gruppo di famiglia in un interno/Conversation Piece* 1975; *Dune* 1984; *Oci Ciornie* 1987.

Mankiewicz, Herman J. • Screenwriter; also playwright. • Born Herman Jacob Mankiewicz, New York, NY, November 7, 1897; died 1953. *Educ.* Columbia College, New York (philosophy); Columbia; University of Berlin. Capable, veteran Hollywood scenarist whose floundering career was given a temporary boost as co-screenwriter of *Citizen Kane* (1941). Mankiewicz had hit his peak in the early 1930s producing and contributing uncredited dialogue to a number of

Paramount's wildest comedies such as *Million Dollar Legs* (1932) and *Duck Soup* (1933). After *Kane* his career resumed its downward path, hastened by gambling debts and heavy alcohol consumption. Father of writer Don M. Mankiewicz and Canadian-based director Francis Mankiewicz, and brother of Joseph L. Mankiewicz. • *The Road to Mandalay* 1926 (story); *Stranded in Paris* 1926 (adapt); *The City Gone Wild* 1927 (titles); *Fashions For Women* 1927 (adapt); *Figures Don't Lie* 1927 (titles); *The Gay Defender* 1927 (titles); *A Gentleman of Paris* 1927 (titles); *Honeymoon Hate* 1927 (titles); *The Spotlight* 1927 (titles); *Two Flaming Youths* 1927 (titles); *Avalanche* 1928 (sc,titles); *The Barker* 1928 (titles); *The Big Killing* 1928 (titles); *The Dragnet* 1928 (titles); *Gentlemen Prefer Blondes* 1928 (titles); *His Tiger Lady* 1928 (titles); *The Last Command* 1928 (titles); *Love and Learn* 1928 (titles); *The Magnificent Flirt* 1928 (titles); *The Mating Call* 1928 (titles); *A Night of Mystery* 1928 (titles); *Something Always Happens* 1928 (titles); *Take Me Home* 1928 (titles); *Three Week-Ends* 1928 (titles); *The Water Hole* 1928 (titles); *What a Night!* 1928 (titles); *Abie's Irish Rose* 1929 (titles); *The Canary Murder Case* 1929 (titles); *The Dummy* 1929 (sc,adapt,dial); *The Love Doctor* 1929 (titles); *The Man I Love* 1929 (sc,story,dial); *Marquis Preferred* 1929 (titles); *The Mighty* 1929 (titles); *Thunderbolt* 1929 (dial); *Honey* 1930 (sc,dial); *Ladies Love Brutes* 1930 (sc,dial); *Laughter* 1930 (uncred.p); *Love Among the Millionaires* 1930 (dial); *Men Are Like That* 1930 (adapt,dial); *The Royal Family of Broadway* 1930 (sc); *True to the Navy* 1930 (dial); *The Vagabond King* 1930 (sc,adapt,dial); *Dude Ranch* 1931 (add.dial); *The Front Page* 1931 (uncred.a); *Ladies' Man* 1931 (sc); *Man of the World* 1931 (sc,story); *Monkey Business* 1931 (uncred.assoc.p); *Dancers in the Dark* 1932 (sc); *Girl Crazy* 1932 (adapt); *Horse Feathers* 1932 (uncred.assoc.p); *The Lost Squadron* 1932 (add.dial); *Million Dollar Legs* 1932 (uncred.p,uncred.dial); *Another Language* 1933 (sc); *Dinner at Eight* 1933 (sc); *Duck Soup* 1933 (uncred.p,uncred.dial); *Meet the Baron* 1933 (story); *The Show-Off* 1934 (sc); *Stamboul Quest* 1934 (sc); *After Office Hours* 1935 (sc); *Escapade* 1935 (sc); *It's in the Air* 1935 (uncred.sc); *Love in Exile* 1936 (dial); *The Three Maxims* 1936 (sc); *The Emperor's Candlesticks* 1937 (uncred.sc); *John Meade's Woman* 1937 (sc); *My Dear Miss Aldrich* 1937 (p,sc,story); *It's a Wonderful World* 1939 (story); *The Wizard of Oz* 1939 (uncred.sc); *Comrade X* 1940 (uncred.sc); *Congo Maisie* 1940 (uncred.sc); *The Ghost Comes Home* 1940 (uncred.sc); *Keeping Company* 1940 (story); *Citizen Kane* 1941 (sc) **(AABSC)**; *Rise and Shine* 1941 (sc); *The Wild Man of Borneo* 1941 (from play); *The Pride of the Yankees* 1942 (sc) **(AANBSC)**; *Stand By For Action* 1942 (sc); *This Time For Keeps* 1942 (from characters); *The Good Fellows* 1943 (from play); *Christmas Holiday* 1944 (sc); *The Enchanted Cottage* 1945 (sc); *The Spanish Main* 1945 (sc); *Fighting Father Dunne* 1948 (uncred.sc); *A Woman's Secret* 1949 (p,sc); *Androcles and the Lion* 1952 (uncred.sc); *The Pride of St. Louis* 1952 (sc).

Mankiewicz, Joseph L. • *aka* Joseph Mankiewic • Director; also producer, screenwriter. • Born Joseph Leo Mankiewicz, Wilkes-Barre, PA, February 11, 1909. *Educ.* Columbia (English). Like his brother Herman, Mankiewicz entered films as a scenarist, after a stint as a foreign correspondent in Berlin. He began producing in 1936 and turned to directing a decade later, building a reputation as one of Hollywood's more "literary" directors. The staginess of Mankiewicz's films is more than compensated for by the urbane wit of his screenplays; *A Letter to Three Wives* (1948), *House of Strangers* (1949), *All About Eve* (1950) and *Julius Caesar* (1953) are all superb examples of his art. Mankiewicz took over the direction of *Cleopatra* (1963) from Rouben Mamoulian; despite his attempts to salvage the film, it proved to be one of Hollywood's most expensive flops and dealt a serious blow to his directing career. Mankiewicz's son Tom is a screenwriter. • *Close Harmony* 1929 (titles); *The Dummy* 1929 (titles); *Fast Company* 1929 (dial); *The Man I Love* 1929 (titles); *The Mysterious Dr. Fu Manchu* 1929 (titles); *River of Romance* 1929 (titles); *The Saturday Night Kid* 1929 (titles); *The Studio Murder Mystery* 1929 (titles); *The Virginian* 1929 (titles); *Woman Trap* 1929 (a); *Only Saps Work* 1930 (sc,dial); *Slightly Scarlet* 1930 (sc,dial); *The Social Lion* 1930 (adapt,dial); *Finn and Hattie* 1931 (sc,dial); *The Gang Buster* 1931 (dial); *June Moon* 1931 (sc,dial); *Newly Rich* 1931 (sc,dial); *Skippy* 1931 (sc,dial) **(AANBSC)**; *Sooky* 1931 (sc); *If I Had a Million* 1932 (sc,from stories—"The Three Marines," "The China Shop," "The Streetwalker," "The Forger," "Rollo and the Roadhogs"); *Million Dollar Legs* 1932 (sc,dial,story); *Sky Bride* 1932 (sc,dial); *This Reckless Age* 1932 (sc,adapt); *Wild Horse Mesa* 1932 (uncred.sc—love scenes); *Alice in Wonderland* 1933 (sc); *College Humor* 1933 (uncred.sc); *Diplomaniacs* 1933 (sc,story); *Emergency Call* 1933 (sc); *Too Much Harmony* 1933 (sc,story); *Forsaking All Others* 1934 (sc); *Manhattan Melodrama* 1934 (sc); *Our Daily Bread* 1934 (dial); *The Scarlet Empress* 1934 (uncred.sc); *I Live My Life* 1935 (sc); *Fury* 1936 (uncred. from story,p); *The Gorgeous Hussy* 1936 (p); *Love on the Run* 1936 (p); *The Three Godfathers* 1936 (p); *The Bride Wore Red* 1937 (p); *Double Wedding* 1937 (p); *A Christmas Carol* 1938 (p); *Mannequin* 1938 (p); *The Shining Hour* 1938 (p); *The Shopworn Angel* 1938 (p); *Three Comrades* 1938 (p); *The Adventures of Huckleberry Finn* 1939 (p); *The Philadelphia Story* 1940 (p); *Strange Cargo* 1940 (p); *The Feminine Touch* 1941 (p); *The Wild Man of Borneo* 1941 (p); *Cairo* 1942 (p); *Reunion in France* 1942 (p); *Woman of the Year* 1942 (p); *The Keys of the Kingdom* 1945 (p,sc); *Backfire* 1946 (d); *Dragonwyck* 1946 (d,sc); *The Ghost and Mrs. Muir* 1947 (d); *The Late George Apley* 1947 (d); *Escape* 1948 (d); *A Letter to Three Wives* 1948 (d,sc) **(AABD,AABSC)**; *House of Strangers* 1949 (d); *All About Eve* 1950 (d,sc) **(AABD,AABSC)**; *No Way Out* 1950 (d,sc) **(AANBSC)**; *People Will Talk* 1951 (d,sc); *Five Fingers* 1952 (d) **(AANBD)**; *Julius Caesar* 1953 (d,sc.adapt); *The Barefoot Contessa* 1954 (d,p,sc) **(AANBSC)**; *Guys and Dolls* 1955 (d,sc); *The Quiet American* 1958 (d,p,sc); *Suddenly, Last Summer* 1959 (d); *Cleopatra* 1963 (d,sc); *The Directors (short)* 1963 (a); *The Honey Pot* 1967 (d,p,sc); *King: A Filmed Record... Montgomery to Memphis* 1970 (d); *There Was a Crooked Man* 1970 (d,p); *Sleuth* 1972 (d) **(AANBD)**; *George Stevens: A Filmmaker's Journey* 1985 (a); *50 Years of Action!* 1986 (a); *Hello Actors Studio* 1987 (a).

Mankiewicz, Tom • Screenwriter; also director. • Born Los Angeles, CA, June 1, 1942. Prolific Hollywood "script doctor" who has applied his scalpel to several "James Bond" films and two "Superman" sagas. Mankiewicz directed several episodes of the TV series "Hart to Hart" and made his feature debut with the detective spoof, *Dragnet* (1987). He is the son of director Joseph Mankiewicz and nephew of writer Herman Mankiewicz. • *The Best Man* 1964 (prod.assoc); *The Sweet Ride* 1968 (sc); *Diamonds Are Forever* 1971 (sc); *Live and Let Die* 1973 (sc); *The Man With the Golden Gun* 1974 (sc); *The Eagle Has Landed* 1976 (sc); *Mother, Jugs & Speed* 1976 (p,sc,story); *The Cassandra Crossing* 1977 (sc); *Superman* 1978 (creative consultant); *Superman II* 1980 (creative consultant); *Ladyhawke* 1985 (sc); *Dragnet* 1987 (d,sc); *Hot Pursuit* 1987 (exec.p).

Mann, Anthony • *aka* Anton Bundsmann, Anton Mann • Director • Born Emil Anton Bundsmann, San Diego, CA, June 30, 1906; died 1967. New York actor who went to Hollywood in the early 1940s and eventually emerged as one of the leading directors of his day. Beginning with *Desperate* (1947), Mann directed a cycle of taut *films noirs* that displayed an immaculate visual style and introduced one of the director's favorite themes; the intelligent, thoughtful man driven to violence. Of these films, *T-Men* (1947), *Raw Deal* (1948) and *Border Incident* (1949) stand out.

Mann then turned to westerns, making a number of films that are often cited as among the genre's highest achievements. Classics such as *Winchester '73* (1950), *Bend of the River* (1952) and *The Naked Spur* (1953) are noted for their well-crafted screenplays (often by Borden Chase), effective use of landscape and gritty violence. Starring in all three of these was James Stewart, who also appeared in several of the director's non-western movies, notably *The Glenn Miller Story* (1954).

Mann's final films were sprawling, big-budget productions such as *El Cid* (1961) and *The Fall of the Roman Empire* (1964), which remain among the more intelligent and absorbing period spectacles Hollywood has produced. He died during the filming of the spy thriller *A Dandy in Aspic* (1968), which was completed by the film's star, Laurence Harvey. Married to actres Sarita Montiel from 1956 to 1963. • *Dr. Broadway* 1942 (d); *Moonlight in Havana* 1942 (d); *Nobody's Darling* 1943 (d); *My Best Gal* 1944 (d); *Strangers in the Night* 1944 (d); *The Great Flamarion* 1945 (d); *Sing Your Way Home* 1945 (d); *Two O'Clock Courage* 1945 (d); *The Bamboo Blonde* 1946 (d); *Strange Impersonation* 1946 (d); *Desperate* 1947 (d,from unpublished story); *Railroaded* 1947 (d); *T-Men* 1947 (d); *He Walked By Night* 1948 (d); *Raw Deal* 1948 (d); *Border Incident* 1949 (d); *Follow Me Quietly* 1949 (d,from unpublished story); *Reign of Terror* 1949 (d); *Devil's Doorway* 1950 (d); *The Furies* 1950 (d); *Side Street* 1950 (d); *Winchester '73* 1950 (d); *It's a Big Country* 1951 (d); *Quo Vadis* 1951 (d); *The Tall Target* 1951 (d); *Bend of the River* 1952 (d); *The Naked Spur* 1953 (d); *Thunder Bay* 1953 (d); *The Glenn Miller Story* 1954 (d); *The Far Country* 1955 (d); *The Last Frontier* 1955 (d); *The Man From Laramie* 1955 (d); *Serenade* 1955 (d); *Strategic Air Command* 1955 (d); *Men in War* 1956 (d); *Night Passage* 1957 (d); *The Tin Star* 1957 (d); *God's Little Acre* 1958 (d,p); *Man of the West* 1958 (d); *Cimarron* 1960 (d); *Spartacus* 1960 (d); *El Cid* 1961 (d); *The Fall of the Roman Empire* 1964 (d); *The Heroes of Telemark* 1965 (d); *A Dandy in Aspic* 1968 (d,p).

Mann, Daniel • Director • Born Daniel Chugerman, Brooklyn, NY, August 8, 1912. *Educ.* Professional Children's School, New York. "Actors' director" who successfully brought to the screen a number of 50s stage hits, including *Come Back, Little Sheba* (1952), which he also directed on Broadway, *The Rose Tattoo* (1955) and *The Teahouse of the August Moon* (1956). • *The Counterfeiters* 1948 (d); *Come Back, Little Sheba* 1952 (d); *About Mrs. Leslie* 1954 (d); *I'll Cry Tomorrow* 1955 (d); *The Rose Tattoo* 1955 (d); *The Teahouse of the August Moon* 1956 (d); *Hot Spell* 1958 (d); *The Last Angry Man* 1959 (a,d); *Butterfield 8* 1960 (d); *The Mountain Road* 1960 (d); *Ada* 1961 (d); *Five Finger Exercise* 1962 (d); *Who's Got the Action?* 1962 (d); *Who's Been Sleeping in My Bed?* 1963 (d); *Judith* 1966 (d); *Our Man Flint* 1966 (d); *For Love of Ivy* 1968 (d); *A Dream of Kings* 1969 (d); *Willard* 1971 (d); *The Revengers* 1972 (d); *Interval* 1973 (d); *Maurie* 1973 (d); *Lost in the Stars* 1974 (d); *Journey Into Fear* 1976 (d); *Matilda* 1978 (d).

Mann, Delbert • Director • Born Lawrence, KS, January 30, 1920. *Educ.* Vanderbilt University, Nashville TN; Yale School of Drama. Working in TV from 1947, Mann directed over 100 live plays, the best known of which was Paddy Chayefsky's *Marty*. In 1955 he directed a big-screen version, starring Ernest Borgnine as the lonely Bronx butcher in search of love. The success of the film—it took the Palme d'Or at Cannes—paved the way for a number of low-budget movies on "small" subjects that flourished in the mid-1950s.

Mann's other successes include the finely acted *The Bachelor Party* (1957), also scripted by Chayefsky, and *The Dark at the Top of the Stairs* (1960). He made some deft comedies in the 1960s and later directed several competent TV adaptations, such as *Jane Eyre* (1972) and *All Quiet on the Western Front* (1982). • *Marty* 1955 (d) **(AABD)**; *The Bachelor Party* 1957 (d); *Desire Under the Elms* 1957 (d); *Separate Tables* 1958 (d); *Middle of the Night* 1959 (d); *The Dark at the Top of the Stairs* 1960 (d); *The Outsider* 1961 (d); *Lover Come Back* 1962 (d); *That Touch of Mink* 1962 (d); *A Gathering of Eagles* 1963 (d); *Dear Heart* 1964 (d); *Quick, Before It Melts* 1964 (d,p); *Mister Buddwing* 1965 (d,p); *Fitzwilly* 1967 (d); *The Pink Jungle* 1968 (d); *David Copperfield* 1970 (d); *Kidnapped* 1971 (d); *Birch Interval* 1975 (d); *Night Crossing* 1981 (d); *Bronte* 1983 (d).

Mann, Michael • Director, producer • Born Chicago, IL. *Educ.* University of Wisconsin; London Film School. Former writer for TV shows, including "Starsky and Hutch" and "Police Story," who graduated to the director's chair with the TV movie *The Jericho Mile* (1979) and made his feature film debut with *Thief* (1981). Mann is best known for producing TV's popular "Miami Vice" (1984-89), a cop series featuring slick action sequences, driving musical scores and detectives dressed in expensive designer clothes. • *Thief* 1981 (d,exec.p,sc); *The Keep* 1983 (d,sc); *Band of the Hand* 1986 (exec.p); *Manhunter* 1986 (d,p,sc,cam.op).

Mansfield, Jayne • Actress • Born Vera Jayne Palmer, Bryn Mawr, PA, April 19, 1933; died 1967. *Educ.* University of Texas (drama); Southern Methodist University, Dallas, TX (drama, psychology); UCLA (drama). Beauty pageant winner turned voluptuous, blonde leading lady of limited comedic talent. Apart from her starring roles in two notable Frank Tashlin films (*The Girl Can't Help It* 1956, *Will Success Spoil Rock Hunter?* 1957), Mansfield appeared in relatively minor Hollywood fare. In the 1960s she was recruited by European filmmakers who attempted to capitalize on her name and her propensity for camp. Mansfield died in a car accident in Louisiana in 1967. Her second husband was Hungarian actor and "Mr. Universe" Mickey Hargitay and her third, director Matt Cimber. Daughter Mariska Hargitay is an actress. • *Hell on Frisco Bay* 1955; *Illegal* 1955; *Pete Kelly's Blues* 1955; *Female Jungle* 1956; *The Girl Can't Help It* 1956; *The Burglar* 1957; *Kiss Them For Me* 1957; *The Wayward Bus* 1957; *Will Success Spoil Rock Hunter?* 1957; *The Sheriff of Fractured Jaw* 1958; *The Challenge* 1959; *Gli Amori di Ercole/The Loves of Hercules* 1960; *Too Hot to Handle* 1960; *The George Raft Story* 1961; *It Happened in Athens* 1962; *Heimweh nach St. Pauli/Homesick for St. Paul* 1963; *L'Amore primitivo/Primitive Love* 1964; *Dog Eat Dog* 1964; *Panic Button* 1964; *Promises, Promises* 1964; *The Fat Spy* 1966; *Las Vegas Hillbillys* 1966; *A Guide For the Married Man* 1967; *Spree* 1967; *Single Room Furnished* 1968; *The Wild, Wild World of Jayne Mansfield* 1968.

Mantegna, Joe • Actor • Born Chicago, IL, November 13, 1947. *Educ.* Goodman School of Drama. Versatile lead and character player, formerly with Chicago's Organic Theater Company, who has long been associated with playwright-director-screenwriter David Mamet. Mantegna's first widespread recognition came with a Tony award-winning role in the Broadway production of Mamet's *Glengarry Glen Ross*; he consolidated his success with a smoothly compelling performance as a seductive con man in Mamet's first feature as a director, *House of Games* (1987). • *Towing* 1978; *Second Thoughts* 1982; *Compromising Positions* 1985; *The Money Pit* 1986; *Off Beat* 1986; *Three Amigos!* 1986; *Critical Condition* 1987; *House of Games* 1987; *Suspect* 1987; *Weeds* 1987; *Things Change* 1988; *Wait Until Spring, Bandini* 1989; *Alice* 1990; *The Godfather III* 1990; *Queens Logic* 1991.

Marais, Jean • Actor • Born Jean Villain-Marais, Cherbourg, France, December 11, 1913. Handsome leading man who began his screen career as a protégé of Marcel l'Herbier, making his screen debut in 1933's *L'Epervier* and subsequently appearing in five more films by the director. In 1937 Marais teamed with Jean Cocteau, starring in many of his stage productions and giving memorable performances in films either directed by Cocteau or based upon his material. (The actor's good looks and ethereal, vulnerable charm made him the perfect choice to play Cocteau's tragic heroes, and several of the director's scripts and screenplays were written expressly for Marais.) He remained a top box-office star in France from the 1940s through the 60s. • *Dans les rues* 1933; *L'Epervier* 1933 (a,ad); *Etienne* 1933; *Le Scandale* 1934; *Le Bonheur* 1935; *Les Hommes nouveaux* 1936; *Nuits de feu* 1936; *Abus de confiance* 1937; *Drole de Drame* 1937; *Le Diamant noir* 1940; *Le Pavillon brûle* 1941; *Le Lit a Colonnes* 1942; *L'Eternel Retour* 1943; *Voyage sans espoir* 1943; *La Belle et la Bête/Beauty and the Beast* 1945; *Carmen* 1945; *Ruy Blas* 1947; *L'Aigle à Deux Têtes/Eagle With Two Heads* 1948; *Aux yeux du souvenir* 1948; *Les Parents Terribles/The Storm Within* 1948; *Leclerc* 1949; *Le Château de Verre* 1950; *Orphée/Orpheus* 1950; *Les Miracles n'ont lieu qu'une fois* 1951; *Nez de Cuir* 1951; *L' Appel du destin* 1952; *La Maison du silence* 1952; *Les Amants de minuit* 1953; *Dortoir des grandes* 1953; *Julietta* 1953; *Si Versailles m'était conté* 1953; *Le Comte de Monte Cristo* 1954; *Le Guerisseur* 1954; *Napoléon* 1954; *Futures Vedettes* 1955; *Goubbiah* 1955; *Si Paris nous était conté* 1955; *Toute la ville accuse* 1955; *Eléna et les hommes/Paris Does Strange Things* 1956; *S.O.S. Noronha* 1956; *Typhon sur Nagasaki* 1956; *Un Amour de Poche* 1957; *Le Notti Bianche/White Nights* 1957; *La Tour, prends garde!* 1957; *La Vie à deux* 1958; *Le Bossu* 1959; *Le Testament d'Orphée/The Testament of Orpheus* 1959; *Austerlitz* 1960; *Le Capitan* 1960; *La Princesse de Clèves* 1960; *Le Capitaine Fracasse* 1961; *Napoléon II, l'Aiglon* 1961; *Ponzia Pilato* 1961; *Il Ratto delle Sabine* 1961; *Le Masque de fer* 1962; *Les Miracle des loups* 1962; *Les Mystères de Paris* 1962; *L'Honorable Stanislas, agent secret* 1963; *Fantômas* 1964; *Patate* 1964; *Fantômas se déchaine* 1965; *Le Gentleman de Cocody* 1965; *Pleins feux sur Stanislas* 1965; *Thomas l'Imposteur* 1965; *Train d'enfer* 1965; *Le Saint prend l'Affût* 1966; *Sept hommes et une garce* 1966; *Fantômas contre Scotland Yard* 1967; *Le Paria* 1968; *La Provocation* 1969; *Le Jouet criminel* 1970; *Peau d'âne* 1970; *Ombre et secrets (short)* 1982; *Petrochimika, I Kathedrikes Tis Erimou* 1982; *Liens de parente* 1985; *Parking* 1985.

March, Fredric • Actor • Born Frederick Ernest McIntyre Bickel, Racine, WI, August 31, 1897; died April 14, 1975. *Educ.* University of Wisconsin (economics). Distinguished stage actor and one of Hollywood's most celebrated, versatile stars of the 1930s and 40s. March's roles ranged from light comedy (*The Royal Family of Broadway* 1930) to horror (*Dr. Jekyll and Mr. Hyde* 1932) to drama (*The Best Years of Our Lives* 1946). His classically trained voice and engaging good looks highlighted a number of period pieces, such as *Anna Karenina* (1935), but he seemed more at home playing contemporary characters like the fading actor in *A Star Is Born* (1937) and the exploitative reporter in the biting comedy *Nothing Sacred* (1937). March was married to actress Florence Eldridge (d. 1988), opposite whom he appeared on stage and screen, from 1927 until his death. • *The Devil* 1921; *The Great Adventure* 1921; *Paying the Piper* 1921; *The Dummy* 1929; *Footlights and Fools* 1929; *Jealousy* 1929; *The Marriage Playground* 1929; *Paris Bound* 1929; *The Studio Murder Mystery* 1929; *The Wild Party* 1929; *Ladies Love Brutes* 1930; *Laughter* 1930; *Manslaughter* 1930; *Paramount on Parade* 1930; *The Royal Family of Broadway* 1930 **(AANBA)**; *Sarah and Son* 1930; *True to the Navy* 1930; *Honor Among Lovers* 1931; *My Sin* 1931; *The Night Angel* 1931; *Dr. Jekyll and Mr. Hyde* 1932 **(AABA)**; *Make Me a Star* 1932; *Merrily We Go to Hell* 1932; *The Sign of the Cross* 1932; *Smilin' Through* 1932; *Strangers in Love* 1932; *Design For Living* 1933; *The Eagle and the Hawk* 1933; *Tonight Is Ours* 1933; *The Affairs of Cellini* 1934; *All of Me* 1934; *The Barretts of Wimpole Street* 1934; *Death Takes a Holiday* 1934; *Good Dame* 1934; *We Live Again* 1934; *Anna Karenina* 1935; *The Dark Angel* 1935; *Les Miserables* 1935; *Anthony Adverse* 1936; *Mary of Scotland* 1936; *The Road to Glory* 1936; *Nothing Sacred* 1937; *A Star Is Born* 1937 **(AANBA)**; *The 400 Million* 1938; *The Buccaneer* 1938; *There Goes My Heart* 1938; *Trade Winds* 1938; *Lights Out in Europe* 1940; *Susan and God* 1940; *Victory* 1940; *Bedtime Story* 1941; *One Foot in Heaven* 1941; *So Ends Our Night* 1941; *China Fights* 1942; *I Married a Witch* 1942; *The Adventures of Mark Twain* 1944; *A Salute to France* 1944; *Tomorrow the World* 1944; *Valley of the Tennessee (short)* 1945; *The Best Years of Our Lives* 1946 **(AABA)**; *An Act of Murder* 1948; *Another Part of the Forest* 1948; *Christopher Columbus* 1949; *Death of a Salesman* 1951 **(AANBA)**; *It's a Big Country* 1951; *Man on a Tightrope* 1953; *Executive Suite* 1954; *The Bridges at Toko-Ri* 1955; *The Desperate Hours* 1955; *The Man in the Gray Flannel Suit* 1955; *Alexander the Great* 1956; *Albert Schweitzer* 1957; *Middle of the Night* 1959; *Inherit the Wind* 1960; *The Young Doctors* 1961; *I Sequestrati di Altona* 1962; *Seven Days in May* 1964; *Hombre* 1967; *Tick, Tick, Tick* 1970; *The Iceman Cometh* 1973.

Marchal, Georges • Actor • Born Georges Louis Lucot, Nancy, France, January 10, 1920. Handsome leading man in international productions of the 1940s and 50s. Marchand has appeared in several Buñuel films, including *Cela s'appelle l'aurore* (1955), *La mort en ce jardin* (1956), *Belle de jour* (1967) and *The Milky Way* (1969). • *Une Fausse alerte* 1940; *Premier rendez-vous* 1941; *Lumière d'Ete* 1943; *Les Démons de l'Aube* 1946; *Bethsabée* 1947; *Au Grand Balcon* 1949; *Les Dernières jours de Pompei* 1949; *Vautrin* 1949; *La Soif des Hommes* 1950; *Robinson Crusoe* 1951; *Les Amours finissent a l'Aube* 1953; *Les Trois Mousquetaires* 1953; *The Affairs of Messalina* 1954; *Theodore, Imperatrice Byzantine* 1954; *La Castiglione* 1955; *Le Vicomte de Bragelonne* 1955; *Cela s'appelle l'aurore* 1955; *La mort en ce jardin* 1956; *Filles de la Nuit* 1957; *Marchands de filles* 1957; *La Rivolta dei Gladiatori* 1958; *Le Legioni di Cleopatra* 1959; *Nel Segno di Roma* 1959; *Austerlitz* 1960; *El Coloso de Rodas* 1961; *Il Colpo Segreto di D'Artagnan* 1962; *La Guerre secrète* 1965; *Belle de jour* 1967; *La Voie Lactée/The Milky Way* 1969; *Faustine et le bel été* 1971; *Les Enfants du Placard* 1977.

Margheriti, Antonio • Director • Born Rome, September 19, 1930. Prolific engineer of mostly low-budget action and science fiction fare. Often credited as Anthony Dawson. • *Il Pianeta degli uomini spenti* 1961 (d); *Danza macabra* 1964 (d); *La Vergine di Norimberga* 1964 (d); *Da Uomo a Uomo* 1967 (a); *E Dio disse a Caino...* 1969 (d); *Nella stretta morsa del ragno* 1971 (d); *War Between the Planets* 1971 (d); *Take a Hard Ride* 1975 (d); *Killer Fish* 1979 (d); *L'Umanoide* 1979 (sfx sup); *Cannibals in the Streets* 1980 (d,sc); *The Last Hunter* 1980 (d); *The Squeeze* 1980 (d); *Cacciatori del cobra d'oro* 1982 (d); *The Ark of the Sun God* 1983 (d); *Tornado* 1983 (d); *Yor, the Hunter From the Future* 1983 (d,sc); *Geheimcode Wildganse* 1984 (d); *Jungle Raiders* 1984 (d); *Kommando Leopard* 1985 (d,fx); *Indio* 1989 (d).

Marin, Richard "Cheech" • *aka* Cheech Marin • Actor; also writer, director. • Born Richard Marin, Los Angeles, CA, July 13, 1946. *Educ.* California State University at Northridge (English). Mustachioed Latino actor and comic who first worked with Tommy Chong as part of Vancouver's City Works improvisational troupe. The two formed the "Cheech and Chong" comedy duo in 1970 and had released three best-selling albums before bringing their stoned hippy routines to the screen with *Cheech & Chong's Up in Smoke* (1978)—the highest-grossing film of the year—and seven, similarly drug-crazed sequels. Following the team's parting in 1985 Cheech continued to appear in films and wrote, directed and starred in *Born in East L.A.* (1987). • *Cheech & Chong's Up in Smoke* 1978 (a,sc,song); *Cheech & Chong's Next Movie* 1980 (a,sc); *Cheech & Chong's Nice Dreams* 1981 (a,sc,song); *It Came From Hollywood* 1982 (a);

Things Are Tough All Over 1982 (a,sc); *Cheech & Chong's Still Smokin'* 1983 (a,sc); *Yellowbeard* 1983 (a); *Cheech & Chong's the Corsican Brothers* 1984 (a,sc); *After Hours* 1985 (a); *Born in East L.A.* 1987 (a,d,sc,lyrics "Born in East L.A."); *Oliver & Company* 1988 (a); *Ghostbusters II* 1989 (a); *Rude Awakening* 1989 (a); *Troop Beverly Hills* 1989 (a); *The Shrimp on the Barbie* 1990 (a).

Marion, Frances • Screenwriter; also director, author. • Born Frances Marion Owens, San Francisco, CA, November 18, 1887; died 1973. *Educ.* Mark Hopkins Art School; University of California, Berkeley. Wrote, co-wrote or adapted some 150 screenplays from 1915 to 1939, leaving a significant stamp on American movies of both the silent and sound eras. A former journalist (she was one of the first female war correspondents), Marion entered films as an actress and made the transition to writer in 1915. She scripted vehicles for Mary Pickford and Marion Davies, among others, and was especially adept at literary adaptations; the scripts for *Stella Dallas* (1925) and *The Scarlet Letter* (1926) are superb examples of book-to-film restructuring. In the early 1920s Marion directed three films from her own screenplays. Her third husband, from 1919 to his death in 1928, was actor Fred Thomson; her fourth, from 1930 till their divorce the following year, was director George F. Hill. • *A Daughter of the Sea* 1915 (from story "The Fishergirl"); *The Foundling* 1915 (sc); *Mistress Nell* 1915 (sc); *A Battle of Hearts* 1916 (from story "The Iron Man"); *Camille* 1916 (sc); *The Feast of Life* 1916 (sc,story); *The Foundling* 1916 (sc,story); *Friday the 13th* 1916 (sc); *The Gilded Cage* 1916 (sc); *The Hidden Scar* 1916 (sc); *The Revolt* 1916 (sc); *Tangled Fates* 1916 (sc); *A Girl's Folly* 1917 (sc,story); *The Hungry Heart* 1917 (sc); *A Little Princess* 1917 (sc,adapt); *The Poor Little Rich Girl* 1917 (sc); *Rebecca of Sunnybrook Farm* 1917 (sc); *Tillie Wakes Up* 1917 (sc); *A Woman Alone* 1917 (sc); *Amarilly of Clothes-Line Alley* 1918 (sc); *Captain Kidd, Jr.* 1918 (sc); *The City of Dim Faces* 1918 (story,sc); *The Goat* 1918 (sc,story); *He Comes Up Smiling* 1918 (sc); *How Could You Jean?* 1918 (sc); *Johanna Enlists* 1918 (sc); *M'Liss* 1918 (sc); *Stella Maris* 1918 (sc); *The Temple of Dusk* 1918 (sc,story); *Anne of Green Gables* 1919 (sc); *The Cinema Murder* 1919 (sc); *The Misleading Widow* 1919 (sc); *A Regular Girl* 1919 (story,sc); *The World and Its Woman* 1919 (a); *The Flapper* 1920 (story,sc); *Humoresque* 1920 (sc); *Pollyanna* 1920 (sc,adapt); *The Restless Sex* 1920 (sc); *The World and His Wife* 1920 (sc); *Just Around the Corner* 1921 (d,sc,adapt); *Little Lord Fauntleroy* 1921 (a); *The Love Light* 1921 (d,sc,story); *Straight Is the Way* 1921 (sc); *Back Pay* 1922 (sc); *East Is West* 1922 (sc,adapt); *The Eternal Flame* 1922 (sc,adapt); *The Primitive Lover* 1922 (sc); *Sonny* 1922 (sc,adapt); *The Toll of the Sea* 1922 (story); *The Famous Mrs. Fair* 1923 (sc); *The French Doll* 1923 (sc,adapt); *The Love Piker* 1923 (sc); *Nth Commandment* 1923 (sc,prod.sup); *Potash and Perlmutter* 1923 (sc); *The Song of Love* 1923 (d,sc,adapt); *The Voice From the Minaret* 1923 (sc); *Within the Law* 1923 (sc); *Cytherea* 1924 (sc,adapt); *The Dramatic Life of Abraham Lincoln* 1924 (sc); *In Hollywood With Potash and Perlmutter* 1924 (sc,adapt); *Secrets* 1924 (sc,adapt); *Sundown* 1924 (sc); *Tarnish* 1924 (sc); *Through the Dark* 1924 (sc); *The Dark Angel* 1925 (sc); *Graustark* 1925 (sc,adapt); *His Supreme Moment* 1925 (sc,adapt); *The Lady* 1925 (sc); *Lazybones* 1925 (sc); *Lightnin'* 1925 (sc); *Simon the Jester* 1925 (sc,adapt); *Stella Dallas* 1925 (sc,adapt); *Thank You* 1925 (sc); *A Thief in Paradise* 1925 (sc); *Zander the Great* 1925 (sc); *The First Year* 1926 (sc); *Paris at Midnight* 1926 (p,sc,adapt); *Partners Again* 1926 (sc,adapt); *The Scarlet Letter* 1926 (sc,adapt,titles); *The Son of the Sheik* 1926 (sc,adapt); *The Winning of Barbara Worth* 1926 (sc); *The Callahans and the Murphys* 1927 (sc); *Love* 1927 (sc,cont); *The Red Mill* 1927 (sc,cont); *The Awakening* 1928 (story); *Bringing Up Father* 1928 (sc); *The Cossacks* 1928 (sc,adapt,cont); *Excess Baggage* 1928 (sc,cont); *The Masks of the Devil* 1928 (sc,cont); *The Wind* 1928 (sc); *Their Own Desire* 1929 (sc); *Anna Christie* 1930 (sc,adapt—German and Swedish-language versions); *The Big House* 1930 (sc,story,dial) **(AABSC)**; *Good News* 1930 (sc); *Let Us Be Gay* 1930 (sc,cont,dial); *Min and Bill* 1930 (sc,dial); *The Rogue Song* 1930 (sc); *The Champ* 1931 (story) **(AABST)**; *The Secret Six* 1931 (sc,story,dial); *Blondie of the Follies* 1932 (sc,story); *Cynara* 1932 (sc); *Emma* 1932 (story); *Dinner at Eight* 1933 (sc); *Going Hollywood* 1933 (story); *Peg o' My Heart* 1933 (adapt); *The Prizefighter and the Lady* 1933 (story) **(AANBST)**; *Secrets* 1933 (sc); *Riffraff* 1935 (sc,story); *Camille* 1937 (sc); *Jericho* 1937 (sc); *Knight Without Armour* 1937 (sc,adapt); *Love From a Stranger* 1937 (sc); *Green Hell* 1940 (sc,story); *New York Town* 1941 (a); *Molly and Me* 1945 (from novel *Molly, Bless Her*); *The Clown* 1953 (story); *The Champ* 1979 (story) **(AABST)**.

Marker, Chris • Director; also producer. • Born Christian François Bouche-Villeneuve, Neuilly-sur-Seine, France, July 29, 1921. Chris Marker is essentially an audio-visual poet and essayist whose (mainly) non-fiction films are characterized by the use of static images, evocative sound tracks and strong, literate commentary. His directorial perspective has always been that of the alien in foreign territory, his films travel diaries with political overtones.

Marker's early life is shrouded in some mystery, much of it perpetrated by the filmmaker himself. During WWII, he served as a resistance fighter during the occupation of France; some accounts claim he also joined the US Army. As a novelist and critic, he authored an important study of dramatist Jean Giraudoux, with whom Marker shares a talent for the abstract narrative devices of existentialist theater.

In the early 1950s, Marker turned to documentary filmmaking, bringing his radical politics to bear on a variety of subjects, many shot outside of France. In 1952, he filmed the Olympic Games in Finland and later won attention with *Sunday in Peking* (1956), *Letter from Siberia* (1957) and *Cuba Si!* (1961). Marker has also been a motivator of, and collaborator on, a number of politically inspired films such as Patricio Guzman's *The Battle of Chile* (1976) and the 1967 pro-North Vietnam compilation, *Far From Vietnam.* His best-known work, however, is *La Jetée* (completed 1962, released 1964), a haunting time-travel parable which consists—except for one short, and very beautiful, sequence of a woman waking up—of a series of still images accompanied by voice-over narration.

Like *La Jetée*, *Le Joli Mai* (1963), Marker's study of Paris during a time of political turmoil, evinces a preoccupation with the manipulation of time and the paradox of memory. Marker is attempting in these films to do away with conventional storytelling techniques, creating an almost incantatory experience of movement in space and time. It is in this sense that his work comes closest to that of his friend and sometime collaborator, Alain Resnais.

In 1966, Marker established SLON (*Société de Lancement des Oeuvres Nouvelles*), a Marxist-inspired arts collective which gave increased impetus to cinema verité documentary. *Junkopia*, a 1981 short shot at Emeryville beach near San Francisco, reflects Marker's continued use of verité techniques in its recording of a spontaneous creation of "found art" sculpture. Unlike proponents of the "direct cinema" school, however, Marker has always played the role of catalyst—some would say *agent provocateur*—in interviewing his on-camera subjects.

Marker's 1985 film, *A.K.*, is a fascinating portrait of Japanese director Akira Kurosawa. TZ • *Olympia 52 (short)* 1952 (d,ph,commentary); *Les Statues Meurent Aussi* 1953 (d,sc,commentary); *Nuit et Brouillard/Night and Fog* 1955 (uncred.collaboration); *Dimanche à Pekin/Sunday in Peking (short)* 1956 (d,ph,commentary); *Toute la Memoire du Monde* 1956 (collaboration); *Letter From Siberia (short)* 1957 (commentary,d); *Le Mystère de l'atelier Quinze* 1957 (commentary,collaboration); *Django Reinhardt (short)* 1958 (sc); *Des Hommes dans le ciel (short)* 1958 (sc); *Les Hommes de la baleine (short)* 1958 (d);

La Mer et les jours (short) 1958 (sc); *Le Siècle a soif (short)* 1958 (sc); *Les Astronautes* 1959 (collaboration,sc); *Cuba Si!* 1961 (commentary,ph,d); *Description d'un combat* 1960 (commentary,d); *La Jetée (short)* prd. 1962, rel. 1964 (d,sc); *Le Joli Mai* 1963 (a,commentary text,d); *Liberté* 1963 (commentary,ph,d); ... *Valparaiso (short)* 1964 (sc); *Le Mystère Koumiko* 1965 (d,sc,ph,ed); *Rotterdam-Europoort* 1966 (commentary adapt); *Si j'avais quatre dromadaires* 1966 (d,ph,commentary,ed); *Le Volcan Interdit* 1966 (sc,ph); *Le Coeur des pierres (short)* 1967 (sc); *Loin du Vietnam/Far From Vietnam* 1967 (collaboration—sc,p, uncred.sup.ed); *Les Mots ont un sens* 1967 (commentary,d); *La Sixième face du Pentagone (short)* 1967 (d,ph,commentary); *Jour de tournage* 1969 (d); *L'Aveu* 1970 (still photography); *La Bataille des dix millions* 1970 (d,sc,commentary,ed); *Le Train en marche (short)* 1971 (d); *Kashima Paradise* 1973 (a,commentary); *Les Deux Memoires* 1974 (ed); *La Solitude du chanteur de fond* 1974 (a,d,ed); *Carlos Marighela (short)* 1975 (a,d); *On vous parle de Brésil (short)* 1975 (commentary,d); *La Spirale* 1975 (consultant,collaboration,d); *The Battle of Chile* 1976 (collaborator—p,sc); *Le Fond de l'air est rouge* 1977 (d,idea,commentary,sound ed,ed); *Le Recours de la méthode* 1978 (sub-titles—French); *Junkopia (short)* 1981 (d,sc,commentary); *Sans Soleil* 1982 (d,sc,ph,ed,commentary,idea); *2084: video clip pour une réflexion syndicale et pour le plaisir (short)* 1984 (sc,commentary,uncred.ed,d); *A.K.* 1985 (a,d,sc,chief ed,commentary); *Les Pyramides bleues* 1988 (tech.ad—artistic); *L'Heritage de la chouette* 1989 (d,p,sc).

Markle, Peter • American director • Former member of the U.S. National Hockey Team who began his film career directing documentaries and commercials. • *The Personals* 1982 (d,sc,ph); *Hot Dog... The Movie* 1984 (d); *Youngblood* 1986 (d,sc,story,cam.op—Minneapolis); *BAT 21* 1988 (d).

Marquand, Richard • Director • Born Cardiff, Wales, c. 1938; died September 4, 1987. *Educ.* Université d'Aix-Marseille, France; King's College, Cambridge (modern languages). Former director of documentaries whose highly assured feature career was foreshortened by a stroke at the age of 49. At his best with the thrillers *Eye of the Needle* (1981) and *Jagged Edge* (1985). • *Do Yourself Some Good (short)* 1975 (d); *Beowulf* 1976 (a); *Birth of the Beatles* 1979 (d); *The Legacy* 1979 (d); *Eye of the Needle* 1981 (d); *Return of the Jedi* 1983 (d); *Until September* 1984 (d); *Jagged Edge* 1985 (d); *Hearts of Fire* 1987 (d,p).

Marsh, Mae • Actress • Born Mary Wayne Marsh, Madrid, NM, November 9, 1895; died 1968. Sensitive heroine of many D.W. Griffith films. Marsh joined the director's company in 1912 and distinguished herself as the younger sister who plunges to her death in *Birth of a Nation* (1915) and the young wife in the modern episode of *Intolerance* (1916). After a brief retirement in the mid-1920s she played supporting parts in sound films. Sister of actress Marguerite Marsh. • *Fighting Blood (short)* 1911; *The New York Hat* 1912; *Judith of Bethulia* 1913; *The Avenging Conscience* 1914; *The Escape* 1914; *Home, Sweet Home* 1914; *Birth of a Nation* 1915; *A Child of the Paris Streets* 1916; *Hoodoo Ann* 1916; *Intolerance* 1916; *The Little Liar* 1916; *The Wharf Rat (short)* 1916; *The Cinderella Man* 1917; *Polly of the Circus* 1917; *Sunshine Alley* 1917; *All Woman* 1918; *The Beloved Traitor* 1918; *The Face in the Dark* 1918; *Fields of Honor* 1918 (uncred.a); *The Glorious Adventure* 1918; *Hidden Fires* 1918; *Money Mad* 1918; *The Mother and the Law* 1918; *The Racing Strain* 1918; *The Bondage of Barbara* 1919; *Spotlight Sadie* 1919; *The Little 'fraid Lady* 1920; *Nobody's Kid* 1921; *Till We Meet Again* 1922; *The White Rose* 1923; *Daddies* 1924; *Tides of Passion* 1925; *Over the Hill* 1931; *Rebecca of Sunnybrook Farm* 1932; *That's My Boy* 1932; *Alice in Wonderland* 1933; *Paddy the Next Best Thing* 1933; *Bachelor of Arts* 1934; *Little Man, What Now?* 1934; *Black Fury* 1935; *Hollywood Boulevard* 1936; *The Man Who Wouldn't Talk* 1940; *Young People* 1940; *Blue, White and Perfect* 1941; *Great Guns* 1941; *Tales of Manhattan* 1942; *Dixie Dugan* 1943; *Jane Eyre* 1944; *A Tree Grows in Brooklyn* 1945; *My Darling Clementine* 1946; *Deep Waters* 1948; *The Snake Pit* 1948; *The Fighting Kentuckian* 1949; *Impact* 1949; *Three Godfathers* 1949; *The Gunfighter* 1950; *When Willie Comes Marching Home* 1950; *Night Without Sleep* 1952; *A Blueprint For Murder* 1953; *The Robe* 1953; *Prince of Players* 1955; *The Tall Men* 1955; *Girls in Prison* 1956; *Julie* 1956; *While the City Sleeps* 1956; *The Wings of Eagles* 1956; *Sergeant Rutledge* 1960; *Two Rode Together* 1961; *Donovan's Reef* 1963.

Marshall, Alan • Producer • Born London, August 12, 1938. Former editor who co-founded the Alan Parker Film Company in 1970. Marshall has produced a number of critically and commercially successful features, beginning with *Bugsy Malone* (1976). • *Bugsy Malone* 1976 (p); *Midnight Express* 1978 (p) **(AANBP)**; *Fame* 1980 (p); *Shoot the Moon* 1981 (p); *Pink Floyd—The Wall* 1982 (p); *Another Country* 1984 (p); *Birdy* 1984 (p); *Angel Heart* 1987 (p); *Leonard, Part 6* 1987 (exec.p); *Homeboy* 1988 (p); *Jacob's Ladder* 1990 (p).

Marshall, Frank • American producer; also actor • *Educ.* UCLA (political science). Former protégé of director Peter Bogdanovich who served as line producer on projects directed by Orson Welles and Martin Scorsese before teaming up with Steven Spielberg to make *Raiders of the Lost Ark* (1981). Marshall, Spielberg and producer Kathleen Kennedy went on to form Amblin Entertainment, one of the most prolific "mini-studios" in Hollywood, and all three have had a hand in some of the highest-grossing films in cinema history. Marshall made his directorial debut with *Arachnophobia* (1990). • *Targets* 1968 (a); *Nickelodeon* 1976 (a,assoc.p); *The Driver* 1978 (assoc.p); *The Warriors* 1979 (exec.p); *Raiders of the Lost Ark* 1981 (a,p) **(AANBP)**; *E.T., the Extra-Terrestrial* 1982 (prod.sup); *Poltergeist* 1982 (p); *Twilight Zone - the Movie* 1983 (exec.p); *Gremlins* 1984 (exec.p); *Indiana Jones and the Temple of Doom* 1984 (2ud—Great Britain,exec.p); *Back to the Future* 1985 (2ud,exec.p); *The Color Purple* 1985 (2ud,p) **(AANBP)**; *Fandango* 1985 (exec.p); *The Goonies* 1985 (exec.p); *Young Sherlock Holmes* 1985 (exec.p); *An American Tail* 1986 (exec.p); *The Money Pit* 1986 (p); *Batteries Not Included* 1987 (exec.p); *Empire of the Sun* 1987 (2ud,p); *Innerspace* 1987 (co-exec.p); *The Land Before Time* 1988 (co-exec.p); *Who Framed Roger Rabbit* 1988 (2ud—Great Britain,p); *Always* 1989 (2ud,p); *Back to the Future II* 1989 (exec.p); *Dad* 1989 (exec.p); *Indiana Jones and the Last Crusade* 1989 (2ud,exec.p); *Tummy Trouble* 1989 (d,exec.p); *Arachnophobia* 1990 (d,exec.p); *Back to the Future III* 1990 (exec.p); *Gremlins 2: The New Batch* 1990 (exec.p); *Joe Versus the Volcano* 1990 (exec.p); *Rollercoaster Rabbit (short)* 1990 (d,exec.p).

Marshall, Garry • Director; also producer, screenwriter • Born New York, NY, c. 1935. *Educ.* Northwestern University School of Journalism. Wrote and produced popular sitcoms such as "The Dick Van Dyke Show" (with partner Jerry Belson) and "Happy Days" before turning to film directing in the early 1980s. Brother of actress-director Penny Marshall, whom he directed in TV's "Laverne and Shirley." • *How Sweet It Is* 1968 (p,sc); *Psych-Out* 1968 (a); *The Grasshopper* 1970 (p,sc); *Young Doctors in Love* 1982 (d,exec.p); *The Flamingo Kid* 1984 (d,sc); *Nothing in Common* 1986 (d); *Overboard* 1987 (d); *Beaches* 1988 (d); *Pretty Woman* 1990 (d).

Marshall, George • Director; also actor, screenwriter. • Born George E. Marshall, Chicago, IL, December 29, 1891; died 1975. *Educ.* University of Chicago. Competent, highly prolific director (he allegedly made over 400 movies) who entered films in 1912 as an actor and made his directing debut five years later. Marshall's output ranged from comedies (*You Can't Cheat an Honest Man* 1939) to thrillers (*The Blue Dahlia* 1946) and includes the satirical James Stewart-Marlene Dietrich western *Destry Rides Again* (1939). • *Liberty, A Daugh-*

ter of the U.S.A. 1916 (a,ad); *Love's Lariat* 1916 (d,p,sc); *The Man From Montana* 1917 (d,story); *The Adventures of Ruth* 1919 (d); *Prairie Trails* 1920 (d); *Ruth of the Rockies* 1920 (d); *After Your Own Heart* 1921 (d); *Hands Off* 1921 (d); *The Jolt* 1921 (d,story); *The Lady From Longacre* 1921 (d); *A Ridin' Romeo* 1921 (d,sc); *Why Trust Your Husband?* 1921 (d,story); *Smiles Are Trumps* 1922 (d); *Don Quickshot of the Rio Grande* 1923 (d); *Haunted Valley* 1923 (d); *Men in the Raw* 1923 (d); *Where Is This West?* 1923 (d); *The Sea Hawk* 1924 (uncred.2ud); *A Trip to Chinatown* 1926 (prod.sup); *The Gay Retreat* 1927 (prod.sup); *Pack Up Your Troubles* 1932 (a); *Their First Mistake (short)* 1932 (d); *Towed in a Hole (short)* 1932 (a,d); *Hip Action* 1933 (d); *Olsen's Big Moment* 1933 (story); *365 Nights in Hollywood* 1934 (d); *Call It Luck* 1934 (story); *Ever Since Eve* 1934 (d); *She Learned About Sailors* 1934 (d); *Wild Gold* 1934 (d); *10 $ Raise* 1935 (d); *In Old Kentucky* 1935 (d); *Life Begins at Forty* 1935 (d); *Music Is Magic* 1935 (d); *Show Them No Mercy* 1935 (d); *Can This Be Dixie?* 1936 (d,story); *The Crime of Dr. Forbes* 1936 (a,d); *A Message to Garcia* 1936 (d); *Love Under Fire* 1937 (d); *Nancy Steele Is Missing* 1937 (d); *The Battle of Broadway* 1938 (d); *The Goldwyn Follies* 1938 (d); *Hold That Co-ed* 1938 (d); *Destry Rides Again* 1939 (d); *You Can't Cheat an Honest Man* 1939 (d); *The Ghost Breakers* 1940 (d); *When the Daltons Rode* 1940 (d); *Pot o' Gold* 1941 (d); *Texas* 1941 (d); *The Forest Rangers* 1942 (d); *Star Spangled Rhythm* 1942 (d); *Valley of the Sun* 1942 (d); *Riding High* 1943 (d); *True to Life* 1943 (d); *And the Angels Sing* 1944 (d); *Hold That Blonde* 1945 (d); *Incendiary Blonde* 1945 (d); *Murder, He Says* 1945 (d); *The Blue Dahlia* 1946 (d); *Monsieur Beaucaire* 1946 (d); *The Perils of Pauline* 1947 (d); *Variety Girl* 1947 (a,d); *Hazard* 1948 (d); *Tap Roots* 1948 (d); *Lust For Gold* 1949 (d); *My Friend Irma* 1949 (d); *Fancy Pants* 1950 (d); *Never a Dull Moment* 1950 (d); *A Millionaire For Christy* 1951 (d); *The Savage* 1952 (d); *Houdini* 1953 (d); *Money From Home* 1953 (d); *Off Limits* 1953 (d); *Scared Stiff* 1953 (d); *Destry* 1954 (d); *Duel in the Jungle* 1954 (d); *Red Garters* 1954 (d); *The Second Greatest Sex* 1955 (d); *Timberjack* 1955 (a); *Pillars of the Sky* 1956 (d); *Beyond Mombasa* 1957 (d); *The Guns of Fort Petticoat* 1957 (d); *The Sad Sack* 1957 (d); *Imitation General* 1958 (d); *The Sheepman* 1958 (d); *It Started With a Kiss* 1959 (d); *The Mating Game* 1959 (d); *The Gazebo* 1960 (d); *Cry For Happy* 1961 (d); *The Happy Thieves* 1962 (d,exec.p); *How the West Was Won* 1962 (d); *Advance to the Rear* 1963 (d); *Papa's Delicate Condition* 1963 (d); *Dark Purpose* 1964 (d); *Boy, Did I Get a Wrong Number!* 1966 (d); *Eight on the Lam* 1967 (d); *Hook, Line and Sinker* 1968 (d); *The Wicked Dreams of Paula Schultz* 1968 (d); *The Crazy World of Julius Vrooder* 1974 (a).

Marshall, Herbert • Actor • Born Herbert Brough Falcon Marshall, London, May 23, 1890; died 1966. Urbane British leading man whose good looks and finely modulated voice made him an ideal romantic lead. Marshall starred opposite such stars as Marlene Dietrich, in *Blonde Venus* (1932), and Greta Garbo, in *The Painted Veil* (1934), as well as in two Hitchcock films, *Murder* (1930) and *Foreign Correspondent* (1940). The son of actors Percy F. Marshall and Ethel May Turner, he was married to actresses Edna Best (1928-1940) and Boots Mallory. Marshall lost a leg during WWI. • *Mumsie* 1927 (a); *The Letter* 1929 (a); *Murder* 1930 (a); *The Calendar* 1931 (a); *Michael and Mary* 1931 (a); *Secrets of a Secretary* 1931 (a); *Blonde Venus* 1932 (a); *Evenings for Sale* 1932 (a); *The Faithful Heart* 1932 (a); *Trouble in Paradise* 1932 (a); *I Was a Spy* 1933 (a); *The Solitaire Man* 1933 (a); *Four Frightened People* 1934 (a); *Outcast Lady* 1934 (a); *The Painted Veil* 1934 (a); *Riptide* 1934 (a); *Accent on Youth* 1935 (a); *The Dark Angel* 1935 (a); *The Flame Within* 1935 (a); *The Good Fairy* 1935 (a); *If You Could Only Cook* 1935 (a); *Forgotten Faces* 1936 (a); *Girls' Dormitory* 1936 (a); *The Lady Consents* 1936 (a); *Make Way For a Lady* 1936 (a); *Till We Meet Again* 1936 (a); *A Woman Rebels* 1936 (a); *Angel* 1937 (a); *Breakfast For Two* 1937 (a); *Always Goodbye* 1938 (a); *Mad About Music* 1938 (a); *Woman Against Woman* 1938 (a); *Zaza* 1939 (a); *A Bill of Divorcement* 1940 (a); *Foreign Correspondent* 1940 (a); *The Letter* 1940 (a); *Adventure in Washington* 1941 (a); *Kathleen* 1941 (a); *The Little Foxes* 1941 (a); *When Ladies Meet* 1941 (a); *The Moon and Sixpence* 1942 (a); *Flight For Freedom* 1943 (a); *Forever and a Day* 1943 (a); *Young Ideas* 1943 (a); *Andy Hardy's Blonde Trouble* 1944 (a); *The Enchanted Cottage* 1945 (a); *The Unseen* 1945 (a); *Volga-Volga* 1945 (d); *Crack-Up* 1946 (a); *The Razor's Edge* 1946 (a); *Duel in the Sun* 1947 (a); *High Wall* 1947 (a); *Ivy* 1947 (a); *The Secret Garden* 1949 (a); *Black Jack* 1950 (a); *The Underworld Story* 1950 (a); *Anne of the Indies* 1951 (a); *Angel Face* 1952 (a); *The Black Shield of Falworth* 1954 (a); *Gog* 1954 (a); *Riders to the Stars* 1954 (a); *The Virgin Queen* 1955 (a); *Wicked As They Come* 1956 (a); *The Weapon* 1957 (a); *The Fly* 1958 (a); *Stage Struck* 1958 (a); *College Confidential* 1960 (a); *Midnight Lace* 1960 (a); *A Fever in the Blood* 1961 (a); *Five Weeks in a Balloon* 1962 (a); *The Caretakers* 1963 (a); *The List of Adrian Messenger* 1963 (a); *The Third Day* 1965 (a).

Marshall, Penny • Actress, director • Born Bronx, NY, October 15, 1942. *Educ.* University of New Mexico (math, psychology). Best known as Laverne in the popular TV sitcom "Laverne and Shirley" (1976-83), some episodes of which she also directed. Marshall began directing theatrical features with *Jumpin' Jack Flash* (1986) and enjoyed substantial box-office success with *Big* (1988). She is the sister of Garry Marshall and is divorced from director Rob Reiner; daughter Tracy Reiner is an actress and has appeared in films by her father and mother, among others. • *How Sweet It Is* 1968 (a); *The Savage Seven* 1968 (a); *How Come Nobody's on Our Side?* 1975 (a); *1941* 1979 (a); *Movers & Shakers* 1985 (a); *Jumpin' Jack Flash* 1986 (d); *Big* 1988 (d); *Awakenings* 1990 (d,exec.p).

Martin, Dean • Actor; also singer. • Born Dino Paul Crocetti, Steubenville, OH, June 7, 1917. Martin made his name opposite Jerry Lewis as the straight half of one of America's most successful comedy duos of the 1940s and 50s. When the team's ten-year partnership ended in 1956, he sustained his popularity via recordings, TV shows and several competent screen roles. Martin turned in creditable performances in Vincente Minnelli's *Some Came Running* (1958), Howard Hawks's *Rio Bravo* (1959) and Billy Wilder's *Kiss Me, Stupid* (1964) and played a hammy, Americanized version of James Bond in the "Matt Helm" movies of the late 60s. His son, actor-singer Dean Paul Martin, was killed in a plane crash in 1987. • *My Friend Irma* 1949; *At War With the Army* 1950; *My Friend Irma Goes West* 1950; *Sailor Beware* 1951; *That's My Boy* 1951; *Jumping Jacks* 1952; *Road to Bali* 1952; *The Stooge* 1952; *The Caddy* 1953; *Money From Home* 1953; *Scared Stiff* 1953; *Living It Up* 1954; *Three Ring Circus* 1954; *Artists and Models* 1955; *You're Never Too Young* 1955; *Hollywood or Bust* 1956; *Pardners* 1956; *Ten Thousand Bedrooms* 1956; *Some Came Running* 1958; *The Young Lions* 1958; *Career* 1959; *Rio Bravo* 1959; *Bells Are Ringing* 1960; *Ocean's Eleven* 1960; *Pepe* 1960; *Who Was That Lady?* 1960; *Ada* 1961 (a,song); *All in a Night's Work* 1961; *The Road to Hong Kong* 1962; *Sergeants 3* 1962; *Who's Got the Action?* 1962; *Canzoni nel mondo* 1963; *Come Blow Your Horn* 1963; *Four For Texas* 1963; *Toys in the Attic* 1963; *Who's Been Sleeping in My Bed?* 1963; *Kiss Me, Stupid* 1964; *Robin and the Seven Hoods* 1964; *What a Way to Go!* 1964; *Marriage on the Rocks* 1965; *The Sons of Katie Elder* 1965; *Murderers' Row* 1966; *The Silencers* 1966; *Texas Across the River* 1966; *The Ambushers* 1967; *Rough Night in Jericho* 1967; *5 Card Stud* 1968; *Bandolero!* 1968; *How to Save a Marriage and Ruin Your Life* 1968; *The Wrecking Crew* 1968; *Airport* 1970; *Something Big* 1971; *Showdown* 1973; *Mr. Ricco* 1974; *The Cannonball Run* 1980; *Cannonball Run II* 1983.

Martin, Steve • Actor, comedian; also screenwriter, producer. • Born Waco, TX, August, 1945. *Educ.* Long Beach College, CA; UCLA. Began his career as a TV writer, winning an Emmy for his work on the "Smothers Brothers Comedy Hour." Martin started performing his own material in the late 1960s and made his name with recordings, appearances on the "Tonight" show, "Saturday Night Live" and SRO comedy tours. The 1980s saw his emergence as a premier comic actor and capable dramatic player in films such as *Pennies From Heaven* (1981), *Dead Men Don't Wear Plaid* (1982), *Roxanne* (1987) and *Parenthood* (1989). He is married to actress Victoria Tennant. • *Sgt. Pepper's Lonely Hearts Club Band* 1978 (a,song); *The Jerk* 1979 (a,sc,story,song); *The Kids Are Alright* 1979 (a); *The Muppet Movie* 1979 (a); *Pennies From Heaven* 1981 (a); *Dead Men Don't Wear Plaid* 1982 (a,sc); *The Man With Two Brains* 1983 (a,sc); *All of Me* 1984 (a); *The Lonely Guy* 1984 (a); *Movers & Shakers* 1985 (a); *Little Shop of Horrors* 1986 (a); *Three Amigos!* 1986 (a,exec.p,sc,song); *Planes, Trains and Automobiles* 1987 (a); *Roxanne* 1987 (a,exec.p,sc); *Dirty Rotten Scoundrels* 1988 (a); *Parenthood* 1989 (a); *My Blue Heaven* 1990 (a); *L.A. Story* 1991 (a,exec.p,sc,story).

Martin, Strother • Actor • Born Kokomo, IN, 1919; died 1980. Hollywood swimming instructor turned character player; the man who said, "What we have here is a failure to communicate," to Paul Newman in *Cool Hand Luke* (1967). • *The Asphalt Jungle* 1950; *Storm Over Tibet* 1952; *The Big Knife* 1955; *Strategic Air Command* 1955; *Target Zero* 1955; *Attack!* 1956; *The Black Whip* 1956; *Black Patch* 1957; *Copper Sky* 1957; *Cowboy* 1958; *The Horse Soldiers* 1959; *The Shaggy Dog* 1959; *The Wild and the Innocent* 1959; *The Deadly Companions* 1961; *Sanctuary* 1961; *The Man Who Shot Liberty Valance* 1962; *McLintock!* 1963; *Showdown* 1963; *Invitation to a Gunfighter* 1964; *Brainstorm* 1965; *Shenandoah* 1965; *The Sons of Katie Elder* 1965; *An Eye For an Eye* 1966; *Harper* 1966; *Cool Hand Luke* 1967; *The Flim-Flam Man* 1967; *Butch Cassidy and the Sundance Kid* 1969; *True Grit* 1969; *The Wild Bunch* 1969; *The Ballad of Cable Hogue* 1970; *Brotherhood of Satan* 1970; *Fools' Parade* 1971; *Hannie Caulder* 1971; *Red Sky at Morning* 1971; *Pocket Money* 1972; *Sssssss* 1973; *Hard Times* 1975; *Rooster Cogburn* 1975; *The Great Scout & Cathouse Thursday* 1976; *Slap Shot* 1977; *Cheech & Chong's Up in Smoke* 1978; *The End* 1978; *The Champ* 1979; *Love and Bullets* 1979; *Nightwing* 1979; *The Villain* 1979.

Martinelli, Elsa • Actress • Born Trastavere, Italy, 1932. Sultry leading lady whose entree into movies came when Kirk Douglas noticed her photograph in a magazine in 1955. Daughter Cristiana Mancinelli (born 1956) has also appeared in some films. • *Donatella* 1955; *The Indian Fighter* 1955; *La Risaia* 1955; *Four Girls in Town* 1956; *Manuela* 1957; *La Mina* 1957; *I Battellieri del Volga* 1959; *Ciao ciao bambina* 1959; *Costa Azzurra* 1959; *Tunisi Top Secret* 1959; *...Et mourir de plaisir* 1960; *Un Amore a Roma* 1960; *Le Capitan/The Boatmen* 1960; *Il Carro armato dell'8 settembre* 1960; *La Notta Brava* 1960; *Il Piaceri del sabato notte* 1960; *La Menace* 1961; *Hatari!* 1962; *The Pigeon That Took Rome* 1962; *The Trial* 1962; *Pelle viva* 1963; *Rampage* 1963; *The V.I.P.s* 1963; *De l'amour* 1964; *La Decima Vittima/The Tenth Victim* 1965; *La Fabuleuse aventure de Marco Polo* 1965; *Je vous salue Maffia* 1965; *Un Milliard dans un Billiard* 1965; *L' Or du Duc* 1966; *Belle Starr* 1967; *Come imparai ad amare le donne* 1967; *Manon 70* 1967; *Maroc 7* 1967; *Le Plus vieux metier du monde* 1967; *Woman Times Seven* 1967; *Candy* 1968; *Qualcuno ha tradito* 1968; *L' Amica* 1969; *Les Chemins de Katmandou* 1969; *If It's Tuesday, This Must Be Belgium* 1969; *Madigan's Millions* 1969; *Maldonne* 1969; *Una sull'altra* 1969; *OSS 117 Prend des Vacances* 1970; *La Araucana* 1971; *La Part des Lions* 1971; *Il Garofano Rosso* 1976; *Sono un Fenomeno Paranormale* 1986.

Marvin, Lee • Actor • Born New York, NY, February 19, 1924; died August 29, 1987, Tucson, AZ. *Educ.* American Theatre Wing, New York. Durable leading man, in films from 1951. Marvin specialized in playing tough, aggressive characters, memorably in *The Big Heat* (1953), *The Killers* (1964) and *Point Blank* (1967). He first branched out into sympathetic film roles in the early 1960s, partly thanks to the success of TV's "M Squad" (1957-59) in which he played a hard-bitten but honest detective. Marvin demonstrated a flair for comedy with *Donovan's Reef* (1963) and *Cat Ballou* (1965), earning an Oscar for his performance in a dual role in the latter film. • *Teresa* 1951; *U.S.S. Tea Kettle* 1951; *Diplomatic Courier* 1952; *Duel at Silver Creek* 1952; *Eight Iron Men* 1952; *Hangman's Knot* 1952; *We're Not Married* 1952; *The Big Heat* 1953; *Down Among the Sheltering Palms* 1953; *The Glory Brigade* 1953; *Gun Fury* 1953; *Seminole* 1953; *The Stranger Wore a Gun* 1953; *The Wild One* 1953; *Bad Day at Black Rock* 1954; *The Caine Mutiny* 1954; *Gorilla at Large* 1954; *The Raid* 1954; *Violent Saturday* 1954; *I Died a Thousand Times* 1955; *A Life in the Balance* 1955; *Not As a Stranger* 1955; *Pete Kelly's Blues* 1955; *Shack Out on 101* 1955; *Attack!* 1956; *Pillars of the Sky* 1956; *The Rack* 1956; *Seven Men From Now* 1956; *Raintree County* 1957; *Missouri Traveler* 1958; *The Comancheros* 1961; *The Man Who Shot Liberty Valance* 1962; *Donovan's Reef* 1963; *Sergeant Ryker* 1963; *The Killers* 1964; *Cat Ballou* 1965 **(AABA)**; *Ship of Fools* 1965; *Our Time in Hell* 1966; *The Professionals* 1966; *The Dirty Dozen* 1967; *Point Blank* 1967; *Tonite Let's All Make Love in London* 1967; *Hell in the Pacific* 1968; *Paint Your Wagon* 1969; *Monte Walsh* 1970; *Pocket Money* 1972; *Prime Cut* 1972; *The Emperor of the North Pole* 1973; *The Iceman Cometh* 1973; *The Klansman* 1974; *The Spikes Gang* 1974; *The Great Scout & Cathouse Thursday* 1976; *Shout at the Devil* 1976; *Avalanche Express* 1979; *The Big Red One* 1980; *Death Hunt* 1981; *Gorky Park* 1983; *Canicule* 1984; *The Delta Force* 1986.

Marx Brothers, The • Although the Marx Brothers enjoyed long and varied careers in show business, they are best remembered for their anarchic film comedies of the 1930s. Their animated physical and verbal performances, cultivated on the vaudeville and Broadway stages, have proved an enormous influence on subsequent generations of film comedians. The Marxes' essentially irreverent brand of humor never enjoyed the widespread appeal of Chaplin and other silent comics, nor the box-office popularity of less influential talents such as Abbott and Costello. Nevertheless, a folkloric affection for their memorable, idiosyncratic personas (especially Groucho's) has pervaded American popular culture, thanks to the frequent revival of their films and a never-ending stream of imitators.

The original five Marx brothers—Leonard (Chico), Adolph (Harpo), Julius (Groucho), Milton (Gummo), and Herbert (Zeppo)—all followed the family tradition by entering show business at an early age. Specializing in musical comedy, the brothers first gained national attention in the zany revue *I'll Say She Is* (1923-25). Although Harpo made a brief film appearance as early as 1925, in the comedy *Too Many Kisses*, the team honed their craft as a major theatrical attraction throughout the decade. Their long-running hit, *The Cocoanuts* (1925-28), with a script by George S. Kaufman and music by Irving Berlin, gave the Marxes their first step up to Broadway. (Gummo had by now dropped out of the act.) During the run of the play, the brothers, who had already developed their trademark characterizations, independently produced a silent comedy film. The lost picture, *Humorisk*, was made in New York and New Jersey with private financing but never received public release.

On the strength of their next Broadway success, *Animal Crackers* (1928-29), the team was signed to a five-picture contract by Paramount, which was scouting talent for its new sound film productions. Both *Cocoanuts* (1929) and *Animal Crackers* (1930) were filmed on

Paramount's Astoria, New York soundstage. Although the limitations of early sound technology forced the Marxes to subdue their energetic comedy style and penchant for improvised dialogue, the movie public took to the team's brand of comic chaos. Each of the four brothers became identifiable by his unique persona: Groucho, always the leader of the bunch, wore a greasepaint moustache, carried a cigar, and portrayed a tactless social climber who sang and hurled puns, insults, and absurd non sequiturs at every interlocutor; the piano-playing Chico (pronounced "chick-o," after his womanizing) donned a pointy hat with mismatched clothes and spoke in an exaggerated Italian accent; Harpo, with red wig and prop-filled trenchcoat, was the childlike clown who never spoke on film but charmed with his harp solos; and Zeppo was the pitiable stooge of a straight man who only sometimes got the girl.

The final three Marx Brothers releases from Paramount—*Monkey Business* (1931), *Horsefeathers* (1932) and *Duck Soup* (1933)—did not perform well at the box office, although they are now regarded as the team's most inspired film comedies. The writing of George Kaufman and Morrie Ryskind was replaced by that of another brilliant humorist, S.J. Perelman. The boys were also being directed by better handlers of comedy, Norman Z. McLeod and, for *Duck Soup*, Leo McCarey. The team's Paramount vehicles de-emphasized the usual Hollywood storylines and romantic subplots and simply provided screen space for the Marxes to perform their routines. The nearly plotless *Monkey Business* features four nameless stowaway characters who wreak havoc on a luxury liner, then attempt to disembark by peforming four Maurice Chevalier impressions. *Horsefeathers* is a similarly free-form romp through college life, with Professor Wagstaff (Groucho) cuing the mayhem with his anti-establishment anthem "What Ever It Is, I'm Against It." Finally, *Duck Soup*, usually considered the team's absurdist masterpiece, is a satire on the politics of war, casting Groucho as the unlikely president of Freedonia who, with the aid of his brothers, runs the country with the musical slogan "Just Wait 'Til I Get Through With It."

The financially troubled Paramount released the Marx Brothers following *Duck Soup*, but the team (minus Zeppo) was picked up by the glamour studio, Metro-Goldwyn-Mayer, at the behest of its production chief Irving Thalberg. Thalberg recast the irrepressible team in the MGM mold. Reinserting the usual Hollywood storylines, he set the brothers up as more sympathetic figures and offered love stories to appeal to audiences less enamored of the team's destructive humor. With these elements, plus classier production values, the return of Kaufman and Ryskind, better supporting casts, the inclusion of Groucho's grand comic foil Margaret Dumont, and MGM's lengthy pretesting of material, the two Thalberg films, *A Night at the Opera* (1935) and *A Day at the Races* (1937), revived their popularity. But the death of Hollywood's top producer in 1937 also marked the end of the well-crafted Marx films. After a quick loan-out to RKO (for *Room Service* 1938), the aging team did three flat comedies at MGM; after the war, apparently out of financial need, they reunited for the undistinguished *A Night in Casablanca* (1946) and *Love Happy* (1949).

In the 1950s, each of the three brothers continued to perform independently on radio, TV and film, with Groucho remaining the most successful, due to his long-running radio/television quiz show "You Bet Your Life" (1947-61). All three appeared in separate roles in Irwin Allen's *The Story of Mankind* (1957) and were briefly reunited in a telefilm broadcast, *The Incredible Jewel Robbery* (1959). Even after Chico and Harpo died, Groucho continued to write and appear on TV. He accepted an honorary Oscar for the Marx Brothers in 1974, three years before his death. DGS

Marx, Chico • Actor, comedian • Born Leonard Marx, New York, NY, March 26, 1886; died 1961. See Marx Brothers, The. • *The Cocoanuts* 1929 (a); *Animal Crackers* 1930 (a); *Monkey Business* 1931 (a); *Horse Feathers* 1932 (a); *Duck Soup* 1933 (a); *A Night at the Opera* 1935 (a); *A Day at the Races* 1937 (a); *Room Service* 1938 (a); *At the Circus* 1939 (a); *Go West* 1940 (a); *The Big Store* 1941 (a); *A Night in Casablanca* 1946 (a); *Love Happy* 1949 (a); *The Story of Mankind* 1957 (a); *Newsfront* 1978 (a).

Marx, Groucho • Actor, comedian • Born Julius Henry Marx, New York, NY, October 2, 1890; died 1977. See Marx Brothers, The. • *The Cocoanuts* 1929 (a); *Animal Crackers* 1930 (a); *Monkey Business* 1931 (a); *Horse Feathers* 1932 (a); *Duck Soup* 1933 (a); *A Night at the Opera* 1935 (a); *A Day at the Races* 1937 (a); *The King and the Chorus Girl* 1937 (sc,story); *Room Service* 1938 (a); *At the Circus* 1939 (a,song); *Go West* 1940 (a); *The Big Store* 1941 (a); *A Night in Casablanca* 1946 (a); *Copacabana* 1947 (a); *Love Happy* 1949 (a); *Mr. Music* 1950 (a); *Double Dynamite* 1951 (a); *A Girl in Every Port* 1952 (a); *The Story of Mankind* 1957 (a); *Will Success Spoil Rock Hunter?* 1957 (a); *Skidoo* 1968 (a).

Marx, Harpo • *aka* Arthur Marx • Actor, comedian; also harpist. • Born Adolph Marx, New York, NY, November 21, 1888; died 1964. See Marx Brothers, The. • *Too Many Kisses* 1925 (a); *The Cocoanuts* 1929 (a); *Animal Crackers* 1930 (a); *Monkey Business* 1931 (a); *Horse Feathers* 1932 (a); *Duck Soup* 1933 (a); *A Night at the Opera* 1935 (a); *A Day at the Races* 1937 (a); *Room Service* 1938 (a); *At the Circus* 1939 (a); *Go West* 1940 (a); *The Big Store* 1941 (a); *Stage Door Canteen* 1943 (a); *A Night in Casablanca* 1946 (a); *Blondie in the Dough* 1947 (sc,story); *Winter Wonderland* 1947 (sc); *Love Happy* 1949 (a,story); *The Story of Mankind* 1957 (a); *A Global Affair* 1964 (sc); *I'll Take Sweden* 1965 (sc); *Eight on the Lam* 1967 (sc,story); *The Impossible Years* 1968 (from play); *Cancel My Reservation* 1972 (sc); *Going Hollywood: The War Years* 1988 (archival footage).

Marx, Zeppo • Actor, comedian • Born Herbert Marx, New York, NY, February 25, 1901; died 1979. See Marx Brothers, The. • *The Cocoanuts* 1929; *Animal Crackers* 1930; *Monkey Business* 1931; *Horse Feathers* 1932; *Duck Soup* 1933.

Masina, Giulietta • Actress • Born Giulia Anna Masina, Giorgio di Piano, Italy, February 22, 1920. *Educ.* University of Rome. Jaunty Italian screen star, best known for her roles in films directed by husband Federico Fellini. Masina's almost Chaplinesque ability to combine pathos and comedy was put to brilliant use in *La Strada* (1954) and *Nights of Cabiria* (1956); she was also superb as the bored Roman housewife whose escape to the world of fantasy is the subject of Fellini's *Juliet of the Spirits* (1965). • *Paisan* 1946; *Senza Pieta* 1947; *Luci del Varieta/Variety Lights* 1950; *Cameriera Bella Presenza Offresi* (1951); *Europa '51* 1951; *Persiane Chiuse* 1951; *Sette Ore di Guai* 1951; *Romanza della Mia Vita* 1952; *Lo Sceicco Bianco/The White Sheik* 1952; *Wanda la Peccatrice* 1952; *Margini della Metropoli* 1953; *Via Padova 46* 1953; *Donne Proibite* 1954; *La Strada* 1954; *Il Bidone* 1955; *Buonanotte Avvocato* 1955; *Le Notti di Cabiria/Nights of Cabiria* 1956; *Fortunella* 1958; *Nella citta l'inferno* 1958; *La Donna dell'Altro* 1959; *La Grande Vie/La Gran Vita/Das Kunstseidene Mädchen* 1960; *Landru* 1963; *Giulietta degli Spiriti/Juliet of the Spirits* 1965; *Scusi Lei é Favorevole o Contrario?* 1966 *Non Stuzzicate la Zanzara* 1967; *The Madwoman of Chaillot* 1969; *Frau Holle* 1985; *Ginger et Fred* 1986.

Maslansky, Paul • Producer; also director, screenwriter. • Born New York, NY, November 23, 1933. *Educ.* Cinémathèque Française, Paris. Veteran Hollywood producer who began his career as a production manager on European films in the 1960s. Maslansky produced the first Italo-Soviet co-production, Mikhail Kalatozov's *The Red Tent* (1970), and the first joint US-USSR film venture, George Cukor's *The Blue Bird* (1976). Best known for the commercially successful "Police Academy" films. • *The Counterfeit Traitor* 1962 (ad); *Jason* *and the Argonauts* 1963 (prod.man); *The Running Man* 1963 (prod.man); *Il Castello dei morti vivi* 1964 (p,sc); *Eyewitness* 1970 (p); *La Tenda rossa/The Red Tent* 1970 (p); *Sugar Hill* 1974 (d); *Hard Times* 1975 (exec.p); *Race With the Devil* 1975 (exec.p); *The Blue Bird* 1976 (p); *Damnation Alley* 1977 (p); *The Silent Flute* 1978 (p); *Hot Stuff* 1979 (exec.p); *Scavenger Hunt* 1979 (p); *The Villain* 1979 (exec.p); *When You Comin' Back, Red Ryder?* 1979 (p); *The Salamander* 1981 (p); *Love Child* 1982 (p); *Police Academy* 1984 (p); *Police Academy 2: Their First Assignment* 1985 (p); *Return to Oz* 1985 (p); *Police Academy 3: Back in Training* 1986 (p); *Police Academy 4: Citizens on Patrol* 1987 (p); *Police Academy 5: Assignment Miami Beach* 1988 (p); *Police Academy 6: City Under Siege* 1989 (p); *Honeymoon Academy* 1990 (exec.p); *The Russia House* 1990 (p); *Ski Patrol* 1990 (exec.p).

Mason, James • Actor • Born James Neville Mason, Huddersfield, Yorkshire, England, May 15, 1909; died July 27, 1984, Lausanne, Switzerland. *Educ.* Marlborough College; Peterhouse College, Cambridge (architecture). The son of a wealthy merchant, Mason decided he could make more money on the stage than designing buildings, and played with the Old Vic and the Gate Company in Dublin. He first appeared onscreen in British "quota quickies" and caused a sensation as a handsome, sadistic aristocrat in the 1943 costume drama, *The Man in Grey*.

After another triumphant appearance in Carol Reed's Irish suspense thriller, *Odd Man Out* (1947), Mason became Britain's biggest star, moving to Hollywood soon after. Although Southern California softened his rougher edges, he found his niche as an urbane matinee idol with a dark side. This persona was exploited to international success in the Cukor-Garland remake of *A Star Is Born* (1954), with Mason playing complex, Barrymore-style monster Norman Maine (a role which Cary Grant had turned down).

Though gifted with a distinctive, beautiful speaking voice, and with a range much deeper than that of a conventional leading man, Mason nevertheless had trouble finding the kind of quality roles he deserved. His filmography is generally undistinguished, but contains several gems, including: *20,000 Leagues Under the Sea* (1954), as the obsessed Captain Nemo; Hitchcock's *North by Northwest* (1959), this time opposite Cary Grant; Kubrick's *Lolita* (1962), as Humbert Humbert; the Harold Pinter-scripted *The Pumpkin Eater* (1964); and *Georgy Girl* (1966), as the aging roué in pursuit of Lynn Redgrave. He received a best supporting actor nomination for his role in 1982's *The Verdict*. RW • *The Man in Grey* 1934; *Late Extra* 1935; *Blind Man's Bluff* 1936; *Fire Over England* 1936; *Prison Breaker* 1936; *The Secret of Stamboul* 1936; *Troubled Waters* 1936; *Twice Branded* 1936; *Catch as Catch Can* 1937; *The High Command* 1937; *The Mill on the Floss* 1937; *The Return of the Scarlet Pimpernel* 1937; *I Met a Murderer* 1939 (a,p,sc); *Hatter's Castle* 1941; *This Man Is Dangerous* 1941; *The Night Has Eyes* 1942; *Secret Mission* 1942; *Thunder Rock* 1942; *The Alibi* 1943; *Bells Go Down* 1943; *Candlelight in Algeria* 1943; *The Man in Gray* 1943; *They Met in the Dark* 1943; *Fanny By Gaslight* 1944; *Hotel Reserve* 1944; *A Place of One's Own* 1945; *The Seventh Veil* 1945; *They Were Sisters* 1945; *The Wicked Lady* 1945; *Odd Man Out* 1947; *Caught* 1949; *East Side, West Side* 1949; *Madame Bovary* 1949; *The Reckless Moment* 1949; *One Way Street* 1950; *The Desert Fox* 1951; *Pandora and the Flying Dutchman* 1951; *Face to Face* 1952; *Five Fingers* 1952; *Lady Possessed* 1952 (a,p,sc); *The Prisoner of Zenda* 1952; *Botany Bay* 1953; *The Desert Rats* 1953; *Julius Caesar* 1953; *The Man Between* 1953; *The Story of Three Loves* 1953; *20,000 Leagues Under the Sea* 1954; *Prince Valiant* 1954; *A Star Is Born* 1954 **(AANBA)**; *Bigger Than Life* 1956 (a,p); *Forever, Darling* 1956; *Island in the Sun* 1957; *Cry Terror!* 1958; *The Decks Ran Red* 1958; *Journey to the Center of the Earth* 1959; *North by Northwest* 1959; *The Marriage-Go-Round* 1960; *A Touch of Larceny* 1960; *The Trials of Oscar Wilde* 1960; *Escape From Zahrain* 1962; *Finche dura la tempesta* 1962; *Hero's Island* 1962 (a,p); *Lolita* 1962; *Tiara Tahiti* 1962; *The Fall of the Roman Empire* 1964; *The Pumpkin Eater* 1964; *Genghis Khan* 1965; *Lord Jim* 1965; *Los Pianos Mecanicos* 1965; *The Blue Max* 1966; *Georgy Girl* 1966 **(AANBSA)**; *The Deadly Affair* 1967; *The London Nobody Knows* 1967; *Stranger in the House* 1967; *Duffy* 1968; *Mayerling* 1968; *The Sea Gull* 1968; *Age of Consent* 1969 (a,p); *Spring and Port Wine* 1970; *De la Part des Copains* 1971; *Kill* 1971; *Bad Man's River* 1972; *Child's Play* 1972; *The Last of Sheila* 1973; *The Mackintosh Man* 1973; *11 Harrowhouse* 1974; *The Destructors* 1974; *Autobiography of a Princess* 1975; *La Citta sconvolta - caccia spietato ai rapitori* 1975; *Gente di rispetto* 1975; *Inside Out* 1975; *Mandingo* 1975; *Paura in citta* 1976; *People of the Wind* 1976; *Voyage of the Damned* 1976; *Cross of Iron* 1977; *Homage to Chagall—The Colours of Love* 1977; *The Boys From Brazil* 1978; *Heaven Can Wait* 1978; *Bloodline* 1979; *Murder By Decree* 1979; *The Passage* 1979; *The Water Babies* 1979; *ffolkes* 1980; *A Dangerous Summer* 1982; *Evil Under the Sun* 1982; *The Verdict* 1982 **(AANBSA)**; *Alexandre* 1983; *Yellowbeard* 1983; *Dr. Fischer of Geneva* 1984; *The Shooting Party* 1984; *The Assisi Underground* 1985.

Mason, Marsha • Actress • Born St. Louis, MO, April 3, 1942. *Educ.* Webster College. Talented leading lady who earned four best actress Oscar nominations in the 1970s and early 80s. Formerly married to playwright Neil Simon. • *Blume in Love* 1973; *Cinderella Liberty* 1973 **(AANBA)**; *Audrey Rose* 1977; *The Goodbye Girl* 1977 **(AANBA)**; *The Cheap Detective* 1978; *Chapter Two* 1979 **(AANBA)**; *Promises in the Dark* 1979; *Only When I Laugh* 1981 **(AANBA)**; *Max Dugan Returns* 1982; *Heartbreak Ridge* 1986; *Stella* 1990; *Drop Dead Fred* 1991.

Massari, Lea • Actress • Born Anna Maria Massatani, Rome, 1934. Worked as an assistant to art director Piero Gherardi before being spotted by director Mario Monicelli and cast in his *Proibito* (1954). Best known for her roles as Anna, the lady who vanishes in Antonioni's *L'Avventura* (1960), and as the incestuous mother in Louis Malle's *Murmur of the Heart* (1971). • *Proibito* 1954; *L'Avventura* 1960; *El Coloso de Rodas/The Colossus of Rhodes* 1961; *Morte di un bandito* 1961; *I Sogni muoiono all'alba* 1961; *Una Vita Dificile* 1961; *Citta Prigioniera* 1962; *Le Monte-charge* 1962; *Le Quattro giornate di Napoli/Four Days of Naples* 1962; *L'Insoumis* 1964; *Llanto por un bandido* 1964; *La Coda del diavolo* 1965; *Made in Italy* 1965; *Le Soldatesse* 1965; *Volver a vivir* 1967; *Il Giardino delle delizie* 1968; *Lo voglio morto* 1968; *L'Amante* 1970; *Celeste* 1970; *Les Choses de la Vie/The Things of Life* 1970; *Senza via d'uscita* 1971; *Le Souffle au coeur/Murmur of the Heart* 1971; *La Course du lievre a travers les champs* 1972; *Le Fils* 1972; *La Prima Notte di Quiete* 1972; *Le Silencieux* 1972; *La Femme en Bleu* 1973; *Impossible Object* 1973; *La Main a Couper...* 1973; *Escape to Nowhere* 1974; *Allonsanfan* 1975; *Chi dice donna dice... donna* 1975; *Peur sur la Ville* 1975; *La Linea del fiume* 1976; *L'Ordinateur des pompes funebres* 1976; *Antonio Gramsci—I Giorni Del Carcere* 1977; *Faces of Love* 1977; *El Perro* 1977; *Reperages* 1977; *Violette et Francois* 1977; *Cristo si e Fermato a Eboli/Christ Stopped at Eboli* 1978; *Les Rendez-Vous d'Anna* 1978; *Sale Reveur* 1978; *Le Divorcement* 1979; *La Flambeuse* 1981; *Sarah* 1983; *Segreti Segreti* 1984; *Le Septieme Cible* 1984; *La Donna Spezzata* 1988 (a,sc).

Massey, Raymond • Actor • Born Raymond Hart Massey, Toronto, Ontario, Canada, August 30, 1896; died July 29, 1983, Los Angeles, CA. Veteran stage and film star in both England and the US, long associated with his performance as *Abe Linclon in Illinois* (1940), written for Massey by playwright Robert Sherwood. Massey later became widely known as Dr. Gillespie of TV's long-running "Dr. Kildare" series (1961-1966). Father of British actors Daniel and Anna Massey. • *Uncle Tom's Cabin* 1927; *The Speckled Band* 1931; *The Face at the Window* 1932; *The Old Dark House* 1932; *The Scarlet Pimpernel* 1935; *Fire Over England* 1936; *Things to Come* 1936; *Dreaming Lips* 1937; *Hurricane* 1937; *The Prisoner of Zenda* 1937; *Under the Red Robe* 1937; *Black Limelight* 1938; *Drums* 1938; *Abe Lincoln in Illinois* 1940 **(AANBA)**; *The Santa Fe Trail* 1940; *49th Parallel* 1941; *Dangerously They Live* 1941; *Desperate Journey* 1942; *Reap the Wild Wind* 1942; *Action in the North Atlantic* 1943; *Arsenic and Old Lace* 1944; *The Woman in the Window* 1944; *God Is My Co-Pilot* 1945; *Hotel Berlin* 1945; *A Matter of Life and Death* 1946; *Mourning Becomes Electra* 1947; *Possessed* 1947; *The Fountainhead* 1949; *Roseanna McCoy* 1949; *Barricade* 1950; *Chain Lightning* 1950; *Dallas* 1950; *Come Fill the Cup* 1951; *David and Bathsheba* 1951; *Sugarfoot* 1951; *Carson City* 1952; *The Desert Song* 1953; *Battle Cry* 1954; *Seven Angry Men* 1954; *East of Eden* 1955; *Prince of Players* 1955; *The Naked Eye* 1957; *Omar Khayyam* 1957; *The Naked and the Dead* 1958; *The Great Impostor* 1960; *The Fiercest Heart* 1961; *The Queen's Guards* 1961; *How the West Was Won* 1962; *MacKenna's Gold* 1969; *The Traveller* 1989 (p).

Masterson, Mary Stuart • Actress • Born New York, NY, 1967. *Educ.* Sundance Institute, Park City UT; NYU (anthropology, film). Promising young lead who made her screen debut at the age of seven, playing the daughter of her real-life father Peter Masterson in Bryan Forbes's *The Stepford Wives* (1975). Masterson gave mature, considered performances in *Some Kind of Wonderful* (1987) and *Immediate Family* (1989). • *The Stepford Wives* 1975; *Heaven Help Us* 1985; *At Close Range* 1986; *My Little Girl* 1986; *Gardens of Stone* 1987; *Some Kind of Wonderful* 1987; *Mr. North* 1988; *Chances Are* 1989; *Immediate Family* 1989; *Funny About Love* 1990.

Masterson, Peter • Actor, director; also screenwriter. • Born Carlos Bee Masterson, Houston, TX, June 1, 1934. *Educ.* Rice University. Masterson made his New York stage debut in *Call Me By My Rightful Name* in 1961 and has subsequently worked in film, theater and TV. He earned critical acclaim for his first feature as a director, the finely acted *The Trip to Bountiful* (1985). Married to actress Carlin Glynn and father of actress Mary Stuart Masterson. • *Counterpoint* 1967 (a); *In the Heat of the Night* 1967 (a); *Tomorrow* 1971 (a); *Von Richthofen and Brown* 1971 (a); *The Exorcist* 1973 (a); *Man on a Swing* 1974 (a); *The Stepford Wives* 1975 (a); *The Best Little Whorehouse in Texas* 1982 (sc,from book); *The Trip to Bountiful* 1985 (d); *Gardens of Stone* 1987 (a); *Full Moon in Blue Water* 1988 (d); *Blood Red* 1989 (d); *Night Games* 1989 (d).

Mastrantonio, Mary Elizabeth • Actress; also singer. • Born Oak Park, IL, November 17, 1958. *Educ.* University of Illinois, Champagne-Urbana (voice). Classically trained actress who made her screen debut as Gina, the sister of Tony Montana (Al Pacino), in *Scarface* (1983). A small role Mastrantonio had previously played in Martin Scorsese's *The King of Comedy* (1983) failed to make the final cut of the film; the director was so impressed with her performance, however, that he cast her as the female lead in *The Color of Money* (1986), leading to an Oscar nomination for best supporting actress. • *Scarface* 1983 (a); *The Color of Money* 1986 (a) **(AANBSA)**; *Slam Dance* 1987 (a); *The January Man* 1988 (a); *The Abyss* 1989 (a); *Fools of Fortune* 1990 (a); *Class Action* 1991 (a); *Robin Hood: Prince of Thieves* 1991 (a).

Mastroianni, Marcello • Actor • Born Marcello Mastrojanni, Fontana Liri, Italy, September 28, 1923. One of the few Italian actors to achieve the international fame of female compatriots such as Sophia Loren and Gina Lollobrigida. Mastroianni appeared as an extra in several films in the early 1940s, but made his breakthrough in 1948 when a stage appearance in *Angelica* led to his being asked to join Luchino Visconti's Quirino theater company. He went on to gain international acclaim as the world-weary, morally vacant lead of Fellini's *La Dolce Vita* (1959) and has continued to function as the directors's chief protagonist/mouthpiece in films from *8 1/2* (1963) through *Intervista* (1987). Mastroianni proved himself one of the most versatile stars of the 1960s, notably in *Divorce Italian Style* (1961) and Visconti's adaptation of Albert Camus's *The Stranger* (1967). He has brought a similar verve to his more recent, middle-aged parts in films such as *Allonsonfan* (1975), *Gabriela* (1983) and *Dark Eyes* (1987). • *Atto d'accusa* 1950; *Contro la legge* 1950; *Cuori sul mare* 1950; *Domenica d'Agosto* 1950; *Vita da cani* 1950; *L' Eterna catena* 1951; *Paris est toujours Paris* 1951; *Tragico ritorno* 1951; *Altri Tempi* 1952; *Gli Eroi della domenica* 1952; *Lulu* 1952; *Penne nere* 1952; *Ragazze di Piazza di Spagna* 1952; *Sensualitá* 1952; *Il Viale della speranza* 1952; *Febbre di vivere* 1953; *Non e mai troppo tardi* 1953; *Casa Ricordi* 1954; *Cronache di Poveri Amanti* 1954; *Giorni d'Amore* 1954; *La Principessa delle Canarie* 1954; *Schiava del peccato* 1954; *La Bella Mugnaia* 1955; *Il Bigamo/The Bigamist* 1955; *Peccato Che Sia una Canaglia/Too Bad She's Bad* 1955; *Tam-Tam Mayumbe* 1955; *La Fortuna di essere Donna* 1956; *Un Ettaro di cielo* 1957; *Il Medico e lo stregone* 1957; *Il Momento Più Bello* 1957; *Le Notti Bianche/White Nights* 1957; *Padri e Figli* 1957; *La Ragazza della salina/Mädchen und Männer* 1957; *The Big Deal on Madonna Street* 1958; *La Loi* 1958; *Racconti d'estate* 1958; *Tutti innamorati* 1958; *Amore e guai* 1959; *La Dolce Vita* 1959; *Ferdinando I re di Napoli* 1959; *Il Nemico di mia moglie* 1959; *Adua e le compagne* 1960; *Il Bell'Antonio* 1960; *Fantasmi a Roma* 1960; *L' Assassino* 1961; *Divorzio All'Italiano/Divorce Italian Style* 1961 **(AANBA)**; *La Notte* 1961; *Vie Privée/A Very Private Affair* 1961; *Cronaca familiare* 1962; *I Compagni/The Organizer* 1963; *Ieri, Oggi, Domani/* • Yesterday, Today and Tomorrow 1963; *Otto e Mezzo/8 1/2* 1963; *Matrimonio all'italiana/Marriage Italian Style* 1964; *Oggi, domani e dopodomani* 1964; *Casanova '70* 1965; *La Decima Vittima* 1965; *Io, Io, Io... e gli Altri* 1965; *The Poppy Is Also a Flower* 1966; *Spara forte, piu forte... non capisco/Shoot Loud, Louder ... I Don't Understand* 1966; *Break-Up* 1967; *Questi Fantasmi* 1967; *Lo Straniero/The Stranger* 1967; *Diamonds for Breakfast* 1968; *Gli Amanti/A Time for Lovers* 1969; *I Girasoli* 1969; *Dramma della gelosia (tutti i particolari in cronaca)* 1970; *Giochi particolari* 1970; *Leo the Last* 1970; *Scipione detto anche l'Africano* 1970; *Ca n'arrive qu'aux autres/It Only Happens to Others* 1971; *La Cagna* 1971; *La Moglie del Prete/The Priest's Wife* 1971; *Permette? Rocco Papaleo* 1971; *Roma* 1972; *Che?/What?* 1973; *L' Evenement le plus important depuis que l'homme a marche sur la lune* 1973; *La Grande Bouffe* 1973; *Massacre in Rome* 1973; *Mordi e Fuggi* 1973; *Salut l'artiste* 1973; *Touche pas a la femme blanche!* 1973; *C'eravamo tanto amati/We All Loved Each Other So Much* 1974; *La Pupa del gangster* 1974; *Allonsanfan* 1975; *Culastrice nobile veneziano* 1975; *La Divina Creatura* 1975; *Per le Antiche Scale* 1975; *La Donna Della Domenica* 1976; *Signore e Signori, Buonanotte* 1976; *Todo Modo* 1976; *Doppio Delitto* 1977; *Una Giornata Particolare/A Special Day* 1977 **(AANBA)**; *Mogliamante* 1977; *Cosi' come sei* 1978; *Fatto di sangue fra due uomini per causa di una vedova. Si sospettano moventi politici/Blood Feud* 1978; *Giallo napoletano* 1978; *Reve de Singe* 1978; *Le Grand embouteillage* 1979; *La Terrazza* 1979; *La Città Delle Donne* 1980; *Io Sono Anna Magnani* 1980; *Fantasma d'Amore* 1981; *La Pelle* 1981; *La Nuit de Varennes* 1982; *Oltre la Porta* 1982; *Storia di Piera* 1982; *Gabriela* 1983; *Le General de l'Armee Morte* 1983; *Enrico IV* 1984; *The Last Horror Film* 1984; *Le Due vite di Mattia Pascal* 1985; *Maccaroni* 1985; *Ginger et Fred/Ginger and Fred* 1986; *I Soliti Ignoti... Vent'Anni Dopo* 1986; *Melissokomos Petheni—O Alles Mythos, Enas* 1986; *O Melissokomos* 1986; *Federico Fellini's Intervista* 1987; *Oci Ciornie/Dark Eyes*

1987 **(AANBA)**; *Miss Arizona* 1988; *Che ora e* 1989; *Splendor* 1989; *Stanno Tutti Bene* 1990.

Masur, Richard • Actor; also director. • Born New York, NY. *Educ.* NYU (theater). Prolific, engaging supporting player of stage, screen and TV. Masur's 1987 short film, *Love Struck*, received an Academy Award nomination. • *Whiffs* 1975; *Bittersweet Love* 1976; *Semi-Tough* 1977; *Who'll Stop the Rain?* 1978; *Hanover Street* 1979; *Scavenger Hunt* 1979; *Heaven's Gate* 1980; *I'm Dancing As Fast As I Can* 1981; *The Thing* 1982; *Timerider: The Adventure of Lyle Swann* 1982; *Nightmares* 1983; *Risky Business* 1983; *Under Fire* 1983; *The Mean Season* 1985; *My Science Project* 1985; *Heartburn* 1986; *The Believers* 1987; *Love Struck (short)* 1987 (d) **(AANBSF)**; *Walker* 1987; *License to Drive* 1988; *Rent-A-Cop* 1988; *Shoot to Kill* 1988; *Far From Home* 1989; *Flashback* 1990; *Out of Sight, Out of Mind* 1990; *Vietnam, Texas* 1990.

Maté, Rudolph • *aka* Rudy Maté • Director of photography, director • Born Rudolf Matheh, Cracow, Poland, January 21, 1898; died 1964. *Educ.* University of Budapest (philosophy). Distinguished cinematographer of Hungarian parentage who began his career in Germany in the 1920s. Maté shot several films for Carl Theodor Dreyer, notably the dream-like masterpiece *Vampyr* (1932), before moving to Hollywood in 1934. His expressionist sensibility redeemed several lesser films, like Tay Garnett's *Professional Soldier* (1935), as well as making significant contributions to classics such as Charles Vidor's *Gilda* (1946). Maté turned to directing in 1947, with results ranging from the competent to the forgettable; his most famous directorial effort is the 1950 noir standard, *D.O.A.* • *Dunkle Gassen* 1923 (ph); *Mikael* 1924 (ph—exteriors); *Pietro der Korsar* 1925 (ph); *Le Roman d'un jeune homme pauvre* 1926 (ph); *Die Hochstaplerin* 1927 (ph); *La Passion de Jeanne d'Arc/The Passion of Joan of Arc* 1927 (ph); *Unter Ausschluss der Offentlichkeit* 1927 (ph); *Prix de Beaute* 1930 (ph); *Le Costaud des P.T.T.* 1931 (d); *La Couturiere de Luneville* 1931 (ph); *Le Monsieur de minuit* 1931 (ph—French-language version); *Le Roi de Camembert* 1931 (ph); *La Vagabonde* 1931 (ph); *Aren't We All?* 1932 (ph); *La Belle Mariniere* 1932 (ph); *Insult* 1932 (ph); *Paprika* 1932 (ph); *Service For Ladies* 1932 (ph); *Vampyr* 1932 (ph); *Die Abenteuer des Konigs Pausole* 1933 (ph); *Dans les rues* 1933 (ph); *Une Femme au volant* 1933 (ph); *La Mille-et-deuxieme nuit* 1933 (ph); *Le Dernier Milliardaire* 1934 (ph); *Liliom* 1934 (ph); *Pursued* 1934 (ph—Spanish-language version); *Dante's Inferno* 1935 (ph); *Dressed to Thrill* 1935 (ph); *Metropolitan* 1935 (ph); *Navy Wife* 1935 (ph); *Professional Soldier* 1935 (ph); *Charlie Chan's Secret* 1936 (ph); *Come and Get It* 1936 (ph); *Dodsworth* 1936 (ph); *A Message to Garcia* 1936 (ph); *Our Relations* 1936 (ph); *The Girl From Scotland Yard* 1937 (ph); *Outcast* 1937 (ph); *Stella Dallas* 1937 (ph); *The Adventures of Marco Polo* 1938 (ph); *Blockade* 1938 (ph); *Trade Winds* 1938 (ph); *Youth Takes a Fling* 1938 (ph); *The Flying Deuces* 1939 (prod.adv); *Love Affair* 1939 (ph); *The Real Glory* 1939 (ph); *Foreign Correspondent* 1940 (ph) **(AANBPH)**; *My Favorite Wife* 1940 (ph); *Seven Sinners* 1940 (ph); *The Westerner* 1940 (uncred.ph); *The Flame of New Orleans* 1941 (ph); *It Started With Eve* 1941 (ph); *That Hamilton Woman* 1941 (ph) **(AANBPH)**; *The Pride of the Yankees* 1942 (ph) **(AANBPH)**; *To Be or Not to Be* 1942 (ph); *Sahara* 1943 (ph) **(AANBPH)**; *They Got Me Covered* 1943 (ph); *Address Unknown* 1944 (ph); *Cover Girl* 1944 (ph) **(AANBPH)**; *Over 21* 1945 (ph); *Tonight and Every Night* 1945 (ph); *Gilda* 1946 (ph); *Down to Earth* 1947 (ph); *It Had to Be You* 1947 (d,ph); *The Dark Past* 1948 (d); *The Return of October* 1948 (p); *Branded* 1950 (d); *D.O.A.* 1950 (d); *No Sad Songs For Me* 1950 (d); *Union Station* 1950 (d); *The Green Glove* 1951 (d); *The Prince Who Was a Thief* 1951 (d); *When Worlds Collide* 1951 (d); *Paula* 1952 (d); *Sally and Saint Anne* 1952 (d); *Forbidden* 1953 (d); *The Mississippi Gambler* 1953 (d); *Second Chance* 1953 (d); *The Black Shield of Falworth* 1954 (d); *The Siege at Red River* 1954 (d); *The Violent Men* 1954 (d); *The Far Horizons* 1955 (d); *Miracle in the Rain* 1956 (d); *Port Afrique* 1956 (d); *The Rawhide Years* 1956 (d); *Three Violent People* 1956 (d); *The Deep Six* 1957 (d); *Come Prima/For the First Time* 1959 (d); *Revak, Lo Schiavo di Cartagine/Revak the Rebel* 1959 (d); *The 300 Spartans* 1962 (d,p); *Aliki - My Love* 1963 (d,p); *Il Re Dei Sette Mari* 1963 (d).

Mathis, June • Screenwriter • Born Leadville, CO, 1892; died 1927. Female scenarist, with Metro (later MGM) from 1918. Mathis had a significant hand in building the reputation of Rudolph Valentino, via such vehicles as *The Four Horsemen of the Apocalypse* (1921) and *Blood and Sand* (1922). She also helped launch Nazimova to stardom in the late teens and was assigned by Irving Thalberg the task of re-editing Erich von Stroheim's *Greed* (1922) down from three hours to one hour and 50 minutes. • *The Sunbeam* 1916 (sc); *Aladdin's Other Lamp* 1917 (sc); *The Barricade* 1917 (a); *The Beautiful Lie* 1917 (sc); *The Call of Her People* 1917 (sc); *His Father's Son* 1917 (sc); *The Jury of Fate* 1917 (sc); *Lady Barnacle* 1917 (sc); *A Magdalene of the Hills* 1917 (sc); *The Millionaire's Double* 1917 (story); *Miss Robinson Crusoe* 1917 (story); *The Power of Decision* 1917 (sc); *Red, White and Blue Blood* 1917 (sc); *The Rose of the Alley* 1917 (sc); *Threads of Fate* 1917 (sc); *The Trail of the Shadow* 1917 (sc); *The Voice of Conscience* 1917 (sc); *A Wife By Proxy* 1917 (sc); *Blue Jeans* 1918 (sc); *The Brass Check* 1918 (sc); *The Claim* 1918 (sc); *Daybreak* 1918 (sc); *Eye For Eye* 1918 (sc); *The Eyes of Mystery* 1918 (sc); *Five Thousand an Hour* 1918 (sc); *His Bonded Wife* 1918 (sc); *The House of Gold* 1918 (sc); *The House of Mirth* 1918 (sc); *Kildares of Storm* 1918 (sc); *The Legion of Death* 1918 (sc,story); *A Man's World* 1918 (sc); *Secret Strings* 1918 (sc); *The Silent Woman* 1918 (sc); *Social Hypocrites* 1918 (sc); *Social Quicksands* 1918 (sc); *The Successful Adventure* 1918 (sc,story); *Sylvia on a Spree* 1918 (sc); *To Hell With the Kaiser* 1918 (sc); *Toys of Fate* 1918 (sc); *The Trail to Yesterday* 1918 (sc); *Why Germany Must Pay* 1918 (a); *The Winding Trail* 1918 (sc); *The Winning of Beatrice* 1918 (sc); *With Neatness and Dispatch* 1918 (sc); *Almost Married* 1919 (sc); *The Amateur Adventuress* 1919 (sc); *The Blind Man's Eyes* 1919 (sc); *The Brat* 1919 (sc); *The Divorcee* 1919 (sc); *Fair and Warmer* 1919 (sc); *The Great Victory* 1919 (sc); *The Island of Intrigue* 1919 (sc); *Johnny on the Spot* 1919 (sc); *Lombardi, Ltd.* 1919 (sc); *The Man Who Stayed at Home* 1919 (sc); *The Microbe* 1919 (sc); *Out of the Fog* 1919 (sc); *The Parisian Tigress* 1919 (story); *The Red Lantern* 1919 (sc); *Satan Junior* 1919 (sc); *Some Bride* 1919 (sc); *The Way of the Strong* 1919 (sc); *Hearts Are Trumps* 1920 (sc); *Old Lady 31* 1920 (sc); *Parlor, Bedroom and Bath* 1920 (sc); *Polly With a Past* 1920 (sc); *The Price of Redemption* 1920 (sc); *The Right of Way* 1920 (sc); *The Saphead* 1920 (sc); *The Walk-Offs* 1920 (sc); *The Willow Tree* 1920 (sc); *Camille* 1921 (sc); *The Conquering Power* 1921 (sc); *The Four Horsemen of the Apocalypse* 1921 (sc); *Hole in the Wall* 1921 (sc); *The Idle Rich* 1921 (sc); *The Man Who* 1921 (sc); *A Trip to Paradise* 1921 (sc); *Blood and Sand* 1922 (sc); *The Golden Gift* 1922 (story); *Greed* 1922 (add.ed,add.sc); *Hate* 1922 (sc); *Kisses* 1922 (sc); *Turn to the Right* 1922 (sc); *The Young Rajah* 1922 (sc); *Day of Faith* 1923 (sc); *In the Palace of the King* 1923 (sc); *The Spanish Dancer* 1923 (sc); *Three Wise Fools* 1923 (sc); *Ben Hur, A Tale of the Christ* 1925 (sc.adapt); *Classified* 1925 (sc); *The Desert Flower* 1925 (sc); *Greed* 1925 (ed); *Sally* 1925 (sc); *We Moderns* 1925 (sc); *The Greater Glory* 1926 (sc); *Irene* 1926 (sc); *Magic Flame* 1927 (sc); *The Masked Woman* 1927 (sc).

Matlin, Marlee • Actress • Born Morton Grove, IL, August 24, 1965. *Educ.* William Rainey Harper College (criminal justice). Delicately pretty, deaf actress who made a highly acclaimed debut in *Children of a Lesser God* (1986). • *Children of a Lesser God* 1986 **(AABA)**; *Walker* 1987.

Matras, Christian • Director of photography • Born Valence, France, December 29, 1903; died 1977. Began his career as a newsreel cameraman and went on to shoot several French classics of the 1930s, including Renoir's *Grand Illusion* (1937). Matras was responsible for the sumptuous colors and critically celebrated, virtuoso camera movements of Max Ophuls's *La Ronde* (1950), *Le Plaisir* (1951), *The Earrings of Madame de...* (1953) and *Lola Montes* (1955). • *Le Billet de logement* 1932 (ph); *Le Chatelaine du Liban* 1933 (ph); *L'Affaire coquelet* 1934 (ph); *La Maison dans la dune* 1934 (ph); *Maternite* 1934 (ph); *La Paquebot 'Tenacity'* 1934 (ph); *Le Scandale* 1934 (ph); *Les Hommes de la cote* 1935 (ph); *La Marmaille* 1935 (ph); *L'Argent* 1936 (ph); *Les Mutines de l'Elseneur* 1936 (ph); *Les Reprouves* 1936 (ph); *Le Chanteur de minuit* 1937 (ph); *La Grande Illusion/Grand Illusion* 1937 (ph); *Cafe de Paris* 1938 (ph); *Entree des Artistes* 1938 (ph); *Legions d'honneur* 1938 (ph); *Le Paradis perdu* 1938 (ph); *La Piste du sud* 1938 (ph); *Prison sans Barreaux* 1938 (ph); *Le Dernier Tournant* 1939 (ph); *Le Duel* 1939 (ph); *La Fin du Jour* 1939 (ph); *La Nuit merveilleuse* 1940 (ph); *Le Briseur de chaines* 1941 (ph); *La Duchesse de Langeais* 1941 (ph); *Parade en sept nuits* 1941 (ph); *Romance de Paris* 1941 (ph); *La Loi du printemps* 1942 (ph); *Pontacarral Colonel d'Empire* 1942 (ph); *L'Escalier sans fin* 1943 (ph); *Lucrece* 1943 (ph); *Mahlia la metisse* 1943 (ph); *Secrets* 1943 (ph); *Un Seul amour* 1943 (ph); *Le Bossu* 1944 (ph); *Boule de Suif* 1945 (ph); *Mademoiselle X* 1945 (ph); *Seul dans la nuit* 1945 (ph); *Tant que je vivrai* 1945 (ph); *L'Idiot* 1946 (ph); *Il Suffit d'une fois* 1946 (ph); *Le Beau voyage* 1947 (ph); *Eternel conflit* 1947 (ph); *Les Jeux sont faits* 1947 (ph); *L'Aigle a Deux Tetes* 1948 (ph); *D'Homme a Hommes* 1948 (ph); *La Revoltee* 1948 (ph); *Tous les chemins menent a Rome* 1949 (ph); *La Valse de Paris* 1949 (ph); *La Ronde* 1950 (ph); *Le Singoalla* 1950 (ph); *Souvenirs perdus* 1950 (ph); *Barbe-Bleue* 1951 (ph); *Olivia* 1951 (ph); *Le Plaisir* 1951 (ph—"Le Masque," "La Maison Tellier"); *Adorables Creatures* 1952 (ph); *Fanfan la Tulipe* 1952 (ph); *Violettes imperiales* 1952 (ph); *The Earrings of Madame De...* 1953 (ph); *Lucrece Borgia* 1953 (ph); *Destinees* 1954 (ph); *Madame du Barry* 1954 (ph); *Secrets d'Alcove* 1954 (ph—"Le billet de logement" "Le lit de la Pompadour"); *Lola Montes* 1955 (ph); *Nana* 1955 (ph); *Les Aventures de Till l'Espiegel* 1956 (ph); *Les Carnets du Major Thompson* 1956 (ph—Martine Carol sequences); *Rencontre a Paris* 1956 (ph); *Rendez-vous avec Maurice Chevalier* 1956 (ph); *Les Espions* 1957 (ph); *Une Manche et la belle* 1957 (ph); *Oeil pour Oeil* 1957 (ph); *Christine* 1958 (ph); *Maxime* 1958 (ph); *The Mirror Has Two Faces* 1958 (ph); *Montparnasse 19* 1958 (ph); *Pourquoi viens-tu si tard?* 1958 (ph); *What Price Murder* 1958 (ph); *La Bete a l'affut* 1959 (ph); *Le Chemin des ecoliers* 1959 (ph); *Die Schone Lugnerin* 1959 (ph); *Le Coeur battant (short)* 1960 (ph); *Les Magiciennes* 1960 (ph); *Vers l'extase* 1960 (ph); *Le Jeu de la Verite* 1961 (a); *Les Lions sont laches* 1961 (ph); *Paris Blues* 1961 (ph); *Cartouche* 1962 (ph); *Le Crime ne paie pas* 1962 (ph); *Sheherazade* 1962 (ph); *Therese Desqueyroux* 1962 (ph); *Coup de bambou* 1963 (ph); *Le Journal d'un fou* 1963 (ph); *Les Amities particulieres* 1964 (ph); *Casablanca, nid d'espions* 1964 (ph); *Samba* 1964 (ph); *La Dama de Beyrut* 1965 (ph); *Les Fetes galantes* 1965 (ph); *Le Majordome* 1965 (ph); *Rancho de los implacables* 1965 (ph); *La Mujer perdida* 1966 (ph); *Mas alla de las montanas* 1967 (ph); *Les Risques du Metier* 1967 (ph); *Woman Times Seven* 1967 (ph); *Les Oiseaux vont mourir au Perou* 1968 (ph); *La Voie Lactee* 1969 (ph); *Le Bal du Comte d'Orgel* 1970 (ph); *Varietes* 1971 (ph); *Pas folle la guepe* 1972 (ph).

Mattes, Eva • Actress • Born Bavaria, West Germany. Leading German actress of the 1980s who has played characters ranging from Proust's maid (in Percy Adlon's *Celeste* 1981) to Rainer Werner Fassbinder (in the director's "non-realist" self-portrait, *A Man Called Eva* 1984). Daughter of film actress Margret Symo. • *Die Bitteren Tranen der Petra von Kant* 1972; *Wildwechsel* 1972; *Fontane Effi Briest* 1974; *Supermarket* 1974; *Frauen in New York* 1977; *Stroszek* 1977; *Schluchtenflitzer* 1978; *Was Ich Bin, Sind Meine Filme* 1978; *David* 1979; *Deutschland Bleiche Mutter/Germany, Pale Mother* 1979; *In Einem Jahr Mit 13 Monden* 1979; *Woyzeck* 1979; *Celeste* 1981; *Friedliche Tage* 1983; *Rita Ritter* 1983; *Die Wilden Fuenfziger* 1983; *Ein Mann Wie EVA/A Man Called Eva* 1984; *Auf Immer und Ewig* 1986; *Felix* 1987; *Herbstmilch* 1989.

Matthau, Walter • Actor; also producer, director. • Born New York, NY, October 1, 1920. *Educ.* Columbia School of Journalism; Dramatic Workshop of the New School for Social Research, New York. Entered films in 1955 after prolonged stage work and is best known for his wry, comic portrayals in films such as *The Fortune Cookie* (1966), *The Odd Couple* (1968) and *The Survivors* (1983). Matthau was equally memorable in several straight roles, including the cynical, Kissinger-like advisor in *Fail Safe* (1964) and the embittered title character in the ironically named thriller, *The Laughing Policeman* (1973). He has directed one film, *The Gangster Story* (1959), as has his son, Charles Matthau (*Doin' Time on Planet Earth* 1988). • *The Indian Fighter* 1955; *The Kentuckian* 1955; *Bigger Than Life* 1956; *A Face in the Crowd* 1957; *Slaughter on Tenth Avenue* 1957; *King Creole* 1958; *Onionhead* 1958; *Ride a Crooked Trail* 1958; *Voice in the Mirror* 1958; *Gangster Story* 1959 (a,d); *Strangers When We Meet* 1960; *Lonely Are the Brave* 1962; *Who's Got the Action?* 1962; *Charade* 1963; *Island of Love* 1963; *Ensign Pulver* 1964; *Fail Safe* 1964; *Goodbye, Charlie* 1964; *Mirage* 1965; *The Fortune Cookie* 1966 **(AABSA)**; *A Guide For the Married Man* 1967; *Candy* 1968; *The Odd Couple* 1968; *The Secret Life of an American Wife* 1968; *Cactus Flower* 1969; *Hello, Dolly!* 1969; *Kotch* 1971 **(AANBA)**; *A New Leaf* 1971; *Plaza Suite* 1971; *Pete 'n' Tillie* 1972; *Charley Varrick* 1973; *The Laughing Policeman* 1973; *Earthquake* 1974; *The Front Page* 1974; *The Taking of Pelham 1, 2, 3* 1974; *The Sunshine Boys* 1975 **(AANBA)**; *The Bad News Bears* 1976; *Gentleman Tramp* 1976; *California Suite* 1978; *Casey's Shadow* 1978; *House Calls* 1978; *Hopscotch* 1980; *Little Miss Marker* 1980 (a,exec.p); *Portrait of a 60% Perfect Man* 1980; *Buddy Buddy* 1981; *First Monday in October* 1981; *I Ought to Be in Pictures* 1981; *The Survivors* 1983; *Movers & Shakers* 1985; *Pirates* 1986; *The Couch Trip* 1988; *Il Piccolo Diavolo* 1988.

Mature, Victor • Actor • Born Victor John Mature, Louisville, KY, January 29, 1915. *Educ.* Pasadena Playhouse. Hulking, handsome leading man of adventure and action films who wisely never took his own talent too seriously. Memorable as Samson to Hedy Lamarr's Delilah in 1949, and very funny as a has-been movie star not unlike himself in Vittorio De Sica's *After the Fox* (1966). • *The Housekeeper's Daughter* 1939; *Captain Caution* 1940; *No, No, Nanette* 1940; *One Million B.C.* 1940; *I Wake Up Screaming* 1941; *The Shanghai Gesture* 1941; *Footlight Serenade* 1942; *My Gal Sal* 1942; *Seven Days Leave* 1942; *Song of the Islands* 1942; *My Darling Clementine* 1946; *The Kiss of Death* 1947; *Moss Rose* 1947; *Cry of the City* 1948; *Fury at Furnace Creek* 1948; *Easy Living* 1949; *Red, Hot and Blue* 1949; *Samson and Delilah* 1949; *Gambling House* 1950; *I'll Get By* 1950; *Stella* 1950; *Wabash Avenue* 1950; *Androcles and the Lion* 1952; *The Las Vegas Story* 1952; *Million Dollar Mermaid* 1952; *Something For the Birds* 1952; *Affair With a Stranger* 1953; *The Glory Brigade* 1953; *The Robe* 1953; *The Veils of Bagdad* 1953; *Betrayed* 1954; *Chief Crazy Horse* 1954; *Dangerous Mission* 1954; *Demetrius and the Gladiators* 1954; *The Egyptian* 1954; *Violent Saturday* 1954; *The Last Frontier* 1955; *Safari* 1956; *The Sharkfighters* 1956; *Zarak* 1956; *Interpol* 1957; *China Doll* 1958; *No Time to Die* 1958; *Annibale/Hannibal* 1959; *The Bandit of Zhobe* 1959; *The Big Circus* 1959; *Escort West* 1959; *Timbuktu* 1959; *I Tartari* 1960; *After the Fox* 1966; *Head* 1968; *Every Little Crook and Nanny*

1972; *Won Ton Ton, the Dog Who Saved Hollywood* 1976; *Firepower* 1979; *Samson and Delilah* 1984.

Maura, Carmen • Actress • Born Madrid, Spain, 1946. Alluring Spanish actress who began her career in cabaret and café theater and became associated with the cultural flowering, labeled the "Movida Madrileña," which followed the death of General Franco. Maura achieved national fame as host of the TV show "Esta Noche" and has starred in several features directed by Pedro Almodovar, including his breakthrough film, the international hit *Women on the Verge of a Nervous Breakdown* (1988). • *El Hombre Oculto* 1970; *El Love Feroz* 1972; *La Peticion* 1976; *Tigres de Papel* 1977; *Los Ojos Vendados* 1978; *Que Hace una Chica Como Tu en un Sitio Como Este?* 1978; *Aquella Casa En Las Afueras* 1980; *La Mano Negra* 1980; *Pepi, Luci, Bom y Otras Chicas del Monton/Pepi, Luci, Bom and Other Girls Like Mom* 1980; *Gary Cooper, Que Estas en los Cielos/Gary Cooper, Who Art in Heaven* 1981; *El Cid Cabreador* 1983; *Entre Tinieblas/Dark Habits* 1983; *Que He Hecho Yo Para Merecer Esto/What Have I Done to Deserve This?* 1984; *Extramuros* 1985; *Se Infiel y no Mires con Quien* 1985; *Matador* 1986; *Tata Mia* 1986; *La Ley del Deseo/Law of Desire* 1987; *Baton Rouge* 1988; *Mujeres al Borde de un Ataque de Nervios/Women on the Verge of a Nervous Breakdown* 1988; *Mieux Vaut Courir* 1989; *Ay, Carmela* 1990.

Mauro, Humberto • Director; also screenwriter, director of photography, actor. • Born Minas Geraes, Brazil, April 30, 1897; died November 6, 1983, Volta Grande, Brazil. Pioneer of Brazilian cinema. Mauro began his career in the provinces in 1926 and was brought to Rio de Janeiro by producer-director Adhemar Gonzaga in 1930. He went on to direct several features which were praised for their uniquely Brazilian style—notably *Ganga Bruta* (1933)—as well as making over 230 shorts for the National Institute of Educational Cinema. Several of the latter, including *A Velha a Fiar* (1964), became classics of the genre. • *Valadiao O Cratera* 1925 (d); *Na primavera da vida* 1926 (d); *Tesouro Perdido* 1927 (d); *Brasa dormida* 1928 (d); *Sangue mineiro* 1929 (d); *O descobrimento do Brasil* 1932 (d); *Ganga bruta* 1933 (d); *Citade Mulher* 1934 (d); *Argila* 1942 (d); *O canto de Saudade* 1952 (d); *I Am Eight* 1958 (d); *A Velha a Fiar (short)* 1964 (d).

May, Elaine • Director, screenwriter, actress • Born Elaine Berlin, Philadelphia, PA, April 21, 1932. *Educ.* Playwrights Theatre, Chicago. Former cabaret performer whose comic partnership with Mike Nichols culminated in their own Broadway showcase, *An Evening with Mike Nichols and Elaine May* (1960). May made her name as a film director with 1972's hilarious *The Heartbreak Kid* (her only directorial outing to have been scripted by someone else) and also earned critical acclaim for *Mikey and Nicky* (1976), an offbeat study of petty gangsters starring Peter Falk and John Cassavetes. (Like 1987's *Ishtar*, however, *Mikey* was a failure at the box-office.) May wrote Otto Preminger's *Such Good Friends* (1971) under the pseudonym Esther Dale and made an uncredited contribution to the screenplay of *Tootsie* (1982). She is the daughter of Yiddish theater director Jack Berlin and mother of actress Jeannie Berlin. • *Enter Laughing* 1966 (a); *Bach to Bach* 1967 (a); *Luv* 1967 (a); *A New Leaf* 1971 (a,d,sc); *Such Good Friends* 1971 (sc); *The Heartbreak Kid* 1972 (d); *Mikey and Nicky* 1976 (d,sc); *California Suite* 1978 (a); *Heaven Can Wait* 1978 (sc) **(AANBSC)**; *Tootsie* 1982 (uncred.sc); *Ishtar* 1987 (d); *In the Spirit* 1990 (a).

May, Joe • *aka* Joseph Mandel, Fred Majo • Director; also producer. • Born Julius Otto Mandl, Vienna, Austria, November 7, 1880; died 1954. *Educ.* Royal Agricultural College, Berlin. May began his career as a director of low-budget crime films and, by the late 1910s, was running his own film empire comprising studios, laboratories and real-estate concerns. (One of several directors who got their start under contract to May was Fritz Lang.) After inflation put an end to his tycoon status in the mid-20s May worked as a director and producer for other companies; his greatest achievement of this period was the expressionistic *Asphalt* (1929), a classic "street movie" about a prostitute and a policeman. After being forced to leave Germany in 1933 May made quick stops in France and England before moving to the US, where he made mostly forgettable films. With his actress wife Mia May (he adopted her name rather than vice versa) he later ran Hollywood's Blue Danube restaurant. • *In der tiefe des schachtes* 1912 (d,sc); *Ein Ausgestossener 1. Teil: Der junge Chef* 1913 (d,sc); *Die Geheimnisvolle villa* 1913 (d); *Heimat und Fremde* 1913 (d,sc); *Das Panzergewolbe* 1914 (d); *Das Gesetz der mine* 1915 (d,sc); *Nebel und Sonne* 1916 (d,sc); *Die Sunde der Helga Arndt* 1916 (d,sc); *Wie ich detektive wurde* 1916 (d,sc); *Hilde Warren und der Tod* 1917 (d,sc); *Die Hochzeit in Exzentric-Club* 1917 (d); *Die Liebe der Hetty Raymond* 1917 (d); *Der Onyxkopf* 1917 (d); *Der Schwarze chauffeur* 1917 (d); *Die Silhouette des teufels* 1917 (d); *Ihr grosses geheimnis* 1918 (d,sc); *Opfer* 1918 (d,sc); *Die Platonische Ehe* 1918 (sc); *Sein bester Freund* 1918 (d); *Veritas Vincit* 1918 (d,story); *Die Herrin der Welt* 1920 (d,sc); *Das Wandernde Bild* 1920 (prod.sup); *Das Indische Grabmal/The Indian Tomb* 1921 (d); *Tragodie der Liebe* 1923 (d); *Der Farmer aus Texas* 1925 (d); *Dagfin* 1926 (d,sc); *Heimkehr* 1928 (d,sc,uncred.ed); *Ungarische rhapsodie* 1928 (sc); *Asphalt* 1929 (d,sc); *Ihre Majestat die liebe* 1930 (d); *...Und das ist di hauptsache* 1931 (d); *Zwei in einem auto* 1931 (d); *Ein Lied fuer dich* 1933 (d); *Music in the Air* 1934 (d); *Two Hearts in Waltztime* 1934 (d); *No Monkey Business* 1935 (story); *Confession* 1937 (d); *The House of Fear* 1939 (d); *Society Smugglers* 1939 (d); *The House of the Seven Gables* 1940 (d); *The Invisible Man Returns* 1940 (d,story); *You're Not So Tough* 1940 (d); *Hit the Road* 1941 (d); *The Invisible Woman* 1941 (story); *The Strange Death of Adolf Hitler* 1943 (story); *Johnny Doesn't Live Here Anymore* 1944 (d); *Uncertain Glory* 1944 (story); *Buccaneer's Girl* 1950 (story).

May, Mathilda • French actress • Beautiful, promising young French lead who has starred in films by Claude Chabrol, Jacques Demy and Tobe Hooper. • *Nemo* 1983; *Les Rois du Gag* 1984; *Letters to an Unknown Lover* 1985; *Lifeforce* 1985; *La Vie dissolue de Gerard Floque* 1986; *Le Cri du hibou* 1987; *La Passerelle* 1987; *La Barbare* 1988; *Trois places pour le 26* 1988; *Naked Tango* 1990.

Mayer, Carl • Screenwriter • Born Graz, Austria, November 20, 1894; died 1944, London. Highly influential figure of German film whose list of credits—ranging from the seminal, expressionistic *The Cabinet of Dr. Caligari* (1919) to the sophisticated early talkie, *Ariane* (1931)—reads like a history of Weimar cinema. Mayer's work stands out from that of his contemporaries thanks to his concern with social issues; working in a film culture which was more concerned with form than content, he managed to inject a grainy realism into the Expressionist visual style, notably in films such as *Sylvester* (1923) and F.W. Murnau's *The Last Laugh* (1924).

Though he turned down the opportunity to go to Hollywood with Murnau (his most consistent collaborator), Mayer continued to write screenplays for him, notably *Sunrise* (1927). *Sunrise* was one of the few silent features to tell its story almost entirely through images, resorting to intertitles only for occasional dialogue. With the coming of Nazism Mayer moved first to France and then Great Britain, where he wrote several Paul Czinner films and worked uncredited on *Pygmalion* (1938) and *Major Barbara* (1941) before dying of cancer. • *Die Frau im Kafig* 1919 (sc); *Das Kabinett des Dr. Caligari/The Cabinet of Dr. Caligari* 1919 (sc); *Der Bucklige und die Tanzerin* 1920 (sc); *Der Dummkopf* 1920 (sc); *Der Gang in der nacht* 1920 (sc); *Genuine die tragodie eines seltsamen Hauses* 1920 (sc); *Johannes Goth* 1920 (sc); *Danton* 1921 (sc.consult.); *Grausige nachte* 1921 (sc); *Hintertreppe* 1921 (sc); *Scherben* 1921 (sc); *Schloss Vogelod* 1921 (sc); *Verlogene Moral*

1921 (sc); *Vanina oder die galgenhochzeit* 1922 (sc); *Erdgeist* 1923 (sc); *Der Puppenmacher von Nian-King* 1923 (sc); *Sylvester tragodie einer nacht/Sylvester* 1923 (sc); *Der Letzte Mann/The Last Laugh* 1924 (sc); *Tartuff* 1925 (sc); *Berlin die sinfonie der grosstadt/Berlin: A Symphony of a Big City* 1927 (uncred. from concept,sc); *Sunrise* 1927 (sc); *Four Devils* 1928 (sc); *Die Letzte Kompanie* 1930 (sc.consult); *Ariane* 1931 (sc); *Der Mann, der Den Mord Beging* 1931 (sc); *Melo* 1932 (sc); *Der traümende Mund/Dreaming Lips* 1932 (sc); *As You Like It* 1936 (adapt); *Dreaming Lips* 1937 (English-language remake); *Pygmalion* 1938 (uncred.sc); *The Fourth Estate* 1939 (sc.consult); *Major Barbara* 1941 (uncred.sc); *World of Plenty* 1943 (sc.consult); *Dreaming Lips* 1953 (remake, from sc); *Der Letzte Mann* 1955 (remake, from sc).

Mayer, Louis B. • *aka* Lazar Mayer, Louis Mayer • Executive • Born Eliezer Mayer, Minsk, Russia, July 4, 1885; died 1957. One of the most influential figures of Hollywood's golden era who, from 1924 to 1951, guided MGM through its reign as America's greatest studio, with "more stars than there are in the heavens."

Immigrating to Canada, and then the US, Mayer set up a successful chain of movie theaters in New England before moving into distribution, scoring a huge profit with *Birth of a Nation* (1915). He then turned to production with the Alco company, which later changed its name to Metro. Mayer went independent in 1917, forming Louis B. Mayer Productions, but seven years later merged once again with Metro, as well as with Samuel Goldwyn. Mayer was named vice-president and general manager of the freshly-formed MGM, and with "boy genius" Irving Thalberg as his production chief he ran the studio like a family household, dishing out punishments or rewards according to his whim. Relying more on intuition than intellect, Mayer steered the company to its greatest successes with the directing skills of DeMille, the face of Garbo and the finest creative and technical personnel in filmdom.

Mayer won a Special Academy Award "for distinguished service to the motion picture industry" in 1950 but was ousted from MGM the following year by his former assistant, Dore Schary.

Maysles, Albert • Filmmaker • Born Brookline, MA, November 26, 1926. *Educ.* Syracuse University (psychology); Boston University (pyschology). With his brother David, one of the chief exponents of the "direct cinema" school of documentary filmmaking. The brothers began working as a team in 1957, each having previously been involved in film in very different ways—Al making a documentary on Soviet mental institutions and David working as production assistant on two Marilyn Monroe films. The brothers designed their own portable equipment to help in their goal of capturing the raw, spontaneous flow of experience, without intruding into the situations being filmed. The Maysles were influenced by Robert Drew and Richard Leacock, with whom they had worked on *Primary* (1960), and often collaborated with Charlotte Zwerin. They are best known for *Salesman* (1969) and the controversial *Gimme Shelter* (1970), a record of a Rolling Stones concert in which a young man is knifed to death onscreen; the latter film stirred much discussion of the moral issues raised by the filmmaker's "detached observer" status. • (Albert Maysles only): *Psychiatry in Russia* 1955 (d,ph); *Youth of Poland* 1957 (d,ph); *Primary* 1960 (d); *Kenya, Africa* 1961 (d,ph); *Showman* 1962 (d,ph); *What's Happening New York Meets the Beatles/Yeah Yeah Yeah* 1964 (d,ph); *Paris Vu Par...* 1965 (ph—"Montparnasse et Levallois"); *Meet Marlon Brando* 1966 (d,ph); *Monterey Pop* 1968 (ph); *A Journey to Jerusalem* 1969 (ph); *Salesman* 1969 (d,ph); *Gimme Shelter* 1970 (d,ph); *Christo's Valley Curtain* 1973 (d,ph) **(AANSHORTDOC)**; *La Pupa del gangster* 1974 (d); *Grey Gardens* 1975 (a,d,p,ph); *The Grateful Dead* 1977 (ph); *Running Fence* 1977 (d,ph,p); *Ozawa* 1984 (d,ph); *Vladimir Horowitz, The Last Romantic* 1985 (d,ph); *Islands* 1986 (d,ph); *James Baldwin: The Price of the Ticket* 1989 (exec.p).

Maysles, David • Filmmaker • Born Boston, MA, January 10, 1932; died January 3, 1987, New York. *Educ.* Boston University (pyschology). See Maysles, Albert. • *Bus Stop* 1956 (uncred.prod.asst.); *The Prince and the Showgirl* 1957 (uncred.prod.asst.); *Youth of Poland* 1957 (d,sound); *Showman* 1962 (d,sound); *What's Happening New York Meets the Beatles* 1964 (d,sound); *Meet Marlon Brando* 1966 (d,sound); *A Journey to Jerusalem* 1969 (ph); *Salesman* 1969 (d,ed,sound); *Gimme Shelter* 1970 (a,d,ph); *Christo's Valley Curtain* 1973 (d,sound) **(AANSHORTDOC)**; *La Pupa del gangster* 1974 (d); *Grey Gardens* 1975 (a,d,p,ph); *Running Fence* 1977 (d,sound,p); *Ozawa* 1984 (d,sound); *Vladimir Horowitz, The Last Romantic* 1985 (d,ph); *Islands* 1986 (d,sound).

Mazursky, Paul • Director, screenwriter; also actor, producer. • Born Irwin Mazursky, Brooklyn, NY, April 25, 1930. *Educ.* Brooklyn College; UCLA (film production). Mazursky began his career as an actor and comedian on the New York nightclub scene, graduating to writing duties on TV series such as the "Danny Kaye Show" and "The Monkees" in the mid-1960s. He scored a critical and commercial success with his directorial debut, *Bob & Carol & Ted & Alice* (1969), a now-tame study of middle-class sexual attitudes that seemed risqué at the time.

Throughout the 1970s and 80s, Mazursky produced a series of elegant comedies, each characterized by interesting and witty commentary on middle-class mores. Taken together, the films add up to an oeuvre of considerable attractiveness.

Alex in Wonderland (1970), Mazursky's *8 1/2*, comments on the "new" Hollywood of the late 60s. Donald Sutherland is the confused auteur/director. *Blume in Love* (1973) is a self-conscious romance, a 15-years-early model for "thirtysomething." *Harry and Tonto* (1974) revived Art Carney's career with his role as the old man in search of an ending, trekking across America. *Next Stop, Greenwich Village* (1976) celebrated, not only Mazursky's own roots in the coffee houses and clubs of the Village of the 50s, but also that important wellspring of contemporary culture. *An Unmarried Woman* (1978), Mazursky's greatest success of the 70s, became a beacon of the women's movement, with Jill Clayburgh winning an Oscar nomination for her depiction of a woman rebuilding her life after a divorce.

Willie and Phil (1980) deals with a contemporary love triangle, again set in Greenwich Village, still Mazursky's home at the time. *Tempest* (1982), an audacious reworking of Shakespeare's swan song, again attempted to limn the life of the artist. John Cassavetes starred and his own distinct viewpoint pervades the film.

Moscow on the Hudson (1984), a bittersweet portrait of a Soviet defector's adaptation to life in America, gave Robin Williams a chance to expand his repertoire in a study of contemporary migration. *Down and Out in Beverly Hills* (1986) is Mazursky's version of the Jean Renoir classic, *Boudu Saved From Drowning*. It marked Mazursky's return to West Coast subjects after a 15-year absence. It was also his first real box-office hit in nearly as many years, proving perhaps that Beverly Hills lifestyles far outsell Greeenwich Village funk.

Moon Over Parador (1988) deals, less insightfully, with a parody of banana republic politics. *Enemies, A Love Story* (1989), much more ambitious, speaks eloquently of resilience, humor and passion in the shadow of the Holocaust in 1940s New York.

Mazursky continues to act, in his own films and others, and, like his contemporary and late colleague John Cassavetes, regards filmmaking as a family matter. Wife Betsy and daughters Jill and Meg have appeared in a number of his films, as has his psychiatrist, Donald F. Muhich. In 1990 Mazursky executive-produced daughter Jill's screenplay, *Taking Care of Business*. JM • *Fear and Desire* 1953 (a); *Blackboard Jungle* 1955 (a); *Deathwatch* 1966 (a); *I Love You, Alice B. Toklas* 1968 (a,exec.p,sc,song); *Bob & Carol & Ted & Alice* 1969 (a,d,sc) **(AANBSC)**; *Alex in Wonderland*

1970 (a,d,sc); *Blume in Love* 1973 (a,d,p,sc); *Harry and Tonto* 1974 (a,d,p,sc) **(AANBSC)**; *Next Stop, Greenwich Village* 1976 (d,p,sc); *A Star Is Born* 1976 (a); *An Unmarried Woman* 1978 (a,d,p,sc) **(AANBP,AANBSC)**; *An Almost Perfect Affair* 1979 (a); *A Man, a Woman and a Bank* 1979 (a); *Willie & Phil* 1980 (a,d,p,sc); *History of the World Part I* 1981 (a); *Tempest* 1982 (a,d,p,sc); *Moscow on the Hudson* 1984 (a,d,p,sc); *Into the Night* 1985 (a); *Down and Out in Beverly Hills* 1986 (a,d,p,sc); *Moon Over Parador* 1988 (a,d,p,sc); *Punchline* 1988 (a); *Enemies, A Love Story* 1989 (a,d,p,sc) **(AANBSC)**; *Scenes From the Class Struggle in Beverly Hills* 1989 (a); *Taking Care of Business* 1990 (exec.p); *Scenes From a Mall* 1991 (d,p,sc).

McAlpine, Donald • Australian director of photography • Photographed two of the finest Australian films of recent years, *My Brilliant Career* (1979) and *Breaker Morant* (1980); the latter marked the beginning of a fruitful association with director Bruce Beresford. McAlpine has also collaborated on several movies directed by Paul Mazursky. • *Or Forever Hold Your Peace* 1970 (ph); *The Adventures of Barry McKenzie* 1972 (ph); *The Man Who Can't Stop* 1973 (ph); *Whatever Happened to Green Valley* 1973 (ph); *A Voice to be Heard* 1974 (ph); *Surrender in Paradise* 1975 (a,ph); *Don's Party* 1976 (ph); *The Getting of Wisdom* 1977 (ph); *Money Movers* 1978 (ph); *Patrick* 1978 (ph); *The Journalist* 1979 (ph); *My Brilliant Career* 1979 (ph); *The Odd Angry Shot* 1979 (ph); *Breaker Morant* 1980 (ph); *The Club* 1980 (ph,cam.op); *The Earthling* 1980 (ph); *Don't Cry, It's Only Thunder* 1981 (ph); *Puberty Blues* 1981 (ph,cam.op); *The Man From Snowy River* 1982 (ph); *Now and Forever* 1982 (ph); *On the Run* 1982 (ph); *Tempest* 1982 (ph); *Blue Skies Again* 1983 (ph); *Barry McKenzie Holds His Own* 1984 (ph); *Harry & Son* 1984 (ph); *Moscow on the Hudson* 1984 (ph); *The Fringe Dwellers* 1985 (ph); *King David* 1985 (ph); *My Man Adam* 1985 (ph); *Down and Out in Beverly Hills* 1986 (ph); *Orphans* 1987 (ph); *Predator* 1987 (ph); *Moon Over Parador* 1988 (ph); *Moving* 1988 (ph); *Parenthood* 1989 (ph); *See You in the Morning* 1989 (ph); *Stanley and Iris* 1990 (ph); *Career Opportunities* 1991 (ph); *The Hard Way* 1991 (ph).

McAnally, Ray • Actor • Born County Donegal, Ireland, c. 1926; died June 15, 1989, County Wicklow, Ireland. Versatile, prolific character player of film, stage and TV. McAnally began his screen career in the 1930s but is best known for his roles of the 80s, notably as the sympathetic papal envoy in *The Mission* (1986) and the beleagured father in *My Left Foot* (1989). He was separated from his wife, actress Ronnie Masterson. • *Shake Hands With the Devil* 1959; *Billy Budd* 1962; *The Looking Glass War* 1970; *Fear Is the Key* 1972; *Angel* 1982; *Cal* 1984; *The Mission* 1986; *Empire State* 1987; *The Fourth Protocol* 1987; *The Sicilian* 1987; *White Mischief* 1987; *High Spirits* 1988; *Taffin* 1988; *My Left Foot* 1989; *We're No Angels* 1989.

McBride, Jim • Director; also writer. • Born New York, NY, September 16, 1941. *Educ.* NYU. McBride received widespread acclaim for his debut feature, *David Holzman's Diary* (1967), which was shot on a budget of only $2,500 and influenced both by the *cinéma vérité* movement and the French New Wave. *Diary* recorded a day in the life of filmmaker David Holzman, who in turn was recording a day in his own life as part of an obsessive desire to capture "the truth" through the lens of his camera. McBride made intermittent excursions into film in the 1970s, trying his hand at sci-fi (*Glen and Randa* 1971) and comedy (*Hot Times* 1974). After a misguided attempt to update Godard's *Breathless* (1983), he joined the Hollywood mainstream with the atmospheric, New Orleans-set thriller, *The Big Easy* (1986). *Great Balls of Fire* (1989), which, like *The Big Easy*, starred Dennis Quaid, was somewhat less successful. • *David Holzman's Diary* 1968 (d,p); *My Girlfriend's Wedding* 1969 (d); *Glen and Randa* 1971 (d,sc); *Hot Times* 1974 (a,d,sc); *Last Embrace* 1979 (a); *Breathless* 1983 (d,sc); *The Big Easy* 1986 (d); *Great Balls of Fire* 1989 (d,sc,m).

McCambridge, Mercedes • Actress • Born Carlotta Mercedes Agnes McCambridge, Joliet, IL, March 17, 1918. *Educ.* Mundelein College, Chicago. Noted radio performer who won an Oscar for her screen debut in *All the King's Men* (1949) and was again nominated for 1956's *Giant*. McCambridge specialized in forceful or domineering roles and provided the memorable voice-over for the demon-child in *The Exorcist* (1973). • *All the King's Men* 1949 **(AABSA)**; *The Scarf* 1950; *Inside Straight* 1951; *Lightning Strikes Twice* 1951; *Johnny Guitar* 1954; *Giant* 1956 **(AANBSA)**; *A Farewell to Arms* 1957; *Touch of Evil* 1958; *Suddenly, Last Summer* 1959; *Cimarron* 1960; *Angel Baby* 1961; *99 Mujeres* 1968; *The Counterfeit Killer* 1968; *The Exorcist* 1973; *Like a Crow on a June Bug* 1974; *Thieves* 1977; *The Concorde—Airport '79* 1979; *Echoes* 1980.

McCarey, Leo • Director; also producer, screenwriter. • Born Thomas Leo McCarey, Los Angeles, CA, October 3, 1898; died 1969. *Educ.* USC Law School, Los Angeles. Entered films as an assistant and script supervisor in 1918 after unsuccessful forays into business and law. In 1923 McCarey joined the Hal Roach studio, where he produced and wrote Laurel and Hardy shorts and directed numerous Charlie Chase vehicles before beginning to work in features in 1929. Over the next three decades McCarey directed landmark comedies such as *Duck Soup* (1933) and *The Milky Way* (1936) as well as wistful melodramas like the Oscar-winning *Going My Way* (1944). • *Society Secrets* 1921 (d); *Eve's Love Letters (short)* 1927 (d); *We Faw Down (short)* 1928 (d); *Liberty (short)* 1929 (d,sc,prod.sup); *Red Hot Rhythm* 1929 (d,story); *The Sophomore* 1929 (d); *Wrong Again (short)* 1929 (d,story); *Let's Go Native* 1930 (d); *Part Time Wife* 1930 (d,sc); *Wild Company* 1930 (d); *Indiscreet* 1931 (d,from story "Obey That Impulse"); *The Kid From Spain* 1932 (d); *Duck Soup* 1933 (d); *Belle of the Nineties* 1934 (d); *Six of a Kind* 1934 (d); *Ruggles of Red Gap* 1935 (d); *The Milky Way* 1936 (d); *The Awful Truth* 1937 (d,p) **(AABD)**; *Make Way For Tomorrow* 1937 (a,d,p); *The Cowboy and the Lady* 1938 (story); *Love Affair* 1939 (d,p,story) **(AANBST)**; *My Favorite Wife* 1940 (from story,p) **(AANBST)**; *Once Upon a Honeymoon* 1942 (d,p,story); *Going My Way* 1944 (d,p,story) **(AABD,AABST)**; *The Bells of St. Mary's* 1945 (d,p,story) **(AANBD)**; *Good Sam* 1948 (d,p,story); *My Son John* 1952 (d,p,sc,story) **(AANBST)**; *An Affair to Remember* 1956 (d,sc,story,song) **(AANBS)**; *Rally Round the Flag, Boys!* 1958 (d,p,sc); *Satan Never Sleeps* 1962 (d,p,sc,lyrics); *Move Over, Darling* 1963 (from story "My Favorite Wife").

McCarthy, Andrew • Actor • Born Westfield, NJ, 1962. *Educ.* NYU (drama). Blandly handsome, intense young lead who appeared in a number of coming-of-age films during the 1980s. • *Class* 1983; *Heaven Help Us* 1985; *St. Elmo's Fire* 1985; *Pretty in Pink* 1986; *Less Than Zero* 1987; *Mannequin* 1987; *Waiting For the Moon* 1987; *Fresh Horses* 1988; *Kansas* 1988; *Weekend at Bernie's* 1989; *Docteur M.* 1990; *Jours tranquilles a Clichy* 1990.

McCarthy, Kevin • Actor • Born Seattle, WA, February 15, 1914. *Educ.* University of Minnesota. Stage actor who made his screen debut as Biff in *Death of a Salesman* (1951) and starred in Don Siegel's sci-fi classic, *Invasion of the Body Snatchers* (1956). McCarthy later appeared in TV series such as "The Survivors" (1969-70). Brother of novelist Mary McCarthy. • *Death of a Salesman* 1951; *Drive a Crooked Road* 1954; *The Gambler From Natchez* 1954; *Stranger on Horseback* 1954; *An Annapolis Story* 1955; *Invasion of the Body Snatchers* 1956; *Nightmare* 1956; *Diamond Safari* 1957; *The Misfits* 1961; *40 Pounds of Trouble* 1962; *An Affair of the Skin* 1963; *A Gathering of Eagles* 1963; *The Prize* 1963; *The Best Man* 1964; *The Three Sisters* 1964; *Mirage* 1965; *A Big Hand For the Little Lady* 1966; *Hotel* 1967; *The Hell With Heroes* 1968; *If He*

Hollers, Let Him Go! 1968; *I Quattro dell'Ave Maria* 1968; *Between Time and Timbuktu* 1972; *Kansas City Bomber* 1972; *Richard* 1972; *El Clan de los Inmorales* 1973; *Buffalo Bill and the Indians, or Sitting Bull's History Lesson* 1976; *Invasion of the Body Snatchers* 1978; *Piranha* 1978; *Hero at Large* 1980; *The Howling* 1980; *Those Lips Those Eyes* 1980; *Montgomery Clift* 1982; *My Tutor* 1982; *Twilight Zone—the Movie* 1983; *Hostage* 1987; *Innerspace* 1987; *Dark Tower* 1989; *Fast Food* 1989; *UHF* 1989; *Love or Money* 1990; *Sleeping Car* 1990; *Eve of Destruction* 1991.

McCowen, Alec • Actor • Born Tunbridge Wells, England, May 26, 1925. *Educ.* RADA, London. British stage actor who began appearing in supporting film roles in the late 1950s; latterly much in demand as a character player. • *The Deep Blue Sea* 1955; *Time Without Pity* 1957; *The Doctor's Dilemma* 1958; *A Night to Remember* 1958; *The One That Got Away* 1958; *The Silent Enemy* 1958; *The Loneliness of the Long Distance Runner* 1962; *In the Cool of the Day* 1963; *The Hawaiians* 1970; *Frenzy* 1972; *Travels With My Aunt* 1972; *Stevie* 1978; *Hanover Street* 1979; *Never Say Never Again* 1983; *Forever Young* 1984; *The Young Visitors* 1984; *The Assam Garden* 1985; *Cry Freedom* 1987; *Personal Services* 1987; *Henry V* 1989.

McCrea, Joel • Actor • Born Joel Albert McCrea, South Pasadena, CA, November 5, 1905; died October 20, 1990, Woodland Hills, California. *Educ.* Pomona State College, CA. Likeable, ruggedly handsome figure who first made his name in adventures and melodramas of the 1930s. McCrea gave one of his finest performances in Hitchcock's *Foreign Correspondent* (1940) and brought an amiable, relaxed charm to his comic roles, especially when directed by Preston Sturges (*Sullivan's Travels* 1941, *The Palm Beach Story* 1942).

Beginning with William Wellman's *Buffalo Bill* (1944) McCrea made the transition to western star, a role that mirrored his own frontier roots as well as his personal life (a passionate outdoorsman, he listed his occupation as "rancher" and his hobby as "acting"). McCrea was married to actress Frances Dee from 1933 until his death; their son Jody McCrea (b. 1934) appeared with him on his TV series "Wichita Town" (1959-60) and in the film *Cry Blood, Apache* (1970). • *A Self-Made Failure* 1924; *The Torrent* 1926 (stunts); *Dynamite* 1929; *The Jazz Age* 1929; *Lightnin'* 1930; *The Silver Horde* 1930; *Born to Love* 1931; *The Common Law* 1931; *Girls About Town* 1931; *Kept Husbands* 1931; *Once a Sinner* 1931; *Bird of Paradise* 1932; *Business and Pleasure* 1932; *The Lost Squadron* 1932; *The Most Dangerous Game* 1932; *Rockabye* 1932; *The Sport Parade* 1932; *Bed of Roses* 1933; *Chance at Heaven* 1933; *One Man's Journey* 1933; *The Silver Cord* 1933; *Gambling Lady* 1934; *Half a Sinner* 1934; *The Richest Girl in the World* 1934; *Barbary Coast* 1935; *Our Little Girl* 1935; *Private Worlds* 1935; *Splendor* 1935; *Woman Wanted* 1935; *Adventure in Manhattan* 1936; *Banjo on My Knee* 1936; *Come and Get It* 1936; *These Three* 1936; *Two in a Crowd* 1936; *Dead End* 1937; *Internes Can't Take Money* 1937; *Wells Fargo* 1937; *Woman Chases Man* 1937; *Three Blind Mice* 1938; *Youth Takes a Fling* 1938; *Espionage Agent* 1939; *They Shall Have Music* 1939; *Union Pacific* 1939; *Foreign Correspondent* 1940; *He Married His Wife* 1940; *The Primrose Path* 1940; *Reaching For the Sun* 1941; *Sullivan's Travels* 1941; *The Great Man's Lady* 1942; *The Palm Beach Story* 1942; *The More the Merrier* 1943; *Buffalo Bill* 1944; *The Great Moment* 1944; *The Unseen* 1945; *The Virginian* 1946; *Ramrod* 1947; *Four Faces West* 1948; *Colorado Territory* 1949; *South of St. Louis* 1949; *Frenchie* 1950; *The Outriders* 1950; *Saddle Tramp* 1950; *Stars in My Crown* 1950; *Cattle Drive* 1951; *The San Francisco Story* 1952; *The Lone Hand* 1953; *Rough Shoot* 1953; *Black Horse Canyon* 1954; *Border River* 1954; *Stranger on Horseback* 1954; *Wichita* 1955; *The First Texan* 1956; *Cattle Empire* 1957; *Gunsight Ridge* 1957; *The Oklahoman* 1957; *The Tall Stranger* 1957; *Trooper Hook* 1957; *Fort Massacre* 1958; *The Gunfight at Dodge City* 1959; *Ride the High Country* 1962; *Cry Blood, Apache* 1970; *Great American Cowboy* 1973; *Mustang Country* 1976; *George Stevens: A Filmmaker's Journey* 1985.

McDaniel, Hattie • Actress; also singer. • Born Wichita, KS, June 10, 1895; died 1952. The first black woman to win an Academy Award and to sing on the radio in the US, McDaniel was also much in demand to play sassy maid/housekeeper types in Hollywood films of the 1930s and 40s. • *Blonde Venus* 1932; *The Golden West* 1932; *I'm No Angel* 1933; *Operator 13* 1933; *The Story of Temple Drake* 1933; *Imitation of Life* 1934; *Judge Priest* 1934; *Little Men* 1934; *Lost in the Stratosphere* 1934; *Alice Adams* 1935; *Another Face* 1935; *China Seas* 1935; *The Little Colonel* 1935; *Music Is Magic* 1935; *The Bride Walks Out* 1936; *Can This Be Dixie?* 1936; *The First Baby* 1936; *Gentle Julia* 1936; *Hearts Divided* 1936; *High Tension* 1936; *Postal Inspector* 1936; *Reunion* 1936; *Show Boat* 1936; *Star For a Night* 1936; *Valiant Is the Word For Carrie* 1936; *45 Fathers* 1937; *The Crime Nobody Saw* 1937; *Don't Tell the Wife* 1937; *Nothing Sacred* 1937; *Over the Goal* 1937; *Racing Lady* 1937; *Saratoga* 1937; *True Confession* 1937; *The Battle of Broadway* 1938; *The Mad Miss Manton* 1938; *The Shining Hour* 1938; *Shopworn Angel,The* 1938; *Everybody's Baby* 1939; *Gone With the Wind* 1939 **(AABSA)**; *Zenobia* 1939; *Maryland* 1940; *Affectionately Yours* 1941; *The Great Lie* 1941; *They Died With Their Boots On* 1941; *George Washington Slept Here* 1942; *In This Our Life* 1942; *The Male Animal* 1942; *Johnny Come Lately* 1943; *Thank Your Lucky Stars* 1943; *Hi, Beautiful!* 1944; *Janie* 1944; *Since You Went Away* 1944; *Three Is a Family* 1944; *Janie Gets Married* 1946; *Margie* 1946; *Never Say Goodbye* 1946; *Song of the South* 1946; *The Flame* 1947; *Family Honeymoon* 1948; *Mickey* 1948.

McDormand, Frances • Actress • Born U.S.A., c. 1957. *Educ.* Yale (drama). Intelligent, versatile lead and character player who has given two outstanding performances as troubled Southern wives: in the Coen brothers' *Blood Simple* (1984), as an adulteress caught in a web of murder and suspicion; and in Alan Parker's *Mississippi Burning* (1988), as the long-suffering wife who finally helps the FBI convict her Klansman husband and his cronies. • *Blood Simple* 1984; *Raising Arizona* 1987; *Mississippi Burning* 1988 **(AANBSA)**; *Chattahoochee* 1990; *Darkman* 1990; *Hidden Agenda* 1990.

McDowall, Roddy • Actor • Born Roderick Andrew Anthony Jude McDowall, London, September 17, 1928. Former child model and prolific juvenile actor who took a break from films in 1951 and returned, after a decade of theater work, in the early 1960s. McDowall's roles ranged from apes (1968's *Planet of the Apes* and its three sequels) to apostles (*The Greatest Story Ever Told* 1965). He has directed one film, *The Devil's Widow* (1970), and published *Double Exposure* and *Double Exposure Take Two*, collections of his photographs, in 1966 and 1989 respectively. • *Convict 99* 1937 (a); *Murder in the Family* 1938 (a); *Yellow Sands* 1938 (a); *His Brother's Keeper* 1939 (a); *Murder Will Out* 1939 (a); *Confirm or Deny* 1941 (a); *How Green Was My Valley* 1941 (a); *Man Hunt* 1941 (a); *On the Sunny Side* 1942 (a); *The Pied Piper* 1942 (a); *Son of Fury* 1942 (a); *Lassie Come Home* 1943 (a); *My Friend Flicka* 1943 (a); *The White Cliffs of Dover* 1944 (a); *Hangover Square* 1945 (a); *The Keys of the Kingdom* 1945 (a); *Molly and Me* 1945 (a); *Thunderhead* 1945 (a); *Holiday in Mexico* 1946 (a); *Kidnapped* 1948 (a,assoc.p); *Macbeth* 1948 (a); *Rocky* 1948 (a,assoc.p); *Black Midnight* 1949 (a,assoc.p); *Tuna Clipper* 1949 (a,assoc.p); *Everybody's Dancing* 1950 (a); *Killer Shark* 1950 (a,assoc.p); *Tall Timber* 1950 (a); *The Steel Fist* 1952 (a); *Midnight Lace* 1960 (a); *The Subterraneans* 1960 (a); *The Longest Day* 1962 (a); *Cleopatra* 1963 (a); *Shock Treatment* 1964 (a); *The Greatest Story Ever Told* 1965 (a); *Inside Daisy Clover* 1965 (a); *The Loved One* 1965 (a); *That Darn Cat* 1965 (a); *The Third Day* 1965 (a); *The Defector* 1966 (a); *Lord Love a Duck* 1966 (a); *The Adventures of Bullwhip Griffin* 1967 (a); *The Cool Ones* 1967 (a); *It!* 1967 (a); *5 Card Stud* 1968 (a); *Planet of the Apes* 1968 (a); *Angel, Angel Down We Go* 1969 (a); *Hello Down There* 1969 (a); *A Run on Gold* 1969 (a); *The Devil's Widow* 1970 (d); *Bedknobs and Broomsticks* 1971 (a); *Escape From the Planet of the Apes* 1971 (a); *Pretty Maids All in a Row* 1971 (a); *Tam Lin* 1971 (d); *Conquest of the Planet of the Apes* 1972 (a); *The Life and Times of Judge Roy Bean* 1972 (a); *The Poseidon Adventure* 1972 (a); *Arnold* 1973 (a); *Battle For the Planet of the Apes* 1973 (a); *The Legend of Hell House* 1973 (a); *Dirty Mary, Crazy Larry* 1974 (a); *Funny Lady* 1975 (a); *Embryo* 1976 (a); *Mean Johnny Barrows* 1976 (a); *Sixth and Main* 1977 (a); *The Cat From Outer Space* 1978 (a); *Laserblast* 1978 (a); *Rabbit Test* 1978 (a); *The Silent Flute* 1978 (a); *The Thief of Bagdad* 1978 (a); *The Black Hole* 1979 (a); *Nutcracker Fantasy* 1979 (a); *Scavenger Hunt* 1979 (a); *Charlie Chan and the Curse of the Dragon Queen* 1981 (a); *Class of 1984* 1982 (a); *Evil Under the Sun* 1982 (a); *Fright Night* 1985 (a); *Gobots: Battle of the Rock Lords* 1986 (a); *Dead of Winter* 1987 (a); *Overboard* 1987 (a,exec.p); *Doin' Time on Planet Earth* 1988 (a); *Fright Night, Part II* 1988 (a); *Going Hollywood: The War Years* 1988 (a); *The Big Picture* 1989 (a); *Cutting Class* 1989 (a); *Shakma* 1990 (a).

McDowell, Malcolm • Actor • Born Leeds, England, June 15, 1943. Boyish, blue-eyed lead of the English stage who made a striking debut as a rebellious schoolboy in Lindsay Anderson's *If....* (1968). McDowell also played the lead in the subsequent installments of Anderson's surreal trilogy attacking corrupt British institutions, *O Lucky Man!* (1973) and *Britannia Hospital* (1982). His blithely amoral, anti-authoritarian persona was perhaps put to best use by Stanley Kubrick in the controversial *A Clockwork Orange* (1971). McDowell is divorced from actresses Margot Dullea and Mary Steenburgen. • *If...* 1968 (a); *Figures in a Landscape* 1970 (a); *The Raging Moon* 1970 (a); *A Clockwork Orange* 1971 (a); *O Lucky Man!* 1973 (a,idea,p); *Royal Flash* 1975 (a); *Aces High* 1976 (a); *Voyage of the Damned* 1976 (a); *Caligula* 1979 (a); *The Passage* 1979 (a); *Tigers Are Better Looking (short)* 1979 (a); *Time After Time* 1979 (a); *Britannia Hospital* 1982 (a); *Cat People* 1982 (a); *Blue Thunder* 1983 (a); *Cross Creek* 1983 (a); *Get Crazy* 1983 (a); *The Compleat Beatles* 1984 (a); *The Caller* 1987 (a); *Buy and Cell* 1988 (a); *Sunset* 1988 (a); *Il Maestro* 1989 (a); *Class of 1999* 1990 (a); *Disturbed* 1990 (a); *Happily Ever After* 1990 (a); *Jezebel's Kiss* 1990 (a); *Maggio Musicale* 1990 (a); *Moon 44* 1990 (a); *Schweitzer* 1990 (a).

McGann, Paul • Actor • Born Liverpool, England. *Educ.* RADA, London. Handsome, stage-trained English actor who first made his name in *Withnail and I* (1986), Bruce Robinson's wry look at the less "swinging" side of 1960s London. • *Withnail & I* 1986; *Empire of the Sun* 1987; *Dealers* 1989; *Drowning in the Shallow End* 1989; *The Rainbow* 1989; *Streets of Yesterday* 1989; *Tree of Hands* 1989; *Paper Mask* 1990.

McGillis, Kelly • Actress • Born Newport Beach, CA, 1958. *Educ.* Juilliard (drama). Leading lady whose first two film appearances, as the love interest in *Reuben, Reuben* (1983) and the soft-spoken Amish widow in *Witness* (1985) displayed a promising mix of talent and earthy beauty. McGillis's attempts at more straightforwardly glamorous roles have earned luke-warm critical responses. • *Reuben, Reuben* 1983; *Witness* 1985; *Top Gun* 1986; *Made in Heaven* 1987; *Unsettled Land* 1987; *The Accused* 1988; *The House on Carroll Street* 1988; *Cat Chaser* 1989; *Winter People* 1989.

McGovern, Elizabeth • Actress • Born Evanston, IL, July 18, 1961. *Educ.* American Conservatory Theater, San Francisco; Juilliard (drama). Large-eyed, dark-haired stage and screen performer who first gained attention as Conrad Jarrett's (Timothy Hutton) girlfriend in the Oscar-winning *Ordinary People* (1980). • *Ordinary People* 1980; *Ragtime* 1981 **(AANBSA)**; *Lovesick* 1983; *Once Upon a Time in America* 1984; *Racing With the Moon* 1984; *Native Son* 1986; *The Bedroom Window* 1987; *Dear America* 1987; *She's Having a Baby* 1988; *The Handmaid's Tale* 1989; *Johnny Handsome* 1989; *A Shock to the System* 1990; *Tune in Tomorrow* 1990.

McGuire, Dorothy • Actress • Born Omaha, NE, June 14, 1918. Wholesome, reserved leading lady of the 1940s and 50s, later a respected character actress. McGuire was memorable as *Claudia* (1943), in a reprisal of her successful Broadway role; as the mother in *A Tree Grows in Brooklyn* (1945); and as the mute servant in Robert Siodmak's classic thriller, *The Spiral Staircase* (1946). McGuire's daughter, by photographer husband John Swope, is actress Topo Swope. • *Claudia* 1943; *The Enchanted Cottage* 1945; *A Tree Grows in Brooklyn* 1945; *Claudia and David* 1946; *The Spiral Staircase* 1946; *Till the End of Time* 1946; *Gentleman's Agreement* 1947 **(AANBA)**; *Mister 880* 1950; *Mother Didn't Tell Me* 1950; *Callaway Went Thataway* 1951; *I Want You* 1951; *Invitation* 1952; *Make Haste To Live* 1954; *Three Coins in the Fountain* 1954; *Trial* 1955; *Friendly Persuasion* 1956; *Old Yeller* 1958; *The Remarkable Mr. Pennypacker* 1958; *A Summer Place* 1959; *This Earth Is Mine* 1959; *The Dark at the Top of the Stairs* 1960; *The Swiss Family Robinson* 1960; *Susan Slade* 1961; *Summer Magic* 1963; *The Greatest Story Ever Told* 1965; *Flight of the Doves* 1971; *Jonathan Livingston Seagull* 1973.

McKellen, Ian • Actor • Born Burnley, England, May 25, 1939. *Educ.* St. Catherine's College, Cambridge (English). Primarily known for his numerous stage roles, and considered one of the finest Shakesperean actors of his generation, McKellen is most familiar to American audiences for his role as philandering English cabinet minister John Profumo in 1988's *Scandal.* • *Alfred the Great* 1969; *The Promise* 1969; *Priest of Love* 1980; *The Keep* 1983; *Loving Walter* 1983; *Plenty* 1985; *Zina* 1985; *Scandal* 1988.

McKern, Leo • Actor • Born Reginald McKern, Sydney, Australia, March 16, 1920. In England since 1946. Popular character player of stage, TV and film, often in garrulous, blustery roles. • *All For Mary* 1955; *Time Without Pity* 1957; *A Tale of Two Cities* 1958; *Beyond This Place* 1959; *The Mouse That Roared* 1959; *Yesterday's Enemy* 1959; *Scent of Mystery* 1960; *Mr. Topaze* 1961; *Lisa* 1962; *Agent 8 3/4* 1964; *King and Country* 1964; *The Amorous Adventures of Moll Flanders* 1965; *Help!* 1965; *A Man For All Seasons* 1966; *Assignment K* 1968; *Decline and Fall... of a Bird Watcher* 1968; *The Shoes of the Fisherman* 1968; *Ryan's Daughter* 1970; *Massacre in Rome* 1973; *The Adventure of Sherlock Holmes' Smarter Brother* 1975; *The Omen* 1976; *Candleshoe* 1977; *Damien: Omen II* 1978; *The House on Garibaldi Street* 1979; *The Last Tasmanian* 1979; *The Blue Lagoon* 1980; *Country* 1981; *The French Lieutenant's Woman* 1981; *Voyage of Bounty's Child* 1983; *The Chain* 1985; *Ladyhawke* 1985; *Travelling North* 1987.

McLaglen, Andrew V. • Director • Born Andrew Victor McLaglen, London, July 28, 1920. *Educ.* University of Virginia. Capable director, mostly of westerns; better films include *McLintock!* (1963), with John Wayne, and *Shenandoah* (1965), starring James Stewart. McLaglen has also directed a number of TV movies and hundreds of episodes for TV shows such as "Perry Mason," "Have Gun—Will Travel" and "Rawhide." Son of actor Victor McLaglen. • *Track of the Cat* 1954 (ad); *Blood Alley* 1955 (ad); *Gun the Man Down* 1956 (d); *Man in the Vault* 1956 (d); *Seven Men From Now* 1956 (p); *The Abductors* 1957 (d); *Freckles* 1960 (d); *The Little Shepherd of Kingdom Come* 1961 (d); *McLintock!* 1963 (d); *Shenandoah* 1965 (d); *The Rare Breed* 1966 (d); *The Ballad of Josie* 1967 (d); *Monkeys, Go Home!* 1967 (d); *The Way West* 1967 (d); *Bandolero!* 1968 (d); *The Devil's Brigade*

1968 (d); *The Undefeated* 1969 (d); *Chisum* 1970 (d); *Fools' Parade* 1971 (d,p); *One More Train to Rob* 1971 (d); *Something Big* 1971 (d,p); *Cahill, United States Marshal* 1973 (d); *Mitchell* 1975 (d); *The Last Hard Men* 1976 (d); *The Wild Geese* 1978 (d); *Steiner—Das Eiserne Kreuz 2, Teil* 1979 (d); *The Sea Wolves* 1980 (d); *ffolkes* 1980 (d); *Sahara* 1984 (d,exec.p); *Return to the River Kwai* 1989 (d); *Eye of the Widow* 1991 (d).

McLaglen, Victor • Actor • Born Tunbridge Wells, England, December 10, 1886; died 1959. Former prizefighter (he once went six rounds against the great Jack Johnson) who entered British films in 1920 and moved to the USA five years later. McLaglen's blunt features were a familiar sight in films by John Ford, and he won an Oscar as the heavy-drinking title character of the director's gripping classic, *The Informer* (1935). Father of director Andrew McLaglen and brother of actors Clifford, Cyril, Kenneth, Arthur and Leopold. • *Carnival* 1921; *The Glorious Adventure* 1922; *The Beloved Brute* 1924; *The Fighting Heart* 1925; *The Hunted Woman* 1925; *Percy* 1925; *The Unholy Three* 1925; *Winds of Chance* 1925; *Beau Geste* 1926; *The Isle of Retribution* 1926; *Men of Steel* 1926; *What Price Glory* 1926; *Loves of Carmen* 1927; *A Girl in Every Port* 1928; *Hangman's House* 1928; *Mother Machree* 1928; *The River Pirate* 1928; *The Black Watch* 1929; *Captain Lash* 1929; *The Cockeyed World* 1929; *Happy Days* 1929; *Hot For Paris* 1929; *Strong Boy* 1929; *A Devil With Women* 1930; *On the Level* 1930; *Annabelle's Affairs* 1931; *Dishonored* 1931; *Not Exactly Gentlemen* 1931; *Wicked* 1931; *Women of All Nations* 1931; *Devil's Lottery* 1932; *The Gay Caballero* 1932; *Guilty As Hell* 1932; *Rackety Rax* 1932; *While Paris Sleeps* 1932; *Hot Pepper* 1933; *Laughing at Life* 1933; *The Captain Hates the Sea* 1934; *The Lost Patrol* 1934; *Murder at the Vanities* 1934; *No More Women* 1934; *The Wharf Angel* 1934; *The Great Hotel Murder* 1935; *The Informer* 1935 **(AABA)**; *Professional Soldier* 1935; *Under Pressure* 1935; *Klondike Annie* 1936; *The Magnificent Brute* 1936; *Under Two Flags* 1936; *Nancy Steele Is Missing* 1937; *Sea Devils* 1937; *This Is My Affair* 1937; *Wee Willie Winkie* 1937; *The Battle of Broadway* 1938; *The Devil's Party* 1938; *The Big Guy* 1939; *Captain Fury* 1939; *Ex-Champ* 1939; *Full Confession* 1939; *Gunga Din* 1939; *Let Freedom Ring* 1939; *Pacific Liner* 1939; *Rio* 1939; *Diamond Frontier* 1940; *South of Pago-Pago* 1940; *Broadway Limited* 1941; *Call Out the Marines* 1941; *China Girl* 1942; *Powder Town* 1942; *Forever and a Day* 1943; *The Princess and the Pirate* 1944; *Roger Touhy, Gangster* 1944; *Tampico* 1944; *Love, Honor, and Goodbye* 1945; *Rough, Tough and Ready* 1945; *Calendar Girl* 1946; *Whistle Stop* 1946; *The Foxes of Harrow* 1947; *The Michigan Kid* 1947; *Fort Apache* 1948; *She Wore a Yellow Ribbon* 1949; *Rio Grande* 1950; *The Quiet Man* 1952 **(AANBSA)**; *Fair Wind to Java* 1953; *Trouble in the Glen* 1953; *Many Rivers to Cross* 1954; *Prince Valiant* 1954; *Bengazi* 1955; *City of Shadows* 1955; *Lady Godiva* 1955; *Around the World in 80 Days* 1956; *The Abductors* 1957; *Sea Fury* 1958.

McLaren, Norman • *aka* W. N. Mclaren • Animator, filmmaker • Born Stirling, Scotland, April 11, 1914; died January 27, 1987, Quebec, Canada. *Educ.* Glasgow School of Art (interior design). Celebrated pioneer of animation techniques including stop motion and drawing directly onto celluloid. McLaren was put on the staff of the British GPO Film Unit by John Grierson in 1937 and followed Grierson to Canada in 1941. Working under the auspices of the National Film Board, he produced several outstanding works which pushed Len Lye's approach of drawing directly onto celluloid into new and breathtaking dimensions. McLaren is noted for his inventive and eclectic use of music, disdain for the boundaries of the film frame, and meticulous working methods. • *Fiddle-De-Dee* 1947 (anim,d); *Begone Dull Care* 1949 (anim,d); *Stars and Stripes* 1949 (anim,d); *Neighbours (short)* 1952 (d,p) **(AASHORT DOC)**; *Blinkety Blank* 1955 (anim,d); *A Chairy Tale (short)* 1957 (d) **(AANBSF)**; *Canon (short)* 1964 (d); *Mosaic (short)* 1965 (d); *Pas de deux* 1967 (anim,d); *Synchromy (short)* 1971 (d).

McLeod, Norman Z. • Director • Born Norman Zenos McLeod, Grayling, MI, September 20, 1898; died 1964. *Educ.* University of Washington, Seattle (science). Former animator who directed several memorable comedies, most notably the Marx Brothers classics *Monkey Business* (1931) and *Horse Feathers* (1932). "He was a very nice guy and a fairly good director," said Groucho Marx, "but no genius." • *The Air Circus* 1928 (sc); *Taking a Chance* 1929 (d); *Along Came Youth* 1930 (d); *Finn and Hattie* 1931 (d); *Monkey Business* 1931 (d); *Skippy* 1931 (sc); *Sooky* 1931 (sc); *Touchdown* 1931 (d); *Horse Feathers* 1932 (d); *If I Had a Million* 1932 (d); *The Miracle Man* 1932 (d); *Alice in Wonderland* 1933 (d); *A Lady's Profession* 1933 (d); *Mama Loves Papa* 1933 (d); *It's a Gift* 1934 (d); *Many Happy Returns* 1934 (d); *Melody in Spring* 1934 (d); *Coronado* 1935 (d); *Here Comes Cookie* 1935 (d); *Redheads on Parade* 1935 (d); *Early to Bed* 1936 (d); *Pennies From Heaven* 1936 (d); *Mind Your Own Business* 1937 (d); *Topper* 1937 (d); *Merrily We Live* 1938 (d); *There Goes My Heart* 1938 (d); *Remember?* 1939 (d,sc,story); *Topper Takes a Trip* 1939 (d); *Little Men* 1940 (d); *Lady Be Good* 1941 (d); *The Trial of Mary Dugan* 1941 (d); *Jackass Mail* 1942 (d); *Panama Hattie* 1942 (d); *The Powers Girl* 1943 (d); *Swing Shift Maisie* 1943 (d); *The Kid From Brooklyn* 1946 (d); *Road to Rio* 1947 (d); *The Secret Life of Walter Mitty* 1947 (d); *Isn't It Romantic* 1948 (d); *The Paleface* 1948 (d); *Let's Dance* 1950 (d); *My Favorite Spy* 1951 (d); *Never Wave at a Wac* 1952 (d); *Casanova's Big Night* 1954 (d); *Public Pigeon No. 1* 1957 (d); *Alias Jesse James* 1959 (d).

McMillan, Kenneth • Actor • Born Brooklyn, NY, 1932; died January 8, 1989, Santa Monica, CA. *Educ.* High School for the Performing Arts, New York. Craggy-faced, rotund supporting player, often in brutal or overbearing roles; memorable as the bullying, racist fire chief in *Ragtime* (1981). • *Serpico* 1973; *The Taking of Pelham 1, 2, 3* 1974; *The Stepford Wives* 1975; *Bloodbrothers* 1978; *Girlfriends* 1978; *Oliver's Story* 1978; *Head Over Heels* 1979; *Borderline* 1980; *Carny* 1980; *Eyewitness* 1980; *Hide in Plain Sight* 1980; *Little Miss Marker* 1980; *Heartbeeps* 1981; *The Killing Hour* 1981; *Ragtime* 1981; *True Confessions* 1981; *Whose Life Is It Anyway?* 1981; *Partners* 1982; *Blue Skies Again* 1983; *The Pope of Greenwich Village* 1984; *Protocol* 1984; *Reckless* 1984; *Dune* 1985; *Runaway Train* 1985; *Stephen King's Cat's Eye* 1985; *Armed and Dangerous* 1986; *Malone* 1987; *Three Fugitives* 1989.

McMullen, Ken • Director, screenwriter; also producer. • Born Manchester, England, 1948. Art-house director whose films deal mainly with political themes. *Ghost Dance* (1983) was a whimsical exercise featuring a cameo appearance by French philosopher Jacques Derrida; *Zina* (1985), based on the life of Trotsky's daughter, was a stylish, intriguing blend of personal, psychological concerns with wider social issues; *1871*, a visually sumptuous, multi-layered account of the Paris Commune, was selected for the *Un Certain Regard* section of the 1990 Cannes festival. • *Resistance* 1976 (d); *Ghost Dance* 1983 (a,d,p,sc); *Being and Doing* 1984 (d,p,ph); *Zina* 1985 (d,p,sc); *Partition* 1988 (d,sc); *1871* (d,exec.p).

McNichol, Kristy • Actress • Born Los Angeles, CA, September 11, 1962. Perky, Emmy Award-winning juvenile lead, best known as the young tomboy of the Lawrence clan on TV's "Family" (1976-80) and as police officer Barbara Weston on the sitcom "Empty Nest" (1988-). Brother Jimmy McNichol is an actor. • *The End* 1978; *Little Darlings* 1980; *The Night the Lights Went Out in Georgia* 1981; *Only When I Laugh* 1981; *The Pirate Movie* 1982; *White Dog* 1982; *Just the Way You Are* 1984; *Dream Lover* 1986; *Two Moon Junction* 1988; *You Can't Hurry Love* 1988; *The Forgotten One* 1990.

McQueen, Steve • Actor • Born Terrence Steven McQueen, Beech Grove, IN, March 24, 1930; died 1980. *Educ.* Neighborhood Playhouse, New York; Actors Studio. Ex-reform school boy, marine and drifter who gravitated to the Actors Studio in the 1950s and made his name starring in TV's "Wanted: Dead or Alive" (1958-1960). McQueen established his screen career—and his cool, charismatic persona—with his role as the motorcycle-riding POW in *The Great Escape* (1963). He went on to become one of the biggest screen attractions of the decade, starring in such fashionable gems as *Love With the Proper Stranger* (1963), *The Cincinnati Kid* (1965), *The Thomas Crown Affair* and *Bullitt* (both 1968). McQueen was married to actresses Neile Adams (1957-72), Ali McGraw (1973-78) and Barbara Minty. Son Chad McQueen is also an actor. • *The Blob* 1958; *The Great St. Louis Bank Robbery* 1958; *Never So Few* 1959; *The Magnificent Seven* 1960; *The Honeymoon Machine* 1961; *Hell Is For Heroes* 1962; *The Great Escape* 1963; *Love With the Proper Stranger* 1963; *Soldier in the Rain* 1963; *Baby, the Rain Must Fall* 1965; *The Cincinnati Kid* 1965; *Nevada Smith* 1966; *The Sand Pebbles* 1966 **(AANBA)**; *Bullitt* 1968; *The Thomas Crown Affair* 1968; *The Reivers* 1969; *Le Mans* 1971; *On Any Sunday* 1971; *The Getaway* 1972; *Junior Bonner* 1972; *Papillon* 1973; *The Towering Inferno* 1974; *An Enemy of the People* 1978; *The Hunter* 1980; *Tom Horn* 1980 (a,exec.p).

McTiernan, John • Director; also screenwriter. • Born New York. *Educ.* Juilliard; SUNY (film); AFI. Former writer and director of TV commercials whose first feature, *Nomads*, was well received at the 1985 Cannes Film Festival. McTiernan scored a major commercial success with *Die Hard*, one of 1988's more entertaining summer "blockbusters." • *Nomads* 1985 (d,sc); *Death of a Soldier* 1986 (a); *Predator* 1987 (d); *Die Hard* 1988 (d); *The Hunt For Red October* 1990 (d); *Flight of the Intruder* 1991 (exec.p).

Medak, Peter • Director • Born Budapest, Hungary. Began directing in the late 1960s and was responsible for one of the most deliriously vicious satires of English upper-crust folly, *The Ruling Class* (1972). The best known of Medak's subsequent films is *The Krays* (1990), a violent look at a different segment of English society with pop singers Gary and Martin Kemp in the roles of Britain's most notorious gangsters. • *The Phantom of the Opera* 1962 (ad); *Funeral in Berlin* 1966 (2u d); *Kaleidoscope* 1966 (assoc.p); *Negatives* 1968 (d); *A Day in the Death of Joe Egg* 1970 (d); *The Ruling Class* 1972 (d); *Ghost in the Noonday Sun* 1973 (d); *The Odd Job* 1978 (d); *The Changeling* 1979 (d); *Zorro, The Gay Blade* 1981 (d); *The Men's Club* 1986 (d); *The Krays* 1990 (d).

Meeker, Ralph • Actor; also producer. • Born Ralph Rathgeber, Minneapolis, MN, November 21, 1920; died August 5, 1988, Woodland Hills, CA. *Educ.* Northwestern University. Rugged, nononsense character actor (usually in action films) who made his screen debut in 1951; memorable as Mike Hammer in the Robert Aldrich classic, *Kiss Me Deadly* (1955). • *Shadow in the Sky* 1951 (a); *Teresa* 1951 (a); *Glory Alley* 1952 (a); *Somebody Loves Me* 1952 (a); *Code Two* 1953 (a); *Jeopardy* 1953 (a); *The Naked Spur* 1953 (a); *Big House, U.S.A.* 1955 (a); *Desert Sands* 1955 (a); *Kiss Me Deadly* 1955 (a); *A Woman's Devotion* 1956 (a); *The Fuzzy Pink Nightgown* 1957 (a); *Paths of Glory* 1957 (a); *Run of the Arrow* 1957 (a); *Ada* 1961 (a); *Something Wild* 1961 (a); *Wall of Noise* 1963 (a); *The Dirty Dozen* 1967 (a); *Gentle Giant* 1967 (a); *The St. Valentine's Day Massacre* 1967 (a); *The Detective* 1968 (a); *The Devil's Eight* 1968 (a); *I Walk the Line* 1970 (a); *The Anderson Tapes* 1971 (a); *The Happiness Cage* 1972 (a); *Angela* 1973 (a); *Brannigan* 1975 (a); *The Food Of the Gods* 1975 (a); *Johnny Firecloud* 1975 (a); *The Alpha Incident* 1977 (a); *The Hi-Riders* 1978 (a); *My Boys Are Good Boys* 1978 (a); *Winter Kills* 1979 (a); *Without Warning* 1980 (a).

Meerson, Lazare • Production designer • Born Russia, 1900; died 1938, England. Influential art director who left Russia after the revolution and, after a spell in Germany, joined Alexandre Kamenka's *Société des Films Albatros* in 1924. Starting out as an assistant to Alberto Cavalcanti, Meerson went on to transform French production design with his work on films by René Clair (*A Nous La Liberté* 1931, *Le Million* 1931, etc.) and Jacques Feyder (*La Kermesse Héroïque* 1935). Meerson was a major influence on the "poetic realism" movement of which his apprentice, Alexandre Trauner, would become the preeminent designer. He worked from 1936 for Alexander Korda but, unhappy with Korda's Hollywood-style production methods, was planning to to return to France when he died of meningitis at the age of 38. • *Les Aventures de Robert Macaire* 1925 (art d); *Feu Mathias Pascal* 1925 (asst.art d); *Gribiche* 1925 (art d); *Le Negre blanc* 1925 (art d); *Paris en 5 jours* 1925 (art d); *Carmen* 1926 (art d); *L' Argent* 1927 (sets); *Un Chapeau de Paille d'Italie/An Italian Straw Hat* 1927 (art d); *Le Chasseur de chez Maxim's* 1927 (art d); *La Proie du Vent* 1927 (art d); *La Comtesse Marie* 1928 (art d); *Les Deux Timides* 1928 (art d); *Les Nouveaux messieurs* 1928 (art d); *Souris d'hotel* 1928 (art d); *Cagliostro* 1929 (art d); *Le Requin* 1929 (art d); *David Golder* 1930 (art d); *L' Etrangere* 1930 (art d); *La Fin du monde* 1930 (art d); *Le Mystere de la chambre jaune* 1930 (art d); *Sous les toits de Paris/Under the Roofs of Paris* 1930 (pd); *A Nous la Liberte* 1931 (pd) **(AANBAD)**; *Le Bal* 1931 (art d); *Jean de la lune* 1931 (art d); *Le Million* 1931 (art d); *Le Monsieur de minuit* 1931 (art d); *Prisonnier de mon coeur* 1931 (art d); *Les Cinq Gentlemen maudits* 1932 (art d); *Conduisez-moi, Madame* 1932 (art d); *La Femme en homme* 1932 (art d); *La Femme nue* 1932 (art d); *L' Ange gardien* 1933 (art d); *Ciboulette* 1933 (art d); *La Femme invisible* 1933 (art d); *Le Grand jeu* 1933 (art d); *L' Hotel du Libre-Echange* 1933 (art d); *Quatorze Juillet* 1933 (art d); *Amok* 1934 (art d); *La Banque Nemo* 1934 (art d); *Justin de Marseille* 1934 (art d); *Lac aux Dames* 1934 (art d); *Pension Mimosas* 1934 (art d); *Poliche* 1934 (art d); *Zouzou* 1934 (art d); *Les Beaux jours* 1935 (art d); *La Kermesse heroique* 1935 (art d); *Princess Tam Tam* 1935 (art d); *As You Like It* 1936 (pd,cost); *Fire Over England* 1936 (art d); *Knight Without Armour* 1937 (sets); *The Return of the Scarlet Pimpernel* 1937 (art d); *Break the News* 1938 (art d); *The Citadel* 1938 (art d); *The Divorce of Lady X* 1938 (art d); *South Riding* 1938 (art d).

Mehta, Ketan • Indian director; also screenwriter. • *Educ.* Film and Television Institute of India. Indian director and screenwriter who began his career as a TV producer. Mehta earned critical accolades for his 1980 feature debut, *A Folk Tale*, which took an uncompromising, yet humorous look at the inequities of the Indian caste system. He reached a wider Western audience with *Spices* (1987). • *Bhavni Bhavai/A Folk Tale* 1980 (d,sc); *Holi* 1984 (d,p,sc,from play *Festival of Fire*); *Mirch Masala/Spices* 1987 (d,sc).

Melato, Mariangela • Italian actress • Striking blond actress of the Italian stage who made her screen debut in 1970 and was acclaimed for her role in Elio Petri's *The Working Class Goes to Heaven* (1971). Melato has appeared in several films directed by Lina Wertmuller—she turned in a superb comic performance as a spoiled aristocrat in the social comedy, *Swept Away* (1974)—and has also worked with Vittorio de Sica, Claude Chabrol and Mario Monicelli. She made her American screen debut opposite Ryan O'Neal in the farcical *So Fine* (1981). • *Il Generale Dorme in Piedi* 1971; *Grazia Ricevuta, Per* 1971; *Orlando Furioso* 1971; *La Classe Operaia Va In Paradise* 1972; *Lo Chiameremo Andrea* 1972; *Mimi Metallurgico Ferito Nell 'Onore* 1972; *La Polizia Ringrazia* 1972; *Film d'Amore e d'Anarchia/Love and Anarchy* 1973; *Nada* 1974; *Par Le sang des autres* 1974; *La Poliziotta* 1974; *Travolti da un insolito destino nell'azzuro mare d'Agosto/Swept Away* 1974; *L' Arbre de Guernica* 1975; *Attenti al Buffone* 1975; *Caro Michele* 1976; *Todo Modo* 1976; *Il*

Casotto 1977; *Il Gatto* 1978; *Dimenticare Venezia* 1979; *I Giorni Cantati* 1979; *By the Blood of Others* 1980; *Flash Gordon* 1980; *Oggetti Smarriti* 1980; *Aiutami a sognare* 1981; *So Fine* 1981; *Bello Mio Bellezza Mia* 1982; *Il Buon Soldato* 1982; *Domani Si Balla* 1982; *Il Petomane* 1983; *Segreti Segreti* 1984; *Figlio Mio Infinitamente Caro* 1985; *Notte d'Estate con Profilo Greco, Occhi a Mandorla e Odore di Basilico* 1986; *Dancers* 1987.

Méliès, Georges • Director, producer; also actor. • Born Marie Georges Jean Méliès, Paris, December 8, 1861; died 1938. *Educ.* Lycée Imperial, Paris; Lycée Louis Le Grand; Ecole des Beaux Arts, Paris. One of the visionary pioneers of the cinema, Georges Méliès was born to a boot manufacturer and passed through adolescence exhibiting two talents: for drawing and for making cardboard Punch & Judy shows. During his military service he was stationed near the home of Robert Houdin, the magician whose optical illusions had captivated Méliès as a child, and whose theater he would eventually buy after he escaped from his family job as overseer of factory machinery.

When the Lumière brothers unveiled their Cinématographe in public on December 28, 1895, Méliès was not only present, but clearly the most affected member of the audience. Frustrated when the Lumières would not sell him the machine, he sought out R.W. Paul and his Animatographe in London. Méliès then built his own camera-projector and was able to present his first film screening on April 4, 1896.

Méliès began by screening the films of others, mainly those made on the Edison Kinetoscope, but within months he was showing his own works; these were apparently one-reel views, usually consisting of one shot lasting sixty seconds. Although Méliès is often credited with inventing the narrative film by relating stories as opposed to simply depicting landscapes or single events, this is not strictly true; many of the Lumière brothers' films were also much more than simple, static views. Méliès's signal contribution to the cinema was to combine his experience as a magician and theater owner with the new invention of motion pictures in order to present spectacles of a kind not possible in the live theater.

Within nine months, Méliès had increased the length of the filmed entertainment (his last film of 1896 consisted of three, three-minute reels) and was making regular use of previously unimaginable special effects, such as making performers disappear by stopping his camera in mid-shot. As the year ended he was also completing a glass-walled studio where he could make films without fear of the elements.

From 1897 to 1904 Méliès made hundreds of films, the great majority now lost. The scores of prints which survive show why his contemporaries were both initially impressed, and ultimately bored. Méliès regarded the story in his films to be a mere "thread intended to link the 'effects'...I was appealing to the spectator's eyes alone." Failing to develop any consistent ideas, his entertainments consisted only of a succession of magical tableaux peopled by Méliès (who often dressed as the conjurer or the devil) and young women recruited from the theaters of Paris, performing against flat, painted backdrops.

Méliès's own resources and interest in these films apparently began to dwindle after 1905, partly due to competition from other filmmakers and rising costs, partly because of the growing industrialization of the French film industry, and partly due to his wish to continue presenting live programs at the Théâtre Robert Houdin. By 1911 he had ceased independent distribution; by the time France entered WWI in 1914 his career as a producer-director had ended. His best-known surviving works are *A Trip to the Moon* (1902), *The Melomaniac* (1903), *An Impossible Voyage* (1904) and *The Conquest of the Pole* (1912, his last year of production). RAH

Melville, Jean-Pierre • Director; also producer, actor. • Born Jean-Pierre Grumbach, Paris, October 20, 1917; died August 1, 1973. *Educ.* Lycée de Condorcet; Lycée de Michelet; Lycée de Charlemagne. Director whose economical production methods were a major influence on the French New Wave. Forced to work outside France's studio system, Melville set up his own production company in 1946 and two years later turned out his first feature, *Le Silence de la mer*, beginning his long-term association with cameraman Henri Decaë. Melville's adaptation of Jean Cocteau's novel, *Les Enfants Terrible* (1950), is considered among the finest film renderings of a literary work; other notable films include *Bob le flambeur* (1955), an homage to American film noir, and *Léon Morin Prêtre* (1961), which saw Jean-Paul Belmondo in a surprisingly effective role as a priest. Much of Melville's output reflected his passion for American culture (he took his name from novelist Herman Melville) and Hollywood movies of the hard-boiled style. • *Le Silence de la mer* 1948 (d); *Les Enfants Terribles* 1949 (d,p); *Bob le Flambeur* 1955 (d); *L'A.F.P. nous communique* 1958 (d); *A bout de souffle/Breathless* 1959 (a); *Léon Morin Prêtre/Leon Morin Priest* 1961 (d); *Landru* 1962 (a); *L'Aine des Ferchaux* 1963 (d,sc); *Le Doulos* 1963 (d,sc,adapt,dial); *Le Samourai/The Samurai* 1967 (d); *L'Armée des ombres/The Shadow Army* 1969 (d,sc); *Le Cercle rouge/The Red Circle* 1970 (d); *Un Flic* 1972 (d,sc).

Menges, Chris • Director of photography; also director. • Born Herefordshire, England, 1940. Former documentary cameraman whose first feature work was for socially conscious director, Ken Loach. Menges graduated to big-budget international films in the 1980s (*The Empire Strikes Back* 1980, *The Mission* 1986) but re-affirmed his social and political concerns with *A World Apart* (1988), a sensitive directorial debut based on the life of murdered South African activist Ruth First. • *If...* 1968 (cam.op); *Kes* 1970 (ph); *Gumshoe* 1971 (ph); *Before the Monsoon* 1979 (ph); *Black Jack* 1979 (ph); *Bloody Kids* 1979 (ph); *Babylon* 1980 (ph); *The Empire Strikes Back* 1980 (cam.op); *The Gamekeeper* 1980 (ph); *Couples & Robbers* 1981 (ph); *Looks and Smiles* 1981 (ph); *Angel* 1982 (ph); *Warlords of the 21st Century* 1982 (ph); *East 103rd Street* 1983 (d,p,ph); *Local Hero* 1983 (ph); *Loving Walter* 1983 (ph); *Comfort and Joy* 1984 (ph); *The Killing Fields* 1984 (ph) **(AABPH)**; *Winter Flight* 1984 (ph); *MARIE* 1985 (ph); *A Sense of Freedom* 1985 (ph); *The Mission* 1986 (ph) **(AABPH)**; *Singing the Blues in Red* 1986 (ph); *High Season* 1987 (ph); *Shy People* 1987 (ph); *A World Apart* 1988 (d).

Menjou, Adolphe • Actor • Born Adolphe Jean Menjou, Pittsburgh, PA, February 18, 1890; died 1963. *Educ.* Culver Military Academy, Indiana; Stiles Preparatory School; Cornell, New York (mechanical engineering). Natty lead and secondary player who first came to prominence in Charlie Chaplin's *Woman of Paris* (1923). Menjou played debonair lotharios, slick manipulators and, on occasion, beady-eyed villains through the 1950s. • *The Moth* 1917; *The Valentine Girl* 1917; *Courage* 1921; *The Faith Healer* 1921; *Queenie* 1921; *The Sheik* 1921; *The Three Musketeers* 1921; *Through the Back Door* 1921; *Clarence* 1922; *The Eternal Flame* 1922; *The Fast Mail* 1922; *Head Over Heels* 1922; *Is Matrimony a Failure?* 1922; *Pink Gods* 1922; *Singed Wings* 1922; *Bella Donna* 1923; *Rupert of Hentzau* 1923; *The Spanish Dancer* 1923; *A Woman of Paris* 1923; *The World's Applause* 1923; *Broadway After Dark* 1924; *Broken Barriers* 1924; *The Fast Set* 1924; *For Sale* 1924; *The Marriage Cheat* 1924; *The Marriage Circle* 1924; *Open All Night* 1924; *Shadows of Paris* 1924; *Sinners in Silk* 1924; *Are Parents People?* 1925; *The King on Main Street* 1925; *A Kiss in the Dark* 1925; *Lost—a Wife* 1925; *The Swan* 1925; *The Ace of Cads* 1926; *Fascinating Youth* 1926; *The Grand Duchess and the Waiter* 1926; *A Social Celebrity* 1926; *The Sorrows of Satan* 1926; *Blonde or Brunette* 1927; *Evening Clothes* 1927; *A Gentleman of Paris* 1927; *Serenade* 1927;

Service For Ladies 1927; *His Private Life* 1928; *His Tiger Lady* 1928; *A Night of Mystery* 1928; *Fashions in Love* 1929; *Marquis Preferred* 1929; *L'Enigmatique M. Parkes* 1930; *Morocco* 1930; *New Moon* 1930; *The Easiest Way* 1931; *Friends and Lovers* 1931; *The Front Page* 1931 **(AANBA)**; *The Great Lover* 1931; *Men Call It Love* 1931; *The Parisian* 1931; *Bachelor's Affairs* 1932; *A Farewell to Arms* 1932; *Forbidden* 1932; *The Night Club Lady* 1932; *Prestige* 1932; *Two White Arms* 1932; *The Circus Queen Murder* 1933; *Convention City* 1933; *Morning Glory* 1933; *The Worst Woman in Paris* 1933; *Easy to Love* 1934; *The Great Flirtation* 1934; *The Human Side* 1934; *Journal of a Crime* 1934; *Little Miss Marker* 1934; *The Mighty Barnum* 1934; *The Trumpet Blows* 1934; *Broadway Gondolier* 1935; *Gold Diggers of 1935* 1935; *The Milky Way* 1936; *One in a Million* 1936; *Sing, Baby, Sing* 1936; *Wives Never Know* 1936; *Cafe Metropole* 1937; *One Hundred Men and a Girl* 1937; *Stage Door* 1937; *A Star Is Born* 1937; *The Goldwyn Follies* 1938; *Letter of Introduction* 1938; *Thanks For Everything* 1938; *Golden Boy* 1939; *The Housekeeper's Daughter* 1939; *King of the Turf* 1939; *That's Right, You're Wrong* 1939; *A Bill of Divorcement* 1940; *Turnabout* 1940; *Father Takes a Wife* 1941; *Road Show* 1941; *Roxie Hart* 1942; *Syncopation* 1942; *You Were Never Lovelier* 1942; *Hi, Diddle Diddle* 1943; *Sweet Rosie O'Grady* 1943; *Step Lively* 1944; *Man Alive* 1945; *The Bachelor's Daughters* 1946; *Heartbeat* 1946; *The Hucksters* 1947; *I'll Be Yours* 1947; *Mr. District Attorney* 1947; *State of the Union* 1948; *Dancing in the Dark* 1949; *My Dream Is Yours* 1949; *To Please a Lady* 1950; *Across the Wide Missouri* 1951; *The Tall Target* 1951; *The Sniper* 1952; *Man on a Tightrope* 1953; *Timberjack* 1955; *The Ambassador's Daughter* 1956; *Bundle of Joy* 1956; *The Fuzzy Pink Nightgown* 1957; *I Married a Woman* 1957; *Paths of Glory* 1957; *Pollyanna* 1960; *Hollywood on Trial* 1976.

Menzel, Jirí • Director; also actor. • Born Czechoslovakia, February 23, 1938. *Educ.* FAMU, Prague. At the age of 28, Jirí Menzel won an Oscar for his debut feature, *Closely Watched Trains* (1966), one of the important films of the Czech New Wave. Menzel's vision combined a devotion to the poetry of the commonplace with his own special brand of slapstick.

Menzel's first outing as a director was the episode, "The Death of Mr. Baltazar," in *Pearls of the Deep* (1965), devoted to the work of Czech writer Bohumil Hrabal. Another episodic film, based on works by writer Josef Skvorecky, featured a Menzel-directed title episode, *Crime at the Girls School* (1965), in which characteristically quixotic details—a statue blowing smoke, potted plants camouflaging potty teachers—enlivened the narrative.

Naïveté led him to accept the direction of *Closely Watched Trains*, an adaptation of a Bohumil Hrabal novel offered to, but refused by, several other filmmakers. After Menzel convinced the author to make changes in the interest of cinema, the completed work appealed more to Hrabal than his own book. This story illustrates Menzel's ability to work in close creative collaboration and still maintain artistic integrity; it also indicates his modesty in offering others the credit for work bearing his own distinctive signature. *Closely Watched Trains* celebrates the primitive but life-affirming sexuality of the Czech peasantry as well as exploding the popular conception of the heroic WWII resistance fighter.

In 1968, Menzel adapted another literary masterpiece, Vladislav Vancura's *Capricious Summer*. Menzel himself plays the interloping tightrope walker, Arnostek, in an astonishing performance full of enthusiastic amateurism and the split-second timing and balance of circus professionals. (It is an act Menzel is wont to repeat on stage, where he still performs nightly when not directing films. He has also appeared in movies by other directors.)

Menzel's 1969 masterpiece *Larks on a String*, an outstpoken satire on the Communist "reeducation" of the bourgeoisie, was banned upon completion but released to critical acclaim in the West in 1990.

By 1974, Menzel had managed to work again on the conventional *Who Looks for Gold?*, a film he now disowns as simply a reward for having recanted his political beliefs (he vigorously resumed his political activities in 1989). His comedy became more physical, drawing on the styles of the American silent era. *Those Wonderful Men with a Crank* (1978) and *Short Cut* (1980) defend nonconformity from within the safety of nostalgia. The latter was again written by Hrabal, as was *The Snowdrop Festival* (1983). This film and *Seclusion Near a Forest* (1976) poke fun at the idyllic notions cherished by urban Czechs of the countryside to which they retreat every weekend.

In 1986, *My Sweet Little Village* elaborated on this theme and became an international hit. Subsequently, Menzel developed "Lullaby" for David Puttnam and Columbia Pictures; it was never made in Hollywood but is on Menzel's Czech agenda under the title "Fade Out." KJ • *Perlicky Na Dne/Pearls of the Deep* ("The Death of Mr. Baltazar" episode) 1965 (d); *Zlocin v dívcí škole/Crime at the Girls School* (title episode) 1965 (d,sc); *Navrat Ztracencho Syna* 1966 (a); *Ostre sledované vlaky/Closely Watched Trains* 1966 (a,d,sc); *Rozmarné Léto/Capricious Summer* 1968 (a,d,sc); *Skrivánci Na Nitich/Larks on a String* 1969 (d,sc); *Kdo hledá zlaté dno/Who Looks For Gold?* 1974 (d,sc); *Na Samote u Lesa/Seclusion Near a Forest* 1976 (d); *Hra o jablko* 1977 (a); *Bájecní Muzi S Klikou/Those Wonderful Men With a Crank* 1978 (a,ad,d); *Postriziny/Short Cut* 1980 (a,d); *Une Blonde Emoustillante/A High-Spirited Blonde* 1980 (d); *Koportos* 1980 (a); *Szivzur* 1982 (a); *Fandy* 1983 (a); *Slavnosti Snezenek/The Snowdrop Festival* 1983 (d); *Upir z Feratu* 1983 (a); *Prague* 1985 (d); *Vesnicko má Strediskovâ/My Sweet Little Village* 1986 (d); *Konec Starych Casu/The End of the Good Old Days* 1989 (d,sc); *Martha und Ich/Martha and I* 1990 (a).

Menzies, William Cameron • *aka* William Menzies • Production designer; also director, producer. • Born New Haven, CT, July 29, 1896; died 1957. One of the most influential designers in the history of cinema and one of the first to earn the title of "production designer" (the individual responsible for coordinating all the design-related elements of a film including sets, costumes, etc.). Menzies's artistry encompassed everything from the opulent appointments of *Gone With the Wind* (1939) to the cramped, shadowy interiors of Anthony Mann's *Reign of Terror* (1949). His directorial career was relatively undistinguished, one exception being the landmark sci-fi drama, *Things to Come* (1936). Tobe Hooper's 1986 remake of *Invaders from Mars* (1953) used some of Menzies's original designs for the project. • *The Thief of Bagdad* 1924 (art d); *The Eagle* 1925 (art d); *The Dove* 1927 (art d); *The Tempest* 1927 (art d) **(AABAD)** (joint award for both 1927 films); *The Iron Mask* 1928 (art d) **(AANBAD)**; *Alibi* 1929 (art d); *Bulldog Drummond* 1929 (art d) **(AANBAD)**; *The Taming of the Shrew* 1929 (pd); *Always Goodbye* 1931 (d); *The Spider* 1931 (d); *Almost Married* 1932 (d); *Chandu the Magician* 1932 (d); *Alice in Wonderland* 1933 (sc); *I Loved You Wednesday* 1933 (d); *The Wharf Angel* 1934 (d); *Things to Come* 1936 (d); *Four Dark Hours* 1937 (d); *Gone With the Wind* 1939 (pd) **(AAHON)**; *The Conquest of the Air* 1940 (d); *The Thief of Bagdad* 1940 (assoc.p); *Address Unknown* 1944 (d,p); *Ivy* 1947 (p); *Reign of Terror* 1949 (p); *Drums in the Deep South* 1951 (d); *The Man He Found* 1951 (d); *Invaders From Mars* 1953 (d); *The Maze* 1953 (d); *Around the World in 80 Days* 1956 (assoc.p).

Mercer, Johnny • Lyricist; also composer, actor. • Born Savannah, GA, November 18, 1909; died 1976. Writer of songs such as "That Old Black Magic" and "Jeepers Creepers" who contributed the score for the Broadway musical *Top Banana* and collaborated with some of America's most distinguished tunesmiths, including Hoagy Carmichael, Jerome

Kern and Henry Mancini. Beginning in the 1930s, Mercer contributed a number of songs to the screen, notably "Moon River" for *Breakfast at Tiffany's* (1961). • *Gambling* 1934 (song); *Old Man Rhythm* 1935 (a,song); *To Beat the Band* 1935 (a,song); *Hollywood Hotel* 1937 (song); *Ready, Willing and Able* 1937 (song); *Varsity Show* 1937 (song); *Cowboy From Brooklyn* 1938 (song); *Garden of the Moon* 1938 (song); *Going Places* 1938 (song) **(AANBS)**; *Gold Diggers in Paris* 1938 (song); *Hard to Get* 1938 (song); *Naughty But Nice* 1939 (song); *Blues in the Night* 1941 (song) **(AANBS)**; *Second Chorus* 1941 (song) **(AANBS)**; *Navy Blues* 1941 (song); *Star Spangled Rhythm* 1942 (song) **(AANBS)**; *You Were Never Lovelier* 1942 (lyrics) **(AANBS)**; *The Sky's the Limit* 1943 (song) **(AANBS)**; *True to Life* 1943 (song); *Here Come the Waves* 1944 (song) **(AANBS)**; *To Have and Have Not* 1944 (song); *The Harvey Girls* 1946 (song) **(AABS)**; *Dark City* 1950 (song); *The Petty Girl* 1950 (song); *Here Comes the Groom* 1951 (song) **(AABS)**; *Macao* 1952 (song); *Seven Brides For Seven Brothers* 1954 (m,lyrics); *Top Banana* 1954 (m,lyrics); *Daddy Long Legs* 1955 (m) **(AANBS)**; *Timberjack* 1955 (song); *Autumn Leaves* 1956 (song); *You Can't Run Away From It* 1956 (song); *Bernadine* 1957 (song); *Spring Reunion* 1957 (song); *Merry Andrew* 1958 (lyrics); *Missouri Traveler* 1958 (lyrics); *Hey Boy! Hey Girl!* 1959 (song); *Li'l Abner* 1959 (lyrics); *The Facts of Life* 1960 (song) **(AANBS)**; *Breakfast at Tiffany's* 1961 (song) **(AABS)**; *Days of Wine and Roses* 1962 (song) **(AABS)**; *Hatari!* 1962 (song); *How the West Was Won* 1962 (lyrics); *Charade* 1963 (song) **(AANBS)**; *The Americanization of Emily* 1964 (song); *Man's Favorite Sport?* 1964 (song); *The Great Race* 1965 (song) **(AANBS)**; *Alvarez Kelly* 1966 (song); *Barefoot in the Park* 1967 (song); *The Brotherhood* 1968 (song); *Alex in Wonderland* 1970 (song); *Darling Lili* 1970 (song) **(AANBS,AANBSS)**; *Kotch* 1971 (lyrics) **(AANBS)**; *The Long Goodbye* 1973 (lyrics); *The Parallax View* 1974 (song).

Merchant, Ismail • Producer; also director. • Born Bombay, India, December 25, 1936. *Educ.* St. Xavier's University, Bombay; New York University (business administration). Director of an acclaimed short, *The Creation of Woman* (1961), who began his long-term association with director James Ivory that same year. Merchant's financial and marketing expertise have greatly contributed to the team's commercial success and enhanced their international profile. He has also directed two films for TV. See also Ivory, James. • *Venice: Theme and Variations* 1957 (p); *The Sword and the Flute* 1959 (p); *The Householder* 1963 (p); *The Delhi Way* 1964 (p); *Shakespeare Wallah* 1965 (p); *The Guru* 1969 (a,p); *Bombay Talkie* 1970 (p); *Adventures of a Brown Man in Search of Civilization* 1972 (p); *Helen, Queen of the Nautch Girls* 1972 (p); *Savages* 1972 (p); *Mahatma and the Mad Boy (short)* 1973 (d,p); *Autobiography of a Princess* 1975 (exec.p); *The Wild Party* 1975 (p); *Sweet Sounds* 1976 (p); *Roseland* 1977 (exec.p); *The Europeans* 1979 (p); *Hullabaloo Over Georgie and Bonnie's Pictures* 1979 (p); *Jane Austen in Manhattan* 1980 (p); *Quartet* 1981 (p); *The Courtesans of Bombay* 1982 (d,p,sc); *Heat and Dust* 1983 (p); *The Bostonians* 1984 (p); *My Little Girl* 1986 (exec.p); *A Room With a View* 1986 (p) **(AANBP)**; *Maurice* 1987 (p); *The Deceivers* 1988 (p); *The Perfect Murder* 1988 (exec.p); *Slaves of New York* 1989 (p); *Mr. & Mrs. Bridge* 1990 (p); *The Ballad of the Sad Cafe* 1991 (p).

Mercouri, Melina • Actress • Born Athens, GA, October 18, 1923. Fiery Greek stage actress, adept at both drama and comedy, who made her film debut in 1955. Mercouri gained prominence in a number of features directed by husband Jules Dassin, notably *Never on Sunday* (1960) and *Phaedra* (1962). Long a political activist, she was expelled from Greece by the notorious Colonels' Junta in 1967 but eventually returned to win a parliamentary seat for the Socialist party in 1977. Mercouri recently lost her bid to become mayor of Athens. • *Celui Qui Doit Mourir* 1957 (a); *The Gypsy and the Gentleman* 1958 (a); *La Loi* 1958 (a); *Pote Tin Kyriaki/Never on Sunday* 1960 (a) **(AANBA)**; *Phaedra* 1962 (a); *The Victors* 1963 (a); *Topkapi* 1964 (a); *10:30 P.M. Summer* 1966 (a); *A Man Could Get Killed* 1966 (a); *Gaily, Gaily* 1969 (a); *La Promesse de l'aube/Promise at Dawn* 1970 (a); *Once Is Not Enough* 1975 (a); *Nasty Habits* 1976 (a); *A Dream of Passion* 1978 (a); *Keine Zufallige Geschichte/Not By Coincidence* 1983 (a).

Meredith, Burgess • Actor; also director, producer. • Born Oliver Burgess Meredith, Cleveland, OH, November 16, 1908. *Educ.* Amherst College. Former child soprano who became a leading figure in American theater of the 1930s and made his film debut in *Winterset* (1936), reprising his earlier stage role in a play written for him by Maxwell Anderson. Versatile and highly accomplished, Meredith gave outstanding performances in *Of Mice and Men* (1939), *The Story of G.I. Joe* (1945) and *The Day of the Locust* (1975), among others. He reached a wide audience as Sylvester Stallone's crusty trainer in *Rocky* (1976) and as the monocled "Penguin" in the TV series "Batman" (1966-68). Meredith's distinctive, sing-song rasp has also been enlisted for countless commercial voice-overs. Married to actress Paulette Goddard (1944-49). • *Winterset* 1936 (a); *There Goes the Groom* 1937 (a); *Spring Madness* 1938 (a); *Idiot's Delight* 1939 (a); *Of Mice and Men* 1939 (a); *Castle on the Hudson* 1940 (a); *Second Chorus* 1940 (a); *San Francisco Docks* 1941 (a); *That Uncertain Feeling* 1941 (a); *Tom, Dick and Harry* 1941 (a); *Street of Chance* 1942 (a); *Welcome to Britain* 1943 (d); *The Story of G.I. Joe* 1945 (a); *The Diary of a Chambermaid* 1946 (a,p,sc); *Magnificent Doll* 1946 (a); *A Miracle Can Happen* 1948 (a,p); *Jigsaw* 1949 (a); *The Man on the Eiffel Tower* 1949 (a,d); *Albert Schweitzer* 1957 (a); *Joe Butterfly* 1957 (a); *The Sorcerer's Village* 1958 (a); *Advise and Consent* 1962 (a); *The Cardinal* 1963 (a); *In Harm's Way* 1965 (a); *Batman* 1966 (a); *A Big Hand For the Little Lady* 1966 (a); *Madame X* 1966 (a); *Hurry Sundown* 1967 (a); *Skidoo* 1968 (a); *Stay Away, Joe* 1968 (a); *Hard Contract* 1969 (a); *MacKenna's Gold* 1969 (a); *The Reivers* 1969 (a); *There Was a Crooked Man* 1970 (a); *Clay Pigeon* 1971 (a); *A Fan's Notes* 1972 (a); *The Man* 1972 (a); *Golden Needles* 1974 (a); *92 in the Shade* 1975 (a); *The Day of the Locust* 1975 (a) **(AANBSA)**; *The Hindenburg* 1975 (a); *The Master Gunfighter* 1975 (a); *Burnt Offerings* 1976 (a); *Rocky* 1976 (a) **(AANBSA)**; *Golden Rendezvous* 1977 (a); *The Manitou* 1977 (a); *The Sentinel* 1977 (a); *Shenanigans* 1977 (a); *The Amazing Captain Nemo* 1978 (a); *Foul Play* 1978 (a); *Magic* 1978 (a); *Rocky II* 1979 (a); *Final Assignment* 1980 (a); *When Time Ran Out* 1980 (a); *Acting: Lee Strasberg and The Actors Studio* 1981 (a); *Clash of the Titans* 1981 (a); *The Last Chase* 1981 (a); *True Confessions* 1981 (a); *Rocky III* 1982 (a); *Twilight Zone—the Movie* 1983 (a); *Broken Rainbow* 1985 (a); *Santa Claus: The Movie* 1985 (a); *Mr. Corbett's Ghost* 1986 (a); *G.I. Joe: The Movie* 1987 (a); *King Lear* 1987 (a); *Full Moon in Blue Water* 1988 (a); *John Huston* 1988 (a); *Rocky V* 1990 (a); *State of Grace* 1990 (a).

Meszaros, Marta • Director; also screenwriter. • Born Budapest, Hungary, 1934. *Educ.* VGIK, Moscow. Key figure of Hungarian cinema who has dealt almost exclusively with the situation of women in contemporary society. Meszaros began her career working on newsreels in Budapest and joined the Mafilm Group 4 film unit in 1966. She made her feature debut with *The Girl* (1968), a poignant study of a young woman's search for affection which staked out several of the director's main concerns. Here, and in later features such as *Riddance* (1973) and *Adoption* (1975), Meszaros brings stylish camerawork and finely tuned powers of observation to bear on contemporary sexual, psychological, social and inter-generational relationships. She is perhaps best known for her autobiographical account of the Stalinist period, *Diary for My Children* (1982), which uses newsreel footage and clips from 1950s features to weave a complex, personal and political portrait of the era. Witheld from distribution in the West for two years, *Diary* finally won a Special Jury Prize at the Cannes Film Festival in 1984.

Meszaros has been married three times: to documentarist Laszlo Karda; to director Miklós Jancsó (1962-81); and, most recently, to Polish actor Jan Nowicki, who has appeared in films by his wife as well as several other leading directors. • *Eladas muveszete, Az/The Art of Salesmanship (short)* 1960 (d); *The Girl* 1968 (d); *Riddance* 1973 (d); *Orokbefogadas/Adoption* 1975 (d,sc); *Kilenc honap/Nine Months* 1976 (d,sc); *Ok ketten/The Two of Them* 1977 (d); *Olyan mint otthon/Just Like Home* 1978 (d); *Utkozben/On the Move* 1979 (d,sc); *Orokseg/The Inheritance* 1980 (d,sc); *Nema Kialtas/Silent Cry* 1982 (d,sc); *Diary For My Children* 1982 (d); *Naplo Szerelmeimnek/Diary For My Loved Ones* 1987 (d); *Piroska es a farkas, Bye Bye, Red Riding Hood* 1989 (d,sc); *Naplo apamnak, anyammnak/Diary For My Father and Mother* 1990 (d,sc).

Metty, Russell • Director of photography • Born Los Angeles, CA, 1906; died 1978. Best known for his work on Orson Welles's *The Stranger* (1946) and *A Touch of Evil* (1958), and for his multi-film association with director Douglas Sirk. • *West of the Pecos* 1934; *Night Waitress* 1936; *Annapolis Salute* 1937; *Behind the Headlines* 1937; *Forty Naughty Girls* 1937; *They Wanted to Marry* 1937; *You Can't Beat Love* 1937; *The Affairs of Annabel* 1938; *Annabel Takes a Tour* 1938; *Bringing Up Baby* 1938; *Next Time I Marry* 1938; *The Sunset Trail* 1938; *The Great Man Votes* 1939; *The Spellbinder* 1939; *That's Right, You're Wrong* 1939; *Three Sons* 1939; *Curtain Call* 1940; *Dance, Girl, Dance* 1940; *Irene* 1940; *No, No, Nanette* 1940; *Four Jacks and a Jill* 1941; *A Girl, a Guy and a Gob* 1941; *Sunny* 1941; *Week-End For Three* 1941; *Army Surgeon* 1942; *The Big Street* 1942; *Falcon's Brother* 1942; *Joan of Paris* 1942; *Mexican Spitfire Sees a Ghost* 1942; *Around the World* 1943; *Behind the Rising Sun* 1943; *Forever and a Day* 1943; *Hitler's Children* 1943; *The Sky's the Limit* 1943; *Tender Comrade* 1943; *The Master Race* 1944; *Music in Manhattan* 1944; *Seven Days Ashore* 1944; *Betrayal From the East* 1945; *Breakfast in Hollywood* 1945; *It's in the Bag* 1945; *Pardon My Past* 1945; *The Story of G.I. Joe* 1945; *The Perfect Marriage* 1946; *The Stranger* 1946; *Whistle Stop* 1946; *Ivy* 1947; *The Private Affairs of Bel Ami* 1947; *Ride the Pink Horse* 1947; *All My Sons* 1948; *Arch of Triumph* 1948; *Kiss the Blood Off My Hands* 1948; *Mr. Peabody and the Mermaid* 1948; *A Woman's Vengeance* 1948; *You Gotta Stay Happy* 1948; *Bagdad* 1949; *The Lady Gambles* 1949; *We Were Strangers* 1949; *Buccaneer's Girl* 1950; *Curtain Call At Cactus Creek* 1950; *The Desert Hawk* 1950; *Peggy* 1950; *Sierra* 1950; *Wyoming Mail* 1950; *Flame of Araby* 1951; *The Golden Horde* 1951; *Katie Did It* 1951; *Little Egypt* 1951; *The Raging Tide* 1951; *Up Front* 1951; *Against All Flags* 1952; *Because of You* 1952; *Scarlet Angel* 1952; *The Treasure of Lost Canyon* 1952; *The World in His Arms* 1952; *Yankee Buccaneer* 1952; *It Happens Every Thursday* 1953; *The Man From the Alamo* 1953; *Seminole* 1953; *Take Me to Town* 1953; *Tumbleweed* 1953; *The Veils of Bagdad* 1953; *Four Guns to the Border* 1954; *Magnificent Obsession* 1954; *Man Without a Star* 1954; *Naked Alibi* 1954; *Sign of the Pagan* 1954; *Taza, Son of Cochise* 1954; *Crashout* 1955; *Cult of the Cobra* 1955; *The Man From Bitter Ridge* 1955; *All That Heaven Allows* 1956; *Battle Hymn* 1956; *Congo Crossing* 1956; *Miracle in the Rain* 1956; *There's Always Tomorrow* 1956; *Written on the Wind* 1956; *Man Afraid* 1957; *Man of a Thousand Faces* 1957; *The Midnight Story* 1957; *Mister Cory* 1957; *The Female Animal* 1958; *Monster on the Campus* 1958; *The Thing That Couldn't Die* 1958; *A Time to Love and a Time to Die* 1958; *Touch of Evil* 1958; *Imitation of Life* 1959; *Step Down to Terror* 1959; *This Earth Is Mine* 1959; *Midnight Lace* 1960; *Portrait in Black* 1960; *Spartacus* 1960 **(AABPH)**; *By Love Possessed* 1961; *Flower Drum Song* 1961 **(AANBPH)**; *The Misfits* 1961; *If a Man Answers* 1962; *The Interns* 1962; *That Touch of Mink* 1962; *Tammy and the Doctor* 1963; *The Thrill of It All* 1963; *Captain Newman, M.D.* 1964; *I'd Rather Be Rich* 1964; *The Art of Love* 1965; *Bus Riley's Back in Town* 1965; *The War Lord* 1965; *The Appaloosa* 1966; *Madame X* 1966; *Texas Across the River* 1966; *Counterpoint* 1967; *Thoroughly Modern Millie* 1967; *Madigan* 1968; *The Pink Jungle* 1968; *The Secret War of Harry Frigg* 1968; *Change of Habit* 1969; *How Do I Love Thee?* 1970; *The Omega Man* 1971; *Ben* 1972; *That's Entertainment!* 1974.

Metz, Christian • Theorist • Born Bézier, France, December 12, 1931. Influential thinker whose pioneering work in cine-semiotics (film as a system of signs) has not only been of lasting importance to an understanding of how meaning in the cinema is made, but—by linking film studies to an established critical discipline like semiotics—helped solidify the place of cinema studies as a "serious" academic discipline in American universities.

Metz brought his background in linguistics to bear on film theory in *Essais sur la signification au cinema* (two volumes, published 1968 and 1972, with the first translated into English as *Film Language: A Semiotics of the Cinema* in 1974); he embraced a broader, more cultural and historical approach in *Language and Cinema* (1974, originally published in French in 1971) and began to incorporate psychoanalytic theory into his work in *The Imaginary Signifier* (1982, originally published in French in 1977).

Metzger, Radley • *aka* Henry Paris • Director, producer • Born U.S.A., 1930. Preeminent figure in the soft-core erotica field (*The Lickerish Quartet* 1970) who has also ventured into deeper, murkier waters under his "hard-core" pseudonym, Henry Paris. • *Gangster Story* 1959 (ed); *The Flesh Eaters* 1966 (ed); *Carmen, Baby* 1967 (d,p); *Therese and Isabelle* 1968 (d,p); *Camille 2000* 1969 (d); *The Lickerish Quartet* 1970 (d,from story *Hide and Seek*,p); *Don't Cry For Me Little Mother* 1972 (a,d,p); *Little Mother* 1972 (d,p); *Score* 1973 (d,p); *The Private Afternoons of Pamela Mann* 1974 (d); *Naked Came the Stranger* 1975 (d); *L'Image* 1976 (d); *The Opening of Misty Beethoven* 1976 (d,p); *Barbara Broadcast* 1977 (d); *The Cat and the Canary* 1979 (d,sc); *The Princess and the Call Girl* 1984 (d,sc).

Meyer, Nicholas • Director; also novelist, screenwriter. • Born U.S.A., December 24, 1945. *Educ.* University of Iowa. Capable engineer of mainstream entertainments who began his career as a Hollywood publicist before his best-selling novel, *The Seven Percent Solution*, was made into a popular film in 1977. Meyer's *The Day After* (1983), an overwrought TV movie depicting post-nuclear holocaust "life," sparked months of controversy before and after the broadcast. He has since shown a talent for bright comedy with his satire of Kennedy era can-doism, *Volunteers* (1985). • *The Seven Per-Cent Solution* 1976 (sc,from novel) **(AANBSC)**; *Time After Time* 1979 (d,sc); *Star Trek II: The Wrath of Khan* 1982 (d); *Volunteers* 1985 (d); *Star Trek IV: The Voyage Home* 1986 (sc); *The Deceivers* 1988 (d).

Meyer, Russ • Producer, director; also actor, screenwriter. • Born Russell Albion Meyer, Oakland, CA, March 21, 1922. WWII newsreel photographer who snapped centerfolds for Playboy before turning out his first "skin flicks" in the 1950s. *The Immortal Mr. Teas* (1959) marked the first of a series of soft-core sex romps featuring Meyer's now notorious trademarks: a predilection for oversized breasts; high-speed, disjointed camerawork; anarchic humor; and overblown violence. The huge commercial success of *Vixen* (1968) led to Meyer being invited by 20th Century-Fox to direct trashy spectacles like *Beyond the Valley of the Dolls* (1970), which was scripted by film critic Roger Ebert. After a ten-year hiatus, Meyer announced his return to film directing—again with an Ebert-scripted project—in July 1990. • *Roogie's Bump* 1954 (a); *The Immoral Mr. Teas* 1959 (d); *Eroticon, Eve and the Handyman* 1961 (d); *Heavenly Bodies* 1963 (d); *Lorna* 1964 (d,story,ph);

Fanny Hill: Memoirs of a Woman of Pleasure 1965 (d); *Motor Psycho* 1965 (d,p,sc,ph); *Rope of Flesh* 1965 (d,p); *Faster Pussycat! Kill! Kill!* 1966 (d,p,story,ed); *Mondo Topless* 1966 (d); *Good Morning, and Goodbye!* 1967 (d,p,story,ph,ed); *Finders Keepers, Lovers Weepers* 1968 (d,p,story,ph,ed); *Cherry, Harry & Raquel* 1969 (d,p,sc,story,ph,ed); *Beyond the Valley of the Dolls* 1970 (d,p,story); *The Seven Minutes* 1971 (d,p); *Sweet Suzy* 1973 (d,p,sc,story,cam.op); *Super Vixens* 1974 (d,p,sc,ph); *Up* 1976 (d,p,story,ph,ed); *Beneath the Valley of the Ultravixens* 1979 (a,d,p,sc,story,ph,ed); *Amazon Women on the Moon* 1987 (a).

Micheaux, Oscar • Director; also writer, producer. • Born Metropolis, IL, 1884; died April 1, 1951, North Carolina. The most prolific black—if not independent—filmmaker in American cinema, Oscar Micheaux wrote, produced and directed nearly forty feature-length films between 1919 and 1948. Despite his importance to black cinema, Micheaux remains an enigmatic and ignored figure; few of his films have survived. In addition, his controversial racial beliefs and technically inferior films make him difficult to interpolate within mainstream film history.

The fifth child in a family of thirteen, Micheaux worked as a shoeshine boy, farm laborer and Pullman porter until 1904, when he purchased a homestead in South Dakota. Within nine years, he had expanded his holdings to 500 acres and also written, published and distributed the first of ten semi-autobiographical novels, *The Conquest* (1913).

In 1918, the Lincoln Film Company in Nebraska—one of the first all-black companies that arose in response to D.W. Griffith's *The Birth of a Nation* (1915)—offered to film Micheaux's 1917 novel, *The Homesteader*. But when Lincoln refused to produce the film on the scale that he desired, Micheaux responded by founding his own production company and shooting the work himself in the abandoned Selig studio in Chicago. The film opened in Chicago in 1919.

Micheaux worked successfully and prolifically throughout the next decade, largely thanks to the promotional techniques he had developed in selling his own novels. With script in hand he would tour ghetto theaters across the nation, soliciting advances from owners and thus circumventing the cash-flow and distribution problems that limited other all-black companies to producing only one or two pictures.

When the advent of sound (with its attendant high costs), Hollywood's move into the production of all-black musicals and the Depression combined to bring about the demise of independent black cinema in the early 1930s, Micheaux alone survived. (He did declare bankruptcy in 1928, forcing him thereafter to depend increasingly on white backers.) He released his first "talkie," *The Exile*, in 1931.

The increasing controversy surrounding Micheaux's films, especially *God's Step Children* (1938), and his unsuccessful attempts to imitate Hollywood genre movies brought his career to a halt in 1940. He staged a disastrous comeback in 1948 with *The Betrayal* and died three years later while on a promotional tour of the South.

Micheaux offered audiences a black version of Hollywood fare, complete with actors typecast as the "black Valentino" or the "sepia Mae West." But because he operated under financial and technical restraints, his films were poorly lighted and edited. Non-professional actors were used, and scenes were often shot in one take, leading to inevitable "flubs." Micheaux incorportated these limitations into a unique style that added a self-conscious element to his films: errors were included "to give the audience a laugh," continuity defied expectation, and narrative was often abandoned in favor of sheer excess.

Above all, Micheaux saw his films as "propaganda" designed to "uplift the race." In the 1930s, however, black critics and audiences rejected his message as racially ambivalent. His bourgeois ideology of the "self-made man" found expression in all-black casts in which the light-skinned blacks succeeded, while the rest were blamed for their own oppression. Nevertheless, his films represented a radical departure from Hollywood's portrayal of blacks as servants and brought diverse images of ghetto life and related social issues to the screen for the first time. CAN • *The Homesteader* 1919 (d,p,sc,from novel); *The Gunsaulus Mystery* 1921 (d,p,sc); *The Millionaire* 1927 (d,p,sc,story); *Thirty Years Later* 1928 (d,sc); *The Exile* 1931 (d,sc); *Harlem After Midnight* 1935 (d,sc); *Lem Hawkins' Confession* 1935 (d,p,sc); *God's Step Children* 1938 (d); *The Betrayal* 1948 (d,p,sc,story).

Midler, Bette • Actress; also singer. • Born Honolulu, Hawaii, December 1, 1945. *Educ.* University of Hawaii; Herbert Berghof Studio, New York. Bawdy, gifted revue performer and recording artist who made her first impact onscreen as a dissolute rock star in *The Rose* (1979), a role that fully exploited her singing talents and yen for the outrageous. Her film career in ruins after the spectacular failure of 1982's *Jinxed!* (her battles with director Don Siegel and costar Ken Wahl are legendary), Midler's fortunes began to improve with the hit *Down and Out in Beverly Hills* (1986) and, aided by the formulaic Disney machine, continued, transforming her into one of the industry's most bankable stars. • *Hawaii* 1965 (a); *The Rose* 1979 (a) **(AANBA)**; *Divine Madness* 1980 (a,sc,add.lyrics "Big Noise From Winnetka"); *Jinxed!* 1982 (a); *Down and Out in Beverly Hills* 1986 (a); *Ruthless People* 1986 (a); *Outrageous Fortune* 1987 (a); *Beaches* 1988 (a,p,songs); *Big Business* 1988 (a); *Oliver & Company* 1988 (a,song); *Stella* 1990 (a); *Scenes From a Mall* 1991 (a).

Mifune, Toshiro • Actor; also producer. • Born Tsingtao, China, April 1, 1920. Although he had originally planned to work in films as an assistant cameraman, Toshiro Mifune was auditioned as an actor instead, a fortuitous career shift which helped change the course of Japanese cinematic history. He has appeared in many of the great post-war Japanese films, most notably those of director Akira Kurosawa.

Collaborations between Kurosawa and Mifune began with the film *Drunken Angel* (1948) and continued with such notable works as *Rashomon* (1950), *Seven Samurai* (1954), *Throne of Blood* (1957), *Yojimbo* (1961) and *Red Beard* (1965). Mifune's career is not, however, limited to films directed by Kurosawa. He also appeared in such varied Japanese films as Senkichi Taniguchi's *Snow Trail* (1947), Kenji Mizoguchi's *The Life of Oharu* (1952), Hiroshi Inagaki's samurai trilogy on Miyamoto Musashi (1954-56) and his *The Rickshaw Man* (1958), in addition to Masaki Kobayashi's *Rebellion* (1967). Mifune has also starred in films by non-Japanese directors, including Ismael Rodriguez's *The Important Man* (1961), John Frankenheimer's *Grand Prix* (1966) and *The Challenge* (1982), John Boorman's *Hell in the Pacific* (1968), Terence Young's *Red Sun* (1971), Spielberg's *1941* (1979) and Jerry London's TV miniseries *Shogun* (1980).

Mifune's roles tend to fall within the area described in kabuki terms as the *tateyaku* style, i.e., that of the forceful, disciplined leading man, in contrast to the softer and more weak-willed *nimaime* male. His fast-paced and explosive style is not, however, all bluster and swordplay. He infuses a subtle degree of sensitivity and psychological complexity into even the most thick-skinned warrior characters. In the course of his career, he has undertaken roles ranging from a modern-day cop to a wandering, masterless samurai (*ronin*), from a Japanese version of Macbeth to a drunken Indian peasant. He has also excelled at playing a wealthy industrialist, a ruthless bandit, a compassionate physician, an aged obsessive and a day laborer.

With a talent for both drama and comedy, Mifune has refined, but never totally lost, his earlier "angry young man" demeanor. He is the only performer to have twice received the best actor Award at the Venice Film Festival and is also the recipient of the 1988 Kawakita Award, presented to those who have contributed significantly to Japanese cinema. Since 1963, Mifune has owned his own production company, Mifune Productions. He tried his hand at directing with a film entitled *The Legacy of the 500,000* (1963), but its failure persuaded him to concentrate his energies on performing. Mifune Productions now specializes in making films for TV. LCE • *Ginrei no hate/Snow Trail* 1947; *Yoidore Tenshi/Drunken Angel* 1948; *Nora Inu* 1949; *Shizukanaru naru ketto* 1949; *Rashomon* 1950; *Shuban* 1950; *Hakuchi* 1951; *Saikaku ichidai onna/The Life of Oharu* 1952; *Miyamoto Musashi* 1954; *Shichinin no Samurai/Seven Samurai* 1954; *Ikimono no Kiroku* 1955; *Donzoko* 1957; *Kumonosujo/Throne of Blood* 1957; *Kakushi Toride no San-Akunin* 1958; *Muhomatsu no issho/The Rickshaw Man* 1958; *The Important Man* 1961; *Yojimbo* 1961; *Chushingura* 1962; *Daitozoku* 1962; *Tsubaki Sanjuro* 1962; *Gojuman-nin no isan/Legacy of the 500,000* 1963 (a,d,p); *Tengoku to Jigoku* 1963; *The Lost World of Sinbad* 1964; *Akahige/Red Beard* 1965; *Grand Prix* 1966; *Jiouchi/Rebellion* 1967; *Hell in the Pacific* 1968; *Yamamoto Isoroku* 1968; *Nihonkai Daikaisen* 1969; *Machi-buse* 1970 (a,exec.p); *Shinsengumi* 1970 (a,p); *Soleil Rouge/Red Sun* 1971; *Zato-ichi to Yojimbo* 1971; *Paper Tiger* 1975; *Battle of Midway* 1976; *1941* 1979; *Oginsaga* 1979; *Winter Kills* 1979; *The Bushido Blade* 1981; *The Challenge* 1982; *Inchon* 1982; *Jinsei Gekijo* 1983; *Seiha* 1984; *Umi Isubame Joe No Kiseki* 1984; *Taketori Monogatari* 1987.

Mikhalkov, Nikita • Director; also actor. • Born Nikita Sergeyevich Mikhalkov-Konchalovsky, Moscow USSR, October 21, 1945. *Educ.* Shchukin Theatre; VGIK. Began his career as an actor before emerging in the mid-1970s as one of his country's leading directors. Mikhalkov's varied output has ranged from adventure spectacles to well-nuanced character studies; like his brother, director Andrei Mikhalkov-Konchalovsky, he has earned a reputation as an actors' director, adroitly steering his players through complex material and extracting some of the finest performances in contemporary Soviet cinema. His affinity for the subtle characterizations and earthy humor of Chekhov is evident in 1977's *An Unfinished Piece for Mechanical Piano*, drawn from several of the master's stories, and *Dark Eyes* (1987), also based on Chekhov material and featuring a landmark performance by Marcello Mastroianni. • *At Home Among Strangers, a Stranger at Home* 1974 (a,d,sc); *A Slave Of Love* 1976 (d); *An Unfinished Piece for Mechanical Piano* 1977 (a,d,sc); *Siberiade* 1978 (a); *Oblomov* 1979 (d,sc); *Pyat' Vecherov/Five Evenings* 1979 (d,sc); *Polioty Vo Sne Naiavou/Flights of Fancy* 1983 (a); *Rodnia/Family Relations* 1983 (d); *Vokzal dla dvoish/Station for Two* 1983 (a); *Bez svidetelei/Without Witnesses* 1983 (d,sc); *Oci Ciornie/Dark Eyes* 1987 (d,sc).

Milchan, Arnon • Producer • Born Israel. Former Israeli stage producer who has been responsible for some 14 features, including films by directors Sergio Leone (*Once Upon a Time in America* 1984), Martin Scorsese (*The King of Comedy* 1983) and Terry Gilliam (*Brazil* 1985). • *Black Joy* 1977 (p); *The Medusa Touch* 1978 (exec.p); *Dizengoff 99* 1979 (p); *Can She Bake a Cherry Pie?* 1983 (a); *The King of Comedy* 1983 (p); *Once Upon a Time in America* 1984 (a,p); *Brazil* 1985 (p); *Legend* 1985 (p); *Stripper* 1985 (exec.p); *Man on Fire* 1987 (p); *Big Man on Campus* 1989 (p); *The War of the Roses* 1989 (p); *Who's Harry Crumb?* 1989 (p); *Pretty Woman* 1990 (p); *Q&A* 1990 (p); *Switch* 1991 (exec.p).

Miles, Sarah • Actress • Born Ingatestone, Essex, England, December 31, 1941. *Educ.* RADA, London. Stage-trained actress whose big eyes and modish bob featured in several prominent films of the 1960s, especially Joseph Losey's *The Servant* (1963) and Michelangelo Antonioni's *Blow-Up* (1966). Miles has worked on stage and screen with screenwriter-director Robert Bolt, whom she married in 1967, divorced in 1976 and re-married in 1988. She began making effective character appearances in the 1980s, as with *Hope and Glory* (1987), in which she plays a harried mother-of-three in blitz-torn London. Sister of Christopher Miles, who has directed several films (e.g. *Priest of Love* 1980). • *The Ceremony* 1963; *The Servant* 1963; *Those Magnificent Men in Their Flying Machines* 1965; *Blow-Up* 1966; *Ryan's Daughter* 1970 **(AANBA)**; *Lady Caroline Lamb* 1972; *The Man Who Loved Cat Dancing* 1973; *The Sailor Who Fell From Grace With the Sea* 1975; *The Big Sleep* 1978; *Priest of Love* 1980; *Venom* 1981; *Loving Walter* 1983; *Ordeal By Innocence* 1985; *Steaming* 1985; *Hope and Glory* 1987; *White Mischief* 1987.

Miles, Sylvia • Actress • Born New York, NY, September 9, 1932. Educ. Actors Studio. Stage-trained actress who first gained attention with a brief appearance in *Midnight Cowboy* (1969). Miles often plays brassy, vulgar types, and gave notable performances in *Wall Street* (1987) and *Crossing Delancey* (1988). • *Murder, Inc.* 1960; *Parrish* 1961; *Pie in the Sky* 1963; *Violent Midnight* 1964; *Terror in the City* 1965; *Midnight Cowboy* 1969 **(AANBSA)**; *The Last Movie* 1971; *Who Killed Mary Whats'ername?* 1971; *Heat* 1972; *92 in the Shade* 1975; *Farewell, My Lovely* 1975 **(AANBSA)**; *The Great Scout & Cathouse Thursday* 1976; *The Sentinel* 1977; *Zero to Sixty* 1978; *The Funhouse* 1981; *Evil Under the Sun* 1982; *Critical Condition* 1987; *Sleeping Beauty* 1987; *Wall Street* 1987; *Crossing Delancey* 1988; *Spike of Bensonhurst* 1988; *She-Devil* 1989; *Superstar* 1990.

Milestone, Lewis • Director; also screenwriter. • Born Lewis Milstein, Chisinau, Ukraine, Russia, September 30, 1895; died 1980. *Educ.* University of Ghent, Belgium (engineering). Former assistant to cinematographer Lucien Andriot (with the US Army Signal Corps) who moved to Hollywood in 1919 and began working as an assistant cutter the following year. Milestone began directing in 1925 and assured himself a place in cinema history with *All Quiet on the Western Front* (1930), a landmark anti-war work, and *The Front Page* (1931), still considered a yardstick of films about journalism, and the topical depression musical *Hallelujah, I'm a Bum* (1933). Milestone was one of Hollywood's most technically accomplished early directors and had a reputation for meticulous pre-production planning and preparation; he continued directing until the 1960s (mostly, by then, in TV), though he too frequently squandered his talents on inferior vehicles. Later works of note include: *Of Mice and Men* (1939), notable for a rare "straight" performance by Lon Chaney, Jr.; *Our Russian Front* (1941), a documentary co-directed with Joris Ivens; and *A Walk in the Sun* (1945), another poignant study of war. Married to actress Kendall Lee Glaezner from 1935 until her death in 1978. • *Up and at 'Em* 1922 (story); *The Yankee Consul* 1924 (adapt); *Bobbed Hair* 1925 (sc); *Dangerous Innocence* 1925 (adapt); *Seven Sinners* 1925 (d,sc,story); *The Teaser* 1925 (adapt); *The Caveman* 1926 (d); *Fascinating Youth* 1926 (a); *The New Klondike* 1926 (d); *Two Arabian Knights* 1927 (d) **(AABD)**; *The Garden of Eden* 1928 (d); *The Racket* 1928 (d); *Betrayal* 1929 (d); *New York Nights* 1929 (d); *All Quiet on the Western Front* 1930 (d) **(AABD)**; *The Front Page* 1931 (d) **(AANBD)**; *Rain* 1932 (d,p); *Hallelujah, I'm a Bum* 1933 (d); *The Captain Hates the Sea* 1934 (d); *Paris in Spring* 1935 (d); *Anything Goes* 1936 (d); *The General Died at Dawn* 1936 (d); *The Night of Nights* 1939 (d); *Of Mice and Men* 1939 (d,p); *Lucky Partners* 1940 (d); *The Westerner* 1940 (d); *My Life With Caroline* 1941 (d,p); *Our Russian Front* 1941 (d,ed); *Edge of Darkness* 1943 (d); *The North Star* 1943 (d); *The Purple Heart* 1944 (d); *A Walk in the Sun* 1945 (d,p); *The Strange Love of Martha Ivers* 1946 (d); *Arch of Triumph* 1948 (d,sc); *No Minor Vices* 1948 (d,p); *The Red Pony* 1949 (d,p); *Halls of Montezuma* 1950 (d); *Kangaroo* 1952 (d); *Les Miserables* 1952 (d); *Melba* 1953 (d); *They Who Dare* 1954 (d); *La Vedova X* 1955 (d); *Pork Chop Hill* 1959 (d); *Ocean's Eleven* 1960 (d,p); *Mutiny on the Bounty* 1962 (d).

Milius, John • Director, screenwriter; also producer. • Born John Frederick Milius, St. Louis, MO, April 11, 1944. *Educ.* Los Angeles City College (English); University of Southern California (film). Began his career as an assistant to producer Lawrence Gordon at Roger Corman's American International Pictures. Milius has demonstrated a flair for writing and directing fast-paced, bloody action films such as *Dillinger* (1973) and *Conan the Barbarian* (1982). Married to actress Celia Kaye. • *Marcello, I'm So Bored (short)* 1967 (d); *The Devil's Eight* 1968 (sc); *Evel Knievel* 1971 (sc); *Jeremiah Johnson* 1972 (sc); *The Life and Times of Judge Roy Bean* 1972 (sc); *Dillinger* 1973 (d,sc); *Magnum Force* 1973 (sc,story); *The Wind and the Lion* 1975 (d,sc); *Big Wednesday* 1978 (d,sc); *1941* 1979 (exec.p,story); *Apocalypse Now* 1979 (sc) (**AANBSC**); *Hardcore* 1979 (exec.p); *Used Cars* 1980 (exec.p); *Conan the Barbarian* 1982 (d,sc); *Deadhead Miles* 1982 (a); *Lone Wolf McQuade* 1982 (tech.adviser); *Uncommon Valor* 1983 (p); *Red Dawn* 1984 (d,sc); *Extreme Prejudice* 1987 (story); *Fatal Beauty* 1987 (exec.p); *Farewell to the King* 1989 (d,sc); *Flight of the Intruder* 1991 (d,sc).

Milland, Ray • *aka* Reginald Mullane, Spike Milland, Raymond Milland • Actor • Born Reginald Alfred Truscott-Jones, Neath, Glamorganshire, Wales, January 3, 1905; died March 10, 1986, Torrance, CA. Former jockey turned romantic leading man of the 1930s, predominantly in light comedies and occasional mysteries. Milland proved his serious dramatic abilities with an Oscar-winning role as an alcoholic writer in Billy Wilder's *The Lost Weekend* (1945), but failed to match his success in later years due to choices of lifeless scripts. He concentrated on directing for TV and film in the 1960s and returned as a character actor in the 70s, notably in *Love Story* (1970). • *Ambassador Bill* 1931; *The Bachelor Father* 1931; *Blonde Crazy* 1931; *Bought* 1931; *Just a Gigolo* 1931; *Strangers May Kiss* 1931; *The Man Who Played God* 1932; *Payment Deferred* 1932; *Polly of the Circus* 1932; *Bolero* 1934; *Charlie Chan in London* 1934; *Many Happy Returns* 1934; *Menace* 1934; *We're Not Dressing* 1934; *Alias Mary Dow* 1935; *Four Hours to Kill* 1935; *The Gilded Lily* 1935; *The Glass Key* 1935; *One Hour Late* 1935; *The Big Broadcast of 1937* 1936; *The Jungle Princess* 1936; *Next Time We Love* 1936; *The Return of Sophie Lang* 1936; *Bulldog Drummond Escapes* 1937; *Easy Living* 1937; *Ebb Tide* 1937; *Three Smart Girls* 1937; *Wings Over Honolulu* 1937; *Wise Girl* 1937; *Her Jungle Love* 1938; *Men With Wings* 1938; *Say It in French* 1938; *Tropic Holiday* 1938; *Beau Geste* 1939; *Everything Happens at Night* 1939; *Hotel Imperial* 1939; *Arise, My Love* 1940; *The Doctor Takes a Wife* 1940; *Irene* 1940; *Untamed* 1940; *I Wanted Wings* 1941; *Skylark* 1941; *Are Husbands Necessary?* 1942; *The Lady Has Plans* 1942; *The Major and the Minor* 1942; *Reap the Wild Wind* 1942; *Star Spangled Rhythm* 1942; *The Crystal Ball* 1943; *Forever and a Day* 1943; *Lady in the Dark* 1944; *Ministry of Fear* 1944; *Till We Meet Again* 1944; *The Uninvited* 1944; *The Lost Weekend* 1945 (**AABA**); *Kitty* 1946; *The Well-Groomed Bride* 1946; *California* 1947; *Golden Earrings* 1947; *The Imperfect Lady* 1947; *The Trouble With Women* 1947; *Variety Girl* 1947; *Alias Nick Beal* 1948; *The Big Clock* 1948; *Sealed Verdict* 1948; *So Evil My Love* 1948; *It Happens Every Spring* 1949; *Copper Canyon* 1950; *A Life of Her Own* 1950; *A Woman of Distinction* 1950; *Circle of Danger* 1951; *Close to My Heart* 1951; *Night Into Morning* 1951; *Rhubarb* 1951; *Bugles in the Afternoon* 1952; *Something to Live For* 1952; *The Thief* 1952; *Jamaica Run* 1953; *Let's Do It Again* 1953; *Dial M For Murder* 1954; *The Girl in the Red Velvet Swing* 1955; *A Man Alone* 1955 (a,d); *Lisbon* 1956 (a,assoc.p,d); *Three Brave Men* 1956; *High Flight* 1957; *The River's Edge* 1957; *The Safecracker* 1957 (a,d); *Panic in Year Zero* 1962 (a,d); *The Premature Burial* 1962; *X* 1963; *Quick, Let's Get Married* 1964; *Hostile Witness* 1968 (a,d); *Company of Killers* 1970; *Love Story* 1970; *Embassy* 1971; *Frogs* 1972; *The Thing With Two Heads* 1972; *Terror in the Wax Museum* 1973; *Escape to Witch Mountain* 1974; *Gold* 1974; *The Swiss Conspiracy* 1975; *Aces High* 1976; *The Last Tycoon* 1976; *La Ragazza del Piagiame Gialle* 1977; *Slavers* 1977; *The Uncanny* 1977; *Battlestar Galactica* 1978; *Et la terreur commence* 1978; *Oliver's Story* 1978; *Spree* 1978; *Game For Vultures* 1979; *Survival Run* 1980; *The Sea Serpent* 1984; *Hitchcock, Il Brivido del Genio* 1985.

Miller, Arthur C. • Director of photography • Born Arthur Charles Miller, Roslyn, NY, July 8, 1895; died 1970. Former child actor, lab technician and camera assistant (for director Edwin S. Porter) who graduated to director of photography in 1918. Miller went on to become one of Hollywood's foremost cinematographers of the 1940s, working on a host of acclaimed 20th Century-Fox productions including John Ford's *How Green Was My Valley* (1941). His active career was cut short by tuberculosis in 1951. • *Stranded in Arcady* 1917; *Sylvia of the Secret Service* 1917; *The Hillcrest Mystery* 1918; *The Naulahka* 1918; *Paying the Piper* 1921; *Kick In* 1922; *Three Live Ghosts* 1922; *To Have and to Hold* 1922; *Bella Donna* 1923; *The Cheat* 1923; *The Eternal City* 1923; *In Hollywood With Potash and Perlmutter* 1924; *Tarnish* 1924; *His Supreme Moment* 1925; *A Thief in Paradise* 1925; *For Alimony Only* 1926; *Made For Love* 1926; *The Volga Boatman* 1926; *The Angel of Broadway* 1927; *The Fighting Eagle* 1927; *Nobody's Widow* 1927; *Vanity* 1927; *The Blue Danube* 1928; *Hold 'Em Yale* 1928; *The Spieler* 1928; *Big News* 1929; *The Flying Fool* 1929; *His First Command* 1929; *Sailor's Holiday* 1929; *Strange Cargo* 1929; *The Lady of Scandal* 1930; *Officer O'Brien* 1930; *See America Thirsty* 1930; *The Truth About Youth* 1930; *The Big Shot* 1931; *Father's Son* 1931; *Me and My Gal* 1932; *Okay America* 1932; *Panama Flo* 1932; *Young Bride* 1932; *Hold Me Tight* 1933; *The Last Trail* 1933; *The Mad Game* 1933; *The Man Who Dared* 1933; *My Weakness* 1933; *Sailor's Luck* 1933; *Bright Eyes* 1934; *Ever Since Eve* 1934; *Handy Andy* 1934; *The White Parade* 1934; *It's a Small World* 1935; *The Little Colonel* 1935; *Paddy O'Day* 1935; *Welcome Home* 1935; *Stowaway* 1936; *White Fang* 1936; *Heidi* 1937; *Wee Willie Winkie* 1937; *The Baroness and the Butler* 1938; *Rebecca of Sunnybrook Farm* 1938; *Submarine Patrol* 1938; *Here I Am a Stranger* 1939; *Susannah of the Mounties* 1939; *Brigham Young, Frontiersman* 1940; *Johnny Apollo* 1940; *On Their Own* 1940; *The Mark of Zorro* 1940; *How Green Was My Valley* 1941; *Man Hunt* 1941; *The Men in Her Life* 1941; *Tobacco Road* 1941; *This Above All* 1942; *Immortal Sergeant* 1943; *The Moon Is Down* 1943; *The Ox-Bow Incident* 1943; *The Song of Bernadette* 1943; *The Purple Heart* 1944; *The Keys of the Kingdom* 1945; *A Royal Scandal* 1945; *Anna and the King of Siam* 1946; *Dragonwyck* 1946; *The Razor's Edge* 1946; *Gentleman's Agreement* 1947; *A Letter to Three Wives* 1948; *The Walls of Jericho* 1948; *Whirlpool* 1949; *The Gunfighter* 1950; *The Prowler* 1951.

Miller, George • Director; also screenwriter. • Born Brisbane, Queensland, Australia, 1945. *Educ.* University of New South Wales Medical School; Melbourne University (film); UCLA (acting). Studied first medicine and then film, the latter under director Philip Noyce at Melbourne University. Miller practiced as a doctor while raising the money to finance his first feature, *Mad Max* (1979), a low-budget biker/exploitation movie set in an arid, post-industrial wasteland. Together with its first sequel, *The Road Warrior* (1981), the film earned cult and critical acclaim for Miller and partner Byron Kennedy, as well as launching Mel Gibson on the road to international stardom. (Producer and co-writer Kennedy died in a helicopter crash in 1983.) Miller has subsequently enjoyed success in Hollywood, notably with his stylish adaptation of John Updidke's novel, *The Witches of Eastwick* (1987). • *Mad Max* 1979 (d,sc,story); *The Road Warrior* 1981 (d,sc); *Twilight Zone—the Movie* 1983 (d); *Anzacs* 1985 (d); *Mad Max Beyond Thunderdome* 1985 (d,p,sc); *The*

Witches of Eastwick 1987 (d); *The Year My Voice Broke* 1987 (p); *Dead Calm* 1989 (2u d,p).

Miller, George • Director • Born George Trumbull Miller, Scotland, c. 1943. Former TV director best known for his theatrical debut, *The Man from Snowy River* (1982). • *In Search of Anna* 1978 (ad); *The Chain Reaction* 1980 (2ud,assoc.p); *The Man From Snowy River* 1982 (d); *The Aviator* 1985 (d); *Cool Change* 1985 (d); *Les Patterson Saves the World* 1987 (d); *Neverending Story II* 1990 (d).

Miller, Penelope Ann • Actress • Born Los Angeles, CA, January 13, 1964. *Educ.* Menlo College. Attractive, pixie-ish actress who made her Broadway debut as Daisy in Neil Simon's *Biloxi Blues*, a role she reprised in Mike Nichols' 1988 film adaptation. • *Adventures in Babysitting* 1987; *Big Top Pee-Wee* 1988; *Biloxi Blues* 1988; *Miles From Home* 1988; *Dead-Bang* 1989; *Awakenings* 1990; *Downtown* 1990; *The Freshman* 1990; *Kindergarten Cop* 1990.

Miller, Robert Ellis • Director • Born U.S.A., 1927. *Educ.* Harvard. TV director of the late 1950s and early 60s who made his feature directorial debut with the engaging romantic comedy, *Any Wednesday* (1966), starring Jane Fonda and Jason Robards. Miller went on to demonstrate a flair for literary adaptations with a well-received version of Carson McCullers's novel, *The Heart is a Lonely Hunter* (1968), and a canny reworking of Peter Devries' comedy, *Reuben, Reuben* (1983). • *Any Wednesday* 1966; *The Heart Is a Lonely Hunter* 1968; *Sweet November* 1968; *The Buttercup Chain* 1970; *The Girl From Petrovka* 1974; *The Baltimore Bullet* 1980; *Reuben, Reuben* 1983; *Hawks* 1988; *Brenda Starr* 1989.

Mills, Hayley • Actress • Born London, April 18, 1946. Wholesome child actress whose highly praised debut in *Tiger Bay* (1959) landed her a five-year contract with Walt Disney, where she played a succession of sweet, ingratiating innocents. Mills's nude appearance in *The Family Way* (1967), and her marrige to a man three decades her senior (director Roy Boulting) put her career on a decidely different and somewhat less successful path. Daughter of actor John Mills and sister of actress Juliet Mills. • *Tiger Bay* 1959; *Pollyanna* 1960 **(AAHON)**; *The Parent Trap* 1961; *Whistle Down the Wind* 1961; *In Search of the Castaways* 1962; *Summer Magic* 1963; *The Chalk Garden* 1964; *The Moon-Spinners* 1964; *That Darn Cat* 1965; *The Truth About Spring* 1965; *The Trouble With Angels* 1966; *Africa, Texas Style* 1967; *The Family Way* 1967; *Pretty Polly* 1967; *Twisted Nerve* 1968; *Take a Girl Like You* 1970; *Mr. Forbush and the Penguins* 1971; *Endless Night* 1972; *Appointment With Death* 1988.

Mills, Sir John • *aka* John Mills • Actor • Born Lewis Ernest Watts Mills, North Elmham, England, February 22, 1908. Diminutive, distinguished star of some of the finest mainstream British features of the 1930s, 40s and 50s. Mills's repeated casting as a stoic, often wartime hero (*In Which We Serve* 1942, *We Dive at Dawn* 1943, *Scott of the Antarctic* 1948) tended to obscure the range of his talent, although he appeared in more diverse character roles later in his career. (He won an Oscar for his performance as the village idiot in the 1970 film, *Ryan's Daughter*.) Married to actress Aileen Raymond and, from 1941, writer Mary Hayley Bell, in some of whose plays Mills has appeared. Father of actresses Hayley and Juliet Mills. • *The Ghost Camera* 1933; *Blind Justice* 1934; *Tudor Rose* 1936; *Four Dark Hours* 1937; *O.H.M.S.* 1937; *Goodbye, Mr. Chips* 1939; *In Which We Serve* 1942; *We Dive at Dawn* 1943; *This Happy Breed* 1944; *Great Expectations* 1946; *So Well Remembered* 1947; *Scott of the Antarctic* 1948; *The Rocking Horse Winner* 1949 (a,p); *Hobson's Choice* 1954; *The End of the Affair* 1955; *Around the World in 80 Days* 1956; *War and Peace* 1956; *Dunkirk* 1958; *Tiger Bay* 1959; *The Vicious Circle* 1959; *The Singer Not the Song* 1960; *Summer of the Seventeenth Doll* 1960; *Swiss Family Robinson* 1960; *Tiara Tahiti* 1962; *The Chalk Garden* 1964; *King Rat* 1965; *Operation Crossbow* 1965; *The Truth About Spring* 1965; *The Wrong Box* 1966; *Africa, Texas Style* 1967; *Chuka* 1967; *Les Amours de Lady Hamilton/Emma Hamilton* 1968; *La Morte non ha sesso* 1968; *Oh! What a Lovely War* 1969; *Philip* 1969; *Adam's Woman* 1970; *Ryan's Daughter* 1970 **(AABSA)**; *Dulcima* 1971; *Lady Caroline Lamb* 1972; *Young Winston* 1972; *Oklahoma Crude* 1973; *The Human Factor* 1975; *A Choice of Weapons* 1976; *Des Teufels Advokat/The Devil's Advocate* 1977; *The 39 Steps* 1978; *The Big Sleep* 1978; *The Quatermass Conclusion* 1979; *Zulu Dawn* 1979; *Gandhi* 1982; *Sahara* 1984; *Tribute to Her Majesty* 1986; *When the Wind Blows* 1986; *Who's That Girl* 1987; *Night of the Fox* 1990.

Milner, Victor • *aka* Victor Miller • Director of photography • Born New York, NY, December 15, 1893; died 1972. Newsreel cameraman from 1913 to 1918, when he arrived in Hollywood and began working as an assistant photographer. Milner went on to become one of Hollywood's foremost cinematographers of the 1930s through the 40s, mostly with Paramount. He enjoyed a fruitful multi-film association with directors Ernst Lubitsch, Henry King, Raoul Walsh and C.B. DeMille. • *Haunting Shadows* 1919 (ph); *The Cave Girl* 1921 (ph); *Live Wires* 1921 (ph); *Play Square* 1921 (ph); *Shadows of Conscience* 1921 (ph); *What Love Will Do* 1921 (ph); *When We Were Twenty-One* 1921 (ph); *A Dangerous Game* 1922 (ph); *Her Night of Nights* 1922 (ph); *Human Hearts* 1922 (ph); *The Kentucky Derby* 1922 (ph); *The Lavender Bath Lady* 1922 (ph); *Cause For Divorce* 1923 (ph); *Gossip* 1923 (ph); *The Love Letter* 1923 (ph); *The Town Scandal* 1923 (ph); *What Love Will Do* 1923 (ph); *Her Night of Romance* 1924 (ph); *On the Stroke of Three* 1924 (ph); *The Red Lily* 1924 (ph); *Thy Name Is Woman* 1924 (ph); *East of Suez* 1925 (ph); *Learning to Love* 1925 (ph); *The Spaniard* 1925 (ph); *The Cat's Pajamas* 1926 (ph); *Kid Boots* 1926 (ph); *The Lady of the Harem* 1926 (ph); *The Lucky Lady* 1926 (ph); *The Wanderer* 1926 (ph); *You Never Know Women* 1926 (ph); *Blonde or Brunette* 1927 (ph); *Children of Divorce* 1927 (ph); *Rolled Stockings* 1927 (ph); *The Spotlight* 1927 (ph); *The Way of All Flesh* 1927 (ph); *Half a Bride* 1928 (ph); *Loves of an Actress* 1928 (ph); *The Showdown* 1928 (ph); *Sins of the Fathers* 1928 (ph); *Three Sinners* 1928 (ph); *The Woman From Moscow* 1928 (ph); *Charming Sinners* 1929 (ph); *The Love Parade* 1929 (ph) **(AANBPH)**; *The Marriage Playground* 1929 (ph); *River of Romance* 1929 (ph); *The Studio Murder Mystery* 1929 (ph); *The Wild Party* 1929 (ph); *The Wolf of Wall Street* 1929 (ph); *Let's Go Native* 1930 (ph); *Monte Carlo* 1930 (ph); *Paramount on Parade* 1930 (ph); *The Texan* 1930 (ph); *True to the Navy* 1930 (ph); *Daughter of the Dragon* 1931 (ph); *I Take This Woman* 1931 (ph); *Kick In* 1931 (ph); *Ladies' Man* 1931 (ph); *Man of the World* 1931 (ph); *No Limit* 1931 (ph); *Broken Lullaby* 1932 (ph); *Love Me Tonight* 1932 (ph); *One Hour With You* 1932 (ph); *This Is the Night* 1932 (ph); *Trouble in Paradise* 1932 (ph); *Undercover Man* 1932 (ph); *Design For Living* 1933 (ph); *Luxury Liner* 1933 (ph); *One Sunday Afternoon* 1933 (ph); *Song of Songs* 1933 (ph); *All of Me* 1934 (ph); *Cleopatra* 1934 (ph) **(AABPH)**; *The Wharf Angel* 1934 (ph); *The Crusades* 1935 (ph) **(AANBPH)**; *The Gilded Lily* 1935 (ph); *So Red the Rose* 1935 (ph); *Desire* 1936 (ph); *The General Died at Dawn* 1936 (ph) **(AANBPH)**; *Give Us This Night* 1936 (ph); *Till We Meet Again* 1936 (ph); *Artists and Models* 1937 (ph); *Bulldog Drummond Escapes* 1937 (ph); *High, Wide, And Handsome* 1937 (ph); *The Plainsman* 1937 (ph); *The Buccaneer* 1938 (ph) **(AANBPH)**; *College Swing* 1938 (ph); *Give Me a Sailor* 1938 (ph); *Hunted Men* 1938 (ph); *Say It in French* 1938 (ph); *Touchdown Army* 1938 (ph); *The Great Victor Herbert* 1939 (ph); *Our Leading Citizen* 1939 (ph); *Union Pacific* 1939 (ph); *What a Life* 1939 (ph); *Christmas in July* 1940 (ph); *North West Mounted Police* 1940 (ph) **(AANBPH)**; *Those Were The Days* 1940 (ph); *The Lady Eve* 1941 (ph); *The Man Who Lost Himself* 1941 (ph); *The Monster and the Girl* 1941 (ph); *My Life With Caroline*

1941 (ph); *The Palm Beach Story* 1942 (ph); *Reap the Wild Wind* 1942 (ph) **(AANBPH)**; *Hostages* 1943 (ph); *The Great Moment* 1944 (ph); *The Princess and the Pirate* 1944 (ph); *The Story of Dr. Wassell* 1944 (ph); *The Wonder Man* 1945 (ph); *The Strange Love of Martha Ivers* 1946 (ph); *The Other Love* 1947 (ph); *Unfaithfully Yours* 1948 (ph); *You Were Meant For Me* 1948 (ph); *Dark City* 1950 (ph); *The Furies* 1950 (ph) **(AANBPH)**; *My Favorite Spy* 1951 (ph); *September Affair* 1951 (ph); *Carrie* 1952 (ph); *Jeopardy* 1953 (ph).

Mineo, Sal • Actor • Born Salvatore Mineo, Bronx, NY, January 10, 1939; died 1976, California. Broadway child actor (*The Rose Tattoo*) turned swarthy juvenile character and lead player of the 1950s, often as troubled, violence-prone youths. Mineo earned the first of two Oscar nominations for his role as James Dean's sidekick in *Rebel Without a Cause* (1955). Mineo was murdered in West Hollywood after returning home from a play rehearsal (*P.S. Your Cat is Dead*) by an assailant whose motive was robbery. • *Six Bridges to Cross* 1954; *The Private War of Major Benson* 1955; *Rebel Without a Cause* 1955 **(AANBSA)**; *Crime in the Streets* 1956; *Giant* 1956; *Rock, Pretty Baby* 1956; *Somebody Up There Likes Me* 1956; *Dino* 1957; *The Young Don't Cry* 1957; *Tonka* 1958; *The Gene Krupa Story* 1959; *A Private's Affair* 1959; *Exodus* 1960 **(AANBSA)**; *Escape From Zahrain* 1962; *The Longest Day* 1962; *Cheyenne Autumn* 1964; *The Greatest Story Ever Told* 1965; *Who Killed Teddy Bear?* 1965; *Eighty Steps to Jonah* 1969; *Krakatoa, East of Java* 1969; *Escape From the Planet of the Apes* 1971.

Minnelli, Liza • Actress; also singer. • Born Liza May Minnelli, Los Angeles, CA, March 12, 1946. *Educ.* Sorbonne, Paris; Herbert Berghof Studio. Vivacious, multi-talented performer who made her screen debut at the age of two-and-a-half in *In the Good Old Summertime* (1949), starring her mother Judy Garland. Minnelli established herself as a charismatic, energetic singer, dancer and actress on the Broadway stage in the 1960s and won widespread acclaim for her role in the 1969 film, *The Sterile Cuckoo*. Although she emerged as a leading star in her own right with a sensational performace as Nazi-era chanteuse Sally Bowles in Bob Fosse's landmark *Cabaret* (1972), her career as a whole has been erratic and hampered by a lack of suitable vehicles. She had a popular hit with the 1981 Dudley Moore comedy, *Arthur*, and enjoyed enormous success as a concert performer throughout the 1970s and 80s. She is the daughter of director Vincente Minnelli and has been married to singer Peter Allen, film executive Jack Haley, Jr., and, from 1979, sculptor Mark Gero. • *In the Good Old Summertime* 1949; *Charlie Bubbles* 1967; *The Sterile Cuckoo* 1969 **(AANBA)**; *Tell Me That You Love Me, Junie Moon* 1970; *Cabaret* 1972 **(AABA)**; *That's Entertainment!* 1974; *Lucky Lady* 1975; *A Matter of Time* 1976; *New York, New York* 1977; *Arthur* 1981; *The Muppets Take Manhattan* 1984; *That's Dancing!* 1985; *Arthur 2 on the Rocks* 1988; *Rent-A-Cop* 1988; *Stepping Out* 1991.

Minnelli, Vincente • Director; also actor, producer. • Born Chicago, IL, February 28, 1910; died July 25, 1986, Beverly Hills, CA. Vincente Minnelli directed some of the most celebrated entertainments in cinema history, including *Meet Me in St. Louis* (1944), *Father of the Bride* (1950), *An American in Paris* (1951), *The Bad and the Beautiful* (1952), *The Band Wagon* (1953), *Lust for Life* (1956) and *Gigi* (1958). Nevertheless, serious commentary on his work has, until recently, been sparse, partly because of the "glossy" nature of his films. Minnelli's first jobs in show business were as costume and set designer; the sophistication he would bring to the American stage and film musical was always redolent of *Vogue* or *Vanity Fair*, and it is no accident that he once directed a charming comedy entitled *Designing Woman* (1957). Even one of his dramatic films, *The Cobweb* (1955), involves neurotic tensions that begin to break out in a psychiatric clinic when new drapes are selected for the common room.

Minnelli was born into a theatrical family; his parents and his uncle operated a tent show that toured the Midwest. As a young man he became a costume and set designer for the Balaban and Katz theater chain in Chicago and in 1931 he moved to New York, where he worked for Radio City Music Hall, eventually graduating in 1935 to directing Broadway musicals. After a brief, abortive stay as a producer at Paramount in the late thirties, he was brought permanently to Hollywood in 1940 by producer Arthur Freed, who was assembling his own unit at MGM. Under Freed's sponsorship, he directed his first film, the underrated all-black musical *Cabin in the Sky* (1943). Minnelli remained at MGM for two decades, specializing in musicals, domestic comedies, and melodramas.

Minnelli kept files on different styles of painting, and he liked to run through them for inspiration. He particularly admired the surrealists and was among the first Hollywood directors to appropriate their motifs. He was not, however, a painterly filmmaker. He loved flamboyant color, costume, and decor, but he never allowed those elements to freeze into static compositions. A master of changing patterns and complex movements, he filled his pictures with swooping crane shots, swirling patterns of fabric and light, with a skillful orchestration of background detail. A sensitive director of actors, he elicited some of the best performances from such diverse players as Judy Garland (his wife from 1945-51 and mother of his daughter, Liza Minnelli), Spencer Tracy and Kirk Douglas.

The imagination or one of its surrogates, such as show business or dreaming, was Minnelli's favorite subject. His central female characters live in fantasy worlds, finding happiness only when they exchange dreams for artifice; his leading men usually play writers, painters, or performers, and if they are not artistic types by profession they tend to be dandies or sensitive youths. By the same token, his films generally take place in studio-manufactured settings, where the boundaries between fantasy and everyday life are blurred. Even when his films are set in small-town America, they tend to burst into remarkable dream-like passages, such as the Halloween sequence in *Meet Me in St. Louis*, the berserk carnival in *Some Came Running* (1958) and the mythic boar hunt in *Home From the Hill* (1960). The ultimate tribute to Minnelli is that few directors in the history of Hollywood have made so many consistently enjoyable, diverse films. JN • *Cabin in the Sky* 1943 (d); *I Dood It* 1943 (d); *Meet Me in St. Louis* 1944 (d); *The Clock* 1945 (d); *Yolanda and the Thief* 1945 (d); *Undercurrent* 1946 (d); *Ziegfeld Follies* 1946 (d); *The Pirate* 1948 (d); *Madame Bovary* 1949 (d); *Father of the Bride* 1950 (d); *An American in Paris* 1951 (d) **(AANBD)**; *Father's Little Dividend* 1951 (d); *The Bad and the Beautiful* 1952 (d); *The Band Wagon* 1953 (d); *The Story of Three Loves* 1953 (d); *Brigadoon* 1954 (d); *The Long, Long Trailer* 1954 (d); *The Cobweb* 1955 (d); *Kismet* 1955 (d); *Lust For Life* 1956 (d); *Tea and Sympathy* 1956 (d); *Designing Woman* 1957 (d); *Gigi* 1958 (d) **(AABD)**; *The Reluctant Debutante* 1958 (d); *Some Came Running* 1958 (d); *Bells Are Ringing* 1960 (d); *Home From the Hill* 1960 (d); *The Four Horsemen of the Apocalypse* 1962 (d); *Two Weeks in Another Town* 1962 (d); *The Courtship of Eddie's Father* 1963 (d); *Goodbye, Charlie* 1964 (d); *The Sandpiper* 1965 (d); *On a Clear Day You Can See Forever* 1970 (d); *A Matter of Time* 1976 (d).

Miou-Miou • Actress • Born Sylvette Hery, Paris, February 22, 1950. Former leading light of the Paris café-theater scene who has brought poise and intelligence to several screen roles of the 1970s and 80s. Miou-Miou has proven adept at both drama and comedy and has worked with a distinguished roster of international directors including Bertrand Blier, Marco Bellochio, Alain Tanner, Joseph Losey and Diane Kurys. • *La Cavale* 1971; *Elle Court, Elle Court la Banlieue* 1972; *Quelques messieurs trop tranquilles* 1972; *Themroc* 1972; *Les Aventures de Rabbi Jacob* 1973; *Les Granges Brulées* 1973; *La Grande Trouille* 1974; *Lily Aime-Moi* 1974; *Les*

Valseuses/Going Places 1974; *D'amour et d'eau fraiche* 1975; *Un Genio, Due Compari, Un Pollo* 1975; *La Marche Triomphale* 1975; *Pas de Problème!* 1975; *F comme Fairbanks* 1976; *Jonas qui aura 25 ans en l'an 2000/Jonah Who Will Be 25 in the Year 2000* 1976; *On aura tout vu* 1976; *Dites-lui que je l'aime* 1977; *Les Routes du Sud* 1978; *Au revoir, à lundi/Bye—See You Monday* 1979; *La Dérobade* 1979; *Le Grand embouteillage* 1979; *Est-ce bien raisonnable?* 1980; *La Femme Flic* 1980; *La Gueule du Loup* 1981; *Josepha* 1981; *Guy De Maupassant* 1982; *Attention! Une femme peut en cacher une autre* 1983; *Entre Nous* 1983; *Canicule/Dog Day* 1984; *Le Vol du Sphinx/The Flight of the Phoenix* 1984; *Blanche et Marie* 1985; *Ménage/Evening Dress* 1986; *La Lectrice/The Reader* 1988; *Les Portes tournantes/Revolving Doors* 1988; *Milou en mai/May Fools* 1990.

Miranda, Carmen • Singer, dancer, actress • Born Maria do Carmo Miranda Da Cunha, Marco de Canavezes, Portugal, February 9, 1909; died 1955. Vibrant star of the Brazilian stage and screen whose colorful performance in the Broadway musical *Streets of Paris* (1939) helped land her a film contract with Fox. "The Brazilian Bombshell," as she was called, enlivened a number of Hollywood musicals from the early 1940s, often appearing in outlandish outfits and her trademark fruit-laden headgear. • *Down Argentine Way* 1940 (a); *That Night in Rio* 1941 (a); *Week-End in Havana* 1941 (a); *Springtime in the Rockies* 1942 (a); *Four Jills in a Jeep* 1943 (a); *The Gang's All Here* 1943 (a); *Greenwich Village* 1944 (a); *Something For the Boys* 1944 (a); *Doll Face* 1945 (a); *If I'm Lucky* 1946 (a); *Copacabana* 1947 (a); *A Date With Judy* 1948 (a); *Nancy Goes to Rio* 1950 (a); *Scared Stiff* 1953 (a); *Os Herdeiros* 1969 (a).

Mirisch, Walter • Producer; also executive. • Born New York, NY, November 8, 1921. *Educ.* CCNY; University of Wisconsin; Harvard Graduate School of Business. Produced low-budget features for Monogram and served as executive producer with its subsidiary, Allied Artists, before forming an independent production company with brother Marvin (born 1918) and half-brother Harold (born 1907) in 1957. The Mirisch Company, Inc., soon emerged as the preeminent independent production outfit of the period following the decline of the major Hollywood studios. Key directors associated with the company included Billy Wilder, John Huston, Blake Edwards and Norman Jewison; notable films included *Some Like it Hot* (1959), *The Magnificent Seven* (1960) and *In the Heat of the Night* (1967). • *Fall Guy* 1947 (p); *I Wouldn't Be in Your Shoes* 1948 (p); *Bomba on Panther Island* 1949 (p); *Bomba, The Jungle Boy* 1949 (p); *Bomba and the Hidden City* 1950 (p); *County Fair* 1950 (p); *The Lost Volcano* 1950 (p); *Cavalry Scout* 1951 (p); *Elephant Stampede* 1951 (p); *Flight to Mars* 1951 (p); *The Lion Hunters* 1951 (p); *Rodeo* 1951 (p); *African Treasure* 1952 (p); *Flat Top* 1952 (p); *Fort Osage* 1952 (p); *Hiawatha* 1952 (p); *Jungle Girl* 1952 (p); *Wild Stallion* 1952 (p); *An Annapolis Story* 1955 (p); *The Warriors* 1955 (p); *Wichita* 1955 (p); *The First Texan* 1956 (p); *The Oklahoman* 1957 (p); *The Tall Stranger* 1957 (p); *Fort Massacre* 1958 (p); *Man of the West* 1958 (p); *Some Like it Hot* 1959 (p); *Cast a Long Shadow* 1959 (p); *The Gunfight at Dodge City* 1959 (p); *The Man in the Net* 1959 (p); *The Magnificent Seven* 1960 (p); *By Love Possessed* 1961 (p); *Two For the Seesaw* 1962 (p); *Toys in the Attic* 1963 (p); *Hawaii* 1966 (p); *Fitzwilly* 1967 (p); *In the Heat of the Night* 1967 (p) **(AABP)**; *Sinful Davey* 1969 (exec.p); *Some Kind of a Nut* 1969 (p); *The Hawaiians* 1970 (p); *The Organization* 1971 (p); *Scorpio* 1973 (p); *Mr. Majestyk* 1974 (p); *The Spikes Gang* 1974 (p); *Battle of Midway* 1976 (p); *Gray Lady Down* 1977 (p); *Same Time, Next Year* 1978 (p); *Dracula* 1979 (p); *The Prisoner of Zenda* 1979 (p); *Romantic Comedy* 1983 (p).

Mirren, Helen • Actress • Born London, 1946. *Educ.* National Youth Theatre; International Centre for Theatre Research, Paris. Leading English stage and screen actress who has worked with acclaimed theater director Peter Brook and made her film debut as Hermia in Peter Hall's screen adaptation of *A Midsummer Night's Dream* (1968). Mirren has brought intelligence and intensity to her roles in films such as Pat O'Connor's *Cal* (1984) and Peter Greenaway's *The Cook, the Thief, his Wife and her Lover* (1989). • *A Midsummer Night's Dream* 1968; *Age of Consent* 1969; *Savage Messiah* 1972; *O Lucky Man!* 1973; *Hamlet* 1976; *Caligula* 1979; *Hussy* 1979; *The Fiendish Plot of Dr. Fu Manchu* 1980; *The Long Good Friday* 1980; *Excalibur* 1981; *2010* 1984; *Cal* 1984; *White Nights* 1985; *Heavenly Pursuits* 1986; *The Mosquito Coast* 1986; *Invocation Maya Deren* 1987; *Pascali's Island* 1988; *People of the Forest* 1988; *The Cook, the Thief, his Wife and her Lover* 1989; *When the Whales Came* 1989; *Bethune: The Making of a Hero* 1990; *The Comfort of Strangers* 1990; *Where Angels Fear to Tread* 1991.

Mitchum, Robert • Actor • Born Robert Charles Durman Mitchum, Bridgeport, CT, August 6, 1917. Heavy-lidded, broad-chested performer who began his film career in 1942 and played a string of heavies in western features before coming to prominence with his role as Lt. Walker in *The Story of G.I. Joe* (1945).

Mitchum's relaxed style and ability to combine insolence with charm has produced some memorable performances, notably in *Pursued, Out of the Past* (both 1947) and, as Philip Marlowe, in *Farewell My Lovely* (1975). He was also outstanding in two psychologically complex roles where he came to seem the personification of evil: as a brutal ex-con who seeks to destroy the lawyer responsible for his conviction, in *Cape Fear* (1962); and as a murderous itinerant preacher who preys upon two defenseless children, in *Night of the Hunter* (1955).

One of the most durable of Hollywood leading men, Mitchum has continued to appear in films and on TV through the 1980s. His sons Christopher and James, and grandson Bentley, have also acted. • *Bar 20* 1943; *Beyond the Last Frontier* 1943; *The Dancing Masters* 1943; *Doughboys in Ireland* 1943; *False Colors* 1943; *Follow the Band* 1943; *Gung Ho!* 1943; *Hoppy Serves a Writ* 1943; *Riders of the Deadline* 1943; *Girl Rush* 1944; *Johnny Doesn't Live Here Anymore* 1944; *Nevada* 1944; *Thirty Seconds Over Tokyo* 1944; *When Strangers Marry* 1944; *The Story of G.I. Joe* 1945 **(AANBSA)**; *West of the Pecos* 1945; *The Locket* 1946; *Till the End of Time* 1946; *Undercurrent* 1946; *Crossfire* 1947; *Desire Me* 1947; *Out of the Past* 1947; *Pursued* 1947; *Blood on the Moon* 1948; *Rachel and the Stranger* 1948; *The Big Steal* 1949; *Holiday Affair* 1949; *The Red Pony* 1949; *Where Danger Lives* 1950; *His Kind of Woman* 1951; *My Forbidden Past* 1951; *The Racket* 1951; *Angel Face* 1952; *The Lusty Men* 1952; *Macao* 1952; *One Minute to Zero* 1952; *Second Chance* 1953; *She Couldn't Say No* 1953; *White Witch Doctor* 1953; *River of No Return* 1954; *Track of the Cat* 1954; *Man Without a Gun* 1955; *The Night of the Hunter* 1955; *Not As a Stranger* 1955; *Bandido* 1956; *Foreign Intrigue* 1956; *The Enemy Below* 1957; *Fire Down Below* 1957; *Heaven Knows, Mr. Allison* 1957; *The Hunters* 1958; *Thunder Road* 1958 (a,exec.p,story,m); *The Angry Hills* 1959; *The Wonderful Country* 1959 (a,exec.p); *The Grass Is Greener* 1960; *Home From the Hill* 1960; *The Sundowners* 1960; *A Terrible Beauty* 1960; *The Last Time I Saw Archie* 1961; *Cape Fear* 1962; *The Longest Day* 1962; *Two For the Seesaw* 1962; *The List of Adrian Messenger* 1963; *Rampage* 1963; *What a Way to Go!* 1964; *Mister Moses* 1965; *El Dorado* 1967; *The Way West* 1967; *5 Card Stud* 1968; *Anzio* 1968; *Secret Ceremony* 1968; *Villa Rides* 1968; *The Good Guys and the Bad Guys* 1969; *Young Billy Young* 1969; *Going Home* 1971; *The Wrath of God* 1972; *The Friends of Eddie Coyle* 1973; *Farewell, My Lovely* 1975; *The Yakuza* 1975; *Battle of Midway* 1976; *The Last Tycoon* 1976; *The Amsterdam Kill* 1977; *The Big Sleep* 1978; *Matilda* 1978; *Steiner—Das Eiserne Kreuz 2, Teil* 1979; *Agency* 1980; *Nightkill* 1980; *That Championship Season* 1982; *The Ambassador* 1984; *Maria's*

Lovers 1985; *John Huston* 1988; *Mr. North* 1988; *Scrooged* 1988; *Presume Dangereux* 1990.

Mitry, Jean • Theoretician; also filmmaker, critic, historian, actor. • Born Jean-René-Pierre Goetgheluck Le Rouge Rillard des Acres De Presfontaines, Soissons, France, November 7, 1907; died January 18, 1988, outside Paris. Began his career as an assistant to, and screenwriter for, both Marcel L'Herbier and Abel Gance during the early 1920s. Mitry spent the next decade writing on film and, in 1929, co-directed *Paris Cinéma*, the first of a series of experimental shorts. With Henri Langlois and Georges Franju he founded the Cinémathèque Française in 1936. Following the dismal failure of his first and only fictional feature, *Enigme aux Folies-Bergère* (1959), Mitry procceeded to produce an impressive body of theoretical and historical writing, culminating in one of the landmark works in film scholarship, the two-volume *Esthétique et Psychologie du Cinéma* (1963).

Mix, Tom • Actor; also director, producer. • Born Thomas Hezikiah Mix, Mix Run, PA, January 6, 1880; died 1940. Rodeo performer who became one of the leading cowboy stars of the silent era, directing, producing and appearing in over 100 two-reelers for Selig Polyscope in the teens. Mix signed on with Fox in 1917 and gained wide popularity for his action-packed, stunt-filled features. He later toured with the Ringling Bros. Circus but returned to the screen in 1932 to make a string of sound westerns for Universal. • *Ace High* 1918; *Cupid's Round-Up* 1918; *Fame and Fortune* 1918; *Mr. Logan, U.S.A.* 1918; *Six Shooter Andy* 1918; *Western Blood* 1918 (a,story); *The Coming of the Law* 1919; *The Feud* 1919; *Fighting For Gold* 1919; *Hell Roarin' Reform* 1919; *Rough Riding Romance* 1919; *The Speed Maniac* 1919; *Treat 'Em Rough* 1919; *Wilderness Trail* 1919; *The Cyclone* 1920; *The Daredevil* 1920 (a,d,sc,story); *Desert Love* 1920 (a,story); *Prairie Trails* 1920; *The Terror* 1920 (a,story); *The Texan* 1920; *Three Gold Coins* 1920; *The Untamed* 1920; *After Your Own Heart* 1921 (a,adapt); *Big Town Round-Up* 1921; *Hands Off* 1921; *The Night Horsemen* 1921; *A Ridin' Romeo* 1921 (a,story); *The Road Demon* 1921; *The Rough Diamond* 1921 (a,story); *Trailin'* 1921; *Arabia* 1922 (a,story); *Catch My Smoke* 1922; *Chasing the Moon* 1922 (a,story); *Do and Dare* 1922; *The Fighting Streak* 1922; *For Big Stakes* 1922; *Just Tony* 1922; *Sky High* 1922; *Up and Going* 1922 (a,story); *Eyes of the Forest* 1923; *The Lone Star Ranger* 1923; *Mile-a-Minute Romeo* 1923; *North of Hudson Bay* 1923; *Romance Land* 1923; *Soft Boiled* 1923; *Stepping Fast* 1923; *Three Jumps Ahead* 1923; *The Deadwood Coach* 1924; *The Heart Buster* 1924; *Ladies to Board* 1924; *The Last of the Duanes* 1924; *Oh, You Tony!* 1924; *Teeth* 1924; *The Trouble Shooter* 1924; *The Best Bad Man* 1925; *A Child of the Prairie* 1925 (a,d,sc); *Dick Turpin* 1925; *The Everlasting Whisper* 1925; *The Lucky Horseshoe* 1925; *The Rainbow Trail* 1925; *Riders of the Purple Sage* 1925; *The Canyon of Light* 1926; *The Great K & A Train Robbery* 1926; *Hard Boiled* 1926; *My Own Pal* 1926; *No Man's Gold* 1926; *Tony Runs Wild* 1926; *The Yankee Senor* 1926; *The Broncho Twister* 1927; *The Circus Ace* 1927; *The Last Trail* 1927; *Outlaws of Red River* 1927; *Silver Valley* 1927; *Tumbling River* 1927; *The Arizona Wildcat* 1928; *Daredevil's Reward* 1928; *Hello Cheyenne* 1928; *A Horseman of the Plains* 1928; *King Cowboy* 1928; *Painted Post* 1928; *Son of the Golden West* 1928; *The Big Diamond Robbery* 1929; *The Drifter* 1929; *Outlawed* 1929; *The Cohens and Kellys in Hollywood* 1932; *Destry Rides Again* 1932; *Flaming Guns* 1932; *The Fourth Horseman* 1932; *Hidden Gold* 1932; *My Pal, the King* 1932; *The Rider of Death Valley* 1932; *The Texas Bad Man* 1932; *Rustlers' Round-Up* 1933; *Terror Trail* 1933; *The Miracle Rider* 1935; *It's Showtime* 1976.

Miyagawa, Kazuo • Director of photography • Born Kyoto, Japan, February 25, 1908. Premier Japanese cinematographer who was once known as "the comic cameraman" for his work on early slapstick features. Miyagawa first distinguished himself with his work for director Hiroshi Inagaki, for whom he developed sophisticated tracking and crane techniques that were influenced by traditional Japanese painting. He is best known in the West for his work on Kurosawa's *Rashomon* (1950) and has also photographed films for Ozu (*Floating Weeds* 1959), Mizoguchi (*Ugetsu* 1953) and Ichikawa (*Conflagration* 1958). Awarded the Imperial Order of Culture in 1978. • *Rashomon* 1950; *Ugetsu* 1953; *Conflagration* 1958; *Floating Weeds* 1959; *Yojimbo* 1961; *The Sin* 1962; *Money Talks* 1964; *Tokyo Olympiad* 1965; *MacArthur's Children* 1985; *Die Tänzerin* 1990.

Mizoguchi, Kenji • Director; also actor, assistant director. • Born Tokyo, Japan, May 16, 1898; died 1956. *Educ.* Aohashi Western Painting Research Institute, Tokyo. Mizoguchi Kenji's life spanned the most important years of the development of the Japanese cinema. Although he made over 85 films in a career that spanned more than 30 years, over 50 of them have been lost, primarily through studio fires, the ravages of war or poor preservation methods. Those that remain include leftist-inspired "tendency films," literary adaptations, historical dramas, proto-feminist critiques, Meiji-period pieces and—from the later stage of his career—works of a more transcendental and symphonic nature.

Although there are no obvious connecting threads in Mizoguchi's varied oeuvre, one common theme is a sympathy for the exploited and marginalized members of society, whether they be women, traveling artists, feudal servants or slaves. While often turning the camera away from moments of extreme violence, Mizoguchi rarely turned away from difficult social themes. His films have been praised for the way in which they harmonize seeming opposites—light and shadow, harshness and beauty, societal pulls and individual needs.

Mizoguchi grew up in the rougher *shitamachi* (downtown) area of Tokyo, but subsequently moved to the more genteel city of Kyoto following the 1923 Kanto earthquake. The unusual degree of empathy he felt toward women was undoubtedly influenced by his having seen both his older sister, Suzu, and his mother suffer from his father's callous treatment of them. Mizoguchi's father undoubtedly influenced the director's portrayal of the male characters in his films, who tend to be self-serving and manipulative. Similarly, his depiction of women, which had been cool and objective in early films like *Sisters of the Gion* (1936) and *Osaka Elegy* (1936), became much less so following the onset of his wife's madness due to syphilis in 1941.

Mizoguchi's training as a painter is apparent in the exquisite pictorial quality of his films, especially in his subtle treatment of light and in his asymmetrical composition (common to the Japanese visual arts in general). Stylistically, he is best known for his elegant use of the long take ("one scene, one shot") which was inspired by his love for the theater, by his respect for the integrity of an actor's performance and by the Japanese horizontal picture scroll (*emakimono*) in which the eye gazes at each section in turn, but then moves on in an irreversible forward progression. This technique causes the viewer to vacillate between a sense of involvement in the characters on the screen, and a sense of distance which invites objective contemplation.

As a director, Mizoguchi was known as a perfectionist; the demands he made on his staff and cast are legendary. This perfectionism was tied in with his desire to immerse his actors in as perfect a setting as possible, in order to help them forget their daily existence and thus draw out of them their best performances. He attracted a loyal group of collaborators, including screenwriter Yoshikata Yoda, cameraman Kazuo Miyagawa, art director Hiroshi Mizutani, music director Fumio Hayasaka and actress Kinuyo Tanaka.

Mizoguchi earned international renown when his films *The Life of Oharu* (1952), *Ugetsu* (1953) and *Sansho the Bailiff* (1954) won top prizes at the Venice Film Festivals of those respective years. He died a few years later, in 1956, with the script for his next work, *Osaka*

Story, at his bedside. The film was subsequently realized by director Kozaburo Yoshimura. LCE • *The Resurrection of Love* 1923 (d); *Among the Ruins* 1923 (d); *Blood and Soul* 1923 (d); *Dreams of Youth* 1924 (d); *Foggy Harbor* 1923 (d); *Native Country* 1923 (d); *The Night* 1923 (d); *Chronicle of the May Rain* 1924 (d); *Death at Dawn* 1924 (d); *Woman of Pleasure* 1924 (d); *Women Are Strong* 1924 (d); *The Man* 1925 (d); *The Smiling Earth* 1925 (d); *Children of the Sea* 1926 (d); *The Passion of a Woman Teacher* 1926 (d); *The Life of a Man* (trilogy) 1928 (d); *Metropolitan Symphony* 1929 (d); *Tokyo March* 1929 (d); *Hometown* 1930 (d); *And Yet They Go On* 1931 (d); *The Man of the Moment* 1932 (d); *The White Threads of the Waterfall* 1933 (d); *Gion Festival* 1933 (d); *The Passing of Love and Hate* 1934 (d); *The Poppies* 1935 (d); *The Virgin From Oyuki* 1935 (d); *Osaka Elegy* 1936 (d); *Sisters of the Gion* 1936 (d); *The Story of the Last Chrysanthemums* 1939 (d); *A Woman of Osaka* 1940 (d); *The Life of an Artist* 1941 (d); *The Loyal Forty-Seven Ronin* 1941-42 (d); *Musashi Miyamoto* 1944 (d); *Utamaro o meguru go-nin no onna/Utamaro and His Five Women* 1946 (d); *Women's Victory* 1946 (d); *The Love of Actress Sumako* 1947 (d); *Women of the Night* 1948 (d); *Waga Koi Wa Moenu/Flame of My Love* 1949 (d); *The Picture of Madame Yuki* 1950 (d); *Woman of Musashino* 1951 (d); *The Life of Oharu* 1952 (d); *A Geisha* 1953 (d); *Ugetsu Monogatari/Ugetsu* 1953 (d); *Gion Festival Music* 1953 (d); *Chikamatzu Monogatari/A Story From Chikamatzu* 1954 (d); *Sansho dayu/Sansho the Bailiff* 1954 (d); *The Woman in the Rumor* 1954 (d); *The Empress Yang Kwei-Fei* 1955 (d); *Shin Heike Monogatari* 1955 (d); *Tales of the Taira Clan* 1955 (d); *Yokihi* 1955 (d); *Akasen Chitai/Street of Shame* 1956 (d).

Mocky, Jean-Pierre • Director; also actor, producer, screenwriter. • Born Jean Mokiejewski, Nice, France, July 6, 1929. *Educ.* Strasbourg University (law). Theater and film star from the 1940s who is probably best known for his performance in Jean Cocteau's *Orpheus* (1950). Mocky began his directorial career with the 1959 release, *The Chasers*, and has subsequently turned out some twenty loosely constructed features noted for their broad black humor and cynicism. Although he is in some sense a kindred spirit to the directors of the New Wave, he is rarely associated with that movement by critics or public. Few of his films have reached international audiences. • *I Vinti* 1952 (a); *Les Dragueurs/The Chasers* 1959 (d); *Snobs!* 1961 (d); *Un Drôle de paroissien/Thank Heaven for Small Favors* 1963 (d); *Les Vierges* 1963 (d); *La Bourse et la vie* 1966 (d); *Les Compagnons de la marguerite* 1966 (d); *La Grande Lessive (!)* 1968 (d); *L'Etalon* 1970 (d,sc); *Solo* 1970 (a,d,sc); *L'Albatros* 1971 (a,d,sc); *Chut!* 1972 (d,sc); *L'Ombre d'une chance* 1973 (a,d,sc); *Un Linceul n'a pas de poches* 1974 (a,d,sc); *L'Ibis Rouge* 1975 (d,sc); *Le Roi des bricoleurs* 1977 (d,sc); *Le Temoin* 1978 (d,sc.adapt); *Le Piège à cons* 1979 (a,d,sc,ed); *Y'a-t-il un Français dans la salle?* 1982 (d); *A Mort l'Arbitre* 1983 (a,d,sc,ed); *La Machine à découdre* 1985 (a,d,p,sc); *Le Pactole* 1985 (d,sc); *Grandeur et décadence d'un petit commerce de cinéma* 1986 (a); *Le Miracule* 1986 (d,sc,ed); *Agent Trouble* 1987 (a,d,sc,ed); *Les Saisons du plaisir* 1987 (d,sc,ed); *Une Nuit à l'assemblée nationale* 1988 (d,sc,ed); *Divine enfant* 1989 (a,d,sc,adapt,dial,ed); *Il gêle en enfer* 1990 (a,d,p,sc).

Modine, Matthew • Actor • Born Loma Linda, CA, March 22, 1959. Engaging, fresh-faced actor who made his screen debut in John Sayles' *Baby, It's You* (1983) but first won acclaim for his starring performance as a severely withdrawn, schizophrenic Vietnam veteran in Alan Parker's *Birdy* (1984). Modine was at his self-effacing, ironic best in Stanley Kubrick's *Full Metal Jacket* (1987) and Jonathan Demme's *Married to the Mob* (1988). He earned a Venice Film Festival best actor award for *Streamers* (1983). • *Baby, It's You* 1983; *Private School* 1983; *Streamers* 1983; *Birdy* 1984; *The Hotel New Hampshire* 1984; *Mrs. Soffel* 1984; *Vision Quest* 1985; *Full Metal Jacket* 1987; *Orphans* 1987; *Married to the Mob* 1988; *La Partita* 1988; *Gross Anatomy* 1989; *Memphis Belle* 1990; *Pacific Heights* 1990.

Mohr, Hal • Director of photography; also director. • Born San Francisco, CA, August 2, 1894; died 1974. Innovative cinematographer best known for the sopisticated crane shots in *Broadway* (1929) and as one of the first cameramen to regularly and fluently use dolly and boom shots. Mohr demonstrated his technical proficiency on a number of highly regarded films, but from the mid-1950s did the bulk of his work in TV. He was married to actress Evelyn Venable. • *The Big Idea (short)* 1918 (d); *The Unfoldment* 1921 (ph); *Watch Him Step* 1922 (ph); *Bag and Baggage* 1923 (ph); *Vanity's Price* 1924 (ph); *A Woman Who Sinned* 1924 (ph); *He Who Laughs Last* 1925 (ph); *Little Annie Rooney* 1925 (ph); *The Monster* 1925 (ph); *Playing With Souls* 1925 (ph); *The High Hand* 1926 (ph); *The Marriage Clause* 1926 (ph); *Sparrows* 1926 (ph); *Bitter Apples* 1927 (ph); *The Girl From Chicago* 1927 (ph); *Heart of Maryland* 1927 (ph); *The Jazz Singer* 1927 (ph); *The Last Performance* 1927 (ph); *A Million Bid* 1927 (ph); *Old San Francisco* 1927 (ph); *Slightly Used* 1927 (ph); *The Third Degree* 1927 (ph); *Glorious Betsy* 1928 (ph); *Tenderloin* 1928 (ph); *The Wedding March* 1928 (ph); *Broadway* 1929 (ph); *The Last Warning* 1929 (ph); *Noah's Ark* 1929 (ph); *Shanghai Lady* 1929 (ph); *Big Boy* 1930 (ph); *Captain of the Guard* 1930 (ph); *The Cat Creeps* 1930 (ph); *The Cohens and Kellys in Africa* 1930 (ph); *The Czar of Broadway* 1930 (ph); *Free Love* 1930 (ph); *King of Jazz* 1930 (ph); *Outward Bound* 1930 (ph); *The Big Gamble* 1931 (ph); *The Common Law* 1931 (ph); *Devotion* 1931 (ph); *A Woman of Experience* 1931 (ph); *The First Year* 1932 (ph); *Lady With a Past* 1932 (ph); *Tess of the Storm Country* 1932 (ph); *Week-Ends Only* 1932 (ph); *A Woman Commands* 1932 (ph); *As Husbands Go* 1933 (ph); *The Devil's in Love* 1933 (ph); *I Loved You Wednesday* 1933 (ph); *State Fair* 1933 (ph); *The Warrior's Husband* 1933 (ph); *The Worst Woman in Paris* 1933 (ph); *Carolina* 1934 (ph); *Charlie Chan's Courage* 1934 (ph); *David Harum* 1934 (ph); *Servant's Entrance* 1934 (ph); *Captain Blood* 1935 (ph); *The County Chairman* 1935 (ph); *A Midsummer Night's Dream* 1935 (ph) **(AABPH)**; *Under Pressure* 1935 (ph); *Bullets or Ballots* 1936 (ph); *The Green Pastures* 1936 (ph); *Ladies in Love* 1936 (ph); *The Walking Dead* 1936 (ph); *When Love Is Young* 1937 (d); *I Met My Love Again* 1938 (ph); *Back Door to Heaven* 1939 (ph); *Destry Rides Again* 1939 (ph); *Rio* 1939 (ph); *The Under-Pup* 1939 (ph); *When the Daltons Rode* 1940 (ph); *Cheers For Miss Bishop* 1941 (ph); *International Lady* 1941 (ph); *Pot o' Gold* 1941 (ph); *Twin Beds* 1942 (ph); *The Phantom of the Opera* 1943 (ph) **(AABPH)**; *Top Man* 1943 (ph); *Watch on the Rhine* 1943 (ph); *The Climax* 1944 (ph); *Enter Arsene Lupin* 1944 (ph); *I'm From Arkansas* 1944 (ph); *The Impatient Years* 1944 (ph); *Ladies Courageous* 1944 (ph); *My Gal Loves Music* 1944 (ph); *San Diego, I Love You* 1944 (ph); *This Is the Life* 1944 (ph); *Her Lucky Night* 1945 (ph); *Salome—Where She Danced* 1945 (ph); *Shady Lady* 1945 (ph); *Because of Him* 1946 (ph); *A Night in Paradise* 1946 (ph); *I'll Be Yours* 1947 (ph); *The Lost Moment* 1947 (ph); *Pirates of Monterey* 1947 (ph); *The Song of Scheherazade* 1947 (ph); *An Act of Murder* 1948 (ph); *Another Part of the Forest* 1948 (ph); *Johnny Holiday* 1949 (ph); *Woman on the Run* 1950 (ph); *The Big Night* 1951 (ph); *The Second Woman* 1951 (ph); *The Four Poster* 1952 (ph) **(AANBPH)**; *The Member of the Wedding* 1952 (ph); *Rancho Notorious* 1952 (ph); *The Wild One* 1953 (ph); *The Boss* 1956 (ph); *Baby Face Nelson* 1957 (ph); *The Gun Runners* 1958 (ph); *The Lineup* 1958 (ph); *The Last Voyage* 1960 (ph); *Underworld, U.S.A.* 1961 (ph); *The Creation of the Humanoids* 1962 (ph); *The Man From the Diner's Club* 1963 (ph); *The Bamboo Saucer* 1968 (ph); *Topaz* 1969 (ph.consultant); *The Man You Loved to Hate* 1979 (a).

Mokae, Zakes • Actor • Born Johannesburg, South Africa, August 5, 1935. *Educ.* RADA, London. One of South Africa's most famous black actors.

Mokae's quiet strength and resilient good humor have animated the searing theatrical productions of his white countryman, Athol Fugard. Since he left South Africa and settled in the US in 1969 Mokae has turned in powerful supporting roles in films including *Cry Freedom* (1987) and *A Dry White Season* (1989). • *The Island* 1980; *Roar* 1981; *Cry Freedom* 1987; *The Serpent and the Rainbow* 1988; *Dad* 1989; *A Dry White Season* 1989; *Gross Anatomy* 1989; *A Rage in Harlem* 1991.

Molander, Gustaf • *aka* Gustav Molander • Director; also screenwriter. • Born Helsinki, Finland, November 18, 1888; died June 21, 1973. Began his career as a stage actor in 1911 before turning his hand to scriptwriting, chiefly for directors Victor Sjostrom and Mauritz Stiller. (Molander also taught acting at Stockholm's Royal Dramatic Theater Academy, where Greta Garbo was among his students.) Molander directed his first film in 1920 and continued to engineer melodramas until the 1930s, when he earned critical acclaim for *One Night* (1931)—considered his finest work—and provided Ingrid Bergman with her breakthrough vehicle, *Intermezzo* (1936). Husband of actress Karin Molander (1910-1918) and brother of director/actor Olof Molander. • *Herr Arnes pengar* 1919 (sc); *Erotikon* 1920 (sc); *King of Boda* 1920 (d); *Thomas Graals* 1922 (d,sc); *Constable Paulus's Easter Bomb* 1924 (d,sc); *His English Wife* 1927 (d); *Sin* 1928 (d); *One Night* 1931 (d); *Swedenhielms* 1935 (d); *Intermezzo* 1936 (d,sc); *Pa solsidan* 1936 (d); *Sara lar sig folkvett* 1937 (d); *Dollar* 1938 (d,sc); *En enda natt* 1938 (d); *En kvinnas ansikte* 1938 (d); *Emilie Hogqvist* 1939 (d); *Intermezzo* 1939 (story); *Jacobs stege* 1942 (d); *Kvinna utan ansikte* 1947 (d); *Eva* 1948 (d); *Franskild* 1951 (add.dial,d); *Stimulantia* 1967 (d).

Molina, Alfred • Actor • Born London. *Educ.* Guildhall School of Music and Drama, London. Stocky English actor best known for his appearances as a Soviet seaman in *Letter to Brezhnev* (1985) and as the lover of playwright Joe Orton in *Prick up Your Ears* (1987). • *Raiders of the Lost Ark* 1981; *Meantime* 1983; *Number One* 1984; *Water* 1984; *Eleni* 1985; *Ladyhawke* 1985; *A Letter to Brezhnev* 1985; *Prick Up Your Ears* 1987; *Manifesto* 1988; *Drowning in the Shallow End* 1989; *Not Without My Daughter* 1991.

Molinaro, Edouard • Director; also screenwriter. • Born Bordeaux, France, May 13, 1928. Former industrial and documentary filmmaker who made his feature debut with *Back to the Wall* (1958). Molinaro's fluid camera technique and light directorial touch were put to good use in his sensitive, humorous portrait of gay life, *La Cage aux Folles* (1978). • *Le Dos au Mur/Back to the Wall* 1958 (d); *Un Témoin dans la ville* 1958 (d); *Les Sept péchés capitaux* 1962 (d); *La Chasse à l'Homme* 1964 (d); *Une Ravissante Idiote/A Ravishing Idiot* 1964 (d); *Quand passent les faisans* 1965 (d); *Oscar* 1967 (d,sc); *Hibernatus* 1969 (d); *La Liberté en croupe* 1970 (d); *Les Aveux les plus doux* 1971 (d); *La Mandarine* 1971 (d,sc); *Le Gang des Otages/The Hostages* 1972 (d,sc); *L'Emmerdeur/A Pain in the A . . .* 1973 (d,sc); *L'Ironie du Sort* 1974 (d,sc); *Le Téléphone Rose/The Pink Telephone* 1975 (d); *Dracula Père et Fils* 1976 (d,sc); *L'Homme pressé/Man in a Hurry* 1977 (d); *La Cage aux folles* 1978 (d,sc,adapt) **(AANBD,AANBSC)**; *Cause toujours... tu m'intéresses!* 1979 (d,sc); *La Cage aux folles II* 1980 (d); *Sunday Lovers* 1980 (d); *Pour 100 Briques, T'as plus rien maintenant* 1982 (d,sc); *L'Amour en Douce* 1984 (d,sc); *Just the Way You Are* 1984 (d); *Palace* 1984 (d); *A Gauche en sortant de l'ascenseur* 1988 (d).

Monicelli, Mario • Director, screenwriter • Born Viareggio, Tuscany, Italy, May 15, 1915. *Educ.* University of Pisa (history, philosophy); University of Milan (history, philosophy). Former film critic whose writing and directing career began in earnest after the end of WWII. Monicelli first gained attention with his satirical 1958 treatment of a bungled heist, *The Big Deal on Madonna Street.* He has proved himself a master of satirical black comedy, notably in films such as *The Great War* (1959) and *The Organizer* (1963), and has elicited fine performances from some of Italy's best actors, notably Vittorio Gassman and Marcello Mastroianni. Monicelli also has a reputation for turning out uninspired commercial vehicles such as *Casanova '70* (1965) and *Lady Liberty* (1972) in between his more "personal" projects. • *Vita da cani* 1950 (d); *Le Infedeli* 1952 (d); *Proibito* 1954 (d); *Donatella* 1955 (d); *La Donna piu bella del mondo* 1955 (sc); *Un Eroe dei nostri tempi* 1955 (d); *Padri e Figli/The Tailor's Maid* 1957 (d,sc); *The Big Deal on Madonna Street* 1958 (d); *La Grande Guerra/The Great War* 1959 (d); *Risate di Gioia/The Passionate Thief* 1960 (d); *Boccaccio '70* 1962 (d); *I Compagni/The Organizer* 1963 (d,sc) **(AANBSC)**; *Casanova '70* 1965 (d,sc) **(AANBSC)**; *L' Armata Brancaleone* 1966 (d); *Le Fate/The Queens* 1966 (d); *To'è morta la nonna!* 1969 (d); *Brancaleone Alle Crociate* 1970 (d); *La Mortadella/Lady Liberty* 1972 (d,sc); *Vogliamo I Colonnelli* 1972 (d,sc); *Romanzo Popolare* 1974 (d,sc); *Amici Miei/My Friends* 1975 (d); *Caro Michele* 1976 (d); *Signore e Signori, Buonanotte* 1976 (d,sc); *Un Borghese Piccolo Piccolo* 1977 (d,sc); *I Nuovi Mostri/The New Monsters* 1977 (d); *Travels With Anita* 1978 (d,sc); *Rosy la Bourrasque/Hurricane Rosy* 1979 (d); *Rue du Pied-De-Grue* 1979 (a); *Sono Fotogenico* 1980 (a); *Il Marchese del Grillo* 1981 (d,sc); *Amici miei atto II/My Friends 2* 1983 (d,sc,story); *Bertoldo, Bertoldino e Cacasenno* 1984 (d,sc); *Le Due vite di Mattia Pascal/The Two Lives of Mattia Pascal* 1985 (d,sc); *Pourvu que ce soit une fille/Let's Hope It's a Girl* 1986 (d,sc); *I Picari/The Rogues* 1987 (d,sc); *Il Male Oscuro/The Obscure Illness* 1990 (d,sc).

Monroe, Marilyn • *aka* Norma Jean Baker • Actress • Born Norma Jean Mortenson, Los Angeles, CA, June 1, 1926; died August 5, 1962, Los Angeles, CA. *Educ.* Actors Studio; Morris Carnovsky Actor's Lab. An illegitimate child whose father (Edward Mortenson) had deserted her mother (Gladys Baker, née Monroe) before she was born, Norma Jean endured a childhood of poverty and misery, sexual abuse (at the age of eight) and years in foster homes and orphanages after her mother suffered a nervous breakdown and was institutionalized. Escape from this cycle came at the age of sixteen with an arranged marriage to a 21-year-old aircraft plant worker.

While working at the Radio Plane Company factory in Burbank, she had her picture taken by a visiting Army photographer. Norma Jean then began modeling bathing suits and, after bleaching her hair blonde, began posing for pinups and glamour photos. Howard Hughes saw some of her photographs and expressed an interest in giving her a screen test for RKO, but Ben Lyon of 20th Century-Fox beat Hughes to the punch, signing Norma Jean Baker to a contract and changing her name to Marilyn Monroe.

After appearing in small parts in films including *Love Happy* (1949) and *All About Eve* (1950), Monroe achieved celebrity with starring roles in three 1953 features—*Niagara, Gentlemen Prefer Blondes* and *How To Marry a Millionaire*—as well as a series of nude calendar photos, taken in 1948, which appeared in the December 1953 debut issue of *Playboy* magazine. By the end of the year, Monroe had been voted the top star of 1953 by American film distributors.

In all her film roles, from *Niagara* to *The Misfits* (1961), Monroe portrayed an object of desire and exhibition. Her basic character grew out of the dumb blonde archetype, but Monroe's dumb blonde could not be pinned down to any particular origin or social class. She was defined only by what was shown on the screen, with neither a previous history nor seemingly a future. Frequently her characters were namelesss (*Love Happy,* 1955's *The Seven Year Itch*), further accentuating her status as an object. She usually had no discernable job and when she did, it was a female-relegated profession such as chorus girl, actress or secretary.

But to the dumb blonde stereotype, Monroe added a sense of innocence, naturalism and overt sexuality. Her sexuality was never seen as a threat, but as something harmless and benevolent. *Time* magazine's sanguine response to Monroe's *Playboy* centerfold summed up her appeal: "Marilyn believes in doing what comes naturally."

Along with this kindly, innocent sexuality went a vulnerability; Monroe's characters were often humiliated at the expense of a voyeuristic pleasure, whether being lassoed like a cow in *Bus Stop* (1956) or exposing herself unknowingly in *Some Like It Hot* (1959). At the height of her fame, Monroe sensed the limited range of her screen persona and clearly desired to change it: "To put it bluntly, I seem to be a whole superstructure without a foundation." Forming Marilyn Monroe Productions in 1956, she produced *Bus Stop* and *The Prince and The Showgirl* (1957). But her personal problems, with failed marriages to baseball star Joe DiMaggio and playwright Arthur Miller and increasing reliance on drugs to combat depression and physical ailments, served to forestall any serious change in her career.

The public wanted Marilyn as they had discovered her in 1953, and that was what they got in *Let's Make Love* (1960). She was still capable of memorable work, especially with top directors like Billy Wilder (*Some Like It Hot*) and John Huston (*The Misfits*), but her personal demons, or precarious involvement with people in high places, eventually overwhelmed her. On August 5, 1962, she was found dead of an overdose of sleeping pills. Monroe's was a tragedy in which her public, the media and the Hollywood power brokers all share blame. As Laurence Olivier once remarked, "Popular opinion and all that goes to promote it is a horribly unsteady conveyance for life, and she was exploited beyond anyone's means." PB • *Dangerous Years* 1947; *Scudda-Hoo! Scudda-Hay!* 1948; *Ladies of the Chorus* 1949; *Love Happy* 1949; *All About Eve* 1950; *The Asphalt Jungle* 1950; *The Fireball* 1950; *Right Cross* 1950; *A Ticket to Tomahawk* 1950; *As Young As You Feel* 1951; *Home Town Story* 1951; *Let's Make It Legal* 1951; *Love Nest* 1951; *Clash By Night* 1952; *Don't Bother to Knock* 1952; *Monkey Business* 1952; *O. Henry's Full House* 1952; *We're Not Married* 1952; *Gentlemen Prefer Blondes* 1953; *How to Marry a Millionaire* 1953; *Niagara* 1953; *River of No Return* 1954; *There's No Business Like Show Business* 1954; *The Seven Year Itch* 1955; *Bus Stop* 1956; *The Prince and the Showgirl* 1957; *Some Like It Hot* 1959; *Let's Make Love* 1960; *The Misfits* 1961; *Marilyn* 1963 (archival footage).

Montagu, Ivor • Filmmaker; also writer, producer. • Born Ivor Goldsmid Samuel Montagu, London, April 23, 1904; died 1984. *Educ.* Royal College of Science, London (zoology, botany); King's College, Cambridge (zoology). Leftist theoretician and critic (Montagu accompanied Eisenstein during his 1930 trip to Hollywood) who also worked as an exhibitor, editor and director of short films. Montagu collaborated on a number of Hitchcock films during the 1930s and made propoganda films for the Republicans during the Spanish Civil War (he documented the experience in his 1939 film, *Peace and Plenty*). Following WWII Montagu worked for the Ealing Studios, where he collaborated on the script of the acclaimed feature, *Scott of the Antarctic* (1948). • *The Lodger* 1926 (ed); *Downhill* 1927 (ed); *Easy Virtue* 1927 (ed); *Bluebottles (short)* 1928 (d); *Day-Dreams (short)* 1928 (d); *The Tonic (short)* 1928 (d); *Sturm uber la Sarraz (short)* 1929 (d); *The Man Who Knew Too Much* 1934 (p); *The 39 Steps* 1935 (p); *Sabotage* 1936 (p); *Secret Agent* 1936 (p); *Behind the Spanish Lines* 1938 (p); *Spanish ABC* 1938 (p); *Peace and Plenty* 1939 (d); *Scott of the Antarctic* 1948 (story,sc); *The Last Man to Hang* 1956 (sc); *Before Hindsight* 1977 (archival footage).

Montand, Yves • Actor, singer • Born Ivo Livi, Monsummano Alto, outside Florence, Italy, October 13, 1921. Former music-hall singer who was "discovered" by Edith Piaf and made his screen debut in 1946 in the Piaf vehicle, *Star Without Light* (he gained more attention for his fine performance, the same year, in Marcel Carne's *Les Portes de la Nuit*). Henri Clouzot's *The Wages of Fear* (1953) launched Montand as an international star, though in his two 1960 Hollywood outings—*Let's Make Love*, opposite Marilyn Monroe, and *Sanctuary*—he was fairly forgettable. From the late 1960s, Montand was able to integrate his political convictions with his acting career by starring in several films by Costa-Gavras, especially *Z* (1969) and *The Confession* (1970). He gave a canny performance as the scheming old uncle, César, in Claude Berri's *Jean de Florette* and *Manon of the Spring* (both 1986). Montand co-starred several times with Simone Signoret, his wife from 1951 until her death in 1985. • *Etoile sans lumière/Star Without Light* 1946; *Les Portes de la nuit* 1946; *L'Auberge Rouge* 1951 (singing commentary); *Paris est toujours Paris* 1951; *Le Salaire de la Peur/The Wages of Fear* 1953; *Les Héros sont fatigués/Heroes and Sinners* 1955; *Les Sorcières de Salem/The Crucible* 1956; *La Loi* 1958; *Premier Mai* 1958; *Let's Make Love* 1960; *Sanctuary* 1960; *Aimez-vouz Brahms?/Goodbye Again* 1961; *Le Joli Mai* 1962; *My Geisha* 1962; *Compartiment tueurs/The Sleeping Car Murder* 1965; *Grand Prix* 1966; *La Guerre est finie/Is Paris Burning?* 1966; *Vivre pour vivre/Live for Life* 1967; *Mister Freedom* 1968; *Un Soir...un Train* 1968; *Le Diable par la Queue/The Devil by the Tail* 1969; *Z* 1969; *L'Aveu/The Confession* 1970; *On a Clear Day You Can See Forever* 1970; *La Folie des grandeurs/Delusions of Grandeur* 1971; *Cesar et Rosalie* 1972; *Le Fils* 1972; *Tout va bien* 1972; *Etat de siège* 1973; *Le Hasard Et La Violence* 1973; *Vincent, François, Paul... et les autres/Vincent, François, Paul... and the Others* 1974; *Police Python.357* 1975; *Le Sauvage* 1975; *Le Fond de l'air est rouge* 1977; *Le Grand Escogriffe* 1977; *La Menace* 1977; *Les Routes du Sud/The Roads to the South* 1978; *Clair de Femme/Womanlight* 1979; *I Comme Icare* 1979; *Carné: l'Homme à la Caméra* 1980; *Le Choix des armes* 1981; *Tout feu, tout flamme/All Fired Up* 1981; *L'Eté meurtrier* 1982 (song); *Garçon!/Waiter!* 1983; *Jean de Florette* 1986; *Manon des sources/Manon of the Spring* 1986; *Nadie Escuchaba/Nobody Listened* 1988; *Trois places pour le 26* 1988; *Netchaiev est de Retour* 1991.

Montgomery, Robert • Actor; also director. • Born Henry Montgomery, Jr., Fishkill Landing, NY, May 21, 1904; died 1981. MGM contract player from 1929, primarily cast as upper-crust playboys opposite stars such as Greta Garbo (*Inspiration* 1931) and Joan Crawford (*The Last of Mrs. Cheyney* 1937). Montgomery developed a tougher image after WWII, during which he had distinguished himself in naval action in Europe. He made his directorial debut when an ailing John Ford was unable to complete *They Were Expendable* (1945), and attracted considerable attention with his screen adaptation of Raymond Chandler's *Lady in the Lake* (1946). The film was related entirely from a "subjective" camera perspective, and is considered one of the more interesting failed experiments in cinematic narrative. Montgomery was a friendly witness before HUAC in 1947 and subsequently trained his sights on TV, the stage and, ultimately, politics, serving as a communications consultant to President Eisenhower following the 1952 campaign. Father of actress Elizabeth Montgomery and Robert Montgomery, Jr. • *So This Is College* 1929; *Their Own Desire* 1929; *Three Live Ghosts* 1929; *Untamed* 1929; *The Big House* 1930; *The Divorcee* 1930; *Free and Easy* 1930; *Love in the Rough* 1930; *Our Blushing Brides* 1930; *Sins of the Children* 1930; *War Nurse* 1930; *The Easiest Way* 1931; *Inspiration* 1931; *The Man in Possession* 1931; *Private Lives* 1931; *Shipmates* 1931; *Strangers May Kiss* 1931; *Transatlantic* 1931; *Blondie of the Follies* 1932; *But the Flesh Is Weak* 1932; *Faithless* 1932; *Letty Lynton* 1932; *Lovers Courageous* 1932; *Another Language* 1933; *Hell Below* 1933; *Made on Broadway* 1933; *Night Flight* 1933; *When Ladies Meet* 1933; *Biography of a Bachelor Girl* 1934; *Forsaking All Others* 1934; *Fugitive Lovers* 1934; *Hide-Out* 1934; *The Mystery of Mr. X* 1934; *Riptide* 1934; *No More Ladies* 1935; *Vanessa, Her Love Story* 1935; *Petticoat*

Fever 1936; *Piccadilly Jim* 1936; *Trouble For Two* 1936; *Ever Since Eve* 1937; *The Last of Mrs. Cheyney* 1937; *Live, Love and Learn* 1937; *Night Must Fall* 1937 **(AANBA)**; *The First Hundred Years* 1938; *Three Loves Has Nancy* 1938; *Yellow Jack* 1938; *Fast and Loose* 1939; *The Earl of Chicago* 1940; *Here Comes Mr. Jordan* 1941 **(AANBA)**; *Mr. & Mrs. Smith* 1941; *Rage in Heaven* 1941; *Unfinished Business* 1941; *They Were Expendable* 1945 (a,d); *Lady in the Lake* 1946 (a,d); *Ride the Pink Horse* 1947 (a,d); *June Bride* 1948; *The Saxon Charm* 1948; *Once More, My Darling* 1949 (a,d); *Your Witness* 1950 (a,d); *The Gallant Hours* 1960 (d,p).

Monti, Felix • Director of photography • Cinematographer in Latin American and Europe since 1970 who gained prominence for his work on Luis Puenza's *The Official Story* (1985) and Fernando Solanas's *Sur* (1988). Monti again collaborated with Puenza on the director's ill-received adaptation of the Carlos Fuentes novel, *Old Gringo* (1989). • *Esperame Mucho* 1983; *La Historia Oficial/The Official Story* 1985; *Tangos—L'exil de Gardel* 1985; *Sur* 1988; *Old Gringo* 1989; *Yo, la Peor de Todas* 1990.

Moore, Demi • Actress • Born Demi Guynes, Roswell, NM, November 11, 1962. Throaty young star of the TV soap, "General Hospital," who graduated to roles in several "brat pack" films during the 1980s. Married to actor Bruce Willis. • *Choices* 1981; *Parasite* 1982; *Young Doctors in Love* 1982; *Blame It on Rio* 1984; *No Small Affair* 1984; *St. Elmo's Fire* 1985; *About Last Night* 1986; *One Crazy Summer* 1986; *Wisdom* 1986; *The Seventh Sign* 1988; *We're No Angels* 1989; *Ghost* 1990; *Mortal Thoughts* 1991; *Nothing But Trouble* 1991.

Moore, Dudley • Actor; also pianist, composer. • Born London, April 19, 1935. *Educ.* Guildhall School of Music and Drama; Magdalen College, Oxford. Diminutive, quick-witted performer who teamed up with fellow Oxford graduates Peter Cook, Jonathan Miller and Alan Bennett to form the comedy troupe *Beyond the Fringe*, an early 1960s precursor to the "Monty Python" group. Moore and "Fringe" colleague Peter Cook went on to form their own two-man act, enjoying popular success with their stage shows and somewhat ribald albums and making their first movie appearances in *The Wrong Box* (1966). Moore became an unlikely Hollywood star with his performance in *Arthur* (1981) and has gone on to appear in a string of saccharine comedies. A proficient pianist, he has recorded several albums of light jazz and appeared in concert with the Los Angeles Philharmonic Orchestra. Divorced from actresses Suzy Kendall and Tuesday Weld. • *The Wrong Box* 1966; *Bedazzled* 1967 (a,story,m); *Inadmissible Evidence* 1968 (m,songs); *The Bed Sitting Room* 1969; *Monte Carlo or Bust!* 1969; *Staircase* 1969 (m); *Alice's Adventures in Wonderland* 1972; *Pleasure at Her Majesty's* 1976; *Foul Play* 1978; *The Hound of the Baskervilles* 1978 (a,sc,m); *10* 1979; *To Russia... With Elton* 1979; *Derek and Clive Get the Horn* 1980 (a,exec.p,m); *Wholly Moses!* 1980; *Arthur* 1981 **(AANBA)**; *Six Weeks* 1982 (a,m,m.perf); *Lovesick* 1983; *Romantic Comedy* 1983; *Unfaithfully Yours* 1983; *Best Defense* 1984; *Micki & Maude* 1984; *Santa Claus: The Movie* 1985; *Koneko Monogatari* 1986; *Like Father, Like Son* 1987; *Arthur 2 on the Rocks* 1988 (a,exec.p); *Crazy People* 1990.

Moore, Mary Tyler • Actress • Born Brooklyn, NY, December 29, 1937. Vivacious, toothsome actress who first gained attention as the quintessential suburban housewife on TV's "The Dick Van Dyck Show" (1961-65) and proved herself one of the small screen's finest comediennes with the popular and critical success, "The Mary Tyler Moore Show" (1970-77). Moore's major screen appearances, beginning with her 1967 role in *Thoroughly Modern Millie*, traded on her TV image but met with limited success. Her performance as the neurotic, repressed wife and mother in *Ordinary People* (1981) tapped a previously unexplored talent for drama. • *X-15* 1961; *Don't Just Stand There!* 1967; *Thoroughly Modern Millie* 1967; *What's So Bad About Feeling Good?* 1968; *Change of Habit* 1969; *Ordinary People* 1981 **(AANBA)**; *Six Weeks* 1982; *Just Between Friends* 1986.

Moore, Michael • Filmmaker; also journalist. • Born Davison, MI, c. 1954. *Educ.* University of Michigan. Former editor of *The Michigan Voice* and, briefly, *Mother Jones* magazine who traded in his pen for a movie camera and concocted the piercing, scathingly funny *Roger and Me* (1989), which documented the effects on Flint, Michigan, of plant closures carried out by auto giant General Motors. The film was a huge commercial success despite concerted attempts by GM to discredit it, largely through claims that Moore had "re-arranged" some of the events he recorded. • *Roger and Me* 1989 (a,d,p,sc).

Moore, Roger • Actor • Born London, October 14, 1927. *Educ.* RADA, London. Suave, unflappable star who first made his mark in the TV series, "The Saint." Moore achieved international celebrity in 1973 when he became a somewhat wooden successor to Sean Connery in *Live and Let Die*, the first of seven "James Bond" films. • *The Last Time I Saw Paris* 1954; *Interrupted Melody* 1955; *The King's Thief* 1955; *Diane* 1956; *The Miracle* 1959; *Gold of the Seven Saints* 1961; *The Sins of Rachel Cade* 1961; *The Man Who Haunted Himself* 1970; *Live and Let Die* 1973; *Gold* 1974; *The Man With the Golden Gun* 1974; *That Lucky Touch* 1975; *Shout at the Devil* 1976; *Street People* 1976; *The Spy Who Loved Me* 1977; *The Wild Geese* 1978; *Escape to Athena* 1979; *Moonraker* 1979; *The Cannonball Run* 1980; *The Sea Wolves* 1980; *Sunday Lovers* 1980; *ffolkes* 1980; *For Your Eyes Only* 1981; *Curse of the Pink Panther* 1983; *Octopussy* 1983; *The Naked Face* 1985; *A View to a Kill* 1985; *The Magic Snowman* 1987; *Bullseye!* 1990; *Fire, Ice and Dynamite* 1990.

Moorehead, Agnes • Actress • Born Clinton, MA, December 6, 1906; died 1974. *Educ.* University of Wisconsin; Bradley University (literature); AADA, New York. Angular, versatile performer who first received acclaim for her roles in two Orson Welles films: as Kane's mother in *Citizen Kane* (1941) and as the forbidding spinster in *The Magnificent Ambersons* (1942). Moorehead subsequently played primarily unpleasant or neurotic characters, and is perhaps best known as Endora in the TV series, "Bewitched" (1964-72). • *Citizen Kane* 1941; *The Big Street* 1942; *Journey Into Fear* 1942; *The Magnificent Ambersons* 1942 **(AANBSA)**; *Government Girl* 1943; *The Youngest Profession* 1943; *Dragon Seed* 1944; *Jane Eyre* 1944; *Mrs. Parkington* 1944 **(AANBSA)**; *The Seventh Cross* 1944; *Since You Went Away* 1944; *Tomorrow the World* 1944; *Her Highness and the Bellboy* 1945; *Keep Your Powder Dry* 1945; *Our Vines Have Tender Grapes* 1945; *Dark Passage* 1947; *The Lost Moment* 1947; *Johnny Belinda* 1948 **(AANBSA)**; *Station West* 1948; *Summer Holiday* 1948; *The Woman in White* 1948; *The Great Sinner* 1949; *The Stratton Story* 1949; *Without Honor* 1949; *Caged* 1950; *Adventures of Captain Fabian* 1951; *The Blue Veil* 1951; *Fourteen Hours* 1951; *Show Boat* 1951; *The Blazing Forest* 1952; *Main Street to Broadway* 1953; *Scandal at Scourie* 1953; *The Story of Three Loves* 1953; *Those Redheads From Seattle* 1953; *Magnificent Obsession* 1954; *The Left Hand of God* 1955; *The Revolt of Mamie Stover* 1955; *Untamed* 1955; *All That Heaven Allows* 1956; *The Conqueror* 1956; *Meet Me in Las Vegas* 1956; *The Opposite Sex* 1956; *Pardners* 1956; *The Swan* 1956; *Jeanne Eagels* 1957; *Raintree County* 1957; *The Story of Mankind* 1957; *The True Story of Jesse James* 1957; *Night of the Quarter Moon* 1958; *La Tempesta* 1958; *The Bat* 1959; *Pollyanna* 1960; *Bachelor in Paradise* 1961; *Jessica* 1961; *Twenty Plus Two* 1961; *How the West Was Won* 1962; *Who's Minding the Store?* 1963; *Hush ... Hush, Sweet Charlotte* 1964 **(AANBSA)**; *The Singing Nun* 1966; *What's The Matter With Helen?* 1971; *Charlotte's Web* 1972; *Dear Dead Delilah* 1975.

Moranis, Rick • Actor • Born Toronto, Canada. Comic actor who specializes in playing gawky, maladroit characters. Moranis demonstrated his versatility and talent for mimicry on the frenetic Canadian comedy show "SCTV" before gaining wider recognition for his role in *Ghostbusters* (1984). He enjoyed considerable box-office success with *Honey, I Shrunk the Kids* (1989). • *Strange Brew* 1983 (a,d,sc); *Ghostbusters* 1984; *Streets of Fire* 1984; *The Wild Life* 1984; *Brewster's Millions* 1985; *Club Paradise* 1986; *Head Office* 1986; *Little Shop of Horrors* 1986; *Spaceballs* 1987; *Ghostbusters II* 1989; *Honey, I Shrunk the Kids* 1989; *Parenthood* 1989; *My Blue Heaven* 1990; *L.A. Story* 1991.

Moreau, Jeanne • Actress; also director, screenwriter. • Born Paris, January 23, 1928. *Educ.* Paris Conservatoire. Leading French stage actress whose austere beauty and cool intelligence graced some of the finest films of the late 1950s and 60s, especially those of New Wave directors Louis Malle and François Truffaut. Moreau came to prominence in Malle's *Elevator to the Gallows* (1957) and *The Lovers* (1958), but it was her free-sprited performance in Truffaut's *Jules and Jim* (1961) that made her an international star. She has distinguished herself in the films of such directors as Antonioni, Welles, Bunuel and Losey, and has used her standing in the French industry to foster the careers of young directors such as Bertrand Blier (in whose 1974 feature, *Going Places*, she gave a cryptic but memorable performance) and André Téchine. Moreau made a well-received directing debut in 1976 with *Lumière*. • *Julietta* 1953; *Touchez Pas au Grisbi* 1953; *Secrets d'Alcove/The Bed* 1954; *Ascenseur pour l'échafaud/Elevator to the Gallows* 1957; *Les Louves* 1957; *Les Amants/The Lovers* 1958; *Le Dos au Mur/Back to the Wall* 1958; *Les Liaisons Dangereuses* 1959; *Les Quatre cents coups/The 400 Blows* 1959; *Five Branded Women* 1960; *Une Femme est une femme* 1961; *Jules et Jim* 1961; *La Notte* 1961; *Eva* 1962; *The Trial* 1962; *La Baie des anges/Bay of Angels* 1963; *Le Feu Follet/The Fire Within* 1963; *Le Journal d'une femme de chambre/Diary of a Chambermaid* 1963; *The Victors* 1963; *Peau de banane* 1964; *The Train* 1964; *Viva Maria* 1965; *Chimes at Midnight* 1966; *Great Catherine* 1968; *Histoire Immortelle* 1968; *La Mariée était en noir/The Bride Wore Black* 1968; *Le Petit Théâtre de Jean Renoir* 1969; *Alex in Wonderland* 1970; *Langlois (short)* 1970; *Monte Walsh* 1970; *Comptes A Rebours* 1971; *L' Humeur Vagabonde* 1971; *Chère Louise* 1972; *Nathalie Granger* 1972; *Je t'aime* 1973; *Race des "Seigneurs," La* 1973; *Les Valseuses/Going Places* 1974; *Hu-Man* 1975; *Le Jardin Qui Bascule* 1975; *Souvenirs d'en France* 1975; *The Last Tycoon* 1976; *Lumière* 1976 (a,d,sc); *Mr. Klein* 1976; *L'Adoléscente* 1978 (d,sc); *Plein Sud* 1980; *Joana Francesa* 1981; *Querelly—ein Pakt mit dem Teufel/Querelle* 1982; *La Truite/The Trout* 1982; *The Wizard of Babylon* 1982; *Jean-Louis Barrault—A Man of the Theater* 1984; *Lillian Gish* 1984 (a,d,p); *Francois Simon—La Présence* 1986; *Le Miracule* 1986; *Le Paltoquet* 1986; *Sauve-toi Lola* 1986; *Calling the Shots* 1988; *Hotel Terminus: Klaus Barbie, His Life and Times* 1988; *La Nuit de l'ocean* 1988; *Alberto Express* 1990; *La Femme fardée* 1990; *Nikita* 1990; *Jusqu'au bout du monde/Till the End of the World* 1991.

Moreno, Rita • *aka* Rosita Moreno • Actress; also singer, dancer. • Born Rosita Dolores Alverio, Humacao, Puerto Rico, December 11, 1931. Fiery Latin performer who made her Hollywood debut in 1945 at the age of 14 and garnered acclaim for her performance in *West Side Story* (1961). First actress to be recipient of an Oscar, a Tony and an Emmy. • *A Medal For Benny* 1945; *Pagan Love Song* 1950; *So Young, So Bad* 1950; *The Toast of New Orleans* 1950; *Cattle Town* 1952; *The Fabulous Senorita* 1952; *The Ring* 1952; *Singin' in the Rain* 1952; *El Alamein* 1953; *Fort Vengeance* 1953; *Jack London's Tales of Adventure* 1953; *Latin Lovers* 1953; *Ma and Pa Kettle on Vacation* 1953; *Garden of Evil* 1954; *Jivaro* 1954; *The Yellow Tomahawk* 1954; *The Lieutenant Wore Skirts* 1955; *Seven Cities of Gold* 1955; *Untamed* 1955; *The King and I* 1956; *The Vagabond King* 1956; *The Deerslayer* 1957; *This Rebel Breed* 1960; *One-Eyed Jacks* 1961 (tech.adv); *Summer and Smoke* 1961; *West Side Story* 1961 **(AABSA)**; *Samar* 1962; *Cry of Battle* 1963; *The Night of the Following Day* 1968; *Marlowe* 1969; *Popi* 1969; *Carnal Knowledge* 1971; *The Ritz* 1976; *The Boss' Son* 1978; *Happy Birthday, Gemini* 1980; *The Four Seasons* 1981; *Life in the Food Chain* 1991.

Morgan, Michèle • Actress • Born Simone Roussel, Neuilly-sur-Seine, France, February 29, 1920. Elegant leading lady of French cinema from 1935 who has worked with directors including René Clair, Marcel Carné and Carol Reed. • *Quai des Brumes/Port of Shadows* 1938; *Joan of Paris* 1942; *Higher and Higher* 1943; *Two Tickets to London* 1943; *Passage to Marseille* 1944; *The Chase* 1946; *La Symphonie Pastorale* 1946; *The Naked Heart* 1949; *La Minute de Vérité/The Moment of Truth* 1952; *Les Sept péchés capitaux* 1952; *Les Orgueilleux/The Proud and the Beautiful* 1953; *Oasis* 1955; *Les Grandes Maneuvres* 1956; *Retour de Manivelle/There's Always a Price Tag* 1957; *The Vintage* 1957; *The Mirror Has Two Faces* 1958; *Landru/Bluebeard* 1962; *Lost Command* 1966; *Benjamin, ou les mémoires d'un puceau* 1968; *Le Chat et la Souris/Cat and Mouse* 1975; *Stanno Tutti Bene* 1990.

Moriarty, Michael • Actor • Born Detroit, MI, April 5, 1941. *Educ.* Dartmouth; LAMDA, London. Stage, screen and TV actor who came to prominence for his sensitive performance in the acclaimed 1973 drama, *Bang the Drum Slowly* (1973). Little of Moriarty's subsequent work has lived up to his early promise. • *Glory Boy* 1971 (a); *Hickey and Boggs* 1972 (a); *Bang the Drum Slowly* 1973 (a); *The Last Detail* 1973 (a); *Shoot It: Black, Shoot It: Blue* 1974 (a); *Report to the Commissioner* 1975 (a); *Who'll Stop the Rain?* 1978 (a); *Renacida* 1981 (a); *Q* 1982 (a,song); *The Link* 1985 (a); *Odd Birds* 1985 (a); *Pale Rider* 1985 (a); *The Stuff* 1985 (a); *Troll* 1986 (a); *The Hanoi Hilton* 1987 (a); *It's Alive III: Island of the Alive* 1987 (a); *My Old Man's Place* 1988 (a); *Dark Tower* 1989 (a); *Full Fathom Five* 1990 (a).

Morita, Pat • Actor • Born Noriyuki Morita, Berkely, CA, 1930. Japanese-American character player. • *Thoroughly Modern Millie* 1967 (a); *Cancel My Reservation* 1972 (a); *Every Little Crook and Nanny* 1972 (a); *Where Does It Hurt?* 1972 (a); *Battle of Midway* 1976 (a); *When Time Ran Out* 1980 (a); *Full Moon High* 1981 (a); *Jimmy the Kid* 1982 (a); *Savannah Smiles* 1982 (a); *The Karate Kid* 1984 (a); *Night Patrol* 1984 (a); *Slapstick of Another Kind* 1984 (a); *The Karate Kid Part II* 1986 (a); *Captive Hearts* 1987 (a,sc); *The Karate Kid Part III* 1989 (a); *Collision Course* 1990 (a).

Morley, Robert • Actor; also playwright. • Born Semley, England, May 25, 1908. *Educ.* Wellington College; RADA, London. Rotund English actor who gained acclaim in 1938 playing the title role in *Oscar Wilde* on the London and Broadway stage. Morley made an Oscar-nominated film debut the same year in *Marie Antoinette* and went on to become a popular screen character actor through the 1980s. • *Marie Antoinette* 1938 **(AANBSA)**; *Return to Yesterday* 1940 (from play *Goodness How Sad*); *Major Barbara* 1941; *Edward, My Son* 1948 (from play); *The African Queen* 1951; *Outcast of the Islands* 1951; *Beat the Devil* 1953; *Melba* 1953; *Beau Brummell* 1954; *The Good Die Young* 1954; *Quentin Durward* 1955; *Around the World in 80 Days* 1956; *Law and Disorder* 1956; *The Doctor's Dilemma* 1958; *The Sheriff of Fractured Jaw* 1958; *The Journey* 1959; *Libel* 1959; *Giuseppe Venduto Dai Fratelli* 1960; *Oscar Wilde* 1960; *The Boys* 1962; *The Road to Hong Kong* 1962; *Nine Hours to Rama* 1963; *The Old Dark House* 1963; *Take Her, She's Mine* 1963; *Agent 8 3/4* 1964; *Of*

Human Bondage 1964; *Topkapi* 1964; *Genghis Khan* 1965; *Life at the Top* 1965; *The Loved One* 1965; *Those Magnificent Men in Their Flying Machines* 1965; *The Alphabet Murders* 1966; *Way... Way Out* 1966; *Woman Times Seven* 1967; *Sinful Davey* 1969; *Cromwell* 1970; *Doctor in Trouble* 1970; *Song of Norway* 1970; *Twinky* 1970; *When Eight Bells Toll* 1971; *Theatre of Blood* 1973; *Hugo the Hippo* 1975; *The Blue Bird* 1976; *Who Is Killing the Great Chefs of Europe?* 1978; *The Human Factor* 1979; *Scavenger Hunt* 1979; *Oh Heavenly Dog* 1980; *The Great Muppet Caper* 1981; *Loophole* 1981; *High Road to China* 1983; *Second Time Lucky* 1984; *The Trouble With Spies* 1987; *The Wind* 1987; *Little Dorrit* 1988; *Istanbul: Keep Your Eyes Open* 1990.

Morley, Ruth • Costume designer • Born Vienna; died New York, February 12, 1991. Renowned costume designer for film, theater, TV and opera whose baggy outfits for Diane Keaton in *Annie Hall* (1977) first brought her to widespread public attention. Morley's first Broadway production was 1951's *Billy Budd*. Daughters Emily and Melissa Hacker are both directors; the latter was working on a documentary about her mother's WWII experiences at the time of Morley's death. • *Never Love a Stranger* 1958 (cost); *The Hustler* 1961 (cost); *The Connection* 1962 (cost); *The Miracle Worker* 1962 (cost) **(AANBCOST)**; *Lilith* 1964 (cost); *The Brotherhood* 1968 (cost); *Diary of a Mad Housewife* 1970 (cost); *Taxi Driver* 1976 (cost); *Annie Hall* 1977 (cost); *The Brink's Job* 1978 (cost); *Slow Dancing in the Big City* 1978 (cost); *Superman* 1978 (add.cost); *Kramer vs. Kramer* 1979 (cost); *Little Miss Marker* 1980 (cost); *The Chosen* 1981 (cost); *I Ought to Be in Pictures* 1981 (cost); *Hammett* 1982 (cost); *One From the Heart* 1982 (cost); *Tootsie* 1982 (cost); *Grace Quigley* 1985 (cost); *Key Exchange* 1985 (cost. consultant); *The Money Pit* 1986 (cost); *Hello, Again* 1987 (cost); *The Dream Team* 1989 (cost); *Parenthood* 1989 (cost); *See No Evil, Hear No Evil* 1989 (cost); *Winter People* 1989 (cost); *Ghost* 1990 (cost).

Moroder, Giorgio • Composer • Born Ortisei, Italy, April 26, 1940. Producer of albums for popular artists such as Donna Summer and composer of pulsing, synthesized scores for films such as *Midnight Express* (1978). • *Midnight Express* 1978 (m) **(AABM)**; *Thank God It's Friday* 1978 (songs); *The Bitch* 1979 (song); *Sunburn* 1979 (song); *American Gigolo* 1980 (m); *Foxes* 1980 (m,m.dir,song); *Cat People* 1982 (m); *Partners* 1982 (song); *D.C. Cab* 1983 (m,songs); *Flashdance* 1983 (m,song) **(AABS)**; *Scarface* 1983 (m,m.arr,songs); *Superman III* 1983 (song); *Electric Dreams* 1984 (a,m,songs); *Metropolis* 1984 (reconstruction and adaptation,m,intertitles,songs); *The Neverending Story* 1984 (song); *Thief of Hearts* 1984 (m); *American Anthem* 1986 (song); *The Money Pit* 1986 (song); *Quicksilver* 1986 (songs); *Top Gun* 1986 (songs) **(AABS)**; *Beverly Hills Cop II* 1987 (songs); *Over the Top* 1987 (m,m.prod,songs); *Another Way—D Kikan Joho* 1988 (m); *Mamba* 1988 (assoc.p,m,m.prod,song); *Let It Ride* 1989 (m,songs); *Navy Seals* 1990 (song); *Stella* 1990 (song).

Morricone, Ennio • *aka* Leo Nichols, Nicola Piovani • Composer • Born Rome, October 11, 1928. *Educ.* Accademia di Santa Cecilia, Rome (music). Prolific composer whose hypnotic scores have graced a wide range of international films from the early 1960s to the present. Morricone began composing for the screen in his native Italy and came to prominence for the haunting score that whined and whistled through Sergio Leone's classic spaghetti western, *A Fistful of Dollars* (1964)—the first of many collaborations between the two. Leone has also worked with Italian directors Bertolucci (*1900* 1977) and Passolini (*The Decameron* 1971) and lent his considerable talent to a host of international productions. To date, he has written scores for some 350 films, and has worked with leading figures such as Terrence Malick (*Days of Heaven* 1978), Brian DePalma (*The Untouchables* 1987) and Roman Polanski (*Frantic* 1988). • *I Basilischi/The Lizards* 1963; *Gringo* 1963 (m,m.dir); *Per un Pugno di Dollari/A Fistful of Dollars* 1964; *Prima Della Rivoluzione/Before the Revolution* 1964; *Amanti d'Oltretomba* 1965; *I Pugni in Tasca/Fist in His Pocket* 1965; *Il Ritorno di Ringo* 1965; *La Battaglia di Algeri/The Battle of Algiers* 1966; *Buono, il Brutto, il Cattivo, Il/The Good, the Bad and the Ugly* 1966; *I Crudeli* 1966; *Navajo Joe* 1966; *Per qualche dollaro in piu/For a Few Dollars More* 1966; *La Resa dei Conti* 1966; *Uccellacci e Uccellini/The Hawks and the Sparrows* 1966 (m; also sang the credit sequences); *Un Uomo a Meta* 1966; *La Cina e vicina* 1967; *Da Uomo a Uomo/Death Rides a Horse* 1967; *Escalation* 1967; *Faccia a Faccia* 1967; *Arabella* 1967; *Quien Sabe?* 1967 (m.sup); *La Ragazza e il Generale* 1967; *Un Bellissimo Novembre* 1968; *Diabolik* 1968; *Dirty Heroes* 1968; *Fraulein Doktor* 1968; *Galileo* 1968; *Grazie Zia* 1968; *Partner* 1968 (m,song); *Roma Come Chicago* 1968; *Teorema* 1968; *Vergogna, Schifosi!* 1968; *L'Assoluto Naturale* 1969; *C'era una Volta il West/Once Upon a Time in the West* 1969 (m,m.dir); *Le Clan des Siciliens* 1969; *Un Esercito di 5 Uomini* 1969; *Gli Intoccabili* 1969; *Metti, una Sera a Cena* 1969; *Quemada!/Burn* 1969; *Ruba al Prossimo Tuo* 1969; *L'Uccello dalle Piume di Cristallo* 1969; *I Cannibali* 1970; *Hornet's Nest* 1970; *Indagine su un Cittadino al di Sopra di Ogni Sospetto/Investigation of a Citizen Above Suspicion* 1970; *The Mercenary* 1970; *Metello* 1970; *Sacco and Venzetti* 1970; *La Tenda rossa* 1970; *Two Mules For Sister Sara* 1970; *Violent City* 1970; *Addio, Fratello Crudele* 1971; *Anche Se Volessi Lavorare, Che Faccio?* 1971; *La Califfa* 1971; *Le Casse* 1971; *Cat O' Nine Tails* 1971; *Chi l'ha Vista Morire?* 1971; *La Cosa Buffa* 1971; *Il Decamerone* 1971; *Il Giro del Mondo degli "Innamorati" di Peynet* 1971; *In Nome del Padre* 1971; *Una Lucertola con la Pelle di Donna* 1971; *Maddalena* 1971; *N.P. Il Segreto* 1971; *Oceano* 1971; *Quattro Mosche di Velluto Grigio* 1971; *Sans Mobile Apparent/Without Apparent Motive* 1971; *Le Tueur* 1971; *L'Attentat* 1972; *Bluebeard* 1972; *La Classe Operaia Va In Paradise/The Working Class Goes to Heaven* 1972; *D'Amore Si Muore* 1972; *Les Deux Saisons de la Vie* 1972; *Duck, You Sucker!* 1972; *Das Geheimnis der Gruenen Stecknadel* 1972; *Il Maestro e Margherita* 1972; *I Racconti di Canterbury/Canterbury Tales* 1972; *Sbatti Il Mostro In Prima Pagina* 1972 (m,uncred.); *Sonny & Jed* 1972; *La Tarantola dal Ventre Nero* 1972; *Un Uomo da Rispettare* 1972; *La Vita, a Volte e Molto Dura, Vero Provvidenza?* 1972; *Giordano Bruno* 1973; *Massacre in Rome* 1973; *Il Mio nome e Nessuno* 1973 (m,m.dir); *Le Moine* 1973; *La Proprieta' non e piu' un furto* 1973; *Questa Specie d'Amore* 1973; *Le Serpent* 1973; *Il Sorriso del Grande Tentatore* 1973; *Il Fiore Delle Mille e Una Notte* 1974; *L'Invenzione di Morel* 1974; *Libera, Amore Mio* 1974; *Mussolini: Ultimo Atto* 1974; *Le Secret* 1974; *L'Ultimo Uomo di Sara* 1974; *Allonsanfan* 1975; *Attenti al Buffone* 1975; *Blood in the Streets* 1975; *La Divina Creatura* 1975; *La Faille* 1975; *Fatti di Gente Perbene* 1975; *Un Genio, Due Compari, Un Pollo* 1975; *The Human Factor* 1975; *Leonor* 1975; *La Marche Triomphale* 1975; *Matti da slegare* 1975; *Per le Antiche Scale* 1975; *Peur sur la Ville* 1975; *Der Richter und Sein Henker* 1975 (m,m.cond); *Salo o le Centiventi Giornate di Sodoma/Salo—120 Days of Sodom* 1975; *Autostop rosso sangue* 1976; *La Donna Della Domenica* 1976; *Eredita' Ferramonti* 1976; *Rene la Canne* 1976; *Todo Modo* 1976; *L'Arriviste* 1977; *Exorcist II: The Heretic* 1977 (m,m.dir); *Il Gabbiano* 1977; *Holocaust 2000* 1977; *Novecento/1900* 1977; *Orca... Killer Whale* 1977 (m,m.dir,song); *Il Prefetto di Ferro* 1977; *Soleil des Hyenes* 1977; *Gli Ultimi Tre Giorni* 1977; *122 rue de provence* 1978; *L'Anti Cristo* 1978 (m,m.perf); *La Cage aux folles* 1978; *The Chosen* 1978; *Corleone* 1978; *Cosi' come sei* 1978; *Days of Heaven* 1978 (m,m.dir) **(AANBM)**; *Deutschland im Herbst* 1978 (song); *Il Gatto* 1978; *The Rise and Fall of Ivor Dickie* 1978; *Travels With Anita* 1978; *Bloodline* 1979 (m,orch,m.cond); *Buone Notizie* 1979; *I*

Comme Icare 1979; *Il Ladrone* 1979; *Ogro* 1979; *Il Prato* 1979; *Un Sacco Bello* 1979; *A Time to Die* 1979 (add.m); *L'Umanoide* 1979; *When You Comin' Back, Red Ryder?* 1979 (song); *Windows* 1979; *La Banquière* 1980; *La Cage aux folles II* 1980 (m,m.dir); *The Island* 1980 (m,m.dir); *Milano Odia: La Polizia non Puo' Sparare* 1980; *Il Minestrone* 1980; *Salto Nel Vuoto* 1980; *Uomini e No* 1980; *Vacanze in Val Trebbia* 1980; *Bianco Rosso e Verdone* 1981; *Butterfly* 1981; *Il Marchese del Grillo* 1981; *Het Meisje met het rode haar* 1981; *La Notte di San Lorenzo* 1981; *So Fine* 1981; *La Tragedia di un Uomo Ridicolo/The Tragedy of a Ridiculous Man* 1981; *Vera Storia Della Signora Delle Camelie* 1981; *Nana* 1982 (m,m.dir); *El Tesora de las Cuatro Coronas* 1982 (m,m.dir); *The Thing* 1982; *White Dog* 1982; *La Chiave* 1983 (m,m.cond); *Copkiller* 1983; *Le Marginal* 1983; *Porca vacca!* 1983; *Le Ruffian* 1983; *La Trace* 1983; *Bertoldo, Bertoldino e Cacasenno* 1984; *Desiderio* 1984; *Don't Kill God* 1984; *Hundra* 1984; *Kaos* 1984 (m,m.dir); *Once Upon a Time in America* 1984; *Partir Revenir* 1984; *Sahara* 1984 (m,m.dir); *De Schorpioen* 1984; *Segreti Segreti* 1984; *Les Voleurs de la nuit* 1984; *La Cage aux folles III: "Elles" se marient* 1985 (m,m.dir); *Le Due vite di Mattia Pascal/The Two Lives of Mattia Pascal* 1985; *Die Forstenbuben* 1985; *La Gabbia* 1985; *Kommando Leopard* 1985; *The Link* 1985; *La Messa E Finita* 1985; *Il Pentito* 1985; *Red Sonja* 1985; *Il Camorrista* 1986; *Ginger et Fred* 1986; *Good Morning Babylon* 1986 (m,m.dir); *The Mission* 1986 (m,m.dir,orch) **(AANBM)**; *Pourvu que ce soit une fille/Let's Hope It's a Girl* 1986 (m,m.dir); *La Venexiana* 1986; *Les Exploits d'un jeune Don Juan* 1987; *Federico Fellini's Intervista* 1987; *Il Giorno Prima* 1987; *Mosca Addio* 1987; *Gli Occhiali d'Oro* 1987; *Quartiere* 1987; *Rampage* 1987; *La Sposa Era Bellissima* 1987; *Strana la Vita* 1987; *The Untouchables* 1987 (m,m.cond,orch) **(AANBM)**; *I Cammelli* 1988; *Domani Accadra* 1988; *Drole d'endroit pour une rencontre/A Strange Place to Meet* 1988 (song); *Frantic* 1988 (m,m.cond,orch); *Manifesto* 1988 (m,m.dir); *Cinema Paradiso* 1988; *La Soule* 1988; *Strange Life!* 1988; *A Time of Destiny* 1988 (m,m.cond,orch); *Young Einstein* 1988 (song); *L'Appassionata* 1989; *Australia* 1989; *Casualties of War* 1989 (m,m.cond,orch); *La Cintura* 1989; *Disamistade* 1989; *Fat Man and Little Boy* 1989; *O Re* 1989; *Palombella Rossa* 1989; *Tempo di Uccidere* 1989; *Atame!/Tie Me Up, Tie Me Down* 1990; *The Big Man* 1990; *Dimenticare Palermo* 1990; *Hamlet* 1990; *Il Male Oscuro* 1990; *Il Sole anche di notte* 1990 (m,m.cond); *Stanno Tutti Bene* 1990; *State of Grace* 1990 (m,orch,m.cond); *Tracce di una vita amorosa* 1990; *Tre Colonne in Cronaca* 1990; *Le Voce della Luna/Voices of the Moon* 1990 .

Morris, Errol • filmmaker • Born Hewlett, NY, 1948. *Educ.* University of Wisconsin (history); University of California, Berkeley (philosophy). Innovative documentary filmmaker who made two off-beat, critically acclaimed studies (1978's *Gates of Heaven*, about pet cemeteries, and 1981's *Vernon, Florida*, about small-town American eccentrics) before achieving his breakthrough with the feature-length *The Thin Blue Line* (1988). The film was an unsettling investigation into the case of Randall Adams, a Texas man who claimed he had been wrongfully convicted of murder. It mixed deadpan interviews, stylized re-creations of conflicting accounts of the crime and alienating close-ups of documents and objects related to the case, all underpinned by a driving, hypnotic score provided by composer Phillip Glass. *The Thin Blue Line* was influential in securing the ultimate overturning of Adams's conviction. • *Gates of Heaven* 1978 (d,p,sc,ed); *Vernon, Florida* 1981 (d,p); *The Thin Blue Line* 1988 (d,sc).

Morris, Oswald • *aka* Ossie Morris • Director of photography • Born Ruislip, England, November 22, 1915. Leading British cinematographer since 1950 who came to international prominence for his work on John Huston's atmospheric *Moulin Rouge* (1952), the first of their many fruitful collaborations. • *Circle of Danger* 1951 (ph); *Moulin Rouge* 1952 (ph); *The Promoter* 1952 (ph); *Beat the Devil* 1953 (ph); *Beau Brummell* 1954 (ph); *Monsieur Ripois* 1954 (ph); *Moby Dick* 1956 (ph); *A Farewell to Arms* 1957 (ph); *Heaven Knows, Mr. Allison* 1957 (ph); *The Key* 1958 (ph); *The Roots of Heaven* 1958 (ph); *Look Back in Anger* 1959 (ph); *The Entertainer* 1960 (ph); *The Guns of Navarone* 1961 (ph); *Lolita* 1962 (ph); *Satan Never Sleeps* 1962 (ph); *The Ceremony* 1963 (ph); *Of Human Bondage* 1964 (ph); *The Pumpkin Eater* 1964 (ph); *The Battle of the Villa Fiorita* 1965 (ph); *The Hill* 1965 (ph); *Life at the Top* 1965 (ph); *Mister Moses* 1965 (ph); *The Spy Who Came in From the Cold* 1965 (ph); *Stop the World—I Want to Get Off* 1966 (ph); *The Winter's Tale* 1966 (ph); *The Taming of the Shrew* 1967 (ph); *Great Catherine* 1968 (ph); *Oliver!* 1968 (ph) **(AANBPH)**; *Goodbye, Mr. Chips* 1969 (ph); *Fragment of Fear* 1970 (ph); *Scrooge* 1970 (ph); *Fiddler on the Roof* 1971 (ph) **(AABPH)**; *Lady Caroline Lamb* 1972 (ph); *Sleuth* 1972 (ph); *The Mackintosh Man* 1973 (ph); *The Man With the Golden Gun* 1974 (ph); *The Odessa File* 1974 (ph); *The Man Who Would Be King* 1975 (ph); *The Seven Per-Cent Solution* 1976 (ph); *Equus* 1977 (ph); *The Wiz* 1978 (ph) **(AANBPH)**; *Just Tell Me What You Want* 1980 (ph); *The Great Muppet Caper* 1981 (ph); *The Dark Crystal* 1982 (ph); *John Huston* 1988 (a).

Morrissey, Paul • Director; also screenwriter, producer. • Born New York, NY, 1939. *Educ.* Fordham. Underground director of the 1960s and sometime manager of rock group The Velvet Underground who worked with Andy Warhol from 1964 to 1972 as producer, writer or photographer on films such as *Bike Boy* (1967) and *Blue Movie* (1968). Morrissey introduced a degree of coherence and accessibility into the artist's celluloid productions which had previously been lacking. After parting from Warhol, he made three Gothic horror films in Europe in the 1970s before returning to the US to continue his independent directing career. • *Bike Boy* 1967 (ph); *Blue Movie* 1968 (d,p,sc,ph); *Flesh* 1968 (d,sc,ph); *Lonesome Cowboys* 1968 (exec.p); *Trash* 1970 (d,story,ph); *Andy Warhol's Women* 1971 (d,ph); *L'Amour* 1972 (d,p); *Heat* 1972 (d,sc,ph); *Andy Warhol's Frankenstein* 1973 (d,sc); *Blood For Dracula* 1974 (d,sc); *The Hound of the Baskervilles* 1978 (d,sc); *Forty Deuce* 1981 (d); *Madame Wang's* 1981 (d,sc); *Rich and Famous* 1981 (a); *Chambre 666* 1982 (a); *Beethoven's Nephew* 1985 (d,sc); *Mixed Blood* 1985 (d,sc); *Spike of Bensonhurst* 1988 (d,sc); *Resident Alien* 1990 (a); *Superstar* 1990 (a).

Mostel, Zero • Actor; also comedian. • Born Samuel Joel Mostel, Brooklyn, NY, February 28, 1915; died 1977. *Educ.* CCNY (art, English); NYU. Volatile, stage-trained comic actor who made his film debut playing dual roles in *Du Barry Was a Lady* (1943). Mostel's solid build and heavy-lidded eyes made him a convincing heavy, but his promising film career was cut short when he was blacklisted following his testimony before the House Un-American Activities Committe in 1951. His fortunes revived in the early 1960s with his maniacally comic Broadway performances in *A Funny Thing Happened on the Way to the Forum* (1963) and, as Tevye, in *Fiddler on the Roof* (1964). Mostel turned in a landmark screen performance as bamboozling Broadway producer Max Bialystock in Mel Brooks's *The Producers* (1967), making regular film appearances into the late 1970s. Son Josh Mostel is an actor. • *Du Barry Was a Lady* 1943 (a); *Panic in the Streets* 1950 (a); *The Enforcer* 1951 (a); *The Guy Who Came Back* 1951 (a); *The Model and the Marriage Broker* 1951 (a); *Mr. Belvedere Rings the Bell* 1951 (a); *Sirocco* 1951 (a); *A Funny Thing Happened on the Way to the Forum* 1966 (a); *The Producers* 1967 (a); *Great Catherine* 1968 (a); *Monsieur Lecoq* 1968 (a,sc); *The Great Bank Robbery* 1969 (a,song); *The Angel Levine* 1970 (a); *The Hot Rock* 1972 (a); *Rhinoceros* 1972 (a); *Marco* 1973 (a); *Once Upon a Scoundrel*

1973 (a); *Foreplay* 1974 (a); *The Front* 1976 (a); *Hollywood on Trial* 1976 (a); *Journey Into Fear* 1976 (a); *Mastermind* 1976 (a); *Watership Down* 1978 (a); *Best Boy* 1979 (a,prod.assistance).

Mozhukhin, Ivan • *aka* Ivan Mosjoukine, Ivan Mosjukine, Ivan Moskine • Actor • Born Penza, Russia, September 26, 1889; died 1939. Strapping star of the Czarist era who fled Russia in the wake of the Revolution and eventually settled in Paris, where his enigmatic presence made him a popular performer of French silents. One of Mozhukhin's tangential contributions to cinema history is as the subject of the "Kuleshov effect": Kuleshov used one repeated shot of the actor, interspersed with footage of crying babies, plates of food, etc., to demonstrate that the same individual image (Mozhukhin's face) could take on different meanings and emotional charges depending on its filmic context. • *Pikovaya dama/The Queen of Spades* 1916 (a); *Otets Sergey/Father Sergius* 1918 (a); *Le Brasier ardent* 1923 (d); *Feu Mathias Pascal/The Late Mathias Pascal* 1925 (a); *Michel Strogoff* 1926 (a,sc); *Surrender* 1927 (a).

Mueller-Stahl, Armin • Actor • Born Tilsit, East Prussia, December 17, 1920. Stage-trained character actor, with East Berlin's Theater am Schiffbauerdamm from 1952 to 1977, who began appearing in films in 1950. Mueller-Stahl has appeared in several features directed by Rainer Werner Fassbinder and won the Montreal Film Festival best actor prize for his performance in Agnieszka Holland's *Angry Harvest* (1985). He immigrated to the West in 1980 and is best known for his role as a dissembling war criminal in Costa-Gavras's *Music Box* (1989). • *Konigskinder* 1962; *Nackt unter Wolfen* 1963; *Der Dritte* 1972; *Kit und Co-Lockruf des Goldes* 1974; *Jakob der Luegner* 1975; *Die Flucht* 1977; *Lola* 1981; *Der Westen Leuchtet* 1981; *Un Dimanche de Flics* 1982; *Flucht aus Pommern* 1982; *Die Fluegel Der Nacht* 1982; *Veronika Voss* 1982; *Viadukt* 1982; *Glut* 1983; *L'Homme blesse* 1983; *Eine Liebe in Deutschland/A Love in Germany* 1983; *Rita Ritter* 1983; *Tausend Augen* 1984; *Trauma* 1984; *An uns glaubt Gott nicht mehr* 1985; *Der Angriff der Gegenwart auf die ubrige Zeit* 1985; *Bittere Ernte/Angry Harvest* 1985; *Hautnah* 1985; *Die Mitlaufer* 1985; *Redl Ezredes/Colonel Redl* 1985; *Vergesst Mozart/Forget Mozart* 1985; *Der Fall Franza* 1986; *Jokehnen* 1986; *Momo* 1986; *Unser Mann im Dschungel* 1986; *Der Joker/Lethal Obsession* 1987; *Der Gorilla* 1988; *Midnight Cop* 1988; *A Hecc* 1989; *Music Box* 1989; *Schweinegeld, Ein Marchen der Gebruder Nimm* 1989; *Das Spinnennetz* 1989; *Avalon* 1990; *Bronsteins Kinder/Bronstein's Children* 1991.

Mulcahy, Russell • Director • Born Melbourne, Australia, 1953. Made his feature debut with the British-produced *Derek and Clive Get the Horn* (1980), starring Peter Cooke and Dudley Moore, and scored a moderate critical success with the Sean Connery/Christopher Lambert vehicle, *Highlander* (1986). • *Derek and Clive Get the Horn* 1980 (d,ed); *Razorback* 1984 (d); *Highlander* 1986 (d); *Highlander II - the Quickening* 1991 (d).

Müller, Robby • Director of photography • Born Netherlands, April 4, 1940. Leading European cinematographer noted for the haunting color vistas of Wim Wenders's *Paris, Texas* (1984) and the poignant, black-and-white compositions of Jim Jarmusch's *Down By Law* (1986). Müller began his career as an assistant photographer in Holland before moving to Germany, where he shot several Wenders films including *Kings of the Road* (1975) and *The American Friend* (1977). He has remained Jarmusch's cinematographer of choice since 1986 and has also worked with Peter Bogdanovich and Barbet Schroeder. • *Summer in the City* 1970 (ph); *Die Angst des Tormanns bein Elfmeter* 1972 (ph); *Der Scharlachrote Buchstabe* 1972 (ph); *Jonathan* 1973 (ph); *Alice in den Stadten/Alice in the Cities* 1974 (ph); *Falsche Bewegung/Wrong Movement* 1975 (ph); *Im Lauf der Zeit/Kings of the Road* 1975 (ph); *Der Amerikanische Freund/The American Friend* 1977 (ph); *Die Linkshandige Frau/The Left-handed Woman* 1977 (ph); *Mysteries* 1978 (ph); *Opname* 1979 (ph); *Saint Jack* 1979 (ph); *Honeysuckle Rose* 1980 (ph); *They All Laughed* 1981 (ph); *Un Dimanche de Flics* 1982 (ph); *Les Tricheurs* 1983 (a,ph); *Body Rock* 1984 (ph); *Paris, Texas* 1984 (ph); *Repo Man* 1984 (ph); *To Live and Die in L.A.* 1985 (ph); *Down By Law* 1986 (ph); *The Longshot* 1986 (ph); *Barfly* 1987 (ph); *The Believers* 1987 (ph); *Coffee and Cigarettes Part Two (short)* 1988 (ph); *Il Piccolo Diavolo* 1988 (ph); *Aufzeichnungen zu Kleidern und Stadten* 1989 (ph); *Mystery Train* 1989 (ph); *Korczak* 1990 (ph); *Motion and Emotion* 1990 (a); *Jusqu'au bout du monde/Till the End of the World* 1991 (ph).

Mulligan, Robert • Director • Born Bronx, NY, August 23, 1925. *Educ.* Fordham University (radio communications). Former divinity student who worked his way up the ranks of CBS and established himself in the 1950s as a leading TV director, noted for his deft handling of actors and leisurely, unobtrusive style. Mulligan made his feature debut with *Fear Strikes Out* (1956), an absorbing account of the personal problems which led baseball star Jim Piersall (Anthony Perkins) to a nervous breakdown. He again collaborated with *Fear* producer Alan Pakula on several fine films of the 1960s, notably *To Kill A Mockingbird* (1962), for which Gregory Peck earned a best actor Oscar, *Love With the Proper Stranger* (1963) and *Up the Down Staircase* (1967). Since the mid-1970s, Mulligan's ouput has been sporadic and uninspired. • *Fear Strikes Out* 1956 (d); *The Great Impostor* 1960 (d); *The Rat Race* 1960 (d); *Come September* 1961 (d); *The Spiral Road* 1962 (d); *To Kill a Mockingbird* 1962 (d) **(AANBD)**; *Love With the Proper Stranger* 1963 (d); *Baby, the Rain Must Fall* 1965 (d); *Inside Daisy Clover* 1965 (d); *Up the Down Staircase* 1967 (d); *The Stalking Moon* 1968 (d); *The Pursuit of Happiness* 1971 (d); *Summer of '42* 1971 (d); *The Other* 1972 (d,p); *The Nickel Ride* 1975 (d,p); *Bloodbrothers* 1978 (d); *Same Time, Next Year* 1978 (d,p); *Kiss Me Goodbye* 1982 (d,p); *Clara's Heart* 1988 (d).

Münch, Jacob Friedrich • Born Switzerland, November 15, 1942. Influential critic and writer during the 1970s (although not widely known outside his own country) who wrote prolifically about film and other media, attempting to provide a scientific foundation for a phenomenon that was—he eventually discovered—more or less immune to the scientific method. Like countryman Hans Lucas in the 50s, whose work he admired and with whom he shares several intellectual positions, Münch believed profoundly that criticism was more a work of art itself—and an end in itself—than a valid commentary on other works of art. In his major work, *Beobachtungen über das Gefühl des Schönen und Erhabenen in Filmrealität* (1973), he revived the Renaissance theory of *sprezzatura*, life as a work of art. Like his friend François Truffaut, he was immersed as a boy in the alternate reality of film; unlike Truffaut, he eventually decided that "life is more important than film." Since the 70s, he has earned his living as a business manager.

Muni, Paul • Actor • Born Muni Weisenfreund, Lemberg, Austria, September 22, 1895; died 1967. Dynamic actor from the Yiddish stage who earned an Oscar nomination for his 1929 film debut in *The Valiant.* Muni's performance as the volatile mob boss in *Scarface* (1932) lead to a long-term contract with Warner Bros. where he made his mark in a series of critically acclaimed biopics, portraying the likes of Louis Pasteur and Emile Zola. He subsequently divided his time among the stage and screen, making intermittent film appearances until faltering eyesight ended his career in 1959. • *Seven Faces* 1929; *The Valiant* 1929 **(AANBA)**; *I Am a Fugitive From a Chain Gang* 1932 **(AANBA)**; *Scarface* 1932; *The World Changes* 1933; *Bordertown* 1934; *Hi, Nellie!* 1934; *Black Fury* 1935; *Dr. Socrates* 1935; *The Story of Louis Pasteur* 1936 **(AABA)**; *The Good Earth* 1937; *The Life of Emile Zola* 1937 **(AANBA)**; *The Woman I Love* 1937; *Juarez* 1939; *Hudson's Bay* 1940; *Commandos Strike* *at Dawn* 1942; *Stage Door Canteen* 1943; *Counter-Attack* 1945; *A Song to Remember* 1945; *Angel on My Shoulder* 1946; *Imbarco a Mezzanotte* 1952; *The Last Angry Man* 1959 **(AANBA)**.

Munk, Andrzej • Director • Born Cracow, Poland, October 16, 1921; died 1961. *Educ.* Lodz Film School. Began his career making acclaimed documentaries and directed his first feature, *Man on the Track*, in 1956. A pioneer of the Polish New Wave along with director Andrzej Wajda, Munk turned a quizzical, ironic eye on subjects such as military heroism (*Eroica* 1958) and Party careerism (*Bad Luck* 1960). He died in 1961 during the filming of *The Passenger*, which was completed by his friend Witold Lesiewicz and released two years later. • *Man on the Track* 1956 (d,sc); *Eroica* 1958 (d); *Zezowate szczescie/Bad Luck* 1960 (d); *Pasazerka/The Passenger* 1963 (d,sc).

Murch, Walter • Sound designer, editor; also screenwriter, director. • Born New York, NY. *Educ.* USC, Los Angeles (film). Acclaimed figure who has enjoyed a long-term collaboration with filmmakers Francis Ford Coppola and George Lucas. Murch's sound editing was central to the success of *The Conversation* (1974), Coppola's brilliant study of eavesdropping, and he won an Oscar for the aural design of the director's Vietnam epic, *Apocalypse Now* (1979). • *The Rain People* 1969 (sound montage); *Gimme Shelter* 1970 (sound); *THX 1138* 1971 (sc,sound); *American Graffiti* 1973 (sound mixer); *The Conversation* 1974 (ed,sound) **(AANSOUND)**; *The Godfather, Part II* 1974 (sound mixer,sound montage); *Julia* 1977 (ed) **(AANBED)**; *Apocalypse Now* 1979 (sound design,sound montage,sound rerecording) **(AASOUND)**; *The Adventures of Mark Twain* 1985 (special creative consultant); *Return to Oz* 1985 (d,sc); *The Unbearable Lightness of Being* 1988 (ed); *Call From Space* 1989 (ed); *Ghost* 1990 (ed,sound rerecording); *The Godfather III* 1990 (ed).

Murnau, F. W. • Director; also actor. • Born Friedrich Wilhelm Plumpe, Bielefeld, Westphalia, December 28, 1888; died March 11, 1931, Southern California. *Educ.* University of Heidelberg (literature, art history). F.W. Murnau's brief career remains an emblem of the darkly romantic Hollywood of the 1920s. Between 1919 and his death in 1931, he completed 22 films. Arriving in Hollywood from Germany in 1926 with an "enviable reputation" based on *Der Letzte Mann/The Last Laugh* (1924) and *Faust* (1926), Murnau immediately began to run afoul of the developing studio system as he started a five-picture contract with Fox Film. In February 1929, as he was completing the third film (*City Girl*), Fox severed the relationship. Although *Sunrise* (1927) had been a great success, *Four Devils* (1928) had failed to match it. With the coming of sound, and Murnau's contract scale increasing, Fox became anxious about the work of this European artist and began to interfere with his projects.

Like so many Europeans in Hollywood at the time, he had come to the new world to harness the enticing technical apparatus of the Hollywood studio system, and, he declared, to make "finer films with an international appeal." But more than most of his compatriots, Murnau failed at the politics of Hollywood. His untimely accidental death marked the end of an era, completing the myth of the romantic artist destroyed by the "well-meaning cruelty of a mighty industry," as one critic described it.

Murnau had first attracted attention after WWI as an exponent of the German expressionist style which evoked the instability, disorientation and despair of the period. His films deal with universal themes of human frailty, decline, self-conflict and redemption in a tragic world. His characters struggle to find psychological peace and self-revelation, external love and commitment. Like much of the best in silent film, it is a Victorian world.

Since only a few of Murnau's films made in 1919 and 1920 exist, it is difficult to establish a thematic framework before *Nosferatu* (1922). Lotte Eisner's description of Murnau's first film, *Der Knabe In Blau* (1919), indicates that the protagonist's obsessive quest for a cursed family jewel leads to tragedy, meliorated finally by a woman's love. From the melodramatic plot twists of *Der Gang in die Nacht* (1920) emerges a failed quest to capture a love.

In *Nosferatu* (1922), Jonathan's quest to contain external evil fails; he realizes that the evil within himself is the cause. Nora, his wife, must sacrifice herself to redeem mankind. In *The Last Laugh* a proud doorman is stripped of status and self-esteem, reduced to a lavatory attendant. Murnau transforms this simple drama into a a psychological quest for self-integrity. The quest of *Faust*, on the other hand, is for world redemption. He must fall from grace and experience his own internal demon before realizing a potential for love and sacrifice.

In *Sunrise* Murnau builds a "city from nowhere," a universal setting. The film abounds with dramatic oppositions: family versus illicit love; life versus death; urban civilization versus nature. The husband in *Sunrise* finds internal salvation by returning to the commitment of a relationship and the sanctuary of marriage.

For Murnau, the natural world is as passionate and volatile as his characters. In *Nosferatu*, darkness struggles with light. In *Sunrise*, the violent storm leads to resolution. In *City Girl*, a hailstorm almost destroys the family but also acts as a catalyst for self-realization.

If natural elements are characters for Murnau, so is the camera. Few other filmmakers of the 1920s revel so in *mise-en-scène*. The opening title of *Faust* announces a "poem in pictures." (Murnau generally disdained intertitles, claiming, "I'd do away with all film titles. They are really unnecessary if the continuity runs smoothly.") In *The Last Laugh*, *City Girl* and *Sunrise* the characters are constricted within a cramped frame which conveys the harsh social reality of their lives. The continuously gliding camera of *The Last Laugh* captures the silent dignity, joyous abandon, and—finally—internal torment of the doorman.

Murnau's camera finds its most eloquent expression in *Sunrise*. Camera movement entraps characters, intensifying conflict. The great tracking shot on the tram, as the husband and wife enter the city, remains a subject of study for student filmmakers even today. RCB • *Der Knabe in Blau/The Blue Boy* 1919 (d); *Satanas* 1919 (d); *Der Bucklige und die Tänzerin/The Hunchback and the Dancer* 1920 (d); *Der Gang in die nacht/Journey into the Night* 1920 (d); *Der Januskopf/The Janus Head* 1920 (d); *Sehnsucht/Longing* 1920 (d); *Marizza, gennant die Schmugglermadonna/Marizza, Called the Smugglers' Madonna* 1921 (d); *Schloss Vogelöd/The Haunted Castle* 1921 (d); *Der Brennende Acker/The Burning Path* 1922 (d); *Nosferatu, eine Symphonie des Grauens/Nosferatu the Vampire* 1922 (d); *Phantom* 1922 (d); *Die Austreibung—die Macht der zweiten Frau/The Expulsion* 1923 (d); *Die Finanzen des Grossherzogs/The Finances of the Grand Duke* 1923 (d); *Der Letzte Mann/The Last Laugh* 1924 (d); *Tartüff* 1925 (d); *Faust* 1926 (d); *Sunrise* 1927 (d); *Four Devils* 1928 (d); *City Girl* 1930 (d,p); *Tabu* 1931 (d,story).

Murphy, Audie • Actor • Born Texas, June 20, 1924; died 1971. Parlayed his experiences as the most decorated American soldier of WWII into a less glorious film career, beginining in 1948. The majority of Murphy's roles were as wholesome youths, on the battlefield or out on the range, in low-budget productions. He starred in John Huston's adaptation of Stephen Crane's Civil War novel, *The Red Badge of Courage* (1951), and in the film version of his autobiography, *To Hell and Back* (1955). • *Bad Boy* 1948 (a); *Beyond Glory* 1948 (a); *Texas, Brooklyn and Heaven* 1948 (a); *Kansas Raiders* 1950 (a); *The Kid From Texas* 1950 (a); *Sierra* 1950 (a); *The Cimarron Kid* 1951 (a); *The Red Badge of Courage* 1951 (a); *Duel at Silver Creek* 1952 (a); *Column South* 1953 (a); *Gunsmoke* 1953 (a); *Tumbleweed* 1953 (a); *Destry* 1954 (a); *Drums Across the River* 1954 (a); *Ride Clear of Diablo* 1954 (a); *To Hell* *and Back* 1955 (a,from book); *World in My Corner* 1955 (a); *Walk the Proud Land* 1956 (a); *The Guns of Fort Petticoat* 1957 (a); *Joe Butterfly* 1957 (a); *Night Passage* 1957 (a); *The Gun Runners* 1958 (a); *The Quiet American* 1958 (a); *Ride a Crooked Trail* 1958 (a); *Cast a Long Shadow* 1959 (a); *No Name on the Bullet* 1959 (a); *The Wild and the Innocent* 1959 (a,song); *Hell Bent For Leather* 1960 (a); *Seven Ways From Sundown* 1960 (a); *The Unforgiven* 1960 (a); *Battle at Bloody Beach* 1961 (a); *Posse From Hell* 1961 (a); *Six Black Horses* 1962 (a); *Showdown* 1963 (a); *Apache Rifles* 1964 (a); *Bullet For a Badman* 1964 (a); *Gunfight at Comanche Creek* 1964 (a); *The Quick Gun* 1964 (a); *Arizona Raiders* 1965 (a); *Gunpoint* 1966 (a); *Texas Kid* 1966 (a); *Forty Guns to Apache Pass* 1967 (a); *A Time For Dying* 1971 (a,p).

Murphy, Eddie • Actor, comedian; also producer, director, screenwriter. • Born Hempstead, NY, April 3, 1961. Leading black comedy star who, at the age of 19, had become a cornerstone of the popular "Saturday Night Live" TV show. Murphy made his feature debut opposite Nick Nolte in *48 Hrs.* (1982), a huge commercial success which established him as a highly bankable Hollywood property. He has colorfully one-lined his way through comedy features (*Trading Places* 1983, *Beverly Hills Cop* 1984) as well as a successful film version of a live stand-up performance, *Eddie Murphy Raw* (1987). Murphy made a less-than-auspicious directorial debut with the violent, profanity-riddled *Harlem Nights* (1989). • *48 Hrs.* 1982 (a); *Trading Places* 1983 (a); *Best Defense* 1984 (a); *Beverly Hills Cop* 1984 (a); *The Golden Child* 1986 (a); *Beverly Hills Cop II* 1987 (a,story); *Eddie Murphy Raw* 1987 (a,exec.p,sc,sketches,song); *Hollywood Shuffle* 1987 (a); *Coming to America* 1988 (a,song); *Harlem Nights* 1989 (a,d,exec.p,sc); *Another 48 Hrs.* 1990 (a).

Murphy, Fred • American director of photography • Co-cinematographer (with Henri Alekan) of Wim Wenders's *The State of Things* (1982), also noted for his work on John Huston's elegant swan song, *The Dead* (1987), and Paul Mazursky's *Enemies, A Love Story* (1989). • *Not a Pretty Picture* 1975 (ph); *Local Color* 1977 (ph); *Girlfriends* 1978 (ph); *The Scenic Route* 1978 (ph); *Imposters* 1979 (ph); *Heartland* 1980 (ph); *Tell Me a Riddle* 1980 (ph); *Martha Clarke, Light and Dark* 1981 (ph); *Q* 1982 (ph); *Der Stand der Dinge/The State of Things* 1982 (ph); *Eddie and the Cruisers* 1983 (ph); *Touched* 1983 (ph); *Death of an Angel* 1985 (ph); *Key Exchange* 1985 (ph); *Hoosiers* 1986 (ph); *The Trip to Bountiful* 1986 (ph); *Best Seller* 1987 (ph); *Cross My Heart* 1987 (Panaglide op); *The Dead* 1987 (ph); *Five Corners* 1987 (ph); *Three O'Clock High* 1987 (Steadicam op); *Fresh Horses* 1988 (ph); *Full Moon in Blue Water* 1988 (ph); *Dead-Bang* 1989 (Steadicam op); *Enemies, A Love Story* 1989 (ph); *Night Games* 1989 (ph); *Funny About Love* 1990 (ph); *Scenes From a Mall* 1991 (ph).

Murphy, Michael • Actor • Born Los Angeles, CA, May 5, 1938. *Educ.* University of Arizona; UCLA. High school teacher turned character actor who made the first of several appearances in Robert Altman movies with *That Cold Day in the Park* (1969). Murphy specializes in playing angst-ridden urban types and is probably best known for his role as Erica Benton's (Jill Clayburgh) cheating husband in Paul Mazursky's *An Unmarried Woman* (1978). • *Double Trouble* 1967; *Countdown* 1968; *The Legend of Lylah Clare* 1968; *The Arrangement* 1969; *That Cold Day in the Park* 1969; *Brewster McCloud* 1970; *Count Yorga, Vampire* 1970; *M*A*S*H* 1970; *McCabe & Mrs. Miller* 1971; *What's Up, Doc?* 1972; *The Thief Who Came to Dinner* 1973; *Gettin' Back* 1974; *Phase IV* 1974; *Nashville* 1975; *The Front* 1976; *Shenanigans* 1977; *The Class of Miss MacMichael* 1978; *An Unmarried Woman* 1978; *Manhattan* 1979; *Dead Kids* 1981; *Talk to Me* 1982; *The Year of Living Dangerously* 1982; *Cloak and Dagger* 1984; *Mesmerized* 1986; *Salvador* 1986; *Hot Money* 1989; *Shocker* 1989.

Murray, Bill • Actor, comedian; also screenwriter. • Born Chicago, IL, September 21, 1950. *Educ.* Regis College. Former member, with his brother Brian Doyle-Murray, of Chicago's Second City improvisational troupe. Murray first gained national prominence for the gallery of characters he portrayed on TV's "Saturday Night Live" from 1977 to 1980. He has turned in some effective film performances, particularly opposite Dustin Hoffman in *Tootsie* (1982) and in the highly successful *Ghostbusters* (1984), directed by frequent Murray collaborator, Ivan Reitman. Murray's 1990 directorial debut, *Quick Change*, met with a mixed critical reception. • *La Honte de la jungle* 1975; *The Dogs* 1978; *A Bird for all Seasons* 1979; *First Love* 1979; *Meatballs* 1979; *Mr. Mike's Mondo Video* 1979; *Caddyshack* 1980; *Where the Buffalo Roam* 1980; *Loose Shoes* 1981; *Stripes* 1981; *Nothing Lasts Forever* 1982; *Tootsie* 1982; *Ghostbusters* 1984; *The Razor's Edge* 1984 (a,sc); *Little Shop of Horrors* 1986; *Scrooged* 1988; *Ghostbusters II* 1989; *Quick Change* 1990 (a,d,p); *What About Bob?* 1991.

Muti, Ornella • Actress • Born Francesca Rivelli, Italy, 1955. Prolific performer, in films since the age of 15. Muti's career has run the gamut from low-budget Italian erotica to glossy US TV movies and she has played important parts in several prestigious European productions, including Volker Schlondorff's *Swann in Love* (1982) and Francesco Rosi's *Chronicle of a DeathForetold* (1987). Combining sophisticated sensuality with an innocent, child-like quality, Muti was particularly effective in two of Marco Ferreri's psychosexual onslaughts, *The Last Woman* (1976) and *The Future Is Woman* (1984). • *La Moglie piu Bella/Most Beautiful Wife* 1970; *La Casa de las Palomas/The House of the Doves* 1971; *Le Monache di Sant'Archangelo/The Nuns of Sant'Archangelo* 1972; *Paolo Il Caldo/Sensual Man* 1973; *Appassionata* 1974; *Italian Graffiti* 1974; *Romanzo Popolare/Come Home and Meet My Wife* 1974; *Leonor* 1975; *La Dernière Femme/L'Ultima Donna*; *The Last Woman* 1976; *I Nuovi Mostri*; *Viva Italia* 1977; *Mort d'un pourri/Death of a Corrupt Man* 1977; *La Stanza del Vescovo/The Bishop's Bedroom* 1977; *Primo Amore/First Love* 1978; *Eutanasia di un amore/Break Up* 1978; *Ritratto di Borghesia in Nero/Nest of Vipers* 1978; *Flash Gordon* 1980; *Il Bisbetico Domato* 1980; *Love & Money* 1980; *Storie di Ordinaria Follia/Tales of Ordinary Madness* 1981; *La Vita e bella* 1982; *Bonnie e Clyde all'italiana/Bonnie and Clyde—Italian Style* 1983; *Un Povero Ricco/A Poor Rich Man* 1983; *La Ragazza di Trieste/The Girl From Trieste* 1983; *Un Amour de Swann/Swann in Love* 1984; *Il Futuro e Donna/The Future Is Woman* 1984; *Tutta Colpa del Paradiso/Blame It on Paradise* 1985; *Grandi Magazzini/Department Store* 1985; *Stregati/Bewitched* 1986; *Cronaca di una morte annunciata/Chronicle of a Death Foretold* 1987; *Io e Mia Sorella/Me and My Sister* 1987; *Codice Privato* 1988; *La Femme de mes amours*; *Il Frutto del Passero*; *L'Envol du moineau* 1988; *O Re/The King of Naples* 1989; *Wait Until Spring, Bandini* 1989; *Il Viaggio di Capitan Fracassa* 1990; *Stasera a Casa di Alice* 1991.

Muybridge, Eadweard James • Director of photography, inventor • Born Edward James Muggeridge, Kingston-on-Thames, England, April 4, 1830; died 1904. Pioneering figure whose sequential photographs of a galloping horse formed an important bridge between still photography and motion pictures, strongly influencing the subsequent innovations of Thomas Edison. Encouraged by California Governor Leland Stanford, Muybridge began his photographic studies of animal movement in 1872. He arranged 24 cameras along a race track so that each one was successively activated by a galloping horse as it passed the corresponding trip wires. Muybridge continued to refine his techniques and toured the U.S. and abroad, projecting his image sequences with a device he dubbed the *Zoopraxiscope*, a forerunner of the movie projector.

Myers, Stanley • American composer • Noted composer for over 60 British and American films who scored his first movie in 1966. Among Myers's more notable credits are Jerzy Skolimoskwi's *Moonlighting* (1982) and Stephen Frears's *Prick Up Your Ears* (1987). • *Kaleidoscope* 1966 (m,m.cond); *Ulysses* 1967 (m); *The Night of the Following Day* 1968 (m,song); *No Way to Treat a Lady* 1968 (m); *Otley* 1968 (m,m.dir,song); *Age of Consent* 1969 (m); *Two Gentlemen Sharing* 1969 (m); *The Raging Moon* 1970 (m,m); *A Severed Head* 1970 (m); *Take a Girl Like You* 1970 (m); *Tropic of Cancer* 1970 (m,m.dir); *The Walking Stick* 1970 (m); *Tam Lin* 1971 (m,m.dir); *King, Queen, Knave* 1972 (m); *Sitting Target* 1972 (m); *X Y & Zee* 1972 (m); *The Blockhouse* 1973 (m); *The Apprenticeship of Duddy Kravitz* 1974 (m); *Caravan to Vaccares* 1974 (m); *Little Malcolm and His Struggle Against the Eunuchs* 1974 (m); *Conduct Unbecoming* 1975 (m); *House of Mortal Sin* 1975 (m,m.dir); *The Wilby Conspiracy* 1975 (m,song); *Der Fangschuss* 1976 (m); *A Portrait of the Artist As a Young Man* 1977 (m,m.dir); *The Class of Miss MacMichael* 1978 (m); *The Comeback* 1978 (m); *The Deer Hunter* 1978 (m); *The Greek Tycoon* 1978 (m,orch); *Absolution* 1979 (m,m.dir); *The Secret Policeman's Ball* 1979 (m); *Yesterday's Hero* 1979 (m.dir); *Watcher in the Woods* 1980 (m,m.dir); *Lady Chatterley's Lover* 1981 (m); *The Incubus* 1982 (m,m.dir); *Moonlighting* 1982 (m); *Beyond the Limit* 1983 (m); *Eureka* 1983 (m,m.cond); *Blind Date* 1984 (m,m.dir); *The Next One* 1984 (m); *Success Is the Best Revenge* 1984 (m); *The Chain* 1985 (m,song); *Dreamchild* 1985 (m); *Insignificance* 1985 (m,song); *The Lightship* 1985 (m); *My Beautiful Laundrette* 1985 (m.perf); *Castaway* 1986 (m); *New World* 1986 (m); *The Second Victory* 1986 (m); *Prick Up Your Ears* 1987 (m); *Sammy and Rosie Get Laid* 1987 (m); *Track 29* 1987 (m); *The Wind* 1987 (m); *Wish You Were Here* 1987 (m,m); *The Zero Boys* 1987 (m); *The Boost* 1988 (m,orch); *The Nature of the Beast* 1988 (m); *Paperhouse* 1988 (m); *Stars and Bars* 1988 (m); *Taffin* 1988 (m); *Ladder of Swords* 1989 (m); *Scenes From the Class Struggle in Beverly Hills* 1989 (m); *Torrents of Spring* 1989 (m); *The Witches* 1990 (m).

Nair, Mira • Director; also producer. • Born Bhubaneswar, Orissa, India, 1957. *Educ.* Delhi University (sociology); Harvard. Nair has made four nonfiction films examining aspects of Indian life and won a best documentary prize at the American Film Festival for *India Cabaret* (1985), a controversial portrait of strippers in a Bombay nightclub. Her highly acclaimed first feature, *Salaam Bombay!* (1988), was a riveting and uncompromising tale of urban street life in the tradition of Buñuel's *Los Olvidados* and Hector Babenco's *Pixote*. *Salaam Bombay!* featured fine performances from non-professional child actors and won both the Camera D'Or, for best first feature, and the Prix du Publique for most popular entry at Cannes. • *Jama Masjid Street Journal* 1979 (d); *So Far From India* 1982 (d); *India Cabaret* 1985 (d); *Children of a Desired Sex* 1987 (d); *Salaam Bombay!* 1987 (d,p,story); *Mississippi Masala* 1991 (d,p,sc,story).

Nakadai, Tatsuya • Actor • Born Tokyo, 1932. Lean, wiry leading man who began his career in the 1950s and established himself in the films of director Masaki Kobayashi, notably as the hero of Kobayashi's great trilogy, *The Human Condition* (1959-61). Nakadai has also appeared in films by Mizoguchi, Ozu and Kurosawa; he is probably best known to Western audiences as Toshiro Mifune's vain, gun-toting nemesis in *Yojimbo* (1961) and as the Lear character in *Ran* (1985). • *Enjo* 1959; *Ningen no joken/The Human Condition I/No Greater Love* 1959; *Ningen no joken II/The Human Condition II/Road to Eternity* 1959; *Aoi vaju* 1960; *Ningen no joken III/The Human Condition III/A Soldier's Prayer* 1961; *Yojimbo* 1961; *Harakiri* 1962; *Tsubaki Sanjuro* 1962; *Tengoku to Jigoku* 1963; *Kwaidan* 1964; *Jiouchi* 1967; *Oggi a Me... Domani a Te!* 1968; *Inochi Bonifuro* 1971; *The Wolves* 1972; *Belladonna* 1973; *The Human Revolution* 1973; *Asayake No Uta* 1974; *Battle Cry* 1978; *Daughters, Wives and a Mother* 1978; *Jo-bachi* 1978; *Kagemusha* 1980; *Bosatsu, Shimoyama Jiken* 1982; *Onimasa* 1982; *Kiryuin Hanako No Shogai* 1983; *Tohno Monogatari* 1983; *A.K.* 1985; *Ran* 1985; *Shokutaku No Nai Ie* 1985; *Hachi-Ko* 1988; *226* 1989; *Return to the River Kwai* 1989.

Napier, Charles • *aka* Chuck Napier • American actor • Character player, often in tough-guy roles, who began his screen career in a series of Russ Meyer exploitation movies. Napier has appeared in several films directed by Jonathan Demme, but is probably best known as Sylvester Stallone's bureaucratic nemesis in *Rambo: First Blood Part II* (1985). • *Cherry, Harry & Raquel* 1969 (a); *Beyond the Valley of the Dolls* 1970 (a); *Love and Kisses* 1970 (a); *Super Vixens* 1974 (a); *Citizens Band* 1977 (a); *Thunder and Lightning* 1977 (a); *Last Embrace* 1979 (a); *The Blues Brothers* 1980 (a); *Melvin and Howard* 1980 (a); *Wacko* 1983 (a); *Swing Shift* 1984 (a); *The Night Stalker* 1985 (a); *Rambo: First Blood Part II* 1985 (a); *Body Count* 1986 (a); *Something Wild* 1986 (a,songs); *Instant Justice* 1987 (a); *Kidnapped* 1987 (a); *Deep Space* 1988 (a); *Married to the Mob* 1988 (a); *Hit List* 1989 (a); *One Man Force* 1989 (a); *Ernest Goes to Jail* 1990 (a); *Future Zone* 1990 (a); *The Grifters* 1990 (a); *Miami Blues* 1990 (a); *The Silence of the Lambs* 1991 (a).

Naughton, David • Actor • Born Hartford, CT, February 13, 1951. *Educ.* University of Pennsylvania; LAMDA, London. TV, stage and film performer best known for his lead role in *An American Werewolf in London* (1981). Brother of actor James Naughton. • *Meatballs* 1979 (song); *Separate Ways* 1979 (a); *Midnight Madness* 1980 (a); *An American Werewolf in London* 1981 (a); *Hot Dog... The Movie* 1984 (a); *Not For Publication* 1984 (a); *The Boy in Blue* 1986 (a); *Separate Vacations* 1986 (a); *Kidnapped* 1987 (a); *Ti Presento un'Amica* 1988 (a); *Overexposed* 1990 (a); *Sleeping Car* 1990 (a).

Naughton, James • Actor • Born Middletown, CT, December 6, 1945. *Educ.* Brown University; Yale School of Drama. Dependable, stage-trained character player who made his Broadway debut in *Long Day's Journey into Night* in 1971 and his first screen appearance, in *The Paper Chase*, two years later. Brother of actor David Naughton. • *The Paper Chase* 1973; *Second Wind* 1975; *A Stranger Is Watching* 1981; *Stephen King's Cat's Eye* 1985; *The Glass Menagerie* 1987; *The Good Mother* 1988.

Nava, Gregory • Director; also producer, screenwriter, director of photography. • Born San Diego, CA, April 10, 1949. *Educ.* UCLA (film). Nava won critical acclaim for his first two features, both produced on minimal budgets and both co-written by his wife, filmmaker Anna Thomas: *The Confessions of Amans* (1976), a medieval drama, won the best first feature award at the Chicago International Film Festival; and *El*

Norte (1983), a gripping account of Guatemalan émigrés struggling to survive in Southern California, earned an Oscar nomination for best screenplay. He fared less happily with his first attempt at big-budget Hollywood filmmaking, the overblown *A Time of Destiny* (1988). • *The Confessions of Amans* 1976 (d,p,sc,ph); *The Haunting of M* 1979 (assoc.p,ph); *El Norte* 1983 (d,sc,story,add.ph—USA) **(AANBSC)**; *A Time of Destiny* 1988 (d,sc).

Nazimova, Alla • *aka* Nazimova • Actress; also producer. • Born Yalta, Crimea, Russia, June 4, 1879; died 1945. *Educ.* St. Petersburg Conservatory (music). Enigmatic Russian star of the silent era who emigrated to the US in 1905. Nazimova became a major Broadway and Hollywood star, producing some of her own films and often being directed by husband Charles Bryant. She appeared in some character roles in the 1940s. • *War Brides* 1916 (a); *Eye For Eye* 1918 (a,p); *Revelation* 1918 (a); *Toys of Fate* 1918 (a); *The Brat* 1919 (a); *Out of the Fog* 1919 (a); *The Red Lantern* 1919 (a,p); *Billions* 1920 (a); *The Heart of a Child* 1920 (a); *Madame Peacock* 1920 (a,sc); *Stronger Than Death* 1920 (a); *Camille* 1921 (a,p); *A Doll's House* 1922 (a); *Salome* 1923 (a,p); *Madonna of the Streets* 1924 (a); *My Son* 1925 (a); *The Redeeming Sin* 1925 (a); *Escape* 1940 (a); *Blood and Sand* 1941 (a); *The Bridge of San Luis Rey* 1944 (a); *In Our Time* 1944 (a); *Since You Went Away* 1944 (a).

Neagle, Dame Anna • *aka* Marjorie Robertson • Actress; also producer. • Born Florence Marjorie Robertson, Forest Gate, England, October 20, 1904; died June 3, 1986, Surrey, England. Ballerina who was molded into one of Britain's leading screen heroines of the 1930s by producer-director Herbert Wilcox, whom she married in 1943. Neagle enjoyed a measure of success in Hollywood during the 1940s. • *Victoria the Great* 1937 (a); *Nurse Edith Cavell* 1939 (a); *Irene* 1940 (a); *No, No, Nanette* 1940 (a); *Sunny* 1941 (a); *Forever and a Day* 1943 (a); *Odette* 1950 (a); *Four Against Fate* 1952 (a); *Let's Make Up* 1954 (a); *My Teenage Daughter* 1956 (a); *Dangerous Youth* 1957 (p).

Neal, Patricia • Actress • Born Packard, KY, January 20, 1926. *Educ.* Northwestern University (drama). Talented, stage-trained actress (*Another Part of the Forest*) who gave a memorable performance opposite Gary Cooper in King Vidor's adaptation of Ayn Rand's *The Fountainhead* (1949). (Neal's affair with the then-married Cooper generated unrelenting publicity and caused her a nervous breakdown.) In 1953 she married writer Roald Dahl, returning to the screen in 1957 in Elia Kazan's acid portrait of political demagoguery, *A Face in the Crowd.* Neal's career was interrupted by a series of strokes in the mid-1960s; her comeback appearance in *The Subject was Roses* (1968) earned her an Oscar nomination, but subsequent appearances have been intermittent. Her physical recovery was deftly handled in the 1981 TV movie *The Patricia Neal Story,* in which Neal was expertly played by Glenda Jackson. • *The Fountainhead* 1949; *The Hasty Heart* 1949; *It's a Great Feeling* 1949; *John Loves Mary* 1949; *The Breaking Point* 1950; *Bright Leaf* 1950; *Three Secrets* 1950; *The Day the Earth Stood Still* 1951; *Operation Pacific* 1951; *Raton Pass* 1951; *Weekend With Father* 1951; *Diplomatic Courier* 1952; *Something For the Birds* 1952; *Washington Story* 1952; *A Face in the Crowd* 1957; *Breakfast at Tiffany's* 1961; *Hud* 1963 **(AABA)**; *Psyche '59* 1964; *In Harm's Way* 1965; *The Subject Was Roses* 1968 **(AANBA)**; *The Night Digger* 1971; *Baxter* 1972; *Happy Mother's Day... Love, George* 1973; *Widows' Nest* 1977; *The Passage* 1979; *Ghost Story* 1981.

Neame, Ronald • Director; also director of photography, producer. • Born London, 1911. Began his career as an assistant cameraman in the late 1920s and graduated to director of photography in 1934. Neame shot a number of prestigious British productions over the next decade, including *Pygmalion* (1938) and *Blithe Spirit* (1945). He produced three films for David Lean and himself made the transition to directing in 1947, most successfully with *The Prime of Miss Jean Brodie* (1969). • *Pygmalion* 1938 (ph); *In Which We Serve* 1942 (ph); *One of Our Aircraft Is Missing* 1942 (ph); *This Happy Breed* 1944 (adapt,ph); *Blithe Spirit* 1945 (adapt,ph); *Brief Encounter* 1945 (prod.man); *Great Expectations* 1946 (p,sc); *Take My Life* 1947 (d); *Oliver Twist* 1948 (p); *The Golden Salamander* 1949 (d); *The Promoter* 1952 (d,p); *The Man With a Million* 1953 (d); *The Man Who Never Was* 1955 (d); *The Seventh Sin* 1957 (d); *Windom's Way* 1957 (d); *The Horse's Mouth* 1958 (d); *Tunes of Glory* 1960 (d); *Escape From Zahrain* 1962 (d,p); *I Could Go on Singing* 1963 (d); *The Chalk Garden* 1964 (d); *Mister Moses* 1965 (d); *Gambit* 1966 (d); *A Man Could Get Killed* 1966 (d); *The Prime of Miss Jean Brodie* 1969 (d); *Scrooge* 1970 (d); *The Poseidon Adventure* 1972 (d); *The Odessa File* 1974 (d); *Meteor* 1979 (d); *Hopscotch* 1980 (d); *First Monday in October* 1981 (d); *Foreign Body* 1986 (d).

Needham, Hal • Director; also stunt coordinator • Born Memphis, TN, March 6, 1937. Former stuntperson who parlayed his talent for organized mayhem into a career as an action-film director. Needham has engineered a number of Burt Reynolds vehicles, making his directorial debut with the popular *Smokey and the Bandit* (1977). • *McLintock!* 1963 (a); *The Ballad of Josie* 1967 (stunt coordinator); *Bandolero!* 1968 (stunt coordinator); *One More Train to Rob* 1971 (a); *The Culpepper Cattle Co.* 1972 (a,stunt coordinator); *The Longest Yard* 1974 (2u d); *Three the Hard Way* 1974 (stunt coordinator); *W. W. and the Dixie Dancekings* 1974 (a,stunt coordinator); *French Connection II* 1975 (stunt coordinator); *Peeper* 1975 (stunt coordinator); *Take a Hard Ride* 1975 (2u d); *Gator* 1976 (2u d); *Jackson County Jail* 1976 (a); *Nickelodeon* 1976 (stunt coordinator,stunts); *Semi-Tough* 1977 (stunt coordinator); *Smokey and the Bandit* 1977 (d,story); *The End* 1978 (stunt coordinator); *Foul Play* 1978 (a,stunts); *Hooper* 1978 (d); *The Villain* 1979 (d); *The Cannonball Run* 1980 (d); *Smokey and the Bandit II* 1980 (d,from characters); *Megaforce* 1982 (d,sc); *Cannonball Run II* 1983 (d,sc); *Stroker Ace* 1983 (d,sc); *Southern Voices, American Dreams* 1985 (a); *RAD* 1986 (d); *Body Slam* 1987 (d).

Neeson, Liam • Actor • Born Ballymena, Northern Ireland, 1953. *Educ.* Lyric Players' Theatre, Belfast; Abbey Theatre, Dublin. Ruggedly handsome Irish actor who made his feature film debut in John Boorman's *Excalibur* (1981) after the director had spotted him onstage in a Dublin production of *Of Mice and Men.* Neeson played a pompous director of low-rent horror movies in Clint Eastwood's *The Dead Pool* (1988), Diane Keaton's lover in *The Good Mother* (1988) and the title character of Sam Raimi's first mainstream venture, *Darkman* (1990). • *Excalibur* 1981; *The Bounty* 1984; *The Innocent* 1984; *Lamb* 1985; *Duet For One* 1986; *The Mission* 1986; *A Prayer For the Dying* 1987; *Suspect* 1987; *The Dead Pool* 1988; *The Good Mother* 1988; *High Spirits* 1988; *Satisfaction* 1988; *Next of Kin* 1989; *The Big Man* 1990; *Darkman* 1990.

Negoda, Natalia • Actress • Born Russia, 1964. *Educ.* Moscow Art Theater Institute (drama, voice, dance). Became an overnight *cause célèbre* in the Soviet Union for her role—which featured an explicit sex scene—in Vasily Pichul's *Little Vera* (1988). The film excited considerable controversy for its uncompromisingly grim portrait of contemporary life in a small Ukrainian town. • *Zavtra Bila Voina* 1987; *Malenkaya Vera/Little Vera* 1988; *V Gorode Sochi Temnye Nochi* 1990.

Negri, Pola • Actress • Born Barbara Appolonia Chalupiec, Janowa, Prussia (now Poland), December 31, 1894; died August 1, 1987, San Antonio, TX. *Educ.* Imperial Ballet School, Russia; Imperial Academy of Dramatic Arts, Warsaw. Leading German stage actress whose appearances in the early films of Ernst Lubitsch attracted the attention of Hollywood, where she moved in 1923. Negri lent her exotic charms to a number of films until the advent of sound exposed her thick accent and effectively ended her colorful career. (She had enjoyed a much-publicized affair with Valentino and a bitter feud with Gloria Swanson.) Negri returned to Germany, although she made a second tour of Hollywood in the 1940s and landed occasional character parts through the 1960s. • *Die Augen der Mummie Ma/The Eyes of the Mummy* 1918; *Carmen* 1918; *Madame Du Barry/Passion* 1919; *Sumurun* 1920; *Die Bergkatze* 1921; *Vendetta* 1921; *Die Flamme* 1922; *Bella Donna* 1923; *The Cheat* 1923; *Hollywood* 1923; *The Spanish Dancer* 1923; *Lily of the Dust* 1924; *Men* 1924; *Shadows of Paris* 1924; *The Charmer* 1925; *East of Suez* 1925; *Flower of Night* 1925; *A Woman of the World* 1925; *The Crown of Lies* 1926; *Good and Naughty* 1926; *Barbed Wire* 1927; *Hotel Imperial* 1927; *The Woman on Trial* 1927; *Loves of an Actress* 1928; *The Secret Hour* 1928; *Three Sinners* 1928; *The Woman From Moscow* 1928; *A Woman Commands* 1932; *Hi Diddle Diddle* 1943; *The Moon-Spinners* 1964.

Negulesco, Jean • Director; also screenwriter. • Born Craiova, Romania, February 26, 1900. Former painter who moved to the US in 1927 and began his film career as an assistant producer, second unit director and co-screenwriter. Negulesco did his finest directing work (notably *Johnny Belinda* 1948) for Warner Bros. in the 40s, but tended to squander his talents on insipid Technicolor melodramas in the following decade. • *Expensive Husbands* 1937 (sc); *Fight For Your Lady* 1937 (story); *The Beloved Brat* 1938 (story); *Swiss Miss* 1938 (story); *Rio* 1939 (story); *Singapore Woman* 1941 (d); *The Conspirators* 1944 (d); *The Mask of Dimitrios* 1944 (d); *Humoresque* 1946 (d); *Nobody Lives Forever* 1946 (d); *Three Strangers* 1946 (d); *Deep Valley* 1947 (d); *Johnny Belinda* 1948 (d) (**AANBD**); *Road House* 1948 (d); *Britannia Mews* 1949 (d); *The Mudlark* 1950 (d); *Three Came Home* 1950 (d); *Under My Skin* 1950 (d); *Take Care of My Little Girl* 1951 (d); *Lure of the Wilderness* 1952 (d); *Lydia Bailey* 1952 (d); *O. Henry's Full House* 1952 (d); *Phone Call From a Stranger* 1952 (d); *How to Marry a Millionaire* 1953 (d); *Scandal at Scourie* 1953 (d); *Titanic* 1953 (d); *Three Coins in the Fountain* 1954 (d); *Woman's World* 1954 (d); *Daddy Long Legs* 1955 (d); *The Rains of Ranchipur* 1955 (d); *Boy on a Dolphin* 1957 (d); *A Certain Smile* 1958 (d); *The Gift of Love* 1958 (d); *The Best of Everything* 1959 (d); *Count Your Blessings* 1959 (d); *Jessica* 1961 (d,p); *The Pleasure Seekers* 1964 (d); *Hello-Goodbye* 1970 (d); *The Heroes* 1970 (d); *Un Officier de Police sans Importance* 1973 (a).

Neill, Sam • Actor • Born Northern Ireland, 1948. *Educ.* University of Canterbury, New Zealand. Cool, refined leading man who first gained acclaim for his performance in Gillian Armstrong's *My Brilliant Career* (1979). Neill has starred opposite Meryl Streep in two films directed by Fred Schepisi; *A Cry in the Dark* (1988) and *Plenty* (1985). • *Sleeping Dogs* 1977; *The Journalist* 1979; *Just Out of Reach* 1979; *My Brilliant Career* 1979; *Attack Force Z* 1981; *The Final Conflict* 1981; *Possession* 1981; *Enigma* 1982; *The Country Girls* 1983; *Robbery Under Arms* 1984; *Le Sang des Autres* 1984; *For Love Alone* 1985; *Plenty* 1985; *The Good Wife* 1986; *A Cry in the Dark* 1988; *Dead Calm* 1989; *La Revolution Francaise* 1989; *Death in Brunswick* 1990; *The Hunt For Red October* 1990; *Jusqu'au bout du monde/Till the End of the World* 1991.

Nelligan, Kate • Actress • Born Patricia Colleen Nelligan, London, Ontario, Canada, March 16, 1951. *Educ.* York University, Canada; Central School of Speech and Drama, London. Three-time Tony nominee who has appeared intermittently in films since the mid-1970s. Memorable in the title role of *Eleni* (1985), based on the life of American writer Nicholas Gage and his attempts to unravel the truth about his mother's execution by Greek communists after WWII. • *The Romantic Englishwoman* 1975; *Licking Hitler* 1977; *Dracula* 1979; *Mr. Patman* 1980; *Eye of the Needle* 1981; *Without a Trace* 1983; *Eleni* 1985; *The Mystery of Henry Moore* 1985; *Il Giorno Prima* 1987; *The White Room* 1990.

Nelson, Craig T. • Actor • Born Spokane, WA, April 4, 1946. *Educ.* University of Arizona; Oxford Theatre, Los Angeles. Began his career working with Barry Levinson as a radio writer-performer and stand-up comic. Nelson made his feature debut in the Levinson-scripted *And Justice For All* (1979) and became a popular character player in the 1980s. • *And Justice For All* 1979; *The Formula* 1980; *Private Benjamin* 1980; *Stir Crazy* 1980; *Where the Buffalo Roam* 1980; *Man, Woman and Child* 1982; *Poltergeist* 1982; *All the Right Moves* 1983; *The Osterman Weekend* 1983; *Silkwood* 1983; *The Killing Fields* 1984; *Poltergeist II: The Other Side* 1986; *Rachel River* 1987; *Red Riding Hood* 1987; *Action Jackson* 1988; *Me and Him* 1988; *Troop Beverly Hills* 1989; *Turner and Hooch* 1989.

Nelson, Judd • Actor • Born Portland, ME, 1959. *Educ.* Haverford College, PA; Stella Adler Conservatory, New York. "Brat-packer" who made his film debut in *Making the Grade* (1984) and cornered the market on playing smugly contentious, troubled young men, as in John Hughes's coming-of-age opus, *The Breakfast Club* and Joel Schumacher's *St. Elmo's Fire* (both 1985). • *Making the Grade* 1984; *The Breakfast Club* 1985; *Fandango* 1985; *St. Elmo's Fire* 1985; *Blue City* 1986; *Transformers—The Movie* 1986; *Dear America* 1987; *From the Hip* 1987; *Never on Tuesday* 1989; *Relentless* 1989; *New Jack City* 1991.

Nemec, Jan • Director; also screenwriter. • Born Prague, July 2, 1936. *Educ.* FAMU, Prague. Leading filmmaker of the Czech new wave who made literary-inspired shorts before crafting his first feature, *Diamonds of the Night*, in 1964. Nemec is known for his intense psychological studies of familial and/or political oppression, perhaps best represented by *A Report on the Party and the Guests* (1966). Long a critic of the totalitarian Communist state, Nemec celebrated the short-lived Dubcek regime—and documented the Soviet invasion which crushed it—in *Oratorio for Prague* (1968). His career was stifled during the post-invasion years years and, in 1974, he was permitted to emigrate to France. Briefly married to costume designer/screenwriter Ester Krumbachova. • *Diamonds of the Night* 1964 (d,sc); *Perlicky Na Dne/Pearls of the Deep* 1965 (d—"The Poseurs"); *Mucednici Lasky/Martyrs of Love* 1966 (d,sc); *O Slavnosti a Hostech/A Report on the Party and the Guests* 1966 (d,sc); *Oratorio For Prague (short)* 1968 (d); *Geheimcode Wildganse* 1984 (m); *'68* 1987 (a); *The Unbearable Lightness of Being* 1988 (a,special consultant).

Nero, Franco • Actor • Born Italy, 1942. Dashing Italian leading man, in international films from the late 1960s; best known as Lancelot in *Camelot* (1967). Nero has a child by actress Vanessa Redgrave. • *La Bibbia/The Bible* 1966 (a); *Tempo di massacro* 1966 (a); *Camelot* 1967 (a); *Texas, Addio* 1968 (a); *The Mercenary* 1970 (a); *Tristana* 1970 (a); *The Virgin and the Gypsy* 1970 (a); *Confessione di un Commissario di Polizia al Procuratore Della Repubblica* 1971 (a); *La Vacanza* 1971 (a); *Pope Joan* 1972 (a); *Senza Ragione* 1972 (a); *Deaf Smith and Johnny Ears* 1973 (a); *Il Delitto Matteotti* 1973 (a); *Don't Turn the Other Cheek* 1973 (a); *Le Moine* 1973 (a); *Il Cittadino Si Ribella* 1974 (a); *Corruzione al Palazzo di Giustizia* 1974 (a); *Mussolini: Ultimo Atto* 1974 (a); *Perche si uccide un Magistrato* 1974 (a); *La Marche Triomphale* 1975 (a); *Autostop rosso sangue* 1976 (a); *Keoma* 1976 (a); *Submission* 1977 (a); *Force 10 From Navarone* 1978 (a); *Un Dramma Borghese* 1979 (a); *Le Rose di Danzica* 1979 (a); *The Day of the Cobra* 1980 (a); *The Man With Bogart's Face* 1980 (a); *Enter the Ninja* 1981 (a); *The Salamander* 1981 (a); *Kamikaze '89* 1982 (a); *Querelly—ein Pakt mit dem Teufel/Querelle* 1982 (a); *Der Falke* 1983 (a); *Grog* 1983 (a); *Red Bells: I've Seen the Birth of the New World* 1983 (a); *Wagner* 1983 (a); *Die Forstenbuben* 1985 (a); *Il Pentito* 1985 (a); *Garibaldi-the General* 1986 (a); *The Girl* 1986 (a); *Sweet Country* 1986 (a); *Un Altare per la Madre* 1987 (a); *Il Giovane Tosca-*

nini/The Young Toscanini 1988 (a); *Silent Night* 1988 (a); *Diceria dell'untore* 1990 (a,p); *Die Hard 2: Die Harder* 1990 (a).

Nesmith, Michael • Actor, producer, musician • Born Texas. *Educ.* San Antonio College. Best known as the guy with the knit ski-cap in the "manufactured" 1960s comedy-pop band "The Monkees." Drawing on his experiences with the "The Monkees" (1966-68) TV show—in which the group's music was secondary to their visual packaging—Nesmith became an influential figure in the music video field in the late 1970s, developing the idea which led to the formation of the *MTV* (Music Television) cable channel. He produced over 50 early episodes for MTV as well as several feature films, and is also a successful entrepreneur, through his Pacific Arts Video company, in the video publishing field. • *Head* 1968 (song); *Timerider: The Adventure of Lyle Swann* 1982 (exec.p,sc,m.perf); *Repo Man* 1984 (exec.p); *Burglar* 1987 (a); *Square Dance* 1987 (exec.p); *Tapeheads* 1988 (a,exec.p).

Newell, Mike • Director • Born England, 1942. TV and stage director who made his feature debut with *The Awakening* (1980), a tawdry adaptation of a Bram Stoker novel. Newell's best work to date is *Dance With a Stranger* (1985), a poignant and finely observed account of the life and death of Ruth Ellis, the last woman to be sentenced to death in England. • *The Awakening* 1980; *Bad Blood* 1982; *Dance With a Stranger* 1985; *The Good Father* 1986; *Amazing Grace and Chuck* 1987; *Soursweet* 1988.

Newman, Alfred • Composer; also conductor. • Born New Haven, CT, March 17, 1901; died 1970. Versatile composer whose scores enlivened some of Hollywood's finest films from the early 1930s through the late 60s. Newman was equally at home with musicals (*Broadway Melody of 1936* 1935), melodramas (*Stella Dallas* 1937), comedies (*The Seven Year Itch* 1955) and spectacular period pieces (*The Greatest Story Ever Told* 1965). He collaborated several times with director John Ford (*Drums Along the Mohawk* 1939, *The Grapes of Wrath* 1940, etc.). Son David Newman is also a film composer. • *Whoopee* 1930 (m.dir); *Arrowsmith* 1931 (m); *Reaching For the Moon* 1931 (m.dir); *Tonight or Never* 1931 (m.dir); *The Greeks Had a Word For Them* 1932 (m); *Night World* 1932 (m); *Advice to the Lovelorn* 1933 (m.dir); *Blood Money* 1933 (m.dir); *The Bowery* 1933 (m.dir); *Broadway Thru a Keyhole* 1933 (m.dir); *Roman Scandals* 1933 (m); *Born to Be Bad* 1934 (m.dir); *The Cat's Paw* 1934 (m.dir); *The Count of Monte Cristo* 1934 (m.dir); *Gallant Lady* 1934 (m.dir); *The House of Rothschild* 1934 (m); *Kid Millions* 1934 (m.dir); *Looking For Trouble* 1934 (m.dir); *The Mighty Barnum* 1934 (m); *Moulin Rouge* 1934 (m.dir); *Transatlantic Merry-Go-Round* 1934 (m.dir); *We Live Again* 1934 (m.dir); *Barbary Coast* 1935 (m,m.dir); *Broadway Melody of 1936* 1935 (m); *The Call of the Wild* 1935 (m); *Clive of India* 1935 (m); *The Dark Angel* 1935 (m.dir); *Folies Bergere* 1935 (m.dir); *The Melody Lingers On* 1935 (m.dir); *Metropolitan* 1935 (m.dir); *Splendor* 1935 (m.dir); *Beloved Enemy* 1936 (m.dir); *Born to Dance* 1936 (m.dir); *Come and Get It* 1936 (m); *Dancing Pirate* 1936 (m.dir); *Dodsworth* 1936 (m.dir,m); *The Gay Desperado* 1936 (m.dir); *Modern Times* 1936 (m.dir); *One Rainy Afternoon* 1936 (m.dir); *Ramona* 1936 (m); *Strike Me Pink* 1936 (m.dir); *These Three* 1936 (m.dir); *52nd Street* 1937 (m.dir); *Dead End* 1937 (m.dir); *Hurricane* 1937 (m.dir) **(AANBM)**; *The Prisoner of Zenda* 1937 (m) **(AANBM)**; *Slave Ship* 1937 (m.dir); *Stella Dallas* 1937 (m.dir); *Wee Willie Winkie* 1937 (m.dir); *When You're in Love* 1937 (m.dir); *Woman Chases Man* 1937 (m.dir); *You Only Live Once* 1937 (m.dir); *Alexander's Ragtime Band* 1938 (m.dir) **(AABM)**; *The Cowboy and the Lady* 1938 (m.dir) **(AANBM)**; *The Goldwyn Follies* 1938 (m.dir) **(AANBM)**; *Trade Winds* 1938 (m); *Beau Geste* 1939 (m); *Drums Along the Mohawk* 1939 (m); *Gunga Din* 1939 (m); *The Hunchback of Notre Dame* 1939 (m) **(AANBM)**; *The Rains Came* 1939 (m) **(AANBM)**; *They Shall Have Music* 1939 (a,m) **(AANBM)**; *Wuthering Heights* 1939 (m,m.dir) **(AANBM)**; *Young Mr. Lincoln* 1939 (m.dir); *The Blue Bird* 1940 (m.dir); *Brigham Young, Frontiersman* 1940 (m); *Broadway Melody of 1940* 1940 (m.dir); *Earthbound* 1940 (m.dir); *Foreign Correspondent* 1940 (m); *The Grapes of Wrath* 1940 (m.dir); *Hudson's Bay* 1940 (m.dir); *Lillian Russell* 1940 (m.dir); *Little Old New York* 1940 (m.dir); *The Mark of Zorro* 1940 (m.dir) **(AANBM)**; *Maryland* 1940 (m.dir); *Public Deb No. 1* 1940 (m.dir); *They Knew What They Wanted* 1940 (m); *Tin Pan Alley* 1940 (m.dir) **(AABM)**; *Vigil in the Night* 1940 (m); *Young People* 1940 (m.dir); *Ball of Fire* 1941 (m) **(AANBM)**; *Belle Starr* 1941 (m); *Blood and Sand* 1941 (m.dir); *Charley's Aunt* 1941 (m); *The Great American Broadcast* 1941 (m.dir); *How Green Was My Valley* 1941 (m.dir) **(AANBM)**; *Man Hunt* 1941 (m); *Moon Over Miami* 1941 (m.dir); *Remember the Day* 1941 (m.dir); *That Night in Rio* 1941 (m.dir); *Week-End in Havana* 1941 (m.dir); *Wild Geese Calling* 1941 (m.dir); *A Yank in the R.A.F.* 1941 (m.dir); *The Black Swan* 1942 (m) **(AANBM)**; *China Girl* 1942 (m); *Girl Trouble* 1942 (m.dir); *Life Begins at Eight-Thirty* 1942 (m); *My Gal Sal* 1942 (m.dir) **(AANBM)**; *Orchestra Wives* 1942 (m.dir); *The Pied Piper* 1942 (m); *Roxie Hart* 1942 (m.dir); *Son of Fury* 1942 (m); *Song of the Islands* 1942 (m.dir); *Springtime in the Rockies* 1942 (m.dir); *Ten Gentlemen From West Point* 1942 (m.dir); *This Above All* 1942 (m); *Claudia* 1943 (m); *Coney Island* 1943 (m.dir) **(AANBM)**; *The Gang's All Here* 1943 (m.dir); *The Moon Is Down* 1943 (m); *My Friend Flicka* 1943 (m); *The Song of Bernadette* 1943 (m) **(AABM)**; *Sweet Rosie O'Grady* 1943 (m.dir); *Wintertime* 1943 (m.dir); *Irish Eyes Are Smiling* 1944 (m.dir) **(AANBM)**; *The Purple Heart* 1944 (m); *Sunday Dinner For a Soldier* 1944 (m); *Wilson* 1944 (m) **(AANBM)**; *A Bell For Adano* 1945 (m.dir); *Diamond Horseshoe* 1945 (m.dir); *The Dolly Sisters* 1945 (m.dir); *The Keys of the Kingdom* 1945 (m) **(AANBM)**; *Leave Her to Heaven* 1945 (m); *A Royal Scandal* 1945 (m); *State Fair* 1945 (m.dir) **(AANBM)**; *A Tree Grows in Brooklyn* 1945 (m); *Centennial Summer* 1946 (m.dir) **(AANBM)**; *Dragonwyck* 1946 (m.dir); *Margie* 1946 (m.dir); *The Razor's Edge* 1946 (m); *Three Little Girls in Blue* 1946 (m.dir); *13 Rue Madeleine* 1947 (m); *Boomerang* 1947 (m.dir); *The Brasher Doubloon* 1947 (m.dir); *Captain From Castile* 1947 (m.dir); *Forever Amber* 1947 (m.dir); *Gentleman's Agreement* 1947 (m); *I Wonder Who's Kissing Her Now* 1947 (m.dir); *Mother Wore Tights* 1947 (m.dir) **(AABM)**; *The Shocking Miss Pilgrim* 1947 (m.dir); *Call Northside 777* 1948 (m.dir); *Chicken Every Sunday* 1948 (m); *Cry of the City* 1948 (m); *Fury at Furnace Creek* 1948 (m.dir); *The Iron Curtain* 1948 (m.dir); *A Letter to Three Wives* 1948 (m); *Sitting Pretty* 1948 (m); *The Snake Pit* 1948 (m.dir) **(AANBM)**; *That Lady in Ermine* 1948 (m.dir); *Unfaithfully Yours* 1948 (m.dir); *When My Baby Smiles at Me* 1948 (m.dir) **(AANBM)**; *Yellow Sky* 1948 (m.dir); *Dancing in the Dark* 1949 (m.dir); *Down to the Sea in Ships* 1949 (m.dir); *Everybody Does It* 1949 (m.dir); *Mother Is a Freshman* 1949 (m.dir); *Mr. Belvedere Goes to College* 1949 (m); *Oh, You Beautiful Doll!* 1949 (m.dir); *Pinky* 1949 (m); *Prince of Foxes* 1949 (m); *Thieves' Highway* 1949 (ed); *Twelve O'Clock High* 1949 (m); *You're My Everything* 1949 (m.dir); *All About Eve* 1950 (m) **(AANBM)**; *The Big Lift* 1950 (m); *Broken Arrow* 1950 (m.dir); *For Heaven's Sake* 1950 (m); *The Gunfighter* 1950 (m); *My Blue Heaven* 1950 (m.dir); *No Way Out* 1950 (m); *Panic in the Streets* 1950 (m); *When Willie Comes Marching Home* 1950 (m); *Call Me Mister* 1951 (m.dir); *David and Bathsheba* 1951 (m) **(AANBM)**; *Fourteen Hours* 1951 (m); *Half Angel* 1951 (m,m.dir); *On the Riviera* 1951 (m.dir) **(AANBM)**; *People Will Talk* 1951 (m.dir); *Take Care of My Little Girl* 1951 (m); *O. Henry's Full House* 1952 (m); *The Prisoner of Zenda* 1952 (m) **(AANBM)**; *Stars and Stripes Forever* 1952 (m.dir); *Viva Zapata!* 1952 (m.dir); *Wait Till the Sun Shines, Nellie* 1952 (m); *What Price Glory* 1952 (m.dir); *With a Song in My Heart* 1952 (m.dir) **(AABM)**; *How to*

Marry a Millionaire 1953 (m); *The President's Lady* 1953 (m); *The Robe* 1953 (m); *Tonight We Sing* 1953 (m.dir); *Demetrius and the Gladiators* 1954 (m); *The Egyptian* 1954 (m); *Hell and High Water* 1954 (m); *A Man Called Peter* 1954 (m,m.dir); *There's No Business Like Show Business* 1954 (m.dir) **(AANBM)**; *Daddy Long Legs* 1955 (m.dir) **(AANBM)**; *Love Is a Many Splendored Thing* 1955 (m) **(AABM)**; *The Seven Year Itch* 1955 (m); *Anastasia* 1956 (m) **(AANBM)**; *Bus Stop* 1956 (m); *Carousel* 1956 (m.dir); *The King and I* 1956 (m) **(AABM)**; *A Certain Smile* 1958 (m); *South Pacific* 1958 (m.cond,m.sup) **(AANBM)**; *The Best of Everything* 1959 (m,song) **(AANBS)**; *The Diary of Anne Frank* 1959 (m) **(AANBM)**; *Flower Drum Song* 1961 (m.dir) **(AANBM)**; *The Pleasure of His Company* 1961 (m); *The Counterfeit Traitor* 1962 (m); *How the West Was Won* 1962 (m,song) **(AANBM)**; *State Fair* 1962 (m,m.cond,m.sup) **(AANBM)**; *The Greatest Story Ever Told* 1965 (m,m.cond) **(AANBM)**; *Nevada Smith* 1966 (m); *Camelot* 1967 (m.dir) **(AABM)**; *Firecreek* 1968 (m); *Airport* 1970 (m,m.dir) **(AANBM)**; *Players* 1979 (m).

Newman, David • Composer; also conductor. • Born Los Angeles, CA. *Educ.* USC, Los Angeles. Successful contemporary composer of film scores (*The War of the Roses* 1989, *The Freshman* 1990) and classical works (*Phos Hilaron*) who has conducted some of the world's finest orchestras. Newman is also the music director of Robert Redford's Sundance Institute. Son of celebrated film composer Alfred Newman and cousin of singer/songwriter Randy Newman, also a successful composer (*Ragtime* 1981, *Avalon* 1990). • *The Worm Eaters* 1977 (song); *Critters* 1986 (m); *The Kindred* 1986 (m); *Vendetta* 1986 (m); *Wise Guys* 1986 (orch); *The Brave Little Toaster* 1987 (m); *Dragnet* 1987 (add.m,orch); *Malone* 1987 (m); *My Demon Lover* 1987 (m); *Pass the Ammo* 1987 (m); *Throw Momma From the Train* 1987 (m); *Bill and Ted's Excellent Adventure* 1989 (m); *Disorganized Crime* 1989 (m); *Gross Anatomy* 1989 (m); *Heathers* 1989 (m); *Little Monsters* 1989 (m); *The War of the Roses* 1989 (m); *DuckTales: The Movie* 1990 (m); *Fire Birds* 1990 (m); *The Freshman* 1990 (m); *Madhouse* 1990 (m); *Mr. Destiny* 1990 (m,orch); *The Marrying Man* 1991 (m).

Newman, David • Screenwriter • Born New York, NY, February 4, 1937. Former magazine writer and editor who, with partner Robert Benton, was responsible for the trend-setting *Bonnie and Clyde* (1967), one of the seminal American films of the 60s. Their friendship with French New Wave directors Truffaut and Godard was evident in the genre films which followed. *What's Up, Doc?* (1972), an homage to the 30s screwball comedy, revived that genre.

Since the mid-60s, when he and Benton wrote the book for the Charles Strouse-Lee Adams musical *It's a Bird. .It's a Plane. . . It's Superman* (1966), Newman has been fascinated with the pop culture of the comic book. With his wife Leslie Newman, he scripted the first three "Superman" movies. In the early 70s, he and Benton co-wrote "Hubba-Hubba," a very funny paean to the Hollywood of the 1940s which remains one of the more notorious unproduced screenplays. In 1974, Newman wrote (with Leslie) and directed *The Crazy American Girl/La Fille d'Amérique* (1975), an unusual "reverse New Wave" effort—a thoroughly French 70s movie but made by Americans in English. (Being so European, the film was never released in the US.) He is also known for his script for the best-selling Michael Jackson music video *Moonwalker.* While other screenwriters come and go, Newman has remained both productive and influential for 25 years and holds a unique position in the American industry. • *Bonnie and Clyde* 1967 (sc) **(AANBSC)**; *There Was a Crooked Man* 1970 (sc); *Bad Company* 1972 (sc); *Oh! Calcutta!* 1972 (sc); *What's Up, Doc?* 1972 (sc); *Superman* 1978 (sc); *Superman II* 1980 (sc); *Jinxed!* 1982 (sc); *Still of the Night* 1982 (story); *Superman III* 1983 (sc); *Sheena* 1984 (sc,story); *Santa Claus: The Movie* 1985 (sc,story); *The Running Man* 1987 (uncred.sc); *Moonwalker* 1988 (sc).

Newman, Leslie • Screenwriter • Born US. Wife of screenwriter David Newman who collaborated on a number of films with her husband in the 70s and 80s before turning an avocation, cooking, into another successful career as a food expert and cookbook author and columnist. The best-seller *Feasts* appeared in 1991, based on her long-running and well-reviewed series of New York New Year's Eve parties for the film industry. No relation to Paul Newman, another film figure who became enamoured of the art of food later in life. • *The Crazy American Girl* 1975 (sc); *Superman* 1978 (sc); *Superman II* 1980 (sc); *Superman III* 1983 (sc); *Santa Claus: The Movie* 1985 (story).

Newman, Lionel • Composer; also conductor, music director. • Born Los Angeles, CA, 1916; died February 2, 1989, Los Angeles, CA. Prolific, versatile figure who began his career as Mae West's piano accompanist before joining 20th Century-Fox as a rehearsal pianist in 1943. Newman stayed with Fox for more than 40 years, working in various capacities on over 250 films. He wrote the score for Elvis Presley's first film, *Love Me Tender* (1956), and won an Academy Award for the Barbra Streisand vehicle, *Hello, Dolly!* (1969). • *Cry of the City* 1948 (m.dir); *Give My Regards to Broadway* 1948 (m.dir); *Green Grass of Wyoming* 1948 (m.dir); *Road House* 1948 (m); *The Street With No Name* 1948 (m.dir); *You Were Meant For Me* 1948 (m.dir); *Father Was a Fullback* 1949 (m.dir); *Cheaper By the Dozen* 1950 (m.dir); *Halls of Montezuma* 1950 (m); *I'll Get By* 1950 (m.dir) **(AANBM)**; *The Jackpot* 1950 (m); *Mother Didn't Tell Me* 1950 (m.dir); *Wabash Avenue* 1950 (m.dir); *Where the Sidewalk Ends* 1950 (m.dir); *Fixed Bayonets* 1951 (m.dir); *Follow the Sun* 1951 (m.dir); *The Frogmen* 1951 (m.dir); *The Guy Who Came Back* 1951 (m.dir); *I Can Get It For You Wholesale* 1951 (m.dir); *I'd Climb the Highest Mountain* 1951 (m.dir); *Meet Me After the Show* 1951 (m.dir); *U.S.S. Tea Kettle* 1951 (m); *Bloodhounds of Broadway* 1952 (m.dir); *Diplomatic Courier* 1952 (m.dir); *Don't Bother to Knock* 1952 (m.dir); *City of Bad Men* 1953 (m); *Gentlemen Prefer Blondes* 1953 (m.dir); *The Kid From Left Field* 1953 (m); *Man in the Attic* 1953 (m.dir); *Niagara* 1953 (m.dir,song); *Pickup on South Street* 1953 (m.dir); *Powder River* 1953 (m.dir); *The Silver Whip* 1953 (m.dir); *The Gambler From Natchez* 1954 (m); *Garden of Evil* 1954 (song); *Princess of the Nile* 1954 (m); *River of No Return* 1954 (song); *Rocket Man* 1954 (m); *The Siege at Red River* 1954 (m); *There's No Business Like Show Business* 1954 (m.dir) **(AANBM)**; *Three Young Texans* 1954 (m.dir); *How to Be Very, Very Popular* 1955 (m.dir); *The Killer Is Loose* 1955 (m); *The Girl Can't Help It* 1956 (m.dir); *A Kiss Before Dying* 1956 (m,song); *The Last Wagon* 1956 (m); *Love Me Tender* 1956 (m); *The Proud Ones* 1956 (m); *Teenage Rebel* 1956 (song); *April Love* 1957 (m.dir); *Bernardine* 1957 (m); *Kiss Them For Me* 1957 (m,song); *Sing Boy Sing* 1957 (m); *The Way to the Gold* 1957 (m); *The Bravados* 1958 (m); *The Gift of Love* 1958 (m.cond); *In Love and War* 1958 (m.cond); *The Long, Hot Summer* 1958 (m.cond); *Mardi Gras* 1958 (m.sup,m.cond) **(AANBM)**; *A Nice Little Bank That Should Be Robbed* 1958 (m); *Rally Round the Flag, Boys!* 1958 (m.cond); *The Remarkable Mr. Pennypacker* 1958 (m.cond); *The Sound and the Fury* 1958 (m.cond); *Ten North Frederick* 1958 (m.cond); *Villa!* 1958 (song); *The Young Lions* 1958 (m.cond); *Compulsion* 1959 (m); *Holiday For Lovers* 1959 (m.cond); *Hound Dog Man* 1959 (m.cond); *Journey to the Center of the Earth* 1959 (m.cond); *A Private's Affair* 1959 (m.cond); *Say One For Me* 1959 (m.sup,m.cond) **(AANBM)**; *Warlock* 1959 (m.cond); *Woman Obsessed* 1959 (m.cond); *Flaming Star* 1960 (m.dir); *Let's Make Love* 1960 (m.dir) **(AANBM)**; *North to Alaska* 1960 (m); *Cleopatra* 1963 (m); *Move Over, Darling* 1963 (m); *The Pleasure Seekers* 1964 (m) **(AANBM)**; *Do Not Disturb* 1965 (m); *I Deal in Danger* 1966 (m.sup); *The Sand Pebbles* 1966 (m.cond); *Doctor Dolittle* 1967 (m) **(AANBM)**; *The St. Valentine's Day Massacre* 1967 (m.cond); *The Bos-*

ton Strangler 1968 (m); *Hello, Dolly!* 1969 (m.dir,m.adapt) **(AABM)**; *The Great White Hope* 1970 (m); *Myra Breckinridge* 1970 (m); *The Salzburg Connection* 1972 (m.sup); *The Blue Bird* 1976 (m); *Alien* 1979 (m.dir); *Breaking Away* 1979 (m.dir,m.cond); *The Final Conflict* 1981 (m.dir); *Cross Creek* 1983 (m.cond); *Unfaithfully Yours* 1983 (m.sup).

Newman, Paul • Actor; also director, producer. • Born Cleveland, OH, January 26, 1925. *Educ.* Kenyon College, Ohio (economics); Yale Drama School; Actors Studio. Newman briefly ran his family's sporting goods store in Cleveland before venturing, in 1950, into stage work at the Williams Bay, Wisconsin, Repertory Company. He attended Yale from 1951-52, during which time he also worked in TV in New York and attended the Actors Studio. Newman was signed by Warner Bros. after attracting critical attention with his 1953 Broadway debut, in *Picnic*. His first screen appearance came as the star of *The Silver Chalice* (1954), a curious biblical epic which brought him as much attention for his miscasting as for his talent. His first positive film notices were for his performance as boxer Rocky Graziano in *Somebody Up There Likes Me* (1956).

Early in his career, Newman was often labeled a Brando imitator, more thanks to the characters he played than to any conscious mimicry. Several of his early performances—in *Cat On a Hot Tin Roof* (1958), *The Long Hot Summer* (1958), and *Sweet Bird of Youth* (1962)—developed his screen image as that of a cynical opportunist whose sex appeal was balanced by his seeming contempt for women.

Some of Newman's finest early portrayals were of anti-heroic, alienated misfits, characterizations which he tuned to perfection in a series of popular star vehicles including *The Left Handed Gun* (1958), *The Hustler (1961), Hud* (1963) and *Cool Hand Luke* (1967).

The late 1960s saw Newman branch out into both production and direction. Fueled by commercial success and a degree of artistic dissatisfaction, he joined with Sidney Poitier, Barbra Streisand, Steve McQueen and several other stars to form the First Artists production company in 1969. The venture, though much imitated, did little for the careers of its founders. His directorial debut, *Rachel, Rachel*, (1968), starring his second wife Joanne Woodward, garnered the best director award from the New York Film Critics Circle.

Newman continued to enjoy popular success in front of the camera, scoring at the box-office with films such as *Butch Cassidy and the Sundance Kid* (1969) and *The Sting* (1973), both opposite Robert Redford. The late 70s saw some bold project choices which enjoyed varying degrees of success, from *Buffalo Bill and the Indians* (1976) and *Slap Shot* (1977) to *The Drowning Pool* (1975) and *Quintet* (1979).

Newman proved highly effective in a number of senior roles in the 1980s and 90s, in films ranging from *Absence of Malice* (1981) to *The Verdict* (1982) to *Mr. and Mrs. Bridge* (1990). He won an honorary Academy Award in 1985 and a best actor oscar the following year for *The Color of Money*. He also earned acclaim for his fifth directorial outing, an adaptation of Tennessee Williams's *The Glass Menagerie* (1987), again starring Woodward.

For each of his directors, from Mark Robson to Arthur Penn to John Huston to Robert Altman, Newman has been able to find a nuance of character and a lightness of being which has maintained his standing as a prime box-office attraction. This extraordinary versatility, combined with a charismatic aloofness, is the hallmark of his craft. TZ • *The Silver Chalice* 1954; *The Rack* 1956; *Somebody Up There Likes Me* 1956; *The Helen Morgan Story* 1957; *Until They Sail* 1957; *Cat on a Hot Tin Roof* 1958 **(AANBA)**; *The Left Handed Gun* 1958; *The Long, Hot Summer* 1958; *Rally Round the Flag, Boys!* 1958; *The Young Philadelphians* 1959; *Exodus* 1960; *From the Terrace* 1960; *The Hustler* 1961 **(AANBA)**; *Paris Blues* 1961; *Adventures of a Young Man* 1962; *Sweet Bird of Youth* 1962; *Hud* 1963 **(AANBA)**; *A New Kind of Love* 1963; *The Prize* 1963; *The Outrage* 1964; *What a Way to Go!* 1964; *Lady L* 1965; *Harper* 1966; *Torn Curtain* 1966; *Cool Hand Luke* 1967 **(AANBA)**; *Hombre* 1967; *Rachel, Rachel* 1968 (d,p) **(AANBP)**; *The Secret War of Harry Frigg* 1968; *Butch Cassidy and the Sundance Kid* 1969; *Winning* 1969; *King: A Filmed Record... Montgomery to Memphis* 1970; *WUSA* 1970 (a,p); *Sometimes a Great Notion* 1971 (a,d); *They Might Be Giants* 1971 (p); *The Effect of Gamma Rays on Man-in-the-Moon Marigolds* 1972 (d,p); *The Life and Times of Judge Roy Bean* 1972; *Pocket Money* 1972; *The Mackintosh Man* 1973; *The Sting* 1973; *The Towering Inferno* 1974; *The Drowning Pool* 1975; *Buffalo Bill and the Indians, or Sitting Bull's History Lesson* 1976; *Slap Shot* 1977; *Quintet* 1979; *When Time Ran Out* 1980; *Absence of Malice* 1981 **(AANBA)**; *Fort Apache, the Bronx* 1981; *The Verdict* 1982 **(AANBA)**; *Harry & Son* 1984 (a,d,p,sc); *The Color of Money* 1986 **(AABA)**; *The Glass Menagerie* 1987 (d); *Hello Actors Studio* 1987; *John Huston* 1988; *Blaze* 1989; *Fat Man and Little Boy* 1989; *Mr. & Mrs. Bridge* 1990.

Niblo, Fred • Director; also producer, actor. • Born Frederico Nobile, York, NB, January 6, 1874; died 1948. Former vaudevillian (his first wife, Josephine, was the sister of George M. Cohan) and stage director who began working for the Ince studio in 1917. Niblo began his screen career turning out silent films starring his second wife, Enid Bennett. He directed Rudolph Valentino, Douglas Fairbanks and Norma Talmadge during the 1920s and is best known for *Ben Hur* (1925) and the classic Garbo showcase, *Camille* (1927). Niblo's career declined with the introduction of sound, although his direction on *The Good Earth* (1937) showed he could rise to the occasion if assigned a good script. • *Princess of the Dark* 1917 (d); *Fuss and Feathers* 1918 (d); *The Marriage Ring* 1918 (d); *When Do We Eat?* 1918 (d); *Dangerous Hours* 1919 (d); *Happy Though Married* 1919 (d); *The Haunted Bedroom* 1919 (d); *The Law of Men* 1919 (d); *Partners Three* 1919 (d); *Stepping Out* 1919 (d); *The Virtuous Thief* 1919 (d); *What Every Woman Learns* 1919 (d); *The Woman in the Suitcase* 1919 (d); *The False Road* 1920 (d); *Hairpins* 1920 (d); *Her Husband's Friend* 1920 (d); *The Mark of Zorro* 1920 (d); *Sex* 1920 (d); *Silk Hosiery* 1920 (d); *Greater Than Love* 1921 (d); *Mother o' Mine* 1921 (d); *The Three Musketeers* 1921 (d); *Blood and Sand* 1922 (d); *The Bootlegger's Daughter* 1922 (a); *Rose o' the Sea* 1922 (d); *Scandalous Tongues* 1922 (a); *The Woman He Married* 1922 (d); *The Famous Mrs. Fair* 1923 (d); *Souls For Sale* 1923 (a); *Strangers of the Night* 1923 (d,p); *The Red Lily* 1924 (d,story); *Thy Name Is Woman* 1924 (d); *Ben Hur, A Tale of the Christ* 1925 (d); *The Temptress* 1926 (d); *Camille* 1927 (d); *The Devil Dancer* 1927 (d); *The Devil Danger* 1927 (d); *Dream of Love* 1928 (d); *The Enemy* 1928 (d); *The Mysterious Lady* 1928 (d); *Two Lovers* 1928 (d,p); *Free and Easy* 1930 (a); *Redemption* 1930 (d); *Way Out West* 1930 (d); *The Big Gamble* 1931 (d); *Young Donovan's Kid* 1931 (d); *Diamond Cut Diamond* 1932 (d); *Two White Arms* 1932 (d); *The Good Earth* 1937 (d); *Ellery Queen, Master Detective* 1940 (a); *I'm Still Alive* 1940 (a); *Father's Son* 1941 (sc); *Life With Henry* 1941 (a).

Nichols, Dudley • Screenwriter; also director. • Born Wapakoneta, OH, April 6, 1895; died 1960. Premier Hollywood screenwriter of the 1930s and 40s best known for his collaborations with John Ford, notably *Stagecoach* (1939). Nichols also worked with Howard Hawks, Jean Renoir, Rene Clair, George Cukor and Fritz Lang. His directorial efforts met with limited success. • *Born Reckless* 1930 (sc); *A Devil With Women* 1930 (sc); *Men Without Women* 1930 (sc); *On the Level* 1930 (adapt); *El Precio de un Beso* 1930 (sc); *Not Exactly Gentlemen* 1931 (sc); *Seas Beneath* 1931 (sc); *Skyline* 1931 (sc); *This Sporting Age* 1932 (sc); *Hot Pepper* 1933 (story); *The Man Who Dared* 1933 (sc,story); *Robbers' Roost* 1933 (sc); *Call It Luck* 1934 (sc,story); *Hold That Girl* 1934 (sc); *Judge Priest* 1934 (sc); *The Lost Patrol* 1934 (sc); *Wild Gold* 1934 (story);

You Can't Buy Everything 1934 (story); *The Arizonian* 1935 (sc,story); *The Crusades* 1935 (sc,story); *The Informer* 1935 (sc) **(AABSC)**; *The Mystery Woman* 1935 (story); *She* 1935 (add.dial); *Steamboat 'Round the Bend* 1935 (sc); *The Three Musketeers* 1935 (sc); *Mary of Scotland* 1936 (sc); *The Plough and the Stars* 1936 (sc); *Hurricane* 1937 (sc); *The Toast of New York* 1937 (sc); *Bringing Up Baby* 1938 (sc); *Carefree* 1938 (story); *Stagecoach* 1939 (sc); *The Long Voyage Home* 1940 (sc) **(AANBSC)**; *Man Hunt* 1941 (sc); *Swamp Water* 1941 (sc); *Air Force* 1943 (sc) **(AANBSC)**; *For Whom the Bell Tolls* 1943 (sc); *Government Girl* 1943 (d,p,sc); *This Land Is Mine* 1943 (p,sc); *It Happened Tomorrow* 1944 (sc); *And Then There Were None* 1945 (sc); *The Bells of St. Mary's* 1945 (sc); *Scarlet Street* 1945 (sc); *Sister Kenny* 1946 (d,p,sc); *The Fugitive* 1947 (sc); *Mourning Becomes Electra* 1947 (d,p,sc); *Pinky* 1949 (sc); *Rawhide* 1951 (sc); *The Big Sky* 1952 (sc); *Return of the Texan* 1952 (sc); *Prince Valiant* 1954 (sc); *Run For the Sun* 1956 (sc); *The Tin Star* 1957 (sc) **(AANBSC)**; *The Hangman* 1959 (sc); *Heller in Pink Tights* 1960 (sc).

Nichols, Mike • Director; also producer. • Born Michael Igor Peschkowsky, Berlin, Germany, November 6, 1931. *Educ.* University of Chicago. Mike Nichols first rose to fame in the late 1950s as one half of a popular comedy act with Elaine May. The team's humor was distinguished by a sharp eye for the foibles of male-female relationships and a bitingly satirical attention to contemporary social pressures. Following the team's breakup, Nichols first turned his attention to directing for the Broadway stage, where he was an immediate success (*Barefoot in the Park, Luv, The Odd Couple*).

Nichols earned similar acclaim for his film directing debut, 1966's *Who's Afraid of Virginia Woolf*, the finest dramatic pairing of Elizabeth Taylor and Richard Burton. The film put the final nail in the coffin of the outmoded Motion Picture Production Code, demonstrating that adult themes could be sensitively handled and—not incidentally—draw a large audience.

Nichols consolidated his reputation with *The Graduate* (1967), which won him the Academy Award for best director. The film established Dustin Hoffman as a star and became the plaintive cry of an entire generation, giving life to otherwise inchoate feelings of alienation and disaffection. A box-office sensation, *The Graduate* also inaugurated (along with Arthur Penn's *Bonnie and Clyde* and Dennis Hopper's *Easy Rider*) a new cycle of youth-oriented films which resurrected the moribund American film industry. Some of the film's satirical elements were overlooked at the time; Nichols was prescient enough to realize that the younger generation had little with which to replace the empty values of their parents.

Nichols next chose to adapt Joseph Heller's complex, cult novel *Catch-22* (1970) to film. A box-office disappointment (in a year which saw Robert Altman's *M*A*S*H* emerge as the ultimate anti-authority comedy), *Catch-22* now seems a noble, if failed, attempt. Nichols and screenwriter Jules Feiffer enjoyed more success with *Carnal Knowledge* (1971), a film which confirmed the star status of Jack Nicholson and resurrected the career of Ann-Margret. *Carnal Knowledge* was ahead of its time in its trenchant examination of sexual politics—a theme to which Nichols has often returned, most notably in another Nicholson collaboration, *Heartburn* (1986).

Although best known for his comic work, including the deftly handled satire on office politics, *Working Girl* (1988), Nichols has also made a substantial contribution to serious screen drama. *Silkwood* (1983) demonstrates a keen sensitivity to the plight of women in a male-dominated society, as well as a strong sense of how any member of that society can be imperiled by dehumanizing systems, whether they be big business or government. DD • *Who's Afraid of Virginia Woolf?* 1966 (d) **(AANBD)**; *Bach to Bach* 1967 (a); *The Graduate* 1967 (d) **(AABD)**; *Catch-22* 1970 (d); *Carnal Knowledge* 1971 (d,p); *The Day of the Dolphin* 1973 (d); *The Fortune* 1975 (d,p); *Gilda Live* 1980 (d); *Silkwood* 1983 (d,p) **(AANBD)**; *Heartburn* 1986 (d,p); *The Longshot* 1986 (exec.p); *Biloxi Blues* 1988 (d); *Working Girl* 1988 (d) **(AANBD)**; *Postcards From the Edge* 1990 (d,p); *Regarding Henry* 1991 (d,p).

Nicholson, Jack • Actor; also producer, screenwriter, director. • Born Neptune, NJ, April 22, 1937. Jack Nicholson was a 32-year-old veteran of low-budget movies, most of them produced by Roger Corman, when he captured the attention of Hollywood and film audiences in the cult hit *Easy Rider* (1969). In an Oscar-nominated role, Nicholson portrayed a dissipated Southern lawyer who finds a temporary kind of freedom on the road with two long-haired bikers. Nicholson's breakthrough role established an instant rapport with both male and female filmgoers and set a pattern which many subsequent parts would follow: beneath the exterior of a normal nerd existed the heart and soul of a maniac.

In *Five Easy Pieces* (1970), Nicholson portrayed a rebellious soul sending out cries of distress about the banality of a life pursued without artistic ambition or love. Nicholson's naturalistic performance, with its minimal gestures and occasional explosions of temper, seemed to re-define screen cynicism for the decade. A series of extraordinary collaborations with strong directors followed: with Mike Nichols in *Carnal Knowledge* (1971), with Hal Ashby in *The Last Detail* (1973) and with Roman Polanski in *Chinatown* (1974)—a role that had him wearing a bandage around his nose through torrid love scenes. Oscar nominations for these last two films inched him toward his receipt of the award, for his powerhouse performance in Milos Forman's *One Flew Over the Cuckoo's Nest* (1975). (As usual, in a world of madmen, the Nicholson character was seen to suffer from his own sanity.)

Nicholson is known as an actor's actor, a professional who takes on unlikely and challenging roles. For Stanley Kubrick, he became a writer blocked into madness in *The Shining* (1980) and for Michelangelo Antonioni, he portrayed an American reporter drifting through a revolution, the alienated alien of *The Passenger* (1975). He claims to choose his roles as much for the opportunity of working with actors he admires as for directors, and he has given some unusual character turns: as a rustler with Marlon Brando in *The Missouri Breaks* (1976); as an ex-astronaut with Shirley MacLaine in *Terms of Endearment* (1983); as a TV anchorman with William Hurt in *Broadcast News* (1987); and as a bleary bum with Meryl Streep in *Ironweed* (1987). (It was reported that during the filming of *Ironweed* Nicholson's contract guaranteed breaks for him to attend every Los Angeles Lakers basketball game. He is an ardent and highly visible fan, even rumored to be an investor in the team.)

Nicholson's fee has reportedly reached $10 million per film, but his fame and good fortune may have affected his career for the worse. His roles as the laughable lothario in *The Witches of Eastwick* (1987) or as "The Joker" in Tim Burton's *Batman* (1989) enhanced the productions and permitted him to explore his comedic talents. Yet Nicholson's success seems to have banned him from the roles that "make his feelings come through his skin," as Pauline Kael once wrote. His feelings have been insulated by the money and system his characters once tried to buck. KJ • *Cry Baby Killer* 1958; *Studs Lonigan* 1960; *Too Soon to Love* 1960; *The Wild Ride* 1960; *Little Shop of Horrors* 1961; *The Broken Land* 1962; *The Raven* 1963; *The Terror* 1963; *Thunder Island* 1963 (sc); *Back Door to Hell* 1964; *Flight to Fury* 1966 (a,sc); *Ride in the Whirlwind* 1966 (a,p,sc); *Hell's Angels on Wheels* 1967; *The Shooting* 1967 (a,p); *The Trip* 1967 (sc); *Head* 1968 (a,p,sc); *Psych-Out* 1968; *Easy Rider* 1969 **(AANBSA)**; *Five Easy Pieces* 1970 **(AANBA)**; *On a Clear Day You Can See Forever* 1970; *Rebel Rousers* 1970; *Carnal Knowledge* 1971; *Drive, He Said* 1971 (d,p,sc); *A Safe Place* 1971; *The King of Marvin Gardens* 1972; *The Last Detail* 1973 **(AANBA)**; *Chinatown* 1974

(AANBA); *The Fortune* 1975; *One Flew Over the Cuckoo's Nest* 1975 **(AABA)**; *The Passenger* 1975; *Tommy* 1975; *The Last Tycoon* 1976; *The Missouri Breaks* 1976; *Goin' South* 1978 (a,d); *The Shining* 1980; *The Border* 1981; *The Postman Always Rings Twice* 1981; *Reds* 1981 **(AANBSA)**; *Terms of Endearment* 1983 **(AABSA)**; *Prizzi's Honor* 1985 **(AANBA)**; *Heartburn* 1986; *Broadcast News* 1987; *Ironweed* 1987 **(AANBA)**; *The Witches of Eastwick* 1987; *Batman* 1989; *The Two Jakes* 1990 (a,d).

Nielsen, Asta • Actress • Born Copenhagen, Denmark, September 11, 1883; died 1972. *Educ.* Childrens' School of the Royal Theater, Copenhagen. Danish stage star who entered films in 1910 under the auspices of director August Blom. The following year, with first husband, director Urban Gad, Nielsen moved to Germany, where her intense, expressive features and naturalistic acting style earned her international fame. By the early 1920s Nielsen had established herself as the greatest tragedienne of the European silent cinema. She played landmark title roles in such films as *Miss Julie* (1922), *Hedda Gabler* (1924) and even *Hamlet* (1920), the latter directed by her second husband, Sven Gade, and produced by Nielsen. Nielsen's career declined with the advent of sound and she published a memoir, *The Silent Muse*, in 1946. • *The Abyss* 1910; *Der Fremde Vogel* 1911; *Engelein* 1913; *Kurfurstendamm* 1918; *Rausch/Intoxication* 1919; *The Idiot* 1920; *Hamlet* 1920; *Miss Julie* 1922; *Vanina Vanini* 1922; *Erdgeist* 1923; *Hedda Gabler* 1924; *Street of Sorrow/Joyless Street* 1925; *Secrets of a Soul* 1926; *Women Without Men* 1927; *Unmögliche Liebe* 1932.

Nilsson, Rob • American director, actor, writer • Independent, San Francisco-based filmmaker whose debut feature, *Northern Lights* (1978), grew out of a series of documentaries he had made for left-wing film cooperative Cine Manifest. A gritty period drama about Norwegian farmers in pre-WWI Dakota, *Northern Lights* won the Camera D'Or at Cannes in 1979 and the American Film Festival Award the following year. Nilsson went on to develop an improvisational filmmaking style, influenced by the techniques of *cinéma vérité* and facilitated by modern video equipment, which he has dubbed "direct action cinema." His films in this mode include *Signal 7* (1983), which follows a day in the life of San Francisco cabbies, and *On the Edge* (1985), starring Bruce Dern. Nilsson played his first leading film role in *Heat and Sunlight* (1987), which he also wrote and directed. • *Northern Lights* 1978 (d,p,sc,ed,casting); *Signal 7* 1983 (d,story); *On the Edge* 1985 (d,p,sc); *Heat and Sunlight* 1987 (a,d,sc); *The Method* 1987 (sc).

Nimoy, Leonard • Actor; also director. • Born Boston, MA, March 26, 1931. *Educ.* Boston College; Antioch College; Pasadena Playhouse. Best known as the unflappable Mr. Spock on the TV series "Star Trek" (1966-69). Nimoy appeared in a number of feature films during the 1970s before making a logical transition to directing with *Star Trek III: The Search for Spock* (1984). • *Queen For a Day* 1951 (a); *Francis Goes to West Point* 1952 (a); *Kid Monk Baroni* 1952 (a); *Zombies of the Stratosphere* 1952 (a); *Old Overland Trail* 1953 (a); *The Brain Eaters* 1958 (a); *The Balcony* 1963 (a); *Deathwatch* 1966 (a,p); *Catlow* 1971 (a); *Invasion of the Body Snatchers* 1978 (a); *Star Trek: The Motion Picture* 1979 (a); *Star Trek II: The Wrath of Khan* 1982 (a); *Star Trek III: The Search For Spock* 1984 (a,d); *Star Trek IV: The Voyage Home* 1986 (a,d,story); *Transformers—The Movie* 1986 (a); *Three Men and a Baby* 1987 (d); *The Good Mother* 1988 (d); *Just One Step: The Great Peace March* 1988 (a); *Star Trek V: The Final Frontier* 1989 (a); *Funny About Love* 1990 (d).

Niven, David • Actor; also author. • Born James David Graham Niven, Kirriemuir, Scotland, March 1, 1910; died July 29, 1983, Chateau d'Oex, Switzerland. *Educ.* Royal Military College, Sandhurst. Dapper leading man who drifted into Hollywood in the mid-1930s. Despite his lack of acting experience Niven rapidly graduated from bit parts to supporting and lead roles which showcased his polished British diction. His first major success came with Edmund Goulding's *The Dawn Patrol* (1938), in which he played a courageous, devil-may-care WWI pilot. Over the next three decades Niven appeared in numerous films in England and America. Though most adept at comedic roles—ranging from the dashing, romantic hero of *Bachelor Mother* (1939) to the unflappable Englishman, Phileas Hogg, in *Around the World in 80 Days* (1956)—he also proved a capable dramatic player, winning critical acclaim for his performance as Major Pollock in *Separate Tables* (1958). In the 1970s Niven published several books, including two best-selling autobiographies, *The Moon's a Balloon* and *Bring On the Empty Horses*, and the novel, *Go Slowly, Come Back Quickly*. • *Eyes of Fate* 1933; *A Feather in Her Hat* 1935; *Splendor* 1935; *Without Regret* 1935; *Beloved Enemy* 1936; *The Charge of the Light Brigade* 1936; *Dodsworth* 1936; *Palm Springs* 1936; *Rose Marie* 1936; *Thank You, Jeeves* 1936; *Dinner at the Ritz* 1937; *The Prisoner of Zenda* 1937; *We Have Our Moments* 1937; *Bluebeard's Eighth Wife* 1938; *The Dawn Patrol* 1938; *Four Men and a Prayer* 1938; *Three Blind Mice* 1938; *Bachelor Mother* 1939; *Eternally Yours* 1939; *The Real Glory* 1939; *Wuthering Heights* 1939; *Raffles* 1940; *The First of the Few* 1942; *Magnificent Doll* 1946; *The Perfect Marriage* 1946; *The Bishop's Wife* 1947; *The Other Love* 1947; *Enchantment* 1948; *A Kiss in the Dark* 1949; *A Kiss For Corliss* 1950; *The Toast of New Orleans* 1950; *Happy Go Lovely* 1951; *The Lady Says No* 1951; *Soldiers Three* 1951; *The Moon Is Blue* 1953; *Carrington V.C.* 1954; *Happy Ever After* 1954; *The King's Thief* 1955; *Around the World in 80 Days* 1956; *The Birds and the Bees* 1956; *Oh, Men! Oh, Women!* 1956; *Bonjour Tristesse* 1957; *The Little Hut* 1957; *My Man Godfrey* 1957; *Separate Tables* 1958 **(AABA)**; *Ask Any Girl* 1959; *Happy Anniversary* 1959; *Please Don't Eat the Daisies* 1960; *The Guns of Navarone* 1961; *Citta Prigioniera* 1962; *55 Days at Peking* 1963; *Bedtime Story* 1964; *The Pink Panther* 1964; *Lady L* 1965; *Eye of the Devil* 1966; *Casino Royale* 1967; *Before Winter Comes* 1968; *The Impossible Years* 1968; *Prudence and the Pill* 1968; *Le Cerveau* 1969; *The Extraordinary Seaman* 1969; *The Statue* 1970; *King, Queen, Knave* 1972; *Old Dracula* 1975; *Paper Tiger* 1975; *Murder By Death* 1976; *No Deposit, No Return* 1976; *Candleshoe* 1977; *Death on the Nile* 1978; *Escape to Athena* 1979; *Rough Cut* 1980; *The Sea Wolves* 1980; *Trail of the Pink Panther* 1982; *Better Late Than Never* 1983.

Noiret, Philippe • Actor • Born Lille, France, October 1, 1930. *Educ.* Centre Dramatique de l'Ouest. One of the most highly acclaimed of contemporary French screen actors. Noiret had enjoyed ten successful years with the Théâtre Nationale Populaire in Paris before he made his film debut in Agnes Varda's *La Pointe Courte* in 1956. He first attracted attention for his portrayal of the unhappy uncle in Louis Malle's *Zazie dans le Métro* (1960) and, on the strength of a delightfully slothful performance in Yves Robert's *Very Happy Alexander* (1968), spent a brief period in Hollywood in the late 1960s. On his return to France, Noiret established himself as one of Europe's most versatile performers, winning a best actor Cesar for his role in Robert Enrico's *Le Vieux Fusil* (1975) and beginning his long-standing, celebrated association with Bertrand Tavernier. Described by Tavernier as "believable in any social context," Noiret has appeared in seven of the director's films to date. He was memorable as a deceptively bumbling colonial police chief in Tavernier's *Clean Slate* (1981). • *La Pointe Courte* 1956; *Zazie dans le Métro* 1960; *Tout l'Or du Monde* 1961; *Thérèse Desqueyroux/Thérèse* 1962; *Cyrano et d'Artagnan* 1963; *Lady L* 1965; *The Night of the Generals* 1966; *L'Une et l'autre* 1967; *Woman Times Seven* 1967; *Adolphe ou l'Age Tendre* 1968; *Alexandre le Bienheureux/Very Happy Alexander* 1968; *Mister Freedom* 1968; *The Assassination Bureau* 1969; *Justine* 1969; *Topaz* 1969; *Murphy's War*

1970; *Les Aveux les plus doux* 1971; *La Mandarine* 1971; *Le Vieille Fille* 1971; *L'Attentat* 1972; *Le Trèfle à Cinq Feuilles* 1972; *Les Gaspards* 1973; *La Grande Bouffe* 1973; *L'Horloger de St Paul/The Clockmaker* 1973; *Poil de Carotte* 1973; *Le Serpent* 1973; *Touche pas à la femme blanche!* 1973; *Le Jeu avec le feu* 1974; *Un Nuage entre les dents* 1974; *Que la fête commence.../Let Joy Reign Supreme* 1974; *Le Secret* 1974; *Amici Miei/My Friends* 1975; *Monsieur Albert* 1975; *Le Vieux Fusil* 1975; *Le Desert des tartares* 1976; *Une Femme A Sa Fenêtre* 1976; *Le Juge et l'assassin* 1976; *Un Taxi mauve* 1977; *Tendre Poulet/Dear Inspector* 1977; *La Barricade du point du Jour* 1978; *Le Témoin* 1978; *Who Is Killing the Great Chefs of Europe?* 1978; *Due pezzi di Pane* 1979; *On a volé la cuisse de Jupiter* 1979; *Rue du Pied-De-Grue* 1979; *Pile ou Face* 1980; *Une Semaine de vacances* 1980; *I Tre fratelli* 1980; *Coup de Torchon/Clean Slate* 1981; *l' Etoile du nord* 1982; *L'Africain* 1983; *L'Ami de Vincent* 1983; *Amici miei atto II* 1983; *Le Grand Carnaval* 1983; *L'Eté Prochain* 1984; *Fort Saganne* 1984; *Souvenirs, Souvenirs* 1984; *Hitchcock, Il Brivido del Genio* 1985; *Le Quatrième Pouvoir* 1985; *Les Ripoux* 1985; *Autour de Minuit/'Round Midnight* 1986; *La Femme secrète* 1986; *Pourvu que ce soit une fille/Let's Hope It's a Girl* 1986; *Twist Again à Moscou* 1986; *La Famiglia* 1987; *L'Homme qui plantait des arbres* 1987; *Masques* 1987; *Noyade interdite* 1987; *Gli Occhiali d'Oro* 1987; *Chouans!* 1988; *La Femme de mes amours* 1988; *Il Giovane Toscanini* 1988; *Nuovo Cinema Paradiso/Cinema Paradiso* 1988; *The Return of the Musketeers* 1989; *La Vie et rien d'autre/Life and Nothing But* 1989; *Dimenticare Palermo* 1990; *Faux et usage de faux* 1990; *Ripoux Contre Ripoux* 1990; *Uranus* 1990.

Nolan, Lloyd • Actor • Born San Francisco, CA, August 11, 1902. Died 1985. *Educ.* Stanford. No-nonsense lead of the 1930s and 40s, primarily in low-budget action films; subsequently in character roles. One latter day gem: the father in *A Hatful of Rain* (1957). • *Atlantic Adventure* 1935; *G-Men* 1935; *One Way Ticket* 1935; *She Couldn't Take It* 1935; *Stolen Harmony* 1935; *15 Maiden Lane* 1936; *Big Brown Eyes* 1936; *Counterfeit* 1936; *Devil's Squadron* 1936; *Lady of Secrets* 1936; *The Texas Rangers* 1936; *You May Be Next* 1936; *Ebb Tide* 1937; *Exclusive* 1937; *Internes Can't Take Money* 1937; *King of Gamblers* 1937; *Wells Fargo* 1937; *Dangerous to Know* 1938; *Every Day's a Holiday* 1938; *Hunted Men* 1938; *King of Alcatraz* 1938; *Tip-Off Girls* 1938; *Ambush* 1939; *The Magnificent Fraud* 1939; *St. Louis Blues* 1939; *Undercover Doctor* 1939; *Behind the News* 1940; *Charter Pilot* 1940; *Gangs of Chicago* 1940; *The Golden Fleecing* 1940; *The House Across the Bay* 1940; *Johnny Apollo* 1940; *The Man I Married* 1940; *The Man Who Wouldn't Talk* 1940; *Michael Shayne, Private Detective* 1940; *Pier 13* 1940; *Blue, White and Perfect* 1941; *Blues in the Night* 1941; *Buy Me That Town* 1941; *Dressed to Kill* 1941; *Mr. Dynamite* 1941; *Sleeping West* 1941; *Steel Against the Sky* 1941; *It Happened in Flatbush* 1942; *Just Off Broadway* 1942; *The Man Who Wouldn't Die* 1942; *Manila Calling* 1942; *Time to Kill* 1942; *Apache Trail* 1943; *Guadalcanal Diary* 1943; *Captain Eddie* 1945; *Circumstantial Evidence* 1945; *The House on 92nd Street* 1945; *A Tree Grows in Brooklyn* 1945; *Backfire* 1946; *Lady in the Lake* 1946; *Two Smart People* 1946; *Wild Harvest* 1947; *Bad Boy* 1948; *Green Grass of Wyoming* 1948; *The Street With No Name* 1948; *Easy Living* 1949; *The Sun Comes Up* 1949; *The Lemon Drop Kid* 1951; *Crazylegs* 1953; *Island in the Sky* 1953; *The Last Hunt* 1955; *Santiago* 1956; *Toward the Unknown* 1956; *Abandon Ship!* 1957; *A Hatful of Rain* 1957; *Peyton Place* 1957; *Girl of the Night* 1960; *Portrait in Black* 1960; *Susan Slade* 1961; *We Joined the Navy* 1962; *The Girl Hunters* 1963; *Sergeant Ryker* 1963; *Circus World* 1964; *Never Too Late* 1965; *An American Dream* 1966; *The Double Man* 1967; *Ice Station Zebra* 1968; *Airport* 1970; *Earthquake* 1974; *The November Plan* 1976; *The Private Files of J. Edgar Hoover* 1977; *My Boys Are Good Boys* 1978; *Prince Jack* 1984; *Hannah and Her Sisters* 1986.

Nolte, Nick • Actor • Born Omaha, NB, February 8, 1941. *Educ.* Arizona State College; Eastern Arizona Junior College; Pasadena City College; Phoenix City College. Heavy-set blond lead who first received attention for his role in the TV miniseries "Rich Man, Poor Man" (1976). Nolte established himself on the big screen in the late 1970s, primarily in action-oriented roles, but subsequently proved his worth across a wider range of genres. He demonstrated a flair for comedy as the straight man in *48 Hrs.* (1982) and as an eccentric bum in *Down and Out in Beverly Hills* (1986), and gave a compelling performance as racist, boorish cop Mike Brennan in Sidney Lumet's *Q&A* (1990). • *Return to Macon County* 1975; *The Deep* 1977; *Who'll Stop the Rain?* 1978; *Heart Beat* 1979; *North Dallas Forty* 1979; *48 Hrs.* 1982; *Cannery Row* 1982; *Under Fire* 1983; *Teachers* 1984; *Grace Quigley* 1985; *Down and Out in Beverly Hills* 1986; *Extreme Prejudice* 1987; *Weeds* 1987; *Farewell to the King* 1989; *New York Stories* 1989; *Three Fugitives* 1989; *Another 48 Hrs.* 1990; *Everybody Wins* 1990; *Q&A* 1990.

Normand, Mabel • *aka* Muriel Fortescue • Actress • Born Boston, MA, November 16, 1894; died 1930. Beautiful teenage model who joined Biograph at the age of 16 and, following a brief stint at Vitagraph, was taken under the wing of director Mack Sennett. Normand emerged as the finest comedienne of the silent era, as well as a capable director of short films—she orchestrated several early Chaplin efforts, including *Tillie's Punctured Romance* (1914), in which they both starred. In 1916 Sennett and his partners, Kessel and Bauman, formed the Mabel Normand Feature Film Company. Normand demonstrated an impressive dramatic range in the company's first feature, *Mickey*, which was not released until 1918. By that time Normand had signed with Samuel Goldwyn; her increasingly dissipated lifestyle, however, made her increasingly unreliable as an actress. She was linked to two prominent Hollywood scandals (including the William Desmond Taylor murder case) and, though cleared of any involvement, was unable to salvage her reputation. Normand made her last feature in 1923, subsequently appearing in a handful of Hal Roach two-reelers. • *The Water Nymph* 1912 (a); *Caught in a Cabaret* 1914 (d,sc); *The Fatal Mallet (short)* 1914 (d,sc); *Her Friend the Bandit (short)* 1914 (d,sc); *Mabel at the Wheel (short)* 1914 (d); *Mabel's Busy Day* 1914 (d,sc); *Mabel's Married Life* 1914 (d,sc); *Tillie's Punctured Romance* 1914 (a); *Dodging a Million* 1918 (a); *The Floor Below* 1918 (a); *Joan of Plattsburg* 1918 (a); *Mickey* 1918 (a); *Peck's Bad Girl* 1918 (a); *A Perfect 36* 1918 (a); *The Venus Model* 1918 (a); *Jinx* 1919 (a); *The Pest* 1919 (a); *Sis Hopkins* 1919 (a); *Upstairs* 1919 (a); *When Doctors Disagree* 1919 (a); *Pinto* 1920 (a); *The Slim Princess* 1920 (a); *What Happened to Rosa* 1920 (a); *Molly O'* 1921 (a); *Back to the Woods* 1922 (a); *Head Over Heels* 1922 (a); *Oh, Mabel Behave* 1922 (a); *The Extra Girl* 1923 (a); *Suzanna* 1923 (a).

Norris, Chuck • Actor • Born Carlos Ray, Ryan, OK, 1939. Former karate champion who entered film under the auspices of Bruce Lee and has parlayed his martial arts prowess into a career in gung-ho action movies. • *Return of the Dragon* 1973 (a); *Breaker, Breaker* 1976 (a); *Good Guys Wear Black* 1978 (a,martial arts chor); *A Force of One* 1979 (a,chor—fight); *Game of Death* 1979 (a); *The Octagon* 1980 (a,chor—karate fights); *An Eye For an Eye* 1981 (a); *Forced Vengeance* 1982 (a); *Lone Wolf McQuade* 1982 (a); *Silent Rage* 1982 (a); *Missing in Action* 1984 (a); *Code of Silence* 1985 (a); *Invasion U.S.A.* 1985 (a,sc); *Missing in Action 2—The Beginning* 1985 (a); *The Delta Force* 1986 (a); *Firewalker* 1986 (a); *Braddock: Missing in Action III* 1988 (a,sc); *Hero and the Terror* 1988 (a); *Delta Force II* 1990 (a).

North, Alex • Composer • Born Chester, PA, December 4, 1910. *Educ.* Curtis Institute; Juilliard School of Music; Moscow Conservatory of Music. Composer of ballets, symphonies and stage music whose work on Elia Kazan's theater production of *Death of a Salesman* moved the director to bring him to Hollywood to score *A Streetcar Named Desire* (1951). The film earned North the first of 15 Oscar nominations and introduced the sparer, more economic style of orchestration that eventually displaced the lusher scores of the 1930s and 40s. North's subsequent work ranged from intimate dramas (*The Member of the Wedding* 1953) to period epics (*Spartacus* 1960) to westerns (*Cheyenne Autumn* 1964). In 1985 he was awarded an honorary Oscar for his cumulative work in motion pictures. • *The 13th Letter* 1951 (m); *A Streetcar Named Desire* 1951 (m) **(AANBM)**; *The Member of the Wedding* 1953 (m); *Les Miserables* 1952 (m); *Pony Soldier* 1952 (m); *Viva Zapata!* 1952 (m) **(AANBM)**; *Desiree* 1954 (m); *Go, Man, Go!* 1954 (m); *Unchained* 1954 (m) **(AANBS)**; *Daddy Long Legs* 1955 (m); *I'll Cry Tomorrow* 1955 (m); *The Racers* 1955 (m); *The Rose Tattoo* 1955 (m) **(AANBM)**; *The Bad Seed* 1956 (m); *The King and Four Queens* 1956 (m); *The Rainmaker* 1956 (m) **(AANBM)**; *Hot Spell* 1958 (m); *The Long, Hot Summer* 1958 (m,song); *The Sound and the Fury* 1958 (m); *South Seas Adventure* 1958 (m,m.cond); *Stage Struck* 1958 (m); *The Wonderful Country* 1959 (m,m.cond); *Spartacus* 1960 (m) **(AANBM)**; *The Children's Hour* 1961 (m); *The Misfits* 1961 (m); *Sanctuary* 1961 (m); *All Fall Down* 1962 (m); *Cleopatra* 1963 (m,m.cond) **(AANBM)**; *Cheyenne Autumn* 1964 (m); *The Outrage* 1964 (m); *The Agony and the Ecstasy* 1965 (m,m.cond) **(AANBM)**; *Who's Afraid of Virginia Woolf?* 1966 (m,m.cond) **(AANBM)**; *The Devil's Brigade* 1968 (m); *The Shoes of the Fisherman* 1968 (m) **(AANBM)**; *A Dream of Kings* 1969 (m,m.dir); *Hard Contract* 1969 (m); *Willard* 1971 (m); *Pocket Money* 1972 (m); *Once Upon a Scoundrel* 1973 (m); *Lost in the Stars* 1974 (m.sup); *Shanks* 1974 (m) **(AANBM)**; *Bite the Bullet* 1975 (m) **(AANBM)**; *Journey Into Fear* 1976 (m); *The Passover Plot* 1976 (m); *Somebody Killed Her Husband* 1978 (m,m.dir,m.adapt); *Wise Blood* 1979 (m,m.dir); *Carny* 1980 (m); *Dragonslayer* 1981 (m) **(AANBM)**; *Baby, It's You* 1983 (song); *Under the Volcano* 1984 (m) **(AANBM)**; *Prizzi's Honor* 1985 (m); *The Dead* 1987 (m); *Good Morning, Vietnam* 1987 (m); *John Huston & The Dubliners* 1987 (m); *The Penitent* 1988 (m); *Ghost* 1990 (song); *Le Dernier papillon* 1991 (m).

Novak, Kim • Actress • Born Marilyn Pauline Novak, Chicago, IL, February 13, 1933. *Educ.* Los Angeles City College. Frosty blonde beauty who broke into films in 1954. Signed and molded by Columbia Pictures mogul Harry Cohn, Novak soon became a popular Hollywood star, with her off-screen romances (Sammy Davis, Frank Sinatra, Cary Grant and Aly Khan were among her partners) attracting as much publicity as her film roles. Probably best known for her cryptic performance in Alfred Hitchcock's dizzying thriller, *Vertigo* (1958). • *Phffl* 1954; *Pushover* 1954; *Five Against the House* 1955; *The Man With the Golden Arm* 1955; *The Eddy Duchin Story* 1956; *Picnic* 1956; *Jeanne Eagels* 1957; *Pal Joey* 1957; *Bell, Book and Candle* 1958; *Vertigo* 1958; *Middle of the Night* 1959; *Pepe* 1960; *Strangers When We Meet* 1960; *Boys' Night Out* 1962; *The Notorious Landlady* 1962; *Kiss Me, Stupid* 1964; *Of Human Bondage* 1964; *The Amorous Adventures of Moll Flanders* 1965; *The Legend of Lylah Clare* 1968; *The Great Bank Robbery* 1969; *Tales That Witness Madness* 1973; *The White Buffalo* 1977; *An American Gigolo* 1979; *The Mirror Crack'd* 1980; *Es Hat Mich Sehr Gefreut* 1987; *The Children* 1990; *Liebestraum* 1991.

Novarro, Ramon • Actor; also director. • Born Ramon Samaniegos, Durango, Mexico, February 6, 1899; died 1968. Mexican vaudevillian who made his film debut in 1917 and emerged as a romantic star of the silent era. Best known for his starring role in *Ben-Hur* (1925). Novarro was brutally murdered in his own home by two teenaged hustlers. • *The Jaguar's Claws* 1917; *The Little American* 1917; *Mr. Barnes of New York* 1922; *The Prisoner of Zenda* 1922; *Trifling Women* 1922; *Scaramouche* 1923; *Where the Pavement Ends* 1923; *The Arab* 1924; *The Red Lily* 1924; *Thy Name Is Woman* 1924; *Ben-Hur, A Tale of the Christ* 1925; *A Lover's Oath* 1925; *The Midshipman* 1925; *Lovers?* 1927; *The Road to Romance* 1927; *The Student Prince in Old Heidelberg* 1927; *Across to Singapore* 1928; *A Certain Young Man* 1928; *Forbidden Hours* 1928; *Devil May Care* 1929; *The Flying Fleet* 1929; *The Pagan* 1929; *Call of the Flesh* 1930; *In Gay Madrid* 1930; *Daybreak* 1931; *Son of India* 1931; *Huddle* 1932; *Mata Hari* 1932; *The Son-Daughter* 1932; *The Barbarian* 1933; *The Cat and the Fiddle* 1934; *Laughing Boy* 1934; *The Night Is Young* 1935; *The Sheik Steps Out* 1937; *The Desperate Adventure* 1938; *The Big Steal* 1949; *We Were Strangers* 1949; *Crisis* 1950; *The Outriders* 1950; *Heller in Pink Tights* 1960.

Noyce, Phillip • Director • Born Griffith, New South Wales, Australia, 1950. *Educ.* Sydney Film School. Began making short films in the late 1960s and became manager of the Sydney Filmaker's Co-operative in 1980. Most of Noyce's work in the 1980s has been for George "Mad Max" Miller's Kennedy Miller Productions; he is best known for the Hitchcock-style thriller, *Dead Calm* (1989). • *The Golden Cage* 1975 (ad); *Let the Balloon Go* 1976 (ad); *Backroads* 1977 (d,p,sc); *Newsfront* 1978 (d,sc); *Heatwave* 1981 (d,sc,special makeup effects); *Shadows of the Peacock* 1986 (d); *Echoes of Paradise* 1988 (d); *Blind Fury* 1989 (d); *Dead Calm* 1989 (d).

Nuytten, Bruno • Director of photography; also director, screenwriter. • Born Paris, August 28, 1945. *Educ.* Académie Charpentier, Paris (art); IDHEC, Paris; Institut des Arts du Spectacle, Brussels. Award-winning cinematographer who apprenticed with two of the world's finest lighting cameramen, Ghislain Cloquet and Ricardo Aronovich, before making his mark shooting Bertrand Blier's bawdy comedy, *Going Places* (1974). Nuytten has since established himself as one of his country's leading directors of photography, winning Cesars for his work on Andre Techine's *Barocco* (1976) and Claude Berri's *Tchao Pantin* (1983) and a British Academy Award for Berri's *Jean de Florette* (1986). Nuytten made an acclaimed directorial debut with *Camille Claudel* (1988), which earned five Cesars and an Oscar nomination as best foreign feature. The film turned on a passionate central performance by Isabelle Adjani, Nuytten's former companion and the mother of his young son. • *Nathalie Granger* 1972 (asst.cam.op.); *Les Valseuses/Going Places* 1974 (ph); *L'Asassin Musicien* 1975 (ph); *India Song* 1975 (ph); *La Meilleure Façon de Marcher/The Best Way to Walk* 1975 (ph); *Souvenirs d'en France* 1975 (ph); *Barocco* 1976 (ph); *Le Camion* 1977 (ph); *L'Exercice du Pouvoir* 1977 (ph); *Mon coeur est rouge* 1977 (ph); *Les Soeurs Brontë/The Brontë Sisters* 1978 (ph); *La Tortue sur le dos* 1978 (ph); *Zoo-Zéro* 1978 (ph); *French Postcards* 1979 (ph); *The Best Way* 1980 (ph); *Brubaker* 1980 (ph); *Garde à Vue/The Inquisitor* 1981 (ph); *Possession* 1981 (ph); *Hotel des Ameriques* 1982 (ph); *Tchao Pantin* 1983 (ph); *La Vie est un roman/Life is a Bed of Roses* 1983 (ph); *Les Enfants* 1984 (ph); *Fort Saganne* 1984 (ph); *La Pirate* 1984 (ph); *Détéctive* 1985 (ph); *Double Messieurs* 1986 (sc,ph); *Jean de Florette* 1986 (ph); *Manon des sources/Manon of the Spring* 1986 (ph); *Camille Claudel* 1988 (d,sc,dial,adapt).

Nykvist, Sven • Director of photography; also director. • Born Moheda, Sweden, December 3, 1922. *Educ.* Stockholm Municipal School for Photographers. Sven Nykvist joined Sandrews studios as an assistant in 1941, his goal being to follow in the footsteps of the great Swedish cameramen, Julius Jaenzon, Goran Strindberg and Gunnar Fischer. He first earned attention during the 1950s for his work with Alf Sjöberg, notably on *Barabbas* (1953), before embarking on his justly renowned series of collaborations with director Ingmar Bergman.

Nykvist's first project with Bergman was *Gycklarnas Afton/Sawdust and Tinsel* 1953; he was assigned the difficult interior shots by his former teacher, director of photography Hilding Bladh, as a final test of his skill. From their first full collaboration, *The Virgin Spring* (1960), the partnership between Bergman and Nykvist flourished.

Influenced by the Swedish tradition of stark, psychologically meaningful landscape and minimalist shot composition, Nykvist and Bergman share a preference for location shooting and natural light. They also agree that subtle changes of light can alter the meaning of a character's actions.

Nykvist designs his cinematography in meticulous detail. Tests are done at all times of the day for the entire film before shooting begins. When working with Bergman and their close-knit group of technicians, Nykvist lights the sets and works the camera himself. He manipulates the light itself, rather than relying on laboratory techniques or distorting filters and lenses, and favors a soft "bounce" lighting that will contour and flatter an actor's face. His camera work is typified by *Scenes from a Marriage* (1973); the film is composed of long takes, some of which last ten minutes and include as many as twenty zooms.

For many years, Nykvist and Bergman favored black-and-white, considering color to be a source of superficial beauty. In 1964, they experimented with color in *All These Women.* Typically, they tested the entire technical crew for color blindness and shot 18,000 feet of color experiments before shooting of the film even began. Both men were nevertheless dissatisfied with the final product, citing its lack of atmosphere and excessive lighting. Their second color film, *En Passion/The Passion of Anna* (1969), was acclaimed for its minimum color saturation and muted tones, which would become Nykvist's trademark. Nykvist won an Academy Award for his color cinematography on Bergman's *Cries and Whispers* (1972).

While Nykvist is most often connected with Bergman, with whom he has made 20 films, he has worked with other Scandinavian directors such as Arne Mattsson and Gunnar Hellstrom in the 1950s and Vilgot Sjöman, Mai Zetterling and Jörn Donner in the 1960s. In the 1970s and 1980s, Nykvist shot films for a variety of international directors, including Roman Polanski, Louis Malle, Volker Schlöndorff and Andrei Tarkovsky, and a number of American filmmakers such as Alan Pakula, Paul Mazursky and Norman Jewison. He won a second Academy Award for Bergman's *Fanny and Alexander* in 1982 and a prize at Cannes in 1986.

In 1964, Nykvist directed his first feature, *The Vine Bridge,* with Harriet Andersson, Folke Sundquist and Mai Zetterling. The film draws on some elements of his own life, featuring a protagonist who, like Nykvist, was raised by missionary parents in Africa.

Nykvist has described his own work as the emulation of the great silent storytellers, particularly Stiller, Sjöstrom, Eisenstein and Lang, who all mastered the art of telling stories with pictures rather than words. RJB • *Barabbas* 1953 (ph); *Gycklarnas Afton/Sawdust and Tinsel* 1953 (ph—interiors); *Karin Mansdotter* 1954 (ph); *The Judge* 1960 (ph); *Jungfrukallan/The Virgin Spring* 1960 (ph); *A Matter of Morals* 1960 (ph); *Sasom i en Spegel/Through a Glass Darkly* 1961 (ph); *Nattvardsgasterna* 1963 (ph); *Tystnaden/The Silence* 1963 (ph); *Att Alska* 1964 (ph); *For att Inte Tala om Alla Dessa Kvinnor/All These Women* 1964 (ph); *Persona* 1966 (ph); *Brant Barn* 1967 (ph); *Roseanna* 1967 (ph); *Skammen/The Shame* 1968 (ph); *Vargtimmen* 1968 (ph); *En Passion/The Passion of Anna* 1969 (ph); *Riten* 1969 (ph); *First Love* 1970 (ph); *Beroringen* 1971 (ph); *The Last Run* 1971 (ph); *One Day in the Life of Ivan Denisovich* 1971 (ph); *Cries and Whispers* 1972 (ph) **(AABPH)**; *Siddhartha* 1972 (ph); *Strohfeuer* 1972 (ph); *Scenes From a Marriage* 1973 (ph); *The Dove* 1974 (ph); *Ransom* 1974 (ph); *Black Moon* 1975 (ph); *Monismanien 1995* 1975 (ph); *Trollflojten/The Magic Flute* 1975 (ph); *Ansikte mot ansikte/Face to Face* 1976 (ph); *Le Locataire/The Tenant* 1976 (ph); *Das Schlangenei/The Serpent's Egg* 1977 (ph); *En och En* 1978 (d,p,ph); *Hostsonaten/Autumn Sonata* 1978 (ph); *King of the Gypsies* 1978 (ph); *Pretty Baby* 1978 (ph); *Hurricane* 1979 (ph); *Starting Over* 1979 (ph); *Aus dem Leben der Marionetten* 1980 (ph); *Marmeladupproret* 1980 (d,p,ph); *Willie & Phil* 1980 (ph); *The Postman Always Rings Twice* 1981 (ph); *Cannery Row* 1982 (ph); *Fanny och Alexander/Fanny and Alexander* 1982 (ph) **(AABPH)**; *Star 80* 1983 (ph); *La Tragedie de Carmen* 1983 (ph); *After the Rehearsal* 1984 (ph); *Un Amour de Swann/Swann in Love* 1984 (ph); *Agnes of God* 1985 (ph); *Dream Lover* 1986 (ph); *Offret-Sacrificatio/The Sacrifice* 1986 (ph); *Another Woman* 1988 (ph); *Katinka* 1988 (ph); *The Unbearable Lightness of Being* 1988 (ph) **(AANBPH)**; *Crimes and Misdemeanors* 1989 (ph); *New York Stories* 1989 (ph—"Oedipus Wrecks"); *The Ox* 1991 (d,sc).

O'Brien, Edmond • Actor; also producer, director. • Born New York, NY, September 10, 1915; died May 9, 1985, Inglewood, CA. *Educ.* Fordham University, New York; Neighborhood Playhouse, New York; Columbia. Leading man of the 1940s turned veteran Hollywood character player. O'Brien joined Orson Welles's Mercury Players in 1937 and worked in film and on stage through the 1940s, turning primarily to the screen after WWII. He is best remembered as the lead in the noir classic, *D.O.A.* (1950), for his role as a sycophantic Hollywood press agent in *The Barefoot Contessa* (1954) and for a string of weather-beaten character parts in the 70s. O'Brien was married to actresses Nancy Kelly and Olga San Juan; Maria O'Brien, his daughter by the latter, has appeared in several films. • *The Hunchback of Notre Dame* 1939 (a); *Girl, a Guy and a Gob, A* 1941 (a); *Obliging Young Lady* 1941 (a); *Parachute Battalion* 1941 (a); *Powder Town* 1942 (a); *The Amazing Mrs. Holliday* 1943 (a); *Winged Victory* 1944 (a); *The Killers* 1946 (a); *A Double Life* 1947 (a); *The Web* 1947 (a); *An Act of Murder* 1948 (a); *Another Part of the Forest* 1948 (a); *Fighter Squadron* 1948 (a); *White Heat* 1949 (a); *711 Ocean Drive* 1950 (a); *The Admiral Was a Lady* 1950 (a); *Backfire* 1950 (a); *Between Midnight and Dawn* 1950 (a); *D.O.A.* 1950 (a); *The Redhead and the Cowboy* 1950 (a); *Silver City* 1951 (a); *Two of a Kind* 1951 (a); *Warpath* 1951 (a); *The Denver and Rio Grande* 1952 (a); *The Turning Point* 1952 (a); *The Bigamist* 1953 (a); *China Venture* 1953 (a); *Cow Country* 1953 (a); *The Hitch-Hiker* 1953 (a); *Julius Caesar* 1953 (a); *Man in the Dark* 1953 (a); *The Barefoot Contessa* 1954 (a) **(AABSA)**; *The Shanghai Story* 1954 (a); *Shield For Murder* 1954 (a,d); *Pete Kelly's Blues* 1955 (a); *1984* 1956 (a); *A Cry in the Night* 1956 (a); *D-Day the Sixth of June* 1956 (a); *The Girl Can't Help It* 1956 (a); *The Rack* 1956 (a); *The Big Land* 1957 (a); *Sing Boy Sing* 1957 (a); *Stopover Tokyo* 1957 (a); *The World Was His Jury* 1957 (a); *Up Periscope* 1959 (a); *The Great Impostor* 1960 (a); *The Last Voyage* 1960 (a); *The Third Voice* 1960 (a); *Man-Trap* 1961 (d,p); *Birdman of Alcatraz* 1962 (a); *The Longest Day* 1962 (a); *The Man Who Shot Liberty Valance* 1962 (a); *Moon Pilot* 1962 (a); *The Hanged Man* 1964 (a); *Rio Conchos* 1964 (a); *Seven Days in May* 1964 (a) (**AANBSA**); *Sylvia* 1965 (a); *Synanon* 1965 (a); *Fantastic Voyage* 1966 (a); *Le Vicomte Regle ses Comptes* 1967 (a); *The Love God?* 1969 (a); *The Wild Bunch* 1969 (a); *They Only Kill Their Masters* 1972 (a); *Re: Lucky Luciano* 1973 (a); *99 and 44/100% Dead* 1974 (a).

O'Brien, Pat • Actor • Born William Joseph Patrick O'Brien, Milwaukee, WI, November 11, 1899; died October 15, 1983, Santa Monica, CA. *Educ.* Marquette University (law); AADA, New York. Veteran Irish-American character player, best known for his title role (opposite Ronald Reagan) in *Knute Rockne—All American* (1940) and as Jimmy Cagney's clerical confidante in *Angels With Dirty Faces* (1938); childhood friend of Spencer Tracy. • *Shadows of the West* 1921; *The Freckled Rascal* 1929; *Fury of the Wild* 1929; *Consolation Marriage* 1931; *Flying High* 1931; *The Front Page* 1931; *Honor Among Lovers* 1931; *Personal Maid* 1931; *Air Mail* 1932; *American Madness* 1932; *The Final Edition* 1932; *Hell's House* 1932; *Hollywood Speaks* 1932; *Scandal For Sale* 1932; *The Strange Case of Clara Deane* 1932; *Virtue* 1932; *The Blonde Bombshell* 1933; *Bureau of Missing Persons* 1933; *College Coach* 1933; *Destination Unknown* 1933; *Flaming Gold* 1933; *Laughter in Hell* 1933; *The World Gone Mad* 1933; *Flirtation Walk* 1934; *Gambling Lady* 1934; *Here Comes the Navy* 1934; *I Sell Anything* 1934; *I've Got Your Number* 1934; *The Personality Kid* 1934; *Twenty Million Sweetharts* 1934; *Ceiling Zero* 1935; *Devil Dogs of the Air* 1935; *In Caliente* 1935; *The Irish in Us* 1935; *Oil For the Lamps of China* 1935; *Outlawed Guns* 1935; *Page Miss Glory* 1935; *The Roaring West* 1935; *Stars Over Broadway* 1935; *China Clipper* 1936; *I Married a Doctor* 1936; *Public Enemy's Wife* 1936; *Back in Circulation* 1937; *The Great O'Malley* 1937; *San Quentin* 1937; *Slim* 1937; *Submarine D-1* 1937; *Women Are Like That* 1937; *Angels With Dirty Faces* 1938; *Bar 20 Justice* 1938; *Boy Meets Girl* 1938; *Cowboy From Brooklyn* 1938; *Garden of the Moon* 1938; *Hawaiian Buckaroo* 1938; *Panamint's Bad Man* 1938; *Indianapolis Speedway* 1939; *The Kid From Kokomo* 1939; *The Night of Nights* 1939; *Off the Record* 1939; *'Til We Meet Again* 1940; *Castle on the Hudson* 1940; *Escape to Glory* 1940; *The Fighting 69th* 1940; *Flowing Gold* 1940; *Knute Rockne—All American* 1940; *Slightly Honorable* 1940; *Torrid Zone* 1940; *Broadway* 1942; *The Navy Comes Through* 1942; *Two Yanks in Trinidad* 1942; *Bombardier* 1943; *His Butler's Sister* 1943; *The Iron Major* 1943; *Marine Raiders* 1944; *Secret Command* 1944; *Having Wonderful Crime* 1945; *Man Alive* 1945; *Crack-Up* 1946; *Perilous Holiday* 1946; *The Boy With Green Hair* 1948; *Fighting Father Dunne* 1948; *A Dangerous Profession* 1949; *Johnny One-Eye* 1949; *The Fireball* 1950; *Criminal Lawyer* 1951; *The People Against O'Hara* 1951; *Okinawa* 1952; *Jubilee Trail* 1954; *Ring of Fear* 1954; *Inside Detroit* 1955; *The Last Hurrah* 1958; *Some Like It Hot* 1959; *Town Tamer* 1965; *The Phynx* 1970; *Billy Jack Goes to Washington* 1976; *The End* 1978; *Ragtime* 1981.

O'Brien, Willis H. • Special effects artist • Born Oakland, CA, 1886; died 1962. Former marble-cutter and cartoonist who began using stop-motion photography to make short films, often featuring models of dinosaurs, in the early teens. O'Brien's efforts attracted the attention of the Edison company, for whom he made ten five-minute shorts on Stone Age subjects before applying his talents to feature films in the 20s. O'Brien pioneered the use of rubber, rather than clay, models, an innovation that first reached the screen in *The Lost World* (1925). Other outstanding examples of his work include the oversized apes of *King Kong* (1933) and *Mighty Joe Young* (1949). • *The Ghost of Slumber Mountain* 1920 (fx); *The Lost World* 1925 (fx); *King Kong* 1933 (fx); *Son of Kong* 1933 (fx); *Mighty Joe Young* 1949 (fx); *The Animal World* 1956 (fx); *El Monstrud de la Montana Huela* 1956 (story); *The Black Scorpion* 1958 (fx).

O'Connor, Donald • Actor; also composer. • Born Chicago, IL, August 30, 1925. Bubbly, youthful lead of several minor Universal musicals in the 1940s. O'Connor later co-starred opposite Gene Kelly and Debbie Reynolds in *Singin' in the Rain* (1952) and—to somewhat less critical acclaim—a trained mule in the "Francis, the Talking Mule" series. • *Melody For Two* 1937; *Men With Wings* 1938; *Sing, You Sinners* 1938; *Sons of the Legion* 1938; *Tom Sawyer, Detective* 1938; *Beau Geste* 1939; *Death of a Champion* 1939; *Million Dollar Legs* 1939; *Night Work* 1939; *On Your Toes* 1939; *Unmarried* 1939; *Get Hep to Love* 1942; *Give Out, Sisters* 1942; *Private Buckaroo* 1942; *When Johnny Comes Marching Home* 1942; *It Comes Up Love* 1943; *Mister Big* 1943; *Top Man* 1943; *Bowery to Broadway* 1944; *Chip Off the Old Block* 1944; *Follow the Boys* 1944; *The Merry Monahans* 1944; *This Is the Life* 1944; *Patrick the Great* 1945; *Something in the Wind* 1947; *Are You With It?* 1948; *Feudin', Fussin', and A-Fightin'* 1948; *Francis* 1949; *Yes, Sir, That's My Baby* 1949; *Curtain Call At Cactus Creek* 1950; *Double Crossbones* 1950; *The Milkman* 1950; *Francis Goes to the Races* 1951; *Francis Goes to West Point* 1952; *Singin' in the Rain* 1952; *Call Me Madam* 1953; *Francis Covers the Big Town* 1953; *I Love Melvin* 1953; *Walking My Baby Back Home* 1953; *Francis Joins the WACS* 1954; *There's No Business Like Show Business* 1954; *Francis in the Navy* 1955; *Anything Goes* 1956; *The Buster Keaton Story* 1957; *Cry For Happy* 1961; *The Wonders of Aladdin* 1961; *That Funny Feeling* 1965; *That's Entertainment!* 1974; *The Big Fix* 1978; *Pandemonium* 1981; *Ragtime* 1981; *A Time to Remember* 1990.

O'Connor, Kevin J. • Actor • Born Illinois. *Educ.* DePaul University; Goodman School of Drama, Chicago. Versatile young lead who made his feature debut immediately upon leaving college, as the bohemian poet who takes Peggy Sue for a ride in Francis Coppola's *Peggy Sue Got Married* (1986). O'Connor has also worked with Robert Altman, in TV's "Tanner '88" and *The Caine Mutiny Court Martial* (both 1988), and with former Altman associate Alan Rudolph, in *The Moderns* (1988) and *Love at Large* (1990). • *Peggy Sue Got Married* 1986; *Candy Mountain* 1987; *The Moderns* 1988; *Signs of Life* 1989; *Steel Magnolias* 1989; *Love at Large* 1990.

O'Connor, Pat • Director • Born Ardmore, Ireland. *Educ.* UCLA; Ryerson Institute, Toronto (film, TV). Began his career as a producer and director of documentaries with Ireland's Radio Telefis Eirann (RTE) and won a British Academy Award for his 1981 TV drama, *A Ballroom of Romance*. O'Connor was subsequently enlisted by David Puttnam to direct *Cal* (1984), an uncompromising political thriller set in the context of the Northern Irish "troubles." The film won widespread critical acclaim and earned Helen Mirren a best actress award at the Cannes Film Festival. With the exception of the studied, atmospheric *A Month in the Country* (1987), most of O'Connor's subsequent work has been disappointing. • *Cal* 1984 (d); *A Month in the Country* 1987 (d); *The January Man* 1988 (d); *Stars and Bars* 1988 (d); *Fools of Fortune* 1990 (d).

O'Hagan, Colo Tavernier • See Tavernier, Colo

O'Hara, Maureen • Actress • Born Maureen Fitzsimmons, Millwall, near Dublin, Ireland, August 17, 1920. *Educ.* Abbey School, Dublin. Radiant, red-haired Irish beauty who played a number of benevolent yet headstrong heroines in the 1940s and 50s. O'Hara was at her liveliest and most appealing in a number of John Ford films, notably opposite John Wayne in *The Quiet Man* (1952). • *The Hunchback of Notre Dame* 1939 (a); *Jamaica Inn* 1939 (a); *A Bill of Divorcement* 1940 (a); *Dance, Girl, Dance* 1940 (a); *How Green Was My Valley* 1941 (a); *They Met in Argentina* 1941 (a); *The Black Swan* 1942 (a); *Ten Gentlemen From West Point* 1942 (a); *To the Shores of Tripoli* 1942 (a); *Fallen Sparrow* 1943 (a); *Immortal Sergeant* 1943 (a); *This Land Is Mine* 1943 (a); *Buffalo Bill* 1944 (a); *The Spanish Main* 1945 (a); *Do You Love Me?* 1946 (a); *Sentimental Journey* 1946 (a); *The Foxes of Harrow* 1947 (a); *The Homestretch* 1947 (a); *Miracle on 34th Street* 1947 (a); *Sinbad the Sailor* 1947 (a); *Sitting Pretty* 1948 (a); *Bagdad* 1949 (a); *Father Was a Fullback* 1949 (a); *A Woman's Secret* 1949 (a); *Comanche Territory* 1950 (a); *Rio Grande* 1950 (a); *Tripoli* 1950 (a); *Flame of Araby* 1951 (a); *Against All Flags* 1952 (a); *At Sword's Point* 1952 (a); *Kangaroo* 1952 (a); *The Quiet Man* 1952 (a); *The Redhead From Wyoming* 1952 (a); *Malaga* 1954 (a); *War Arrow* 1954 (a); *Lady Godiva* 1955 (a); *The Long Gray Line* 1955 (a); *The Magnificent Matador* 1955 (a); *Everything But the Truth* 1956 (a); *Lisbon* 1956 (a); *The Wings of Eagles* 1956 (a); *The Deadly Companions* 1961 (a,song); *The Parent Trap* 1961 (a); *Mr. Hobbs Takes a Vacation* 1962 (a); *McLintock!* 1963 (a); *Spencer's Mountain* 1963 (a); *The Battle of the Villa Fiorita* 1965 (a); *The Rare Breed* 1966 (a); *How Do I Love Thee?* 1970 (a); *Big Jake* 1971 (a); *Only the Lonely* 1991 (a).

O'Herlihy, Dan • Actor • Born Wexford, Ireland, May 1, 1919. *Educ.* National University of Ireland (architecture). Character actor and idiosyncratic leading man who performed with the Gate Theatre and the Abbey Players in Dublin before immigrating to the US in the late 1940s. O'Herlihy joined Orson Welles's Mercury Theatre and played MacDuff opposite Welles's Macbeth in both the stage and (1948) screen version of the play. He is known for his title role in Buñuel's *The Adventures of Robinson Crusoe* (1952) and continues to appear in character parts on film and TV. • *Odd Man Out* 1947; *Kidnapped* 1948; *Larceny* 1948; *Macbeth* 1948; *The Blue Veil* 1951; *The Desert Fox* 1951; *The Highwayman* 1951; *Soldiers Three* 1951; *Actors and Sin* 1952; *Adventures of Robinson Crusoe* 1952 **(AANBA)**; *At Sword's Point* 1952; *Invasion U.S.A.* 1952; *Operation Secret* 1952; *Sword of Venus* 1953; *Bengal Brigade* 1954; *The Black Shield of Falworth* 1954; *The Purple Mask* 1955; *The Virgin Queen* 1955; *That Woman Opposite* 1957; *Home Before Dark* 1958; *Imitation of Life* 1959; *The Young Land* 1959; *One Foot in Hell* 1960; *A Terrible Beauty* 1960; *King of the Roaring 20's—The Story of Arnold Rothstein* 1961; *The Cabinet of Caligari* 1962; *Fail Safe* 1964; *How to Steal the World* 1968; *100 Rifles* 1969; *The Big Cube* 1969; *Waterloo* 1970; *The Carey Treatment* 1972; *The Tamarind Seed* 1974; *MacArthur the Rebel General* 1977; *Halloween III: Season of the Witch* 1982; *The Last Starfighter* 1984; *The Whoopee Boys* 1986; *The Dead* 1987; *John Huston & The Dubliners* 1987.

O'Neal, Ron • Actor; also director. • Born Utica, NY, September 1, 1937. *Educ.* Ohio State University. Impeccably cool lead of several 1970s "blaxploitation" movies, best known as the hip, high-stepping drug pusher in *Superfly* (1972). • *Move* 1970 (a); *The Organization* 1971 (a); *Superfly* 1972 (a); *Super Fly TNT* 1973 (a,d,story); *The Master Gunfighter* 1975 (a); *Brothers* 1977 (a); *A Force of One* 1979 (a); *When a Stranger Calls* 1979 (a); *The Final Countdown* 1980 (a); *St. Helens* 1981 (a); *Red Dawn* 1984 (a); *Freedom Fighter* 1988 (a); *Hero and the Terror* 1988 (a).

O'Neal, Ryan • Actor • Born Patrick Ryan O'Neal, Los Angeles, CA, April 20, 1941. Ruggedly handsome, sandy-haired lead who appeared, often opposite Mia Farrow, in over 500 episodes of TV's seminal soap opera, "Peyton Place" (1964-69) before boosting national handkerchief sales with his starring role in Erich Segal's soggy melodrama, *Love Story* (1970). O'Neal is at his best in light comedies, often as an abstracted bumbler—or, in the case of his most memorable role, an inept hustler (*Paper Moon* 1973). He is the son of screenwriter Charles O'Neal and actress Patricia Callaghan O'Neal and is married to actress Farrah Fawcett (former wives are actresses Joanna Moore and Leigh Taylor-Young). O'Neal's brother Kevin and son Griffin are both actors and daughter Tatum starred opposite her father in *Paper Moon*. • *The Big Bounce* 1969; *The Games* 1970; *Love Story* 1970 **(AANBA)**; *Wild Rovers* 1971; *What's Up, Doc?* 1972; *Paper Moon* 1973; *The Thief Who Came to Dinner* 1973; *Barry Lyndon* 1975; *Nickelodeon* 1976; *A Bridge Too Far* 1977; *The Driver* 1978; *Oliver's Story* 1978; *The Main Event* 1979; *Green Ice* 1981; *So Fine* 1981; *Partners* 1982; *Fever Pitch* 1985; *Tough Guys Don't Dance* 1987; *Chances Are* 1989.

O'Neal, Tatum • Actress • Born Los Angeles, CA, November 5, 1963. Juvenile star of the 1970s, best remembered for her Oscar-winning performance opposite her father, Ryan O'Neal, in *Paper Moon* (1973) and as the headstrong little-league pitching ace in *The Bad News Bears* (1976). Married tennis star John McEnroe in 1986. • *Paper Moon* 1973 **(AABSA)**; *The Bad News Bears* 1976; *Nickelodeon* 1976; *International Velvet* 1978; *Circle of Two* 1980; *Little Darlings* 1980; *Prisoners* 1983; *Certain Fury* 1984; *Little Noises* 1991.

O'Neill, Pat • American filmmaker; also special effects artist. • Experimental filmmaker whose many 16mm shorts make innovative and unusual use of special optical effects. Among O'Neill's better known films are *Saugus Series* (1974, 19 mins) and *Let's Make a Sandwich* (1982, 20 mins), the title of which refers to part of the optical printing process. Perhaps uniquely among contemporary avant-garde filmmakers, O'Neill has also applied his talents to several Hollywood features. • *The Groove Tube* 1974 (anim); *Saugus Series* 1974 (d,idea); *Piranha* 1978 (fx); *The Adventures of Mark Twain* 1985 (fx); *Phantasm II* 1988 (add.fx); *Water and Power* 1989 (d,p).

O'Steen, Sam • Editor; also director. • Born U.S.A., November 6, 1923. Began his career as an assistant editor in 1956 and, since the early 1960s, has cut several superbly crafted Hollywood productions. O'Steen is particularly known for his long-running association with Mike Nichols; he has edited nine of the director's films, from *Who's Afraid of Virginia Woolf?* (1966) through *Working Girl* (1988). O'Steen made his directorial debut with the TV movie *A Brand New Life* (1973) and directed his first feature film, the cult fave *Sparkle*, in 1976. • *Kisses For My President* 1964 (ed); *Robin and the Seven Hoods* 1964 (ed); *Youngblood Hawke* 1964 (ed); *Marriage on the Rocks* 1965 (ed); *None But the Brave* 1965 (ed); *Who's Afraid of Virginia Woolf?* 1966 (ed) **(AANBED)**; *Cool Hand Luke* 1967 (ed); *The Graduate* 1967 (ed); *Hotel* 1967 (ed); *Rosemary's Baby* 1968 (ed); *The Sterile Cuckoo* 1969 (ed); *Catch-22* 1970 (ed); *Carnal Knowledge* 1971 (ed); *Portnoy's Complaint* 1972 (ed); *The Day of the Dolphin* 1973 (ed); *Chinatown* 1974 (ed) **(AANBED)**; *Sparkle* 1976 (d); *Straight Time* 1978 (ed); *Hurricane* 1979 (ed); *Amityville II: The Possession* 1982 (ed); *Silkwood* 1983 (ed) **(AANBED)**; *Heartburn* 1986 (ed); *Nadine* 1987 (ed); *Biloxi Blues* 1988 (ed); *Frantic* 1988 (ed); *Working Girl* 1988 (ed); *A Dry White Season* 1989 (ed); *Postcards From the Edge* 1990 (ed); *Regarding Henry* 1991 (ed).

O'Sullivan, Maureen • Actress • Born Boyle, Ireland, May 17, 1911. Petite, attractive ingenue who entered film in the early 1930s, first with Fox and then at MGM. O'Sullivan is best known for her roles as Jane, opposite Johnny Weissmuller, in a number of "Tarzan" features of the 30s and early 40s. She married director John Farrow in 1936 and her screen appearances became more intermittent from the mid-50s.

O'Sullivan has lately enjoyed something of a comeback as a character player, notably opposite her daughter Mia Farrow in Woody Allen's *Hannah and Her Sisters* (1986). Daughter Tisa Farrow is also an actress. • *Just Imagine* 1930; *The Princess and the Plummer* 1930; *So This Is London* 1930; *Song O' My Heart* 1930; *The Big Shot* 1931; *Connecticut Yankee* 1931; *Skyline* 1931; *Fast Companions* 1932; *Okay America* 1932; *Payment Deferred* 1932; *The Silver Lining* 1932; *Skyscraper Souls* 1932; *Strange Interlude* 1932; *Tarzan, the Ape Man* 1932; *The Cohens and Kellys in Trouble* 1933; *Robbers' Roost* 1933; *Stage Mother* 1933; *Tugboat Annie* 1933;

The Barretts of Wimpole Street 1934; *Hide-Out* 1934; *Tarzan and His Mate* 1934; *The Thin Man* 1934; *Anna Karenina* 1935; *The Bishop Misbehaves* 1935; *Cardinal Richelieu* 1935; *David Copperfield* 1935; *The Flame Within* 1935; *West Point of the Air* 1935; *Woman Wanted* 1935; *The Devil-Doll* 1936; *Tarzan Escapes* 1936; *The Voice of Bugle Ann* 1936; *Between Two Women* 1937; *A Day at the Races* 1937; *The Emperor's Candlesticks* 1937; *My Dear Miss Aldrich* 1937; *The Crowd Roars* 1938; *Hold That Kiss* 1938; *Port of Seven Seas* 1938; *Spring Madness* 1938; *A Yank at Oxford* 1938; *Let Us Live* 1939; *Tarzan Finds a Son* 1939; *Pride and Prejudice* 1940; *Sporting Blood* 1940; *Maisie Was a Lady* 1941; *Tarzan's Secret Treasure* 1941; *Tarzan's New York Adventure* 1942; *The Big Clock* 1948; *Where Danger Lives* 1950; *Bonzo Goes to College* 1952; *All I Desire* 1953; *Mission Over Korea* 1953; *Duffy of San Quentin* 1954; *The Steel Cage* 1954; *The Tall T* 1957; *Wild Heritage* 1958; *Never Too Late* 1965; *The Phynx* 1970; *Traveller* 1981; *Too Scared to Scream* 1982; *Hannah and Her Sisters* 1986; *Peggy Sue Got Married* 1986; *Stranded* 1987.

O'Toole, Annette • Actress • Born Houston, TX, April 1, 1953. *Educ.* UCLA. Vivacious, red-haired character player who began her career as a dancer on "The Danny Kaye Show." • *The First Nudie Musical* 1975 (song); *Smile* 1975 (a); *One on One* 1977 (a); *King of the Gypsies* 1978 (a); *Foolin' Around* 1979 (a); *48 Hrs.* 1982 (a); *Cat People* 1982 (a); *Superman III* 1983 (a); *Cross My Heart* 1987 (a); *Love at Large* 1990 (a).

O'Toole, Peter • Actor • Born Connemara, Ireland, August 2, 1932. *Educ.* RADA, London. Blond, blue-eyed British actor whose acclaimed work with the Royal Shakespeare Theater at Stratford-upon-Avon led to a starring role in David Lean's *Lawrence of Arabia* (1962) and overnight, international fame. O'Toole's peculiar flair for portraying abstracted, visionary characters led to some superb performances in the 1960s and early 70s, notably opposite Richard Burton in *Becket* (1964) and in the title role of Richard Brooks's Conrad adaptation, *Lord Jim* (1965). (Both features were co-produced by O'Toole's Keep Films company.) He was also superb as the personification of upper-class English eccentricity in the screen adaptation of Peter Barnes's play, *The Ruling Class* (1972). O'Toole's well-publicized bout with alcoholism sent his career on a downward spiral in the 1970s but he made a creditable comeback in *The Stunt Man* (1980) and followed it up with a fine performance as an over-the-hill swashbuckler in the riotous comedy, *My Favorite Year* (1982). Although he has been known to sqaunder his talents on unworthy vehicles and has earned something of a reputation as a ham, O'Toole remains a performer of exceptional charisma and charm. He turned in an engaging character role as "RJ" Johnson, private tutor to Pu Yi, in Bertolucci's award-winning epic, *The Last Emperor* (1987). • *The Day They Robbed the Bank of England* 1960 (a); *Kidnapped* 1960 (a); *The Savage Innocents* 1960 (a); *Lawrence of Arabia* 1962 (a) **(AANBA)**; *Becket* 1964 (a) **(AANBA)**; *Lord Jim* 1965 (a); *What's New, Pussycat?* 1965 (a); *La Bibbia* 1966 (a); *How to Steal a Million* 1966 (a); *The Night of the Generals* 1966 (a); *Great Catherine* 1968 (a,p); *The Lion in Winter* 1968 (a) **(AANBA)**; *Goodbye, Mr. Chips* 1969 (a) **(AANBA)**; *Country Dance* 1970 (a); *Murphy's War* 1970 (a); *Under Milk Wood* 1971 (a); *The Ruling Class* 1972 (a) **(AANBA)**; *Man of La Mancha* 1972 (a); *Foxtrot* 1975 (a); *Man Friday* 1975 (a); *Rosebud* 1975 (a); *Power Play* 1978 (a); *Caligula* 1979 (a); *Zulu Dawn* 1979 (a); *The Stunt Man* 1980 (a) **(AANBA)**; *My Favorite Year* 1982 (a) **(AANBA)**; *Buried Alive* 1984 (a); *Supergirl* 1984 (a); *Creator* 1985 (a); *Sherlock Holmes and a Study in Scarlet* 1985 (a); *Sherlock Holmes and the Baskerville Curse* 1985 (a); *Sherlock Holmes and the Sign of Four* 1985 (a); *Sherlock Holmes and the Valley of Fear* 1985 (a); *Club Paradise* 1986 (a); *The Last Emperor* 1987 (a); *High Spirits* 1988 (a); *In una notte di chiaro di luna/Crystal or Ash, Fire or Wind, As Long As Its Love* 1989 (a); *The Nutcracker Prince* 1990 (a); *Wings of Fame* 1990 (a); *King Ralph* 1991 (a).

Oates, Warren • Actor • Born Depoy, KY, July 5, 1928; died 1982. *Educ.* University of Louisville. Craggy-faced character actor in mostly routine films of the 1960s who began playing more significant roles from the early 70s. Memorable in two typically gritty Sam Peckinpah films, *The Wild Bunch* (1969) and, as the American piano player at the center of a Mexican bloodbath, *Bring Me the Head of Alfredo Garcia* (1974). • *Yellowstone Kelly* 1959; *Private Property* 1960; *The Rise and Fall of Legs Diamond* 1960; *Hero's Island* 1962; *Ride the High Country* 1962; *Mail Order Bride* 1964; *Major Dundee* 1965; *Return of the Seven* 1966; *In the Heat of the Night* 1967; *The Shooting* 1967; *Welcome to Hard Times* 1967; *The Split* 1968; *Crooks and Coronets* 1969; *Smith* 1969; *The Wild Bunch* 1969; *Barquero* 1970; *There Was a Crooked Man* 1970; *Chandler* 1971; *The Hired Hand* 1971; *Two-Lane Blacktop* 1971; *Badlands* 1973; *Dillinger* 1973; *Kid Blue* 1973; *The Thief Who Came to Dinner* 1973; *Tom Sawyer* 1973; *Bring Me the Head of Alfredo Garcia* 1974; *Cockfighter* 1974; *The White Dawn* 1974; *92 in the Shade* 1975; *Race With the Devil* 1975; *Dixie Dynamite* 1976; *Drum* 1976; *Sleeping Dogs* 1977; *The Brink's Job* 1978; *China 9, Liberty 37* 1978; *1941* 1979; *The Border* 1981; *Stripes* 1981; *Tough Enough* 1982; *Blue Thunder* 1983.

Oberon, Merle • Actress • Born Estelle Merle O'Brien Thompson, Tasmania, Australia, February 19, 1911; died 1979. Exotic brunette actress whose primary asset can be summed up in one word: style. She is best-remembered for one of her worst performances, opposite Olivier (who wanted Vivien Leigh) in Goldwyn's *Wuthering Heights* (1939). Her best work came later in *Desirée* (1954) as Empress Josephine to Brando's Napoleon, then much later—and fleetingly—in admirable cameos in *The Oscar* (1965) and *Hotel* (1966). Married to Alexander Korda from 1939 until their divorce in 1945. • *Ebb Tide* 1932 (a); *The Private Life of Henry VIII* 1933 (a); *The Battle* 1934 (a); *The Broken Melody* 1934 (a); *The Private Life of Don Juan* 1934 (a); *The Dark Angel* 1935 (a) **(AANBA)**; *Folies Bergere* 1935 (a); *The Scarlet Pimpernel* 1935 (a); *Beloved Enemy* 1936 (a); *These Three* 1936 (a); *Over the Moon* 1937 (a); *The Cowboy and the Lady* 1938 (a); *The Divorce of Lady X* 1938 (a); *Wuthering Heights* 1939 (a); *'Til We Meet Again* 1940 (a); *Affectionately Yours* 1941 (a); *Lydia* 1941 (a); *That Uncertain Feeling* 1941 (a); *First Comes Courage* 1943 (a); *Forever and a Day* 1943 (a); *Stage Door Canteen* 1943 (a); *Dark Waters* 1944 (a); *The Lodger* 1944 (a); *A Song to Remember* 1945 (a); *This Love of Ours* 1945 (a); *A Night in Paradise* 1946 (a); *Temptation* 1946 (a); *Night Song* 1947 (a); *Berlin Express* 1948 (a); *Pardon My French* 1951 (a); *Deep in My Heart* 1954 (a); *Desiree* 1954 (a); *The Price of Fear* 1956 (a); *Of Love and Desire* 1963 (a); *The Epic That Never Was (I, Claudius)* 1965 (a); *The Oscar* 1966 (a); *Hotel* 1967 (a); *Interval* 1973 (a,p).

Ogier, Bulle • Actress • Born Boulogne-sur-Seine, France, 1939. Distinguished blonde performer who began her career in experimental theater and made her screen debut in Jacques Rivette's mammoth, engrossing *L'amour fou* (1968). Ogier has since played the schizophrenic heroine of Alain Tanner's *La salamandre* (1971), one of the wandering dinner guests in Buñuel's *The Discreet Charm of the Bourgeoisie* (1972) and the whip-toting sadist in Barbet Schroeder's *Maitresse* (1976).

Ogier has appeared in most of Rivette's films, including *Le Pont du Nord* (1981), opposite her sister, the late actress Pascale Ogier. • *L'Amour Fou* 1968; *Pierre et Paul* 1969; *Cinéma Different 3* 1970; *La Salamandre* 1971; *Rendez-Vous à Bray/Appointment in Bray* 1971; *M comme Mathieu/M As in Mathieu* 1971; *Out 1: Noli Me Tangere/Out One* 1971; *La Vallée/The Valley* 1972; *Le Charme Discret de la Bourgeoisie/The Discreet Charm of the Bourgeoisie* 1972; *Le Gang des Otages/The Hostage Gang*

1972; *Out 1: Spectre* 1972; *Bel Ordure* 1973; *Projection Privée/Private Projection* 1973; *Céline et Julie vont en bâteau/Céline and Julie Go Boating* 1973; *Mariage/Marriage* 1974; *La Paloma* 1974; *Un Divorce Heureux/A Happy Divorce* 1975; *Maîtresse/Mistress* 1975; *Jamais plus toujours/Never Again Always* 1975; *Des Journées entières dans les arbres/Entire Days in the Trees* 1976; *Sérail* 1976; *Duelle* 1976; *Flocons d'Or* 1978; *La Mémoire courte/Short Memory* 1979; *Die Dritte Generation/The Third Generation* 1979; *Le Navire Night/The Navire Night* 1979; *Le Pont du Nord* 1981; *Aspern* 1981; *Les Tricheurs* 1983; *La Derelitta* 1983; *Mon cas/My Case* 1986; *Das Weite Land/Unknown Country* 1987; *Candy Mountain* 1987; *La Bande des quatre* 1989.

Olbrychski, Daniel • Actor • Born Poland, 1945. Young, athletic lead who established himself in Poland as the star of Jerzy Lipman's *Ashes* (1965) and went on to become a prominent supporting player of European films of the 1970s and 80s. Superb at playing both inflexible figures of authority and benign, sympathetic types, Olbrychski has appeared in films by Andrzej Wajda, Miklos Jancso, Margarethe von Trotta and Joseph Losey. His first performance in an American film was as the devious bureaucrat in Philip Kaufman's *The Unbearable Lightness of Being* (1988). • *Popioly* 1965 (a); *Wszystko Na Sprzedaz* 1967 (a); *Pan Wolodyjowski* 1968 (a); *Polowanie Na Muchy* 1969 (a,ad); *Brzezina* 1970 (a); *Krajobraz Po Bitwie* 1970 (a); *La Pacifista* 1971 (a); *Zycie Rodzinne* 1971 (a); *Pilatus und Andere* 1972 (a); *Wesele* 1972 (a); *Roma Rivuole Cesare* 1973 (a); *Potop* 1974 (a); *Ziemia Obiecana* 1975 (a); *Dagny* 1976 (a); *Panny z Wilka* 1979 (a); *Les Uns et les autres* 1981 (a); *Roza* 1982 (a); *La Truite/The Trout* 1982 (a); *La Derelitta* 1983 (a); *Eine Liebe in Deutschland/A Love in Germany* 1983 (a); *La Diagonale du Fou* 1984 (a); *Lieber Karl* 1984 (a); *Der Bulle und das Mädchen* 1985 (a); *Objection* 1985 (a); *Rosa Luxemburg* 1985 (a); *Siekierezada* 1986 (a); *Mosca Addio* 1987 (a); *Dekalog 3* 1988 (a); *Et moi! Et moi!* 1988 (a); *Notturno* 1988 (a); *The Unbearable Lightness of Being* 1988 (a); *Zoo* 1988 (a); *La Boutique de l'orfèvre* 1989 (a); *L'Orchestre Rouge* 1989 (a); *To Teleftaio Stoixima* 1989 (a).

Oldman, Gary • Actor • Born New Cross, South London, England, March 21, 1958. *Educ.* Greenwich Young People's Theater; Rose Bruford Drama College (theater arts). Award-winning stage performer who established himself in the front rank of British screen actors with his two roles as doomed, iconoclastic figures of very different kinds: punk performer Sid Vicious, in Alex Cox's poignant, uncompromising *Sid and Nancy* (1986); and irreverent gay playwright Joe Orton, in Stephen Frears's *Prick up Your Ears* (1987). Married to actress Uma Thurman. • *Remembrance* 1981 (a); *Meantime* 1983 (a); *Honest, Decent and True* 1985 (a); *Sid and Nancy* 1986 (a,song); *Prick Up Your Ears* 1987 (a); *Track 29* 1987 (a); *Criminal Law* 1988 (a); *We Think the World of You* 1988 (a); *Chattahoochee* 1990 (a); *Rosencrantz and Guildenstern Are Dead* 1990 (a); *State of Grace* 1990 (a).

Olin, Lena • Actress • Born Stockholm, Sweden, 1955. Olin has enjoyed a long-standing association, primarily as a stage actress, with Ingmar Bergman, of whose Royal Dramatic Theatre in Stockholm she remains a member. (Bergman wrote the part of Anna in 1984's *After the Rehearsal* expressly for her.) She became an international screen star with two compelling, sexually charged roles, in *The Unbearable Lightness of Being* (1988) and *Enemies, A Love Story* (1989). Olin's father, actor-director Stig Olin, also worked with Bergman. • *Picassos Aventyr/The Adventures of Picasso* 1978; *Karleken* 1980; *Fanny och Alexander/Fanny and Alexander* 1982; *Grasanklingar* 1982; *After the Rehearsal* 1984; *Pa liv och dod* 1986; *Friends* 1987; *The Unbearable Lightness of Being* 1988; *Enemies, A Love Story* 1989 **(AANBSA)**; *S/Y Gladjen* 1989; *Havana* 1990.

Olivier, Lord Laurence • *aka* Sir Laurence Olivier • Actor, director; also producer. • Born Laurence Kerr Olivier, Dorking, Surrey, England, May 22, 1907; died July 11, 1989, Steyning, West Sussex, England. *Educ.* Saint Edward's School, Oxford. Laurence Olivier is widely regarded as this century's consummate English-speaking theatrical actor, a performer who was bedecked with awards and honors and was both knighted and granted a lordship by the British crown.

Olivier was born into a severe, confining religious household, presided over by a cleric who moved his family through a number of parish districts. Young Laurence took refuge in play-acting and had played several Shakesperean roles by his mid-teens. So successful was his portrayal of Puck in *A Midsummer's Night Dream* at the School of St. Edward that even his pious father encouraged him to apply to London's Central School of Speech Training and Dramatic Arts. As a student there, Olivier secured his first professional acting credits—as a stage manager and understudy in *Through the Crack* and as Lennox in *Macbeth.* Upon graduation, Olivier became a member of Sir Barry Vincent Jackson's Birmingham Repertory Company. He landed his first leading role, in *Harold,* at the age of twenty.

At first, Olivier's athleticism and elegant features typecast him as a young innocent hero. Although he appeared in a spate of London successes, such as *Journey's End, The Last Enemy* and *Private Lives,* he still struggled for serious recognition. His early film work was unimpressive, with no depth or passion beneath his matinee-idol looks; his outspoken disdain for film in general undoubtedly contributed to his wooden performances in *The Yellow Ticket* (1931) and *Perfect Understanding* (1933).

It was Shakespeare and Freud who turned Olivier's career around in the mid-1930s. In 1935, London was undergoing a Shakespeare revival, largely thanks to John Gielgud's successful production of *Hamlet.* For his next production, Gielgud chose Olivier to play Romeo in *Romeo and Juliet* and, in spite of complaints that his performance was shallow and athletic, the play was another huge hit. In 1937, Olivier was offered the role of *Hamlet.* Given a copy of Ernest Jones's *Essays in Applied Psychoanalysis* by the play's director, Tyrone Guthrie, Olivier became fascinated with the idea of adapting Freudian psychology to his character. Eschewing the flowery phrasing and artificial pretenses of previous Shakespearean performances, Olivier invented a new, staccato rhythm to reflect the psychological torment of the character. Audiences responded enthusiastically to his electrifying portrait of the doomed prince.

Olivier would bring this psychological intensity to bear upon his next important film performance, in *Wuthering Heights* (1939). Instead of a stock-in-trade doomed lover, Olivier played Heathcliff with a smouldering, dangerous undercurrent, one that carried over into his subsequent performances in *Rebecca* (1940), *Pride and Prejudice* (1940) and *That Hamilton Woman* (1941).

As a director, Olivier adapted this duality of artifice and immediacy to cinematic techniques in his Shakespearean films. *Henry V* (1944) begins in a blatantly false Globe Theatre and gradually opens out into an intensely cinematic battle at Agincourt. *Hamlet* (1948) employs voice-over interior monologues for Hamlet's soliloquies and enlists Wellesian deep focus and ominous moving-camera shots to convey the fetid atmosphere of the restricted castle setting of Elsinore. And *Richard III* (1955) uses eye contact with the camera to permit the audience to become accomplices in the comically maniacal Richard's conspiracies.

From the end of WWII to the early 70s, Olivier made sporadic film appearances, largely owing to his involvement in the administration of London's St. James Theatre in the late 40s and the National Theatre at the Old Vic from 1963 to 1973.

With the film version of John Osborne's play *The Entertainer* (1960), Olivier bade farewell to his romantic screen persona and introduced Olivier the character actor in the role of Archie Rice, the seedy, pathetic vaudevillian. Now he began making film appearances in small character roles, often virtually unrecognizable beneath heavy makeup. Most notable among these performances were the Madhi in *Khartoum* (1966), the reclusive mystery writer in *Sleuth* (1972), and the evil Nazi dentist in *Marathon Man* (1976). In declining health, Olivier mustered his old fire in 1984 for a bittersweet, reflective television production of *King Lear*, a fitting swan song for an actor dedicated to depicting the life-spark of humanity. Married to Vivien Leigh from 1940 to 1960 and Joan Plowright until his death in 1989. PB • *Friends and Lovers* 1931 (a); *The Yellow Ticket* 1931 (a); *Westward Passage* 1932 (a); *Perfect Understanding* 1933 (a); *Moscow Nights* 1935 (a); *As You Like It* 1936 (a); *Fire Over England* 1936 (a); *21 Days* 1937 (a); *The Divorce of Lady X* 1938 (a); *Wuthering Heights* 1939 (a) **(AANBA)**; *The Conquest of the Air* 1940 (a); *Pride and Prejudice* 1940 (a); *Rebecca* 1940 (a) **(AANBA)**; *49th Parallel* 1941 (a); *That Hamilton Woman* 1941 (a); *Henry V* 1944 (a,adapt,d,p) **(AANBA,AAHON)**; *Hamlet* 1948 (a,adapt,d,p) **(AANBD,AABA)**; *Carrie* 1952 (a); *Richard III* 1955 (a,adapt,d,p) **(AANBA)**; *The Prince and the Showgirl* 1957 (a,d,p); *The Devil's Disciple* 1959 (a); *The Entertainer* 1960 (a) **(AANBA)**; *Spartacus* 1960 (a); *Bunny Lake Is Missing* 1965 (a); *Othello* 1965 (a) **(AANBA)**; *Khartoum* 1966 (a); *The Dance of Death* 1968 (a); *Romeo and Juliet* 1968 (a); *The Shoes of the Fisherman* 1968 (a); *Battle of Britain* 1969 (a); *Oh! What a Lovely War* 1969 (a); *David Copperfield* 1970 (a); *Three Sisters* 1970 (a,d); *Nicholas and Alexandra* 1971 (a); *Lady Caroline Lamb* 1972 (a); *Sleuth* 1972 (a) **(AANBA)**; *Gentleman Tramp* 1976 (a); *Marathon Man* 1976 (a) **(AANBSA)**; *The Seven Per-Cent Solution* 1976 (a); *A Bridge Too Far* 1977 (a); *The Betsy* 1978 (a); *The Boys From Brazil* 1978 (a) **(AANBA)**; *Dracula* 1979 (a); *A Little Romance* 1979 (a); *The Jazz Singer* 1980 (a); *Clash of the Titans* 1981 (a); *Inchon* 1982 (a); *Wagner* 1983 (a); *The Bounty* 1984 (a); *The Jigsaw Man* 1984 (a); *Wild Geese II* 1985 (a); *Directed By William Wyler* 1986 (a); *War Requiem* 1988 (a).

Olmi, Ermanno • Director; also producer. • Born Bergamo, Italy, July 24, 1931. *Educ.* Accademia d'Arte Drammatica, Milan. A largely unheralded director, Olmi's simple technical style and concern for the issues facing working people have made his films poetic insights into human strength and integrity. Olmi's parents were peasants who moved to the city to find jobs. For several years, his mother worked for the Edison-Volta company, where Olmi landed his first job as a clerk. Through his participation in company theater and film events, he was eventually put in charge of Edison's film department.

Over a period of seven years he was involved in the production of over 40 films at Edison-Volta, mainly industrial documentaries and docudramas. Olmi's final film for Edison, *Il tempo si è fermato* (1959), ostensibly about the building of a dam in the Alps, is really a story of the relationship that develops between an aging watchman and his student assistant. Olmi's ability to portray subtle actions revealing deeper personal significance was first evident here.

With *Il tempo si è fermato*'s success, Olmi quit Edison to devote himself to theatrical filmmaking. In Milan he helped form an independent film cooperative known as "The Twenty-Four Horses," which provided financial assistance for his first independent effort, *Il posto* (1961). Partially autobiographical, *Il Posto*'s minimal plot follows a young man who comes to the city to work his first job as a clerk for a large company. He becomes accustomed to daily routines while harboring simple dreams of acceptance and romance. Finally, he becomes yet another cog in the wheel of his impersonal factory. Olmi's next feature, *The Fiancés* (1963), was also made on a minuscule budget with the assistance of the film cooperative "December 12." Though technically simple, *The Fiancés*'s complex narrative weaves past and present as it studies the unstable relationship between a couple whose plans for marriage are interrupted by an 18-month separation. These two features were impressive enough to merit Olmi the direction of his first and only commercial endeavor, *And There Came A Man* (1965), a big-budget biography of Pope John XXIII starring Rod Steiger. Poorly received, this effort did little to help Olmi's marginal reputation. Olmi made one more feature, *One Fine Day* (1968), before turning his attention for a time to TV.

With his reputation as a director worthy of international recognition almost completely dissipated, Olmi then made an auspicious return to form with *The Tree of Wooden Clogs* (1978). The winner of several major awards at the 1978 Cannes Film Festival, including the Golden Palm, the film is set on a farm where five peasant families glean existence from the land. A series of vignettes vividly portrays the sorrows, joys and resilience of the peasants, making the film a moving tribute to the strength of the human spirit and a notable record of the rhythms of everyday Italian country life.

With only a handful of credits, Olmi's position is unique in modern film in that he retains complete control over his movies by producing, directing, shooting and editing them. With one exception, *And There Came A Man*, he has employed only nonprofessional actors. Unlike many of his fellow countymen who have become world figures in the film industry, Olmi has remained a practicing Catholic throughout his life. PP • *Il tempo si è fermato/Time Stood Still* 1959 (d,sc) ; *Il posto/The Sound of Trumpets* 1961 (d,sc); *I Fidanzati/The Fiancés* 1963 (d,sc); *E Venne un uomo/And There Came a Man* 1965 (d,sc); *Un Certo Giorno/One Fine Day* 1968 (d,sc,ed); *I Recuperanti/The Scavengers* 1970 (d,sc,ph,ed,art d); *Durante l'estate/During the Summer* 1971 (d,sc,ph,ed); *La Circostanza/The Circumstance* 1974 (d,sc,ph,ed); *L'Albero degli zoccoli/The Tree of Wooden Clogs* 1978 (d,sc,ph,ed); *Camminacammina/Cammina Cammina* 1983 (d,p,sc,ph,ed,art d,cost); *Milano '83/Milan '83* 1983 (d,sc,ph,ed); *Lunga Vita alla Signora!* 1987 (d,sc,ph,ed); *La Leggenda del Santo Bevitore* 1988 (d,sc,ed).

Olmos, Edward James • Actor; also composer, producer. • Born Los Angeles, CA, February 24, 1947. *Educ.* East Los Angeles College; California State University. Ruggedly handsome Latino actor who began his career as a rock singer and earned a Los Angeles Drama Critics Circle Award for his performance in Luis Valdez's musical drama, *Zoot Suit*. (He reprised his role on Broadway and in Valdez's 1981 film version.) Olmos first became known to national audiences as the no-nonsense police chief in TV's "Miami Vice" (1984-89) and was memorable as the sinister, origami-practising police detective in *Blade Runner* (1982). He was nominated for a best actor Oscar for his role as a charismatic, inspirational math teacher in the 1986 feature film, *Stand and Deliver* (1988). • *Aloha, Bobby And Rose* 1975 (a); *Fukkatsu no hi* 1980 (a); *Wolfen* 1981 (a); *Zoot Suit* 1981 (a); *Blade Runner* 1982 (a); *The Ballad of Gregorio Cortez* 1983 (a,assoc.p,m,m.adapt,m.dir); *Saving Grace* 1986 (a); *Stand and Deliver* 1988 (a) **(AANBA)**; *Triumph of the Spirit* 1989 (a,sc); *Maria's Story* 1990 (a); *A Talent For the Game* 1991 (a).

Ondrícek, Miroslav • *aka* Ondrícek, Mirek • Director of photography • Born Czechoslovakia, 1933. *Educ.* Barrandov Studio Training School. Cinematographer who began his career with the emergence of the Czech New Wave in the early 1960s. Ondrícek made his professional debut with Miloš Forman's 1962 feature, *Talent Competition*, beginning an association with the director which has lasted for over 25 years. Ondrícek has also worked with countrymen Jan Nemec and Ivan Passer and shot three films for Lindsay Anderson, including his landmark feature, *If...* (1968). He left Czechoslovakia with Forman to make *Taking Off* (1971) and has worked regularly in the US since then, winning acclaim for his richly textured work on Forman's *Ragtime* (1981) and *Valmont* (1989).

• *Talent Competition* 1962; *Intimni Osvetleni/Intimate Lighting* 1965; *Lasky Jedne Plavovlasky* 1965; *Mucednici Lasky* 1966; *Hori, Ma Panenko* 1967; *The White Bus (short)* 1967; *If...* 1968; *Slaughterhouse-Five* 1971; *Taking Off* 1971; *O Lucky Man!* 1973; *Hair* 1979; *Boszka Ema* 1980; *Temne Slunce* 1980; *Ragtime* 1981 **(AANBPH)**; *The World According to Garp* 1982; *The Divine Emma* 1983; *Silkwood* 1983; *Amadeus* 1984 **(AANBPH)**; *Heaven Help Us* 1985; *F/X* 1986; *Big Shots* 1987; *Distant Harmony* 1987; *Funny Farm* 1988; *Valmont* 1989; *Awakenings* 1990.

Ontkean, Michael • Actor • Born Canada, January 24, 1950. *Educ.* University of New Hampshire. Former child actor with the National Shakespeare Festival who who first came to prominence in the TV series "The Rookies." Ontkean has appeared in several films, notably opposite Paul Newman in *Slap Shot* (1977). He is best known to today's audiences as straight-arrow police chief Harry S. Truman in David Lynch's soap-opera-with-a-twist, "Twin Peaks." • *The Peace Killers* 1971; *Necromancy* 1972; *Pickup on 101* 1972; *Hot Summer Week* 1973; *Slap Shot* 1977; *Voices* 1979; *Willie & Phil* 1980; *Making Love* 1982; *Just the Way You Are* 1984; *Le Sang des Autres* 1984; *The Allnighter* 1987; *Maid to Order* 1987; *Clara's Heart* 1988; *Bye Bye Blues* 1989; *Cold Front* 1989; *Street Justice* 1989; *Postcards From the Edge* 1990.

Ophuls, Marcel • *aka* Marcel Wall • Director; also producer. • Born Frankfurt, Germany, November 21, 1927. *Educ.* Occidental College, Los Angeles; University of California, Berkeley; Sorbonne, Paris (philosophy). Like his father, director Max Ophuls (*Letter From an Unknown Woman, Lola Montes*), Marcel Ophuls explores the nature of oppression and prejudice in his work. Rather than making fiction films, Marcel has concentrated on using the medium to document historical events and to disrupt people's complacency.

Ophuls came to American with his family as a teenager, attending Hollywood High School and college in California. He began his film career in 1951 in France as an assistant to Julien Duvivier, John Huston, Anatole Litvak and his father. He also worked in a variety of capacities for German and French television. Ophuls made a quiet debut as a director with a sketch for the anthology film, *Love at Twenty* (1962), followed by *Peau de banane* (1963), a successful if routine detective film starring Jean-Paul Belmondo. But it was his *The Sorrow and the Pity* (1970) which brought him considerable international attention.

This monumental documentary, a profoundly moving indictment of collaboration, uses interviews and Nazi newsreel footage to chronicle events in occupied France, focusing on the town of Clermont-Ferrand. One of the striking qualities of the work is the remarkably relaxed and candid manner in which people recall extraordinary events. The film won numerous awards, including the Prix Georges Sadoul and an Oscar nomination, but in depicting a period in French history which many wanted to let fade from memory, it was considered so disturbing—some went as far as to label it "antigaullist"—that was it was banned from French TV until 1981. (The unstated fact that French cowardice and duplicity were being presented by a German Jew didn't help matters.)

While continuing to produce historical documentaries for televison and theaters on subjects ranging from the My Lai massacre to the Nuremberg war crimes trials and the civil war in Northern Ireland, Ophuls also pursued acting and writing for magazines such as *American Film* and *Positif* and served on the board of the French Filmmakers' Society. His most recent work rivals *The Sorrow and the Pity* for its unrelenting examination of another concrete instance of the horrors of war.

Hotel Terminus (1988) takes as its subject the wartime activities of Klaus Barbie and the forty-year search for this Nazi collaborator known as the "Butcher of Lyon." In the process, Ophuls's film exposes the governmental collusion that allowed this man to remain hidden until 1983, when he was finally brought to trial. *Hotel Terminus* won the 1988 Academy Award for best documentary, as well as the International Critics Prize at the Cannes Film Festival the same year. RDH • *Henri Matisse ou Le talent du bonheur (short)* 1961 (d); *L'Amour a vingt ans/Love at Twenty* 1962 (d,screenplay "Munich"); *Peau de banane/Banana Peel* 1963 (d,sc); *Fea à volonté/Fire at Will* 1964 (d); *Munich, ou la Prix pour Cent Ans* 1967 (d); *Le Chagrin et la Pitié/The Sorrow and the Pity* 1970 (d,p,sc) **(AANBDOC)**; *The Harvest at Mai Lai* 1970 (d); *A Sense of Loss* 1972 (d,p); *The Memory of Justice* 1976 (d); *Kortner Geschichte* 1980 (d); *Hotel Terminus: Klaus Barbie, His Life and Times* 1988 (d,p) **(AABDOC)**.

Ophuls, Max • *aka* Max Opuls • Director, screenwriter • Born Max Oppenheimer, Saarbrucken, Germany, May 6, 1902; died March 26, 1957, Hamburg, Germany. Much of Max Ophuls's life was spent dealing with a series of adverse experiences: being a Jew in Nazi Germany, forced eviction from two countries, unemployment in America, innumerable terminated projects, limited distribution of his pictures, and lack of critical appreciation in his lifetime. However, Ophuls perserved and drew strength from this adversity. In his 25 years of filmmaking he completed 22 films, at least a third of which are now considered masterpieces, and Ophuls has finally been recognized as one of the great directors.

Following an unsuccessful career as a stage actor, Ophuls began directing plays in 1923 and directed his first film in 1930. Four more films followed in the next two years, of which *Liebelei* (1932) is the most notable. Ophuls left Nazi Germany for Paris in 1933 and became a French citizen five years later. Between 1933 and 1940 Ophuls directed 10 feature-length films in France, Italy and Holland. *La Signora di Tutti* (1934) is the most notable of these.

With the fall of France in 1940, Ophuls and his family fled to Switzerland. A dispute with the Swiss government over his status in France resulted in termination of a film project and his expulsion from Switzerland. Ophuls eventually arrived in Hollywood in 1941.

Ophuls was unemployed until 1946, when Preston Sturges, impressed by *Liebelei*, arranged for him to direct *Vendetta* for RKO. However, disagreements with Sturges caused Ophuls's early removal. He then directed four more films in America for different studios: *The Exile* (1947) and his American masterpieces: *Letter from an Unknown Woman* (1948), and the two films noirs, *Caught* and *The Reckless Moment* (both 1949).

Ophuls then returned to France and directed four more films: *La Ronde* (1950), *Le Plaisir* (1951), *Madame de...* (1953), and *Lola Montes* (1955). He died of a heart attack at the age of 54 in Hamburg.

Ophuls's reputation rests on both his choice of subject matter and its presentation. Most of his pictures take place in "fin-de-siècle" Vienna. Against this historical and cultural background, Ophuls focused on women in love. However, this love is neither sweet nor romantic but fraught with unhappiness, obsession, betrayal, male mistreatment and exploitation, misfortune and tragedy. All of this unfolds in an environment of opulent and luxurious décor: palatial buildings containing ornate furnishings, chandeliers, staircases and mirrors. (Even his three American films have the same feel as his European work: *Letter From an Unknown Woman* has the same setting, while *Caught* and *The Reckless Moment* are contemporary treatments of the same themes set in America.)

Technically, an Ophuls film is characterized by complex and dramatic camera work which emphasizes fluidity and motion and is accomplished by masterful use of framing, lighting, tilts, tracking shots, crane shots and pan shots. The effect of this fusion of content and style is to produce an intensely personal and emotional encounter which transports the viewer to a timeless world in which basic human experiences, feelings, emotions and states of mind are compellingly presented. LPM • *Liebelei* 1932 (d); *Une Histoire d'Amour* 1933 (d); *On a volé un Homme* 1934 (d); *La Signora di Tutti* 1934 (d,sc); *Komedie om Geld* 1936 (d,sc); *La Tendre Ennemie/The Tender Enemy* 1936 (d,sc); *Yoshiwara* 1937 (d,sc); *Le Roman de Werther* 1938 (d); *Sans Lendemain* 1940 (d); *The Exile* 1947 (d); *Letter From an Unknown Woman* 1948 (d); *Caught* 1949 (d); *The Reckless Moment* 1949 (d); *La Ronde* 1950 (d,sc) **(AANBSC)**; *Le Plaisir* 1951 (d,p,adapt—"La maison Madame Teller") **(AANBAD)**; *Madame de.../The Earrings of Madame de...* 1953 (d,sc); *Lola Montes* 1955 (d,sc).

Orbach, Jerry • Actor • Born Bronx, NY, October 20, 1935. *Educ.* University of Illinois (drama); Northwestern University (drama). Sleepy-eyed character actor from the musical stage (*The Fantasticks*) whose film career gained momentum in the mid-1980s. He contributed a memorable performance as Martin Landau's shady, mob-connected brother in Woody Allen's *Crimes and Misdemeanors* (1989). • *Cop Hater* 1958; *Mad Dog Coll* 1961; *John Goldfarb, Please Come Home* 1964; *The Gang That Couldn't Shoot Straight* 1971; *A Fan's Notes* 1972; *Foreplay* 1974; *The Sentinel* 1977; *Prince of the City* 1981; *Brewster's Millions* 1985; *The Imagemaker* 1985; *F/X* 1986; *Dirty Dancing* 1987; *I Love N.Y.* 1987; *Someone to Watch Over Me* 1987; *Crimes and Misdemeanors* 1989; *Last Exit to Brooklyn* 1989; *Dead Women in Lingerie* 1990.

Ornitz, Arthur J. • Director of photography • Born US, 1916; died July 10, 1985, New York, NY. *Educ.* UCLA (film). Has worked with independent filmmakers such as Shirley Clarke (*The Connection* 1962) and Russ Meyer (*Sweet Suzy/Blacksnake* 1973) and is is best known for his many captivating images of New York City, in both black-and-white (*A Thousand Clowns* 1965) and color (*Serpico* 1973). • *The Goddess* 1958; *The Pusher* 1960; *The Young Doctors* 1961; *The Connection* 1962; *Requiem For a Heavyweight* 1962; *Act One* 1963; *The World of Henry Orient* 1964; *A Thousand Clowns* 1965; *The Tiger Makes Out* 1967; *Me, Natalie* 1969; *The Anderson Tapes* 1971; *Minnie and Moskowitz* 1971; *Serpico* 1973; *Sweet Suzy/Blacksnake* 1973; *Law and Disorder* 1974; *E'Lollipop* 1975; *Thieves* 1977.

Orry-Kelly • Costume designer • Born John Kelley, Sydney, Australia, December 31, 1897; died 1964. Prolific, Australian-born designer who worked on Broadway before moving to Hollywood in 1923; won Academy Awards for his work on *An American in Paris* (1951) and *Some Like It Hot* (1959). • *The Man Hunter* 1930 (a); *I Am a Fugitive From a Chain Gang* 1932 (cost); *Armored Car* 1937 (a); *Exposed* 1938 (a); *The Dark Corner* 1946 (a); *Berlin Express* 1948 (cost—Merle Oberon); *An American in Paris* 1951 (cost) **(AABCD)**; *Oklahoma!* 1955 (cost); *Les Girls* 1957 (cost) **(AABCD)**; *Auntie Mame* 1958 (cost); *Some Like It Hot* 1959 (cost—Monroe) **(AABCD)**; *Gypsy* 1962 (cost) **(AANBCD)**.

Oshima, Nagisa • Director, screenwriter; also producer. • Born Kyoto, Japan, March 31, 1932. *Educ.* University of Kyoto (law, political history). Nagisa Oshima's career extends from the initiation of the "Nuberu bagu" (New Wave) movement in Japanese cinema in the late 1950s and early 1960s, to the contemporary use of cinema and television to express paradoxes in modern society.

After an early involvement with the student protest movement in Kyoto, Oshima rose rapidly in the Shochiku company from the status of apprentice in 1954 to that of director. By 1960, he had grown disillusioned with the traditional studio production policies and broke away from Shochiku to form his own independent production company, Sozosha, in 1965. With other Japanese New Wave filmmakers like Masahiro Shinoda, Shohei Imamura and Yoshishige Yoshida, Oshima reacted against the humanistic style and subject matter of directors like Yasujiro Ozu, Kenji Mizoguchi and Akira Kurosawa, as well as against established left-wing political movements.

Oshima has been primarily concerned with depicting the contradictions and tensions of postwar Japanese society. His films tend to expose contemporary Japanese materialism, while also examining what it means to be Japanese in the face of rapid industrialization and Westernization. Many of Oshima's earlier films, such as *Ai To Kibo No Machi/A Town of Love and Hope* (1959) and *Taiyo No Hakaba/The Sun's Burial* (1960), feature rebellious, underprivileged youths in anti-heroic roles. The film for which he is probably best known in the West, *Ai No Corrida/In the Realm of the Senses* (1976), centers on an obsessive sexual relationship. Like several other Oshima works, it gains additional power by being based on an actual incident.

Other important Oshima films include *Koshikei/Death by Hanging* (1968), an examination of the prejudicial treatment of Koreans in Japan; *Shonen/Boy* (1969), which deals with the cruel use of a child for extortion purposes, and with the child's subsequent escapist fantasies; *Tokyo Senso Sengo Hiwa/The Man Who Left His Will on Film* (1970), about another ongoing concern of Oshima's, the art of filmmaking itself; and *Gishiki/The Ceremony* (1971), which presents a microcosmic view of Japanese postwar history through the lives of one wealthy family.

In recent years, Oshima has repeatedly turned to sources outside Japan for the production of his films. This was the case with *Realm of the Senses* (1976), *Merry Christmas, Mr. Lawrence* (1983), and *Max mon Amour* (1987). It is less well known in the West that Oshima has also been a prolific documentarist, film theorist and television personality. He is the host of a long-running television talk show, "The School for Wives", in which female participants (kept anonymous by a distorting glass) present their personal problems, to which he responds from offscreen.LCE • *Ai To Kibo No Machi* 1959 (d,sc); *Nihon No Yoru To Kiri* 1960 (d,sc); *Seishun Zankoku Monogatari* 1960 (d,sc); *Taiyo No Hakaba* 1960 (d,sc); *Shiiku* 1961 (d); *Amakusa Shiro Tokisada* 1962 (d,sc); *Etsuraku* 1965 (d,sc); *Hakuchu No Torima* 1966 (d); *Muri Shinju Nihon No Natsu* 1967 (d,sc); *Nihon Shunka-Ko* 1967 (d,sc); *Ninja Bugeicho* 1967 (d,p,sc); *Kaettekita Yopparai* 1968 (d,sc); *Koshikei/Death by Hanging* 1968 (a,d,p,sc); *Shinjuku Dorobo Nikki* 1968 (d,sc,ed); *Shonen* 1969 (d); *The Man Who Left His Will on Film* 1970 (d,sc); *Gishiki* 1971 (d,sc); *Tokyo Senso Sengo Hiwa* 1971 (d,sc); *Natsu No Omoto/Dear Summer Sister* 1972 (d,sc); *Ai No Corrida/In the Realm of the Senses* 1976 (d,sc); *Ai No Borei/The Empire of Passion* 1978 (d,sc); *Merry Christmas, Mr. Lawrence* 1982 (d,sc); *Max mon amour* 1987 (d,sc,dial); *Yunbogi No Nikki* 1986 (d,sc,ph).

Oury, Gérard • Director, screenwriter; also actor. • Born Max-Gérard Houry Tannenbaum, Paris, 1919. Spruce character player who began directing light entertainments in the late 1950s and, within a decade, was making some of France's highest-grossing films. Oury is best known to English-speaking audiences for the superb slapstick of *The Mad Adventures of Rabbi Jacob* (1973), starring Louis De Funes. Oury's daughter, scenarist Danielle Thompson, has worked frequently with her father as well as on productions such as Jean-Charles Tacchella's *Cousin Cousine* (1975) and Claude Pinoteau's *La boum* (1980). • *The Heart of the Matter* 1953 (a); *Sea Devils* 1953 (a); *La Donna del Fiume* 1954 (a); *Eterna Femmina* 1954 (a); *They Who Dare* 1954 (a); *Les Héros sont fatigués* 1955 (a); *Mefiez-vous Fillettes* 1957 (a); *Le Dos au Mur* 1958 (a); *The Journey* 1959 (a); *La Main chaude* 1959 (d); *La Ménace* 1961 (d); *Le Crime ne paie pas* 1962 (d); *The Prize* 1963 (a); *La Grande vadrouille* 1966 (d); *Le Cerveau* 1969 (d,sc); *La Folie des grandeurs* 1971 (d); *Les Aventures de Rabbi Jacob/The Mad Adventures of Rabbi Jacob* 1973 (d,sc); *La Carapate* 1978 (d); *Le Coup du Parapluie* 1980 (d,sc); *L'As des As* 1982 (d,sc); *Le Vengeance du serpent à plumes* 1984 (d,sc); *Levy et Goliath* 1986 (d,sc); *Vanille Fraise* 1989 (d,sc).

Oz, Frank • Director, screenwriter, actor, puppeteer • Born Frank Oznowicz, England, May 25, 1944. First became known for his work on the "Sesame Street" and "Muppet Show" TV series, where he created, and provided the voices for, widely loved characters such as Fozzy Bear, Miss Piggy and Animal. Oz's first feature film, *The Dark Crystal* (1982), was co-directed with the late "Muppet" mastermind Jim Henson; he has since proved himself an adroit handler of comedy, adventure and fantasy material. • *The Muppet Movie* 1979 (a,creative consultant,song); *The Blues Brothers* 1980 (a); *The Empire Strikes Back* 1980 (a); *An American Werewolf in London* 1981 (a); *The Great Muppet Caper* 1981 (Muppet performer,a,p); *The Dark Crystal* 1982 (a,d); *Return of the Jedi* 1983 (a); *Trading Places* 1983 (a); *The Muppets Take Manhattan* 1984 (a,d,sc); *Sesame Street Presents: Follow That Bird* 1985 (a); *Spies Like Us* 1985 (a); *Labyrinth* 1986 (a); *Little Shop of Horrors* 1986 (d); *Dirty Rotten Scoundrels* 1988 (d); *What About Bob?* 1991 (d).

Ozu, Yasujiro • Director; also screenwriter. • Born Tokyo, December 12, 1903; died December 11, 1963. *Educ.* Waseda University. Few filmmakers outside the avant-garde have developed a personal style as rigorous as Yasujiro Ozu. While his films are in a sense experimental, he worked exclusively in the mainstream Japanese film industry, making extraordinary movies about quite ordinary events. His early films include a ghost story, a thriller, and a period piece, but Ozu is best known and admired for his portraits of everyday family life shot in what one critic has called a most "unreasonable style."

Ozu's early fascination with cinema soon turned into an obsession; as a student he reportedly went to great lengths to skip school and watch movies, usually Hollywood fare. His own filmmaking career began with his entry in 1923 into the newly formed Shochiku Studios, where he worked as an assistant cameraman and an assistant director. He directed his first film in 1927, and over the next four years directed twenty-one more.

The years 1931 to 1940 saw some of his greatest films, and he received the Best Film award from Kinema Jumpo three consecutive times, for *I Was Born, But...* (1932), *Passing Fancy* (1933) and *A Story of Floating Weeds* (1934). During the war, he directed two relatively successful films before being sent to Singapore to make propaganda pictures. There, he had the opportunity to screen captured prints of American films; later he would comment: "Watching *Fantasia* made me suspect that we were going to lose the war. These guys look like trouble, I thought."

Upon his return to Japan, he directed several unexceptional films before returning to form with *Late Spring* (1949). From this point onward, Ozu scaled down his output to about one film a year, while maintaining the high standards he had set during the thirties.

The most distinctive aspect of Ozu cinema is its self-imposed restraint. The elements of his unique style were in place by the mid-1930s and are deceptively easy to list. They represent a range of "unreasonable" choices, which the director continually refined (or reduced) throughout his career. Ozu's signature feature is his camera placement, which is usually (but not always) close to the ground. Its position is actually proportional: the height can change, as long as it stays lower than the object being shot.

Ozu also developed a curious form of transition, which various critics have labeled "pillow shots" or "curtain shots." Between scenes, he would always place carefully framed shots of the surroundings to signal changes in setting, as well as for less obvious reasons. Basically a hybrid of the cutaway and placing shots, these transitions were considered unusual for extended length; they sometimes seem motivated more by graphic composition and pacing than by the demands of the narrative.

Ozu's most radical departure from classical style was his use of 360-degree space. By convention, Hollywood style dictates that the camera should stay within a 180-degree space to one side of the action. This is to provide proper "screen direction" and a sense of homogenous space. Ozu's camera, on the other hand, orbits around the characters. Furthermore, this 360-degree space is broken down into multiples of 45 degrees, into which the camera angles generally fall. This produces a number of unusual effects, but Ozu's stories are so engrossing that they don't disrupt the story.

One effect of jumping over the 180-degree stage line is that actors facing each other seem to look off in the same direction. Ozu's response to this was to place characters in identical positions between (as well as within) shots. He favored a sitting position with the actor's body "torqued" to face the camera. Frustrated actors found their bodies treated as objects to be carefully manipulated within the frame, their lines to be delivered with a minimum of emotion and movement.

Ozu pushed this "graphic matching" between shots to notorious extremes: it is not unusual to see props such as beer bottles moved across tables or closer to the camera to preserve their size and screen position from shot to shot. Any effects that interfered with composition were cast away; Ozu never used a zoom and only one dissolve (in *Life of an Office Worker*, 1929). He also subordinated camera movement to composition; he never used pans because they disturbed his framing. The few Ozu tracking shots were designed to maintain a static composition (by moving along a road with a character, for example). When Ozu began shooting in color (with *Higanbana*, 1958), he did away with camera movement altogether.

While Ozu's films are not flashy, they are exceedingly complex. An essay this brief cannot begin to suggest the extent to which all these stylistic features are systematically choreographed. The permutations of form and variation become so minute they are visible only on close, multiple viewings.

The motives for Ozu's style have been the subject of rigorous debate. Because he was thought "too Japanese" for foreigners to accept or understand, for many years his films were not exported. When critics in the West finally discovered his work, his "unreasonable style" was usually explained in thematic, anthropomorphic and even religious terms. His low camera, for example, was described as the point of view of a child, a dog, a god or a person sitting Japanese style. Some critics attempted to explain the Ozu style through questionable comparisons to Zen Buddhism. Marxist critic Noel Burch, on the other hand, felt Ozu exemplified a rejection of Hollywood style and its ideological baggage. To date, the most convincing explanation has been offered by Kristin Thompson and David Bordwell, who suggest that in Ozu's cinema questions of style may be detached from theme and narrative. Ozu's films feature a playful, overt narration in which stylistic features do not have to mean anything and can be appreciated for their own sake.

Despite their restraint, Ozu's films, with their families in the throes of marriage and death, are among the most touching of melodramas. As important and influential as Ozu was, no other filmmaker has ever adopted his style, leaving his 53 films quite unique in the history of cinema. Ironically, the influence of Ozu's visual style may be more readily noticeable in a number of non-Japanese filmmakers, including Wayne Wang, Jim Jarmusch and Wim Wenders, who called Ozu's films "a sacred treasure of the cinema." MN • *Zange no Yaiba/The Sword of Penitence* 1927 (d); *Wakodo no Yume/The Dreams of Youth* 1928 (d); *Nyobo Funshitsu/Wife Lost* 1928 (d); *Kabocha/Pumpkin* 1928 (d); *Hikkoshi Fufu/A Couple on the Move* 1928 (d); *Nikutaibi/Body Beautiful* 1928 (d); *Takara no Yama/Treasure Mountain* 1929 (d); *Wakaki Hi/Days of Youth* 1929 (d); *Wasei Kenka Tomodachi/Fighting Friends—Japanese Style* 1929 (d); *Daigaku wa Deta Keredo/I Graduated, But ...* 1929 (d); *Kaishain Seikatsu/The Life of an Office Worker* 1929 (d); *Tokkan Kozo/A Straightforward Boy* 1929 (d); *Kekkon Gaku Nyumon/An Introduction to Marriage* 1930 (d); *Hogaraka ni Ayume/Walk Cheerfully* 1930 (d); *Rakudai wa Shita Keredo/I Flunked, But ...* 1930 (d); *Sono Yo no Tsuma/That Night's Wife* 1930 (d);

Erogami no Onryo/The Revengful Spirit of Eros 1930 (d); *Ashi ni Sawatta Koun/Lost Luck/Luck Touched My Legs* 1930 (d); *Ojosan/Young Miss* 1931 (d); *Shukujo to Hige/The Lady and the Beard/The Lady and Her Favorite* 1931 (d); *Bijin Aishu/Beauty's Sorrows* 1931 (d); *Tokyo no Gassho/Tokyo Chorus* 1931 (d); *Haru wa Gofujin Kara/Spring Comes From the Ladies* 1932 (d); *Umarete wa Mita Keredo/I Was Born, But ...* 1932 (d); *Seishun no Yume Ima Izuko/Where Now Are the Dreams of Youth* 1932 (d); *Mata Au Hi Made/Until the Day We Meet Again* 1932 (d); *Tokyo no Onna/Woman of Tokyo* 1933 (d); *Hijosan no Onna/Dragnet Girl/Women On the Firing Line* 1933 (d); *Dekigokoro/Passing Fancy* 1933 (d); *Haha o Kawazuya/A Mother Should Be Loved* 1934 (d); *Ukigusa Monogatari/A Story of Floating Weeds* 1934 (d); *Hakoiri Musume/An Innocent Maid/The Young Virgin* 1935 (d); *Tokyo no Yado/An Inn in Tokyo* 1935 (d); *Daigaku Yoi Toko/College Is a Nice Place* 1936 (d): *Hitori Musuko/The Only Son* 1936 (d); *Shukujo wa Nani o Wasuretaka/What Did the Lady Forget?* 1937 (d); *Toda-ke no Kyodai/The Brothers and Sisters of the Toda Family* 1941 (d); *Chichi Ariki/There Was a Father* 1942 (d); *Nagaya no Shinshi Roku/The Record of a Tenement Gentleman* 1947 (d); *Kaze no Naka no Mendori/A Hen In the Wind* 1948 (d); *Banshun/Late Spring* 1949 (d,sc); *Munekata Shimai/The Munekata Sisters* 1948 (d); *Bakushu/Early Summer* 1951 (d); *Ochazuke No Aji/The Flavor of Green Tea Over Rice/Tea and Rice* 1952 (d,sc); *Tokyo Monogatari/Tokyo Story* 1953 (d,sc); *Soshun/Early Spring* 1956 (d); *Tokyo Boshoku/Tokyo Twilight/Twilight in Tokyo* 1957 (d); *Higanbana/Equinox Flower* 1958 (d); *Ohayo/Good Morning* 1959 (d); *Ukigusa/Floating Weeds* 1959 (d); *Akibiyori/Late Autumn* 1960 (d); *Kohayagawa-ke no Aki/The End of Summer/Early Autumn/The Last of Summer* 1961 (d); *Samma No Aji/An Autumn Afternoon* 1963 (d,sc).

P

Pabst, G. W. • Director; also actor, screenwriter. • Born Georg Wilhelm Pabst, Raudnitz, Bohemia, August 27, 1885; died 1967. *Educ.* Academy of Decorative Arts, Vienna. Georg Wilhelm Pabst's greatest contribution to filmmaking is his not being limited by a dominant style. Though his films have been criticized for their lack of stylistic unity, rather than diminishing their impact, that eclectic approach pushed him beyond the aesthetic norm to break away from convention. This experimentation contributed to the evolution of the "Neue Sachlichkeit" (New Objectivity) in German films, a movement which rejected the extremist values of Expressionism for a less intrusive, quasi-documentary style.

Pabst began his academic career in engineering but his interests gravitated to the theater and in 1904, he entered the Vienna Academy of Decorative Arts. He made his directorial debut in New York in 1910 on a tour with a German-language theatrical troupe. Upon his return to Europe in 1914, he was detained as an enemy alien in a French prison camp, where he organized a theater company. After the war, he directed theater in Prague and later in Vienna. The German cinematographer and film pioneer, Carl Froelich, coaxed Pabst into filmmaking, offering him a job as assistant director.

In 1923, Pabst directed his first film, *Der Schatz/The Treasure.* His use of "chiaroscuro" and his ability to arrange physical objects in highly expressive (though seemingly objective) ways demonstrated his technical prowess. His next film, *Gräfin Donelli/Countess Donelli* (1924) was a commercial success but it was *Die Freudlose Gasse/The Joyless Street* (1925) which established Pabst as an important director. *The Joyless Street* is a gritty look at how the residents of Melchoir Street are affected by the postwar ills of corruption, prostitution and inflation. Among the film's accomplishments is its creation of a prototype for the naturalistic "street film" genre. One of the first directors to shoot on location, Pabst developed a photographic style that effectively depicted the stark realities of the streets. Among the cast of *The Joyless Street* was a young Greta Garbo; when Hollywood executive Louis B. Mayer saw the film, he recruited her to a contract with MGM.

Always fascinated by the human psyche, Pabst's next film, *Geheimnise Einer Seele/Secrets of a Soul* (1926) dramatized a Freudian case history. The extraordinary dream sequences, which utilized optical distortion and other special effects, were prototypes of surrealism. *Die Liebe Der Jeanne Ney/The Love of Jeanne Ney* (1927), with its undercurrent of modern angst, marked an important advance in Pabst's technique. The editing reveals Pabst's technical adeptness, the rapid cutting on movement occupying the viewer's attention on movement, thus making the cuts "invisible." This method, especially useful with reverse cuts, where a shift of speaker could be implied, foreshadowed the dialogue cutting of sound film and accounts in part for why Pabst's silent films seem surprisingly modern today.

One of his most controversial films was *Die Buchse Der Pandora/Pandora's Box* (1928). Criticized for its inconsistent style and its blatant sexuality, including a lesbian scene, the film received a hostile reception. Recent critics have praised the film, especially Louise Brooks's performance as Lulu, whose primitive sexuality is heightened by Pabst's careful closeups. Pabst's masterful direction of actors, especially women, inspired provocative, remarkable performances in many of his films.

The coming of sound further enhanced Pabst's artistry. His ingenuity with the new technology is especially evident in *Westfront 1918* (1930) and *Kameradschaft/Comradeship* (1931).

Although he continued to work in film into the 1950s, making movies in France, Austria, the United States and Italy, as well his native Germany, Pabst is best known for his early work. In general, Pabst refused to be defined. His constant drive to experiment reflected his restless vision, a vision which has influenced other directors and produced an inspired body of work. MCJ • *Der Schatz/The Treasure* 1923 (d); *Gräfin Donelli* 1924 (d); *Die Freudlose gasse/The Joyless Street* 1925 (d); *Geheimnisse einer Seele/Secrets of a Soul* 1926 (d); *Die Liebe der Jeanne Ney/The Love of Jeanne Ney* 1927 (d); *Abwege/Begierde/Crisis/Desire* 1928 (d); *Buchse der Pandora/Pandora's Box* 1928 (d,sc); *Das Tagebuch einer Verlorenen/Diary of a Lost Girl* 1929 (d,p); *Die Weisse Hölle Piz Palü/The White Hell of Piz Palü* 1929 (d); *Westfront 1918/Comrades of 1918* 1930 (d); *Die Dreigroschenoper/The Threepenny Opera* 1931 (d); *Kameradschaft/Comradeship* 1931 (d); *L'Atlantide/Die Herrin von Atlantis* 1932 (d); *Don Quichotte/Don Quixote* 1933 (d); *De Haut en bas* 1933 (d); *A Modern Hero* 1934 (d); *Mademoiselle Docteur/Street of Shadows/Spies from Salonika* 1936 (d); *Le Drame de Shanghai* 1937 (d); *Jeunes filles en détresse* 1939 (d); *Paracelsus* 1943 (d,sc); *Der Prozess/The Trial* 1947 (d); *Geheimnisvolle Tiefen/Mysterious Shadows* 1949 (d); *La Voce del Silenzio/The Voice of Silence* 1952 (d); *Cose da Pazzi/Droll Stories* 1953 (d); *Das Bekenntnis der Ina Kahr/Afraid to Love* 1954 (d); *Der letzte Akt/The Last Ten Days/Ten Days to Die* 1955 (d); *Es Geschah am 20 Juli/The Jackboot Mutiny* 1956 (d); *Rosen Für Bettina/Ballerina* 1956 (d); *Durch die Wälder, durch di Auen* 1956 (d).

Pacino, Al • Actor • Born Alberto Pacino, New York, NY, April 25, 1940. *Educ.* High School for the Performing Arts, New York; Herbert Berghof Studio, New York; Actors Studio. Award-winning, Italian-American stage actor who first gained screen prominence for his finely calibrated performance as a war-hero-turned-mob-heir in Francis Ford Coppola's *The Godfather* (1972). Pacino went on to become a major star of the 1970s, playing a series of brooding, anti-authoritarian figures which seemed to reflect the cynical mood of the times. He was acclaimed for his roles as the incorruptible cop in *Serpico* (1973) and as the fiery, unwittingly comical bank robber in *Dog Day Afternoon* (1975). Pacino's career went into a tailspin following a string of less controlled performances in the late 70s and early 80s, though he made an effective comeback as a volatile police detective in *Sea of Love* (1989), produced by long-term associate Martin Bregman. • *Me, Natalie* 1969; *Panic in Needle Park* 1971; *The Godfather* 1972 **(AANBSA)**; *Scarecrow* 1973; *Serpico* 1973 **(AANBA)**; *The Godfather, Part II* 1974 **(AANBA)**; *Dog Day Afternoon* 1975 **(AANBA)**; *Bobby Deerfield* 1977; *And Justice For All* 1979 **(AANBA)**; *Cruising* 1980; *Acting: Lee Strasberg and The Actors Studio* 1981; *Author! Author!* 1982; *Scarface* 1983; *Revolution* 1985; *Sea of Love* 1989; *Dick Tracy* 1990; *The Godfather Part III* 1990; *The Local Stigmatic (short)* 1990.

Page, Geraldine • Actress • Born Kirskville, MO, November 22, 1924; died June 13, 1987, New York. *Educ.* Chicago Academy of Fine Arts; Goodman Theater School of Drama. Acclaimed method actress whose rich performances on stage and screen displayed an unparalleled repertoire of neurotic tics and mannerisms. Page's highly strung, eccentric persona was put to fine use in films such as Richard Brooks's adaptation of Tennessee Williams's *Sweet Bird of Youth* (1962) and the tender, atmospheric drama, *The Trip to Bountiful* (1986). Married from 1961 to actor Rip Torn, opposite whom she frequently performed on stage. • *Hondo* 1953 **(AANBSA)**; *Summer and Smoke* 1961 **(AANBA)**; *Sweet Bird of Youth* 1962 **(AANBA)**; *Toys in the Attic* 1963; *Dear Heart* 1964; *The Three Sisters* 1964; *The Happiest Millionaire* 1967; *You're a Big Boy Now* 1967 **(AANBSA)**; *Trilogy* 1969; *Whatever Happened to Aunt Alice?* 1969; *The Beguiled* 1971; *J.W. Coop* 1971; *Pete 'n' Tillie* 1972 **(AANBSA)**; *Happy As the Grass Was Green* 1973; *The Day of the Locust* 1975; *Nasty Habits* 1976; *The Rescuers* 1977; *Interiors* 1978 **(AANBA)**; *Harry's War* 1981; *Honky Tonk Freeway* 1981; *I'm Dancing As Fast As I Can* 1981; *The Pope of Greenwich Village* 1984 **(AANBSA)**; *The Bride* 1985; *Flanagan* 1985; *White Nights* 1985; *My Little Girl* 1986; *Native Son* 1986; *The Trip to Bountiful* 1986 **(AABA)**.

Pagnol, Marcel • Director, screenwriter, producer, playwright • Born Aubagne, France, February 28, 1895; died April 28, 1974. Marcel Pagnol is often dismissed in film histories as an author of "canned theater" whose appeal is limited to a certain regional quaintness. This attitude is partly due to the fact that he first found fame as a playwright, but Pagnol did play a central role in developing and popularizing sound film in France. At a time when the French film industry was being radically transformed by the introduction of sound, Pagnol emerged as a major writer, director and producer of hugely successful films. Like Sacha Guitry, another homme du theatre with whom he is often compared, Pagnol initially assigned film a dubious artistic status, but once he became interested in the medium, he abandoned the theater altogether and in 1933 founded his own production company, Les Films Marcel Pagnol. In the process Pagnol became one of the few French directors of the period to control virtually every aspect of film production.

Pagnol's name is virtually synonymous with Marseilles, the southern port which provided him with his cultural roots, the setting for much of his work, a host of Provençal character types portrayed in his films by a remarkable group of actors including Raimu and Fernandel, and the region's unique accent—"introduced" at the moment when its originality would be most striking, when film was beginning to talk. Pagnol shared with the writer Jean Giono a profound respect for the region's people and traditions and an affinity for simple morality tales concerning family honor. Simple, austere and often sensual, his characters' authentic lives are portrayed through richly poetic language and an attention to authentic details of setting and speech.

Pagnol's first vocation was teaching, but even before he took his first job, he had published poems, written a play and founded the review "Fortunio" (which later became the prestigious "Cahiers du Sud"). In 1922 he obtained a teaching position in Paris, where he wrote *Pirouettes,* his first novel. But theater preoccupied him. With Paul Nivoix, he wrote three unremarkable plays, one of which (*Direct au Coeur*) was later filmed (1933). Pagnol's first success came with his satirical comedy *Topaze* (1928), and, after he gave up teaching altogher, he solidified his reputation with his memorable Marseilles trilogy: *Marius, Fanny* and *César.*

Here begins Pagnol's transition to film. *Topaze* (1933), directed by Louis Gasnier, was adapted for the screen, while *Marius* (1931, Alexander Korda) and *Fanny* (1932, Marc Allegret) were also filmed. For the film version of *César* (1935), Pagnol took over the directorial reins himself and scored his first film triumph. Pagnol would direct two more versions of *Topaze,* in 1936 and 1950, as well as adapting the work of other regional authors, especially Alphonse Daudet (*Les Lettres de mon Moulin,* 1954) and Giono (*Regain,* 1937; *La Femme du boulanger,* 1938). Pagnol also occasionally played the role of independent producer, notably on Jean Renoir's *Toni* (1934).

It is in the best sense that Pagnol is generally regarded as a creator of regional works representing a simpler time. Still, the recent success of Claude Berri's *Jean de Florette* and *Manon des sources* (both 1986), based on a Pagnol story which he filmed as *Manon des sources* (1952), demonstrates a continued interest in his work. RDH • *Topaze* 1933 (from play); *Angèle* 1934 (d,p,sc); *Le Gendre de Monsieur Poirier* 1934 (d); *Jofroi/Ways of Love* 1934 (d); *César* 1935 (d,sc,adapt,dial); *Cigalon* 1935 (d); *Merlusse* 1935 (d); *Regain/Harvest* 1937 (d); *Le Schpountz/Heartbeat* 1938 (d); *La Femme du boulanger/The Baker's Wife* 1938 (d); *Port of Seven Seas* 1938 (from play *Fanny*); *Le Schpountz* 1938 (d,p,sc); *La Fille du puisatier/The Welldigger's Daughter* 1940 (d); *La Belle meunière* 1948 (d); *Topaze* 1950 (d); *Manon des sources/Manon of the Spring* 1952 (d,p,sc,from novel); *Les Lettres de mon Moulin/Letters From My Windmill* 1954 (d,p,sc); *Fanny* 1961 (from play); *Mr. Topaze/I Like Money* 1961 (from play); *Jean de Florette* 1986 (from novel *L'eau des collines*,dial); *Manon des sources* 1986 (from novel); *Le Chateau de ma mere* 1990 (from autobiography); *La Gloire de mon pere* 1990 (from autobiography).

Pakula, Alan J. • Director, producer • Born New York, NY, April 7, 1928. *Educ.* Yale School of Drama. Began his career as an assistant in the Warner Bros. cartoon department in 1949 and graduated to producer status at Paramount with the 1956 baseball psychodrama, *Fear Strikes Out.* The film marked the first of seven collaborations with director Robert Mulligan which included *To Kill a Mockingbird* (1962), *Inside Daisy Clover* (1965) and *Up the Down Staircase* (1967). Pakula launched his own directorial career with the sensitive, if somewhat static melodrama, *The Sterile Cuckoo* (1969) and hit his stride two years later with *Klute* (1971), a moody psychological thriller in which Donald Sutherland and Jane Fonda each gave one of the best performances of their careers. Pakula consolidated his position as one of Hollywood's most bankable directors with his fine adaptation of the Watergate expose, *All the President's Men* (1976), and has continued to demonstrate a flair for intelligent and literate, if sometimes earnest, filmmaking. Pakula earned critical acclaim for his translation of William Styron's Holocaust drama, *Sophie's Choice* (1982), and for the screen version of Scott Turow's bestselling thriller, *Presumed Innocent* (1990). • *Fear Strikes Out* 1956 (p); *To Kill a Mockingbird* 1962 (p) **(AANBP)**; *Love With the Proper Stranger* 1963 (p);

Baby, the Rain Must Fall 1965 (p); *Inside Daisy Clover* 1965 (p); *Up the Down Staircase* 1967 (p); *The Stalking Moon* 1968 (p); *The Sterile Cuckoo* 1969 (d,p); *Klute* 1971 (d,p); *Liebe, Schmerz und das Danze Verdammte Zeug* 1973 (d,p); *The Parallax View* 1974 (d,p); *All the President's Men* 1976 (d) **(AANBD)**; *Comes a Horseman* 1978 (d); *Starting Over* 1979 (d,p); *Rollover* 1981 (d); *Sophie's Choice* 1982 (d,p,sc) **(AANBSC)**; *George Stevens: A Filmmaker's Journey* 1985 (a); *Dream Lover* 1986 (d,p); *Orphans* 1987 (d,p); *See You in the Morning* 1989 (d,p,sc); *Presumed Innocent* 1990 (d).

Pal, George • Producer; also director, special effects artist. • Born Cegled, Hungary, February 1, 1908; died 1980. Set desiger with UFA before moving in the 1930s to Western Europe, where he produced ingenious short advertising films featuring wire-jointed, stylized puppets. In 1940 Pal moved to Hollywood, where he produced the "Puppetoons" series for Paramount and began directing and/or producing special-effects oriented features including *War of the Worlds* (1953) and *The Time Machine* (1960). He received a special Academy Award in 1943 for developing a technique which combined animation with live action. • *Destination Moon* 1950 (p) **(AABFX)**; *The Great Rupert* 1950 (p); *When Worlds Collide* 1951 (p); *Houdini* 1953 (p); *War of the Worlds* 1953 (p); *Conquest of Space* 1954 (p); *The Naked Jungle* 1954 (p); *Tom Thumb* 1958 (d,p); *The Time Machine* 1960 (d,p); *Atlantis, the Lost Continent* 1961 (d,p); *The Wonderful World of the Brothers Grimm* 1962 (d,p); *The 7 Faces of Dr. Lao* 1964 (d,p); *The Power* 1968 (p); *Doc Savage, The Man of Bronze* 1975 (p,sc); *The Fantasy Film World of George Pal* 1986 (a).

Palance, Jack • Actor • Born Walter Jack Palahnuik, Lattimer, PA, February 18, 1919. *Educ.* University of North Carolina; Stanford University. Stage actor whose gaunt, leathery features (partially the result of a WWII bomber accident) were first seen on film in 1950, when Elia Kazan, who had previously directed Palance in the Broadway production of *A Streetcar Named Desire*, cast him as a plague-ridden gangster in *Panic in the Streets* (1950). Palance went on to earn two Oscar nominations, for *Sudden Fear* (1952) and *Shane* (1953), and seemed subsequently fixed in the public mind as a menacing bad guy. He began appearing in foreign films from the late 1950s, turning in a superb performance as a crass American movie producer in Jean-Luc Godard's *Contempt* (1963). Palance gave a fine performance against type as a vulnerable ex-fighter in the TV movie, *Requiem for a Heavyweight* (1965). • *Halls of Montezuma* 1950; *Panic in the Streets* 1950; *Sudden Fear* 1952 **(AANBSA)**; *Arrowhead* 1953; *Flight to Tangier* 1953; *Man in the Attic* 1953; *Second Chance* 1953; *Shane* 1953 **(AANBSA)**; *Sign of the Pagan* 1954; *The Silver Chalice* 1954; *The Big Knife* 1955; *I Died a Thousand Times* 1955; *Kiss of Fire* 1955; *Attack!* 1956; *House of Numbers* 1957; *The Lonely Man* 1957; *The Man Inside* 1958; *Ten Seconds to Hell* 1959; *I Mongoli/The Mongols* 1960; *Barabbas* 1962; *Le Mepris/Contempt* 1963; *Temoignage sur Bardot-Godard ou Le parti des choses (short)* 1964; *Once a Thief* 1965; *The Professionals* 1966; *The Spy in the Green Hat* 1966; *Kill a Dragon* 1967; *The Desperados* 1968; *Las Vegas 500 Milliones* 1968; *L'Urlo dei Giganti* 1968; *Che!* 1969; *The McMasters* 1970; *The Mercenary* 1970; *Monte Walsh* 1970; *The Horsemen* 1971; *Chato's Land* 1972; *Craze* 1973; *Oklahoma Crude* 1973; *Eva Nera* 1976; *The Four Deuces* 1976; *Squadra antiscippo* 1976; *Welcome to Blood City* 1977; *One Man Jury* 1978; *Cocaine Cowboys* 1979; *The Shape of Things to Come* 1979; *Hawk the Slayer* 1980; *Without Warning* 1980; *Alone in the Dark* 1982; *George Stevens: A Filmmaker's Journey* 1985; *Gor* 1987; *Out of Rosenheim/Baghdad Cafe* 1987; *Young Guns* 1988; *Batman* 1989; *Outlaw of Gor* 1989; *Tango and Cash* 1989; *Solar Crisis* 1990; *City Slickers* 1991.

Palcy, Euzhan • Director; also screenwriter. • Born Martinique, 1957. *Educ.* Sorbonne, Paris (literature); Vaugirard Film School, Paris. Began her career as a TV writer and director in Martinique before moving to Paris in the mid-1970s. Palcy's first feature, *Sugar Cane Alley*, was shot in 1983 on a budget of only $800,000. The film is a remarkably polished account of Martiniquan sugar-cane workers whose condition still approaches that of slavery; it recounts the efforts of a young orphan to escape her background via a classical education that—ironically—is also part of the legacy of colonialism. The film marked an auspicious debut for Palcy, winning a César (the French Oscar) for best first film as well as a Silver Lion at Venice. Her next feature, *A Dry White Season* (1989), was adapted from André Brink's novel about the persecution of a black family by the South African police. Despite a cast which included Donald Sutherland, Susan Sarandon and—in a highly effective cameo—Marlon Brando, the result was a somewhat wooden, formulaic indictment of the horrors of apartheid. • *Safrana ou le droit à la parole* 1978 (asst.ed); *La Rue cases nègres/Sugar Cane Alley/Black Shack Alley* 1983 (d,sc); *Dionysos* 1984 (sc); *A Dry White Season* 1989 (d,sc).

Palin, Michael • Actor; also screenwriter. • Born Sheffield, England, May 5, 1943. *Educ.* Brasenose College, Oxford (history). Made his West End stage debut in *Hang Down Your Head and Die*, a 1964 production by Oxford's satirical Experimental Theatre Club. After graduation, Palin wrote for and appeared in a number of comic programs, including "The Complete and Utter History of Britain," before becoming part of "Monty Python's Flying Circus" in 1969. He co-scripted the successful fantasy feature, *Time Bandits* (1981), and made a memorable appearance as the stuttering bumbler in Michael Crichton's homage to Ealing comedy, *A Fish Called Wanda* (1988). • *And Now For Something Completely Different* 1971 (a,sc,idea); *Monty Python and the Holy Grail* 1975 (a,sc); *Jabberwocky* 1976 (a); *Pleasure at Her Majesty's* 1976 (a); *Monty Python's Life of Brian* 1979 (a,sc); *The Secret Policeman's Ball* 1979 (a,sc); *The Missionary* 1981 (a,p,sc); *The Secret Policeman's Other Ball* 1981 (a); *Time Bandits* 1981 (a,sc); *Monty Python Live at the Hollywood Bowl* 1982 (a,sc); *Monty Python's The Meaning of Life* 1983 (a,sc,song); *A Private Function* 1984 (a); *Brazil* 1985 (a); *Consuming Passions* 1988 (from play *Secrets*); *A Fish Called Wanda* 1988 (a).

Palmer, Lilli • Actress; also writer. • Born Lillie Marie Peiser, Posen, Germany, May 24, 1914; died January 27, 1986, Los Angeles, CA. *Educ.* Ilka Gruning School of Acting, Berlin. Poised, sophisticated leading lady who arrived in Paris from her native Germany in 1932 and eventually landed in England, where she made her screen debut in 1935. Palmer touched down in Hollywood in 1945 with her first husband, actor Rex Harrison, and returned to Europe nine years later, where she continued to appear in a number of international features. • *Crime Unlimited* 1935; *Secret Agent* 1936; *Wolf's Clothing* 1936; *Beware of Pity* 1946; *Cloak and Dagger* 1946; *Body and Soul* 1947; *My Girl Tisa* 1948; *No Minor Vices* 1948; *The Four Poster* 1952; *Main Street to Broadway* 1953; *Teufel in Seide* 1955; *Der Glaserne Turm* 1957; *Wie ein Sturmwind* 1957; *Montparnasse 19* 1958; *But Not For Me* 1959; *The Pleasure of His Company* 1961; *The Counterfeit Traitor* 1962; *Julia, du bist zauberhaft* 1962; *Miracle of the White Stallions* 1963; *The Amorous Adventures of Moll Flanders* 1965; *Jack of Diamonds* 1967; *Oedipus the King* 1968; *Sebastian* 1968; *Das Ausschweifende Leben des Marquis De Sade* 1969; *Hard Contract* 1969; *Murders in the Rue Morgue* 1971; *Lotte in Weimar* 1975; *The Boys From Brazil* 1978; *The Holcroft Covenant* 1985.

Palmer, Patrick • Producer • Born Los Angeles, CA. *Educ.* California State University, Northbridge (economics). Began his film career with The Mirisch Company and worked as a production manager on films such as *West Side Story* (1961) and *Seven Days in May* (1964). Palmer is best known for a long-running association with director Norman Jewison which has encompassed features such as *The Landlord* (1970), *Fiddler on the Roof* (1971) and *Moonstruck* (1987). • *West Side Story* 1961 (prod. man); *Seven Days in May* 1964 (prod. man); *The Landlord* 1970 (assoc.p); *Fiddler on the Roof* 1971 (assoc.p); *F.I.S.T.* 1978 (assoc.p); *And Justice For All* 1979 (p); *The Dogs of War* 1980 (exec.p); *Best Friends* 1982 (p); *Iceman* 1984 (p); *A Soldier's Story* 1984 (p) **(AANBP)**; *Agnes of God* 1985 (p); *Children of a Lesser God* 1986 (2u d,p) **(AANBP)**; *Moonstruck* 1987 (p) **(AANBP)**; *Mermaids* 1990 (2u d,p); *Stanley and Iris* 1990 (2u d,exec.p).

Panfilov, Gleb • Director • Born Magnitogorsk, USSR, December 21, 1934. *Educ.* Urals Polytechnic Institute (chemical engineering); VGIK (film). Gleb Panfilov first worked as a factory foreman after graduating from the Urals Polytechnic Institute. After seeing Mikhail Kalatazov's *The Cranes Are Flying* (1957), he became interested in film and started a correspondence course at VGIK (the State Cinema Institute) in 1960. In 1968 Panfilov made his first feature film, *No Ford in the Fire*, which also marked the beginning of an ongoing collaboration with his wife, Inna Churikova. The star of all his films, Churikova has been described as "a Russian Giulietta Masina" for her endearing, comic awkwardness.

In 1970 Panfilov made the financially successful *The Beginning*, which intercuts the story of Joan of Arc with a contemporary narrative. Not satisfied with depicting only part of the French heroine's life, Panfilov and Churikova tried for the next six years to film her entire story. The simplicity of Joan's peasant roots combined with her extraordinary sensibility and her faith in her cause fascinated the filmmakers, who learned French and traveled to France in order to study records about her. Although they wrote and even published a script, they never received the financial backing needed to make the film on location.

In his early works, Panfilov explored the interplay of life and art. *No Ford in the Fire* is a civil war story in which a nurse who cares for wounded soldiers is also an artist whose work has displeased a cultural commissar. A comment on the stifled talents and creativity of the Russian people, the film also reviles socialist realism. *The Beginning* deals with a young factory worker involved in amateur theatricals who gets the opportunity to play Joan of Arc in a film. The complex interplay between the two lives reveals the richness behind ordinary existence; Panfilov suggests this by juxtaposing the funny and the tragic, the great and the small. Despite the vast differences in the historical scale of events and destinies, both the heroine of the film and Joan of Arc gather their strength from a national spirit.

With *I Want the Floor* (1975), Panfilov began to examine the increasing conservatism of Soviet life. This film relates the difficulties faced by the female mayor of a large town who is overwhelmed by party politics. *The Theme* (1980), based on problems encountered by a writer, suggests the difficulty of emigration from the Soviet Union; this film was screened a few times and ultimately banned. These later works suffer from mechanical plots and flat characters, due perhaps to the imposition of veteran screenwriters. In response to the increasingly conservative reactions to his films, Panfilov adapted two plays in 1981. The Chekhovian *Valentine* (1983), from Alexander Vampilov's *Last Summer in Tchoulimsk*, chronicles the interactions among ten characters in a village inn. Maxim Gorky's *Vassa Gelznova* is the basis of *Vassa* (1983), a tale of a decaying petit bourgeois family. Although these later films are not on a par with his earlier work, Panfilov is still considered to be one of the Soviet Union's most promising filmmakers. RJB • *Vognye broda nyet/No Crossing Under Fire/No Ford in the Fire* 1968 (d,sc); *Nachalo/The Beginning/The Debut* 1970 (d,sc); *Proshu Slova/I Wish to Speak/I Want the Floor* 1975 (d,sc); *Tema/The Theme* 1980 (d,sc); *Valentina/Valentine* 1983 (d,sc); *Vassa* 1983 (d,sc); *Matj (Zaprechtchionnye Lioudi)* 1990 (d,sc).

Papas, Irene • Actress • Born Chilimodion, Greece, 1926. Began her career as a variety performer and started appearing in Greek films in the early 1950s. Papas made her US debut in *Tribute to a Bad Man* (1955) and established her international reputation with Michael Cacoyannis's *Zorba the Greek* (1964). Her dark, intense features are well suited to tragic roles; she made an indelible impression as the widow of the slain political activist in Costa-Gavras's *Z* (1969). • *The Man From Cairo* 1953; *Théodore, Imperatrice Byzantine/ Theodora, Slave Empress* 1954; *Attila* 1955; *Tribute to a Bad Man* 1955; *Antigone* 1961; *The Guns of Navarone* 1961; *The Moon-Spinners* 1964; *Zorba the Greek* 1964; *The Brotherhood* 1968; *Anne of the Thousand Days* 1969; *A Dream of Kings* 1969; *Z* 1969; *N.P. Il Segreto* 1971; *Non Si Sevizia un Paperino* 1971; *The Trojan Women* 1971; *Le Faro da Padre* 1974; *Mohammad Messenger of God* 1976; *Iphigenia* 1977; *Cristo si è Fermato a Eboli/Christ Stopped at Eboli* 1978; *Bloodline* 1979; *Lion of the Desert* 1980; *Erendira* 1982; *Il Disertore* 1983; *The Assisi Underground* 1985; *Into the Night* 1985; *Sweet Country* 1986; *Cronaca di una morte annunciata/Chronicle of a Death Foretold* 1987; *High Season* 1987; *Island* 1989.

Paradzhanov, Sergei • *aka* Sergei Paradjanov, Sergei Paradjanian • Director • Born Sarkis Paradzhanov, Tbilisi, Georgia, Russia, January 1, 1924; died July 21, 1990, Yerevan, Armenia. *Educ.* Tbilisi Conservatory, Georgia, USSR; VGIK, Moscow (directing). Born to a well-to-do Armenian family, Paradzhanov played violin and studied in the music conservatory before enrolling in the Directing Department of VGIK (All-Union Institute of Cinematography), from which he graduated in 1951. Beginning in 1949, he worked as an assistant director, then director at the Kiev film studios. Paradzhanov's first feature as a director, *Andriesh* (1955), co-directed with Ya. Bazelyan, was noteworthy for its unusual use of surealistic elements. In 1957 Paradzhanov made three shorts: *Dumka, Golden Hands* and *Ataliva Uzhvii*, followed by several undistinguished comedies and melodramas of the socialist-realist type: *The First Lad* (1959), *Ukrainian Rhapsody* (1961), *Flower on the Stone* (1963).

In 1964 he completed *Shadows of Our Forgotten Ancestors*, a striking departure from his previous work as well from all of postwar Soviet cinema. With this film, Paradzhanov and his cameraman Yuri Ilyenko, soon to become a leading director himself, recovered and developed the tradition of Ukrainian poetic cinema rooted in the work of Dovzhenko. Based on turn-of-the-century Ukrainian writer Kotzyubinsky's stories and on Carpathian folklore, the film made a significant contribution to the theory and practice of film language with its use of color and camera to convey complex psychological states of the heroes, a bold rejection of conventional narrative, and its director's lyricism, mysticism and ecstatic emotionalism. These characteristics were all but revolutionary and invited comparison not only with Dovzhenko but with Eisenstein. Although *Shadows* won over a dozen international awards, Paradzhanov was not allowed to accompany the film abroad. The intense Ukrainian nationalism of both the film and its Armenian director (Paradzhanov refused to dub *Shadows* into Russian) granted him the patronage of Pyotr Shelest, the communist party boss of the Ukraine.

After the success of *Shadows*, Paradzhanov's Kiev apartment became an intellectual center; to the great displeasure of the authorities he was visited by people from all over the country, as well as foreigners. Moreover, the outspoken Paradzhanov took part in human rights campaigns of the late 1960s, signing letters of protest and sending angry telegrams to Moscow. Soon, a number of his projects submitted to Dovzhenov studios were rejected. He did manage to make a film in Armenia, *Sayat Nova* (1969), the story of an 18th-century Armenian monk, poet, and national hero killed by the invading Persians for his refusal to renounce Christ. However, *Sayat Nova* was no conventional biopic; it was an attempt to convey the visual equivalent of Sayat Nova's poetry embodying the beauty and tragedy of the ancient Armenian culture, history and landscape. A series of tableaux composed like Oriental miniatures, it is far from static: there is a permanent movement of an image within each frame.

Sayat Nova was an even greater triumph than *Shadows*, although its impact was not immediately felt. The film was not seen abroad until 1977, when the screening of a 16mm bootleg print was arranged in Paris. In 1980 it was shown at the New York Film Festival and proclaimed by many critics the best Soviet film of the postwar period. Such belated international acclaim for *Sayat Nova* was due to drastic political and cultural changes in the USSR around 1968. To screen the film in Armenia upon its initial release was permissible, but for it to be shown all over the country, authorities insisted it be cut to become "understandable to the people." Paradzhanov refused to butcher his film and it was edited by another filmmaker. Finally, it was released in the Soviet Union in 1972 as *The Color of Pomegranates*, although in limited distribution.

By that time Paradzhanov had had other serious confrontations with the regime. His situation became especially precarious when his next project, *Kievan Frescos*, containing some footage on destruction of Christian monuments, was shelved. In January 1974, while Paradzhanov was working on a TV film on Hans Christian Andersen, he was arrested and accused of homosexuality, hard currency dealing, distributing pornography and trafficking in art objects. Most of the charges were fabricated; as for homosexuality, considered a crime according to Soviet law, Paradzhanov had never concealed his sexual preferences and it was never an issue with the authorities until he became politically active. Paradzhanov was sentenced to five years of hard labor, and his films and mention of his name in print was banned for ten years. Due to an unprecedented international campaign in his defense (virtually all European filmmakers of renown signed petitions on his behalf), he was released a year early.

A sick and broken man, Paradzhanov moved into his parents' house in Tbilisi. He was not allowed to return to cinema, so he wrote scripts and stories based on his prison experiences, creating surrealistic collages, assemblages and drawings, which he claims he started making in prison out of junk. In 1982 Paradzhanov was arrested again, and only an appeal from the French government saved him from a prison sentence of five years. Fortunately, the Brezhnev regime had come to an end, and shortly after his ordeal Paradzhanov could return to filmmaking. Perhaps as a final act of mistrust he was assigned a co-director, the famous Georgian actor Dodo Abashidze.

Paradzhanov made his next three films at the Georgia-Film studios in Tbilisi: *The Legend of Suram Fortress* (1984), the short *Arabesques on the Pirosmani Theme* (1985), and *Ashik Kerib* (1988). *Suram Fortress*, based on an ancient Georgian legend, demonstrated Paradzhanov's unique ability to create a true national art deeply rooted in folklore. The film, a pictorial spectacle, presents a series of exquisite tableaux with a wonderful sense of color, line, composition, all shot with a static camera but with an enormous visual power and metaphoric richness within every shot.

With his last film, *Ashik Kerib*, Paradzhanov revealed his enchantment not only with the two Christian civilizations of the Caucasus—Armenian and Georgian—but also with the third civilization—the Muslim. Based on Lermontov's Oriental tale, Paradzhanov's film considerably enhances its fantastic, grotesque potential. With its conglomeration of props, both medieval and modern, its kitschy make-up and cumbersome mise-en-scène, the film could be seen as a homage to Mèliés. It is also filled with quotations from Paradzhanov's own films, as if he was evoking his earlier achievements and presenting them as self-parody to say goodbye to a certain kind of filmmaking he had been practicing for over twenty years. The film ends with an image of a dove sitting on the movie camera. The inscription says, "Dedicated to the memory of Andrei Tarkovsky." Both the late Tarkovsky and Paradzhanov could be viewed as symbolic *Ashik Kerib*, or "traveling artists."

Unlike Paradzhanov's other films, *Kerib* has a happy ending: the wanderer returns home after prevailing over his enemies. *Ashik Kerib* was shown at the 1988 New York Film Festival and Paradzhanov was allowed for the first time to come to the US to attend the premiere. Back home, he started working on a long-delayed project, the autobiographic *Confession*, but was hospitalized with lung cancer and died in July 1990. Meanwhile, Ilyenko has finished a film based on Paradzhanov's prison stories, *Swan Lake—The Zone*. AB • *Andriesch* 1955 (d); *Ataliva Uzhvii (short)* 1957 (d); *Dumka (short)* 1957 (d); *Golden Hands (short)* 1957 (d); *Perwyi Paren/The First Lad* 1959 (d); *Ukrainskaja Rapsodija/Ukranian Rhapsody* 1961 (d); *Zwetok na Kamne/Flower on the Stone* 1962 (d); *Teni zabytykh predkov/Shadows of Our Forgotten Ancestors* 1964 (d,sc); *Nran Gouyne/Sayat Nova/The Color of Pomegranates* 1968 (d,sc,ed,chor—pantomime); *Legenda Suramskoi Kreposti/The Legend of Suram Fortress* 1984 (d); *Arabeski Na temu Pirosmani/Arabesques on the Pirosmani Theme (short)* 1985 (d); *Ashik Kerib* 1988 (d); *Lebedyne Ozero-Zona/Swan Lake—The Zone* 1990 (sc).

Pare, Michael • Actor • Born Brooklyn, NY, 1959. *Educ.* Culinary Institute of America, Hyde Park, New York. Handsome young lead who made his screen debut in the title role of Martin Davidson's *Eddie and the Cruisers* (1983). • *Eddie and the Cruisers* 1983; *The Philadelphia Experiment* 1984; *Streets of Fire* 1984; *Undercover* 1984; *Instant Justice* 1987; *Space Rage* 1987; *The Women's Club* 1987; *World Gone Wild* 1988; *Eddie and the Cruisers II: Eddie Lives* 1989; *The Closer* 1990; *Moon 44* 1990; *Il Sole Buio* 1990.

Parker, Alan • Director; also writer. • Born Islington, England, February 14, 1944. Alan Parker began his career when he and partner Alan Marshall founded a production company to make industrial films and commercials. Between 1969 and 1978, Parker churned out over 500 television commercials, winning every major industry award, while he was cited as an important influence on both fashion and film style of that time. Parker adeptly used lighting, and his sense of drama as a feature film director seems to come as much from his early need to convey a message in 30 seconds as from a sense of pictorial grace.

In 1973, Parker wrote and directed a 50-minute film, *No Hard Feelings*, which the BBC bought and eventually aired several years later. *Evacuees* (1975), his first film produced for the BBC, brought attention from the theatrical marketplace, and in 1976 he and producer David Puttnam collaborated on Parker's debut as a director/writer, *Bugsy Malone*, a musical spoof of gangster films with an all-children cast. His second feature, *Midnight Express* (1978), based on the true story of an American arrested in Turkey for drug smuggling, earned six Oscar nominations and won for best screenplay adaptation and score. Parker has a knack for turning diverse subjects into uniquely personal statements. After his popular success with the stylish *Fame* (1980), he turned to a sensitively detailed examination of relationships in *Shoot the Moon* (1981), and in *Pink Floyd—The Wall* (1982) he expanded the themes of the bestselling rock concept album, employing innovative animation techniques.

The quirky *Birdy* (1984) and the controversial *Angel Heart* (1987) solidified Parker's position as a highly visual storyteller whose pallette makes use of the soundtrack as well as strong imagery. *Mississippi Burning*, his 1988 exploration of a famous civil rights murder, represents less an artistic success than an act of directorial courage in trying to delve into the mysteries of a foreign culture. Here, Parker's detached perspective served more to castigate than to soothe.

Always fiercely independent, Parker has often lambasted the British film establishment and film critics. No stranger to controversy, he took on the ratings board of the MPAA and personally challenged their "X" rating of *Angel Heart.* Parker has also authored a compiliation of satirical cartoons, *Hares in the Gate* (1982), and in 1984 produced *A Turnip Head's Guide to British Cinema,* a sarcastic documentary which ridiculed the critical mentality, a film that delighted his filmmaking contemporaries as well as his four children, whom he has cited as his chief inspiration. TZ • *S.W.A.L.K. Melody* 1970 (sc,story); *Evacuees* 1975 (d); *Bugsy Malone* 1976 (d,sc); *Midnight Express* 1978 (d) **(AANBD)**; *Fame* 1980 (d); *Shoot the Moon* 1981 (d); *Pink Floyd—The Wall* 1982 (d); *Jaws 3-D* 1983 (m); *Birdy* 1984 (d); *Angel Heart* 1987 (d,sc); *Mississippi Burning* 1988 (d) **(AANBD)**; *Come See the Paradise* 1990 (d,sc,lyrics "Jack's Theatre Song").

Parker, Eleanor • Actress • Born Cedarville, OH, June 26, 1922. Sultry leading lady of the 1940s and 50s, probably best known as the innocent turned hardened con in *Caged* (1950) and as Kirk Douglas's neglected wife in *Detective Story* (1951). Parker continued to appear in secondary roles through the 1970s. • *Busses Roar* 1942; *Mission to Moscow* 1943; *The Mysterious Doctor* 1943; *Between Two Worlds* 1944; *Crime By Night* 1944; *Hollywood Canteen* 1944; *The Last Ride* 1944; *The Very Thought of You* 1944; *Pride of the Marines* 1945; *Never Say Goodbye* 1946; *Of Human Bondage* 1946; *Escape Me Never* 1947; *The Voice of the Turtle* 1947; *The Woman in White* 1948; *It's a Great Feeling* 1949; *Caged* 1950 **(AANBA)**; *Chain Lightning* 1950; *Three Secrets* 1950; *Detective Story* 1951 **(AANBA)**; *A Millionaire For Christy* 1951; *Valentino* 1951; *Above and Beyond* 1952; *Scaramouche* 1952; *Escape From Fort Bravo* 1953; *Many Rivers to Cross* 1954; *The Naked Jungle* 1954; *Valley of the Kings* 1954; *Interrupted Melody* 1955 **(AANBA)**; *The Man With the Golden Arm* 1955; *The King and Four Queens* 1956; *Lizzie* 1956; *The Seventh Sin* 1957; *A Hole in the Head* 1959; *Home From the Hill* 1960; *Return to Peyton Place* 1961; *Madison Avenue* 1962; *Panic Button* 1964; *The Sound of Music* 1965; *An American Dream* 1966; *The Oscar* 1966; *How to Steal the World* 1968; *Eye of the Cat* 1969; *Sunburn* 1979.

Parks, Gordon • Director, photographer; also writer, composer. • Born Fort Scott, KS, November 30, 1912. *Educ.* Kansas State University. Preeminent black photojournalist. Parks was acclaimed for his work at *Life* magazine from 1948 to 1968. He made his directorial debut with *The Learning Tree* (1969), a visually stunning adaptation of his autobiographical novel about growing up in Kansas. In 1989 *The Learning Tree* was selected by the Library of Congress as among the first 25 works to be preserved in the national film registry.

Parks scored a box-office success with his second feature, the gritty black exploitation classic, *Shaft* (1971). *Leadbelly* (1976), a fine account of the life of the legendary blues singer, failed to find the audience it deserved, partially due to poor marketing and distribution. Father of the late director Gordon Parks, Jr., who was best known for *Superfly* (1972). • *The Learning Tree* 1969 (d); *Shaft* 1971 (d); *Shaft's Big Score* 1972 (d,m); *The Super Cops* 1973 (d); *Aaron Loves Angela* 1975 (d); *Leadbelly* 1976 (d); *50 Years of Action!* 1986 (a); *Moments Without Proper Names* 1986 (d,sc,m).

Parks, Larry • Actor • Born Lawrence Klausman Parks, Olathe, KS, December 13, 1914; died 1975. *Educ.* Illinois University. Fringe player in numerous B productions of the 1940s who came to prominence as the lead in *The Jolson Story* (1946). Parks's career was ruined when he admitted his past Communist affiliations to the House Committee on Un-American Activities. Married to actress Betty Garrett from 1944. • *Harmon of Michigan* 1941; *Harvard, Here I Come* 1941; *Mystery Ship* 1941; *Alias Boston Blackie* 1942; *Atlantic Convoy* 1942; *Blondie Goes to College* 1942; *The Boogie Man Will Get You* 1942; *Canal Zone* 1942; *Flight Lieutenant* 1942; *Hello, Annapolis* 1942; *North of the Rockies* 1942; *Submarine Raider* 1942; *You Were Never Lovelier* 1942; *Deerslayer* 1943; *Is Everybody Happy?* 1943; *Power of the Press* 1943; *Reveille With Beverly* 1943; *The Black Parachute* 1944; *Hey, Rookie* 1944; *The Racket Man* 1944; *Sergeant Mike* 1944; *She's a Sweetheart* 1944; *Stars on Parade* 1944; *Counter-Attack* 1945; *The Jolson Story* 1946 **(AANBA)**; *Renegades* 1946; *Down to Earth* 1947; *High Conquest* 1947; *The Swordsman* 1947; *The Gallant Blade* 1948; *Jolson Sings Again* 1949; *Emergency Wedding* 1950; *Love Is Better Than Ever* 1952; *Tiger By the Tail* 1957; *Freud* 1962.

Parsons, Estelle • Actress • Born Marblehead, MA, January 20, 1927. *Educ.* Connecticut College for Women (political science); Boston University Law School. Former TV writer and producer who began appearing on stage in the late 1950s and established herself as a leading screen character actress in the following decade. Parsons was memorable as the shrewish Blanche Barrow in Arthur Penn's *Bonnie and Clyde* (1967) and as the lesbian religious fanatic in *Rachel, Rachel* (1968). She recently played Mrs. Trueheart in Warren Beatty's *Dick Tracy* (1990). • *Ladybug, Ladybug* 1963; *Bonnie and Clyde* 1967 **(AABSA)**; *Rachel, Rachel* 1968 **(AANBSA)**; *Don't Drink the Water* 1969; *I Never Sang For My Father* 1970; *I Walk the Line* 1970; *Watermelon Man* 1970; *Two People* 1973; *For Pete's Sake* 1974; *Foreplay* 1974; *The Lemon Sisters* 1989; *Dick Tracy* 1990.

Parton, Dolly • Actress, singer, composer • Born Dolly Rebecca Parton, Sevierville, TN, January 19, 1946. Began her entertainment career as a teenager in Nashville and rose to fame singing alongside Porter Wagoner before going solo in 1974. Parton had become one of the genre's biggest stars when she branched out into film in 1980, giving an engaging performance as a Southern secretary opposite Jane Fonda and Lily Tomlin in *9 to 5*. She also wrote the film's title song, which earned an Oscar nomination and won a Grammy.

Parton is well known for her role as the owner of a hair salon in the 1989 film adaptation of Robert Harling's play, *Steel Magnolias*. An astute businesswoman, she is the joint owner, with manager Sandy Gallin, of the Sandollar production company and has her own theme park, Dollywood, located in the Smoky Mountains. • *9 to 5* 1980 (a,song) **(AANBS)**; *The Best Little Whorehouse in Texas* 1982 (a,m.sup,songs); *Rhinestone* 1984 (a,m,m.sup,songs); *Steel Magnolias* 1989 (a).

Pasdar, Adrian • Actor • Born Pittsfield, MA. *Educ.* University of Central Florida; People's Light and Theatre Company, Philadelphia; Lee Strasberg Theatre Institute. The handsome young lead, widely seen in *Top Gun* (1986), gained cult recognition for his performance as a reluctant, latter-day vampire in Kathyrn Bigelow's *Near Dark* (1987). • *Solarbabies* 1986; *Streets of Gold* 1986; *Top Gun* 1986; *Made in U.S.A.* 1987; *Near Dark* 1987; *Cookie* 1989; *Torn Apart* 1990; *Vital Signs* 1990.

Pasolini, Pier Paolo • Director, screenwriter; also poet, novelist, theorist. • Born Bologna, Italy, March 5, 1922; died 1975. *Educ.* University of Bologna. Pier Paolo Pasolini considered himself first and foremost a poet. But his poetic vision was of people who lived on the edge of society or outside the law, a vision that carried over into his filmmaking.

The son of a committed Fascist officer, he graduated from the university in his hometown of Bologna and in rebellion against his father's political beliefs turned to communism. Conscripted for the army, he was taken prisoner by German forces following the Italian surrender to the Allies. He escaped and hid out with his family; being on the run and hiding out would become recurrent themes in his life and work.

In 1947 Pasolini became secretary of the communist party cell at Casarsa. Two years later, after he was accused of corrupting minors and fired from the Casarsa school where he taught, he moved to Rome with his beloved mother. Though he was an avowed atheist, communist and homosexual, he had great respect for his mother's simple beliefs, a respect which probably played a role in the making of his most celebrated film, *Il Vangelo Secondo Matteo/The Gospel According to St. Matthew*, which won the special jury prize at the 1964 Venice Film Festival.

During the early 1950s, Pasolini was indicted for obscenity for his first novel, *Ragazzi di Vita.* Though he continued writing fiction and poetry, he began to turn to film scripts as well, working under Federico Fellini on *Le Notti di Cabiria* (1956). His first film as a director was *Accatone* (1961), based on his own novel of a low-life crook and pimp in the slums of Rome. Two years later, he was back in trouble with the law when he was prosecuted for vilification of the Church for directing the "La Ricotta" segment of the anthology film *RoGoPag.* Other Pasolini films of the 1960s included *Teorema* (1968), an allegory with Terence Stamp, and *Medea* (1970), with opera diva Maria Callas.

In the 70s Pasolini embarked on a series of films based on ribald classical literary works such as *The Decameron* (1971) and *The Canterbury Tales* (1972). His last film was the controversial *Salo* (1975): subtitled *The 120 Days of Sodom.* This allegory of Fascist Italy was filled with savage violence, sado-masochism and a variety of other sexual depravities.

On November 2, 1975, Pasolini was murdered in a manner bizarre enough to come out of one of his films. He was bludgeoned to death near a soccer field by a 17-year old boy, who was later arrested for speeding in Pasolini's Alfa Romeo. The killer claimed Pasolini had made sexual advances to him.

Regarded abroad as one of the foremost filmmakers of his generation, Pasolini, was also, according to Susan Sontag, "indisputably the most remarkable figure to have emerged in Italian arts and letters since the Second World War." His personal vision was of a world of violence and sexuality, ranging from the shanty towns and city streets of contemporary Rome to the moral fantasies of Boccaccio and the Arabian Nights. His films are portraits of outsiders in violent struggle with their society, much of that concern reflecting his own inner turmoil. DLY • *La Donna del Fiume* 1954 (sc); *Le Notti di Cabiria* 1956 (add.dial); *Giovani Mariti* 1958 (sc); *Morte di un amico* 1959 (sc); *Il Bell'Antonio* 1960 (sc); *Una Giornata Balorda* 1960 (sc,story); *La Notta Brava* 1960 (sc,from novel *Ragazza di vita*); *Accattone* 1961 (d,sc); *La Canta delle Marane* 1961 (sc,from novel *Ragazzi di vita*); *La Commare Secca* 1962 (sc,story); *Mamma Roma* 1962 (d,sc); *RoGoPag* 1962 (d,sc,from subject—"La Ricotta"); *La Rabbia* 1963 (d,sc,story,commentary,ed); *Comizi d'Amore* 1964 (a,commentary writer,d); *Il Vangelo Secondo Matteo/The Gospel According to St. Matthew* 1964 (d,sc,adapt); *Sopraluoghi in Palestina* 1965 (d); *Uccellacci e Uccellini* 1966 (d,sc);*La Sequenza del fiore di carta/ The Episode of the Paper Flower* in *Amore e rabbia* 1967 (d); *Edipo Re/Oedipus Rex* 1967 (a,d,sc,m,m); *Appunti per un'film sull'India* 1968 (a,d,story,commentary); *Capriccio all'italiana* 1968 (d); *Le Streghe* 1968 (d,sc—"La terra vista dalla luna"/"The Earth Seen From the Moon"); *Teorema* 1968 (d,sc,from novel); *Porcile* 1969 (d,sc); *Appunti per un romanzo dell'immondeza* 1970 (d); *Appunti per un'orestiade African/Notes for an African Oresteia* 1970 (d,sc,commentary,ph); *Medea* 1970 (d,sc); *Le mura di Sana/The Walls of Sana (short)* 1970 (a,commentary,d); *Il Decamerone/The Decameron* 1971 (a,d,sc,m); *Dodici dicembre 1972* 1972 (d); *I Racconti di Canterbury/The Canterbury Tales* 1972 (a,d,sc,m); *Storie Scellerate* 1973 (sc); *Il Fiore Delle Mille e Una Notte/The Arabian Nights/The Flower of the Arabian Nights/A Thousand and One Nights* 1974 (d,sc); *Salo o le Centiventi Giornate di Sodoma/Salo/The 120 days of Sodom* 1975 (d,sc); *Castelporziano, Ostia Dei Poeti* 1981 (lyrics); *Calderon* 1983 (sc,from play); *A Futura Memoria di Pier Paolo Pasolini* 1987 (docu).

Passer, Ivan • Director; also writer. • Born Prague, Czechlosvakia, July 10, 1933. *Educ.* FAMU, Prague. Leading figure of the Czech new wave who co-scripted all of Milos Forman's native films before making his directorial debut with the acclaimed medium-length study of football fanaticism, *A Boring Afternoon* (1964). Passer's subsequent output displayed a Forman-like ability to capture the absurdity of everyday life and—as evinced by his highly regarded first feature, *Intimate Lighting* (1965)—a sure feel for the uses of music in film. Following the Soviet invasion in 1968 Passer moved, first to Western Europe at the invitation of Carlo Ponti, and then to the US. There he made a number of modest, quirky films, the most successful of which was *Cutter's Way* (1981), an offbeat study of a group of drifters, which has become something of a cult favorite. • *Fádní odpoledne/A Boring Afternoon* 1964 (sc);*Intimni Osvetleni/Intimate Lightning* 1965 (d,sc); *Lasky Jedne Plavovlasky* 1965 (sc); *Hori, Ma Panenko* 1967 (sc); *Born to Win/Born to Lose* 1971 (d,sc); *Law and Disorder* 1974 (d,sc); *Crime and Passion/An Ace Up My Sleeve* 1976 (d); *Silver Bears* 1977 (d); *Cutter's Way/Cutter and Bone* 1981 (d); *Creator* 1985 (d).

Pasternak, Joe • Producer • Born Joseph Pasternak, Szilagy-Somlyo, Hungary, September 19, 1901. Worked his way up through the ranks to become an assistant director at Paramount in 1923. After producing several successful films in Europe, Pasternak revived the flagging fortunes of Universal with a series of hit musicals starring Deanna Durbin in the mid-1930s. He is also credited with discovering Judy Garland and Mario Lanza and rejuvenating the career of Marlene Dietrich. • *Ludwig der Zweite, Koenig von Bayern* 1929; *Three Smart Girls* 1937; *Mad About Music* 1938; *That Certain Age* 1938; *Youth Takes a Fling* 1938; *Destry Rides Again* 1939; *First Love* 1939; *Three Smart Girls Grow Up* 1939; *The Under-Pup* 1939; *It's a Date* 1940; *A Little Bit of Heaven* 1940; *Seven Sinners* 1940; *Spring Parade* 1940; *The Flame of New Orleans* 1941; *It Started With Eve* 1941; *Nice Girl?* 1941; *Seven Sweethearts* 1942; *Presenting Lily Mars* 1943; *Song of Russia* 1943; *Thousands Cheer* 1943; *Music For Millions* 1944; *Two Girls and a Sailor* 1944; *Anchors Aweigh* 1945; *Her Highness and the Bellboy* 1945; *Thrill of a Romance* 1945; *Holiday in Mexico* 1946; *No Leave, No Love* 1946; *Two Sisters From Boston* 1946; *This Time For Keeps* 1947; *The Unfinished Dance* 1947; *Big City* 1948; *A Date With Judy* 1948; *The Kissing Bandit* 1948; *Luxury Liner* 1948; *On an Island With You* 1948; *Three Daring Daughters* 1948; *In the Good Old Summertime* 1949; *That Midnight Kiss* 1949; *Duchess of Idaho* 1950; *Nancy Goes to Rio* 1950; *Summer Stock* 1950; *The Toast of New Orleans* 1950; *The Great Caruso* 1951; *Rich, Young and Pretty* 1951; *The Strip* 1951; *Because You're Mine* 1952; *The Merry Widow* 1952; *Skirts Ahoy!* 1952; *Easy to Love* 1953; *Latin Lovers* 1953; *Small Town Girl* 1953; *Athena* 1954; *Flame and the Flesh* 1954; *The Student Prince* 1954; *Hit the Deck* 1955; *Love Me or Leave Me* 1955; *Meet Me in Las Vegas* 1956; *The Opposite Sex* 1956; *Ten Thousand Bedrooms* 1956; *This Could Be the Night* 1957; *Party Girl* 1958; *Ask Any Girl* 1959; *Please Don't Eat the Daisies* 1960; *Where the Boys Are* 1960; *Billy Rose's Jumbo* 1962; *The Horizontal Lieutenant* 1962; *The Courtship of Eddie's Father* 1963; *A Ticklish Affair* 1963; *Looking For Love* 1964; *Girl Happy* 1965; *Made in Paris* 1966; *Spinout* 1966; *The Sweet Ride* 1968.

Paterson, Bill • Actor • Born Scotland. *Educ.* Royal Scottish Academy of Music and Drama. Stage, TV and film performer who began his career with the Glasgow Citizens Theatre and was a founding member of the radical 7:84 company (the name derives from the fact that 7% of the population of Britain own 84% of the country's wealth). Paterson first gained attention on screen for his role as a lonely D.J. in Bill Forsyth's *Comfort and Joy* (1984) and has since turned in finely controlled performances in films by Roland Joffe, Hugh Hudson and Malcolm Mowbray. • *Licking Hitler* 1977; *Licensed to Love and Kill* 1978; *The Odd Job* 1978; *The Ploughman's Lunch* 1983; *Comfort and Joy* 1984; *The Killing Fields* 1984; *A Private Function* 1984; *Defence of the Realm* 1985; *Rhosyn a Rhith* 1986;

Friendship's Death 1987; *Hidden City* 1987; *The Adventures of Baron Munchausen* 1988; *Just Ask For Diamond* 1988; *The Singing Detective* 1988; *Bearskin: An Urban Fairytale* 1989; *The Return of the Musketeers* 1989; *Cello* 1990; *The Witches* 1990; *The Object of Beauty* 1991.

Pathé, Charles • Film pioneer • Born Chevry-Cossigny, France, December 25, 1863; died 1957. Pathe first enjoyed success as a businessman by exhibiting the Edison phonograph at French fairgrounds. He established his own phonograph business in 1894 and two years later formed the Pathé Frères company with brothers Emile, Jacques and Théophile. The brothers at first concentrated on marketing a camera and projector designed by Henri Joly, but ventured into film production in 1900. By 1902 the company had constructed a large studio at Vincennes and assembled a team of directors, most notably Ferdinand Zecca; by 1907 it had become an industrial empire with interests in every aspect of production, distribution and exhibition with offices, factories and studios spread across the world. Among the company's innovations were the replacement of fairground booths with permanent cinemas and the practice of renting, rather than selling, films to exhibitors. Pathé's output encompassed everything from light comedy to the Film d'Art series, with its creative personnel including figures such as Louis Gasnier and Max Linder. Pathé's virtual monopoly of the film industry was eroded by the onset of WWI, escalating production costs and the eventual shriveling of the international market; a slow dismemberment of the empire began in 1918, with Charles Pathé finally selling his interests and retiring in 1929.

Patinkin, Mandy • Actor; also singer. • Born Chicago, IL, November 20, 1947. *Educ.* University of Kansas; Juilliard School of Drama. Versatile stage and screen performer who first came to prominence as Che Guevara in the Broadway musical, *Evita*. Patinkin has subsequently appeared in musical, dramatic and comic features, notably *Ragtime* (1981). • *The Big Fix* 1978 (a); *French Postcards* 1979 (a); *Last Embrace* 1979 (a); *Night of the Juggler* 1980 (a); *Ragtime* 1981 (a); *Daniel* 1983 (a); *Yentl* 1983 (a); *Maxie* 1985 (a); *The Princess Bride* 1987 (a); *Alien Nation* 1988 (a); *The House on Carroll Street* 1988 (a); *Dick Tracy* 1990 (a,song); *Impromptu* 1991 (a); *True Colors* 1991 (a).

Patton, Will • Actor • Born Charleston, SC. *Educ.* North Carolina School of the Arts. Veteran of over 40 New York stage plays who won an Obie for his performance as Eddie in the 1982 Circle Repertory production of Sam Shepard's *Fool for Love*. Patton turned in a fine screen performance as Gene Hackman's oily, officious aide in Roger Donaldson's Washington thriller, *No Way Out* (1987). • *King Blank* 1982; *Silkwood* 1983; *Variety* 1983; *Chinese Boxes* 1984; *After Hours* 1985; *Belizaire the Cajun* 1985; *Desperately Seeking Susan* 1985; *No Way Out* 1987; *Stars and Bars* 1988; *Wildfire* 1988; *Signs of Life* 1989; *Everybody Wins* 1990; *A Shock to the System* 1990; *The Rapture* 1991.

Pearce, Richard • Director, director of photography • Born San Diego, CA. *Educ.* Yale (English); New School for Social Research, New York (political economics). After meeting D.A. Pennebaker during his senior year in college, Pearce got his first taste of filmmaking helping out on Pennebaker's Bob Dylan documentary, *Don't Look Back* (1967). He went on to shoot such documentaries as Emile de Antonio's *America Is Hard to See* and Michael Wadleigh's *Woodstock* (1970) before making his feature directorial debut with *Heartland* (1980), an unromanticized story of Midwestern life in the 1910s. The film won a Golden Bear at the Berlin festival and established the themes of rural hardship and resilience which Pearce would again explore in *Country* (1984), starring Sam Shepard and Jessica Lange. • *Woodstock* 1970 (ph); *Marjoe* 1972 (ph); *Let the Good Times Roll* 1973 (ph); *Hearts and Minds* 1974 (assoc.p,ph); *Running Fence* 1977 (asst.cam.op); *Baby Snakes* 1979 (ph); *Hair* 1979 (add.ph); *Rust Never Sleeps* 1979 (ph); *Heartland* 1980 (d); *Threshold* 1981 (d); *Country* 1984 (d); *No Mercy* 1986 (d); *The Long Walk Home* 1990 (d).

Peck, Gregory • Actor; also producer. • Born Eldred Gregory Peck, La Jolla, CA, April 5, 1916. *Educ.* San Diego State College; University of California, Berkeley (pre-med, English); Neighborhood Playhouse School of Dramatics. While enrolled in the pre-med program at Berkeley, Peck took a trip to New York City, where he saw Vera Zorina in *I Married an Angel*, and changed his priorities: he withdrew from pre-med and joined a small theater group on campus. In 1939, Peck returned to New York City and, after winning a scholarship to the prestigious Neighborhood Playhouse School of Dramatics, his acting career caught on. The plays themselves (*Morning Star, The Willow and I, Sons and Soldiers*) were less than successful, but Peck's excellent notices attracted the attention of Hollywood.

The scarcity of leading men in Hollywood during the war years (Peck was exempt from service because of a spinal injury), the glowing reviews of his Broadway performances and savvy manipulation on the part of his agent, Leland Hayward, all contributed to Peck's being in great demand. In fact, the young actor soon found himself starting his Hollywood career under contract to four studios: R.K.O, 20th Century-Fox, Selznick Productions and MGM.

His first film, *Days of Glory* (1944), an over-ripe tribute to Russian peasant resistance against the Nazis, featured Peck as a strong-boned resistance leader. But it was *The Keys of the Kingdom*, with Peck as a dedicated Roman Catholic missionary to China, that made him a star. This was the first of his incarnations as an authority figure of quiet dignity and uncompromising singlemindedness; the next four decades saw him play variations of that character in *The Yearling* (1946), *The Macomber Affair* (1947) *Gentleman's Agreement* (1947), *The Gunfighter* (1950), *The Man in the Gray Flannel Suit* (1956), *The Guns of Navarone* (1961), *To Kill a Mockingbird* (1962), *The Omen* (1976) and *Old Gringo* (1989). Interspersed among these films were others depicting a darker side of his persona, a man fatalistically obssessed (even possessed) by hidden demons that push him toward the brink of madness, as in *Spellbound* (1945), *Duel in the Sun* (1947), *Yellow Sky* (1948), *Twelve O'Clock High* (1949), *Moby Dick* (1956), *MacArthur the Rebel General* (1977) and *The Boys From Brazil* (1978).

Peck's zenith as a film actor was *To Kill A Mockingbird*, for which he won an Academy Award for his portrayal of Atticus Finch, a small-town Southern lawyer whose quiet intensity and moral courage became a summary of Peck's screen persona. After that film, however, Peck found himself embroiled in such post-studio era potboilers as *Mackenna's Gold* (1969), *The Chairman* (1969), *Billy Two Hats* (1973) and *The Boys From Brazil* (1978).

Even as his film career declined, his philanthropic efforts in support of arts organizations flowered, with Peck working tirelessly as a founder of the American Film Institute, three-term president of the Academy of Motion Picture Arts and Sciences and member of the National Council of Arts—making him seem less an actor than a politician. As such, it seemed fitting that the two Pecks finally melded in the 1982 television production of *The Blue and the Grey*, with Peck at last playing Abraham Lincoln. Daughter Cecilia Peck is an actress. PB • *Days of Glory* 1944 (a); *The Keys of the Kingdom* 1945 (a) **(AANBA)**; *Spellbound* 1945 (a); *The Valley of Decision* 1945 (a); *The Yearling* 1946 (a) **(AANBA)**; *Duel in the Sun* 1947 (a); *Gentleman's Agreement* 1947 (a) **(AANBA)**; *The Macomber Affair* 1947 (a); *The Paradine Case* 1947 (a); *Yellow Sky* 1948 (a); *The Great Sinner* 1949 (a); *Twelve O'Clock High* 1949 (a) **(AANBA)**; *The Gunfighter* 1950 (a); *Captain Horatio Hornblower* 1951 (a); *David and Bathsheba* 1951 (a); *Only the Valiant* 1951 (a); *The Snows of Kilimanjaro* 1952 (a); *The World in His Arms* 1952 (a); *The Man With a Million* 1953 (a); *Roman Holiday* 1953 (a); *Night People* 1954 (a); *The Purple Plain* 1954 (a); *The Man in the Gray Flannel Suit* 1955 (a); *Moby Dick* 1956 (a); *Designing Woman* 1957 (a); *The Big Country* 1958 (a,p); *The Bravados* 1958 (a); *Beloved Infidel* 1959 (a); *On the Beach* 1959 (a); *Pork Chop Hill* 1959 (a,exec.p); *The Guns of Navarone* 1961 (a); *Cape Fear* 1962 (a); *How the West Was Won* 1962 (a); *To Kill a Mockingbird* 1962 (a) **(AABA)**; *Behold a Pale Horse* 1964 (a); *Captain Newman, M.D.* 1964 (a); *Mirage* 1965 (a); *Arabesque* 1966 (a); *The Stalking Moon* 1968 (a); *The Chairman* 1969 (a); *MacKenna's Gold* 1969 (a); *Marooned* 1969 (a); *I Walk the Line* 1970 (a); *Shoot Out* 1971 (a); *The Trial of the Catonsville Nine* 1972 (p); *Billy Two Hats* 1973 (a); *The Dove* 1974 (p); *It's Showtime* 1976 (a); *The Omen* 1976 (a); *MacArthur the Rebel General* 1977 (a); *The Boys From Brazil* 1978 (a); *The Sea Wolves* 1980 (a); *Directed By William Wyler* 1986 (a); *Amazing Grace and Chuck* 1987 (a); *Old Gringo* 1989 (a).

Peckinpah, Sam • Director, screenwriter; also actor. • Born Fresno, CA, February 21, 1925; died December 28, 1984, Inglewood, CA. *Educ.* USC, Los Angeles (drama). Sam Peckinpah was a paradox who both cultivated and disdained his own legend as one of Hollywood's most difficult directors, his often violent films evoked strong responses and varied, almost contradictory, readings. Born to a California legal clan, Peckinpah served in the Marine Corps and earned a master's degree from U.S.C. in 1950. He spent his early career as a theater and television director before becoming an assistant on five films to director Don Siegel, famed for his hard-bitten action films (Peckinpah even played a small part in Siegel's *Invasion of the Body Snatchers*, 1956). Peckinpah soon became associated with the western genre, writing and directing episodes of "Gunsmoke," "The Rifleman," "The Westerner" and other TV series. His 1957 script on the legend of Billy the Kid eventually became, without his participation and with many changes, Marlon Brando's eccentric *One-Eyed Jacks* (1961).

Peckinpah's first film as a director, *The Deadly Companions* (1961), plus *Ride the High Country* (1962), *Major Dundee* (1965), *The Wild Bunch* (1969) and *Pat Garrett and Billy the Kid* (1973) form an arc in the stylistic span of outlaw mythology; among other accomplishments, they raised to the level of perverse sacrament the male gesture of mutual respect that supersedes fear of death. His "semi-westerns," *The Ballad of Cable Hogue* (1970) and the director's personal favorite, *Junior Bonner* (1972), extended his theme of the demise of a noble way of life in the face of a modern world. *The Getaway* (1972) and *Convoy* (1978) put contemporary anti-heroes ahead of as well as outside the law. Perhaps his most controversial film was *Straw Dogs* (1971); the inevitable brutality of its protagonist, ostensibly a man of reason, offers a metaphor on the ancient bent of the human psyche vis-à-vis personal territory and blood rites. *Bring Me the Head of Alfredo Garcia* (1974), reputedly autobiographical, was a psychodrama refracted through a tequila haze, a saga of a loner/artiste who reaps the grotesque wages of sin on a desperate trek of atonement. Peckinpah's distrust of policymakers was reflected in *The Killer Elite* (1975) and his last film, *The Osterman Weekend*, (1983), both essays on vicious tactics and dissolute friendship in the CIA. *Cross of Iron* (1977), Peckinpah's largest production, is a fiercely edited view of World War II slaughter where the Wehrmacht wear the patented scars of his honorable killers.

Few directors have had more conflict with studio heads and producers than Peckinpah. Feuds over the content and final cuts of *Major Dundee* (after which Peckinpah was blacklisted for three years), *The Wild Bunch* and *Pat Garrett* are the stuff of Hollywood legend. Critical response to his work has often been as violent as the films themselves, with Peckinpah frequently berated for demeaning women and excessively glorifying male exploits. On an aesthetic level, Peckinpah is celebrated for his slow motion furies, first employed in a 1963 entry of TV's "Dick Powell Theater" called "The Losers," exercised to startling effect in *The Wild Bunch*, but somewhat overused in subsequent work. "Cathartic violence" was a term that seemed coined to define his iconoclastic postures. In Peckinpah's Conradian scheme that mixes nobility with tragedy, all are guilty to some degree and all have their reasons. His work typically exists on a skewed moral plane between eras and cultures, with ambiguous quests for identity and redemption undertaken by hopelessly lost outcasts and enemies. He vividly defines the thin line between internal conflict and external action, and, perhaps most importantly, the violent displacement of a false code of honor (and law itself) by another more enduring and devout.

As thorny as his relationships with producers and executives were, Peckinpah could inspire extraordinary loyalty among actors and technicians. An ensemble of notable Peckinpah players would include David Warner, Warren Oates, L.Q. Jones, Strother Martin, James Coburn, Kris Kristofferson and Ben Johnson. Peckinpah also enjoyed repeated and fruitful collaborations with cinematographers Lucien Ballard and John Coquillon and composer Jerry Fielding. MDM • *Private Hell 36* 1954 (dial.d); *Invasion of the Body Snatchers* 1956 (a); *The Deadly Companions* 1961 (d); *Ride the High Country* 1962 (d); *The Glory Guys* 1965 (sc); *Major Dundee* 1965 (d,sc); *Villa Rides* 1968 (sc); *The Wild Bunch* 1969 (d,sc) **(AANBSC)**; *The Ballad of Cable Hogue* 1970 (d,p); *Straw Dogs* 1971 (d,sc,from novel *Trencher's Farm*); *The Getaway* 1972 (d); *Junior Bonner* 1972 (d); *Pat Garrett and Billy the Kid* 1973 (d,p); *Bring Me the Head of Alfredo Garcia* 1974 (d,sc,story,song); *The Killer Elite* 1975 (d); *Cross of Iron* 1977 (d); *China 9, Liberty 37* 1978 (a); *Convoy* 1978 (d); *The Visitor* 1979 (a); *The Osterman Weekend* 1983 (d); *Hollywood Mavericks* 1990 (a).

Peerce, Larry • Director • Born Bronx, NY. *Educ.* North Carolina University (drama); Columbia (drama). Began his career as a TV director and earned critical acclaim for his feature debut, *One Potato, Two Potato* (1964), shot on a budget of only $230,000. A sensitive and compelling account of an interracial marriage, the film earned star Barbara Barrie a best actress award at Cannes. Peerce's subsequent film work has been erratic, though he scored another hit with *Goodbye, Columbus* (1969), adapted from the novel by Philip Roth. He continues to work in TV. • *One Potato, Two Potato* 1964 (d); *The Big T.N.T. Show* 1966 (d); *The Incident* 1967 (d); *Goodbye, Columbus* 1969 (d); *The Sporting Club* 1971 (d); *A Separate Peace* 1972 (d); *Ash Wednesday* 1973 (d); *The Other Side of the Mountain* 1974 (d); *Two-Minute Warning* 1976 (d); *The Other Side of the Mountain - Part 2* 1977 (d); *The Bell Jar* 1979 (d,exec.p); *Why Would I Lie?* 1980 (d); *Love Child* 1982 (d); *Hard to Hold* 1983 (d); *Wired* 1989 (d).

Peña, Elizabeth • Actress • Born Elizabeth, NJ. *Educ.* High School for the Performing Arts. Sultry, stage-trained actress, best known for her TV work ("Shannon's Deal") and as Lou Diamond Phillips's fiery, over-protective mother in *La Bamba* (1987). • *El Super* 1979; *Times Square* 1980; *They All Laughed* 1981; *Crossover Dreams* 1985; *Down and Out in Beverly Hills* 1986; *Batteries Not Included* 1987; *La Bamba* 1987; *Vibes* 1988; *Blue Steel* 1989; *Jacob's Ladder* 1990.

Pendleton, Austin • Actor; also stage director. • Born U.S.A., 1940. Diminutive, stage-trained character actor, in films since 1968. • *Skidoo* 1968; *Catch-22* 1970; *Every Little Crook and Nanny* 1972; *What's Up, Doc?* 1972; *The Thief Who Came to Dinner* 1973; *The Front Page* 1974; *The Great Smokey Roadblock* 1976; *The Muppet Movie* 1979; *Starting Over* 1979; *First Family* 1980; *Simon* 1980; *Talk to Me* 1982; *My Man Adam* 1985; *Off Beat* 1986; *Short Circuit* 1986; *Hello, Again* 1987; *Mr. & Mrs. Bridge* 1990.

Penn, Arthur • Director • Born Philadelphia, PA, September 27, 1922. *Educ.* Black Mountain College, NC; University of Perugia, Italy; University of Florence, Italy; Actors Studio, Los Angeles. An actor's director, Penn is adept at establishing supportive relationships with his actors and eliciting an incredible range of expression from them. Because he is technically astute, he understands the poetry of close camera work. As he contends, in film you don't have to say it: "A look, a simple look, will do it." Penn's use of lighting and sound are stylistically and intellectually sophisticated, but it is his themes, rather than his style, which empower his oeuvre. Using myth, violence and moral ambiguity, Penn often deals with contemporary issues through the lives of social outcasts.

His interest in dramatics began in high school. In the army during WWII, he directed a theater company in Europe and after his discharge he attended Black Mountain College in North Carolina and later taught acting.

In 1951, Penn was hired as a third floor manager for TV's "Colgate Comedy Hour." Fred Coe, a friend from his army days, later hired him to direct a live dramatic series called "Gulf Playhouse: First Person." Penn continued to work in television through the 50s, on such dramatic programs as "Philco Playhouse" and "Playhouse 90," and he branched out to Broadway as well, with *Blue Denim* (1954) and *Two for the Seesaw* (1957).

In 1958, as a favor to Coe, Penn directed his first film, *The Left Handed Gun*, based on Gore Vidal's television play, a psychological interpretation of the legend of Billy the Kid. Received with indifference in the US, the film won the Grand Prix at the Brussels Film Festival. Most importantly, it identified several themes which would recur throughout his work: the dichotomy of father-son relationships; the function of myth in reconciling reality; the arbitrary nature of violence; and the outcast as a reflection of society.

Penn's next film was *The Miracle Worker* (1962), based on a play he had successfully directed for television and on Broadway. The film relied little on the conventions of the medium to complement the narrative. The acting of Oscar winners Anne Bancroft and Patty Duke, however, was superlative and Penn received his first Academy Award nomination for Best Director.

Penn's next film, *Mickey One* (1965) is a noteworthy addition to the film noir genre. Its fragmented tale of a nightclub comic on the run from mobsters received decidedly mixed reivews, although the film does retain a strong cult following.

Bonnie and Clyde (1967), Penn's next significant film, is a complex, romantic myth based on the real Barrow Gang of the American Depression-era Southwest. When the film was criticized for its graphic brutality, Penn characterized violence as an element of human nature. His startling juxtaposition of comedy and mayhem supports his assertion that violence often erupts arbitrarily. Eliminating violence from film, Penn said, is "like eliminating one of the primary colors from the palette of the painter." The film received ten Oscar nominations, including one for Penn.

His next two films sustained the theme of the outcast's relationship with conventional society. *Alice's Restaurant* (1969), for which Penn received his third Oscar nomination, portrays a metaphorical death of 1960s idealism in its story about a commune of hippies. *Little Big Man* (1970) attacks the romantic myths of the American West in a sometimes lyric, often brutal story told in flashback by a 121-year-old man (Dustin Hoffman) who claims he is the only white survivor of Custer's Last Stand. Another Penn western, *The Missouri Breaks* (1976), reiterates his themes in its tale of a rustler (Jack Nicholson) caught on the fence between the outlaw life and respectability; the film demonstrates a mature, beautifully composed visual style.

More recently, Penn's films have lacked the energy of his earlier works. Movies like *Four Friends* (1981) and *Dead of Winter* (1987) are not up the standards Penn set with *Bonnie and Clyde*, but he remains a vital filmmaker, and his filmic contributions have not been fully realized. MCJ • *The Left Handed Gun* 1958 (d); *The Miracle Worker* 1962 (d) **(AANBD)**; *Mickey One* 1965 (d,p); *The Chase* 1966 (d); *Bonnie and Clyde* 1967 (d) **(AANBD)**; *Alice's Restaurant* 1969 (d,sc) **(AANBD)**; *Little Big Man* 1970 (d); *Visions of Eight* 1973 (d—"The Highest"); *Night Moves* 1975 (d); *The Missouri Breaks* 1976 (d); *Four Friends* 1981 (d,p); *Target* 1985 (d); *Dead of Winter* 1987 (d); *Hello Actors Studio* 1987 (a); *Penn & Teller Get Killed* 1989 (d,p).

Penn, Sean • Actor • Born Burbank, CA, August 17, 1960. Made his film debut in *Taps* (1981), playing Timothy Hutton's military academy roommate, and consolidated his popularity with his role as surfer Jeff Spicoli in Amy Heckerling's *Fast Times at Ridgemont High* (1982). Penn has gone on to establish himself as one of Hollywood's finest young stars, with an intense, volatile screen presence that has frequently—and very publicly—spilled over into his off-screen life. Penn is divorced from pop performer Madonna and is the brother of actor Christopher and musician Michael. His father Leo Penn is an actor and director of stage, film and TV and mother Eileen Ryan is an actress (she played Sean's grandmother in 1986's *At Close Range*). • *Taps* 1981; *Fast Times at Ridgemont High* 1982; *Bad Boys* 1983; *Crackers* 1984; *Racing With the Moon* 1984; *The Falcon and the Snowman* 1985; *At Close Range* 1986; *Shanghai Surprise* 1986; *Dear America* 1987; *Colors* 1988; *Judgment in Berlin* 1988; *Casualties of War* 1989; *We're No Angels* 1989; *State of Grace* 1990.

Pennebaker, D.A. • Filmmaker • Born Donn Alan Pennebaker, Evanston, IL, 1930. *Educ.* Yale; MIT. Former engineer, advertising copywriter and painter who began making experimental and documentary films in the 1950s. Beginning with *Daybreak Express* (1953), Pennebaker emerged as one of the foremost proponents of direct cinema, a style of filmmaking which favored the immediate recording of reality in as unobtrusive a manner as possible. He worked for a time at Drew Associates with Richard Leacock and Albert Maysles; although he left in 1963, he continued to collaborate on joint ventures with Leacock. Pennebaker is best known for *Don't Look Back* (1967), documenting Bob Dylan's first tour of England, *Monterey Pop* (1968) and for completing and editing *1 A.M.* (1971), a film begun by Jean-Luc Godard. • *Daybreak Express (short)* 1953 (d); *Primary* 1960 (d); *On the Road to Button Bay* 1962 (d); *Timothy Leary's Wedding Day* 1964 (d); *Elizabeth and Mary* 1965 (d); *Don't Look Back* 1967 (d,p,ph); *Beyond the Law* 1968 (ph); *Goin' to San Francisco (short)* 1968 (d); *Monterey Pop* 1968 (d,sc,ph); *Maidstone* 1970 (ph); *Original Cast Album: Company (short)* 1970 (d,ph,ed); *Sweet Toronto* 1970 (d,ph); *One American Movie/1 A.M.* 1971 (p,sc,ph,ed); *Ziggy Stardust and the Spiders From Mars* 1973 (d,ph); *Town Bloody Hall* 1979 (d,p,sc,ph); *Elliott Carter* 1980 (d); *Before the Nickelodeon: The Early Cinema Of Edwin S. Porter* 1982 (a); *Dance Black America* 1985 (d,ph,ed,commentary); *Jimi Plays Monterey* 1986 (d); *Shake (Otis Redding)* 1986 (d); *Dal polo all'equatore* 1987 (ed); *Depeche Mode 101* 1989 (d,ed).

Peploe, Clare • British screenwriter, director • Co-screenwriter of Michelangelo Antonioni's *Zabriskie Point* (1970) and husband Bernardo Bertolucci's *La Luna* (1979) who reached feature directorial acclaim with *High Season* (1987), a comedy starring James Fox and Jacqueline Bissett. Sister of screenwriter Mark Peploe. • *Zabriskie Point* 1970 (sc); *La Luna* 1979 (sc,ad); *Couples & Robbers* 1981 (d,sc); *High Season* 1987 (d,sc).

Peploe, Mark • British screenwriter • Collaborative scenarist who has worked with Jacques Demy, Michelangelo Antonioni and brother-in-law Bernardo Bertolucci, among others. Co-wrote sister Clare Peploe's *High Season* (1987). • *The Pied Piper* 1972; *Baby Sitter—Un maledetto pasticcio* 1975; *The Passenger* 1975; *High Season* 1987; *The Last Emperor* 1987 **(AABSC)**; *The Sheltering Sky* 1990.

Peppard, George • Actor; also director, producer. • Born Detroit, MI, October 1, 1928. *Educ.* Purdue; Carnegie Tech; Actors Studio. Silver-haired leading man, in a number of action films and romantic comedies since the late 1950s. Peppard was memorable opposite Audrey Hepburn in Blake Edward's fine adaptation of Truman Capote's novella, *Breakfast at Tiffany's* (1961). He has also done extensive TV work and is probably best known as the leader of "The A-Team" (1982-87). Married to actress Elizabeth Ashley from 1966 until their divorce in 1972. • *The Strange One* 1957 (a); *Pork Chop Hill* 1959 (a); *Home From the Hill* 1960 (a); *The Subterraneans* 1960 (a); *Breakfast at Tiffany's* 1961 (a); *How the West Was Won* 1962 (a); *The Victors* 1963 (a); *The Carpetbaggers* 1964 (a); *Operation Crossbow* 1965 (a); *The Third Day* 1965 (a); *The Blue Max* 1966 (a); *Rough Night in Jericho* 1967 (a); *Tobruk* 1967 (a); *P.J.* 1968 (a); *What's So Bad About Feeling Good?* 1968 (a); *Pendulum* 1969 (a); *Cannon For Cordoba* 1970 (a); *The Executioner* 1970 (a); *One More Train to Rob* 1971 (a); *The Groundstar Conspiracy* 1972 (a); *Newman's Law* 1974 (a); *Damnation Alley* 1977 (a); *Five Days From Home* 1977 (a,d,p); *De l'enfer à la Victoire* 1979 (a); *Battle Beyond the Stars* 1980 (a); *Race For the Yankee Zephyr* 1981 (a); *Target Eagle* 1982 (a); *Zwei Frauen* 1989 (a); *Night of the Fox* 1990 (a).

Pereira, Hal • Production designer • Born Chicago, IL, 1905; died December 17, 1983, Los Angeles, CA. *Educ.* University of Illinois. One of Hollywood's most distinguished art directors. Pereira began his career designing film theaters in Chicago, moved to the West Coast in 1942 and was made supervising art director at Paramount in 1950—a post he held for 18 years. Pereira worked on over 150 films and received 23 Academy nominations, each earned with at least one collaborator. • *Double Indemnity* 1944; *Ministry of Fear* 1944; *The Big Carnival* 1951; *Detective Story* 1951; *Carrie* 1952 **(AANBAD)**; *Roman Holiday* 1953 **(AANBAD)**; *The Country Girl* 1954 **(AANBAD)**; *Rear Window* 1954; *Red Garters* 1954 **(AANBAD)**; *Sabrina* 1954 **(AANBAD)**; *White Christmas* 1954; *The Rose Tattoo* 1955 **(AABAD)**; *The Scarlet Hour* 1955; *To Catch a Thief* 1955 **(AANBAD)**; *The Trouble With Harry* 1955; *We're No Angels* 1955; *The Man Who Knew Too Much* 1956; *The Proud and the Profane* 1956 **(AANBAD)**; *The Ten Commandments* 1956 **(AANBAD)**; *Desire Under the Elms* 1957; *Funny Face* 1957 **(AANBAD)**; *As Young As We Are* 1958; *The Black Orchid* 1958; *The Buccaneer* 1958; *The Colossus of New York* 1958; *The Geisha Boy* 1958; *Hot Spell* 1958; *Houseboat* 1958; *King Creole* 1958; *Maracaibo* 1958; *The Matchmaker* 1958; *The Party Crashers* 1958; *Rock-a-Bye Baby* 1958; *The Space Children* 1958; *St Louis Blues* 1958; *Teacher's Pet* 1958; *Vertigo* 1958 **(AANBAD)**; *The Young Captives* 1958; *Alias Jesse James* 1959; *But Not For Me* 1959; *Career* 1959 **(AANBAD)**; *Don't Give Up the Ship* 1959; *The Five Pennies* 1959; *The Jayhawkers* 1959; *Li'l Abner* 1959; *The Trap* 1959; *It Started in Naples* 1960 **(AANBAD)**; *Visit to a Small Planet* 1960 **(AANBAD)**; *All in a Night's Work* 1961; *Blueprint For Robbery* 1961; *Breakfast at Tiffany's* 1961 **(AANBAD)**; *One-Eyed Jacks* 1961; *Summer and Smoke* 1961 **(AANBAD)**; *Hatari!* 1962; *The Pigeon That Took Rome* 1962 **(AANBAD)**; *Come Blow Your Horn* 1963 **(AANBAD)**; *Hud* 1963 **(AANBAD)**; *Love With the Proper Stranger* 1963 **(AANBAD)**; *Billie* 1965; *The Family Jewels* 1965; *Red Line 7000* 1965; *The Slender Thread* 1965 **(AANBAD)**; *The Sons of Katie Elder* 1965; *The Spy Who Came In From the Cold* 1965 **(AANBAD)**; *Apache Uprising* 1966; *Assault on a Queen* 1966; *The Last of the Secret Agents* 1966; *Nevada Smith* 1966; *The Oscar* 1966 **(AANBAD)**; *Barefoot in the Park* 1967; *The Busy Body* 1967; *El Dorado* 1967; *Arizona Bushwhackers* 1968; *The Odd Couple* 1968; *Project X* 1968.

Périnal, Georges • Director of photography • Born Paris, 1897; died 1965. Began his career as a projectionist in 1913 and went on to photograph some of the finest French films of the early 1930s, by directors including Jean Cocteau (*Blood of a Poet* 1930) and René Clair (*A nous la Liberté* 1931, *Le Million* 1932). Périnal began working with Alexander Korda in London in 1933 and applied his talents to a succession of fine English films, notably *The Thief of Bagdad* (1940). He worked in France and Hollywood in the late 1950s. • *Blood of a Poet* 1930 (ph); *Sous les toits de Paris* 1930 (ph); *A Nous la Liberté* 1931 (ph); *Le Million* 1931 (ph); *The Private Life of Henry VIII* 1933 (ph); *Things to Come* 1936 (ph); *Dark Journey* 1937 (ph); *The Squeaker* 1937 (ph); *Prison Without Bars* 1938 (ph); *The Thief of Bagdad* 1940 (ph); *Dangerous Moonlight* 1941 (ph); *That Dangerous Age* 1949 (ph); *The Mudlark* 1950 (ph); *My Daughter Joy* 1950 (ph); *I'll Never Forget You* 1951 (ph); *No Highway* 1951 (ph); *Three Cases of Murder* 1953 (ph); *L'Amant de Lady Chatterley* 1955 (ph); *Bonjour Tristesse* 1957 (ph); *A King in New York* 1957 (ph); *Saint Joan* 1957 (ph); *Tom Thumb* 1958 (ph); *The Day They Robbed the Bank of England* 1960 (ph); *Once More, With Feeling* 1960 (ph); *Oscar Wilde* 1960 (ph); *The Epic That Never Was (I, Claudius)* 1965 (ph—"I, Claudius").

Perkins, Anthony • Actor; also director. • Born New York, NY, April 4, 1932. *Educ.* Columbia; Rollins College, Winter Park FL. Began his career as a juvenile lead in the early 1950s and distinguished himself in films including *Tin Star* (1957) and, as baseball star Jim Piersall, *Fear Strikes Out* (1956). Perkins's gripping re-creation of Piersall's mental problems made him a suitable choice for what would become his signature role, the mother-fixated Norman Bates in Hitchcock's classic thriller, *Psycho* (1960). He went on to appear in a number of interesting works, including Orson Welles's adaptation of Kafka's *The Trial* (1962), but could never quite shake the "Psycho" mantle. In the mid-1980s Perkins returned to the scene of his early triumph, reprising the Bates role in two progressively campy sequels, the latter of which also marked his directorial debut. He is the son of actor Osgood Perkins and husband of Berry Berenson, who has appeared opposite him in two films. • *The Actress* 1953 (a); *Fear Strikes Out* 1956 (a); *Friendly Persuasion* 1956 (a) **(AANBSA)**; *Barrage contre le Pacifique* 1957 (a,song); *Desire Under the Elms* 1957 (a); *The Lonely Man* 1957 (a); *The Tin Star* 1957 (a); *The Matchmaker* 1958 (a); *Green Mansions* 1959 (a,song); *On the Beach* 1959 (a); *Psycho* 1960 (a); *Tall Story* 1960 (a); *Goodbye Again* 1961 (a); *Phaedra* 1962 (a); *The Trial* 1962 (a); *Five Miles to Midnight* 1963 (a); *Le Scandale* 1966 (a); *Pretty Poison* 1968 (a); *Catch-22* 1970 (a); *WUSA* 1970 (a); *La Décade Prodigieuse* 1971 (a); *Quelqu'un derrière la porte* 1971 (a); *The Life and Times of Judge Roy Bean* 1972 (a); *Play It As It Lays* 1972 (a); *The Last of Sheila* 1973 (sc); *Lovin' Molly* 1974 (a); *Murder on the Orient Express* 1974 (a); *Mahogany* 1975 (a); *Remember My Name* 1978 (a); *The Black Hole* 1979 (a); *Twee Vrouwen/Twice a Woman* 1979 (a); *Winter Kills* 1979 (a); *Double Negative* 1980 (a); *ffolkes* 1980 (a); *Psycho II* 1983 (a); *Crimes of Passion* 1984 (a,song); *For the Term of His Natural Life* 1985 (a); *Hitchcock, Il Brivido del Genio* 1985 (a); *Psycho III* 1986 (a,d); *Destroyer* 1988 (a); *Edge of Sanity* 1989 (a); *Lucky Stiff* 1989 (d).

Perkins, Elizabeth • Actress • Born Queens, NY, 1961. *Educ.* Goodman School of Drama, Chicago. Versatile actress who made her film debut in *About Last Night* (1986), the bratpack film adaptation of David Mamet's play, *Sexual Perversity in Chicago*. Perkins turned in a well-received performance opposite Tom Hanks in the popular 1988 comedy, *Big*. • *About Last Night* 1986; *From the Hip* 1987; *Big* 1988; *Sweet Hearts Dance* 1988; *Teach 109 (short)* 1988; *Avalon* 1990; *Enid Is Sleeping* 1990; *Love at Large* 1990; *He Said, She Said* 1991.

Perrin, Jacques • Actor; also producer, screenwriter. • Born Paris, July 13, 1941. Educ. Paris Conservatoire. Made his screen debut in 1957 and appeared in several key French and Italian films of the 1960s, winning the best actor award at the Venice Film Festival for his role in Vittorio De Seta's *Half a Man* (1966). Perrin began a second career as a producer in 1968, beginning with Costa-Gavras's landmark political thriller, Z (1969). (He had earlier appeared in the director's first film, *The Sleeping Car Murders* 1965). • *Le Soleil dans l'oeil* 1961 (a); *La 317ème Section* 1964 (a); *Compartiment tueurs/The Sleeping Car Murders* 1965 (a); *L'Horizon* 1966 (a); *La Ligne de Demarcation* 1966 (a); *Un Uomo a Metà/Half a Man* 1966 (a); *Les Démoiselles de Rochefort* 1967 (a); Z 1969 (a,p) **(AANBP)**; *L'Etrangleur* 1970 (a); *Goya* 1970 (a); *Peau d'ane* 1970 (a); *Blanche* 1971 (a); *La Guerre d'Algerie* 1972 (p); *Home Sweet Home* 1973 (a); *Section Speciale* 1975 (a); *La Spirale* 1975 (p); *Le Desert des tartares* 1976 (a,p); *La Victoire en chantant* 1976 (p); *Le Crabe-Tambour* 1977 (a); *Adoption* 1978 (a,p); *La Part du feu* 1978 (a); *La Legion saute sur kolwezi* 1979 (a); *Raoni: The Fight For the Amazon* 1979 (commentary); *Une Robe noire pour un tueur* 1981 (a); *L'Annee des Méduses* 1984 (a); *Le Juge* 1984 (a); *Paroles et Musique* 1984 (a); *Parole de Flic* 1985 (a); *Garibaldi-the General* 1986 (a); *Nuovo Cinema Paradiso* 1988 (a); *Le Peuple singe* 1989 (p); *Vanille Fraise* 1989 (a).

Perrine, Valerie • Actress • Born Galveston, TX, September 3, 1944. *Educ.* University of Arizona; University of Nevada. Brash, provocative leading lady of the 1970s; memorable in *Lenny* (1974) as the controversial comedian's drug-taking, stripper wife. • *Slaughterhouse-Five* 1971; *The Last American Hero* 1973; *Lenny* 1974 **(AANBA)**; *W.C. Fields and Me* 1976; *Mr. Billion* 1977; *Superman* 1978; *The Electric Horseman* 1979; *The Magician of Lublin* 1979; *Agency* 1980; *Can't Stop the Music* 1980; *Superman II* 1980; *The Border* 1981; *Water* 1984; *Maid to Order* 1987; *Mask of Murder* 1989.

Perry, Frank • Director • Born New York, NY, 1930. *Educ.* University of Miami. TV producer who made a highly acclaimed directorial debut with *David and Lisa* (1962), co-written by his wife Eleanor. A sensitive, finely acted portrait of two mentally disturbed teenagers, the film was shot on a minimal budget and possessed a distinctly independent tone. Perry and his wife collaborated on several more savvy studies of social mores, notably their adaptation of the John Cheever short story, *The Swimmer* (1968). Perry's work suffered somewhat following his divorce in 1970 but he returned to form with the spoof western, *Rancho Deluxe* (1974), scripted by novelist Thomas McGuane. He scored another popular success with the suburban comedy, *Compromising Positions* (1985). • *Island Women* 1958 (art d); *David and Lisa* 1962 (d) **(AANBD)**; *Ladybug, Ladybug* 1963 (d,p); *The Swimmer* 1968 (d); *Last Summer* 1969 (d) **(AANBSA)**; *My Side of the Mountain* 1969 (a); *Trilogy* 1969 (d,p); *Diary of a Mad Housewife* 1970 (d,p); *Doc* 1971 (d,p); *Play It As It Lays* 1972 (d,p); *The Neptune Factor* 1973 (a); *Man on a Swing* 1974 (d); *Rancho Deluxe* 1974 (d); *Mommie Dearest* 1981 (d,sc); *Monsignor* 1982 (d); *Compromising Positions* 1985 (d,p); *Hello Again* 1987 (d,p).

Pesci, Joe • Actor • Born Newark, NJ. Italian-American character player, best known as Jake La Motta's long-suffering brother in *Raging Bull* (1980). Pesci again appeared opposite Robert De Niro in *Once Upon a Time in America* (1984) and *Goodfellas* (1990). He also played the evil drug lord, "Mr. Big," in Michael Jackson's hugely successful "Moonwalker" music video. • *Death Collector* 1976 (a); *Raging Bull* 1980 (a) **(AANBSA)**; *I'm Dancing As Fast As I Can* 1981 (a); *Dear Mr. Wonderful* 1982 (a,song); *Easy Money* 1983 (a); *Eureka* 1983 (a); *Once Upon a Time in America* 1984 (a); *Tutti Dentro* 1984 (a); *Man on Fire* 1987 (a); *Moonwalker* 1988 (a); *Lethal Weapon 2* 1989 (a); *Backtrack* 1990 (a); *Betsy's Wedding* 1990 (a); *GoodFellas* 1990 (a); *Home Alone* 1990 (a).

Peters, Bernadette • Actress • Born Bernadette Lazzara, Queens, NY, February 28, 1948. First gained prominence at the age of 19 for her role in the off-Broadway musical parody, *Dames at Sea.* Peters went on to distinguish herself in the musical theater, winning a Tony award for her role in Andrew Lloyd Webber's *Song and Dance* in 1985, and has proved a capable comic performer on both the large and small screens. She also enjoys a successful career as a recording artist and nightclub performer. • *Ace Eli and Rodger of the Skies* 1973; *The Longest Yard* 1974; *Vigilante Force* 1975; *Silent Movie* 1976; *W.C. Fields and Me* 1976; *The Jerk* 1979; *Heartbeeps* 1981; *Pennies From Heaven* 1981; *Annie* 1982; *Pink Cadillac* 1989; *Slaves of New York* 1989; *Alice* 1990; *Impromptu* 1991.

Peters, Brock • Actor, singer; also producer. • Born Brock Fisher, New York, NY, July 2, 1927. *Educ.* University of Chicago; CCNY. One of the leading black film actors of the 1960s and 70s. Peters made his stage debut in a 1943 production of "Porgy and Bess" and first appeared on screen in *Carmen Jones* (1954). He was memorable as Tom Robinson, the man wrongfully accused of raping a white woman, in Robert Mulligan's *To Kill a Mockingbird* (1962). • *Carmen Jones* 1954 (a); *Porgy and Bess* 1959 (a,song); *The L-Shaped Room* 1962 (a); *To Kill a Mockingbird* 1962 (a); *Major Dundee* 1965 (a); *The Pawnbroker* 1965 (a); *The Incident* 1967 (a); *The Daring Game* 1968 (a); *P.J.* 1968 (a); *I Quattro dell'Ave Maria* 1968 (a); *The McMasters* 1970 (a); *Black Girl* 1972 (a); *Five on the Black Hand Side* 1973 (p); *Slaughter's Big Rip-Off* 1973 (a); *Soylent Green* 1973 (a); *From These Roots (short)* 1974 (a); *Lost in the Stars* 1974 (a); *Framed* 1975 (a); *Two-Minute Warning* 1976 (a); *Joe Louis - For All Time* 1984 (a); *Diggers* 1985 (a); *Star Trek IV: The Voyage Home* 1986 (a).

Peters, Jon • Producer • Born Van Nuys, CA, 1947. Peters had established a highly lucrative beauty parlor empire before entering the film world as lover-turned-personal manager to Barbra Streisand. His first film as a producer, the Streisand vehicle *A Star Is Born* (1976), took a critical drubbing but was a commercial smash, yielding over $100 million at the box-office and earning four Oscar nominations. (He also produced a string of best-selling Streisand albums.) Peters launched one of the most successful production ventures of the 1980s when he joined with Peter Guber in 1982 to form the Guber-Peters company. The team was responsible for such blockbuster successes as *Flashdance* (1983), *Rain Man* (1988) and *Batman* (1989) before being hired to run Columbia after Sony's costly purchase of the studio in 1989. • *For Pete's Sake* 1974 (wig design); *A Star Is Born* 1976 (p); *Eyes of Laura Mars* 1978 (p,story); *The Main Event* 1979 (p); *Caddyshack* 1980 (exec.p); *Die Laughing* 1980 (exec.p); *An American Werewolf in London* 1981 (exec.p); *Missing* 1982 (exec.p); *Six Weeks* 1982 (p); *D.C. Cab* 1983 (exec.p); *Flashdance* 1983 (exec.p); *Sheena* 1984 (a); *Clue* 1985 (exec.p); *The Color Purple* 1985 (exec.p); *The Legend of Billie Jean* 1985 (exec.p); *Vision Quest* 1985 (p); *The Clan of the Cave Bear* 1986 (exec.p); *Head Office* 1986 (exec.p); *Youngblood* 1986 (exec.p); *Innerspace* 1987 (exec.p); *Who's That Girl* 1987 (exec.p); *The Witches of Eastwick* 1987 (p); *Caddyshack II* 1988 (p); *Gorillas in the Mist* 1988 (exec.p); *Rain Man* 1988 (exec.p); *Batman* 1989 (p); *Missing Link* 1989 (exec.p); *Tango and Cash* 1989 (p,story); *Bonfire of the Vanities* 1990 (exec.p).

Petersen, Wolfgang • Director • Born Emden, Germany, March 14, 1941. German director from the stage who received acclaim for his gripping U-boat drama, *Das Boot* (1981). Peterson's subsequent output, with the exception of the charming children's fantasy, *The Neverending Story* (1984), has been disappointing. • *Die Konsequenz/The Consequence* 1977 (d,sc); *Einer von uns Beiden* 1978 (d,p); *Schwarz und Weiss Wie Tage und Naechte* 1978 (d,sc); *Das Boot/The Boat* 1981 (d,sc) **(AANBSC)**; *Reifezeugnis* 1982 (d,sc); *The Neverending Story* 1984 (d,sc); *Enemy Mine* 1985 (d).

Petri, Elio • Director • Born Rome, January 29, 1929; died 1982. *Educ.* University of Rome (literature). Former critic who turned out a handful of documentaries and contributed to the scripts of several films (notably by Guiseppe De Santis) before directing his first feature in 1961. Petri used stylish visuals and a knack for finely paced storytelling to communicate his pointed social and political satire. His best films include *The Tenth Victim* (1965), a futuristic fantasy in which men and women are trained to kill each other for sport; *Investigation of a Citizen Above Suspicion* (1970), an Oscar-winning parable about a Fascist police chief; and *Lulu the Tool* (1972), a complex and absorbing account of a factory worker's political awakening. • *La Strada lunga un Anno* 1958 (sc); *I Giorni contati* 1961 (d); *Il Maestro di Vigevano* 1963 (d); *Alta Infedelta* 1964 (d); *La Decima Vittimae/The Tenth Victim* 1965 (d); *Ciascuno il suo* 1967 (d); *Un Tranquillo Posto di Campagna/A Quiet Place in the Country* 1968 (d); *Indagine su un Cittadino al di Sopra di Ogni Sospetto/Investigation of a Citizen Above Suspicion* 1970 (d,sc) **(AANBSC)**; *La Classe Operaia Va In Paradisee/Lulu the Tool/The Working Class Goes to Heaven* 1972 (d,sc); *La Proprietà non e più un furto* 1973 (d,sc); *Todo Modo* 1976 (d,sc); *Buone Notizie/Good News* 1979 (d,p,sc).

Petrie, Daniel • Director; also actor. • Born Glace Bay, Nova Scotia, Canada, November 26, 1920. *Educ.* St. Francis Xavier University, Nova Scotia (communications); Columbia (adult education); Northwestern. TV and stage director who won acclaim for his second film, a sensitive 1961 adaptation of the Lorraine Hansbury play, *A Raisin in the Sun*. Some of Petrie's finest subsequent work was done for the small screen, notably *The Dollmaker* (1984). He won a Genie (the Canadian Oscar) for his semi-autobiographical feature, *Bay Boy* (1984), starring Liv Ullmann and Kiefer Sutherland. Petrie's wife Dorothea is a producer and both their sons, Daniel Jr. and Donald, are directors. • *The Bramble Bush* 1960 (d); *A Raisin in the Sun* 1961 (d); *The Main Attraction* 1962 (d); *Stolen Hours* 1963 (d); *The Idol* 1966 (d); *The Spy With a Cold Nose* 1966 (d); *The Neptune Factor* 1973 (d); *Lifeguard* 1976 (d); *The Betsy* 1978 (d); *Resurrection* 1980 (d); *Fort Apache, the Bronx* 1981 (d); *Six Pack* 1982 (d); *Bay Boy* 1984 (d,sc); *Into the Night* 1985 (a); *Half a Lifetime* 1986 (d); *Square Dance* 1987 (d,p); *Cocoon: The Return* 1988 (d); *Rocket Gibraltar* 1988 (d).

Petrie, Daniel, Jr. • American screenwriter, producer • *Educ.* University of Redlands, CA (psychology, creative writing). Literary agent turned screenwriter who scored with the popular Eddie Murphy vehicle, *Beverly Hills Cop* (1984). Petrie began a second career as a producer with *Shoot to Kill* (1988). Son of Daniel Petrie and brother of AFI-trained director Donald Petrie (*Mystic Pizza* 1988). • *Beverly Hills Cop* 1984 (sc); *The Big Easy* 1987 (sc); *Shoot to Kill* 1988 (p,sc); *Turner and Hooch* 1989 (sc).

Pfeiffer, Michelle • Actress • Born Santa Ana, CA, 1957. *Educ.* Golden West College, CA; Whitley College, CA (court reporting). Alluring beauty who landed roles in several low-budget features before gaining attention for her part in *Grease 2* (1982). Pfeiffer joined the front rank of Hollywood actresses with her performances in *The Witches of Eastwick* (1987), opposite Cher and Susan Sarandon, and *Dangerous Liaisons* (1988), as prim-wife-turned-passionate-lover Madame de Tourvel. Sister of actress Dedee Pfeiffer (*The Allnighter* 1987, *Brothers in Arms* 1989) and former wife of actor Peter Horton. • *Falling in Love Again* 1980 (a); *The Hollywood Knights* 1980 (a); *Charlie Chan and the Curse of the Dragon Queen* 1981 (a); *Grease 2* 1982 (a); *Scarface* 1983 (a); *Into the Night* 1985 (a); *Ladyhawke* 1985 (a); *Sweet Liberty* 1986 (a); *Amazon Women on the Moon* 1987 (a); *The Witches of Eastwick* 1987 (a); *Dangerous Liaisons* 1988 (a) **(AANBSA)**; *Married to the Mob* 1988 (a); *Tequila Sunrise* 1988 (a); *The Fabulous Baker Boys* 1989 (a,m,song) **(AANBA)**; *The Russia House* 1990 (a).

Philipe, Gérard • Actor • Born Cannes, France, December 4, 1922; died 1959. First gained attention as the young student smitten by an older woman (Micheline Presle) in Claude Autant-Lara's *Devil in the Flesh* (1947) and went on to become one of France's most charming and popular romantic leads of the late 1940s and 50s. Philipe's career was foreshortened by a heart attack at the age of 36. • *Le Diable au corps/Devil in the Flesh* 1947 (a); *La Ronde* 1950 (a); *Les Sept peches capitaux* 1952 (a); *Les Orgueilleux* 1953 (a); *Villa Borghese* 1953 (a); *Monsieur Ripois* 1954 (a); *Rouge et Noir* 1954 (a); *Les Aventures de Till l'Espiegle* 1956 (d); *Les Grandes Manoeuvres* 1956 (a); *Pot Bouille* 1957 (a); *Montparnasse 19* 1958 (a); *La Fièvre Monte à El Pao* 1959 (a); *Les Liaisons Dangereuses* 1959 (a).

Phillips, Lou Diamond • Actor • Born Philippines, 1962. *Educ.* University of Texas, Arlington (drama). Handsome young lead who first came to prominence as doomed 1950s rock-and-roll star Richie Valens in *La Bamba* (1987). A charismatic and conscientious performer, Phillips subsequently distinguished himself as gang member "Angel" in Ramon Menendez's high school drama, *Stand and Deliver* (1988). • *Trespasses* 1983 (a,sc); *La Bamba* 1987 (a); *Dakota* 1988 (a,assoc.p); *Stand and Deliver* 1988 (a); *Young Guns* 1988 (a); *Disorganized Crime* 1989 (a); *Renegades* 1989 (a); *The First Power* 1990 (a); *A Show of Force* 1990 (a); *Young Guns II* 1990 (a).

Phoenix, River • Actor • Born Madras, OR, August 23, 1971. Impressively mature young performer who had a winning film role in Rob Reiner's poignant coming-of-age drama, *Stand By Me* (1986). Phoenix subsequently distinguished himself in Peter Weir's *Mosquito Coast* and Sidney Lumet's *Running on Empty* (1988). Brother of actor Leaf Phoenix and actresses Summer, Rainbow and Liberty Phoenix. • *Explorers* 1985; *The Mosquito Coast* 1986; *Stand By Me* 1986; *Little Nikita* 1988; *A Night in the Life of Jimmy Reardon* 1988; *Running on Empty* 1988 **(AANBSA)**; *Indiana Jones and the Last Crusade* 1989; *I Love You to Death* 1990; *Dogfight* 1991.

Pialat, Maurice • Director; also screenwriter, actor. • Born Cunlhat, Puy-de-Dome, France, August 21, 1925. *Educ.* L'Ecole des Arts Décoratifs, Paris; L'Ecole des Beaux-Arts. Former painter who made a number of 16mm shorts and spent ten years working in TV before directing his acclaimed first feature, *Me* (1968). A poignant, unromanticized study of adolescence, the film staked out Pialat's concern with the realistic depiction of everyday issues and events. He continued in this vein with *We Will Not Grow Old Together* (1972), an uncompromising account of the disintegration of a marriage, and *La Gueule ouverte* (1974), which charts a man's reaction to the death of his mother. Pialat enjoyed international recognition with two films starring Gérard Dépardieu, the melodramatic *Loulou* (1979) and the fast-paced, violence-riddled *Police* (1985). He took the Palme d'Or at Cannes with *Under the Sun of Satan* (1989). • *La Fleur de l'age, ou les adolescentes* 1964 (a); *L' Enfance Nue/Me* 1968 (d,sc,adapt,dial); *Que la Bête Meure* 1969 (a); *Nous ne vieillirons pas ensemble/We Will Not Grow Old Together* 1972 (d,sc,dial); *La Gueule ouverte* 1974 (d,sc); *Mes Petites Amoureuses* 1974 (a); *Loulou* 1979 (adapt,dial,d); *Passe ton bac d'abord/Graduate First* 1979 (d,sc,dial); *A nos amours* 1983 (a,d,sc); *Police* 1985 (d,sc,story); *Sous le soleil de Satan/Under the Sun of Satan* 1987 (a,d,sc,adapt,dial).

Piccoli, Michel • Actor • Born Jacques Daniel Michel Piccoli, Paris, December 27, 1925. Urbane Franco-Italian performer, on stage from the late 1940s and in routine screen character roles through the 50s. Piccoli gained prominence in the following decades with roles as sophisticated bourgeois types in films by Bunuel, Hitchcock and Chabrol. He has since cemented his reputation as one of France's most prolific and acclaimed performers, working through the 1990s with directors including Bertrand Tavernier (*Spoiled Children* 1977), Louis Malle (*Atlantic City* 1980) and Leos Carax (*Bad Blood* 1986). • *La Mort en ce jardin* 1956 (a); *Nathalie Agent Secret* 1957 (a); *Les Vièrges de Rome* 1961 (a);

Le Doulos 1963 (a); *Le Journal d'une femme de chambre* 1963 (a); *Le Mépris* 1963 (a); *Compartiment tueurs* 1965 (a); *Les Créatures* 1965 (a); *La Guerre est finie* 1966 (a); *Belle de Jour* 1967 (a); *Mon Amour, Mon Amour* 1967 (a); *Benjamin, ou les mémoires d'un puceau* 1968 (a); *La Chamade* 1968 (a); *Diabolik* 1968 (a); *Dillinger E Morto* 1968 (a); *La Prisonnière* 1968 (a); *Topaz* 1969 (a); *La Voie Lactée* 1969 (a); *L' Amante* 1970 (a); *L'Invasion* 1970 (a); *Max et les Ferrailleurs* 1970 (a); *La Cagna* 1971 (a); *La Décade Prodigieuse* 1971 (a); *La Poudre d'escampette* 1971 (a); *L'Udienza* 1971 (a); *L'Attentat* 1972 (a); *Le Charme Discret de la Bourgeoisie* 1972 (a); *Themroc* 1972 (a); *La Grande Bouffe* 1973 (a); *Les Noces Rouges* 1973 (a); *Touche pas à la femme blanche!* 1973 (a); *Le Fantôme de la Liberté* 1974 (a); *Grandeur Nature* 1974 (a); *Le Trio Infernal* 1974 (a); *Vincent, François, Paul... et les Autres* 1974 (a); *7 Morts sur Ordonnance* 1975 (a); *La Faille* 1975 (a); *Léonor* 1975 (a); *La Dernière Femme* 1976 (a); *F comme Fairbanks* 1976 (a); *Mado* 1976 (a); *René la Canne* 1976 (a); *Todo Modo* 1976 (a); *Des Enfants Gâtés/Spoiled Children* 1977 (a); *L'Etat sauvage* 1977 (a,p); *Strauberg Ist Da* 1977 (a); *La Part du feu* 1978 (a); *La Petite fille en velours bleu* 1978 (a); *Le Sucre* 1978 (a); *Le Divorcement* 1979 (a); *Le Mors aux dents* 1979 (a); *Atlantic City* 1980 (a); *Der Preis fuers uberleben* 1980 (a); *Salto Nel Vuoto* 1980 (a); *La Fille Prodigue* 1981 (a); *Une Chambre en Ville* 1982 (a); *La Nuit de Varennes* 1982 (a); *Gli Occhi, la Bocca* 1982 (a); *Oltre la Porta* 1982 (a); *Passion* 1982 (a); *Que les gros salaires levent le doigt!!!* 1982 (a); *Le General de l'Armée Morte* 1983 (a,p,sc); *La Passante* 1983 (a); *Le Prix du Danger* 1983 (a); *La Diagonale du Fou* 1984 (a); *Le Matelot 512* 1984 (a); *Partir Revenir* 1984 (a); *Péril en la Demeure* 1984 (a); *Success Is the Best Revenge* 1984 (a); *Viva la Vie!* 1984 (a); *Adieu, Bonaparte* 1985 (a); *Mon beau-frère a tué ma soeur* 1985 (a); *Mauvais sang/Bad Blood* 1986 (a); *Le Paltoquet* 1986 (a); *La Puritaine* 1986 (a); *La Rumba* 1986 (a); *L'Homme voilé* 1987 (a); *Das Weite Land* 1987 (a); *Y'a bon les blancs* 1987 (a); *Blanc de chine* 1988 (a); *Le Peuple singe* 1989 (a); *La Révolution Française* 1989 (a); *Martha und Ich* 1990 (a); *Milou en mai/May Fools* 1990 (a).

Pickens, Slim • Actor • Born Louis Bert Lindley Jr., Kingsberg, CA, June 29, 1919; died December 8, 1983, Modesto, CA. Rodeo circuit veteran who became a favorite Hollywood cowboy of the 1950s through the 70s; perhaps best known as the B-52 pilot who, at the end of Stanley Kubrick's *Dr. Strangelove* (1964), "rides" a hydrogen bomb to destruction. • *Rocky Mountain* 1950; *Border Saddlemates* 1952; *Colorado Sundown* 1952; *The Last Musketeer* 1952; *Old Oklahoma Plains* 1952; *South Pacific Trail* 1952; *The Story of Will Rogers* 1952; *Thunderbirds* 1952; *Down Laredo Way* 1953; *Iron Mountain Trail* 1953; *Old Overland Trail* 1953; *Red River Shore* 1953; *Shadows of Tombstone* 1953; *The Boy From Oklahoma* 1954; *The Outcast* 1954; *Phantom Stallion* 1954; *The Last Command* 1955; *Santa Fe Passage* 1955; *Stranger at My Door* 1955; *When Gangland Strikes* 1955; *The Great Locomotive Chase* 1956; *Gun Brothers* 1956; *Gunsight Ridge* 1957; *The Sheepman* 1958; *Tonka* 1958; *Escort West* 1959; *Chartroose Caboose* 1960; *One-Eyed Jacks* 1961; *A Thunder of Drums* 1961; *Savage Sam* 1963; *Dr. Strangelove. Or, How I Learned to Stop Worrying and Love the Bomb* 1964; *The Glory Guys* 1965; *In Harm's Way* 1965; *Major Dundee* 1965; *Up From the Beach* 1965; *An Eye For an Eye* 1966; *Stagecoach* 1966; *The Flim-Flam Man* 1967; *Rough Night in Jericho* 1967; *Never a Dull Moment* 1968; *Skidoo* 1968; *Will Penny* 1968; *The Ballad of Cable Hogue* 1970; *The Cowboys* 1971; *The Honkers* 1971; *La Spina Dorsale del Diavola* 1971; *The Getaway* 1972; *J.C.* 1972; *Ginger in the Morning* 1973; *Pat Garrett and Billy the Kid* 1973; *Blazing Saddles* 1974; *Bootleggers* 1974; *Rancho Deluxe* 1974; *The Apple Dumpling Gang* 1975; *The Legend of Earl Durand* 1975; *Poor Pretty Eddie* 1975; *Sweet Punkin'* 1975; *White Line Fever* 1975; *Hawmps* 1976; *Pony Express Rider* 1976; *Mr. Billion* 1977; *The White Buffalo* 1977; *Smokey and the Goodtime Outlaws* 1978; *The Swarm* 1978; *The Sweet Creek County War* 1978; *Wishbone Cutter* 1978; *1941* 1979; *Beyond the Poseidon Adventure* 1979; *The Good-Time Outlaws* 1979; *Spirit of the Wind* 1979; *Honeysuckle Rose* 1980; *The Howling* 1980; *Tom Horn* 1980; *Pink Motel* 1982.

Pickford, Mary • Actress • Born Gladys Smith, Toronto, Canada, April 8, 1893; died 1979. Mabel Normand, before her career was ruined by scandal, responded to an interviewer who asked her hobby as follows: "Say anything you like, but don't say I like to work. That sounds too much like Mary Pickford, that prissy bitch."

The pretty little blonde who inspired this remark had led a hard life by the time she became "America's Sweetheart." Born into genteel poverty (her childhood was much like Lillian Gish's), her mother had been widowed by the time she became four. But the family income was saved when the child began acting in a local stock company. Years later, when the fanzines asked likes and dislikes, Pickford invaribly listed crimson as the color she detested. The color reminded her of the train seats smelling of coal dust on which she and her family spent hundreds of long hours, barnstorming the country up until 1907.

In New York, Pickford cornered producer David Belasco, who gave her touring and Broadway parts until 1909, when her family's fortunes went bust (by this time mother and brother were trying to act as well). Mary went to Biograph where Griffith interviewed her, made her up and ushered her onto her first set. At the end of the day he asked her to return the next day for $5 per day. She asked for $10, and got it.

Thus was launched Mary Pickford—if popularity were all, the greatest star there has ever been. Her first big hit, *The Little Teacher* (1910), identified her as "Little Mary" in the sub-titles, and audiences began referring to her likewise. Little Mary became the industry's chief focus and biggest asset, as well as the draw of draws—bigger, even, than Chaplin—and was the subject of the first cinematic close-up in *Friends* (1912). Some titles in her filmography speak for themselves: *A Little Princess* (1917), *Rebecca of Sunnybrook Farm* (1917), *Pollyanna* (1920), *Little Lord Fauntleroy* (1921), *Tess of the Storm Country* (1922), *Little Annie Rooney* (1925). But in all fairness to Pickford, she played her heroines with idealism and spunk, with subtle suggestions of the nymphet. While other actors used the Delsartan "French School of pantomime," Mary's expressions were restrained, her gestures small and drawn-out, and therefore all the more expressive. She moved only when movement was called for, and her stillness drew audience attention. Griffith said, "She never stopped listening and learning." Soon she was telling Adolph Zukor (after moving to Famous Players), "I can't afford to work for only ten thousand dollars a week."

Pickford was not overestimating the power of her box-office draw. The quality of her films was, in a sense, immaterial; for millions of people who had never been to a theater it was an entirely new experience to see a "star," someone to identify with and love from a distance.

United Artists was formed in 1919 by Pickford, D.W. Griffith, Chaplin and Fairbanks (to whom she was married that year); it was rumored this was in reaction against industry word that moguls were going to put a ceiling on star salaries ("It took longer to make one of Mary's contracts than it did to make one of Mary's pictures," said Sam Goldwyn). Pickford, now endowed with creative control, found herself saddled by her "glad girl" image. By the mid-20s, she was hiding a defiantly bobbed head of hair under the required wig of golden curls.

With the coming of sound Pickford wisely chose George Abbot's *Coquette* (1929—from a Broadway hit starring Helen Hayes) and gained a best actress Academy Award. But in playing a flapper, Pickford put herself into competition with the likes of Clara Bow and Joan Crawford; the uniqueness of Little Mary was gone for good.

Perhaps a crossover success made her over-confident. At any rate, fans had clamored for years for King Doug and Queen Mary to star together. They did, in *The Taming of the Shrew* (1929), a disaster of monstrous porportions. Two more costly failures followed, and Mary Pickford allowed the curtain to fall for good.

In the 30s Pickford made a vaudeville appearance, published two books (a novel and something called *Why Not Try God?*) and frequently broadcast on radio. After her marriage to Fairbanks fell apart in 1935 she wed actor Charles "Buddy" Rogers, by all accounts a happy union. Chaplin and Pickford bought out (and eventually outlived) Griffith and Fairbanks, and sold UA (also 1935). In the 50s, she was set to appear in *Storm Center* (1956), but changed her mind and was replaced by Bette Davis.

Mary Pickford was honored with a special Academy Award in 1976 and died peacefully at Pickfair in 1979. The appeal of her ever-childlike, spirited moppet image may not be well understood today, but Pickford's mere presence entranced the world. Spoiled by riches she may have been, but underneath the romantic golden vision of youth's innocence lurked a critical faculty reminiscent of a steel trap: "I never liked one of my pictures in its entirety." RW • *The Little Teacher* 1910 (a); *The Dream* 1911 (a,sc); *Friends* 1912 (a); *The Informer* 1912 (a); *The Old Actor* 1912 (a); *Behind the Scenes* 1914 (a); *The Eagle's Mate* 1914 (a); *A Good Little Devil* 1914 (a); *Such a Little Queen* 1914 (a); *Tess of the Storm Country* 1914 (a); *The Dawn of a Tomorrow* 1915 (a); *Fanchon, the Cricket* 1915 (a); *The Foundling* 1915 (a,p); *Little Pal* 1915 (a); *Madame Butterfly* 1915 (a); *Mistress Nell* 1915 (a); *Rags* 1915 (a); *The Eternal Grind* 1916 (a); *The Foundling* 1916 (a); *Hulda From Holland* 1916 (a); *Less Than the Dust* 1916 (a); *Poor Little Peppina* 1916 (a); *The Little American* 1917 (a); *A Little Princess* 1917 (a); *The Poor Little Rich Girl* 1917 (a); *The Pride of the Clan* 1917 (a); *Rebecca of Sunnybrook Farm* 1917 (a); *A Romance of the Redwoods* 1917 (a); *Amarilly of Clothes-Line Alley* 1918 (a); *Captain Kidd, Jr.* 1918 (a); *How Could You Jean?* 1918 (a); *Johanna Enlists* 1918 (a); *M'Liss* 1918 (a); *Stella Maris* 1918 (a); *Daddy Long Legs* 1919 (a); *Heart O' the Hills* 1919 (a); *The Hoodlum* 1919 (a); *Pollyanna* 1920 (a); *Suds* 1920 (a); *Little Lord Fauntleroy* 1921 (a); *The Love Light* 1921 (a); *Through the Back Door* 1921 (a); *Tess of the Storm Country* 1922 (a); *Rosita* 1923 (a); *Dorothy Vernon of Haddon Hall* 1924 (a); *Little Annie Rooney* 1925 (a); *Sparrows* 1926 (a); *My Best Girl* 1927 (a); *The Gaucho* 1928 (a); *Coquette* 1929 (a) **(AABA)**; *The Taming of the Shrew* 1929 (a); *Kiki* 1931 (a); *Secrets* 1933 (a); *The Gay Desperado* 1936 (p); *Sleep, My Love* 1948 (p).

Pidgeon, Walter • Actor • Born East St. John, New Brunswick, Canada, September 23, 1897. *Educ.* University of New Brunswick; New England Conservatory of Music. Handsome, dignified performer, in lead and supporting film roles from the 1930s. Pidgeon is best known for his roles as Maureen O'Hara's suitor in John Ford's *How Green Was My Valley* (1941) and, opposite Greer Garson, in the English WWII melodrama *Mrs. Miniver* (1942). He was also memorable in the engaging sci-fi feature, *Forbidden Planet* (1956). • *Mannequin* 1926; *Marriage License?* 1926; *Miss Nobody* 1926; *Old Loves and New* 1926; *The Outsider* 1926; *The Girl From Rio* 1927; *The Gorilla* 1927; *The Heart of Salome* 1927; *The Thirteenth Juror* 1927; *Clothes Make the Woman* 1928; *The Gateway to the Moon* 1928; *Melody of Love* 1928; *Turn Back the Hours* 1928; *Woman Wise* 1928; *Her Private Life* 1929; *A Most Immoral Lady* 1929; *The Voice Within* 1929; *Bride of the Regiment* 1930; *Going Wild* 1930; *The Gorilla* 1930; *Sweet Kitty Bellairs* 1930; *Viennese Nights* 1930; *The Hot Heiress* 1931; *Kiss Me Again* 1931; *Rockabye* 1932; *The Kiss Before the Mirror* 1933; *Journal of a Crime* 1934; *Big Brown Eyes* 1936; *Fatal Lady* 1936; *As Good as Married* 1937; *Girl Overboard* 1937; *A Girl With Ideas* 1937; *My Dear Miss Aldrich* 1937; *Saratoga* 1937; *She's Dangerous* 1937; *The Girl of the Golden West* 1938; *Listen, Darling* 1938; *Man-Proof* 1938; *Shopworn Angel,The* 1938; *Too Hot to Handle* 1938; *Nick Carter, Master Detective* 1939; *Six Thousand Enemies* 1939; *Society Lawyer* 1939; *Stronger Than Desire* 1939; *Dark Command* 1940; *Flight Command* 1940; *The House Across the Bay* 1940; *It's a Date* 1940; *Phantom Raiders* 1940; *Sky Murder* 1940; *Blossoms in the Dust* 1941; *Design For Scandal* 1941; *How Green Was My Valley* 1941; *Man Hunt* 1941; *Mrs. Miniver* 1942 **(AANBA)**; *White Cargo* 1942; *Madame Curie* 1943 **(AANBA)**; *The Youngest Profession* 1943; *Mrs. Parkington* 1944; *Weekend at the Waldorf* 1945; *Holiday in Mexico* 1946; *The Secret Heart* 1946; *If Winter Comes* 1947; *Command Decision* 1948; *Julia Misbehaves* 1948; *The Red Danube* 1949; *That Forsyte Woman* 1949; *The Miniver Story* 1950; *Calling Bulldog Drummond* 1951; *The Sellout* 1951; *Soldiers Three* 1951; *The Unknown Man* 1951; *The Bad and the Beautiful* 1952; *Million Dollar Mermaid* 1952; *Dream Wife* 1953; *Scandal at Scourie* 1953; *Deep in My Heart* 1954; *Executive Suite* 1954; *The Last Time I Saw Paris* 1954; *Men of the Fighting Lady* 1954; *Hit the Deck* 1955; *Forbidden Planet* 1956; *The Rack* 1956; *These Wilder Years* 1956; *Voyage to the Bottom of the Sea* 1961; *Advise and Consent* 1962; *Big Red* 1962; *Funny Girl* 1968; *Rascal* 1969; *Skyjacked* 1972; *Harry in Your Pocket* 1973; *The Neptune Factor* 1973; *Two-Minute Warning* 1976; *Sextette* 1978.

Pillsbury, Sarah • Producer • Born New York, NY. *Educ.* Yale. Began her career as a producer of documentaries (including the Oscar-nominated *The California Reich* 1976) before teaming up with Midge Sanford in 1980. Sanford/Pillsbury productions have since been responsible for a string of acclaimed independent features by directors including Susan Seidelman, Tim Hunter and John Sayles. • *The California Reich* 1976 (p) **(AANBDOC)**; *Board and Care* 1979 (p) **(AABSF)**; *Desperately Seeking Susan* 1985 (p); *River's Edge* 1987 (p); *Eight Men Out* 1988 (p); *Immediate Family* 1989 (p).

Pinter, Harold • *aka* David Baron • Playwright, screenwriter; also novelist, poet, director, actor. • Born Hackney, East London, October 10, 1930. *Educ.* RADA, London. Former actor turned preeminent playwright of his generation. Pinter gained attention in 1960 with *The Caretaker*, the first in a series of celebrated plays whose spare, oblique, mordantly humorous dialogue reflects the influence of Samuel Beckett. His first screen work came with a typically cryptic adaptation of Robert Maugham's novel, *The Servant* (1963), marking the beginning of a multi-film association with director Joseph Losey. Pinter has subsequently written movie versions of several literary works—he was responsible for the acclaimed film-within-a-film adaptation of John Fowles's *The French Lieutenant's Woman* (1981)—as well as translating his own stage plays into film form, notably with *Betrayal* (1983). Pinter, formerly married to the late actress Vivien Merchant, is currently married to the writer Lady Antonia Fraser. • *The Caretaker* 1963 (sc,from play); *The Servant* 1963 (sc); *The Pumpkin Eater* 1964 (sc); *The Quiller Memorandum* 1966 (sc); *Accident* 1967 (a,sc); *The Birthday Party* 1968 (sc,from play); *The Rise and Rise of Michael Rimmer* 1970 (a); *The Go-Between* 1971 (sc); *The Homecoming* 1973 (sc,from play); *Butley* 1974 (d); *The Tamarind Seed* 1974 (a); *The Last Tycoon* 1976 (sc); *The French Lieutenant's Woman* 1981 (sc) **(AANBSC)**; *Doll's Eye* 1982 (a); *Betrayal* 1983 (sc,from play) **(AANBSC)**; *Turtle Diary* 1985 (a,sc); *The Handmaid's Tale* 1989 (sc); *Reunion* 1989 (sc); *The Comfort of Strangers* 1990 (sc).

Pisier, Marie-France • Actress; also screenwriter, director, author. • Born Dalat, Indochina, May, 1944. *Educ.* University of Paris (law, political science). Slight, attractive leading lady, born to French parents in Indochina. Pisier moved to Paris with her family at the age of 12 and began acting in films five years later. She appeared in a number of interesting, low-budget productions before gaining widespread public recognition in 1975 as the star of the popular comedy *Cousin Cousine*—a role which earned her a best actress Cesar. Pisier has collaborated on two screenplays—Jacques Rivette's *Celine and Julie Go Boating* (1973) and Francois Truffaut's *Love on the Run* (1979)—and made her directorial debut in 1990 with *Le Bal du Gouverneur*, which she adapted from her own best-selling novel. • *L'Amour a vingt ans* 1962 (a); *Trans-Europ-Express* 1966 (a); *Baisers volés* 1968 (a); *Le Journal D'Un Suicide* 1972 (a); *Céline et Julie vont en bateau* 1973 (a,sc); *Feminin-Feminin* 1973 (a); *Cousin, Cousine* 1975 (a); *Souvenirs d'en France* 1975 (a); *Barocco* 1976 (a); *Le Corps de Mon Ennemi* 1976 (a); *Serail* 1976 (a); *Les Apprentis Sorciers* 1977 (a); *The Other Side of Midnight* 1977 (a); *Les Soeurs Brontë* 1978 (a); *L'Amour en Fuite/Love on the Run* 1979 (a,sc); *French Postcards* 1979 (a); *La Banquiere* 1980 (a); *Chanel Solitaire* 1981 (a); *Miss Right* 1981 (a); *L'As des As* 1982 (a); *Hot Touch* 1982 (a); *Der Stille Ozean* 1982 (a); *Der Zauberberg* 1982 (a); *L'Ami de Vincent* 1983 (a); *Le Prix du Danger* 1983 (a); *Les Nanas* 1984 (a); *44 ou les recits de la nuit* 1985 (a); *Parking* 1985 (a); *L'Inconnu de Vienne* 1986 (a); *L'Oeuvre au noir* 1988 (a); *Le Bal du Gouverneur* 1990 (d,sc,from novel).

Pitts, Zasu • Actress • Born Parsons, KA, January 3, 1898; died 1963. Lead and supporting player from 1917 who first gained attention for her performance in Erich Von Stoheim's mammoth *Greed* (1925). With the emergence of sound Pitts established herself as an endearingly daffy comedienne, often in support of Thelma Todd or in tandem with Slim Summerville. Pitts's trademark wailing voice and fluttering hands were last seen on screen in Stanley Kramer's 1963 film, *It's a Mad, Mad, Mad, Mad World*. • *A Little Princess* 1917; *A Modern Musketeer* 1917; *Rebecca of Sunnybrook Farm* 1917; *How Could You Jean?* 1918; *A Lady's Name* 1918; *A Society Sensation* 1918; *As the Sun Went Down* 1919; *Better Times* 1919; *Men, Women and Money* 1919; *The Other Half* 1919; *Poor Relations* 1919; *Bright Skies* 1920; *Heart of Twenty* 1920; *Seeing It Through* 1920; *Patsy* 1921; *A Daughter of Luxury* 1922; *For the Defense* 1922; *Is Matrimony a Failure?* 1922; *Youth to Youth* 1922; *The Girl Who Came Back* 1923; *Mary of the Movies* 1923; *Poor Men's Wives* 1923; *Souls For Sale* 1923; *Tea—With a Kick* 1923; *Three Wise Fools* 1923; *Changing Husbands* 1924; *Daughters of Today* 1924; *The Fast Set* 1924; *The Goldfish* 1924; *The Legend of Hollywood* 1924; *Triumph* 1924; *West of the Water Tower* 1924; *The Business of Love* 1925; *The Great Divide* 1925; *The Great Love* 1925; *Greed* 1925; *Lazybones* 1925; *Old Shoes* 1925; *Pretty Ladies* 1925; *The Re-Creation of Brian Kent* 1925; *Secrets of the Night* 1925; *Thunder Mountain* 1925; *Wages For Wives* 1925; *What Happened to Jones* 1925; *A Woman's Faith* 1925; *Early to Wed* 1926; *Her Big Night* 1926; *Mannequin* 1926; *Monte Carlo* 1926; *Risky Business* 1926; *Sunny Side Up* 1926; *Casey at the Bat* 1927; *13 Washington Square* 1928; *Buck Privates* 1928; *Sins of the Fathers* 1928; *The Wedding March* 1928; *Wife Savers* 1928; *The Argyle Case* 1929; *The Dummy* 1929; *Her Private Life* 1929; *The Locked Door* 1929; *Oh, Yeah!* 1929; *Paris* 1929; *The Squall* 1929; *This Thing Called Love* 1929; *Twin Beds* 1929; *The Devil's Holiday* 1930; *Free Love* 1930; *Honey* 1930; *The Little Accident* 1930; *The Lottery Bride* 1930; *Monte Carlo* 1930; *No, No, Nanette* 1930; *Passion Flower* 1930; *River's End* 1930; *Sin Takes a Holiday* 1930; *The Squealer* 1930; *War Nurse* 1930; *Bad Sister* 1931; *Beyond Victory* 1931; *The Big Gamble* 1931; *Finn and Hattie* 1931; *The Guardsman* 1931; *Penrod and Sam* 1931; *The Secret Witness* 1931; *Seed* 1931; *Their Mad Moment* 1931; *The Unexpected Father* 1931; *A Woman of Experience* 1931; *Back Street* 1932; *Blondie of the Follies* 1932; *Broken Lullaby* 1932; *The Crooked Circle* 1932; *Destry Rides Again* 1932; *Is My Face Red?* 1932; *Madison Square Garden* 1932; *Make Me a Star* 1932; *Once in a Lifetime* 1932; *Roar of the Dragon* 1932; *Shopworn* 1932; *Steady Company* 1932; *Strangers of the Evening* 1932; *They Just Had to Get Married* 1932; *The Trial of Vivienne Ware* 1932; *The Vanishing Frontier* 1932; *Walking Down Broadway* 1932; *Westward Passage* 1932; *Aggie Appleby, Maker of Men* 1933; *Her First Mate* 1933; *Love, Honor, and Oh, Baby!* 1933; *Meet the Baron* 1933; *Mr. Skitch* 1933; *Out All Night* 1933; *Professional Sweetheart* 1933; *Dames* 1934; *The Gay Bride* 1934; *Love Birds* 1934; *The Meanest Gal in Town* 1934; *Mrs. Wiggs of the Cabbage Patch* 1934; *Private Scandal* 1934; *Sing and Like it* 1934; *Their Big Moment* 1934; *Three on a Honeymoon* 1934; *Two Alone* 1934; *The Affair of Susan* 1935; *Going Highbrow* 1935; *Hot Tip* 1935; *Ruggles of Red Gap* 1935; *She Gets Her Man* 1935; *Spring Tonic* 1935; *13 Hours By Air* 1936; *Mad Holiday* 1936; *The Plot Thickens* 1936; *Sing Me a Love Song* 1936; *52nd Street* 1937; *Forty Naughty Girls* 1937; *Eternally Yours* 1939; *The Lady's From Kentucky* 1939; *Mickey the Kid* 1939; *Naughty But Nice* 1939; *Nurse Edith Cavell* 1939; *It All Came True* 1940; *No, No, Nanette* 1940; *Broadway Limited* 1941; *Mexican Spitfire's Baby* 1941; *Miss Polly* 1941; *Niagara Falls* 1941; *Week-End For Three* 1941; *The Bashful Bachelor* 1942; *Meet the Mob* 1942; *Mexican Spitfire at Sea* 1942; *So's Your Aunt Emma* 1942; *Tish* 1942; *Let's Face It* 1943; *Breakfast in Hollywood* 1945; *The Perfect Marriage* 1946; *Life With Father* 1947; *Francis* 1949; *The Denver and Rio Grande* 1952; *Francis Joins the WACS* 1954; *This Could Be the Night* 1957; *Teenage Millionaire* 1961; *It's a Mad, Mad, Mad, Mad World* 1963; *The Thrill of It All* 1963.

Placido, Michele • Actor • Born Foggia (near Naples), Italy. Ruggedly handsome Italian lead who has appeared in films by some of his country's finest directors, including Lina Wertmuller, Marco Bellochio, Mario Monicelli, Francesco Rosi and the Taviani brothers. Placido made his American debut in the Bette Midler vehicle, *Big Business* (1988). • *Teresa la Ladra* 1973 (a); *Mio Dio, come sono Caduta in Basso* 1974 (a); *Romanzo Popolare* 1974 (a); *La Divina Creatura* 1975 (a); *La Marche Triomphale* 1975 (a); *La Orca* 1976 (a); *Il Casotto* 1977 (a); *Io Sono Mia* 1977 (a); *La Ragazza del Piagiame Gialle* 1977 (a); *Corleone* 1978 (a); *Ernesto* 1978 (a); *Letti Selvaggi* 1978 (a); *Tigers in Lipstick* 1978 (a); *Il Prato* 1979 (a); *Fontamara* 1980 (a); *Lulu* 1980 (a); *Salto Nel Vuoto* 1980 (a); *I Tre fratelli* 1980 (a); *Les Ailes de la Colombe* 1981 (a); *Colpire Al Cuore* 1982 (a); *Till Marriage Do Us Part* 1982 (a); *L'Art d'Aimer* 1983 (a); *Dear Maestro* 1983 (a); *Sciopen* 1983 (a); *Les Amants Terribles* 1984 (a); *Attacco alla Piovra* 1984 (a); *Grandi Magazzini* 1985 (a); *Notte d'Estate con Profilo Greco, Occhi à Mandorla e Odore di Basilico* 1986 (a); *Y'a bon les blancs* 1987 (a); *Big Business* 1988 (a); *Ti Presento un'Amica* 1988 (a); *Cavalli Si Nasce* 1989 (a); *Mery Per Sempre* 1989 (a); *Pummaro* 1990 (d,sc).

Planer, Franz • *aka* Frank F. Planer • Director of photography • Born Karlsbad (now Karlovy Vary), Czechoslovakia, March 29, 1894; died 1963. Began photographing films in Germany in 1919 and worked throughout Europe before arriving in Hollywood in 1937. Planer's mobile, sinuous style chimed perfectly with that of director Max Ophuls, with whom he collaborated on *Liebelei* (1932), *The Exile* (1947) and *Letter from an Unknown Woman* (1948). He was also responsible for some fine color cinematography, notably on William Wyler's *The Big Country* (1958) and Blake Edwards's *Breakfast at Tiffany's* (1961). • *Nie Wieder Liebe* 1931; *Liebelei* 1932; *Beloved Vagabond* 1936; *Adventure in Sahara* 1938; *Girl's School* 1938; *Holiday* 1938; *Glamour For Sale* 1940; *The Face Behind the Mask* 1941; *Harvard, Here I Come* 1941; *Honolulu Lu* 1941; *Meet Boston Blackie* 1941; *Our Wife* 1941; *Sweetheart of the Campus* 1941; *They Dare Not Love* 1941; *Three Girls About Town* 1941; *Time Out For Rhythm* 1941; *The Adventures of Martin Eden* 1942; *Flight Lieutenant* 1942; *Sabotage Squad* 1942; *The Spirit of Stanford* 1942; *The Wife Takes a Flyer* 1942; *Appointment in Berlin* 1943; *Destroyer* 1943; *The Heat's* on 1943; *My Kingdom For a Cook* 1943; *Something to Shout About* 1943; *Carolina Blues* 1944; *Once Upon a Time* 1944; *Secret Command* 1944; *Strange Affair* 1944; *I Love a Bandleader* 1945; *Leave It to Blondie* 1945; *Snafu* 1945; *Her Sister's Secret* 1946; *The Exile* 1947; *Criss Cross* 1948; *Letter From an Unknown Woman* 1948; *One Touch of Venus* 1948; *Champion* 1949; *Once More, My Darling* 1949; *Take One False Step* 1949; *711 Ocean Drive* 1950; *Cyrano De Bergerac* 1950; *The Scarf* 1950; *Three Husbands* 1950; *Vendetta* 1950; *The Blue Veil* 1951; *Death of a Salesman* 1951; *Decision Before Dawn* 1952; *The 5,000 Fingers of Dr. T.* 1953; *99 River Street* 1953; *Roman Holiday* 1953; *20,000 Leagues Under the Sea* 1954; *The Caine Mutiny* 1954; *The Long Wait* 1954; *The Left Hand of God* 1955; *Not As a Stranger* 1955; *The Mountain* 1956; *The Pride and the Passion* 1957; *The Big Country* 1958; *Stage Struck* 1958; *The Nun's Story* 1959 **(AANBPH)**; *The Unforgiven* 1960; *Breakfast at Tiffany's* 1961; *The Children's Hour* 1961; *King of Kings* 1961.

Platt, Polly • Producer, production designer; also screenwriter • Born US. Acclaimed designer (notably of films directed by former husband Peter Bogdanovich) who wrote the screenplay for Louis Malle's *Pretty Baby* in 1978 and earned her first executive producer credit on James Brooks's *Broacast News* (1987). • *Targets* 1968 (story,pd); *The Last Picture Show* 1971 (pd); *What's Up, Doc?* 1972 (pd); *Paper Moon* 1973 (pd); *The Thief Who Came to Dinner* 1973 (pd); *The Bad News Bears* 1976 (pd); *A Star Is Born* 1976 (pd); *Pretty Baby* 1978 (sc,story); *Good Luck, Miss Wyckoff* 1979 (sc); *Young Doctors in Love* 1982 (pd); *The Man With Two Brains* 1983 (pd); *Terms of Endearment* 1983 (pd) **(AANBAD)**; *Broadcast News* 1987 (exec.p); *The Witches of Eastwick* 1987 (pd); *Say Anything* 1989 (a,p); *The War of the Roses* 1989 (exec.p).

Pleasence, Donald • Actor • Born Worksop, Nottinghamshire, England, October 5, 1919. First gained attention on the London stage, notably in plays directed by Peter Brook, and began appearing in films in the mid-1950s. Pleasence reprised an award-winning stage role in the film adaptation of Harold Pinter's *The Caretaker* (1963) and was also memorable in Roman Polanski's black comedy, *Cul-de-Sac* (1966). Although effective in benign, avuncular roles, it is his ability to exude an oily menace that filmmakers have tended to exploit, lately in fairly second-rate horror thrillers. • *The Beachcomber* 1954; *Value For Money* 1955; *1984* 1956; *All at Sea* 1957; *The Man Inside* 1958; *A Tale of Two Cities* 1958; *The Two-Headed Spy* 1958; *Look Back in Anger* 1959; *Sons and Lovers* 1960; *Lisa* 1962; *The Caretaker* 1963; *The Great Escape* 1963; *The Greatest Story Ever Told* 1965; *The Hallelujah Trail* 1965; *Cul-de-Sac* 1966; *Eye of the Devil* 1966; *Fantastic Voyage* 1966; *Matchless* 1966; *The Night of the Generals* 1966; *You Only Live Twice* 1967; *Mister Freedom* 1968; *Will Penny* 1968; *The Madwoman of Chaillot* 1969; *Soldier Blue* 1970; *The Jerusalem File* 1971; *Kidnapped* 1971; *Outback* 1971; *THX 1138* 1971; *Innocent Bystanders* 1972; *The Pied Piper* 1972; *The Rainbow Boys* 1972; *Wedding in White* 1972; *La Loba y la Paloma* 1973; *Tales That Witness Madness* 1973; *The Black Windmill* 1974; *Escape to Witch Mountain* 1974; *The Mutation* 1974; *Hearts of the West* 1975; *A Choice of Weapons* 1976; *The Devil Within Her* 1976; *The Eagle Has Landed* 1976; *Journey Into Fear* 1976; *The Last Tycoon* 1976; *The Passover Plot* 1976; *Les Liens de sang* 1977; *Night Creature* 1977; *Oh, God!* 1977; *Telefon* 1977; *The Uncanny* 1977; *Halloween* 1978; *L'Ordre et la sécurité du monde* 1978; *Out of the Darkness* 1978; *Power Play* 1978; *Sgt. Pepper's Lonely Hearts Club Band* 1978; *Tomorrow Never Comes* 1978; *Dracula* 1979; *Good Luck, Miss Wyckoff* 1979; *L'Homme en colère* 1979; *Jaguar Lives!* 1979; *Escape From New York* 1981; *Halloween II* 1981; *The Monster Club* 1981; *Race For the Yankee Zephyr* 1981; *Alone in the Dark* 1982; *The Devonsville Terror* 1982; *The Ambassador* 1984; *Barry McKenzie Holds His Own* 1984; *A Breed Apart* 1984; *Terror in the Aisles* 1984; *Where Is Parsifal?* 1984; *Creepers* 1985; *Frankenstein's Great-Aunt Tillie* 1985; *Sotto il Vestito Niente* 1985; *El Tesoro del Amazones* 1985; *To Kill a Stranger* 1985; *Warrior of the Lost World* 1985; *Warrior Queen* 1986; *Cobra Mission* 1987; *Fuga Dall'inferno* 1987; *Nosferatu a Venezia* 1987; *Prince of Darkness* 1987; *Spettri* 1987; *Ground Zero* 1988; *Halloween 4: The Return of Michael Myers* 1988; *Hanna's War* 1988; *Phantom of Death* 1988; *Halloween 5: The Revenge of Michael Meyers* 1989; *Paganini Horror* 1989; *River of Death* 1989; *Ten Little Indians* 1989; *American Riscio* 1990; *Buried Alive* 1990; *Casablanca Express* 1990.

Plimpton, Martha • Actress • Born New York, NY. Effervescent young performer who made her mark opposite Tommy Lee Jones in *The River Rat* (1984) and gave a fine performance as the girlfriend of River Phoenix in Sidney Lumet's *Running on Empty* (1988). Daughter of actors Keith Carradine and Shelley Plimpton. • *Rollover* 1981; *The River Rat* 1984; *The Goonies* 1985; *The Mosquito Coast* 1986; *Shy People* 1987; *Another Woman* 1988; *Running on Empty* 1988; *Stars and Bars* 1988; *Parenthood* 1989; *Zwei Frauen* 1989; *Stanley and Iris* 1990.

Plowright, Joan • Actress; also stage director. • Born Brigg, England, October 28, 1929. *Educ.* Laban Art of Movement Studio; Old Vic Theatre School. One of the finest stage actresses of her generation, Plowright has played almost every major role in the classical repertory. She made her screen debut in John Huston's *Moby Dick* (1956) and was acclaimed for her performance in the film adaptation of John Osborne's play, *The Entertainer* (1960), starring her future husband Laurence Olivier. Plowright has subsequently made selective appearances in films including *Equus* (1977) and *Britannia Hospital* (1982). • *Moby Dick* 1956; *Time Without Pity* 1957; *The Entertainer* 1960; *Three Sisters* 1970; *Equus* 1977; *Brimstone and Treacle* 1982; *Britannia Hospital* 1982; *Wagner* 1983; *Revolution* 1985; *The Dressmaker* 1988; *Drowning By Numbers* 1988; *Avalon* 1990; *I Love You to Death* 1990.

Plummer, Amanda • Actress • Born US, March 23, 1957. *Educ.* Middlebury College. Made an impressive screen debut opposite Burt Lancaster in the offbeat western *Cattle Annie and Little Britches* (1981), and has continued to turn in fine performances on both stage and screen. Plummer won a Tony and a Drama Desk award for her title role in the 1982 Broadway play, *Agnes of God*. Daughter of actors Christopher Plummer and Tammy Grimes. • *Cattle Annie and Little Britches* 1981; *The World According to Garp* 1982; *Daniel* 1983; *The Hotel New Hampshire* 1984; *Courtship* 1986; *Static* 1986; *Made in Heaven* 1987; *Prisoners of Inertia* 1989; *Joe Versus the Volcano* 1990; *The Fisher King* 1991.

Plummer, Christopher • Actor • Born Arthur Christopher Orme Plummer, Montreal, Canada, December 13, 1927. Began his career in Canadian theater and TV and made his Broadway debut in 1954. Plummer went on to establish himself as one of the finest stage actors of his generation, particularly in Shakesperean roles, and has won a number of theater awards on both sides of the Atlantic. He made his film debut in Sidney Lumet's *Stage Struck* (1958) and is probably best known for his roles as Baron Von Trapp in *The Sound of Music* (1965) and Rudyard Kipling in John Huston's *The Man Who Would Be King* (1975). Father (by actress Tammy Grimes) of Amanda Plummer. • *Stage Struck* 1958; *Wind Across the Everglades* 1958; *The Fall of the Roman Empire* 1964; *Inside Daisy Clover* 1965; *The Sound of Music* 1965; *The Night of the Generals* 1966; *Oedipus the King* 1968; *Battle of Britain* 1969; *Lock Up Your Daughters!* 1969; *The Royal Hunt of the Sun* 1969; *Waterloo* 1970; *The Pyx* 1973; *Conduct Unbecoming* 1975; *The Man Who Would Be King* 1975; *The Return of the Pink Panther* 1975; *Aces High* 1976; *Atentat u Sarajevu* 1976; *Dis-*

appearance 1977; *Uppdraget* 1977; *International Velvet* 1978; *The Silent Partner* 1978; *Arthur Miller on Home Ground* 1979; *Hanover Street* 1979; *Highpoint* 1979; *Murder By Decree* 1979; *Starcrash* 1979; *Eyewitness* 1980; *Somewhere in Time* 1980; *The Amateur* 1981; *Being Different* 1981; *Dreamscape* 1984; *Jatszani Kell* 1985; *Ordeal By Innocence* 1985; *An American Tail* 1986; *The Boss' Wife* 1986; *The Boy in Blue* 1986; *Dragnet* 1987; *L'Homme qui plantait des arbres* 1987; *I Love N.Y.* 1987; *Nosferatu a Venezia* 1987; *Souvenir* 1987; *Light Years* 1988; *Shadow Dancing* 1988; *Kingsgate* 1989; *Mind Field* 1989; *Red-Blooded American Girl* 1990; *Where the Heart Is* 1990; *Rock-A-Doodle* 1991.

Poitier, Sidney • Actor; also director, producer. • Born Miami, FL, February 20, 1924. Gifted, handsome leading man, generally acknowledged as Hollywood's first black movie star. After stage work with the American Negro Theater, Poitier entered movies in 1950 and turned in a number of memorable supporting roles, as in *The Blackboard Jungle* (1955), before gaining international attention for his Oscar-nominated appearance in *The Defiant Ones* (1958). He came into his own with a string of commanding performances in the 1960s, both in films which turned upon the issue of color—*A Patch of Blue* (1965), *In the Heat of the Night* (1967), *Guess Who's Coming to Dinner* (1967)—as well as some which didn't—*A Slender Thread, The Bedford Incident* (both 1965).

Poitier's international popularity in the 1960s helped pave the way for the commercial black cinema of the early 70s and was instrumental in allowing blacks to appear in less stereotypical screen roles. He began a second career as a director in the early 70s and has made a number of entertaining movies, in some of which he has also appeared. He is probably best known to younger audiences for his role opposite Tom Berenger in Roger Spottiswoode's 1988 thriller, *Shoot to Kill.* Married to actress Joanna Shimkus since 1976. • *No Way Out* 1950 (a); *Red Ball Express* 1952 (a); *Go, Man, Go!* 1954 (a); *The Blackboard Jungle* 1955 (a); *Good-Bye, My Lady* 1956 (a); *Band of Angels* 1957 (a); *Edge of the City* 1957 (a); *The Mark of the Hawk* 1957 (a); *Something of Value* 1957 (a); *The Defiant Ones* 1958 (a) **(AANBA)**; *Virgin Island* 1958 (a); *Porgy and Bess* 1959 (a); *All the Young Men* 1960 (a); *Paris Blues* 1961 (a); *A Raisin in the Sun* 1961 (a); *Pressure Point* 1962 (a); *Lilies of the Field* 1963 (a) **(AABA)**; *The Bedford Incident* 1965 (a); *The Greatest Story Ever Told* 1965 (a); *A Patch of Blue* 1965 (a); *The Slender Thread* 1965 (a); *Duel at Diablo* 1966 (a); *Guess Who's Coming to Dinner?* 1967 (a); *In the Heat of the Night* 1967 (a); *To Sir With Love* 1967 (a); *For Love of Ivy* 1968 (a,story); *The Lost Man* 1969 (a); *Brother John* 1970 (a); *King: A Filmed Record...Montgomery to Memphis* 1970 (a); *They Call Me Mr. Tibbs* 1970 (a); *The Organization* 1971 (a); *Buck and the Preacher* 1972 (a,d); *A Warm December* 1972 (a,d); *Uptown Saturday Night* 1974 (a,d); *Let's Do It Again* 1975 (a,d); *The Wilby Conspiracy* 1975 (a); *A Piece of the Action* 1977 (a,d); *Stir Crazy* 1980 (d); *Hanky Panky* 1982 (d); *Fast Forward* 1985 (d); *Little Nikita* 1988 (a); *Shoot to Kill* 1988 (a); *Ghost Dad* 1990 (d).

Polanski, Roman • Director, screenwriter; also actor. • Born Paris, August 18, 1933. *Educ.* Lòdz Film School. Roman Polanski was born in Paris of Polish-Jewish parents. At the age of three, he and his family returned to their native Poland. A few years later, with the onset of WWII, Polanski's parents were taken to a Nazi concentration camp, where his mother perished. Growing up in war-torn Poland, the young Polanski found solace in trips to the cinema and acting in radio dramas, on stage and in films. His early screen acting credits included work with famed Polish director Andrzej Wajda. In 1954, he was accepted to an intensive five-year program at the Lodz Film School. One of his student films, *Two Men and a Wardrobe* (1958), won five international awards, including a Bronze Medal at the Brussels World's Fair. In 1962, Polanski directed his first feature-length film, *Knife in the Water.* Poorly received by Polish state officials and some domestic critics, the film was a sensation in the West, awarded the Critics' Prize at the Venice Film Festival and nominated for an Academy Award.

Polanski moved to England to make his next three films: *Repulsion* (1965), a psychological terror story of a young woman's disintegration; *Cul-de-Sac* (1966), a dark comedy of mobsters and a mismatched couple set in an isolated castle; and a horror film parody, *Dance of the Vampires/The Fearless Vampire Killers* (1967), in which Polanski costarred with American actress Sharon Tate. In 1968, Polanski and Tate were married; that same year saw Polanski's American film debut, the enormously successful "gynecological horror story," *Rosemary's Baby.* The following summer, Polanski's new-found success was dealt a shattering blow when Tate and three of Polanski's friends were murdered by members of the Charles Manson cult.

Polanski made his next film, *Macbeth,* in 1971. A brutally realistic adaptation of an already violent play, it was seen by many critics as a form of catharsis for Polanski after the Manson slayings. Polanski himself, however, downplayed the link between the film and the tragic murders.

In 1974, Polanski was back in Hollywood for his greatest triumph, *Chinatown,* a tale of greed, corruption and incest set in 1930s Los Angeles. The director made a memorable impression onscreen, too, as the cocky gangster who slices Jack Nicholson's nose. Two years later, Polanski undertook his most arduous acting role, the lead in his film *The Tenant.* Like *Repulsion,* this was a harrowing tale of psychological disintegration, with the director playing a man who comes unraveled when he moves into the apartment of a woman who recently committed suicide.

In 1979, Polanski was arrested in California on charges of unlawful sexual intercourse with a thirteen-year-old girl. He spent forty-two days in prison under observation. Before further criminal proceedings could get underway, Polanski fled the United States. He made his next film, *Tess* (1979), an acclaimed version of the Thomas Hardy novel *Tess of the d'Urbervilles,* in France. In 1981, he returned to Poland to direct and star in a stage production of *Amadeus.* Polanski's most recent film, shot in Paris, was the suspenseful *Frantic* (1988), with Harrison Ford as an American visitor searching for his abducted wife.

As an artist who exerts tremendous control over his films, often co-writing the screenplays and sometimes acting in them, Polanski is able to instill in his work his unique personal view of the world. Recurring Polanski preoccupations include violence and victimization, isolation and alienation, and a profound sense of the absurd.

The relationship between Polanski's personal life and his work has received a great deal of attention. While there are some strong parallels, focusing on this relationship has unfortunately tended to overshadow the surprising diversity of his films and eclipse his achievements as a filmmaker. DFD • *Pokolenie* 1954 (a); *Dwaj Ludzie z Szafa/Two Men and a Wardrobe (short)* 1958 (a,d,sc); *Gdy Spadaja Anioly/When Angels Fall (short)* 1959 (a,d,sc); *Lotna* 1959 (a); *Niewinni Czarodzieje* 1960 (a); *Le Gros et le Maigre/The Fat and the Lean (short)* 1961 (a,d,sc,ed); *Samson* 1961 (a); *Noz w Wodzie/Knife in the Water* 1962 (d,sc); *Ssaki/Mammals (short)* 1962 (a,d,sc); *Les Plus belles escroqueries du monde/The World's Most Beautiful Swindlers* • 1964 (d,sc—"Amsterdam"); *Repulsion* 1965 (a,d,sc); *Cul-de-Sac* 1966 (d,sc); *The Fearless Vampire Killers* 1967 (a,d,sc); *Rosemary's Baby* 1968 (d,sc) **(AANBSC)**; *Cinéma Different 3* 1970 (d,sc—"La riviere de diamants"); *The Magic Christian* 1970 (a); *Macbeth* 1971 (d,sc); *Weekend of a Champion* 1972 (a,p); *Che?* 1973 (a,d,sc,ed); *Blood For Dracula* 1974 (a); *Chinatown* 1974 (a,d) **(AANBD)**; *The Evolution of Snuff* 1976 (a); *Le Locataire/The Tenant* 1976 (a,d,sc); *Tess* 1979 (d,sc) **(AANBD)**; *Pirates* 1986 (d,sc); *Frantic* 1988 (d,sc).

Poledouris, Basil • Composer • Born Kansas City, MO. *Educ.* Long Beach State University, CA (music, composition); USC, Los Angeles (film); AFI, Los Angeles. Classmate (at USC) of John Milius who has subsequently scored most of the director's features. Poledouris's TV credits include the 14-hour miniseries *Amerika* (1987) and *Lonesome Dove* (1989), for which he earned an Emmy. • *Extreme Close-Up* 1973 (m); *Big Wednesday* 1978 (m); *Dolphin* 1979 (m); *The House of God* 1979 (m); *The Blue Lagoon* 1980 (m,m.dir,m.cond); *Defiance* 1980 (m); *Conan the Barbarian* 1982 (m,m.dir); *Summer Lovers* 1982 (m); *Conan the Destroyer* 1984 (m); *Making the Grade* 1984 (m); *Protocol* 1984 (m); *Red Dawn* 1984 (m); *Flesh + Blood* 1985 (m,m.dir); *Iron Eagle* 1986 (m); *No Man's Land* 1987 (m); *Robocop* 1987 (m); *Cherry 2000* 1988 (m); *Spellbinder* 1988 (m); *Split Decisions* 1988 (m); *Farewell to the King* 1989 (m); *Un Plan d'enfer* 1989 (m); *Wired* 1989 (m); *The Hunt For Red October* 1990 (m,song); *Quigley Down Under* 1990 (m).

Pollack, Sydney • Director; also producer. • Born Lafayette, IN, July 1, 1934. *Educ.* Neighborhood Playhouse, New York. Sydney Pollack is best known for the fine performances he has elicited from Hollywood stars such as Robert Redford, Jane Fonda, Dustin Hoffman, Barbra Streisand, Paul Newman and Burt Lancaster. Pollack began his own career as an actor. After studying at New York's Neighborhood Playhouse School of the Theatre with Sanford Meisner, he stayed on at Meisner's request as an acting coach, while also appearing on Broadway, in summer stock and on television. A role in a "Playhouse 90" production of *For Whom the Bell Tolls*, directed by John Frankenheimer, led to an introduction to Burt Lancaster. It was through Lancaster that Pollack got his chance to begin directing for television. In the next five years he would direct over 80 shows, most notably 15 episodes of the popular "Ben Casey" series.

Pollack's first feature as a director was *The Slender Thread* (1965), featuring Anne Bancroft as a suicidal woman and Sidney Poitier as a crisis center worker trying to keep her on the telephone while emergency services track her down. This taut drama, shot on location in Seattle in black and white, opened with an aerial shot which would soon become one of the director's trademarks.

After consolidating his film career with *This Property Is Condemned* (1966), *The Scalphunters* (1968) and *Castle Keep* (1969), Pollack achieved his first major success with *They Shoot Horses, Don't They?* (1970), a harrowing drama set during a Depression-era dance marathon. Although the film was criticized for toning down the harsher, more abrasive qualities of the Horace McCoy novel on which it was based, it did earn Gig Young an Oscar as Best Supporting Actor and Pollack a nomination for Best Director.

Pollack next scored at the box office with *The Way We Were* (1973), an old-fashioned love story starring Robert Redford and Barbra Streisand. After several missteps, Pollack returned to form with *The Electric Horseman* (1979), this time pairing Redford with Jane Fonda in a romantic comedy about a modern-day cowboy and a reporter. His biggest commercial success to date has been *Tootsie* (1982), in which he also had a small role as the agent of an intransigent actor, played by Dustin Hoffman. Pollack's career reached a zenith with *Out of Africa* (1985), a sumptuous love story of writer Isak Dinesen (Meryl Streep) and Denys Finch Hatton (Redford) which Pollack produced and directed, winning an Oscar for both. TZ • *War Hunt* 1962 (a); *Il Gattopardo/The Leopard* 1963 (voice dubbing supervisor—American version); *The Slender Thread* 1965 (d); *This Property Is Condemned* 1966 (d); *The Scalphunters* 1968 (d); *The Swimmer* 1968 (d); *Castle Keep* 1969 (d); *They Shoot Horses, Don't They?* 1969 (d,p) **(AANBD)**; *Jeremiah Johnson* 1972 (d); *The Way We Were* 1973 (d,p); *Three Days of the Condor* 1975 (d); *The Yakuza* 1975 (d,p); *Bobby Deerfield* 1977 (d,p); *The Electric Horseman* 1979 (d); *Honeysuckle Rose* 1980 (exec.p); *Absence of Malice* 1981 (d,p); *Tootsie* 1982 (a,d,p) **(AANBD,AANBP)**; *Songwriter* 1984 (p); *Out of Africa* 1985 (d,p) **(AABD,AABP)**; *Hello Actors Studio* 1987 (a); *Bright Lights, Big City* 1988 (p); *The Fabulous Baker Boys* 1989 (exec.p); *Major League* 1989 (exec.p); *Havana* 1990 (d,p); *Presumed Innocent* 1990 (p); *White Palace* 1990 (exec.p).

Pollard, Michael J. • Actor • Born Michael J. Pollack, Passaic, NJ, May 30, 1939. *Educ.* Actors Studio. Diminutive, engaging character player, best known for his Oscar-nominated performance as getaway-car driver C.W. Moss in *Bonnie and Clyde* (1967). • *Adventures of a Young Man* 1962; *The Stripper* 1963; *Summer Magic* 1963; *Enter Laughing* 1966; *The Wild Angels* 1966; *Bonnie and Clyde* 1967 **(AANBSA)**; *Caprice* 1967; *Hannibal Brooks* 1968; *Jigsaw* 1968; *Little Fauss and Big Halsy* 1970; *Les Pétroleuses* 1971; *Dirty Little Billy* 1972; *Between the Lines* 1977; *Melvin and Howard* 1980; *America* 1982; *Heated Vengeance* 1985; *The American Way* 1986; *The Patriot* 1986; *American Gothic* 1987; *Roxanne* 1987; *Scrooged* 1988; *Fast Food* 1989; *Next of Kin* 1989; *Night Visitor* 1989; *Un Plan d'enfer* 1989; *Season of Fear* 1989; *Sleepaway Camp 3: Teenage Wasteland* 1989; *Tango and Cash* 1989; *Dick Tracy* 1990; *Enid Is Sleeping* 1990; *I Come in Peace* 1990; *The Art of Dying* 1991.

Polonsky, Abraham • Director; also screenwriter, novelist. • Born New York, NY, December 5, 1910. *Educ.* CCNY; Columbia Law School. Former journalist and radio writer whose first notable film work was as screenwriter on Robert Rossen's *Body and Soul* (1947), starring John Garfield. Polonsky was then hired by the film's producer, Bob Robertson, to direct his next feature, another Garfield vehicle called *Force of Evil* (1948). The result was a gritty, socially conscious gangster drama which has since come to be regarded as a classic of its kind.

Blacklisted after a 1951 HUAC hearing, Polonsky was temporarily unable to continue working in Hollywood. He supported himself by writing TV scripts under an assumed name before returning to big-screen work in the late 1960s. His second feature, 1969's *Tell Them Willie Boy Is Here*, was one of the few Hollywood westerns to deal honestly with the white man's persecution of the American Indian. *Romance of a Horsethief* (1971), a farcical account of Jewish ghetto life in pre-Revolutionary Russia, was generally received as a kind of thinking person's *Fiddler on the Roof.* Polonsky's subsequent film work has been intermittent. • *Body and Soul* 1947 (sc,story) **(AANBSC)**; *Golden Earrings* 1947 (sc); *Force of Evil* 1948 (d,sc); *I Can Get It For You Wholesale* 1951 (sc); *Madigan* 1968 (sc); *Tell Them Willie Boy Is Here* 1969 (d,sc); *Romance of a Horse Thief* 1971 (d); *Avalanche Express* 1979 (sc); *Body and Soul* 1981 (from story) **(AANBSC)**; *Monsignor* 1982 (sc).

Pommer, Erich • Producer • Born Hildesheim, Germany, July 20, 1889; died 1966, Hollywood, CA. Highly influential figure of the German silent cinema. Pommer began his career working for Gaumont in Paris at the age of 18 and had set up his own Berlin-based production company, Decla, by 1915. Pommer merged the company with Bioscop four years later and went on to produce such expressionist classics as Robert Wiene's *The Cabinet of Dr. Caligari* (1919) and Fritz Lang's *Dr. Mabuse, Der Spieler* (1922). In 1923 his company was absorbed within UFA, with Pommer taking over as chief of production for the giant studio. His keen eye for new talent and ability to detect commercial appeal led him to back early works by F.W. Murnau, Carl Theodor Dreyer and Josef von Sternberg, as well as other Lang films, particularly the classic *Metropolis* (1926)—a big-budget extravaganza which, in fact, contributed to UFA's demise.

Pommer left Germany in 1933 and subsequently worked in both the US and England, where he formed Mayflower Productions with actor-director Charles Laughton. Among the company's more notable productions were Hitchcock's *Jamaica Inn* (1939), Dorothy Arzner's

Dance, Girl, Dance (1940) and Pommer's only film as a director, *Vessel of Wrath* (1938). He spent the war years in the US, becoming an American citizen in 1944. After WWII he again worked in Germany, first as a film production supervisor for the Allied authorities; he finally returned to the US in 1956. • *The Cabinet of Dr. Caligari* 1919 (p); *Der Mude Tod/Destiny* 1921 (p); *Dr. Mabuse, Der Spieler* 1922 (p); *Mikael* 1924 (p); *Die Nibelungen* 1924 (p); *Metropolis* 1926 (p); *Barbed Wire* 1927 (p); *Hotel Imperial* 1927 (p); *Die Wunderbare Lüge der Nina Petrowna* 1929 (p); *Der Blaue Engel/The Blue Angel* 1930 (p); *Liliom* 1934 (p); *Fire Over England* 1936 (p); *Farewell Again* 1937 (p); *St. Martin's Lane W.C.2* 1938 (p); *Vessel of Wrath* 1938 (d,p); *Jamaica Inn* 1939 (p); *Dance, Girl, Dance* 1940 (p); *They Knew What They Wanted* 1940 (p); *Illusion in Moll* 1952 (p); *Kinder, Mutter und ein General* 1955 (p); *Eine Liebesgeschichte* 1958 (p).

Pontecorvo, Gillo • Director • Born Gilberto Pontecorvo, Pisa, Italy, November 19, 1919. Leftist filmmaker who worked as a foreign correspondent in Paris, assistant to Yves Allegret, and documentarist before gaining attention with the grim concentration camp melodrama, *Kapo* (1960). Pontecorvo's best-known film is the *The Battle of Algiers* (1966), a gripping account of the Algerian rebellion against French rule. Shot in a grainy, neo-documentary style and featuring non-professional actors, the film won the Golden Lion at the Venice Film Festival and remains a landmark political drama. Pontecorvo's only subsequent feature of note was *Burn!* (1969), another critique of colonialism set in the 19th-century Antilles. Perhaps because of its upscale production values and star cast—which included Marlon Brando—the film lacked the edge of Pontecorvo's earlier work. • *Die Windrose* 1956 (d); *La Grande strada azzurra* 1957 (d); *Il Medico e lo stregone* 1957 (d); *Kapo* 1960 (d); *La Battaglia di Algeri/Battle of Algiers* 1966 (d,story,m) **(AANBD,AANBSC)**; *Quemada!/Burn!* 1969 (d,story); *Ogro* 1979 (d,sc).

Ponti, Carlo • Producer • Born Milan, Italy, December 11, 1910. *Educ.* University of Milan (law). Worked for Lux Films in Rome from 1945 to 1949, where he oversaw several features by directors including Mario Camerini and Alberto Lattuada. In 1950 Ponti began a successful partnership with Dino De Laurentiis, producing a number of noted films such as Federico Fellini's *La Strada* (1954). He then branched out on his own in the mid-1950s, scoring critical and popular success with international productions by directors such as Vittorio De Sica, Jean-Luc Godard and David Lean.

Ponti's 1957 marriage to Sophia Loren sparked off a string of Italian legal complications (a previous divorce was still being contested) which resulted in his taking French citizenship in 1964. In 1979 he was sentenced, in absentia, to a jail term and a multi-million dollar fine, for charges involving the smuggling of currency and art. • *Ulysses* 1953 (p); *La Lupa* 1954 (p); *Mambo* 1954 (p); *L'Oro di Napoli/The Gold of Naples* 1954 (p); *La Strada* 1954 (p) **(AABFP)**; *Attila* 1955 (p); *Il Ferroviere/The Railroad Man* 1955 (p); *Guendalina* 1955 (p); *Outlaw Girl* 1955 (p); *The Black Orchid* 1958 (p); *That Kind of Woman* 1959 (p); *A Breath of Scandal* 1960 (p); *La Ciociara/Two Women* 1960 (p); *Heller in Pink Tights* 1960 (p); *Une Femme est une femme/A Woman is a Woman* 1961 (p); *Boccaccio '70* 1962 (p); *Cléo de 5 à 7/Cleo From 5 to 7* 1962 (exec.p); *L'Isola di Arturo* 1962 (p); *Landru/Bluebeard* 1962 (p); *L'Oeil du Malin/The Third Lover* 1962 (p); *I Sequestrati di Altona/The Condemned of Altona* 1962 (p); *Les Carabiniers* 1963 (p); *Le Doulos* 1963 (p); *Le Mepris* 1963 (p); *La Donna Scimmia* 1964 (p); *Matrimonio all'italiana/Marriage Italian Style* 1964 (p); *Casanova '70* 1965 (p); *Doctor Zhivago* 1965 (p) **(AANBP)**; *Lady L* 1965 (p); *Blow-Up* 1966 (p); *C'era una Volta...* 1967 (p); *La Ragazza e il Generale/The Girl and the General* 1967 (p); *Gli Amanti/A Place For Lovers* 1969 (p); *The Best House in London* 1969 (p); *I Girasoli* 1969 (p); *Zabriskie Point* 1970 (p); *Bianco, Rosso e...* 1971 (p); *La Moglie del Prete/The Priest's Wife* 1971 (exec.p); *La Mortadella/Lady Liberty* 1972 (p); *Andy Warhol's Frankenstein* 1973 (p); *Giordano Bruno* 1973 (p); *Massacre in Rome* 1973 (p); *Mordi e Fuggi* 1973 (p); *Il Bestione/The Beast* 1974 (p); *Blood For Dracula* 1974 (p); *I Corpi Presentano Tracce Di Violenza Carnale* 1974 (p); *Permette signora che ami vostra figlia/Claretta and Ben* 1974 (p); *La Poliziotta/Policewoman* 1974 (p); *Baby Sitter—Un maledetto pasticcio* 1975 (p); *Loving Cousins* 1975 (p); *Il Padrone e l'Operaio/The Boss and the Worker* 1975 (p); *The Passenger* 1975 (p); *Virilità* 1975 (p); *Brutti, Sporchi e Cattivi/Ugly, Dirty and Bad* 1976 (p); *The Cassandra Crossing* 1977 (p); *Una Giornata Particolare/A Special Day* 1977 (exec.p); *Running Away* 1989 (p); *Sabato, Domenica e Lunedi/Saturday, Sunday and Monday* 1990 (exec.p); *Oscar* 1991 (p).

Porter, Edwin S. • Filmmaker • Born Edwin Stanton Porter, Scozia, Italy, April 21, 1869; died April 30, 1941. Preeminent figure among early American filmmakers and one of the first to use techniques such as closeups and intercutting for narrative purposes. Porter was a projectionist, inventor and entrepreneur before starting work in 1900 for the Edison company, where he was soon promoted to head of film production. By 1901 he was making multi-shot films such as *The Execution of Czolgosz*, a drama about the execution of President McKinley's assassin which juxtaposed documentary footage of the prison with a staged dramatization of the execution itself.

Porter's first major achievement was *The Life of an American Fireman* (1902), usually considered a landmark work thanks to its sophisticated editing techniques. The film cuts back and forth between the interior and exterior of a burning building in order to heighten dramatic effect, and is thus frequently cited as the first American use of editing in order to "drive" a narrative. (An alternative print of the film was recently discovered in which the exterior and interior scenes are juxtaposed as two continuous sequences, leading to speculation that the intercut version may have been a later development.)

Porter is probably best known for *The Great Train Robbery* (1903), a sophisticated, 12-minute narrative broken up into separate scenes and using camera movement and continuity editing to advance the story. His last important contribution to film was to give an unknown actor and playwright named David Wark Griffith his debut role in the 1907 production, *Rescued From an Eagle's Nest*. Porter formed his own company, Rex Films, in 1911, but soon afterward went to work for Famous Players. There he directed several competent but unexceptional features as well as experimenting with various aspects of the filmic process. • *Smashing a Jersey Mosquito (short)* 1901 (p,ph); *Trapeze Disrobing Act (short)* 1901 (p,ph); *What Happened on 23rd Street, N.Y.C. (short)* 1901 (ph); *The Burning of Durland's Riding Academy (short)* 1902 (ph); *The Life of an American Fireman* 1902 (d); *The Messenger Boy's Mistake* 1902 (d); *Electrocuting an Elephant (short)* 1903 (ph); *The Great Train Robbery* 1903 (d); *Rube and Mandy at Coney Island (short)* 1903 (ph); *What Happened in the Tunnel (short)* 1903 (ph); *The European Rest-Cure* 1904 (p,ph); *Strenuous Life* 1904 (p,ph); *Coney Island at Night* 1905 (ph,title animation); *The Miller's Daughter* 1905 (d,ph); *Getting Evidence* 1906 (p,ph); *Three American Beauties* 1906 (p,ph); *Rescued From an Eagle's Nest* 1907 (d); *The Count of Monte Cristo* 1913 (d,sc); *A Good Little Devil* 1914 (d,ph); *Tess of the Storm Country* 1914 (d,ph); *Bella Donna* 1915 (d); *The Eternal City* 1915 (d); *Sold* 1915 (d); *Zaza* 1915 (d); *Lydia Gilmore* 1916 (d).

Potter, Dennis • Screenwriter, playwright; also novelist. • Born Forest of Dean, Gloucester, England, May 17, 1935. *Educ.* New College, Oxford. Leading contemporary English playwright who has adapted several of his works for film as well as contributing original screenplays. Potter first gained acclaim for his musical TV drama, *Pennies From Heaven*, in which popular songs from the 1940s were used as an inventive and ironic means of commenting on the narrative. The English version, which starred Bob Hoskins, was transferred to the American screen by Herbert Ross in 1981 with Steve Martin and Bernadette Peters in the leading roles. Potter was similarly acclaimed for "The Singing Detective" (1986, released theatrically in US in 1988), a multi-layered drama in which the hospital experiences of an ailing author mirror the adventures of one of his fictional protagonists. The success of the mini-series led to its release in theatrical form in the US in 1988. • *Pennies From Heaven* 1981 (sc,from television series) (**AANBSC**); *Brimstone and Treacle* 1982 (sc,from television play "Pennies From Heaven"); *Gorky Park* 1983 (sc); *Dreamchild* 1985 (exec.p,sc); *Emma's War* 1985 (a); *Track 29* 1987 (sc); *The Singing Detective* 1988 (p,sc).

Potts, Annie • Actress • Born Nashville, TN, October 28, 1952. *Educ.* Stevens College, MO. Perky, attractive character player, best known for her roles as daffy secretary Janine Melnitz in *Ghostbusters* (1984) and wry Mary Jo Shively on the popular TV sitcom "Designing Women" (1986-). Potts recently charmed critics in the otherwise lackluster *Texasville* (1990). • *Corvette Summer* 1978; *King of the Gypsies* 1978; *Heartaches* 1981; *Crimes of Passion* 1984; *Ghostbusters* 1984; *Jumpin' Jack Flash* 1986; *Pretty in Pink* 1986; *Pass the Ammo* 1987; *Ghostbusters II* 1989; *Who's Harry Crumb?* 1989; *Texasville* 1990.

Powell, Dick • Actor; also director, producer. • Born Richard E. Powell, Mountain View, AR, November 14, 1904; died 1963. Romantic lead of Warner Bros. musicals of the 1930s who later moved into straight comedies such as Preston Sturges's *Christmas in July* (1940) before becoming a key interpreter of tough-guy film noir roles in the mid-40s. Powell's definitive "hard boiled" role was as Raymond Chandler's private eye Philip Marlowe, in Edward Dmytryk's *Murder, My Sweet* (1944). Powell later directed and produced several unexceptional films in the 1950s and was portrayed by his son, Dick Powell, Jr., in *Day of the Locust* (1975). Married to Joan Blondell from 1936 to 1945 and June Allyson until his death in 1963. • *Blessed Event* 1932 (a); *Too Busy to Work* 1932 (a); *42nd Street* 1933 (a); *College Coach* 1933 (a); *Convention City* 1933 (a); *Footlight Parade* 1933 (a); *Gold Diggers of 1933* 1933 (a); *The King's Vacation* 1933 (a); *Dames* 1934 (a); *Flirtation Walk* 1934 (a); *Happiness Ahead* 1934 (a); *Twenty Million Sweethearts* 1934 (a); *Wonder Bar* 1934 (a); *Broadway Gondolier* 1935 (a); *Gold Diggers of 1935* 1935 (a); *A Midsummer Night's Dream* 1935 (a); *Page Miss Glory* 1935 (a); *Shipmates Forever* 1935 (a); *Thanks a Million* 1935 (a); *Colleen* 1936 (a); *Gold Diggers of 1937* 1936 (a); *Hearts Divided* 1936 (a); *Stage Struck* 1936 (a); *Hollywood Hotel* 1937 (a); *On the Avenue* 1937 (a); *The Singing Marine* 1937 (a); *Varsity Show* 1937 (a); *Cowboy From Brooklyn* 1938 (a); *Going Places* 1938 (a); *Hard to Get* 1938 (a); *Naughty But Nice* 1939 (a); *Christmas in July* 1940 (a); *I Want a Divorce* 1940 (a); *In the Navy* 1941 (a); *Model Wife* 1941 (a); *Star-Spangled Rhythm* 1942 (a); *Happy Go Lucky* 1943 (a); *Riding High* 1943 (a); *True to Life* 1943 (a); *It Happened Tomorrow* 1944 (a); *Meet the People* 1944 (a); *Murder, My Sweet* 1944 (a); *Cornered* 1945 (a); *Johnny O'Clock* 1947 (a); *Pitfall* 1948 (a); *Rogue's Regiment* 1948 (a); *Station West* 1948 (a); *To the Ends of the Earth* 1948 (a); *Mrs. Mike* 1949 (a); *The Reformer and the Redhead* 1950 (a); *Right Cross* 1950 (a); *Cry Danger* 1951 (a); *The Tall Target* 1951 (a); *You Never Can Tell* 1951 (a); *The Bad and the Beautiful* 1952 (a); *Split Second* 1953 (d); *Susan Slept Here* 1954 (a); *The Conqueror* 1956 (d,p); *You Can't Run Away From It* 1956 (d,p); *The Enemy Below* 1957 (d,p); *The Hunters* 1958 (d,p).

Powell, Eleanor • Actress • Born Springfield, MA, November 21, 1912; died 1982. World-class tap artist who danced her way through a dozen successful MGM musicals in the late 1930s and early 40s before retiring from the screen in 1945—save for a guest role in *The Duchess of Idaho* (1950). Married to actor Glenn Ford from 1943 to 1959. • *George White's Scandals* 1935; *Born to Dance* 1936; *Broadway Melody of 1936* 1936; *Rosalie* 1937; *Broadway Melody of 1938* 1938; *Honolulu* 1939; *Broadway Melody of 1940* 1940; *Lady Be Good* 1941; *Ship Ahoy* 1942; *I Dood It* 1943; *Thousands Cheer* 1943; *Sensations* 1945; *The Great Morgan* 1946; *Duchess of Idaho* 1950.

Powell, Michael • Director, screenwriter, producer • Born Bekesbourne, Kent, England, September 30, 1905; died February 19, 1990, Avening, Gloucestershire, England. Michael Powell's introduction to the film business came at the age of 20, when, with the assistance of his father, he secured a job with Rex Ingram's film unit based in Nice, France. In the late 1920s, Powell worked at Elstree Studios for Harry Lachman and Alfred Hitchcock. During the early 1930s, Powell cut his directorial teeth on a number of forgettable, low budget "quota quickies" for independent production companies in England.

In 1938, after making *The Edge of the World* (1937), a personal exploration of man's battle with nature on an isolated island off the coast of Scotland, Powell was brought together with German scriptwriter Emric Pressburger to develop *The Spy in Black* (1939) as a vehicle for Conrad Veidt. Powell made two more films without Pressburger, including *The Thief of Bagdad* (1940), a remarkable children's fantasy film, before forming a partnership with Pressburger in their own production company, the Archers.

Some of the most notable Powell-Pressburger achievements include *The Life and Death of Colonel Blimp* (1944), whose satiric view of the British military incurred the wrath of Winston Churchill; *A Canterbury Tale* (1944) and *I Know Where I'm Going* (1945), films which were, according to Powell, "a crusade against materialism"; *A Matter of Life and Death/Stairway to Heaven* (1946), an epic fantasy film; and *The Red Shoes* (1948), the Archers' most prestigious effort, still cited as the best film ever made about the ballet.

The essence of Powell's visual style and his attitude towards art and life, however, are best displayed in *Black Narcissus* (1947) and *The Tales of Hoffmann* (1951). *Black Narcissus* chronicles the failure of a group of Anglican nuns to establish a mission in the Himalayan mountains. Powell shot virtually all of the film in a studio to maintain complete control over color, setting and atmosphere, which he employed to reveal character and theme. With its constant undercurrent of repressed sexuality and the mystical power of nature, the film also reveals the paganism of Powell's personal philosophy. Finally, it illustrates his preoccupation with mastering technique to achieve what he calls "the unity of art." For the film's dramatic climax, Powell first used what he calls "composed film." Brian Easdale wrote the music for the scene, even before the dramatic action was plotted out and measured with a stop watch. The sequence was then shot and edited to mirror the rhythms of the music. *The Tales of Hoffmann*, an eccentric, astonishingly expressionistc ballet-opera version of Offenbach's last work, stands as Powell's most magnificent attempt to fuse the arts into film form. Perhaps its only rival in this context is Disney's *Fantasia*.

After Powell and Pressburger dissolved their partnership in 1956, Powell's most notorious work was the controversial *Peeping Tom* (1960). This self-reflexive film is the story of a killer who stalks his female victims with a spear-and-mirror-equipped camera, to film them as they watch themselves die. At the time of its release the critical attacks on *Peeping Tom* were so vicious and extreme that they virtually terminated Powell's career. The film has since been revived and praised by Martin Scorsese, among others, as one of the great movies about the psychology of filmmaking and film viewing.

Although he is now acknowledged as one of England's foremost filmmakers, Michael Powell paid an enormous price for cultivating his personal vision within the context of a national cinema almost totally at odds with his artistic concerns. His emphasis on the bold uses of imagery and color has inspired a whole generation of filmmakers, including Ken Russell, Nicolas Roeg, John Boorman, and Derek Jarman. Married to editor Thelma Schoonmaker from 1984 until his death in 1990. JAG • *The Garden of Allah* 1927 (a); *The Fire Raisers* 1933 (d); *Perfect Understanding* 1933 (sc); *The Night of the Party* 1934 (d); *Red Ensign* 1934 (d); *The Love Test* 1935 (d); *Some Day* 1935 (d); *The Edge of the World* 1937 (d); *The Lion Has Wings* 1939 (d); *The Spy in Black* 1939 (d); *Contraband* 1940 (d,sc); *The Thief of Bagdad* 1940 (d); *49th Parallel* 1941 (d,p); *One of Our Aircraft Is Missing* 1942 (d,p,sc) **(AANBSC)**; *The Volunteer (short)* 1943 (d); *The Life and Death of Colonel Blimp* 1944 (d); *A Canterbury Tale* 1944 (d,p,sc,story); *I Know Where I'm Going* 1945 (d,p,story); *A Matter of Life and Death/Stairway to Heaven* 1946 (d); *Black Narcissus* 1947 (d,p,sc); *The Red Shoes* 1948 (d,sc); *The Small Back Room* 1948 (d); *The Elusive Pimpernel* 1950 (d); *Gone to Earth* 1950 (d,p,sc); *The Tales of Hoffmann* 1951 (d,p,sc); *The Sorcerer's Apprentice (short)* 1955 (d); *Battle of the River Plate* 1956 (d); *Ill Met By Moonlight* 1957 (d,p); *Peeping Tom* 1960 (d); *The Queen's Guards* 1961 (d); *Sebastian* 1968 (p); *Age of Consent* 1969 (d,p); *Pavlova* 1983 (sup—Western version).

Powell, William • Actor • Born William Horatio Powell, Pittsburgh, PA, July 29, 1892; died March 5, 1984, Palm Springs, CA. *Educ.* University of California; AADA, New York. Best remembered as Nick Charles of the "Thin Man" series, Powell was the epitome of the suave and debonair Hollywood leading man. He first appeared on screen in 1922's *Sherlock Holmes*, opposite Basil Rathbone, and made a smooth transition to talkies with hits such as *One Way Passage* (1932). With MGM for much of his career, Powell starred opposite some of Hollywood's greatest leading ladies, including Marilyn Monroe, Jean Harlow, Carole Lombard, to whom he was married from 1931 to 1933, and especially Myrna Loy. • *Sherlock Holmes* 1922 (a); *Outcast* 1922 (a); *When Knighthood Was in Flower* 1922 (a); *The Bright Shawl* 1923 (a); *Under the Red Robe* 1923 (a); *Dangerous Money* 1924 (a); *Romola* 1924 (a); *The Beautiful City* 1925 (a); *Faint Perfume* 1925 (a); *My Lady's Lips* 1925 (a); *Too Many Kisses* 1925 (a); *Aloma of the South Seas* 1926 (a); *Beau Geste* 1926 (a); *Desert Gold* 1926 (a); *The Great Gatsby* 1926 (a); *The Runaway* 1926 (a); *Sea Horses* 1926 (a); *Tin Gods* 1926 (a); *White Mice* 1926 (a); *Love's Greatest Mistake* 1927 (a); *Nevada* 1927 (a); *New York* 1927 (a); *Paid to Love* 1927 (a); *Senorita* 1927 (a); *She's a Sheik* 1927 (a); *Special Delivery* 1927 (a); *Time to Love* 1927 (a); *Beau Sabreur* 1928 (a); *The Dragnet* 1928 (a); *Feel My Pulse* 1928 (a); *Forgotten Faces* 1928 (a); *The Last Command* 1928 (a); *Partners in Crime* 1928 (a); *The Vanishing Pioneer* 1928 (a); *The Canary Murder Case* 1929 (a); *Charming Sinners* 1929 (a); *The Four Feathers* 1929 (a); *The Greene Murder Case* 1929 (a); *Interference* 1929 (a); *Pointed Heels* 1929 (a); *Behind the Make-Up* 1930 (a); *The Benson Murder Case* 1930 (a); *For the Defense* 1930 (a); *Paramount on Parade* 1930 (a); *Shadow of the Law* 1930 (a); *Street of Chance* 1930 (a); *Dishonored* 1931 (a); *Ladies' Man* 1931 (a); *Man of the World* 1931 (a); *The Road to Singapore* 1931 (a); *High Pressure* 1932 (a); *Jewel Robbery* 1932 (a); *Lawyer Man* 1932 (a); *One Way Passage* 1932 (a); *Double Harness* 1933 (a); *The Kennel Murder Case* 1933 (a); *Private Detective 62* 1933 (a); *Evelyn Prentice* 1934 (a); *The Key* 1934 (a); *Manhattan Melodrama* 1934 (a); *The Thin Man* 1934 (a) **(AANBA)**; *Escapade* 1935 (a); *Reckless* 1935 (a); *The Rendezvous* 1935 (a); *Star of Midnight* 1935 (a); *After the Thin Man* 1936 (a); *The Ex-Mrs. Bradford* 1936 (a); *The Great Ziegfeld* 1936 (a); *Libeled Lady* 1936 (a); *My Man Godfrey* 1936 (a) **(AANBA)**; *Double Wedding* 1937 (a); *The Emperor's Candlesticks* 1937 (a); *The Last of Mrs. Cheyney* 1937 (a); *The Baroness and the Butler* 1938 (a); *Another Thin Man* 1939 (a); *I Love You Again* 1940 (a); *Love Crazy* 1941 (a); *Shadow of the Thin Man* 1941 (a); *Crossroads* 1942 (a); *The Heavenly Body* 1943 (a); *The Youngest Profession* 1943 (a); *The Thin Man Goes Home* 1944 (a); *The Hoodlum Saint* 1946 (a); *Ziegfeld Follies* 1946 (a); *Life With Father* 1947 (a) **(AANBA)**; *The Senator Was Indiscreet* 1947 (a); *Song of the Thin Man* 1947 (a); *Mr. Peabody and the Mermaid* 1948 (a); *Dancing in the Dark* 1949 (a); *Take One False Step* 1949 (a); *It's a Big Country* 1951 (a); *The Treasure of Lost Canyon* 1952 (a); *The Girl Who Had Everything* 1953 (a); *How to Marry a Millionaire* 1953 (a); *Mister Roberts* 1955 (a); *It's Showtime* 1976 (archival footage).

Power, Tyrone • Actor • Born Tyrone Edmund Power, Jr., Cincinnati, OH, May 5, 1913; died 1958. Handsome romantic lead of the late 1930s and 40s whose affability and charm was put to good use in a number of stylish dramas. Power was memorable as a man searching for faith in *The Razor's Edge* (1946) and as the earnest, but ultimately caddish, defendant in *Witness For the Prosecution* (1957). Son of early American actor Tyrone Power, Sr.; husband of actresses Annabella (1939-48) and Linda Christian (1949-55); and father of Tyrone, Jr., and Romina, both of whom have appeared in films. • *Red Kimono* 1925 (a); *Ladies in Love* 1936 (a); *Cafe Metropole* 1937 (a); *Love Is News* 1937 (a); *Second Honeymoon* 1937 (a); *Thin Ice* 1937 (a); *Alexander's Ragtime Band* 1938 (a); *In Old Chicago* 1938 (a); *Marie Antoinette* 1938 (a); *Suez* 1938 (a); *Day-Time Wife* 1939 (a); *Jesse James* 1939 (a); *The Rains Came* 1939 (a); *Rose of Washington Square* 1939 (a); *Second Fiddle* 1939 (a); *Brigham Young, Frontiersman* 1940 (a); *Johnny Apollo* 1940 (a); *The Mark of Zorro* 1940 (a); *Blood and Sand* 1941 (a); *A Yank in the R.A.F.* 1941 (a); *The Black Swan* 1942 (a); *Son of Fury* 1942 (a); *This Above All* 1942 (a); *Crash Dive* 1943 (a); *The Razor's Edge* 1946 (a); *Captain From Castile* 1947 (a); *Nightmare Alley* 1947 (a); *The Luck of the Irish* 1948 (a); *That Wonderful Urge* 1948 (a); *Prince of Foxes* 1949 (a); *An American Guerrilla in the Philippines* 1950 (a); *The Black Rose* 1950 (a); *I'll Never Forget You* 1951 (a); *Rawhide* 1951 (a); *Diplomatic Courier* 1952 (a); *Pony Soldier* 1952 (a); *The Mississippi Gambler* 1953 (a); *King of the Khyber Rifles* 1954 (a); *The Long Gray Line* 1955 (a); *Untamed* 1955 (a); *The Eddy Duchin Story* 1956 (a); *Abandon Ship!* 1957 (a); *Rising of the Moon* 1957 (a); *The Sun Also Rises* 1957 (a); *Witness For the Prosecution* 1957 (a); *Going Hollywood: The War Years* 1988 (archival footage).

Praunheim, Rosa Von • See Von Praunheim, Rosa.

Preminger, Otto • Director, producer; also actor. • Born Otto Ludwig Preminger, Austria, December 5, 1906; died April 23, 1986, New York, NY. *Educ.* University of Vienna (law). Former assistant to German stage producer Max Reinhardt who began his directing career with the 1935 Broadway melodrama, *Libel*. Preminger then directed a couple of B films at 20th Century-Fox before a dispute with Darryl Zanuck temporary halted his behind-the-camera career. When he found himself in demand as an actor—Preminger's stern features and Viennese accent made him the perfect screen Nazi—he used this new popularity to maneuver his way back into the director's chair. Preminger made his breakthrough with the critical and commercial smash, *Laura* (1944), on which he took over the direction from Rouben Mamoulian. His subsequent work at Fox was disappointing and he began independently producing his own films, through his Carlyle Productions company, in the early 1950s. Preminger soon earned a reputation for turning out controversial works which broached previously taboo subjects such as drug addiction (*The Man With the Golden Arm* 1955). A skilled technician who lacked any consistently discernable style, his career encompassed polished successes including *Anatomy of a Murder* (1959), *Exodus* (1960), *Advise and Consent* (1962) and *Bunny Lake Is Missing* (1965), alongside notable flops such as *Saint Joan* (1957) and *Rosebud* (1975). Father, by stripper

Gypsy Rose Lee, of producer-screenwriter Eric Lee Preminger and brother of agent-turned-producer Ingo Preminger. • *Die Grosse Liebe* 1932 (d); *Under Your Spell* 1936 (d); *Danger - Love at Work* 1937 (d); *The Pied Piper* 1942 (a); *Margin For Error* 1943 (a,d); *They Got Me Covered* 1943 (a); *In the Meantime, Darling* 1944 (d,p); *Laura* 1944 (d,p) **(AANBD)**; *Fallen Angel* 1945 (d,p); *A Royal Scandal* 1945 (d); *Centennial Summer* 1946 (d,p); *Daisy Kenyon* 1947 (d,p); *Forever Amber* 1947 (d); *The Fan* 1949 (d,p); *Whirlpool* 1949 (d,p); *Where the Sidewalk Ends* 1950 (d,p); *The 13th Letter* 1951 (d,p); *Angel Face* 1952 (d,p); *The Moon Is Blue* 1953 (d,p); *Stalag 17* 1953 (a); *Carmen Jones* 1954 (d,p); *River of No Return* 1954 (d); *The Court Martial of Billy Mitchell* 1955 (d); *The Man With the Golden Arm* 1955 (d,p); *Bonjour Tristesse* 1957 (d,p); *Saint Joan* 1957 (d,p); *Anatomy of a Murder* 1959 (d,p); *Porgy and Bess* 1959 (d); *Exodus* 1960 (d,p); *Advise and Consent* 1962 (d,p); *The Cardinal* 1963 (d,p) **(AANBD)**; *Bunny Lake Is Missing* 1965 (d,p); *In Harm's Way* 1965 (d,p); *Hurry Sundown* 1967 (d,p); *Skidoo* 1968 (d,p); *Tell Me That You Love Me, Junie Moon* 1970 (d,p); *Such Good Friends* 1971 (d,p); *Rosebud* 1975 (d,p); *Hollywood on Trial* 1976 (a); *The Human Factor* 1979 (d,p).

Presley, Elvis • Singer, actor • Born Elvis Aron Presley, Tupelo, MS, January 8, 1935; died August 16, 1977, Memphis, TN. When Elvis Presley's identical twin died at birth, his mother interpreted it as a divine omen of her surviving son's destiny. The family moved to Memphis, Tennessee, when he was 13, and there, in 1953, the 17-year-old Presley went into the recording studio at Sun Records and paid five dollars to record a two-sided single as a birthday present for his mother. "I don't sing like nobody," he told the engineer. An impressed secretary made a note of his name and passed it along to the owner of Sun Records, Sam Phillips.

Presley was by far the most charismatic of the phenomenal first wave of rock'n'rollers recorded by Sam Phillips—along with the likes of Carl Perkins, Johnny Cash, Jerry Lee Lewis, Roy Orbison and Charlie Rich. According to legend, Phillips, who had produced a string of R&B hits by such artists as Howlin' Wolf and Rufus Thomas in the early 1950s, had proclaimed that if he could find a young white singer with the sound and spirit of a black man, he would make a billion dollars (Phillips himself staked his money on Carl Perkins, selling Presley's contract, along with the rights to his 5 Sun singles to RCA for $35,000). Presley went on to achieve explosive success with RCA.

In 1956, his hometown of Tupelo, Mississippi, declared an "Elvis Presley Day" on the occasion of his first return performance since winning second prize for singing "Old Shep" at the Mississippi-Alabama Fair and Dairy Show in 1945. This time, the National Guard had to be called in to maintain order. Teenagers screamed and fainted at his concerts. According to troubled experts of the day, Presley had single-handedly unleashed the pent-up sexual energy of McCarthy-era middle America. The end of Western civilization and free enterprise could not be far behind. TV cameramen were instructed to film "Elvis the Pelvis" only from the waist up.

Presley himself, however, considered his singing career primarily as a means to an end. His real ambition all along was to be a movie star. From 1956 to 1969, Presley starred in 33 feature films, most of them following nearly identical scripts, tailored to showcase Presley, and all subject to approval by Presley's tyrannical manager, "Colonel" Tom Parker. There were several exceptions. *Jailhouse Rock* (1957), captures Presley in all his snarling, shaking teen-idol glory, and features his choreography for the terrific title number. *Flaming Star* (1960) features Elvis as a half-breed Indian who must choose sides, and shows the instinctive actor within him that might have flourished had he escaped Parker's greedy machinations. And *Viva Las Vegas* (1964), despite being hampered by the typical Presley-pic plot, pairs Elvis with the explosive Ann-Margret, the only co-star he ever had who equaled him in musical talent and sexual charisma (rumor has it that Parker was made uncomfortable seeing Presley's talent played off of someone who measured up to him).

Although his movies consistently made money at the box office, Presley's artistic reputation suffered. With the emergence of such artists as Bob Dylan, the Beatles and the Rolling Stones in the early 1960s, Presley all but vanished from the rock'n'roll scene. In 1968, friends persuaded Elvis to veto Colonel Parker's concept for a sappy TV Christmas special. Instead, Elvis made a triumphant comeback in the "Singer Special," where he literally wiggled out of the "wholesome" movie persona that had so severely constrained him for more than a decade (not until 1968's *Live a Little, Love a Little* did an Elvis character "go all the way"). The "Singer Special" was followed by a smash comeback album, concert appearances and hit singles such as "In the Ghetto" and "Suspicious Minds." Presley's regained popularity continued to grow, even as his health declined. He died of a heart attack at his "Graceland" mansion in Memphis at the age of 42.

Although Elvis Presley's greatest contribution unquestionably came from his earliest recordings, circa 1955-57, when he was the young, sneering rebel, his later image as well remains a strong presence in the popular consciousness. Since his death, the adoration of his fans has been known to reach cultish, even religious, proportions. Theories and rumors concerning his death—even the reality of his death—continue as a staple of tabloid journalism. (Well, why *is* his name misspelled "Elvis Aaron Presley" on his tombstone? His middle name was "Aron," with only one "a"). DH • *Love Me Tender* 1956 (a,song); *Jailhouse Rock* 1957 (a); *Loving You* 1957 (a); *King Creole* 1958 (a,song); *Flaming Star* 1960 (a); *G.I. Blues* 1960 (a); *Blue Hawaii* 1961 (a); *Wild in the Country* 1961 (a); *Follow That Dream* 1962 (a); *Girls! Girls! Girls!* 1962 (a); *Kid Galahad* 1962 (a); *Fun in Acapulco* 1963 (a); *It Happened at the World's Fair* 1963 (a); *Scorpio Rising* 1963 (song); *Kissin' Cousins* 1964 (a); *Roustabout* 1964 (a); *Viva Las Vegas* 1964 (a); *Girl Happy* 1965 (a); *Harum Scarum* 1965 (a,song); *Tickle Me* 1965 (a); *Frankie and Johnnie* 1966 (a); *Paradise Hawaiian Style* 1966 (a); *Spinout* 1966 (a); *Clambake* 1967 (a); *Double Trouble* 1967 (a); *Easy Come, Easy Go* 1967 (a); *Live a Little, Love a Little* 1968 (a); *Speedway* 1968 (a); *Stay Away, Joe* 1968 (a); *Change of Habit* 1969 (a); *Charro!* 1969 (a); *The Trouble With Girls* 1969 (a); *Elvis That's the Way It Is* 1970 (a,songs); *Warnung Vor Einer Heiligen Nutte* 1971 (m); *Elvis on Tour* 1972 (a,songs); *Faustrecht der Freiheit* 1975 (song); *Hempa's Bar* 1977 (m); *Touched By Love* 1979 (song); *Out of the Blue* 1980 (songs); *Shifshuf Naim* 1981 (song); *This Is Elvis* 1981 (songs); *Diner* 1982 (songs); *This Is Spinal Tap* 1984 (song); *Desert Hearts* 1985 (song); *Porky's Revenge* 1985 (song); *Static* 1986 (song); *Dear America* 1987 (song); *Cocktail* 1988 (song); *Heartbreak Hotel* 1988 (songs); *Catch Me If You Can* 1989 (song); *Great Balls of Fire* 1989 (song); *Heart of Dixie* 1989 (song); *She-Devil* 1989 (song); *Joe Versus the Volcano* 1990 (song); *Wild at Heart* 1990 (song).

Pressburger, Emeric • Producer, screenwriter; also director. • Born Imre Pressburger, Miskolc, Hungary, December 5, 1902; died February 5, 1988, Saxstead, England. *Educ.* University of Prague, Czechoslovakia; University of Stuttgart, Germany. Began his career writing screenplays in both Germany and France, notably for Robert Siodmak, before arriving in England in 1936. Pressburger contributed to several Alexander Korda projects before collaborating with director Michael Powell for the first time on the entertaining, somewhat convoluted thriller, *The Spy in Black/U-Boat 29* (1939). Powell and Pressburger became official partners in 1942, forming the Archers production company and co-writing, co-producing and co-directing 14 films between 1942 and 1956. Among their most outstanding productions were

Black Narcissus (1947), *The Red Shoes* (1948) and *The Tales of Hoffmann* (1951).

Pressburger's later efforts, including his only film as a solo director, *Twice Upon a Time* (1953), were generally less effective than his earlier work. He wrote Michael Anderson's adroitly handled WWII thriller *Operation Crossbow* (1965) under the pseudonym Richard Imrie and briefly re-teamed with Powell on the 1972 British children's film, *The Boy Who Turned Yellow*. See also Powell, Michael. • *La Vie Parisienne* 1935 (sc); *One Rainy Afternoon* 1936 (from play "Monsieur Sans Gène"); *The Challenge* 1938 (sc); *The Spy In Black/U-Boat 29* 1939 (sc); *Contraband* 1940 (d,story); *49th Parallel* 1941 (sc,scenario,story); *The Invaders* 1942 **(AANBSC)**; *One of Our Aircraft Is Missing* 1942 (d,p,sc) **(AANBSC)**; *The Volunteer (short)* 1943 (d); *A Canterbury Tale* 1944 (d,p,sc,story); *I Know Where I'm Going* 1945 (d,p,story); *A Matter of Life and Death* 1946 (d); *Black Narcissus* 1947 (d,p,sc); *The Red Shoes* 1948 (d,sc) **(AANBST)**; *The Small Back Room* 1948 (d); *The Elusive Pimpernel* 1950 (d); *Gone to Earth* 1950 (p,sc); *The Tales of Hoffmann* 1951 (d,p,sc); *Twice Upon a Time* 1953 (d); *Battle of the River Plate* 1956 (d); *Ill Met By Moonlight* 1957 (d,p); *Behold a Pale Horse* 1964 (from story "Killing a Mouse on Sunday"); *Operation Crossbow* 1965 (sc); *The Boy Who Turned Yellow* 1972 (p).

Pressman, Edward R. • *aka* Edward Pressman • Producer • Born New York, NY. *Educ.* Stanford; London School of Economics. Began his career in England in partnership with director Paul Williams and has since produced a wide range of films which have introduced unknown or unproven talents to American audiences. Pressman produced the early Brian DePalma feature, *Sisters* (1973), Terrence Malick's acclaimed debut, *Badlands* (1973), R.W. Fassbinder's first English-language film, *Despair* (1978), and three Oliver Stone movies, including his directorial debut, *The Hand* (1981). He has also worked with Wolfgang Peterson, David Hare, Bob Swaim, David Byrne and Alex Cox. • *Out of It* 1969 (p); *The Revolutionary* 1970 (p); *Dealing: Or the Berkeley-to-Boston Forty-Brick Lost-Bag Blues* 1972 (p); *Badlands* 1973 (exec.p); *Sisters* 1973 (p); *Phantom of the Paradise* 1974 (p); *Despair* 1978 (exec.p); *Old Boyfriends* 1978 (p); *Paradise Alley* 1978 (exec.p); *Heart Beat* 1979 (exec.p); *Victoria* 1979 (exec.p); *You Better Watch Out* 1980 (p); *Das Boot* 1981 (exec.p); *Flicks* 1981 (exec.p); *The Hand* 1981 (p); *Conan the Barbarian* 1982 (exec.p); *The Pirates of Penzance* 1982 (exec.p); *Crimewave* 1985 (a,exec.p); *Plenty* 1985 (p); *Good Morning Babylon* 1986 (exec.p); *Half Moon Street* 1986 (exec.p); *True Stories* 1986 (exec.p); *Masters of the Universe* 1987 (exec.p); *Walker* 1987 (exec.p); *Wall Street* 1987 (p); *Cherry 2000* 1988 (p); *Paris By Night* 1988 (exec.p); *Talk Radio* 1988 (p); *Blue Steel* 1989 (p); *Martians Go Home* 1990 (exec.p); *Reversal of Fortune* 1990 (p); *To Sleep With Anger* 1990 (exec.p); *Waiting For the Light* 1990 (exec.p).

Preston, Kelly • Actress • Born Honolulu, HI. *Educ.* UCLA (drama); USC, Los Angeles (drama). Attractive young actress of the 1980s. Preston played the young woman whose brutal murder Roy Scheider (her lover) is forced to witness on film in *52 Pick-Up* (1986). • *Christine* 1983; *Metalstorm: The Destruction of Jared-Syn* 1983; *Mischief* 1985; *Secret Admirer* 1985; *52 Pick-Up* 1986; *SpaceCamp* 1986; *Amazon Women on the Moon* 1987; *Love at Stake* 1987; *A Tiger's Tale* 1987; *Spellbinder* 1988; *Twins* 1988; *The Experts* 1989; *Run* 1991.

Preston, Robert • Actor • Born Robert Preston Meservey, Newton Highlands, MA, June 8, 1918; died March 21, 1987, Santa Barbara, CA. *Educ.* Pasadena Playhouse. Dynamic song-and-dance man from the stage who began appearing in B films in the late 1930s. Preston is best known as the effusive huckster in *The Music Man* (1962) and for two highly amusing performances in the Blake Edwards farces, *S.O.B.* (1981) and *Victor/Victoria* (1982). • *Illegal Traffic* 1938; *King of Alcatraz* 1938; *Beau Geste* 1939; *Disbarred* 1939; *Union Pacific* 1939; *Moon Over Burma* 1940; *North West Mounted Police* 1940; *Typhoon* 1940; *The Lady From Cheyenne* 1941; *Midnight Angel* 1941; *New York Town* 1941; *The Night of January 16th* 1941; *Parachute Battalion* 1941; *Pacific Blackout* 1942; *Reap the Wild Wind* 1942; *This Gun For Hire* 1942; *Wake Island* 1942; *Night Plane From Chungking* 1943; *The Macomber Affair* 1947; *Variety Girl* 1947; *Wild Harvest* 1947; *Big City* 1948; *Blood on the Moon* 1948; *The Lady Gambles* 1949; *Tulsa* 1949; *Whispering Smith* 1949; *The Sundowners* 1950; *Best of the Badmen* 1951; *My Outlaw Brother* 1951; *When I Grow Up* 1951; *Face to Face* 1952; *The Last Frontier* 1955; *The Dark at the Top of the Stairs* 1960; *How the West Was Won* 1962; *The Music Man* 1962; *All the Way Home* 1963; *Island of Love* 1963; *Child's Play* 1972; *Junior Bonner* 1972; *Mame* 1974; *Semi-Tough* 1977; *S.O.B.* 1981; *Victor/Victoria* 1982 **(AANBSA)**; *The Last Starfighter* 1984.

Prévert, Jacques • Poet, screenwriter; also actor. • Born Neuilly-sur-Seine, France, February 4, 1900; died 1977. Noted French surrealist poet and one of the most influential scenarists of the 1930s and 40s. Prévert contributed to most of the landmark films of "poetic realism," collaborating with Jean Renoir (*Le Crime de Monsieur Lange* 1936), Jean Gremillon (*Stormy Waters* 1941) and, most notably, Marcel Carné (*Quai des brumes* 1938, *Le jour se lève* 1939, *Children of Paradise* 1945). His last collaboration with Carné was on the underrated *Les portes de la nuit* (1946), for which Prévert wrote the now-famous song "Autumn Leaves," used again in Robert Aldrich's 1956 film of the same name.

Prévert later collaborated in a more surrealistic, satirical vein with his director brother Pierre on three films—*L'Affaire est dans le sac* (1932), *Adieu Leonard* (1943) and *Voyage Surprise* (1946)—which all failed miserably at the box office. • *L'Affaire est dans le sac* 1932 (sc); *L'Atalante* 1934 (a); *Le Crime de Monsieur Lange* 1936 (sc); *Quai des brumes* 1938 (sc); *Le jour se lève* 1939 (sc); *Stormy Waters* 1941 (sc); *Les Visiteurs du soir* 1942 (sc); *Adieu Leonard* 1943 (sc); *Children Of Paradise* 1945 (sc) **(AANBSC)**; *Les portes de la nuit* 1946 (sc); *Voyage Surprise* 1946 (sc); *Autumn Leaves* 1956 (song).

Previn, Andre • Composer; also conductor, arranger, musical director. • Born Berlin, April 6, 1929. Began working in film in the late 1940s and contributed memorable scores to a number of powerful dramas as well as musical direction/supervision on several big budget musicals of the 1950s and 60s, notably *Gigi* (1958) and *Porgy and Bess* (1959). Formerly married to actress Mia Farrow. • *She's For Me* 1943 (m.dir); *Act of Violence* 1948 (m.cond); *Border Incident* 1949 (m.dir); *Challenge to Lassie* 1949 (m); *Scene of the Crime* 1949 (m); *The Secret Garden* 1949 (m.dir); *The Sun Comes Up* 1949 (m); *Tension* 1949 (m); *Dial 1119* 1950 (m); *Kim* 1950 (m); *The Outriders* 1950 (m); *Shadow on the Wall* 1950 (m); *Three Little Words* 1950 (m.dir) **(AANBM)**; *Cause For Alarm* 1951 (m); *Give a Girl a Break* 1953 (m.dir); *Kiss Me Kate* 1953 (m) **(AANBM)**; *Small Town Girl* 1953 (m.dir); *Bad Day at Black Rock* 1954 (m); *It's Always Fair Weather* 1955 (m,m.dir) **(AANBM)**; *Kismet* 1955 (m.dir); *The Catered Affair* 1956 (m); *The Fastest Gun Alive* 1956 (m); *Invitation to the Dance* 1956 (m,m.dir); *Designing Woman* 1957 (m); *Hot Summer Night* 1957 (m); *House of Numbers* 1957 (m); *Silk Stockings* 1957 (m.dir); *Gigi* 1958 (m.sup,m.cond) **(AABM)**; *Porgy and Bess* 1959 (m.dir) **(AABM)**; *Elmer Gantry* 1960 (m) **(AANBM)**; *Pepe* 1960 (a) **(AANBS)**; *The Subterraneans* 1960 (a,m); *All in a Night's Work* 1961 (m); *One, Two, Three* 1961 (m); *The Four Horsemen of the Apocalypse* 1962 (m); *Long Day's Journey Into Night* 1962 (m); *Two For the Seesaw* 1962 (m) **(AANBS)**; *Irma la Douce* 1963 (m) **(AABM)**; *Dead Ringer* 1964 (m); *Goodbye, Charlie* 1964 (m,song); *Kiss Me, Stupid* 1964 (m); *My Fair Lady* 1964 (m.dir) **(AABM)**; *Inside Daisy Clover*

1965 (m); *The Fortune Cookie* 1966 (m); *Harper* 1966 (song); *Thoroughly Modern Millie* 1967 (m) **(AANBM)**; *Valley of the Dolls* 1967 (song); *Paint Your Wagon* 1969 (add.m,song); *The Music Lovers* 1971 (m.dir); *Jesus Christ Superstar* 1973 (m.cond) **(AANBSS)**; *Rollerball* 1975 (m.sup); *The Elephant Man* 1980 (m); *Six Weeks* 1982 (m); *Romeo and Juliet* 1990 (m.cond).

Price, Richard • American screenwriter, novelist; also actor. • Price had two of his popular, streetwise novels adapted for film (*Bloodbrothers* 1978, *The Wanderers* 1979) before embarking on a successful career as an original screenwriter, notably with *The Color of Money* (1986) and *Sea of Love* (1989). • *Bloodbrothers* 1978 (from novel); *The Wanderers* 1979 (a,from novel); *The Color of Money* 1986 (a,sc) **(AANBSC)**; *Streets of Gold* 1986 (sc); *Arena Brains (short)* 1987 (a,sc); *New York Stories* 1989 (a,screenplay "Life Lessons"); *Sea of Love* 1989 (sc).

Price, Vincent • Actor • Born St. Louis, MO, May 27, 1911. *Educ.* Yale (art history, English); University of London (fine arts); Nuremberg University. Cultured, debonair stage star who gained initial attention in England and made his Hollywood debut in 1938. Although he turned in strong performances in straight dramas—notably Otto Preminger's *Laura* (1944) and Anatole Litvak's *The Long Night* (1947)—Price was soon associated almost exclusively with horror films. From the early 1950s he starred in a host of chillers, the best of which include *House of Wax* (1953), *The Fly* (1958), *House on Haunted Hill* (1958), *The Abominable Dr. Phibes* (1971) and a series of Edgar Allen Poe adaptations produced by Roger Corman in the early 1960s.

Price is also a fine arts lecturer of some note and has published books on art and cuisine, ranging from *Drawings of Delacroix* (1962) to *The Come Into the Kitchen Cook Book* (1969), co-authored with second wife Mary Price (nee Grant). His third wife is actress Coral Browne. • *Service De Luxe* 1938 (a); *The Private Lives of Elizabeth and Essex* 1939 (a); *Tower of London* 1939 (a); *Brigham Young, Frontiersman* 1940 (a); *Green Hell* 1940 (a); *The House of the Seven Gables* 1940 (a); *Hudson's Bay* 1940 (a); *The Invisible Man Returns* 1940 (a); *The Song of Bernadette* 1943 (a); *The Eve of St. Mark* 1944 (a); *Laura* 1944 (a); *Wilson* 1944 (a); *The Keys of the Kingdom* 1945 (a); *Leave Her to Heaven* 1945 (a); *A Royal Scandal* 1945 (a); *Dragonwyck* 1946 (a); *Shock* 1946 (a); *The Long Night* 1947 (a); *Moss Rose* 1947 (a); *The Web* 1947 (a); *Rogue's Regiment* 1948 (a); *The Three Musketeers* 1948 (a); *Up in Central Park* 1948 (a); *Bagdad* 1949 (a); *The Bribe* 1949 (a); *The Baron of Arizona* 1950 (a); *Champagne For Caesar* 1950 (a); *Curtain Call At Cactus Creek* 1950 (a); *Adventures of Captain Fabian* 1951 (a); *His Kind of Woman* 1951 (a); *The Las Vegas Story* 1952 (a); *House of Wax* 1953 (a); *Dangerous Mission* 1954 (a); *The Mad Magician* 1954 (a); *Serenade* 1955 (a); *Son of Sinbad* 1955 (a); *The Ten Commandments* 1956 (a); *While The City Sleeps* 1956 (a); *The Story of Mankind* 1957 (a); *The Fly* 1958 (a); *House on Haunted Hill* 1958 (a); *The Bat* 1959 (a); *The Big Circus* 1959 (a); *Return of the Fly* 1959 (a); *The Tingler* 1959 (a); *House of Usher* 1960 (a); *Master of the World* 1961 (a); *The Pit and the Pendulum* 1961 (a); *Confessions of an Opium Eater* 1962 (a); *Convicts Four* 1962 (a); *Tales of Terror* 1962 (a); *Tower of London* 1962 (a); *Beach Party* 1963 (a); *Diary of a Madman* 1963 (a); *The Haunted Palace* 1963 (a); *The Raven* 1963 (a); *Twice Told Tales* 1963 (a); *The Comedy of Terrors* 1964 (a); *The Last Man on Earth* 1964 (a); *The Masque of the Red Death* 1964 (a); *Dr. Goldfoot and the Bikini Machine* 1965 (a); *The Tomb of Ligeia* 1965 (a); *War Gods of the Deep* 1965 (a); *The Jackals* 1967 (a); *Conqueror Worm* 1968 (a); *More Dead Than Alive* 1969 (a); *The Oblong Box* 1969 (a); *The Trouble With Girls* 1969 (a); *Cry of the Banshee* 1970 (a); *Scream and Scream Again* 1970 (a); *The Abominable Doctor Phibes* 1971 (a); *Doctor Phibes Rises Again* 1972 (a); *Theatre of Blood* 1973 (a); *It's Not the Size That Counts* 1974 (a); *Madhouse* 1974 (a); *Journey Into Fear* 1976 (a); *Scavenger Hunt* 1979 (a); *The Monster Club* 1981 (a); *House of the Long Shadows* 1982 (a); *Making Michael Jackson's Thriller* 1983 (narration—"Thriller"); *Bloodbath at the House of Death* 1984 (a); *The Great Mouse Detective* 1986 (a); *The Offspring* 1987 (a); *The Whales of August* 1987 (a); *Dead Heat* 1988 (a); *Backtrack* 1990 (a); *Edward Scissorhands* 1990 (a).

Prince • Singer, songwriter, actor, director • Born Prince Rogers Nelson, Minneapolis, MN, 1960. Dynamic, innovative composer and performer whose best-selling albums blend rock, jazz, funk and rap and have confirmed him as one of the most influential forces in contemporary popular music. Prince's forays into film have been somewhat less fortunate; he made his screen acting debut in the semi-autobiographical *Purple Rain* (1984) and went on to direct, star in and score three highly stylized, narcissistic flops, *Under the Cherry Moon* (1986), *Sign o'the Times* (1987) and *Graffiti Bridge* (1990). • *Purple Rain* 1984 (a,m,m.prod,songs) **(AABSS)**; *Under the Cherry Moon* 1986 (a,d,m,m.perf,songs); *Sign o' the Times* 1987 (a,d,sc,m,m.arr,m.prod,songs); *Batman* 1989 (songs); *Graffiti Bridge* 1990 (a,d,sc,m,songs).

Prochnow, Jurgen • Actor • Born Berlin. *Educ.* Volkswanschule, Essen. Stage and screen performer who came to international prominence with his roles in Volker Schlondorff ad Margarethe Von Trotta's *The Lost Honor of Katharina Blum* (1975) and, as the captain of the ill-fated submarine, in Wolfgang Peterson's gripping WWII drama, *Das Boot* (1981). Prochnow began appearing in American features in 1982. • *Zoff* 1971; *Zartlichkeit der Wolfe* 1973; *Die Verrohung des Franz Blum* 1974; *Die Verlorene Ehre der Katharina Blum/The Lost Honor of Katharina Blum* 1975; *Die Konsequenz/The Consequence* 1977; *Einer von uns Beiden* 1978; *Unter Verschluss* 1979; *Soweit das Auge reicht* 1980; *Das Boot* 1981; *Comeback* 1982; *Krieg und Frieden* 1982; *The Keep* 1983; *Der Bulle und das Mädchen* 1985; *Dune* 1985; *Killing Cars* 1985; *Terminus* 1986; *Beverly Hills Cop II* 1987; *Devil's Paradise* 1987; *The Seventh Sign* 1988; *A Dry White Season* 1989; *The Fourth War* 1990; *The Man Inside* 1990.

Prosky, Robert • Actor • Born Philadelphia, PA. *Educ.* Temple University, PA; American Theatre Wing, New York. Likeable, craggy-faced stage veteran who came to prominence as the endearing Sgt. Jablonski in TV's "Hill Street Blues." Prosky made his film debut in 1981 and turned in a memorable performance as the avuncular mob boss in David Mamet's *Things Change* (1988). • *Thief* 1981; *Hanky Panky* 1982; *Monsignor* 1982; *Christine* 1983; *The Keep* 1983; *The Lords of Discipline* 1983; *The Natural* 1984; *Big Shots* 1987; *Broadcast News* 1987; *Outrageous Fortune* 1987; *The Great Outdoors* 1988; *Things Change* 1988; *Loose Cannons* 1989; *Dangerous Pursuit* 1990; *Funny About Love* 1990; *Green Card* 1990; *Gremlins 2: The New Batch* 1990; *Life in the Food Chain* 1991.

Pryce, Jonathan • Actor • Born North Wales, June 1, 1947. *Educ.* RADA, London. Intelligent, disciplined performer of stage, screen and TV who won a best supporting actor Tony for his 1977 Broadway debut, in *Comedians*. Price is best known on film for his roles as a manipulative journalist, in *The Ploughman's Lunch* (1983), and as the hapless clerk at the center of Terry Gilliam's dystopian epic, *Brazil* (1985). He became a figure of controversy in August 1990, when Actors' Equity barred Pryce from reprising his acclaimed role in the smash West End musical *Miss Saigon* in the play's New York version. (Equity objected to a Caucasian actor portraying a Eurasian character.) The ruling was subsequently overturned. • *Voyage of the Damned* 1976; *Breaking Glass* 1980; *Loophole* 1981; *Praying Mantis* 1982; *The Ploughman's Lunch* 1983; *Something Wicked This Way Comes* 1983; *Brazil* 1985; *The Doctor and the Devils* 1985; *Haunted Honeymoon* 1986; *Jumpin' Jack Flash* 1986; *Hotel London*

1987; *Man on Fire* 1987; *The Adventures of Baron Munchausen* 1988; *Consuming Passions* 1988; *The Rachel Papers* 1989.

Pryor, Richard • Actor, comedian; also screenwriter, producer, director. • Born Peoria, IL, December 1, 1940. The foremost black comedian of his generation, Pryor's searing, profane, socially astute routines have provoked thought and anger as well as laughter. He established himself as a successful nightclub performer and TV writer in the mid-1960s and made his film debut in the 1967 comedy, *The Busy Body.* Pryor's first memorable role was as "The Piano Man" in *Lady Sings the Blues* (1972) and he went on to enliven a host of urban romps such as *Uptown Saturday Night* (1974) and *Car Wash* (1976). He co-scripted the classic Mel Brooks western spoof, *Blazing Saddles* (1974), and teamed with Gene Wilder in a series of popular buddy movies including *Silver Streak* (1976) and *Stir Crazy* (1980). His first feature as a director was *Richard Pryor Here and Now* (1983), one of three films to have been made of his standup performances. Pryor has also won five Grammy awards for his comic albums. • *The Busy Body* 1967 (a); *Wild in the Streets* 1968 (a); *The Phynx* 1970 (a); *You've Got to Walk It Like You Talk It or You'll Lose That Beat* 1971 (a); *Dynamite Chicken* 1972 (a); *Lady Sings the Blues* 1972 (a); *Wattstax* 1972 (a); *Hit* 1973 (a); *The Mack* 1973 (a); *Some Call It Loving* 1973 (a); *Blazing Saddles* 1974 (sc); *Uptown Saturday Night* 1974 (a); *Adios Amigo* 1976 (a); *The Bingo Long Traveling All-Stars and Motor Kings* 1976 (a); *Car Wash* 1976 (a); *Silver Streak* 1976 (a); *Greased Lightning* 1977 (a); *Which Way Is Up?* 1977 (a); *Blue Collar* 1978 (a); *California Suite* 1978 (a); *The Wiz* 1978 (a); *The Muppet Movie* 1979 (a); *Richard Pryor Live in Concert* 1979 (a,sc); *In God We Trust* 1980 (a); *Stir Crazy* 1980 (a); *Wholly Moses!* 1980 (a); *Bustin' Loose* 1981 (a,p,story); *Richard Pryor Live on the Sunset Strip* 1982 (a,p,sc); *Some Kind of Hero* 1982 (a); *The Toy* 1982 (a); *Richard Pryor Here and Now* 1983 (a,d,sc); *Superman III* 1983 (a); *Brewster's Millions* 1985 (a); *Jo Jo Dancer, Your Life Is Calling* 1986 (a,d,p,sc); *Critical Condition* 1987 (a); *Moving* 1988 (a); *Harlem Nights* 1989 (a); *See No Evil, Hear No Evil* 1989 (a).

Pudovkin, Vsevolod • Director, screenwriter; also actor, theorist. • Born Vsevolod Illarianovich Pudovkin, Penza, Russia, February 16, 1893; died June 20, 1953, Riga, Latvia, USSR. *Educ.* University of Moscow (chemistry); GIK, Moscow. Pudovkin is often designated as the second great artist of the Soviet silent film; his accomplishments have often taken a back seat to those of his more bellicose contemporary, Sergei Eisenstein. The difference between the two directors is typified in the oft-quoted statement of French critic Léon Moussinac: "Pudovkin's films resemble a song, Eisenstein's a scream." But if Eisenstein gained notoriety as the more resolutely avant-garde film artist, it was Pudovkin who arguably made the more enduring contributions to the medium, refining the body of techniques—pioneered by D.W. Griffith—which today compose the seamless continuity of the psychological film.

Pudovkin's entrance into the arts came at the relatively late age of 27. After studying chemistry, he was drafted into the military service, was wounded in 1915 and spent three years in a prisoner of war camp. During that time he learned to speak English, German and Polish. Upon his release, Pudovkin went to work in the laboratory of a military plant, but a viewing of Griffith's *Intolerance* had a profound effect on him and in 1920 he decided to abandon chemistry in favor of a career in cinema.

Pudovkin began to study under Vladimir Gardin, one of the few successful prewar directors to continue working after the Revolution. Working as both actor and assistant director, Pudovkin's projects with Gardin included *Sickle and Hammer* and *Hunger...Hunger...Hunger* (both 1921), the latter a film which attempted to increase public awareness about a famine devastating the Ukraine.

In 1922 Pudovkin left Gardin to join the seminal group of film talents—which included Eisenstein—working under Lev Kuleshov at the State Film School. There he participated in the famous series of editing experiments designed to demonstrate how montage is responsible for the psychological coherence of cinematic cognition. For the group's first feature, *The Extraordinary Adventures of Mr. West in the Land of the Bolsheviks* (1924), Pudovkin wrote the screenplay, was an assistant director, and played a role. He also wore several hats, as writer, designer, and actor, in the workshop's next project, *The Death Ray* (1925)—a film intended to showcase the collective's comprehensive knowledge of the medium.

Pudovkin was commissioned by "Mezraboom-Russ" to make an educational film popularizing the principles of Pavlov's studies in reflex conditioning. *Mechanics of the Brain* (1926) allowed the director to practice a disciplined application of his principles of film exposition; it also initiated his career-long relationship with cameraman Anatoli Golovnya, who worked almost exclusively with Pudovkin. Before this project was completed, Pudovkin directed a short, *Chess Fever* (1925), a comedy which incorporated footage from Moscow's International Chess Tournament of 1925.

Pudovkin's next film would secure his place in the history of cinema. Adapted from Maxim Gorky's novel by Pudovkin's frequent scenarist, Nathan Zarkhi, *Mother* (1926) distinguishes Pudovkin as a director of economy and precision. The film demonstrates his methodological differences with Eisenstein; Pudovkin advocated a theory of "linkage," in which montage "builds" not for an Eisensteinian abstraction but the impact of emotional identification. To support that theory, Pudovkin choses to structure his tale of the Revolution around its effect on an individual.

His next project, *The End of St. Petersburg* (1927), was, like Eisenstein's *October* (1928), commissioned in celebration of the tenth anniversary of the Revolution. The Russian public, familiar with the rivalry between the two men, saw the films as a way of comparing the virtues of their philosophies. Pudovkin's film, the first of many to benefit from the assistance of Mikhail Doller, was well-received and its sophisticated analysis of the Revolution is considered by some critics to be superior to Eisenstein's effort.

Pudovkin's later films saw the director "increasingly seduced by the charm of the image," as in *The Heir of Genghis Khan/Storm Over Asia* (1928), a film on which Pudovkin also began to run afoul of the stringent and constricting ideological specifications of the Party. Although popular with audiences and well-received abroad, the film was officially condemned for the "formalist indulgence" of its cinematic sheen. Pudovkin's last silent film, *The Heir of Genghis Khan* achieved a level of accomplishment and recognition that the director would never reach again.

To contemporary film students, Pudovkin is perhaps best known for his books of film theory, *Film Director and Film Material* (1926) and *Film Scenario and Its Theory* (1926), which were later combined into one volume, *Film Technique.* Although many of his ideas are tied to the techniques of silent film, Pudovkin's writing is still studied in many film courses all over the world. RH • *In Days of Struggle* 1920 (a); *Sickle and Hammer* 1921 (d,a); *Hunger...Hunger...Hunger* 1921 (d,sc); *The Locksmith and the Chancellor* 1923 (sc); *The Extraordinary Adventures of Mr. West in the Land of Bolsheviks* 1924 (a,ad,sc); *Bricklayers* 1925 (a); *Chess Fever* 1925 (d); *The Death Ray* 1925 (a,d); *Mechanics of the Brain* 1926 (d,sc); *Mother* 1926 (d,sc); *The End of St. Petersburg* 1927 (d); *The Heir of Genghis Khan/Storm Over Asia* 1928 (d); *The Living Corpse* 1929 (a); *The Happy Canary* 1929 (a); *The New Babylon* 1929 (a); *Zhivoi Trup* 1929 (a,ed); *The Deserter* 1933 (d); *A Simple Case* 1938 (d); *Victory* 1938 (d); *Minin and Pozharski* 1939 (d); *Twenty Years of Cinema* 1940 (d); *Suvorov* 1940 (d); *The Feast at Zhirmunka* 1941 (d); *Murderers Are on Their Way* 1942 (d) (shelved); *In the Name of the Homeland* 1943 (d,s); *Ivan Grozny Part I/Ivan the Terrible Part I*

1945 (a); *Admiral Nakhimov* 1946 (a,d); *Ivan Grozny Part II/Ivan the Terrible Part II* 1946 (a); *Tri vstrechi* 1948 (d); *Zhukovsky* 1950 (d); *Vozvrashchenie Vasiliya Bortnikova* 1953 (d).

Puenzo, Luis • Director; also screenwriter, producer. • Born Argentina, c. 1946. Leading figure of the Argentianian film industry who began directing commercials at the age of 19 and directed, produced and co-wrote his first feature, *Lights of My Shoes*, in 1973. Puenzo earned international recognition for *The Official Story* (1985), a subtle and moving account of a middle-class woman who gradually becomes aware of her own complicity in a corrupt political regime. The film earned Norma Aleandro a best actress award at Cannes in 1985 and itself took home the Oscar for best foreign film the following year; Puenzo was also nominated for best screenplay.

On the strength of his ability to make an intimate, character-driven drama reflect wider social and political issues, Puenzo was chosen to direct *Old Gringo* (1989), adapted from the novel by Carlos Fuentes. Despite a $25 million budget and the presence of stars Jane Fonda and Gregory Peck, the film proved a rambling critical and commercial flop. • *Lights of My Shoes* 1973 (d,p,sc); *La Historia Oficial/The Official Story* 1985 (d,sc) **(AANBSC)**; *Old Gringo* 1989 (d,sc).

Purviance, Edna • Actress • Born Lovelock, NV, 1894; died 1958, Hollywood, CA. Former secretary discovered by Charlie Chaplin at the age of 17 while she was visiting his studios. Purviance, a full-figured blonde, co-starred with Chaplin in over 30 films, beginning with *A Night Out* (1915) and including *The Tramp* (1915), *The Immigrant* (1917) and *The Kid* (1921). Purviance contributed sensitivity and enchantment to Chaplin's films, fitting beautifully into the pathos and forlorn mood of his settings; she remained on his payroll for years after her retirement from the movies. • *The Bank* 1915; *A Night Out* 1915; *The Tramp* 1915; *Behind the Screen* 1916; *The Pawnshop (short)* 1916; *The Rink (short)* 1916; *The Adventurer* 1917; *The Immigrant* 1917; *A Day's Pleasure (short)* 1919; *Sunnyside* 1919; *The Kid* 1921; *A Woman of Paris* 1923; *A Woman of the Sea* 1926.

Puttnam, David • Producer, executive • Born London, 1941. David Puttnam rose from a working-class background into the advertising business as a photographer's agent during London's Swinging 60s. After a few false starts in film, Puttnam hit his stride as a producer in two collaborations with director Alan Parker: *Bugsy Malone* (1976) and the Oscar-winning hit *Midnight Express* (1978). Puttnam would publicly regret the latter film's exploitative affect on audiences, and this unlikely "mea culpa" launched him as a responsible renegade willing to collide with stars or bankers. His eye for directors with panache gave several promising talents their debuts or breakthroughs, including Ridley Scott (*The Duellists* 1977), Roland Joffe (*The Killing Fields* 1984) and Bill Forsyth (*Local Hero* 1983). Puttnam's star never shone brighter than after his production of Hugh Hudson's *Chariots of Fire* (1981) won the Academy Award for best picture.

In 1986 the Coca-Cola Co. hired Puttnam as chief of production for its Columbia Pictures division. Puttnam's reputation was for modestly budgeted productions which achieved critical acclaim and moderate box-office receipts, while dealing with socially and politically sensitive subjects. With an impressive network to support his ambitions in Hollywood, Puttnam created enormous expectations. He promised to keep costs down with leaner, lower-budgeted fare that would also serve an international rather than simply American audience. He gave European filmmakers such as Emir Kusturica, Jirí Menzel, Doris Dörrie and Bernardo Bertolucci the opportunity to exercise artistic approaches to filmmaking under the aegis of a product-oriented system.

Simultaneously, Puttnam demonstrated an aggressive candor. He announced that if someone wrote him a check for the $150 million that *Rambo* would bring in at the box office, he still would not make that film. He would claim that remarks disparaging Bill Murray (star of the studio's smash hit *Ghostbusters*, 1984) were misunderstood, yet his statements were never designed to court talent agents, longtime Columbia producers such as Ray Stark (who is said to have been a prime mover in the "Dump Puttnam" movement) or the public itself, whose taste he disdained. This Savonarola with an English accent was eventually deemed tiresome; even those who had hopes of succeeding through him were angered at a style that spelled doom. When Puttnam left Columbia with a $3 million golden parachute, he left behind colleagues made vulnerable by his arrogance. Whether a more politic Puttnam could have succeeded is a moot point. His productions were neither marketed nor distributed with care by his successors at Columbia, who had to restore peace.

Puttnam returned to England to resume film- and speech-making. "We in the arts and those who employ us have to regain a true sense of collective responsibility," he said in 1988. "I try to make films about morally accountable individuals, trying to hold true to their beliefs....What I find offensive in films like *Rambo* is the illusion of an individual facing a complex world with nothing but his own brute force—and prevailing, as though all we have to do for the triumph of moral virtue is to summon up the violent animal impulse that may well exist deep within all of us." KJ • *S.W.A.L.K. Melody* 1970 (p); *The Pied Piper* 1972 (p); *The Last Days of Man on Earth* 1973 (exec.p); *Mahler* 1973 (exec.p); *Swastika* 1973 (p); *That'll Be the Day* 1973 (p); *Brother, Can You Spare a Dime?* 1974 (p); *Stardust* 1974 (m.prod,m.arr,p); *James Dean, the First American Teenager* 1975 (p); *Lisztomania* 1975 (p); *Bugsy Malone* 1976 (exec.p); *The Duellists* 1977 (p); *Midnight Express* 1978 (p) **(AANBP)**; *Foxes* 1980 (p); *Chariots of Fire* 1981 (p) **(AABP)**; *Experience Preferred But Not Essential* 1982 (exec.p); *Kipperbang* 1982 (exec.p); *Secrets* 1982 (exec.p); *Arthur's Hallowed Ground* 1983 (exec.p); *Local Hero* 1983 (p); *Red Monarch* 1983 (exec.p); *Sharma and Beyond* 1983 (exec.p); *Those Glory Glory Days* 1983 (exec.p); *Cal* 1984 (p); *Forever Young* 1984 (exec.p); *The Killing Fields* 1984 (p) **(AANBP)**; *Winter Flight* 1984 (exec.p); *Defence of the Realm* 1985 (exec.p); *The Frog Prince* 1985 (exec.p); *Mr. Love* 1985 (exec.p); *Knights and Emeralds* 1986 (exec.p); *The Mission* 1986 (exec.p) **(AANBP)**; *Memphis Belle* 1990 (p).

Quaid, Dennis • Actor; also singer, songwriter. • Born Houston, TX, April 9, 1954. *Educ.* Bellaire High School, Bellaire, TX; University of Houston. Handsome, homespun younger brother of actor Randy Quaid, opposite whom he appeared off-Broadway in *True West* in 1984. Quaid began appearing in films in the mid-1970s and first gained attention for his role as a frustrated Midwestern teenager in *Breaking Away* (1979). Though his career has been somewhat uneven, his easy-going charm and Texan drawl have been put to good use in films by Philip Kaufman (*The Right Stuff* 1983) and Jim McBride (*The Big Easy* 1986). Quaid's second career as a singer-songwriter has made him an appropriate—though not always successful—choice to portray musicians on screen, as in *The Night the Lights Went Out in Georgia* (1981), *Tough Enough* (1982) and—as Jerry Lee Lewis—in *Great Balls of Fire* (1989). He has also written songs for the soundtracks of several of his films. Formerly married to actress P.J. Soles. Quaid married actress Meg Ryan in 1991. • *9/30/55* 1977; *Our Winning Season* 1978; *Seniors* 1978; *Breaking Away* 1979; *G.O.R.P.* 1980; *The Long Riders* 1980; *All Night Long* 1981; *Caveman* 1981; *The Night the Lights Went Out in Georgia* 1981 (a,songs); *Tough Enough* 1982; *Jaws 3-D* 1983; *The Right Stuff* 1983; *Dreamscape* 1984; *Enemy Mine* 1985; *The Big Easy* 1986 (a,songs); *Innerspace* 1987; *Suspect* 1987; *D.O.A.* 1988; *Everybody's All-American* 1988; *Great Balls of Fire* 1989; *Come See the Paradise* 1990; *Postcards From the Edge* 1990.

Quaid, Randy • Actor • Born Houston, TX, 1953. *Educ.* University of Houston (drama). Heavyset, earnest-faced actor, discovered by Peter Bogdanovich while still a drama student, who made his screen debut in the director's superbly acted ensemble piece, *The Last Picture Show* (1971). He went on to establish himself as a versatile, talented character player of stage, screen and TV, winning an Oscar nomination for his role opposite Jack Nicholson in *The Last Detail* (1973). Quaid earned a Golden Globe award for his portrayal of Lyndon Johnson on TV's *LBJ: The Early Years* (1987) and turned in a wonderfully sly performance as a cannibalistic suburban father in Bob Balaban's underrated black comedy, *Parents* (1989). • *The Last Picture Show* 1971; *What's Up, Doc?* 1972; *The Last Detail* 1973 (**AANBSA**); *Lolly-Madonna XXX* 1973; *Paper Moon* 1973; *The Apprenticeship of Duddy Kravitz* 1974; *Breakout* 1975; *Bound For Glory* 1976; *The Missouri Breaks* 1976; *The Choirboys* 1977; *Three Warriors* 1977; *Midnight Express* 1978; *Foxes* 1980; *The Long Riders* 1980; *Heartbeeps* 1981; *National Lampoon's Vacation* 1983; *The Wild Life* 1984; *Fool For Love* 1985; *The Slugger's Wife* 1985; *Sweet Country* 1986; *The Wraith* 1986; *Dear America* 1987; *No Man's Land* 1987; *Caddyshack II* 1988; *Moving* 1988; *Out Cold* 1988; *Bloodhounds of Broadway* 1989; *National Lampoon's Christmas Vacation* 1989; *Parents* 1989; *Cold Dog Soup* 1990; *Days of Thunder* 1990; *Martians Go Home* 1990; *Quick Change* 1990; *Texasville* 1990.

Quayle, Sir Anthony • Actor • Born John Anthony Quayle, Ainsdale, England, September 7, 1913; died October 20, 1989, London. *Educ.* RADA, London. Distinguished stage actor who had a non-speaking part in *Pygmalion* (1938) and made his screen debut proper in Olivier's *Hamlet* (1948), playing Marcellus. Quayle subsequently turned in memorable supporting roles in films ranging from the period drama, *Anne of the Thousand Days* (1969), to Woody Allen's farcical *Everything You Always Wanted to Know About Sex* (*but were afraid to ask)* (1972). • *Pygmalion* 1938; *Hamlet* 1948; *Saraband For Dead Lovers* 1948; *The Wrong Man* 1956; *Tarzan's Greatest Adventure* 1959; *The Guns of Navarone* 1961; *Lawrence of Arabia* 1962; *East of Sudan* 1964; *The Fall of the Roman Empire* 1964; *Operation Crossbow* 1965; *The Poppy Is Also a Flower* 1966; *Before Winter Comes* 1968; *Anne of the Thousand Days* 1969; *MacKenna's Gold* 1969; *Everything You Always Wanted to Know About Sex* (*but were afraid to ask)* 1972; *The Nelson Affair* 1973; *The Tamarind Seed* 1974; *The Eagle Has Landed* 1976; *Holocaust 2000* 1977; *The Chosen* 1978; *Murder By Decree* 1979; *Buster* 1988; *La Leggenda del Santo Bevitore* 1988; *Silent Night* 1988; *King of the Wind* 1990.

Quine, Richard • Director, actor; also producer, screenwriter. • Born Detroit, MI, November 12, 1920; died June 10, 1989, Los Angeles, CA. Former child actor who played some leading roles in the 1940s, notably in *For Me and My Gal* (1942) and *We've Never Been Licked* (1943). Quine began his behind-the-camera career in 1948, when he co-directed *Leather Gloves* with William Asher. He went on to direct several fine films in the 1950s, proving himself adept with thrillers (*Pushover* 1954), musicals (*My Sister Eileen* 1955) and comedies (*The Solid Gold Cadillac* 1956). His later output, despite the bigger budgets he was able to command, were generally less satisfactory.

Quine's wife from 1943 to 1948 was actress Susan Peters (nee Carnahan, 1921), who earned an Oscar nomination for *Random Harvest* (1943). Her promising career was foreshortened by a spinal injury that eventually led to her death in 1953. • *Jane Eyre* 1934 (a); *Little Men* 1934 (a); *Dinky* 1935 (a); *A Dog of Flanders* 1935 (a); *Life Returns* 1935 (a); *Babes on Broadway* 1941 (a); *Dr. Gillespie's New Assistant* 1942 (a); *For Me and My Gal* 1942 (a); *My Sister Eileen* 1942 (a); *Stand By For Action* 1942 (a); *Tish* 1942 (a); *We've Never Been Licked* 1943 (a); *The Cockeyed Miracle* 1946 (a); *Command Decision* 1948 (a); *Leather Gloves* 1948 (d,p); *Words and Music* 1948 (a); *The Clay Pigeon* 1949 (a); *The Flying Missile* 1950 (a); *No Sad Songs For Me* 1950 (a); *Rookie Fireman* 1950 (a); *Purple Heart Diary* 1951 (d); *Sunny Side of the Street* 1951 (d); *Rainbow 'Round My Shoulder* 1952 (d,sc); *Sound Off* 1952 (d,sc,story); *All Ashore* 1953 (d); *Cruisin' Down the River* 1953 (d,sc,story); *Siren of Bagdad* 1953 (d); *Drive a Crooked Road* 1954 (d,sc.adapt); *Pushover* 1954 (d); *So This Is Paris* 1954 (d); *Bring Your Smile Along* 1955 (story); *My Sister Eileen* 1955 (d,sc); *He Laughed Last* 1956 (sc,story); *The Solid Gold Cadillac* 1956 (d); *Full of Life* 1957 (d); *Going Steady* 1957 (song); *Operation Mad Ball* 1957 (d,song); *Bell, Book and Candle* 1958 (d); *Gunman's Walk* 1958 (song); *It Happened to Jane* 1959 (d,lyrics,p); *Juke Box Rhythm* 1959 (song); *Strangers When We Meet* 1960 (p); *The World of Suzie Wong* 1960 (d); *The Notorious Landlady* 1962 (d); *Paris When It Sizzles* 1963 (d,p); *Sex and the Single Girl* 1964 (d); *How to Murder Your Wife* 1965 (d); *Synanon* 1965 (d,p); *Hotel* 1967 (d); *Oh Dad, Poor Dad, Mamma's Hung You in the Closet and I'm Feelin' So Sad* 1967 (d); *A Talent For Loving* 1969 (d); *The Moonshine War* 1970 (d); *W* 1974 (d); *The Prisoner of Zenda* 1979 (d).

Quinlan, Kathleen • Actor • Born Pasadena, CA, November 19, 1954. Engaging lead and supporting actress of the 1970s and 80s who landed her first major role in *Lifeguard* (1976), opposite Sam Elliott. Quinlan was acclaimed for her performance as a schizophrenic teenager in the absorbing 1977 drama, *I Never Promised You A Rose Garden.* • *Lifeguard* 1976; *Airport 77* 1977; *I Never Promised You a Rose Garden* 1977; *The Promise* 1979; *The Runner Stumbles* 1979; *Sunday Lovers* 1980; *Hanky Panky* 1982; *Independence Day* 1982; *Twilight Zone—the Movie* 1983; *Warning Sign* 1985; *Man Outside* 1987; *Wild Thing* 1987; *Clara's Heart* 1988; *Sunset* 1988; *The Doors* 1991.

Quinn, Aidan • Actor • Born Chicago, IL, March 8, 1959. Handsome, blue-eyed lead who first gained attention for his role as a loft-dwelling cinema projectionist in *Desperately Seeking Susan* (1985). Quinn was acclaimed for his role in the 1985 TV drama, *An Early Frost*, as a young man stricken with AIDS. • *Reckless* 1984; *Desperately Seeking Susan* 1985; *The Mission* 1986; *Stakeout* 1987; *Crusoe* 1988; *The Handmaid's Tale* 1989; *The Lemon Sisters* 1989; *Avalon* 1990.

Quinn, Anthony • Actor • Born Chihuahua, Mexico, April 21, 1915. Imposing Irish-Mexican performer who began his film career in 1936. Quinn played assorted exotic heavies through the 1940s before hitting his stride with two landmark roles, as Zapata's (Marlon Brando's) brother in *Viva Zapata!* (1952) and as Gauguin, opposite Kirk Douglas's Van Gogh, in *Lust for Life* (1956). He went on to give several memorable performances which emphasized his brooding machismo, notably as the vicious circus peformer in Fellini's *La Strada* (1954) and the opportunistic Bedouin, Auda Abu Tayi, in *Lawrence of Arabia* (1962). Although he continues to appear in films and and on TV—frequently in roles that verge on self-parody—he remains best known for his title part in *Zorba the Greek* (1964). Quinn's first wife was Katherine DeMille, the adopted daughter of C.B. DeMille. He is the father of actors Francesco, Valentina and Danielle Quinn. • *Parole* 1936; *Daughter of Shanghai* 1937; *The Last Train From Madrid* 1937; *Partners in Crime* 1937; *The Plainsman* 1937; *Swing High, Swing Low* 1937; *Waikiki Wedding* 1937; *The Buccaneer* 1938; *Bulldog Drummond in Africa* 1938; *Dangerous to Know* 1938; *Hunted Men* 1938; *King of Alcatraz* 1938; *Tip-Off Girls* 1938; *Island of Lost Men* 1939; *King of Chinatown* 1939; *Television Spy* 1939; *Union Pacific* 1939; *City For Conquest* 1940; *Emergency Squad* 1940; *The Ghost Breakers* 1940; *Parole Fixer* 1940; *Road to Singapore* 1940; *Blood and Sand* 1941; *Bullets For O'Hara* 1941; *Knockout* 1941; *Manpower* 1941; *The Perfect Snob* 1941; *Texas Rangers Ride Again* 1941; *They Died With Their Boots On* 1941; *Thieves Fall Out* 1941; *The Black Swan* 1942; *Larceny, Inc.* 1942; *Road to Morocco* 1942; *Guadalcanal Diary* 1943; *The Ox-Bow Incident* 1943; *Buffalo Bill* 1944; *Irish Eyes Are Smiling* 1944; *Ladies of Washington* 1944; *Roger Touhy, Gangster* 1944; *Back to Bataan* 1945; *China Sky* 1945; *Where Do We Go From Here?* 1945; *Black Gold* 1947; *California* 1947; *The Imperfect Lady* 1947; *Sinbad the Sailor* 1947; *Tycoon* 1947; *The Brave Bulls* 1951; *The Mask of the Avenger* 1951; *Against All Flags* 1952; *The Brigand* 1952; *Viva Zapata!* 1952 **(AABSA)**; *The World in His Arms* 1952; *Blowing Wild* 1953; *City Beneath the Sea* 1953; *Donne Proibite* 1953; *East of Sumatra* 1953; *Ride, Vaquero* 1953; *Seminole* 1953; *Ulysses* 1953; *The Beachcomber* 1954; *The Long Wait* 1954; *La Strada* 1954; *Attila* 1955; *The Magnificent Matador* 1955; *The Naked Street* 1955; *Seven Cities of Gold* 1955; *The Last Man to Hang* 1956; *Lust For Life* 1956 **(AABSA)**; *Man From Del Rio* 1956; *The Wild Party* 1956; *Notre-Dame de Paris* 1957; *The Ride Back* 1957; *Rising of the Moon* 1957; *The River's Edge* 1957; *The Story of Esther Costello* 1957; *Wild Is the Wind* 1957 **(AANBA)**; *The Black Orchid* 1958; *The Buccaneer* 1958 (d); *Hot Spell* 1958; *Alive and Kicking* 1959; *Last Train From Gun Hill* 1959; *Warlock* 1959; *Heller in Pink Tights* 1960; *Portrait in Black* 1960; *The Savage Innocents* 1960; *Circle of Deception* 1961; *The Guns of Navarone* 1961; *Barabbas* 1962; *Lawrence of Arabia* 1962; *Requiem For a Heavyweight* 1962; *Behold a Pale Horse* 1964; *Zorba the Greek* 1964 (a,assoc.p) **(AANBA)**; *A High Wind in Jamaica* 1965; *Lost Command* 1966; *The Happening* 1967; *Guns For San Sebastian* 1968; *The Magus* 1968; *The Shoes of the Fisherman* 1968; *A Dream of Kings* 1969; *The Secret of Santa Vittoria* 1969; *Flap* 1970; *R.P.M.* 1970; *A Walk in the Spring Rain* 1970; *Arruza* 1971; *Across 110th Street* 1972 (a,exec.p); *Deaf Smith and Johnny Ears* 1973; *The Don Is Dead* 1973; *The Destructors* 1974; *Eredita' Ferramonti* 1976; *Mohammad Messenger of God* 1976; *Caravans* 1978; *The Children of Sanchez* 1978; *The Greek Tycoon* 1978; *The Passage* 1979; *Lion of the Desert* 1980; *High Risk* 1981; *Mystique* 1981 (exec.p); *The Salamander* 1981; *Valentina/1919* 1982; *Ingrid* 1985; *Pasion de Hombre* 1989; *Stradivari* 1989; *Ghosts Can't Do It* 1990; *Revenge* 1990; *Only the Lonely* 1991.

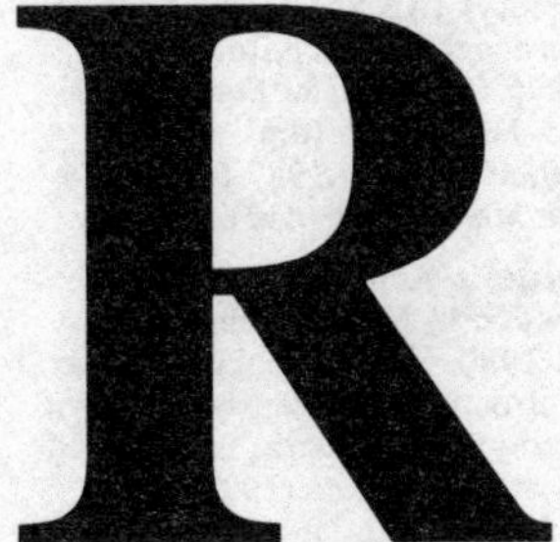

Rabal, Francisco • Actor • Born Aguilas, Spain, March 8, 1925. Handsome, athletic performer who played numerous supporting roles in the 1940s and came to prominence as the title character of Luis Bunuel's *Nazarin* (1958). Rabal has appeared in over 100 international films, by directors including Michelangelo Antonioni, Jacques Rivette, Arne Mattsson and Pedro Almodovar, and is one of Spain's most popular and prolific actors. He made his American feature debut in 1977, in William Friedkin's *Sorcerer*, and won a best actor award at Cannes for his role in Mario Camus's *The Holy Innocents* (1984). • *Nazarin* 1958; *Viridiana* 1961; *L' Eclisse/The Eclipse* 1962; *Marie-Chantal Contre le Docteur Kha* 1965; *Suzanne Simonin, la Religieuse de Denis Diderot/The Nun* 1965; *Belle de Jour* 1967; *Cervantes* 1967; *El "Che" Guevara/Rebel With a Cause* 1968; *Le Streghe* 1968; *Ann and Eve* 1969; *Goya* 1970; *Le Soldat Laforet* 1970; *Laia* 1972; *Las Melancolicas* 1972; *Planeta Venere* 1972; *Il Consigliori* 1973; *Il Sorriso del Grande Tentatore* 1973; *Metralleta Stein* 1974; *Tormento* 1974; *Las Largas Vacaciones del 36* 1975; *El Muerto* 1975; *Battle Command* 1976; *Sorcerer* 1977; *Corleone* 1978; *Cosi' come sei/Stay As You Are* 1978; *City of the Walking Dead* 1980; *El Tesora de las Cuatro Coronas* 1982; *La Colmena* 1983; *Victoria* 1983; *Un Delitto* 1984; *Los Santos Inocentes/The Holy Innocents* 1984; *Los Zancos* 1984; *Un Complicato Intrigo di Donne, Vicoli e Delitti* 1985; *La Hora Bruja* 1985; *Luces de Bohemia* 1985; *Padre Nuestro* 1985; *Los Paraises Perdidos* 1985; *Tiempo de Silencio* 1985; *La Vieja Musica* 1985; *El Disputado Voto del Sr. Cayo* 1986; *El Hermano Bastardo de Dios* 1986; *La Storia* 1986; *Divinas Palabras* 1987; *Gallego* 1988; *A Time of Destiny* 1988; *Barroco* 1989; *Atame!/Tie Me Up, Tie Me Down* 1990.

Rabier, Jean • Director of photography • Born Paris, April 21, 1927. Former assistant to, and camera operator for, Henri Decae who went on to succeed his former boss as Claude Chabrol's cinematographer of choice. Rabier has shot all except three of Chabrol's features since *Les Godelureaux* (1960), as well as doing noted work for Agnes Varda (*Cleo From 5 to 7* 1962) and Jacques Demy (*The Umbrellas of Cherbourg* 1964). • *Le Beau Serge* 1958 (cam.op); *Les Godelureaux* 1960 (ph); *Cleo de 5 a 7/Cleo From 5 to 7* 1962 (ph); *Landru* 1962 (ph); *L'Oeil du Malin* 1962 (ph); *Ophelia* 1962 (ph); *RoGoPag* 1962 (ph—"Le Nouveau Monde"); *Les Sept peches capitaux/The Seven Deadly Sins* 1962 (ph—"Greed"); *La Baie des anges* 1963 (ph); *Les Parapluies de Cherbourg/The Umbrellas of Cherbourg* 1964 (ph); *Peau de banane* 1964 (ph); *Les Plus belles escroqueries du monde* 1964 (ph—"L'homme qui vendit la tour eiffel"); *Le Tigre Aime la Chair Fraiche* 1964 (ph); *Le Bonheur* 1965 (ph); *Marie-Chantal Contre le Docteur Kha* 1965 (ph); *Paris Vu Par...* 1965 (ph—"La Muette"); *Le Tigre se parfume a la dynamite* 1965 (ph); *La Ligne de Demarcation* 1966 (ph); *Le Scandale* 1966 (ph); *Les Biches* 1967 (ph); *La Route de Corinthe* 1967 (ph); *La Femme Infidele* 1968 (ph); *Le Boucher* 1969 (ph); *Que la Bete Meure* 1969 (ph); *L'Homme Orchestre* 1970 (ph); *La Rupture* 1970 (ph); *Comptes A Rebours* 1971 (ph); *De la Part des Copains* 1971 (ph); *La Decade Prodigieuse* 1971 (ph); *Juste avant la nuit* 1971 (ph); *Docteur Popaul* 1972 (ph); *Les Noces Rouges/Blood Wedding* 1973 (ph); *Nada* 1974 (ph); *Une Partie de Plaisir* 1974 (ph); *Les Innocents aux mains Sales* 1975 (ph); *Alice ou la derniere Fugue* 1976 (ph); *Folies bourgeoises* 1976 (ph); *Violette Noziere/Violette* 1977 (ph); *Le Cheval d'orgueil* 1979 (ph); *Les Fantomes du Chapelier* 1982 (ph); *Inspector Lavardin* 1986 (ph); *Le Cri du hibou* 1987 (ph); *Masques* 1987 (ph); *A notre regrettable epoux* 1988 (ph); *Une Affaire de femmes* 1988 (ph); *En toute innocence* 1988 (ph); *Docteur M.* 1990 (ph); *Jours tranquilles a Clichy/Quiet Days in Clichy* 1990 (ph); *Madame Bovary* 1991 (ph).

Rademakers, Fons • Director; also producer, actor. • Born Roosendael, Netherlands, September 5, 1920. *Educ.* Academy of Dramatic Art, Amsterdam. Stage actor and director who apprenticed under Vittorio De Sica and Jean Renoir before making his feature debut with the Bergmanesque, Oscar-nominated *Village on the River* (1959). Rademakers went on to establish himself as the preeminent Dutch director of the next two decades, turning out a string of finely executed, psychologically complex dramas such as

The Knife (1960) and *Mira* (1970). He also produced several films for other directors, particularly his wife, Lili Rademakers (*Menuet* 1972, *Diary of a Mad Old Man* 1987). Rademakers's 1986 political thriller, *The Assault*, won the Oscar for best foreign film. • *Dorp Aan de Rivier/Village on the River* 1959 (d,sc); *The Knife* 1960 (d); *Als twee druppels water/The Spitting Image* 1963 (d,p); *De Dans van de Reiger* 1966 (d); *Bezeten-het gat in de muur* 1969 (a); *Mira* 1970 (a,d,p); *Daughters of Darkness* 1971 (a); *Menuet* 1972 (p); *Niet voor de poesen* 1973 (d); *Keetje Tippel* 1975 (a); *Lifespan* 1975 (a); *Max Havelaar* 1976 (d,p); *Mysteries* 1978 (a); *Mijn Vriend* 1979 (d); *De Aanslag/The Assault* 1986 (d,p); *Dagboek van een oude dwaas/Diary of a Mad Old Man* 1987 (p); *The Rose Garden* 1989 (d).

Radford, Michael • Director, screenwriter • Born New Delhi, India, November 14, 1950. Made his directorial debut with a music documentary, *Van Morrison in Ireland* (1981), and received mixed reviews for his adaptation of George Orwell's *1984* (1984), in which Richard Burton gave his last screen performance. • *Love Is Like a Violin* 1977 (p); *Van Morrison in Ireland* 1981 (d); *Another Time, Another Place* 1983 (d,sc); *1984* 1984 (d,sc); *White Mischief* 1987 (d,sc).

Rafelson, Bob • Director; also screenwriter, producer. • Born New York, NY, 1935. *Educ.* Dartmouth (philosophy); University of Benares, India (philosophy). Began his career as a TV story editor, script writer and producer. Rafelson scored an early commercial success in 1966 when, with partner Bert Schneider, he created the popular series, "The Monkees" (1966-68), featuring a pop group manufactured especially for the show. Together with Schneider and Steve Blauner he then formed the BBS production company to produce his first film as a director, *Head* (1968), which also starred the Monkees and was cowritten by Jack Nicholson. The film has been widely praised as a madcap, almost surrealistic satire of the process by which pop icons such as the Monkees are created and marketed. After BBS had enjoyed further success with 1969's *Easy Rider*, Rafelson went on to direct *Five Easy Pieces* (1970), still considered by many to be his finest work. An absorbing study in contemporary alienation featuring fine central performances by Nicholson and Karen Black, the movie stands as a landmark of the American filmmaking renaissance of the late 1960s and 70s. Rafelson received mixed reviews for *The King of Marvin Gardens* (1972), another exposé of pop culture which again starred Nicholson.

Rafelson's output since the mid-70s has been sporadic, partly due to his reputation as a "difficult" director. (He was fired from the set of 1979's *Brubaker* after allegedly attacking a visiting studio executive). The last decade has seen two glossy, if unexceptional, thrillers (*The Postman Always Rings Twice* 1981, *Black Widow* 1987) and a more personally inspired project—1990's *Mountains of the Moon*, based on the life of 19th-century explorer Sir Richard Burton—which generated limited critical enthusiasm. • Rafelson is the nephew of playwright-screenwriter Samson Raphaelson. • *Head* 1968 (a,d,p,sc); *Easy Rider* 1969 (uncred.exec.p); *Five Easy Pieces* 1970 (d,p,story) **(AANSC)**; *The King of Marvin Gardens* 1972 (d,p,story); *Stay Hungry* 1975 (d,p,sc); *The Postman Always Rings Twice* 1981 (d,p); *Always* 1985 (a); *Black Widow* 1987 (d); *Mountains of the Moon* 1990 (d,sc).

Raft, George • Actor • Born George Ranft, New York, NY, September 26, 1895; died 1980. Sinister-looking former boxer and Broadway dancer, best known for his portrayals of smooth, underworld characters, as in *Scarface* (1932). Raft also starred in several dance films of the 1930s and 40s. • *Queen of the Night Clubs* 1929; *Hush Money* 1931; *Palmy Days* 1931; *Quick Millions* 1931; *Dancers in the Dark* 1932; *If I Had a Million* 1932; *Love Is a Racket* 1932; *Madame Racketeer* 1932; *Night After Night* 1932; *Night World* 1932; *Scarface* 1932; *Undercover Man* 1932; *The Bowery* 1933; *Midnight Club* 1933; *Pick Up* 1933; *All of Me* 1934; *Bolero* 1934; *Limehouse Blues* 1934; *The Trumpet Blows* 1934; *Every Night at Eight* 1935; *The Glass Key* 1935; *Rumba* 1935; *She Couldn't Take It* 1935; *Stolen Harmony* 1935; *It Had to Happen* 1936; *Yours For the Asking* 1936; *Souls at Sea* 1937; *Spawn of the North* 1938; *You and Me* 1938; *Each Dawn I Die* 1939; *I Stole a Million* 1939; *The Lady's From Kentucky* 1939; *The House Across the Bay* 1940; *Invisible Stripes* 1940; *They Drive By Night* 1940; *Manpower* 1941; *Broadway* 1942; *Background to Danger* 1943; *Stage Door Canteen* 1943; *Follow the Boys* 1944; *Johnny Angel* 1945; *Nob Hill* 1945; *Mr. Ace* 1946; *Nocturne* 1946; *Whistle Stop* 1946; *Christmas Eve* 1947; *Intrigue* 1947; *Sinner's Holiday* 1947; *Race Street* 1948; *A Dangerous Profession* 1949; *Johnny Allegro* 1949; *Outpost in Morocco* 1949; *Red Light* 1949; *I'll Get You For This* 1951; *Loan Shark* 1952; *I'll Get You* 1953; *The Man From Cairo* 1953; *Black Widow* 1954; *Rogue Cop* 1954; *A Bullet For Joey* 1955; *Around the World in 80 Days* 1956; *Some Like It Hot* 1959; *Jet Over the Atlantic* 1960; *Ocean's Eleven* 1960; *The Ladies' Man* 1961; *For Those Who Think Young* 1964; *Casino Royale* 1967; *Skidoo* 1968; *Hammersmith Is Out* 1972; *Sextette* 1978; *The Man With Bogart's Face* 1980; *Deadhead Miles* 1982; *Entertaining the Troops* 1989 (archival footage).

Railsback, Steve • Actor • Born Dallas, TX, 1948. Supporting player who has also played leading roles, mostly in minor films. Railsback turned in creditable performances in *The Stunt Man* (1980), opposite Peter O'Toole, and in Tobe Hooper's sci-fi chiller, *Lifeforce* (1985). • *The Visitors* 1972; *Cockfighter* 1974; *Who Fell Asleep?* 1979; *The Stunt Man* 1980; *Turkey Shoot* 1981; *The Golden Seal* 1983; *Angela* 1984; *Torchlight* 1984; *Lifeforce* 1985; *Armed and Dangerous* 1986; *Blue Monkey* 1987; *Distortions* 1987; *Scenes From the Goldmine* 1987; *The Survivalist* 1987; *The Wind* 1987; *Deadly Intent* 1988; *Nukie* 1989; *The Assassin* 1990.

Raimi, Sam M. • American director, screenwriter; also producer, actor. • *Educ.* Michigan State University. Enjoyed critical success at the 1983 Cannes Film Festival with *The Evil Dead*, a kinetic exercise in camp horror which went on to become an international cult favorite. Raimi delivered an even more tongue-in-cheek sequel, confirming his taste for camera pyrotechnics and severed body parts, in 1987, and made his first stab at mainstream filmmaking with 1990's *Darkman*.

A stylish, witty transposition of the comic-book aesthetic to the screen, *Darkman* also paid satiric tribute to the Universal horror features of the 1930s; it was a success at the box-office and introduced a wider audience to Raimi's work.

As a child Raimi made 8mm shorts influenced by his favorite comic books, and, in his college days, he formed creative partnerships which have lasted through four feature films. At Michigan State he founded the Society of Creative Filmmaking with brother Ivan, who later co-scripted *Darkman*, and actor Robert Tapert, who has produced all Raimi's features to date. On graduating, Raimi formed Renaissance Pictures with Tapert and another student performer, Bruce Campbell, who has appeared in all of his films, notably as Ash in the *Evil Dead* stories. Raimi has also been associated with the Coen Brothers: producer Ethan was an assistant editor on *The Evil Dead* and both brothers scripted *Crimewave* (1985). • *The Evil Dead* 1980 (d,sc); *Crimewave* 1985 (d,sc); *Spies Like Us* 1985 (a); *Evil Dead 2: Dead By Dawn* 1987 (d,sc); *Thou Shall Not Kill... Except* 1987 (a); *Maniac Cop* 1988 (a); *Easy Wheels* 1989 (exec.p); *Intruder* 1989 (a); *Darkman* 1990 (d,sc,story).

Rainer, Yvonne • Director, screenwriter; also producer, actress. • Born San Francisco, CA, 1934. Noted modern dance choreographer of the 1960s (she co-founded the influential Judson Dance Theater in 1962) who turned her attention to feature films in the early 70s, subsequently emerging as a critically lauded practitioner of politically challenging, avant-garde cinema.

Rainer began integrating slides and short films into her dance work as early as 1968, and made her feature debut with *Lives of Performers* (1972), an outgrowth of her dance background. A politically committed artist, her film work evolved away from the influences of the so-called American avant-garde to concern itself not only with the film medium, but with its modes of representation of gender, race, class, etc. Rainer's films break with the illusionism of Hollywood, disrupting narrative expectations, relying heavily on verbal—as opposed to visual—language, and dealing most often with power relations, particularly between the sexes. Her use of Brechtian distancing effects (extended voice-overs, the combination of documentary and staged footage) brings to mind the work of Jean-Luc Godard.

Rainer's multi-layered collage, *The Man Who Envied Women* (1985), is perhaps her most ambitious film, dealing with psychoanalytic and narrative theory, aging, US policy in Central America and New York's housing crisis, while quoting from theorists and critics such as Michel Foucault, Frederic Jameson and Julia Kristeva. SKK • *Lives of Performers* 1972 (a,d,ed,sc); *Film About a Woman Who...* 1974 (d,ed,narr,sc); *Underground and Emigrants* 1976 (a); *The Man Who Envied Women* 1985 (d,ed,sc); *Amy!* 1980 (voice); *Working Title: Journeys From Berlin/1971* 1980 (a,d,ed,sc);*Privilege* 1990 (a,d,ed,p,sc).

Rains, Claude • Actor • Born London, November 10, 1889; died 1967. Character player whose impeccable charm and finely modulated voice graced some of the finest Hollywood films of the 1930s and 40s. Rains began appearing on the London stage at age 11, was one of the leading members of New York's Theatre Guild by the mid-1920s and made a sensational screen debut as *The Invisible Man* in 1933. Primarily at Warner Bros. from 1936, he turned in a string of memorable performances opposite Bette Davis (*Now, Voyager* 1942, *Mr. Skeffington* 1945, *Deception* 1946) and is perhaps best remembered as the dapper, opportunistic police chief in *Casablanca* (1942). He was also outstanding in Alfred Hitchcock's *Notorious* (1946), as Ingrid Bergman's child-like, Nazi-conspiring husband—one of four roles to earn him an Oscar nomination for best supporting actor. The first of Rains's five marriages was to British actress Isabel Jeans. • *The Invisible Man* 1933; *Crime Without Passion* 1934; *The Man Who Reclaimed His Head* 1934; *The Last Outpost* 1935; *Mystery of Edwin Drood* 1935; *Anthony Adverse* 1936; *Hearts Divided* 1936; *Stolen Holiday* 1936; *The Prince and the Pauper* 1937; *They Won't Forget* 1937; *Four Daughters* 1938; *Gold Is Where You Find It* 1938; *Robin Hood* 1938; *White Banners* 1938; *Daughters Courageous* 1939; *Four Wives* 1939; *Juarez* 1939; *Mr. Smith Goes to Washington* 1939 **(AANBSA)**; *They Made Me a Criminal* 1939; *Lady With Red Hair* 1940; *Saturday's Children* 1940; *Four Mothers* 1941; *Here Comes Mr. Jordan* 1941; *King's Row* 1941; *The Wolf Man* 1941; *Casablanca* 1942 **(AANBSA)**; *Moontide* 1942; *Now, Voyager* 1942; *Strange Holiday* 1942; *Forever and a Day* 1943; *The Phantom of the Opera* 1943; *Passage to Marseille* 1944; *Mr. Skeffington* 1945 **(AANBSA)**; *This Love of Ours* 1945; *Angel on My Shoulder* 1946; *Deception* 1946; *Notorious* 1946 **(AANBSA)**; *The Unsuspected* 1947; *The Passionate Friends* 1949; *Rope of Sand* 1949; *Song of Surrender* 1949; *Where Danger Lives* 1950; *The White Tower* 1950; *Sealed Cargo* 1951; *Lisbon* 1956; *The Pied Piper of Hamelin* 1957; *This Earth Is Mine* 1959; *The Lost World* 1960; *Il Pianeta degli uomini spenti* 1961; *Lawrence of Arabia* 1962; *Twilight of Honor* 1963; *The Greatest Story Ever Told* 1965.

Ramis, Harold • Screenwriter, director, actor • Born Chicago, IL, November 21, 1944. *Educ.* Washington University, St. Louis. Versatile comic talent who wrote for Chicago's renowned Second City troupe and the National Lampoon radio show before co-scripting the antic fraternity house romp, *Animal House* (1978). Ramis made his directorial debut with the equally madcap *Caddyshack* (1980) and appeared opposite Bill Murray in the military farce, *Stripes* (1981), which he also co-wrote. He has since carved out a successful multi-faceted career, most notably with his participation in the lucrative *Ghostbusters* films. Ramis is a frequent collaborator with producer-director Ivan Reitman. • *National Lampoon's Animal House* 1978 (sc); *Meatballs* 1979 (sc); *Caddyshack* 1980 (d,sc); *Heavy Metal* 1981 (a); *Stripes* 1981 (a,sc); *National Lampoon's Vacation* 1983 (d); *Ghostbusters* 1984 (a,sc); *Armed and Dangerous* 1986 (exec.p,sc,story); *Back to School* 1986 (exec.p,sc); *Club Paradise* 1986 (d,sc); *Baby Boom* 1987 (a); *Caddyshack II* 1988 (sc); *Stealing Home* 1988 (a); *Ghostbusters II* 1989 (a,sc,from characters).

Rampling, Charlotte • Actress • Born Sturmer, England, February 5, 1946. Leading lady of international films who began her screen career in the mid-1960s. Rampling has proved a highly competent dramatic actress but remains primarily associated with sensual, and often controversial, characterizations, in films such as Luchino Visconti's *The Damned* (1969) and Liliana Caviani's erotically explicit *The Night Porter* (1974). In Nagisa Oshima's 1986 black comedy, *Max, My Love*, she plays a diplomat's wife who takes a chimpanzee for a lover. • *The Knack... and How to Get It* 1965; *Georgy Girl* 1966; *The Long Duel* 1967; *La Caduta degli dei/The Damned* 1969; *How to Make It* 1969; *Three* 1969; *The Ski Bum* 1970; *Vanishing Point* 1970; *Addio, Fratello Crudele* 1971; *Asylum* 1972; *Corky* 1972; *Giordano Bruno* 1973; *Caravan to Vaccares* 1974; *La Chair de l'orchidee* 1974; *The Night Porter* 1974; *Yuppi Du* 1974; *Zardoz* 1974; *Farewell, My Lovely* 1975; *Foxtrot* 1975; *Orca... Killer Whale* 1977; *Un Taxi mauve* 1977; *Stardust Memories* 1980; *The Verdict* 1982; *Viva la Vie!* 1984; *On Ne Meurt Que 2 Fois* 1985; *Tristesse et Beaute* 1985; *Max mon amour/Max, My Love* 1986; *Angel Heart* 1987; *Mascara* 1987; *D.O.A.* 1988; *Paris By Night* 1988; *Helmut Newton: Frames From the Edge* 1989; *Rebus* 1989.

Rank, Lord J. Arthur • Executive • Born Joseph Arthur Rank, Hull, England, December 22, 1888; died 1972. Heir to a flour and milling fortune who entered films in the mid-1930s and, within a decade, had become Britain's most powerful film magnate. Initially interested in the medium as a means of promoting his Methodist beliefs, Rank efficiently acquired production, distribution and exhibition interests to a point where he owned over half of his country's film studios (including Pinewood, Islington and Denham) as well as its two leading theater circuits, Gaumont British and Odeon. The Rank organization also supported such lauded production companies as the Archers (*The Life and Death of Colonel Blimp* 1943, *Black Narcissus* 1946), Two Cities (*Henry V* 1945, *Odd Man Out* 1947) and Cineguild (*Great Expectations* 1945, *Oliver Twist* 1948).

In response to a declining market, the Rank Organization began scaling down its film operations in the early 1950s. Much of its production empire has been dismantled, though it still owns Pinewood Studios and through Rank Film Distributors, Rank Laboratories (a leading film processing service) and several Rank-owned theater chains are still in operation. In recent years the organization has diversified into other interests such as hotel chains, bowling alleys and computer/mimeograph technologies. J. Arthur Rank was awarded a peerage in 1957.

Ransohoff, Martin • Producer • Born New Orleans, LA, 1927. *Educ.* Colgate University. Prolific and successful independent producer who was responsible, through his Filmways company, for popular TV series including "The Beverly Hillbillies," "Green Acres" and "The Addams Family." Ransohoff produced his first feature in 1962 and has subsequently been responsible for such films as *The Cincinatti Kid* (1965), *Catch-22* (1970), *Silver Streak* (1976) and *Jagged Edge* (1985). • *Boys' Night Out* 1962 (p); *The Wheeler Dealers* 1963 (p); *The Americanization of Emily* 1964 (p); *The Cincinnati Kid* 1965 (p); *The Sandpiper* 1965 (p,story); *Don't Make Waves* 1967 (p); *The Fearless Vampire Killers* 1967 (exec.p); *Ice Station Zebra* 1968 (p); *A Midsummer Night's Dream* 1968 (exec.p); *Castle Keep* 1969 (p); *10 Rillington Place* 1970 (p); *Catch-22* 1970 (p); *Hamlet* 1970 (exec.p); *The Moonshine War* 1970 (p); *See No Evil* 1971 (p); *Fuzz* 1972 (p); *Save the Tiger* 1973 (p); *The White Dawn* 1974 (adapt,p); *Silver Streak* 1976 (exec.p); *Nightwing* 1979 (p); *The Wanderers* 1979 (p); *A Change of Seasons* 1980 (p,story); *American Pop* 1981 (p); *Hanky Panky* 1982 (p); *Class* 1983 (p); *Jagged Edge* 1985 (p); *The Big Town* 1987 (p); *Physical Evidence* 1988 (p); *Switching Channels* 1988 (p); *Welcome Home* 1989 (p).

Raphael, Frederic • Screenwriter, novelist • Born Chicago, IL, August 14, 1931. *Educ.* St. John's College, Cambridge. British-educated writer who made several significant contributions to 1960s English cinema, including the overlooked comedy, *Nothing But the Best* (1964). Raphael subsequently wrote original screenplays for John Schlesinger's *Darling* (1965) and Stanley Donen's *Two For the Road* (1967) and has adapted several literary works—including his own novel, *Richard's Things* (1980)—for the screen. Raphael is also an acclaimed TV writer ("The Glittering Prizes" 1976) and has directed for the small screen. • *Bachelor of Hearts* 1958 (sc); *Don't Bother to Knock* 1961 (sc); *Nothing But the Best* 1964 (sc,song); *Darling* 1965 (sc,story) **(AABSC)**; *Far From the Madding Crowd* 1967 (sc); *Two For the Road* 1967 (sc) **(AANBSC)**; *A Severed Head* 1970 (sc); *Daisy Miller* 1974 (sc); *Richard's Things* 1980 (sc,from book); *Sleeps Six* 1984 (sc); *The King's Whore* 1990 (sc).

Raphaelson, Samson • Screenwriter, playwright • Born New York, NY, March 30, 1896; died July 16, 1983, New York, NY. *Educ.* University of Illinois. Raphaelson had many of his plays adapted for the screen (*The Jazz Singer* made the transition three times) as well as writing sparkling original screenplays, notably for the sophisticated comedies of Ernst Lubitsch (*Trouble in Paradise* 1932, *Heaven Can Wait* 1943). Uncle of writer-director-producer Bob Rafelson. • *The Jazz Singer* 1927 (from play); *The Magnificent Lie* 1931 (sc); *Broken Lullaby* 1932 (sc); *One Hour With You* 1932 (sc); *Trouble in Paradise* 1932 (sc); *Caravan* 1934 (sc); *The Merry Widow* 1934 (sc); *Servant's Entrance* 1934 (sc); *Accent on Youth* 1935 (from play); *Dressed to Thrill* 1935 (sc); *Angel* 1937 (sc); *The Last of Mrs. Cheyney* 1937 (sc); *The Shop Around the Corner* 1940 (sc); *Skylark* 1941 (from play); *Suspicion* 1941 (sc); *Heaven Can Wait* 1943 (sc); *The Harvey Girls* 1946 (sc); *The Perfect Marriage* 1946 (from play); *Green Dolphin Street* 1947 (sc); *That Lady in Ermine* 1948 (sc); *In the Good Old Summertime* 1949 (sc); *Mr. Music* 1950 (from play "Accent on Youth"); *Bannerline* 1951 (story); *The Jazz Singer* 1953 (from play); *Main Street to Broadway* 1953 (sc); *The Jazz Singer* 1980 (from play).

Rappaport, David • Actor • Born Britain, c. 1952; died May 1990, Los Angeles. *Educ.* University of Bristol (psychology). English dwarf actor best known for his roles in *Time Bandits* (1981) and, as "Mighty Mouth," on TV's "LA Law". Rappaport committed suicide at the age of 38. • *Mysteries* 1978; *Black Jack* 1979; *Cuba* 1979; *The Secret Policeman's Ball* 1979; *The Secret Policeman's Other Ball* 1981; *Time Bandits* 1981; *Sword of the Valiant—The Legend of Gawain and the Green Knight* 1984; *Unfair Exchanges* 1984; *The Bride* 1985; *Luigi's Ladies* 1989.

Rapper, Irving • Director • Born London, 1898. *Educ.* NYU. Moved to the US at the age of eight and directed for the New York stage before beginning his film career in the mid-1930s. Rapper worked as a dialogue coach and assistant director on several William Dieterle films before making his directorial debut in 1941. Though his films tended to be stagey, his theatrical experience helped him elicit fine performances from his actors, notably in the Claude Rains/Bette Davis classics *Now, Voyager* (1942) and *Deception* (1946). • *City For Conquest* 1940 (dial.d); *One Foot in Heaven* 1941 (d); *Shining Victory* 1941 (d); *The Gay Sisters* 1942 (d); *Now, Voyager* 1942 (d); *The Adventures of Mark Twain* 1944 (d); *The Corn Is Green* 1945 (d); *Rhapsody in Blue* 1945 (d); *Deception* 1946 (d); *The Voice of the Turtle* 1947 (d); *Anna Lucasta* 1949 (d); *The Glass Menagerie* 1950 (d); *Another Man's Poison* 1952 (d); *Forever Female* 1953 (d); *Bad For Each Other* 1954 (d); *The Brave One* 1956 (d); *Strange Intruder* 1956 (d); *Marjorie Morningstar* 1958 (d); *The Miracle* 1959 (d); *Giuseppe Venduto Dai Fratelli* 1960 (d); *Ponzia Pilato* 1961 (d); *The Christine Jorgensen Story* 1970 (d); *Born Again* 1978 (d).

Rath, Franz • German director of photography • Leading cinematographer who first came to prominence with the emergence of the New German Cinema. Rath shot Volker Schlöndorff's first two films, *Young Törless* (1966) and *The Sudden Wealth of the Poor People of Kombach* (1971), and is also known for his work on Margarethe von Trotta's *Sisters, Or The Balance of Happiness* (1979) and *Rosa Luxemburg* (1985). • *Der Junge Törless/Young Törless* 1966 (ph); *Mord und Totschlag* 1966 (ph); *Der Plötzliche Reichtum der Armen Leute Von Kombach/The Sudden Wealth of the Poor People of Kombach* 1971 (ph); *Studenten Aufs Schafott* 1972 (ph); *Die Ploetzliche Einsamkeit des Konrad Steiner* 1976 (ph); *Das Zweite Erwachen der Christa Klages* 1977 (ph); *Schwestern, Oder Die Balance Des Gluecks/Sisters, Or The Balance of Happiness* 1979 (ph); *Pilgrim, Farewell* 1980 (ph); *Die Bleierne Zeit/Marianne and Julianne* 1981 (ph); *Die Falschung/Circle of Deceit* 1981 (cam.op); *Krieg und Frieden* 1982 (ph—Engstfeld); *Haunted* 1983 (ph); *Mann Ohne Gedachtnis* 1984 (ph); *The Neverending Story* 1984 (cam.op); *Rosa Luxemburg* 1985 (ph); *Felix* 1987 (ph); *Der Unsichtbare* 1987 (ph).

Rathbone, Basil • Actor • Born Philip St. John Basil Rathbone, Johannesburg, South Africa, June 13, 1892; died 1967, New York. Rathbone was an established stage star on both sides of the Atlantic before making his US film debut in 1924. With the emergence of sound his precise, clipped diction, combined with his suave, somewhat pointed features, confirmed him as Hollywood's debonair villain of choice. He played elegant, sardonic and thoroughly worthless characters in films such as 1938's *Robin Hood*, opposite Errol Flynn, and 1940's *The Mark of Zorro*, opposite Tyrone Power. Rathbone is best remembered as Sherlock Holmes in two fine 1939 films—*The Hound of the Baskervilles* and *The Adventures of Sherlock Holmes*—which were followed by 12 highly inferior variations on the same theme. • *Trouping With Ellen* 1924; *The Masked Bride* 1925; *The Great Deception* 1926; *The Last of Mrs. Cheyney* 1929; *The Bishop Murder Case* 1930; *The Flirting Widow* 1930; *A Lady Surrenders* 1930; *The Lady of Scandal* 1930; *A Notorious Affair* 1930; *Sin Takes a Holiday* 1930; *This Mad World* 1930; *A Woman Commands* 1932; *Anna Karenina* 1935; *Captain Blood* 1935; *David Copperfield* 1935; *A Feather in Her Hat* 1935; *Kind Lady* 1935; *The Last Days of Pompeii* 1935; *A Tale of Two Cities* 1935; *The Garden of Allah* 1936; *Private Number* 1936; *Romeo and Juliet* 1936 **(AANBSA)**; *Confession* 1937; *Love From a Stranger* 1937; *Make a Wish* 1937; *Tovarich* 1937; *The Adventures of Marco Polo* 1938; *The Dawn Patrol* 1938; *If I Were King* 1938 **(AANBSA)**; *Robin Hood* 1938; *The Adventures of Sherlock Holmes* 1939; *The Hound of the Baskervilles* 1939; *Rio* 1939; *Son of Frankenstein* 1939; *The Sun Never Sets* 1939; *Tower of London* 1939; *The Mark of Zorro* 1940; *Rhythm on the River* 1940; *The Black Cat* 1941; *International Lady* 1941; *The Mad Doctor* 1941; *Crossroads* 1942; *Fingers at the Window* 1942; *Paris Calling* 1942; *Sherlock Holmes and the Secret Weapon* 1942; *Sherlock Holmes and the Voice of Terror* 1942; *Above Suspicion* 1943; *Sherlock Holmes Faces Death* 1943; *Sherlock Holmes in Washington* 1943; *Bathing Beauty* 1944; *Frenchman's Creek* 1944; *The Pearl of Death* 1944; *The Scarlet Claw* 1944; *The Spider Woman* 1944; *The House of Fear* 1945; *Pursuit to Algiers* 1945; *The Woman in Green* 1945; *Dressed to Kill* 1946; *Heartbeat* 1946; *Terror By Night* 1946; *Casanova's Big*

Night 1954; *We're No Angels* 1955; *The Black Sleep* 1956; *The Court Jester* 1956; *The Last Hurrah* 1958; *Ponzia Pilato* 1961; *The Magic Sword* 1962; *Tales of Terror* 1962; *The Comedy of Terrors* 1964; *The Ghost in the Invisible Bikini* 1966; *Queen of Blood* 1966; *Hillbillys in a Haunted House* 1967; *The Great Mouse Detective* 1986.

Ratoff, Gregory • Director; also Actor • Born St. Petersburg, Russia, April 20, 1897; died 1960, Hollywood, CA. *Educ.* University of St. Petersburg (law, drama). Czarist émigré who worked on Broadway before being typecast as a heavily accented foreigner in Hollywood films from the early 1930s. Ratoff made his directorial debut in 1936 and turned out mostly unexceptional pictures, first in Hollywood and then, from the late 1940s, in England. He is best known for *Intermezzo* (1939)—Ingrid Bergman's first English-language film—and *Oscar Wilde* (1960), starring Robert Morley, in addition to his numerous character roles, most memorably *All About Eve* (1950). • *Once in a Lifetime* 1932 (a); *Secrets of the French Police* 1932 (a); *Skyscraper Souls* 1932 (a); *Symphony of Six Million* 1932 (a); *Undercover Man* 1932 (a); *What Price Hollywood?* 1932 (a); *Broadway Thru a Keyhole* 1933 (a); *Girl Without a Room* 1933 (a); *Headline Shooter* 1933 (a); *I'm No Angel* 1933 (a); *Sitting Pretty* 1933 (a); *Sweepings* 1933 (a); *George White's Scandals* 1934 (a); *The Great Flirtation* 1934 (from story "I Love an Actress"); *Let's Fall in Love* 1934 (a); *King of Burlesque* 1935 (a); *Remember Last Night?* 1935 (a); *Here Comes Trouble* 1936 (a); *The Road to Glory* 1936 (a); *Sing, Baby, Sing* 1936 (a); *Sins of Man* 1936 (d); *Under Two Flags* 1936 (a); *Under Your Spell* 1936 (a); *Cafe Metropole* 1937 (a,story); *The Lancer Spy* 1937 (d); *Seventh Heaven* 1937 (a); *Top of the Town* 1937 (a); *You Can't Have Everything* 1937 (story); *Gateway* 1938 (a); *Sally, Irene and Mary* 1938 (a); *Barricade* 1939 (d); *Hotel For Women* 1939 (d); *Intermezzo* 1939 (d); *Rose of Washington Square* 1939 (d); *Wife, Husband, and Friend* 1939 (d); *The Great Profile* 1940 (a); *I Was an Adventuress* 1940 (d); *Public Deb No. 1* 1940 (d); *Adam Had Four Sons* 1941 (d); *The Corsican Brothers* 1941 (d); *The Men in Her Life* 1941 (d,p); *Footlight Serenade* 1942 (d); *Two Yanks in Trinidad* 1942 (d); *The Heat's on* 1943 (d); *Something to Shout About* 1943 (d,p); *Song of Russia* 1943 (d); *Irish Eyes Are Smiling* 1944 (d); *Paris Underground* 1945 (d); *Where Do We Go From Here?* 1945 (d); *Do You Love Me?* 1946 (d); *Carnival in Costa Rica* 1947 (d); *Moss Rose* 1947 (d); *Black Magic* 1949 (d,p); *That Dangerous Age* 1949 (d,p); *All About Eve* 1950 (a); *My Daughter Joy* 1950 (d,p); *O. Henry's Full House* 1952 (a); *Taxi* 1953 (d); *Abdullah the Great* 1955 (a,d,p); *The Sun Also Rises* 1957 (a); *Exodus* 1960 (a); *Once More, With Feeling* 1960 (a); *Oscar Wilde* 1960 (d); *The Big Gamble* 1961 (a).

Ray, Aldo • Actor • Born Aldo DaRe, Pen Argyl, PA, September 25, 1926. *Educ.* University of California. Gravel-voiced, thick-set former Navy frogman who was running for sheriff of Crockett, CA, when he was discovered by director David Miller. Ray played one of the reminiscing lovers in George Cukor's *The Marrying Kind* (1952) and also worked for directors Michael Curtiz and Raoul Walsh; he has subsequently been typecast as a hot-blooded, gung-ho character, primarily in action films. • *My True Story* 1951; *Saturday's Hero* 1951; *The Marrying Kind* 1952; *Pat and Mike* 1952; *Let's Do It Again* 1953; *Miss Sadie Thompson* 1953; *Battle Cry* 1954; *Three Stripes in the Sun* 1955; *We're No Angels* 1955; *Men in War* 1956; *Nightfall* 1956; *God's Little Acre* 1958; *The Naked and the Dead* 1958; *The Day They Robbed the Bank of England* 1960; *Nightmare in the Sun* 1965; *Sylvia* 1965; *Dead Heat on a Merry-Go-Round* 1966; *What Did You Do in the War, Daddy?* 1966; *Kill a Dragon* 1967; *Riot on Sunset Strip* 1967; *The Violent Ones* 1967; *Welcome to Hard Times* 1967; *The Green Berets* 1968; *The Power* 1968; *Angel Unchained* 1970; *La Course du lièvre à travers les champs* 1972; *Tom* 1973; *The Centerfold Girls* 1974; *The Dynamite Brothers* 1974; *Seven Alone* 1974; *Inside Out* 1975; *The Man Who Would Not Die* 1975; *Psychic Killer* 1975; *Stud Brown* 1975; *The Bad Bunch* 1976; *The Glove* 1976; *Haunted* 1977; *Haunts* 1977; *Kino, the Padre on Horseback* 1977; *Bog* 1978; *Death Dimension* 1978; *Little Moon & Jud McGraw* 1978; *Samuel Fuller & The Big Red One* 1979; *Human Experiments* 1980; *Boxoffice* 1982; *The Executioner Part II* 1982; *The Secret of Nimh* 1982; *Biohazard* 1983; *Prison Ship* 1984; *Evils of the Night* 1985; *Flesh and Bullets* 1985; *To Kill a Stranger* 1985; *Hollywood Cop* 1987; *The Sicilian* 1987; *Star Slammer, the Escape* 1988; *Blood Red* 1989; *Dark Sanity* 1989; *Swift Justice* 1989; *The Shooters* 1990.

Ray, Nicholas • Director; also actor. • Born Raymond Nicholas Kienzle, Galesville, WI, August 7, 1911; died June 16, 1979. *Educ.* University of Chicago; University of Wisconsin. "I'm a stranger here myself," is the epigram most closely associated with Nicholas Ray. The phrase is spoken by the title character in Ray's *Johnny Guitar* (1954) and is also a concise expression of Ray's relationship to the Hollywood studio system and of his central concerns as a filmmaker.

Prior to becoming a film director, Ray studied architecture with Frank Lloyd Wright and then worked with Elia Kazan and John Houseman on stage projects. His film directing debut, produced by Houseman, was *They Live By Night* (1948), a convincing version of the now-familiar lovers-on-the-run-from-the-law theme. This was followed by two middling melodramas, *A Woman's Secret* and *Knock on Any Door* (both 1949). The latter made a forceful social statement about juvenile delinquency, but its emphasis on polemics rather than drama blunted the overall effect. The film starred Humphrey Bogart, who returned for Ray's next production, *In a Lonely Place* (1950), among the best work ever done by both star and director.

Ray was already concentrating on disaffected loners—individuals who, by choice or fate, could not be integrated into society's mainstream. *In a Lonely Place* explored the life of an asocial screenwriter suspected of murder. Ray extracted Bogart's most passionate performance, placing it in a spare, direct framework. *In a Lonely Place* is not only one of the best movies about Hollywood and the fallacy of romance but also a bitter parable about the postwar condition. It remains a very contemporary motion picture.

On Dangerous Ground (1951) starred Robert Ryan as a disillusioned city cop infected with the violence which surrounds him. Ray's careening camera served as an apt metaphor for the instability of an atomized urban existence. Despite the studio-imposed happy ending, with Ryan returning to the blind Ida Lupino in a bleak rural landscape, the film's evocation of the paralyzing angst of modern life could not be evaded. Alienated protagonists populated Ray's films of the early 1950s—Robert Mitchum's ex-rodeo star searching for home and security in *The Lusty Men* (1952); Joan Crawford as the embattled saloon owner in *Johnny Guitar* (1954); and of course, James Dean—along with Natalie Wood and Sal Mineo—in *Rebel Without a Cause* (1955).

It was in *Rebel* that Ray's allegiance with the marginalized was most evident and most sympathetic. The teenagers in the story are at the mercy of a society that demands conformity and saps individuality. Integration or destruction are the only options available and, though Dean and Wood are reintegrated into society by film's end, Ray makes it clear that this action is tantamount to a slow death.

In *Bigger Than Life* (1956) James Mason plays a teacher whose addiction to cortisone leads to neuroses that foreground a number of the era's dominant concerns—conformity, consumption, education and religion. The film is not only excellent drama, but, like most Ray movies, it is also an important social document. Furthermore, *Bigger Than Life*, like *Rebel*, demonstrated that Ray was one of the few directors to use CinemaScope in an accomplished way. His time with Frank Lloyd Wright had given him a keen sense of space and horizontal line.

Ray's films had been largely taken for granted in his native country until the critics of *Cahiers du Cinéma* embarked upon a concerted process of deification. Concurrent with the spread of the Ray cult to the US in the early 1960s, the director's output underwent a significant change, as he undertook two period epics, *King of Kings* (1961) and *55 Days at Peking* (1963). Though both films featured Ray flourishes, they lacked the intensity of his earlier, more emotionally compact works.

Ray subsequently abandoned Hollywood and spent some time in Europe before returning to the States in the late 1960s to take a job teaching film at New York State University at Binghampton. A unique collaborative project with his students resulted, usually known as *You Can't Go Home Again* (1973). Ray's increasingly poor health limited his activities to several cameo appearances in films of other directors; he himself was the subject of his last directorial effort, in collaboration with Wim Wenders, *Lighting Over Water* (1980), about the final months of Ray's battle with cancer. It was a difficult but fitting epitaph, as the director (like so many of his characters) was shown searching for peace and a sense of place. ES • *A Tree Grows in Brooklyn* 1945 (ad); *They Live By Night* 1948 (adapt,d); *Knock on Any Door* 1949 (d); *A Woman's Secret* 1949 (d); *Born to Be Bad* 1950 (d); *In a Lonely Place* 1950 (d); *Flying Leathernecks* 1951 (d); *On Dangerous Ground* 1951 (d); *The Lusty Men* 1952 (d); *Johnny Guitar* 1954 (d); *Run For Cover* 1954 (d); *Rebel Without a Cause* 1955 (d,story) **(AANBST)**; *Bigger Than Life* 1956 (d); *Hot Blood* 1956 (d); *The True Story of Jesse James* 1957 (d); *Bitter Victory* 1958 (d,sc); *Party Girl* 1958 (d); *Wind Across the Everglades* 1958 (d); *The Savage Innocents* 1960 (d,sc); *King of Kings* 1961 (d); *55 Days at Peking* 1963 (a,d); *Circus World* 1964 (story); *You Can't Go Home Again* (1973); *I'm a Stranger Here Myself* 1974 (a); *Der Amerikanische Freund/The American Friend* 1977 (a); *Hair* 1979 (a); *Lightning Over Water* 1980 (a,d); *Crystal Gazing* 1982 (a).

Ray, Satyajit • Director; also screenwriter. • Born Calcutta, India, May 2, 1921. *Educ.* Presidency College, University of Calcutta (science, economics); Santiniketan University (art history). Satyajit Ray, India's only internationally renowned filmmaker, was born into a family prominent in Bengali arts and letters for fifteen generations. In 1940, after receiving his degree in science and economics, he attended Rabindranath Tagore's "world university" in rural Santiniketan. Tangore, the dominant figure in India's cultural renaissance, had a strong influence on Ray, whose humanist films reaffirm his Bengali heritage within a modern context.

In 1942, Ray returned to Calcutta, where he spent the next ten years as layout artist and art director for a British-run advertising agency. In his spare time he wrote film scenarios, among them an adaptation of Tagore's novel, *Ghare Baire*, which producers rejected when Ray refused to make changes. With India's independence in 1947, Ray cofounded Calcutta's first film society with Chidananda Das Gupta and wrote articles calling for a new cinema.

His reputation as a graphic artist brought offers to illustrate books, including an abridged edition of Bibhuti Bhusan Banerjee's classic novel, *Pather Panchali*, in 1946. After an influential encounter with Jean Renoir in Calcutta in 1949 and a business trip to London in 1950, where he saw Vittorio De Sica's *The Bicycle Thief* (1948), Ray set out to script and direct *Pather Panchali*. The film, shot on location on weekends, failed to attract backers and could not be completed until a request from the Museum of Modern Art in New York to include it in their Indian art exhibit led the West Bengal government—in an unprecendented move—to provide funds.

Pather Panchali (1956) won several international awards and established Ray as a world-class director, as well as being a box-office hit at home. Artistic and financial success gave Ray total control over his subsequent films; in his numerous functions—writer, director, casting director, composer (since 1961) and cinematographer (since 1963)—he was able to continue Tagore's example in theater of welding the arts into a unified entity. Two sequels also based on the novel (*Aparajito* 1957, *The World of Apu* 1959) completed the acclaimed *Apu* trilogy, whose slow-paced realism broke with the song-and-dance melodramas of Indian cinema. Using long takes and reaction shots, slow camera movements, and—in *Kanchanjangha* (1962)—real-time narrative, Ray allows the meticulous accumulation of details to reveal the inner lives and humanity of diverse Bengali characters.

In 1961, Ray revived *Sandesh*, a children's magazine founded by his grandfather, and he continues to contribute illustrations, verses and stories. Since 1969, he has also made four popular children's films which contain an unobtrusive yet distinct political awareness. Earlier in his career, Ray was criticized by Indian critics for failing to deal with Calcutta's immediate social problems. And although he defended his humanist (versus ideological) approach, *Pratidwandi* (1971) signaled a shift toward political themes. In the 1970s, Ray's films acquired a bitter tone and deviated from his usual classical style, with the abrupt use of montage, including jump cuts and flashbacks.

Ray's *Ghaire Baire/The Home and the World* (1984) was a return to his first screen adaptation. While shooting, he suffered two heart attacks and his son, Sandip, completed the project from his father's detailed instructions. Ray continues to be a prolific writer, having finished 13 half-hour TV screenplays to be directed by Sandip, and returned to directing in 1989 with *Enemy of the People*. CAN • *Pather Panchali* 1956 (d,sc); *Aparajito* 1957 (d,sc); *The World of Apu* 1959 (d,sc); *Kanchanjangha* 1962 (d,sc,m); *Mahanagar/The Great City* 1963 (d,sc,m); *Charulata* 1964 (d,sc,m); *Shakespeare Wallah* 1965 (m); *Aranyer Din Ratri/Days and Nights in the Forest* 1969 (d,sc,m); *Pratidwandi/The Adversary* 1971 (d,sc,m); *Simbaddha/Company* 1972 (d,sc,m); *Ashani Sanket/Distant Thunder* 1973 (d,sc,m); *Jana-Aranya/The Middleman* 1976 (d,sc,m); *Shatranj ke Khilari/The Chess Players* 1977 (d,sc,dial,m); *Baba Felunath, Joi/The Elephant God* 1979 (d,sc,m); *Sadgati/Deliverance* 1982 (d,m,sc); *Satyajit Ray* 1982 (a); *Ghare Baire/The Home and the World* 1984 (d,sc,m,m.dir); *Ganashatru/Enemy of the People* 1989 (d,sc,m).

Reagan, Ronald • Actor; also politician. • Born Tampico, IL, February 6, 1911. *Educ.* Eureka College. Began his career as a sportscaster for a Des Moines radio station and wound up serving as President of the United States of America from 1981 to 1989.

An affable actor possessed of minimal talent but undeniable charisma, Reagan proved a popular romantic lead in numerous minor films from the late 1930s. He turned in the odd creditable performance and certainly delivered some lines which have passed into contemporary folklore (a gift he would later perfect as a politician): in *Knute Rockne—All American* (1940), he intones "Win just one for the Gipper"; and in *King's Row* (1942), playing a character who has just had both legs amputated, he laments, "Where's the rest of me?" (the title of his 1965 autobiography).

After WWII, in which he served with the Air Force making training films, Reagan became immersed in Hollywood politics. Known as a firm liberal, he served as head of the Screen Actors Guild from 1947 to 1952, and again in 1959. Though his big-screen star had faded, he remained popular on TV as host of the "General Electric Theater" and other shows. By the early 1960s he had shifted his political stance and become an increasingly conservative member of the Republican party. In the same year that he sponsored the conservative presidential candidate Barry Goldwater, Reagan starred as a woman-slapping, white-collar criminal in one of his final films, *The Killers* (1964). Most of his subsequent appearances in front of cameras were in the capacity of professional politician, first as governor of California (1967-1975) and then as one of

America's most popular presidents. Married to actresses Jane Wyman (1940-1948) and, since 1952, Nancy Reagan (formerly Nancy Davis). • *Hollywood Hotel* 1937 (a); *Love Is on the Air* 1937 (a); *Accidents Will Happen* 1938 (a); *Boy Meets Girl* 1938 (a); *Brother Rat* 1938 (a); *Cowboy From Brooklyn* 1938 (a); *Girls on Probation* 1938 (a); *Going Places* 1938 (a); *Sergeant Murphy* 1938 (a); *Swing Your Lady* 1938 (a); *Angels Wash Their Faces* 1939 (a); *Code of the Secret Service* 1939 (a); *Dark Victory* 1939 (a); *Hell's Kitchen* 1939 (a); *Naughty But Nice* 1939 (a); *Secret Service of the Air* 1939 (a); *Smashing the Money Ring* 1939 (a); *An Angel From Texas* 1940 (a); *Brother Rat and a Baby* 1940 (a); *Knute Rockne—All American* 1940 (a); *Murder in the Air* 1940 (a); *The Santa Fe Trail* 1940 (a); *Tugboat Annie Sails Again* 1940 (a); *The Bad Man* 1941 (a); *International Squadron* 1941 (a); *Million Dollar Baby* 1941 (a); *Nine Lives Are Not Enough* 1941 (a); *Desperate Journey* 1942 (a); *Juke Girl* 1942 (a); *King's Row* 1942 (a); *This Is the Army* 1943 (a); *Stallion Road* 1947 (a); *That Hagen Girl* 1947 (a); *The Voice of the Turtle* 1947 (a); *The Girl From Jones Beach* 1949 (a); *The Hasty Heart* 1949 (a); *John Loves Mary* 1949 (a); *Night Unto Night* 1949 (a); *Louisa* 1950 (a); *Bedtime For Bonzo* 1951 (a); *Hong Kong* 1951 (a); *The Last Outpost* 1951 (a); *Storm Warning* 1951 (a); *She's Working Her Way Through College* 1952 (a); *The Winning Team* 1952 (a); *Law and Order* 1953 (a); *Tropic Zone* 1953 (a); *Cattle Queen of Montana* 1954 (a); *Prisoner of War* 1954 (a); *Tennessee's Partner* 1955 (a); *Hellcats of the Navy* 1957 (a); *The Killers* 1964 (a).

Redford, Robert • Actor; also director, producer. • Born Charles Robert Redford, Jr., Santa Monica, CA, August 18, 1937. Educ. University of Colorado; Pratt Institute, Brooklyn NY (art); AADA, New York. • Once Robert Redford, according to screenwriter William Goldman, was called "just another California blond—throw a stick at Malibu, you'll hit six of him." It is unlikely, however, that any of the six would combine Redford's charm, intelligence, talent and looks. Redford attended the University of Colorado on a baseball scholarship but dropped out in 1957 to spend a year traveling and painting in Europe. Back in the States, he studied theatrical design and acting in New York.

Redford enjoyed his first Broadway success in 1963 in *Barefoot in the Park* (he had made his movie debut a year earlier in *War Hunt*, an anti-war film set during the Korean conflict). The success of the play led to four more films of varying quality, but in none did Redford make a strong impression. His career took a major leap when he reprised his stage role in the film version of *Barefoot* (1967) opposite Jane Fonda. The phenomenal success of his pairing with Paul Newman in *Butch Cassidy and the Sundance Kid* (1969, scripted by Goldman) made him a bankable stars and cemented his screen image as an intelligent, reliable, sometimes sardonic good guy.

Redford's career saw no major milestones for the next four years, though *Downhill Racer* (1969), on which he served as executive producer, was an interesting look at the world of competitive skiing. *Jeremiah Johnson* and *The Candidate* (both 1972) were admirable, but it was his next two films, *The Way We Were* and *The Sting* (both 1973) that solidified his box-office appeal. About the first film he joked: "Nice Jewish girl (Barbra Streisand) gets nice blond WASP." Of the second: "Nice Jewish boy (Paul Newman) gets nice blond WASP."

All the President's Men (1976) was a landmark film for Redford. Again, he was executive producer, and the film's serious subject matter, the Watergate scandal, reflected the actor's offscreen concerns for political and environmental causes. In 1980, his first outing as a director won him an Oscar for *Ordinary People*, a drama about the slow disintegration of a middle-class family. More recently, he was behind the camera on *The Milagro Beanfield War* (1988), a screen version of John Nichols's acclaimed novel of the Southwest.

Redford also made a fine romantic lead opposite Meryl Streep in *Out of Africa* (1985); although many critics complained that his portrayal of Isak Dinesen's lover wasn't particularly realistic, Redford's characterization was more substantial than the ghostly figure of Dinesen's book.

In 1981, Redford founded the nonprofit Sundance Institute in Park City, Utah which, through its various workshops and the popular United States Film Festival, has proved much-needed support for independent film production. DLY • *War Hunt* 1962 (a); *Inside Daisy Clover* 1965 (a); *Situation Hopeless-But Not Serious* 1965 (a); *The Chase* 1966 (a); *This Property Is Condemned* 1966 (a); *Barefoot in the Park* 1967 (a); *Butch Cassidy and the Sundance Kid* 1969 (a); *Downhill Racer* 1969 (a); *Tell Them Willie Boy Is Here* 1969 (a); *Little Fauss and Big Halsy* 1970 (a); *The Candidate* 1972 (a); *The Hot Rock* 1972 (a); *Jeremiah Johnson* 1972 (a); *The Sting* 1973 (a) **(AANBA)**; *The Way We Were* 1973 (a); *Broken Treaty at Battle Mountain* 1974 (a); *The Great Gatsby* 1974 (a); *The Great Waldo Pepper* 1975 (a); *Three Days of the Condor* 1975 (a); *All the President's Men* 1976 (a); *A Bridge Too Far* 1977 (a); *The Electric Horseman* 1979 (a); *Brubaker* 1980 (a); *Ordinary People* 1980 (d) **(AABD)**; *The Natural* 1984 (a); *Out of Africa* 1985 (a); *Legal Eagles* 1986 (a); *Promised Land* 1987 (exec.p); *The Milagro Beanfield War* 1988 (d,p); *Some Girls* 1988 (exec.p); *Yosemite: The Fate of Heaven* 1988 (a,exec.p); *To Protect Mother Earth* 1989 (a); *Havana* 1990 (a).

Redgrave, Lynn • Actress • Born London, March 8, 1943. *Educ.* Central School of Speech and Drama, London. Stage, screen and TV performer who first came to prominence for her title role in *Georgy Girl* (1966), playing a frumpy young woman who shares a London apartment with a glamorous, attractive roommate (Charlotte Rampling). Redgrave subsequently slimmed down and moved to the US where, though she remains active on the stage, she is best known for her numerous TV shows and "Weight Watchers" commercials. Daughter of Michael Redgrave and Rachel Kempson and sister of Corin and Vanessa Redgrave. • *Tom Jones* 1963; *Georgy Girl* 1966 **(AANBA)**; *The Deadly Affair* 1967; *Last of the Mobile Hot-Shots* 1969; *Every Little Crook and Nanny* 1972; *Everything You Always Wanted To Know About Sex* (*but were afraid to ask)* 1972; *Don't Turn the Other Cheek* 1973; *The National Health* 1973; *The Happy Hooker* 1975; *The Big Bus* 1976; *Sunday Lovers* 1980; *Morgan Stewart's Coming Home* 1987; *Death of a Son* 1988; *Midnight* 1988; *Getting It Right* 1989.

Redgrave, Sir Michael • Actor; also author. • Born Bristol, England, 1908; died March 21, 1985, Denham, England. *Educ.* Cambridge. Tall, distinguished star of the English stage and screen, and a member of the generation of British actors which included Laurence Olivier, Ralph Richardson and John Gielgud. A versatile and polished performer, Redgrave made a superb screen debut as the musician hero of the classic Hitchcock thriller, *The Lady Vanishes* (1938). He demonstrated a fine talent for comedy, as in Anthony Asquith's *The Importance of Being Earnest* (1952), as well as playing reserved, upper-class characters in films such as *The Browning Version* (1950) and *The Loneliness of the Long Distance Runner* (1962). He was knighted in 1959 for his services to the theater.

Redgrave wrote two plays and several books, including his autobiography, *Face or Mask* (1958), and was the father, by his actress wife Rachel Kempson, of Vanessa, Corin and Lynn Redgrave. • *The Lady Vanishes* 1938; *Lady In Distress* 1942; *Dead of Night* 1945; *Mourning Becomes Electra* 1947 **(AANBA)**; *Secret Beyond the Door* 1948; *The Browning Version* 1950; *The Importance of Being Earnest* 1952; *The Green Scarf* 1954; *The Sea Shall Not Have Them* 1954; *The Dam Busters* 1955; *Mr. Arkadin* 1955; *The Night My Number Came Up* 1955; *1984* 1956; *The Happy Road* 1956; *Law and Disorder* 1956; *Time Without Pity* 1957; *Behind the Mask* 1958; *The Quiet American* 1958; *Shake Hands With the Devil* 1959; *The*

Wreck of the Mary Deare 1959; *The Innocents* 1961; *No, My Darling Daughter* 1961; *The Loneliness of the Long Distance Runner* 1962; *The Heroes of Telemark* 1965; *The Hill* 1965; *Young Cassidy* 1965; *Assignment K* 1968; *Battle of Britain* 1969; *Goodbye, Mr. Chips* 1969; *Oh! What a Lovely War* 1969; *David Copperfield* 1970; *Goodbye Gemini* 1970; *The Go-Between* 1971; *Nicholas and Alexandra* 1971.

Redgrave, Vanessa • Actress • Born London, January 30, 1937. *Educ.* Central School of Speech and Drama, London. One of the foremost actresses of her generation and a strong-willed, independent figure whose portrayal of similar characters on screen has helped redefine contemporary perceptions of women. Redgrave established herself on the English stage in the early 1960s and made her first significant film appearance in *Morgan—A Suitable Case for Treatment* (1966). She went on to give acclaimed performances as Guinevere in *Camelot* (1967), as legendary dancer Isadora Duncan in *Isadora* (1968) and as *Julia*, the political activist friend of Lillian Hellman in the 1977 film of the same name. She has recently been praised for her 1989 performances in Tennessee Williams's *Orpheus Descending* on the London and New York stage.

Redgrave has at times attracted as much attention for her political beliefs as for her brilliant film performances. She has been an outspoken member of the Workers' Revolutionary Party and used her speech at the 1978 Oscar ceremony to attack Israel's policy toward the Lebanon. (Jewish groups subsequently protested when Redgrave was cast to play concentration-camp survivor Fania Fenelon in the Arthur Miller-scripted 1980 TV movie, *Playing for Time*).

The daughter of Michael Redgrave and Rachel Kempson and sister of actors Corin and Lynn, Redgrave has two daughters, Natasha and Joely, who are also actresses. (She divorced their father, director Tony Richardson, in 1967.) She also has a son, Carlo Nero, fathered by her *Camelot* co-star, Franco Nero. • *Behind the Mask* 1958; *Blow-Up* 1966; *A Man For All Seasons* 1966; *Morgan—A Suitable Case for Treatment* 1966 **(AANBA)**; *Camelot* 1967; *Tonite Let's All Make Love in London* 1967; *The Charge of the Light Brigade* 1968; *Isadora* 1968 **(AANBA)**; *The Sea Gull* 1968; *Oh! What a Lovely War* 1969; *The Body* 1970; *The Devils* 1971; *Mary, Queen of Scots* 1971 **(AANBA)**; *The Trojan Women* 1971; *La Vacanza* 1971; *Murder on the Orient Express* 1974; *Out of Season* 1975; *The Seven Per-Cent Solution* 1976; *Julia* 1977 **(AABSA)**; *Agatha* 1979; *Bear Island* 1979; *Yanks* 1979; *Wagner* 1983; *The Bostonians* 1984 **(AANBA)**; *Steaming* 1985; *Wetherby* 1985; *Comrades* 1987; *Prick Up Your Ears* 1987; *Consuming Passions* 1988; *Diceria dell'untore* 1990; *Romeo-Juliet* 1990; *The Ballad of the Sad Cafe* 1991.

Reed, Sir Carol • Director; also producer. • Born London, December 30, 1906; died April 25, 1976. Reed began his film career in 1927 as an assistant to Edgar Wallace at British Lion films, supervising the adaptation of Wallace's works into film. After a spell as dialogue director and assistant director for Basil Dean, he made his own directing debut with *Men of the Sea* (1935).

Reed soon earned a reputation for his finely observed portrayals of working-class life, such as *Bank Holiday* (1937), *The Stars Look Down* (1939)—the film which established Reed as a major director—and *Kipps* (1941), adapted from the novel by H.G. Wells. He also earned attention for *Night Train to Munich* (1940), a wartime comedy-thriller which borrowed heavily—but creditably—from Hitchcock's *The Lady Vanishes.* (Both films were written by Frank Launder and Sidney Gilliat.) These early features confirmed Reed as a capable craftsman with a sharp eye for detail, an unpretentious style and a knack for extracting fine performances from his actors.

During WWII Reed worked as a director for the Army Kinematograph Service and directed the acclaimed propaganda feature, *The Way Ahead* (1944), starring David Niven. He also co-directed, with Garson Kanin, *The True Glory* (1945), an Oscar-winning documentary compiled from footage shot by Allied army cameramen.

Reed hit his peak in the post-war years with a string of features which remain landmarks in English film history. These began with *Odd Man Out* (1947), a suberb hunt drama which follows a wounded Irish revolutionary (James Mason) through the final encounters of his life. The success of *Odd Man Out* led to a contract with Alexander Korda, for whom Reed made five films, beginning with *The Fallen Idol* (1948). A superbly crafted thriller which turns on a child's misconception of adult emotional entanglements, it was followed in 1949 by the director's acknowledged masterpiece, *The Third Man*. Justly regarded as the finest of the many films to have been adapted from the works of Graham Greene, this atmospheric thriller made superb use of its postwar Viennese locations and featured fine performances from Joseph Cotten, Trevor Howard and Orson Welles.

Reed's critical reputation took a downward turn in the 1950s and early 60s, when he turned out a number of more expensive, but less meticulously crafted productions such as the Hollywood-made *Trapeze* (1956) and *The Agony and the Ecstacy* (1965). His fortunes revived with *Oliver!* (1968), an exhuberant musical version of Dicken's *Oliver Twist* which won six Academy Awards, including best picture and best director. • Reed's first marriage (1943-47) was to the distinguished stage and screen actress Diana Wynyard; he married another actress, Penelope Ward, in 1948. He was knighted in 1952 for his service to the British film industry. SKK • *Men of the Sea* 1935 (d); *Midshipman Easy* 1935 (d); *Bank Holiday* 1937 (d); *Who's Your Lady Friend?* 1937 (d); *Climbing High* 1938 (d); *Penny Paradise* 1938 (d); *A Girl Must Live* 1939 (d); *The Stars Look Down* 1939 (d); *The Girl in the News* 1940 (d); *Night Train to Munich* 1940 (d); *Kipps* 1941 (d); *The Young Mr. Pitt* 1942 (d); *The Way Ahead* 1944 (d); *The True Glory* 1945 (d); *Odd Man Out* 1947 (d); *The Fallen Idol* 1948 (d) **(AANBD)**; *The Third Man* 1949 (d) **(AANBD)**; *Outcast of the Islands* 1951 (d,p); *The Man Between* 1953 (d); *A Kid For Two Farthings* 1954 (d,p); *Trapeze* 1956 (d); *The Key* 1958 (d); *Our Man in Havana* 1959 (d); *Mutiny on the Bounty* 1962 (d); *The Running Man* 1963 (d,p); *The Agony and the Ecstasy* 1965 (d,p); *Oliver!* 1968 (d) **(AABD)**; *Flap* 1970 (d); *Follow Me!* 1972 (d).

Reed, Oliver • Actor • Born Wimbledon, London, England, February 13, 1938. Bull-necked, muscular leading man who made his film debut in *The Bulldog Breed* (1959) and first starred in *The Curse of the Werewolf* (1961). Initially typecast in surly, rebellious roles, Reed soon proved his versatility in films such as Joseph Losey's *The Damned* (1963) and Michael Winner's *The Jokers* (1966). He achieved international prominence with his performances as Bill Sikes, in uncle Carol Reed's *Oliver!* (1968); as arrogant and intransigent mine owner Gerald Crich in Ken Russell's *Women in Love* (1969); and as the hot-blooded Athos in Richard Lester's "Musketeers" movies of the 1970s. Reed continues to appear in films and, increasingly, on TV. • *The Bulldog Breed* 1959; *The Curse of the Werewolf* 1961; *The Rebel* 1961; *The Damned/These Are the Damned* 1963; *The Bridge of Kandahar* 1965; *The Jokers* 1966; *I'll Never Forget What's 'Is Name* 1967; *Hannibal Brooks* 1968; *Oliver!* 1968; *The Assassination Bureau* 1969; *Women in Love* 1969; *La Dame dans l'auto avec des lunettes et un fusil/The Lady in the Car With Glasses and a Gun* 1970; *Take a Girl Like You* 1970; *The Devils* 1971; *The Hunting Party* 1971; *Sitting Target* 1972; *Z.P.G.* 1972; *Mordi e Fuggi* 1973; *The Three Musketeers* 1973; *The Triple Echo* 1973; *And Then There Were None* 1975; *Blood in the Streets* 1975; *The Four Musketeers* 1975; *Royal Flash* 1975; *Tommy* 1975; *Burnt Offerings* 1976; *The Great Scout & Cathouse Thursday* 1976; *The Sell Out* 1976; *Crossed Swords* 1977; *Maniac* 1977; *The Big Sleep* 1978; *The Class of Miss MacMichael* 1978; *Tomorrow Never*

Comes 1978; *The Brood* 1979; *Dr. Heckyl & Mr. Hype* 1980; *Lion of the Desert* 1980; *Condorman* 1981; *Venom* 1981; *Spasms* 1982; *The Sting II* 1982; *Fanny Hill* 1983; *Two of a Kind* 1983; *Captive* 1986; *Castaway* 1986; *The Misfit Brigade* 1986; *Dragonard* 1987; *Gor* 1987; *The Adventures of Baron Munchausen* 1988; *Captive Rage* 1988; *Skeleton Coast* 1988; *Rage to Kill* 1989; *The Return of the Musketeers* 1989; *Panama Sugar* 1990; *The Revenger* 1990.

Reed, Pamela • Actress • Born Tacoma, WA, April 2, 1949. *Educ.* University of Washington (drama). First appeared on Broadway in 1978 and made her screen debut two years later, playing Belle Starr in Walter Hill's stylish western, *The Long Riders.* Reed turned in an effective performances as wife of astronaut Gordon Cooper (Dennis Quaid) in Philip Kaufman's *The Right Stuff* (1983) and as campaign manager for candidate Jack Tanner in Robert Altman's TV series on HBO, "Tanner '88" (1988). • *Eyewitness* 1980; *The Long Riders* 1980; *Melvin and Howard* 1980; *Young Doctors in Love* 1982; *The Right Stuff* 1983; *The Goodbye People* 1984; *The Best of Times* 1986; *The Clan of the Cave Bear* 1986; *Rachel River* 1987; *Cadillac Man* 1990; *Chattahoochee* 1990; *Kindergarten Cop* 1990.

Reeve, Christopher • Actor • Born New York, September 25, 1952. *Educ.* Cornell; Juilliard (drama). Handsome, classically trained actor who shot to stardom as *Superman* (1978), a role he reprised in three decreasingly inventive sequels. Reeve's continued association with the superhero has hampered the development of his film career, though he he continues to do respected work on stage, notably with the Williamstown Theatre Festival in Massachusetts. • *Gray Lady Down* 1977 (a); *Superman* 1978 (a); *Somewhere in Time* 1980 (a); *Superman II* 1980 (a); *Deathtrap* 1982 (a); *Monsignor* 1982 (a); *Superman III* 1983 (a); *The Bostonians* 1984 (a); *The Aviator* 1985 (a); *Street Smart* 1987 (a); *Superman IV: The Quest For Peace* 1987 (a,story,2u d); *Switching Channels* 1988 (a).

Reeves, Keanu • Actor • Born Beirut, Lebanon, 1965. *Educ.* High School for the Performing Arts, Toronto; Second City; Hedgerow Theatre, PA. Talented young lead of the 1980s whose variations on the role of a confused teenager have ranged from Matt in *River's Edge* (1987)—in which he has to beg his nine-year-old brother not to shoot him—to Ted in *Bill and Ted's Excellent Adventure* (1989)—in which he resorts to time travel in an attempt to pass a high-school history test. • *Flying* 1986; *Youngblood* 1986; *River's Edge* 1987; *Dangerous Liaisons* 1988; *The Night Before* 1988; *Permanent Record* 1988; *The Prince of Pennsylvania* 1988; *Bill and Ted's Excellent Adventure* 1989; *Parenthood* 1989; *I Love You to Death* 1990; *Tune in Tomorrow* 1990.

Reggio, Godfrey • Director; also screenwriter, producer. • Born New Orleans, LA. *Educ.* College of Santa Fe, NM. Former Roman Catholic priest who was asked to leave his order in 1968 because of his political activites; Reggio eventually moved into TV as a means of spotlighting problems he was encountering as a social worker. His non-narrative feature films have continued to explore social issues, though they are primarily seen as hallucinatory visual feasts, making liberal use of slow-motion and stop-motion techniques and set to the hypnotic music of Philip Glass. • *Koyaanisqatsi* 1982 (d,p,sc,concept); *Powaqqatsi* 1988 (d,p,sc); *Songlines* 1989 (d).

Reid, Wallace • Actor; also director, screenwriter. • Born William Wallace Reid, St. Louis, MO, April 15, 1891; died 1923. Handsome, clean-cut star of the mid-1910s who frequently directed, and sometimes wrote, his own vehicles. After being treated with morphine following a 1919 train accident, Reid became addicted to the drug and died at age 32. Husband of actress Dorothy Davenport (from 1913) and son of screenwriter-director-actor James Hallek Reid (1860-1920). • *Dead Man's Shoes* 1913 (a,d); *The Foreign Spy* 1913 (a,d); *The Gratitude of Wanda* 1913 (a,d); *The Harvest of Flame* 1913 (a,d); *The Kiss* 1913 (a,d); *The Lightning Bolt* 1913 (a,d,sc); *Love and the Law* 1913 (a,d); *The Modern Snare* 1913 (a,d); *Pride of Lonesome* 1913 (a,d); *The Tattooed Arm* 1913 (a,d); *Via Cabaret* 1913 (a,d); *The Ways of Fate* 1913 (a,d); *When Jim Returned* 1913 (a,d); *The Den of Thieves* 1914 (a,d); *Fires of Conscience* 1914 (a,d); *A Flash in the Dark* 1914 (a,d); *The Fruit of Evil* 1914 (a,d); *The Heart of the Hills* 1914 (a,d); *The Intruder* 1914 (a,d); *Passing of the Beast* 1914 (a,d); *Regeneration* 1914 (a,d); *The Skeleton* 1914 (a,d); *The Siren* 1914 (a,d); *The Test* 1914 (a,d); *The Way of a Woman* 1914 (a,d); *Birth of a Nation* 1915 (a); *Carmen* 1915 (a); *The Chorus Lady* 1915 (a); *Enoch Arden* 1915 (a); *The Golden Chance* 1915 (a); *The Lost House* 1915 (a); *Old Heidelberg* 1915 (a); *The House With the Golden Windows* 1916 (a); *Intolerance* 1916 (a); *Joan the Woman* 1916 (a); *The Love Mask* 1916 (a); *Maria Rosa* 1916 (a); *The Prison Without Walls* 1916 (a); *The Selfish Woman* 1916 (a); *To Have and to Hold* 1916 (a); *The Yellow Pawn* 1916 (a); *Big Timber* 1917 (a); *The Devil Stone* 1917 (a); *The Golden Fetter* 1917 (a); *The Hostage* 1917 (a); *Nan of Music Mountain* 1917 (a); *The Squaw Man's Son* 1917 (a); *The Things We Love* 1917 (a); *The Woman God Forgot* 1917 (a); *The World Apart* 1917 (a); *Believe Me Xantippe* 1918 (a); *The Dub* 1918 (a); *The Firefly of France* 1918 (a); *The House of Silence* 1918 (a); *Less Than Kin* 1918 (a); *The Man From Funeral Range* 1918 (a); *Rimrock Jones* 1918 (a); *The Source* 1918 (a); *Too Many Millions* 1918 (a); *Alias Mike Moran* 1919 (a); *Hawthorne of the U.S.A.* 1919 (a); *The Lottery Man* 1919 (a); *The Love Burglar* 1919 (a); *The Roaring Road* 1919 (a); *The Valley of the Giants* 1919 (a); *You're Fired* 1919 (a); *Always Audacious* 1920 (a); *The Dancin' Fool* 1920 (a); *Double Speed* 1920 (a); *Excuse My Dust* 1920 (a); *Sick Abed* 1920 (a); *What's Your Hurry?* 1920 (a); *The Affairs of Anatol* 1921 (a); *The Charm School* 1921 (a); *Don't Tell Everything* 1921 (a); *Forever* 1921 (a); *The Hell Diggers* 1921 (a); *The Love Special* 1921 (a); *Too Much Speed* 1921 (a); *Across the Continent* 1922 (a); *Clarence* 1922 (a); *The Dictator* 1922 (a); *The Ghost Breaker* 1922 (a); *Nice People* 1922 (a); *Night Life in Hollywood* 1922 (a); *Rent Free* 1922 (a); *Thirty Days* 1922 (a); *The World's Champion* 1922 (a).

Reiner, Carl • Actor, screenwriter; also director, producer. • Born Bronx, NY, March 20, 1923. Gifted comedian who appeared on Sid Caesar's classic "Your Show of Shows" (1950-54) and helped create the hugely popular "The Dick Van Dyke Show" (1961-66) before moving into films. Reiner made an impressive directorial debut with an adaptation of his autobiographical novel, *Enter Laughing* (1966), and has subsequently made several offbeat comedy gems including *Where's Poppa?* (1970) and *Dead Men Don't Wear Plaid* (1982). He wrote the screenplays for two Norman Jewison movies (*The Thrill of it All* 1963, *The Art of Love* 1965) and has directed four films starring Steve Martin (*The Jerk* 1979, *Dead Men Don't Wear Plaid* 1982, *The Man With Two Brains* 1983, *All of Me* 1984). Father, by entertainer Estelle Reiner, of actor-director-screenwriter Rob Reiner. • *Happy Anniversary* 1959 (a); *The Gazebo* 1960 (a); *Gidget Goes Hawaiian* 1961 (a); *It's a Mad, Mad, Mad, Mad World* 1963 (a); *The Thrill of It All* 1963 (sc,story); *The Art of Love* 1965 (a,sc); *Alice of Wonderland in Paris* 1966 (a); *Don't Worry, We'll Think of a Title* 1966 (a); *Enter Laughing* 1966 (d,p,sc,from novel); *The Russians Are Coming, the Russians Are Coming* 1966 (a); *A Guide For the Married Man* 1967 (a); *The Comic* 1969 (d,p,sc); *Generation* 1969 (a); *Where's Poppa?* 1970 (d); *10 From Your Show of Shows* 1973 (a); *Oh, God!* 1977 (a,d); *The End* 1978 (a); *The One and Only* 1978 (d); *The Jerk* 1979 (a,d); *Dead Men Don't Wear Plaid* 1982 (a,d,sc); *The Man With Two Brains* 1983 (d,sc); *All of Me* 1984 (d); *Summer Rental* 1985 (d); *Summer School* 1987 (d); *Bert Rigby, You're a Fool* 1989 (d,sc); *Sibling Rivalry* 1990 (d); *Spirit of '76* 1990 (a).

Reiner, Rob • Director; also screenwriter, actor. • Born New York, NY, March 6, 1945. Reiner began his career as an actor and appeared in two films directed by his father, Carl (*Enter Laughing* 1966, *Where's Poppa* 1970) before gaining national prominence for his role as Archie Bunker's liberal son-in-law, Mike Stivic, on TV's landmark "All in the Family." He made a hilarious directorial debut with the "rockumentary" parody, *This Is Spinal Tap* (1984), and has since established himself as a leading comedic director with films such as *The Princess Bride* (1987) and *When Harry Met Sally...* (1989). Reiner demonstrated a sure feel for dramatic material with his poignant adaptation of Stephen King's adolescent thriller, *Stand By Me* (1986). Daughter Tracy Reiner (by actress-director Penny Marshall, from whom he is divorced) has appeared in films directed by both her parents; son Lucas directed his first feature, *Spirit of '76*, in 1990. • *Enter Laughing* 1966 (a); *Halls of Anger* 1970 (a); *Where's Poppa?* 1970 (a); *Summertree* 1971 (a); *How Come Nobody's on Our Side?* 1975 (a); *Fire Sale* 1977 (a); *This Is Spinal Tap* 1984 (a,d,sc,m,lyrics,song); *The Sure Thing* 1985 (d); *Stand By Me* 1986 (d); *The Princess Bride* 1987 (d,p); *Throw Momma From the Train* 1987 (a); *When Harry Met Sally...* 1989 (d,p); *Misery* 1990 (d,p); *Postcards From the Edge* 1990 (a); *Spirit of '76* 1990 (a); *Regarding Henry* 1991 (a).

Reinhardt, Max • Director • Born Maximilian Goldman, Baden, Austria, September 8, 1873; died 1943. One of the most prolific and influential figures of German theater in the early 20th century. Reinhardt was director of Berlin's Deutsches Theater from 1903, co-founded the annual Salzburg Festival in 1920 and owned and operated a string of theaters throughout Germany and Austria. Though he made only four films in Europe, he brought to the stage the expressionist aesthetic which greatly influenced the burgeoning German cinema. He also trained some of the greatest talents of Weimer cinema, including directors William Dieterle, Paul Leni, Ernst Lubitsch and F.W. Murnau, and actors Elisabeth Bergner, Curt Bois, Marlene Dietrich, Emil Jannings and Conrad Veidt.

In 1933 Reinhardt left Europe for the US, where he co-directed (with Dieterle) one more film, an adaptation of his famous stage production of *A Midsummer Night's Dream* (1935). One son, Gottfried, began working as a Hollywood scenarist in the mid-1930s and later produced and directed films in both the US and Europe; another, Wolfgang, was a screenwriter, producer and occasional actor. • *Sumurun* 1908 (d); *Das Mirakel* 1912 (d); *Insel der Seligen* 1913 (d); *Eine Venezianische Nacht* 1914 (d); *A Midsummer Night's Dream* 1935 (d,p).

Reinhold, Judge • Actor • Born Wilmington, DE, 1956. *Educ.* Mary Washington College; North Carolina School of the Arts, Winston-Salem. Engaging comic actor who began his career in regional theater. Reinhold made his mark as the blundering senior in *Fast Times at Ridgemont High* (1982) and is perhaps best known as the ineffectual detective in *Beverly Hills Cop* (1984). • *Pandemonium* 1981 (a); *Stripes* 1981 (a); *Fast Times at Ridgemont High* 1982 (a); *The Lords of Discipline* 1983 (a); *Beverly Hills Cop* 1984 (a); *Gremlins* 1984 (a); *Roadhouse 66* 1984 (a); *Head Office* 1986 (a); *Off Beat* 1986 (a); *Ruthless People* 1986 (a); *Beverly Hills Cop II* 1987 (a); *A Soldier's Tale* 1988 (a); *Vice Versa* 1988 (a); *Rosalie Goes Shopping* 1989 (a); *Daddy's Dyin'... Who's Got the Will?* 1990 (a); *Enid Is Sleeping* 1990 (a); *Zandalee* 1991 (a,p).

Reisz, Karel • Director; also author, critic, producer. • Born Ostrava, Czechoslovakia, July 21, 1926. *Educ.* Emmanuel College, Cambridge (science). Arrived in England at the age of 12, having narrowly escaped the Nazi invasion of Czechoslovakia (both his parents later died in concentration camps). Reisz's first involvement with film came in the early 1950s, when he wrote for the influential journals *Sequence* and *Sight and Sound*, coming into contact with figures such as Tony Richardson and Lindsay Anderson. In 1953 he published *The Technique of Film Editing* (co-authored with Gavin Millar), a landmark study encompassing the theory, history and practice of editing which has gone into 27 editions to date.

In the mid-1950s Reisz and some of his *Sequence* colleagues translated their critical theories to the screen. The result was a short-lived documentary movement known as Free Cinema, to which Reisz contributed *Momma Don't Allow* (1956, co-directed with Tony Richardson) and the award-winning *We Are the Lambeth Boys* (1958). This was followed by his first feature, *Saturday Night and Sunday Morning* (1960), a fine example of the influence of Free Cinema on narrative film. *Saturday Night* enjoyed critical and commercial success for its gritty portrayal of the frustrations of working-class life and, together with Jack Clayton's *Room at the Top* and Richardson's *Look Back in Anger* (both 1959), heralded the renaissance of British cinema. Reisz directed three more British films (most notably *Morgan—A Suitable Case for Treatment* 1966) before beginning his Hollywood career with 1974's *The Gambler*, starring James Caan. Most of his US-produced movies have been unexceptional, though well acted. *The French Lieutenant's Woman* (1981) was a finely realized, intelligent version of John Fowles' novel, adapted for the screen by Harold Pinter. • *Momma Don't Allow (short)* 1956 (d); *Every Day Except Christmas* 1957 (p); *We Are the Lambeth Boys* 1958 (d); *Saturday Night and Sunday Morning* 1960 (d); *This Sporting Life* 1963 (p); *Night Must Fall* 1964 (d); *Morgan—A Suitable Case for Treatment* 1966 (d); *Isadora* 1968 (d); *The Gambler* 1974 (d); *Who'll Stop the Rain?* 1978 (d); *The French Lieutenant's Woman* 1981 (d); *Sweet Dreams* 1985 (d); *Everybody Wins* 1990 (d).

Reitman, Ivan • Producer, director; also composer. • Born Czechoslovakia, October 26, 1946. *Educ.* McMaster University, Hamilton, Ontario, Canada. In Canada from the age of four, Reitman began his career as a stage and TV producer and turned out his first feature film in 1971. Among his early, low-budget ventures were two films, *They Came from Within* (1975) and *Rabid* (1977), directed by David Cronenberg. He has played a significant role in the careers of Dan Aykroyd, who featured in the Reitman-produced TV show, "Greed," and Bill Murray, who starred in *Meatballs* (1979) and *Stripes* (1981). Both actors appeared in *Ghostbusters* (1984), Reitman's biggest commercial success to date.

The *Ghostbusters* quickly became part of 80s popular culture. Although less well known than contemporaries George (*Star Wars*) Lucas and Steven (*E.T.*) Spielberg, Reitman has had nearly as profound an effect on contemporary myth. • *Foxy Lady* 1971 (d,m,ed,p); *Cannibal Girls* 1972 (d,exec.p); *The Parasite Murders* 1975 (m,p); *Death Weekend* 1976 (m.sup,p); *They Came from Within* 1975 (p); *Rabid* 1977 (exec.p,m); *Et la terreur commence* 1978 (exec.p); *National Lampoon's Animal House* 1978 (p); *Meatballs* 1979 (d); *Heavy Metal* 1981 (p); *Stripes* 1981 (d,p); *Spacehunter: Adventures in the Forbidden Zone* 1983 (exec.p); *Ghostbusters* 1984 (d,p); *The Canadian Conspiracy* 1986 (a); *Legal Eagles* 1986 (d,p,story); *Big Shots* 1987 (exec.p); *Casual Sex?* 1988 (exec.p); *Feds* 1988 (exec.p); *Twins* 1988 (d,p); *Ghostbusters II* 1989 (d,p); *Kindergarten Cop* 1990 (d,p).

Remar, James • American actor • *Educ.* Neighborhood Playhouse. Rugged character player, adept in vicious, sometimes psychopathic roles. Best known for his roles as a homicidal maniac in *48 Hrs.* (1982) and a no-nonsense cop in *Drugstore Cowboy* (1989). • *On the Yard* 1978; *The Warriors* 1979; *Cruising* 1980; *The Long Riders* 1980; *Windwalker* 1980; *48 Hrs.* 1982; *Partners* 1982; *The Cotton Club* 1984; *Band of the Hand* 1986; *The Clan of the Cave Bear* 1986; *Quiet Cool* 1986; *Rent-A-Cop* 1988; *The Dream Team* 1989; *Drugstore Cowboy* 1989; *Zwei Frauen* 1989; *Tales From the Darkside, The Movie* 1990.

Remick, Lee • Actress • Born Boston, MA, December 14, 1935. *Educ.* Barnard College, New York. Talented leading lady of the 1950s and 60s who combines genteel respectability with alluring sensuality. Remick has been effective in flirtatious, manipulative roles (*The Long Hot Summer* 1958, *Anatomy of a Murder* 1959) and as pathetic or victimized women (*Sanctuary* 1961, *Days of Wine and Roses* 1962). She demonstrated a flair for comedy in *A Severed Head* and *Loot* (both 1970). Remick began her career on stage and TV and continues to appear in both media. • *A Face in the Crowd* 1957; *The Long, Hot Summer* 1958; *Anatomy of a Murder* 1959; *These Thousand Hills* 1959; *Sanctuary* 1961; *Days of Wine and Roses* 1962 **(AANBA)**; *Experiment in Terror* 1962; *The Running Man* 1963; *The Wheeler Dealers* 1963; *Baby, the Rain Must Fall* 1965; *The Hallelujah Trail* 1965; *The Detective* 1968; *No Way to Treat a Lady* 1968; *Hard Contract* 1969; *Loot* 1970; *A Severed Head* 1970; *Sometimes a Great Notion* 1971; *A Delicate Balance* 1973; *Hennessy* 1975; *The Omen* 1976; *Telefon* 1977; *The Medusa Touch* 1978; *The Europeans* 1979; *The Competition* 1980; *Tribute* 1980; *Montgomery Clift* 1982; *Emma's War* 1985; *The Vision* 1987.

Rennahan, Ray • Director of photography • Born Raymond Rennahan, Las Vegas, NM, May 1, 1896; died 1980. Pioneer of color photography who began his career as a cameraman in 1917. Rennahan produced striking color images for films such as *The Mystery of the Wax Museum* (1933) and *Wings of the Morning* (1937)—the first British Technicolor film, co-shot with Jack Cardiff. He switched to working in TV in the late 1950s. • *Blood Test* 1923 (ph); *Gold Diggers of Broadway* 1929 (ph); *King of Jazz* 1930 (ph); *The Vagabond King* 1930 (ph); *Whoopee* 1930 (ph); *Fanny Foley Herself* 1931 (ph); *The Runaround* 1931 (ph); *Doctor X* 1932 (ph—Technicolor); *The Mystery of the Wax Museum* 1933 (ph); *Becky Sharp* 1935 (ph); *Ebb Tide* 1937 (ph); *Wings of the Morning* 1937 (ph); *Her Jungle Love* 1938 (ph); *Kentucky* 1938 (ph); *Drums Along the Mohawk* 1939 (ph); *Gone With the Wind* 1939 (ph,Technicolor associate) **(AABPH)**; *The Blue Bird* 1940 (ph) **(AANBPH)**; *Chad Hanna* 1940 (ph); *Down Argentine Way* 1940 (ph) **(AANBPH)**; *Maryland* 1940 (ph); *Belle Starr* 1941 (ph); *Blood and Sand* 1941 (ph) **(AABPH)**; *Louisiana Purchase* 1941 (ph) **(AANBPH)**; *For Whom the Bell Tolls* 1943 (ph) **(AANBPH)**; *Victory Through Air Power* 1943 (ph); *Belle of the Yukon* 1944 (ph); *Lady In The Dark* 1944 (ph) **(AANBPH)**; *The Three Caballeros* 1944 (ph); *Up in Arms* 1944 (ph); *Incendiary Blonde* 1945 (ph); *It's a Pleasure* 1945 (ph); *A Thousand and One Nights* 1945 (ph); *California* 1947 (ph); *Duel in the Sun* 1947 (ph); *The Perils of Pauline* 1947 (ph); *Unconquered* 1947 (ph); *The Paleface* 1948 (ph); *A Connecticut Yankee in King Arthur's Court* 1949 (ph); *Streets of Laredo* 1949 (ph); *Whispering Smith* 1949 (ph); *The White Tower* 1950 (ph); *Flaming Feather* 1951 (ph); *The Great Missouri Raid* 1951 (ph); *Silver City* 1951 (ph); *Warpath* 1951 (ph); *At Sword's Point* 1952 (ph); *The Denver and Rio Grande* 1952 (ph); *Hurricane Smith* 1952 (ph); *Arrowhead* 1953 (ph); *Flight to Tangier* 1953 (ph); *Pony Express* 1953 (ph); *Stranger on Horseback* 1954 (ph); *A Lawless Street* 1955 (ph); *Rage at Dawn* 1955 (ph); *Texas Lady* 1955 (ph); *The Halliday Brand* 1956 (ph); *Seventh Cavalry* 1956 (ph); *The Guns of Fort Petticoat* 1957 (ph); *Terror in a Texas Town* 1958 (ph).

Renoir, Claude • Director of photography • Born Paris, December 4, 1914. Apprenticed under noted cinematographers Christian Matras and Boris Kaufman and shot or co-shot several films directed by his uncle, Jean Renoir (*La Grande Illusion* 1937; *La Bête Humaine* 1938; *The River* 1951, *The Golden Coach* 1953, *Elena and Her Men* 1955). Renoir was also responsible for the stark black-and-white compositions of Maurice Cloche's *Monsieur Vincent* (1947) and the psychedelic 1960s colors of Roger Vadim's *Barbarella* (1968). Son of character actor Pierre Renoir (1885-1952) and not to be confused with his other uncle, Claude Renoir, who worked in a production capacity on several Jean Renoir films. • *Toni* 1934 (ph); *Un Partie de Campagne/A Day in the Country* 1936 (ph); *La Grande Illusion/Grand Illusion* 1937 (ph); *La Bête Humaine* 1938 (ad); *La Marseillaise* 1938 (ad); *Prison sans Barreaux* 1938 (ph); *Opéra-Musette* 1942 (d); *Monsieur Vincent* 1947 (ph); *Impasse des deux anges* 1948 (ph); *Alice in Wonderland* 1951 (ph—French version); *The Green Glove* 1951 (ph); *The River* 1951 (ph); *The Golden Coach* 1952 (ph); *Crime et Chatiment* 1956 (ph); *Eléna et les Hommes/Elena and Her Men* 1956 (ph); *Le Mystère Picasso/The Mystery of Picasso* 1956 (ph); *Les Sorcières de Salem* 1956 (ph); *...Et mourir de plaisir* 1960 (ph); *Cleopatra* 1963 (2u ph); *Circus World* 1964 (2u ph); *Barbarella* 1968 (ph); *The Madwoman of Chaillot* 1969 (ph); *La Dame dans l'auto avec des lunettes et un fusil/The Lady in the Car With Glasses and a Gun* 1970 (ph); *Les Mariés de l'an Deux* 1970 (ph); *Le Casse* 1971 (ph); *The Horsemen* 1971 (ph); *Le Tueur* 1971 (ph); *Helle* 1972 (ph); *Impossible Object* 1973 (ph); *Le Serpent/The Serpent* 1973 (ph); *Paul et Michelle* 1974 (ph); *Calmos* 1975 (ph); *Docteur Françoise Gailland* 1975 (ph); *French Connection II* 1975 (ph); *La Traque* 1975 (ph); *L'Aile et la Cuisse* 1976 (ph); *Une Femme Fidèle* 1976 (ph); *L'Animal* 1977 (ph); *The Spy Who Loved Me* 1977 (ph); *Attention, les enfants regardent* 1978 (ph); *La Zizanie* 1978 (ph); *Le Toubib* 1979 (ph).

Renoir, Jean • Director, screenwriter; also producer, actor. • Born Montmartre, Paris, September 15, 1894; died February 12, 1979, Hollywood. *Educ.* Collège Saint-Croix, Neuilly, France; Ecole Sainte-Marie de Monceau; Ecole Massena, Nice; Univerity of Aix-en-Provence (mathematics, philosophy). Renoir is arguably the greatest artist that the cinema has ever known, simply because he was able to work effectively in virtually all genres without sacrificing his individuality or bowing to public or commercial conventions. Although the son of the famed impressionist painter Auguste Renoir, his visual sensibility was entirely his own, and the technical facility that marks his films is the result of long and assiduous study.

Renoir's first serious interest in cinema developed during a period of recuperation after he had been wounded by a stray bullet while serving with the Alpine infantry in 1915. His first active involvement came in 1924, when money raised by the sale of some of his father's paintings (Auguste Renoir had died in 1919) allowed him to began production on *Catherine/Une Vie Sans Joie* in 1924. Renoir provided the screenplay and Albert Dieudonné the direction; Renoir's young wife Andrée Madeleine Heuchling, a former model of his father's, was the star, with her name changed to Catherine Hessling for billing purposes.

Renoir's first film as director, *La Fille de L'eau,* was shot in 1924, with Renoir also functioning as producer and art director and Catherine Hessling again starring. Anticipating Jean Vigo's *L'Atalante* (1934), the film's plot centered on a young woman who lives and works on a river boat. It's modest success led Renoir to plunge, somewhat impulsively, into the direction of *Nana* (1926), an adaptation from the Zola novel which now looks uncharacteristically stagebound.

Nearly bankrupt, Renoir had to take out a loan to finance his next film, *Charleston* (1927), a 24-minute fantasy that featured Hessling teaching the popular title dance in costumes that were as brief as possible. After it attained only limited success, Renoir accepted a straight commercial directing job on *Marquitta* (1927).

Renoir's next significant film was *Tire-au-Flanc* (1928), a military comedy that François Truffaut would later call a visual "tour de force" and which marked the director's first collaboration with actor Michel Simon. The working relationship between Renoir and Hessling, meanwhile, had taken its toll; the couple separated in 1930, though Hessling continued to appear in Renoir's films through *Crime et Châtiment/Crime and Punishment* (1935).

To prove that he understood the new medium of the sound film, Renoir directed a down-and-dirty comedy based on a farce by Georges Feydeau, *On*

Purge Bébé (1931). The film was shot on a very brief schedule, with Renoir apparently letting the camera run for as long as possible during each take, in order to work around the clumsy sound-on-disc recording apparatus. He also inserted a number of instances of mild "blue humor" (for example, the sound of a toilet heard flushing off-screen). Perhaps because he had aimed so resolutely for commercial success, Renoir's first talkie was a huge hit, allowing him to rush into production on his first major sound film, *La Chienne/The Bitch* (1931). This was the first of his films to be edited by Marguerite Mathieu, with whom Renoir became romantically involved at this time and who would later take the name Marguerite Renoir, though the couple never married. It was on this film, too, that Renoir developed his early strategy of sound shooting. In the face of objections from his producers down to his sound technicians, he insisted on using only natural sync-sound, recorded for the most part in actual locations. He also made extensive use of a moving camera, particularly in one sequence where the camera "waltzes" around the dance floor, keeping perfect time with the actors.

Renoir next directed his brother Pièrre in *La Nuit du Carrefour/Night at the Crossroads* (1932), a brilliant but little-seen detective film based on one of Georges Siménon's Inspector Maigret novels. He followed it with the delightful comedy, *Boudu Sauvé des Eaux/Boudu Saved From Drowning* (1932). The film uses Renoir's by now polished on-location sync-sound shooting technique to tell the tale of Boudu (Michel Simon), a bum who is fished out of the Seine after a suicide attempt by a well-meaning bourgeois bookseller, Lestingois (Charles Granval). Taken into the Lestingois household, Boudu wreaks havoc until he escapes during a boating accident, free to wander again. The charm and invention of this beautiful film make it one of the glories of the early sound cinema. (It was remade in 1986 by director Paul Mazursky as *Down and Out in Beverly Hills.*)

With the critical and popular success of *Boudu*, Renoir embarked upon a project reminiscent of *Nana. Madame Bovary* (1934) starred Pièrre Renoir as Charles Bovary and Valentine Tessier as Emma Bovary. The first cut of the film ran three hours and thirty minutes, but it was eventually trimmed to two hours. Still, the film met with little commercial success; undeterred, Renoir began shooting *Toni* (1934) almost entirely on location in Martigues, using non-professional actors in most of the roles. *Toni* thus presages the Italian Neorealist movement by more than a decade, and in following his inherent bent for "naturalism," Renoir created a beautiful and tragic film which is now recognized as one of his finest works. Nevertheless, the film met with little public or critical favor, a pattern which was becoming increasingly familiar.

Renoir's next film, *The Crime of Monsieur Lange* (1936), marked the director's only collaboration with writer Jacques Prévert, and gave ample evidence of the director's increasing politicization. Marked by beautiful, fluid, yet carefully precise camera work, as well as the excellent ensemble acting of the Groupe Octobre, *The Crime of Monsieur Lange* is one of Renoir's finest and most accessible films. It was followed by *La Vie est à nous/People of France* (1936), a political tract which bears a striking resemblance to Godard's 16mm "ciné tracts" of the late 1960s and early 70s. Initially withheld by the censor, the film enjoyed a limited release in the US in 1937 but was not shown to the paying French public until 1969, as a result of the student riots in France the previous May.

Renoir was now nearing the end of his first great stage of directorial activity, and in rapid succession he created a series of unforgettable films: *Une Partie de Compagne/A Day in the Country* (1936), based on a short story by Guy de Maupassant, completed in the face of considerable production difficulties, and not released in France until 1946 and the US in 1950; *Les Bas Fonds/The Lower Depths* (1936), an adaptation of the Maxim Gorky play; *La Grande Illusion/Grand Illusion* (1937), one of the best known and beloved films of all time, as compelling an anti-war document as has ever been created; *La Marseillaise* (1938), an examination of the events of the French Revolution, characteristically reduced to human scale, despite impressive production values; *La Bête Humaine/The Human Beast* (1938), an adaptation of Zola's novel (remade by Fritz Lang in 1954 as *Human Desire*); and finally, *La Règle du jeu/The Rules of the Game* (1939), now universally recognized as the director's masterwork, although, amazingly enough, it was reviled upon its initial release. This astutely observed tale of romance among the aristocrats and working class during a sporting weekend in the country was a complete box-office failure on its initial release. The film was withdrawn after a brief run and not revived until 1945, and later 1948—and then only in a mutilated version which gave no sense of the original. It was not until 1965 that the "definitive" version of the film was painfully reconstructed from various archival materials.

Renoir spent much of 1939 in Rome, teaching at the Centro Sperimental di Cinematografia. He co-wrote, with Carl Koch and Luchino Visconti, a screen version of *La Tosca* and began production on it in the spring of 1940, only to be interrupted by Italy's entry into WWII. Koch completed the film, and Renoir returned to France.

In 1940, however, Renoir came to America at the behest of documentarian Robert Flaherty. His "American period" would be marked by a number of uneven films, but saw the production of at least two of great beauty and accomplishment. Renoir enjoyed modest success with his first American film, *Swamp Water* (1941), starring Dana Andrews, Walter Huston, John Carradine and Walter Brennan and filmed on location in Georgia. Meanwhile, however, his admirers in France had turned on him. At a crucial moment in his country's history, they complained, the director had "gone Hollywood." Disregarding the controversy for the moment, Renoir signed to shoot a Deanna Durbin musical, then abandoned the project nearly two-thirds of the way through shooting.

This misadventure was followed by *This Land Is Mine* (1943), a story of the French resistance shot entirely on studio sets, starring Charles Laughton, Kent Smith, George Sanders and Maureen O'Hara. The film did acceptable business in the US, but received a truly hostile reception in France. Renoir attempted to make amends with a 20-minute short, *Salute to France* (1944), which was produced by the Office of War Information from a script by Philip Dunne, Renoir and Burgess Meredith, who also acted in the film. Kurt Weill supplied the music for this well-intentioned effort, which did nothing to salvage Renoir's reputation at home, although it was well received in the US.

Renoir's next film was an independent production, *The Southerner* (1945), starring Zachary Scott, Betty Field, J. Carrol Naish and Percy Kilbride. Working with his old associate Eugène Lourié as set designer, Robert Aldrich as assistant director and William Faulkner as dialogue consultant, Renoir created one of his most satisfying American films, a tale of the trials and tribulations of an Southern cotton farmer. *The Southerner* received the best contemporary critical notices of any of its director's American efforts.

The Diary of a Chambermaid (1946) was a curious choice for Renoir, and the result was a highly uneven film. The cast included Paulette Goddard, Burgess Meredith (who also co-produced and co-authored the screenplay), Hurd Hatfield, Reginald Owen, Judith Anderson, Irene Ryan and Francis Lederer. Shot on severely stylized studio sets, the film is overtly theatrical and eschews almost entirely the style Renoir had so carefully developed in his early sound films of the 1930s.

Renoir's last American film, *The Woman on the Beach* (1947), was directed for RKO. He originally developed the idea for the film with producer Val Lewton, justly famous for his series of horror films for RKO in the 1940s. However, Lewton left the production before shooting commenced and the film was substantially cut before its release. At least two versions now circulate; the most complete edition begins with a long undersea nightmare sequence reminiscent of *La Fille de L'eau,* in which the film's protagonists, Robert Ryan and Joan Bennett, encounter each other at the bottom of the ocean. Jacques Rivette, Manny Farber and other critics have hailed the film as a masterpiece. Mutilated as it is, it displays a maturity of vision equal to the precise grace of *The Rules of the Game* or *The Crime of Monsieur Lange.* In truncated versions running as short as 71 mimutes, the film is only a fragment of what it might have been, but Rivette has aptly compared it to Erich von Stroheim's *Greed* (1925).

Renoir's third and final period as a director begins with *The River* (1950), an independently produced film based on Rumer Godden's novel. Shot entirely in Calcutta, it won first prize at the Venice Film Festival in 1951. This relaxed and contemplative coming-of-age story, beautifully photographed in Technicolor, represents a return to the naturalism of Renoir's early work. *Le Carosse d'or/The Golden Coach* (1952) shares with *Diary of a Chambermaid* an intense interest in theatrical film style, and gave Anna Magnani one of her greatest roles as Camilla, the fiery diva of a traveling theater troupe. Though Eric Rohmer has called *Le Carosse d'or* "the 'open sesame' of all of Renoir's work," the film was not well received upon its initial release.

Renoir was unable to find backing for another film until *French Cancan* (1954, sometimes known in the US as *Only the French Can*), his first made in France in over 15 years. This valentine to the Moulin Rouge met with great public success and featured a number of French music hall performers in cameo roles, including a very brief appearance by Edith Piaf. *Elena et les Hommes/Paris Does Strange Things* (1956) starred Ingrid Bergman, Jean Marais and Mel Ferrer in another, lightweight love letter to a bygone age.

Le Testament du Dr. Cordelier (1959), though not regarded as one of Renoir's finest works, has him using multiple cameras for the first time, blocking the film as though it were a stage play in the manner now routinely used by TV sitcoms. Based on *Dr. Jekyll & Mr. Hyde,* the film stars Jean-Louis Barrault as Dr. Cordelier and his mad alter ego, Opale, and is shot in stark black-and-white, in contrast to the lush coloring of Renoir's other film of this final period.

Le Déjeuner sur l'herbe/Picnic on the Grass (1959) followed, a topical fantasy film which has much in common with *Une Partie de Campagne.* Shot in delicious pastel colors, the film is at once ephemeral and melancholic, as if the director were acknowledging his bewilderment in the face of the "civilizing" forces of modern society. *Le Caporal épinglé/The Elusive Corporal* (1962) is a return to the drabness of *Le Testament du Dr. Cordelier;* it recalls *La Grande Illusion* in its WWII tale of the numerous escape attempts of a corporal (Jean-Pierre Cassel) who is incarcerated in a series of German prison camps.

In 1968, Renoir appeared in and directed a short film, *La Direction D'Acteur par Jean Renoir* which shows him directing the actress Gisèle Braunberger in a scene from a Rumer Godden novel, *Breakfast with Nicolaides.* Shot in a half-day, the film's direction credit is sometimes given to Ms. Braunberger. The following year, Renoir directed his last feature, *Le Petit Théâtre de Jean Renoir,* which was released in 1971. Jeanne Moreau is featured in four sketches which Renoir wrote, directed and narrated for French TV; when released theatrically in the US, it was warmly received, even though it was far from the director's most accomplished work.

At last, the public had caught up with Jean Renoir. *The Rules of the Game* had long since been reconstituted and enshrined as one of the greatest films of all time, and its director was pleased to accept an honorary Oscar in 1975 for his lifetime achievement in the cinema. The year before, Renoir had completed his memoirs, *Ma Vie et Mes Films/My Life and My Films,* which contain valuable insights into the director's method of scripting, direction and his ability to retain a sense of "self" in a highly commercial and competitive industry. In 1977, Renoir received his final major honor, the French Legion of Honor. WWD • *Un Vie Sans Joie/Catherine* 1924 (sc); *La Fille de l'eau* 1924 (art d,d,p); *Nana* 1926 (d,ed,p); *Charleston (short)* 1927 (d,p); *Marquitta* 1927 (d); *La P'Tite Lili* 1927 (d); *La Petite marchande d'allumettes/The Little Match Girl* 1928 (d,p,sc); *Tire-au-Flanc* 1928 (d,sc); *Le Bled* 1929 (d); *La Chienne* 1931 (d,sc,ed); *On Purge Bébé* 1931 (d); *Boudu Sauvé des Eaux/Boudu Saved From Drowning* 1932 (d,sc); *Chotard et Compagnie* 1932 (d,sc); *La Nuit du Carrefour* 1932 (d); *Madame Bovary* 1934 (d,sc); *Toni* 1934 (d,sc,dial); *Crime et Châtiment/Crime and Punishment* 1935 (d); *Les Bas-Fonds/The Lower Depths* 1936 (d,sc); *Le Crime de Monsieur Lange* 1936 (d,sc); *Un Partie de Campagne/A Day in the Country* 1936 (a,d,sc); *La Vie est à nous/People of France* 1936 (d,sc); *La Grande Illusion/The Grande Illusion* 1937 (d,sc); *La Bête Humaine* 1938 (d); *La Marseillaise* 1938 (d,sc,dial); *La Règle du jeu/The Rules of the Game* 1939 (a,d,sc,adapt,dial); *Swamp Water* 1941 (d); *La Tosca* 1941 (co-sc,d); *The Amazing Mrs. Holliday* 1943 (d); *This Land Is Mine* 1943 (d,p); *A Salute to France* 1944 (d); *The Southerner* 1945 (d,sc) **(AANBD)**; *The Diary of a Chambermaid* 1946 (d); *The Woman on the Beach* 1947 (d,sc); *The River* 1950 (d); *La Carrozza d'Oro/The Golden Coach* 1952 (d); *French Cancan* 1954 (d,p,sc); *Elena et les hommes/Paris Does Strange Things* 1956 (d); *Le Dejéuner sur l'herbe* 1959 (d); *Le Testament du Dr. Cordelier* 1959 (d); *Le Caporal épinglé* 1962 (d); *Jean Renoir, le Patron* 1966 (a); *Le Petit Théâtre de Jean Renoir* 1969 (d,sc); *The Christian Licorice Store* 1971 (a); *Vivement Truffaut!* 1985 (a).

Resnais, Alain • Director; also screenwriter, editor. • Born Vannes, France, June 3, 1922. *Educ.* IDHEC, Paris. An important modern figure whose films consistently deal with the effects of the past on the present, Alain Resnais began making documentary shorts in the late 1940s, often on art subjects (*Van Gogh* 1948, *Gauguin* and *Guernica,* both 1950). Resnais's most memorable documentary achievement is the 31-minute elegy *Night and Fog* (1956), called by then-critic François Truffaut the greatest film ever made. A harrowing look at concentration camps and the Holocaust, it carefully juxtaposes documentary footage shot in black-and-white by the Allied troops who liberated the camps with contemporary color footage. The poetic refrain of the narrator—"Who is responsible?"—forces us to confront the Holocaust as a continuing potentiality.

Although Resnais's rise to prominence coincided with that of the other New Wave directors, he was older than Godard, Truffaut, Chabrol, *et al.* And unlike those figures, who had worked as critics before turning to directing, Resnais, along with the other members of the "Left Bank School"—Agnès Varda, Chris Marker, Jacques Demy—had already gained experience within the traditional film industry. His debut feature, *Hiroshima, Mon Amour* (1959), won the International Critics Prize at the same Cannes Film Festival that named François Truffaut best director for *The 400 Blows.* Expanding on the stylistic experiments of *Night and Fog,* this collaboration with screenwriter Marguerite Duras details the affair between a Japanese man and a French actress who has come to Hiroshima to make a film about the atomic holocaust. Particularly notable is the long opening sequence which juxtaposes the images of the nude, intertwined lovers with horrific documentary footage of the aftermath of the bombing. Resnais's montage allows him to travel from one place to another and from the "present" to a variety of past times. Like *Night and Fog, Hiroshima, Mon Amour* asks if we are destined to forget the past and thus be forced, in some way, to relive it.

In 1961 came Resnais's experimental feature, *Last Year at Marienbad,* scripted by Alain Robbe-Grillet. An expressionist exercise in the manipulation of time and memory, *Marienbad* places three characters, enigmatically named A, X and M, within the endless corridors and grounds of a huge castle resort, where they may or may not have previously met. Throughout the film, the camera lovingly and sensuously dollies through the corridors to reveal the physical realities of the castle's objects and geometrically choreographed movements of characters, who act more like automatons than people—even though (in one of the most famous images from the film) they have shadows, whereas the trees and gardens do not.

Two films more concretely grounded in specific social and political realities followed: *Muriel* (1963), about one family's moral dilemnas within the context of the Algerian War; and *La Guerre est finie* (1966), about an aging revolutionary in contemporary France. Both films embedded their plots within typically intricate and convoluted narratives and stylistic devices, with the flashforwards in *La Guerre est finie* particularly notable. With a script by Jorge Semprun, *La Guerre est finie* remains Resnais's most fully realized effort. As the 20th-century battle between Left and Right comes to an end, this intelligent essay gains in importance.

Je T'aime, je t'aime (1968), one of Resnais's rarely screened films, continued his interest in time and memory—this time in the context of a love story which included the science-fiction element of a time machine in which the protagonist gets trapped. Resnais takes a real editor's joy in intercutting shots from various arbitrary time periods in his protagonist's mundane life, creating an exhilarating visual music based on and celebrating the rhythms of everyday life.

Stavisky. . . (1974), with a score by Stephen Sondheim, is Resnais's most approachable film. Jean-Paul Belmondo stars in this commercial and romantic story of the 1930s adventurer/con-man, as Resnais enjoys recreating a time when the media (popular newspapers, radio) not only colored but sometimes created the reality it reported. *Providence* (1977), the director's first English-language film, explores the workings of the creative process. With a script by playwright David Mercer and a cast including John Gielgud, Dirk Bogarde, Elaine Stritch and Ellen Burstyn, *Providence* is an almost perverse undertaking, with Resnais using the English language to explore particularly French (and particularly dry) ideas about writing.

Mon Oncle d'Amerique (1980) is a provocative, humorous expansion of biologist Henri Laborit's theories on the human condition, intercutting the stories of three people suffering from stress with footage from a lecture about the effects of frustration on rats. *Life Is a Bed of Roses* (1983) is set in a French chateau occupied, at different points during a 70-year period, by three groups of people: a hedonistic count and his friends who attempt to achieve perfect happiness in the 1920s; a group of international scholars who debate "The Education of the Imagination" in the 1980s; and a group of schoolchildren on summer vacation who conjure up a fairytale romance. Whimsical and gently satirical, it is one of Resnais's more accessible works. *L'Amour à Mort* (1984) is a rather dry meditation on resurrection, in which an architect literally comes back from the dead to experience life and love with a new intensity.

Resnais turned to more conventional—and much less interesting—material in *Mélo* (1987), an adaptation of a 1929 stage play about a romantic triangle. In general, his more recent work, though continuing to experiment with narrative conventions, has lacked the emotional power and vision of his early, groundbreaking films. CD, JM • *Van Gogh (short)* 1948 (d,ed); *Gauguin (short)* 1950 (d,ed); *Guernica (short)* 1950 (d,ed); *Les Statues Meurent Aussi (short)* 1953 (d,sc,commentary,ed); *Nuit et Brouillard/Night and Fog (short)* 1955 (d); *Toute la Mémoire du Monde (short)* 1956 (d,ed); *Le Mystère de l'atelier Quinze (short)* 1957 (d); *Le Chant du Styrène (short)* 1958 (d,ed); *Hiroshima, Mon Amour* 1959 (d); *L' Année dernière a Marienbad/Last Year at Marienbad* 1961 (d); *Muriel* 1963 (d); *La Guerre est finie* 1966 (d); *Loin du Vietnam* 1967 (d); *Je T'aime, je t'aime* 1968 (adapt,dial,d); *Stavisky* 1973 (d); *Providence* 1977 (d); *Mon oncle d'Amerique* 1979 (d); *La Vie est un roman* 1983 (d); *L'Amour à mort* 1984 (d); *Mélo* 1986 (d,sc); *Je veux rentrer à la maison* 1989 (d).

Reville, Alma • Screenwriter • Born England, 1900; died 1982. Continuity superviser and assistant editor who worked in minor capacities on Alfred Hitchcock's first two films, married him in 1926, and subsequently collaborated on many of his scripts. Reville also contributed to other features, notably the Fred Allen vehicle, *It's in the Bag* (1945). • *The Ring* 1927 (adapt); *The Constant Nymph* 1928 (cont); *Juno and the Paycock* 1930 (sc); *Murder* 1930 (sc); *The Outsider* 1931 (sc); *The Skin Game* 1931 (sc); *Rich and Strange* 1932 (sc); *Waltzes From Vienna* 1934 (sc); *The 39 Steps* 1935 (sc,cont); *Sabotage* 1936 (adapt); *Secret Agent* 1936 (sc); *Young and Innocent* 1937 (sc); *Suspicion* 1941 (sc); *Shadow of a Doubt* 1943 (sc); *It's in the Bag* 1945 (sc,story); *The Paradine Case* 1947 (adapt); *Stage Fright* 1950 (adapt).

Rey, Fernando • Actor • Born Fernando Casado Arambillet, La Coruna, Spain, September 20, 1917. *Educ.* Madrid School of Architecture. Versatile talent who has appeared in several English-language features. Rey is best known for his usually deadpan peformances in the later films of countryman Luis Buñuel, particularly *That Obscure Object of Desire* (1977). He played Worcester in Orson Welles's *Chimes at Midnight* (1966) and the elusive drug kingpin in the *French Connection* movies. His role in Carlos Saura's *Elisa, Vida mia* earned him a best actor award at Cannes in 1977. • *The Siege* 1954; *Marcelino* 1955; *Pantaloons* 1956; *Mission in Morocco* 1959; *Viridiana* 1961; *The Ceremony* 1963; *The Running Man* 1963; *El Valle de las espadas/The Castilian* 1963; *Echappement libre* 1964; *Chimes at Midnight/Falstaff* 1966; *Navajo Joe* 1966; *Son of a Gunfighter* 1966; *Cervantes* 1967; *Le Vicomte Règle ses Comptes* 1967; *Histoire Immortelle/The Immortal Story* 1968; *Villa Rides* 1968; *Guns of the Magnificent Seven* 1969; *Land Raiders* 1969; *Antony and Cleopatra* 1970; *La Colera Del Viento* 1970; *Tristana* 1970; *Bianco, Rosso e...* 1971; *The French Connection* 1971; *The Light at the Edge of the World* 1971; *A Town Called Hell* 1971; *Le Charme Discret de la Bourgeoisie/The Discreet Charm of the Bourgeoisie* 1972; *La Duda* 1972; *La Chute D'Un Corps* 1973; *Questa Specie d'Amore* 1973; *Corruzione al Palazzo di Giustizia* 1974; *Dites-Le avec des fleurs* 1974; *La Femme aux Bottes Rouges* 1974; *Fatti di Gente Perbene/Drama of the Rich* 1975; *French Connection II* 1975; *Pasqualino Settebellezze* 1975; *Cadaveri Eccellenti* 1976; *A Matter of Time* 1976; *Voyage of the Damned* 1976; *Cet obscur objet du désir/That Obscure Object of Desire* 1977; *Elisa, Vida mia/Elisa, My Life* 1977; *El Segundo Poder* 1977; *Uppdraget/The Assignment* 1977; *Le Dernier Amant Romantique* 1978; *El Crimen de Cuenca* 1979; *Le Grand embouteillage* 1979; *Quintet* 1979; *Caboblanco* 1980; *Vera Storia Della Signora Delle Camelie* 1981; *Bearn* 1982; *Cercasi Gesu* 1982; *Monsignor* 1982; *La Straniera* 1982; *The Hit* 1984; *Una Strana Passione/A Strange Passion* 1984; *Padre Nuestro* 1985; *Rustler's Rhapsody* 1985; *El Caballero del Dragon* 1986; *Saving Grace* 1986; *El Bosque Animado* 1987; *Hotel du Paradis* 1987; *Mi General* 1987; *Les Predateurs de la nuit/Angel of Death* 1987; *El Aire de un Crimen* 1988; *Diario de Invierno* 1988; *Esmeralda Bay* 1988; *Moon Over Parador* 1988; *Pasodoble* 1988; *El Tunel* 1988; *Hard to Be a God* 1989; *Diceria dell'untore* 1990; *Naked Tango* 1990.

Reynolds, Burt • Actor; also director. • Born Burton Leon Reynolds, Jr., Waycross, GA, February 11, 1936. *Educ.* Florida State University; Hyde Park Playhouse, New York. Handsome, muscular leading man who first achieved prominence on TV's "Riverboat" in the late 1950s. Although he made his film debut in 1961 Reynolds remained best known for his small-screen work, notably on "Gunsmoke" (1962-65) and "Hawk" (1966-67). His movie breakthrough came in 1972 with a role in John Boorman's powerful backwoods drama, *Deliverance*, that pushed him into the front rank of

Hollywood stars. Reynolds's career as an actor-director began in 1976 with *Gator* and reached a peak with the taut cop drama, *Sharkey's Machine*, in 1981.

Reynolds made a successful transition to middle-aged parts with Bill Forsyth's engaging 1989 comedy, *Breaking In*. He has latterly turned his attention to TV production and to directing and teaching at the Burt Reynolds Dinner Theatre and Institute for Theatre Training in Jupiter, FL (founded 1978). Divorced from "Laugh-In" star Judy ("Sock it to me") Carne and married, since 1988, to TV actress Loni Anderson. • *Angel Baby* 1961 (a); *Armored Command* 1961 (a); *Operation C.I.A.* 1965 (a); *Navajo Joe* 1966 (a); *Fade-In* 1968 (a); *100 Rifles* 1969 (a); *Impasse* 1969 (a); *Sam Whiskey* 1969 (a); *Shark* 1969 (a); *Skullduggery* 1970 (a); *Deliverance* 1972 (a); *Everything You Always Wanted To Know About Sex* (*but were afraid to ask)* 1972 (a); *Fuzz* 1972 (a); *Shamus* 1972 (a); *The Man Who Loved Cat Dancing* 1973 (a); *White Lightning* 1973 (a); *The Longest Yard* 1974 (a); *W. W. and the Dixie Dancekings* 1974 (a); *At Long Last Love* 1975 (a); *Hustle* 1975 (a,exec.p); *Lucky Lady* 1975 (a,song); *Gator* 1976 (a,d); *Nickelodeon* 1976 (a); *Semi-Tough* 1977 (a); *Smokey and the Bandit* 1977 (a); *The End* 1978 (a,d); *Hooper* 1978 (a); *Starting Over* 1979 (a); *The Cannonball Run* 1980 (a); *Rough Cut* 1980 (a); *Smokey and the Bandit II* 1980 (a); *Paternity* 1981 (a); *Sharky's Machine* 1981 (a,d); *Best Friends* 1982 (a); *The Best Little Whorehouse in Texas* 1982 (a); *Cannonball Run II* 1983 (a); *The Man Who Loved Women* 1983 (a); *Smokey and the Bandit Part 3* 1983 (a); *Stroker Ace* 1983 (a); *City Heat* 1984 (a); *Uphill All the Way* 1984 (a); *Southern Voices, American Dreams* 1985 (a); *Stick* 1985 (a,d); *Heat* 1987 (a); *Malone* 1987 (a); *Physical Evidence* 1988 (a); *Rent-A-Cop* 1988 (a); *Switching Channels* 1988 (a); *All Dogs Go to Heaven* 1989 (a,song); *Breaking In* 1989 (a); *Modern Love* 1990 (a).

Reynolds, Debbie • Actress • Born Mary Frances Reynolds, El Paso, TX, April 1, 1932. Bubbly, wholesome star of the 1950s and 60s, primarily in MGM musicals and light comedies. Reynolds was at her best in the classic *Singin' in the Rain* (1952), as the spirited title character of Frank Tashlin's *Susan Slept Here* (1954) and—appropriately—as *The Unsinkable Molly Brown* (1964). Her daughter by first husband (1955-59) Eddie Fisher is actress Carrie Fisher, whose semi-autobiographical novel, *Postcards From the Edge*, was adapted for the screen in 1990; the Reynolds character was portrayed by Shirley MacLaine. • *The Daughter of Rosie O'Grady* 1950 (a); *Three Little Words* 1950 (a); *Two Weeks With Love* 1950 (a); *Mr. Imperium* 1951 (a); *Singin' in the Rain* 1952 (a); *The Affairs of Dobie Gillis* 1953 (a); *Give a Girl a Break* 1953 (a); *I Love Melvin* 1953 (a); *Athena* 1954 (a); *Susan Slept Here* 1954 (a); *Hit the Deck* 1955 (a); *The Tender Trap* 1955 (a); *Bundle of Joy* 1956 (a); *The Catered Affair* 1956 (a); *Tammy and the Bachelor* 1957 (a); *This Happy Feeling* 1958 (a,song); *It Started With a Kiss* 1959 (a,song); *The Mating Game* 1959 (a,song); *Say One For Me* 1959 (a,song); *The Gazebo* 1960 (a); *Pepe* 1960 (a); *The Rat Race* 1960 (a); *The Pleasure of His Company* 1961 (a); *The Second Time Around* 1961 (a); *How the West Was Won* 1962 (a); *Mary, Mary* 1963 (a); *My Six Loves* 1963 (a); *Goodbye, Charlie* 1964 (a); *The Unsinkable Molly Brown* 1964 (a) **(AANBA)**; *The Singing Nun* 1966 (a); *Divorce American Style* 1967 (a); *How Sweet It Is* 1968 (a); *What's The Matter With Helen?* 1971 (a); *Charlotte's Web* 1972 (a); *That's Entertainment!* 1974 (a).

Reynolds, Norman • Production designer • Born London. Began his career in the art department at the British branch of MGM. Reynolds worked his way through several British studios before becoming a full-fledged art director in 1976, when he earned an Oscar nomination for *The Incredible Sarah*. He began working on big-budget US productions in the late 1970s and is best known for *Star Wars* (1977) and *Raiders of the Lost Ark* (1981). • *A Warm December* 1972 (sets); *The Little Prince* 1974 (art d); *Lucky Lady* 1975 (art d); *Mr. Quilp* 1975 (art d); *The Incredible Sarah* 1976 (art d) **(AANBAD)**; *Star Wars* 1977 (art d); *Superman* 1978 (art d); *The Empire Strikes Back* 1980 (pd) **(AANBAD)**; *Superman II* 1980 (art d); *Raiders of the Lost Ark* 1981 (pd) **(AABAD)**; *Return of the Jedi* 1983 (fxpd) **(AANBAD)**; *Return to Oz* 1985 (pd); *Young Sherlock Holmes* 1985 (pd); *Empire of the Sun* 1987 (pd) **(AANBAD)**; *Avalon* 1990 (pd); *Mountains of the Moon* 1990 (pd); *William Peter Blatty's The Exorcist III* 1990 (fx d—Los Angeles).

Reynolds, William H. • Editor • Born Elmira, NY, 1910. Hollywood veteran who began his editing career in the late 1930s. Reynolds won Oscars for *The Sound of Music* (1965) and *The Sting* (1973) and was nominated for *Fanny* (1961), *The Sand Pebbles* (1966), *Hello, Dolly!* (1969), *The Godfather* (1972) and *The Turning Point* (1977). He also served as post-production executive on Michael Cimino's ill-fated *Heaven's Gate* (1980). • *52nd Street* 1937 (ed); *Algiers* 1938 (ed); *So Ends Our Night* 1941 (ed); *Moontide* 1942 (ed); *Carnival in Costa Rica* 1947 (ed); *Give My Regards to Broadway* 1948 (ed); *The Street With No Name* 1948 (ed); *You Were Meant For Me* 1948 (ed); *Come to the Stable* 1949 (ed); *Mother Is a Freshman* 1949 (ed); *The Day the Earth Stood Still* 1951 (ed); *The Frogmen* 1951 (ed); *Take Care of My Little Girl* 1951 (ed); *The Outcasts of Poker Flat* 1952 (ed); *Red Skies of Montana* 1952 (ed); *Beneath the 12 Mile Reef* 1953 (ed); *Dangerous Crossing* 1953 (ed); *The Kid From Left Field* 1953 (ed); *Desiree* 1954 (ed); *Three Coins in the Fountain* 1954 (ed); *Daddy Long Legs* 1955 (ed); *Good Morning, Miss Dove* 1955 (ed); *Love Is a Many Splendored Thing* 1955 (ed); *Bus Stop* 1956 (ed); *Carousel* 1956 (ed); *Time Limit!* 1957 (p); *In Love and War* 1958 (ed); *South Pacific* 1958 (prod.assoc); *Beloved Infidel* 1959 (ed); *Blue Denim* 1959 (ed); *Compulsion* 1959 (ed); *Chartroose Caboose* 1960 (d); *Wild River* 1960 (ed); *Fanny* 1961 (ed) **(AANBED)**; *Taras Bulba* 1962 (ed); *Tender Is the Night* 1962 (ed); *Kings of the Sun* 1963 (ed); *Ensign Pulver* 1964 (ed); *The Sound of Music* 1965 (ed) **(AABED)**; *Our Man Flint* 1966 (ed); *The Sand Pebbles* 1966 (ed) **(AANBED)**; *Star!* 1968 (ed); *Hello, Dolly!* 1969 (ed) **(AANBED)**; *What's The Matter With Helen?* 1971 (ed); *The Godfather* 1972 (ed) **(AANBED)**; *The Sting* 1973 (ed) **(AABED)**; *Two People* 1973 (ed); *The Great Waldo Pepper* 1975 (ed); *The Master Gunfighter* 1975 (ed); *The Seven Per-Cent Solution* 1976 (ed); *The Turning Point* 1977 (ed) **(AANBED)**; *Old Boyfriends* 1978 (ed); *A Little Romance* 1979 (ed); *Heaven's Gate* 1980 (post-prod.exec,ed); *Nijinsky* 1980 (ed); *Author! Author!* 1982 (ed); *Making Love* 1982 (ed); *Yellowbeard* 1983 (ed); *The Little Drummer Girl* 1984 (ed); *The Lonely Guy* 1984 (ed); *Pirates* 1986 (ed); *Dancers* 1987 (ed); *Ishtar* 1987 (ed); *A New Life* 1988 (ed); *Rooftops* 1989 (ed); *Taking Care of Business* 1990 (ed).

Rhys-Davies, John • Actor • Born Salisbury, Wiltshire, England, 1944. *Educ.* University of East Anglia (English, history); RADA, London. Heavy-set supporting player; memorable as Indiana Jones's accomplice, Sallah, in *Raiders of the Lost Ark* (1981). • *The Black Windmill* 1974 (a); *Sphinx* 1980 (a); *Raiders of the Lost Ark* 1981 (a); *Victor/Victoria* 1982 (a); *Best Revenge* 1984 (a); *In the Shadow of Kilimanjaro* 1984 (a); *Sahara* 1984 (a); *King Solomon's Mines* 1985 (a); *Firewalker* 1986 (a); *The Living Daylights* 1987 (a); *Il Giovane Toscanini* 1988 (a); *Waxwork* 1988 (a); *Indiana Jones and the Last Crusade* 1989 (a); *Rising Storm* 1989 (a); *Tusks* 1990 (a,sc).

Richards, Beah • Actress • Born Vicksburg, MS. *Educ.* Dillard University, New Orleans. Seasoned, understated black actress who began her career in the theater; best known for her roles as Sidney Poitier's mother in *Guess Who's Coming to Dinner?* (1967) and on TV series including "Frank's Place" and "Hill St. Blues." • *Take a Giant Step* 1959; *The Miracle Worker* 1962; *Gone Are the Days* 1963; *Guess Who's Coming to Dinner?* 1967 **(AANBSA)**; *Hurry Sundown* 1967; *In the Heat of the Night* 1967; *The*

Great White Hope 1970; *The Biscuit Eater* 1972; *Mahogany* 1975; *Inside Out* 1986; *Drugstore Cowboy* 1989.

Richardson, Miranda • Actress • Born Lancashire, England, 1958. *Educ.* Bristol University (drama). Began her career in regional theater and on British TV before making a stunning impression as Ruth Ellis, the last woman to be hanged in Britain, in Mike Newell's haunting *Dance With a Stranger* (1985). Richardson is also known for her comic portrayal of Queen Elizabeth I on TV's "Blackadder." • *The Innocent* 1984; *Dance With a Stranger* 1985; *After Pilkington* 1986; *The Death of the Heart* 1986; *Underworld* 1986; *Eat the Rich* 1987; *Empire of the Sun* 1987; *Ball-Trap on the Cote Sauvage* 1989; *El Mono Loco/The Mad Monkey* 1989; *The Fool* 1990.

Richardson, Natasha • Actress • Born London, May 11, 1963. *Educ.* Central School of Speech and Drama, London. Gifted stage and screen actress who has turned in fine performances in otherwise disappointing films (*Patty Hearst* 1988, *The Handmaid's Tale* 1989). Sister of actress Joely Richardson (who appeared opposite their mother Vanessa Redgrave in 1985's *Wetherby*) and daughter of director Tony Richardson. • *Every Picture Tells a Story* 1984; *Gothic* 1986; *A Month in the Country* 1987; *Patty Hearst* 1988; *Fat Man and Little Boy* 1989; *The Handmaid's Tale* 1989; *The Comfort of Strangers* 1990.

Richardson, Sir Ralph • Actor • Born Ralph David Richardson, Cheltenham, England, December 19, 1902; died October 10, 1983, London. *Educ.* Brighton School of Art. Illustrious British stage actor who made his professional debut in 1921 and first gained prominence—like John Gielgud and Alec Guiness—for his Shakesperean performances with the Old Vic. Richardson's film career was always secondary to his work in the theater, though he turned in several fine supporting roles, notably in the films of Carol Reed. He was memorable as the manservant in *The Fallen Idol* (1948), as Buckingham in *Richard III* (1955) and as the father in Sidney Lumet's *Long Day's Journey Into Night* (1962). Twice Oscar-nominated, for *The Heiress* (1949) and his final film, *Greystoke* (1984). • *Java Head* 1934 (a); *The Man Who Could Work Miracles* 1936 (a); *Things to Come* 1936 (a); *Thunder in the City* 1937 (a); *The Citadel* 1938 (a); *The Divorce of Lady X* 1938 (a); *Clouds Over Europe* 1939 (a); *The Four Feathers* 1939 (a); *Anna Karenina* 1948 (a); *The Fallen Idol* (1948); *The Heiress* 1949 (a) **(AANBSA)**; *Home at Seven* 1951 (d); *Outcast of the Islands* 1951 (a); *The Holly and the Ivy* 1952 (a); *The Sound Barrier* 1952 (a); *Richard III* 1955 (a); *The Passionate Stranger* 1957 (a); *Exodus* 1960 (a); *Oscar Wilde* 1960 (a); *The 300 Spartans* 1962 (a); *Long Day's Journey Into Night* 1962 (a); *Woman of Straw* 1964 (a); *Doctor Zhivago* 1965 (a); *Khartoum* 1966 (a); *The Wrong Box* 1966 (a); *Battle of Britain* 1969 (a); *The Bed Sitting Room* 1969 (a); *Oh! What a Lovely War* 1969 (a); *A Run on Gold* 1969 (a); *David Copperfield* 1970 (a); *The Looking Glass War* 1970 (a); *Upon This Rock* 1970 (a); *Eagle in a Cage* 1971 (a); *Who Slew Auntie Roo?* 1971 (a); *Alice's Adventures in Wonderland* 1972 (a); *Lady Caroline Lamb* 1972 (a); *Tales From The Crypt* 1972 (a); *A Doll's House* 1973 (a); *O Lucky Man!* 1973 (a); *Rollerball* 1975 (a); *Watership Down* 1978 (a); *Dragonslayer* 1981 (a); *Time Bandits* 1981 (a); *Give My Regards to Broad Street* 1983 (a); *Invitation to the Wedding* 1983 (a); *Wagner* 1983 (a); *Greystoke: The Legend of Tarzan, Lord of the Apes* 1984 (a) **(AANBSA)**; *Directed By William Wyler* 1986 (a).

Richardson, Robert • American director of photography • Richardson has shot all of Oliver Stone's films since first teaming up with him on the acclaimed independent production, *Salvador* (1986). • *Repo Man* 1984 (add.ph); *Platoon* 1986 (ph) **(AANBPH)**; *Salvador* 1986 (ph); *Dudes* 1987 (ph); *Wall Street* 1987 (ph); *Eight Men Out* 1988 (ph); *Talk Radio* 1988 (ph); *Born on the Fourth of July* 1989 (ph) **(AANBPH)**; *To the Moon, Alice (short)* 1990 (2u ph,visual consultant); *The Doors* 1991 (ph).

Richardson, Tony • Director; also producer. • Born Cecil Antonio Richardson, Shipley, Yorkshire, England, June 5, 1928. *Educ.* Wadham College, Oxford (English). Theater and film director primarily associated with the "Angry Young Man" movement of the late 1950s and early 60s. Richardson worked as a producer with the BBC from 1952 to 1955 and co-directed a short documentary about working-class youths, *Momma Don't Allow*, with Karel Reisz in 1955. The film was well received when shown at the first "Free Cinema" program in 1956—the same year that *Look Back in Anger*, a play written by John Osborne and directed by Richardson, shook up the English theatrical establishment with its bitter indictment of postwar culture.

Richardson continued to work with Osborne in the theater and, in 1958, the two formed Woodfall Film Productions in an attempt to bring the new theatrical sensibility to the screen. The company's first two features were adaptations of Richardson's and Osborne's stage collaborations—*Look Back in Anger* (1959) and *The Entertainer* (1960). Both featured fine performances, the first from Richard Burton and the second from Laurence Olivier, but failed to attract much interest at the box-office. (Woodfall's first commercial success came with 1960's *Saturday Night and Sunday Morning*, directed by Reisz.)

Richardson scored his first major hit with *A Taste of Honey* (1961), a realistic yet lyrical tale of working-class life in Manchester. Both critics and public responded to a fine central performance from Rita Tushingham and to the industrial landscapes poetically photographed by Walter Lassally.

The influence of the French New Wave was particularly noticeable in Richardson's next two films, *The Loneliness of the Long Distance Runner* (1962)—which used a flashback narrative structure to weave a *400 Blows*-style story of adolescent rebellion—and *Tom Jones* (1963), considered by many the director's masterpiece. *Tom Jones* is a hilarious, bawdy romp through 18th-century England, adapted by Osborne from the Joseph Fielding novel and superbly acted by, among others, Albert Finney and Susannah York. It was particularly noted for its inventive, imaginative location camerawork, again by Lassally. The film earned nearly $40 million and won three Oscars, including best film and best director.

Little of Richardson's subsequent work has matched up to his earlier achievements. *The Charge of the Light Brigade* (1968) earned measured praise for its unromanticized portrait of Victorian military life; *Hamlet* (1970) was an effective example of a stage production transposed to the screen; and *Joseph Andrews* (1977) was an unsuccessful attempt to repeat the *Tom Jones* formula. His most recent features have been produced in the US. *The Border* (1982) is more noted for Jack Nicholson's performance than for Richardson's direction; *The Hotel New Hampshire* (1984), a faithful adaptation of John Irving's novel featuring a star-studded cast (Jodie Foster, Beau Bridges, Nastassja Kinski *et al*), met with only limited critical and commercial success.

Richardson is the father, by Vanessa Redgrave (divorced 1967), of actresses Natasha and Joely Richardson. JDP • *Look Back in Anger* 1959 (d); *The Entertainer* 1960 (d); *Saturday Night and Sunday Morning* 1960 (p); *Sanctuary* 1961 (d); *A Taste of Honey* 1961 (d,p,sc); *The Loneliness of the Long Distance Runner* 1962 (d); *Tom Jones* 1963 (d,p) **(AABD)**; *The Loved One* 1965 (d); *Red and Blue* 1967 (d); *The Sailor From Gibraltar* 1967 (d); *The Charge of the Light Brigade* 1968 (d); *Laughter in the Dark* 1969 (d); *Hamlet* 1970 (d); *Ned Kelly* 1970 (d,sc); *A Delicate Balance* 1973 (d); *Joseph Andrews* 1977 (d,from screenplay); *The Border* 1982 (d); *The Hotel New Hampshire* 1984 (d,sc); *Blue Sky* 1991 (d).

Richter, Hans • Painter; also filmmaker, theoretician, author. • Born Berlin, 1888; died 1976. Dadaist painter who began making avant-garde films in the late 1910s. Richter pioneered the technique of painting directly onto rolls of film, creating abstract, rhythmic works which emphasized the two-dimensional nature of the film frame (*Rhythmus 21* 1921, *Rhythmus 25* 1925). He collaborated with Eisenstein and others on *Sturm über la Sarraz* in 1929 and made primarily commercial and industrial films in Switzerland and France before immigrating to the US in 1941. The following year, Richter was appointed Director of the Institute of Film Techniques at the City College of New York, where he taught for nearly 15 years. His best known American work is *Dreams That Money Can Buy* (1946), featuring sequences contributed by himself, Fernand Leger, Man Ray, Marcel Duchamp, Max Ernst and Alexander Calder. Richter continued to collaborate with some of these artists in Switzerland, where he settled in 1952. • *Rhythmus 21 (short)* 1921 (d); *Rhythmus 25 (short)* 1925 (d); *Everyday (short)* 1929 (d); *Sturm über la Sarraz (short)* 1929 (d); *Brennendes Geheimnis* 1933 (a); *Das Hofkonzert* 1936 (a); *Dreams That Money Can Buy* 1946 (d,dial,ed,p,pd,sc,story—"Narcissus"); *8 x 8* 1956 (d); *Neues vom Rauber Hotzenplotz* 1979 (a); *He Stands in a Desert Counting the Seconds of His Life* 1985 (a).

Richter, W.D. • Screenwriter; also director. • Born New Britain, CT, December 7, 1945. *Educ.* Dartmouth; USC Film School, Los Angeles. Successful, versatile writer who made his directorial debut with *The Adventures of Buckaroo Banzai* (1984), a madcap, tongue-in-cheek sci-fi thriller starring Peter "Robocop" Weller, Jeff Goldblum and Christopher Lloyd. The film has become something of a cult favorite. • *Slither* 1973 (sc); *Peeper* 1975 (sc); *Nickelodeon* 1976 (sc); *Invasion of the Body Snatchers* 1978 (sc); *Dracula* 1979 (sc); *Brubaker* 1980 (sc,story) **(AANBSC)**; *All Night Long* 1981 (sc,song); *Hang Tough* 1982 (sc); *The Adventures of Buckaroo Banzai: Across the 8th Dimension* 1984 (d,p); *Big Trouble in Little China* 1986 (uncred.sc,adapt); *Hang Tough* 1990 (sc).

Riefenstahl, Leni • Director; also actress, screenwriter, dancer, photographer. • Born Helene Berta Amalie Riefenstahl, Berlin, August 22, 1902. *Educ.* Russian Ballet School (Berlin). Considered in some quarters the nearest thing to a war criminal and in others a film genius, Leni Riefenstahl symbolizes the fate of a naive actress and director prompted to deal with devils—devils on the order of Adolf Hitler, who sparked her film career, and Joseph Goebbels, who almost as quickly curtailed it.

As a young woman, Riefenstahl initially studied and performed modern dance (an avocation that would surface in some of her own films) before she was asked by director Arnold Fanck to appear in his dramatic features about skiers and mountain climbers braving avalanches and gorges. While starring in these films, she learned production techniques, especially the value of location shooting and aerial photography, for which Fanck's films were well known.

In 1932 Riefenstahl's first directorial effort, *The Blue Light*, was released. The film, co-scripted by and starring the director, was about a mountain girl whose natural innocence is ruined by greedy businessmen eager for the wealth they connect to her mysterious home. Riefenstahl was praised for her work and, most importantly, attracted the notice of Adolf Hitler.

Hitler chose her to film the first Nazi Party Rally following his accession to power, but his jealous propaganda minister, Joseph Goebbels, stymied her efforts in 1933. By 1934, Riefenstahl had learned to outmaneuver Goebbels in the vipers' nest of rival Nazi chieftains. The Nazi Party rally had by now become a well-honed and rehearsed event, and Riefenstahl was granted 36 cameramen and assistants to chronicle it in perhaps the most notorious documentary ever filmed, *Triumph of the Will* (1935). After the war, she was to excuse her effort as pure documentary—yet one section, Hitler's motorcade to Munich, was compiled from several different events and the closeups of Nazi leaders at the podium were shot in a staged studio sequence.

With its serried ranks passing in review before the Führer, the sea of flags and ecstatic Aryan faces, *Triumph of the Will* extolls the unity of the German people. Although the imagery of an imperious Hitler atop the reviewing block and the goose-stepping SS regiments is intertwined in the popular mind with wartime atrocities, it should be remembered that the film was made a year before the promulgation of the Nazi racial laws, four years before the Kristallnacht pogrom and five years before the invasion of Poland.

Riefenstahl's second most famous film is her documemntary of the 1936 Berlin Olympic Games. The film opens with an intriguing prologue of stylized nude dancers linking the Olympian spirit of ancient Greece with that of contemporary Berlin. Another sequence repeats this imagery, pulling back from a shot of three young women swinging exercise clubs to show an aerial view of the stadium filled with gymnasts from the Nazi League of German Girls.

Riefenstahl's technical virtuosity—her use of automatic and hand-held cameras, jump-cuts and impressionistic sound effects—influenced later German newsreels and films by the German Army Propaganda Companies, whose members were composed in part of her *Olympia* cameramen.

Her naïveté was remarkable throughout the Nazi years. The Berlin film critic, Lotte Eisner, reported how Riefenstahl once invited her to a luncheon with Hitler, despite the fact that Eisner had been condemned as a "Jewish Bolshevik" by the Nazi press. In 1941, her cameraman Heinz "Harry" von Jaworsky claimed that she admitted that the men around Hitler were criminals, but she still believed in the Führer. To her credit, she was shocked by the sight of a punitive operation in occupied Poland.

Riefenstahl returned in 1944 to Berlin to begin a film, *Tiefland*, in the tradition of *The Blue Light*. Goebbels got his revenge, holding up the necessary state support, and Riefenstahl was not able to complete the film until 1954. It was to be her last; she spent four years in a French detention camp after the war for her Nazi activities and was never able to raise financing for a film again. She became an acclaimed still photographer instead, working in Africa and, on assignment for the *Times* of London, at the 1972 Munich Olympics.

Her association with the Third Reich continued to dog Riefenstahl; when she was honored in 1974 at the Telluride Film Festival, anti-Nazi pickets demonstrated against her. LR • *The Blue Light* 1932 (d); *S.O.S. Eisberg* 1933 (a); *Triumph des Willens/Triumph of the Will* 1935 (art.p,d,p); *Olympia* 1938 (d,ed,p); *Tiefland* 1954 (d).

Riegert, Peter • Actor • Born New York, NY, April 11, 1947. *Educ.* University of Buffalo (English). Engaging, low-key performer who began his career with the improvisational comedy troupe, War Babies, and made his film debut in the successful fraternity-house romp, *Animal House* (1978). Riegert turned in memorable, understated performances in Bill Forsyth's wry satire, *Local Hero* (1983), and Joan Micklin Silver's romantic comedy, *Crossing Delancey* (1988). • *National Lampoon's Animal House* 1978; *Americathon* 1979; *Head Over Heels* 1979; *National Lampoon Goes to the Movies* 1982; *The City Girl* 1983; *Le Grand Carnaval* 1983; *Local Hero* 1983; *Un Homme amoureux* 1987; *The Stranger* 1987; *Crossing Delancey* 1988; *That's Adequate* 1989; *Beyond the Ocean* 1990; *A Shock to the System* 1990; *The Object of Beauty* 1991; *Oscar* 1991.

Ringwald, Molly • Actress • Born Sacramento, CA, 1968. Young lead of the 1980s who made her film debut in Paul Mazursky's *Tempest* (1982), a role which earned her a Golden Globe nomination. Ringwald established herself in a series of "brat pack" movies directed by John Hughes, beginning with 1984's *Sixteen Candles*. Daughter of musician Bob Ringwald, with whose Great Pacific Jazz Band she began singing at the age of four. • *P.K. and the Kid* 1982; *Tempest* 1982; *Spacehunter: Adventures in the Forbidden Zone* 1983; *Sixteen Candles* 1984; *The Breakfast Club* 1985; *Pretty in Pink* 1986; *King Lear* 1987; *The Pick-*

Up Artist 1987; *For Keeps* 1988; *Fresh Horses* 1988; *Strike It Rich* 1989; *Betsy's Wedding* 1990.

Riskin, Robert • Screenwriter, playwright • Born New York, NY, 1897; died 1955. *Educ.* Columbia. Distinguished, prolific writer of stage plays in the 1920s and original and adapted screenplays from 1931. Riskin provided Frank Capra with some of his best material, including *It Happened One Night* (1934), *Mr. Deeds Goes to Town* (1936) and *Meet John Doe* (1941). He later tried his hand as a producer. Riskin married actress Fay Wray in 1942. • *Arizona* 1931 (sc); *Illicit* 1931 (from play); *Many a Slip* 1931 (from play); *Men Are Like That* 1931 (sc); *Men in Her Life* 1931 (sc); *The Miracle Woman* 1931 (from play *Bless You Sister*); *American Madness* 1932 (story); *The Big Timer* 1932 (sc,story); *The Night Club Lady* 1932 (sc); *Virtue* 1932 (sc); *Ann Carver's Profession* 1933 (sc,from story "Rules for Wives"); *Ex-Lady* 1933 (story); *Lady For a Day* 1933 (sc) **(AANBSC)**; *Broadway Bill* 1934 (sc); *It Happened One Night* 1934 (sc) **(AABSC)**; *Carnival* 1935 (sc,story); *The Whole Town's Talking* 1935 (sc); *Mr. Deeds Goes to Town* 1936 (sc) **(AANBSC)**; *Lost Horizon* 1937 (sc); *When You're in Love* 1937 (d,sc); *You Can't Take It With You* 1938 (sc) **(AANBSC)**; *Meet John Doe* 1941 (sc); *The Thin Man Goes Home* 1944 (sc,story); *Magic Town* 1947 (p,sc,story); *Mister 880* 1950 (sc); *Riding High* 1950 (sc); *Half Angel* 1951 (sc); *Here Comes the Groom* 1951 (story) **(AANBST)**; *You Can't Run Away From It* 1956 (sc).

Ritchie, Michael • Director • Born Waukesha, WI, November 28, 1938. *Educ.* Harvard (history, literature). Ritchie gained early directorial experience as an undergraduate at Harvard, staging the original production of classmate Arthur Kopit's *Oh Dad, Poor Dad, Mama's Hung You in the Closet and I'm Feelin' So Sad.* Following graduation he worked in TV, directing episodes of series including "The Man From U.N.C.L.E." and "Dr. Kildare." Ritchie's first feature, *Downhill Racer* (1969), was noted for its gripping ski sequences, shot with hand-held 16mm cameras. His third film, *The Candidate* (1972), also starred Robert Redford and remains one of the finest filmic exposés of the American political system. Ritchie's subsequent output has been primarily in the comedic vein. • *Downhill Racer* 1969 (d); *The Candidate* 1972 (d); *Prime Cut* 1972 (d); *Smile* 1975 (d,lyrics,p); *The Bad News Bears* 1976 (d); *Semi-Tough* 1977 (d); *The Bad News Bears Go to Japan* 1978 (p); *An Almost Perfect Affair* 1979 (d,story); *Divine Madness* 1980 (d,p); *The Island* 1980 (d); *The Survivors* 1983 (d); *Fletch* 1985 (d); *The Golden Child* 1986 (d); *Wildcats* 1986 (d); *The Couch Trip* 1988 (d); *Fletch Lives* 1989 (d).

Ritt, Martin • Director; also actor. • Born New York, NY, March 2, 1914; died December 8, 1990, Santa Monica, CA. *Educ.* Elon College, Burlington; St. John's University, Brooklyn (law). Stage and screen actor who began directing for theater and TV after WWII. When Ritt's small-screen career was curtailed by blacklisting, he began teaching at the Actors Studio, where his students included Paul Newman, Joanne Woodward, Rod Steiger and Lee Remick. His 1956 stage production of Robert Aurthur's *A Very Special Baby* caught the attention of Hollywood and he directed his first feature, *Edge of the City*, the next year. A gritty waterfront drama starring Sidney Poitier and John Cassavetes, the film earned high critical praise and established Ritt as a director of note.

Ritt went on to demonstrate his skill as a meticulous craftsman capable of eliciting fine ensemble performances and tackling important and controversial social issues in an intelligent—if sometimes heavy-handed—manner.

Highlights of his career include the Faulkner adaptation, *The Long Hot Summer* (1958), which marked the first of many collaborations with writers Irving Ravetch and Harriet Frank, Jr.; *Hud* (1963), which helped popularize the concept of the "anti-hero" (Paul Newman) and earned James Wong Howe an Oscar for best cinematography and Patricia Neal and Melvyn Douglas Oscars for best actress and best supporting actor, respectively; and *The Spy Who Came in From the Cold* (1965), an unglamorized adaptation of the Le Carré novel featuring a fine central performance by Richard Burton.

Ritt's seriocomic film on the travails of blacklisted writers, *The Front* (1976), drew on his own experiences in the early 1950s. He continued to direct dramas on themes such as union organizing (*Norma Rae* 1978) and illiteracy (*Stanley and Iris* 1990) until his death, from heart disease complications in 1990. • *Winged Victory* 1944 (a); *Edge of the City* 1957 (d); *No Down Payment* 1957 (d); *The Black Orchid* 1958 (d); *The Long, Hot Summer* 1958 (d); *The Sound and the Fury* 1958 (d); *Five Branded Women* 1960 (d); *Paris Blues* 1961 (d); *Adventures of a Young Man* 1962 (d); *Hud* 1963 (d,p) **(AANBD)**; *The Outrage* 1964 (d); *The Spy Who Came in From the Cold* 1965 (d,p); *Hombre* 1967 (d,p); *The Brotherhood* 1968 (d); *The Great White Hope* 1970 (d); *The Molly Maguires* 1970 (d,p); *Pete 'n' Tillie* 1972 (d); *Sounder* 1972 (d); *Conrack* 1973 (d,p); *Der Richter und Sein Henker* 1975 (a); *The Front* 1976 (d,p); *Hollywood on Trial* 1976 (a); *Casey's Shadow* 1978 (d); *Norma Rae* 1978 (d); *Back Roads* 1981 (d,p); *Cross Creek* 1983 (d,p); *Murphy's Romance* 1985 (d,exec.p); *The Slugger's Wife* 1985 (a); *50 Years of Action!* 1986 (a); *Nuts* 1987 (d); *Stanley and Iris* 1990 (d).

Ritter, John • Actor; also producer. • Born Jonathan Ritter, Hollywood, CA, September 17, 1948. *Educ.* USC, Los Angeles. Engaging comic performer who made his film acting debut in 1970 and came to prominence on TV's popular "Three's Company" (1977-84). Ritter went on to appear in a number of light comedies through the 1980s and has served as executive producer of two TV series. Son of actor Tex Ritter (1905-74) and husband of actress Nancy Morgan. • *The Barefoot Executive* 1970; *Scandalous John* 1971; *The Other* 1972; *The Stone Killer* 1973; *Nickelodeon* 1976; *Breakfast in Bed* 1977; *Americathon* 1979; *Hero at Large* 1980; *Wholly Moses!* 1980; *They All Laughed* 1981; *Real Men* 1987; *Skin Deep* 1989; *Problem Child* 1990.

Ritter, Thelma • Actress • Born Brooklyn, NY, February 14, 1905; died 1969. Character actress from the stage who enjoyed almost immediate, and enduring, success following her film debut in the late 1940s. Usually in the role of the sardonic choric figure, strewing films with witty asides and cynical observations, Ritter enlivened a host of excellent productions including *All About Eve* (1950), *Pickup on South Street* (1953), in a heartbreaking departure from type, and *Rear Window* (1954). • *A Letter to Three Wives* 1948; *City Across the River* 1949; *Father Was a Fullback* 1949; *All About Eve* 1950 **(AANBSA)**; *I'll Get By* 1950; *The Mating Season* 1950 **(AANBSA)**; *Perfect Strangers* 1950; *As Young As You Feel* 1951; *The Model and the Marriage Broker* 1951; *With a Song in My Heart* 1952 **(AANBSA)**; *The Farmer Takes a Wife* 1953; *Pickup on South Street* 1953 **(AANBSA)**; *Titanic* 1953; *Rear Window* 1954; *Daddy Long Legs* 1955; *Lucy Gallant* 1955; *The Proud and the Profane* 1956; *A Hole in the Head* 1959; *Pillow Talk* 1959 **(AANBSA)**; *The Misfits* 1961; *The Second Time Around* 1961; *Birdman of Alcatraz* 1962 **(AANBSA)**; *How the West Was Won* 1962; *For Love or Money* 1963; *Move Over, Darling* 1963; *A New Kind of Love* 1963; *Boeing Boeing* 1965; *The Incident* 1967.

Rivette, Jacques • Director • Born Pierre Louis Rivette, Rouen, France, March 1, 1928. Although François Truffaut has written that the New Wave began "thanks to Rivette," the films of this masterful French director are not well known. Rivette, like his *Cahiers du Cinéma* colleagues Truffaut, Jean-Luc Godard, Claude Chabrol and Eric Rohmer, did graduate to filmmaking but, like Rohmer, was something of a late bloomer as a director. He made two shorts (*Aux Quatre Coins* 1949 and *Le Quadrille* 1950, starring Jean-Luc Godard); in the mid-1950s he served as an assistant to Jean Renoir and Jacques Becker; and in 1958 he was, along with Chabrol, the first of the five to begin production on a feature-length film. Without the financial benefit of a producer, Rivette took to the streets with his friends, a 16mm camera, and film stock purchased on borrowed money. It was only, however, after the commercial success of Truffaut's *The 400 Blows*, Resnais' *Hiroshima Mon Amour* and Godard's *Breathless* that the resulting film, the elusive, intellectual, and somehwat lengthy (135 minutes) *Paris Nous Appartient*, saw its release in 1960.

In retrospect, Rivette's debut sketched out the path which all his subsequent films would follow; *Paris Nous Appartient* was a monumental undertaking for the critic-turned-director, with some 30 actors (including Chabrol, Godard and Jacques Demy), almost as many locations, and an impenetrably labyrinthine narrative.

His next film, the considerably more commercial *La Religieuse* (1965), was an adaptation of the Diderot novel which Rivette had staged in 1963. The least characteristic of all his features, it was also his first and only commercial success, becoming a "succèss de scandale" when the government blocked its release for a year.

Rivette's true talents first made themselves visible during the fruitful period, 1968-74. During this time he directed the 4-hour *L'Amour Fou* (1968), the now legendary 13-hour *Out 1* (made for French TV in 1971 but never broadcast; edited to a 4-hour feature and retitled *Out 1:Spectre*, 1972), and the 3-hour *Céline and Julie Go Boating* (1973), his most entertaining and widely seen picture. In these three films, Rivette began to construct what has come to be called his "House of Fiction"—an enigmatic filmmaking style influenced by the work of Louis Feuillade and involving improvisation, ellipsis and considerable narrative experimentation.

Unfortunately, Rivette seems to have no place in contemporary cinema. On the one hand, his work is considered too inaccessible for theatrical distribution; on the other, although his revolutionary theories have influenced figures such as Jean-Marie Straub & Danielle Huillet and Chantal Akerman, he is deemed too commercial to be accepted by the underground cinema; he still employs a narrative and uses "name" actors such as Jean-Pierre Léaud, Juliet Berto, Anna Karina and Maria Schneider.

Since *Céline and Julie*, Rivette's career has been as mysterious as one of his plots. In 1976 he received an offer to make a series of four films, *Les Filles du Feu. Duelle* (1976), the first entry, received such negative response that the second, *Noroit* (1976)—which some critics call his greatest picture—was held from release. The final two installments (one of which was due to star Leslie Caron and Albert Finney) were never filmed. The 1980s proved no kinder. He made five films, but only one of them, 1984's *Love on the Ground*, opened in the US (it received disastrous reviews). Although he continues to be an innovative and challenging artist, Rivette has failed to find the type of audience that has contributed to the commercial success of his New Wave compatriots. DC • *Aux Quatre Coins (short)* 1949; *Le Quadrille (short)* 1950 (d); *Le Coup du Berger (short)* 1956 (a,d,sc); *Paris Nous Appartient* 1960 (a,d,sc); *Suzanne Simonin, la Religieuse de Denis Diderot/The Nun* 1965 (d,sc,adapt); *Jean Renoir, le Patron* 1966 (d); *L'Amour Fou* 1968 (d,sc); *Out 1: Noli Me Tangere* 1971 (d,sc); *Out 1: Spectre* 1972 (d,sc); *Céline et Julie vont en bateau/Céline and Julie Go Boating* 1973 (d,sc); *Duelle* 1976 (d,sc); *Noroit* 1976 (d,sc,dial); *La Mémoire courte* 1979 (a); *Le Pont du Nord* 1981 (d,sc); *Merry Go Round* 1983 (d,sc); *L'Amour par terre/Love on the Ground* 1984 (d,sc); *Hurlevent* 1985 (d,sc); *La Bande des quatre/The Gang of Four* 1989 (d,sc).

Roach, Hal • Producer; also screenwriter, director. • Born Elmira, NY, January 14, 1892. Former mule skinner and gold prospector who stumbled into film in 1912, serving as stuntman and bit player in a number of Universal action films and westerns. With backing from Pathé, Roach and former Universal cohort Harold Lloyd formed the Rolin company in 1914 and commenced production on a series of comic shorts starring Lloyd. Such was the success of the "Lonesome Luke" films that Roach was able to take over a large, fully equipped studio in Culver City in 1919. There he continued to turn out successful comedies, distinguished from the Keystone company's product by an emphasis on narrative structure as opposed to sight gags. In 1921 Roach inaugurated the "Our Gang" series, which remained popular over the next two decades. Other notable productions included *Safety Last* (1923), starring Lloyd; *From Soup to Nuts* (1928), starring Laurel and Hardy (whom Roach had first teamed the previous year); and *Of Mice and Men* (1939), directed by Lewis Milestone. Although Roach became increasingly involved with the administration of his organization, he continued to enjoy occasional stints as a director. Actors who developed their careers under Roach's guidance included Mickey Rooney, Charlie Chase and Zasu Pitts; directors included George Stevens, Norman Z. McLeod and Leo McCarey. Adept at staying abreast of developments within the industry, Roach moved into sound films in the early 1930s, switched to feature production (in partnership with his son, Hal Roach, Jr.) later in the decade, and turned his attention to TV in the late 1940s. The Hal Roach Television Corporation, formed in 1948, enjoyed intermittent success until its eventual demise in the late 1950s. • *Bumping Into Broadway (short)* 1919 (d); *Captain Kidd's Kids (short)* 1919 (d); *His Royal Slyness (short)* 1919 (d); *Hoot Mon (short)* 1919 (d); *An Eastern Westerner (short)* 1920 (d); *Get Out and Get Under (short)* 1920 (d); *Haunted Spooks (short)* 1920 (d); *High and Dizzy (short)* 1920 (d); *Number, Please (short)* 1920 (d); *Now or Never* 1921 (d); *A Sailor-Made Man* 1921 (p,story); *Doctor Jack* 1922 (p,story); *Grandma's Boy* 1922 (story); *Safety Last* 1923 (p,sc,story); *The Battling Orioles* 1924 (story); *The King of the Wild Horses* 1924 (p,story); *The White Sheep* 1924 (d,story); *Black Cyclone* 1925 (story); *The Devil Horse* 1926 (story); *From Soup to Nuts* 1928 (p); Men of the North 1930 (d); *On the Loose (short)* 1931 (d); *The Music Box* 1932 (p) **(AABSF)**; *The Devil's Brother* 1933 (d,p); *Heroes of the Regiment* 1935 (p); *Tit For Tat* 1935 (p) **(AANBSF)**; *The Bohemian Girl* 1936 (p); *General Spanky* 1936 (p); *Kelly the Second* 1936 (p); *Mr. Cinderella* 1936 (p); *Neighborhood House* 1936 (p); *Nobody's Baby* 1937 (p); *Pick a Star* 1937 (p); *Topper* 1937 (p); *Way Out West* 1937 (p); *Swiss Miss* 1938 (p); *There Goes My Heart* 1938 (p) **(AANBSF)**; *Captain Fury* 1939 (d,p); *The Housekeeper's Daughter* 1939 (d,p); *Of Mice and Men* 1939 (p); *Topper Takes a Trip* 1939 (p); *Captain Caution* 1940 (p); *A Chump at Oxford* 1940 (p); *One Million B.C.* 1940 (d,p); *Saps at Sea* 1940 (p); *Turnabout* 1940 (d,p); *All American Co-Ed* 1941 (p); *Broadway Limited* 1941 (p); *Miss Polly* 1941 (p); *Niagara Falls* 1941 (p); *Road Show* 1941 (d,p); *Tanks a Million* 1941 (p); *Topper Returns* 1941 (p); *Brooklyn Orchid* 1942 (p); *Dudes Are Pretty People* 1942 (p); *Flying With Music* 1942 (p) **(AANBSF)**; *The Crazy World of Laurel and Hardy* 1964 (p); *George Stevens: A Filmmaker's Journey* 1985 (a).

Robards, Jason • *aka* Jason Robards, Jr. • Actor • Born Jason Nelson Robards, Jr., Chicago, IL, July 22, 1922. *Educ.* AADA, New York. Leading interpreter of the works of Eugene O'Neill in the 1950s and 60s. Robards first achieved theatrical prominence in the 1956 Circle in the Square production of *The Iceman Cometh* and followed up his success the following year with an acclaimed Broadway performance as Jamie Tyrone in *Long Day's Journey Into Night*—a role he reprised in the 1962 film version directed by Sidney Lumet. Robards proved a versatile screen lead through the 60s and 70s and has turned in several memorable performances based on real-life figures; he played Washington editor Ben Bradlee in *All the President's Men* (1976), novelist Dashiell Hammett in *Julia* (1977) and Howard Hughes in Jonathan Demme's engaging *Melvin and Howard* (1980). (He won Oscars for the first two of these films and was nominated for the third.) Robards continues to appear in films, on Broadway and on TV and won an Emmy in 1988 for his role in the miniseries, *Inherit the Wind.* He is the son of stage and screen star Jason Robards (1892-1963) and father of two actors, Jason Robards, III (from his first marriage) and Sam Robards (by his third wife, Lauren Bacall). • *The Journey* 1958; *By Love Possessed* 1959; *Tender Is the Night* 1961; *Long Day's Journey Into Night* 1962; *A Thousand Clowns* 1965; *A Big Hand For the Little Lady* 1966; *Any Wednesday* 1966; *Divorce American Style* 1967; *The Hour of the Gun* 1967; *The St. Valentine's Day Massacre* 1967; *The Night They Raided Minsky's* 1968; *Isadora* 1968; *Once Upon a Time in the West* 1969; *Tora! Tora! Tora!* 1970; *Julius Caesar* 1970; *The Ballad of Cable Hogue* 1970; *Murders in the Rue Morgue* 1971; *Johnny Got His Gun* 1971; *The War Between Men and Women* 1972; *Pat Garrett and Billy the Kid* 1973; *Play It as It Lays* 1973; *All the President's Men* 1976 **(AABSA)**; *Washington Behind Closed Doors* 1977; *Julia* 1977 **(AABSA)**; *Comes a Horseman* 1978; *Hurricane* 1979; *Melvin and Howard* 1980 **(AABSA)**; *Raise the Titanic* 1980; *Caboblanco* 1981; *The Legend of the Lone Ranger* 1981; *Max Dugan Returns* 1983; *Something Wicked This Way Comes* 1983; *Square Dance* 1986.

Robbe-Grillet, Alain • Screenwriter, novelist; also director. • Born Brest, France, August 18, 1922. Leading figure of the French Nouveau Roman ("New Novel") movement of the late 1950s. Robbe-Grillet's screenplay for Alain Resnais' labyrinthine *Last Year at Marienbad* (1961) incorporated many of the characteristic features of his novels: an undermining of chronological and narrative structure; an "objective" style supposedly free from authorial involvement; an investigation of the nature of memory and repetition; and a stylized eroticism. The film remains a landmark of European art cinema. Robbe-Grillet made his directorial debut with *L'Immortelle* (1963) and has continued to navigate similar thematic and stylistic terrain, though to decreasingly innovative and successful effect. His introduction to the published screenplay of *Last Year* raises interesting theoretical questions on the differences between the novel and the film as media. JDP • *L'Année dernière à Marienbad/Last Year at Marienbad* 1961 (sc,dial,from book) **(AANBSC)**; *L'Immortelle* 1963 (d,story,sc); *Trans-Europ-Express* 1966 (a,d,sc); *Glissements progressifs du plaisir* 1973 (d,sc); *Le Jeu avec le feu* 1974 (d,sc); *Guerres civiles en France* 1978 (consultant); *La Belle Captive* 1982 (d,sc).

Robbins, Tim • Actor • Born West Covina, CA, October 16, 1958. *Educ.* NYU; UCLA (theater). Co-founder of the Los Angeles theater co-op, The Actors Gang, which also includes actor John Cusack. Robbins is best known as the eccentric minor league baseball pitcher, "Nuke" Laloosh, in *Bull Durham* (1988). Robbins has a child with actress Susan Sarandon. • *No Small Affair* 1984 (a); *Fraternity Vacation* 1985 (a); *The Sure Thing* 1985 (a); *Howard the Duck* 1986 (a); *Top Gun* 1986 (a); *Five Corners* 1987 (a); *Bull Durham* 1988 (a); *Tapeheads* 1988 (a,songs); *Erik the Viking* 1989 (a); *Miss Firecracker* 1989 (a); *Cadillac Man* 1990 (a); *Jacob's Ladder* 1990 (a).

Roberts, Eric • Actor • Born Eric Anthony Roberts, Biloxi, MS, April 18, 1956. *Educ.* RADA, London; AADA, New York. Talented, stage-trained lead who made an auspicious feature debut in the title role of *King of the Gypsies* (1978). Roberts has given generally fine performances in films of uneven quality; he was memorable in *Raggedy Man* (1981), opposite Sissy Spacek, *The Coca-Cola Kid* (1985), directed by Dusan Makavejev, and *Runaway Train* (1985), co-starring John Voight and directed by Andrei Konchalovsky. Sister of actresses Julia and Lisa and son of Walter Roberts, who founded the Atlanta Actors and Writers Workshop in 1963. • *King of the Gypsies* 1978 (a); *The Alternative Miss World* 1980 (a,commentary); *Raggedy Man* 1981 (a); *Miss Lonelyhearts* 1983 (a); *Star 80* 1983 (a); *The Pope of Greenwich Village* 1984 (a); *The Coca-Cola Kid* 1985 (a); *Runaway Train* 1985 (a) **(AANBSA)**; *Nobody's Fool* 1986 (a); *Dear America* 1987 (a); *Best of the Best* 1989 (a); *Options* 1989 (a); *Rude Awakening* 1989 (a); *Blood Red* 1989 (a).

Roberts, Julia • Actress • Born Smyrna, GA, 1967. Ingenuous beauty introduced to her craft at an early age by her parents, who ran the Atlanta-based Actors and Writers Workshop. Roberts made her screen debut opposite brother Eric in *Blood Red*, though the 1986-produced film went unreleased for three years. She scored a huge box-office hit opposite Richard Gere in the saccharine rags-to-riches saga, *Pretty Woman* (1990). Sister Lisa is also an actress. • *Mystic Pizza* 1988; *Satisfaction* 1988; *Blood Red* 1989; *Steel Magnolias* 1989 **(AANBSA)**; *Flatliners* 1990; *Pretty Woman* 1990; *Sleeping With the Enemy* 1991.

Roberts, Rachel • Actress • Born Llanelly, Carmarthen, Wales, September 20, 1927; died Los Angeles, 1980. Distinguished stage actress who made intermittent film appearances, beginning in 1953. Married to actors Alan Dobie (1955-61) and Rex Harrison (1962-71). *No Bells on Sunday*, the actress's posthumously published journal, offers a harrowing account of her desertion by Harrison, her slide into substance abuse and her subsequent suicide. • *The Limping Man* 1953; *Saturday Night and Sunday Morning* 1960; *This Sporting Life* 1963 **(AANBA)**; *A Flea in Her Ear* 1968; *The Reckoning* 1969; *Doctors' Wives* 1970; *Wild Rovers* 1971; *Alpha Beta* 1973; *The Belstone Fox* 1973; *O Lucky Man!* 1973; *Murder on the Orient Express* 1974; *Picnic at Hanging Rock* 1975; *Foul Play* 1978; *When a Stranger Calls* 1979; *Yanks* 1979; *Charlie Chan and the Curse of the Dragon Queen* 1981.

Roberts, Tony • Actor • Born David Anthony Roberts, New York, NY, October 22, 1939. *Educ.* Northwestern University (drama). Tall, curly-haired wiseguy from the stage who entered films in 1965. Roberts made his mark as the abstracted businessman whose wife (Diane Keaton) is coveted by Woody Allen in *Play It Again, Sam* (1972). His command of upwardly mobile mannerisms and affectations made him the perfect WASP foil to Allen's "nebbish" persona in films such as *Annie Hall* (1977). • *Beach Girls and the Monster* 1965; *$1,000,000 Duck* 1971; *Star Spangled Girl* 1971; *Play It Again, Sam* 1972; *Serpico* 1973; *The Taking of Pelham 1, 2, 3* 1974; *Le Sauvage* 1975; *Annie Hall* 1977; *Opening Night* 1977; *Just Tell Me What You Want* 1980; *Stardust Memories* 1980; *A Midsummer Night's Sex Comedy* 1982; *Amityville 3-D* 1983; *Key Exchange* 1985; *Hannah and Her Sisters* 1986; *Seize the Day* 1986; *Radio Days* 1987; *18 Again!* 1988; *Painting the Town: The Illusionistic Murals of Richard Haas* 1989; *Popcorn* 1991; *Switch* 1991.

Robertson, Cliff • Actor • Born Clifford Parker Robertson III, La Jolla, CA, September 9, 1925. *Educ.* Antioch College. Solid, earnest leading man from the stage who made his screen debut in 1956 and was selected by then-president JFK to portray him in the adaption of his wartime memoir, *PT 109* (1963). Robertson was acclaimed for his poignant characterization of a mentally retarded bakery worker in *Charly* (1968) and has contributed a number of workmanlike performances to the small and big screen through the 1980s. Married since 1966 to actress Dina Merrill. • *Autumn Leaves* 1956 (a); *Picnic* 1956 (a); *Girl Most Likely* 1958 (a,song); *The Naked and the Dead* 1958 (a); *Battle of the Coral Sea* 1959 (a); *Gidget* 1959 (a); *All in a Night's Work* 1961 (a); *The Big Show* 1961 (a); *Underworld, U.S.A.* 1961 (a); *The Interns* 1962 (a); *My Six Loves* 1963 (a); *PT 109* 1963 (a); *Sunday in New York* 1963 (a); *633 Squadron* 1964 (a); *The Best Man* 1964 (a); *Love Has Many Faces* 1965 (a); *Up From the Beach* 1965 (a); *The Honey Pot* 1967 (a); *Charly* 1968 (a) **(AABA)**; *The Devil's Brigade* 1968 (a); *Too Late the Hero* 1970 (a); *J.W. Coop* 1971 (a,d,p,sc); *The Great Northfield Minnesota Raid* 1972 (a); *Ace Eli and Rodger of the Skies* 1973 (a); *Man on a Swing* 1974 (a); *Out of Season* 1975 (a); *Three Days of the Condor* 1975 (a); *Battle of Midway* 1976 (a); *Obses-*

sion 1976 (a); *Shoot* 1976 (a); *Dominique* 1977 (a); *Fraternity Row* 1977 (a); *The Pilot* 1980 (d); *Brainstorm* 1983 (a); *Class* 1983 (a); *Star 80* 1983 (a); *Shaker Run* 1985 (a); *Malone* 1987 (a); *Wild Hearts Can't Be Broken* 1991 (a).

Robeson, Paul • Actor; also singer. • Born Princeton, NJ, April 9, 1898; died 1976. *Educ.* Rutgers University, NJ; Columbia Law School. Distinguished black athlete and scholar who played pro football while atttending law school and deferred his entry into the New York bar when Eugene O'Neill persuaded him to star in a production of *The Emperor Jones.* A singularly versatile talent, Robeson went on to charm international audiences with his distinctive baritone voice and his signature song, "Ole Man River." He made his film debut in the 1933 adaption of the O'Neill play and continued to appear in films until the early 1940s. Robeson achieved star status with *Show Boat* (1936) but was frustrated by the stereotypical nature of the roles available for blacks; one exception was *The Proud Valley* (1940), in which he played a heroic miner in Wales. Robeson's leftist political views brought him into conflict with the US goverment and his passport was revoked in 1950. He was eventually able to leave the country in 1958, traveling to the USSR to receive the Stalin Peace Prize and playing *Othello* with the Royal Shakespeare Company (he had enjoyed great success in the role on Broadway in the 40s). • *The Emperor Jones* 1933 (a); *Sanders of the River* 1935 (a); *Show Boat* 1936 (a); *Jericho* 1937 (a); *King Solomon's Mines* 1937 (a); *The Proud Valley* 1940 (a,song) *Tales of Manhattan* 1942 (a); *Killer of Sheep* 1977 (song); *Daniel* 1983 (song).

Robinson, Amy • Producer; also actress. • Born Trenton, NJ, April 13, 1948. *Educ.* Sarah Lawrence College, Bronxville NY. Actress—best known for her role in Martin Scorsese's *Mean Streets* (1973)—turned independent producer. Robinson has worked primarily in partnership with Griffin Dunne, forming Triple Play Productions with Dunne and Mark Metcalfe in 1977, and Double Play Productions, sans Metcalfe, in 1982. She enjoyed critical and commercial success with *After Hours* (1985), which reunited her with director Scorsese. Robinson is also active with Robert Redford's Sundance Institute. • *Mean Streets* 1973 (a); *Head Over Heels* 1979 (p); *A Taste of Sin* 1981 (a); *Baby, It's You* 1983 (p,story); *After Hours* 1985 (p); *Running on Empty* 1988 (p); *White Palace* 1990 (p); *Once Around* 1991 (p).

Robinson, Bruce • Director; also screenwriter, actor, novelist. • Born Broadstairs, Kent, England, 1946. *Educ.* Central School of Speech and Drama, London. Robinson was chosen to appear in Franco Zeffirelli's *Romeo and Juliet* during his third year of drama school and acted in several films—notably *The Story of Adèle H.* (1975), as Lieutenant Pinson—before giving up performing in 1975 to concentrate on writing. It took ten years and 20 screenplays before his work reached the screen in the shape of the Oscar-winning *The Killing Fields* (1984), directed by Roland Joffe.

Robinson then parlayed the success of *Fields* into his first directing assignment, the critically acclaimed *Withnail & I* (1987). A laconic study of two "resting" actors set in the late 1960s, the film demonstrated Robinson's wry sense of humor, keen powers of social observation and ability to coax fine performances from his actors. He confirmed his talents with *How to Get Ahead in Advertising* (1988), a blazing satire in which a boil on an ad exec's neck develops a life of its own and begins to spout apocalyptic right-wing ideology. Despite moments of brilliant high farce, the film failed to draw as wide an audience as *Withnail.* JDP • *Romeo and Juliet* 1968 (a); *The Music Lovers* 1971 (a); *Private Road* 1971 (a); *Tam Lin* 1971 (a); *L'Histoire d'Adèle H./The Story of Adèle H.* 1975 (a); *Beyond and Back* 1977 (a); *The Killing Fields* 1984 (sc) **(AANBSC)**; *Withnail & I* 1987 (d,sc,from novel) *How to Get Ahead in Advertising* 1988 (d,sc); *Fat Man and Little Boy* 1989 (sc,story).

Robinson, Edward G. • Actor • Born Emmanuel Goldenberg, Bucharest, Rumania, December 12, 1893; died 1973. *Educ.* CCNY; AADA, New York. Sneering, dough-faced character player whose defining role as trigger-happy mob boss Cesare Bandello in *Little Caesar* (1931) established him as one of the screen's greatest heavies. Robinson began his career on the stage, made his film debut in 1923 and played a string of underworld types in Warner Bros. ganster films of the 1930s. He then branched out into a wider range of roles, playing the title character in the 1940 biopic, *Dr. Ehrlich's Magic Bullet,* and the assiduous insurance agent in *Double Indemnity* (1944). Robinson was also memorable opposite Joan Bennett in two films directed by Fritz Lang, *The Woman in the Window* (1944) and *Scarlet Street* (1945). Other notable films include Orson Welles's *The Stranger* (1946), John Huston's *Key Largo* (1948), the 1959 comedy *A Hole in the Head* and *The Cincinnati Kid* (1965), in which he gave a memorable characterization as cultured poker kingpin Lancy Howard.

Robinson suffered a series of personal setbacks in the 1950s, including a hearing before the House Un-American Activities Committee (he was eventually exonerated of Communist affiliiations) and the selling of his extensive art collection as a condition of his divorce settlement. By the time he made his final film in 1973, he had become one of the most identifiable and imitated stars of all time. • *The Bright Shawl* 1923 (a); *A Hole in the Wall* 1929 (a); *East Is West* 1930 (a); *The Kibitzer* 1930 (from play); *A Lady to Love* 1930 (a); *Night Ride* 1930 (a); *Outside the Law* 1930 (a); *The Widow From Chicago* 1930 (a); *Five Star Final* 1931 (a); *Little Ceasar* 1931 (a); *Smart Money* 1931 (a); *The Hatchet Man* 1932 (a); *Silver Dollar* 1932 (a); *Tiger Shark* 1932 (a); *Two Seconds* 1932 (a); *I Loved a Woman* 1933 (a); *The Little Giant* 1933 (a); *Dark Hazard* 1934 (a); *The Man With Two Faces* 1934 (a); *Barbary Coast* 1935 (a); *The Whole Town's Talking* 1935 (a); *Bullets or Ballots* 1936 (a); *Kid Galahad* 1937 (a); *The Last Gangster* 1937 (a); *Thunder in the City* 1937 (a); *The Amazing Dr. Clitterhouse* 1938 (a); *I Am the Law* 1938 (a); *A Slight Case of Murder* 1938 (a); *Blackmail* 1939 (a); *Confessions of a Nazi Spy* 1939 (a); *Brother Orchid* 1940 (a); *A Dispatch From Reuters* 1940 (a); *Dr. Ehrlich's Magic Bullet* 1940 (a); *Manpower* 1941 (a); *The Sea Wolf* 1941 (a); *Unholy Partners* 1941 (a); *Larceny, Inc.* 1942 (a); *Tales of Manhattan* 1942 (a); *Destroyer* 1943 (a); *Flesh and Fantasy* 1943 (a); *Double Indemnity* 1944 (a); *Mr. Winkle Goes to War* 1944 (a); *Tampico* 1944 (a); *The Woman in the Window* 1944 (a); *Journey Together* 1945 (a); *Our Vines Have Tender Grapes* 1945 (a); *Scarlet Street* 1945 (a); *The Stranger* 1946 (a); *The Red House* 1947 (a); *All My Sons* 1948 (a); *Key Largo* 1948 (a); *The Night Has a Thousand Eyes* 1948 (a); *House of Strangers* 1949 (a); *It's a Great Feeling* 1949 (a); *My Daughter Joy* 1950 (a); *Actors and Sin* 1952 (a); *Big Leaguer* 1953 (a); *The Glass Web* 1953 (a); *Vice Squad* 1953 (a); *Black Tuesday* 1954 (a); *The Violent Men* 1954 (a); *A Bullet For Joey* 1955 (a); *Hell on Frisco Bay* 1955 (a); *Illegal* 1955 (a); *Tight Spot* 1955 (a); *Nightmare* 1956 (a); *The Ten Commandments* 1956 (a); *A Hole in the Head* 1959 (a); *Pepe* 1960 (a); *Seven Thieves* 1960 (a); *My Geisha* 1962 (a); *Two Weeks in Another Town* 1962 (a); *The Prize* 1963 (a); *Sammy Going South* 1963 (a); *Cheyenne Autumn* 1964 (a); *Good Neighbor Sam* 1964 (a); *The Outrage* 1964 (a); *The Cincinnati Kid* 1965 (a); *The Biggest Bundle of Them All* 1968 (a); *Never a Dull Moment* 1968 (a); *MacKenna's Gold* 1969 (a); *Neither By Day Nor By Night* 1972 (a); *Soylent Green* 1973 (a); *Entertaining the Troops* 1989 (a).

Robinson, Phil Alden • American director, screenwriter • *Educ.* Union College, Schenectady, NY. Screenwriter who made his directorial mark with *Field of Dreams* (1989), adapted from the novel by W.P. Kinsella. The film's combination of baseball, fantasy and nostalgia proved irresistable to American audiences and generated over $60 million at the box-office. • *All of Me* 1984 (assoc.p,sc); *Rhinestone* 1984 (sc,story,song); *In the Mood* 1987 (d,sc,story,song); *Field of Dreams* 1989 (d,sc) **(AANBSC)**.

Robson, Dame Flora • Actress • Born Flora McKenzie Robson, South Shields, England, March 28, 1902; died July 7, 1984, Brighton, England. Sharp-faced leading light of the English stage for over fifty years; in films from the early 1930s. Her greatest stage triumph: as the tragic Edinburgh prostitute in *The Anatomist*. Robson became a Dame of the British Empire in 1970. • *Fire Over England* 1936; *Farewell Again* 1937; *We Are Not Alone* 1939; *Wuthering Heights* 1939; *Invisible Stripes* 1940; *The Sea Hawk* 1940; *Bahama Passage* 1941; *Great Day* 1945; *Saratoga Trunk* 1945 **(AANBSA)**; *Black Narcissus* 1947; *Saraband For Dead Lovers* 1948; *Malta Story* 1953; *Romeo and Juliet* 1954; *The Gypsy and the Gentleman* 1958; *55 Days at Peking* 1963; *Guns at Batasi* 1964; *The Epic That Never Was (I, Claudius)* 1965; *Seven Women* 1965; *Those Magnificent Men in Their Flying Machines* 1965; *Young Cassidy* 1965; *Eye of the Devil* 1966; *Fragment of Fear* 1970; *Alice's Adventures in Wonderland* 1972; *Dominique* 1977; *Clash of the Titans* 1981.

Robson, Mark • Director; also producer. • Born Montreal, Canada, December 4, 1913; died 1978, London. *Educ.* UCLA (political science, economics); Pacific Coast University (law). Respected craftsman who began his career as a prop man at Fox in 1932 and became an editor at RKO three years later, assisting Robert Wise on the cutting of two Orson Welles projects (*Citizen Kane* 1941 and *The Magnificent Ambersons* 1942). Robson moved into the director's chair at the behest of horror producer Val Lewton, for whom he engineered two powerful Boris Karloff vehicles, *Isle of the Dead* (1945) and *Bedlam* (1946). Robson's subsequent output as a director included two fine boxing films (*Champion* 1949, *The Harder They Fall* 1956), a probing drama on race relations (*Home of the Brave* 1949), the classy trash of *Home of the Brave* (1957) and *Valley of the Dolls* (1967), and a brace of hyperactive blockbusters, including *Earthquake* (1974). • *Cat People* 1942 (ed); *Falcon's Brother* 1942 (ed); *Journey Into Fear* 1942 (ed); *The Ghost Ship* 1943 (d); *I Walked With a Zombie* 1943 (ed); *The Leopard Man* 1943 (ed); *The Seventh Victim* 1943 (d); *Youth Runs Wild* 1944 (d); *Isle of the Dead* 1945 (d); *Bedlam* 1946 (d,sc); *Champion* 1949 (d); *Home of the Brave* 1949 (d); *Roughshod* 1949 (d); *Edge of Doom* 1950 (d); *My Foolish Heart* 1950 (d); *Bright Victory* 1951 (d); *I Want You* 1951 (d); *Return to Paradise* 1953 (d); *Hell Below Zero* 1954 (d); *Phfft* 1954 (d); *The Bridges at Toko-Ri* 1955 (d); *Prize of Gold* 1955 (d); *Trial* 1955 (d); *The Harder They Fall* 1956 (d); *The Little Hut* 1957 (d,p); *Peyton Place* 1957 (d) **(AANBD)**; *The Inn of the Sixth Happiness* 1958 (d) **(AANBD)**; *From the Terrace* 1960 (d,p); *Lisa* 1962 (p); *Nine Hours to Rama* 1963 (d,p); *The Prize* 1963 (d); *Von Ryan's Express* 1965 (d); *Lost Command* 1966 (d,p); *Valley of the Dolls* 1967 (d); *Daddy's Gone A-Hunting* 1969 (d,p); *Happy Birthday, Wanda June* 1971 (d); *Women in Limbo* 1972 (d); *Earthquake* 1974 (d,p); *Avalanche Express* 1979 (d,p).

Rocha, Glauber • Director; also producer, critic. • Born Victoria da Conquista, Bahia, Brazil, March 14, 1938; died August 22, 1981, Brazil. Except for two years in which he studied law (1959-61), Glauber Rocha devoted his life to cinema, starting at the age of 16 when he began organizing film clubs. In 1957, he founded a production company, Lemanja-Filmes, and directed several short films before making his feature debut with *Barravento* (1962).

As filmmaker, theoretician and critic, Rocha was the leader of Brazil's influential *cinema nôvo* movement. "The Brazilian public," Rocha noted, "is enslaved by the language of foreign films—particularly North American movies." Such cultural imperialism fostered an inferiority complex on the part of Brazilian cinema, which thus failed to confront the social realities of a country in which unemployment and illiteracy reached fifty percent.

Rocha's aim was to instill cultural nationalism through a polemical, noncommercial cinema. The message in his films was that violence could transform a social order whose "essence" was hunger. As he explained in his 1965 manifesto, *The Aesthetic of Hunger:* "The moment of violence is the moment when the coloniser becomes aware of the existence of the colonised."

Rocha developed his lyrical, allegorical and self-reflexive style in reaction to Euro-American cinematic realism. His films feature a highly baroque *mise-en-scène*, frenetic camera movement, and an Eisensteinian use of montage. His characters do not reflect moral absolutes but are instead complex and protean, while also representative of larger historical forces.

Rocha, however, was not above practical considerations in his desire for an authentic Brazilian film culture. He shot *Antonio das Mortes* (1969) in color to broaden its appeal and drew upon Brazilian popular culture and established artistic movements. Rocha also incorporated elements of an indigenous "culture of resistance," such as *candomble*, African magic with an appropriated Christian guise. He also allowed his cast (which included non-actors) to improvise and determine scenes.

After the overthrow of the leftist regime of Joao Goulart in 1964, Rocha set out "to fight back," using the camera—"the only weapon I could master." In *Terra Em Transe* (1967), a masterpiece of political cinema, he examined the failure of both the populist left and fascist right, with their established solutions and false prophets. In 1968, Brazil's military regime suspended civil rights under its Fifth Institutional Act, and Rocha went abroad to direct two films: *Der Leon Have Sept Cabecas* (Zaire, 1970) and *Cabezas Cortadas* (Spain, 1971). While these films were part of a larger Third World project he envisioned from a Hispanic perspective, Rocha's influences were noticeably European: Brecht, Godard and Eisenstein. After a brief return to Brazil in 1969, Rocha went into exile, where he completed three films that went unnoticed.

In 1976, with Brazil's move toward democratic liberties, Rocha returned and directed his most ambitious and challenging film, *La Idade Da Terra* (1980), an allegorical history of colonialism and liberation in Brazil. The "moment of violence"—conveyed in a chaotic blend of styles, histories, myths and deologies—resurrects a Third World Christ, played in typical Rocha fashion by four characters (black, Indian, militant and peasant) to represent the people. In 1980, after unfavorable reception of the film and the death of his sister, Rocha again went into exile. He published a novel and a book on *cinema nôvo* but, on August 19, 1981, suffering from pulmonary disease, he returned to Brazil, where he died three days later. CAN • *Barravento/The Turning Wind* 1962 (d,sc); *Deus e o Diabo na Terra do Sol/Black God, White Devil* 1964 (assoc.p,d,sc,art d,lyrics,sets); *Terra Em Transe* 1967 (assoc.p,d,sc); *Antonio das Mortes* 1969 (d,sc); *O Dragao da maldade contra o santo guerreiro* 1969 (d,p,sc,art d); *Le Vent d'est/East Wind* 1969 (a); *Der Leone Have Sept Cabecas/The Lion Has Seven Heads* 1970 (d,sc,ed); *Cabezas Cortadas* 1971 (d); *A Idade Da Terra/The Age of the Earth* 1980 (d,p,sc).

Roddam, Franc • Director • Born England, 1946. *Educ.* London Film School. Former advertising copywriter and maker of documentary films for the BBC. Roddam's first feature was *Quadrophenia* (1979), a finely observed coming-of-age saga set against a backdrop of teenage gang rivalry in 1950s Britain and based on a song cycle by rock group The Who. *Lords of Discipline* (1983) is a tense military drama and *The Bride* (1985) an atmospheric reworking of 1935's *The Bride of Frankenstein.* • *Quadrophenia* 1979 (d,sc); *The Lords of Discipline* 1983 (d); *The Bride* 1985 (d); *Aria* 1987 (d,sc—"Tristan und Isolde"); *War Party* 1988 (d,exec.p).

Rodgers, Richard • Composer • Born New York, NY, June 28, 1902; died 1979. *Educ.* Columbia; Juilliard. Prolific writer of show tunes who enjoyed fruitful collaborations with lyricists Lorenz Hart and Oscar Hammerstein. Rogers confected some of Hollywood's most enduring musicals, via Broadway, including *Oklahoma!* (1955), *The King and I* (1956) and *The Sound of Music* (1965) and contributed numerous scores and songs to films through the 1960s. • *Heads Up* 1930 (from play); *Leatherneck-ing* 1930 (from play *Present Arms*); *The Melody Man* 1930 (from play); *Spring Is Here* 1930 (from play); *The Hot Heiress* 1931 (song); *The Phantom President* 1932 (song); *Hallelujah, I'm a Bum* 1933 (song); *Mississippi* 1935 (song); *Fools for Scandal* 1938 (song); *Babes in Arms* 1939 (from play); *On Your Toes* 1939 (from play); *The Boys From Syracuse* 1940 (from play); *Too Many Girls* 1940 (from play,song); *They Met in Argentina* 1941 (song); *I Married an Angel* 1942 (from play,song); *State Fair* 1945 (song) **(AABS)**; *Words and Music* 1948 (song); *Oklahoma!* 1955 (from play,exec.p,song); *Carousel* 1956 (from play,song); *Gaby* 1956 (song); *The King and I* 1956 (from play,m,libretto); *Pal Joey* 1957 (from play,m); *Slaughter on Tenth Avenue* 1957 (song); *South Pacific* 1958 (from play,m); *Flower Drum Song* 1961 (from play,m); *Billy Rose's Jumbo* 1962 (from play,song); *State Fair* 1962 (m,song) **(AABS)**; *The Sound of Music* 1965 (from play,song).

Roeg, Nicolas • Director; also director of photography, producer, screenwriter. • Born London, August 15, 1928. Nicolas Roeg started working in the film industry at the age of 19 at the Marylebone Studio, where he was a teaboy and assisted in the dubbing of French films. Roeg then went to work for MGM's London studios, where he slowly moved his way up the ladder to become a camera operator. He did second-unit photography for *Lawrence of Arabia* (1962) and finally became a director of photography on such films as *The Caretaker* (1963), *Farenheit 451* (1966), *Far From the Madding Crowd* (1967) and *Petulia* (1968).

In 1968, Roeg co-directed *Performance* with screenwriter Donald Cammell, but Warner Bros. was so dismayed with the film that they initially refused to release it. (The plot involved two characters—James Fox as a gangster on the run and Mick Jagger as a reclusive rock singer—whose identities merge.) When *Performance* was finally released in 1970, reactions were hardly tepid; critic Richard Schickel called it "the most disgusting, the most completely worthless film I have seen since I began reviewing." The film postulates the frightening concept that individualized, integrated personality is a fiction; it remains one of the most boldly experimental features made within the commercial confines of the English film industry.

With *Walkabout* (1971), Roeg transformed a didactic children's novel about a teenaged girl and her young brother lost in the Australian outback into a film about missed opportunities and different ways of seeing the world. *Don't Look Now* (1973), perhaps his most carefully structured work, is also about perception and perspective and can even be analyzed as a self-reflexive work about how we watch films. Roeg's visionary philosophy and his disavowal of traditional narrative conventions reached their most extreme form in *The Man Who Fell to Earth* (1976), in which he attempted, in his words, "to push the structure of film grammar into a different area...by taking away the crutch of time which the audience holds onto." Unlike his previous films, where ambiguities can be best understood through multiple viewings and careful analysis of correspondences, *The Man Who Fell to Earth* can't be fully grasped because Roeg refuses to give his viewers all the necessary information; it is his most open-ended work.

Bad Timing (1980) and the rarely screened *Eureka* (produced 1983, released 1985) both reflect the director's concerns with convoluted narrative, the merging of disparate identities and the "interconnectedness" of all things, in a style characterized by frenzied editing and shifting camera angles. Like many of Roeg's subsequent films, they starred his wife, actress Theresa Russell.

After *Eureka*, Roeg seemed to be moving away from some of these themes and techniques, perhaps finding it increasingly difficult to balance his unique personal vision with the overriding commercial considerations of the 1980s. *Insignificance* (1985), *Castaway* (1986), *Track 29* (1987) and *The Witches* (1990) pale in comparison to his early, groundbreaking films. JAG • *Lawrence of Arabia* 1962 (cam.op); *The Caretaker* 1963 (ph); *Nothing But the Best* 1964 (ph); *Code 7, Victim 5!* 1965 (ph); *Fahrenheit 451* 1966 (ph); *A Funny Thing Happened on the Way to the Forum* 1966 (ph); *Casino Royale* 1967 (add.ph); *Far From the Madding Crowd* 1967 (ph); *Petulia* 1968 (ph); *Performance* 1970 (d,ph); *Walkabout* 1971 (d,ph); *Don't Look Now* 1973 (d); *The Man Who Fell to Earth* 1976 (d); *Bad Timing* 1980 (d,song); *Eureka* 1983 (d); *Insignificance* 1985 (d); *Castaway* 1986 (d); *Aria* 1987 (d,sc—"Un Ballo in Maschera"); *Track 29* 1987 (d); *The Witches* 1990 (d); *Without You I'm Nothing* 1990 (exec.p).

Roemer, Michael • Director; also screenwriter. • Born Berlin, January 1, 1928. *Educ.* Harvard. Made a feature-length documentary while at Harvard and worked in various production capacities for Louis De Rochemont before establishing himself as a director of educational shorts. Roemer directed his first fiction feature, *Nothing But a Man*, in 1964, receiving critical plaudits for his intelligent treatment of a racial theme. His sardonic comedy, *The Plot Against Harry*, was produced in 1969 but languished in post-production limbo for twenty years before being released to widespread acclaim in 1989. • *The Inferno* 1962 (d); *Nothing But a Man* 1964 (d,p,sc); *Pilgrim, Farewell* 1980 (d,sc); *Haunted* 1983 (d,sc); *The Plot Against Harry* 1989 (d,p,sc).

Rogers, Ginger • Actress; also dancer, singer. • Born Virginia Katherine McMath, Independence, MO, July 16, 1911. Prodded by a protypical "stage mother," Rogers made her performing debut as a dancer at the age of 14 and soon became a regular on the vaudeville circuit. She acheived her breakthough in 1929 when she was prominently cast in the Broadway musical, *Top Speed*, and began landing feature film roles soon thereafter. Rogers moved to Hollywood in 1931 and eventually joined RKO (via "discovery" by her mother Lela, who had become a talent scout for the studio), where she began her legendary partnership with Fred Astaire. The duo glided through many a gilded 1930s musical including *Top Hat* (1935) and *Swing Time* (1936), forming one of the most memorable pairings since Rolls and Royce.

Rogers subsequently expanded her range, earning an Oscar for her dramatic performance in *Kitty Foyle* (1940) and turning in a fine comic performance in Billy Wilder's *The Major and the Minor* (1942). She made regular film appearances through the late 1950s and returned to the spotlight in 1965 in the lead role of the hit Broadway musical, *Hello Dolly!* Husbands have included actors Lew Ayres and Jacques Bergerac and actor-director-producer William Marshall. • *Follow the Leader* 1930; *Queen High* 1930; *The Sap From Syracuse* 1930; *Young Man of Manhattan* 1930; *Honor Among Lovers* 1931; *Suicide Fleet* 1931; *The Tip-Off* 1931; *Carnival Boat* 1932; *Hat Check Girl* 1932; *The Tenderfoot* 1932; *The Thirteenth Guest* 1932; *You Said a Mouthful* 1932; *42nd Street* 1933; *Broadway Bad* 1933; *Chance at Heaven* 1933; *Don't Bet on Love* 1933; *Flying Down to Rio* 1933; *Gold Diggers of 1933* 1933; *Professional Sweetheart* 1933; *Rafter Romance* 1933; *A Shriek in the Night* 1933; *Sitting Pretty* 1933; *Change of Heart* 1934; *Finishing School* 1934; *The Gay Divorcee* 1934; *Romance in Manhattan* 1934; *Twenty Million Sweethearts* 1934; *Upperworld* 1934; *In Person* 1935; *Roberta* 1935; *Star of Midnight* 1935; *Top Hat* 1935; *Follow the Fleet* 1936; *Swing Time* 1936; *Shall We Dance* 1937; *Stage Door* 1937; *Carefree* 1938; *Having Wonderful Time* 1938; *Vivacious Lady* 1938; *Bachelor Mother* 1939; *Fifth Avenue Girl* 1939; *The Story of Vernon and Irene Castle* 1939; *Kitty Foyle* 1940 **(AABA)**; *Lucky Partners* 1940; *The Primrose Path* 1940; *Tom, Dick and Harry* 1941; *The Major and the Minor* 1942; *Once Upon a Honeymoon* 1942; *Roxie Hart* 1942; *Tales of Manhattan* 1942; *Tender Comrade* 1943; *I'll Be Seeing You* 1944; *Lady in the Dark* 1944; *Weekend at the Waldorf* 1945; *Heartbeat* 1946; *Magnificent Doll* 1946; *It Had to Be You* 1947; *The Barkleys of Broadway* 1949; *Perfect Strangers* 1950; *The Groom Wore Spurs* 1951; *Storm Warning* 1951; *Dreamboat* 1952; *Monkey Business* 1952; *We're Not Married* 1952; *The Beautiful Stranger* 1954; *Black Widow* 1954; *Tight Spot* 1955; *The First Traveling Saleslady* 1956; *Oh, Men! Oh, Women!* 1956; *Teenage Rebel* 1956; *Quick, Let's Get Married* 1964; *Harlow* 1965; *George Stevens: A Filmmaker's Journey* 1985.

Rogers, Mimi • Actress • Born Coral Gables, FL. Elegant leading lady who first became known for her role in the short-lived TV series, "Paper Dolls" (1984). Rogers turned in a creditable performance opposite Tom Berenger in Ridley Scott's stylish thriller, *Someone to Watch Over Me* (1987). Divorced from actor Tom Cruise. • *Blue Skies Again* 1983; *Gung Ho* 1986; *Someone to Watch Over Me* 1987; *Street Smart* 1987; *Hider in the House* 1989; *The Mighty Quinn* 1989; *Desperate Hours* 1990; *Dimenticare Palermo* 1990; *The Doors* 1991; *The Rapture* 1991.

Rohmer, Eric • *aka* Gilbert Cordier • Director, screenwriter • Born Jean-Marie Maurice Scherer, Nancy, France, April 4, 1920. • Along with François Truffaut, Jean-Luc Godard, Jean Rivette and Claude Chabrol, Eric Rohmer was one of the founding contributors of the influential film magazine, *Cahiers du Cinéma*, where he also served as editor from 1956 to 1963. Born Jean-Marie Scherer, he had written a novel during the Occupation under the name Gilbert Cordier and went on to write film criticism in the 1950s under the name Eric Rohmer. Among his critical writings were a monograph on Alfred Hitchcock (co-written by Chabrol) and a dissertation on F.W. Murnau, whose "rich imagination" he expressly admires.

Rohmer tested his own talent in short films through the 1950s, abandoning his first feature, *Les petites Filles modeles*, in 1952. Chabrol's company produced Rohmer's first feature, *La Signe du lion* (1960), but it was hardly a revolutionary manifesto in terms of cinematic language. Indeed, Rohmer took a more literary, philosophical turn in his art, conceiving his *Six Moral Tales*, not as the moralistic fables implied in the English translation, but as stories which, as Rohmer describes them, "deal less with what people do than with what is going on in their minds while they're doing it. A cinema of thoughts rather than actions."

The first two of the six *Tales* films, *La Boulangère de Monceau* (1962) and *La Carrière de Suzanne* (1963), were minor efforts, but the third, *My Night at Maud's* (1969), a talkative chamber drama dealing with ethics, religion and hypocrisy, was a surprise hit that garnered Rohmer an Oscar nomination for best screenplay. The fourth to be released in the series (but third to be filmed) was *La Collectionneuse* (1967). Though not as successful as *Maud*, it is nevertheless an engaging tale about a young woman "collecting" one-night-stands. *Claire's Knee* (1970) and *Chloe in the Afternoon* (1972) completed the cycle and established Rohmer, and his cameraman Nestor Almendros, as creators of a unique cinematic world firmly rooted in ethical concerns and suffused by the director's devout Catholicism.

In the mid-1970s, Rohmer turned to literary adaptations and historical subjects with *The Marquise of O...* (1975), a well-received tale of unrestrained passion, *Perceval le Gallois* (1978), his interpretation of medieval codes of gallantry, and a TV film, *Catherine de Heilbronn.*

For the 1980s Rohmer embarked on a new series of six films, *Comedies and Proverbs*, launched by *The Aviator's Wife* (1980). These droll, intimate stories, set in ever-shifting contemporary French society, revolve around quirky characters whose emotional problems almost overwhelm them but who finally discover the resources for survival. *Le Rayon Vert/Summer* (1986) is about a young girl on vacation hoping for a romantic revelation without compromise. She idealistically struggles against a companion's more relaxed approach, until at the end she is rewarded with the indescribably beautiful, ephemeral "green ray" of a perfect sunset. This fragile study of youthful yearning and confusion won the Golden Lion prize at the Venice Film Festival.

Youth continues to be the preoccupation of this aging director, although his attention is focused on the struggle to grow up—or, at least, to behave that way. This focus has broadened Rohmer's audience, yet he still makes talky, spare, low-budget films with unknown actors and little background music, preferring to shoot in sequence at the place and during the season of the narrative. In 1987, when the Montreal Film Festival honored him for his entire *Comedies and Proverbs* series, he announced, "I'm lucky to have practically complete independence, which is rare. That's because I make films in which there is no waste." An elegant simplicity is his achievement. KJ • *La Sonate à Kreutzer* 1956 (medium) (d); *Tous les Garcons s'appèllent Patrick/All Boys Are Called Patrick (short)* 1957 (sc); *Le Signe du lion* 1960 (d,sc); *Presentation ou Charlotte et son steack (short)* 1961 (d); *Paris Vu Par.../Six in Paris* 1965 (d,sc—"Place de l'Etoile"); *La Collectionneuse* 1967 (d,sc); *Ma nuit chez Maud/My Night at Maud's* 1969 (d,sc) **(AANBSC)**; *Le Genou de Claire/Claire's Knee* 1970 (d,sc); *Out 1: Noli Me Tangere* 1971 (a); *L'Amour l'apres-midi/Chloe in the Afternoon* 1972 (d,sc); *Out 1: Spectre* 1972 (a); *La Marquise d'O.../The Marquise of O...* 1976 (d,sc); *Perceval le Gallois/Perceval* 1978 (d,sc,adapt); *La Femme de l'aviateur/The Aviator's Wife* 1980 (d,sc); *Le Beau Mariage/A Good Marriage* 1982 (d,sc); *Pauline a la Plage/Pauline at the Beach* 1983 (d,sc); *Les Nuits de la pleine lune/Nights of the Full Moon* 1984 (d,sc); *Le Rayon Vert/Summer* 1986 (d,sc); *L'Ami de mon amie/Girlfriends and Boyfriends* 1987 (d,sc); *Quatre aventures de Reinette et Mirabelle/Four Adventures of Reinette and Mirabelle* 1987 (d,p,sc); *Les Pyramides bleues/The Novice* 1988 (tech.adv—art); *Conte de printemps/A Tale of Springtime* 1990 (d,sc).

Röhrig, Walter • Production designer • Born Germany, 1893; deceased. Prominent figure in the German Expressionist movement and a member of the Berlin Sturm group. Röhrig graduated from stage to film design following WWI and collaborated with Hermann Warm and Walther Reimann on the sets for *The Cabinet of Dr. Caligari* (1919). He later worked, frequently in collaboration with Robert Herlth, on landmark German silent productions including Lang's *Destiny* (1921) and Murnau's *The Last Laugh* (1924). • *Das Kabinett des Dr. Caligari/The Cabinet of Dr. Caligari* 1919 (sets); *Die Pest von Florenz* 1919 (art d); *Der Golem/The Golem* 1920 (art d); *Das Lachende Grauen* 1920 (art d); *Das Geheimnis von Bombay* 1920 (art d); *Der Idiot/The Idiot* 1920 (art d); *Der Mude Tod/Destiny* 1921 (art d—German tale); *Satansketten* 1921 (art d); *Fräulein Julie/Miss Julie* 1922 (art d); *Komödie des Herzens* 1924 (art d); *Der Letzte Mann/The Last Laugh* 1924 (art d); *Zur Chronik von Grieshuus - Um das Erbe von Greishuus/The Chronicles of the Grey House* 1925 (art d); *Tartüff/Tartuffe* 1925 (art d); *Faust* 1926 (sets); *Luther* 1927 (art d); *Looping the Loop* 1928 (art d); *Die Wunderbare Luge der Nina Petrowna/The Wonderful Lie of Nina Petrovna* 1929 (sets); *Hokuspokus/Hocuspocus* 1930 (art d); *Der Kongress Tanzt/The Congress Dances* 1931 (art d); *Die Gräfin von Monte Cristo* 1932 (art d); *Walzerkrieg/Waltz Time in Vienna* 1933 (art d); *Prinzessin Tournadot* 1934 (art d); *Bacarole* 1935 (art d); *Amphytrion* 1935 (art d); *Hans im Glück* 1936 (art d); *Capriccio* 1938 (art d); *Heimkehr* 1941 (art d); *Rembrandt* 1942 (art d).

Roizman, Owen • Director of photography • Born Brooklyn, NY, September 22, 1936. *Educ.* Gettysburg College, PA (mathematics, physics). Began his career working on TV commercials in New York and shot his first feature, Bill Gunn's *Stop*, in 1970. Roizman soon became known for his gritty, documentary-influenced urban compositions, particularly in films such as *The French Connection* (1971) and *The Taking of Pelham 1,2,3* (1974). Roizman formed a commercial production company, Roizman and Associates, in 1983 but returned to feature-film making in 1990 with Lawrence Kasdan's *I Love You To Death*. His father, Sol, was a cinematographer for Fox Movietone News and his uncle, Morris, a film editor. • *Stop* 1970 (ph); *The French Connection* 1971 (ph) **(AANBPH)**; *The Gang That Couldn't Shoot Straight* 1971 (ph); *The Heartbreak Kid* 1972 (ph); *Play It Again, Sam* 1972 (ph); *The Exorcist* 1973 (ph) **(AANBPH)**; *The Taking of Pelham 1, 2, 3* 1974 (ph); *The Stepford Wives* 1975 (ph); *Three Days of the Condor* 1975 (ph); *Independence* 1976 (ph); *Network* 1976 (ph) **(AANBPH)**; *The Return of a Man Called Horse* 1976 (ph); *Sgt. Pepper's Lonely Hearts Club Band* 1978 (ph); *Straight Time* 1978 (ph); *The Black Marble* 1979 (ph); *The Electric Horseman* 1979 (ph); *The Rose* 1979 (add.ph); *Absence of Malice* 1981 (ph); *Taps* 1981 (ph); *True Confessions* 1981 (ph); *Tootsie* 1982 (ph) **(AANBPH)**; *Vision Quest* 1985 (ph); *Havana* 1990 (a,ph); *I Love You to Death* 1990 (ph).

Rollins, Howard, Jr. • Actor • Born Baltimore, MD, October 17, 1950. *Educ.* Towson State College, Baltimore. Commanding black actor who came to prominence as Coalhouse Walker, Jr., in Milos Forman's adaptation of the E. L. Doctorow novel, *Ragtime* (1981). Rollins was also memorable in Norman Jewison's tightly wound drama, *A Soldier's Story* (1984), and has earned widespread recognition for his role in the TV series, "In the Heat of the Night" (1987-). • *The House of God* 1979; *Ragtime* 1981 **(AANBSA)**; *Chytilova vs. Forman* 1983; *A Soldier's Story* 1984; *Dear America* 1987; *On the Block* 1989.

Romero, George • Director, producer, screenwriter • Born George Andrew Romero, New York, NY, February 4, 1940. *Educ.* Carnegie-Mellon Institute (art, theater, design). Key figure, along with Roger Corman, in the introduction of explicit violence and gore into the horror genre. Romero had made 8mm shorts and industrial and commercial films (through his Pittsburgh-based Latent Image company) before directing his first feature, *Night of the Living Dead*, in 1968. Produced, like many early Romero films, on a minimal budget, *Living Dead* was a tongue-in-cheek essay in zombie carnage which proved a landmark in the development of the "cult" film—movies played at late-night screenings to young audiences, primarily in American college towns.

The director secured his position as schlock horror king of the 1970s with *Dawn of the Dead* (1978), a *Living Dead* sequel which takes some satirical potshots at consumerism, and *Martin* (1978), a vampire/sex-fiend tale guaranteed to do little for the Pittsburgh tourist trade.

Romero's later work has tended more toward the mainstream: *Creepshow* (1982) was an uninspired hommage to the EC horror comics Romero and writer Stephen King had read as children; *Monkey Shines* (1988) fared poorly with critics and public alike. • *Night of the Living Dead* 1968 (d); *There's Always Vanilla* 1971 (d,ph,ed); *Hungry Wives* 1972 (d,sc,ph,ed); *The Crazies* 1973 (d,sc); *Martin* 1978 (d); *Dawn of the Dead* 1978 (d,sc,ed,a); *Knightriders* 1981 (d,sc,ed); *Creepshow* 1982 (d,ed—"Something to Tide You Over"); *Day of the Dead* 1985 (d,sc); *Flight of the Spruce Goose* 1986 (a); *Creepshow 2* 1987 (sc); *Lightning Over Braddock: A Rustbowl Fantasy* 1988 (a); *Monkey Shines: An Experiment in Fear* 1988 (d,sc); *Two Evil Eyes* 1990 (d,sc—"The Facts in the Case of Mr. Valdemar"); *Tales From the Darkside, The Movie* 1990 (sc—"Cat From Hell"); *Night of the Living Dead* 1990 (exec.p,sc).

Romm, Mikhail • Director; also screenwriter. • Born Irkutsk, Russia, January 24, 1901; died 1971. Journalist and translator who became a screenwriter and assistant director in the 1930s and made an acclaimed directorial debut with the Maupassant adaptation, *Pushka/Boule de Suif* (1934). During his early career, Romm's vision chimed with the prevailing political climate. He directed two intelligent, sensitive biographical portraits, *Lenin in October* (1937) and *Lenin in 1918* (1938); and, when commissioned to make a socialist version of John Ford's *Lost Patrol*, turned out a gripping and compassionate desert drama, *The Thirteen* (1937). His films of the late 1940s and 50s unfortunately suffered from the pressures of Stalinism; he returned to form, however, with *Nine Days of One Year* (1961) and *Ordinary Fascism* (1965), a compilation feature about the rise of Nazism. • *Pushka/Boule de Suif* 1934 (d,sc); *Lenin in October* 1937 (d); *The Thirteen* 1937 (d); *Lenin in 1918* 1938 (d); *Dream* 1943 (d); *Russkii vopros* 1948 (d,sc); *Admiral Ushakov* 1953 (d); *Poprigunya* 1955 (p); *Chelkash* 1957 (art.sup); *Nine Days of One Year* 1961 (d); *Obyknovennyi fashizm/Ordinary Fascism* 1965 (a,d,sc,narrative text,ed).

Rooney, Mickey • Actor; also singer, dancer. • Born Joe Yule, Jr., Brooklyn, NY, September 23, 1920. Compact, energetic performer who made his stage debut at the age of 18 months as part of his family's vaudeville act. Rooney made his film debut at age six and, from 1927 to 1933, starred in over 50 episodes of the two-reel comedy series, "Mickey McGuire." He adopted the name "Mickey Rooney" in 1932 and began landing bit parts in feature films, signing with MGM in 1934. Rooney was loaned out to Warner Bros. in 1935 and played a memorable Puck in the Max Reinhardt/William Dieterle production of *A Midsummer Night's Dream*. He enjoyed a popular, 15-film tenure as the brash title character in the "Andy Hardy" series (1937-47), turned in a fine performance in *Boys Town* (1938) and enjoyed great success opposite Judy Garland in a number of breezy musicals. His roles in *The Human Comedy* (1943) and *National Velvet* (1944) confirmed his status as the nation's most popular film star.

Rooney established himself as a solid character actor in the postwar period, particularly with his roles in *Baby Face Nelson* (1957) and *Breakfast at Tiffany's* (1961). He made a triumphant stage debut in the late 1970s in the glitzy Broadway musical, *Sugar Babies*, and won widespread acclaim for his sensitive portrait of a retarded man in the 1981 TV drama, *Bill*. Rooney's eight wives have included actresses Ava Gardner and Martha Vickers. • *The Beast of the City* 1932 (a); *Fast Companions* 1932 (a); *My Pal, the King* 1932 (a); *The Big Cage* 1933 (a); *The Big Chance* 1933 (a); *Broadway to Hollywood* 1933 (a); *The Chief* 1933 (a); *The Life of Jimmy Dolan* 1933 (a); *Beloved* 1934 (a); *Blind Date* 1934 (a); *Death on the Diamond* 1934 (a); *Half a Sinner* 1934 (a); *Hide-Out* 1934 (a); *I Like It That Way* 1934 (a); *The Lost Jungle* 1934 (a); *Love Birds* 1934 (a); *Manhattan Melodrama* 1934 (a); *Upperworld* 1934 (a); *Ah, Wilderness!* 1935 (a); *The County Chairman* 1935 (a); *The Healer* 1935 (a); *A Midsummer Night's Dream* 1935 (a); *Riffraff* 1935 (a); *Devil Is a Sissy* 1936 (a); *Down the Stretch* 1936 (a); *Little Lord Fauntleroy* 1936 (a); *Captains Courageous* 1937 (a); *A Family Affair* 1937 (a); *The Hoosier Schoolboy* 1937 (a); *Live, Love and Learn* 1937 (a); *Slave Ship* 1937 (a); *Thoroughbreds Don't Cry* 1937 (a); *Boys Town* 1938 (a); *Hold That Kiss* 1938 (a); *Judge Hardy's Children* 1938 (a); *Lord Jeff* 1938 (a); *Love Finds Andy Hardy* 1938 (a); *Love Is a Headache* 1938 (a); *Out West With the Hardys* 1938 (a); *Stablemates* 1938 (a); *You're Only Young Once* 1938 (a); *The Adventures of Huckleberry Finn* 1939 (a); *Andy Hardy Gets Spring Fever* 1939 (a); *Babes in Arms* 1939 (a) **(AANBA)**; *The Hardys Ride High* 1939 (a); *Judge Hardy and Son* 1939 (a); *Andy Hardy Meets a Debutante* 1940 (a); *Strike Up the Band* 1940 (a); *Young Tom Edison* 1940 (a); *Andy Hardy's Private Secretary* 1941 (a); *Babes on Broadway* 1941 (a); *Life Begins For Andy Hardy* 1941 (a); *Men of Boys Town* 1941 (a); *Andy Hardy's Double Life* 1942 (a); *The Courtship of Andy Hardy* 1942 (a); *A Yank at Eton* 1942 (a); *Girl Crazy* 1943 (a); *The Human*

Comedy 1943 (a) **(AANBA)**; *Thousands Cheer* 1943 (a); *Andy Hardy's Blonde Trouble* 1944 (a); *National Velvet* 1944 (a); *Love Laughs at Andy Hardy* 1946 (a); *Killer McCoy* 1947 (a); *Summer Holiday* 1948 (a); *Words and Music* 1948 (a); *The Big Wheel* 1949 (a); *The Fireball* 1950 (a); *He's a Cockeyed Wonder* 1950 (a); *Quicksand* 1950 (a); *My Outlaw Brother* 1951 (a); *My True Story* 1951 (d); *The Strip* 1951 (a); *Sound Off* 1952 (a); *All Ashore* 1953 (a); *Off Limits* 1953 (a); *A Slight Case of Larceny* 1953 (a); *The Atomic Kid* 1954 (a); *Drive a Crooked Road* 1954 (a); *The Bold and the Brave* 1955 (a,song) **(AANBSA)**; *The Bridges at Toko-Ri* 1955 (a); *Jaguar* 1955 (assoc.p); *The Twinkle in God's Eye* 1955 (a,song); *Francis in the Haunted House* 1956 (a); *Magnificent Roughnecks* 1956 (a); *Baby Face Nelson* 1957 (a); *Operation Mad Ball* 1957 (a); *Andy Hardy Comes Home* 1958 (a,song); *A Nice Little Bank That Should Be Robbed* 1958 (a); *The Big Operator* 1959 (a); *The Last Mile* 1959 (a); *Platinum High School* 1960 (a); *The Private Lives of Adam and Eve* 1960 (a,d); *Breakfast at Tiffany's* 1961 (a); *Everything's Ducky* 1961 (a); *King of the Roaring 20's—The Story of Arnold Rothstein* 1961 (a); *Requiem For a Heavyweight* 1962 (a); *It's a Mad, Mad, Mad, Mad World* 1963 (a); *The Secret Invasion* 1964 (a); *How to Stuff a Wild Bikini* 1965 (a); *Ambush Bay* 1966 (a); *Skidoo* 1968 (a); *The Comic* 1969 (a); *Eighty Steps to Jonah* 1969 (a); *The Extraordinary Seaman* 1969 (a); *The Cockeyed Cowboys of Calico County* 1970 (a); *B.J. Presents* 1971 (a); *Pulp* 1972 (a); *Richard* 1972 (a); *That's Entertainment!* 1974 (a); *Bon Baisers de Hong Kong* 1975 (a); *The Domino Killings* 1977 (a); *Pete's Dragon* 1977 (a); *The Magic of Lassie* 1978 (a); *Arabian Adventure* 1979 (a); *The Black Stallion* 1979 (a) **(AANBSA)**; *The Fox and the Hound* 1981 (a); *La Traversée de la Pacific* 1982 (a); *The Care Bears Movie* 1985 (a); *Lightning—The White Stallion* 1986 (a); *Rudolph & Frosty's Christmas in July* 1988 (a); *Erik the Viking* 1989; *My Heroes Have Always Been Cowboys* 1991 (a).

Rose, William • Screenwriter • Born Jefferson City, MO, 1918; died February 10, 1987, Isle of Jersey, UK. American-born writer who, from the late 1940s, wrote several quintessentially English comedies including *Genevieve* (1953), *The Maggie* 1954 and *The Ladykillers* (1955). Rose returned to America in the late 1950s and wrote several entertaining Hollywood romps, making a successful foray into drama with *Guess Who's Coming to Dinner?* (1967). • *My Daughter Joy* 1950 (sc); *I'll Get You For This* 1951 (sc); *Genevieve* 1953 (sc,story) **(AANBSC)**; *The Maggie* 1954 (sc); *The Ladykillers* 1955 (sc,from story) **(AANBSC)**; *Touch and Go* 1955 (sc,story); *It's a Mad, Mad, Mad, Mad World* 1963 (sc,story); *The Russians Are Coming, the Russians Are Coming* 1966 (sc) **(AANBSC)**; *The Flim-Flam Man* 1967 (sc); *Guess Who's Coming to Dinner?* 1967 (sc) **(AABSC)**; *The Secret of Santa Vittoria* 1969 (sc).

Rosenberg, Philip • American production designer • *Educ.* Brooklyn College; Yale School of Drama (stage design). Successful and prolific designer who began his career working on New York stage productions. Rosenberg has designed several features directed by Sidney Lumet, from 1971's *The Anderson Tapes* through 1990's *Q&A*. • *The Owl and the Pussycat* 1970 (art d); *The Anderson Tapes* 1971 (art d); *Child's Play* 1972 (pd); *The Possession of Joel Delaney* 1972 (art d); *Shamus* 1972 (art d); *Badge 373* 1973 (art d); *From the Mixed-Up Files of Mrs. Basil E. Frankweiler* 1973 (art d); *The Gambler* 1974 (pd); *E'Lollipop* 1975 (art d—New York); *Network* 1976 (art d); *Next Stop, Greenwich Village* 1976 (pd); *The Sentinel* 1977 (pd); *The Wiz* 1978 (art d) **(AANBAD)**; *All That Jazz* 1979 (pd) **(AABAD)**; *Eyewitness* 1980 (pd); *Soup For One* 1982 (pd); *Daniel* 1983 (pd); *Lovesick* 1983 (original paintings,pd); *Garbo Talks* 1984 (pd); *Scream For Help* 1984 (design consultant—USA); *The Manhattan Project* 1986 (pd); *Moonstruck* 1987 (pd); *The January Man* 1988 (pd); *Running on Empty* 1988 (pd); *Family Business* 1989 (pd); *Q&A* 1990 (pd).

Rosenberg, Stuart • Director • Born New York, NY, 1927. *Educ.* NYU (Irish literature). Prolific director of 1950s TV series such as "The Untouchables" and "Naked City" who turned to features in the early 1960s. Rosenberg distinguished himself with *Cool Hand Luke* (1967), a tightly wound prison drama starring Paul Newman. He returned to similar terrain, though from a somewhat different perspective, with the Robert Redford vehicle, *Brubaker* (1980). Rosenberg has also tried his hand, with varying degrees of success, at neo-Gothic thrillers (*The Amityville Horror* 1979) and ethnic portraits (*The Pope of Greenwich Village* 1984). • *Murder, Inc.* 1960 (d); *Question 7* 1961 (d); *Cool Hand Luke* 1967 (d); *The Counterfeit Killer* 1968 (d); *The April Fools* 1969 (d); *Move* 1970 (d); *WUSA* 1970 (d); *Pocket Money* 1972 (d); *The Laughing Policeman* 1973 (d,p); *The Drowning Pool* 1975 (d); *Voyage of the Damned* 1976 (d); *The Amityville Horror* 1979 (d); *Love and Bullets* 1979 (d); *Brubaker* 1980 (d); *The Pope of Greenwich Village* 1984 (d); *Let's Get Harry* 1987 (d); *My Heroes Have Always Been Cowboys* 1991 (d).

Rosenblum, Ralph • Editor; also director. • Born New York, NY, October 13, 1925. Entered film in the early 1960s and is known for his work with Sidney Lumet (*Fail Safe* 1964, *The Pawnbroker* 1965) and Woody Allen. Rosenblum has also directed for TV. In 1979 he published *When the Shooting Stops...the Cutting Begins*, an engaging account of his experiences in—and out of—the editing room. • *Murder, Inc.* 1960 (ed); *Pretty Boy Floyd* 1960 (ed); *Mad Dog Coll* 1961 (ed); *Long Day's Journey Into Night* 1962 (ed); *Pie in the Sky* 1963 (ed); *Fail Safe* 1964 (ed); *The Pawnbroker* 1965 (ed); *Terror in the City* 1965 (ed); *A Thousand Clowns* 1965 (ed); *Bach to Bach* 1967 (ed); *Bye Bye Braverman* 1968 (ed); *Don't Drink the Water* 1969 (ed); *Goodbye, Columbus* 1969 (ed); *Trilogy* 1969 (ed); *Bananas* 1971 (assoc.p); *Bad Company* 1972 (ed); *Sleeper* 1973 (ed); *Love and Death* 1975 (ed); *Annie Hall* 1977 (ed); *Shenanigans* 1977 (ed,p); *Interiors* 1978 (ed); *By Design* 1981 (consultant ed); *America* 1982 (creative consultant); *Marvin and Tige* 1983 (creative consultant); *Stuck on You!* 1983 (ed); *Forever, Lulu* 1986 (consultant ed).

Rosenfeld, Hilary • Costume designer • Born US. *Educ.* New School for Social Research; NYU. One of the more successful of the new generation of costume designers, best known for *Dirty Dancing* (1987). New York-based, Rosenfeld began her career with the New York Shakespeare Festival and continues to work in New York theater. She has done some of her best work with Robert M. Young (*The Ballad of Gregorio Cortez* 1983). • *Rich Kids* 1979; *Heartland* 1980; *One-Trick Pony* 1980; *The Janitor*; *The Ballad of Gregorio Cortez* 1983; *Desert Bloom* 1986; *At Close Range* 1986; *No Mercy* 1986; *Dirty Dancing* 1987; *Dominick and Eugene* 1988; *Triumph of the Spirit* 1989.

Rosenman, Leonard • Composer • Born Brooklyn, NY, September 7, 1924. Protégé of influential avant-garde composer Arnold Schoenberg who contributed his first film score to the 1955 release, *The Cobweb*. Rosenman earned wide recognition for his work on Stanley Kubrick's opulent costume drama, *Barry Lyndon* (1975). • *The Cobweb* 1955 (m); *East of Eden* 1955 (m,m.dir); *Rebel Without a Cause* 1955 (m); *Bombers B-52* 1957 (m); *Edge of the City* 1957 (m); *The Young Stranger* 1957 (m); *Lafayette Escadrille* 1958 (m); *Pork Chop Hill* 1959 (m,m.cond); *The Bramble Bush* 1960 (m); *The Crowded Sky* 1960 (m); *The Plunderers* 1960 (m); *The Rise and Fall of Legs Diamond* 1960 (m); *The Savage Eye* 1960 (m); *The Outsider* 1961 (m); *The Chapman Report* 1962 (m); *Convicts Four* 1962 (m); *Hell Is For Heroes* 1962 (m); *Fantastic Voyage* 1966 (m); *A Covenant With Death* 1967 (m); *Countdown* 1968 (m); *Beneath the Planet of the Apes* 1970 (m); *A Man Called Horse* 1970 (m); *The Todd Killings* 1971 (m); *Battle For the Planet of the Apes* 1973 (m); *Barry Lyndon* 1975 (m.sup,m.adapt,m.dir) **(AABSS)**; *Birch*

Interval 1975 (m); *Race With the Devil* 1975 (m); *Bound For Glory* 1976 (m.sup) **(AABSS)**; *9/30/55* 1977 (m); *The Car* 1977 (m); *An Enemy of the People* 1978 (m); *The Lord of the Rings* 1978 (m,m.dir,song); *Promises in the Dark* 1979 (m); *Prophecy* 1979 (m); *Hide in Plain Sight* 1980 (m); *The Jazz Singer* 1980 (m,add.m); *Making Love* 1982 (m); *Cross Creek* 1983 (m) **(AANBM)**; *Miss Lonelyhearts* 1983 (m); *Heart of the Stag* 1984 (m); *Sylvia* 1984 (m); *Star Trek IV: The Voyage Home* 1986 (m,add.m) **(AANBM)**; *Robocop 2* 1990 (m).

Rosher, Charles, Jr. • American director of photography • Best known for his work with director Robert Altman. Son of Charles Rosher. • *Adam at 6 A.M.* 1970; *The Baby Maker* 1970; *Pretty Maids All in a Row* 1971 (ph); *Hex* 1972; *Together Brothers* 1974 (ph); *Semi-Tough* 1977; *The Late Show* 1977 (ph); *Three Women* 1977 (ph); *Movie Movie* 1978 (ph—"Dynamite Hands"); *A Wedding* 1978 (ph); *Nightwing* 1979 (ph); *The Onion Field* 1979 (ph); *Heartbeeps* 1981 (ph); *Independence Day* 1982 (ph).

Rosher, Charles • Director of photography • Born England, 1885; died 1974. Pioneering cinematographer who began his career in London film laboratories, moved to the US in 1908 and settled in Hollywood in 1911. Rosher enjoyed two exceptionally creative periods during his 40-year career. In the silent era he was responsible for several important technical innovations, shot several Mary Pickford vehicles (including *Little Lord Fauntleroy* 1921 and *Sparrows* 1926), and was co-photographer, with Karl Struss, of F.W. Murnau's visually haunting *Sunrise* (1927). In the 1940s and 50s he again asserted himself as one of the foremost artists in his field with the lush color compositions of features such as *The Yearling* (1946), *Ziegfeld Follies* (1946) and *Show Boat* (1951). Father of cinematographer Charles Rosher, Jr., and actress Joan Marsh. • *The Ghost House* 1917; *The Secret Game* 1917; *The Widow's Might* 1917; *Captain Kidd, Jr.* 1918; *The Honor of His House* 1918; *How Could You Jean?* 1918; *Johanna Enlists* 1918; *One More American* 1918; *The White Man's Law* 1918; *Daddy Long Legs* 1919; *Heart O' the Hills* 1919; *The Hoodlum* 1919; *Pollyanna* 1920; *Suds* 1920; *Latin Love* 1921; *Little Lord Fauntleroy* 1921; *The Love Light* 1921; *Through the Back Door* 1921; *Smilin' Through* 1922; *Tess of the Storm Country* 1922; *Rosita* 1923; *Tiger Rose* 1923; *Dorothy Vernon of Haddon Hall* 1924; *Little Annie Rooney* 1925; *Sparrows* 1926; *My Best Girl* 1927 **(AANBPH)**; *Sunrise* 1927 **(AABPH)**; *Tempest* 1928 **(AANBPH)**; *Paid* 1930; *La Route est belle* 1930; *War Nurse* 1930; *The Beloved Bachelor* 1931; *Dance, Fools, Dance* 1931; *Husband's Holiday* 1931; *Laughing Sinners* 1931; *Silence* 1931; *This Modern Age* 1931; *Rockabye* 1932; *Two Against the World* 1932; *What Price Hollywood?* 1932; *After Tonight* 1933; *Bed of Roses* 1933; *Flaming Gold* 1933; *Our Betters* 1933; *The Past of Mary Holmes* 1933; *The Silver Cord* 1933; *The Affairs of Cellini* 1934 **(AANBPH)**; *Moulin Rouge* 1934; *Outcast Lady* 1934; *What Every Woman Knows* 1934; *After Office Hours* 1935; *The Call of the Wild* 1935; *Broadway Melody of 1936* 1936; *Little Lord Fauntleroy* 1936; *Small Town Girl* 1936; *Hollywood Hotel* 1937; *The Perfect Specimen* 1937; *The Woman I Love* 1937; *Hard to Get* 1938; *White Banners* 1938; *Espionage Agent* 1939; *Off the Record* 1939; *Yes, My Darling Daughter* 1939; *Brother Rat and a Baby* 1940; *A Child Is Born* 1940; *My Love Came Back* 1940; *Three Cheers For the Irish* 1940; *Four Mothers* 1941; *Million Dollar Baby* 1941; *One Foot in Heaven* 1941; *Mokey* 1942; *Pierre of the Plains* 1942; *Stand By For Action* 1942; *Assignment in Brittany* 1943; *Swing Fever* 1943; *Kismet* 1944 **(AANBPH)**; *Yolanda and the Thief* 1945; *The Yearling* 1946 **(AABPH)**; *Ziegfeld Follies* 1946; *Dark Delusion* 1947; *Fiesta* 1947; *Song of the Thin Man* 1947; *On an Island With You* 1948; *Words and Music* 1948; *East Side, West Side* 1949; *Neptune's Daughter* 1949; *The Red Danube* 1949; *Annie Get Your Gun* 1950 **(AANBPH)**; *Pagan Love Song* 1950; *Show Boat* 1951 **(AANBPH)**; *Scaramouche* 1952; *Kiss Me Kate* 1953; *The Story of Three Loves* 1953; *Young Bess* 1953; *Jupiter's Darling* 1955.

Rosi, Francesco • Director; also screenwriter. • Born Naples, Italy, November 15, 1922. Leading figure in political cinema of the 1960s who began his film career as an assistant (along with Franco Zeffirelli) on Visconti's *La Terra Trema* (1948). Rosi then worked in a similar capacity for figures such as Antonioni and Monicelli, and contributed to the scripts of several films, before taking over the direction of *Red Shirts* (1952) after Goffredo Alessandrini had quit the project. He made a solid, if unexceptional, solo directing debut with the Neapolitan gangster film, *The Challenge* (1958), but landed squarely in the international spotlight with 1962's *Salvatore Guiliano*. The film is an oblique, quasi-documentary account of a real-life Sicilian bandit, told largely in flashbacks and featuring, in true neorealist style, a non-professional cast shot almost entirely on location. It earned critical plaudits, including the Silver Bear at Berlin, and stirred considerable controversy for pointing out—as have several of Rosi's films—the explicit links between Mafia and state. The director continued in a similar vein with *Hands Over the City* (1963), a powerful exposé of corrupt real-estate developers, and *The Moment of Truth* (1965), an indictment of exploitation in the world of bull-fighting.

Rosi began to shed the journalistic elements of his style in films such as *Re: Lucky Luciano* (1973) and *Illustrious Corpses* (1976), two visually polished dramas which use the conventions of the gangster and thriller genres to paint searing portraits of institutional and political corruption. (In this respect, his work bears fruitful comparison with that of his countryman, Elio Petri.) The director's subsequent work has been generally mellower in tone and more leisurely paced. *Christ Stopped at Eboli* (1979) and *Chronicle of a Death Foretold* (1987) were both adapted from literary sources and star Gian Maria Volonte. The first is a lyrical account of writer Carlo Levi's Fascist-imposed exile in a primitive southern village in the 1930s; the second is a beautifully shot but somewhat static adaptation of the best-selling novel by Gabriel Garcia Marquez. *Carmen* (1984) is a relatively faithful, visually sumptuous translation of Bizet's opera to the screen. JDP • *La Terra Trema* 1948 (ad); *Bellissima* 1951 (sc,ad); *I Vinti* 1952 (ad); *Camicie rosse/Red Shirts/Anita Garibaldi* 1952 (d); *Senso* 1954 (ad); *Il Bigamo* 1955 (sc); *Kean* 1956 (d); *The Challenge* 1958 (d); *Salvatore Giuliano* 1962 (d,sc); *Le Mani sulla Città/Hands Over the City* 1963 (d,sc); *The Moment of Truth* 1965 (d); *C'era una Volta...* 1967 (d,sc); *Uomini Contro* 1970 (d,sc); *Il Caso Mattei* 1972 (d,sc); *Re: Lucky Luciano* 1973 (d,sc); *Cadaveri Eccellenti* 1976 (d,sc); *Cristo si è Fermato a Eboli/Christ Stopped at Eboli* 1979 (d,sc,adapt); *I Tre fratelli* 1980 (d,sc); *Bizet's Carmen* 1984 (art d,d,sc); *Cronaca di una morte annunciata/Chronicle of a Death Foretold* 1987 (d,sc,adapt); *Dimenticare Palermo* 1990 (d,sc).

Ross, Herbert • Director; also choreographer, dancer, actor. • Born New York, NY, May 13, 1927. *Educ.* Herbert Berghof Studio, New York. Began his career as a dancer and started choreographing Broadway shows in the early 1950s. Ross soon graduated to directing musical sequences and did the choreography for his first film, *Carmen Jones*, in 1954. He directed *Goodbye, Mr. Chips*, a musical remake of the Robert Donat classic, in 1969, and hit his stride with the delirious Woody Allen vehicle, *Play It Again, Sam* (1972), and a string of collaborations with playwright/screenwriter Neil Simon. To date, Ross has directed five features scripted by Simon, three of which have been adaptations of successful Broadway plays (*The Sunshine Boys* 1975, *California Suite* 1978, *I Ought to Be in Pictures* 1981). Ross returned to his dancing roots with an acclaimed study of the ballet world, *The Turning Point* (1977). Like several of his films it was co-produced by his wife, Nora Kaye, a former prima ballerina who died of cancer in 1987. He enjoyed critical and box-office success in the 1980s with solidly crafted entertainments such as *Pennies From Heaven* (1981) and *Steel Magnolias* (1989). Ross married Lee Radziwill in 1989. • *Carmen Jones* 1954 (chor); *Summer Holiday* 1963 (d); *Doctor Dolittle* 1967 (chor); *Funny Girl* 1968 (chor); *Goodbye, Mr. Chips* 1969 (d); *The Owl and the Pussycat* 1970 (d,p); *T. R. Baskin* 1971 (d); *Play It Again, Sam* 1972 (d); *The Last of Sheila* 1973 (d,p); *Funny Lady* 1975 (d); *The Sunshine Boys* 1975 (d); *The Seven Per-Cent Solution* 1976 (d,p); *The Goodbye Girl* 1977 (d); *The Turning Point* 1977 (d,p) **(AANBD,AANBP)**; *California Suite* 1978 (d); *Nijinsky* 1980 (d); *I Ought to Be in Pictures* 1981 (d,p); *Pennies From Heaven* 1981 (d,p); *Max Dugan Returns* 1982 (d,p); *Footloose* 1984 (d); *Protocol* 1984 (d); *Dancers* 1987 (d); *The Secret of My Success* 1987 (d,p); *Steel Magnolias* 1989 (d); *My Blue Heaven* 1990 (d,p); *True Colors* 1991 (d,p).

Ross, Katharine • Actress • Born Los Angeles, CA, January 29, 1942. *Educ.* Santa Rosa College, CA; San Francisco Actor's Workshop. Promising star of the mid-to-late 1960s, best known for her performances in *The Graduate* (1967) and *Butch Cassidy and the Sundance Kid* (1969). Since then, Ross's talents seem to have been squandered in mostly inferior film and TV vehicles. Married to actor Sam Elliot. • *Mister Buddwing* 1965; *Shenandoah* 1965; *The Singing Nun* 1966; *Games* 1967; *The Graduate* 1967 **(AANBSA)**; *Butch Cassidy and the Sundance Kid* 1969; *Tell Them Willie Boy Is Here* 1969; *Fools* 1970; *Get to Know Your Rabbit* 1972; *They Only Kill Their Masters* 1972; *Le Hasard et la Violence* 1973; *The Stepford Wives* 1975; *Voyage of the Damned* 1976; *The Betsy* 1978; *The Swarm* 1978; *The Legacy* 1979; *The Final Countdown* 1980; *Wrong Is Right* 1982; *Red-Headed Stranger* 1986.

Rossellini, Isabella • Actress; also model. • Born Rome, Italy, June 18, 1952. *Educ.* Finch College; New School for Social Research, New York. Former translator and TV journalist who made her film debut opposite her mother, Ingrid Bergman, in Vincente Minnelli's best-forgotten *A Matter of Time* (1976). Rossellini came to prominence as the abused, abstracted chanteuse in *Blue Velvet* (1986), directed by long-term companion David Lynch, though she is best known—and better renumerated—for her career as a model. (Her contract as the official "face" of the Lancôme cosmetics empire has earned her more than $2 million to date.) Daughter of director Roberto Rossellini and formerly married (1979-82) to director Martin Scorsese. • *A Matter of Time* 1976; *Il Prato* 1979; *Il Pap'Occhio* 1981; *White Nights* 1985; *Blue Velvet* 1986; *Red Riding Hood* 1987; *Siesta* 1987; *Tough Guys Don't Dance* 1987; *Zelly and Me* 1988; *Cousins* 1989; *Dames Galantes* 1990; *Wild at Heart* 1990.

Rossellini, Roberto • Director • Born Rome, May 8, 1906; died June 4, 1977. Often identified with the constrictive "neorealist" label, Roberto Rossellini stands as one of the greatest directors in the history of Italian film: the man responsible for the postwar rebirth of Italian cinema and one of the few truly great humanists (along with Jean Renoir) to work in the medium.

Born into a bourgeois Roman family, Rossellini spent his formative years under Mussolini's fascist fist and, by his early 30s, had drifted into filmmaking—a common pattern amongst the idle Italian rich. He worked with his friend, producer Vittorio Mussolini, the son of *il Duce*, on the script for *Luciano Serra Pilota* (1938), a propaganda film which showed some early marks of a neorealist style. After directing a handful of pictures under the official government banner, Rossellini, the stereotypically apolitical Roman, made an indelible mark on world cinema in 1945 with *Open City*. Despite a lukewarm response in Italy, the film was a sensation in France and the US with its raw, near-documentary style: grainy black-and-white photography, amateur performers and real locations. These were elements that audiences had not previously seen in feature films, and *Open City* was hailed as bringing a new kind of realism, "neorealism," to the screen.

While his two subsequent films—*Paisan* (1946) and *Germany, Year Zero* (1947)—bore the hallmarks of the neorealist style, Rossellini drew increasing critical fire for his use of melodrama (especially through his brother Renzo's musical scores) and Hollywood narrative conventions. He had never been a strict neorealist, however. His aim was to show "people as they are," to understand rather than recreate reality, and he incorporated other expressionistic elements into nearly all his work. These elements are particularly evident in films such as the underappreciated *Fear* (1954), with its psychologically based visuals, but had already been partially present in *Open City*.

In 1949, Rossellini further challenged the film community's expectations by forming a creative and personal—not to mention scandalous—union with one of Hollywood's greatest stars, Ingrid Bergman. Beginning with *Stromboli* (1949), the pair collaborated over a six-year period on seven films, all of which proved disastrous with both critics and public. By 1958, the two had separated, following revelations of Rossellini's affair with Indian screenwriter Somali Das Gupta. Rossellini's documentary *India* (1958) was a box-office failure, although its critical reputation remains high. Commercial success finally returned with *General Della Rovere* (1959), a wartime Resistance story which also marked a return to the familiar neorealist style; Rossellini would later see the film as a retread of the ideas and forms of his previous successes.

By 1964, Rossellini had been canonized by numerous critics, as well as fellow filmmakers like Jean-Luc Godard and Bernardo Bertolucci (in the latter's *Before the Revolution* 1964, a character declares, "One cannot live without Rossellini!"). Concerned chiefly with the state of cinema and its function as an artistic and educational tool, Rossellini decided to remove himself from the commercial arena. Viewing himself as a craftsman and not an artist, he devoted his creative energies to TV films on science and history: the five-hour *L'Eté del Ferro/The Age of Iron* (1964), the twelve-hour *Lotta Dell'Uomo per la Sua Sopravvivenza/Man's Struggle for Survival* (1967) and the six-hour *Atti Degli Apostoli/The Acts of the Apostles* (1968), as well as biographies of Socrates, Blaise Pascal, Augustine of Hippo, Descartes, Jesus and Louis XIV. Only the latter, *The Rise of Louis XIV* (1966), has received its due acclaim, chiefly because it is one of the few to have been screened theatrically. DC • *Daphne* (short) 1936 (d); *Prelude a l'àprès-Midi d'un Faune* (short) 1938 (d); *Luciano Serra Pilota* 1938 (assoc.d,sc); *La Nave Bianca* 1941 (d,sc); *Una Pilota Ritorna* 1942 (d,sc); *L'Uomo della Croce* 1943 (d,sc); *Roma, città aperta/Open City* 1945 (d); *Desiderio* 1946 (d); *Paisan* 1946 (d,sc) **(AANBSC)**; *Germania, Anno Zero/Germany Year Zero* 1947 (d,sc,story); *L'Amore* 1948 (d,p,sc,from play—*Il Miracolo*); *La Macchina ammazzacattivi* 1948 (d,p,sc); *Stromboli* 1949 (d,sc); *Francesco Giullare di Dio* 1950 (d); *Europa '51* 1951 (d,p,sc); *Les Sept péchés capitaux/The Seven Deadly Sins* 1952 (d,sc—"Envy"); *Siamo Donne* 1953 (d); *Viaggio in Italia* 1953 (d); *Die Angst/Fear* 1954 (d); *Giovanna d'Arco al Rogo* 1954 (d); *India* 1958 (d,sc); *Il Generale Della Rovere/General Della Rovere* 1959 (d,sc); *Era Notte a Roma* 1960 (d,sc); *Vanina Vanini* 1961 (d); *Anima nera* 1962 (d,sc); *RoGoPag* 1962 (d,sc—"Illibatezza"); *Les Carabiniers* 1963 (sc); *L'Eté del Ferro/The Age of Iron* 1964 (sc); *La Prise de pouvoir par Louis XIV/The Rise of Louis XIV* 1966 (d); *Lotta Dell'Uomo per la Sua Sopravvivenza/Man's Struggle for Survival* 1967 (p,sc); *Atti Degli Apostoli/The Acts of the Apostles* 1968 (d,p,sc); *The Night of Counting the Years* 1970 (p); *Socrates* 1971 (d,sc,ed); *Agostino d'Ippona* 1972 (d); *E ta di Cozimo de'Medici* 1972 (d); *Anno Uno* 1974 (d,sc); *Blaise Pascal* 1974 (d,sc); *Il Messia* 1978 (d,sc); *He Stands in a Desert Counting the Seconds of His Life* 1985 (a).

Rossen, Robert • Director; also screenwriter, producer. • Born Robert Rosen, New York, NY, March 16, 1908; died 1966. *Educ.* NYU. Former boxer whose work as a writer and director of socially conscious plays such as *The Body Beautiful* led to a writing contract with Warner Bros. in 1936. Rossen scripted some ten features over the next seven years for directors including Lloyd Bacon, Mervyn Leroy and Lewis Milestone. His writing was influenced by his Communist affiliations and, although he had left the party in 1945, his involvement led to a subpoena from the House Un-American Activities Committee in 1947. In the four years that elapsed before Rossen was eventually tried and blacklisted, he established himself as an independent producer and director of note with films such as *Body and Soul* (1947), scripted by Abraham Polonsky, and *All the King's Men* (1949), an incisive indictment of political corruption.

After "naming names" in 1953 Rossen was allowed to continue working, but chose not to return to Hollywood. His subsequent output was uneven, but not without successes. *The Hustler* (1961) is a moody poolroom drama with its roots in an unproduced Rossen play, "Corner Pocket"; it was nominated for Academy Awards in every major category and inspired a Martin Scorsese-directed sequel, *The Color of Money* (1986), which again starred Paul Newman. *Lilith* (1964) is a tragic study of obsession set in a mental hospital and starring Warren Beatty and Jean Seberg; shot, like *The Hustler*, by Eugene Shuftan, it was dismissed by US critics at the time of its release but is now regarded by many as Rossen's masterpiece. • *Marked Woman* 1937 (sc); *They Won't Forget* 1937 (sc); *Racket Busters* 1938 (sc); *Dust Be My Destiny* 1939 (sc); *The Roaring Twenties* 1939 (sc); *A Child Is Born* 1940 (sc); *Blues in the Night* 1941 (sc); *Out of the Fog* 1941 (sc); *The Sea Wolf* 1941 (sc); *Edge of Darkness* 1943 (sc); *A Walk in the Sun* 1945 (sc); *The Strange Love of Martha Ivers* 1946 (sc); *Body and Soul* 1947 (d); *Desert Fury* 1947 (sc); *Johnny O'Clock* 1947 (d,sc); *All the King's Men* 1949 (d,p,sc) **(AANBSC)**; *Undercover Man* 1949 (p); *The Brave Bulls* 1951 (d,p); *Mambo* 1954 (d,sc,story); *Alexander the Great* 1956 (d,p,sc); *Island in the Sun* 1957 (d); *They Came to Cordura* 1959 (d,sc); *The Hustler* 1961 (d,p,sc) **(AANBD,AANBP,AANBSC)**; *Billy Budd* 1962 (sc); *The Cool World* 1963 (from play); *Lilith* 1964 (d,p,sc).

Rossif, Frédéric • Director • Born Cetinje, Montenegro, Yugoslavia, August 14, 1922; died April 18, 1990, Paris. Compilation filmmaker who began his career working for the Cinémathèque Française and directed several programs for French TV in the 1950s. Rossif chronicled some of the most significant events of modern European history, including the Spanish Civil War (*To Die in Madrid* 1963, which earned him the Prix Jean Vigo), the Russian Revolution (*Revolution d'Octobre* 1967, which incorporated footage from Vertov's *Man with a Movie Camera* 1929) and the rise and fall of German National Socialism (*From Nuremberg to Nuremberg*). His later work included studies of Jacques Brel and Pablo Picasso. • *Vel' d'hiv' (short)* 1960 (d); *Le Temps du Ghetto* 1961 (d,sc—English language version); *Les Animaux* 1963 (d); *Encore Paris (short)* 1963 (d); *Mourir à Madrid/To Die in Madrid* 1963 (d,p) **(AANBDOC)**; *Pour l'Espagne (short)* 1963 (d); *Behold a Pale Horse* 1964 (opening montage *To Die in Madrid*); *Révolution d'Octobre* 1967 (d); *Aussi Loin Que l'Amour* 1971 (d); *La Fête Sauvage* 1975 (d,idea); *Brel* 1982 (d,sc); *Picasso, Pablo* 1982 (d); *Sauvage et Beau* 1984 (d,sc); *Le Coeur Musicien* 1987 (d,sc).

Rota, Nino • Composer • Born Milan, December 31, 1911; died 1979. *Educ.* Accademia di Santa Cecilia, Rome; Curtis Institute, Philadelphia PA. Acclaimed symphonic and operatic composer who began writing film scores in the mid-1940s and enjoyed consistent success in the field. Rota is best known for his 25-year association with Fellini—notably on *La Strada* (1954), *La Dolce Vita* (1959) and *8 1/2* (1963)—and for his work on Visconti's *The Leopard* (1963) and Coppola's "Godfather" films (His music, composed directly for the first two in the series, was incorporated into the score for the third installment after his death). • *Sotte il Sole di Roma* 1948 (m); *Obsession* 1949 (m); *The Pirates of Capri* 1949 (m); *Lo Sceicco Bianco* 1952 (m); *La Grande Speranza* 1953 (m); *I Vitelloni* 1953 (m); *Eterna Femmina* 1954 (m); *Mambo* 1954 (m); *I Sette dell'orsa Maggiore* 1954 (m); *Side Street Story* 1954 (m); *La Strada* 1954 (m); *Amici Per la Belle* 1955 (m); *Il Bidone* 1955 (m); *Le Notti di Cabiria/Nights of Cabiria* 1956 (m); *Star of India* 1956 (m); *War and Peace* 1956 (m); *The Wild Oat* 1956 (m); *Barrage contre le Pacifique* 1957 (m); *Londra Chiama Polo Nord* 1957 (m); *Le Notti Bianche* 1957 (m); *La Loi c'est la loi* 1958 (m); *La Dolce Vita* 1959 (m); *Sotto dieci bandiere* 1960 (m); *Boccaccio '70* 1962 (m); *L'Isola di Arturo* 1962 (m); *The Reluctant Saint* 1962 (m); *I Sequestrati di Altona/The Condemned of Altona* 1962 (m); *Il Gattopardo/The Leopard* 1963 (m); *Otto e Mezzo* 1963 (m); *Giulietta degli Spiriti/Juliet of the Spirits* 1965 (m); *The Taming of the Shrew* 1967 (m); *Histoires Extraordinaires/Spirits of the Dead* 1968 (m); *Romeo and Juliet* 1968 (m,song); *Satyricon* 1969 (m); *Alex in Wonderland* 1970 (song); *I Clowns/The Clowns* 1970 (m); *Waterloo* 1970 (m,m.dir); *The Godfather* 1972 (m); *Roma* 1972 (m); *Amarcord* 1973 (m); *Film d'Amore e d'Anarchia* 1973 (m,song); *The Abdication* 1974 (m); *The Godfather, Part II* 1974 (m) **(AABM)**; *Caro Michele* 1976 (m); *Il Casanova di Federico Fellini/Fellini's Casanova* 1976 (m); *Ragazzo di Borgata* 1976 (m); *Death on the Nile* 1978 (m); *Prova d'Orchestra/Orchestra Rehearsal* 1978 (m); *Hurricane* 1979 (m); *I Soliti Ignoti... Vent'Anni Dopo* 1986 (m); *Federico Fellini's Intervista* 1987 (m); *The Godfather Part III* 1990 (m).

Roth, Ann • Costume designer • Born Pennsylvania. *Educ.* Carnegie Tech. Highly regarded costume designer who amassed over 30 Broadway credits before entering film with George Roy Hill's *The World of Henry Orient* (1964). Roth earned her first solo credit on John Schlesinger's *Midnight Cowboy* (1969) and went on to collaborate with filmmakers including Herbert Ross, Brian De Palma, Milos Forman, Karel Reisz and Alan Pakula. She designed the costumes for the original Broadway production of *The Odd Couple* and has continued to work with Mike Nichols ever since. • *A Fine Madness* 1966 (cost); *Pretty Poison* 1968 (cost); *Midnight Cowboy* 1969 (cost); *The Owl and the Pussycat* 1970 (cost); *They Might Be Giants* 1971 (cost); *The Happy Hooker* 1975 (cost); *Independence* 1976 (cost); *Coming Home* 1977 (cost); *The Goodbye Girl* 1977 (cost); *Nunzio* 1977 (cost); *California Suite* 1978 (cost); *Hair* 1979 (cost); *Promises in the Dark* 1979 (cost); *9 to 5* 1980 (cost); *Dressed to Kill* 1980 (cost); *The Island* 1980 (cost); *Blow Out* 1981 (cost—Nancy Allen); *Honky Tonk Freeway* 1981 (cost); *Only When I Laugh* 1981 (cost); *Rollover* 1981 (cost); *The World According to Garp* 1982 (cost); *Silkwood* 1983 (cost); *The Survivors* 1983 (cost); *Places in the Heart* 1984 (cost) **(AANBCD)**; *Jagged Edge* 1985 (cost); *Maxie* 1985 (cost); *The Slugger's Wife* 1985 (cost); *Sweet Dreams* 1985 (cost); *Heartburn* 1986 (cost); *The Morning After* 1986 (cost); *Biloxi Blues* 1988 (cost); *Funny Farm* 1988 (cost); *The January Man* 1988 (cost); *Stars and Bars* 1988 (cost); *The Unbearable Lightness of Being* 1988 (cost); *Working Girl* 1988 (cost); *Family Business* 1989 (cost); *Her Alibi* 1989 (cost); *Bonfire of the Vanities* 1990 (cost); *Everybody Wins* 1990 (cost); *Pacific Heights* 1990 (cost); *Postcards From the Edge* 1990 (cost); *Q&A* 1990 (cost); *Regarding Henry* 1991 (cost).

Roth, Joe • Producer, director • Born New York, NY, 1948. *Educ.* Boston University (public communications). Former production assistant and producer of the improvisational comedy group, the Pitchell Players, who produced his first film, *Tunnelvision*, in 1976. A spoof on TV programming made for $250,000 and starring then-unknown actors such as Chevy Chase and Larraine Newman, the film grossed around $17 million. Roth went on to produce a string of commercially successful features and made his directorial debut with the boxing melodrama, *Streets of Gold* (1986). In 1987 he co-founded, with James G. Robinson, the Morgan Creek independent production company, responsible for films including *Dead Ringers* (1988) and *Major League* (1989). In 1989 he was named chairman of the Fox Film Corporation, the newly formed theatrical film unit of the 20th Century-Fox Film Corporation. • *Tunnelvision* 1976 (p); *Cracking Up* 1977 (exec.p); *Our Winning Season* 1978 (p); *Americathon* 1979 (p); *The Final Terror* 1981 (p); *Ladies and Gentlemen, the Fabulous Stains* 1982 (p); *P.K. and the Kid* 1982 (p); *Bachelor Party* 1983 (exec.p); *The Stone Boy* 1983 (p); *Moving Violations* 1985 (p); *Off Beat* 1986 (p); *Streets of Gold* 1986 (d,p); *Where the River Runs Black* 1986 (p); *Revenge of the Nerds II* 1987 (d,exec.p); *Young Guns* 1988 (p); *Enemies, A Love Story* 1989 (exec.p); *Renegades* 1989 (exec.p); *Skin Deep* 1989 (exec.p); *Coupe De Ville* 1990 (d,exec.p); *Nightbreed* 1990 (exec.p); *Pacific Heights* 1990 (exec.p); *William Peter Blatty's The Exorcist III* 1990 (exec.p).

Roth, Tim • British actor • Rising young lead of British film and TV; adept at playing sneering, street-wise types. • *Meantime* 1983; *Return to Waterloo* 1983; *The Hit* 1984; *Popielusko* 1988; *A World Apart* 1988; *The Cook, the Thief, His Wife and Her Lover* 1989; *Farendj* 1990; *Rosencrantz and Guildenstern Are Dead* 1990; *Vincent and Theo* 1990; *Backsliding* 1991.

Rotha, Paul • Filmmaker; also author. • Born Paul Thompson, London, June 3, 1907; died March 7, 1984, Oxfordshire, England. *Educ.* Slade School of Fine Arts, London (graphics). Painter and designer who was commissioned at the age of 20 to write *The Film Till Now* (1930, revised 1949), a pioneering work of cinema history that established many of the parameters for future study. He began making films in the 1930s, initially under the guidance of John Grierson, and was widely acclaimed for his industrial works such as *Shipyard* and *The Face of Britain* (both 1935). Rotha turned increasingly to production in the 40s but continued to direct noted documentaries including *World of Plenty* (1943) and *The World is Rich* (1947), both about food policy, and *World Without End* (1953), co-directed with Basil Wright for UNESCO. He made three feature films in the late 1950s and 60s which, though influenced by his documentary style, were unexceptional. The compilation film, *The Life of Adolf Hitler* (1962), remains one of the finest screen histories of Nazism. • *Australian Wine* 1931 (d); *Shipyard* 1935 (d); *The Face of Britain* 1935 (d); *The Fourth Estate* 1939 (d); *World of Plenty* 1943 (d); *The World Is Rich* 1947 (d,p) **(AANBDOC)**; *Valley of the Headhunters* 1953 (a); *White Witch Doctor* 1953 (a); *World Without End* 1953 (d); *Jungle Man-Eaters* 1954 (a); *Untamed* 1955 (a); *The Disembodied* 1957 (a); *Watusi* 1959 (a); *The Life of Adolf Hitler* 1962 (d); *Maggie & Pierre* 1984 (creative consultant).

Rotunno, Giuseppe • Director of photography • Born Rome, March 19, 1923. Former still photographer who worked as a camera operator for figures such as G.R. Aldo before graduating to director of photography in 1955. Rotunno became one of Europe's leading cinematographers in the 1960s, with his work ranging from the epic, operatic compositions of Visconti's *The Leopard* (1963) to the daguerrotype-influenced style of Monicelli's *The Organizer* (1963). He has shot several of Fellini's films as well as features directed by Mike Nichols (*Carnal Knowledge* 1971), Bob Fosse (*All That Jazz* 1979) and Terry Gilliam (*The Adventures of Baron Munchausen* 1988). • *Tosca* 1956 (ph); *The Monte Carlo Story* 1957 (ph); *Le Notti Bianche* 1957 (ph); *La Ragazza del Palio* 1957 (ph); *Fast and Sexy* 1958 (ph); *The Naked Maja* 1959 (ph); *On the Beach* 1959 (ph); *The Angel Wore Red* 1960 (ph); *Five Branded Women* 1960 (ph); *Rocco e i suoi Fratelli/Rocco and His Brothers* 1960 (ph); *Boccaccio '70* 1962 (ph—"Il lavoro"); *I Compagni* 1963 (ph); *Il Gattopardo/The Leopard* 1963 (ph); *I Compagni/The Organizer* 1963 (ph); *La Bibbia/The Bible* 1966 (ph); *Anzio* 1968 (ph); *Candy* 1968 (ph); *Histoires Extraordinaires/Spirits of the Dead* 1968 (ph); *I Girasoli* 1969 (ph); *Satyricon* 1969 (ph); *The Secret of Santa Vittoria* 1969 (ph); *Carnal Knowledge* 1971 (ph); *Roma* 1972 (ph); *L'Uomo della Mancha/Man of La Mancha* 1972 (ph); *Amarcord* 1973 (ph); *Film d'Amore e d'Anarchia/Love and Anarchy* 1973 (ph); *Il Bestione* 1974 (ph); *Tutto a Posto e Niente In Ordine* 1974 (ph); *La Divina Creatura* 1975 (ph); *Il Casanova di Federico Fellini/Fellini's Casanova* 1976 (ph); *Sturmtruppen* 1976 (ph); *The End of the World in Our Usual Bed in a Night Full of Rain* 1977 (ph); *Prova d'Orchestra/Orchestra Rehearsal* 1978 (ph); *All That Jazz* 1979 (ph) **(AANBPH)**; *La Città Delle Donne/City of Women* 1980 (ph); *Popeye* 1980 (ph); *Rollover* 1981 (ph); *Bello Mio Bellezza Mia* 1982 (ph); *Five Days One Summer* 1982 (ph); *E la nave Va/And the Ship Sails On* 1983 (ph); *American Dreamer* 1984 (ph—Paris); *Desiderio* 1984 (ph); *Non ci resta che piangere* 1984 (ph); *The Assisi Underground* 1985 (ph); *Red Sonja* 1985 (ph); *Hotel Colonial* 1986 (ph); *Julia and Julia* 1987 (ph); *The Adventures of Baron Munchausen* 1988 (ph); *Haunted Summer* 1988 (ph); *Rent-A-Cop* 1988 (ph); *Rebus* 1989 (ph); *Regarding Henry* 1991 (ph).

Rouch, Jean • Filmmaker • Born Paris, May 31, 1917. Ethnographer who began using film to record African rituals and customs in 1947. Rouch documented several aspects of African life before developing an interest in the film medium itself and experimenting with techniques which would later become central to cinéma vérité. Rouch's *Chronicle of a Summer* (1960) is seen by many as marking the beginning of the vérité movement; co-directed by sociologist Edgar Morin, it used the new lightweight film equipment to capture the diversity and variety of Parisian life. Rouch later returned to filming African subjects, frequently addressing the conflicts between European and African cultures. • *Chronique d'un été/Chronicle of a Summer* 1960 (a,d,sc); *La Punition* 1962 (d); *La Fleur de l'age, ou les adolescentes* 1964 (d,sc—"Marie-France and Veronica"); *La Chasse au Lion à l'arc* 1965 (a,d,sc); *Paris Vu Par...* 1965 (d,sc—"Gare du Nord"); *Petit à Petit* 1970 (d,sc.conception,ph); *Chantons sous l'occupation* 1976 (add.ph); *Cocorico Monsieur Poulet* 1977 (d,sc); *Funerailles à Bongo: Le Vieux Anai* 1979 (d); *Dionysos* 1984 (d,sc,ph); *Brise-glace* 1987 (d,ph); *Enigma* 1987 (d,sc,ph); *Boulevards d'Afrique* 1988 (d,ph); *Folie ordinaire d'une fille de Cham* 1988 (d,ph); *Chine, ma douleur* 1989 (tech.ad); *Cantate pour deux généraux* 1990 (d).

Roud, Richard • Critic, author. Born Boston, MA, July 6, 1929; died January 15, 1989, Nimes, France. Co-founder in 1963 (with Amos Vogel) of the New York Film Festival and long-time director of that venue, Roud was American by birth and European by choice, living all of his adult life in London and Paris. More than any other single individual, he was responsible for exposing American audiences to European cinema of the 60s and 70s through showings at the New York Film Festival. Godard, Truffaut, Resnais, Chabrol, Rohmer, Rivette, Antonioni, Bertolucci, Fassbinder, Wenders, Straub, Tanner and others all owed a debt to Roud and the Festival.

"Richard was the right man in the right place at the right time," writer Susan Sontag told The New York Times. "He got to know all the innovative New Wave directors and became a spokesperson for a whole new generation of young filmmakers.... He was an impresario for those continental filmmakers and the films he promoted changed people's taste in this country," she observed.

The New York Film Festival and Roud also showcased the work of young American directors outside the Hollywood orbit. Martin Scorsese's *Mean Streets* (1973) debuted there, for example. According to Scorsese, "Richard Roud shaped the very look of American movies, because so many filmmakers saw, and were influenced by, what he chose since 1963."

A critic as well as impresario, Roud became the London correspondent for *Cahiers du Cinéma* in the 1950s and wrote for *The Manchester Guardian* from 1963 until his death. His monograph on *Godard* (1968) was not only influential in establishing the reputation of that director, it was also one of the first of a series of essays which helped form contemporary film culture. Roud was also the author of *A Passion for Films* (1983), a history of the Cinémathèque Française and its founder, Henri Langlois, and editor of *A Critical Dictionary of Cinema* (1979). He was as dedicated to promoting the work of younger critics in both the US and the UK as he was to advancing the careers of filmmakers whom he admired.

In October 1987, little more than a year before his death, Roud was fired as Director of the New York Film Festival in a small scandal which resulted in the resignations of a number of film critics from the Festival's program committee in protest.

During the more than thirty years he split his time between Europe and the US, Roud seldom availed himself of modern air travel. This idiosyncracy became increasingly difficult to satisfy as, one by one throughout the 60s and 70s, the great ocean liners retired from the North Atlantic routes. He had flown the route—once—in the early 1950s, to return to the US for his father's funeral. He avoided planes after that. Like the ships he preferred, by the late 1980s he was a relic of an earlier, perhaps more civilized time.

Roud was made a chevalier of the French Légion d'honneur in 1979, one of few foreigners to wear the rosette. JM

Roundtree, Richard • Actor • Born New Rochelle, NY, September 7, 1942. *Educ.* Southern Illinois University. Handsome black lead who got his start with New York City's esteemed Negro Ensemble Company and made his name as the smooth title character in the classic black exploitation film, *Shaft* (1971). Roundtree repeated the role in two sequels and a small-screen spinoff and has since divided his time between film and TV. • *What Do You Say to a Naked Lady?* 1970; *Embassy* 1971; *Shaft* 1971; *Charley-One-Eye* 1972; *Shaft's Big Score* 1972; *Shaft in Africa* 1973; *Earthquake* 1974; *Diamonds* 1975; *Man Friday* 1975; *Escape to Athena* 1979; *Game For Vultures* 1979; *An Eye For an Eye* 1981; *Inchon* 1982; *One Down Two to Go* 1982; *Q* 1982; *The Big Score* 1983; *Young Warriors* 1983; *City Heat* 1984; *Killpoint* 1984; *Jocks* 1986; *Opposing Force* 1986; *Angel III: The Final Chapter* 1988; *Maniac Cop* 1988; *Party Line* 1988; *Bad Jim* 1989; *The Banker* 1989; *Crack House* 1989; *Night Visitor* 1989.

Rourke, Mickey • Actor • Born Schenectady, NY, 1950. *Educ.* Actors Studio. Ruggedly appealing, soft-spoken lead with a talent for playing world-weary or marginalized characters. Rourke first came to attention with his roles in two films by emerging young directors; he played a professional arsonist in Lawrence Kasdan's *Body Heat* (1981) and a debt-ridden hairdresser/lothario in Barry Levinson's *Diner* (1982). His subsequent career has seen somewhat uneven, encompassing an excellent performance as an alcohol-sodden writer, in *Barfly* (1987), as well as two glorified soft-porn roles, in *9 1/2 Weeks* (1986) and *Wild Orchid* (1989). *Homeboy* (1988) was based on a story by Rourke. • *1941* 1979 (a); *Fade to Black* 1980 (a); *Heaven's Gate* 1980 (a); *Body Heat* 1981 (a); *Diner* 1982 (a); *Eureka* 1983 (a); *Rumble Fish* 1983 (a); *The Pope of Greenwich Village* 1984 (a); *Year of the Dragon* 1985 (a); *9 1/2 Weeks* 1986 (a); *Angel Heart* 1987 (a); *Barfly* 1987 (a); *A Prayer For the Dying* 1987 (a); *Homeboy* 1988 (a,story); *Francesco* 1989 (a); *Johnny Handsome* 1989 (a); *Wild Orchid* 1989 (a); *Desperate Hours* 1990 (a).

Rousselot, Philippe • Director of photography • Born Meurthe et Moselle, France, 1945. *Educ.* Vaugirard Film School, Paris. Assisted Nestor Almendros on three films directed by Eric Rohmer before graduating to director of photography in 1972. Rousselot had already enjoyed fruitful collaborations with directors Diane Kurys and Claude Goretta before landing in the international spotlight with Jean-Jacques Beineix's slick, stylish thriller, *Diva* (1982). The film won him his first César (the French Oscar) and paved the way for a prestigious international career. Rousselot won a second César for Alain Cavalier's *Thérèse* (1986) and has worked with John Boorman (*The Emerald Forest* 1985, *Hope and Glory* 1987), Stephen Frears (*Dangerous Liaisons* 1988) and Philip Kaufman (*Henry & June* 1990). • *Ma nuit chez Maud/My Night at Maud's* 1969 (cam.op. 2nd asst); *Absences Repetees* 1972 (ph); *Il pleut toujours ou c'est mouille* 1974 (ph); *Adom ou le sang d'abel* 1977 (ph); *Le Couple Temoin* 1977 (ph); *Diabolo Menthe/Peppermint Soda* 1977 (ph); *Paradiso* 1977 (ph); *Pauline et l'Ordinateur* 1977 (ph); *Pour Clemence* 1977 (ph); *Les Chemins de l'exil, ou les dernières années de Jean Jacques Rousseau* 1978 (ph); *Cocktail Molotov* 1979 (ph); *La Drolesse* 1979 (ph); *La Provinciale* 1980 (ph); *La Gueule du Loup* 1981 (ph); *Diva* 1982 (ph); *Guy De Maupassant* 1982 (ph); *La Lune dans le caniveau* 1983 (ph); *Némo* 1983 (ph); *Des Terroristes à la retraite* 1983 (cam.collaboration); *Les Voleurs de la nuit* 1984 (ph); *The Emerald Forest* 1985 (ph); *La Nuit Magique* 1985 (ph); *Thérèse* 1986 (ph); *Hope and Glory* 1987 (ph) **(AANBPH)**; *Dangerous Liaisons* 1988 (ph); *L'Ours/The Bear* 1988 (ph); *Trop belle pour toi/Too Beautiful For You* 1989 (ph); *We're No Angels* 1989 (ph); *Henry & June* 1990 (ph);

Rowlands, Gena • Actress • Born Cambria, WI, June 19, 1936. *Educ.* University of Wisconsin; AADA, New York. Talented, alluring blonde star of stage, screen and TV whose success on Broadway (*Middle of the Night*) in 1956 led to her film debut in *The High Cost of Loving* (1958). Rowlands, whose appearances onscreen have been infrequent but seldom unmemorable, is best known for her roles in films directed by her late husband, John Cassavetes; among the highlights of their association are *Faces* (1968), *A Woman Under the Influence* (1974), *Opening Night* (1977) and *Gloria* (1980), which earned her a Golden Lion Award at the Venice Film Festival. • *The High Cost of Loving* 1958 (a); *A Child Is Waiting* 1962 (a); *Lonely Are the Brave* 1962 (a); *The Spiral Road* 1962 (a); *Tony Rome* 1967 (a); *Faces* 1968 (a); *Gli Intoccabili* 1969 (a); *Minnie and Moskowitz* 1971 (a); *A Woman Under the Influence* 1974 (a) **(AANBA)**; *Two-Minute Warning* 1976 (a); *Opening Night* 1977 (a); *The Brink's Job* 1978 (a); *Gloria* 1980 (a) **(AANBA)**; *Tempest* 1982 (a); *"I'm Almost Not Crazy..." John Cassavetes: The Man and His Work* 1983 (a); *Love Streams* 1984 (a,song); *Light of Day* 1987 (a); *Another Woman* 1988 (a); *Once Around* 1991 (a).

Rozema, Patricia • Director, screenwriter • Born Canada, c. 1959. Stirred considerable critical interest at the 1987 Cannes Film Festival with her refreshing debut feature *I've Heard the Mermaids Singing*, an engaging chronicle of a secretary's disillusioning brush with the art world. Due to a strict Calvinist upbringing, Rozema had seen no films before the age of 16; before embarking on her breakthrough project she had made only one short, *Passion: A Letter in 16mm* (1986), and worked as an assistant on two features. • *Unfinished Business* 1983 (asst. to Don Owen); *The Fly* 1986 (3rd ad); *Passion: A Letter in 16mm (short)* 1986 (d); *I've Heard the Mermaids Singing* 1987 (d,p,sc,ed); *The White Room* 1990 (d,exec.p,sc,ed).

Rozsa, Miklos • Composer • Born Budapest, Hungary, April 18, 1907. *Educ.* Leipzig Conservatory. Symphonic and chamber composer who began scoring films for Alexander Korda in England in the 1930s and went with him to Hollywood to make *The Thief of Bagdad* (1940). A prolific and versatile figure, Rosa's work ranges from the intimate, disturbing accompaniment for *Spellbound* (1945) to the epic, sweeping scores of *Ben-Hur* (1959) and *El Cid* (1961). • *Knight Without Armour* 1937 (m); *The Squeaker* 1937 (m); *The Thief of Bagdad* 1940 (m) **(AANBM)**; *Lydia* 1941 (m) **(AANBM)**; *Sundown* 1941 (m) **(AANBM)**; *That Hamilton Woman*

1941 (m); *Jacare* 1942 (m); *The Jungle Book* 1942 (m) **(AANBM)**; *Five Graves to Cairo* 1943 (m); *Sahara* 1943 (m); *So Proudly We Hail* 1943 (m); *The Woman of the Town* 1943 (m) **(AANBM)**; *Dark Waters* 1944 (m); *Double Indemnity* 1944 (m,m.arr) **(AANBM)**; *The Hour Before the Dawn* 1944 (m); *The Man in Half Moon Street* 1944 (m); *A Song To Remember* 1945 (m) **(AANBM)**; *Blood on the Sun* 1945 (m); *Lady on a Train* 1945 (m); *The Lost Weekend* 1945 (m) **(AANBM)**; *Spellbound* 1945 (m) **(AABM)**; *Because of Him* 1946 (m); *The Killers* 1946 (m,song) **(AANBM)**; *The Strange Love of Martha Ivers* 1946 (m); *Brute Force* 1947 (m); *Desert Fury* 1947 (m); *A Double Life* 1947 (m) **(AABM)**; *The Macomber Affair* 1947 (m); *The Other Love* 1947 (m); *The Red House* 1947 (m); *The Song of Scheherazade* 1947 (m.dir); *Time Out of Mind* 1947 (m); *Command Decision* 1948 (m); *Criss Cross* 1948 (m); *Kiss the Blood Off My Hands* 1948 (m); *The Naked City* 1948 (m); *Secret Beyond the Door* 1948 (m); *A Woman's Vengeance* 1948 (m); *Adam's Rib* 1949 (m); *The Bribe* 1949 (m); *East Side, West Side* 1949 (m); *Madame Bovary* 1949 (m); *The Red Danube* 1949 (m); *The Asphalt Jungle* 1950 (m); *Crisis* 1950 (m); *The Miniver Story* 1950 (m); *The Light Touch* 1951 (m.dir); *Quo Vadis* 1951 (m) **(AANBM)**; *Ivanhoe* 1952 (m) **(AANBM)**; *Plymouth Adventure* 1952 (m); *Julius Caesar* 1953 (m) **(AANBM)**; *Knights of the Round Table* 1953 (m); *Crest of the Wave* 1954 (m); *Green Fire* 1954 (m); *Men of the Fighting Lady* 1954 (m); *Valley of the Kings* 1954 (m); *The King's Thief* 1955 (m); *Moonfleet* 1955 (m); *Tribute to a Bad Man* 1955 (m); *Bhowani Junction* 1956 (m,m.dir); *Diane* 1956 (m); *Lust For Life* 1956 (m); *The Seventh Sin* 1957 (m); *Something of Value* 1957 (m); *Tip on a Dead Jockey* 1957 (m); *A Time to Love and a Time to Die* 1958 (m); *Ben-Hur* 1959 (m) **(AABM)**; *The World, the Flesh and the Devil* 1959 (m); *El Cid* 1961 (m) **(AANBM,AANBS)**; *King of Kings* 1961 (m); *Sodoma e Gomorra/Sodom and Gomorrah* 1962 (m); *The V.I.P.s* 1963 (m); *The Green Berets* 1968 (m); *The Power* 1968 (m); *The Private Life of Sherlock Holmes* 1970 (m); *The Golden Voyage of Sinbad* 1973 (m); *The Private Files of J. Edgar Hoover* 1977 (m); *Fedora* 1978 (m); *Last Embrace* 1979 (m); *Time After Time* 1979 (m); *Eye of the Needle* 1981 (m); *The Atomic Cafe* 1982 (m,cond); *Dead Men Don't Wear Plaid* 1982 (m,song); *Dragnet* 1987 (song); *Gesucht: Monika Ertl* 1989 (m).

Ruben, Joseph • Director • Born Briarcliff, NY, 1951. *Educ.* University of Michigan (theater, film); Brandeis University, Waltham, MA. Ruben made his feature directorial debut at the ripe age of 24 with the bleak psychodrama *The Sister-in-Law* (1975). His subsequent work has included two takes on high school life (*The Pom Pom Girls* 1976, *Our Winning Season* 1978), a road movie (*Joyride* 1977) and an engaging thriller, *True Believer* (1989), starring James Woods and Robert Downey, Jr. Ruben seems at his best, however, when exploring the dark underbelly of that most sacred of American institutions, the family: cult favorite *The Stepfather* (1987) has "family man" Terry O'Quinn moving from town to town, settling in with a fatherless family, and then slaying them; in *Sleeping with the Enemy* (1991), Ruben's first big commercial hit, Julia Roberts fakes her own death in order to escape her violently possessive husband. • *The Sister-in-Law* 1975 (d,p,sc); *The Pom Pom Girls* 1976 (d,p,sc,story); *Joyride* 1977 (d,sc); *Our Winning Season* 1978 (d,sc); *G.O.R.P.* 1980 (d); *Dreamscape* 1984 (d,sc); *The Stepfather* 1987 (d); *True Believer* 1989 (d); *Sleeping With the Enemy* 1991 (d).

Rudolph, Alan • Director, screenwriter; also producer, actor. • Born Los Angeles, CA, December 18, 1943. *Educ.* UCLA (business studies). The son of director Oscar Rudolph, Alan Rudolph grew up in the film industry, quitting college to learn about filmmaking by watching studio people at work. He consistently points out that he successfully avoided film school, although he eventually did enter the Director's Guild training program for assistant directors.

By 1970, Rudolph was writing screenplays for low-budget features and had made several short films set to rock-and-roll hits—an early indication of his concern with musical themes and desire to use music as an inspirational element for his screenplays. During a long association with Robert Altman, Rudolph worked as an assistant director on *The Long Goodbye, California Split* and *Nashville* and wrote the script for *Buffalo Bill and the Indians.* Altman, in turn, produced Rudolph's first "official" feature, *Welcome to L.A.* (1976). (His first feature was 1972's pretentious *Premonition*, virtually forgotten until its appearance on home video.) *Welcome* offered an ironic view of laid-back L.A. hustling, though its dark sensibility was not appreciated in all quarters.

In his second film, *Remember My Name* (1978), Rudolph gave Geraldine Chaplin full rein to create a mysterious character study of a woman released from prison to haunt the man who has abandoned her; the film's sense of menace was underlined by a soundtrack featuring celebrated blues singer Alberta Hunter. *Roadie* (1980), a look at life on the road for pop performers, abandoned laid-back stylishness for funky, chaotic comedy and marked the beginning of Rudolph's long association with producer Carolyn Pfeiffer. Though it left critics puzzled, Rudolph claims it is his favorite film.

Endangered Species (1982), a political thriller, was an unhappy experience for Rudolph; he was locked out of the editing room during the film's postproduction. Its resulting, impersonal quality was echoed in later hired-gun efforts such as *Songwriter* (1984) and *Made in Heaven* (1987).

Return Engagement (1983), a documentary of the debates between 1960s guru Dr. Timothy Leary and Watergate conspirator G. Gordon Liddy, was provocative and bizarre. Rudolph then enjoyed his first big success with *Choose Me* (1984), a moody musing on the convoluted romantic entanglements of a bar owner and her lovelorn patrons, including a radio talk show hostess called Dr. Love. The film was inspired by soul singer Teddy Pendergrass's song of the same name. By his next film, *Trouble in Mind* (1985), Rudolph had gathered a following dedicated to his meditations on love and loneliness in peculiar settings, this time a town called Rain City in an unspecified dystopian future. The Rudolph brew had also come to mean cryptic performances by, typically, Chaplin, Keith Carradine and Genevieve Bujold, and a whimsical absurdity that could sometimes sabotage narrative flow. (1990's *Love at Large*, starring Tom Berenger and Anne Archer, suffered from this problem.)

The Moderns (1988) marked the realization of a long-cherished project, a story of an American artist in 1920s Paris who witnesses the transformation of "art" into a commodity. The film mixes fictional characters with historical figures such as Gertrude Stein, who sums up Rudolph's approach in one line: "I'm not interested in the abnormal; the normal is so much more simply complicated." KJ • *Premonition* 1972 (d,p,sc,story); *The Long Goodbye* 1973 (ad); *California Split* 1974 (ad); *Nashville* 1975 (ad); *Barn of the Naked Dead* 1976 (d); *Buffalo Bill and the Indians, or Sitting Bull's History Lesson* 1976 (sc); *Welcome to L.A.* 1976 (d,sc); *Remember My Name* 1978 (d,sc); *Roadie* 1980 (d,story); *Endangered Species* 1982 (d,sc); *Return Engagement* 1983 (d); *Choose Me* 1984 (d); *Songwriter* 1984 (d); *Trouble in Mind* 1985 (d,sc); *Made in Heaven* 1987 (d); *The Moderns* 1988 (d,sc); *Hollywood Mavericks* 1990 (a); *Love at Large* 1990 (d,sc); *Mortal Thoughts* 1991 (d).

Ruehl, Mercedes • Actress • Born Queens, NY. *Educ.* College of New Rochelle (English Literature). Regional theater veteran who first received attention for her Obie award-winning performance in Christopher Durang's *The Marriage of Bette and Boo* and came to screen prominence as Dean Stockwell's possessive, crazed Mafia wife in the Jonathan Demme spoof, *Married to the Mob* (1988). • *The Warriors* 1979; *Four Friends* 1981; *84 Charing Cross Road* 1986; *Heartburn* 1986; *Leader of the*

Band 1987; *Radio Days* 1987; *The Secret of My Success* 1987; *Big* 1988; *Married to the Mob* 1988; *Slaves of New York* 1989; *Crazy People* 1990; *The Fisher King* 1991.

Ruiz, Raúl • Director; also playwright. • Born Puerto Montt, Chile, July 25, 1941. *Educ.* University of Chile (theology, law). Rising to international prominence in the early 1980s, Raul Ruiz has proved one of the most exciting and innovative filmmakers of recent years, providing more intellectual fun and artistic experimentation, shot for shot, than any filmmaker since Jean-Luc Godard. Slashing his way through celluloid with machete-sharp sounds and images, Ruiz is a guerrilla who uncompromisingly assaults the preconceptions of film art. This frightfully prolific figure—he has made over 50 films in twenty years—does not adhere to any one style of filmmaking. He has worked in 35mm, 16mm and video, for theatrical release and for European TV, and on documentary and fiction features.

Ruiz's career began in the avant-garde theater where, from 1956 to 1962, he wrote over 100 plays. Although he never directed any of these productions, he did dabble in filmmaking in 1960 and 1964 with two short, unfinished films. In 1968, with the release of his first completed feature, *Très tristes tigres*, Ruiz, along with Miguel Littin and Aldo Francia, was placed in the forefront of Chilean film. A committed leftist who supported the Marxist government of Salvador Allende, Ruiz was forced to flee his country during the fascist coup of 1973. Living in exile in Paris since that time, he has found a forum for his ideas in European TV. His first great European success came with *The Hypothesis of the Stolen Painting* (1978); a puzzling black-and-white film adapted from a novel by Pierre Koslowski, constructed in a "tableaux vivants" style that tells the enigmatic story of a missing 19th-century painting.

Influenced by the fabulist tradition that runs through much Latin American literature (Gabriel García Márquez, Jorge Luis Borges, and Alfonso Reyes have all been cited as influences), Ruiz is a poet of fantastic images whose films slip effortlessly from reality to imagination and back again. A manipulator of wild, intellectual games in which the rules are forever changing, Ruiz's techniques are as varied as film itself—a collection of odd Wellesian angles and close-ups, bewildering p.o.v. shots, dazzling colors, and labyrinthine narratives which weave and dodge the viewer's grasp with every shot. As original as Ruiz is, one can tell much about him by the diversity of his influences; in addition to adapting Klossowski, he has been inspired by Franz Kafka (*La Colonia Penal* 1971 is a Chilean reworking of *The Penal Colony*), Racine (*Bérenice* 1984), Calderon (*Memory of Appearances: Life Is a Dream* 1986), Shakespeare (*Richard III* 1986), Robert Louis Stevenson (*Treasure Island* 1985), Orson Welles (whose *F For Fake* is a precursor of *The Hypothesis of the Stolen Painting* 1978), and Hollywood B movies (Roger Corman was executive producer on *The Territory* 1983). Like Godard (whom Ruiz names as an early influence and who also owes a debt to B films), Ruiz makes no differentiation between the "high art" of Racine or Calderon and the "low art" of Roger Corman.

Unfortunately, only a handful of Ruiz's films are available for viewing in the US, and it is on these few films that his reputation here is built. The few works that are available, however, bear witness to the genius that informs his entire body of work. DC • *Tres tristes tigres* 1968 (d,sc); *La Colonia Penal* 1971 (d,sc); *Que Hacer?* 1972 (d,idea); *Dialogue d'exiles* 1974 (d); *Le Colloque de chiens (short)* 1977 (d); *Dora et la lanterne magique* 1977 (sc); *La Vocation Suspendue* 1977 (d,sc,dial); *De Grands Evenements et des Gens Ordinaires* 1978 (d,sc); *L'Hypothese du Tableau Vole/The Hypothesis of the Stolen Painting* 1978 (d,sc); *Le Jeu de l'oie (short)* 1980 (d); *The Territory* 1983 (d,sc); *Het Dak van de Walvis* 1982 (d); *Les Trois couronnes du matelot* 1983 (d,sc); *La Ville des Pirates* 1983 (d,sc); *Bérenice* 1984 (d); *Notre Mariage* 1984 (sc); *Les Destins de Manoel* 1985 (d,sc); *L'Eveille du Pont d'Alma* 1985 (d,sc); *L'Ile au Tresor/Treasure Island* 1985 (d,sc); *Los Naufragos del Liguria* 1985 (a); *La Présence réele* 1985 (d); *Dans un Miroir* 1986 (d); *Mammame* 1986 (d,sc,pd); *Mémoire des apparences: la vie est un songe/Memory of Appearances: Life Is a Dream* 1986 (d,sc); *Regime sans pain* 1986 (d,sc); *Richard III* 1986 (d,sc); *Brise-glace* 1987 (d); *Palombella Rossa* 1989 (a); *The Golden Boat* 1990 (d,sc).

Ruiz-Anchia, Juan • Director of photography • Born Bilbao, Spain. *Educ.* Escuela Oficial de Cinematografia, Madrid; AFI, Los Angeles. Outstanding young cinematographer; particularly adept at creating a mood of tension, as with the harshly lit *At Close Range* (1986) and *House of Games* (1987). • *El Desencanto* 1976; *Renacida* 1981; *Valentina/1919* 1982; *1919* 1983; *Miss Lonelyhearts* 1983; *Pares y Nones* 1983; *Soldados De Plomo* 1983; *The Stone Boy* 1983; *George Stevens: A Filmmaker's Journey* 1985; *Maria's Lovers* 1985; *That Was Then... This Is Now* 1985; *At Close Range* 1986; *Where the River Runs Black* 1986; *House of Games* 1987; *Surrender* 1987; *The Seventh Sign* 1988; *Things Change* 1988; *The Last of the Finest* 1989; *Lost Angels* 1989; *Naked Tango* 1990.

Russell, Ken • Director • Born Henry Kenneth Alfred Russell, Southampton, England, July 3, 1927. *Educ.* Pangbourne Nautical College; Walthamstow Art School, London (photography). Ken Russell is a controversial British director noted primarily for his exploration of sexual themes and his stylistic excesses. He first drew notice between 1959 and 1962 for a series of unorthodox biographical films made for the BBC's "Monitor" series on such artists as Bartok, Debussy, Isadora Duncan and Dante Rossetti. In these early works Russell was already exhibiting an unconventional approach to biography that combined historical fact, aesthetic interpretation and personal vision. As a result of his extraordinarily successful film on British composer Edward Elgar in 1962, Russell was given the opportunity to move into feature filmmaking. His first two features, the underrated offbeat comedy, *French Dressing* (1964), and his adaptation of a Len Deighton thriller, *Billion Dollar Brain* (1967), starring Michael Caine, were commercial flops.

Russell's career changed dramatically with his next film, an adaptation of D.H. Lawrence's *Women in Love* (1969). A commercial and critical success, the film garnered an Oscar for actress Glenda Jackson, establishing her as a major star of the 70s. The film's fine period evocation and its bold erotic sensibility, particularly in the famous nude wrestling scene between Alan Bates and Oliver Reed, encouraged Russell to continue exploring the related themes of art and sensuality. He maintained his particular interest in the erotics of music with *The Music Lovers* (1971), *The Boy Friend* (1971), *Mahler* (1973), *Tommy* (1975), and *Lisztomania* (1975). *The Music Lovers*, focusing on Tchaikovsky's homosexuality, struck many viewers as inappropriate, while *Lisztomania*'s unrestrained use of Nazi and pop-culture iconography seemed to demonstrate a complete loss of aesthetic control. With the exception of *Tommy*, a virtually guaranteed success because of the popularity of The Who and their source "rock opera" and an all-star cast, none of these films achieved a success comparable to *Women in Love*. Indeed, since the commercial failure of *Valentino* (1977), Russell's career seems to have foundered.

Russell's most recent work, while still of considerable interest, shows him searching for a form to contain his themes, just as the protagonist of *Altered States* (1980) almost loses his body in pursuit of his mystic vision. *The Lair of the White Worm* (1988), adapted from a novel by Bram Stoker, shows Russell once again employing the imagery of sexual excess, if only in self-parody.

Russell returns again and again to themes of sexuality, primarily issues involving the burdens of masculine identity. His examination of Tchaikovsky concentrates on the composer's conflict between homoerotic desire and the dominant ideology of heterosexualtiy. Similarly, his Valentino is a man destroyed by his very popularity, since his appeal for women is seen as a threat to the power of the American male. Russell's biographical films are unorthodox because he often dispenses with history in favor of psychological speculation. These films freely blend fact and fantasy, implying that the significance of the artist's work lies as much in the perception of the listener or spectator as in the work itself. Hence the orgiastic release, a historical fact chronicled in *The Devils* (1971), has become for Russell a paradigm of the potency of art. For him aesthetics, sexuality, and the imagination are inseparable: the films are, in effect, the cinematic equivalent of a musical fantasia.

In retrospect, it is clear why Russell was so attracted to D.H. Lawrence's novel, and why that film became a turning point in the director's career: like the Laurentian alter-ego Birkin, Russell is a romantic visionary who has sought to liberate repressed sexuality through his work. The prostitute of *Crimes of Passion* (1984), in her ability to act out a variety of male sexual fantasies, is a performance artist who, like so many of Russell's characters, seeks to artfully transcend social and sexual constraints through her body.

Although he has his defenders, for the most part critics have not been kind to Russell's work. He is frequently considered tasteless, vulgar, unrestrained, even misanthropic. Pauline Kael has called him "a shrill, screaming gossip," and his movies have been described as "hyperthyroid camp circuses." Ultimately, though, much of this critical hostility can be explained as either a matter of taste or stock response to the material. Russell consciously refuses to make movies in the genteel British tradition, and he readily admits that, because of its subject and style, his work often makes viewers uncomfortable. BKG • *French Dressing* 1964 (d); *Billion Dollar Brain* 1967 (d); *Women in Love* 1969 (d) **(AANBD)**; *The Boy Friend* 1971 (d,p,sc); *The Devils* 1971 (d,p,sc); *The Music Lovers* 1971 (d,p); *Savage Messiah* 1972 (d,p); *Mahler* 1973 (d,sc); *Lisztomania* 1975 (d,sc); *Tommy* 1975 (d,p,sc); *Valentino* 1977 (d,sc,new lyrics "The Sheik of Araby"); *Altered States* 1980 (d); *Crimes of Passion* 1984 (d); *Gothic* 1986 (d); *Aria* 1987 (d,screenplay "Turandot"); *The Lair of the White Worm* 1988 (d,p,sc); *Salome's Last Dance* 1988 (d,sc); *The Rainbow* 1989 (d,p,sc); *The Russia House* 1990 (a); *Whore* 1991 (d,sc).

Russell, Kurt • Actor • Born Springfield, MA, March 17, 1951. Athletic, handsome lead who began his career as a juvenile performer in the early 1960s. Russell starred in his own TV series, "The Travels of Jamie McPheeters" (1963-64), and appeared in a string of Disney family features through the mid-1970s. He attracted attention for his title role in John Carpenter's TV movie, *Elvis* (1979), and went on to become a bankable Hollywood star of the 80s. He has proved adept at both comedy and straight drama and appeared opposite his long-time companion, Goldie Hawn, in the films *Swing Shift* (1984) and *Overboard* (1987). • *Follow Me, Boys!* 1966; *The Horse in the Gray Flannel Suit* 1968; *The One and Only, Genuine, Original Family Band* 1968; *The Computer Wore Tennis Shoes* 1969; *Guns in the Heather* 1969; *The Barefoot Executive* 1970; *Fools' Parade* 1971; *Charley and the Angel* 1972; *Now You See Him, Now You Don't* 1972; *Superdad* 1973; *The Strongest Man in the World* 1975; *Used Cars* 1980; *Escape From New York* 1981; *The Fox and the Hound* 1981; *The Thing* 1982; *Silkwood* 1983; *Swing Shift* 1984; *The Mean Season* 1985; *The Best of Times* 1986; *Big Trouble in Little China* 1986; *Overboard* 1987; *Tequila Sunrise* 1988; *Tango and Cash* 1989; *Winter People* 1989.

Russell, Rosalind • Actress • Born Waterbury, CT, June 4, 1908; died 1976. *Educ.* Marymount College; AADA, New York. Brash, appealing leading lady who hit her stride in the 1940s playing wisecracking, no-nonsense career women in a string of breezy comedies. Russell was unforgettable racing through *His Girl Friday* (1940), opposite Cary Grant, and *My Sister Eileen* (1942), in a role she would later reprise on the musical stage. Her straight dramatic roles were generally less successful, though one of her four Oscar nominations was for Dudley Nichols's *Mourning Becomes Electra* (1947), and she stole the spotlight from a star-studded cast in *Picnic* (1956). Russell was married to producer Frederick Brisson. • *Evelyn Prentice* 1934 (a); *Forsaking All Others* 1934 (a); *The President Vanishes* 1934 (a); *The Casino Murder Case* 1935 (a); *China Seas* 1935 (a); *The Night Is Young* 1935 (a); *Reckless* 1935 (a); *The Rendezvous* 1935 (a); *West Point of the Air* 1935 (a); *Craig's Wife* 1936 (a); *It Had to Happen* 1936 (a); *Trouble For Two* 1936 (a); *Under Two Flags* 1936 (a); *Live, Love and Learn* 1937 (a); *Night Must Fall* 1937 (a); *The Citadel* 1938 (a); *Four's a Crowd* 1938 (a); *Man-Proof* 1938 (a); *Fast and Loose* 1939 (a); *The Women* 1939 (a); *Hired Wife* 1940 (a); *His Girl Friday* 1940 (a); *No Time For Comedy* 1940 (a); *Design For Scandal* 1941 (a); *The Feminine Touch* 1941 (a); *They Met in Bombay* 1941 (a); *This Thing Called Love* 1941 (a); *My Sister Eileen* 1942 (a) **(AANBA)**; *Take a Letter, Darling* 1942 (a); *Flight For Freedom* 1943 (a); *What a Woman!* 1943 (a); *Roughly Speaking* 1945 (a); *She Wouldn't Say Yes* 1945 (a); *Sister Kenny* 1946 (a) **(AANBA)**; *The Guilt of Janet Ames* 1947 (a); *Mourning Becomes Electra* 1947 (a) **(AANBA)**; *The Velvet Touch* 1948 (a); *Tell It to the Judge* 1949 (a); *A Woman of Distinction* 1950 (a); *Never Wave at a Wac* 1952 (a); *The Girl Rush* 1955 (a); *Picnic* 1956 (a); *The Unguarded Moment* 1956 (story); *Auntie Mame* 1958 (a) **(AANBA)**; *A Majority of One* 1961 (a); *Five Finger Exercise* 1962 (a); *Gypsy* 1962 (a); *The Trouble With Angels* 1966 (a); *Oh Dad, Poor Dad, Mamma's Hung You in the Closet and I'm Feelin' So Sad* 1967 (a); *Rosie* 1967 (a); *Where Angels Go... Trouble Follows* 1968 (a); *Mrs. Pollifax—Spy* 1969 (a).

Russell, Theresa • Actress • Born Theresa Paup, San Diego, CA, 1957. *Educ.* Lee Strasberg Theatre Institute, Hollywood. Alluring, enigmatic actress who made her film debut in Elia Kazan's adaptation of the F. Scott Fitzgerald novel, *The Last Tycoon* (1976). Russell, who's displayed a predilection for unusual roles, was first directed by her future husband, Nicolas Roeg, in *Bad Timing* (1980) and has appeared in five of his films to date. Probably best known for her portrayal of a Marilyn Monroe-type figure in Roeg's *Insignificance* (1985) and a seductive serial killer in Bob Rafelson's *Black Widow* (1987). • *The Last Tycoon* 1976; *Straight Time* 1978; *Bad Timing* 1980; *Eureka* 1982; *The Razor's Edge* 1984; *Insignificance* 1985; *Aria* 1987; *Black Widow* 1987; *Track 29* 1987; *Physical Evidence* 1988; *Impulse* 1990; *Whore* 1991.

Rutherford, Dame Margaret • Actress • Born London, May 11, 1892; died 1972. *Educ.* Old Vic, London. Hilarious, endearing character player, in films since the mid-1930s. Rutherford personified the eccentric English spinster in a number of memorable movies, including *Blithe Spirit* (1945) and *The Happiest Days of Your Life* (1950). She is perhaps best known as the indomitable title character in four "Miss Marple" films of the 60s. • *Dusty Ermine* 1936; *Talk of the Devil* 1936; *Beauty and the Barge* 1937; *Catch as Catch Can* 1937; *Quiet Wedding* 1940; *The Demi-Paradise/Adventure for Two* 1943; *The Yellow Canary* 1943; *English Without Tears/Her Man Gilbey* 1944; *Blithe Spirit* 1945; *Meet Me at Dawn* 1946; *While the Sun Shines* 1947; *Miranda* 1948; *Passport to Pimlico* 1949; *The Happiest Days of Your Life* 1950; *Her Favorite Husband* 1950; *The Magic Box* 1951; *Castle in the Air* 1952; *Curtain Up* 1952; *The Importance of Being Earnest* 1952; *Miss Robin Hood* 1952; *Innocents in Paris* 1953; *Trouble in Store* 1953; *Aunt Clara* 1954; *Mad About Men* 1954; *The Runaway Bus* 1954; *An Alligator Named Daisy* 1955; *Just My Luck* 1957; *The Smallest Show on Earth* 1957; *I'm All Right Jack* 1959; *Murder She Said* 1961; *On the Double* 1961; *The Mouse on the Moon* 1963; *Murder at the Gallop* 1963; *The V.I.P.s* 1963 **(AABSA)**; *Murder Ahoy* 1964; *Murder Most Foul* 1964; *The Alphabet Murders* 1966; *Chimes at Midnight/Falstaff* 1966; *A*

Countess From Hong Kong 1967; *Arabella* 1967; *The Wacky World of Mother Goose* 1967.

Ruttenberg, Joseph • Director of photography • Born St. Petersberg, Russia, July 4, 1889; died May 1, 1983, Los Angeles, CA. Former photojournalist and newsreel photographer-producer who served as a cinematographer with Fox (1915-26), MGM (1926-62) and Paramount. Ruttenberg was one of Hollywood's foremost directors of photography from the late 1930s through the 50s. • *The Painted Madonna* 1917; *Thou Shalt Not Steal* 1917; *The Debt of Honor* 1918; *Doing Our Bit* 1918; *From Now On* 1920; *Beyond Price* 1921; *Know Your Men* 1921; *The Mountain Woman* 1921; *A Virgin Paradise* 1921; *My Friend, the Devil* 1922; *Silver Wings* 1922; *The Town That Forgot God* 1922; *Does It Pay?* 1923; *If Winter Comes* 1923; *The Fool* 1925; *School For Wives* 1925; *Summer Bachelors* 1926; *The Struggle* 1931; *Woman in the Dark* 1934; *Frankie and Johnnie (short)* 1935; *Gigolette* 1935; *The People's Enemy* 1935; *Fury* 1936; *Mad Holiday* 1936; *Man Hunt* 1936; *Piccadilly Jim* 1936; *The Three Godfathers* 1936; *The Big City* 1937; *A Day at the Races* 1937; *Everybody Sing* 1938; *The First Hundred Years* 1938; *The Great Waltz* 1938 **(AABPH)**; *The Shopworn Angel* 1938; *Spring Madness* 1938; *Three Comrades* 1938; *Balalaika* 1939; *Ice Follies of 1939* 1939; *On Borrowed Time* 1939; *Tell No Tales* 1939; *The Women* 1939; *Broadway Melody of 1940* 1940; *Comrade X* 1940; *The Philadelphia Story* 1940; *Waterloo Bridge* 1940 **(AANBPH)**; *Dr. Jekyll and Mr. Hyde* 1941 **(AANBPH)**; *Two-Faced Woman* 1941; *Crossroads* 1942; *Mrs. Miniver* 1942 **(AABPH)**; *Random Harvest* 1942; *Woman of the Year* 1942; *Madame Curie* 1943 **(AANBPH)**; *Presenting Lily Mars* 1943; *Gaslight* 1944 **(AANBPH)**; *Mrs. Parkington* 1944; *Adventure* 1945; *The Valley of Decision* 1945; *B.F.'s Daughter* 1947; *Desire Me* 1947; *Killer McCoy* 1947; *Julia Misbehaves* 1948; *The Bribe* 1949; *That Forsyte Woman* 1949; *The Magnificent dYankee* 1950; *The Miniver Story* 1950; *Side Street* 1950; *Cause For Alarm* 1951; *The Great Caruso* 1951; *It's a Big Country* 1951; *Kind Lady* 1951; *Too Young to Kiss* 1951; *Because You're Mine* 1952; *Young Man With Ideas* 1952; *Julius Caesar* 1953 **(AANBPH)**; *Latin Lovers* 1953; *Small Town Girl* 1953; *The Great Diamond Robbery* 1954; *Her Twelve Men* 1954; *The Last Time I Saw Paris* 1954; *Interrupted Melody* 1955; *Kismet* 1955; *Invitation to the Dance* 1956; *Somebody Up There Likes Me* 1956 **(AANBPH)**; *The Swan* 1956; *Man on Fire* 1957; *Until They Sail* 1957; *The Vintage* 1957; *Gigi* 1958 **(AABPH)**; *Green Mansions* 1959; *The Wreck of the Mary Deare* 1959; *Butterfield 8* 1960 **(AANBPH)**; *The Subterraneans* 1960; *Ada* 1961; *Bachelor in Paradise* 1961; *Two Loves* 1961; *Who's Got the Action?* 1962; *The Hook* 1963; *It Happened at the World's Fair* 1963; *Who's Been Sleeping in My Bed?* 1963; *A Global Affair* 1964; *Harlow* 1965; *Love Has Many Faces* 1965; *Sylvia* 1965; *The Oscar* 1966; *Speedway* 1968.

Ruttmann, Walter • Director, director of photography, editor • Born Frankfurt, Germany, December 28, 1887; died 1941. Ruttman trained as an architect and painter and worked as a poster designer before beginning to experiment with avant-garde film in the early 1920s. He directed the dream sequence for Fritz Lang's *Die Nibelungen* (1924) and worked with Lotte Reiniger on *The Adventures of Prince Achmed* (1926), the world's first full-length animated film. Ruttman exerted a tremendous influence on the documentary movement with *Berlin—Symphony of a City* (1927), a rhythmically edited celebration of the German capital which inspired a spate of similar "city symphonies," including his own *World Melody* (1929). He later assisted Leni Riefenstahl with the editing of *Olympia* (1938), made an unsuccessful foray into fiction films with the Pirandello-scripted *Steel* (1933) and engineered Nazi propaganda documentaries such as *German Tanks* (1940). • *Die Nibelungen* 1924 (anim); *Berlin die sinfonie der grosstadt/Berlin—Symphony of a City* 1927 (d); *Melodie der Welt/World Melody* 1929 (d); *Arbeit Macht Frei/Steel* 1933 (d); *Deutsche Panzer/German Tanks* 1940 (d).

Ryan, Meg • Actress • Born Fairfield, CT, 1962. *Educ.* NYU (journalism). Attractive, personable performer who first gained attention with an effective cameo appearance as the wife of Anthony Edwards in *Top Gun* (1986). Ryan's first leading role came opposite Billy Crystal in Rob Reiner's successful comedy, *When Harry Met Sally...* (1989). Married since 1991 to actor Dennis Quaid. • *Rich and Famous* 1981; *Amityville 3-D* 1983; *Armed and Dangerous* 1986; *Top Gun* 1986; *Innerspace* 1987; *Promised Land* 1987; *D.O.A.* 1988; *The Presidio* 1988; *When Harry Met Sally...* 1989; *Joe Versus the Volcano* 1990; *The Doors* 1991.

Ryan, Robert • Actor • Born Chicago, IL, November 11, 1909; died 1973. *Educ.* Loyola Academy, Chicago; Dartmouth; Max Reinhardt Theatrical Workshop, Hollywood. Imposing, ruggedly handsome lead who made his film debut in *Golden Gloves* (1940) and signed with RKO two years later. Ryan hit his stride in the late 1940s playing a string of psychopathic or hard-boiled types, notably the anti-Semitic murderer in *Crossfire* (1947) and the over-the-hill pug in the classic boxing drama, *The Set-Up* (1949). He went on to appear in a host of films through the mid-70s, often giving fine performances in decidedly mediocre vehicles. Ryan was memorable as the lusty, violent patriarch of Erskine Caldwell's *God's Little Acre* (1958) and William Holden's buddy-turned-nemesis in Sam Peckinpah's *The Wild Bunch* (1969). • *Golden Gloves* 1940; *North West Mounted Police* 1940; *Queen of the Mob* 1940; *Behind the Rising Sun* 1943; *Bombardier* 1943; *Gangway For Tomorrow* 1943; *The Iron Major* 1943; *The Sky's the Limit* 1943; *Tender Comrade* 1943; *Marine Raiders* 1944; *Crossfire* 1947 **(AANBSA)**; *Dead Reckoning* 1947; *Trail Street* 1947; *The Woman on the Beach* 1947; *Act of Violence* 1948; *Berlin Express* 1948; *The Boy With Green Hair* 1948; *Return of the Bad Men* 1948; *Caught* 1949; *I Married a Communist* 1949; *The Set-Up* 1949; *Born to Be Bad* 1950; *The Secret Fury* 1950; *Best of the Badmen* 1951; *Flying Leathernecks* 1951; *On Dangerous Ground* 1951; *The Racket* 1951; *Beware, My Lovely* 1952; *Clash By Night* 1952; *Horizons West* 1952; *City Beneath the Sea* 1953; *Inferno* 1953; *The Naked Spur* 1953; *About Mrs. Leslie* 1954; *Alaska Seas* 1954; *Bad Day at Black Rock* 1954; *Escape to Burma* 1954; *Her Twelve Men* 1954; *House of Bamboo* 1955; *The Tall Men* 1955; *Back From Eternity* 1956; *Men in War* 1956; *The Proud Ones* 1956; *God's Little Acre* 1958; *Lonelyhearts* 1958; *Day of the Outlaw* 1959; *Odds Against Tomorrow* 1959; *Ice Palace* 1960; *The Canadians* 1961; *King of Kings* 1961; *Billy Budd* 1962; *The Longest Day* 1962; *Battle of the Bulge* 1965; *The Professionals* 1966; *The Busy Body* 1967; *Custer of the West* 1967; *The Dirty Dozen* 1967; *Hour of the Gun* 1967; *Anzio* 1968; *Captain Nemo and the Underwater City* 1969; *The Wild Bunch* 1969; *Lawman* 1971; *The Love Machine* 1971; *La Course du lièvre a travers les champs/And Hope to Die* 1972; *Executive Action* 1973; *The Iceman Cometh* 1973; *Lolly-Madonna XXX* 1973; *The Outfit* 1973.

Rydell, Mark • Director; also actor, producer. • Born New York, NY, March 23, 1934. *Educ.* NYU (English, philosophy); Juilliard (music); University of Chicago; Chicago Music College; Neighborhood Playhouse (acting); Actors Studio. Former jazz pianist who appeared on Broadway and TV before beginning his directing career with series such as "Ben Casey," "I Spy" and "Gunsmoke." Rydell earned critical acclaim for his debut feature, *The Fox* (1968), and for *Cinderella Liberty* (1973). *On Golden Pond* (1981) earned him an Oscar nomination as best director. • *Crime in the Streets* 1956 (a); *The Fox* 1967 (d); *The Reivers* 1969 (d); *The Cowboys* 1971 (d,p); *Cinderella Liberty* 1973 (d,p); *The Long Goodbye* 1973 (a); *Harry and Walter Go to New York* 1976 (d); *The Rose* 1979 (d); *On Golden Pond* 1981 (d) **(AANBD)**; *The River* 1984 (d); *Punchline* 1988 (a); *Havana* 1990 (a).

Ryder, Winona • Actress • Born Winona Laura Horowitz, Winona, MN, October, 1971. *Educ.* American Conservatory Theatre, San Francisco. Teenage star of the late 1980s who enjoyed a "classic" alternative upbringing, spending some of her childhood on a Northern California commune. (Ryder boasts acid culture guru Timothy Leary as her godfather.) Discovered by a talent scout at the age of 13, during a performance at San Francisco's American Conservatory Theatre, Ryder has turned in some impressively mature roles, notably in Michael Lehmann's black "teen suicide" comedy, *Heathers* (1989) and the otherwise lackluster *Mermaids* (1990). • *Lucas* 1986; *Square Dance* 1987; *1969* 1988; *Beetlejuice* 1988; *Great Balls of Fire* 1989; *Heathers* 1989; *Edward Scissorhands* 1990; *Mermaids* 1990; *Welcome Home, Roxy Carmichael* 1990.

Ryskind, Morrie • Playwright, screenwriter • Born Brooklyn, NY, October 20, 1895; died August 24, 1985, Washington, DC. *Educ.* Columbia (journalism). Collaborated with George S. Kaufman on several Broadway hits including the Marx Brothers vehicle *Cocoanuts* (1925) and 1932's Pulitzer prize-winning *Of Thee I Sing* (with Ira Gershwin). A former socialist, in 1947 he testified before the House Committee on Un-American Activities and later became an extreme rightist and member of the John Birch Society. • *The Cocoanuts* 1929 (sc); *Animal Crackers* 1930 (sc,from play); *Palmy Days* 1931 (sc); *A Night at the Opera* 1935 (sc); *My Man Godfrey* 1936 (sc); *Stage Door* 1937 (sc); *Room Service* 1938 (sc); *Man About Town* 1939 (sc,story); *Louisiana Purchase* 1941 (from play); *Penny Serenade* 1941 (sc); *Claudia* 1943 (sc); *Where Do We Go From Here?* 1945 (sc,story); *My Man Godfrey* 1957 (from screenplay).

S

Sadoul, Georges • Historian; also critic. • Born Nancy, France, February 4, 1904; died 1967. Distinguished, Marxist-oriented scholar and the author of *Histoire générale du cinéma*, which remains a standard of its kind, as well as a definitive study of film pioneer Georges Méliès. A sometime professor at the Sorbonne and the French film school, IDHEC, Sadoul is best known for his twin *Dictionnaires* (one covering around 10,000 films, the other some 1,000 filmmakers), published in French in 1965 and English in 1972.

Sägebrecht, Marianne • Actress • Born Starnberg, Bavaria, Germany, August, 1945. Leading producer and performer of Germany's alternative theater/cabaret scene who first earned international recognition in the films of Percy Adlon. Sägebrecht gave memorable performances in *Sugarbaby* (1985), as an overweight mortician in love with a subway conductor, and *Bagdad Cafe* (1987), as a hausfrau who transforms the life of a Southwestern desert community where she is abandoned by her husband. • *Irrsee* 1984; *Zuckerbaby/Sugarbaby* 1985; *Crazy Boys* 1987; *Baghdad Cafe* 1987; *Moon Over Parador* 1988; *Rosalie Goes Shopping* 1989; *The War of the Roses* 1989; *Martha und Ich/Martha and I* 1990.

Saint, Eva Marie • Actress • Born Newark, NJ, July 4, 1924. *Educ.* Bowling Green State University, OH. Ethereal, blonde beautiful leading lady from the stage who made a stunning debut as Marlon Brando's sensitive girlfriend in *On the Waterfront* (1954). Aside from the gripping drug-addiction drama, *Hatful of Rain* (1957) and Hitchcock's *North by Northwest* (1959), few of Saint's subsequent vehicles have been worthy of her talent. She is known to younger audiences for her role on TV's "Moonlighting." • *On the Waterfront* 1954 **(AABSA)**; *That Certain Feeling* 1956; *A Hatful of Rain* 1957; *Raintree County* 1957; *North By Northwest* 1959; *All Fall Down* 1962; *36 Hours* 1964; *The Sandpiper* 1965; *Grand Prix* 1966; *The Russians Are Coming, the Russians Are Coming* 1966; *The Stalking Moon* 1968; *Loving* 1970; *Cancel My Reservation* 1972; *Nothing in Common* 1986.

Sakamoto, Ryuichi • Japanese composer, actor, musician • *Educ.* University of the Arts, Tokyo (music). One of the few figures in contemporary Japanese popular music to have found an international audience, first with the successful Yellow Magic Orchestra. Ryuichi began composing for films in 1983 with *Merry Christmas, Mr. Lawrence*, in which he also portrayed Captain Yonoi, and won an Oscar for the haunting score of *The Last Emperor* (1987), co-written with David Byrne and Cong Su. • *Merry Christmas, Mr. Lawrence* 1982 (a,m); *Tokyo Melody, A Film About Ryuichi Sakamoto* 1985 (a); *Brand New Day* 1987 (a); *The Last Emperor* 1987 (a,m) **(AABM)**; *The Laserman* 1988 (song); *Black Rain* 1989 (songs).

Saks, Gene • Director; also actor. • Born New York, November 8, 1921. *Educ.* Cornell; Dramatic Workshop of New School for Social Research; Actors Studio. Former stage and TV actor who directed his first Broadway play in 1963 and his first film in 1967. Saks remains best known for his theater work, notably with the Neil Simon-penned *Barefoot in the Park*, *The Odd Couple*, *Broadway Bound* and *Rumors*. Most of his films have been adaptations of plays. • *A Thousand Clowns* 1965 (a); *Barefoot in the Park* 1967 (d); *The Odd Couple* 1968 (d); *Cactus Flower* 1969 (d); *Last of the Red Hot Lovers* 1972 (d); *Mame* 1974 (d); *The Prisoner of Second Avenue* 1974 (a); *The One and Only* 1978 (a); *Lovesick* 1983 (a); *The Goodbye People* 1984 (a); *Brighton Beach Memoirs* 1986 (d); *Funny* 1988 (a).

Salkind, Alexander • Producer • Born Gdansk, Poland, c. 1915. International figure whose productions have ranged from Orson Welles's *The Trial* (1962) to big-budget spectacles such as Richard Lester's *The Three Musketeers* (1973). *Superman* (1978) was produced in collaboration with his son, Ilya (born 1948), who has since built his career around a series of sequels starring the cape-clad hero. • *The Trial* 1962 (p); *Cervantes* 1967 (p); *Kill* 1971 (p); *Bluebeard* 1972 (p); *The Three Musketeers* 1973 (p); *The Four Musketeers* 1975 (p); *Crossed Swords* 1977 (p); *Superman* 1978 (p); *Superman II* 1980 (p); *Superman III* 1983 (exec.p); *Santa Claus: The Movie* 1985 (p).

Salomon, Mikael • Director of photography • Born Copenhagen, Denmark. Leading Danish cinematographer whose impressive credits include Henning Carlsen's biopic of Gaugin, *The Wolf at the Door* (1986), James Cameron's underwater spectacle, *The Abyss* (1989), and Steven Spielberg's *Always* (1989). • *Fantasterne* 1967 (ph); *Mig og min lillebror og Boelle* 1970 (ph); *Et doegn med Ilse* 1971 (ph); *Hvorfor goer de det?* 1971 (ph); *Mine Soestres Hoern, Naar de Er Vaerst* 1971 (ph); *Welcome to the Club* 1971 (ph); *Motorvejdpaa Sengekanten* 1972 (ph); *Rektor paa sengekanten* 1972 (ph); *Z.P.G.* 1972 (add.ph); *The Hottest Show in Town* 1974 (ph); *Hjerter er Trumf* 1975 (ph); *Kun Sandheden* 1975 (ph); *Violer er bla/Violets Are Blue* 1975 (ph); *Stroemer* 1976 (ph); *Elvis! Elvis!* 1977 (ph); *Pas paa ryggen, professor* 1977 (ph); *Slaegten/The Heritage* 1979 (ph); *The Flying Devils* 1985 (ph); *Barndommens gade* 1986 (ph); *The Wolf at the Door* 1986 (ph); *Peter von Scholten* 1987 (ph); *Time Out* 1987 (aerial ph); *Stealing Heaven* 1988 (ph); *Torch Song Trilogy* 1988 (ph); *Zelly and Me* 1988 (ph); *The Abyss* 1989 (ph,underwater lighting sup.) **(AANBPH)**; *Always* 1989 (ph); *Arachnophobia* 1990 (ph,Gyrosphere op).

Salt, Waldo • Screenwriter • Born Chicago, IL, October 18, 1914; died March 7, 1987, Los Angeles, CA. *Educ.* Stanford. Entered film as a scriptwriter in the late 1930s but did not find his stride until 30 years later, following a period of inactivity caused by his 1951 blacklisting. Salt's gritty, socially informed work includes one of the emblematic dramas of the 60s, *Midnight Cowboy* (1969), and the highly acclaimed post-Vietnam drama, *Coming Home* (1978). His daughter, actress Jennifer Salt, began appearing in films in the late 60s. • *Shopworn Angel,The* 1938 (sc); *The Wild Man of Borneo* 1941 (sc); *Tonight We Raid Calais* 1943 (sc); *Mr. Winkle Goes to War* 1944 (sc); *Rachel and the Stranger* 1948 (sc); *The Flame and the Arrow* 1950 (sc,story); *Taras Bulba* 1962 (sc); *Wild and Wonderful* 1964 (sc); *Midnight Cowboy* 1969 (sc) **(AABSC)**; *The Gang That Couldn't Shoot Straight* 1971 (sc); *Serpico* 1973 (sc) **(AANBSC)**; *The Day of the Locust* 1975 (sc); *Coming Home* 1978 (sc) **(AABSC)**; *Into the Night* 1985 (a).

Saltzman, Harry • Producer • Born St. John, New Brunswick, Canada, October 27, 1915. Made his name with socially informed, "Angry Young Man" dramas such as *Look Back in Anger* (1959) and *Saturday Night and Sunday Morning* (1960); made his fortune with several "James Bond" features co-produced by Albert R. "Cubby" Broccoli. • *The Iron Petticoat* 1956 (story); *Look Back in Anger* 1959 (p); *Saturday Night and Sunday Morning* 1960 (exec.p); *Dr. No* 1962 (p); *From Russia With Love* 1963 (p); *The Ipcress File* 1965 (p); *Thunderball* 1965 (p); *Funeral in Berlin* 1966 (p); *Billion Dollar Brain* 1967 (p); *You Only Live Twice* 1967 (p); *Play Dirty* 1968 (p); *Battle of Britain* 1969 (p); *On Her Majesty's Secret Service* 1969 (p); *Tomorrow* 1970 (p); *Diamonds Are Forever* 1971 (p); *Live and Let Die* 1973 (p); *The Man With the Golden Gun* 1974 (p); *Nijinsky* 1980 (exec.p); *Dom Za Vesanje* 1988 (p).

San Giacomo, Laura • Actress • Born New Jersey, c. 1962. *Educ.* Carnegie-Mellon University, Pittsburgh (acting). Experienced stage performer who made an auspicious debut as the brassy, hedonistic Cynthia in Steven Soderbergh's low-budget 1989 hit, *sex, lies, and videotape*. • *sex, lies, and videotape* 1989; *Pretty Woman* 1990; *Quigley Down Under* 1990; *Vital Signs* 1990; *Once Around* 1991.

Sanda, Dominique • Actress • Born Dominique Varaigne, Paris, March 11, 1951. *Educ.* Saint Vincent de Paul, Paris. Former model who made a memorable screen debut in Robert Bresson's *Une Femme douce* (1969), playing a pawnbroker's wife who is eventually driven to suicide. Unlike many of Bresson's "discoveries," Sanda went on to become an actress of note, appearing in films by several leading international directors in the 1970s and 80s. She gave a memorable performance in *The Garden of the Finzi-Continis* (1971). • *Une Femme douce* 1969; *Il Conformista/The Conformist* 1970; *First Love* 1970; *Il Giardino del Finzi-Continis/The Garden of the Finzi-Continis* 1971; *Sans Mobile Apparent* 1971; *Night of the Flowers* 1972; *Impossible Object* 1973; *The Mackintosh Man* 1973; *Steppenwolf* 1974; *Gruppo di famiglia in un interno* 1975; *Novecento/1900* 1976; *Al di la del bene e del male* 1977; *Damnation Alley* 1977; *La Chanson de Roland* 1978; *Utopia* 1978; *Le Navire Night* 1979; *Le Voyage en Douce* 1979; *Caboblanco* 1980; *Les Ailes de la Colombe* 1981; *Une Chambre en Ville* 1982; *Poussière d'Empire* 1983; *Le Matelot 512* 1984; *De Weg Naar Bresson* 1984; *Corps et biens* 1986; *Les Mendiants* 1987; *Il Decimo Clandestino* 1989; *Guerriers et captives* 1989; *In una notte di chiaro di luna* 1989; *Yo, la Peor de Todas* 1990.

Sanders, George • Actor • Born St. Petersburg, Russia, July 3, 1906; died 1972, Barcelona, Spain. *Educ.* Brighton College; Manchester Technical College. The suave, supercilious scoundrel in a host of English, American and European productions from the 1930s through the 70s. Born to British parents in Russia, Sanders was educated in England and based in Hollywood from the late 30s. He enjoyed occasional success in roles against type (*Rage in Heaven* 1941, *The Moon and Sixpence* 1942), but is best known as the acidulous drama critic, Addison DeWitt, in *All About Eve* (1950). Sanders died from an overdose of sleeping pills. • *Lloyd's of London* 1936 (a); *The Lady Escapes* 1937 (a); *The Lancer Spy* 1937 (a); *Love Is News* 1937 (a); *Slave Ship* 1937 (a); *Four Men and a Prayer* 1938 (a); *International Settlement* 1938 (a); *Allegheny Uprising* 1939 (a); *Confessions of a Nazi Spy* 1939 (a); *Mr. Moto's Last Warning* 1939 (a); *Nurse Edith Cavell* 1939 (a); *The Saint Strikes Back* 1939 (a); *The Saint in London* 1939 (a); *So This Is London* 1939 (a); *Bitter Sweet* 1940 (a); *Foreign Correspondent* 1940 (a); *Green Hell* 1940 (a); *The House of the Seven Gables* 1940 (a); *Rebecca* 1940 (a); *The Saint Takes Over* 1940 (a); *Saint's Double Trouble* 1940 (a); *The Son of Monte Cristo* 1940 (a); *A Date With the Falcon* 1941 (a); *The Gay Falcon* 1941 (a); *Man Hunt* 1941 (a); *Rage in Heaven* 1941 (a); *The Saint in Palm Springs* 1941 (a); *Sundown* 1941 (a); *The Black Swan* 1942 (a); *The Falcon Takes Over* 1942 (a); *Falcon's Brother* 1942 (a); *Her Cardboard Lover* 1942 (a); *The Moon and Sixpence* 1942 (a); *Quiet, Please, Murder* 1942 (a); *Son of Fury* 1942 (a); *Tales of Manhattan* 1942 (a); *Appointment in Berlin* 1943 (a); *Paris After Dark* 1943 (a); *They Came to Blow Up America* 1943 (a); *This Land Is Mine* 1943 (a); *Action in Arabia* 1944 (a); *The Lodger* 1944 (a); *Summer Storm* 1944 (a); *Hangover Square* 1945 (a); *The Picture of Dorian Gray* 1945 (a); *The Strange Affair of Uncle Harry* 1945 (a); *The Strange Woman* 1946 (a); *Thieves' Holiday* 1946 (a); *Forever Amber* 1947 (a); *The Ghost and Mrs. Muir* 1947 (a); *Lured* 1947 (a); *The Private Affairs of Bel Ami* 1947 (a); *The Fan* 1949 (a); *Samson and Delilah* 1949 (a); *All About Eve* 1950 (a) **(AABSA)**; *I Can Get It For You Wholesale* 1951 (a); *The Light Touch* 1951 (a); *Assignment—Paris* 1952 (a); *Ivanhoe* 1952 (a); *Call Me Madam* 1953 (a); *Viaggio in Italia* 1953 (a); *King Richard and the Crusaders* 1954 (a); *A Stranger Came Home/The Unholy Four* 1954 (from novel); *Witness to Murder* 1954 (a); *The Big Tip Off* 1955 (a); *Jupiter's Darling* 1955 (a); *The King's Thief* 1955 (a); *Moonfleet* 1955 (a); *Never Say Goodbye* 1955 (a); *Night Freight* 1955 (a); *The Scarlet Coat* 1955 (a); *Death of a Scoundrel* 1956 (a); *That Certain Feeling* 1956 (a); *While The City Sleeps* 1956 (a); *Outcasts of the City* 1957 (a); *The Seventh Sin* 1957 (a); *From the Earth to the Moon* 1958 (a); *The Whole Truth* 1958 (a); *Solomon and Sheba* 1959 (a); *That Kind of Woman* 1959 (a); *Bluebeard's Ten Honeymoons* 1960 (a); *The Last Voyage* 1960 (a); *The Rebel* 1961 (a); *In Search of the Castaways* 1962 (a); *Cairo* 1963 (a); *Dark Purpose* 1964 (a); *A Shot in the Dark* 1964 (a); *The Amorous Adventures of Moll Flanders* 1965 (a); *The Quiller Memorandum* 1966 (a); *The Golden Head* 1967 (a); *Good Times* 1967 (a); *The Jungle Book* 1967 (a); *Rey de Africa* 1967 (a); *The Best House in London* 1969 (a); *The Body Stealers* 1969 (a); *The Candy Man* 1969 (a); *The Kremlin Letter* 1970 (a); *Endless Night* 1972 (a).

Sanders-Brahms, Helma • Director, screenwriter; also producer. • Born Emden, Germany, November 20, 1940. *Educ.* Cologne University (theater, literature). Key figure of the New German Cinema and, alongside Margarethe Von Trotta, the only woman of the group to achieve international recognition. Unlike most other New German directors, Sanders-Brahms has remained a radical in terms of both her content (Marxist- and feminist-inspired canvases on life, politics and love) and form (use of alienation techniques, symbolism, interweaving of past/present and dream/reality).

Sanders-Brahms (she is related to the famed composer on her mother's side) began her career as a TV announcer and turned to directing several years later. Through the 1970s she turned out a series of prize-winning documentaries and features dealing invariably with such contemporary German ills as capitalist exploitation and machine-driven alienation. A highlight of this period is *Shirin's Wedding* (1976), which deals both with the "guest worker" question (a preoccupation for the New German Cinema) and the place of women within that schema.

In 1979 Sanders-Brahms made *Germany, Pale Mother*, the film for which she remains best known. Freely based on recollections of life with her mother in war-torn and post-war Germany, the film was coolly received in her native land but earned substantial international acclaim; it features a riveting performance by Eva Mattes and masterful black-and-white photography by Jurgen Jurges. SKK • *Unterm Pflaster ist der Strand/Under the Pavement Lies the Strand* 1975 (d,sc); *Heinrich* 1976 (d,sc); *Deutschland Bleiche Mutter/Germany, Pale Mother* 1979 (d,p,sc); *Die Beruhrte/No Mercy No Future* 1981 (d,p,sc); *Der Subjektive Faktor/The Subjective Factor* 1981 (a); *Flugel und Felleln/L'Avenir d'Emilie; The Future of Emily* 1984 (d); *Laputa* 1986 (d,sc); *Felix* 1987 (d,sc); *Geteilte Liebe/Divided Love* 1988 (d,p,sc).

Sandrelli, Stefania • Actress • Born Viareggio, Italy, 1946. Popular, innocent-looking Italian actress who has starred in films since her teens. Sandrelli is best known in the US for her roles in the films of Bertolucci, including *Partner* (1968) and *The Conformist* (1970), in which she dances with Dominique Sanda in one of the key set pieces of the film. Sandrelli was also in *Divorce Italian Style* (1961), as the teen sexpot who drives Marcello Mastroaianni to murder; *Seduced and Abandoned* (1964); *We All Loved Each Other So Much* (1974), as the actress that all the men fall for; and Ettore Scola's leisurely portrait of *The Family* (1987). • *Divorzio All'Italiano/Divorce Italian Style* 1961; *L'Aîne des Ferchaux/Magnet of Doom* 1963; *Sedotta e Abbandonata/Seduced and Abandoned* 1964; *L'Immorale* 1967; *Partner* 1968; *Brancaleone Alle Crociate* 1970; *Il Conformista/The Conformist* 1970; *La Tarantola dal Ventre Nero* 1972; *Alfredo, Alfredo* 1973; *Delitto d'Amore* 1974; *C'eravamo tanto amati/We All Loved Each Other So Much* 1974; *Police Python.357* 1975; *Quelle Strane Occasioni; Strange Events* 1976; *Novecento/1900* 1976; *Le Voyage de Noces* 1976; *Io Sono Mia* 1977; *Dove vai in vacanza?* 1978; *Le Grand embouteillage* 1979; *La Verdad Sobre el Caso Savolta* 1979; *Desideria, La Vita Interiore* 1980; *Bello Mio Bellezza Mia* 1982; *La Chiave* 1983; *Eccezzziunale...Veramente* 1983; *Vaconze di Natale* 1984; *Magic Moments* 1984; *Una Donna Allo Specchio/A Woman In the Mirror* 1984; *Segreti Segreti/Secrets Secrets* 1984; *L'Attenzione* 1985; *Mamma Ebe* 1985; *Pourvu que ce soit une fille/Let's Hope It's a Girl* 1986; *D'Annunzio* 1986; *La Famiglia/The Family* 1987; *La Sposa Era Bellissima/The Bride Was Beautiful* 1987; *Gli Occhiali d'Oro/The Gold-Rimmed Glasses* 1987; *Noyage interdite* 1987; *Secondo Ponzio Pilato* 1987; *Mignon e Partita* 1988; *Il Piccolo Diavolo/The Little Devil* 1988; *Zio Indegno/The Sleazy Uncle* 1989; *Il Male Oscuro* 1990; *Evelina e i suoi figli* 1990; *L'Africana* 1990.

Sands, Julian • Actor • Born Yorkshire, England, 1958. *Educ.* Central School of Speech and Drama, London. Handsome, blonde lead who first received attention as photographer Jon Swain in *The Killing Fields* (1984) and achieved stardom opposite Helena Bonham Carter in James Ivory's E.M. Forster adaptation, *A Room With a View* (1986). • *Privates on Parade* 1982; *The Killing Fields* 1984; *Oxford Blues* 1984; *After Darkness* 1985; *The Doctor and the Devils* 1985; *Gothic* 1986; *A Room With a View* 1986; *Siesta* 1987; *Gdzieskolwiek jest, jeslis jest/Wherever You Are* 1988; *Manika* 1988; *Vibes* 1988; *Tennessee Nights* 1989; *Warlock* 1989; *Arachnophobia* 1990; *Il Sole anche di notte* 1990; *Impromptu* 1991; *Wicked* 1991.

Sanford, Midge • Producer • Born New York, NY. *Educ.* Sarah Lawrence College, Bronxville NY; California State University, Los Angeles (education). Formed Sanford/Pillsbury productions with Sarah Pillsbury in 1982 and has been responsible for several critically and/or financially successful independent films, beginning with *Desperately Seeking Susan* (1985). • *Desperately Seeking Susan* 1985; *River's Edge* 1987; *Eight Men Out* 1988; *Immediate Family* 1989.

Sanjines, Jorge • Filmmaker • Born Bolivia, 1936. *Educ.* Catholic University, Santiago, Chile (philosophy, film). Sanjines made his first feature film, *Ukamau* (1966), under the auspices of the Bolivian Film Institute, of which he was named director in 1965. A landmark in the history of Bolivian cinema, *Ukamau* is a sympathetic depiction of the social problems of the Andean peasantry shot exclusively in Aymara, an indigenous language. Because of the controversy surrounding the film, Sanjines was fired from his post, but went on to become one of the most successful of Latin America's leftist filmmakers.

Sanjines has attempted to forge a genuinely popular cinema capable of presenting a revolutionary political agenda in a form accessible to working-class and peasant audiences. His most famous feature, the controversial *Yawar Mallku/Blood of the Condor* (1969), is an impassioned defense of Bolivia's Indian cultures and an attack on US imperialism (symbolized by a covert sterilization program). The nonfiction film *El coraje del pueblo/The Courage of the People* (1971) features a documentary reconstruction, enacted by survivors, of the infamous "Night of San Juan" massacre of Bolivian miners. In *El enemígo principál/The Principal Enemy* (1973, released in Peru), Sanjines worked with members of an Andean peasant community to dramatize the brutal exploitation of the peasantry. Even when he has worked in exile, Sanjines has shown an exceptional ability to make artistically innovative and politically powerful films in spite of low budgets and the difficulties attendant on nonindustrial film production in Latin America. DW • *Yawar Mallku/Ukamau* 1966 (d); *Blood of the Condor* 1969 (d); *El Coraje del Pueblo/The Courage of the People* 1971 (d,ed); *El enemígo principál/The Principal Enemy* 1973 (d); *La Nación Clandestina* 1989 (d,sc).

Sarandon, Chris • Actor • Born Beckley, WV, July 24, 1942. *Educ.* University of West Virginia; Catholic University, Washington, DC. Character actor who first came to attention as Al Pacino's overwrought gay lover in *Dog Day Afternoon* (1975). Formerly married to actress Susan Sarandon. • *Dog Day Afternoon* 1975 **(AANBSA)**; *Lipstick* 1976; *The Sentinel* 1977; *Cuba* 1979; *The Osterman Weekend* 1983; *Protocol* 1984; *Fright Night* 1985; *The Princess Bride* 1987; *Child's Play* 1988; *Forced March* 1989; *Slaves of New York* 1989; *Collision Course* 1990.

Sarandon, Susan • Actress • Born Susan Tomaling, New York, NY, October 4, 1946. *Educ.* Catholic University, Washington, DC (drama). Former Ford model who appeared in several secondary film roles in the 1970s, notably in the campy cult classic, *The Rocky Horror Picture Show* (1975). Sarandon played Brooke Shields's mother in Louis Malle's *Pretty Baby* (1978) and brought candor and intelligence to her finely nuanced, unglamorous role as a casino worker in Malle's seedy elegy, *Atlantic City* (1980). She has since proved herself a versatile, talented lead, enjoying box-office success with her roles in *The Witches of Eastwick* (1987) and *Bull Durham* (1988). Formerly married to actor Chris Sarandon. Has a child with actor Tim Robbins. • *Joe* 1970; *The Front Page* 1974; *Lovin' Molly* 1974; *Dragonfly* 1975; *The Great Waldo Pepper* 1975; *The Rocky Horror Picture Show* 1975; *Crash* 1976; *The Great Smokey Roadblock* 1976; *Checkered Flag or Crash* 1977; *The Other Side of Midnight* 1977; *King of the Gypsies* 1978; *Pretty Baby* 1978; *Something Short of Paradise* 1979; *Atlantic City* 1980 **(AANBA)**; *Loving Couples* 1980; *Tempest* 1982; *The Hunger* 1983; *The Buddy System* 1984; *In Our Hands* 1984; *Compromising Positions* 1985; *The Witches of Eastwick* 1987; *Bull Durham* 1988; *The January Man* 1988; *Sweet Hearts Dance* 1988; *A Dry White Season* 1989; *Through the Wire* 1990; *White Palace* 1990; *Thelma and Louise* 1991.

Sarde, Philippe • Composer • Born Neuilly-sur-Seine, Paris, June 21, 1948. *Educ.* Paris Conservatoire. Versatile, prolific composer who has written the music for over 120 films since 1969, when he scored his first feature, Claude Sautet's *The Things of Life.* Sarde has enjoyed multi-film associations with Robert Bresson, Bertrand Tavernier and Roman Polanski. In 1976 he earned a double César (the French Oscar) for his work on Tavernier's *The Judge and the Assassin* and Andre Techine's *Barocco.* • *Les Choses de la Vie/The Things of Life* 1969 (m); *La Cagna* 1971 (m); *Le Fils* 1972 (m); *Charlie et ses deux nenettes* 1973 (m); *Les Corps Celestes* 1973 (m); *La Grande Bouffe* 1973 (m); *L'Horloger de St. Paul* 1973 (m); *Le Mariage à la Mode* 1973 (m); *La Race des "Seigneurs"* 1973 (m); *Touche pas à la femme blanche!* 1973 (m); *Le Train* 1973 (m); *La Valise* 1973 (m); *Lancelot du Lac* 1974 (m); *Les Seins de Glace* 1974 (m); *Vincent, François, Paul... et les Autres* 1974 (m); *7 Morts sur Ordonnance* 1975 (m); *Un Divorce Heureux* 1975 (m); *Histoire d'O* 1975 (m); *Un Sac de Billes* 1975 (m); *Souvenirs d'en France* 1975 (m); *Barocco* 1976 (m); *La Dernière Femme* 1976 (m); *Le Juge et l'assassin* 1976 (m); *Le Locataire* 1976 (m); *Mado* 1976 (m); *Marie—Poupée* 1976 (m); *Comme la Lune* 1977 (m); *Le Crabe-Tambour* 1977 (m); *Le Diable Probablement* 1977 (m); *Des Enfants Gatés* 1977 (m.adapt,m); *Le Juge Fayard dit le "sheriff"* 1977 (m); *Madame Rosa* 1977 (m); *Un Moment d'Egarement* 1977 (m); *Mort d'un pourri* 1977 (m); *Un Taxi mauve* 1977 (m); *Violette et François* 1977 (m); *L'Adolescente* 1978 (m); *La Clé Sur la Porte* 1978 (m); *Une Histoire simple* 1978 (m); *Ils sont fous ces sorciers* 1978 (m); *Passe-Montagne* 1978 (m); *Rêve de Singe* 1978 (m); *Les Soeurs Bronte* 1978 (m); *Le Sucre* 1978 (m); *Chiedo Asilo* 1979 (m); *Flic ou voyou* 1979 (m); *Loulou* 1979 (m.adapt,songs); *Tess* 1979 (m) **(AANBM)**; *Le Toubib* 1979 (m); *Chère Inconnue/I Sent a Letter to My Love* 1980 (m); *Est-ce bien raisonnable?* 1980 (m); *La Femme Flic* 1980 (m); *Un Mauvais Fils* 1980 (m); *Les Ailes de la Colombe/Wings of the Dove* 1981 (m); *Beau Père* 1981 (m); *Le Choix des armes/Choice of Weapons* 1981 (m); *Coup de Torchon* 1981 (m); *Ghost Story* 1981 (m); *Quest For Fire* 1981 (m); *Storie di Ordinaria Follia/Tales of Ordinary Madness* 1981 (m); *Le Choc* 1982 (m); *L'Etoile du nord* 1982 (m); *Hôtel des Amériques* 1982 (m); *J'ai Epousé Une Ombre* 1982 (m); *Que les gros salaires lèvent le doigt!!!* 1982 (m); *Storia di Piera* 1982 (m); *L'Ami de Vincent* 1983 (m); *Attention! Une femme peut en cacher une autre* 1983 (m); *Garçon!* 1983 (m); *Lovesick* 1983 (m); *Premiers Desirs* 1983 (m); *Stella* 1983 (m); *Ca n'arrive qu'à Moi* 1984 (m); *Un Dimanche à la Campagne/A Sunday in the Country* 1984 (m.arr); *L'Eté Prochain* 1984 (m); *Fort Saganne* 1984 (m); *La Garce* 1984 (m); *Joyeuses Pâques* 1984 (m); *La Pirate* 1984 (m); *Signé Charlotte* 1984 (m); *Le Cowboy* 1985 (m); *Devil in the Flesh* 1985 (m); *Harem* 1985 (m); *L'Homme aux yeux d'argent* 1985 (m); *Hors-la-loi* 1985 (m); *Joshua Then and Now* 1985 (m); *Mon beau-frère a tué ma soeur* 1985 (m); *Rendezvous* 1985 (m); *La Tentation d'Isabelle* 1985 (m); *Cours privé* 1986 (m); *L'Etat de grace* 1986 (m); *Everytime We Say Goodbye* 1986 (m); *Le Lieu du Crime/Scene of the Crime* 1986 (m); *The Manhattan Project* 1986 (m); *Pirates* 1986 (m); *La Puritaine* 1986 (m); *Comédie!* 1987 (m); *De guerre lasse* 1987 (m); *Les Deux crocodiles* 1987 (m); *Ennemis intimes* 1987 (m); *Funny Boy* 1987 (m); *Les Innocents* 1987 (m); *L'été dernier à Tanger* 1987 (m); *La Maison assassinée* 1987 (m); *Les Mois d'avril sont meurtriers* 1987 (m); *Noyade interdite* 1987 (m); *Poker* 1987 (m); *La Couleur du vent* 1988 (m); *La Maison de Jade* 1988 (m); *Mangeclous* 1988 (m); *L'Ours/The Bears* 1988 (m); *Quelques jours avec moi* 1988 (m); *La Travestie* 1988 (m); *Chambre à part* 1989 (m); *Hiver 54, l'abbé Pierre* 1989 (m); *L'Invité surprise* 1989 (m); *Lost Angels* 1989 (m,m.adapt,m); *Music Box* 1989 (m); *Reunion* 1989 (m); *La Baule les pins* 1990 (m); *Faux et usage de faux* 1990 (m); *Lord of the Flies* 1990 (m); *Lung Ta: Les cavaliers du vent* 1990 (m); *Le Petit Criminel* 1990 (m).

Sargent, Alvin • Screenwriter • Born U.S.A.. Former TV writer who began a successful film career in the mid-1960s. Sargent's deft, sentimental treatments of "serious" topics have earned him three Oscar nominations; he won the award for *Julia* (1977) and *Ordinary People* (1980). • *Gambit* 1966; *The Stalking Moon* 1968; *The Sterile Cuckoo* 1969; *I Walk the Line* 1970; *The Effect of Gamma Rays on Man-in-the-Moon Marigolds* 1972; *Liebe, Schmerz und das Danze Verdammte Zeug* 1973; *Paper Moon* 1973 **(AANBSC)**; *Bobby Deerfield* 1977; *Julia* 1977 **(AABSC)**; *Straight Time* 1978; *Ordinary People* 1980 **(AABSC)**; *Nuts* 1987; *Dominick and Eugene* 1988; *White Palace* 1990; *What About Bob?* 1991 (story,creative consultant).

Sarrazin, Michael • Actor • Born Jacques Michel André Sarrazin, Québec City, Canada, May 22, 1940. *Educ.* Actors Studio. Charismatic young lead of the late 1960s and early 70s, memorable in *They Shoot Horses, Don't They?* (1969), whose career has not lived up to its early promise. • *The Flim-Flam Man* 1967; *Gunfight in Abilene* 1967; *Journey to Shiloh* 1968; *The Sweet Ride* 1968; *Eye of the Cat* 1969; *A Man Called Gannon* 1969; *They Shoot Horses, Don't They?* 1969; *In Search of Gregory* 1970; *Believe in Me* 1971; *The Pursuit of Happiness* 1971; *Sometimes a Great Notion* 1971; *The Groundstar Conspiracy* 1972; *Harry in Your Pocket* 1973; *For Pete's Sake* 1974; *The Loves and Times of Scaramouche* 1975; *The Reincarnation of Peter Proud* 1975; *The Gumball Rally* 1976; *Caravans* 1978; *Double Negative* 1980; *The Seduction* 1981; *Fighting Back* 1982; *Viadukt* 1982; *Joshua Then and Now* 1985; *Captive Hearts* 1987; *Keeping Track* 1987; *Mascara* 1987; *Malarek* 1989; *The Phone Call* 1990.

Sarris, Andrew • Critic; also author • Born Brooklyn, NY, October 31, 1928. *Educ.* Columbia College. Long-time film critic for *The Village Voice* (1960-89) who was influential in the 1960s in introducing the auteur theory to the US, both in his columns and his best-known book, *The American Cinema: Directors and Directions 1929-1968* (1968). At a time when film critics and their personal tastes were news, Sarris battled publicly with Pauline Kael, John Simon and others. The coverage of these intellectual debates was an important element in the development of the new film culture in the US in the 1960s and 70s.

Saura, Carlos • Director, screenwriter • Born Huesca, Aragon, Spain, January 4, 1932. *Educ.* Instituto de Investigaciones y Experiencias Cinematograficas, Madrid. • A leading figure of Spanish cinema in the 1970s and 80s, Saura is known mainly for his explorations of the repressive effects of the Franco regime on Spanish society. Saura was already establishing himself as a still photographer when his brother talked him into attending film school in Madrid. Here he came into contact with the works of the Italian neorealists, whose influences were evident in his first feature, *Los Golfos* (1960), with its location shooting, use of nonprofessional actors and concern with social issues.

Los Golfos was poorly received and it was not until Saura's third feature, *La Caza/The Hunt* (1966) that his abilities were noticed. With *La Caza,* Saura established a crew (including Elias Querejeta as producer, Luis Cuadrado as photographer, and Pablo G. del Amo as editor) which would work with him on a number of features.

Saura's films of the next ten years were much influenced by the Spanish artistic tradition of *esperpento,* an absurdist type of black humor in which fact and fantasy are intermixed. *Peppermint Frappé* (1967), *Garden of Delights* (1970), *La Prima Angelíca* (1973) and *Cría Cuervos* (1976) were virtually the only films emerging from Spain during this period to receive any form of world recognition. *Peppermint Frappe* received the Silver Bear at the 1968 Berlin Festival, *La Prima Angelíca* the Jury Prize at the 1974 Cannes Festival, and *Cría* the 1976 Special Jury Prize at Cannes. Often in allegorical terms, these films showed ways in which the repressiveness of Franco's regime manifested itself in areas of society not normally considered "political." One common theme was how sexual repression could develop into forms of abnormal and destructive behavior.

Actress Geraldine Chaplin, with whom Saura had a son, frequently starred in these works.

After the death of Franco in 1975, Saura felt free to deal with themes and issues which had previously been taboo. *Deprisa, Deprisa* (1980), a winner of the Golden Bear at the 1981 Berlin Festival, looks at adolescent street life in Madrid and marks a return to the issues Saura had explored in *Los Golfos.* To achieve a greater sense of realism, Saura had four youngsters from the streets work with him on the script.

Next, Saura embarked on his acclaimed dance trilogy: *Blood Wedding* (1981), *Carmen* (1983) and *El Amor Brujo* (1986). These films, among the most popular in Spanish box-office history, were adapted with choreographer Antonio Gades from classical ballets and placed in contemporary settings. The trilogy earned a special award at the 1988 Montreal Film Festival. In between these dance features, Saura directed *Dulces Horas* (1982), *Antonieta* (1982) and *Los Zancos* (1984), soul-searching stories all dealing with the impact of suicide.

Saura's latest works include *El Dorado,* a lavish historical epic based upon the life of Conquestador Pedro de Ursuo (which also formed the basis for Werner Herzog's *Aguirre Wrath of God*) and *Ay, Carmela* (1990), for which Carmen Maura received best actress honors from the European Film Awards. PP • *Los Golfos* 1960 (d); *Llanto por un bandido* 1964 (d); *La Caza/The Hunt* 1966 (d,sc); *Peppermint Frappé* 1967 (d); *El Jardín de las Delicias/The Garden of Delights* 1970 (d,sc); *Ana y Los Lobos* 1973 (d,sc); *La Prima Angelica* 1973 (d); *Cría Cuervos/Cria* 1976 (d,sc); *Elisa, Vida Mía* 1977 (d,sc); *Los Ojos Vendados* 1978 (d,sc); *Mama Cumple 100 Anos* 1979 (d,sc); *Deprisa, Deprisa* 1980 (d); *Bodas de Sangre/Blood Wedding* 1981 (d); *Antonieta* 1982 (d,sc); *Dulces Horas/Sweet Hours* 1982 (d); *Carmen* 1983 (d,sc,chor); *Los Zancos* 1984 (d,sc); *El Amor Brujo* 1986 (d,sc,chor); *El Dorado* 1988 (d,sc); *La Noche Oscura* 1989 (d,sc); *Ay, Carmela* 1990 (d,sc).

Sautet, Claude • Director, screenwriter • Born Montrouge, France, February 23, 1924. *Educ.* School of Decorative Arts, Paris (sculpture); IDHEC, Paris. One of France's leading chroniclers of middle-class, and especially middle-aged, life. Sautet began his career as an assistant (e.g. to Jacques Becker on the classic gangster yarn, *Touchez pas au Grisbi* 1954), served as a TV producer and earned a reputation as a superior scenarist before directing his first feature in 1955. His first significant achievement, the craftily handled underworld melodrama *The Big Risk* (1960), was overshadowed by the activities of the younger, New Wave directors. Sautet came into his own, however, with *The Things of Life* (1970), a keenly observed study of a mid-life crisis triggered by an automobile accident. Like many of the director's subsequent films, it starred Romy Schneider and Michel Piccoli.

Sautet has subsequently turned out a number of finely observed social studies, often documenting the relations between large numbers of characters. He is best known in the US for *Vincent, Francois, Paul and the Others* (1974), *A Simple Story* (1978) and *A Few Days with Me* (1988), a relatively uncharacteristic departure into more youthful territory. • *Bonjour sourire* 1955 (d); *Classe tous risques/The Big Risk* 1960 (d,sc); *Echappement libre* 1964 (sc,adapt); *Peau de banane* 1964 (sc); *Borsalino* 1970 (sc); *L'Amante/Les Choses de la Vie/The Things of Life* 1970 (d,sc); *Max et les Ferrailleurs* 1970 (d); *Cesar et Rosalie* 1972 (d,sc); *Vincent, Francois, Paul... et les Autres/Vincent, Francois, Paul... and the Others* 1974 (d,sc); *Mado* 1976 (d,sc); *Une Histoire simple/A Simple Story* 1978 (d,sc); *Un Mauvais Fils* 1980 (d,sc); *Garcon!* 1983 (d,sc); *Mon ami le traitre* 1988 (sc); *Quelques jours avec moi/A Few Days With Me* 1988 (d,sc,adapt,dial).

Savage, Fred • Actor • Born Highland Park, IL, July 9, 1976. Juvenile lead apt at appearing wise beyond his years—a talent put to good use in *Vice Versa* (1988), the story of a father (Judge Reinhold) and son who switch bodies. Savage, whose younger siblings Kala and Ben are also actors, is best known as the star of TV's popular "The Wonder Years." • *The Boy Who Could Fly* 1986; *The Princess Bride* 1987; *Vice Versa* 1988; *Little Monsters* 1989; *The Wizard* 1989.

Savage, John • Actor • Born Long Island, NY, August 25, 1949. *Educ.* AADA, New York. Sensitive, stage-trained performer who gained recognition for his gripping performances in *The Deer Hunter* (1978) and *The Onion Field* (1979). Savage's subsequent appearances, in films and on TV, have been less enthralling. • *Bad Company* 1972; *The Killing Kind* 1973; *Steelyard Blues* 1973; *The Sister-in-Law* 1975; *The Deer Hunter* 1978; *Hair* 1979; *The Onion Field* 1979; *Inside Moves* 1980; *The Amateur* 1981; *Cattle Annie and Little Britches* 1981; *The Long Ride* 1984; *Soldier's Revenge* 1984; *Maria's Lovers* 1985; *Hotel Colonial* 1986; *Salvador* 1986; *The Beat* 1987; *Beauty and the Beast* 1987; *Dear America* 1987; *Caribe* 1988; *Do the Right Thing* 1989; *Hunting* 1989; *Point of View* 1989; *Any Man's Death* 1990; *The Godfather Part III* 1990.

Sayles, John • Director, screenwriter; also producer, author, actor, editor. • Born Schenectady, NY, September 28, 1950. *Educ.* Williams College, Williamstown, MA (psychology). One of America's best known independent filmmakers, John Sayles is primarily concerned with personal and political relationships. "My main interest is making films about people," he admits. "I'm not interested in cinematic art." Nonetheless, he has developed a distinctive personal style, utilizing ensemble acting as well as his own performing skills.

After appearing in school plays and summer stock while at Williams College, Sayles embarked on a career as a fiction writer, submitting stories to magazines and supporting himself as an orderly, day laborer and meat packer. His two novels, *Pride of the Bimbos* (1975) and *Union Dues* (1977), and his short story anthology, *The Anarchist's Convention* (1979), received critical acclaim for their honest characterizations and authentic use of dialect, although they did not meet with financial success.

In the mid-70s, Sayles joined Roger Corman's stable of B-movie scriptwriters, penning *Piranha* (1978), *The Lady in Red* (1979) and *Battle Beyond the Stars* (1980). His first film as director, *Return of the Secaucus Seven* (1979), was shot in four weeks during 1978 at a reported cost of $40,000. A witty, poignant look at a reunion of 1960s activists on the verge of adulthood, the film has been praised as a more authentic and charming portrait of the same territory explored in the more commercially successful *The Big Chill* (1983). Almost a "talking heads" film, *Secaucus* used few sets, sparse camera movement and little action, but it won the Best Screenplay award from the Los Angeles Film Critics and was Oscar-nominated in the same category.

Lianna (1982) is a daring yet subtle examination of the changes a married woman undergoes following her discovery that she is a lesbian. This low-budget film (shot for $300,000) has been both praised for its sensitivity and derided as exploitative. *Baby, It's You* (1983), the story of a doomed high-school romance between a college-bound Jewish girl and a working class Italian youth, was an uncharacteristically frothy departure for Sayles.

In 1983 Sayles was awarded a prestigious MacArthur Foundation "genius" grant which provided him with $34,000 per year, tax-free, for five years. One of the results was *The Brother From Another Planet* (1984), an unlikely story of a mute, black alien adrift in Harlem. A captivating look at a variety of issues, including racial prejudice and drug addiction, the film relies on brilliant performances from a tightly knit cast to bring to life a talk-heavy script.

Matewan (1987) explores the personal and political dimensions of union-making and breaking in the West Virginia coal mines of the 1920s. A complex study of individual integrity and community solidarity, the film is, typically for Sayles, largely dialogue-driven—although the director does succeed, with the help of Appalachian locations, Haskell Wexler's cinematography and Mason Daring's lively bluegrass soundtrack, in creating an evocative setting for his narrative.

Eight Men Out (1988) is Sayles's most ambitious film to date. An account of the 1919 Black Sox scandal that rocked the baseball world,it examines the controversy through the eyes of individual ball players. Rather than simple caricatures, each man is seen as having complex reasons for agreeing or refusing to throw the World Series. Here, Sayles relies even more on visuals: impressionistic lighting and scrupulous production design help capture this pivotal period of American history. CSE • *Piranha* 1978 (sc,story); *The Lady in Red* 1979 (sc); *The Return of the Secaucus Seven* 1979 (a,d,sc,ed) **(AANBSC)**; *Alligator* 1980 (sc,story); *Battle Beyond the Stars* 1980 (sc,story); *The Howling* 1980 (a,sc); *The Challenge* 1982 (sc); *Lianna* 1982 (a,d,sc,ed); *Baby, It's You* 1983 (d,sc); *Enormous Changes at the Last Minute* 1983 (sc); *The Brother From Another Planet* 1984 (a,d,sc,ed,song); *Hard Choices* 1984 (a); *The Clan of the Cave Bear* 1986 (sc); *Something Wild* 1986 (a); *Matewan* 1987 (a,d,sc); *Wild Thing* 1987 (sc,story); *Eight Men Out* 1988 (a,d,sc,song); *Breaking In* 1989 (sc); *Untamagiru* 1989 (a); *Little Vegas* 1990 (a); *City of Hope* 1991 (d,sc,ed).

Scacchi, Greta • Actress • Born Milan, Italy, 1960. *Educ.* University of Western Australia; Bristol Old Vic Theatre School. Beautiful blonde lead of several international films of the 1980s. Scacchi first gained attention as the spirited grandmother in the flashback sequence of *Heat and Dust* (1983) and was memorable as the daffy secretary in Dusan Makavejev's *The Coca-Cola Kid* (1985). She seemed trapped in two-dimensional, femme fatale-type roles in *White Mischief* (1987) and *Presumed Innocent* (1990). • *Heat and Dust* 1983 (a); *Dr. Fischer of Geneva* 1984 (a); *Burke & Wills* 1985 (a); *The Coca-Cola Kid* 1985 (a); *Defence of the Realm* 1985 (a,cost); *Good Morning Babylon* 1986 (a); *Un Homme amoureux/A Man in Love* 1987 (a); *White Mischief* 1987 (a); *La Donna della Luna* 1988 (a); *Paura e Amore/Fear and Love* 1988 (a); *Waterfront* 1988 (a); *Presumed Innocent* 1990 (a).

Scales, Prunella • Actress • Born Sutton Abinger, Surrey, England. *Educ.* Old Vic, London; Herbert Berghof Studio, New York. Gifted comedienne, best known as the bane of husband/hotel manager Basil Fawlty (John Cleese) in TV's "Fawlty Towers" series. Scales is primarily a stage actress but has made intermittent, and highly effective, appearances in several films. • *Laxdale Hall* 1953; *Hobson's Choice* 1954; *Waltz of the Toreadors* 1962; *Escape From the Dark* 1976; *The Boys From Brazil* 1978; *The Hound of the Baskervilles* 1978; *The Wicked Lady* 1983; *The Lonely Passion of Judith Hearne* 1987; *Consuming Passions* 1988; *A Chorus of Disapproval* 1989.

Scarwid, Diana • Actress • Born Savannah, GA, August 27, 1955. *Educ.* University of Georgia Theatre Workshop, Athens; National Shakespeare Conservatory, Woodstock, NY; AADA, New York; Pace University; Film Actor's Workshop, Burbank Studios. Homespun blonde character player who appeared in several interesting features of the late 1970s through the mid-80s, making her debut in Louis Malle's *Pretty Baby* (1978) and playing Christina Crawford in *Mommie Dearest* (1981). • *Pretty Baby* 1978; *Honeysuckle Rose* 1980; *Inside Moves* 1980 **(AANBSA)**; *Mommie Dearest* 1981; *Rumble Fish* 1983; *Silkwood* 1983; *Strange Invaders* 1983; *Extremities* 1986; *The Ladies Club* 1986; *Psycho III* 1986; *Heat* 1987; *Brenda Starr* 1989.

Schaffner, Franklin J. • Director; also screenwriter, producer. • Born Franklin James Schaffner, Tokyo, May 30, 1920; died July 2, 1989, Santa Monica, CA. *Educ.* Franklin & Marshall College, Lancaster, PA. One of the leading directors of the "Golden Age" of live TV who later proved himself a capable handler of both epic action features and intimate dramas. Schaffner began his career as an assistant on "The March of Time" documentary series and directed over 150 TV plays, including the original broadcasts of *Twelve Angry Men* (1954) and *The Caine Mutiny Court Martial* (1955). He enjoyed success with his 1960 Broadway production of *Advise and Consent* and made his first feature film, *The Stripper*—adapted from a play by William Inge—in 1963.

Schaffner is best known for *Planet of the Apes* (1968), *Patton* (1970) and *Papillon* (1973), which yielded one of Dustin Hoffman's finest performances. • *The Stripper* 1963 (d); *The Best Man* 1964 (d); *The Double Man* 1967 (d); *Planet of the Apes* 1968 (d); *Patton* 1970 (d) **(AABD)**; *Nicholas and Alexandra* 1971 (d,p); *Papillon* 1973 (d,p); *Islands in the Stream* 1976 (d); *The Boys From Brazil* 1978 (d); *Sphinx* 1980 (d,exec.p); *Yes, Giorgio* 1982 (d); *Lionheart* 1987 (d); *Welcome Home* 1989 (d).

Schary, Dore • Producer, screenwriter; also playwright, director. • Born Newark, NJ, August 31, 1905; died 1980. Former actor and journalist who began writing screenplays in the 1930s and worked as executive producer of MGM's B productions (1941-43), producer for David O. Selznick (1943-47), executive vice president of production for RKO (1947-48) and, most notably, chief of production at MGM (1948-1956). Schary was unable to save MGM from its TV-induced decline in the 1950s and, after being ousted from the company, wrote plays and made occasional independent films. • *Fog* 1933 (sc); *Fury of the Jungle* 1933 (sc); *He Couldn't Take It* 1933 (sc,story); *Let's Talk It Over* 1934 (story); *Most Precious Thing in Life* 1934 (sc); *Murder in the Clouds* 1934 (sc,story); *Young and Beautiful* 1934 (sc); *Chinatown Squad* 1935 (sc); *Silk Hat Kid* 1935 (sc); *Your Uncle Dudley* 1935 (adapt); *Her Master's Voice* 1936 (sc); *Timothy's Quest* 1936 (sc); *The Big City* 1937 (sc); *The Girl From Scotland Yard* 1937 (sc); *Mind Your Own Business* 1937 (sc); *Outcast* 1937 (sc); *Boys Town* 1938 (sc,story) **(AANBSC,AABST)**; *Behind the News* 1940 (story); *Broadway Melody of 1940* 1940 (story); *Edison, the Man* 1940 (story) **(AANBST)**; *Young Tom Edison* 1940 (sc); *Married Bachelor* 1941 (sc); *I'll Be Seeing You* 1944 (p); *The Spiral Staircase* 1946 (p); *Till the End of Time* 1946 (p); *The Bachelor and the Bobby Soxer* 1947 (p); *Crossfire* 1947 (exec.p); *The Farmer's Daughter* 1947 (p); *Berlin Express* 1948 (exec.p); *Battleground* 1949 (p); *The Next Voice You Hear* 1950 (p); *Go For Broke* 1951 (p); *It's a Big Country* 1951 (story); *Westward the Women* 1951 (p); *The Hoaxters* 1952 (p) **(AANBDOC)**; *Plymouth Adventure* 1952 (p); *Washington Story* 1952 (p); *Dream Wife* 1953 (p); *Take the High Ground* 1953 (p); *Bad Day at Black Rock* 1954 (p); *The Last Hunt* 1955 (p); *The Battle of Gettysburg* 1955 (p) **(AANBSF)**; *The Swan* 1956 (p); *Designing Woman* 1957 (p); *Lonelyhearts* 1958 (p,sc); *Sunrise at Campobello* 1960 (p,sc,from play); *Act One* 1963 (d,p,sc).

Schatzberg, Jerry • Director • Born New York, NY, June 26, 1927. *Educ.* University of Miami; worked as assistant to photographer Bill Helburn (1954-56); freelance still photographer and director of TV commercials (1956-69). Former fashion photographer who scored with his second directorial effort, the gripping, finely acted, *Panic in Needle Park* (1971). A capable technician with a knack for extracting well-rounded performances, Schatzberg earned praise for *Scarecrow* (1973), a moody tale of two drifters (Gene Hackman and Al Pacino), and *Street Smart* (1987), an intriguing drama featuring fine performances from Morgan Freeman and Kathy Baker. • *Puzzle of a Downfall Child* 1970 (d,story); *Panic in Needle Park* 1971 (d); *Scarecrow* 1973 (d); *Dandy, the All American Girl* 1976 (d,p); *The Seduction of Joe Tynan* 1979 (d); *Honeysuckle Rose* 1980 (d); *Misunderstood* 1984 (d); *No Small Affair* 1984 (d); *Street Smart* 1987 (d); *Reunion* 1989 (d).

Scheider, Roy • Actor • Born Orange, NJ, November 10, 1935. *Educ.* Franklin & Marshall College, PA (history). Versatile, classically trained lead who made his film debut in the mid-1960s and made his mark with finely nuanced roles in the atmospheric thriller, *Klute* (1971), and the gritty urban action film, *The French Connection* (1971). Scheider received wide attention for his role in Steven Spielberg's box-office success, *Jaws* (1975), and contributed a powerful turn in *Marathon Man* (1976). He gave what was possibly his richest performance as director Bob Fosse's alter ego in the semi-autobiographical *All That Jazz* (1979). Few of Scheider's roles in the 80s matched up to his earlier triumphs. • *The Curse of the Living Corpse* 1964; *Stiletto* 1969; *Loving* 1970; *Puzzle of a Downfall Child* 1970; *The French Connection* 1971 **(AANBSA)**; *Klute* 1971; *L'Attentat* 1972; *Un Homme Est Mort* 1973; *The Seven Ups* 1973; *Jaws* 1975; *Sheila Levine Is Dead and Living in New York* 1975; *Marathon Man* 1976; *Sorcerer* 1977; *Jaws 2* 1978; *All That Jazz* 1979 **(AANBA)**; *Last Embrace* 1979; *Still of the Night* 1982; *Blue Thunder* 1983; *2010* 1984; *In Our Hands* 1984; *Mishima: A Life in Four Chapters* 1985; *52 Pick-Up* 1986; *The Men's Club* 1986; *Cohen and Tate* 1988; *Listen to Me* 1989; *Night Games* 1989; *The Fourth War* 1990; *The Russia House* 1990.

Schell, Maximilian • Actor; also director, producer, screenwriter. • Born Vienna, Austria, December 8, 1930. *Educ.* University of Zurich (art history); University of Munich. Darkly handsome Austrian-born lead who made his screen debut in the mid-1950s and appeared in a number of German films before arriving in Hollywood in 1958. Schell earned a best actor Oscar for his role as a defense attorney in *Judgment at Nuremberg* (1961), though it was some time before he would receive similar acclaim, for his character roles in films such as *The Man in the Glass Booth* (1974) and *Julia* (1977). In the meantime he turned to production, with a 1968 adaption of Franz Kafka's *The Castle*, and direction, with *First Love* (1970), based on a story by Turgenev. He wrote, produced and starred in his second feature as a director, *The Pedestrian* (1974), which was nominated for an Oscar as best foreign film. Schell's fascinating 1984 documentary, *Marlene*, centered on an "interview" with Marlene Dietrich, in which the legendary star (who refused to appear on camera) continued to stage-manage her career with a combination of charm, guile and deliberate obfuscation. Schell is the son of poet and playwright Ferdinand Hermann Schell and actress Margarethe Noe; his sister is actress Maria Schell (*The Last Bridge* 1954, *Gervaise* 1956). • *Kinder, Mutter und ein General* 1955 (a); *The Young Lions* 1958 (a); *Judgment at Nuremberg* 1961 (a) **(AABA)**; *Five Finger Exercise* 1962 (a); *The Reluctant Saint* 1962 (a); *I Sequestrati di Altona* 1962 (a); *Topkapi* 1964 (a); *Return From the Ashes* 1965 (a); *Counterpoint* 1967 (a); *The Deadly Affair* 1967 (a); *The Castle* 1968 (a,p); *Krakatoa, East of Java* 1969 (a); *First Love* 1970 (a,d,p,sc); *Trotta* 1971 (sc); *Paulina 1880* 1972 (a); *Pope Joan* 1972 (a); *The Man in the Glass Booth* 1974 (a) **(AANBA)**; *The Odessa File* 1974 (a); *The Pedestrian* 1974 (a,d,p,sc); *Ansichten Eines Clowns* 1975 (p); *Der Richter und Sein Henker* 1975 (d,p,sc); *Atentat u Sarajevu* 1976 (a); *St. Ives* 1976 (a); *A Bridge Too Far* 1977 (a); *Cross of Iron* 1977 (a); *Julia* 1977 (a) **(AANBSA)**; *Geschichten aus dem Wienerwald* 1978 (d,p,sc); *Amo Non Amo* 1979 (a); *Avalanche Express* 1979 (a); *The Black Hole* 1979 (a); *Players* 1979 (a); *The Chosen* 1981 (a); *Marlene* 1984 (a,d,sc); *Morgen in Alabama* 1984 (a); *The Assisi Underground* 1985 (a); *The Rose Garden* 1989 (a); *The Freshman* 1990 (a).

Schenck, Joseph M. • Executive; also producer. • Born Rybinsk, Russia, December 25, 1878; died 1961. Russian immigrant who began acquiring amusement parks with his brother Nicholas in the teens and bankrolling Broadway musicals in the 20s. Schenck soon became allied with the Loew organization, where he graduated to a senior executive position. Schenck left Loew's in 1917 to become an independent film producer, turning out vehicles for Norma Talmadge (his wife), Buster Keaton and Fatty Arbuckle. After a spell at United Artists he co-founded the 20th Century corporation with Darryl Zanuck, becoming chairman of the board of 20th Century-Fox after the 1935 merger. Schenck was forced to resign in 1941 when he was indicted for income tax irregularies, but returned to the fold as an executive producer after four months in jail. In 1953 he formed the Magna Corporation with Michael Todd, inventor of the Todd-AO widescreen process. Brother Nicholas, meanwhile, had remained with Loew's—he was appointed chairman of the board in 1955—and exerted a tremendous influence over the output of their production and distribution subsidiary, MGM. • *Mama's Affair* 1921 (p); *East Is West* 1922 (p); *Ashes of Vengeance* 1923 (p); *Our Hospitality* 1923 (p); *The Three Ages* 1923 (p); *Secrets* 1924 (p); *Sherlock, Jr.* 1924 (p); *The General* 1927 (p); *Steamboat Bill, Jr.* 1928 (p); *Spite Marriage* 1929 (exec.p); *Kiki* 1931 (p).

Schepisi, Fred • Director; also producer, screenwriter. • Born Melbourne, Australia, December 26, 1939. Former director of TV commercials who made his mark in the late 1970s and early 80s with sensitively handled dramas such as the probing race study, *The Chant of Jimmie Blacksmith* (1978), and the haunting sci-fi parable, *Iceman* (1984). Schepisi continued to demonstrate his mastery of atmosphere and dramatic rhythm in the intriguing, if slightly overwrought, adaption of the David Hare play, *Plenty* (1985); he teamed with Steve Martin on *Roxanne* (1987), a witty update of the "Cyrano" story, and directed *Plenty* star Meryl Streep for the second time in *A Cry in the Dark* (1988). • *Libido* 1973 (d); *The Devil's Playground* 1976 (d,p,sc); *The Chant of Jimmie Blacksmith* 1978 (d,p,sc); *Barbarosa* 1982 (d); *Iceman* 1984 (d); *Plenty* 1985 (d); *Roxanne* 1987 (d); *A Cry in the Dark* 1988 (d,sc); *The Russia House* 1990 (d,p).

Schiffman, Suzanne • French director, screenwriter • *Educ.* Sorbonne, Paris (art history). Former continuity supervisor for Jean-Luc Godard and François Truffaut who eventually became the latter's assistant director and co-scenarist. The Nathalie Baye character in Truffaut's *Day for Night* (1973)—which earned Schiffman an Oscar nomination for best original screenplay—is a recognizable fictional version of herself. Schiffman has also contributed to the screenplays of several films directed by Jacques Rivette and made her own directorial debut with the coolly assured medieval saga, *Sorceress* (1987). • *Paris Nous Appartient* 1960 (ad); *Baisers voles/Stolen Kisses* 1968 (script supervisor); *Domicile conjugal/Bed and Board* (ad); *L'Enfant sauvage/The Wild Child* 1970 (ad); *Les Deux Anglaises et le Continent/Two English Girls* 1971 (ad); *Out 1: Noli Me Tangere* 1971 (sc); *Une Belle fille come moi/Such a Lovely Kid Like Me* 1972 (ad); *Out 1: Spectre* 1972 (sc); *La Nuit Americaine/Day For Night* 1973 (sc,ad) **(AANBSC)**; *L'Argent de poche/Small Change* 1975 (sc); *L'Histoire d'Adele H./The Story of Adele H.* 1975 (sc,ad); *La Chambre Verte/The Green Room* 1978 (ad); *L'Amour en Fuite/Love on the Run* 1979 (sc,ad); *Le Dernier Metro/The Last Metro* 1980 (ad,sc,dial); *La Femme d'à côté/The Woman Next Door* 1981 (sc,ad); *Le Pont du Nord* 1981 (sc); *Vivement Dimanche/Confidentially Yours* 1982 (sc,ad); *Merry Go Round* 1983 (sc); *L'Amour par terre/Love on the Ground* 1984 (sc,ad); *Hurlevent/Wuthering Heights* 1985 (sc); *Rouge Gorge* 1985 (sc); *Le Moine et la sorciere/Sorceress* 1987 (d,sc,adapt,dial); *Corps Perdus* 1989 (sc); *Femme de papier* 1989 (d,sc).

Schifrin, Lalo • Composer; also arranger, pianist. • Born Buenos Aires, Argentina, June 21, 1932. *Educ.* Paris Conservatoire. Former pianist with the Dizzy Gillespie band who entered film in 1964 and went on to score a number of fine, often action-oriented productions, including *The Cincinatti Kid* (1965), *Cool Hand Luke* (1967), *Bullitt* (1968) and a handful of Clint Eastwood vehicles. Schifrin also wrote the infectious theme music for the TV series, "Mission Impossible." • *Rhino!* 1964 (m); *The Cincinnati Kid* 1965 (m); *The Dark Intruder* 1965 (m); *Once a Thief* 1965 (m); *Blindfold* 1966 (m); *Murderers' Row* 1966 (m); *Way... Way Out* 1966 (m); *Cool Hand Luke* 1967 (m) **(AANBM)**; *The Fox* 1967 (m,m.cond) **(AANBM)**; *The*

President's Analyst 1967 (m); *Sullivan's Empire* 1967 (m); *The Venetian Affair* 1967 (m); *Who's Minding the Mint?* 1967 (m); *The Brotherhood* 1968 (m); *Bullitt* 1968 (m); *Coogan's Bluff* 1968 (m,song); *Hell in the Pacific* 1968 (m); *Sol Madrid* 1968 (m); *Where Angels Go... Trouble Follows* 1968 (m); *Che!* 1969 (m); *Mission Impossible Vs. the Mob* 1969 (m); *I Love My Wife* 1970 (m); *Imago* 1970 (m); *Kelly's Heroes* 1970 (m,m.dir,song); *Pussycat, Pussycat, I Love You* 1970 (m); *WUSA* 1970 (m); *The Beguiled* 1971 (m); *The Christian Licorice Store* 1971 (m); *Dirty Harry* 1971 (m); *The Hellstrom Chronicle* 1971 (m); *Pretty Maids All in a Row* 1971 (m); *THX 1138* 1971 (m); *Joe Kidd* 1972 (m); *Prime Cut* 1972 (m); *Rage* 1972 (m); *To Be Free* 1972 (m); *The Wrath of God* 1972 (m,original score); *Charley Varrick* 1973 (m); *Enter the Dragon* 1973 (m); *Harry in Your Pocket* 1973 (m); *Hit* 1973 (m); *Magnum Force* 1973 (m); *The Neptune Factor* 1973 (m); *Golden Needles* 1974 (m); *Man on a Swing* 1974 (m); *The Four Musketeers* 1975 (m); *Hustle* 1975 (m); *The Master Gunfighter* 1975 (m); *Day of the Animals* 1976 (m); *The Eagle Has Landed* 1976 (m); *Sky Riders* 1976 (m); *Special Delivery* 1976 (m); *St. Ives* 1976 (m); *Voyage of the Damned* 1976 (m) **(AANBM)**; *The Manitou* 1977 (m); *Nunzio* 1977 (m); *Rollercoaster* 1977 (m,m.dir); *Telefon* 1977 (m); *The Cat From Outer Space* 1978 (m); *Return From Witch Mountain* 1978 (m); *The Amityville Horror* 1979 (m) **(AANBM)**; *Boulevard Nights* 1979 (m,song); *The Concorde—Airport '79* 1979 (m); *Escape to Athena* 1979 (m); *Love and Bullets* 1979 (m); *The Big Brawl* 1980 (m); *Brubaker* 1980 (m); *The Competition* 1980 (m,m.dir,song) **(AANBS)**; *The Nude Bomb* 1980 (m,song); *Serial* 1980 (m,song); *When Time Ran Out* 1980 (m); *Buddy Buddy* 1981 (m); *Caveman* 1981 (m); *Loophole* 1981 (m); *The Seduction* 1981 (m); *A Stranger Is Watching* 1981 (m); *Los Viernes de la Eternidad* 1981 (m); *Airplane II: The Sequel* 1982 (song); *Amityville II: The Possession* 1982 (m); *Class of 1984* 1982 (m,song); *Doctor Detroit* 1982 (m); *Fast Walking* 1982 (m); *The Sting II* 1982 (m,m.adapt,orch) **(AANBSS)**; *The Osterman Weekend* 1983 (m); *Sudden Impact* 1983 (m,song); *Tank* 1984 (m); *Bad Medicine* 1985 (m); *The Mean Season* 1985 (m); *The New Kids* 1985 (m); *Black Moon Rising* 1986 (m); *The Ladies Club* 1986 (m); *The Fourth Protocol* 1987 (m,m.dir); *The Silence at Bethany* 1987 (m); *Berlin Blues* 1988 (m,song); *The Dead Pool* 1988 (m); *Little Sweetheart* 1988 (m); *Return to the River Kwai* 1989 (m); *Naked Tango* 1990 (m).

Schildkraut, Joseph • Actor • Born Vienna, Austria, March 22, 1895; died 1964. *Educ.* AADA, New York. Son of renowned Viennese actor Rudolph Schildkraut who studied at the American Academy of Dramatic Arts before joining Max Reinhart's company in 1913, where he soon emerged as a star. Schildkraut set down in the US in 1920 and almost immediately established himself as a matinee idol on Broadway. He pursued a simultaneous screen career, first in debonair leading roles and later in a number of oily, villainous characterizations. He gave notable performances in *The Life of Emile Zola* (1937) and *The Diary of Anne Frank* (1959). • *Orphans of the Storm* 1921; *The Song of Love* 1923; *The Road to Yesterday* 1925; *Meet the Prince* 1926; *Shipwrecked* 1926; *Young April* 1926; *The Forbidden Woman* 1927; *The Heart Thief* 1927; *King of Kings* 1927; *The Blue Danube* 1928; *Tenth Avenue* 1928; *The Mississippi Gambler* 1929; *Show Boat* 1929; *Cock O' the Walk* 1930; *Night Ride* 1930; *Cleopatra* 1934; *Sisters Under the Skin* 1934; *Viva Villa* 1934; *The Crusades* 1935; *The Garden of Allah* 1936; *Lady Behave* 1937; *The Lancer Spy* 1937; *The Life of Emile Zola* 1937 **(AABSA)**; *Slave Ship* 1937; *Souls at Sea* 1937; *The Baroness and the Butler* 1938; *Marie Antoinette* 1938; *Suez* 1938; *Idiot's Delight* 1939; *Lady of the Tropics* 1939; *The Man in the Iron Mask* 1939; *Mr. Moto Takes a Vacation* 1939; *Pack Up Your Troubles* 1939; *The Rains Came* 1939; *The Three Musketeers* 1939; *Meet the Wildcat* 1940; *Phantom Raiders* 1940; *Rangers of Fortune* 1940; *The Shop Around the Corner* 1940; *The Parson of Panamint* 1941; *The Cheaters* 1945; *Flame of the Barbary Coast* 1945; *Monsieur Beaucaire* 1946; *The Plainsman and the Lady* 1946; *Northwest Outpost* 1947; *The Gallant Legion* 1948; *Old Los Angeles* 1948; *The Diary of Anne Frank* 1959; *King of the Roaring 20's - The Story of Arnold Rothstein* 1961; *The Greatest Story Ever Told* 1965.

Schlesinger, John • Director; also actor. • Born London, February 16, 1926. John Schlesinger is celebrated for his ability to elicit sensitive performances from his actors, a skill which draws on his own experience on the British stage in the 1950s. His style is also influenced by techniques he developed while directing TV documentaries—a period of his career characterized by extensive location shooting, tight production schedules and an emphasis on the role of editing in shaping narrative structure.

Schlesinger first became interested in film at the age of 11, when he received a 9.5 mm movie camera as a gift. While serving with the Royal Engineers during WWII he made an amateur film, *Horrors*, and performed as a magician in the Combined Services Entertainment Unit. When he resumed his education in 1945 he immersed himself in the theater, joining the Oxford University Dramatic Society and soon becoming president of the Oxford Experimental Theatre Company. (He would continue to direct for the stage, in between movie assignments, throughout the 1960s and 70s.)

From 1952 to 1957 Schlesinger worked in England, Australia and New Zealand, appearing in five feature films, acting in nearly 20 plays with various repertory companies and performing on TV and radio. During this period, a chance meeting with director/producer Roy Boulting catalyzed his interest in photography and filmmaking and led to the creation, with theatrical agent Basil Appleby, of a 15-minute documentary, *Sunday in the Park* (1956). The film brought Schlesinger a series of documentary assignments for the BBC. After a stint as a second unit director, he was commissioned to make an industrial documentary of daily life in London's Waterloo Station. The poignant result, *Terminus* (1961), achieved nationwide commercial distribution and earned him a Venice Festival Gold Lion and a British Academy Award.

Motivated in part by the festival success of *Terminus*, producer Joseph Janni offered Schlesinger his first shot at a feature film with *A Kind of Loving* (1962). The result was a critical and financial success which won the Golden Bear at the Berlin Festival and propelled its director into the front rank of young British filmmakers. In *Billy Liar* (1963), Schlesinger continued to examine the themes of inarticulate ambition and frustrated tenderness he had explored in *A Kind of Loving*. Both films showed the influence of the British Free Cinema movement, with its emphasis on the constraints and restrictions of working-class life. Schlesinger then moved into very different terrain with *Darling* (1965), a flashy satire of "swinging London" that certified its lead actress, Julie Christie, as an international star when she won the Academy Award for best actress.

Midnight Cowboy (1969) was perhaps Schlesinger's greatest success commercially and critically, winning Oscars for best picture and best director and launching a long but rather turbulent Hollywood career for Schlesinger. Films such as *Sunday, Bloody Sunday* (1971), *The Day of the Locust* (1975) and *Marathon Man* (1976) all bear witness to Schlesinger's remarkable ability to weave meticulously observed, realistic backgrounds into his complex studies of human relationships.

Schlesinger's later films have included *The Believers* (1987), a gripping contemporary horror story starring Martin Sheen and Helen Shaver, *Madame Sousatzka* (1988), about a London piano teacher (Shirley MacLaine) and her gifted young student, and *Pacific Heights* (1990), possibly the first thriller to weave its plot around the problems faced by landlords in their attempt to evict a bad tenant. TZ • *The Last Man to Hang* 1956 (a); *Terminus* 1961 (d); *A Kind of Loving* 1962 (d); *Billy Liar* 1963 (d);

Darling 1965 (d,story) **(AANBD)**; *Far From the Madding Crowd* 1967 (d); *Midnight Cowboy* 1969 (d) **(AABD)**; *Sunday Bloody Sunday* 1971 (d) **(AANBD)**; *Visions of Eight* 1973 (d); *The Day of the Locust* 1975 (d); *Marathon Man* 1976 (d); *Yanks* 1979 (d); *Honky Tonk Freeway* 1981 (d); *Privileged* 1982 (consultant d); *An Englishman Abroad* 1983 (d); *The Falcon and the Snowman* 1985 (d,p); *50 Years of Action!* 1986 (a); *The Believers* 1987 (d,p); *Madame Sousatzka* 1988 (d,sc); *Pacific Heights* 1990 (d).

Schlöndorff, Volker • Director; also screenwriter, producer. • Born Wiesbaden, Germany, March 31, 1939. *Educ.* Sorbonne, Paris (political science); IDHEC, Paris. Volker Schlöndorff is one of the major directors of the New German Cinema, the group of fimmakers who, in the late 1960s and early 70s, revitalized a moribund German film culture. He studied at the *Institut des Hautes Etudes Cinématographiques* in Paris in the late 1950s and, between 1960 and 1964, worked as an assistant to directors including Louis Malle, Alain Resnais and Jean-Pierre Mélville.

Schlöndorff's first feature, *Young Torless* (1966), based on a classic novel by Robert Musil about coming of age in an elite Austrian military academy, is considered a milestone of the New German cinema. Greeted with critical acclaim at a number of international film festivals, it also gained a small but devoted popular following at home. It was the first of many literary adaptations by the director, evincing a continuing predeliction for highly structured narrative films with a leftist political perspective, directed at a mass audience.

Schlöndorff's next two films, *A Degree of Murder* (1967), starring Anita Pallenberg with a score by Brian Jones of the Rolling Stones, and *Michael Kohlhaas* (1969), based on a novella by Heinrich von Kleist, were both action dramas that were critical and box-office failures. His 1969 adaptation of Brecht's *Baal (1969)*, starring Rainer Werner Fassbinder, and *The Sudden Wealth of the Poor People of Kombach* (1970), his best film since *Torless* and one of the few not adapted from a literary source, fared better with the critics. During this period, he married a young actress who had appeared in both films, Margarethe von Trotta, forming a fruitful writer-director collaboration which would last until von Trotta began directing her own films in 1977.

The von Trotta-Schlöndorff collaboration produced the director's best films of the early and mid-1970s: *A Free Woman* (1972), an ironic feminist commentary on divorce; *The Lost Honor of Katharina Blum* (1975), adapted from Heinrich Böll's bestseller about a woman falsely accused of terrorism; and *Coup de Grace* (1976), based upon a 1936 Marguerite Yourcenar novel concerning the radicalization of a young aristocratic woman during the revolutionary period following WWII.

Schlöndorff's best known, and most successful, work to date is his 1979 adaptation of Günter Grass's *The Tin Drum*, a rollicking account of the rise of fascism as seen through the eyes of a boy who literally and figuratively refuses to grow up. *Katharina Blum* and *Tin Drum* became two of the most financially successful German films ever made, with the latter winning the Academy Award for best foreign film.

Although Schlöndorff lacks the innovative skill or visionary power of such colleagues as Fassbinder, Kluge, Wenders and Herzog, he has, unlike them, adapted well to the international film market and to working in the US. His 1985 adaptation for American TV of *Death of a Salesman*, starring Dustin Hoffman, was well-received, and his most recent film is an adaptation of Margaret Atwood's futurist/feminist parable, *The Handmaid's Tale* (1990), featuring an all-star cast and a screenplay by Harold Pinter. At his best, like Bertolucci and Oliver Stone, Schlöndorff is a polished filmmaker capable of presenting sensitive and controversial social issues to a mass audience in an entertaining and enlightening manner. RM • *Le Doulos* 1963 (ad,ass. p,uncred.a); *Der Junge Torless/Young Torless* 1966 (d,sc); *Mord und Totschlag/A Degree of Murder* 1967 (d,sc); *Baal* 1969 (d); *Michael Kohlhaas - Der Rebell* 1969 (d); *Rio das Mortes* 1970 (idea); *Die Moral der Ruth Halbfass* 1972 (d,sc); *Der Plötzliche Reichtum der Armen Leute Von Kombach/The Sudden Wealth of the Poor People of Kombach* 1970 (d,sc); *Strohfeuer/A Free Woman* 1972 (d,sc); *Die Verlorene Ehre der Katharina Blum/The Lost Honor of Katharina Blum* 1975 (d,sc); *Der Fangschus/The Coup de Grace* 1976 (d); *Deutschland im Herbst* 1978 (d); *Die Blechtrommel/The Tin Drum* 1979 (d,sc); *Kaleidoskop: Valeska Gert, Nur zum Spass-nur zum Spiel* 1979 (d,p,sc); *Der Kandidat* 1980 (d); *Die Falschung* 1981 (d,sc); *Krieg und Frieden/War and Peace* 1982 (d); *Un Amour de Swann/Swann in Love* 1984 (d,sc.adapt); *Private Conversations* 1985 (a); *Vermischte Nachrichten* 1986 (d); *The Handmaid's Tale* 1990 (d); *Voyager* 1991 (d,sc).

Schneider, Maria • Actress • Born Paris, March 27, 1952. Sultry actress who began appearing in secondary parts in 1971 and came to prominence opposite Marlon Brando in Bernardo Bertolucci's study of existential eroticism, *Last Tango in Paris* (1972). Schneider starred opposite Jack Nicholson in Antonioni's *The Passenger* (1975), but has done little of note since. Daughter of actor Daniel Gelin. • *Last Tango in Paris* 1972; *Baby Sitter—Un maledetto pasticcio* 1975; *The Passenger* 1975; *Violanta* 1976; *Io Sono Mia* 1977; *La Derobade* 1979; *Haine* 1979; *Een Vrouw Als Eva* 1979; *Mamma Dracula* 1980; *Cercasi Gesu* 1982; *Balles Perdues* 1983; *The Song For Europe* 1985; *Residence surveillee* 1987; *Mama Dracula* 1988; *Bunker Palace Hotel* 1989.

Schneider, Romy • Actress • Born Rosemarie Albach-Retty, Vienna, September 23, 1938; died 1982. Sensual, intelligent leading lady who first earned international attention with her role in the Visconti-directed episode of *Boccaccio '70* (1962). Schneider became something of a fixture in Claude Sautet's studies of French middle-class life; she also appeared in films by Orson Welles (*The Trial* 1962), Clive Donner (*What's New, Pussycat?* 1965), Joseph Losey (*The Assassination of Trotsky* 1972) and Bertrand Tavernier (the underrated *Death Watch* 1979). Her career, still in full bloom, was cut tragically short by a heart attack in 1982. Daughter of a leading Austrian theatrical family; actors Wolf Albach-Retty and Magda Schneider, both born in 1908. • *Der Letzte Mann* 1955; *Montpi* 1957; *The Story of Vickie* 1957; *Ein Engel auf Erden* 1959; *Katia* 1960; *Boccaccio '70* 1962; *The Trial* 1962; *The Cardinal* 1963; *The Victors* 1963; *Good Neighbor Sam* 1964; *What's New, Pussycat?* 1965; *10:30 P.M. Summer* 1966; *Otley* 1968; *My Lover, My Son* 1969; *La Piscine* 1969; *L'Amante* 1970; *Max et les Ferrailleurs* 1970; *Qui?* 1970; *Bloomfield* 1971; *La Califfa* 1971; *The Assassination of Trotsky* 1972; *Cesar et Rosalie* 1972; *Ludwig* 1972; *Le Train* 1973; *Un Amour de pluie* 1974; *Le Mouton Enrage* 1974; *Le Trio Infernal* 1974; *L'Important c'est d'aimer* 1975; *Les Innocents aux mains Sales* 1975; *Le Vieux Fusil* 1975; *Mado* 1976; *Gruppenbild Mit Dame* 1977; *Une Histoire simple* 1978; *Bloodline* 1979; *Clair de Femme* 1979; *La Mort en Direct/Death Watch* 1979; *La Banquiere* 1980; *Fantasma d'Amore* 1981; *Garde a Vue* 1981; *La Passante* 1983.

Schoonmaker, Thelma • Editor • Born US, 1945. Distinguished editor who has enjoyed a lengthy association with Martin Scorsese, whom she met at a New York University film class. Schoonmaker cut Scorsese's debut feature, *Who's That Knocking at My Door* (1968), collaborated with him on the editing of Michael Wadleigh's monumental *Woodstock* (1970), and has worked on all of his films since *Raging Bull* (1980). Married to director Michael Powell from 1984 until his death in 1990. • *Passages From James Joyce's Finnegans Wake* 1965 (ed); *Who's That Knocking at My Door?* 1968 (ed); *Woodstock* 1970 (ad,ed) **(AANBED)**; *The Kids Are Alright* 1979 (special consultant); *Raging Bull* 1980 (ed) **(AABED)**; *The King of Comedy* 1983 (ed,prod.sup); *After Hours* 1985 (ed); *The Color of Money* 1986 (ed); *The Last Temptation of Christ* 1988 (ed); *New York Stories* 1989 (ed—"Life Lessons"); *GoodFellas* 1990 (ed).

Schorm, Evald • Director; also actor. • Born Prague, Czechoslovakia, December 15, 1931; died December 14, 1988, Prague. *Educ.* FAMU, Prague. Highly acclaimed figure whose films, though more traditional in form than those of contemporaries such as Jan Nemec and Vera Chytilová, have been seen as the moral and philosophical center of the Czech New Wave. Schorm began making documentaries while a student at FAMU and turned to features in 1964, repeatedly examing the conflict between individual ideals and social structures. Schorm's central characters, as in his impressive debut *Everyday Courage* (1964), his most celebrated film, *The Return of the Prodigal Son* (1966), and the Josef Skvorecky-scripted farce, *End of a Priest* (1968), are often alienated outsiders, or people cut off from their usual environs, who must face the consequences of their societal maladjustment. Not surprisingly, all three films encountered trouble with the Communist authorities.

Heavy-lidded, tall and prematurely gray, Schorm acted in a number of films directed by his colleagues. The most interesting of these roles was in Nemec's surrealistic allegory, *A Report on the Party and the Guests* (1966), in which Schorm is symbolically cast as the only "guest" who takes action and leaves the notorious "party."

Remaining in his country after the Soviet invasion, Schorm worked primarily as an opera director and occasionally for TV. He died of a heart attack one day before his 57th birthday. • *Everyday Courage* 1964 (d); *Navrat Ztracencho Syna/Return of the Prodigal Son* 1966 (d); *O Slavnosti a Hostech/A Report on the Party and the Guests* 1966 (a); *Fararuv Konec/The End of a Priest* 1968 (d); *Zert/The Joke* 1968 (a); *Den Sedmy Osma Noc/The Seventh Day, the Eighth Night* 1969 (d); *Singing on the Treadmill* 1974 (a); *Vlastne Se Nic Nestalo/Killing With Kindness* 1989 (d).

Schrader, Paul • Screenwriter; also director. • Born Grand Rapids, MI, July 22, 1946. *Educ.* Calvin College, Grand Rapids (theology, philosophy); Columbia; UCLA (cinema studies). Former critic of renown whose contributions to American cinema include three striking screenplays for Martin Scorsese and a directorial output that has unrelentingly and inventively examined both true-life stories and controversial social issues.

Schrader began his career as a film critic in Los Angeles and published a still-influential study, *Transcendental Style in Film: Ozu, Bresson, Dreyer*, in 1972. His first produced screenplay, cowritten with his brother Leonard (*Kiss of the Spider Woman* 1985) and Robert Towne, was for the Japanese underworld thriller, *The Yakuza* (1975). Schrader collaborated with Scorsese for the first time on *Taxi Driver* (1976), a classic study of urban alienation, and made his directorial debut with *Blue Collar* (1978), a gripping, muckraking account of autoworker exploitation in Detroit. After several flawed but interesting films, he attracted attention with the ambitious, multi-layered biopic, *Mishima* (1985), a portrait of controversial Japanese author Yukio Mishima. The film took the "artistic merit" prize at Cannes for "John Bailey's visual conception, Eiko Ishioka's designs and the music of Philip Glass."

Schrader's subsequent work has encompassed controversial subjects ranging from the life of Jesus, in the Scorsese-directed *The Last Temptation of Christ* (1988), to terrorism, in 1988's *Patty Hearst*. Married to actress Mary Beth Hurt. • *The Yakuza* 1975 (sc); *Obsession* 1976 (sc,story); *Taxi Driver* 1976 (sc); *Rolling Thunder* 1977 (sc,story); *Blue Collar* 1978 (d,sc,song); *Old Boyfriends* 1978 (exec.p,sc); *Hardcore* 1979 (d,sc); *American Gigolo* 1980 (d,sc); *Raging Bull* 1980 (sc); *Cat People* 1982 (d); *De Weg Naar Bresson* 1984 (a); *Mishima: A Life in Four Chapters* 1985 (d,sc); *The Mosquito Coast* 1986 (sc); *Light of Day* 1987 (d,sc); *The Last Temptation of Christ* 1988 (sc); *Patty Hearst* 1988 (d); *The Comfort of Strangers* 1990 (d); *Hollywood Mavericks* 1990 (a).

Schroder, Rick • *aka* Ricky Schroder, Ricky Schroeder • Actor • Born Staten Island, NY, April 3, 1970. Blonde juvenile model and actor who came to prominence with a heart-rending performance in the 1979 remake of *The Champ*. Schroder went on to star in the popular TV series, "Silver Spoons" (1982-86) and has appeared in several TV movies and miniseries, notably 1989's *Lonesome Dove*. • *The Champ* 1979; *The Earthling* 1980; *The Last Flight of Noah's Ark* 1980; *Across the Tracks* 1990.

Schroeder, Barbet • Director, producer; also actor, critic. • Born Teheran, Iran, April 26, 1941. *Educ.* Sorbonne, Paris (philosophy). Former film critic (for *Cahiers du Cinema*), photojournalist (in India) and jazz impresario who formed the *Les Films du Losange* production company with director Eric Rohmer in 1962. Schroeder produced all of Rohmer's early films, beginning with the as-yet-unreleased short, *La Boulangère de Monceau* (1962), which he also narrated. After producing, appearing in and assisting with several other New Wave films, Schroeder directed his first feature, *More*, in 1969. He has been acclaimed for his feature-length documentaries, notably *General Idi Amin Dada* (1974), a portrait of the former Ugandan despot.

Schroeder first attracted attention in the US for *Barfly* (1987), an engaging account of a low-life, alcohol-sodden writer (Mickey Rourke) modelled not-too-loosely on Charles Bukowski. His *The Charles Bukowski Tapes*, a series of fascinating and highly entertaining "interviews" with the author made during early work on *Barfly*, was shown on French TV and at New York's Public Theater in 1989.

Schroeder's most recent project was *Reversal of Fortune* (1990), a darkly humorous, multi-layered account of the Claus and Sunny von Bulow scandal based on the book by Harvard law professor Alan Dershowitz. The film featured finely turned performances from Jeremy Irons, Glenn Close and Ron Silver. • *Les Carabiniers* 1963 (a); *Paris Vu Par...* 1965 (a,p); *La Collectionneuse* 1966 (p); *Ma nuit chez Maud/My Night at Maud's* 1969 (p); *More* 1969 (d,sc,story); *L'Amour, l'après-midi/Chloe in the Afternoon* 1972 (p); *La Vallée* 1972 (d,sc); *Céline et Julie vont en bateau/Céline and Julie Go Boating* 1973 (a,exec.p); *General Idi Amin Dada* 1974 (d,sc,idea); *Maîtresse* 1975 (d,sc); *Koko le gorille qui parle* 1978 (d,sc,commentary); *Perceval le gallois* 1978 (p); *Roberte* 1978 (a); *Sauve qui peut la vie* 1980 (subtitles); *Passion* 1982 (subtitles); *Mauvaise Conduite* 1983 (p); *Les Tricheurs* 1983 (d,sc); *The Charles Bukowski Tapes* 1985 (d); *Barfly* 1987 (d,p); *Wait Until Spring, Bandini* 1989 (a); *The Golden Boat* 1990 (a); *Reversal of Fortune* 1990 (d).

Schüfftan, Eugen • *aka* Eugene Shuftan • Director of photography • Born Breslau, Germany, July 21, 1893; died 1977. Former architect, painter and sculptor who entered film in the early 1920s as a special effects artist. He invented the Schüfftan Process, a technique which allowed a single camera to combine live action with shots of miniature models by means of a specially adapted mirror. The process was used in films including Fritz Lang's *Metropolis* (1926) and Hitchcock's *Blackmail* (1929) before being supplanted by the less time-consuming "matte" technique.

Schüftan made several innovations in documentary techniques, particularly with his photography on *Menschen am Sonntag* (1929) for Robert Siodmak, with whom he would later collaborate in Hollywood. After fleeing Germany in 1933 he became one of the most influential, and cosmopolitan, of cinematographers, working with directors including Marcel Carne (*Drole de drame* 1937, *Quai des brumes* 1938), Max Ophuls, Rene Clair, George Franju (*La Tete contre les murs* 1958) and Robert Rossen (*The Hustler* 1961, *Lilith* 1964). • *Metropolis* 1926 (fx,ph); *Konigin Luise/Queen Louise* 1927 (ph); *Menschen am Sonntag/People on Sunday* 1929 (ph); *Abschied* 1930 (ph); *Das Ekel* 1931 (ph); *Die Herrin von Atlantis* 1932 (ph); *Der Läufer von Marathon* 1933 (ph); *La Crise Est Finie* 1934 (ph); *Du Haut en Bas* 1934 (ph); *La Tendre Ennemie, Le Scandale* 1936 (ph); *Bizarre Bizarre, Mademoiselle Docteur* 1937 (ph); *Mollenard* 1937 (ph); *The Shanghai*

Drama 1938 (ph); *Port of Shadows* 1938 (ph); *Sans Landmain, Les Musiciens du Ciel* 1939 (ph); *L'Emigrante* 1940 (ph); *It Happened Tomorrow* 1944 (tech.d); *The Dark Mirror* 1946 (tech.d); *Women in the Night* 1948 (ph); *Gunman in the Streets* 1950 (ph); *The Respectable Prostitute* 1952 (ph); *The Crimson Curtain* 1952 (ph); *Marianne de ma Jeunesse* 1954 (ph); *Ulysses* 1955 (fx,ph); *La Tete contre les Murs* 1958 (ph); *The Bloody Brood* 1959 (ph); *The Horror Chamber of Dr. Faustus* 1960 (ph); *Un Couple* 1960 (ph); *The Hustler* 1961 (ph) **(AABPH)**; *Something Wild* 1961 (ph); *Captain Sinbad* 1963 (ph); *Lilith* 1964 (ph); *Trois Chambres a Manhattan* 1965 (ph); *The Doctor Says* 1966 (ph).

Schulberg, Budd • Author; also screenwriter. • Born Budd Wilson Schulberg, New York, NY, March 27, 1914. *Educ.* Dartmouth. Son of producer and publicist B.P. Schulberg who began his career with Paramount, working as a publicist from the age of 17 and a screenwriter two years later. He was dismissed from the studio in 1939 after the failure of *Winter Carnival*, on which he collaborated with an ailing F. Scott Fitzgerald. In 1941 Schulberg penned the controversial roman à clef, *What Makes Sammy Run?*, a classic satire of Hollywood power, corruption and pretention. He joined John Ford's documentary unit during WWII and "named names" before the House Un-American Activities Committee in 1951 (an experience that he obliquely examined in his screenplay for Elia Kazan's gripping 1954 social drama, *On the Waterfront*).

Schulberg also wrote the cynical boxing novel *The Harder They Fall* (1947), which provided the basis for the 1956 film of the same name; he again collaborated with Kazan on his blistering exposé of media demagoguery, *A Face in the Crowd* (1957). Husband of actresses Virginia Ray (1936-42), Virginia Anderson (1943-64) and Geraldine Brooks (1964-77). • *Little Orphan Annie* 1938 (sc); *Winter Carnival* 1939 (sc,adapt); *Week-End For Three* 1941 (story); *Cinco Fueron Escogidos* 1942 (story); *City Without Men* 1943 (story); *Government Girl* 1943 (adapt); *On the Waterfront* 1954 (sc,story) **(AABSC)**; *The Harder They Fall* 1956 (from novel); *A Face in the Crowd* 1957 (sc,from short story "Your Arkansas Traveler" in book *Some Faces in the Crowd*,song); *Wind Across the Everglades* 1958 (sc,story); *Joe Louis—For All Time* 1984 (p,sc).

Schumacher, Joel • Director; also screenwriter. • Born New York, NY, 1939. *Educ.* Parson's School of Design. Former window display artist and fashion designer who entered film as a costume artist and went on to contribute screenplays to such films as *Car Wash* (1976) and *The Wiz* (1978). Schumacher made his feature directorial debut with *The Incredible Shrinking Woman* (1981), a quasi-feminist spoof starring Lily Tomlin. Most of his subsequent output has been mainstream Hollywood fare, ranging from the "brat pack" vehicles, *St. Elmo's Fire* (1985) and *Flatliners* (1990), to the saccharine romantic comedy *Cousins* (1989), a remake of the popular French film, *Cousin, Cousine* (1975). • *Car Wash* 1976 (sc); *Sparkle* 1976 (sc,story); *The Wiz* 1978 (sc); *The Incredible Shrinking Woman* 1981 (d); *D.C. Cab* 1983 (d,sc,story); *St. Elmo's Fire* 1985 (d,sc); *The Lost Boys* 1987 (d); *Cousins* 1989 (d); *Flatliners* 1990 (d).

Schwarzenegger, Arnold • Actor; also bodybuilder. • Born Graz, Austria, July 30, 1947. *Educ.* University of Wisconsin (business, economics). Three-time Mr. Universe and seven-time Mr. Olympia who, in the course of 20 years, has become one of the world's leading box-office attractions, married into one of America's foremost families and built a thriving business and real estate empire.

Schwarzenegger played forgettable roles in several 1970s movies, first gaining attention as the subject of George Butler's fine documentary, *Pumping Iron* (1976). He earned a Golden Globe as best newcomer for his role in Bob Rafelson's *Stay Hungry* (1975) and starred in two ludicrous swordplay sagas, *Conan the Barbarian* (1982) and *Conan the Destroyer* (1984), each of which grossed over $100 million worldwide. Schwarzenegger's screen persona—a physique that strains the imagination combined with a thick Austrian accent—took a major credibility boost with *The Terminator* (1984), which cast him as an alien übermensch and established his trademark, automaton-like delivery of minimal lines such as "I'll be back." The film made him an international star, established the careers of director James Cameron and producer Gale Ann Hurd and set the pace for many of the action-adventure, special effects-driven movies that would dominate the global market in the 1980s. Schwarzenegger has continued to star in such films, with the exception of the preposterous, but successful, *Twins*, a 1988 comedy which paired him with Danny DeVito. The odd turkey notwithstanding, his films have grossed over $1 billion worldwide over the last decade. (He has also killed over 275 people onscreen.)

Schwarzenegger's has been a carefully orchestrated career, reflecting an aggressive business and marketing acumen which has also brought him success in other fields (he now produces the "Mr. Universe" and "Mr. Olympia" pageants he once dominated). With an eagerness to adapt reminiscent of some of the earlier immigrants who founded America's entertainment industry, he has wholeheartedly embraced the American way, becoming a naturalized citizen in 1983 and joining the country's nobility with his 1986 marriage to Maria Shriver. Schwarzenegger was appointed Chairman of the President's Council on Physical Fitness and Sports in 1990. JDP • *Stay Hungry* 1975; *Pumping Iron* 1976; *The Villain* 1979; *Conan the Barbarian* 1982; *Conan the Destroyer* 1984; *The Terminator* 1984; *Commando* 1985; *Red Sonja* 1985; *Raw Deal* 1986; *Predator* 1987; *The Running Man* 1987; *Red Heat* 1988; *Twins* 1988; *Kindergarten Cop* 1990; *Total Recall* 1990; *Terminator 2: Judgment Day* 1991 (a).

Schygulla, Hanna • Actress • Born Kattowitz, Germany (now Poland), December 25, 1943. One of the most celebrated European leading ladies of the last two decades. Schygulla's career was sparked by Rainer Werner Fassbinder, whom she met while taking an acting class in Munich and with whom she worked at the Munich Action Theater. A luminous, enigmatic beauty in the classic Teutonic mold, Schygulla provided the dramatic cornerstone of many of Fassbinder's finest films, appearing in nearly 20 features directed by him between 1969 (*Love is Colder than Death*) and 1981 (*Lili Marleen*). She has also worked with Volker Schlöndorff (*Circle of Deceit* 1981), Jean-Luc Godard (*Passion* 1982) and Andrzej Wajda (*A Love in Germany* 1983). • *Der Brautigam, die Komodiantin und der Zuhalter* 1968; *Gotter der Pest* 1969; *Katzelmacher* 1969; *Liebe Ist Kälter als der Tod/Love is Colder Than Death* 1969; *Das Kaffeehaus* 1970; *Die Niklashauser Fahrt* 1970; *Pioniere in Ingolstadt* 1970; *Rio das Mortes* 1970; *Warum Lauft Herr R. Amok?* 1970; *Warnung Vor Einer Heiligen Nutte* 1971; *Die Bitteren Tränen der Petra von Kant/The Bitter Tears of Petra von Kant* 1972; *Bremer Freiheit* 1972; *Der Handler der vier Jahreszeiten* 1972; *Wildwechsel* 1972; *Fontane Effi Briest/Effi Briest* 1974; *Ansichten Eines Clowns* 1975; *Falsche Bewegung* 1975; *Die Ehe der Maria Braun/The Marriage of Maria Braun* 1978; *Die Dritte Generation* 1979; *Berlin Alexanderplatz* 1980; *Die Falschung/Circle of Deceit* 1981; *Lili Marleen* 1981; *Antonieta* 1982; *Heller Wahn* 1982; *La Nuit de Varennes* 1982; *Passion* 1982; *Storia di Piera* 1982; *Eine Liebe in Deutschland/A Love in Germany* 1983; *Il Futuro è Donna* 1984; *The Delta Force* 1986; *Forever, Lulu* 1986; *Miss Arizona* 1988; *El Verano de la Señora Forbes* 1988; *Abraham's Gold* 1990.

Scofield, Paul • Actor • Born Hurstpierpoint, England, January 21, 1922. Commanding English stage actor who began appearing in films in 1954. Scofield garnered acclaim for his performance as Sir Thomas More in the adaptation of the Robert Bolt play, *A Man For All Seasons* (1966); he was also effective in the title role of Peter Brook's *King Lear* (1971). • *That Lady* 1955; *Carve Her Name With Pride* 1964; *The Train* 1964; *A Man For All Seasons* 1966

(AABA); *King Lear* 1971; *A Delicate Balance* 1973; *Scorpio* 1973; *1919* 1984; *Mr. Corbett's Ghost* 1986; *Henry V* 1989; *When the Whales Came* 1989; *Hamlet* 1990.

Scola, Ettore • Director, screenwriter • Born Trevico, Italy, May 10, 1931. *Educ.* University of Jurisprudence, Rome (law). A director and screenwriter, working in the traditions of postwar Italian comedy, who makes films marked by psychological insight and political awareness. A member of the Italian Communist Party, he celebrates the underdog without taking his eyes off the wider social landscape.

Scola grew up in Rome, the son of a doctor, living in a house with a large extended family much like the one he would later portray in *The Family* (1987). His interest in humorous writing began at an early age; by 21 he had already contributed jokes, illustrations and articles to satirical magazines, written for radio and worked as an uncredited collaborator on some 50 comedy screenplays, including vehicles for Italian comedians Alberto Sordi and Toto. Although he studied at the University of Jurisprudence in Rome, he never seriously considered practicing law. Scola received his first screen credit in 1954 and went on to collaborate on several dozen comedic scripts with such writers as Ruggero Maccari, Agenore Incrocci, Furio Scarpelli and Rodolfo Sonego, for directors that included Dino Risi and Antonio Pietrangeli.

Scola's directorial debut came with the episodic comedy *Let's Talk About Women* (1964), in which Vittorio Gassman encounters nine females of various types. In 1969, *Inspector Pepe* marked a shift in the director's interests toward more substantial topics. The popular dark comedy, *The Pizza Triangle* (1970), had Monica Vitti choosing between Marcello Mastroianni and Giancarlo Giannini. The bittersweet epic, *We All Loved Each Other So Much* (1974), about three very different men who become friends during the Resistance and later go their separate ways, examines a generation's disillusionment—summed up in the line, "We thought we could change the world, but the world has changed us."

The late 1970s saw Scola working on a variety of successful films, including *Down and Dirty* (1976), about lowlifes in Rome's shanty towns; *A Special Day* (1977), set in 1938 Rome, about a lonely housewife (Sophia Loren) and an anti-Fascist homosexual (Marcello Mastroianni); and *The Terrace* (1980), where a group of intellectuals regularly meet and discuss their disappointments in life and work. His most ambitious film to date was *La nuit de Varennes* (1982), a historical fable that examines politics and romance during the French Revolution; it fancifully brings together such figures as Casanova and Thomas Paine.

The stylish *Le Bal* (1983), wholly set in a Parisian dance hall, depicts changes in the establishment and its customers through eight key moments in French history between 1936 and 1983—without one line of dialogue. Changing styles of dress and uniform, music, dance and modes of behavior tell all. Scola suffered a heart attack during production of the film, but production was only briefly delayed while he made a speedy recovery.

The Family, Scola's most autobiographical film, warmly depicts the life of an extended family living in a large house through five generations. It chronicles 70 years of European history, starting with WWI, without ever leaving the confines of the house. The tremors of family life reflect the changes in society throughout the years; by the end, the family has changed but is still intact.

Having directed some 25 feature films, Scola continues to explore his fascination with history and with the relationship between society and the individual. He prefers to work with a familiar group of associates, including actors Marcello Mastroianni and Vittorio Gassman, screenwriter Ruggero Maccari, production designer Luciano Ricceri, composer Armando Trovaioli and his daughter Paola as assistant director. VMC • *La Congiuntura* 1964 (d); *Se Permettete parliamo di donna/Let's Talk About Women* 1964 (d); *Made in Italy* 1965 (sc,story); *Thrilling* 1965 (d); *L'Arcidiavolo* 1966 (d); *Le Dolci signore* 1967 (sc); *Il Profeta* 1967 (sc,story); *Riusciranno i nostri eroi a ritrovare l'amico misteriosamente scomparso in Africa?* 1968 (d); *Il Commissario Pepe* 1969 (d); *Dramma della gelosia (tutti i particolari in cronaca/The Pizza Triangle)* 1970 (d); *Permette? Rocco Papaleo* 1971 (d,sc); *La Più Bella Serata Della Mia Vita* 1972 (d,sc); *C'eravamo tanto amati/We All Loved Each Other So Much* 1974 (d,sc); *Brutti, Sporchi e Cattivi/Down and Dirty* 1976 (d,sc); *Signore e Signori, Buonanotte* 1976 (d,sc); *Una Giornata Particolare* 1977 (d,sc,story); *I Nuovi Mostri* 1977 (d); *La Terrazza/The Terrace* 1980 (d,sc); *Passione d'amore* 1981 (d,sc); *La Nuit de Varennes* 1982 (d,sc); *Le Bal* 1983 (d,sc); *Macaroni* 1985 (d,sc); *La Famiglia/The Family* 1987 (d,sc,ed); *Che ora e* 1989 (d,sc); *Splendor* 1989 (d,sc); *Il Viaggio di Capitan Fracass* 1990 (d,p,sc).

Scorsese, Martin • Director; also screenwriter, producer, actor. • Born Queens, NY, November 17, 1942. *Educ.* Cathedral College (Seminary); NYU. Martin Scorsese is the most consistently passionate, committed and inventive director to have worked in the American cinema over the past 20 years. His films are often rooted in his own experience, exploring his Italian-American Catholic heritage and confronting the themes of sin and redemption in a fiercely contemporary, yet universally resonant fashion. Scorsese has worked largely outside the traditional Hollywood establishment, making films on relatively small budgets which attract relatively small, yet dedicated, audiences. Although he has never enjoyed the box-office success of a *Godfather* or a *Star Wars*, he has earned an almost uninterrupted run of critical kudos that has made him the envy of many of his peers.

Scorsese was raised in New York's Little Italy and flirted with the idea of the priesthood, even studying at Cathedral College, a junior seminary. Rather than devote himself to the Church, he enrolled in New York University and soon discovered the religion of film. By 1966, Scorsese had received his master's degree, shot several successful short films including *It's Not Just You, Murray*, an ironic portrait of a gangster, and commenced production on a feature titled *Who's That Knocking at My Door?*. The film was shown at the 1967 Chicago Film Festival but failed to gain theatrical release at the time.

In 1969, after having spent some time in the Netherlands, Scorsese was teaching film history classes at NYU and helping fellow student Michael Wadleigh edit the mammoth rock documentary *Woodstock*. His career was boosted when producer Joseph Brenner offered to distribute *Who's That Knocking?*. With a gratuitous sex scene thrown in, the film was released in New York that year. It stars Harvey Keitel as J.R., an Italian-American who has been conditioned by his strict Catholic upbringing to see all women as either "girls" (virgins who make good wives and mothers) or "broads" (purely sexual creatures about whom he fantasizes). The film was critically praised for its realism and inspired camera work.

After working on the documentary *Street Scenes* (1970), Scorsese was assigned by Roger Corman to direct *Boxcar Bertha* (1972), a Depression-era allegory which parallels—within the limitations of an exploitation picture—the relationship between Mary Magdalene and Jesus Christ. Barbara Hershey (who gave Scorsese a copy of the novel *Last Temptation of Christ* during filming and would play Mary Magdalene in Scorsese's film of that book) plays Bertha, a good-natured whore, and David Carradine is labor leader Bill Shelley who, at the film's end, is literally crucified on the side of a boxcar. The film introduced one of Scorsese's central thematic concerns, the figure of the "sinner" who has temporarily slipped from grace, only to enjoy a final, if ambiguous, redemption.

In 1973 came the film that assured Scorsese a starring role in contemporary film history: *Mean Streets*, the story of a group of young hoods living and dying on the streets of New York (shot, surprisingly, almost entirely in Los Angeles). Charlie (Keitel), the film's central character, juggles his concern for his crazy friend Johnny Boy (Robert De Niro), a secret romance with Johnny's cousin, and his ambition to run an uptown restaurant. At his best here, Scorsese combines a cineaste's passion for film noir with an actor's obsession with rich characters and a loving sense of time and place. The film was Scorsese's first with De Niro (the two were raised in the same neighborhood) and marked the beginning of one of the most creative pairings in contemporary American cinema. De Niro would star in five more Scorsese features: *Taxi Driver* (1976), *New York, New York* (1977), *Raging Bull* (1980), *King of Comedy* (1983) and *GoodFellas* (1990).

Alice Doesn't Live Here Anymore (1974) marked a departure, if not an act of penance, for Scorsese—it is his only film with a woman protagonist and one of very few that isn't suffused with a particularly masculine point of view. The story of a woman (Ellen Burstyn) who takes off with her young son in search of America and a job ironically became a favorite of the nascent women's movement of the early 1970s; it also spawned a successful sitcom.

As if in reaction to the feminism of *Alice*, Scorsese returned with a vengeance to the macho world of *Mean Streets* with *Taxi Driver* (1976). Scripted by Paul Schrader, *Taxi Driver* was an iconographic street opera which gave De Niro an opportunity for a tour-de-force performance as Travis Bickle, a Vietnam vet turned psychotic vigilante. The film generated considerable controversy, largely thanks to its bloody denouement—a sustained, hallucinatory, brilliantly edited piece of carnage centering around a 12-year-old prostitute (Jodie Foster).

The pendulum swung the other way with *New York, New York* (1977), an extravagant, uneven 1940s-style musical rooted in Scorsese's childhood memories of the "Make-Believe-Ballroom" era. *Raging Bull* (1980) remains Scorsese's acknowledged masterpiece. Based on the autobiography of Jake La Motta and scripted by Schrader and Mardik Martin, the film afforded De Niro the greatest performance of his career in this story of the rise and fall of a middleweight boxing champion (De Niro gained 70 pounds to play La Motta later in life, as a nightclub performer). Shot in black-and-white save for some poignant "home movie" sequences, *Raging Bull* won Academy Awards for De Niro and editor Thelma Schoonmaker. (Schoonmaker has stated that her much-praised work in editing the film's horrific, but compelling slow-motion fight sequences was all predetermined by Scorsese's fastidious shot composition.) *King of Comedy* (1983), with De Niro as Rupert Pupkin, an obsessed fan/would-be comic, Sandra Bernhardt as his wacko accomplice and Jerry Lewis as a Johnny Carson-type figure in perhaps Scorsese's most underrated film, a dark but pointed social comedy.

Layered between these features were several documentary projects, most notably *Italianamerican* (1974), a short but rich portrait of his parents, Charles and Catherine Scorsese (who later went on to make memorable cameo appearances in a number of their son's movies), and *The Last Waltz* (1978), a meticulously shot and edited record of the 1976 farewell concert by rock group The Band.

After a false start on his long-planned adaptation of Nikos Kazantzakis's *The Last Temptation of Christ*, Scorsese temporarily turned away from high-rolling, big-budget filmmaking to make *After Hours* (1985), a nightmarish black comedy set entirely on the streets of New York during one night. In 1986 he abandoned New York for the streets of Chicago to direct *The Color of Money*, a bloodless but stylish sequel to Robert Rossen's 1961 classic, *The Hustler*. Part of his reason for directing the film, said Scorsese, was to prove that he could make a "studio picture," with a big budget ($15 million) and stars—Paul Newman, Tom Cruise—to match.

The Last Temptation of Christ (1988) gave Scorsese the chance to dramatize the historical figure whose struggle between the spiritual and the secular is the most celebrated of all. Scorsese's Christ begins as a social outcast, reviled for making crucifixes, who wavers between good and evil, between the spirit and the flesh, before eventually choosing the path to redemption. In this sense, Christ has an affinity with Keitel's J.R. and Charlie, DeNiro's Travis Bickle and Rupert Pupkin, and David Carradine's Bill Shelley. Yet despite superbly shot, exotic locations and an infectious "world music" score contributed by Peter Gabriel, the film lacked the emotional power of Scorsese's earlier, smaller-scale productions.

Adapted from Nicholas Pileggi's book *Wiseguys*, about the experiences of small-time gangster-turned-Federal-witness Henry Hill, *Goodfellas* (1990) marked a return to classic Scorsese form and content. The film captures both the undeniable excitement as well as the tawdry, daily details of life on the fringes of "the mob," pushing audience manipulation to the extreme by juxtaposing moments of graphic violence with scenes of high humor. Superb camerawork, including several extended tracking shots, and consummate performances by De Niro, Joe Pesci, Ray Liotta and Lorraine Bracco, make the film among the finest of Scorsese's achievements, a virtuoso memory of the 40s, 50s, 60s, 70s and 80s on the Mean Streets of New York. DC, JM • *What's a Nice Girl Like You Doing in a Place Like This? (short)* 1963 (d); *It's Not Just You, Murray (short)* 1964 (d); *The Big Shave (short)* 1967 (d); *Who's That Knocking at My Door?* 1967 (d,sc); *Bezeten—het gat in de muur* 1969 (sc); *Street Scenes* 1970, unreleased (prod.sup,post-prod.d); *Woodstock* 1970 (ad,ed); *Medicine Ball Caravan* 1971 (assoc.p,post-prod.sup); *Boxcar Bertha* 1972 (d); *Elvis on Tour* 1972 (ed.sup—montage); *Mean Streets* 1973 (d,sc); *Alice Doesn't Live Here Anymore* 1974 (d); *Italianamerican (short)* 1974 (a,d); *Cannonball* 1976 (a); *Taxi Driver* 1976 (a,d); *American Boy* 1977 (a,d); *New York, New York* 1977 (d); *The Last Waltz* 1978 (a,d); *Roger Corman: Hollywood's Wild Angel* 1978 (a); *Raging Bull* 1980 (a,d) **(AANBD)**; *The King of Comedy* 1983 (a,d); *Pavlova* 1983 (a); *After Hours* 1985 (d); *Autour de Minuit/Round Midnight* 1986 (a); *The Color of Money* 1986 (d); *Not Just Any Flower (short)* 1987 (assistance); *The Last Temptation of Christ* 1988 (d) **(AANBD)**; *New York Stories* 1989 (d); *Akira Kurosawa's Dreams* 1990 (a); *GoodFellas* 1990 (d,sc); *The Grifters* 1990 (p).

Scott, Adrian • Producer, writer • Born Arlington, NJ, February 6, 1912; died 1973. *Educ.* Amherst. Magazine editor turned screenwriter who became a producer with RKO in 1943. Scott was reponsible for such films as the Raymond Chandler adaptation, *Murder, My Sweet* (1944, from *Farewell My Lovely*), and the biting indictment of anti-semitism, *Crossfire* (1947). His career was ended when he refused to testify before the House Un-American Activities Commitee in 1947 and he served a year in prison as one of the "Hollywood Ten". His fate was sealed by the damning testimony of Edward Dmytryk, who directed the majority of Scott's films. • *Keeping Company* 1940 (sc); *The Parson of Panamint* 1941 (sc); *We Go Fast* 1941 (sc); *Mr. Lucky* 1943 (sc); *Murder, My Sweet* 1944 (p); *My Pal Wolf* 1944 (p); *Cornered* 1945 (p); *Miss Susie Slagle's* 1945 (adapt); *Deadline at Dawn* 1946 (p); *Crossfire* 1947 (p); *So Well Remembered* 1947 (p).

Scott, George C. • Actor • Born George Campbell Scott, Wise, VA, October 18, 1927. *Educ.* University of Missouri. Gruff, commanding, stage-trained actor who made his film debut in *The Hanging Tree* (1959). Scott proved a riveting screen presence with roles as the hard-boiled manager in *The Hustler* (1963) and, in a wildly comic turn, the mad general in *Dr. Strangelove* (1964). A reluctant star, he earned a best actor Oscar for his performance as the crusty title character in *Patton* (1970) but refused to accept the award. Scott directed two films in the early 1970s and continues to appear in features and, primarily, on TV. Divorced from actress Colleen Dewhurst and married to actress Trish Van Devere. • *Anatomy of a Murder* 1959 (a) **(AANBSA)**; *The Hanging Tree*

1959 (a); *The Hustler* 1963 (a) **(AANBSA)**; *The List of Adrian Messenger* 1963 (a); *Dr. Strangelove; or, How I Learned to Stop Worrying and Love the Bomb* 1964 (a); *La Bibbia* 1966 (a); *Not With My Wife, You Don't* 1966 (a); *The Flim-Flam Man* 1967 (a); *Petulia* 1968 (a); *Patton* 1970 (a) **(AABA)**; *The Hospital* 1971 (a) **(AANBA)**; *The Last Run* 1971 (a); *They Might Be Giants* 1971 (a); *The New Centurions* 1972 (a); *Rage* 1972 (a,d); *The Day of the Dolphin* 1973 (a); *Oklahoma Crude* 1973 (a); *Bank Shot* 1974 (a); *The Savage Is Loose* 1974 (a,d,p); *The Hindenburg* 1975 (a); *Islands in the Stream* 1976 (a); *Crossed Swords* 1977 (a); *Movie Movie* 1978 (a); *Arthur Miller on Home Ground* 1979 (a); *The Changeling* 1979 (a); *Hardcore* 1979 (a); *The Formula* 1980 (a); *Taps* 1981 (a); *The Beastmaster* 1982 (a); *Firestarter* 1984 (a); *The Indomitable Teddy Roosevelt* 1984 (a); *The Rescuers Down Under* 1990 (a); *William Peter Blatty's The Exorcist III* 1990 (a).

Scott, Randolph • Actor • Born Randolph Crane, Orange County, VA, January 23, 1898; died March 2, 1987, Los Angeles, CA. *Educ.* Georgia Institute of Technology, Atlanta; University of North Carolina; Pasadena Playhouse. Ruggedly handsome star who entered film as a bit player in 1929 as a result of a chance meeting with Howard Hughes. Scott proved himself a versatile lead in the mid-1930s and played several military heroes during and after the war years, before settling into a popular niche as a weathered, quiet-talking cowboy who was, above all, a lover. Some of Scott's best work came in the late 50s, when he formed the Ranown production company with Harry Joe Brown and starred in a series of adult-oriented westerns directed by Budd Boetticher. He turned in an engagingly self-effacing swansong as the aging gunslinger in Sam Peckinpah's valentine to the genre, *Ride the High Country* (1962). • *The Far Call* 1929 (a); *Women Men Marry* 1931 (a); *Heritage of the Desert* 1932 (a); *Hot Saturday* 1932 (a); *Wild Horse Mesa* 1932 (a); *Broken Dreams* 1933 (a); *Cocktail Hour* 1933 (a); *Hello, Everybody!* 1933 (a); *Man of the Forest* 1933 (a); *Murders in the Zoo* 1933 (a); *Sunset Pass* 1933 (a); *Supernatural* 1933 (a); *The Thundering Herd* 1933 (a); *To the Last Man* 1933 (a); *The Last Round-Up* 1934 (a); *Wagon Wheels* 1934 (a); *Home on the Range* 1935 (a); *Roberta* 1935 (a); *Rocky Mountain Mystery* 1935 (a); *She* 1935 (a); *So Red the Rose* 1935 (a); *Village Tale* 1935 (a); *And Sudden Death* 1936 (a); *Follow the Fleet* 1936 (a); *Go West, Young Man* 1936 (a); *The Last of the Mohicans* 1936 (a); *High, Wide, and Handsome* 1937 (a); *Rebecca of Sunnybrook Farm* 1938 (a); *The Road to Reno* 1938 (a); *The Texans* 1938 (a); *Coast Guard* 1939 (a); *Frontier Marshal* 1939 (a); *Jesse James* 1939 (a); *Susannah of the Mounties* 1939 (a); *My Favorite Wife* 1940 (a); *Virginia City* 1940 (a); *When the Daltons Rode* 1940 (a); *Belle Starr* 1941 (a); *Western Union* 1941 (a); *Paris Calling* 1942 (a); *Pittsburgh* 1942 (a); *The Spoilers* 1942 (a); *To the Shores of Tripoli* 1942 (a); *Bombardier* 1943 (a); *Corvette K-225* 1943 (a); *The Desperadoes* 1943 (a); *Gung Ho!* 1943 (a); *Belle of the Yukon* 1944 (a); *Follow the Boys* 1944 (a); *Captain Kidd* 1945 (a); *China Sky* 1945 (a); *Abilene Town* 1946 (a); *Badman's Territory* 1946 (a); *Home, Sweet Homicide* 1946 (a); *Albuquerque* 1947 (a); *Christmas Eve* 1947 (a); *Gunfighters* 1947 (a); *Sinner's Holiday* 1947 (a); *Trail Street* 1947 (a); *Canadian Pacific* 1948 (a); *Coroner Creek* 1948 (a); *Return of the Bad Men* 1948 (a); *The Doolins of Oklahoma* 1949 (a); *Fighting Man of the Plains* 1949 (a); *The Walking Hills* 1949 (a); *The Cariboo Trail* 1950 (a); *Colt .45* 1950 (a); *The Nevadan* 1950 (a); *Forth Worth* 1951 (a); *Man in the Saddle* 1951 (a); *Santa Fe* 1951 (a); *Starlift* 1951 (a); *Sugarfoot* 1951 (a); *Carson City* 1952 (a); *Hangman's Knot* 1952 (a); *The Man Behind the Gun* 1952 (a); *The Stranger Wore a Gun* 1953 (a); *Thunder Over the Plains* 1953 (a); *The Bounty Hunter* 1954 (a); *Riding Shotgun* 1954 (a); *A Lawless Street* 1955 (a,assoc.p); *Rage at Dawn* 1955 (a); *Tall Man Riding* 1955 (a); *Ten Wanted Men* 1955 (a,assoc.p); *Seven Men From Now* 1956 (a); *Seventh Cavalry* 1956 (a,assoc.p); *Decision at Sundown* 1957 (a); *Shoot-Out at Medicine Bend* 1957 (a); *The Tall T* 1957 (a); *Buchanan Rides Alone* 1958 (a,assoc.p); *Ride Lonesome* 1959 (a,exec.p); *Westbound* 1959 (a); *Comanche Station* 1960 (a); *Ride the High Country* 1962 (a).

Scott, Ridley • Director, producer • Born South Shields, Northumberland, England, 1939. *Educ.* West Hartlepool College of Art; Royal College of Art, London (art, film). In the mid-1960s, Ridley Scott worked for BBC Television as a set designer, an experience that has colored much of his subsequent work as a director. From his first film, *The Duellists* (1977), through *Black Rain* (1989), Scott has consistently turned out visually spectacular features. Though some critics feel this is at the expense of well-rounded characters and coherent stories, Danny Peary, for example, counters that in *Blade Runner* (1982) at least, the "awesome visuals...help tell the story and advance the themes."

Scott began his directing career in TV, working on episodes of such series as "Z Cars" and "The Informer." In 1967 he left the BBC and spent the next ten years as a freelance director, turning out hundreds of commercials.

Scott spent a total of five years, from conception through financing and production, on his first feature, *The Duellists* (1977). Although it won a special jury prize at Cannes, some criticised *The Duellists* as little more than carefully posed tableaux of the Napoleonic era that rarely illuminated the human aspects of the two central characters (Keith Carradine and Harvey Keitel). Scott's next feature was the influential, stomach-churningly tense sci-fi thriller, *Alien* (1979). The film enjoyed considerable box-office success, made a star of Sigourney Weaver and spawned an unusually good sequel (*Aliens II* 1986, directed by James Cameron).

Blade Runner presents a bleak, stunning vision of an over-populated and media-saturated Los Angeles in the year 2019. The story, about a bounty hunter (Harrison Ford) tracking down a gang of outlaw androids, offers an unusually sympathetic treatment of the "replicants" as they search for their maker, hoping he can extend their four-year life span. The film has developed a significant cult following, though some critics had problems with Ford's wooden, cliched voice-over and a tacked-on happy ending which sees him soaring into a rural paradise accompanied by his android lover (Sean Young).

Critical reception for *Legend* (1985) was generally poor, centering on a weak, fairy-tale storyline that was swamped by sumptuous production design (impressively enough, the entire film was shot on a soundstage at London's Pinewood Studios). *Someone to Watch Over Me* (1987) was a well-structured, straightforward suspense thriller; finely acted by Tom Berenger and Lorraine Bracco, and untypically devoid of flashy visual effects, it performed poorly at the box-office. Scott then scored his biggest hit since *Alien* with *Black Rain* (1989), a police corruption thriller set in New York and Japan; though the narrative was somewhat confused—a romantic sub-plot between a detective (Michael Douglas) and a nightclub hostess (Kate Capshaw) seemed to get dropped and resumed virtually at random—the Tokyo skyline afforded Scott some of his finest urban compositions to date. DLY • *The Duellists* 1977 (d); *Alien* 1979 (d); *Blade Runner* 1982 (d); *Legend* 1985 (d); *Someone to Watch Over Me* 1987 (d,exec.p); *Black Rain* 1989 (d); *Thelma and Louise* 1991 (d,p).

Scott, Tony • Director • Born Newcastle, England. *Educ.* Leeds College of Art; Royal College of Art, London (film). One of a generation of British figures (including brother Ridley Scott, Alan Parker and Adrian Lyne) whose background in TV commercials has led to a career directing glossy, mainstream Hollywood fare. Scott made his feature directorial debut with the slick, stylish thriller, *The Hunger* (1983), and hit the box-office jackpot with films such as *Top Gun* (1986) and *Beverly Hills Cop II* (1987). • *The Hunger* 1983 (d); *Top*

Gun 1986 (d); *Beverly Hills Cop II* 1987 (d); *Days of Thunder* 1990 (d); *Revenge* 1990 (d).

Seagrove, Jenny • Actress • Born Kuala Lumpur, Malaysia. Promising, attractive young performer of stage, screen and TV. Seagrove was Peter Riegert's love interest in Bill Forsyth's whimsical comedy, *Local Hero* (1983). • *Moonlighting* 1982; *Local Hero* 1983; *Nate and Hayes* 1983; *Appointment With Death* 1988; *A Chorus of Disapproval* 1989; *The Guardian* 1990.

Seale, John • Director of photography • Born Warwick, Queensland, Australia. Worked as camera operator to Russel Boyd on a number of Peter Weir films before graduating to cinematographer in 1980. Seale has shot all of Weir's American features, notably *Witness* (1985), with its memorable compositions of both the Philadelphia train station and the rolling Pennsylvania landscape. He has also photographed such handsome, big-budget productions as *Rain Man* (1988) and *Dead Poets Society* (1989). • *Alvin Purple* 1973 (ph); *Deathcheaters* 1976 (ph); *The Irishman* 1978 (cam.op); *Stunt Rock* 1978 (cam.op 2u—Australia); *The Odd Angry Shot* 1979 (cam.op); *Fatty Finn* 1980 (ph,cam.op); *By Design* 1981 (2u ph); *Doctors and Nurses* 1981 (ph); *Fighting Back* 1981 (ph); *Gallipoli* 1981 (cam.op); *Goose Flesh* 1981 (ph); *Horror Movie* 1981 (ph); *The Survivor* 1981 (ph); *Ginger Meggs* 1982 (ph); *Goodbye Paradise* 1982 (ph); *The Year of Living Dangerously* 1982 (2u ph); *BMX Bandits* 1983 (ph); *Careful, He Might Hear You* 1983 (ph); *Silver City* 1984 (ph); *The Empty Beach* 1985 (ph,cam.op); *Witness* 1985 (ph) **(AANBPH)**; *Children of a Lesser God* 1986 (ph); *The Hitcher* 1986 (ph); *The Mosquito Coast* 1986 (ph,cam.op); *Stakeout* 1987 (ph); *Gorillas in the Mist* 1988 (ph); *Rain Man* 1988 (ph) **(AANBPH)**; *Dead Poets Society* 1989 (ph).

Seberg, Jean • Actress • Born Marshalltown, IA, November 13, 1938; died September 8, 1979. *Educ.* Iowa University. Gamine blonde actress who landed the title role in Otto Preminger's *Saint Joan* (1957) after a much-publicized contest involving some 18,000 hopefuls. The failure of that film, and the only moderate success of her next, *Bonjour Tristesse* (1958), combined to stall Seberg's career, until her role in Jean-Luc Godard's landmark New Wave feature, *Breathless* (1959), brought her renewed international attention. Seberg gave a memorable performance as a schizophrenic in the title role of Robert Rossen's *Lilith* (1964) and was directed by husbands François Moreuil, in *Playtime* (1962), and Romain Gary, in *Les Oiseaux vont mourir au Pérou* (1968). Seberg was found dead under mysterious circumstances in a Paris suburb in 1979. • *Bonjour Tristesse* 1957; *Saint Joan* 1957; *A bout de souffle/Breathless* 1959; *The Mouse That Roared* 1959; *Let No Man Write My Epitaph* 1960; *La Récréation/Playtime* 1962; *A la Française* 1963; *Echappement libre* 1964; *Lilith* 1964; *Les Plus belles escroqueries du monde* 1964; *Un Milliard dans un Billiard* 1965; *Estouffade à la Caraibe* 1966; *A Fine Madness* 1966; *La Ligne de Démarcation* 1966; *Moment to Moment* 1966; *La Route de Corinthe* 1967; *Les Oiseaux vont mourir au Pérou* 1968; *Paint Your Wagon* 1969; *Pendulum* 1969; *Airport* 1970; *Macho Callahan* 1970; *Ondata di Calore* 1970; *Camorra* 1971; *Kill* 1971; *L'Attentat* 1972; *La Corrupcion de Chris Miller* 1973; *Questa Specie d'Amore* 1973; *Le Grand Délire* 1975; *Die Wildente/The Wild Duck* 1976.

Segal, George • Actor • Born Great Neck, Long Island, NY, February 13, 1934. *Educ.* Columbia. Began his career on the New York stage and made his film debut in *The Young Doctors* (1961). A thoughtful, versatile performer with a talent for wry, understated humor, Segal appeared in several notable films of the 1960s and 70s, distinguishing himself in *Who's Afraid of Virginia Woolf?* (1966), *The Owl and the Pussycat* (1970), the uproarious *Where's Poppa?* (1970) and the gentle 1973 comedy, *A Touch of Class.* • *The Young Doctors* 1961 (a); *Act One* 1963 (a); *Invitation to a Gunfighter* 1964 (a); *The New Interns* 1964 (a); *King Rat* 1965 (a); *Ship of Fools* 1965 (a); *Lost Command* 1966 (a); *The Quiller Memorandum* 1966 (a); *Who's Afraid of Virginia Woolf?* 1966 (a) **(AANBSA)**; *The St. Valentine's Day Massacre* 1967 (a); *Bye Bye Braverman* 1968 (a); *No Way to Treat a Lady* 1968 (a); *The Bridge at Remagen* 1969 (a); *Loving* 1970 (a); *The Owl and the Pussycat* 1970 (a); *Where's Poppa?* 1970 (a); *Born to Win* 1971 (a,p); *The Hot Rock* 1972 (a); *Blume in Love* 1973 (a); *A Touch of Class* 1973 (a); *California Split* 1974 (a); *The Terminal Man* 1974 (a); *The Black Bird* 1975 (a,exec.p); *Russian Roulette* 1975 (a); *The Duchess and the Dirtwater Fox* 1976 (a); *Fun With Dick and Jane* 1976 (a); *Rollercoaster* 1977 (a); *Who Is Killing the Great Chefs of Europe?* 1978 (a); *The Last Married Couple in America* 1979 (a); *Lost and Found* 1979 (a); *Carbon Copy* 1981 (a); *Killing 'em Softly* 1981 (a); *Stick* 1985 (a); *All's Fair* 1989 (a); *Look Who's Talking* 1989 (a).

Seidelman, Susan • Director • Born near Philadelphia, PA, December 11, 1952. *Educ.* Drexel Institute of Technology, Philadelphia (art); NYU (film). In an arid comedy landscape, the films of Susan Seidelman seem like a teeming oasis. Her relentlessly contemporary features are knowing satires that examine contemporary issues of fame, self-fulfillment and relations between the sexes.

Seidelman grew up in a middle-class New Jersey neighborhood and studied art in Philadelphia and film at New York University. Her satiric flair earned student film awards for her shorts, *And You Act Like One Too, Deficit* and *Yours Truly, Andrea G. Stern.* On the strength of these productions she managed to raise $80,000 to make her first feature, *Smithereens* (1982), the story of a selfish hustler (Susan Berman) with ambitions to become the manager of a punk rock band. The success of *Smithereens* success in America and Europe brought her the attention of the major studios and the chance to direct *Desperately Seeking Susan* (1985), a hit comedy of an identity mixup between a New Jersey housewife (Rosanna Arquette) and a downtown New York rocker (Madonna).

Seidelman's next three films gathered some critical support but were less successful at the box-office. *Making Mr. Right* (1987) focused on a savvy public relations expert and her attempts to promote an android astronaut (John Malkovich). *Cookie* (1989) was the comic story of a mob hood (Peter Falk) and his wacky daughter (Emily Lloyd). With *She-Devil* (1989), Seidelman explored the vengeance a dumpy housewife (Roseanne Barr) wreaks on her romantic rival (Meryl Streep). • *Chambre 666* 1982 (a); *Smithereens* 1982 (d,ed,p,story); *Desperately Seeking Susan* 1985 (d); *50 Years of Action!* 1986 (a); *Making Mr. Right* 1987 (d,exec.p); *Cookie* 1989 (d,exec.p); *She-Devil* 1989 (d,p).

Seitz, John F. • Director of photography • Born Chicago, IL, June 23, 1893; died 1979. Influential cinematographer of both the silent and sound eras. Seitz began his career as a lab technician with the St. Louis Motion Picture Company, joined American Mutual in 1916 and had graduated to cinematographer by 1919. His best work was done at Metro (1920-28), especially for director Rex Ingram, and at Paramount (1941-52), notably in collaboration with Preston Sturges (*Sullivan's Travels* 1941, *The Miracle of Morgan's Creek* 1944, etc.) and Billy Wilder (*The Lost Weekend* 1945, *Sunset Boulevard* 1950, etc.). Seitz also invented several key photographic techniques, including the matte shot. Brother of director George B. Seitz (1888-1944). • *Beauty and the Rogue* 1918; *Shore Acres* 1920; *The Conquering Power* 1921; *The Four Horsemen of the Apocalypse* 1921; *Uncharted Seas* 1921; *The Prisoner of Zenda* 1922; *Trifling Women* 1922; *Turn to the Right* 1922; *Scaramouche* 1923; *Where the Pavement Ends* 1923; *The Arab* 1924; *Classmates* 1924; *The Price of a Party* 1924; *The Magician* 1926; *Mare Nostrum* 1926; *The Fair Co-ed* 1927; *The Patsy* 1927; *Across to Singapore* 1928; *Adoration* 1928; *Outcast* 1928; *The Trail of '98* 1928; *Careers* 1929; *The Divine Lady* 1929 **(AANBPH)**; *Hard to Get* 1929; *Her Private Life* 1929; *A Most Immoral Lady* 1929; *The Painted Angel* 1929;

Saturday's Children 1929; *The Squall* 1929; *Back Pay* 1930; *The Bad Man* 1930; *In the Next Room* 1930; *Kismet* 1930; *Murder Will Out* 1930; *Road to Paradise* 1930; *Sweethearts and Wives* 1930; *The Age For Love* 1931; *East Lynne* 1931; *Hush Money* 1931; *Men of the Sky* 1931; *Merely Mary Ann* 1931; *Misbehaving Ladies* 1931; *Over the Hill* 1931; *The Right of Way* 1931; *Young Sinners* 1931; *The Careless Lady* 1932; *A Passport to Hell* 1932; *She Wanted a Millionaire* 1932; *Six Hours to Live* 1932; *The Woman in Room 13* 1932; *Adorable* 1933; *Dangerously Yours* 1933; *Ladies They Talk About* 1933; *Mr. Skitch* 1933; *Paddy the Next Best Thing* 1933; *All Men Are Enemies* 1934; *Coming Out Party* 1934; *Helldorado* 1934; *Marie Galante* 1934; *Springtime For Henry* 1934; *Curly Top* 1935; *The Littlest Rebel* 1935; *Navy Wife* 1935; *One More Spring* 1935; *Our Little Girl* 1935; *15 Maiden Lane* 1936; *Captain January* 1936; *The Country Doctor* 1936; *The Poor Little Rich Girl* 1936; *Between Two Women* 1937; *Madame X* 1937; *Navy, Blue and Gold* 1937; *The Crowd Roars* 1938; *Lord Jeff* 1938; *Love Is a Headache* 1938; *Stablemates* 1938; *Young Dr. Kildare* 1938; *The Adventures of Huckleberry Finn* 1939; *Bad Little Angel* 1939; *Sergeant Madden* 1939; *Six Thousand Enemies* 1939; *Thunder Afloat* 1939; *Dr. Kildare's Crisis* 1940; *Dr. Kildare's Strange Case* 1940; *A Little Bit of Heaven* 1940; *Sullivan's Travels* 1941; *Fly By Night* 1942; *Lucky Jordan* 1942; *The Moon and Sixpence* 1942; *This Gun For Hire* 1942; *Five Graves to Cairo* 1943 **(AANBPH)**; *Casanova Brown* 1944; *Double Indemnity* 1944 **(AANBPH)**; *Hail the Conquering Hero* 1944; *The Hour Before the Dawn* 1944; *The Miracle of Morgan's Creek* 1944; *The Lost Weekend* 1945 **(AANBPH)**; *The Unseen* 1945; *Home, Sweet Homicide* 1946; *The Well-Groomed Bride* 1946; *Calcutta* 1947; *The Imperfect Lady* 1947; *Wild Harvest* 1947; *Beyond Glory* 1948; *The Big Clock* 1948; *A Miracle Can Happen* 1948; *The Night Has a Thousand Eyes* 1948; *Saigon* 1948; *Chicago Deadline* 1949; *The Great Gatsby* 1949; *Captain Carey, U.S.A.* 1950; *Molly* 1950; *Sunset Boulevard* 1950 **(AANBPH)**; *Appointment With Danger* 1951; *Dear Brat* 1951; *When Worlds Collide* 1951 **(AANBPH)**; *The Iron Mistress* 1952; *The San Francisco Story* 1952; *The Savage* 1952; *Botany Bay* 1953; *Desert Legion* 1953; *Invaders From Mars* 1953; *Many Rivers to Cross* 1954; *Rocket Man* 1954; *Rogue Cop* 1954 **(AANBPH)**; *Saskatchewan* 1954; *Hell on Frisco Bay* 1955; *The McConnell Story* 1955; *A Cry in the Night* 1956; *Santiago* 1956; *The Big Land* 1957; *The Deep Six* 1957; *The Badlanders* 1958; *Island of Lost Women* 1959; *The Man in the Net* 1959; *Guns of the Timberland* 1960.

Selleck, Tom • Actor • Born Detroit, MI, January 29, 1945. *Educ.* USC, Los Angeles. Ruggedly handsome, affable lead who appeared in several TV and feature films in the 1970s before making his mark as the title character of the popular TV series, "Magnum P.I." (1980-88). With the exception of *Three Men and a Baby* (1987), a saccharine but highly profitable remake of Coline Serreau's 1985 French comedy, most of Selleck's subsequent big-screen outings have been flops. • *Myra Breckinridge* 1970; *The Seven Minutes* 1971; *Daughters of Satan* 1972; *Coma* 1978; *High Road to China* 1983; *Lassiter* 1984; *Runaway* 1984; *Three Men and a Baby* 1987; *Her Alibi* 1989; *An Innocent Man* 1989; *Quigley Down Under* 1990; *Three Men and a Little Lady* 1990.

Sellers, Peter • Actor • Born Richard Henry Sellers, Southsea, England, September 8, 1925; died 1980. Protean comic actor who first came to attention on the popular radio series "The Goon Show," a precursor to both "Beyond the Fringe" and "Monty Python's Flying Circus." Sellers made his screen debut in 1951 and demonstrated a remarkable gift for character transformation in films such as *The Mouse That Roared* (1959), a political spoof in which he played three very different roles. In 1964, Sellers starred in the first installment of the hugely popular "Pink Panther" series, introducing the lovable bumbler, Inspector Clouseau. (In that same year, he again assumed multiple identities in Stanley Kubrick's barbed satire, *Dr. Strangelove.*) Although the Clouseau character made him a rich, international star, Sellers expressed frustration with the limitations of the role. One of his final roles was a triumphant performance as the gardener-turned-statesman in Hal Ashby's gentle political satire, *Being There* (1979). He was married to actresses Britt Eckland and Lynne Frederick. • *The Ladykillers* 1955 (a); *The Naked Truth* 1957 (a); *Tom Thumb* 1958 (a); *Up the Creek!* 1958 (a); *The Battle of the Sexes* 1959 (a); *I'm All Right Jack* 1959 (a); *The Mouse That Roared* 1959 (a); *The Millionairess* 1960 (a); *Mr. Topaze* 1961 (a,d); *Lolita* 1962 (a); *Waltz of the Toreadors* 1962 (a); *The Wrong Arm of the Law* 1962 (a); *Heaven's Above!* 1963 (a); *Dr. Strangelove; or, How I Learned to Stop Worrying and Love the Bomb* 1964 (a) **(AANBA)**; *The Pink Panther* 1964 (a); *A Shot in the Dark* 1964 (a); *The World of Henry Orient* 1964 (a); *What's New, Pussycat?* 1965 (a); *After the Fox* 1966 (a,song); *The Bobo* 1967 (a); *Casino Royale* 1967 (a); *Woman Times Seven* 1967 (a); *I Love You, Alice B. Toklas* 1968 (a); *The Party* 1968 (a); *Hoffman* 1970 (a); *The Magic Christian* 1970 (a,sc); *There's a Girl in My Soup* 1970 (a); *Alice's Adventures in Wonderland* 1972 (a); *Where Does It Hurt?* 1972 (a); *The Blockhouse* 1973 (a); *Ghost in the Noonday Sun* 1973 (a); *The Optimists* 1973 (a); *The Great McGonagall* 1974 (a); *The Return of the Pink Panther* 1975 (a); *Undercovers Hero* 1975 (a); *Murder By Death* 1976 (a); *The Pink Panther Strikes Again* 1976 (a); *Revenge of the Pink Panther* 1978 (a); *Being There* 1979 (a) **(AANBA)**; *The Prisoner of Zenda* 1979 (a); *The Fiendish Plot of Dr. Fu Manchu* 1980 (a); *Trail of the Pink Panther* 1982 (a).

Seltzer, David • Screenwriter, director • Born Highland Park, IL, 1940. *Educ.* Northwestern University School for Film and TV. Versatile scenarist who co-adapted Vladimir Nabokov's *King, Queen, Knave* (1972), wrote a couple of sophisticated horror films—the best of which was *The Omen* (1976)—and turned out several adroit tearjerkers, before making his directorial debut with *Lucas* (1986), a winning, low-key portrait of adolescence. • *The Hellstrom Chronicle* 1971 (sc); *King, Queen, Knave* 1972 (sc); *One Is a Lonely Number* 1972 (sc); *The Other Side of the Mountain* 1974 (sc); *The Omen* 1976 (sc); *Damien: Omen II* 1978 (from characters); *Prophecy* 1979 (sc); *Six Weeks* 1982 (sc); *Table For Five* 1983 (sc); *Lucas* 1986 (d,sc); *Punchline* 1988 (d,sc); *Bird on a Wire* 1990 (sc).

Selznick, David O. • Producer • Born David Oliver Selznick in Pittsburgh, PA, May 10, 1902; died 1965. *Educ.* Columbia. As the flamboyant director-producers of the early days of American cinema (Griffith, Von Stroheim, Neilan) were squeezed out by the emerging studio system, the focus of power shifted to the studio production supervisor, whose main responsiblity was to grind out formulaic product to exhibit in studio-owned theaters. These producers were often paint-by-the-numbers administrators who saw efficiency and profitability as their main objectives. David O. Selznick was one of the few who broke this mold; he considered himself a creative producer concerned with the most minute details of film production. He also thought himself something of a maverick—a tub-thumping independent turning out prestigious, quality motion pictures smack in the middle of the omnipotent Hollywood studio system. In fact, Selznick produced some of Hollywood's most renowned productions (*Gone With the Wind* 1939; *Rebecca* 1940) and, for all his talk of independence, these films are now considered exemplars of the Golden Age of the studio system.

Selznick made his reputation as a perceptive story analyst and a top-notch studio efficiency expert. He began his career in his teens, working for his father, independent film distributor Lewis Selznick, in publicity and as a story analyst. In 1926, young Selznick joined the newly born MGM as a script reader and shortly rose to the head of the scenario department and then to production supervisor. But after a disagreement with Irving Thalberg, who prefered another supervisor to Selznick on *White Shadows in the South Seas* (1928), Selznick was fired. This was during the advent of sound films, when the studios were consolidating their power and seeking economic and efficient ways of adapting to the new technology. Producers like Selznick were in great demand and B.P. Schulberg of Paramount Pictures hired him in 1927 to supervise the story department and writing staff. Before long, Selznick was promoted to supervising the routine Paramount productions.

But Selznick chafed at Paramount's strict regimentation and, when he was asked to take a heavy salary cut during the depths of the Depression in 1931, he resigned. Selznick's next stop was RKO, where he instituted a unit production scheme in which he would oversee the studio's top productions while the more routine features were supervised by a staff of seven assistant producers. At RKO Selznick's predilection for glossily produced stories about self-sufficient females was first displayed in films like *A Bill of Divorcement* (1932), *What Price Hollywood?* (1932), and *Little Women* (1933). When Thalberg fell ill at MGM and Louis B. Mayer sought Selznick as a unit producer, Selznick readily accepted. Back at MGM Selznick once again promoted strong production values and a strong storyline (which usually meant an adaptation of a classic novel or popular play), as in *Dancing Lady* (1933), *Dinner at Eight* (1933), *Manhattan Melodrama* (1934) and *David Copperfield* (1935).

Selznick left MGM in 1936 to form his own, independent company, Selznick International Pictures. His intention was to produce only a few, prestige films each year, allowing him to meticulously follow the progress of every project—from selecting the properties to overseeing the shooting and supervising the editing and retakes—and thus to achieve a perfectionism unattainable in a studio environment. Without studio front office restrictions, however, Selznick's perfectionist ways went unchecked and the films emerged at a sluggish pace. When they were released, however, they were not merely films; they were major events.

A Star Is Born was the first film released through S.I.P.; it was soon followed by such critical and popular successes as *Nothing Sacred* (1937), *The Prisoner of Zenda* (1937) and *Rebecca*. Selznick's ultimate triumph was *Gone With the Wind*, on which he enlisted the services of six directors (George Cukor, Sam Wood, William Cameron Menzies, King Vidor, Victor Fleming and himself) and countless screenwriters. But the film was such a hit that in 1940 S.I.P. was the top money-making studio in Hollywood, even with only three pictures—*Gone With the Wind, Rebecca,* and *Intermezzo* (1939)—in release.

S.I.P.'s astounding success ironically spelled the end of the company. Without a major studio set up to back him, Selznick had no place to re-invest his tremendous profits and thus faced a huge tax burden. In August 1940, the stockholders voted to dissolve Selznick International Pictures.

Selznick immediately formed David Selznick Productions but, understandably exhausted after the strain of *Gone With The Wind*, was unable to match his earlier success. The company soon became more a glorified talent agency than a production outfit; Selznick spent less time on making movies and more on making loan-out deals for the talent he had under contract (which included Alfred Hitchcock, Joan Fontaine, Gregory Peck and Ingrid Bergman), as well as preparing story/director/actor packages for sale to other studios. When he did return to feature production, the resulting films were either mawkishly sentimental (*Since You Went Away* 1944, *A Farewell to Arms* 1957) or overblown and operatic (*Duel in the Sun*, 1946).

Selznick played a significant role in creating the mystique and glamour of the classical Hollywood film. Moreover, he showed that it was possible, however briefly, to work outside the studio system and still produce films of technical polish and timeless appeal. Married to actress Jennifer Jones from 1949 until his death in 1965. PB • *The Age of Consent* 1932 (exec.p); *The Animal Kingdom* 1932 (p); *A Bill of Divorcement* 1932 (p); *Half Naked Truth* 1932 (p); *Men of America* 1932 (p); *The Phantom of Crestwood* 1932 (p); *The Roadhouse Murder* 1932 (p); *State's Attorney* 1932 (p); *Symphony of Six Million* 1932 (exec.p); *Westward Passage* 1932 (p); *What Price Hollywood?* 1932 (p); *Young Bride* 1932 (p); *Dancing Lady* 1933 (exec.p); *Dinner at Eight* 1933 (p); *Little Women* 1933 (uncred.p); *Lucky Devils* 1933 (exec.p); *Meet the Baron* 1933 (p); *The Monkey's Paw* 1933 (p); *No Other Woman* 1933 (exec.p); *Our Betters* 1933 (p); *Topaze* 1933 (p); *Manhattan Melodrama* 1934 (p); *Viva Villa* 1934 (p); *Anna Karenina* 1935 (p); *David Copperfield* 1935 (p); *Reckless* 1935 (p); *A Tale of Two Cities* 1935 (p); *Vanessa, Her Love Story* 1935 (p); *The Garden of Allah* 1936 (p); *Little Lord Fauntleroy* 1936 (p); *Nothing Sacred* 1937 (p); *The Prisoner of Zenda* 1937 (p); *A Star Is Born* 1937 (p); *The Adventures of Tom Sawyer* 1938 (p); *The Young in Heart* 1938 (p); *Gone With the Wind* 1939 (p); *Intermezzo* 1939 (p); *Made For Each Other* 1939 (p); *Rebecca* 1940 (p); *Since You Went Away* 1944 (p,sc); *Spellbound* 1945 (p); *Duel in the Sun* 1947 (sc); *The Paradine Case* 1947 (p,sc); *Portrait of Jennie* 1948 (p,sc); *The Third Man* 1949 (p); *Gone to Earth* 1950 (exec.p); *A Farewell to Arms* 1957 (p).

Sembene, Ousmane • Director, screenwriter; also producer, author. • Born Ziguenchor, Casamance, Senegal, January 1, 1923. *Educ.* Ecole de Céramique, Marsassoum; VGIK. The first film director from an African country to achieve international recognition, Ousmane Sembene remains the major figure in the rise of an independent post-colonial African cinema. Sembene's roots were not, as might be expected, in the educated élite. After working as a mechanic and bricklayer, he joined the Free French forces in 1942, serving in Africa and France. In 1946, he returned to Dakar, where he participated in the great railway strike of 1947. The next year he returned to France, where he worked in a Citröen factory in Paris, and then, for ten years, on the dock in Marseilles. During this time Sembene became very active in trade union struggles and began an extraordinarily successful writing career. His first novel, *Le Docker Noir*, was published in 1956 to critical acclaim. Since then, he has produced a number of works which have placed him in the foreground of the international literary scene.

Long an avid filmgoer, Sembene became aware that to reach a mass audience of workers and preliterate Africans outside urban centers, cinema was a more effective vehicle than the written word. In 1961, he traveled to Moscow to study film at VGIK and then to work at the Gorky Studios. Upon his return to Senegal, Sembene turned his attention to filmmaking and, after two short films, he wrote and directed his first feature, *Black Girl* (1965). Received with great enthusiasm at a number of international film festivals, it also won the prestigious Jean Vigo Prize for its director.

Shot in a simple, quasi-documentary style probably influenced by the French New Wave, *Black Girl* tells the tragic story of a young Senegalese woman working as a maid for an affluent French family on the Riviera, focusing on her sense of isolation and growing despair. Her country may have been "decolonized," but she is still a colonial—a non-person in the colonizers' world. Sembene's next film, *Mandabi/The Money Order* (1968), marked a sharp departure. Based on his novel of the same name and shot in color in two language versions—French and Wolof, the main dialect of Senegal—*Mandabi* is a trenchant and often delightfully witty satire of the new bourgeoisie, torn between outmoded patriarchal traditions and an uncaring, rapacious and inefficient bureaucracy.

Emitai (1971) records the struggle of the Diola people of the Casamance region of Senegal (where Sembene grew up) against the French authorities during WWII. Shot in Diola dialect and French from an original script, *Emitai* offers a respectful but unromanticized depiction of an ancient tribal culture, while highlighting the role of women in the struggle against colonialist oppression. In *Xala* (1974), Sembene again takes on the native bourgeoisie, this time in the person of a rich, partially Westernized Moslem businessman afflicted by "xala" (impotence) on the night of his wedding to a much younger third wife. *Ceddo* (1977), considered by many to be Sembene's masterpiece, departs from the director's customary realist approach, documenting the struggle over the last centuries of an unspecified African society against the incursions of Islam and European colonialism. Featuring a strong female central character, *Ceddo* is a powerful evocation of the African experience. KJ • *Black Girl* 1965 (d,sc); *Mandabi/The Money Order* 1968 (d,sc); *Emitai* 1971 (d,sc); *Xala* 1974 (d,sc); *Ceddo* 1977 (a,d,sc); *Camera d'Afrique: Twenty Years of African Cinema* 1983 (a); *Camp de Thiaroye/The Camp at Thiaroye* 1988 (d,sc).

Semler, Dean • Australian director of photography • Former news and documentary cameraman who first gained attention for his work on the arid wastelands of George Miller's *The Road Warrior* (1981). • *Let the Balloon Go* 1976 (ph); *The Earthling* 1980 (cam.op); *Stepping Out* 1980 (ph); *Hoodwink* 1981 (ph); *The Road Warrior* 1981 (ph); *Kitty and the Bagman* 1982 (ph); *In Memory of Malawan* 1983 (ph); *Razorback* 1984 (ph); *Undercover* 1984 (ph); *The Coca-Cola Kid* 1985 (ph); *Mad Max Beyond Thunderdome* 1985 (ph); *Bullseye* 1986 (ph); *Going Sane* 1986 (ph); *The Lighthorsemen* 1987 (ph); *Cocktail* 1988 (ph); *Young Guns* 1988 (ph); *Dead Calm* 1989 (ph); *Farewell to the King* 1989 (cam.op,ph); *K-9* 1989 (ph); *Dances With Wolves* 1990 (ph); *Impulse* 1990 (ph); *Young Guns II* 1990 (ph); *City Slickers* 1991 (ph).

Semprun, Jorge • Screenwriter, novelist • Born Jorge Maura Semprun, Madrid, Spain, December 10, 1923. *Educ.* Sorbonne, Paris (philosophy, literature). A son of the embattled Spanish Republic and the French Resistance who spent two years in Buchenwald, Jorge Semprun has used his wartime and post-war experience as the source of several novels and screenplays. His first venture into the film world came with the script for Alain Resnais's *La Guerre est finie* (1966); another notable collaboration was on Costa-Gavras's *Z* (1969). Semprun has also directed one film, *The Two Memories* (1974). He was appointed Spanish Minister of Culture in July 1988. • *La Guerre est finie* 1966 (a,sc,dial) (**AANBSC**); *Z* 1969 (sc); *L'Aveu* 1970 (sc); *L'Attentat* 1972 (sc); *Stavisky* 1973 (sc); *Les Deux Mèmoires* 1974 (d,sc,idea); *Section Speciale* 1975 (sc); *Une Femme A Sa Fentre* 1976 (sc); *Le Fond de l'air est rouge* 1977 (a); *Les Routes du Sud* 1978 (sc); *Les Trottoirs de Saturne* 1985 (sc).

Sen, Mrinal • Director • Born East Bengal (now Bangladesh), May 4, 1923. Sen is one of his nation's most politically active filmakers.

After having studied physics at university in Calcutta, Sen worked as a freelance journalist, a salesman of patent medicines and a sound technician in a film studio. In the mid-1940s he joined the Indian People's Theatre Association and at that time began to read about and study film. The association had links to the Communist Party of India and this heralded the beginning of Sen's involvement with Marxist politics.

In 1956 Sen made his debut with *Raat Bhore/The Dawn*, the first of his 25 feature films. Although his first film was openly political, he achieved national status as the director of a comedy, *Bhuvan Shome*, in 1969.

Influenced by Italian neorealism and the work of fellow countryman Satyajit Ray, Sen used location shooting and nonprofessional casts in his early films. By the 1970s he was making wider use of symbolism and allegory. Although he remains politically committed, Sen feels that the "difference between party Marxists and a private Marxist like me is that others think they pocketed truth, whereas I am always in search of truth..."

Sen's films have won numerous international awards. *Kharij/The Case is Closed* (1982), a scathing look at the hypocritical reaction of a bourgeois Calcutta family to the death of a servant boy, took home the Jury Prize from the 1983 Cannes Film Festival. • *Raat Bhore/The Dawn* 1956 (d,sc); *Bhuvan Shome* 1969 (d,p,sc); *Calcutta 71* 1972 (d,sc); *Padatik* 1974 (d,sc); *Oka Oorie Katha* 1977 (d,sc); *Parasuram* 1978 (d,sc); *Ekdin Pratidin* 1979 (d,p,sc); *Aakaler Sandhaney* 1980 (d,sc); *Kharij/The Case is Closed* 1982 (d,sc); *Khandar* 1983 (d,sc); *Kharij* 1983 (d,sc); *Tasveer Apni Apni* 1984 (d,p,sc); *Genesis* 1986 (d,sc,m); *Ek Din Achanak* 1988 (d,sc); *City Life* 1990 (d,p—"Calcutta, My Eldorado").

Sennett, Mack • Director, producer, actor • Born Mikall Sinnott, Danville, Quebec, Canada, January 17, 1880; died 1960. Mack Sennett was often known by his self-endowed title "The King of Comedy." In truth, Sennett was not so much a king as a ringmaster for a motley menagerie of otherworldy grotesques that slipped, slid and slapped their way at breakneck speeds across American movie screens of the 1910s. The anarchic world of cross-eyed rubes, nightmare-bearded villains, pulchritudinous bathing beauties and bumbling cops falling off cliffs, out of buildings, and into and out of cars was the quite unexpected creation of a gentleman whose first ambition in life was to be an opera star.

Born in Canada, Sennett moved with his family at the age of 17 to Connecticut. An encounter with fellow Canadian Marie Dressler led to an introduction to producer David Belasco and a new career for young Sennett on the vaudeville stage. In New York, he met the formidable film producer-director D.W. Griffith, for whom he played a bevy of roles, including the lead in *The Curtain Pole* (1909), Griffith's only directorial attempt at a comedy. Sennett stumbled into directing by accident: when a director fell ill at the last minute, he was told to replace him. Griffith then assigned Sennett to supervise production of his comedy unit and, by 1912, Sennett had set up his own studio in Hollywood and had become America's self-appointed comic showman—"a producer of laughs."

And a producer he was. Sennett's Keystone operation became a California version of Henry Ford's automobile plant in Michigan. Comedies were cranked out at bracing, production-line speed, with several produced in one day from an outline prepared under Sennett's supervision. The formula was unrepentently drawn from French models; as Sennett put it, "I stole my first ideas from the Pathés."

In spite of the appearance of frenzied freedom in Sennett's slapstick orgies, the formula was in fact strict and unbending. Characterization was eschewed in favor of stereotypes with whom the audience could make an immediate identification. Sennett also issued strict rules governing the type of gags that could be used; in fact, he declared, there were only two real categories of gags: "the fall of dignity and the mistaken identity."

The roster of Sennett talent was impressive. At one point Charlie Chaplin, Gloria Swanson, Fatty Arbuckle, Mabel Normand, Harry Langdon, Harold Lloyd, Raymond Griffith and Frank Capra worked for Sennett. But, for an innovator, Keystone was a graveyard, and any comic talent with ideas bolted at the first opportunity.

Sennett, however, refused to change and clung to his threadbare formula through the 1920s and into the 30s, churning out tired, low-budget variations of his successes of the teens. He had, nevertheless, created the ground rules for American screen comedy. Among the pratfalls, chases, stereotypes and pantomime, Sennett set the tone and composed the basic melody. It was left to other, more inspired artists, to pick up that tune and transform it into a symphony. PB • *The Black Viper (short)* 1908 (a); *The Curtain Pole* 1909 (a); *The Water Nymph* 1912 (a,d,p); *A Film Johnnie (short)* 1914 (d); *Mabel at the Wheel (short)* 1914 (d); *Mabel's Strange Predicament (short)* 1914 (d); *Tango Tangles (short)* 1914 (d); *Tillie's Punctured Romance* 1914 (d); *Home Talent* 1921 (d,p); *Molly O'* 1921 (story); *A Small Town Idol* 1921 (sc); *The Crossroads of*

New York 1922 (sc,story); *Oh, Mabel Behave* 1922 (a,d); *The Extra Girl* 1923 (story); *The Shriek of Araby* 1923 (p,story); *Suzanna* 1923 (sc); *The Goodbye Kiss* 1928 (d,sc); *The Old Barn* 1928 (d); *Midnight Daddies* 1930 (d,p); *I Surrender Dear (short)* 1931 (d); *One More Chance (short)* 1931 (d); *Hypnotized* 1932 (d,sc,story); *The Timid Young Man (short)* 1935 (d); *Hollywood Cavalcade* 1939 (a); *Down Memory Lane* 1949 (archival footage).

Serreau, Coline • French director, screenwriter; also actress. • Versatile figure of French theater, film and TV, who gained international recognition with her witty and wise gender comedy, *Three Men and a Cradle* (1985). Written and directed by Serreau, the film won two Césars (the French Oscar) and was remade with great commercial success in America as *Three Men and a Baby* (1987). Many of Serreau's films, including the feature-length documentary, *But What Do These Women Want?* (1977), center on the situation of women in contemporary French society. • *On s'est trompé d'histoire d'amour* 1974 (a); *Le Fou de mai* 1977 (a); *Mais qu'est-ce qu'elles veulent/But What Do These Women Want?* 1977 (d,sc,sound engineer); *Pourquoi Pas!* 1978 (d,sc,dial); *Qu'est-ce qu'on attend pour être heureux!* 1982 (d,sc); *Trois hommes et un couffin/Three Men and a Cradle* 1985 (d,sc); *Three Men and a Baby* 1987 (from film *Trois hommes et un couffin*,tech.adv); *Romuald et Juliette/Mama, There's a Man in Your Bed* 1989 (d,sc); *Three Men and a Little Lady* 1990 (from screenplay *Trois hommes et un couffin*).

Seyrig, Delphine • Actress • Born Beirut, Lebanon, 1932; died October 15, 1990, Paris. *Educ.* Comédie de Saint-Etienne; Centre Dramatique de l'Est; Actors Studio. Coolly elegant leading lady who graced several important international productions of the 1960s and 70s.

Seyrig first came to prominence in Alain Resnais's styish, labyrinthine *Last Year at Marienbad* (1961) and won a best actress award at Venice for her role in his *Muriel* (1963). Her aloof charm was well used by directors including Francois Truffaut, Joseph Losey and Luis Bunuel.

By the mid-1970s she had become an active feminist and began working with female directors in such films as Marguerite Duras's *India Song* (1975) and Chantal Akerman's *Jeanne Dielman, 23 Quai du Commerce, 1080 Bruxelles* (1975). • *L'Année dernière a Marienbad/Last Year at Marienbad* 1961 (a); *Muriel* 1963 (a); *La Musica* 1966 (a); *Accident* 1967 (a); *Baisers volés/Stolen Kisses* 1968 (a); *Mister Freedom* 1968 (a); *La Voie Lactée/The Milky Way* 1969 (a); *Peau d'âne/Donkey Skin* 1970 (a); *Daughters of Darkness* 1971 (a); *Le Charme Discret de la Bourgeoisie/Discreet Charm of the Bourgeoisie* 1972 (a); *The Day of the Jackal* 1973 (a); *A Doll's House* 1973 (a); *The Black Windmill* 1974 (a); *Le Cri Du Coeur* 1974 (a); *Dites-Le avec des fleurs* 1974 (a); *Aloise* 1975 (a); *India Song* 1975 (a); *Le Jardin Qui Bascule* 1975 (a); *Jeanne Dielman, 23 quai du Commerce, 1080 Bruxelles* 1975 (a); *Caro Michele* 1976 (a); *Der Letzte Schrei* 1976 (a); *Baxter, Vera Baxter* 1977 (a); *Faces of Love* 1977 (a); *Repérages* 1977 (a); *Sois belle et tais-toi* 1977 (d); *Utkozben* 1979 (a); *Le Chemin Perdu* 1980 (a); *Chère Inconnue* 1980 (a); *Freak Orlando* 1981 (a); *Dorian Gray im Speigel der Boulevardpresse/Dorian Grey in the Mirror of the Popular Press* 1983 (a); *Le Grain de Sable* 1983 (a); *Golden Eighties* 1986 (a,song); *Letters Home* 1986 (a); *Seven Women-Seven Sins* 1987 (a—"Superbia"); *Johanna d'Arc of Mongolia/Joan of Arc of Mongolia* 1989 (a).

Shamroy, Leon • Director of photography • Born New York, NY, July 16, 1901; died 1974. *Educ.* Cooper Union; CCNY; Columbia. Distinguished American cinematographer, best known for his lavish color work on epics and musicals of the 1940s and 50s. Shamroy began shooting features in the late 1920s and, after a seven-year stint with Paramount (1932-39), spent most of his career at 20th Century-Fox. He worked primarily with Henry King and Walter Lang in the 1940s and was influential in the development of Cinemascope in the 50s. (Shamroy photographed the first film to use the new process, *The Robe*, in 1953.) He also worked with Otto Preminger on films such as *Daisy Kenyon* (1947), *Porgy and Bess* (1959) and *The Cardinal* (1963). • *Hidden Aces* 1927; *Land of the Lawless* 1927; *The Last Moment* 1927; *Pirates of the Sky* 1927; *Tongues of Scandal* 1927; *The Trunk Mystery* 1927; *Bitter Sweets* 1928; *Out With the Tide* 1928; *Alma de Gaucho* 1930; *Women Men Marry* 1931; *Stowaway* 1932; *Her Bodyguard* 1933; *Jennie Gerhardt* 1933; *Three Cornered Moon* 1933; *Good Dame* 1934; *Kiss and Make Up* 1934; *Ready For Love* 1934; *Thirty Day Princess* 1934; *Accent on Youth* 1935; *Behold My Wife* 1935; *Mary Burns, Fugitive* 1935; *Private Worlds* 1935; *She Couldn't Take It* 1935; *She Married Her Boss* 1935; *Fatal Lady* 1936; *Soak the Rich* 1936; *Spendthrift* 1936; *Wedding Present* 1936; *Blossoms on Broadway* 1937; *The Great Gambini* 1937; *Her Husband Lies* 1937; *She Asked For It* 1937; *You Only Live Once* 1937; *The Young in Heart* 1938 **(AANBPH)**; *The Adventures of Sherlock Holmes* 1939; *Made For Each Other* 1939; *Second Fiddle* 1939; *The Story of Alexander Graham Bell* 1939; *Down Argentine Way* 1940 **(AANBPH)**; *Four Sons* 1940; *I Was an Adventuress* 1940; *Lillian Russell* 1940; *Little Old New York* 1940; *Tin Pan Alley* 1940; *Confirm or Deny* 1941; *The Great American Broadcast* 1941; *Moon Over Miami* 1941; *That Night in Rio* 1941; *A Yank in the R.A.F.* 1941; *The Black Swan* 1942 **(AABPH)**; *Roxie Hart* 1942; *Ten Gentlemen From West Point* 1942 **(AANBPH)**; *Claudia* 1943; *Crash Dive* 1943; *Stormy Weather* 1943; *Buffalo Bill* 1944; *Greenwich Village* 1944; *Wilson* 1944 **(AABPH)**; *Leave Her to Heaven* 1945 **(AABPH)**; *State Fair* 1945; *A Tree Grows in Brooklyn* 1945; *Where Do We Go From Here?* 1945; *Daisy Kenyon* 1947; *Forever Amber* 1947; *The Shocking Miss Pilgrim* 1947; *That Lady in Ermine* 1948; *Prince of Foxes* 1949 **(AANBPH)**; *Twelve O'Clock High* 1949; *Cheaper By the Dozen* 1950; *Two Flags West* 1950; *David and Bathsheba* 1951 **(AANBPH)**; *On the Riviera* 1951; *The Snows of Kilimanjaro* 1952 **(AANBPH)**; *Wait Till the Sun Shines, Nellie* 1952; *With a Song in My Heart* 1952; *Call Me Madam* 1953; *Down Among the Sheltering Palms* 1953; *The Girl Next Door* 1953; *The Robe* 1953 **(AANBPH)**; *Tonight We Sing* 1953; *White Witch Doctor* 1953; *The Egyptian* 1954 **(AANBPH)**; *King of the Khyber Rifles* 1954; *Daddy Long Legs* 1955; *Good Morning, Miss Dove* 1955; *Love Is a Many Splendored Thing* 1955 **(AANBPH)**; *The Best Things in Life Are Free* 1956; *The Girl Can't Help It* 1956; *The King and I* 1956 **(AANBPH)**; *Desk Set* 1957; *The Bravados* 1958; *Rally Round the Flag, Boys!* 1958; *South Pacific* 1958 **(AANBPH)**; *Beloved Infidel* 1959; *The Blue Angel* 1959; *Porgy and Bess* 1959 **(AANBPH)**; *North to Alaska* 1960; *Wake Me When It's Over* 1960; *Snow White and the Three Stooges* 1961; *Tender Is the Night* 1962; *The Cardinal* 1963 **(AANBPH)**; *Cleopatra* 1963 **(AABPH)**; *John Goldfarb, Please Come Home* 1964; *What a Way to Go!* 1964; *The Agony and the Ecstasy* 1965 **(AANBPH)**; *Do Not Disturb* 1965; *The Glass Bottom Boat* 1966; *Caprice* 1967; *Planet of the Apes* 1968; *The Secret Life of an American Wife* 1968; *Skidoo* 1968; *Justine* 1969.

Shanley, John Patrick • Screenwriter, playwright; also director. • Born New York, NY, 1950. *Educ.* NYU (educational theater). Earned almost overnight recognition for his first play, *Danny and the Deep Blue Sea*, and has continued to win acclaim for his stage work, which often revolves around working-class, ethnic concerns. Shanley made his Hollywood reputation with *Moonstruck* (1987), a deftly constructed romantic comedy set in Brooklyn's Italian-American community. The film won three Oscars (one for best original screenplay) and was a huge box-office success. His subsequent film efforts—notably his script for the confused crime thriller, *January Man* (1989), and his directorial debut with the overblown *Joe Versus the Volcano* (1989)—have been somewhat disappointing. • *Five Corners* 1987 (assoc.p,sc); *Moonstruck* 1987 (sc)

(AABSC); *Crossing Delancey* 1988 (a); *The January Man* 1988 (sc); *Joe Versus the Volcano* 1990 (sc,song,d).

Sharaff, Irene • Costume designer • Born Boston, Massachussetts, 1910. Began her career in the theater and first made her mark in film with the precisely realized period musical, *Meet Me in St. Louis* (1944). Sharaff subsequently lent her talents to a host of meticulously detailed productions, including *An American in Paris* (1951), *West Side Story* (1961) and *Cleopatra* (1963). • *Meet Me in St. Louis* (cost) 1944; *An American in Paris* 1951 (cost—ballet) **(AABCD)**; *Call Me Madam* 1953 (cost) **(AANBCD)**; *A Star Is Born* 1954 (cost) **(AANBCD)**; *Brigadoon* 1954 (cost) **(AANBCD)**; *Guys and Dolls* 1955 (cost) **(AANBCD)**; *The King and I* 1956 (cost) **(AABCD)**; *Porgy and Bess* 1959 (cost) **(AANBCD)**; *Can-Can* 1960 (cost) **(AANBCD)**; *Flower Drum Song* 1961 (cost) **(AANBCD)**; *West Side Story* 1961 (cost) **(AABCD)**; *Cleopatra* 1963 (cost—Elizabeth Taylor) **(AABCD)**; *Who's Afraid of Virginia Woolf?* 1966 (cost) **(AABCD)**; *The Taming of the Shrew* 1967 (cost—Elizabeth Taylor) **(AANBCD)**; *Funny Girl* 1968 (cost); *Hello, Dolly!* 1969 (cost) **(AANBCD)**; *The Great White Hope* 1970 (cost); *The Other Side of Midnight* 1977 (cost) **(AANBCD)**; *Mommie Dearest* 1981 (cost).

Sharif, Omar • *aka* Omar El-Sharif • Actor • Born Michel Shahoub, Alexandria, Egypt, April 10, 1932. *Educ.* Victoria College, Cairo. Soulful, Egyptian-born romantic lead who appeared in several Middle Eastern films during the 1950s before achieving his international breakthrough in the David Lean epic, *Lawrence of Arabia* (1962). Sharif went on to distinguish himself in a number of big-budget productions, notably as the title character in Lean's adaptation of the Pasternak novel, *Dr. Zhivago* (1965). He appeared in several TV movies in the 1980s. Formerly married to popular Egyptian actress, Faten Hamama. • *Lawrence of Arabia* 1962 **(AANBSA)**; *Behold a Pale Horse* 1964; *The Fall of the Roman Empire* 1964; *Doctor Zhivago* 1965; *Genghis Khan* 1965; *The Night of the Generals* 1966; *The Poppy Is Also a Flower* 1966; *C'era una Volta...* 1967; *Funny Girl* 1968; *Mayerling* 1968; *The Appointment* 1969; *Che!* 1969; *MacKenna's Gold* 1969; *Le Casse* 1971; *The Horsemen* 1971; *The Last Valley* 1971; *L'Ile Mystérieuse/The Mysterious Island* 1973; *Juggernaut* 1974; *The Tamarind Seed* 1974; *Funny Lady* 1975; *Crime and Passion* 1976; *Ashanti* 1979; *Bloodline* 1979; *The Baltimore Bullet* 1980; *Oh Heavenly Dog* 1980; *Green Ice* 1981; *Return to Eden* 1982; *Ayoub* 1983; *Top Secret!* 1984; *Les Possédés* 1987; *Les Pyramides bleues* 1988; *Viaggio d'amore* 1990.

Sharkey, Ray • Actor • Born Brooklyn, NY, 1952. Lead and character player who began his career on TV in the 1970s and acheived his movie breakthrough in *The Idolmaker* (1980), Taylor Hackford's stinging look at exploitation in the music business. Sharkey has appeared in several Paul Mazursky films, notably as Phil D'Amico in the engaging *Willie & Phil* (1980). He excels in tough, urban roles and is known for his role as mob boss Sonny Steelgrave in the popular TV series, "Wiseguy." • *Hot Tomorrows* 1977 (a); *Stunts* 1977 (a); *Paradise Alley* 1978 (a); *Who'll Stop the Rain?* 1978 (a); *Heart Beat* 1979 (a); *The Idolmaker* 1980 (a,song); *Love & Money* 1980 (a); *Willie & Phil* 1980 (a); *Some Kind of Hero* 1982 (a); *Body Rock* 1984 (a); *Hellhole* 1984 (a); *duBEAT-e-o* 1984 (a); *No Mercy* 1986 (a); *Wise Guys* 1986 (a); *Private Investigations* 1987 (a); *Act of Piracy* 1988 (a); *Scenes From the Class Struggle in Beverly Hills* 1989 (a); *Wired* 1989 (a); *The Rain Killer* 1990 (a).

Shatner, William • Actor; also director. • Born Montreal, Quebec, Canada, March 22, 1931. *Educ.* McGill University, Montreal (business studies). Best known as the indomitable Captain Kirk in the popular TV series, "Star Trek" (1966-69) and its several movie spin-offs. Shatner's feature directorial debut came with the fifth—somewhat wooden—installment of these, 1989's *Star Trek V: The Final Frontier.* (He had previously directed several episodes of the TV show "T.J. Hooker" (1982-86), in which he also starred.) Shatner's wife, Marcy Lafferty, and daughter, Melanie, are both actresses. • *The Brothers Karamazov* 1958 (a); *The Explosive Generation* 1961 (a); *Judgment at Nuremberg* 1961 (a); *The Intruder* 1962 (a); *The Outrage* 1964 (a); *Incubus* 1965 (a); *Big Bad Mama* 1974 (a); *The Devil's Rain* 1975 (a); *Impulse* 1975 (a); *A Whale of a Tale* 1976 (a); *Kingdom of the Spiders* 1977 (a); *The Land of No Return* 1978 (a); *Star Trek: The Motion Picture* 1979 (a); *The Kidnapping of the President* 1980 (a); *Visiting Hours* 1981 (a); *Airplane II: The Sequel* 1982 (a); *Star Trek II: The Wrath of Khan* 1982 (a); *Star Trek III: The Search For Spock* 1984 (a); *The Bradbury Trilogy* 1985 (a); *The Canadian Conspiracy* 1986 (a); *Star Trek IV: The Voyage Home* 1986 (a); *Star Trek V: The Final Frontier* 1989 (a,d,story).

Shaver, Helen • Actress • Born St. Thomas, Ontario, Canada, February 24, 1952. *Educ.* Banff School of Fine Arts, Alberta (acting). Cool blonde beauty who played several effective lead and character roles in the 1980s. Shaver was outstanding as a prim East Coast college professor who makes a wary, but liberating foray into lesbianism in Donna Deitch's moving *Desert Hearts* (1985); she is perhaps best known for her role opposite Paul Newman in *The Color of Money* (1986). • *Shoot* 1976; *The Supreme Kid* 1976; *In Praise of Older Women* 1977; *Outrageous* 1977; *Starship Invasions* 1977; *Who Has Seen the Wind* 1977; *High-ballin'* 1978; *The Amityville Horror* 1979; *Gas* 1981; *Harry Tracy* 1981; *The Osterman Weekend* 1983; *Best Defense* 1984; *Desert Hearts* 1985; *The Color of Money* 1986; *Lost!* 1986; *The Believers* 1987; *The Land Before Time* 1988; *Walking After Midnight* 1988; *Tree of Hands* 1989; *Bethune: The Making of a Hero* 1990.

Shaw, Robert • Actor; also novelist, playwright. • Born Westhoughton, England, August 9, 1927; died 1978. *Educ.* RADA, London. Rough-hewn British character actor who made his stage debut in 1949 and began appearing in films in the mid-1950s. Originally typecast in tough, villainous roles, he proved his versatility with an exuberant, Oscar-nominated performance as Henry VIII in the fine Robert Bolt adaptation, *A Man For All Seasons* (1966). Shaw gained international renown in the 1970s for his curmudgeonly roles in blockbuster hits such as *The Sting* (1973) and *Jaws* (1975). He also wrote a play and a number of novels, including *The Man in the Glass Booth*, which he adapted for the stage and for a 1975 film. His second of three wives was actress Mary Ure. • *A Hill in Korea* 1956 (a); *Sea Fury* 1958 (a); *Libel* 1959 (a); *The Caretaker* 1963 (a); *From Russia With Love* 1963 (a); *The Luck of Ginger Coffey* 1964 (a); *Battle of the Bulge* 1965 (a); *Situation Hopeless-But Not Serious* 1965 (from novel *The Hiding Place*); *A Man For All Seasons* 1966 (a) **(AANBSA)**; *Custer of the West* 1967 (a); *The Birthday Party* 1968 (a); *Battle of Britain* 1969 (a); *The Royal Hunt of the Sun* 1969 (a); *Figures in a Landscape* 1970 (a,sc); *A Reflection of Fear* 1971 (a); *A Town Called Hell* 1971 (a); *Young Winston* 1972 (a); *The Sting* 1973 (a); *The Taking of Pelham 1, 2, 3* 1974 (a); *Diamonds* 1975 (a); *Jaws* 1975 (a); *The Man in the Glass Booth* 1975 (from play); *Der Richter und Sein Henker* 1975 (a); *Robin and Marian* 1976 (a); *Swashbuckler* 1976 (a); *Black Sunday* 1977 (a); *The Deep* 1977 (a); *Force 10 From Navarone* 1978 (a); *Avalanche Express* 1979 (a).

Shawn, Wallace • Playwright, screenwriter, actor • Born New York, NY, November 12, 1943. *Educ.* Harvard; Oxford. Made his stage debut in his own translation of Machiavelli's *The Mandrake* in 1977 and turned in a memorable screen performance two years later as Diane Keaton's ex-husband in Woody Allen's *Manhattan* (1979). Shawn scored a surprise hit with his thinly veiled autobiographical turn in the Louis Malle-directed talkathon, *My Dinner With Andre* (1981), which he co-wrote with fellow star Andre Gregory. An accomplished playwright (*Marie and Bruce, Aunt Dan and Lemon*), he is probably best known as the preposterous evil mastermind in Rob Reiner's engaging fairy tale, *The Princess Bride* (1987). • *All That Jazz* 1979 (a); *Manhattan* 1979 (a); *Starting Over* 1979 (a); *Atlantic City* 1980 (a); *Simon* 1980 (a); *A Little Sex* 1981 (a); *My Dinner With Andre* 1981 (a,sc); *The First Time* 1982 (a); *Deal of the Century* 1983 (a); *Lovesick* 1983 (a); *Saigon-Year of the Cat* 1983 (a); *Strange Invaders* 1983 (a); *The Bostonians* 1984 (a); *Crackers* 1984 (a); *The Hotel New Hampshire* 1984 (a); *Micki & Maude* 1984 (a); *Heaven Help Us* 1985 (a); *Head Office* 1986 (a); *The Bedroom Window* 1987 (a); *Nice Girls Don't Explode* 1987 (a); *Prick Up Your Ears* 1987 (a); *The Princess Bride* 1987 (a); *Radio Days* 1987 (a); *The Moderns* 1988 (a); *Scenes From the Class Struggle in Beverly Hills* 1989 (a); *She's Out of Control* 1989 (a); *We're No Angels* 1989 (a).

Shea, John • Actor • Born Conway, NH, April 14, 1949. *Educ.* Bates College, Lewiston, ME; Yale School of Drama (directing). Began a successful stage career in 1975 and has also appeared in several films, most notably in the role of Jack Lemmon's abducted son in the Costa-Gavras thriller, *Missing* (1982). Shea is also a popular TV actor and won an Emmy for his performance in the 1988 "surrogate mother" miniseries, *Baby M.* • *Hussy* 1979; *Missing* 1982; *In Our Hands* 1984; *Windy City* 1984; *Lune de Miel* 1985; *Coast to Coast* 1986; *Unsettled Land* 1987; *Light Years* 1988; *A New Life* 1988; *Stealing Home* 1988.

Shearer, Norma • Actress • Born Edith Norma Shearer, Montreal, Canada, August 10, 1900; died 1983. Child model and bit player in New York-based films whose appearance in *The Stealers* (1920) caught the attention of producer Irving Thalberg. Thalberg signed Shearer to a long-term contract with MGM in 1923 and married her in 1927, after which she had her pick of films, parts, directors and one cameraman who even photographed her costume tests. Compensating for a lack of natural beauty with great poise and charm, she played a narrow range of romantic roles in a glittering array of films, including *Their Own Desire* (1929), *The Divorcee* (1930), *The Barretts of Wimpole Street* (1934), *Romeo and Juliet* (1936) and *Marie Antoinette* (1938). Shearer's career faltered after Thalberg's death in 1936. Her brother, Douglas Shearer (1899-1971), was a pioneering sound technician who won 12 Oscars and developed several key technical innovations. • *The Flapper* 1920; *The Stealers* 1920; *Trail of the Law* 1921; *Blue Waters* 1922; *Bootleggers* 1922; *Channing of the Northwest* 1922; *The Man Who Paid* 1922; *A Clouded Name* 1923; *The Devil's Partner* 1923; *Lucretia Lombard* 1923; *Man and Wife* 1923; *Pleasure Mad* 1923; *The Wanters* 1923; *Broadway After Dark* 1924; *Broken Barriers* 1924; *Empty Hands* 1924; *He Who Gets Slapped* 1924; *Married Flirts* 1924; *The Snob* 1924; *The Wolf Man* 1924; *Excuse Me* 1925; *His Secretary* 1925; *Lady of the Night* 1925; *Pretty Ladies* 1925; *A Slave of Fashion* 1925; *The Tower of Lies* 1925; *Waking Up the Town* 1925; *The Devil's Circus* 1926; *Upstage* 1926; *The Waning Sex* 1926; *After Midnight* 1927; *The Demi-Bride* 1927; *The Student Prince in Old Heidelberg* 1927; *The Actress* 1928; *A Lady of Chance* 1928; *The Latest From Paris* 1928; *The Hollywood Revue of 1929* 1929; *The Last of Mrs. Cheyney* 1929; *Their Own Desire* 1929 **(AANBA)**; *The Trial of Mary Dugan* 1929; *The Divorcee* 1930 **(AABA)**; *Let Us Be Gay* 1930; *A Free Soul* 1931 **(AANBA)**; *Private Lives* 1931; *Strangers May Kiss* 1931; *Smilin' Through* 1932; *Strange Interlude* 1932; *The Barretts of Wimpole Street* 1934 **(AANBA)**; *Riptide* 1934; *Romeo and Juliet* 1936 **(AANBA)**; *Marie Antoinette* 1938 **(AANBA)**; *Idiot's Delight* 1939; *The Women* 1939; *Escape* 1940; *Her Cardboard Lover* 1942; *We Were Dancing* 1942.

Sheedy, Ally • Actress; also writer. • Born Alexandra Sheedy, New York, NY, June 13, 1962. *Educ.* USC, Los Angeles (drama). Made her film debut as Sean Penn's loyal girlfriend in the delinquent youth drama, *Bad Boys* (1983), and appeared in a number of "brat-pack" vehicles through the 1980s. Before pursuing an acting career, Sheedy (at age 12) wrote a best-selling children's book, *She Was Nice to Mice*, and performed with the American Ballet Theater. • *Bad Boys* 1983; *WarGames* 1983; *Oxford Blues* 1984; *The Breakfast Club* 1985; *St. Elmo's Fire* 1985; *Twice in a Lifetime* 1985; *Blue City* 1986; *Short Circuit* 1986; *Maid to Order* 1987; *Heart of Dixie* 1989; *Betsy's Wedding* 1990; *Only the Lonely* 1991.

Sheen, Charlie • Actor • Born Carlos Estevez, Los Angeles, CA, September 3, 1965. Clean-cut young lead who made his first film appearance as an extra in *Apocalypse Now* (1979), starring his father, Martin Sheen. Sheen junior first attracted attention for his role as the sensitive high school jock in *Lucas* (1986) and has since emerged as one of the leading actors of his generation. He gave fine performances in two films directed by Oliver Stone: *Platoon* (1986), in which he served as the first-person narrator; and *Wall Street* (1987)—again starring Martin Sheen—in which he played a young trader whose unscrupulous ambition leads him into conflict with his blue-collar father. Brother Emilio Estevez is also an actor. • *Red Dawn* 1984 (a); *The Boys Next Door* 1985 (a); *Ferris Bueller's Day Off* 1986 (a); *Lucas* 1986 (a); *Platoon* 1986 (a); *Wisdom* 1986 (a); *The Wraith* 1986 (a); *No Man's Land* 1987 (a); *Three For the Road* 1987 (a); *Wall Street* 1987 (a); *Eight Men Out* 1988 (a); *Young Guns* 1988 (a); *Beverly Hills Brats* 1989 (a); *Courage Mountain* 1989 (a); *Major League* 1989 (a); *Never on Tuesday* 1989 (a); *Tale of Two Sisters* 1989 (a,from poetry,narrative text); *Backtrack* 1990 (a); *Cadence* 1990 (a); *Men at Work* 1990 (a); *Navy Seals* 1990 (a); *The Rookie* 1990 (a).

Sheen, Martin • Actor • Born Ramon Estevez, Dayton, OH, August 3, 1940. One of the finest American actors of his generation and one of the most socially engaged of contemporary Hollywood figures.

Sheen began his career on the New York stage, first gaining attention for his leading role in the 1964 Broadway production, *The Subject Was Roses*. He began appearing in films in 1967 and has turned in several landmark performances; he was outstanding in Terrence Malick's *Badlands* (1973), as an alienated, amoral killer on the run, and in Francis Ford Coppola's *Apocolypse Now* (1979), during the shooting of which he suffered a serious heart attack.

Sheen's TV work includes his celebrated title role in the 1974 docudrama, *The Execution of Private Slovik*, as well as characterizations of several political figures such as President John Kennedy (in the *Kennedy* miniseries), his brother Robert (*The Missiles of October*) and Watergate principal John Dean (*Blind Ambition*). He made his directorial debut with the well-regarded TV production, *Babies Having Babies*.

An active campaigner in various liberal and charitable causes, Sheen has been arrested during several anti-nuclear demonstrations. His three sons—Emilio and Ramon Estevez and Charlie Sheen—are all actors, as is his daughter, Renee Estevez. • *The Incident* 1967 (a); *The Subject Was Roses* 1968 (a); *Catch-22* 1970 (a); *No Drums, No Bugles* 1971 (a); *Pickup on 101* 1972 (a); *Rage* 1972 (a); *Badlands* 1973 (a); *The Legend of Earl Durand* 1975 (a); *The Cassandra Crossing* 1977 (a); *The Little Girl Who Lives Down the Lane* 1977 (a); *Eagle's Wing* 1978 (a); *Apocalypse Now* 1979 (a); *The Final Countdown* 1980 (a); *Loophole* 1981 (a); *Enigma* 1982 (a); *Gandhi* 1982 (a); *In the King of Prussia* 1982 (a); *Man, Woman and Child* 1982 (a); *That Championship Season* 1982 (a); *The Dead Zone* 1983 (a); *Firestarter* 1984 (a); *In the Name of the People* 1984 (a); *Broken Rainbow* 1985 (a); *A State of Emergency* 1986 (a); *The Believers* 1987 (a); *Dear America* 1987 (a); *Siesta* 1987 (a); *Wall Street* 1987 (a); *Da* 1988 (a,exec.p); *Judgment in Berlin* 1988 (a,exec.p); *Just One Step: The Great Peace March* 1988 (a); *Personal Choice* 1988 (a); *Promises to Keep* 1988 (a); *Walking After Midnight* 1988 (a); *Beverly Hills Brats* 1989 (a); *Cold Front* 1989 (a); *Cadence* 1990 (a,d,sc).

Shelton, Ron • Screenwriter • Born Whittier, CA, September 15, 1945. *Educ.* Westmont College, Santa Barbara, CA; University of Arizona, Tuscon (sculpture). Former minor league baseball player who wrote two scripts for director Roger Spottiswoode (including 1983's *Under Fire*) before establishing himself as a writer-director with the 1988 sleeper hit, *Bull Durham*, a witty and literate insider's account of both love and hardball. Shelton was also responsible for the well-received *Blaze* (1989), based on Louisiana governor Huey Long's notorious relationship with stripper Blaze Starr. • *The Pursuit of D.B. Cooper* 1981 (assoc.p); *Under Fire* 1983 (sc,2u d); *The Best of Times* 1986 (sc); *Bull Durham* 1988 (d,sc) **(AANBSC)**; *Blaze* 1989 (d,sc).

Shepard, Sam • Playwright, screenwriter, actor • Born Samuel Shepard Rogers, Fort Sheridan, IL, November 5, 1943. Emerged as a leading American playwright in the late 1960s and early 70s with a number of powerful dramas which reworked American mythology, especially that of the "old west." Among Shepard's eight Obie-winning plays are *Curse of the Starving Class* (1977), *Buried Child* (1979), *Fool for Love* (1984) and *True West* (1985).

Shepard contributed to the screenplay of Michelangelo Antonioni's interesting, if poorly receieved, *Zabriskie Point* (1970) and scripted Wim Wenders's atmospheric American odyssey, *Paris, Texas* (1984). Tall, with weathered good looks, he made his first film appearance in Bob Dylan's *Renaldo & Clara* (1977) and went on to establish himself as an able supporting and lead player, notably in Terrence Malick's *Days of Heaven* (1978), as the legendary Chuck Yeager in *The Right Stuff* (1983) and in Robert Altman's film adaptation of *Fool for Love* (1985). He made his directorial debut with the elliptical drama, *Far North* (1988), which he also wrote. Shepard has two children by actress Jessica Lange. • *Bronco Bullfrog* 1970 (a); *Zabriskie Point* 1970 (sc); *Renaldo & Clara* 1977 (a); *Days of Heaven* 1978 (a); *Resurrection* 1980 (a); *Raggedy Man* 1981 (a); *Frances* 1982 (a); *The Right Stuff* 1983 (a) **(AANBSA)**; *Country* 1984 (a); *Paris, Texas* 1984 (sc,from story "Motel Chronicles"); *Fool For Love* 1985 (a,sc,from play); *Crimes of the Heart* 1986 (a); *Baby Boom* 1987 (a); *Far North* 1988 (d,sc); *Steel Magnolias* 1989 (a); *Bright Angel* 1991 (a); *Defenseless* 1991 (a); *Voyager* 1991 (a).

Shepherd, Cybill • Actress; also singer. • Born Memphis, TN, February 18, 1950. *Educ.* Hunter College; NYU; USC, Los Angeles. Former Miss Teenage Memphis and fashion model who gained immediate attention with her first screen role, as the teenage coquette in Peter Bogdanovich's *The Last Picture Show* (1971). Shepherd became Bogdanovich's romantic partner, but her roles in his subsequent films attracted critical scorn. Despite a creditable performance in *Taxi Driver* (1976), her Hollywood career had petered out by the late 1970s. She revived it in 1985 as star, alongside newcomer Bruce Willis, of the popular TV series "Moonlighting" (1985-89). Shepherd appeared in *Texasville*, the sequel to *Picture Show*, in 1990. • *The Last Picture Show* 1971; *The Heartbreak Kid* 1972; *Daisy Miller* 1974; *At Long Last Love* 1975; *Special Delivery* 1976; *Taxi Driver* 1976; *Silver Bears* 1977; *The Lady Vanishes* 1979; *Chances Are* 1989; *Alice* 1990; *Texasville* 1990.

Sheridan, Ann • Actress, singer • Born Clara Lou Sheridan, Denton, TX, February 21, 1915; died 1967. *Educ.* North Texas State Teachers College. Former beauty queen who appeared in several Paramount features before signing in 1936 with Warner Bros., where her smart, no-nonsense persona was put to good use in a number of crime melodramas. Sheridan made her mark in the haunting small town saga, *King's Row* (1942), and continued to showcase her talent in comedies and musicals through the early 1950s. She was subsequently known for her roles on the TV series, "Another World" and "Pistols and Petticoats" (1966-67). Actors Edward Norris, George Brent and Scott McKay were her husbands. • *The Bandit's Son* 1927 (a); *Casey Jones* 1927 (a); *Casey at the Bat* 1927 (a); *Galloping Thunder* 1927 (a); *The Way of All Flesh* 1927 (a); *Wedding Bills* 1927 (a); *Come on Marines* 1934 (a); *Ladies Should Listen* 1934 (a); *Behold My Wife* 1935 (a); *Car 99* 1935 (a); *Fighting Youth* 1935 (a); *Home on the Range* 1935 (a); *Red Blood of Courage* 1935 (a); *Rocky Mountain Mystery* 1935 (a); *Black Legion* 1936 (a); *Sing Me a Love Song* 1936 (a); *Alcatraz Island* 1937 (a); *The Footloose Heiress* 1937 (a); *The Great O'Malley* 1937 (a); *San Quentin* 1937 (a); *Wine, Women, and Horses* 1937 (a); *Angels With Dirty Faces* 1938 (a); *Broadway Musketeers* 1938 (a); *Cowboy From Brooklyn* 1938 (a); *Letter of Introduction* 1938 (a); *Little Miss Thoroughbred* 1938 (a); *Mystery House* 1938 (a); *The Patient in Room 18* 1938 (a); *She Loved a Fireman* 1938 (a); *Angels Wash Their Faces* 1939 (a); *Dodge City* 1939 (a); *Indianapolis Speedway* 1939 (a); *Naughty But Nice* 1939 (a); *They Made Me a Criminal* 1939 (a); *Winter Carnival* 1939 (a); *Castle on the Hudson* 1940 (a); *City For Conquest* 1940 (a); *It All Came True* 1940 (a); *They Drive By Night* 1940 (a); *Torrid Zone* 1940 (a); *Honeymoon For Three* 1941 (a); *The Man Who Came to Dinner* 1941 (a); *Navy Blues* 1941 (a); *George Washington Slept Here* 1942 (a); *Juke Girl* 1942 (a); *King's Row* 1942 (a); *Wings For the Eagle* 1942 (a); *Edge of Darkness* 1943 (a); *Thank Your Lucky Stars* 1943 (a); *The Doughgirls* 1944 (a); *Shine on Harvest Moon* 1944 (a); *One More Tomorrow* 1946 (a); *Nora Prentiss* 1947 (a); *The Unfaithful* 1947 (a); *Good Sam* 1948 (a); *Silver River* 1948 (a); *I Was a Male War Bride* 1949 (a); *Stella* 1950 (a); *Woman on the Run* 1950 (a); *Steel Town* 1951 (a); *Just Across the Street* 1952 (a); *Appointment in Honduras* 1953 (a); *Take Me to Town* 1953 (a,song); *Come Next Spring* 1955 (a); *The Opposite Sex* 1956 (a); *The Woman and the Hunter* 1957 (a).

Sheridan, Jim • Director, screenwriter • Born Dublin, Ireland, 1949. *Educ.* University College, Dublin; NYU (film). An acomplished director of the Dublin and New York stage who has had eight of his own plays produced, including the highly regarded *Spike in the First World War* (1983). Sheridan's debut feature, *My Left Foot* (1989), based on the life of paralyzed writer-painter Christy Brown and bolstered by Daniel Day-Lewis's Oscar-wining performance, earned international praise. • *My Left Foot* 1989 (d,sc) **(AANBD)**; *The Field* 1990 (d,sc).

Sherwood, Bill • Filmmaker; also screenwriter. • Born Washington, DC, 1952; died February 10, 1990, New York. *Educ.* Interlochen Arts Academy; Juilliard (composition); Hunter College, New York (film); USC, Los Angeles (film). Made the well-received low-budget feature, *Parting Glances* (1986), which rates among the most engaging big-screen portraits of New York gay life. Sherwood died at 37 due to complications resulting from the AIDS virus. • *Parting Glances* 1986 (d,sc,ed,sound ed,m).

Shields, Brooke • Actress; also model. • Born New York, NY, May 31, 1965. *Educ.* Princeton. Former child model (discovered by fashion photographer Francesco Scavullo before the age of one) who made a strong impression—if only for the innocent nude scenes—as a juvenile prostitute in Louis Malle's *Pretty Baby* (1978). Beautiful but wooden, Shields spent her adolescent years starring in disappointing features such as the *The Blue Lagoon* (1980) and Franco Zeffirelli's overwrought *Endless Love* (1981). • *Communion* 1977; *King of the Gypsies* 1978; *Pretty Baby* 1978; *Just You and Me, Kid* 1979; *Tilt* 1979; *Wanda Nevada* 1979; *The Blue Lagoon* 1980; *Endless Love* 1981; *The Muppets Take Manhattan* 1984; *Sahara* 1984; *Brenda Starr* 1989; *Speed Zone* 1989; *Backstreet Dreams* 1990.

Shindo, Kaneto • Director; also screenwriter, production designer. • Born Hiroshima, Japan, April 28, 1912. Art director of the late 1930s who became a scriptwriter in the mid-1940s, establishing a multi-film relationship with director Kimibasuro Yoshimura and contributing to the films of Kenji Mizoguchi, Kon Ichikawa and others. Shindo formed a production company in

1950 with Yoshimura and actress Nobuko Otowa (who starred in many of his films) and turned out works ranging from comedies to horror films.

Shindo made his directorial debut with *The Story of a Beloved Wife* (1951) and received international acclaim for his highly personal examination of post-nuclear trauma, *Children of Hiroshima* (1952). Though effective, the film was marred by a heavy-handed sentimentality that has also plagued many of his other efforts.

In 1960 Shindo crafted his finest achievement, *The Island*, a stark portrait of the daily struggles of an island-dwelling farmer shot almost entirely without dialogue. Shindo has continued to write, direct and produce mostly glossy, commercially oriented features. • *Waga Koi Wa Moenu* 1949 (sc); *The Story of a Beloved Wife* 1951 (d,sc); *Children of Hiroshima* 1952 (d,sc); *Avalanche* 1952 (d,sc); *Epitome* 1953 (d,sc); *A Woman's Life* 1953 (d,sc); *Gutter* 1954 (d,sc); *Wolves* 1955 (d,sc); *A Geisha's Suicide* 1956 (d,sc); *The Fishing Boat* 1956 (d,sc); *Harbor Rats* 1957 (d,sc); *Kanashimi wa onna dakeni/Only Women Have Trouble* 1958 (d,sc); *The Lucky Dragon No.5* 1959 (d,sc); *The Bride From Japan* 1959 (d,sc); *The Island* 1960 (d,sc); *The Man* 1962 (d,sc); *Mother* 1963 (d,sc); *Onibaba/The Demon/The Hole* 1964 (d,sc); *Conquest* 1965 (d,sc); *Lost Sex* 1966 (d,sc); *Libido* 1967 (d,sc); *Kuroneko/Black Cat* 1967 (d,sc); *Operation Negligee* 1968 (d,sc); *Strange Affinity* 1969 (d,sc); *Heat Wave Island* 1969 (d,sc); *Live Today—Die Tomorrow* 1971 (d,sc); *The Life of a Film Director* 1975 (d,sc); *My Way* 1975 (d,sc); *Chikuzan Travels Alone/The Life of Chikuzan* 1977 (d,sc); *Jiken* 1979 (sc); *Hokusai Manga* 1982 (d); *Chiheisen* 1984 (d,sc); *Eiga Joyu* 1987 (sc,from novel *Kinuyo Tanaka*); *Hachi-Ko* 1988 (sc).

Shire, David • Composer, songwriter • Born Buffalo, NY, July 3, 1937. *Educ.* Yale. Prolific composer who has divided his time among theater, TV and movies, hitting a peak in the 1970s with scores for such films as *The Conversation* (1974), *All the President's Men* (1976) and *Saturday Night Fever* (1977) and his Oscar-winning song for *Norma Rae* (1978), "It Goes Like It Goes." Formerly married to actress Talia Shire and currently wed to actress Didi Cohn. • *Drive, He Said* 1971 (m); *One More Train to Rob* 1971 (m); *Skin Game* 1971 (m); *Summertree* 1971 (m,song); *To Find a Man* 1972 (m); *Class of '44* 1973 (m); *Showdown* 1973 (m); *Steelyard Blues* 1973 (m); *Two People* 1973 (m); *The Conversation* 1974 (m); *The Taking of Pelham 1, 2, 3* 1974 (m); *Farewell, My Lovely* 1975 (m); *The Fortune* 1975 (m.sup); *The Hindenburg* 1975 (m); *All the President's Men* 1976 (m); *The Big Bus* 1976 (m); *Harry and Walter Go to New York* 1976 (a,m); *Saturday Night Fever* 1977 (m,add.m); *Norma Rae* 1978 (m,song) **(AABS)**; *Old Boyfriends* 1978 (m); *Straight Time* 1978 (m,song); *Fast Break* 1979 (m,song); *I'll Never Say Goodbye* 1979 (song) **(AANBS)**; *The Promise* 1979 (m,song); *The Earthling* 1980 (song); *The Night the Lights Went Out in Georgia* 1981 (m,song); *Only When I Laugh* 1981 (m); *Paternity* 1981 (m,song); *Max Dugan Returns* 1982 (m); *The World According to Garp* 1982 (m.adapt); *2010* 1984 (m); *Oh, God! You Devil* 1984 (m); *Return to Oz* 1985 (m,m.cond); *'night, Mother* 1986 (m); *Short Circuit* 1986 (m,song); *Backfire* 1987 (m); *Monkey Shines: An Experiment in Fear* 1988 (m); *Vice Versa* 1988 (m).

Shire, Talia • *aka* Talia Shire Schwartzman • Actress • Born Talia Rose Coppola, Jamaica, NY, April 25, 1946. *Educ.* Yale School of Drama. Waif-like actress who first gained attention as Don Corleone's abused daughter in *The Godfather* (1972) and came to prominence as Sylvester Stallone's demure, faithful wife in the "Rocky" series. Sister of director Francis Ford Coppola, formerly married to composer David Shire and currently wed to producer Jack Schwartzman, with whom she co-founded the Taliafilm II production company. • *Gas-s-s-s!* 1970 (a); *The Godfather* 1972 (a); *The Godfather, Part II* 1974 (a) **(AANBSA)**; *Rocky* 1976 (a) **(AANBA)**; *Old Boyfriends* 1978 (a); *Prophecy* 1979 (a); *Rocky II* 1979 (a); *Windows* 1980 (a); *Rocky III* 1982 (a); *Never Say Never Again* 1983 (consultant to producer); *Rocky IV* 1985 (a); *RAD* 1986 (a); *From Another Star* 1987 (a,exec.p); *Lionheart* 1987 (p); *New York Stories* 1989 (a); *The Godfather Part III* 1990 (a); *Rocky V* 1990 (a).

Short, Martin • Actor • Born Hamilton, Ontario, Canada, 1951. *Educ.* McMaster University, Hamilton, Ontario (social work, writing). Diminutive comedic performer who displayed his gift for zany characterizations with Toronto's Second City troupe, where he became known for his "Ed Grimley" and "Jackie Rogers, Jr." personae. Short was a regular on New York's "Saturday Night Live" (1984-85) before moving into features. Brother of comedy writer Michael Short and husband of actress Nancy. • *Lost and Found* 1979 (a); *The Outsider* 1979 (a); *The Canadian Conspiracy* 1986 (a); *Three Amigos!* 1986 (a,song); *Cross My Heart* 1987 (a); *Innerspace* 1987 (a); *Three Fugitives* 1989 (a); *Clifford* 1991 (a).

Shostakovich, Dmitri • Composer • Born St. Petersburg (now Lenigrad), Russia, September 25, 1906; died 1975. One of the foremost composers of the 20th century, Shostakovich began his career playing piano accompaniment for silent films. He wrote the first of many memorable film scores in 1929, for Kozintsev and Trauberg's *New Babylon*, and later scored the pair's famous "Maxim" trilogy. Shostakovich worked mainly at the Lenfilm studio from 1935-47 and at Mosfilm thereafter. • *New Babylon* 1929 (m); *Prostiye lyudi* 1945 (m); *Pirogov* 1947 (m); *Michurin* 1948 (m); *Molodaya gvardiya* 1948 (m); *Padeniye Berlina* 1949 (m); *Vstrecha na Elbe* 1949 (m); *Nezabyvayemyi 1919 god* 1952 (m); *Pervi eshelon* 1955 (m); *Khovanshchina* 1959 (sc,m,orch) **(AANBM)**; *Pyat dnei—pyat nochei* 1960 (m); *I Sequestrati di Altona/The Condemned of Altona* 1962 (m); *Sibirska Ledi Magbet* 1962 (m); *Hamlet* 1964 (m); *Katerina Izmailova* 1967 (from opera); *King Lear* 1971 (m); *First Time Round* 1972 (m); *Jacques Duclos ou le triomphe de la vie* 1977 (m); *The Eye of the Heart* 1978 (m); *Rikos ja Rangaistus/Crime and Punishment* 1983 (m); *Parad Planyet/Parade of the Planets* 1984 (m); *Ce fou de peuple Russe* 1985 (m); *Fandango* 1985 (m); *Half Life* 1985 (m); *Jour et Nuit* 1986 (m); *Eine Bewegung der Zeit* 1987 (m); *Dmitri Schostakowitsch Altowaja Sonata/Dmitri Shostakovich—Sonata For Viola* 1987 (m); *La Ley del Deseo/The Law of Desire* 1987 (m); *Testimony* 1987 (from memoirs,m); *Ariel* 1988 (m); *The Cow* 1989 (m).

Shub, Esther • Editor, compilation filmmaker • Born Ukraine, Russia, 1894; died 1949. The most prominent Soviet woman filmmaker of her generation, Shub carries the distinction of having singlehandedly created a film genre. With Dziga Vertov, the filmmaker with whom whe was to maintain a lifelong—and frequently stormy—professional relationship, Shub took the established form of the documentary film and managed to recreate it wholly in the image of the Soviet Revolution, creating what is now known as the historical compilation film. She was also a painstaking archivist and an editor of great intuitive ability.

Born into a family of landowners, Shub studied literature in Moscow in the years before the Revolution. She immersed herself in the salon-like atmosphere of the city, making the acquaintance of, among others, the poet Mayakovsky. With the Revolution came a corresponding change in attitude for Shub, who enrolled in classes at the Institute for Women's Higher Education and subsequently landed a job as a "theater officer" at the State Commissariat of Education. Initially involved in collaborations with Meyerhold and Mayakovsky, she soon joined the Goskino film company, where she developed her technical expertise by re-editing foreign films for Soviet distribution.

Shub shared with Vertov a belief in film's intrinsic ability to reveal aspects of reality not visible to the naked eye. But unlike Vertov, whose interest lay in contemporary matters, she became engaged in the interpretation of the historical world. Her reputation is based on a film trilogy which traces the birth of the Soviet Socialist Republic through to the tenth anniversary of the October Revolution. The first of the series, *The Fall of the Romanov Dynasty* (1927), covers the years 1912-17; its successor, *The Great Road* (1927) chronicles the first ten years of the Revolution; and the final film, *Lev Tolstoi and the Russia of Nikolai II* (1928), commemorates the centenary of Tolstoi's birth, with an examination of the years 1897-1912. Produced under the auspices of Sovkino, in cooperation with the Museum of the Revolution, the trilogy reflects a formidable amount of research; it is estimated that Shub viewed close to three million feet of newsreel footage.

In the process of compiling her films Shub had to contend with not only an overwhelming volume of material but also the problem of locating relevant footage. She often found that valuable documents of the pre-war period had been sold abroad or had deteriorated beyond repair in ill-equipped newsreel archives. She compensated for lack of material by using newly shot footage. *Lev Tolstoi*, for example, is constructed around fewer than 80 meters of footage of the author and his family. Unlike Vertov, who was an outspoken critic of the "staged" film, Shub did not consider the use of contrived material a compromise of the authenticity of her work. She later claimed her desire was to create "editorialized newsreels." Her films derive much of their power from this technique of providing a contemporary context for archival footage.

Because she managed to negotiate a middle path between narrative and documentary forms, Shub's work was admired by theorists of both camps. It was also highly regarded by both Constructivists and Futurists, who often praised her films within their attacks against the bourgeois indulgences of "imaginative art." But, like her contemporaries, Shub was the victim of Party philistines and ideological prejudice against "formal experimentation." Sovkino denied Shub authorial rights for her trilogy on the grounds that she was "just an editor" and that the construction of the films had required "no special ability."

Despite this indignity, Shub was in 1935 awarded the title Honored Artist of the Republic. She went on to collaborate with Pudovkin on the successful *Twenty Years of Soviet Cinema* (1940). In 1942 Shub left Goskino to become chief editor of *The News of the Day* at the Central Studio for Documentary film in Moscow. Although she produced and directed several documentaries, most of her later years were confined to editing duties. She wrote two books, *In Close Up* (1959) and *My Life—Cinematograph* (1972). RH • *The Fall of the Romanov Dynasty* 1927; *The Great Road* 1927; *Lev Tolstoi and the Russia of Nikolai II* 1928; *Twenty Years of Soviet Cinema* 1940.

Shue, Elisabeth • Actress • Born US, 1963. Attractive lead who earned praise as the determined child-watcher in 1987's *Adventures in Babysitting* before playing Tom Cruise's love interest in *Cocktail* (1988). Shue also took over the role of Marty McFly's marooned girlfriend, Jennifer, in the second and third installments of the "Back to the Future" films. • *The Karate Kid* 1984; *Link* 1986; *Adventures in Babysitting* 1987; *Cocktail* 1988; *Back to the Future II* 1989; *Back to the Future III* 1990; *The Marrying Man* 1991.

Sidney, Sylvia • Actress • Born Sophia Kosow, Bronx, NY, August 8, 1910. *Educ.* Theatre Guild School, New York. Exceptional emotional actress and Broadway lead who entered films in 1927 and joined Paramount in 1931, carving out a niche as a Depression-era working-class heroine, notably in *An American Tragedy* (1931), Fritz Lang's *Fury* and Hitchcock's *Sabotage* (both 1936).

Sidney proved unable to shake her typecast and retired from movies in the mid-1950s to concentrate on her theater work; she returned to the big screen in 1973, winning acclaim for her performance in *Summer Wishes, Winter Dreams*. Married to Bennett Cerf and Luther Adler. • *Thru Different Eyes* 1929; *An American Tragedy* 1931; *City Streets* 1931; *Confessions of a Co-ed* 1931; *Ladies of the Big House* 1931; *Street Scene* 1931; *Madame Butterfly* 1932; *Merrily We Go to Hell* 1932; *The Miracle Man* 1932; *Jennie Gerhardt* 1933; *Pick Up* 1933; *Good Dame* 1934; *Thirty Day Princess* 1934; *Accent on Youth* 1935; *Behold My Wife* 1935; *Mary Burns, Fugitive* 1935; *Fury* 1936; *Sabotage* 1936; *The Trail of the Lonesome Pine* 1936; *Dead End* 1937; *You Only Live Once* 1937; *You and Me* 1938; *One Third of a Nation* 1939; *The Wagons Roll at Night* 1941; *Blood on the Sun* 1945; *Mr. Ace* 1946; *The Searching Wind* 1946; *Love From a Stranger* 1947; *Les Miserables* 1952; *Violent Saturday* 1954; *Behind the High Wall* 1956; *Summer Wishes, Winter Dreams* 1973 (**AANBSA**); *God Told Me To* 1976; *I Never Promised You a Rose Garden* 1977; *Damien: Omen II* 1978; *Hammett* 1982; *Copkiller* 1983; *Beetlejuice* 1988; *Going Hollywood: The War Years* 1988.

Siegel, Don • Director • Born Donald Siegel, Chicago, IL, October 26, 1912. *Educ.* Jesus College, Cambridge; RADA, London. Former actor who joined Warner Bros. in 1933 as an assistant film librarian and worked his way up to head of the montage department. Siegel directed a number of shorts in the 1940s, notably the Oscar-winning *Star in the Night* (cartoon) and *Hitler Lives?* (documentary), both in 1945. He made his feature debut the following year with *The Verdict*.

By the late 50s Siegel had established himself as an inspired orchestrator of tense, action-packed thrillers, including the controversially violent *Riot in Cell Block 11* (1954), the classic sci-fi parable, *Invasion of the Body Snatchers* (1956), the crime melodrama, *Baby Face Nelson* (1957) and *The Killers* (1964), an uncompromising remake of Robert Siodmak's 1946 underworld saga featuring a hot-tempered Ronald Reagan in his last screen apppearance. These films attracted the attention of the French *Cahiers du Cinéma* critics, who praised Siegel's technical finesse and no-nonsense approach to a quintessentially American genre.

Siegel went on to enjoy a prolific and productive association with Clint Eastwood, which included *Coogan's Bluff* (1968) and *The Beguiled* (1971) as well as the classic urban crime series which began with *Dirty Harry* (1971), in which Eastwood became the ultimate embodiment of one of Siegel's favorite trademarks, the "rogue cop." Siegel also appeared (as Murphy the bartender) in the Eastwood-directed *Play Misty for Me* (1971) and in the 1978 remake of *Invasion of the Body Snatchers*. His son Kristoffer Tabori-Siegel, from his marriage (1945-53) to actress Viveca Lindfors, is an actor. • *Hitler Lives?* 1945 (d); *Star in the Night* 1945 (d); *The Verdict* 1946 (d); *The Big Steal* 1949 (d); *Night Unto Night* 1949 (d); *Duel at Silver Creek* 1952 (d); *No Time For Flowers* 1952 (d); *China Venture* 1953 (d); *Count the Hours* 1953 (d); *Private Hell 36* 1954 (d); *Riot in Cell Block 11* 1954 (d); *An Annapolis Story* 1955 (d); *Crime in the Streets* 1956 (d); *Invasion of the Body Snatchers* 1956 (d); *Baby Face Nelson* 1957 (d); *The Gun Runners* 1958 (d); *The Lineup* 1958 (d); *A Spanish Affair* 1958 (d); *Edge of Eternity* 1959 (a,assoc.p,d); *Hound Dog Man* 1959 (d); *Flaming Star* 1960 (d); *Hell Is For Heroes* 1962 (d); *The Hanged Man* 1964 (d); *The Killers* 1964 (d,p); *Coogan's Bluff* 1968 (d,p); *Madigan* 1968 (d); *Death of a Gunfighter* 1969 (d); *Two Mules For Sister Sara* 1970 (d); *The Beguiled* 1971 (d,p); *Dirty Harry* 1971 (d,p); *Play Misty For Me* 1971 (a); *Charley Varrick* 1973 (a,d,p); *The Black Windmill* 1974 (d,p); *The Shootist* 1976 (d); *Telefon* 1977 (d); *Invasion of the Body Snatchers* 1978 (a); *Escape From Alcatraz* 1979 (a,d,p); *Rough Cut* 1980 (d); *Jinxed!* 1982 (d); *Into the Night* 1985 (a).

Siemaszko, Casey • Actor • Born Kazimierz Siemaszko, Chicago, IL, March 17, 1961. *Educ.* Goodman Theatre School of Drama, Chicago. Juvenile lead of the 1980s, notable as the doomed high school student in *Three O'Clock*

High (1987) and Burt Reynolds's youthful partner-in-crime in *Breaking In* (1989). • *Class* 1983; *Back to the Future* 1985; *Secret Admirer* 1985; *Stand By Me* 1986; *Gardens of Stone* 1987; *Three O'Clock High* 1987; *Biloxi Blues* 1988; *Young Guns* 1988; *Back to the Future II* 1989; *Breaking In* 1989.

Signoret, Simone • Actress • Born Simone Kaminker, Wiesbaden, Germany, March 25, 1921; died September 30, 1985, Normandy, France. Steamy, unique beauty who took to film work during WWII as a means of supporting her family after her father, a Jewish linguist, had fled to London to join the Free French Army. Projecting both hard-bitten cynicism and earthy sensuality, Signoret was appearing in featured roles by the mid-1940s, typically playing fallen, grasping or luckless women and unbeatable as a woman in love. Notable early films include the sophisticated romantic comedy, *La Ronde* (1950), Henri-Georges Clouzot's classic thriller, *Diabolique* (1955) and the gritty British social drama, *Room at the Top* (1958), which earned her numerous honors, including a best actress Oscar.

In later years Signoret grew convincingly into more matronly roles, contributing a memorable turn opposite Oskar Werner in Stanley Kramer's classy soap-opera, *Ship of Fools* (1965). Mother, by one time husband Yves Allegret, of actress Catherine Allegret. Married to Yves Montand from 1951 until her death. • *Les Demons de l'Aube* 1946; *Dédée/Dédée d'Anvers* 1948; *Impasse des deux anges* 1948; *La Ronde* 1950; *Time Running Out* 1950; *Casque d'or* 1952; *Thérèse Raquin* 1953; *Les Diaboliques/Diabolique* 1955; *La Mort en ce jardin* 1956; *Les Sorcières de Salem* 1956; *Room at the Top* 1958 **(AABA)**; *Le Joli Mai* 1962; *Dragées au Poivre* 1963; *Compartiment tueurs/The Sleeping Car Murders* 1965; *Ship of Fools* 1965 **(AANBA)**; *The Deadly Affair* 1967; *Games* 1967; *The Sea Gull* 1968; *L'Armée des ombres* 1969; *L'Aveu* 1970; *Langlois (short)* 1970; *Le Chat* 1971; *Comptes A Rebours* 1971; *La Veuve Couderc* 1971; *Les Granges Brulées* 1973; *Rude journée pour la reine* 1973; *La Chair de l'orchidée* 1974; *Police Python.357* 1975; *Le Fond de l'air est rouge* 1977; *Madame Rosa* 1977; *L'Adolescente* 1978; *Judith Therpauve* 1978; *Chère Inconnue/I Sent a Letter to My Love* 1980; *L'Etoile du nord* 1982; *Guy De Maupassant* 1982; *Des Terroristes à la retraite* 1983.

Silberman, Serge • Producer • Born Poland, May 13, 1917. A significant force in French feature production since 1966, when he founded the Greenwich Film Production company. Silberman backed all of Bunuel's late films, including the Oscar-winning *The Discreet Charm of the Bourgeoisie* (1972). Other notable credits include Jean-Jacques Beineix's *Diva* (1981), Akira Kurosawa's epic *Ran* (1985) and Nagisa Oshima's *Max, mon amour* (1986). • *Le Journal d'une femme de chambre/Diary of a Chambermaid* 1963 (p); *La Voie Lactée/The Milky Way* 1969 (p); *La Course du lièvre à travers les champs* 1972 (p); *Le Charme discret de la bourgeoisie/The Discreet Charm of the Bourgeoisie* 1972 (p); *Le Fantôme de la liberté/The Phantom of Liberty* 1974 (exec.p); *Les Mal Partis* 1975 (p); *Cet obscur objet du désir/That Obscure Object of Desire* 1977 (p); *Exposed* 1983 (exec.p); *A.K./Akira Kurosawa* 1985 (p); *Ran* 1985 (p); *Max mon amour/Max, My Love* 1986 (p); *Jeniec Europy/Hostage of Europe* 1989 (p).

Silliphant, Stirling • Screenwriter; also producer. • Born Detroit, MI, January 16, 1918. Advertising executive with Disney and Fox who turned to producing and screenwriting in the mid-1950s. Silliphant won a best screenplay Oscar for the tense racial drama, *In the Heat of the Night* (1967), and was noted for his work on such TV series as "Naked City" and "Route 66." Later work includes *The Enforcer* (1976) and 1987's *Over the Top*, co-written with Sylvester Stallone. • *The Joe Louis Story* 1953 (p); *Five Against the House* 1955 (p,sc); *Huk!* 1956 (sc,from novel); *Nightfall* 1956 (sc); *Damn Citizen!* 1957 (sc,story); *The Lineup* 1958 (sc); *Maracaibo* 1958 (from novel); *The Slender Thread* 1965 (sc); *In the Heat of the Night* 1967 (sc) **(AABSC)**; *Charly* 1968 (sc); *Marlowe* 1969 (sc); *The Liberation of L.B. Jones* 1970 (sc); *Murphy's War* 1970 (sc); *A Walk in the Spring Rain* 1970 (p,sc); *Shaft* 1971 (p); *The New Centurions* 1972 (sc); *The Poseidon Adventure* 1972 (sc); *Shaft's Big Score* 1972 (p); *Shaft in Africa* 1973 (sc); *The Towering Inferno* 1974 (sc); *The Killer Elite* 1975 (sc); *The Enforcer* 1976 (sc); *Telefon* 1977 (sc); *The Silent Flute* 1978 (sc,story); *The Swarm* 1978 (sc); *When Time Ran Out* 1980 (sc); *Feel the Heat* 1987 (exec.p,sc); *Over the Top* 1987 (sc).

Silver, Joan Micklin • Director; also screenwriter, producer. • Born Omaha, NB, May 24, 1935. *Educ.* Sarah Lawrence College, Bronxville, NY. Consistently effective director whose films have been noted for their emotional depth, fine acting (often by unknown performers) and deftly drawn characters.

Silver began her career writing educational films and made her feature directing debut with the keenly observed immigrant tale, *Hester Street* (1975). Made for under $400,000 and rejected by distributors, it was eventually released by Silver's husband Raphael and earned $5 million as well as an Oscar nomination for actress Carol Kane. Silver battled with United Artists over her first studio film, *Chilly Scenes of Winter*—UA changed the ending and released it as *Head Over Heels* in 1979, though it finally saw the light in its original form in 1982—and earned her first notable commercial success with *Crossing Delancey* (1988), the story of a love affair between a sophisticated New York literary type (Amy Irving) and a reticent Lower East Side pickle seller (Peter Riegert).

Silver's husband has produced several of her films (the two switched functions for *On the Yard* 1978) and their daughter Marisa made a promising directorial debut at age 24 with *Old Enough* (1984), which was produced by her sister, Dina. • *Women in Limbo* 1972 (sc,story); *Hester Street* 1975 (d,sc); *Between the Lines* 1977 (d); *On the Yard* 1978 (p); *Head Over Heels* 1979 (d,sc); *50 Years of Action!* 1986 (a); *Crossing Delancey* 1988 (d); *Loverboy* 1989 (d).

Silver, Joel • American producer • *Educ.* NYU. Leading producer of the action-adventure style films that dominated Hollywood movie production in the 1980s. Silver began his career as an assistant to producer Lawrence Gordon, with whom he continues to work (*Predator* 1987, *Die Hard* 1988); he has also enjoyed multi-film collaborations with directors Walter Hill (*48 Hrs.* 1982) and Richard Donner (*Lethal Weapon* 1987). • *The Warriors* 1979 (assoc.p); *Xanadu* 1980 (p); *48 Hrs.* 1982 (p); *Jekyll and Hyde... Together Again* 1982 (exec.p); *Streets of Fire* 1984 (p); *Brewster's Millions* 1985 (p); *Commando* 1985 (p); *Weird Science* 1985 (p); *Jumpin' Jack Flash* 1986 (p); *Lethal Weapon* 1987 (p); *Predator* 1987 (p); *Action Jackson* 1988 (p); *Die Hard* 1988 (p); *Who Framed Roger Rabbit?* 1988 (a); *Lethal Weapon 2* 1989 (p); *Road House* 1989 (p); *The Adventures of Ford Fairlane* 1990 (p); *Die Hard 2: Die Harder* 1990 (p); *Predator 2* 1990 (p).

Silver, Ron • Actor • Born New York, NY, July 2, 1946. *Educ.* State University of New York at Buffalo (Chinese); Herbert Berghof Studio; Actors Studio. Intense, quixotic lead and supporting player of stage, TV and—from 1976—film. Silver came to prominence with a Tony Award-winning role as a sleazy film producer in the Broadway production of David Mamet's *Speed-the-Plow.* He received widespread acclaim for his film performances as a resourceful Holocaust survivor in Paul Mazursky's *Enemies, A Love Story* (1989) and as Harvard law professor Alan Dershowitz in Barbet Schroeder's black comedy of manners based on the von Bulow murder trial, *Reversal of Fortune* (1990). Active in many political causes, he is a co-founder of liberal advocacy group, the Creative Coalition. • *Tunnelvision* 1976; *Semi-Tough* 1977; *Best Friends* 1982; *The Entity* 1982; *Silent Rage* 1982; *Lovesick* 1983; *Silkwood* 1983; *Garbo Talks* 1984; *The Goodbye People* 1984; *Oh, God! You Devil* 1984; *Romancing the Stone* 1984; *Eat and Run* 1985; *Blue*

Steel 1989; *Enemies, A Love Story* 1989; *Fellow Traveller* 1990; *Reversal of Fortune* 1990.

Silvestri, Alan • Composer • Born New York, NY. *Educ.* Berklee College of Music, Boston MA. Leading contemporary composer who began his career scoring low-budget films and worked on the TV series "CHiPS" before graduating to prestigious Hollywood productions including *Romancing the Stone* (1984), *Back to the Future* (1985) and *Who Framed Roger Rabbit* (1988). • *Las Vegas Lady* 1975 (m); *The Amazing Dobermans* 1976 (m); *Par ou t'es rentré? On t'as vu Sortir* 1984 (m); *Romancing the Stone* 1984 (m); *Fandango* 1985 (m); *Stephen King's Cat's Eye* 1985 (m); *Back to the Future* 1985 (m); *Summer Rental* 1985 (m); *American Anthem* 1986 (m); *The Clan of the Cave Bear* 1986 (m); *The Delta Force* 1986 (m); *Flight of the Navigator* 1986 (m); *No Mercy* 1986 (m); *Critical Condition* 1987 (m); *Outrageous Fortune* 1987 (m); *Overboard* 1987 (m); *Predator* 1987 (m); *Mac and Me* 1988 (m,songs); *My Stepmother Is an Alien* 1988 (m); *Who Framed Roger Rabbit* 1988 (m); *The Abyss* 1989 (m); *Back to the Future II* 1989 (m); *She's Out of Control* 1989 (m); *Tummy Trouble* 1989 (m); *Back to the Future III* 1990 (m); *Downtown* 1990 (m); *Predator 2* 1990 (m); *Young Guns II* 1990 (m).

Sim, Alastair • Actor • Born Edinburgh, Scotland, October 9, 1900; died 1976. *Educ.* Edinburgh University. Inimitable Scottish comic performer who made his screen debut in the mid-1930s at the age of 35 and went on to play assorted eccentrics and bumblers through the mid-70s. Sim was especially memorable as the over-taxed headmaster in the prep-school farce, *The Happiest Days of Your Life* (1949), as Scrooge in *A Christmas Carol* (1951) and as a ridiculous clergyman in the outlandish satire, *The Ruling Class* (1972). • *Late Extra* 1935; *The Man in the Mirror* 1936; *The Squeaker* 1937; *Inspector Hornleigh* 1939; *This Man in Paris* 1939; *The Happiest Days of Your Life* 1949; *Stage Fright* 1950; *Scrooge/A Christmas Carol* 1951; *Laughter in Paradise* 1951; *Innocents in Paris* 1953; *The Belles of St. Trinian's* 1954; *An Inspector Calls* 1954; *Wee Geordie* 1955; *Blue Murder at St. Trinian's* 1957; *The Doctor's Dilemma* 1958; *The Anatomist* 1961; *The Ruling Class* 1972; *Royal Flash* 1975; *Escape From The Dark* 1976.

Simmons, Jean • Actress • Born London, January 31, 1929. Gifted, dark-haired English beauty who appeared in some prestigious British productions (notably Lean's *Great Expectations* in 1946 and as Ophelia in Olivier's 1949 *Hamlet*) before moving in 1950 to Hollywood with her husband, Stewart Granger. Simmons soon became a major Hollywood star, appearing opposite leading men including Richard Burton (*The Robe* 1953), Marlon Brando (*Guys and Dolls* 1955), Paul Newman (*Until They Sail* 1957) and Gregory Peck (*The Big Country* 1958).

In 1960 Simmons divorced Granger and married Richard Brooks, who directed her and Burt Lancaster that same year in *Elmer Gantry*, an acclaimed adaptation of the Sinclair Lewis novel. She subsequently appeared in mostly unexceptional films and began performing in high-profile TV productions (*The Thorn Birds, Inherit the Wind*) in the 1980s. • *Great Expectations* 1946; *Black Narcissus* 1947; *Hamlet* 1948 **(AANBSA)**; *So Long at the Fair* 1950; *Trio* 1950; *Androcles and the Lion* 1952; *Angel Face* 1952; *The Actress* 1953; *Affair With a Stranger* 1953; *The Robe* 1953; *She Couldn't Say No* 1953; *Young Bess* 1953; *A Bullet Is Waiting* 1954; *Desiree* 1954; *The Egyptian* 1954; *Footsteps in the Fog* 1955; *Guys and Dolls* 1955; *Hilda Crane* 1956; *This Could Be the Night* 1957; *Until They Sail* 1957; *The Big Country* 1958; *Home Before Dark* 1958; *This Earth Is Mine* 1959; *Elmer Gantry* 1960; *The Grass Is Greener* 1960; *Spartacus* 1960; *All the Way Home* 1963; *Life at the Top* 1965; *Mister Buddwing* 1965; *Divorce American Style* 1967; *Rough Night in Jericho* 1967; *The Happy Ending* 1969 **(AANBA)**; *Say Hello to Yesterday* 1970; *Mr. Sycamore* 1974; *Dominique* 1977; *Going Undercover* 1984; *The Dawning* 1988; *King Ralph* 1991.

Simon, John • Critic • Theater and film critic for various publications in the 1960s who became known as the "critic you love to hate" because of his often vitriolic, yet always entertaining (and usually intelligent) attacks both on filmmakers, other critics, and actors (whom he physically disparaged). While Andrew Sarris championed the auteur/director and Pauline Kael raised the anti-auteur, pro-star, all-American banner in opposition to that foreign theory, Simon castigated both from a broader, older cultural perspective. Their battles were news in the 1960s and 70s and helped to form a new film culture in the US.

Simon, Michel • Actor • Born François Simon, Geneva, Switzerland, April 9, 1895; died 1975. Former boxer and acrobatic clown who metamorphosed into one of the greatest French character players of all time. Simon first earned acclaim in the stage and film versions of *Jean de la Lune* (1931) and gained wide popularity for his commanding, soulful performances—usually as coarse commoners or unscrupulous rustics—in the films of Jean Renoir (*Boudu Saved From Drowning* 1932), Jean Vigo (*L'Atalante* 1934), Marcel Carne (*Quai des Brumes* 1938), Julien Duvivier (*End of a Day* 1939) and Rene Clair (*Beauty and the Devil* 1950). Although Simon's career tailed off in the 1950s after an accident which affected his central nervous system, he resurfaced with a triumphant performance in Claude Berri's poignant *The Two of Us* (1967), winning the prize for best actor at Berlin. Father of actor François Simon. • *Feu Mathias Pascal/The Late Mathias Pascal* 1925 (a); *La Passion de Jeanne d'Arc/The Passion of Joan of Arc* 1927 (a); *Jean de la Lune* 1931 (a); *La Chienne* 1931 (a); *Boudu Sauvé des Eaux/Boudu Saved From Drowning* 1932 (a,p); *L'Atalante* 1934 (a); *Quai des Brumes* 1938 (a); *La Fin du Jour/The End of the Day* 1939 (a); *La Tosca* 1941 (a); *Vautrin* 1949 (a); *La Beauté du Diable/Beauty and the Devil* 1950 (a); *Altri Tempi* 1952 (a); *Saadia* 1954 (a); *Candide, ou l'optimisme au XX siècle* 1960 (a); *Cyrano et d'Artagnan* 1963 (a); *The Train* 1964 (a); *Le Vieil Homme et l'Enfant/The Two of Us* 1967 (a); *Le Fou* 1970 (a); *Mourir d'aimer* 1970 (a); *Blanche* 1971 (a); *Corpo d'Amore* 1972 (a); *La Più Bella Serata Della Mia Vita* 1972 (a); *L'Invitation* 1973 (a); *Der Tod Des Flohzirkusdirektors Oder Ottocaro Weiss Reformiert Seine Firma* 1973 (a); *La Chair de l'orchidée* 1974 (a); *L'Ibis Rouge* 1975 (a).

Simon, Neil • Playwright; also screenwriter, author. • Born Marvin Neil Simon, Bronx, NY, July 4, 1927. *Educ.* NYU. Former staff writer on the signature comedy series of TV's infancy, "Your Show of Shows," who went on to establish himself as one of Broadway's most prolific and consistently successful hit-makers. Many of Simon's plays have been adapted to film, including *Barefoot in the Park* (1967), *The Odd Couple* (1968) and *The Sunshine Boys* (1975). Among his original movie scripts are *The Heartbreak Kid* (1972) and *Murder By Death* (1976). In the 1980s, Simon wrote a cycle of thinly veiled autobiographical plays which he then transposed for the screen, including the coming-of-age tale, *Brighton Beach Memoirs* (1986), and the riotously funny boot camp comedy, *Biloxi Blues* (1988). Divorced from actress Marsha Mason. • *Come Blow Your Horn* 1963 (from play); *After the Fox* 1966 (sc,story); *Barefoot in the Park* 1967 (assoc.p,sc,from play); *The Odd Couple* 1968 (sc,from play) **(AANBSC)**; *Sweet Charity* 1969 (from play,libretto); *The Out-of-Towners* 1970 (sc,from play); *Plaza Suite* 1971 (sc,from play); *Star Spangled Girl* 1971 (from play); *The Heartbreak Kid* 1972 (sc); *Last of the Red Hot Lovers* 1972 (sc,from play); *The Prisoner of Second Avenue* 1974 (sc,from play); *The Sunshine Boys* 1975 (sc,from play) **(AANBSC)**; *Murder By Death* 1976 (sc); *The Goodbye Girl* 1977 (sc) **(AANBSC)**; *California Suite* 1978 (sc,from play) **(AANBSC)**; *The Cheap Detective* 1978 (sc); *Chapter Two* 1979 (sc,from play); *Seems Like Old Times* 1980 (sc); *I Ought to Be in Pictures* 1981 (p,sc,from play); *Only When I Laugh* 1981 (p,sc,from play "The Gingerbread Lady"); *Max Dugan Returns* 1982 (p,sc); *The Lonely Guy* 1984 (adapt); *The Slugger's Wife* 1985 (sc); *Brighton Beach Memoirs* 1986 (sc,from play); *Biloxi Blues* 1988 (sc,from play); *The Marrying Man* 1991 (exec.p,sc).

Simon, Simone • Actress • Born Bethune, France, April 23, 1911. Delicately pretty French-Italian actress whose first stab at a Hollywood career (1936-38) proved inconclusive but who returned for another try, bolstered by her domestic success in Jean Renoir's *La Bête Humaine* (1938). Simon enjoyed better fortune the second time around, distinguishing herself as a vixen from hell (literally) in William Dieterle's *The Devil and Daniel Webster* (1941) and in the atmospheric thrillers, *Cat People* (1942) and *The Curse of the Cat People* (1944). She continued to appear in international productions—notably Max Ophuls's stylish erotic comedy, *La Ronde* (1950)—through the mid-1950s. • *Girls' Dormitory* 1936; *Ladies in Love* 1936; *Love and Hisses* 1937; *Seventh Heaven* 1937; *La Bête Humaine* 1938; *Josette* 1938; *The Devil and Daniel Webster* 1941; *Cat People* 1942; *Tahiti Honey* 1943; *The Curse of the Cat People* 1944; *Johnny Doesn't Live Here Anymore* 1944; *Mademoiselle Fifi* 1944; *La Ronde* 1950; *Olivia* 1951; *Le Plaisir* 1951.

Simpson, Don • Producer; also screenwriter. • Born Anchorage, AK, October 29, 1945. *Educ.* University of Oregon. Former marketing executive who worked his way up through the ranks at Paramount to become president of worldwide production in 1981. In 1983 Simpson cofounded Don Simpson/Jerry Bruckheimer Productions, which was responsible for some of the most commercially successful films of the decade, including *Flashdance* (1983), *Beverly Hills Cop* (1984) and *Top Gun* (1986). • *Flashdance* 1983 (p); *Beverly Hills Cop* 1984 (p); *Thief of Hearts* 1984 (p); *Top Gun* 1986 (p); *Beverly Hills Cop II* 1987 (p); *The Big Bang* 1989 (a); *Days of Thunder* 1990 (a,p); *Young Guns II* 1990 (a).

Sinatra, Frank • Singer, actor • Born Francis Albert Sinatra, Hoboken, NJ, December 12, 1915. Crooner with the Harry James and Tommy Dorsey orchestras who emerged as a pop idol in the early 1940s. Slightly built and possessed of undeniably magnetic charm, Sinatra made his first non-singing film appearance in 1943 and appeared in light, breezy fare through the decade until hemorrhaged vocal chords brought the first phase of his career to an end in 1952.

Sinatra then proved his versatility and resilience by aggressively seeking out dramatic acting roles, giving acclaimed performances as Maggio in *From Here To Eternity* (1953), as a heroin addict in Otto Preminger's *The Man With the Golden Arm* (1955) and as Bennett Marco in the political psychodrama, *The Manchurian Candidate* (1962).

After regaining and developing his vocal powers, Sinatra emerged as a show business institution, turning out pop hits, selling out Vegas nightclubs and starring in an assortment of international films, including some creditable crime thrillers. His fabled fall and dramatic resurgence allegedly served as the basis for the Johnny Fontane character in *The Godfather* (1972), whose floundering career is put right thanks to "mob" muscle. Formerly married to actresses Ava Gardner and Mia Farrow and father of singer/actress Nancy Sinatra (b. 1940) and actor Frank Sinatra, Jr. (b. 1943). • *Las Vegas Nights* 1941 (a); *Ship Ahoy* 1941 (a); *Higher and Higher* 1943 (a); *Reveille With Beverly* 1943 (a); *Step Lively* 1944 (a); *Anchors Aweigh* 1945 (a); *The House I Live In (short)* 1945 (a) **(AAHON)**; *Till the Clouds Roll By* 1946 (a); *It Happened in Brooklyn* 1947 (a); *The Kissing Bandit* 1948 (a); *The Miracle of the Bells* 1948 (a); *On the Town* 1949 (a); *Take Me Out to the Ball Game* 1949 (a); *Double Dynamite* 1951 (a); *Meet Danny Wilson* 1952 (a); *From Here to Eternity* 1953 (a) **(AABSA)**; *Suddenly* 1954 (a); *Three Coins in the Fountain* 1954 (song); *Guys and Dolls* 1955 (a); *The Man With the Golden Arm* 1955 (a) **(AANBA)**; *Not As a Stranger* 1955 (a); *The Tender Trap* 1955 (a); *Young at Heart* 1955 (a); *Around the World in 80 Days* 1956 (a); *High Society* 1956 (a); *Johnny Concho* 1956 (a,p); *The Joker Is Wild* 1957 (a); *Pal Joey* 1957 (a); *The Pride and the Passion* 1957 (a); *Kings Go Forth* 1958 (a); *Some Came Running* 1958 (a); *A Hole in the Head* 1959 (a,p,song); *Never So Few* 1959 (a); *Can-Can* 1960 (a); *Ocean's Eleven* 1960 (a); *Pepe* 1960 (a); *The Devil at 4 O'Clock* 1961 (a); *Advise and Consent* 1962 (song); *The Manchurian Candidate* 1962 (a); *Sergeants 3* 1962 (a,p); *Come Blow Your Horn* 1963 (a); *Four For Texas* 1963 (a); *The List of Adrian Messenger* 1963 (a); *Robin and the Seven Hoods* 1964 (a,p); *Marriage on the Rocks* 1965 (a); *None But the Brave* 1965 (a,d,p); *Von Ryan's Express* 1965 (a); *Assault on a Queen* 1966 (a,exec.p); *Cast a Giant Shadow* 1966 (a); *The Naked Runner* 1967 (a); *Tony Rome* 1967 (a); *The Detective* 1968 (a); *Lady in Cement* 1968 (a); *Dirty Dingus Magee* 1970 (a); *That's Entertainment!* 1974 (a); *First Deadly Sin* 1980 (a,exec.p); *Cannonball Run II* 1983 (a); *Who Framed Roger Rabbit* 1988 (a); *Entertaining the Troops* 1989 (a); *Listen Up* 1990 (a).

Singer, Lori • Actress • Born Corpus Christi, TX, November 6, 1962. Striking, blue-eyed former cellist who graduated from TV's "Fame" to the big screen with a starring role in *Footloose* (1984). Sister of actor Marc Singer (*Go Tell the Spartans* 1978, *If You Could See What I Hear* 1982). • *Footloose* 1984; *The Falcon and the Snowman* 1985; *The Man With One Red Shoe* 1985; *Trouble in Mind* 1985; *Made in U.S.A.* 1987; *Summer Heat* 1987; *Warlock* 1989.

Siodmak, Robert • Director • Born Memphis, TN, August 8, 1900; died 1973. *Educ.* University of Marburg, Germany. Master craftsman of suspense and crime films who, in the mid-1940s, applied his Germanic sensibility to a series of exquisitely crafted Hollywood thrillers including *The Spiral Staircase* and *The Killers* (both 1946).

Raised in Germany (from age one), Siodmak began working for UFA in 1925 and directed his first film, the landmark pseudo-documentary *People on Sunday*, in 1929. The film launched the careers not only of co-directors Siodmak and Edgar Ulmer, but of co-screenwriters Billy Wilder and Curt Siodmak (Robert's younger brother), cinematographer Eugen Schufftan and his assistant, Fred Zinnemann.

Siodmak's first solo feature was *Farewell* (1930), a kind of working-class *Grand Hotel*. Scripted by Emeric Pressburger (whom Siodmak had earlier "discovered" while working as a writing scout), its technical accomplishment and experimental verve heralded an important new talent in German cinema. Three years and three films later, however, the Jewish Siodmak was forced into exile, first in France, where he made, among others, *Personal Column* (1939), and then, in 1941, to Hollywood.

After making B pictures for various studios, Siodmak hit his peak at Universal making deft, noir-ish thrillers like *The Phantom Lady* (1944), *The Suspect* (1944), *The Strange Affair of Uncle Harry* (1945), *The Dark Mirror* (1946) and *Criss Cross* (1946). Central to the succcess of all of these is Siodmak's ability to evoke a sinister mood, a fear of each and every dark shadow, while maintaining a taut narrative drive.

Siodmak's last great Hollywood product was the swashbuckling classic *The Crimson Pirate* (1952). He then returned to Europe and, with the exception of the German-made *The Rats* (1955) and *The Devil Strikes at Night* (1957), turned out mostly unexceptional films.

Siodmak's brother Curt enjoyed success as a writer of horror films (*I walked With a Zombie* 1943, *The Beast With Five Fingers* 1947) but earned less acclaim for his directing work. SKK • *Menschen am Sonntag/People on Sunday* 1929 (d,sc); *Abschied/Farewell* 1930 (d);*Der Mann, der Seinen Morder Sucht* 1931 (d,sc); *Sturme der Leidenschaft/Tempest* 1931 (d); *Voruntersuchung/Inquest* 1931 (d); *Quick, Der Sieger/The Victor* 1932 (d); *Brennendes Geheimnis* 1933 (d); *Le Sexe Faible* 1933 (d); *La Crise Est Finie* 1934 (d); *La Vie Parisienne* 1935 (d); *Mr. Flow* 1936 (d); *Cargaison Blanche* 1937 (d); *Mollenard* 1937 (d); *Pièges/Personal Column* 1939 (d); *West Point Widow* 1941 (d); *Fly By Night* 1942 (d); *My Heart Belongs to Daddy* 1942 (d); *The Night Before the Divorce* 1942 (d); *Someone to Remember* 1943 (d); *Son of Dracula* 1943 (d); *Christmas Holiday* 1944 (d); *Cobra Woman* 1944 (d); *Phantom Lady* 1944 (d); *The Suspect* 1944 (d); *Conflict* 1945 (story); *The Strange Affair of Uncle Harry* 1945 (d); *The Dark Mirror* 1946 (d); *The Killers* 1946 (d) **(AANBD)**; *The Spiral Staircase* 1946 (d); *Time Out of Mind* 1947 (d,p); *Criss Cross* 1948 (d); *Cry of the City* 1948 (d); *The File on Thelma Jordan* 1949 (d); *The Great Sinner* 1949 (d); *Deported* 1950 (d); *The Whistle at Eaton Falls* 1951 (d); *The Crimson Pirate* 1952 (d); *Le Grand Jeu* 1953 (d); *Die Ratten* 1955 (d); *Mein Vater, der Schauspieler* 1956 (d); *Nachts, Wenn Der Teufel Kam/The Devil Strikes at Night* 1957 (d,p); *Dorothea Angermann* 1959 (d); *The Rough and the Smooth* 1959 (d); *Katia* 1960 (d); *Mein Schulefreund* 1960 (d); *L'Affaire Nina B* 1961 (d,sc); *Tunnel 28* 1962 (d); *Die Pyramide des Sonnengottes* 1965 (d); *Der Schatz Der Azteken* 1965 (d); *Custer of the West* 1967 (d); *Kampf um Rom* 1968 (d); *Kampf um Rom II: Der Verrat* 1969 (d).

Sirk, Douglas • *aka* Detlef Sierck • Director; also producer. • Born Claus Detlev Sierk, Hamburg, Germany, April 26, 1900; died January 14, 1987, Lugano, Switzerland. *Educ.* Naval Academy, Munich University, Jena University, University of Hamburg, Germany. Best known for his Hollywood melodramas of the 1950s, Douglas Sirk first achieved success in post-WWI Germany, as a theater director. Under the name Claus Detlef Sierck, he directed for the stage from 1922 to 1937, emphasizing the work of such classic playwrights as Molière, Ibsen, Shaw and Shakespeare. In 1934 he was hired by UFA, which released his first feature film, *'T was een April/It Was in April*, in 1935. Despite his great success, Sirk left Germany in 1937 because of his opposition to the policies of the Third Reich. After a brief stay in France and Holland, where he worked on several scripts and produced two films, Sirk was invited to America to remake *Zu Neuen Ufern/To New Shores* (1937), one of his most successful German films featuring the great star Zarah Leander.

In Hollywood, after several years of aborted projects, Sirk directed his first American feature, *Hitler's Madman* (1943). His early work in Hollywood remains largely undistinguished, although Sirk devotees insist that, like his later, more important films, it contains ironic critiques of American culture. *Lured* (1947) and *Sleep, My Love* (1948) stand out in this period as atypical but competent thrillers.

Sirk's great period was during his association with Universal-International studios, beginning in 1951 and continuing until his retirement from filmmaking in 1959, and particulary with producers Albert Zugsmith and Ross Hunter. The series of melodramas he made for Universal struck a responsive chord with audiences; among the best-remembered are *Magnificent Obsession* (1954), *All That Heaven Allows* (1956), *Written on the Wind* (1956), *A Time to Love and a Time to Die* (1958) and *Imitation of Life* (1959). During its release, *Imitation of Life* became Universal's most commercially successful picture. Yet it also proved to be Sirk's last film: either because of ill health, a distaste for American culture or both, Sirk retired from filmmaking and returned to Europe, living in Switzerland and Germany until his death.

Largely considered merely a director of competent melodramas by critics in North America, Sirk's career was redefined by British criticism in the early 1970s. He became the subject of essays in theoretical film journals such as *Screen* and was given a retrospective at the 1972 Edinburgh Film Festival, along with an accompanying critical anthology. Such Sirk remarks as, "The angles are a director's thoughts. The lighting is his philosophy" endeared him to a new generation of film critics viewing Sirk as a socially conscious artist who criticized Eisenhower America from within mainstream filmmaking.

Sirk's style hinges on a highly developed sense of irony, employing subtle parody, cliche and stylization. At one time Sirk was seen as a filmmaker who simply employed conventional Hollywood rhetoric, but his style is now regarded as a form of Brechtian distancing that drew the viewer's attention to the methods and purposes of Hollywood illusionism. The world of Sirk's melodramas is extremely lavish and artificial, the colors of walls, cars, costumes and flowers harmonizing into a constructed aesthetic unity, providing a comment on the oppressive world of the American bourgeoisie. The false lake, a studio interior in *Written on the Wind*, for example, is presented as "obviously" false, an editorial comment on the self-deceptive, romanticized imagination that Marylee Hadley (Dorothy Malone) brings to the past. Sirk is renowned for his thematic use of mirrors, shadows and glass, as in the opening shot of *Imitation of Life*: behind the credits, chunks of glass, supposedly diamonds, slowly fill the frame from top to bottom, an ironic comment, like the film's very title, about the nature of its own appeal. Later, more obviously political filmmakers like Rainer Werner Fassbinder have been influenced by Sirk's American melodramas, which have been offered as models of ideological critique that may also pass as simple entertainment. BKG • *'T was een April/It Was in April* 1935 (d); *Das Madchen vom Moorhof* 1935 (d); *Stutzen der Gesellschaft* 1935 (d); *La Chanson du Souvenir* 1936 (d); *Das Hofkonzert* 1936 (d,sc); *Schlussakkord* 1936 (d,sc); *La Habanera* 1937 (d,song); *Liebling der Matrosen* 1937 (d,sc); *Zu Neuen Ufern/To New Shores* 1937 (d,sc); *Accord Final* 1939 (uncred.prod.sup); *Boefje* 1939 (d,sc); *Hitler's Hangman/Hitler's Madman* 1943 (d); *Summer Storm* 1944 (d,sc,adapt); *Thieves' Holiday* 1946 (d); *Lured* 1947 (d); *Sleep, My Love* 1948 (d); *Shockproof* 1949 (d); *Slightly French* 1949 (d); *Mystery Submarine* 1950 (d); *The First Legion* 1951 (d,p); *The Lady Pays Off* 1951 (d); *Thunder on the Hill* 1951 (d); *Weekend With Father* 1951 (d); *Has Anybody Seen My Gal?* 1952 (d); *Meet Me at the Fair* 1952 (d); *No Room For the Groom* 1952 (d); *All I Desire* 1953 (d); *Take Me to Town* 1953 (d); *Magnificent Obsession* 1954 (d); *Sign of the Pagan* 1954 (d); *Taza, Son of Cochise* 1954 (d); *Captain Lightfoot* 1955 (d); *Never Say Goodbye* 1955 (d); *All That Heaven Allows* 1956 (d); *Battle Hymn* 1956 (d); *There's Always Tomorrow* 1956 (d); *Written on the Wind* 1956 (d); *Interlude* 1957 (d); *The Tarnished Angels* 1958 (d); *A Time to Love and a Time to Die* 1958 (d); *Imitation of Life* 1959 (d); *My Life For Zarah Leander* 1986 (a).

Siskel, Gene • Critic; also author. • Film critic for the Chicago *Tribune* who is best known as the co-star, with Roger Ebert, of TV's "Siskel and Ebert." Siskel built a classic Chicago newspaper rivalry with Roger Ebert into first, a local TV career, then a national TV series that became the most influential critical benchmark of the 80s. In the process, this engaging pair has reaped a greater financial harvest than any of their peers in the field of film criticism.

Sjöberg, Alf • Director • Born Stockholm, Sweden, June 21, 1903; died April 17, 1980. *Educ.* Royal Dramatic Theatre School, Stockholm. Stage actor and director who made an impressive silent film debut in 1929 with *The Strongest*, a wrenching, documentary-like portrayal of seal hunters. Sjöberg became disillusioned with the film medium after the advent of sound and returned to working in the theater until the 1940s, when he helped revive the Swedish cinema with films such as the pacifist *They Staked Their Lives* (1940) and the Ingmar Bergman-scripted *Torment* (1944), starring future director Mai Zetterling. He subsequently directed a striking version of Strindberg's *Miss Julie* (1951), among several other noted films. • *The Strongest* 1929 (d,story); *They Staked Their Lives* 1940 (d,sc); *Blossom Time* 1940 (d,sc); *Home From Babylon* 1941 (d,sc); *Himlaspelet/The Road to Heaven* 1942 (d,sc); *Hets/Torment* 1944 (d); *Journey Out* 1945 (d,sc); *Iris and the Lieutenant* 1946 (d,sc); *Bare en Mor/Only a Mother* 1949 (d,sc); *Miss Julie* 1951 (d,sc); *Barabbas* 1953 (d,sc); *Karin Daughter of Man* 1954 (d,sc); *Wild Birds* 1955 (d,sc); *Sista Paret Ut/Last Pair Out* 1956 (d); *The Judge* 1960 (d,sc); *The Island* 1966 (d,sc); *The Father* 1969 (d,sc).

Sjöman, Vilgot • Director, screenwriter • Born David Harald Vilgot Sjöman, Stockholm, Sweden, December 2, 1924. *Educ.* • UCLA (filmmaking). Primarily known for his sexually explicit, and formally bold duet, 1967's *I Am Curious—Yellow* and 1968's *I Am Curious—Blue* (the two colors of his national flag). Associated with Swedish theater and cinema circles from the early 1940s, Sjöman only began making films in the 60s. Despite the seemingly liberal social climate of the times he encountered his first censorship problems with his debut feature *491* (1963) and has since continued to experiment with sexually dynamic content and aesthetically bold stylistics. *Yellow*, after much-publicized court proceedings, finally opened in New York in 1969 and was a phenomenal "succès de scandale," paving the way for the explicit sex on American screens in the 1970s. • *491* 1963 (d); *Nattvardsgasterna/Winter Light* 1963 (ad); *Jag ar Nyfiken-Gul/I Am Curious—Yellow* 1967 (a,d,sc); *I Am Curious—Blue* 1968 (d,sc); *Skammen* 1968 (a); *Lyekliga Skitar* 1970 (d,sc); *Ni Ljuger* 1970 (d,sc); *Troll* 1973 (d,p,sc); *En Handfull karlek* 1974 (d,sc); *Till Sex Do Us Part* 1974 (d,sc); *Garaget* 1975 (d,p,sc); *Tabu* 1976 (d,sc); *Kristoffers Hus* 1979 (sc); *Linus Eller Tegelhusets Hemlighet* 1979 (d,sc,from book); *Jag rodnar* 1981 (d,sc,idea); *Malacca* 1986 (d,p,sc); *Fallgropen* 1989 (d,sc).

Sjöström, Victor • *aka* Victor Seastrom • Director; also actor. • Born Silbodal, Varmland, Sweden, September 20, 1879; died January 3, 1960, Linnégatan, Sweden. One of the most influential forces in the development of the Swedish cinema, Sjöström began his career as a professional actor in 1896, as a member of Ernst Ahlbom's travelling theater company. He worked as both an actor and director for a number of Swedish companies during the next 16 years. In 1911 he formed his own company along with Einar Froberg, and, in 1913, was offered a film contract by Svenksa Bio.

Throughout his career, reviewers of Sjöström's performances seldom failed to mention his "distinctive, monumental face, as rich and alive as any landscape." Likewise, Sjöström's films as a director, which he often wrote and starred in, gained their greatest acclaim for his expressive use of landscape and "natural scenery." Sjöström's first great success came during the years 1917-1921, which saw his four film adaptations of novels by Swedish Nobel laureate Selma Lagerlof (three of which he also starred in), and the film that many consider his directorial masterpiece, *Thy Soul Shall Bear Witness* (1920).

Although Sjöström's Swedish films were generally considered too downbeat for American audiences (a trade magazine warned theater owners that they would have a better time attending their own funerals than a screening of *Thy Soul Shall Bear Witness*), the enthusiastic reviews they received for "artistic excellence" and "sheer pictorial power" made Sjöström, along with the likes of Ernst Lubitsch, Erich von Stroheim, and Sjöström's colleague Mauritz Stiller, a prime candidate for American import.

In 1923, Svensk Filmindustri sent Sjöström on a "study trip to America," retaining the Scandinavian distribution rights to the films he would direct for Samuel Goldwyn. During his seven-year residence in Hollywood (1923-1930), "Seastrom," as he was billed in the US, directed top stars of the day such as Lillian Gish (*The Scarlet Letter* 1926, *The Wind* 1927), Greta Garbo (*The Divine Woman* 1927), Lon Chaney and Edward G. Robinson. In a 1924 interview, Charlie Chaplin called him "the greatest director in the world."

Sjöström made his reputation as a master of silent films by virtue of his expressive imagery and minimal use of titles. With the advent of "talkies," however, his style of filmmaking was quickly outdated. He returned to Sweden in 1930 and resumed his career on the stage, although he continued to appear frequently in the films of other directors, concluding with his most memorable role, at the age of 78, as Professor Isak Berg in Ingmar Bergman's *Wild Strawberries* (1957) • *Tradgardsmastaren/The Gardener* 1912 (a); *De svarta maskerna/The Black Masks* 1912 (a); *Ett hemligt giftermal/A Secret Marriage* 1912 (d); *I livets var* 1912 (a); *Aktenskapsbyran/Marraige Bureau* 1912 (d,sc); *Lojen och tarar/Laughter and Tears* 1912 (d); *Lady Marions sommarflirt/Lady Marion's Summer Flirtation* 1912 (d); *Barnet/The Child* 1913 (a); *Vampyren/The Vampire* 1913 (a); *Nar karleken dodar/When Love Kills* 1913 (a); *Blodets rost/The Voice of Passion* 1913 (a,d); *Livets konflikter/The Conflicts of Life* 1913 (a,d); *For sin karleks skull* 1913 (a); *Ingeborg Holm/Margaret Day* 1913 (d,sc); *Miraklet/The Miracle* 1913 (d); *Karlek starkare an hat/The Poacher* 1913 (d); *Halvblod/Half Breed* 1913 (d); *Prasten/The Parson* 1913 (d); *Strejken/The Strike* 1913 (a,d,sc); *Hogfjallets dotter/Daughter of the Peaks* 1914 (a,d,sc); *Domen icke/Judge Not* 1914 (d); *Bra flicka reder sig sjalv/A Good Girl Keeps Herself In Order* 1914 (d,sc); *Gatans barn/Children of the Streets* 1914 (d); *Hjartan som motas/Hearts That Meet* 1914 (d); *En av de manga/One of the Many* 1914 (d,sc); *Sonad skuld/Guilt Redeemed* 1914 (d,sc); *Det var i maj* 1914 (d,sc); *Landshovdingens dottrar* 1915 (d,sc); *Skomakare bliv vid din last/Stick to Your Last, Shoemaker* 1915 (d,sc); *Judaspengar/The Price of Betrayal* 1915 (d); *I provningens stund/In the Hour of Trial* 1915 (a,d); *Skepp som motas/The Ships That Meet* 1915 (d); *Havsgamar/Predators of the Sea* 1915 (d); *Hon segrade/She Triumphs* 1915 (a,d,sc); *Therese* 1916 (d,sc); *Dodskyssen/Kiss of Death* 1916 (a,d,sc); *Terje vigen/A Man There Was* 1916 (a,d); *Thomas Graals basta film/Thomas Graal's Best Film* 1917 (a); *Tosen fran stormyrtorpet/The Girl from the Marsh Croft* 1917 (d,sc); *Berg-Ejvind och hans hustru/The Outlaw and His Wife* 1917 (a,d,sc); *Thomas Graals basta barn/Thomas Graal's First Child* 1918 (a); *Ingmarssonerna I & II/Sons of Ingmar* 1918 (a,d,sc); *Hans nads testamente/His Grace's Will* 1919 (d,sc); *Klostret i Sendomir/The Monastery of Sendomir* 1919 (d,sc); *Karin Ingmarsdotter/Karin Daughter of Ingmar* 1919 (a,d,sc); *Masterman* 1920 (a,d); *Korkarlen/Thy Soul Shall Bear Witness* 1920 (a,d,sc); *Vem domer/Mortal Clay* 1921 (d); *Det omringade huset/The Surrounded House* 1922 (a,d,sc with Ragnar Hylten-Cavallius); *Eld ombord/Fire On Board* 1922 (a,d,sc); *Name the Man* 1923 (d); *He Who Gets Slapped* 1924 (d,sc); *Confessions of a Queen* 1924 (d); *The Tower of Lies* 1925 (d); *The Scarlet Letter* 1926 (d); *The Wind* 1927 (d); *The Divine Woman* 1927 (d); *The Masks of the Devil* 1928 (d); *A Lady to Love* 1929 (d); *Markurells i Wadkoping/The Markurells of Wadkoping* 1930 (a,d); *Synnove Solbakken* 1934 (a); *Valborgsmassoafton/Walpurgis Night* 1935 (a); *Under the Red Robe* 1936 (d); *John Ericsson—Segraren vid Hampton Roads/John Ericson—The Victor of Hampton Roads* 1937 (a); *Gubben kommer/The Old Man's Coming* 1939 (a); *Mot nya tider/Towards New Times* 1939 (a); *Striden gar vidare* 1941 (a); *Det brinner en eld* 1943 (a); *Ordet/The Word* 1943 (a); *Kejsaren av Portugallien* 1944 (a); *Rallare* 1947 (a); *Jag ar med eder...* 1948 (a); *Farlig var* 1949 (a); *Till gladje/To Joy* 1950 (a); *Kvartetten som sprangdes* 1950 (a); *Hard klang* 1952 (a); *Karlek* 1952 (a); *Mannen i morker* 1955 (a); *Les evades/Flyktingarna* 1956 (a); *Smultronstallet/Wild Strawberries* 1957 (a).

Skerritt, Tom • Actor • Born Detroit, MI, August 25, 1933. *Educ.* Wayne State University, Detroit; UCLA. Handsome, rough-hewn lead and supporting player who gained initial attention as the eccentric dentist in *M*A*S*H* (1970). Skerritt then appeared in a series of obscure Italian productions before highlighting such films as *The Turning Point* (1977, as Shirley Maclaine's husband) and *Alien* (1979, as the harried space captain). He has appeared recently in several TV movies and made a few memorable guest appearances on the sitcom "Cheers." • *War Hunt* 1962; *One Man's Way* 1964; *Those Calloways* 1964; *M*A*S*H* 1970; *Wild Rovers* 1971; *Fuzz* 1972; *Big Bad Mama* 1974; *Thieves Like Us* 1974; *The Devil's Rain* 1975; *The Turning Point* 1977; *Cheech & Chong's Up in Smoke* 1978; *Ice Castles* 1978; *Alien* 1979; *Savage Harvest* 1981; *Silence of the North* 1981; *A Dangerous Summer* 1982; *Fighting Back* 1982; *The Dead Zone* 1983; *Opposing Force* 1986; *SpaceCamp* 1986; *Top Gun* 1986; *Wisdom* 1986; *The Big Town* 1987; *Maid to Order* 1987; *Poltergeist III* 1988; *Big Man on Campus* 1989; *Steel Magnolias* 1989; *The Rookie* 1990.

Skolimowski, Jerzy • *aka* Yurek Skolimowski • Director; also screenwriter, actor, poet, playwright. • Born Lódz, Poland, May 5, 1938. *Educ.* Warsaw University (literature, history); Lódz Film School. A sporadic yet highly inventive and original filmmaker, Skolimowski is one of the few directors from the Eastern Bloc to earn a widespread reputation in the West. He attended the University of Warsaw, studying anthropology, history and literature. Early on he proved to be a young man of many talents; he not only published a number of short stories and two volumes of poetry, but was also a practicing jazz musician.

Through a chance meeting with Andrzej Wajda, Skolimowski contributed to the script for the director's film *Innocent Sorcerers* (1960). Wadja's influence enabled Skolimowski to attend the Film School at Lódz, where he and fellow student Roman Polanski wrote the script for Polanski's first feature, the much heralded *Knife in the Water* (1962). Skolimowski's own first feature, *Rysopis/Identification Marks: None* (1964), was made over a four-year period by combining smaller student projects into one film. Like his other films from this period (*Walkover* 1965; *Barrier* 1966; and *Le Départ* 1967), it was concerned with the conflicts in Poland between the postwar generation and their elders. These films illustrate the absence of any strong sense of identity among Polish youth; their style reflects his background in poetry: complexly manipulative narratives combined with stark visuals that perfectly convey the desolation of his characters.

Although his last film in Poland, *Hands Up!*, was, because of its anti-Stalinist theme, banned and not seen in the West until the 1981 Cannes Film Festival, Skolimowski's reputation outside Poland was made when *Le Départ* received the Golden Bear at the 1967 Berlin Film Festival. He was then invited to make *The Adventures of Gerard* (1970), a British-Swiss coproduction with a multimillion dollar budget and big-name cast. This first commercial effort was poorly received and offered little indication of the director's maturing talent. • *Deep End* (1970) and *The Shout* (1978) solidified Skolimowski's reputation as a director capable of handling abstract and metaphorical material in an adroit manner. When martial law was declared in Poland in December 1981, Skolimowski was staying at his home there; this situation provided the basis for *Moonlighting* (1982), his most critically acclaimed and commercially successful film. An insightful probe into the genesis of political repression, *Moonlighting* is a compelling allegory that shies away from preachiness. A group of Polish workmen are refurbishing a home in London when martial law is declared. They are kept from knowing of the events in their homeland by their foreman (Jeremy Irons). Irons resorts to stealing for money and food when funds from Poland fail to arrive. In a metaphorical sense, he becomes as dictatorial to these men as the Soviet Union was to Poland.

Despite the success of *Moonlighting*, Smolimowski's next two films have gone virtually unnoticed. *Success Is the Best Revenge* (1984) is an effective portrayal of complacency, political apathy and artistic integrity. With its complex narrative, *Success* has had virtually no distribution, despite stunning visuals and a compelling story. The same fate has befallen *The Lightship* (1985); although it won the 1987 Venice Film Festival Award for Best Film, it has had extremely limited distribution. In addition to starring in several of his own films, Skolimowski has also acted in *Circle of Deceit* (1981) and *White Nights* (1985). PP • *Niewinni Czarodzieje/Innocent Sorcerers* 1960 (a,sc); *Noz w Wodzie/Knife in the Water* 1962 (sc); *Rysopis/Identification Marks: None* 1964 (a,d,sc,art d,ed,sets); *Walkover* 1965 (a,d,sc,ed); *Bariera/Barrier* 1966 (d,sc); *Le Départ* 1967 (d,sc); *Rece Do Gory/Hands Up!* 1967 (a,d,sc); *Dialog* 1968 (d,sc); *The Adventures of Gerard* 1970 (d,sc); *Deep End* 1970 (d,sc); *King, Queen, Knave* 1972 (d); *Poslizg* 1972 (sc); *The Shout* 1978 (d,sc); *Die Falschung/Circle of Deceit* 1981 (a); *Moonlighting* 1982 (a,d,p,sc); *Success Is the Best Revenge* 1984 (d,p,sc,story); *The Lightship* 1985 (d); *White Nights* 1985 (a); *Mesmerized* 1986 (from treatment); *Big Shots* 1987 (a); *Torrents of Spring* 1989 (a,d,sc).

Skye, Ione • *aka* Ione Skye Leitch • Actress • Born London, 1971. Attractive juvenile player who made her screen debut in Tim Hunter's *River's Edge* (1987) and gave a winning performance as high school hearthrob Diane Court in Cameron Crowe's fine, bittersweet love story, *Say Anything* (1989). Daughter of folksinger Donovan and sister of actor Donovan Leitch. • *River's Edge* 1987; *Stranded* 1987; *A Night in the Life of Jimmy Reardon* 1988; *The Rachel Papers* 1989; *Say Anything* 1989; *Mindwalk* 1990.

Slater, Christian • Actor • Born New York, NY, August 18, 1969. Cool, laconic young lead who first attracted attention for his Jack Nicholson-inspired performance in Michael Lehmann's 1989 cult hit, *Heathers*. • *The Legend of Billie Jean* 1985; *The Name of the Rose* 1986; *Gleaming the Cube* 1988; *Personal Choice* 1988; *Tucker: The Man and His Dream* 1988; *Heathers* 1989; *The Wizard* 1989; *Pump Up the Volume* 1990; *Tales From the Darkside, The Movie* 1990; *Young Guns II* 1990; *Robin Hood: Prince of Thieves* 1991.

Slater, Helen • Actress • Born New York, NY, December 15, 1963. *Educ.* High School for the Performing Arts, New York. Tall blonde lead who literally soared to fame as *Supergirl* (1984) and turned in creditable performances in *The Legend of Billie Jean* (1985) and *Ruthless People* (1986). Slater has also appeared on stage and TV. • *Supergirl* 1984; *The Legend of Billie Jean* 1985; *Ruthless People* 1986; *The Secret of My Success* 1987; *Sticky Fingers* 1988; *Happy Together* 1989; *City Slickers* 1991.

Sloane, Everett • Actor • Born New York, NY, October 1, 1909; died 1965. *Educ.* University of Pennsylvania. Incisive, diminutive character actor who moved to Hollywood with Orson Welles and the Mercury Theater and is perhaps best remembered for playing Kane's loyal, bespectacled sidekick Bernstein in *Citizen Kane* (1941), and the corrupt, crippled lawyer in Welles's *The Lady from Shanghai* (1948). Strong portrayals also in *The Men* (1950) and *Patterns* (1955). • *Citizen Kane* 1941; *Journey Into Fear* 1942; *The Lady From Shanghai* 1948; *Prince of Foxes* 1949; *The Men* 1950; *Bird of Paradise* 1951; *The Blue Veil* 1951; *The Desert Fox* 1951; *The Enforcer* 1951; *The Prince Who Was a Thief* 1951; *The Sellout* 1951; *Sirocco* 1951; *Way of a Gaucho* 1952; *The Big Knife* 1955; *Patterns* 1955; *Lust For Life* 1956; *Somebody Up There Likes Me* 1956; *The Gun Runners* 1958; *Marjorie Morningstar* 1958; *Home From the Hill* 1960; *By Love Possessed* 1961; *Brushfire!* 1962; *The Man From the Diner's Club* 1963; *The Disorderly Orderly* 1964; *The Patsy* 1964; *Ready For the People* 1964.

Slocombe, Douglas • Director of photography • Born London, February 10, 1913. Celebrated English cinematographer who began his career as a newsreel cameraman during WWII, when he filmed the German invasion of Poland and Holland. Douglas subsequently joined Ealing Studios, where he shot such acclaimed films as *Kind Hearts and Coronets* (1949) and *The Man in the White Suit* (1951), and later contributed to landmark British features of the 1960s including *The L-Shaped Room* (1962) and *The Servant* (1963).

Slocombe's more recent credits include *Julia* (1977) for Fred Zinnemann, and *Indiana Jones and the Temple of Doom* (1984) for Steven Spielberg. • *Lights Out in Europe* 1940 (ph—Polish invasion); *Saraband For Dead Lovers* 1948 (ph); *Kind Hearts and Coronets* 1949 (ph); *The Man in the White Suit* 1951 (ph); *The Lavender Hill Mob* 1952 (ph); *All at Sea* 1957 (ph); *Tread Softly Stranger* 1958 (ph); *The Mark* 1961 (ph); *Freud* 1962 (ph); *The L-Shaped Room* 1962 (ph); *The Servant* 1963 (ph); *Guns at Batasi* 1964 (ph); *A High Wind in Jamaica* 1965 (ph); *The Blue Max* 1966 (ph); *Promise Her Anything* 1966 (ph); *Fathom* 1967 (ph); *The Fearless Vampire Killers* 1967 (ph); *Robbery* 1967 (ph); *Boom!* 1968 (ph); *The Lion in Winter* 1968 (ph); *The Italian Job* 1969 (ph); *The Buttercup Chain* 1970 (ph); *Murphy's War* 1970 (ph); *The Music Lovers* 1971 (ph); *Travels With My Aunt* 1972 (ph) **(AANBPH)**; *Jesus Christ Superstar* 1973 (ph); *The Destructors* 1974 (ph); *The Great Gatsby* 1974 (ph); *The Maids* 1974 (ph); *Hedda* 1975 (ph); *Rollerball* 1975 (ph); *The Sailor Who Fell From Grace With the Sea* 1975 (ph); *That Lucky Touch* 1975 (ph); *The Bawdy Adventures of Tom Jones* 1976 (ph); *Nasty Habits* 1976 (ph); *Close Encounters of the Third Kind* 1977 (add.ph—India sequences); *Julia* 1977 (ph) **(AANBPH)**; *Caravans* 1978 (ph); *The Lady Vanishes* 1979 (ph); *Lost and Found* 1979 (ph); *Close Encounters of the Third Kind: Special Edition* 1980 (add.ph—India sequence); *Nijinsky* 1980 (ph); *Raiders of the Lost Ark* 1981 (ph) **(AANBPH)**; *The Pirates of Penzance* 1982 (ph); *Never Say Never Again* 1983 (ph); *Indiana Jones and the Temple of Doom* 1984 (ph); *Water* 1984 (ph); *Lady Jane* 1986 (ph); *Indiana Jones and the Last Crusade* 1989 (ph).

Small, Michael • American composer • Particularly known for his work on thrillers, including *Klute* (1971), *The Parallax View* (1974), *Marathon Man* (1976) and *The Postman Always Rings Twice* (1981). • *Jenny* 1969 (m); *Out of It* 1969 (m); *Puzzle of a Downfall Child* 1970 (m); *Klute* 1971 (m); *The Sporting Club* 1971 (m); *Child's Play* 1972 (m); *Dealing: Or the Berkeley-to-Boston Forty-Brick Lost-Bag Blues* 1972 (m); *Liebe, Schmerz und das Danze Verdammte Zeug* 1973 (m); *The Parallax View* 1974 (m); *The Drowning Pool* 1975 (m); *Night Moves* 1975 (m); *The Stepford Wives* 1975 (m,m.dir); *Marathon Man* 1976 (m); *Pumping Iron* 1976 (m,song); *Audrey Rose* 1977 (m); *Comes a Horseman* 1978 (m,m.dir); *The Driver* 1978 (m); *Girlfriends* 1978 (m); *Going in Style* 1979 (m); *The Lathe of Heaven* 1979 (m); *Those Lips Those Eyes* 1980 (m,m.cond); *Continental Divide* 1981 (m,m.dir,song); *Miss Right* 1981 (m); *The Postman Always Rings Twice* 1981 (m,m.dir); *Rollover* 1981 (m); *The Star Chamber* 1983 (m,m.dir); *Firstborn* 1984 (m); *Kidco* 1984 (m); *Target* 1985 (m); *Brighton Beach Memoirs* 1986 (m); *Dream Lover* 1986 (m); *Black Widow* 1987 (m); *Heat and Sunlight* 1987 (m); *Jaws: The Revenge* 1987 (m,m.arr); *Orphans* 1987 (m); *1969* 1988 (m); *Exit No Exit (short)* 1988 (a); *See You in the Morning* 1989 (m,song); *American Dream* 1990 (m); *Mountains of the Moon* 1990 (m).

Smith, Alexis • Actress • Born Gladys Smith, Penticton, British Columbia, Canada, June 8, 1921. *Educ.* Los Angeles City College. Glamorous lead and supporting player of the 1940s and 50s, initially with Warner Bros., Smith excelled at portraying disarming schemers and beguiling opportunists, and gave one of her finest performances in Joseph Losey's British-produced *The Sleeping Tiger* (1954). She retired in 1959 but re-emerged on stage in 1971 (and later in films), winning a Tony and a New York Drama Critics award for her performance in the Stephen Sondheim musical, *Follies*. Married to actor Craig Stevens. • *Dive Bomber* 1941; *The Smiling Ghost* 1941; *Steel Against the Sky* 1941; *Gentleman Jim* 1942; *The Constant Nymph* 1943; *Thank Your Lucky Stars* 1943; *The Adventures of Mark Twain* 1944; *The Doughgirls* 1944; *Hollywood Canteen* 1944; *Conflict* 1945; *The Horn Blows at Midnight* 1945; *Rhapsody in Blue* 1945; *San Antonio* 1945; *The Two Mrs. Carrolls* 1945; *Night and Day* 1946; *Of Human Bondage* 1946; *One More Tomorrow* 1946; *Stallion Road* 1947; *The Decision of Christopher Blake* 1948; *The Woman in White* 1948; *Any Number Can Play* 1949; *One Last Fling* 1949; *South of St. Louis* 1949; *Whiplash* 1949; *Montana* 1950; *Undercover Girl* 1950; *Wyoming Mail* 1950; *Cave of Outlaws* 1951; *Here Comes the Groom* 1951; *The Turning Point* 1952; *Split Second* 1953; *The Sleeping Tiger* 1954; *The Eternal Sea* 1955; *Beau James* 1957; *This Happy Feeling* 1958; *The Young Philadelphians* 1959; *Once Is Not Enough* 1975; *The Little Girl Who Lives Down the Lane* 1977; *Casey's Shadow* 1978; *La Truite* 1982; *Tough Guys* 1986.

Smith, Bud • Editor; also director, producer. • Born Tulsa, OK. Former race-car driver (Smith is a two-time winner of the Pacific Coast Championship) and veteran editor who has often worked with director William Friedkin. Smith earned a British Academy award for *Flashdance* (1983), has produced several films and directed the teen jock movie, *Johnny Be Good* (1988). • *Greaser's Palace* 1972 (ed); *Rhinoceros* 1972 (ed); *The Exorcist* 1973 (ed) **(AANBED)**; *Sorcerer* 1977 (ed); *The Brink's Job* 1978 (ed); *Cruising* 1980 (ed); *Falling in Love Again* 1980 (ed); *Cat People* 1982 (ed,2u d); *Personal Best* 1982 (ed); *Deal of the Century* 1983 (ed); *Flashdance* 1983 (ed) **(AANBED)**; *The Karate Kid* 1984 (assoc.p,ed); *To Live and Die in L.A.* 1985 (ed,p); *Poltergeist II: The Other Side* 1986 (add.ed); *Some Kind of Wonderful* 1987 (ed); *Johnny Be Good* 1988 (d); *Gross Anatomy* 1989 (ed); *Sing* 1989 (ed); *Darkman* 1990 (ed).

Smith, Sir C. Aubrey • Actor • Born Charles Aubrey Smith, London, July 21, 1863; died 1948. *Educ.* Cambridge. Tall, distinguished stage actor with memorable bushy eyebrows and thick moustache who entered films in 1915 but is best known for his numerous character roles for Hollywood in the 1930s and 40s; often cast as a crusty, blustery upper-class Brit. • *Bohemian Girl* 1922; *The Bachelor Father* 1931; *Daybreak* 1931; *Guilty Hands* 1931; *Just a Gigolo* 1931; *The Man in Possession* 1931; *Never the Twain Shall Meet* 1931; *The Phantom of Paris* 1931; *Son of India* 1931; *Surrender* 1931; *But the Flesh Is Weak* 1932; *Love Me Tonight* 1932; *No More Orchids* 1932; *Polly of the Circus* 1932; *Tarzan, the Ape Man* 1932; *They Just Had to Get Married* 1932; *Trouble in Paradise* 1932; *Adorable* 1933; *The Barbarian* 1933; *Blonde Bombshell* 1933; *Luxury Liner* 1933; *The Monkey's Paw* 1933; *Morning Glory* 1933; *Queen Christina* 1933; *Secrets* 1933; *Bulldog Drummond Strikes Back* 1934; *Caravan* 1934; *Cleopatra* 1934; *Curtain at Eight* 1934; *The Firebird* 1934; *Gambling Lady* 1934; *The House of Rothschild* 1934; *One More River* 1934; *The Scarlet Empress* 1934; *China Seas* 1935; *Clive of India* 1935; *The Crusades* 1935; *The Florentine Dagger* 1935; *The Gilded Lily* 1935; *Jalna* 1935; *The Lives of a Bengal Lancer* 1935; *The Right to Live* 1935; *The Garden of Allah* 1936; *Little Lord Fauntleroy* 1936; *Lloyd's of London* 1936; *Romeo and Juliet* 1936; *Hurricane* 1937; *The Prisoner of Zenda* 1937; *Thoroughbreds Don't Cry* 1937; *Wee Willie Winkie* 1937; *Four Men and a Prayer* 1938; *Kidnapped* 1938; *Another Thin Man* 1939; *Balalaika* 1939; *East Side of Heaven* 1939; *Eternally Yours* 1939; *Five Came Back* 1939; *The Sun Never Sets* 1939; *The Under-Pup* 1939; *Beyond Tomorrow* 1940; *A Bill of Divorcement* 1940; *City of Chance* 1940; *A Little Bit of Heaven* 1940; *Rebecca* 1940; *Waterloo Bridge* 1940; *Dr. Jekyll and Mr. Hyde* 1941; *Free and Easy* 1941; *Maisie Was a Lady* 1941; *Flesh and Fantasy* 1943; *Forever and a Day* 1943; *Madame Curie* 1943; *Two Tickets to London* 1943; *The Adventures of Mark Twain* 1944; *Forever Yours* 1944; *The Secrets of Scotland Yard* 1944; *The White Cliffs of Dover* 1944; *And Then There Were None* 1945; *Scotland Yard Investigator* 1945; *Sensations of 1945* 1945; *Cluny Brown* 1946; *Rendezvous With Annie* 1946; *High Conquest* 1947; *Unconquered* 1947; *Little Women* 1949.

Smith, Charles Martin • Actor; also director. • Born Van Nuys, CA, October 30, 1953. *Educ.* California State University. Diminutive, intense (usually bearded) character actor who turned in a superb performance in the central role of *Never Cry Wolf* (1983). Smith made his directing debut with the rock 'n' roll horror film, *Trick or Treat* (1986). • *American Graffiti* 1973 (a); *Rafferty and the Gold Dust Twins* 1974 (a); *No Deposit, No Return* 1976 (a); *The Hazing* 1977 (a); *The Buddy Holly Story* 1978 (a,song); *More American Graffiti* 1979 (a); *Herbie Goes Bananas* 1980 (a); *Never Cry Wolf* 1983 (a); *Starman* 1984 (a); *Trick or Treat* 1986 (a,d); *The Untouchables* 1987 (a); *The Experts* 1989 (a); *The Hot Spot* 1990 (a).

Smith, Kurtwood • Actor • Born Wisconsin. *Educ.* Stanford (drama). Character player of stage, TV and film, best known as the sadistic killer, Clarence Botticker, in *Robocop* (1987) and the domineering, inflexible father in *Dead Poets Society* (1989). • *Roadie* 1980; *Staying Alive* 1983; *Flashpoint* 1984; *The Delos Adventure* 1985; *Robocop* 1987; *Homesick (short)* 1988; *Rambo III* 1988; *Dead Poets Society* 1989; *Heart of Dixie* 1989; *True Believer* 1989; *12:01 PM* 1990; *Quick Change* 1990; *Oscar* 1991.

Smith, Dame Maggie • Actress • Born Ilford, England, December 28, 1934. *Educ.* Oxford Playhouse School (drama). Sublimely accomplished performer who has racked up numerous stage triumphs over three decades on both sides of the Atlantic, and whose relatively few screen appearences have yielded a number of outstanding performances. Her versatility, her range of acting styles and the variety of her film roles is enormous: from her tour de force as the charismatic title character in *The Prime of Miss Jean Brodie* (1969), her grande dame performance in *Evil Under the Sun* (1982), her farcical comic genius in the wacky black comedy *A Private Function* (1985), to the heartbreaking pathos of her portrait of a desperate, alcoholic spinster in *The Lonely Passion of Judith Hearne* (1987).

Most recently Smith reconquered the London and Broadway stage in the deliciously manipulative vehicle, *Lettice and Lovage*, written for her by Peter Shaffer. • *Nowhere to Go* 1959; *The V.I.P.s* 1963; *The Pumpkin Eater* 1964; *Othello* 1965 **(AANBSA)**; *Young Cassidy* 1965; *The Honey Pot* 1967; *Oh! What a Lovely War* 1969; *The Prime of Miss Jean Brodie* 1969 **(AABA)**; *Hot Circuit* 1971; *Travels With My Aunt* 1972 **(AANBA)**; *Liebe, Schmerz und das Danze Verdammte Zeug/Love, Pain and the Whole Damned Thing* 1973; *Murder By Death* 1976; *California Suite* 1978 **(AABSA)**; *Death on the Nile* 1978; *Clash of the Titans* 1981; *The Missionary* 1981; *Quartet* 1981; *Evil Under the Sun* 1982; *Better Late Than Never* 1983; *Jatszani Kell/Lily in Love* 1985; *A Private Function* 1985; *A Room With a View* 1986 **(AANBSA)**; *The Lonely Passion of Judith Hearne* 1987; *Romeo-Juliet* 1990.

Smith, Mel • Actor; also director, screenwriter. • Born London, 1952. *Educ.* New College, Oxford (psychology). British revue performer who began his career as a stage director. Smith performed in and co-wrote the BBC-TV series "Not the Nine O'Clock News" and, with partner Griff Rhys-Jones, wrote and starred in the series "Alias Smith and Jones" (he also appeared in the stage versions of both these shows). Smith played character parts in films before making the transition to directing with *The Tall Guy* (1989). • *Babylon* 1980 (a); *Bullshot* 1983 (a); *Number One* 1984 (a); *Slayground* 1984 (a); *Morons From Outer Space* 1985 (a,sc,song); *Restless Natives* 1985 (a); *The Princess Bride* 1987 (a); *The Wolves of Willoughby Chase* 1988 (a); *The Tall Guy* 1989 (d); *Wilt* 1989 (a).

Smits, Jimmy • Actor • Born Brooklyn, NY, July 9, 1955. *Educ.* Brooklyn College (education); Cornell (theater). Tall, commanding Latino actor, best known as Victor Sifuentes on TV's "L.A. Law" (1986-). Smits appeared with the New York Shakespeare Festival before entering films and starred opposite Jane Fonda in Luis Puenzo's *Old Gringo* (1989). • *Running Scared* 1986; *The Believers* 1987; *Old Gringo* 1989; *Vital Signs* 1990; *Fires Within* 1991; *Switch* 1991.

Snodgress, Carrie • Actress • Born Caroline Snodgress, Barrington, IL, October 27, 1946. *Educ.* Northern Illinois University; Goodman Theater School. Capable lead who worked in TV and on the Chicago stage before making her screen mark in the riveting drama, *Diary of a Mad Housewife* (1970). Snodgress interrupted her blossoming career to raise her son but returned to the screen in *The Fury* (1978); she has since appeared in a handful of less than memorable productions. • *Diary of a Mad Housewife* 1970 **(AANBA)**; *Rabbit, Run* 1970; *The Fury* 1978; *Homework* 1982; *Trick or Treats* 1982; *A Night in Heaven* 1983; *Pale Rider* 1985; *Rainy Day Friends* 1985; *Murphy's Law* 1986; *Blueberry Hill* 1988; *The Chill Factor* 1989; *Across the Tracks* 1990.

Snow, Michael • Filmmaker; also painter. • Born Michael Aleck James Snow, Toronto, Ontario, Canada, December 10, 1929. *Educ.* Ontario College of Art (design). Central figure of the American avant-garde. An artist who made an isolated animated short, *A to Z*, in 1956, Snow concentrated on his painting career until moving to New York in 1963. After attending avant-garde film screenings organized by critic-filmmaker Jonas Mekas and turning out a second film, the formalist *New York Eye and Ear Control* (1964), he made the highly influential *Wavelength* (1967).

Wavelength consists of a 45-minute zoom across a loft—interruped at several points by a cryptic narrative involving a murder—which ends on a close-up of a photograph of ocean waves. The film quickly earned a reputation in international avant-garde circles and inspired a generation of structuralist filmmakers. It was the first in a series of Snow's works which reduce the film medium to one of its most basic elements—camera movement: *Standard Time* (1967) is made up of 360-degree pans; in *Back and Forth* (1969), the camera moves backwards and forwards at varying speeds, recording events in a classroom; in *La Région centrale* (1971), Snow's remote-controlled camera, mounted on a tripod in the middle of the Quebec tundra, executes 360 degree rotations in three different circular patterns (at various speeds) while zooming in and out. • *A to Z* 1956 (d); *New York Eye and Ear Control* 1964 (d); *Standard Time* 1967 (d,p); *Wavelength* 1967 (d,p); *Back and Forth* 1969 (d,p); *La Région centrale* 1971 (d,p); *So Is This* 1983 (d,p); *Artist on Fire: The Work of Joyce Wieland* 1987 (a); *I Will Not Make Any More Boring Art* 1988 (a); *Seated Figures* 1988 (d).

Sobocinski, Witold • Director of photography • Born Ozorkow, Poland, October 15, 1929. *Educ.* Lódz Film School. Leading Polish cinematographer who has worked repeatedly with such distinguished directors as Jerzy Skolimowski, Andrzej Wajda, Krystoff Zanussi and, most recently, Roman Polanski. • *Rece Do Gory/Hands Up!* 1967; *Wszystko Na Sprzedaz* 1967; *The Adventures of Gerard* 1970; *Zycie Rodzinne* 1971; *Wesele/The Wedding* 1972; *Sanatorium Pod Klepsydra/The Hourglass Sanatorium* 1973; *The Catamount Killing* 1974; *Ziemia Obiecana* 1975; *Moja Wojna-Moja Milosc* 1976; *Szpital Przemienienia* 1978; *Wege in der Nacht* 1979; *Uindii* 1984; *O-Bi, O-Ba - Koniec Cywilizacji* 1985; *Pirates* 1986; *Zjoek* 1987; *Frantic* 1988; *Torrents of Spring* 1989; *Bronsteins Kinder* 1991.

Soderbergh, Steven • Director; also screenwriter. • Born Georgia, January 14, 1963. Soderbergh cut his teeth making short Super-8 mm films with equipment borrowed from Louisiana State University film students. He skipped college in favor of a frustrating spell in Hollywood before returning to Baton Rouge to further develop his craft. His first break came in 1986 when rock group "Yes" enlisted him to shoot concert footage which was eventually shaped into a Grammy-winning video. Soderbergh's first feature project was the low-budget ($1.2 million), finely crafted modern-day morality tale, *sex, lies, and videotape* (1989). The film scored a double triumph at Cannes, winning the Palme d'Or for Soderbergh and the best actor award for James Spader, and established its director as one of the most promising young filmmakers of his generation. • *sex, lies, and videotape* 1989 (d,sc,sound ed,sound rerecording,ed) **(AANBSC)**.

Solanas, Fernando E. • Director, screenwriter; also director of photography. • Born Olivos, Argentina, February 16, 1936. *Educ.* National School of Dramatic Art, Buenos Aires (acting, directing). Before commencing his career as a filmmaker, Fernando Solanas studied music, theater, and law and worked in journalism and advertising. He began making films in 1962 as a producer and director.

From 1966 to 1968 Solanas worked with director Octavio Getino and the Cine Liberacion collective on a clandestine project, the militantly left-Peronist, four hour-twenty minute *La hora de los Hornos/The Hour of the Furnaces*, a classic in the history of documentary film. The members of the collective saw themselves as guerrilla filmmakers whose powerful documentary would alter the course of Argentine history in favor of the left wing of the Peronist movement. The secret screenings of *La hora de los Hornos* became "film-acts" when projection was deliberately halted to force spectators out of their passivity and into debates concerning Argentine history and politics. Part one of the film, and the finest section, is a brilliantly edited collage that draws on opera, archival newsreel and documentary footage, avant-garde film techniques, still photos, pop culture icons, TV-style advertising, and satiric vignettes to make a provocative, revolutionary analysis of Argentine history, politics and culture.

Their work in the Cine Liberacion collective led Solanas and Getino to develop their influential notion of "Third Cinema," which they promoted in numerous writings and interviews. Third Cinema rejected both the Hollywood production model and the European auteurist tradition and called for an anti-imperialist, revolutionary cinema made independently and cheaply by collectives using a variety of film techniques in artisanal contexts.

In their next two documentary features, Solanas and Getino distanced themselves from the Third Cinema concept. *Actualizacion Politica y Doctrinaria Para la Toma del Poder* and *La Revolucion Justicialista* (both 1971) are stylistically conventional examinations of populist leader Juan Peron's political program and his movement, known as Justicialismo. These promotional documentaries were made to support the exiled Peron's return to power.

Solanas's next film, *Los Hijos de Fierro* (1976), is creatively adapted from the great Argentine gaucho poem *Martin Fierro.* This fiction feature is an allegorical epic with a contemporary political theme, Peronism.

Because of political persecution, Solanas fled into exile in France during the early days of the repressive military regime that ruled Argentina from 1976-83. The director was able to channel his prolonged exile experience into a burst of artistic creativity in his next two fiction features, which have been widely hailed as poetic masterpieces: *Tangos: L'exil de Gardel* (1985) and *Sur* (1988). The elements of both these Argentine-French coproductions are a superb tango score, stunning art direction and beautiful cinematography, a mix of allegorical and real characters and elements of humor and magic realism, all creating an attractive spectacle that entertains even as it takes up contemporary Argentine political problems such as repression and exile. With these film Solanas has become a leader among the many Latin American cineastes who seek to escape Hollywood models, draw on their own popular culture, and make artistically and commercially attractive films that boast both entertainment and socially conscious values. DW • *La Hora de los Hornos/The Hour of the Furnaces* 1968 (d,p,sc,ed); *Actualizacion Politica y Doctrinaria Para la Toma del Poder* 1971; *La Revolucion Justicialista* 1971; *Los Hijos de Fierro* 1976; *Tangos: L'exil de Gardel/Tangos: The Exile of Gardel* 1985 (d,p,sc); *Sur* 1988 (d,exec.p,p,sc pd,line p—Argentina,song).

Solo, Robert H. • Executive, producer • Born Waterbury, CT, December 4, 1932. *Educ.* University of Connecticut. Warner Bros. executive whose posts have included vice president of foreign production, where he oversaw such films as François Truffaut's *Day for Night* (1973) and Federico Fellini's *Amarcord* (1974). As an independent producer, Solo has backed films including *Bad Boys* (1983) and *Colors* (1988). • *Scrooge* 1970 (p); *The Devils* 1971 (p); *Invasion of the Body Snatchers* 1978 (p); *The Awakening* 1980 (p); *I, the Jury* 1981 (p); *Bad Boys* 1983 (p); *Above the Law* 1988 (exec.p); *Colors* 1988 (p); *Winter People* 1989 (p); *Blue Sky* 1991 (p).

Sommer, Josef • Actor • Born Maximilian Josef Sommer, Griefswald, Germany, June 26, 1934. *Educ.* Carnegie-Mellon University, Pittsburgh. Sturdy, stage-trained character actor who made his debut as the district attorney in *Dirty Harry* (1971) and went on to lend solid support to a number of excellent productions, including *The Front* (1976), *Reds* (1981), *Silkwood* (1983) and *Witness* (1985). On TV he starred as President Gerald Ford in *The Betty Ford Story* (1987). • *Dirty Harry* 1971; *Man on a Swing* 1974; *The Front* 1976; *Pleasantville* 1976; *Close Encounters of the Third Kind* 1977; *Oliver's Story* 1978; *Hide in Plain Sight* 1980; *Absence of Malice* 1981; *Reds* 1981; *Rollover* 1981; *Hanky Panky* 1982; *Independence Day* 1982; *Sophie's Choice* 1982; *Still of the Night* 1982; *Saigon-Year of the Cat* 1983; *Silkwood* 1983; *Iceman* 1984; *D.A.R.Y.L.* 1985; *Target* 1985; *Witness* 1985; *The Rosary Murders* 1987; *Dracula's Widow* 1988; *Bloodhounds of Broadway* 1989; *Chances Are* 1989; *Forced March* 1989.

Sondergaard, Gale • Actress • Born Edith Holm Sondergaard, Litchfield, MN, February 15, 1899; died August 14, 1985, Woodland Hills, CA. *Educ.* University of Minnesota. Successful stage actress in Hollywood from 1934, primarily as Hollywood's premier exotic villainess. Politically active and married to "Hollywood Ten" member Herbert Biberman, Sondergaard was blacklisted in the late 1940s. Her 1936 best supporting actress Academy Award, for Mervyn LeRoy's *Anthony Adverse* (1936), was the first to be given in that category. • *Anthony Adverse* 1936 **(AABSA)**; *The Life of Emile Zola* 1937; *Maid of Salem* 1937; *Seventh Heaven* 1937; *Dramatic School* 1938; *Lord Jeff* 1938; *The Cat and the Canary* 1939; *Juarez* 1939; *The Llano Kid* 1939; *Never Say Die* 1939; *The Blue Bird* 1940; *The Letter* 1940; *The Mark of Zorro* 1940; *The Black Cat* 1941; *Enemy Agents Meet Ellery Queen* 1942; *My Favorite Blonde* 1942; *A Night to Remember* 1942; *Paris Calling* 1942; *Appointment in Berlin* 1943; *Isle of Forgotten Sins* 1943; *The Strange Death of Adolf Hitler* 1943; *Christmas Holiday* 1944; *The Climax* 1944; *Enter Arsene Lupin* 1944; *Follow the Boys* 1944; *Gypsy Wildcat* 1944; *The Invisible Man's Revenge* 1944; *The Spider Woman* 1944; *Anna and the King of Siam* 1946 **(AANBSA)**; *A Night in Paradise* 1946; *The Spider Woman Strikes Back* 1946; *The Time of Their Lives* 1946; *Pirates of Monterey* 1947; *Road to Rio* 1947; *East Side, West Side* 1949; *Slaves* 1969; *Hollywood on Trial* 1976; *Pleasantville* 1976; *The Return of a Man Called Horse* 1976; *Echoes* 1980.

Sondheim, Stephen • Composer, lyricist; also screenwriter. • Born New York, NY, March 22, 1930. *Educ.* Williams College, Williamstown, MA. Preeminent figure of contemporary American musical theater whose sophisticated lyrics (*West Side Story, Gypsy, A Funny Thing Happened on the Way to the Forum*) and scores (*A Little Night Music, Sunday in the Park With George, Into the Woods*) have virtually spawned a new school of theatrical composition, lifting musicals from rousing banality into a loftier, more cerebral realm. Several of Sondheim's musical efforts have been successfully transposed to the screen and he has contributed fine music to a handful of films, including Alain Resnais's *Stavisky* (1974) and Warren Beatty's *Reds* (1981) and *Dick Tracy* (1990).

Since the 1960s, Sondheim has shown a Joycean fascination with language. He was instrumental in popularizing the British Crossword puzzle in the US in the late 60s. In 1973 he co-wrote with actor Anthony Perkins the comic mystery *The Last of Sheila*; both dialogue and *mise-en-scène* are replete with puns, anagrams and other alliterative wordplays. The solution to the mystery is itself semiotic. The film remains one of the most *significant* inside jokes ever played on the moviegoing public. JM • *West Side Story* 1961 (m,lyrics); *Gypsy* 1962 (lyrics); *A Funny Thing Happened on the Way to the Forum* 1966 (song); *The Last of Sheila* 1973 (sc); *Stavisky* 1974 (m); *The Seven Per-Cent Solution* 1976 (song); *A Little Night Music* 1977 (m,lyrics); *Airplane!* 1980 (song); *Reds* 1981 (m); *Terms of Endearment* 1983 (song); *Rhosyn a Rhith* 1986 (song); *Dick Tracy* 1990 (songs); *Postcards From the Edge* 1990 (song).

Sonnenfeld, Barry • Director of photography • Born US. *Educ.* NYU (political science); NYU Institute of Film and TV. Former NYU classmate of Joel Coen who made his mark with the Coen brothers' contemporary film noir, *Blood Simple* (1984). Sonnenfeld was also responsible for the acrobatic camerawork of the Coens' *Raising Arizona* (1987), as well as more mainstream fare such as Danny De Vito's *Throw Momma from the Train* (1987) and Rob Reiner's *When Harry Met Sally...* (1989). • *In Our Water* 1982 (ph); *Blood Simple* 1984 (ph); *Violated* 1984 (add.ph); *Compromising Positions* 1985 (ph); *Wisdom* 1986 (add.ph); *Raising Arizona* 1987 (ph); *Three O'Clock High* 1987 (ph); *Throw Momma From the Train* 1987 (ph); *Big* 1988 (ph); *When Harry Met Sally...* 1989 (ph); *Miller's Crossing* 1990 (ph); *Misery* 1990 (ph,2u d).

Sordi, Alberto • Actor; also director, screenwriter. • Born Rome, June 15, 1919. Italian leading man who came to prominence in the 1950s, especially in comic or romantic roles. Memorable Sordi performances include one of the young punks in Federico Fellini's *I Vitelloni* (1953), one of the grudging captains in *The Best of Enemies* (1961) and the lovelorn, hot-blooded Italian marooned in frosty Sweden in the finely observed comedy, *To Bed or Not To Bed* (1965). Sordi began screenwriting in the 1950s and directing occasionally in the mid-60s. • *Lo Sceicco Bianco/The White Sheik* 1952 (a); *I Vitelloni* 1953 (a); *A Farewell to Arms* 1957 (a); *Souvenir D'Italie* 1957 (a); *The Virtuous Bigamist* 1957 (a); *Nella città l'inferno* 1958 (a); *Oh, Que Mambo!* 1959 (a); *Crimen* 1960 (a); *The Best of Enemies* 1961 (a); *Made in Italy* 1965 (a); *Those Magnificent Men in Their Flying Machines* 1965 (a); *To Bed or Not To Bed* 1965 (a); *Scusi, lei è favorevole o contrario?* 1966 (d); *Le Streghe* 1968 (a); *Bello Onesto Emigrato Australia Sposerebbe Compaesan Illibata* 1971 (a); *Detenuto in Attesa di Giudizio* 1971 (a); *La Più Bella Serata Della Mia Vita* 1972 (a); *Roma* 1972 (a); *Lo Scopone Scientifico* 1972 (a); *Anastasia mio fratello ovvero il presunto capo dell'aninima assassini* 1973 (a); *Polvere di Stelle* 1973 (a,d,sc); *Finchè C'è Guerra C'è Speranza* 1974 (a,d,sc); *Quelle Strane Occasioni* 1976 (a); *Un Borghese Piccolo Piccolo* 1977 (a); *I Nuovi Mostri* 1977 (a); *Dove vai in vacanza?* 1978 (a,d,sc—"Le vacanze intelligenti"); *Le Temoin* 1978 (a,sc.adapt); *Le Grand embouteillage* 1979 (a); *Il Malato Immaginario* 1979 (a,sc); *Io e Caterina* 1980 (a,d,sc); *Il Marchese del Grillo* 1981 (a,sc); *Io So Che Tu Sai Che Io So* 1982 (a,d,sc); *In Viaggio Con Papa* 1983 (a,d,sc,story); *Il Tassinaro* 1983 (a,d,sc); *Bertoldo, Bertoldino e Cacasenno* 1984 (a); *Tutti Dentro* 1984 (a,d,sc); *Troppo Forte* 1985 (a,sc); *Sono un Fenomeno Paranormale* 1986 (a,sc); *Un Tassinaro a New York* 1987 (a,d,sc); *Les Fanfarons* 1988 (a,sc); *L'Avaro* 1990 (a,sc).

Sorvino, Paul • Actor; also opera singer • Born Brooklyn, NY, 1939. *Educ.* American Musical and Dramatic Academy, New York. Chunky, polished character actor from the stage who made his film debut in the riotous comedy, *Where's Poppa?* (1970). Usually in ethnic, blue-collar roles, Sorvino has turned in dependable performances in a number of fine productions, including *Panic in Needle Park* (1971), *Reds* (1981) and *Goodfellas* (1990). • *Cry Uncle* 1970; *Where's Poppa?* 1970; *Made For Each Other* 1971; *Panic in Needle Park* 1971; *The Day of the Dolphin* 1973; *A Touch of Class* 1973; *The Gambler* 1974; *Shoot It: Black, Shoot It: Blue* 1974; *I Will... I Will... For Now* 1975; *Oh, God!* 1977; *Bloodbrothers* 1978; *The Brink's Job* 1978; *Slow Dancing in the Big City* 1978; *Lost and Found* 1979; *Cruising* 1980; *I, the Jury* 1981; *Melanie* 1981; *Reds* 1981; *That Championship Season* 1982; *Off the Wall* 1983; *Very Close Quarters* 1983; *The Stuff* 1985; *Turk 182* 1985; *A Fine Mess* 1986; *Vasectomy, a Delicate Matter* 1986; *Dick Tracy* 1990; *GoodFellas* 1990; *Jailbait: Betrayed By Innocence* 1990; *Life in the Food Chain* 1991; *The Rocketeer* 1991.

Sothern, Ann • *aka* Harriete Lake • Actress • Born Harriette Lake, Valley City, ND, January 22, 1909. *Educ.* University of Washington. Classically trained singer who briefly appeared in several films from the late 1920s before making her mark on Broadway. Sothern joined Columbia in 1933 and coasted as a star of B vehicles until she signed on with MGM six years later and emerged as the dizzy lead of the popular, long-running comedy-adventure film series that began with *Maisie*. She went on to enliven a number of musical comedies (including *Panama Hattie* 1942) and exhibited a flair for dramatics in such engaging melodramas as *A Letter to Three Wives* (1948).

Sothern turned her attention to TV in the early 1950s, starring in two immensely successful series "Private Secretary" (1953-57) and "The Ann Sothern Show" (1958-61), and intermittently appeared in blowsy character roles from the mid-60s. She made a lauded return to the screen in a supporting role in *The Whales of August* (1987). Married to actors Roger Pryor and Robert Sterling and mother of actress Tisha Sterling. • *The Show of Shows* 1929 (a,song); *Blind Date* 1934 (a); *The Hell Cat* 1934 (a); *Kid Millions* 1934 (a); *Melody in Spring* 1934 (a); *The Party's Over* 1934 (a); *Eight Bells* 1935 (a); *Folies Bergère* 1935 (a); *The Girl Friend* 1935 (a); *Grand Exit* 1935 (a); *Hooray For Love* 1935 (a); *Don't Gamble With Love* 1936 (a); *Hell-Ship Morgan* 1936 (a); *My American Wife* 1936 (a); *The Smartest Girl in Town* 1936 (a); *Walking on Air* 1936 (a); *You May Be Next* 1936 (a); *Danger—Love at Work* 1937 (a); *Dangerous Number* 1937 (a); *Fifty Roads to Town* 1937 (a); *Super Sleuth* 1937 (a); *There Goes My Girl* 1937 (a); *There Goes the Groom* 1937 (a); *She's Got Everything* 1938 (a); *Trade Winds* 1938 (a); *Fast and Furious* 1939 (a); *Hotel For Women* 1939 (a); *Joe and Ethel Turp Call on the President* 1939 (a); *Maisie* 1939 (a); *Brother Orchid* 1940 (a); *Congo Maisie* 1940 (a); *Dulcy* 1940 (a); *Gold Rush Maisie* 1940 (a); *Lady Be Good* 1941 (a); *Maisie Was a Lady* 1941 (a); *Ringside Maisie* 1941 (a); *Maisie Gets Her Man* 1942 (a); *Panama Hattie* 1942 (a); *Cry Havoc* 1943 (a); *Swing Shift Maisie* 1943 (a); *Thousands Cheer* 1943 (a); *Three Hearts For Julia* 1943 (a); *Maisie Goes to Reno* 1944 (a); *Up Goes Maisie* 1946 (a); *Undercover Maisie* 1947 (a); *April Showers* 1948 (a); *A Letter to Three Wives* 1948 (a); *Words and Music* 1948 (a); *The Judge Steps Out* 1949 (a); *Nancy Goes to Rio* 1950 (a); *Shadow on the Wall* 1950 (a); *The Blue Gardenia* 1953 (a); *The Best Man* 1964 (a); *Lady in a Cage* 1964 (a); *Sylvia* 1965 (a); *Chubasco* 1968 (a); *The Killing Kind* 1973 (a); *Golden Needles* 1974 (a); *Crazy Mama* 1975 (a); *The Manitou* 1977 (a); *The Little Dragons* 1980 (a); *The Whales of August* 1987 (a) **(AANBSA)**.

Southern, Terry • *aka* Maxwell Kenton • Screenwriter; also novelist. • Born Alvalrado, TX, May 1, 1926. *Educ.* Southern Methodist University; University of Chicago; Northwestern; Sorbonne, Paris. Author of satirical novels including the then-scandalous erotic adventure, *Candy*, who in the 1960s contributed his incisive wit and intelligence to several screen gems, particularly *Dr. Strangelove* (1964) and *Easy Rider* (1969). • *Dr. Strangelove; or, How I Learned to Stop Worrying and Love the Bomb* 1964 (sc) **(AANBSC)**; *The Cincin-*

nati Kid 1965 (sc); *The Loved One* 1965 (sc); *Barbarella* 1968 (sc); *Candy* 1968 (from novel); *The Queen* 1968 (a); *Easy Rider* 1969 (sc) **(AANBSC)**; *The End of the Road* 1970 (p,sc); *The Magic Christian* 1970 (sc,from novel); *CS Blues* 1972 (a); *Burroughs* 1983 (a); *The Telephone* 1988 (sc).

Spaak, Charles • Screenwriter; also director. • Born Brussels, Belgium, May 25, 1903; died 1975. Flemish screenwriter, in France from 1928. Spaak served as secretary to director Jacques Feyder before contributing scripts to his films, beginning with the effervescent satire, *Les Nouveaux Messieurs* (1928), and went on to write for such directors as Jean Renoir (*Grand Illusion* 1937) and Julien Duvivier (*The End of a Day* 1939), establishing himself as one of the more significant figures of French *poetic realism*. Spaak also lent his talents to the works of André Cayatte and in 1949 directed his one and only film, *Le Mystère Barton* (1949). Father of actresses Agnes and Catherine Spaak. • *Les Nouveaux Messieurs/The Grand Illusion* 1928 (sc); *La Grande Illusion* 1937 (sc); *Mollenard* 1937 (sc); *La Fin du Jour/The End of a Day* 1939 (sc); *Le Mystère Barton* 1949 (d); *Adorables Créatures* 1952 (sc,adapt); *Les Sept péchés capitaux/The Seven Deadly Sins* 1952 (sc—"Avarice and Anger"); *Le Grand Jeu* 1953 (sc,story); *Thérèse Raquin* 1953 (sc); *Crime et Chatiment* 1956 (sc); *Paris Palace Hotel* 1956 (sc); *Katia* 1960 (sc); *Das Brennende Gericht* 1962 (sc,dial); *Cartouche* 1962 (sc); *Un Milliard dans un Billiard* 1965 (sc); *La Main à Couper...* 1973 (sc).

Spacek, Sissy • Actress • Born Mary Elizabeth Spacek, Quitman, TX, December 25, 1949. *Educ.* Actors Studio; Lee Strasberg Theater Institute. Waif-like, honey-haired performer who gained attention in the mid-1970s for her sympathetic performances as disturbed teenagers, in Terrence Malick's poetic *Badlands* (1973) and Brian De Palma's gore show, *Carrie* (1976), before moving on to more adult roles. Spacek was superb as one of Robert Altman's *Three Women* (1977) and as country singer Loretta Lynn in Michael Apted's finely observed biopic, *Coal Miner's Daughter* (1980). She is married to production designer-director Jack Fisk and starred in his films *Raggedy Man* (1981) and *Violets Are Blue* (1986). First cousin of actor Rip Torn. • *Prime Cut* 1972 (a); *Badlands* 1973 (a); *Ginger in the Morning* 1973 (a); *Phantom of the Paradise* 1974 (sets); *Carrie* 1976 (a) **(AANBA)**; *Welcome to L.A.* 1976 (a); *Three Women* 1977 (a); *Heart Beat* 1979 (a); *Coal Miner's Daughter* 1980 (a,song) **(AABA)**; *Raggedy Man* 1981 (a); *Missing* 1982 (a) **(AANBA)**; *The River* 1984 (a) **(AANBA)**; *Marie* 1985 (a); *'night, Mother* 1986 (a); *Crimes of the Heart* 1986 (a) **(AANBA)**; *Violets Are Blue* 1986 (a); *The Long Walk Home* 1990 (a).

Spacey, Kevin • Actor • Born South Orange, NJ, July 26, 1959. *Educ.* Los Angeles Valley College; Juilliard (drama). Engaging, stage-trained actor who made his screen debut in Mike Nichols's *Heartburn* (1986). (He was also featured in the Nichols-directed Broadway play, *Hurlyburly*, and in his 1988 film *Working Girl.*) Although Spacey is best known for his role as Mel Proffit in the TV series "Wiseguy," he was memorable as the struggling standup comic in *Rocket Gibraltar* (1988) and as Jamie Tyrone in the Broadway revival of *Long Day's Journey Into Night* opposite Jack Lemmon. • *Heartburn* 1986; *Rocket Gibraltar* 1988; *Working Girl* 1988; *Dad* 1989; *See No Evil, Hear No Evil* 1989; *Henry & June* 1990; *A Show of Force* 1990.

Spader, James • Actor • Born Boston, MA, February 7, 1960. *Educ.* Michael Chekhov Studio. Attractive, innocent-looking blond lead who has tended to be typecast as a clean-cut young professional (*Baby Boom* 1987, *Wall Street* 1987, *Bad Influence* 1990). Spader won the best actor award at Cannes for his role as Graham, the social outsider who disrupts the life of a young Southern lawyer and his wife, in *sex, lies, and videotape* (1989). • *Endless Love* 1981; *The New Kids* 1985; *Tuff Turf* 1985; *Pretty in Pink* 1986; *Baby Boom* 1987; *Less Than Zero* 1987; *Wall Street* 1987; *Jack's Back* 1988; *The Rachel Papers* 1989; *sex, lies, and videotape* 1989; *Bad Influence* 1990; *White Palace* 1990; *True Colors* 1991.

Spano, Vincent • Actor • Born Brooklyn, NY, October 18, 1962. Darkly handsome young lead who came to prominence as the ingratiating misfit, "The Shiek," opposite Rosanna Arquette in John Sayles's *Baby, It's You* (1983). Spano has proved his versatility in a wide variety of films, from Roger Vadim's remake of *And God Created Woman* (1988) to the Taviani Brothers' valentine to the early days of Hollywood, *Good Morning Babylon* (1986). • *The Double McGuffin* 1979; *Over the Edge* 1979; *Baby, It's You* 1983; *The Black Stallion Returns* 1983; *Rumble Fish* 1983; *Alphabet City* 1984; *Creator* 1985; *Maria's Lovers* 1985; *Good Morning Babylon* 1986; *And God Created Woman* 1988; *High-Frequency* 1988; *Venezia Rosso Sangue* 1989; *The Heart of the Deal* 1990; *City of Hope* 1991; *Oscar* 1991.

Spencer, Dorothy • Editor • Born Covington, KY, February 2, 1909. Acclaimed American editor noted for her collaboration with John Ford on the classic western, *Stagecoach* (1939), and her work on a number of action-packed spectacles including the opulent *Cleopatra* (1963) and the trend-setting disaster film, *Earthquake* (1974). • *Married in Hollywood* 1929; *Nix on Dames* 1929; *As Husbands Go* 1933; *Coming Out Party* 1934; *She Was a Lady* 1934; *The Case Against Mrs. Ames* 1936; *The Luckiest Girl in the World* 1936; *Stand-In* 1937; *Vogues of 1938* 1937; *Blockade* 1938; *Trade Winds* 1938; *Eternally Yours* 1939; *Stagecoach* 1939 **(AANBED)**; *Winter Carnival* 1939; *The House Across the Bay* 1940; *Slightly Honorable* 1940; *Sundown* 1941; *To Be or Not to Be* 1942; *Happy Land* 1943; *Heaven Can Wait* 1943; *Lifeboat* 1944; *Sweet and Low Down* 1944; *A Royal Scandal* 1945; *A Tree Grows in Brooklyn* 1945; *Cluny Brown* 1946; *Dragonwyck* 1946; *My Darling Clementine* 1946; *The Ghost and Mrs. Muir* 1947; *The Snake Pit* 1948; *That Lady in Ermine* 1948; *Down to the Sea in Ships* 1949; *Three Came Home* 1950; *Under My Skin* 1950; *Fourteen Hours* 1951; *Decision Before Dawn* 1952 **(AANBED)**; *Lydia Bailey* 1952; *What Price Glory* 1952; *Man on a Tightrope* 1953; *Tonight We Sing* 1953; *Black Widow* 1954; *Demetrius and the Gladiators* 1954; *Night People* 1954; *The Left Hand of God* 1955; *The Man in the Gray Flannel Suit* 1955; *Prince of Players* 1955; *The Rains of Ranchipur* 1955; *Soldier of Fortune* 1955; *The Best Things in Life Are Free* 1956; *A Hatful of Rain* 1957; *The Young Lions* 1958; *The Journey* 1959; *A Private's Affair* 1959; *From the Terrace* 1960; *North to Alaska* 1960; *Seven Thieves* 1960; *Wild in the Country* 1961; *Cleopatra* 1963 **(AANBED)**; *Circus World* 1964; *Von Ryan's Express* 1965; *Lost Command* 1966; *A Guide For the Married Man* 1967; *Valley of the Dolls* 1967; *Daddy's Gone A-Hunting* 1969; *Happy Birthday, Wanda June* 1971; *Women in Limbo* 1972; *Earthquake* 1974 **(AANBED)**; *The Concorde-Airport '79* 1979.

Spheeris, Penelope • Director; also producer, screenwriter. • Born New Orleans, LA, 1945. *Educ.* UCLA (film); AFI, Los Angeles. After producing Albert Brooks's hilarious *Real Life* (1978) Spheeris turned to directing, making a number of ambitious but mostly undistinguished films. Her "Decline" documentaries chronicle, respectively, the late-70s Los Angeles punk scene and the mid-80s heavy metal phenomenon. • *Real Life* 1978 (p); *The Decline of Western Civilization* 1980 (d,p,sc,add.ph); *Suburbia* 1983 (d,sc); *The Boys Next Door* 1985 (d); *Hollywood Vice Squad* 1986 (d); *Summer Camp Nightmare* 1986 (sc); *Dudes* 1987 (d); *Calling the Shots* 1988 (a); *The Decline of Western Civilization Part II, The Metal Years* 1988 (d); *Wedding Band* 1990 (a).

Spiegel, Sam • *aka* S. P. Eagle • Producer • Born Jaroslau, Austria, November 11, 1903; died December 31, 1985, St. Martin Island. *Educ.* University of Vienna. Austrian producer who began his career as a story translator in Hollywood in 1927. Soon after, Spiegel moved to Berlin, where he worked on French and

German versions of several Universal films. He fled the Nazis in 1933 and independently produced several films before returning to Hollywood in 1935.

Spiegel established himself in the American industry in the early 1940s, using the pseudonym "S.P. Eagle" and scoring with such excellent productions as Orson Welles's *The Stranger* (1946) and John Huston's *The African Queen* (1951). He resumed the use of his real name for his credit on *On the Waterfront* (1954) and the "Spiegel" imprimatur went on to adorn such notable, independently produced films as *The Bridge on the River Kwai* (1957) and *Lawrence of Arabia* (1962). • *Tales of Manhattan* 1942; *The Stranger* 1946; *We Were Strangers* 1949; *The African Queen* 1951; *The Prowler* 1951; *When I Grow Up* 1951; *Melba* 1953; *On the Waterfront* 1954 **(AABP)**; *The Bridge on the River Kwai* 1957 **(AABP)**; *The Strange One* 1957; *Suddenly, Last Summer* 1959; *Lawrence of Arabia* 1962 **(AABP)**; *The Chase* 1966; *The Night of the Generals* 1966; *Nicholas and Alexandra* 1971 **(AANBP)**; *The Last Tycoon* 1976; *Betrayal* 1983.

Spielberg, Steven • Director, producer • Born Cincinnati, OH, December 18, 1947. *Educ.* California State University, Long Beach, CA. As a producer and director, Steven Spielberg's name has become a household word. Six of his movies as director—*Jaws* (1975); *Close Encounters of the Third Kind* (1977); *Raiders of the Lost Ark* (1981) and its two sequels, *Indian Jones and the Temple of Doom* (1984) and *Indiana Jones and the Last Crusade* (1989); and *E.T., The Extra-Terrestrial* (1982)—are among the highest grossing of all time. Astonishingly, Spielberg has managed to combine the intimacy of a personal vision with the epic requirements of the commercial blockbuster.

A Spielberg film frequently uses elements of science fiction and fantasy, eschewing ideas in favor of emotions, particularly childlike awe and trust. Indeed, his work has decisively influenced the emphasis in contemporary science fiction film on the sensibility of youth. His films often succeed in spite of their sentimental limitations, because the director is able to sustain even the shakiest narrative with masterful use of emotionally potent visual imagery. Spielberg possesses, in short, an uncanny knack for eliciting and manipulating audience response.

Unlike George Lucas, John Carpenter and other successful young American filmmakers of the last two decades, Spielberg did not attend one of the major American university film programs. Largely self-taught, he made his first feature, a two-hour science fiction movie entitled *Firelight*, at the age of sixteen, and a local movie house in Phoenix, Arizona, consented to run it for one evening. In 1969 his short film, *Amblin'* (now the name of his production company) earned him a job with Universal Studios' television unit, where he directed episodes of such weekly series as Rod Serling's "Night Gallery," "Columbo" and "Marcus Welby, M.D." He also made three television movies, one of which, *Duel* (1972), was given the honor of a theatrical release in Europe, where it garnered both critical praise and commercial success. Its story, of a salesman pursued by a giant diesel truck whose driver is never seen nor motive explained, is conveyed with a sure handling of suspense. His first theatrical film, *The Sugarland Express* (1974), based on the true story of a Texas woman fighting the law to regain custody of her baby, anticipates the emphasis on family in Spielberg's subsequent work; his choreographed car chases and deft handling of suspense and comedy marked him as a director to watch.

Spielberg pours into his films his personal knowledge of American middle-class suburbia, which he once remarked was like "growing up with three parents—a mother, a father and a TV set." Characters in his films are frequently awash in the detritus of bourgeois America, although they are not always at ease with their surroundings. When the hero of *Close Encounters* has his first encounter, which causes his company truck to shake like one of the many battery-operated toys that fill the film, he acknowledges the existence of greater powers in the universe. In both this film and *E.T.*, alien beings offer the promise of life beyond the restrictions of conventional middle-class life; the spaceships in *Close Encounters* unheedingly pass the toll booths on the state highway, markers of boundaries that signifies the earthbound vision of middle-class America.
Dreyfuss's departure aboard the mother ship for unknown adventures is the film's final grandiloquent embrace of the possible.

Spielberg's ability to portray imaginative possibilities beyond the realm of reason is a result of his kinship with a childlike sense of wonder. In 1982 he admitted, "I feel I'm still a kid. I'm 34 and I really haven't grown up yet." It is no surprise, then, that his episode of *Twilight Zone—the Movie* (1983) is a story of old folks who can become children again if they only wish strongly enough. In *E.T.* the imagination of youth can soar to both literal and poetic heights, as the kids do on their bicycles, despite the obvious narrative inconsistency.
Spielberg cleverly maintains the point of view of the 12-year-old Elliott throughout *E.T.* with camera placement and angles. Spielberg shares this affinity for children with the late French director François Truffaut, who played the scientist in *Close Encounters* with an open faith in the existence of extraterrestrials. The aliens in that film, in fact, look like nothing so much as wondrous children, representing a much more benign presentation than the common view of monstrous conquerors in almost all of the science fiction movies of the 1950s.

In Spielberg's films anything that threatens the family and its routine existence is evil. In *Jaws*, the normally safe harbor of a patrolled public beach becomes threatening because of a great white shark, a giant "eating machine" similar to the truck in *Duel*. The heroes of *The Sugarland Express* and the Indiana Jones trilogy are transported from normal life to a world of exciting adventure. Ultimately, it seems, Spielberg would much prefer the childish world of harmless adventure in his production *The Goonies* (1985) to the violence and hardships of the real world. Thus, Spielberg looks at WWII through the eyes of his youthful protagonist in *Empire of the Sun* (1987) and conjures an Oedipal fantasy as the producer of *Back to the Future* (1985), in which a son remakes his parents from nerds into successful yuppies.

Such a vision, inevitably, is politically naive. *Indiana Jones and the Temple of Doom* (1984), for example, is embarrassingly racist and misogynist. Even his adaptation of Alice Walker's novel *The Color Purple* (1985), although dealing with racism, lesbianism and wife-beating, has the air of an old- fashioned Disney film. (Politically minded critics condemned Spielberg's film for its "whitewashing" of Walker's novel). That Spielberg co-produced and co-wrote but did not direct *Poltergiest* (1982) is significant, for it presents the dark underside of suburbia that is only hinted at in his own films as director—"my personal nightmare," he has remarked—and suggests that Spielberg is, to some extent at least, aware of his own limitations. BKG • *Duel* 1972 (d); *Ace Eli and Rodger of the Skies* 1973 (story); *The Sugarland Express* 1974 (d,story); *Jaws* 1975 (d); *Close Encounters of the Third Kind* 1977 (d,sc,fx) **(AANBD)**; *I Wanna Hold Your Hand* 1978 (exec.p); *1941* 1979 (d); *The Blues Brothers* 1980 (a); *Used Cars* 1980 (exec.p); *Continental Divide* 1981 (exec.p); *Raiders of the Lost Ark* 1981 (d) **(AANBD)**; *Chambre 666* 1982 (a); *E.T., the Extra-Terrestrial* 1982 (d,p) **(AANBD)**; *Poltergeist* 1982 (p,sc,story); *Twilight Zone—the Movie* 1983 (d,exec.p); *Gremlins* 1984 (exec.p); *Indiana Jones and the Temple of Doom* 1984 (d); *Back to the Future* 1985 (exec.p); *The Color Purple* 1985 (d,p) **(AANBP)**; *The Goonies* 1985 (exec.p,story); *Young Sherlock Holmes* 1985 (exec.p); *An American Tail* 1986 (exec.p); *The Money Pit* 1986 (exec.p); *Batteries Not Included* 1987 (exec.p); *Empire of the Sun* 1987 (d,p); *Innerspace* 1987 (exec.p); *The Land Before Time* 1988 (exec.p); *Who Framed Roger Rabbit?* 1988 (exec.p); *Always* 1989 (d,p); *Back to the Future II* 1989 (exec.p); *Dad* 1989 (exec.p); *Indiana Jones and the Last Crusade* 1989 (d); *Tummy Trouble* 1989 (exec.p); *Arachnophobia* 1990 (exec.p); *Back to the Future III* 1990 (exec.p); *Gremlins 2: The New Batch* 1990 (exec.p); *Joe Versus the Volcano* 1990 (exec.p); *Listen Up* 1990 (a); *Rollercoaster Rabbit* 1990 (exec.p).

Spinell, Joe • *aka* Joseph J. Spagnuolo • Actor • Born New York, c. 1938; died January 13, 1989, New York. Husky character player, usually in tough Italian roles ranging from petty mobsters to police officers. Spinell wrote, produced and starred in *Maniac* (1981), an unrelenting portrait of a psychopathic killer and the first of two films in which he appeared opposite Caroline Munro. • *The Godfather, Part II* 1974 (a); *92 in the Shade* 1975 (a); *Stay Hungry* 1975 (a); *Rocky* 1976 (a); *Nunzio* 1977 (a); *Sorcerer* 1977 (a); *Big Wednesday* 1978 (a); *One Man Jury* 1978 (a); *Paradise Alley* 1978 (a); *Last Embrace* 1979 (a); *Rocky II* 1979 (a); *Starcrash* 1979 (a); *Twinkle, Twinkle, "Killer" Kane* 1979 (a); *Winter Kills* 1979 (a); *Brubaker* 1980 (a); *Cruising* 1980 (a); *First Deadly Sin* 1980 (a); *The Little Dragons* 1980 (a); *Maniac* 1981 (a,exec.p,sc); *Nighthawks* 1981 (a); *Monsignor* 1982 (a); *National Lampoon Goes to the Movies* 1982 (a); *Night Shift* 1982 (a); *One Down Two to Go* 1982 (a); *Vigilante* 1982 (a); *Walking the Edge* 1982 (a); *The Big Score* 1983 (a); *Eureka* 1983 (a); *The Last Fight* 1983 (a); *Losin' It* 1983 (a); *The Last Horror Film* 1984 (a); *Hollywood Harry* 1985 (a); *The Whoopee Boys* 1986 (a); *Deadly Illusion* 1987 (a); *The Messenger* 1987 (a); *The Pick-Up Artist* 1987 (a); *Operation Warzone* 1990 (a); *Rapid Fire* 1990 (a).

Spinotti, Dante • Director of photography • Born Italy. Italian cinematographer who has worked with native directors including Lina Wertmuller and Liliana Cavani and shot American films such as Michael Mann's *Manhunter* (1986), Bruce Beresford's *Crimes of the Heart* (1986), Peter Bogdanovich's *Illegally Yours* (1988) and Paul Schrader's *The Comfort of Strangers* (1990). • *Cenerentola '80* 1980 (ph); *Il Minestrone* 1980 (ph); *Le Armi e Gli Amori* 1983 (ph); *Basileus Quartet* 1983 (ph); *I Paladini Storia d'Armi e d'Amori* 1983 (ph); *Sogno di Una Notte d'Estate* 1983 (ph); *Così Parlò Bellavista* 1984 (ph); *Fotografando Patrizia* 1984 (ph); *Interno Berlinese* 1985 (ph); *Sotto, Sotto* 1985 (ph); *Voyage of the Rock Aliens* 1985 (ph—"When the Rain Begins to Fall"); *Choke Canyon* 1986 (ph); *Crimes of the Heart* 1986 (ph); *Manhunter* 1986 (ph); *Aria* 1987 (ph—"Die Tote Stadt); *From the Hip* 1987 (ph); *Beaches* 1988 (ph); *Illegally Yours* 1988 (ph); *La Leggenda del Santo Bevitore* 1988 (ph); *Mamba* 1988 (ph); *Torrents of Spring* 1989 (ph); *Cellini a Violent Life* 1990 (ph); *The Comfort of Strangers* 1990 (ph); *Hudson Hawk* 1991 (ph); *True Colors* 1991 (ph).

Spottiswoode, Roger • Director; also producer, screenwriter, editor. • Born England, c. 1947. Former British TV and documentary editor who cut three Sam Peckinpah films, *Straw Dogs* (1971), *The Getaway* (1972) and *Pat Garrett and Billy the Kid* (1973), before making his directorial debut with *Terror Train* in 1980. Spottiswoode directed the taut political drama *Under Fire* (1983) and has developed into an adaptable, competent Hollywood director of mainstream films such as *Shoot to Kill* (1988), *Turner and Hooch* (1989) and *Air America* (1990). • *Straw Dogs* 1971 (ed); *The Getaway* 1972 (ed); *Pat Garrett and Billy the Kid* 1973 (ed); *The Gambler* 1974 (ed); *Hard Times* 1975 (ed); *Who'll Stop the Rain?* 1978 (assoc.p); *Terror Train* 1980 (d); *The Pursuit of D.B. Cooper* 1981 (d); *48 Hrs.* 1982 (sc); *Under Fire* 1983 (d); *Baby: The Secret of the Lost Legend* 1985 (exec.p); *The Best of Times* 1986 (d); *Shoot to Kill* 1988 (d); *Turner and Hooch* 1989 (d); *Air America* 1990 (d); *Another 48 Hrs.* 1990 (from characters).

St. Jacques, Raymond • Actor • Born James Arthur Johnson, Hartford, CT, March 1, 1930; died August 27, 1990, Los Angeles, CA. *Educ.* Yale (psychology, drama); Actors Studio. Tall, stage-trained actor with a resonant baritone voice, who emerged as one of America's premier black performers of the mid-1960s. St. Jacques, who effectively portrayed heroic characters as well as villians, appeared in films including *The Pawnbroker* (1965), *The Comedians* (1967) and *Cotton Comes to Harlem* (1970) and was well known for his role as a cattle driver in the TV series, "Rawhide." He directed, produced and starred in the 1972 feature, *Book of Numbers*, a comic drama about racketeering in a small Arkansas town in the 1930s. • *Mister Buddwing* 1965 (a); *Mister Moses* 1965 (a); *The Pawnbroker* 1965 (a); *The Comedians* 1967 (a); *The Green Berets* 1968 (a); *If He Hollers, Let Him Go!* 1968 (a); *Madigan* 1968 (a); *Uptight* 1968 (a); *Change of Mind* 1969 (a); *Cotton Comes to Harlem* 1970 (a); *The Final Comedown* 1971 (a); *Book of Numbers* 1972 (a,d,p); *Come Back Charleston Blue* 1972 (a); *Cool Breeze* 1972 (a); *Lost in the Stars* 1974 (a); *Blast* 1976 (a); *The Private Files of J. Edgar Hoover* 1977 (a); *Born Again* 1978 (a); *Cuba Crossing* 1979 (a); *The Evil That Men Do* 1984 (a); *The Wild Pair* 1987 (a); *They Live* 1988 (a); *Voodoo Dawn* 1991 (a).

Stack, Robert • Actor • Born Robert Langford Modini, Los Angeles, CA, January 13, 1919. *Educ.* USC, Los Angeles; Henry Duffy School of Theater. Steely-eyed, resolute leading man, in films from 1939, who hit a peak in the 1950s starring in two Douglas Sirk weepies: *Written on the Wind* (1956) and *The Tarnished Angels* (1958); best known as gangster-buster Eliot Ness on TV's "The Untouchables" (1959-1963). Stack wryly spoofed his humorless tough-guy image in the hilarious 1980 comedy, *Airplane!* • *First Love* 1939; *A Little Bit of Heaven* 1940; *The Mortal Storm* 1940; *Badlands of Dakota* 1941; *Nice Girl?* 1941; *Eagle Squadron* 1942; *Men of Texas* 1942; *To Be or Not to Be* 1942; *A Date With Judy* 1948; *Fighter Squadron* 1948; *Miss Tatlock's Millions* 1948; *Mr. Music* 1950; *Bullfighter and the Lady* 1951; *My Outlaw Brother* 1951; *Bwana Devil* 1952; *Conquest of Cochise* 1953; *Sabre Jet* 1953; *War Paint* 1953; *The High and the Mighty* 1954; *The Iron Glove* 1954; *Good Morning, Miss Dove* 1955; *House of Bamboo* 1955; *Great Day in the Morning* 1956; *Written on the Wind* 1956 **(AANBSA)**; *The Gift of Love* 1958; *The Tarnished Angels* 1958; *John Paul Jones* 1959; *The Last Voyage* 1960; *The Caretakers* 1963; *Le Soleil des voyous* 1967; *Storia di una Donna* 1970; *Un Second Souffle* 1978; *1941* 1979; *Airplane!* 1980; *Big Trouble* 1985; *Transformers—The Movie* 1986; *Caddyshack II* 1988; *Dangerous Curves* 1988; *Plain Clothes* 1988; *Joe Versus the Volcano* 1990.

Stahl, John M. • Director; also producer. • Born New York, NY, January 21, 1886; died January 12, 1950. Capable craftsman, in films from 1914, with a flair for lifting trite, sentimental material to higher ground. A master of the *woman's melodrama*, Stahl directed the original screen versions of several classic weepies, including *Back Street* (1932), *Imitation of Life* (1934) and *Magnificent Obsession* (1935). The latter two were remade in the 1950s, in more florid style, by Douglas Sirk. • *Suspicion* 1918 (d); *Wives of Men* 1918 (d,sc); *Her Code of Honor* 1919 (d); *A Woman Under Oath* 1919 (d); *Greater Than Love* 1920 (d); *The Woman in His House* 1920 (d); *Women Men Forget* 1920 (d); *The Child Thou Gavest Me* 1921 (d); *Sowing the Wind* 1921 (d); *The Dangerous Age* 1922 (d); *One Clear Call* 1922 (d); *The Song of Life* 1922 (d); *Suspicious Wives* 1922 (d); *The Wanters* 1923 (d,p); *Husbands and Lovers* 1924 (d); *Why Men Leave Home* 1924 (d,p); *Fine Clothes* 1925 (d); *The Gay Deceiver* 1926 (d); *Memory Lane* 1926 (d,sc); *In Old Kentucky* 1927 (d); *Lovers?* 1927 (d); *Marriage By Contract* 1928 (p); *A Lady Surrenders* 1930 (d); *Seed* 1931 (d); *Strictly Dishonorable* 1931 (d); *Back Street* 1932 (d); *Only Yesterday* 1933 (d); *Imitation of Life* 1934 (d); *Magnificent Obsession* 1935 (d); *Parnell* 1937 (d,p); *Letter of Introduction* 1938 (d,p); *When Tomorrow Comes* 1939 (d,p); *Our Wife* 1941 (d,p); *Holy Matrimony* 1943 (d); *Immortal Sergeant* 1943 (d); *The Eve of St. Mark* 1944 (d); *The Keys of the Kingdom* 1945 (d); *Leave Her to Heaven* 1945 (d); *The Foxes of Harrow* 1947 (d); *The Walls of Jericho* 1948 (d); *Father Was a Fullback* 1949 (d); *Oh, You Beautiful Doll!* 1949 (d).

Stallone, Sylvester • *aka* Sly Stallone • Actor; also director, screenwriter, producer. • Born New York, NY, July 6, 1946. *Educ.* American College in Switzerland; University of Miami (drama). Italian-American who gained overnight stardom when he starred in and wrote the Oscar-winning sleeper of 1976, *Rocky*. Stallone's early acting credits include a part in the nude play *Score* and in a semi-pornographic film (since retitled *The Italian Stallion* 1971) and a role as one of the thugs who harasses Woody Allen on the subway in *Bananas* (1971).

He subsequently landed parts in other legitimate feature films, but his career only began flying high when he took matters into his own hands and wrote *Rocky*. Though he sold the screenplay for a relatively small sum, Stallone was compensated in the form of percentage points and, more significantly, in his being cast in the title role. He made his directing debut with the flawed, but watchable, *Paradise Alley* (1978), and has written a number of his subsequent vehicles, on occasion even singing a song for the soundtracks.

Excepting *Night Hawks* (1981), which he neither wrote, produced nor directed, Stallone has not been involved with a film as rich and refreshing as his breakthrough. His "Rambo" films, like the *Rockys*, have steadily declined in quality, while cashing in on, and contributing to, the conservative political and social climate of the 1980s.

Stallone was formerly married to actress Brigitte Nielsen. Brother Frank Stallone is a singer-songwriter-actor who has worked on and/or appeared in a number of his brother's films, and was well cast as the belligerent bartender in *Barfly* (1986). • *Bananas* 1971 (a); *The Italian Stallion* 1971 (a); *The Lords of Flatbush* 1974 (a); *Capone* 1975 (a); *Death Race 2000* 1975 (a); *Farewell, My Lovely* 1975 (a); *No Place to Hide* 1975 (a); *Cannonball* 1976 (a); *Rocky* 1976 (a,sc) **(AANBA)**; *F.I.S.T.* 1978 (a,sc); *Paradise Alley* 1978 (a,d,sc,song); *Rocky II* 1979 (a,d,sc,chor—boxing); *Escape to Victory* 1981 (a); *Nighthawks* 1981 (a); *First Blood* 1982 (a,sc); *Rocky III* 1982 (a,d,sc,chor—boxing); *Staying Alive* 1983 (d,p,sc); *Rhinestone* 1984 (sc,song); *Rambo: First Blood Part II* 1985 (a,sc); *Rocky IV* 1985 (a,d,sc); *Cobra* 1986 (a,sc); *Over the Top* 1987 (a,sc); *Rambo III* 1988 (a,sc); *Lock Up* 1989 (a); *Tango and Cash* 1989 (a); *Rocky V* 1990 (a,sc); *Oscar* 1991 (a).

Stamp, Terence • Actor • Born Stepney, East London, July 23, 1939. *Educ.* Webber-Douglas Academy. English leading man with haunting pale eyes and a knack for conveying intense, disturbing characters both evil and benign. Stamp made his film debut as the title character in Peter Ustinov's adaptation of *Billy Budd* (1962) and went on to distinguish himself in the films of Joseph Losey (*Modesty Blaise* 1966), John Schlesinger (*Far From the Madding Crowd* 1967), Ken Loach (*Poor Cow* 1967) and Pier Paolo Pasolini (*Teorema* 1968). In few films of note during the 1970s, Stamp has since re-established himself, primarily as a character actor; he played the arch-villian in *Superman II* (1980) and the sequestered informer whose time has run out in Stephen Frears's offbeat thriller, *The Hit* (1984). • *Billy Budd* 1962 **(AANBSA)**; *The Collector* 1965; *Modesty Blaise* 1966; *Far From the Madding Crowd* 1967; *Poor Cow* 1967; *Blue* 1968; *Histoires Extraordinaires/Spirits of the Dead* 1968; *Teorema* 1968; *The Mind of Mr. Soames* 1970; *La Divina Creatura* 1975; *Hu-Man* 1975; *Black Out* 1977; *Superman* 1978; *The Thief of Bagdad* 1978; *Amo Non Amo* 1979; *Meetings With Remarkable Men* 1979; *Superman II* 1980; *Monster Island* 1981; *Morte in Vaticano* 1982; *The Hit* 1984; *The Company of Wolves* 1985; *Directed By William Wyler* 1986; *Hud* 1986; *Legal Eagles* 1986; *Link* 1986; *The Sicilian* 1987; *Wall Street* 1987; *Alien Nation* 1988; *La Barbare* 1988; *Young Guns* 1988; *Genuine Risk* 1990.

Stander, Lionel • Actor • Born New York, NY, January 11, 1908. *Educ.* University of North Carolina. Craggy-faced character player with a distinctive raspy voice who made his film debut in 1932 and went on to enliven numerous films, usually as an endearing curmudgeon, until he was blacklisted in the early 1950s. Stander supported himself as a stock player and Wall Street broker before resurfacing in international films, particularly "spaghetti westerns," in the 1960s. He later played the eccentric chauffeur on the TV series, "Hart to Hart" (1979-84). Stander was memorable as the cynical press agent in *A Star is Born* (1937) and as an old-time gangster in Roman Polanski's atmospheric *Cul-de-Sac* (1966). • *The Gay Deception* 1935; *Hooray For Love* 1935; *I Live My Life* 1935; *If You Could Only Cook* 1935; *Page Miss Glory* 1935; *The Scoundrel* 1935; *We're in the Money* 1935; *Meet Nero Wolfe* 1936; *The Milky Way* 1936; *More Than a Secretary* 1936; *Mr. Deeds Goes to Town* 1936; *The Music Goes 'Round* 1936; *Soak the Rich* 1936; *They Met in a Taxi* 1936; *The Last Gangster* 1937; *The League of Frightened Men* 1937; *A Star Is Born* 1937; *The Crowd Roars* 1938; *No Time to Marry* 1938; *Professor Beware* 1938; *Ice Follies* 1939; *What a Life* 1939; *The Bride Wore Crutches* 1941; *Hangmen Also Die* 1943; *Tahiti Honey* 1943; *The Big Show-Off* 1944; *A Boy, a Girl and a Dog* 1945; *Gentleman Joe Palooka* 1946; *In Old Sacramento* 1946; *The Kid From Brooklyn* 1946; *Specter of the Rose* 1946; *The Sin of Harold Diddlebock* 1947; *Call Northside 777* 1948; *Texas, Brooklyn and Heaven* 1948; *Trouble Makers* 1948; *Unfaithfully Yours* 1948; *St. Benny the Dip* 1951; *Two Gals and a Guy* 1951; *The Moving Finger* 1963; *The Loved One* 1965; *Cul-de-Sac* 1966; *Promise Her Anything* 1966; *Gates to Paradise* 1967; *A Dandy in Aspic* 1968; *C'era una Volta il West/Once Upon a Time in the West* 1969; *Wie Kommt ein So Reizendes Maedchen zu Diesem Gewerbe?* 1970; *Don Camillo e i Giovani d'Oggi* 1971; *The Gang That Couldn't Shoot Straight* 1971; *Per Grazia Ricevuta* 1971; *Pulp* 1972; *Treasure Island* 1972; *Mordi e Fuggi* 1973; *Paolo Il Caldo* 1973; *The Black Bird* 1975; *The Cassandra Crossing* 1977; *New York, New York* 1977; *Matilda* 1978; *1941* 1979; *The Squeeze* 1980; *Transformers—The Movie* 1986; *Cookie* 1989; *Wicked Stepmother* 1989.

Stanton, Harry Dean • *aka* Dean Stanton • Actor • Born West Irvine, KY, July 14, 1926. *Educ.* University of Kentucky; Pasadena Playhouse. Prolific supporting player, in films from 1957, who has specialized in playing outsiders, psychotics and heavies. Stanton had turned in a battery of finely turned character roles in such films as *Wise Blood*, *Alien* (both 1979) and *Repo Man* (1984) before landing his first romantic lead as the bewildered, wandering father, Travis, in Wim Wenders's bittersweet *Paris, Texas* (1984). • *Revolt at Fort Laramie* 1957 (a); *Tomahawk Trail* 1957 (a); *Proud Rebel* 1958 (a); *Pork Chop Hill* 1959 (a); *The Adventures of Huckleberry Finn* 1960 (a); *Dog's Best Friend* 1960 (a); *Hero's Island* 1962 (a); *The Man From the Diner's Club* 1963 (a); *The Hostage* 1966 (a); *Ride in the Whirlwind* 1966 (a); *Cool Hand Luke* 1967 (a); *The Long Ride Home* 1967 (a); *Day of the Evil Gun* 1968 (a); *The Mini-Skirt Mob* 1968 (a); *Rebel Rousers* 1970 (a); *Cisco Pike* 1971 (a); *Two-Lane Blacktop* 1971 (a); *Count Your Bullets* 1972 (a); *Face to the Wind* 1972 (a); *Dillinger* 1973 (a); *Pat Garrett and Billy the Kid* 1973 (a); *Where the Lilies Bloom* 1973 (a); *Cockfighter* 1974 (a); *The Godfather, Part II* 1974 (a); *Rafferty and the Gold Dust Twins* 1974 (a); *Rancho Deluxe* 1974 (a); *Zandy's Bride* 1974 (a); *92 in the Shade* 1975 (a); *Farewell, My Lovely* 1975 (a); *Win, Place or Steal* 1975 (a); *The Missouri Breaks* 1976 (a); *Renaldo & Clara* 1977 (a); *Straight Time* 1978 (a); *Alien* 1979 (a); *The Black Marble* 1979 (a); *La Mort en Direct* 1979 (a); *The Rose* 1979 (a); *Wise Blood* 1979 (a); *Private Benjamin* 1980 (a); *UFOria* 1980 (a); *Escape From New York* 1981 (a); *One From the Heart* 1982 (a); *Young Doctors in Love* 1982 (a); *Christine* 1983 (a); *The Bear* 1984 (a); *Paris, Texas* 1984 (a); *Red Dawn* 1984 (a); *Repo Man* 1984 (a); *The Care Bears Movie* 1985 (a); *Fool For Love* 1985 (a); *One Magic Christmas* 1985 (a); *Pretty in Pink* 1986 (a); *Slam Dance* 1987 (a); *The Last Temptation of Christ* 1988 (a); *Mr. North* 1988 (a); *Stars and Bars* 1988 (a); *The Bounty*

Hunter 1989 (song); *Dream a Little Dream* 1989 (a); *Twister* 1989 (a); *The Fourth War* 1990 (a); *Motion and Emotion* 1990 (a); *Wild at Heart* 1990 (a).

Stanwyck, Barbara • Actress • Born Ruby Stevens, Brooklyn, NY, July 16, 1907; died January 20, 1990, Santa Monica, CA. Enduring, thoroughly professional star who, despite her share of wicked or malignant characters, remained one of America's most-loved screen personalities.

Originally a stage and cabaret dancer, Stanwyck moved to Hollywood with her first husband, vaudevillian Frank Fay. She made impressive appearances in films such as Frank Capra's *The Miracle Woman* (1931), William Wellman's *Night Nurse* (1931) and, particularly, King Vidor's classic "woman's melodrama," *Stella Dallas* (1937), and was a full-fledged star by the end of the 1930s. Stanwyck hit her peak in the 1940s, alternating between comic roles, in classics such as *The Lady Eve* (1941) and *Ball of Fire* (1941), and tough femme fatale parts in *Double Indemnity* (1944) and *The Strange Love of Martha Ivers* (1946). Most of her characters were strong-willed and feisty, holding their own against, and even dominating, their male counterparts in films such as *Annie Oakley* (1935) and *Cattle Queen of Montana* (1954).

Though her big screen career had faltered by the late 1950s, she remained popular on TV, with shows such as "The Barbara Stanwyck Show" (1960-61) and "Big Valley" (1965-69), both of which won her Emmys. She was lured out of semi-retirement in 1983 to co-star in TV's *The Thorn Birds*, for which she won another Emmy, and "Dynasty II: The Colbys" (1985-86). Married to second husband Robert Taylor from 1939 to 1951. • *Broadway Nights* 1927 (a); *The Locked Door* 1929 (a); *Mexicali Rose* 1929 (a); *Ladies of Leisure* 1930 (a); *Illicit* 1931 (a); *The Miracle Woman* 1931 (a); *Night Nurse* 1931 (a); *Ten Cents a Dance* 1931 (a); *The Bitter Tea of General Yen* 1932 (a); *Forbidden* 1932 (a); *The Purchase Price* 1932 (a); *Shopworn* 1932 (a); *So Big* 1932 (a); *Baby Face* 1933 (a); *Ever in My Heart* 1933 (a); *Ladies They Talk About* 1933 (a); *Gambling Lady* 1934 (a); *A Lost Lady* 1934 (a); *Annie Oakley* 1935 (a); *Red Salute* 1935 (a); *The Secret Bride* 1935 (a); *The Woman in Red* 1935 (a); *Banjo on My Knee* 1936 (a); *The Bride Walks Out* 1936 (a); *His Brother's Wife* 1936 (a); *A Message to Garcia* 1936 (a); *The Plough and the Stars* 1936 (a); *Breakfast For Two* 1937 (a); *Internes Can't Take Money* 1937 (a); *Stella Dallas* 1937 (a) **(AANBA)**; *This Is My Affair* 1937 (a); *Always Goodbye* 1938 (a); *The Mad Miss Manton* 1938 (a); *Golden Boy* 1939 (a); *Union Pacific* 1939 (a); *Remember the Night* 1940 (a); *Ball of Fire* 1941 (a) **(AANBA)**; *The Lady Eve* 1941 (a); *Meet John Doe* 1941 (a); *You Belong to Me* 1941 (a); *The Gay Sisters* 1942 (a); *The Great Man's Lady* 1942 (a); *Flesh and Fantasy* 1943 (a); *Lady of Burlesque* 1943 (a); *Double Indemnity* 1944 (a) **(AANBA)**; *Hollywood Canteen* 1944 (a); *Christmas in Connecticut* 1945 (a); *The Two Mrs. Carrolls* 1945 (a); *The Bride Wore Boots* 1946 (a); *My Reputation* 1946 (a); *The Strange Love of Martha Ivers* 1946 (a); *B.F.'s Daughter* 1947 (a); *California* 1947 (a); *Cry Wolf* 1947 (a); *The Other Love* 1947 (a); *Variety Girl* 1947 (a); *Sorry, Wrong Number* 1948 (a) **(AANBA)**; *East Side, West Side* 1949 (a); *The File on Thelma Jordan* 1949 (a); *The Lady Gambles* 1949 (a); *The Furies* 1950 (a); *No Man of Her Own* 1950 (a); *To Please a Lady* 1950 (a); *The Man With a Cloak* 1951 (a); *Clash By Night* 1952 (a); *All I Desire* 1953 (a); *Blowing Wild* 1953 (a); *Jeopardy* 1953 (a); *The Moonlighter* 1953 (a); *Titanic* 1953 (a); *Cattle Queen of Montana* 1954 (a); *Escape to Burma* 1954 (a); *Executive Suite* 1954 (a); *The Violent Men* 1954 (a); *Witness to Murder* 1954 (a); *The Maverick Queen* 1956 (a); *There's Always Tomorrow* 1956 (a); *These Wilder Years* 1956 (a); *Crime of Passion* 1957 (a); *Forty Guns* 1957 (a); *Trooper Hook* 1957 (a); *Walk on the Wild Side* 1962 (a); *The Night Walker* 1964 (a); *Roustabout* 1964 (a); *Going Hollywood: The War Years* 1988 (archival footage).

Stapleton, Maureen • Actress • Born Troy, NY, June 21, 1925. *Educ.* Siena College; Herbert-Berghof Studio, New York; Actors Studio. Earthy character player who first attracted attention for her portrayal of the Tennessee Williams heroine in *The Rose Tattoo* on Broadway in the early 1950s. Stapleton made an acclaimed film debut in the 1959 adaptation of Nathaniel West's book, *Lonelyhearts*, and has since given effective, wide-ranging performances in films including *The Fugitive Kind* (1960), *Interiors* (1978) and *Reds* (1981) and the affecting TV movie, *Queen of the Stardust Ballroom* (1975). • *Lonelyhearts* 1959 **(AANBSA)**; *The Fugitive Kind* 1960; *A View From the Bridge* 1962; *Trilogy* 1969; *Airport* 1970 **(AANBSA)**; *Plaza Suite* 1971; *Interiors* 1978 **(AANBSA)**; *Arthur Miller on Home Ground* 1979; *Lost and Found* 1979; *The Runner Stumbles* 1979; *On the Right Track* 1980; *The Fan* 1981; *Reds* 1981 **(AABSA)**; *Montgomery Clift* 1982; *America and Lewis Hine* 1984; *Johnny Dangerously* 1984; *Cocoon* 1985; *The Cosmic Eye* 1985; *Heartburn* 1986; *The Money Pit* 1986; *Hello Actors Studio* 1987; *Made in Heaven* 1987; *Nuts* 1987; *Sweet Lorraine* 1987; *Cocoon: The Return* 1988; *Doin' Time on Planet Earth* 1988.

Stark, Ray • American producer • Born c. 1914. *Educ.* Rutgers University, NJ. One of the most influential Hollywood producers who has succeeded in combining serious, ambitious projects with commercial success. Former newsman, press agent, literary agent and high-powered talent agent, Stark co-founded the Seven Arts Production Company, specializing in made-for-TV-movies, with film executive Eliot Hyman in 1957.

He produced his first independent feature in 1960 and, with the formation of Rastar Productions in 1966, embarked on a highly successful career as an independent producer beginning with *Funny Girl*, the first of his many popular Barbra Streisand vehicles. Stark has also enjoyed multi-film collaborations with Neil Simon, Jackie Gleason, John Huston, Herbert Ross and Sydney Pollack. Married to Frances, the daughter of Fanny (*Funny Girl*) Brice. • *The World of Suzie Wong* 1960; *The Night of the Iguana* 1964; *Promise Her Anything* 1966; *Oh Dad, Poor Dad, Mamma's Hung You in the Closet and I'm Feelin' So Sad* 1967; *Reflections in a Golden Eye* 1967; *Funny Girl* 1968 **(AANBP)**; *The Owl and the Pussycat* 1970; *Fat City* 1972; *The Way We Were* 1973; *Funny Lady* 1975; *The Sunshine Boys* 1975; *Murder By Death* 1976; *The Goodbye Girl* 1977 **(AANBP)**; *California Suite* 1978; *Casey's Shadow* 1978; *The Cheap Detective* 1978; *Chapter Two* 1979; *The Electric Horseman* 1979; *Seems Like Old Times* 1980; *Annie* 1982; *The Slugger's Wife* 1985; *Brighton Beach Memoirs* 1986; *Biloxi Blues* 1988; *Steel Magnolias* 1989.

Steadman, Alison • Actress • Born Liverpool, England, August 26, 1946. *Educ.* East 15 Acting School. Blonde British character actress best known as Michael Gambon's wife in the British TV mini-series, "The Singing Detective" (1986, released theatrically in US in 1988) and as the heroine's fickle traveling companion in *Shirley Valentine* (1989). Married to director Mike Leigh. • *Kipperbang* 1982; *Champions* 1983; *Number One* 1984; *A Private Function* 1984; *Clockwise* 1986; *The Short and Curlies (short)* 1987; *The Adventures of Baron Munchausen* 1988; *The Singing Detective* 1988; *Stormy Monday* 1988; *Shirley Valentine* 1989; *Wilt* 1989; *Life Is Sweet* 1991.

Steenburgen, Mary • Actress • Born Newport, AR, 1953. *Educ.* Hendrix College, Conway; Neighborhood Playhouse, New York. Soft-spoken, appealing performer who won raves as Melvin's flustered but caring wife in Jonathan Demme's *Melvin and Howard* (1980). Steenburgen has twice played time-traveling heroines: in *Time After Time* (1979), opposite future husband Malcolm McDowell (they are now separated), and in *Back to the Future III* (1990). • *Goin' South* 1978 (a); *Time After Time* 1979 (a); *Melvin and Howard* 1980 (a) **(AABSA)**; *Ragtime* 1981 (a); *A Midsummer Night's Sex Comedy* 1982 (a); *Cross Creek* 1983 (a); *Romantic Comedy* 1983 (a); *One Magic Christmas* 1985 (a); *Dead* *of Winter* 1987 (a); *End of the Line* 1987 (a,exec.p); *The Whales of August* 1987 (a); *Miss Firecracker* 1989 (a); *Parenthood* 1989 (a); *Back to the Future III* 1990 (a); *The Long Walk Home* 1990 (a); *Clifford* 1991 (a).

Steiger, Rod • Actor • Born Rodney Stephen Steiger, Westhampton, NY, April 14, 1925. *Educ.* Dramatic Workshop of the New School for Social Research, New York; New York Theatre Wing; Actors Studio. Husky, volatile New York stage actor who turned in some memorable tough-guy performances in the 1950s, notably as Marlon Brando's brother in *On the Waterfront* (1954) and as the title character of *Al Capone* (1959). Steiger was outstanding as concentration camp survivor Sol Nazerman in Sidney Lumet's *The Pawnbroker* (1965) and as the redneck Southern sheriff in Norman Jewison's *In the Heat of the Night* (1967). Married to actress Claire Bloom from 1959 to 1969. • *Teresa* 1951; *On the Waterfront* 1954 **(AANBSA)**; *The Big Knife* 1955; *The Court Martial of Billy Mitchell* 1955; *Oklahoma!* 1955; *Back From Eternity* 1956; *The Harder They Fall* 1956; *Jubal* 1956; *Across the Bridge* 1957; *Run of the Arrow* 1957; *The Unholy Wife* 1957; *Cry Terror!* 1958; *Al Capone* 1959; *Seven Thieves* 1960; *The Mark* 1961; *13 West Street* 1962; *Convicts Four* 1962; *The Longest Day* 1962; *Le Mani sulla Citta* 1963; *Doctor Zhivago* 1965; *E Venne un uomo* 1965; *The Loved One* 1965; *The Pawnbroker* 1965 **(AANBA)**; *In the Heat of the Night* 1967 **(AABA)**; *La Ragazza e il Generale* 1967; *The Sergeant* 1968; *The Illustrated Man* 1969; *Three Into Two Won't Go* 1969; *Waterloo* 1970; *Happy Birthday, Wanda June* 1971; *Duck, You Sucker* 1972; *Gli Eroi* 1972; *Lolly-Madonna XXX* 1973; *Re: Lucky Luciano* 1973; *Mussolini: Ultimo Atto* 1974; *Hennessy* 1975; *Les Innocents aux mains Sales* 1975; *W.C. Fields and Me* 1976; *F.I.S.T.* 1978; *Wolf Lake* 1978; *The Amityville Horror* 1979; *Jack London's Klondike Fever* 1979; *Love and Bullets* 1979; *Steiner—Das Eiserne Kreuz 2, Teil* 1979; *Lion of the Desert* 1980; *The Lucky Star* 1980; *Cattle Annie and Little Britches* 1981; *The Chosen* 1981; *Der Zauberberg* 1982; *The Naked Face* 1985; *The Kindred* 1986; *American Gothic* 1987; *Feel the Heat* 1987; *Hello Actors Studio* 1987; *The January Man* 1988; *The Exiles* 1989; *Sauf votre respect* 1989; *Tennessee Nights* 1989; *That Summer of White Roses* 1989; *Men of Respect* 1990; *The Ballad of the Sad Cafe* 1991.

Steiner, Max • Composer; also lyricist, conductor. • Born Maximilian Raoul Steiner, Vienna, Austria, May 10, 1888; died 1971. *Educ.* Imperial Academy of Music, Vienna. Child prodigy and former student of Gustav Mahler who began working professionally as a conductor at the age of 16 and became Hollywood's most prolific film composer, allegedly scoring over 250 films. In the US from 1914, Steiner moved to Hollywood at the beginning of the sound era, working first as a musical director and then a composer. His richly orchestrated scores provided the appropriate emotional resonance for films such as *Gone With the Wind* (1939), *Now Voyager, Casablanca* (both 1942), *The Big Sleep* (1946) and *The Treasure of the Sierra Madre* (1948). Steiner worked on nearly 20 Bette Davis films and was with RKO and Warner Bros. for most of his career. • *The Animal Kingdom* 1932 (m.dir); *A Bill of Divorcement* 1932 (m.dir); *Is My Face Red?* 1932 (m.dir); *Little Orphan Annie* 1932 (m.dir); *The Sport Parade* 1932 (m.dir); *Symphony of Six Million* 1932 (m); *Westward Passage* 1932 (m.dir); *Ace of Aces* 1933 (m.dir); *After Tonight* 1933 (m.dir); *Aggie Appleby, Maker of Men* 1933 (m.dir); *Ann Vickers* 1933 (m.dir); *Bed of Roses* 1933 (m.dir,m); *Before Dawn* 1933 (m.dir); *Blind Adventure* 1933 (m.dir); *Chance at Heaven* 1933 (m.dir); *Christopher Strong* 1933 (m.dir); *Diplomaniacs* 1933 (m.dir); *Double Harness* 1933 (m.dir); *Flying Devils* 1933 (m.dir); *The Great Jasper* 1933 (m.dir); *Headline Shooter* 1933 (m.dir); *If I Were Free* 1933 (m.dir); *King Kong* 1933 (m.dir); *Lucky Devils* 1933 (m.dir); *Melody Cruise* 1933 (m.dir); *Midshipman Jack* 1933 (m.dir); *The Monkey's Paw* 1933 (m.dir); *Morning Glory* 1933 (m); *No Marriage Ties* 1933 (m.dir); *No Other Woman* 1933 (m.dir); *One Man's Journey* 1933 (m); *Our Betters* 1933 (m); *Professional Sweetheart* 1933 (m.dir); *Rafter Romance* 1933 (m.dir); *The Silver Cord* 1933 (m.dir); *Son of Kong* 1933 (m); *Sweepings* 1933 (m.dir); *Topaze* 1933 (m.dir); *The Age of Innocence* 1934 (m.dir); *Anne of Green Gables* 1934 (m.dir); *Bachelor Bait* 1934 (m.dir); *By Your Leave* 1934 (m.dir); *The Crime Doctor* 1934 (m.dir); *Dangerous Corner* 1934 (m.dir); *Down to Their Last Yacht* 1934 (m.dir); *Finishing School* 1934 (m.dir); *The Fountain* 1934 (m); *The Gay Divorcee* 1934 (m.dir) **(AANBM)**; *Gridiron Flash* 1934 (m.dir); *Hat, Coat, and Glove* 1934 (m.dir); *His Greatest Gamble* 1934 (m.dir); *Keep 'Em Rolling* 1934 (m.dir); *Let's Try Again* 1934 (m.dir); *The Life of Vergie Winters* 1934 (m); *The Little Minister* 1934 (m); *Long Lost Father* 1934 (m.dir); *The Lost Patrol* 1934 (m) **(AANBM)**; *Man of Two Worlds* 1934 (m.dir); *The Meanest Gal in Town* 1934 (m.dir); *Murder on the Blackboard* 1934 (m.dir); *Of Human Bondage* 1934 (m); *The Richest Girl in the World* 1934 (m.dir); *Sing and Like it* 1934 (m.dir); *Spitfire* 1934 (m.dir); *Stingaree* 1934 (m.dir); *Strictly Dynamite* 1934 (m.dir); *Success at Any Price* 1934 (m.dir); *Their Big Moment* 1934 (m); *This Man Is Mine* 1934 (m.dir); *Two Alone* 1934 (m.dir); *We're Rich Again* 1934 (m.dir); *Wednesday's Child* 1934 (m.dir); *Where Sinners Meet* 1934 (m.dir); *Alice Adams* 1935 (m,song); *Becky Sharp* 1935 (m.dir); *Break of Hearts* 1935 (m.dir); *I Dream Too Much* 1935 (m.dir); *The Informer* 1935 (ph) **(AABM)**; *Roberta* 1935 (m.dir); *She* 1935 (m); *Star of Midnight* 1935 (m.dir); *The Three Musketeers* 1935 (m); *Top Hat* 1935 (m.dir); *The Charge of the Light Brigade* 1936 (m) **(AANBM)**; *Follow the Fleet* 1936 (m.dir); *The Garden of Allah* 1936 (m) **(AANBM)**; *God's Country and the Woman* 1936 (m); *Little Lord Fauntleroy* 1936 (m); *Green Light* 1937 (m); *The Life of Emile Zola* 1937 (m) **(AANBM)**; *Lost Horizon* 1937 (m.dir); *A Star Is Born* 1937 (m); *Submarine D-1* 1937 (m); *That Certain Woman* 1937 (m); *Tovarich* 1937 (m); *Angels With Dirty Faces* 1938 (m); *Crime School* 1938 (m); *The Dawn Patrol* 1938 (m); *Four Daughters* 1938 (m); *Gold Is Where You Find It* 1938 (m); *Jezebel* 1938 (m); *The Sisters* 1938 (m); *Valley of the Giants* 1938 (m); *White Banners* 1938 (m); *Dark Victory* 1939 (m) **(AANBM)**; *Daughters Courageous* 1939 (m); *Dodge City* 1939 (m); *Four Wives* 1939 (m); *Gone With the Wind* 1939 (m) **(AANBM)**; *The Old Maid* 1939 (m); *They Made Me a Criminal* 1939 (m); *We Are Not Alone* 1939 (m); *All This, and Heaven Too* 1940 (m); *City For Conquest* 1940 (m); *A Dispatch From Reuters* 1940 (m); *Dr. Ehrlich's Magic Bullet* 1940 (m); *The Letter* 1940 (m) **(AANBM)**; *The Santa Fe Trail* 1940 (m); *Tugboat Annie Sails Again* 1940 (m); *Virginia City* 1940 (m); *The Bride Came C.O.D.* 1941 (m); *The Great Lie* 1941 (m); *Sergeant York* 1941 (m) **(AANBM)**; *Shining Victory* 1941 (m); *They Died With Their Boots On* 1941 (m); *Casablanca* 1942 (m) **(AANBM)**; *Desperate Journey* 1942 (m); *The Gay Sisters* 1942 (m); *In This Our Life* 1942 (m); *Now, Voyager* 1942 (m) **(AABM)**; *Mission to Moscow* 1943 (m); *Watch on the Rhine* 1943 (m); *The Adventures of Mark Twain* 1944 (m) **(AANBM)**; *Arsenic and Old Lace* 1944 (m); *The Conspirators* 1944 (m); *Passage to Marseille* 1944 (m); *Since You Went Away* 1944 (m) **(AABM)**; *The Corn Is Green* 1945 (m); *Mildred Pierce* 1945 (m); *Rhapsody In Blue* 1945 (m) **(AANBM)**; *Roughly Speaking* 1945 (m); *San Antonio* 1945 (m); *Saratoga Trunk* 1945 (m); *The Beast With Five Fingers* 1946 (m); *The Big Sleep* 1946 (m); *Cloak and Dagger* 1946 (m); *My Reputation* 1946 (m); *Night and Day* 1946 (m) **(AANBM)**; *One More Tomorrow* 1946 (m); *A Stolen Life* 1946 (m); *Tomorrow Is Forever* 1946 (m); *Cheyenne* 1947 (m); *Deep Valley* 1947 (m); *Life With Father* 1947 (m) **(AANBM)**; *My Wild Irish Rose* 1947 (m) **(AANBM)**; *Pursued* 1947 (m); *The Unfaithful* 1947 (m); *The Voice of the Turtle* 1947 (m); *Adventures of Don Juan* 1948 (m); *The Decision of Christopher Blake* 1948 (m); *Fighter Squadron* 1948 (m); *Johnny Belinda* 1948 (m); *Key Largo* 1948 (m); *My Girl Tisa* 1948 (m); *Silver River* 1948 (m); *The Treasure* *of the Sierra Madre* 1948 (m); *Winter Meeting* 1948 (m); *The Woman in White* 1948 (m); *Beyond the Forest* 1949 (m) **(AANBM)**; *Flamingo Road* 1949 (m); *The Fountainhead* 1949 (m); *A Kiss in the Dark* 1949 (m); *The Lady Takes a Sailor* 1949 (m); *South of St. Louis* 1949 (m); *White Heat* 1949 (m); *Without Honor* 1949 (m); *Caged* 1950 (m); *Dallas* 1950 (m); *The Flame and the Arrow* 1950 (m) **(AANBM)**; *The Glass Menagerie* 1950 (m); *Rocky Mountain* 1950 (m); *Close to My Heart* 1951 (m); *Distant Drums* 1951 (m); *Force of Arms* 1951 (m); *Jim Thorpe—All American* 1951 (m); *On Moonlight Bay* 1951 (m); *Operation Pacific* 1951 (m); *Raton Pass* 1951 (m); *Sugarfoot* 1951 (m); *The Jazz Singer* 1952 (m) **(AANBM)**; *The Iron Mistress* 1952 (m); *Mara Maru* 1952 (m); *The Miracle of Our Lady of Fatima* 1952 (m) **(AANBM)**; *Room For One More* 1952 (m); *Springfield Rifle* 1952 (m); *By the Light of the Silvery Moon* 1953 (m.adapt); *The Charge at Feather River* 1953 (m); *The Desert Song* 1953 (m.adapt); *So Big* 1953 (m); *So This Is Love* 1953 (m.adapt); *Trouble Along the Way* 1953 (m); *Battle Cry* 1954 (m) **(AANBM)**; *The Boy From Oklahoma* 1954 (m); *The Caine Mutiny* 1954 (m) **(AANBM)**; *King Richard and the Crusaders* 1954 (m); *The Violent Men* 1954 (m); *Come Next Spring* 1955 (m,song); *Hell on Frisco Bay* 1955 (m); *Illegal* 1955 (m,m.dir); *The Last Command* 1955 (m,song); *The McConnell Story* 1955 (m); *Bandido* 1956 (m,m.dir); *Death of a Scoundrel* 1956 (m); *Helen of Troy* 1956 (m); *The Searchers* 1956 (m); *All Mine to Give* 1957 (m); *Band of Angels* 1957 (m); *Escapade in Japan* 1957 (m); *Darby's Rangers* 1958 (m); *Fort Dobbs* 1958 (m); *Marjorie Morningstar* 1958 (m); *Cash McCall* 1959 (m); *The F.B.I. Story* 1959 (m); *The Hanging Tree* 1959 (m); *John Paul Jones* 1959 (m); *A Summer Place* 1959 (m); *The Dark at the Top of the Stairs* 1960 (m); *Ice Palace* 1960 (m); *A Majority of One* 1961 (m); *Parrish* 1961 (m); *Portrait of a Mobster* 1961 (m); *The Sins of Rachel Cade* 1961 (m); *Susan Slade* 1961 (m); *Rome Adventure* 1962 (m); *Spencer's Mountain* 1963 (m); *A Distant Trumpet* 1964 (m); *FBI Code 98* 1964 (m); *Those Calloways* 1964 (m); *Youngblood Hawke* 1964 (m); *Two on a Guillotine* 1965 (m); *Friday on My Mind* 1970 (m); *Play It Again, Sam* 1972 (m); *Angel Number 9* 1974 (m); *Real Life* 1978 (song); *Running Brave* 1983 (song); *The Flamingo Kid* 1984 (song); *Mr. Love* 1985 (m); *My American Cousin* 1986 (song); *Orphans* 1987 (song); *Batman* 1989 (m); *Great Balls of Fire* 1989 (song); *UHF* 1989 (m); *When Harry Met Sally...* 1989 (m).

Steinkamp, Fredric • *aka* Frederic Steinkamp • American editor • Entered film as an apprentice film editor at MGM in 1951, cut his first film, *The Adventures of Huckleberry Finn*, in 1960 and began a productive collaboration with Sydney Pollack in 1969 with *They Shoot Horses, Don't They*? Steinkamp began co-editing with his son, William Robert Steinkamp, in the 1980s, and the pair have gained recognition for their work on films such as Pollack's *Tootsie* (1982), *Out of Africa* (1985) and *Havana* (1990). • *The Adventures of Huckleberry Finn* 1960; *Two Loves* 1961; *All Fall Down* 1962; *Period of Adjustment* 1962; *It Happened at the World's Fair* 1963; *Quick, Before It Melts* 1964; *The Unsinkable Molly Brown* 1964; *Mister Buddwing* 1965; *Once a Thief* 1965; *Grand Prix* 1966 **(AABED)**; *Duel at Diablo* 1966; *Charly* 1968; *The Extraordinary Seaman* 1969; *A Run on Gold* 1969; *They Shoot Horses, Don't They?* 1969 **(AANBED)**; *The Strawberry Statement* 1970; *The Marriage of a Young Stockbroker* 1971; *A New Leaf* 1971; *Nightmare Honeymoon* 1972; *Freebie and the Bean* 1974; *Three Days of the Condor* 1975 **(AANBED)**; *The Yakuza* 1975; *Harry and Walter Go to New York* 1976; *Bobby Deerfield* 1977; *Hide in Plain Sight* 1980; *Tootsie* 1982 **(AANBED)**; *Against All Odds* 1983; *Out of Africa* 1985 **(AANBED)**; *White Nights* 1985; *Adventures in Babysitting* 1987; *Burglar* 1987; *Scrooged* 1988; *Havana* 1990.

Stern, Daniel • Actor • Born Bethesda, MD, August 28, 1957. *Educ.* H.B. Studios. Lanky, affable second lead, memorable as "one of the guys" in both *Breaking Away* (1979) and *Diner* (1982). Stern has appeared in two Woody Allen movies and supplies the reminiscing voice-over narration for the hit TV series, "The Wonder Years" (1988-), episodes of which he has also directed. • *Breaking Away* 1979; *Starting Over* 1979; *It's My Turn* 1980; *One-Trick Pony* 1980; *A Small Circle of Friends* 1980; *Stardust Memories* 1980; *Honky Tonk Freeway* 1981; *I'm Dancing As Fast As I Can* 1981; *Diner* 1982; *Blue Thunder* 1983; *Get Crazy* 1983; *C.H.U.D.* 1984; *Key Exchange* 1985; *The Boss' Wife* 1986; *Hannah and Her Sisters* 1986; *Born in East L.A.* 1987; *D.O.A.* 1988; *The Milagro Beanfield War* 1988; *Friends, Lovers & Lunatics* 1989; *Leviathan* 1989; *Little Monsters* 1989; *Coupe De Ville* 1990; *Home Alone* 1990; *My Blue Heaven* 1990; *City Slickers* 1991.

Sternhagen, Frances • Actress • Born Washington, DC, January 13, 1930. *Educ.* Vassar College, Poughkeepsie, NY; Perry-Mansfield School of Theater; Neighborhood Playhouse. Respected stage lead (*Equus*, *On Golden Pond*) who made her film debut in *Up the Down Staircase* (1967) and has since played a wide range of supporting roles. On screen, Sternhagen has convincingly portrayed prim, slightly disapproving characters as well as warmly maternal women. • *The Tiger Makes Out* 1967; *Up the Down Staircase* 1967; *Two People* 1973; *Fedora* 1978; *Starting Over* 1979; *Outland* 1981; *Independence Day* 1982; *Romantic Comedy* 1983; *Bright Lights, Big City* 1988; *Communion, A True Story* 1989; *See You in the Morning* 1989; *Misery* 1990; *Sibling Rivalry* 1990.

Stevens, George • Director; also producer, actor. • Born Oakland, CA, December 18, 1904; died March 8, 1975, Paris. Leading Hollywood craftsman, responsible for some fine films of the 1930s and 40s, but whose later output tended toward the over-ambitious and excessive. The son of performers, Stevens entered films at age 17 as a cameraman and later worked for the Hal Roach company, where he directed his first shorts. He joined RKO in 1934 and proceeded to churn out a series of crafty comedies and light musicals, scoring his first major success with *Alice Adams* (1935), which was followed by the Astaire-Rogers classic *Swing Time* (1936), the action-packed *Gunga Din* (1939) and the brilliantly realized debut pairing of Katharine Hepburn and Spencer Tracy, *Woman of the Year* (1942).

After heading the Army Signal Corps Special Motion Picture Unit during WWII, Stevens re-entered civilian life in 1945 and hit his peak with *I Remember Mama* (1948) and *A Place in the Sun* (1951). His subsequent work, including *Shane* (1953) and *Giant* (1956), strove for epic status but came off as overblown and excessive. Stevens's final effort, *The Only Game in Town* (1970), was a refreshing, if flawed, return to his earlier, more modest, style.

Son George Stevens, Jr., is a producer who made a well-received documentary on his father, *George Stevens, Filmmaker* (1984), served as chief of the United States Information Service's motion picture division from 1962 to 1967 and was named the first head of the American Film Institute in 1977. • *A Million Bid* 1914 (a); *My Lady's Slipper* 1916 (a); *Love Without Question* 1920 (a); *The New York Idea* 1920 (uncred.a); *Oh, Mary Be Careful* 1921 (a); *Trail of the Law* 1921 (a); *The Battling Orioles* 1924 (ph); *The White Sheep* 1924 (ph); *Black Cyclone* 1925 (ph); *The Desert's Toll* 1926 (ph); *The Devil Horse* 1926 (ph); *The Girl From Gay Paree* 1927 (ph); *Lightning* 1927 (ph); *No Man's Law* 1927 (ph); *The Valley of Hell* 1927 (ph); *The Cohens and Kellys in Trouble* 1933 (d); *Bachelor Bait* 1934 (d); *Hollywood Party* 1934 (d); *Kentucky Kernels* 1934 (d); *Alice Adams* 1935 (d); *Annie Oakley* 1935 (d); *Laddie* 1935 (d); *The Nitwits* 1935 (d); *Swing Time* 1936 (d); *A Damsel in Distress* 1937 (d); *Quality Street* 1937 (d); *Vivacious Lady* 1938 (d,p); *Gunga Din* 1939 (d,p); *Vigil in the Night* 1940 (d,p); *Penny Serenade* 1941 (d,p); *Talk of the Town* 1942 (d,p); *Woman of the Year* 1942 (d); *The More the Merrier* 1943 (d,p) **(AANBD)**; *I Remember Mama* 1948 (d); *A Place in the

Sun 1951 (d,p) **(AANBP,AABD)**; *Something to Live For* 1952 (d,p); *Shane* 1953 (d,p) **(AANBD,AANBP)**; *Giant* 1956 (d,p) **(AANBP,AABD)**; *The Diary of Anne Frank* 1959 (d,p) **(AANBD,AANBP)**; *The Greatest Story Ever Told* 1965 (d,p,sc); *The Only Game in Town* 1970 (d).

Stevens, Stella • Actress • Born Estelle Egglestone, Yazoo City, MS, October 1, 1936. *Educ.* Memphis State University. Beautiful, talented performer who unfortunately—perhaps because she was a former *Playboy* centerfold—was typecast in undemanding, sexpot roles through the 1960s. Although Stevens first gained attention as the vamp, Appassionata von Climax, in the film *Li'l Abner* (1959), it wasn't until John Cassavetes's *Too Late Blues* (1961) and Sam Peckinpah's lyrical *The Ballad of Cable Hogue* (1970) that she was able to showcase her dramatic and comedic gifts. She later produced and directed a feature-length documentary, *The American Heroine* (1979), and has appeared on numerous TV shows. She directed her first feature, *The Ranch*, starring her son Andrew Stevens, in 1989. • *Li'l Abner* 1959 (a); *Say One For Me* 1959 (a); *Man-Trap* 1961 (a); *Too Late Blues* 1961 (a); *Girls! Girls! Girls!* 1962 (a); *Advance to the Rear* 1963 (a); *The Courtship of Eddie's Father* 1963 (a); *The Nutty Professor* 1963 (a); *The Secret of My Success* 1965 (a); *Synanon* 1965 (a); *Rage* 1966 (a); *The Silencers* 1966 (a); *How to Save a Marriage and Ruin Your Life* 1968 (a); *The Last Shot You Hear* 1968 (songs); *Sol Madrid* 1968 (a); *Where Angels Go... Trouble Follows* 1968 (a); *The Mad Room* 1969 (a); *The Ballad of Cable Hogue* 1970 (a,song); *A Town Called Hell* 1971 (a); *The Poseidon Adventure* 1972 (a); *Slaughter* 1972 (a); *Stand Up and Be Counted* 1972 (a); *Arnold* 1973 (a); *Cleopatra Jones and the Casino of Gold* 1975 (a); *Las Vegas Lady* 1975 (a); *Nickelodeon* 1976 (a); *The Manitou* 1977 (a); *The American Heroine* 1979 (d); *Chained Heat* 1983 (a); *Monster in the Closet* 1983 (a); *Wacko* 1983 (a); *The Longshot* 1986 (a); *Adventures Beyond Belief* 1988 (a); *The Ranch* 1989 (d); *Down the Drain* 1990 (a); *The Terror Within II: The Fight For Mojave Lab* 1991 (a).

Stevenson, Robert • Director; also screenwriter. • Born Buxton, Derbyshire, England, 1905; died 1986. *Educ.* St. John's College, Cambridge. Veteran director who moved to Hollywood in 1939 on the strength of his success with British films like *King Solomon's Mines* (1937). Stevenson was responsible for such accomplished, atmospheric delights as *Jane Eyre* (1944) and *To the Ends of the Earth* (1948) but, after directing a spate of unsuccessful films for Howard Hughes at RKO in the late 1940s and early 50s, he worked in TV from 1952 to 1956.

Stevenson then joined Walt Disney, where he pioneered the studio's live-action attempts and became one of the most commercially successful directors of the 1950s and 60s, thanks to projects such as *Mary Poppins* (1964). Married (1934-44) to actress Anna Lee (nee Joan Boniface Winnifrith), who appeared in a number of his films in both England and the US. • *Falling For You* 1933 (d); *The Battle* 1934 (sc); *White Heat* 1934 (a); *Jack of All Trades* 1936 (d); *The Man Who Lived Again* 1936 (d); *Tudor Rose* 1936 (d,story,adapt); *King Solomon's Mines* 1937 (d); *Non-Stop New York* 1937 (d); *Owd Bob* 1938 (d); *The Ware Case* 1938 (d,sc); *Young Man's Fancy* 1939 (d,story); *Return to Yesterday* 1940 (d,sc); *Tom Brown's School Days* 1940 (d); *Back Street* 1941 (d); *Joan of Paris* 1942 (d); *Valley of Hunted Men* 1942 (a); *Forever and a Day* 1943 (d,p); *Jane Eyre* 1944 (d,sc); *The American Creed (short)* 1946 (d); *Dishonored Lady* 1947 (d); *Bonnie Prince Charlie* 1948 (d); *To the Ends of the Earth* 1948 (d); *I Married a Communist* 1949 (d); *I Was a Male War Bride* 1949 (a); *Walk Softly, Stranger* 1950 (d); *All That I Have* 1951 (a); *My Forbidden Past* 1951 (d); *The Las Vegas Story* 1952 (d); *Fangs of the Wild* 1954 (a); *Johnny Tremain* 1957 (d); *Zero Hour!* 1957 (a); *Gun Fever* 1958 (a); *Old Yeller* 1958 (d); *Darby O'Gill and the Little People* 1959 (d); *The Absent-Minded Professor* 1960 (d); *Kidnapped* 1960 (d,sc); *Boy Who Caught a Crook* 1961 (a); *In Search of the Castaways* 1962 (d); *Son of Flubber* 1963 (d); *Mary Poppins* 1964 (d) **(AANBD)**; *The Misadventures of Merlin Jones* 1964 (d); *The Monkey's Uncle* 1965 (d); *That Darn Cat* 1965 (d); *The Gnome-Mobile* 1967 (d); *Blackbeard's Ghost* 1968 (d); *The Love Bug* 1968 (d); *My Dog, the Thief* 1969 (d); *Bedknobs and Broomsticks* 1971 (d); *Herbie Rides Again* 1974 (d); *The Island at the Top of the World* 1974 (d); *One of Our Dinosaurs Is Missing* 1975 (d); *The Shaggy D.A.* 1976 (d).

Stewart, Donald Ogden • Screenwriter; also playwright, novelist. • Born Columbus, OH, November 30, 1894; died 1980. *Educ.* Yale (English). Novelist, playwright and stage actor who adapted the play *Brown of Harvard* to the screen in 1926. Stewart arrived in Hollywood in 1930 and began turning out scripts noted for their polish and satirical wit, particularly the sophisticated costume drama, *The Prisoner of Zenda* (1937), and the swank romantic comedy, *The Philadelphia Story* (1940). He joined the Hollywood Anti-Nazi league and wrote the anti-fascist script for *Keeper of the Flame* (1947) which led to his being blacklisted in the early 1950s. The following year Stewart moved to England, where he wrote scripts and, in 1970, an autobiography. • *Brown of Harvard* 1926 (adapt); *Laughter* 1930 (sc) **(AANBST)**; *Not So Dumb* 1930 (a); *Finn and Hattie* 1931 (from story "Mr. and Mrs. Haddock Abroad"); *Rebound* 1931 (from play); *Tarnished Lady* 1931 (sc,story); *Another Language* 1933 (sc); *Going Hollywood* 1933 (sc); *The White Sister* 1933 (sc); *The Barretts of Wimpole Street* 1934 (sc); *No More Ladies* 1935 (sc); *The Prisoner of Zenda* 1937 (sc); *Holiday* 1938 (sc); *Marie Antoinette* 1938 (sc); *Love Affair* 1939 (sc); *The Night of Nights* 1939 (sc); *The Philadelphia Story* 1940 (sc) **(AABSC)**; *Smilin' Through* 1941 (sc); *That Uncertain Feeling* 1941 (sc); *A Woman's Face* 1941 (sc); *Keeper of the Flame* 1942 (sc); *Tales of Manhattan* 1942 (sc,story); *Forever and a Day* 1943 (sc); *Without Love* 1945 (sc); *Cass Timberlane* 1947 (sc,adapt); *Keeper of the Flame* 1947 (sc); *Life With Father* 1947 (sc); *Edward, My Son* 1948 (sc); *Escapade* 1955 (sc); *Moment of Danger/Malaga* 1960 (sc).

Stewart, James • Actor; also author. • Born Indiana, PA, May 20, 1908. *Educ.* Princeton (architecture). James Stewart is arguably the most loved actor ever to have appeared on screen. Certainly, he is the last of the great men who captured audience hearts in the throes of the Depression and became, in the words of Andrew Sarris, "the most complete actor-personality in the American cinema."

Stewart's origins read like cliches; he was born in 1908 in Indiana, Pennsylvania, the son of the local hardware store owner (his Oscar has permanently resided in the store, which has been in the family for generations). While studying architecture at Princeton (his father's alma mater), he met Joshua Logan, who convinced him to begin acting. Billy O'Grady, MGM's chief talent scout, saw his performance in a line of female impersonators and remembered him as "the only one who didn't ham it up." Bitten at last by the drama bug, Stewart moved with Logan to summer stock work with the University Players in Falmouth, MA, joining Henry Fonda and Margaret Sullavan.

That summer a production had a pre-Broadway tryout at Falmouth and Stewart, as a chaffeur, had two lines: "Mrs. Mainwaring's car is waiting" and, after being delayed, "Mrs. Mainwaring's going to be sore as hell." It tore down the house and was noticed and written up by a visiting New York critic. Stewart and Fonda moved to New York, where Hedda Hopper recommended Jimmy for a screen test, resulting in a long-term MGM contract.

From the first, Stewart's performances stood out: raw, edgy, full of nervous energy. While his rivals played with masculine understatement, Stewart mirrored the vital excesses of those most American of rising actresses—Crawford, Davis, Hepburn.

Audiences first took note of him as Eleanor Powell's leading man in 1936's *Born to Dance* (everyone at Metro at least had to *try* musicals; Stewart, singing—sort of—introduced Cole Porter's "Easy to Love". He was hopeless, but the public found him adorable).

Most of Stewart's big breaks came away from MGM: Steven's *Vivacious Lady*, at RKO, and Capra's *You Can't Take it With You*, at Columbia (both 1938); David O. Selznick's *Made For Each Other* (1939), opposite Carole Lombard; *Mr. Smith Goes to Washington*, with Jean Arthur, at Columbia; and *Destry Rides Again*, taming Dietrich and the west at Universal (both 1939). MGM rallied with two winners, both costarring Sullavan: Lubitsch's *The Shop Around the Corner* and Borzage's haunting *The Mortal Storm* (both 1940). Cukor's *The Philadelphia Story* followed. Stewart surprised the industry and himself, winning a best actor Oscar, despite being second lead to Cary Grant.

At age 33, he enlisted as private and rose to colonel in the Air Force, leading one thousand plane strikes against Germany; Stewart won the Air Medal and the Distinguished Flying Cross.

After the war, Stewart contributed what is undoubtedly his best-known performance, in Capra's *It's a Wonderful Life* (1946). He would later deliver a speech before Congress protesting the film's colorization.

Postwar audiences no longer wanted sentiment. Stewart vigorously changed his image, turning hard-bitten for *Call Northside 777* and working for Hitchcock in *Rope* (both 1948). He returned to Broadway to replace Frank Fay in the whimsical *Harvey* and, before filming the 1950 movie version, made the first two westerns of his career, both of which were hugely popular. Stewart also turned in a heart-tugging performance as a clown in Demille's *The Greatest Show on Earth* (1951).

In 1952, Stewart's agent Leland Hayward successfully negotiated an agreement with Universal for Stewart to work on a percentage basis—a first for the sound era. Every star in the business stampeded to do the same, something which Stewart felt signified the last hurrah for the studio system. He still looks back on his "factory years" with clear nostalgia and gratitude.

The next phase of Stewart's career saw some of his most complex roles, for directors such as Hitchcock, Preminger (1959's *Anatomy of a Murder* earned him a best actor award from the New York Critics—his second—and the Venice Film Festival), Ford, Aldrich and Anthony Mann. His famous gawky, stammering mannerisms took on an extra interest for being filtered through toughness, cynicism and world-weariness. Though there have been occasional flops, he has undoubtedly proved his ability to transcend bad material.

Stewart married his wife Gloria in 1949 and had four children. In 1970, he revived *Harvey* on Broadway with Helen Hayes and has done occasional TV work, notably "The Jimmy Stewart Show" (1971-72) and 1983's powerful TV-movie *Right of Way*, with Bette Davis. In 1990 he was honored by the Film Society of Lincoln Center for lifetime achievement. RW • *Art Trouble* 1934 (a); *The Murder Man* 1935 (a); *After the Thin Man* 1936 (a); *Born to Dance* 1936 (a); *The Gorgeous Hussy* 1936 (a); *Next Time We Love* 1936 (a); *Rose Marie* 1936 (a); *Small Town Girl* 1936 (a); *Speed* 1936 (a); *Wife vs. Secretary* 1936 (a); *The Last Gangster* 1937 (a); *Navy, Blue and Gold* 1937 (a); *Seventh Heaven* 1937 (a); *Of Human Hearts* 1938 (a); *The Shopworn Angel* 1938 (a); *Vivacious Lady* 1938 (a); *You Can't Take It With You* 1938 (a); *Destry Rides Again* 1939 (a); *Ice Follies* 1939 (a); *It's a Wonderful World* 1939 (a); *Made For Each Other* 1939 (a); *Mr. Smith Goes to Washington* 1939 (a) **(AANBA)**; *The Mortal Storm* 1940 (a); *No Time For Comedy* 1940 (a); *The Philadelphia Story* 1940 (a) **(AABA)**; *The Shop Around the Corner* 1940 (a); *Come Live With Me* 1941 (a); *Pot o' Gold* 1941 (a); *Ziegfeld Girl* 1941 (a); *It's a Wonderful Life* 1946 (a) **(AANBA)**; *Magic Town* 1947 (a); *Call Northside 777* 1948 (a); *A Miracle Can Happen* 1948 (a); *Rope* 1948 (a); *You Gotta Stay Happy* 1948 (a); *Malaya* 1949 (a); *The Stratton Story* 1949 (a); *Broken Arrow* 1950 (a); *Harvey* 1950 (a) **(AANBA)**; *The Jackpot* 1950 (a); *Winchester '73* 1950 (a); *Bend of the River* 1952 (a); *Carbine Williams* 1952 (a); *The Greatest Show on Earth* 1952 (a); *The Naked Spur* 1953 (a); *Thunder Bay* 1953 (a); *The Glenn Miller Story* 1954 (a); *Rear Window* 1954 (a); *The Far Country* 1955 (a); *The Man From Laramie* 1955 (a); *Strategic Air Command* 1955 (a); *The Man Who Knew Too Much* 1956 (a); *Night Passage* 1957 (a); *The Spirit of St. Louis* 1957 (a); *Bell, Book and Candle* 1958 (a); *Vertigo* 1958 (a); *Anatomy of a Murder* 1959 (a) **(AANBA)**; *The F.B.I. Story* 1959 (a); *The Mountain Road* 1960 (a); *Two Rode Together* 1961 (a); *How the West Was Won* 1962 (a); *The Man Who Shot Liberty Valance* 1962 (a); *Mr. Hobbs Takes a Vacation* 1962 (a); *Take Her, She's Mine* 1963 (a); *Cheyenne Autumn* 1964 (a); *Dear Brigitte* 1965 (a); *The Flight of the Phoenix* 1965 (a); *Shenandoah* 1965 (a); *The Rare Breed* 1966 (a); *Bandolero!* 1968 (a); *Firecreek* 1968 (a); *The Cheyenne Social Club* 1970 (a); *Directed By John Ford* 1971 (a); *Fools' Parade* 1971 (a); *That's Entertainment!* 1974 (a); *The Shootist* 1976 (a); *Airport 77* 1977 (a); *The Big Sleep* 1978 (a); *The Magic of Lassie* 1978 (a); *Going Hollywood: The War Years* 1988 (archival footage).

Stiller, Mauritz • *aka* Mosche Katzman, Mowscha Stiller • Director; also screenwriter. • Born Mosche Stiller, Helsinki, Finland, July 17, 1883; died November 8, 1928, Stockholm, Sweden. One of the two dominant figures of the "golden age" of Swedish silent cinema (the other being Victor Sjöstrom), whose reputation as a director has been somewhat overshadowed by his fame as mentor and "discoverer" of Greta Garbo.

Of Russian-Jewish parentage, Stiller moved from Finland to Sweden at the age of 20 (fleeing service in the Russian Army) and with little acting talent and good looks became a leading stage actor and later director. Charles Magnusson hired both Stiller and Sjöstrom in 1912 to work at Svensk Biograf (later Svensk Filmindustri) and together they produced some of the most exquisite and sophisticated works of the silent era, propelling the Swedish cinema into the European vanguard.

Stiller possessed an exquisite visual sensibility, combining naturalism and lyricism to great effect. Though a versatile talent, he is best known for his astute social comedies, from *Love and Journalism* (1916) to the internationally successful *Erotikon* (1920), both starring Karin Molander. Stiller also made a number of fine literary adaptations, including three from the novels of Selma Lagerlöf: *Sir Arne's Treasure* (1919), *Gunnar Hede's Saga* (1922) and *The Atonement of Gösta Berling* (1924). The latter film introduced the world to Garbo and earned Stiller an invitation to Hollywood from Louis B. Mayer—which the director accepted on the condition that his protégé accompany him.

Garbo was immediately groomed for stardom while Stiller experienced constant conflicts with the constraints of the American studio system. The first Garbo vehicle he directed, *The Temptress* (1926), was taken out of his hands, and despite the relative success of *Hotel Imperial* and *The Woman on Trial*, two 1927 films starring Pola Negri, his Hollywood sojourn was an overall disappointment. He was credited as director for *The Street of Sin* (1928), but the film was actually completed by scenarist Josef von Sternberg. Suffering from acute rheumatism, Stiller returned to Sweden, where he died at age 45. • *The Black Masks* 1912 (d,sc); *Mother and Daughter* 1912 (d,sc,a); *The Tyrannical Fiancée* 1912 (d,sc,a); *The Child* 1913 (d); *The Modern Suffragette* 1913 (d,sc); *On the Fateful Roads of Life* 1913 (d,sc); *The Unknown Woman* 1913 (d,sc); *The Vampire* 1913 (d,sc); *When the Alarm Bell Rings* 1913 (d); *When Love Kills* 1913 (d,sc,from story); *Because of Her Love* 1914 (d,sc); *Brothers* 1914 (d,from story,sc); *The Chamberlain* 1914 (d,sc); *People of the Border* 1914 (d); *The Red Tower* 1914 (d,sc); *The Shot* 1914 (d); *Stormy Petrel* 1914 (d); *When the Mother-in-Law Reigns* 1914 (d,sc,a); *Ace of Thieves* 1915 (d); *The Dagger* 1915 (d); *His Wife's Past* 1915 (d); *Madame de Thebes* 1915 (d); *Playmates* 1915 (d,sc); *When Artists Love* 1915 (d); *The Avenger* 1916 (d); *The Ballet Primadonna* 1916 (d); *The Fight For His Heart* 1916 (d,sc); *His Wedding Night* 1916 (d); *Love and Journalism* 1916 (d); *The Lucky Brooch* 1916 (d); *The Mine Pilot* 1916 (d); *The Wings* 1916 (d,sc); *Alexander the Great* 1917 (d,sc); *Thomas Graals Bästa Film/Thomas Graal's Best Film* 1917 (d); *Thomas Graal's First Child* 1918 (d,sc); *Herr Arnes pengar/Sir Arne's Treasure* 1919 (d,sc); *Song of the Scarlet Flower* 1919 (d); *Erotikon* 1920 (d,sc); *The Fishing Village* 1920 (d); *The Exiles* 1921 (d,sc); *Johan* 1921 (d,sc); *Gunnar Hede's Saga* 1922 (d,sc); *Gösta Berlings Saga/The Atonement of Gösta Berling* 1924 (d); *The Temptress* 1926 (d); *Hotel Imperial* 1927 (d); *The Woman on Trial* 1927 (d); *The Street of Sin* 1928 (d).

Sting • Musician, actor • Born Gordon Matthew Sumner, Newcastle-upon-Tyne, England, October 2, 1951. *Educ.* Warwick University. Multi-talented peformer who came to prominence as the singer, bass player and songwriter of *The Police*, one of the more influential New Wave bands of the late 1970s and mid-80s. Sting scored with his first film role in *Quadrophenia* (1979), based on The Who's rock album, and established himself as a forceful screen presence in such features as David Lynch's *Dune* (1985), Fred Schepisi's *Plenty* (1985) and Mike Figgis's *Stormy Monday* (1988). • *Quadrophenia* 1979 (a); *Radio On* 1979 (a,song); *Riding High* 1980 (song); *Remembrance* 1981 (song); *The Secret Policeman's Other Ball* 1981 (a,guitarist,song); *Urgh! A Music War* 1981 (song); *48 Hrs.* 1982 (song); *Brimstone and Treacle* 1982 (a,m,song); *The Bride* 1985 (a); *Bring on the Night* 1985 (a,m,m.prod,song); *Dune* 1985 (a); *Plenty* 1985 (a); *Dudes* 1987 (song); *Julia and Julia* 1987 (a); *The Adventures of Baron Munchausen* 1988 (a); *Dance of Hope* 1988 (m); *Stormy Monday* 1988 (a); *Resident Alien* 1990 (a,m).

Stockwell, Dean • Actor • Born North Hollywood, CA, March 5, 1936. *Educ.* UCLA. Prolific performer whose career has come in several waves, each punctuated by a "retirement" from the screen. As a child actor under contract to MGM from 1945, Stockwell specialized in "sensitive child" roles like the title character of Joseph Losey's *The Boy With Green Hair* (1948). After five years spent traveling around the US and working at odd jobs, he matured into a a strikingly attractive, introverted young adult lead, winning acclaim as the son in *Sons and Lovers* (1960) and the Eugene O'Neill character in *Long Day's Journey Into Night* (1962).

Stockwell dropped out of acting again in the early 1960s, to embrace a hippy lifestyle, and yet again in the mid-70s, to pursue a career as a real-estate broker. He revitalized his screen career in the mid-1980s, specializing in spooky and eccentric characterizations such as the suavely perverse Ben in *Blue Velvet* (1986), mafia don Tony "The Tiger" Russo in *Married to the Mob* (1988) and Howard Hughes (a particularly eerie cameo) in *Tucker: The Man and His Dream* (1988). Stockwell wrote and directed his first feature film, *Human Highway*, in 1982. Son of actor Harry Stockwell (who provided the voice of Prince Charming in Disney's 1937 *Snow White and the Seven Dwarfs*), brother of actor Guy Stockwell and former husband of actress Millie Perkins. • *Anchors Aweigh* 1945 (a); *The Valley of Decision* 1945 (a); *The Green Years* 1946 (a); *Home, Sweet Homicide* 1946 (a); *Mighty McGurk* 1946 (a); *The Arnelo Affair* 1947 (a); *Gentleman's Agreement* 1947 (a); *The Romance of Rosy Ridge* 1947 (a); *Song of the Thin Man* 1947 (a); *The Boy With Green Hair* 1948 (a); *Deep Waters* 1948 (a); *Down to the Sea in Ships* 1949 (a); *The Secret Garden* 1949 (a); *The Happy Years* 1950 (a); *Kim* 1950 (a); *Stars in My Crown* 1950 (a); *Cattle Drive* 1951 (a); *The Careless Years* 1957 (a); *A Gun For a Coward* 1957 (a); *Compulsion* 1959 (a); *Sons and Lovers* 1960 (a); *Long Day's Journey Into Night* 1962 (a); *Rapture* 1965 (a); *Psych-Out* 1968 (a); *The Dunwich Horror* 1970 (a); *The Last Movie* 1971 (a); *The Loners* 1971 (a); *Werewolf of Washington* 1973 (a); *Win, Place or Steal* 1975 (a); *Eadweard Muybridge, Zoopraxographer* 1976 (a); *Tracks* 1976 (a); *She Came to the Valley* 1979 (a); *Alsino y el Condor* 1982 (a); *Human Highway* 1982 (a,d,sc); *Wrong Is Right* 1982 (a); *Sweet Scene of Death* 1983 (a); *Paris, Texas* 1984 (a); *Dune* 1985 (a); *The Legend of Billie Jean* 1985 (a); *To Kill a Stranger* 1985 (a); *To Live and Die in L.A.* 1985 (a); *Blue Velvet* 1986 (a); *Banzai Runner* 1987 (a); *Beverly Hills Cop II* 1987 (a); *Gardens of Stone* 1987 (a); *The Time Guardian* 1987 (a); *The Blue Iguana* 1988 (a); *Buying Time* 1988 (a); *The Long Haul* 1988 (a); *Married to the Mob* 1988 (a) **(AANBSA)**; *Palais Royale* 1988 (a); *Tucker: The Man and His Dream* 1988 (a); *Limit Up* 1989 (a); *Stickfighter* 1989 (a); *Backtrack* 1990 (a); *Sandino* 1990 (a).

Stoltz, Eric • Actor • Born American Samoa, 1961. *Educ.* USC, Los Angeles (theater). Amiable, red-headed juvenile lead who made his film debut in *Fast Times at Ridgemont High* (1982) and came to prominence playing the spunky, disfigured son of Cher in *Mask* (1985). • *Fast Times at Ridgemont High* 1982 (a); *Running Hot* 1984 (a); *Surf II* 1984 (a); *The Wild Life* 1984 (a); *Code Name: Emerald* 1985 (a); *Mask* 1985 (a); *The New Kids* 1985 (a); *Lionheart* 1987 (a); *Sister, Sister* 1987 (a); *Some Kind of Wonderful* 1987 (a); *Haunted Summer* 1988 (a); *Manifesto* 1988 (a); *The Fly II* 1989 (a); *Say Anything* 1989 (a,prod.asst); *Memphis Belle* 1990 (a).

Stone, Dee Wallace • *aka* Dee Wallace • Actress • Born Deanna Bowers, Kansas City, MO, December 14, 1948. *Educ.* University of Kansas (theater, education). TV lead who has appeared in occasional films, most notably as the distressed single mother trying to raise a family and an alien, in *E.T., the Extra-Terrestrial* (1982). Married to actor Christopher Stone, with whom she co-starred in *Cujo* (1983). • *The Stepford Wives* 1975 (a); *The Hills Have Eyes* 1977 (a); *10* 1979 (a); *The Howling* 1980 (a); *E.T., the Extra-Terrestrial* 1982 (a); *Jimmy the Kid* 1982 (a); *Cujo* 1983 (a); *Club Life* 1985 (a,song); *Secret Admirer* 1985 (a); *Critters* 1986 (a); *Shadow Play* 1986 (a); *Popcorn* 1991 (a).

Stone, Oliver • Director; also screenwriter, producer. • Born New York, NY, September 15, 1946. *Educ.* Yale; NYU (film). First made his name as a writer, winning an Oscar, a Writer's Guild Award and a Golden Globe for his screenplay of *Midnight Express* (1978). Stone has gone on to become one of Hollywood's most forceful directors, tackling difficult social and political themes with evident skill and commitment. He received a second Oscar and a Directors Guild Award for *Platoon* (1986), one of the starkest treatments of the Vietnam war to have reached American screens, and brought a similarly uncompromising gaze to bear on the world of high finance in *Wall Street* (1987).

Born on the Fourth of July (1989), based on the true story of Vietnam veteran Ron Kovac and featuring Tom Cruise in his first "heavyweight" dramatic role, earned Stone a second DGA Award but fared less successfully at the box-office. • *Street Scenes 1970* 1970 (d,ph); *Seizure* 1974 (d,sc,ed); *Midnight Express* 1978 (sc) **(AABSC)**; *The Hand* 1981 (a,d,sc,from book *The Lizard's Tail*); *Conan the Barbarian* 1982 (sc); *Scarface* 1983 (sc); *Year of the Dragon* 1985 (sc); *8 Million Ways to Die* 1986 (sc); *Platoon* 1986 (d,sc) **(AANBSC,AABD)**; *Salvador* 1986 (d,p,sc) **(AANBSC)**; *Wall Street* 1987 (a,d,sc); *Talk Radio* 1988 (d,sc); *Blue Steel* 1989 (p); *Born on the Fourth of July* 1989 (a,d,p,sc) **(AANBP,AABD)**; *Reversal of Fortune* 1990 (p); *The Doors* 1991 (d,sc).

Stoppard, Tom • Playwright; also screenwriter. • Born Tomas Straussler, Zlin (now Gottwaldov), Czechoslovakia, July 3, 1937. English-language playwright celebrated for his verbal acrobatics and madcap intellectual conceits. Stoppard first made his name in 1968 with the playful, breathlessly inventive

Rosencrantz and Guildenstern Are Dead, a play loosely related to *Hamlet* but with its feet firmly in the absurdist tradition of Beckett and Pinter. He consolidated his reputation with the philosophical whodunnit, *Jumpers*, and the Wildean historical farce, *Travesties*, and collaborated on the film adaptation of *The Romantic Englishwoman*, in 1975.

Stoppard's script for Fassbinder's *Despair* (1978) was transposed from the Nabokov novel, and *The Human Factor* (1979) was based on the Graham Greene work. He earned plaudits for his contribution to Terry Gilliam's *Brazil* (1985) and made an acclaimed film directorial debut with his own adaptation of *Rosencrantz and Guildenstern* in 1990. • *The Engagement* 1970 (sc); *The Romantic Englishwoman* 1975 (sc); *Despair* 1978 (sc); *The Human Factor* 1979 (sc); *Squaring the Circle* 1983 (sc); *Brazil* 1985 (sc) **(AANBSC)**; *Empire of the Sun* 1987 (sc); *Rosencrantz and Guildenstern Are Dead* 1990 (d,sc,from play); *The Russia House* 1990 (sc).

Storaro, Vittorio • Director of photography • Born Rome, 1940. *Educ.* Duca D'Aosta Technical Photographic Institute; Italian Cinemagraphic Training Center; Centro Sperimentale di Cinematografia, Rome. Modern master of his art who came to prominence for his work on the films of Bernardo Bertolucci, including *The Conformist* (1970) and *Last Tango in Paris* (1972). Storaro has shot a number of English-language films, including several directed by Francis Ford Coppola (*Apocalypse Now* 1979, *One From the Heart* 1982, *Tucker: The Man and His Dream* 1988). • *Delitto al Circolo del Tennis* 1969 (ph); *L'Uccello dalle Piume di Cristallo* 1969 (ph); *Il Conformista/The Conformist* 1970 (ph); *Giovinezza Giovinezza* 1970 (ph); *La Strategia del Ragno/The Spider's Strategem* 1970 (ph); *Addio, Fratello Crudele* 1971 (ph); *Orlando Furioso* 1971 (ph); *Corpo d'Amore* 1972 (ph); *Last Tango in Paris* 1972 (ph); *Giordano Bruno* 1973 (ph); *Malizia* 1973 (ph); *Novecento/1900* 1976 (ph); *Submission* 1977 (ph); *Agatha* 1979 (ph); *Apocalypse Now* 1979 (ph) **(AABPH)**; *La Luna* 1979 (ph); *Reds* 1981 (ph) **(AABPH)**; *One From the Heart* 1982 (ph); *Wagner* 1983 (ph); *Ladyhawke* 1985 (ph); *Captain Eo (short)* 1986 (lighting consultant,photographic consultant); *Ishtar* 1987 (ph); *The Last Emperor* 1987 (ph) **(AABPH)**; *Tucker: The Man and His Dream* 1988 (ph); *New York Stories* 1989 (ph—"Life Without Zoe"); *Dick Tracy* 1990 (ph); *The Sheltering Sky* 1990 (ph).

Stowe, Madeleine • Actress • Born Eagle Rock, CA. *Educ.* USC, Los Angeles (film, journalism). Alluring, Latinate performer with stage and TV credits who made her feature debut as the object of surveillance in *Stakeout* (1987), co-starring Richard Dreyfuss and Emilio Estevez. Stowe went on to co-star in *Revenge* and *The Two Jakes* (both 1990). • *Stakeout* 1987; *Tropical Snow* 1989; *Worth Winning* 1989; *Revenge* 1990; *The Two Jakes* 1990; *Closet Land* 1991.

Stradling, Harry, Jr. • Director of photography • Born New York, January 7, 1925. Began his career as a camera assistant and camera operator (he assisted his father, cinematographer Harry Stradling, on 1955's *Guys and Dolls*) and shot his first feature film, *Welcome to Hard Times*, in 1967. Stradling, Jr., has been noted for his outdoor color photography and has contributed to productions including *Little Big Man* (1970), *The Way We Were* (1973) and several films directed by Blake Edwards. • *Welcome to Hard Times* 1967; *The Mad Room* 1969; *Support Your Local Sheriff* 1969; *Dirty Dingus Magee* 1970; *Little Big Man* 1970; *There Was a Crooked Man* 1970; *Fools' Parade* 1971; *The Late Liz* 1971; *Something Big* 1971; *Support Your Local Gunfighter* 1971; *1776* 1972 **(AANBPH)**; *Nightmare Honeymoon* 1972; *Skyjacked* 1972; *Thumb Tripping* 1972; *The Man Who Loved Cat Dancing* 1973; *The Way We Were* 1973 **(AANBPH)**; *Bank Shot* 1974; *McQ* 1974; *Bite the Bullet* 1975; *Mitchell* 1975; *Rooster Cogburn* 1975; *Battle of Midway* 1976; *The Big Bus* 1976; *Special Delivery* 1976; *Damnation Alley* 1977; *The Greatest* 1977; *Born Again* 1978; *Convoy* 1978; *Go Tell the Spartans* 1978; *Prophecy* 1979; *Carny* 1980; *Up the Academy* 1980; *Buddy Buddy* 1981; *The Pursuit of D.B. Cooper* 1981; *S.O.B.* 1981; *O'Hara's Wife* 1982; *Micki & Maude* 1984; *A Fine Mess* 1986; *Blind Date* 1987; *Caddyshack II* 1988.

Stradling, Harry • Director of photography • Born Newark, NJ, September 1, 1901; died February, 1970. Entered film in the early 1920s as a Hollywood cameraman and emerged as a prominent cinematographer following his work in France on director Jacques Feyder's *Carnival in Flanders* (1935). Stradling gained renown for his work on a number of British productions, including *Knight Without Armour* (1937) and *Pygmalion* (1938), before returning to Hollywood in 1940. He contributed to such outstanding black-and-white productions as *The Picture of Dorian Gray* (1945), *A Streetcar Named Desire* (1951) and *Who's Afraid of Virginia Woolf?* (1966) and was responsible for the lush color of films including *Guys and Dolls* (1955) and *My Fair Lady* (1964). Stradling shot Barbra Streisand's first four movies and died while filming *The Owl and the Pussycat* (1970). • *The Great Adventure* 1921 (ph); *Jim the Penman* 1921 (ph); *Fair Lady* 1922 (ph); *His Wife's Husband* 1922 (ph); *How Women Love* 1922 (ph); *The Secrets of Paris* 1922 (ph); *Wandering Fires* 1924 (ph); *The Substitute Wife* 1925 (ph); *Burnt Fingers* 1927 (ph); *The Nest* 1927 (ph); *Lucky in Love* 1929 (ph); *Mother's Boy* 1929 (ph); *Mistigri* 1932 (ph); *Carnival in Flanders/La Kermesse Héroïque* 1935 (ph); *Action For Slander* 1937 (ph); *Knight Without Armour* 1937 (ph); *Over the Moon* 1937 (ph); *The Citadel* 1938 (ph); *Pygmalion* 1938 (ph); *South Riding* 1938 (ph); *Clouds Over Europe* 1939 (ph); *Jamaica Inn* 1939 (ph); *My Son, My Son* 1940 (ph); *They Knew What They Wanted* 1940 (ph); *The Corsican Brothers* 1941 (ph); *The Devil and Miss Jones* 1941 (ph); *The Men in Her Life* 1941 (ph); *Mr. & Mrs. Smith* 1941 (ph); *Mr. and Mrs. North* 1941 (ph); *Suspicion* 1941 (ph); *Fingers at the Window* 1942 (ph); *Her Cardboard Lover* 1942 (ph); *Maisie Gets Her Man* 1942 (ph); *Nazi Agent* 1942 (ph); *White Cargo* 1942 (ph); *The Human Comedy* 1943 (ph) **(AANBPH)**; *Song of Russia* 1943 (ph); *Swing Shift Maisie* 1943 (ph); *Bathing Beauty* 1944 (ph); *Her Highness and the Bellboy* 1945 (ph); *The Picture of Dorian Gray* 1945 (ph) **(AABPH)**; *Thrill of a Romance* 1945 (ph); *Easy to Wed* 1946 (ph); *Holiday in Mexico* 1946 (ph); *Till the Clouds Roll By* 1946 (ph); *Sea of Grass* 1947 (ph); *Song of Love* 1947 (ph); *Easter Parade* 1948 (ph); *The Pirate* 1948 (ph); *Words and Music* 1948 (ph); *The Barkleys of Broadway* 1949 (ph) **(AANBPH)**; *In the Good Old Summertime* 1949 (ph); *Tension* 1949 (ph); *Edge of Doom* 1950 (ph); *The Yellow Cab Man* 1950 (ph); *I Want You* 1951 (ph); *A Millionaire For Christy* 1951 (ph); *A Streetcar Named Desire* 1951 (ph) **(AANBPH)**; *Valentino* 1951 (ph); *Androcles and the Lion* 1952 (ph); *Angel Face* 1952 (ph); *Hans Christian Andersen* 1952 (ph) **(AANBPH)**; *My Son John* 1952 (ph); *Forever Female* 1953 (ph); *A Lion Is in the Streets* 1953 (ph); *Johnny Guitar* 1954 (ph); *Guys and Dolls* 1955 (ph); *The Eddy Duchin Story* 1956 (ph) **(AANBPH)**; *Helen of Troy* 1956 (ph); *A Face in the Crowd* 1957 (ph); *The Pajama Game* 1957 (ph); *Auntie Mame* 1958 (ph); *Marjorie Morningstar* 1958 (ph); *The Crowded Sky* 1960 (ph); *The Dark at the Top of the Stairs* 1960 (ph); *Who Was That Lady?* 1960 (ph); *A Majority of One* 1961 (ph); *On the Double* 1961 (ph); *Parrish* 1961 (ph); *Five Finger Exercise* 1962 (ph); *Gypsy* 1962 (ph); *Island of Love* 1963 (ph); *Mary, Mary* 1963 (ph); *My Fair Lady* 1964 (ph) **(AABPH)**; *How to Murder Your Wife* 1965 (ph); *Synanon* 1965 (ph); *Moment to Moment* 1966 (ph); *Penelope* 1966 (ph); *Walk, Don't Run* 1966 (ph); *Who's Afraid of Virginia Woolf?* 1966 (ph); *Funny Girl* 1968 (ph) **(AANBPH)**; *With Six You Get Eggroll* 1968 (ph); *The Good Guys and the Bad Guys* 1969 (ph); *Hello, Dolly!* 1969 (ph); *Young Billy Young* 1969 (ph); *On a Clear Day You Can See Forever* 1970 (ph); *The Owl and the Pussycat* 1970 (ph).

Straithairn, David • Actor • Born San Francisco, CA, c. 1950. *Educ.* Williams College, Williamstown, MA; Ringling Bros. Clown College, FL. Affable character player who has appeared in four of college-mate John Sayles's films, most notably as morally flawed baseball pitcher Eddie Cicotte in *Eight Men Out* (1988). A veteran stage actor, Straithairn has also been prominent on TV, as J. Robert Oppenheimer in the movie *Day One* (1989) and as the bookseller in the series "The Days and Nights of Molly Dodd." • *The Return of the Secaucus Seven* 1979; *When Nature Calls* 1982; *Enormous Changes at the Last Minute* 1983; *Lovesick* 1983; *Silkwood* 1983; *The Brother From Another Planet* 1984; *Iceman* 1984; *At Close Range* 1986; *Matewan* 1987; *Call Me* 1988; *Dominick and Eugene* 1988; *Eight Men Out* 1988; *Stars and Bars* 1988; *The Feud* 1989; *Memphis Belle* 1990.

Strasberg, Lee • Actor; also stage director. • Born Israel Strasberg, Budzanow, Austria, November 17, 1901; died 1982. *Educ.* American Laboratory Theatre. One of America's leading proponents of "Method" acting. Strasberg arrived in the US at age nine, co-founded the influential, left-leaning Group Theater in 1930 and became artistic director of the newly formed Actors Studio in 1948. Strasberg and his associates, through their teaching of the Method at the Studio, heavily influenced the course of American screen acting; students included Marlon Brando, Rod Steiger, Marilyn Monroe, Paul Newman and Shelley Winters. In 1969 he set up the Lee Strasberg Institute, with chapters in Los Angeles and New York. He himself acted in only a handful of films (his first and best part was as a workaday Jewish mobster in 1974's *The Godfather, Part II*). Father of actress Susan Strasberg. • *Backfire* 1946 (adapt); *The Godfather, Part II* 1974 (a) (**AANBSA**); *The Cassandra Crossing* 1977 (a); *And Justice For All* 1979 (a); *Boardwalk* 1979 (a); *Going in Style* 1979 (a); *Acting: Lee Strasberg and The Actors Studio* 1981 (a).

Straub, Jean-Marie • Director; also screenwriter, producer. • Born Metz, France, January 8, 1933. *Educ.* University of Strasbourg (literature); University of Nancy (literature). Jean-Marie Straub and Daniele Huillet form one of the few husband-and-wife production teams of any real consequence or true equality. Together they have created some of the most demanding and interesting films of the 1960s and 70s, beginning in 1963 with their short film *Machorka-Muff* (sometimes spelled "Majorka-Muff").

Straub ran a local cineclub in his birthplace of Metz, and later worked in varous assistant capacities for such directors as Jean Renoir, Abel Gance and Robert Bresson, all of whom had an enormous influence on his work. He and Huillet met in 1954 in Paris and immediately became artistic partners. In 1958 Straub, fleeing conscription into the French armed forces, moved to Munich, Germany, with Huillet, and they soon became involved with radical theater groups in that city. Among Straub's early collaborators was Rainer Werner Fassbinder, who appears as an actor in Straub's short film, *The Bridegroom, the Comedienne and the Pimp* (1968), which combines the story of the murder of a pimp (Fassbinder) with a drastically condensed theatrical piece and a lengthy tracking shot from an automobile of prostitutes plying their trade on an ill-lit German thoroughfare.

Perhaps the couple's most famous early film is *Chronicle of Anna Magdalena Bach* (1968), which the director shot on the actual locations of Joahnn Sebastian Bach's life, featuring Gustav Maria Leonhardt, the renowned harpsichordist, as Bach, and instruments borrowed from various museums for a more accurate sound. The film almost collapsed before production: Straub insisted on recording all the sync-sound on location, eschewing the use of any post-dubbing, to get the most natural and authentic performances from the ensemble of excellent musicians he had assembled. This horrified the original backers, who withdrew their funding at the last moment. Jean-Luc Godard came through with emergency funding, but the film had to be shot in black-and-white rather than in color, which Straub would have preferred. Nevertheless, it was a surprise hit at the 1968 New York Film Festival and remains a stunning artistic achievement.

In *Chronicle*, as in all his works, Straub insisted upon lengthy takes, which were used virtually without editing in the final film; some shots of nearly ten minutes' duration appear in *Chronicle*. Coupled with the use of natural lighting, austere sets and subdued performances, this minimalist shooting technique results in a an extraordinary sense of "place," as if one is watching the incidents of Bach's life as they occur, rather than a re-creation of them.

Other early successes include an adaptation of Heinrich Böll's *Billiards at Half Past Nine*, which became the astoundingly rich and perverse film, *Not Reconciled, or Only Violence Helps Where Violence Rules* (1965). By the late 1960s and early 1970s, Straub preferred to function more as a producer than a director; often working in 16mm film, Huillet and Straub created such films as *Othon* (1971), *History Lessons* (1972), *Moses and Aaron* (1975) and most recently *Class Relations* (1984), based on Franz Kafka's *Amerika*.

In all these films, Huillet and Straub demand a great deal from the viewer, refusing to create films of easy visual reconstruction. Given the proper attention, however, Straub-Huillet films remain among the most haunting and visually resonant of the German filmmaking renaissance. Certainly the two are worthy of wider appreciation, particularly in light of recent attention paid to the works of Fassbinder and Wim Wenders. WWD • *Machorka-Muff* 1963 (d,sc,ed,sound); *Nicht Versohnt oder es hilft nur gewalt, wo gewalt herrscht/Not Reconciled, or Only Violence Helps Where Violence Rules* 1965 (d,p,sc,cam.op,ed); *Der Brautigam, die Komodiantin und der Zuhalter/The Bridegroom, the Comedienne and the Pimp* 1968 (d,sc,ed); *Chronik der Anna Magdalena Bach/Chronicle of Anna Magdalena Bach* 1968 (d,sc,ed); *Les Yeux ne veulent pas en tout temps se fermer ou peut-être qu'un jour Rome se permettra de choisir à son tour* 1970 (a,dsc,ed,d); *Othon* 1971 (d,sc,e,a); *Geschichtsunterricht/History Lessons* 1972 (d,p,sc,e); *Einleitung zu Arnold Schönberg's Begleitmusik zu einer Lichtspielscene (short)* 1973 (a,d,sc,e); *Moses und Aaron/Moses and Aaron* 1975 (d,sc,e); *Fortini/Cani* 1976 (d,p,sc,e); *Toute révolution est un coup de dès (short)* 1977 (d,p,sc,e); *Dalla nube alla resistenza* 1979 (d,p,sc,e); *Too Early, Too Late* 1981 (d); *Klassenverhaltnisse/Class Relations* 1984 (d,sc,e); *Der Tod des Empedokles/The Death of Empedocles* 1986 (d,sc,e); *Schwarze Sunde* 1989 (d,p,sc,e).

Streep, Meryl • Actress • Born Mary Louise Streep, Summit, NJ, June 22, 1949. *Educ.* Vassar College, Poughkeepsie, NY (English, drama); Dartmouth (set and costume design, playwrighting); Yale School of Drama. Cool and controlled, elegant and graceful, Streep has reigned as the American cinema's leading serious actress since the early 1980s.

Attracting professional interest while still a graduate student at Yale (where she became something of a legend, performing in over 40 productions), Streep quickly established herself in the New York theater world with impressive turns in *27 Wagons Full of Cotton* and *Trelawny of the Wells*.

After making her screen debut in *Julia* (1977), Streep was Oscar-nominated (the first of nine times) for *The Deer Hunter* (1978). In the watershed year of 1979 she played the seductress in *The Seduction of Joe Tynan* and Woody Allen's lesbian ex-wife in *Manhattan* and won her first Oscar, for *Kramer vs. Kramer*. Two years after her first screen appearance, she had become one of the most widely praised actresses working in the medium.

Streep turned in a bravura performance opposite Jeremy Irons in *The French Lieutenant's Woman* (1981) and cemented her reputation with a riveting tour de force as the title character of *Sophie's Choice* (1982)—a role that combined flawless technique with raw emotional intensity and earned her another Oscar. She went on to give a succession of performances that aggressively proved her mastery of any idiom, accent or social milieu, playing a blue-collar political activist in *Silkwood* (1983), transplanted Danish writer Karen Blixen in *Out of Africa* (1988) and Lindy Chamberlain—the woman whose claim that dingos had made off with her baby made her "the most maligned woman in Australia"—in *A Cry in the Dark* (1988).

Streep's career took a new turn in the late 1980s with several comedic roles, including Susan Seidelman's lackluster *She-Devil* (1989) and the more successful *Postcards From the Edge* (1990), in which she played a character loosely modeled on actress Carrie Fisher. • *Julia* 1977; *The Deer Hunter* 1978 **(AANBSA)**; *Kramer vs. Kramer* 1979 **(AABSA)**; *Manhattan* 1979; *The Seduction of Joe Tynan* 1979; *The French Lieutenant's Woman* 1981 **(AANBA)**; *Sophie's Choice* 1982 **(AABA)**; *Still of the Night* 1982; *Silkwood* 1983 **(AANBA)**; *Falling in Love* 1984; *In Our Hands* 1984; *Out of Africa* 1985 **(AANBA)**; *Plenty* 1985; *Heartburn* 1986; *Ironweed* 1987 **(AANBA)**; *A Cry in the Dark* 1988 **(AANBA)**; *She-Devil* 1989; *Postcards From the Edge* 1990; *Defending Your Life* 1991.

Streisand, Barbra • Singer, actress; also producer, director, songwriter. • Born Barbara Joan Streisand, Brooklyn, NY, April 24, 1942. Multi-talented performer who conquered Broadway with her energetic stage presence in the musicals, *I Can Get It for You Wholesale* (1962) and *Funny Girl* (1964), recorded a string of best-selling albums and powered a number of award-winning TV specials ("My Name is Barbara", "Color Me Barbara") before moving into films. Equally magnetic on the big screen, Streisand starred in musicals before moving on to, and proving herself more than capable in, screwball comedies and romances.

Compensating for her "imperfect" beauty with unbounded energy and immense talent, she turned several mediocre movies into box-office successes, and appeared in such first-rate films as *What's Up, Doc?* (1972) and *The Way We Were* (1973), making her the biggest female star of the 1970s.

Increasingly criticized for her sometimes megalomaniac tendencies, Streisand responded by branching out into producing (beginning with 1976's *A Star Is Born*) and then directing (beginning with 1983's *Yentl*, which she also wrote); she has since produced most of her own vehicles. Formerly married to *I Can Get It For You Wholeseale* co-star Elliot Gould and mother of actor Jason Gould. • *Funny Girl* 1968 (a) **(AABA)**; *Hello, Dolly!* 1969 (a); *On a Clear Day You Can See Forever* 1970 (a); *The Owl and the Pussycat* 1970 (a); *Up the Sandbox* 1972 (a); *What's Up, Doc?* 1972 (a); *The Way We Were* 1973 (a) **(AANBA)**; *For Pete's Sake* 1974 (a); *Funny Lady* 1975 (a); *A Star Is Born* 1976 (a,exec.p,m,song) **(AABS)**; *The Main Event* 1979 (a,p,song); *All Night Long* 1981 (a); *Yentl* 1983 (a,d,p,sc); *Directed By William Wyler* 1986 (a); *Nuts* 1987 (a,m,p); *Listen Up* 1990 (a).

Stritch, Elaine • Actress • Born Detroit, MI, February 2, 1926. *Educ.* Dramatic Workshop of the New School for Social Research. Raspy-voiced stage star, known for her wry, ironic comic delivery, who made made her film debut in 1956. Stritch has starred on Broadway, most notably in the musicals *Goldilocks*, Noel Coward's *Sail Away!* and, saluting "the ladies who lunch," in Stephen Sondheim's *Company*; she has also appeared on numerous TV series since the early 1950s, including the British sitcom "Two's Company" (1975-76) with late husband John M. Bay. • *The Scarlet Hour* 1955; *Three Violent People* 1956; *A Farewell to Arms* 1957; *The Perfect Furlough* 1959; *Who Killed Teddy Bear?* 1965; *Original Cast Album: Company (short)* 1970; *Pigeons* 1970; *Providence* 1977; *September* 1987; *Cocoon: The Return* 1988; *Cadillac Man* 1990.

Strode, Woody • Actor • Born Woodrow Strode, Los Angeles, CA, 1914. *Educ.* UCLA. Black actor and former pro football player and wrestler who made his film debut in the early 1940s. Strode lent his imposing presence to a number of peripheral roles, such as Kirk Douglas's sparring partner in *Spartacus* (1960), though he got a chance to flex his underused acting muscles as a wrongly accused soldier in John Ford's *Sergeant Rutledge* (1960). • *The Lion Hunters* 1951; *Caribbean* 1952; *City Beneath the Sea* 1953; *The Gambler From Natchez* 1954; *The Ten Commandments* 1956; *The Buccaneer* 1958; *Tarzan's Fight For Life* 1958; *Pork Chop Hill* 1959; *The Last Voyage* 1960; *Sergeant Rutledge* 1960; *Spartacus* 1960; *The Sins of Rachel Cade* 1961; *Two Rode Together* 1961; *The Man Who Shot Liberty Valance* 1962; *Tarzan's Three Challenges* 1963; *Genghis Khan* 1965; *Seven Women* 1965; *The Professionals* 1966; *Shalako* 1968; *C'era una Volta il West/Once Upon a Time in the West* 1969; *Che!* 1969; *Tarzan's Deadly Silence* 1970; *Last Rebel* 1971; *La Spina Dorsale del Diavola* 1971; *Black Rodeo* 1972; *The Italian Connection* 1972; *The Revengers* 1972; *The Gatling Gun* 1973; *Winterhawk* 1975; *Keoma/The Violent Breed* 1976; *Kingdom of the Spiders* 1977; *Cuba Crossing* 1979; *Jaguar Lives!* 1979; *Ravagers* 1979; *Angkor-Cambodia Express* 1981; *Scream* 1981; *Vigilante* 1982; *The Black Stallion Returns* 1983; *The Final Executioner* 1983; *Jungle Warriors* 1983; *The Cotton Club* 1984; *Lust in the Dust* 1984.

Struss, Karl • Director of photography • Born New York, NY, 1891; died 1981. *Educ.* Columbia (photography). Began his career as a commercial photographer and entered film in 1919, serving a three-year stint as cameraman for Cecil B. DeMille. Struss then went freelance and gained renown for his work on *Ben Hur* (1925), particularly in his use of filters to effect visual transformations—a technique he repeated to great effect in *Dr. Jekyll and Mr. Hyde* (1932).

Struss received widespread recognition for his collaboration with Charles Rosher on F. W. Murnau's *Sunrise* (1927) and, following several collaborations with D.W. Griffith, began a fruitful 18-year association with Paramount. Other memorable work includes his contributions to the atmospheric thriller, *Island of Lost Souls* (1933) and Charlie Chaplin's *Limelight* (1952). • *Something to Think About* 1920; *The Affairs of Anatol* 1921; *Fool's Paradise* 1921; *Fools First* 1922; *The Hero* 1922; *The Law and the Woman* 1922; *Minnie* 1922; *Rich Men's Wives* 1922; *Saturday Night* 1922; *Thorns and Orange Blossoms* 1922; *Daughters of the Rich* 1923; *Maytime* 1923; *Mothers-in-Law* 1923; *Poor Men's Wives* 1923; *Idle Tongues* 1924; *The Legend of Hollywood* 1924; *Poisoned Paradise* 1924; *White Man* 1924; *Ben Hur, A Tale of the Christ* 1925; *The Winding Stair* 1925; *Forever After* 1926; *Hell's 400* 1926; *Meet the Prince* 1926; *Sparrows* 1926; *Babe Comes Home* 1927; *Sunrise* 1927 **(AABPH)**; *The Battle of the Sexes* 1928; *Drums of Love* 1928 **(AANBPH)**; *The Night Watch* 1928; *Lady of the Pavements* 1929; *The Taming of the Shrew* 1929; *Abraham Lincoln* 1930; *The Bad One* 1930; *Be Yourself!* 1930; *Lummox* 1930; *One Romantic Night* 1930; *Kiki* 1931; *Murder By the Clock* 1931; *The Road to Reno* 1931; *Skippy* 1931; *Up Pops the Devil* 1931; *Women Love Once* 1931; *Dancers in the Dark* 1932; *Dr. Jekyll and Mr. Hyde* 1932 **(AANBPH)**; *Forgotten Commandments* 1932; *Guilty As Hell* 1932; *The Man From Yesterday* 1932; *The Sign of the Cross* 1932 **(AANBPH)**; *Two Kinds of Women* 1932; *The World and the Flesh* 1932; *Disgraced* 1933; *The Girl in 419* 1933; *Island of Lost Souls* 1933; *The Story of Temple Drake* 1933; *Tonight Is Ours* 1933; *Torch Singer* 1933; *The Woman Accused* 1933; *Belle of the Nineties* 1934; *Four Frightened People* 1934; *Here Is My Heart* 1934; *The Pursuit of Happiness* 1934; *Goin' to Town* 1935; *Two For Tonight* 1935; *Anything Goes* 1936; *Go West, Young Man* 1936; *Hollywood Boulevard* 1936; *Let's Make a Million* 1936; *The Preview Murder Case* 1936; *Rhythm on the Range* 1936; *Too Many Parents* 1936; *Double or Nothing* 1937; *Mountain Music* 1937; *Thunder Trail* 1937; *Waikiki Wedding* 1937; *Every Day's a Holiday* 1938; *Sing, You Sinners* 1938; *Thanks For the Memory* 1938; *Island of Lost Men* 1939; *Paris*

Honeymoon 1939; *Some Like It Hot* 1939; *The Star Maker* 1939; *Zenobia* 1939; *The Great Dictator* 1940; *Aloma of the South Seas* 1941 **(AANBPH)**; *Caught in the Draft* 1941; *Journey Into Fear* 1942; *Happy Go Lucky* 1943; *Riding High* 1943; *And the Angels Sing* 1944; *Rainbow Island* 1944; *Bring on the Girls* 1945; *Mr. Ace* 1946; *Suspense* 1946; *Tarzan and the Leopard Woman* 1946; *Heaven Only Knows* 1947; *The Macomber Affair* 1947; *Bad Boy* 1948; *The Dude Goes West* 1948; *Siren of Atlantis* 1948; *Tarzan's Magic Fountain* 1949; *Father's Wild Game* 1950; *It's a Small World* 1950; *The Return of Jesse James* 1950; *Rocket Ship X-M* 1950; *The Texan Meets Calamity Jane* 1950; *Tarzan's Peril* 1951; *Limelight* 1952; *Mesa of Lost Women* 1952; *Rose of Cimarron* 1952; *Tarzan's Savage Fury* 1952; *Tarzan and the She-Devil* 1953; *Attila* 1955; *Mohawk* 1956; *The Deerslayer* 1957; *Kronos* 1957; *She Devil* 1957; *The Fly* 1958; *The Hot Angel* 1958; *Machete* 1958; *The Rawhide Trail* 1958; *The Alligator People* 1959; *Counterplot* 1959; *Here Come the Jets* 1959; *The Rebel Set* 1959; *The Sad Horse* 1959.

Stubbs, Imogen • Actress • Born Newcastle-upon-Tyne, England, 1961. *Educ.* Exeter College, Oxford (English); RADA, London. Classically trained performer whose few screen appearances, like her stage work, have garnered excellent reviews. Highly effective in the title role of the British-French co-production, *Nanou* (1987). • *Privileged* 1982; *Nanou* 1987; *A Summer Story* 1988; *Erik the Viking* 1989; *True Colors* 1991.

Sturges, John • Director • Born John Eliot Sturges, Oak Park, IL, January 3, 1910. *Educ.* Marin Junior College. Reliable Hollywood craftsman who established his reputation in the mid-1950s with a series of intense, morally charged features such as *Bad Day at Black Rock* (1954) and *Gunfight at the O.K. Corral* (1957), before moving on to bigger—though not especially better—productions.

Sturges began his career as an editor, co-directed the war documentary, *Thunderbolt* (1945), with William Wyler, and subsequently specialized in action and western features. Other notable films include *The Magnificent Seven* (1960), *The Great Escape* (1963) and—Howard Hughes's favorite movie—*Ice Station Zebra* (1968). • *They Knew What They Wanted* 1940 (ed); *Scattergood Meets Broadway* 1941 (ed); *Tom, Dick and Harry* 1941 (ed); *Syncopation* 1942 (ed); *Thunderbolt* 1945 (d); *Alias Mr. Twilight* 1946 (d); *The Man Who Dared* 1946 (d); *Shadowed* 1946 (d); *For the Love of Rusty* 1947 (d); *Keeper of the Bees* 1947 (d); *The Best Man Wins* 1948 (d); *The Sign of the Ram* 1948 (d); *The Walking Hills* 1949 (d); *The Capture* 1950 (d); *The Magnificent Yankee* 1950 (d); *Mystery Street* 1950 (d); *Right Cross* 1950 (d); *It's a Big Country* 1951 (d); *Kind Lady* 1951 (d); *The People Against O'Hara* 1951 (d); *The Girl in White* 1952 (d); *Escape From Fort Bravo* 1953 (d); *Fast Company* 1953 (d); *Jeopardy* 1953 (d); *Bad Day at Black Rock* 1954 (d) **(AANBD)**; *The Scarlet Coat* 1955 (d); *Underwater* 1955 (d); *Backlash* 1956 (d); *Gunfight at the O.K. Corral* 1957 (d); *The Law and Jake Wade* 1958 (d); *The Old Man and the Sea* 1958 (d); *Last Train From Gun Hill* 1959 (d); *Never So Few* 1959 (d); *The Magnificent Seven* 1960 (d,p); *By Love Possessed* 1961 (d); *A Girl Named Tamiko* 1962 (d); *Sergeants 3* 1962 (d); *The Great Escape* 1963 (d,p); *The Hallelujah Trail* 1965 (d,p); *The Satan Bug* 1965 (d,p); *Hour of the Gun* 1967 (d,p); *Ice Station Zebra* 1968 (d); *Marooned* 1969 (d); *Joe Kidd* 1972 (d); *Valdez il Mezzosangue* 1973 (d,p); *McQ* 1974 (d); *The Eagle Has Landed* 1976 (d).

Sturges, Preston • Director, screenwriter; also playwright. • Born Edmund Preston Biden, Chicago, IL, August 29, 1898; died August 6, 1959, New York, NY. *Educ.* School of Military Aeronautics, Austin, TX. One of the great satiric wits of the cinema, Preston Sturges demonstrated a rare ability in both his writing and his directing to combine cynicism with sentiment. The result was fresh, sharp films, filled with witty, fast-moving conversation. His targets were often living models of empty wealth and moral hypocrisy—the inevitable graduates, as he saw them, of a system that showcased material success. While heaping scorn on popular tastes and mass conformity, he regularly used the standard ingredients of popular comedy (mistaken or withheld identity, rags to riches, etc.) to deliver his satire.

Sturges's mother, Mary Desti, left her traveling salesman husband while her son was an infant and went to Paris, where she befriended Isadora Duncan and began a career as a bohemian and socialite. Upon returning to Chicago, she divorced her first husband and married Solomon Sturges, a kindly broker who legally adopted the four-year-old child in 1902. As a young man Preston assisted his mother with her cosmetics business, but after WWI he began writing plays, one of which, *Strictly Dishonorable*, was a Broadway hit in 1929. Two years later, he adapted it for the movies.

Sturges remained in Hollywood as a writer during the Great Depression, scoring several successes. Most notable were *The Power and the Glory* (1933), William K. Howard's drama that featured a narrative structure that may have influenced *Citizen Kane*, and Mitchell Leisen's excellent screwball comedy, *Easy Living* (1937).

Sturges earned his fame during a short period between 1940 and 1944, when the world was preoccupied with the devastations of war, although his pictures dealt only obliquely, if at all, with the military campaigns. His first hit as both writer and director was *The Great McGinty* (1940), a dramatic comedy about graft and corruption, as well as love and sacrifice. He won the Oscar for best original screenplay with this vigorous, quick-moving study of a tough guy (played by Brian Donlevy) who sells his vote in a Chicago mayoral election 37 times over, and is eventually elected governor of Illinois.

The film succeeded financially, as did his more wildly comical satires *The Palm Beach Story* (1942), about a struggling inventor (Joel McCrea) and his dizzy wife (Claudette Colbert); *Hail the Conquering Hero* (1944), which made light of bravery when few people dared to; and *The Miracle of Morgan's Creek* (1944), concerning a small town girl named Trudy Kockenlocker who winds up pregnant by a soldier she can't remember.

Most critics agree, however, that Sturges's best films were *The Lady Eve* (1941), a sometimes farcical romance which pits an extremely skilled gold-digger (Barbara Stanwyck) against a multimillionaire (Henry Fonda) with a love for snakes, and *Sullivan's Travels* (1941), with Joel McCrea playing a comedy-film director in search of poverty so he can make a philosophically profound picture, one of the most intelligent and comically adroit films about the Hollywood frame of mind.

After WWII Sturges's star faded. Later pictures such as *The Beautiful Blonde From Bashful Bend* (1949) and the French project, *Les Carnets du Major Thompson* (1956), were poorly received by patrons and critics alike. But his reputation as a great shaper of dialogue continues, enhanced in recent years by the availability of several of his best screenplays in published form. ATJ • *Strictly Dishonorable* 1931 (from play); *Child of Manhattan* 1933 (from play); *The Power and the Glory* 1933 (sc,story); *Thirty Day Princess* 1934 (sc); *We Live Again* 1934 (sc); *Diamond Jim* 1935 (sc); *The Good Fairy* 1935 (sc); *One Rainy Afternoon* 1936 (song); *Easy Living* 1937 (sc); *Hotel Haywire* 1937 (sc,story); *If I Were King* 1938 (sc); *Port of Seven Seas* 1938 (sc); *Never Say Die* 1939 (sc); *Christmas in July* 1940 (d,sc); *The Great McGinty* 1940 (d,sc) **(AABSC)**; *Remember the Night* 1940 (sc,story); *The Lady Eve* 1941 (d,sc); *Sullivan's Travels* 1941 (d,sc,story); *The Palm Beach Story* 1942 (d,sc); *Star Spangled Rhythm* 1942 (a); *The Great Moment* 1944 (d,sc); *Hail the Conquering Hero* 1944 (d,sc) **(AANBSC)**; *The Miracle of Morgan's Creek* 1944 (d,sc) **(AANBSC)**; *I'll Be Yours* 1947 (sc); *The Sin of Harold Diddlebock* 1947 (d,p,sc); *Unfaithfully Yours* 1948 (d,p,sc,story); *The Beautiful Blonde From Bashful Bend* 1949 (d,p,sc); *Strictly Dishonorable* 1951 (from play); *The Birds and the Bees* 1956 (sc); *Les Carnets du Major*

Thompson 1956 (d,sc); *Paris Holiday* 1958 (a); *Rock-a-Bye Baby* 1958 (from story "The Miracle of Morgan's Creek"); *Unfaithfully Yours* 1983 (from screenplay).

Sturridge, Charles • Director • Born London, June 24, 1951. Gifted young talent who was directing TV's "Coronation Street" (1972) by his early 20s and gained international recognition for his work on the much-praised, 11-part *Brideshead Revisited* (1981-83). Sturridge has made three assured forays into feature films, including the lyrically sculpted black-and-white segment, "La Forza del Destino" from *Aria* (1987), and two other Evelyn Waugh adaptations. • *If...* 1968 (a); *Runners* 1983 (d); *Aria* 1987 (d,screenplay — "La Forza del Destino"); *A Handful of Dust* 1988 (d,sc); *Where Angels Fear to Tread* 1991 (d).

Styne, Jule • Composer; also producer, music publisher. • Born Julius Kerwin Stein, London, December 31, 1905. *Educ.* Chicago College of Music (piano, composition, theory); Northwestern University. Brilliant, prolific tunesmith who was playing solo piano with the Chicago Symphony at age eight and entered films in the 1930s as a vocal coach, arranger and conductor. Styne wrote a number of classic film songs ("It Seems I Heard That Song Before" from *Youth on Parade* 1942, "I'll Walk Alone" from *Tonight and Every Night* 1945, "It's Magic" from *Romance on the High Seas* 1948) and lent his talent for infectious, buoyant melodies to such film scores as *Anchors Aweigh* (1945), *The Kid From Brooklyn* (1946), *It Happened in Brooklyn* (1947) and *My Sister Eileen* (1955). His genius for writing brassy Broadway hits for strong leading women has been captured in the film versions of his musicals: *Gentlemen Prefer Blondes* (1953), *Bells Are Ringing* (1960), *Gypsy* (1962) and *Funny Girl* (1968). • *Hit Parade of 1941* 1940 (song); *Melody and Moonlight* 1940 (song); *Sailors on Leave* 1941 (song); *Priorities on Parade* 1942 (song); *Youth on Parade* 1942 (song) **(AANBS)**; *Let's Face It* 1943 (song); *Thumbs Up* 1943 (song); *Follow the Boys* 1944 (song) **(AANBS)**; *Anchors Aweigh* 1945 (song) **(AANBS)**; *Tonight and Every Night* 1945 (song) **(AANBS)**; *The Kid From Brooklyn* 1946 (m); *Tars and Spars* 1946 (song); *It Happened in Brooklyn* 1947 (m); *Romance on the High Seas* 1948 (song) **(AANBS)**; *Two Guys From Texas* 1948 (song); *It's a Great Feeling* 1949 (song) **(AANBS)**; *The West Point Story* 1950 (song); *Meet Me After the Show* 1951 (song); *Macao* 1952 (song); *Gentlemen Prefer Blondes* 1953 (m); *Living It Up* 1954 (m); *Three Coins in the Fountain* 1954 (song) **(AABS)**; *How to Be Very, Very Popular* 1955 (song); *My Sister Eileen* 1955 (m); *Bells Are Ringing* 1960 (m); *Gypsy* 1962 (song); *Funny Girl* 1968 (m,song) **(AANBS)**.

Sucksdorff, Arne • Filmmaker • Born Stockholm, Sweden, February 3, 1917. *Educ.* University of Stockholm (natural history). Renowned documentarist who began making short, poetic nature films in his native Sweden, progressing in the 1950s to feature-length works filmed in distant locales such as India and Brazil. Sucksdorff's command of image and mood and his ability to lend an unobtrusive narrative quality to his studies have invited comparisons to the work of American master Robert Flaherty.

Aside from the restrained and beautifully photographed *The Great Adventure* (1953), Sucksdorff's later, increasingly fictionalized, features have been less successful than his shorts. He has scripted, photographed and edited all of his films. • *The Great Adventure* 1953 (a,d,p,sc,ph); *The Flute and the Arrow* 1957 (d,sc,ph); *Pojken i tradet/The Boy in a Tree* 1960 (d); *My Home Is Copacabana* 1966 (d,sc,ph).

Sukowa, Barbara • Actress • Born Bremen, Germany, February 2, 1950. *Educ.* Max Reinhardt Schauspielschule, Berlin. Striking, versatile stage actress whose relatively few screen appearances have yielded several memorable performances. Sukowa played the title character of Rainer Werner Fassbinder's *Lola* (1982), for which she was named best actress at the Berlin Film Festival, and had leading roles in Margarethe von Trotta's *Marianne and Julianne* (1981) and *Rosa Luxemburg* (1985). • *Frauen in New York* 1977; *Berlin Alexanderplatz* 1980; *Die Bleierne Zeit/Marianne and Julianne* 1981; *Un Dimanche de Flics* 1982; *Lola* 1982; *Equateur* 1983; *Rosa Luxemburg* 1985; *Die Verliebten* 1986; *The Sicilian* 1987; *L'Africana/The African Woman* 1990; *Voyager* 1991.

Sullavan, Margaret • Actress • Born Margaret Brooke Sullavan, Norfolk, VA, May 16, 1911; died January 1, 1960, New Haven, CT. *Educ.* Sullins College, Bristol; Denishawn School of Dance, Boston; E.E. Clive's Copley Theatre Dramatic School, Boston. Made her stage debute with the University Players (which included James Stewart and Henry Fonda) in Falmouth, MA, and entered films in 1933. With her husky voice, subtle talent and unique, magnetic charm Sullavan was an immediate success, but her critical disdain for the Hollywood establishment significantly reduced her screen output, facilitating her many returns to Broadway. She was married to Henry Fonda, William Wyler and producer-agent Leland Hayward. Sullavan died of a drug overdose and a family memoir, *Haywire* (1977), was written by her daughter, Brooke Hayward. • *Only Yesterday* 1933; *Little Man, What Now?* 1934; *The Good Fairy* 1935; *So Red the Rose* 1935; *The Moon's Our Home* 1936; *Next Time We Love* 1936; *The Shining Hour* 1938; *The Shopworn Angel* 1938; *Three Comrades* 1938 **(AANBA)**; *The Mortal Storm* 1940; *The Shop Around the Corner* 1940; *Appointment for Love* 1941; *Back Street* 1941; *So Ends Our Night* 1941; *Cry Havoc* 1943; *No Sad Songs For Me* 1950.

Surtees, Bruce • Director of photography • Born Los Angeles, CA, July 23, 1937. Has worked on several Clint Eastwood films, though some of his best work was done in the mid-1970s for other directors including Bob Fosse (*Lenny* 1974), Gordon Parks (*Leadbelly* 1976) and Arthur Penn (*Night Moves* 1975). Surtees's preference for low-key lighting has earned him the nickname "Prince of Darkness." Son of cinematographer Robert L. Surtees. • *The Beguiled* 1971 (ph); *Dirty Harry* 1971 (ph); *Play Misty For Me* 1971 (ph); *Conquest of the Planet of the Apes* 1972 (ph); *The Great Northfield Minnesota Raid* 1972 (ph); *Joe Kidd* 1972 (ph); *Blume in Love* 1973 (ph); *High Plains Drifter* 1973 (ph); *Lost Horizon* 1973 (cam.op); *The Outfit* 1973 (ph); *Lenny* 1974 (ph) **(AANBPH)**; *Night Moves* 1975 (ph); *The Outlaw Josey Wales* 1975 (ph); *Leadbelly* 1976 (ph); *The Shootist* 1976 (ph); *Sparkle* 1976 (ph); *Three Warriors* 1977 (ph); *Big Wednesday* 1978 (ph); *Movie Movie* 1978 (ph—"Baxter's Beauties of 1933"); *Dreamer* 1979 (ph); *Escape From Alcatraz* 1979 (ph); *Firefox* 1982 (ph); *Honkytonk Man* 1982 (ph); *Inchon* 1982 (ph); *Ladies and Gentlemen, the Fabulous Stains* 1982 (ph); *White Dog* 1982 (ph); *Bad Boys* 1983 (ph); *Risky Business* 1983 (ph); *Sudden Impact* 1983 (ph); *Beverly Hills Cop* 1984 (ph); *Tightrope* 1984 (ph); *Pale Rider* 1985 (ph); *Out of Bounds* 1986 (ph); *Psycho III* 1986 (ph); *Ratboy* 1986 (ph); *Back to the Beach* 1987 (ph); *License to Drive* 1988 (ph); *Men Don't Leave* 1990 (ph).

Surtees, Robert L. • Director of photography • Born Covington, KY, August 9, 1906; died 1985. Began career as an assistant to Gregg Toland in the late 1920s and had established himself as a dependable Hollywood craftsman by the end of the 40s. Surtees distinguished himself with his lush, vibrant color cinematography, notably on *King Solomon's Mines* (1950), *Oklahoma!* (1955), *Ben-Hur* (1959) and *The Collector* (1965); he made a triumphant return to black-and-white to shoot Peter Bogdanovich's *The Last Picture Show* (1971). Father of cinematographer Bruce Surtees. • *Strange Holiday* 1942 (ph); *Meet the People* 1944 (ph); *Music For Millions* 1944 (ph); *Thirty Seconds Over Tokyo* 1944 (ph) **(AANBPH)**; *Two Girls and a Sailor* 1944 (ph); *Our Vines Have Tender Grapes* 1945 (ph); *No Leave, No Love* 1946 (ph); *Two Sisters From Boston* 1946 (ph); *The Unfinished Dance* 1947 (ph); *Act of Violence* 1948 (ph); *Big City* 1948 (ph); *Big Jack* 1948 (ph); *A Date With Judy* 1948 (ph); *The Kissing Bandit* 1948 (ph); *Tenth Avenue Angel* 1948 (ph); *Intruder in the Dust* 1949 (ph); *That Midnight Kiss* 1949 (ph); *King Solomon's Mines* 1950 (ph) **(AABPH)**; *The Light Touch* 1951 (ph); *Quo Vadis* 1951 (ph) **(AANBPH)**; *The Strip* 1951 (ph); *The Bad and the Beautiful* 1952 (ph) **(AABPH)**; *The Merry Widow* 1952 (ph); *The Wild North* 1952 (ph); *Escape From Fort Bravo* 1953 (ph); *Mogambo* 1953 (ph); *Ride, Vaquero* 1953 (ph); *The Long, Long Trailer* 1954 (ph); *Valley of the Kings* 1954 (ph); *Oklahoma!* 1955 (ph) **(AANBPH)**; *Trial* 1955 (ph); *Tribute to a Bad Man* 1955 (ph); *The Swan* 1956 (ph); *Les Girls* 1957 (ph); *Raintree County* 1957 (ph); *The Law and Jake Wade* 1958 (ph); *Merry Andrew* 1958 (ph); *Ben-Hur* 1959 (ph) **(AABPH)**; *Cimarron* 1960 (ph); *It Started in Naples* 1960 (ph); *Mutiny on the Bounty* 1962 (ph) **(AANBPH)**; *PT 109* 1963 (ph); *Kisses For My President* 1964 (ph); *The Collector* 1965 (ph); *The Hallelujah Trail* 1965 (ph); *The Satan Bug* 1965 (ph); *The Third Day* 1965 (ph); *The Chase* 1966 (add.ph); *Lost Command* 1966 (ph); *Doctor Dolittle* 1967 (ph) **(AANBPH)**; *The Graduate* 1967 (ph) **(AANBPH)**; *The Arrangement* 1969 (ph); *Sweet Charity* 1969 (ph); *The Liberation of L.B. Jones* 1970 (ph); *The Cowboys* 1971 (ph); *The Last Picture Show* 1971 (ph) **(AANBPH)**; *Summer of '42* 1971 (ph) **(AANBPH)**; *The Other* 1972 (ph); *Lost Horizon* 1973 (ph); *Oklahoma Crude* 1973 (ph); *The Sting* 1973 (ph) **(AANBPH)**; *The Great Waldo Pepper* 1975 (ph); *The Hindenburg* 1975 (ph) **(AANBPH)**; *A Star Is Born* 1976 (ph) **(AANBPH)**; *The Turning Point* 1977 (ph) **(AANBPH)**; *Bloodbrothers* 1978 (ph); *Same Time, Next Year* 1978 (ph).

Sutherland, Donald • Actor • Born St. John, New Brunswick, Canada, July 17, 1934. *Educ.* University of Toronto (engineering, drama); LAMDA, London; RADA, London. Tall, gaunt leading man with British repertory stage experience who played in several 1960s horror films before winning his first plaudits as irreverent surgeon Hawkeye Pierce in Robert Altman's breakthrough feature, *M*A*S*H* (1970).

The politically active Canadian then made the transition from anti-hero character parts to starring roles. Landmark performances include the reserved detective in *Klute* (1971), opposite Jane Fonda (with whom he co-wrote, co-produced and co-starred in the 1972 anti-war film, *FTA*); Jesus Christ in Dalton Trumbo's *Johnny Got His Gun* (1971); a clairvoyant, death-obsessed parent in Nicolas Roeg's eerie masterpiece, *Don't Look Now* (1973); and the father in Robert Redford's *Ordinary People* (1980). Sutherland continues to make regular film appearances, though few of his later roles have matched his earlier successes; he gave a convincing portrayal of a South African schoolteacher whose conscience prods him into anti-apartheid activism in Euzhan Palcy's *A Dry White Season* (1989). Sutherland is divorced from actresses Lois Hardwick and Shirley Douglas; his son by the latter, actor Kiefer Sutherland, was named after Warren Kiefer, the screenwriter on Sutherland elder's first film, *Castle of the Living Dead*. • *Il Castello dei morti vivi/Castle of the Living Dead* 1964 (a); *Dr. Terror's House of Horrors* 1964 (a); *The Bedford Incident* 1965 (a); *Die! Die! My Darling!* 1965 (a); *Promise Her Anything* 1966 (a); *The Dirty Dozen* 1967 (a); *Joanna* 1968 (a); *Oedipus the King* 1968 (a); *Sebastian* 1968 (a); *The Split* 1968 (a); *Act of the Heart* 1970 (a); *Alex in Wonderland* 1970 (a); *Kelly's Heroes* 1970 (a); *M*A*S*H* 1970 (a); *Start the Revolution Without Me* 1970 (a); *Johnny Got His Gun* 1971 (a); *Klute* 1971 (a); *Little Murders* 1971 (a); *FTA* 1972 (a,p,sc "FTA Show",song); *Don't Look Now* 1973 (a); *Lady Ice* 1973 (a); *Steelyard Blues* 1973 (a,exec.p); *Spys* 1974 (a); *The Day of the Locust* 1975 (a); *Il Casanova di Federico Fellini/Fellini's Casanova* 1976 (a); *The Eagle Has Landed* 1976 (a); *Novecento/1900* 1976 (a); *Disappearance* 1977 (a); *The Kentucky Fried Movie* 1977 (a); *Les Liens de sang* 1977 (a); *Invasion of the Body Snatchers* 1978 (a); *National Lampoon's Animal House* 1978 (a); *Bear Island* 1979 (a); *The First Great Train Robbery* 1979 (a); *A Man, a Woman and a Bank* 1979 (a); *Murder By Decree* 1979 (a); *North China Commune* 1979 (a); *Nothing Personal* 1979 (a); *Ordinary People* 1980 (a); *Eye of the Needle* 1981 (a); *Gas* 1981 (a); *Threshold* 1981 (a); *Max Dugan Returns* 1982 (a); *A War Story* 1982 (a); *Crackers* 1984 (a); *Heaven Help Us* 1985 (a); *Ordeal By Innocence* 1985 (a); *Revolution* 1985 (a); *The Wolf at the Door* 1986 (a); *The Rosary Murders* 1987 (a); *The Trouble With Spies* 1987 (a); *A Dry White Season* 1989 (a); *Lock Up* 1989 (a); *Lost Angels* 1989 (a); *Bethune: The Making of a Hero* 1990 (a); *Eminent Domain* 1991 (a).

Sutherland, Kiefer • Actor • Born London, England, 1967. Talented young lead who made his film acting debut in 1984 and came to attention for his performances as a small-town bully in *Stand By Me* (1986), a teenage vampire in *The Lost Boys* (1987) and an unctuous yuppie in *Bright Lights, Big City* (1988). Son of actor Donald Sutherland. • *Bay Boy* 1984; *At Close Range* 1986; *Crazy Moon* 1986; *Stand By Me* 1986; *The Killing Time* 1987; *The Lost Boys* 1987; *Promised Land* 1987; *1969* 1988; *Bright Lights, Big City* 1988; *Young Guns* 1988; *Renegades* 1989; *Chicago Joe and the Showgirl* 1990; *Flashback* 1990; *Flatliners* 1990; *The Nutcracker Prince* 1990; *Young Guns II* 1990.

Suzman, Janet • Actress • Born Johannesburg, South Africa, February 9, 1939. *Educ.* Kingsmead College University of Witwaterstrand (English, French); LAMDA, London. South African- born actress who honed her craft on the London stage as a member of the Royal Shakespeare Company. Suzman made her film debut opposite Alan Bates in *A Day in the Death of Joe Egg* (1970), received an Oscar nomination for her next role—as the Czarina Alexandra in *Nicholas and Alexandra* (1971)—and contributed an excellent turn in Euzhan Palcy's anti-apartheid drama, *A Dry White Season* (1989). • *A Day in the Death of Joe Egg* 1970; *Nicholas and Alexandra* 1971 **(AANBA)**; *The Black Windmill* 1974; *Voyage of the Damned* 1976; *The House on Garibaldi Street* 1979; *Nijinsky* 1980; *Priest of Love* 1980; *The Draughtsman's Contract* 1982; *E la nave Va/And the Ship Sails On* 1983; *The Singing Detective* 1988; *A Dry White Season* 1989; *Nuns on the Run* 1990.

Svankmajer, Jan • Animator • Born Czechoslovakia. Major figure of contemporary East European animation whose surrealistic, often macabre work owes more to the nightmarish visions of Kafka and Buñuel than to the sunny daydreams of Walt Disney and his creative progeny. Noted for investing otherwise ordinary objects with ominous overtones, Svankmajer reached his widest audience to date with a feature-length adaptation of Lewis Carroll's *Alice* (1988) which blended animated and live-action footage—a technique he had earlier used to hair-raising effect in *Down to the Cellar* (1983). He is a major influence on the somewhat better known animation artists, the brothers Quay, as evinced by their 1984 tribute, *The Cabinet of Jan Svankmajer*. • *Posledni Trik Pana Schwarcewalldea a Pana Edgara/The Last Trick* (short) 1964 (d,sc,layout artist); *Rakvickarna/The Coffin House (short)* 1966 (d,sc,layout artist); *Byt/The Flat (short)* 1968 (d,sc,story); *Historia Naturae (short)* 1968 (d); *Zahrada/Garden (short)* 1968 (d,sc); *Don Sanche (short)* 1969 (d,sc,storyboard artist); *Tichy Tyden v Dome/A Quiet Week in the House (short)* 1969 (d,sc,story,storyboard artist); *Kostnice/The Ossuary (short)* 1970 (d,sc,story); *Jabberwocky (short)* 1971 (d,sc,pd); *Moznosti Dialogu/Dimensions of Dialogue (short)* 1982 (d,sc,layout artist); *Do Pivnice/Down to the Cellar (short)* 1983 (d,sc,story,layout artist); *Kyvaldo, Jama a Nadeje/The Pit, the Pendulum and Hope (short)* 1983 (d,sc,storyboard artist); *Alice* 1988 (art d,d,sc,ed,pd); *Leonarduv Denik/Leonardo's Diary (short)* 1988 (d,sc); *Animated Self-Portraits (short)* 1989 (d); *Muzne hry/The Male Game* 1989 (d).

Swaim, Bob • Director; also screenwriter. • Born Robert Frank Swaim, Jr., Evanston, IL, November 2, 1943. *Educ.* California State University; L'Ecole Nationale de la Cinématographie, Paris. Gifted director who first established himself in France, where he had originally gone as a graduate student in anthropology. Swaim's most successful films to date have effectively been American-style crime movies shot in Parisian locales. He made his feature directing debut with *La Nuit de Saint-Germain des Près* (1977) and scored both critically and at the box-office with the terse, uncompromising crime thriller *La Balance* (1982). • *La Nuit de Saint-Germain des Près* 1977 (d,sc); *La Balance* 1982 (d,sc,dial); *Spies Like Us* 1985 (a); *Half Moon Street* 1986 (d,sc); *Masquerade* 1988 (d); *Visioni Privati/Private Screenings* 1990 (a).

Swanson, Gloria • *aka* Gloria Mae • Actress; also producer. • Born Gloria Josephine Mae Swenson, Chicago, IL, March 27, 1897; died April 4, 1983. Imperious silent screen legend and epitome of early Hollywood glamour who began her career at Chicago's Essanay Studios in 1913. Swanson married Wallace Beery, another Essanay performer, in 1916, and the pair moved to Hollywood. After appearing in a series of Mack Sennett's romantic comedies at Triangle, Swanson moved to Paramount, back to Triangle, and then back again to Paramount, where she reached stardom in the snappy, sophisticated bedroom farces of C.B. DeMille.

By the mid-20s Swanson was at the peak of her popularity. In 1927, with financial assistance from investor and lover Joseph P. Kennedy, she began producing her own films; these included the two features for which she received her first Oscar nominations, *Sadie Thompson* (1928) and *The Trespasser* (1929). Her company ran into massive fiscal problems, however, due to director Erich von Stroheim's extravagant *Queen Kelly* (1928).

Swanson retired from the screen in 1934 after having made an only moderately successful transition to sound films. She made numerous comebacks before her death in 1983, the most fruitful being her Oscar-nominated performance as a reclusive, aging silent screen star in Billy Wilder's *Sunset Boulevard* (1950). • *Teddy at the Throttle* 1916 (a); *Every Woman's Husband* 1918 (a); *Her Decision* 1918 (a); *The Secret Code* 1918 (a); *Shifting Sands* 1918 (a); *Society For Sale* 1918 (a); *Station Content* 1918 (a); *Wife or Country* 1918 (a); *You Can't Believe Everything* 1918 (a); *Don't Change Your Husband* 1919 (a); *For Better, For Worse* 1919 (a); *Male and Female* 1919 (a); *Something to Think About* 1920 (a); *Why Change Your Wife?* 1920 (a); *The Affairs of Anatol* 1921 (a); *Don't Tell Everything* 1921 (a); *The Great Moment* 1921 (a); *Under the Lash* 1921 (a); *Beyond the Rocks* 1922 (a); *Her Gilded Cage* 1922 (a); *Her Husband's Trademark* 1922 (a); *The Impossible Mrs. Bellew* 1922 (a); *Bluebeard's Eighth Wife* 1923 (a); *Hollywood* 1923 (a); *My American Wife* 1923 (a); *Prodigal Daughters* 1923 (a); *Zaza* 1923 (a); *Her Love Story* 1924 (a); *The Humming Bird* 1924 (a); *Manhandled* 1924 (a); *A Society Scandal* 1924 (a); *Wages of Virtue* 1924 (a); *The Coast of Folly* 1925 (a); *Madame Sans-Gêne* 1925 (a); *Stage Struck* 1925 (a); *Fine Manners* 1926 (a); *The Untamed Lady* 1926 (a); *The Love of Sunya* 1927 (a); *Queen Kelly* 1928 (a); *Sadie Thompson* 1928 (a) **(AANBA)**; *The Trespasser* 1929 (a) **(AANBA)**; *What a Widow!* 1930 (a); *Indiscreet* 1931 (a); *Tonight or Never* 1931 (a); *Perfect Understanding* 1933 (a); *Music in the Air* 1934 (a); *Father Takes a Wife* 1941 (a); *Sunset Boulevard* 1950 (a) **(AANBA)**; *Three For Bedroom C* 1952 (a); *Chaplinesque, My Life and Hard Times* 1972 (a); *Airport 1975* 1975 (a).

Swayze, Patrick • Actor; also dancer. • Born Houston, TX, August 18, 1954. *Educ.* Harkness Ballet School; Joffrey Ballet School; San Jacinto College, Houston. Athletic lead and classically trained dancer who performed on Broadway in *Grease* before making his film debut in 1979. After several films and TV work on "Renegades" and *North and South, Books I and II*, Swayze became widely known for his role as a swaggering, hotheaded dance champion in the 1987 box-office hit *Dirty Dancing*. • *Skatetown, USA* 1979 (a); *The Outsiders* 1983 (a); *Uncommon Valor* 1983 (a); *Grandview, U.S.A.* 1984 (a,chor); *Red Dawn* 1984 (a); *Youngblood* 1986 (a); *Dirty Dancing* 1987 (a,songs); *Steel Dawn* 1987 (a); *Tiger Warsaw* 1988 (a); *Next of Kin* 1989 (a); *Road House* 1989 (a,songs); *Ghost* 1990 (a).

Sweet, Blanche • Actress • Born Sarah Blanche Sweet, Chicago, IL, June 18, 1895; died September 6, 1986, New York, NY. Child stage actress who began her screen career at the age of 14 and appeared in movies consistently through the silent era. Sweet is best known for her roles in the Biograph films of D.W. Griffith, for whom she played a number of strong-willed heroines. Her two most famous Griffith films are *The Lonedale Operator* (1911), in which she picks up a gun to defend herself against thieves, and the epic Biblical spectacle, *Judith of Bethulia* (1913), in which she plays the title character who attempts to save her city by assassinating the conquerer Holofernes.

Sweet's first husband, Marshall Nielan, directed her in a number of films, including *Tess of the D'Urbervilles* (1924). Her second husband was her stage co-star, Raymond Hackett. • *The Lonedale Operator* 1911; *Judith of Bethulia* 1913; *The Avenging Conscience* 1914; *The Escape* 1914; *Home, Sweet Home* 1914; *The Captive* 1915; *The Case of Becky* 1915; *The Clue* 1915; *The Secret Orchard* 1915; *The Secret Sin* 1915; *Stolen Goods* 1915; *The Warrens of Virginia* 1915; *The Dupe* 1916; *The Sowers* 1916; *The Storm* 1916; *The Thousand Dollar Husband* 1916; *Unprotected* 1916; *The Evil Eye* 1917; *The Silent Partner* 1917; *The Hushed Hour* 1919; *The Unpardonable Sin* 1919; *A Woman of Pleasure* 1919; *The Deadlier Sex* 1920; *Fighting Cressy* 1920; *The Girl in the Web* 1920; *Help Wanted—Male* 1920; *Her Unwilling Husband* 1920; *Simple Souls* 1920; *That Girl Montana* 1921; *Quincy Adams Sawyer* 1922; *Anna Christie* 1923; *In the Palace of the King* 1923; *The Meanest Man in the World* 1923; *Souls For Sale* 1923; *Tess of the D'Urbervilles* 1924; *Those Who Dance* 1924; *His Supreme Moment* 1925; *The New Commandment* 1925; *The Sporting Venus* 1925; *Why Women Love* 1925; *Bluebeard's Seven Wives* 1926; *Diplomacy* 1926; *The Far Cry* 1926; *The Lady From Hell* 1926; *Singed* 1927; *Showgirl in Hollywood* 1930; *The Silver Horde* 1930; *The Woman Racket* 1930; *Before the Nickelodeon: The Early Cinema of Edwin S. Porter* 1982.

Swinton, Tilda • British actress • Born c. 1961. *Educ.* Cambridge (social science, political science). Delicately beautiful performer who has chosen to appear only in non-mainstream films, notably those of director Derek Jarman. Film theoretician Peter Wollen put Swinton's ethereal, somewhat androgynous presence to good use in his directorial debut, *Friendship's Death* (1987), in which she played an alien android shipwrecked on earth. • *Caravaggio* 1986 (a); *Aria* 1987 (a); *Friendship's Death* 1987 (a); *The Last of England* 1987 (a); *War Requiem* 1988 (a); *Melancholia* 1989 (m.perf); *Play Me Something* 1989 (a); *The Garden* 1990 (a).

Syberberg, Hans-Jürgen • Director; also screenwriter, producer. • Born Nossendorf, Germany, December 8, 1935. *Educ.* Munich University (German literature, art). Flamboyant, ingenious "chronicler of the German soul" who has made some of the most formally arresting films of the New German Cinema. Syberberg made numerous shorts and TV documentaries before directing his first narrative features, *Scarabea* (1968) and *San Domingo* (1970). Both films foreshadow, to a limited extent, the formal experimentation of his later, better known works, *Ludwig—Requiem for a Virgin King* (1972) and the seven-hour *Hitler, a Film From Germany* (1977). Low-budget, studio-bound features employing Brechtian theatrics, backdrops and rear-screen projection, these films juggle myth, history and psychology to evoke, respectively, the mad King of Bavaria and the mad Führer from Austria.

In 1982 Syberberg directed a much-praised, though highly idiosyncratic adaptation of Richard Wagner's *Parsifal*.

Constantly critical of his native film industry, Syberberg is regarded as a renegade in German film circles and has gained most of his critical (and financial) support from abroad, particularly from France. • *Scarabea* 1968 (d); *San Domingo* 1970 (d); *Ludwig—Requiem Für einen jungfraulichen König/Ludwig—Requiem For a Virgin King* 1972 (d,p); *Nach Meinem Letzten Umzug* 1972 (d,p,sc,ed,ph); *Karl May* 1974 (d,p,sc); *Winifred Wagner und die Geschichte des Hauses Wahnfried 1914-1975* 1975 (d,p); *Hitler, Ein film aus Deutschland/Hitler, a Film From Germany* 1977 (d,sc); *Parsifal* 1982 (d); *Die Nacht* 1985 (d,sc).

Sylbert, Richard • Production designer • Born Brooklyn, NY, 1928. Leading American art director who studied his craft under the legendary William Cameron Menzies and has worked on some of the best American movies of the past four decades. Sylbert began his career in TV and did his first significant feature work for Elia Kazan on films such as *Baby Doll* (1956), *A Face in the Crowd* (1957) and *Splendor in the Grass* (1961). Subsequent credits of note include *The Manchurian Candidate* (1962) for John Frankenheimer, *The Pawnbroker* (1965) for Sidney Lumet, *Who's Afraid of Virginia Woolf?* (1966) for Mike Nichols, *Chinatown* (1974) for Roman Polanski and, most recently, *Dick Tracy* (1990) for Warren Beatty. Divorced from costume designer-turned-producer Anthea Sylbert and twin brother of art director Paul Sylbert. • *Crowded Paradise* 1955 (art d); *Patterns* 1955 (art d); *Baby Doll* 1956 (art d); *Edge of the City* 1957 (art d); *A Face in the Crowd* 1957 (art d); *Wind Across the Everglades* 1958 (art d); *The Fugitive Kind* 1960 (art d); *Murder, Inc.* 1960 (art d); *Splendor in the Grass* 1961 (pd); *The Connection* 1962 (pd); *Long Day's Journey Into Night* 1962 (pd); *The Manchurian Candidate* 1962 (pd); *All the Way Home* 1963 (art d,pd); *Lilith* 1964 (pd); *How to Murder Your Wife* 1965 (pd); *The Pawnbroker* 1965 (art d); *Grand Prix* 1966 (pd); *Who's Afraid of Virginia Woolf?* 1966 (pd) **(AABAD)**; *The Graduate* 1967 (pd); *Rosemary's Baby* 1968 (pd); *The April Fools* 1969 (pd); *Catch-22* 1970 (pd); *Carnal Knowledge* 1971 (pd); *Fat City* 1972 (pd); *The Heartbreak Kid* 1972 (art d); *The Day of the Dolphin* 1973 (pd); *Chinatown* 1974 (pd) **(AANBAD)**; *The Fortune* 1975 (pd); *Shampoo* 1975 (pd) **(AANBAD)**; *Players* 1979 (pd); *Reds* 1981 (pd) **(AANBAD)**; *Frances* 1982 (pd); *Partners* 1982 (pd); *Breathless* 1983 (pd); *The Cotton Club* 1984 (pd) **(AANBAD)**; *Under the Cherry Moon* 1986 (pd); *Shoot to Kill* 1988 (pd); *Tequila Sunrise* 1988 (pd); *Bonfire of the Vanities* 1990 (pd); *Dick Tracy* 1990 (pd).

Szabó, István • Director, screenwriter • Born Budapest, Hungary, February 18, 1938. *Educ.* Academy for Theater and Film Art, Budapest (directing). The Central European experience, from the Austro-Hungarian Empire to the Warsaw Pact, is key to the content of István Szabó's films as well as their symbolic structure. There may even be an implied metaphor in a film like *Colonel Redl* (1985) between the complex social atmosphere and political issues in the old imperial dynasty and the modern people's republic.

In Szabó's films, the illusory hopes and dreadful realities of the past are always presented in the most immediate human terms, whether the fanciful imaginings of a son for a dead parent in *Father* (1966), the memory of Nazi deportations in *25 Fireman's Street* (1974), the failed 1956 rebellion of *Love Film* (1970) or the memory of betrayal by a lover to one's enemies in *Confidence* (1979).

Szabó's use of symbols and devices can be bewilderingly complex, as in *25 Fireman's Street*, or exceedingly droll, as in *Budapest Tales* (1977), where a tram is set working again by a group of displaced people at the war's close. In this allegory of socialist reconstruction, tyranny and deceit rival heroism and honesty in an effort to reach Budapest.

Szabó was catapulted to international success and fame in 1981, when *Mephisto* received an Academy Award. Starring an Austrian, Klaus Maria Brandauer, with Hungarian and Polish performers, *Mephisto* chronicled the moral quandry and professional success of an actor befriended by a high-ranking Nazi, modeled after Hermann Goering, whose wide powers extend to the Prussian State Theater. A disturbingly likable careerist, the actor ends his marriage to a leftist, yet can give work to a Jewish employee and insult a Nazi colleague. Still, he stages an aryan *Hamlet* and ends an affair with a dancer because of her one African parent. At the film's close, it is clear that despite his success and celebrity, he is no match for his ruthless patron.

For his next film, Szabó delved deeper into the past and the twilight of the Austro-Hungarian Empire. The figure in a celebrated pre-WWI espionage case and the subject of a novel and play, *Colonel Redl* may also be Szabo's metaphor for contemporary Communist relations. Again, Brandauer starred as the professional army officer who is caught up in the swirl of ethnic hatreds, class prejudices and dynastic intrigue. Internally driven by homosexual impulses and fears of his provincial origins, Redl is lured into the kind of counter-espionage trap he has used on others.

Szabó's most recent film, *Hanussen* (1988), completes a trilogy on similar themes, begun with *Mephisto* and *Colonel Redl*. Based on the experiences of a clairvoyant famous in pre-Nazi Berlin, the film attempted to portray its main character as a mixture of conscious showman and tormented mystic who ends up a political victim. Due to either inadequate scripting or acting, *Hanussen* did not enjoy the success of the director's earlier work. LR • *Almodozasok Kora/Age of Illusions* 1964 (d,sc); *Apa/Father* 1966 (d,sc); *Szerelmesfilm/Love Film* 1970 (d,sc); *Tuzolto Utca 25/25 Fireman's Street* 1974 (d,sc); *Budapest Tales* 1977 (d,sc); *Magyarok/The Hungarians* 1978 (a); *Bizalom/Confidence* 1979 (d,sc,story); *Fabian Balint Talalkozasa Istennel/Fabian Balint Meets God* 1980 (a); *Mephisto* 1981 (d,sc); *Redl Ezredes/Colonel Redl* 1985 (d,sc); *Hanussen* 1988 (d,sc); *Tusztortenet/Stand Off* 1989 (a); *Iskolakerulok/Truants* 1990 (a).

Szwarc, Jeannot • Director • Born Paris, France, November 21, 1937. French director who has worked mostly in the US, primarily on mainstream commercial features. • *Extreme Close-Up* 1973; *Bug* 1975; *Jaws 2* 1978; *Somewhere in Time* 1980; *Enigma* 1982; *Supergirl* 1984; *Santa Claus: The Movie* 1985.

Tacchella, Jean-Charles • Director; also screenwriter. • Born France, 1925. Worked as a journalist and TV writer before making two noted shorts in the early 1970s, and his debut feature in 1973. Tacchella's films are generally sentimental, understated character studies which on occasion, as with the internationally acclaimed *Cousin Cousine* (1975), rise above their superfical treatments. A smooth technician, Tacchella's camera work is fluid and precise. *Travelling avant* (1987)—the title roughly equivalent to the American film term "tracking shot"—is a semi-autobiographical paean to his youth as a cinema fanatic and ciné-club enthusiast in post-war Paris. • *La Loi c'est la loi* 1958 (sc,adapt); *The Last Winters (short)* 1971 (d); *Une Belle journée (short)* 1972 (d); *Voyage en grande Tartarie* 1973 (d,sc); *Cousin, Cousine* 1975 (d,sc) **(AANBSC)**; *Le Pays Bleu* 1977 (d,sc,dial); *Il y a longtemps que j'taime* 1979 (d,sc,dial); *Croque la Vie* 1981 (d,sc); *Escalier C* 1985 (d,sc); *Travelling avant* 1987 (d,sc); *Cousins* 1989 (from sc,from film *Cousin, Cousine*); *Dames Galantes* 1990 (d,sc).

Talbot, Daniel • Distributor; also author. • Editor of *Film: An Anthology* (1959), a seminal collection of essays by figures such as Eisenstein and Kracauer which helped form the new film culture of the 1960s in the US. Talbot was also founder of New Yorker Films, a distribution company active in importing the French New Wave in the 60s, the New German Cinema in the 70s, much Third World cinema (Sembene, Diegues, Gutierrez Alea) and works by various Japanese masters (Mizoguchi, Ozu, Oshima).

Talmadge, Norma • Actress • Born Niagara Falls, NY, May 26, 1897; died 1957, Las Vegas, NV. Elder sister of actresses Natalie (1898-1969) and Constance Talmadge (1900-73), and the first of them to enter films, in 1910. Norma was prolific but unexceptional at both Vitagraph and Triangle before marrying producer Joseph Schenck, who set up the Norma Talmadge Film Corporation and guided her to a career peak in the early 1920s with a series of weepy melodramas. They divorced in 1926, though Schenck continued to work with Talmadge, but she made a poor transition to sound films and retired in 1930. She later married and divorced singer-actor George Jessel.

Constance Talmadge developed into a superb player of sophisticated comedy, and rivaled Norma's fame. Also managed for a time by Schenck, she retired from film in 1929, and never took a stab at sound films. Natalie Talmadge was a competent but undistinguished performer who appeared in a number of films. She is best known for her troubled marriage to Buster Keaton, and the few movies she made with him, notably *Our Hospitality* (1923). • *The Battle Cry of Peace* 1915; *The Crown Prince's Double* 1915; *The Children in the House* 1916; *The Devil's Needle* 1916; *Fifty-Fifty* 1916; *Going Straight* 1916; *Martha's Vindication* 1916; *The Missing Links* 1916; *The Social Secretary* 1916; *The Law of Compensation* 1917; *The Moth* 1917; *Panthea* 1917; *Poppy* 1917; *The Secret of Storm Country* 1917; *By Right of Purchase* 1918; *De Luxe Annie* 1918; *Forbidden City* 1918; *The Ghosts of Yesterday* 1918; *The Heart of Wetona* 1918; *Her Only Way* 1918; *The Safety Curtain* 1918; *The Isle of Conquest* 1919; *The New Moon* 1919; *The Probation Wife* 1919; *The Way of a Woman* 1919; *The Branded Woman* 1920; *A Daughter of Two Worlds* 1920; *She Loves and Lies* 1920; *The Woman Gives* 1920; *Yes or No* 1920; *Love's Redemption* 1921; *The Passion Flower* 1921; *The Sign on the Door* 1921; *The Eternal Flame* 1922; *Smilin' Through* 1922; *Ashes of Vengeance* 1923; *The Song of Love* 1923; *The Voice From the Minaret* 1923; *Within the Law* 1923; *In Hollywood With Potash and Perlmutter* 1924; *The Only Woman* 1924; *Secrets* 1924; *Graustark* 1925; *The Lady* 1925; *Kiki* 1926; *Camille* 1927; *The Dove* 1927; *Show People* 1928; *The Woman Disputed* 1928; *New York Nights* 1929; *Du Barry, Woman of Passion* 1930.

Tan, Fred • Director; also screenwriter. • Born Taiwan, c. 1955; died March 7, 1990, Taipei, Taiwan. *Educ.* National Taiwan University (law); UCLA Film School. Chinese-born filmmaker who arrived in the US in 1975 and served as the Hollywood editor and film critic of *China Times* before making his directorial debut in 1986 with *Dark Night*. Tan received attention for his third feature, *Rouge of the North* (1988), centering on the life of an opium-addicted mother during the first half of the 20th century. His death at age 35 was due to acute hepatitis. • *Dark Night* 1986 (d,sc); *Yuan nu/Rouge of the North* 1988 (d,sc); *Split of the Spirit* 1989 (d,sc).

Tandy, Jessica • Actress • Born London, June 7, 1909. *Educ.* University of Western Ontario (law). Versatile, patrician stage performer, in occasional films. Tandy made her Hollywood debut, with husband Hume Cronyn, in Fred Zinnemann's first-rate thriller *The Seventh Cross* (1944), and gained prominence for her performance in the original 1947 production of Tennessee Williams's *A Streetcar Named Desire*. Since winning her second Tony in 1978 for the Pulitzer prize-winning play *The Gin Game*, Tandy has reignited her film career, costarring in *Cocoon* (1985), *Batteries Not Included* (1987), *Cocoon: The Return* (1988) and winning her first Oscar as the crusty Southern matron opposite Morgan Freeman in *Driving Miss Daisy* (1989). • *Murder in the Family* 1938; *The Seventh Cross* 1944; *The Valley of Decision* 1945; *Dragonwyck* 1946; *The Green Years* 1946; *Forever Amber* 1947; *A Woman's Vengeance* 1948; *The Desert Fox* 1951; *September Affair* 1951; *The Light in the Forest* 1958; *Adventures of a Young Man* 1962; *The Birds* 1963; *Butley* 1974; *Honky Tonk Freeway* 1981; *Best Friends* 1982; *Still of the Night* 1982; *The World According to Garp* 1982; *The Bostonians* 1984; *Cocoon* 1985; *Hitchcock, Il Brivido del Genio* 1985; *Batteries Not Included* 1987; *Cocoon: The Return* 1988; *The House on Carroll Street* 1988; *Driving Miss Daisy* 1989 **(AABA)**.

Tangerine Dream • German composers; also musicians. • Seminal synthesizer ensemble formed in psychedelic 1967, who achieved cult followings in Europe, Japan and the US with a succession of ethereal, electronically driven albums in the 1970s.

Their atmospheric conjurings made them ideal composers for film. Beginning with William Friedkin's *Sorcerer* (1977), Tangerine Dream has contributed either scores or songs to such notable features as Michael Mann's *Thief* (1981), Antonioni's *Identification of a Woman* (1982), Andrei Konchalovski's *Shy People* and Kathryn Bigelow's *Near Dark* (both 1987). • *Sorcerer* 1977 (m); *Kneuss* 1978 (m); *Take It to the Limit* 1979 (m); *Thief* 1981 (m); *Identificazione di una donna/Identification of a Woman* 1982 (song); *Kamikaze '89* 1982 (m); *The Soldier* 1982 (song); *Spasms* 1982 (songs); *The Keep* 1983 (m); *Risky Business* 1983 (m,m.perf); *Wavelength* 1983 (m); *Firestarter* 1984 (m,m.perf); *Flashpoint* 1984 (m); *Heartbreakers* 1984 (m); *Legend* 1985 (m,song); *Rote Hitze* 1985 (m); *Vision Quest* 1985 (m,m.perf); *Zoning* 1986 (m); *Near Dark* 1987 (m,m.perf); *Shy People* 1987 (m,m.perf,songs); *Three O'Clock High* 1987 (m,m.perf); *Miracle Mile* 1988 (m,m.perf); *Red Nights* 1988 (m); *Catch Me If You Can* 1989 (m,m.perf); *City of Shadows* 1989 (m,song); *The Man Inside* 1990 (m).

Tanner, Alain • Director; also screenwriter. • Born Geneva, Switzerland, December 6, 1929. *Educ.* Calvin College (economics). Alain Tanner, with his portraits of life among Geneva's marginal and harmless rebels, can easily be considered the director who introduced American audiences to the fact that not only bankers and diplomats live in Geneva. Influenced by his involvement with the British Free Cinema movement in London in the early 1960s and with the French New Wave during his Paris years, Tanner's films, often co-scripted with the English art critic John Berger, combine a cinéma-vérité documentary style and with fable-like story telling. A gentle, idiosyncratic anarchy, tinged with irony, suffuses both *La Salamandre* and *Jonah Who Will Be 25 in the Year 2000*. His later films, however, have been darker, and in the case of *No Man's Land*, the whimsical optimism of the late 1970s has been totally reversed. • *La Salamandre* 1971 (d,sc); *Le Retour d'Afrique* 1972 (d,p,sc); *Le Milieu du Monde* 1974 (d,sc,adapt,dial); *Jonas qui aura 25 ans en l'an 2000/Jonah Who Will Be 25 in the Year 2000* 1976 (d,sc,adapt,dial); *Messidor* 1978 (d,sc); *Les Années lumières* 1981 (d,sc); *Dans la ville blanche* 1982 (d,exec.p,p,sc,sound); *No Man's Land* 1985 (d,p,sc); *François Simon—La Prèsence* 1986 (a); *Une Flamme dans mon coeur* 1987 (d,sc); *La Vallée fantôme* 1987 (d,exec.p,sc); *La Femme de Rose Hill* 1989 (d,p,sc); *Les Anges* 1990 (assoc.p).

Taradash, Daniel • Screenwriter; also director. • Born Louisville, KY, January 29, 1913. *Educ.* Harvard; Harvard Law School. Smart, capable scenarist who left a career in law after winning a playwrighting contest. Often worked in collaboration and particularly skilled with adaptations, such as *From Here to Eter-*

nity (for which he won an Academy Award in 1953), *Picnic* (1956) and *Bell, Book and Candle* (1958). • *For Love or Money* 1939 (story); *Golden Boy* 1939 (sc); *A Little Bit of Heaven* 1940 (sc); *The Noose Hangs High* 1948 (story); *Knock on Any Door* 1949 (sc); *Don't Bother to Knock* 1952 (sc); *Rancho Notorious* 1952 (sc); *From Here to Eternity* 1953 (sc) (**AABSC**); *Desiree* 1954 (sc); *Picnic* 1956 (sc); *Storm Center* 1956 (d,sc,story); *Bell, Book and Candle* 1958 (sc); *Morituri* 1965 (sc); *Hawaii* 1966 (sc); *Castle Keep* 1969 (sc); *Doctors' Wives* 1970 (sc); *The Other Side of Midnight* 1977 (sc).

Tarkovsky, Andrei • *aka* Andrei Tarkovski • Director; also screenwriter. • Born Laovrazhe, Ivanova, USSR, April 4, 1932; died December 29, 1986, Paris. *Educ.* Soviet School of Music; Institute of Oriental Languages (Arabic); VGIK, Moscow. Distinguished Soviet director whose austerely poetic, deeply personal films made him one of the most treasured artists of his generation.

Tarkovsky followed his prize-winning short diploma piece, *The Steamroller and the Violin* (1960), with a lyrical feature debut *My Name is Ivan/Ivan's Childhood* (1962). The film portrays a young boy's espionage activities with partisans during WWII and was awarded top honors at the Venice Film Festival. Tarkovsky followed it with the epic, allegorical *Andrei Roublev* (1966).

Over three years in the making, *Andrei Roublev* follows the life of a 15th-century icon painter as he loses faith in society, God and art, finally achieving spiritual revitalization in the famous, concluding bell-making scene. Shelved for several years for its references to the plight of the contemporary Soviet artist, the film was released to wide acclaim in the West in 1969. Like most of Tarkovsky's work, it is a slow-moving, sumptuously textured canvas with a richly emotional climax.

Most of Tarkovsky's subsequent films deal in some degree with the otherworldly: in *Solaris* (1972), a space-traveler's fantasies are conjured into reality; *Stalker* (1979) takes place in "the zone," a mysterious, forbidden wasteland; and *The Sacrifice* (1986) unfolds in the final hours before a nuclear armageddon. *The Mirror* (1974), an intensely personal, multi-layered aural and visual poem, recalls an artist's youth in the Soviet Union during WWII. Tarkovsky's real-life mother plays the mother of the artist and his father, the esteemed poet Arseniy Tarkovsky, reads his own works on the soundtrack.

Tarkovsky began working outside the USSR in the early 1980s, making *Nostalgia* (which he himself described as "tedious") in Italy in 1983. He then employed several members of Ingmar Bergman's filmmaking team, including actor Erland Josephson and cinematographer Sven Nykvist, to make *The Sacrifice* in Sweden. Josephson plays a celebrated, retired artist/intellectual who can only avert a worldwide holocaust by making a supreme personal sacrifice. Visually sumptuous and extremely slow-paced (the opening shot is nearly ten minutes long), the film is a supreme summation of what Tarkovsky considered his most crucial concern: "the absence in our culture of room for spiritual existence." *The Sacrifice* won a Special Jury Prize at Cannes in the same year that Tarkovsky died of lung cancer in Paris at age 54. SKK • *The Steamroller and the Violin* 1960 (d,sc); *Ivanovo detstvo/Ivan's Childhood/My Name Is Ivan* 1962 (d); *Andrei Rublyov/Andrei Roublev* 1966 (d,sc); *Solaris* 1972 (d,sc); *The Mirror* 1974 (d,sc); *Stalker* 1979 (d,pd); *Nostalghia/Nostalgia* 1983 (d,sc); *Andrei Tarkovsky* 1984 (a); *De Weg Naar Bresson* 1984 (a); *Offret-Sacrificatio/The Sacrifice* 1986 (d,sc,ed); *Directed By Andrei Tarkovsky* 1988 (a); *Gruppa Tovariscej (short)* 1988 (a).

Tashlin, Frank • Director, screenwriter • Born Weehawken, NJ, February 19, 1913; died May 5, 1972. Former cartoonist who entered features as a comedy writer (*The Paleface* 1948, etc.) and turned to directing with *The First Time* (1952), bringing his exuberant, exhilarating comic-strip style with him. Besides his eight films with the appropriately cast Jerry Lewis, Tashlin's name is chiefly connected with Jayne Mansfield, whose only notable films—*The Girl Can't Help It* (1956) and the brilliant satire of the advertising business, *Will Success Spoil Rock Hunter?* (1957)—he engineered.

Tashlin tried to repeat similar formulas with Anita Ekberg and Doris Day, but their personae did not lend themselves to parody as readily as Mansfield's. He was praised for his inventiveness by several French critics, particularly Godard and Truffaut. • *Delightfully Dangerous* 1945 (story); *Variety Girl* 1947 (sc,story); *The Fuller Brush Man* 1948 (sc); *One Touch of Venus* 1948 (sc); *The Paleface* 1948 (sc); *Love Happy* 1949 (sc); *Miss Grant Takes Richmond* 1949 (sc); *The Fuller Brush Girl* 1950 (sc); *The Good Humor Man* 1950 (sc); *Kill the Umpire* 1950 (sc,story); *The First Time* 1952 (d,sc); *Son of Paleface* 1952 (d,sc); *Marry Me Again* 1954 (d,sc); *Susan Slept Here* 1954 (d,sc); *Artists and Models* 1955 (d,sc); *The Lieutenant Wore Skirts* 1955 (d,sc); *The Scarlet Hour* 1955 (sc,from story "The Kiss Off"); *The Girl Can't Help It* 1956 (d,p,sc); *Hollywood or Bust* 1956 (d); *Will Success Spoil Rock Hunter?* 1957 (d,p,sc,story); *The Geisha Boy* 1958 (d,sc); *Rock-a-Bye Baby* 1958 (d,sc); *Say One For Me* 1959 (d,p); *Cinderfella* 1960 (d,sc); *Bachelor Flat* 1961 (d,sc); *It's Only Money* 1962 (d); *The Man From the Diner's Club* 1963 (d); *Who's Minding the Store?* 1963 (d,sc); *The Disorderly Orderly* 1964 (d,sc); *The Alphabet Murders* 1966 (d); *The Glass Bottom Boat* 1966 (d); *Caprice* 1967 (d,sc); *The Private Navy of Sgt. O'Farrell* 1968 (d,sc); *The Shakiest Gun in the West* 1968 (from story "The Paleface").

Tati, Jacques • *aka* Jacques Tatischeff • Director, actor, screenwriter • Born Le Pecq, France, October 9, 1908; died November 5, 1982. • Jacques Tati is a chessmaster of modern film comedy, a creator of complex comic structures in which gag constructions and audience expectations become pawns on his cinematic board. The recurring figure in these games is Monsieur Hulot (played by the director), a blank-faced comic cypher garbed in a crumbled raincoat and ill-fitting trousers, an ever-present pipe muffling any words he may say, an umbrella clutched in indecisive hands. His determinedly irresolute stride across Tati's expansive canvases is the unlikely spark that sets the comic machinery afire. On the basis of a mere four features (*Mr. Hulot's Holiday* 1953; *Mon Oncle* 1958; *Playtime* 1967; and *Traffic* 1971) over a 20-year period, Tati managed to reshape slapstick comedy, turning it into an intellectual parlor game.

Tati began performing in French music halls and cafes as a pantomimist and impersonator. In 1931, he filmed a comedy short, *Oscar, Champion de Tennis*, but it was never completed. Following were a number of short films which anticipated his later features in their use of natural and mechanical sounds—*On Demande une Brute* (1934), *Gai Dimanche* (1935), and *Soigne ton Gauche* (1936). After WWII, Tati appeared in the features *Sylvie et le Fantôme* (1945) and *Le Diable au Corps* (1946). In his short film, *L'Ecole de Facteurs* (1947), Tati created the character of François the postman, a character he would play himself in his first self-directed feature, *Jour de Fête* (1948). *Jour* used the riffing gag structure Tati would explore more fully in his later features, plus creative sound as a source for gags.

Unhappy with the François character, Tati sought a persona with a more universal appeal. With Monsieur Hulot, Tati found his cosmic archetype: a zero who creates comic anarchy in his wake. In *Mr.Hulot's Holiday*, Tati applies Hulot to the gag structures of *Jour de Fête. Mon Oncle* deals with the tension between Hulot's old world sensibilities and the new world of modern mechanization and consumerism. *Playtime*, Tati's masterpiece, released in 70mm and stereophonic sound, examines the disappearance of humanity within the maze-like confines of post-industrial society. *Trafic* portrays the anthropomorphism of automobiles and the mechanization of human beings.

Tati's cold, crisp examinations are a result of his re-inventing film comedy structures. Hulot has no purpose except to ignite the gag machinery. He is never the center of a gag sequence and frequently disappears from the gag situation once the perpetual motion machine takes hold. (In one sequence in *Playtime*, Hulot appears merely as a reflection in a glass window.) Once the gag machinery begins, Tati subverts the punchline by either delaying it or ignoring it altogether. The result creates a tension for audience expectations: will the punchline continue to be prolonged or simply demolished? Tati does not allow his audience to identify with the main character in the scene; as a result, the subject of the shot becomes everything that appears within the frame. A Tati film is characterized by a tangled texture (especially on his densely packed soundtracks) that requires many viewings to unravel.

This complexity was Tati's commercial undoing; because of the prolonged preparations required to plan his films, Tati lost his audience. The nine-year gap between *Mon Oncle* and *Playtime* crippled the momentum of his career, and after the extravagances of *Playtime*, Tati never recovered financially. When *Trafic* was released, it seemed a throwback to his films before *Playtime* and was a financial failure. In 1974, Tati released his final film, *Parade*, a low-budget celebration of pantomime recalling his shorts from the thirties.

Although Tati influenced filmmakers as diverse as Jerry Lewis and Robert Altman, his career seems in a way to be both the beginning and the end of a comic tradition. Nevertheless, Tati's structural experiments did breathe life for a time into a moribund form. PB • *On Demande une Brute (short)* 1934 (ad(,sc); *Gai Dimanche (short)* 1935 (a,d,sc); *Soigne ton Gauche (short)* 1936 (a,d,sc); *Sylvie et le Fantôme* 1945 (a); *Le Diable au Corps* 1946 (a); *L'Ecole de Facteurs (short)* 1947 (a,d,sc); *Jour de Fête* 1949 (a,d,sc); *Les Vacances de Monsieur Hulot/Mr. Hulot's Holiday* 1953 (a,d,sc,story,adapt) **(AANBSC)**; *Mon Oncle* 1958 (a,d,sc); *Playtime* 1967 (a,d,sc); *Trafic* 1971 (a,d,sc); *Parade* 1974 (a,d,sc).

Taurog, Norman • Director; also actor. • Born Chicago, IL, February 23, 1899; died April 7, 1981, Palm Desert, CA. Archetypal "contract" studio director who entered films as an actor, began making comedy shorts, and moved up to features in the late 1920's. Working most often for MGM and Paramount, Taurog specialized in comedies and other light entertainments, though he made several dramas as well, such as *The Beginning or the End* (1946), about the birth of the atomic bomb. By the mid-50s he was directing formula vehicles for box-office stars such as Dean Martin and Jerry Lewis and Elvis Presley. • *The Rent Collector (short)* 1921; *The Farmer's Daughter* 1928; *The Ghetto* 1928; *Lucky Boy* 1929; *Follow the Leader* 1930; *Hot Curves* 1930; *Sunny Skies* 1930; *Troopers Three* 1930; *Finn and Hattie* 1931; *Huckleberry Finn* 1931; *Newly Rich* 1931; *Skippy* 1931 **(AABD)**; *Sooky* 1931; *Hold 'Em Jail* 1932; *If I Had a Million* 1932; *The Phantom President* 1932; *A Bedtime Story* 1933; *The Way to Love* 1933; *College Rhythm* 1934; *Mrs. Wiggs of the Cabbage Patch* 1934; *We're Not Dressing* 1934; *The Big Broadcast of 1936* 1935; *Reunion* 1936; *Rhythm on the Range* 1936; *Strike Me Pink* 1936; *Fifty Roads to Town* 1937; *You Can't Have Everything* 1937; *The Adventures of Tom Sawyer* 1938; *Boys Town* 1938 **(AANBD)**; *The Girl Downstairs* 1938; *Mad About Music* 1938; *Lucky Night* 1939; *Broadway Melody of 1940* 1940; *Little Nellie Kelly* 1940; *Young Tom Edison* 1940; *Design For Scandal* 1941; *Men of Boys Town* 1941; *Are Husbands Necessary?* 1942; *A Yank at Eton* 1942; *Girl Crazy* 1943; *Presenting Lily Mars* 1943; *The Beginning or the End* 1946; *The Hoodlum Saint* 1946; *Big City* 1948; *The Bride Goes Wild* 1948; *Words and Music* 1948; *That Midnight Kiss* 1949; *Mrs. O'Malley and Mr. Malone* 1950; *Please Believe Me* 1950; *The Toast of New Orleans* 1950; *Rich, Young and Pretty* 1951; *Jumping Jacks* 1952; *Room For One More* 1952; *The Stooge* 1952; *The Caddy* 1953; *The Stars Are Singing* 1953; *Living It Up* 1954; *You're Never Too Young* 1955; *The Birds and the Bees* 1956; *Bundle of Joy* 1956; *Pardners* 1956; *The Fuzzy Pink Nightgown* 1957; *Onionhead* 1958; *Don't Give Up the Ship* 1959; *G.I. Blues* 1960; *Visit to a Small Planet* 1960; *All Hands on Deck* 1961; *Blue Hawaii* 1961; *Girls! Girls! Girls!* 1962; *It Happened at the World's Fair* 1963; *Palm Springs Weekend* 1963; *Dr. Goldfoot and the Bikini Machine* 1965; *Sergeant Deadhead* 1965; *Tickle Me* 1965; *Spinout* 1966; *Double Trouble* 1967; *Live a Little, Love a Little* 1968; *Speedway* 1968.

Tavernier, Bertrand • Director; also critic. • Born Lyons, France, April 25, 1941. *Educ.* Sorbonne, Paris. Tavernier quit law school to write film criticism for *Cahiers du Cinéma* and other major journals, worked as an assistant director and publicist (e.g., for Jean-Pierre Melville) and authored a couple of books on American cinema before making his first feature, *L'Horloge de St. Paul* (1973). Adapted from a Georges Siménon novel (and transposed from the US to Tavernier's hometown), it is an intelligent, studied debut with finely tuned performances, which won a Special Jury Prize at the 1974 Berlin Film Festival, the Prix Louis Delluc in France, and established Tavernier's reputation. His subsequent works have been equally well-crafted, displaying an affecting confluence of French and American cinematic styles. Tavernier's other noted films include *Coup de Torchon* (1981), a bold adaptation of Jim Thompson's *Pop. 1280*, set not in the US South, but in French North Africa, and *'Round Midnight* (1986), a smooth, pseudo-biopic of an American jazz musician in 1950s Paris. Separated from screenwriter Colo Tavernier O'Hagan, who has worked on several of his films, and father of actor Nils Tavernier, who appeared in, among others, *Beatrice* (1987). • *Les Baisers* 1963 (d); *Le Doulos* 1963 (publicist); *L'Horloger de St. Paul* 1973 (d,sc); *Que la fête commence.../Let Joy Reign Supreme* 1974 (d,sc); *Le Juge et l'assassin* 1976 (d,sc); *La Question* 1976 (p); *Des Enfants Gatés* 1977 (d,sc,dial); *La Mort en Direct* 1979 (d,p,sc); *Une Semaine de vacances* 1980 (d,p,sc); *Coup de Torchon/Clean Slate* 1981 (d,sc,song); *Mississippi Blues* 1983 (d,p); *La Trace* 1983 (p,sc); *Un Dimanche à la Campagne/A Sunday in the Country* 1984 (d,sc); *Autour de Minuit/'Round Midnight* 1986 (d,sc); *La Passion Béatrice/Beatrice* 1986 (d); *Les Mois d'avril sont meurtriers* 1987 (sc); *Hotel Terminus: Klaus Barbie, His Life and Times* 1988 (a); *La Vie et rien d'autre* 1989 (d,sc); *Daddy Nostalgie* 1990 (d).

Tavernier O'Hagan, Colo • *aka* Colo Tavernier • Screenwriter • Born Colo O'Hagan, England. Particularly adept at literary adaptations (she won a César for her work on husband Bertrand Tavernier's *Sunday in the Country* 1984) and period dramas such as Claude Chabrol's *Story of Women* (1988). O'Hagan married Tavernier in 1965 but did not begin her working relationship with him until the couple separated in 1980. Son Nils Tavernier is an actor. • *Une Semaine de vacances* 1980 (sc); *Un Dimanche à la Campagne/A Sunday in the Country* 1984 (sc); *Autour de Minuit/'Round Midnight* 1986 (French translation); *La Passion Beatrice/Beatrice* 1986 (sc); *Une Affaire de femmes/Story of Women* 1988 (sc); *Comedie d'ete* 1989 (sc); *Daddy Nostalgie* 1990 (sc,dial).

Taviani, Paolo and Vittorio • Directors; also screenwriters • Born San Miniato, Pisa, Italy, November 8, 1931 (Paolo) and September 20, 1929 (Vittorio). *Educ.* University of Pisa (Paolo: liberal arts; Vittorio: law). During their student days, Paolo and Vittorio started shooting documentary films. Their first completed short, *San Miniato, July 1944* (1954), a collaboration with Cesare Zavattini, concerned a Nazi massacre in their hometown. Working as a team from the start, their early films were influenced by and often made with Valentino Orsini, a resistance fighter. A turning point in their work, as well as Italian political cinema in general, was *Subversives* (1967), which combined documentary footage of a prominent Communist leader's funeral and the story of four people for whom this death raises numerous questions about their political future.

The Tavianis work together on the writing, design, and direction of all their feature films. Their primary inspiration was Roberto Rossellini's *Paisan* (1946), a film which treated contemporaneous life honestly and suggested means for its improvement. Although their first films used non-professional actors, natural lighting, location shooting, ambient sound and working-class situations, the Tavianis have altered this approach in search of a style adequate to their own times. Using ambiguity of character and motivation to suggest the impossibility of portraying historical truth, they present subjective views of history based on objective fact. They have rejected the neorealist aesthetic in favor of a more metaphoric film language.

Perhaps because their childhoods were dominated by plays and concerts rather than movies, the Tavianis are strongly influenced by the theater. Their tendency to emphasize invention and staging calls narrative perspective into question and proclaims their work as interpretations of history rather than documentaries. *The Night of San Lorenzo* (1981), a feature-length remake of *San Miniato, July 1944*, exemplifies this quality and its effect. A flat, painted mural of a window opening out to a starry night is accompanied by a poetic voice-over describing the film as a wish-fulfillment fantasy. A child narrator, whose memories are corrected by adults, suggests the collective nature of memory and the capriciousness of individual recollection. Similarly, *Kaos* (1984), an adaptation of four Pirandello stories, each intended to be shown separately on television, describes how an uncomprehended childhood memory blossoms forth in its full significance only as it is told and envisioned on film.

Music, and sound in general, are very important to the Tavianis' work. Both men are musicians who use their knowledge and appreciation of folk music and instruments, oratorio and classical presentation and the modern symphony of voices, radios and record players to reinforce their themes. In *Under the Sign of Scorpio* (1969), the camera's rhythm is determined by the music's pace to enforce the balletic, antinaturalistic structure of the film.

Padre Padrone (1977), the only film to win both the Grand Prix and the Critics International Prize at Cannes, is the Tavianis' best known work. Using a highly mobile camera, with elaborate aerial and pull-back shots, they scrutinize the relationship of a father and son who both suffer under a system of cruel domination. The film alternates extreme long shots of field, roads, or church interiors with close-ups in order to isolate characters in their determinant time and place as a means of explaining motivation. Within this dialectic of peasant and modern laws, silence and communication, father and child, the son learns to save himself through the telling of his story.

The theme of resistance and communal action in an ongoing, revolutionary effort is evident in all of the Tavianis' films. They often use an allegorical structure to discuss current events and relate them to the past, referring to anarchists of the 1870s in *Saint Michael Had a Rooster* (1971) and to revolutionaries of 1816 in *Allonsanfan* (1975). They question the possibility of a "good" revolution, since upheaval is inevitably marked by bloodshed, injustice and innocent victims. In the Tavianis' view of history, one revolution replaces another in an everlasting struggle between the collective and the individual.

The Night of San Lorenzo best exemplifies the Tavianis' belief in history as a continual utopian rebirth based on military liberation and domestic reform. A deft combining of emotional involvement with characters who reflect the Tavianis' own lives and an ironic distancing through the use of slapstick, the film narrates the past through a variety of perspectives to illuminate the present. This film and *Kaos* stress how Italian folk myth and popular religion define people's lives and their place in history. The Tavianis believe that retelling history in a style appropriate to current needs, whether within a community or in a film, acts as an incantation to prevent the repetition of history's worst aspects. RJB • *I Fuorilegge del matrimonio* 1963 (d); *Sovversivi/Subversives* 1967 (d); *Sotto il Segno dello scorpione/Under the Sign of Scorpio* 1969 (sc,d); *San Michele Aveva un Gallo/Saint Michael Had a Rooster* 1971 (d,sc); *Allonsanfan* 1975 (d,sc); *Padre Padrone* 1977 (d,sc,dial); *Il Prato* 1979 (d,sc); *La Notte di San Lorenzo/The Night of San Lorenzo* 1981 (d,sc); *Kaos* 1984 (d,sc); *Good Morning Babylon* 1986 (d,sc,story); *Il Sole anche di notte* 1990 (d,sc).

Tavoularis, Dean • Production designer • Born Lowell, MA, 1932. Established himself on several noted films (e.g., *Bonnie and Clyde* 1967, *Zabriskie Point* 1970) before designing *The Godfather* (1972), the first of many impeccable productions for Francis Ford Coppola (including *The Conversation, Apocalype Now* and *Tucker: The Man and His Dream*). Brother Alex Tavoularis is also an art director. Married to actress Aurore Clément. • *Bonnie and Clyde* 1967 (art d); *Candy* 1968 (art d); *Little Big Man* 1970 (pd); *Zabriskie Point* 1970 (pd); *The Godfather* 1972 (pd); *The Conversation* 1974 (pd); *The Godfather, Part II* 1974 (pd) **(AABAD)**; *Farewell, My Lovely* 1975 (pd); *The Brink's Job* 1978 (art d) **(AANBAD)**; *Apocalypse Now* 1979 (pd) **(AANBAD)**; *The Escape Artist* 1982 (pd); *Hammett* 1982 (pd); *One From the Heart* 1982 (pd); *The Outsiders* 1983 (pd,sets); *Rumble Fish* 1983 (pd,title design); *Peggy Sue Got Married* 1986 (pd); *Gardens of Stone* 1987 (pd); *Heat* 1987 (visual consultant); *Un Homme amoureux* 1987 (pd); *Tucker: The Man and His Dream* 1988 (pd) **(AANBAD)**; *New York Stories* 1989 (pd "Life Without Zoe"); *The Godfather Part III* 1990 (pd).

Taylor, Elizabeth • Actress • Born London, February 27, 1932. Strikingly beautiful, quintessential movie star of the 1950s and 60s whose on-screen talent has often been overshadowed by her much-publicized personal life. Within three years after arriving in the US, Taylor was cast as the young heroine opposite Roddy McDowall in *Lassie Come Home* (1943), which led to a long-term contract with MGM. Before reaching her late teens, she had physically outgrown juvenile parts and was playing young adults. *Father of the Bride* (1950) and the much-lauded *A Place in the Sun* (1951) firmly established her as a major adult star and over the next decade she developed into one of the most glamorous and highly paid movie performers in the world.

Married numerous times (including twice to her most prominent leading man, Richard Burton, and once each to crooner Eddie Fisher, actor Michael Wilding and producer Michael Todd), Taylor's off-screen persona undoubtably contributed to her popularity, but somewhat limited her critical reputation. She was nominated three times before winning the first of her two Oscars, for *Butterfield 8* (1960), as a disillusioned, high-class call girl.

Taylor has been particularly adept throughout her career at playing somewhat neurotic beauties and in several ideal roles (*Cat on a Hot Tin Roof* 1958, *Who's Afraid of Virginia Woolf?* 1966) has given full expression to her immense, untrained and unbridled talent. • *There's One Born Every Minute* 1942 (a); *Lassie Come Home* 1943 (a); *Jane Eyre* 1944 (a); *National Velvet* 1944 (a); *Courage of Lassie* 1946 (a); *Cynthia* 1947 (a); *Life With Father* 1947 (a); *A Date With Judy* 1948 (a); *Julia Misbehaves* 1948 (a); *Conspirator* 1949 (a); *Little Women* 1949 (a); *The Big Hangover* 1950 (a); *Father of the Bride* 1950 (a); *Father's Little Dividend* 1951 (a); *A Place in the Sun* 1951 (a); *Ivanhoe* 1952 (a); *Love Is Better Than Ever* 1952 (a); *The Girl Who Had Everything* 1953 (a); *Beau Brummell* 1954 (a); *Elephant Walk* 1954 (a); *The Last Time I Saw Paris* 1954 (a); *Rhapsody* 1954 (a); *Giant* 1956 (a); *Raintree County* 1957 (a) **(AANBA)**; *Cat on a Hot Tin Roof* 1958 (a) **(AANBA)**; *Suddenly, Last Summer* 1959 (a) **(AANBA)**; *Butterfield 8* 1960 (a) **(AABA)**; *Cleopatra* 1963 (a); *The V.I.P.s* 1963 (a); *The Sandpiper* 1965 (a); *Who's Afraid of Virginia Woolf?* 1966 (a) **(AABA)**; *The Comedians in Africa (short)* 1967 (a);

The Comedians 1967 (a); *Doctor Faustus* 1967 (a); *Reflections in a Golden Eye* 1967 (a); *The Taming of the Shrew* 1967 (a,p); *Boom!* 1968 (a); *Secret Ceremony* 1968 (a); *The Only Game in Town* 1970 (a); *Under Milk Wood* 1971 (a); *Hammersmith Is Out* 1972 (a); *X Y & Zee* 1972 (a); *Ash Wednesday* 1973 (a); *Night Watch* 1973 (a); *Identikit* 1974 (a); *That's Entertainment!* 1974 (a); *The Blue Bird* 1976 (a); *It's Showtime* 1976 (a); *A Little Night Music* 1977 (a); *Winter Kills* 1979 (a); *The Mirror Crack'd* 1980 (a); *Genocide* 1981 (a); *George Stevens: A Filmmaker's Journey* 1985 (a); *Il Giovane Toscanini/Young Toscanini* 1988 (a).

Taylor, Gil • Director of photography • Born Gilbert Taylor, Bushey Heath, England, April 12, 1914. Entered films at age 15, and by the early 1960s—following a succession of J. Lee Thompson movies—developed into a leading cinematographer, capable in black-and-white and color. After his outstanding work on Stanley Kubrick's *Dr. Strangelove* (1964), Richard Lester's *A Hard Day's Night* (1964)—both employing a wide variety of photographic modes—and his three exceptional collaborations with Polanski (*Repulsion* 1965, *Cul-de-Sac* 1966, *Macbeth* 1971), Taylor began working consistently in Hollywood. • *Seven Days to Noon* 1950 (ph); *Alive and Kicking* 1959 (ph); *The Full Treatment* 1961 (ph); *The Rebel* 1961 (ph); *Dr. Strangelove; or, How I Learned to Stop Worrying and Love the Bomb* 1964 (ph); *A Hard Day's Night* 1964 (ph); *Hide and Seek* 1964 (ph); *The Bedford Incident* 1965 (ph); *Repulsion* 1965 (ph); *Cul-de-Sac* 1966 (ph); *Blood Fiend* 1967 (ph); *Before Winter Comes* 1968 (ph); *A Nice Girl Like Me* 1969 (ph); *Quackser Fortune Has a Cousin in the Bronx* 1970 (ph); *Macbeth* 1971 (ph); *Frenzy* 1972 (ph); *Undercovers Hero* 1975 (ph); *The Omen* 1976 (ph); *Star Wars* 1977 (ph); *Damien: Omen II* 1978 (ph— Israel); *Dracula* 1979 (ph); *Escape to Athena* 1979 (ph); *Meetings With Remarkable Men* 1979 (ph); *Flash Gordon* 1980 (ph); *Green Ice* 1981 (ph); *Venom* 1981 (ph); *Losin' It* 1983 (ph); *Lassiter* 1984 (ph); *Voyage of the Rock Aliens* 1985 (ph); *The Bedroom Window* 1987 (ph).

Taylor, John Russell • Critic • Born Dover, England, 1935. Prolific film critic during the 1960s and author of *Cinema Eye, Cinema Ear* (1964), a seminal work in the introduction of the new film culture that emerged in the 60s. Also a noted theater critic, Taylor's other film-related works include *Directors and Directions: Cinema for the Seventies* (1975) and *Strangers in Paradise: Hollywood Emigrés, 1935-1950* (1983).

Taylor, Lili • Actress • Born Glencoe, IL, c. 1967. *Educ.* Goodman Theatre School of DePaul University, Chicago. Gifted, compact performer who splits her time among theater, TV and film. Taylor gained well-deserved praise and wide recognition as the feisty bride-to-be in *Mystic Pizza* (1988) and the musically inclined, emotionally scarred lover in *Say Anything* (1989). • *Mystic Pizza* 1988; *She's Having a Baby* 1988; *Born on the Fourth of July* 1989; *Say Anything* 1989; *Bright Angel* 1990; *Dogfight* 1991.

Taylor, Robert • Actor • Born Spangler Arlington Brugh, Filley, NE, August 5, 1911; died 1969. *Educ.* Doane College, NE (music); Pomona College, CA (medicine). Dependable, clean-cut star who was signed by MGM while still in school and spent most of his subsequent career with the company. Boyishly handsome, with a "perfect profile," Taylor highlighted many a light romance and was immensely popular for years after starring in *Magnificent Obsession* (1935). He eventually grew out of his pretty-boy good looks and made up for any lack of talent with a much-noted professionalism in a succession of epics (*Ivanhoe* 1952, *Knights of the Round Table 1953*) and westerns (*The Hangman 1959, Return of the Gunfighter 1966*) that punctuated his mature screen work. Married to Barbara Stanwyck from 1939 to 1951. • *Handy Andy* 1934 (a); *There's Always Tomorrow* 1934 (a); *A Wicked Woman* 1934 (a); *Magnificent Obsession* 1935 (a); *Only Eight Hours* 1935 (a); *Times Square Lady* 1935 (a); *West Point of the Air* 1935 (a); *Broadway Melody of 1936* 1936 (a); *The Gorgeous Hussy* 1936 (a); *His Brother's Wife* 1936 (a); *Private Number* 1936 (a); *Small Town Girl* 1936 (a); *Camille* 1937 (a); *Personal Property* 1937 (a); *This Is My Affair* 1937 (a); *Broadway Melody of 1938* 1938 (a); *The Crowd Roars* 1938 (a); *Three Comrades* 1938 (a); *A Yank at Oxford* 1938 (a); *Lady of the Tropics* 1939 (a); *Lucky Night* 1939 (a); *Remember?* 1939 (a); *Stand Up and Fight* 1939 (a); *Escape* 1940 (a); *Flight Command* 1940 (a); *Waterloo Bridge* 1940 (a); *Billy the Kid* 1941 (a); *Johnny Eager* 1941 (a); *When Ladies Meet* 1941 (a); *Her Cardboard Lover* 1942 (a); *Stand By For Action* 1942 (a); *Bataan* 1943 (a); *Song of Russia* 1943 (a); *The Youngest Profession* 1943 (a); *Undercurrent* 1946 (a); *High Wall* 1947 (a); *Ambush* 1949 (a); *The Bribe* 1949 (a); *Conspirator* 1949 (a); *Devil's Doorway* 1950 (a); *Quo Vadis* 1951 (a); *Westward the Women* 1951 (a); *Above and Beyond* 1952 (a); *Ivanhoe* 1952 (a); *All the Brothers Were Valiant* 1953 (a); *I Love Melvin* 1953 (a); *Knights of the Round Table* 1953 (a); *Ride, Vaquero* 1953 (a); *Many Rivers to Cross* 1954 (a); *Rogue Cop* 1954 (a); *Valley of the Kings* 1954 (a); *The Last Hunt* 1955 (a); *Quentin Durward* 1955 (a); *D-Day the Sixth of June* 1956 (a); *The Power and the Prize* 1956 (a); *Tip on a Dead Jockey* 1957 (a); *The Law and Jake Wade* 1958 (a); *Party Girl* 1958 (a); *Saddle the Wind* 1958 (a); *The Hangman* 1959 (a); *The House of the Seven Hawks* 1959 (a); *Killers of Kilimanjaro* 1960 (a); *Cattle King* 1963 (a); *Miracle of the White Stallions* 1963 (a); *A House Is Not a Home* 1964 (a); *The Night Walker* 1964 (a); *Hondo and the Apaches* 1966 (a); *Johnny Tiger* 1966 (a); *Pampa Salvaje* 1966 (a); *Return of the Gunfighter* 1966 (a); *The Glass Sphinx* 1967 (a); *Where Angels Go... Trouble Follows* 1968 (a); *Hollywood on Trial* 1976 (archival footage).

Taylor, Rod • *aka* Rodney Taylor • Actor • Born Sydney, Australia, January 11, 1929. *Educ.* East Sydney Art College (art). Theater-exprienced, ruggedly handsome performer who went to Hollywood in 1955 and hit a peak in the early 1960s as a tough but endearing lead of adventure-thrillers, including George Pal's first-rate adaptation of H.G. Wells's *The Time Machine* (1960) and Hitchcock's *The Birds* (1963). • *King of the Coral Sea* 1953 (a); *Long John Silver* 1954 (a); *Hell on Frisco Bay* 1955 (a); *Top Gun* 1955 (a); *The Virgin Queen* 1955 (a); *World Without End* 1955 (a); *The Catered Affair* 1956 (a); *Giant* 1956 (a); *Raintree County* 1957 (a); *Separate Tables* 1958 (a); *Ask Any Girl* 1959 (a); *Step Down to Terror* 1959 (a); *The Time Machine* 1960 (a); *The Birds* 1963 (a); *A Gathering of Eagles* 1963 (a); *Il Re Dei Sette Mari* 1963 (a); *Sunday in New York* 1963 (a); *The V.I.P.s* 1963 (a); *36 Hours* 1964 (a); *Fate Is the Hunter* 1964 (a); *Do Not Disturb* 1965 (a); *Young Cassidy* 1965 (a); *The Glass Bottom Boat* 1966 (a); *Chuka* 1967 (a,p); *Hotel* 1967 (a); *The Hell With Heroes* 1968 (a); *Darker Than Amber* 1970 (a); *The Man Who Had Power Over Women* 1970 (a); *Zabriskie Point* 1970 (a); *Gli Eroi* 1972 (a); *The Deadly Trackers* 1973 (a); *Trader Horn* 1973 (a); *The Train Robbers* 1973 (a); *Partisani* 1974 (a); *Blondy* 1975 (a); *The Picture Show Man* 1976 (a); *Hell River* 1978 (a); *A Time to Die* 1979 (a); *On the Run* 1982 (a); *The Fantasy Film World of George Pal* 1986 (a); *Mask of Murder* 1989 (a).

Taylor, William Desmond • Director; also actor. • Born William Cunningham Dean Tanner, Ireland, April 26, 1877; died February 2, 1922, Hollywood, CA. Dashing actor who starred in Vitagraph's *Captain Alvarez* (1914) before turning to directing over 40 silent films. Though he rose to prominence as the director of several Mary Pickford vehicles, today Taylor is far better known as the victim of one of Hollywood's most sensational unsolved murders: he was shot to death in his Hollywood mansion under mysterious circumstances. Director King Vidor attempted to solve the mystery and his notes became the basis of *Cast of Killers*, one of the recent books written about the murder and its cover-up. The resulting scandal, with its hints of sexual intrigue and Hollywood narcotics use, virtually put an end to the careers of film stars Mabel Normand and Mary Miles Minter (who separately had visited Taylor the night of the murder) and paved the way for industry efforts to improve its image by self-censorship. • *Billy's Rival (short)* 1914 (d); *Captain Alvarez* 1914 (a); *When the Road Parts (short)* 1914 (d); *The Diamond From the Sky* 1915 (d); *The American Beauty* 1916 (d); *Ben Blair* 1916 (d); *Davy Crockett* 1916 (d); *The Happiness of Three Women* 1916 (d,p); *He Fell in Love With His Wife* 1916 (d); *Her Father's Son* 1916 (d); *The Parson of Panamint* 1916 (d); *Redeeming Love* 1916 (d); *Big Timber* 1917 (d); *Jack and Jill* 1917 (d); *Out of the Wreck* 1917 (d); *The Spirit of '17* 1917 (d); *Tom Sawyer* 1917 (d); *The Varmint* 1917 (d); *The World Apart* 1917 (d); *Captain Kidd, Jr.* 1918 (d); *His Majesty, Bunker Bean* 1918 (d); *How Could You Jean?* 1918 (d); *Huck and Tom* 1918 (d); *Johanna Enlists* 1918 (d); *Mile-a-Minute Kendall* 1918 (d); *Up the Road With Sallie* 1918 (d); *Anne of Green Gables* 1919 (d); *The Furnace* 1920 (d); *Huckleberry Finn* 1920 *(d); Jenny Be Good* 1920 (d); *Judy of Rogues' Harbor* 1920 (d); *Nurse Marjorie* 1920 (d); *The Soul of Youth* 1920 (d); *Beyond* 1921 (d); *Morals* 1921 (d); *Sacred and Profane Love* 1921 (d); *Wealth* 1921 (d); *The Witching Hour* 1921 (d); *The Green Temptation* 1922 (d); *The Top of New York* 1922 (d).

Teague, Lewis • Director • Born US, 1941. *Educ.* NYU. Edited a number of low-budget productions for Roger Corman's New World Pictures, before directing similar fare such as *Alligator* (1980), *Death Vengeance* (1982), *Cujo* (1983) and *Cat's Eye* (1985) with evident panache. Teague scored a commerical success with the romantic adventure *The Jewel of the Nile* (1985). • *Cockfighter* 1974 (ed); *Dirty O'Neil* 1974 (d); *Forgotten Island Of Santosha* 1974 (ed); *Summer Run* 1974 (ed); *Crazy Mama* 1975 (ed); *Death Race 2000* 1975 (2u d,assoc.ed); *Thunder and Lightning* 1977 (2u d); *Avalanche* 1978 (avalanche sequence d,ed); *Fast Charlie—The Moonbeam Rider* 1978 (2u d); *The Lady in Red* 1979 (d,ed); *Alligator* 1980 (d); *The Big Red One* 1980 (2u d); *Death Vengeance* 1982 (d); *Fighting Back* 1982 (d); *Cujo* 1983 (d); *The Jewel of the Nile* 1985 (d); *Stephen King's Cat's Eye* 1985 (d); *Collision Course* 1990 (d); *Navy Seals* 1990 (d).

Téchiné, André • Director • Born France, 1943. *Cahiers du Cinéma* critic-turned-filmmaker who demonstrated his flair for richly textured, atmospheric storytelling with the aptly titled thriller *Barocco* (1977). Téchiné followed it with the sluggish, but well-crafted *The Bronte Sisters* (1978)—worthwhile mainly for the superlative performances of Isabelle Huppert, Marie-France Pisier and Isabelle Adjani, as well the sole dramatic outing of literary theorist Roland Barthes (a fan of Téchiné's) in the role of William Thackery. Téchiné has since sculpted several other stylish, psychological thrillers, particularly *Rendezvous* (1985), starring Juliette Binoche, which earned him a best director award at Cannes. • *Aloise* 1975 (sc); *Souvenirs d'en France* 1975 (d,sc); *Barocco* 1977 (d,sc); *Les Soeurs Bronte/The Bronte Sisters* 1978 (d,sc); *Hotel des Ameriques* 1982 (d,sc); *Rendezvous* 1985 (d,sc); *Le Lieu du Crime* 1986 (d,sc,adapt,dial); *Les Innocents* 1987 (d,sc,lyrics); *Les Ministères de l'art* 1988 (a); *Mauvaise Fille* 1991 (sc).

Temple, Julien • Director; also writer. • Born London, November 26, 1953. *Educ.* Kings College, Cambridge (architecture, history); National Film School. Gained notice with *The Great Rock 'n' Roll Swindle* (1979), a gripping, anarchic account of the quintessential punk rock band, *The Sex Pistols*. Temple continued to rock with music videos for the likes of Mick Jagger and David Bowie and filmed the raucous two-day concert/comedy fest, *The Secret Policeman's Other Ball* (1981). He went on to create several music-driven features, notably the daffy *Earth Girls Are Easy* (1989). • *The Great Rock 'n' Roll Swindle* 1979 (d); *The Secret Policeman's Other Ball* 1981 (d); *Undercover* 1983 (d,sc); *Mantrap* 1984 (d,sc); *Running Out of Luck* 1985 (d,sc); *Absolute Beginners* 1986 (d,song); *Aria* 1987 (d,sc "Rigoletto"); *Earth Girls Are Easy* 1989 (d).

Temple, Shirley • *aka* Shirley Temple Black • Actress, singer • Born Santa Monica, CA, April 23, 1928. Beloved child performer who appeared in films consistently through the 1940s, but is best remembered for her many cutesy roles of the 30s. A genuine talent, Temple entered movies at age three, but was only definitively established at six with *Stand Up and Cheer* (1934). Her bouncing blonde curls, effervescence and impeccable charm were the basis for a Depression-era phenomenon. Portraying a doll-like model daughter, she helped ease the pain of audiences the world over, while virtually keeping 20th Century-Fox afloat with her astounding profitability. Temple earned a Special 1934 Oscar "in grateful recognition of her outstanding contribution to screen entertainment," but as she reached adolescence her popularity evaporated. She entered politics in the late 60s, and has served several posts for the US government, including as Ambassador to Ghana from 1974 to 1976 and as Ambassador to Czechoslovakia since 1989. • *The Red Haired Alibi* 1932 (a); *Baby Takes a Bow* 1934 (a); *Bright Eyes* 1934 (a); *Change of Heart* 1934 (a); *Little Miss Marker* 1934 (a); *Now I'll Tell* 1934 (a); *Now and Forever* 1934 (a); *Stand Up and Cheer* 1934 (a); *Curly Top* 1935 (a); *The Little Colonel* 1935 (a); *The Littlest Rebel* 1935 (a); *Our Little Girl* 1935 (a); *Captain January* 1936 (a); *Dimples* 1936 (a); *The Poor Little Rich Girl* 1936 (a); *Stowaway* 1936 (a); *Heidi* 1937 (a); *Wee Willie Winkie* 1937 (a); *Just Around the Corner* 1938 (a); *Little Miss Broadway* 1938 (a); *Rebecca of Sunnybrook Farm* 1938 (a); *The Little Princess* 1939 (a); *Susannah of the Mounties* 1939 (a); *The Blue Bird* 1940 (a); *Young People* 1940 (a); *Kathleen* 1941 (a); *Miss Annie Rooney* 1942 (a); *I'll Be Seeing You* 1944 (a); *Since You Went Away* 1944 (a); *Kiss and Tell* 1945 (a); *The Bachelor and the Bobby Soxer* 1947 (a); *Honeymoon* 1947 (a); *That Hagen Girl* 1947 (a); *Adventure in Baltimore* 1948 (a); *Fort Apache* 1948 (a); *Mr. Belvedere Goes to College* 1949 (a); *The Story of Seabiscuit* 1949 (a); *A Kiss For Corliss* 1950 (a); *Going Hollywood: The War Years* 1988 (archival footage).

Tennant, Victoria • Actress • Born London, September 30, 1953. *Educ.* Central School of Speech and Drama, London. Lead and supporting player, memorable opposite husband Steve Martin (and Lily Tomlin) in *All of Me* (1984) and opposite Robert Mitchum in the TV miniseries *Winds of War* and *War and Remembrance.* Daughter of former prima ballerina Irina Baronova and Cecil Tennant, the late talent agent whose clients included John Gielgud, Michael Redgrave and her godfather, Laurence Olivier. • *The Ragman's Daughter* 1972 (a); *Hussy* 1979 (lyrics); *The Dogs of War* 1980 (a); *Horror Planet* 1980 (a); *Sphinx* 1980 (a); *Stranger's Kiss* 1983 (a); *All of Me* 1984 (a); *The Holcroft Covenant* 1985 (a); *Best Seller* 1987 (a); *Flowers in the Attic* 1987 (a); *Zugzwang* 1989 (a); *Whispers* 1990 (a); *L.A. Story* 1991 (a).

Terry-Thomas • *aka* Terry Thomas, Thomas Terry • Actor • Born Thomas Terry Hoar Stevens, Finchley, Enland, July 14, 1911; died January 8, 1990, Godalming, Surrey, England. *Educ.* Ardingly College. Gap-toothed comic player who used his expressive eyes, mobile eyebrows and Royal Guards' mustache to create a variety of asinine British characters, usually in supporting roles, occasionally in leads. His comic personae ranged from the comically malevolent to the naive in such films as *I'm All Right, Jack* (1959), *It's a Mad, Mad, Mad, Mad World* (1963) and, perhaps his signature role, Sir Percival War-Armitage in *Those Magnificent Men in Their Flying Machines* (1965). • *The Brass Monkey* 1948; *Private's Progress* 1956; *Blue Murder at St. Trinian's* 1957; *Lucky Jim* 1957; *The Naked Truth* 1957; *Happy Is the Bride* 1958; *Tom Thumb* 1958; *I'm All Right, Jack* 1959; *Too Many Crooks* 1959; *Bachelor Flat* 1961; *The Wonderful World of the Brothers Grimm* 1962; *It's a Mad, Mad, Mad, Mad World* 1963; *How to Murder Your Wife* 1965; *Strange Bedfellows* 1965;

Those Magnificent Men in Their Flying Machines 1965; *Munster, Go Home* 1966; *Our Man in Marrakesh* 1966; *A Guide For the Married Man* 1967; *The Karate Killers* 1967; *Arabella* 1967; *The Perils of Pauline* 1967; *Se Tutte le Donne Del Mondo* 1967; *Diabolik* 1968; *Don't Raise the Bridge, Lower the River* 1968; *How Sweet It Is* 1968; *Where Were You When the Lights Went Out?* 1968; *2,000 Years Later* 1969; *Monte Carlo or Bust!* 1969; *Le Mur de l'Atlantique* 1970; *The Abominable Doctor Phibes* 1971; *Doctor Phibes Rises Again* 1972; *Gli Eroi* 1972; *Robin Hood* 1973; *The Vault of Horror* 1973; *Who Stole the Shah's Jewels?* 1974; *Side By Side* 1975; *The Bawdy Adventures of Tom Jones* 1976; *The Mysterious House of Dr. C* 1976; *Spanish Fly* 1976; *The Last Remake of Beau Geste* 1977; *The Hound of the Baskervilles* 1978; *See No Evil* 1988.

Tesich, Steve • Screenwriter; also playwright. • Born Stoyan Tesich, Titovo Utice, Yugoslavia, September 29, 1942. *Educ.* Indiana University, Bloomington; Columbia (Russian literature). In the US from 1955, Tesich established himself as a playwright before entering films with his Oscar-winning screenplay *Breaking Away* (1979). His finely observed scripts range from original New York thrillers (*Eyewitness* 1980) to deft literary adaptations (*The World According to Garp* 1982, *Eleni* 1985), effectively combining personal and social issues. Tesich has worked several times with director Peter Yates. • *Breaking Away* 1979 (**AABSC**); *Eyewitness* 1980; *Four Friends* 1981; *The World According to Garp* 1982; *American Flyers* 1985; *Eleni* 1985.

Thalberg, Irving G. • Executive • Born Brooklyn, NY, May 30, 1899; died September 14, 1936. From the late 1920s until his death in 1936, Irving Thalberg was the stuff of legend, regarded in the American film industry with a mixture of respect, awe, envy and fear. Unknown to the general public, Thalberg, through his obssesive concern with quality film production and his unwavering faith in public opinion, became the paragon of the studio factory system and an exemplar of public taste. As production head at MGM, Thalberg trod the delicate line between commerce and art and in the process transformed the studio into the pinnacle of the Hollywood system.

Thalberg began his career in film as a teenager fresh out of high school, joining Universal in 1918 as a secretary at their New York offices. Working exclusively for studio patriarch Carl Laemmle, he worked his way up the corporate ladder and by the time he was 21 had become executive in charge of production at Universal City in California.

At Universal, Thalberg sought to upgrade the quality of the studio's product and to rein in profligate costs on its "Jewel" productions. In the first instance, Thalberg oversaw Universal's first major production, *The Hunchback of Notre Dame* (1923), from pre-production planning to editing and promotion, resulting in a tremendous success for the studio. In the second instance, he clashed with autocratic director-star Erich Von Stroheim, ordering substantial cuts in *Foolish Wives* (1922) and removing him from the helm of *Merry-Go-Round* (1923). But Thalberg's efforts went unrewarded by the parsimonious Laemmle and the young executive resigned in 1923 to take a production position with fledgling Louis B. Mayer Productions.

Soon after Thalberg's defection from Universal, Marcus Loew and Nicholas Schenck of Metro Pictures merged with Louis B. Mayer Productions to become a fully integrated film company, Metro-Goldwyn-Mayer. Thalberg came along with the package and was named supervisor of production. Once again, he clashed with Von Stroheim, cutting his mammoth version of *Greed* (1923) down to two hours and overseeing every aspect of production on *The Merry Widow* (1925). This muzzling of Von Stroheim marked the demise of the era of the flamboyant producer-director and heralded the birth of a new order with the studio production system. The litmus test for the "new order" was *The Big Parade* (1925); its spectacular success (it reportedly became the most profitable film of the silent era) validated Thalberg's production methods.

Thalberg's strategy became synonymous with the MGM house style that held sway into the late 1940s: he combined intensive pre-production preparation with a post-production system of previews designed to gauge audience reactions and determine ensuing retakes. Working with Louis B. Mayer and facilities supervisor Eddie Mannix, Thalberg oversaw every MGM production until 1932 to ensure that the highest standards were maintained. Sustaining a virtual highwire act between the money men in New York and the studio artists and technicians in Los Angeles, Thalberg transformed MGM into the most profitable and respected studio in the industry with such prestige successes as *The Broadway Melody* (1929), *Grand Hotel* (1932) and *Red Dust* (1932).

In 1932, Thalberg was dealt a crushing blow when one of his associate producers, Paul Bern, committed suicide. His reaction was to pour himself pell-mell into MGM's upcoming productions. Never in strong health following a sickly childhood, he suffered a physical collapse at the end of the year, creating a power vacuum that Mayer, smoldering with resentment over Thalberg's power, readily filled, hiring David Selznick and Walter Wanger as unit producers. When Thalberg returned in August of 1933, it was as another unit producer, with his system of production supervision scrapped. Even as a unit producer, Thalberg helped create such hits as *Mutiny on the Bounty* (1935), *A Night at the Opera* (1935), *San Francisco* (1936) and *The Good Earth* (1937). But his health continued to deteriorate and, during pre-production on *A Day At The Races* (1937), he contracted pneumonia and died at the age of 37. Married to actress Norma Shearer. PB

Theodorakis, Mikis • Composer • Born Khios, Greece, 1925. *Educ.* Conservatory of Patras; Athens Conservatory; Paris Conservatoire. Committed leftist whose turbulent political activity resulted in multiple jailings and exiles between 1943 and 1973. Theodorakis made a name for himself in Paris in the mid-1950s and gained international recognition with his infectious score for Michael Cacoyannis's *Zorba the Greek* (1964). He has worked on a number of subsequent times with Cacoyannis as well as with Constantin Costa-Gavras (*Z* 1969, *State of Siege* 1973) and Sidney Lumet (*Serpico* 1973). • *The Barefoot Battalion* 1954 (m,m.cond); *Ill Met By Moonlight* 1957 (m); *Phaedra* 1962 (m); *Five Miles to Midnight* 1963 (m); *Zorba the Greek* 1964 (m,m.cond); *Z* 1969 (m); *Biribi* 1971 (m); *The Trojan Women* 1971 (m); *Etat de siège/State of Siege* 1973 (m); *Serpico* 1973 (m); *Actas de Marusia* 1976 (m); *Iphigenia* 1977 (m); *Hell River* 1978 (add.m); *Easy Road* 1979 (m); *Kostas* 1979 (m); *O Anthropos Me To Garyfallo* 1980 (m); *Nela* 1980 (m); *Belladonna* 1981 (m); *The Savage Hunt* 1981 (song); *Mod att leva* 1983 (m); *Les Clowns de Dieu* 1986 (m); *Sis* 1989 (m).

Thomas, Jeremy • Producer • Born Ealing, London, July 27, 1949. Served a brief stint as an editor before producing his first film, Phillipe Mora's *Mad Dog*, in 1976. Thomas has since worked with such directors as Jerzy Skolimowski, Nicolas Roeg, Nagisa Oshima and Stephen Frears, gaining his widest acclaim for producing Bernardo Bertolucci's epic, *The Last Emperor* (1987). He is the son of Ralph Thomas, who directed the farcical English "Doctor" series, and nephew of director Gerald Thomas, who helmed the "Carry On" comedies. • *Brother, Can You Spare a Dime?* 1974 (ed); *Mad Dog* 1976 (p); *The Shout* 1978 (p); *The Great Rock 'n' Roll Swindle* 1979 (exec.p); *The Kids Are Alright* 1979 (special consultant); *Bad Timing* 1980 (p); *Merry Christmas, Mr. Lawrence* 1982 (p); *Eureka* 1983 (p); *The Hit* 1984 (p); *Insignificance* 1985 (p); *Good to Go* 1986 (exec.p); *The Last Emperor* 1987 (p) (**AABP**); *Everybody Wins* 1990 (p); *The Sheltering Sky* 1990 (p).

Thompson, J. Lee • Director; also actor, screenwriter, producer. • Born John Lee Thompson, Bristol, England, 1914. Multi-talented figure from the stage who landed his first screen role in 1935. A competent technician, Thompson made his directorial debut in 1950 and went on to produce a considerable volume of British and American features, notably *The Guns of Navarone* (1961) and *Cape Fear* (1962). Thompson has also directed nine Charles Bronson vehicles. • *The Strangler* 1941 (sc); *For Better For Worse* 1954 (d); *The Weak and the Wicked* 1954 (d,sc); *An Alligator Named Daisy* 1955 (d); *As Long As They're Happy* 1955 (d); *Blonde Sinner* 1956 (d); *No Trees in the Street* 1959 (d); *North West Frontier* 1959 (d); *Tiger Bay* 1959 (d); *I Aim at the Stars* 1960 (d); *The Guns of Navarone* 1961 (d) **(AANBD)**; *Cape Fear* 1962 (d); *Taras Bulba* 1962 (d); *Kings of the Sun* 1963 (d); *John Goldfarb, Please Come Home* 1964 (d); *What a Way to Go!* 1964 (d); *Return From the Ashes* 1965 (d,p); *Eye of the Devil* 1966 (d); *Before Winter Comes* 1968 (d); *The Chairman* 1969 (d); *MacKenna's Gold* 1969 (d); *Country Dance* 1970 (d); *Conquest of the Planet of the Apes* 1972 (d); *Battle For the Planet of the Apes* 1973 (d); *Huckleberry Finn* 1974 (d); *The Reincarnation of Peter Proud* 1975 (d); *St. Ives* 1976 (d); *The White Buffalo* 1977 (d); *The Greek Tycoon* 1978 (d); *The Passage* 1979 (d); *Caboblanco* 1980 (d); *Happy Birthday to Me* 1980 (d); *10 to Midnight* 1983 (d,story); *The Ambassador* 1984 (d); *The Evil That Men Do* 1984 (d); *King Solomon's Mines* 1985 (d); *Firewalker* 1986 (d); *Murphy's Law* 1986 (d); *Death Wish 4: The Crackdown* 1987 (d); *Messenger of Death* 1988 (d); *Kinjite* 1989 (d).

Thompson, Jack • Actor • Born John Payne, Sydney, Australia, August 31, 1940. *Educ.* Queensland University. Star of several major films of the Australian film renaissance of the 1970s and 80s, including Fred Schepisi's *The Chant of Jimmie Blacksmith* (1978) and Bruce Beresford's *Breaker Morant* (1979). Thompson also appeared in Nagisa Oshima's *Merry Christmas, Mr. Lawrence* (1983). • *The Savage Wild* 1970 (a); *Outback* 1971 (a); *Libido* 1973 (a); *Petersen* 1974 (a); *Scobie Malone* 1975 (a); *Sunday Too Far Away* 1975 (a); *The Taking of Christina* 1975 (a); *Caddie* 1976 (a); *Mad Dog* 1976 (a); *The Chant of Jimmie Blacksmith* 1978 (a); *The Journalist* 1979 (a); *Breaker Morant* 1979 (a); *The Club* 1980 (a); *The Earthling* 1980 (a); *Bad Blood* 1982 (a); *The Man From Snowy River* 1982 (a); *Merry Christmas, Mr. Lawrence* 1983 (a); *Burke & Wills* 1985 (a); *Flesh + Blood* 1985 (a); *Ground Zero* 1988 (a); *Waterfront* 1988 (a).

Thompson, Lea • Actress • Born Rochester, MN, 1962. Comely brunette character player who gave up a ballet career for acting. After appearing in some 20 Burger King commercials, Thompson gained attention in *All the Right Moves* (1983) as the girlfriend of Tom Cruise. She played three versions of Lorraine (Bates) McFly in *Back to the Future* (1985), rose above lackluster material in *Howard the Duck* (1986) and demonstrated her ability to play more complex characters in *The Wizard of Loneliness* (1988). • *All the Right Moves* 1983; *Jaws 3-D* 1983; *Going Undercover* 1984; *Red Dawn* 1984; *The Wild Life* 1984; *Back to the Future* 1985; *Howard the Duck* 1986; *SpaceCamp* 1986; *Some Kind of Wonderful* 1987; *Casual Sex?* 1988; *The Wizard of Loneliness* 1988; *Back to the Future II* 1989; *Back to the Future III* 1990.

Thomson, Alex • Director of photography • Born London, January 12, 1929. Former assistant to Nicolas Roeg who has shot such first-rate, visually challenging films as John Boorman's *Excalibur* (1981) and Roeg's *Eureka* (1983). • *Code 7, Victim 5!* 1965 (cam.op); *A Funny Thing Happened on the Way to the Forum* 1966 (cam.op); *Here We Go 'Round the Mulberry Bush* 1968 (ph); *Alfred the Great* 1969 (ph); *The Best House in London* 1969 (ph); *I Start Counting* 1969 (ph); *The Rise and Rise of Michael Rimmer* 1970 (ph); *The Night Digger* 1971 (ph); *Doctor Phibes Rises Again* 1972 (ph); *Fear Is the Key* 1972 (ph); *The Man Who Would Be King* 1975 (2u ph); *The Seven Per-Cent Solution* 1976 (cam.op); *The Class of Miss MacMichael* 1978 (ph); *Superman* 1978 (add.ph); *The Cat and the Canary* 1979 (ph); *Game For Vultures* 1979 (ph); *Excalibur* 1981 (ph) **(AANBPH)**; *Bullshot* 1983 (ph); *Eureka* 1983 (ph); *The Keep* 1983 (ph); *Electric Dreams* 1984 (ph); *Legend* 1985 (ph); *Year of the Dragon* 1985 (ph); *Duet For One* 1986 (ph); *Labyrinth* 1986 (ph); *Raw Deal* 1986 (ph); *Date With an Angel* 1987 (ph); *The Sicilian* 1987 (ph,cam.op); *Track 29* 1987 (ph); *High Spirits* 1988 (ph); *Leviathan* 1989 (ph); *The Rachel Papers* 1989 (ph); *Mr. Destiny* 1990 (cam.op); *Wings of Fame* 1990 (ph).

Thornton, Sigrid • Actress • Born Canberra, New South Wales, Australia, 1959. Attractive performer, in films from her late teens; since *The Man From Snowy River* (1982), Thornton has been one of Australia's most popular actresses. • *The Getting of Wisdom* 1977 (a); *Snap-Shot* 1978 (a); *The King of the Two Day Wonder* 1979 (a); *Partners* 1981 (a); *The Man From Snowy River* 1982 (a); *Street Hero* 1984 (a); *Niel Lynne* 1985 (a); *The Lighthorsemen* 1987 (a); *Slate, Wyn & Me* 1987 (a); *Return to Snowy River Part II* 1988 (a); *Great Expectations—The Untold Story* 1990 (a,assoc.p).

Thorpe, Richard • Director; also actor. • Born Rollo Smolt Thorpe, Hutchinson, KS, February 24, 1896; died 1986. Former actor who turned to directing, mostly of low-budget fare, in 1923. Thorpe began working on more prestigious productions, notably the MGM "Tarzan" cycle, from the mid-1930s. Proficient to the point of boredom ("His reputaton for only needing one take is why we don't remember his films," quipped James Mason), Thorpe was immensely prolific and capable in all genres. Highlights include *Night Must Fall* (1937), *The Great Caruso* (1951), *Ivanhoe* (1952) and *Jailhouse Rock* (1957). • *Burn 'Em Up Barnes* 1921 (a); *Battling Buddy* 1924 (d); *Bringin' Home the Bacon* 1924 (d); *Fast and Fearless* 1924 (d); *Flames of Desire* 1924 (a); *Hard Hittin' Hamilton* 1924 (d); *Rarin' to Go* 1924 (d); *Restless Wives* 1924 (a); *Rip Roarin' Roberts* 1924 (d); *Rough Ridin'* 1924 (a,d); *Three O'Clock in the Morning* 1924 (a); *Thundering Romance* 1924 (d); *Walloping Wallace* 1924 (d); *The Desert Demon* 1925 (d); *Double Action Daniels* 1925 (d); *Fast Fightin'* 1925 (d); *Full Speed* 1925 (d); *Galloping On* 1925 (d); *Gold and Grit* 1925 (d); *On the Go* 1925 (d); *Quicker'n Lightnin'* 1925 (d); *Tearin' Loose* 1925 (d); *The Bandit Buster* 1926 (d,sc); *The Bonanza Buckaroo* 1926 (d); *College Days* 1926 (d); *Coming An' Going* 1926 (d); *The Dangerous Dub* 1926 (d); *Deuce High* 1926 (d); *Double Daring* 1926 (d); *Easy Going* 1926 (d); *The Fighting Cheat* 1926 (d); *Josselyn's Wife* 1926 (d); *Rawhide* 1926 (d); *Riding Rivals* 1926 (d); *The Roaring Rider* 1926 (d); *The Saddle Cyclone* 1926 (d); *Speedy Spurs* 1926 (d); *A Streak of Luck* 1926 (d); *Trumpin' Trouble* 1926 (d); *Twin Triggers* 1926 (d); *Twisted Triggers* 1926 (d); *Between Dangers* 1927 (d,sc); *The Cyclone Cowboy* 1927 (d); *The Desert of the Lost* 1927 (d); *The First Night* 1927 (d); *The Galloping Gobs* 1927 (d); *The Interferin' Gent* 1927 (d); *The Meddlin' Stranger* 1927 (d); *The Obligin' Buckaroo* 1927 (d); *Pals in Peril* 1927 (d); *Ride 'Em High* 1927 (d); *The Ridin' Rowdy* 1927 (d); *Roarin' Broncs* 1927 (d); *Skedaddle Gold* 1927 (d); *Soda Water Cowboy* 1927 (d); *Tearin' Into Trouble* 1927 (d); *White Pebbles* 1927 (d); *The Ballyhoo Buster* 1928 (d); *The Cowboy Cavalier* 1928 (d); *Desperate Courage* 1928 (d); *The Flying Buckaroo* 1928 (d); *Saddle Mates* 1928 (d); *The Valley of Hunted Men* 1928 (d); *The Vanishing West* 1928 (d); *Vultures of the Sea* 1928 (d); *The Bachelor Girl* 1929 (d); *The Fatal Warning* 1929 (d); *King of the Kongo* 1929 (d); *Border Romance* 1930 (d); *The Dude Wrangler* 1930 (d); *The Lone Defender* 1930 (d); *The Thoroughbred* 1930 (d); *Under Montana Skies* 1930 (d); *The Utah Kid* 1930 (d); *Wings of Adventure* 1930 (d); *The Devil Plays* 1931 (d,ed); *Grief Street* 1931 (d,ed); *King of the Wild* 1931 (d); *The Lady From Nowhere* 1931 (d,ed); *The Lawless Woman* 1931 (d,story); *Neck and Neck* 1931 (d); *The Sky Spider* 1931 (d); *Wild Horse* 1931 (d); *The Beauty Parlor* 1932 (d); *Cross Examination* 1932 (d); *Escapade* 1932 (d); *Forbidden Company* 1932 (d); *Forgotten Women* 1932 (d); *The King Murder* 1932 (d); *The Midnight Lady* 1932 (d); *Mur-*

der at Dawn 1932 (d); *Probation* 1932 (d,ed); *The Secrets of Wu Sin* 1932 (d); *Slightly Married* 1932 (d); *The Thrill of Youth* 1932 (d); *Women Won't Tell* 1932 (d); *Forgotten* 1933 (d); *I Have Lived* 1933 (d); *Love Is Dangerous* 1933 (d); *A Man of Sentiment* 1933 (d); *Notorious But Nice* 1933 (d); *Rainbow Over Broadway* 1933 (d); *Strange People* 1933 (d); *Cheating Cheaters* 1934 (d); *City Park* 1934 (d,ed); *Green Eyes* 1934 (d); *Murder on the Campus* 1934 (d); *The Quitter* 1934 (d); *Secret of the Chateau* 1934 (d); *Stolen Sweets* 1934 (d); *Last of the Pagans* 1935 (d); *Strange Wives* 1935 (d); *Tarzan Escapes* 1936 (d); *The Voice of Bugle Ann* 1936 (d); *Dangerous Number* 1937 (d); *Double Wedding* 1937 (d); *Night Must Fall* 1937 (d); *The Crowd Roars* 1938 (d); *The First Hundred Years* 1938 (d); *Love Is a Headache* 1938 (d); *Man-Proof* 1938 (d); *Three Loves Has Nancy* 1938 (d); *The Toy Wife* 1938 (d); *The Adventures of Huckleberry Finn* 1939 (d); *Tarzan Finds a Son* 1939 (d); *The Earl of Chicago* 1940 (d); *Twenty Mule Team* 1940 (d); *Wyoming* 1940 (d); *The Bad Man* 1941 (d); *Barnacle Bill* 1941 (d); *Tarzan's Secret Treasure* 1941 (d); *Joe Smith, American* 1942 (d); *Tarzan's New York Adventure* 1942 (d); *White Cargo* 1942 (d); *Above Suspicion* 1943 (d); *Apache Trail* 1943 (d); *Cry Havoc* 1943 (d); *Three Hearts For Julia* 1943 (d); *The Thin Man Goes Home* 1944 (d); *Two Girls and a Sailor* 1944 (d); *Her Highness and the Bellboy* 1945 (d); *Thrill of a Romance* 1945 (d); *What Next, Corporal Hargrove?* 1945 (d); *Fiesta* 1947 (d); *This Time For Keeps* 1947 (d); *Big Jack* 1948 (d); *A Date With Judy* 1948 (d); *On an Island With You* 1948 (d); *Black Hand* 1949 (d); *Challenge to Lassie* 1949 (d); *Malaya* 1949 (d); *The Sun Comes Up* 1949 (d); *Three Little Words* 1950 (d); *The Great Caruso* 1951 (d); *It's a Big Country* 1951 (d); *The Unknown Man* 1951 (d); *Vengeance Valley* 1951 (d); *Carbine Williams* 1952 (d); *Ivanhoe* 1952 (d); *The Prisoner of Zenda* 1952 (d); *All the Brothers Were Valiant* 1953 (d); *The Girl Who Had Everything* 1953 (d); *Knights of the Round Table* 1953 (d); *Athena* 1954 (d); *The Student Prince* 1954 (d); *The Prodigal* 1955 (d); *Quentin Durward* 1955 (d); *Ten Thousand Bedrooms* 1956 (d); *Jailhouse Rock* 1957 (d); *Tip on a Dead Jockey* 1957 (d); *The House of the Seven Hawks* 1959 (d); *Killers of Kilimanjaro* 1960 (d); *I Tartari* 1960 (d); *The Honeymoon Machine* 1961 (d); *The Horizontal Lieutenant* 1962 (d); *Follow the Boys* 1963 (d); *Fun in Acapulco* 1963 (d); *That Funny Feeling* 1965 (d); *The Truth About Spring* 1965 (d); *The Golden Head* 1967 (d); *The Last Challenge* 1967 (d,p).

Thulin, Ingrid • Actress; also director. • Born Solleftea, Sweden, January 27, 1929. *Educ.* Royal Dramatic Theater School, Stockholm. Member of Ingmar Bergman's distinguished acting troupe who made a successful transition to international films. Piercing as the sexually frustrated sister in *The Silence* (1963), she was equally superb in Jorge Semprun's and Alain Resnais's *La Guerre est finie* (1966) and Luchino Visconti's *The Damned* (1969). In conjunction with other Bergman regulars, Erland Josephson and Sven Nykvist, Thulin made her directing debut with *One and One* (1978). • *Foreign Intrigue* 1956 (a); *Smultronstallet/Wild Strawberries* 1957 (a); *Ansiktet/The Magician* 1958 (a); *Nara Livet/Brink of Life* 1958 (a); *The Four Horsemen of the Apocalypse* 1962 (a); *Nattvardsgasterna/Winter Light* 1963 (a); *Tystnaden/The Silence* 1963 (a); *Return From the Ashes* 1965 (a); *La Guerre est finie* 1966 (a); *Adelaide* 1968 (a); *Badarna* 1968 (a); *Vargtimmen/The Hour of the Wolf* 1968 (a); *La Caduta degli dei/The Damned* 1969 (a); *Riten/The Ritual* 1969 (a); *N.P. Il Segreto* 1971 (a); *Cries and Whispers* 1972 (a); *La Sainte Famille* 1972 (a); *En Handfull karlek* 1974 (a); *La Cage* 1975 (a); *Madam Kitty* 1975 (a); *Monismanien 1995* 1975 (a); *Comincio il viaggio nella vertigini, E* 1976 (a); *The Cassandra Crossing* 1977 (a); *En och En/One and One* 1978 (a,d); *Brusten Himmsel* 1982 (d,sc); *After the Rehearsal* 1984 (a); *Il Giorno Prima* 1987 (a); *La Casa del Sorriso/House of Smiles* 1991 (a).

Thurman, Uma • Actress • Born Uma Karuna Thurman, Boston, MA, April 29, 1970. Sultry young actress who made her film debut in 1987 and came to attention as the duplicitous virgin in Stephen Frears's *Dangerous Liaisons* (1988). Married to actor Gary Oldman. • *Kiss Daddy Good Night* 1987; *The Adventures of Baron Munchausen* 1988; *Dangerous Liaisons* 1988; *Johnny Be Good* 1988; *Henry & June* 1990; *Where the Heart Is* 1990.

Ticotin, Rachel • Actress • Born New York, NY, November 1, 1958. Attractive brunette who made her film debut in *Fort Apache, the Bronx* (1981) and is probably most widely identified as the enigmatic Melina in Arnold Schwarznegger's *Total Recall* (1990). Married to actor David Caruso. • *King of the Gypsies* 1978 (a); *Dressed to Kill* 1980 (prod.asst); *Raging Bull* 1980 (prod.asst); *Fort Apache, the Bronx* 1981 (a); *Four Friends* 1981 (dance asst); *Critical Condition* 1987 (a); *Total Recall* 1990 (a); *F/X II* 1991 (a).

Tierney, Gene • Actress • Born Brooklyn, NY, November 20, 1920. Exotic, strikingly beautiful debutante whose Broadway and then film career was fueled and promoted, through a family-owned company, by her insurance-broker father. (He sued his daughter for breach of "contract" in the early 1940s.) Tierney's best roles include the neurotically possessive bride in John M. Stahl's lusciously photographed 1945 melodrama, *Leave Her to Heaven*, as well as memorable performances in noir thrillers such as Otto Preminger's *Laura* (1944) and Joseph Mankiewicz's *Dragonwyck* (1946).

Divorced from designer Oleg Cassini in 1952, Tierney became associated with Aly Khan and suffered a nervous breakdown when he left her during the filming of *The Left Hand of God* (1955). She was put on suspension by Fox and did not return to acting until 1962. In 1960 she married Texas oilman W. Howard Lee, former husband of Hedy Lamarr. • *Hudson's Bay* 1940; *The Return of Frank James* 1940; *Belle Starr* 1941; *The Shanghai Gesture* 1941; *Sundown* 1941; *Tobacco Road* 1941; *China Girl* 1942; *Rings on Her Fingers* 1942; *Son of Fury* 1942; *Thunder Birds* 1942; *Heaven Can Wait* 1943; *Laura* 1944; *A Bell For Adano* 1945; *Leave Her to Heaven* 1945 **(AANBA)**; *Dragonwyck* 1946; *The Razor's Edge* 1946; *The Ghost and Mrs. Muir* 1947; *The Iron Curtain* 1948; *That Wonderful Urge* 1948; *Whirlpool* 1949; *The Mating Season* 1950; *Night and the City* 1950; *Where the Sidewalk Ends* 1950; *Close to My Heart* 1951; *On the Riviera* 1951; *The Secret of Convict Lake* 1951; *Plymouth Adventure* 1952; *Way of a Gaucho* 1952; *Never Let Me Go* 1953; *Personal Affair* 1953; *Black Widow* 1954; *The Egyptian* 1954; *The Left Hand of God* 1955; *Advise and Consent* 1962; *Toys in the Attic* 1963; *The Pleasure Seekers* 1964.

Tilly, Meg • Actress • Born California, 1960. Innocent-faced former dancer, raised in Canada, who first came to prominence as the girlfriend-of-the-deceased in *The Big Chill* (1983). Tilly proved herself a capable lead in the title role of *Agnes of God* (1985) and as the initially virtuous wife in Miloš Forman's *Valmont* (1989). Sister of actress Jennifer Tilly (b. 1958). • *Fame* 1980; *One Dark Night* 1982; *Tex* 1982; *The Big Chill* 1983; *Psycho II* 1983; *Impulse* 1984; *Agnes of God* 1985 **(AANBSA)**; *Off Beat* 1986; *The Girl in a Swing* 1988; *Masquerade* 1988; *Valmont* 1989; *The Two Jakes* 1990.

Tiomkin, Dimitri • *aka* Dmitri Tiomkin • Composer; also conductor, songwriter. • Born St. Petersburg, Russia, May 10, 1899; died 1979. *Educ.* St. Petersburg Conservatory of Music; St. Petersburg University; University of St. Mary's (law). Accomplished, prolific composer, in the US from 1925, whose lush, often sentimental scores proved effective across a wide range of genres. Tiomkin first gained prominence in the 1930s for his accompaniments to films such as Frank Capra's *Lost Horizon* (1937) and *Mr. Smith Goes to Washington* (1939). Highlights of his work include the poignant lone harmonica segment from *High Noon* (1952)—the film won him two Oscars, one for his score and one, in collaboration with lyricist Ned Washington, for the song "Do Not Forsake Me, Oh My Darlin'"—and his more fully orchestrated scores for *Red River* (1948), *Giant* (1956) and *The High and the Mighty* (1954).

In 1970 Tiomkin realized a long-cherished project, serving as executive producer on the Oscar-winning, US-USSR co-production, *Tchaikovsky*. • *The Rogue Song* 1930 (m); *Resurrection* 1931 (m); *Alice in Wonderland* 1933 (m); *The Casino Murder Case* 1935 (m); *I Live My Life* 1935 (m); *Mad Love* 1935 (m); *Lost Horizon* 1937 (m) **(AANBM)**; *The Road Back* 1937 (m); *You Can't Take It With You* 1938 (m); *Mr. Smith Goes to Washington* 1939 (m) **(AANBM)**; *Only Angels Have Wings* 1939 (m); *Lucky Partners* 1940 (m); *The Westerner* 1940 (m); *The Corsican Brothers* 1941 (m) **(AANBM)**; *Flying Blind* 1941 (m); *Forced Landing* 1941 (m.sup); *Meet John Doe* 1941 (m); *Our Russian Front* 1941 (m); *Scattergood Meets Broadway* 1941 (m); *A Gentleman After Dark* 1942 (m); *The Moon and Sixpence* 1942 (m) **(AANBM)**; *Twin Beds* 1942 (m); *Why We Fight* 1942 (m); *Shadow of a Doubt* 1943 (m); *The Unknown Guest* 1943 (m); *The Bridge of San Luis Rey* 1944 (m.dir) **(AANBM)**; *The Impostor* 1944 (m); *When Strangers Marry* 1944 (m); *Let There Be Light* 1945 (m); *Pardon My Past* 1945 (m); *Angel on My Shoulder* 1946 (m); *Black Beauty* 1946 (m); *The Dark Mirror* 1946 (m); *It's a Wonderful Life* 1946 (m); *Duel in the Sun* 1947 (m); *The Long Night* 1947 (m); *Canadian Pacific* 1948 (m); *The Dude Goes West* 1948 (m); *Portrait of Jennie* 1948 (m); *Red River* 1948 (m); *So This Is New York* 1948 (m); *Tarzan and the Mermaids* 1948 (m); *Champion* 1949 (m) **(AANBM)**; *Home of the Brave* 1949 (m); *Red Light* 1949 (m); *Champagne For Caesar* 1950 (m.dir); *Cyrano De Bergerac* 1950 (m); *D.O.A.* 1950 (m); *Dakota Lil* 1950 (m); *Guilty Bystander* 1950 (m); *The Men* 1950 (m,m.dir); *Drums in the Deep South* 1951 (m.dir); *Mr. Universe* 1951 (m); *Peking Express* 1951 (m); *Strangers on a Train* 1951 (m); *The Thing* 1951 (m); *The Well* 1951 (m); *Angel Face* 1952 (m,m.cond); *The Big Sky* 1952 (m); *Bugles in the Afternoon* 1952 (m); *The Four Poster* 1952 (a); *The Happy Time* 1952 (m); *High Noon* 1952 (m,m.dir,song) **(AABM,AABS)**; *The Lady in the Iron Mask* 1952 (m); *Mutiny* 1952 (m); *My Six Convicts* 1952 (m); *The Steel Trap* 1952 (m); *Blowing Wild* 1953 (m); *His Majesty O'Keefe* 1953 (m); *I Confess* 1953 (m); *Return to Paradise* 1953 (m); *Take the High Ground* 1953 (m); *A Bullet Is Waiting* 1954 (m); *The Command* 1954 (m); *Dial M For Murder* 1954 (m); *The High and the Mighty* 1954 (m,song) **(AANBS,AABM)**; *Strange Lady in Town* 1954 (m); *The Court Martial of Billy Mitchell* 1955 (m); *Land of the Pharaohs* 1955 (m); *Friendly Persuasion* 1956 (m,song) **(AANBS)**; *Giant* 1956 (m,song) **(AANBM)**; *Tension at Table Rock* 1956 (m,song); *Gunfight at the O.K. Corral* 1957 (m,song); *Night Passage* 1957 (m,song); *Search For Paradise* 1957 (m); *Wild Is the Wind* 1957 (m,song) **(AANBS)**; *The Old Man and the Sea* 1958 (m,m.cond) **(AABM)**; *Last Train From Gun Hill* 1959 (m); *Rio Bravo* 1959 (m,m.cond); *The Young Land* 1959 (m,song) **(AANBS)**; *The Alamo* 1960 (m,song) **(AANBM,AANBS)**; *The Sundowners* 1960 (m); *The Unforgiven* 1960 (m); *The Guns of Navarone* 1961 (m,m.cond) **(AANBM)**; *Town Without Pity* 1961 (m,song) **(AANBS)**; *55 Days at Peking* 1963 (m,m.cond,song) **(AANBM,AANBS)**; *Circus World* 1964 (m); *The Fall of the Roman Empire* 1964 (m) **(AANBM)**; *The War Wagon* 1967 (m); *MacKenna's Gold* 1969 (p); *Tchaikovsky* 1970 (p) **(AANBFLF)**.

Tissé, Edouard • Director of photography • Born Eduard Kazimirovich Tissé, Stockholm, Sweden, April 1, 1897; died 1961, Moscow. Highly regarded cinematographer who came to prominence as Sergei Eisenstein's cameraman of choice. Tissé, born to a Swedish mother and Russian father, got his start as a newsreel photographer covering the Russian Revolution and shot the first Soviet-sponsored feature, *Signal*, in 1918. After photographing Eisenstein's silent classics, he accompanied the director and his assistant, Grigor Alexandrov, on their trip to the West, collaborating with the latter on the short *Romance sentimentale* (1931) in France, as well as shooting Eisenstein's celebrated Mexican footage.

A formidable technician, Tissé was noted for his speed, precision, and for the exquisite luminosity he achieved in black-and-white features such as *Alexander Nevsky* (1938).

Tissé also worked with V.I. Pudovkin (*Hunger, Hunger, Hunger* 1921) and Alexander Dovzhenko (*Aerograd* 1935), as well as on Alexandrov's *Glinka* (1952). He co-directed one film, the Swiss-produced *Woman Happy, Woman Unhappy* (1929), on the subject of abortion. • *Signal* 1918 (ph); *Hunger, Hunger, Hunger* 1921 (ph); *Bronenosets Potyomkin/Battleship Potemkin* 1925 (ph); *Oktyabar/October/Ten Days That Shook the World* 1928 (a,ph); *Woman Happy, Woman Unhappy* 1929 (d); *Romance sentimentale* (short) 1931 (ph); *Que Viva Mexico* 1932 (ph); *Aerograd* 1935 (ph); *Bezhin Lug/Bezhin Meadow* 1937 (ph); *Alexander Nevsky* 1938 (ph); *Ivan Grozny Part I/Ivan the Terrible Part I* 1945 (ph); *In the Mountains of Yugoslavia* 1946 (ph); *Ivan Grozny Part II/Ivan the Terrible Part II* 1946 (ph); *Vstrecha na Elbe/Meeting on the Elbe* 1949 (ph); *Kompozitor Glinka/Glinka* 1952 (ph).

Toback, James • Director, screenwriter; also producer. • Born New York, NY, November 23, 1944. *Educ.* Harvard; Columbia. Former journalist and literature professor who began his film career by scripting Karel Reisz's *The Gambler* (1974) and made a haunting directorial debut with *Fingers* (1977). (Toback had previously published a profile of the film's star, actor-athlete Jim Brown.) Toback's subsequent films, particularly the erotic thriller *Exposed* (1983)—in which he appears as Nastassja Kinski's professor/lover—have all been lesser outings, though the self-reflexive documentary, *The Big Bang* (1989) is a diverting, off-beat look at the meaning of life. • *The Gambler* 1974 (sc); *Fingers* 1977 (d,sc); *Love & Money* 1980 (d,p,sc); *Exposed* 1983 (a,d,p,sc); *The Pick-Up Artist* 1987 (d,sc); *The Big Bang* 1989 (a,d,sc); *Alice* 1990 (a).

Todd, Ann • Actress • Born Ann Todd Mayfield, Hartford, England, January 24, 1909. *Educ.* Central School of Speech and Drama, London. Blonde stage actress best known as the central character of Compton Bennett's landmark psychodrama, *The Seventh Veil* (1945). Married to David Lean from 1949 to 1957, Todd starred in several of his films, notably the first-rate melodramas, *The Passionate Friends* (1948) and *Madeleine* (1949). She began writing, producing and directing travel films in the 1950s • *The Ghost Train* 1931; *Action For Slander* 1937; *The Squeaker* 1937; *South Riding* 1938; *All This, and Heaven Too* 1940; *Bad Men of Missouri* 1941; *Blood and Sand* 1941; *The Seventh Veil* 1945; *Vacation From Marriage* 1945; *The Paradine Case* 1947; *The Passionate Friends* 1948; *So Evil My Love* 1948; *Madeleine* 1949; *The Sound Barrier* 1952; *The Green Scarf* 1954; *Time Without Pity* 1957; *The Human Factor* 1979; *Hitchcock, Il Brivido del Genio* 1985; *Ingrid* 1985; *The McGuffin* 1985.

Tognazzi, Ugo • Actor; also director. • Born Cremona, Italy, March 23, 1922; died October 27, 1990;, Rome, Italy. Former accountant who entered film in the 1950s and gained recognition for his roles in the dark, misanthropic comedies of Marco Ferreri, notably *Queen Bee* (1963) and *The Ape Woman* (1964). Tognazzi has also featured in the works of Mario Monicelli and Dino Risi and is best known to international audiences as one of the owners of *La Cage aux Folles* (1978). He won a best actor award at Cannes for Bernardo Bertolucci's *Tragedy of a Ridiculous Man* (1981). Son Ricky Tognazzi is also an actor. • *RoGoPag* 1962 (a); *Una Storia moderna/Queen Bee* 1963 (a); *La Donna Scimmia/The Ape Woman* 1964 (a); *Liola* 1964 (a); *Il Fischio al nasio* 1967 (d); *L'Immorale* 1967 (a); *Barbarella* 1968 (a); *Sissignore* 1968 (d); *Porcile* 1969 (a); *Cuori Solitari* 1970 (a); *La Califfa* 1971 (a); *Il Generale Dorme in*

Piedi 1971 (a); *In Nome del Popolo Italiano* 1971 (a); *L'Udienza* 1971 (a); *Il Maestro e Margherita* 1972 (a); *Vogliamo I Colonnelli* 1972 (a); *La Grande Bouffe* 1973 (a); *La Proprietà non e più un furto* 1973 (a); *Questa Specie d'Amore* 1973 (a); *Touche pas à la femme blanche!* 1973 (a); *Permette signora che ami vostra figlia* 1974 (a); *Romanzo Popolare* 1974 (a); *Amici Miei* 1975 (a); *La Faille* 1975 (a); *L'Anatra all'Arancia* 1976 (a); *Signore e Signori, Buonanotte* 1976 (a); *Il Casotto* 1977 (a); *I Nuovi Mostri* 1977 (a); *La Stanza del Vescovo* 1977 (a); *La Cage aux folles* 1978 (a); *Dove vai in vacanza?* 1978 (a); *Il Gatto* 1978 (a); *La Mazzetta* 1978 (a); *Primo Amore* 1978 (a); *Le Grand embouteillage* 1979 (a); *La Terrazza* 1979 (a); *La Cage aux folles II* 1980 (a); *Sono Fotogenico* 1980 (a); *Sunday Lovers* 1980 (a); *La Tragedia di un Uomo Ridicolo/Tragedy of a Ridiculous Man* 1981 (a); *Amici miei atto II* 1983 (a); *Il Petomane* 1983 (a); *Scherzo del Destino in Agguato Dietro L'Angolo Come un Brigante di Strada* 1983 (a); *Scusa se è poco* 1983 (a); *Trenta Minuti D'Amore* 1983 (a); *Bertoldo, Bertoldino e Cacasenno* 1984 (a); *Le Bon Roi Dagobert* 1984 (a); *La Cage aux folles III: "Elles" se marient* 1985 (a); *Amici Miei Atto III* 1986 (a); *Yiddish Connection* 1986 (a); *Ultimo Momento* 1987 (a); *Arrivederci e Grazie* 1988 (a); *I Giorni del commissario Ambrosio* 1988 (a); *Tolerance* 1989 (a); *La Batalla de los Tres Reyes* 1990 (a).

Toland, Gregg • Director of photography • Born Charleston, IL, May 29, 1904; died September 28, 1948, Hollywood, CA. During the deeply entrenched days of the Hollywood studio system, cinematographer Gregg Toland's technical and visual innovations set him apart from the flock of doctrinaire technicians and engineers embedded in the formulaic studio factories. He was that rarity among technicians—a cinematographer eager to accept technological advances and apply them creatively to the narrative film form. Toland's talent was readily accepted by the Hollywood establishment, who graced him with a charmed life amid the workmanlike atmosphere pervading most studio productions. Contracted throughout his career to Samuel Goldwyn (although he was lent to other producers), Toland was permitted more freedom than most cinematographers of his time, from being allowed his choice of crew and story properties to converting studio cameras to his own specifications. Working with such outstanding directors as Howard Hawks, William Wyler, John Ford and Orson Welles, Toland was in the unique position of incorporating technological innovations into equally innovative narrative frameworks.

As a child, Toland attended technical school to study electrical engineering. At 15, Toland left school for Hollywood, where he found a position as an office boy for a Hollywood film studio. Developing an interest in camerawork, it wasn't long before he became an assistant to George Barnes. By the time Toland was 27, he had become a first cameraman, the youngest in Hollywood.

In Toland's early work, in films such as *Les Miserables* (1935), *Dead End* (1937), *Intermezzo* (1939), *The Grapes of Wrath* (1940), *The Long Voyage Home* (1940), and *Wuthering Heights* (1939), he consciously rejected the soft focus, one-plane depth of the established Hollywood house style and strove for a more jarring, razor-sharp black-and-white, employing recent advances in photography that included the use of high-powered Technicolor arc lamps for black-and-white productions, Super XX film stock (a 1938 Kodak stock four times faster than its previous stock without any increase in graininess), lens coating (to cut down on glare) and self-blimped cameras (permitting filming in confined spaces). *The Long Voyage Home* is a milestone in the evolution of Toland's technical experimentation, enlisting high contrast black-and-white film, deep focus (with foreground, middle-ground, and background all in sharp focus), the self-blimped camera, ceilinged sets, low-angle lighting, shots composed into light sources and Germanic expressionism. But John Ford's turgid Eugene O'Neill mood piece was not an ideal showcase for Toland's technical wizardry, which required a bright, high-voltage directorial presence in which to display his innovations.

Toland once said, "I want to work with someone who's never made a movie. That's the only way to learn anything—from someone who doesn't know anything." In Orson Welles, Toland found a fresh perspective and vision outside of the Hollywood mainstream and in *Citizen Kane* (1941), he consolidated his bone-crisp look into a personal style, upsetting Hollywood cinematographic conventions in its wake. *Kane* synthesized Toland's deep focus experiments with Welles's directorial flourishes of fluid, moving camera shots and long takes, rejecting the standard Hollywood technique of intercutting. Welles and Toland achieved a heightened reality of space and time that exposed the artifice of the Hollywood house style, revitalizing Hollywood narrative forms and shaking up complacent technical and creative personnel.

At first Toland's deep-focus technique was considered too radical a departure from Hollywood norms. Moreover, Toland's fellow cinematographers found the films that succeeded *Kane, The Little Foxes* and *Ball of Fire* (both 1941), too visually dense and confusing, and they complained that Toland's exaggerated depth-of-field sacrificed compositional roundness and rendered the image cartoonish.

After completing *Ball of Fire*, Toland was drafted into wartime service with John Ford's OSS photographic unit, with which he shot Ford's memorable documentary, *December 7th* (1943). Toland was in the process of toning down his bravura technique into a more adaptable style, when, at 44, he suffered a fatal heart attack in 1948.

Where Toland rebeled in the 1930s against the prevalent style, by the end of the 1940s, Toland's technique had become the "new" Hollywood style, a transformation that invigorated a moribund classical cinema through the late 1940s and into the 1950s, until the advent of television and cheap cinematic gimmicks marked the fragmentation of the Hollywood system. PB • *Bulldog Drummond* 1929 (ph); *Condemned* 1929 (ph); *The Trespasser* 1929 (ph); *One Heavenly Night* 1930 (ph); *Raffles* 1930 (ph); *Whoopee* 1930 (ph); *The Devil to Pay* 1931 (ph); *Indiscreet* 1931 (ph); *Palmy Days* 1931 (ph); *Tonight or Never* 1931 (ph); *The Unholy Garden* 1931 (ph); *The Kid From Spain* 1932 (ph); *Man Wanted* 1932 (ph); *Play Girl* 1932 (ph); *The Tenderfoot* 1932 (ph); *The Washington Masquerade* 1932 (ph); *The Masquerader* 1933 (ph); *The Nuisance* 1933 (ph); *Roman Scandals* 1933 (ph); *Tugboat Annie* 1933 (ph); *Forsaking All Others* 1934 (ph); *Lazy River* 1934 (ph); *Nana* 1934 (ph); *We Live Again* 1934 (ph); *The Dark Angel* 1935 (ph); *Mad Love* 1935 (ph); *Les Miserables* 1935 (ph) **(AANBPH)**; *Public Hero Number One* 1935 (ph); *Splendor* 1935 (ph); *The Wedding Night* 1935 (ph); *Beloved Enemy* 1936 (ph); *Come and Get It* 1936 (ph); *The Road to Glory* 1936 (ph); *Strike Me Pink* 1936 (ph); *These Three* 1936 (ph); *Dead End* 1937 (ph) **(AANBPH)**; *History Is Made at Night* 1937 (ph); *Woman Chases Man* 1937 (ph); *The Cowboy and the Lady* 1938 (ph); *The Goldwyn Follies* 1938 (ph); *Kidnapped* 1938 (ph); *Intermezzo* 1939 (ph); *They Shall Have Music* 1939 (ph); *Wuthering Heights* 1939 (ph) **(AABPH)**; *The Grapes of Wrath* 1940 (ph); *The Long Voyage Home* 1940 (ph) **(AANBPH)**; *Raffles* 1940 (ph); *The Westerner* 1940 (ph); *Ball of Fire* 1941 (ph); *Citizen Kane* 1941 (ph) **(AANBPH)**; *The Little Foxes* 1941 (ph); *December 7th (short)* 1943 (d); *The Outlaw* 1943 (ph); *The Best Years of Our Lives* 1946 (ph); *The Kid From Brooklyn* 1946 (ph); *Song of the South* 1946 (ph—live-action); *The Bishop's Wife* 1947 (ph); *Enchantment* 1948 (ph); *A Song Is Born* 1948 (ph).

Tomasini, George • American editor • Born 1909; died 1964. Best known for his work with Alfred Hitchcock on films such as *Rear Window* (1954), *North By Northwest* (1959), *Psycho* (1960) and

The Birds (1963). Tomasini also contributed to films by directors including George Pal (*The Time Machine* 1960), John Huston (*The Misfits* 1961) and J. Lee Thompson (*Cape Fear* 1962); on *Elephant Walk* (1954), he was faced with the peculiar challenge of matching long-shot footage of Vivien Leigh to close-ups of Elizabeth Taylor, after the former had withdrawn from the project. • *Wild Harvest* 1947; *The Turning Point* 1952; *Houdini* 1953; *Elephant Walk* 1954; *Rear Window* 1954; *To Catch a Thief* 1955; *The Man Who Knew Too Much* 1956; *The Wrong Man* 1956; *Hear Me Good* 1957; *I Married a Monster From Outer Space* 1958; *Vertigo* 1958; *North By Northwest* 1959 **(AANBED)**; *Psycho* 1960; *The Time Machine* 1960; *The Misfits* 1961; *Cape Fear* 1962; *The Birds* 1963; *Who's Been Sleeping in My Bed?* 1963; *Marnie* 1964; *In Harm's Way* 1965.

Tomlin, Lily • Actress, comedienne • Born Mary Jean Tomlin, Detroit, MI, September 1, 1939. *Educ.* Wayne State University, Detroit (pre-med); studied acting with Peggy Feury. Multi-talented performer and writer who came to attention in 1969 as a featured performer on the kaleidoscopic TV comedy show, "Laugh In." A gifted comedienne and actress, Tomlin created a memorable gallery of characters such as the snide telephone operator, Ernestine, and the mischievous child, Edith Ann, during her memorable TV appearances through the 1970s and made an acclaimed film debut in Robert Altman's penetrating *Nashville* (1975).

Her subsequent film work has been uneven, with sympathetic performances in Robert Benton's off-beat mystery, *The Late Show* (1977) and in the title role of Joel Schumacher's underrated comedy, *The Incredible Shrinking Woman* (1981), alongside starring roles in a number of forgettable features. Tomlin, who has co-authored most of her material with long-time collaborator Jane Wagner, has showcased her remarkable talent as a sketch performer in two award-winning, one-woman Broadway shows, *Appearing Nitely* (1977) and *The Search for Signs of Intelligent Life in the Universe* (1986). • *Nashville* 1975 (a,songs) **(AANBSA)**; *The Late Show* 1977 (a); *Moment By Moment* 1978 (a); *9 to 5* 1980 (a); *The Incredible Shrinking Woman* 1981 (a); *All of Me* 1984 (a); *Lily Tomlin* 1986 (a); *Big Business* 1988 (a).

Tone, Franchot • Actor; also director, producer. • Born Stanislas Pascal Franchot Tone, Niagara Falls, NY, February 27, 1905; died September 18, 1968. *Educ.* Cornell; University of Rennes, France. Stage-trained actor who made his film debut in 1932. Owing to his upper-class poise and polish, Tone was pigeonholed as a tuxedoed, cafe society sophisticate in a host of MGM comedies and dramas. By 1937 he was one of Hollywood's leading stars, receiving recognition for his roles in *Mutiny on the Bounty* (1935), *The Lives of a Bengal Lancer* (1935) and *Three Comrades* (1938).

Save for an occasional success such as *Five Graves to Cairo* (1943), Tone made few memorable films during the 1940s, and his screen career was all but washed up by the early part of the next decade. He repaired to the stage and intermittently surfaced in character parts in films through the 1960s. (He was especially fine as the seedy, menacing nightclub owner in Arthur Penn's offbeat 1965 drama, *Mickey One*.) Tone was also featured in the popular TV series, "Ben Casey".

He was married to actresses Joan Crawford, Jean Wallace, Barbara Payton and Dolores Dorn-Heft. • *The Wiser Sex* 1932 (a); *Blonde Bombshell* 1933 (a); *Dancing Lady* 1933 (a); *Gabriel Over the White House* 1933 (a); *Midnight Mary* 1933 (a); *Stage Mother* 1933 (a); *The Stranger's Return* 1933 (a); *Today We Live* 1933 (a); *Gentlemen Are Born* 1934 (a); *The Girl From Missouri* 1934 (a); *Moulin Rouge* 1934 (a); *Sadie McKee* 1934 (a); *Straight Is the Way* 1934 (a); *The World Moves On* 1934 (a); *Dangerous* 1935 (a); *The Lives of a Bengal Lancer* 1935 (a); *Mutiny on the Bounty* 1935 (a) **(AANBA)**; *No More Ladies* 1935 (a); *One New York Night* 1935 (a); *Reckless* 1935 (a); *Exclusive Story* 1936 (a); *The Gorgeous Hussy* 1936 (a); *The King Steps Out* 1936 (a); *Love on the Run* 1936 (a); *Suzy* 1936 (a); *The Unguarded Hour* 1936 (a); *Between Two Women* 1937 (a); *The Bride Wore Red* 1937 (a); *Quality Street* 1937 (a); *They Gave Him a Gun* 1937 (a); *The Girl Downstairs* 1938 (a); *Love Is a Headache* 1938 (a); *Man-Proof* 1938 (a); *Three Comrades* 1938 (a); *Three Loves Has Nancy* 1938 (a); *Fast and Furious* 1939 (a); *Trail of the Vigilantes* 1940 (a); *Nice Girl?* 1941 (a); *She Knew All the Answers* 1941 (a); *This Woman Is Mine* 1941 (a); *Star Spangled Rhythm* 1942 (a); *The Wife Takes a Flyer* 1942 (a); *Five Graves to Cairo* 1943 (a); *His Butler's Sister* 1943 (a); *Pilot No. 5* 1943 (a); *True to Life* 1943 (a); *Dark Waters* 1944 (a); *The Hour Before the Dawn* 1944 (a); *Phantom Lady* 1944 (a); *That Night With You* 1945 (a); *Because of Him* 1946 (a); *Her Husband's Affairs* 1947 (a); *Honeymoon* 1947 (a); *I Love Trouble* 1947 (a); *Lost Honeymoon* 1947 (a); *Every Girl Should Be Married* 1948 (a); *Jigsaw* 1949 (a); *The Man on the Eiffel Tower* 1949 (a); *Without Honor* 1949 (a); *Here Comes the Groom* 1951 (a); *Uncle Vanya* 1958 (a,d,p); *Advise and Consent* 1962 (a); *La Bonne Soupe* 1964 (a); *In Harm's Way* 1965 (a); *Mickey One* 1965 (a).

Tonti, Aldo • Director of photography. • Born Rome, March 2, 1910; died July 7, 1988, outside Rome. Beginning as a camera assistant in 1934, he emerged as a cinematographer in 1939 and gained prominence for his contribution to the groundbreaking film of Italian neo-realism, Luchino Viscounti's *Ossessione* (1942). Tonti went on to collaborate on such classic works as Federico Fellini's *Nights of Cabiria* (1956), Alberto Lattuada's *The Bandit* (1946) and Mario Monicelli's *Casanova '70* (1965).

Tonti also worked in the US on such features as Nicholas Ray's *The Savage Innocents* (1960), John Huston's *Reflections in a Golden Eye* (1967) and Terence Young's *The Valachi Papers* (1972). • *Ossessione* 1942; *The Bandit* 1946; *L'Amore* 1948 (ph—"Il Miracolo"); *Molti Sogni per le Strade* 1949; *Attila* 1955; *Le Notti di Cabiria/Nights of Cabiria* 1956; *War and Peace* 1956; *Souvenir D'Italie* 1957; *La Tempesta* 1958; *Come Prima* 1959; *The Savage Innocents* 1960; *Sotto dieci bandiere* 1960; *Barabbas* 1962; *La Donna Scimmia/The Ape Woman* 1964; *Casanova '70* 1965; *Cast a Giant Shadow* 1966; *Reflections in a Golden Eye* 1967; *Lo Scatenato* 1967; *Se Tutte le Donne Del Mondo* 1967; *Roma Come Chicago* 1968; *Brancaleone Alle Crociate* 1970; *Upon This Rock* 1970; *Violent City* 1970; *Bello Onesto Emigrato Australia Sposerebbe Compaesan Illibata* 1971; *Il Prode Anselmo* 1971; *La Spina Dorsale del Diavola* 1971; *The Valachi Papers* 1972; *Crazy Joe* 1973; *Three Tough Guys* 1973; *Quelle Strane Occasioni* 1976; *Rene la Canne* 1976; *Ashanti* 1979.

Topol • *aka* Haym Topol • Actor • Born Chaim Topol, Tel Aviv, Israel, September 9, 1935. Zestful, vigorous lead and supporting player, best known for his Tevye in the screen version of *Fiddler on the Roof* (1971)—a role he had previously played on the Tel Aviv and London stage. Topol has worked primarily in the theater, making infrequent appearances in such other films as *Before Winter Comes* (1968), *The Public Eye* (1972) and *Galileo* (1974) and on TV in *Winds of War* (1982) and *War and Remembrance* (1988). • *Sallah Shabati* 1964; *Cast a Giant Shadow* 1966; *Before Winter Comes* 1968; *A Talent For Loving* 1969; *Hatarnegol* 1970; *Fiddler on the Roof* 1971 **(AANBA)**; *Follow Me!* 1972; *The Public Eye* 1972; *Galileo* 1974; *The House on Garibaldi Street* 1979; *Flash Gordon* 1980; *For Your Eyes Only* 1981; *Roman Behemshechim* 1985.

Torn, Rip • Actor; also director. • Born Elmore Rual Torn, Jr., Temple, TX, February 6, 1931. *Educ.* Texas A & M, College Station (animal husbandry); University of Texas, Austin (architecture, drama); Actors Studio. Versatile character player whose occasional leading roles have showcased an explosive talent, as in *Tropic of Cancer* (1970), *Payday* (1971) and the made-for-TV *Blind Ambition* (1979, as Richard Nixon). Usually cast as Southern good-ole-boy or redneck, Torn has played volatile supporting characters in several Tennessee Williams plays—*Orpheus Descending* (1958), *Sweet Bird of Youth* (1958) and *The Glass Menagerie* (1975)—and films: *Baby Doll* (1956) and *Sweet Bird of Youth* (1962).

Torn also appeared in a couple of Norman Mailer's cinematic improvisations of the late 1960s and was perhaps at his most manic playing himself in the ill-fated, rarely seen Jean-Luc Godard/D.A. Pennebaker experiment, *1 A.M.* (1971). He made his film directing debut with the Whoopi Goldberg vehicle, *The Telephone* (1988).

Married to actresses Anne Wedgeworth and Geraldine Page (from 1961 until her death in 1987). • *Baby Doll* 1956 (a); *A Face in the Crowd* 1957 (a); *Time Limit!* 1957 (a); *Pork Chop Hill* 1959 (a); *King of Kings* 1961 (a); *Hero's Island* 1962 (a); *Sweet Bird of Youth* 1962 (a); *Critic's Choice* 1963 (a); *The Cincinnati Kid* 1965 (a); *One Spy Too Many* 1966 (a); *Beach Red* 1967 (a); *You're a Big Boy Now* 1967 (a); *Beyond the Law* 1968 (a); *Sol Madrid* 1968 (a); *Coming Apart* 1969 (a); *Maidstone* 1970 (a); *Tropic of Cancer* 1970 (a); *One American Movie/1 A.M.* 1971 (a); *Payday* 1971 (a); *Slaughter* 1972 (a); *Crazy Joe* 1973 (a); *Birch Interval* 1975 (a); *The Man Who Fell to Earth* 1976 (a); *Nasty Habits* 1976 (a); *The Private Files of J. Edgar Hoover* 1977 (a); *Coma* 1978 (a); *The Seduction of Joe Tynan* 1979 (a); *The Wobblies* 1979 (a); *First Family* 1980 (a); *Heartland* 1980 (a); *One-Trick Pony* 1980 (a); *A Stranger Is Watching* 1981 (a); *Airplane II: The Sequel* 1982 (a); *The Beastmaster* 1982 (a); *Jinxed!* 1982 (a); *Cross Creek* 1983 (a) (**AANBSA**); *City Heat* 1984 (a); *Flashpoint* 1984 (a); *Misunderstood* 1984 (a); *Songwriter* 1984 (a); *Beer* 1985 (a); *Summer Rental* 1985 (a); *Extreme Prejudice* 1987 (a); *Nadine* 1987 (a); *Blind Curve (short)* 1988 (a); *The Telephone* 1988 (d); *Cold Feet* 1989 (a); *Hit List* 1989 (a); *Zwei Frauen* 1989 (a); *Beautiful Dreamers* 1990 (a); *Defending Your Life* 1991 (a).

Tornatore, Guiseppe • Director; also screenwriter. • Born Bagheria, Sicily, Italy, 1956. Prize-winning still photographer turned TV director who made numerous film documentaries before crafting his first feature in 1986, *Il Camorrista/The Professor.* Tornatore scored with his second film, the warmly nostalgic *Cinema Paradiso* (1989) which was shot on location in the director's native village, near Palermo. • *Il Camorrista* 1986 (d,sc); *Nuovo Cinema Paradiso/Cinema Paradiso* 1989 (d,sc,story); *Stanno Tutti Bene* 1990 (d,sc).

Torre-Nilsson, Leopoldo • *aka* Leopoldo Torre Nilsson • Director • Born Buenos Aires, Argentina, May 5, 1924; died September 8, 1978. Trailblazing Latin American director whose *The House of Angel* (1957) put the post-war Argentine cinema on the map. Born to a Spanish Catholic father (film director Leopoldo Torre-Rios) and a Protestant Swedish mother, Torre-Nilsson proclaimed himself "an atheist, and profoundly Argentinian." He entered films at 15 as his father's assistant, sidetracked his film career by pursuing an interest in writing and returned to the cinema in 1950.

After directing his first two features with his father, Torre-Nilsson made his solo debut in 1954 and gained worldwide acclaim with *The House of Angel.* A number of his subsequent films owe much of their success to his wife, novelist, playwright and scenarist Beatriz Guido, who collaborated on many of them. Torre-Nilsson's films are almost Buñuelian in their consistency of attack on established orders, particularly Catholicism and the family structure. • *Para Vestir Santos* 1954 (d); *La Casa del Angel/The House of Angel* 1957 (d,sc); *La Terraza* 1963 (d); *El Ojo de la Cerradura* 1964 (sc,story); *La Chica del Lunes* 1966 (d); *Y Que Patatin y Que Patatan* 1971 (p); *La Maffia* 1972 (d,p,sc); *Los Siete Locos* 1973 (d,sc); *Boquitas Pintadas* 1974 (d,p,sc).

Totheroh, Rollie • Director of photography • Born Roland H. Totheroh, San Francisco, CA, 1890; died 1967. Former newspaper illustrator who entered film in 1910 as a cameraman with Essanay studios in Chicago. Totheroh's multi-film association with Charlie Chaplin began when the latter left Keystone for Essanay in 1915. Their collaboration spanned over three decades and included most of Chaplin's masterpieces: *The Tramp* (1915), *The Kid* (1921), *The Gold Rush* (1925) and (as co-cinematographer) *City Lights* (1931), *Modern Times* (1936), *The Great Dictator* (1940) and *Limelight* (1952). • *The Bank (short)* 1915; *The Tramp* 1915; *Behind the Screen (short)* 1916; *One A.M. (short)* 1916; *The Pawnshop (short)* 1916; *The Rink (short)* 1916; *The Adventurer* 1917; *A Day's Pleasure (short)* 1919; *Sunnyside* 1919; *The Kid* 1921; *A Woman of Paris* 1923; *The Gold Rush* 1925; *The Circus* 1928; *City Lights* 1931; *Modern Times* 1936; *The Great Dictator* 1940; *Monsieur Verdoux* 1947; *Song of My Heart* 1947; *Limelight* 1952.

Tourneur, Jacques • Director; also editor. • Born Paris, November 12, 1904; died December 19, 1977, Bergerac, France. Master of macabre suspense who hit his peak in the 1940s with such atmospheric gems as *Cat People* (1942), *Experiment Perilous* (1944) and *Out of the Past* (1947). Tourneur worked on the films of his father, Maurice Tourneur, in the US and then in Paris, where he made his directorial debut in 1931. He returned to America in 1935, making shorts and B features at MGM before hitting his stride with several brilliantly understated features for producer Val Lewton at RKO: *Cat People, I Walked With a Zombie* (1943), and *The Leopard Man* (1943).

Tourneur inherited his father's gift for atmospheric, evocative compositions and put it to good use in westerns (*Canyon Passage* 1946), films noirs (*Out of the Past* 1947) and thrillers (*Berlin Express* 1948). His films from the mid-1950s, for various studios, were less effective, though the British-made *Curse of the Demon* (1958) marked a notable return to his earlier form. • *Accusée, Levez-vous* 1930 (ed); *Maison de danses* 1930 (ed); *Partir* 1931 (ed); *Tout ça ne vaut pas l'amour* 1931 (d); *Au Nom de la Loi* 1932 (ed); *Les Gaietés de l'Escadron* 1932 (ed); *Les Deux Orphélines* 1933 (ed); *Pour être aimé* 1933 (d); *Toto* 1933 (d); *Les Filles de la Concièrge* 1934 (d); *Le Voleur* 1934 (ed); *A Tale of Two Cities* 1935 (prod. sup—revolutionary scenes); *Nick Carter, Master Detective* 1939 (d); *They All Come Out* 1939 (d); *Phantom Raiders* 1940 (d); *Doctors Don't Tell* 1941 (d); *Cat People* 1942 (d); *I Walked With a Zombie* 1943 (d); *The Leopard Man* 1943 (d); *Days of Glory* 1944 (d); *Experiment Perilous* 1944 (d); *Canyon Passage* 1946 (d); *Out of the Past* 1947 (d); *Berlin Express* 1948 (d); *Easy Living* 1949 (d); *The Flame and the Arrow* 1950 (d); *Stars in My Crown* 1950 (d); *Anne of the Indies* 1951 (d); *Circle of Danger* 1951 (d); *Way of a Gaucho* 1952 (d); *Appointment in Honduras* 1953 (d); *Stranger on Horseback* 1954 (d); *Wichita* 1955 (d); *Great Day in the Morning* 1956 (d); *Nightfall* 1956 (d); *Curse of the Demon* 1958 (d); *The Fearmakers* 1958 (d); *Fury River* 1958 (d); *Mission of Danger* 1959 (d); *Timbuktu* 1959 (d); *La Battaglia di Maratona* 1960 (d); *The Comedy of Terrors* 1964 (d); *War Gods of the Deep* 1965 (d).

Tourneur, Maurice • Director • Born Maurice Thomas, Paris, February 2, 1876; died August 4, 1961, Paris. Former student of Auguste Rodin who turned his attention to the theater and then moved into films as an actor and assistant director at the Eclair studios. Tourneur moved to the US in 1914, initially as head of Eclair's Fort Lee, N.J., subsidiary. He soon became known as one of the most stylish directors of his time, partly thanks to his collaboration with art director Ben Carre, who designed some 35 features for Tourneur through 1920. The pair's best work was in the mystery and fantasy genres.

Tourneur returned to Europe in 1927 and, aside from one German film, continued his career in France through 1948, when he lost a leg in a car accident. He subsequently translated English-language mystery novels into French. Father of director Jacques Tourneur. • *The Man of the Hour* 1914 (d,sc); *Mother* 1914 (d); *The Pit* 1914 (d); *The Wishing Ring*

1914 (d,sc); *Alias Jimmy Valentine* 1915 (d,sc); *A Butterfly on the Wheel* 1915 (d); *The Cub* 1915 (d); *The Ivory Snuff Box* 1915 (d,sc); *Trilby* 1915 (d); *The Closed Road* 1916 (d,sc); *The Hand of Peril* 1916 (d,sc); *The Pawn of Fate* 1916 (d); *The Rail Rider* 1916 (d); *The Velvet Paw* 1916 (d); *Barbary Sheep* 1917 (d); *Exile* 1917 (d); *A Girl's Folly* 1917 (d,sc,story); *The Law of the Land* 1917 (d); *The Poor Little Rich Girl* 1917 (d); *The Pride of the Clan* 1917 (d); *The Rise of Jennie Cushing* 1917 (d); *The Undying Flame* 1917 (d); *The Whip* 1917 (d); *The Blue Bird* 1918 (d); *A Doll's House* 1918 (d); *Prunella* 1918 (d); *Rose of the World* 1918 (d); *Sporting Life* 1918 (d,p); *Woman* 1918 (d,p); *The Broken Butterfly* 1919 (d,sc); *The Life Line* 1919 (d); *Victory* 1919 (d); *The White Heather* 1919 (d); *The County Fair* 1920 (d); *Deep Waters* 1920 (d); *The Great Redeemer* 1920 (p); *The Last of the Mohicans* 1920 (d); *My Lady's Garter* 1920 (d); *Treasure Island* 1920 (d); *While Paris Sleeps* 1920 (d); *The White Circle* 1920 (d,p); *The Bait* 1921 (d); *The Foolish Matrons* 1921 (d); *Lorna Doone* 1922 (d,p,sc); *The Brass Bottle* 1923 (d,p); *The Christian* 1923 (d); *The Isle of Lost Ships* 1923 (d); *Jealous Husbands* 1923 (d); *Mary of the Movies* 1923 (a); *Torment* 1924 (d); *The White Moth* 1924 (d); *Clothes Make the Pirate* 1925 (d); *Never the Twain Shall Meet* 1925 (d); *Sporting Life* 1925 (d); *Aloma of the South Seas* 1926 (d); *Old Loves and New* 1926 (d); *L'Equipage* 1928 (d,sc); *Das Schiff der Verlorenen Menschen* 1929 (d); *Accusée, Levez-vous* 1930 (d); *Maison de danses* 1930 (d,sc); *Partir* 1931 (d); *Au Nom de la Loi* 1932 (d,sc); *Les Gaiétes de l'Escadron* 1932 (d); *Les Deux Orphelines* 1933 (d); *Justin de Marseille* 1934 (d); *Obsession* 1934 (d); *Le Voleur* 1934 (d); *Koenigsmark* 1935 (d); *Samson* 1936 (d); *Avec le Sourire* 1937 (d); *Katia* 1938 (d); *Le Patriote* 1938 (d); *Volpone* 1940 (d); *Mam'zelle Bonaparte* 1941 (d); *Péchés de Jeunesse* 1941 (d); *La Main du Diable* 1942 (d); *Cécile est Morte* 1943 (d); *Le Val d'Enfer* 1943 (d); *Après L'Amour* 1947 (d); *Impasse des deux anges* 1948 (d).

Towne, Robert • American screenwriter; also director, producer, actor. • Born 1936. *Educ.* Pomona College, Clairmont, CA (literature, philosophy). Graduated from writing low-budget Roger Corman curiosities to become one of Hollywood's most acclaimed scenarists of the mid-1970s, sculpting such compelling works as *The Last Detail* (1973), *Chinatown* (1974) and *Shampoo* (1975). Towne made an impressive directorial debut with *Personal Best* (1982), a character study of a lesbian athlete, but the slick romantic thriller *Tequila Sunrise* (1988) fared less successfully with the critics.

Towne is also known in the film industry as a "script doctor," having done uncredited work on movies including *Marathon Man* (1976), *The Missouri Breaks* (1976) and *Frantic* (1989). He used the pseudonym P.H. Vazak (his dog's name) for his contribution to the screenplay of *Greystoke: The Legend of Tarzan, Lord of the Apes* (1984). • *The Last Woman on Earth* 1960 (sc); *The Tomb of Ligeia* 1965 (sc); *Bonnie and Clyde* 1967 (special consultant); *Villa Rides* 1968 (sc); *Drive, He Said* 1971 (a); *The Last Detail* 1973 (sc) **(AANBSC)**; *Chinatown* 1974 (sc) **(AABSC)**; *Shampoo* 1975 (sc) **(AANBSC)**; *The Yakuza* 1975 (sc); *Personal Best* 1982 (d,p,sc); *Greystoke: The Legend of Tarzan, Lord of the Apes* 1984 (sc); *The Bedroom Window* 1987 (exec.p,sc); *The Pick-Up Artist* 1987 (a); *Tough Guys Don't Dance* 1987 (assistance); *Tequila Sunrise* 1988 (d,sc); *Days of Thunder* 1990 (sc,story); *The Two Jakes* 1990 (sc,from characters *Chinatown*).

Townsend, Robert • Director, actor; also writer, producer, comedian. • Born Chicago, IL, February 6, 1957. *Educ.* Illinois State University; Hunter College; Negro Ensemble Company (acting); Second City comedy workshop. Multi-talented figure who graduated from stand-up comedy to film, making his screen acting debut in Paul Mazursky's *Willie & Phil* (1980) and contributing a fine dramatic performance in *A Soldier's Story* (1984).

Frustrated at the dearth of significant screen roles for blacks, Townsend scraped together some $100,000 (putting most of it on his assortment of credit cards) to produce, direct, write and star in his witty lampoon of the travails of an aspiring minority actor, *Hollywood Shuffle* (1987). Having since directed Eddie Murphy's concert movie, *Raw* (1987), as well as several cable TV comedy shows, Townsend's first major studio effort was *The Five Heartbeats* (1991), a bittersweet drama about the rise of a fictional '60s soul group. • *Willie & Phil* 1980 (a); *A Soldier's Story* 1984 (a); *Streets of Fire* 1984 (a); *American Flyers* 1985 (a); *Odd Jobs* 1986 (a); *Ratboy* 1986 (a); *Eddie Murphy Raw* 1987 (d); *Hollywood Shuffle* 1987 (a,d,p,sc); *The Mighty Quinn* 1989 (a); *That's Adequate* 1989 (a); *The Five Heartbearts* (a,d,p,sc).

Tracy, Lee • Actor • Born William Lee Tracy, Atlanta, GA, April 14, 1898; died October 18, 1968. *Educ.* Union College. Dynamic actor from the Broadway stage who entered film in 1929 and parlayed his success as the antic, fast-talking Hildy Johnson in the 1930 theatrical production of *The Front Page* into a number of screen roles as a hyperactive reporter. Noted for his staccato, nasal delivery, Tracy played a host of commanding leads and suporting roles through the 1940s and won an Oscar nomination for his perfomance in the 1964 drama, *The Best Man.* He also starred in the TV series "Martin Kane—Private Eye" (1952-53) and, again as a reporter, on "New York Confidential" (1958-59). • *Big Time* 1929; *Born Reckless* 1930; *Liliom* 1930; *She Got What She Wanted* 1930; *Blessed Event* 1932; *Doctor X* 1932; *Half Naked Truth* 1932; *Love Is a Racket* 1932; *The Night Mayor* 1932; *The Strange Love of Molly Louvain* 1932; *Washington Merry-Go-Round* 1932; *Advice to the Lovelorn* 1933; *Blonde Bombshell* 1933; *Clear All Wires* 1933; *Dinner at Eight* 1933; *The Nuisance* 1933; *Private Jones* 1933; *Turn Back the Clock* 1933; *I'll Tell the World* 1934; *The Lemon Drop Kid* 1934; *You Belong to Me* 1934; *Carnival* 1935; *Two Fisted* 1935; *Sutter's Gold* 1936; *Wanted! Jane Turner* 1936; *Behind the Headlines* 1937; *Criminal Lawyer* 1937; *Crashing Hollywood* 1938; *Fixer Dugan* 1939; *The Spellbinder* 1939; *Millionaires in Prison* 1940; *The Pay-Off* 1942; *Power of the Press* 1943; *Betrayal From the East* 1945; *I'll Tell the World* 1945; *High Tide* 1947; *The Best Man* 1964 **(AANBSA)**.

Tracy, Spencer • Actor • Born Milwaukee, WI, April 5, 1900; died June 10, 1967. *Educ.* Northwestern Military Academy; Ripon College, Wisconsin; AADA, New York. In the early 1930s, Spencer Tracy's truculent attitude and thunderingly aberrant behavior were his only defenses against studio power brokers who cast him as stereotypical con men, buddies and gangsters. But by the end of the decade the actor's on-screen style—seamless naturalism and subtle inflections—had proved the ticket to stardom. A Tracy performance was always more than just action; there was always an undercurrent of mental activity beneath the surface. Stanley Kramer, who directed him in several films, recalls: "I was afraid to say, 'Spencer, you're a great actor. He'd only say, 'Now what the hell kind of thing is that to come out with?' He wanted to know it; he needed to know it. But he didn't want you to say it—just think it. And maybe that was one of the reasons he was a great actor. He thought and listened better than anyone in the history of motion pictures. A silent close-up reaction of Spencer Tracy said it all." Tracy's seemingly effortless approach earned him the respect of his peers, helping him to become one of the most distinguished and venerated actors of his generation.

Tracy's early childhood was one of intense rebelliousness—he was expelled from a total of fifteen grade schools. By the time he reached high school, he had had a change of attitude, achieving good grades and even aspiring to the priesthood. But at Ripon College Tracy became involved with college theatrical productions, and before long he found himself in New York City, enrolled in the American Academy of Dramatic Arts.

The 1920s were a decade of struggle, as he fended off poverty by taking any acting job that came along, from traveling road companies and one-nighters to repertory work in towns as far-flung as White Plains and Grand Rapids. He first achieved Broadway notice in *Yellow* (1926) and critical and audience praise in *Baby Cyclone* (1927). But three flops in a row in 1929 (*Conflict, Nigger Rich* and *Veneer*) saw his career come to a standstill. In 1930, Tracy appeared in two low-budget short films: *Taxi Talks,* as a gangster, and *Hard Guy,* as a World War I veteran. But the films were unimpressive and Tracy still struggled until *The Last Mile.* Playing killer John Mears in this Broadway crime drama, Tracy had his first major success. One audience member impressed by Tracy's performance was director John Ford, who persuaded Fox to sign him for Ford's upcoming film *Up the River* (1930).

Up the River, a comic crime film, was a hit for Fox and Tracy was put under contract. But before long Tracy despaired of the studio's ever casting him in the right vehicles. Although he received critical praise for *Quick Millions* (1931), *Society Girl* (1932), and *20,000 Years in Sing Sing* (1933), most of his films were financial failures and Fox was reluctant to promote him in quality features. A frustrated Tracy responded with heavy drinking, fighting with producers and directors and disappearing from film sets for days at a time. Fox did cast him in its prestige production, *The Power and the Glory* (1933), Tracy's most challenging role yet, as a ruthless business tycoon, but the film's meager box-office convinced Fox that Tracy would never be a box-office star and he played out his contract in second-rate productions.

Although Louis B. Mayer felt Spencer Tracy lacked box-office fire, Irving Thalberg pushed for Tracy to come to MGM, feeling that he could make it at a studio top-heavy with female stars. Signing with MGM in 1935, Tracy was featured the next year in two successes, *San Francisco* and *Libeled Lady,* although more as a glorified supporting player to Clark Gable and William Powell than a force who could carry his own film. Tracy more than proved his star power and earned industry respect with back-to-back Academy Award-winning performances in *Captains Courageous* (1937) and *Boys Town* (1938). Having proved his mettle in dramatic roles, Tracy solidified his reputation for versatility by costarring in a long-running series of romantic comedies with Katharine Hepburn, beginning with *Woman of the Year* (1942) and continuing with such classics as *State of the Union* (1948), *Adam's Rib* (1949), and *Pat and Mike* (1952). Tracy's unsophisticated gruffness provided a perfect counterpoint to Hepburn's ethereal cosmopolitanism.

Tracy continued at MGM until problems developed on the set of *Tribute to a Bad Man* (1956), where his imperious and confusing behavior caused the production to shut down. Director Robert Wise was forced to fire Tracy from the film, effectively ending his twenty years with the studio.

In declining health, Tracy became reclusive, never venturing from his rented home. But he developed a friendship with director Stanley Kramer, who guided him through the final decade of his life in such crowning performances as the Clarence Darrow-inspired lawyer in *Inherit the Wind* (1960) and the transcendental judge in *Judgment at Nuremberg* (1961). Suffering from emphysema, Tracy made his last screen appearance opposite Hepburn in Kramer's *Guess Who's Coming to Dinner?* (1967). Struggling through the production, Tracy died two weeks after filming was completed.

Tracy's presence was a strong, quiet, reliable one. He gave the American cinema some of its most enduring and undeterred portrayals of stolid honesty and thoughtful scrupulousness. The inner strength and self-assurance he projected are in stark contrast to the cinema's current stars. PB • *Up the River* 1930; *Goldie* 1931; *Quick Millions* 1931; *Six Cylinder Love* 1931; *Disorderly Conduct* 1932; *Me and My Gal* 1932; *The Painted Woman* 1932; *She Wanted a Millionaire* 1932; *Sky Devils* 1932; *Society Girl* 1932; *Young America* 1932; *20,000 Years in Sing Sing* 1933; *The Face in the Sky* 1933; *The Mad Game* 1933; *A Man's Castle* 1933; *The Power and the Glory* 1933; *Shanghai Madness* 1933; *Bottoms Up* 1934; *Looking For Trouble* 1934; *Marie Galante* 1934; *Now I'll Tell* 1934; *The Show-Off* 1934; *Dante's Inferno* 1935; *It's a Small World* 1935; *The Murder Man* 1935; *Riffraff* 1935; *Whipsaw* 1935; *Fury* 1936; *Libeled Lady* 1936; *San Francisco* 1936 **(AANBA)**; *The Big City* 1937; *Captains Courageous* 1937 **(AABA)**; *They Gave Him a Gun* 1937; *Boys Town* 1938 **(AABA)**; *Mannequin* 1938; *Test Pilot* 1938; *Stanley and Livingstone* 1939; *Boom Town* 1940; *Edison, the Man* 1940; *I Take This Woman* 1940; *Northwest Passage* 1940; *Dr. Jekyll and Mr. Hyde* 1941; *Men of Boys Town* 1941; *Keeper of the Flame* 1942; *Tortilla Flat* 1942; *Woman of the Year* 1942; *A Guy Named Joe* 1943; *The Seventh Cross* 1944; *Thirty Seconds Over Tokyo* 1944; *Without Love* 1945; *Cass Timberlane* 1947; *Sea of Grass* 1947; *Edward, My Son* 1948; *State of the Union* 1948; *Adam's Rib* 1949; *Malaya* 1949; *Father of the Bride* 1950 **(AANBA)**; *Father's Little Dividend* 1951; *The People Against O'Hara* 1951; *Pat and Mike* 1952; *Plymouth Adventure* 1952; *The Actress* 1953; *Bad Day at Black Rock* 1954 **(AANBA)**; *Broken Lance* 1954; *The Mountain* 1956; *Desk Set* 1957; *The Last Hurrah* 1958; *The Old Man and the Sea* 1958 **(AANBA)**; *Inherit the Wind* 1960 **(AANBA)**; *The Devil at 4 O'Clock* 1961; *Judgment at Nuremberg* 1961 **(AANBA)**; *How the West Was Won* 1962; *It's a Mad, Mad, Mad, Mad World* 1963; *Guess Who's Coming to Dinner?* 1967 **(AANBA)**; *George Stevens: A Filmmaker's Journey* 1985 (archival footage); *Going Hollywood: The War Years* 1988 (archival footage).

Trauner, Alexander • *aka* Alexandre Trauner • Production designer • Born Budapest, Hungary, August 3, 1906. Renowned art director who came to prominence with the French "poetic realism" movement of the 1930s. Trauner, who apprenticed under Lazare Meerson and espoused a studio-bound aesthetic, produced textured, finely detailed sets for such Marcel Carné classics as *Quai des brumes* (1938) and *Le jour se lève* (1939).

During the German Occupation, though Jewish, Trauner managed to work uncredited on films such as Carne's *The Devil's Envoys* (1942) and *Children of Paradise* (1945). He then created the stunning, baroque designs for Orson Welles's *Othello* (1952) and, at the invitation of Billy Wilder, moved to Hollywood. Notable collaborations with Wilder include *The Apartment* (1960) and *Irma La Douce* (1963); Trauner has also enjoyed enjoyed extended working relationships with Joseph Losey, Claude Berri and Bertrand Tavernier and was more prolific in the 1980s than he had been in the 30s and 40s. • *A Nous la Liberté* 1931 (art d); *Quai des brumes* 1938 (art d); *Le jour se leve* 1939 (art d); *Othello* 1952 (design); *L'Amant de Lady Chatterley* 1955 (sets); *The Nun's Story* 1959 (art d); *The Apartment* 1960 (art d) **(AABAD)**; *Romanoff and Juliet* 1961 (art d); *Irma La Douce* 1963 (art d); *Behold a Pale Horse* 1964 (assoc.p,pd); *Uptight* 1968 (pd); *Les Mariés de l'an II* 1971 (art d); *Impossible Object* 1973 (art d); *Grandeur Nature* 1974 (doll design director); *The Man Who Would Be King* 1975 (pd) **(AANBAD)**; *Mr. Klein* 1976 (art d); *La Première Fois* 1976 (art d); *Fedora* 1978 (pd); *Les Routes du Sud* 1978 (art d); *Don Giovanni* 1979 (asst.art d); *The Fiendish Plot of Dr. Fu Manchu* 1980 (pd); *Coup de Torchon* 1981 (pd); *Tchao Pantin* 1983 (art d); *Vive les Femmes!* 1984 (art d); *Harem* 1985 (pd); *Subway* 1985 (art d); *Autour de Minuit/Round Midnight* 1986 (pd); *Le Moustachu* 1987 (artistic tech.ad); *La Nuit Bengali* 1988 (pd); *Comédie d'amour* 1989 (artistic tech.ad); *Réunion* 1989 (a,pd).

Travolta, John • Actor • Born Englewood, NJ, February 18, 1954. Bright-eyed, boyish lead who graduated from TV's "Welcome Back Kotter"(1975-78) to "hustling" his way to stardom in one of the signature films of the late 1970s, *Saturday Night Fever* (1977). Travolta cemented his popularity with *Grease* (1978) but subsequently languished in several forgettable films before scoring in the sleeper hit of 1989, *Look Who's Talking*. Sister Ellen and brother Joey are both actors. • *The Devil's Rain* 1975 (a); *Carrie* 1976 (a); *Saturday Night Fever* 1977 (a) **(AANBA)**; *Grease* 1978 (a,song); *Moment By Moment* 1978 (a); *Urban Cowboy* 1980 (a); *Blow Out* 1981 (a); *Staying Alive* 1983 (a); *Two of a Kind* 1983 (a,song); *Perfect* 1985 (a); *The Experts* 1989 (a); *Look Who's Talking* 1989 (a); *Chains of Gold* 1990 (a); *Look Who's Talking Too* 1990 (a).

Trevor, Claire • Actress • Born Claire Wemlinger, New York, NY, March 8, 1909. *Educ.* Columbia; AADA, New York. Actress from the New York stage who made forays to Brooklyn to appear in Vitaphone shorts in the early 1930s before making her feature film debut in 1933. Trevor typically toiled as a hardened but sympathetic victim or gun moll in a host of B productions until she gained recognition for her fine performance as the classic, gold-hearted saloon gal in John Ford's classic western, *Stagecoach* (1939).

In the 1940s and 50s, Trevor emerged as a star of several top-shelf works, notably *Key Largo* (1948) and *The High and the Mighty* (1954); she also appeared in a number of TV productions, receiving an Emmy for her performance opposite Fredric March in *Dodsworth* (1956). • *Jimmy and Sally* 1933; *The Last Trail* 1933; *Life in the Raw* 1933; *The Mad Game* 1933; *Baby Takes a Bow* 1934; *Elinor Norton* 1934; *Hold That Girl* 1934; *Wild Gold* 1934; *Black Sheep* 1935; *Dante's Inferno* 1935; *My Marriage* 1935; *Navy Wife* 1935; *Spring Tonic* 1935; *15 Maiden Lane* 1936; *Career Woman* 1936; *Human Cargo* 1936; *The Song and Dance Man* 1936; *Star For a Night* 1936; *To Mary—With Love* 1936; *Big Town Girl* 1937; *Dead End* 1937 **(AANBSA)**; *King of Gamblers* 1937; *One Mile From Heaven* 1937; *Second Honeymoon* 1937; *Time Out For Romance* 1937; *The Amazing Dr. Clitterhouse* 1938; *Five of a Kind* 1938; *Valley of the Giants* 1938; *Walking Down Broadway* 1938; *Allegheny Uprising* 1939; *I Stole a Million* 1939; *Stagecoach* 1939; *Dark Command* 1940; *Honky Tonk* 1941; *Texas* 1941; *The Adventures of Martin Eden* 1942; *Crossroads* 1942; *Street of Chance* 1942; *The Desperadoes* 1943; *Good Luck, Mr. Yates* 1943; *The Woman of the Town* 1943; *Murder, My Sweet* 1944; *Johnny Angel* 1945; *The Bachelor's Daughters* 1946; *Crack-Up* 1946; *Born to Kill* 1947; *The Babe Ruth Story* 1948; *Key Largo* 1948 **(AABSA)**; *Raw Deal* 1948; *The Velvet Touch* 1948; *Borderline* 1949; *The Lucky Stiff* 1949; *Best of the Badmen* 1951; *Hard, Fast and Beautiful* 1951; *Hoodlum Empire* 1952; *My Man and I* 1952; *Stop, You're Killing Me* 1952; *The Stranger Wore a Gun* 1953; *The High and the Mighty* 1954 **(AANBSA)**; *Man Without a Star* 1954; *Lucy Gallant* 1955; *The Mountain* 1956; *Marjorie Morningstar* 1958; *Two Weeks in Another Town* 1962; *The Stripper* 1963; *How to Murder Your Wife* 1965; *The Cape Town Affair* 1967; *Kiss Me Goodbye* 1982.

Trintignant, Jean-Louis • Actor; also director. • Born Fiolenc, France, December 11, 1930. Handsome, contemplative lead who was catapulted to stardom opposite Brigitte Bardot in *And God Created Woman* (1956), fell out of the spotlight after being drafted into the Algerian War and regained his prominence in the Oscar-winning *A Man and a Woman* (1966). Experienced on stage, Trintignant has been most effective in romances and political films, such as Costa-Gavras's *Z* (1969), which earned him a best actor award at Cannes, and Bertolucci's *The Conformist* (1970). He made a surprisingly impressive directing debut with *A Well-Filled Day* (1973). Divorced from actress Stephane Audran, he has been married to director-screenwriter Nadine Trintignant (nee Marquand) since 1960. Father of actress Marie Trintignant. • *Et Dieu... Crea la Femme/And God Created Woman* 1956 (a); *Si Tous les Gars du Monde...* 1956 (a); *Les Liaisons Dangereuses* 1959 (a); *Antinea, L'Amante della Citta Sepolta* 1961 (a); *Una Vita Dificile* 1961 (a); *Les Sept péchés capitaux/The Seven Deadly Sins* 1962 (a); *Chateau en Suede* 1963 (a); *Compartiment tueurs/The Sleeping Car Murders* 1965 (a); *Un Homme et une femme/A Man and a Woman* 1966 (a); *Trans-Europ-Express* 1966 (a); *Les Biches* 1967 (a); *Mon Amour, Mon Amour* 1967 (a); *La Matriarca* 1968 (a); *Ma nuit chez Maud/My Night at Maud's* 1969 (a); *Metti, una Sera a Cena* 1969 (a); *Z* 1969 (a); *Il Conformista/The Conformist* 1970 (a); *Las Secretas Intenciones* 1970 (a); *Sans Mobile Apparent* 1971 (a); *L'Attentat* 1972 (a); *La Course du lièvre à travers les champs* 1972 (a); *Defense de savoir* 1973 (a); *L'Escapade* 1973 (a); *Un Homme Est Mort* 1973 (a); *Une Journée bien remplie/A Well-Filled Day* 1973 (d,sc); *Le Train/The Train* 1973 (a); *Les Violons du Bal* 1973 (a); *L'Agression* 1974 (a); *Le Jeu avec le feu* 1974 (a); *Le Mouton Enragé* 1974 (a); *Le Secret* 1974 (a); *Flic Story* 1975 (a); *Il Pleut sur Santiago* 1975 (a); *Le Desert des tartares* 1976 (a); *La Donna Della Domenica* 1976 (a); *L'Ordinateur des pompes funebres* 1976 (a); *Le Voyage de Noces* 1976 (a); *Faces of Love* 1977 (a); *Les Passagers* 1977 (a); *Reperages* 1977 (a); *L'Argent des autres* 1978 (a); *Le Maître-Nageur* 1979 (a,d,sc); *Melancolie Baby* 1979 (a); *La Terrazza* 1979 (a); *La Banquière* 1980 (a); *Je vous aime* 1980 (a); *Une Affaire d'Hommes* 1981 (a); *Eaux Profondes* 1981 (a); *Le Grand Pardon* 1981 (a); *Passione d'amore* 1981 (a); *Colpire Al Cuore* 1982 (a); *La Nuit de Varennes* 1982 (a); *Vivement Dimanche/Confidentially Yours* 1982 (a); *Le Bon Plaisir* 1983 (a); *La Crime* 1983 (a); *Femmes de personne* 1983 (a); *Under Fire* 1983 (a); *L'Eté Prochain* 1984 (a); *Partir Revenir* 1984 (a); *Surtuz Egy Fekete Bivalyert* 1984 (a); *Viva la Vie!* 1984 (a); *L'Homme aux yeux d'argent* 1985 (a); *Rendezvous* 1985 (a); *La Femme de ma vie* 1986 (a); *Un Homme et une femme: Vingt ans deja/A Man and a Woman: 20 Years Later* 1986 (a); *Quinze Août (short)* 1986 (a); *Le Moustachu* 1987 (a); *La Vallée fantôme* 1987 (a); *Bunker Palace Hotel* 1989 (a); *Merci, la vie* 1991 (a).

Trintignant, Nadine • Director; also screenwriter. • Born Nadine Marquand, Nice, France, November 11, 1934. The sister of actor Serge Marquand and actor-director Christian Marquand, Trintignant worked as an editor with such directors as Jacques Doniol-Valcroze and Jean-Luc Godard before turning to directing. Her films typically deal with the problems of familial and sexual relationships. Wife, since 1960, of Jean-Louis Trintignant and mother of Marie Trintignant; both have appeared in her films. • *Le Petit Soldat* 1960 (ed); *Mon Amour, Mon Amour* 1967 (d,sc); *Le Voleur de crimes* 1969 (d); *Ça n'arrive qu'aux autres* 1971 (d,sc); *Défense de savoir* 1973 (d,sc); *Le Voyage de Noces* 1976 (d,sc); *Premier Voyage* 1979 (d,sc); *L'Eté Prochain* 1984 (d,sc); *La Maison de Jade* 1988 (d,sc).

Trnka, Jirí • Animation director; also screenwriter. • Born Pilsen, Czechoslovakia, February 24, 1912; died December 30, 1969. *Educ.* School of Arts and Crafts (UMPRUM), Prague. World-renowned figure who began his career working on cartoons but is best known for his ingenious puppet animation. Notable achievements include the anti-Nazi parable *The Devil of the Springs* (1945), the western satire *Song of the Prairie* (1949), *Old Czech Legends* (1953) and the feature-length *A Midsummer Night's Dream* (1959). • *Grandpa Planted a Beet* 1945 (d); *The Devil of the Springs* 1945 (d); *The Gift* 1946 (d); *The Animals and the Brigands* 1946 (d); *Spalícek/The Czech Year* 1947 (d); *Císaruv Slavík/The Emporer's Nightingale* 1948 (d); *Song of the Prairie* 1949 (d); *Prince Bayaya* 1950 (d); *The Golden Fish* 1951 (d); *Old Czech Legends* 1953 (d); *The Good Soldier Schweik* 1954 (d); *A Midsummer Night's Dream* 1959 (d); *Obsession* 1960 (d); *Cybernetic Grandma* 1962 (d); *The Archangel Gabriel and Mrs. Goose* 1965 (d); *The Hand (short)* 1965 (d).

Troell, Jan • Director; also director of photography, screenwriter, editor. • Born Limhamn, Skåne, Sweden, July 23, 1931. Former elementary school teacher who began collaborating on films with director Bo Widerberg in the early 1960s. Troell made his own feature directing debut in 1965 and went on to become one of his country's leading filmmakers. His best-known work outside Sweden is the sweeping dyptich *The Emigrants* (1972) and *The New Land* (1972), based on novels by Vilhelm Moberg and starring Liv Ullmann and Max Von Sydow. He has made two US films, the disappointing *Zandy's Bride* (1974) and *Hurricane* (1979). • *Barnvagnen* 1962 (ph); *Har Har Du Ditt Liv* 1966 (d,sc,ph,ed); *Ole Dole Doff* 1967 (d,sc,ph,ed); *Utvandrarna/The Emigrants* 1970 (d,sc,ph,ed) **(AANBD)**; *Nybyggarna/The New Land* 1972 (d,sc,ph,ed); *Zandy's Bride* 1974 (d); *Bang!* 1977 (d,sc,ph,ed); *Hurricane* 1979 (d); *Ingenjor Andrees Luftfard* 1982 (d,sc,ph,ed); *Sagolandet* 1986 (a,d,sc,ph,ed).

Truffaut, François • Director, screenwriter, critic; also actor, producer. • Born Paris, February 6, 1932; died October 21, 1984, Neuilly, France. Influential film critic, leading New Wave director and heir to the humanistic cinematic tradition of Jean Renoir, François Truffaut made films that reflected his three professed passions: a love of cinema, an interest in male-female relationships and a fascination with children.

After a troubled childhood, Truffaut joined the French army, deserted and was sentenced to a prison term. Critic André Bazin helped secure his release and encouraged his interest in film. In Bazin's influential journal, *Cahiers du Cinéma*, Truffaut published "Une Certaine Tendance du Cinéma Français" ("A Certain Tendency in French Cinema") in 1954, proposing what came to be known as the auteur theory. A reaction against the bloated "Tradition of Quality" cinema in France, the article was a plea for a more personal cinema and an informal manifesto for the New Wave, which had not yet broken on the shores of French film.

As a filmmaker, Truffaut began by making shorts (*Une Visite* 1954, *Les Mistons* 1957) and working as an assistant to Roberto Rossellini. In 1959 he completed his first feature-length film, the semi-autobiographical childhood story *The 400 Blows*, about a troubled adolescent, Antoine Doinel. Truffaut went on to chronicle Doinel's youth and young adulthood in the "Antoine and Colette" episode of *Love at Twenty* (1962), *Stolen Kisses* (1968), *Bed and Board* (1970) and *Love on the Run* (1979), all films featuring the same actor, Jean-Pierre Léaud, as Antoine.

Two diverging strains characterize most of Truffaut's work from the early 1960s on. On the one hand, the director celebrated life in the humanistic tradition of Jean Renoir. These films include that masterwork of 60s cinema, *Jules and Jim* (1961), which defined the modern romantic triangle for a generation—it is the bittersweet story, not of Jules and Jim, the two men, but of Catherine (Jeanne Moreau), the woman who dominates their lives and is free, at least, to choose; *The Wild Child* (1970), an essay in signs and meaning in which Truffaut himself starred as the historical Dr. Jean Itard, obsessed with understanding how to establish human communication with a boy raised outside of society; the ebullient *Such a Gorgeous Kid Like Me* (1972); *Day For Night* (1973), an exuberant celebration of the joy of filmmaking, the ultimate communal art; the joyous depiction of childhood, *Small Change* (1975); the celebration of women and love in *The Man Who Loved Women* (1977); and the gentle thriller *Confidentially Yours* (1982).

On the other hand, many of Truffaut's films are fatalistic or even cynical, displaying a Hitchcockian fascination with life's darker side. This group includes *The Bride Wore Black* (1968), his most explicit homage to Hitchcock, scored by the master's regular composer, Bernard Herrmann; *Two English Girls* (1971), about a writer (Léaud) and his affairs with two sisters; *The Story of Adèle H.* (1975), one of the most harrowing examinations of unrequited love ever filmed; *The Green Room* (1978), about the love of death; and *The Woman Next Door* (1981).

Yet another group of films reflect an uneasy balance of these two divergent tendencies, as in his anatomy of adultery, *The Soft Skin* (1964); the romantic but brooding *Mississippi Mermaid* (1968), which Truffaut described as being about "degradation, by love"; and *The Last Metro* (1980).

"I want a film I watch to express either the joy of making cinema or the anguish of making cinema," Truffaut once said. "I am not interested in all the films that don't vibrate." In 1976, Truffaut accepted the invitation of the wildly successful young American director Steven Spielberg to star in *Close Encounters of the Third Kind* as the scientist in search of communication with extra-terrestrials. His stoic portrait in that film is an emblem of Truffaut's . . .pain; the arduous difficulty a born outsider encounters in communicating. This pain suffuses his lesser films, and cramps them, but it also lurks never far from the heart of his great films. It's what makes them "vibrate."

Always concerned with the process as well as the product of his profession, Truffaut maintained his role as critic and commentator throughout his filmmaking career, as proud of his books as he was of his films. Among his publications is a book-length interview with Hitchcock, *Hitchcock-Truffaut* (1967), a perennial critical classic which he revised in 1983, shortly before his death. His critical essays were collected in *Les Films de ma Vie* (1975) and his letters—posthumously—in *François Truffaut Correspondance* (1990), with a foreword by Jean-Luc Godard.

Truffaut died—dramatically, arbitrarily—of a brain tumor in the American Hospital in Neuilly in 1984. He is the father of Laura Truffaut (born 1959) and Eva Truffaut (born 1961), both of whom appeared in their father's film *L'Argent de Poche* (1975) and whose mother is his former wife, Madeleine Morgenstern; and of Joséphine (born 1983), whose mother is Fanny Ardant. CRB, JM • *Une Visite* (short) 1954 (d); *Le Mistons* 1957 (d); *Le Coup du Berger (short)* 1956 (a); *Une Histoire d'Eau (short)* 1958 (d); *Les Mistons* 1958 (d,sc); *A bout de souffle/Breathless* 1959 (idea); *Les Quatre cents coups/The 400 Blows* 1959 (d,sc,story) **(AANBSC)**; *Paris Nous Appartient/Paris Belongs to Us* 1960 (p); *Tirez Sur le Pianiste/Shoot the Piano Player* 1960 (d,sc,dial); *Jules et Jim/Jules and Jim* 1961 (d,sc); *Tire au flanc 62/The Army Game* 1961 (a,d,sc); *L'Amour à vingt ans/Love at Twenty* 1962 (d,screenplay "Paris—Antoine et Colette"); *La Peau Douce/The Soft Skin* 1964 (d,sc); *Fahrenheit 451* 1966 (d,sc); *Baisers volés/Stolen Kisses* 1968 (d,sc,story); *La Mariée était en noir/The Bride Wore Black* 1968 (d,sc,adapt,dial); *La Sirène du Mississipi/Mississippi Mermaid* 1968 (d,sc); *Domicile conjugal/Bed and Board* 1970 (d,sc); *L'Enfant sauvage/The Wild Child* 1970 (a,d,sc); *Langlois (short)* 1970 (a); *Les Deux Anglaises et le Continent/Two English Girls* 1971 (d,sc); *Une Belle fille come moi/Such a Gorgeous Kid Like Me* 1972 (d,sc); *La Nuit Américaine/Day For Night* 1973 (a,d,sc) **(AANBD,AANBSC)**; *L'Argent de poche/Small Change* 1975 (a,d,sc); *L'Histoire d'Adèle H./The Story of Adele H.* 1975 (d,sc); *Les Lolos de Lola* 1975 (p); *Close Encounters of the Third Kind* 1977 (a); *L'Homme qui aimait les femmes/The Man Who Loved Women* 1977 (a,d,sc); *La Chambre Verte/The Green Room* 1978 (a,d,sc); *L'Amour en Fuite/Love on the Run* 1979 (d,sc); *Close Encounters of the Third Kind: Special Edition* 1980 (a); *Le Dernier Metro/The Last Metro* 1980 (d,sc,dial); *La Femme d'à côté/The Woman Next Door* 1981 (d,sc); *Vivement Dimanche/Confidentially Yours* 1982 (d,p,sc); *Breathless* 1983 (story); *The Man Who Loved Women* 1983 (from film); *Vivement Truffaut!* 1985 (a); *La Petite voleuse/The Little Thief* 1988 (from sc).

Trumbo, Dalton • Screenwriter • Born James Dalton Trumbo, Montrose, CO, December 9, 1905; died 1976. *Educ.* University of Colorado; UCLA; USC, Los Angeles. Journalist who turned to screenwriting in the mid-1930s and became one of the "Hollywood Ten" some fifteen years later. Jailed for ten months because of his refusal to cooperate with HUAC and subsequently blacklisted,

Trumbo nonetheless turned out a substantial number of screenplays under various pseudonyms, notably *The Brave One* (1956) as Robert Rich, which won an Oscar for Best Writing.

Though the event was a great embarrassment to the industry and had the potential to undermine the blacklist, it was not until 1960, with the support of producers Kirk Douglas (*Spartacus*) and Otto Preminger (*Exodus*), that Trumbo's name again began appearing in film credits. He made an electrifying directing debut (at age 65!) with a harrowing adaptation of his 1939 anti-war novel, *Johnny Got His Gun* (1971). • *Love Begins at Twenty* 1936 (sc); *Road Gang* 1936 (sc); *Tugboat Princess* 1936 (story); *Devil's Playground* 1937 (sc); *Fugitives For a Night* 1938 (sc); *A Man to Remember* 1938 (sc); *Career* 1939 (sc); *Five Came Back* 1939 (sc); *The Flying Irishman* 1939 (sc); *Heaven With a Barbed Wire Fence* 1939 (sc,story); *The Kid From Kokomo* 1939 (story); *Sorority House* 1939 (sc); *A Bill of Divorcement* 1940 (sc); *Curtain Call* 1940 (sc); *Half a Sinner* 1940 (story); *Kitty Foyle* 1940 (sc) **(AANBSC)**; *The Lone Wolf Strikes* 1940 (story); *We Who Are Young* 1940 (sc,story); *Accent on Love* 1941 (story); *You Belong to Me* 1941 (story); *The Remarkable Andrew* 1942 (sc,from novel); *A Guy Named Joe* 1943 (sc); *Tender Comrade* 1943 (sc); *Thirty Seconds Over Tokyo* 1944 (sc); *Jealousy* 1945 (story); *Our Vines Have Tender Grapes* 1945 (sc); *Emergency Wedding* 1950 (story); *The Brave One* 1956 (from story "The Boy and the Bull") **(AABST)**; *Exodus* 1960 (sc); *Spartacus* 1960 (sc); *The Last Sunset* 1961 (sc); *Lonely Are the Brave* 1962 (sc); *The Sandpiper* 1965 (sc); *Hawaii* 1966 (sc); *The Fixer* 1968 (sc); *The Horsemen* 1971 (sc); *Johnny Got His Gun* 1971 (d,sc,from novel); *FTA* 1972 (sc—"FTA Show",novel extract *Johnny Got His Gun*); *Executive Action* 1973 (sc); *Papillon* 1973 (a,sc); *Hollywood on Trial* 1976 (a); *Always* 1989 (from sc *A Guy Named Joe*).

Trumbull, Douglas • Special effects artist, director of photography; also inventor. • Born Los Angeles, CA, 1942. First came to the fore with his groundbreaking work as co-special effects supervisor on Stanley Kubrick's *2001: A Space Odyssey* (1968). Trumbull made a small gem of a directorial debut with *Silent Running* (1971), a sci-fi tale starring Bruce Dern, and also directed the intriguing but ill-fated *Brainstorm* (1983), remembered mainly because star Natalie Wood died during production (1981). • *2001: A Space Odyssey* 1968 (fx); *Candy* 1968 (ph—opening and closing sequences); *The Andromeda Strain* 1971 (fx); *Silent Running* 1971 (d,fx); *Close Encounters of the Third Kind* 1977 (cam.op,fx) **(AANBFX)**; *Star Trek: The Motion Picture* 1979 (fx d) **(AANBFX)**; *Close Encounters of the Third Kind: Special Edition* 1980 (fx sup); *Blade Runner* 1982 (fx sup) **(AANBFX)**; *Brainstorm* 1983 (d,p).

Turman, Lawrence • Producer • Born Los Angeles, CA, November 28, 1926. *Educ.* UCLA. Former talent agent who emerged as an independent producer in the early 1960s, siring such critically recognized works as *The Best Man* (1964) and *The Graduate* (1967). Turman's prolific collaboration with fellow producer David Foster resulted in a number of well regarded Broadway-based films, including *Tribute* (1980) and *Mass Appeal* (1984), as well the youth films, *Short Circuit* (1986) and *Gleaming the Cube* (1988).

Turman ventured into directing with *The Marriage of a Young Stockbroker* (1971) and *Second Thoughts* (1982), which he also scripted. • *The Young Doctors* 1961 (p); *The Best Man* 1964 (p); *The Flim-Flam Man* 1967 (p); *The Graduate* 1967 (p) **(AANBP)**; *Pretty Poison* 1968 (exec.p); *The Great White Hope* 1970 (p); *The Marriage of a Young Stockbroker* 1971 (d,p); *The Drowning Pool* 1975 (p); *The Nickel Ride* 1975 (exec.p); *First Love* 1977 (p); *Heroes* 1977 (p); *Walk Proud* 1979 (p); *Tribute* 1980 (p); *Caveman* 1981 (p); *Second Thoughts* 1982 (d,p); *The Thing* 1982 (p); *Mass Appeal* 1984 (p); *The Mean Season* 1985 (p); *Running Scared* 1986 (p); *Short Circuit* 1986 (p); *Full Moon in Blue Water* 1988 (p); *Gleaming the Cube* 1988 (p); *Short Circuit 2* 1988 (p).

Turner, Kathleen • Actress • Born Springfield, MO, June 19, 1954. *Educ.* Southwest Missouri State University; University of Maryland; Central School of Speech and Drama, London. Sultry blonde leading lady who graduated from daytime soaps ("The Doctors") to almost overnight big screen stardom with a show-stopping film debut in Lawrence Kasdan's contemporary film noir, *Body Heat* (1981). With looks and poise reminiscent of the Hollywood stars of old, Turner has proved herself a gifted comedienne in films ranging from the old-fashioned adventure yarn *Romancing the Stone* (1984) to Danny De Vito's blackly humorous study in marital breakdown, *The War of the Roses* (1989). She was also effective as a cold-hearted hit-woman in the mafia comedy, *Prizzi's Honor* (1985), and as a mature woman inhabiting the body of a teenager in Francis Ford Coppola's time-travel yarn, *Peggy Sue Got Married* (1986). Turner earned acclaim on Broadway, starring in the 1989 revival of Tennessee Williams's *Cat On a Hot Tin Roof.* • *Body Heat* 1981; *The Man With Two Brains* 1983; *A Breed Apart* 1984; *Crimes of Passion* 1984; *Romancing the Stone* 1984; *The Jewel of the Nile* 1985; *Prizzi's Honor* 1985; *Peggy Sue Got Married* 1986 **(AANBA)**; *Dear America* 1987; *Julia and Julia* 1987; *The Accidental Tourist* 1988; *Switching Channels* 1988; *Who Framed Roger Rabbit?* 1988; *Tummy Trouble* 1989; *The War of the Roses* 1989; *Rollercoaster Rabbit* 1990.

Turner, Lana • Actress • Born Julia Jean Mildred Frances Turner, Wallace, ID, February 8, 1920. Quintessential rags-to-riches blonde lead of the 1940s, allegedly "discovered" while playing hooky from school and sipping a soda at Schwab's. A popular pin-up during the war and packaged as "The Sweater Girl," Turner's glamorous poise and elegant beauty assured her stardom. Her personal life was torridly publicized, particularly her love affairs, which included marriages to band leader Artie Shaw and cinematic Tarzan Lex Barker. In 1958, between Turner's superb performance in *Peyton Place* (1957) and her equally memorable role in Douglas Sirk's masterful weepy, *Imitation of Life* (1959), her daughter, Cheryl Crane, stabbed to death Turner's then-boyfriend, gangster Johnny Stompanato. Though Crane was acquitted on grounds of justifiable homicide, the fiasco included public readings of Turner's heated correspondence with the deceased, which only served to heighten her oversexed image.

A veteran of seven marriages, Turner dressed the set in most of her movies, but rose to the fore when a strong director guided her performances. Highlights of her career include: *Ziegfeld Girl* (1941), *Johnny Eager* (1941), *The Postman Always Rings Twice* (1946), *The Bad and the Beautiful* (1952, in a role based on Diana Barrymore) and *Madame X* (1966). Turner has also done occasional TV work, notably on the night-time soap, "Falcon Crest." • *The Great Garrick* 1937 (a); *They Won't Forget* 1937 (a); *The Adventures of Marco Polo* 1938 (a); *Dramatic School* 1938 (a); *Love Finds Andy Hardy* 1938 (a); *Rich Man, Poor Girl* 1938 (a); *Calling Dr. Kildare* 1939 (a); *Dancing Co-ed* 1939 (a); *These Glamour Girls* 1939 (a); *Two Girls on Broadway* 1940 (a); *We Who Are Young* 1940 (a); *Dr. Jekyll and Mr. Hyde* 1941 (a); *Honky Tonk* 1941 (a); *Johnny Eager* 1941 (a); *Ziegfeld Girl* 1941 (a); *Somewhere I'll Find You* 1942 (a); *Slightly Dangerous* 1943 (a); *The Youngest Profession* 1943 (a); *Marriage Is a Private Affair* 1944 (a); *Keep Your Powder Dry* 1945 (a); *Weekend at the Waldorf* 1945 (a); *The Postman Always Rings Twice* 1946 (a); *Cass Timberlane* 1947 (a); *Green Dolphin Street* 1947 (a); *Homecoming* 1948 (a); *The Three Musketeers* 1948 (a); *A Life of Her Own* 1950 (a); *Mr. Imperium* 1951 (a); *The Bad and the Beautiful* 1952 (a); *The Merry Widow* 1952 (a); *Latin Lovers* 1953 (a); *Betrayed* 1954 (a); *Flame and the Flesh* 1954 (a); *The Prodigal* 1955 (a); *The Rains of Ranchipur* 1955 (a); *The Sea Chase* 1955 (a); *Diane* 1956 (a); *The Lady Takes a Flyer* 1957 (a); *Peyton Place* 1957 (a) **(AANBA)**; *Another Time, Another Place* 1958 (a,p); *Imitation of*

Life 1959 (a); *Portrait in Black* 1960 (a); *Bachelor in Paradise* 1961 (a); *By Love Possessed* 1961 (a); *Who's Got the Action?* 1962 (a); *Love Has Many Faces* 1965 (a); *Madame X* 1966 (a); *The Big Cube* 1969 (a); *Persecution* 1973 (a); *Bittersweet Love* 1976 (a); *Witches' Brew* 1978 (a).

Turturro, John • Actor • Born Brooklyn, NY, February 28, 1957. *Educ.* SUNY, New Paltz; Yale Drama School. Stage-trained actor with a dark intensity which has served him well in roles such as the psychopathic parolee in *Five Corners* (1987) and the racist pizza-man in Spike Lee's *Do the Right Thing* (1989). Turturro made his film debut in Martin Scorsese's *Raging Bull* (1980) and has also shown a flair for sly comedy, playing a double-crossing gangster in the Coen brothers' *Miller's Crossing* and a greedy music promoter in Lee's *Mo' Better Blues* (both 1990). • *Raging Bull* 1980; *Exterminator 2* 1984; *The Flamingo Kid* 1984; *Desperately Seeking Susan* 1985; *To Live and Die in L.A.* 1985; *The Color of Money* 1986; *Gung Ho* 1986; *Hannah and Her Sisters* 1986; *Off Beat* 1986; *Five Corners* 1987; *The Sicilian* 1987; *Do the Right Thing* 1989; *Making "Do the Right Thing"* 1989; *Backtrack* 1990; *Men of Respect* 1990; *Miller's Crossing* 1990; *Mo' Better Blues* 1990; *State of Grace* 1990.

Tushingham, Rita • Actress • Born Liverpool, England, March 14, 1940. *Educ.* Liverpool Playhouse. Unorthodox, waif-like lead of the 1960s who burst into the public eye with a starring role in Tony Richardson's *A Taste of Honey* (1961). After numerous first-rate outings in the 1960s, during which she was typecast as the female equivalent of the British *angry young man*, Tushingham's career faltered in the bleak 70s and she made several mediocre Italian films. She resurfaced in the 80s, starring in the 1986 thriller, *A Judgment in Stone* (directed by her second husband, Ousama Rawi) and *Resurrected* (1989). • *A Taste of Honey* 1961; *The Leather Boys* 1963; *Doctor Zhivago* 1965; *The Knack... and How to Get It* 1965; *The Bed Sitting Room* 1969; *The Guru* 1969; *The Human Factor* 1975; *Rachel's Man* 1975; *Ragazzo di Borgata* 1976; *Mysteries* 1978; *Spaghetti House* 1982; *Flying* 1986; *A Judgment in Stone* 1986; *The Housekeeper* 1987; *Resurrected* 1989; *Hard Days, Hard Nights* 1990.

Tyson, Cicely • Actress • Born New York, NY, December 19, 1933. *Educ.* NYU; Actors Studio. Former model and New York stage lead who gained widespread attention for her role as a secretary on the hard-hitting TV series, "East Side/West Side" (1963-64), opposite George C. Scott. Like many gifted black performers, Tyson finally began landing worthy film roles in the 1970s, earning an Oscar nomination for her role in *Sounder* (1972). She turned in a bravura performance in the title role of the award-winning TV movie, *The Autobiography of Miss Jane Pittman* (1974), and has continued to appear as strong, courageous women, mostly on TV. Divorced from jazz legend Miles Davis, whom she married in 1981. • *Odds Against Tomorrow* 1959; *A Man Called Adam* 1966; *The Comedians* 1967; *The Heart Is a Lonely Hunter* 1968; *Sounder* 1972 **(AANBA)**; *The River Niger* 1975; *The Blue Bird* 1976; *A Hero Ain't Nothin' But a Sandwich* 1977; *The Concorde—Airport '79* 1979; *Bustin' Loose* 1981.

Ullman, Tracey • Actress; also singer, dancer. • Born Slough, Berkshire, England, December 29, 1959. *Educ.* Italia Conti School, London. Multi-faceted performer best known for her Emmy award-winning American TV series, "The Tracey Ullman Show" (1987-90). Ullman earned acclaim on the British stage (*Four in a Million* 1981) and TV ("A Kick Up the Eighties" 1983), recorded a top-selling album, *You Broke My Heart in Seventeen Places*, and made her first big-screen mark in *Plenty* (1985), co-starring Meryl Streep, Charles Dance and Sting. In 1991 she made her Broadway debut in Jay Presson Allen's *The Big Love*. Ullman is married to British TV producer Allan McKeown. • *Give My Regards to Broad Street* 1983 (a); *The Young Visitors* 1984 (a); *Plenty* 1985 (a); *Jumpin' Jack Flash* 1986 (a); *I Love You to Death* 1990 (a).

Ullmann, Liv • Actress • Born Tokyo, December 16, 1939. *Educ.* Webster-Douglas Academy, London. Born to Norwegian parents in the Orient. A luminously beautiful, consummately talented performer, Ullmann is chiefly associated with the work of Ingmar Bergman, by whom she has a daughter, Linn. She was an established Norwegian stage talent before being chosen by Bergman—partly due to her resemblance to Bibi Andersson—to co-star in *Persona* (1966). For the next decade and a half, though frequently in international productions, Ullmann's best work was in Swedish films, where her gift for interpreting emotionally wrought characters was displayed in Bergman films such as *The Shame* (1968), *Scenes From a Marriage* (1973), *Face to Face* (1976) and *Autumn Sonata* (1978), as well as Jan Troell's *The Emigrants* (1971) and its sequel *The New Land* (1973).

Ullmann reached the peak of her worldwide popularity in the late 1970s, making her Broadway debut in *A Doll's House* (1975) and publishing her autobiography, *Changing*, in 1977; she was also the subject of a feature-length documentary, *A Look at Liv* (1977). Ullmann has since made a successful transition to middle-aged roles and in the 1980s continued as a reigning talent of both cinema and theater. • *Persona* 1966; *Skammen/The Shame* 1968; *Vargtimmen/Hour of the Wolf* 1968; *En Passion/The Passion of Anna* 1969; *De la Part des Copains/The Night Visitor* 1971; *Utvandrarna/The Emigrants* 1971 **(AANBA)**; *Cries and Whispers* 1972; *Ingmar Bergman* 1972; *Pope Joan* 1972; *40 Carats* 1973; *Lost Horizon* 1973; *Nybyggarna/The New Land* 1973; *Scenes From a Marriage* 1973; *The Abdication* 1974; *Zandy's Bride* 1974; *Leonor* 1975; *Ansikte mot ansikte/Face to Face* 1976 **(AANBA)**; *A Bridge Too Far* 1977; *A Look at Liv* 1977; *Das Schlangenei/The Serpent's Egg* 1977; *Hostsonaten/Autumn Sonata* 1978; *Players* 1979; *Richard's Things* 1980; *Love* 1981 (d,sc—"Parting"); *The Wild Duck* 1982; *Bay Boy* 1984; *La Diagonale du Fou* 1984; *Ingrid* 1985; *Pourvu que ce soit une fille* 1986; *Gaby - A True Story* 1987; *Mosca Addio* 1987; *La Amiga* 1988; *The Rose Garden* 1989; *Mindwalk* 1990; *The Ox* 1991.

Ulmer, Edgar G. • *aka* John Warner • Director; also screenwriter, production designer. • Born Edgar Georg Ulmer, Vienna, Austria, September 17. 1900; died September 30, 1972, Woodland Hills, CA. *Educ.* Academy of Arts, Vienna (architecture); University of Vienna (philosophy). Prolific director of relatively minor fare who nevertheless created a wide assortment of odd, low-budget gems. Originally a stage actor and set designer, Ulmer did his first film work as an art director as early as 1919, became an assistant to theater impressario Max Reinhardt and crossed the Atlantic several times, working in both theater and film. After serving as F.W. Murnau's assistant for six years, he made his feature debut in Germany, co-directing with Robert Siodmak the landmark pseudo-documentary, *People on Sunday* (1929).

In 1931 Ulmer settled in the US, working first as a production designer and then a director of second features. He made one major studio picture, the Universal horror classic, *The Black Cat* (1934), but otherwise worked for a variety of low-budget outfits known collectively and colloquially as Poverty Row studios. He turned out a number of fast-paced programmers, including the highly entertaining *Detour* (1945), *Bluebeard* (1944) and *Ruthless* (1948). Ulmer himself declared that he preferred to work in this milieu ("I did not want to be ground up in the Hollywood hash machine") and, despite budgetary constraints, he was awarded a degree of creative freedom that he would not have had with the major studios. The result is a distinctive personal stamp present on many of his films, partly thanks to his roots in the German expressionist movement and his experience in design. • *Menschen am Sonntag/People on Sunday* 1929 (d); *Damaged Lives* 1933 (d,sc,story); *The Black Cat* 1934 (adapt,d); *From Nine to Nine* 1935 (d); *Green Fields* 1937 (d,p); *Yankel dem Schmidt* 1938 (d,p); *Americaner Schädchen* 1939 (d,p); *Cossacks in Exile* 1939 (d); *Die Klatsche* 1939 (d,p); *Moon Over Harlem* 1939 (d); *Prisoner of Japan* 1942 (story); *Tomorrow We Live* 1942 (d); *Corregidor* 1943 (sc,story); *Danger! Women At Work* 1943 (story); *Girls in Chains* 1943 (d,story); *Isle of Forgotten Sins* 1943 (d,story); *Jive Junction* 1943 (d); *Bluebeard* 1944 (d); *Club Havana* 1945 (d); *Detour* 1945 (d); *Strange Illusion* 1945 (d); *Her Sister's Secret* 1946 (d); *The Strange Woman* 1946 (d); *The Wife of Monte Cristo* 1946 (d,story); *Carnegie Hall* 1947 (d); *Ruthless* 1948 (d); *The Pirates of Capri* 1949 (d); *The Man From Planet X* 1951 (d); *St. Benny the Dip* 1951 (d); *Babes in Baghdad* 1952 (d); *Eterna Femmina* 1954 (d); *Murder Is My Beat* 1954 (d); *The Naked Dawn* 1955 (d); *Daughter of Dr. Jekyll* 1957 (d); *Annibale* 1959 (d); *The Amazing Transparent Man* 1960 (d); *Beyond the Time Barrier* 1960 (d); *Antinea, L'Amante della Citta Sepolta* 1961 (d); *The Cavern* 1965 (d,p).

Unsworth, Geoffrey • Director of photography • Born London, 1914; died 1978, Brittany, France. Former camera operator who graduated to cinematographer in the mid-1940s. Unsworth demonstrated a deft command of black-and-white in films such the documentary-like *A Night to Remember* (1958) but was chiefly noted for his lush color work, particularly on period films. Unsworth won a British Film Academy award (Stella) for *Becket* (1964) and, in addition to shooting *2001: A Space Odyssey* (1968), is credited with helping devise some of its ground-breaking special effects. Unsworth's other outstanding credits include *Cabaret* (1972), for which he won his first Oscar, and Roman Polanski's sumptuous *Tess* (1979), during the production of which he died of a heart attack. His Oscar for *Tess* was shared with Ghislain Cloquet. • *Trio* 1950; *The Purple Plain* 1954; *A Town Like Alice* 1956; *Hell Divers* 1957; *Bachelor of Hearts* 1958; *Dangerous Exile* 1958; *A Night to Remember* 1958; *The World of Suzie Wong* 1960; *Don't Bother to Knock* 1961; *The 300 Spartans* 1962; *The Main Attraction* 1962; *Becket* 1964 **(AANBPH)**; *Genghis Khan* 1965; *Othello* 1965; *Oh Dad, Poor Dad, Mamma's Hung You in the Closet and I'm Feelin' So Sad* 1967; *2001: A Space Odyssey* 1968; *The Bliss of Mrs. Blossom* 1968; *The Dance of Death* 1968; *Half a Sixpence* 1968; *The Assassination Bureau* 1969; *The Reckoning* 1969; *Cromwell* 1970; *Goodbye Gemini* 1970; *The Magic Christian* 1970; *Say Hello to Yesterday* 1970; *Three Sisters* 1970; *Umman, Wittering and Zigo* 1971; *Alice's Adventures in Wonderland* 1972; *Baxter* 1972; *Cabaret* 1972 **(AABPH)**; *Don Quixote* 1973; *Liebe, Schmerz und das Danze Verdammte Zeug* 1973; *The Abdication* 1974; *The Internecine Project* 1974; *Murder on the Orient Express* 1974 **(AANBPH)**; *Zardoz* 1974; *Lucky Lady* 1975; *The Return of the Pink Panther* 1975; *Royal Flash* 1975; *A Matter of Time* 1976; *A Bridge Too Far* 1977; *Superman* 1978; *The First Great Train Robbery* 1979; *Tess* 1979 **(AABPH)**; *Superman II* 1980.

Ure, Mary • Actress • Born Glasgow, Scotland, February 18, 1933; died 1975. *Educ.* Central School of Speech and Drama, London. Fiery lead of the London stage, in occasional films. Ure's first husband was playwright John Osborne, for whom she starred in both the stage (1956) and screen (1959) versions of *Look Back in Anger*; she received her widest acclaim for her sensual performance as Clara in *Sons and Lovers* (1960). Her second husband was Robert Shaw, whom she later divorced. Ure died of an accidental overdose of alcohol and barbituates at age 42. • *Storm Over the Nile* 1955; *Windom's Way* 1957; *Look Back in Anger* 1959; *Sons and Lovers* 1960 **(AANBSA)**; *The Mind Benders* 1963; *The Luck of Ginger Coffey* 1964; *Custer of the West* 1967; *Where Eagles Dare* 1968; *A Reflection of Fear* 1971.

Ustinov, Sir Peter • Actor; also director, screenwriter, playwright, author. • Born Swiss Cottage, London, April 16, 1921. *Educ.* London Theatre Studio. Burly, multi-faceted talent who, by his mid-20s, had achieved considerable success in both theater and cinema directing, writing and acting in cultivated, witty comedies.

Ustinov reached the peak of his fame in the early 1960s with two Oscars for best supporting actor and a couple of superb directorial efforts (which he also produced, starred in and wrote): *Romanoff and Juliet* (1961), a biting Cold War satire based on his own play, and the bracing *Billy Budd* (1962). Since the late 70s he has been chiefly known for his performances as Belgian sleuth Hercule Poirot in a series of Agatha Christie mysteries. • *The True Glory* 1945 (sc); *School For Secrets* 1946 (d); *Vice Versa* 1948 (d,p,sc); *Private Angelo* 1949 (d); *Le Plaisir* 1951 (a); *Quo Vadis* 1951 (a) **(AANBSA)**; *Beau Brummell* 1954 (a); *The Egyptian* 1954 (a); *Lola Montès* 1955 (a); *We're No Angels* 1955 (a); *I Girovaghi* 1956 (a); *Spartacus* 1960 (a) **(AABSA)**; *The Sundowners* 1960 (a); *Romanoff and Juliet* 1961 (a,d,p,sc,from play); *Billy Budd* 1962 (a,d,p,sc); *John Goldfarb, Please Come Home* 1964 (a); *Topkapi* 1964 (a) **(AABSA)**; *Lady L* 1965 (a,d,sc); *The Comedians* 1967 (a); *Blackbeard's Ghost* 1968 (a); *Hot Millions* 1968 (a); *Viva Max!* 1970 (a); *Hammersmith Is Out* 1972 (a,d); *Robin Hood* 1973 (a); *One of Our Dinosaurs Is Missing* 1975 (a); *Logan's Run* 1976 (a); *Treasure of Matecumbe* 1976 (a); *Doppio Delitto* 1977 (a); *The Last Remake of Beau Geste* 1977 (a); *The Mouse and His Child* 1977 (a); *Un Taxi mauve* 1977 (a); *Death on the Nile* 1978 (a); *The Thief of Bagdad* 1978 (a); *Ashanti* 1979 (a); *Nous maigrirons ensemble* 1979 (a); *Players* 1979 (a); *Tarka the Otter* 1979 (a); *Grendel, Grendel, Grendel* 1980 (a); *Charlie Chan and the Curse of the Dragon Queen* 1981 (a); *The Great Muppet Caper* 1981 (a); *Evil Under the Sun* 1982 (a); *Memed My Hawk* 1983 (a,d,sc); *Appointment With Death* 1988 (a); *Peep and the Big Wide World (short)* 1988 (a); *La Révolution Française* 1989 (a); *C'era un castello con 40 cani* 1990 (a).

Uys, Jamie • Director; also screenwriter, producer. • Born Jacobus Johannes Uys, Boksburg, South Africa, 1921. *Educ.* Pretoria University. One of South Africa's most prolific and prominent filmmakers. Uys gained worldwide attention with *The Gods Must Be Crazy* (1981), a comedy about African cultural clashes which became the highest-grossing foreign film of all time when released in the US in 1984. He attempted to repeat his success with *The Gods Must Be Crazy II* (1989) but attracted fewer filmgoers, and more criticism for his stereotypical racial portraits, the second time around. • *Animals Are Beautiful People* 1974 (d,p,sc,ph,ed); *The Gods Must Be Crazy* 1981 (a,d,p,sc,ph,ed); *The Gods Must Be Crazy II* 1989 (d,exec.p,sc).

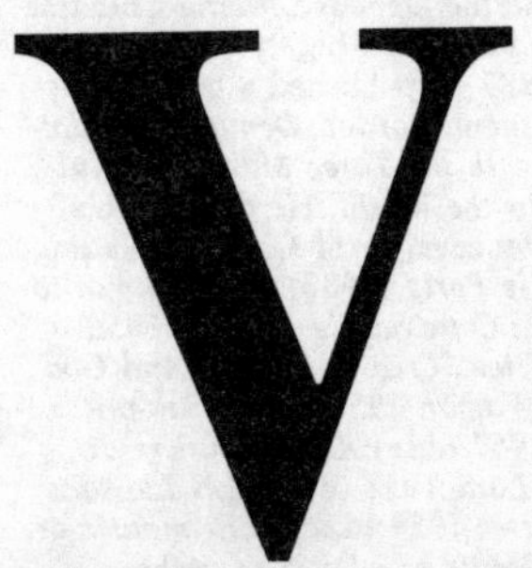

Vacano, Jost • German director of photography • Born March 15, 1934. Chiefly associated with Dutch director Paul Verhoeven, for whom he has created several exquisite canvases, from the melancholic hues of *Soldier of Orange* (1979) and *Spetters* (1980) to the hard-edged, high-tech worlds of *Robocop* (1987) and *Total Recall* (1990). Vacano is noted for his crisp color and fluid, mobile camera work; other notable credits include Volker Schlöndorff's *The Lost Honor of Katharina Blum* (1975) and Wolfgang Petersen's *Das Boot* (1981). • *Supermarket* 1974; *Die Verlorene Ehre der Katharina Blum/The Lost Honor of Katherina Blum* 1975; *Die Brueder* 1976; *Tod Oder Freiheit* 1977; *Das Fuenfte Gebot* 1979; *Soldier of Orange* 1979; *Spetters* 1980; *Das Boot* 1981 **(AANBPH)**; *Die Wilden Fuenfziger* 1983; *The Neverending Story* 1984; *52 Pick-Up* 1986; *Robocop* 1987; *Rocket Gibraltar* 1988; *Total Recall* 1990.

Vadim, Roger • Director; also screenwriter, actor. • Born Roger Vadim Plemiannikov, Paris, January 26, 1928. Formidable presence in French cinema of the late 1950s and 60s, as well known for his capacity to mold wives and lovers into starlets as for his occasional cinematic flourishes.

A former stage actor, assistant to director Marc Allegret and journalist, Vadim—with his then wife Brigitte Bardot—gained worldwide attention with the release of *And God Created Woman* (1956). The film's striking wide-screen color and erotic frankness (including shots of a semi-clad Bardot) earned it vast commercial success and paved the way for the subsequent New Wave breakthrough by convincing French producers of the viability of young directors.

Vadim enjoyed continued success with films such as the superb *Les Liaisons Dangereuses* (1959, with Jeanne Moreau), a flawed but engaging reworking of *La Ronde* (1964) and the comic-strip Jane Fonda vehicle *Barbarella* (1968). Since the early 70s, when outright nudity became commonplace, his teasingly erotic works have been fewer and much less successful.

Vadim's relationships with wives (Bardot, Annette Stroyberg, Fonda) and lovers (Catherine Deneuve, Marie-Christine Barrault) have been highly publicized, and in 1987 he published a book about three of them, *Bardot, Denueve, Fonda: My Life with the Three Most Beautiful Women in the World*. He directed his son by Deneuve, actor Christian Vadim, in *Surprise Party* (1983). • *Blackmailed* 1951 (sc); *Cette Sacrée Gamine* 1956 (sc); *Et Dieu...Créa la Femme/And God Created Woman* 1956 (d,sc); *Sait-on-Jamais* 1957 (d,sc); *Les Bijoutiers du Clair de Lune* 1958 (d,sc); *Les Liaisons Dangereuses* 1959 (d,sc); *...Et mourir de plaisir* 1960 (d,sc); *Les Sept péchés capitaux/The Seven Deadly Sins* 1962 (d,sc—"Pride"/"L'orgueil"); *Le Vice et la vertu* 1962 (d); *Château en Suède* 1963 (d,sc); *Dragées au Poivre* 1963 (a); *La Ronde* 1964 (d); *La Curée* 1966 (d); *Barbarella* 1968 (d,sc); *Pretty Maids All in a Row* 1971 (d); *Ciao! Manhattan* 1972 (a); *Helle* 1972 (d,sc); *Don Juan 1973 ou si Don Juan etait une femme* 1973 (d,sc); *La Jeune Fille assassinee* 1974 (a,d,p,sc); *Une Femme Fidèle* 1976 (d,sc); *Night Games* 1979 (d); *Rich and Famous* 1981 (a); *Hot Touch* 1982 (d); *Surprise Party* 1983 (d,sc); *Into the Night* 1985 (a); *And God Created Woman* 1988 (d,from sc).

Valdez, Luis • Director, playwright; also screenwriter. • Born June 26, 1940. *Educ.* San Jose State University (theater). Born to parents of Mexican descent, Luis Valdez spent his childhood as a migrant farmworker. After graduating from San Jose State College he spent a year with the San Francisco Mime Troupe which culminated in a cultural exchange trip to Cuba. Upon his return to the US, Valdez returned to his hometown of Delano and joined Cesar Chavez's United Farmworkers. There he formed a workers' theatre company, "El Teatro Campesino," which developed original material in the form of short agit-prop skits called "actos." "El Teatro Campesino" also produced several short films of their plays.

After several years with "Teatro Campesino," Valdez decided to expand into more conventionial theatrical venues. He wrote and directed the musical drama *Zoot Suit,* which opened in August 1978 in Los Angeles and was an immediate hit. On a budget of $2.5 million, Valdez filmed the play. Released in 1981, *Zoot Suit* is based loosely on the infamous Sleepy Lagoon case in 1942 Los Angeles. Daniel Valdez (Luis' brother and the talented composer of the film's musical numbers) plays the leader of a gang of 'pachucos' (streetwise chicano kids wearing zoot suits) named Henry Reyna, who is is arrested and convicted by a racist court for a murder he did not commit.

Valdez' second feature, *La Bamba* (1987), was tremendously successful in both mainstream and Hispanic markets. To chronicle the life of the first Mexican-American rock star, Ritchie Valens (ne Valenzuela), Valdez used the classical Hollywood narrative style, and some reviewers criticized him for becoming too conventional. Valdez responded that his style was appropriate for communicating the theme of acculturation to a national audience.

More recently, Valdez wrote and directed for TV an adaptation of his play, *Corridos! Tales of Passion and Revolution* (1987), a series of vignettes based on Mexican-American folk ballads. Using both English and Spanish dialogue, *Corridos* raises the consciousness of Chicano and non-Chicano viewers who usually have little contact with Mexican-American history. It is clear from the diversity of formats Valdez has successfully worked in that he is a director of outstanding talent. CL • *Which Way Is Up?* 1977 (a); *Zoot Suit* 1981 (d,sc,from play); *La Bamba* 1987 (d,sc).

Valentino, Rudolph • *aka* Rodolph Valentino • Actor • Born Rodolfo Alfonzo Raffaele Pierre Philibert Guglielmi, Castellaneta, Italy, May 6, 1895; died August 23, 1926. The original "latin lover" whose exotic, erotic presence earned him the adoration of female filmgoers the world over, making him, for a brief period, one of the silent cinema's greatest stars.

In New York from 1913, Valentino worked as a gardener, waiter and dancer before landing in California. For two years he played bits and minor parts, often as a Latinate villain. June Mathis, a screenwriter and influential force at Metro, saw Valentino's potential and secured him the lead in Rex Ingram's *Four Horsemen of the Apocalypse* (1921); the film was an immense success and established him as a star.

A graceful, good-looking performer possessed of enormous sensuality, Valentino exuded sex like no other actor of his day, much to the delight of women and the ire of Anglo men. After continued success with such films as *The Sheik* (1921) and *Monsieur Beaucaire* (1924) his reputation began to suffer, due in part to the machinations of his second wife Natasha Rambova (nee Winifred Shaunessy, 1897-1969). A set designer and minor actress, Rambova's domineering presence soiled Valentino's reputation as a forceful male; she was also responsible for his increasingly effete screen appearances, which finally prompted a scathing critique in the Chicago *Tribune* that called the great screen lover a "painted pansy."

Valentino's sudden death at age 31, due to a perforated ulcer, produced an emotional outpouring that has rarely been equalled, including near riots and alleged suicides by distressed women fans and a grandstanding, cross-country performance-in-mourning by Pola Negri. Though it has diminished in recent decades, for years after his demise a Valentino cult made its presence felt worldwide. • *My Official Wife* 1914; *Alimony* 1917; *All Night* 1918; *A Society Sensation* 1918; *The Big Little Person* 1919; *The Delicious Little Devil* 1919; *The Eyes of Youth* 1919; *The Home Breaker* 1919; *Out of Luck* 1919; *A Rogue's Romance* 1919; *Virtuous Sinners* 1919; *An Adventuress* 1920; *The Cheater* 1920; *The Married Virgin* 1920; *Once to Every Woman* 1920; *Passion's Playground* 1920; *Stolen Moments* 1920; *The Wonderful Chance* 1920; *Camille* 1921; *The Conquering Power* 1921; *The Four Horsemen of the Apocalypse* 1921; *The Sheik* 1921; *Uncharted Seas* 1921; *Beyond the Rocks* 1922; *Blood and Sand* 1922; *Moran of the Lady Letty* 1922; *The Young Rajah* 1922; *Monsieur*

Beaucaire 1924; *A Sainted Devil* 1924; *Cobra* 1925; *The Eagle* 1925; *The Son of the Sheik* 1926.

Valli, Alida • *aka* Valli • Actress • Born Alida Maria Altenburger, Pola, Italy, May 3, 1921. *Educ.* Centro Sperimentale di Cinematografia, Rome (drama). Strikingly beautiful Italian actress who began her career in the mid-1930s at the age of 15. Valli starred in mostly uninspired works until her temporary retirement in 1944, due to her refusal to appear in Fascist propaganda films (in 1945 her mother was shot as a collaborator). Following the war, Valli landed a contract with David O. Selnzick, but her career did not really take off until her appearance as Harry Lime's faithful paramour in the Carol Reed classic *The Third Man* (1949). Often billed simpy as *Valli*, she shined in films including Visconti's *Senso* (1954), Henri Colpi's *Une Aussi Longue Absence* (1961) and Bertolucci's *The Spider's Stratagem* (1970). Formerly married to pianist-composer Oscar de Mejo ("All I Want for Christmas Is My Two Front Teeth"). • *Noi Vivi/We the Living* 1942 (a); *The Paradine Case* 1947 (a); *The Miracle of the Bells* 1948 (a); *The Third Man* 1949 (a); *Walk Softly, Stranger* 1950 (a); *The White Tower* 1950 (a); *Senso/The Wanton Contessa* 1954 (a); *Barrage contre le Pacifique* 1957 (a); *Il Grido* 1957 (a); *Les Bijoutiers du Clair de Lune* 1958 (a); *Une Aussi Longue Absence* 1961 (a); *Il Disordine* 1962 (a); *The Happy Thieves* 1962 (a); *Ophelia* 1962 (a); *El Valle de las espadas* 1963 (a); *Edipo Re* 1967 (a); *La Strategia del Ragno/The Spider's Strategem* 1970 (a); *Diario di un Italiano* 1972 (a); *La Prima Notte di Quiete* 1972 (a); *La Chair de l'orchidée* 1974 (a); *La Grande Trouille* 1974 (a); *La Casa dell'Exorcismo* 1975 (a); *Ce Cher Victor* 1975 (a); *Le Jeu de Solitaire* 1975 (a); *Novecento/1900* 1976 (a); *Suspiria* 1976 (a); *The Cassandra Crossing* 1977 (a); *L'Anti Cristo* 1978 (a); *Un Cuore Semplice* 1978 (a); *Zoo-Zero* 1978 (a); *Der Landvogt von Griefensee* 1979 (a); *La Luna/Luna* 1979 (a); *Aquella Casa En Las Afueras* 1980 (a); *Inferno* 1980 (a); *Aspern* 1981 (a); *Sogni Mostruosamente Proibiti* 1983 (a); *Segreti Segreti* 1984 (a); *Hitchcock, Il Brivido del Genio* 1985 (a); *Le Jupon rouge* 1987 (a); *A notre regrettable epoux* 1988 (a).

Vallone, Raf • Actor • Born Raffaele Vallone, Tropea, Italy, February 17, 1916. *Educ.* University of Turin (liberal arts, philosophy). Former journalist who became handsome, muscle-bound lead of international films. Vallone came to prominence co-starring in Giuseppe De Santis's eroticized neorealist landmark, *Bitter Rice* (1949); a second highlight of his otherwise limited career was *A View From the Bridge* (1962), adapted from the play by Arthur Miller. • *Riso Amaro/Bitter Rice* 1949; *Thérèse Raquin* 1953; *Don Juan's Night of Love* 1955; *Guendalina* 1955; *Les Possedées* 1955; *Le Piège* 1958; *Rose Bernd* 1958; *La Ciociara* 1960; *Recours en Grace* 1960; *El Cid* 1961; *Phaedra* 1962; *A View From the Bridge* 1962; *The Cardinal* 1963; *The Secret Invasion* 1964; *Harlow* 1965; *Nevada Smith* 1966; *Se Tutte le Donne Del Mondo* 1967; *The Italian Job* 1969; *Cannon For Cordoba* 1970; *The Kremlin Letter* 1970; *A Gunfight* 1971; *The Summertime Killer* 1972; *The Human Factor* 1975; *Rosebud* 1975; *That Lucky Touch* 1975; *The Other Side of Midnight* 1977; *Des Teufels Advokat/The Devil's Advocate* 1977; *The Greek Tycoon* 1978; *An Almost Perfect Affair* 1979; *Arthur Miller on Home Ground* 1979; *A Time to Die* 1979; *Lion of the Desert* 1980; *Retour à Marseille* 1980; *Le Pouvoir du Mal* 1985; *The Godfather Part III* 1990; *La Leyenda del Cura Bargota* 1990.

Van Cleef, Lee • Actor • Born Somerville, NJ, January 9, 1925; died December 14, 1989, Oxnard, CA. Lean, cool character player whose angular features marked him as a villain and who found his fortune as the hero of "spaghetti westerns" such as *For a Few Dollars More* (1966) and *The Good, the Bad and the Ugly* (1966). • *High Noon* 1952; *Kansas City Confidential* 1952; *Untamed Frontier* 1952; *Arena* 1953; *The Bandits of Corsica* 1953; *The Beast From 20,000 Fathoms* 1953; *Jack Slade* 1953; *The Lawless Breed* 1953; *The Nebraskan* 1953; *Tumbleweed* 1953; *Vice Squad* 1953; *White Lightning* 1953; *Arrow in the Dust* 1954; *Dawn at Socorro* 1954; *The Desperado* 1954; *Gypsy Colt* 1954; *Princess of the Nile* 1954; *Rails Into Laramie* 1954; *Treasure of Ruby Hills* 1954; *The Yellow Tomahawk* 1954; *The Big Combo* 1955; *I Cover the Underworld* 1955; *A Man Alone* 1955; *The Road to Denver* 1955; *Ten Wanted Men* 1955; *Tribute to a Bad Man* 1955; *The Vanishing American* 1955; *Accused of Murder* 1956; *The Conqueror* 1956; *It Conquered the World* 1956; *Pardners* 1956; *The Badge of Marshal Brennan* 1957; *China Gate* 1957; *Day of the Badman* 1957; *Gun Battle at Monterey* 1957; *Gunfight at the O.K. Corral* 1957; *Joe Dakota* 1957; *Last Stagecoach West* 1957; *The Lonely Man* 1957; *The Quiet Gun* 1957; *Raiders of Old California* 1957; *The Tin Star* 1957; *The Bravados* 1958; *Guns, Girls and Gangsters* 1958; *Machete* 1958; *The Young Lions* 1958; *Ride Lonesome* 1959; *Posse From Hell* 1961; *How the West Was Won* 1962; *The Man Who Shot Liberty Valance* 1962; *Il Buono, il Brutto, il Cattivo/The Good, the Bad, and the Ugly* 1966; *Per qualche dollaro in più/For a Few Dollars More* 1966; *La Resa dei Conti* 1966; *Da Uomo a Uomo* 1967; *I Giorni dell' Ira* 1967; *Barquero* 1970; *Ehi Amico... c'e Sabata* 1970; *El Condor* 1970; *Captain Apache* 1971; *The Magnificent Seven Ride* 1972; *Take a Hard Ride* 1975; *Kid Vengeance* 1977; *The Octagon* 1980; *The Squeeze* 1980; *Escape From New York* 1981; *Geheimcode Wildganse* 1984; *Jungle Raiders* 1984; *Killing Machine* 1985; *Armed Response* 1986; *Speed Zone* 1989; *Thieves of Fortune* 1990.

Van Damme, Jean-Claude • Actor • Born Brussels, Belgium. Former European karate champion, aptly nicknamed "Muscles from Brussels", turned star of action movies. • *No Retreat, No Surrender* 1986; *Bloodsport* 1988; *Kickboxer* 1988; *Black Eagle* 1988; *Cyborg* 1989; *Marquis* 1989; *Death Warrant* 1990; *Lionheart* 1990.

Van de Sande, Theo • Director of photography • Born Tilburg, Netherlands, 1947. *Educ.* Dutch Film Academy. Leading Dutch cinematographer whose outstanding work on two Jos Stelling films (*The Illusionist* 1983 and *The Pointsman* 1988) and on Fons Rademakers's Oscar-winning *The Assault* (1986) has led to international recognition. Van de Sande made his US debut with the subdued hues of *Crossing Delancey* (1988). • *Dakota* 1974 (ph); *Zwaarmoedige Verhalen* 1975 (ph); *Doctor Vlimmen* 1977 (ph); *Soleil des Hyenes* 1977 (ph); *Kasper in de Onderwereld* 1978 (ph); *Mijn Vriend* 1979 (ph); *De Plaats van de Vreemdeling* 1979 (ph); *De Witte Van Sichem* 1980 (cam.op); *Charlotte* 1981 (ph); *Meisje met het rode haar, Het* 1981 (ph); *De Anna* 1983 (ph); *Giovanni* 1983 (ph); *De Illusionist/The Illusionist* 1983 (ph); *Schatjes!* 1984 (ph); *De Schorpioen* 1984 (ph); *Bittere Kruid, Het* 1985 (ph); *De Ijssalon* 1985 (ph); *Stranger at Home* 1985 (ph); *De Aanslag/The Assault* 1986 (ph); *Mama Is boos!* 1986 (ph); *De Wisselwachter* 1986 (ph); *Der Madonna Mann* 1987 (ph); *Zoeken naar Eileen* 1987 (ph); *Crossing Delancey* 1988 (ph); *Miracle Mile* 1988 (ph); *The Pointsman* 1988 (ph); *Rooftops* 1989 (ph); *The First Power* 1990 (ph); *Once Around* 1991 (ph).

Van Dyke, W. S. • *aka* William S. Van Dyke II, Woody Van Dyke • Director • Born Woodbridge Strong Van Dyke II, San Diego, CA, March 21, 1889; died February 5, 1943. Van Dyke began his career as an assistant director, notably under D.W. Griffith on *Intolerance* (1916). He rose to prominence after he took over the direction of *White Shadows in the South Seas* from Robert Flaherty in 1928 and, by the 1930s, had developed into one of MGM's most reliable directors. Van Dyke was a capable craftsman whose nonchalant approach to filming earned him the nickname "One-Shot Woody"; it also brought him success at the box-office, particulary with the "Thin Man" series, starring William Powell and Myrna Loy. His deft touch is evident in films such as *Trader Horn* (1931), *Manhattan Melodrama* (1934) and *Sweethearts* (1938). • *Intolerance*

1916 (ad); *Gift o' Gab* 1917 (d); *The Land of Long Shadows* 1917 (sc,d); *The Men of the Desert* 1917 (d,sc); *The Open Places* 1917 (d,sc); *The Range Boss* 1917 (d,sc); *Sadie Goes to Heaven* 1917 (d); *Lady of the Dugout* 1919 (d); *Daredevil Jack* 1920 (d); *The Hawk's Trail* 1920 (d); *The Avenging Arrow* 1921 (d); *Double Adventure* 1921 (d); *According to Hoyle* 1922 (d); *The Boss of Camp 4* 1922 (d); *Forget Me Not* 1922 (d); *White Eagle* 1922 (d); *The Destroying Angel* 1923 (d); *The Little Girl Next Door* 1923 (d); *The Miracle Makers* 1923 (d); *Barriers Burned Away* 1924 (d); *The Battling Fool* 1924 (d); *The Beautiful Sinner* 1924 (d); *Half-a-Dollar Bill* 1924 (d); *Loving Lies* 1924 (d); *Winner Take All* 1924 (d); *The Desert's Price* 1925 (d); *Gold Heels* 1925 (d); *Hearts and Spurs* 1925 (d); *Ranger of the Big Pines* 1925 (d); *Timber Wolf* 1925 (d); *The Trail Rider* 1925 (d); *The Gentle Cyclone* 1926 (d); *War Paint* 1926 (d); *California* 1927 (d); *Eyes of the Totem* 1927 (d); *Foreign Devils* 1927 (d); *The Heart of the Yukon* 1927 (d,story); *Spoilers of the West* 1927 (d); *Winners of the Wilderness* 1927 (d); *Riders of the Dark* 1928 (sc,story); *Under the Black Eagle* 1928 (d); *White Shadows in the South Seas* 1928 (d); *Wyoming* 1928 (d,story); *The Pagan* 1929 (d); *The Cuban Love Song* 1931 (d); *Guilty Hands* 1931 (d); *Never the Twain Shall Meet* 1931 (d); *Trader Horn* 1931 (d); *Night Court* 1932 (d); *Tarzan, the Ape Man* 1932 (d); *Eskimo* 1933 (d); *Penthouse* 1933 (d); *The Prizefighter and the Lady* 1933 (d,p); *Forsaking All Others* 1934 (d); *Hide-Out* 1934 (d); *Laughing Boy* 1934 (d); *Manhattan Melodrama* 1934 (d); *The Thin Man* 1934 (d) **(AANBD)**; *I Live My Life* 1935 (d); *Naughty Marietta* 1935 (d); *After the Thin Man* 1936 (d); *Devil Is a Sissy* 1936 (d); *His Brother's Wife* 1936 (d,p); *Love on the Run* 1936 (d); *Rose Marie* 1936 (d); *San Francisco* 1936 (d) **(AANBD)**; *The Good Earth* 1937 (d); *Personal Property* 1937 (d); *Rosalie* 1937 (d); *They Gave Him a Gun* 1937 (d); *Marie Antoinette* 1938 (d); *Sweethearts* 1938 (d); *Andy Hardy Gets Spring Fever* 1939 (d); *Another Thin Man* 1939 (d); *It's a Wonderful World* 1939 (d); *Stand Up and Fight* 1939 (d); *Bitter Sweet* 1940 (d); *I Love You Again* 1940 (d); *I Take This Woman* 1940 (d); *Dr. Kildare's Victory* 1941 (d); *The Feminine Touch* 1941 (d); *Rage in Heaven* 1941 (d); *Shadow of the Thin Man* 1941 (d); *Cairo* 1942 (d); *I Married an Angel* 1942 (d); *Journey For Margaret* 1942 (d).

Van Dyke, Willard • Filmmaker, photographer • Born Denver, CO, December 5, 1906; died January 23, 1986, Jackson, TN. *Educ.* University of California. Eminent American documentarist who began his career as a still photographer, co-founding the renowned "f.64 Group" (which included Edward Weston, Ansel Adams and Imogen Cunningham) in 1932 and earning acclaim for his portraits of migrant workers. Van Dyke entered film as the co-photographer of Pare Lorentz's celebrated history of the Mississippi Basin, *The River* (1937). He then set up American Documentary Films Inc. with Ralph Steiner and together they directed, photographed and produced another monumental documentary, *The City* (1939), with an outline by Lorentz and an affecting score by Aaron Copland. Van Dyke's other notable works include *Valley Town* (1940), with music by Marc Blitzstein, a series of films made for the Office of War Information during WWII (such as *Steel Town* 1945), *San Francisco* (1945)—the official film on the founding of the United Nations—and *The Skyscraper* (1958), described by co-director Shirley Clarke as "a musical comedy about the building of a skyscraper." Van Dyke served as director of the Museum of Modern Art's film department from 1965 to 1973. • *The River* 1937 (ph); *The City* 1939 (d); *Valley Town* 1940 (ph); *San Francisco* 1945 (ph); *Steel Town (short)* 1945 (d); *Journey Into Medicine* 1946 (d); *Osmosis (short)* 1948 (d); *To Hear Your Banjo Play (short)* 1948 (d); *Mount Vernon (short)* 1949 (d); *New Frontier (short)* 1950 (d); *Years of Change (short)* 1950 (d); *New York University (short)* 1952 (d); *American Frontier (short)* 1953 (d); *Recollections of Boyhood: An Interview With Joseph Welch (short)* 1954 (d); *The Skyscraper (short)* 1958 (d) **(AANBSF)**; *Conversations With Willard Van Dyke* 1981 (a); *He Stands in a Desert Counting the Seconds of His Life* 1985 (a).

Van Heusen, Jimmy • *aka* James Van Heusen • Songwriter; also composer. • Born Edward Chester Babcock, Syracuse, NY, January 26, 1913; died February 7, 1990, Rancho Mirage, CA. *Educ.* Syracuse University, NY (piano, voice). Van Heusen (he took his name from the shirt manufacturer) began writing songs for films in 1940, first in partnership with Johnny Burke and then, from 1954, Sammy Cahn. Oscar-winning compositions include "Swinging on a Star" from *Going My Way* (1944) and "High Hopes" from *A Hole in the Head* (1959). He wrote 76 tunes recorded by Frank Sinatra (more than any other composer) and the songs for six of the seven Crosby-Hope "Road" pictures. • *Playmates* 1941 (m); *My Favorite Spy* 1942 (song); *Road to Morocco* 1942 (song); *Dixie* 1943 (song); *Going My Way* 1944 (song) **(AABS)**; *Belle of the Yukon* 1945 (song) **(AANBS)**; *The Bells of St. Mary's* 1945 (song) **(AANBS)**; *Cross My Heart* 1946 (song); *Road to Bali* 1952 (song); *Not As a Stranger* 1955 (song); *The Tender Trap* 1955 (song) **(AANBS)**; *Anything Goes* 1956 (song); *Pardners* 1956 (song); *The Joker Is Wild* 1957 (song) **(AABS)**; *Indiscreet* 1958 (song); *Night of the Quarter Moon* 1958 (song); *Some Came Running* 1958 (m) **(AANBS)**; *Career* 1959 (song); *A Hole in the Head* 1959 (song) **(AABS)**; *Holiday For Lovers* 1959 (song); *Journey to the Center of the Earth* 1959 (m,song); *Say One For Me* 1959 (m); *This Earth Is Mine* 1959 (m); *High Time* 1960 (song) **(AANBS)**; *Ocean's Eleven* 1960 (song); *A Pocketful of Miracles* 1961 (song) **(AANBS)**; *The Road to Hong Kong* 1962 (song); *Papa's Delicate Condition* 1963 (song) **(AABS)**; *Honeymoon Hotel* 1964 (song); *The Pleasure Seekers* 1964 (song); *Robin and the Seven Hoods* 1964 (song) **(AANBS)**; *Where Love Has Gone* 1964 (song) **(AANBSC)**; *Thoroughly Modern Millie* 1967 (song) **(AANBS)**; *Star!* 1968 (song) **(AANBS)**; *The Great Bank Robbery* 1969 (song).

Van Peebles, Melvin • Director; also screenwriter, producer, composer, novelist, broker. • Born Melvin Peebles, Chicago, IL, August 21, 1932. *Educ.* Ohio Wesleyan University, Delaware; West Virginia State College. Van Peebles began writing novels while living in France in the 60s and made his feature debut in that country with an adaptation of one of them, *La Permission/The Story of a Three-Day Pass*; the story of a romance between an American soldier and a French girl, it was selected as the French entry in the 1968 San Francisco Film Festival. Van Peebles then received various offers from American studios, returning to the US to direct the hilarious *Watermelon Man* (1970), about a white bigot who one day wakes up black.

Next Van Peebles independently produced, directed, wrote, scored and starred in his best known film, the tough, controversial *Sweet Sweetback's Baadasssss Song* (1971). A violent, frenzied tale of a superstud on the run from the police, *Sweetback* cost $500,000 to make (including $50,000 borrowed from Bill Cosby) and grossed over $14 million. It remains one of the very few films to define an African-American esthetic.

After having mastered three vastly different styles (European, American studio, angry independent), Van Peebles moved on to other interests: first the musical stage with the 1970s hits *Ain't Supposed to Die a Natural Death* and *Don't Play Us Cheap*, which helped to build the continuing black presence on Broadway, then commodities trading, where he enjoyed success in the 1980s. He is the author of *Bold Money: A New Way to Play the Options Market* (1986).

Though none of his subsequent work has had an equal impact, Van Peebles has remained a significant figure in contemporary American cinema—due less to his artistic finesse than to his grittier-than-Hollywood portraits of black Americans. In 1990 New York's Museum of Modern Art held a retrospective of his works. Son Mario Van Peebles is a successful TV actor-director who co-produced, co-scripted and starred in his father's *Identity Crisis* (1989) before making his feature directorial debut solo with *New Jack City* (1991). JM • *Sunlight (short)* 1958 (d,p,sc); *Three Pickup Men For Herrick (short)* 1958 (d,p,sc); *La Permission/The Story of a Three Day Pass* 1967 (d,sc,m); *Watermelon Man* 1970 (d,m,m.dir); *Sweet Sweetback's Baadasssss Song* 1971 (a,d,p,sc,ed,m); *Don't Play Us Cheap* 1973 (d,p,sc,from play,ed,m,song); *Greased Lightning* 1977 (sc); *America* 1982 (a); *Jaws: The Revenge* 1987 (a); *O.C. and Stiggs* 1987 (a); *Identity Crisis* 1989 (d,ed,p); *Making "Do the Right Thing"* 1989 (a).

Van Runkle, Theodora • American costume designer • Born c. 1940. *Educ.* Chouinard Art Institute, Los Angeles. Especially noted for her work on period films such as *Bonnie and Clyde* (1967, her debut), Francis Ford Coppola's *The Godfather Part II* (1974), Peter Bogdanovich's *Nickleodeon* (1976) and Martin Scorsese's *New York, New York* (1977). • *Bonnie and Clyde* 1967 **(AANBCD)**; *Bullitt* 1968; *The Reivers* 1969; *Ace Eli and Rodger of the Skies* 1973; *Kid Blue* 1973; *The Godfather, Part II* 1974 **(AANBCD)**; *Mame* 1974; *Nickelodeon* 1976; *New York, New York* 1977; *Heaven Can Wait* 1978; *Same Time, Next Year* 1978; *The Jerk* 1979; *Heartbeeps* 1981; *S.O.B.* 1981; *The Best Little Whorehouse in Texas* 1982; *Rhinestone* 1984; *Native Son* 1986; *Peggy Sue Got Married* 1986 **(AANBCD)**; *Everybody's All-American* 1988; *Wildfire* 1988; *Troop Beverly Hills* 1989; *Stella* 1990.

Van Sant, Gus • Director; also screenwriter. • Born Gus Van Sant, Jr., Louisville, KY, c. 1952. *Educ.* Rhode Island School of Design, Providence. Former commercials producer whose explorations of America's seamy, skid-row underbelly have yielded two of the more potent independent productions of the late 1980s. *Mala Noche* (1985), about the doomed relationship between a Mexican migrant worker and a liquor-store clerk, won a Los Angeles Film Critics Award for best independent film; *Drugstore Cowboy* (1989) chronicled the exploits of a heroin-addicted hustler (Matt Dillon) and his "crew" who survive by robbing West Coast pharmacies. Lyrically shot, and boasting superb performances from Dillon and co-star Kelly Lynch, the film marked Van Sant as a director of considerable promise. Since 1984, he has been making an annual, autobiographical short film that he ultimately plans to assemble into a cinematic diary; Van Sant also paints, plays guitar and writes for his own Portland, Oregon, rock band, "Destroy All Blondes." • *Property* 1978 (sound); *Mala Noche* 1985 (d,p,sc,ed,song); *Five Ways to Kill Yourself (short)* 1987 (d); *Ken Death Gets Out of Jail (short)* 1987 (d,p,sc); *My New Friends (short)* 1987 (d); *Junior (short)* 1988 (d); *Drugstore Cowboy* 1989 (d,sc).

Vanderbeek, Stan • Filmmaker • Born Manhattan, NY; died September 19, 1984, Columbia, MD. *Educ.* Cooper Union, New York (art); Black Mountain College, NC. Experimental filmmaker whose *Science Friction* (1960) was cited by the Creative Film Foundation as contributing to the recognition of film "as a fine art form." • *Science Friction* 1960 (d); *Breathdeath* 1964 (d,idea,p); *Super-Imposition* 1965 (d,idea,p); *See Saw Seems (short)* 1967 (d); *Poem Field No. 1 (short)* 1968 (d); *Dreaming* 1980 (d,idea,p).

Vangelis • Greek composer; also conductor. • Born Vangelis Papathanassiou, March 23, 1943. Specializes in synthesizer-driven yet atmospheric scores and enjoyed his biggest popular success to date with *Chariots of Fire* (1981). In the watershed year of 1982 Vangelis collaborated with Ridley Scott (*Blade Runner*), Peter Weir (*The Year of Living Dangerously*) and Costa-Gavras (*Missing*); more recent work includes Liliana Cavani's *Francesco* (1989). • *Salut, Jerusalem* 1972 (m); *Amore* 1973 (m); *No Oyes Ladrar los Perros?* 1975 (m); *Chariots of Fire* 1981 (m,m.arr,m.perf) **(AABM)**; *Die Todesgottin des Liebescamps* 1981 (asst.cam.op); *Blade Runner* 1982 (m,m.perf,m.arr); *Missing* 1982 (m,m.arr); *Pablo Picasso* 1982 (m); *The Year of Living Dangerously* 1982 (m); *Wonders of Life* 1983 (m); *The Bounty* 1984 (m,m.perf); *Sauvage et Beau* 1984 (m); *Nosferatu a Venezia* 1987 (m); *Someone to Watch Over Me* 1987 (song); *Le Diner des Bustes (short)* 1988 (m); *Francesco* 1989 (m); *Russicum* 1989 (song).

Varda, Agnès • Director, screenwriter • Born Brussels, Belgium, May 30, 1928. *Educ.* Sorbonne, Paris (literature); Ecole du Louvre, Paris (art history); Vaugirard school of photography. Agnès Varda is often called the "grandmother of the New Wave." Although not a member of the *Cahiers du Cinéma* critical fraternity which formed the core of this movement, the Belgian-born Varda completed her first feature, *La Pointe Courde*, in 1954, five years before the New Wave's first films. With almost no academics or technical knowledge of film, though she had been a still photographer for Jean Vilar's Theatre National Populaire, Varda tells two parallel tales (inspired by William Faulkner's *Wild Palms*): the jagged romance of a young married couple and the struggles of the fishermen in the village of La Pointe Courte. Critic Georges Sadoul calls this work "certainly the first film of the Nouvelle Vague" and it set the tone for Varda's career to come, combining fiction with documentary and also (in its debt to Faulkner) illustrating Varda's desire to expand the language of film. "I had the feeling," she said later, "that the cinema was not free, above all in its form, and that annoyed me. I wanted to make a film exactly as one writes a novel."

Unfortunately for Varda, *La Pointe Courte* (which was edited by Alain Resnais, who initially refused to work on it because Varda's techniques were close to those which he was developing) would be the only feature she would make in the 1950s. Although she lit the fuse under the New Wave, it was not until the explosive feature debuts of her male counterparts that Varda received another opportunity to direct a feature, *Cleo From 5 to 7* (1961), which established her as a significant talent on the international film scene. In *Cleo*, we witness the emergence of a great Varda theme, borrowed from Simone de Beauvoir: "One isn't born a woman, one becomes one."

From her first film to her most recent projects, Varda has shown a strong connection to the Earth, becoming a kind of cinematic Mother Nature, whose characters have been personifications of wood and iron (*La Pointe Courte*), sickly trees (*Vagabond*, 1985), animals (*Les Créatures*, 1966) and food ("Apple" of *One Sings, The Other Doesn't* 1977). The world of Agnès Varda is one expansive Garden of Eden, where characters can live without the human burden of morality or sin, whether that world is the French Riviera (*Du côté de la côté* 1958), the city (*Cleo from 5 to 7*), or the country (*Le Bonheur*, 1965; *Les Créatures, Vagabond*). Varda knows that this Eden is a mythical place which exists only in the minds of her main characters and for this reason, her films also contain contrasting elements: troubled characters (the struggling fishermen of *La Pointe Courte* or the suicidal wife of *Le Bonheur*) or less picturesque surroundings (the frozen landscape of *Vagabond*).

Although Varda's initial impact on cinema was a powerful one, by the mid-1960s her career as a commercial filmmaker began to wane. After the improvisational and obscure *Lions Love* (1969), Varda completed only one more fictional commercial feature over the next fifteen years—the epic tale of womanhood and motherhood, *One Sings, the Other Doesn't*. She remained active by directing numerous shorts and documentaries, but much of her work went unseen or unnoticed.

It was not until 1985 that she reemerged in the commercial realm with *Vagabond*, a documentary-style feature about a young French female wanderer which is arguably her best work to date. It deals with all her major concerns: the independence of women, the coexistence with nature, the need for freedom, the acceptance of chance, the cyclical nature of birth and death, the personification of nature, and the seamless blending of documentary and fiction. DC • *La Pointe Courte* 1954 (d); *Toute la Mémoire du*

Monde 1956 (collaboration); *Du côté de la côté (short)* 1958 (d); *La Cocotte d'azur (short)* 1959 (d); *Les Fiancés du Pont Macdonald (short)* 1961 (d); *Cleo de 5 à 7/Cleo From 5 to 7* 1961 (d,sc,adapt,dial,lyrics); *Salut les Cubains (short)* 1963 (d); *Le Bonheur* 1965 (d,sc); *Christmas Carol (short)* 1965 (d); *Les Créatures/The Creatures* 1966 (d,sc); *Loin du Vietnam/Far From Vietnam* 1967 (d); *Uncle Yanco (short)* 1968 (d); *Lions Love* 1969 (d,p,sc); *L'Une chante, l'autre pas/One Sings, the Other Doesn't* 1977 (d,p,sc,song); *Sans toit ni loi/Vagabond* 1985 (d,sc,ed); *La Petit Amor/Kung Fu Master!* 1987 (d,p,sc); *Jane B. par Agnès V./Jane B. by Agnès V.* 1988 (a,d,p,sc,ed).

Veber, Francis • Director, screenwriter; also playwright, producer. • Born Neuilly-sur-Seine, France, 1937. Former journalist who scripted a number of fine comedies for the likes of Yves Robert (*A Tall Blonde Man with One Black Shoe* 1972) and Eduard Molinaro (*A Pain in the A—* 1973) before making his own directing debut with *Le Jouet* (1976). Veber's infectious comedies—including three pairings of Pierre Richard and Gerard Depardieu (*The Goat* 1982, *Les Compères* 1983, *Les Fugitifs* 1986)—proved so successful in his native France that several of his films have been remade in Hollywood. Veber made his US directing debut with one of these, *Three Fugitives* (1989). • *Il Etait une fois un flic* 1971 (sc); *Le Grand Blond avec une Chaussure Noire/A Tall Blonde Man with One Black Shoe* 1972 (sc); *L'Emmerdeur/A Pain in the A—* 1973 (sc,from play *The Contract*); *La Valise* 1973 (sc); *Le Retour du Grand Blond* 1974 (sc); *Adieu Poulet* 1975 (sc); *Peur sur la Ville* 1975 (sc); *Le Telephone Rose* 1975 (sc); *Le Jouet* 1976 (d); *On aura tout vu* 1976 (sc); *La Cage aux folles* 1978 (sc,adapt) **(AANBSC)**; *Cause toujours... tu m'interesses!* 1979 (adapt); *Coup de Tete* 1979 (sc,adapt,dial); *La Cage aux folles II* 1980 (sc); *Sunday Lovers* 1980 (sc—French segment); *Buddy Buddy* 1981 (from play); *La Chevre/The Goat* 1982 (d,sc); *Partners* 1982 (exec.p,sc); *The Toy* 1982 (from film *Le Jouet*); *Les Compères* 1983 (d,sc); *Hold-Up* 1985 (sc,dial); *The Man With One Red Shoe* 1985 (orig. French sc); *Les Fugitifs* 1986 (d,sc); *Three Fugitives* 1989 (d,exec.p,sc,from film *Les Fugitifs*).

Veidt, Conrad • Actor; also director, producer. • Born Hans Walter Konrad Veidt, Potsdam, Germany, January 22, 1893; died April 3, 1943, Hollywood, CA. With his spare frame, high cheekbones and wide, thin-lipped mouth, Conrad Veidt seemed destined to play sinister roles, and to many filmgoers, he is primarily known for his two roles: Cesare, the sleep-walking killer in *The Cabinet of Dr. Caligari* (1919), and Nazi Major Strasser in *Casablanca* (1942). Before his role as Cesare, however, he had made dozens of screen appearances, and before Strasser he had played many sympathetic, even romantic, figures in German and British films.

Veidt studied under the legendary Max Reinhardt in Berlin's Deutsches Theater, before being drafted to serve in the WWI. Invalided out of the army due to jaundice, he found acting work in the front-line theaters organized by actress Lucie Mannheim. With his experience and the wartime shortage of talent, he was eventually asked to perform in motion pictures. In the light of his later career, it is ironic that his first role was in a 1917 film entitled *The Spy/Der Spion*.

Although he did play tyrants and mad killers from Ivan the Terrible to Mr. Hyde in the German silent cinema, Veidt later portrayed Fréderic Chopin, Lord Nelson and Don Carlos. In his British films he often portrayed German officers torn between their sense of duty and personal desires. His reputation for playing disturbed characters was augmented by his role in *Anders Als Die Anderen/Different From the Others* (1919), a film that argued for reform of the laws regarding homosexuality.

Invited to Hollywood in the mid-1920s, Veidt returned with the advent of sound films to Germany, where his voice consolidated his position. By 1930, Veidt had already worked in British co-productions and his unease at the looming Nazi political victory prompted him to emigrate to England. His marriage to a half-Jewish woman must have influenced his decision, although Nazi propaganda minister Joseph Goebbels tried to reassure him about her safety. The Nazis briefly tried to keep him in Germany under the pretext of poor health, until British producer Michael Balcon sent a British doctor to Berlin to retrieve him.

In England, Veidt starred in a number of films, most notably *I Was A Spy* (1933) *Jew Suss* (1934), *Dark Journey* (1937), and *The Spy in Black* (1939). Despite the nuances of character Veidt was able to impart to his roles as WWI German officers and spies, one critic lamented that "the man who is built by nature to petrify kings and emperors with a look, rot the marrow in their bones with a sibilant whisper," took such insubstanial roles.

Still, he did receive top billing in the fantasy classic, *The Thief of Baghdad* (1940), adding immeasurably with his role as the demonic magician and grand vizier Jaffar. At this time, the British government persuaded him to go to Hollywood, since he would be protected from a German invasion and, like other British film personalities, he could help the war effort.

Of the eight films he made in Hollywood before his death, *Casablanca* is the best known, but there was also *Nazi Agent* (1942), in which he played two roles, that of a Nazi agent and his adversary. LR • *Der Spion/The Spy* 1917 (a); *Anders Als die Anderen/Different From the Others* 1919 (a); *Das Kabinett des Dr. Caligari/The Cabinet of Dr. Caligari* 1919 (a); *Liebe Macht Blind* 1923 (a); *The Beloved Rogue* 1927 (a); *The Last Performance* 1927 (a); *A Man's Past* 1927 (a); *The Man Who Laughs* 1928 (a); *Die Letzte Kompanie* 1930 (a); *Der Mann, der Den Mord Beging* 1931 (a); *I Was a Spy* 1933 (a); *Bella Donna* 1934 (a); *Jew Suss* 1934 (a); *Dark Journey* 1937 (a); *The Spy in Black/U-Boat 29* 1939 (a); *Contraband* 1940 (a); *Escape* 1940 (a); *The Thief of Bagdad* 1940 (a); *The Men in Her Life* 1941 (a); *Whistling in the Dark* 1941 (a); *A Woman's Face* 1941 (a); *All Through the Night* 1942 (a); *Casablanca* 1942 (a); *Nazi Agent* 1942 (a); *Above Suspicion* 1943 (a).

Venora, Diane • Actress • Born Hartford, CT, 1952. *Educ.* Juilliard (drama). New York stage actress who first attacted notice as an unlikely Prince of Denmark in the New York Shakespeare Festival's 1983 production of *Hamlet.* Venora had a bit part in *All That Jazz* (1979) and contributed a powerful performance as the strong-willed wife of jazzman Charlie Parker in Clint Eastwood's *Bird* (1988). • *All That Jazz* 1979; *Wolfen* 1981; *The Cotton Club* 1984; *Terminal Choice* 1985; *F/X* 1986; *Ironweed* 1987; *Bird* 1988.

Ventura, Lino • Actor • Born Lino Borrini, Parma, Italy, July 14, 1919; died October 23, 1987, Saint-Cloud, France. Solidly built, husky-voiced performer whose background as a boxer initially landed him numerous roles as tough cops or bad guys. Ventura made a competent debut in Jacques Becker's gangster study *Touchez pas au Grisbi* (1953) and, after supporting parts in several other films starring Jean Gabin, was turning in immaculately nuanced lead performances by the end of the decade. Superb as the title character of Claude Pinoteau's taut spy thriller *Le Silencieux* (1972). • *Touchez Pas au Grisbi* 1953; *Razzia* 1954; *Crime et Chatiment* 1956; *Ascenseur pour l'échafaud* 1957; *Le Rouge est mis* 1957; *Montparnasse 19* 1958; *Classe tous risques* 1960; *Herrin der Welt* 1960; *La Métamorphose des cloportes* 1965; *Les Aventuriers* 1967; *L'Armée des ombres* 1969; *Le Clan des Siciliens/The Sicilian Clan* 1969; *Boulevard du Rhum* 1971; *Fantasia Chez Les Ploucs* 1971; *L'Aventure c'est l'aventure* 1972; *Le Silencieux* 1972; *Le Dossier Valachi/The Valachi Papers* 1972; *La Bonne Année* 1973; *L'Emmerdeur* 1973; *Three Tough Guys* 1973; *Escape to Nowhere* 1974; *La Gifle* 1974; *Adieu Poulet* 1975; *La Cage* 1975; *Cadaveri Eccellenti* 1976; *The Medusa Touch* 1978; *Un Papillon sur l'Epaule* 1978; *L'Homme en colère* 1979; *Sunday Lovers* 1980; *Garde à Vue* 1981; *Le Ruffian* 1983; *Cento Giorni A Palermo* 1984; *Le Septième Cible* 1984; *La Rumba* 1986.

Verhoeven, Paul • Director • Born Amsterdam, Netherlands, 1938. *Educ.* University of Leiden (mathematics, physics). Verhoeven began his career making documentaries for the Royal Dutch Navy and for Dutch TV, where he moved into fiction and gained attention for the series, "Floris," starring Rutger Hauer. His feature debut came in 1971 with *Business is Business* but it was *Turkish Delight* (1973) which made his name—an erotic, satirical study of a marriage between a sculptor (Hauer) and a middle-class girl (Monique Van de Ven) which scored at the domestic and international box-office.

Verhoeven then turned out a trio of fine, Dutch-produced films—the episodic WWII tale *Soldier of Orange* (1979), the contemporary slice-of-life drama *Spetters* (1980) and the erotic thriller, *The Fourth Man* (1982)—which generated little critical enthusiasm at home but earned international attention for the director, his actors of choice (Jeroen Krabbe, Renée Soutendijk and Rutger Hauer) and cinematographer Jost Vacano.

Verhoeven's first international co-production was the brutal, US/Netherlands-produced tale of the middle ages, *Flesh + Blood* (1985). He has gone on to become one of Holland's best-known exports to the US, garnering both critical and commercial success with the witty sci-fi thriller *Robocop* (1987) and directing one of the more entertaining summer blockbusters of 1990, *Total Recall*. • *Wat Zien Ik/Business Is Business* 1971 (d); *Oh Jonathan, Oh Jonathan* 1973 (a); *Turkish Delight* 1973 (d); *Keetje Tippel* 1975 (d); *Soldier of Orange* 1979 (d,sc); *Spetters* 1980 (d); *De Vierde Man/The Fourth Man* 1982 (d); *Flesh + Blood* 1985 (d,sc); *Robocop* 1987 (d); *Total Recall* 1990 (d).

Vertov, Dziga • Director, editor; also theoretician. • Born Denis Arkadievitch Kaufman, Bialystok, Poland, January 2, 1896; died February 12, 1954. *Educ.* Bialystok Music Conservatory. Dziga Vertov was born as Denis Abramovich (later changed to Arkadievich) Kaufman to a Jewish book-dealer's family. His younger brothers, renowned Soviet documentary filmmaker Mikhail Kaufman and cameraman Boris Kaufman, would later establish their own niches in film history. As a child he studied piano and violin, and at the age of ten began to write poetry; Vertov's films would reflect these early interests.

After WWI started the Kaufman family fled to Moscow. In 1916 Vertov enrolled in Petrograd Psychoneurological Institute. For his studies of human perception, he recorded and edited natural sounds in his "Laboratory of Hearing," trying to create new sound effects by means of rhythmic grouping of phonetic units. Familiar with the Russian Futurist movement, he took on the pseudonym "Dziga Vertov" (loosely translated as "spinning top"). In 1918 Mikhail Koltstov, who headed Moscow Film Committee's newsreel section, hired Vertov as his assistant. Among Vertov's colleagues were Lev Kuleshov, who was conducting his legendary montage experiments, and Eduard Tisse, Eisenstein's future cameraman. Vertov would recall later that they were most strongly influenced by Griffith's *Intolerance*.

Vertov began to edit documentary footage and soon was appointed editor of *Kinonedelya*, the first Soviet weekly newsreel. His first film as a director was *The Anniversary of the Revolution* (1919), followed by two shorts, *Battle of Tsaritsyn* (1920) and *The Agit-Train VTSIK* (1921), and the thirteen-reel *History of Civil War* (1922). In editing those documentaries, Vertov was discovering the possibilities of montage. He began joining pieces of film without regard for chronology or location to achieve an expressiveness which would politically engage the viewers.

In 1919 Vertov and his future wife, the talented film editor Elisaveta Svilova, plus several other young filmmakers created a group called "Kinoks" ("kino-oki," meaning cinema-eyes). In 1922 they were joined by Mikhail Kaufman, who had just returned from the civil war. From 1922 to 1923 Vertov, Kaufman, and Svilova published a number of manifestos in avant-garde journals which clarified the Kinoks' positions vis-à-vis other leftist groups. The Kinoks rejected "staged" cinema with its stars, plots, props and studio shooting. They insisted that the cinema of the future be the cinema of fact: newsreels recording the real world, "life caught unawares." Vertov proclaimed the primacy of camera ("Kino-Eye") over the human eye. The camera lens was a machine that could be perfected infinitely to grasp the world in its entirety and organize visual chaos into a coherent, objective picture. At the same time Vertov emphasized that his Kino-Eye principle was a method of "communist" deciphering of the world. For Vertov there was no contradiction here; as a true believer he considered Marxism the only objective and scientific tool of analysis and even called a series of the 23 newreels he directed between 1922 and 1925 *Kino-Pravda*, "pravda" being not only the Russian word for the truth but also the title of the official party newspaper.

Nevertheless, Vertov's films weren't mere propoganda. Created from documentary footage, they represented an intricate blend of art and rhetoric, achieved with a sophistication that, among Vertov's contemporaries, would be rivaled only by Leni Riefenstahl. Vertov's achievement was also his tragedy. He considered his films documentaries, but they also strongly reflected his personal, highly emotional poetic vision of Soviet reality, a vision he maintained throughout his life. As early as the mid-1920s Vertov was arousing suspicion from party authorities with his utopian and ecstatic cine-tracts and his pioneering techniques, including slow and reverse motion, "candid camera" tricks, bizarre angles, shooting in motion, split screens and multiple superimpositions, the inventive use of still photography, constructivist graphics, animation and most importantly rapid montage that sometimes consisted of only several frames. All these advances also left the masses indifferent. Among filmmakers Vertov acquired the reputation of an eccentric, an extremist who rejected everything in cinema except for the Kinoks' work. Fortunately Vertov, like Eisenstein, received the support of the influential European avant-garde. His feature-length *Kino-Eye—Life Caught Unawares* (1924) was awarded a silver medal and honorary diploma at the World Exhibit in Paris, and that success led to two more films commissioned by Moscow: *Stride, Soviet!* and *A Sixth of the World* (both 1926).

By now, the central authorities were fed up with Vertov's formal experimenting, and they refused to support his most ambitious project, *The Man With a Movie Camera* (1929). To make the film, Vertov had to accept the invitation of the film studio VUFKU in the Ukraine, where he moved with Svilova and Kaufman. These changes resulted in the collapse of the Kinoks group and by the time the project was finally realized there were already several similar "city symphonies" completed by such innovative filmmakers as Alberto Cavalcanti (in Paris), Mikhail Kaufman (in Moscow) and Walter Ruttman (in Berlin). Then too, Vertov's youngest brother Boris Kaufman, who lived in France, was about to start shooting *A Propos de Nice* for Jean Vigo. However, Vertov's film was significantly different from its brethren: its goal was not only to present a mosaic of the life of a city (a combination of Kiev, Moscow and Odessa) by use of the most advanced cinematic means, but also to engage spectators in theoretical discourse on the relationship between film and reality, on the nature of cinematic language and human perception.

In so doing Vertov was at least 30 years ahead of his time: his ideas of the self-reflective cinema, of the viewer identifying himself with the filmmaking process, would reemerge only at the end of the fifties in the work of Chris Marker, Jean-Luc Godard, Michael Snow and Stan Brakhage. But in 1929, when *The Man With a Movie Camera* was publicly released, it was too obscure, even for Eisenstein. Mikhail Kaufman was also dissatisfied by the final version of the film and it marked the end of his collaboration with Vertov.

In the transition to sound Vertov outstripped Eisenstein and most of the other silent cinema masters. He was prepared for the sound revolution because of his early experiments with noise recording, and in *A Sixth of the World* he had even discovered substitutes for the human voice: by using various prints in his intertitles and by rhythmically alternating the phrases with images, Vertov achieved the illusion of off-screen narration. His first sound picture, *Enthusiasm: Donbass Symphony* (1931), was an instant success abroad; Chaplin wrote that he had never imagined that industrial sounds could be organized in such a beautiful way and named *Enthusiasm* the best film of the year. Yet at home it was widely ridiculed as cacophony, in spite of its ideological fervor. Vertov's next film, *Three Songs of Lenin* (1934), made in commemoration of the tenth anniversary of Lenin's death, had to wait six months for its official release, allegedly because it had failed to emphasize the "important role" of Stalin in the Russian Revolution. Subsequently, the proper footage was added. In spite of these complications, the film turned out to be a popular success both at home and abroad. Even those who had little reason to adore Lenin couldn't help praising the overall elegance of its structure, the elegiac fluidity of montage, the lyrical inner monologue and the highly expressive and technologically innovative synchronous-sound shots of people talking.

In spite of such success, by the end of the 1930s Vertov was deprived of any serious independent work. He was not persecuted, like many of his avant-garde friends; he lived for almost 20 years in obscurity, editing conventional newsreels, the same kind of films he had once proven so capable of transforming into art.

Six years after his death, French documentary filmmakers Jean Rouch and Edgar Morin adopted Vertov's theory and practice into their method of Cinéma-Vérité. In recent years Vertov's heritage of poetic documentary has influenced many young filmmakers all over the world. In 1962 the first Soviet monograph on Vertov was published, followed by *Dziga Vertov: Articles, Diaries, Projects,* which was published in English as *Kino-Eye, The Writings of Dziga Vertov.* In 1984, in commemoration of the 30th anniversary of Vertov's death, three New York organizations—Anthology Film Archives, the Collective for Living Cinema and Joseph Papp's Film at the Public—mounted the first American retrospective of Vertov's work, with panels and lectures by leading Vertov scholars and screenings of films by Vertov's contemporaries and his followers from all over the world. AB • *Kino-nedelya/Cinema Week* 1918-19; *Godouschine revolyutsii/Anniversary of the Revolution* 1919; *Istoriya grazhdanskoy voyny/History of the Civil War* 1922; *Kino-Pravda/Cinema-Truth* 1922-25; *Kino-Glaz/Kino-Eye—Life Caught Unawares* 1924; *Shagai, Soviet/Stride, Soviet* 1926; *Shestaya chast mira/A Sixth of the World* 1926; *Odinnadtsatyi/The Eleventh Year* 1928; *Chelovek s kinoapparatom/The Man With a Movie Camera* 1929; *Entuziasm: Simfoniya Donbasa/Enthusiasm: Donbass Symphony* 1931; *Tri pesni o Lenine/Three Songs of Lenin* 1934; *Kolibelnaya/Lullaby* 1937; *Serge Ordjonikidze* 1937; *Tri geroini/Three Heroines* 1938; *Novostni Dnia/News of the Day* 1944-54.

Vidor, Charles • Director; also screenwriter. • Born Budapest, Hungary, July 27, 1900; died June 5, 1959, Vienna, Austria. *Educ.* University of Budapest (civil engineering); University of Berlin (civil engineering). Editor and assistant director with UFA who arrived in the US in 1924 and, after a stint with a Wagnerian opera company and in a Broadway chorus, left for Hollywood. Vidor made his directorial debut in 1931 with the self-financed short, *The Bridge,* which landed him a contract with MGM. In 1932 he co-directed his first feature, *The Mask of Fu Manchu,* one of the finest screen adaptions of the Sax Rohmer novels. Vidor was noted for his ability to impart a technical fluency to routine subjects. Among the best of his prolific output were *Ladies in Retirement* (1941), *Love Me or Leave Me* (1955) and *The Joker Is Wild* (1957). Vidor was also responsible for the trailblazing psychological study, *Blind Alley* (1939), and the two Rita Hayworth vehicles that cemented her stardom: the arresting musical, *Cover Girl* (1944), and the steamy noir thriller, *Gilda* (1946). • *The Mask of Fu Manchu* 1932 (d); *Sensation Hunters* 1933 (d); *The Double Door* 1934 (d); *The Arizonian* 1935 (d); *His Family Tree* 1935 (d); *Strangers All* 1935 (d); *Muss 'Em Up* 1936 (d); *A Doctor's Diary* 1937 (d); *The Great Gambini* 1937 (d); *She's No Lady* 1937 (d); *Blind Alley* 1939 (d); *Romance of the Redwoods* 1939 (d); *Those High Grey Walls* 1939 (d); *The Lady in Question* 1940 (d); *My Son, My Son* 1940 (d); *Ladies in Retirement* 1941 (d); *New York Town* 1941 (d); *The Tuttles of Tahiti* 1942 (d); *The Desperadoes* 1943 (d); *Cover Girl* 1944 (d); *Together Again* 1944 (d); *Over 21* 1945 (d); *A Song to Remember* 1945 (d); *Gilda* 1946 (d); *The Loves of Carmen* 1948 (d,p); *Edge of Doom* 1950 (d); *It's a Big Country* 1951 (d); *Hans Christian Andersen* 1952 (d); *Thunder in the East* 1952 (d); *Rhapsody* 1954 (d); *Love Me or Leave Me* 1955 (d); *The Swan* 1956 (d); *A Farewell to Arms* 1957 (d); *The Joker Is Wild* 1957 (d); *Song Without End* 1960 (d).

Vidor, King • Director; also actor. • Born King Wallis Vidor, Galveston, TX, February 8, 1894; died November 1, 1982. King Vidor's films range across all genres, but they are unified by a concern with the struggle for selfhood in a pluralistic, mass society. Influenced both by D.W. Griffith's realism and Sergei Eisenstein's montage aesthetic, Vidor has come closer to reconciling these strains than any other American director.

Raised in Texas, Vidor shot local events for national newsreel companies before forming the Hotex Motion Picture Company in Houston in 1914. Moving to Hollywood with his actress wife Florence, he supported himself with a variety of production jobs before settling at Universal as a writer. His first directing work in Hollywood was independently produced. He made a series of ten inspirational shorts in 1918, followed by *The Turn in the Road* (1919), an extremely successful feature with Vidor's Christian Science beliefs as thematic material.

After a series of further successes released through Robertson-Cole and First National between 1919 and 1921, the director founded "Vidor Village," a small studio from which he planned to produce independently. The experiment failed, but in the meantime Florence Vidor had become a star, and Vidor directed several films featuring her before beginning work for the Metro and Goldwyn studios in 1922. The merger which created MGM in 1924 also made Vidor a senior director for the company, and his fifth film for the young studio, *The Big Parade* (1925), was a landmark critical and popular success.

The Big Parade was the first serious screen treatment of WWI, and its harrowing story of a disinterested heir (John Gilbert) experiencing passion, fear and loss in wartime struck a responsive chord. The film, reportedly one of the most profitable silent films ever produced, made Gilbert a star, vaulted MGM to front-rank studio status and gave Vidor unheard-of creative control.

Vidor's record as a bankable director accounts for the freedom with which he was able to make the unusual urban parable, *The Crowd* (1928). Though a financial failure, the film garnered further prestige for MGM and reinforced Vidor's now international reputation for stylistic experimentation and uncompromising concern for social issues. Subsequent critical milestones were *Hallelujah* (1929), a pioneering black film; *Street Scene* (1931), an adaption of Elmer Rice's socially conscious drama; and *Our Daily Bread* (1934), the story of a Depression agricultural cooperative, clearly indebted to Soviet montage filmmaking. Notable box-office successes for Vidor were *The Champ* (1931) and *Stella Dallas* (1937). Vidor was instrumental in founding the Screen Directors' Guild in 1936, and alongside John Ford, Frank Capra and Ernst Lubitsch, was a central figure in 30s American filmmaking.

After some three weeks' work on *The Wizard of Oz* (1939) and the spectacular and innovative location Technicolor photography of *Northwest Passage* (1940), Vidor became frustrated with MGM's apparent lack of commitment to his increasingly epochal vision of American life. His *An American Romance* (1944) was drastically cut by MGM and led him to sever ties with the studio where, except for prestigious loan-outs, he had been directing for over 20 years.

Vidor's epic *Duel in the Sun* (1947) pioneered the "adult" western genre, but he quit the project before completion and the final result is the product of several directorial hands, as well as producer David O. Selznick. After his episode of the omnibus film *On Our Merry Way* (1948) was cut by producer Benedict Bogeaus, Vidor signed with Warner Bros. for what would eventually be a three-picture deal. The first of these projects was *The Fountainhead* (1949), which skillfully combined novelist Ayn Rand's radical egoism with the director's own, more quizzical, individualism. The story of an architect's battle with professional and social hypocrisy, the film was among Vidor's most fully realized productions of the postwar period. Although equally striking, *Beyond the Forest* (1949) was thematically bizarre: the tale of a small-town doctor's wife (Bette Davis) and her ambitions ended Davis's 20-year career at Warners amid poor box-office returns and much resentment.

On concluding his deal with Warners, Vidor experimented as an independent producer with two films, *Japanese War Bride* (1952) and, in the same year, *Ruby Gentry*—the last picture to fully manifest his bleak point of view and operatic visual style. His last three features were the inconclusive and bloodless *Man Without a Star* (1955) and the spectacles *War and Peace* (1956) and *Solomon and Sheba* (1959).

Vidor spent his last years producing two short films on metaphysics, lecturing at film schools and retrospectives of his work, and trying to interest producers in various projects, including a film based on his investigation of the 1924 William Desmond Taylor murder case.

Vidor's darkly humanistic vision, accompanied (especially in the 1925-35 period) by a striking and eclectic visual style, made him one of the most influential directors of his time. His oeuvre is as rich, diverse and intelligent as any in the history of cinema. KJH • *The Intrigue* 1916 (a); *Better Times* 1919 (d,sc); *The Other Half* 1919 (d,sc); *Poor Relations* 1919 (d,sc); *The Turn in the Road* 1919 (d,sc); *The Family Honor* 1920 (d); *The Jack-Knife Man* 1920 (d); *Love Never Dies* 1921 (d,sc); *The Sky Pilot* 1921 (d); *Conquering the Woman* 1922 (d); *Dusk to Dawn* 1922 (d); *Peg o' My Heart* 1922 (d); *The Real Adventure* 1922 (d); *Souls For Sale* 1923 (a); *Three Wise Fools* 1923 (adapt,d); *The Woman of Bronze* 1923 (d); *Happiness* 1924 (d); *His Hour* 1924 (d); *Wife of the Centaur* 1924 (d); *Wild Oranges* 1924 (d,sc); *Wine of Youth* 1924 (d,p); *The Big Parade* 1925 (d,p); *Proud Flesh* 1925 (d); *Bardelys the Magnificent* 1926 (d); *La Boheme* 1926 (d); *The Patsy* 1927 (d); *The Crowd* 1928 (d,sc,story) **(AANBD)**; *Show People* 1928 (d,p); *Hallelujah* 1929 (d,story) **(AANBD)**; *Billy the Kid* 1930 (d,p); *Not So Dumb* 1930 (d); *The Champ* 1931 (d,p) **(AANBD)**; *Street Scene* 1931 (d); *Bird of Paradise* 1932 (d,p); *Cynara* 1932 (d); *The Stranger's Return* 1933 (d,p); *Our Daily Bread* 1934 (d,story); *So Red the Rose* 1935 (d); *The Wedding Night* 1935 (d); *The Texas Rangers* 1936 (d,story); *Stella Dallas* 1937 (d); *The Citadel* 1938 (d) **(AANBD)**; *Comrade X* 1940 (d); *Northwest Passage* 1940 (d); *H. M. Pulham, Esq.* 1941 (d,sc); *An American Romance* 1944 (d,p,story); *Duel in the Sun* 1947 (d); *A Miracle Can Happen* 1948 (d); *Beyond the Forest* 1949 (d); *The Fountainhead* 1949 (d); *Lightning Strikes Twice* 1951 (d); *Japanese War Bride* 1952 (d); *Ruby Gentry* 1952 (d,p); *Man Without a Star* 1954 (d); *War and Peace* 1956 (d,sc,adapt) **(AANBD)**; *Solomon and Sheba* 1959 (d).

Vierny, Sacha • Director of photography • Born Bois-le-Roi, France, August 10, 1919. *Educ.* IDHEC, Paris. Began his film career making news documentaries in Africa and shot his first feature, *Le Bel Age*, in 1958. Vierny is known for his crisp lighting and deep-focus photography and has often worked with Alain Resnais, notably on *Hiroshima, mon Amour* (1959) and *Last Year at Marienbad* (1961). He has lately become director Peter Greenaway's cinematographer of choice, reaching American audiences with the strikingly shot *The Cook, the Thief, His Wife and Her Lover* (1989). • *Nuit et Brouillard/Night and Fog* 1955 (ph); *Le Mystère de l'atelier Quinze* 1957 (ph); *Le Bel Age* 1958 (ph); *Le Chant du Styrène* 1958 (ph); *Hiroshima, mon amour* 1959 (ph (France)); *L'Année dernière à Marienbad/Last Year at Marienbad* 1961 (ph); *Muriel* 1963 (ph); *De Dans van de Reiger* 1966 (ph); *La Guerre est finie* 1966 (ph); *La Musica* 1966 (ph); *Belle de Jour* 1967 (ph); *Bof! L'Anatomie d'un livreur* 1971 (ph); *La Sainte Famille* 1972 (ph); *Les Granges Brulées* 1973 (ph); *Le Moine* 1973 (ph); *Stavisky* 1973 (ph); *Baxter, Vera Baxter* 1977 (ph); *Le Diable dans la boîte* 1977 (ph); *La Vocation Suspendue* 1977 (ph); *La Bravade Legendaire* 1978 (ph); *L'Hypothèse du Tableau Volé* 1978 (ph); *Mon oncle d'Amerique* 1979 (ph); *Le Chemin Perdu* 1980 (ph); *Beau Père* 1981 (ph); *Les Trois couronnes du matelot* 1983 (ph); *L'Amour à mort* 1984 (ph); *Clash* 1984 (ph); *La Femme Publique* 1984 (ph); *Flugel und Felleln* 1984 (ph); *A Zed and Two Noughts* 1985 (ph); *The Belly of an Architect* 1987 (ph); *Drowning By Numbers* 1988 (ph); *Le Cuisinier, le voleur, sa femme et son amant/The Cook, the Thief, His Wife and Her Lover* 1989 (ph); *Prospero's Books* 1991.

Vigne, Daniel • Director, screenwriter • Born France, 1942. Meticulous craftsman who directed his first film in 1972 and earned widespread acclaim for the medieval drama, *The Return of Martin Guerre* (1982), starring Gérard Dépardieu. Vigne's acute attention to detail has been cited as the reason for his relatively limited output. • *Les Hommes* 1973 (d,sc); *Le Retour de Martin Guerre/The Return of Martin Guerre* 1982 (d,p,sc); *Une Femme ou deux* 1985 (d,sc,idea); *Comédie d'été* 1989 (d,sc,ed); *The King's Whore* 1990 (sc).

Vigo, Jean • Director • Born Jean Bonaventure de Vigo, Paris, April 26, 1905; died October 26, 1934, Paris. Battling chronic lung disease throughout his life, branded a traitor's son by his fellow countrymen, dead at the untimely age of 29, Jean Vigo left a truncated cinema legacy of four films. Despite his meager output, Vigo has become one of the most influential French filmmakers of the century, even if it was an honor he would never live to see. At the time of their release, the films now considered Vigo's three masterpieces, *A propos de Nice* (1929), *Zero de conduite* (1933) and *L'Atalante* (1934), were largely vilified by the critics, ignored by the public, recut and butchered by producers and exhibitors. Not until the late 1940s, during the postwar art cinema movement, was Vigo's work rediscovered and finally appreciated for its lyric realism and poetic simplicity.

Vigo's life was one of constant turmoil. A sickly child who suffered from respiratory disease, Vigo was constantly shuttled in and out of hospitals and sanitoriums. Both his parents were intensely involved in politics, leaving no time for the care of a child, and Jean found himself passed from relative to relative and boarding school to boarding school. During Jean's young adulthood, his father, Eugène Bonaventure de Vigo (*aka* Miguel Almereyda), a left-wing political activist, was accused by the French government of collaborating with Germany in a scheme to end WWI, and he was put on trial as a traitor. But before Almereyda was to appear at his trial, he was found strangled in his jail cell. Embittered over the questionable circumstances behind his father's death, Vigo became embroiled in a campaign to clear his father's name, but frequent relapses of his illness somewhat diluted his efforts. In 1926, Vigo began to attend classes at the Sorbonne, sparking his interest in cinema.

In 1928, Vigo traveled to Paris, where, through meetings with Claude Autant-Lara and Germaine Dulac, he became an assistant cameraman to the noted French cinematographer Burel on *Venus*. After receiving a 100,000 franc gift from his father-in-law, Vigo purchased a Debrie camera and proceeded to shoot an independent documentary, *A propos de Nice*.

As with such innovators as Griffith and Welles, Vigo's genius was in incorporating past trends and reshaping them into a new film style that future filmmakers can adopt and amend. With *A propos de Nice, Zero de conduite* and *L'Atalante,* Vigo consolidated the formalistic expressiveness of the silent French avant-garde, the open naturalism of the American silent cinema of von Stroheim and Chaplin, and the blasting immediacy of Dziga Vertov's Kino Pravda newsreel. Vigo reshaped these strands into a cinema of stylized realism. His films were poetic studies of small details and processes transformed into celebrations of mythic moments.

A propos de Nice uses satirical exagerations and sexual imagery to explode a seemingly gentle travelogue into a subversive expose of a way of life. *Taris Champion de Natation* (1931), his second film, enlisted a toned-down surrealism which undercut a celebratory profile of a famous swimmer. In its depiction of an authoritarian adult world in a French boarding school, *Zero de conduite* employed an opposition between formalist caricature and a hyper-real depiction of a child's world view to criticize stifling regimentation and conservatism. And in *L'Atalante,* Vigo wove a simple, graceful narrative into a celebratory ode to movement and the present tense. In these films, Vigo strove to create a new, immediate style that was later to achieve full expression in the open cinema of Welles and Renoir and retooled into the French New Wave essays of Jean-Luc Godard.

But the bright promise of Vigo in pursuit of a new film style was suddenly crushed when, on October 5, 1934, a few days after the opening of *L'Atlante,* Jean Vigo succumbed to rheumatic septicameia. However, by its lyrical grace and sparkling immediacy, Vigo's scant filmwork has endured and reshaped cinema, its towering contradictions and poetic sensibility ever fresh and new. PB • *A propos de Nice (short)* 1929 (d); *La Natation par Jean Taris champion de France/Taris champion de Natation (short)* 1931 (d); *Zero de conduite* 1933 (d); *L'Atalante* 1934 (add.dial,d).

Visconti, Luchino • Director • Born Count Don Luchino Visconti DiModrone, Milan, Italy, November 2, 1906; died March 17, 1976, Rome. Luchino Visconti occupies a unique place in the history of world cinema; he is the most Italian of internationalists, the most operatic of realists, and the most aristocratic of Marxists. Although one of the progenitors of the Italian neorealist movement, Visconti, with his love of spectacle and historical panorama, would seem to have more in common with Orson Welles or even Erich von Stroheim than with Rossellini or De Sica. Directors as diverse as Bertolucci, Scorsese, Coppola and Fassbinder have named him as a major influence.

Born to an aristocratic family, Visconti spent the pre-WWII years in Paris, soaking up the intellectual, cultural and poltical currents of the time. His close association with Jean Renoir led to his decision to become a filmmaker, although he continued throughout his life to devote part of his considerable energies to the theater and opera. An active anti-fascist, he managed to escape persecution by the Mussolini government until the final days of the war. He directed his first film, *Ossessione* (1942) during the war years. An unauthorized adapatation of the James M. Cain novel, *The Postman Always Rings Twice,* the film avoided overt political content but was still censored by the Fascists for "obscenity," perhaps because of its raw and naturalistic portrayal of the lovers' affair.

Immediately after the war, Visconti turned his attention to opera and theater, but in 1948, he made his most overtly Marxist film, *La Terra Trema,* an adaptation of Giovanni Verga's classic novel about life in a poor Sicilian fishing village. In 1951, Visconti changed pace again, with one of his few attempts at satire, *Bellissima,* which records the attempts of an indefatigable stage mother, brilliantly played by Anna Magnani, to get her little daughter into the movies.

Another complete turn, this time to the period of the Risorgimento, produced *Senso* (1954), a filmic opera of revolution, illicit love and betrayal which even incorporates sections from Verdi's *Il Travaotre.* In 1957, Visconti offered a very theatrical version of Dostoevsky's *White Nights,* starring Marcello Mastroianni and Maria Schell, and in 1960 he made his final foray into working-class life, *Rocco and His Brothers,* a domestic tragedy portraying the difficulties encountered by a Sicilian peasant family transplanted because of economic need to the industrial North. Visconti's next film, an adaptation of Giuseppe di Lampedusa's novel *The Leopard* (1963), was an account of an arsitocratic Sicilian family faced with enormous social changes during the late 19th century. Although awarded the Golden Palm at Cannes, it was severely edited for US audiences and not restored for almost twenty years.

In *Sandra* (1965), Visconti deals for the first time with the Italian Resistance, through the story of a wealthy woman haunted by an incestuous relationship with her brother and the knowledge that her mother had betrayed her father, a Jew, to the Nazis. Following an excellent adaptation of Camus' *The Stranger* (1967), Visconti abandoned himself finally to his greatest loves—opera and politics—in *The Damned* (1969), a truly Wagnerian account of the fall of a German industrial family in its capitulation to the evils of Hitler and the SS. Two more "German decadence" films followed: *Death in Venice* (1971), far more Visconti than Thomas Mann, and *Ludwig* (1972), a colorful rendition of the life of the "mad" King Ludwig of Bavaria.

Visconti made two final films, *Conversation Piece* (1975), a semi-autobiographical story of an elderly intellectual confounded by a new Italy in which the vulgar materialism of the new bourgeoisie clashes with the sometimes desperate alienation and militancy of radicalized youth, and *L'Innocente* (1976), based on Gabrielle d'Annunzio's novel of upper-class adultery. They reveal signs of his declining powers but still testify to a dedication to art, beauty, social justice and human values that were the motivating forces behind this extraordinary talent. RM • *Toni* 1934 (prod.asst); *Un Partie de Campagne* 1936 (props,uncred costumes); *La Tosca* 1941 (sc,ad); *Ossessione* 1942 (d,sc,adapt); *Giorni di Gloria* 1945 (d); *La Terra Trema* 1948 (d,sc,story,commentary,m); *Bellissima* 1951 (d,sc); *Appunti su un fatto di Cronaca* 1953 (d,narrative text); *Siamo Donne* 1953 (d); *Senso/The Wanton Contessa* 1954 (d,sc); *Le Notti Bianche/White Nights* 1957 (d,sc); *Of Life and Love* 1958 (d); *Rocco e i suoi Fratelli/Rocco and His Brothers* 1960 (d,sc,dial,idea); *Boccaccio '70* 1962 (d,sc—"Il lavoro"); *Il Gattopardo/The Leopard* 1963 (d,sc); *Vaghe stelle dell'orsa/Sandra* 1965 (d,sc); *Lo Straniero/The Stranger* 1967 (d); *Le Streghe* 1968 (d); *La Caduta degli dei/The Damned* 1969 (d,sc,story) **(AANBSC)**; *Morte a Venezia/Death in Venice* 1971 (d,p,sc); *Ludwig* 1972 (d,sc,story); *Gruppo di famiglia in un interno/Conversation Piece* 1975 (d,sc); *L'Innocente/The Innocent* 1976 (d,sc).

Vitti, Monica • Actress; also director. • Born Maria Louisa Ceciarelli, Rome, November 3, 1931. *Educ.* National Academy of Dramatic Arts, Rome. Cool, elegant beauty who began appearing in films in the mid-1950s, playing characters far from her spritely self. Vitti was cast in several stage plays directed by Michelangelo Antonioni in the later part of the decade and gained international recognition for her performances in his films. With a presence as distant and forlorn as the landscape that figures so prominently in Antonioni's work, Vitti was perfectly suited to his singular vision, contributing memorably to the the classic trilogy, *L'Avventura* (1959), *La Notte* (1961) and *L'Eclisse* (1962) and to the neurotic study of angst and alienation, *Red Desert* (1964). Vitti made her own directing debut in 1989 with *Scandalo Segreto/Secret Scandal.* • *L'Avventura* 1959 (a); *La Notte* 1961 (a); *L'Eclisse* 1962 (a); *Chateau en Suède* 1963 (a); *Dragées au Poivre* 1963 (a); *Deserto Rosso/Red Desert* 1964 (a); *Le Bambole* 1965 (a); *Modesty Blaise* 1966 (a); *La Cintura di Castita* 1967 (a); *Nini Tirabuscle* 1970 (a); *Gli Ordini Sono Ordini* 1971 (a); *La Pacifista* 1971 (a); *Polvere di Stelle* 1973 (a); *Teresa la Ladra* 1973 (a); *Le Fantôme de la Liberté/The Phantom of Liberty* 1974 (a); *A Mezzanotte va la ronda del Piacere* 1975 (a); *L'Anatra all'Arancia* 1976 (a); *Letti Selvaggi* 1978 (a); *La Raison d'etat* 1978 (a); *Tigers in Lipstick* 1978 (a); *An Almost Perfect Affair* 1979 (a); *Il Mistero di Oberwald/The Mystery of Oberwald* 1980 (a); *Il Tango della Gelosia* 1981 (a); *Io So Che Tu Sai Che Io So* 1982 (a); *The Flirt* 1983 (a,sc); *Scusa se è poco* 1983 (a); *Trenta Minuti D'Amore* 1983 (a); *Scandalo Segreto/Secret Scandal* 1989 (a,d,sc).

Vlady, Marina • *aka* Marina Versois • Actress • Born Marina De Poliakoff-Baidaroff, Clichy, France, March 10, 1938. Refined, striking beauty who entered films as a child and had become an established international lead by the mid-1960s. Vlady was named best actress at Cannes for her performance as the sexually insatiable wife in Marco Ferreri's *The Conjugal Bed* (1963) and gave a suitably Brechtian performance in Jean-Luc Godard's essay on Paris, prostitution and moving pictures, *Two or Three Things I Know About Her* (1966). The sister of actresses Helene Vellier and Odile Versois, she has been married to actor-director Robert Hossein, from whom she is divorced, and actor/singer Vladimir Vysotsky, who died in 1980. • *Pardon My French* 1951; *Sophie et le Crime* 1955; *Crime et Châtiment* 1956; *La Sorcière* 1956; *Les Sept péchés capitaux/The Seven Deadly Sins* 1962; *Dragées au Poivre* 1963; *Una Storia moderna/The Conjugal Bed* 1963; *Campanidas a Medianoche/Chimes at Midnight/Falstaff* 1966; *Deux ou trois choses que je sais d'elle/Two or Three Things I Know About Her* 1966; *Tout le monde il est beau, tout le monde il est gentil* 1972; *Le Complot* 1973; *Que la fête commence.../Let Joy Reign Supreme...* 1974; *7 Morts sur Ordonnance* 1975; *Ok ketten* 1977; *The Thief of Bagdad* 1978; *Duos sur Canape* 1979; *Il Malato Immaginario* 1979; *L'Oeil du Maître* 1979; *Les Jeux de la Comtesse Dolingen de Gratz* 1981; *Bordello* 1985; *Tangos—L'exil de Gardel/Tangos: The Exile of Gardel* 1985; *Una Casa in Bilico* 1986; *Sapore del Grano* 1986; *Twist Again à Moscou* 1986; *Les Exploits d'un jeune Don Juan* 1987; *Migrations* 1988; *Notes pour Debussy* 1988; *Follow Me* 1989; *Splendor* 1989.

Voight, Jon • Actor; also producer. • Born Yonkers, NY, December 29, 1938. *Educ.* Catholic University, Washington, DC; Neighborhood Playhouse, New York. Tall, blond lead who first appeared on Broadway in 1961 in *The Sound of Music* and made his film debut in *Fearless Frank* (shot in 1964, shown at Cannes in 1967 and released in the US in 1969). Voight achieved stardom with his poignant portrait of a naive, failed hustler in one of the signature films of the 1960s, *Midnight Cowboy* (1969). Handsome and engaging, he brings a rare sensitivity and well-rounded craft to nearly every role he undertakes. Memorable performances include the voice of reason in *Deliverance* (1972), the maimed Vietnam vet opposite Jane Fonda in *Coming Home* (1977) and the escaped convict in Andrei Konchalovsky's relentless 1985 thriller, *Runaway Train*. (Voight was instrumental in getting Konchalovsky to work in the West, having seen and admired the director's *Siberiade* at Cannes in 1979.) He produced and co-wrote his own 1982 vehicle, *Lookin' to Get Out*. • *Hour of the Gun* 1967 (a); *Fearless Frank* 1969 (a); *Midnight Cowboy* 1969 (a) **(AANBA)**; *Out of It* 1969 (a); *Catch-22* 1970 (a); *The Revolutionary* 1970 (a); *Deliverance* 1972 (a); *The All-American Boy* 1973 (a); *Conrack* 1973 (a); *The Odessa File* 1974 (a); *Der Richter und Sein Henker* 1975 (a); *Coming Home* 1977 (a) **(AABA)**; *The Champ* 1979 (a); *Lookin' to Get Out* 1982 (a,p,sc); *Table For Five* 1983 (a,p); *Runaway Train* 1985 (a) **(AANBA)**; *Desert Bloom* 1986 (a); *Eternity* 1990 (a,sc).

Volonte, Gian Maria • *aka* John Wells • Actor • Born Milan, Italy, April 9, 1933. *Educ.* Accademia Nazionale di Arti Drammatica. Thoughtful, stage-trained leading man who appeared in a couple of classic "spaghetti westerns" in the mid-1960s and gained worldwide fame as the title character of Elio Petri's *Investigation of a Citizen Above Suspicion* (1970). A committed leftist, Volonte appeared in subsequent Petri outings such as *The Working Class Goes to Heaven* (1973) and a number of films by Francesco Rosi. He gave a finely nuanced portrayal of exiled, anti-fascist writer Carlo Levi in Rosi's *Christ Stopped at Eboli* (1978). • *Rafter Romance* 1933 (story); *Living on Love* 1937 (from novel); *Per un Pugno di Dollari* 1964 (a); *Per qualche dollaro in piu* 1966 (a); *The Bobo* 1967 (a); *Faccia a Faccia* 1967 (a); *Quien Sabe?* 1967 (a); *Le Vent d'est* 1969 (a); *Every Home Should Have One* 1970 (a); *Indagine su un Cittadino al di Sopra di Ogni Sospetto/Investigation of a Citizen Above Suspicion* 1970 (a); *Sacco and Venzetti* 1970 (a); *Uomini Contro* 1970 (a); *L'Attentat* 1972 (a); *Il Caso Mattei* 1972 (a); *La Classe Operaia Va In Paradise/The Working Class Goes to Heaven* 1973 (a); *Sbatti Il Mostro In Prima Pagina* 1972 (a); *Giordano Bruno* 1973 (a); *Lucky Luciano* 1973 (a); *Il Sospetto* 1975 (a); *Actas de Marusia* 1976 (a); *Todo Modo* 1976 (a); *Cristo si è Fermato a Eboli/Christ Stopped at Eboli* 1978 (a); *Ogro* 1979 (a); *For Your Eyes Only* 1981 (a); *The Secret Policeman's Other Ball* 1981 (a); *Vera Storia Della Signora Delle Camelie* 1981 (a); *Bullshot* 1983 (a); *La Mort de Mario Ricci* 1983 (a); *Scherzo del Destino in Agguato Dietro L'Angolo Come un Brigante di Strada* 1983 (a); *Greystoke: The Legend of Tarzan, Lord of the Apes* 1984 (a); *Revolution* 1985 (a); *Il Caso Moro* 1986 (a); *Cronaca di una morte annunciata/Chronicle of a Death Foretold* 1987 (a).

Von Harbou, Thea • Screenwriter; also novelist, director. • Born Tauperlitz, Bavaria, December 12, 1888; died 1954. Novelist who became a pivotal contributor to the German Expressionist movement during the 1920s, collaborating with Murnau, May, Dreyer and, from 1920, Fritz Lang. Von Harbou married Lang in 1924 but the two were later divorced, largely due to her joining the Nazi Party in the early 30s. • *Das Wandernde Bild* 1920 (sc); *Der Müde Tod/Destiny* 1921 (sc); *Vier um die Frau* 1921 (sc); *Dr. Mabuse der Spieler* 1922 (sc); *Mikael* 1924 (sc); *Die Nibelungen* 1924 (sc); *Zur Chronik von Grieshuus—Um das Erbe von Greishuus* 1925 (sc); *Metropolis* 1926 (sc,from novel); *Spione/Spies* 1928 (sc,from novel); *Die Frau im Mond* 1929 (sc,from novel); *M* 1931 (sc,story); *Das Testament des Dr. Mabuse* 1933 (sc); *M* 1951 (story); *Angelika* 1954 (sc); *Das Indische Grabmal* 1959 (from novel).

Von Praunheim, Rosa • Director • Born Holger Mischwitzki, Riga (German-occupied Latvia), November 25, 1942. *Educ.* Hochschule fur Bildende Kunste, West Berlin. One of the more eccentric figures to make his name with the emergence of the New German Cinema movement. Praunheim made several short films in the late 1960s—the first was *Von Rosa von Praunheim* in 1967—and made his first feature, *Berliner Bettwurst*, in 1973. Von Praunheim has remained a more marginal figure than contemporaries such as Volker Schlöndorff and Wim Wenders, preferring to address specific issues of politics and sexuality than to reach a broader, mainstream audience. • *Von Rosa von Pranheim* 1967 (d); *Leidenschaften* 1972 (p,sc,ph,m,ed); *Berliner Bettwurst* 1973 (d,p,sc,ph); *Ich Bin ein Antistar...* 1976 (d,p,sc,ed); *Underground and Emigrants* 1976 (a,d,p,ph); *Armee der Liebenden oder Aufstand der Perversen* 1978 (a,d,p,sc,ph,ed); *Tally Brown, N.Y.* 1979 (d,p,sc,ph); *Stadt der Verlorenen Seelen* 1983 (d,p,sc,ed); *Der Biss* 1985 (a); *Ein Virus Kennt Keine Moral* 1986 (a,d,p,sc,ed); *Anita—Tanze des Lasters/Anita—Dances of Vice* 1987 (d,p,sc,ed); *Dolly, Lotte und Maria* 1988 (d,ed,p); *Positiv* 1989 (d,p,sc,ed); *Silence = Death* 1990 (d,p,sc,ed); *Uberleben in New York/Surviving in New York* 1990 (d,ed).

Von Sternberg, Josef • Director; also screenwriter. • Born Jonas Sternberg, Vienna, Austria, May 29, 1894; died December 22, 1969, Hollywood, CA. Once considered one of Hollywood's premier directors, Josef von Sternberg is now remembered chiefly for his seven films with Marlene Dietrich. Actually, his main contribution to cinema is probably his handling of lighting. Sternberg (the "von" was added, as with his fellow Austrian Erich von Stroheim, to lend glamour to his name) was first and foremost a master cinematographer. He never made a color film, but the rich textures of his cinematic spaces attained a color of their own; if he learned anything from the experiments of early German cinema, it was the establishment, through "expressionist" use of light and dark, of "Stimmung" (atmosphere). Even when the plot line of his film was diffuse, its stunning visuals took on a life of their own. Whether a Sternberg film is set in a small German town or an outpost in Morocco, sunny Spain or a misty Japanese island, the Russian Imperial court or the California coast, it is part of a distinct universe.

Sternberg's first films were made in Hollywood, and his very first, *The Salvation Hunters* (1925), was an immediate success. The great German actor Emil Jannings, whom Sternberg brought to the US to star in *The Last Command* (1928) as a Russian general dispossessed by the Revolution, recommended that he return to Europe to direct the film version of Heinrich Mann's *The Blue Angel* (1930). The film, Germany's first sound production, made an international star not only of Dietrich but of Sternberg himself, and the two were welcomed back to Hollywood with great fanfare, initiating a collaboration that would, in the space of five years, make film history with *Morocco* (1930), *Dishonored* (1931), *Shanghai Express* (1932), *Blonde Venus* (1932), *The Scarlet Empress* (1934) and *The Devil Is a Woman* (1935).

While *The Blue Angel*, based on a literary source, employed a certain degree of realism to tell its tale of an authoritarian schoolmaster smitten with a free-spirited cabaret entertainer, the Hollywood films seem to deal with aspects of the Eternal Feminine, as personified by the sometimes glamorous and mysterious, sometimes mischievious and witty, sometimes earthy, always feisty Dietrich, whose very presence gives a decidedly feminist cast to all these films.

Of Sternberg's post-Dietrich films, three are notable: 1937's uncompleted *I, Claudius*, which might have been his finest film he had not run into problems with financial backers; *The Shanghai Gesture* (1941), a delightfully dark piece of suspense and exoticism in which Gene Tierney and Gale Sondergaard together assume the Dietrich persona; and the director's own favorite project, *The Saga of Anatahan* (1952), a poetic study of Japanese soldiers isolated on an island at the end of WWII. *Anatahan* can be seen as a virtual encyclopedia of the possibilities inherent in black-and-white cinematography. RM • *The Masked Bride* 1925 (d); *The Salvation Hunters* 1925 (d,sc,ed); *The Exquisite Sinner* 1926 (d,sc); *A Woman of the Sea* 1926 (d,sc); *Underworld* 1927 (d); *The Docks of New York* 1928 (d); *The Dragnet* 1928 (d); *The Last Command* 1928 (d); *The Street of Sin* 1928 (story); *The Case of Lena Smith* 1929 (d); *Thunderbolt* 1929 (d); *Der Blaue Engel/The Blue Angel* 1930 (d); *Morocco* 1930 (d) **(AANBD)**; *An American Tragedy* 1931 (d,p); *Dishonored* 1931 (d,from story "X-27," add.m); *Blonde Venus* 1932 (d,story); *Shanghai Express* 1932 (d) **(AANBD)**; *The Scarlet Empress* 1934 (add.m,d,sc,add.m); *Crime and Punishment* 1935 (d); *The Devil Is a Woman* 1935 (d,ph); *The King Steps Out* 1936 (d); *The Great Waltz* 1938 (d); *Sergeant Madden* 1939 (d); *The Shanghai Gesture* 1941 (d,sc); *The Town* 1944 (d); *Macao* 1952 (d); *The Saga of Anatahan* 1952 (a,d,sc,ph); *Jet Pilot* 1957 (d); *The Epic That Never Was (I, Claudius)* 1965 (a,d).

Von Stroheim, Erich • *aka* Erich Oswald Hans Carl Maria Stroheim • Director; also actor, screenwriter. • Born Erich Oswald Stroheim, Vienna, September 22, 1885; died May 12, 1957, Maurepas, France. Erich Stroheim adopted his "von," the mark of nobility, somewhere between his native Vienna, where he grew up working in his father's straw hat factory, and Hollywood, where he joined D.W. Griffith's ensemble around 1914, playing mainly villains. As America entered WWI and anti-German sentiment grew, Stroheim cultivated the image of the implacable, autocratic Hun, which inspired the studio tag line, "the man you love to hate."

In fact, his true aspiration was directing. *Blind Husbands* (1919) provided Stroheim with a successful debut—he not only directed, but wrote, designed the sets and starred. The film earned him a reputation as a master of physical detail and psychological sophistication flavored by a European sensibility. *The Devil's Passkey* (1920) and *Foolish Wives* (1922) also amplified his reputation for tales of adultery, as well as spendthrift production. To the Hollywood establishment, Stroheim's most annoying trait was his penchant for lengthy, psychologically intricate movies, and he invariably fell afoul of studio editing and interference. *Foolish Wives* was reduced by a third, and he was fired from *Merry-Go-Round* (1923) by Universal production chief Irving Thalberg. In perhaps the most famous case of a mangled masterpiece, Stroheim filmed Frank Norris's novel *McTeague* in obsessive detail, producing a 9 1/2 hour masterwork, *Greed* (1925). The horrified studio forced the director to cut the film, but that version was still over 4 hours, so the film was taken out of Stroheim's hands and given first to director Rex Ingram and eventually to editor June Mathis, who pruned it to its present 140-minute running time. Search for the missing footage spawned a virtual cottage industry among devoted archivists and Stroheim devotees.

Hired by MGM to direct the operetta *The Merry Widow* (1925), Stroheim perversely adapted it as a black comedy, replete with the sadism of the decadent Hapburg empire. He returned to the same subject for *The Wedding March* (1928), a film so long it had to be released in two parts—the second part called *The Honeymoon* in Europe. As brillaint as Stroheim's films were, he seemed willfully ignorant of the havoc his painstaking and expensive production methods wreaked in his relations with financial backers. His most profligate escapade was with Joseph P. Kennedy's money, on the Gloria Swanson vehicle *Queen Kelly* (1928). Stroheim's high-handedness also failed to endear him to stars, and Swanson fired him from the picture, which was never completed, although a "reconstructed" version was issued in 1985. Stroheim's directing career virtually ended with the swashbuckling silent era, as sound and budget-conscious production changed the tenor of filmmaking.

In the 1930s, with the Germans once again on the march, Stroheim returned to acting the horrible Hun. As the commandant of the POW camp in Jean Renoir's *Grand Illusion* (1937), his disdainful demeanor, complete with monocle, would stand as an indelible symbol of the tragic decline of the European aristocracy. Although typecast, he did seem the only actor to inhabit that persona, and it was used with particularly poignant effect in *Sunset Boulevard* (1950). By his death in 1957, he had become an icon of another era, one whose image he had helped create by living up to his self-imposed "von." KJ • *Old Heidelberg* 1915 (a); *Intolerance* 1916 (a); *The Social Secretary* 1916 (a); *Hearts of the World* 1917 (a,military tech.ad); *Panthea* 1917 (a); *Vengeance Is Mine* 1917 (a); *The Hun Within* 1918 (a); *Blind Husbands* 1919 (a,d,sc,from story "The Pinnacle"); *The Devil's Passkey* 1920 (d,sc,story); *Foolish Wives* 1922 (a,d,sc,story); *Merry-Go-Round* 1923 (d); *Souls For Sale* 1923 (a); *Greed* 1925 (d,sc); *The Merry Widow* 1925 (d,sc,art d,cost); *Queen Kelly* 1928 (d,sc,story); *The Wedding March* 1928 (a,d,sc,story,cont,m.sup,print restoration); *The Great Gabbo* 1929 (a); *Three Faces East* 1930 (a); *Friends and Lovers* 1931 (a); *As You Desire Me* 1932 (a); *The Lost Squadron* 1932 (a); *Walking Down Broadway* 1932 (d,sc); *Crimson Romance* 1934 (a); *Fugitive Road* 1934 (a); *The Crime of Dr. Crespi* 1935 (a); *The Devil-Doll* 1936 (sc); *Between Two Women* 1937 (story); *Grand Illusion* 1937 (a); *Pieges* 1939 (a); *I Was an Ad-*

venturess 1940 (a); *So Ends Our Night* 1941 (a); *Five Graves to Cairo* 1943 (a); *The North Star* 1943 (a); *The Lady and the Monster* 1944 (a); *Storm Over Lisbon* 1944 (a); *The Great Flamarion* 1945 (a); *Scotland Yard Investigator* 1945 (a); *The Mask of Diijon* 1946 (a); *Sunset Boulevard* 1950 (a) **(AANBSA)**.

Von Sydow, Max • Actor; also director. • Born Carl Adolf Von Sydow, Lund, Sweden, April 10, 1929. *Educ.* Royal Dramatic Theater School, Stockholm. Max von Sydow, internationally recognized Swedish screen star, studied acting at the Royal Dramatic Theater School, where he met and married Kerstin Olin in 1951. He made his film debut in Victor Sjöberg's *Bara en Mor* (1949), but it was his devotion to the theatre in Halsingborg from 1953 to 1955 and then at Malmö from 1955 to 1960 that earned him a reputation as a fine classical stage actor.

Director Ingmar Bergman saw in von Sydow the embodiment of the tormented, angst-ridden souls of many of his great psycho-social dramas. The two began a long-running relationship with *The Seventh Seal* (1957), and von Sydow soon became the cornerstone of Bergman's repertory group of performers. Their astonishing series of early collaborations included *Wild Strawberries* (1957), *Brink of Life* (1958), *The Magician* (1958), *The Virgin Spring* (1960), *Through a Glass Darkly* (1961) and *Winter Light* (1963).

In 1960, von Sydow became a member of the Royal Dramatic Theater of Stockholm, and he has continued his ties to the stage to this day. In the mid-1960s, von Sydow was drawn to Hollywood, debuting as Christ in George Stevens's mammoth *The Greatest Story Ever Told* (1965). American producers seized upon his strange physicality to cast him in a variety of roles, often unsympathetic; he played a Nazi in *The Quiller Memorandum* (1966), a minister in *Hawaii* (1966) and a priest in *The Exorcist* (1973).

In the late 60s, von Sydow returned to the Bergman fold for one more memorable series of films, including *Hour of the Wolf* and *Shame* (both 1968), *The Passion of Anna* (1970), and *The Touch* (1971). The 70s saw von Sydow making frequent screen appearances in films as varied as *Steppenwolf* (1974), *Three Days of the Condor* (1975) and *The Hurricane* (1979).

More recently, von Sydow scored triumphs as the psychotherapist in the stage and screen productions of *Duet for One* (1987) and his Oscar-nominated role in *Pelle the Conqueror* (1987)—thoughtful, intense performances which recalled the best of his years with Bergman TZ • *Bara en Mor* 1949; *Det Sjunde Inseglet/The Seventh Seal* 1957; *Smultronstallet/Wild Strawberries* 1957; *Ansiktet/The Magician* 1958; *Nara Livet/Brink of Life* 1958; *Jungfrukallan/The Virgin Spring* 1960; *Sasom i en Spegel/Through a Glass Darkly* 1961; *Nattvardsgasterna/Winter Light* 1963; *The Greatest Story Ever Told* 1965; *The Reward* 1965; *Har Har Du Ditt Liv* 1966; *Hawaii* 1966; *The Quiller Memorandum* 1966; *Skammen/Shame* 1968; *Vargtimmen/Hour of the Wolf* 1968; *En Passion/The Passion of Anna* 1970; *The Kremlin Letter* 1970; *Utvandrarna/The Emigrants* 1970; *Beroringen/The Touch* 1971; *Embassy* 1971; *The Night Visitor* 1971; *Appelkriget* 1972; *Ingmar Bergman* 1972; *Nybyggarna/The New Land* 1972; *The Exorcist* 1973; *Steppenwolf* 1974; *Aegget ar Lost* 1975; *Cuore Di Cane* 1975; *Foxtrot* 1975; *Three Days of the Condor* 1975; *Trompe L'oeil* 1975; *The Ultimate Warrior* 1975; *Cadaveri Eccellenti* 1976; *Le Desert des tartares* 1976; *Voyage of the Damned* 1976; *Exorcist II: The Heretic* 1977; *March or Die* 1977; *Brass Target* 1978; *The Hurricane* 1979; *La Mort en Direct* 1979; *Flash Gordon* 1980; *Escape to Victory* 1981; *She Dances Alone* 1981; *Conan the Barbarian* 1982; *Ingenjor Andrees Luftfard* 1982; *Target Eagle* 1982; *Le Cercle des Passions* 1983; *Never Say Never Again* 1983; *Strange Brew* 1983; *Dreamscape* 1984; *Code Name: Emerald* 1985; *Dune* 1985; *George Stevens: A Filmmaker's Journey* 1985; *Il Pentito* 1985; *Duet For One* 1986; *Hannah and Her Sisters* 1986; *The Second Victory* 1986; *The Wolf at the Door* 1986; *Duet For One* 1987; *Pelle Erobreren/Pelle the Conqueror* 1987 **(AANBA)**; *Katinka* 1988 (d); *Quo Vadis* 1988; *Samson and Delilah* 1988; *Awakenings* 1990; *Cellini a Violent Life* 1990; *Father* 1990; *Jusqu'au bout du monde/Till the End of the World* 1991; *A Kiss Before Dying* 1991: *The Ox* 1991.

Von Trotta, Margarethe • Director; also screenwriter, actress. • Born Berlin, February 21, 1942. Perhaps the best known female director to emerge from the New German Cinema, Von Trotta began her career as a stage actress and, in the late 1960s, appeared in films by Rainer Werner Fassbinder and Volker Schlöndorff (whom she married in 1971). She then co-scripted (and narrated) Schlöndorff's *The Sudden Wealth of the Poor People of Kolmbach* (1971), turned in a precise, riveting performance in the lead role of *Coup de Grace* (1974) and co-directed *The Lost Honor of Katharina Blum* (1975) with her husband. Von Trotta made an impressive solo directing debut with *The Second Awakening of Christa Klages* (1977). The film introduces many of the themes that recur in her later work: the complexities of female bonding; the dimensions and dilemmas of liberalism; and the uses and effects of violence. *Sisters, or the Balance of Happiness* (1979) is an intricate examination of the relationship between a destructive, confused Hamburg secretary and her two "sisters"—one by birth and one whom she "adopts"; *Marianne and Julianne* (1981) is a compelling study of terrorism, viewed via the relationship between a Baader Meinhof activist and her journalist sister (the two are based on the real-life characters, Gudrun and Christiane Ensslin. *Rosa Luxemburg* (1985) is an accomplished, multi-leveled biography of the early 20th-century radical. • *Rece Do Gory* 1967 (a); *Gotter der Pest* 1969 (a); *Der Amerikanische Soldat* 1970 (a); *Die Moral der Ruth Halbfass* 1971 (a); *Der Plötzliche Reichtum der Armen Leute Von Kombach/The Sudden Wealth of the Poor People of Kombach* 1971 (a,sc); *Warnung Vor Einer Heiligen Nutte* 1971 (a); *Strohfeuer* 1972 (a,sc); *Coup de Grace* 1974 (a); *Die Verlorene Ehre der Katharina Blum/The Lost Honor of Katharina Blum* 1975 (d,sc); *Die Atlantikschwinner* 1976 (a); *Der Fangschuss* 1976 (a); *Das Zweite Erwachen der Christa Klages/The Second Awakening of Christa Klages* 1977 (d,sc); *Schwestern, Oder Die Balance Des Gluecks/Sisters, or the Balance of Happiness* 1979 (d,sc); *Die Bleierne Zeit/Marianne and Julianne* 1981 (d,sc); *Die Falschung* 1981 (sc); *Heller Wahn* 1982 (d,sc); *Blaubart* 1984 (a); *Unerreichbare Naehe* 1984 (sc); *Rosa Luxemburg* 1985 (d,sc); *Felix* 1987 (d,sc); *Calling the Shots* 1988 (a); *Paura e Amore/Three Sisters* 1988 (d,sc); *L'Africana/The African Woman* 1990 (d,sc).

Wagner, Fritz Arno • Director of photography • Born Schmiedefeld am Rennsteig, Germany, December 5, 1889; died 1958. *Educ.* University of Leipzig, Germany; Académie des Beaux-Arts, Paris. While attending the Academy of Fine Art in Paris, Wagner clerked at the Pathé film company, where he nurtured his interest in cinematography. He was dispatched to New York as a newsreel cameraman and, in 1919, was enlisted by Decla-Bioscop of Berlin to shoot features. Along with Karl Freund, Wagner became Germany's leading cinematographer of the 1920s and 30s, a master of the moody, Gothic lighting that characterized the expressionist movement. Among his finest achievements are Murnau's *Nosferatu* (1922) and Lang's *Spies* (1928); notable sound films include Pabst's *Westfront 1918* (1930) and *Kammeradschaft* (1931), and Lang's *M* (1931).

The virtual exodus of German directors after the Nazi ascendance in 1933 deprived Wagner of vehicles equal to his talent, although he remained relatively prolific until his death in 1958. • *Der Müde Tod/Destiny* 1921; *Nosferatu, eine Symphonie des Grauens* 1922; *Zur Chronik von Grieshuus—Um das Erbe von Greishuus* 1925; *Das Letzte Port* 1928; *Spione/Spies* 1928; *Dolly Macht Karriere* 1929; *Westfront 1918* 1930; *Kammeradschaft* 1931; *M* 1931; *Das Testament des Dr. Mabuse/The Testament of Dr. Mabuse* 1933; *Geliebte Corinna* 1958.

Waits, Tom • Singer, songwriter, composer, musician; also actor. • Born Pomona, CA, December 7, 1949. Raspy-voiced singer-songwriter whose down-at-the-heels musical persona and colorful, jazz-tinged narratives have led to a second, successful career as a film composer and actor. Waits cut his first critically praised album, *Closing Time*, in 1973, made his screen debut in *Paradise Alley* (1978) and subsequently played supporting roles in a number of movies, notably several by Francis Ford Coppola.

Waits's songs have highlighted films ranging from Coppola's *One From the Heart* (1982), to Jean-Luc Godard's *First Name: Carmen* (1983), which makes mesmerizing use of "Ruby's Arms," to Jim Jarmusch's *Down By Law* (1986), in which Waits also turned in a fine comic performance.

Waits was aptly cast as Jack Nicholson's hobo sidekick in *Ironweed* (1987) and was the subject of the film *Big Time* (1988), an unfortunate attempt to juxtapose concert footage with "dramatized" sequences inspired by his songs. • *On the Yard* 1978 (a); *Paradise Alley* 1978 (a); *On the Nickel* 1979 (songs); *Bad Timing* 1980 (songs); *Divine Madness* 1980 (song); *Den Tuchtigen Gehort Die Welt* 1981 (m); *Wolfen* 1981 (song); *One From the Heart* 1982 (m,songs) **(AANBM)**; *Poetry in Motion* 1982 (a); *The King of Comedy* 1983 (song); *The Outsiders* 1983 (a); *Prenom Carmen/First Name: Carmen* 1983 (songs); *Rumble Fish* 1983 (a); *The Cotton Club* 1984 (a); *Streetwise* 1985 (songs); *Down By Law* 1986 (a,songs); *Candy Mountain* 1987 (a,m); *Ironweed* 1987 (a,m); *Wohin?* 1987 (m); *Big Time* 1988 (a,sc,stage show concept,lighting designer—tour,m,songs); *Let's Get Lost* 1988 (song); *Bearskin: An Urban Fairytale* 1989 (a,songs); *Cold Feet* 1989 (a); *In una notte di chiaro di luna* 1989 (m); *Mystery Train* 1989 (a); *Sea of Love* 1989 (song); *Wait Until Spring, Bandini* 1989 (m); *Queens Logic* 1991 (a); *The Fisher King* 1991 (a).

Wajda, Andrzej • Director; also screenwriter. • Born Suwalki, Poland, March 6, 1927. *Educ.* Cracow Academy of Fine Arts (painting); Lódz Film School. By far the best-known film director working in Poland, Andrzej Wajda has achieved the status, both in his life and his work, of a symbol for his beleaguered country.

The son of a cavalry officer killed in WWII, Wajda joined the Resistance as a teenager. Later, he studied at the Fine Arts Academy in Krakow for three years before transferring in 1950 to the newly opened Lódz State Film School.

Wajda's first feature film, *A Generation* (1954), traced the fate of several young people living under the Nazi Occupation. It was followed in 1957 by *Kanal*, a grim tribute to the Warsaw Uprising of 1944, when Red Army units were unable or unwilling to come to the aid of the city. Wajda completed this trilogy on the effects of WWII with his best-known early film, the controversial *Ashes and Diamonds* (1958), which dealt with the undeclared civil war of 1945-46 between elements of the anticommunist Home Army and the security forces established by the Communist Party-dominated government. Based on a Jerzy Andrzejewski novel, the film incisively depicted the corruption and idealism coloring both sides of the struggle. In keeping with Wajda's tragic sense of Polish history, the idealistic representative of each faction is killed, and both sides remain controlled by the corrupt—whether greedy politicians or arrogant aristocrats.

In addition to adapting literary works to the screen (*The Birch-Wood* 1970, *The Wedding* 1972, *The Young Girls of Wilko* 1979), Wajda has consistently drawn on Polish history for material suited to his tragic sensibility—from the fate of lancers serving under Napoleon in *Ashes* (1965) to the harsh industrialization of Lodz in *Land of Promise* (1975). It was in the late 1970s, however, that his films became a virtual barometer of social unrest and rebellion.

Man of Marble (1977) and *Without Anesthesia* (1979) depict the oppression, respectively, of the worker and the intellectual in contemporary Poland. In the later film, a journalist discovers that he has taken the wrong side in a literary prize discussion and subsequently loses his university lectureship, as well as such special privileges as the opportunity to read foreign news magazines. Unable to cope with the simultaneous collapse of his marriage, he is driven to suicide. *Man of Marble*, with a plot which echoes *Citizen Kane*, traces a student filmmaker's attempt to reconstruct the story of Birkut, a Stakhanovite bricklayer and former propaganda hero who mysteriously fell from favor and went to an unmarked grave after the 1967 unrest.

That film's sequel, *Man of Iron* (1981), charted the beginnings of the Solidarity movement, using newsreel footage and featuring Solidarity leader Lech Walesa in both its documentary and directed segments. The events of August 1980 are seen through the eyes of Winkiel, an alcoholic reporter whom the secret police try to use in order to defame the movement. Although essentially a tribute to Solidarity's success, the film ends with a Party official laughingly dismissing the accord between union and government as a mere piece of paper.

Following the military crackdown of the winter of 1981, Wajda moved to France to make *Danton* (1982), a consideration of the dual nature of revolution. The grim tone of the film is hardly surprising given the fate of Solidarity, and of his own "Unit X" film production unit, which was to be dismantled in 1983.

In 1989, with the astounding liberalization in Poland, Andrzej Wajda was not only elected as Solidarity candidate to the Sejm (the Polish parliament), but was able to realize a long-cherished project about Jewish-Polish pedagogue Janusz Korczak, who died, along with his wards, in a Nazi death camp. LR • *Ceramika Ilzecka (short)* 1951 (d); *Pokolenie/A Generation* 1954 (d); *Ide ku Sloncu* 1955 (d,sc); *Kanal* 1957 (d); *Popiol i Diament/Ashes and Diamonds* 1958 (d,sc); *Lotna* 1959 (d,sc); *Niewinni Czarodzieje* 1960 (d); *Samson* 1961 (d,sc); *L'Amour a vingt ans/Love at Twenty* 1962 (d); *Sibirska Ledi Magbet/Siberian Lady Macbeth* 1962 (d); *Popioly/Ashes* 1965 (d); *Gates to Paradise* 1967 (d,sc); *Wszystko Na Sprzedaz/Everything for Sale* 1967 (d,sc); *Przekladaniec* 1968 (d); *Polowanie Na Muchy/Hunting Flies* 1969 (d); *Brzezina/The Birch-Wood* 1970 (sc); *Krajobraz Po Bitwie* 1970 (d); *Pilatus und Andere* 1972 (d,sc,art d,cost); *Wesele/The Wedding* 1972 (d); *Ziemia Obiecana/Land of Promise* 1975 (d,sc); *Czlowiek z Marmuru/Man of Marble* 1977 (d); *Zdjecia Probne* 1977 (a); *Bez Znieczulenia/Without Anesthesia* 1979 (d,sc); *Panny z Wilka/The Young Girls of Wilko* 1979 (d); *Dyrygent/The Orchestra Conductor* 1980 (d); *Cziowiek z Zelaza/Man of Iron* 1981 (d); *Danton* 1982 (d,sc); *Przesluchanie/Interrogation* 1982 (exec.p); *Eine Liebe in Deutschland/A Love in Germany* 1983 (d,sc); *Wajda's Danton* 1983 (a); *Visage de Chien* 1985 (tech.ad—artistic); *Kronika wypadkow milosnych/A Chronicle of Amorous Accidents* 1986 (d,sc); *Les Possédés/The Possessed* 1987 (d,sc); *Korczak/Dr. Korczak* 1990 (d).

Wakhevitch, Georges • Production designer • Born Odessa, Ukraine, Russia, August 18, 1907; died February 11, 1984, Paris. Distinguished scenic designer who collaborated with Jean Renoir (*La Grande Illusion* 1937, *Diary of a Chambermaid* 1963), Marcel Carné

(*The Devil's Envoys* 1942) and Jean Cocteau (*Eagle With Two Heads* 1948), among others. • *La Grande Illusion/Grand Illusion* 1937 (pd); *Les Visiteurs du Soir/The Devil's Envoys* 1942 (pd); *L'Aigle a Deux Têtes/Eagle With Two Heads* 1948 (pd); *Paris Holiday* 1958 (pd); *Un, deux, trois, quatre!* 1960 (art d,sets and cost—"The Diamond Cruncher"); *Le Journal d'une femme de chambre/Diary of a Chambermaid* 1963 (art d,cost); *Echappement libre* 1964 (art d); *Monnaie de Singe* 1965 (art d); *Carmen* 1967 (art d,cost); *Giselle* 1968 (sets); *Mayerling* 1968 (pd); *La Folie des grandeurs* 1971 (art d); *King Lear* 1971 (pd); *Meetings With Remarkable Men* 1979 (pd); *La Tragédie de Carmen* 1983 (art d).

Walas, Chris • Special effects artist; also director. • Born Christopher Walas, Chicago, IL. *Educ.* William Peterson College, NJ; Los Angeles City College (film). Leading FX wizard who first attracted attention for his makeup design on David Cronenberg's *Scanners* and Steven Spielberg's *Raiders of the Lost Ark* (both 1981). In the mid-1980s he formed Chris Walas Inc., the company responsible for creating beings such as the *Gremlins* (1984) and the over-sized spiders of *Arachnophobia* (1990). After his ingenious work on *The Fly* (1986), Walas made his directing debut with the 1989 sequel, *The Fly II*. • *L'Isola degli uomini Pesce* 1979 (makeup fx); *Airplane!* 1980 (fx); *Galaxina* 1980 (makeup fx); *Caveman* 1981 (creature design—Abominable Snowman); *Dragonslayer* 1981 (dragon mover); *Raiders of the Lost Ark* 1981 (makeup fx); *Scanners* 1981 (makeup fx); *Return of the Jedi* 1983 (creature consultant); *Gremlins* 1984 (creature designer); *Enemy Mine* 1985 (creature fx); *The Fly* 1986 (fx,makeup) **(AAMAKEUP)**; *House II: The Second Story* 1987 (creature fx, makeup); *The Kiss* 1988 (creature fx,makeup); *The Fly II* 1989 (d); *Arachnophobia* 1990 (creature fx).

Walbrook, Anton • *aka* Adolf Wohlbruck • Actor • Born Vienna, Austria, November 19, 1900; died 1967. Suave, polished performer who broke with 10 generations of his family's circus tradition to make his mark on the Austrian and German stage. Walbrook entered German film in the early 1920s and emerged as a star a decade later, billed as Adolf Wohlbruck. He arrived in Hollywood to appear in the 1937 production, *The Soldier and the Lady*, reprising his starring role in the earlier French and German versions.

Walbrook went on to establish himself on the English stage and screen as an upper-crust Continental charmer. He was memorable as the affable German officer in *The Life and Times of Colonel Blimp* (1943) and turned in graceful, sophisticated performances in two swank Max Ophuls features, *La Ronde* (1950) and *Lola Montès* (1955). • *The Soldier and the Lady* 1937; *Victoria the Great* 1937; *Gaslight* 1940; *49th Parallel* 1941; *Dangerous Moonlight* 1941; *The Life and Times of Colonel Blimp* 1943; *The Red Shoes* 1948; *La Ronde* 1950; *Lola Montès* 1955; *I Accuse!* 1957; *Saint Joan* 1957.

Walken, Christopher • Actor • Born Queens, NY, March 31, 1943. *Educ.* Hofstra University, Hempstead, NY (English). Angular, blue-eyed, stage-trained actor who first came to attention as a young electronics expert in the intriguing *Anderson Tapes* (1971) and gained acclaim for his portrayal of a catatonic Vietnam vet in *The Deer Hunter* (1978). Adept at projecting both sensitivity and menace, Walken was memorable as a man capable of seeing into the future, in David Cronenberg's *The Dead Zone* (1983), and contributed a hilarious comic turn as an eccentric drill sergeant in *Biloxi Blues* (1988). • *The Anderson Tapes* 1971; *The Happiness Cage* 1972; *Next Stop, Greenwich Village* 1976; *Annie Hall* 1977; *Roseland* 1977; *The Sentinel* 1977; *The Deer Hunter* 1978 **(AABSA)**; *Last Embrace* 1979; *The Dogs of War* 1980; *Heaven's Gate* 1980; *Pennies From Heaven* 1981; *Brainstorm* 1983; *The Dead Zone* 1983; *A View to a Kill* 1985; *At Close Range* 1986; *War Zone* 1986; *Biloxi Blues* 1988; *Homeboy* 1988; *The Milagro Beanfield War* 1988; *Puss in Boots* 1988; *Communion, A True Story* 1989; *The Comfort of Strangers* 1990; *King of New York* 1990.

Walker, Joseph • Director of photography • Born Denver, CO, 1892; died August 1, 1985, Las Vegas, NV. Leading Hollywood cinematographer who worked on 18 pictures with Frank Capra, including *Lost Horizon* (1937) and *It's a Wonderful Life* (1946). Walker won a special Academy Award in 1982 for his "outstanding technical contributions" to the medium, which included pioneering work with zoom lenses undertaken after his retirement. • *The Girl From God's Country* 1921; *Danger* 1923; *The Grub State* 1923; *Richard, the Lion-Hearted* 1923; *Chalk Marks* 1924; *The Girl on the Stairs* 1924; *What Shall I Do?* 1924; *The Wise Virgin* 1924; *Clash of the Wolves* 1925; *Fighting Courage* 1925; *Let Women Alone* 1925; *My Neighbor's Wife* 1925; *North Star* 1925; *The Pleasure Buyers* 1925; *Baited Trap* 1926; *The Dixie Flyer* 1926; *Flaming Fury* 1926; *Temporary Sheriff* 1926; *Tentacles of the North* 1926; *Aflame in the Sky* 1927; *The College Hero* 1927; *Death Valley* 1927; *Fire and Steel* 1927; *The Flying U Ranch* 1927; *The Great Mail Robbery* 1927; *Isle of Forgotten Women* 1927; *The Outlaw Dog* 1927; *Shanghaied* 1927; *Stage Kisses* 1927; *Tarzan and the Golden Lion* 1927; *The Tigress* 1927; *After the Storm* 1928; *Beware of Blondes* 1928; *Court-Martial* 1928; *Driftwood* 1928; *Lady Raffles* 1928; *Modern Mothers* 1928; *Nothing to Wear* 1928; *Ransom* 1928; *Say It With Sables* 1928; *The Sideshow* 1928; *The Street of Illusion* 1928; *Submarine* 1928; *That Certain Thing* 1928; *Virgin Lips* 1928; *The Bachelor Girl* 1929; *Broadway Hoofer* 1929; *The Eternal Woman* 1929; *Flight* 1929; *Object—Alimony* 1929; *The Quitter* 1929; *Restless Youth* 1929; *The Song of Love* 1929; *Trial Marriage* 1929; *Around the Corner* 1930; *Ladies Must Play* 1930; *Ladies of Leisure* 1930; *Midnight Mystery* 1930; *The Murder on the Roof* 1930; *Rain or Shine* 1930; *The Deceiver* 1931; *Fifty Fathoms Deep* 1931; *Lover Come Back* 1931; *The Miracle Woman* 1931; *Platinum Blonde* 1931; *Subway Express* 1931; *American Madness* 1932; *The Bitter Tea of General Yen* 1932; *By Whose Hand?* 1932; *Forbidden* 1932; *Shopworn* 1932; *Virtue* 1932; *Air Hostess* 1933; *Below the Sea* 1933; *Lady For a Day* 1933; *Broadway Bill* 1934; *It Happened One Night* 1934; *The Best Man Wins* 1935; *Eight Bells* 1935; *A Feather in Her Hat* 1935; *The Girl Friend* 1935; *Let's Live Tonight* 1935; *Love Me Forever* 1935; *Mr. Deeds Goes to Town* 1936; *The Music Goes 'Round* 1936; *Theodora Goes Wild* 1936; *The Awful Truth* 1937; *It Happened in Hollywood* 1937; *Lost Horizon* 1937; *When You're in Love* 1937; *Joy of Living* 1938; *Start Cheering* 1938; *There's That Woman Again* 1938; *You Can't Take It With You* 1938 **(AANBPH)**; *Mr. Smith Goes to Washington* 1939; *Only Angels Have Wings* 1939; *Arizona* 1940; *He Stayed For Breakfast* 1940; *His Girl Friday* 1940; *Too Many Husbands* 1940; *Bedtime Story* 1941; *Here Comes Mr. Jordan* 1941 **(AANBPH)**; *Penny Serenade* 1941; *This Thing Called Love* 1941; *You Belong to Me* 1941; *My Sister Eileen* 1942; *A Night to Remember* 1942; *Tales of Manhattan* 1942; *They All Kissed the Bride* 1942; *First Comes Courage* 1943; *What a Woman!* 1943; *What's Buzzin' Cousin?* 1943; *Mr. Winkle Goes to War* 1944; *Together Again* 1944; *Roughly Speaking* 1945; *She Wouldn't Say Yes* 1945; *It's a Wonderful Life* 1946; *The Jolson Story* 1946 **(AANBPH)**; *Tars and Spars* 1946; *The Guilt of Janet Ames* 1947; *The Dark Past* 1948; *The Mating of Millie* 1948; *The Velvet Touch* 1948; *Mr. Soft Touch* 1949; *Tell It to the Judge* 1949; *Born Yesterday* 1950; *Never a Dull Moment* 1950; *No Sad Songs For Me* 1950; *A Woman of Distinction* 1950; *The Mob* 1951; *Affair in Trinidad* 1952; *The Marrying Kind* 1952.

Walker, Robert • Actor • Born Salt Lake City, UT, October 13, 1918; died August 28, 1951, Brentwood, CA. *Educ.* Pasadena Playhouse; AADA, New York. Fresh-faced actor who carved a niche as a wholesome lead in several MGM productions, notably *Bataan* (1943) and, opposite Judy Garland, Vincente Minnelli's charming *The Clock* (1945). An emotionally unstable figure, Walker was devastated when his wife, actress Jennifer Jones, left him for producer David O. Selznick. (His pain is documented in 1944's *Since You Went Away*, produced by Selznick and, with cruel irony, featuring Jones as Walker's estranged sweetheart.) Walker then took to drinking and suffered several nervous breakdowns; in 1948 he entered into a marriage with Barbara Ford, daughter of director John Ford, which was annulled after five weeks. After a memorable performance as a disarming psychopathic murderer in *Strangers on a Train* (1951), Walker died at 32, suffering respiratory failure after receiving a sedative injection of sodium amytal from his psychiatrist. He was the father, by Jones, of actors Robert Walker, Jr., and Michael Walker. • *I'll Sell My Wife* 1941; *Bataan* 1943; *Madame Curie* 1943; *Slightly Dangerous* 1943; *See Here, Private Hargrove* 1944; *Since You Went Away* 1944; *Thirty Seconds Over Tokyo* 1944; *The Clock* 1945; *Her Highness and the Bellboy* 1945; *The Sailor Takes a Wife* 1945; *What Next, Corporal Hargrove?* 1945; *The Beginning or the End* 1946; *Till the Clouds Roll By* 1946; *Song of Love* 1947; *One Touch of Venus* 1948; *Please Believe Me* 1950; *The Skipper Suprised His Wife* 1950; *Strangers on a Train* 1951; *Vengeance Valley* 1951; *My Son John* 1952.

Wallach, Eli • Actor • Born Brooklyn, NY, December 7, 1915. *Educ.* University of Texas; CCNY (education); Neighborhood Playhouse, New York. Prominent method actor of the 1950s who had made his Broadway debut in 1945, following his wartime service. Wallach's first screen role came in *Baby Doll* (1956) adapted from works by Tennessee Williams. He went on to portray numerous, often hot-headed characters, from the Mexican bandito in *The Magnificent Seven* (1960) to the contemptible pistolero in the landmark "spaghetti western," *The Good, the Bad and the Ugly* (1966). Wallach gradually mellowed into more sober, avuncular roles, often appearing in tandem with his wife, actress Anne Jackson. Father of special effects director Peter Wallach. • *Baby Doll* 1956; *The Lineup* 1958; *The Magnificent Seven* 1960; *Seven Thieves* 1960; *The Misfits* 1961; *Adventures of a Young Man* 1962; *How the West Was Won* 1962; *Act One* 1963; *The Victors* 1963; *Kisses For My President* 1964; *The Moon-Spinners* 1964; *Genghis Khan* 1965; *Lord Jim* 1965; *Il Buono, il Brutto, il Cattivo/The Good, the Bad and the Ugly* 1966; *How to Steal a Million* 1966; *The Poppy Is Also a Flower* 1966; *The Tiger Makes Out* 1967; *How to Save a Marriage and Ruin Your Life* 1968; *A Lovely Way to Die* 1968; *I Quattro dell'Ave Maria* 1968; *Le Cerveau* 1969; *MacKenna's Gold* 1969; *The Adventures of Gerard* 1970; *The Angel Levine* 1970; *The People Next Door* 1970; *Zigzag* 1970; *Romance of a Horse Thief* 1971; *Cinderella Liberty* 1973; *Crazy Joe* 1973; *Don't Turn the Other Cheek* 1973; *Il Bianco, Il Giallo, Il Nero* 1974; *Attenti al Buffone* 1975; *Independence* 1976; *Nasty Habits* 1976; *The Deep* 1977; *The Domino Killings* 1977; *The Sentinel* 1977; *Girlfriends* 1978; *Movie Movie* 1978; *The Silent Flute* 1978; *Firepower* 1979; *Winter Kills* 1979; *The Hunter* 1980; *Acting: Lee Strasberg and The Actors Studio* 1981; *The Salamander* 1981; *Sam's Son* 1984; *Tough Guys* 1986; *Hello Actors Studio* 1987; *Nuts* 1987; *Funny* 1988; *Terezin Diary* 1989; *The Godfather Part III* 1990.

Wallis, Hal • *aka* Hal B. Wallis • Producer, executive • Born Hal Brent Wallis, Chicago, IL, September 14, 1898; died October 5, 1986, Rancho Mirage, CA. Former office boy and salesman who entered film as the manager of a Los Angeles movie theater in 1922. Wallis's success attracted the notice of the Brothers Warner, who hired him as assistant to the director of publicity; he became director of the department within three months. Wallis was appointed studio manager in 1928 and named production executive soon thereafter, but was supplanted by Darryl Zanuck in 1931.

Wallis recaptured his former post when Zanuck left to found 20th Century in 1933; he went on to oversee numerous fine productions, including several 1930s musicals and many of the gangster pictures with which the studio would become synonymous.

Wallis formed his own production company in 1944, releasing through Paramount and, in the 1960s, Universal. Over the course of his prolific career, he was responsible for some 400 films produced both within and without the studio system, ranging from *Little Casear* (1930) to *The Story of Louis Pasteur* (1936) to *Casablanca* (1942) to *Becket* (1964). Wallis was married to actresses Louise Fazenda and Martha Hyer. • *Little Caesar* 1930 (exec.p); *Doctor X* 1932 (prod.sup); *Scarlet Dawn* 1932 (p); *The Charge of the Light Brigade* 1936 (p); *God's Country and the Woman* 1936 (p); *Gold Diggers of 1937* 1936 (p); *The Story of Louis Pasteur* 1936; *Back in Circulation* 1937 (p); *Call It a Day* 1937 (p); *Confession* 1937 (p); *Ever Since Eve* 1937 (p); *First Lady* 1937 (p); *The Go Getter* 1937 (p); *Green Light* 1937 (p); *Hollywood Hotel* 1937 (p); *It's Love I'm After* 1937 (p); *Kid Galahad* 1937 (p); *The Life of Emile Zola* 1937 (p); *Marry the Girl* 1937 (p); *The Perfect Specimen* 1937 (p); *The Prince and the Pauper* 1937 (p); *Slim* 1937 (p); *Tovarich* 1937 (p); *Boy Meets Girl* 1938 (p); *Brother Rat* 1938 (p); *Cowboy From Brooklyn* 1938 (p); *The Dawn Patrol* 1938 (p); *Four Daughters* 1938 (p); *Going Places* 1938 (p); *Gold Diggers in Paris* 1938 (p); *Gold Is Where You Find It* 1938 (p); *Hard to Get* 1938 (p); *Love, Honor, and Behave* 1938 (p); *Robin Hood* 1938 (p); *The Sisters* 1938 (p); *A Slight Case of Murder* 1938 (p); *Swing Your Lady* 1938 (p); *White Banners* 1938 (p); *Daughters Courageous* 1939 (p); *Four Wives* 1939 (p); *Juarez* 1939 (p); *The Old Maid* 1939 (p); *The Private Lives of Elizabeth and Essex* 1939 (p); *The Roaring Twenties* 1939 (p); *They Made Me a Criminal* 1939 (p); *Wings of the Navy* 1939 (p); *Yes, My Darling Daughter* 1939 (p); *'Til We Meet Again* 1940 (p); *All This, and Heaven Too* 1940 (p); *Brother Orchid* 1940 (p); *Brother Rat and a Baby* 1940 (p); *A Child Is Born* 1940 (p); *City For Conquest* 1940 (p); *A Dispatch From Reuters* 1940 (p); *Dr. Ehrlich's Magic Bullet* 1940 (p); *The Fighting 69th* 1940 (p); *Invisible Stripes* 1940 (p); *It All Came True* 1940 (p); *Knute Rockne—All American* 1940 (p); *The Letter* 1940 (p); *My Love Came Back* 1940 (p); *No Time For Comedy* 1940 (p); *The Santa Fe Trail* 1940 (p); *Saturday's Children* 1940 (p); *The Sea Hawk* 1940 (p); *They Drive By Night* 1940 (p); *Three Cheers For the Irish* 1940 (p); *Torrid Zone* 1940 (p); *Virginia City* 1940 (p); *Affectionately Yours* 1941 (p); *The Bride Came C.O.D.* 1941 (p); *Dive Bomber* 1941 (p); *Footsteps in the Dark* 1941 (p); *The Great Lie* 1941 (p); *High Sierra* 1941 (p); *King's Row* 1941 (p); *The Maltese Falcon* 1941 (p); *The Man Who Came to Dinner* 1941 (p); *Million Dollar Baby* 1941 (p); *Navy Blues* 1941 (p); *One Foot in Heaven* 1941 (p); *Out of the Fog* 1941 (p); *The Sea Wolf* 1941 (p); *Sergeant York* 1941 (p); *Shining Victory* 1941 (p); *The Strawberry Blonde* 1941 (p); *They Died With Their Boots On* 1941 (p); *Underground* 1941 (p); *The Wagons Roll at Night* 1941 (p); *Captains of the Clouds* 1942 (p); *Casablanca* 1942 (p); *Desperate Journey* 1942 (p); *In This Our Life* 1942 (p); *Juke Girl* 1942 (p); *Larceny, Inc.* 1942 (p); *The Male Animal* 1942 (p); *Now, Voyager* 1942 (p); *Yankee Doodle Dandy* 1942 (p); *Air Force* 1943 (p); *Princess O'Rourke* 1943 (p); *This Is the Army* 1943 (p); *Watch on the Rhine* 1943 (p); *Passage to Marseille* 1944 (p); *The Affairs of Susan* 1945 (p); *Love Letters* 1945 (p); *Saratoga Trunk* 1945 (p); *You Came Along* 1945 (p); *The Perfect Marriage* 1946 (p); *The Searching Wind* 1946 (p); *The Strange Love of Martha Ivers* 1946 (p); *Desert Fury* 1947 (p); *I Walk Alone* 1947 (p); *The Accused* 1948 (p); *So Evil My Love* 1948 (p); *Sorry, Wrong Number* 1948 (p); *The File on Thelma Jordan* 1949 (p); *My Friend Irma* 1949 (p); *Paid in Full* 1949 (p); *Rope of Sand* 1949 (p); *Dark City* 1950 (p); *The Furies* 1950 (p); *My Friend Irma Goes West* 1950 (p); *Peking Express* 1951 (p); *Red Mountain* 1951 (p); *Sailor Beware* 1951 (p); *September Affair* 1951 (p); *That's My Boy* 1951 (p); *Come Back Little Sheba* 1952 (p); *Jumping Jacks* 1952 (p); *The Stooge* 1952 (p);

Money From Home 1953 (p); *Scared Stiff* 1953 (p); *About Mrs. Leslie* 1954 (p); *Cease Fire* 1954 (p); *Three Ring Circus* 1954 (p); *Artists and Models* 1955 (p); *The Rose Tattoo* 1955 (p) **(AANBP)**; *Hollywood or Bust* 1956 (p); *The Rainmaker* 1956 (p); *Gunfight at the O.K. Corral* 1957 (p); *Loving You* 1957 (p); *The Sad Sack* 1957 (p); *Wild Is the Wind* 1957 (p); *Hot Spell* 1958 (p); *King Creole* 1958 (p); *Career* 1959 (p); *Don't Give Up the Ship* 1959 (p); *Last Train From Gun Hill* 1959 (p); *G.I. Blues* 1960 (p); *Visit to a Small Planet* 1960 (p); *All in a Night's Work* 1961 (p); *Blue Hawaii* 1961 (p); *Summer and Smoke* 1961 (p); *A Girl Named Tamiko* 1962 (p); *Girls! Girls! Girls!* 1962 (p); *Fun in Acapulco* 1963 (p); *Wives and Lovers* 1963 (p); *Becket* 1964 (p) **(AANBP)**; *Roustabout* 1964 (p); *Boeing Boeing* 1965 (p); *The Sons of Katie Elder* 1965 (p); *Paradise Hawaiian Style* 1966 (p); *Barefoot in the Park* 1967 (p); *Easy Come, Easy Go* 1967 (p); *5 Card Stud* 1968 (p); *Anne of the Thousand Days* 1969 (p) **(AANBP)**; *True Grit* 1969 (p); *Norwood* 1970 (p); *Mary, Queen of Scots* 1971 (p); *Red Sky at Morning* 1971 (p); *Shoot Out* 1971 (p); *Follow Me!* 1972 (p); *The Don Is Dead* 1973 (p); *The Nelson Affair* 1973 (p); *Rooster Cogburn* 1975 (p).

Walsh, David M. • American director of photography • Began his career in 1955 as an assistant animation cameraman at Disney and graduated to feature cinematographer with *Monte Walsh* (1970). Walsh has often worked with directors Arthur Hiller and Herbert Ross. • *Paint Your Wagon* 1969 (cam.op); *I Walk the Line* 1970 (ph); *Monte Walsh* 1970 (ph); *Evel Knievel* 1971 (ph); *A Gunfight* 1971 (ph); *Corky* 1972 (ph); *Everything You Always Wanted To Know About Sex* (*but were afraid to ask)* 1972 (sc,ph); *Ace Eli and Rodger of the Skies* 1973 (ph); *Cleopatra Jones* 1973 (ph); *The Laughing Policeman* 1973 (ph); *Sleeper* 1973 (ph); *The Crazy World of Julius Vrooder* 1974 (ph); *The Other Side of the Mountain* 1974 (ph); *The Sunshine Boys* 1975 (ph); *Whiffs* 1975 (ph); *Murder By Death* 1976 (ph); *Silver Streak* 1976 (ph); *W.C. Fields and Me* 1976 (ph); *The Goodbye Girl* 1977 (ph); *Rollercoaster* 1977 (ph); *Scott Joplin* 1977 (ph); *California Suite* 1978 (ph); *Foul Play* 1978 (ph); *House Calls* 1978 (ph); *Chapter Two* 1979 (ph); *The In-Laws* 1979 (ph); *Just You and Me, Kid* 1979 (ph); *Hero at Large* 1980 (ph); *Private Benjamin* 1980 (ph); *Seems Like Old Times* 1980 (ph); *I Ought to Be in Pictures* 1981 (ph); *Only When I Laugh* 1981 (ph); *Making Love* 1982 (ph); *Max Dugan Returns* 1982 (ph); *Romantic Comedy* 1983 (ph); *Unfaithfully Yours* 1983 (ph); *Country* 1984 (ph); *Johnny Dangerously* 1984 (ph); *Teachers* 1984 (ph); *My Science Project* 1985 (ph); *Fatal Beauty* 1987 (ph); *Outrageous Fortune* 1987 (ph); *Summer School* 1987 (ph); *Stella* 1990 (add.ph); *Taking Care of Business* 1990 (ph).

Walsh, J. T. • Actor • Born San Francisco, CA. Began acting at the age of 30 and has since racked up numerous screen credits, often as calculating executives. Walsh also earned a Tony nomination for David Mamet's *Glengarry Glen Ross* (1984). • *Hard Choices* 1984; *Hannah and Her Sisters* 1986; *Power* 1986; *Good Morning, Vietnam* 1987; *House of Games* 1987; *Tin Men* 1987; *Tequila Sunrise* 1988; *Things Change* 1988; *The Big Picture* 1989; *Dad* 1989; *Un Plan d'enfer* 1989; *Wired* 1989; *Crazy People* 1990; *The Grifters* 1990; *Narrow Margin* 1990; *The Russia House* 1990.

Walsh, M. Emmet • Actor • Born Michael Emmet Walsh, Ogdensburg, NY, March 22, 1935. *Educ.* Clarkson College of Technology, Potsdam, NY (business administration); AADA, New York. Husky, heavyweight character player who specializes in playing villains or unsympathetic authority figures. Walsh made an uncredited screen debut in *Midnight Cowboy* (1969) and, over the last two decades, has become one of the most prolific supporting actors in Hollywood. He was memorable as the callous police captain in *Blade Runner* (1982) and the crooked Southern private eye in *Blood Simple* (1984). • *Alice's Restaurant* 1969; *Midnight Cowboy* 1969; *Little Big Man* 1970; *The Traveling Executioner* 1970; *Get to Know Your Rabbit* 1972; *What's Up, Doc?* 1972; *Serpico* 1973; *The Gambler* 1974; *At Long Last Love* 1975; *Mikey and Nicky* 1976; *Nickelodeon* 1976; *Airport 77* 1977; *Slap Shot* 1977; *Straight Time* 1978; *The Fish That Saved Pittsburgh* 1979; *The Jerk* 1979; *Brubaker* 1980; *Ordinary People* 1980; *Raise the Titanic* 1980; *Back Roads* 1981; *Reds* 1981; *Blade Runner* 1982; *Cannery Row* 1982; *The Escape Artist* 1982; *Fast Walking* 1982; *Silkwood* 1983; *Blood Simple* 1984; *Courage* 1984; *Missing in Action* 1984; *The Pope of Greenwich Village* 1984; *Scandalous* 1984; *Fletch* 1985; *Back to School* 1986; *The Best of Times* 1986; *Critters* 1986; *Wildcats* 1986; *Harry and the Hendersons* 1987; *No Man's Land* 1987; *Raising Arizona* 1987; *Clean and Sober* 1988; *The Milagro Beanfield War* 1988; *Sunset* 1988; *War Party* 1988; *Red Scorpion* 1989; *Sundown, the Vampire in Retreat* 1989; *Thunderground* 1989; *Narrow Margin* 1990.

Walsh, Raoul • Director • Born New York, NY, March 11, 1887; died 1981. *Educ.* Seton Hall University, South Orange, NJ. Raoul Walsh's film career spanned more than half a century, encompassing acting, writing scenarios and directing. He began as an actor in 1909 in westerns made by the Pathé brothers. He signed with D.W. Griffith in 1912, appearing as the young Pancho Villa in Christy Cabanne's *The Life of General Villa* (1912) and as John Wilkes Booth in *Birth of a Nation* (1915). *Villa* also marked Walsh's first directing experience; he shot the Mexican documentary sequence for the film, persuading Villa himself to restage the battle of Durango. From there, it was on to one- and two-reelers and then features, most of them under contract to Fox between 1916 and 1928. Many of these films were minor efforts, but several are among his better accomplishments: *Evangeline* (1919); *The Thief of Bagdad*, with Douglas Fairbanks (1924); the WWI classic *What Price Glory?* (1926); *Sadie Thompson*, with Gloria Swanson (1928); and *Me, Gangster* (1928).

Walsh's career took a dramatic turn in 1939 when he assumed direction of *The Roaring Twenties* for Warner Bros. It began a fruitful 15-year association with that studio, in whose productive and creative environment Walsh flourished. At Warners, Walsh associated with first-rate talent at all levels. From these collaborations emerged a body of films that demonstrated Walsh's remarkable talent for different genres.

Walsh directed four first-rate examples of film noir: *They Drive By Night* (1940), *High Sierra* (1941), *The Man I Love* (1946) and *White Heat* (1949). *High Sierra* and *White Heat*, among the very best gangsgter films, demonstrate Walsh's mastery of action; his style is wonderfully straightforward and unpretentious but not without flair and bravura. *They Drive By Night* and *The Man I Love* focus more on relationships than on action. Ida Lupino's role in the latter film calls attention to Walsh's continued interest in, and sympathy with, strong women characters.

Most of Walsh's westerns are skillfully made if traditional action-oriented films such as *They Died With Their Boots On* (1941). However, *Pursued* (1947), with its strong Freudian undertones, introduced the psychological western and belies the notion that Walsh's style and technique were always simple and direct. *Colorado Territory* (1949) is an affecting and effective reworking of *High Sierra*.

Objective Burma! (1945) is one of the outstanding war films of the 1940s and amply showcases Walsh's talents. Critic Jean-Pierre Couroson has observed of this film: "Seen purely in terms of direction...Walsh's control over pace and space, narrative and detail, performance and logistics, is total."

After his contract with Warners expired in 1953, Walsh continued working for another 11 years, but his successes were limited. Still, his long and productive career surely mark him for consideration among the best craftsman working in the heyday of the Hollywood studio system. LPM • *The Life of General Villa* (a) 1912; *The Birth of a Nation* 1915 (a,ad); *Carmen* 1915 (d,sc); *The Re-*

generation 1915 (d,p,sc); *Blue Blood and Red* 1916 (d,sc); *The Honor System* 1916 (d); *The Serpent* 1916 (d,p,sc); *Betrayed* 1917 (d,sc,story); *The Conqueror* 1917 (d,sc); *The Innocent Sinner* 1917 (d,sc); *The Pride of New York* 1917 (d,sc); *The Silent Lie* 1917 (d); *This Is the Life* 1917 (d); *I'll Say So* 1918 (d); *On the Jump* 1918 (d,sc); *The Prussian Cur* 1918 (d,sc,story); *Woman and the Law* 1918 (d,sc); *Evangeline* 1919 (d,sc); *Every Mother's Son* 1919 (d,sc); *Should a Husband Forgive?* 1919 (d,sc); *The Deep Purple* 1920 (d); *From Now On* 1920 (d); *The Strongest* 1920 (d,sc); *The Oath* 1921 (d); *Serenade* 1921 (d); *Kindred of the Dust* 1922 (d); *Lost and Found on a South Sea Island* 1923 (d); *The Thief of Bagdad* 1924 (d); *East of Suez* 1925 (d); *The Spaniard* 1925 (d); *The Lady of the Harem* 1926 (d); *The Lucky Lady* 1926 (d); *The Wanderer* 1926 (d,p); *What Price Glory?* 1926 (d); *Loves of Carmen* 1927 (d); *The Monkey Talks* 1927 (d); *Me, Gangster* 1928 (d,sc); *The Red Dance* 1928 (d); *Sadie Thompson* 1928 (a,d,sc); *The Cockeyed World* 1929 (d,sc); *Hot For Paris* 1929 (d,story); *In Old Arizona* 1929 (d); *The Big Trail* 1930 (d); *The Man Who Came Back* 1931 (d); *Women of All Nations* 1931 (d); *The Yellow Ticket* 1931 (d); *Me and My Gal* 1932 (d); *Walking Down Broadway* 1932 (d); *Wild Girl* 1932 (d); *The Bowery* 1933 (d); *Going Hollywood* 1933 (d,p,sc); *Sailor's Luck* 1933 (d); *Baby Face Harrington* 1935 (d); *Every Night at Eight* 1935 (d); *Under Pressure* 1935 (d); *Big Brown Eyes* 1936 (d,sc); *Klondike Annie* 1936 (d); *Spendthrift* 1936 (d,sc); *Artists and Models* 1937 (d); *Hitting a New High* 1937 (d); *Jump For Glory* 1937 (d); *O.H.M.S.* 1937 (d); *College Swing* 1938 (d); *The Roaring Twenties* 1939 (d); *St. Louis Blues* 1939 (d); *Dark Command* 1940 (d); *They Drive By Night* 1940 (d); *High Sierra* 1941 (d); *Manpower* 1941 (d); *The Strawberry Blonde* 1941 (d); *They Died With Their Boots On* 1941 (d); *Desperate Journey* 1942 (d); *Gentleman Jim* 1942 (d); *Background to Danger* 1943 (d); *Northern Pursuit* 1943 (d); *Uncertain Glory* 1944 (d); *The Horn Blows at Midnight* 1945 (d); *Objective Burma!* 1945 (d); *Salty O'Rourke* 1945 (d); *The Man I Love* 1946 (d); *Cheyenne* 1947 (d); *Pursued* 1947 (d); *Fighter Squadron* 1948 (d); *One Sunday Afternoon* 1948 (d); *Silver River* 1948 (d); *Colorado Territory* 1949 (d); *White Heat* 1949 (d); *Along the Great Divide* 1951 (d); *Captain Horatio Hornblower* 1951 (d); *Distant Drums* 1951 (d); *The Enforcer* 1951 (d); *Blackbeard the Pirate* 1952 (d); *Glory Alley* 1952 (d); *The World in His Arms* 1952 (d); *Gun Fury* 1953 (d); *The Lawless Breed* 1953 (d); *A Lion Is in the Streets* 1953 (d); *Sea Devils* 1953 (d); *Battle Cry* 1954 (d); *Saskatchewan* 1954 (d); *The Revolt of Mamie Stover* 1955 (d); *The Tall Men* 1955 (d); *The King and Four Queens* 1956 (d); *Band of Angels* 1957 (d); *The Naked and the Dead* 1958 (d); *The Sheriff of Fractured Jaw* 1958 (d); *A Private's Affair* 1959 (d); *Esther and the King* 1960 (d,p,sc); *Marines, Let's Go* 1961 (d,p,story); *A Distant Trumpet* 1964 (d); *75 Years of Cinema Museum* 1972 (a).

Walters, Julie • Actress • Born Birmingham, England, February 22, 1950. *Educ.* Manchester Polytechnic (drama). Feisty, forthright actress who first came to screen attention opposite Michael Caine in *Educating Rita* (1983); in the same year, Walters won a best actress Tony for her role in the original stage play. • *Educating Rita* 1983 **(AANBA)**; *Unfair Exchanges* 1984; *Car Trouble* 1985; *Dreamchild* 1985; *She'll Be Wearing Pink Pyjamas* 1985; *Personal Services* 1987; *Prick Up Your Ears* 1987; *Buster* 1988; *Killing Dad* 1989; *Mack the Knife* 1989; *Stepping Out* 1991.

Walton, Tony • Production designer, costume designer • Born Walton-on-Thames, Surrey, England, October 24, 1934. Noted British art director who did his first screen work in 1964, on the musical *Mary Poppins*. Walton has been acclaimed for his theatrical and film projects, notably *All That Jazz* (1979). • *Mary Poppins* 1964 (cost consultant,design consultant); *Fahrenheit 451* 1966 (design consultant,cost consultant); *A Funny Thing Happened on the Way to the Forum* 1966 (pd,cost); *The Sea Gull* 1968 (pd,cost); *The Boy Friend* 1971 (sets); *Murder on the Orient Express* 1974 (pd,cost) **(AANBCD)**; *Equus* 1977 (cost,pd); *The Wiz* 1978 (pd,cost) **(AANBCD)**; *All That Jazz* 1979 (fantasy design) **(AABAD)**; *Just Tell Me What You Want* 1980 (pd,cost); *Prince of the City* 1981 (pd); *Deathtrap* 1982 (pd,cost); *Star 80* 1983 (visual consultant); *The Goodbye People* 1984 (pd,cost); *Heartburn* 1986 (pd); *The Glass Menagerie* 1987 (pd,cost); *Regarding Henry* 1991 (pd).

Wanamaker, Sam • Actor; also director. • Born Chicago, IL, June 14, 1919. *Educ.* Drake University, Des Moines, IA; Goodman Theater School of Drama, Chicago. Left-leaning actor who made his screen debut in 1948 before moving to England to avoid any possible repercussions for his political commitments. After appearing in two British productions, however, Wanamaker found that the tentacles of the Hollywood blacklist reached across the Atlantic, making it impossible for him to continue working in film. He subsequently made a name for himself as a stage actor, director and producer, and reemerged in screen roles in the 1960s. Wanamaker's occasional directorial outings have yielded mostly unexceptional results. • *My Girl Tisa* 1948 (a); *Give Us This Day* 1949 (a); *The Secret* 1955 (a); *The Criminal* 1960 (a); *Taras Bulba* 1962 (a); *The Spy Who Came in From the Cold* 1965 (a); *Those Magnificent Men in Their Flying Machines* 1965 (a); *The File of the Golden Goose* 1969 (d); *The Executioner* 1970 (d); *Catlow* 1971 (d); *Billy Jack Goes to Washington* 1976 (a); *The Sell Out* 1976 (a); *Voyage of the Damned* 1976 (a); *Sinbad and the Eye of the Tiger* 1977 (d); *De l'enfer a la Victoire* 1979 (a); *The Competition* 1980 (a); *Private Benjamin* 1980 (a); *Irreconcilable Differences* 1984 (a); *The Aviator* 1985 (a); *Raw Deal* 1986 (a); *Baby Boom* 1987 (a); *Superman IV: The Quest For Peace* 1987 (a); *Judgment in Berlin* 1988 (a); *Cognac* 1990 (a); *Guilty By Suspicion* 1991 (a).

Wang, Peter • Director, screenwriter; also producer, actor, author. • Born Taiwan. *Educ.* University of Pennsylvania, Philadelphia (electro-optics). Founding member of the San Francisco-based Asian Living Theater, with which he wrote and staged several productions before turning to film. Wang made a number of documentaries centering on Chinese culture and history, including the acclaimed *Old Treasures From New China* (1977). He appeared in Wayne Wang's *Chan is Missing* (1981) as a short order cook and co-wrote (with director Allen Fong) and starred in the highly regarded feature, *Ah Ying* (1984).

Wang received widespread recognition for his first feature, *A Great Wall* (1985), a gently amusing, intelligent probe of a Chinese-American family visiting the land of their origins. The film, produced by the director's own Peter Wang Films company, was also notable as the first American feature to be shot in China.

Wang drew on his background in electro-optics to make *The Laserman* (1988), the story of a Chinese-Jewish laser specialist and his problems in finding a new job after he accidentally kills a friend during an experiment.

Wang is also known as an essayist and short story-writer in Asia. • *Old Treasures From New China* (d) 1977; *Chan Is Missing* 1981 (a); *Ah Ying* (a,sc) 1984; *A Great Wall* 1985 (a,d,p,sc); *The Laserman* 1988 (a,d,p,sc); *First Date* 1989 (a,d,exec.p,sc).

Wang, Wayne • Director; also producer, screenwriter. • Born Hong Kong, 1949. *Educ.* College of Arts and Crafts, Oakland CA (film). Hong Kong native who studied photography, film, TV and painting in the US before landing several directorial assignments in his homeland; these included the Chinese episodes of Robert Clouse's *The Golden Needles* (1974) and a popular TV show based on "All in the Family."

Wang then returned to the US and scraped together the $22,000 needed to complete *Chan is Missing* (1981), a hip, Zen-inspired detective story which also carefully dissected prevailing Oriental stereotypes. His next film, *Dim Sum* (1985), again centered on San Francisco's Chinese-American community, playfully examining familial relationships while simultaneously celebrating Asian cuisine (almost every scene of the film features someone eating something).

Wang confirmed his status as one of America's most interesting independent directors with *Eat a Bowl of Tea* (1989), about the arranged marriage of a Chinese couple and how they deal with their meddling families. Married to actress Cora Miao. • *Man, a Woman and a Killer* 1975 (d); *Chan Is Missing* 1981 (a,d,p,sc,ed); *Dim Sum: A Little Bit of Heart* 1985 (d,p,story); *Slam Dance* 1987 (d); *Eat a Bowl of Tea* 1989 (d); *Life Is Cheap... But Toilet Paper Is Expensive* 1989 (d,exec.p,story).

Wanger, Walter • Producer; also executive. • Born Walter Feuchtwanger, San Francisco, CA, July 11, 1894; died 1968. *Educ.* Dartmouth. Produced a Broadway play before serving as an officer with Army Intelligence in WWI and a staffer with President Wilson's negotiating team at the Paris Peace Conference.

Wanger went on to become a producer with Paramount, finally attaining the position of production chief. He served in similar posts with Columbia and MGM before establishing himself as an independent producer, shepherding such excellent films as the Garbo vehicle, *Queen Christiana* (1933), John Ford's classic western, *Stagecoach* (1939), Hitchcock's *Foreign Correspondent* (1940), Fritz Lang's *Scarlet Street* (1945) and the sci-fi melodrama, *Invasion of the Body Snatchers* (1956).

Wanger was married to second wife Joan Bennett from 1940, a union not without scandal. In 1951, a jealous Wanger shot Bennett's agent, Jennings Lang, in the groin; Wanger was convicted and served a short jail sentence. He and Bennett were reconciled in 1953 and he widowed her in 1968. • *Queen Christina* 1933; *The President Vanishes* 1934; *Stamboul Quest* 1934; *Every Night at Eight* 1935; *Mary Burns, Fugitive* 1935; *Private Worlds* 1935; *Shanghai* 1935; *Smart Girl* 1935; *Big Brown Eyes* 1936; *The Case Against Mrs. Ames* 1936; *Fatal Lady* 1936; *Her Master's Voice* 1936; *The Moon's Our Home* 1936; *Palm Springs* 1936; *Spendthrift* 1936; *The Trail of the Lonesome Pine* 1936; *52nd Street* 1937; *History Is Made at Night* 1937; *Stand-In* 1937; *Vogues of 1938* 1937; *You Only Live Once* 1937; *Algiers* 1938; *Blockade* 1938; *I Met My Love Again* 1938; *Trade Winds* 1938; *Eternally Yours* 1939; *Stagecoach* 1939; *Winter Carnival* 1939; *Foreign Correspondent* 1940; *The House Across the Bay* 1940; *The Long Voyage Home* 1940; *Sundown* 1941; *Arabian Nights* 1942; *Eagle Squadron* 1942; *Gung Ho!* 1943; *We've Never Been Licked* 1943; *Ladies Courageous* 1944; *Salome - Where She Danced* 1945; *Scarlet Street* 1945; *Canyon Passage* 1946; *A Night in Paradise* 1946; *The Lost Moment* 1947; *Smash-Up, the Story of a Woman* 1947; *Joan of Arc* 1948 **(AAHON)**; *Secret Beyond the Door* 1948; *Tap Roots* 1948; *The Reckless Moment* 1949; *Tulsa* 1949; *Aladdin and His Lamp* 1952; *Battle Zone* 1952; *The Lady in the Iron Mask* 1952; *Fort Vengeance* 1953; *Kansas Pacific* 1953; *The Adventures of Hajji Baba* 1954; *Riot in Cell Block 11* 1954; *Invasion of the Body Snatchers* 1956; *Navy Wife* 1956; *I Want to Live!* 1958; *Cleopatra* 1963 **(AANBP)**.

Ward, Fred • Actor; also producer. • Born San Diego, CA, 1943. *Educ.* Herbert Berghof Studio, New York. Character and lead player who appeared in two TV movies directed by Roberto Rosselini in Rome—*The Power of Cosimo* (1974) and *Cartesia* (1975)—before earning his first widespread recognition as astronaut Gus Grissom in Philip Kaufman's *The Right Stuff* (1983); Ward played Henry Miller in the same director's *Henry & June* (1990). He served as co-executive producer on *Miami Blues* (1990), in which he also starred. • *Escape From Alcatraz* 1979 (a); *Tilt* 1979 (a); *Carny* 1980 (a); *UFOria* 1980 (a); *Southern Comfort* 1981 (a); *Timerider: The Adventure of Lyle Swann* 1982 (a); *The Right Stuff* 1983 (a); *Silkwood* 1983 (a); *Uncommon Valor* 1983 (a); *Swing Shift* 1984 (a); *Remo Williams: The Adventure Begins...* 1985 (a); *Secret Admirer* 1985 (a); *Big Business* 1988 (a); *Off Limits* 1988 (a); *The Price of Life* 1988 (a); *The Prince of Pennsylvania* 1988 (a); *Backtrack* 1990 (a); *Henry & June* 1990 (a); *Miami Blues* 1990 (a,exec.p); *Tremors* 1990 (a).

Ward, Rachel • Actress • Born London, 1957. Former model, best known for her role opposite Richard Chamberlain in the blustery TV mini-series *The Thorn Birds* (1983). Ward has turned in several creditable screen performances, notably in Burt Reynolds's *Sharky's Machine* (1981), Bruce Robinson's blistering satire, *How to Get Ahead in Advertising* (1988) and James Foley's *After Dark, My Sweet* (1990). Married to actor Bryan Brown. • *The Final Terror* 1981; *Fortress* 1981; *Sharky's Machine* 1981; *Terror Eyes* 1981; *Dead Men Don't Wear Plaid* 1982; *Against All Odds* 1983; *The Good Wife* 1986; *Hotel Colonial* 1986; *How to Get Ahead in Advertising* 1988; *After Dark, My Sweet* 1990.

Ward, Simon • Actor • Born Beckenham, England, October 19, 1941. Blond, classically handsome English lead who made his film debut in Lindsay Anderson's *If...* (1968) and has typically played dashing aristocratic types in films such as *Young Winston* (1972), *The Three Musketeers* (1973) and *Zulu Dawn* (1979). • *If...* 1968 (a); *Frankenstein Must Be Destroyed* 1969 (a); *I Start Counting* 1969 (a); *Young Winston* 1972 (a); *Hitler: The Last Ten Days* 1973 (a); *The Three Musketeers* 1973 (a); *Butley* 1974 (sc,from play); *Children of Rage* 1974 (a); *The Four Musketeers* 1975 (a); *Aces High* 1976 (a); *Dominique* 1977 (a); *Holocaust 2000* 1977 (a); *Die Standarte* 1977 (a); *The Chosen* 1978 (a); *La Sabina* 1979 (a); *Zulu Dawn* 1979 (a); *The Monster Club* 1981 (a); *L'Etincelle* 1983 (a); *Supergirl* 1984 (a); *Leave All Fair* 1985 (a).

Ward, Vincent • Director; also screenwriter. • Born Greytown, New Zealand, 1956. *Educ.* Ilam School of Fine Art, Christchurch (film). Ward made acclaimed short films and won praise for his debut feature, *Vigil* (1984), the first New Zealand-produced film to be shown in competition at Cannes.

He then spent four years making *The Navigator* (1988), a visually stunning fantasy about a group of men from plague-ridden, medieval England who tunnel through the earth—and time—into 20th-Century Australia in an attempt to save their village. • *A State of Siege (short)* 1977 (d); *In Spring One Plants Alone (short)* 1982 (d); *Vigil* 1983 (d,sc); *The Navigator* 1988 (d,sc).

Warden, Jack • Actor • Born Newark, NJ, September 18, 1920. Gruff, craggy-faced character actor who abandoned a career as a prizefighter for the stage. Warden appeared in several Broadway productions and made his screen debut in the early 1950s, often playing hard-boiled military types; he made his mark in *The Bachelor Party* and, as the impatient juror, in *Twelve Angry Men* (both 1957). Warden developed a talent for vulgarly comedic roles, contributing memorable turns as the football coach in *Heaven Can Wait* (1978) and as a garment district hustler in *So Fine* (1981). • *The Man With My Face* 1951; *U.S.S. Tea Kettle* 1951; *Red Ball Express* 1952; *The Bachelor Party* 1957; *Edge of the City* 1957; *Twelve Angry Men* 1957; *Darby's Rangers* 1958; *Run Silent, Run Deep* 1958; *The Sound and the Fury* 1958; *That Kind of Woman* 1959; *Wake Me When It's Over* 1960; *The Lawbreakers* 1961; *Escape From Zahrain* 1962; *Donovan's Reef* 1963; *The Thin Red Line* 1964; *Blindfold* 1966; *Bye Bye Braverman* 1968; *The Sporting Club* 1971; *Summertree* 1971; *Welcome to the Club* 1971; *Who Is Harry Kellerman, and Why Is He Saying Those Terrible Things About Me?* 1971; *Billy Two Hats* 1973; *The Man Who Loved Cat Dancing* 1973; *The Apprenticeship of Duddy Kravitz* 1974; *Shampoo* 1975 **(AANBSA)**; *All the President's Men* 1976; *The White Buffalo* 1977; *Death on the Nile* 1978; *Heaven Can Wait* 1978 **(AANBSA)**; *And Justice For All* 1979; *Being There* 1979; *Beyond the Poseidon Adventure* 1979; *The Champ* 1979; *Dreamer* 1979; *Used Cars* 1980; *Carbon Copy* 1981; *Chu Chu and the Philly Flash* 1981; *The Great Muppet Caper* 1981; *So Fine* 1981; *The Verdict* 1982;

Crackers 1984; *The Aviator* 1985; *September* 1987; *The Presidio* 1988; *Everybody Wins* 1990; *Problem Child* 1990.

Warhol, Andy • Artist, filmmaker; also author, publisher. • Born Andrew Warhola, Cleveland, OH, August 8, 1927; died February 22, 1987, New York, NY. *Educ.* Carnegie Institute of Technology, Pittsburgh, PA (art). Pioneer of the Pop Art movement of the 1960s who transplanted his sometimes witty, sometimes boring explorations of popular culture from the canvas to the screen. Warhol acquired a 16mm camera in 1963 and made his first "underground" film, *Kiss*, the same year. It combined the amateurish techniques endorsed by the American avant-garde with Warhol's own camp sensibility and the ironic banality of his "serial" artwork.

Warhol's film work falls into a silent and a sound phase, the first of which reached its apex in *Sleep* (1963), a six-hour study of a slumbering man conveyed via a virtually stationary camera. Glacially indifferent to the question of viewer involvement, *Sleep* is not so much "watched" as it is "experienced."

Warhol was prolific in his idiosyncratic, voyeuristic brand of *cinéma vérité*, churning out product at an assembly-line clip of roughly one film a week during the period 1964-65. He trained his camera on the motley band of freaks, musicians and social register slummers that trooped through his Felliniesque "Factory." In an ironic inversion of the Hollywood studio system, Warhol elevated the more prominent "players" into underground "superstars": the beautiful, tragic Candy Darling, Joe Dallesandro, Holly Woodlawn, Jackie Curtis, et al.

Although all of Warhol's films were governed by his peculiar sensibility, he assembled a nucleus of capable tehcnicians, such as Paul Morrissey and Chuck Wein, who made various—uncredited—contributions, often in the master's absence.

Warhol entered his "sound phase" with *Harlot* (1964) and continued to crank out such influential films as *Vinyl* (1965), based upon Anthony Burgess's *A Clockwork Orange*, which launched the tragic career and cruel exploitation of socialite/superstar Edie Sedgewick. In 1966 he produced his most enduring and definitive work, *The Chelsea Girls*, a crazed showcase of Factory stalwarts which synthesized the enthusiasms and strategies encompassed by his previous work. The film was projected on two adjacent screens, each of which depicted unrelated situations. Its relative popularity (*The Chelsea Girls* was the first Warhol film to surface in "real" movie houses) inspired a more commercial, or at least less arcane approach to filmmaking.

While such post-*Chelsea Girls* films as *Lonesome Cowboys* (1968) continued to use typically Warholian alienation effects (extreme long takes, "strobe" cuts, etc.), they also relied on previously disdained qualities such as plot and characterization. By the time the Factory closed, after an attempt on Warhol's life in June of 1968, Morrissey had inserted his more formal concerns into the Warhol formula, producing a series of bizarre sex farces that proved more accessible to a popular audience (although they gradually reverted into self-parody). By the mid-1970s, Morrissey was turning out Gothic romps with the Warhol brand name, although they were only vaguely indebted to the Factory style.

Though he had effectively closed the filmmaking chapter of his career after the release of *Andy Warhol's Bad* (directed by Jed Johnson, 1976), Warhol continued to satisfy his voyeuristic appetites with a Polaroid camera that he toted on his late-night revels until his untimely death in 1987. • *Blow Job* 1963 (d); *Dance Movie* 1963 (d,p); *Eat* 1963 (d,p); *Kiss* 1963 (d,p); *Sleep* 1963 (d,p); *Batman Dracula* 1964 (d,p); *Couch* 1964 (d,p); *Empire* 1964 (d,p); *Harlot* 1964 (d,p); *Henry Geldzahler* 1964 (d,p); *Soap Opera* 1964 (d,p); *Tarzan and Jane Regained... Sort of* 1964 (d,p); *Taylor Mead's Ass* 1964 (d,p); *The Thirteen Most Beautiful Women* 1964 (d,p); *Afternoon* 1965 (d,p); *Beauty #2* 1965 (d,p); *Bitch* 1965 (d,p); *Camp* 1965 (d,p); *Drunk* 1965 (d,p); *Face* 1965 (d,p); *Hedy* 1965 (d,p); *Horse* 1965 (d,p); *Kitchen* 1965 (d,p); *The Life of Juanita Castro* 1965 (d,p); *Lupe* 1965 (d,p); *More Milk Yvette* 1965 (d,p); *My Hustler* 1965 (p,ph); *Outer and Inner Space* 1965 (d,p); *Paul Swan* 1965 (d,p); *Poor Little Rich Girl* 1965 (d,p); *Prison* 1965 (d,p); *Restaurant* 1965 (d,p); *Screen Test #1* 1965 (d,p); *Screen Test #2* 1965 (d,p); *Space* 1965 (d,p); *Suicide* 1965 (d,p); *The Thirteen Most Beautiful Boys* 1965 (d,p); *Vinyl* 1965 (d,p); *The Chelsea Girls* 1966 (d,p,sc,ph); *Eating Too Fast* 1966 (d,p); *The Velvet Underground and Nico* 1966 (d,p); *Bike Boy* 1967 (d,p,sc); *Four Stars* 1967 (d,p,ph,ed); *I, a Man* 1967 (d,p,ph); *The Loves of Ondine* 1967 (d,p); *Nude Restaurant* 1967 (d,p,sc,ph,ed); *Flesh* 1968 (p); *Lonesome Cowboys* 1968 (d,p,sc); *The Queen* 1968 (a); *Diaries, Notes and Sketches* 1969 (a); *Imitation of Christ* 1970 (p); *Trash* 1970 (p); *Andy Warhol's Women* 1971 (p); *L'Amour* 1972 (d,sc); *CS Blues* 1972 (a); *Dynamite Chicken* 1972 (a); *Heat* 1972 (exec.p); *Andy Warhol's Frankenstein* 1973 (p); *Painters Painting* 1973 (a); *Blood For Dracula* 1974 (p); *Identikit* 1974 (a); *Andy Warhol's Bad* 1976 (exec.p); *Underground and Emigrants* 1976 (a); *An Unmarried Woman* 1978 (art collaboration); *Cocaine Cowboys* 1979 (a); *The Look* 1985 (a); *Vamp* 1986 (contributing artist); *Superstar: The Life and Times of Andy Warhol* 1991 (a).

Warner, David • Actor • Born Manchester, England, July 29, 1941. *Educ.* RADA, London. Gangly British stage-trained lead who entered film in the early 1960s and came to attention in the title role of Karel Reisz's eccentric drama, *Morgan* (1966), playing an unbalanced artist driven to the edge by his divorce. Warner has worked for many directors, including John Frankenheimer, Sidney Lumet, Joseph Losey, Alain Resnais, Ivan Passer and—on three occasions—Sam Peckinpah.

Several of Warner's more notable recent appearances have been as villains, including Jack the Ripper to Malcolm McDowell's H.G. Wells in *Time After Time* (1979), the Evil Genius in Terry Gilliam's *Time Bandits* (1981) and the sinister doctor in *Mr. North* (1988). • *Tom Jones* 1963; *Morgan* 1966; *The Deadly Affair* 1967; *The Bofors Gun* 1968; *The Fixer* 1968; *A Midsummer Night's Dream* 1968; *The Sea Gull* 1968; *The Ballad of Cable Hogue* 1970; *The Engagement* 1970; *Perfect Friday* 1970; *A Doll's House* 1973; *Little Malcolm and His Struggle Against the Eunuchs* 1974; *Mr. Quilp* 1975; *The Omen* 1976; *Age of Innocence* 1977; *Cross of Iron* 1977; *Providence* 1977; *Silver Bears* 1977; *The 39 Steps* 1978; *The Concorde—Airport '79* 1979; *Nightwing* 1979; *Time After Time* 1979; *The Island* 1980; *The French Lieutenant's Woman* 1981; *Time Bandits* 1981; *Tron* 1982; *The Man With Two Brains* 1983; *The Company of Wolves* 1985; *Hansel and Gretel* 1987; *Hanna's War* 1988; *Mr. North* 1988; *My Best Friend Is a Vampire* 1988; *Office Party* 1988; *Silent Night* 1988; *Waxwork* 1988; *Mortal Passions* 1989; *Star Trek V: The Final Frontier* 1989; *Grave Secrets* 1990; *Tripwire* 1990; *Teenage Mutant Ninja Turtles II: The Secret of the Ooze* 1991.

Warschilka, Edward A. • Editor • Born Sopron, Hungary. Capable Hollywood craftsman who has worked on a number of off-beat gems including *Harold and Maude* (1971, his first film as an editor), *Hearts of the West* (1975) and *Brainstorm* (1983). Son Edward Warschilka, Jr., is also an editor. • *Harold and Maude* 1971 (ed); *Child's Play* 1972 (ed); *The Last of Sheila* 1973 (ed); *The Education of Sonny Carson* 1974 (ed); *Hearts of the West* 1975 (ed); *The Big Bus* 1976 (ed); *House Calls* 1978 (ed); *The Main Event* 1979 (ed); *Cheaper to Keep Her* 1980 (ed); *Raggedy Man* 1981 (ed); *Brainstorm* 1983 (ed); *Sixteen Candles* 1984 (ed); *Big Trouble in Little China* 1986 (ed); *Howard the Duck* 1986 (add.ed); *Violets Are Blue* 1986 (ed); *Hiding Out* 1987 (ed); *The Running Man* 1987 (ed); *Child's Play* 1988 (ed); *Rambo III* 1988 (ed).

Washington, Denzel • Actor • Born Mount Vernon, NY, December 28, 1954. *Educ.* Fordham University, Bronx NY (journalism); American Conservatory Theatre, San Francisco. Handsome, stage-trained black actor who first received notice as Dr. Chandler in the popular TV series, "St. Elsewhere" (1982-88). Washington's film career, after a dreary debut as George Segal's illegitimate son in the inane comedy *Carbon Copy* (1981), was spurred by his riveting performance as the outspoken recruit in *A Soldier's Story* (1984).

Washington also garnered critical praise playing South African activist Steven Biko in *Cry Freedom* (1987), earned a best supporting actor Oscar for *Glory* (1989) and turned in yet another powerful performance as trumpeter Bleek Gilliam in Spike Lee's *Mo' Better Blues* (1990). • *Carbon Copy* 1981 (a); *A Soldier's Story* 1984 (a); *Power* 1986 (a); *Cry Freedom* 1987 (a) **(AANBSA)**; *For Queen & Country* 1988 (a); *Reunion* 1988 (a); *Glory* 1989 (a) **(AABSA)**; *The Mighty Quinn* 1989 (a,song); *Heart Condition* 1990 (a); *Mo' Better Blues* 1990 (a,song); *Mississippi Masala* 1991 (a).

Wasson, Craig • Actor • Born Eugene, OR, March 15, 1954. Unassuming, stage-trained performer who made his film acting debut in *The Boys in Company C* (1977—he also contributed a song), was featured in the fine adaptation of Peter Straub's *Ghost Story* (1981) and was widely seen as the voyeur-in-over-his-head in Brian De Palma's lurid thriller *Body Double* (1984). • *The Boys in Company C* 1977 (a,song); *Rollercoaster* 1977 (a); *Go Tell the Spartans* 1978 (a); *The Outsider* 1979 (a); *Carny* 1980 (a); *Nights at O'Rear's* 1980 (a); *Schizoid* 1980 (a); *Four Friends* 1981 (a); *Ghost Story* 1981 (a); *Second Thoughts* 1982 (a,m); *Body Double* 1984 (a); *The Men's Club* 1986 (a); *A Nightmare on Elm Street 3: Dream Warriors* 1987 (a); *Bum Rap* 1988 (a).

Waters, John • Director, screenwriter; also director of photography, producer, editor, essayist. • Born Baltimore, MD, 1946. John Waters once stated that having someone vomit while watching one of his movies was like getting a standing ovation. Although a slow but steady integration into mainstream filmmaking has tempered that kind of thinking, Waters remains one of cinema's most audacious practitioners.

Born into an upper-middle-class Catholic family, Waters grew up in Baltimore, which serves as the locale of all his movies. Childhood interests in car accidents and murders marked him as a unique personality. As a teenager, he began making 8mm films, largely influenced by the experimental and exploitation films that he sought out while skipping school. His crude early short films, sporting titles like *Hag in a Black Leather Jacket* and *Eat Your Makeup*, were screened only in the Baltimore area, but did spark the genesis of Waters's Dreamland Productions stock company. Made up of his friends and neighbors, the Dreamlanders came to include Divine, a 300-pound transvestite, and Edith Massey, a snaggle-toothed barmaid and thrift shop owner, as well as Mink Stole, Cookie Mueller, Mary Vivian Pearce, Danny Mills and David Lochary.

Waters's first 16mm sound feature, *Multiple Maniacs* (1971), established the pattern for most of his work: a complex plot involving a "family"; vicious attacks on middle-class manners and morals, religion and other sacred cows; and an overriding mission to offend even the most jaded moviegoer. *Pink Flamingos* (1972), made for $10,000, was Waters's first film to receive national distribution, becoming a hit on the midnight movie circuit. Divine played "the filthiest person alive"; she finds her title challenged by the Marbles (Stole and Lochary), who kidnap women, have their servant rape them with a syringe and then sell the babies to lesbian couples. The film assaults the viewer with a barrage of repellent images, such as the hefty Massey splayed out in a play pen wearing a bra and girdle and covered with the half-eaten eggs that are her passion. The notorious finale, in which Divine eats dog excrement, remains one of the most sickening sights captured on film. Nonetheless, Waters plays everything on a broadly comic scale. Dialogue is ridiculously melodramatic and performances are overblown. The sets, designed by Waters's regular art director Vincent Peranio, are the essence of kitsch. As bad taste is elevated to a new aesthetic, the audience must laugh to keep from gagging. The act of attending and professing to enjoy one of Waters's midnight movies became a safe way to thumb one's nose at the establishment during the Me Decade.

Divine returned to star in *Female Trouble* (1975), Waters's rumination on fashion, fame and criminality. The film demonstrated that the director had discovered the last exploitable subject in film—the idea of taste itself. In *Desperate Living* (1977), Waters's satire became sharper. Mink Stole starred as Peggy Gravel, a suburban housewife recovering from a breakdown. When Peggy's husband is killed, she and her maid escape to Mortville, a community of criminals presided over by the despotic Queen Carlotta (Massey). The expected disgusting gags are present—sex changes, rabies injections, roach eating, death-by-dog-food. But the anarchistic tone of Waters's earlier films has given way to more pointed commentary on class and gender roles, as Peggy is stripped of her middle-class pretensions.

Waters made his move out of the midnight movie ghetto in 1981 with *Polyester*. He toned down the visually gross elements but compensated with a gimmick worthy of one of his heroes, producer/director William Castle. Audience members were given scratch 'n' sniff "Odorama" cards, which they were cued to use by numbers flashing on the screen. Scents ranged from roses to dirty sneakers. Divine played Francine Fishpaw, a housewife beset by family problems; her philandering husband owns a porn theater, her daughter is a high school harlot and her son is the dreaded Baltimore Foot Stomper. Francine goes over the edge but is rescued by drive-in owner Tod Tomorrow, played by former teen idol Tab Hunter in a delightfully mannered performance. The film plays like a hyperbolic "woman's picture" from Hollywood's golden age, complete with a ludicrous happy ending. Once again, bourgeois attitudes are Waters's favorite target.

Throughout the 1980s Waters has published numerous cheeky articles in film and music magazines, extolling the virtues of Pia Zadora, the *National Enquirer* and other campy topics. *Hairspray* (1988), a light musical about the racial intergration of a popular Baltimore teen TV program in the early 1960s, established Waters as a bankable mainstream director. His assaults on good taste have largely dissipated, but Waters continues to be one of cinema's most potent satirists. ES • *Mondo Trasho* 1970 (d,p,sc,ph,ed); *Multiple Maniacs* 1971 (d); *Pink Flamingos* 1972 (d,p,sc,ph,ed); *Female Trouble* 1975 (d,p,sc,ph,song); *Desperate Living* 1977 (d,p,sc,ph); *Polyester* 1981 (d,p,sc); *Something Wild* 1986 (a); *Hairspray* 1988 (a,d,p,sc); *Homer and Eddie* 1989 (a); *Cry-Baby* 1990 (d,sc,lyric adaptations).

Waterston, Sam • Actor • Born Cambridge, MA, November 15, 1940. *Educ.* Yale; Sorbonne, Paris. Lanky, intense, classically trained actor who entered film in the mid-1960s. Waterston languished in several forgettabble features while piling up impressive credits on the New York stage until he scored as Nick Carraway in the glossy adaptation of F. Scott Fitzgerald's *The Great Gatsby* (1974). He has appeared in a series of Woody Allen films, begining with *Interiors* (1978) and, most recently, as the rabbi with failing eyesight in *Crimes and Misdemeanors* (1989), and gained acclaim as journalist Sidney Schanberg in Roland Joffe's *The Killing Fields* (1984). • *Fitzwilly* 1967; *Generation* 1969; *Three* 1969; *Cover Me Babe* 1970; *Who Killed Mary Whats'ername?* 1971; *Savages* 1972; *The Great Gatsby* 1974; *Rancho Deluxe* 1974; *Dandy, the All American Girl* 1976; *Journey Into Fear* 1976; *Capricorn One* 1978; *Eagle's Wing* 1978; *Interiors* 1978; *Sweet William* 1979; *Heaven's Gate* 1980; *Hopscotch* 1980; *The Killing Fields* 1984 **(AANBA)**; *Warning Sign* 1985; *Flagrant Désir* 1986; *Hannah and Her Sisters* 1986; *Just Between Friends* 1986; *Devil's Paradise* 1987; *September* 1987; *Crimes and Misdemeanors* 1989; *Welcome Home* 1989; *Mindwalk* 1990.

Watkin, David • Director of photography • Born Margate, England, March 23, 1925. Former documentary cameraman with British Transport Films who graduated to cinematographer on Richard Lester's *The Knack* (1965). Watkin has since enjoyed a distinguished international career, working with such directors as Mike Nichols (*Catch-22* 1970) and Tony Richardson (*The Charge of the Light Brigade* 1968) and earning acclaim for the lush, luxuriant colors of *Chariots of Fire* (1981) and *Out of Africa* (1985). • *Help!* 1965 (ph); *The Knack... and How to Get It* 1965 (ph); *Marat/Sade/The Persecution and Assassination of Jean-Paul Marat As Performed By the Inmates of the Asylum of Charenton Under the Direction of the Marquis de Sade* 1966 (ph); *How I Won the War* 1967 (ph); *The Charge of the Light Brigade* 1968 (ph); *The Bed Sitting Room* 1969 (ph); *Catch-22* 1970 (ph; *The Boy Friend* 1971 (ph); *The Devils* 1971 (ph); *A Delicate Balance* 1973 (ph); *The Homecoming* 1973 (ph); *The Three Musketeers* 1973 (ph); *Mahogany* 1975 (ph); *Joseph Andrews* 1976 (ph); *Robin and Marian* 1976 (ph); *To the Devil, a Daughter* 1976 (ph); *Cuba* 1979 (ph); *Hanover Street* 1979 (ph); *That Summer* 1979 (ph); *Chariots of Fire* 1981 (ph); *Endless Love* 1981 (ph); *Yentl* 1983 (ph); *The Hotel New Hampshire* 1984 (ph); *Out of Africa* 1985 (ph) **(AABPH)**; *Return to Oz* 1985 (ph,fx tech); *White Nights* 1985 (ph); *Journey to the Center of the Earth* 1986 (ph); *Sky Bandits* 1986 (ph); *Moonstruck* 1987 (ph); *The Good Mother* 1988 (ph); *Last Rites* 1988 (ph); *Masquerade* 1988 (ph); *Hamlet* 1990 (ph); *Memphis Belle* 1990 (ph); *The Cabinet of Dr. Ramirez* 1991 (ph); *The Object of Beauty* 1991 (ph).

Watkins, Peter • Director; also screenwriter, editor. • Born Norbiton, Surrey, England, October 29, 1935. *Educ.* Christ College, Cambridge; RADA, London. Began his career in advertising as an assistant producer and turned to amateur filmmaking in the late 1950s. In the mid-60s Watkins was commissioned by BBC-TV to make two feature-length "docudramas" incorporating a quasi-newsreel style and nonprofessional actors. The second of these, *The War Game* (1966), graphicaly portrayed the nightmare of nuclear war and was banned from broadcast. It was subsequently released in theaters and earned a best documentary Oscar in 1966.

Watkins enjoyed modest success with the commercial feature film, *Privilege* (1967), but has subsequently worked primarily in the documentary genre, based in various Scandanavian countries. His most recent film, *The Journey* (1986), is a 14 1/2 hour epic that addresses such issues as the arms race and global hunger. • *Culloden* 1964 (d,p,sc); *The War Game* 1966 (d,p,sc) **(AABDOC)**; *Privilege* 1967 (d); *Gladiatorerna* 1969 (d,sc); *Punishment Park* 1971 (d,sc,ed); *Edvard Munch* 1975 (a,d,sc,ed); *Aftenlandet* 1976 (d,sc,story,ed); *The Journey* 1986 (d,p,sc,ed,sound ed).

Waxman, Franz • Composer • Born Franz Wachsmann, Königshütte, Germany, December 24, 1906; died 1967. *Educ.* Dresden Music Academy; Berlin Music Conservatory. Began his film career with UFA in 1930 and scored a number of German films before leaving the country in 1934. Waxman subsequently moved to the US, where he emerged as one of Hollywood's finest and most prolific composers of the 1940s and 50s. Adept at psychologically laden scores, Waxman contributed to several Hitchcock films, notably *Rebecca* (1940) and *Rear Window* (1954); other outstanding credits include *The Philadelphia Story* (1940), *Mr. Skeffington* (1944), *Humoresque* (1946) and *Sunset Boulevard* (1950). • *Der Mann, der Seinen Mörder Sucht* 1931 (m); *La Crise Est Finie* 1934 (m); *Liliom* 1934 (m); *Mauvaise Graine* 1934 (m); *Bride of Frankenstein* 1935 (m); *Diamond Jim* 1935 (m); *The Great Impersonation* 1935 (m); *Absolute Quiet* 1936 (m); *The Devil-Doll* 1936 (m); *Fury* 1936 (m); *His Brother's Wife* 1936 (m); *Love Before Breakfast* 1936 (m.dir); *Love on the Run* 1936 (m); *Next Time We Love* 1936 (m); *The Bride Wore Red* 1937 (m); *Captains Courageous* 1937 (m); *A Day at the Races* 1937 (m.dir); *The Emperor's Candlesticks* 1937 (m); *Personal Property* 1937 (m); *Arsene Lupin Returns* 1938 (m); *A Christmas Carol* 1938 (m); *Dramatic School* 1938 (m); *Man-Proof* 1938 (m); *Port of Seven Seas* 1938 (m); *The Shining Hour* 1938 (m); *Test Pilot* 1938 (m); *Three Comrades* 1938 (m); *Too Hot to Handle* 1938 (m); *The Young in Heart* 1938 (m) **(AANBM)**; *The Adventures of Huckleberry Finn* 1939 (m); *Ice Follies* 1939 (m.dir); *Lady of the Tropics* 1939 (m); *Lucky Night* 1939 (m.dir); *On Borrowed Time* 1939 (m); *Boom Town* 1940 (m); *Flight Command* 1940 (m); *Florian* 1940 (m); *I Love You Again* 1940 (m.dir); *The Philadelphia Story* 1940 (m); *Rebecca* 1940 (m) **(AANBM)**; *Sporting Blood* 1940 (m); *Strange Cargo* 1940 (m); *Design For Scandal* 1941 (m); *Dr. Jekyll and Mr. Hyde* 1941 (m) **(AANBM)**; *The Feminine Touch* 1941 (m); *Honky Tonk* 1941 (m); *Kathleen* 1941 (m); *Suspicion* 1941 (m) **(AANBM)**; *Her Cardboard Lover* 1942 (m.dir); *Journey For Margaret* 1942 (m); *Reunion in France* 1942 (m); *Seven Sweethearts* 1942 (m); *Tortilla Flat* 1942 (m); *Woman of the Year* 1942 (m); *Air Force* 1943 (m); *Destination Tokyo* 1943 (m); *Old Acquaintance* 1943 (m); *In Our Time* 1944 (m); *Mr. Skeffington* 1944 (m); *The Very Thought of You* 1944 (m); *Confidential Agent* 1945 (m); *God Is My Co-Pilot* 1945 (m); *The Horn Blows at Midnight* 1945 (m); *Hotel Berlin* 1945 (m); *Objective Burma!* 1945 (m); *Pride of the Marines* 1945 (m); *The Two Mrs. Carrolls* 1945 (m); *Her Kind of Man* 1946 (m); *Humoresque* 1946 (m); *Cry Wolf* 1947 (m); *Dark Passage* 1947 (m); *Nora Prentiss* 1947 (m); *The Paradine Case* 1947 (m); *Possessed* 1947 (m); *That Hagen Girl* 1947 (m); *The Unsuspected* 1947 (m); *Alias Nick Beal* 1948 (m); *No Minor Vices* 1948 (m); *Sorry, Wrong Number* 1948 (m); *Johnny Holiday* 1949 (m); *Night Unto Night* 1949 (m); *Rope of Sand* 1949 (m); *Task Force* 1949 (m); *Whiplash* 1949 (m); *Dark City* 1950 (m.dir); *The Furies* 1950 (m); *Night and the City* 1950 (m); *Sunset Boulevard* 1950 (m) **(AABM)**; *Anne of the Indies* 1951 (m); *He Ran All the Way* 1951 (m); *Only the Valiant* 1951 (m); *A Place in the Sun* 1951 (m) **(AABM)**; *Red Mountain* 1951 (m); *Come Back Little Sheba* 1952 (m); *Decision Before Dawn* 1952 (m); *Lure of the Wilderness* 1952 (m); *My Cousin Rachel* 1952 (m); *Phone Call From a Stranger* 1952 (m); *A Lion Is in the Streets* 1953 (m); *Stalag 17* 1953 (m); *Demetrius and the Gladiators* 1954 (m); *Elephant Walk* 1954 (m); *Prince Valiant* 1954 (m); *Rear Window* 1954 (m); *The Silver Chalice* 1954 (m) **(AANBM)**; *This Is My Love* 1954 (m); *The Indian Fighter* 1955 (m); *Untamed* 1955 (m); *The Virgin Queen* 1955 (m.dir); *Back From Eternity* 1956 (m); *Crime in the Streets* 1956 (m); *Miracle in the Rain* 1956 (m); *Love in the Afternoon* 1957 (m.adapt); *Peyton Place* 1957 (m); *Sayonara* 1957 (m); *The Spirit of St. Louis* 1957 (m); *Home Before Dark* 1958 (m); *Run Silent, Run Deep* 1958 (m); *Beloved Infidel* 1959 (m,song); *Career* 1959 (m); *Count Your Blessings* 1959 (m,m.cond); *The Nun's Story* 1959 (m,m.cond) **(AANBM)**; *Cimarron* 1960 (m); *The Story of Ruth* 1960 (m); *Sunrise at Campobello* 1960 (m); *King of the Roaring 20's - The Story of Arnold Rothstein* 1961 (m); *Return to Peyton Place* 1961 (m); *Adventures of a Young Man* 1962 (m,m.cond); *My Geisha* 1962 (m); *Taras Bulba* 1962 (m) **(AANBM)**; *Lost Command* 1966 (m).

Wayans, Keenan • *aka* Keenan Ivory Wayans • Director, screenwriter, actor; also producer, comedian. • Born New York, NY. *Educ.* Tuskegee Institute, AL (engineering). Co-wrote, co-produced and appeared in Robert Townsend's *Hollywood Shuffle* (1987), a telling satire of the compromises made by aspiring black actors fighting for precious few screen roles. Wayans again collaborated with Townsend on the latter's HBO series, "Partners in Crime," and on the production and writing of Eddie Murphy's concert film, *Raw* (1987). One of the brightest of America's emerging comic talents, he wrote, directed and starred in *I'm Gonna Git You Sucka* (1988), a sporadically funny satire of 1970s "blaxploitation" films.

Wayans also conceived the TV show "In Living Color" (1990-) a compilation of comedy sketches featuring his sister

Kim and brother Damon (Damon has been a featured performer on "Saturday Night Live" and has appeared in several films, including *Punchline* and *Colors*, both 1988). • *Hollywood Shuffle* 1987 (a,p,sc); *Raw* 1987 (p,sc); *I'm Gonna Git You Sucka* 1988 (a,d,sc).

Wayne, John • *aka* Duke Morrison • Actor; also producer, director. • Born Marion Michael Morrison, Winterset, IA, May 26, 1907; died 1979. *Educ.* USC, Los Angeles. John Wayne, one of the cinema's greatest stars, is also one of the cinema's greatest problems. His image as an icon of American individualism and the frontier spirit has overshadowed his career to such an extent that it is almost impossible for viewers and writers to separate Wayne the legend from Wayne the actor and Wayne the man.

As Marion Michael Morrison, he played football for USC and held several behind-the-scenes jobs at Fox before moving in front of the cameras in the late 1920s in a series of bit roles. Director John Ford, who had befriended "Duke" Wayne, recommended him for the lead in Raoul Walsh's 1930 western epic, *The Big Trail.* But stardom did not materialize and Wayne spent the rest of the decade slogging through a series of low-budget oaters whose meager budgets and rapid shooting schedules did little to sharpen his acting skills. Still, even in the unsophisticated world of the Poverty Row studios, his easygoing authority and physical presence could command attention.

John Ford gave Wayne another career break in 1939 by casting him as the Ringo Kid in *Stagecoach,* thus rescuing the actor from a life in serials and cheap action pictures. The role propelled Wayne into the top ranks of box-office stars and during the 1940s his legend began to take shape. Excused from military service because of physical ailments, Wayne became the film industry's exemplar of the hard-bitten, decisive soldier who could be compassionate when necessary. Wartime releases such as *Flying Tigers* (1942), *The Fighting Seabees* (1944) and *Back to Bataan* (1945) placed Wayne squarely in the larger-than-life, heroic mold.

But it was the movies he made at the end of the decade that established him as an actor of merit, something more than just a star of tremendous stature. Howard Hawks emphasized the willful side of Wayne's screen persona, taking it to extremes in *Red River* (1948). As the inflexible Tom Dunson, Wayne was able to eschew mock heroics and concentrate on the psychology of a man obsessed. Giving an uncompromisingly hard-edged performance, Wayne created a difficult, unlikable, yet compelling character. Two other John Ford films from the period gave Wayne the opportunity for greater depth—*Fort Apache* (1948) and *She Wore a Yellow Ribbon* (1949)—the latter a particularly moving portrait of a man and an era reaching a turning point.

For most of the 1950s and 60s Wayne ambled through a number of mediocre pictures, standard westerns and action movies made watchable, and financially successful, because of his participation. When the script was poor and the role ill-considered, the results could be disatrous: witness *The Conqueror* (1956), which featured the unfortunate Duke as Genghis Khan. But with a carefully tailored part and a director at the top of his form, Wayne always rose to the occasion—*Rio Bravo* (1959) for Hawks, and *The Searchers* (1956) and *The Man Who Shot Liberty Valance* (1962) for Ford. *The Searchers,* now considered by many to be Ford's greatest picture, also features Wayne's best performance, perhaps because in the driven character of Ethan Edwards viewers can negotiate their private terms with Wayne the man, super patriot and defender of the conservative faith. Ethan is a grotesque figure, the essence of patriarchy, a victim of his personal prejudices and blinded by an extremist code. But at the same time his skill and tenacity are admirable. Finally, one must feel compassion for him, realizing that he will never be integrated into the mainstream, will never be thought of in terms of human scale. Understanding the character of Ethan helps demystify Wayne the icon.

Although he won the 1969 Best Actor Oscar for *True Grit,* a lighthearted if not particularly impressive performance, Wayne's best role in his last decade on screen was also his last. In *The Shootist* (1976) he played a dying gunman who is just beginning to understand his own life and legend. It was the perfect elegy for Wayne, who was himself dying of cancer, and a role which he investd with a touching simplicity and directness—the hallmarks of both his acting career and personal popularity. ES • *Salute* 1929 (a); *Words and Music* 1929 (a); *The Big Trail* 1930 (a); *Men Without Women* 1930 (a); *Arizona* 1931 (a); *Girls Demand Excitement* 1931 (a); *Maker of Men* 1931 (a); *Men Are Like That* 1931 (a); *The Range Feud* 1931 (a); *Three Girls Lost* 1931 (a); *The Big Stampede* 1932 (a); *Haunted Gold* 1932 (a); *The Hurricane Express* 1932 (a); *Lady and Gent* 1932 (a); *Ride Him Cowboy* 1932 (a); *The Shadow of the Eagle* 1932 (a); *Texas Cyclone* 1932 (a); *Two Fisted Law* 1932 (a); *Baby Face* 1933 (a); *His Private Secretary* 1933 (a); *The Life of Jimmy Dolan* 1933 (a); *The Man From Monterey* 1933 (a); *Riders of Destiny* 1933 (a); *Sagebrush Trail* 1933 (a); *Somewhere in Sonora* 1933 (a); *The Telegraph Trail* 1933 (a); *The Three Musketeers* 1933 (a); *'Neath the Arizona Skies* 1934 (a); *Blue Steel* 1934 (a); *The Lucky Texan* 1934 (a); *The Man From Utah* 1934 (a); *Randy Rides Alone* 1934 (a); *The Star Packer* 1934 (a); *The Trail Beyond* 1934 (a); *West of the Divide* 1934 (a); *The Dawn Rider* 1935 (a); *The Desert Trail* 1935 (a); *The Lawless Frontier* 1935 (a); *Lawless Range* 1935 (a); *The New Frontier* 1935 (a); *Paradise Canyon* 1935 (a); *Rainbow Valley* 1935 (a); *Texas Terror* 1935 (a); *Westward Ho* 1935 (a); *Conflict* 1936 (a); *King of the Pecos* 1936 (a); *The Lawless Nineties* 1936 (a); *The Lonely Trail* 1936 (a); *The Oregon Trail* 1936 (a); *Sea Spoilers* 1936 (a); *Winds of the Wasteland* 1936 (a); *Adventure's End* 1937 (a); *California Straight Ahead* 1937 (a); *I Cover the War* 1937 (a); *Idol of the Crowds* 1937 (a); *Born to the West* 1938 (a); *Overland Stage Raiders* 1938 (a); *Pals of the Saddle* 1938 (a); *Red River Range* 1938 (a); *Santa Fe Stampede* 1938 (a); *Allegheny Uprising* 1939 (a); *The New Frontier* 1939 (a); *The Night Riders* 1939 (a); *Stagecoach* 1939 (a); *Three Texas Steers* 1939 (a); *Wyoming Outlaw* 1939 (a); *Dark Command* 1940 (a); *The Long Voyage Home* 1940 (a); *Seven Sinners* 1940 (a); *Three Faces West* 1940 (a); *Lady For a Night* 1941 (a); *Lady From Louisiana* 1941 (a); *The Shepherd of the Hills* 1941 (a); *Flying Tigers* 1942 (a); *In Old California* 1942 (a); *Pittsburgh* 1942 (a); *Reap the Wild Wind* 1942 (a); *Reunion in France* 1942 (a); *The Spoilers* 1942 (a); *In Old Oklahoma* 1943 (a); *A Lady Takes a Chance* 1943 (a); *The Fighting Seabees* 1944 (a); *Tall in the Saddle* 1944 (a); *Back to Bataan* 1945 (a); *Dakota* 1945 (a); *Flame of the Barbary Coast* 1945 (a); *They Were Expendable* 1945 (a); *Without Reservations* 1946 (a); *Angel and the Badman* 1947 (a,p); *Tycoon* 1947 (a); *Fort Apache* 1948 (a); *Red River* 1948 (a); *Wake of the Red Witch* 1948 (a); *The Fighting Kentuckian* 1949 (a,p); *Sands of Iwo Jima* 1949 (a) **(AANBA)**; *She Wore a Yellow Ribbon* 1949 (a); *Three Godfathers* 1949 (a); *Rio Grande* 1950 (a); *Bullfighter and the Lady* 1951 (p); *Flying Leathernecks* 1951 (a); *Operation Pacific* 1951 (a); *Big Jim McLain* 1952 (a); *The Quiet Man* 1952 (a); *Hondo* 1953 (a); *Island in the Sky* 1953 (a); *Trouble Along the Way* 1953 (a); *The High and the Mighty* 1954 (a); *Blood Alley* 1955 (a); *The Sea Chase* 1955 (a); *The Conqueror* 1956 (a); *The Searchers* 1956 (a); *The Wings of Eagles* 1956 (a); *I Married a Woman* 1957 (a); *Jet Pilot* 1957 (a); *Legend of the Lost* 1957 (a); *The Barbarian and the Geisha* 1958 (a); *China Doll* 1958 (exec.p); *The Horse Soldiers* 1959 (a); *Rio Bravo* 1959 (a); *The Alamo* 1960 (a,d,p) **(AANBP)**; *North to Alaska* 1960 (a); *The Comancheros* 1961 (a); *Hatari!* 1962 (a); *How the West Was Won* 1962 (a); *The Longest Day* 1962 (a); *The Man Who Shot Liberty Valance* 1962 (a); *Donovan's Reef* 1963 (a); *McLintock!* 1963 (a); *Circus World* 1964 (a); *The Greatest Story Ever Told* 1965 (a); *In Harm's Way* 1965 (a); *The Sons of Katie Elder* 1965 (a); *Cast a Giant Shadow* 1966 (a); *El Dorado* 1967 (a); *The War*

Wagon 1967 (a); *The Green Berets* 1968 (a,d); *True Grit* 1969 (a) **(AABA)**; *The Undefeated* 1969 (a); *Chisum* 1970 (a); *Rio Lobo* 1970 (a); *Big Jake* 1971 (a); *The Cowboys* 1971 (a); *Directed By John Ford* 1971 (a); *Cahill, United States Marshal* 1973 (a); *The Train Robbers* 1973 (a); *McQ* 1974 (a); *Brannigan* 1975 (a); *Rooster Cogburn* 1975 (a); *It's Showtime* 1976 (a); *The Shootist* 1976 (a); *Going Hollywood: The War Years* 1988 (archival footage).

Weathers, Carl • Actor • Born New Orleans, LA. *Educ.* San Diego State University, CA (drama). Strapping actor who graduated from the gridiron to the screen, first gaining prominence as the showboating heavyweight champ in *Rocky* (1976). Weathers has since featured in a number of action films and landed his first starring role in the chaotic demolition derby, *Action Jackson* (1988). • *Bucktown* 1975; *Friday Foster* 1975; *Rocky* 1976; *Close Encounters of the Third Kind* 1977; *Semi-Tough* 1977; *The Bermuda Depths* 1978; *Force 10 From Navarone* 1978; *Rocky II* 1979; *Death Hunt* 1981; *Rocky III* 1982; *Rocky IV* 1985; *Predator* 1987; *Action Jackson* 1988.

Weaver, Sigourney • Actress • Born Susan Weaver, New York, NY, October 8, 1949. *Educ.* Stanford; Yale School of Drama. Tall, handsome actress who began using the name Sigourney (after a character mentioned in *The Great Gatsby*) in the early 1960s. The daughter of former NBC president Sylvester "Pat" Weaver and actress Elizabeth Inglis, Weaver graduated from Yale drama school one year before Meryl Streep and cut her teeth on the New York stage before making her film debut in the Israeli-produced feature *Madman* (1976). She gained almost overnight stardom as the tenacious heroine of Ridley Scott's sci-fi thriller, *Alien* (1979), and proved her serious dramatic credentials opposite Mel Gibson in the political drama, *The Year of Living Dangerously* (1982).

Weaver went on to become one of Hollywood's biggest female stars of the 1980s. She reached her widest audience as a comic foil to Bill Murray in the hugely successful *Ghostbusters* (1984) and made the cover of *Time* magazine with one of her co-stars of the blockbuster 1986 sequel, *Aliens*. Weaver has earned three Oscar nominations, two of them in 1989: for best supporting actress (as a model of WASP snobbery) opposite Melanie Griffith in *Working Girl*; and for best actress, portraying Dian Fossey in *Gorillas in the Mist*. Weaver married stage director Jim Simpson in 1984. • *Madman* 1976; *Annie Hall* 1977; *Alien* 1979; *Eyewitness* 1980; *The Year of Living Dangerously* 1982; *Deal of the Century* 1983; *Ghostbusters* 1984; *Une Femme ou deux/One Woman or Two* 1985; *Aliens* 1986 **(AANBA)**; *Half Moon Street* 1986; *Gorillas in the Mist* 1988 **(AANBA)**; *Working Girl* 1988 **(AANBSA)**; *Ghostbusters II* 1989; *Helmut Newton: Frames From the Edge* 1989; *Aliens III* 1991.

Webb, Chloe • Actress • Born New York, NY. *Educ.* Boston Conservatory of Music and Drama. Stage-trained performer who garnered wide critical acclaim (including a best actress award from the National Society of Film Critics) for her impassioned portrayal of drug-addicted, punk rock groupie Nancy Spungeon in Alex Cox's *Sid and Nancy* (1986). Webb smoothly shifted gears to play Brian Dennehy's adultorous wife in Peter Greenaway's Pythagorean *The Belly of an Architect* (1987) and reached a wide audience as the girlfriend of Danny DeVito in the entertaining piece of Hollywood fluff, *Twins* (1988). • *Sid and Nancy* 1986; *The Belly of an Architect* 1987; *Twins* 1988; *Heart Condition* 1990; *Queens Logic* 1991.

Webb, Clifton • Actor • Born Webb Parmallee Hollenbeck, Indianapolis, IN, November 19, 1891; died 1966. Multi-talented child performer who graduated to the legitimate stage in 1917 and made sporadic appearances in silent films from 1920. Webb was often cast as an effete, waspish snob; he played a mordant columnist in Otto Preminger's *Laura* (1944) and was memorably pompous in *Razor's Edge, The Dark Corner* (both 1946) and *Sitting Pretty* (1948). Other notable films include *Cheaper By the Dozen* (1950) and *Three Coins in the Fountain* (1954). • *Polly With a Past* 1920; *Heart of a Siren* 1925; *New Toys* 1925; *Laura* 1944 **(AANBSA)**; *The Dark Corner* 1946; *The Razor's Edge* 1946 **(AANBSA)**; *Sitting Pretty* 1948 **(AANBA)**; *Mr. Belvedere Goes to College* 1949; *Cheaper By the Dozen* 1950; *For Heaven's Sake* 1950; *Elopement* 1951; *Mr. Belvedere Rings the Bell* 1951; *Dreamboat* 1952; *Stars and Stripes Forever* 1952; *Mister Scoutmaster* 1953; *Titanic* 1953; *Three Coins in the Fountain* 1954; *Woman's World* 1954; *The Man Who Never Was* 1955; *Boy on a Dolphin* 1957; *The Remarkable Mr. Pennypacker* 1958; *Holiday For Lovers* 1959; *Satan Never Sleeps* 1962.

Webber, Robert • Actor • Born Santa Ana, CA, October 14, 1924; died May 19, 1989, Malibu, CA. Character player, often of suave, insidious types, who entered film in 1951 and received attention for his role in Sidney's Lumet's *Twelve Angry Men* (1957). Webber appeared primarily in action films and intrigues, though he ended his career in several succesful farces (*10* 1979, *Private Benjamin* 1980, *S.O.B.* 1981). • *Highway 301* 1950; *Twelve Angry Men* 1957; *The Nun and the Sergeant* 1962; *The Stripper* 1963; *The Sandpiper* 1965; *The Third Day* 1965; *Dead Heat on a Merry-Go-Round* 1966; *Harper* 1966; *The Silencers* 1966; *The Dirty Dozen* 1967; *Don't Make Waves* 1967; *The Big Bounce* 1969; *The Great White Hope* 1970; *Macedoine* 1970; *$* 1971; *Pacific Challenge* 1973; *Bring Me the Head of Alfredo Garcia* 1974; *Battle of Midway* 1976; *The Choirboys* 1977; *L'Imprecateur* 1977; *Madame Claude* 1977; *Casey's Shadow* 1978; *Revenge of the Pink Panther* 1978; *10* 1979; *Courage Fuyons* 1979; *Private Benjamin* 1980; *Sunday Lovers* 1980; *Tous Vedettes* 1980; *S.O.B.* 1981; *Who Dares Wins* 1982; *Wrong Is Right* 1982; *Wild Geese II* 1985; *Nuts* 1987.

Weill, Claudia • Director; also screenwriter, producer. • Born New York, NY, 1947. *Educ.* Radcliffe; Yale (photography). Made amateur films while a Radcliffe student and, after graduating in 1969, studied painting with Oskar Kokoschka and still photography at Yale with Walker Evans. Weill engineered a number of documentary shorts and experimental films and gained acclaim for her feature-length documentary, *The Other Half of the Sky: A China Memoir* (1975), made in collaboration with Shirley MacLaine. She directed her attentions toward the mainstream with two likeable but uneven dramas, *Girlfriends* (1978) and *It's My Turn* (1980), centering on the plight of contempoarary women. Weill has reached her widest audience to date as director of the popular TV series, "thirtysomething." • *The Year of the Woman* 1973 (ph); *The Other Half of the Sky: A China Memoir* 1975 (d,ph,ed); *Girlfriends* 1978 (d,p,story); *The Scenic Route* 1978 (a); *It's My Turn* 1980 (d); *Calling the Shots* 1988 (a).

Weir, Peter • Director; also screenwriter. • Born Peter Lindsay Weir, Sydney, Australia, August 8, 1944. *Educ.* University of Sydney (art, law). Peter Weir briefly attended Sydney University, dropped out to join his father's real estate business, and left that job for a trip to Europe in 1966. Upon his return, he took a job at a television station and, in his free time, began making short films full of anti-establishment attitudes. In 1969, he signed on with the Commonwealth Film Unit as an assistant camerman and production designer, which led to opportunities to direct a number of short films and eventually features.

Weir's contribution to the Australian film renaissance of the late 1970s lies in his ability to portray the imminent disruption of the rational world by irrational forces hovering just beyond our mundane lives. His reputation as the most stylish of the new Australian directors is built on his charting of that country's landscape and cultural oddities with a sense of wonder.

Weir's first feature, *The Cars That Ate Paris* (1974), portrayed the terror lurking beneath a sleepy Outback town called Paris which profits from highway disasters. It is a Gothic horror story laced with fetishistic black humor. He created another kind of haunting atmosphere for *Picnic at Hanging Rock* (1975), in which a turn-of-the-century girls' school picnic in the Australian bush turns tragic. Weir contrasted the imported and repressive cultural values of the English-style boarding school with the liberating influence of the natural environment of Hanging Rock, where the girls' sexuality is stirred by the phallic and frankly unrefined rock.

The accumulation of details around a motif also shaped *The Last Wave* (1977), in which water is used functionally in the narrative as well as thematically, until all civilization seems at the mercy of an enormous tidal wave prophesied by an ignored aborigine. All of Weir's films portray a stable society about to collapse both from fear and from events beyond its control, and never more so than in *Gallipoli* (1981). A culturally underdeveloped society, made strong by the values of camaraderie and loyalty, is forced by duty into war in service of an empire devoid of concern for anything but its privileged classes. The film makes the isolationism of Australia comprehensible in the context of snobbish, exploitative and incompetent British rule.

Australian films have tended to avoid male/female psychology and romance, but in *The Year of Living Dangerously* (1982), Weir dealt with the animal attraction of an endangered species, Caucasian observers in the Third World. An Australian journalist (Mel Gibson) and an embassy employee (Sigourney Weaver) fall in love in the midst of political unrest in 1965 Jakarta. Once again, Weir sharply evokes a palpable sense of place and time in this underrated film which, although mishandled by its American distributor, did land Weir his first Hollywood picture.

In the thriller *Witness* (1985), he sensitively re-created the simple but disciplined virtues of the Amish, in contrast to the corrupt world of urban police politics. Its soft edges were as surprising as the comic edges around *Dead Poets Society* (1989), in which he came full circle to depict an American private boys' school and its repressive response to ideas about individuality and sensitivity. The film's lectures on the value of poetry and a new way of seeing seem addressed more to Hollywood than an educational elite. KJ • *Three to Go* 1970 (d,sc—"Michael"); *Whatever Happened to Green Valley? (short)* 1973 (d); *The Cars That Ate Paris* 1974 (d,sc,story); *Picnic at Hanging Rock* 1975 (d); *The Last Wave* 1977 (d,sc,idea); *The Plumber* 1979 (d,sc); *Gallipoli* 1981 (d,idea); *The Year of Living Dangerously* 1982 (d,sc); *Witness* 1985 (d) **(AANBD)**; *The Mosquito Coast* 1986 (d); *Dead Poets Society* 1989 (d) **(AANBD)**; *Green Card* 1990 (d,p,sc).

Weissmuller, Johnny • Actor • Born Peter John Weissmuller, Windber, PA, June 2, 1904; died January 20, 1984, Acapulco, Mexico. *Educ.* University of Chicago. Former Olympic swimming champion turned *Tarzan the Ape Man* (1932). Weissmuller was Hollywood's longest-running loincloth-clad creeper-swinger and also appeared in the not-unrelated role of "Jungle Jim" in late 1940s and early 50s B movies and on TV. • *Glorifying the American Girl* 1929; *Tarzan, the Ape Man* 1932; *Tarzan and His Mate* 1934; *Tarzan Escapes* 1936; *Tarzan Finds a Son* 1939; *Tarzan's Secret Treasure* 1941; *Tarzan's New York Adventure* 1942; *Stage Door Canteen* 1943; *Tarzan Triumphs* 1943; *Tarzan's Desert Mystery* 1943; *Tarzan and the Amazons* 1945; *Swamp Fire* 1946; *Tarzan and the Leopard Woman* 1946; *Tarzan and the Huntress* 1947; *Jungle Jim* 1948; *Tarzan and the Mermaids* 1948; *The Lost Tribe* 1949; *Captive Girl* 1950; *Fury of the Congo* 1950; *Mark of the Gorilla* 1950; *Pygmy Island* 1950; *Jungle Manhunt* 1951; *Jungle Jim in the Forbidden Land* 1952; *Voodoo Tiger* 1952; *Killer Ape* 1953; *Savage Mutiny* 1953; *Valley of the Headhunters* 1953; *Cannibal Attack* 1954; *Jungle Man-Eaters* 1954; *Devil Goddess* 1955; *Jungle Moon Men* 1955; *The Phynx* 1970.

Welch, Raquel • Actress • Born Raquel Tejada, Chicago, IL, September 5, 1940. *Educ.* San Diego State College (drama). The archetypal manufactured sex symbol, Welch began appearing in films in the mid-1960s and first caught the public imagination clad in a well-tailored animal skin in the prehistoric fantasy, *One Million Years B.C.* (1966). She ornamented a number of lightweight vehicles before bombing in the title role of *Myra Breckinridge* (1970—Mae West walked off with most of the publicity).

Most of Welch's films have been comic romps and action films, though she earned some credibility for her performances in *Kansas City Bomber* (1972) and in the Broadway production of *Woman of the Year* (succeeding Lauren Bacall). She is the mother of actress Tahnee Welch (born 1962). • *A Swingin' Summer* 1965 (a); *Fantastic Voyage* 1966 (a); *One Million Years B.C.* 1966 (a); *Bedazzled* 1967 (a); *Fathom* 1967 (a); *Bandolero!* 1968 (a); *The Biggest Bundle of Them All* 1968 (a); *Lady in Cement* 1968 (a); *100 Rifles* 1969 (a); *Flareup* 1969 (a); *The Magic Christian* 1970 (a); *Myra Breckinridge* 1970 (a); *The Beloved* 1971 (a); *Hannie Caulder* 1971 (a,p); *Bluebeard* 1972 (a); *Fuzz* 1972 (a); *Kansas City Bomber* 1972 (a); *The Last of Sheila* 1973 (a); *The Three Musketeers* 1973 (a); *The Four Musketeers* 1975 (a); *The Wild Party* 1975 (a); *Mother, Jugs & Speed* 1976 (a); *L'Animal* 1977 (a); *Crossed Swords* 1977 (a).

Weld, Tuesday • Actress • Born Susan Ker Weld, New York, NY, August 27, 1943. *Educ.* Hollywood Professional School, CA. Luminous, ageless beauty who supported her family as a highly successful child model and TV performer; the strains precipitated a nervous breakdown at the age of 9, an alcohol problem at 10 and a suicide attempt at 12. Weld appeared in her first film in 1956 at the age of 13 and, drawing on experience beyond her years, played various oversexed and underaged nymphets in a bevy of low-rent productions and the TV series "The Many Loves of Dobie Gillis." Her tempestuous off-screen adventures made her fodder for the gossip columnists, but she went on to display a quirky, unique talent in several fine dramas, including *The Cincinatti Kid* (1965) and *Pretty Poison* (1968)—in which she suggested both innocence and evil as no one had since Louise Brooks. Her reputation fully rehabilitated, Weld carved a niche as a dependable lead in a number of fine films, including *Lord Love a Duck* (1966), *A Safe Place* (1971), with Orson Welles and Jack Nicholson, and *Play It As It Lays* (1972).

Weld has one son by former husband Dudley Moore and is currently married to violinist Pinchas Zuckerman. • *Rally Round the Flag, Boys!* 1958; *The Five Pennies* 1959; *Because They're Young* 1960; *High Time* 1960; *The Private Lives of Adam and Eve* 1960; *Sex Kittens Go to College* 1960; *Bachelor Flat* 1961; *Return to Peyton Place* 1961; *Wild in the Country* 1961; *Soldier in the Rain* 1963; *The Cincinnati Kid* 1965; *I'll Take Sweden* 1965; *Lord Love a Duck* 1966; *Pretty Poison* 1968; *I Walk the Line* 1970; *A Safe Place* 1971; *Play It As It Lays* 1972; *Looking For Mr. Goodbar* 1977 **(AANBSA)**; *Who'll Stop the Rain?* 1978; *Serial* 1980; *Thief* 1981; *Author! Author!* 1982; *Once Upon a Time in America* 1984; *Heartbreak Hotel* 1988.

Welland, Colin • Screenwriter, actor • Born Liverpool, England, July 4, 1934. Wrote, and performed in, several British TV shows including "Z Cars" before entering film in 1969 and garnering acclaim for his supporting role in Ken Loach's *Kes*. Welland scripted John Schlesinger's *Yanks* (1979) and has since worked consistently as a screenwriter and occasionally as an actor. He appeared in *Straw Dogs* (1971) and won a best screenplay Oscar for *Chariots of Fire* (1981). • *Kes* 1970 (a); *Straw Dogs* 1971 (a); *Villain* 1971 (a); *Sweeney* 1976 (a); *Yanks* 1979 (sc,story); *Chariots of Fire* 1981 (sc) **(AABSC)**; *Farmers Arms* 1983 (a); *Twice in a Lifetime* 1985 (sc,from teleplay "Kisses at 50"); *A Dry White Season* 1989 (sc); *Dancin' Thru the Dark* 1990 (a).

Weller, Peter • Actor • Born Stevens Point, WI, June 24, 1947. *Educ.* North Texas State University, Denton (theater); AADA, New York. Contemplative, blue-eyed lead with classically sculpted features. Weller's stage experience includes notable performances in David Rabe's

Streamers and David Mamet's *The Woods.* He entered film in 1979 and, though best known for his roles in the deadpan cult favorite *The Adventures of Buckaroo Banzai* (1984) and as the armor-clad title character of *Robocop* (1987), Weller has also been effective in more character-driven dramas such as *Shoot the Moon* (1981) and *Firstborn* (1984). • *Butch and Sundance: The Early Days* 1979; *Just Tell Me What You Want* 1980; *Shoot the Moon* 1981; *Of Unknown Origin* 1982; *The Adventures of Buckaroo Banzai: Across the 8th Dimension* 1984; *Firstborn* 1984; *My Sister's Keeper* 1986; *Robocop* 1987; *Shakedown* 1988; *El Tunel* 1988; *Cat Chaser* 1989; *Leviathan* 1989; *Robocop 2* 1990.

Welles, Orson • Director, producer, screenwriter, actor; also author. • Born George Orson Welles, Kenosha, WI, May 6, 1915; died October 9, 1985. Orson Welles's pioneering, influential cinema was imaginative, ambitious and technically daring. His baroque cinematic style created a dense moral universe in which every action had tangled—and usually tragic—human repercussions. Before his dramatic arrival in Hollywood, Welles had carved a considerable reputation in theater and radio. At 18 he was a successful actor at the experimental Gate Theatre in Ireland; at 19, he made his Broadway debut as Tybalt in *Romeo and Juliet.* A series of collaborations with director/producer John Houseman led to their participation in the New York Federal Theatre Project. Their first great success was Welles's staging of an all-black "voodoo" *Macbeth,* which demonstrated Welles's penchant for stretching existing forms beyond established limits. Welles and Houseman eventually formed their own repertory company, the Mercury Theatre, enjoying success with their 1937 production of *Julius Caesar,* which Welles rewrote and set in contemporary Fascist Italy.

Soon Welles was also directing the Mercury players in weekly, hour-long radio dramas for CBS. Once again he stretched the medium, exploiting radio's intimacy to heighten narrative immediacy, most notoriously with the Halloween 1938 broadcast of H.G. Wells's *War of the Worlds.* Concocted news bulletins and eyewitness accounts were so authentic in "reporting" the landing of hostile Martians in New Jersey that the broadcast caused a panic among unsuspecting listeners. Seeking to capitalize on Welles's notoriety, RKO brought him to Hollywood to produce, direct, write and act in two films for $225,000 plus total creative freedom and a percentage of the profits. It was the most generous offer a Hollywood studio had ever made to an untested filmmaker.

After several projects (among them an adaptation of Joseph Conrad's *Heart of Darkness*) came to naught, the 25 year-old Welles made what is generally described as the most stunning debut in the history of film. Initially called *American* and later retitled *Citizen Kane,* Welles's film was a bold, brash and inspired tour-de-force that told its story from several different perspectives, recounting the rise and corruption of an American tycoon, Charles Foster Kane (modeled on publishing magnate William Randolph Hearst). With the brashness of someone new to Hollywood, Welles pushed existing filmmaking techniques as far as they would go, creating a new and distinctive film aesthetic.

Among the innovative elements of Welles's style exhibited in *Citizen Kane* were: 1. composition in depth: the use of extreme deep focus cinematography to connect distant figures in space; 2. complex "mise-en-scène," in which the frame overflowed with action and detail; 3. low-angle shots that revealed ceilings and made characters, especially Kane, seem simultaneously dominant and trapped; 4. long takes; 5. a fluid, moving camera that expanded the action beyond the frame and increased the importance of off-screen space; and 6. the creative use of sound as a transition device (Thatcher wishes a young Charles "Merry Christmas..." and completes the phrase "...and a Happy New Year" to a grown Charles years later) and to create visual metaphors (as in the opera montage where the image of the flickering backstage lamp combined with Susan Kane's faint singing and a whirring noise to symbolize her imminent breakdown and subsequent suicide attempt).

Although well received by the critics, *Citizen Kane* faced distribution and exhibition problems exacerbated by Hearst's negative campaign, and it fared poorly at the box office. Welles's second film for RKO, an adaptation of Booth Tarkington's *The Magnificent Ambersons* (1942), was a more conventional, less flamboyant film that utilized many of the same techniques Welles had developed for *Kane* to evoke a richly textured recollection of turn-of-the-century America. But with Welles off to South America to shoot a semi-documentary (the never-completed *It's All True*) jointly sponsored by RKO and the US government, the studio severely edited the film, deleting 43 minutes. Even in its truncated form, *Ambersons* remains a dark, compelling look at nature of wealth, class and progress in America. Before he left for South America, Welles supervised the filming of *Journey Into Fear* (1942), whose direction is credited to Norman Foster. Welles co-starred and co-wrote the screenplay with Joseph Cotten; the result was an intriguing but muddled thriller. When *Ambersons* proved a commercial failure, it was a blow from which Welles's reputation would never recover. Welles and the Mercury Players were dismissed from RKO. *The Stranger* (1946), produced by independent Sam Spiegel, had Welles directing himself as a Nazi war criminal hiding in a small town, but it was devoid of the characteristic Welles touch. He regained his filmmaking flair with *The Lady From Shanghai* (1948), a stunning film noir in which Welles and his wife Rita Hayworth co-starred. (Already separated before the collaboration began, she filed for divorce once filming was completed.) The hall-of-mirrors finale is a superb example of Welles's gift for the audacious visual image.

Welles's next film proved to be the first of an informal, impressive Shakespeare trilogy, an eccentric, atmospheric version of *Macbeth* (1948) in which the actors were encouraged to speak with thick Scottish burrs. Its centerpiece—a sequence that begins with Macbeth's decision to kill the king, includes the murder and ends with the discovery of the crime by Macduff—was captured in a single ten-minute take. The film, however, was not successful and was dismissed at the Venice Film Festival. Four years later, he answered his critics with a striking version of *Othello* (1952), which won the Grand Prix at Cannes. The final film in the trilogy was the triumphant *Chimes at Midnight/Falstaff* (1966) which Welles, who by this time was of the correct girth to play Falstaff, fashioned from five of Shakespeare's historical plays. As a separate narrative, Falstaff's tale is a bitter one of deteriorating friendship passing from privilege to neglect. It ranks among Welles's greatest achievements.

After the failure of *Macbeth,* Welles began a self-imposed, ten-year exile from Hollywood. His follow-up to *Othello, Mr. Arkadin/Confidential Report* (1955), was an acerbic profile of a powerful man that showed signs of the brilliance that marked *Kane,* but was hindered by an episodic narrative and spotty acting. Welles returned to Hollywood to act in and direct *Touch of Evil* (1958), a film noir masterpiece. From its stunning long-take opening of a car bombing to its tragic denouement, it reiterated his overarching vision of the world as an exacting moral network where each human act has endless and unforseen moral consequences. His adaptation of Kafka's *The Trial* (1962), a nightmarish extension of that vision, depicted a society completely devoid of a moral sense, where empty procedure replaced principle. *The Immortal Story* (1968) was a satisfying, minor work made for French televison, an adaptation of an Isak Dinesen story. His final completed film, *F For Fake* (1973), a diverting collage of documentary and staged footage that investigated the line separating reality and illusion, celebrated all tricksters—including its director, who sometimes stated that if he had not become a director, he would have been a magician.

At the time of his death, *The Other Side of the Wind,* a project he had begun filming in the 1970s, remained unfinished. Obviously autobiographical, it was the story of a famous filmmaker (played by Welles's good friend, John Huston) struggling to find financing for his film, just as Welles was forced to do many times. As an unseen fragment, it was a sad and ironic end for a filmmaking maverick who set the standards for the modern narrative film and the man who was, in the words of Martin Scorsese, "responsible for inspiring more people to be film directors than anyone else in history of the cinema." CRB • *The Hearts of Age (short)* 1934 (a,d); *Too Much Johnson (short)* 1938 (d); *Citizen Kane* 1941 (a,d,p,sc) **(AANBA,AABSC)**; *It's All True* 1942 (d); *Journey Into Fear* 1942 (a,p); *The Magnificent Ambersons* 1942 (d,p,sc); *Follow the Boys* 1944 (a); *Jane Eyre* 1944 (a); *The Stranger* 1946 (a,d); *Tomorrow Is Forever* 1946 (a); *The Lady From Shanghai* 1948 (a,d,sc); *Macbeth* 1948 (a,adapt,d,p); *Black Magic* 1949 (a); *Prince of Foxes* 1949 (a); *The Third Man* 1949 (a); *The Black Rose* 1950 (a); *Othello* 1952 (a,d,p,sc,adapt); *Trent's Last Case* 1952 (a); *Three Cases of Murder* 1953 (a); *Trouble in the Glen* 1953 (a); *Mr. Arkadin/Confidential Report* 1955 (a,d,sc); *Moby Dick* 1956 (a); *Man in the Shadow* 1957 (a); *The Long, Hot Summer* 1958 (a); *The Roots of Heaven* 1958 (a); *South Seas Adventure* 1958 (a); *Touch of Evil* 1958 (a,d,sc); *Compulsion* 1959 (a); *Crack in the Mirror* 1960 (a); *I Tartari* 1960 (a); *RoGoPag* 1962 (a); *The Trial* 1962 (a,d,sc); *The V.I.P.s* 1963 (a); *Campanidas a Medianoche/Chimes at Midnight/Falstaff* 1966 (a,d,p,sc,adapt); *A Man For All Seasons* 1966 (a); *Casino Royale* 1967 (a); *I'll Never Forget What's 'Is Name* 1967 (a); *Histoire Immortelle/The Immortal Story* 1968 (a,d,sc); *Oedipus the King* 1968 (a); *Catch-22* 1970 (a); *The Kremlin Letter* 1970 (a); *Start the Revolution Without Me* 1970 (a); *Upon This Rock* 1970 (a); *Waterloo* 1970 (a); *La Decade Prodigieuse/Ten Days Wonder* 1971 (a); *Directed By John Ford* 1971 (a); *A Safe Place* 1971 (a); *Get to Know Your Rabbit* 1972 (a); *Malpertuis: Histoire d'une maison Maudite* 1972 (a); *Necromancy* 1972 (a); *The Other Side of the Wind* 1972 (d); *Treasure Island* 1972 (a,sc); *Vérités et Mensonges/F For Fake* 1973 (a,d,sc,idea,add.ph); *And Then There Were None* 1975 (a); *The Challenge* 1976 (a); *Voyage of the Damned* 1976 (a); *Rime of the Ancient Mariner* 1977 (a); *Filming Othello* 1978 (a,d); *The Late Great Planet Earth* 1978 (a); *The Muppet Movie* 1979 (a); *Butterfly* 1981 (a); *Genocide* 1981 (a); *History of the World Part I* 1981 (a); *The Man Who Saw Tomorrow* 1981 (a); *Orson Welles à la Cinémathèque* 1982 (a); *Almonds and Raisins* 1983 (a); *In Our Hands* 1984 (a); *Slapstick of Another Kind* 1984 (a); *Where Is Parsifal?* 1984 (a); *Transformers—The Movie* 1986 (a); *Someone to Love* 1987 (a); *Hot Money* 1989 (a); *Hollywood Mavericks* 1990 (a).

Wellman, William A. • *aka* "Wild Bill" • Director; also producer, screenwriter. • Born William Augustus Wellman, Brookline, MA, February 29, 1896; died December 9, 1975. Versatile director whose prolific output was mostly unexceptional but which included a number of cinematic gems.

After an aimless, misspent youth, including a stint in the foreign legion, Wellman became an ace pilot in WWI. He was discharged as a war hero after his plane was shot down and, in 1918, was stationed as a flight instructor at an air base in Southern California. He was then invited to Hollywood by Douglas Fairbanks, whom he had met and befriended before the war.

Garbed in full military splendor, Wellman greeted Fairbanks and was promptly offered a substantial part in *Knickerbocker Buckaroo* (1919); he found the experience unbearable, and acting an unmanly undertaking. He opted instead for a directing career and worked his way up the ranks; has first job, as a messenger, involved delivering fan notices to his estranged first wife, Helene Chadwick. Wellman made his directorial debut with Fox in 1923 and, over the course of four years, graduated from low-profile westerns to major productions; in 1927 he directed *Wings* (1927), the first film to win an Academy Award.

Wellman went on to prove a capable, well-rounded technician, and was responsible for such excellent, diverse films as *The Public Enemy* (1931), the definitive Cagney gangster film; the original *A Star Is Born* (1937), for which he earned a best screenplay Oscar; *Nothing Sacred* (1937), a scathingly funny screwball comedy; and *The Ox-Bow Incident* (1943), a didactic drama about lynching. He also directed two fine war films, *The Story of GI Joe* (1945) and *Battleground* (1949). Among his later wives were singer-dancer Margery Chapin and actress Dorothy Coonan, whom he directed in *Wild Boys of the Road* (1933). • *Knickerbocker Buckaroo* 1919 (a); *Big Dan* 1923 (d); *Cupid's Fireman* 1923 (d); *The Man Who Won* 1923 (d); *Second Hand Love* 1923 (d); *The Circus Cowboy* 1924 (d); *Not a Drum Was Heard* 1924 (d); *Vagabond Trail* 1924 (d); *When Husbands Flirt* 1925 (d); *The Boob* 1926 (d); *The Cat's Pajamas* 1926 (d); *You Never Know Women* 1926 (d); *Wings* 1927 (d); *Beggars of Life* 1928 (d,p); *Ladies of the Mob* 1928 (d); *The Legion of the Condemned* 1928 (d); *Chinatown Nights* 1929 (d); *The Man I Love* 1929 (d); *Woman Trap* 1929 (d); *Dangerous Paradise* 1930 (d); *Maybe It's Love* 1930 (d); *Young Eagles* 1930 (d); *Night Nurse* 1931 (d); *Other Men's Women* 1931 (d); *The Public Enemy* 1931 (d); *Safe in Hell* 1931 (d); *The Star Witness* 1931 (d); *The Conquerors* 1932 (d); *The Hatchet Man* 1932 (d); *Love Is a Racket* 1932 (d); *The Purchase Price* 1932 (d); *So Big* 1932 (d); *Central Airport* 1933 (d); *College Coach* 1933 (d); *Frisco Jenny* 1933 (d); *Heroes For Sale* 1933 (d); *Lilly Turner* 1933 (d); *Midnight Mary* 1933 (d); *Wild Boys of the Road* 1933 (d); *Looking For Trouble* 1934 (d); *The President Vanishes* 1934 (d); *Stingaree* 1934 (d); *The Call of the Wild* 1935 (d); *The Robin Hood of El Dorado* 1936 (d,sc); *Small Town Girl* 1936 (d); *The Last Gangster* 1937 (story); *Nothing Sacred* 1937 (d); *A Star Is Born* 1937 (d,story) **(AABST)**; *Men With Wings* 1938 (d,p); *Beau Geste* 1939 (d,p); *The Light That Failed* 1939 (d,p); *Reaching For the Sun* 1941 (d,p); *The Great Man's Lady* 1942 (d,p); *Roxie Hart* 1942 (d); *Thunder Birds* 1942 (d); *Lady of Burlesque* 1943 (d); *The Ox-Bow Incident* 1943 (d); *Buffalo Bill* 1944 (d); *The Story of G.I. Joe* 1945 (d); *This Man's Navy* 1945 (d); *Gallant Journey* 1946 (d,p,sc); *Magic Town* 1947 (d); *The Iron Curtain* 1948 (d); *Yellow Sky* 1948 (d); *Battleground* 1949 (d) **(AANBD)**; *The Happy Years* 1950 (d); *The Next Voice You Hear* 1950 (d); *Across the Wide Missouri* 1951 (d); *It's a Big Country* 1951 (d); *Westward the Women* 1951 (d); *My Man and I* 1952 (d); *Island in the Sky* 1953 (d); *The High and the Mighty* 1954 (d); *A Star Is Born* 1954 (story) **(AABST)**; *Track of the Cat* 1954 (d); *Blood Alley* 1955 (d); *Good-Bye, My Lady* 1956 (d); *Darby's Rangers* 1958 (d); *Lafayette Escadrille* 1958 (d,p,story).

Wenders, Wim • Director, screenwriter; also producer. • Born Wilhelm Ernst Wenders, Düsseldorf, Germany, August 14, 1945. *Educ.* University of Freiburg (philosophy, medicine); Hochschule für Film und Fernsehen, Munich. One of the best known directors of the New German Cinema, Wenders is often characterized as the "existentialist" of the movement. Stylistically, his films blend Hollywood forms and genres with elements of counter-cinema. Thematically, his films attempt to disclose states of consciousness—loneliness, irresolution, anxiety—and explore the ambivalent impact of American culture on post-WWII German life. "All my films," Wenders claims, "have as their underlying current the Americanization of Germany." No other German filmmaker has dealt more extensively or more obssesively with the American presence in the European unconscious.

Wenders's fascination with American culture began in his childhood. He grew up at a time when American culture provided a diversion for West Germans eager to forget their own past. Extremely shy and introspective as a teenager, Wenders planned to study for the priesthood, but this desire soon gave away to an interest in American music and American film. After studying medicine and philosophy at the University of Freiburg and painting in Paris, Wenders enrolled in Munich's film school, where he made several student films between 1967 and 1970.

His first professional feature, *The Goalie's Anxiety at the Penalty Kick* (1972), attracted considerable critical attention. The film is based on a novel by Peter Handke, a Wenders friend who would write *Wrong Move* (1975) and collaborate with Wenders on *Wings of Desire* (1987). After a film of Hawthorne's *The Scarlet Letter* (1972), his least satisfying work, Wenders made *Alice in the Cities* (1974), *Wrong Move* and *Kings of the Road* (1975)—a trilogy of "road movies" that exemplifies his formal and thematic concerns. The best of the three, *Kings,* focuses on the relationship that develops between two men as they travel in a van along the border between East and West Germany. Lonely and introspective, they both long for the company of women. By the end of their journey, they derive comfort from the fact that "in the course of time" (the film's German title) their lives have taken on some shape and some significance.

Kings of the Road is a quiet, almost lyrical film that disdains psychological motivation, suspense and dramatic tension. In that sense, it reflects Wenders's admiration for the films of Yasujiro Ozu. But in its intricate allusions and resonant implications, it evokes Wenders's favorite themes: the difficulties of communication, the Americanization of German life ("The Yanks have colonized our subconscious," one of the characters says) and the fate of German cinema.

In *The American Friend* (1977), a film that won Wenders international attention, the director continues to explore these themes. Based on Patricia Highsmith's novel, *Ripley's Game,* the film depicts the last few weeks in the life of Jonathan (Bruno Ganz), a picture restorer and framemaker living quietly in Hamburg. The real interest of the film, however, is the friendship that develops between Jonathan and Ripley (Dennis Hopper), an American underworld figure who manipulates Jonathan into committing a series of murders. Jonathan finds himself irresistibly drawn to Ripley, even as he is gradually corrupted and destroyed by the friendship. This story allows Wenders to focus on German/American cultural tensions and to explore the exigencies of international filmmaking dominated by Hollywood and American interests. (Two of Wenders's American idols, directors Nicholas Ray and Sam Fuller, play minor roles in the film.)

In 1978 Wenders came to the United States under contract to direct *Hammett* for Francis Ford Coppola. After numerous problems with the script and conflicts with Coppola, less than 30 percent of Wenders's original film was retained in the final version, released in 1983. Wenders indirectly documented his problems with *Hammett* in *The State of Things* (1982), a self-referential film that contrasts European and American ways of making films. *Paris, Texas* (1984), based on a script by Sam Shepard about a reunion between a drifter and his family, won the Palm d'Or at Cannes in 1984 and represents in many ways the culmination of themes that run through Wenders's earlier films. Wenders returned to Berlin to make *Wings of Desire,* a fantasy/meditation on that city shot largely in black-and-white, for which he won the Best Director Award at Cannes in 1987. PR • *Summer in the City* 1970 (a,d,p,sc); *Die Angst des Tormanns beim Elfmeter/The Goalie's Anxiety at the Penalty Kick* 1972 (d,sc,dial); *Der Scharlachrote Buchstabe/The Scarlet Letter* 1972 (d,sc); *Alice in den Stadten/Alice in the Cities* 1974 (d,sc); *Falsche Bewegung/Wrong Move* 1975 (d); *Im Lauf der Zeit/Kings of the Road* 1975 (d,p,sc); *Der Amerikanische Freund/The American Friend* 1977 (d,sc); *Die Linkshandige Frau/The Left-Handed Woman* 1977 (p); *Long Shot* 1978 (a); *Radio On* 1979 (assoc.p); *Lightning Over Water* 1980 (a,d,sc); *Als Diesel Geboren* 1982 (exec.p); *Chambre 666* 1982 (a,d); *Der Stand der Dinge/The State of Things* 1982 (d,sc); *Hammett* 1983 (d); *Aus der Familie der Panzereschen (short)* 1984 (d); *Paris, Texas* 1984 (d); *I Played It For You* 1985 (a,add.ph); *King Kongs Faust* 1985 (a); *Tokyo-Ga* 1985 (d,sc,ed); *Der Himmel uber Berlin/Wings of Desire* 1987 (d,p,sc,dial); *Yer demir, gok bakir* 1987 (p); *Helsinki Napoli All Night Long* 1988 (a); *Aufzeichnungen zu Kleidern und Stadten/A Notebook on Clothes and Cities* 1989 (a,d,sc,ph); *Motion and Emotion* 1990 (a); *Jusqu'au bout du monde/Till the End of the World* 1991 (d,sc,story).

Wendkos, Paul • Director • Born Philadelphia, PA, September 20, 1922. *Educ.* Columbia. Capable technician who directed episodes of TV's "Naked City" and "Mr. Novak" and made several documentaries before moving on to feature work in 1957. Wendkos's first film was *The Burglar*, an offbeat film noir which has generated some cult interest, partly thanks to an atypically restrained performance by Jayne Mansfield. Other early features, such as *Angel Baby* (1961), displayed some visual flair but later work was increasingly routine. Since the early 1970s, Wendkos has done the bulk of his directing for TV; among his well-received dramas are *Honor Thy Father* (1973), *79 Park Avenue* (1978) and *The Ordeal of Patty Hearst* (1979). • *The Burglar* 1957; *The Case Against Brooklyn* 1958; *Tarawa Beachead* 1958; *Battle of the Coral Sea* 1959; *Face of a Fugitive* 1959; *Gidget* 1959; *Because They're Young* 1960; *Angel Baby* 1961; *Gidget Goes Hawaiian* 1961; *Gidget Goes to Rome* 1963; *Johnny Tiger* 1966; *Attack on the Iron Coast* 1968; *Guns of the Magnificent Seven* 1969; *Hell Boats* 1969; *Cannon For Cordoba* 1970; *The Mephisto Waltz* 1970; *Special Delivery* 1976.

Werner, Oskar • Actor • Born Oskar Josef Bschliessmayer, Vienna, Austria, November 13, 1922; died October 23, 1984, Marburg, West Germany. Member of Vienna's renowned Burgtheater who alternated between stage and screen work from the late 1940s. Werner scored leads in several European productions but, save for his poignant performance in *Decision Before Dawn* (1952), remained better known for his theater work; he was generally considered his country's greatest talent.

Fair-haired and slight, Werner re-emerged in the 1960s in a string of excellent film roles, including Jules in Francois Truffaut's classic *Jules and Jim* (1961), the world-weary counterspy in *The Spy Who Came in From the Cold* and the ship's physician in *Ship of Fools* (both 1965). • *The Angel With the Trumpet* 1950; *Decision Before Dawn* 1952; *Lola Montès* 1955; *Mozart* 1958; *Jules et Jim/Jules and Jim* 1961; *Ship of Fools* 1965 **(AANBA)**; *The Spy Who Came in From the Cold* 1965; *Fahrenheit 451* 1966; *The Shoes of the Fisherman* 1968; *Voyage of the Damned* 1976.

Wertmuller, Lina • Director, screenwriter; also actress, playwright. • Born Arcangela Felice Assunta Wertmuller von Elgg Spanol Von Brauchich, Rome, August 14, 1928. *Educ.* Stanislavskyan Academy of Theater, Rome. European director whose grotesque/comic treatments of weighty political, social and sexual themes earned her a sizeable cult following in the mid-1970s.

Wertmuller was born to a family of Swiss aristocrats; her father, a lawyer, dominated his family and young Lina constantly fought with him. A product of a Roman Catholic education, Wertmuller brought her domestic battles into the classroom and, as she approached college age, could boast of having been thrown out of fifteen schools. Her father wanted her to attend law school but Wertmuller decided, at the instigation of a friend, to enroll in theater school. After her graduation in 1951 she became an itinerant theatrical jack-of-all-trades, traveling through Europe as a producer of avant-garde plays, puppeteer, stage manager, set designer, publicist and radio/TV scriptwriter. Through an acquaintance with Marcello Mastroianni, Wertmuller was introduced to Federico Fellini, who offered her a production position on his film *8 1/2* (1962).

Through her work on this production Wertmuller developed a desire to direct her own film. Enlisting the services of several technicians from *8 1/2*, Wertmuller (with the financial backing of Fellini) made her first film, *The Lizards,* in 1963. A second film, *Let's Talk About Men* (1965), performed decently at the box office, but when she had difficulty obtaining funding for a third film, Wertmuller returned to her work in the theater and TV.

Wertmuller re-emerged as a major film director through her friendship with actor Giancarlo Giannini, who had already established a reputation as a popular stage star. Wertmuller directed him in a TV production, *Rita the Mosquito* (1966); Giannini then recommended a play she had written, *Two Plus Two Are No Longer Four*, to Franco Zefferelli, who agreed to produce it with Giannini starring. The critical and financial success of this production was the breakthrough Wertmuller needed.

Giannini and Wertmuller now agreed to collaborate on films. Their first production, *The Seduction of Mimi*, a comic examination of sexual role-playing and political maneuvering, garnered Wertmuller the best director award at the 1972 Cannes Film Festival. Their next film, *Love and Anarchy* (1973), won Giannini the best actor award at Cannes and, booked for distribution in New York in 1974, gave American critics a first look at a new directorial sensibility. Its success prompted the release of *The Seduction of Mimi* in the US.

The release of these films created an almost instantaneous cult around Wertmuller, which was fueled by the release of *All Screwed Up* (1974) and *Let's Talk About Men* and culminated with the release of *Swept Away* (1974) and *Seven Beauties* (1975). These films combined heavy-handed caricature with extended, often violent, political and sexual debate. Wertmuller's satirical thrust was so broad that both feminists and anti-feminists, liberals and conservatives flocked to her films. On the whole, however, Wertmuller's women characters were treated with contempt—from the shrill, ultra-chic Mariangelo Melato in *Swept Away* and *Summer Night* (1986) to the Felliniesque, wide-angle exaggerations of *The Seduction of Mimi* and *Seven Beauties*. Her male characters were not much more sympathetic, but their broad, macho posturing and chauvinism was tempered by the Chaplinesque pathos of Giannini's performances—particularly his pathologically comic Pasqualino in *Seven Beauties*.

After *Seven Beauties*, Wertmuller's reputation took a sharp downward turn. Her first American film, *The End of the World in Our Usual Bed in a Night Full of Rain* (1978), was both a critical and financial flop and her subsequent, sporadic productions have failed to recapture her audience. PB • *I Basilischi/The Lizards* 1963 (d,sc); *Questa volta parliamo di uomini/Let's Talk About Men* 1965 (d); *Rita La Zanzara* 1966 (d, as "George Brown"; m.dir); *Non stuzzicate la zanzara* 1967 (d,sc); *Violent City* 1970 (sc); *Mimi Metallurgico Ferito Nell 'Onore/The Seduction of Mimi* 1972 (d,sc); *Brother Sun, Sister Moon* 1973 (sc); *Un Film d'Amore e d'Anarchia/Love and Anarchy* 1973 (d,sc); *Travolti da un insolito destino nell'azzuro mare d'Agosto/Swept Away...By an Unusual Destiny in the Blue Sea of August* 1974 (d,sc,story); *Tutto a Posto e Niente In Ordine/All Screwed Up* 1974 (d,sc); *Pasqualino Settebellezze/Seven Beauties* 1975 (d,p,sc); *Which Way Is Up?* 1977 (from sc—*The Seduction of Mimi*); *The End of the World in Our Usual Bed in a Night Full of Rain* 1978 (d,sc); *Fatto di sangue fra due uomini per causa di una vedova. Si sospettano moventi politici/Blood Feud* 1979 (sc,d); *Scherzo del Destino in Agguato Dietro L'Angolo Come un Brigante di Strada/A Joke of Destiny Lying in Wait Around the Corner Like a Robber* 1983 (sc,story,d); *Un Complicato Intrigo di Donne, Vicoli e Delitti/A Complex Plot About Women, Alleys and Crimes* 1985 (d,sc,story); *Sotto, Sotto/Softly, Softly* 1985 (d,sc,story); *Notte d'Estate con Profilo Greco, Occhi a Mandorla e Odore di Basilico/Summer Night With Greek Profile, Almond Eyes and Scent of Basil* 1986 (d,sc); *Il Decimo Clandestino/The Tenth One in Hiding* 1989 (d,sc); *In una Notte di Chiaro di Luna, o Di Cristallo o ol Genere, ol Fuoco o di Vento, Purche sia Amore/Of Crystal or Cinders, Fire or Wind, As Long As It's Love* 1989 (d,sc); *Sabato, Domenica e Lunedi/Saturday, Sunday and Monday* 1990 (d,sc).

West, Mae • Actress, screenwriter; also playwright, vaudevillian. • Born Brooklyn, NY, August 17, 1892; died November 23, 1980. The first great sex clown of film, whose purring asides and salacious eye-rolling fueled a string of risque comedies from the early 1930s.

A vaudevilian from the age of 14, West wrote, produced and directed the 1926 Broadway show, *Sex*, which led to her being jailed on obscenity charges. She staged her next play, *Drag*, the following year; despite its suceess in Paterson, NJ, it was banned on Broadway owing to its subject matter—homosexuality.

With *Diamond Lil* (1928), West became the toast of Broadway and in 1932 she signed with Paramount. Her first film role was supporting George Raft in *Night After Night* (1932), in which Raft said "She stole everything but the cameras." The first film to star West, *She Done Him Wrong* (1933), the film version of *Diamond Lil*, broke box-office records and saved Paramount from selling out to MGM. The Hays office brought in a new censorship code in 1934, largely to combat the code of the West, but she led them a merry chase through several more blockbusters: *I'm No Angel* (1933), *Belle of the Nineties* (1934), *Goin' to Town* (1935) and *Klondike Annie* (1936). Her popularity declined in the late 30s and, afer the failure of *The Heat's On* (1943, the first West film she didn't script herself) she returned to the stage and, later, the nightclub circuit. She turned down numerous film offers, including *Sunset Boulevard* (1950), but finally made a comeback of sorts in *Myra Breckenridge* (1970).

West skirted the delicate sensibilities of Hollywood censors with sexual innuendo and double entendre and her witty observations were as widely quoted as Ben Franklin bromides: "It's better to be looked over than overlooked"; "I used to be Snow White but it drifted," etc. Although she cultivated the image of the "tough broad," West always conveyed a curious Victorian innocence coupled with a winking, self-effacing amusement at her own preposterous creation. Her popularity reached such peaks that sailors were inspired to name their inflatable life jackets after her overemphasised 43-inch "assets," ensuring West a place, like no other actress to date, in Webster's Dictionary. RW • *Night After Night* 1932 (a); *I'm No Angel* 1933 (a,sc,story); *She Done Him Wrong* 1933 (a,from play *Diamond Lil*); *Belle of the Nineties* 1934 (a,sc,story); *Goin' to Town* 1935 (a,sc); *Go West, Young Man* 1936 (a,sc); *Klondike Annie* 1936 (a,sc); *Every Day's a Holiday* 1938 (a,sc); *My Little Chickadee* 1940 (a,sc); *The Heat's On* 1943 (a); *Myra Breckinridge* 1970 (a); *It's Showtime* 1976 (a); *Sextette* 1978 (a,from play).

Weston, Jack • Actor • Born Jack Weinstein, Cleveland, OH, August 21, 1924. *Educ.* Cleveland Playhouse; American Theater Wing, New York. Durable, heavy-set charcter player, often cast as bumbling bad guys. Weston made his stage and TV debuts in 1950 and has appeared in a number of Neil Simon plays; memorable films include *Mirage* (1965), *Wait Until Dark* (1967) and Alan Alda's *The Four Seasons* (1981), as a neurotic dentist. • *Stage Struck* 1958; *Imitation of Life* 1959; *Please Don't Eat the Daisies* 1960; *All in a Night's Work* 1961; *The Honeymoon Machine* 1961; *It's Only Money* 1962; *Palm Springs Weekend* 1963; *The Incredible Mr. Limpet* 1964; *The Cincinnati Kid* 1965; *Mirage* 1965; *Wait Until Dark* 1967; *The Counterfeit Killer* 1968; *The Thomas Crown Affair* 1968; *The April Fools* 1969; *Cactus Flower* 1969; *A New Leaf* 1971; *Fuzz* 1972; *Marco* 1973; *Gator* 1976; *The Ritz* 1976; *Cuba* 1979; *Can't Stop the Music* 1980; *The Four Seasons* 1981; *High Road to China* 1983; *The Longshot* 1986; *RAD* 1986; *Dirty Dancing* 1987; *Ishtar* 1987; *Short Circuit 2* 1988.

Wexler, Haskell • Director of photography; also director, producer, screenwriter. • Born Chicago, IL, 1926. *Educ.* University of California, Berkeley. Acclaimed cinematographer who began his feature filmmaking career in the late 1950s, having previously shot educational and industrial shorts.

A passionate liberal, Wexler produced, directed, wrote and photographed one of the most devastating and technically sophisticated anti-establishment films ever made, *Medium Cool* (1969). Drawing on the stylistic and theoretical advances made by such vanguard figures as Jean-Luc Godard, and taking its title almost straight from mouth of media guru Marshall McLuhan, *Medium Cool* was set and filmed during the 1968 Chicago Democratic convention. It chronicles—in striking, neo-documentary style—the affairs, both professional and amorous, of a detached TV news cameraman (Robert Forster) as he becomes increasingly aware of the political ramifications of his work. The film remains a landmark of political cinema and an insightful essay on the "cool medium."

As a director of photography Wexler has lent his talent to a number of important features, tackling such charged issues as racism (*In the Heat of the Night* 1967), Vietnam (*Coming Home* 1978), union busting (*Matewan* 1987) and urban gang warfare (*Colors* 1988). Other highlights of his work include *Who's Afraid of Virginia Woolf?* (1966) and *The Thomas Crown Affair* (1968). • *Stakeout on Dope Street* 1958 (uncred.ph); *Five Bold Women* 1959 (ph); *Angel Baby* 1961 (ph); *The Hoodlum Priest* 1961 (ph); *The Intruder* 1962 (cam.op); *America, America* 1963 (ph); *A Face in the Rain* 1963 (ph); *The Best Man* 1964 (ph); *The Bus* 1965 (d,p,ph); *The Loved One* 1965 (p); *Who's Afraid of Virginia Woolf?* 1966 (ph) **(AABPH)**; *In the Heat of the Night* 1967 (ph); *The Thomas Crown Affair* 1968 (ph); *Medium Cool* 1969 (d,p,sc,ph); *Gimme Shelter* 1970 (ph); *Brazil: A Report on Torture* 1971 (d,p); *The Trial of the Catonsville Nine* 1972 (ph); *American Graffiti* 1973 (ph); *Introduction to the Enemy* 1974 (d,ph); *One Flew Over the Cuckoo's Nest* 1975 (ph) **(AANBPH)**; *Bound For Glory* 1976 (ph) **(AABPH)**; *Underground* 1976 (a,p); *CIA: Case Officer* 1978 (ph); *Coming Home* 1978 (ph); *Days of Heaven* 1978 (add.ph); *The Rose* 1979 (add.ph); *No Nukes* 1980 (documentary footage director,ph); *Second-Hand Hearts* 1980 (ph); *Lookin' to Get Out* 1982 (ph); *Richard Pryor Live on the Sunset Strip* 1982 (ph); *The Black Stallion Returns* 1983 (add.ph); *Bus II* 1983 (d,p); *The Man Who Loved Women* 1983 (ph); *Latino* 1985 (d,sc); *Matewan* 1987 (ph) **(AANBPH)**; *Colors* 1988 (ph); *Blaze* 1989 (ph) **(AANBPH)**; *Three Fugitives* 1989 (ph); *Through the Wire* 1990 (ph); *To the Moon, Alice (short)* 1990 (2u ph).

Whale, James • Director • Born Dudley, England, July 22, 1896; died 1957. Former newspaper cartoonist who embarked on a stage career, trying his hand at acting, set designing and directing. Whale arrived in Hollywod in 1930 to bring his stage version of *Journey's End* to the screen. He went on to craft some of the most intelligent and witty films of the horror genre, including the three classics, *Frankenstein* (1931), *The Invisible Man* (1933) and *Bride of Frankenstein* (1935). Whale brought a similar grace and humor to several literary and stage adaptations, including *Showboat* (1936) and *The Man In the Iron Mask* (1939). He abandoned film in the early 1940s (save for a segment of a never-released omnibus film produced in 1949) to try his hand at painting. Whale drowned in his swimming pool under suspicious circumstances in 1957. • *Journey's End* 1930; *Frankenstein* 1931; *Waterloo Bridge* 1931; *The Impatient Maiden* 1932; *The Old Dark House* 1932; *By Candlelight* 1933; *The Invisible Man* 1933; *The Kiss Before the Mirror* 1933; *One More River* 1934; *Bride of Frankenstein* 1935; *Remember Last Night?* 1935; *Show Boat* 1936; *The Great Garrick* 1937; *The Road Back* 1937; *Port of Seven Seas* 1938; *Sinners in Paradise* 1938; *Wives Under Suspicion* 1938; *The Man in the Iron Mask* 1939; *Green Hell* 1940; *They Dare Not Love* 1941.

Whalley-Kilmer, Joanne • Actress • Born Joanne Whalley, Salford, England, 1964. Petite, attractive performer who first gained attention on the London stage and in the British TV miniseries, *Edge of Darkness*. Whalley-Kilmer first received international attention as the beatific Nurse Mills in Dennis Potter's award-winning TV mini-series "The Singing Detective" (1986, released theatrically in the US in 1988) and she brought a winning candor to her starring role as Christine Keeler in *Scandal* (1989). She is married to actor Val Kilmer, with whom she co-starred in the films *Willow* (1988) and *Kill Me Again* (1989). • *Pink Floyd The Wall* 1982; *Dance With a Stranger* 1985; *The Good Father* 1986; *No Surrender* 1986; *Popielusko* 1988; *The Singing Detective* 1988; *Willow* 1988; *Kill Me Again* 1989; *Scandal* 1989; *A TV Dante* 1989; *The Big Man* 1990; *Navy Seals* 1990.

Wheeler, Lyle • art director • Born Woburn, MA, February 2, 1905; died January 10, 1990, Woodland Hills, CA. *Educ.* USC School of Architecture, Los Angeles. Former magazine illustrator and industrial designer who began his film career in the mid-1930s. Wheeler was named supervising art director at 20th Century-Fox in 1944 and promoted to the head of the art department three years later. His distinguished work adorned everything from lush period melodramas (*Gone With the Wind* 1939), to dank film noirs (*Call Northside 777* 1948) to swank musicals (*South Pacific* 1958). Son W. Brooke Wheeler is a production designer and has worked on several recent J. Lee Thompson films. • *Nothing Sacred* 1937 (art d); *The Prisoner of Zenda* 1937 (art d) **(AANBAD)**; *A Star Is Born* 1937 (sets); *The Adventures of Tom Sawyer* 1938 (art d) **(AANBAD)**; *Gone With the Wind* 1939 (art d) **(AABAD)**; *Rebecca* 1940 (art d) **(AANBAD)**; *Laura* 1944 (art d) **(AANBAD)**; *Fallen Angel* 1945 (art d); *Leave Her to Heaven* 1945 (art d) **(AANBAD)**; *A Tree Grows in Brooklyn* 1945 (art d); *Anna and the King of Siam* 1946 (art d) **(AABAD)**; *The Foxes of Harrow* 1947 (art d) **(AANBAD)**; *Gentleman's Agreement* 1947 (art d); *Call Northside 777* 1948 (art d); *Come to the Stable* 1949 (art d) **(AANBAD)**; *Cry of the City* 1948 (art d); *I Was a Male War Bride* 1949 (art d); *Pinky* 1949 (art d); *All About Eve* 1950 (art d) **(AANBAD)**; *An American Guerrilla in the Philippines* 1950 (art d); *Panic in the Streets* 1950 (art d); *David and Bathsheba* 1951 (art d) **(AANBAD)**; *The Desert Fox* 1951 (art d); *Fourteen Hours* 1951 (art d) **(AANBAD)**; *House on Telegraph Hill* 1951 (art d) **(AANBAD)**; *On the Riviera* 1951 (art d) **(AANBAD)**; *Rawhide* 1951 (art d); *U.S.S. Tea Kettle* 1951 (art d); *Diplomatic Courier* 1952 (art d); *My Cousin Rachel* 1952 (art d) **(AANBAD)**; *The Snows of Kilimanjaro* 1952 (art d) **(AANBAD)**; *Viva Zapata!* 1952 (art d) **(AANBAD)**; *Niagara* 1953 (art d); *Pickup on South Street* 1953 (art d); *The President's Lady* 1953 (art d) **(AANBAD)**; *The Robe* 1953 (art d) **(AABAD)**; *The Titanic* 1953 (art d) **(AANBAD)**; *White Witch Doctor* 1953 (art d); *Desiree* 1954 (art d) **(AANBAD)**; *The Egyptian* 1954 (art d); *Garden of Evil* 1954 (art d); *Prince Valiant* 1954 (art d); *Daddy Long Legs* 1955 (art d) **(AANBAD)**; *Love Is a Many Splendored Thing* 1955 (art d) **(AANBAD)**; *The Racers* 1955 (art d); *23 Paces to Baker Street* 1956 (art d); *The King and I* 1956 (art d) **(AABAD)**; *Sing Boy Sing* 1957 (art d); *The Barbarian and the Geisha* 1958 (art d); *The Bravados* 1958 (art d); *A Certain Smile* 1958 (art d) **(AANBAD)**; *The Fiend Who Walked the West* 1958 (art d); *The Fly* 1958 (art d); *Fraulein* 1958 (art d); *From Hell to Texas* 1958 (art d); *The Gift of Love* 1958 (art d); *The Hunters* 1958 (art d); *In Love and War* 1958 (art d); *The Long, Hot Summer* 1958 (art d); *Mardi Gras* 1958 (art d); *A Nice Little Bank That Should Be Robbed* 1958 (art d); *Rally Round the Flag, Boys!* 1958 (art d); *The Remarkable Mr. Pennypacker* 1958 (art d); *The Sound and the Fury* 1958 (art d); *South Pacific* 1958 (ph); *Ten North Frederick* 1958 (art d); *The Young Lions* 1958 (art d); *The Alligator People* 1959 (art d); *Beloved Infidel* 1959 (art d); *The Best of Everything* 1959 (art d); *Blue Denim* 1959 (art d); *Compulsion* 1959 (art d); *The Diary of Anne Frank* 1959 (art d) **(AABAD)**; *Five Gates to Hell* 1959 (art d); *Here Come the Jets* 1959 (art d); *Holiday For Lovers* 1959 (art d); *Hound Dog Man* 1959 (art d); *Journey to the Center of the Earth* 1959 (art d) **(AANBAD)**; *The Man Who Understood Women* 1959 (art d); *The Miracle of the Hills* 1959 (art d); *A Private's Affair* 1959 (art d); *Return of the Fly* 1959 (art d); *The Sad Horse* 1959 (art d); *Say One For Me* 1959 (art d); *These Thousand Hills* 1959 (art d); *Warlock* 1959 (art d); *Woman Obsessed* 1959 (art d); *Seven Thieves* 1960 (art d); *Wild River* 1960 (art d); *Advise and Consent* 1962 (pd); *The Cardinal* 1963 (art d) **(AANBAD)**; *The Best Man* 1964 (art d); *The Big Mouth* 1967 (pd); *Marooned* 1969 (pd); *Doctors' Wives* 1970 (pd); *The Love Machine* 1971 (pd); *Stand Up and Be Counted* 1972 (pd); *Posse* 1975 (pd).

Whitaker, Forest • Actor • Born Longview, TX, 1961. *Educ.* California Polytechnic, Pomona; USC, Los Angeles (music). Imposing, stage-trained performer who first came to notice as Paul Newman's duplicitous billiards opponent in *The Color of Money* (1986). Whitaker was named best actor at Cannes for his portrayal of jazz legend Charlie Parker in Clint Eastwood's *Bird* (1988). (Brother Damon Whitaker played "Bird" as a young boy.) • *Fast Times at Ridgemont High* 1982; *Vision Quest* 1985; *The Color of Money* 1986; *Platoon* 1986; *Good Morning, Vietnam* 1987; *Stakeout* 1987; *Bird* 1988; *Bloodsport* 1988; *Johnny Handsome* 1989; *Downtown* 1990; *A Rage in Harlem* 1991 (a,p).

Whitelaw, Billie • Actress • Born Coventry, England, June 6, 1932. Distinguished actress who worked extensively in radio during childhood and made her mark as one of the leading young performers of British TV in the 1960s.

Whitelaw made her big-screen debut in Terence Hanbury's (aka, Joseph Losey's) *The Sleeping Tiger* (1954) and gained acclaim, including a British Academy best actress award, for Albert Finney's *Charlie Bubbles* (1967). She has since turned in highly effective, if intermittent, movie performances; she was memorable as the ill-fated nanny in 1976's *The Omen* and was recently seen by US audiences as the mother of British gangsters, *The Krays* (1990). On the stage, Whitelaw is widely considered the preeminent interpreter of the work of Samuel Beckett. • *The Sleeping Tiger* 1954; *Gideon's Day* 1958; *Mr. Topaze* 1961; *Charlie Bubbles* 1967; *Twisted Nerve* 1968; *The Adding Machine* 1969; *Leo the Last* 1970; *Start the Revolution Without Me* 1970; *Eagle in a Cage* 1971; *Gumshoe* 1971; *Frenzy* 1972; *Night Watch* 1973; *The Omen* 1976; *The Water Babies* 1979; *An Unsuitable Job For a Woman* 1981; *The Dark Crystal* 1982; *Samuel Beckett: Silence to Silence* 1984; *Slayground* 1984; *The Chain* 1985; *Shadey* 1985; *Maurice* 1987; *The Dressmaker* 1988; *Joyriders* 1988; *The Krays* 1990.

Wicki, Bernhard • *aka* Bernhardt Wicki • Actor, director; also screenwriter. • Born St. Polten, Austria, October 28, 1919. Key figure of post-war German cinema whose preoccupation with recent German history anticipated the work of the New German Cinema.

As an actor, Wicki's memorable early screen roles include the Yogoslav partisan in Helmut Kautner's anti-war film *The Last Bridge* (1953), one of the officers conspiring against Hitler in G.W. Pabst's *It Happened in Broad Daylight* (1956) and the dying friend in Michelangelo Antonioni's *La Notte* (1961). After a 15-year hiatus, Wicki returned to screen acting in 1976, appearing mostly in character parts (he played the Germanic Dr. Ulmer—in the middle of Texas—in Wim Wenders's *Paris, Texas* 1984).

As a director, Wicki first gained international attention with the adroitly handled anti-war film, *The Bridge* (1959) and was named best director at Berlin for *The Miracle of Malachias* (1961). He also directed the German section of the Hollywood WWII epic *The Longest Day* (1962) and the Marlon Brando spy thriller *Morituri* (1965).

Zwicki's more recent work includes two films adapted from Joseph Roth: *The False Weight* (1971), about the fall of the Hapsburg Dynasty, and *The Spider's Web* (1989), on the rise of Nazism. His wife, actress Agnes Fink, has appeared in films by various directors, including her husband and Margarethe von Trotta. • *Die Letze Brucke/The Last Bridge* 1953 (a); *Ewiger Walzer/The Eternal Waltz* 1954 (a); *Rummelplatz Der Liebe* 1954 (a); *Kinder, Mutter und ein General* 1955 (a); *Es Geschah am 20.Juli/It Happened in Broad Daylight* 1956 (a); *Die Zürcher Verlobung* 1957 (a); *Die Brücke/The Bridge* 1959 (d); *La Chatte* 1959 (a); *La Notte* 1961 (a); *Das Wunder des Malachias/The Miracle of Malachias* 1961 (d,p,sc); *The Longest Day* 1962 (d); *Der Besuch* 1964 (d); *Morituri* 1965 (d); *Das Falsche Gewicht/The Wanting Weight/The False Weight* 1971 (d,sc); *Crime and Passion* 1976 (a); *Die Eroberung der Zitadelle* 1977 (d,sc); *Die Linkshändige Frau/The Left-Handed Woman* 1977 (a); *Despair* 1978 (a); *Die Glaeserne Zelle* 1978 (a); *La Mort en Direct/Deathwatch* 1979 (a); *Domino* 1982 (a); *Eine Liebe in Deutschland/A Love in Germany* 1983 (a); *La Diagonale du Fou/Dangerous Moves* 1984 (a); *Frühlingssinfonie/Spring Symphony* 1984 (a); *Die Grünstein-Variante* 1984 (d,sc); *Paris, Texas* 1984 (a); *Killing Cars* 1985 (a); *Marie Ward* 1985 (a); *Das Spinnennetz/The Spider's Web* 1989 (d,sc).

Widerberg, Bo • Director, screenwriter; also novelist, critic, producer. • Born Bo Gunnar Widerberg, Malmö, Sweden, June 8, 1930. Already acclaimed as one of the leading novelists of his generation, Widerberg turned to film criticism in the early 1960s. In 1962 he published a collection of essays, *Vision in the Swedish Cinema*, which vociferously denounced Swedish film as rarified and oblivious to everyday, contemporary issues; Ingmar Bergman was singled out as the primary offender. The following year, Widerberg turned from fiery prose to practice, directing his first feature, *The Baby Carriage* (1962).

Widerberg gained international acclaim with the lyrically photographed *Elvira Madigan* (1967), which tells the true story of a doomed love affair in morally oppressive 19th-century Sweden. He subsequently made two glossy but effective films centered on the plight of the working class; *Adalen '31* (1968), about a bloody strike in Northern Sweden, which won a Special Jury Prize at Cannes, and *Joe Hill* (1971), a biopic of the legendary American labor leader.

A punctilious craftsman, Widerberg has since made only a handful of films, none of which have garnered the acclaim of his earlier efforts. • *Barnvagnen/The Baby Carraige* 1962 (d,sc); *Kvarteret Korpen/Raven's End* 1964 (d,sc); *Karlek 65/Love 65* 1965 (d,sc,ed); *Elvira Madigan* 1967 (d,sc,ed); *Adalen '31* 1968 (d,sc,ed); *Joe Hill* 1971 (d,p,sc,ed); *Fimpen* 1973 (d,p,sc,story,ed); *Mannen pa taket* 1976 (d,sc,ed,cost); *Victoria* 1979 (d,sc,ed); *Mannen Fran Mallorca* 1984 (d,sc,ed); *Ormen's vag pa halleberget* 1986 (d,ed,sc,ed).

Widmark, Richard • Actor; also producer. • Born Sunrise, MN, December 26, 1914. *Educ.* Lake Forrest College, IL (law, drama). Broadway actor whose early roles were often as tough guys or heavies. Widmark earned an Oscar nomination for his 1947 screen debut in the gangster saga *Kiss of Death* (as a giggling psychopathic killer, he pushed a crippled old lady down a flight of stairs); he played the disinterested hero of Sam Fuller's ambiguous cold-war thriller *Pickup on South Street* (1953) and was superb in the title role of Don Siegel's New York cop tale *Madigan* (1968).

Blonde, handsome and athletic, Widmark is also noted for his many westerns (e.g. John Ford's *Two Rode Together* 1961), and played noted character roles in *Judgment at Nuremberg* (1961) and *The Bedford Incident* (1965). Widmark has also produced several films, including the spy thriller *The Secret Ways* (1961), scripted by wife Jean Hazelwood. • *The Kiss of Death* 1947 (a) **(AANBSA)**; *Road House* 1948 (a); *The Street With No Name* 1948 (a); *Yellow Sky* 1948 (a); *Down to the Sea in Ships* 1949 (a); *Slattery's Hurricane* 1949 (a); *Halls of Montezuma* 1950 (a); *Night and the City* 1950 (a); *No Way Out* 1950 (a); *Panic in the Streets* 1950 (a); *The Frogmen* 1951 (a); *Don't Bother to Knock* 1952 (a); *My Pal Gus* 1952 (a); *O. Henry's Full House* 1952 (a); *Red Skies of Montana* 1952 (a); *Destination Gobi* 1953 (a); *Pickup on South Street* 1953 (a); *Take the High Ground* 1953 (a); *Broken Lance* 1954 (a); *Garden of Evil* 1954 (a); *Hell and High Water* 1954 (a); *The Cobweb* 1955 (a); *Prize of Gold* 1955 (a); *Backlash* 1956 (a); *The Last Wagon*

1956 (a); *Run For the Sun* 1956 (a); *Saint Joan* 1957 (a); *Time Limit!* 1957 (a,p); *The Law and Jake Wade* 1958 (a); *The Tunnel of Love* 1958 (a); *The Trap* 1959 (a,p); *Warlock* 1959 (a); *The Alamo* 1960 (a); *Judgment at Nuremberg* 1961 (a); *The Secret Ways* 1961 (a,p); *Two Rode Together* 1961 (a); *How the West Was Won* 1962 (a); *Cheyenne Autumn* 1964 (a); *Flight From Ashiya* 1964 (a); *The Bedford Incident* 1965 (a,p); *Alvarez Kelly* 1966 (a); *The Way West* 1967 (a); *Madigan* 1968 (a); *Death of a Gunfighter* 1969 (a); *A Talent For Loving* 1969 (a); *The Moonshine War* 1970 (a); *When the Legends Die* 1972 (a); *Murder on the Orient Express* 1974 (a); *The Sell Out* 1976 (a); *To the Devil, a Daughter* 1976 (a); *The Domino Killings* 1977 (a); *Rollercoaster* 1977 (a); *Twilight's Last Gleaming* 1977 (a); *Coma* 1978 (a); *The Swarm* 1978 (a); *Bear Island* 1979 (a); *Hanky Panky* 1982 (a); *National Lampoon Goes to the Movies* 1982 (a); *Who Dares Wins* 1982 (a); *Against All Odds* 1983 (a); *True Colors* 1991 (a).

Wiene, Robert • Director; also actor, screenwriter. • Born Sasku, Germany, 1881; died July 17, 1938, Paris. *Educ.* University of Vienna (theater history). German expressionist director who began his career in the theater, entered films as a scenarist and is best known for the expressionist classic, *The Cabinet of Dr. Caligari* (1919). Wiene was the second choice to direct the film (producer Erich Pommer originally offered the job to Fritz Lang), which was scripted by Carl Mayer and Hans Janowitz; his subsequent work casts doubt on the extent of his contribution to the project. Wiene's later German films include *Raskolnikov* (1923) and the biblical spectacle, *INRI* (1923); he moved to France when the Nazis took power and his final film, *Ultimatum* (1938), was completed by Robert Siodmak. Brother Conrad Wiene was also a director, chiefly known for *The Power of Darkness* (1923), based on a Tolstoy tale and scripted by Robert. • *Das Kabinett des Dr. Caligari/The Cabinet of Dr. Caligari* 1919 (d); *Genuine die tragödie eines seltsamen Hauses* 1920 (d); *INRI* 1923 (d); *Der Puppenmacher von Nian-King* 1923 (d); *Raskolnikov* 1923 (d); *Unfug der Liebe* 1928 (d); *Ultimatum* 1938 (d).

Wiest, Dianne • Actress • Born Kansas City, MO, March 28, 1948. *Educ.* University of Maryland. Exuberant, engaging character player who first gained attention for her appearances in a string of Woody Allen films, notably as one of "Hannah's" sisters and as the lovelorn aunt in *Radio Days* (1987). Wiest has since played a number of mothers-under-pressure, as in *Cookie* (1989) and, especially, *Parenthood* (1989). She won a best actress Obie for *The Art of Dining* in 1983 and made her stage directing debut with *Not About Heroes* at the Williamstown Playhouse in 1985. • *It's My Turn* 1980; *I'm Dancing As Fast As I Can* 1981; *Independence Day* 1982; *Falling in Love* 1984; *Footloose* 1984; *The Purple Rose of Cairo* 1985; *Hannah and Her Sisters* 1986 **(AABSA)**; *The Lost Boys* 1987; *Radio Days* 1987; *September* 1987; *Bright Lights, Big City* 1988; *Cookie* 1989; *Parenthood* 1989 **(AANBSA)**; *Edward Scissorhands* 1990; *Little Man Tate* 1991.

Wilcox, Herbert • Producer, director • Born Cork, Ireland, April 19, 1892; died 1977. Film impressario responsible for a number of competent biopics and bubbly comedies.

Originally a film salesman, Wilcox turned to producing in 1922, founded Elstree Studios in 1926 and was one of the central figures of British cinema by the end of the decade. Combining a keen sense for public taste with a flair for promotion, Wilcox produced numerous hits and guided the career of Anna Neagle, whom he would marry in 1943. Neagle's genteel charm, not any special talent, made her England's biggest female draw for seven years. Beginning with *Goodnight in Vienna* (1933), Wilcox directed her in a series of hugely successful, mostly historical films, including *Odette* (1950) and the Queen Victoria diptych, *Victoria the Great* (1937) and *Sixty Glorious Years* (1938).

Wilcox enjoyed modest success during a Hollywood sojourn in the late 1930s, returned to Britain in the early 40s and continued to dominate the British industry with a string of saccharine comedies starring Neagle and Michael Wilding, such as *Piccadily Incident* (1946) and *Spring in Park Lane* (1948). His producing prowess began to falter in the early 50s and he was bankrupt by 1964. He published an autobiography, *Twenty Five Thousand Sunsets*, in 1967. • *London* 1926 (d); *Nell Gwyn* 1926 (d); *Madame Pompadour* 1927 (d); *Mumsie* 1927 (d); *Tiptoes* 1927 (d); *When Knights Were Bold* 1929 (p,sc); *Rookery Nook* 1930 (p); *The Blue Danube* 1932 (d); *Bitter Sweet* 1933 (d); *Goodnight in Vienna* 1933 (d); *Sorrell and Son* 1933 (p); *That's a Good Girl* 1933 (d,p); *Brewster's Millions* 1935 (p); *Escape Me Never* 1935 (p); *Peg of Old Drury* 1935 (d); *The Three Maxims* 1936 (d); *Victoria the Great* 1937 (d,p); *Sixty Glorious Years* 1938 (d); *Nurse Edith Cavell* 1939 (d,p); *Irene* 1940 (d,p); *No, No, Nanette* 1940 (d,p); *Sunny* 1941 (d,p); *Forever and a Day* 1943 (d,p); *Piccadily Incident* 1946 (d); *Spring in Park Lane* 1948 (d); *Odette* 1950 (d); *Four Against Fate* 1952 (d); *Trent's Last Case* 1952 (d,p); *Laughing Anne* 1953 (d); *Trouble in the Glen* 1953 (d,p); *Let's Make Up* 1954 (d,p); *King's Rhapsody* 1955 (d); *My Teenage Daughter* 1956 (d,p); *Dangerous Youth* 1957 (d).

Wilde, Cornel • Actor, director; also producer. • Born Cornelius Louis Wilde, New York, NY, October 13, 1915; died October 16, 1989, Los Angeles, CA. *Educ.* CCNY (pre-med). Athletic, darkly handsome lead who abandoned a medical career and a berth on the 1936 Olympic fencing team to pursue his acting career.

From Broadway (notably as Tybalt in Olivier's 1940 production of *Romeo and Juliet*), Wilde entered films in 1940 and made his name playing Frederic Chopin in *A Song to Remember* (1945). Of limited charm and talent, he fluctuated between A and B pictures (including a number of swashbucklers) before beginning to direct and star in his own independent productions in the mid-1950s. Among his more inspired directorial efforts is the striking adventure feature, *The Naked Prey* (1966).

Wilde was married to actress Patricia Wright from 1937 to 1951 and to Jean Wallace from 1951 to 1981; he costarred with Wallace in several films (*The Big Combo* 1955, *Sword of Lancelot* 1963). • *High Sierra* 1941 (a); *Kisses For Breakfast* 1941 (a); *Knockout* 1941 (a); *The Perfect Snob* 1941 (a); *Life Begins at Eight-Thirty* 1942 (a); *Manila Calling* 1942 (a); *Wintertime* 1943 (a); *The Bandit of Sherwood Forest* 1945 (a); *Leave Her to Heaven* 1945 (a); *A Song to Remember* 1945 (a) **(AANBA)**; *A Thousand and One Nights* 1945 (a); *Centennial Summer* 1946 (a); *Forever Amber* 1947 (a); *The Homestretch* 1947 (a); *It Had to Be You* 1947 (a); *The Walls of Jericho* 1948 (a); *Shockproof* 1949 (a); *Two Flags West* 1950 (a); *At Sword's Point* 1952 (a); *California Conquest* 1952 (a); *The Greatest Show on Earth* 1952 (a); *Operation Secret* 1952 (a); *Treasure of the Golden Condor* 1953 (a); *Passion* 1954 (a); *Saadia* 1954 (a); *Woman's World* 1954 (a); *The Big Combo* 1955 (a); *The Scarlet Coat* 1955 (a); *Storm Fear* 1955 (a,d,p); *Hot Blood* 1956 (a); *Star of India* 1956 (a); *Beyond Mombasa* 1957 (a); *The Devil's Hairpin* 1957 (a,d,p,sc); *Omar Khayyam* 1957 (a); *Maracaibo* 1958 (a,d,p); *Edge of Eternity* 1959 (a); *Constantino il Grande* 1961 (a); *Sword of Lancelot* 1963 (a,d,p); *The Naked Prey* 1966 (a,d,p); *Beach Red* 1967 (a,d,p); *The Comic* 1969 (a); *No Blade of Grass* 1970 (d,p); *Shark's Treasure* 1975 (a,d,p,sc); *The Norseman* 1978 (a); *The 5th Musketeer* 1979 (a); *Flesh and Bullets* 1985 (a).

Wilder, Billy • Director, screenwriter; also producer. • Born Samuel Wilder, Vienna, Austria, June 22, 1906. *Educ.* University of Vienna (law). Billy Wilder's work as a director in Hollywood runs an erratic, colorful course. Early in his directorial career, Wilder proved adept at turning out major films in established genres, including farce (*The Major and the Minor*, 1942), film noir (*Double Indemnity*, 1944) and the social problem film (*The Lost Weekend*, 1945). With experience, Wilder created a variation on the Lubitsch comedy of manners and seduction in films such as *Sabrina* (1954) and *Love in the Afternoon* (1957). And finally, beginning with the vastly underrated *A Foreign Affair* (1948), Wilder developed a strain of harsh black-comic expression in such films as *Ace in the Hole/The Big Carnival*, 1951) and *The Seven Year Itch* (1955), a strain which found its apotheosis in works that were critically despised on their initial release: *One, Two, Three* (1961) and the disastrous *Kiss Me, Stupid* (1964).

After leaving law school in his native Vienna and working as a tabloid journalist, Wilder drifted into screenwriting. From 1929 to 1933, he wrote screenplays for a number of important German films in which he began to develop the tightly woven, intricate narrative structures, marked by incredible reversals, paradoxes and inversions, that would characterize his best American work. Important in this regard is his work on two 1931 films. *Emil Und Die Detektive* utilized the streets of a large city as a psychological labyrinth, prefiguring the complex use of physical settings in *Foreign Affair* and *The Apartment* (1960). The script for Robert Siodmak's *Der Mann, Der Seinen Mörder Sucht* (which inspired two American films under the title *D.O.A.*) is successfully built around a seemingly impossible premise: a man solves his own murder. Wilder's American films often begin with characters in similar narrative cul-de-sacs. In *The Major and the Minor*, the heroine is forced to play a person half her own age; the musicians-on-the-run in *Some Like It Hot* (1959) are forced to live in drag; Sefton, the American prisoner-of-war at the center of *Stalag 17* (1953), is accused of being a collaborator.

In 1933, after co-directing a film in France, Wilder arrived in Hollywood, part of the large emigre influx of German and Austrian film talent. During the 1930s, Wilder roomed for a time with Peter Lorre and apprenticed under Ernst Lubitsch. In 1938 he and screenwriter Charles Brackett formed a writing tandem that quickly became one of Hollywood's hottest teams. Their writing credits included *Bluebeard's Eighth Wife* (1938), *Midnight*, *Ninotchka* (both 1939) and *Ball of Fire* (1941). Even after he began directing with *The Major and the Minor*, Wilder continued to write his own screenplays, mostly with Brackett producing, in a relationship that lasted until 1950. Films such as *Double Indemnity*, *The Lost Weekend*, and *Sunset Boulevard* (1950) won Wilder a reputation as a cynic, but also notable was the bleak *A Foreign Affair*, a film that Wilder, a colonel during WWII, chose to direct in recently captured Berlin; it brilliantly captured the bewildering moral climate of the late 1940s.

Sunset Boulevard marked the end of Wilder's years with Brackett, and for the next seven years he wrote scripts with several co-authors. Interestingly, *Sunset Boulevard* also marks the apogee of Wilder's career as a visual stylist. None of his later films match his early work for its chiaroscuro lighting or self-conscious use of camera angles. Beginning with *The Seven Year Itch*, however, Wilder utilized highly symbolic art direction and set design as a way of exaggerating his characters' psychological predicaments; in particular, *The Apartment* and *Irma La Douce* (1963) represent one of the most significant director-designer collaborations in the history of the American cinema.

In 1957, Wilder began writing his with I.A.L. Diamond, who shared many of Wilder's thematic interests, such as the use of interlocking acts of deception practiced by large ensembles of characters (*The Apartment*, *The Fortune Cookie* 1966) and the tangled connections of sex and economics (*The Apartment*, *Irma La Douce*, *Kiss Me, Stupid*).

Wilder's career reached its zenith in the early 1960s. Writing, directing and producing his own films for release by the Mirisch Corporation through United Artists, he reaped a healthy share of the profits of such blockbusters as *Some Like It Hot* and *Irma la Douce;* he also enjoyed virtually total control over his films. A series of setbacks began with *Kiss Me, Stupid*, a film which was castigated by critics and moral guardians such as Cardinal Spellman for its dry, unflinching sexual humor. *The Private Life of Sherlock Holmes* (1970) was drastically cut and failed to earn back its cost. The 1970s saw Wilder struggling with a remake of *The Front Page* (1974) and the misbegotten *Fedora* (1978). Wilder's most recent film, with his frequent stars Jack Lemmon and Walter Matthau, was the farcical *Buddy Buddy* (1981).

If the later years of his career were less than successful, the consolations have been many; seven Academy Awards for writing, directing and producing; the Cannes festival Palme d'Or for *The Lost Weekend;* the Irving Thalberg Award; the Life Achievement Awards of the Director's Guild and the American Film Institute. Billy Wilder has brought to the screen an outsider's sharp eye for American absurdity and cruelty, and a master scenarist's skill at rendering those absurdities within a dozen variations, some bitter, some sweet, but all with intelligence, clarity and even affection. KJH

• *Menschen am Sonntag/People on Sunday* 1929 (sc); *Emil Und Die Detektive/Emil and the Detective* 1931 (sc); *Der Mann, der Seinen Mörder Sucht* 1931 (sc); *Adorable* 1933 (story); *Mauvaise Graine* 1934 (d,sc); *Music in the Air* 1934 (sc); *One Exciting Adventure* 1934 (story); *The Lottery Lover* 1935 (sc); *Champagne Waltz* 1937 (story); *Bluebeard's Eighth Wife* 1938 (sc); *That Certain Age* 1938 (sc); *Midnight* 1939 (sc); *Ninotchka* 1939 (sc) **(AANBSC)**; *What a Life* 1939 (sc); *Arise, My Love* 1940 (sc); *Rhythm on the River* 1940 (story); *Ball of Fire* 1941 (sc,from story "A to Z") **(AANBST)**; *Hold Back the Dawn* 1941 (sc) **(AANBSC)**; *The Major and the Minor* 1942 (d,sc); *Five Graves to Cairo* 1943 (d,sc); *Double Indemnity* 1944 (d,sc) **(AANBD,AANBSC)**; *The Lost Weekend* 1945 (d,sc) **(AABD,AABSC)**; *The Emperor Waltz* 1948 (d,sc,story); *A Foreign Affair* 1948 (d,sc) **(AANBSC)**; *A Song Is Born* 1948 (from story "From A to Z"); *Sunset Boulevard* 1950 (d,sc) **(AANBD,AABSC)**; *Ace in the Hole/The Big Carnival* 1951 (d,p,sc,story); *Stalag 17* 1953 (d,p,sc) **(AABD)**; *Sabrina* 1954 (d,p,sc) **(AANBD,AANBSC)**; *The Seven Year Itch* 1955 (d,sc); *Love in the Afternoon* 1957 (d,p,sc); *The Spirit of St. Louis* 1957 (d,sc); *Witness For the Prosecution* 1957 (d,sc) **(AANBD)**; *Some Like It Hot* 1959 (d,p,sc) **(AANBD,AANBSC)**; *The Apartment* 1960 (d,p,sc) **(AABP,AABD,AABSC)**; *One, Two, Three* 1961 (d,p,sc); *Irma la Douce* 1963 (d,p,sc); *Kiss Me, Stupid* 1964 (d,p,sc); *The Fortune Cookie* 1966 (d,p,sc) **(AANBSC)**; *The Private Life of Sherlock Holmes* 1970 (d,p,sc); *Avanti!* 1972 (d,p,sc); *The Front Page* 1974 (d,sc); *Fedora* 1978 (d,p,sc); *Portrait of a 60% Perfect Man* 1980 (a); *Buddy Buddy* 1981 (d,sc); *Directed By William Wyler* 1986 (a); *The Exiles* 1989 (a).

Wilder, Gene • Actor, director, screenwriter; also producer. • Born Jerry Silberman, Milwaukee, WI, June 11, 1935. *Educ.* University of Iowa; Bristol Old Vic; Actors Studio. Wilder was an established stage actor when his performance as the endearingly frantic Leo Bloom in *The Producers* (1967) kicked off a celebrated collaboration with Mel Brooks, culminating with the inspired lunacy of *Blazing Saddles* and *Young Frankenstein* (both 1974). Spurred by these triumphs, Wilder made his directorial debut with *The Adventures of Sherlock Holmes' Smarter Brother* (1975). His subsequent behind-the-camera efforts have, on the whole, been disappointing. As an actor, Wilder has teamed with comedian Richard Pryor in a series of commercially successful, if predictable, comic romps.

Wilder was married to the late comedienne Gilda Radner from 1984 until her premature death in 1989. • *Bonnie and Clyde* 1967 (a); *The Producers* 1967 (a) **(AANBSA)**; *Quackser Fortune Has a Cousin in the Bronx* 1970 (a); *Start the Revolution Without Me* 1970 (a); *Willy Wonka and the Chocolate Factory* 1971 (a); *Everything You Always Wanted To Know About Sex* (*but were afraid to ask)* 1972 (a); *Rhinoceros* 1972 (a); *Blazing Saddles* 1974 (a); *The Little Prince* 1974 (a); *Young Frankenstein* 1974 (a,sc) **(AANBSC)**; *The Adventure of Sher-*

lock Holmes' Smarter Brother 1975 (a,d,sc); *Silver Streak* 1976 (a); *The World's Greatest Lover* 1977 (a,d,p,sc,song); *The Frisco Kid* 1979 (a); *Stir Crazy* 1980 (a,song); *Sunday Lovers* 1980 (a,d,sc—American segment); *Hanky Panky* 1982 (a); *The Woman in Red* 1984 (a,d,sc); *Haunted Honeymoon* 1986 (a,d,p,sc); *Hello Actors Studio* 1987 (a); *See No Evil, Hear No Evil* 1989 (a,sc); *Funny About Love* 1990 (a).

Williams, Billy • Director of photography • Born Walthamstow, England, June 3, 1929. Cinematographer who established himself in the 1960s with his work on two Ken Russel films, *Billion Dollar Brain* (1967) and *Women in Love* (1969). Outstanding credits include *Sunday Bloody Sunday* (1971), *On Golden Pond* (1981) and *Ghandi* (1982), for which he won an Oscar. Son of British director of photography Billie Williams. • *Billion Dollar Brain* 1967 (ph; *The Magus* 1968 (ph); *Two Gentlemen Sharing* 1969 (ph); *Women in Love* 1969 (ph) **(AANBPH)**; *The Mind of Mr. Soames* 1970 (ph); *Sunday Bloody Sunday* 1971 (ph); *Tam Lin* 1971 (ph); *Pope Joan* 1972 (ph); *X Y & Zee* 1972 (ph); *The Exorcist* 1973 (ph—Iraq); *Kid Blue* 1973 (ph); *Night Watch* 1973 (ph); *The Wind and the Lion* 1975 (ph); *Voyage of the Damned* 1976 (ph); *Des Teufels Advokat* 1977 (ph); *Eagle's Wing* 1978 (ph); *The Silent Partner* 1978 (ph); *Boardwalk* 1979 (ph); *Going in Style* 1979 (ph); *Saturn 3* 1980 (ph); *On Golden Pond* 1981 (ph) **(AANBPH)**; *Gandhi* 1982 (ph) **(AABPH)**; *Monsignor* 1982 (ph); *The Survivors* 1983 (ph); *Dreamchild* 1985 (ph); *Eleni* 1985 (ph); *Ordeal By Innocence* 1985 (ph); *The Manhattan Project* 1986 (ph); *Suspect* 1987 (ph); *Just Ask For Diamond* 1988 (ph); *The Rainbow* 1989 (ph); *Stella* 1990 (ph).

Williams, Billy Dee • Actor • Born New York, NY, April 6, 1937. *Educ.* National Academy of Design School of Fine Arts, New York. Handsome, suave leading man who succeeded Sidney Poitier as (white) America's favorite black actor in the 1970s.

On stage from age seven, Williams made his screen debut in 1959 in *The Last Angry Man* and worked in theater through the 1960s. After gaining attention in the TV movie *Brian's Song* (1971), he soared to stardom in two overblown Diana Ross vehicles, *Lady Sings the Blues* (1972) and *Mahogany* (1975), and was superb as ragtime kingpin *Scott Joplin* (1977).

Since the 1980s Williams has contributed his poise and polish to a number of obscure works as well as to quality blockbusters like the later "Star Wars" installments, as Lando Calrissian, and *Batman* (1989), as a crusading district attorney. • *The Last Angry Man* 1959; *The Out-of-Towners* 1970; *The Final Comedown* 1971; *Lady Sings the Blues* 1972; *Hit* 1973; *The Take* 1974; *Mahogany* 1975; *The Bingo Long Traveling All-Stars and Motor Kings* 1976; *Blast* 1976; *Scott Joplin* 1977; *The Empire Strikes Back* 1980; *Nighthawks* 1981; *Marvin and Tige* 1983; *Return of the Jedi* 1983; *Fear City* 1985; *Number One With a Bullet* 1986; *Deadly Illusion* 1987; *The Imposter* 1988; *Batman* 1989.

Williams, Esther • Actress; also swimmer. • Born Los Angeles, CA, August 8, 1923. *Educ.* Los Angeles City College. Teenage swimming champion who made her film debut in a 1942 Andy Hardy short, *Andy Hardy's Double Life.* Two years later Williams starred in the first of a series of effervescent swimming musicals—a curious, if lucrative sub-genre, created especially for her—which continued to pull large, enthusiastic audiences into the early 1950s.

Williams's subsequent attempts at dramatic roles were less than inspiring and she wisely retired from the movies in the 1960s. Her third husband (from 1967) was actor Fernando Lamas. • *Andy Hardy's Double Life* 1942; *A Guy Named Joe* 1943; *Bathing Beauty* 1944; *Thrill of a Romance* 1945; *Easy to Wed* 1946; *The Hoodlum Saint* 1946; *Ziegfeld Follies* 1946; *Fiesta* 1947; *This Time For Keeps* 1947; *On an Island With You* 1948; *Neptune's Daughter* 1949; *Take Me Out to the Ball Game* 1949; *Duchess of Idaho* 1950; *Pagan Love Song* 1950; *Texas Carnival* 1951; *Million Dollar Mermaid* 1952; *Dangerous When Wet* 1953; *Easy to Love* 1953; *Jupiter's Darling* 1955; *The Unguarded Moment* 1956; *Raw Wind in Eden* 1958; *The Big Show* 1961.

Williams, Jobeth • Actress • Born Houston, TX, 1953. *Educ.* Brown University, Providence, RI (English). Stage actress who graduated from daytime soaps to the big screen with *Kramer Vs. Kramer* (1979). Dark-haired and attractive (but not flashy), Williams has an honest charm which, combined with her evident talent, has proved an effective combination; memorable in such films as *Poltergeist* (1982), *The Big Chill* (1983) and *Desert Bloom* (1986) and in the TV movie, *My Name Is Bill W.* (1989). Williams is married to TV director John Pasquin. • *Kramer vs. Kramer* 1979; *The Dogs of War* 1980; *Stir Crazy* 1980; *Endangered Species* 1982; *Poltergeist* 1982; *The Big Chill* 1983; *American Dreamer* 1984; *Teachers* 1984; *Desert Bloom* 1986; *Poltergeist II: The Other Side* 1986; *Memories of Me* 1988; *Welcome Home* 1989; *Switch* 1991.

Williams, John • *aka* Johnny Williams • Composer; also conductor. • Born Long Island, NY, February 8, 1932. *Educ.* UCLA; Juilliard (music). Perhaps the best-known composer working in contemporary American film, Williams entered the industry in the 1950s but only came to prominence in the mid-70s, scoring such blockbusters as *Jaws* (1975), *Star Wars* (1977) and *Raiders of the Lost Ark* (1981). Not noted for the subtlety of his scores, Williams has become synonymous with the big-budget spectacles which have dominated Hollywood's output in recent years (*E.T.* 1982, *Empire of the Sun* 1987). He has scored most of Steven Spielberg's films and, since 1980, has been the conductor of the Boston Pops Orchestra. • *Daddy-'O'* 1959 (m); *Gidget* 1959 (orch); *Because They're Young* 1960 (m); *I Passed For White* 1960 (m); *Bachelor Flat* 1961 (m); *The Secret Ways* 1961 (m); *Diamond Head* 1962 (m); *Gidget Goes to Rome* 1963 (m); *Sergeant Ryker* 1963 (m); *John Goldfarb, Please Come Home* 1964 (m); *The Killers* 1964 (m); *None But the Brave* 1965 (m); *How to Steal a Million* 1966 (m); *Not With My Wife, You Don't* 1966 (m); *Penelope* 1966 (m); *The Plainsman* 1966 (m); *Fitzwilly* 1967 (m); *Valley of the Dolls* 1967 (m.dir) **(AANBM)**; *Daddy's Gone A-Hunting* 1969 (m,m.cond,song); *Goodbye, Mr. Chips* 1969 (m.sup,m.dir) **(AANBM)**; *The Reivers* 1969 (m) **(AANBM)**; *Storia di una Donna* 1970 (m); *The Cowboys* 1971 (m); *Fiddler on the Roof* 1971 (m.arr,m.cond) **(AABM)**; *Images* 1972 (m) **(AANBM)**; *Pete 'n' Tillie* 1972 (m); *The Poseidon Adventure* 1972 (m) **(AANBM)**; *Cinderella Liberty* 1973 (m) **(AANBM,AANBS)**; *Conrack* 1973 (m); *The Long Goodbye* 1973 (m,m.cond,song); *The Man Who Loved Cat Dancing* 1973 (m); *The Paper Chase* 1973 (m); *Tom Sawyer* 1973 (m.sup) **(AANBSS)**; *Earthquake* 1974 (m); *The Sugarland Express* 1974 (m); *The Towering Inferno* 1974 (m) **(AANBM)**; *The Eiger Sanction* 1975 (m); *Jaws* 1975 (m) **(AABM)**; *Battle of Midway* 1976 (m); *Family Plot* 1976 (m); *The Missouri Breaks* 1976 (m); *Black Sunday* 1977 (m); *Close Encounters of the Third Kind* 1977 (m) **(AANBM)**; *Star Wars* 1977 (m) **(AABM)**; *The Deer Hunter* 1978 (main title theme perf); *The Fury* 1978 (m); *Jaws 2* 1978 (m); *The Stud* 1978 (song); *Superman* 1978 (m,song) **(AANBM)**; *1941* 1979 (m); *Dracula* 1979 (m,m.dir); *Airplane!* 1980 (m); *The Empire Strikes Back* 1980 (m) **(AANBM)**; *Superman II* 1980 (m); *Heartbeeps* 1981 (m); *Raiders of the Lost Ark* 1981 (m) **(AANBM)**; *E.T., the Extra-Terrestrial* 1982 (m) **(AABM)**; *Monsignor* 1982 (m); *Yes, Giorgio* 1982 (song) **(AANBS)**; *Beyond the Limit* 1983 (m); *The Big Chill* 1983 (m); *Jaws 3-D* 1983 (m); *Return of the Jedi* 1983 (m) **(AANBM)**; *Superman III* 1983 (m); *Best Defense* 1984 (songs); *Indiana Jones and the Temple of Doom* 1984 (m) **(AANBM)**; *The River* 1984 (m) **(AANBM)**; *Terror in the Aisles* 1984 (m); *Top Secret!* 1984 (m); *Emma's War* 1985 (m,m.perf); *Ferris Bueller's Day Off* 1986 (song); *SpaceCamp* 1986 (m); *Empire of the Sun* 1987 (m); *Jaws: The Revenge* 1987 (m); *Superman IV: The Quest For Peace* 1987 (m); *The Witches of*

Eastwick 1987 (m,m.cond); *The Accidental Tourist* 1988 (m) **(AANBM)**; *Always* 1989 (m); *Born on the Fourth of July* 1989 (m) **(AANBM)**; *Indiana Jones and the Last Crusade* 1989 (m) **(AANBM)**; *Home Alone* 1990 (m); *Presumed Innocent* 1990 (m); *Stanley and Iris* 1990 (m).

Williams, Robin • Actor, comedian • Born Chicago, IL, July 21, 1952. *Educ.* Claremont Men's College, CA (political science); College of Marin, Kentfield, CA (acting); Juilliard (drama). Hyperkinetic performer who made his name as part of the burgeoning West Coast comedy scene in the late 1970s. Williams first seized the nation's imagination as the ad-libbing extra-terrestrial, Mork from Ork, on the popular sitcom "Happy Days," which quickly led to the spin-off show, "Mork and Mindy" (1978-82). Although his launch as a film lead, in *Popeye* (1980), was a disappointment—audiences were thrown by director Robert Altman's purist vision—box-office success came two years later with George Roy Hill's *The World According to Garp* (1982).

Williams, who divides his time among live SRO comedy appearances, TV specials and film work, is renowned for his free-associative comic rants. Although some of his finest moments in *Good Morning, Vietnam* (1987) were the result of on-set improvisations, his unpredictability was at one point seen as a barrier to a dramatic screen career. He has, however, defied initial scepticism and proven himself capable of disciplined work in such films as *Dead Poets Society* (1989) and *Awakenings* (1990). • *Can I Do It... Till I Need Glasses?* 1979; *Popeye* 1980; *The World According to Garp* 1982; *The Survivors* 1983; *Moscow on the Hudson* 1984; *The Best of Times* 1986; *Club Paradise* 1986; *Seize the Day* 1986; *Dear America* 1987; *Good Morning, Vietnam* 1987 **(AANBA)**; *The Adventures of Baron Munchausen* 1988; *Dead Poets Society* 1989 **(AANBA)**; *Awakenings* 1990; *Cadillac Man* 1990; *The Fisher King* 1991.

Williams, Treat • Actor • Born Richard Williams, Rowayton, CT, 1952. *Educ.* Franklin and Marshall College, Lancaster PA. Muscular lead who has worked steadily in films since 1976. To date, Williams is best known for his boisterous caterwauling in the musical *Hair* (1979), as a New York police detective turned Justice Department informant in *Prince of the City* (1981) and as the seducer Arnold Friend in Joyce Chopra's *Smooth Talk* (1985). • *Deadly Hero* 1976; *The Eagle Has Landed* 1976; *The Ritz* 1976; *1941* 1979; *Hair* 1979; *Why Would I Lie?* 1980; *Prince of the City* 1981; *The Pursuit of D.B. Cooper* 1981; *Stangata napoletana—La trastola* 1983; *Flashpoint* 1984; *Once Upon a Time in America* 1984; *Smooth Talk* 1985; *The Men's Club* 1986; *La Notte degli Squali* 1987; *Dead Heat* 1988; *Burro* 1989; *Heart of Dixie* 1989; *Russicum* 1989; *Sweet Lies* 1989; *Beyond the Ocean* 1990.

Williamson, Nicol • Actor • Born Hamilton, Scotland, September 14, 1938. Forceful performer who made an auspicious feature debut reprising his performance as the promiscuous, boorish lawyer whose world collapses in John Osborne's stage hit *Inadmissable Evidence* (1968). Williamson starred in another stage-to-screen translation, Tony Richardson's *Hamlet* in 1970.

Primarily a stage actor, Williamson's screen output has been relatively spare, though he's turned in several outstanding performances: he played an angry young businessman in *The Reckoning* (1969), a cocaine-sniffing Sherlock Holmes in *The Seven Per-Cent Solution* (1976) and a scatterbrained Merlin in John Boorman's *Excalibur* (1981). • *The Bofors Gun* 1968; *Inadmissible Evidence* 1968; *Laughter in the Dark* 1969; *The Reckoning* 1969; *Hamlet* 1970; *The Jerusalem File* 1971; *Le Moine* 1973; *The Wilby Conspiracy* 1975; *Robin and Marian* 1976; *The Seven Per-Cent Solution* 1976; *The Goodbye Girl* 1977; *The Cheap Detective* 1978; *The Human Factor* 1979; *Excalibur* 1981; *I'm Dancing As Fast As I Can* 1981; *Venom* 1981; *Return to Oz* 1985; *Black Widow* 1987; *William Peter Blatty's The Exorcist III* 1990.

Willis, Bruce • Actor; also singer. • Born West Germany, March 19, 1955. *Educ.* Montclair State College, NJ. Relaxed, raffish performer who shot to stardom as private investigator David Addison on TV's smash series "Moonlighting" (1985-89) and graduated to feature roles with a lead in Blake Edwards's *Blind Date* (1987).

Willis's brand of wise-guy machismo has made him immensely popular with commercial audiences, notably in his role as New York cop John McClane in *Die Hard* (1988) and its 1990 sequel. His restrained performance as a troubled Vietnam vet in Norman Jewison's *In Country* (1989) suggests a broader range, though the same could not be said for his portrayal of sleazy tabloid journalist Peter Fallow in *Bonfire of the Vanities* (1990). Willis married actress Demi Moore in 1987. • *Blind Date* 1987 (a); *Die Hard* 1988 (a); *Sunset* 1988 (a,co-exec.p); *In Country* 1989 (a); *Look Who's Talking* 1989 (a); *That's Adequate* 1989 (a); *Bonfire of the Vanities* 1990 (a); *Die Hard 2: Die Harder* 1990 (a); *Look Who's Talking Too* 1990 (a,song); *Hudson Hawk* 1991 (a,story); *Mortal Thoughts* 1991 (a).

Willis, Gordon • American director of photography • First came to prominence for his contribution to Francis Ford Coppola's *The Godfather* (1972) and *The Godfather Part II* (1974), casting both the Sicilian countryside and the streets of Little Italy in a rich, nostalgic glow.

Willis has subsequently become best known for his collaborations with Woody Allen, beginning in 1977 with *Annie Hall*. Highlights of the teaming include bleak, understated hues of *Interiors* (1978), the sumptuous, impressionistic colors of *A Midsummer Night's Sex Comedy* (1982), the melancholic grays of *Manhattan* (1979) and the striking black-and-white of *Stardust Memories* (1980).

Since ending his creative partenerhip with Allen, Willis has continued to produce exceptional work, as with Alan Pakula's *Presumed Innocent* and Coppola's *The Godfather Part III* (both 1990). • *The End of the Road* 1970 (ph); *The Landlord* 1970 (ph); *Loving* 1970 (ph); *The People Next Door* 1970 (ph); *Klute* 1971 (ph); *Little Murders* 1971 (ph); *Bad Company* 1972 (ph); *The Godfather* 1972 (ph); *Up the Sandbox* 1972 (ph); *The Paper Chase* 1973 (ph); *The Godfather, Part II* 1974 (ph); *The Parallax View* 1974 (ph); *The Drowning Pool* 1975 (ph); *All the President's Men* 1976 (ph); *9/30/55* 1977 (ph); *Annie Hall* 1977 (ph); *Comes a Horseman* 1978 (ph); *Interiors* 1978 (ph); *Manhattan* 1979 (ph); *Stardust Memories* 1980 (ph); *Windows* 1980 (d,ph); *Pennies From Heaven* 1981 (ph); *A Midsummer Night's Sex Comedy* 1982 (ph); *Zelig* 1983 (ph) **(AANBPH)**; *Broadway Danny Rose* 1984 (ph); *Perfect* 1985 (ph); *The Purple Rose of Cairo* 1985 (ph); *The Money Pit* 1986 (ph); *The Pick-Up Artist* 1987 (ph); *Bright Lights, Big City* 1988 (ph); *The Godfather Part III* 1990 (ph); *Presumed Innocent* 1990 (ph).

Wilson, Lambert • Actor • Born France. Lanky leading man who has emerged as one of France's more prominent exports of the 1980s, starring as the destructive Quentin in André Téchiné's psychodrama *Rendezvous*, as the cynical photographer in Vera Belmont's nostalgic *Rouge Baiser* (both 1985) and as the adulterous Caspasian Speckler in Peter Greenaway's *The Belly of an Architect* (1987). Son of actor Georges Wilson, in whose directorial debut, *La vouivre* (1988), Lambert starred. • *New Generation* 1978; *Chanel Solitaire* 1981; *Five Days One Summer* 1982; *La Femme Publique* 1984; *Sahara* 1984; *Le Sang des Autres/The Blood of Others* 1984; *Bleu Comme l'enfer* 1985; *L'Homme aux yeux d'argent* 1985; *Rendezvous* 1985; *Rouge Baiser/Red Kiss* 1985; *Corps et biens* 1986; *La Storia* 1986; *The Belly of an Architect* 1987; *Les Possédés/The Possessed* 1987; *Chouans!* 1988; *El Dorado* 1988; *La Vouivre* 1988; *Hiver 54, l'abbe Pierre* 1989; *Suivez cet avion* 1989.

Wilson, Michael • Screenwriter • Born McAlester, OK, July 1, 1914; died 1978. *Educ.* University of California. Talented writer whose career was interrupted by the HUAC hearings of 1951—the year he earned an Oscar for co-adapting *A Place in the Sun*. Wilson subsequently wrote fellow blacklistee Herbert Biberman's independently produced leftist classic *Salt of the Earth* (1954) and worked uncredited on such films as *Friendly Persuasion* (1956), *The Bridge on the River Kwai* (1957) and *Lawrence of Arabia* (1962). He publicly resurfaced in the mid-1960s, contributing to Franklin Schaffner's sci-fi classic *Planet of the Apes* (1968) and Richard Fleischer's much-maligned biopic, *Che!* (1969). • *The Men in Her Life* 1941 (sc); *Bar 20* 1943 (sc); *Border Patrol* 1943 (sc,story); *Colt Comrades* 1943 (sc); *Forty Thieves* 1944 (sc); *A Place in the Sun* 1951 (sc) **(AABSC)**; *Five Fingers* 1952 (sc) **(AANBSC)**; *Salt of the Earth* 1954 (sc,story); *Lawrence of Arabia* 1962 (uncred.sc); *The Sandpiper* 1965 (sc); *Planet of the Apes* 1968 (sc); *Che!* 1969 (sc).

Wimperis, Arthur • Screenwriter • Born London, December 3, 1874; died 1953. *Educ.* University College, London. Former graphic artist and librettist who co-scripted (mostly with Lajos Biro) several outstanding Alexander Korda productions of the 1930s, notably *The Private Life of Henry VIII* (1933) and *The Four Feathers* (1939). After sharing an Oscar for his work on *Mrs. Miniver* (1942), Wimperis worked chiefly in Hollywood, on films including *Random Harvest* (1942) and *Young Bess* (1953). • *Wife Savers* 1928 (from play *Louie the Fourteenth*); *Song of Soho* 1930 (sc); *That Night in London* 1932 (sc); *Counsel's Opinion* 1933 (sc); *The Private Life of Henry VIII* 1933 (sc,dial,story); *Brewster's Millions* 1935 (dial); *Sanders of the River* 1935 (sc); *The Scarlet Pimpernel* 1935 (sc,dial,cont); *Beloved Vagabond* 1936 (sc); *Dark Journey* 1937 (dial); *Four Dark Hours* 1937 (sc); *Knight Without Armour* 1937 (sc,dial); *The Return of the Scarlet Pimpernel* 1937 (sc); *Drums* 1938 (sc); *Prison Without Bars* 1938 (sc); *Clouds Over Europe* 1939 (story); *The Four Feathers* 1939 (sc); *Mrs. Miniver* 1942 (sc) **(AABSC)**; *Random Harvest* 1942 (sc) **(AANBSC)**; *If Winter Comes* 1947 (sc); *Julia Misbehaves* 1948 (sc); *The Red Danube* 1949 (sc); *Young Bess* 1953 (sc).

Winfield, Paul • Actor • Born Los Angeles, CA, May 22, 1940. *Educ.* University of Portland, OR; Stanford; Los Angeles City College; UCLA. Powerhouse supporting player and occasional lead. Winfield appeared on TV's "Julia" (1968-71), starring Diahann Carroll, and gained international recognition opposite Cicely Tyson in Martin Ritt's *Sounder* (1972).

Winfield consistently works in theater and TV, and two of his finest performances have come in the latter medium: as The Reverend Dr. Martin Luther King, Jr., in *King* (1978) and as the main character of *Go Tell It On the Mountain* (1984), from the semi-autobiographical book by James Baldwin. • *The Lost Man* 1969; *Brother John* 1970; *R.P.M.* 1970; *Sounder* 1972 **(AANBA)**; *Trouble Man* 1972; *Conrack* 1973; *Gordon's War* 1973; *Huckleberry Finn* 1974; *Hustle* 1975; *Damnation Alley* 1977; *The Greatest* 1977; *A Hero Ain't Nothin' But a Sandwich* 1977; *High Velocity* 1977; *Twilight's Last Gleaming* 1977; *Carbon Copy* 1981; *Mike's Murder* 1982; *On the Run* 1982; *Star Trek II: The Wrath of Khan* 1982; *White Dog* 1982; *Go Tell It on the Mountain* 1984; *The Terminator* 1984; *Blue City* 1986; *Big Shots* 1987; *Death Before Dishonor* 1987; *The Serpent and the Rainbow* 1988; *James Baldwin: The Price of the Ticket* 1989; *Presumed Innocent* 1990.

Winger, Debra • Actress • Born Cleveland, OH, May 17, 1955. *Educ.* California State University, Northridge (sociology). Winger spent two years in Israel as a teenager (including three months in the Israeli army) and decided to pursue acting full-time after recovering from a coma brought on by an accident at a California amusement park where she was performing as a troll. She made her TV debut playing Drusilla the Wonder Girl on "Wonder Woman" (1976-77) and her feature debut in *Slumber Party '57* (1977).

A consummate technician capable of projecting fiery intensity, Winger became both a critics' darling and a major box-office draw during the early 1980s. She turned in forceful, delicately shaded performances in *Urban Cowboy* (1980), *An Officer and a Gentleman* (1982) and *Terms of Endearment* (1983), the last two of which earned her Oscar nominations.

After this early, spectacular ascent, Winger's career began to falter. She exercises considerable care in her choice of roles, but recent outings in films by two of Europe's most celebrated directors—Costa-Gavras for *Betrayed* (1988) and Bertolucci for *The Sheltering Sky* (1990)—have yielded disappointing results.

Winger is separated from actor Timothy Hutton, with whom she has a son. • *Slumber Party '57* 1977; *Thank God It's Friday* 1978; *French Postcards* 1979; *Urban Cowboy* 1980; *Cannery Row* 1982; *Mike's Murder* 1982; *An Officer and a Gentleman* 1982 **(AANBA)**; *Terms of Endearment* 1983 **(AANBA)**; *Legal Eagles* 1986; *Black Widow* 1987; *Made in Heaven* 1987; *Betrayed* 1988; *Everybody Wins* 1990; *The Sheltering Sky* 1990.

Winkler, Irwin • Producer • Born New York, NY, May 28, 1931. *Educ.* NYU. In partnership with Robert I. Chartoff from the late 1960s, Winkler produced an impressive array of modern American gems, such as *They Shoot Horses, Don't They?* (1969), *Rocky* (1976) and *Raging Bull* (1980). Since *Revolution* (1985) he has worked mostly on his own, continuing to shepherd such noteworthy features as Bertrand Tavernier's *'Round Midnight* (1986) and Costa-Gavras's *Music Box* (1990). Winkler made his directorial debut in 1991 with the McCarthy-era drama *Guilty By Suspicion*, starring Robert DeNiro. • *Double Trouble* 1967 (p); *Point Blank* 1967 (p); *Blue* 1968 (p); *The Split* 1968 (p); *They Shoot Horses, Don't They?* 1969 (p); *Leo the Last* 1970 (p); *The Strawberry Statement* 1970 (p); *Believe in Me* 1971 (p); *The Gang That Couldn't Shoot Straight* 1971 (p); *The Mechanic* 1972 (p); *The New Centurions* 1972 (p); *Thumb Tripping* 1972 (p); *Up the Sandbox* 1972 (p); *Busting* 1973 (p); *The Gambler* 1974 (p); *Spys* 1974 (p); *Breakout* 1975 (p); *Peeper* 1975 (p); *Nickelodeon* 1976 (p); *Rocky* 1976 (p) **(AABP)**; *New York, New York* 1977 (p); *Valentino* 1977 (p); *Comes a Horseman* 1978 (exec.p); *Uncle Joe Shannon* 1978 (p); *Rocky II* 1979 (p); *Raging Bull* 1980 (p) **(AANBP)**; *True Confessions* 1981 (p); *Author! Author!* 1982 (p); *Rocky III* 1982 (p); *The Right Stuff* 1983 (p) **(AANBP)**; *Revolution* 1985 (p); *Rocky IV* 1985 (p); *Autour de Minuit/'Round Midnight* 1986 (p); *Betrayed* 1988 (p); *Music Box* 1990 (p); *Goodfellas* 1990 (p); *Rocky V* 1990 (p); *Guilty By Suspicion* 1991 (d,p,sc).

Winner, Michael • Director; also producer, screenwriter. • Born London, October 30, 1935. *Educ.* Cambridge (law, economics). A critic from age 16, Winner began making films for BBC-TV in the 1950s and had ventured into theatrical features by the end of the decade. He hit his peak in the mid-60s with a series of taut, cynical films starring Oliver Reed, including *The System/The Girl-Getters* (1964) and *The Jokers* (1967). Winner then moved to Hollywood and directed several ambitious, but mostly unexceptional films; he is probably best known for the first of his *Death Wish* (1974) installments. • *Play It Cool* 1962 (d); *West 11* 1963 (d); *The System/The Girl-Getters* 1964 (d); *I'll Never Forget What's 'is Name* 1967 (d,p); *The Jokers* 1967 (d); *Hannibal Brooks* 1968 (d,p,story); *The Games* 1970 (d); *Lawman* 1971 (d,p); *The Nightcomers* 1971 (d); *Chato's Land* 1972 (d,p); *The Mechanic* 1972 (d); *Scorpio* 1973 (d); *The Stone Killer* 1973 (d,p); *Death Wish* 1974 (d,p); *Won Ton Ton, the Dog Who Saved Hollywood* 1976 (d,p); *The Sentinel* 1977 (d,p,sc); *The Big Sleep* 1978 (d,p,sc); *Firepower* 1979 (d,p,story,ed); *Death Wish II* 1981 (d,ed); *The Wicked Lady* 1983 (d,sc,ed); *Scream For Help* 1984 (d,p); *Death Wish 3* 1985 (d,ed,p); *Appointment With Death* 1988 (d,p,sc,ed); *A Chorus of Disapproval* 1989 (d,p,sc); *Bullseye!* 1990 (d,p).

Winters, Shelley • Actress • Born Shirley Schrift, St. Louis, IL, August 18, 1922. *Educ.* Wayne State University, Detroit MI; Dramatic Workshop of the New School for Social Research, New York; Actors Studio. Indomitable, highly prolific lead and character player. Raised in Brooklyn, Winters made her Broadway debut in 1941 and entered films two years later, gaining attention as Ronald Colman's victimized mistress in *A Double Life* (1947). Not conventionally beautiful, she exuded a strong, earthy sensuality and played a number of flashy roles which capitalized on this trait. In 1951, Winters convinced George Stevens she could alter herself to play the factory worker who vies with upper-class Elizabeth Taylor for Montgomery Clift in *A Place in the Sun* (1951). The role won Winters her first Oscar nomination and acclaimed performances followed in *The Big Knife, Night of the Hunter* (having earlier made an indelible impression on Charles Laughton as his star pupil) and *I Am a Camera* (all 1955).

In the late 1950s, though only in her 30s, Winters studied under Lee Strasberg and made the transition to character roles, winning Oscars for brilliant performances in *The Diary of Anne Frank* (1959) and *A Patch of Blue* (1965) and making an indelible impression as the pathetically lovelorn Charlotte Haze in Stanley Kubrick's *Lolita* (1962).

A galvanic presence both on- and offscreen, Winters has maintained a prolific schedule into the 1990s, working in TV and occasionally on stage and turning in straight and camp performances in both obscure and memorable films. Among her cult classics are *What's the Matter With Helen?* (1971) and Roger Corman's *Bloody Mama* (1970). She has also become, through her work at the Actors Studio, one of the country's top acting instructors. Winters authored her first autobiography, *Shelley*, in 1980, and her second, *Shelley II*, in 1989—both recount her numerous assignations with a number of Hollywood leading men. She was married to Vittorio Gassman from 1952 to 1954 and Anthony Franciosa from 1957 to 1960. • *Knickerbocker Holiday* 1944 (a); *Sailor's Holiday* 1944 (a); *She's a Soldier Too* 1944 (a); *A Thousand and One Nights* 1945 (a); *Tonight and Every Night* 1945 (a); *A Double Life* 1947 (a); *The Gangster* 1947 (a); *Cry of the City* 1948 (a); *Larceny* 1948 (a); *The Great Gatsby* 1949 (a); *Johnny Stool Pigeon* 1949 (a); *Take One False Step* 1949 (a); *Frenchie* 1950 (a); *South Sea Sinner* 1950 (a); *Winchester '73* 1950 (a); *Behave Yourself* 1951 (a); *He Ran All the Way* 1951 (a); *A Place in the Sun* 1951 (a) **(AANBA)**; *The Raging Tide* 1951 (a); *Meet Danny Wilson* 1952 (a); *My Man and I* 1952 (a); *Phone Call From a Stranger* 1952 (a); *Untamed Frontier* 1952 (a); *Executive Suite* 1954 (a); *Mambo* 1954 (a); *Playgirl* 1954 (a); *Saskatchewan* 1954 (a); *Tennessee Champ* 1954 (a); *The Big Knife* 1955 (a); *I Am a Camera* 1955 (a); *I Died a Thousand Times* 1955 (a); *The Night of the Hunter* 1955 (a); *The Treasure of Pancho Villa* 1955 (a); *The Diary of Anne Frank* 1959 (a) **(AABSA)**; *Odds Against Tomorrow* 1959 (a); *Let No Man Write My Epitaph* 1960 (a); *The Young Savages* 1961 (a); *The Chapman Report* 1962 (a); *Lolita* 1962 (a); *The Balcony* 1963 (a); *Wives and Lovers* 1963 (a); *A House Is Not a Home* 1964 (a); *The Three Sisters* 1964 (a); *The Greatest Story Ever Told* 1965 (a); *A Patch of Blue* 1965 (a) **(AABSA)**; *Alfie* 1966 (a); *Enter Laughing* 1966 (a); *Harper* 1966 (a); *Buona Sera, Mrs. Campbell* 1968 (a); *The Scalphunters* 1968 (a); *Wild in the Streets* 1968 (a); *The Mad Room* 1969 (a); *Bloody Mama* 1970 (a); *Flap* 1970 (a); *How Do I Love Thee?* 1970 (a); *Something to Hide* 1971 (a); *What's The Matter With Helen?* 1971 (a); *Who Slew Auntie Roo?* 1971 (a); *The Poseidon Adventure* 1972 (a) **(AANBSA)**; *Blume in Love* 1973 (a); *Cleopatra Jones* 1973 (a); *Diamonds* 1975 (a); *Poor Pretty Eddie* 1975 (a); *That Lucky Touch* 1975 (a); *Journey Into Fear* 1976 (a); *Le Locataire* 1976 (a); *Next Stop, Greenwich Village* 1976 (a); *Un Borghese Piccolo Piccolo* 1977 (a); *Pete's Dragon* 1977 (a); *Tentacoli* 1977 (a); *King of the Gypsies* 1978 (a); *City on Fire* 1979 (a); *The Magician of Lublin* 1979 (a); *The Visitor* 1979 (a); *Looping* 1981 (a); *My Mother, My Daughter* 1981 (a); *S.O.B.* 1981 (a); *Fanny Hill* 1983 (a); *Over the Brooklyn Bridge* 1983 (a); *Very Close Quarters* 1983 (a); *Deja Vu* 1984 (a); *Ellie* 1984 (a); *Witchfire* 1984 (a,assoc.p); *George Stevens: A Filmmaker's Journey* 1985 (a); *The Delta Force* 1986 (a); *Hello Actors Studio* 1987 (a); *Purple People Eater* 1988 (a); *Rudolph & Frosty's Christmas in July* 1988 (a); *An Unremarkable Life* 1989 (a); *Superstar: The Life and Times of Andy Warhol* 1990 (a); *Touch of a Stranger* 1990 (a); *Stepping Out* 1991 (a).

Wise, Robert • Director, producer • Born Winchester, IN, September 10, 1914. *Educ.* Franklin College, IN. Veteran Hollywood craftsman whose prolific body of work contains a number of startlingly original gems.

Wise made cinematic history at RKO before ever having directed a film, as editor of Orson Welles's *Citizen Kane* (1941) and *The Magnificent Ambersons* (1942). Two years later he made an auspicious behind-the-camera debut under the aegis of producer Val Lewton, with the stylish, atmospheric horror film, *The Curse of the Cat People* (1944).

Wise's last film at RKO, the landmark boxing feature *The Set-Up* (1949), established him as a leading Hollywood talent. He went on to direct consistently through the mid-1960s for various studios, notably with the sci-fi favorite *The Day the Earth Stood Still* (1951), the classic submarine drama *Run Silent, Run Deep* (1958), the Shakespearean musical update *West Side Story* (1961) and the eternally popular Julie Andrews vehicle, *The Sound of Music* (1965).

Since the 1970s Wise has directed only a handful of films, mostly big-budget spectacles that have fallen short of his earlier achievements. He was married to actress Patricia Doyle from 1942 until her death in 1975. • *Bachelor Mother* 1939 (ed); *Fifth Avenue Girl* 1939 (ed); *The Hunchback of Notre Dame* 1939 (ed); *Dance, Girl, Dance* 1940 (ed); *My Favorite Wife* 1940 (ed); *Citizen Kane* 1941 (ed) **(AANBED)**; *The Devil and Daniel Webster* 1941 (ed); *The Magnificent Ambersons* 1942 (ed); *Seven Days Leave* 1942 (ed); *Bombardier* 1943 (ed); *The Fallen Sparrow* 1943 (ed); *The Iron Major* 1943 (ed); *The Curse of the Cat People* 1944 (d); *Mademoiselle Fifi* 1944 (d); *The Body Snatcher* 1945 (d); *A Game of Death* 1945 (d); *Criminal Court* 1946 (d); *Born to Kill* 1947 (d); *Blood on the Moon* 1948 (d); *Mystery in Mexico* 1948 (d); *The Set-Up* 1949 (d); *Three Secrets* 1950 (d); *Two Flags West* 1950 (d); *The Day the Earth Stood Still* 1951 (d); *The House on Telegraph Hill* 1951 (d); *The Captive City* 1952 (d); *Something For the Birds* 1952 (d); *The Desert Rats* 1953 (d); *Destination Gobi* 1953 (d); *So Big* 1953 (d); *Executive Suite* 1954 (d); *Tribute to a Bad Man* 1955 (d); *Helen of Troy* 1956 (d); *Somebody Up There Likes Me* 1956 (d); *This Could Be the Night* 1957 (d); *Until They Sail* 1957 (d); *I Want to Live!* 1958 (d); *Run Silent, Run Deep* 1958 (d); *Odds Against Tomorrow* 1959 (d,p); *West Side Story* 1961 (d,p) **(AABD,AABP)**; *Two For the Seesaw* 1962 (d); *The Haunting* 1963 (d,p); *The Sound of Music* 1965 (d,p) **(AABD,AABP)**; *The Sand Pebbles* 1966 (d,p) **(AANBP)**; *Star!* 1968 (d,p); *The Andromeda Strain* 1971 (d,p); *Two People* 1973 (d,p); *The Hindenburg* 1975 (d,p) *Audrey Rose* 1977 (d); *Star Trek: The Motion Picture* 1979 (d); *50 Years of Action!* 1986 (a); *The Fantasy Film World of George Pal* 1986 (a); *Rooftops* 1989 (d).

Wiseman, Frederick • Filmmaker; also producer. • Born Boston, MA, January 1, 1930. *Educ.* Williams College, Williamstown MA; Yale Law School; University of Paris (law). A former lawyer, Wiseman has captured American institutional life more fully than any other documentarist. Of all the filmmakers who emerged in the heydey of direct cinema in the 1960s, Wiseman remains the most consistently active.

Since 1968 Wiseman has produced over 20 films, each of which (with the exception of his first documentary, *Titicut Follies*) has been broadcast nationally on PBS. From 1971 to 1981, Wiseman had two successive five-year contracts to make one film a year, with no constraints as to subject or running time, and to premiere them on New York's PBS station, WNET. Since the expiration of the second contract, Wiseman has financed his work through money from his MacArthur Foundation Grant and fees from the rentals of his films through his own distribution company, Zipporah Films, based in Cambridge, MA.

Wiseman began his career by producing a fiction feature about Harlem teenagers, *The Cool World* (1963), adapted from the novel by Warren Miller and directed by New York filmmaker Shirley Clarke. Four years later, he inaugrated his "institutional series" of documentaries with *Titicut Follies* (1967), about life in a prison for the criminally insane in Bridgewater, MA. The film quickly became mired in lengthy litigation with state authorities, and the ensuing controversy established Wiseman's somewhat inaccurate reputation as an uncompromising muckraker.

Wiseman's other early films did seem to fulfill this promise, tending to work as exposés of public, tax-supported intitutions. *High School* (1969), *Law and Order* (1969), *Hospital* (1970), *Juvenile Court* (1973) and *Welfare* (1975) show the institutions of public health, education and welfare, the police force and the legal system, collapsing under their own bureaucratic weight and dehumanizing their clients.

With time, however, Wiseman's films have become less didactic and more complex. Motivated early in his career by reformist optimism, Wiseman has grown less sure of film's ability to stimulate social change. Beginning with *Primate* (1974), Wiseman began to express more sweeping thematic concerns about both American culture and the film experience itself. His handling of • point-of-view and montage, and his ability to discover symbolic • potential in everyday events, marks *Primate* as a maturation of Wiseman's style.

His more recent films tend to expand the idea of institution from a limited geographical space to the physically unbounded operations of ideology. *Model* (1980) and *The Store* (1983) take as their subjects advertising and consumerism, continuing the filmmaker's exploration of the nature of visual imagery, while *Canal Zone* and *Sinai Field Mission* (both 1977) indirectly examine American society by depicting the presence of US citizens in foreign settings: Panama and the Middle East, respectively.

Wiseman's films are not structured chronologically, as is usually the case with both direct cinema and cinéma vérité. They are structured thematically, with sequences connected by comparison, contrast, parallelism, inversion, irony or other rhetorical devices, creating what critic Bill Nichols has called a "mosaic" structure. Narration—whether by someone speaking to the camera or in voice-over—is never provided. Viewers are forced to participate in the films, since they must actively contemplate the subtle relationships between sequences. Wiseman edits his own films, devoting a considerable amount of time to the task. For each film, he spends from four to six weeks on location shooting, but much longer in the editing room (*High School* took a relatively short four months, *Primate* fourteen).

Wiseman has also ventured into fiction filmmaking, writing an early script for *The Stunt Man* (directed by Richard Rush in 1979), which he claims bears no relation to the final film, and writing and directing *Seraphita's Diary* (1982), an experimental feature that flopped commercially. BKG • *The Cool World* 1963 (p); *Titicut Follies* 1967 (d,p); *High School* 1969 (d,ed,p); *Law and Order* 1969 (d,ed,p); *Basic Training* 1971 (d,ed,p); *Hospital* 1971 (d,ed,p); *Essene* 1972 (d,ed,p); *Juvenile Court* 1973 (d,ed,p); *Primate* 1974 (d,ed,p); *Welfare* 1975 (d,p,sc,ed); *Meat* 1976 (d); *Canal Zone* 1977 (d,p,sc); *Sinai Field Mission* 1977 (d); *Manoeuvre* 1979 (d,ed,p); *Model* 1980 (d,p,sc,ed,sound recording mixer); *Seraphita's Diary* 1982 (d,sc); *The Store* 1983 (d,ed,p); *Racetrack* 1985 (d,p,sc,ed,sound); *Adjustment and Work* 1987 (d,ed,sound,p); *Blind* 1987 (d,p,sound,ed); *Deaf* 1987 (d,ed,sound,p); *Missile* 1987 (d,sc,ed,sound); *Multi-Handicapped* 1987 (d,ed,sound,p); *Near Death* 1989 (d,ed,sound,p).

Wollen, Peter • Theorist, director; also screenwriter, producer. • Key British film theorist who first gained attention with the publication of the relatively accessible, still-relevant and still-selling book of structuralist theory, *Signs and Meaning in the Cinema* (1969; revised 1972).

Wollen began his career in film production as co-writer of Michelangelo Antonioni's *The Passenger* (1975) and then co-directed a series of experimental features, produced under the aegis of the British Film Institute, with wife and fellow theorist Laura Mulvey (the two are now separated). Wollen made his solo directing debut with the cerebral science fiction feature, *Friendship's Death* (1987), about a female alien (Tilda Swinton) who crash-lands in strife-torn Jordan during "Black September" and strikes up a relationship with a male journalist (Bill Paterson). • *The Passenger* 1975 (sc); *Riddles of the Sphinx* 1976 (d,p,sc); *Amy!* 1980 (a,d,sc); *Crystal Gazing* 1982 (d,sc); *The Man Who Envied Women* 1985 (from writings); *Friendship's Death* 1987 (d,sc,from story).

Wolsky, Albert • Costume designer • Born Paris, November 24, 1930. Began his career working on New York stage productions and entered film in 1968, designing the costumes for *The Heart Is a Lonely Hunter* (1968). Wolsky has worked often with Paul Mazursky and won an Oscar for *All That Jazz* (1979), the second of his three collaborations with Bob Fosse. • *The Heart Is a Lonely Hunter* 1968 (cost); *Lovers and Other Strangers* 1970 (cost); *Born to Win* 1971 (cost); *Little Murders* 1971 (cost); *Harry and Tonto* 1974 (cost); *Lenny* 1974 (cost); *Next Stop, Greenwich Village* 1976 (cost); *Fingers* 1977 (cost); *Thieves* 1977 (cost,cost); *The Turning Point* 1977 (cost); *Grease* 1978 (cost); *Moment By Moment* 1978 (cost); *An Unmarried Woman* 1978 (cost,cost); *All That Jazz* 1979 (cost) **(AABCD)**; *Manhattan* 1979 (cost); *Meteor* 1979 (cost); *The Jazz Singer* 1980 (cost); *Willie & Phil* 1980 (cost); *All Night Long* 1981 (cost—Barbra Streisand); *Paternity* 1981 (cost); *Sophie's Choice* 1982 (cost) **(AANBCD)**; *Still of the Night* 1982 (cost); *Tempest* 1982 (cost); *Star 80* 1983 (cost); *To Be or Not to Be* 1983 (cost); *Moscow on the Hudson* 1984 (cost); *The Falcon and the Snowman* 1985 (cost); *The Journey of Natty Gann* 1985 (cost) **(AANBCD)**; *Crimes of the Heart* 1986 (cost); *Down and Out in Beverly Hills* 1986 (cost); *Legal Eagles* 1986 (cost); *Nadine* 1987 (cost); *Moon Over Parador* 1988 (cost); *Chances Are* 1989 (cost); *Cookie* 1989 (cost); *Enemies, A Love Story* 1989 (cost); *She-Devil* 1989 (cost); *Funny About Love* 1990 (cost); *Scenes From a Mall* 1991 (cost).

Wood, Natalie • Actress • Born Natasha Gurdin, San Francisco, CA, July 20, 1938; died November 29, 1981, off Santa Catalina Island, CA. Heart-tugging child actress in films such as *Tomorrow Is Forever* (1946), *Miracle on 34th Street* and *The Ghost and Mrs. Muir* (both 1947) who made an effective transition to teenage roles in the mid-1950s. Although somewhat limited in range, Wood gave sympathetic performances as neurotic young women in *Rebel Without a Cause* (1955), *Marjorie Morningstar* (1958) and *Splendor in the Grass* (1961) and starred (her singing voice was dubbed) in the musical films *West Side Story* (1961) and *Gypsy* (1962).

Wood played a succession of contemporary, modish heroines in the 60s (*Love with the Proper Stranger* 1963, *Sex and the Single Girl* 1964, *Bob & Carol & Ted & Alice* 1969), but made only intermittent appearances in the 70s; she played herself in 1980's *Willie and Phil* but was drowned in a mysterious incident on her own yacht toward the end of the filming of *Brainstorm* (released 1983). Wood was the daughter of architect and set designer Nicholas Gurdin and ballet dancer Maria Gurdin and the sister of actress Lana Wood. She was married to actor Robert Wagner (from 1957 to 1963), British producer Richard Gregson (from 1969) and to Wagner for the second time from 1972. During their second marriage, Wagner adopted Wood's daughter by Gregson, actress Natasha Wagner. • *The Bride Wore*

Boots 1946; *Tomorrow Is Forever* 1946; *Driftwood* 1947; *The Ghost and Mrs. Muir* 1947; *Miracle on 34th Street* 1947; *Chicken Every Sunday* 1948; *Scudda-Hoo! Scudda-Hay!* 1948; *Father Was a Fullback* 1949; *The Green Promise* 1949; *The Jackpot* 1950; *Never a Dull Moment* 1950; *No Sad Songs For Me* 1950; *Our Very Own* 1950; *The Blue Veil* 1951; *Dear Brat* 1951; *Just For You* 1952; *The Rose Bowl Story* 1952; *The Star* 1952; *The Silver Chalice* 1954; *One Desire* 1955; *Rebel Without a Cause* 1955 **(AANBSA)**; *The Burning Hills* 1956; *A Cry in the Night* 1956; *The Girl He Left Behind* 1956; *The Searchers* 1956; *Bombers B-52* 1957; *Kings Go Forth* 1958; *Marjorie Morningstar* 1958; *Cash McCall* 1959; *All the Fine Young Cannibals* 1960; *Splendor in the Grass* 1961 **(AANBA)**; *West Side Story* 1961; *Gypsy* 1962; *Love With the Proper Stranger* 1963 **(AANBA)**; *Sex and the Single Girl* 1964; *The Great Race* 1965; *Inside Daisy Clover* 1965; *Penelope* 1966; *This Property Is Condemned* 1966; *Bob & Carol & Ted & Alice* 1969; *Peeper* 1975; *The Last Married Couple in America* 1979; *Meteor* 1979; *Willie & Phil* 1980; *Brainstorm* 1983.

Wood, Sam • *aka* Chad Applegate • Director; also producer. • Born Samuel Grosvenor Wood, Philedalphia, PA, July 18, 1883; died 1949. Began his career as an actor, moved behind the camera as assistant to C.B. DeMille in 1915 and made his directorial debut in 1920 with *Double Speed*. Wood displayed a flair for complementing the talents of whatever stars he was handed, turning out a number of Gloria Swanson vehicles at Paramount in the early 1920s (*Bluebeard's Eighth Wife*, 1923 etc.), and finding his stride at MGM in the 30s and 40s. His output includes two Marx Brothers films, the durable soap opera *Madame X* (1937), the poignant *Goodbye Mr. Chips* (1939) and the literary adaptations, *Our Town* (1940) and *For Whom the Bell Tolls* (1943).

A conservative in politics as well as in film practice, Wood testified before HUAC in 1947. Father of actress K.T. Stevens, who enjoyed short-lived leading lady status in the 1940s. • *A City Sparrow* 1920 (d); *The Dancin' Fool* 1920 (d); *Double Speed* 1920 (d); *Excuse My Dust* 1920 (d); *Her Beloved Villain* 1920 (d); *Her First Elopement* 1920 (d); *Sick Abed* 1920 (d); *What's Your Hurry?* 1920 (d); *Don't Tell Everything* 1921 (d); *The Great Moment* 1921 (d); *Peck's Bad Boy* 1921 (d,sc); *The Snob* 1921 (d); *Under the Lash* 1921 (d); *Beyond the Rocks* 1922 (d,p); *Her Gilded Cage* 1922 (d); *Her Husband's Trademark* 1922 (d); *The Impossible Mrs. Bellew* 1922 (d); *Bluebeard's Eighth Wife* 1923 (d); *His Children's Children* 1923 (d); *My American Wife* 1923 (d,p); *Prodigal Daughters* 1923 (d); *Bluff* 1924 (d); *The Female* 1924 (d); *The Mine With the Iron Door* 1924 (d); *The Next Corner* 1924 (d); *The Re-Creation of Brian Kent* 1925 (d); *Fascinating Youth* 1926 (d); *One Minute to Play* 1926 (d); *The Fair Co-ed* 1927 (d); *A Racing Romeo* 1927 (d); *Rookies* 1927 (d); *The Latest From Paris* 1928 (d); *Telling the World* 1928 (d,p); *It's a Great Life* 1929 (d); *So This Is College* 1929 (d,p); *The Girl Said No* 1930 (d); *Paid* 1930 (d,p); *Sins of the Children* 1930 (d); *They Learned About Women* 1930 (d); *Way For a Sailor* 1930 (d,p); *The Man in Possession* 1931 (d,p); *New Adventures of Get Rich Quick Wallingford* 1931 (d,p); *A Tailor Made Man* 1931 (d,p); *Wallingford* 1931 (d); *Huddle* 1932 (d,p); *Prosperity* 1932 (d,p); *The Barbarian* 1933 (d,p); *Christopher Bean* 1933 (d); *Hold Your Man* 1933 (d,p); *Hollywood Party* 1934 (d); *Stamboul Quest* 1934 (d); *Let 'Em Have It* 1935 (d); *A Night at the Opera* 1935 (d); *Whipsaw* 1935 (d); *The Unguarded Hour* 1936 (d); *A Day at the Races* 1937 (d,p); *Madame X* 1937 (d); *Navy, Blue and Gold* 1937 (d); *Lord Jeff* 1938 (d); *Stablemates* 1938 (d); *Goodbye, Mr. Chips* 1939 (d) **(AANBD)**; *Kitty Foyle* 1940 (d) **(AANBD)**; *Our Town* 1940 (d); *Raffles* 1940 (d); *Rangers of Fortune* 1940 (d); *The Devil and Miss Jones* 1941 (d); *King's Row* 1941 (d) **(AANBD)**; *The Pride of the Yankees* 1942 (d); *For Whom the Bell Tolls* 1943 (d,p); *Casanova Brown* 1944 (d); *Guest Wife* 1945 (d); *Saratoga Trunk* 1945 (d); *Heartbeat* 1946 (d); *Ivy* 1947 (d); *Command Decision* 1948 (d); *Ambush* 1949 (d); *The Stratton Story* 1949 (d).

Woodard, Alfre • Actress • Born Tulsa, OK, November 8, 1953. *Educ.* Boston University. Versatile black character actress who pushed the art of deadpan to new heights as the hotel manager in Robert Altman's droll satire, *Health* (1980); best known as Geechee in *Cross Creek* (1983) and hilarious as Popeye Jackson in *Miss Firecracker* (1989). Woodard works often in theater and TV. • *Remember My Name* 1978; *Health* 1980; *Cross Creek* 1983 **(AANBSA)**; *Go Tell It on the Mountain* 1984; *Extremities* 1986; *Scrooged* 1988; *Miss Firecracker* 1989.

Woods, James • Actor • Born Vernal, UT, April 18, 1947. *Educ.* MIT (political science). Lean, intense, stage-trained lead who made his screen debut in 1972 in Elia Kazan's *The Visitors* and attracted widespread attention as a volatile cop-killer in *The Onion Field* (1979).

Woods projects menace like few other contemporary actors and has been particularly effective playing heavies—a calculating gangster in Sergio Leone's *Once Upon a Time in America* (1984) or a Gordon Liddy-like psychopath in *Best Seller* (1987). A talented and intelligent performer, he demonstrated a wider range portraying a conniving journalist in *Salvador* (1986), the crusading cofounder of Alcoholics Anonymous in the TV movie *My Name is Bill W.* (1989) and an aging hippy lawyer in *True Believer* (1989). • *Hickey and Boggs* 1972 (a); *The Visitors* 1972 (a); *The Way We Were* 1973 (a); *The Gambler* 1974 (a); *Distance* 1975 (a); *Night Moves* 1975 (a); *Alex & the Gypsy* 1976 (a); *The Choirboys* 1977 (a); *The Black Marble* 1979 (a); *The Onion Field* 1979 (a); *Eyewitness* 1980 (a); *Fast Walking* 1982 (a); *Split Image* 1982 (a); *Against All Odds* 1983 (a); *Videodrome* 1983 (a); *Once Upon a Time in America* 1984 (a); *Joshua Then and Now* 1985 (a); *Stephen King's Cat's Eye* 1985 (a); *Salvador* 1986 (a) **(AANBA)**; *Best Seller* 1987 (a); *The Boost* 1988 (a); *Cop* 1988 (a,p); *Immediate Family* 1989 (a); *True Believer* 1989 (a); *The Hard Way* 1991 (a).

Woodward, Edward • Actor; also singer. • Born Croydon, England, June 1, 1930. *Educ.* RADA, London. Critically acclaimed British stage and TV performer, top-selling recording artist and occasional film actor; best known in the US for TV's "The Equalizer" (1986-89) and for his title role in Bruce Beresford's *Breaker Morant* (1979). • *Becket* 1964 (a); *The File of the Golden Goose* 1969 (a); *Sitting Target* 1972 (a); *Young Winston* 1972 (a); *The Wicker Man* 1973 (a); *Stand Up Virgin Soldiers* 1977 (a); *Breaker Morant* 1980 (a,song); *Comeback* 1982 (a); *Who Dares Wins* 1982 (a); *Champions* 1983 (a); *King David* 1985 (a); *Mister Johnson* 1991 (a).

Woodward, Joanne • Actress • Born Thomasville, GA, February 27, 1930. *Educ.* Louisiana State University, Baton Rouge; Neighborhood Playhouse, New York; Actors Studio; Sarah Lawrence College, Bronxville, NY. Talented, engaging performer from the New York stage who made her mark as the schizophrenic title character of *The Three Faces of Eve* (1957), in a role that earned her an Oscar for best actress.

Not conventionally beautiful, Woodward specialized in portraying frustrated, emotionally wrought characters over the next decade, giving compelling performances in *The Long Hot Summer* (1958), *The Fugitive Kind* (1960) and, in a difficult part originally planned for Monroe, *The Stripper* (1963). She received widespread acclaim as a spinster trying to change her introverted ways in *Rachel, Rachel* (1968), the first directorial outing for Paul Newman, her husband since 1958. Woodward has appeared in 11 films opposite Newman, including *Rally Round the Flag, Boys!* (1958), *From the Terrace* (1960), *Paris Blues* (1961), *The Drowning Pool* (1975) and, most recently, *Mr. and Mrs. Bridge* (1990). She was directed by him in *The Effect of Gamma Rays on Man-in-the-Moon Marigolds* (1972), *The Shadow Box* (1980, for TV), *Harry & Son* (1984) and *The Glass Menagerie* (1987). • *Count Three and Pray* 1955; *A Kiss Before Dying* 1956; *No Down Payment*

1957; *The Three Faces of Eve* 1957 **(AABA)**; *The Long, Hot Summer* 1958; *Rally Round the Flag, Boys!* 1958; *The Sound and the Fury* 1958; *From the Terrace* 1960; *The Fugitive Kind* 1960; *Paris Blues* 1961; *A New Kind of Love* 1963; *The Stripper* 1963; *Signpost to Murder* 1964; *A Big Hand For the Little Lady* 1966; *A Fine Madness* 1966; *Rachel, Rachel* 1968 **(AANBA)**; *Winning* 1969; *King: A Filmed Record... Montgomery to Memphis* 1970; *WUSA* 1970; *They Might Be Giants* 1971; *The Effect of Gamma Rays on Man-in-the-Moon Marigolds* 1972; *Summer Wishes, Winter Dreams* 1973 **(AANBA)**; *The Drowning Pool* 1975; *The End* 1978; *Harry & Son* 1984; *The Glass Menagerie* 1987; *Mr. & Mrs. Bridge* 1990.

Woolley, Stephen • Producer; also executive. • Born London, September 3, 1956. Prominent figure of the beleaguered British film industry. In 1981 Woolley and Nik Powell co-founded Palace Pictures, a successful distribution company which brought to England such films as *Diva* (1982) and *Blood Simple* (1984). He then moved into production with Powell and Chris Brown and has enjoyed critical and commercial success with features including Chris Bernard's *A Letter to Brezhnev* (1985) and Neil Jordan's *Mona Lisa* (1986). • *Chinese Boxes* 1984 (exec.p); *The Company of Wolves* 1985 (exec.p,p); *A Letter to Brezhnev* 1985 (p); *Absolute Beginners* 1986 (p); *Mona Lisa* 1986 (p); *The Courier* 1987 (p); *Siesta* 1987 (exec.p); *Dream Demon* 1988 (exec.p); *High Spirits* 1988 (p); *Shag* 1988 (p); *Lenny Live* 1989 (exec.p); *Scandal* 1989 (p); *The Big Man* 1990 (p); *Dancin' Thru the Dark* 1990 (co-exec.p); *Hardware* 1990 (exec.p); *The Miracle* 1991 (p); *The Pope Must Die* 1991 (p); *A Rage in Harlem* 1991 (p).

Woronov, Mary • American actress; also artist. • Born c. 1943. *Educ.* Cornell. Striking performer who has starred in a series of off-beat films, often directed by Paul Bartel.

Woronov began her career as an aspiring New York artist, hooked up with Andy Warhol's Factory and featured as a "superstar" in several of Warhol's 1960s films, notably *The Chelsea Girls* (1966). After winning acclaim on Broadway with *In the Boom Boom Room* (1974) she made the transition to slightly more mainstream films, via Roger Corman productions such as *Death Race 2000* (1975). Woronov was memorable in Bartel's *Eating Raoul* (1982) and *Scenes from the Class Struggle in Beverly Hills* (1988). She has recently resumed her art career, with exhibits in New York and London. • *Hedy* 1965; *The Chelsea Girls* 1966; *Kemek* 1970; *Sugar Cookies* 1973; *Seizure* 1974; *Cover Girl Models* 1975; *Death Race 2000* 1975; *Cannonball* 1976; *Death Threat* 1976; *Hollywood Boulevard* 1976; *Jackson County Jail* 1976; *Bad Georgia Road* 1977; *Mr. Billion* 1977; *The One and Only* 1978; *The Lady in Red* 1979; *Rock 'n' Roll High School* 1979; *Angel of H.E.A.T.* 1981; *Eating Raoul* 1982; *National Lampoon Goes to the Movies* 1982; *Get Crazy* 1983; *Hellhole* 1984; *Movie House Massacre* 1984; *Night of the Comet* 1984; *My Man Adam* 1985; *Nomads* 1985; *Chopping Mall* 1986; *TerrorVision* 1986; *Black Widow* 1987; *Mortuary Academy* 1988; *Scenes From the Class Struggle in Beverly Hills* 1988; *Let It Ride* 1989; *Warlock* 1989; *Dick Tracy* 1990; *Watchers II* 1990.

Wright, Amy • Actress • Born Chicago, IL. *Educ.* Beloit College, WI. Gap-toothed, off-beat stage actress who played juveniles in the 70s and graduated to droll, oddball parts during the next decade. Wright played the calm, collected groupie who slips into Woody Allen's bed in *Stardust Memories* (1980) and William Hurt's spinster sister in *The Accidental Tourist* (1988). She has a child by actor Rip Torn. • *Not a Pretty Picture* 1975; *The Deer Hunter* 1978; *Girlfriends* 1978; *The Amityville Horror* 1979; *Breaking Away* 1979; *Wise Blood* 1979; *Heartland* 1980; *Inside Moves* 1980; *Stardust Memories* 1980; *Off Beat* 1986; *The Accidental Tourist* 1988; *Crossing Delancey* 1988; *The Telephone* 1988; *Miss Firecracker* 1989; *Daddy's Dyin'... Who's Got the Will?* 1990; *Love Hurts* 1990.

Wright, Basil • Director, producer; also author. • Born London, June 12, 1907. *Educ.* Cambridge (classics, economics). Pioneering British documentarist who helped John Grierson forge the movement in the early 1930s, first at the Empire Marketing Board and then at its successor, the GPO film unit. In the mid-1930s Wright directed *Song of Ceylon* (1935) and *Nightmail* (1936, with words by W.H. Auden); the films combined lyricism (the influence of Robert Flaherty) and social realism (the influence of Grierson) and remain landmarks of the documentary genre.

Wright then turned his attention to producing (under his Realist Film Unit, founded 1938) and writing, but returned to directing in the late 1940s, again blending poetic and realist strains in films such as *Waters of Time* (1951), on the River Thames, and *The Immortal Land* (1958), about Greece.

A noted film critic and noted lecturer, Wright has authored two books: *The Use of Film* (1948) and *The Long View* (1974), a history of the cinema. • *Conquest* 1930 (d); *Country Comes to Town (short)* 1931 (d); *The Country Comes to Town* 1931 (d); *Industrial Britain (short)* 1931 (ph); *Lumber* 1931 (d); *O'er Hill and Dale* 1932 (d); *Cargo From Jamaica* 1933 (d); *Liner Cruising South* 1933 (d); *Windmill in Barbados* 1933 (d); *Song of Ceylon* 1935 (d); *Children at School* 1936 (d); *Nightmail* 1936 (d); *The Face of Scotland* 1938 (d); *Waters of Time* 1951 (d); *The Stained Glass at Fairford (short)* 1956 (d); *The Immortal Land* 1958 (d).

Wright, Teresa • Actress • Born Muriel Teresa Wright, New York, NY, October 27, 1918. Quiet, sweetly compelling stage actress who appeared in a number of first-rate movies of the 1940s and 50s, notably *The Little Foxes* (1941, her debut), *Mrs. Miniver* (1942), which earned her a best supporting actress Oscar, *Shadow of a Doubt* (1943), *The Best Years of Our Lives* (1946) and *The Men* (1950), opposite a debuting Marlon Brando.

Wright retired from the screen at the end of the decade but returned in 1969 to play occasional character parts. She resumed her stage career in the early 1960s and has made sporadic TV appearances. Married to screenwriter Niven Busch from 1942 to 1952 and subsequently married to, divorced from and remarried to playwright Robert Anderson. • *The Little Foxes* 1941 **(AANBSA)**; *Mrs. Miniver* 1942 **(AABSA)**; *The Pride of the Yankees* 1942 **(AANBA)**; *Shadow of a Doubt* 1943; *Casanova Brown* 1944; *The Best Years of Our Lives* 1946; *The Imperfect Lady* 1947; *Pursued* 1947; *The Trouble With Women* 1947; *Enchantment* 1948; *The Capture* 1950; *The Men* 1950; *California Conquest* 1952; *Something to Live For* 1952; *The Steel Trap* 1952; *The Actress* 1953; *Count the Hours* 1953; *Track of the Cat* 1954; *The Search For Bridey Murphy* 1956; *Escapade in Japan* 1957; *The Restless Years* 1958; *Hail, Hero!* 1969; *The Happy Ending* 1969; *Roseland* 1977; *Somewhere in Time* 1980; *The Good Mother* 1988.

Wu Tianming • Producer, executive; also director. • Born Shaanxi Province, China, October 1939. *Educ.* Beijing Film Academy (directing). Central figure of China's "Fifth Generation" filmmakers who, after being named head of Xi'an Studios in 1984, has backed two of the group's most prominent and impressive works; Zhang Yimou's *Red Sorghum* (1987) and Chen Kaige's *King of the Children* (1988). Wu has himself directed several films, notably *The Old Well* (1987), which won the grand prize at the 2nd Tokyo International Film Festival. • *Hei Pao Shi Jian/The Black Cannon Incident* 1985 (exec.p); *Rensheng/Life* 1985 (d); *Daomi Zei/Horse Thief* 1986 (exec.p); *Hong Gaoliang/Red Sorghum* 1987 (exec.p); *Lao Jing/The Old Well* 1987 (d); *King of the Children* 1988 (exec.p).

Wurtzel, Stuart • American production designer • *Educ.* Carnegie-Mellon University, Pittsburgh PA (scenic design). Wurtzel began his career designing for the stage, spending four years with San Francisco's American Conservatory Theater before commencing film work in the mid-1970s. His designs have ranged from Brooklyn's Jewish neighborhoods of the 40s (*Brighton Beach Memoirs* 1986) to Manhattan in the late 70s (*Times Square* 1980) to revolutionary Mexico (*Old Gringo* 1989). He is married to another leading production designer, Patrizia von Brandenstein. • *The Next Man* 1976 (art d); *Between the Lines* 1977 (pd); *Hair* 1979 (pd); *Night of the Juggler* 1980 (pd); *Simon* 1980 (pd); *Times Square* 1980 (pd); *The Chosen* 1981 (pd); *Tattoo* 1981 (pd); *The Ballad of Gregorio Cortez* 1983 (pd); *The Purple Rose of Cairo* 1985 (pd); *Brighton Beach Memoirs* 1986 (pd); *Hannah and Her Sisters* 1986 (pd) **(AANBAD)**; *Suspect* 1987 (pd); *The House on Carroll Street* 1988 (pd); *An Innocent Man* 1989 (pd); *Old Gringo* 1989 (pd); *Mermaids* 1990 (pd); *Three Men and a Little Lady* 1990 (pd).

Wyler, William • Director; also producer. • Born Mulhausen, Germany, July 1, 1902; died 1981. *Educ.* Paris Conservatoire (violin). Few film directors have demonstrated the depth, range, longevity, and sensitivity that William Wyler gave to the American screen. Yet like many of the early Hollywood destiny shapers, Wyler possessed neither a background in the arts nor even an all-American upbringing. Born in Alsace-Lorraine of German-Swiss-Jewish parentage, he was schooled in Switzerland and prepared for a career as a haberdasher in Paris. During a visit to his parents' home in 1920 he met Carl Laemmle, his mother's cousin from America and president of Universal Studios. Laemmle, a former clothing merchant himself, had no problem coaxing young Willie into working for him in America.

Wyler spent the next year in the publicity department of Universal's New York offices. He was then transferred to Hollywood and accepted several menial studio jobs until 1925, when he was offered the chance to cut his directorial teeth on low-budget westerns. By 1928 he had completed two dozen two-reelers, seven feature-length westerns and one comedy. He was also granted his United States citizenship that year.

Over the next decade Wyler built a reputation as a director of popular and respectable film adaptations of classic literary works and contemporary theater. In 1936 he signed with Samuel Goldwyn Productions and established a working relationship with playwright Lillian Hellman. They reworked her controversial Broadway drama, *The Children's Hour,* into a sensitive (if sanitized) film titled *These Three* (1936). At this time Wyler also teamed with cameraman Gregg Toland, who would develop the deep-focus technique that would enhance such Wyler films as *The Little Foxes* (1941), another Hellman collaboration. *Dodsworth* (1936), *Dead End* (1937) and *Jezebel* (1938) followed, all critical and commercial successes. Wyler's amazing string of hits continued with *Wuthering Heights* (1939), *The Letter* (1940) and *The Little Foxes.* Oscar-nominated for all three films, Wyler won his first Academy Award for *Mrs. Miniver* (1942), an uplifting tale of a British family's fortitude in the face of the hardships of WWII.

Ironically, later that year Wyler was commissioned as a major in the US Army Air Force. While stationed in England he produced documentaries and undertook several dangerous missions to gather air combat footage. Over Italy he suffered injuries that left him partially deaf. Following the war he ended his long association with Goldwyn on an exceptionally high note with *The Best Years Of Our Lives* (1946), a story of three returning American war veterans which won Wyler his second Oscar and proved to be the top box office draw of the decade. In 1947 he rallied to counteract the stinging accusations of the Congressional HUAC investigations of Hollywood by helping to form, along with John Huston and Phillip Dunne, the Committee for the First Amendment. In 1948, he and fellow directors Frank Capra, George Stevens and Samuel Briskin formed their own production company, Liberty Films, which was later taken over by Paramount.

The Heiress (1949) found Wyler demonstrating his knack for bringing rich, visual staging to the literary classics. During the 1950s Wyler's work embraced several genres: urban melodrama (*Detective Story* 1951), romantic comedy (*Roman Holiday* 1953), and western (*The Big Country* 1958). He capped the decade with *Ben-Hur* (1959), the Bibilical spectacle that garnered a record 11 Academy Awards including best picture and best director—Wyler's third Oscar.

The next ten years presented a variety of cinematic challenges for Wyler, including his first musical, *Funny Girl* (1968). That Barbra Streisand won an Oscar in this, her debut film, owed something to the Wyler touch which had guided so many other performers to award-winning performances. His last film, *The Liberation of L.B. Jones* (1970), proved a critical and box-office disappointment and Wyler retired shortly thereafter. In 1976 he became the third recipient of the prestigious Life Achievement Award from the American Film Institute. KG • *Lazy Lightning* 1926 (d); *The Stolen Ranch* 1926 (d); *Blazing Days* 1927 (d); *The Border Cavalier* 1927 (d); *Desert Dust* 1927 (d); *Hard Fists* 1927 (d); *Straight Shootin'* 1927 (d); *Anybody Here Seen Kelly?* 1928 (d); *Thunder Riders* 1928 (d); *Hell's Heroes* 1929 (d); *The Love Trap* 1929 (d); *The Shakedown* 1929 (d); *The Storm* 1930 (d); *A House Divided* 1932 (d); *Tom Brown of Culver* 1932 (d); *Counsellor at Law* 1933 (d); *Her First Mate* 1933 (d); *Glamour* 1934 (d); *The Gay Deception* 1935 (d); *The Good Fairy* 1935 (d); *Come and Get It* 1936 (d); *Dodsworth* 1936 (d) **(AANBD)**; *These Three* 1936 (d); *Dead End* 1937 (d); *Jezebel* 1938 (d); *Wuthering Heights* 1939 (d) **(AANBD)**; *The Letter* 1940 (d) **(AANBD)**; *The Westerner* 1940 (d); *The Little Foxes* 1941 (d) **(AANBD)**; *Mrs. Miniver* 1942 (d) **(AABD)**; *The Fighting Lady* 1944 (d); *Thunderbolt* 1945 (d); *The Best Years of Our Lives* 1946 (d) **(AABD)**; *The Heiress* 1949 (d,p) **(AANBD)**; *Detective Story* 1951 (d,p) **(AANBD)**; *Carrie* 1952 (d,p); *Roman Holiday* 1953 (d,p) **(AANBD,AANBP)**; *The Desperate Hours* 1955 (d,p); *Friendly Persuasion* 1956 (d,p) **(AANBD,AANBP)**; *The Big Country* 1958 (d,p); *Ben-Hur* 1959 (d) **(AABD)**; *The Children's Hour* 1961 (d,p); *The Collector* 1965 (d) **(AANBD)**; *How to Steal a Million* 1966 (d); *Funny Girl* 1968 (d); *The Liberation of L.B. Jones* 1970 (d); *Directed By William Wyler* 1986 (a).

Wyman, Jane • *aka* Jane Durrell • Actress; also painter. • Born Sarah Jane Fulks, St. Joseph, MO, January 4, 1914. *Educ.* University of Missouri. Button-nosed actress who began her career as a radio singer and entered films in the mid-1930s as a bit player and chorine (using the name Jane Durrell).

Wyman was pigeonholed as a peppy blonde in mostly low-budget fare until garnering recognition for her sensitive performance in Billy Wilder's harrowing *The Lost Weekend* (1945), opposite Ray Milland. She went on to distinguish herself in several fine dramas, earning plaudits for her roles in *The Yearling* (1946), as a deaf-mute rape victim in *Johnny Belinda* (1948) and as the object of Rock Hudson's *Magnificent Obsession* in the 1954 Douglas Sirk melodrama.

From 1955 until its cancellation in 1958 Wyman appeared regularly on TV as hostess and star of "Fireside Theatre" (renamed "The Jane Wyman Show" in her honor). Following an absence of several years, she resurfaced in a number of TV movies and emerged as one of America's favorite matriarchs in the popular soap, "Falcon Crest" (1981-90)

Wyman was formerly married to actor and future President Ronald Reagan, with whom she collaborated to produce daughter Maureen Reagan, sometime actress, singer and White House adviser. Her second husband (1952-54) was Fred Karger, Fox musician and vocal coach. • *Gold Diggers of 1937* 1936; *My Man Godfrey* 1936; *Smart Blonde* 1936; *The King and the Chorus Girl* 1937; *Mr. Dodd Takes the Air* 1937; *Public Wedding* 1937; *Ready, Willing and Able* 1937; *The Singing Marine* 1937; *Slim* 1937; *Brother Rat* 1938; *The Crowd Roars* 1938; *He Couldn't Say No* 1938; *The Spy Ring* 1938; *Wide Open Faces* 1938; *The Kid From Kokomo* 1939; *Kid Nightingale* 1939; *Private Detective* 1939; *Tail Spin* 1939; *Torchy*

Plays With Dynamite 1939; *An Angel From Texas* 1940; *Brother Rat and a Baby* 1940; *Flight Angels* 1940; *Gambling on the High Seas* 1940; *My Love Came Back* 1940; *Tugboat Annie Sails Again* 1940; *Bad Men of Missouri* 1941; *The Body Disappears* 1941; *Honeymoon For Three* 1941; *You're in the Army Now* 1941; *Footlight Serenade* 1942; *Larceny, Inc.* 1942; *My Favorite Spy* 1942; *Princess O'Rourke* 1943; *Crime By Night* 1944; *The Doughgirls* 1944; *Hollywood Canteen* 1944; *Make Your Own Bed* 1944; *The Lost Weekend* 1945; *Night and Day* 1946; *One More Tomorrow* 1946; *The Yearling* 1946 **(AANBA)**; *Cheyenne* 1947; *Magic Town* 1947; *Johnny Belinda* 1948 **(AABA)**; *It's a Great Feeling* 1949; *A Kiss in the Dark* 1949; *The Lady Takes a Sailor* 1949; *The Glass Menagerie* 1950; *Stage Fright* 1950; *The Blue Veil* 1951 **(AANBA)**; *Here Comes the Groom* 1951; *Starlift* 1951; *Three Guys Named Mike* 1951; *Just For You* 1952; *The Story of Will Rogers* 1952; *Let's Do It Again* 1953; *So Big* 1953; *Magnificent Obsession* 1954; *Lucy Gallant* 1955; *All That Heaven Allows* 1956; *Miracle in the Rain* 1956; *Holiday For Lovers* 1959; *Pollyanna* 1960; *Bon Voyage!* 1962; *How to Commit Marriage* 1969.

Wynn, Keenan • Actor • Born Francis Xavier Aloysius Wynn, New York, NY, July 27, 1916; died 1986. Veteran character player from the stage, memorable as the absurdly earnest Army man who gives Peter Sellers a scare at the telephone booth in *Dr. Strangelove* (1964). Son of vaudevillian-turned-character-actor Ed Wynn (*The Diary of Anne Frank* 1959, *Mary Poppins* 1964, etc.) and father of Tracy Keenan Wynn (b. 1945), who wrote several films in the mid-1970s (*The Longest Yard* 1974, etc.). • *For Me and My Gal* 1942; *Northwest Rangers* 1942; *Lost Angel* 1943; *Between Two Women* 1944; *Marriage Is a Private Affair* 1944; *See Here, Private Hargrove* 1944; *Since You Went Away* 1944; *The Clock* 1945; *Weekend at the Waldorf* 1945; *What Next, Corporal Hargrove?* 1945; *Without Love* 1945; *The Cockeyed Miracle* 1946; *Easy to Wed* 1946; *No Leave, No Love* 1946; *The Thrill of Brazil* 1946; *Ziegfeld Follies* 1946; *B.F.'s Daughter* 1947; *The Hucksters* 1947; *Song of the Thin Man* 1947; *My Dear Secretary* 1948; *The Three Musketeers* 1948; *Neptune's Daughter* 1949; *That Midnight Kiss* 1949; *Annie Get Your Gun* 1950; *Love That Brute* 1950; *Three Little Words* 1950; *Angels in the Outfield* 1951; *It's a Big Country* 1951; *Royal Wedding* 1951; *Texas Carnival* 1951; *The Belle of New York* 1952; *Desperate Search* 1952; *Fearless Fagan* 1952; *Holiday For Sinners* 1952; *Phone Call From a Stranger* 1952; *Sky Full of Moon* 1952; *All the Brothers Were Valiant* 1953; *Battle Circus* 1953; *Code Two* 1953; *Kiss Me Kate* 1953; *The Glass Slipper* 1954; *The Long, Long Trailer* 1954; *Men of the Fighting Lady* 1954; *Tennessee Champ* 1954; *The Man in the Gray Flannel Suit* 1955; *The Marauders* 1955; *Running Wild* 1955; *Shack Out on 101* 1955; *The Great Man* 1956; *Johnny Concho* 1956; *The Naked Hills* 1956; *The Deep Six* 1957; *Don't Go Near the Water* 1957; *The Fuzzy Pink Nightgown* 1957; *Joe Butterfly* 1957; *A Time to Love and a Time to Die* 1958; *A Hole in the Head* 1959; *The Perfect Furlough* 1959; *That Kind of Woman* 1959; *The Absent-Minded Professor* 1960; *The Crowded Sky* 1960; *King of the Roaring 20's—The Story of Arnold Rothstein* 1961; *Son of Flubber* 1963; *The Americanization of Emily* 1964; *Bikini Beach* 1964; *Dr. Strangelove; or, How I Learned to Stop Worrying and Love the Bomb* 1964; *Honeymoon Hotel* 1964; *The Patsy* 1964; *Stage to Thunder Rock* 1964; *The Great Race* 1965; *Nightmare in the Sun* 1965; *Around the World Under the Sea* 1966; *The Night of the Grizzly* 1966; *Promise Her Anything* 1966; *Stagecoach* 1966; *Point Blank* 1967; *The War Wagon* 1967; *Welcome to Hard Times* 1967; *The Falling Man* 1968; *Finian's Rainbow* 1968; *C'era una Volta il West/Once Upon a Time in the West* 1969; *Eighty Steps to Jonah* 1969; *MacKenna's Gold* 1969; *The Monitors* 1969; *Smith* 1969; *Loving* 1970; *Viva Max!* 1970; *The Animals* 1971; *B.J. Presents* 1971; *Black Jack* 1971; *Padella Calibro 38* 1971; *Pretty Maids All in a Row* 1971; *Cancel My Reservation* 1972; *The Mechanic* 1972; *Snowball Express* 1972; *Wild in the Sky* 1972; *Herbie Rides Again* 1974; *The Internecine Project* 1974; *The Devil's Rain* 1975; *The Legend of Earl Durand* 1975; *The Man Who Would Not Die* 1975; *Nashville* 1975; *A Woman For All Men* 1975; *The Glove* 1976; *He Is My Brother* 1976; *The Killer Inside Me* 1976; *The Shaggy D.A.* 1976; *High Velocity* 1977; *Kino, the Padre on Horseback* 1977; *Orca... Killer Whale* 1977; *Coach* 1978; *Laserblast* 1978; *Piranha* 1978; *The Dark* 1979; *Parts: The Clonus Horror* 1979; *Sunburn* 1979; *Just Tell Me What You Want* 1980; *Best Friends* 1982; *The Last Unicorn* 1982; *Hysterical* 1983; *Wavelength* 1983; *Prime Risk* 1985; *Black Moon Rising* 1986; *Hyper Sapien: People From Another Star* 1986.

Yamamoto, Satsuo • Director; also actor. • Born Japan, July 15, 1910; died August 11, 1983, Tokyo. *Educ.* Waseda University (theater). Former student activist and stage talent whose film directing career (his first success was *La Symphonie pastorale* 1938) was interrupted when he was drafted into WWII. In the post-war years Yamamoto came into his own as one of Japan's leading political directors, with a series of engaging left-wing exercises, notably *The Street Without Sun* (1954). • *La Symphonie pastorale* 1938 (d); *The Street* 1939 (d); *End of Engagement* 1940 (d); *Tsubasa no gaika* 1942 (d); *Hot Wind* 1943 (d); *War and Peace* 1945 (d); *The Street of Violence* 1950 (d); *Storm Clouds Over Mount Hakone* 1951 (d); *Vacuum Zone* 1952 (d); *The Street Without Sun* 1954 (d); *Avalanche* 1956 (d); *Typhoon* 1956 (d); *The Human Wall* 1959 (d); *Battle Without Arms* 1960 (d); *A Band of Assassins* 1962 (d); *Red Water* 1963 (d); *Tycoon* 1964 (d); *The Spy* 1965 (d); *Freezing Point* 1966 (d); *The Bride From Hades* 1968 (d); *The Family* 1974 (d); *Annular Eclipse* 1975 (d); *The Story of Yugaku Ohara* 1976 (d); *The Barren Ground* 1977 (d); *August Without the Emperor* 1978 (d); *Ah! Nomugi Toge* 1980 (d).

Yang, Edward • Director; also screenwriter. • Born Yang Te-ch'ang, Shanghai, 1947. *Educ.* Florida State University (computer science); USC, Los Angeles (film). Edward Yang is often cited, along with Hou Hsiao-hsien, as one of the central figures of New Taiwan Cinema. Born in Shanghai, he moved with his family at the age of two to Taiwan. After studying engineering in Taiwan, he received an advanced degree in computer science in Florida, before entering USC's film school in 1974. Yang left before graduating, but never gave up the idea of making films. He took a computer job in Seattle until 1980, when a friend from USC asked him to write a screenplay for *The Winter of 1905.* He went to Japan for the shoot, then returned to Taiwan in 1981, an opportune time for a budding filmmaker. Almost immediately, he directed "Duckweed"

(1981), an episode from the groundbreaking TV series "11 Women." The following year, he was one of four young filmmakers to participate in *In Our Time* (1983), the film which inaugurated the new cinema. It introduced important new directors and represented what Yang considered the first attempt to recover the Taiwanese past, to "open up questions about our origins, our politics, our relationship to Mainland China."

Yang's first full-fledged feature film was *That Day on the Beach* (1983), a dark, brooding look at the relationship between two women. Their conversation at a bar frames an elaborate structure of flashbacks (and flashbacks within flashbacks) which probe their shared childhood and the choices that led one to a music career and the other to a more traditional role. Visually stunning and structurally complex, *That Day on the Beach* treats a number of issues which Yang would return to in subsequent films.

Taipei Story (1985) brought Yang—and Taiwanese cinema—world-wide attention. As in his previous films, the focus is primarily on urban women and their ability to adapt better than men to a society in flux. The new cinema's tendency towards literary adaptation forms a reflexive subtext for Yang's third feature, *The Terrorizers* (1986). A woman author is one of a number of characters around which Yang spins a fabric of intertwining narratives. The relationships among their stories develop slowly; some don't connect until near the end. The film's main concern is with the interconnectedness of modern life and how even random actions reverberate throughout society.

Yang's visual and narrative style is among the most distinctive and spectacular in recent Chinese film. His films are quiet, slow, and use a minimum of dialogue. Western critics often invoke Antonioni, although Yang appears to resent the comparison. In Taiwan, where "different" is read as "foreign," his departure from the norms of classical style are considered a symptom of Western influence. The director, however, attributes his stark style to Chinese origins, particularly his early education in Chinese brush painting. In any case, Yang's films are passionately connected to place, as he consistently addresses the problems posed by modern Taiwanese life. MN • *The Winter of 1905* 1980 (sc); *Feng-Kuei-Lai-Te jen/All the Beautiful Days* 1983 (m); *Hai-t'an-shang-te Yi T'ien/That Day on the Beach* 1983 (d,sc); *Kuang-Yin-Te Kushih/In Our Time* 1983 (d,sc—"Desires"); *Dongdong de Jiaqi/A Summer at Grandpa's* 1984 (m,m.sup); *Taipei Story* 1985 (d); *K'ung-pu fen-tzu/The Terrorizers* 1986 (d,sc).

Yanne, Jean • Actor, director; also producer, screenwriter. • Born Jean Gouyé, France, 1933. Effective lead of the late 1960s, memorable as the bourgeois protagonist of Godard's *Weekend* (1967) and the psychopathic title character of Chabrol's *Le Boucher* (1969). Since 1972, Yanne has split his time between acting in other people's films and directing, writing and producing his own anarchic satires on subjects ranging from the occupation of France by the Chinese (*Les Chinois à Paris* 1973) to a contemporary version of the birth of Christ (*Deux heures moins le quart avant Jesus Christ* 1982). • *La Vie à l'Envers* 1964 (a); *Monnaie de Singe* 1965 (a); *La Ligne de Demarcation* 1966 (a); *Le Vicomte Régle ses Comptes* 1967 (a); *Weekend* 1967 (a); *Le Boucher* 1969 (a); *Erotissimo* 1969 (a); *Que la Bête Meure* 1969 (a); *Laisse Aller, c'est une valse* 1970 (a); *Fantasia Chez Les Ploucs* 1971 (a); *Le Saut de l'ange* 1971 (a); *Moi y'en a vouloir des Sous* 1972 (a,d,sc); *Nous ne vieillirons pas ensemble* 1972 (a); *Tout le monde il est beau, tout le monde il est gentil* 1972 (a,d,p,sc); *Andy Warhol's Frankenstein* 1973 (p); *Les Chinois à Paris* 1973 (a,d,p,sc); *Touche pas à la femme blanche!* 1973 (p); *Blood For Dracula* 1974 (p); *Lancelot du Lac* 1974 (p); *Chobizenesse* 1975 (a,d,sc,m); *Armaguedon* 1977 (a); *L'Imprecateur* 1977 (a); *Moi, Fleur Bleue* 1977 (a); *La Raison d'état* 1978 (a); *Je te tiens, tu me tiens par la Barbichette* 1979 (a,d,exec.p,sc,dial); *Asphalte* 1981 (a); *Deux heures moins le quart avant Jesus Christ* 1982 (a,d,sc,m); *Une Journée en Taxi* 1982 (a); *Hannah K* 1983 (a); *Papy Fait de la Résistance* 1983 (a); *Le Téléphone sonne toujours deux fois!!* 1984 (a); *Liberté, Egalité, Choucroute* 1985 (a,d,sc,m); *Le Paltoquet* 1986 (a); *The Wolf at the Door* 1986 (a); *Attention Bandits* 1987 (a); *Cayenne-Palace* 1987 (a); *Fucking Fernand* 1987 (a); *Quicker Than the Eye* 1988 (a); *Madame Bovary* 1991 (a).

Yates, Peter • Director • Born Ewshott, Surrey, England, July 24, 1929. *Educ.* RADA, London. Began staging plays in the British provinces from the age of 19 and worked as an assistant to J. Lee Thompson and Tony Richardson in the early 1960s. Yates then alternated between film and TV work and made his feature debut with *Summer Holiday* (1963).

Yates's early work exhibits a talent for fast-paced action, reflected in such films as *Bullitt* (1968), which includes one of the most harrowing car chases ever filmed, and *The Friends of Eddie Coyle* (1973). In the 1980s he crafted a number of fine, character-driven studies such as *The Dresser* (1983), *Eleni* (1985) and *Suspect* (1987). • *The Guns of Navarone* 1961 (ad); *The Roman Spring of Mrs. Stone* 1961 (ad); *A Taste of Honey* 1961 (ad); *Summer Holiday* 1963 (d); *One Way Pendulum* 1964 (d); *Robbery* 1967 (d,sc); *Bullitt* 1968 (d); *John and Mary* 1969 (d); *Murphy's War* 1970 (d); *The Hot Rock* 1972 (d); *The Friends of Eddie Coyle* 1973 (d); *For Pete's Sake* 1974 (d); *Mother, Jugs & Speed* 1976 (d,p); *The Deep* 1977 (d); *Breaking Away* 1979 (d,p) **(AANBD,AANBP)**; *Eyewitness* 1980 (d,p); *The Dresser* 1983 (d,p) **(AANBD,AANBP)**; *Krull* 1983 (d); *Eleni* 1985 (d); *Suspect* 1987 (d); *The House on Carroll Street* 1988 (d,p); *An Innocent Man* 1989 (d).

Yordan, Philip • Screenwriter, producer; also playwright, novelist. • Born Chicago, IL, 1913. *Educ.* University of Illinois; Kent College (law). Novelist and playwright who entered films in 1941 (working uncredited on *The Devil and Daniel Webster* 1941) and went on to script such riveting features as *House of Strangers* (1949) and *Detective Story* (1951). Yordan was also responsible for a brace of sophisticated westerns, notably *Johnny Guitar* and *Broken Lance* (both 1954) and allegedly lent his name to a number of scripts penned by blacklisted writers during the Hollywood witch-hunt.

Yordan produced his first film in 1949 (an adaptation of his stage hit *Anna Lucasta*, which he adapted again for an all-black remake in 1958), and his second, the stinging boxing drama, *The Harder They Fall* in 1956. He went on to write or produce a number of increasingly top-heavy extravaganzas, including *El Cid* (1961) and *Battle of the Bulge* (1965). • *Syncopation* 1942 (sc); *The Unknown Guest* 1943 (sc); *Johnny Doesn't Live Here Anymore* 1944 (sc); *When Strangers Marry* 1944 (sc); *Dillinger* 1945 (sc,story) **(AANBSC)**; *The Chase* 1946 (sc); *Suspense* 1946 (sc,story); *Whistle Stop* 1946 (sc); *Bad Men of Tombstone* 1948 (sc); *Anna Lucasta* 1949 (p,sc,from play); *House of Strangers* 1949 (sc); *Reign of Terror* 1949 (sc); *Edge of Doom* 1950 (sc); *Detective Story* 1951 (sc) **(AANBSC)**; *Drums in the Deep South* 1951 (sc); *Mara Maru* 1952 (story); *Mutiny* 1952 (sc); *Blowing Wild* 1953 (sc,story); *Houdini* 1953 (sc); *Man Crazy* 1953 (p,sc,story); *Broken Lance* 1954 (from novel) **(AABST)**; *Conquest of Space* 1954 (adapt); *Johnny Guitar* 1954 (sc); *The Naked Jungle* 1954 (sc); *The Big Combo* 1955 (sc); *Joe Macbeth* 1955 (sc); *The Last Frontier* 1955 (sc); *The Man From Laramie* 1955 (sc); *The Harder They Fall* 1956 (p,sc); *Men in War* 1956 (sc); *Four Boys and a Gun* 1957 (sc); *Gun Glory* 1957 (from novel *Man of the West*); *No Down Payment* 1957 (sc); *Street of Sinners* 1957 (story); *Anna Lucasta* 1958 (sc,from play); *The Bravados* 1958 (sc); *The Fiend Who Walked the West* 1958 (sc); *God's Little Acre* 1958 (sc); *Island Women* 1958 (sc); *Day of the Outlaw* 1959 (sc); *The Bramble Bush* 1960 (sc); *Studs Lonigan* 1960 (p,sc); *El Cid* 1961 (sc); *King of Kings* 1961 (sc); *The Day of the Triffids* 1962 (exec.p,sc); *55 Days at Peking* 1963 (sc); *Circus World* 1964 (story); *The Fall of the Roman Empire* 1964 (sc); *Battle of* *the Bulge* 1965 (p,sc); *Crack in the World* 1965 (exec.p); *The Royal Hunt of the Sun* 1969 (p,sc); *Captain Apache* 1971 (p,sc); *Savage Journey* 1983 (p,sc); *Night Train to Terror* 1985 (sc); *Bloody Wednesday* 1987 (p,sc); *Cry Wilderness* 1987 (p,sc); *The Unholy* 1988 (sc).

York, Michael • Actor • Born Michael York-Johnson, Fulmer, Buckinghamshire, England, March 27, 1942. *Educ.* National Youth Theatre; University College, Oxford (English). Handsome blond lead who made made his London stage debut in Franco Zeffirelli's stage production of *Much Ado About Nothing* in 1965 and his film debut in the same director's opulent adaptation of *The Taming of the Shrew* (1967). York has typically played charming, well-bred characters, such as the struggling, sexually confused writer opposite Liza Minnelli in *Cabaret* (1972) and the dashing D'Artagnan in *The Three Musketeers* (1973) and its sequels. York played himself in Billy Wilder's *Fedora* (1978). • *Accident* 1967 (a); *The Taming of the Shrew* 1967 (a); *Romeo and Juliet* 1968 (a); *Alfred the Great* 1969 (a); *The Guru* 1969 (a); *Justine* 1969 (a); *Something For Everyone* 1970 (a); *Zeppelin* 1970 (a); *La Poudre d'escampette* 1971 (a); *Cabaret* 1972 (a); *England Made Me* 1973 (a); *Lost Horizon* 1973 (a); *The Three Musketeers* 1973 (a); *Murder on the Orient Express* 1974 (a); *Conduct Unbecoming* 1975 (a); *The Four Musketeers* 1975 (a); *Logan's Run* 1976 (a); *Seven Nights in Japan* 1976 (a); *The Island of Dr. Moreau* 1977 (a); *The Last Remake of Beau Geste* 1977 (a); *Fedora* 1978 (a); *The Riddle of the Sands* 1979 (a,assoc.p); *Final Assignment* 1980 (a); *Au nom de tous les Miens* 1983 (a); *The Weather in the Streets* 1983 (a); *Success Is the Best Revenge* 1984 (a); *L'Aube* 1986 (a); *Der Joker* 1987 (a); *Midnight Cop* 1988 (a); *Phantom of Death* 1988 (a); *The Return of the Musketeers* 1989 (a); *Come See the Paradise* 1990 (a).

York, Susannah • Actress • Born Susannah Yolande Fletcher, London, January 9, 1941. *Educ.* RADA, London. Respected stage and TV actress who first gained prominence as the winsome object of Albert Finney's affection in *Tom Jones* (1963) and turned in fine performances in *A Man For All Seasons* (1966) and *They Shoot Horses, Don't They?* (1969).

York's career was briefly fueled by starring roles in two controversial films dealing with lesbianism, *The Killing of Sister George* (1968) and *X Y & Zee* (1972). She has since appeared in mainstream fare such as the "Superman" series as well as art-house features including Jerzy Skolimowski's *The Shout* (1978) and Andi Engel's *Melancholia* (1989). York co-wrote her 1980 feature, *Falling in Love Again*. • *Tunes of Glory* 1960 (a); *Freud* 1962 (a); *Tom Jones* 1963 (a); *Sands of the Kalahari* 1965 (a); *Kaleidoscope* 1966 (a); *A Man For All Seasons* 1966 (a); *Duffy* 1968 (a); *The Killing of Sister George* 1968 (a); *Sebastian* 1968 (a); *Battle of Britain* 1969 (a); *Lock Up Your Daughters!* 1969 (a); *Oh! What a Lovely War* 1969 (a); *They Shoot Horses, Don't They?* 1969 (a) **(AANBSA)**; *Happy Birthday, Wanda June* 1971 (a); *Images* 1972 (a); *X Y & Zee* 1972 (a); *Gold* 1974 (a); *The Maids* 1974 (a); *Conduct Unbecoming* 1975 (a); *That Lucky Touch* 1975 (a); *Eliza Fraser* 1976 (a); *Sky Riders* 1976 (a); *Long Shot* 1978 (a); *The Shout* 1978 (a); *The Silent Partner* 1978 (a); *Superman* 1978 (a); *The Awakening* 1980 (a); *Falling in Love Again* 1980 (a,sc); *Superman II* 1980 (a); *Loophole* 1981 (a); *Montgomery Clift* 1982 (a); *Nelly's Version* 1983 (a); *Yellowbeard* 1983 (a); *Daemon* 1986 (a); *Barbablu Barbablu* 1987 (a); *Mio min Mio* 1987 (a); *PrettyKill* 1987 (a); *Superman IV: The Quest For Peace* 1987 (a); *American Roulette* 1988 (a); *Just Ask For Diamond* 1988 (a,song); *A Summer Story* 1988 (a); *En Handfull tid* 1989 (a); *Melancholia* 1989 (a); *Fate* 1991 (a).

Yorkin, Bud • Director; also producer. • Born Alan David Yorkin, Washington, PA, February 22, 1926. *Educ.* Carnegie Institute of Technology, Pittsburgh, PA; Columbia. Yorkin first made his name as a director and producer of TV comedy and variety shows in the 1950s. In 1959 he teamed up with Norman Lear to found Tandem Productions and made his feature directing debut four years later with the Neil Simon adaptation *Come Blow Your Horn* (1963).

Yorkin has directed several first-rate comedies (usually produced by Lear), notably *Start the Revolution Without Me* (1970); he was also responsible for the finely observed family drama, *Twice in a Lifetime* (1985). His TV hits with Lear include "All in the Family" (1971-79) and the seminal black family sitcom, "Good Times" (1974-79). • *Come Blow Your Horn* 1963 (d,p); *Never Too Late* 1965 (d); *Divorce American Style* 1967 (d); *Inspector Clouseau* 1968 (d); *Start the Revolution Without Me* 1970 (d,p); *Cold Turkey* 1971 (exec.p); *The Thief Who Came to Dinner* 1973 (d,p); *Deal of the Century* 1983 (p); *Twice in a Lifetime* 1985 (d,p); *Arthur 2 on the Rocks* 1988 (d); *Love Hurts* 1990 (d,p).

Young, Burt • Actor • Born New York, NY, April 30, 1940. Stout, stage-trained character player who began appearing in films in the early 1970s. Young has generally been typecast as a thug and gained attention for his role as Paulie opposite Sylvester Stallone in *Rocky* (1976). He wrote and starred in *Uncle Joe Shannon* (1978), a critical and commercial flop about a down-and-out trumpeter. • *The Gang That Couldn't Shoot Straight* 1971 (a); *Cinderella Liberty* 1973 (a); *Chinatown* 1974 (a); *The Gambler* 1974 (a); *Live a Little, Steal a Lot* 1974 (a); *The Killer Elite* 1975 (a); *Harry and Walter Go to New York* 1976 (a); *Rocky* 1976 (a) **(AANBSA)**; *The Choirboys* 1977 (a); *Twilight's Last Gleaming* 1977 (a); *Convoy* 1978 (a); *Uncle Joe Shannon* 1978 (a,sc); *Rocky II* 1979 (a); *Blood Beach* 1980 (a); *All the Marbles* 1981 (a); *Amityville II: The Possession* 1982 (a); *Lookin' to Get Out* 1982 (a); *Rocky III* 1982 (a); *Over the Brooklyn Bridge* 1983 (a); *Once Upon a Time in America* 1984 (a); *The Pope of Greenwich Village* 1984 (a); *Rocky IV* 1985 (a); *Back to School* 1986 (a); *Beverly Hills Brats* 1989 (a); *Blood Red* 1989 (a); *Last Exit to Brooklyn* 1989 (a); *Medium Rare* 1989 (a); *Wait Until Spring, Bandini* 1989 (a); *Backstreet Dreams* 1990 (a); *Betsy's Wedding* 1990 (a); *Bright Angel* 1990 (a); *Diving In* 1990 (a); *Rocky V* 1990 (a).

Young, Freddie • Director of photography • Born Frederick A. Young, England, 1902. Began his career in British film at the age of 15 and graduated to cinematographer in the late 1920s. Young went on to illuminate a host of British and Anglo-American productions and enjoyed a productive long-term association with director David Lean, earning Oscars for his color photography on such lush spectacles as *Lawrence of Arabia* (1962), *Doctor Zhivago* (1965) and *Ryan's Daughter* (1970).

Young also shot Vincente Minnelli's richly textured *Lust For Life* and Gene Kelly's *Invitation to the Dance* (both 1956), a film that integrated live action with animated footage. An octogenarian, Young directed his first film, *Arthur's Hallowed Ground*, in 1985. • *Escape Me Never* 1935 (ph); *Goodbye, Mr. Chips* 1939 (ph); *Nurse Edith Cavell* 1939 (ph); *49th Parallel* 1941 (ph); *So Well Remembered* 1947 (ph); *Edward, My Son* 1948 (ph); *Escape* 1948 (ph); *The Winslow Boy* 1948 (ph); *Conspirator* 1949 (ph); *Treasure Island* 1950 (ph); *Calling Bulldog Drummond* 1951 (ph); *Ivanhoe* 1952 (ph); *Knights of the Round Table* 1953 (ph); *Mogambo* 1953 (ph); *Terror on a Train* 1953 (ph); *Bedevilled* 1954 (ph); *Betrayed* 1954 (ph); *Bhowani Junction* 1956 (ph); *Invitation to the Dance* 1956 (ph); *Lust For Life* 1956 (ph); *Beyond Mombasa* 1957 (ph); *I Accuse!* 1957 (ph); *Island in the Sun* 1957 (ph); *The Little Hut* 1957 (ph); *Indiscreet* 1958 (ph); *The Inn of the Sixth Happiness* 1958 (ph); *Solomon and Sheba* 1959 (ph); *The Wreck of the Mary Deare* 1959 (add.ph); *Macbeth* 1960 (ph); *Lawrence of Arabia* 1962 (ph) **(AABPH)**; *Doctor Zhivago* 1965 (ph) **(AABPH)**; *Lord Jim* 1965 (ph); *The Deadly Affair* 1967 (ph); *You Only Live Twice* 1967 (ph); *Battle of Britain* 1969 (ph); *Sinful Davey* 1969 (ph); *Ryan's Daughter* 1970 (ph) **(AABPH)**; *Nicholas and Alexandra* 1971 (ph) **(AANBPH)**; *The Asphyx* 1972 (ph); *Luther* 1974 (ph); *The Tamarind Seed* 1974 (ph); *Permission to Kill* 1975 (ph);

The Blue Bird 1976 (ph); *Stevie* 1978 (ph); *Bloodline* 1979 (ph); *Richard's Things* 1980 (ph); *Rough Cut* 1980 (ph); *Invitation to the Wedding* 1983 (ph); *Sword of the Valiant—The Legend of Gawain and the Green Knight* 1984 (ph); *Arthur's Hallowed Ground* 1985 (d).

Young, Gig • *aka* Bryant Fleming • Actor • Born Byron Elsworth Barr, St. Cloud, MN, November 4, 1913; died 1978, Manhattan, NY. *Educ.* Pasadena Playhouse. Amiable supporting player and occasional lead who broke into film in the early 1940s. Young appeared in several bit parts under his given name, Byron Barr, and the pseudonym, Bryant Fleming, before adopting the name of his character in the 1942 feature, *The Gay Sisters* (1942). While he proved capable in several dramatic parts (notably as the sleazy emcee in the haunting *They Shoot Horses, Don't They?* 1969), Young seemed destined to play debonair cads in sophisticated light comedies such as *Teacher's Pet* (1958) and *That Touch of Mink* (1962). Young's third and fourth wives were actresses Elizabeth Montgomery and Kim Schmidt; he allegedly shot Schmidt three weeks into the marriage before killing himself. • *The Gay Sisters* 1942; *Air Force* 1943; *Old Acquaintance* 1943; *Escape Me Never* 1947; *The Three Musketeers* 1948; *Wake of the Red Witch* 1948; *The Woman in White* 1948; *Lust For Gold* 1949; *Tell It to the Judge* 1949; *Hunt the Man Down* 1950; *Come Fill the Cup* 1951 **(AANBSA)**; *Only the Valiant* 1951; *Slaughter Trail* 1951; *Target Unknown* 1951; *Too Young to Kiss* 1951; *Holiday For Sinners* 1952; *You For Me* 1952; *Arena* 1953; *City That Never Sleeps* 1953; *The Girl Who Had Everything* 1953; *Torch Song* 1953; *The Desperate Hours* 1955; *Young at Heart* 1955; *Desk Set* 1957; *Teacher's Pet* 1958 **(AANBSA)**; *The Tunnel of Love* 1958; *Ask Any Girl* 1959; *The Story on Page One* 1959; *Kid Galahad* 1962; *That Touch of Mink* 1962; *Five Miles to Midnight* 1963; *For Love or Money* 1963; *A Ticklish Affair* 1963; *Strange Bedfellows* 1965; *They Shoot Horses, Don't They?* 1969 **(AABSA)**; *Lovers and Other Strangers* 1970; *Bring Me the Head of Alfredo Garcia* 1974; *The Hindenburg* 1975; *The Killer Elite* 1975; *Game of Death* 1979.

Young, Loretta • Actress • Born Gretchen Michaela Young, Salt Lake City, UT, January 6, 1913. After the rigors of a covent education interrupted her nascent career (she had broken into film as a bit player at the age of three), Loretta Young resurfaced at the age of 14 to play a supporting role in *Naughty But Nice* (1927), netting herself a contract with First National.

By the mid-1930s Young, having made a strategic switch to the Fox lot, had blossomed into one of Hollywood's loveliest and most prominent leading ladies, capably adorning a number of (mostly mediocre) productions. Her career reached its peak during the late 1940s in such carefully mounted vehicles as *The Farmer's Daughter* (1947) and *Come to the Stable* (1949), playing put-upon heroines.

By 1954 Young had abandoned the screen in favor of a successful second career as the crisp, glamorous hostess, and frequent star, of TV's long-running anthology series "The Loretta Young Show" (1954-63). Her second husband was producer-writer Thomas Lewis. • *Sweet Kitty Bellairs* 1916 (a); *Naughty But Nice* 1927 (a); *The Head Man* 1928 (a); *Laugh, Clown, Laugh* 1928 (a); *The Magnificent Flirt* 1928 (a); *Scarlet Seas* 1928 (a); *The Whip Woman* 1928 (a); *The Careless Age* 1929 (a); *Fast Life* 1929 (a); *The Forward Pass* 1929 (a); *The Girl in the Glass Cage* 1929 (a); *The Show of Shows* 1929 (a,song); *The Squall* 1929 (a); *Kismet* 1930 (a); *Loose Ankles* 1930 (a); *The Man From Blankley's* 1930 (a); *Road to Paradise* 1930 (a); *The Second Floor Mystery* 1930 (a); *The Truth About Youth* 1930 (a); *Beau Ideal* 1931 (a); *Big Business Girl* 1931 (a); *The Devil to Pay* 1931 (a); *I Like Your Nerve* 1931 (a); *Platinum Blonde* 1931 (a); *The Right of Way* 1931 (a); *The Ruling Voice* 1931 (a); *Three Girls Lost* 1931 (a); *Too Young to Marry* 1931 (a); *The Hatchet Man* 1932 (a); *Life Begins* 1932 (a); *Play Girl* 1932 (a); *Taxi* 1932 (a); *They Call It Sin* 1932 (a); *Week-End Marriage* 1932 (a); *The Devil's in Love* 1933 (a); *Employees' Entrance* 1933 (a); *Grand Slam* 1933 (a); *Heroes For Sale* 1933 (a); *The Life of Jimmy Dolan* 1933 (a); *A Man's Castle* 1933 (a); *Midnight Mary* 1933 (a); *She Had to Say Yes* 1933 (a); *Zoo in Budapest* 1933 (a); *Born to Be Bad* 1934 (a); *Bulldog Drummond Strikes Back* 1934 (a); *Caravan* 1934 (a); *The House of Rothschild* 1934 (a); *The White Parade* 1934 (a); *The Call of the Wild* 1935 (a); *Clive of India* 1935 (a); *The Crusades* 1935 (a); *Shanghai* 1935 (a); *Ladies in Love* 1936 (a); *Private Number* 1936 (a); *Ramona* 1936 (a); *The Unguarded Hour* 1936 (a); *Cafe Metropole* 1937 (a); *Love Is News* 1937 (a); *Love Under Fire* 1937 (a); *Second Honeymoon* 1937 (a); *Wife, Doctor, and Nurse* 1937 (a); *Four Men and a Prayer* 1938 (a); *Kentucky* 1938 (a); *Suez* 1938 (a); *Eternally Yours* 1939 (a); *The Story of Alexander Graham Bell* 1939 (a); *Wife, Husband, and Friend* 1939 (a); *The Doctor Takes a Wife* 1940 (a); *He Stayed For Breakfast* 1940 (a); *Bedtime Story* 1941 (a); *The Lady From Cheyenne* 1941 (a); *The Men in Her Life* 1941 (a); *A Night to Remember* 1942 (a); *China* 1943 (a); *And Now Tomorrow* 1944 (a); *Ladies Courageous* 1944 (a); *Along Came Jones* 1945 (a); *The Perfect Marriage* 1946 (a); *The Stranger* 1946 (a); *The Bishop's Wife* 1947 (a); *The Farmer's Daughter* 1947 (a) **(AABA)**; *The Accused* 1948 (a); *Rachel and the Stranger* 1948 (a); *Come to the Stable* 1949 (a) **(AANBA)**; *Mother Is a Freshman* 1949 (a); *Key to the City* 1950 (a); *Cause For Alarm* 1951 (a); *Half Angel* 1951 (a); *Because of You* 1952 (a); *Paula* 1952 (a); *It Happens Every Thursday* 1953 (a); *Going Hollywood: The War Years* 1988 (archival footage).

Young, Robert • Actor • Born Chicago, IL, February 22, 1907. Affable, forthright leading man who broke into film in 1931 and went on to appear in some 100 productions, notably Hitchcock's *Secret Agent* (1936), Fritz Lang's *Western Union* (1941) and Edward Dmytryk's *Crossfire* (1947).

Young is best known as the title characters of TV's "Father Knows Best" (1954-60) and "Marcus Welby M.D." (1969-76) and has parlayed his avuncular image into a profitable second career in commercials. • *The Black Camel* 1931; *Guilty Generation* 1931; *The Sin of Madelon Claudet* 1931; *The Kid From Spain* 1932; *New Morals For Old* 1932; *Strange Interlude* 1932; *Unashamed* 1932; *The Wet Parade* 1932; *Hell Below* 1933; *Men Must Fight* 1933; *The Right to Romance* 1933; *Saturday's Millions* 1933; *Today We Live* 1933; *Tugboat Annie* 1933; *The Band Plays on* 1934; *Carolina* 1934; *Death on the Diamond* 1934; *The House of Rothschild* 1934; *Lazy River* 1934; *Paris Interlude* 1934; *Spitfire* 1934; *Whom the Gods Destroy* 1934; *Calm Yourself* 1935; *Red Salute* 1935; *Remember Last Night?* 1935; *Vagabond Lady* 1935; *West Point of the Air* 1935; *The Bride Comes Home* 1936; *The Bride Walks Out* 1936; *The Longest Night* 1936; *Secret Agent* 1936; *Stowaway* 1936; *Sworn Enemy* 1936; *The Three Wise Guys* 1936; *The Bride Wore Red* 1937; *Dangerous Number* 1937; *The Emperor's Candlesticks* 1937; *I Met Him in Paris* 1937; *Married Before Breakfast* 1937; *Navy, Blue and Gold* 1937; *Josette* 1938; *Paradise For Three* 1938; *Rich Man, Poor Girl* 1938; *The Shining Hour* 1938; *Three Comrades* 1938; *The Toy Wife* 1938; *Bridal Suite* 1939; *Honolulu* 1939; *Maisie* 1939; *Miracles For Sale* 1939; *Dr. Kildare's Crisis* 1940; *Florian* 1940; *The Mortal Storm* 1940; *Northwest Passage* 1940; *Sporting Blood* 1940; *H. M. Pulham, Esq.* 1941; *Lady Be Good* 1941; *Married Bachelor* 1941; *The Trial of Mary Dugan* 1941; *Western Union* 1941; *Cairo* 1942; *Joe Smith, American* 1942; *Journey For Margaret* 1942; *Claudia* 1943; *Sweet Rosie O'Grady* 1943; *The Canterville Ghost* 1944; *The Enchanted Cottage* 1945; *Those Endearing Young Charms* 1945; *Claudia and David* 1946; *Lady Luck* 1946; *The Searching Wind* 1946; *Crossfire* 1947; *They Won't Believe Me* 1947; *Adventure in Baltimore* 1948; *Relentless* 1948; *Sitting Pretty* 1948; *And Baby Makes Three* 1949; *Bride For Sale* 1949; *That Forsyte Woman* 1949; *Goodbye, My Fancy* 1951; *The Second Woman* 1951; *The Half-Breed* 1952; *Secret of the Incas* 1954.

Young, Robert M. • Director; also producer. • Born Robert Milton Young, New York, NY, November 22, 1924. *Educ.* Harvard (English). New York filmmaker who collaborated on a number of documentaries with Michael Roemer in the 1960s, notably *Cortile Cascino/The Inferno* (1962), shot for the NBC series "White Paper" but deemed too controversial to air. Young's first fiction feature as a director was the 1977 adaptation of Miguel Pinhero's harrowing stage play *Short Eyes*.

Young's films are noted for their gritty, unglamorous qualities and fine use of locations. Highlights include *Rich Kids* (1979), a realistic portrait of two upper-class Manhattan juveniles watching their parents' world fall apart; *Alambrista!* (1978), about the exploitation of a naïve Mexican after he has crossed the border to the US, and *The Ballad of Gregorio Cortez* (1983), based on the true story of a Mexican who killed a US sheriff in 1901.

Young has begun to reach a wider audience in the 1980s with films such as the Farrah Fawcett vehicle *Extremities* (1986) and the concentration camp drama *Triumph of the Spirit* (1989), starring Willem Dafoe. • *Secrets of the Reef* 1956 (d,sc,ph,ed); *Cortile Cascino/The Inferno* 1962 (d,sc,ph,ed); *Nothing But a Man* 1964 (p,sc,ph); *The Plot Against Harry* 1969 (p,ph); *Deal* 1977 (d,ph); *Short Eyes* 1977 (d); *Alambrista!* 1978 (d,sc,ph); *Rich Kids* 1979 (d); *One-Trick Pony* 1980 (d); *The Ballad of Gregorio Cortez* 1983 (d,sc.adapt); *Extremities* 1986 (d); *Saving Grace* 1986 (d); *Dominick and Eugene* 1988 (d); *Triumph of the Spirit* 1989 (d).

Young, Roland • Actor • Born London, November 11, 1887; died 1953. *Educ.* London University; RADA, London. Slight, mild-mannered British character actor who played a host of lower-middle-class types, from Uriah Heep in *David Copperfield* (1935) to the meek sales clerk invested with God-like powers in *The Man Who Could Work Miracles* (1936). Best known to American audiences for his starring roles in three of the "Topper" films (1937-41). • *Sherlock Holmes* 1922; *Grit* 1924; *Her Private Life* 1929; *The Unholy Night* 1929; *Wise Girls* 1929; *The Bishop Murder Case* 1930; *Madam Satan* 1930; *New Moon* 1930; *Annabelle's Affairs* 1931; *Don't Bet on Women* 1931; *The Guardsman* 1931; *Pagan Lady* 1931; *The Prodigal* 1931; *The Squaw Man* 1931; *Lovers Courageous* 1932; *One Hour With You* 1932; *Street of Women* 1932; *They Just Had to Get Married* 1932; *This Is the Night* 1932; *A Woman Commands* 1932; *Blind Adventure* 1933; *His Double Life* 1933; *A Lady's Profession* 1933; *Pleasure Cruise* 1933; *Here Is My Heart* 1934; *David Copperfield* 1935; *Ruggles of Red Gap* 1935; *Give Me Your Heart* 1936; *The Man Who Could Work Miracles* 1936; *One Rainy Afternoon* 1936; *The Unguarded Hour* 1936; *Ali Baba Goes to Town* 1937; *Call It a Day* 1937; *Gypsy* 1937; *King Solomon's Mines* 1937; *Topper* 1937 (**AANBSA**); *The Young in Heart* 1938; *Here I Am a Stranger* 1939; *The Night of Nights* 1939; *Topper Takes a Trip* 1939; *Yes, My Darling Daughter* 1939; *He Married His Wife* 1940; *Irene* 1940; *No, No, Nanette* 1940; *The Philadelphia Story* 1940; *Private Affairs* 1940; *Star Dust* 1940; *The Flame of New Orleans* 1941; *Topper Returns* 1941; *Two-Faced Woman* 1941; *The Lady Has Plans* 1942; *Tales of Manhattan* 1942; *They All Kissed the Bride* 1942; *Forever and a Day* 1943; *Standing Room Only* 1944; *And Then There Were None* 1945; *You Gotta Stay Happy* 1948; *The Great Lover* 1949; *Let's Dance* 1950; *St. Benny the Dip* 1951; *That Man From Tangier* 1953.

Young, Sean • Actress • Born Louisville, KY, November 20, 1959. *Educ.* Interlochen Arts Academy, MI (dance). Former model who has ornamented a number of feature films since the early 1980s, notably *Blade Runner* (1982), as Harrison Ford's android lover, and *No Way Out* (1987). • *Jane Austen in Manhattan* 1980; *Stripes* 1981; *Blade Runner* 1982; *Young Doctors in Love* 1982; *Baby: The Secret of the Lost Legend* 1985; *Dune* 1985; *Arena Brains (short)* 1987; *No Way Out* 1987; *Wall Street* 1987; *The Boost* 1988; *Cousins* 1989; *Fire Birds* 1990; *A Kiss Before Dying* 1991; *Love Crimes* 1991.

Young, Terence • Director; also screenwriter. • Born Shanghai, China, June 20, 1915. *Educ.* St. Catherine's College, Cambridge (history). Began his career as a screenwriter in the mid-1930s and, following WWII service, made his fiction directorial debut with *One Night With You* (1948). Young directed a number of routine British action films before hitting his stride in the 1960s with a series of James Bond extravaganzas, beginning with *Dr. No* (1962). His recent credits include *Inchon* (1982), one of the biggest commercial disasters in the history of cinema. • *Corridor of Mirrors* 1948 (d); *One Night With You* 1948 (d); *Woman Hater* 1948 (d); *They Were Not Divided* 1950 (d); *Valley of the Eagles* 1951 (d); *The Red Beret* 1953 (d); *Storm Over the Nile* 1955 (d); *That Lady* 1955 (d); *Safari* 1956 (d); *Zarak* 1956 (d); *Action of the Tiger* 1957 (d); *No Time to Die* 1958 (d,sc); *Too Hot to Handle* 1960 (d); *Un, deux, trois, quatre!* 1960 (d); *Orazi e Curiazi* 1961 (p); *Dr. No* 1962 (d); *From Russia With Love* 1963 (d); *The Amorous Adventures of Moll Flanders* 1965 (d); *La Guerre secréte* 1965 (d); *Thunderball* 1965 (d); *The Poppy Is Also a Flower* 1966 (d); *Triple Cross* 1966 (d); *L'Avventuriero* 1967 (d); *Wait Until Dark* 1967 (d); *Mayerling* 1968 (d,sc); *L'Arbre de Noël* 1969 (d,sc); *De la Part des Copains* 1971 (d); *Soleil Rouge/Red Sun* 1971 (d); *Valachi Papers* 1972 (d); *The Klansman* 1974 (d); *Bloodline* 1979 (d); *Inchon* 1982 (d); *The Jigsaw Man* 1984 (d); *Where Is Parsifal?* 1984 (exec.p).

Yutkevich, Sergei • Director; also screenwriter, educator. • Born St. Petersburg, Russia, December 28, 1904; died April 23, 1985, Moscow. Versatile, highly regarded veteran of the Soviet film industry who began his career in his mid-teens designing stage sets for fellow student Sergei Eisenstein. Yutkevich then co-founded the experimental Factory of the Eccentric Actor (FEX) in 1921, worked as assistant to Abram Room and made his feature directing debut with *Lace* (1928), one of the earliest Soviet sound films.

Yutkevich went on to make a series of fine films about V.I. Lenin, featuring justly famed performances by Maxim Strauch, and earned prizes at Cannes in the mid-1950s for *Skanderbeg* (1953; special jury prize) and *Othello* (1955; best director). He also made some documentaries and, in 1962, devised and executed an animated screen adaptation of Mayakovsky's *The Bath House*, which he had previously directed for the stage. Among Yutkevich's published works include a biography of Max Linder, a book on adapting Shakespeare to the screen and the theoretical study, *Film—Truth at 24 Frames per Second* (1974). • *Lace* 1928 (d); *The Black Sail* 1929 (d); *Golden Mountains* 1931 (d,sc); *Counterplan/Pozor/Shame* 1932 (d,sc); *The Miners* 1937 (d); *The Man With the Gun* 1938 (d); *Yakov Sverdlov* 1940 (d,sc); *The New Adventures of Schweik* 1943 (d); *Tri vstrechi* 1948 (d); *Przhevalsky* 1951 (d); *Veliki voin Albanii Skanderbeg/The Great Warrior Skanderbeg* 1953 (d); *Othello* 1955 (d,sc); *Poprigunya* 1955 (p); *Rasskazi o Lenine* 1957 (d); *Banya/The Bath House* 1962 (d,sc); *Lenin v Polshe* 1965 (d,sc); *Nran Gouyne* 1968 (add.ed).

Zaentz, Saul • Producer • Born Passaic, NJ. After popular groups such as Creedence Clearwater Revival earned his Berkeley-based label, Fantasy Records, a fortune during the 1960s,

Zaentz made an auspicious entry into feature film production with *One Flew Over the Cuckoo's Nest* (1975). Starring Jack Nicholson and based on Ken Kesey's underground classic, the film became one of the biggest—and least likely—critical and commercial smashes of the day, earning a best picture Oscar for Zaentz and co-producer Michael Douglas.

Zaentz's subsequent efforts, often literary adaptations, have usually been worth the wait, particularly *Amadeus* (1984), another Oscar champion, and *The Unbearable Lightness of Being* (1988), which introduced Lena Olin to American audiences.

The Saul Zaentz Company Film Center, a post-production sound facility, opened its doors in the early 80s. • *One Flew Over the Cuckoo's Nest* 1975 (p) **(AABP)**; *Three Warriors* 1977 (p); *The Lord of the Rings* 1978 (p); *Amadeus* 1984 (p) **(AABP)**; *The Mosquito Coast* 1986 (exec.p); *The Unbearable Lightness of Being* 1988 (p).

Zanuck, Darryl F. • Producer, executive; also screenwriter. • Born Wahoo, NE, September 5, 1902; died 1979. Studio founder whose dynamism and gift for gauging audience appeal made him one of the most durable and influential executives in Hollywood history.

Zanuck began submitting stories to film studios in the early 1920s and was a staff screenwriter for Warner Bros. by 1924. He had a knack for catchy, crafty narratives, including a series of Rin Tin Tin vehicles; more importantly, he displayed energy and a talent for administration which led to his being named production chief in 1929. In this position, Zanuck oversaw the transition to sound (which made Warner Bros. a major studio overnight) and put into production the cycle of gangster movies, bitter social melodramas and musicals for which the studio became renowned.

Zanuck formed 20th Century Pictures with Joseph Schenck in 1933; a year later, the company merged with Fox, with Zanuck positioned as head of production. A shrewd leader, with the ablity to inspire awe and respect from those around him, Zanuck would guide the studio to many a commercial bonanza.

At 20th Century-Fox, Zanuck concentrated first on profit and entertainment and second on ethical or artistic concerns. As he had done at Warner Bros., Zanuck gave audiences what they wanted when they wanted it, from the simple morale-boosting of Shirley Temple vehicles to the superior, war-time Americana of John Ford (*The Grapes of Wrath* 1940) and Henry King (*Wilson* 1944) to post-war "problem" films like *Gentleman's Agreement* (1947) and *No Way Out* (1950).

Zanuck went independent in 1956 and suffered a string of flops before scoring a huge success with the WWII epic *The Longest Day* (1962). In the same year, he was called back by 20th Century-Fox to save the company from the impending financial disaster brought on by *Cleopatra* (1962). Zanuck took over as president and named his son, Richard Zanuck, executive vice president of production. In 1969 he became chairman and CEO and elevated his son to president, only to fire him a year later due to continuing fiscal problems. Zanuck himself resigned in 1971. • *Find Your Man* 1924 (sc,story); *The Lighthouse By the Sea* 1924 (sc); *The Millionaire Cowboy* 1924 (story); *The Telephone Girl* 1924 (sc); *A Broadway Butterfly* 1925 (sc,story); *Eve's Lover* 1925 (sc); *Hogan's Alley* 1925 (sc); *The Limited Mail* 1925 (sc); *On Thin Ice* 1925 (sc); *Seven Sinners* 1925 (sc,story); *Across the Pacific* 1926 (sc); *The Better 'Ole* 1926 (sc); *The Caveman* 1926 (sc); *Footloose Widows* 1926 (sc); *The Little Irish Girl* 1926 (sc); *Oh, What a Nurse!* 1926 (sc); *The Social Highwayman* 1926 (story); *Three Weeks in Paris* 1926 (sc); *The First Auto* 1927 (story); *Good Time Charley* 1927 (story); *Ham and Eggs at the Front* 1927 (story); *The Missing Link* 1927 (sc,story); *Old San Francisco* 1927 (story); *Wolf's Clothing* 1927 (sc); *Noah's Ark* 1929 (story); *Say It With Songs* 1929 (story); *The Show of Shows* 1929 (p); *Little Caesar* 1930 (p); *The Public Enemy* 1931 (p); *Advice to the Lovelorn* 1933 (p); *Born to Be Bad* 1934 (p); *Gallant Lady* 1934 (p); *The House of Rothschild* 1934 (p); *Looking For Trouble* 1934 (p); *The Mighty Barnum* 1934 (p); *Moulin Rouge* 1934 (p); *The Call of the Wild* 1935 (p); *Clive of India* 1935 (p); *Folies Bergere* 1935 (p); *Metropolitan* 1935 (p); *Les Miserables* 1935 (p); *Professional Soldier* 1935 (p); *Thanks a Million* 1935 (p); *Captain January* 1936 (p); *The Country Doctor* 1936 (p); *Dimples* 1936 (p); *Girls' Dormitory* 1936 (p); *Half Angel* 1936 (p); *It Had to Happen* 1936 (p); *A Message to Garcia* 1936 (p); *One in a Million* 1936 (p); *The Poor Little Rich Girl* 1936 (p); *The Prisoner of Shark Island* 1936 (p); *The Road to Glory* 1936 (p); *Sing, Baby, Sing* 1936 (p); *Sins of Man* 1936 (p); *To Mary - With Love* 1936 (p); *Under Two Flags* 1936 (p); *White Fang* 1936 (p); *White Hunter* 1936 (p); *Ali Baba Goes to Town* 1937 (p); *Heidi* 1937 (p); *Love Is News* 1937 (p); *Love Under Fire* 1937 (p); *Love and Hisses* 1937 (p); *Second Honeymoon* 1937 (p); *Slave Ship* 1937 (p); *Wake Up and Live* 1937 (p); *You Can't Have Everything* 1937 (p); *Alexander's Ragtime Band* 1938 (p); *The Baroness and the Butler* 1938 (p); *Four Men and a Prayer* 1938 (p); *Gateway* 1938 (p); *Happy Landing* 1938 (p); *Hold That Co-ed* 1938 (p); *In Old Chicago* 1938 (p); *Just Around the Corner* 1938 (p); *Kentucky* 1938 (p); *Kentucky Moonshine* 1938 (p); *Kidnapped* 1938 (p); *Little Miss Broadway* 1938 (p); *Rebecca of Sunnybrook Farm* 1938 (p); *Sally, Irene and Mary* 1938 (p); *Straight, Place, and Show* 1938 (p); *Suez* 1938 (p); *Day-Time Wife* 1939 (p); *Hollywood Cavalcade* 1939 (p); *Jesse James* 1939 (p); *The Little Princess* 1939 (p); *The Rains Came* 1939 (p); *The Return of the Cisco Kid* 1939 (p); *Stanley and Livingstone* 1939 (p); *Swanee River* 1939 (p); *Tail Spin* 1939 (p); *The Blue Bird* 1940 (p); *Brigham Young, Frontiersman* 1940 (p); *Chad Hanna* 1940 (p); *Down Argentine Way* 1940 (p); *Four Sons* 1940 (p); *The Grapes of Wrath* 1940 (p); *The Great Profile* 1940 (p); *He Married His Wife* 1940 (p); *Johnny Apollo* 1940 (p); *Lillian Russell* 1940 (p); *Little Old New York* 1940 (p); *The Return of Frank James* 1940 (p); *Star Dust* 1940 (p); *Tin Pan Alley* 1940 (p); *Blood and Sand* 1941 (p); *How Green Was My Valley* 1941 (p); *That Night in Rio* 1941 (p); *Tobacco Road* 1941 (p); *A Yank in the R.A.F.* 1941 (p); *Son of Fury* 1942 (p); *This Above All* 1942 (p); *To the Shores of Tripoli* 1942 (p); *The Purple Heart* 1944 (p); *Wilson* 1944 (p); *Winged Victory* 1944 (p); *Dragonwyck* 1946 (p); *The Razor's Edge* 1946 (p); *Boomerang* 1947 (exec.p); *Gentleman's Agreement* 1947 (p); *Pinky* 1949 (p); *Twelve O'Clock High* 1949 (p); *All About Eve* 1950 (p); *No Way Out* 1950 (p); *David and Bathsheba* 1951 (p); *People Will Talk* 1951 (p); *The Snows of Kilimanjaro* 1952 (p); *Viva Zapata!* 1952 (p); *The Egyptian* 1954 (p); *The Man in the Gray Flannel Suit* 1955 (p); *Island in the Sun* 1957 (p); *The Sun Also Rises* 1957 (p); *The Roots of Heaven* 1958 (p); *Compulsion* 1959 (p); *Crack in the Mirror* 1960 (p); *The Big Gamble* 1961 (p); *Sanctuary* 1961 (p); *The Longest Day* 1962 (p).

Zanuck, Richard D. • Producer, executive • Born Richard Darryl Zanuck, Los Angeles, CA, December 13, 1934. *Educ.* Stanford. The son of legendary studio head Darryl F. Zanuck, Richard Zanuck entered the film business while still in college and produced his first feature, *Compulsion* (1959), at age 24. During his reign as head of production at 20th Century-Fox, the studio accumulated over 150 Oscar nominations, as well as three best picture awards. (See also Zanuck, Darryl F.)

Zanuck formed the Zanuck/Brown company with former Fox colleague David Brown in 1972; among the team's successful collaborations were *The Sting* (1973), *Jaws* (1975) and *Cocoon* (1985, also co-produced with third wife Lili Fini Zanuck). He dissolved his partnership with Brown in 1988 and formed the Zanuck Company the following year, sharing an Oscar with his wife for the company's first feature, *Driving Miss Daisy* (1989). • *Compulsion* 1959 (p); *The Chapman Report* 1962 (p); *Sssssss* 1973 (exec.p); *The Sting* 1973 (p); *The Black Windmill* 1974 (exec.p); *The Girl From Petrovka* 1974 (p); *The Sugarland Express* 1974 (p); *Willie Dynamite* 1974 (p); *The Eiger Sanction* 1975 (exec.p);

Jaws 1975 (p) **(AANBP)**; *MacArthur the Rebel General* 1977 (exec.p); *Jaws 2* 1978 (p); *The Island* 1980 (p); *Neighbors* 1981 (p); *The Verdict* 1982 (p); *Cocoon* 1985 (p); *Target* 1985 (p); *Cocoon: The Return* 1988 (p); *Driving Miss Daisy* 1989 (p) **(AABP)**.

Zanussi, Krzysztof • Director, screenwriter • Born Warsaw, Poland, July 17, 1939. *Educ.* University of Warsaw (physics); University of Cracow (philosophy); Lódz Film School, Poland. Zanussi's 1966 diploma film, *The Death of a Provincial*, won a number of international awards, setting him on the way to becoming Poland's premier film director, after Andrjez Wajda.

Zanussi's first feature film, *The Structure of Crystals* (1969), set like many of his works in the scientific community, concerns the divergent paths taken by two school friends pursuing their scientific careers. It received the best picture award from Polish Film critics that year. *Family Life* (1971) is a meditative study of a young technocrat whose return to his family roots precipitates an emotional and intellectual crisis, while *Behind The Wall* (also 1971) further analyzes the conflict between professional duty and personal emotion, which has been a major theme in all of the director's work, probably most directly in his acclaimed 1973 effort, *Illumination*. During this time, Zanussi also found time to make a number of short films for Polish and West German television, and in 1974, he further expanded his horizons with *The Catamount Killing*, shot in the US with an American and West German cast.

Zanussi's concern with the conflict between public and private morality, official corruption and the delicate balance between intellect and intuition are further explored in *A Woman's Decision* (1977), *Camouflage* (1977) and *Spirale/Spiral/Quarterly Balance*, 1978). In a cameo appearance as himself in Krzysztof Kieslowski's *Camera Buff* (1979), Zanussi expresses his interest in the workings of corruption and the dilemma we face when it becomes apparent that success in the world is usually achieved only when our values are compromised. This philosophical and moral dilemma is fully explored in *Ways In The Night* (1979), in which a basically decent German officer is called on to uphold the policies of National Socialism, and in *The Constant Factor* (1980), one of Zanussi's finest films, where the problem is further complicated by the workings of chance: the young protagonist loses his opportunities for a successful career because of his refusal to compromise his ideals, only to become the unwitting cause of a tragedy.

In 1980, Zanussi turned to black comedy in another of his best films, *Contract*, a merciless depiction of the Polish ruling class in which a son, disgusted by his family's decadent, materialistic lifestyle, burns down the family home. In the same year, he also turned his talents to quite another kind of project when he was chosen to direct *From A Far Country*, the biography of Pope John Paul II. Although a staunch supporter of the Solidarity movement, Zanussi would seem to be philosophically far from the conservative Catholic orthodoxy of the Polish Pope, but his customary objectivity and sharp eye for various social forces at work yield an enlightening portrait of Polish society in transition.

After the temporary defeat of the Solidarity movement in the mid-1980s, Zanussi worked abroad, mostly for German television. With the latest political developments in his native country it will be interesting to see where this most intellectual and provocative of filmmakers will turn his attention. Zanussi has always been an artist more likely to pose questions than to propose answers, and will most certainly continue to challenge his audience in films to come. KJ • *Death of a Provincial* 1966 (d,sc); *Struktura krysztalu/The Structure of Crystals* 1969 (d,sc); *Za Sciana/Behind the Wall* 1971 (d,sc); *Zycie Rodzinne/Family Life* 1971 (d,sc); *Iluminacja/Illumination* 1973 (d,sc); *The Catamount Killing* 1974 (d); *Barwy Ochronne/Camouflage* 1977 (d,sc); *A Woman's Decision* 1977 (d,sc); *Spirale* 1978 (d,sc); *Amator/Camera Buff* 1979 (a); *Wege in der Nacht/Ways in the Night* 1979 (d,sc); *The Constant Factor* 1980 (d); *Contract* 1980 (d); *From a Far Country* 1980 (d); *Imperativ* 1982 (d,sc); *Die Unerreichbare* 1982 (d,sc,from plays *The Unapproachable* and *Scout's Honor*); *Blaubart/Bluebeard* 1984 (d,sc); *Rok Spokonjnego Slonca/The Year of the Quiet Sun* 1984 (d,sc); *Le Pouvoir du Mal* 1985 (d,sc); *Le Jeune magicien* 1987 (p); *Gdzieskolwiek jest, jeslis jest* 1988 (d,sc); *The Road Home* 1988 (art.d); *And the Violins Stopped Playing* 1989 (exec.p); *Stan Posiadania* 1989 (d,sc).

Zavattini, Cesare • Screenwriter; also author, director. • Born Luzzara Emilia, Italy, September 29, 1902; died October 13, 1989, Rome. Central architect of Italian neorealist cinema who layed down the blueprint for the movement with writings ranging from screenplays and novels to theory and poetry.

After an uneventful screenwriting debut with *I'll Give a Million* (1938), Zavattini, a committed Marxist, began to formulate his vision of a cinema of truth, free of artificiality and pretense, which would concern itself with the problems of everyday people. He collaborated with another key figure of the movement, Vittorio De Sica, as early as *Teresea Venerdi* (1941), but it was with *The Children are Watching Us* (1943), about a young boy who experiences the separation of his parents, that the foundations for the movement were laid. Zavattini and De Sica went on collaborate on such classic films as *Shoeshine* (1946), *The Bicycle Thief* (1948), *Miracle in Milan* (1950), *Umberto D* (1952), *The Roof* (1957) and *Two Women* (1960).

Zavattini also wrote several books (some of which were turned into films) as well as screenplays for other directors, among them Allesandro Blasetti (*Four Steps in the Clouds* 1942), René Clément (*The Walls of Malapaga* 1949) and Luchino Visconti (*Bellisima* 1951). At the age of 80 he directed his first film, the surrealistic *The Truth* (1982). • *Daro un Milione/I'll Give a Million* 1938 (story); *Teresea Venerdi* 1941 (sc); *Quattro Passi fra la Nuvole/Four Steps in the Clouds* 1942 (sc); *I Bambini Ci Guardano/The Children Are Watching Us* 1943 (sc); *Sciuscia/Shoeshine* 1946 (sc) **(AANBSC)**; *Ladri di Biciclette/The Bicycle Thief* 1948 (sc) **(AANBSC)**; *La Mura di Malapaga/The Walls of Malapaga* 1949 (sc,story); *Domenica d'Agosto* 1950 (sc); *Miracolo a Milano/Miracle in Milan* 1950 (sc,story); *Bellissima* 1951 (from story "La bambina più bella del mondo"); *Buongiorno Elefante!* 1952 (from subject,scenes); *Umberto D* 1952 (sc,story) **(AANBST)**; *Amore in Città/Love in the City* 1953 (d,p,sc,from story—"Tentato Suicidio"—"When Love Fails"); *Indiscretion of an American Wife* 1953 (sc,from story "Stazione Termini"); *Siamo Donne* 1953 (sc,idea); *L'Oro di Napoli/The Gold of Naples* 1954 (sc); *Suor Letizia* 1957 (sc,story); *Il Tetto/The Roof* 1957 (sc); *The Virtuous Bigamist* 1957 (from orig.sc—*Four Steps in the Cloud*); *La Ciociara/Two Women* 1960 (sc); *Boccaccio '70* 1962 (from idea—*Il lavoro*,prod.); *L'Isola di Arturo* 1962 (sc); *I Sequestrati di Altona* 1962 (sc); *After the Fox* 1966 (sc); *Woman Times Seven* 1967 (sc); *Le Streghe* 1968 (sc,from story—"The Witch Burned Alive," "A Night Like Any Other"); *Gli Amanti* 1969 (sc); *I Girasoli* 1969 (sc); *Lo Chiameremo Andrea* 1972 (sc); *Una Breve Vacanza* 1973 (sc); *The Children of Sanchez* 1978 (sc); *Un Cuore Semplice* 1978 (sc); *Ligabue* 1978 (sc,from text); *La Veritaaà/The Truth* 1982 (a,d,sc,m); *Strand—Under the Dark Cloth* 1989 (a).

Zea, Kristi • Production designer; also costume designer. • Born New York, NY, October 24, 1948. *Educ.* Middlebury College, VT; Columbia (English). Designed the costumes for four Alan Parker films before graduating to art director on his stylish psychodrama, *Angel Heart* (1987). Zea has since worked as production designer on films by Jonathan Demme and Martin Scorsese. • *Interiors* 1978 (design coordinator); *Fame* 1980 (cost); *Endless Love* 1981 (cost); *Shoot the Moon* 1981 (cost); *Tattoo* 1981 (cost); *Exposed* 1983 (cost); *Lovesick* 1983 (cost); *Terms of Endearment* 1983 (cost); *Unfaithfully Yours* 1983 (cost); *Beat Street* 1984 (cost); *Best Defense* 1984 (cost); *Birdy* 1984 (cost); *The Little Drummer Girl* 1984 (cost—Diane Keaton); *Silverado* 1985 (cost); *Dead End Kids* 1986 (cost); *Lucas* 1986 (assoc.p); *Angel Heart* 1987 (art d); *Broadcast News* 1987 (art d,assoc.p); *Married to the Mob* 1988 (pd); *Miss Firecracker* 1989 (pd); *New York Stories* 1989 (pd—"Life Lessons"); *GoodFellas* 1990 (pd); *The Silence of the Lambs* 1991 (pd).

Zeffirelli, Franco • Director, screenwriter; also production designer. • Born Florence, Italy, February 12, 1923. *Educ.* Accademia di Belle Arti, Florence; Florence University (architecture). Franco Zeffirelli's distinctive career reflects his reverence for the classics of music and literature. Nearly all his films are adaptations, lavish productions utilizing lush locations, extravagant sets and sumptuous costumes. In fact, the very qualities which embellish also tend to impair his work. His films are so well researched that the audience is often overwhelmed with detail. A daring filmmaker, Zeffirelli is not afraid to pursue risky projects which challenge the predictable world of commercial filmmaking.

Zeffirelli's roots are in the theater, especially opera. Ironically, his name is taken from a Mozart aria in *Così fan tutte.* His mother chose the name "Zeffiretti" or "little breezes" from the aria, but his name was misspelled in the birth register as "Zeffirelli."

His formal education was in architecture at the University of Florence. However, after seeing Laurence Olivier's film of *Henry V* (1945), Zeffirelli decided it was the stage which truly ignited him. That same year, he began his career as a theatrical set designer, working as an assistant to a scenic painter in the Teatro della Pergola in Florence. It was here that he met his mentor, Luchino Visconti, who hired him as an assistant director on *La Terra Trema* (1948). Visconti's influence over Zeffirelli was profound, especially in their passionate attention to detail.

Although Zeffirelli would work with Visconti on two other films, *Bellissima* (1951) and *Senso* (1954), he spent much of the 1950s and 1960s immersed in the theater, designing costumes and sets and directing a variety of productions, from Tennesse Williams to Shakespeare, as well as guiding opera diva Maria Callas through some of her greatest performances. In 1967 Zeffirelli caught the attention of the film world with *The Taming of the Shrew.* He managed to maintain a delicate equilibrium between his two stars, Richard Burton and Elizabeth Taylor, and in the process created a film which was true to the spirit of the original play, though it was criticized as a bowdlerization.

In November 1966, while editing *The Taming of the Shrew*, Zeffirelli heard of widespread destruction caused by flooding in Florence. He and a hastily assembled crew shot a documentary for Italian television depicting the devastation, and Richard Burton did the narration. The film helped raise over $20 million toward the restoration of the city and its valuable works of art.

Zeffirelli's name is still most closely associated with his next film, *Romeo and Juliet* (1968). In a bit of inspired casting, Zeffirelli chose two teenage actors, Olivia Hussey and Leonard Whiting, to play the leads. This version of Shakespeare's tragedy was consonant with the 1960s and included a nude love scene. A box-office smash, *Romeo and Juliet* also earned Academy Awards for cinematography and costume design.

Few Zeffirelli films since *Romeo and Juliet* have realized such widespread popularity. *Brother Sun, Sister Moon* (1973), the life of St. Francis of Assisi, was a box-office failure, although a recent resurgence of interest has elevated the film to a kind of cult status. Zeffirelli's television presentation, *Jesus of Nazareth*, first broadcast in 1977, exhibited his masterful ability to direct spectacle and to render a sensitive subject intelligently. These qualities were also evident in *La Traviata* (1983). In this extraordinary film, his decision to deconstruct the images of the famed opera while sustaining the melody serves the opera most eloquently. Applying the same techniques to his next cinematic opera, *Otello* (1986), however, failed to produce the same results.

Though film critics have chastised him for his unabashed sentimentality (especially in his remake of *The Champ*, 1979) and extravagant productions, these are also the qualities that have made him popular with film audiences, as well as theater and opera patrons around the world. MCJ • *La Terra Trema* 1948 (ad); *Bellissima* 1951 (ad); *Senso/The Wanton Contessa* 1954 (ad); *Camping* 1957 (d); *La Bohème* 1965 (d,pd); *The Taming of the Shrew* 1967 (d,p,sc); *Romeo and Juliet* 1968 (d,sc) **(AANBD)**; *Brother Sun, Sister Moon* 1973 (d,sc); *The Champ* 1979 (d); *Endless Love* 1981 (d); *La Traviata* 1983 (d,sc,pd) **(AANBAD)**; *Otello* 1986 (d,sc); *Il Giovane Toscanini/Young Toscanini* 1988 (d,story); *Hamlet* 1990 (d,sc).

Zemeckis, Robert • Director; also screenwriter. • Born Chicago, IL, 1952. *Educ.* Northern Illinois University; USC, Los Angeles (film). One of the preeminent directors of mainstream Hollywood entertainment since the mid-1980s.

While studying at USC, Zemeckis met future partner Bob Gale, with whom he went on to work in TV. The team cowrote their first feature, the nostalgic teen romp *I Wanna Hold Your Hand* (1978), with Zemeckis directing and Steven Spielberg debuting as executive producer. (They also collaborated on the screenplay of Spielberg's 1979 feature, *1941.*) Neither *Hold Your Hand* nor *Used Cars* (1980) stimulated much box-office action; they did, however, draw the attention of Michael Douglas, who hired Zemeckis to direct the hit romantic adventure, *Romancing the Stone* (1984).

With Gale usually producing and co-writing, Zemeckis has gone on to turn out some of the most popular films of the 1980s, including the clever time warp adventure/comedy *Back to the Future* (1985) and the bravura piece of live action/animation integration, *Who Framed Roger Rabbit?* (1988). • *I Wanna Hold Your Hand* 1978 (d,sc); *1941* 1979 (sc,story); *Used Cars* 1980 (d,sc); *Romancing the Stone* 1984 (d); *Back to the Future* 1985 (d,sc) **(AANBSC)**; *Who Framed Roger Rabbit?* 1988 (d); *Back to the Future II* 1989 (d,story,from characters); *Back to the Future III* 1990 (d,story).

Zetterling, Mai • Actress, director; also screenwriter, novelist. • Born Vasteras, Sweden, May 24, 1925. *Educ.* Royal Dramatic Theater School, Stockholm. Mai Zetterling came to feminism gradually. In her autobiography, *All Those Tomorrows,* she notes, "When the reviews of my first full-length feature movie came out, I was horrified to read that 'Mai Zetterling directs like a man.' What did that mean?" As an actress she was considered no threat. But when she decided to become a film director, she was "not the same any more in the eyes of men." It took years to realize "the change I had made was positive and, in the end, the only way."

As a teenager, Zetterling joined a children's theater club and at 16 played the lead in a play by Pär Lagerkvist. At 17, she joined the Swedish National Theater, where Alf Sjöberg became her mentor and directed her in her first major film, *Frenzy/Torment* (1944), written by Ingmar Bergman.

For British film director Basil Dearden she played the title role in *Frieda* (1947), which led to a successful British film career with Rank. Back in Sweden, she also made one film under Ingmar Bergman, *Music in the Dark* (1948).

In the early 1950s, she accepted an offer to be Danny Kaye's leading lady in *Knock on Wood* (1954). It was to be her only film in Hollywood, a place she hated. She returned to England and starred on the stage in a production of *A Doll's House.*

After she married British writer David Hughes, Zetterling made plans toward becoming a film director. She and Hughes collaborated for BBC-TV on a series of documentaries: *The Polite Invasion* (1960), about the problems of the Lapps and the Swedes; *Little Lords of Egypt* (1961), concerning the plight of

Gypsies; and *The War Game* (1961), an anti-war short about two boys playing a game that turns nasty. The latter film won the Golden Lion Prize at the 1963 Venice Film Festival.

Her directing career went into high gear with her feature, *Loving Couples* (1964). Its poster won a prize in Vienna but it was banned in Cannes as obscene. *Night Games* (1966), based on her own novel, was even more of a cause célèbre. Banned from the Venice Festival, it was censured by critics for scenes of sexuality, childbirth, and vomiting in detailing the story of a 35-year-old man's attempts to deal with childhood memories marked by depravity and perversity. Three films later, her marriage with Hughes came to an end.

Most notable among her more recent films are *We Have Many Faces* (1975), which drew on "the pain and misery of the break-up of my marriage"; *Of Seals and Man* (1978), detailing the disappearing breed of Eskimo seal hunters; and *Scrubbers* (1982), which dealt with young female offenders sent to Britain's Borstal prison.

Zetterling's work shows a fascination with outsiders, whether Eskimos, Gypies or girl delinquents. "Perhaps I am a madhatter Swede," she says, "who got lost in the world...I feel very far from the norm of just about everything." DLY • *Hets/Frenzy/Torment* 1944 (a); *Frieda* 1947 (a); *Musik i morker/Music in the Dark* 1948 (a); *Blackmailed* 1951 (a); *The Ringer* 1952 (a); *Knock on Wood* 1954 (a); *Giftas* 1955 (a); *Prize of Gold* 1955 (a); *Abandon Ship!* 1957 (a); *The Truth About Women* 1958 (a); *Jet Storm* 1959 (a); *The Main Attraction* 1962 (a); *Alksande Par/Loving Couples* 1964 (d,sc); *Night Games* 1966 (d,sc,from novel); *Flickorna/The Girls* 1968 (d,sc); *Visions of Eight* 1973 (d); *We Have Many Faces* 1975 (d,sc); *Of Seals and Man* 1978 (d); *Love* 1981 (d,sc); *Scrubbers* 1982 (d,sc); *Amarosa* 1986 (d,sc,story,ed); *Hidden Agenda* 1990 (a); *The Witches* 1990 (a).

Zhang Yimou • Director of photography, director • Born Shaanxi Province, China, 1950. *Educ.* Beijing Film Academy (cinematography). Leading cinematographer of China's "Fifth Generation" filmmakers who has shot films by directors Chen Kaige and Wu Tianming. Zhang made an auspicious directorial debut with *Red Sorghum* (1987), which won the Golden Bear at the 1988 Berlin Festival. Set in the remote Shandong province in the 1930s and rich with mythical overtones, *Red Sorghum* uses minimal dialogue, haunting music and stunning visuals to tell the story of a meek young bride who develops into the forceful head of her husband's winery after his death. • *Huang Tudi* 1984 (ph); *Yi Ge Yu Ba Ge* 1985 (ph); *Da Yue Bing* 1986 (ph); *Hong Gaoliang/Red Sorghum* 1987 (d,song); *Lao Jing* 1987 (a,ph); *Judou* 1989 (d); *The Terra-Cotta Warrior* 1990 (a,p).

Zieff, Howard • Director • Born Chicago, IL, 1943. *Educ.* Los Angeles Art Center (photography). Leading director of TV commercials who turned to features in 1973 and has proved adept at handling light comedy. Zieff directed the enjoyable Jeff Bridges vehicle, *Hearts of the West* (1975), about the making of B westerns in 1930s Hollywood. • *Slither* 1973; *Hearts of the West* 1975; *House Calls* 1978; *The Main Event* 1979; *Private Benjamin* 1980; *Unfaithfully Yours* 1983; *The Dream Team* 1989.

Zimmer, Hans • Composer • Former London-based jingles composer who pioneered the use of computer-driven film scores. Zimmer collaborated with Stanley Myers on a string of films between 1982 and 1988, including Jerzy Skolomowski's *Moonlighting* (1982) and Nicholas Roeg's *Insignificance* (1985). Subsequent credits have ranged from Ridley Scott's *Black Rain* (1989) to Bruce Beresford's *Driving Miss Daisy* (1989). Zimmer also co-produced the soundtrack album for Bertolucci's *The Last Emperor* (1987). • *Moonlighting* 1982 (electronic effects); *Success Is the Best Revenge* 1984 (m); *Insignificance* 1985 (m); *The Lightship* 1985 (m); *My Beautiful Laundrette* 1985 (m.perf); *Castaway* 1986 (add.m); *Double Exposure* 1987 (m); *The Wind* 1987 (m); *The Zero Boys* 1987 (m); *Arcadia (short)* 1988 (m); *Burning Secret* 1988 (m); *The Fruit Machine* 1988 (m); *The Nature of the Beast* 1988 (m); *Paperhouse* 1988 (m); *Prisoner of Rio* 1988 (add.m); *Rain Man* 1988 (m) **(AANBM)**; *Taffin* 1988 (m); *A World Apart* 1988 (m); *Black Rain* 1989 (m,song); *Diamond Skulls* 1989 (m); *Driving Miss Daisy* 1989 (m); *Twister* 1989 (m); *Bird on a Wire* 1990 (m); *Chicago Joe and the Showgirl* 1990 (m); *Days of Thunder* 1990 (m,song); *Fools of Fortune* 1990 (m); *Green Card* 1990 (m); *The Neverending Story II The Next Chapter* 1990 (m); *Pacific Heights* 1990 (m).

Zinnemann, Fred • Director; also producer. • Born Vienna, Austria, April 29, 1907. *Educ.* University of Vienna (law); Ecole Technique de Photographie et de Cinématographie, Paris. Director Fred Zinnemann has had an outstanding career spanning six decades, during which he has directed 22 features, 19 short subjects and won three Oscars.Perhaps his best-known work is *High Noon* (1952), one of the first 25 American film classics chosen in 1989 for the National Film Registry. With its psychological and moral examinations of its lawman hero, played by Gary Cooper, its allegorical political commentary (on McCarthy-era witch-hunting) and its innovative chronology whereby screen time approximated the tense 80-minute countdown to the confrontational hour, *High Noon* shattered the mold of the formulaic shoot-em-up western.

The director's other eminent films, all compelling dramas of lone and principled individuals tested by tragic events, include *From Here to Eternity* (1953); *The Nun's Story* (1959); *A Man For All Seasons* (1966); and *Julia* (1977). Regarded as a consummate craftsman, Zinnemann has traditionally endowed his work with meticulous attention to detail, an intuitive gift for brilliant casting and a preoccupation with the moral dilemmas of his characters.

Zinnemann's penchant for realism and authenticity is evident in his first feature *Redes/The Wave* (1935), shot on location in Mexico with mostly non-professional actors recruited among the locals, which is one of the earliest examples of realism in narrative film. Earlier in the decade, in fact, Zinnemann had worked with documentarian Robert Flaherty, an association he considered "the most important event of my professional life."

The filmmaker also used authentic locales and extras in *The Search* (1948), which won an Oscar for screenwriting and secured his position in the Hollywood establishment. Shot in war-ravaged Germany, the film stars Montgomery Clift in his screen debut as a G.I. who cares for a lost Czech boy traumatized by the war. In the critically acclaimed *The Men* (1950), starring newcomer Marlon Brando as a paraplegic vet, Zinnemann filmed many scenes in a California hospital where real patients served as extras.

Besides Clift and Brando, other Zinnemann discoveries included Pier Angeli and John Ericson, who co-starred in *Teresa* (1951), with Rod Steiger and Ralph Meeker debuting in secondary roles. And in *Oklahoma!* (1955), Zinnemann's version of the Rodgers and Hammerstein musical, the wide screen format Todd-AO made its debut, as did the film's young star Shirley Jones.

Zinnemann's casting choices were often as daring as they were judicious. For his screen adaptation of the play *The Member of the Wedding* (1952), Zinnemann chose the 26-year-old Julie Harris as the film's 12-year-old protagonist. In *From Here to Eternity* (1953), which brought Zinnemann his first Oscar for feature directing, he cast Frank Sinatra, who was at the lowest point of his popularity. As the likable loser Maggio, Sinatra won an Oscar for best supporting actor. *From Here to Eternity* also featured Deborah Kerr, best known for prim and proper roles, as a philandering Army wife. And Audrey Hepburn, previously cast in delightful comedic roles, gave the performance of her career as the anguished Sister Luke in the highly acclaimed *The Nun's Story.*

Throughout his career Zinnemann has favored a protagonist morally impelled to act heroically in defense of his or her beliefs. Hepburn in *The Nun's Story* and Cooper in *High Noon*, determined to confront savage outlaws hungry for revenge, are two prominent examples. Paul Scofield as Sir Thomas More in *A Man For All Seasons* (1966), which earned Zinnemann his second Oscar for feature film direction, gave a brilliant portrayal of a man driven by conscience to his ultimate fate.

And in *Julia* (1977), another of Zinnemann's crowning achievements, Vanessa Redgrave is a doomed American heiress who forsakes the safety and comfort of great wealth to devote her life to the anti-Nazi cause in Germany. Perhaps the most unusual and perversely engaging loner in Zinnemann's films is Edward Fox as the cold-blooded antihero assassin in the taut thriller *Day of the Jackal* (1973), a man who is impelled by greed rather than politics to try to kill French president DeGaulle.

In spite of the many consistencies and high quality that characterize his work, Zinnemann has been perceived by some critics—citing the many different genres he has embraced—to be a director for all seasons rather than an "auteur." Even his less sure-footed forays into film noir, melodrama, musicals and panoramic romance cannot outweigh Zinnemann's major efforts, which assure his reputation as one of America's most accomplished directors. DT • *Menschen am Sonntag* 1929 (prod.asst); *All Quiet on the Western Front* 1930 (a); *Redes/The Wave* 1935 (d); *Eyes in the Night* 1942 (d); *Kid Glove Killer* 1942 (d); *The Seventh Cross* 1944 (d); *Little Mr. Jim* 1946 (d); *My Brother Talks to Horses* 1946 (d); *Act of Violence* 1948 (d); *The Search* 1948 (d) **(AANBD)**; *The Men* 1950 (d); *Benjy (short)* 1951 (d); *Teresa* 1951 (d); *High Noon* 1952 (d) **(AANBD)**; *The Member of the Wedding* 1952 (d); *From Here to Eternity* 1953 (d) **(AABD)**; *Oklahoma!* 1955 (d); *A Hatful of Rain* 1957 (d); *The Nun's Story* 1959 (d) **(AANBD)**; *The Sundowners* 1960 (d,p) **(AANBD,AANBP)**; *Behold a Pale Horse* 1964 (d,p); *A Man For All Seasons* 1966 (d,p) **(AABD,AABP)**; *The Day of the Jackal* 1973 (d); *Julia* 1977 (d) **(AANBD)**; *Five Days One Summer* 1982 (d,p); *George Stevens: A Filmmaker's Journey* 1985 (a).

Zsigmond, Vilmos • *aka* William Zsigmond • Director of photography • Born Czeged, Hungary, June 16, 1930. *Educ.* Academy for Theater and Film Art, Budapest (cinematography). Along with Laszlo Kovacs, a fellow student who also fled Hungary in 1956, Zsigmond rose to prominence in the 1970s. He is known for his fluid camerawork and vivid use of color on such features as John Boorman's *Deliverance* (1972), Robert Altman's *The Long Goodbye* (1973) and Steven Spielberg's *Close Encounters of the Third Kind* (1977). Zsigmond has also worked with directors Brian DePalma, Michael Cimino and Martin Scorsese. • *The Incredibly Strange Creatures Who Stopped Living and Became Mixed-Up Zombies!!?* 1962 (cam.op); *The Sadist* 1963 (ph); *The Nasty Rabbit* 1964 (ph); *The Time Travelers* 1964 (ph); *Deadwood '76* 1965 (ph); *The Name of the Game Is Kill* 1968 (ph); *Futz* 1969 (ph); *Hot Rod Action* 1969 (ph); *The Lonely Man* 1969 (ph); *The Monitors* 1969 (ph); *Horror of the Blood Monsters* 1970 (ph); *The Hired Hand* 1971 (ph); *McCabe & Mrs. Miller* 1971 (ph); *Red Sky at Morning* 1971 (ph); *Deliverance* 1972 (ph); *Images* 1972 (ph); *Cinderella Liberty* 1973 (ph); *The Long Goodbye* 1973 (ph); *Scarecrow* 1973 (ph); *The Girl From Petrovka* 1974 (ph); *The Sugarland Express* 1974 (ph); *Dandy, the All American Girl* 1976 (ph); *Death Riders* 1976 (ph); *Obsession* 1976 (ph); *Close Encounters of the Third Kind* 1977 (ph) **(AABPH)**; *The Deer Hunter* 1978 (ph) **(AANBPH)**; *The Last Waltz* 1978 (ph); *The Rose* 1979 (ph); *Winter Kills* 1979 (ph); *Heaven's Gate* 1980 (ph); *Blow Out* 1981 (ph); *The Border* 1981 (add.ph); *Jinxed!* 1982 (ph); *Table For Five* 1983 (ph); *No Small Affair* 1984 (ph); *The River* 1984 (ph) **(AANBPH)**; *Real Genius* 1985 (ph); *The Witches of Eastwick* 1987 (ph); *Journey to Spirit Island* 1988 (ph); *Fat Man and Little Boy* 1989 (ph); *Bonfire of the Vanities* 1990 (ph); *The Two Jakes* 1990 (ph).

Zucker, David • Director, producer, screenwriter; also actor. • Born Milwaukee, WI, October 16, 1947. *Educ.* University of Wisconsin (film). Responsible, with brother Jerry Zucker and college friend Jim Abrahams, for a series of corny, but often hilarious, spoofs of popular movie genres. After a raunchy debut with *The Kentucky Fried Movie* (1977), the team first enjoyed mainstream success with *Airplane!* (1980) and followed it with *Top Secret!* (1984), about an Elvis-like surfer (Val Kilmer) battling Nazi-Communists in East Germany with the aid of the French Resistance.

David Zucker made his solo directing debut with *The Naked Gun* (1988), based on the team's short-lived TV series "Police Squad" (1981), and younger brother Jerry, in his own solo debut, scored a huge success with the supernatural thriller-romance, *Ghost* (1990). See also Abrahams, Jim. • *The Kentucky Fried Movie* 1977 (a,sc); *Airplane!* 1980 (a,d,exec.p,sc); *Top Secret!* 1984 (d,exec.p,lyrics "Spend This Night With Me,"sc); *Ruthless People* 1986 (d); *The Naked Gun—From the Files of Police Squad!* 1988 (d,exec.p,sc).

Zucker, Jerry • Director, producer, screenwriter • Born Milwaukee, WI, March 11, 1950. *Educ.* University of Wisconsin (film). See David Zucker. • *The Kentucky Fried Movie* 1977 (a,sc); *Rock 'n' Roll High School* 1979 (2u d); *Airplane!* 1980 (a,d,exec.p,sc); *Top Secret!* 1984 (d,exec.p,lyrics "Spend This Night With Me,"sc); *Ruthless People* 1986 (d); *The Naked Gun - From the Files of Police Squad!* 1988 (exec.p,sc); *Ghost* 1990 (d).

Zukor, Adolph • Executive; also distributor, exhibitor. • Born Risce, Hungary, January 7, 1873; died 1976. One of the original studio "moguls." Zukor arrived in the US at 16, got one of his first jobs as a furrier's apprentice and, over 80 years later, was still going to work every day—at Paramount Pictures.

Zukor worked his way up to become a well-heeled Chicago furrier and, in 1903, teamed with Marcus Loew to open the first of a series of penny arcades. Two years later the team formed Loew's Consolidated, with Zukor as treasurer of the far-flung empire of theaters.

Zukor went into films on his own in 1912 and reaped a windfall as the US distributor of the four-reel European production *Queen Elizabeth.* With his profits he formed Famous Players, a production and distribution company modelled after France's Film d'Art, which filmed popular plays starring renowned stage performers. The resultant "canned theater" proved a resounding financial success, which was compounded by his signing of Mary Pickford, "America's Sweetheart," later that year.

In 1916 Famous Players joined forces with the Jesse Lasky Feature Play Company to form the Famous Players-Lasky Company, with Zukor as president. They soon took the name of a minor company they had bought (Paramount), snapped up a chain of movie theaters and hired two soon-to-be distinguished impresarios (Samuel Goldwyn, C.B. De Mille) to run the operation, which would emerge as one of the industry's leading studios.

With Zukor at the helm, Paramount weathered the financial downturn of the early 1930s. He fended off a number of attempts to unseat him until, in 1936, he was replaced as president by Barney Balaban. Zukor assumed the token position of chairman of the board and received a special Academy Award in 1948 for his "contribution to the industry." He published a memoir, *The Public is Never Wrong*, in 1953 and remained as Paramount's chairman of the board emeritus until his death at the age of 103. • *The Sorrows of Satan* 1926 (p); *Glorifying the American Girl* 1929 (a); *The Scarlet Empress* 1934 (p).

Zuniga, Daphne • Actress • Born San Francisco, CA, c. 1963. *Educ.* American Conservatory Theater, San Francisco; UCLA (theater). Best known as John Cusack's reluctant traveling companion in Rob Reiner's winning collegiate romance, *The Sure Thing* (1985).

• *The Dorm That Dripped Blood* 1981; *The Initiation* 1983; *The Sure Thing* 1985; *Vision Quest* 1985; *Modern Girls* 1986; *Spaceballs* 1987; *Last Rites* 1988; *The Fly II* 1989; *Gross Anatomy* 1989; *Staying Together* 1989.

Zwerin, Charlotte • American filmmaker; also editor. • Before going solo with *Thelonius Monk: Straight, No Chaser* (1988), a portrait of the renowned jazz artist, Zwerin was best known for her long-term collaboration with filmmakers David and Albert Maysles, having worked as an editor on such landmark documentary features as *Salesman* (1969) and *Gimme Shelter* (1970). • *Showman* 1962 (ed); *What's Happening New York Meets the Beatles* 1964 (d,ed); *Meet Marlon Brando* 1966 (ed); *Salesman* 1969 (d,ed); *Gimme Shelter* 1970 (d,ed); *Running Fence* 1977 (d,ed,p); *Islands* 1986 (d,ed,p); *Thelonius Monk: Straight, No Chaser* 1988 (d,ed,p).

Zwick, Edward • Director; also producer, screenwriter. • Born Winnetka, IL, October 8, 1952. *Educ.* Harvard (literature); AFI, Los Angeles. A former journalist and editor for *The New Republic* and *Rolling Stone*, the precocious Zwick first enjoyed mainstream success as a writer, story editor, producer and director of the warmhearted TV series "Family" (1976-80).

After making his feature directorial debut with *About Last Night...* (1986), a tepid adaptation of David Mamet's play *Sexual Perversity in Chicago*, Zwick returned to the small screen as creator and executive producer of the award-winning "thirtysomething" (1987-), a polished paean to yuppie angst.

His second feature, *Glory* (1989), a stirring Civil War drama about the formation of the first black regiment, firmly established him as a director of scope and ambition. • *About Last Night* 1986 (d); *Glory* 1989 (d).